Peterson's
Two-Year
Colleges
2015

About Peterson's

Peterson's provides the accurate, dependable, high-quality education content and guidance you need to succeed. No matter where you are on your academic or professional path, you can rely on Peterson's print and digital publications for the most up-to-date education exploration data, expert test-prep tools, and top-notch career success resources—everything you need to achieve your goals.

For more information, contact Peterson's Publishing, 3 Columbia Circle, Suite 205, Albany, NY 12203-5158; 800-338-3282 Ext. 54229; or find us on the World Wide Web at www.petersonsbooks.com.

ISSN 0894-9328
ISBN: 978-0-7689-3869-2

Printed in the United States of America

10 9 8 7 6 5 4 3 2 1   16 15 14

Forty-fifth Edition

Sustainability—Its Importance to Peterson's

What does sustainability mean to Peterson's? As a leading publisher, we are aware that our business has a direct impact on vital resources—most importantly the raw material used to make our books. Peterson's is proud that its products are printed at SFI Chain-of-Custody certified facilities and that all of its books are printed on SFI certified paper with 10 percent post-consumer waste using vegetable-based ink.

Supporting the Sustainable Forestry Initiative® (SFI®) means that we only use vendors—from paper suppliers to printers—who have undergone rigorous certification audits by independent parties to demonstrate that they meet the standards.

Peterson's continuously strives to find new ways to incorporate responsible sourcing throughout all aspects of its business.

Contents

A Note from the Peterson's Editors

For more than 40 years, Peterson's has given students and parents the most comprehensive, up-to-date information on undergraduate institutions in the United States. Peterson's researches the data published in *Peterson's Two-Year Colleges* each year. The information is furnished by the colleges and is accurate at the time of publishing.

This guide also features advice and tips on the college search and selection process, such as how to decide if a two-year college is right for you, how to approach transferring between colleges, and what's in store for adults returning to college. If you seem to be getting more, not less, anxious about choosing and getting into the right college, *Peterson's Two-Year Colleges* provides just the right help, giving you the information you need to make important college decisions and ace the admission process.

Opportunities abound for students, and this guide can help you find what you want in a number of ways:

"What You Need to Know About Two-Year Colleges" outlines the basic features and advantages of two-year colleges. "Surviving Standardized Tests" gives an overview of the common examinations students take prior to attending college. "Who's Paying for This? Financial Aid Basics" provides guidelines for financing your college education. "Frequently Asked Questions About Transferring" takes a look at the two-year college scene from the perspective of a student who is looking toward the day when he or she may pursue additional education at a four-year institution. "Returning to School: Advice for Adult Students" is an analysis of the pros and cons (mostly pros) of returning to college after already having begun a professional career. "What International Students Need to Know About Admission to U.S. Colleges and Universities" is an article written particularly for students overseas who are considering a U.S. college education. "Community Colleges and the New Green Economy" offers information on some exciting "green" programs at community colleges throughout the United States, as well as two insightful essays by Mary F. T. Spilde, President, Lane Community College and James DeHaven, V.P. of Economic and Business Development, Kalamazoo Valley Community College. Finally, "How to Use This Guide"

gives details on the data in this guide: what terms mean and why they're here.

- If you already have specifics in mind, such as a particular institution or major, turn to the easy-to-use **Two-Year Colleges At-a-Glance Chart** or **Indexes.** You can look up a particular feature—location and programs offered—or use the alphabetical index and immediately find the colleges that meet your criteria.

- For information about particular colleges, turn to the **Profiles of Two-Year Colleges** section. Here, our comprehensive college profiles are arranged alphabetically by state. They provide a complete picture of need-to-know information about every accredited two-year college—from admission to graduation, including expenses, financial aid, majors, and campus safety. All the information you need to apply is placed together at the conclusion of each college **Profile.** Display ads, which appear near some of the institutions' profiles, have been provided and paid for by those colleges or universities that wished to supplement their profile data with additional information about their institution.

- In addition, two-page narrative descriptions, which appear as **College Close-Ups,** are paid for and written by college officials and offer great detail about each college. They are edited to provide a consistent format across entries for your ease of comparison.

Peterson's publishes a full line of books—education exploration, test prep, financial aid, and career preparation. Peterson's publications can be found at high school guidance offices, college libraries and career centers, and your local bookstore and library. Peterson's books are also available as eBooks and online at www.petersonsbooks.com.

We welcome any comments or suggestions you may have about this publication. Your feedback will help us make educational dreams possible for you—and others like you.

Colleges will be pleased to know that Peterson's helped you in your selection. Admissions staff members are more than happy to answer questions, address specific problems and help in any way they can. The editors at Peterson's wish you great success in your college search.

The College Admissions Process: An Overview

What You Need to Know About Two-Year Colleges

David R. Pierce

Two-year colleges—better known as community colleges—are often called "the people's colleges." With their open-door policies (admission is open to individuals with a high school diploma or its equivalent), community colleges provide access to higher education for millions of Americans who might otherwise be excluded from higher education. Community college students are diverse and of all ages, races, and economic backgrounds. While many community college students enroll full-time, an equally large number attend on a part-time basis so they can fulfill employment and family commitments as they advance their education.

Community colleges can also be referred to as either technical or junior colleges, and they may either be under public or independent control. What unites two-year colleges is that they are regionally accredited, postsecondary institutions, whose highest credential awarded is the associate degree. With few exceptions, community colleges offer a comprehensive curriculum, which includes transfer, technical, and continuing education programs.

IMPORTANT FACTORS IN A COMMUNITY COLLEGE EDUCATION

The student who attends a community college can count on receiving high-quality instruction in a supportive learning community. This setting frees the student to pursue his or her own goals, nurture special talents, explore new fields of learning, and develop the capacity for lifelong learning.

From the student's perspective, four characteristics capture the essence of community colleges:

1. They are community-based institutions that work in close partnership with high schools, community groups, and employers in extending high-quality programs at convenient times and places.

2. Community colleges are cost effective. Annual tuition and fees at public community colleges average approximately half those at public four-year colleges and less than 15 percent of private four-year institutions. In addition, since most community colleges are generally close to their students' homes, these students can also save a significant amount of money on the room, board, and transportation expenses traditionally associated with a college education.

3. Community colleges provide a caring environment, with faculty members who are expert instructors, known for excellent teaching and meeting students at the point of their individual needs, regardless of age, sex, race, current job status, or previous academic preparation. Community colleges join a strong curriculum with a broad range of counseling and career services that are intended to assist students in making the most of their educational opportunities.

4. Many offer comprehensive programs, including transfer curricula in such liberal arts programs as chemistry, psychology, and business management, that lead directly to a baccalaureate degree and career programs that prepare students for employment or assist those already employed in upgrading their skills. For those students who need to strengthen their academic skills, community colleges also offer a wide range of developmental programs in mathematics, languages, and learning skills, designed to prepare the student for success in college studies.

GETTING TO KNOW YOUR TWO-YEAR COLLEGE

The first step in determining the quality of a community college is to check the status of its accreditation. Once you have established that a community college is appropriately accredited, find out as much as you can about the programs and services it has to offer. Much of that information can be found in materials the college provides. However, the best way to learn about a college is to visit in person.

During a campus visit, be prepared to ask a lot of questions. Talk to students, faculty members, administrators, and counselors about the college and its programs, particularly those in which you have a special interest. Ask about available certificates and associate degrees. Don't be shy. Do what you can to dig below the surface. Ask college officials about the transfer rate to four-year colleges. If a college emphasizes student services, find out what particular assistance is offered, such as educational or career guidance. Colleges are eager to provide you with the information you need to make informed decisions.

3

COMMUNITY COLLEGES CAN SAVE YOU MONEY

If you are able to live at home while you attend college, you will certainly save money on room and board, but it does cost something to commute. Many two-year colleges offer you instruction in your own home through online learning programs or through home study courses that can save both time and money. Look into all the options, and be sure to add up all the costs of attending various colleges before deciding which is best for you.

FINANCIAL AID

Many students who attend community colleges are eligible for a range of federal financial aid programs, state aid, and on-campus jobs. Your high school counselor or the financial aid officer at a community college will also be able to help you. It is in your interest to apply for financial aid months in advance of the date you intend to start your college program, so find out early what assistance is available to you. While many community colleges are able to help students who make a last-minute decision to attend college, either through short-term loans or emergency grants, if you are considering entering college and think you might need financial aid, it is best to find out as much as you can as early as you can.

WORKING AND GOING TO SCHOOL

Many two-year college students maintain full-time or part-time employment while they earn their degrees. Over the years, a steadily growing number of students have chosen to attend community colleges while they fulfill family and employment responsibilities. To enable these students to balance the demands of home, work, and school, most community colleges offer classes at night and on weekends.

For the full-time student, the usual length of time it takes to obtain an associate degree is two years. However, your length of study will depend on the course load you take: the fewer credits you earn each term, the longer it will take you to earn a degree. To assist you in moving more quickly toward earning your degree, many community colleges now award credit through examination or for equivalent knowledge gained through relevant life experiences. Be certain to find out the credit options that are available to you at the college in which you are interested. You may discover that it will take less time to earn a degree than you first thought.

PREPARATION FOR TRANSFER

Studies have repeatedly shown that students who first attend a community college and then transfer to a four-year college or university do at least as well academically as the students who entered the four-year institutions as freshmen. Most community colleges have agreements with nearby four-year institutions to make transfer of credits easier. If you are thinking of transferring, be sure to meet with a counselor or faculty adviser before choosing your courses. You will want to map out a course of study with transfer in mind. Make sure you also find out the credit-transfer requirements of the four-year institution you might want to attend.

ATTENDING A TWO-YEAR COLLEGE IN ANOTHER REGION

Although many community colleges serve a specific county or district, they are committed (to the extent of their ability) to the goal of equal educational opportunity without regard to economic status, race, creed, color, sex, or national origin. Independent two-year colleges recruit from a much broader geographical area—throughout the United States and, increasingly, around the world.

Although some community colleges do provide on-campus housing for their students, most do not. However, even if on-campus housing is not available, most colleges do have housing referral services.

NEW CAREER OPPORTUNITIES

Community colleges realize that many entering students are not sure about the field in which they want to focus their studies or the career they would like to pursue. Often, students discover fields and careers they never knew existed. Community colleges have the resources to help students identify areas of career interest and to set challenging occupational goals.

Once a career goal is set, you can be confident that a community college will provide job-relevant, technical education. About half of the students who take courses for credit at community colleges do so to prepare for employment or to acquire or upgrade skills for their current job. Especially helpful in charting a career path is the assistance of a counselor or a faculty adviser, who can discuss job opportunities in your chosen field and help you map out your course of study.

In addition, since community colleges have close ties to their communities, they are in constant contact with leaders in business, industry, organized labor, and public life. Community colleges work with these individuals and their organizations to prepare students for direct entry into the world of work. For example, some community colleges have established partnerships with local businesses and industries to provide specialized training programs. Some also provide the academic portion of apprenticeship training, while others offer extensive job-shadowing and cooperative education opportunities. Be sure to examine all of the career-preparation opportunities offered by the community colleges in which you are interested.

David R. Pierce is the former President of the American Association of Community Colleges.

Surviving Standardized Tests

WHAT ARE STANDARDIZED TESTS?

Colleges and universities in the United States use tests to help evaluate applicants' readiness for admission or to place them in appropriate courses. The tests that are most frequently used by colleges are the ACT® of American College Testing, Inc., and the College Board's SAT®. In addition, the Educational Testing Service (ETS) offers the TOEFL® test, which evaluates the English-language proficiency of nonnative speakers. The tests are offered at designated testing centers located at high schools and colleges throughout the United States and U.S. territories and at testing centers in various countries throughout the world.

Upon request, special accommodations for students with documented visual, hearing, physical, or learning disabilities are available. Examples of special accommodations include tests in Braille or large print and such aids as a reader, recorder, magnifying glass, or sign language interpreter. Additional testing time may be allowed in some instances. Contact the appropriate testing program or your guidance counselor for details on how to request special accommodations.

THE ACT

The ACT is a standardized college entrance examination that measures knowledge and skills in English, mathematics, reading, and science reasoning and the application of these skills to future academic tasks. The ACT consists of four multiple-choice tests.

Test 1: English
- 75 questions, 45 minutes
- Usage and mechanics
- Rhetorical skills

Test 2: Mathematics
- 60 questions, 60 minutes
- Pre-algebra
- Elementary algebra
- Intermediate algebra
- Coordinate geometry
- Plane geometry
- Trigonometry

Test 3: Reading
- 40 questions, 35 minutes
- Prose fiction
- Humanities
- Social studies
- Natural sciences

Test 4: Science
- 40 questions, 35 minutes
- Data representation
- Research summary
- Conflicting viewpoints

Each section is scored from 1 to 36 and is scaled for slight variations in difficulty. Students are not penalized for incorrect responses. The composite score is the average of the four scaled scores. The ACT Plus Writing includes the four multiple-choice tests and a writing test, which measures writing skills emphasized in high school English classes and in entry-level college composition courses.

- To prepare for the ACT, ask your guidance counselor for a free guidebook called "Preparing for the ACT." Besides providing general test-preparation information and additional test-taking strategies, this guidebook describes the content and format of the four ACT subject area tests, summarizes test administration procedures followed at ACT test centers, and includes a practice test. Peterson's publishes *The Real ACT* that includes five official ACT tests.

DON'T FORGET TO . . .

- ❏ Take the SAT or ACT before application deadlines.
- ❏ Note that test registration deadlines precede test dates by about six weeks.
- ❏ Register to take the TOEFL test if English is not your native language and you are planning on studying at a North American college.
- ❏ Practice your test-taking skills with *Peterson's Master the SAT and The Real ACT*
- ❏ Contact the College Board or American College Testing, Inc., in advance if you need special accommodations when taking tests.

THE SAT

The SAT measures developed critical reading and mathematical reasoning abilities as they relate to successful performance in college. It is intended to supplement the secondary school record and other information about the student in assessing readiness for college. There is one unscored, experimental section on the exam, which is used for equating and/or pretesting purposes and can cover either the mathematics or critical reading area.

Critical Reading
- 67 questions, 70 minutes
- Sentence completion
- Passage-based reading

Mathematics
- 54 questions, 70 minutes
- Multiple-choice
- Student-produced response (grid-ins)

Writing

- 49 questions plus essay, 60 minutes
- Identifying sentence errors
- Improving paragraphs
- Improving sentences
- Essay

Students receive one point for each correct response and lose a fraction of a point for each incorrect response (except for student-produced responses). These points are totaled to produce the raw scores, which are then scaled to equalize the scores for slight variations in difficulty for various editions of the test. The critical reading, writing, and mathematics scaled scores range from 200–800 per section. The total scaled score range is from 600–2400.

Changes to the SAT

The SAT is changing in 2016! According to the College Board, the new exam will have these sections: Evidence-Based Reading and Writing, Math, and the Essay. It will be based on 1600 points—the top scores for the Math section and the Evidence-Based Reading and Writing section will be 800, and the Essay score will be reported separately.

According to the College Board's website, the "Eight Key Changes" are the following:

- **Relevant Words in Context:** Students will need to interpret the meaning of words based on the context of the passage in which they appear. The focus will be on "relevant" words—not obscure ones.
- **Command of Evidence:** In addition to demonstrating writing skills, students will need to show that they're able to interpret, synthesize, and use evidence found in a wide range of sources.
- **Essay Analyzing a Source:** Students will read a passage and explain how the author builds an argument, supporting support their claims with actual data from the passage.
- **Math Focused on Three Key Areas:** Problem Solving and Data Analysis (using ratios, percentages, and proportional reasoning to solve problems in science, social science, and career contexts), the Heart of Algebra (mastery of linear equations and systems), and Passport to Advanced Math (more complex equations and the manipulation they require).
- **Problems Grounded in Real-World Contexts:** All of the questions will be grounded in the real world, directly related to work performed in college.
- **Analysis in Science and in Social Studies:** Students will need to apply reading, writing, language, and math skills to answer questions in contexts of science, history, and social studies.
- **Founding Documents and Great Global Conversation:** Students will find an excerpt from one of the Founding Documents—such as the Declaration of Independence, the Constitution, and the Bill of Rights—or a text from the "Great Global Conversation" about freedom, justice, and human dignity.

- **No Penalty for Wrong Answers:** Students will earn points for the questions they answer correctly.

If you'll be taking the test after March 2016, you should check out the College Board's website at https://www.collegeboard.org/delivering-opportunity/sat/redesign for the most up-to-date information.

Top 10 Ways Not to Take the Test
10. Cramming the night before the test.
9. Not becoming familiar with the directions before you take the test.
8. Not becoming familiar with the format of the test before you take it.
7. Not knowing how the test is graded.
6. Spending too much time on any one question.
5. Second-guessing yourself.
4. Not checking spelling, grammar, and sentence structure in essays.
3. Writing a one-paragraph essay.
2. Forgetting to take a deep breath to keep from—
1. Losing It!

SAT SUBJECT TESTS

Subject Tests are required by some institutions for admission and/or placement in freshman-level courses. Each Subject Test measures one's knowledge of a specific subject and the ability to apply that knowledge. Students should check with each institution for its specific requirements. In general, students are required to take three Subject Tests (one English, one mathematics, and one of their choice).

Subject Tests are given in the following areas: biology, chemistry, Chinese, French, German, Italian, Japanese, Korean, Latin, literature, mathematics, modern Hebrew, physics, Spanish, U.S. history, and world history. These tests are 1 hour long and are primarily multiple-choice tests. Three Subject Tests may be taken on one test date.

Scored like the SAT, students gain a point for each correct answer and lose a fraction of a point for each incorrect answer. The raw scores are then converted to scaled scores that range from 200 to 800.

THE TOEFL INTERNET-BASED TEST (IBT)

The Test of English as a Foreign Language Internet-Based Test (TOEFL iBT) is designed to help assess a student's grasp of English if it is not the student's first language. Performance on the TOEFL test may help interpret scores on the critical reading sections of the SAT. The test consists of four integrated sections: speaking, listening, reading, and writing. The TOEFL iBT emphasizes integrated skills. The paper-based versions of the TOEFL will continue to be administered in certain countries where the Internet-based version has not yet been introduced. For further information, visit www.toefl.org.

WHAT OTHER TESTS SHOULD I KNOW ABOUT?

The AP Program

This program allows high school students to try college-level work and build valuable skills and study habits in the process. Subject matter is explored in more depth in AP courses than in other high school classes. A qualifying score on an AP test— which varies from school to school—can earn you college credit or advanced placement. Getting qualifying grades on enough exams can even earn you a full year's credit and sophomore standing at more than 1,500 higher-education institutions. There are more than thirty AP courses across multiple subject areas, including art history, biology, and computer science. Speak to your guidance counselor for information about your school's offerings.

College-Level Examination Program (CLEP)

The CLEP enables students to earn college credit for what they already know, whether it was learned in school, through independent study, or through other experiences outside of the classroom. More than 2,900 colleges and universities now award credit for qualifying scores on one or more of the 33 CLEP exams. The exams, which are 90 minutes in length and are primarily multiple choice, are administered at participating colleges and universities. For more information, check out the website at www.collegeboard.com/clep.

WHAT CAN I DO TO PREPARE FOR THESE TESTS?

Know what to expect. Get familiar with how the tests are structured, how much time is allowed, and the directions for each type of question. Get plenty of rest the night before the test and eat breakfast that morning.

There are a variety of products, from books to software to videos, available to help you prepare for most standardized tests. Find the learning style that suits you best. As for which products to buy, there are two major categories— those created by the test-makers and those created by private companies. The best approach is to talk to someone who has been through the process and find out which product or products he or she recommends.

Some students report significant increases in scores after participating in coaching programs. Longer-term programs (40 hours) seem to raise scores more than short-term programs (20 hours), but beyond 40 hours, score gains are minor. Math scores appear to benefit more from coaching than critical reading scores.

Resources

There is a variety of ways to prepare for standardized tests— find a method that fits your schedule and your budget. But you should definitely prepare. Far too many students walk into these tests cold, either because they find standardized tests frightening or annoying or they just haven't found the time to study. The key is that these exams are standardized. That means these tests are largely the same from administration to administration; they always test the same concepts. They have to, or else you couldn't compare the scores of people who took the tests on different dates. The numbers or words may change, but the underlying content doesn't.

So how do you prepare? At the very least, you should review relevant material, such as math formulas and commonly used vocabulary words, and know the directions for each question type or test section. You should take at least one practice test and review your mistakes so you don't make them again on the test day. Beyond that, you know best how much preparation you need. You'll also find lots of material in libraries or bookstores to help you: books and software from the test- makers and from other publishers (including Peterson's) or live courses that range from national test-preparation companies to teachers at your high school who offer classes.

Who's Paying for This?
Financial Aid Basics

A college education can be expensive—costing more than $150,000 for four years at some of the higher priced private colleges and universities. Even at the lower-cost state colleges and universities, the cost of a four-year education can approach $60,000. Determining how you and your family will come up with the necessary funds to pay for your education requires planning, perseverance, and learning as much as you can about the options that are available to you. But before you get discouraged, College Board statistics show that 53 percent of full-time students attend four-year public and private colleges with tuition and fees less than $9000, while 20 percent attend colleges that have tuition and fees more than $36,000. College costs tend to be less in the western states and higher in New England.

Paying for college should not be looked at as a four-year financial commitment. For many families, paying the total cost of a student's college education out of current income and savings is usually not realistic. For families that have planned ahead and have financial savings established for higher education, the burden is a lot easier. But for most, meeting the cost of college requires the pooling of current income and assets and investing in longer-term loan options. These family resources, together with financial assistance from state, federal, and institutional sources, enable millions of students each year to attend the institution of their choice.

FINANCIAL AID PROGRAMS

There are three types of financial aid:

1. Gift-aid—Scholarships and grants are funds that do not have to be repaid.

2. Loans—Loans must be repaid, usually after graduation; the amount you have to pay back is the total you've borrowed plus any accrued interest. This is considered a source of self-help aid.

3. Student employment—Student employment is a job arranged for you by the financial aid office. This is another source of self-help aid.

The federal government has four major grant programs—the Federal Pell Grant, the Federal Supplemental Educational Opportunity Grant, Academic Competitiveness Grants (ACG), and SMART grants. ACG and SMART grants are limited to students who qualify for a Pell grant and are awarded to a select group of students. Overall, these grants are targeted to low-to-moderate income families with significant financial need. The federal government also sponsors a student employment program called the Federal Work-Study Program, which offers jobs both on and off campus, and

several loan programs, including those for students and for parents of undergraduate students.

There are two types of student loan programs: subsidized and unsubsidized. The subsidized Federal Direct Loan and the Federal Perkins Loan are need-based, government-subsidized loans. Students who borrow through these programs do not have to pay interest on the loan until after they graduate or leave school. The unsubsidized Federal Direct Loan and the Federal Direct PLUS Loan Program are not based on need, and borrowers are responsible for the interest while the student is in school. These loans are administered by different methods. Once you choose your college, the financial aid office will guide you through this process.

After you've submitted your financial aid application and you've been accepted for admission, each college will send you a letter describing your financial aid award. Most award letters show estimated college costs, how much you and your family are expected to contribute, and the amount and types of aid you have been awarded. Most students are awarded aid from a combination of sources and programs. Hence, your award is often called a financial aid "package."

SOURCES OF FINANCIAL AID

Millions of students and families apply for financial aid each year. Financial aid from all sources exceeds $143 billion per year. The largest single source of aid is the federal government, which will award more than $100 billion this year.

The next largest source of financial aid is found in the college and university community. Most of this aid is awarded to students who have a demonstrated need based on the Federal Methodology. Some institutions use a different formula, the Institutional Methodology (IM), to award their own funds in conjunction with other forms of aid. Institutional aid may be either need-based or non-need based. Aid that is not based on need is usually awarded for a student's academic performance (merit awards), specific talents or abilities, or to attract the type of students a college seeks to enroll.

Another source of financial aid is from state government. All states offer grant and/or scholarship aid, most of which is need-based. However, more and more states are offering substantial merit-based aid programs. Most state programs award aid only to students attending college in their home state.

Other sources of financial aid include:

- Private agencies
- Foundations
- Corporations
- Clubs
- Fraternal and service organizations

- Civic associations
- Unions
- Religious groups that award grants, scholarships, and low-interest loans
- Employers that provide tuition reimbursement benefits for employees and their children

More information about these different sources of aid is available from high school guidance offices, public libraries, college financial aid offices, directly from the sponsoring organizations, and online at www.petersons.com/college-search/scholarship-search.aspx.

HOW NEED-BASED FINANCIAL AID IS AWARDED

When you apply for aid, your family's financial situation is analyzed using a government-approved formula called the Federal Methodology. This formula looks at five items:

1. Demographic information of the family
2. Income of the parents
3. Assets of the parents
4. Income of the student
5. Assets of the student

This analysis determines the amount you and your family are expected to contribute toward your college expenses, called your Expected Family Contribution, or EFC. If the EFC is equal to or more than the cost of attendance at a particular college, then you do not demonstrate financial need. However, even if you don't have financial need, you may still qualify for aid, as there are grants, scholarships, and loan programs that are not need-based.

If the cost of your education is greater than your EFC, then you do demonstrate financial need and qualify for assistance. The amount of your financial need that can be met varies from school to school. Some are able to meet your full need, while others can only cover a certain percentage of need. Here's the formula:

Cost of Attendance
− Expected Family Contribution
= Financial Need

The EFC remains constant, but your need will vary according to the costs of attendance at a particular college. In general, the higher the tuition and fees at a particular college, the higher the cost of attendance will be. Expenses for books and supplies, room and board, transportation, and other miscellaneous items are included in the overall cost of attendance. It is important to remember that you do not have to be "needy" to qualify for financial aid. Many middle and upper-middle income families qualify for need-based financial aid.

APPLYING FOR FINANCIAL AID

Every student must complete the Free Application for Federal Student Aid (FAFSA) to be considered for financial aid. The FAFSA is available from your high school guidance office,

many public libraries, colleges in your area, or directly from the U.S. Department of Education.

Students are encouraged to apply for federal student aid on the Web. The electronic version of the FAFSA can be accessed at http://www.fafsa.ed.gov. Both the student and at least one parent must apply for a federal PIN at http://www.pin.ed.gov. The PIN serves as your electronic signature when applying for aid on the Web.

To award their own funds, some colleges require an additional application, the CSS/Financial Aid PROFILE® form. The PROFILE asks supplemental questions that some colleges and awarding agencies feel provide a more accurate assessment of the family's ability to pay for college. It is up to the college to decide whether it will use only the FAFSA or both the FAFSA and the PROFILE. PROFILE applications are available from the high school guidance office and on the Web. Both the paper application and the website list those colleges and programs that require the PROFILE application.

If Every College You're Applying to for Fall 2015 Requires the FAFSA

. . . then it's pretty simple: Complete the FAFSA after January 1, 2015, being certain to send it in before any college-imposed deadlines. (You are not permitted to send in the 2015–16 FAFSA before January 1, 2015.) Most college FAFSA application deadlines are in February or early March. It is easier if you have all your financial records for the previous year available, but if that is not possible, you are strongly encouraged to use estimated figures.

After you send in your FAFSA, either with the paper application or electronically, you'll receive a Student Aid Report (SAR) that includes all of the information you reported and shows your EFC. If you provided an e-mail address, the SAR is sent to you electronically; otherwise, you will receive a paper copy in the mail. Be sure to review the SAR, checking to see if the information you reported is accurately represented. If you used estimated numbers to complete the FAFSA, you may have to resubmit the SAR with any corrections to the data. The college(s) you have designated on the FAFSA will receive the information you reported and will use that data to make their decision. In many instances, the colleges to which you've applied will ask you to send copies of your and your parents' federal income tax returns for 2014, plus any other documents needed to verify the information you reported.

If a College Requires the PROFILE

Step 1: Register for the CSS/Financial Aid PROFILE in the fall of your senior year in high school. You can apply for the PROFILE online at http://profileonline.collegeboard.com/prf/index.jsp. Registration information with a list of the colleges that require the PROFILE is available in most high school guidance offices. There is a fee for using the Financial Aid PROFILE application ($25 for the first college, which includes the $9 application fee, and $16 for each additional college). You must pay for the service by credit card when you register. If you do not have a credit card, you will be billed. A limited number of fee waivers are automatically granted to first-time applicants based on the financial information provided on the PROFILE.

Step 2: Fill out your customized CSS/Financial Aid PROFILE. Once you register, your application will be immediately available online and will have questions that all students must complete, questions which must be completed by the student's parents (unless the student is independent and the colleges or programs selected do not require parental information), and *may* have supplemental questions needed by one or more of your schools or programs. If required, those will be found in Section Q of the application.

In addition to the PROFILE application you complete online, you may also be required to complete a Business/ Farm Supplement via traditional paper format. Completion of this form is not a part of the online process. If this form is required, instructions on how to download and print the supplemental form are provided. If your biological or adoptive parents are separated or divorced and your colleges and programs require it, your noncustodial parent may be asked to complete the Noncustodial PROFILE.

Once you complete and submit your PROFILE application, it will be processed and sent directly to your requested colleges and programs.

IF YOU DON'T QUALIFY FOR NEED-BASED AID

If you are not eligible for need-based aid, you can still find ways to lessen your burden.

Here are some suggestions:

- Search for merit scholarships. You can start at the initial stages of your application process. College merit awards are increasingly important as more and more colleges award these to students they especially want to attract. As a result, applying to a college at which your qualifications put you at the top of the entering class may give you a larger merit award. Another source of aid to look for is private scholarships that are given for special skills and talents. Additional information can be found at www.finaid.org.

- Seek employment during the summer and the academic year. The student employment office at your college can help you locate a school-year job. Many colleges and local businesses have vacancies remaining after they have hired students who are receiving Federal Work-Study Program financial aid.

- Borrow through the unsubsidized Federal Direct Loan program. This is generally available to all students. The terms and conditions are similar to the subsidized loans. The biggest difference is that the borrower is responsible for the interest while still in college, although the government permits students to delay paying the interest right away and add the accrued interest to the total amount owed. You must file the FAFSA to be considered.

- After you've secured what you can through scholarships, working, and borrowing, you and your parents will be expected to meet your share of the college bill (the Expected Family Contribution). Many colleges offer monthly payment plans that spread the cost over the academic year. If the monthly payments are too high, parents can borrow through the Federal Direct PLUS Loan Program, through one of the many private education loan programs available, or through home equity loans and lines of credit. Families seeking assistance in financing college expenses should inquire at the financial aid office about what programs are available at the college. Some families seek the advice of professional financial advisers and tax consultants.

Frequently Asked Questions About Transferring

Muriel M. Shishkoff

Among the students attending two-year colleges are a large number who began their higher education knowing they would eventually transfer to a four-year school to obtain their bachelor's degree. There are many reasons why students go this route. Upon graduating from high school, some simply do not have definite career goals. Although they don't want to put their education on hold, they prefer not to pay exorbitant amounts in tuition while trying to "find themselves." As the cost of a university education escalates—even in public institutions—the option of spending the freshman and sophomore years at a two-year college looks attractive to many students. Others attend a two-year college because they are unable to meet the initial entrance standards—a specified grade point average (GPA), standardized test scores, or knowledge of specific academic subjects—required by the four-year school of their choice. Many such students praise the community college system for giving them the chance to be, academically speaking, "born again." In addition, students from other countries often find that they can adapt more easily to language and cultural changes at a two-year school before transferring to a larger, more diverse four-year college.

If your plan is to attend a two-year college with the ultimate goal of transferring to a four-year school, you will be pleased to know that the increased importance of the community college route to a bachelor's degree is recognized by all segments of higher education. As a result, many two-year schools have revised their course outlines and established new courses in order to comply with the programs and curricular offerings of the universities. Institutional improvements to make transferring easier have also proliferated at both the two-and four-year levels. The generous transfer policies of the Pennsylvania, New York, and Florida state university systems, among others, reflect this attitude; these systems accept all credits from students who have graduated from accredited community colleges.

If you are interested in moving from a two-year college to a four-year school, the sooner you make up your mind that you are going to make the switch, the better position you will be to transfer successfully (that is, without having wasted valuable time and credits). The ideal point at which to make such a decision is **before** you register for classes at your two-year school; a counselor can help you plan your course work with an eye toward fulfilling the requirements needed for your major course of study.

Naturally, it is not always possible to plan your transferring strategy that far in advance, but keep in mind that the key to a successful transfer is **preparation,** and preparation takes time—time to think through your objectives and time to plan the right classes to take.

As students face the prospect of transferring from a two-year to a four-year school, many thoughts and concerns about this complicated and often frustrating process race through their minds. Here are answers to the questions that are most frequently asked by transferring students.

Q Does every college and university accept transfer students?

A Most four-year institutions accept transfer students, but some do so more enthusiastically than others. Graduating from a community college is an advantage at, for example, Arizona State University and the University of Massachusetts Boston; both accept more community college transfer students than traditional freshmen. At the State University of New York at Albany, graduates of two-year transfer programs within the State University of New York System are given priority for upper-division (i.e., junior- and senior-level) vacancies.

Schools offering undergraduate work at the upper division only are especially receptive to transfer applications. On the other hand, some schools accept only a few transfer students; others refuse entrance to sophomores or those in their final year. Princeton University requires an "excellent academic record and particularly compelling reasons to transfer." Check the catalogs of several colleges for their transfer requirements before you make your final choice.

Q Do students who go directly from high school to a four-year college do better academically than transfer students from community colleges?

A On the contrary: some institutions report that transfers from two-year schools who persevere until graduation do *better* than those who started as freshmen in a four-year college.

Q Why is it so important that my two-year college be accredited?

A Four-year colleges and universities accept transfer credits only from schools formally recognized by a regional, national, or professional educational agency. This accreditation signifies that an institution or program of study meets or exceeds a minimum level of educational quality necessary for meeting stated educational objectives.

Q After enrolling at a four-year school, may I still make up necessary courses at a community college?

A Some institutions restrict credit after transfer to their own facilities. Others allow students to take a limited number of transfer courses after matriculation, depending on the subject matter. A few provide opportunities for cross-registration or dual enrollment, which means taking classes on more than one campus.

Q What do I need to do to transfer?

A First, send for your high school and college transcripts. Having chosen the school you wish to transfer to, check its admission requirements against your transcripts. If you find that you are admissible, file an application as early as possible before the deadline. Part of the process will be asking your former schools to send official transcripts to the admission office, i.e., not the copies you used in determining your admissibility.

Plan your transfer program with the head of your new department as soon as you have decided to transfer. Determine the recommended general education pattern and necessary preparation for your major. At your present school, take the courses you will need to meet transfer requirements for the new school.

Q What qualifies me for admission as a transfer student?

A Admission requirements for most four-year institutions vary. Depending on the reputation or popularity of the school and program you wish to enter, requirements may be quite selective and competitive. Usually, you will need to show satisfactory test scores, an academic record up to a certain standard, and completion of specific subject matter.

Transfer students can be eligible to enter a four-year school in a number of ways: by having been eligible for admission directly upon graduation from high school, by making up shortcomings in grades (or in subject matter not covered in high school) at a community college, or by satisfactory completion of necessary courses or credit hours at another postsecondary institution. Ordinarily, students coming from a community college or from another four-year institution must meet or exceed the receiving institution's standards for freshmen and show appropriate college-level course work taken since high school. Students who did not graduate from high school can present proof of proficiency through results on the General Educational Development (GED) test.

Q Are exceptions ever made for students who don't meet all the requirements for transfer?

A Extenuating circumstances, such as disability, low family income, refugee or veteran status, or athletic talent, may permit the special enrollment of students who would not otherwise be eligible but who demonstrate the potential for academic success. Consult the appropriate office—the Educational Opportunity Program, the disabled students' office, the athletic department, or the academic dean—to see whether an exception can be made in your case.

Q How far in advance do I need to apply for transfer?

A Some schools have a rolling admission policy, which means that they process transfer applications as they are received, all year long. With other schools, you must apply during the priority filing period, which can be up to a year before you wish to enter. Check the date with the admission office at your prospective campus.

Q Is it possible to transfer courses from several different institutions?

A Institutions ordinarily accept the courses that they consider transferable, regardless of the number of accredited schools involved. However, there is the danger of exceeding the maximum number of credit hours that can be transferred from all other schools or earned through credit by examination, extension courses, or correspondence courses. The limit placed on transfer credits varies from school to school, so read the catalog carefully to avoid taking courses you won't be able to use. To avoid duplicating courses, keep attendance at different campuses to a minimum.

Q What is involved in transferring from a semester system to a quarter or trimester system?

A In the semester system, the academic calendar is divided into two equal parts. The quarter system is more aptly named trimester, since the academic calendar is divided into three equal terms (not counting a summer session). To convert semester units into quarter units or credit hours, simply multiply the semester units by one and a half. Conversely, multiply quarter units by two thirds to come up with semester units. If you are used to a semester system of fifteen- to sixteen-week courses, the ten-week courses of the quarter system may seem to fly by.

Q Why might a course be approved for transfer credit by one four-year school but not by another?

A The beauty of postsecondary education in the United States lies in its variety. Entrance policies and graduation requirements are designed to reflect and serve each institution's mission. Because institutional policies vary so widely, schools may interpret the subject matter of a course from quite different points of view. Given that the granting of transfer credit indicates that a course is viewed as being, in effect, parallel to one offered by the receiving institution, it is easy to see how this might be the case at one university and not another.

Q Must I take a foreign language to transfer?

A Foreign language proficiency is often required for admission to a four-year institution; such proficiency also often figures in certain majors or in the general education pattern. Often, two or three years of a single language in high school will do the trick. Find out if scores received on Advanced Placement (AP) examinations, placement examinations given by the foreign language department, or SAT Subject Tests will be accepted in lieu of college course work.

Q Will the school to which I'm transferring accept pass/no pass, pass/fail, or credit/no credit grades in lieu of letter grades?

A Usually, a limit is placed on the number of these courses you can transfer, and there may be other restrictions as well. If you want to use other-than-letter grades for the fulfillment of general education requirements or lower-division (freshman and sophomore) preparation for the major, check with the receiving institution.

Q Which is more important for transfer—my grade point average or my course completion pattern?

A Some schools believe that your past grades indicate academic potential and overshadow prior preparation for a specific degree program. Others require completion of certain introductory courses before transfer to prepare you for upper-division work in your major. In any case, appropriate course selection will cut down the time to graduation and increase your chances of making a successful transfer.

Q What happens to my credits if I change majors?

A If you change majors after admission, your transferable course credit should remain fairly intact. However, because you may need extra or different preparation for your new major, some of the courses you've taken may now be useful only as electives. The need for additional lower-level preparation may mean you're staying longer at your new school than you originally planned. On the other hand, you may already have taken courses that count toward your new major as part of the university's general education pattern.

Excerpted from *Transferring Made Easy: A Guide to Changing Colleges Successfully,* by Muriel M. Shishkoff, © 1991 by Muriel M. Shishkoff (published by Peterson's).

Returning to School: Advice for Adult Students

Sandra Cook, Ph.D.
Associate Vice President for Enrollment Management,
San Diego State University

Many adults think for a long time about returning to school without taking any action. One purpose of this article is to help the "thinkers" finally make some decisions by examining what is keeping them from action. Another purpose is to describe not only some of the difficulties and obstacles that adult students may face when returning to school but also tactics for coping with them.

If you have been thinking about going back to college, and believing that you are the only person your age contemplating college, you should know that approximately 7 million adult students are currently enrolled in higher education institutions. This number represents 50 percent of total higher education enrollments. The majority of adult students are enrolled at two-year colleges.

There are many reasons why adult students choose to attend a two-year college. Studies have shown that the three most important criteria that adult students consider when choosing a college are location, cost, and availability of the major or program desired. Most two-year colleges are public institutions that serve a geographic district, making them readily accessible to the community. Costs at most two-year colleges are far less than at other types of higher education institutions. For many students who plan to pursue a bachelor's degree, completing their first two years of college at a community college is an affordable means to that end. If you are interested in an academic program that will transfer to a four-year institution, most two-year colleges offer the "general education" courses that compose most freshman and sophomore years. If you are interested in a vocational or technical program, two-year colleges excel in providing this type of training.

SETTING THE STAGE

There are three different "stages" in the process of adults returning to school. The first stage is uncertainty. Do I really want to go back to school? What will my friends or family think? Can I compete with those 18-year-old whiz kids? Am I too old? The second stage is choice. Once the decision to return has been made, you must choose where you will attend. There are many criteria to use in making this decision. The third stage is support. You have just added another role to your already-too-busy life. There are, however, strategies that will help you accomplish your goals—perhaps not without struggle, but with grace and humor nonetheless. Let's look at each of these stages.

UNCERTAINTY

Why are you thinking about returning to school? Is it to

- fulfill a dream that had to be delayed?
- become more educationally well-rounded?
- fill an intellectual void in your life?

These reasons focus on personal growth.

If you are returning to school to

- meet people and make friends
- attain and enjoy higher social status and prestige among friends, relatives, and associates
- understand/study a cultural heritage
- have a medium in which to exchange ideas

You are interested in social and cultural opportunities.

If you are like most adult students, you want to

- qualify for a new occupation
- enter or reenter the job market
- increase earnings potential
- qualify for a more challenging position in the same field of work

You are seeking career growth.

Understanding the reasons why you want to go back to school is an important step in setting your educational goals and will help you to establish some criteria for selecting a college. However, don't delay your decision because you have not been able to clearly define your motives. Many times, these aren't clear until you have already begun the process, and they may change as you move through your college experience.

Assuming you agree that additional education will benefit you, what is it that keeps you from returning to school? You may have a litany of excuses running through your mind:

- I don't have time.
- I can't afford it.
- I'm too old to learn.
- My friends will think I'm crazy.

- I'll be older than the teachers and other students.
- My family can't survive without me to take care of them every minute.
- I'll be X years old when I finish.
- I'm afraid.
- I don't know what to expect.

And that is just what these are—excuses. You can make school, like anything else in your life, a priority or not. If you really want to return, you can. The more you understand your motivation for returning to school and the more you understand what excuses are keeping you from taking action, the easier your task will be.

If you think you don't have time: The best way to decide how attending class and studying can fit into your schedule is to keep track of what you do with your time each day for several weeks. Completing a standard time-management grid (each day is plotted out by the half hour) is helpful for visualizing how your time is spent. For each 3-credit-hour class you take, you will need to find 3 hours for class plus 6 to 9 hours for reading-studying-library time. This study time should be spaced evenly throughout the week, not loaded up on one day. It is not possible to learn or retain the material that way. When you examine your grid, see where there are activities that could be replaced with school and study time. You may decide to give up your bowling league or some time in front of the TV. Try not to give up sleeping, and don't cut out every moment of free time. Here are some suggestions that have come from adults who have returned to school:

- Enroll in a time-management workshop. It helps you rethink how you use your time.
- Don't think you have to take more than one course at a time. You may eventually want to work up to taking more, but consider starting with one. (It is more than you are taking now!)
- If you have a family, start assigning to them those household chores that you usually do—and don't redo what they do.
- Use your lunch hour or commuting time for reading.

If you think you cannot afford it: As mentioned earlier, two-year colleges are extremely affordable. If you cannot afford the tuition, look into the various financial aid options. Most federal and state funds are available to full- and part-time students. Loans are also available. While many people prefer not to accumulate a debt for school, these same people will think nothing of taking out a loan to buy a car. After five or six years, which is the better investment? Adult students who work should look into whether their company has a tuition-reimbursement policy. There are also private scholarships, available through foundations, service organizations, and clubs, that are focused on adult learners. Your public library, the Web, and a college financial aid adviser are three excellent sources for reference materials regarding financial aid.

If you think you are too old to learn: This is pure myth. A number of studies have shown that adult learners perform as well as, or better than, traditional-age students.

If you are afraid your friends will think you're crazy: Who cares? Maybe they will, maybe they won't. Usually, they will admire your courage and be just a little jealous of your ambition (although they'll never tell you that). Follow your dreams, not theirs.

If you are concerned because the teachers or students will be younger than you: Don't be. The age differences that may be apparent in other settings evaporate in the classroom. If anything, an adult in the classroom strikes fear into the hearts of some 18-year-olds because adults have been known to be prepared, ask questions, be truly motivated, and be there to learn!

If you think your family will have a difficult time surviving while you are in school: If you have done everything for them up to now, they might struggle. Consider this an opportunity to help them become independent and self-sufficient. Your family can only make you feel guilty if you let them. You are not abandoning them; you are becoming an educational role model. When you are happy and working toward your goals, everyone benefits. Admittedly, it sometimes takes time for them to realize this. For single parents, there are schools that offer support groups, child care, and cooperative babysitting.

If you're appalled at the thought of being X years old when you graduate in Y years: How old will you be in Y years if you don't go back to school?

If you are afraid or don't know what to expect: Know that these are natural feelings when one encounters any new situation. Adult students find that their fears usually dissipate once they begin classes. Fear of trying is usually the biggest roadblock to the reentry process.

No doubt you have dreamed up a few more reasons for not making the decision to return to school. Keep in mind that what you are doing is making up excuses, and you are using these excuses to release you from the obligation to make a decision about your life. The thought of returning to college can be scary. Anytime anyone ventures into unknown territory, there is a risk, but taking risks is a necessary component of personal and professional growth. It is your life, and you alone are responsible for making the decisions that determine its course. Education is an investment in your future.

CHOICE

Once you have decided to go back to school, your next task is to decide where to go. If your educational goals are well defined (e.g., you want to pursue a degree in order to change careers), then your task is a bit easier. But even if your educational goals are still evolving, do not defer your return. Many students who enter higher education with a specific major in mind change that major at least once.

Most students who attend a public two-year college choose the community college in the district in which they live. This is generally the closest and least expensive option if the school offers the programs you want. If you are planning to begin your education at a two-year college and then transfer to a four-year school, there are distinct advantages to choosing your four-year school early. Many community and four-year colleges have "articulation" agreements that designate what credits from the two-year school will transfer to the four-year college and how. Some four-year institutions accept an associate degree as equivalent to the freshman and sophomore years, regardless of the courses you have taken. Some four-year schools accept two-year college work only on a course-by-course basis. If you can identify which school you will transfer to, you can know in advance exactly how your two-year credits will apply, preventing an unexpected loss of credit or time.

Each institution of higher education is distinctive. Your goal in choosing a college is to come up with the best student-institution fit—matching your needs with the offerings and characteristics of the school. The first step in choosing a college is to determine what criteria are most important to you in attaining your educational goals. Location, cost, and program availability are the three main factors that influence an adult student's college choice. In considering location, don't forget that some colleges have conveniently located branch campuses. In considering cost, remember to explore your financial aid options before ruling out an institution because of its tuition. Program availability should include not only the major in which you are interested, but also whether or not classes in that major are available when you can take them.

Some additional considerations beyond location, cost, and programs are:

- Does the school have a commitment to adult students and offer appropriate services, such as child care, tutoring, and advising?
- Are classes offered at times when you can take them?
- Are there academic options for adults, such as credit for life or work experience, credit by examination (including CLEP), credit for military service, or accelerated programs?
- Is the faculty sensitive to the needs of adult learners?

Once you determine which criteria are vital in your choice of an institution, you can begin to narrow your choices. There are myriad ways for you to locate the information you desire. Many newspapers publish a "School Guide" several times a year in which colleges and universities advertise to an adult student market. In addition, schools themselves publish catalogs, class schedules, and promotional materials that contain much of the information you need, and they are yours for the asking. Many colleges sponsor information sessions and open houses that allow you to visit the campus and ask questions. An appointment with an adviser is a good way to assess the fit between you and the institution. Be sure to bring your questions with you to your interview.

SUPPORT

Once you have made the decision to return to school and have chosen the institution that best meets your needs, take some additional steps to ensure your success during your crucial first semester. Take advantage of institutional support and build some social support systems of your own. Here are some ways of doing just that:

- Plan to participate in any orientation programs. These serve the threefold purpose of providing you with a great deal of important information, familiarizing you with the campus and its facilities, and giving you the opportunity to meet and begin networking with other students.
- Take steps to deal with any academic weaknesses. Take mathematics and writing placement tests if you have reason to believe you may need some extra help in these areas. It is not uncommon for adult students to need a math refresher course or a program to help alleviate math anxiety. Ignoring a weakness won't make it go away.
- Look into adult reentry programs. Many institutions offer adults workshops focusing on ways to improve study skills, textbook reading, test-taking, and time-management skills.
- Build new support networks by joining an adult student organization, making a point of meeting other adult students through workshops, or actively seeking out a "study buddy" in each class—that invaluable friend who shares and understands your experience.
- Incorporate your new status as "student" into your family life. Doing your homework with your children at a designated "homework time" is a valuable family activity and reinforces the importance of education.
- Make sure you take a reasonable course load in your first semester. It is far better to have some extra time on your hands and to succeed magnificently than to spend the entire semester on the brink of a breakdown. Also, whenever possible, try to focus your first courses not only on requirements, but also on areas of personal interest.
- Faculty members, advisers, and student affairs personnel are there to help you during difficult times—let them assist you as often as necessary.

After completing your first semester, you will probably look back in wonder at why you thought going back to school was so imposing. Certainly, it's not without its occasional exasperations. But, as with life, keeping things in perspective and maintaining your sense of humor make the difference between just coping and succeeding brilliantly.

What International Students Need to Know About Admission to U.S. Colleges and Universities

Kitty M. Villa

There are two principles to remember about admission to a university in the United States. First, applying is almost never a one-time request for admission but an ongoing process that may involve several exchanges of information between applicant and institution. "Admission process" or "application process" means that a "yes" or "no" is usually not immediate, and requests for additional information are to be expected. To successfully manage this process, you must be prepared to send additional information when requested and then wait for replies. You need a thoughtful balance of persistence to communicate regularly and effectively with your selected universities and patience to endure what can be a very long process.

The second principle involves a marketplace analogy. The most successful applicants are alert to opportunities to create a positive impression that sets them apart from other applicants. They are able to market themselves to their target institution. Institutions are also trying to attract the highest-quality student that they can. The admissions process presents you with the opportunity to analyze your strengths and weaknesses as a student and to look for ways to present yourself in the most marketable manner.

FIRST STEP—SELECTING INSTITUTIONS

With thousands of institutions of higher education in the United States, how do you begin to narrow your choices down to the institutions that are best for you? There are many factors to consider, and you must ultimately decide which factors are most important to you.

Location

You may spend several years studying in the United States. Do you prefer an urban or rural campus? Large or small metropolitan area? If you need to live on campus, will you be unhappy at a university where most students commute from off-campus housing? How do you feel about extremely hot summers or cold winters? Eliminating institutions that do not match your preferences in terms of location will narrow your choices.

Recommendations from Friends, Professors, or Others

There are valid academic reasons to consider the recommendations of people who know you well and have firsthand knowledge about particular institutions. Friends and contacts may be able to provide you with "inside information" about the campus or its academic programs to which published sources have no access. You should carefully balance anecdotal information with your own research and your own impressions. However, current and former students, professors, and others may provide excellent information during the application process.

Your Own Academic and Career Goals

Consideration of your academic goals is more complex than it may seem at first glance. All institutions do not offer the same academic programs. The application form usually provides a definitive listing of the academic programs offered by an institution. A course catalog describes the degree program and all the courses offered. In addition to printed sources, there is a tremendous amount of institutional information available on the Web. Program descriptions, even course descriptions and course syllabi, are often available to peruse online.

You may be interested in the rankings of either the university or of a program of study. Keep in mind, however, that rankings usually assume that quality is quantifiable. Rankings are usually based on presumptions about how data relate to quality and are likely to be unproven. It is important to carefully consider the source and the criteria of any ranking information before believing and acting upon it.

Your Own Educational Background

You may be concerned about the interpretation of your educational credentials, since your country's degree nomenclature and the grading scale may differ from those in the United States. Universities use reference books about the educational systems of other countries to help them understand specific educational credentials. Generally, these credentials are interpreted by each institution; there is not a single interpretation that applies to every institution. The lack of uniformity is good news for most students, since it means that students from a wide variety of educational backgrounds can find a U.S. university that is appropriate to their needs.

To choose an appropriate institution, you can and should do an informal self-evaluation of your educational background. This self-analysis involves three important questions:

1. How Many Years of Study Have You Completed?

Completion of secondary school with at least twelve total years of education usually qualifies students to apply for undergraduate (bachelor's) degree programs. Completion of a university degree program that involves at least sixteen years of total education qualifies one to apply for admission to graduate (master's) degree programs in the United States.

2. Does the Education That You Have Completed in Your Country Provide Access to Further Study in the United States?

Consider the kind of institution where you completed your previous studies. If educational opportunities in your country are limited, it may be necessary to investigate many U.S. institutions and programs in order to find a match.

3. Are Your Previous Marks or Grades Excellent, Average, or Poor?

Your educational record influences your choice of U.S. institutions. If your grades are average or poor, it may be advisable to apply to several institutions with minimally difficult or non-competitive entrance levels.

YOU are one of the best sources of information about the level and quality of your previous studies. Awareness of your educational assets and liabilities will serve you well throughout the application process.

SECOND STEP—PLANNING AND ASSEMBLING THE APPLICATION

Planning and assembling a university application can be compared to the construction of a building. First, you must start with a solid foundation, which is the application form itself. The application, often available online as well as in paper form, usually contains a wealth of useful information, such as deadlines, fees, and degree programs available at that institution. To build a solid application, it is best to begin well in advance of the application deadline.

How to Obtain the Application Form

Application forms and links to institutional Web sites may also be available at a U.S. educational advising center associated with the American Embassy or Consulate in your country. These centers are excellent resources for international students and provide information about standardized test administration, scholarships, and other matters to students who are interested in studying in the United States. Your local U.S. Embassy or Consulate can guide you to the nearest educational advising center.

What Are the Key Components of a Complete Application?

Institutional requirements vary, but the standard components of a complete application include the following:

- Transcript
- Required standardized examination scores
- Evidence of financial support
- Letters of recommendation
- Application fee

Transcript

A complete academic record or transcript includes all courses completed, grades earned, and degrees awarded. Most universities require an official transcript to be sent directly from the school or university. In many other countries, however, the practice is to issue official transcripts and degree certificates directly to the student. If you have only one official copy of your transcript, it may be a challenge to get additional certified copies that are acceptable to U.S. universities. Some institutions will issue additional official copies for application purposes.

If your institution does not provide this service, you may have to seek an alternate source of certification. As a last resort, you may send a photocopy of your official transcript, explain that you have only one original, and ask the university for advice on how to deal with this situation.

Required Standardized Examination Scores

Arranging to take standardized examinations and earning the required scores seem to cause the most anxiety for international students.

The university application form usually indicates which examinations are required. The standardized examination required most often for undergraduate admission is the Test of English as a Foreign Language (TOEFL). Institutions may also require the SAT of undergraduate applicants. These standardized examinations are administered by the Educational Testing Service (ETS).

These examinations are offered in almost every country of the world. It is advisable to begin planning for standardized examinations at least six months prior to the application deadline of your desired institutions. Test centers fill up quickly, so it is important to register as soon as possible. Information about the examinations is available at U.S. educational advising centers associated with embassies or consulates.

Most universities require that the original test scores, not a student copy, be sent directly by the testing service. When you register for the test, be sure to indicate that the testing service should send the test scores directly to the universities.

You should begin your application process before you receive your test scores. Delaying submission of your application until the test scores arrive may cause you to miss deadlines and negatively affect the outcome of your application. If you want to know your scores in order to assess your chances of admission to an institution with rigorous admission standards, you should take the tests early.

Many universities in the United States set minimum required scores on the TOEFL or other standardized examinations. Test scores are an important factor, but most institutions also look at a number of other factors in their consideration of a candidate for admission.

For More Information

Questions about test formats, locations, dates, and registration may be addressed to:

ETS Corporate Headquarters
Rosedale Road
Princeton, New Jersey 08541
Web sites: http://www.ets.org
          http://www.ets.org/toefl/
Phone: 609-921-9000
Fax: 609-734-5410

Evidence of Financial Support

Evidence of financial support is required to issue immigration documents to admitted students. This is part of a complete application package but usually plays no role in determining admission. Most institutions make admissions decisions without regard to the source and amount of financial support.

Letters of Recommendation

Most institutions require one or more letters of recommendation. The best letters are written by former professors, employers, or others who can comment on your academic achievements or professional potential.

Some universities provide a special form for the letters of recommendation. If possible, use the forms provided. If you are applying to a large number of universities, however, or if your recommenders are not available to complete several forms, it may be necessary for you to duplicate a general recommendation letter.

Application Fee

Most universities also require an application fee, ranging from $25 to $100, which must be paid to initiate consideration of the application.

Completing the Application Form

Whether sent by mail or electronically, the application form must be neat and thoroughly filled out. Although parts of the application may not seem to apply to you or your situation, do your best to answer all the questions.

Remember that this is a process. You provide information, and your proposed university then may request clarification and further information. If you have questions, it is better to initiate the entire process by submitting the application form rather than asking questions before you apply. The university will be better able to respond to you after it has your application. Always complete as much as you can. Do not permit uncertainty about the completion of the application form to cause unnecessary delays.

THIRD STEP—DISTINGUISH YOUR APPLICATION

To distinguish your application—to market yourself successfully—is ultimately the most important part of the application process. As you select your prospective universities, begin to analyze your strengths and weaknesses as a prospective student. As you complete your application, you should strive to create a positive impression and set yourself apart from other applicants, to highlight your assets and bring these qualities to the attention of the appropriate university administrators and professors. Applying early is a very easy way to distinguish your application.

Deadline or Guideline?

The application deadline is the last date that an application for a given semester will be accepted. Often, the application will specify that all required documents and information be submitted before the deadline date. To meet the deadlines, start the application process early. This also gives you more time to take—and perhaps retake and improve—the required standardized tests.

Admissions deliberations may take several weeks or months. In the meantime, most institutions accept additional information, including improved test scores, after the posted deadline.

Even if your application is initially rejected, you may be able to provide additional information to change the decision. You can request reconsideration based on additional information, such as improved test scores, strong letters of recommendation, or information about your class rank. Applying early allows more time to improve your application. Also, some students may decide not to accept their offers of admission, leaving room for offers to students on a waiting list. Reconsideration of the admission decisions can occur well beyond the application deadline.

Think of the deadline as a guideline rather than an impermeable barrier. Many factors—the strength of the application, your research interests, the number of spaces available at the proposed institution—can override the enforcement of an application deadline. So, if you lack a test score or transcript by the official deadline, you may still be able to apply and be accepted.

Statement of Purpose

The statement of purpose is your first and perhaps best opportunity to present yourself as an excellent candidate for admission. Whether or not a personal history essay or statement of purpose is required, always include a carefully written statement of purpose with your applications. A compelling statement of purpose does not have to be lengthy, but it should include some basic components:

- Part One—Introduce yourself and describe your educational background. This is your opportunity to describe any facet of your educational experience that you wish to emphasize. Perhaps you attended a highly ranked secondary school or university in your home country. Mention the name and any noteworthy characteristics of the secondary school or university from which you graduated. Explain the grading scale used at your university. Do not forget to mention your rank in your graduating class and any honors you may have received. This is not the time to be modest.

- Part Two—Describe your current academic and career interests and goals. Think about how these will fit into those of the institution to which you are applying, and mention the reasons why you have selected that institution.

- Part Three—Describe your long-term goals. When you finish your program of study, what do you plan to do next? If you already have a job offer or a career plan, describe it. Give some thought to how you'll demonstrate that studying in the United States will ultimately benefit others.

Use Personal Contacts When Possible

Appropriate and judicious use of your own network of contacts can be very helpful. Friends, former professors, former students of your selected institutions, and others may be willing to advise you during the application process and provide you with introductions to key administrators or professors. If suggested, you may wish to contact certain professors or administrators by mail, phone, or e-mail. A personal visit to discuss your interest in the institution may be appropriate. Whatever your choice of communication, try to make the encounter pleasant and personal. Your goal is to make a positive impression, not to rush the admission decision.

There is no single right way to be admitted to U.S. universities. The same characteristics that make the educational choice in the United States so difficult—the number of institutions and the variety of programs of study—are the same attributes that allow so many international students to find the institution that's right for them.

Kitty M. Villa is the former Assistant Director, International Office, at The University of Texas at Austin.

Community Colleges and the New Green Economy

Community colleges are a focal point for state and national efforts to create a green economy and workforce. As the United States transforms its economy into a "green" one, community colleges are leading the way—filling the need for both educated technicians whose skills can cross industry lines as well as those technicians who are able to learn new skills as technologies evolve.

Community colleges have been at the heart of the Obama administration's economic recovery strategy, with $12 billion allocated over this decade. President Obama has extolled community colleges as "the unsung heroes of America's education system," essential to our country's success in the "global competition to lead in the growth of industries of the twenty-first century." With the support of state governments, and, more importantly, local and international business partners, America's community colleges are rising to meet the demands of the new green economy. Community colleges are training individuals to work in fields such as renewable energy, energy efficiency, wind energy, green building, and sustainability. The programs are as diverse as the campuses housing them.

Here is a quick look at just some of the exciting "green" programs available at community colleges throughout the United States.

At Mesalands Community College in Tucumcari, New Mexico, the North American Wind Research and Training Center provides state-of-the-art facilities for research and training qualified technicians in wind energy technology to help meet the need for an estimated 170,000 new positions in the industry by 2030. The Center includes a facility for applied research in collaboration with Sandia National Laboratories—the first-ever such partnership between a national laboratory and a community college. It also provides associate degree training for wind energy technicians, meeting the fast-growing demand for "windsmiths" in the western part of the country—jobs that pay $45,000–$60,000 per year. For more information, visit http://www.mesalands.edu.

Cape Cod Community College (CCCC) in Massachusetts has become one of the nation's leading colleges in promoting and integrating sustainability and green practices throughout all campus operations and technical training programs. Ten years ago, Cape Wind Associates, Cape Cod's first wind farm, provided $50,000 to jumpstart CCCC's wind technician program—considered a state model for community-based clean energy workforce development and education. In addition, hundreds of CCCC students have earned associate degrees in environmental technology and environmental studies, as well as certificate programs in coastal zone management, environmental site assessment, solar thermal tech-

nology, and more. Visit http://www.capecod.edu/web/natsci/env/programs for more information.

At Oakland Community College in Michigan, more than 350 students are enrolled in the college's Renewable Energies and Sustainable Living program and its related courses. Students gain field experience refurbishing public buildings with renewable materials, performing energy audits for the government, and working with small businesses and hospitals to reduce waste and pollution. To learn more, visit http://www.oaklandcc.edu/est/.

In 2007, Columbia Gorge Community College in Oregon became the first community college in the Pacific Northwest to offer training programs for the windpower generation industry. The college offers a one-year certificate and a two-year Associate of Applied Science (A.A.S.) degree in renewable energy technology. The Renewable Energy Technology program was designed in collaboration with industry partners from the wind energy industry and the power generation industry. Students are prepared for employment in a broad range of industries, including hydro-generation, wind-generation, automated manufacturing, and engineering technology, and the College plans to add solar array technology to this list as well. For more information, visit http://www.cgcc.cc.or.us/Academics/WindTechnologyPage.cfm.

Central Carolina Community College (CCCC) in Pittsboro, North Carolina, has been leading the way in "green" programs for more than a decade. It offered a sustainable agriculture class at its Chatham campus in 1996 and soon became the first community college in the nation to offer an Associate in Applied Science degree in sustainable agriculture and the first in North Carolina to offer an associate degree in biofuels. In addition, it was the first North Carolina community college to offer a North American Board of Certified Energy Practitioners (NABCEP)–approved solar PV panel installation course as part of its green building/renewable energy program. In 2010, CCCC added an associate degree in sustainable technology and launched its new Natural Chef culinary arts program. The College also offers an ecotourism certificate as well as certificates in other green programs. For more information about Central Carolina Community College's green programs, visit http://www.cccc.edu/green.

The Green Jobs Academy at Bucks County Community College in Pennsylvania is an exciting new venture that includes a variety of academic and private industry partners that include Gamesa, Lockheed Martin, Dow, Veterans Green Jobs, and PECO, an Excelon Company. The Green Jobs Academy provides both long- and short-term training programs that are geared toward workers, who are looking for new skill sets in the green and sustainability industries. Courses include Hazardous Site Remediation & Preliminary Assessments, PV Solar Design, NABCEP (*North American Board of Certified Energy Practitioners*) PV Solar Entry Level Program (40 hours), Electric Vehicle Conversion Workshop, Wind Energy Apprentice, Certified Green Supply Chain Professional, Certified Indoor Air Quality Manager, a Veterans' Weatherization Training Program, and many others. For details, visit http://www.bucks.edu/academics/cwd/green/.

At Cascadia Community College in Bothell, Washington, thanks to a grant from Puget Sound Energy (PSE), students in the Energy Informatics class designed a kiosk screen that shows the energy usage and solar generation at the local 21 Acres Center for Local Food and Sustainable Living. The PSE grant supports the classroom materials for renewable energy education and the Web-based monitoring software that allows students and interested community members to track how much energy is being generated as the weather changes. For more information, visit http://www.cascadia.edu/Default.aspx.

At Grand Rapids Community College, the federally funded Pathways to Prosperity program has successfully prepared low-income residents for jobs in fields such as renewable energy. More than 200 people have completed the program, which began in 2010 thanks to a $4-million grant from the Department of Labor, and found jobs in industries ranging from energy-efficient building construction to alternative energy and sustainable manufacturing. For additional information, check out http://cms.grcc.edu/workforce-training/pathways-prosperity.

Established in 2008, the Green Institute at Heartland Community College in Normal, Illinois, supports a wide range of campus initiatives, educational programs, and community activities that are related to sustainability, energy conservation, renewable energy, recycling, retro-commissioning, and other environmental technologies. For more information, visit http://www.heartland.edu/greenInstitute/.

Most of California's 112 community colleges offer some type of green-tech classes. These include photovoltaic panel installation and repair, green construction practices, and biotechnology courses leading to careers in agriculture, medicine, and environmental forensics. For additional information, check out http://www.californiacommunitycolleges.cccco.edu/ProgramstoWatch/MoreProgramstoWatch/GreenTechnology.aspx.

Linn-Benton Community College (LBCC) in Albany, Oregon, is now offering training for the Oregon Green Technology Certificate. Oregon Green Tech is a federally funded program that is designed to prepare entry-level workers with foundational skills for a variety of industries associated with or in support of green jobs. Students learn skills in green occupations that include green energy production; manufacturing, construction, installation, monitoring, and repair of equipment for solar, wind, wave, and bio-energy; building retro-fitting; process recycling; hazardous materials removal work; and

more. LBCC is one of ten Oregon community colleges to provide training for the Green Technology Certificate, offered through the Oregon Consortium and Oregon Workforce Alliance. Visit http://www.linnbenton.edu for additional information.

The Santa Fe Community College Sustainable Technology Center in New Mexico offers several green jobs training programs along with various noncredit courses. It also provides credit programs from certificates in green building systems, environmental technology training, and solar energy training as well as an Associate in Applied Science (A.A.S.) degree in environmental technology. For more information, go online to http://www.sfcc.edu/sustainable_technologies_center.

In Colorado, Red Rocks Community College (RRCC) offers degree and certificate programs in renewable energy (solar photovoltaic, solar thermal, and wind energy technology), energy and industrial maintenance, energy operations and process technology, environmental technology, water quality management, and energy audit. RRCC has made a commitment to the national challenge of creating and sustaining a green workforce and instructs students about the issues of energy, environmental stewardship, and renewable resources across the college curriculum. For more information, visit http://www.rrcc.edu/green/.

At GateWay Community College in Phoenix, Arizona, graduates of the Environmental Science program now work for the U.S. Geological Survey (USGS), the Arizona Department of Environmental Quality (ADEQ), the Occupational Safety and Health Administration (OSHA), and municipalities across the state and region, as well as private consultants and environmental organizations. For additional information, check out http://www.gatewaycc.edu/environment.

Next you'll find two essays about other green community college programs. The first essay was written by the president of Lane Community College in Eugene, Oregon, about the role Lane and other community colleges are playing in creating a workforce for the green economy. Then, read a first-hand account of the new Wind Turbine Training Program at Kalamazoo Valley Community College in Kalamazoo, Michigan—a program that has more applicants than spaces and one whose students are being hired BEFORE they even graduate. It's clear that there are exciting "green" programs at community colleges throughout the United States.

The Role of Community Colleges in Creating a Workforce for the Green Economy

by Mary F.T. Spilde, President
Lane Community College

Community colleges are expected to play a leadership role in educating and training the workforce for the green economy. Due to close connections with local and regional labor markets, colleges assure a steady supply of skilled workers by developing and adapting programs to respond to the needs of business and industry. Further, instead of waiting for employers to create job openings, many colleges are actively engaged in local economic development to help educate potential employers to grow their green business opportunities and to participate in the creation of the green economy.

As the green movement emerges there has been confusion about what constitutes a green job. It is now clear that many of the green jobs span several economic sectors such as renewable energy, construction, manufacturing, transportation and agriculture. It is predicted that there will be many middle skill jobs requiring more than a high school diploma but less than a bachelor's degree. This is precisely the unique role that community colleges play. Community colleges develop training programs, including pre-apprenticeship, that ladder the curriculum to take lower skilled workers through a relevant and sequenced course of study that provides a clear pathway to career track jobs. As noted in *Going Green: The Vital Role of Community Colleges in Building a Sustainable Future and Green Workforce* by the National Council for Workforce Education and the Academy for Educational Development, community colleges are strategically positioned to work with employers to redefine skills and competencies needed by the green workforce and to create the framework for new and expanded green career pathways.

While there will be new occupations such as solar and wind technologists, the majority of the jobs will be in the energy management sector—retrofitting the built environment. For example, President Obama called for retrofitting more than 75 percent of federal buildings and more than 2 million homes to make them more energy-efficient. The second major area for growth will be the "greening" of existing jobs as they evolve to incorporate green practices. Both will require new knowledge, skills and abilities. For community colleges, this means developing new programs that meet newly created industry standards and adapting existing programs and courses to integrate green skills. The key is to create a new talent pool of environmentally conscious, highly skilled workers.

These two areas show remarkable promise for education and training leading to high wage/high demand jobs:

- Efficiency and energy management: There is a need for auditors and energy efficiency experts to retrofit existing buildings. Consider how much built environment we have in this country, and it's not difficult to see that this is where the vast amount of jobs are now and will be in the future.
- Greening of existing jobs: There are few currently available jobs that environmental sustainability will not impact. Whether it is jobs in construction, such as plumbers, electricians, heating and cooling technicians, painters, and building supervisors, or chefs, farmers, custodians, architects, automotive technicians and interior designers, all will need to understand how to lessen their impact on the environment.

Lane Community College offers a variety of degree and certificate programs to prepare students to enter the energy efficiency fields. Lane has offered an Energy Management program since the late 1980s—before it was hip to be green! Students in this program learn to apply basic principles of physics and analysis techniques to the description and measurement of energy in today's building systems, with the goal of evaluating and recommending alternative energy solutions that will result in greater energy efficiency and energy cost savings. Students gain a working understanding of energy systems in today's built environment and the tools to analyze and quantify energy efficiency efforts. The program began with an emphasis in residential energy efficiency/solar energy systems and has evolved to include commercial energy efficiency and renewable energy system installation technology.

The Renewable Energy Technician program is offered as a second-year option within the Energy Management program. Course work prepares students for employment designing and installing solar electric and domestic hot water systems. Renewable Energy students, along with Energy Management students, take a first-year curriculum in commercial energy efficiency giving them a solid background that includes residential energy efficiency, HVAC systems, lighting, and physics and math. In the second year, Renewable Energy students diverge from the Energy Management curriculum and take course work that starts with two courses in electricity fundamentals and one course in energy economics. In the following terms, students learn to design, install, and develop a thorough understanding of photovoltaics and domestic hot water systems.

Recent additions to Lane's offerings are Sustainability Coordinator and Water Conservation Technician degrees. Both programs were added to meet workforce demand.

Lane graduates find employment in a wide variety of disciplines and may work as facility managers, energy auditors, energy program coordinators, or control system specialists, for such diverse employers as engineering firms, public and private utilities, energy equipment companies, and departments of energy and as sustainability leaders within public and private sector organizations.

Lane Community College also provides continuing education for working professionals. The Sustainable Building Advisor (SBA) Certificate Program is a nine-month, specialized training program for working professionals. Graduate are able to advise employers or clients on strategies and tools for implementing sustainable building practices. Benefits from participating in the SBA program often include saving long-term building operating costs; improving the environmental, social, and economic viability of the region; and reducing environmental impacts and owner liability—not to mention the chance to improve one's job skills in a rapidly growing field.

The Building Operators Certificate is a professional development program created by The Northwest Energy Efficiency Council. It is offered through the Northwest Energy Education Institute at Lane. The certificate is designed for operations and maintenance staff working in public or private commercial buildings. It certifies individuals in energy and resource-efficient operation of building systems at two levels: Level I–Building System Maintenance and Level II–Equipment Troubleshooting and Maintenance.

Lane Community College constantly scans the environment to assess workforce needs and develop programs that provide highly skilled employees. Lane, like most colleges, publishes information in its catalog on workforce demand and wages so that students can make informed decisions about program choice.

Green jobs will be a large part of a healthy economy. Opportunities will abound for those who take advantage of programs with a proven record of connecting with employers and successfully educating students to meet high skills standards.

Establishing a World-Class Wind Turbine Technician Academy

by James DeHaven, Vice President of Economic & Business Development
Kalamazoo Valley Community College

When Kalamazoo Valley Community College (KVCC) decided it wanted to become involved in the training of utility-grade technicians for wind-energy jobs, early on the choice was made to avoid another "me too" training course.

Our program here in Southwest Michigan, 30 miles from Lake Michigan, had to meet industry needs and industry standards.

It was also obvious from the start that the utility-grade or large wind industry had not yet adopted any uniform training standards in the United States.

Of course, these would come, but why should the college wait when European standards were solidly established and working well in Germany, France, Denmark and Great Britain?

As a result, in 2009, KVCC launched its Wind Turbine Technician Academy, the first of its kind in the United States. The noncredit academy runs 8 hours a day, five days a week, for twenty-six weeks of intense training in electricity, mechanics, wind dynamics, safety, and climbing. The college developed this program rather quickly—in eight months—to fast-track individuals into this emerging field.

KVCC based its program on the training standards forged by the Bildungszentrum fur Erneuerebare Energien (BZEE)—the Renewable Energy Education Center. Located in Husum, Germany, the BZEE was created and supported by major wind-turbine manufacturers, component makers, and enterprises that provide operation and maintenance services.

As wind-energy production increased throughout Europe, the need for high-quality, industry-driven, international standards emerged. The BZEE has become the leading trainer for wind-turbine technicians across Europe and now in Asia.

With the exception of one college in Canada, the standards are not yet available in North America. When Kalamazoo Valley

realized it could be the first college or university in the United States to offer this training program—that was enough motivation to move forward.

For the College to become certified by the BZEE, it needed to hire and send an electrical instructor and a mechanical instructor to Germany for six weeks of "train the trainer." The instructors not only had to excel in their respective fields, they also needed to be able to climb the skyscraper towers supporting megawatt-class turbines—a unique combination of skills to possess. Truly, individuals who fit this job description don't walk through the door everyday—but we found them! Amazingly, we found a top mechanical instructor who was a part-time fireman and comfortable with tall ladder rescues and a skilled electrical instructor who used to teach rappelling off the Rockies to the Marine Corps.

In addition to employing new instructors, the College needed a working utility-grade nacelle that could fit in its training lab that would be located in the KVCC Michigan Technical Education Center. So one of the instructors traveled to Denmark and purchased a 300-kilowatt turbine.

Once their own training was behind them and the turbine was on its way from the North Sea, the instructors quickly turned to crafting the curriculum necessary for our graduates to earn both an academy certificate from KVCC and a certification from the BZEE.

Promoting the innovative program to qualified potential students across the country was the next step. News releases were published throughout Michigan, and they were also picked up on the Internet. Rather quickly, KVCC found itself with more than 500 requests for applications for a program built for 16 students.

Acceptance into the academy includes a medical release, a climbing test, reading and math tests, relevant work experience, and, finally, an interview. Students in the academy's pioneer class, which graduated in spring 2010, ranged in age from their late teens to early 50s. They hailed from throughout Michigan, Indiana, Ohio, and Illinois as well as from Puerto Rico and Great Britain.

The students brought with them degrees in marketing, law, business, science, and architecture, as well as entrepreneurial experiences in several businesses, knowledge of other languages, military service, extensive travel, and electrical, computer, artistic, and technical/mechanical skills.

Kalamazoo Valley's academy has provided some high-value work experiences for the students in the form of two collaborations with industry that has allowed them to maintain and/or repair actual utility-grade turbines, including those at the 2.5 megawatt size. This hands-on experience will add to the attractiveness of the graduates in the market place. Potential employers were recently invited to an open house where they could see the lab and meet members of this pioneer class.

The College's Turbine Technician Academy has also attracted a federal grant for $550,000 to expand its program through additional equipment purchases. The plan is to erect our own climbing tower. Climbing is a vital part of any valid program, and yet wind farms cannot afford to shut turbines down just for climb-training.

When the students are asked what best distinguishes the Kalamazoo Valley program, their answers point to the experienced instructors and the working lab, which is constantly changing to offer the best training experiences.

Industry continues to tell us that community colleges need to offer fast-track training programs of this caliber if the nation is to reach the U.S. Department of Energy's goal of 20 percent renewable energy by 2030. This would require more than 1,500 new technicians each year.

With that in mind, KVCC plans to host several BZEE orientation programs for other community colleges in order to encourage them to consider adopting the European training standards and start their own programs.

Meanwhile, applications are continuing to stream in from across the country for the next Wind Turbine Technician Academy program at Kalamazoo Valley Community College. For more information about the program, visit http://groves-center.kvcc.edu/career/wtta/.

How to Use This Guide

Peterson's Two-Year Colleges 2015 contains a wealth of information for anyone interested in colleges offering associate degrees. This section details the criteria that institutions must meet to be included in this guide and provides information about research procedures used by Peterson's.

QUICK-REFERENCE CHART

The **Two-Year Colleges At-a-Glance Chart** is a geographically arranged table that lists colleges by name and city within the state, or country in which they are located. Areas listed include the United States, Canada, and other countries; the institutions are included because they are accredited by recognized U.S. accrediting bodies (see **Criteria for Inclusion** section).

The At-a-Glance chart contains basic information that enables you to compare institutions quickly according to broad characteristics such as degrees awarded, enrollment, application requirements, financial aid availability, and numbers of sports and majors offered. A dagger (†) after the institution's name indicates that an institution has an entry in the **College Close-Ups** section.

Column 1: Degrees Awarded

C= *college transfer associate degree:* the degree awarded after a "university-parallel" program, equivalent to the first two years of a bachelor's degree.

T= *terminal associate degree:* the degree resulting from a one- to three-year program providing training for a specific occupation.

B= *bachelor's degree (baccalaureate):* the degree resulting from a liberal arts, science, professional, or preprofessional program normally lasting four years, although in some cases an accelerated program can be completed in three years.

M= *master's degree:* the first graduate (postbaccalaureate) degree in the liberal arts and sciences and certain professional fields, usually requiring one to two years of full-time study.

D= *doctoral degree* (research/scholarship, professional practice, or other)

Column 2: Institutional Control

Private institutions are designated as one of the following:

Ind = *independent* (nonprofit)

I-R = *independent-religious:* nonprofit; sponsored by or affiliated with a particular religious group or having a nondenominational or interdenominational religious orientation.

Prop = *proprietary* (profit-making)

Public institutions are designated by the source of funding, as follows:

Fed = *federal*

St = *state*

Comm = *commonwealth* (Puerto Rico)

Terr = *territory* (U.S. territories)

Cou = *county*

Dist = *district:* an administrative unit of public education, often having boundaries different from units of local government.

City = *city*

St-L = *state and local:* local may refer to county, district, or city.

St-R = *state-related:* funded primarily by the state but administratively autonomous.

Column 3: Student Body

M= *men only* (100% of student body)

PM = *coed, primarily men*

W= *women only* (100% of student body)

PW = *coed, primarily women*

M/W = *coeducational*

Column 4: Undergraduate Enrollment

The figure shown represents the number of full-time and part-time students enrolled in undergraduate degree programs as of fall 2013.

Columns 5–7: Enrollment Percentages

Figures are shown for the percentages of the fall 2013 undergraduate enrollment made up of students attending part-time (column 5) and students 25 years of age or older (column 6). Also listed is the percentage of students in the last graduating class who completed a college-transfer associate program and went directly on to four-year colleges (column 7).

For columns 8 through 15, the following letter codes are used: Y = yes; N = no; R = recommended; S = for some.

Columns 8–10: Admission Policies

The information in these columns shows whether the college has an open admission policy (column 8) whereby virtually all applicants are accepted without regard to standardized test scores, grade average, or class rank; whether a high school equivalency certificate is accepted in place of a high school diploma for admission consideration (column 9); and whether a high school transcript (column 10) is required as part of the application process. In column 10, the combination of the codes R and S indicates that a high school transcript is recommended for all applicants (R) or required for some (S).

Columns 11–12: Financial Aid

These columns show which colleges offer the following types of financial aid: need-based aid (column 11) and part-time jobs (column 12), including those offered through the federal government's Federal Work-Study program.

Columns 13–15: Services and Facilities

These columns show which colleges offer the following: career counseling (column 13) on either an individual or group basis, job placement services (column 14) for individual students, and college-owned or -operated housing facilities (column 16) for noncommuting students.

Column 16: Sports

This figure indicates the number of sports that a college offers at the intramural and/or intercollegiate levels.

Column 17: Majors

This figure indicates the number of major fields of study in which a college offers degree programs.

PROFILES OF TWO-YEAR COLLEGES AND SPECIAL MESSAGES

The **Profiles of Two-Year Colleges** contain basic data in capsule form for quick review and comparison. The following outline of the **Profile** format shows the section headings and the items that each section covers. Any item that does not apply to a particular college or for which no information was supplied is omitted from that college's **Profile**. Display ads, which appear near some of the institution's profiles, have been provided and paid for by those colleges that chose to supplement their profile with additional information.

Bulleted Highlights

The bulleted highlights section features important information, for quick reference and comparison. The number of possible bulleted highlights that an ideal **Profile** would have if all questions were answered in a timely manner follow. However, not every institution provides all of the information necessary to fill out every bulleted line. In such instances, the line will not appear.

First Bullet

Institutional control: Private institutions are designated as independent (nonprofit), proprietary (profit-making), or independent, with a specific religious denomination or affiliation. Nondenominational or interdenominational religious orientation is possible and would be indicated.

Public institutions are designated by the source of funding. Designations include federal, state, province, commonwealth (Puerto Rico), territory (U.S. territories), county, district (an administrative unit of public education, often having boundaries different from units of local government), city, state and local (local may refer to county, district, or city), or state-related (funded primarily by the state but administratively autonomous).

Religious affiliation is also noted here.

Institutional type: Each institution is classified as one of the following:

Primarily two-year college: Awards baccalaureate degrees, but the vast majority of students are enrolled in two-year programs.

Four-year college: Awards baccalaureate degrees; may also award associate degrees; does not award graduate (postbaccalaureate) degrees.

Upper-level institution: Awards baccalaureate degrees, but entering students must have at least two years of previous college-level credit; may also offer graduate degrees.

Comprehensive institution: Awards baccalaureate degrees; may also award associate degrees; offers graduate degree programs, primarily at the master's, specialist's, or professional level, although one or two doctoral programs may be offered.

University: Offers four years of undergraduate work plus graduate degrees through the doctorate in more than two academic or professional fields.

Founding date: If the year an institution was chartered differs from the year when instruction actually began, the earlier date is given.

System or administrative affiliation: Any coordinate institutions or system affiliations are indicated. An institution that has separate colleges or campuses for men and women but shares facilities and courses is termed a coordinate institution. A formal administrative grouping of institutions, either private or public, of which the college is a part, or the name of a single institution with which the college is administratively affiliated, is a system.

Second Bullet

Setting: Schools are designated as urban (located within a major city), suburban (a residential area within commuting distance of a major city), small-town (a small but compactly settled area not within commuting distance of a major city), or rural (a remote and sparsely populated area). The phrase *easy access to...* indicates that the campus is within an hour's drive of the nearest major metropolitan area that has a population greater than 500,000.

Third Bullet

Endowment: The total dollar value of funds and/or property donated to the institution or the multicampus educational system of which the institution is a part.

Fourth Bullet

Student body: An institution is coed (coeducational—admits men and women), primarily (80 percent or more) women, primarily men, women only, or men only.

Undergraduate students: Represents the number of full-time and part-time students enrolled in undergraduate degree programs as of fall 2013. The percentage of full-time undergraduates and the percentages of men and women are given.

Category Overviews

Undergraduates

For fall 2013, the number of full- and part-time undergraduate students is listed. This list provides the number of states and U.S. territories, including the District of Columbia and Puerto Rico (or for Canadian institutions, provinces and territories), and other countries from which undergraduates come. Percentages of undergraduates who are part-time or full-time students; transfers in; live on campus; out-of-state; Black or African American, non-Hispanic/Latino; Hispanic/Latino; Asian, non-Hispanic/Latino; Native Hawaiian or other Pacific Islander, non-Hispanic/Latino; American Indian or Alaska Native, non-Hispanic/Latino are given.

Retention: The percentage of freshmen (or, for upper-level institutions, entering students) who returned the following year for the fall term.

Freshmen

Admission: Figures are given for the number of students who applied for fall 2013 admission, the number of those who were admitted, and the number who enrolled. Freshman statistics include the average high school GPA; the percentage of freshmen who took the SAT and received critical reading, writing, and math scores above 500, above 600, and above 700; as well as the percentage of freshmen taking the ACT who received a composite score of 18 or higher.

Faculty

Total: The total number of faculty members; the percentage of full-time faculty members as of fall 2013; and the percentage of full-time faculty members who hold doctoral/first professional/ terminal degrees.

Student-faculty ratio: The school's estimate of the ratio of matriculated undergraduate students to faculty members teaching undergraduate courses.

Majors

This section lists the major fields of study offered by the college.

Academics

Calendar: Most colleges indicate one of the following: 4-1-4, 4-4-1, or a similar arrangement (two terms of equal length plus an abbreviated winter or spring term, with the numbers referring to months); semesters; trimesters; quarters; 3-3 (three courses for each of three terms); modular (the academic year is divided into small blocks of time; courses of varying lengths are assembled according to individual programs); or standard year (for most Canadian institutions).

Degrees: This names the full range of levels of certificates, diplomas, and degrees, including prebaccalaureate, graduate, and professional, that are offered by this institution:

Associate degree: Normally requires at least two but fewer than four years of full-time college work or its equivalent.

Bachelor's degree (baccalaureate): Requires at least four years but not more than five years of full-time college-level work or its equivalent. This includes all bachelor's degrees in which the normal four years of work are completed in three years and bachelor's degrees conferred in a five-year cooperative (work-study plan) program. A cooperative plan provides for alternate class attendance and employment in business, industry, or government. This allows students to combine actual work experience with their college studies.

Master's degree: Requires the successful completion of a program of study of at least the full-time equivalent of one but not more than two years of work beyond the bachelor's degree.

Doctoral degree (doctorate; research/scholarship, professional, or other): The highest degree in graduate study. The doctoral degree classification includes Doctor of Education, Doctor of Juridical Science, Doctor of Public Health, Doctor of Philosophy, Doctor of Podiatry, Doctor of Veterinary Medicine, and many more.

Post-master's certificate: Requires completion of an organized program of study of 24 credit hours beyond the master's degree but does not meet the requirements of academic degrees at the doctoral level.

Special study options: Details are next given here on study options available at each college:

Accelerated degree program: Students may earn a bachelor's degree in three academic years.

Academic remediation for entering students: Instructional courses designed for students deficient in the general competencies necessary for a regular postsecondary curriculum and educational setting.

Adult/continuing education programs: Courses offered for nontraditional students who are currently working or are returning to formal education.

Advanced placement: Credit toward a degree awarded for acceptable scores on College Board Advanced Placement (AP) tests.

Cooperative (co-op) education programs: Formal arrangements with off-campus employers allowing students to combine work and study in order to gain degree-related experience, usually extending the time required to complete a degree.

Distance learning: For-credit courses that can be accessed off-campus via cable television, the Internet, satellite, DVD, correspondence course, or other media.

Double major: A program of study in which a student concurrently completes the requirements of two majors.

English as a second language (ESL): A course of study designed specifically for students whose native language is not English.

External degree programs: A program of study in which students earn credits toward a degree through a combination of independent study, college courses, proficiency examinations, and personal experience. External degree programs require minimal or no classroom attendance.

Freshmen honors college: A separate academic program for talented freshmen.

Honors programs: Any special program for very able students offering the opportunity for educational enrichment, independent study, acceleration, or some combination of these.

Independent study: Academic work, usually undertaken outside the regular classroom structure, chosen or designed by the student with departmental approval and instructor supervision.

Internships: Any short-term, supervised work experience usually related to a student's major field, for which the student earns academic credit. The work can be full-or part-time, on or off-campus, paid or unpaid.

Off-campus study: A formal arrangement with one or more domestic institutions under which students may take courses at the other institution(s) for credit.

Part-time degree program: Students may earn a degree through part-time enrollment in regular session (daytime) classes or evening, weekend, or summer classes.

Self-designed major: Program of study based on individual interests, designed by the student with the assistance of an adviser.

Services for LD students: Special help for learning-disabled students with resolvable difficulties, such as dyslexia.

Study abroad: An arrangement by which a student completes part of the academic program studying in another country. A college may operate a campus abroad or it may have a cooperative agreement with other U.S. institutions or institutions in other countries.

Summer session for credit: Summer courses through which students may make up degree work or accelerate their program.

Tutorials: Undergraduates can arrange for special in-depth academic assignments (not for remediation) working with faculty members one-on-one or in small groups.

ROTC: Army, Naval, or Air Force Reserve Officers' Training Corps programs offered either on campus, at a branch campus [designated by a (b)], or at a cooperating host institution [designated by (c)].

Unusual degree programs: Nontraditional programs such as a 3-2 degree program, in which three years of liberal arts study is followed by two years of study in a professional field at another institution (or in a professional division of the same institution), resulting in two bachelor's degrees or a bachelor's and a master's degree.

Student Life

Housing options: The institution's policy about whether students are permitted to live off-campus or are required to live on campus for a specified period; whether freshmen-only, coed, single-sex, cooperative, and disabled student housing options are available; whether campus housing is leased by the school and/or provided by a third party; whether freshman applicants are given priority for college housing. The phrase *college housing not available* indicates that no college-owned or -operated housing facilities are provided for undergraduates and that noncommuting students must arrange for their own accommodations.

Activities and organizations: Lists information on drama-theater groups, choral groups, marching bands, student-run campus newspapers, student-run radio stations, and social organizations (sororities, fraternities, eating clubs, etc.) and how many are represented on campus.

Campus security: Campus safety measures including 24-hour emergency response devices (telephones and alarms) and patrols by trained security personnel, student patrols, late-night transport-escort service, and controlled dormitory access (key, security card, etc.).

Student services: Information provided indicates services offered to students by the college, such as legal services, health clinics, personal-psychological counseling, and women's centers.

Athletics

Membership in one or more of the following athletic associations is indicated by initials.

NCAA: National Collegiate Athletic Association

NAIA: National Association of Intercollegiate Athletics

NCCAA: National Christian College Athletic Association

NJCAA: National Junior College Athletic Association

USCAA: United States Collegiate Athletic Association

CIS: Canadian Interuniversity Sports

The overall NCAA division in which all or most intercollegiate teams compete is designated by a roman numeral I, II, or

III. All teams that do not compete in this division are listed as exceptions.

Sports offered by the college are divided into two groups: intercollegiate (**M** or **W** following the name of each sport indicates that it is offered for men or women) and intramural. An **s** in parentheses following an **M** or **W** for an intercollegiate sport indicates that athletic scholarships (or grants-in-aid) are offered for men or women in that sport, and a c indicates a club team as opposed to a varsity team.

Standardized Tests

The most commonly required standardized tests are the ACT, SAT, and SAT Subject Tests. These and other standardized tests may be used for selective admission, as a basis for counseling or course placement, or for both purposes. This section notes if a test is used for admission or placement and whether it is required, required for some, or recommended.

In addition to the ACT and SAT, the following standardized entrance and placement examinations are referred to by their initials:

ABLE: Adult Basic Learning Examination

ACT ASSET: ACT Assessment of Skills for Successful Entry and Transfer

ACT PEP: ACT Proficiency Examination Program

CAT: California Achievement Tests

CELT: Comprehensive English Language Test

CPAt: Career Programs Assessment

CPT: Computerized Placement Test

DAT: Differential Aptitude Test

LSAT: Law School Admission Test

MAPS: Multiple Assessment Program Service

MCAT: Medical College Admission Test

MMPI: Minnesota Multiphasic Personality Inventory

OAT: Optometry Admission Test

PAA: Prueba de Aptitud Académica (Spanish-language version of the SAT)

PCAT: Pharmacy College Admission Test

PSAT/NMSQT: Preliminary SAT National Merit Scholarship Qualifying Test

SCAT: Scholastic College Aptitude Test

SRA: Scientific Research Association (administers verbal, arithmetical, and achievement tests)

TABE: Test of Adult Basic Education

TASP: Texas Academic Skills Program

TOEFL: Test of English as a Foreign Language (for international students whose native language is not English)

WPCT: Washington Pre-College Test

Costs

Costs are given for the 2014–15 academic year or for the 2013–14 academic year if 2014–15 figures were not yet available. Annual expenses may be expressed as a comprehensive fee (including full-time tuition, mandatory fees, and college room and board) or as separate figures for full-time tuition, fees, room and board, or room only. For public institutions where tuition differs according to residence, separate figures are given for area or state residents and for nonresidents. Part-time tuition is expressed in terms of a per-unit rate (per credit, per semester hour, etc.) as specified by the institution.

The tuition structure at some institutions is complex in that freshmen and sophomores may be charged a different rate from that for juniors and seniors, a professional or vocational division may have a different fee structure from the liberal arts division of the same institution, or part-time tuition may be prorated on a sliding scale according to the number of credit hours taken. Tuition and fees may vary according to academic program, campus/location, class time (day, evening, weekend), course/credit load, course level, degree level, reciprocity agreements, and student level. Room and board charges are reported as an average for one academic year and may vary according to the board plan selected, campus/location, type of housing facility, or student level. If no college-owned or -operated housing facilities are offered, the phrase *college housing not available* will appear in the Housing section of the Student Life paragraph.

Tuition payment plans that may be offered to undergraduates include tuition prepayment, installment payments, and deferred payment. A tuition prepayment plan gives a student the option of locking in the current tuition rate for the entire term of enrollment by paying the full amount in advance rather than year by year. Colleges that offer such a prepayment plan may also help the student to arrange financing.

The availability of full or partial undergraduate tuition waivers to minority students, children of alumni, employees or their children, adult students, and senior citizens may be listed.

Financial Aid

The number of Federal Work Study and/or part-time jobs and average earnings are listed. Financial aid deadlines are given as well.

Applying

Application and admission options include the following:

Early admission: Highly qualified students may matriculate before graduating from high school.

Early action plan: An admission plan that allows students to apply and be notified of an admission decision well in advance of the regular notification dates. If accepted, the candidate is not committed to enroll; students may reply to the offer under the college's regular reply policy.

Early decision plan: A plan that permits students to apply and be notified of an admission decision (and financial aid offer, if applicable) well in advance of the regular notification date. Applicants agree to accept an offer of admission and to withdraw their applications from other colleges. Candidates who are not accepted under early decision are automatically considered with the regular applicant pool, without prejudice.

Deferred entrance: The practice of permitting accepted students to postpone enrollment, usually for a period of one academic term or year.

Application fee: The fee required with an application is noted. This is typically nonrefundable, although under certain specified conditions it may be waived or returned.

Requirements: Other application requirements are grouped into three categories: required for all, required for some, and recommended. They may include an essay, standardized test scores, a high school transcript, a minimum high school grade point average (expressed as a number on a scale of 0 to 4.0, where 4.0 equals A, 3.0 equals B, etc.), letters of recommendation, an interview on campus or with local alumni, and, for certain types of schools or programs, special requirements such as a musical audition or an art portfolio.

Application deadlines and notification dates: Admission application deadlines and dates for notification of acceptance or rejection are given either as specific dates or as **rolling** and **continuous.** Rolling means that applications are processed as they are received, and qualified students are accepted as long as there are openings. Continuous means that applicants are notified of acceptance or rejection as applications are processed up until the date indicated or the actual beginning of classes. The application deadline and the notification date for transfers are given if they differ from the dates for freshmen. Early decision and early action application deadlines and notification dates are also indicated when relevant.

Admissions Contact

The name, title, and phone number of the person to contact for application information are given at the end of the Profile. The admission office address is listed in most cases. Toll-free phone numbers may also be included. The admission office fax number and e-mail address, if available, are listed, provided the school wanted them printed for use by prospective students. Finally, the URL of the institution's Web site is provided.

Additional Information

Each college that has a **College Close-Up** in the guide will have a cross-reference appended to the Profile, referring you directly to that **College Close-Up.**

COLLEGE CLOSE-UPS

These narrative descriptions provide an inside look at certain colleges, shifting the focus to a variety of other factors that should also be considered. The descriptions provide a wealth of statistics that are crucial components in the college decision-making equation—components such as tuition, financial aid, and major fields of study. Prepared exclusively by college officials, the descriptions are designed to help give students a better sense of the individuality of each institution, in terms that include campus environment, student activities, and lifestyle. Such quality-of-life intangibles can be the deciding factors in the college selection process. The absence of any college or university does not constitute an editorial decision on the part of Peterson's. In essence, these descriptions are an open forum for colleges, on a voluntary basis, to communicate their particular message to prospective college students. The colleges included have paid a fee to Peterson's to provide this information. The **College Close-Ups** are edited to provide a consistent format across entries for your ease of comparison.

INDEXES

2013–14 Changes in Institutions

Here you will find an alphabetical listing of institutions that have recently closed, merged with other institutions, or changed their name or status.

Associate Degree Programs at Two-and Four-Year Colleges

These indexes present hundreds of undergraduate fields of study that are currently offered most widely according to the colleges' responses on *Peterson's Annual Survey of Undergraduate Institutions.* The majors appear in alphabetical order, each followed by an alphabetical list of the schools that offer an associate-level program in that field. Liberal Arts and Studies indicates a general program with no specified major. The terms used for the majors are those of the U.S. Department of Education Classification of Instructional Programs (CIPs). Many institutions, however, use different terms. Readers should refer to the **College Close-Up** in this book for the school's exact terminology. In addition, although the term "major" is used in this guide, some colleges may use other terms, such as "concentration," "program of study," or "field."

DATA COLLECTION PROCEDURES

The data contained in the **Profiles** of Two-Year Colleges and **Indexes** were researched in winter and spring 2014 through *Peterson's Annual Survey of Undergraduate Institutions.* Questionnaires were sent to the more than 1,900 colleges that meet the outlined inclusion criteria. All data included in this edition have been submitted by officials (usually admission and financial aid officers, registrars, or institutional research personnel) at the colleges themselves. All usable information received in time for publication has been included. The omission of any particular item from the **Profiles** of Two-Year Colleges and **Indexes** listing signifies either that the item is not applicable to that institution or that data were not available. Because of the comprehensive editorial review that takes place in our offices and because all material comes directly from college officials, Peterson's has every reason to believe that the information presented in this guide is accurate at the time of printing. However, students should check with a specific college or university at the time of application to verify such figures as tuition and fees, which may have changed since the publication of this volume.

CRITERIA FOR INCLUSION IN THIS BOOK

Peterson's Two-Year Colleges 2015 covers accredited institutions in the United States, U.S. territories, and other countries that award the associate degree as their most popular undergraduate offering (a few also offer bachelor's, master's, or doctoral degrees). The term two-year college is the commonly used designation for institutions that grant the associate degree, since two years is the normal duration of the traditional associate degree program. However, some programs may be completed in one year, others require three years, and, of course, part-time programs may take a considerably longer period. Therefore, "two-year college" should be understood as a conventional term that accurately describes most of the institutions included in this guide but which should not be taken literally in all cases. Also included are some non-degree-granting institutions, usually branch campuses of a multicampus system, which offer the equivalent of the first two years of a bachelor's degree, transferable to a bachelor's degree–granting institution.

To be included in this guide, an institution must have full accreditation or be a candidate for accreditation (preaccreditation) status by an institutional or specialized accrediting body recognized by the U.S. Department of Education or the Council for Higher Education Accreditation (CHEA). Institutional accrediting bodies, which review each institution as a whole, include the six regional associations of schools and colleges (Middle States, New England, North Central, Northwest, Southern, and Western), each of which is responsible for a specified portion of the United States and its territories. Other institutional accrediting bodies are national in scope and accredit specific kinds of institutions (e.g., Bible colleges, independent colleges, and rabbinical and Talmudic schools). Program registration by the New York State Board of Regents is considered to be the equivalent of institutional accreditation, since the board requires that all programs offered by an institution meet its standards before recognition is granted. This guide also includes institutions outside the United States that are accredited by these U.S. accrediting bodies. There are recognized specialized or professional accrediting bodies in more than forty different fields, each of which is authorized to accredit institutions or specific programs in its particular field. For specialized institutions that offer programs in one field only, we designate this to be the equivalent of institutional accreditation. A full explanation of the accrediting process and complete information on recognized, institutional (regional and national), and specialized accrediting bodies can be found online at www.chea.org or at www.ed.gov/admins/finaid/accred/index.html.

Quick-Reference Chart

Two-Year Colleges At-a-Glance

This chart includes the names and locations of accredited two-year colleges in the United States, Canada, and other countries and shows institutions' responses to the *Peterson's Annual Survey of Undergraduate Institutions.* If an institution submitted incomplete data, one or more columns opposite the institution's name is blank. A dagger after the school name indicates that the institution has one or more entries in the *College Close-Ups* section. If a school does not appear, it did not report any of the information.

Column key — Degrees Awarded: College Transfer Associate (C), Terminal Associate (T), Bachelor's (B), Master's (M), Doctoral (D). Institutional Control abbreviations. Student Body: Men, Primarily Men, Women, Primarily Women, Coed (M/W). Y—Yes; N—No; R—Recommended; S—For Some.

Institution	Location	Degrees Awarded	Institutional Control	Student Body	Undergraduate Enrollment	Percent Attending Part-Time	Percent 25 Years of Age or Older	Percent of Grads Going on to Four-Year Colleges	High School Equivalency Certificate Accepted	Open Admissions	High School Transcript Required	Need-Based Aid Available	Part-Time Jobs Available	Career Counseling Available	Job Placement Services Available	College Housing Available	Number of Sports Available	Number of Majors Offered
UNITED STATES																		
Alabama																		
Alabama Southern Community College	Monroeville	C,T	St	M/W	1,349	29			Y	Y	Y	Y	Y	Y	Y	N	3	30
Bevill State Community College	Jasper	C,T	St	M/W	3,734	48	38	18	Y	Y	Y	Y	Y	Y	Y	N		13
Bishop State Community College	Mobile	C,T	St	M/W	3,900	44	60		Y	Y	Y	Y	Y	Y	Y	N	4	16
Brown Mackie College–Birmingham†	Birmingham	T,B	Prop	M/W														10
Community College of the Air Force	Maxwell Gunter Air Force Base	T	Fed	M/W	314,962													
Gadsden State Community College	Gadsden	C,T	St	M/W	5,797	45	37	15	Y	Y	Y		Y	Y	Y	Y	4	23
ITT Technical Institute	Bessemer	T,B	Prop	M/W						Y		Y	Y			N		16
ITT Technical Institute	Madison	T,B	Prop	M/W												N		13
ITT Technical Institute	Mobile	T,B	Prop	M/W												N		12
Jefferson State Community College	Birmingham	C,T	St	M/W	8,542	66	35		Y	Y	S	Y	Y	Y	Y	N		19
J. F. Drake State Technical College	Huntsville	C,T	St	M/W	1,258	40												
Lawson State Community College	Birmingham	C,T	St	M/W	3,031	41	35	2	Y	Y	Y	Y	Y	Y	Y	Y	4	15
Lurleen B. Wallace Community College	Andalusia	C,T	St	M/W	1,570	38	25		Y	Y	Y	Y	Y	Y		N	3	10
Marion Military Institute	Marion	C	St	M/W	418	2	0.4	86	N	Y	Y	Y	Y			Y	11	4
Northwest-Shoals Community College	Muscle Shoals	C	St	M/W	3,854	52	26	2	Y	Y	Y	Y	Y	Y		N	3	15
Reid State Technical College	Evergreen	T	St	M/W	517	50	39		Y	Y	Y	Y	Y	Y	Y	N		4
Shelton State Community College	Tuscaloosa	C,T	St	M/W	5,068	51	23		Y	Y	Y	Y	Y			N	4	18
Snead State Community College	Boaz	C,T	St	M/W	2,161	29			Y	Y	Y	Y	Y			Y	5	5
Alaska																		
Ilisagvik College	Barrow	C	St	M/W	257	81	66		Y	Y	Y			Y	Y	Y	1	7
University of Alaska Anchorage, Kenai Peninsula College	Soldotna	C,T,B	St	M/W	2,733													
University of Alaska, Prince William Sound Community College	Valdez	C,T	St	M/W	527	87												
American Samoa																		
American Samoa Community College	Pago Pago	C,T,B	Terr	M/W	1,488	51			Y	Y		Y	Y	Y	Y	N	8	25
Arizona																		
Arizona Western College	Yuma	C,T	St-L	M/W	7,979	65	32		Y			Y	Y	Y	Y	Y	7	55
Brown Mackie College–Phoenix†	Phoenix	T,B	Prop	M/W														9
Brown Mackie College–Tucson†	Tucson	T,B	Prop	M/W														11
Carrington College–Mesa	Mesa	T	Prop	M/W	691	10	46		N	Y	Y	Y				N		5
Carrington College–Phoenix	Phoenix	T	Prop	M/W	676		27			Y	Y	Y				N		6
Carrington College–Phoenix Westside	Phoenix	T	Prop	M/W	513	30	65		Y	Y	Y					N		6
Carrington College–Tucson	Tucson	T	Prop	M/W	440	1	36		N	Y	Y					N		2
Chandler-Gilbert Community College	Chandler	C,T	St-L	M/W	14,399	69			Y			Y	Y		Y	N	6	37
Cochise College	Sierra Vista	C,T	St-L	M/W	3,787	59	45		Y		R	Y	Y	Y	Y	Y	3	49
Coconino Community College	Flagstaff	C,T	St	M/W	3,698	73	40	5	Y			Y	Y	Y	Y	N		39
CollegeAmerica–Flagstaff	Flagstaff	C,T,B	Priv	M/W	255		0		Y	Y								5
Eastern Arizona College	Thatcher	C,T	St-L	M/W	6,502	72	30		Y		R	Y	Y	Y	Y	Y	10	52
Glendale Community College	Glendale	C,T	St-L	M/W	21,361	66			Y		S	Y	Y	Y	Y	N	11	32
ITT Technical Institute	Phoenix	T,B	Prop	M/W						Y		Y	Y			N		12
ITT Technical Institute	Phoenix	T,B	Prop	M/W												N		11
ITT Technical Institute	Tucson	T,B	Prop	M/W						Y		Y	Y			N		13
Mesa Community College	Mesa	C,T	St-L	M/W	22,000				Y			Y	Y	Y	Y	N	11	36
Mohave Community College	Kingman	C,T	St	M/W	5,227	73	51		Y			Y	Y			N		34
Phoenix College	Phoenix	C,T	Cou	M/W	12,228				Y			Y	Y	Y	Y	N	6	56
Pima Community College	Tucson	C,T	St-L	M/W	26,613				Y			Y	Y	Y		N		63
Scottsdale Community College	Scottsdale	C,T	St-L	M/W	10,313	69	31		Y			Y	Y	Y		N	13	25
Sessions College for Professional Design	Tempe	T	Prop	M/W					N	Y	Y							4
Arkansas																		
Arkansas State University–Mountain Home	Mountain Home	T	St	M/W														
Arkansas State University–Newport	Newport	C,T	St	M/W	2,057	53	32		Y	Y		Y	Y			N		16
College of the Ouachitas	Malvern	C,T	St	M/W	1,501	61			Y	Y		Y	Y			N		16
Cossatot Community College of the University of Arkansas	De Queen	C,T	St	M/W	1,575		30		Y	Y	R	Y	Y			N	1	17
ITT Technical Institute	Little Rock	T,B	Prop	M/W						Y		Y	Y			N		11
Mid-South Community College	West Memphis	C,T	St.	M/W	1,793	61	35	11	Y	Y		Y	Y			N		7
NorthWest Arkansas Community College	Bentonville	C,T	St-L	M/W	8,020	65	51		Y	Y		Y	Y	Y		N	6	23
Ozarka College	Melbourne	C,T	St	M/W	1,600													
University of Arkansas Community College at Hope	Hope	C,T	St	M/W	1,460	50	38		Y		Y.	Y	Y			N		14
University of Arkansas Community College at Morrilton	Morrilton	C,T	St	M/W	2,149	41	41		Y	Y		Y	Y			N	5	17
California																		
Academy of Couture Art	Beverly Hills	C,T,B	Prop	M/W								Y	Y			N		2
Antelope Valley College	Lancaster	C,T	St-L	M/W	15,108	68	32		Y			Y	Y			N	12	45
Bakersfield College	Bakersfield	C,T	St-L	M/W	15,001													
Barstow Community College	Barstow	C,T	St-L	M/W	4,791		56		Y		R	Y	Y	Y		N	3	21
Berkeley City College	Berkeley	C,T	St-L	M/W	7,645		65	0			R	Y	Y	Y	Y			32
Butte College	Oroville	C,T	St-L	M/W	12,290	57			Y		S	Y	Y	Y	Y	N	9	55

This chart includes the names and locations of accredited two-year colleges in the United States, Canada, and other countries and shows institutions' responses to the *Peterson's Annual Survey of Undergraduate Institutions.* If an institution submitted incomplete data, one or more columns opposite the institution's name is blank. A dagger after the school name indicates that the institution has one or more entries in the *College Close-Ups* section. If a school does not appear, it did not report any of the information.

Legend: Y—Yes; N—No; R—Recommended; S—For Some

Column key:
- **Degrees Awarded:** College Transfer Associate (C), Terminal Associate (T), Bachelor's (B), Master's (M), Doctoral (D)
- **Institutional Control:** County District City, Federal, State and Local, State-Related; Independent, State, Commonwealth, Proprietary; Independent-Religious
- **Student Body:** Men, Primarily Men; Women, Primarily Women; Coed

Institution	Location	Degrees Awarded	Institutional Control	Student Body	Undergraduate Enrollment	Percent Attending Part-Time	Percent 25 or Older	Percent of Grads Going on to Four-Year Colleges	High School Equivalency Certificate Accepted	Open Admissions	High School Transcript Required	Need-Based Aid Available	Part-Time Jobs Available	Career Counseling Available	Job Placement Services Available	College Housing Available	Number of Sports Offered	Number of Majors Offered
Cañada College	Redwood City	C,T	St-L	M/W	6,658				Y	Y		Y	Y	Y	Y	N	4	44
Carrington College California–Citrus Heights	Citrus Heights	T	Prop	M/W	451	7			Y	Y						N		10
Carrington College California–Pleasant Hill	Pleasant Hill	T	Prop	M/W	589	13	43		Y	Y						N		16
Carrington College California–Pomona	Pomona	T	Prop	M/W	301	20	29		Y	Y								
Carrington College California–Sacramento	Sacramento	T	Prop	M/W	1,267	10	52		Y	Y								11
Carrington College California–San Jose	San Jose	T	Prop	M/W	693	4	46		Y	Y						N		19
Carrington College California–San Leandro	San Leandro	T	Prop	M/W	521	3	35		Y	Y						N		10
Carrington College California–Stockton	Stockton	T	Prop	M/W	465	8	26											1
College of Marin	Kentfield	C,T	St-L	M/W	7,000				Y			Y	Y	Y	Y	N	8	55
College of the Canyons	Santa Clarita	C,T	St-L	M/W	16,997				Y		R	Y	Y	Y	Y	N	11	54
College of the Desert	Palm Desert	C,T	St-L	M/W	9,259	61	33		Y	Y		Y	Y	Y		N	11	61
Columbia College	Sonora	C,T	St-L	M/W	2,667	69	25	17	Y	Y	S	Y	Y	Y	Y	N	2	32
Copper Mountain College	Joshua Tree	C,T	St	M/W	2,500	32	52		Y							N		23
Cosumnes River College	Sacramento	C,T	Dist	M/W	14,545		41		Y	Y		Y	Y	Y	Y	N		60
De Anza College	Cupertino	C,T	St-L	M/W	23,833	57	52					Y	Y	Y	Y	N	13	63
Deep Springs College	Deep Springs	C	Ind	M	26													
Feather River College	Quincy	C,T	St-L	M/W	1,785	64	22		Y			Y	Y	Y			8	22
FIDM/The Fashion Institute of Design & Merchandising, Los Angeles Campus†	Los Angeles	C,T,B	Prop	M/W	3,459	11	14		N	Y	Y		Y	Y	Y	Y		10
FIDM/The Fashion Institute of Design & Merchandising, Orange County Campus	Irvine	C,T	Prop	PW	214	4	7		N	Y	Y			Y	Y	Y		9
FIDM/The Fashion Institute of Design & Merchandising, San Diego Campus	San Diego	C,T	Prop	PW	169	11	12		N	Y	Y			Y	Y	Y		7
FIDM/The Fashion Institute of Design & Merchandising, San Francisco Campus	San Francisco	C,T	Prop	M/W	637	9	17		N	Y	Y			Y	Y	N		8
Foothill College	Los Altos Hills	C,T	St-L	M/W	15,765													
Fullerton College	Fullerton	C,T	St-L	M/W	24,423	65	21		Y			Y	Y	Y	Y	N	13	75
Gavilan College	Gilroy	C,T	St-L	M/W	5,267	66	46	13	Y	Y		Y	Y	Y	Y	N	6	42
Golden West College	Huntington Beach	C,T	St-L	M/W	12,333	64	29		Y	Y	R	Y	Y	Y	Y	N	9	31
Imperial Valley College	Imperial	C,T	St-L	M/W	7,413				Y		R,S	Y	Y	Y	Y	N	5	35
ITT Technical Institute	Culver City	T,B	Prop	M/W														11
ITT Technical Institute	Lathrop	T,B	Prop	M/W								Y		Y	Y	N		12
ITT Technical Institute	National City	T,B	Prop	M/W								Y		Y	Y	N		11
ITT Technical Institute	Oakland	T,B	Prop	M/W								Y		Y	Y			10
ITT Technical Institute	Orange	T,B	Prop	M/W								Y		Y	Y	N		13
ITT Technical Institute	Oxnard	C,T,B	Prop	M/W								Y		Y	Y	N		12
ITT Technical Institute	Rancho Cordova	T,B	Prop	M/W								Y		Y	Y	N		14
ITT Technical Institute	San Bernardino	T,B	Prop	M/W								Y		Y	Y	N		12
ITT Technical Institute	San Dimas	T,B	Prop	M/W								Y		Y	Y	N		11
ITT Technical Institute	Sylmar	T,B	Prop	M/W								Y		Y	Y	N		13
ITT Technical Institute	Torrance	T,B	Prop	M/W								Y		Y	Y	N		9
Lake Tahoe Community College	South Lake Tahoe	C,T	St-L	M/W	5,700				Y		R	Y	Y	Y	Y	N	1	27
Los Angeles Film School	Hollywood	C,T	Prop	M/W					Y		Y			Y	Y			4
Los Angeles Mission College	Sylmar	C,T	St-L	M/W	8,990	78	35		Y			Y	Y	Y		N		25
Mendocino College	Ukiah	C,T	St-L	M/W	3,614	64												
MiraCosta College	Oceanside	C,T	St	M/W	14,537	56	30		Y			Y	Y	Y	Y	N	2	80
Mt. San Antonio College	Walnut	C,T	St-L	M/W	28,481	63			Y		S	Y	Y	Y	Y	N	15	77
Mt. San Jacinto College	San Jacinto	C,T	St-L	M/W	14,170	64	36	18	Y		R	Y	Y	Y	Y	N	8	33
Orange Coast College	Costa Mesa	C,T	St-L	M/W	21,088	63	28		Y			Y	Y	Y	Y	N	14	99
Oxnard College	Oxnard	C	St	M/W	6,867	72	34		Y	Y	R	Y	Y	Y		N	5	37
Palomar College	San Marcos	C	St-L	M/W	22,535	64	37		Y			Y	Y	Y	Y	N	14	98
Pasadena City College	Pasadena	C,T	St-L	M/W	23,814	68	17		Y			Y	Y	Y	Y	N	13	74
Professional Golfers Career College	Temecula	T	Ind	PM	282													
Rio Hondo College	Whittier	C,T	St-L	M/W	29,281		40		Y			Y	Y	Y		N	10	4
The Salvation Army College for Officer Training at Crestmont	Rancho Palos Verdes	C,T	I-R	M/W	124	51												
San Diego City College	San Diego	C	St-L	M/W	16,930			61	Y		S	Y	Y	Y		N	16	66
San Diego Mesa College	San Diego	C	St-L	M/W	25,464													
San Joaquin Valley College	Bakersfield	T	Prop	M/W	743		40		N	Y	S			Y				9
San Joaquin Valley College	Chula Vista	T	Prop	M/W	25													
San Joaquin Valley College	Fresno	T	Prop	M/W	738		37				Y			Y	Y			8
San Joaquin Valley College	Hanford	T	Prop	M/W														19
San Joaquin Valley College	Hesperia	T	Prop	M/W	694		30											19
San Joaquin Valley College	Lancaster		Prop	M/W														
San Joaquin Valley College	Ontario	T	Prop	M/W	746		27		N	Y				Y	Y	N		10
San Joaquin Valley College	Rancho Cordova	T	Prop	M/W	114		72		N	Y					Y	N		2
San Joaquin Valley College	Salida	T	Prop	M/W	322		38		N	Y								6
San Joaquin Valley College	Temecula	T	Prop	M/W	314		40											19
San Joaquin Valley College	Visalia	T	Prop	M/W	1,892		53		N	Y	S	Y		Y	Y			16
San Joaquin Valley College–Fresno Aviation Campus	Fresno	T	Prop	PM	83		65		N	Y	S	S		Y	Y			1
San Joaquin Valley College–Online	Visalia	T	Prop	M/W	529		53		N	Y				Y	Y			5
Santa Monica College	Santa Monica	C,T	St-L	M/W	30,000	64	22		Y	Y	Y	Y	Y	Y	Y	N	10	36
Santa Rosa Junior College	Santa Rosa	C,T	St-L	M/W	22,008		46		Y			Y	Y	Y		N	15	76
Santiago Canyon College	Orange	C,T	St	M/W	14,083	43												
Sierra College	Rocklin	C,T	St	M/W	19,416	72												
Taft College	Taft	C,T	St-L	M/W	9,500	95												
Victor Valley College	Victorville	C	St	M/W	4,118	100	33		Y			Y	Y	Y		N	12	41
Colorado																		
Arapahoe Community College	Littleton	C,T	St	M/W	11,900	79	53		Y			Y	Y	Y		N	15	24

This chart includes the names and locations of accredited two-year colleges in the United States, Canada, and other countries and shows institutions' responses to the *Peterson's Annual Survey of Undergraduate Institutions*. If an institution submitted incomplete data, one or more columns opposite the institution's name is blank. A dagger after the school name indicates that the institution has one or more entries in the *College Close-Ups* section. If a school does not appear, it did not report any of the information.

Y—Yes; N—No; R—Recommended; S—For Some

Column legend: Degrees Awarded — College Transfer Associate (C), Terminal Associate (T), Bachelor's (B), Master's (M), Doctoral (D). Institutional Control — County, District, City; Federal; State, Commonwealth, Territory; Independent; Independent Religious; Proprietary; State and Locally Related; Men Primarily; Women Primarily. Student Body — Men Primarily; Women Primarily; Coed.

Institution	Location	Degrees Awarded	Institutional Control	Student Body	Undergraduate Enrollment	Percent Attending Part-Time	Percent 25 Years of Age or Older	Percent of Grads Going on to Four-Year Colleges	High School Equivalency Certificate Accepted	High School Transcript Required	Open Admissions	Need-Based Aid Available	Part-Time Jobs Available	Career Counseling Available	Job Placement Services Available	College Housing Available	Number of Sports Offered	Number of Majors Offered
Colorado Northwestern Community College	Rangely	C,T	St	M/W	1,158	55	26		Y	Y		Y	Y	Y		Y	11	14
Colorado School of Trades	Lakewood	T	Prop	M/W	134													
Institute of Business & Medical Careers	Fort Collins	T	Priv	M/W	302		20		Y	Y	Y	Y	Y	Y	Y	N		15
ITT Technical Institute	Aurora	T,B	Prop	M/W														10
ITT Technical Institute	Westminster	T,B	Prop	M/W						Y			Y	Y		N		10
Lamar Community College	Lamar	C,T	St	M/W	916	46	16		Y	Y		Y	Y	Y		Y	7	29
Lincoln College of Technology	Denver	T	Prop	PM	952		25		N	Y			Y	Y	Y	N		2
Northeastern Junior College	Sterling	C,T	St	M/W	1,962	51	22		Y		R	Y	Y	Y	Y	Y	15	58
Otero Junior College	La Junta	C,T	St	M/W	1,449		32	11	Y	Y	R	Y	Y	Y	Y	Y	6	24
Pueblo Community College	Pueblo	C,T	St	M/W	6,717	62	43	8	Y	Y						N		37
Red Rocks Community College	Lakewood	C,T	St	M/W	9,028	68												37
Connecticut																		
Goodwin College	East Hartford	C,T,B	Ind	M/W	3,388	82	67		Y	Y	Y	Y	Y	Y	Y	N	4	28
Housatonic Community College	Bridgeport	C,T	St	M/W	5,813				Y	Y	Y	Y	Y	Y	Y	N		24
Manchester Community College	Manchester	C,T	St	M/W	7,571	64	32		Y	Y	Y	Y	Y	Y	Y	N	4	31
Northwestern Connecticut Community College	Winsted	C,T	St	M/W	1,549	70	43		Y	Y	Y	Y	Y	Y	Y	N		35
Norwalk Community College	Norwalk	C,T	St	M/W	6,556	67	39	35	Y	Y	Y	Y	Y	Y	Y	N		34
Three Rivers Community College	Norwich	C,T	St	M/W	4,749	66	41		Y	Y	R	Y	Y	Y	Y	N	2	39
Tunxis Community College	Farmington	C,T	St	M/W	4,590	63	38	25	Y	Y	Y		Y	Y	Y	N		23
Delaware																		
Delaware Technical & Community College, Jack F. Owens Campus	Georgetown	C,T	St	M/W	4,429	55			Y	Y	S	Y	Y			N	4	52
Delaware Technical & Community College, Stanton/Wilmington Campus	Newark	C,T	St	M/W	7,035	63			Y	Y	S	Y	Y			N	5	64
Delaware Technical & Community College, Terry Campus	Dover	C,T	St	M/W	3,032	52			Y	Y	S	Y	Y			N	3	44
Florida																		
Broward College	Fort Lauderdale	C,T,B	St	M/W	43,715	70	37		Y	Y	S	Y	Y	Y	Y	N	5	157
Brown Mackie College–Miami†	Miramar	T,B	Prop	M/W														10
Chipola College	Marianna	C,T,B	St	M/W	2,189	57	37		Y	Y	Y	Y	Y	Y	Y	N	4	19
College of Central Florida	Ocala	C,T,B	St-L	M/W	8,114	66	31		Y	Y	Y	Y	Y	Y	Y	N	4	19
Daytona State College	Daytona Beach	C,T,B	St	M/W	15,708	59	40		Y	Y	Y	Y	Y	Y	Y	N	11	52
Eastern Florida State College	Cocoa	C,T,B	St	M/W	16,711	65	33		Y	Y	Y	Y	Y	Y	Y	N	5	26
Florida Gateway College	Lake City	C,T,B	St	M/W	3,057	69	34		Y	Y	S	Y	Y		Y	N		20
Florida State College at Jacksonville	Jacksonville	C,T,B	St	M/W	28,134	67	49		Y	Y	Y		Y	Y	Y		11	93
Hillsborough Community College	Tampa	C,T	St	M/W	26,590	57	37		Y	Y	Y	Y	Y	Y	Y	Y	5	38
ITT Technical Institute	Fort Lauderdale	T,B	Prop	M/W					Y			Y	Y		N			12
ITT Technical Institute	Fort Myers	T,B	Prop	M/W														12
ITT Technical Institute	Jacksonville	T,B	Prop	M/W					Y			Y	Y		N			13
ITT Technical Institute	Lake Mary	T,B	Prop	M/W					Y			Y	Y					12
ITT Technical Institute	Miami	T,B	Prop	M/W					Y			Y	Y					13
ITT Technical Institute	Orlando	T,B	Prop	M/W														10
ITT Technical Institute	Pensacola		Prop	M/W														7
ITT Technical Institute	St. Petersburg	T,B	Prop	M/W												N		12
ITT Technical Institute	Tallahassee	T,B	Prop	M/W														11
ITT Technical Institute	Tampa	T,B	Prop	M/W					Y			Y	Y		N			12
Miami Dade College	Miami	C,T,B	St-L	M/W	66,298	60	35		Y	Y	Y	Y	Y	Y	Y	N	4	143
Northwest Florida State College	Niceville	C,T,B	St-L	M/W	6,938	60	45	60	Y	Y	Y	Y	Y	Y	Y	N	4	42
Pasco-Hernando State College	New Port Richey	C,T	St	M/W	10,206	61			Y	Y	Y	Y	Y	Y		N	6	18
Pensacola State College	Pensacola	C,T,B	St	M/W	11,235	60	38		Y	Y	Y	Y	Y	Y	Y	N	16	95
Seminole State College of Florida	Sanford	C,T,B	St-L	M/W	18,427	63	40		Y	Y	Y	Y	Y	Y	Y	N	3	50
South Florida State College	Avon Park	C,T,B	St	M/W	2,699	64	35		Y	Y	Y	Y	Y	Y	Y	Y	6	164
Tallahassee Community College	Tallahassee	C,T	St-L	M/W	13,661	54	25		Y	Y	Y		Y	Y	Y	N	6	38
Georgia																		
Albany Technical College	Albany	T	St	M/W	3,894	46			Y	Y	Y					N		17
Altamaha Technical College	Jesup	T	St	M/W	1,244	71			Y	Y	Y					N		9
Athens Technical College	Athens	T	St	M/W	4,563	72			Y	Y	Y	Y	Y			N		27
Atlanta Technical College	Atlanta	T	St	M/W	4,859	64			Y	Y	Y					N		11
Augusta Technical College	Augusta	T	St	M/W	4,379	60			Y	Y	Y					N		24
Bainbridge State College	Bainbridge	C,T	St	M/W	2,705			50		Y	S	Y	Y	Y	Y	N	2	33
Brown Mackie College–Atlanta†	Atlanta	T	Prop	M/W														8
Central Georgia Technical College	Warner Robins	T	St	M/W	7,796	59			Y	Y	Y	Y				N		27
Chattahoochee Technical College	Marietta	T	St	M/W	10,470	67			Y	Y	Y					N		22
Columbus Technical College	Columbus	T	St	M/W	3,739	62			Y	Y	Y	Y				N		24
Darton State College	Albany	C,T,B	St	M/W	6,396	51			Y	Y	S	Y	Y	Y	Y	Y	14	67
Georgia Highlands College	Rome	C,T,B	St	M/W	5,487	48	22		N	Y	Y	Y	Y	Y		N	12	36
Georgia Military College	Milledgeville	C	St-L	M/W	7,069	46	40		Y	Y	S	Y	Y			N	7	22
Georgia Northwestern Technical College	Rome	T	St	M/W	6,051	65			Y	Y	Y	Y				N		13
Georgia Piedmont Technical College	Clarkston	T	St	M/W	4,431	67			Y	Y	Y	Y				N		27
Gordon State College	Barnesville	C,T,B	St	M/W	4,189		26		Y	Y	Y	Y	Y	Y		N	5	42
Gwinnett Technical College	Lawrenceville	T	St	M/W	7,180	68			Y	Y	Y	Y				N		27
ITT Technical Institute	Atlanta	T,B	Prop	M/W												N		11
ITT Technical Institute	Duluth	T,B	Prop	M/W					Y			Y				N		13
ITT Technical Institute	Kennesaw	T,B	Prop	M/W														12
Lanier Technical College	Oakwood	T	St	M/W	3,579	71			Y	Y	Y					N		21
Moultrie Technical College	Moultrie	T	St	M/W	2,058	62			Y	Y	Y					N		10
North Georgia Technical College	Clarkesville	T	St	M/W	2,441	58			Y	Y	Y					N		10

This chart includes the names and locations of accredited two-year colleges in the United States, Canada, and other countries and shows institutions' responses to the *Peterson's Annual Survey of Undergraduate Institutions*. If an institution submitted incomplete data, one or more columns opposite the institution's name is blank. A dagger after the school name indicates that the institution has one or more entries in the *College Close-Ups* section. If a school does not appear, it did not report any of the information.

Legend: Y—Yes; N—No; R—Recommended; S—For Some

Column headings (left to right): **Degrees Awarded** — College Transfer Associate (C), Terminal Associate (T), Bachelor's (B), Master's (M), Doctoral (D); **Institutional Control** — County, District, City, Federal, State, Commonwealth, Territory, Independent, Independent-Religious, Proprietary, State and Locally Supported; **Student Body** — Men, Primarily Men, Women, Primarily Women, Coed; Undergraduate Enrollment; Percent Attending Part-Time; Percent 25 Years of Age or Older; Percent of Grads Going on to Four-Year Colleges; High School Equivalency Certificate Accepted; Open Admissions; High School Transcript Required; Need-Based Aid Required; Part-Time Jobs Available; Career Counseling Available; Job Placement Services Available; College Housing Available; Number of Sports Offered; Number of Majors Offered.

Institution	Location	Degrees	Control	Student Body	UG Enroll	% PT	% 25+	% to 4-Yr	HS Equiv	Open Adm	HS Transcript	Need-Based Aid	PT Jobs	Career Couns	Job Placement	Housing	Sports	Majors
Oconee Fall Line Technical College	Sandersville	T	St	M/W	1,869	70			Y	Y	Y					N		5
Ogeechee Technical College	Statesboro	T	St	M/W	2,216	61			Y	Y	Y					N		24
Okefenokee Technical College	Waycross	T	St	M/W	1,180	68			Y	Y	Y					N		11
Savannah Technical College	Savannah	T	St	M/W	4,784	63			Y	Y	Y		Y			N		16
Southeastern Technical College	Vidalia	T	St	M/W	1,533	71			Y	Y	Y					N		13
Southern Crescent Technical College	Griffin	T	St	M/W	5,177	59			Y	Y	Y	Y						23
South Georgia State College	Douglas	C,B	St	M/W	2,579	27	19		N	Y	Y	Y	Y	Y		Y	10	24
South Georgia Technical College	Americus	T	St	M/W	1,828	47			Y	Y	Y							15
Southwest Georgia Technical College	Thomasville	T	St	M/W	1,546	71			Y	Y	Y	Y	Y			N		11
West Georgia Technical College	Waco	T	St	M/W	6,915	68			Y	Y	Y	Y	Y			N		17
Wiregrass Georgia Technical College	Valdosta	T	St	M/W	3,966	65			Y	Y	Y					N		15
Hawaii																		
Hawaii Tokai International College	Honolulu	C,T	Ind	M/W	64													
Honolulu Community College	Honolulu	C,T	St	M/W	4,368	63			Y			S	Y	Y	Y	N	Y		21
University of Hawaii Maui College	Kahului	C,T,B	St	M/W	4,071	64			Y		S	Y	Y	Y	Y	Y	4	17
Idaho																		
Brown Mackie College–Boise†	Boise	T,B	Prop	M/W														8
Carrington College–Boise	Boise	T	Prop	M/W	552	10	56		N	Y	Y	Y		Y		Y	N		9
College of Southern Idaho	Twin Falls	T	St-L	M/W	8,330	67	43		Y	Y	Y	Y	Y	Y	Y	Y	13	72
College of Western Idaho	Nampa	C,T	St	M/W	9,204				Y	Y	Y			Y	Y	N		38
Eastern Idaho Technical College	Idaho Falls	T	St	M/W	756	57	60		Y	Y	Y		Y	Y	Y	N		12
ITT Technical Institute	Boise	T,B	Prop	M/W						Y			Y	Y		N		11
Illinois																		
College of Lake County	Grayslake	C,T	Dist	M/W	17,577	72										N	5	30
Danville Area Community College	Danville	C,T	St-L	M/W	4,031	71	44		Y	Y	Y	Y	Y	Y		N	5	30
Elgin Community College	Elgin	C,T	St-L	M/W	11,285	67	42		Y		S		Y	Y	Y	N	8	35
Fox College	Bedford Park	T	Priv	M/W	400											N		6
Harper College	Palatine	C,T	St-L	M/W	14,827	63	38		Y	Y	Y		Y	Y	Y	N	12	66
Highland Community College	Freeport	C,T	St-L	M/W	2,031	48	37		Y	Y	R,S	Y	Y	Y		N	6	22
Illinois Central College	East Peoria	C,T	St-L	M/W	11,125	63												
Illinois Eastern Community Colleges, Frontier Community College	Fairfield	C,T	St-L	M/W	2,194	90	60		Y	Y	Y	Y	Y	Y	Y	N		14
Illinois Eastern Community Colleges, Lincoln Trail College	Robinson	C,T	St-L	M/W	972	57	39		Y	Y	Y	Y	Y	Y	Y	N	3	12
Illinois Eastern Community Colleges, Olney Central College	Olney	C,T	St-L	M/W	1,470	54	37		Y	Y	Y	Y	Y	Y	Y	N	3	15
Illinois Eastern Community Colleges, Wabash Valley College	Mount Carmel	C,T	St-L	M/W	4,512	88	49		Y	Y	Y	Y	Y	Y	Y	N	3	19
ITT Technical Institute	Arlington Heights	T,B	Prop	M/W						Y			Y	Y		N		10
ITT Technical Institute	Oak Brook	T,B	Prop	M/W						Y			Y	Y	Y	N		9
ITT Technical Institute	Orland Park	T,B	Prop	M/W						Y			Y	Y	Y	N		10
Kankakee Community College	Kankakee	C,T	St-L	M/W	3,825	58	45	24	Y	Y	Y	Y	Y	Y	Y	N	5	42
Kaskaskia College	Centralia	C,T	St-L	M/W	5,258	63	42		Y			Y	Y	Y	Y	N	9	40
Lake Land College	Mattoon	C,T	St-L	M/W	6,351	56			Y		R	Y	Y	Y	Y	N	9	37
Lincoln Land Community College	Springfield	C,T	Dist	M/W	7,020	57	32		Y		R	Y	Y	Y	Y	N	5	42
McHenry County College	Crystal Lake	C,T	St-L	M/W	6,976	63	34		Y		R	R	Y	Y	Y	N	6	27
Moraine Valley Community College	Palos Hills	C,T	St-L	M/W	16,106	58	28	85	Y	Y	R	Y	Y	Y	Y	N	9	42
Oakton Community College	Des Plaines	C,T	Dist	M/W	10,016		39		Y	Y	R	Y		Y		N	10	30
Parkland College	Champaign	C,T	Dist	M/W	9,368	63												
Rend Lake College	Ina	C,T	St	M/W	2,714	46	47		Y	Y	Y	Y	Y	Y	Y	N	8	28
Rock Valley College	Rockford	C,T	Dist	M/W	8,849	51	40		Y			Y	Y	Y	Y	N	9	32
Sauk Valley Community College	Dixon	C,T	Dist	M/W	2,220	55	37	78	Y		R	Y	Y	Y	Y	N	5	45
Shawnee Community College	Ullin	C,T	St-L	M/W	1,579	45	47		Y		R	Y	Y	Y	Y	N	5	31
South Suburban College	South Holland	C,T	St-L	M/W	5,508		52		Y	Y		Y	Y	Y	Y	N	5	23
Southwestern Illinois College	Belleville	C,T	Dist	M/W	11,331	57	41		Y	Y	Y	Y	Y	Y	Y	N	5	60
Spoon River College	Canton	C,T	St	M/W	1,784	60	41		Y	Y	Y	Y	Y	Y	Y	N	4	47
Vet Tech Institute at Fox College	Tinley Park	T	Priv	M/W	153							Y				N		1
Waubonsee Community College	Sugar Grove	C,T	Dist	M/W	10,721	68			Y				Y	Y	Y	N	11	39
Indiana																		
Ancilla College	Donaldson	C,T	I-R	M/W	424	33	31		Y	Y	Y	Y	Y	Y	Y	N	7	14
Brown Mackie College–Fort Wayne†	Fort Wayne	T,B	Prop	M/W														10
Brown Mackie College–Indianapolis†	Indianapolis	T,B	Prop	M/W														9
Brown Mackie College–Merrillville†	Merrillville	T,B	Prop	M/W														8
Brown Mackie College–South Bend†	South Bend	T,B	Prop	PW														8
International Business College	Indianapolis	T	Priv	M/W	403				Y			Y				Y		11
ITT Technical Institute	Fort Wayne	T,B	Prop	M/W						Y			Y	Y	Y	N		13
ITT Technical Institute	Merrillville	T,B	Prop	M/W						Y								10
ITT Technical Institute	Newburgh	T,B	Prop	M/W						Y			Y	Y	Y	N		13
Ivy Tech Community College–Bloomington	Bloomington	C,T	St	M/W	6,477	61	54		Y		Y	Y	Y	Y	Y	N		27
Ivy Tech Community College–Central Indiana	Indianapolis	C,T	St	M/W	21,978	68	53		Y		Y	Y	Y	Y	Y	N	6	42
Ivy Tech Community College–Columbus	Columbus	C,T	St	M/W	4,578	72	47		Y		Y	Y	Y	Y	Y	N		32
Ivy Tech Community College–East Central	Muncie	C,T	St	M/W	7,466	56	47		Y		Y	Y	Y	Y	Y	N		38
Ivy Tech Community College–Kokomo	Kokomo	C,T	St	M/W	3,948	60	58		Y		Y	Y	Y	Y	Y	N		31
Ivy Tech Community College–Lafayette	Lafayette	C,T	St	M/W	6,398	56	42		Y		Y	Y	Y	Y	Y	N		42
Ivy Tech Community College–North Central	South Bend	C,T	St	M/W	7,182	71	60		Y		Y	Y	Y	Y	Y	N		42
Ivy Tech Community College–Northeast	Fort Wayne	C,T	St	M/W	9,102	65	54		Y		Y	Y	Y	Y	Y	N		39
Ivy Tech Community College–Northwest	Gary	C,T	St	M/W	9,942	65	56		Y		Y	Y	Y	Y	Y	N		42
Ivy Tech Community College–Richmond	Richmond	C,T	St	M/W	3,095	66	72		Y		Y	Y	Y	Y	Y	N	1	30

This chart includes the names and locations of accredited two-year colleges in the United States, Canada, and other countries and shows institutions' responses to the *Peterson's Annual Survey of Undergraduate Institutions.* If an institution submitted incomplete data, one or more columns opposite the institution's name is blank. A dagger after the school name indicates that the institution has one or more entries in the *College Close-Ups* section. If a school does not appear, it did not report any of the information.

Y—Yes; N—No; R—Recommended; S—For Some

		Degrees Awarded	Institutional Control	Student Body	Undergraduate Enrollment	Percent Attending Part-Time	Percent 25 Years of Age or Older	Percent of Grads Going on to Four-Year Colleges	Open Admissions	High School Equivalency Certificate Accepted	High School Transcript Required	Need-Based Aid Required	Career Counseling Available	Part-Time Jobs Available	Job Placement Services Available	College Housing Available	Number of Sports Offered	Number of Majors Offered
Ivy Tech Community College–Southeast	Madison	C,T	St	M/W	2,881	66	51		Y		Y		Y	Y	Y	Y	N		18
Ivy Tech Community College–Southern Indiana	Sellersburg	C,T	St	M/W	4,892	74	58		Y		Y		Y	Y	Y	Y	N		31
Ivy Tech Community College–Southwest	Evansville	C,T	St	M/W	5,475	67	56		Y		Y		Y	Y	Y	Y	N		42
Ivy Tech Community College–Wabash Valley	Terre Haute	C,T	St	M/W	5,364	64	52		Y		Y		Y	Y	Y	Y	N	2	44
Vet Tech Institute at International Business College	Fort Wayne	T	Priv	M/W	128											Y	Y	1	1
Vet Tech Institute at International Business College	Indianapolis	T	Priv	M/W	124					Y						Y	Y	1	1
Vincennes University	Vincennes	C,T,B	St	M/W	18,383	67			Y	Y		Y	Y			Y		8	125
Iowa																		
Brown Mackie College–Quad Cities†	Bettendorf	T	Prop	M/W														5
Hawkeye Community College	Waterloo	C,T	St-L	M/W	5,803	47	29		Y	Y	Y		Y	Y	Y	Y	N	8	36
Iowa Lakes Community College	Estherville	C,T	St-L	M/W	2,574	48	25		Y	Y		Y	Y	Y	Y	Y	18	193
ITT Technical Institute	Clive	T,B	Prop	M/W								Y				N		11
Northeast Iowa Community College	Calmar	C,T	St-L	M/W	5,201	64	21		Y		R		Y	Y	Y	N	7	29
North Iowa Area Community College	Mason City	C	St-L	M/W	3,207	51			Y	Y		Y	Y	Y	Y	Y	10	40
St. Luke's College	Sioux City	T,B	Ind	M/W	187	25	41	25	N	Y	Y	Y	Y	Y	Y	N		3
Southeastern Community College	West Burlington	C	St-L	M/W	3,225	50	27		Y				Y	Y	Y		6	29
Western Iowa Tech Community College	Sioux City	C,T	St	M/W	6,425	58												
Kansas																		
Allen Community College	Iola	C,T	St-L	M/W	2,852		20		Y	Y	Y		Y	Y	Y	Y	12	66
Barton County Community College	Great Bend	C,T	St-L	M/W														
Brown Mackie College–Kansas City†	Lenexa	T,B	Prop	M/W														11
Brown Mackie College–Salina†	Salina	T,B	Prop	M/W														10
Cloud County Community College	Concordia	C,T	St-L	M/W	2,318	62	33		Y	Y	Y		Y	Y	Y	Y	8	20
Colby Community College	Colby	C,T	St-L	M/W	1,451	50												
Cowley County Community College and Area Vocational–Technical School	Arkansas City	C,T	St-L	M/W	4,328	46												
Donnelly College	Kansas City	C,T,B	I-R	M/W	419	47	60	2	Y	Y	R	Y	Y	Y	Y	Y		4
Garden City Community College	Garden City	C,T	Cou	M/W	1,997	46	20		Y	Y	Y		Y	Y	Y	Y	16	42
Hutchinson Community College and Area Vocational School	Hutchinson	C,T	St-L	M/W	6,126	61	30	70	Y	Y	S	Y	Y			Y	13	55
Independence Community College	Independence	C,T	St	M/W	1,031	44	27	39		Y	Y		Y	Y		N	5	29
Manhattan Area Technical College	Manhattan	C,T	St-L	M/W	825	40	46		Y	Y	Y	S			Y	Y	N		24
Wichita Area Technical College	Wichita	C,T	Dist	M/W	2,936	63	59					S			Y	Y	N		26
Wright Career College	Overland Park	C,T,B	Prop	M/W	71	73		0	Y	Y					Y	Y	N		13
Wright Career College	Wichita	T,B	Prop	M/W	362	65	65	0	Y	Y					Y	Y	N		9
Kentucky																		
Brown Mackie College–Hopkinsville†	Hopkinsville	T	Prop	M/W														4
Brown Mackie College–Louisville†	Louisville	T,B	Prop	M/W														10
Brown Mackie College–Northern Kentucky†	Fort Mitchell	C,B	Prop	M/W														10
Elizabethtown Community and Technical College	Elizabethtown	C,T	St	M/W	7,586	58													
Gateway Community and Technical College	Florence	C	St	M/W	4,789	69			Y	Y	Y				Y		N		15
Hopkinsville Community College	Hopkinsville	C,T	St	M/W	3,609	55			Y	Y	R	Y	Y	Y	Y	N	5	20
ITT Technical Institute	Louisville	T,B	Prop	M/W						Y		Y	Y	Y		N		12
Owensboro Community and Technical College	Owensboro	C,T	St	M/W	4,297	57	39	7	Y	Y	Y	Y	Y	Y	Y	N		21
Somerset Community College	Somerset	C,T	St	M/W	7,878		45		Y	Y	Y	Y	Y	Y	Y	N		18
Spencerian College	Louisville	T	Prop	M/W	532	43			Y	Y	Y	Y	Y	Y	Y	Y		11
Spencerian College–Lexington	Lexington	T	Prop	M/W	160		45			Y	Y	Y	Y	Y	Y	Y		12
Sullivan College of Technology and Design	Louisville	C,T,B	Prop	M/W	457	32	52		N	Y	Y		Y	Y	Y	Y		45
West Kentucky Community and Technical College	Paducah	C,T	St	M/W	4,668	49	45		Y	Y	S		Y	Y	Y	N	1	14
Louisiana																		
Bossier Parish Community College	Bossier City	C,T	St	M/W	8,512	40	32		Y	Y		Y				N	10	21
Career Technical College	Monroe	T	Prop	M/W	576	22	56		N	Y	Y			Y	Y	N		12
ITI Technical College	Baton Rouge	T	Prop	M/W	585		50	1	Y	Y	Y				Y	N		8
ITT Technical Institute	Baton Rouge	T,B	Prop	M/W												N		13
ITT Technical Institute	St. Rose	T,B	Prop	M/W						Y			Y	Y	Y	N		13
Nunez Community College	Chalmette	C,T	St	M/W	2,506	63	52		Y			S	Y	Y	Y	N	2	6
Southern University at Shreveport	Shreveport	C,T	St	M/W	3,018	30	41				Y	Y	Y	Y	Y	Y	2	36
South Louisiana Community College	Lafayette	C,T	St	M/W	7,563	57	28		Y	Y			Y	Y	Y	N		31
Sowela Technical Community College	Lake Charles	T	St	M/W	3,225	47	29		Y	Y	Y		Y	Y	Y	N		7
Maine																		
Beal College	Bangor	T	Prop	M/W	464	22	53		Y	Y			Y	Y	Y	N		11
Central Maine Community College	Auburn	C,T	St	M/W	3,109	53	39		N	Y	Y		Y	Y	Y	Y	7	25
Central Maine Medical Center College of Nursing and Health Professions	Lewiston	T	Ind	M/W	227	73	74		N	Y	Y				Y			3
Kennebec Valley Community College	Fairfield	C,T	St	M/W	2,470	71												
Southern Maine Community College	South Portland	C,T	St	M/W	7,131	58	43		Y	Y		Y	Y	Y	Y	Y	10	29
York County Community College	Wells	C,T	St	M/W	1,583	60	44		Y	Y			Y	Y	Y	N	10	17
Maryland																		
Anne Arundel Community College	Arnold	C,T	St-L	M/W	17,650	71												
Carroll Community College	Westminster	C,T	St-L	M/W	3,794	62	29		Y		Y		Y	Y	Y	N		33
Cecil College	North East	C	Cou	M/W	2,527	67	22		Y		Y		Y	Y		N	7	42
College of Southern Maryland	La Plata	C,T	St-L	M/W	8,781	62	33		Y			R	Y	Y	Y	N	7	32
The Community College of Baltimore County	Baltimore	C,T	Cou	M/W	24,275	67					Y	Y	Y			N	8	54
Garrett College	McHenry	C,T	St-L	M/W	769	22	14		Y		Y		Y	Y		Y	9	13
Hagerstown Community College	Hagerstown	C,T	St-L	M/W	4,903	75	40		Y			S	Y	Y	Y		12	29

This chart includes the names and locations of accredited two-year colleges in the United States, Canada, and other countries and shows institutions' responses to the *Peterson's Annual Survey of Undergraduate Institutions*. If an institution submitted incomplete data, one or more columns opposite the institution's name is blank. A dagger after the school name indicates that the institution has one or more entries in the *College Close-Ups* section. If a school does not appear, it did not report any of the information.

Column legend (Y—Yes; N—No; R—Recommended; S—For Some):

- **Degrees Awarded:** College Transfer Associate (C), Terminal Associate (T), Bachelor's (B), Master's (M), Doctoral (D)
- **Institutional Control:** County District City, Federal, State and Local, State-Related (St-L, St, Dist, Cou); Independent (Ind), Independent-Religious; Proprietary (Prop, Priv)
- **Student Body:** Men, Primarily Men (PM); Women, Primarily Women; Coed (M/W)
- Undergraduate Enrollment
- Percent Attending Part-Time (% PT)
- Percent 25 Years of Age or Older (% 25+)
- Percent of Grads Going on to Four-Year Colleges (% →4yr)
- Open Admissions (OA)
- High School Equivalency Certificate Accepted (HSE)
- High School Transcript Required (HST)
- Need-Based Aid Available (NB)
- Part-Time Jobs Available (PTJ)
- Career Counseling Available (CC)
- Job Placement Services Available (JP)
- College Housing Available (CH)
- Number of Sports Offered (Sports)
- Number of Majors Offered (Majors)

Institution	Location	Degrees	Control	Student Body	Enroll	% PT	% 25+	% →4yr	OA	HSE	HST	NB	PTJ	CC	JP	CH	Sports	Majors
Harford Community College	Bel Air	C,T	St-L	M/W	7,039	63	32	47	Y				Y	Y	Y		13	65
Howard Community College	Columbia	C,T	St-L	M/W	10,223	64	37		Y			S	Y	Y	Y	N	6	52
ITT Technical Institute	Owings Mills	T,B	Prop	M/W												N		9
Montgomery College	Rockville	C,T	St-L	M/W	26,155	65	31	68	Y			R	Y	Y	Y		9	44
Wor-Wic Community College	Salisbury	C,T	St-L	M/W	3,419	68	42		Y			R		Y	Y	N		23
Massachusetts																		
Bay State College †	Boston	C,T,B	Ind	M/W	1,098		48		N	Y	Y		Y	Y	Y	Y		13
Benjamin Franklin Institute of Technology	Boston	C,T,B	Ind	M/W	470	12	21		Y	Y	Y		Y	Y	Y	Y	3	16
Berkshire Community College	Pittsfield	C,T	St	M/W	2,400	66	51	42	Y	Y	Y	Y	Y	Y	Y	N		20
Bristol Community College	Fall River	C,T	St	M/W	9,335	53	36		Y	Y	Y	Y	Y	Y	Y	N	3	59
Bunker Hill Community College	Boston	C,T	St	M/W	14,023	67			Y	Y		Y	Y	Y	Y	N	6	57
Dean College	Franklin	C,T,B	Ind	M/W	1,300	17	1		N		Y		Y	Y	Y	Y	11	13
Greenfield Community College	Greenfield	C,T	St	M/W	2,243	64	43		Y	Y		S	Y	Y	Y	N		34
Holyoke Community College	Holyoke	C,T	St	M/W	6,688	52	34		Y			Y	Y	Y	Y	N	7	22
ITT Technical Institute	Norwood	T,B	Prop	M/W							Y		Y	Y		N		8
ITT Technical Institute	Wilmington	T,B	Prop	M/W							Y		Y	Y		N		9
Massachusetts Bay Community College	Wellesley Hills	C,T	St	M/W	5,377	64	59		Y	Y			Y	Y	Y	N	9	30
Middlesex Community College	Bedford	C,T	St	M/W	9,664													
Mount Wachusett Community College	Gardner	C,T	St	M/W	4,734	58	46	44	Y	Y		Y	Y	Y	Y	N	8	29
Northern Essex Community College	Haverhill	C,T	St	M/W	7,352	67	34		Y	Y		Y	Y	Y	Y	N	10	58
North Shore Community College	Danvers	C,T	St	M/W	7,750	61	41	45	Y	Y		S	Y	Y	Y	N	2	40
Quinsigamond Community College	Worcester	C,T	St	M/W	8,583	60	35		Y	Y		Y	Y	Y	Y	N	6	42
Springfield Technical Community College	Springfield	C,T	St	M/W	6,792	53	42		Y	Y		Y	Y	Y	Y	N	8	55
Michigan																		
Alpena Community College	Alpena	C,T	St-L	M/W	1,950												6	64
Delta College	University Center	C,T	Dist	M/W	10,273	62	35	33	Y			R	Y	Y	Y	N	6	64
Glen Oaks Community College	Centreville	C,T	St-L	M/W	1,221	57			Y			Y	Y	Y	Y	N	5	7
Gogebic Community College	Ironwood	C,T	St-L	M/W	1,199	46	40		Y	Y	Y	Y	Y	Y	Y	Y	10	19
Grand Rapids Community College	Grand Rapids	C,T	Dist	M/W	16,590	66	33		Y	Y			Y	Y	Y	N	6	33
ITT Technical Institute	Canton	T,B	Prop	M/W							Y		Y	Y				14
ITT Technical Institute	Dearborn	T,B	Prop	M/W														12
ITT Technical Institute	Swartz Creek	C,B	Prop	M/W														12
ITT Technical Institute	Troy	T,B	Prop	M/W							Y		Y	Y		N		13
ITT Technical Institute	Wyoming	T,B	Prop	M/W							Y		Y	Y		N		13
Jackson College	Jackson	C,T	Cou	M/W	5,665	58	39		Y				Y	Y	Y	Y	7	26
Kirtland Community College	Roscommon	C,T	Dist	M/W	1,805	62	45		Y	Y			Y	Y	Y	N	3	35
Lake Michigan College	Benton Harbor	C,T	Dist	M/W	4,548	67												
Lansing Community College	Lansing	C,T	St-L	M/W	17,562	62	38		Y			S	Y	Y	Y	N	6	114
Macomb Community College	Warren	C,T	Dist	M/W	23,446	68	36		Y				Y	Y	Y	N	11	72
Monroe County Community College	Monroe	C,T	Cou	M/W			45		Y	Y	Y		Y	Y	Y	N	2	42
Montcalm Community College	Sidney	C,T	St-L	M/W	2,011	66												
Mott Community College	Flint	C,T	Dist	M/W	9,683	70	48		Y				Y	Y	Y	N	7	48
Oakland Community College	Bloomfield Hills	C,T	St-L	M/W	26,405	69	46	51	Y				Y	Y	Y	N	5	82
Saginaw Chippewa Tribal College	Mount Pleasant	C,T	Ind	M/W	127	64						Y		Y				3
St. Clair County Community College	Port Huron	C,T	St-L	M/W	4,324	59	32		Y				Y	Y	Y	N	5	26
Schoolcraft College	Livonia	C,T	Dist	M/W	12,384	65	36		Y	Y		R,S	Y	Y	Y	N	5	48
Southwestern Michigan College	Dowagiac	C,T	St-L	M/W	2,801	50	29		Y	Y		Y	Y	Y		Y	8	27
Wayne County Community College District	Detroit	C,T	St-L	M/W	18,119	79	47		Y	Y		Y	Y	Y	Y	N	1	37
Minnesota																		
Alexandria Technical and Community College	Alexandria	C,T	St	M/W	2,630		22		Y	Y		Y	Y	Y	Y	N	4	26
Anoka-Ramsey Community College	Coon Rapids	C,T	St	M/W	7,807		24		Y	Y		S	Y	Y	Y	N	11	24
Anoka-Ramsey Community College, Cambridge Campus	Cambridge	C,T	St	M/W	2,313		26		Y	Y		S	Y	Y	Y	N	7	23
Anoka Technical College	Anoka	C,T	St	M/W	2,152		44		Y	Y		Y	Y	Y	Y	N		22
Century College	White Bear Lake	C,T	St	M/W	10,009	60	44		Y	Y		Y	Y	Y	Y	N	11	42
Dunwoody College of Technology	Minneapolis	T,B	Ind	PM	1,071	20	51		N	Y	Y		Y	Y	Y	N		25
The Institute of Production and Recording	Minneapolis	T	Prop	M/W	242	37	27					Y	Y	Y		N		2
ITT Technical Institute	Brooklyn Center	T,B	Prop	M/W														8
ITT Technical Institute	Eden Prairie	T,B	Prop	M/W														10
Lake Superior College	Duluth	C,T	St	M/W	5,050	58	41		Y			S	Y	Y	Y			34
Mesabi Range Community and Technical College	Virginia	C,T	St	M/W	1,451	39	37		Y	Y		Y	Y	Y	Y	Y	13	16
Minneapolis Business College	Roseville	T	Priv	M/W	267							Y			Y			9
Minneapolis Community and Technical College	Minneapolis	C,T	St	M/W	9,718	65	55		Y	Y		Y	Y	Y	Y	N	4	46
Minnesota School of Business–Brooklyn Center	Brooklyn Center	C,T,B	Prop	M/W	169	41	68		Y	Y		Y	Y	Y		N		11
Minnesota School of Business–Plymouth	Plymouth	C,T,B	Prop	M/W	190	44	62		Y	Y		Y	Y	Y		N		11
Minnesota State College–Southeast Technical	Winona	C,T	St	M/W	2,184	48	49		Y	Y		Y	Y	Y		Y		27
Minnesota West Community and Technical College	Pipestone	C,T	St	M/W	3,467	62												
Normandale Community College	Bloomington	C,T	St	M/W	9,296	57			Y	Y		S	Y	Y	Y	N	10	23
North Hennepin Community College	Brooklyn Park	C,T	St	M/W	7,657	70												16
Northwest Technical College	Bemidji	T	St	M/W	1,203	64	51					Y		Y	Y	Y			
Rainy River Community College	International Falls	C,T	St	M/W	304	22	54		Y			R	Y	Y	Y	Y	16	5
St. Cloud Technical & Community College	St. Cloud	C,T	St	M/W	4,751	53												
Mississippi																		
Copiah-Lincoln Community College	Wesson	C,T	St-L	M/W	3,157	21	6		Y			Y	Y	Y	Y	Y	8	42
Hinds Community College	Raymond	C,T	St-L	M/W	11,893	29	32					Y	Y	Y	Y	Y	14	111
Mississippi Delta Community College	Moorhead	C,T	Dist	M/W	2,950	22	20		N	Y		Y	Y	Y	Y	Y	6	44

This chart includes the names and locations of accredited two-year colleges in the United States, Canada, and other countries and shows institutions' responses to the *Peterson's Annual Survey of Undergraduate Institutions*. If an institution submitted incomplete data, one or more columns opposite the institution's name is blank. A dagger after the school name indicates that the institution has one or more entries in the *College Close-Ups* section. If a school does not appear, it did not report any of the information.

Y—Yes; N—No; R—Recommended; S—For Some

Institution	Location	Degrees Awarded	Institutional Control	Student Body	Undergraduate Enrollment	Percent Women, Coed	Percent Attending Part-Time	Percent 25 Years of Age or Older	Percent of Grads Going on to Four-Year Colleges	High School Equivalency Certificate Accepted	Open Admissions	High School Transcript Required	Need-Based Aid Required	Part-Time Jobs Available	Career Counseling Available	Job Placement Services Available	College Housing Available	Number of Sports Offered	Number of Majors Offered
Mississippi Gulf Coast Community College	Perkinston	C,T	Dist	M/W	10,074		31					Y	Y	Y	Y	Y	Y	Y	9	45
Northwest Mississippi Community College	Senatobia	C,T	St-L	M/W	6,300					Y	Y	Y	Y	Y	Y		Y	7	48
Missouri																			
Brown Mackie College–St. Louis†	Fenton	T,B	Prop	M/W																9
Cottey College	Nevada	C,B	Ind	CW	284			1	95			Y		Y	Y	Y	Y	Y	5	1
Crowder College	Neosho	C,T	St-L	M/W	5,845		56			Y	Y	Y	Y	Y	Y	Y	Y	4	46
Culinary Institute of St. Louis at Hickey College	St. Louis	T	Priv	M/W	91						Y					Y				1
East Central College	Union	C,T	Dist	M/W	3,900		53	35		Y	Y	Y	Y	Y	Y		N		3	32
ITT Technical Institute	Arnold	T,B	Prop	M/W							Y		Y	Y			N			13
ITT Technical Institute	Earth City	T,B	Prop	M/W							Y		Y	Y			N			13
ITT Technical Institute	Kansas City	T,B	Prop	M/W							Y									12
Jefferson College	Hillsboro	C,T	Dist	M/W	5,194		48	25	Y″	Y	Y	Y	Y	Y	Y	Y	Y	6	26
Metro Business College	Jefferson City	T	Prop	M/W	142		20	62				Y		Y	Y	Y	N			2
Metropolitan Community College–Kansas City	Lee's Summit	C,T	St-L	M/W	19,234		60	37	Y	Y		Y	Y	Y	Y	Y	N	6	46
Mineral Area College	Park Hills	C,T	Dist	M/W	4,508		36	23	Y		Y	Y	Y	Y	Y	Y	Y	5	33
Missouri State University–West Plains	West Plains	C,T	St	M/W	2,123		38	38	Y	Y	S	Y	Y	Y	Y	Y	Y	2	21
Ozarks Technical Community College	Springfield	C,T	Dist	M/W	14,798					Y	Y	Y	Y	Y	Y	Y	N			34
St. Louis Community College	St. Louis	C,T	Pub	M/W	24,005		58	44	Y	Y	S			Y	Y	N		5	
State Fair Community College	Sedalia	C,T	Dist	M/W	5,185		47	34	Y	Y	Y	Y	Y	Y	Y	Y		1	29
Vet Tech Institute at Hickey College	St. Louis	T	Priv	M/W	126											Y				1
Montana																			
Flathead Valley Community College	Kalispell	C,T	St-L	M/W	2,216		51	49	45	Y	Y	Y	Y	Y	Y	Y	Y	7	28
Great Falls College Montana State University	Great Falls	C,T	St	M/W	1,875		52	53		Y	Y	Y	Y	Y	Y	Y			20
Helena College University of Montana	Helena	C,T	St	M/W	1,430		53	46	12	Y	Y	S	Y	Y	Y	Y	N		17
Miles Community College	Miles City	C,T	St-L	M/W	441		37													
Nebraska																			
ITT Technical Institute	Omaha	T,B	Prop	M/W							Y		Y				N			12
Little Priest Tribal College	Winnebago	C	Ind	M/W	122		34													
Mid-Plains Community College	North Platte	C,T	Dist	M/W	2,491		61	36	Y	Y	Y	Y	Y	Y	Y	Y	Y	5	18
Wright Career College	Omaha	T,B	Prop	M/W	306		69	54	Y	Y					Y	Y	N			10
Nevada																			
Carrington College–Las Vegas	Las Vegas	T	Prop	M/W	255		12	64			Y	Y					N			2
Carrington College–Reno	Reno	T	Prop	M/W	333		24	66			Y	Y					N			1
Great Basin College	Elko	C,T,B	St	M/W	3,185					Y			Y	Y	Y	Y	Y	Y	3	30
ITT Technical Institute	Henderson	T,B	Prop	M/W							Y		Y	Y						12
ITT Technical Institute	North Las Vegas	T,B	Prop	M/W							Y		Y							10
Truckee Meadows Community College	Reno	C,T	St	M/W	11,204		74	40	34	Y			Y	Y	Y	Y	N		2	51
Western Nevada College	Carson City	C,T,B	St	M/W	3,976		72	52		Y		S	Y	Y	Y	Y	N	2	27
New Hampshire																			
Lakes Region Community College	Laconia	C,T	St	M/W	1,179		58	39	Y	Y	Y	Y	Y				N			23
NHTI, Concord's Community College	Concord	C	St	M/W	3,700															16
River Valley Community College	Claremont	C,T	St	M/W	982		64	53	Y	Y	Y	Y	Y				N			16
New Jersey																			
Burlington County College	Pemberton	C,T	Cou	M/W	10,071		49													
County College of Morris	Randolph	C,T	Cou	M/W	8,447			23	Y	Y	Y	Y	Y	Y	Y	Y	N	12	30
Cumberland County College	Vineland	C,T	St-L	M/W	3,919			35	Y	Y	Y	Y	Y	Y	Y	Y	N	7	20
Essex County College	Newark	C,T	Cou	M/W	11,979		45										N			17
Hudson County Community College	Jersey City	C,T	St-L	M/W	9,036		33	34	Y				Y	Y	Y	Y	N			17
ITT Technical Institute	Marlton	T	Prop	M/W																3
Mercer County Community College	Trenton	C,T	St-L	M/W	8,501		64	39	Y		Y	Y	Y	Y	Y	Y	N	9	51
Middlesex County College	Edison	C,T	Cou	M/W	12,611				Y	Y	Y	Y	Y	Y	Y		N	7	40
Ocean County College	Toms River	C,T	Cou	M/W	9,477		46	26	55	Y		S	Y	Y	Y	Y	N	12	19
Raritan Valley Community College	Branchburg	C,T	St-L	M/W	8,405		57	23				Y	Y	Y	Y	Y	N	6	57
Sussex County Community College	Newton	C,T	St-L	M/W	3,732		45	60	Y			Y	Y	Y			N	4	17
Union County College	Cranford	C,T	St-L	M/W	12,146		52													
New Mexico																			
Brown Mackie College–Albuquerque†	Albuquerque	T,B	Prop	M/W																12
Carrington College–Albuquerque	Albuquerque	T	Prop	M/W	647		16	60					Y							3
Central New Mexico Community College	Albuquerque	C,T	St	M/W	28,323		67													13
ITT Technical Institute	Albuquerque	T,B	Prop	M/W							Y		Y	Y		N				13
New Mexico State University–Alamogordo	Alamogordo	C,T	St	M/W	3,371		70	47	Y	Y	Y	Y	Y	Y	Y	Y	N		20
San Juan College	Farmington	C,T	St	M/W	8,491		71	58	Y	Y	Y	Y	Y	Y	Y	N	N	14	52
Southwestern Indian Polytechnic Institute	Albuquerque	C,T	Fed	M/W	480		15	38	N	Y	Y	Y	Y	Y	Y	N	Y	3	12
University of New Mexico–Los Alamos Branch	Los Alamos	C,T	St	M/W	744		74	48	35				Y	Y	Y	Y	Y			18
New York																			
Adirondack Community College	Queensbury	C,T	St-L	M/W	3,987		43													
American Academy of Dramatic Arts–New York	New York	T	Ind	M/W	258															
The Art Institute of New York City	New York	T	Prop	M/W																3
The Belanger School of Nursing	Schenectady	C,T	Ind	PW	124		70	78				Y	Y				N			1
Borough of Manhattan Community College of the City University of New York	New York	C,T	St-L	M/W	24,186		34	25	Y	Y	Y	Y			Y	Y	N	5	25
Bronx Community College of the City University of New York	Bronx	C,T	St-L	M/W	11,368		42	35	Y	Y		Y	Y	Y	Y			6	27
Cayuga County Community College	Auburn	C,T	St-L	M/W	4,619		52	30	Y	Y	Y	Y	Y	Y	Y	Y	Y	8	34

This chart includes the names and locations of accredited two-year colleges in the United States, Canada, and other countries and shows institutions' responses to the *Peterson's Annual Survey of Undergraduate Institutions*. If an institution submitted incomplete data, one or more columns opposite the institution's name is blank. A dagger after the school name indicates that the institution has one or more entries in the *College Close-Ups* section. If a school does not appear, it did not report any of the information.

Y—Yes; N—No; R—Recommended; S—For Some

Column legend (left to right): Degrees Awarded [College Transfer Associate (C); Terminal Associate (T); Bachelor's (B); Master's (M); Doctoral (D)] · Institutional Control · Student Body · Undergraduate Enrollment · Percent Attending Part-Time · Percent 25 Years of Age or Older · Percent of Grads Going on to Four-Year Colleges · Open Admissions · High School Equivalency Certificate Accepted · High School Transcript Required · Need-Based Aid Available · Part-Time Jobs Available · Career Counseling Available · Job Placement Services Available · College Housing Available · Number of Sports Offered · Number of Majors Offered

Institution	Location	Degrees	Inst. Control	Student Body	Enroll.	% PT	% 25+	% to 4-yr	Open Adm.	HS Equiv.	HS Transc.	Need Aid	PT Jobs	Career Couns.	Job Place.	Housing	Sports	Majors
Clinton Community College	Plattsburgh	C,T	St-L	M/W	1,997		16	36	Y		Y	Y	Y	Y	Y	N	5	17
Columbia-Greene Community College	Hudson	C,T	St-L	M/W	2,112	54	26				Y	Y	Y	Y		N	5	21
Corning Community College	Corning	C,T	St-L	M/W	4,957	54												
Dutchess Community College	Poughkeepsie	C,T	St-L	M/W	10,232	52	18		Y	Y	Y	Y	Y	Y	Y	Y	6	31
Elmira Business Institute	Elmira	C,T	Priv	PW	98	24			Y	Y	Y	Y		Y	Y	N		4
Erie Community College	Buffalo	C,T	St-L	M/W	3,281	25	42	81	Y	Y	Y	Y	Y	Y	Y	N	11	15
Erie Community College, North Campus	Williamsville	C,T	St-L	M/W	6,466	35	35	81	Y	Y	Y	Y	Y	Y	Y	N	11	27
Erie Community College, South Campus	Orchard Park	C,T	St-L	M/W	3,902	39	20	81	Y	Y	Y	Y	Y	Y	Y	N	11	19
Fashion Institute of Technology†	New York	C,T,B,M	St-L	PW	9,566	24	22		N	Y	Y	Y	Y	Y	Y	Y	8	21
Finger Lakes Community College	Canandaigua	C,T	St-L	M/W	6,389	47	32		Y	Y	Y	Y	Y	Y	Y	Y	9	57
Fiorello H. LaGuardia Community College of the City University of New York	Long Island City	C,T	St-L	M/W	19,586	47	28	51	Y	Y		Y	Y	Y	Y	N	7	43
Genesee Community College	Batavia	C,T	St-L	M/W	7,087	53	36		Y	Y		Y	Y	Y	Y	Y	13	91
Herkimer County Community College	Herkimer	C,T	St-L	M/W	3,223	35	27					Y	Y	Y	Y	Y	13	29
Institute of Design and Construction	Brooklyn	C,T	Ind	M/W	103	58	54		Y		Y	Y	Y		Y	N		4
Island Drafting and Technical Institute	Amityville	C,T	Prop	PM	116		45	0	Y	Y	R	Y		Y	Y	N		8
ITT Technical Institute	Albany	T	Prop	M/W						Y		Y	Y			N		5
ITT Technical Institute	Getzville	T	Prop	M/W						Y		Y	Y			N		9
ITT Technical Institute	Liverpool	T	Prop	M/W						Y		Y				N		6
Jamestown Business College	Jamestown	T,B	Prop	M/W	294	2	47		N	Y	Y	Y		Y	Y	N	8	4
Jamestown Community College	Jamestown	C,T	St-L	M/W	3,600	26	31	53	Y	Y	Y	Y	Y	Y	Y	N	10	30
Jefferson Community College	Watertown	C,T	St-L	M/W	4,127	45			N	Y	Y	Y	Y	Y	Y	N	6	36
Kingsborough Community College of the City University of New York	Brooklyn	C,T	St-L	M/W	18,794	43	28		Y	Y	Y	Y		Y		N	7	40
Long Island Business Institute	Flushing	C	Prop	PW	443	26	76	0	Y	Y	Y			Y	Y	N		7
Mohawk Valley Community College	Utica	C,T	St-L	M/W	7,419	38	35		Y		S	Y	Y	Y	Y	Y	13	48
Monroe Community College	Rochester	C,T	St-L	M/W	16,458	38	41		Y	Y	Y	Y	Y	Y	Y	Y	18	67
Nassau Community College	Garden City	C,T	St-L	M/W	23,034	40	23		Y	Y	Y	Y	Y	Y	Y	N	18	53
New York Career Institute	New York	T	Prop	PW	702				N	Y	Y			Y		N		3
Niagara County Community College	Sanborn	C,T	St-L	M/W	6,648	37	23		Y	Y	Y	Y	Y	Y	Y	Y	11	42
Onondaga Community College	Syracuse	C,T	St-L	M/W	12,841	49	24		Y	Y	Y	Y	Y		Y	N	13	39
St. Elizabeth College of Nursing	Utica	T	Ind	M/W	159	55	47		N	Y		Y			Y	N		1
State University of New York College of Technology at Alfred	Alfred	C,T,B	St	M/W	3,549	9	15		N	Y	Y	Y	Y	Y	Y	Y	17	79
Sullivan County Community College	Loch Sheldrake	C,T	St-L	M/W	1,585	36	20	45	Y	Y	Y	Y	Y	Y	Y	Y	14	37
TCI–The College of Technology	New York	C,T	Prop	M/W	3,020				Y	Y	Y	Y	Y	Y		N		13
Tompkins Cortland Community College	Dryden	C,T	St-L	M/W	5,450	51	27		Y	Y	Y	Y	Y	Y	Y	N	22	35
Westchester Community College	Valhalla	C,T	St-L	M/W	13,781	45	27		Y	Y	Y	Y	Y	Y	Y	N	11	50
Wood Tobe–Coburn School	New York	T	Priv	M/W	523				N	Y		Y				N		9
North Carolina																		
Alamance Community College	Graham	C,T	St	M/W	4,648	53	44		Y	Y	Y	Y	Y	Y	Y	N	4	28
Beaufort County Community College	Washington	C,T	St	M/W	1,933													
Cape Fear Community College	Wilmington	C,T	St	M/W	9,246	51	38		Y	Y	S	Y	Y	Y	Y	N	6	35
Carolinas College of Health Sciences	Charlotte	T	Pub	M/W	438	87	61		N	Y	S	Y	Y	Y	Y	Y		3
Catawba Valley Community College	Hickory	C,T	St-L	M/W	4,561	61	35		Y	Y	Y	Y	Y	Y	Y	N	4	34
Central Carolina Community College	Sanford	C,T	St-L	M/W	4,900	56	53		Y	Y	Y	Y	Y	Y	Y	N	3	29
Cleveland Community College	Shelby	C,T	St	M/W	3,371	65			Y	Y	Y	Y	Y	Y	Y	N		32
Fayetteville Technical Community College	Fayetteville	C,T	St	M/W	12,383	59	60	13	Y	Y	S	Y	Y	Y	Y	N	5	49
Forsyth Technical Community College	Winston-Salem	C,T	St	M/W	9,941	53												
Guilford Technical Community College	Jamestown	C,T	St-L	M/W	14,793	47												
Halifax Community College	Weldon	C,T	St-L	M/W	1,510		47		Y	Y	Y	Y		Y	Y	N		15
Harrison College	Morrisville	C,T	Prop	M/W	200	21	62		N	Y	Y			Y	Y	N		2
ITT Technical Institute	Cary	T,B	Prop	M/W												N		8
ITT Technical Institute	Charlotte	T,B	Prop	M/W												N		9
ITT Technical Institute	High Point	T,B	Prop	M/W												N		10
James Sprunt Community College	Kenansville	C,T	St	M/W	1,291	46	32	1	Y	Y	Y	Y	Y	Y	Y	N	2	17
Johnston Community College	Smithfield	C,T	St	M/W	4,235	48	40		Y	Y	Y	Y	Y	Y	Y	N	1	13
King's College	Charlotte	T	Priv	M/W	501											Y		9
Lenoir Community College	Kinston	C,T	St	M/W	2,813	52	40		Y	Y	Y	Y	Y	Y	Y	N	3	25
Living Arts College	Raleigh	B	Prop	M/W	578		33		N	Y	Y			Y	Y	N		6
Mitchell Community College	Statesville	C,T	St	M/W	3,514	56	41		Y	Y	Y	Y	Y	Y	Y	N		32
Montgomery Community College	Troy	C,T	St	M/W	837	54												
Piedmont Community College	Roxboro	C,T	St	M/W	1,591				Y	Y	S	Y	Y	Y	Y	N	1	24
Pitt Community College	Greenville	C,T	St-L	M/W	8,902	48			Y	Y	Y	Y	Y	Y	Y	N	5	55
Randolph Community College	Asheboro	C,T	St	M/W	3,024	62	34	53	Y	Y	Y	Y	Y			N	4	30
Richmond Community College	Hamlet	C,T	St	M/W	2,664	58	42		Y	Y		Y	Y			N		23
Robeson Community College	Lumberton	C,T	St	M/W	2,869													
Southeastern Community College	Whiteville	C,T	St	M/W	1,402	45	62		Y	Y	Y	Y	Y	Y	Y	N	4	21
South Piedmont Community College	Polkton	C,T	St	M/W	2,773		62		Y	Y	Y	Y	Y	Y	Y	N		29
Southwestern Community College	Sylva	C,T	St	M/W	2,689				Y	Y	Y	Y	Y			N		32
Tri-County Community College	Murphy	C,T	St	M/W	1,353													
Wayne Community College	Goldsboro	C,T	St-L	M/W	3,837	53	45		Y	Y	Y	Y	Y	Y	Y	N	1	33
Wilson Community College	Wilson	C,T	St	M/W	1,837	51												
North Dakota																		
Bismarck State College	Bismarck	C,T,B	St	M/W	4,062	42	34		Y	Y	Y	Y	Y	Y	Y	Y	8	40
Dakota College at Bottineau	Bottineau	C,T	St	M/W	793		33		Y	Y	Y	Y	Y	Y	Y	Y	9	72
Lake Region State College	Devils Lake	C,T	St	M/W	1,898	74	19		Y	Y	S	Y	Y	Y	Y	Y	4	15
North Dakota State College of Science	Wahpeton	C,T	St	M/W	3,168	46	17		Y	Y	Y	Y	Y	Y	Y	Y	6	41
Williston State College	Williston	C,T	St	M/W	909		23		Y	Y	Y	Y	Y	Y	Y	Y	5	26

This chart includes the names and locations of accredited two-year colleges in the United States, Canada, and other countries and shows institutions' responses to the *Peterson's Annual Survey of Undergraduate Institutions.* If an institution submitted incomplete data, one or more columns opposite the institution's name is blank. A dagger after the school name indicates that the institution has one or more entries in the *College Close-Ups* section. If a school does not appear, it did not report any of the information.

Y—Yes; N—No; R—Recommended; S—For Some

Column headings: Degrees Awarded — College Transfer Associate (C); Terminal Associate (T); Bachelor's (B); Master's (M); Doctoral (D). Institutional Control. Student Body — Men, Primarily Men, Women, Primarily Women, Coed. Undergraduate Enrollment. Percent Women, Coed. Percent Attending Part-Time. Percent 25 Years of Age or Older. Percent of Grads Going on to Four-Year Colleges. Open Admissions. High School Equivalency Certificate Accepted. High School Transcript Required. Need-Based Aid Required. Part-Time Jobs Available. Career Counseling Available. Job Placement Services Available. College Housing Available. Number of Sports Offered. Number of Majors Offered.

Institution	Location	Degrees	Control	Student Body	Undergrad Enroll.	% Part-Time	% 25+	% Grads to 4-Yr	Open Adm.	HS Equiv.	HS Transcript	Need-Based Aid	Part-Time Jobs	Career Couns.	Job Place.	College Housing	# Sports	# Majors
Ohio																		
The Art Institute of Cincinnati	Cincinnati	C,B	Ind	M/W	35	14	26	20	N	Y	Y		Y	Y	N	N		1
Bowling Green State University–Firelands College	Huron	C,T,B	St	M/W	2,441	49	42		N	Y	Y		Y	Y	Y	N	5	25
Bradford School	Columbus	T	Priv	PW	541									Y			N	5
Brown Mackie College–Akron†	Akron	T,B	Prop	M/W										Y			N	5
Brown Mackie College–Cincinnati†	Cincinnati	T,B	Prop	M/W														11
Brown Mackie College–Findlay†	Findlay	T,B	Prop	M/W					*									9
Brown Mackie College–North Canton†	Canton	T,B	Prop	M/W														7
Central Ohio Technical College	Newark	T	St	M/W	3,648	73	51		Y	Y	Y		Y	Y	Y	N	8	28
Cincinnati State Technical and Community College	Cincinnati	C,T	St	M/W	11,167	63	52	54	Y	Y	Y	Y	Y	Y	Y	N	4	63
Clark State Community College	Springfield	C,T	St	M/W	5,653	70	57		Y	Y	Y	Y	Y	Y		N	5	56
Cleveland Institute of Electronics	Cleveland	T	Prop	PM	1,477		85		Y	Y	Y							3	1
Columbus Culinary Institute at Bradford School	Columbus	T	Priv	M/W	150											Y		1
Columbus State Community College	Columbus	C,T	St	M/W	25,249	65	45	51	Y			R,S	Y	Y	Y	N	10	62
Cuyahoga Community College	Cleveland	C,T	St-L	M/W	30,065	65												
Davis College	Toledo	T	Prop	M/W	218	76	55		N	Y	Y	Y	Y	Y	Y	N		20
Eastern Gateway Community College	Steubenville	C,T	St-L	M/W	2,929	52			Y	Y	S	Y	Y	Y	Y	N	2	21
Edison Community College	Piqua	C,T	St	M/W	2,993	71	56	62	Y	Y	Y		Y	Y	Y	N	3	41
Hocking College	Nelsonville	C,T	St	M/W	4,094		28		Y	Y	Y		Y			Y	10	39
International College of Broadcasting	Dayton	C,T	Priv	M/W	88		35		Y	Y	Y			Y	Y	N		1
ITT Technical Institute	Akron	T,B	Prop	M/W														14
ITT Technical Institute	Columbus	T,B	Prop	M/W														12
ITT Technical Institute	Dayton	T,B	Prop	M/W								Y		Y	Y	N		14
ITT Technical Institute	Hilliard	T,B	Prop	M/W														15
ITT Technical Institute	Maumee	T,B	Prop	M/W														12
ITT Technical Institute	Norwood	C,B	Prop	M/W								Y		Y	Y	N		13
ITT Technical Institute	Strongsville	T,B	Prop	M/W								Y		Y	Y	N		14
ITT Technical Institute	Warrensville Heights	T,B	Prop	M/W								Y		Y	Y	N		14
ITT Technical Institute	Youngstown	T,B	Prop	M/W								Y		Y	Y	N		14
James A. Rhodes State College	Lima	C,T	St	M/W	3,883	60												
Kent State University at Ashtabula	Ashtabula	C,B	St	M/W	2,339	47	51		Y	Y	Y	Y	Y	Y		N		25
Kent State University at East Liverpool	East Liverpool	C,B,M	St	M/W	1,671	47	46		Y	Y	Y	Y	Y	Y	Y	N		14
Kent State University at Salem	Salem	C,B	St	M/W	1,844	33	41		Y	Y	Y	Y	Y	Y	Y	N	5	21
Kent State University at Trumbull	Warren	C,B	St	M/W	3,061	39	44		Y	Y	Y	Y	Y	Y	Y	N		26
Kent State University at Tuscarawas	New Philadelphia	C,B	St	M/W	2,375	43	40		Y	Y	Y	Y	Y	Y	Y	N	2	25
Lakeland Community College	Kirtland	C,T	St-L	M/W	8,839	64			Y	Y	Y	Y	Y	Y	Y	N	6	39
Lorain County Community College	Elyria	C,T	St-L	M/W	12,280	72	42		Y	Y	S	Y	Y	Y	Y	N	6	72
Marion Technical College	Marion	C,T	St	M/W	2,765													
Northwest State Community College	Archbold	C,T	St	M/W	4,244	79					Y							
Ohio Business College	Hilliard	T	Prop	M/W					Y	Y	Y							
The Ohio State University Agricultural Technical Institute	Wooster	C,T	St	M/W	694		10		Y	Y	Y	Y	Y	Y	Y	Y	8	35
Owens Community College	Toledo	C,T	St	M/W	14,674	65	46		Y		R,S	Y	Y	Y	N	N	11	53
Southern State Community College	Hillsboro	C,T	St	M/W	2,431	52		25	Y	Y	R	Y	Y	Y	N	N	4	29
Stark State College	North Canton	C,T	St-R	M/W	15,450	71	50				Y	Y	Y	Y	N		49
Terra State Community College	Fremont	C,T	St	M/W	3,172	61												
The University of Akron–Wayne College	Orrville	C,T,B	St	M/W	2,353	53	33		Y	Y	S	Y	Y	Y	Y	N	4	8
Vet Tech Institute at Bradford School	Columbus	T	Priv	M/W	156											Y		1
Oklahoma																		
Brown Mackie College–Oklahoma City†	Oklahoma City	T,B	Prop	M/W														9
Brown Mackie College–Tulsa†	Tulsa	T,B	Prop	M/W													9	9
Carl Albert State College	Poteau	C,T	St	M/W	2,460	44	35		Y	Y		Y		Y		Y	6	29
Clary Sage College	Tulsa	T	Prop	PW	228		64		Y	Y	Y		Y	Y		N		3
Community Care College	Tulsa	T	Prop	PW	942		51		Y	Y	Y	Y	Y	Y		N		12
ITT Technical Institute	Tulsa	T,B	Prop	M/W												N		14
Oklahoma City Community College	Oklahoma City	C,T	St	M/W	13,026	65	44		Y			S	Y	Y	Y	N	9	72
Oklahoma State University Institute of Technology	Okmulgee	C,T,B	St	M/W	2,877	28	17		Y	Y	S	Y	Y	Y	Y	Y	7	3
Oklahoma State University, Oklahoma City	Oklahoma City	C,T,B	St	M/W	6,996	68	51		Y	Y	Y	Y	Y	Y	Y	N		46
Oklahoma Technical College	Tulsa	T	Prop	M/W	84		50		Y	Y	Y			Y	Y	N		5
Redlands Community College	El Reno	C,T	St	M/W	2,560	64												
Seminole State College	Seminole	C,T	St	M/W	2,123	44	33		Y	Y		Y		Y		Y	7	28
Tulsa Community College	Tulsa	C,T	St	M/W	17,876	64	46		Y	Y	Y	Y	Y	Y	Y	N	10	87
Western Oklahoma State College	Altus	C,T	St	M/W	1,690	60	35		Y	Y	Y	Y	Y	Y	Y	Y	6	10
Wright Career College	Oklahoma City	C,T,B	Prop	M/W	254	29	65		Y	Y			Y	Y		N		9
Wright Career College	Tulsa	C,T,B	Prop	M/W	309	64	67		Y	Y			Y	Y		N		9
Oregon																		
Central Oregon Community College	Bend	C,T	Dist	M/W	6,760	56	47		*Y	Y		Y	Y	Y	Y	Y	11	56
Chemeketa Community College	Salem	C,T	St-L	M/W	12,371	50												
Clatsop Community College	Astoria	C,T	Cou	M/W	1,071	58	44		Y		R	Y	Y	Y	N		5
Columbia Gorge Community College	The Dalles	C,T	St	M/W	1,245	56	48		Y			Y	Y			N		9
ITT Technical Institute	Portland	T,B	Prop	M/W						Y		Y	Y		N		14
Klamath Community College	Klamath Falls	C,T	St	M/W	1,148	66												
Lane Community College	Eugene	C,T	St-L	M/W	11,002	55	46		Y			Y	Y	Y	Y	N	15	35
Linn-Benton Community College	Albany	C,T	St-L	M/W	5,617	54	37		Y			Y	Y	Y	N	N	4	44
Oregon Coast Community College	Newport	C,T	Pub	M/W	540	71	54	36	Y		Y			Y		N		5
Rogue Community College	Grants Pass	C,T	St-L	M/W	5,530	57	50		Y			Y	Y	Y	Y	N	5	53
Treasure Valley Community College	Ontario	C,T	St-L	M/W	2,443	50	38		Y			Y	Y	Y	Y	Y	11	63
Umpqua Community College	Roseburg	C,T	St-L	M/W	2,114	57	49	10	Y		R	Y	Y	Y	Y	N	2	53

This chart includes the names and locations of accredited two-year colleges in the United States, Canada, and other countries and shows institutions' responses to the *Peterson's Annual Survey of Undergraduate Institutions.* If an institution submitted incomplete data, one or more columns opposite the institution's name is blank. A dagger after the school name indicates that the institution has one or more entries in the *College Close-Ups* section. If a school does not appear, it did not report any of the information.

Y—Yes; N—No; R—Recommended; S—For Some

Column key (left to right): **Degrees Awarded** — College Transfer Associate (C), Terminal Associate (T), Bachelor's (B), Masters (M), Doctoral (D); **Institutional Control** — County/District City, Federal, State, Commonwealth, Territory, Independent, Independent-Religious, Proprietary, State and Local, State-Related; **Student Body** — Men, Primarily Men, Women, Primarily Women, Coed; Undergraduate Enrollment; Percent Attending Part-Time; Percent 25 Years of Age or Older; Percent of Grade Going on to Four-Year Colleges; High School Equivalency Certificate Accepted; High School Transcript Required; Open Admissions; Need-Based Aid Required; Part-Time Jobs Available; Job Placement Services Available; Career Counseling Available; College Housing Available; Number of Sports Offered; Number of Majors Offered.

Institution	Location	Degrees Awarded	Institutional Control	Student Body	Undergrad Enrollment	% Part-Time	% 25+ yrs	% to 4-yr	HS Equiv Accepted	HS Transcript Req	Open Admissions	Need-Based Aid	Part-Time Jobs	Job Placement	Career Counseling	College Housing	# Sports	# Majors
Pennsylvania																		
Antonelli Institute	Erdenheim	T	Prop	M/W	176				Y	Y				Y	Y			2
Bradford School	Pittsburgh	T	Priv	M/W	387				Y	Y				Y	Y			11
Bucks County Community College	Newtown	C,T	Cou	M/W	9,880	67	31	49	Y	Y	Y	Y	Y	Y	Y	N	8	61
Butler County Community College	Butler	C,T	Cou	M/W	3,686		29		Y	Y		Y	Y	Y	Y	N	8	62
Cambria-Rowe Business College	Indiana	C,T	Prop	M/W	105			0						Y	Y			7
Cambria-Rowe Business College	Johnstown	C,T	Prop	PW	142	1	47		N	Y	Y		Y		Y	N		10
Career Training Academy	Pittsburgh	T	Prop	M/W	70													
Commonwealth Technical Institute	Johnstown	T	St	M/W	208		50		Y	Y	R,S	Y	Y	Y		Y		6
Community College of Allegheny County	Pittsburgh	C,T	Cou	M/W	18,207	65	46		Y	R	Y	Y				N	15	115
Community College of Beaver County	Monaca	C,T	St	M/W	2,779													
Community College of Philadelphia	Philadelphia	C,T	St-L	M/W	39,500		53	71	Y	Y	S		Y	Y	Y	N	8	38
Harrisburg Area Community College	Harrisburg	C,T	St-L	M/W	20,780	69	43		Y		S	Y	Y	Y		N	5	86
ITT Technical Institute	Dunmore	T	Prop	M/W														5
ITT Technical Institute	Harrisburg	T	Prop	M/W														7
ITT Technical Institute	Levittown	T	Prop	M/W						Y				Y	Y			5
ITT Technical Institute	Philadelphia		Prop	M/W														3
ITT Technical Institute	Pittsburgh	T	Prop	M/W										Y	Y			6
ITT Technical Institute	Plymouth Meeting	T	Prop	M/W										Y	Y			5
ITT Technical Institute	Tarentum	T	Prop	M/W						Y				Y	Y			5
JNA Institute of Culinary Arts	Philadelphia	T	Prop	M/W	65													
Lehigh Carbon Community College	Schnecksville	C,T	St-L	M/W	7,128	64	39	54	Y		S	Y	Y	Y	Y	N	7	61
Luzerne County Community College	Nanticoke	C,T	Cou	M/W	6,411	51	37		Y		R	Y	Y	Y	Y	N	10	74
Manor College	Jenkintown	C,T	I-R	M/W	926													
McCann School of Business & Technology	Pottsville	C,T	Prop	M/W	1,657													
Montgomery County Community College	Blue Bell	C,T	Cou	M/W	13,122	65	35	62	Y	Y	Y	Y	Y	Y		N	13	59
Northampton Community College	Bethlehem	C,T	St-L	M/W	10,666	56	34	68	Y	Y	R,S	Y	Y	Y	Y	Y	9	61
Penn State Beaver	Monaca	B	St-R	M/W	703	11	10		N	Y	Y	Y	Y			Y	10	118
Penn State Brandywine	Media	C,T,B	St-R	M/W	1,492	16	14		N	Y	Y	Y				N	10	120
Penn State DuBois	DuBois	C,T,B	St-R	M/W	704	21	22		N	Y	Y	Y				N	7	127
Penn State Fayette, The Eberly Campus	Uniontown	C,T,B	St-R	M/W	846	23	24		N	Y	Y	Y				N	11	124
Penn State Greater Allegheny	McKeesport	C,T,B,M	St-R	M/W	623	10	10		N	Y	Y	Y				Y	12	119
Penn State Hazleton	Hazleton	C,T,B	St-R	M/W	951	7	10		N	Y	Y	Y				Y	8	125
Penn State Lehigh Valley	Fogelsville	C,T,B	St-R	M/W	889	19	12		N	Y	Y	Y		Y	Y	N	13	119
Penn State Mont Alto	Mont Alto	C,T,B	St-R	M/W	1,022	28	22		N	Y	Y	Y				Y	10	120
Penn State New Kensington	New Kensington	C,T,B,M	St-R	M/W	680	23	21		N	Y	Y	Y	Y				13	124
Penn State Schuylkill	Schuylkill Haven	C,T,B	St-R	M/W	837	21	19		N	Y	Y	Y					8	124
Penn State Wilkes-Barre	Lehman	C,T,B	St-R	M/W	606	14	9		N	Y	Y	Y				N	11	122
Penn State Worthington Scranton	Dunmore	C,T,B	St-R	M/W	1,178	20	24		N	Y	Y	Y				N	10	119
Penn State York	York	C,T,B,M	St-R	M/W	1,141	28	23		N	Y	Y	Y				N		126
Pennsylvania College of Health Sciences	Lancaster	T,B	Ind	PW	1,429	64	54			Y	S				Y	N	2	11
Pennsylvania Highlands Community College	Johnstown	C,T	St-L	M/W	2,506				Y	Y	Y	Y	Y	Y	Y	N	2	5
Pennsylvania Institute of Technology	Media	C,T	Ind	M/W	743	36	40		Y	Y	Y	Y	Y	Y	Y	N	1	7
Pittsburgh Technical Institute	Oakdale	T	Prop	M/W	1,841		21		Y	Y	Y			Y	Y	Y	5	15
Reading Area Community College	Reading	C,T	Cou	M/W	4,538	78	43		Y	Y	R,S	Y	Y	Y	Y	N		39
Triangle Tech, Inc.–Pittsburgh School	Pittsburgh	C,T	Prop	PM	103		44			Y	Y	Y	Y	Y		N		6
University of Pittsburgh at Titusville	Titusville	C,T	St-R	M/W	388	19												
Vet Tech Institute	Pittsburgh	T	Priv	M/W	337						Y			Y		Y		1
Westmoreland County Community College	Youngwood	C,T	Cou	M/W	6,104	51	37		Y				Y	Y	Y	N	10	72
The Williamson Free School of Mechanical Trades	Media	T	Ind	CM	270		0		N	Y	Y	Y		Y	Y	Y	12	8
Rhode Island																		
Community College of Rhode Island	Warwick	C,T	St	M/W	17,699	69	38		Y	Y		Y	Y	Y	Y	N	8	48
South Carolina																		
Brown Mackie College–Greenville†	Greenville	T,B	Prop	M/W														9
Denmark Technical College	Denmark	C,T	St	M/W	2,003	9												
Forrest College	Anderson	C,T	Prop	M/W	120	28												
Greenville Technical College	Greenville	C,T	St	M/W	13,448	59	41		Y	Y	Y	Y	Y	Y	Y	N	7	38
Horry-Georgetown Technical College	Conway	C,T	St-L	M/W	7,698	62												
ITT Technical Institute	Columbia	T,B	Prop	M/W												N		9
ITT Technical Institute	Greenville	T,B	Prop	M/W						Y				Y		N		8
ITT Technical Institute	Myrtle Beach	T,B	Prop	M/W														8
ITT Technical Institute	North Charleston	T,B	Prop	M/W														7
Northeastern Technical College	Cheraw	C,T	St-L	M/W	976	54	43		Y	Y	Y	Y	Y	Y	Y	N		12
Spartanburg Community College	Spartanburg	C,T	St	M/W	5,864	52	36		Y	Y	Y	Y	Y	Y	Y			19
Spartanburg Methodist College	Spartanburg	C,T	I-R	M/W	818	2	1	81	N	Y	Y	Y	Y	Y	Y	Y	12	5
Technical College of the Lowcountry	Beaufort	C,T	St	M/W	2,427					Y	Y	Y		Y		N		19
Trident Technical College	Charleston	C,T	St-L	M/W	17,489	57	54		Y	Y	S	Y	Y	Y	Y	N		39
University of South Carolina Salkehatchie	Allendale	C,T	St	M/W	1,173													
University of South Carolina Union	Union	C	St	M/W	500	50												
South Dakota																		
Kilian Community College	Sioux Falls	C,T	Ind	M/W	253	87	55	60	Y	Y	Y	Y	Y	Y	Y	N		16
Lake Area Technical Institute	Watertown	T	St	M/W	1,600				Y	Y	Y	Y	Y	Y	Y	Y	3	33
Mitchell Technical Institute	Mitchell	T	St	M/W	1,221	23	27		Y	Y	Y	Y	Y	Y	Y	N	6	26
Southeast Technical Institute	Sioux Falls	T	St	M/W	2,467	32	27		N	Y	Y	Y	Y	Y	Y	N	3	53
Western Dakota Technical Institute	Rapid City	T	St	M/W	1,088	27	49		Y	Y	Y	Y	Y	Y	Y	N		19

This chart includes the names and locations of accredited two-year colleges in the United States, Canada, and other countries and shows institutions' responses to the *Peterson's Annual Survey of Undergraduate Institutions.* If an institution submitted incomplete data, one or more columns opposite the institution's name is blank. A dagger after the school name indicates that the institution has one or more entries in the *College Close-Ups* section. If a school does not appear, it did not report any of the information.

Key to columns: Y—Yes; N—No; R—Recommended; S—For Some

Degrees Awarded: College Transfer Associate (C); Terminal Associate (T); Bachelor's (B); Master's (M); Doctoral (D)

Institution	Location	Degrees Awarded	Institutional Control	Student Body	Undergrad Enrollment	% Part-Time	% 25 or Older	% Grads to 4-Yr	HS Equiv Accepted	Open Admissions	HS Transcript Required	Need-Based Aid	Part-Time Jobs	Career Counseling	Job Placement	College Housing	# Sports	# Majors
Tennessee																		
Chattanooga College–Medical, Dental and Technical Careers	Chattanooga	C	Prop	M/W	330				Y			Y		Y	Y	Y	N		1
Cleveland State Community College	Cleveland	C,T	St	M/W	3,790	50	32	60	Y	Y	Y	Y	Y	Y	Y	Y	N	8	13
Dyersburg State Community College	Dyersburg	C,T	St	M/W	3,258	60	30				Y	Y	Y	Y	Y	Y	N	8	20
Fountainhead College of Technology	Knoxville	C,T,B	Prop	M/W	230												N		11
ITT Technical Institute	Chattanooga	T,B	Prop	M/W													N		11
ITT Technical Institute	Cordova	T,B	Prop	M/W							Y		Y	Y			N		12
ITT Technical Institute	Johnson City	T,B	Prop	M/W															12
ITT Technical Institute	Knoxville	T,B	Prop	M/W							Y		Y	Y			N		13
ITT Technical Institute	Nashville	T,B	Prop	M/W							Y		Y	Y			N		14
Jackson State Community College	Jackson	C,T	St	M/W	4,585				Y	Y	S	Y	Y	Y	Y		N	3	13
John A. Gupton College	Nashville	C,T	Ind	M/W	122	41	54		N	Y	Y		Y		Y	Y	Y		1
Motlow State Community College	Tullahoma	C,T	St	M/W	4,732	62	24		Y	Y	Y	Y	Y	Y	Y	Y	N	8	5
Nossi College of Art	Nashville	T,B	Ind	M/W	279		61		N	Y	Y		Y		Y	Y	N		5
Roane State Community College	Harriman	C,T	St	M/W	6,214	59	35		Y	Y	Y	Y	Y	Y	Y	Y	N	8	42
Volunteer State Community College	Gallatin	C,T	St	M/W	8,153	58	29		Y	Y	Y	Y	Y	Y	Y	Y	N	5	18
Walters State Community College	Morristown	C,T	St	M/W	6,265	49	29		Y	Y	Y	Y	Y	Y	Y	Y	N	5	20
Texas																		
Alvin Community College	Alvin	C,T	St-L	M/W	5,794	73	35		Y	Y	S	Y	Y	Y	Y	Y	N	3	33
Amarillo College	Amarillo	C,T	St-L	M/W	11,530		36		Y	Y	Y	Y	Y	Y	Y	Y	N	5	83
Austin Community College	Austin	C,T	St-L	M/W	41,627		43		Y	Y	Y	Y	Y	Y	Y		N	3	90
Brookhaven College	Farmers Branch	C,T	Cou	M/W	12,319	81	46		Y		Y		Y	Y	Y		N	5	27
Brown Mackie College–Dallas/Ft. Worth†	Bedford	T,B	Prop	M/W															11
Brown Mackie College–San Antonio†	San Antonio	T,B	Prop	M/W															10
College of the Mainland	Texas City	C,T	St-L	M/W	4,188	73	33		Y	Y	S	Y	Y	Y	Y		N	5	22
Collin County Community College District	McKinney	C,T	St-L	M/W	27,972	66	32	25	Y	Y	Y	Y	Y	Y	Y	Y	N	2	49
Culinary Institute LeNotre	Houston	T	Prop	M/W	403		55				Y	Y		Y	Y	N			3
El Centro College	Dallas	C,T	Cou	M/W	10,101	77													
Frank Phillips College	Borger	C,T	St-L	M/W	1,148	56	20		Y	Y	Y	Y	Y	Y	Y	Y	Y	6	20
Galveston College	Galveston	C,T	St-L	M/W	2,131	73	38		Y	Y	S	Y	Y	Y	Y	Y	Y	4	32
Grayson College	Denison	C,T	St-L	M/W	5,014	58	39	36	Y	Y		Y	Y	Y	Y	Y	Y	2	45
Hallmark College of Technology	San Antonio	C,B,M	Ind	M/W	356		49			Y	Y	Y		Y	Y	N			13
Hallmark Institute of Aeronautics	San Antonio	C	Priv	M/W	227		54			Y	Y	Y		Y	Y	Y			2
Houston Community College System	Houston	C,T	St-L	M/W	57,978	69	44		Y	Y	S	Y	Y	Y	Y		N		61
ITT Technical Institute	Arlington	T,B	Prop	M/W							Y		Y	Y			N		11
ITT Technical Institute	Austin	T,B	Prop	M/W							Y		Y	Y			N		11
ITT Technical Institute	DeSoto	T,B	Prop	M/W															12
ITT Technical Institute	Houston	T,B	Prop	M/W							Y		Y	Y			N		12
ITT Technical Institute	Houston	T,B	Prop	M/W							Y		Y	Y			N		10
ITT Technical Institute	Richardson	T,B	Prop	M/W							Y								9
ITT Technical Institute	San Antonio	T,B	Prop	M/W							Y		Y	Y			N		11
ITT Technical Institute	San Antonio	T,B	Prop	M/W															11
ITT Technical Institute	Waco	T,B	Prop	M/W							Y		Y	Y			N		11
ITT Technical Institute	Webster	T,B	Prop	M/W							Y		Y	Y			N		12
Kilgore College	Kilgore	C,T	St-L	M/W	5,867	55	31		Y	Y	Y	Y	Y	Y	Y	Y	Y	7	62
Lamar State College–Orange	Orange	C,T	St	M/W	2,426	59	38		Y	Y	Y	Y	Y	Y	Y		N	4	16
Lone Star College–CyFair	Cypress	C,T	St-L	M/W	19,544	68	29		Y	Y					Y		N		26
Lone Star College–Kingwood	Kingwood	C,T	St-L	M/W	11,943	65	36		Y	Y		Y	Y	Y	Y		N	1	17
Lone Star College–Montgomery	Conroe	C,T	St-L	M/W	12,758	66	36		Y	Y		Y	Y	Y	Y		N		13
Lone Star College–North Harris	Houston	C,T	St-L	M/W	17,217	68	42		Y	Y		Y	Y	Y	Y	Y		15	16
Lone Star College–Tomball	Tomball	C,T	St-L	M/W	8,862	67	37		Y	Y		Y	Y	Y	Y		N		13
Lone Star College–University Park	Houston	C,T	St-L	M/W	7,297	68	31				R		Y						4
Mountain View College	Dallas	C,T	St-L	M/W	9,068	77	37		Y	Y		Y	Y	Y			N	4	11
Northeast Texas Community College	Mount Pleasant	C,T	St-L	M/W	3,282	66	26		Y	Y		Y	Y	Y		Y		8	50
Panola College	Carthage	C,T	St-L	M/W	2,699	51	32		Y	Y	R,S	Y	Y	Y		Y	Y	7	14
Paris Junior College	Paris	C,T	St-L	M/W	5,301	53	28		Y	Y	Y	Y		Y			Y	11	62
St. Philip's College	San Antonio	C,T	Dist	M/W	10,710	79													
San Jacinto College District	Pasadena	C,T	St-L	M/W	28,385	73	31	22	Y	Y		Y	Y	Y	Y		N	10	96
South Plains College	Levelland	C,T	St-L	M/W	9,444	54	39	95	Y	Y		Y	Y	Y	Y		Y	11	58
Tarrant County College District	Fort Worth	C,T	Cou	M/W	50,439	65	38					Y	Y	Y	Y	Y	N	6	42
Temple College	Temple	C,T	Dist	M/W	5,506	67	40	0	Y	Y		Y	Y	Y	Y	Y	Y	5	20
Texarkana College	Texarkana	C,T	St-L	M/W	4,111				Y	Y		Y	Y	Y	Y	Y	Y	6	41
Texas State Technical College Harlingen	Harlingen	C,T	St	M/W	5,509	57													
Texas State Technical College Waco	Waco	C,T	St	M/W	7,269	26	32		Y	Y		Y	Y	Y	Y	Y	Y	7	38
Trinity Valley Community College	Athens	C,T	St-L	M/W	5,172	62	35		Y	Y	Y	Y	Y	Y	Y	Y	Y	7	55
Tyler Junior College	Tyler	C,T	St-L	M/W	11,308	45	27		Y	Y	Y	Y	Y	Y	Y		Y	9	56
Vet Tech Institute of Houston	Houston	T	Priv	M/W	256												N		1
Victoria College	Victoria	C,T	Cou	M/W	4,419	69	32		Y	Y		Y	Y	Y	Y		N	3	16
Western Texas College	Snyder	C,T	St-L	M/W	2,473	72	26	50	Y	Y		Y	Y	Y	Y	Y		14	22
Utah																		
ITT Technical Institute	Murray	T,B	Prop	M/W							Y		Y	Y			N		13
LDS Business College	Salt Lake City	C,T	I-R	M/W	2,191	27	21		Y	Y	Y	Y	Y	Y	Y	Y	N		15
Salt Lake Community College	Salt Lake City	C,T	St	M/W	31,137	72	39		Y	Y	Y	Y	Y	Y	Y		N	6	69
Snow College	Ephraim	C,T	St	M/W	4,605	39	14		Y	Y	Y	Y	Y	Y	Y	Y	Y	16	56
Vermont																		
Community College of Vermont	Montpelier	C,T	St	M/W	6,619		50	36	Y	Y	Y	Y	Y				N		26

This chart includes the names and locations of accredited two-year colleges in the United States, Canada, and other countries and shows institutions' responses to the *Peterson's Annual Survey of Undergraduate Institutions*. If an institution submitted incomplete data, one or more columns opposite the institution's name is blank. A dagger after the school name indicates that the institution has one or more entries in the *College Close-Ups* section. If a school does not appear, it did not report any of the information.

Column key: Degrees Awarded — Bachelor's (B), Terminal Associate (T), College Transfer Associate (C), Master's (M), Doctoral (D). Institutional Control — County/District/City, State/Commonwealth/Territory, Federal, Independent, Independent-Religious, Proprietary, State-Related. Student Body — Men, Primarily Men; Women, Primarily Women; Coed. Y—Yes; N—No; R—Recommended; S—For Some.

Institution	City	Degrees	Control	Student Body	Undergrad Enrollment	% Part-Time	% 25 or Older	% Grads to 4-Yr	HS Equiv. Accepted	Open Admissions	HS Transcript Req.	Need-Based Aid	Part-Time Jobs	Job Placement	Career Counseling	College Housing	# Sports	# Majors
Landmark College	Putney	T,B	Ind	M/W	487	1	4	88	N	Y	Y	Y	Y	Y		Y	13	6
New England Culinary Institute	Montpelier	T,B	Prop	M/W	425		32		N	N	Y	Y	Y	Y	Y	Y		3
Virginia																		
Central Virginia Community College	Lynchburg	C,T	St	M/W	4,767		26		Y	Y		Y	Y	Y	Y	N	1	19
Dabney S. Lancaster Community College	Clifton Forge	C,T	St	M/W	1,284	76	29				R	Y	Y	Y	Y	N	4	17
Eastern Shore Community College	Melfa	C,T	St	M/W	857				Y	R	Y	Y	Y	Y	Y	N		9
ITT Technical Institute	Chantilly	T,B	Prop	M/W					Y		Y	Y						13
ITT Technical Institute	Norfolk	T,B	Prop	M/W					Y		Y	Y						15
ITT Technical Institute	Richmond	T,B	Prop	M/W					Y		Y	Y						13
ITT Technical Institute	Salem	T,B	Prop	M/W							Y							13
ITT Technical Institute	Springfield	T,B	Prop	M/W					Y		Y	Y						12
John Tyler Community College	Chester	C,T	St	M/W	10,157	73			Y		R	Y	Y	Y	Y	N		22
J. Sargeant Reynolds Community College	Richmond	C,T	St	M/W	12,469	71	39	60	Y	Y	Y	R	Y	Y	Y	N		55
Mountain Empire Community College	Big Stone Gap	C,T	St	M/W	2,924		28	59	Y	Y	Y	Y	Y	Y	Y	N	3	16
Patrick Henry Community College	Martinsville	C,T	St	M/W	3,163		29		Y	Y	Y	Y	Y	Y	Y	N	8	17
Paul D. Camp Community College	Franklin	C,T	St	M/W	1,579													
Piedmont Virginia Community College	Charlottesville	C,T	St	M/W	5,630	79	33		Y		S	Y	Y	Y	Y	N	8	17
Rappahannock Community College	Glenns	C,T	St-L	M/W	3,555				Y			Y	Y	Y	Y		1	11
Southwest Virginia Community College	Richlands	C,T	St	M/W	2,766	58	33		Y	Y	Y		Y	Y	Y	N		12
Thomas Nelson Community College	Hampton	C,T	St	M/W	10,942													
Virginia Western Community College	Roanoke	C,T	St	M/W	8,652	83	38	72	Y	Y	R,S	Y	Y	Y	Y	N	3	25
Wytheville Community College	Wytheville	C,T	St	M/W	3,468		33		Y		Y	Y	Y	Y	Y	N	3	21
Washington																		
Bellingham Technical College	Bellingham	C,T	St	M/W	2,864		61		Y		S	Y	Y	Y	Y	N		25
Big Bend Community College	Moses Lake	C,T	St	M/W	1,840	29	35		Y		S	S	Y	Y	Y	Y	4	18
Carrington College–Spokane	Spokane	T	Prop	M/W	538		55			Y	Y					N		3
Cascadia Community College	Bothell	C,T	St	M/W	2,670	60			Y							N		3
Clark College	Vancouver	C,T	St	M/W	11,462	51	38				Y	Y				N	8	37
Grays Harbor College	Aberdeen	C,T	St	M/W	1,966	33	54		Y	Y	R	Y	Y	Y	Y	N	6	16
ITT Technical Institute	Everett	T,B	Prop	M/W														11
ITT Technical Institute	Seattle	T,B	Prop	M/W					Y		Y	Y						12
ITT Technical Institute	Spokane Valley	T,B	Prop	M/W					Y		Y	Y						13
Lower Columbia College	Longview	C,T	St	M/W	3,199	45	53		Y		R	Y	Y	Y		N	5	20
Olympic College	Bremerton	C,T,B	St	M/W	7,951		48		Y		S	Y	Y	Y	Y	N	9	17
Pierce College at Puyallup	Puyallup	C,T	St	M/W	13,294													
Shoreline Community College	Shoreline	C	St	M/W	8,591		45		Y		Y	Y	Y	Y	Y	N	15	41
South Puget Sound Community College	Olympia	C,T	St	M/W	4,955	46												
Walla Walla Community College	Walla Walla	C,T	St	M/W	5,109	42	54		Y		R	Y	Y	Y	Y	N	6	36
Wenatchee Valley College	Wenatchee	C,T	St-L	M/W	4,102				Y		R	S	Y	Y	Y	Y	10	39
West Virginia																		
Blue Ridge Community and Technical College	Martinsburg	C,T	St	M/W	5,021	76	56		Y	Y	Y			Y	Y	N		25
ITT Technical Institute	Huntington	T	Prop	M/W														9
Mountain State College	Parkersburg	T	Prop	M/W	176	1	55		N	Y	Y	Y	Y		Y	N		7
Potomac State College of West Virginia University	Keyser	C,T,B	St	M/W	1,660	22	13		Y	Y	Y	Y	Y		Y	Y	10	53
West Virginia Junior College–Bridgeport	Bridgeport	C,T	Prop	M/W	389		30		Y	Y	R	Y	Y	Y		N		8
West Virginia Northern Community College	Wheeling	C,T	St	M/W	2,505	54												
Wisconsin																		
Blackhawk Technical College	Janesville	C,T	Dist	M/W	2,522	60	53	0	Y	Y	Y	Y	Y	Y	Y	N		29
Chippewa Valley Technical College	Eau Claire	C,T	Dist	M/W	5,617	56	44		Y	Y	S	Y	Y	Y	Y	N		28
Fox Valley Technical College	Appleton	T	St-L	M/W	10,502	72	48		Y	Y	Y	Y	Y	Y	Y	N	6	56
Gateway Technical College	Kenosha	T	St-L	M/W	8,720	80												
ITT Technical Institute	Green Bay	T,B	Prop	M/W					Y		Y	Y						11
ITT Technical Institute	Greenfield	T,B	Prop	M/W					Y		Y	Y						13
ITT Technical Institute	Madison	T,B	Prop	M/W														9
Moraine Park Technical College	Fond du Lac	C,T	Dist	M/W	6,613	83	55				Y		Y		Y	N		37
Northcentral Technical College	Wausau	C,T	Dist	M/W	4,373	57	51		Y	Y	Y	Y	Y	Y	Y	Y	8	29
University of Wisconsin–Fox Valley	Menasha	C,T	St	M/W	1,797	42	25	70			Y	Y	Y	Y		N	7	1
University of Wisconsin–Richland	Richland Center	C	St	M/W	519	44												
University of Wisconsin–Sheboygan	Sheboygan	C	St	M/W	747				Y	Y	Y	Y	Y	Y		N	7	1
University of Wisconsin–Waukesha	Waukesha	C,B	St	M/W	2,155	53	28		N	Y	Y	Y	Y	Y		N	10	1
Waukesha County Technical College	Pewaukee	T	St-L	M/W	8,799	78	51		Y		Y	Y	Y	Y		N		40
Wisconsin Indianhead Technical College	Shell Lake	T	Dist	M/W	3,418	57	55		Y							N		21
Wyoming																		
Casper College	Casper	C,T	St-L	M/W	4,179	53	36	40	Y		Y	Y	Y	Y	Y	Y	10	101
Central Wyoming College	Riverton	C,T	St-L	M/W	2,265	63	42	53	Y		R	Y	Y	Y	Y	Y	15	57
Eastern Wyoming College	Torrington	C,T	St-L	M/W	1,876	64					R	Y	Y	Y	Y	Y	4	43
Laramie County Community College	Cheyenne	C,T	Dist	M/W	4,632	57	10	57	Y		S	Y	Y	Y	Y	Y	11	62
Northwest College	Powell	C,T	St-L	M/W	1,881	43	27		Y	Y	Y	Y	Y	Y	Y	Y	10	62
Sheridan College	Sheridan	C,T	St-L	M/W	4,437	68	35		Y		R,S	Y	Y	Y	Y	Y	10	48
Western Wyoming Community College	Rock Springs	C,T	St-L	M/W	3,621				Y	Y	Y	Y	Y	Y	Y	Y	15	84

Profiles
of Two-Year
Colleges

ALABAMA

Alabama Southern Community College
Monroeville, Alabama

- **State-supported** 2-year, founded 1965, part of Alabama Community College System
- **Rural** 80-acre campus
- **Coed,** 1,349 undergraduate students

Undergraduates 28% Black or African American, non-Hispanic/Latino; 0.4% Hispanic/Latino; 0.3% Asian, non-Hispanic/Latino; 0.8% American Indian or Alaska Native, non-Hispanic/Latino; 0.1% Two or more races, non-Hispanic/Latino; 0.5% Race/ethnicity unknown; 0.1% international. *Retention:* 57% of full-time freshmen returned.
Faculty *Student/faculty ratio:* 17:1.
Majors Agricultural business and management; agriculture; art; biology/biological sciences; biomedical technology; chemistry; computer science; criminal justice/law enforcement administration; dramatic/theater arts; early childhood education; elementary education; forest technology; health information/medical records administration; health services/allied health/health sciences; kindergarten/preschool education; liberal arts and sciences/liberal studies; mathematics; music; physical education teaching and coaching; pre-dentistry studies; pre-engineering; pre-law studies; premedical studies; pre-pharmacy studies; pre-veterinary studies; registered nursing/registered nurse; rhetoric and composition; secondary education; social sciences; special education.
Academics *Calendar:* semesters. *Degree:* certificates and associate. *Special study options:* academic remediation for entering students, adult/continuing education programs, advanced placement credit, part-time degree program, summer session for credit.
Library Dennis Stone Forte Library plus 1 other with 43,000 titles, 670 serial subscriptions.
Student Life *Housing:* college housing not available. *Activities and Organizations:* choral group. *Campus security:* 24-hour patrols.
Athletics Member NJCAA. *Intercollegiate sports:* baseball M(s), basketball M(s)/W(s), softball W(s).
Standardized Tests *Recommended:* ACT (for admission).
Costs (2014–15) *Tuition:* state resident $3616 full-time; nonresident $7232 full-time. Full-time tuition and fees vary according to course load. Part-time tuition and fees vary according to course load. *Required fees:* $928 full-time. *Waivers:* senior citizens and employees or children of employees.
Applying *Options:* electronic application, early admission. *Required:* high school transcript. *Application deadlines:* 9/10 (freshmen), 9/10 (transfers).
Freshman Application Contact Alabama Southern Community College, PO Box 2000, Monroeville, AL 36461. *Phone:* 251-575-3156 Ext. 8252. *Website:* http://www.ascc.edu/.

Bevill State Community College
Jasper, Alabama

- **State-supported** 2-year, founded 1969, part of Alabama Community College System
- **Rural** 245-acre campus with easy access to Birmingham
- **Endowment** $147,298
- **Coed,** 3,734 undergraduate students, 52% full-time, 64% women, 36% men

Undergraduates 1,954 full-time, 1,780 part-time. 15% Black or African American, non-Hispanic/Latino; 1% Hispanic/Latino; 0.5% Asian, non-Hispanic/Latino; 0.3% American Indian or Alaska Native, non-Hispanic/Latino; 0.9% Two or more races, non-Hispanic/Latino; 2% Race/ethnicity unknown. *Retention:* 53% of full-time freshmen returned.
Freshmen *Admission:* 883 enrolled.
Faculty *Total:* 329, 35% full-time, 12% with terminal degrees. *Student/faculty ratio:* 16:1.
Majors Administrative assistant and secretarial science; child-care and support services management; computer and information sciences; drafting and design technology; electrician; emergency medical technology (EMT paramedic); general studies; heating, ventilation, air conditioning and refrigeration engineering technology; industrial electronics technology; legal assistant/paralegal; liberal arts and sciences/liberal studies; registered nursing/registered nurse; tool and die technology.
Academics *Calendar:* semesters. *Degree:* certificates and associate. *Special study options:* academic remediation for entering students, adult/continuing education programs, advanced placement credit, cooperative education, distance learning, honors programs, off-campus study, part-time degree program, services for LD students, summer session for credit.

Library 579,344 titles, 3,021 serial subscriptions, an OPAC, a Web page.
Student Life *Housing Options:* coed. Campus housing is university owned. *Activities and Organizations:* drama/theater group, choral group, Student Government Association, Campus Ministries, Circle K, Outdoors men Club, Students Against Destructive Decisions. *Campus security:* 24-hour emergency response devices.
Costs (2013–14) *Tuition:* state resident $2664 full-time, $111 per credit hour part-time; nonresident $5328 full-time, $222 per credit hour part-time. Full-time tuition and fees vary according to course load and program. Part-time tuition and fees vary according to course load and program. *Required fees:* $711 full-time, $29 per credit hour part-time. *Room and board:* $1850. Room and board charges vary according to board plan and location. *Payment plan:* installment. *Waivers:* employees or children of employees.
Financial Aid Of all full-time matriculated undergraduates who enrolled in 2012, 88 Federal Work-Study jobs (averaging $1807).
Applying *Options:* electronic application, early admission, deferred entrance. *Required:* high school transcript. *Application deadlines:* rolling (freshmen), rolling (transfers).
Freshman Application Contact Bevill State Community College, 1411 Indiana Avenue, Jasper, AL 35501. *Phone:* 205-387-0511 Ext. 5813. *Website:* http://www.bscc.edu/.

Bishop State Community College
Mobile, Alabama

- **State-supported** 2-year, founded 1965, part of Alabama Community College System
- **Urban** 9-acre campus
- **Coed,** 3,900 undergraduate students, 56% full-time, 60% women, 40% men

Undergraduates 2,175 full-time, 1,725 part-time. Students come from 8 states and territories; 32 other countries; 3% are from out of state; 62% Black or African American, non-Hispanic/Latino; 1% Hispanic/Latino; 2% Asian, non-Hispanic/Latino; 0.2% Native Hawaiian or other Pacific Islander, non-Hispanic/Latino; 0.7% American Indian or Alaska Native, non-Hispanic/Latino; 0.9% Two or more races, non-Hispanic/Latino; 0.4% Race/ethnicity unknown; 2% international; 10% transferred in. *Retention:* 41% of full-time freshmen returned.
Freshmen *Admission:* 965 enrolled.
Faculty *Total:* 187, 63% full-time. *Student/faculty ratio:* 23:1.
Majors Accounting technology and bookkeeping; administrative assistant and secretarial science; child-care and support services management; civil engineering technology; computer and information sciences; drafting and design technology; electrical, electronic and communications engineering technology; emergency medical technology (EMT paramedic); food service systems administration; funeral service and mortuary science; general studies; graphic communications; health information/medical records technology; multi/interdisciplinary studies related; physical therapy technology; registered nursing/registered nurse.
Academics *Calendar:* semesters. *Degree:* certificates and associate. *Special study options:* academic remediation for entering students, accelerated degree program, adult/continuing education programs, advanced placement credit, cooperative education, distance learning, independent study, internships, part-time degree program, services for LD students, summer session for credit.
Library Minnie Slade Bishop Library plus 3 others with 70,398 titles, 76 serial subscriptions, 4,483 audiovisual materials, an OPAC, a Web page.
Student Life *Housing:* college housing not available. *Activities and Organizations:* drama/theater group, choral group. *Campus security:* 24-hour emergency response devices and patrols, 24-hour electronic alert system.
Athletics Member NJCAA. *Intercollegiate sports:* baseball M(s)/W(s), basketball M(s)/W(s), cheerleading W(s), softball W(s).
Costs (2014–15) *Tuition:* state resident $1332 full-time, $111 per credit hour part-time; nonresident $2664 full-time, $222 per credit hour part-time. Full-time tuition and fees vary according to course load. Part-time tuition and fees vary according to course load. *Required fees:* $348 full-time, $29 per credit hour part-time. *Waivers:* senior citizens and employees or children of employees.
Financial Aid Of all full-time matriculated undergraduates who enrolled in 2012, 299 Federal Work-Study jobs (averaging $2400).
Applying *Options:* electronic application, early admission, deferred entrance. *Required:* high school transcript. *Application deadlines:* rolling (freshmen), rolling (transfers). *Notification:* continuous until 9/17 (freshmen), continuous until 9/17 (transfers).
Freshman Application Contact Bishop State Community College, 351 North Broad Street, Mobile, AL 36603-5898. *Phone:* 251-405-7000. *Toll-free phone:* 800-523-7235.
Website: http://www.bishop.edu/.

Brown Mackie College–Birmingham

Birmingham, Alabama

- **Proprietary** 4-year, part of Education Management Corporation
- **Coed**

Majors Biomedical technology; business administration and management; computer support specialist; drafting and design technology; graphic design; health/health-care administration; legal assistant/paralegal; medical office management; occupational therapist assistant; surgical technology.

Academics *Degrees:* diplomas, associate, and bachelor's.

Freshman Application Contact Brown Mackie College–Birmingham, 105 Vulcan Road, Suite 100, Birmingham, AL 35209. *Phone:* 205-909-1500. *Toll-free phone:* 888-299-4699.

Website: http://www.brownmackie.edu/birmingham.

See display below and page 382 for the College Close-Up.

Calhoun Community College

Decatur, Alabama

Freshman Application Contact Admissions Office, Calhoun Community College, PO Box 2216, Decatur, AL 35609-2216. *Phone:* 256-306-2593. *Toll-free phone:* 800-626-3628. *Fax:* 256-306-2941. *E-mail:* admissions@calhoun.edu.

Website: http://www.calhoun.edu/.

Central Alabama Community College

Alexander City, Alabama

Freshman Application Contact Ms. Donna Whaley, Central Alabama Community College, 1675 Cherokee Road, Alexander City, AL 35011-0699. *Phone:* 256-234-6346 Ext. 6232. *Toll-free phone:* 800-634-2657.

Website: http://www.cacc.edu/.

Chattahoochee Valley Community College

Phenix City, Alabama

Freshman Application Contact Chattahoochee Valley Community College, 2602 College Drive, Phenix City, AL 36869-7928. *Phone:* 334-291-4929.

Website: http://www.cv.edu/.

Community College of the Air Force

Maxwell Gunter Air Force Base, Alabama

- **Federally supported** 2-year, founded 1972, part of Air University
- **Suburban** campus
- **Coed**

Undergraduates 314,962 full-time.

Academics *Calendar:* continuous. *Degrees:* certificates and associate (courses conducted at 125 branch locations worldwide for members of the U.S. Air Force). *Special study options:* academic remediation for entering students, adult/continuing education programs, advanced placement credit, distance learning, independent study, internships.

Student Life *Campus security:* 24-hour emergency response devices and patrols.

Standardized Tests *Required:* Armed Services Vocational Aptitude Battery (for admission).

Costs (2013–14) *Tuition:* $0 full-time. Air Force Tuition Assistance (TA) provides 100% tuition and fees for courses taken by active duty personnel.

Applying *Options:* electronic application. *Required:* high school transcript, interview, military physical, good character, criminal background check.

Freshman Application Contact Ms. Teresa Amatuzzi, Director of Enrollment Management/Registrar, Community College of the Air Force, 100 South Turner Blvd., Maxwell Air Force Base, Maxwell - Gunter AFB, AL 36114-3011. *Phone:* 334-649-5080. *Fax:* 334-649-5015. *E-mail:* teresa.amatuzzi@maxwell.af.mil.

Website: http://www.au.af.mil/au/ccaf/.

Enterprise State Community College

Enterprise, Alabama

Director of Admissions Mr. Gary Deas, Associate Dean of Students/Registrar, Enterprise State Community College, PO Box 1300, Enterprise, AL 36331-1300. *Phone:* 334-347-2623 Ext. 2233. *E-mail:* gdeas@eocc.edu.

Website: http://www.escc.edu/.

Fortis College

Montgomery, Alabama

Admissions Office Contact Fortis College, 3470 Eastdale Circle, Montgomery, AL 36117. *Toll-free phone:* 855-4-FORTIS.

Website: http://www.fortis.edu/.

Gadsden State Community College
Gadsden, Alabama

- **State-supported** 2-year, founded 1965, part of Alabama Community College System
- **Small-town** 275-acre campus with easy access to Birmingham
- **Coed,** 5,797 undergraduate students, 55% full-time, 59% women, 41% men

Undergraduates 3,185 full-time, 2,612 part-time. Students come from 10 states and territories; 24 other countries; 9% are from out of state; 20% Black or African American, non-Hispanic/Latino; 3% Hispanic/Latino; 0.6% Asian, non-Hispanic/Latino; 0.1% Native Hawaiian or other Pacific Islander, non-Hispanic/Latino; 0.7% American Indian or Alaska Native, non-Hispanic/Latino; 2% Two or more races, non-Hispanic/Latino; 4% Race/ethnicity unknown; 2% international; 51% transferred in; 2% live on campus.
Freshmen *Admission:* 1,388 enrolled.
Faculty *Total:* 324, 46% full-time. *Student/faculty ratio:* 20:1.
Majors Accounting technology and bookkeeping; administrative assistant and secretarial science; child-care and support services management; civil engineering technology; clinical/medical laboratory technology; communication and journalism related; computer and information sciences; court reporting; criminal justice/police science; drafting and design technology; electrical, electronic and communications engineering technology; emergency medical technology (EMT paramedic); general studies; heating, ventilation, air conditioning and refrigeration engineering technology; industrial mechanics and maintenance technology; legal assistant/paralegal; liberal arts and sciences/liberal studies; manufacturing engineering technology; radiologic technology/science; registered nursing/registered nurse; sales, distribution, and marketing operations; substance abuse/addiction counseling; tool and die technology.
Academics *Calendar:* semesters. *Degree:* certificates and associate. *Special study options:* academic remediation for entering students, adult/continuing education programs, advanced placement credit, cooperative education, distance learning, English as a second language, external degree program, honors programs, internships, part-time degree program, services for LD students, study abroad, summer session for credit. *ROTC:* Army (b).
Library Meadows Library with 115,901 titles, 144 serial subscriptions, 7,080 audiovisual materials, an OPAC, a Web page.
Student Life *Housing Options:* coed. Campus housing is university owned. *Activities and Organizations:* drama/theater group, choral group, National Society of Leadership and Success, Student Government Association, Circle K, International Club, Cardinal Spirit Club. *Campus security:* 24-hour patrols. *Student services:* personal/psychological counseling.
Athletics Member NJCAA. *Intercollegiate sports:* basketball M(s)/W(s), softball W(s), tennis M(s), volleyball W(s).
Costs (2013–14) *Tuition:* state resident $3330 full-time, $111 per credit hour part-time; nonresident $6660 full-time, $222 per credit hour part-time. Full-time tuition and fees vary according to reciprocity agreements. Part-time tuition and fees vary according to reciprocity agreements. *Required fees:* $570 full-time, $19 per credit hour part-time. *Room and board:* $3200. *Waivers:* minority students, adult students, senior citizens, and employees or children of employees.
Applying *Options:* electronic application, early admission, deferred entrance. *Required:* high school transcript. *Application deadlines:* rolling (freshmen), rolling (transfers).
Freshman Application Contact Mrs. Jennie Dobson, Admissions and Records, Gadsden State Community College, Allen Hall, Gadsden, AL 35902-0227. *Phone:* 256-549-8210. *Toll-free phone:* 800-226-5563. *Fax:* 256-549-8205. *E-mail:* info@gadsdenstate.edu.
Website: http://www.gadsdenstate.edu/.

George Corley Wallace State Community College
Selma, Alabama

Director of Admissions Ms. Sunette Newman, Registrar, George Corley Wallace State Community College, PO Box 2530, Selma, AL 36702. *Phone:* 334-876-9305.
Website: http://www.wccs.edu/.

George C. Wallace Community College
Dothan, Alabama

Freshman Application Contact Mr. Keith Saulsberry, Director, Enrollment Services/Registrar, George C. Wallace Community College, 1141 Wallace Drive, Dothan, AL 36303. *Phone:* 334-983-3521 Ext. 2470. *Toll-free phone:* 800-543-2426. *Fax:* 334-983-3600. *E-mail:* ksaulsberry@wallace.edu.
Website: http://www.wallace.edu/.

H. Councill Trenholm State Technical College
Montgomery, Alabama

Freshman Application Contact Mrs. Tennie McBryde, Registrar, H. Councill Trenholm State Technical College, Montgomery, AL 36108. *Phone:* 334-420-4306. *Toll-free phone:* 866-753-4544. *Fax:* 334-420-4201. *E-mail:* tmcbryde@trenholmstate.edu.
Website: http://www.trenholmstate.edu/.

ITT Technical Institute
Bessemer, Alabama

- **Proprietary** primarily 2-year, founded 1994, part of ITT Educational Services, Inc.
- **Suburban** campus
- **Coed**

Majors Business administration and management; computer programming (specific applications); computer software technology; computer systems networking and telecommunications; construction management; cyber/computer forensics and counterterrorism; drafting and design technology; electrical, electronic and communications engineering technology; forensic science and technology; game and interactive media design; graphic communications; industrial technology; information technology project management; network and system administration; project management; registered nursing/registered nurse.
Academics *Calendar:* quarters. *Degrees:* associate and bachelor's.
Student Life *Housing:* college housing not available. *Campus security:* 24-hour emergency response devices.
Freshman Application Contact Director of Recruitment, ITT Technical Institute, 6270 Park South Drive, Bessemer, AL 35022. *Phone:* 205-497-5700. *Toll-free phone:* 800-488-7033.
Website: http://www.itt-tech.edu/.

ITT Technical Institute
Madison, Alabama

- **Proprietary** primarily 2-year, part of ITT Educational Services, Inc.
- **Coed**

Majors Business administration and management; computer programming (specific applications); computer software technology; construction management; cyber/computer forensics and counterterrorism; drafting and design technology; electrical, electronic and communications engineering technology; forensic science and technology; industrial technology; information technology project management; network and system administration; project management; registered nursing/registered nurse.
Academics *Degrees:* associate and bachelor's.
Student Life *Housing:* college housing not available.
Freshman Application Contact Director of Recruitment, ITT Technical Institute, 9238 Madison Boulevard, Suite 500, Madison, AL 35758. *Phone:* 256-542-2900. *Toll-free phone:* 877-628-5960.
Website: http://www.itt-tech.edu/.

ITT Technical Institute
Mobile, Alabama

- **Proprietary** primarily 2-year, part of ITT Educational Services, Inc.
- **Coed**

Majors Business administration and management; computer programming (specific applications); construction management; cyber/computer forensics and counterterrorism; drafting and design technology; electrical, electronic and communications engineering technology; forensic science and technology; industrial technology; information technology project management; network and system administration; project management; registered nursing/registered nurse.
Academics *Degrees:* associate and bachelor's.
Student Life *Housing:* college housing not available.
Freshman Application Contact Director of Recruitment, ITT Technical Institute, Office Mall South, 3100 Cottage Hill Road, Building 3, Mobile, AL 36606. *Phone:* 251-472-4760. *Toll-free phone:* 877-327-1013.
Website: http://www.itt-tech.edu/.

James H. Faulkner State Community College
Bay Minette, Alabama

Freshman Application Contact Ms. Carmelita Mikkelsen, Director of Admissions and High School Relations, James H. Faulkner State Community College, 1900 Highway 31 South, Bay Minette, AL 36507. *Phone:* 251-580-

2213. *Toll-free phone:* 800-231-3752. *Fax:* 251-580-2285. *E-mail:* cmikkelsen@faulknerstate.edu.
Website: http://www.faulknerstate.edu/.

Jefferson Davis Community College
Brewton, Alabama

Director of Admissions Ms. Robin Sessions, Registrar, Jefferson Davis Community College, PO Box 958, Brewton, AL 36427-0958. *Phone:* 251-867-4832.
Website: http://www.jdcc.edu/.

Jefferson State Community College
Birmingham, Alabama

- **State-supported** 2-year, founded 1965, part of Alabama Community College System
- **Suburban** 351-acre campus
- **Endowment** $1.2 million
- **Coed,** 8,542 undergraduate students, 34% full-time, 61% women, 39% men

Undergraduates 2,891 full-time, 5,651 part-time. Students come from 59 other countries; 3% are from out of state; 22% Black or African American, non-Hispanic/Latino; 4% Hispanic/Latino; 2% Asian, non-Hispanic/Latino; 0.1% Native Hawaiian or other Pacific Islander, non-Hispanic/Latino; 0.3% American Indian or Alaska Native, non-Hispanic/Latino; 3% Two or more races, non-Hispanic/Latino; 0.8% international; 6% transferred in. *Retention:* 53% of full-time freshmen returned.
Freshmen *Admission:* 3,929 applied, 3,929 admitted, 1,658 enrolled. *Average high school GPA:* 2.84.
Faculty *Total:* 383, 36% full-time, 16% with terminal degrees. *Student/faculty ratio:* 22:1.
Majors Accounting technology and bookkeeping; administrative assistant and secretarial science; child-care and support services management; clinical/medical laboratory technology; computer and information sciences; construction engineering technology; criminal justice/police science; emergency medical technology (EMT paramedic); engineering technology; fire services administration; funeral service and mortuary science; general studies; hospitality administration; liberal arts and sciences/liberal studies; office management; physical therapy technology; radiologic technology/science; registered nursing/registered nurse; veterinary/animal health technology.
Academics *Calendar:* semesters. *Degree:* certificates and associate. *Special study options:* academic remediation for entering students, adult/continuing education programs, advanced placement credit, distance learning, English as a second language, honors programs, independent study, internships, part-time degree program, services for LD students, summer session for credit. *ROTC:* Army (c), Air Force (c).
Library Jefferson State Libraries plus 4 others with 217,609 titles, 301 serial subscriptions, 1,478 audiovisual materials, an OPAC, a Web page.
Student Life *Housing:* college housing not available. *Activities and Organizations:* choral group, Student Government Association, Phi Theta Kappa, Sigma Kappa Delta, Jefferson State Ambassadors, Students in Free Enterprise (SIFE). *Campus security:* 24-hour patrols.
Costs (2013–14) *Tuition:* state resident $4260 full-time, $142 per semester hour part-time; nonresident $7590 full-time, $253 per semester hour part-time. Full-time tuition and fees vary according to course load. Part-time tuition and fees vary according to course load. *Waivers:* senior citizens and employees or children of employees.
Applying *Options:* electronic application, early admission, early action, deferred entrance. *Required for some:* high school transcript. *Application deadline:* rolling (freshmen). *Notification:* continuous (freshmen), continuous (transfers).
Freshman Application Contact Mrs. Lillian Owens, Director of Admissions and Retention, Jefferson State Community College, 2601 Carson Road, Birmingham, AL 35215-3098. *Phone:* 205-853-1200 Ext. 7990. *Toll-free phone:* 800-239-5900. *Fax:* 205-856-6070. *E-mail:* lowens@jeffstateonline.com.
Website: http://www.jeffstateonline.com/.

J. F. Drake State Technical College
Huntsville, Alabama

- **State-supported** 2-year, founded 1961, part of Alabama Community College System of the Alabama Department of Postsecondary Education
- **Urban** 6-acre campus
- **Coed**

Undergraduates 754 full-time, 504 part-time. Students come from 1 other state; 2 other countries; 4% are from out of state; 23% transferred in.

Faculty *Student/faculty ratio:* 17:1.
Academics *Calendar:* semesters. *Degree:* certificates and associate. *Special study options:* academic remediation for entering students, cooperative education, internships, part-time degree program, services for LD students.
Student Life *Campus security:* 24-hour patrols.
Costs (2013–14) *Tuition:* state resident $3330 full-time, $111 per credit hour part-time; nonresident $6660 full-time, $222 per credit hour part-time. *Required fees:* $840 full-time, $28 per credit hour part-time.
Financial Aid Of all full-time matriculated undergraduates who enrolled in 2012, 15 Federal Work-Study jobs (averaging $2679).
Applying *Options:* electronic application, deferred entrance. *Required:* high school transcript.
Freshman Application Contact Mrs. Kristin Treadway, Pre-Admissions Coordinator, J. F. Drake State Technical College, Huntsville, AL 35811. *Phone:* 256-551-3111 Ext. 704. *Toll-free phone:* 888-413-7253. *E-mail:* sudeall@drakestate.edu.
Website: http://www.drakestate.edu/.

Lawson State Community College
Birmingham, Alabama

- **State-supported** 2-year, founded 1949, part of Alabama Community College System
- **Urban** 30-acre campus
- **Coed,** 3,031 undergraduate students, 59% full-time, 59% women, 41% men

Undergraduates 1,791 full-time, 1,240 part-time. Students come from 14 states and territories; 1 other country; 1% are from out of state; 75% Black or African American, non-Hispanic/Latino; 1% Hispanic/Latino; 0.4% Asian, non-Hispanic/Latino; 0.2% Native Hawaiian or other Pacific Islander, non-Hispanic/Latino; 0.1% American Indian or Alaska Native, non-Hispanic/Latino; 0.8% Two or more races, non-Hispanic/Latino; 8% Race/ethnicity unknown; 0.1% international; 7% transferred in; 1% live on campus. *Retention:* 52% of full-time freshmen returned.
Freshmen *Admission:* 1,596 applied, 1,311 admitted, 699 enrolled.
Faculty *Total:* 209, 39% full-time. *Student/faculty ratio:* 17:1.
Majors Accounting technology and bookkeeping; administrative assistant and secretarial science; automotive engineering technology; building/construction finishing, management, and inspection related; business administration and management; child-care and support services management; computer and information sciences; criminal justice/police science; drafting and design technology; general studies; industrial electronics technology; liberal arts and sciences/liberal studies; manufacturing engineering technology; registered nursing/registered nurse; social work.
Academics *Calendar:* semesters. *Degree:* certificates and associate. *Special study options:* academic remediation for entering students, adult/continuing education programs, advanced placement credit, cooperative education, distance learning, honors programs, internships, part-time degree program, services for LD students, summer session for credit.
Library Lawson State Library with 51,579 titles, 265 serial subscriptions, 2,068 audiovisual materials, an OPAC.
Student Life *Housing Options:* coed. Campus housing is university owned. *Activities and Organizations:* choral group, Student Government Association, Phi Theta Kappa, Kappa Beta Delta Honor Society, Phi Beta Lambda, Social Work Club. *Campus security:* 24-hour emergency response devices and patrols, controlled dormitory access. *Student services:* personal/psychological counseling.
Athletics Member NJCAA. *Intercollegiate sports:* baseball M, basketball M/W, volleyball W. *Intramural sports:* weight lifting M.
Costs (2014–15) *Tuition:* state resident $3420 full-time, $114 per credit hour part-time; nonresident $6840 full-time, $228 per credit hour part-time. *Required fees:* $850 full-time, $28 per credit hour part-time. *Room and board:* $4760; room only: $3000. *Payment plan:* installment. *Waivers:* senior citizens and employees or children of employees.
Financial Aid Of all full-time matriculated undergraduates who enrolled in 2012, 91 Federal Work-Study jobs (averaging $3000).
Applying *Options:* electronic application. *Required:* high school transcript. *Application deadlines:* rolling (freshmen), rolling (transfers). *Notification:* continuous (freshmen), continuous (transfers).
Freshman Application Contact Mr. Jeff Shelley, Director of Admissions and Records, Lawson State Community College, 3060 Wilson Road, SW, Birmingham, AL 35221-1798. *Phone:* 205-929-6361. *Fax:* 205-923-7106. *E-mail:* jshelley@lawsonstate.edu.
Website: http://www.lawsonstate.edu/.

Lurleen B. Wallace Community College
Andalusia, Alabama

- **State-supported** 2-year, founded 1969, part of Alabama Community College System
- **Small-town** 200-acre campus
- **Coed,** 1,570 undergraduate students, 62% full-time, 61% women, 39% men

Undergraduates 972 full-time, 598 part-time. Students come from 7 states and territories; 3 other countries; 5% are from out of state; 23% Black or African American, non-Hispanic/Latino; 0.9% Hispanic/Latino; 0.7% Asian, non-Hispanic/Latino; 0.2% American Indian or Alaska Native, non-Hispanic/Latino; 0.4% Two or more races, non-Hispanic/Latino; 0.2% Race/ethnicity unknown; 0.1% international; 6% transferred in.
Freshmen *Admission:* 464 enrolled.
Faculty *Total:* 97, 58% full-time, 9% with terminal degrees. *Student/faculty ratio:* 17:1.
Majors Administrative assistant and secretarial science; child-care and support services management; computer and information sciences; diagnostic medical sonography and ultrasound technology; emergency medical technology (EMT paramedic); forest technology; general studies; industrial electronics technology; liberal arts and sciences/liberal studies; registered nursing/registered nurse.
Academics *Calendar:* semesters. *Degree:* certificates and associate. *Special study options:* academic remediation for entering students, cooperative education, distance learning, honors programs, independent study, part-time degree program, summer session for credit.
Library Lurleen B. Wallace Library plus 2 others with 38,368 titles, 6,336 serial subscriptions, 2,114 audiovisual materials, an OPAC, a Web page.
Student Life *Housing:* college housing not available. *Activities and Organizations:* drama/theater group, choral group, Student Government Association, Student Ambassadors, Interclub Council, Campus Civitan, Christian Student Ministries. *Student services:* personal/psychological counseling.
Athletics Member NJCAA. *Intercollegiate sports:* baseball M(s), basketball M(s)/W(s), softball W(s).
Costs (2013–14) *Tuition:* state resident $3330 full-time, $111 per credit hour part-time; nonresident $6660 full-time, $222 per credit hour part-time. Full-time tuition and fees vary according to course load. Part-time tuition and fees vary according to course load. *Required fees:* $840 full-time. *Waivers:* senior citizens and employees or children of employees.
Financial Aid Of all full-time matriculated undergraduates who enrolled in 2010, 903 were judged to have need.
Applying *Required:* high school transcript. *Application deadlines:* rolling (freshmen), rolling (transfers).
Freshman Application Contact Lurleen B. Wallace Community College, PO Box 1418, Andalusia, AL 36420-1418. *Phone:* 334-881-2273.
Website: http://www.lbwcc.edu/.

Marion Military Institute
Marion, Alabama

- **State-supported** 2-year, founded 1842, part of Alabama Community College System
- **Rural** 130-acre campus with easy access to Birmingham
- **Coed,** 418 undergraduate students, 98% full-time, 19% women, 81% men

Undergraduates 411 full-time, 7 part-time. Students come from 40 states and territories; 66% are from out of state; 23% Black or African American, non-Hispanic/Latino; 10% Hispanic/Latino; 4% Asian, non-Hispanic/Latino; 0.5% Native Hawaiian or other Pacific Islander, non-Hispanic/Latino; 1% American Indian or Alaska Native, non-Hispanic/Latino; 3% Two or more races, non-Hispanic/Latino; 1% Race/ethnicity unknown; 6% transferred in; 100% live on campus. *Retention:* 38% of full-time freshmen returned.
Freshmen *Admission:* 696 applied, 420 admitted, 249 enrolled. *Average high school GPA:* 3.19. *Test scores:* SAT critical reading scores over 500: 60%; SAT math scores over 500: 66%; ACT scores over 18: 83%; SAT critical reading scores over 600: 24%; SAT math scores over 600: 26%; ACT scores over 24: 38%; SAT critical reading scores over 700: 2%; SAT math scores over 700: 5%; ACT scores over 30: 4%.
Faculty *Total:* 40, 45% full-time, 18% with terminal degrees. *Student/faculty ratio:* 16:1.
Majors Biological and physical sciences; engineering; general studies; liberal arts and sciences/liberal studies.
Academics *Calendar:* semesters. *Degree:* associate. *Special study options:* academic remediation for entering students, English as a second language, services for LD students. *ROTC:* Army (b), Air Force (c).
Library Baer Memorial Library with 22,000 titles, 75 serial subscriptions, 600 audiovisual materials, an OPAC, a Web page.
Student Life *Housing:* on-campus residence required through sophomore year. *Options:* coed, men-only. Campus housing is university owned. *Activities and*

Organizations: drama/theater group, choral group, marching band, Honor Guard, White Knights Precision Drill Team, Swamp Foxes, Marching Band, Scabbard and Blade. *Campus security:* night patrols by trained security personnel. *Student services:* health clinic, personal/psychological counseling.
Athletics Member NJCAA. *Intercollegiate sports:* baseball M(s), basketball M(s), softball W(s), tennis M(s)/W(s), wrestling M(c). *Intramural sports:* basketball M/W, football M/W, soccer M/W, softball M/W, table tennis M/W, ultimate Frisbee M/W, volleyball M/W, water polo M/W.
Standardized Tests *Required:* SAT or ACT (for admission).
Costs (2014–15) *Tuition:* state resident $6000 full-time; nonresident $12,000 full-time. *Required fees:* $2570 full-time. *Room and board:* $3950. *Waivers:* employees or children of employees.
Financial Aid Of all full-time matriculated undergraduates who enrolled in 2012, 29 Federal Work-Study jobs (averaging $210).
Applying *Options:* electronic application, deferred entrance. *Application fee:* $30. *Required:* high school transcript, minimum 2.0 GPA. *Application deadlines:* rolling (freshmen), rolling (transfers). *Notification:* continuous (freshmen), continuous (transfers).
Freshman Application Contact Mrs. Brittany Crawford, Director of Admissions, Marion Military Institute, 1101 Washington Street, Marion, AL 36756. *Phone:* 800-664-1842. *Toll-free phone:* 800-664-1842. *Fax:* 334-683-2383. *E-mail:* bcrawford@marionmilitary.edu.
Website: http://www.marionmilitary.edu/.

Northeast Alabama Community College
Rainsville, Alabama

Freshman Application Contact Northeast Alabama Community College, PO Box 159, Rainsville, AL 35986-0159. *Phone:* 256-228-6001 Ext. 2325.
Website: http://www.nacc.edu/.

Northwest-Shoals Community College
Muscle Shoals, Alabama

- **State-supported** 2-year, founded 1963, part of Alabama Department of Postsecondary Education
- **Small-town** 210-acre campus
- **Endowment** $331,223
- **Coed,** 3,854 undergraduate students, 48% full-time, 57% women, 43% men

Undergraduates 1,840 full-time, 2,014 part-time. Students come from 3 states and territories; 1 other country; 1% are from out of state; 11% Black or African American, non-Hispanic/Latino; 4% Hispanic/Latino; 0.4% Asian, non-Hispanic/Latino; 0.1% Native Hawaiian or other Pacific Islander, non-Hispanic/Latino; 0.6% American Indian or Alaska Native, non-Hispanic/Latino; 0.6% Two or more races, non-Hispanic/Latino; 0.1% Race/ethnicity unknown; 6% transferred in.
Freshmen *Admission:* 1,222 applied, 1,222 admitted, 811 enrolled.
Faculty *Total:* 153, 50% full-time, 6% with terminal degrees. *Student/faculty ratio:* 25:1.
Majors Administrative assistant and secretarial science; child-care and support services management; child development; computer and information sciences; criminal justice/police science; drafting and design technology; emergency medical technology (EMT paramedic); environmental engineering technology; general studies; industrial electronics technology; industrial mechanics and maintenance technology; liberal arts and sciences/liberal studies; medical/clinical assistant; multi/interdisciplinary studies related; registered nursing/registered nurse.
Academics *Calendar:* semesters. *Degree:* certificates and associate. *Special study options:* academic remediation for entering students, accelerated degree program, adult/continuing education programs, advanced placement credit, cooperative education, distance learning, honors programs, independent study, part-time degree program, services for LD students, summer session for credit.
Library Larry W. McCoy Learning Resource Center and James Glasgow Library with 103,323 titles, 50 serial subscriptions, 1,499 audiovisual materials, an OPAC.
Student Life *Housing:* college housing not available. *Activities and Organizations:* choral group, Student Government Association, Science Club, Phi Theta Kappa, Baptist Campus Ministry, Northwest-Shoals Singers. *Campus security:* 24-hour emergency response devices. *Student services:* personal/psychological counseling.
Athletics *Intramural sports:* basketball M/W, football M/W, tennis M/W.
Standardized Tests *Required:* COMPASS Placement Test for English and Math (for admission).
Costs (2014–15) *Tuition:* state resident $3390 full-time, $113 per credit hour part-time; nonresident $6780 full-time, $226 per credit hour part-time. *Required fees:* $810 full-time, $27 per credit hour part-time. *Waivers:* senior citizens and employees or children of employees.
Financial Aid Of all full-time matriculated undergraduates who enrolled in 2012, 31 Federal Work-Study jobs (averaging $1601). *Financial aid deadline:* 6/1.

Applying *Options:* electronic application. *Required:* high school transcript. *Application deadlines:* rolling (freshmen), rolling (transfers). *Notification:* continuous (transfers).

Freshman Application Contact Mr. Tom Carter, Assistant Dean of Recruitment, Admissions and Financial Aid, Northwest-Shoals Community College, PO Box 2545, Muscle Shoals, AL 35662. *Phone:* 256-331-5263. *Toll-free phone:* 800-645-8967. *Fax:* 256-331-5366. *E-mail:* tom.carter@ nwscc.edu.

Website: http://www.nwscc.edu/.

Prince Institute of Professional Studies

Montgomery, Alabama

Freshman Application Contact Kellie Brescia, Director of Admissions, Prince Institute of Professional Studies, 7735 Atlanta Highway, Montgomery, AL 35117. *Phone:* 334-271-1670. *Toll-free phone:* 877-853-5569. *Fax:* 334-271-1671. *E-mail:* admissions@princeinstitute.edu.

Website: http://www.princeinstitute.edu/.

Reid State Technical College

Evergreen, Alabama

- **State-supported** 2-year, founded 1966, part of Alabama Community College System
- **Rural** 26-acre campus
- **Coed,** 517 undergraduate students, 50% full-time, 62% women, 38% men

Undergraduates 260 full-time, 257 part-time. Students come from 2 states and territories; 1% are from out of state; 48% Black or African American, non-Hispanic/Latino; 1% Hispanic/Latino; 0.6% Asian, non-Hispanic/Latino; 0.4% Native Hawaiian or other Pacific Islander, non-Hispanic/Latino; 1% American Indian or Alaska Native, non-Hispanic/Latino; 0.2% Two or more races, non-Hispanic/Latino.

Freshmen *Admission:* 77 applied, 77 admitted, 77 enrolled.

Faculty *Total:* 37, 73% full-time, 11% with terminal degrees. *Student/faculty ratio:* 12:1.

Majors Administrative assistant and secretarial science; child-care and support services management; computer and information sciences; electrical, electronic and communications engineering technology.

Academics *Calendar:* semesters. *Degree:* certificates and associate. *Special study options:* academic remediation for entering students, adult/continuing education programs, double majors, independent study, internships, part-time degree program, services for LD students, summer session for credit.

Library Edith A. Gray Library with 4,157 titles, 99 serial subscriptions, 298 audiovisual materials, a Web page.

Student Life *Housing:* college housing not available. *Activities and Organizations:* Student Government Association, Phi Beta Lambda, National Vocational-Technical Society, Ambassadors, Who's Who. *Campus security:* 24-hour emergency response devices, day and evening security guard. *Student services:* personal/psychological counseling.

Costs (2014–15) *Tuition:* state resident $3996 full-time, $111 per credit part-time; nonresident $7992 full-time, $222 per credit part-time. Full-time tuition and fees vary according to course load and program. Part-time tuition and fees vary according to course load and program. *Required fees:* $1110 full-time, $30 per credit part-time. *Payment plan:* deferred payment. *Waivers:* senior citizens and employees or children of employees.

Financial Aid Of all full-time matriculated undergraduates who enrolled in 2012, 35 Federal Work-Study jobs (averaging $1500).

Applying *Options:* early admission. *Required:* high school transcript. *Application deadlines:* rolling (freshmen), rolling (transfers).

Freshman Application Contact Dr. Alesia Stuart, Public Relations/Marketing/Associate Dean of Workforce Development, Reid State Technical College, Evergreen, AL 36401-0588. *Phone:* 251-578-1313 Ext. 108. *E-mail:* akstuart@rstc.edu.

Website: http://www.rstc.edu/.

Remington College–Mobile Campus

Mobile, Alabama

Freshman Application Contact Remington College–Mobile Campus, 828 Downtowner Loop West, Mobile, AL 36609-5404. *Phone:* 251-343-8200. *Toll-free phone:* 800-560-6192.

Website: http://www.remingtoncollege.edu/.

Shelton State Community College

Tuscaloosa, Alabama

- **State-supported** 2-year, founded 1979, part of Alabama Community College System
- **Small-town** 202-acre campus with easy access to Birmingham
- **Coed,** 5,068 undergraduate students, 49% full-time, 56% women, 44% men

Undergraduates 2,468 full-time, 2,600 part-time. 5% are from out of state; 34% Black or African American, non-Hispanic/Latino; 0.5% Hispanic/Latino; 1% Asian, non-Hispanic/Latino; 0.3% American Indian or Alaska Native, non-Hispanic/Latino; 1% Two or more races, non-Hispanic/Latino; 7% Race/ethnicity unknown; 0.4% international; 9% transferred in. *Retention:* 58% of full-time freshmen returned.

Freshmen *Admission:* 1,356 enrolled.

Faculty *Total:* 222, 41% full-time, 13% with terminal degrees. *Student/faculty ratio:* 25:1.

Majors Administrative assistant and secretarial science; business/commerce; culinary arts; diesel mechanics technology; drafting and design technology; electrical, electronic and communications engineering technology; electrician; general studies; heating, ventilation, air conditioning and refrigeration engineering technology; industrial electronics technology; liberal arts and sciences/liberal studies; machine tool technology; medical administrative assistant and medical secretary; precision metal working related; registered nursing/registered nurse; respiratory care therapy; tool and die technology; welding technology.

Academics *Calendar:* semesters. *Degree:* certificates, diplomas, and associate. *Special study options:* academic remediation for entering students, accelerated degree program, adult/continuing education programs, advanced placement credit, cooperative education, distance learning, double majors, part-time degree program, services for LD students, summer session for credit. *ROTC:* Army (c), Air Force (c).

Library Brooks-Cork Library plus 1 other with an OPAC, a Web page.

Student Life *Housing:* college housing not available. *Activities and Organizations:* drama/theater group, choral group, Phi Theta Kappa, Student Government Association, African American Cultural Association, Red Cross Club. *Campus security:* 24-hour emergency response devices and patrols.

Athletics Member NJCAA. *Intercollegiate sports:* baseball M(s), basketball M(s)/W(s), cheerleading M(s)/W(s), softball W(s).

Costs (2014–15) *Tuition:* state resident $3330 full-time, $111 per credit part-time; nonresident $6660 full-time, $222 per credit part-time. Full-time tuition and fees vary according to course load and reciprocity agreements. Part-time tuition and fees vary according to course load and reciprocity agreements. *Required fees:* $570 full-time, $19 per credit part-time. *Waivers:* senior citizens and employees or children of employees.

Applying *Options:* electronic application. *Required:* high school transcript. *Application deadlines:* rolling (freshmen), rolling (transfers).

Freshman Application Contact Ms. Sharon Chastine, Secretary to the Associate Dean of Student Services Enrollment, Shelton State Community College, 9500 Old Greensboro Road, Tuscaloosa, AL 35405. *Phone:* 205-391-2309. *Fax:* 205-391-3910. *E-mail:* schastine@sheltonstate.edu.

Website: http://www.sheltonstate.edu/.

Snead State Community College

Boaz, Alabama

- **State-supported** 2-year, founded 1898, part of Alabama College System
- **Small-town** 42-acre campus with easy access to Birmingham
- **Coed,** 2,161 undergraduate students, 71% full-time, 61% women, 39% men

Undergraduates 1,538 full-time, 623 part-time.

Freshmen *Admission:* 716 enrolled.

Faculty *Student/faculty ratio:* 23:1.

Majors Business administration and management; child-care and support services management; computer and information sciences; engineering technology; general studies.

Academics *Calendar:* semesters. *Degree:* certificates and associate. *Special study options:* academic remediation for entering students, accelerated degree program, adult/continuing education programs, advanced placement credit, distance learning, independent study, internships, part-time degree program, services for LD students, student-designed majors, summer session for credit.

Library Learning Resource Center with an OPAC, a Web page.

Student Life *Housing Options:* coed. Campus housing is university owned. *Activities and Organizations:* choral group, Phi Theta Kappa, Ambassadors, Student Government Association. *Campus security:* 24-hour patrols.

Athletics Member NJCAA. *Intercollegiate sports:* baseball M(s), basketball M(s)/W(s), softball W(s), tennis W(s), volleyball W(s).

Financial Aid Of all full-time matriculated undergraduates who enrolled in 2012, 45 Federal Work-Study jobs.

Applying *Options:* electronic application, early admission, deferred entrance. *Required:* high school transcript. *Required for some:* interview.
Freshman Application Contact Dr. Jason Watts, Chief Academic Officer, Snead State Community College, PO Box 734, Boaz, AL 35957-0734. *Phone:* 256-840-4118. *Fax:* 256-593-7180. *E-mail:* jwatts@snead.edu.
Website: http://www.snead.edu/.

Southern Union State Community College
Wadley, Alabama

Freshman Application Contact Admissions Office, Southern Union State Community College, PO Box 1000, Roberts Street, Wadley, AL 36276. *Phone:* 256-395-5157. *E-mail:* info@suscc.edu.
Website: http://www.suscc.edu/.

Virginia College in Huntsville
Huntsville, Alabama

Freshman Application Contact Director of Admission, Virginia College in Huntsville, 2021 Drake Avenue SW, Huntsville, AL 35801. *Phone:* 256-533-7387. *Fax:* 256-533-7785.
Website: http://www.vc.edu/.

Virginia College in Mobile
Mobile, Alabama

Admissions Office Contact Virginia College in Mobile, 3725 Airport Boulevard, Suite 165, Mobile, AL 36608.
Website: http://www.vc.edu/.

Virginia College in Montgomery
Montgomery, Alabama

Admissions Office Contact Virginia College in Montgomery, 6200 Atlanta Highway, Montgomery, AL 36117-2800.
Website: http://www.vc.edu/.

Wallace State Community College
Hanceville, Alabama

Director of Admissions Jennifer Hill, Director of Admissions, Wallace State Community College, PO Box 2000, 801 Main Street, Hanceville, AL 35077-2000. *Phone:* 256-352-8278. *Toll-free phone:* 866-350-9722.
Website: http://www.wallacestate.edu/.

ALASKA

Alaska Career College
Anchorage, Alaska

Admissions Office Contact Alaska Career College, 1415 East Tudor Road, Anchorage, AK 99507.
Website: http://www.alaskacareercollege.edu/.

Charter College
Anchorage, Alaska

Director of Admissions Ms. Lily Sirianni, Vice President, Charter College, 2221 East Northern Lights Boulevard, Suite 120, Anchorage, AK 99508. *Phone:* 907-277-1000. *Toll-free phone:* 888-200-9942.
Website: http://www.chartercollege.edu/.

Ilisagvik College
Barrow, Alaska

- **State-supported** 2-year, founded 1995
- **Rural** 7-acre campus
- **Endowment** $3.5 million
- **Coed,** 257 undergraduate students, 19% full-time, 63% women, 37% men

Undergraduates 50 full-time, 207 part-time. Students come from 3 states and territories; 3 other countries; 2% Black or African American, non-Hispanic/Latino; 2% Hispanic/Latino; 7% Asian, non-Hispanic/Latino; 4% Native Hawaiian or other Pacific Islander, non-Hispanic/Latino; 58% American Indian or Alaska Native, non-Hispanic/Latino; 1% Race/ethnicity unknown; 0.8% international; 3% transferred in; 10% live on campus.
Freshmen *Admission:* 93 applied, 77 admitted, 30 enrolled.
Faculty *Total:* 51, 24% full-time. *Student/faculty ratio:* 6:1.

Majors Accounting technology and bookkeeping; American Indian/Native American studies; business administration and management; fire science/firefighting; health services/allied health/health sciences; liberal arts and sciences/liberal studies; office management.
Academics *Calendar:* semesters. *Degree:* certificates, diplomas, and associate. *Special study options:* academic remediation for entering students, cooperative education, distance learning, double majors, English as a second language, independent study, internships, off-campus study, part-time degree program, services for LD students, summer session for credit.
Library Tuzzy Consortium Library with 65,000 titles, 175 serial subscriptions, 4,500 audiovisual materials, an OPAC, a Web page.
Student Life *Housing Options:* coed. Campus housing is leased by the school. *Activities and Organizations:* Student Government, Barrow Camera Club, Ilisagvik Green Team, Aglaun Literary Journal. *Campus security:* 24-hour emergency response devices and patrols, controlled dormitory access. *Student services:* personal/psychological counseling.
Athletics *Intramural sports:* basketball M/W.
Standardized Tests *Recommended:* ACT ASSET or COMPASS Test.
Costs (2014–15) *Tuition:* state resident $3000 full-time, $125 per credit part-time; nonresident $3000 full-time, $125 per credit part-time. Full-time tuition and fees vary according to course load and program. Part-time tuition and fees vary according to course load and program. *Required fees:* $460 full-time, $60 per term part-time, $60 per term part-time. *Room and board:* $6600; room only: $4000. Room and board charges vary according to housing facility. *Payment plans:* installment, deferred payment. *Waivers:* senior citizens and employees or children of employees.
Applying *Options:* deferred entrance. *Required:* high school transcript, minimum 2.0 GPA. *Required for some:* copy of Alaska Native Shareholder/Native American Tribal Affiliation card if native. *Application deadlines:* 8/2 (freshmen), 8/2 (out-of-state freshmen), 8/2 (transfers). *Notification:* continuous (freshmen), continuous (out-of-state freshmen), continuous (transfers).
Freshman Application Contact Janelle Everett, Recruiter, Ilisagvik College, PO BOX 749, Barrow, AK 99723. *Phone:* 907-852-1799. *Toll-free phone:* 800-478-7337. *Fax:* 907-852-2729. *E-mail:* janelle.everett@ilisagvik.edu.
Website: http://www.ilisagvik.edu/.

University of Alaska Anchorage, Kenai Peninsula College
Soldotna, Alaska

- **State-supported** primarily 2-year, founded 1964, part of University of Alaska System
- **Rural** 360-acre campus
- **Coed**

Academics *Calendar:* semesters. *Degrees:* certificates, associate, and bachelor's. *Special study options:* academic remediation for entering students, adult/continuing education programs, advanced placement credit, cooperative education, distance learning, English as a second language, part-time degree program, services for LD students.
Student Life *Campus security:* 24-hour emergency response devices.
Standardized Tests *Required:* ACT, SAT or ACCUPLACER scores (for admission).
Applying *Options:* electronic application. *Application fee:* $40. *Required:* high school transcript.
Freshman Application Contact Ms. Shelly Love Blatchford, Admission and Registration Coordinator, University of Alaska Anchorage, Kenai Peninsula College, 156 College Road, Soldotna, AK 99669-9798. *Phone:* 907-262-0311. *Toll-free phone:* 877-262-0330.
Website: http://www.kpc.alaska.edu/.

University of Alaska Anchorage, Kodiak College
Kodiak, Alaska

Freshman Application Contact University of Alaska Anchorage, Kodiak College, 117 Benny Benson Drive, Kodiak, AK 99615-6643. *Phone:* 907-486-1235. *Toll-free phone:* 800-486-7660.
Website: http://www.koc.alaska.edu/.

University of Alaska Anchorage, Matanuska-Susitna College
Palmer, Alaska

Freshman Application Contact Ms. Sandra Gravley, Student Services Director, University of Alaska Anchorage, Matanuska-Susitna College, PO Box 2889, Palmer, AK 99645-2889. *Phone:* 907-745-9712. *Fax:* 907-745-9747. *E-mail:* info@matsu.alaska.edu.
Website: http://www.matsu.alaska.edu/.

University of Alaska, Prince William Sound Community College

Valdez, Alaska

- **State-supported** 2-year, founded 1978, part of University of Alaska System
- **Small-town** campus
- **Endowment** $62,630
- **Coed**

Undergraduates 69 full-time, 458 part-time. Students come from 1 other state; 1 other country; 4% are from out of state; 4% Hispanic/Latino; 3% Asian, non-Hispanic/Latino; 5% American Indian or Alaska Native, non-Hispanic/Latino; 0.5% Two or more races, non-Hispanic/Latino; 42% Race/ethnicity unknown; 0.5% international; 2% live on campus.

Faculty *Student/faculty ratio:* 8:1.

Academics *Calendar:* semesters. *Degree:* certificates, diplomas, and associate. *Special study options:* academic remediation for entering students, adult/continuing education programs, advanced placement credit, cooperative education, distance learning, double majors, English as a second language, independent study, internships, summer session for credit.

Student Life *Campus security:* student patrols, controlled dormitory access, housing manager supervision.

Standardized Tests *Recommended:* SAT or ACT (for admission), ACCUPLACER.

Costs (2013–14) *Tuition:* state resident $3480 full-time, $145 per credit part-time; nonresident $3480 full-time, $145 per credit part-time. Full-time tuition and fees vary according to course load, location, and program. Part-time tuition and fees vary according to course load, location, and program. *Required fees:* $300 full-time, $32 per credit part-time. *Room and board:* room only: $4230. Room and board charges vary according to housing facility. *Payment plans:* installment, deferred payment.

Applying *Options:* electronic application, early admission. *Application fee:* $25. *Required:* high school transcript.

Freshman Application Contact Shelia Mann, University of Alaska, Prince William Sound Community College, PO Box 97, Valdez, AK 99686-0097. *Phone:* 907-834-1600. *Toll-free phone:* 800-478-8800. *Fax:* 907-834-1691. *E-mail:* studentservices@pwscc.edu. *Website:* http://www.pwscc.edu/.

University of Alaska Southeast, Ketchikan Campus

Ketchikan, Alaska

Freshman Application Contact Admissions Office, University of Alaska Southeast, Ketchikan Campus, 2600 7th Avenue, Ketchikan, AK 99901-5798. *Phone:* 907-225-6177. *Toll-free phone:* 888-550-6177. *Fax:* 907-225-3895. *E-mail:* ketch.info@uas.alaska.edu. *Website:* http://www.ketch.alaska.edu/.

University of Alaska Southeast, Sitka Campus

Sitka, Alaska

Freshman Application Contact Cynthia Rogers, Coordinator of Admissions, University of Alaska Southeast, Sitka Campus, 1332 Seward Avenue, Sitka, AK 99835-9418. *Phone:* 907-747-7705. *Toll-free phone:* 800-478-6653. *Fax:* 907-747-7793. *E-mail:* cynthia.rogers@uas.alaska.edu. *Website:* http://www.uas.alaska.edu/.

AMERICAN SAMOA

American Samoa Community College

Pago Pago, American Samoa

- **Territory-supported** primarily 2-year, founded 1969
- **Rural** 20-acre campus
- **Endowment** $3.1 million
- **Coed,** 1,488 undergraduate students, 49% full-time, 61% women, 39% men

Undergraduates 735 full-time, 753 part-time. Students come from 5 other countries; 1% Asian, non-Hispanic/Latino; 92% Native Hawaiian or other Pacific Islander, non-Hispanic/Latino; 0.1% Race/ethnicity unknown; 7% international; 0.1% transferred in.

Freshmen *Admission:* 278 applied, 176 admitted, 490 enrolled. *Test scores:* SAT critical reading scores over 500: 5%; SAT math scores over 500: 4%; SAT writing scores over 500: 6%; SAT critical reading scores over 600: 2%; SAT math scores over 600: 2%; SAT writing scores over 600: 3%; SAT critical reading scores over 700: 1%; SAT math scores over 700: 1%; SAT writing scores over 700: 1%.

Faculty *Total:* 89, 70% full-time, 11% with terminal degrees.

Majors Accounting; agricultural business and management; agriculture; architectural drafting and CAD/CADD; art; autobody/collision and repair technology; automobile/automotive mechanics technology; business administration and management; civil engineering; construction trades; criminal justice/safety; education; electrical, electronic and communications engineering technology; family and consumer economics related; forensic science and technology; health services/allied health/health sciences; human services; liberal arts and sciences/liberal studies; marine science/merchant marine officer; music; natural resources/conservation; office occupations and clerical services; political science and government; pre-law studies; welding technology.

Academics *Calendar:* semesters. *Degrees:* certificates, associate, and bachelor's. *Special study options:* academic remediation for entering students, adult/continuing education programs, cooperative education, double majors, English as a second language, honors programs, independent study, internships, off-campus study, part-time degree program, services for LD students, student-designed majors, summer session for credit. *ROTC:* Army (b).

Library ASCC Learning Resource Center/ Library plus 1 other with 40,000 titles, 50 serial subscriptions, an OPAC.

Student Life *Housing:* college housing not available. *Activities and Organizations:* student-run newspaper, Student Government Association, Phi Theta Kappa, ASCC Research Foundation Student Club, Fa'aSamoa (Samoan Culture) Club, Journalism Club. *Campus security:* 24-hour patrols. *Student services:* personal/psychological counseling.

Athletics *Intramural sports:* basketball M/W, football M/W, golf M/W, rugby M, soccer M, tennis M/W, track and field M/W, volleyball M/W.

Standardized Tests *Recommended:* SAT (for admission), ACT (for admission), SAT or ACT (for admission), SAT and SAT Subject Tests or ACT (for admission), SAT Subject Tests (for admission).

Financial Aid Of all full-time matriculated undergraduates who enrolled in 2012, 929 applied for aid, 929 were judged to have need. 125 Federal Work-Study jobs (averaging $471). *Average percent of need met:* 50%. *Average financial aid package:* $5550.

Applying *Options:* early admission, deferred entrance. *Application deadline:* 8/1 (freshmen).

Freshman Application Contact American Samoa Community College, PO Box 2609, Pago Pago, AS 96799-2609. *Phone:* 684-699-1141. *Website:* http://www.amsamoa.edu/.

ARIZONA

Acacia University

Tempe, Arizona

Admissions Office Contact Acacia University, 7665 South Research Drive, Tempe, AZ 85284. *Website:* http://www.acacia.edu/.

Anthem College–Phoenix

Phoenix, Arizona

Freshman Application Contact Mr. Glen Husband, Vice President of Admissions, Anthem College–Phoenix, 1515 East Indian School Road, Phoenix, AZ 85014-4901. *Phone:* 602-279-9700. *Toll-free phone:* 855-331-7767. *Website:* http://anthem.edu/phoenix-arizona/.

Arizona Automotive Institute

Glendale, Arizona

Director of Admissions Director of Admissions, Arizona Automotive Institute, 6829 North 46th Avenue, Glendale, AZ 85301-3597. *Phone:* 623-934-7273 Ext. 211. *Toll-free phone:* 800-321-5861 (in-state); 800-321-5961 (out-of-state). *Fax:* 623-937-5000. *E-mail:* info@azautoinst.com. *Website:* http://www.aai.edu/.

Arizona College

Glendale, Arizona

Freshman Application Contact Admissions Department, Arizona College, 4425 West Olive Avenue, Suite 300, Glendale, AZ 85302-3843. *Phone:* 602-222-9300. *E-mail:* lhicks@arizonacollege.edu. *Website:* http://www.arizonacollege.edu/.

Arizona Western College
Yuma, Arizona

- **State and locally supported** 2-year, founded 1962, part of Arizona State Community College System
- **Rural** 640-acre campus
- **Coed,** 7,979 undergraduate students, 35% full-time, 57% women, 43% men

Undergraduates 2,801 full-time, 5,178 part-time. Students come from 27 states and territories; 32 other countries; 3% are from out of state; 3% Black or African American, non-Hispanic/Latino; 64% Hispanic/Latino; 1% Asian, non-Hispanic/Latino; 0.4% Native Hawaiian or other Pacific Islander, non-Hispanic/Latino; 1% American Indian or Alaska Native, non-Hispanic/Latino; 0.1% Two or more races, non-Hispanic/Latino; 3% Race/ethnicity unknown; 7% international; 6% live on campus.

Freshmen *Admission:* 2,046 enrolled.

Faculty *Total:* 449, 28% full-time. *Student/faculty ratio:* 22:1.

Majors Accounting; agricultural business and management; agriculture; architectural technology; biology/biological sciences; business administration and management; business/commerce; carpentry; chemistry; civil engineering technology; computer and information sciences; computer graphics; construction trades related; criminal justice/law enforcement administration; crop production; culinary arts; data entry/microcomputer applications; dramatic/theater arts; early childhood education; electrical/electronics equipment installation and repair; elementary education; emergency medical technology (EMT paramedic); engineering; English; environmental science; fine/studio arts; fire science/firefighting; general studies; geology/earth science; health services/allied health/health sciences; heating, air conditioning, ventilation and refrigeration maintenance technology; history; hospitality administration; industrial technology; legal administrative assistant/secretary; logistics, materials, and supply chain management; marketing/marketing management; massage therapy; mass communication/media; mathematics; music; office management; parks, recreation and leisure facilities management; philosophy; physics; plumbing technology; political science and government; radio and television broadcasting technology; radiologic technology/science; secondary education; social sciences; solar energy technology; Spanish; welding technology; work and family studies.

Academics *Calendar:* semesters. *Degree:* certificates and associate. *Special study options:* academic remediation for entering students, adult/continuing education programs, advanced placement credit, cooperative education, distance learning, English as a second language, honors programs, independent study, part-time degree program, services for LD students, summer session for credit.

Library Arizona Western College and NAU-Yuma Library with 108,994 titles, 434 serial subscriptions, 5,259 audiovisual materials, an OPAC, a Web page.

Student Life *Housing Options:* coed, men-only, women-only. Campus housing is university owned. *Activities and Organizations:* drama/theater group, student-run newspaper, radio and television station, choral group, Student Government Association, Spirit Squad, Dance Team, Students in Free Enterprise (SIFE), International Students Team, national fraternities, national sororities. *Campus security:* 24-hour emergency response devices and patrols, student patrols, late-night transport/escort service. *Student services:* health clinic, personal/psychological counseling.

Athletics Member NJCAA. *Intercollegiate sports:* baseball M(s), basketball M(s)/W(s), football M(s), soccer M(s)/W(s), softball W(s), volleyball W(s). *Intramural sports:* cheerleading M(c)/W(c).

Standardized Tests *Required for some:* SAT or ACT (for admission).

Costs (2014–15) *Tuition:* state resident $1830 full-time, $76 per credit hour part-time; nonresident $7440 full-time, $310 per credit hour part-time. Full-time tuition and fees vary according to course load, program, and reciprocity agreements. Part-time tuition and fees vary according to course load, program, and reciprocity agreements. *Room and board:* $6200; room only: $2262. Room and board charges vary according to board plan and housing facility. *Payment plan:* installment. *Waivers:* senior citizens and employees or children of employees.

Financial Aid Of all full-time matriculated undergraduates who enrolled in 2012, 350 Federal Work-Study jobs (averaging $1500). 100 state and other part-time jobs (averaging $1800).

Applying *Options:* electronic application, early admission, deferred entrance. *Application deadlines:* rolling (freshmen), rolling (out-of-state freshmen), rolling (transfers).

Freshman Application Contact Amy Pignatore, Director of Admissions/Registrar, Arizona Western College, PO Box 929, Yuma, AZ 85366. *Phone:* 928-317-6092. *Toll-free phone:* 888-293-0392. *Fax:* 928-344-7712. *E-mail:* amy.pignatore@azwestern.edu. *Website:* http://www.azwestern.edu/.

Brown Mackie College–Phoenix
Phoenix, Arizona

- **Proprietary** primarily 2-year, part of Education Management Corporation
- **Coed**

Majors Biomedical technology; business administration and management; corrections and criminal justice related; health/health-care administration; legal assistant/paralegal; medical office management; occupational therapist assistant; registered nursing/registered nurse; surgical technology.

Academics *Degrees:* diplomas, associate, and bachelor's.

Freshman Application Contact Brown Mackie College–Phoenix, 13430 North Black Canyon Highway, Suite 190, Phoenix, AZ 85029. *Phone:* 602-337-3044. *Toll-free phone:* 866-824-4793. *Website:* http://www.brownmackie.edu/phoenix/.

See display on next page and page 414 for the College Close-Up.

Brown Mackie College–Tucson
Tucson, Arizona

- **Proprietary** primarily 2-year, founded 1972, part of Education Management Corporation
- **Suburban** campus
- **Coed**

Majors Biomedical technology; business administration and management; business/commerce; computer and information sciences and support services related; computer support specialist; corrections and criminal justice related; graphic design; health/health-care administration; medical office management; occupational therapist assistant; surgical technology.

Academics *Degrees:* diplomas, associate, and bachelor's.

Freshman Application Contact Brown Mackie College–Tucson, 4585 East Speedway, Suite 204, Tucson, AZ 85712. *Phone:* 520-319-3300. *Website:* http://www.brownmackie.edu/tucson/.

See display on next page and page 426 for the College Close-Up.

The Bryman School of Arizona
Phoenix, Arizona

Freshman Application Contact Admissions Office, The Bryman School of Arizona, 2250 West Peoria Avenue, Phoenix, AZ 85029. *Phone:* 602-274-4300. *Toll-free phone:* 866-381-6383 (in-state); 866-391-6383 (out-of-state). *Fax:* 602-248-9087. *Website:* http://www.brymanschool.edu/.

Carrington College–Mesa
Mesa, Arizona

- **Proprietary** 2-year, founded 1977, part of Carrington Colleges Group, Inc.
- **Suburban** campus
- **Coed,** 691 undergraduate students, 90% full-time, 81% women, 19% men

Undergraduates 624 full-time, 67 part-time. 1% are from out of state; 5% Black or African American, non-Hispanic/Latino; 33% Hispanic/Latino; 3% Asian, non-Hispanic/Latino; 0.7% Native Hawaiian or other Pacific Islander, non-Hispanic/Latino; 12% American Indian or Alaska Native, non-Hispanic/Latino; 0.7% Two or more races, non-Hispanic/Latino; 1% Race/ethnicity unknown; 9% transferred in.

Freshmen *Admission:* 100 enrolled.

Faculty *Total:* 50, 24% full-time. *Student/faculty ratio:* 26:1.

Majors Dental hygiene; medical office management; physical therapy technology; respiratory care therapy; respiratory therapy technician.

Academics *Calendar:* semesters. *Degree:* certificates and associate.

Student Life *Housing:* college housing not available.

Applying *Required:* essay or personal statement, high school transcript, interview.

Freshman Application Contact Carrington College–Mesa, 1001 West Southern Avenue, Suite 130, Mesa, AZ 85210. *Website:* http://carrington.edu/.

Carrington College–Phoenix
Phoenix, Arizona

- **Proprietary** 2-year, founded 1976, part of Carrington Colleges Group, Inc.
- **Urban** campus
- **Coed,** 676 undergraduate students, 100% full-time, 84% women, 16% men

Undergraduates 676 full-time. 1% are from out of state; 8% Black or African American, non-Hispanic/Latino; 54% Hispanic/Latino; 0.4% Asian, non-Hispanic/Latino; 0.6% Native Hawaiian or other Pacific Islander, non-

Hispanic/Latino; 8% American Indian or Alaska Native, non-Hispanic/Latino; 1% Two or more races, non-Hispanic/Latino; 1% Race/ethnicity unknown; 8% transferred in.

Freshmen *Admission:* 132 enrolled.

Faculty *Total:* 28, 54% full-time. *Student/faculty ratio:* 35:1.

Majors Massage therapy; medical office management; occupational therapy; radiologic technology/science; registered nursing/registered nurse; respiratory care therapy.

Academics *Calendar:* continuous. *Degree:* certificates and associate.

Student Life *Housing:* college housing not available.

Applying *Required:* essay or personal statement, high school transcript, interview.

Freshman Application Contact Carrington College–Phoenix, 8503 North 27th Avenue, Phoenix, AZ 85051.

Website: http://carrington.edu/.

Carrington College–Phoenix Westside

Phoenix, Arizona

- **Proprietary** 2-year, part of Carrington Colleges Group, Inc.
- **Urban** campus
- **Coed,** 513 undergraduate students, 70% full-time, 64% women, 36% men

Undergraduates 358 full-time, 155 part-time. 2% are from out of state; 9% Black or African American, non-Hispanic/Latino; 27% Hispanic/Latino; 4% Asian, non-Hispanic/Latino; 1% Native Hawaiian or other Pacific Islander, non-Hispanic/Latino; 4% American Indian or Alaska Native, non-Hispanic/Latino; 1% Two or more races, non-Hispanic/Latino; 3% Race/ethnicity unknown; 2% transferred in.

Freshmen *Admission:* 12 enrolled.

Faculty *Total:* 45, 36% full-time. *Student/faculty ratio:* 16:1.

Majors Clinical/medical laboratory technology; hospital and health-care facilities administration; medical radiologic technology; occupational therapist assistant; registered nursing/registered nurse; respiratory therapy technician.

Academics *Calendar:* semesters. *Degree:* certificates and associate.

Student Life *Housing:* college housing not available.

Applying *Required:* essay or personal statement, high school transcript, interview.

Freshman Application Contact Carrington College–Phoenix Westside, 2701 West Bethany Home Road, Phoenix, AZ 85017.

Website: http://carrington.edu/.

Carrington College–Tucson

Tucson, Arizona

- **Proprietary** 2-year, founded 1984, part of Carrington Colleges Group, Inc.
- **Suburban** campus
- **Coed,** 440 undergraduate students, 99% full-time, 79% women, 21% men

Undergraduates 437 full-time, 3 part-time. 0.5% are from out of state; 4% Black or African American, non-Hispanic/Latino; 61% Hispanic/Latino; 0.2% Asian, non-Hispanic/Latino; 0.5% Native Hawaiian or other Pacific Islander, non-Hispanic/Latino; 5% American Indian or Alaska Native, non-Hispanic/Latino; 1% Two or more races, non-Hispanic/Latino; 2% Race/ethnicity unknown; 8% transferred in.

Freshmen *Admission:* 84 enrolled.

Faculty *Total:* 19, 42% full-time. *Student/faculty ratio:* 38:1.

Majors Clinical/medical laboratory technology; medical office management.

Academics *Calendar:* semesters modular courses are offered. *Degree:* certificates and associate.

Student Life *Housing:* college housing not available. *Student services:* personal/psychological counseling, legal services.

Applying *Required:* essay or personal statement, high school transcript, interview.

Freshman Application Contact Carrington College–Tucson, 3550 North Oracle Road, Tucson, AZ 85705.

Website: http://carrington.edu/.

Central Arizona College

Coolidge, Arizona

Freshman Application Contact Dr. James Moore, Dean of Records and Admissions, Central Arizona College, 8470 North Overfield Road, Coolidge, AZ 85128. *Phone:* 520-494-5261. *Toll-free phone:* 800-237-9814. *Fax:* 520-426-5083. *E-mail:* james.moore@centralaz.edu.

Website: http://www.centralaz.edu/.

Chandler-Gilbert Community College
Chandler, Arizona

- **State and locally supported** 2-year, founded 1985, part of Maricopa County Community College District System
- **Suburban** 80-acre campus with easy access to Phoenix
- **Coed,** 14,399 undergraduate students, 31% full-time, 53% women, 47% men

Undergraduates 4,467 full-time, 9,932 part-time. 4% Black or African American, non-Hispanic/Latino; 21% Hispanic/Latino; 5% Asian, non-Hispanic/Latino; 0.3% Native Hawaiian or other Pacific Islander, non-Hispanic/Latino; 1% American Indian or Alaska Native, non-Hispanic/Latino; 2% Two or more races, non-Hispanic/Latino; 13% Race/ethnicity unknown; 0.5% international; 4% transferred in. *Retention:* 63% of full-time freshmen returned.

Freshmen *Admission:* 2,004 enrolled.

Faculty *Total:* 617, 21% full-time. *Student/faculty ratio:* 25:1.

Majors Accounting; accounting technology and bookkeeping; airline pilot and flight crew; business administration and management; business administration, management and operations related; business/commerce; business, management, and marketing related; computer and information sciences; computer and information sciences and support services related; computer programming; computer programming (vendor/product certification); computer systems analysis; computer systems networking and telecommunications; criminal justice/safety; data entry/microcomputer applications; data modeling/warehousing and database administration; dietetic technology; dietitian assistant; dramatic/theater arts; electromechanical technology; elementary education; fine/studio arts; general studies; information technology; kinesiology and exercise science; liberal arts and sciences and humanities related; liberal arts and sciences/liberal studies; lineworker; massage therapy; mechanic and repair technologies related; music management; organizational behavior; physical sciences; psychology; registered nursing/registered nurse; social work; visual and performing arts.

Academics *Calendar:* semesters. *Degree:* certificates, diplomas, and associate. *Special study options:* academic remediation for entering students, advanced placement credit, English as a second language, freshman honors college, honors programs, independent study, part-time degree program, services for LD students, study abroad, summer session for credit.

Library Chandler-Gilbert Community College Library with an OPAC.

Student Life *Housing:* college housing not available. *Activities and Organizations:* student-run newspaper, radio station, choral group. *Campus security:* 24-hour emergency response devices and patrols, late-night transport/escort service. *Student services:* personal/psychological counseling.

Athletics Member NJCAA. *Intercollegiate sports:* baseball M, basketball M/W, golf M/W, soccer M/W, softball W, volleyball W.

Costs (2014–15) *Tuition:* area resident $1944 full-time, $81 per credit hour part-time; state resident $7728 full-time, $334 per credit hour part-time; nonresident $8016 full-time, $322 per credit hour part-time. Full-time tuition and fees vary according to reciprocity agreements. Part-time tuition and fees vary according to reciprocity agreements. *Required fees:* $30 full-time, $15 part-time. *Payment plans:* installment, deferred payment. *Waivers:* employees or children of employees.

Applying *Options:* electronic application.

Freshman Application Contact Ryan Cain, Coordinator of Enrollment Services, Chandler-Gilbert Community College, 2626 East Pecos Road, Chandler, AZ 85225-2479. *Phone:* 480-732-7044. *E-mail:* ryan.cain@cgc.edu.

Website: http://www.cgc.maricopa.edu/.

Cochise College
Sierra Vista, Arizona

- **State and locally supported** 2-year, founded 1977
- **Small-town** 518-acre campus with easy access to Tucson
- **Coed,** 3,787 undergraduate students, 41% full-time, 53% women, 47% men

Undergraduates 1,567 full-time, 2,220 part-time. 9% are from out of state; 6% Black or African American, non-Hispanic/Latino; 44% Hispanic/Latino; 2% Asian, non-Hispanic/Latino; 0.6% Native Hawaiian or other Pacific Islander, non-Hispanic/Latino; 0.7% American Indian or Alaska Native, non-Hispanic/Latino; 2% Two or more races, non-Hispanic/Latino; 2% Race/ethnicity unknown; 0.4% international; 3% live on campus. *Retention:* 56% of full-time freshmen returned.

Freshmen *Admission:* 2,248 applied, 2,248 admitted, 803 enrolled. *Average high school GPA:* 2.76.

Faculty *Total:* 334, 25% full-time. *Student/faculty ratio:* 15:1.

Majors Administrative assistant and secretarial science; adult and continuing education; agricultural business and management; air and space operations technology; airline pilot and flight crew; air transportation related; art; art teacher education; automobile/automotive mechanics technology; avionics maintenance technology; biology/biological sciences; building construction technology; business administration and management; chemistry; computer and information systems security; computer programming; computer science; computer systems networking and telecommunications; criminal justice/police science; culinary arts; digital communication and media/multimedia; dramatic/theater arts; early childhood education; economics; electrical, electronic and communications engineering technology; elementary education; emergency medical technology (EMT paramedic); engineering; English; fire science/firefighting; general studies; health and physical education/fitness; history teacher education; humanities; information science/studies; intelligence; journalism; logistics, materials, and supply chain management; mathematics; music; philosophy; physics; psychology; registered nursing/registered nurse; respiratory care therapy; social sciences; social work; speech communication and rhetoric; welding technology.

Academics *Calendar:* semesters. *Degree:* certificates and associate. *Special study options:* academic remediation for entering students, adult/continuing education programs, advanced placement credit, cooperative education, distance learning, English as a second language, honors programs, independent study, internships, part-time degree program, services for LD students, summer session for credit.

Library an OPAC, a Web page.

Student Life *Housing Options:* coed, special housing for students with disabilities. Campus housing is university owned. *Activities and Organizations:* drama/theater group, student-run newspaper, choral group, Student Nurses, Phi Theta Kappa, Strong Oak. *Campus security:* 24-hour emergency response devices and patrols. *Student services:* personal/psychological counseling.

Athletics Member NJCAA. *Intercollegiate sports:* baseball M(s), basketball M(s)/W(s), soccer W(s).

Costs (2014–15) *Tuition:* state resident $2250 full-time, $75 per credit hour part-time; nonresident $7500 full-time, $250 per credit hour part-time. Full-time tuition and fees vary according to course load and program. Part-time tuition and fees vary according to course load and program. *Room and board:* $6300.

Financial Aid Of all full-time matriculated undergraduates who enrolled in 2012, 1,017 applied for aid, 826 were judged to have need. In 2012, 27 non-need-based awards were made. *Average financial aid package:* $5635. *Average need-based loan:* $3095. *Average need-based gift aid:* $3335. *Average non-need-based aid:* $1527.

Applying *Options:* electronic application, deferred entrance. *Recommended:* high school transcript. *Application deadlines:* rolling (freshmen), rolling (out-of-state freshmen), rolling (transfers). *Notification:* continuous (freshmen), continuous (out-of-state freshmen), continuous (transfers).

Freshman Application Contact Ms. Debbie Quick, Director of Admissions and Records, Cochise College, 901 North Colombo Avenue, Sierra Vista, AZ 85635-2317. *Phone:* 520-515-3640. *Toll-free phone:* 800-593-9567. *Fax:* 520-515-5452. *E-mail:* quickd@cochise.edu.

Website: http://www.cochise.edu/.

Coconino Community College
Flagstaff, Arizona

- **State-supported** 2-year, founded 1991
- **Small-town** 5-acre campus
- **Endowment** $322,526
- **Coed,** 3,698 undergraduate students, 27% full-time, 58% women, 42% men

Undergraduates 1,009 full-time, 2,689 part-time. Students come from 10 states and territories; 1% are from out of state; 1% Black or African American, non-Hispanic/Latino; 14% Hispanic/Latino; 1% Asian, non-Hispanic/Latino; 0.4% Native Hawaiian or other Pacific Islander, non-Hispanic/Latino; 21% American Indian or Alaska Native, non-Hispanic/Latino; 4% Two or more races, non-Hispanic/Latino; 2% Race/ethnicity unknown.

Freshmen *Admission:* 608 enrolled.

Faculty *Total:* 207, 19% full-time. *Student/faculty ratio:* 18:1.

Majors Accounting technology and bookkeeping; anthropology; architectural drafting and CAD/CADD; architectural engineering technology; architectural technology; area studies related; building construction technology; business administration and management; business/commerce; carpentry; computer software technology; computer technology/computer systems technology; construction management; construction trades related; corrections; corrections and criminal justice related; criminal justice/law enforcement administration; desktop publishing and digital imaging design; early childhood education; electrical, electronic and communications engineering technology; elementary education; emergency care attendant (EMT ambulance); environmental science; fine/studio arts; fire science/firefighting; forensic science and technology; general studies; hospitality administration; medical insurance/medical billing; medical office assistant; nursing assistant/aide and patient care assistant/aide; phlebotomy technology; psychology; registered nursing/registered nurse; sheet metal technology; sign language interpretation and translation; sociology; solar energy technology; visual and performing arts.

Academics *Calendar:* semesters. *Degree:* certificates and associate. *Special study options:* academic remediation for entering students, adult/continuing education programs, distance learning, honors programs, independent study, internships, part-time degree program, study abroad, summer session for credit. *ROTC:* Army (b), Air Force (b).

Library Information Resources and Library Services with 5,905 titles, 3,515 serial subscriptions, 2,358 audiovisual materials, an OPAC, a Web page.

Student Life *Housing:* college housing not available. *Activities and Organizations:* Art Club, Clay Club, Dance Club, Native American Club, Video Gaming Club. *Campus security:* 24-hour emergency response devices, student patrols, late-night transport/escort service, security patrols while campuses are open; electronic access throughout the campuses with security cards.

Costs (2014–15) *Tuition:* state resident $2208 full-time, $87 per credit hour part-time; nonresident $7428 full-time, $305 per credit hour part-time. *Payment plan:* installment. *Waivers:* senior citizens and employees or children of employees.

Financial Aid Of all full-time matriculated undergraduates who enrolled in 2012, 25 Federal Work-Study jobs (averaging $4000).

Applying *Options:* electronic application. *Application deadlines:* rolling (freshmen), rolling (transfers). *Notification:* continuous (freshmen), continuous (transfers).

Freshman Application Contact Veronica Hipolito, Director of Student Services, Coconino Community College, 2800 South Lone Tree Road, Flagstaff, AZ 86001. *Phone:* 928-226-4334 Ext. 4334. *Toll-free phone:* 800-350-7122. *Fax:* 928-226-4114. *E-mail:* veronica.hipolito@coconino.edu. *Website:* http://www.coconino.edu/.

CollegeAmerica–Flagstaff
Flagstaff, Arizona

- **Private** primarily 2-year, part of Center for Excellence in Higher Education, Stevens-Henager College, CollegeAmerica, California College San Diego, Independence University
- **Coed,** 255 undergraduate students, 100% full-time, 77% women, 23% men

Undergraduates 255 full-time.
Freshmen *Admission:* 111 enrolled.
Faculty *Student/faculty ratio:* 20:1.
Majors Business administration and management; computer science; computer systems networking and telecommunications; health/health-care administration; medical/health management and clinical assistant.
Academics *Degrees:* associate and bachelor's.
Library Main Library plus 1 other.
Freshman Application Contact CollegeAmerica–Flagstaff, 3012 East Route 66, Flagstaff, AZ 86004. *Phone:* 928-213-6060 Ext. 1402. *Toll-free phone:* 800-622-2894.
Website: http://www.collegeamerica.edu/.

Diné College
Tsaile, Arizona

Freshman Application Contact Mrs. Louise Litzin, Registrar, Diné College, PO Box 67, Tsaile, AZ 86556. *Phone:* 928-724-6633. *Toll-free phone:* 877-988-DINE. *Fax:* 928-724-3349. *E-mail:* louise@dinecollege.edu. *Website:* http://www.dinecollege.edu/.

Eastern Arizona College
Thatcher, Arizona

- **State and locally supported** 2-year, founded 1888, part of Arizona State Community College System
- **Small-town** campus
- **Endowment** $3.6 million
- **Coed,** 6,502 undergraduate students, 28% full-time, 55% women, 45% men

Undergraduates 1,853 full-time, 4,649 part-time. Students come from 24 other countries; 4% are from out of state; 3% Black or African American, non-Hispanic/Latino; 20% Hispanic/Latino; 1% Asian, non-Hispanic/Latino; 0.3% Native Hawaiian or other Pacific Islander, non-Hispanic/Latino; 7% American Indian or Alaska Native, non-Hispanic/Latino; 0.9% Two or more races, non-Hispanic/Latino; 4% Race/ethnicity unknown; 0.5% international; 1% transferred in; 5% live on campus.
Freshmen *Admission:* 618 applied, 618 admitted, 1,197 enrolled.
Faculty *Total:* 384, 24% full-time, 7% with terminal degrees. *Student/faculty ratio:* 17:1.
Majors Anthropology; art; art teacher education; automobile/automotive mechanics technology; biology/biological sciences; business administration

and management; business, management, and marketing related; business operations support and secretarial services related; business teacher education; chemistry; civil engineering technology; commercial and advertising art; cosmetology; criminal justice/law enforcement administration; criminal justice/police science; diesel mechanics technology; drafting and design technology; dramatic/theater arts; early childhood education; elementary education; emergency medical technology (EMT paramedic); English; entrepreneurship; environmental biology; fire science/firefighting; foreign languages and literatures; forestry; geology/earth science; health and physical education/fitness; health/medical preparatory programs related; history; industrial electronics technology; industrial mechanics and maintenance technology; information science/studies; liberal arts and sciences/liberal studies; machine shop technology; mathematics; mining technology; multi/interdisciplinary studies related; music; pharmacy technician; physics; political science and government; premedical studies; pre-pharmacy studies; psychology; registered nursing/registered nurse; secondary education; sociology; technology/industrial arts teacher education; welding technology; wildlife biology.

Academics *Calendar:* semesters. *Degree:* certificates and associate. *Special study options:* academic remediation for entering students, adult/continuing education programs, advanced placement credit, cooperative education, distance learning, double majors, independent study, internships, part-time degree program, services for LD students, study abroad, summer session for credit.

Library Alumni Library with an OPAC, a Web page.

Student Life *Housing Options:* men-only, women-only. Campus housing is university owned. *Activities and Organizations:* drama/theater group, choral group, marching band, Latter-Day Saints Student Association, Criminal Justice Student Association, Multicultural Council, Phi Theta Kappa, Mark Allen Dorm Club. *Campus security:* 24-hour emergency response devices, late-night transport/escort service, controlled dormitory access, 20-hour patrols by trained security personnel. *Student services:* personal/psychological counseling.

Athletics Member NJCAA. *Intercollegiate sports:* baseball M(s), basketball M(s)/W(s), football M(s), golf M/W, softball W(s), volleyball W(s). *Intramural sports:* basketball M/W, racquetball M/W, swimming and diving M/W, table tennis M/W, tennis M/W, volleyball M/W.

Costs (2014–15) *One-time required fee:* $150. *Tuition:* state resident $1920 full-time, $90 per credit part-time; nonresident $8820 full-time, $180 per credit part-time. Full-time tuition and fees vary according to program. Part-time tuition and fees vary according to program. *Room and board:* $5890. Room and board charges vary according to board plan. *Waivers:* senior citizens and employees or children of employees.

Financial Aid Of all full-time matriculated undergraduates who enrolled in 2010, 1,610 applied for aid, 1,468 were judged to have need, 72 had their need fully met. In 2010, 133 non-need-based awards were made. *Average percent of need met:* 56%. *Average financial aid package:* $5999. *Average need-based gift aid:* $5241. *Average non-need-based aid:* $3122.

Applying *Options:* electronic application, early admission, deferred entrance. *Recommended:* high school transcript. *Application deadlines:* rolling (freshmen), rolling (transfers). *Notification:* continuous (freshmen).

Freshman Application Contact Suzette Udall, Records Assistant, Eastern Arizona College, 615 North Stadium Avenue, Thatcher, AZ 85552-0769. *Phone:* 928-428-8904. *Toll-free phone:* 800-678-3808. *Fax:* 928-428-3729. *E-mail:* admissions@eac.edu. *Website:* http://www.eac.edu/.

Estrella Mountain Community College
Avondale, Arizona

Freshman Application Contact Estrella Mountain Community College, 3000 North Dysart Road, Avondale, AZ 85392. *Phone:* 623-935-8812. *Website:* http://www.emc.maricopa.edu/.

Everest College
Phoenix, Arizona

Freshman Application Contact Mr. Jim Askins, Director of Admissions, Everest College, 10400 North 25th Avenue, Suite 190, Phoenix, AZ 85021. *Phone:* 602-942-4141. *Toll-free phone:* 888-741-4270. *Fax:* 602-943-0960. *E-mail:* jaskins@cci.edu. *Website:* http://www.everest.edu/.

GateWay Community College
Phoenix, Arizona

Freshman Application Contact Director of Admissions and Records, GateWay Community College, 108 North 40th Street, Phoenix, AZ 85034. *Phone:* 602-286-8200. *Fax:* 602-286-8200. *E-mail:* enroll@gatewaycc.edu. *Website:* http://www.gatewaycc.edu/.

Glendale Community College

Glendale, Arizona

- **State and locally supported** 2-year, founded 1965, part of Maricopa County Community College District System
- **Suburban** 222-acre campus with easy access to Phoenix
- **Coed,** 21,361 undergraduate students, 34% full-time, 54% women, 46% men

Undergraduates 7,335 full-time, 14,026 part-time. *Retention:* 58% of full-time freshmen returned.

Freshmen *Admission:* 3,700 enrolled.

Faculty *Total:* 923, 30% full-time.

Majors Accounting technology and bookkeeping; administrative assistant and secretarial science; architectural drafting and CAD/CADD; automobile/automotive mechanics technology; behavioral sciences; biotechnology; business administration and management; business/commerce; CAD/CADD drafting/design technology; cinematography and film/video production; commercial and advertising art; computer and information sciences; computer and information systems security; computer systems analysis; computer systems networking and telecommunications; criminal justice/safety; data entry/microcomputer applications; early childhood education; educational leadership and administration; emergency medical technology (EMT paramedic); engineering technology; family and community services; fire science/firefighting; graphic design; homeland security, law enforcement, firefighting and protective services related; kinesiology and exercise science; marketing/marketing management; music management; public relations/image management; recording arts technology; registered nursing/registered nurse; web page, digital/multimedia and information resources design.

Academics *Calendar:* semesters. *Degree:* certificates and associate. *Special study options:* academic remediation for entering students, adult/continuing education programs, advanced placement credit, cooperative education, distance learning, double majors, English as a second language, freshman honors college, honors programs, internships, off-campus study, part-time degree program, services for LD students, study abroad, summer session for credit. *ROTC:* Army (c), Air Force (c).

Library Library/Media Center plus 1 other with 97,768 titles, 30,094 serial subscriptions, 6,032 audiovisual materials, an OPAC, a Web page.

Student Life *Housing:* college housing not available. *Activities and Organizations:* drama/theater group, student-run newspaper, choral group, marching band, Phi Theta Kappa, M.E.Ch.A. (Movimiento Estudiantil Chicano de Aztlan), Associated Student Government, Biotechnology Club, Compass. *Campus security:* 24-hour patrols, student patrols, late-night transport/escort service. *Student services:* personal/psychological counseling, legal services.

Athletics Member NJCAA. *Intercollegiate sports:* baseball M(s), basketball M(s)/W(s), cross-country running M(s)/W(s), football M(s), golf M(s), soccer M(s)/W(s), softball W(s), tennis M(s)/W(s), track and field M(s)/W(s), volleyball W(s). *Intramural sports:* golf M, racquetball M/W, softball W, tennis M/W, volleyball W.

Costs (2014–15) *Tuition:* state resident $1944 full-time; nonresident $7608 full-time. Full-time tuition and fees vary according to course load, program, and reciprocity agreements. Part-time tuition and fees vary according to course load, program, and reciprocity agreements. *Required fees:* $30 full-time. *Payment plan:* installment. *Waivers:* employees or children of employees.

Financial Aid Of all full-time matriculated undergraduates who enrolled in 2012, 150 Federal Work-Study jobs (averaging $2300).

Applying *Options:* electronic application. *Required for some:* high school transcript. *Application deadlines:* 8/20 (freshmen), 8/20 (transfers). *Notification:* continuous until 8/20 (freshmen), continuous until 8/20 (transfers).

Freshman Application Contact Ms. Mary Blackwell, Dean of Enrollment Services, Glendale Community College, 6000 West Olive Avenue, Glendale, AZ 85302. *Phone:* 623-435-3305. *Fax:* 623-845-3303. *E-mail:* admissions.recruitment@gccaz.edu.

Website: http://www.gc.maricopa.edu/.

Golf Academy of America

Chandler, Arizona

Admissions Office Contact Golf Academy of America, 2031 N. Arizona Avenue, Suite 2, Chandler, AZ 85225.

Website: http://www.golfacademy.edu/.

ITT Technical Institute

Tucson, Arizona

- **Proprietary** primarily 2-year, founded 1984, part of ITT Educational Services, Inc.
- **Urban** campus
- **Coed**

Majors Business administration and management; computer programming (specific applications); construction management; cyber/computer forensics and counterterrorism; drafting and design technology; electrical, electronic and communications engineering technology; forensic science and technology; game and interactive media design; graphic communications; industrial technology; information technology project management; network and system administration; project management.

Academics *Calendar:* quarters. *Degrees:* associate and bachelor's.

Student Life *Housing:* college housing not available.

Freshman Application Contact Director of Recruitment, ITT Technical Institute, 1455 West River Road, Tucson, AZ 85704. *Phone:* 520-408-7488. *Toll-free phone:* 800-870-9730.

Website: http://www.itt-tech.edu/.

Le Cordon Bleu College of Culinary Arts in Scottsdale

Scottsdale, Arizona

Director of Admissions Le Cordon Bleu College of Culinary Arts in Scottsdale, 8100 East Camelback Road, Suite 1001, Scottsdale, AZ 85251-3940. *Toll-free phone:* 888-557-4222.

Website: http://www.chefs.edu/Scottsdale/.

Mesa Community College

Mesa, Arizona

- **State and locally supported** 2-year, founded 1965, part of Maricopa County Community College District System
- **Urban** 160-acre campus with easy access to Phoenix
- **Coed,** 22,000 undergraduate students

Majors Accounting; administrative assistant and secretarial science; agricultural business and management; agricultural mechanization; agronomy and crop science; art; automobile/automotive mechanics technology; biology/biological sciences; business administration and management; child development; criminal justice/law enforcement administration; data processing and data processing technology; drafting and design technology; electrical, electronic and communications engineering technology; engineering technology; family and consumer sciences/human sciences; fashion merchandising; finance; fire science/firefighting; heavy equipment maintenance technology; horticultural science; industrial technology; insurance; interior design; liberal arts and sciences/liberal studies; library and information science; marketing/marketing management; mathematics; medical administrative assistant and medical secretary; music; ornamental horticulture; pre-engineering; quality control technology; real estate; registered nursing/registered nurse; teacher assistant/aide.

Academics *Calendar:* semesters. *Degree:* certificates and associate. *Special study options:* academic remediation for entering students, adult/continuing education programs, advanced placement credit, cooperative education, distance learning, English as a second language, freshman honors college, honors programs, independent study, off-campus study, part-time degree program, services for LD students, student-designed majors, study abroad, summer session for credit. *ROTC:* Army (c), Air Force (c).

Library Information Commons with an OPAC, a Web page.

Student Life *Housing:* college housing not available. *Activities and Organizations:* drama/theater group, student-run newspaper, choral group, MECHA, International Student Association, American Indian Association, Asian/Pacific Islander Club. *Campus security:* 24-hour emergency response devices and patrols, student patrols. *Student services:* personal/psychological counseling, legal services.

Athletics Member NJCAA. *Intercollegiate sports:* baseball M, basketball M/W, cross-country running M, football M, golf M/W, soccer M/W, softball W, tennis M/W, track and field M/W, volleyball W, wrestling M. *Intramural sports:* basketball M/W, cross-country running M, football M/W, tennis M/W, track and field M/W, volleyball M/W, wrestling M/W.

Costs (2014–15) *Tuition:* area resident $1944 full-time; state resident $7728 full-time; nonresident $7728 full-time. Full-time tuition and fees vary according to course load and reciprocity agreements. Part-time tuition and fees vary according to course load and reciprocity agreements. *Required fees:* $30 full-time. *Payment plan:* installment. *Waivers:* employees or children of employees.

Applying *Options:* electronic application, early admission, deferred entrance. *Application deadlines:* 8/18 (freshmen), 8/18 (transfers). *Notification:* continuous (freshmen).

Freshman Application Contact Dr. Barbara Boros, Dean, Enrollment Services, Mesa Community College, 1833 West Southern Avenue, Mesa, AZ 85202-4866. *Phone:* 480-461-7342. *Toll-free phone:* 866-532-4983. *Fax:* 480-844-3117. *E-mail:* admissionsandrecords@mesacc.edu.

Website: http://www.mesacc.edu/.

Mohave Community College

Kingman, Arizona

- **State-supported** 2-year, founded 1971
- **Small-town** 160-acre campus
- **Coed,** 5,227 undergraduate students, 27% full-time, 64% women, 36% men

Undergraduates 1,433 full-time, 3,794 part-time. Students come from 16 states and territories; 4% are from out of state; 1% Black or African American, non-Hispanic/Latino; 18% Hispanic/Latino; 1% Asian, non-Hispanic/Latino; 0.7% Native Hawaiian or other Pacific Islander, non-Hispanic/Latino; 2% American Indian or Alaska Native, non-Hispanic/Latino; 2% Two or more races, non-Hispanic/Latino; 1% Race/ethnicity unknown.

Freshmen *Admission:* 981 enrolled.

Faculty *Total:* 361, 22% full-time. *Student/faculty ratio:* 16:1.

Majors Accounting; art; automobile/automotive mechanics technology; building/construction finishing, management, and inspection related; business administration and management; computer and information sciences related; computer programming (specific applications); computer science; criminal justice/police science; culinary arts; dental assisting; dental hygiene; drafting and design technology; education; emergency medical technology (EMT paramedic); English; fire science/firefighting; heating, air conditioning, ventilation and refrigeration maintenance technology; history; information technology; legal assistant/paralegal; liberal arts and sciences/liberal studies; mathematics; medical/clinical assistant; personal and culinary services related; pharmacy technician; physical therapy technology; psychology; registered nursing/registered nurse; sociology; substance abuse/addiction counseling; surgical technology; truck and bus driver/commercial vehicle operation/instruction; welding technology.

Academics *Calendar:* semesters. *Degree:* certificates and associate. *Special study options:* academic remediation for entering students, adult/continuing education programs, cooperative education, distance learning, English as a second language, independent study, part-time degree program, summer session for credit.

Library Mohave Community College Library with 45,849 titles, 476 serial subscriptions, an OPAC, a Web page.

Student Life *Housing:* college housing not available. *Activities and Organizations:* Art Club, Phi Theta Kappa, Computer Club (MC4), Science Club, student government. *Campus security:* late-night transport/escort service.

Costs (2013–14) *Tuition:* state resident $2340 full-time, $78 per credit hour part-time; nonresident $9360 full-time, $312 per credit hour part-time. Full-time tuition and fees vary according to program. Part-time tuition and fees vary according to program. *Required fees:* $210 full-time, $7 per credit hour part-time. *Payment plans:* installment, deferred payment. *Waivers:* employees or children of employees.

Applying *Options:* electronic application, early admission, deferred entrance. *Application deadlines:* rolling (freshmen), rolling (transfers). *Notification:* continuous (freshmen), continuous (transfers).

Freshman Application Contact Ms. Ana Masterson, Dean of Student Services, Mohave Community College, 1971 Jagerson Ave, Kingman, AZ 86409. *Phone:* 928-757-0803. *Toll-free phone:* 888-664-2832. *Fax:* 928-757-0808. *E-mail:* amasterson@mohave.edu.

Website: http://www.mohave.edu/.

Northland Pioneer College

Holbrook, Arizona

Freshman Application Contact Ms. Suzette Willis, Coordinator of Admissions, Northland Pioneer College, PO Box 610, Holbrook, AZ 86025. *Phone:* 928-536-6271. *Toll-free phone:* 800-266-7845. *Fax:* 928-536-6212. *Website:* http://www.npc.edu/.

Paradise Valley Community College

Phoenix, Arizona

Freshman Application Contact Paradise Valley Community College, 18401 North 32nd Street, Phoenix, AZ 85032-1200. *Phone:* 602-787-7020. *Website:* http://www.pvc.maricopa.edu/.

The Paralegal Institute, Inc.

Scottsdale, Arizona

Freshman Application Contact Patricia Yancy, Director of Admissions, The Paralegal Institute, Inc., 2933 West Indian School Road, Drawer 11408, Phoenix, AZ 85061-1408. *Phone:* 602-212-0501. *Toll-free phone:* 800-354-1254. *Fax:* 602-212-0502. *E-mail:* paralegalinst@mindspring.com.

Website: http://www.theparalegalinstitute.edu/.

Phoenix College

Phoenix, Arizona

- **County-supported** 2-year, founded 1920, part of Maricopa County Community College District System
- **Urban** 56-acre campus
- **Coed,** 12,228 undergraduate students, 27% full-time, 62% women, 38% men

Undergraduates 3,341 full-time, 8,887 part-time. 12% Black or African American, non-Hispanic/Latino; 39% Hispanic/Latino; 3% Asian, non-Hispanic/Latino; 0.2% Native Hawaiian or other Pacific Islander, non-Hispanic/Latino; 4% American Indian or Alaska Native, non-Hispanic/Latino; 1% Two or more races, non-Hispanic/Latino; 11% Race/ethnicity unknown; 0.4% international.

Faculty *Total:* 738, 22% full-time. *Student/faculty ratio:* 17:1.

Majors Accounting; administrative assistant and secretarial science; architectural drafting and CAD/CADD; art; banking and financial support services; building/home/construction inspection; business administration and management; business/commerce; child-care and support services management; civil engineering technology; clinical/medical laboratory technology; commercial and advertising art; commercial photography; computer and information sciences; computer graphics; computer systems analysis; construction management; criminal justice/safety; culinary arts; dental assisting; dental hygiene; dramatic/theater arts; elementary education; emergency medical technology (EMT paramedic); family and community services; family and consumer sciences/human sciences; fashion/apparel design; fashion merchandising; fine/studio arts; fire science/firefighting; food service systems administration; forensic science and technology; general studies; graphic design; health information/medical records technology; histologic technology/histotechnologist; human services; interior design; legal assistant/paralegal; liberal arts and sciences/liberal studies; marketing/marketing management; massage therapy; medical/clinical assistant; medical office assistant; music management; natural sciences; organizational behavior; parks, recreation and leisure; physical sciences; recording arts technology; registered nursing/registered nurse; sign language interpretation and translation; surveying technology; teacher assistant/aide; visual and performing arts; web page, digital/multimedia and information resources design.

Academics *Calendar:* semesters. *Degree:* certificates, diplomas, and associate. *Special study options:* academic remediation for entering students, adult/continuing education programs, advanced placement credit, cooperative education, distance learning, English as a second language, freshman honors college, honors programs, independent study, internships, off-campus study, part-time degree program, services for LD students, study abroad, summer session for credit. *ROTC:* Army (c), Navy (c), Air Force (c).

Library Fannin Library with 192,868 titles, 74,832 serial subscriptions, 7,010 audiovisual materials, an OPAC, a Web page.

Student Life *Housing:* college housing not available. *Activities and Organizations:* drama/theater group, choral group, Student Leadership Council (SLC), MEChA Movimiento Estudiantil Chicanos de Aztlan, ALE Asociacion Latina Estudiantil, Rainbow Spectrum - Gay, Straight, Whatever alliance, International Club. *Campus security:* 24-hour emergency response devices and patrols, student patrols, late-night transport/escort service. *Student services:* personal/psychological counseling.

Athletics Member NCAA, NJCAA. All NCAA Division II. *Intercollegiate sports:* baseball M(s), basketball M(s)/W(s), football M(s), soccer M(s)/W(s), softball W(s), volleyball W(s).

Costs (2013–14) *Tuition:* area resident $1944 full-time, $81 per credit hour part-time; state resident $8016 full-time, $334 per credit hour part-time; nonresident $8016 full-time, $334 per credit hour part-time. Full-time tuition and fees vary according to reciprocity agreements. Part-time tuition and fees vary according to course load and reciprocity agreements. *Required fees:* $30 full-time, $15 per term part-time. *Payment plan:* installment. *Waivers:* employees or children of employees.

Financial Aid Of all full-time matriculated undergraduates who enrolled in 2012, 220 Federal Work-Study jobs (averaging $4800).

Applying *Options:* electronic application, early admission, deferred entrance. *Application deadlines:* rolling (freshmen), rolling (out-of-state freshmen), rolling (transfers). *Notification:* continuous (freshmen), continuous (out-of-state freshmen), continuous (transfers).

Freshman Application Contact Ms. Brenda Stark, Director of Admissions, Registration, and Records, Phoenix College, 1202 West Thomas Road, Phoenix, AZ 85013. *Phone:* 602-285-7503. *Fax:* 602-285-7813. *E-mail:* kathy.french@pcmail.maricopa.edu.
Website: http://www.pc.maricopa.edu/.

Pima Community College

Tucson, Arizona

- **State and locally supported** 2-year, founded 1966
- **Urban** 486-acre campus with easy access to Tucson
- **Coed,** 26,613 undergraduate students

Undergraduates 5% Black or African American, non-Hispanic/Latino; 41% Hispanic/Latino; 3% Asian, non-Hispanic/Latino; 0.3% Native Hawaiian or other Pacific Islander, non-Hispanic/Latino; 2% American Indian or Alaska Native, non-Hispanic/Latino; 3% Two or more races, non-Hispanic/Latino.
Majors Accounting; administrative assistant and secretarial science; airframe mechanics and aircraft maintenance technology; American Indian/Native American studies; American Sign Language (ASL); anthropology; automobile/automotive mechanics technology; building/property maintenance; business/commerce; CAD/CADD drafting/design technology; cinematography and film/video production; clinical/medical laboratory assistant; clinical/medical laboratory technology; clinical/medical social work; clinical research coordinator; computer systems analysis; computer systems networking and telecommunications; criminal justice/police science; criminal justice/safety; dental hygiene; dental laboratory technology; design and visual communications; digital arts; digital communication and media/multimedia; early childhood education; education; electrical/electronics equipment installation and repair; electrical/electronics maintenance and repair technology related; elementary education; emergency medical technology (EMT paramedic); executive assistant/executive secretary; fashion/apparel design; fashion merchandising; fire science/firefighting; game and interactive media design; general studies; health information/medical records technology; hospitality administration; hotel, motel, and restaurant management; interior design; language interpretation and translation; legal assistant/paralegal; liberal arts and sciences/liberal studies; logistics, materials, and supply chain management; machine tool technology; massage therapy; mining and petroleum technologies related; pharmacy technician; political science and government; pre-engineering; professional, technical, business, and scientific writing; psychology; radiologic technology/science; registered nursing/registered nurse; respiratory care therapy; restaurant, culinary, and catering management; social work; sociology; substance abuse/addiction counseling; veterinary/animal health technology; visual and performing arts; welding technology; youth services.
Academics *Calendar:* semesters. *Degrees:* certificates, diplomas, associate, and postbachelor's certificates. *Special study options:* academic remediation for entering students, adult/continuing education programs, advanced placement credit, cooperative education, distance learning, English as a second language, honors programs, independent study, internships, off-campus study, part-time degree program, services for LD students, student-designed majors, summer session for credit. *ROTC:* Army (c), Navy (c), Air Force (c).
Library Pima Community College Library with an OPAC, a Web page.
Student Life *Housing:* college housing not available. *Activities and Organizations:* drama/theater group, student-run newspaper, choral group. *Student services:* health clinic.
Athletics Member NJCAA.
Applying *Options:* electronic application.
Freshman Application Contact Terra Benson, Director of Admissions and Registrar, Pima Community College, 4905B East Broadway Boulevard, Tucson, AZ 85709-1120. *Phone:* 520-206-4640. *Fax:* 520-206-4790. *E-mail:* tbenson@pima.edu.
Website: http://www.pima.edu/.

Pima Medical Institute

Mesa, Arizona

Freshman Application Contact Pima Medical Institute, 2160 S. Power Road, Mesa, AZ 85209. *Phone:* 480-898-9898.
Website: http://www.pmi.edu/.

Pima Medical Institute

Mesa, Arizona

Freshman Application Contact Admissions Office, Pima Medical Institute, 957 South Dobson Road, Mesa, AZ 85202. *Phone:* 480-644-0267 Ext. 225. *Toll-free phone:* 800-477-PIMA (in-state); 888-477-PIMA (out-of-state).
Website: http://www.pmi.edu/.

Pima Medical Institute

Tucson, Arizona

Freshman Application Contact Admissions Office, Pima Medical Institute, 3350 East Grant Road, Tucson, AZ 85716. *Phone:* 520-326-1600 Ext. 5112. *Toll-free phone:* 800-477-PIMA (in-state); 888-477-PIMA (out-of-state).
Website: http://www.pmi.edu/.

The Refrigeration School

Phoenix, Arizona

Freshman Application Contact Ms. Heather Haskell, The Refrigeration School, 4210 East Washington Street. *Phone:* 602-275-7133. *Toll-free phone:* 888-943-4822. *Fax:* 602-267-4811. *E-mail:* heather@rsiaz.edu.
Website: http://www.refrigerationschool.com/.

Rio Salado College

Tempe, Arizona

Freshman Application Contact Laurel Redman, Director, Instruction Support Services and Student Development, Rio Salado College, 2323 West 14th Street, Tempe 85281. *Phone:* 480-517-8563. *Toll-free phone:* 800-729-1197. *Fax:* 480-517-8199. *E-mail:* admission@riomail.maricopa.edu.
Website: http://www.rio.maricopa.edu/.

Scottsdale Community College

Scottsdale, Arizona

- **State and locally supported** 2-year, founded 1969, part of Maricopa County Community College District System
- **Urban** 160-acre campus with easy access to Phoenix
- **Coed,** 10,313 undergraduate students, 31% full-time, 53% women, 47% men

Undergraduates 3,177 full-time, 7,136 part-time. Students come from 44 other countries; 4% are from out of state; 5% Black or African American, non-Hispanic/Latino; 16% Hispanic/Latino; 3% Asian, non-Hispanic/Latino; 0.4% Native Hawaiian or other Pacific Islander, non-Hispanic/Latino; 5% American Indian or Alaska Native, non-Hispanic/Latino; 2% Two or more races, non-Hispanic/Latino; 7% Race/ethnicity unknown; 1% international; 76% transferred in.
Faculty *Total:* 744, 22% full-time, 13% with terminal degrees. *Student/faculty ratio:* 16:1.
Majors Accounting; administrative assistant and secretarial science; business administration and management; criminal justice/law enforcement administration; culinary arts; dramatic/theater arts; electrical, electronic and communications engineering technology; emergency medical technology (EMT paramedic); environmental design/architecture; equestrian studies; fashion merchandising; finance; fire science/firefighting; hospitality administration; hotel/motel administration; information science/studies; interior design; kindergarten/preschool education; mathematics; medical administrative assistant and medical secretary; photography; public administration; real estate; registered nursing/registered nurse; special products marketing.
Academics *Calendar:* semesters. *Degree:* certificates, diplomas, and associate. *Special study options:* academic remediation for entering students, adult/continuing education programs, advanced placement credit, cooperative education, English as a second language, honors programs, internships, off-campus study, part-time degree program, services for LD students, study abroad, summer session for credit.
Library Scottsdale Community College Library with an OPAC, a Web page.
Student Life *Housing:* college housing not available. *Activities and Organizations:* drama/theater group, student-run newspaper, radio station, choral group, Student Leadership Forum, International Community Club, Phi Theta Kappa, Music Industry Club, SCC ASID-Interior Design group. *Campus security:* 24-hour emergency response devices and patrols, student patrols, late-night transport/escort service, 24-hour automatic surveillance cameras. *Student services:* personal/psychological counseling.
Athletics Member NCAA, NJCAA. All NCAA Division II. *Intercollegiate sports:* baseball M, basketball M/W, cross-country running M/W, football M, golf M/W, soccer M/W, softball W, tennis M/W, track and field M/W, volleyball W. *Intramural sports:* archery M/W, badminton M/W, basketball M/W, racquetball M/W, track and field M/W, volleyball M/W.
Costs (2013–14) *Tuition:* area resident $2430 full-time, $81 per credit hour part-time; state resident $9660 full-time, $322 per credit hour part-time; nonresident $9660 full-time, $322 per credit hour part-time. Full-time tuition and fees vary according to program and reciprocity agreements. Part-time tuition and fees vary according to program and reciprocity agreements. *Required fees:* $30 full-time. *Payment plan:* deferred payment. *Waivers:* employees or children of employees.

Financial Aid Of all full-time matriculated undergraduates who enrolled in 2012, 75 Federal Work-Study jobs (averaging $2000). *Financial aid deadline:* 7/15.

Applying *Options:* electronic application, early admission. *Application deadline:* rolling (freshmen). *Notification:* continuous (freshmen).

Freshman Application Contact Ms. Fran Watkins, Director of Admissions and Records, Scottsdale Community College, 9000 East Chaparral Road, Scottsdale, AZ 85256. *Phone:* 480-423-6133. *Fax:* 480-423-6200. *E-mail:* fran.watkins@scottsdalecc.edu.
Website: http://www.scottsdalecc.edu/.

Sessions College for Professional Design
Tempe, Arizona
- **Proprietary** 2-year
- **Coed**

Majors Animation, interactive technology, video graphics and special effects; graphic design; illustration; web page, digital/multimedia and information resources design.

Academics *Degree:* certificates and associate. *Special study options:* adult/continuing education programs, part-time degree program.

Costs (2014–15) *Comprehensive fee:* $17,000 includes full-time tuition ($7800), mandatory fees ($200), and room and board ($9000). Full-time tuition and fees vary according to course load. Part-time tuition: $350 per credit. Part-time tuition and fees vary according to course load. No tuition increase for student's term of enrollment. *Payment plan:* installment.

Applying *Options:* early admission. *Application fee:* $50. *Required:* essay or personal statement, high school transcript, portfolio. *Application deadline:* 7/15 (freshmen). *Notification:* continuous (freshmen).

Freshman Application Contact Mhelanie Hernandez, Director of Admissions, Sessions College for Professional Design, 350 South Mill Avenue, Suite B-104, Tempe, AZ 85281. *Phone:* 480-212-1704. *Toll-free phone:* 800-258-4115. *E-mail:* admissions@sessions.edu.
Website: http://www.sessions.edu/.

South Mountain Community College
Phoenix, Arizona

Director of Admissions Dean of Enrollment Services, South Mountain Community College, 7050 South Twenty-fourth Street, Phoenix, AZ 85040. *Phone:* 602-243-8120.
Website: http://www.southmountaincc.edu/.

Southwest Institute of Healing Arts
Tempe, Arizona

Director of Admissions Katie Yearous, Student Advisor, Southwest Institute of Healing Arts, 1100 East Apache Boulevard, Tempe, AZ 85281. *Phone:* 480-994-9244. *Toll-free phone:* 888-504-9106. *E-mail:* joannl@swiha.net.
Website: http://www.swiha.org/.

Tohono O'odham Community College
Sells, Arizona

Freshman Application Contact Admissions, Tohono O'odham Community College, PO Box 3129, Sells, AZ 85634. *Phone:* 520-383-8401. *E-mail:* info@tocc.cc.az.us.
Website: http://www.tocc.edu/.

Universal Technical Institute
Avondale, Arizona

Freshman Application Contact Director of Admission, Universal Technical Institute, 10695 West Pierce Street, Avondale, AZ 85323. *Phone:* 623-245-4600. *Toll-free phone:* 800-510-5072. *Fax:* 623-245-4601.
Website: http://www.uti.edu/.

Yavapai College
Prescott, Arizona

Freshman Application Contact Mrs. Sheila Jarrell, Admissions, Registration, and Records Manager, Yavapai College, 1100 East Sheldon Street, Prescott, AZ 86301-3297. *Phone:* 928-776-2107. *Toll-free phone:* 800-922-6787. *Fax:* 928-776-2151. *E-mail:* registration@yc.edu.
Website: http://www.yc.edu/.

ARKANSAS

Arkansas Northeastern College
Blytheville, Arkansas

Freshman Application Contact Mrs. Leslie Wells, Admissions Counselor, Arkansas Northeastern College, PO Box 1109, Blytheville, AR 72316. *Phone:* 870-762-1020 Ext. 1118. *Fax:* 870-763-1654. *E-mail:* lwells@anc.edu.
Website: http://www.anc.edu/.

Arkansas State University–Beebe
Beebe, Arkansas

Freshman Application Contact Mr. Ronald Hudson, Coordinator of Student Recruitment, Arkansas State University–Beebe, PO Box 1000, Beebe, AR 72012. *Phone:* 501-882-8860. *Toll-free phone:* 800-632-9985. *E-mail:* rdhudson@asub.edu.
Website: http://www.asub.edu/.

Arkansas State University–Mountain Home
Mountain Home, Arkansas
- **State-supported** 2-year, founded 2000, part of Arkansas State University System
- **Small-town** 136-acre campus
- **Coed**

Academics *Calendar:* semesters. *Degree:* certificates and associate. *Special study options:* academic remediation for entering students, advanced placement credit, cooperative education, distance learning, English as a second language, honors programs, independent study, internships, part-time degree program, services for LD students, summer session for credit. *ROTC:* Army (b).

Student Life *Campus security:* during operation hours security is present and available as needed.

Standardized Tests *Recommended:* SAT or ACT (for admission), COMPASS, ASSET.

Costs (2013–14) *Tuition:* state resident $2088 full-time, $87 per credit hour part-time; nonresident $3576 full-time, $149 per credit hour part-time. Full-time tuition and fees vary according to course load and program. Part-time tuition and fees vary according to course load and program. *Required fees:* $504 full-time, $21 per credit hour part-time.

Financial Aid Of all full-time matriculated undergraduates who enrolled in 2012, 645 applied for aid, 608 were judged to have need, 45 had their need fully met. 14 Federal Work-Study jobs (averaging $3500). In 2012, 10. *Average percent of need met:* 62. *Average financial aid package:* $8217. *Average need-based loan:* $3154. *Average need-based gift aid:* $4308. *Average non-need-based aid:* $1772.

Applying *Options:* electronic application. *Required:* high school transcript. *Recommended:* placement scores, GED scores accepted.

Freshman Application Contact Ms. Delba Parrish, Admissions Coordinator, Arkansas State University–Mountain Home, 1600 South College Street, Mountain Home, AR 72653. *Phone:* 870-508-6180. *Fax:* 870-508-6287. *E-mail:* dparrish@asumh.edu.
Website: http://www.asumh.edu/.

Arkansas State University–Newport
Newport, Arkansas
- **State-supported** 2-year, founded 1989, part of Arkansas State University System
- **Rural** 189-acre campus
- **Endowment** $2.0 million
- **Coed,** 2,057 undergraduate students, 47% full-time, 59% women, 41% men

Undergraduates 963 full-time, 1,094 part-time. Students come from 4 states and territories; 2 other countries; 8% are from out of state; 13% Black or African American, non-Hispanic/Latino; 3% Hispanic/Latino; 0.3% Asian, non-Hispanic/Latino; 0.1% Native Hawaiian or other Pacific Islander, non-Hispanic/Latino; 0.4% American Indian or Alaska Native, non-Hispanic/Latino; 3% Two or more races, non-Hispanic/Latino; 5% Race/ethnicity unknown; 0.7% international; 21% transferred in.

Freshmen *Admission:* 355 enrolled. *Average high school GPA:* 2.8.

Faculty *Total:* 144, 43% full-time, 3% with terminal degrees. *Student/faculty ratio:* 14:1.

Majors Autobody/collision and repair technology; automobile/automotive mechanics technology; business/commerce; computer technology/computer systems technology; criminal justice/law enforcement administration; early childhood education; education (multiple levels); emergency medical technology (EMT paramedic); forensic science and technology; general studies; health/medical preparatory programs related; heating, ventilation, air conditioning and refrigeration engineering technology; liberal arts and sciences/liberal studies; management information systems; multi/interdisciplinary studies related; registered nursing/registered nurse.

Academics *Calendar:* semesters. *Degree:* certificates, diplomas, and associate. *Special study options:* academic remediation for entering students, adult/continuing education programs, advanced placement credit, cooperative education, distance learning, external degree program, independent study, internships, off-campus study, part-time degree program, services for LD students, summer session for credit.

Library Harryette M. Hodges and Kaneaster Hodges, Sr. Library plus 2 others with 11,759 titles, 61 serial subscriptions, 627 audiovisual materials, an OPAC.

Student Life *Activities and Organizations:* Phil Theta Kappa, Student Veterans Organization.

Standardized Tests *Required:* SAT or ACT or COMPASS (for admission).

Costs (2014–15) *Tuition:* state resident $88 full-time; nonresident $144 full-time. *Required fees:* $288 full-time. *Waivers:* senior citizens and employees or children of employees.

Financial Aid Of all full-time matriculated undergraduates who enrolled in 2012, 19 Federal Work-Study jobs (averaging $4500).

Applying *Options:* electronic application. *Required:* high school transcript. *Application deadlines:* rolling (freshmen), rolling (out-of-state freshmen), rolling (transfers), rolling (early action). *Early decision deadline:* rolling (for plan 1), rolling (for plan 2). *Notification:* continuous (freshmen), continuous (out-of-state freshmen), continuous (transfers), rolling (early decision plan 1), rolling (early decision plan 2), rolling (early action).

Freshman Application Contact Arkansas State University–Newport, 7648 Victory Boulevard, Newport, AR 72112. *Phone:* 870-512-7800. *Toll-free phone:* 800-976-1676.

Website: http://www.asun.edu/.

Black River Technical College
Pocahontas, Arkansas

Director of Admissions Director of Admissions, Black River Technical College, 1410 Highway 304 East, Pocahontas, AR 72455. *Phone:* 870-892-4565.

Website: http://www.blackrivertech.edu/.

College of the Ouachitas
Malvern, Arkansas

- **State-supported** 2-year, founded 1972
- **Small-town** 11-acre campus with easy access to Little Rock
- **Coed,** 1,501 undergraduate students, 39% full-time, 63% women, 37% men

Undergraduates 584 full-time, 917 part-time. 12% Black or African American, non-Hispanic/Latino; 4% Hispanic/Latino; 0.7% Asian, non-Hispanic/Latino; 0.1% Native Hawaiian or other Pacific Islander, non-Hispanic/Latino; 0.5% American Indian or Alaska Native, non-Hispanic/Latino; 3% Two or more races, non-Hispanic/Latino; 0.2% international.

Freshmen *Admission:* 147 enrolled. *Test scores:* ACT scores over 18: 62%; ACT scores over 24: 9%.

Faculty *Total:* 98, 40% full-time, 9% with terminal degrees.

Majors Accounting; administrative assistant and secretarial science; automobile/automotive mechanics technology; business administration and management; child-care and support services management; computer and information sciences; electromechanical technology; industrial technology; legal administrative assistant/secretary; legal assistant/paralegal; liberal arts and sciences/liberal studies; licensed practical/vocational nurse training; machine tool technology; management information systems; marketing/marketing management; medical administrative assistant and medical secretary.

Academics *Calendar:* semesters. *Degree:* certificates and associate. *Special study options:* academic remediation for entering students, accelerated degree program, advanced placement credit, cooperative education, distance learning, double majors, freshman honors college, honors programs, independent study, internships, part-time degree program, services for LD students, summer session for credit.

Library College of the Ouachitas Library/Learning Resource Center with 8,000 titles, 100 serial subscriptions, 1,200 audiovisual materials, an OPAC, a Web page.

Student Life *Housing:* college housing not available. *Activities and Organizations:* student-run newspaper. *Campus security:* 24-hour patrols. *Student services:* personal/psychological counseling.

Standardized Tests *Recommended:* SAT or ACT (for admission), ACT COMPASS or ASSET.

Costs (2014–15) *Tuition:* state resident $2550 full-time, $85 per credit part-time; nonresident $5100 full-time, $170 per credit part-time. Full-time tuition and fees vary according to program. Part-time tuition and fees vary according to program. No tuition increase for student's term of enrollment. *Required fees:* $950 full-time, $24 per credit part-time, $21 per term part-time. *Payment plan:* installment. *Waivers:* senior citizens and employees or children of employees.

Financial Aid Of all full-time matriculated undergraduates who enrolled in 2012, 18 Federal Work-Study jobs (averaging $2400).

Applying *Options:* electronic application, early admission, deferred entrance. *Required:* high school transcript. *Application deadlines:* rolling (freshmen), rolling (transfers).

Freshman Application Contact Mrs. Shanea Nelson, Student Success Coordinator, College of the Ouachitas, One College Circle, Malvern, AR 72104. *Phone:* 501-337-5000 Ext. 1177. *Toll-free phone:* 800-337-0266. *Fax:* 501-337-9382. *E-mail:* snelson@coto.edu.

Website: http://www.coto.edu/.

Cossatot Community College of the University of Arkansas
De Queen, Arkansas

- **State-supported** 2-year, founded 1991, part of University of Arkansas System
- **Rural** 30-acre campus
- **Endowment** $76,785
- **Coed,** 1,575 undergraduate students

Undergraduates Students come from 8 states and territories; 1 other country; 2% are from out of state; 11% Black or African American, non-Hispanic/Latino; 18% Hispanic/Latino; 0.9% Asian, non-Hispanic/Latino; 0.3% Native Hawaiian or other Pacific Islander, non-Hispanic/Latino; 3% American Indian or Alaska Native, non-Hispanic/Latino.

Faculty *Total:* 84, 43% full-time, 2% with terminal degrees. *Student/faculty ratio:* 15:1.

Majors Aeronautics/aviation/aerospace science and technology; agricultural business and management; automobile/automotive mechanics technology; business administration and management; business/commerce; criminal justice/law enforcement administration; criminal justice/safety; early childhood education; forensic science and technology; general studies; liberal arts and sciences/liberal studies; management information systems; medical/clinical assistant; middle school education; multi/interdisciplinary studies related; physical education teaching and coaching; psychology.

Academics *Calendar:* semesters. *Degree:* certificates and associate. *Special study options:* academic remediation for entering students, accelerated degree program, advanced placement credit, cooperative education, distance learning, double majors, honors programs, independent study, internships, off-campus study, part-time degree program, services for LD students, summer session for credit.

Library Kimbell Library in now "The Educational Resource Center" with 9,620 titles, 6 serial subscriptions, 2,212 audiovisual materials, an OPAC, a Web page.

Student Life *Housing:* college housing not available. *Activities and Organizations:* student-run radio station, Student Ambassadors, Phi Theta Kappa, ALPNA, VICA (Vocational Industrial Clubs of America), Multi Diversity. *Campus security:* Daytime campus police force. Evening patrol by city police force. *Student services:* health clinic, personal/psychological counseling.

Athletics *Intercollegiate sports:* soccer M/W.

Costs (2014–15) *Tuition:* area resident $1710 full-time, $61 per credit hour part-time; state resident $2010 full-time, $72 per credit hour part-time; nonresident $4560 full-time, $157 per credit hour part-time. *Required fees:* $502 full-time, $251 per term part-time. *Payment plan:* installment. *Waivers:* senior citizens and employees or children of employees.

Financial Aid Of all full-time matriculated undergraduates who enrolled in 2012, 14 Federal Work-Study jobs (averaging $2700).

Applying *Options:* electronic application. *Recommended:* high school transcript.

Freshman Application Contact Mrs. Tommi Cobb, Admissions Coordinator, Cossatot Community College of the University of Arkansas, 183 College Drive, DeQueen, AR 71832. *Phone:* 870-584-4471 Ext. 1158. *Toll-free phone:* 800-844-4471. *Fax:* 870-642-5088. *E-mail:* tcobb@cccua.edu.

Website: http://www.cccua.edu/.

Crowley's Ridge College
Paragould, Arkansas

Freshman Application Contact Amanda Drake, Director of Admissions, Crowley's Ridge College, 100 College Drive, Paragould, AR 72450-9731. *Phone:* 870-236-6901. *Toll-free phone:* 800-264-1096. *Fax:* 870-236-7748. *E-mail:* njoneshi@crc.pioneer.paragould.ar.us.

Website: http://www.crc.edu/.

East Arkansas Community College
Forrest City, Arkansas

Freshman Application Contact Ms. Sharon Collier, Director of Enrollment Management/Institutional Research, East Arkansas Community College, 1700 Newcastle Road, Forrest City, AR 72335-2204. *Phone:* 870-633-4480. *Toll-free phone:* 877-797-3222. *Fax:* 870-633-3840. *E-mail:* dadams@eacc.edu. *Website:* http://www.eacc.edu/.

ITT Technical Institute
Little Rock, Arkansas

- **Proprietary** primarily 2-year, founded 1993, part of ITT Educational Services, Inc.
- **Urban** campus
- **Coed**

Majors Business administration and management; construction management; cyber/computer forensics and counterterrorism; drafting and design technology; electrical, electronic and communications engineering technology; forensic science and technology; graphic communications; industrial technology; information technology project management; network and system administration; project management.

Academics *Calendar:* quarters. *Degrees:* associate and bachelor's.

Student Life *Housing:* college housing not available.

Freshman Application Contact Director of Recruitment, ITT Technical Institute, 12200 Westhaven Drive, Little Rock, AR 72211. *Phone:* 501-565-5550. *Toll-free phone:* 800-359-4429. *Website:* http://www.itt-tech.edu/.

Mid-South Community College
West Memphis, Arkansas

- **State-supported** 2-year, founded 1993
- **Suburban** 80-acre campus with easy access to Memphis
- **Endowment** $967,261
- **Coed,** 1,793 undergraduate students, 39% full-time, 62% women, 38% men

Undergraduates 703 full-time, 1,090 part-time. Students come from 3 states and territories; 3 other countries; 5% are from out of state; 53% Black or African American, non-Hispanic/Latino; 0.4% Hispanic/Latino; 0.6% Asian, non-Hispanic/Latino; 0.1% Native Hawaiian or other Pacific Islander, non-Hispanic/Latino; 0.3% American Indian or Alaska Native, non-Hispanic/Latino; 4% Two or more races, non-Hispanic/Latino; 0.5% international; 7% transferred in. *Retention:* 34% of full-time freshmen returned.

Freshmen *Admission:* 336 applied, 336 admitted, 326 enrolled.

Faculty *Total:* 104, 34% full-time, 6% with terminal degrees. *Student/faculty ratio:* 14:1.

Majors Computer and information sciences; education (multiple levels); liberal arts and sciences/liberal studies; management information systems and services related; manufacturing engineering technology; multi/interdisciplinary studies related; web/multimedia management and webmaster.

Academics *Calendar:* semesters. *Degree:* certificates and associate. *Special study options:* academic remediation for entering students, adult/continuing education programs, advanced placement credit, distance learning, independent study, internships, part-time degree program, services for LD students, summer session for credit.

Library Mid-South Community College Library/Media Center with 14,672 titles, 88 serial subscriptions, 2,151 audiovisual materials, an OPAC, a Web page.

Student Life *Housing:* college housing not available. *Activities and Organizations:* Phi Theta Kappa, Baptist Collegiate Ministry, Skills USA - VICA. *Campus security:* 24-hour emergency response devices, security during class hours. *Student services:* health clinic, personal/psychological counseling.

Standardized Tests *Required:* SAT, ACT or Compass (for admission).

Costs (2014–15) *Tuition:* area resident $1080 full-time; state resident $1320 full-time; nonresident $3600 full-time. *Required fees:* $144 full-time. *Payment plan:* installment. *Waivers:* senior citizens and employees or children of employees.

Financial Aid Of all full-time matriculated undergraduates who enrolled in 2012, 39 Federal Work-Study jobs (averaging $1676).

Applying *Options:* early admission. *Application deadlines:* rolling (freshmen), rolling (transfers). *Notification:* continuous (freshmen), continuous (transfers).

Freshman Application Contact Jeremy Reece, Director of Admissions, Mid-South Community College, 2000 West Broadway, West Memphis, AR 72301.

Phone: 870-733-6786. *Toll-free phone:* 866-733-6722. *Fax:* 870-733-6719. *E-mail:* jreece@midsouthcc.edu. *Website:* http://www.midsouthcc.edu/.

National Park Community College
Hot Springs, Arkansas

Director of Admissions Dr. Allen B. Moody, Director of Institutional Services/Registrar, National Park Community College, 101 College Drive, Hot Springs, AR 71913. *Phone:* 501-760-4222. *E-mail:* bmoody@npcc.edu. *Website:* http://www.npcc.edu/.

North Arkansas College
Harrison, Arkansas

Freshman Application Contact Mrs. Charla Jennings, Director of Admissions, North Arkansas College, 1515 Pioneer Drive, Harrison, AR 72601. *Phone:* 870-391-3221. *Toll-free phone:* 800-679-6622. *Fax:* 870-391-3339. *E-mail:* charlam@northark.edu. *Website:* http://www.northark.edu/.

NorthWest Arkansas Community College
Bentonville, Arkansas

- **State and locally supported** 2-year, founded 1989
- **Urban** 77-acre campus
- **Coed,** 8,020 undergraduate students, 35% full-time, 58% women, 42% men

Undergraduates 2,843 full-time, 5,177 part-time. Students come from 21 states and territories; 2% are from out of state; 7% transferred in. *Retention:* 50% of full-time freshmen returned.

Freshmen *Admission:* 1,559 enrolled. *Average high school GPA:* 2.85. *Test scores:* ACT scores over 18: 74%; ACT scores over 24: 17%; ACT scores over 30: 1%.

Faculty *Total:* 455, 32% full-time. *Student/faculty ratio:* 19:1.

Majors Accounting; business administration and management; commercial and advertising art; computer programming; criminal justice/law enforcement administration; criminal justice/safety; culinary arts; data processing and data processing technology; drafting and design technology; early childhood education; education; electrical, electronic and communications engineering technology; emergency medical technology (EMT paramedic); environmental science; finance; fire services administration; homeland security, law enforcement, firefighting and protective services related; legal assistant/paralegal; liberal arts and sciences/liberal studies; occupational safety and health technology; physical therapy; registered nursing/registered nurse; respiratory care therapy.

Academics *Calendar:* semesters. *Degree:* certificates and associate. *Special study options:* academic remediation for entering students, accelerated degree program, adult/continuing education programs, advanced placement credit, cooperative education, distance learning, double majors, English as a second language, honors programs, independent study, internships, part-time degree program, services for LD students, student-designed majors, summer session for credit. *ROTC:* Army (c), Air Force (c).

Library Pauline Whitaker Library plus 1 other with 45,000 titles, 159 serial subscriptions, an OPAC, a Web page.

Student Life *Housing:* college housing not available. *Activities and Organizations:* drama/theater group, student-run newspaper, choral group, Student Advisory Activity Council, Gamma Beta Phi, Phi Beta Lambda, Student Nurses Association, Students in Free Enterprise (SIFE). *Campus security:* 24-hour emergency response devices and patrols. *Student services:* personal/psychological counseling.

Athletics *Intramural sports:* basketball M(c)/W(c), bowling M(c)/W(c), golf M(c), soccer M(c)/W(c), softball M(c)/W(c), volleyball W(c).

Costs (2014–15) *Tuition:* area resident $2250 full-time, $75 per credit hour part-time; state resident $3675 full-time, $123 per credit hour part-time; nonresident $5250 full-time, $175 per credit hour part-time. *Required fees:* $837 full-time, $24 per credit hour part-time, $55 per term part-time. *Payment plan:* installment. *Waivers:* senior citizens and employees or children of employees.

Applying *Options:* electronic application. *Application fee:* $10. *Required:* high school transcript. *Application deadline:* rolling (freshmen). *Notification:* continuous (freshmen).

Freshman Application Contact NorthWest Arkansas Community College, One College Drive, Bentonville, AR 72712. *Phone:* 479-636-9222. *Toll-free phone:* 800-995-6922. *Fax:* 479-619-4116. *E-mail:* admissions@nwacc.edu. *Website:* http://www.nwacc.edu/.

Ozarka College

Melbourne, Arkansas

- **State-supported** 2-year, founded 1973
- **Rural** 40-acre campus
- **Coed**

Undergraduates 1% are from out of state.

Faculty *Student/faculty ratio:* 20:1.

Academics *Calendar:* semesters. *Degree:* certificates and associate. *Special study options:* academic remediation for entering students, advanced placement credit, distance learning, external degree program, internships, services for LD students, summer session for credit.

Student Life *Campus security:* security patrols after business hours.

Applying *Options:* electronic application, deferred entrance. *Required:* high school transcript. *Required for some:* essay or personal statement, interview. *Recommended:* minimum 2.0 GPA.

Freshman Application Contact Ms. Dylan Mowery, Director of Admissions, Ozarka College, PO Box 10, Melbourne, AR 72556. *Phone:* 870-368-7371 Ext. 2013. *Toll-free phone:* 800-821-4335. *E-mail:* dmmowery@ozarka.edu. *Website:* http://www.ozarka.edu/.

Phillips Community College of the University of Arkansas

Helena, Arkansas

Director of Admissions Mr. Lynn Boone, Registrar, Phillips Community College of the University of Arkansas, PO Box 785, Helena, AR 72342-0785. *Phone:* 870-338-6474. *Website:* http://www.pccua.edu/.

Pulaski Technical College

North Little Rock, Arkansas

Freshman Application Contact Mr. Clark Atkins, Director of Admissions, Pulaski Technical College, 3000 West Scenic Drive, North Little Rock, AR 72118. *Phone:* 501-812-2734. *Fax:* 501-812-2316. *E-mail:* catkins@pulaskitech.edu. *Website:* http://www.pulaskitech.edu/.

Remington College–Little Rock Campus

Little Rock, Arkansas

Director of Admissions Brian Maggio, Director of Recruitment, Remington College–Little Rock Campus, 19 Remington Drive, Little Rock, AR 72204. *Phone:* 501-312-0007. *Fax:* 501-225-3819. *E-mail:* brian.maggio@remingtoncollege.edu. *Website:* http://www.remingtoncollege.edu/.

Rich Mountain Community College

Mena, Arkansas

Director of Admissions Dr. Steve Rook, Dean of Students, Rich Mountain Community College, 1100 College Drive, Mena, AR 71953. *Phone:* 479-394-7622 Ext. 1400. *Website:* http://www.rmcc.edu/.

Shorter College

North Little Rock, Arkansas

Director of Admissions Mr. Keith Hunter, Director of Admissions, Shorter College, 604 Locust Street, North Little Rock, AR 72114-4885. *Phone:* 501-374-6305. *Website:* http://www.shortercollege.edu/.

South Arkansas Community College

El Dorado, Arkansas

Freshman Application Contact Dr. Stephanie Tully-Dartez, Director of Enrollment Services, South Arkansas Community College, PO Box 7010, El Dorado, AR 71731-7010. *Phone:* 870-864-7142. *Toll-free phone:* 800-955-2289. *Fax:* 870-864-7109. *E-mail:* dinman@southark.edu. *Website:* http://www.southark.edu/.

Southeast Arkansas College

Pine Bluff, Arkansas

Freshman Application Contact Ms. Barbara Dunn, Director of Admissions, Southeast Arkansas College, 1900 Hazel Street, Pine Bluff, AR 71603. *Phone:*

870-543-5957. *Toll-free phone:* 888-SEARK TC (in-state); 888-SEARC TC (out-of-state). *Fax:* 870-543-5957. *E-mail:* bdunn@seark.edu. *Website:* http://www.seark.edu/.

Southern Arkansas University Tech

Camden, Arkansas

Freshman Application Contact Mrs. Beverly Ellis, Admissions Analyst, Southern Arkansas University Tech, PO Box 3499, Camden, AR 71711-1599. *Phone:* 870-574-4558. *Fax:* 870-574-4478. *E-mail:* bellis@sautech.edu. *Website:* http://www.sautech.edu/.

University of Arkansas Community College at Batesville

Batesville, Arkansas

Freshman Application Contact Ms. Sharon Gage, Admissions Coordinator, University of Arkansas Community College at Batesville, PO Box 3350, Batesville, AR 72503. *Phone:* 870-612-2042. *Toll-free phone:* 800-508-7878. *Fax:* 870-612-2129. *E-mail:* sgage@uaccb.edu. *Website:* http://www.uaccb.edu/.

University of Arkansas Community College at Hope

Hope, Arkansas

- **State-supported** 2-year, founded 1966, part of University of Arkansas System
- **Rural** 60-acre campus
- **Coed**, 1,460 undergraduate students, 50% full-time, 67% women, 33% men

Undergraduates 732 full-time, 728 part-time. 5% are from out of state; 38% Black or African American, non-Hispanic/Latino; 6% Hispanic/Latino; 0.5% Asian, non-Hispanic/Latino; 0.1% Native Hawaiian or other Pacific Islander, non-Hispanic/Latino; 0.9% American Indian or Alaska Native, non-Hispanic/Latino; 0.3% Two or more races, non-Hispanic/Latino; 3% Race/ethnicity unknown; 7% transferred in. *Retention:* 40% of full-time freshmen returned.

Freshmen *Admission:* 885 applied, 885 admitted, 306 enrolled. *Average high school GPA:* 2.77. *Test scores:* ACT scores over 18: 49%; ACT scores over 24: 9%; ACT scores over 30: 1%.

Faculty *Total:* 91, 44% full-time, 11% with terminal degrees. *Student/faculty ratio:* 17:1.

Majors Business/commerce; child-care and support services management; computer and information sciences; education (multiple levels); electrical, electronic and communications engineering technology; emergency medical technology (EMT paramedic); funeral service and mortuary science; general studies; human services; liberal arts and sciences/liberal studies; medical office management; multi/interdisciplinary studies related; registered nursing/registered nurse; respiratory care therapy.

Academics *Calendar:* semesters. *Degree:* certificates, diplomas, and associate. *Special study options:* academic remediation for entering students, accelerated degree program, advanced placement credit, distance learning, double majors, independent study, internships, off-campus study, part-time degree program, services for LD students, summer session for credit.

Library University of Arkansas Community College at Hope Library with a Web page.

Student Life *Housing:* college housing not available. *Activities and Organizations:* Phi Theta Kappa, Arkansas Licensed Practical Nursing Association, Campus Crusaders for Christ, Technical and Industrial Club, Fine Arts Club. *Campus security:* 24-hour emergency response devices, on-campus security during class hours.

Costs (2014–15) *Tuition:* area resident $1815 full-time, $61 per credit part-time; state resident $1965 full-time, $66 per credit part-time; nonresident $3930 full-time, $131 per credit part-time. *Required fees:* $466 full-time, $15 per credit part-time, $8 per term part-time. *Payment plan:* installment. *Waivers:* senior citizens and employees or children of employees.

Financial Aid *Average indebtedness upon graduation:* $2625.

Applying *Options:* early admission. *Required:* high school transcript. *Application deadlines:* rolling (freshmen), rolling (out-of-state freshmen), rolling (transfers). *Notification:* continuous (freshmen), continuous (out-of-state freshmen), continuous (transfers).

Freshman Application Contact University of Arkansas Community College at Hope, PO Box 140, Hope, AR 71802. *Phone:* 870-772-8174. *Website:* http://www.uacch.edu/.

University of Arkansas Community College at Morrilton
Morrilton, Arkansas

- **State-supported** 2-year, founded 1961, part of University of Arkansas System
- **Rural** 79-acre campus
- **Coed,** 2,149 undergraduate students, 59% full-time, 58% women, 42% men

Undergraduates 1,270 full-time, 879 part-time. Students come from 8 states and territories; 1 other country; 0.5% are from out of state; 10% Black or African American, non-Hispanic/Latino; 0.7% Hispanic/Latino; 0.8% Asian, non-Hispanic/Latino; 0.4% American Indian or Alaska Native, non-Hispanic/Latino; 5% Two or more races, non-Hispanic/Latino; 6% Race/ethnicity unknown; 2% international; 10% transferred in.
Freshmen *Admission:* 1,564 applied, 913 admitted, 586 enrolled. *Average high school GPA:* 2.87. *Test scores:* ACT scores over 18: 75%; ACT scores over 24: 15%; ACT scores over 30: 1%.
Faculty *Total:* 108, 63% full-time, 6% with terminal degrees. *Student/faculty ratio:* 19:1.
Majors Autobody/collision and repair technology; automobile/automotive mechanics technology; business/commerce; child development; commercial and advertising art; computer and information sciences; computer technology/computer systems technology; criminal justice/law enforcement administration; drafting and design technology; education (multiple levels); forensic science and technology; general studies; heating, air conditioning, ventilation and refrigeration maintenance technology; liberal arts and sciences/liberal studies; petroleum technology; registered nursing/registered nurse; surveying technology.
Academics *Calendar:* semesters. *Degree:* certificates and associate. *Special study options:* academic remediation for entering students, advanced placement credit, cooperative education, distance learning, double majors, internships, part-time degree program, services for LD students, summer session for credit.
Library E. Allen Gordon Library with 24,767 titles, 53 serial subscriptions, 1,814 audiovisual materials, an OPAC, a Web page.
Student Life *Housing:* college housing not available. *Activities and Organizations:* drama/theater group, Student Government Association, Phi Beta Lambda, Student Practical Nurses Organization, Computer Information Systems Organization, Early Childhood Development Organization. *Campus security:* 24-hour emergency response devices, campus alert system through phone call, text message and/or e-mail. *Student services:* personal/psychological counseling.
Athletics *Intramural sports:* basketball M/W, football M/W, table tennis M/W, ultimate Frisbee M/W, volleyball M/W.
Standardized Tests *Recommended:* SAT or ACT (for admission), ACT COMPASS.
Costs (2014–15) *Tuition:* area resident $1680 full-time; state resident $1827 full-time; nonresident $2604 full-time. *Required fees:* $890 full-time. *Payment plan:* installment. *Waivers:* senior citizens and employees or children of employees.
Financial Aid Of all full-time matriculated undergraduates who enrolled in 2013, 1,113 applied for aid, 994 were judged to have need, 60 had their need fully met. 23 Federal Work-Study jobs (averaging $1826). In 2013, 62 non-need-based awards were made. *Average percent of need met:* 52%. *Average financial aid package:* $6027. *Average need-based loan:* $2667. *Average need-based gift aid:* $4063. *Average non-need-based aid:* $2883. *Financial aid deadline:* 7/1.
Applying *Options:* electronic application, early admission, deferred entrance. *Required:* high school transcript. *Required for some:* immunization records and prior college transcript(s). *Application deadlines:* rolling (freshmen), rolling (transfers). *Notification:* continuous (freshmen), continuous (transfers).
Freshman Application Contact Ms. Rachel Mullins, Coordinator of Recruitment, University of Arkansas Community College at Morrilton, 1537 University Boulevard, Morrilton, AR 72110. *Phone:* 501-977-2174. *Toll-free phone:* 800-264-1094. *Fax:* 501-977-2123. *E-mail:* mullins@uaccm.edu. *Website:* http://www.uaccm.edu/.

CALIFORNIA

Academy of Couture Art
Beverly Hills, California

- **Proprietary** primarily 2-year
- **Urban** campus with easy access to Los Angeles
- **Coed**

Majors Apparel and textile manufacturing; fashion/apparel design.

Academics *Degrees:* associate and bachelor's. *Special study options:* double majors, English as a second language.
Student Life *Housing:* college housing not available. *Campus security:* 24-hour emergency response devices and patrols.
Freshman Application Contact Academy of Couture Art, 8484 Wilshire Boulevard, Suite 730, Beverly Hills, CA 90211. *Phone:* 310-360-8888. *Website:* http://www.academyofccoutureart.edu/.

Allan Hancock College
Santa Maria, California

Freshman Application Contact Ms. Adela Esquivel Swinson, Director of Admissions and Records, Allan Hancock College, 800 South College Drive, Santa Maria, CA 93454-6399. *Phone:* 805-922-6966 Ext. 3272. *Toll-free phone:* 866-342-5242. *Fax:* 805-922-3477. *Website:* http://www.hancockcollege.edu/.

American Academy of Dramatic Arts
Hollywood, California

Freshman Application Contact Steven Hong, Director of Admissions, American Academy of Dramatic Arts, 1336 North La Brea Avenue, Hollywood, CA 90028. *Phone:* 323-464-2777 Ext. 103. *Toll-free phone:* 800-222-2867. *E-mail:* shong@aada.edu. *Website:* http://www.aada.org/.

American Career College
Anaheim, California

Director of Admissions Susan Pailet, Senior Executive Director of Admission, American Career College, 1200 North Magnolia Avenue, Anaheim, CA 92801. *Phone:* 714-952-9066. *Toll-free phone:* 877-832-0790. *E-mail:* info@americancareer.com. *Website:* http://americancareercollege.edu/.

American Career College
Los Angeles, California

Director of Admissions Tamra Adams, Director of Admissions, American Career College, 4021 Rosewood Avenue, Los Angeles, CA 90004-2932. *Phone:* 323-668-7555. *Toll-free phone:* 877-832-0790. *E-mail:* info@americancareer.com. *Website:* http://americancareercollege.edu/.

American Career College
Ontario, California

Director of Admissions Juan Tellez, Director of Admissions, American Career College, 3130 East Sedona Court, Ontario, CA 91764. *Phone:* 951-739-0788. *Toll-free phone:* 877-832-0790. *E-mail:* info@amercancareer.com. *Website:* http://americancareercollege.edu/.

American River College
Sacramento, California

Freshman Application Contact American River College, 4700 College Oak Drive, Sacramento, CA 95841-4286. *Phone:* 916-484-8171. *Website:* http://www.arc.losrios.edu/.

Antelope Valley College
Lancaster, California

- **State and locally supported** 2-year, founded 1929, part of California Community College System
- **Suburban** 135-acre campus with easy access to Los Angeles
- **Endowment** $299,569
- **Coed,** 15,108 undergraduate students, 32% full-time, 60% women, 40% men

Undergraduates 4,802 full-time, 10,306 part-time. Students come from 7 states and territories; 1% are from out of state; 16% transferred in. *Retention:* 68% of full-time freshmen returned.
Freshmen *Admission:* 2,830 applied, 2,830 admitted, 2,830 enrolled.
Faculty *Total:* 618, 32% full-time. *Student/faculty ratio:* 45:1.
Majors Administrative assistant and secretarial science; aircraft powerplant technology; airframe mechanics and aircraft maintenance technology; apparel and textiles; autobody/collision and repair technology; automobile/automotive mechanics technology; avionics maintenance technology; biology/biological sciences; business administration and management; business/commerce; child-care and support services management; child development; cinematography and film/video production; computer and information sciences; computer graphics; computer programming; construction engineering technology;

corrections; criminal justice/law enforcement administration; criminal justice/police science; data processing and data processing technology; drafting and design technology; electrical, electronic and communications engineering technology; engineering; engineering technology; family and consumer sciences/home economics teacher education; fiber, textile and weaving arts; fire prevention and safety technology; foods, nutrition, and wellness; health and physical education/fitness; heating, air conditioning, ventilation and refrigeration maintenance technology; interior design; liberal arts and sciences/liberal studies; marketing/marketing management; mathematics; medical administrative assistant and medical secretary; music; ornamental horticulture; photography; physical sciences; real estate; registered nursing/registered nurse; teacher assistant/aide; welding technology; work and family studies.

Academics *Calendar:* semesters. *Degree:* certificates and associate. *Special study options:* academic remediation for entering students, adult/continuing education programs, advanced placement credit, cooperative education, distance learning, English as a second language, honors programs, independent study, part-time degree program, services for LD students, student-designed majors, summer session for credit. *ROTC:* Air Force (c).

Library Antelope Valley College Library with 43,000 titles, 175 serial subscriptions, an OPAC.

Student Life *Housing:* college housing not available. *Activities and Organizations:* drama/theater group, student-run newspaper, choral group. *Campus security:* 24-hour emergency response devices and patrols, late-night transport/escort service. *Student services:* personal/psychological counseling.

Athletics *Intercollegiate sports:* baseball M, basketball M/W, cross-country running M/W, football M, golf M/W, soccer W, softball W, tennis W, track and field M/W, volleyball W. *Intramural sports:* basketball M/W, golf M/W, swimming and diving M/W, tennis M/W, volleyball M/W, weight lifting M/W.

Applying *Options:* electronic application, early admission. *Required:* high school transcript. *Recommended:* assessment. *Application deadlines:* rolling (freshmen), rolling (transfers). *Notification:* continuous (freshmen), continuous (transfers).

Freshman Application Contact Welcome Center, Antelope Valley College, 3041 West Avenue K, Lancaster, CA 93536-5426. *Phone:* 661-722-6331. *Website:* http://www.avc.edu/.

Anthem College–Sacramento
Sacramento, California

Freshman Application Contact Admissions Office, Anthem College–Sacramento, 9738 Lincoln Village Drive, Suite 100, Sacramento, CA 95827. *Phone:* 916-929-9700. *Toll-free phone:* 855-331-7768. *Website:* http://anthem.edu/sacramento-california/.

APT College
Carlsbad, California

Director of Admissions Monica Hoffman, Director of Admissions/Registrar, APT College, 5751 Palmer Way, Suite D, PO Box 131717, Carlsbad, CA 92013. *Phone:* 800-431-8488. *Toll-free phone:* 800-431-8488. *Fax:* 888-431-8588. *E-mail:* aptc@aptc.com. *Website:* http://www.aptc.edu/.

Aviation & Electronic Schools of America
Colfax, California

Freshman Application Contact Admissions Office, Aviation & Electronic Schools of America, 111 South Railroad Street, PO Box 1810, Colfax, CA 95713-1810. *Phone:* 530-346-6792. *Toll-free phone:* 800-345-2742. *Fax:* 530-346-8466. *E-mail:* aesa@aesa.com. *Website:* http://www.aesa.com/.

Bakersfield College
Bakersfield, California

- **State and locally supported** 2-year, founded 1913, part of California Community College System
- **Urban** 175-acre campus
- **Coed**

Academics *Calendar:* semesters. *Degree:* associate. *Special study options:* academic remediation for entering students, accelerated degree program, adult/continuing education programs, advanced placement credit, cooperative education, English as a second language, internships, part-time degree program, services for LD students, summer session for credit.

Student Life *Campus security:* 24-hour patrols, late-night transport/escort service.

Financial Aid Of all full-time matriculated undergraduates who enrolled in 2012, 300 Federal Work-Study jobs (averaging $2500). 15 state and other part-time jobs (averaging $2500).

Freshman Application Contact Bakersfield College, 1801 Panorama Drive, Bakersfield, CA 93305-1299. *Phone:* 661-395-4301. *Website:* http://www.bakersfieldcollege.edu/.

Barstow Community College
Barstow, California

- **State and locally supported** 2-year, founded 1959, part of California Community College System
- **Small-town** 50-acre campus
- **Coed**, 4,791 undergraduate students

Faculty *Student/faculty ratio:* 35:1.

Majors Accounting technology and bookkeeping; automobile/automotive mechanics technology; biological and physical sciences; business administration and management; business/commerce; child-care provision; cosmetology; criminal justice/police science; diesel mechanics technology; electrical/electronics equipment installation and repair; electrician; emergency medical technology (EMT paramedic); fire science/firefighting; health and physical education/fitness; humanities; information technology; medical/clinical assistant; nursing assistant/aide and patient care assistant/aide; photography; social sciences; welding technology.

Academics *Calendar:* semesters. *Degree:* certificates and associate. *Special study options:* academic remediation for entering students, adult/continuing education programs, cooperative education, English as a second language, external degree program, part-time degree program, services for LD students, student-designed majors, summer session for credit.

Library Thomas Kimball Library with an OPAC, a Web page.

Student Life *Housing:* college housing not available. *Activities and Organizations:* drama/theater group, student-run newspaper. *Campus security:* evening security personnel. *Student services:* personal/psychological counseling.

Athletics *Intercollegiate sports:* baseball M, basketball M/W, cross-country running M/W.

Applying *Options:* early admission, deferred entrance. *Recommended:* high school transcript. *Application deadlines:* rolling (freshmen), rolling (transfers).

Freshman Application Contact Barstow Community College, 2700 Barstow Road, Barstow, CA 92311-6699. *Phone:* 760-252-2411 Ext. 7236. *Website:* http://www.barstow.edu/.

Berkeley City College
Berkeley, California

- **State and locally supported** 2-year, founded 1974, part of California Community College System
- **Urban** campus with easy access to San Francisco, Oakland
- **Coed**, 7,645 undergraduate students

Undergraduates 1% are from out of state; 18% Black or African American, non-Hispanic/Latino; 12% Hispanic/Latino; 16% Asian, non-Hispanic/Latino; 0.5% Native Hawaiian or other Pacific Islander, non-Hispanic/Latino; 0.5% American Indian or Alaska Native, non-Hispanic/Latino; 3% Two or more races, non-Hispanic/Latino; 31% Race/ethnicity unknown.

Faculty *Total:* 312, 20% full-time. *Student/faculty ratio:* 35:1.

Majors Accounting; accounting and business/management; American Sign Language (ASL); art; biology/biotechnology laboratory technician; business administration and management; business administration, management and operations related; business/commerce; business, management, and marketing related; computer and information sciences; computer and information sciences related; computer and information systems security; computer graphics; computer software and media applications related; creative writing; data entry/microcomputer applications related; English; fine/studio arts; general studies; liberal arts and sciences/liberal studies; medical administrative assistant and medical secretary; office management; psychology; public health education and promotion; public health related; sign language interpretation and translation; social sciences related; social work related; sociology; Spanish; web page, digital/multimedia and information resources design; writing.

Academics *Calendar:* semesters. *Degree:* certificates and associate. *Special study options:* academic remediation for entering students, adult/continuing education programs, advanced placement credit, cooperative education, distance learning, double majors, English as a second language, independent study, internships, off-campus study, part-time degree program, services for LD students, student-designed majors, study abroad, summer session for credit.

Library Susan A. Duncan Library plus 1 other with an OPAC, a Web page.

Student Life *Activities and Organizations:* student-run newspaper, choral group, Civic Engagement Club, Global Studies Club, Indigenous Student

Alliance, The National Society of Leadership and Success, The Digital Arts Club (DAC). *Campus security:* 24-hour patrols. *Student services:* health clinic, personal/psychological counseling.

Standardized Tests *Required:* Matriculating students must take a math and English assessment test (for admission).

Costs (2014–15) *Tuition:* state resident $1380 full-time, $46 per credit part-time; nonresident $7770 full-time, $259 per credit part-time. Full-time tuition and fees vary according to class time, course load, and program. Part-time tuition and fees vary according to class time, course load, and program. *Required fees:* $296 full-time, $46 per credit part-time, $296 per year part-time. *Waivers:* minority students, children of alumni, adult students, senior citizens, and employees or children of employees.

Financial Aid Of all full-time matriculated undergraduates who enrolled in 2013, 48 Federal Work-Study jobs (averaging $3000).

Applying *Required:* assessment test in Math and English for matriculating students. *Recommended:* high school transcript.

Freshman Application Contact Dr. May Kuang-chi Chen, Vice President of Student Services, Berkeley City College, 2050 Center Street, Berkeley, CA 94704. *Phone:* 510-981-2820. *Fax:* 510-841-7333. *E-mail:* mrivas@peralta.edu.
Website: http://www.berkeleycitycollege.edu/.

Bryan College
Gold River, California

Freshman Application Contact Bryan College, 2317 Gold Meadow Way, Gold River, CA 95670. *Phone:* 916-649-2400. *Toll-free phone:* 866-649-2400.
Website: http://www.bryancollege.edu/.

Butte College
Oroville, California

- **State and locally supported** 2-year, founded 1966, part of California Community College System
- **Rural** 928-acre campus with easy access to Sacramento
- **Coed,** 12,290 undergraduate students, 43% full-time, 52% women, 48% men

Undergraduates 5,330 full-time, 6,960 part-time. 3% Black or African American, non-Hispanic/Latino; 15% Hispanic/Latino; 6% Asian, non-Hispanic/Latino; 0.4% Native Hawaiian or other Pacific Islander, non-Hispanic/Latino; 2% American Indian or Alaska Native, non-Hispanic/Latino; 0.1% Two or more races, non-Hispanic/Latino; 1% international.

Freshmen *Admission:* 6,239 applied, 6,239 admitted, 1,716 enrolled.

Faculty *Student/faculty ratio:* 25:1.

Majors Accounting; administrative assistant and secretarial science; agribusiness; agricultural mechanics and equipment technology; agriculture; art; automobile/automotive mechanics technology; biology/biological sciences; business administration and management; ceramic arts and ceramics; chemistry; child development; computer science; cosmetology; criminal justice/police science; data entry/microcomputer applications related; digital communication and media/multimedia; drafting and design technology; emergency medical technology (EMT paramedic); engineering; engineering technologies and engineering related; English language and literature related; environmental science; family and consumer sciences/human sciences; fire science/firefighting; foods, nutrition, and wellness; graphic design; hazardous materials management and waste technology; health and physical education/fitness; horticultural science; information technology; interior design; journalism; legal administrative assistant/secretary; liberal arts and sciences/liberal studies; licensed practical/vocational nurse training; mathematics; medical administrative assistant and medical secretary; natural resources management and policy; network and system administration; parks, recreation and leisure facilities management; photography; physical sciences; physics; radio and television; real estate; registered nursing/registered nurse; respiratory care therapy; retailing; sales, distribution, and marketing operations; small business administration; social sciences; substance abuse/addiction counseling; tourism and travel services management; welding technology.

Academics *Calendar:* semesters. *Degree:* certificates and associate. *Special study options:* academic remediation for entering students, accelerated degree program, adult/continuing education programs, advanced placement credit, cooperative education, distance learning, double majors, English as a second language, honors programs, independent study, internships, part-time degree program, services for LD students, study abroad, summer session for credit.

Library Frederick S. Montgomery Library with 70,000 titles, 27,000 serial subscriptions, an OPAC, a Web page.

Student Life *Housing:* college housing not available. *Activities and Organizations:* drama/theater group, student-run newspaper, Phi Theta Kappa - International Honor society for Community College Students, Ag

Ambassadors, Horticulture Club, International Club, Sigma Alpha Pi (National society of Leadership). *Campus security:* 24-hour emergency response devices and patrols, student patrols. *Student services:* health clinic, personal/psychological counseling.

Athletics *Intercollegiate sports:* baseball M, basketball M/W, cross-country running M/W, football M, golf M/W, soccer M/W, softball W, track and field M/W, volleyball W.

Costs (2013–14) *Tuition:* state resident $1104 full-time, $46 per unit part-time; nonresident $5904 full-time, $246 per unit part-time. Full-time tuition and fees vary according to course load, location, and program. Part-time tuition and fees vary according to course load, location, and program. *Required fees:* $252 full-time, $126 per term part-time. *Payment plans:* installment, deferred payment.

Applying *Options:* electronic application, early admission, deferred entrance. *Required for some:* high school transcript. *Application deadlines:* rolling (freshmen), rolling (transfers).

Freshman Application Contact Mr. Brad Zuniga, Director of Recruitment, Outreach and New Student Orientation, Butte College, 3536 Butte Campus Drive, Oroville, CA 95965-8399. *Phone:* 530-895-2948.
Website: http://www.butte.edu/.

Cabrillo College
Aptos, California

Freshman Application Contact Tama Bolton, Director of Admissions and Records, Cabrillo College, 6500 Soquel Drive, Aptos, CA 95003-3194. *Phone:* 831-477-3548. *Fax:* 831-479-5782. *E-mail:* tabolton@cabrillo.edu.
Website: http://www.cabrillo.edu/.

Cambridge Junior College
Yuba City, California

Freshman Application Contact Admissions Office, Cambridge Junior College, 990-A Klamath Lane, Yuba City, CA 95993. *Phone:* 530-674-9199. *Fax:* 530-671-7319.
Website: http://cambridge.edu/.

Cañada College
Redwood City, California

- **State and locally supported** 2-year, founded 1968, part of San Mateo County Community College District System
- **Suburban** 131-acre campus with easy access to San Francisco, San Jose
- **Coed,** 6,658 undergraduate students

Undergraduates *Retention:* 65% of full-time freshmen returned.

Faculty *Total:* 263, 29% full-time. *Student/faculty ratio:* 25:1.

Majors Accounting technology and bookkeeping; administrative assistant and secretarial science; animation, interactive technology, video graphics and special effects; anthropology; apparel and textile manufacturing; archeology; area studies related; art; biological and physical sciences; biology/biological sciences; business administration and management; chemistry; child-care provision; computer science; computer systems networking and telecommunications; dramatic/theater arts; economics; engineering; English; fashion/apparel design; geography; health and physical education/fitness; history; humanities; human services; interior design; international relations and affairs; legal assistant/paralegal; liberal arts and sciences/liberal studies; linguistics; medical/clinical assistant; music; network and system administration; philosophy; physics; political science and government; psychology; radiologic technology/science; retailing; small business administration; sociology; Spanish; speech communication and rhetoric; sport and fitness administration/management.

Academics *Calendar:* semesters. *Degree:* certificates and associate. *Special study options:* academic remediation for entering students, accelerated degree program, adult/continuing education programs, advanced placement credit, cooperative education, distance learning, English as a second language, honors programs, internships, part-time degree program, services for LD students, study abroad, summer session for credit.

Library an OPAC.

Student Life *Housing:* college housing not available. *Activities and Organizations:* drama/theater group, choral group. *Campus security:* 12-hour patrols by trained security personnel. *Student services:* health clinic, personal/psychological counseling.

Athletics *Intercollegiate sports:* baseball M, basketball M, golf M/W, soccer M/W.

Costs (2013–14) *Tuition:* state resident $0 full-time; nonresident $6312 full-time, $263 per credit part-time. *Required fees:* $1104 full-time, $46 per credit part-time, $20 per term part-time. *Payment plan:* installment.

Financial Aid Of all full-time matriculated undergraduates who enrolled in 2012, 35 Federal Work-Study jobs (averaging $2600).

Applying *Options:* early admission. *Application deadlines:* rolling (freshmen), rolling (transfers).
Freshman Application Contact Cañada College, 4200 Farm Hill Boulevard, Redwood City, CA 94061-1099. *Phone:* 650-306-3125.
Website: http://www.canadacollege.edu/.

Carrington College California–Citrus Heights

Citrus Heights, California

- Proprietary 2-year, part of Carrington Colleges Group, Inc.
- Coed, 451 undergraduate students, 93% full-time, 85% women, 15% men

Undergraduates 420 full-time, 31 part-time. 9% Black or African American, non-Hispanic/Latino; 15% Hispanic/Latino; 2% Asian, non-Hispanic/Latino; 1% Native Hawaiian or other Pacific Islander, non-Hispanic/Latino; 0.7% American Indian or Alaska Native, non-Hispanic/Latino; 4% Two or more races, non-Hispanic/Latino; 12% Race/ethnicity unknown; 17% transferred in.
Freshmen *Admission:* 42 enrolled.
Faculty *Total:* 17, 53% full-time. *Student/faculty ratio:* 37:1.
Majors Accounting technology and bookkeeping; business administration and management; criminal justice/safety; dental assisting; health/health-care administration; medical/clinical assistant; medical insurance/medical billing; pharmacy technician; surgical technology; veterinary/animal health technology.
Academics *Degree:* certificates and associate.
Student Life *Housing:* college housing not available.
Applying *Required:* essay or personal statement, high school transcript, interview.
Freshman Application Contact Carrington College California–Citrus Heights, 7301 Greenback Lane, Suite A, Citrus Heights, CA 95621.
Website: http://carrington.edu/.

Carrington College California–Pleasant Hill

Pleasant Hill, California

- Proprietary 2-year, founded 1997, part of Carrington Colleges Group, Inc.
- Coed, 589 undergraduate students, 87% full-time, 79% women, 21% men

Undergraduates 512 full-time, 77 part-time. 14% Black or African American, non-Hispanic/Latino; 28% Hispanic/Latino; 13% Asian, non-Hispanic/Latino; 3% Native Hawaiian or other Pacific Islander, non-Hispanic/Latino; 0.7% American Indian or Alaska Native, non-Hispanic/Latino; 3% Two or more races, non-Hispanic/Latino; 1% Race/ethnicity unknown; 0.3% international; 17% transferred in.
Freshmen *Admission:* 50 enrolled.
Faculty *Total:* 38, 55% full-time. *Student/faculty ratio:* 20:1.
Majors Accounting technology and bookkeeping; business administration and management; criminal justice/police science; criminal justice/safety; dental assisting; graphic communications related; health and medical administrative services related; health/health-care administration; health information/medical records technology; massage therapy; medical/clinical assistant; medical insurance/medical billing; pharmacy technician; physical therapy technology; respiratory therapy technician; veterinary/animal health technology.
Academics *Calendar:* semesters. *Degree:* certificates and associate.
Student Life *Housing:* college housing not available.
Costs (2014–15) *Tuition:* $32,351 per degree program part-time. Total costs vary by program. Tuition provided is for largest program (Veterinary Technology).
Applying *Required:* essay or personal statement, high school transcript, interview.
Freshman Application Contact Carrington College California–Pleasant Hill, 380 Civic Drive, Suite 300, Pleasant Hill, CA 94523.
Website: http://carrington.edu/.

Carrington College California–Pomona

Pomona, California

- Proprietary 2-year
- Coed, 301 undergraduate students, 80% full-time, 89% women, 11% men

Undergraduates 240 full-time, 61 part-time. 4% Black or African American, non-Hispanic/Latino; 59% Hispanic/Latino; 5% Asian, non-Hispanic/Latino; 1% Native Hawaiian or other Pacific Islander, non-Hispanic/Latino; 0.7% American Indian or Alaska Native, non-Hispanic/Latino; 1% Two or more races, non-Hispanic/Latino; 3% Race/ethnicity unknown; 2% international; 14% transferred in.
Freshmen *Admission:* 33 enrolled.

Faculty *Total:* 13, 85% full-time. *Student/faculty ratio:* 22:1.
Academics *Degree:* certificates and associate.
Costs (2014–15) *Tuition:* $32,351 per degree program part-time. Total costs vary by program. Tuition provided is for largest program (Veterinary Technology).
Freshman Application Contact Carrington College California–Pomona, 901 Corporate Center Drive, Suite 300, Pomona, CA 91768. *Toll-free phone:* 877-206-2106.
Website: http://carrington.edu/.

Carrington College California–Sacramento

Sacramento, California

- Proprietary 2-year, founded 1967, part of Carrington Colleges Group, Inc.
- Coed, 1,267 undergraduate students, 90% full-time, 86% women, 14% men

Undergraduates 1,145 full-time, 122 part-time. 10% are from out of state; 13% Black or African American, non-Hispanic/Latino; 20% Hispanic/Latino; 12% Asian, non-Hispanic/Latino; 2% Native Hawaiian or other Pacific Islander, non-Hispanic/Latino; 1% American Indian or Alaska Native, non-Hispanic/Latino; 7% Two or more races, non-Hispanic/Latino; 6% Race/ethnicity unknown; 0.1% international; 13% transferred in.
Freshmen *Admission:* 60 enrolled.
Faculty *Total:* 103, 26% full-time. *Student/faculty ratio:* 23:1.
Majors Dental assisting; dental hygiene; health/health-care administration; licensed practical/vocational nurse training; massage therapy; medical/clinical assistant; medical insurance/medical billing; medical office management; pharmacy technician; registered nursing/registered nurse; veterinary/animal health technology.
Academics *Calendar:* semesters. *Degree:* certificates and associate.
Standardized Tests *Required:* Entrance test administered by Carrington College California (for admission).
Costs (2014–15) *Tuition:* $17,671 per degree program part-time. Total costs vary by program. Tuition provided is for largest program (Medical Assisting).
Applying *Required:* essay or personal statement, high school transcript, interview.
Freshman Application Contact Carrington College California–Sacramento, 8909 Folsom Boulevard, Sacramento, CA 95826.
Website: http://carrington.edu/.

Carrington College California–San Jose

San Jose, California

- Proprietary 2-year, founded 1999, part of Carrington Colleges Group, Inc.
- Coed, 693 undergraduate students, 96% full-time, 86% women, 14% men

Undergraduates 662 full-time, 31 part-time. 1% are from out of state; 2% Black or African American, non-Hispanic/Latino; 45% Hispanic/Latino; 16% Asian, non-Hispanic/Latino; 4% Native Hawaiian or other Pacific Islander, non-Hispanic/Latino; 1% American Indian or Alaska Native, non-Hispanic/Latino; 3% Two or more races, non-Hispanic/Latino; 0.3% Race/ethnicity unknown; 0.6% international; 17% transferred in.
Freshmen *Admission:* 55 enrolled.
Faculty *Total:* 62, 32% full-time. *Student/faculty ratio:* 20:1.
Majors Accounting technology and bookkeeping; allied health and medical assisting services related; architectural drafting and CAD/CADD; biology/biotechnology laboratory technician; business administration and management; computer graphics; criminal justice/safety; dental assisting; dental hygiene; drafting and design technology; health/health-care administration; licensed practical/vocational nurse training; massage therapy; medical/clinical assistant; medical insurance/medical billing; medical office management; pharmacy technician; surgical technology; veterinary/animal health technology.
Academics *Calendar:* semesters. *Degree:* certificates and associate.
Student Life *Housing:* college housing not available.
Standardized Tests *Required:* Entrance test administered by Carrington College California (for admission).
Costs (2014–15) *Tuition:* $32,351 per degree program part-time. Total costs vary by program. Tuition provided is for largest program (Veterinary Technology).
Applying *Required:* essay or personal statement, high school transcript, interview.
Freshman Application Contact Carrington College California–San Jose, 6201 San Ignacio Avenue, San Jose, CA 95119.
Website: http://carrington.edu/.

Carrington College California–San Leandro
San Leandro, California

- **Proprietary** 2-year, founded 1986, part of Carrington Colleges Group, Inc.
- **Coed,** 521 undergraduate students, 97% full-time, 89% women, 11% men

Undergraduates 505 full-time, 16 part-time. 20% Black or African American, non-Hispanic/Latino; 40% Hispanic/Latino; 9% Asian, non-Hispanic/Latino; 5% Native Hawaiian or other Pacific Islander, non-Hispanic/Latino; 0.2% American Indian or Alaska Native, non-Hispanic/Latino; 5% Two or more races, non-Hispanic/Latino; 1% Race/ethnicity unknown; 0.2% international; 17% transferred in.
Freshmen *Admission:* 70 enrolled.
Faculty *Total:* 24, 42% full-time. *Student/faculty ratio:* 35:1.
Majors Accounting technology and bookkeeping; business administration and management; dental assisting; health and medical administrative services related; health/health-care administration; massage therapy; medical/clinical assistant; medical insurance/medical billing; pharmacy technician; veterinary/animal health technology.
Academics *Calendar:* semesters. *Degree:* certificates and associate.
Student Life *Housing:* college housing not available.
Standardized Tests *Required:* Entrance test administered by Carrington Colleges California (for admission).
Costs (2014–15) *Tuition:* $32,351 per degree program part-time. Total costs vary by program. Tuition provided is for largest program (Veterinary Technology).
Applying *Required:* essay or personal statement, high school transcript, interview.
Freshman Application Contact Carrington College California–San Leandro, 15555 East 14th Street, Suite 500, San Leandro, CA 94578.
Website: http://carrington.edu/.

Carrington College California–Stockton
Stockton, California

- **Proprietary** 2-year
- **Coed,** 465 undergraduate students, 92% full-time, 86% women, 14% men

Undergraduates 430 full-time, 35 part-time. 12% Black or African American, non-Hispanic/Latino; 42% Hispanic/Latino; 7% Asian, non-Hispanic/Latino; 2% Native Hawaiian or other Pacific Islander, non-Hispanic/Latino; 2% American Indian or Alaska Native, non-Hispanic/Latino; 3% Two or more races, non-Hispanic/Latino; 1% Race/ethnicity unknown; 12% transferred in.
Freshmen *Admission:* 62 enrolled.
Faculty *Total:* 15, 40% full-time. *Student/faculty ratio:* 49:1.
Majors Veterinary/animal health technology.
Academics *Degree:* certificates and associate.
Costs (2014–15) *Tuition:* $32,351 per degree program part-time. Total costs vary by program. Tuition provided is for largest program (Veterinary Technology).
Freshman Application Contact Carrington College California–Stockton, 1313 West Robinhood Drive, Suite B, Stockton, CA 95207.
Website: http://carrington.edu/.

Cerritos College
Norwalk, California

Director of Admissions Ms. Stephanie Murguia, Director of Admissions and Records, Cerritos College, 11110 Alondra Boulevard, Norwalk, CA 90650-6298. *Phone:* 562-860-2451. *E-mail:* smurguia@cerritos.edu.
Website: http://www.cerritos.edu/.

Cerro Coso Community College
Ridgecrest, California

Freshman Application Contact Mrs. Heather Ootash, Counseling/Matriculation Coordinator, Cerro Coso Community College, 3000 College Heights Boulevard, Ridgecrest, CA 93555. *Phone:* 760-384-6291. *Fax:* 760-375-4776. *E-mail:* hostash@cerrocoso.edu.
Website: http://www.cerrocoso.edu/.

Chabot College
Hayward, California

Director of Admissions Paulette Lino, Director of Admissions and Records, Chabot College, 25555 Hesperian Boulevard, Hayward, CA 94545-5001. *Phone:* 510-723-6700.
Website: http://www.chabotcollege.edu/.

Chaffey College
Rancho Cucamonga, California

Freshman Application Contact Erlinda Martinez, Coordinator of Admissions, Chaffey College, 5885 Haven Avenue, Rancho Cucamonga, CA 91737-3002. *Phone:* 909-652-6610. *E-mail:* erlinda.martinez@chaffey.edu.
Website: http://www.chaffey.edu/.

Citrus College
Glendora, California

Freshman Application Contact Admissions and Records, Citrus College, Glendora, CA 91741-1899. *Phone:* 626-914-8511. *Fax:* 626-914-8613. *E-mail:* admissions@citruscollege.edu.
Website: http://www.citruscollege.edu/.

City College of San Francisco
San Francisco, California

Freshman Application Contact Ms. Mary Lou Leyba-Frank, Dean of Admissions and Records, City College of San Francisco, 50 Phelan Avenue, San Francisco, CA 94112-1821. *Phone:* 415-239-3291. *Fax:* 415-239-3936. *E-mail:* mleyba@ccsf.edu.
Website: http://www.ccsf.edu/.

Coastline Community College
Fountain Valley, California

Freshman Application Contact Jennifer McDonald, Director of Admissions and Records, Coastline Community College, 11460 Warner Avenue, Fountain Valley, CA 92708-2597. *Phone:* 714-241-6163.
Website: http://www.coastline.edu/.

Coleman University
San Marcos, California

Director of Admissions Senior Admissions Officer, Coleman University, 1284 West San Marcos Boulevard, San Marcos, CA 92078. *Phone:* 760-747-3990. *Fax:* 760-752-9808.
Website: http://www.coleman.edu/.

College of Alameda
Alameda, California

Freshman Application Contact College of Alameda, 555 Ralph Appezzato Memorial Parkway, Alameda, CA 94501-2109. *Phone:* 510-748-2204.
Website: http://alameda.peralta.edu/.

College of Marin
Kentfield, California

- **State and locally supported** 2-year, founded 1926, part of California Community College System
- **Suburban** 410-acre campus with easy access to San Francisco
- **Coed,** 7,000 undergraduate students

Undergraduates 7% Black or African American, non-Hispanic/Latino; 19% Hispanic/Latino; 8% Asian, non-Hispanic/Latino; 0.4% Native Hawaiian or other Pacific Islander, non-Hispanic/Latino; 0.4% American Indian or Alaska Native, non-Hispanic/Latino; 5% Two or more races, non-Hispanic/Latino; 5% Race/ethnicity unknown; 0.9% international.
Faculty *Total:* 322.
Majors Accounting technology and bookkeeping; animation, interactive technology, video graphics and special effects; architectural technology; art; autobody/collision and repair technology; automobile/automotive mechanics technology; biological and physical sciences; biology/biological sciences; business administration and management; business/commerce; chemistry; child-care provision; cinematography and film/video production; computer science; computer systems networking and telecommunications; court reporting; criminal justice/police science; dance; data modeling/warehousing and database administration; dental assisting; design and visual communications; dramatic/theater arts; engineering; engineering technology; English; ethnic, cultural minority, gender, and group studies related; film/cinema/video studies; foreign languages and literatures; French; geography; geology/earth science; health and physical education/fitness; history; humanities; interior design; international relations and affairs; landscaping and groundskeeping; liberal arts and sciences/liberal studies; machine tool technology; mass communication/media; mathematics; medical administrative assistant and medical secretary; medical/clinical assistant; music; office management; physical sciences; physics; plant nursery management; political science and government; psychology; real estate; registered nursing/registered nurse; social sciences; Spanish; speech communication and rhetoric.

Academics *Calendar:* semesters. *Degree:* certificates and associate. *Special study options:* academic remediation for entering students, advanced placement credit, cooperative education, distance learning, English as a second language, part-time degree program, services for LD students, summer session for credit.

Library Main Library plus 1 other.

Student Life *Housing:* college housing not available. *Activities and Organizations:* drama/theater group, student-run newspaper. *Campus security:* 24-hour emergency response devices and patrols. *Student services:* health clinic, personal/psychological counseling.

Athletics *Intercollegiate sports:* baseball M, basketball M/W, soccer M/W, softball W, swimming and diving M/W, track and field M/W, volleyball W, water polo M/W.

Costs (2013–14) *Tuition:* state resident $1380 full-time, $46 per credit hour part-time; nonresident $7530 full-time, $251 per credit hour part-time. Full-time tuition and fees vary according to course load. Part-time tuition and fees vary according to course load. *Required fees:* $20 per term part-time. *Payment plan:* installment.

Applying *Options:* electronic application, early admission. *Application deadlines:* rolling (freshmen), rolling (transfers).

Freshman Application Contact College of Marin, 835 College Avenue, Kentfield, CA 94904. *Phone:* 415-485-9414.

Website: http://www.marin.edu/.

College of San Mateo
San Mateo, California

Director of Admissions Mr. Henry Villareal, Dean of Admissions and Records, College of San Mateo, 1700 West Hillsdale Boulevard, San Mateo, CA 94402-3784. *Phone:* 650-574-6590. *E-mail:* csmadmission@smccd.edu. *Website:* http://www.collegeofsanmateo.edu/.

College of the Canyons
Santa Clarita, California

- **State and locally supported** 2-year, founded 1969, part of California Community College System
- **Suburban** 224-acre campus with easy access to Los Angeles
- **Coed,** 16,997 undergraduate students

Undergraduates 5% Black or African American, non-Hispanic/Latino; 44% Hispanic/Latino; 9% Asian, non-Hispanic/Latino; 0.2% Native Hawaiian or other Pacific Islander, non-Hispanic/Latino; 0.2% American Indian or Alaska Native, non-Hispanic/Latino; 0.4% Two or more races, non-Hispanic/Latino; 0.6% Race/ethnicity unknown.

Freshmen *Admission:* 3,113 applied, 3,113 admitted.

Majors Accounting technology and bookkeeping; administrative assistant and secretarial science; animation, interactive technology, video graphics and special effects; architectural drafting and CAD/CADD; art; athletic training; automobile/automotive mechanics technology; biological and physical sciences; building/construction site management; business administration and management; child-care provision; cinematography and film/video production; computer science; computer systems networking and telecommunications; criminal justice/police science; dramatic/theater arts; English; fire prevention and safety technology; French; geography; graphic design; health and physical education/fitness; history; hospitality administration; hotel/motel administration; humanities; interior design; journalism; legal assistant/paralegal; liberal arts and sciences/liberal studies; manufacturing engineering technology; mathematics; music; parks, recreation and leisure; philosophy; photography; physics; political science and government; pre-engineering; psychology; radio and television; real estate; registered nursing/registered nurse; restaurant, culinary, and catering management; sales, distribution, and marketing operations; sign language interpretation and translation; small business administration; social sciences; sociology; Spanish; speech communication and rhetoric; surveying technology; water quality and wastewater treatment management and recycling technology; welding technology.

Academics *Calendar:* semesters. *Degree:* certificates and associate. *Special study options:* academic remediation for entering students, accelerated degree program, adult/continuing education programs, advanced placement credit, cooperative education, distance learning, double majors, English as a second language, honors programs, internships, part-time degree program, services for LD students, summer session for credit.

Library College of the Canyons Library with 61,947 titles, 139 serial subscriptions, 5,954 audiovisual materials, an OPAC, a Web page.

Student Life *Housing:* college housing not available. *Activities and Organizations:* drama/theater group, choral group, COC Film Club, National Student Nurses Association, Grad Club, American Sign Language Club, Parallax Photography Club. *Campus security:* 24-hour emergency response devices, late-night transport/escort service. *Student services:* health clinic, personal/psychological counseling, women's center.

Athletics *Intercollegiate sports:* baseball M, basketball M/W, cross-country running M/W, football M, golf M/W, ice hockey M(c), softball W, swimming and diving M/W, track and field M/W, volleyball W.

Costs (2014–15) *Tuition:* state resident $1154 full-time, $46 per unit part-time; nonresident $5450 full-time, $225 per unit part-time. Full-time tuition and fees vary according to course load. Part-time tuition and fees vary according to course load. *Required fees:* $50 full-time.

Financial Aid Of all full-time matriculated undergraduates who enrolled in 2012, 15,496 applied for aid, 9,185 were judged to have need.

Applying *Options:* electronic application. *Recommended:* high school transcript. *Application deadlines:* rolling (freshmen), rolling (transfers). *Notification:* continuous (freshmen), continuous (transfers).

Freshman Application Contact Ms. Jasmine Ruys, Director, Admissions and Records and Online Services, College of the Canyons, 26455 Rockwell Canyon Road, Santa Clarita, CA 91355. *Phone:* 661-362-3280. *Fax:* 661-254-7996. *E-mail:* jasmine.ruys@canyons.edu. *Website:* http://www.canyons.edu/.

College of the Desert
Palm Desert, California

- **State and locally supported** 2-year, founded 1959, part of California Community College System
- **Small-town** 160-acre campus
- **Endowment** $19.9 million
- **Coed,** 9,259 undergraduate students, 39% full-time, 54% women, 46% men

Undergraduates 3,629 full-time, 5,630 part-time. Students come from 39 other countries; 2% are from out of state; 4% Black or African American, non-Hispanic/Latino; 65% Hispanic/Latino; 3% Asian, non-Hispanic/Latino; 0.2% Native Hawaiian or other Pacific Islander, non-Hispanic/Latino; 0.3% American Indian or Alaska Native, non-Hispanic/Latino; 2% Two or more races, non-Hispanic/Latino; 1% Race/ethnicity unknown; 2% international; 4% transferred in. *Retention:* 75% of full-time freshmen returned.

Freshmen *Admission:* 1,520 enrolled.

Faculty *Total:* 423, 24% full-time, 18% with terminal degrees. *Student/faculty ratio:* 29:1.

Majors Agribusiness; agriculture; anthropology; applied horticulture/horticulture operations; architectural technology; art; automobile/automotive mechanics technology; biological and physical sciences; biology/biological sciences; building/construction site management; business administration and management; business/commerce; chemistry; child-care and support services management; computer graphics; computer science; creative writing; criminal justice/police science; crop production; culinary arts; dietetic technology; drafting and design technology; dramatic/theater arts; economics; English; environmental science; environmental studies; fire science/firefighting; French; geography; geology/earth science; health and physical education/fitness; heating, air conditioning, ventilation and refrigeration maintenance technology; history; hospitality administration; humanities; information technology; Italian; journalism; liberal arts and sciences/liberal studies; licensed practical/vocational nurse training; mass communication/media; mathematics; multi/interdisciplinary studies related; music; natural resources/conservation; office management; parks, recreation and leisure facilities management; philosophy; physics; political science and government; psychology; registered nursing/registered nurse; resort management; social sciences; sociology; Spanish; speech communication and rhetoric; substance abuse/addiction counseling; turf and turfgrass management; vehicle maintenance and repair technologies.

Academics *Calendar:* semesters. *Degree:* certificates, diplomas, and associate. *Special study options:* academic remediation for entering students, adult/continuing education programs, distance learning, double majors, English as a second language, freshman honors college, honors programs, independent study, part-time degree program, services for LD students, study abroad, summer session for credit.

Library College of the Desert Library plus 1 other with an OPAC, a Web page.

Student Life *Housing:* college housing not available. *Activities and Organizations:* drama/theater group, student-run newspaper, radio station, choral group, Student Nursing Association, Phi Theta Kappa, Gay Straight Alliance, International Club, Support and Education for Local Media and Arts (SELMA) SELMA Grows COD. *Campus security:* 24-hour emergency response devices and patrols, late-night transport/escort service. *Student services:* health clinic, personal/psychological counseling.

Athletics Member NJCAA. *Intercollegiate sports:* baseball M, basketball M/W, cross-country running M/W, fencing M/W, football M, golf M/W, soccer M/W, softball W, tennis M/W, track and field M/W, volleyball W.

Costs (2014–15) *Tuition:* state resident $1289 full-time, $46 per unit part-time; nonresident $6609 full-time, $236 per unit part-time. Full-time tuition and fees vary according to course load and program. Part-time tuition and fees vary according to course load and program. *Required fees:* $38 full-time, $0 per unit part-time, $20 per term part-time. *Payment plan:* installment. *Waivers:* employees or children of employees.

Applying *Options:* electronic application. *Application deadlines:* rolling (freshmen), rolling (transfers). *Notification:* continuous (freshmen), continuous (transfers).

Freshman Application Contact College of the Desert, 43-500 Monterey Avenue, Palm Desert, CA 92260-9305. *Phone:* 760-346-8041 Ext. 7441. *Website:* http://www.collegeofthedesert.edu/.

College of the Redwoods
Eureka, California

Freshman Application Contact Director of Enrollment Management, College of the Redwoods, 7351 Tompkins Hill Road, Eureka, CA 95501-9300. *Phone:* 707-476-4100. *Toll-free phone:* 800-641-0400. *Fax:* 707-476-4400. *Website:* http://www.redwoods.edu/.

College of the Sequoias
Visalia, California

Freshman Application Contact Ms. Lisa Hott, Director for Admissions, College of the Sequoias, 915 South Mooney Boulevard, Visalia, CA 93277-2234. *Phone:* 559-737-4844. *Fax:* 559-737-4820. *Website:* http://www.cos.edu/.

College of the Siskiyous
Weed, California

Freshman Application Contact Recruitment and Admissions, College of the Siskiyous, 800 College Avenue, Weed, CA 96094-2899. *Phone:* 530-938-5555. *Toll-free phone:* 888-397-4339. *E-mail:* admissions-weed@siskyous.edu. *Website:* http://www.siskiyous.edu/.

Columbia College
Sonora, California

- **State and locally supported** 2-year, founded 1968, part of Yosemite Community College District System
- **Rural** 200-acre campus
- **Endowment** $296,432
- **Coed,** 2,667 undergraduate students, 31% full-time, 55% women, 45% men

Undergraduates 826 full-time, 1,841 part-time. 1% Black or African American, non-Hispanic/Latino; 14% Hispanic/Latino; 2% Asian, non-Hispanic/Latino; 0.4% Native Hawaiian or other Pacific Islander, non-Hispanic/Latino; 2% American Indian or Alaska Native, non-Hispanic/Latino; 4% Two or more races, non-Hispanic/Latino; 3% Race/ethnicity unknown; 8% transferred in.

Freshmen *Admission:* 2,460 enrolled.

Faculty *Total:* 140, 35% full-time. *Student/faculty ratio:* 19:1.

Majors Administrative assistant and secretarial science; art; automobile/automotive mechanics technology; biological and physical sciences; biology/biological sciences; business administration and management; business/commerce; child-care provision; computer science; cooking and related culinary arts; emergency medical technology (EMT paramedic); English; environmental science; fire science/firefighting; forestry; geography related; geology/earth science; health and physical education/fitness; health services/allied health/health sciences; hotel/motel administration; humanities; human services; information technology; liberal arts and sciences/liberal studies; mathematics; medical administrative assistant and medical secretary; music; natural resources/conservation; photography; physical sciences; restaurant, culinary, and catering management; speech communication and rhetoric.

Academics *Calendar:* semesters. *Degree:* certificates and associate. *Special study options:* academic remediation for entering students, adult/continuing education programs, advanced placement credit, cooperative education, distance learning, double majors, English as a second language, independent study, internships, off-campus study, part-time degree program, services for LD students, summer session for credit.

Library Columbia College Library plus 1 other with an OPAC, a Web page.

Student Life *Housing:* college housing not available. *Activities and Organizations:* drama/theater group, student-run newspaper, choral group. *Campus security:* 24-hour emergency response devices and patrols, late-night transport/escort service. *Student services:* health clinic, personal/psychological counseling.

Athletics *Intercollegiate sports:* basketball M, volleyball W.

Costs (2014–15) *Tuition:* state resident $1150 full-time, $46 per credit part-time; nonresident $6046 full-time, $268 per credit part-time. *Required fees:* $1150 full-time, $46 per credit part-time, $35 per term part-time. *Room and board:* $10,862.

Financial Aid Of all full-time matriculated undergraduates who enrolled in 2010, 2,616 applied for aid, 2,232 were judged to have need. 29 Federal Work-Study jobs (averaging $1672). In 2010, 30 non-need-based awards were made. *Average non-need-based aid:* $100.

Applying *Options:* electronic application, early admission. *Required for some:* high school transcript, All new students are required to complete the matriculation process that may include assessment testing, orientation and advisement. *Application deadlines:* rolling (freshmen), rolling (transfers). *Notification:* continuous (freshmen), continuous (transfers).

Freshman Application Contact Admissions Office, Columbia College, 11600 Columbia College Drive, Sonora, CA 95370. *Phone:* 209-588-5231. *Fax:* 209-588-5337. *E-mail:* ccadmissions@yosemite.edu. *Website:* http://www.gocolumbia.edu/.

Community Christian College
Redlands, California

Freshman Application Contact Enrique D. Melendez, Assistant Director of Admissions, Community Christian College, 251 Tennessee Street, Redlands, CA 92373. *Phone:* 909-222-9556. *Fax:* 909-335-9101. *E-mail:* emelendez@cccollege.edu. *Website:* http://www.cccollege.edu/.

Concorde Career College
Garden Grove, California

Freshman Application Contact Chris Becker, Director, Concorde Career College, 12951 Euclid Street, Suite 101, Garden Grove, CA 92840. *Phone:* 714-703-1900. *Fax:* 714-530-4737. *E-mail:* cbecker@concorde.edu. *Website:* http://www.concorde.edu/.

Concorde Career College
North Hollywood, California

Freshman Application Contact Madeline Volker, Director, Concorde Career College, 12412 Victory Boulevard, North Hollywood, CA 91606. *Phone:* 818-766-8151. *Fax:* 818-766-1587. *E-mail:* mvolker@concorde.edu. *Website:* http://www.concorde.edu/.

Concorde Career College
San Bernardino, California

Admissions Office Contact Concorde Career College, 201 East Airport Drive, San Bernardino, CA 92408. *Website:* http://www.concorde.edu/.

Concorde Career College
San Diego, California

Admissions Office Contact Concorde Career College, 4393 Imperial Avenue, Suite 100, San Diego, CA 92113. *Website:* http://www.concorde.edu/.

Contra Costa College
San Pablo, California

Freshman Application Contact Admissions and Records Office, Contra Costa College, San Pablo, CA 94806. *Phone:* 510-235-7800 Ext. 7500. *Fax:* 510-412-0769. *E-mail:* A&R@contracosta.edu. *Website:* http://www.contracosta.edu/.

Copper Mountain College
Joshua Tree, California

- **State-supported** 2-year, founded 1966
- **Rural** 26-acre campus
- **Endowment** $102,297
- **Coed,** 2,500 undergraduate students, 68% full-time, 57% women, 43% men
- 90% of applicants were admitted

Undergraduates 1,712 full-time, 788 part-time. 7% Black or African American, non-Hispanic/Latino; 13% Hispanic/Latino; 4% Asian, non-Hispanic/Latino; 2% American Indian or Alaska Native, non-Hispanic/Latino; 7% Race/ethnicity unknown.

Freshmen *Admission:* 720 applied, 651 admitted, 2,500 enrolled.

Faculty *Total:* 112, 19% full-time.

Majors Anthropology; art; automobile/automotive mechanics technology; business administration and management; business/commerce; computer science; criminal justice/police science; drawing; economics; English; environmental science; fire science/firefighting; history; information technology; liberal arts and sciences/liberal studies; licensed practical/vocational nurse training; mathematics; philosophy; political science and government; psychology; registered nursing/registered nurse; social sciences; Spanish.

Academics *Calendar:* semesters. *Degree:* certificates and associate. *Special study options:* academic remediation for entering students, advanced placement credit, distance learning, English as a second language, honors programs, independent study, internships, off-campus study, services for LD students, summer session for credit.

Library Greenleaf Library with 9,500 titles, 1,300 serial subscriptions, 1,100 audiovisual materials.

Student Life *Housing:* college housing not available. *Activities and Organizations:* drama/theater group, Student Government, Literary Magazine, Christian Club, Service Club, Culture Club. *Campus security:* 24-hour emergency response devices.

Costs (2014–15) *Tuition:* state resident $1384 full-time; nonresident $8430 full-time. *Payment plan:* deferred payment.

Applying *Options:* electronic application. *Application deadlines:* rolling (freshmen), rolling (out-of-state freshmen), rolling (transfers). *Notification:* continuous (freshmen), continuous (out-of-state freshmen), continuous (transfers).

Freshman Application Contact Greg Brown, Executive Vice President for Academic and Student Affairs, Copper Mountain College, 6162 Rotary Way, Joshua Tree, CA 92252. *Phone:* 760-366-3791. *Toll-free phone:* 866-366-3791. *Fax:* 760-366-5257. *E-mail:* gbrown@cmccd.edu.

Website: http://www.cmccd.edu/.

Cosumnes River College
Sacramento, California

- **District-supported** 2-year, founded 1970, part of Los Rios Community College District System
- **Suburban** 180-acre campus with easy access to Sacramento
- **Coed,** 14,545 undergraduate students, 100% full-time, 51% women, 49% men

Undergraduates 14,545 full-time.

Faculty *Student/faculty ratio:* 34:1.

Majors Accounting technology and bookkeeping; administrative assistant and secretarial science; agribusiness; agriculture; architectural drafting and CAD/CADD; architectural technology; art; automobile/automotive mechanics technology; banking and financial support services; biological and physical sciences; broadcast journalism; building/construction site management; building/home/construction inspection; business administration and management; business/commerce; chemistry; child-care and support services management; child-care provision; computer programming; computer science; computer systems networking and telecommunications; construction trades related; dietetic technology; dramatic/theater arts; engineering; English; environmental studies; ethnic, cultural minority, gender, and group studies related; film/cinema/video studies; fire science/firefighting; geography; geology/earth science; graphic design; health and physical education/fitness; health information/medical records technology; health teacher education; horse husbandry/equine science and management; humanities; human services; information technology; journalism; liberal arts and sciences/liberal studies; mathematics; medical/clinical assistant; music; network and system administration; pharmacy technician; photographic and film/video technology; physics; plant nursery management; public relations/image management; radio and television; real estate; restaurant, culinary, and catering management; sales, distribution, and marketing operations; small business administration; social sciences; Spanish; speech communication and rhetoric; veterinary/animal health technology.

Academics *Calendar:* semesters. *Degree:* certificates and associate. *Special study options:* academic remediation for entering students, accelerated degree program, adult/continuing education programs, advanced placement credit, cooperative education, distance learning, double majors, English as a second language, freshman honors college, honors programs, independent study, internships, off-campus study, part-time degree program, services for LD students, study abroad, summer session for credit.

Library Cosumnes River College Library plus 1 other with an OPAC, a Web page.

Student Life *Housing:* college housing not available. *Activities and Organizations:* drama/theater group, student-run newspaper, radio and television station, choral group. *Campus security:* 24-hour emergency response devices and patrols, student patrols, late-night transport/escort service. *Student services:* health clinic, personal/psychological counseling.

Financial Aid Of all full-time matriculated undergraduates who enrolled in 2012, 139 Federal Work-Study jobs (averaging $2000).

Applying *Options:* electronic application, early admission. *Application deadlines:* 8/1 (freshmen), 8/15 (transfers). *Notification:* continuous until 8/15 (freshmen), continuous until 8/15 (transfers).

Freshman Application Contact Admissions and Records, Cosumnes River College, 8401 Center Parkway, Sacramento, CA 95823-5799. *Phone:* 916-691-7411.

Website: http://www.crc.losrios.edu/.

Crafton Hills College
Yucaipa, California

Director of Admissions Larry Aycock, Admissions and Records Coordinator, Crafton Hills College, 11711 Sand Canyon Road, Yucaipa, CA 92399-1799. *Phone:* 909-389-3663. *E-mail:* laycock@craftonhills.edu.
Website: http://www.craftonhills.edu/.

Cuesta College
San Luis Obispo, California

Freshman Application Contact Cuesta College, PO Box 8106, San Luis Obispo, CA 93403-8106. *Phone:* 805-546-3130 Ext. 2262.
Website: http://www.cuesta.edu/.

Cuyamaca College
El Cajon, California

Freshman Application Contact Ms. Susan Topham, Dean of Admissions and Records, Cuyamaca College, 900 Rancho San Diego Parkway, El Cajon, CA 92019-4304. *Phone:* 619-660-4302. *Fax:* 619-660-4575. *E-mail:* susan.topham@gcccd.edu.
Website: http://www.cuyamaca.net/.

Cypress College
Cypress, California

Freshman Application Contact Admissions Office, Cypress College, 9200 Valley View, Cypress, CA 90630-5897. *Phone:* 714-484-7346. *Fax:* 714-484-7446. *E-mail:* admissions@cypresscollege.edu.
Website: http://www.cypresscollege.edu/.

De Anza College
Cupertino, California

- **State and locally supported** 2-year, founded 1967, part of California Community College System
- **Suburban** 112-acre campus with easy access to San Francisco, San Jose
- **Coed,** 23,833 undergraduate students, 43% full-time, 49% women, 51% men

Undergraduates 10,365 full-time, 13,468 part-time. 4% Black or African American, non-Hispanic/Latino; 23% Hispanic/Latino; 35% Asian, non-Hispanic/Latino; 0.5% Native Hawaiian or other Pacific Islander, non-Hispanic/Latino; 0.5% American Indian or Alaska Native, non-Hispanic/Latino; 5% Two or more races, non-Hispanic/Latino; 6% Race/ethnicity unknown.

Freshmen *Admission:* 23,833 enrolled.

Faculty *Total:* 738, 39% full-time. *Student/faculty ratio:* 36:1.

Majors Accounting; administrative assistant and secretarial science; art; art history, criticism and conservation; automobile/automotive mechanics technology; behavioral sciences; biology/biological sciences; business administration and management; business machine repair; ceramic arts and ceramics; child development; commercial and advertising art; computer graphics; computer programming; computer science; construction engineering technology; corrections; criminal justice/law enforcement administration; criminal justice/police science; developmental and child psychology; drafting/design engineering technologies related; dramatic/theater arts; drawing; economics; engineering; engineering technology; English; environmental studies; film/cinema/video studies; history; humanities; industrial technology; information science/studies; international relations and affairs; journalism; legal assistant/paralegal; liberal arts and sciences/liberal studies; licensed practical/vocational nurse training; machine tool technology; marketing/marketing management; mass communication/media; mathematics; medical/clinical assistant; music; philosophy; photography; physical education teaching and coaching; physical therapy; physics; political science and government; pre-engineering; printmaking; professional, technical, business, and scientific writing; psychology; purchasing, procurement/acquisitions and contracts management; radio and television; real estate; registered nursing/registered nurse; rhetoric and composition; sculpture; social sciences; sociology; Spanish.

Academics *Calendar:* quarters. *Degree:* certificates, diplomas, and associate. *Special study options:* academic remediation for entering students, adult/continuing education programs, advanced placement credit, cooperative education, distance learning, English as a second language, external degree program, honors programs, independent study, internships, part-time degree program, services for LD students, student-designed majors, study abroad, summer session for credit. *ROTC:* Army (c), Air Force (c).

Library A. Robert DeHart Learning Center with 80,000 titles, 927 serial subscriptions, an OPAC, a Web page.

Student Life *Housing:* college housing not available. *Activities and Organizations:* drama/theater group, student-run newspaper, choral group, Student Nurses Association, Phi Theta Kappa, Automotive Club, Vietnamese Club, Filipino Club. *Campus security:* 24-hour emergency response devices, student patrols, late-night transport/escort service. *Student services:* health clinic, personal/psychological counseling, legal services.

Athletics Member NCAA. All Division II. *Intercollegiate sports:* baseball M, basketball M/W, cross-country running M/W, football M, golf M/W, soccer M/W, softball W, swimming and diving M/W, tennis M/W, track and field M/W, volleyball M/W, water polo M. *Intramural sports:* badminton M/W, basketball M, soccer M/W, swimming and diving M/W, volleyball M/W.

Costs (2014–15) *Tuition:* state resident $1494 full-time; nonresident $6048 full-time, $144 per credit part-time. Full-time tuition and fees vary according to course load. Part-time tuition and fees vary according to course load. *Required fees:* $167 full-time, $31 per credit part-time, $58 per term part-time. *Payment plan:* installment. *Waivers:* minority students and adult students.

Freshman Application Contact De Anza College, 21250 Stevens Creek Boulevard, Cupertino, CA 95014-5793. *Phone:* 408-864-8292.

Website: http://www.deanza.fhda.edu/.

Deep Springs College
Deep Springs, California

- **Independent** 2-year, founded 1917
- **Rural** 3000-acre campus
- **Endowment** $18.0 million
- **Men only**

Undergraduates 26 full-time. Students come from 18 states and territories; 3 other countries; 80% are from out of state; 62% transferred in; 100% live on campus. *Retention:* 100% of full-time freshmen returned.

Faculty *Student/faculty ratio:* 5:1.

Academics *Calendar:* 6 seven-week terms. *Degree:* associate. *Special study options:* advanced placement credit, distance learning, freshman honors college, honors programs, independent study, internships, services for LD students, summer session for credit.

Student Life *Campus security:* 24-hour emergency response devices, late-night transport/escort service.

Standardized Tests *Required:* SAT and SAT Subject Tests or ACT (for admission).

Costs (2013–14) *Comprehensive fee:* includes mandatory fees ($800). Every student accepted to Deep Springs receives a scholarship covering tuition, room, and board.

Applying *Required:* essay or personal statement, high school transcript, interview.

Freshman Application Contact David Neidorf, President, Deep Springs College, HC 72, Box 45001, Dyer, NV 89010-9803. *Phone:* 760-872-2000 Ext. 45. *Fax:* 760-874-0314. *E-mail:* apcom@deepsprings.edu.

Website: http://www.deepsprings.edu/.

Diablo Valley College
Pleasant Hill, California

Freshman Application Contact Ileana Dorn, Director of Admissions and Records, Diablo Valley College, Pleasant Hill, CA 94523-1529. *Phone:* 925-685-1230 Ext. 2330. *Fax:* 925-609-8085. *E-mail:* idorn@dvc.edu.

Website: http://www.dvc.edu/.

East Los Angeles College
Monterey Park, California

Freshman Application Contact Mr. Jeremy Allred, Associate Dean of Admissions, East Los Angeles College, 1301 Avenida Cesar Chavez, Monterey Park, CA 91754. *Phone:* 323-265-8801. *Fax:* 323-265-8688. *E-mail:* allredjp@elac.edu.

Website: http://www.elac.edu/.

El Camino College
Torrance, California

Director of Admissions Mr. William Mulrooney, Director of Admissions, El Camino College, 16007 Crenshaw Boulevard, Torrance, CA 90506-0001. *Phone:* 310-660-3418. *Toll-free phone:* 866-ELCAMINO. *Fax:* 310-660-6779. *E-mail:* wmulrooney@elcamino.edu.

Website: http://www.elcamino.edu/.

Empire College
Santa Rosa, California

Freshman Application Contact Ms. Dahnja Barker, Admissions Officer, Empire College, 3035 Cleveland Avenue, Santa Rosa, CA 95403. *Phone:* 707-546-4000. *Toll-free phone:* 877-395-8535.

Website: http://www.empcol.edu/.

Everest College
City of Industry, California

Freshman Application Contact Admissions Office, Everest College, 12801 Crossroads Parkway South, City of Industry, CA 91746. *Phone:* 562-908-2500. *Toll-free phone:* 888-741-4270. *Fax:* 562-908-7656.

Website: http://www.everest.edu/.

Everest College
Los Angeles, California

Admissions Office Contact Everest College, 3000 South Robertson Boulevard, Suite 300, Los Angeles, CA 90034.

Website: http://www.everest.edu/.

Everest College
Ontario, California

Freshman Application Contact Admissions Office, Everest College, 1819 South Excise Avenue, Ontario, CA 91761. *Phone:* 909-484-4311. *Toll-free phone:* 888-741-4270. *Fax:* 909-484-1162.

Website: http://www.everest.edu/.

Evergreen Valley College
San Jose, California

Freshman Application Contact Evergreen Valley College, 3095 Yerba Buena Road, San Jose, CA 95135-1598. *Phone:* 408-270-6423.

Website: http://www.evc.edu/.

Feather River College
Quincy, California

- **State and locally supported** 2-year, founded 1968, part of California Community College System
- **Rural** 150-acre campus
- **Coed,** 1,785 undergraduate students, 36% full-time, 47% women, 53% men

Undergraduates 639 full-time, 1,146 part-time. 15% are from out of state; 13% Black or African American, non-Hispanic/Latino; 20% Hispanic/Latino; 5% Asian, non-Hispanic/Latino; 1% Native Hawaiian or other Pacific Islander, non-Hispanic/Latino; 3% American Indian or Alaska Native, non-Hispanic/Latino; 0.7% Two or more races, non-Hispanic/Latino; 5% Race/ethnicity unknown; 2% international; 16% transferred in. *Retention:* 52% of full-time freshmen returned.

Freshmen *Admission:* 354 enrolled.

Faculty *Total:* 98, 23% full-time. *Student/faculty ratio:* 23:1.

Majors Administrative assistant and secretarial science; agriculture; biology/biological sciences; business/commerce; child-care provision; criminal justice/police science; English; environmental studies; equestrian studies; foods, nutrition, and wellness; health and physical education/fitness; history; humanities; liberal arts and sciences/liberal studies; licensed practical/vocational nurse training; mathematics; natural resources/conservation; parks, recreation and leisure; physical sciences; social sciences; visual and performing arts; wildlife, fish and wildlands science and management.

Academics *Calendar:* semesters. *Degree:* certificates, diplomas, and associate. *Special study options:* academic remediation for entering students, adult/continuing education programs, advanced placement credit, cooperative education, distance learning, double majors, honors programs, independent study, part-time degree program, services for LD students, summer session for credit.

Library Feather River Library with 21,598 titles, 125 serial subscriptions, an OPAC.

Student Life *Housing Options:* Campus housing is university owned. *Activities and Organizations:* drama/theater group. *Campus security:* student patrols. *Student services:* health clinic.

Athletics *Intercollegiate sports:* baseball M, basketball M/W, cross-country running W, equestrian sports M/W, football M, soccer M/W, track and field W, volleyball W.

Costs (2014–15) *Tuition:* state resident $1380 full-time, $46 per credit part-time; nonresident $7230 full-time, $241 per credit part-time. *Room and board:* room only: $4250. *Payment plan:* installment.

Financial Aid Of all full-time matriculated undergraduates who enrolled in 2012, 22 Federal Work-Study jobs (averaging $750). 103 state and other part-time jobs (averaging $1504).

Applying *Options:* electronic application.

Freshman Application Contact Leslie Mikesell, Director of Admissions and Records, Feather River College, 570 Golden Eagle Avenue, Quincy, CA 95971-9124. *Phone:* 530-283-0202. *Toll-free phone:* 800-442-9799. *E-mail:* lmikesell@frc.edu.

Website: http://www.frc.edu/.

FIDM/The Fashion Institute of Design & Merchandising, Los Angeles Campus

Los Angeles, California

- **Proprietary** primarily 2-year, founded 1969, part of The Fashion Institute of Design and Merchandising/FIDM
- **Urban** campus
- **Coed,** 3,459 undergraduate students, 89% full-time, 89% women, 11% men

Undergraduates 3,072 full-time, 387 part-time. Students come from 58 other countries; 41% are from out of state; 6% Black or African American, non-Hispanic/Latino; 23% Hispanic/Latino; 12% Asian, non-Hispanic/Latino; 1% Native Hawaiian or other Pacific Islander, non-Hispanic/Latino; 0.5% American Indian or Alaska Native, non-Hispanic/Latino; 3% Two or more races, non-Hispanic/Latino; 8% Race/ethnicity unknown; 13% international; 16% transferred in. *Retention:* 93% of full-time freshmen returned.

Freshmen *Admission:* 1,624 applied, 802 admitted, 523 enrolled.

Faculty *Total:* 275, 24% full-time. *Student/faculty ratio:* 23:1.

Majors Apparel and accessories marketing; apparel and textiles; business administration and management; commercial and advertising art; consumer merchandising/retailing management; design and visual communications; fashion/apparel design; fashion merchandising; interior design; metal and jewelry arts.

Academics *Calendar:* quarters. *Degrees:* associate and bachelor's (also includes Orange County Campus). *Special study options:* academic remediation for entering students, adult/continuing education programs, advanced placement credit, cooperative education, distance learning, English as a second language, independent study, internships, part-time degree program, services for LD students, study abroad, summer session for credit.

Library FIDM Los Angeles Campus Library plus 1 other with 32,667 titles, 249 serial subscriptions, 7,250 audiovisual materials, an OPAC, a Web page.

Student Life *Activities and Organizations:* Cross-Cultural Student Alliance, Fashion Industry Club, Phi Theta Kappa Honor Society, Student Council, MODE. *Campus security:* 24-hour emergency response devices and patrols, late-night transport/escort service. *Student services:* personal/psychological counseling.

Standardized Tests *Recommended:* SAT or ACT (for admission).

Costs (2014–15) *Tuition:* $27,955 full-time. *Payment plan:* installment. *Waivers:* employees or children of employees.

Financial Aid Of all full-time matriculated undergraduates who enrolled in 2012, 88 Federal Work-Study jobs (averaging $2935).

Applying *Options:* electronic application, deferred entrance. *Application fee:* $225. *Required:* essay or personal statement, high school transcript, minimum 2.0 GPA, 3 letters of recommendation, interview, major-determined project. *Application deadlines:* rolling (freshmen), rolling (out-of-state freshmen), rolling (transfers).

Freshman Application Contact Ms. Susan Aronson, Director of Admissions, FIDM/The Fashion Institute of Design & Merchandising, Los Angeles Campus, Los Angeles, CA 90015. *Phone:* 213-624-1201. *Toll-free phone:* 800-624-1200. *Fax:* 213-624-4799. *E-mail:* saronson@fidm.com.

Website: http://www.fidm.edu/.

See display below and page 432 for the College Close-Up.

FIDM/The Fashion Institute of Design & Merchandising, Orange County Campus

Irvine, California

- **Proprietary** 2-year, founded 1981, part of The Fashion Institute of Design and Merchandising/FIDM
- **Coed, primarily women,** 214 undergraduate students, 96% full-time, 89% women, 11% men

Undergraduates 205 full-time, 9 part-time. Students come from 10 states and territories; 3 other countries; 13% are from out of state; 3% Black or African American, non-Hispanic/Latino; 29% Hispanic/Latino; 14% Asian, non-Hispanic/Latino; 1% Native Hawaiian or other Pacific Islander, non-Hispanic/Latino; 0.9% American Indian or Alaska Native, non-Hispanic/Latino; 3% Two or more races, non-Hispanic/Latino; 2% Race/ethnicity unknown; 4% international; 29% transferred in. *Retention:* 79% of full-time freshmen returned.

Freshmen *Admission:* 294 applied, 198 admitted, 115 enrolled.

Faculty *Total:* 21, 24% full-time. *Student/faculty ratio:* 20:1.

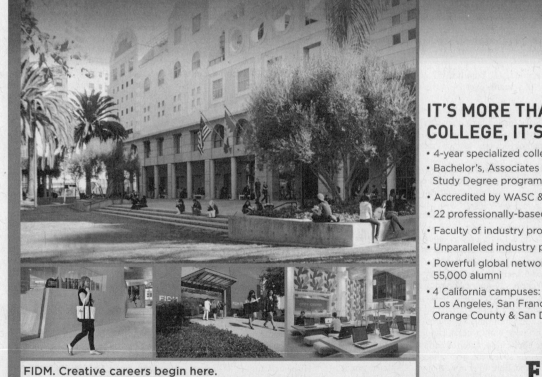

FIDM. Creative careers begin here.

IT'S MORE THAN A COLLEGE, IT'S FIDM.

- 4-year specialized college
- Bachelor's, Associates & Advanced Study Degree programs
- Accredited by WASC & NASAD
- 22 professionally-based majors
- Faculty of industry professionals
- Unparalleled industry partnerships
- Powerful global network of 55,000 alumni
- 4 California campuses: Los Angeles, San Francisco, Orange County & San Diego

FIDM

Visit fidm.edu or call 800.624.1200

Majors Apparel and textiles; commercial and advertising art; consumer merchandising/retailing management; fashion/apparel design; fashion merchandising; fiber, textile and weaving arts; industrial technology; interior design; marketing/marketing management.

Academics *Calendar:* quarters. *Degree:* associate. *Special study options:* academic remediation for entering students, adult/continuing education programs, advanced placement credit, cooperative education, distance learning, English as a second language, independent study, internships, part-time degree program, services for LD students, study abroad, summer session for credit.

Library FIDM Orange County Campus Library plus 1 other with 3,915 titles, 65 serial subscriptions, 3,273 audiovisual materials, an OPAC, a Web page.

Student Life *Activities and Organizations:* MODE, Student Council, Phi Theta Kappa- National Honor Society, Fashion Industry Club, Cross-Cultural Student Alliance. *Campus security:* 24-hour emergency response devices, late-night transport/escort service. *Student services:* personal/psychological counseling.

Costs (2014–15) *Tuition:* $27,955 full-time. *Required fees:* $965 full-time. *Payment plan:* installment. *Waivers:* employees or children of employees.

Applying *Options:* deferred entrance. *Application fee:* $225. *Required:* essay or personal statement, high school transcript, minimum 2.0 GPA, 3 letters of recommendation, interview, entrance requirement project. *Application deadlines:* rolling (freshmen), rolling (out-of-state freshmen), rolling (transfers). *Notification:* continuous (freshmen), continuous (out-of-state freshmen), continuous (transfers).

Freshman Application Contact Admissions, FIDM/The Fashion Institute of Design & Merchandising, Orange County Campus, 17590 Gillette Avenue, Irvine, CA 92614-5610. *Phone:* 949-851-6200. *Toll-free phone:* 888-974-3436. *Fax:* 949-851-6808.
Website: http://www.fidm.edu/.

FIDM/The Fashion Institute of Design & Merchandising, San Diego Campus
San Diego, California

- **Proprietary** 2-year, founded 1985, part of The Fashion Institute of Design and Merchandising/FIDM
- **Urban** campus
- **Coed, primarily women,** 169 undergraduate students, 89% full-time, 95% women, 5% men

Undergraduates 151 full-time, 18 part-time. Students come from 11 states and territories; 5 other countries; 23% are from out of state; 4% Black or African American, non-Hispanic/Latino; 36% Hispanic/Latino; 7% Asian, non-Hispanic/Latino; 2% Native Hawaiian or other Pacific Islander, non-Hispanic/Latino; 1% American Indian or Alaska Native, non-Hispanic/Latino; 2% Two or more races, non-Hispanic/Latino; 4% Race/ethnicity unknown; 4% international; 25% transferred in. *Retention:* 68% of full-time freshmen returned.

Freshmen *Admission:* 187 applied, 112 admitted, 67 enrolled. *Test scores:* ACT scores over 18: 100%; ACT scores over 24: 40%; ACT scores over 30: 10%.

Faculty *Total:* 22, 9% full-time. *Student/faculty ratio:* 19:1.

Majors Apparel and accessories marketing; commercial and advertising art; consumer merchandising/retailing management; design and visual communications; fashion/apparel design; fashion merchandising; interior design.

Academics *Calendar:* quarters. *Degree:* associate. *Special study options:* academic remediation for entering students, adult/continuing education programs, advanced placement credit, cooperative education, distance learning, English as a second language, independent study, internships, part-time degree program, services for LD students, study abroad, summer session for credit.

Library FIDM San Diego Campus Library plus 1 other with 6,856 titles, 119 serial subscriptions, 3,846 audiovisual materials, an OPAC.

Student Life *Activities and Organizations:* MODE, Student Council, Phi Theta Kappa- National Honor Society, Fashion Industry Club, Cross-Cultural Student Alliance. *Campus security:* 24-hour emergency response devices and patrols. *Student services:* personal/psychological counseling.

Standardized Tests *Recommended:* SAT or ACT (for admission).

Costs (2014–15) *Tuition:* $27,955 full-time. *Required fees:* $965 full-time. *Payment plan:* installment. *Waivers:* employees or children of employees.

Applying *Options:* electronic application, deferred entrance. *Application fee:* $225. *Required:* essay or personal statement, high school transcript, minimum 2.0 GPA, 3 letters of recommendation, interview, major-determined project. *Application deadlines:* rolling (freshmen), rolling (out-of-state freshmen), rolling (transfers).

Freshman Application Contact Ms. Susan Aronson, Director of Admissions, FIDM/The Fashion Institute of Design & Merchandising, San Diego Campus, San Diego, CA 92101. *Phone:* 213-624-1200 Ext. 5400. *Toll-free phone:* 800-243-3436. *Fax:* 619-232-4322. *E-mail:* info@fidm.com.
Website: http://www.fidm.edu/.

FIDM/The Fashion Institute of Design & Merchandising, San Francisco Campus
San Francisco, California

- **Proprietary** 2-year, founded 1973, part of The Fashion Institute of Design and Merchandising/FIDM
- **Urban** campus
- **Coed,** 637 undergraduate students, 91% full-time, 93% women, 7% men

Undergraduates 580 full-time, 57 part-time. Students come from 6 states and territories; 13 other countries; 5% are from out of state; 5% Black or African American, non-Hispanic/Latino; 22% Hispanic/Latino; 18% Asian, non-Hispanic/Latino; 2% Native Hawaiian or other Pacific Islander, non-Hispanic/Latino; 0.6% American Indian or Alaska Native, non-Hispanic/Latino; 4% Two or more races, non-Hispanic/Latino; 6% Race/ethnicity unknown; 5% international; 20% transferred in. *Retention:* 100% of full-time freshmen returned.

Freshmen *Admission:* 306 applied, 156 admitted, 112 enrolled. *Test scores:* ACT scores over 18: 100%; ACT scores over 24: 40%; ACT scores over 30: 10%.

Faculty *Total:* 56, 16% full-time. *Student/faculty ratio:* 24:1.

Majors Apparel and accessories marketing; apparel and textiles; commercial and advertising art; consumer merchandising/retailing management; design and visual communications; fashion/apparel design; fashion merchandising; interior design.

Academics *Calendar:* quarters. *Degree:* associate. *Special study options:* academic remediation for entering students, adult/continuing education programs, advanced placement credit, cooperative education, distance learning, English as a second language, honors programs, independent study, internships, off-campus study, part-time degree program, services for LD students, study abroad, summer session for credit.

Library FIDM San Francisco Library plus 1 other with 9,249 titles, 149 serial subscriptions, 3,738 audiovisual materials, an OPAC, a Web page.

Student Life *Housing:* college housing not available. *Activities and Organizations:* MODE, Student Council, Phi Theta Kappa- National Honor Society, Fashion Industry Club, Cross-Cultural Student Alliance. *Campus security:* 24-hour emergency response devices and patrols. *Student services:* personal/psychological counseling.

Standardized Tests *Recommended:* SAT or ACT (for admission).

Costs (2014–15) *Tuition:* $27,955 full-time. *Required fees:* $965 full-time. *Payment plan:* installment. *Waivers:* employees or children of employees.

Applying *Options:* electronic application, deferred entrance. *Application fee:* $225. *Required:* essay or personal statement, high school transcript, 3 letters of recommendation, interview, major-determined project. *Application deadlines:* rolling (freshmen), rolling (out-of-state freshmen), rolling (transfers).

Freshman Application Contact Ms. Susan Aronson, Director of Admissions, FIDM/The Fashion Institute of Design & Merchandising, San Francisco Campus, San Francisco, CA 94108. *Phone:* 213-624-1201. *Toll-free phone:* 800-422-3436. *Fax:* 415-296-7299. *E-mail:* info@fidm.com.
Website: http://www.fidm.edu/.

Folsom Lake College
Folsom, California

Freshman Application Contact Admissions Office, Folsom Lake College, 10 College Parkway, Folsom, CA 95630. *Phone:* 916-608-6500.
Website: http://www.flc.losrios.edu/.

Foothill College
Los Altos Hills, California

- **State and locally supported** 2-year, founded 1958, part of Foothill-DeAnza Community College District
- **Suburban** 122-acre campus with easy access to San Jose
- **Endowment** $15.0 million
- **Coed**

Undergraduates 5,191 full-time, 10,574 part-time. Students come from 16 states and territories; 109 other countries; 1% are from out of state; 4% Black or African American, non-Hispanic/Latino; 19% Hispanic/Latino; 22% Asian, non-Hispanic/Latino; 1% Native Hawaiian or other Pacific Islander, non-Hispanic/Latino; 0.3% American Indian or Alaska Native, non-Hispanic/Latino; 4% Two or more races, non-Hispanic/Latino; 3% Race/ethnicity unknown; 6% international.

Academics *Calendar:* quarters. *Degree:* certificates and associate. *Special study options:* academic remediation for entering students, accelerated degree program, adult/continuing education programs, advanced placement credit, cooperative education, distance learning, English as a second language, honors programs, independent study, internships, off-campus study, part-time degree program, services for LD students, student-designed majors, study abroad, summer session for credit. *ROTC:* Army (c), Air Force (c).

Student Life *Campus security:* 24-hour emergency response devices and patrols, late-night transport/escort service.

Athletics Member NJCAA.

Costs (2013–14) *Tuition:* state resident $1224 full-time; nonresident $6192 full-time. Full-time tuition and fees vary according to course load. Part-time tuition and fees vary according to course load.

Financial Aid Of all full-time matriculated undergraduates who enrolled in 2012, 80 Federal Work-Study jobs (averaging $1300). 210 state and other part-time jobs.

Applying *Options:* electronic application. *Recommended:* high school transcript.

Freshman Application Contact Ms. Shawna Aced, Registrar, Foothill College, Admissions and Records, 12345 El Monte Road, Los Altos Hills, CA 94022. *Phone:* 650-949-7771. *E-mail:* acedshawna@hda.edu.
Website: http://www.foothill.edu/.

Fremont College

Cerritos, California

Admissions Office Contact Fremont College, 18000 Studebaker Road, 9th Floor, Cerritos, CA 90703. *Toll-free phone:* 877-344-2345.
Website: http://www.fremont.edu/.

Fresno City College

Fresno, California

Freshman Application Contact Office Assistant, Fresno City College, 1101 East University Avenue, Fresno, CA 93741-0002. *Phone:* 559-442-4600 Ext. 8604. *Fax:* 559-237-4232. *E-mail:* fcc.admissions@fresnocitycollege.edu.
Website: http://www.fresnocitycollege.edu/.

Fullerton College

Fullerton, California

- **State and locally supported** 2-year, founded 1913, part of California Community College System
- **Suburban** 79-acre campus with easy access to Los Angeles
- **Coed,** 24,423 undergraduate students, 35% full-time, 51% women, 49% men

Undergraduates 8,538 full-time, 15,885 part-time. 4% transferred in. *Retention:* 78% of full-time freshmen returned.

Freshmen *Admission:* 2,360 enrolled.

Faculty *Student/faculty ratio:* 29:1.

Majors Accounting technology and bookkeeping; administrative assistant and secretarial science; anthropology; apparel and textile marketing management; apparel and textiles; applied horticulture/horticulture operations; architectural technology; area studies related; art; astronomy; automobile/automotive mechanics technology; biological and physical sciences; biology/biological sciences; biomedical technology; building/construction site management; building/home/construction inspection; business administration and management; carpentry; chemical technology; chemistry; child-care provision; computer science; construction trades related; cosmetology; criminal justice/police science; dance; drafting and design technology; dramatic/theater arts; economics; electrical/electronics equipment installation and repair; engineering; English; environmental studies; ethnic, cultural minority, gender, and group studies related; fashion/apparel design; foods, nutrition, and wellness; foreign languages and literatures; geography; geology/earth science; graphic and printing equipment operation/production; graphic design; hazardous materials management and waste technology; health and physical education/fitness; health/medical preparatory programs related; history; humanities; information technology; interior design; international business/trade/commerce; journalism; landscaping and groundskeeping; legal administrative assistant/secretary; legal assistant/paralegal; liberal arts and sciences/liberal studies; mass communication/media; mathematics; mechanical engineering/mechanical technology; microbiology; music; parks, recreation and leisure; philosophy; physics; plant nursery management; political science and government; psychology; radio and television; real estate; recording arts technology; religious studies; sales, distribution, and marketing operations; small business administration; sociology; speech communication and rhetoric; sport and fitness administration/management; technology/industrial arts teacher education.

Academics *Calendar:* semesters. *Degree:* certificates and associate. *Special study options:* academic remediation for entering students, adult/continuing education programs, advanced placement credit, cooperative education,

English as a second language, honors programs, part-time degree program, services for LD students, study abroad, summer session for credit. *ROTC:* Army (c), Navy (c), Air Force (c).

Library William T. Boyce Library.

Student Life *Housing:* college housing not available. *Activities and Organizations:* drama/theater group, student-run newspaper, radio station. *Student services:* health clinic, personal/psychological counseling, women's center, legal services.

Athletics *Intercollegiate sports:* badminton W, baseball M, basketball M/W, cross-country running M/W, football M, golf W, soccer M/W, softball W, swimming and diving M/W, tennis M/W, track and field M/W, volleyball W, water polo M/W.

Financial Aid *Financial aid deadline:* 6/30.

Applying *Options:* electronic application, early admission. *Application deadlines:* rolling (freshmen), rolling (transfers).

Freshman Application Contact Fullerton College, 321 East Chapman Avenue, Fullerton, CA 92832-2095. *Phone:* 714-992-7076.
Website: http://www.fullcoll.edu/.

Gavilan College

Gilroy, California

- **State and locally supported** 2-year, founded 1919, part of California Community College System
- **Rural** 150-acre campus with easy access to San Jose
- **Coed,** 5,267 undergraduate students, 34% full-time, 51% women, 49% men

Undergraduates 1,767 full-time, 3,500 part-time. Students come from 5 states and territories; 0.1% are from out of state; 3% Black or African American, non-Hispanic/Latino; 51% Hispanic/Latino; 6% Asian, non-Hispanic/Latino; 0.4% Native Hawaiian or other Pacific Islander, non-Hispanic/Latino; 0.6% American Indian or Alaska Native, non-Hispanic/Latino; 1% Two or more races, non-Hispanic/Latino; 5% Race/ethnicity unknown; 100% transferred in. *Retention:* 69% of full-time freshmen returned.

Freshmen *Admission:* 1,022 enrolled.

Faculty *Total:* 324, 23% full-time, 12% with terminal degrees. *Student/faculty ratio:* 30:1.

Majors Accounting technology and bookkeeping; administrative assistant and secretarial science; airframe mechanics and aircraft maintenance technology; art; biological and physical sciences; biology/biological sciences; business administration and management; business/commerce; carpentry; child-care provision; cinematography and film/video production; computer graphics; computer programming; computer science; computer systems networking and telecommunications; corrections; cosmetology; criminal justice/police science; data entry/microcomputer applications; desktop publishing and digital imaging design; drafting and design technology; dramatic/theater arts; engineering; English; family resource management; general studies; health and physical education/fitness; health/medical preparatory programs related; liberal arts and sciences/liberal studies; licensed practical/vocational nurse training; mathematics; medical administrative assistant and medical secretary; music; network and system administration; physical sciences; real estate; registered nursing/registered nurse; rhetoric and composition; social sciences; Spanish; theater design and technology; visual and performing arts.

Academics *Calendar:* semesters. *Degree:* certificates, diplomas, and associate. *Special study options:* academic remediation for entering students, adult/continuing education programs, advanced placement credit, cooperative education, distance learning, English as a second language, honors programs, independent study, internships, part-time degree program, services for LD students, study abroad, summer session for credit.

Library Gavilan Library with 60,587 titles, 2,541 serial subscriptions, an OPAC, a Web page.

Student Life *Housing:* college housing not available. *Activities and Organizations:* drama/theater group, student-run newspaper, choral group, EOPS, Rho Alpha Mu (Honor Society), Science Alliance, TADAA Drama Club, Vets Club. *Campus security:* 24-hour emergency response devices. *Student services:* health clinic, personal/psychological counseling.

Athletics *Intercollegiate sports:* baseball M, basketball M, football M, soccer M, softball W, volleyball W.

Financial Aid Of all full-time matriculated undergraduates who enrolled in 2012, 50 Federal Work-Study jobs (averaging $2000). *Financial aid deadline:* 6/30.

Applying *Application deadlines:* rolling (freshmen), rolling (out-of-state freshmen), rolling (transfers). *Notification:* continuous (freshmen), continuous (out-of-state freshmen), continuous (transfers).

Freshman Application Contact Gavilan College, 5055 Santa Teresa Boulevard, Gilroy, CA 95020-9599. *Phone:* 408-848-4754.
Website: http://www.gavilan.edu/.

Glendale Community College
Glendale, California

Freshman Application Contact Ms. Sharon Combs, Dean, Admissions, and Records, Glendale Community College, 1500 North Verdugo Road, Glendale, CA 91208. *Phone:* 818-240-1000 Ext. 5910. *E-mail:* scombs@glendale.edu. *Website:* http://www.glendale.edu/.

Golden West College
Huntington Beach, California

- **State and locally supported** 2-year, founded 1966, part of Coast Community College District System
- **Suburban** 122-acre campus with easy access to Los Angeles
- **Endowment** $880,684
- **Coed,** 12,333 undergraduate students, 36% full-time, 54% women, 46% men

Undergraduates 4,408 full-time, 7,925 part-time. 3% are from out of state; 2% Black or African American, non-Hispanic/Latino; 28% Hispanic/Latino; 28% Asian, non-Hispanic/Latino; 4% Two or more races, non-Hispanic/Latino; 4% Race/ethnicity unknown; 1% international. *Retention:* 76% of full-time freshmen returned.

Freshmen *Admission:* 8,323 applied, 8,323 admitted, 2,231 enrolled.

Faculty *Total:* 419, 30% full-time. *Student/faculty ratio:* 32:1.

Majors Accounting; administrative assistant and secretarial science; architectural engineering technology; art; automobile/automotive mechanics technology; biological and physical sciences; biology/biological sciences; business administration and management; commercial and advertising art; consumer merchandising/retailing management; cosmetology; criminal justice/law enforcement administration; criminal justice/police science; drafting and design technology; electrical, electronic and communications engineering technology; engineering technology; graphic and printing equipment operation/production; humanities; journalism; legal administrative assistant/secretary; liberal arts and sciences/liberal studies; marketing/marketing management; mathematics; music; natural sciences; ornamental horticulture; physical sciences; radio and television; real estate; registered nursing/registered nurse; sign language interpretation and translation.

Academics *Calendar:* semesters (summer session). *Degree:* certificates and associate. *Special study options:* academic remediation for entering students, adult/continuing education programs, advanced placement credit, cooperative education, distance learning, English as a second language, external degree program, honors programs, independent study, internships, part-time degree program, services for LD students, student-designed majors, study abroad, summer session for credit. *ROTC:* Air Force (c).

Library Golden West College Library plus 1 other with 95,000 titles, 410 serial subscriptions, an OPAC, a Web page.

Student Life *Housing:* college housing not available. *Activities and Organizations:* drama/theater group, student-run newspaper, choral group. *Campus security:* 24-hour emergency response devices and patrols, late-night transport/escort service. *Student services:* health clinic, personal/psychological counseling, legal services.

Athletics Member NJCAA. *Intercollegiate sports:* baseball M, cross-country running M/W, football M, soccer M/W, softball W, swimming and diving M/W, track and field M/W, volleyball M/W, water polo M/W.

Costs (2013–14) *Tuition:* state resident $1104 full-time, $46 per unit part-time; nonresident $5256 full-time, $219 per unit part-time. Full-time tuition and fees vary according to course load and program. Part-time tuition and fees vary according to course load and program. *Required fees:* $38 full-time, $38 per year part-time. *Waivers:* minority students, children of alumni, adult students, senior citizens, and employees or children of employees.

Applying *Options:* early admission. *Required for some:* essay or personal statement. *Recommended:* high school transcript. *Application deadlines:* rolling (freshmen), rolling (transfers). *Notification:* continuous (freshmen), continuous (transfers).

Freshman Application Contact Golden West College, PO Box 2748, 15744 Golden West Street, Huntington Beach, CA 92647-2748. *Phone:* 714-892-7711 Ext. 58965. *Website:* http://www.goldenwestcollege.edu/.

Golf Academy of America
Carlsbad, California

Director of Admissions Ms. Deborah Wells, Admissions Coordinator, Golf Academy of America, 1950 Camino Vida Roble, Suite 125, Carlsbad, CA 92008. *Phone:* 760-414-1501. *Toll-free phone:* 800-342-7342. *E-mail:* sdga@sdgagolf.com. *Website:* http://www.golfacademy.edu/.

Grossmont College
El Cajon, California

Freshman Application Contact Admissions Office, Grossmont College, 8800 Grossmont College Drive, El Cajon, CA 92020-1799. *Phone:* 619-644-7186. *Website:* http://www.grossmont.edu/.

Hartnell College
Salinas, California

Director of Admissions Director of Admissions, Hartnell College, 411 Central Avenue, Salinas, CA 93901. *Phone:* 831-755-6711. *Fax:* 831-759-6014. *Website:* http://www.hartnell.edu/.

Heald College–Concord
Concord, California

Freshman Application Contact Director of Admissions, Heald College–Concord, 5130 Commercial Circle, Concord, CA 94520. *Phone:* 925-288-5800. *Toll-free phone:* 800-88-HEALD. *Fax:* 925-288-5896. *E-mail:* concordinfo@heald.edu. *Website:* http://www.heald.edu/.

Heald College–Fresno
Fresno, California

Freshman Application Contact Director of Admissions, Heald College–Fresno, 255 West Bullard Avenue, Fresno, CA 93704-1706. *Phone:* 559-438-4222. *Toll-free phone:* 800-88-HEALD. *Fax:* 559-438-0948. *E-mail:* fresnoinfo@heald.edu. *Website:* http://www.heald.edu/.

Heald College–Hayward
Hayward, California

Freshman Application Contact Director of Admissions, Heald College–Hayward, 25500 Industrial Boulevard, Hayward, CA 94545. *Phone:* 510-783-2100. *Toll-free phone:* 800-88-HEALD. *Fax:* 510-783-3287. *E-mail:* harwardinfo@heald.edu. *Website:* http://www.heald.edu/.

Heald College–Modesto
Salida, California

Admissions Office Contact Heald College–Modesto, 5260 Pirrone Court, Salida, CA 95368. *Website:* http://www.heald.edu/.

Heald College–Rancho Cordova
Rancho Cordova, California

Freshman Application Contact Director of Admissions, Heald College–Rancho Cordova, 2910 Prospect Park Drive, Rancho Cordova, CA 95670-6005. *Phone:* 916-638-1616. *Toll-free phone:* 800-88-HEALD. *Fax:* 916-638-1580. *E-mail:* ranchocordovainfo@heald.edu. *Website:* http://www.heald.edu/.

Heald College–Roseville
Roseville, California

Freshman Application Contact Director of Admissions, Heald College–Roseville, 7 Sierra Gate Plaza, Roseville, CA 95678. *Phone:* 916-789-8600. *Toll-free phone:* 800-88-HEALD. *Fax:* 916-789-8606. *E-mail:* rosevilleinfo@heald.edu. *Website:* http://www.heald.edu/.

Heald College–Salinas
Salinas, California

Freshman Application Contact Director of Admissions, Heald College–Salinas, 1450 North Main Street, Salinas, CA 93906. *Phone:* 831-443-1700. *Toll-free phone:* 800-88-HEALD. *Fax:* 831-443-1050. *E-mail:* salinasinfo@heald.edu. *Website:* http://www.heald.edu/.

Heald College–San Francisco
San Francisco, California

Freshman Application Contact Director of Admissions, Heald College–San Francisco, 350 Mission Street, San Francisco, CA 94105. *Phone:* 415-808-

3000. *Toll-free phone:* 800-88-HEALD. *Fax:* 415-808-3005. *E-mail:* sanfranciscoinfo@heald.edu.
Website: http://www.heald.edu/.

Heald College–San Jose

Milpitas, California

Freshman Application Contact Director of Admissions, Heald College–San Jose, 341 Great Mall Parkway, Milpitas, CA 95035. *Phone:* 408-934-4900. *Toll-free phone:* 800-88-HEALD. *Fax:* 408-934-7777. *E-mail:* sanjoseinfo@heald.edu.

Website: http://www.heald.edu/.

Heald College–Stockton

Stockton, California

Freshman Application Contact Director of Admissions, Heald College–Stockton, 1605 East March Lane, Stockton, CA 95210. *Phone:* 209-473-5200. *Toll-free phone:* 800-88-HEALD. *Fax:* 209-477-2739. *E-mail:* stocktoninfo@heald.edu.

Website: http://www.heald.edu/.

ICDC College

Huntington Park, California

Admissions Office Contact ICDC College, 6812 Pacific Boulevard, Huntington Park, CA 33409.

Website: http://icdccollege.edu/.

Imperial Valley College

Imperial, California

- **State and locally supported** 2-year, founded 1922, part of California Community College System
- **Rural** 160-acre campus
- **Endowment** $832,061
- **Coed,** 7,413 undergraduate students

Undergraduates Students come from 12 states and territories; 3% are from out of state.

Majors Accounting; administrative assistant and secretarial science; agricultural business and management; agricultural mechanization; agriculture; anthropology; art; automobile/automotive mechanics technology; behavioral sciences; biological and physical sciences; business administration and management; criminal justice/law enforcement administration; English; fire science/firefighting; French; human development and family studies; humanities; hydrology and water resources science; information science/studies; journalism; kindergarten/preschool education; liberal arts and sciences/liberal studies; licensed practical/vocational nurse training; marketing/marketing management; mathematics; modern languages; music; physical education teaching and coaching; physical sciences; pre-engineering; psychology; registered nursing/registered nurse; social sciences; Spanish; welding technology.

Academics *Calendar:* semesters. *Degree:* certificates and associate. *Special study options:* academic remediation for entering students, accelerated degree program, adult/continuing education programs, advanced placement credit, double majors, English as a second language, part-time degree program, services for LD students, student-designed majors, summer session for credit.

Library Spencer Library with 55,875 titles, 425 serial subscriptions, 3,383 audiovisual materials, an OPAC, a Web page.

Student Life *Housing:* college housing not available. *Activities and Organizations:* drama/theater group, student-run newspaper, choral group, Student Support Services Club, Pre-School Mothers, Care Club, Christian Club, Nursing Club. *Campus security:* student patrols. *Student services:* personal/psychological counseling, women's center.

Athletics *Intercollegiate sports:* baseball M, basketball M/W, soccer M/W, softball W, tennis M/W.

Applying *Application fee:* $23. *Required for some:* high school transcript. *Recommended:* high school transcript. *Application deadlines:* rolling (freshmen), rolling (transfers). *Notification:* continuous (freshmen), continuous (transfers).

Freshman Application Contact Imperial Valley College, 380 East Aten Road, PO Box 158, Imperial, CA 92251-0158. *Phone:* 760-352-8320 Ext. 200.

Website: http://www.imperial.edu/.

Irvine Valley College

Irvine, California

Director of Admissions Mr. John Edwards, Director of Admissions, Records, and Enrollment Services, Irvine Valley College, 5500 Irvine Center Drive, Irvine, CA 92618. *Phone:* 949-451-5416.
Website: http://www.ivc.edu/.

ITT Technical Institute

Culver City, California

- **Proprietary** primarily 2-year, part of ITT Educational Services, Inc.
- **Coed**

Majors Business administration and management; computer programming (specific applications); construction management; cyber/computer forensics and counterterrorism; drafting and design technology; electrical, electronic and communications engineering technology; forensic science and technology; industrial technology; information technology project management; network and system administration; project management.

Academics *Calendar:* quarters. *Degrees:* associate and bachelor's.

Freshman Application Contact Director of Recruitment, ITT Technical Institute, 6101 W. Centinela Avenue, Suite 180, Culver City, CA 90230. *Phone:* 310-417-5800. *Toll-free phone:* 800-215-6151.
Website: http://www.itt-tech.edu/.

ITT Technical Institute

Lathrop, California

- **Proprietary** primarily 2-year, founded 1997, part of ITT Educational Services, Inc.
- **Coed**

Majors Business administration and management; computer programming (specific applications); construction management; cyber/computer forensics and counterterrorism; drafting and design technology; electrical, electronic and communications engineering technology; forensic science and technology; graphic communications; industrial technology; information technology project management; network and system administration; project management.

Academics *Calendar:* quarters. *Degrees:* associate and bachelor's.

Student Life *Housing:* college housing not available.

Freshman Application Contact Director of Recruitment, ITT Technical Institute, 16916 South Harlan Road, Lathrop, CA 95330. *Phone:* 209-858-0077. *Toll-free phone:* 800-346-1786.
Website: http://www.itt-tech.edu/.

ITT Technical Institute

National City, California

- **Proprietary** primarily 2-year, founded 1981, part of ITT Educational Services, Inc.
- **Suburban** campus
- **Coed**

Majors Business administration and management; computer programming (specific applications); construction management; cyber/computer forensics and counterterrorism; drafting and design technology; electrical, electronic and communications engineering technology; forensic science and technology; industrial technology; information technology project management; network and system administration; project management.

Academics *Calendar:* quarters. *Degrees:* associate and bachelor's.

Student Life *Housing:* college housing not available.

Freshman Application Contact Director of Recruitment, ITT Technical Institute, 401 Mile of Cars Way, National City, CA 91950. *Phone:* 619-327-1800. *Toll-free phone:* 800-883-0380.
Website: http://www.itt-tech.edu/.

ITT Technical Institute

Oakland, California

- **Proprietary** primarily 2-year, part of ITT Educational Services, Inc.
- **Coed**

Majors Business administration and management; computer programming (specific applications); construction management; cyber/computer forensics and counterterrorism; drafting and design technology; electrical, electronic and communications engineering technology; industrial technology; information technology project management; network and system administration; project management.

Academics *Calendar:* quarters. *Degrees:* associate and bachelor's.

Freshman Application Contact Director of Recruitment, ITT Technical Institute, 7901 Oakport Street, Suite 3000, Oakland, CA 94621. *Phone:* 510-553-2800. *Toll-free phone:* 877-442-5833.
Website: http://www.itt-tech.edu/.

ITT Technical Institute
Orange, California

- **Proprietary** primarily 2-year, founded 1982, part of ITT Educational Services, Inc.
- **Suburban** campus
- **Coed**

Majors Business administration and management; communications technology; computer programming (specific applications); construction management; cyber/computer forensics and counterterrorism; drafting and design technology; electrical, electronic and communications engineering technology; forensic science and technology; health information/medical records technology; industrial technology; information technology project management; network and system administration; project management.

Academics *Calendar:* quarters. *Degrees:* associate and bachelor's.

Student Life *Housing:* college housing not available.

Financial Aid Of all full-time matriculated undergraduates who enrolled in 2012, 20 Federal Work-Study jobs (averaging $5000).

Freshman Application Contact Director of Recruitment, ITT Technical Institute, 4000 West Metropolitan Drive, Suite 100, Orange, CA 92868. *Phone:* 714-941-2400.

Website: http://www.itt-tech.edu/.

ITT Technical Institute
Oxnard, California

- **Proprietary** primarily 2-year, founded 1993, part of ITT Educational Services, Inc.
- **Urban** campus
- **Coed**

Majors Business administration and management; computer programming (specific applications); construction management; cyber/computer forensics and counterterrorism; drafting and design technology; electrical, electronic and communications engineering technology; forensic science and technology; game and interactive media design; industrial technology; information technology project management; network and system administration; project management.

Academics *Calendar:* quarters. *Degrees:* associate and bachelor's.

Student Life *Housing:* college housing not available.

Freshman Application Contact Director of Recruitment, ITT Technical Institute, 2051 Solar Drive, Suite 150, Oxnard, CA 93036. *Phone:* 805-988-0143. *Toll-free phone:* 800-530-1582.

Website: http://www.itt-tech.edu/.

ITT Technical Institute
Rancho Cordova, California

- **Proprietary** primarily 2-year, founded 1954, part of ITT Educational Services, Inc.
- **Urban** campus
- **Coed**

Majors Business administration and management; computer programming (specific applications); construction management; cyber/computer forensics and counterterrorism; drafting and design technology; electrical, electronic and communications engineering technology; forensic science and technology; graphic communications; industrial technology; information technology project management; medical/clinical assistant; network and system administration; project management; registered nursing/registered nurse.

Academics *Calendar:* quarters. *Degrees:* associate and bachelor's.

Student Life *Housing:* college housing not available.

Freshman Application Contact Director of Recruitment, ITT Technical Institute, 10863 Gold Center Drive, Rancho Cordova, CA 95670-6034. *Phone:* 916-851-3900. *Toll-free phone:* 800-488-8466.

Website: http://www.itt-tech.edu/.

ITT Technical Institute
San Bernardino, California

- **Proprietary** primarily 2-year, founded 1987, part of ITT Educational Services, Inc.
- **Urban** campus
- **Coed**

Majors Business administration and management; computer programming (specific applications); construction management; cyber/computer forensics and counterterrorism; drafting and design technology; electrical, electronic and communications engineering technology; forensic science and technology; health information/medical records technology; industrial technology; information technology project management; network and system administration; project management.

Academics *Calendar:* quarters. *Degrees:* associate and bachelor's.

Student Life *Housing:* college housing not available.

Freshman Application Contact Director of Recruitment, ITT Technical Institute, 670 East Carnegie Drive, San Bernardino, CA 92408. *Phone:* 909-806-4600. *Toll-free phone:* 800-888-3801.

Website: http://www.itt-tech.edu/.

ITT Technical Institute
San Dimas, California

- **Proprietary** primarily 2-year, founded 1982, part of ITT Educational Services, Inc.
- **Suburban** campus
- **Coed**

Majors Business administration and management; computer programming (specific applications); construction management; cyber/computer forensics and counterterrorism; drafting and design technology; electrical, electronic and communications engineering technology; forensic science and technology; industrial technology; information technology project management; network and system administration; project management.

Academics *Calendar:* quarters. *Degrees:* associate and bachelor's.

Student Life *Housing:* college housing not available.

Financial Aid Of all full-time matriculated undergraduates who enrolled in 2012, 20 Federal Work-Study jobs (averaging $4500).

Freshman Application Contact Director of Recruitment, ITT Technical Institute, 650 West Cienega Avenue, San Dimas, CA 91773. *Phone:* 909-971-2300. *Toll-free phone:* 800-414-6522.

Website: http://www.itt-tech.edu/.

ITT Technical Institute
Sylmar, California

- **Proprietary** primarily 2-year, founded 1982, part of ITT Educational Services, Inc.
- **Urban** campus
- **Coed**

Majors Business administration and management; communications technology; computer programming (specific applications); construction management; cyber/computer forensics and counterterrorism; drafting and design technology; electrical, electronic and communications engineering technology; forensic science and technology; health information/medical records technology; industrial technology; information technology project management; network and system administration; project management.

Academics *Calendar:* quarters. *Degrees:* associate and bachelor's.

Student Life *Housing:* college housing not available.

Freshman Application Contact Director of Recruitment, ITT Technical Institute, 12669 Encinitas Avenue, Sylmar, CA 91342-3664. *Phone:* 818-364-5151. *Toll-free phone:* 800-363-2086 (in-state); 800-636-2086 (out-of-state).

Website: http://www.itt-tech.edu/.

ITT Technical Institute
Torrance, California

- **Proprietary** primarily 2-year, founded 1987, part of ITT Educational Services, Inc.
- **Urban** campus
- **Coed**

Majors Business administration and management; construction management; cyber/computer forensics and counterterrorism; drafting and design technology; electrical, electronic and communications engineering technology; forensic science and technology; information technology project management; network and system administration; project management.

Academics *Calendar:* quarters. *Degrees:* associate and bachelor's.

Student Life *Housing:* college housing not available.

Financial Aid Of all full-time matriculated undergraduates who enrolled in 2012, 6 Federal Work-Study jobs (averaging $4000).

Freshman Application Contact Director of Recruitment, ITT Technical Institute, 2555 West 190th Street, Suite 125, Torrance, CA 90504. *Phone:* 310-965-5900.

Website: http://www.itt-tech.edu/.

ITT Technical Institute
West Covina, California

Freshman Application Contact Director of Recruitment, ITT Technical Institute, 1530 W. Cameron Avenue, West Covina, CA 91790. *Phone:* 626-813-3681. *Toll-free phone:* 877-480-2766.

Website: http://www.itt-tech.edu/.

Kaplan College
North Hollywood, California

Freshman Application Contact Ms. Renee Codner, Director of Admissions, Kaplan College, 6180 Laurel Canyon Boulevard, Suite 101, North Hollywood, CA 91606. *Phone:* 818-763-2563 Ext. 240. *Toll-free phone:* 800-935-1857. *E-mail:* rcodner@mariccollege.edu.
Website: http://https://www.kaplancollege.com/north-hollywood-ca/.

Kaplan College, Bakersfield Campus
Bakersfield, California

Freshman Application Contact Kaplan College, Bakersfield Campus, 1914 Wible Road, Bakersfield, CA 93304. *Phone:* 661-836-6300. *Toll-free phone:* 800-935-1857.
Website: http://bakersfield.kaplancollege.com/.

Kaplan College, Chula Vista Campus
Chula Vista, California

Freshman Application Contact Kaplan College, Chula Vista Campus, 555 Broadway, Chula Vista, CA 91910. *Phone:* 877-473-3052. *Toll-free phone:* 800-935-1857.
Website: http://chulavista.kaplancollege.com/.

Kaplan College, Fresno Campus
Clovis, California

Freshman Application Contact Kaplan College, Fresno Campus, 44 Shaw Avenue, Clovis, CA 93612. *Phone:* 559-325-5100. *Toll-free phone:* 800-935-1857.
Website: http://fresno.kaplancollege.com/.

Kaplan College, Modesto Campus
Salida, California

Freshman Application Contact Kaplan College, Modesto Campus, 5172 Kiernan Court, Salida, CA 95368. *Phone:* 209-543-7000. *Toll-free phone:* 800-935-1857.
Website: http://modesto.kaplancollege.com/.

Kaplan College, Palm Springs Campus
Palm Springs, California

Freshman Application Contact Kaplan College, Palm Springs Campus, 2475 East Tahquitz Canyon Way, Palm Springs, CA 92262. *Phone:* 760-778-3540. *Toll-free phone:* 800-935-1857.
Website: http://palm-springs.kaplancollege.com/.

Kaplan College, Riverside Campus
Riverside, California

Freshman Application Contact Kaplan College, Riverside Campus, 4040 Vine Street, Riverside, CA 92507. *Phone:* 951-276-1704. *Toll-free phone:* 800-935-1857.
Website: http://riverside.kaplancollege.com/.

Kaplan College, Sacramento Campus
Sacramento, California

Freshman Application Contact Kaplan College, Sacramento Campus, 4330 Watt Avenue, Suite 400, Sacramento, CA 95821. *Phone:* 916-649-8168. *Toll-free phone:* 800-935-1857.
Website: http://sacramento.kaplancollege.com/.

Kaplan College, San Diego Campus
San Diego, California

Freshman Application Contact Kaplan College, San Diego Campus, 9055 Balboa Avenue, San Diego, CA 92123. *Phone:* 858-279-4500. *Toll-free phone:* 800-935-1857.
Website: http://san-diego.kaplancollege.com/.

Kaplan College, Vista Campus
Vista, California

Freshman Application Contact Kaplan College, Vista Campus, 2022 University Drive, Vista, CA 92083. *Phone:* 760-630-1555. *Toll-free phone:* 800-935-1857.
Website: http://vista.kaplancollege.com/.

Lake Tahoe Community College
South Lake Tahoe, California

- **State and locally supported** 2-year, founded 1975, part of California Community College System
- **Small-town** 164-acre campus
- **Coed,** 5,700 undergraduate students

Freshmen *Admission:* 450 applied, 450 admitted.
Faculty *Total:* 200, 21% full-time.
Majors Accounting; administrative assistant and secretarial science; art; biological and physical sciences; business administration and management; computer science; criminal justice/law enforcement administration; criminal justice/police science; dramatic/theater arts; finance; fire science/firefighting; geography; geology/earth science; humanities; kindergarten/preschool education; liberal arts and sciences/liberal studies; marketing/marketing management; mathematics; medical administrative assistant and medical secretary; medical/clinical assistant; music; natural sciences; physical education teaching and coaching; psychology; real estate; social sciences; Spanish.
Academics *Calendar:* quarters. *Degree:* certificates and associate. *Special study options:* academic remediation for entering students, advanced placement credit, cooperative education, distance learning, double majors, English as a second language, independent study, internships, part-time degree program, services for LD students, study abroad, summer session for credit.
Library Lake Tahoe Community College Library with 20,000 titles, 10,000 serial subscriptions, 5,000 audiovisual materials, an OPAC, a Web page.
Student Life *Housing:* college housing not available. *Activities and Organizations:* drama/theater group, choral group, Associated Student Council, Alpha Gamma Sigma, Foreign Language Club, Art Club, Performing Arts League. *Campus security:* 24-hour emergency response devices, late-night transport/escort service. *Student services:* personal/psychological counseling.
Athletics *Intercollegiate sports:* soccer M/W.
Costs (2014–15) *Tuition:* state resident $1395 full-time; nonresident $7650 full-time. Full-time tuition and fees vary according to course load. Part-time tuition and fees vary according to course load.
Financial Aid Of all full-time matriculated undergraduates who enrolled in 2012, 15 Federal Work-Study jobs (averaging $1500).
Applying *Options:* electronic application, early admission. *Recommended:* high school transcript. *Application deadlines:* rolling (freshmen), rolling (transfers). *Notification:* continuous (freshmen), continuous (transfers).
Freshman Application Contact Office of Admissions and Records, Lake Tahoe Community College, One College Drive, South Lake Tahoe, CA 96150. *Phone:* 530-541-4660 Ext. 211. *Fax:* 530-541-7852. *E-mail:* admissions@ltcc.edu.
Website: http://www.ltcc.edu/.

Laney College
Oakland, California

Freshman Application Contact Mrs. Barbara Simmons, District Admissions Officer, Laney College, 900 Fallon Street, Oakland, CA 94607-4893. *Phone:* 510-466-7369.
Website: http://www.laney.edu/.

Las Positas College
Livermore, California

Director of Admissions Mrs. Sylvia R. Rodriguez, Director of Admissions and Records, Las Positas College, 3000 Campus Hill Drive, Livermore, CA 94551. *Phone:* 925-373-4942.
Website: http://www.laspositascollege.edu/.

Lassen Community College District
Susanville, California

Freshman Application Contact Mr. Chris J. Alberico, Registrar, Lassen Community College District, Highway 139, PO Box 3000, Susanville, CA 96130. *Phone:* 530-257-6181.
Website: http://www.lassencollege.edu/.

Le Cordon Bleu College of Culinary Arts in Los Angeles
Pasadena, California

Director of Admissions Nora Sandoval, Registrar, Le Cordon Bleu College of Culinary Arts in Los Angeles, 530 East Colorado Boulevard, Pasadena, CA 91101. *Phone:* 626-229-1300. *Fax:* 626-204-3905. *E-mail:* nsandoval@la.chefs.edu.
Website: http://www.chefs.edu/Los-Angeles/.

Le Cordon Bleu College of Culinary Arts in San Francisco
San Francisco, California

Director of Admissions Ms. Nancy Seyfert, Vice President of Admissions, Le Cordon Bleu College of Culinary Arts in San Francisco, 350 Rhode Island Street, San Francisco, CA 94103. *Phone:* 800-229-2433 Ext. 275. *Toll-free phone:* 800-229-2433 (in-state); 800-BAYCHEF (out-of-state).
Website: http://www.chefs.edu/San-Francisco/.

Long Beach City College
Long Beach, California

Director of Admissions Mr. Ross Miyashiro, Dean of Admissions and Records, Long Beach City College, 4901 East Carson Street, Long Beach, CA 90808-1780. *Phone:* 562-938-4130.
Website: http://www.lbcc.edu/.

Los Angeles City College
Los Angeles, California

Freshman Application Contact Elaine Geismar, Director of Student Assistance Center, Los Angeles City College, 855 North Vermont Avenue, Los Angeles, CA 90029-3590. *Phone:* 323-953-4340.
Website: http://www.lacitycollege.edu/.

Los Angeles County College of Nursing and Allied Health
Los Angeles, California

Freshman Application Contact Admissions Office, Los Angeles County College of Nursing and Allied Health, 1237 North Mission Road, Los Angeles, CA 90033. *Phone:* 323-226-4911.
Website: http://www.ladhs.org/wps/portal/CollegeOfNursing.

Los Angeles Film School
Hollywood, California

- **Proprietary** primarily 2-year
- **Urban** 250,000-acre campus with easy access to Hollywood
- **Coed**
- 85% of applicants were admitted

Freshmen *Admission:* 1,505 applied, 1,272 admitted.
Majors Computer graphics; film/cinema/video studies; game and interactive media design; recording arts technology.
Academics *Degrees:* associate and bachelor's.
Applying *Options:* electronic application. *Application fee:* $75. *Required:* essay or personal statement, high school transcript, interview.
Freshman Application Contact Los Angeles Film School, 6363 Sunset Boulevard, Hollywood, CA 90028. *Toll-free phone:* 877-952-3456.
Website: http://www.lafilm.edu/.

Los Angeles Harbor College
Wilmington, California

Freshman Application Contact Los Angeles Harbor College, 1111 Figueroa Place, Wilmington, CA 90744-2397. *Phone:* 310-233-4091.
Website: http://www.lahc.edu/.

Los Angeles Mission College
Sylmar, California

- **State and locally supported** 2-year, founded 1974, part of Los Angeles Community College District (LACCD)
- **Urban** 22-acre campus with easy access to Los Angeles
- **Coed,** 8,990 undergraduate students, 22% full-time, 60% women, 40% men

Undergraduates 1,941 full-time, 7,049 part-time. 3% Black or African American, non-Hispanic/Latino; 75% Hispanic/Latino; 4% Asian, non-Hispanic/Latino; 0.1% Native Hawaiian or other Pacific Islander, non-Hispanic/Latino; 0.2% American Indian or Alaska Native, non-Hispanic/Latino; 1% Two or more races, non-Hispanic/Latino; 3% Race/ethnicity unknown; 1% international; 8% transferred in. *Retention:* 70% of full-time freshmen returned.
Freshmen *Admission:* 1,112 enrolled.
Faculty *Total:* 339, 27% full-time.
Majors Accounting; administrative assistant and secretarial science; biology/biological sciences; business administration and management; computer programming; criminal justice/police science; culinary arts; developmental and child psychology; dramatic/theater arts; English; family

and consumer economics related; finance; geography; history; humanities; liberal arts and sciences/liberal studies; mathematics; music; philosophy; physical sciences; psychology; real estate; social sciences; sociology; Spanish.
Academics *Calendar:* semesters. *Degree:* certificates and associate. *Special study options:* academic remediation for entering students, adult/continuing education programs, advanced placement credit, cooperative education, distance learning, double majors, English as a second language, external degree program, independent study, internships, off-campus study, part-time degree program, services for LD students, study abroad, summer session for credit.
Library Los Angeles Mission College Library with an OPAC, a Web page.
Student Life *Housing:* college housing not available. *Activities and Organizations:* drama/theater group, student-run newspaper, choral group. *Campus security:* 24-hour emergency response devices and patrols, late-night transport/escort service. *Student services:* health clinic, personal/psychological counseling.
Financial Aid Of all full-time matriculated undergraduates who enrolled in 2012, 40 Federal Work-Study jobs (averaging $4000).
Applying *Options:* early admission. *Notification:* continuous until 9/25 (freshmen).
Freshman Application Contact Los Angeles Mission College, 13356 Eldridge Avenue, Sylmar, CA 91342-3245.
Website: http://www.lamission.edu/.

Los Angeles Pierce College
Woodland Hills, California

Director of Admissions Ms. Shelley L. Gerstl, Dean of Admissions and Records, Los Angeles Pierce College, 6201 Winnetka Avenue, Woodland Hills, CA 91371-0001. *Phone:* 818-719-6448.
Website: http://www.piercecollege.edu/.

Los Angeles Southwest College
Los Angeles, California

Director of Admissions Dan W. Walden, Dean of Academic Affairs, Los Angeles Southwest College, 1600 West Imperial Highway, Los Angeles, CA 90047-4810. *Phone:* 323-242-5511.
Website: http://www.lasc.edu/.

Los Angeles Trade-Technical College
Los Angeles, California

Director of Admissions Dr. Raul Cardoza, Los Angeles Trade-Technical College, 400 West Washington Boulevard, Los Angeles, CA 90015-4108. *Phone:* 213-763-5301. *E-mail:* CardozaRJ@lattc.edu.
Website: http://www.lattc.edu/.

Los Angeles Valley College
Van Nuys, California

Director of Admissions Mr. Florentino Manzano, Associate Dean, Los Angeles Valley College, 5800 Fulton Avenue, Van Nuys, CA 91401-4096. *Phone:* 818-947-2353. *E-mail:* manzanf@lavc.edu.
Website: http://www.lavc.cc.ca.us/.

Los Medanos College
Pittsburg, California

Freshman Application Contact Ms. Gail Newman, Director of Admissions and Records, Los Medanos College, 2700 East Leland Road, Pittsburg, CA 94565-5197. *Phone:* 925-439-2181 Ext. 7500.
Website: http://www.losmedanos.net/.

Mendocino College
Ukiah, California

- **State and locally supported** 2-year, founded 1973, part of California Community College System
- **Rural** 127-acre campus
- **Endowment** $6.4 million
- **Coed**

Undergraduates 1,296 full-time, 2,318 part-time. Students come from 16 states and territories; 2 other countries; 3% Black or African American, non-Hispanic/Latino; 23% Hispanic/Latino; 3% Asian, non-Hispanic/Latino; 0.6% Native Hawaiian or other Pacific Islander, non-Hispanic/Latino; 5% American Indian or Alaska Native, non-Hispanic/Latino; 3% Race/ethnicity unknown; 4% transferred in.
Faculty *Student/faculty ratio:* 16:1.
Academics *Calendar:* semesters. *Degree:* certificates and associate. *Special study options:* academic remediation for entering students, adult/continuing education programs, advanced placement credit, cooperative education,

distance learning, English as a second language, honors programs, independent study, internships, part-time degree program, services for LD students, summer session for credit.

Student Life *Campus security:* late-night transport/escort service, security patrols 6 pm to 10 pm.

Athletics Member NJCAA.

Costs (2013–14) *Tuition:* state resident $1380 full-time; nonresident $7380 full-time. Full-time tuition and fees vary according to course load. Part-time tuition and fees vary according to course load. *Required fees:* $32 full-time.

Financial Aid *Financial aid deadline:* 5/20.

Applying *Options:* electronic application, early admission, deferred entrance. *Required:* high school transcript.

Freshman Application Contact Mendocino College, 1000 Hensley Creek Road, Ukiah, CA 95482-0300. *Phone:* 707-468-3103.
Website: http://www.mendocino.edu/.

Merced College
Merced, California

Freshman Application Contact Ms. Cherie Davis, Associate Registrar, Merced College, 3600 M Street, Merced, CA 95348-2898. *Phone:* 209-384-6188. *Fax:* 209-384-6339.
Website: http://www.mccd.edu/.

Merritt College
Oakland, California

Freshman Application Contact Ms. Barbara Simmons, District Admissions Officer, Merritt College, 12500 Campus Drive, Oakland, CA 94619-3196. *Phone:* 510-466-7369. *E-mail:* hperdue@peralta.cc.ca.us.
Website: http://www.merritt.edu/.

MiraCosta College
Oceanside, California

- **State-supported** 2-year, founded 1934, part of California Community College System
- **Suburban** 131-acre campus with easy access to San Diego
- **Coed,** 14,537 undergraduate students, 44% full-time, 56% women, 44% men

Undergraduates 6,438 full-time, 8,099 part-time. 1% are from out of state; 4% Black or African American, non-Hispanic/Latino; 32% Hispanic/Latino; 7% Asian, non-Hispanic/Latino; 0.5% Native Hawaiian or other Pacific Islander, non-Hispanic/Latino; 0.4% American Indian or Alaska Native, non-Hispanic/Latino; 6% Two or more races, non-Hispanic/Latino; 2% Race/ethnicity unknown; 1% international.

Freshmen *Admission:* 2,695 enrolled.

Faculty *Total:* 634, 23% full-time. *Student/faculty ratio:* 23:1.

Majors Accounting technology and bookkeeping; administrative assistant and secretarial science; adult development and aging; agribusiness; American studies; anthropology; architectural technology; area studies related; art; astronomy; automobile/automotive mechanics technology; biological and physical sciences; biology/biological sciences; biomedical technology; business administration and management; chemistry; child-care and support services management; child-care provision; computer programming; computer science; computer systems networking and telecommunications; cosmetology; criminal justice/police science; dance; data entry/microcomputer applications; drafting and design technology; dramatic/theater arts; economics; English; environmental science; ethnic, cultural minority, gender, and group studies related; floriculture/floristry management; French; general studies; geography; geology/earth science; German; graphic communications; health and physical education/fitness; health/medical preparatory programs related; health teacher education; history; hospitality administration;' human services; Japanese; landscape architecture; landscaping and groundskeeping; legal studies; liberal arts and sciences/liberal studies; licensed practical/vocational nurse training; mathematics; mechanical drafting and CAD/CADD; medical/clinical assistant; music; office management; philosophy; photographic and film/video technology; physical sciences; physics; plant nursery management; political science and government; psychology; psychology related; real estate; recording arts technology; registered nursing/registered nurse; restaurant, culinary, and catering management; retailing; rhetoric and composition; sales, distribution, and marketing operations; small business administration; social sciences; sociology; Spanish; surgical technology; theater design and technology; tourism and travel services marketing; turf and turfgrass management; visual and performing arts; web/multimedia management and webmaster.

Academics *Calendar:* semesters. *Degree:* certificates, diplomas, and associate. *Special study options:* academic remediation for entering students, accelerated degree program, adult/continuing education programs, advanced placement credit, cooperative education, distance learning, double majors, English as a second language, honors programs, independent study,

internships, part-time degree program, services for LD students, student-designed majors, study abroad, summer session for credit.

Library MiraCosta College Library with an OPAC, a Web page.

Student Life *Housing:* college housing not available. *Activities and Organizations:* drama/theater group, student-run newspaper, choral group, Inter Varsity Christian Fellowship, Accounting and Business Club, Backstage Players (Drama), Gay Straight Alliance, Puente Diversity Network. *Campus security:* 24-hour emergency response devices, student patrols, late-night transport/escort service, trained security personnel during class hours. *Student services:* health clinic, personal/psychological counseling, women's center.

Athletics *Intercollegiate sports:* basketball M/W, soccer M/W.

Costs (2013–14) *Tuition:* state resident $1288 full-time, $46 per unit part-time; nonresident $5180 full-time, $185 per unit part-time. Full-time tuition and fees vary according to course load. Part-time tuition and fees vary according to course load. *Required fees:* $48 full-time, $48 per year part-time.

Applying *Options:* electronic application, early admission, deferred entrance. *Application deadlines:* rolling (freshmen), rolling (transfers).

Freshman Application Contact Alicica G. Terry, Registrar, MiraCosta College, One Barnard Drive, Oceanside, CA 92057. *Phone:* 760-795-6620. *Toll-free phone:* 888-201-8480. *E-mail:* admissions@miracosta.edu.
Website: http://www.miracosta.edu/.

Mission College
Santa Clara, California

Director of Admissions Daniel Sanidad, Dean of Student Services, Mission College, 3000 Mission College Boulevard, Santa Clara, CA 95054-1897. *Phone:* 408-855-5139.
Website: http://www.missioncollege.org/.

Modesto Junior College
Modesto, California

Freshman Application Contact Ms. Susie Agostini, Dean of Matriculation, Admissions, and Records, Modesto Junior College, 435 College Avenue, Modesto, CA 95350. *Phone:* 209-575-6470. *Fax:* 209-575-6859. *E-mail:* mjcadmissions@mail.yosemite.cc.ca.us.
Website: http://www.mjc.edu/.

Monterey Peninsula College
Monterey, California

Director of Admissions Ms. Vera Coleman, Registrar, Monterey Peninsula College, 980 Fremont Street, Monterey, CA 93940-4799. *Phone:* 831-646-4007. *E-mail:* vcoleman@mpc.edu.
Website: http://www.mpc.edu/.

Moorpark College
Moorpark, California

Freshman Application Contact Ms. Katherine Colborn, Registrar, Moorpark College, 7075 Campus Road, Moorpark, CA 93021-2899. *Phone:* 805-378-1415.
Website: http://www.moorparkcollege.edu/.

Moreno Valley College
Moreno Valley, California

Freshman Application Contact Jamie Clifton, Director, Enrollment Services, Moreno Valley College, 16130 Lasselle Street, Moreno Valley, CA 92551. *Phone:* 951-571-6293. *E-mail:* admissions@mvc.edu.
Website: http://www.mvc.edu/.

Mt. San Antonio College
Walnut, California

- **State and locally supported** 2-year, founded 1946, part of California Community College System
- **Suburban** 421-acre campus with easy access to Los Angeles
- **Coed,** 28,481 undergraduate students, 37% full-time, 51% women, 49% men

Undergraduates 10,499 full-time, 17,982 part-time. Students come from 21 states and territories; 139 other countries; 1% are from out of state; 5% Black or African American, non-Hispanic/Latino; 59% Hispanic/Latino; 18% Asian, non-Hispanic/Latino; 0.4% Native Hawaiian or other Pacific Islander, non-Hispanic/Latino; 0.2% American Indian or Alaska Native, non-Hispanic/Latino; 3% Two or more races, non-Hispanic/Latino; 2% Race/ethnicity unknown; 2% international. *Retention:* 79% of full-time freshmen returned.

Freshmen *Admission:* 4,835 enrolled.

Faculty *Total:* 1,260, 30% full-time. *Student/faculty ratio:* 26:1.

Majors Accounting; administrative assistant and secretarial science; advertising; agricultural business and management; agriculture; airframe mechanics and aircraft maintenance technology; airline pilot and flight crew; air traffic control; animal sciences; apparel and textiles; architectural engineering technology; avionics maintenance technology; biological and physical sciences; building/construction finishing, management, and inspection related; business administration and management; business teacher education; child development; civil engineering technology; commercial and advertising art; computer and information sciences; computer engineering technology; computer graphics; computer science; corrections; criminal justice/police science; dairy science; data processing and data processing technology; drafting and design technology; drafting/design engineering technologies related; electrical, electronic and communications engineering technology; emergency medical technology (EMT paramedic); engineering technology; English language and literature related; family and consumer sciences/human sciences; fashion merchandising; finance; fire science/firefighting; forest technology; health and physical education/fitness; heating, air conditioning, ventilation and refrigeration maintenance technology; horticultural science; hotel/motel administration; humanities; industrial and product design; industrial radiologic technology; interior design; journalism; kindergarten/preschool education; landscape architecture; legal administrative assistant/secretary; legal assistant/paralegal; machine tool technology; marketing/marketing management; materials science; mathematics; medical administrative assistant and medical secretary; mental health counseling; music; occupational safety and health technology; ornamental horticulture; parks, recreation and leisure; parks, recreation and leisure facilities management; photography; physical sciences related; pre-engineering; quality control technology; radio and television; real estate; registered nursing/registered nurse; respiratory care therapy; sign language interpretation and translation; social sciences; surveying technology; transportation and materials moving related; visual and performing arts; welding technology; wildlife, fish and wildlands science and management.

Academics *Calendar:* semesters. *Degree:* certificates, diplomas, and associate. *Special study options:* academic remediation for entering students, adult/continuing education programs, advanced placement credit, cooperative education, distance learning, double majors, English as a second language, honors programs, independent study, part-time degree program, services for LD students, study abroad, summer session for credit. *ROTC:* Army (b), Air Force (b).

Library Learning Resources Center with 97,996 titles, 231 serial subscriptions, 9,933 audiovisual materials, an OPAC, a Web page.

Student Life *Housing:* college housing not available. *Activities and Organizations:* drama/theater group, student-run radio station, choral group, Alpha Gamma Sigma, Muslim Student Association, student government, Asian Student Association, Kasama-Filipino Student Organization. *Campus security:* 24-hour emergency response devices and patrols, late-night transport/escort service. *Student services:* health clinic, personal/psychological counseling, women's center.

Athletics *Intercollegiate sports:* badminton W, baseball M, basketball M/W, cheerleading M/W, cross-country running M/W, football M, golf M/W, soccer M/W, softball W, swimming and diving M/W, tennis M/W, track and field M/W, volleyball M/W, water polo M/W, wrestling M.

Costs (2013–14) *Tuition:* state resident $1104 full-time, $46 per unit part-time; nonresident $7364 full-time, $217 per unit part-time. Full-time tuition and fees vary according to course load and program. Part-time tuition and fees vary according to course load and program. *Required fees:* $58 full-time, $58 per term part-time, $58 per term part-time.

Financial Aid Of all full-time matriculated undergraduates who enrolled in 2012, 223 Federal Work-Study jobs (averaging $2728). 69 state and other part-time jobs (averaging $2526).

Applying *Options:* electronic application, early admission, deferred entrance. *Required for some:* high school transcript. *Notification:* continuous (freshmen), continuous (transfers).

Freshman Application Contact Dr. George Bradshaw, Dean of Enrollment Management, Mt. San Antonio College, Walnut, CA 91789. *Phone:* 909-274-5570 Ext. 4505.

Website: http://www.mtsac.edu/.

Mt. San Jacinto College

San Jacinto, California

- **State and locally supported** 2-year, founded 1963, part of California Community College System
- **Suburban** 180-acre campus with easy access to San Diego
- **Endowment** $1.6 million
- **Coed,** 14,170 undergraduate students, 36% full-time, 57% women, 43% men

Undergraduates 5,105 full-time, 9,065 part-time. Students come from 4 states and territories; 8% Black or African American, non-Hispanic/Latino; 43%

Hispanic/Latino; 6% Asian, non-Hispanic/Latino; 0.5% Native Hawaiian or other Pacific Islander, non-Hispanic/Latino; 0.5% American Indian or Alaska Native, non-Hispanic/Latino; 5% Two or more races, non-Hispanic/Latino; 2% Race/ethnicity unknown; 7% transferred in. *Retention:* 70% of full-time freshmen returned.

Freshmen *Admission:* 15,299 applied, 15,299 admitted, 2,536 enrolled.

Faculty *Total:* 671, 20% full-time. *Student/faculty ratio:* 27:1.

Majors Administrative assistant and secretarial science; adult development and aging; art; automobile/automotive mechanics technology; biological and physical sciences; business administration and management; child development; criminal justice/police science; dance; design and visual communications; diagnostic medical sonography and ultrasound technology; digital communication and media/multimedia; drafting and design technology; dramatic/theater arts; fire science/firefighting; geography related; health and physical education/fitness; humanities; information technology; legal assistant/paralegal; liberal arts and sciences/liberal studies; mathematics; medical/clinical assistant; music; music management; photography; real estate; registered nursing/registered nurse; social sciences; substance abuse/addiction counseling; turf and turfgrass management; visual and performing arts; water quality and wastewater treatment management and recycling technology.

Academics *Calendar:* semesters. *Degree:* certificates, diplomas, and associate. *Special study options:* academic remediation for entering students, adult/continuing education programs, advanced placement credit, distance learning, double majors, English as a second language, honors programs, off-campus study, part-time degree program, services for LD students, study abroad, summer session for credit.

Library Milo P. Johnson Library plus 1 other with 28,000 titles, 330 serial subscriptions.

Student Life *Housing:* college housing not available. *Activities and Organizations:* drama/theater group. *Campus security:* part-time trained security personnel. *Student services:* personal/psychological counseling.

Athletics *Intercollegiate sports:* baseball M, basketball M/W, football M, golf M, soccer W, softball W, tennis M/W, volleyball W.

Costs (2014–15) *One-time required fee:* $6. *Tuition:* state resident $1380 full-time, $46 per credit part-time; nonresident $6930 full-time, $231 per credit part-time. *Required fees:* $1380 full-time.

Financial Aid Of all full-time matriculated undergraduates who enrolled in 2012, 109 Federal Work-Study jobs (averaging $1114). 125 state and other part-time jobs (averaging $1000).

Applying *Options:* early admission. *Recommended:* high school transcript. *Application deadlines:* rolling (freshmen), rolling (transfers).

Freshman Application Contact Mt. San Jacinto College, 1499 North State Street, San Jacinto, CA 92583-2399. *Phone:* 951-639-5212.

Website: http://www.msjc.edu/.

MTI College

Sacramento, California

Freshman Application Contact Director of Admissions, MTI College, 5221 Madison Avenue, Sacramento, CA 95841. *Phone:* 916-339-1500. *Fax:* 916-339-0305.

Website: http://www.mticollege.edu/.

Napa Valley College

Napa, California

Director of Admissions Mr. Oscar De Haro, Vice President of Student Services, Napa Valley College, 2277 Napa-Vallejo Highway, Napa, CA 94558-6236. *Phone:* 707-253-3000. *Toll-free phone:* 800-826-1077. *E-mail:* odeharo@napavalley.edu.

Website: http://www.napavalley.edu/.

Norco College

Norco, California

Freshman Application Contact Mark DeAsis, Director, Enrollment Services, Norco College, 2001 Third Street, Norco, CA 92860. *E-mail:* admissionsnorco@norcocollege.edu.

Website: http://www.norcocollege.edu/.

Ohlone College

Fremont, California

Freshman Application Contact Christopher Williamson, Director of Admissions and Records, Ohlone College, 43600 Mission Boulevard, Fremont, CA 94539-5884. *Phone:* 510-659-6518. *Fax:* 510-659-7321. *E-mail:* cwilliamson@ohlone.edu.

Website: http://www.ohlone.edu/.

Orange Coast College
Costa Mesa, California

- **State and locally supported** 2-year, founded 1947, part of Coast Community College District
- **Suburban** 164-acre campus with easy access to Los Angeles
- **Endowment** $10.8 million
- **Coed,** 21,088 undergraduate students, 38% full-time, 49% women, 51% men

Undergraduates 7,908 full-time, 13,180 part-time. Students come from 69 other countries; 2% are from out of state; 1% Black or African American, non-Hispanic/Latino; 31% Hispanic/Latino; 20% Asian, non-Hispanic/Latino; 0.3% Native Hawaiian or other Pacific Islander, non-Hispanic/Latino; 0.3% American Indian or Alaska Native, non-Hispanic/Latino; 4% Two or more races, non-Hispanic/Latino; 5% Race/ethnicity unknown; 3% international; 6% transferred in.

Freshmen *Admission:* 3,352 enrolled.

Faculty *Total:* 587, 42% full-time. *Student/faculty ratio:* 41:1.

Majors Accounting; administrative assistant and secretarial science; aeronautics/aviation/aerospace science and technology; airline pilot and flight crew; anthropology; architectural engineering technology; art; athletic training; avionics maintenance technology; behavioral sciences; biology/biological sciences; building/home/construction inspection; business administration and management; cardiovascular technology; chemistry; child-care and support services management; child-care provision; cinematography and film/video production; clinical laboratory science/medical technology; commercial and advertising art; communications technology; computer engineering technology; computer graphics; computer programming; computer programming (specific applications); computer typography and composition equipment operation; construction engineering technology; culinary arts; dance; data entry/microcomputer applications related; data processing and data processing technology; dental hygiene; dietetics; drafting and design technology; dramatic/theater arts; economics; electrical and power transmission installation; electrical, electronic and communications engineering technology; electrical/electronics equipment installation and repair; emergency medical technology (EMT paramedic); engineering; English; family and consumer economics related; family and consumer sciences/human sciences; fashion merchandising; film/cinema/video studies; food science; foods, nutrition, and wellness; food technology and processing; French; geography; geology/earth science; German; health professions related; heating, air conditioning, ventilation and refrigeration maintenance technology; history; horticultural science; hotel/motel administration; housing and human environments; human development and family studies; humanities; industrial and product design; industrial radiologic technology; information science/studies; interior design; journalism; kindergarten/preschool education; kinesiology and exercise science; liberal arts and sciences/liberal studies; machine shop technology; machine tool technology; marine maintenance and ship repair technology; marketing/marketing management; mass communication/media; mathematics; medical administrative assistant and medical secretary; medical/clinical assistant; music; musical instrument fabrication and repair; music management; natural sciences; nuclear medical technology; ornamental horticulture; philosophy; photography; physical education teaching and coaching; physics; political science and government; religious studies; respiratory care therapy; restaurant, culinary, and catering management; retailing; selling skills and sales; social sciences; sociology; Spanish; special products marketing; welding technology; word processing.

Academics *Calendar:* semesters plus summer session. *Degree:* certificates and associate. *Special study options:* academic remediation for entering students, adult/continuing education programs, advanced placement credit, cooperative education, distance learning, double majors, English as a second language, external degree program, freshman honors college, honors programs, internships, off-campus study, part-time degree program, services for LD students, student-designed majors, study abroad, summer session for credit. *ROTC:* Army (c), Air Force (c).

Library Library with 112,783 titles, 169 serial subscriptions, 3,240 audiovisual materials, an OPAC, a Web page.

Student Life *Housing:* college housing not available. *Activities and Organizations:* drama/theater group, student-run newspaper, choral group, Architecture Club, Circle K, Doctors of Tomorrow, Speech, Theater, and Debate, Vietnamese Student Association. *Campus security:* 24-hour emergency response devices and patrols, student patrols, late-night transport/escort service. *Student services:* health clinic, personal/psychological counseling, legal services.

Athletics *Intercollegiate sports:* baseball M, basketball M/W, bowling M(c)/W(c), crew M/W, cross-country running M/W, football M, golf M/W, soccer M/W, softball W, swimming and diving M/W, tennis M/W, track and field M/W, volleyball W, water polo M/W.

Costs (2014–15) *Tuition:* state resident $1112 full-time, $46 per unit part-time; nonresident $6992 full-time, $219 per unit part-time. *Required fees:* $902 full-time, $61 per term part-time. *Payment plan:* installment.

Financial Aid Of all full-time matriculated undergraduates who enrolled in 2012, 108 Federal Work-Study jobs (averaging $3000). *Financial aid deadline:* 5/28.

Applying *Options:* electronic application. *Application deadlines:* rolling (freshmen), rolling (transfers). *Notification:* continuous (freshmen), continuous (transfers).

Freshman Application Contact Efren Galvan, Director of Admissions, Records and Enrollment Technology, Orange Coast College, 2701 Fairview Road, Costa Mesa, CA 92926. *Phone:* 714-432-5774. *E-mail:* egalvan@occ.cccd.edu.

Website: http://www.orangecoastcollege.edu/.

Oxnard College
Oxnard, California

- **State-supported** 2-year, founded 1975, part of Ventura County Community College District System
- **Urban** 119-acre campus
- **Endowment** $1.7 million
- **Coed,** 6,867 undergraduate students, 28% full-time, 55% women, 45% men

Undergraduates 1,927 full-time, 4,940 part-time. 3% Black or African American, non-Hispanic/Latino; 71% Hispanic/Latino; 5% Asian, non-Hispanic/Latino; 0.3% American Indian or Alaska Native, non-Hispanic/Latino; 2% Two or more races, non-Hispanic/Latino; 0.6% Race/ethnicity unknown; 0.1% international; 3% transferred in.

Freshmen *Admission:* 990 enrolled.

Faculty *Total:* 188, 46% full-time. *Student/faculty ratio:* 30:1.

Majors Administrative assistant and secretarial science; anthropology; art; autobody/collision and repair technology; automobile/automotive mechanics technology; biology/biological sciences; business administration and management; child development; computer and information systems security; computer systems networking and telecommunications; culinary arts; dental hygiene; economics; English; environmental engineering technology; environmental studies; family and community services; fine/studio arts; fire prevention and safety technology; fire science/firefighting; fire services administration; heating, air conditioning, ventilation and refrigeration maintenance technology; history; hotel/motel administration; legal assistant/paralegal; marketing/marketing management; mathematics; philosophy; political science and government; psychology; radio and television; restaurant/food services management; sociology; Spanish; speech communication and rhetoric; substance abuse/addiction counseling; web page, digital/multimedia and information resources design.

Academics *Calendar:* semesters. *Degree:* certificates, diplomas, and associate. *Special study options:* academic remediation for entering students, accelerated degree program, advanced placement credit, distance learning, double majors, English as a second language, honors programs, independent study, part-time degree program, services for LD students, summer session for credit.

Library Oxnard College Library with 31,500 titles, 107 serial subscriptions, an OPAC, a Web page.

Student Life *Housing:* college housing not available. *Activities and Organizations:* drama/theater group, student-run television station. *Campus security:* 24-hour patrols. *Student services:* health clinic, personal/psychological counseling, women's center.

Athletics *Intercollegiate sports:* baseball M, basketball M, cross-country running M/W, soccer M/W, softball W.

Costs (2013–14) *Tuition:* state resident $0 full-time; nonresident $7000 full-time, $250 per unit part-time. *Required fees:* $1316 full-time, $47 per unit part-time, $42 per year part-time. *Payment plan:* installment.

Financial Aid Of all full-time matriculated undergraduates who enrolled in 2012, 80 Federal Work-Study jobs (averaging $3000).

Applying *Options:* electronic application, early admission. *Recommended:* high school transcript. *Application deadlines:* rolling (freshmen), rolling (transfers). *Notification:* continuous (freshmen), continuous (transfers).

Freshman Application Contact Mr. Joel Diaz, Registrar, Oxnard College, 4000 South Rose Avenue, Oxnard, CA 93033-6699. *Phone:* 805-986-5843. *Fax:* 805-986-5943. *E-mail:* jdiaz@vcccd.edu.

Website: http://www.oxnardcollege.edu/.

Palomar College
San Marcos, California

- **State and locally supported** 2-year, founded 1946, part of California Community College System
- **Suburban** 156-acre campus with easy access to San Diego
- **Coed,** 22,535 undergraduate students, 36% full-time, 44% women, 56% men

Undergraduates 8,107 full-time, 14,428 part-time.

Freshmen *Admission:* 4,166 enrolled.

Majors Accounting; administrative assistant and secretarial science; advertising; airline pilot and flight crew; animation, interactive technology, video graphics and special effects; apparel and textile marketing management; archeology; architectural drafting and CAD/CADD; art; astronomy; autobody/collision and repair technology; automobile/automotive mechanics technology; aviation/airway management; biological and physical sciences; biology/biological sciences; building/home/construction inspection; business administration and management; business/commerce; cabinetmaking and millwork; carpentry; ceramic arts and ceramics; chemistry; child development; commercial and advertising art; commercial photography; computer installation and repair technology; computer programming; computer systems networking and telecommunications; cooking and related culinary arts; criminal justice/police science; dance; dental assisting; design and visual communications; desktop publishing and digital imaging design; diesel mechanics technology; digital communication and media/multimedia; drafting and design technology; dramatic/theater arts; drawing; drywall installation; e-commerce; economics; electrical/electronics drafting and CAD/CADD; electrical/electronics equipment installation and repair; electrician; emergency medical technology (EMT paramedic); engineering; English; family and consumer sciences/human sciences; fashion/apparel design; film/cinema/video studies; fire science/firefighting; food service systems administration; forensic science and technology; French; geology/earth science; graphic communications; graphic design; hazardous materials management and waste technology; health and physical education/fitness; humanities; information technology; insurance; interior design; international business/trade/commerce; journalism; legal administrative assistant/secretary; legal assistant/paralegal; legal studies; liberal arts and sciences/liberal studies; library and archives assisting; masonry; mathematics; medical administrative assistant and medical secretary; medical/clinical assistant; metal and jewelry arts; music; network and system administration; parks, recreation and leisure; parks, recreation and leisure facilities management; printing management; psychology; public administration; quality control technology; radio and television; real estate; registered nursing/registered nurse; rhetoric and composition; sculpture; security and loss prevention; sheet metal technology; sign language interpretation and translation; social sciences; substance abuse/addiction counseling; water quality and wastewater treatment management and recycling technology; web page, digital/multimedia and information resources design; welding technology; women's studies.

Academics *Calendar:* semesters. *Degree:* certificates and associate. *Special study options:* academic remediation for entering students, advanced placement credit, cooperative education, distance learning, English as a second language, internships, part-time degree program, services for LD students, study abroad, summer session for credit.

Library Palomar Library with 108,000 titles, an OPAC, a Web page.

Student Life *Housing:* college housing not available. *Activities and Organizations:* drama/theater group, student-run newspaper, radio and television station, choral group, SNAP (Student Nursing Association of Palomar College), Alpha Omega Rho Chapter of Phi Theta Kappa (International Honor Society), Active Minds, Student Veterans Organizaton, MEChA (Chicano Organization). *Campus security:* 24-hour patrols, student patrols, late-night transport/escort service. *Student services:* health clinic, personal/psychological counseling.

Athletics *Intercollegiate sports:* baseball M, basketball M/W, football M, golf M, soccer M/W, softball W, swimming and diving M/W, tennis M/W, track and field M/W, volleyball M/W, water polo M/W, wrestling M. *Intramural sports:* basketball M/W, bowling M, golf M, skiing (downhill) M/W, soccer M, softball W, tennis M, volleyball M, water polo M, wrestling M.

Costs (2013–14) *Tuition:* state resident $1380 full-time, $46 per unit part-time; nonresident $7200 full-time, $240 per unit part-time. *Required fees:* $64 full-time, $1 per unit part-time, $19 per term part-time.

Applying *Options:* electronic application. *Application deadlines:* rolling (freshmen), rolling (transfers). *Notification:* continuous (freshmen), continuous (transfers).

Freshman Application Contact Dr. Kendyl Magnuson, Director of Enrollment Services, Palomar College, 1140 West Mission Road, San Marcos, CA 92069-1487. *Phone:* 760-744-1150 Ext. 2171. *Fax:* 760-744-2932. *E-mail:* kmagnuson@palomar.edu.

Website: http://www.palomar.edu/.

Palo Verde College

Blythe, California

Freshman Application Contact Diana Rodriguez, Vice President of Student Services, Palo Verde College, 1 College Drive, Blythe, CA 92225. *Phone:* 760-921-5428. *Fax:* 760-921-3608. *E-mail:* diana.rodriguez@paloverde.edu.

Website: http://www.paloverde.edu/.

Pasadena City College

Pasadena, California

- **State and locally supported** 2-year, founded 1924, part of California Community College System
- **Urban** 55-acre campus with easy access to Los Angeles
- **Coed,** 23,814 undergraduate students, 32% full-time, 52% women, 48% men

Undergraduates 7,509 full-time, 16,305 part-time. Students come from 15 states and territories; 150 other countries; 5% Black or African American, non-Hispanic/Latino; 46% Hispanic/Latino; 24% Asian, non-Hispanic/Latino; 0.2% Native Hawaiian or other Pacific Islander, non-Hispanic/Latino; 0.1% American Indian or Alaska Native, non-Hispanic/Latino; 6% Two or more races, non-Hispanic/Latino; 6% Race/ethnicity unknown; 2% transferred in. *Retention:* 81% of full-time freshmen returned.

Freshmen *Admission:* 5 applied, 9,135 enrolled.

Faculty *Total:* 1,336, 28% full-time. *Student/faculty ratio:* 18:1.

Majors Accounting; accounting technology and bookkeeping; administrative assistant and secretarial science; animation, interactive technology, video graphics and special effects; anthropology; architecture; art; audiology and speech-language pathology; automobile/automotive mechanics technology; biochemistry; biological and physical sciences; biology/biological sciences; broadcast journalism; building/home/construction inspection; business administration and management; business automation/technology/data entry; chemistry; child development; cinematography and film/video production; classics and classical languages; computer/information technology services administration related; computer science; computer technology/computer systems technology; construction trades; cosmetology; cosmetology, barber/styling, and nail instruction; criminal justice/law enforcement administration; dance; data entry/microcomputer applications related; dental assisting; dental hygiene; dental laboratory technology; desktop publishing and digital imaging design; digital communication and media/multimedia; drafting and design technology; dramatic/theater arts; electrical and electronic engineering technologies related; electrical and electronics engineering; engineering technology; fashion/apparel design; fashion merchandising; fire prevention and safety technology; food service and dining room management; graphic and printing equipment operation/production; graphic design; history; hospitality administration; humanities; industrial electronics technology; international business/trade/commerce; international/global studies; legal assistant/paralegal; liberal arts and sciences/liberal studies; library science related; licensed practical/vocational nurse training; machine shop technology; marketing/marketing management; mathematics; mechanical engineering; medical/clinical assistant; medical insurance/medical billing; medical office assistant; photography; photojournalism; psychology; radio and television; radio and television broadcasting technology; radiologic technology/science; registered nursing/registered nurse; sociology; Spanish; speech communication and rhetoric; theater design and technology; welding technology.

Academics *Calendar:* semesters. *Degree:* certificates and associate. *Special study options:* academic remediation for entering students, adult/continuing education programs, advanced placement credit, distance learning, double majors, English as a second language, honors programs, independent study, internships, part-time degree program, services for LD students, study abroad, summer session for credit.

Library Pasadena City College Library plus 1 other with 137,945 titles, 19,326 serial subscriptions, 12,079 audiovisual materials, an OPAC, a Web page.

Student Life *Housing:* college housing not available. *Activities and Organizations:* drama/theater group, student-run newspaper, choral group, marching band. *Campus security:* 24-hour emergency response devices and patrols, late-night transport/escort service, cadet patrols. *Student services:* health clinic, personal/psychological counseling.

Athletics *Intercollegiate sports:* badminton M/W, baseball M, basketball M/W, cheerleading W(c), cross-country running M/W, football M, soccer M/W, softball W, swimming and diving M/W, tennis M/W, track and field M/W, volleyball W, water polo W. *Intramural sports:* water polo M(c).

Costs (2013–14) *Tuition:* state resident $1152 full-time; nonresident $6120 full-time. *Required fees:* $48 full-time.

Applying *Options:* electronic application. *Application deadlines:* rolling (freshmen), rolling (transfers). *Notification:* continuous (freshmen), continuous (transfers).

Freshman Application Contact Pasadena City College, 1570 East Colorado Boulevard, Pasadena, CA 91106-2041. *Phone:* 626-585-7284. *Fax:* 626-585-7915.

Website: http://www.pasadena.edu/.

Pima Medical Institute
Chula Vista, California

Freshman Application Contact Admissions Office, Pima Medical Institute, 780 Bay Boulevard, Suite 101, Chula Vista, CA 91910. *Phone:* 619-425-3200. *Toll-free phone:* 800-477-PIMA (in-state); 888-477-PIMA (out-of-state). *Website:* http://www.pmi.edu/.

Platt College
Alhambra, California

Director of Admissions Mr. Detroit Whiteside, Director of Admissions, Platt College, 1000 South Fremont A9W, Alhambra, CA 91803. *Phone:* 323-258-8050. *Toll-free phone:* 888-866-6697 (in-state); 888-80-PLATT (out-of-state). *Website:* http://www.plattcollege.edu/.

Platt College
Ontario, California

Director of Admissions Ms. Jennifer Abandonato, Director of Admissions, Platt College, 3700 Inland Empire Boulevard, Suite 400, Ontario, CA 91764. *Phone:* 909-941-9410. *Toll-free phone:* 888-80-PLATT. *Website:* http://www.plattcollege.edu/.

Porterville College
Porterville, California

Director of Admissions Ms. Judy Pope, Director of Admissions and Records/Registrar, Porterville College, 100 East College Avenue, Porterville, CA 93257-6058. *Phone:* 559-791-2222. *Website:* http://www.pc.cc.ca.us/.

Professional Golfers Career College
Temecula, California

- **Independent** 2-year
- **Rural** campus
- **Coed, primarily men**
- 100% of applicants were admitted

Undergraduates 282 full-time. Students come from 50 states and territories; 13 other countries; 75% are from out of state; 1% Black or African American, non-Hispanic/Latino; 4% Hispanic/Latino; 2% Asian, non-Hispanic/Latino; 0.7% Native Hawaiian or other Pacific Islander, non-Hispanic/Latino; 1% American Indian or Alaska Native, non-Hispanic/Latino; 1% Two or more races, non-Hispanic/Latino; 12% international; 26% live on campus. *Retention:* 69% of full-time freshmen returned. **Faculty** *Student/faculty ratio:* 15:1. **Academics** *Calendar:* semesters. *Degree:* associate. *Special study options:* English as a second language. **Costs (2013–14)** *Tuition:* $26,800 full-time. No tuition increase for student's term of enrollment. *Required fees:* $2000 full-time. **Applying** *Options:* early admission, deferred entrance. *Application fee:* $75. *Required:* high school transcript, 3 letters of recommendation. **Freshman Application Contact** Mr. Gary Gilleon, Professional Golfers Career College, 26109 Ynez Road, Temecula, CA 92591. *Phone:* 951-719-2994 Ext. 1021. *Toll-free phone:* 800-877-4380. *Fax:* 951-719-1643. *E-mail:* garygilleon@golfcollege.edu. *Website:* http://www.golfcollege.edu/.

Reedley College
Reedley, California

Freshman Application Contact Admissions and Records Office, Reedley College, 995 North Reed Avenue, Reedley, CA 93654. *Phone:* 559-638-0323. *Fax:* 559-637-2523. *Website:* http://www.reedleycollege.edu/.

Rio Hondo College
Whittier, California

- **State and locally supported** 2-year, founded 1960, part of California Community College System
- **Suburban** 128-acre campus with easy access to Los Angeles
- **Coed,** 29,281 undergraduate students

Undergraduates Students come from 5 states and territories; 40 other countries; 3% Black or African American, non-Hispanic/Latino; 69% Hispanic/Latino; 9% Asian, non-Hispanic/Latino; 0.2% Native Hawaiian or other Pacific Islander, non-Hispanic/Latino; 0.2% American Indian or Alaska Native, non-Hispanic/Latino; 0.9% Two or more races, non-Hispanic/Latino; 7% Race/ethnicity unknown; 0.2% international. **Faculty** *Total:* 523, 34% full-time. *Student/faculty ratio:* 28:1.

Majors Business teacher education; criminal justice/law enforcement administration; liberal arts and sciences/liberal studies; registered nursing/registered nurse. **Academics** *Calendar:* semesters. *Degree:* certificates and associate. *Special study options:* academic remediation for entering students, adult/continuing education programs, advanced placement credit, English as a second language, honors programs, part-time degree program, services for LD students, study abroad, summer session for credit. *ROTC:* Army (c), Navy (c), Air Force (c). **Library** Learning Resource Center plus 1 other with 94,143 titles, 479 serial subscriptions, a Web page. **Student Life** *Housing:* college housing not available. *Activities and Organizations:* drama/theater group, student-run newspaper, radio station, choral group. *Campus security:* 24-hour patrols, late-night transport/escort service. *Student services:* health clinic, personal/psychological counseling, women's center, legal services. **Athletics** *Intercollegiate sports:* baseball M, basketball M/W, cross-country running M/W, softball W, swimming and diving M/W, tennis M/W, volleyball W, water polo M/W, wrestling M. *Intramural sports:* field hockey W, volleyball M/W. **Financial Aid** Of all full-time matriculated undergraduates who enrolled in 2012, 150 Federal Work-Study jobs (averaging $3200). 35 state and other part-time jobs (averaging $3200). *Financial aid deadline:* 5/1. **Applying** *Options:* early admission. *Application deadlines:* 7/10 (freshmen), 7/10 (transfers). *Notification:* continuous (freshmen), continuous (transfers). **Freshman Application Contact** Rio Hondo College, 3600 Workman Mill Road, Whittier, CA 90601-1699. *Phone:* 562-692-0921 Ext. 3415. *Website:* http://www.riohondo.edu/.

Riverside City College
Riverside, California

Freshman Application Contact Joy Chambers, Dean of Enrollment Services, Riverside City College, Riverside, CA 92506. *Phone:* 951-222-8600. *Fax:* 951-222-8037. *E-mail:* admissionsriverside@rcc.edu. *Website:* http://www.rcc.edu/.

Sacramento City College
Sacramento, California

Director of Admissions Mr. Sam T. Sandusky, Dean, Student Services, Sacramento City College, 3835 Freeport Boulevard, Sacramento, CA 95822-1386. *Phone:* 916-558-2438. *Website:* http://www.scc.losrios.edu/.

Saddleback College
Mission Viejo, California

Freshman Application Contact Admissions Office, Saddleback College, 28000 Marguerite Parkway, Mission Viejo, CA 92692. *Phone:* 949-582-4555. *Fax:* 949-347-8315. *E-mail:* earaiza@saddleback.edu. *Website:* http://www.saddleback.edu/.

Sage College
Moreno Valley, California

Admissions Office Contact Sage College, 12125 Day Street, Building L, Moreno Valley, CA 92557-6720. *Toll-free phone:* 888-755-SAGE. *Website:* http://www.sagecollege.edu/.

The Salvation Army College for Officer Training at Crestmont
Rancho Palos Verdes, California

- **Independent Salvation Army** 2-year, founded 1878
- **Suburban** 44-acre campus with easy access to Los Angeles
- **Endowment** $85.5 million
- **Coed**

Undergraduates 61 full-time, 63 part-time. Students come from 14 states and territories; 1 other country; 67% are from out of state; 4% Black or African American, non-Hispanic/Latino; 22% Hispanic/Latino; 7% Asian, non-Hispanic/Latino; 6% Native Hawaiian or other Pacific Islander, non-Hispanic/Latino; 3% Two or more races, non-Hispanic/Latino; 100% live on campus. *Retention:* 98% of full-time freshmen returned. **Faculty** *Student/faculty ratio:* 1:1. **Academics** *Calendar:* quarters. *Degree:* associate. *Special study options:* academic remediation for entering students, accelerated degree program, cooperative education, distance learning, English as a second language, external degree program, independent study, internships, off-campus study, student-designed majors. **Student Life** *Campus security:* 24-hour emergency response devices and patrols.

Applying *Application fee:* $15. *Required:* essay or personal statement, high school transcript, 2 letters of recommendation, interview.

Freshman Application Contact Capt. Brian Jones, Director of Curriculum, The Salvation Army College for Officer Training at Crestmont, 30840 Hawthorne Boulevard, Rancho Palos Verdes, CA 90275. *Phone:* 310-544-6442. *Fax:* 310-265-6520.
Website: http://www.crestmont.edu/.

San Bernardino Valley College
San Bernardino, California

Director of Admissions Ms. Helena Johnson, Director of Admissions and Records, San Bernardino Valley College, 701 South Mount Vernon Avenue, San Bernardino, CA 92410-2748. *Phone:* 909-384-4401.
Website: http://www.valleycollege.edu/.

San Diego City College
San Diego, California

- **State and locally supported** 2-year, founded 1914, part of San Diego Community College District System
- **Urban** 60-acre campus with easy access to San Diego, Tijuana
- **Endowment** $166,270
- **Coed,** 16,930 undergraduate students

Undergraduates 13% Black or African American, non-Hispanic/Latino; 47% Hispanic/Latino; 9% Asian, non-Hispanic/Latino; 0.5% Native Hawaiian or other Pacific Islander, non-Hispanic/Latino; 0.3% American Indian or Alaska Native, non-Hispanic/Latino; 7% Race/ethnicity unknown.

Faculty *Total:* 803, 21% full-time, 16% with terminal degrees. *Student/faculty ratio:* 35:1.

Majors Accounting; administrative assistant and secretarial science; African American/Black studies; anthropology; art; artificial intelligence; automobile/automotive mechanics technology; behavioral sciences; biology/biological sciences; business administration and management; carpentry; commercial and advertising art; computer engineering technology; consumer services and advocacy; cosmetology; court reporting; data processing and data processing technology; developmental and child psychology; drafting and design technology; dramatic/theater arts; electrical, electronic and communications engineering technology; emergency medical technology (EMT paramedic); engineering technology; English; environmental engineering technology; fashion merchandising; finance; graphic and printing equipment operation/production; Hispanic-American, Puerto Rican, and Mexican-American/Chicano studies; hospitality administration; industrial technology; insurance; interior design; journalism; labor and industrial relations; Latin American studies; legal administrative assistant/secretary; legal assistant/paralegal; liberal arts and sciences/liberal studies; licensed practical/vocational nurse training; machine tool technology; marketing/marketing management; mathematics; modern languages; music; occupational safety and health technology; parks, recreation and leisure; photography; physical education teaching and coaching; physical sciences; political science and government; pre-engineering; psychology; radio and television; real estate; registered nursing/registered nurse; rhetoric and composition; social sciences; social work; sociology; special products marketing; teacher assistant/aide; telecommunications technology; tourism and travel services management; transportation and materials moving related; welding technology.

Academics *Calendar:* semesters. *Degree:* certificates and associate. *Special study options:* academic remediation for entering students, adult/continuing education programs, cooperative education, distance learning, English as a second language, external degree program, honors programs, independent study, off-campus study, part-time degree program, services for LD students, student-designed majors, summer session for credit. *ROTC:* Air Force (c).

Library San Diego City College Library with 88,000 titles, 191 serial subscriptions, 950 audiovisual materials, an OPAC.

Student Life *Housing:* college housing not available. *Activities and Organizations:* drama/theater group, student-run newspaper, radio station, choral group, Alpha Gamma Sigma, Association of United Latin American Students, MECHA, Afrikan Student Union, Student Nurses Association. *Campus security:* 24-hour emergency response devices and patrols, late-night transport/escort service. *Student services:* health clinic, personal/psychological counseling.

Athletics *Intercollegiate sports:* baseball M, basketball M/W, cross-country running M/W, football M, golf M/W, soccer M/W, softball W, tennis M/W, track and field M/W, volleyball M/W. *Intramural sports:* archery M/W, badminton M/W, baseball M, basketball M/W, bowling M/W, racquetball M/W, soccer M/W, softball W, swimming and diving M/W, tennis M/W, track and field M/W, volleyball M/W, weight lifting M/W.

Costs (2014–15) *Tuition:* state resident $1380 full-time, $46 per unit part-time; nonresident $7080 full-time, $236 per unit part-time. Full-time tuition and fees vary according to course load. Part-time tuition and fees vary according to course load. *Required fees:* $60 full-time.

Financial Aid Of all full-time matriculated undergraduates who enrolled in 2010, 90 Federal Work-Study jobs (averaging $3844). 19 state and other part-time jobs (averaging $2530).

Applying *Options:* electronic application. *Required for some:* high school transcript. *Application deadlines:* rolling (freshmen), rolling (transfers).

Freshman Application Contact Ms. Lou Humphries, Registrar/Supervisor of Admissions, Records, Evaluations and Veterans, San Diego City College, 1313 Park Boulevard, San Diego, CA 92101-4787. *Phone:* 619-388-3474. *Fax:* 619-388-3505. *E-mail:* lhumphri@sdccd.edu.
Website: http://www.sdcity.edu/.

San Diego Mesa College
San Diego, California

- **State and locally supported** 2-year, founded 1964, part of San Diego Community College District System
- **Suburban** 104-acre campus
- **Coed**

Undergraduates 25,464 full-time. 7% Black or African American, non-Hispanic/Latino; 31% Hispanic/Latino; 16% Asian, non-Hispanic/Latino; 0.7% Native Hawaiian or other Pacific Islander, non-Hispanic/Latino; 0.4% American Indian or Alaska Native, non-Hispanic/Latino; 9% Race/ethnicity unknown.

Academics *Calendar:* semesters. *Degree:* certificates, diplomas, and associate. *Special study options:* academic remediation for entering students, adult/continuing education programs, English as a second language, external degree program, honors programs, independent study, part-time degree program, services for LD students, summer session for credit.

Student Life *Campus security:* 24-hour emergency response devices and patrols, late-night transport/escort service.

Costs (2013–14) *Tuition:* state resident $0 full-time; nonresident $5496 full-time, $229 per unit part-time. *Required fees:* $1104 full-time, $46 per unit part-time.

Financial Aid Of all full-time matriculated undergraduates who enrolled in 2012, 115 Federal Work-Study jobs (averaging $5000). *Financial aid deadline:* 6/30.

Freshman Application Contact Ms. Cheri Sawyer, Admissions Supervisor, San Diego Mesa College, 7250 Mesa College Drive, San Diego, CA 92111. *Phone:* 619-388-2686. *Fax:* 619-388-2960. *E-mail:* csawyer@sdccd.edu.
Website: http://www.sdmesa.edu/.

San Diego Miramar College
San Diego, California

Freshman Application Contact Ms. Dana Andras, Admissions Supervisor, San Diego Miramar College, 10440 Black Mountain Road, San Diego, CA 92126-2999. *Phone:* 619-536-7854. *E-mail:* dmaxwell@sdccd.cc.ca.us.
Website: http://www.sdmiramar.edu/.

San Joaquin Delta College
Stockton, California

Freshman Application Contact Ms. Catherine Mooney, Registrar, San Joaquin Delta College, 5151 Pacific Avenue, Stockton, CA 95207. *Phone:* 209-954-5635. *Fax:* 209-954-5769. *E-mail:* admissions@deltacollege.edu.
Website: http://www.deltacollege.edu/.

San Joaquin Valley College
Bakersfield, California

- **Proprietary** 2-year, founded 1977, part of San Joaquin Valley College
- **Suburban** campus with easy access to Bakersfield
- **Coed,** 743 undergraduate students, 100% full-time, 73% women, 27% men

Undergraduates 743 full-time. 4% Black or African American, non-Hispanic/Latino; 55% Hispanic/Latino; 3% Asian, non-Hispanic/Latino; 0.9% Native Hawaiian or other Pacific Islander, non-Hispanic/Latino; 0.9% American Indian or Alaska Native, non-Hispanic/Latino; 4% Two or more races, non-Hispanic/Latino; 2% Race/ethnicity unknown; 4% international. *Retention:* 60% of full-time freshmen returned.

Faculty *Total:* 76, 51% full-time. *Student/faculty ratio:* 17:1.

Majors Business administration and management; corrections; heating, ventilation, air conditioning and refrigeration engineering technology; homeland security, law enforcement, firefighting and protective services related; medical/clinical assistant; medical insurance/medical billing; pharmacy technician; respiratory care therapy; surgical technology.

Academics *Degree:* certificates and associate.

Student Life *Activities and Organizations:* CAMA Club, RACT Club, Business Club, Student Council, National Technical Honor Society.

Costs (2013–14) *Tuition:* $29,750 per degree program part-time. No tuition increase for student's term of enrollment. *Payment plan:* installment.

Applying *Required for some:* essay or personal statement, high school transcript, interview. *Application deadlines:* rolling (freshmen), rolling (transfers). *Notification:* continuous (freshmen), continuous (transfers).
Freshman Application Contact Enrollment Services Director, San Joaquin Valley College, 201 New Stine Road, Bakersfield, CA 93309. *Phone:* 661-834-0126. *Toll-free phone:* 866-544-7898. *Fax:* 661-834-8124. *E-mail:* admissions@sjvc.edu.
Website: http://www.sjvc.edu/bakersfield.

San Joaquin Valley College
Chula Vista, California
- **Proprietary** 2-year, founded 2012
- **Urban** campus with easy access to San Diego
- **Coed,** 25 undergraduate students

Academics *Degree:* associate.
Costs (2013–14) *Tuition:* $57,650 per degree program part-time. No tuition increase for student's term of enrollment. *Payment plan:* installment.
Freshman Application Contact San Joaquin Valley College, 303 H Street, Chula Vista, CA 91910.
Website: http://www.sjvc.edu/san-diego.

San Joaquin Valley College
Fresno, California
- **Proprietary** 2-year, part of San Joaquin Valley College
- **Urban** campus with easy access to Fresno
- **Coed,** 738 undergraduate students, 100% full-time, 72% women, 28% men

Undergraduates 738 full-time. 4% Black or African American, non-Hispanic/Latino; 56% Hispanic/Latino; 6% Asian, non-Hispanic/Latino; 0.8% Native Hawaiian or other Pacific Islander, non-Hispanic/Latino; 0.9% American Indian or Alaska Native, non-Hispanic/Latino; 6% Two or more races, non-Hispanic/Latino; 2% Race/ethnicity unknown; 4% international. *Retention:* 69% of full-time freshmen returned.
Faculty *Student/faculty ratio:* 18:1.
Majors Corrections; heating, ventilation, air conditioning and refrigeration engineering technology; medical/clinical assistant; medical office assistant; office occupations and clerical services; pharmacy technician; surgical technology; veterinary/animal health technology.
Academics *Degree:* certificates and associate.
Student Life *Housing:* college housing not available. *Activities and Organizations:* Associated Student Body, American Medical Technologists, State and County Dental Assistants Association, Arts and Entertainment.
Costs (2013–14) *Tuition:* $15,500 full-time. Full-time tuition and fees vary according to location and program. *Payment plans:* tuition prepayment, installment.
Applying *Required for some:* essay or personal statement, 1 letter of recommendation, interview. *Application deadlines:* rolling (freshmen), rolling (transfers). *Notification:* continuous (freshmen), continuous (transfers).
Freshman Application Contact Enrollment Services Director, San Joaquin Valley College, 295 East Sierra Avenue, Fresno, CA 93710. *Phone:* 559-448-8282. *Fax:* 559-448-8250. *E-mail:* admissions@sjvc.edu.
Website: http://www.sjvc.edu/fresno.

San Joaquin Valley College
Hanford, California
- **Proprietary** 2-year
- **Small-town** campus with easy access to Fresno
- **Coed**

Majors Avionics maintenance technology; business administration and management; construction management; criminal justice/law enforcement administration; dental hygiene; diagnostic medical sonography and ultrasound technology; heating, air conditioning, ventilation and refrigeration maintenance technology; human resources management; industrial technology; licensed practical/vocational nurse training; massage therapy; medical/clinical assistant; medical insurance/medical billing; pharmacy technician; physician assistant; registered nursing/registered nurse; respiratory care therapy; surgical technology; veterinary/animal health technology.
Academics *Degree:* certificates and associate.
Costs (2013–14) *Tuition:* $29,750 per degree program part-time. No tuition increase for student's term of enrollment. *Payment plan:* installment.
Freshman Application Contact San Joaquin Valley College, 215 West 7th Street, Hanford, CA 93230.
Website: http://www.sjvc.edu/hanford.

San Joaquin Valley College
Hesperia, California
- **Proprietary** 2-year, part of San Joaquin Valley College
- **Suburban** campus with easy access to San Bernadino
- **Coed,** 694 undergraduate students

Undergraduates Students come from 1 other state. *Retention:* 67% of full-time freshmen returned.
Majors Avionics maintenance technology; communication sciences and disorders; criminal justice/law enforcement administration; dental hygiene; diagnostic medical sonography and ultrasound technology; heating, air conditioning, ventilation and refrigeration maintenance technology; human resources management; industrial technology; licensed practical/vocational nurse training; massage therapy; medical/clinical assistant; medical insurance/medical billing; pharmacy; pharmacy technician; physician assistant; registered nursing/registered nurse; respiratory care therapy; surgical technology; veterinary/animal health technology.
Academics *Degree:* certificates and associate.
Costs (2013–14) *Tuition:* $31,950 per degree program part-time. No tuition increase for student's term of enrollment. *Payment plan:* installment.
Freshman Application Contact San Joaquin Valley College, 9331 Mariposa Road, Hesperia, CA 92344.
Website: http://www.sjvc.edu/victor-valley.

San Joaquin Valley College
Lancaster, California
- **Proprietary** 2-year, founded 2012, part of San Joaquin Valley College
- **Suburban** campus
- **Coed**

Costs (2013–14) *Tuition:* $31,950 per degree program part-time. No tuition increase for student's term of enrollment. *Payment plan:* installment.
Freshman Application Contact San Joaquin Valley College, 42135 10th Street West, Lancaster, CA 93534.
Website: http://www.sjvc.edu/antelope-valley.

San Joaquin Valley College
Ontario, California
- **Proprietary** 2-year, part of San Joaquin Valley College
- **Urban** campus with easy access to Los Angeles
- **Coed,** 746 undergraduate students, 100% full-time, 60% women, 40% men

Undergraduates 746 full-time. 6% Black or African American, non-Hispanic/Latino; 61% Hispanic/Latino; 4% Asian, non-Hispanic/Latino; 3% Native Hawaiian or other Pacific Islander, non-Hispanic/Latino; 0.7% American Indian or Alaska Native, non-Hispanic/Latino; 4% Two or more races, non-Hispanic/Latino; 3% Race/ethnicity unknown; 3% international. *Retention:* 70% of full-time freshmen returned.
Faculty *Student/faculty ratio:* 20:1.
Majors Construction management; corrections; dental hygiene; heating, air conditioning, ventilation and refrigeration maintenance technology; industrial mechanics and maintenance technology; medical/clinical assistant; medical office assistant; office occupations and clerical services; pharmacy technician; respiratory therapy technician.
Academics *Degree:* certificates and associate.
Student Life *Housing:* college housing not available. *Activities and Organizations:* Students in Free Enterprise (SIFE), Associated Student Body, Fitness Club, Ambassador Club, Diversity Club.
Costs (2013–14) *Tuition:* $16,650 full-time. Full-time tuition and fees vary according to location and program. *Payment plans:* tuition prepayment, installment.
Applying *Required for some:* essay or personal statement, interview. *Application deadlines:* rolling (freshmen), rolling (transfers). *Notification:* continuous (freshmen), continuous (transfers).
Freshman Application Contact Enrollment Services Director, San Joaquin Valley College, 4580 Ontario Mills Parkway, Ontario, CA 91764. *Phone:* 909-948-7582. *Fax:* 909-948-3860. *E-mail:* admissions@sjvc.edu.
Website: http://www.sjvc.edu/ontario.

San Joaquin Valley College
Rancho Cordova, California
- **Proprietary** 2-year, part of San Joaquin Valley College
- **Suburban** campus with easy access to Sacramento
- **Coed,** 114 undergraduate students, 100% full-time, 54% women, 46% men

Undergraduates 114 full-time. 4% Black or African American, non-Hispanic/Latino; 6% Hispanic/Latino; 21% Asian, non-Hispanic/Latino; 6% Native Hawaiian or other Pacific Islander, non-Hispanic/Latino; 6% Two or more races, non-Hispanic/Latino; 3% Race/ethnicity unknown; 5% international. *Retention:* 67% of full-time freshmen returned.

Faculty *Student/faculty ratio:* 12:1.

Majors Medical/clinical assistant; respiratory therapy technician.

Academics *Degree:* certificates and associate.

Student Life *Housing:* college housing not available. *Activities and Organizations:* Associated Student Body, Diversity Committee.

Costs (2013–14) *Tuition:* $24,250 full-time. Full-time tuition and fees vary according to location and program. *Payment plans:* tuition prepayment, installment.

Applying *Required for some:* essay or personal statement, interview. *Application deadlines:* rolling (freshmen), rolling (transfers). *Notification:* continuous (freshmen), continuous (transfers).

Freshman Application Contact Enrollment Services Director, San Joaquin Valley College, 11050 Olson Drive, Suite 100, Rancho Cordova, CA 95670. *Phone:* 916-638-7582. *Fax:* 916-638-7553. *E-mail:* admissions@sjvc.edu. *Website:* http://www.sjvc.edu/rancho-cordova.

San Joaquin Valley College

Salida, California

- **Proprietary** 2-year, part of San Joaquin Valley College
- **Suburban** campus
- **Coed,** 322 undergraduate students, 100% full-time, 73% women, 27% men

Undergraduates 322 full-time. Students come from 1 other state; 3% Black or African American, non-Hispanic/Latino; 52% Hispanic/Latino; 4% Asian, non-Hispanic/Latino; 2% Native Hawaiian or other Pacific Islander, non-Hispanic/Latino; 0.9% American Indian or Alaska Native, non-Hispanic/Latino; 5% Two or more races, non-Hispanic/Latino; 2% Race/ethnicity unknown; 4% international.

Faculty *Student/faculty ratio:* 17:1.

Majors Industrial technology; massage therapy; medical/clinical assistant; medical office assistant; office occupations and clerical services; pharmacy technician.

Academics *Degree:* certificates and associate.

Student Life *Activities and Organizations:* Associated Student Body, Book Club.

Costs (2013–14) *Tuition:* $15,500 full-time. Full-time tuition and fees vary according to location and program. *Payment plans:* tuition prepayment, installment.

Applying *Required for some:* essay or personal statement, interview. *Application deadlines:* rolling (freshmen), rolling (transfers). *Notification:* continuous (freshmen), continuous (transfers).

Freshman Application Contact Enrollment Services Director, San Joaquin Valley College, 5380 Pirrone Road, Salida, CA 95368. *Phone:* 209-543-8800. *Fax:* 209-543-8320. *E-mail:* admissions@sjvc.edu. *Website:* http://www.sjvc.edu/modesto.

San Joaquin Valley College

Temecula, California

- **Proprietary** 2-year, part of San Joaquin Valley College
- **Urban** campus with easy access to Los Angeles
- **Coed,** 314 undergraduate students, 100% full-time, 78% women, 22% men

Undergraduates 314 full-time. 2% are from out of state. *Retention:* 80% of full-time freshmen returned.

Faculty *Student/faculty ratio:* 24:1.

Majors Avionics maintenance technology; business administration and management; construction management; criminal justice/law enforcement administration; dental hygiene; diagnostic medical sonography and ultrasound technology; heating, air conditioning, ventilation and refrigeration maintenance technology; human resources management; industrial technology; licensed practical/vocational nurse training; massage therapy; medical/clinical assistant; medical insurance/medical billing; pharmacy technician; physician assistant; registered nursing/registered nurse; respiratory care therapy; surgical technology; veterinary/animal health technology.

Academics *Degree:* certificates and associate.

Costs (2013–14) *Tuition:* $31,950 per degree program part-time. No tuition increase for student's term of enrollment. *Payment plan:* installment.

Freshman Application Contact Robyn Whiles, Enrollment Services Director, San Joaquin Valley College, 27270 Madison Avenue, Suite 103, Temecula, CA 92590. *Phone:* 559-651-2500. *E-mail:* admissions@sjvc.edu. *Website:* http://www.sjvc.edu/temecula.

San Joaquin Valley College

Visalia, California

- **Proprietary** 2-year, founded 1977, part of San Joaquin Valley College
- **Suburban** campus with easy access to Fresno
- **Coed,** 1,892 undergraduate students, 100% full-time, 78% women, 22% men

Undergraduates 1,892 full-time. 14% Black or African American, non-Hispanic/Latino; 40% Hispanic/Latino; 4% Asian, non-Hispanic/Latino; 0.7% Native Hawaiian or other Pacific Islander, non-Hispanic/Latino; 0.9% American Indian or Alaska Native, non-Hispanic/Latino; 4% Two or more races, non-Hispanic/Latino; 2% Race/ethnicity unknown; 3% international.

Faculty *Total:* 168. *Student/faculty ratio:* 20:1.

Majors Business/commerce; computer and information sciences and support services related; corrections; dental hygiene; health and medical administrative services related; heating, ventilation, air conditioning and refrigeration engineering technology; human resources management; industrial technology; licensed practical/vocational nurse training; medical administrative assistant and medical secretary; medical/clinical assistant; medical office assistant; pharmacy technician; physician assistant; registered nursing/registered nurse; respiratory care therapy.

Academics *Calendar:* semesters. *Degree:* certificates and associate. *Special study options:* academic remediation for entering students.

Library SJVC Visalia Campus Library.

Student Life *Housing:* college housing not available. *Activities and Organizations:* Associated Student Body, Students in Free Enterprise (SIFE), American Medical Technologists, National and Technical Honor Society. *Campus security:* late-night transport/escort service, full-time security personnel.

Costs (2013–14) *Tuition:* $29,750 per degree program part-time. No tuition increase for student's term of enrollment. *Payment plan:* installment.

Applying *Required for some:* essay or personal statement, high school transcript, interview. *Application deadlines:* rolling (freshmen), rolling (transfers). *Notification:* continuous (freshmen), continuous (transfers).

Freshman Application Contact Susie Topjian, Enrollment Services Director, San Joaquin Valley College, 8400 West Mineral King Boulevard, Visalia, CA 93291. *Phone:* 559-651-2500. *Fax:* 559-734-9048. *E-mail:* admissions@sjvc.edu. *Website:* http://www.sjvc.edu/visalia.

San Joaquin Valley College–Fresno Aviation Campus

Fresno, California

- **Proprietary** 2-year, part of San Joaquin Valley College
- **Coed, primarily men,** 83 undergraduate students, 100% full-time, 6% women, 94% men

Undergraduates 83 full-time. 4% Black or African American, non-Hispanic/Latino; 30% Hispanic/Latino; 12% Asian, non-Hispanic/Latino; 4% Two or more races, non-Hispanic/Latino; 4% Race/ethnicity unknown; 4% international.

Majors Airframe mechanics and aircraft maintenance technology.

Academics *Degree:* associate.

Student Life *Housing:* college housing not available. *Activities and Organizations:* RC Club (radio controlled airplane).

Costs (2013–14) *Tuition:* $30,210 per degree program part-time. No tuition increase for student's term of enrollment. *Payment plan:* installment.

Applying *Required for some:* essay or personal statement, high school transcript, interview. *Application deadlines:* rolling (freshmen), rolling (transfers). *Notification:* continuous (freshmen), continuous (transfers).

Freshman Application Contact Enrollment Services Coordinator, San Joaquin Valley College–Fresno Aviation Campus, 4985 East Anderson Avenue, Fresno, CA 93727. *Phone:* 559-453-0123. *Fax:* 599-453-0133. *E-mail:* admissions@sjvc.edu. *Website:* http://www.sjvc.edu/aviation-campus.

San Joaquin Valley College–Online

Visalia, California

- **Proprietary** 2-year, part of San Joaquin Valley College
- **Suburban** campus
- **Coed,** 529 undergraduate students, 100% full-time, 78% women, 22% men

Undergraduates 529 full-time. 31% Black or African American, non-Hispanic/Latino; 15% Hispanic/Latino; 2% Asian, non-Hispanic/Latino; 0.4% Native Hawaiian or other Pacific Islander, non-Hispanic/Latino; 0.8% American Indian or Alaska Native, non-Hispanic/Latino; 4% Two or more races, non-Hispanic/Latino; 9% Race/ethnicity unknown.

Majors Business administration and management; construction management; human resources management and services related; medical/clinical assistant; medical office management.

Academics *Degree:* certificates and associate.

Costs (2013–14) *Tuition:* $29,620 per degree program part-time. No tuition increase for student's term of enrollment. *Payment plan:* installment.

Applying *Options:* electronic application. *Required for some:* essay or personal statement, interview. *Application deadlines:* rolling (freshmen), rolling (transfers). *Notification:* continuous (freshmen), continuous (transfers).

Freshman Application Contact Enrollment Services Director, San Joaquin Valley College–Online, 801 S. Akers Street, Suite 150, Visalia, CA 93277. *E-mail:* admissions@sjvc.edu.

Website: http://www.sjvc.edu/campus/SJVC_Online/.

San Jose City College
San Jose, California

Freshman Application Contact Mr. Carlo Santos, Director of Admissions/Registrar, San Jose City College, 2100 Moorpark Avenue, San Jose, CA 95128-2799. *Phone:* 408-288-3707. *Fax:* 408-298-1935.

Website: http://www.sjcc.edu/.

Santa Ana College
Santa Ana, California

Freshman Application Contact Mrs. Christie Steward, Admissions Clerk, Santa Ana College, 1530 West 17th Street, Santa Ana, CA 92706-3398. *Phone:* 714-564-6053.

Website: http://www.sac.edu/.

Santa Barbara Business College
Bakersfield, California

Admissions Office Contact Santa Barbara Business College, 5300 California Avenue, Bakersfield, CA 93309.

Website: http://www.sbbcollege.edu/.

Santa Barbara Business College
Santa Maria, California

Admissions Office Contact Santa Barbara Business College, 303 East Plaza Drive, Santa Maria, CA 93454.

Website: http://www.sbbcollege.edu/.

Santa Barbara City College
Santa Barbara, California

Freshman Application Contact Ms. Allison Curtis, Director of Admissions and Records, Santa Barbara City College, Santa Barbara, CA 93109. *Phone:* 805-965-0581 Ext. 2352. *Fax:* 805-962-0497. *E-mail:* admissions@sbcc.edu. *Website:* http://www.sbcc.edu/.

Santa Monica College
Santa Monica, California

- **State and locally supported** 2-year, founded 1929, part of California Community College System
- **Urban** 40-acre campus with easy access to Los Angeles
- **Coed,** 30,000 undergraduate students, 36% full-time, 52% women, 48% men

Undergraduates 10,722 full-time, 19,278 part-time. 6% are from out of state; 9% Black or African American, non-Hispanic/Latino; 37% Hispanic/Latino; 11% Asian, non-Hispanic/Latino; 0.3% Native Hawaiian or other Pacific Islander, non-Hispanic/Latino; 0.2% American Indian or Alaska Native, non-Hispanic/Latino; 4% Two or more races, non-Hispanic/Latino; 1% Race/ethnicity unknown; 11% international. *Retention:* 65% of full-time freshmen returned.

Freshmen *Admission:* 5,159 enrolled.

Faculty *Total:* 1,303, 24% full-time.

Majors Accounting; administrative assistant and secretarial science; animation, interactive technology, video graphics and special effects; anthropology; apparel and textile marketing management; art; biological and physical sciences; business administration and management; child development; commercial photography; computer programming; computer science; cosmetology; dance; data entry/microcomputer applications; data modeling/warehousing and database administration; digital communication and media/multimedia; dramatic/theater arts; fashion/apparel design; film/cinema/video studies; graphic design; health and physical education/fitness; interior design; journalism; legal administrative assistant/secretary; liberal arts and sciences/liberal studies; music; office management; radio and television; registered nursing/registered nurse; respiratory care therapy; rhetoric and composition; sales, distribution, and marketing operations; selling skills and sales; special education–early childhood; women's studies.

Academics *Calendar:* semester plus optional winter and summer terms. *Degree:* certificates and associate. *Special study options:* academic remediation for entering students, adult/continuing education programs, advanced placement credit, cooperative education, distance learning, English as a second language, honors programs, independent study, internships, part-time degree program, services for LD students, study abroad, summer session for credit. *ROTC:* Army (c).

Library Santa Monica College Library with 101,317 titles, 389 serial subscriptions, an OPAC, a Web page.

Student Life *Housing:* college housing not available. *Activities and Organizations:* drama/theater group, student-run newspaper, choral group. *Campus security:* 24-hour emergency response devices and patrols, student patrols, late-night transport/escort service. *Student services:* health clinic, personal/psychological counseling, women's center, legal services.

Athletics Member NJCAA. *Intercollegiate sports:* basketball M/W, cross-country running M/W, football M, soccer W, softball W, swimming and diving M/W, tennis W, track and field M/W, volleyball M/W, water polo M/W.

Costs (2014–15) *Tuition:* state resident $896 full-time, $46 per credit part-time; nonresident $5768 full-time, $315 per credit part-time.

Financial Aid Of all full-time matriculated undergraduates who enrolled in 2012, 450 Federal Work-Study jobs (averaging $3000).

Applying *Options:* early admission. *Required:* high school transcript. *Application deadlines:* 8/30 (freshmen), 8/30 (transfers). *Notification:* continuous until 8/30 (freshmen), continuous until 8/30 (transfers).

Freshman Application Contact Santa Monica College, 1900 Pico Boulevard, Santa Monica, CA 90405-1628. *Phone:* 310-434-4774.

Website: http://www.smc.edu/.

Santa Rosa Junior College
Santa Rosa, California

- **State and locally supported** 2-year, founded 1918, part of California Community College System
- **Urban** 100-acre campus with easy access to San Francisco
- **Endowment** $41.3 million
- **Coed,** 22,008 undergraduate students, 31% full-time, 55% women, 45% men

Undergraduates 6,830 full-time, 15,178 part-time. Students come from 36 other countries; 3% are from out of state; 3% Black or African American, non-Hispanic/Latino; 31% Hispanic/Latino; 4% Asian, non-Hispanic/Latino; 1% Native Hawaiian or other Pacific Islander, non-Hispanic/Latino; 0.8% American Indian or Alaska Native, non-Hispanic/Latino; 4% Two or more races, non-Hispanic/Latino; 6% Race/ethnicity unknown.

Freshmen *Admission:* 5,889 applied, 5,889 admitted.

Faculty *Total:* 1,323, 20% full-time, 13% with terminal degrees. *Student/faculty ratio:* 22:1.

Majors Agricultural business and management; agricultural communication/journalism; agroecology and sustainable agriculture; American Sign Language (ASL); animal sciences; anthropology; art; art history, criticism and conservation; automobile/automotive mechanics technology; behavioral sciences; biology/biological sciences; business administration and management; chemistry; child development; civil engineering technology; communication; community health services counseling; computer science; criminal justice/law enforcement administration; culinary arts; dance; dental hygiene; diesel mechanics technology; dietetic technology; digital communication and media/multimedia; dramatic/theater arts; early childhood education; economics; electrical, electronic and communications engineering technology; emergency medical technology (EMT paramedic); engineering; English; environmental studies; fashion/apparel design; fashion merchandising; fire science/firefighting; floriculture/floristry management; French; graphic design; health and physical education/fitness; history; horse husbandry/equine science and management; humanities; human resources management; human services; interior design; jazz/jazz studies; kinesiology and exercise science; landscaping and groundskeeping; Latin American studies; legal assistant/paralegal; liberal arts and sciences/liberal studies; licensed practical/vocational nurse training; mathematics; medical/clinical assistant; music related; natural resources/conservation; natural sciences; nutrition sciences; parks, recreation and leisure facilities management; pharmacy technician; philosophy; physics; political science and government; psychology; radiologic technology/science; real estate; registered nursing/registered nurse; religious studies; restaurant/food services management; social sciences; sociology; Spanish; surveying technology; viticulture and enology; women's studies.

Academics *Calendar:* semesters. *Degree:* certificates and associate. *Special study options:* academic remediation for entering students, adult/continuing education programs, advanced placement credit, cooperative education, distance learning, English as a second language, independent study, internships, off-campus study, part-time degree program, services for LD students, study abroad, summer session for credit.

Library Doyle Library plus 1 other with 185,461 titles, 29,932 serial subscriptions, 18,173 audiovisual materials, an OPAC, a Web page.

Student Life *Housing:* college housing not available. *Activities and Organizations:* drama/theater group, student-run newspaper, choral group, AG Ambassadors, MECHA, Alpha Gamma Sigma, Phi Theta Kappa, Puente. *Campus security:* 24-hour emergency response devices and patrols, student patrols. *Student services:* health clinic, personal/psychological counseling.

Athletics Member NJCAA. *Intercollegiate sports:* baseball M, basketball M/W, cross-country running M/W, football M, golf M, ice hockey M(c), rugby M(c), soccer M/W, softball W, swimming and diving M/W, tennis M/W, track and field M/W, volleyball W, water polo M/W, wrestling M.

Costs (2014–15) *One-time required fee:* $40. *Tuition:* state resident $0 full-time; nonresident $5832 full-time, $243 per unit part-time. Full-time tuition and fees vary according to course load. Part-time tuition and fees vary according to course load. *Required fees:* $1104 full-time, $46 per unit part-time, $20 per term part-time. *Payment plans:* installment, deferred payment.

Financial Aid Of all full-time matriculated undergraduates who enrolled in 2009, 135 Federal Work-Study jobs (averaging $2210). 43 state and other part-time jobs (averaging $7396).

Applying *Options:* electronic application, early admission. *Application deadlines:* rolling (freshmen), rolling (out-of-state freshmen), rolling (transfers). *Notification:* continuous (freshmen), continuous (out-of-state freshmen), continuous (transfers).

Freshman Application Contact Ms. Freyja Pereira, Director, Admissions, Records and Enrollment Services, Santa Rosa Junior College, 1501 Mendocino Avenue, Santa Rosa, CA 95401. *Phone:* 707-527-4512. *Fax:* 707-527-4798. *E-mail:* admininfo@santarosa.edu.
Website: http://www.santarosa.edu/.

Santiago Canyon College
Orange, California

- **State-supported** 2-year, founded 2000, part of California Community College System
- **Suburban** campus with easy access to Los Angeles
- **Coed**

Undergraduates 7,987 full-time, 6,096 part-time. Students come from 6 other countries; 6% are from out of state; 0.2% transferred in.

Faculty *Student/faculty ratio:* 23:1.

Academics *Calendar:* semesters. *Degree:* certificates and associate. *Special study options:* academic remediation for entering students, adult/continuing education programs, advanced placement credit, cooperative education, distance learning, English as a second language, external degree program, freshman honors college, honors programs, part-time degree program, services for LD students, summer session for credit.

Student Life *Campus security:* 24-hour emergency response devices, late-night transport/escort service.

Costs (2013–14) *Tuition:* state resident $0 full-time; nonresident $5136 full-time, $214 per unit part-time. *Required fees:* $1104 full-time, $46 per unit part-time, $38 per term part-time.

Freshman Application Contact Tuyen Nguyen, Admissions and Records, Santiago Canyon College, 8045 East Chapman Avenue, Orange, CA 92869. *Phone:* 714-628-4902.
Website: http://www.sccollege.edu/.

Shasta College
Redding, California

Director of Admissions Dr. Kevin O'Rorke, Dean of Enrollment Services, Shasta College, PO Box 496006, 11555 Old Oregon Trail, Redding, CA 96049-6006. *Phone:* 530-242-7669.
Website: http://www.shastacollege.edu/.

Sierra College
Rocklin, California

- **State-supported** 2-year, founded 1936, part of California Community College System
- **Suburban** 327-acre campus with easy access to Sacramento
- **Coed**

Undergraduates 5,355 full-time, 14,061 part-time. 1% are from out of state; 4% transferred in; 1% live on campus.

Faculty *Student/faculty ratio:* 25:1.

Academics *Calendar:* semesters. *Degree:* certificates and associate. *Special study options:* academic remediation for entering students, accelerated degree program, advanced placement credit, distance learning, double majors, English as a second language, honors programs, independent study, internships, off-

campus study, part-time degree program, services for LD students, study abroad, summer session for credit.

Student Life *Campus security:* 24-hour emergency response devices and patrols, late-night transport/escort service.

Financial Aid Of all full-time matriculated undergraduates who enrolled in 2012, 150 Federal Work-Study jobs (averaging $2340).

Applying *Options:* electronic application, early admission.

Freshman Application Contact Sierra College, 5000 Rocklin Road, Rocklin, CA 95677-3397. *Phone:* 916-660-7341.
Website: http://www.sierracollege.edu/.

Skyline College
San Bruno, California

Freshman Application Contact Terry Stats, Admissions Office, Skyline College, 3300 College Drive, San Bruno, CA 94066-1698. *Phone:* 650-738-4251. *E-mail:* stats@smccd.net.
Website: http://skylinecollege.net/.

Solano Community College
Fairfield, California

Freshman Application Contact Solano Community College, 4000 Suisun Valley Road, Fairfield, CA 94534. *Phone:* 707-864-7000 Ext. 4313.
Website: http://www.solano.edu/.

South Coast College
Orange, California

Director of Admissions South Coast College, 2011 West Chapman Avenue, Orange, CA 92868. *Toll-free phone:* 877-568-6130.
Website: http://www.southcoastcollege.com/.

Southwestern College
Chula Vista, California

Freshman Application Contact Director of Admissions and Records, Southwestern College, 900 Otay Lakes Road, Chula Vista, CA 91910-7299. *Phone:* 619-421-6700 Ext. 5215. *Fax:* 619-482-6489.
Website: http://www.swc.edu/.

Stanbridge College
Irvine, California

Admissions Office Contact Stanbridge College, 2041 Business Center Drive, Irvine, CA 92612.
Website: http://www.stanbridge.edu/.

SUM Bible College & Theological Seminary
Oakland, California

Freshman Application Contact Admissions, SUM Bible College & Theological Seminary, 735 105th Avenue, Oakland, CA 94603. *Phone:* 510-567-6174. *Toll-free phone:* 888-567-6174. *Fax:* 510-568-1024.
Website: http://www.sum.edu/.

Taft College
Taft, California

- **State and locally supported** 2-year, founded 1922, part of California Community College System
- **Small-town** 15-acre campus
- **Endowment** $14,405
- **Coed**

Undergraduates 505 full-time, 8,995 part-time. Students come from 1 other country; 5% are from out of state; 3% transferred in; 6% live on campus.

Academics *Calendar:* semesters. *Degree:* certificates and associate. *Special study options:* academic remediation for entering students, adult/continuing education programs, advanced placement credit, distance learning, English as a second language, honors programs, independent study, part-time degree program, services for LD students, summer session for credit.

Student Life *Campus security:* 24-hour emergency response devices, controlled dormitory access, parking lot security.

Costs (2013–14) *One-time required fee:* $125. *Tuition:* state resident $1380 full-time, $46 per unit part-time; nonresident $7080 full-time, $190 per unit part-time. Full-time tuition and fees vary according to course load and program. Part-time tuition and fees vary according to course load. *Required fees:* $46 per unit part-time. *Room and board:* $4172; room only: $1576. Room and board charges vary according to board plan and housing facility.

Applying *Options:* electronic application. *Required for some:* high school transcript.
Freshman Application Contact Nichole Cook, Admissions/Counseling Technician, Taft College, 29 Emmons Park Drive, Taft, CA 93268-2317. *Phone:* 661-763-7790. *Fax:* 661-763-7758. *E-mail:* ncook@taftcollege.edu. *Website:* http://www.taftcollege.edu/.

Unitek College
Fremont, California

Admissions Office Contact Unitek College, 4670 Auto Mall Parkway, Fremont, CA 94538.
Website: http://www.unitekcollege.edu/.

Ventura College
Ventura, California

Freshman Application Contact Ms. Susan Bricker, Registrar, Ventura College, 4667 Telegraph Road, Ventura, CA 93003-3899. *Phone:* 805-654-6456. *Fax:* 805-654-6357. *E-mail:* sbricker@vcccd.net.
Website: http://www.venturacollege.edu/.

Victor Valley College
Victorville, California

- **State-supported** 2-year, founded 1961, part of California Community College System
- **Small-town** 253-acre campus with easy access to Los Angeles
- **Coed,** 6,824 undergraduate students, 35% women, 26% men

Undergraduates 4,118 part-time. 3% are from out of state; 2% Black or African American, non-Hispanic/Latino; 0.3% Hispanic/Latino; 0.1% Asian, non-Hispanic/Latino; 0.3% Native Hawaiian or other Pacific Islander, non-Hispanic/Latino; 45% American Indian or Alaska Native, non-Hispanic/Latino; 33% Two or more races, non-Hispanic/Latino; 4% Race/ethnicity unknown; 14% international; 12% transferred in. *Retention:* 66% of full-time freshmen returned.
Freshmen *Admission:* 685 enrolled.
Faculty *Student/faculty ratio:* 24:1.
Majors Administrative assistant and secretarial science; agricultural teacher education; art; automobile/automotive mechanics technology; biological and physical sciences; biology/biological sciences; building/construction finishing, management, and inspection related; business administration and management; business/commerce; child-care and support services management; child development; computer and information sciences; computer programming (specific applications); computer science; construction engineering technology; criminal justice/police science; dramatic/theater arts; electrical, electronic and communications engineering technology; fire prevention and safety technology; fire science/firefighting; food technology and processing; horticultural science; humanities; information science/studies; kindergarten/preschool education; liberal arts and sciences/liberal studies; management information systems; mathematics; music; natural sciences; ornamental horticulture; physical sciences; real estate; registered nursing/registered nurse; respiratory care therapy; science technologies related; social sciences; teacher assistant/aide; trade and industrial teacher education; vehicle maintenance and repair technologies related; welding technology.
Academics *Calendar:* semesters. *Degree:* certificates, diplomas, and associate. *Special study options:* academic remediation for entering students, accelerated degree program, advanced placement credit, cooperative education, distance learning, double majors, English as a second language, honors programs, independent study, internships, off-campus study, part-time degree program, services for LD students, study abroad, summer session for credit.
Library Learning Resource Center with an OPAC, a Web page.
Student Life *Housing:* college housing not available. *Activities and Organizations:* drama/theater group, student-run newspaper, choral group, Black Student Union, Drama Club, rugby, Phi Theta Kappa. *Campus security:* 24-hour emergency response devices and patrols, late-night transport/escort service, part-time trained security personnel. *Student services:* health clinic, personal/psychological counseling.
Athletics Member NCAA, NJCAA. *Intercollegiate sports:* baseball M, basketball M/W, cross-country running M/W, football M, golf M, soccer M/W, softball W, tennis M/W, track and field M/W, volleyball W, wrestling M. *Intramural sports:* rock climbing M/W.
Costs (2013–14) *Tuition:* state resident $1104 full-time, $46 per credit part-time; nonresident $4296 full-time, $179 per credit part-time. *Required fees:* $10 full-time. *Payment plan:* installment.

Financial Aid *Average need-based loan:* $6168. *Average need-based gift aid:* $3707.
Applying *Application deadline:* rolling (freshmen). *Notification:* continuous (freshmen).
Freshman Application Contact Ms. Greta Moon, Director of Admissions and Records (Interim), Victor Valley College, 18422 Bear Valley Road, Victorville, CA 92395. *Phone:* 760-245-4271. *Fax:* 760-843-7707. *E-mail:* moong@vvc.edu.
Website: http://www.vvc.edu/.

West Hills Community College
Coalinga, California

Freshman Application Contact Sandra Dagnino, West Hills Community College, 300 Cherry Lane, Coalinga, CA 93210-1399. *Phone:* 559-934-3203. *Toll-free phone:* 800-266-1114. *Fax:* 559-934-2830. *E-mail:* sandradagnino@westhillscollege.com.
Website: http://www.westhillscollege.com/.

West Los Angeles College
Culver City, California

Director of Admissions Mr. Len Isaksen, Director of Admissions, West Los Angeles College, 9000 Overland Avenue, Culver City, CA 90230-3519. *Phone:* 310-287-4255.
Website: http://www.lacolleges.net/.

West Valley College
Saratoga, California

Freshman Application Contact Ms. Barbara Ogilive, Supervisor, Admissions and Records, West Valley College, 14000 Fruitvale Avenue, Saratoga, CA 95070-5698. *Phone:* 408-741-4630. *E-mail:* barbara_ogilvie@westvalley.edu.
Website: http://www.westvalley.edu/.

Woodland Community College
Woodland, California

Admissions Office Contact Woodland Community College, 2300 East Gibson Road, Woodland, CA 95776.
Website: http://www.yccd.edu/woodland/.

WyoTech Fremont
Fremont, California

Freshman Application Contact Admissions Department, WyoTech Fremont, 200 Whitney Place, Fremont, CA 94539-7663. *Phone:* 510-580-3507. *Toll-free phone:* 888-577-7559. *Fax:* 510-490-8599.
Website: http://www.wyotech.edu/.

WyoTech Long Beach
Long Beach, California

Freshman Application Contact Admissions Office, WyoTech Long Beach, 2161 Technology Place, Long Beach, CA 90810. *Phone:* 562-624-9530. *Toll-free phone:* 888-577-7559. *Fax:* 562-437-8111.
Website: http://www.wyotech.edu/.

Yuba College
Marysville, California

Director of Admissions Dr. David Farrell, Dean of Student Development, Yuba College, 2088 North Beale Road, Marysville, CA 95901-7699. *Phone:* 530-741-6705.
Website: http://www.yccd.edu/.

COLORADO

Aims Community College
Greeley, Colorado

Freshman Application Contact Ms. Susie Gallardo, Admissions Technician, Aims Community College, Box 69, 5401 West 20th Street, Greeley, CO 80632-0069. *Phone:* 970-330-8008 Ext. 6624. *E-mail:* wgreen@chiron.aims.edu.
Website: http://www.aims.edu/.

Anthem College–Aurora
Aurora, Colorado

Director of Admissions Amy Marshall, Director of Admissions, Anthem College–Aurora, 350 Blackhawk Street, Aurora, CO 80011. *Phone:* 720-859-7900. *Toll-free phone:* 855-268-4363.
Website: http://www.anthem.edu/aurora-colorado/.

Arapahoe Community College
Littleton, Colorado

- **State-supported** 2-year, founded 1965, part of Colorado Community College and Occupational Education System
- **Suburban** 52-acre campus with easy access to Denver
- **Coed,** 11,900 undergraduate students, 21% full-time, 54% women, 46% men

Undergraduates 2,479 full-time, 9,421 part-time. Students come from 54 other countries; 8% are from out of state; 3% Black or African American, non-Hispanic/Latino; 12% Hispanic/Latino; 3% Asian, non-Hispanic/Latino; 0.3% Native Hawaiian or other Pacific Islander, non-Hispanic/Latino; 0.7% American Indian or Alaska Native, non-Hispanic/Latino; 4% Two or more races, non-Hispanic/Latino; 5% Race/ethnicity unknown; 1% international; 6% transferred in. *Retention:* 55% of full-time freshmen returned.

Freshmen *Admission:* 2,636 applied, 2,636 admitted, 1,660 enrolled. *Average high school GPA:* 2.81.

Faculty *Total:* 498, 20% full-time. *Student/faculty ratio:* 21:1.

Majors Accounting technology and bookkeeping; architectural engineering technology; automobile/automotive mechanics technology; banking and financial support services; business administration and management; civil engineering technology; clinical/medical laboratory technology; computer and information sciences; computer and information sciences and support services related; criminal justice/law enforcement administration; electrical, electronic and communications engineering technology; emergency medical technology (EMT paramedic); engineering technology; funeral service and mortuary science; graphic design; health and physical education/fitness; health information/medical records technology; interior design; legal assistant/paralegal; liberal arts and sciences/liberal studies; medical office management; physical therapy technology; registered nursing/registered nurse; system, networking, and LAN/WAN management.

Academics *Calendar:* semesters. *Degree:* certificates, diplomas, and associate. *Special study options:* academic remediation for entering students, accelerated degree program, adult/continuing education programs, advanced placement credit, cooperative education, distance learning, double majors, English as a second language, honors programs, independent study, internships, off-campus study, part-time degree program, services for LD students, student-designed majors, study abroad, summer session for credit. *ROTC:* Army (c), Navy (c), Air Force (c).

Library Weber Center for Learning Resources plus 1 other with 48,693 titles, 194 serial subscriptions, an OPAC, a Web page.

Student Life *Housing:* college housing not available. *Activities and Organizations:* drama/theater group, student-run newspaper, choral group, History Club, Science Club, Phi Theta Kappa, Outdoor Club, Frisbee Golf. *Campus security:* 24-hour emergency response devices and patrols, late-night transport/escort service. *Student services:* personal/psychological counseling.

Athletics *Intercollegiate sports:* baseball M, softball W. *Intramural sports:* baseball M(c)/W, basketball M, football M, ice hockey M, rock climbing M/W, skiing (cross-country) M/W, skiing (downhill) M/W, soccer M/W, softball M/W, swimming and diving M/W, table tennis M/W, tennis M/W, ultimate Frisbee M/W, volleyball M/W, weight lifting M.

Standardized Tests *Recommended:* ACT (for admission), SAT or ACT (for admission).

Costs (2014–15) *Tuition:* state resident $3585 full-time, $120 per credit hour part-time; nonresident $14,709 full-time, $490 per credit hour part-time. Full-time tuition and fees vary according to program and reciprocity agreements. Part-time tuition and fees vary according to program and reciprocity agreements. *Required fees:* $195 full-time, $29 per semester hour part-time. *Payment plans:* installment, deferred payment. *Waivers:* senior citizens.

Financial Aid Of all full-time matriculated undergraduates who enrolled in 2012, 100 Federal Work-Study jobs (averaging $4200). 200 state and other part-time jobs (averaging $4200).

Applying *Options:* electronic application, early admission, deferred entrance. *Application deadlines:* rolling (freshmen), rolling (out-of-state freshmen), rolling (transfers). *Notification:* continuous (freshmen), continuous (out-of-state freshmen), continuous (transfers).

Freshman Application Contact Arapahoe Community College, 5900 South Santa Fe Drive, PO Box 9002, Littleton, CO 80160-9002. *Phone:* 303-797-5623.
Website: http://www.arapahoe.edu/.

Bel–Rea Institute of Animal Technology
Denver, Colorado

Director of Admissions Ms. Paulette Kaufman, Director, Bel–Rea Institute of Animal Technology, 1681 South Dayton Street, Denver, CO 80247. *Phone:* 303-751-8700. *Toll-free phone:* 800-950-8001. *E-mail:* admissions@bel-rea.com.
Website: http://www.bel-rea.com/.

CollegeAmerica–Colorado Springs
Colorado Springs, Colorado

Freshman Application Contact CollegeAmerica–Colorado Springs, 2020 N. Academy Boulevard, Colorado Springs, CO 80909. *Phone:* 719-637-0600. *Toll-free phone:* 800-622-2894.
Website: http://www.collegeamerica.edu/.

CollegeAmerica–Denver
Denver, Colorado

Freshman Application Contact Admissions Office, CollegeAmerica–Denver, 1385 South Colorado Boulevard, Denver, CO 80222. *Phone:* 303-300-8740. *Toll-free phone:* 800-622-2894.
Website: http://www.collegeamerica.edu/.

CollegeAmerica–Fort Collins
Fort Collins, Colorado

Director of Admissions Ms. Anna DiTorrice-Mull, Director of Admissions, CollegeAmerica–Fort Collins, 4601 South Mason Street, Fort Collins, CO 80525-3740. *Phone:* 970-223-6060 Ext. 8002. *Toll-free phone:* 800-622-2894.
Website: http://www.collegeamerica.edu/.

Colorado Academy of Veterinary Technology
Colorado Springs, Colorado

Admissions Office Contact Colorado Academy of Veterinary Technology, 2766 Janitell Road, Colorado Springs, CO 80906.
Website: http://www.coloradovettech.com/.

Colorado Northwestern Community College
Rangely, Colorado

- **State-supported** 2-year, founded 1962, part of Colorado Community College and Occupational Education System
- **Rural** 150-acre campus
- **Coed,** 1,158 undergraduate students, 45% full-time, 55% women, 45% men

Undergraduates 516 full-time, 642 part-time. 14% are from out of state; 2% Black or African American, non-Hispanic/Latino; 6% Hispanic/Latino; 1% Asian, non-Hispanic/Latino; 0.3% Native Hawaiian or other Pacific Islander, non-Hispanic/Latino; 1% American Indian or Alaska Native, non-Hispanic/Latino; 3% Two or more races, non-Hispanic/Latino; 9% Race/ethnicity unknown; 0.8% international; 7% transferred in. *Retention:* 49% of full-time freshmen returned.

Freshmen *Admission:* 637 applied, 637 admitted, 220 enrolled.

Faculty *Total:* 38, 100% full-time. *Student/faculty ratio:* 19:1.

Majors Accounting; aircraft powerplant technology; airline pilot and flight crew; banking and financial support services; cosmetology; dental hygiene; early childhood education; emergency medical technology (EMT paramedic); equestrian studies; general studies; liberal arts and sciences/liberal studies; natural resources/conservation; registered nursing/registered nurse; small business administration.

Academics *Calendar:* semesters. *Degree:* certificates and associate. *Special study options:* academic remediation for entering students, adult/continuing education programs, advanced placement credit, distance learning, double majors, independent study, internships, part-time degree program, services for LD students, student-designed majors, summer session for credit.

Library Colorado Northwestern Community College Library plus 1 other with 20,063 titles, 230 serial subscriptions, 3,559 audiovisual materials, an OPAC.

Student Life *Housing:* on-campus residence required for freshman year. *Options:* coed. Campus housing is university owned. Freshman applicants given priority for college housing. *Activities and Organizations:* student-run newspaper, choral group. *Campus security:* student patrols, late-night transport/escort service. *Student services:* personal/psychological counseling.

Athletics Member NJCAA. *Intercollegiate sports:* baseball M(s), basketball M(s)/W(s), softball W(s), volleyball W(s). *Intramural sports:* basketball

M/W, football M/W, golf M/W, racquetball M/W, skiing (cross-country) M/W, skiing (downhill) M/W, softball M/W, table tennis M/W, tennis M/W, volleyball M/W.

Standardized Tests *Recommended:* ACT (for admission).

Costs (2013–14) *Tuition:* state resident $3585 full-time, $120 per credit hour part-time; nonresident $6704 full-time, $223 per credit hour part-time. Full-time tuition and fees vary according to program. Part-time tuition and fees vary according to program. *Required fees:* $250 full-time, $8 per credit hour part-time, $12 per term part-time. *Room and board:* $6124; room only: $2306. Room and board charges vary according to board plan and housing facility. *Payment plan:* installment.

Applying *Options:* electronic application, early admission, deferred entrance. *Required:* high school transcript. *Required for some:* essay or personal statement, 3 letters of recommendation, interview. *Application deadlines:* rolling (freshmen), rolling (out-of-state freshmen), rolling (transfers). *Notification:* continuous (freshmen), continuous (out-of-state freshmen), continuous (transfers).

Freshman Application Contact Colorado Northwestern Community College, 500 Kennedy Drive, Rangely, CO 81648-3598. *Phone:* 970-675-3285. *Toll-free phone:* 800-562-1105.
Website: http://www.cncc.edu/.

Colorado School of Healing Arts
Lakewood, Colorado

Freshman Application Contact Colorado School of Healing Arts, 7655 West Mississippi Avenue, Suite 100, Lakewood, CO 80220. *Phone:* 303-986-2320. *Toll-free phone:* 800-233-7114. *Fax:* 303-980-6594.
Website: http://www.csha.net/.

Colorado School of Trades
Lakewood, Colorado

- **Proprietary** 2-year, founded 1947
- **Suburban** campus
- **Coed**
- 87% of applicants were admitted

Undergraduates 134 full-time. 88% are from out of state.
Faculty *Student/faculty ratio:* 12:1.
Academics *Degree:* associate.
Costs (2013–14) *Tuition:* $19,800 full-time. No tuition increase for student's term of enrollment.
Applying *Application fee:* $25. *Required:* essay or personal statement, high school transcript, interview.
Freshman Application Contact Colorado School of Trades, 1575 Hoyt Street, Lakewood, CO 80215-2996. *Phone:* 303-233-4697 Ext. 44. *Toll-free phone:* 800-234-4594.
Website: http://www.schooloftrades.com/.

Community College of Aurora
Aurora, Colorado

Freshman Application Contact Community College of Aurora, 16000 East Centre Tech Parkway, Aurora, CO 80011-9036. *Phone:* 303-360-4701.
Website: http://www.ccaurora.edu/.

Community College of Denver
Denver, Colorado

Freshman Application Contact Mr. Michael Rusk, Dean of Students, Community College of Denver, PO Box 173363, Campus Box 201, Denver, CO 80127-3363. *Phone:* 303-556-6325. *Fax:* 303-556-2431. *E-mail:* enrollment_services@ccd.edu.
Website: http://www.ccd.edu/.

Concorde Career College
Aurora, Colorado

Admissions Office Contact Concorde Career College, 111 North Havana Street, Aurora, CO 80010.
Website: http://www.concorde.edu/.

Everest College
Aurora, Colorado

Freshman Application Contact Everest College, 14280 East Jewell Avenue, Suite 100, Aurora, CO 80014. *Phone:* 303-745-6244. *Toll-free phone:* 888-741-4270.
Website: http://www.everest.edu/.

Everest College
Colorado Springs, Colorado

Director of Admissions Director of Admissions, Everest College, 1815 Jet Wing Drive, Colorado Springs, CO 80916. *Phone:* 719-630-6580. *Toll-free phone:* 888-741-4270. *Fax:* 719-638-6818.
Website: http://www.everest.edu/.

Everest College
Thornton, Colorado

Freshman Application Contact Admissions Office, Everest College, 9065 Grant Street, Thornton, CO 80229-4339. *Phone:* 303-457-2757. *Toll-free phone:* 888-741-4270. *Fax:* 303-457-4030.
Website: http://www.everest.edu/.

Front Range Community College
Westminster, Colorado

Freshman Application Contact Ms. Yolanda Espinoza, Registrar, Front Range Community College, Westminster, CO 80031. *Phone:* 303-404-5000. *Fax:* 303-439-2614. *E-mail:* yolanda.espinoza@frontrange.edu.
Website: http://www.frontrange.edu/.

Heritage College
Denver, Colorado

Freshman Application Contact Admissions Office, Heritage College, 12 Lakeside Lane, Denver, CO 80212-7413.
Website: http://www.heritage-education.com/.

Institute of Business & Medical Careers
Fort Collins, Colorado

- **Private** 2-year, founded 1987
- **Suburban** campus with easy access to Denver
- **Coed,** 302 undergraduate students, 100% full-time, 89% women, 11% men
- 100% of applicants were admitted

Undergraduates 302 full-time. Students come from 1 other state; 2% are from out of state. *Retention:* 69% of full-time freshmen returned.
Freshmen *Admission:* 366 applied, 366 admitted, 302 enrolled.
Faculty *Total:* 34, 32% full-time. *Student/faculty ratio:* 14:1.
Majors Accounting technology and bookkeeping; aesthetician/esthetician and skin care; business administration and management; computer support specialist; cosmetology, barber/styling, and nail instruction; dental assisting; hair styling and hair design; legal administrative assistant/secretary; legal assistant/paralegal; massage therapy; medical administrative assistant and medical secretary; medical/clinical assistant; nail technician and manicurist; office occupations and clerical services; pharmacy technician.
Academics *Calendar:* continuous. *Degree:* certificates, diplomas, and associate. *Special study options:* accelerated degree program, adult/continuing education programs, cooperative education, honors programs, internships, summer session for credit.
Library IBMC College plus 8 others with 175,000 titles, 40 serial subscriptions, 125 audiovisual materials.
Student Life *Housing:* college housing not available. *Activities and Organizations:* Alpha Beta Kappa, Circle of Hope, Relay for Life, Peer Mentoring, Peer Tutor.
Standardized Tests *Required:* Wonderlic Assessment (for admission).
Costs (2014–15) *One-time required fee:* $25. *Tuition:* $11,340 full-time. Full-time tuition and fees vary according to course load and program. Part-time tuition and fees vary according to course load and program. No tuition increase for student's term of enrollment. *Payment plans:* tuition prepayment, installment. *Waivers:* children of alumni and employees or children of employees.
Financial Aid Of all full-time matriculated undergraduates who enrolled in 2013, 939 applied for aid, 888 were judged to have need, 675 had their need fully met. 38 Federal Work-Study jobs (averaging $2200). *Average percent of need met:* 72%. *Average financial aid package:* $7500. *Average need-based loan:* $3500. *Average need-based gift aid:* $3205.
Applying *Options:* electronic application. *Application fee:* $75. *Required:* high school transcript, interview. *Application deadline:* rolling (freshmen).
Freshman Application Contact Miss Judy Johnson, Admissions Manager, Institute of Business & Medical Careers, 3842 South Mason Street, Fort Collins, CO 80525. *Phone:* 970-223-2669. *Toll-free phone:* 800-495-2669. *E-mail:* jjohnson@ibmc.edu.
Website: http://www.ibmc.edu/.

IntelliTec College
Colorado Springs, Colorado

Director of Admissions Director of Admissions, IntelliTec College, 2315 East Pikes Peak Avenue, Colorado Springs, CO 80909-6030. *Phone:* 719-632-7626. *Toll-free phone:* 800-748-2282.
Website: http://www.intelliteccollege.edu/.

IntelliTec College
Grand Junction, Colorado

Freshman Application Contact Admissions, IntelliTec College, 772 Horizon Drive, Grand Junction, CO 81506. *Phone:* 970-245-8101. *Toll-free phone:* 800-748-2282. *Fax:* 970-243-8074.
Website: http://www.intelliteccollege.edu/.

IntelliTec Medical Institute
Colorado Springs, Colorado

Director of Admissions Michelle Squibb, Admissions Representative, IntelliTec Medical Institute, 2345 North Academy Boulevard, Colorado Springs, CO 80909. *Phone:* 719-596-7400. *Toll-free phone:* 800-748-2282.
Website: http://www.intelliteccollege.edu/.

ITT Technical Institute
Aurora, Colorado

- **Proprietary** primarily 2-year
- **Coed**

Majors Business administration and management; computer programming (specific applications); construction management; cyber/computer forensics and counterterrorism; drafting and design technology; electrical, electronic and communications engineering technology; forensic science and technology; graphic communications; network and system administration; project management.
Academics *Degrees:* associate and bachelor's.
Freshman Application Contact Director of Recruitment, ITT Technical Institute, 12500 East Iliff Avenue, Suite 100, Aurora, CO 80014. *Phone:* 303-695-6317. *Toll-free phone:* 877-832-8460.
Website: http://www.itt-tech.edu/.

ITT Technical Institute
Westminster, Colorado

- **Proprietary** primarily 2-year, founded 1984, part of ITT Educational Services, Inc.
- **Suburban** campus
- **Coed**

Majors Business administration and management; computer programming (specific applications); construction management; cyber/computer forensics and counterterrorism; drafting and design technology; electrical, electronic and communications engineering technology; forensic science and technology; information technology project management; network and system administration; project management.
Academics *Calendar:* quarters. *Degrees:* associate and bachelor's.
Student Life *Housing:* college housing not available.
Freshman Application Contact Director of Recruitment, ITT Technical Institute, 8620 Wolff Court, Suite 100, Westminster, CO 80031. *Phone:* 303-288-4488. *Toll-free phone:* 800-395-4488.
Website: http://www.itt-tech.edu/.

Lamar Community College
Lamar, Colorado

- **State-supported** 2-year, founded 1937, part of Colorado Community College and Occupational Education System
- **Small-town** 125-acre campus
- **Endowment** $136,000
- **Coed,** 916 undergraduate students, 54% full-time, 52% women, 48% men

Undergraduates 494 full-time, 422 part-time. Students come from 6 other countries; 10% are from out of state; 4% Black or African American, non-Hispanic/Latino; 22% Hispanic/Latino; 0.5% Asian, non-Hispanic/Latino; 0.4% Native Hawaiian or other Pacific Islander, non-Hispanic/Latino; 1% American Indian or Alaska Native, non-Hispanic/Latino; 2% Two or more races, non-Hispanic/Latino; 6% Race/ethnicity unknown; 4% international; 7% transferred in; 20% live on campus. *Retention:* 47% of full-time freshmen returned.

Freshmen *Admission:* 429 applied, 429 admitted, 169 enrolled.
Faculty *Total:* 46, 35% full-time. *Student/faculty ratio:* 20:1.
Majors Accounting; agricultural business and management; agriculture; agronomy and crop science; animal sciences; animal training; biological and physical sciences; biology/biological sciences; business administration and management; computer programming; computer science; computer typography and composition equipment operation; construction trades; cosmetology; criminal justice/safety; data processing and data processing technology; emergency medical technology (EMT paramedic); entrepreneurship; equestrian studies; farm and ranch management; history; information science/studies; liberal arts and sciences/liberal studies; licensed practical/vocational nurse training; management information systems; marketing/marketing management; medical office computer specialist; pre-engineering; registered nursing/registered nurse.
Academics *Calendar:* semesters. *Degree:* certificates, diplomas, and associate. *Special study options:* academic remediation for entering students, adult/continuing education programs, advanced placement credit, cooperative education, distance learning, double majors, English as a second language, independent study, internships, part-time degree program, services for LD students, student-designed majors, summer session for credit.
Library Learning Resources Center with 27,729 titles, 172 serial subscriptions, an OPAC.
Student Life *Housing:* on-campus residence required for freshman year. *Options:* coed. Campus housing is university owned. *Campus security:* 24-hour emergency response devices and patrols, student patrols, late-night transport/escort service, controlled dormitory access. *Student services:* health clinic, personal/psychological counseling.
Athletics Member NJCAA. *Intercollegiate sports:* baseball M(s), basketball M(s)/W(s), equestrian sports M(s)/W(s), golf M(s), soccer M(c), softball W(s), volleyball W(s).
Costs (2014–15) *Tuition:* state resident $2706 full-time, $113 per credit hour part-time; nonresident $5363 full-time, $223 per credit hour part-time. *Required fees:* $353 full-time. *Room and board:* $5606. *Payment plan:* installment. *Waivers:* employees or children of employees.
Financial Aid Of all full-time matriculated undergraduates who enrolled in 2012, 16 Federal Work-Study jobs (averaging $2000). 81 state and other part-time jobs (averaging $2000).
Applying *Options:* electronic application, early admission. *Application deadlines:* 9/16 (freshmen), 9/16 (transfers).
Freshman Application Contact Director of Admissions, Lamar Community College, 2401 South Main Street, Lamar, CO 81052-3999. *Phone:* 719-336-1592. *Toll-free phone:* 800-968-6920. *E-mail:* admissions@lamarcc.edu.
Website: http://www.lamarcc.edu/.

Lincoln College of Technology
Denver, Colorado

- **Proprietary** 2-year, founded 1963
- **Urban** campus
- **Coed, primarily men,** 952 undergraduate students

Freshmen *Admission:* 400 applied, 400 admitted.
Majors Automobile/automotive mechanics technology; diesel mechanics technology.
Academics *Calendar:* 8 six-week terms. *Degree:* certificates, diplomas, and associate. *Special study options:* cooperative education, services for LD students, summer session for credit.
Library Denver Automotive and Diesel College Library plus 1 other with 1,050 titles, 8 serial subscriptions, a Web page.
Student Life *Housing:* college housing not available. *Campus security:* 24-hour emergency response devices and patrols. *Student services:* personal/psychological counseling.
Applying *Application fee:* $25. *Application deadlines:* rolling (freshmen), rolling (out-of-state freshmen).
Freshman Application Contact Lincoln College of Technology, 11194 East 45th Avenue, Denver, CO 80239. *Phone:* 800-347-3232 Ext. 43032.
Website: http://www.lincolnedu.com/campus/denver-co/.

Morgan Community College
Fort Morgan, Colorado

Freshman Application Contact Ms. Kim Maxwell, Morgan Community College, 920 Barlow Road, Fort Morgan, CO 80701-4399. *Phone:* 970-542-3111. *Toll-free phone:* 800-622-0216. *Fax:* 970-867-6608. *E-mail:* kim.maxwell@morgancc.edu.
Website: http://www.morgancc.edu/.

Northeastern Junior College
Sterling, Colorado

- **State-supported** 2-year, founded 1941, part of Colorado Community College and Occupational Education System
- **Small-town** 65-acre campus
- **Endowment** $5.6 million
- **Coed,** 1,962 undergraduate students, 49% full-time, 59% women, 41% men

Undergraduates 966 full-time, 996 part-time. Students come from 26 states and territories; 4 other countries; 5% are from out of state; 6% Black or African American, non-Hispanic/Latino; 10% Hispanic/Latino; 0.4% Asian, non-Hispanic/Latino; 0.2% Native Hawaiian or other Pacific Islander, non-Hispanic/Latino; 0.9% American Indian or Alaska Native, non-Hispanic/Latino; 2% Two or more races, non-Hispanic/Latino; 11% Race/ethnicity unknown; 1% international; 4% transferred in; 28% live on campus. *Retention:* 59% of full-time freshmen returned.

Freshmen *Admission:* 1,543 applied, 1,543 admitted, 313 enrolled. *Average high school GPA:* 2.83.

Faculty *Total:* 78, 58% full-time, 5% with terminal degrees. *Student/faculty ratio:* 23:1.

Majors Accounting; agricultural business and management; agricultural economics; agricultural mechanization; agricultural teacher education; agriculture; agronomy and crop science; anatomy; animal sciences; applied mathematics; art; art teacher education; automobile/automotive mechanics technology; biological and physical sciences; biology/biological sciences; business administration and management; business teacher education; child development; clinical laboratory science/medical technology; computer engineering technology; computer science; corrections; cosmetology; criminal justice/police science; dramatic/theater arts; drawing; economics; education; elementary education; emergency medical technology (EMT paramedic); English; equestrian studies; family and consumer sciences/human sciences; farm and ranch management; fine/studio arts; health professions related; history; humanities; journalism; kindergarten/preschool education; legal administrative assistant/secretary; liberal arts and sciences/liberal studies; licensed practical/vocational nurse training; marketing/marketing management; mathematics; medical administrative assistant and medical secretary; music; music teacher education; natural sciences; physical education teaching and coaching; physical sciences; pre-engineering; psychology; registered nursing/registered nurse; social sciences; social work; trade and industrial teacher education; zoology/animal biology.

Academics *Calendar:* semesters. *Degree:* certificates and associate. *Special study options:* academic remediation for entering students, accelerated degree program, adult/continuing education programs, advanced placement credit, cooperative education, distance learning, double majors, English as a second language, honors programs, independent study, internships, part-time degree program, services for LD students, summer session for credit.

Library Monahan Library with 96,871 titles, 116 serial subscriptions, an OPAC, a Web page.

Student Life *Housing:* on-campus residence required for freshman year. *Options:* coed, women-only. Campus housing is university owned. Freshman campus housing is guaranteed. *Activities and Organizations:* drama/theater group, choral group, Associated Student Government, Post Secondary Agriculture (PAS), Crossroads, NJC Ambassadors, Business Club. *Campus security:* 24-hour emergency response devices, late-night transport/escort service, controlled dormitory access. *Student services:* health clinic, personal/psychological counseling.

Athletics Member NCAA, NJCAA. All NCAA Division I. *Intercollegiate sports:* baseball M(s), basketball M(s)/W(s), equestrian sports M(s)/W(s), golf M(s)/W(s), soccer M(s), softball W(s), volleyball W(s). *Intramural sports:* badminton M/W, baseball M/W, basketball M/W, bowling M/W, cheerleading M/W, football M, golf M/W, racquetball M/W, soccer M/W, softball M/W, tennis M/W, ultimate Frisbee M/W, volleyball M/W, weight lifting M/W.

Costs (2014–15) *Tuition:* state resident $3747 full-time, $125 per credit hour part-time; nonresident $5621 full-time, $187 per credit hour part-time. Full-time tuition and fees vary according to course load. Part-time tuition and fees vary according to course load. *Required fees:* $599 full-time, $23 per credit hour part-time, $13 per term part-time. *Room and board:* $6376; room only: $3000. Room and board charges vary according to board plan and housing facility. *Payment plan:* installment. *Waivers:* senior citizens and employees or children of employees.

Applying *Options:* electronic application, early admission, deferred entrance. *Recommended:* high school transcript. *Application deadlines:* rolling (freshmen), rolling (out-of-state freshmen), rolling (transfers). *Notification:* continuous until 8/1 (freshmen), continuous (out-of-state freshmen), continuous until 8/1 (transfers).

Freshman Application Contact Mr. Terry Ruch, Director of Admissions, Northeastern Junior College, 100 College Avenue, Sterling, CO 80751-2399.

Phone: 970-521-7000. *Toll-free phone:* 800-626-4637. *E-mail:* terry.ruch@njc.edu.
Website: http://www.njc.edu/.

Otero Junior College
La Junta, Colorado

- **State-supported** 2-year, founded 1941, part of Colorado Community College System
- **Rural** 40-acre campus
- **Endowment** $1.5 million
- **Coed,** 1,449 undergraduate students

Undergraduates Students come from 20 states and territories; 10 other countries; 9% are from out of state; 3% Black or African American, non-Hispanic/Latino; 29% Hispanic/Latino; 0.8% Asian, non-Hispanic/Latino; 0.5% Native Hawaiian or other Pacific Islander, non-Hispanic/Latino; 1% American Indian or Alaska Native, non-Hispanic/Latino; 6% Race/ethnicity unknown; 3% international. *Retention:* 53% of full-time freshmen returned.

Faculty *Student/faculty ratio:* 11:1.

Majors Administrative assistant and secretarial science; agricultural business and management; automobile/automotive mechanics technology; biological and physical sciences; biology/biological sciences; business administration and management; child development; comparative literature; data processing and data processing technology; dramatic/theater arts; elementary education; history; humanities; kindergarten/preschool education; legal administrative assistant/secretary; liberal arts and sciences/liberal studies; mathematics; medical administrative assistant and medical secretary; modern languages; political science and government; pre-engineering; psychology; registered nursing/registered nurse; social sciences.

Academics *Calendar:* semesters. *Degree:* certificates and associate. *Special study options:* academic remediation for entering students, adult/continuing education programs, advanced placement credit, distance learning, external degree program, honors programs, internships, part-time degree program, summer session for credit.

Library Wheeler Library with 36,701 titles, 183 serial subscriptions, an OPAC.

Student Life *Housing:* on-campus residence required for freshman year. *Options:* men-only, women-only. Campus housing is university owned. *Activities and Organizations:* drama/theater group, student-run newspaper, choral group. *Campus security:* 24-hour patrols, late-night transport/escort service.

Athletics Member NJCAA. *Intercollegiate sports:* baseball M(s), basketball M(s)/W(s), golf M(s)/W(s), soccer M(s)/W(s), softball W(s), volleyball W(s). *Intramural sports:* basketball M/W, volleyball M/W.

Costs (2013–14) *Tuition:* state resident $2868 full-time; nonresident $5363 full-time. *Required fees:* $267 full-time. *Room and board:* $5966. Room and board charges vary according to board plan and housing facility. *Payment plans:* installment, deferred payment. *Waivers:* senior citizens.

Financial Aid Of all full-time matriculated undergraduates who enrolled in 2012, 30 Federal Work-Study jobs (averaging $2000). 100 state and other part-time jobs (averaging $2000).

Applying *Options:* electronic application, early admission. *Recommended:* high school transcript. *Application deadlines:* 8/30 (freshmen), 8/30 (transfers). *Notification:* continuous (freshmen), continuous (transfers).

Freshman Application Contact Mrs. Rana Brown, Registrar, Otero Junior College, 1802 Colorado Ave., La Junta, CO 81050. *Phone:* 719-384-6831. *Fax:* 719-384-6933. *E-mail:* Rana.Brown@ojc.edu.
Website: http://www.ojc.edu/.

Pikes Peak Community College
Colorado Springs, Colorado

Freshman Application Contact Pikes Peak Community College, 5675 South Academy Boulevard, Colorado Springs, CO 80906-5498. *Phone:* 719-540-7041. *Toll-free phone:* 866-411-7722.
Website: http://www.ppcc.edu/.

Pima Medical Institute
Aurora, Colorado

Admissions Office Contact Pima Medical Institute, 13750 E. Mississippi Avenue, Aurora, CO 80012. *Toll-free phone:* 800-477-PIMA.
Website: http://www.pmi.edu/.

Pima Medical Institute
Colorado Springs, Colorado

Freshman Application Contact Pima Medical Institute, 3770 Citadel Drive North, Colorado Springs, CO 80909. *Phone:* 719-482-7462.
Website: http://www.pmi.edu/.

Pima Medical Institute
Denver, Colorado

Freshman Application Contact Admissions Office, Pima Medical Institute, 7475 Dakin Street, Denver, CO 80221. *Phone:* 303-426-1800. *Toll-free phone:* 800-477-PIMA (in-state); 888-477-PIMA (out-of-state).

Website: http://www.pmi.edu/.

Prince Institute–Rocky Mountains Campus
Westminster, Colorado

Director of Admissions Director of Admissions, Prince Institute–Rocky Mountains Campus, 9051 Harlan Street, Unit 20, Westminster, CO 80031. *Phone:* 303-427-5292. *Toll-free phone:* 866-712-2425.

Website: http://www.princeinstitute.edu/.

Pueblo Community College
Pueblo, Colorado

- **State-supported** 2-year, founded 1933, part of Colorado Community College System
- **Urban** 35-acre campus
- **Endowment** $1.1 million
- **Coed,** 6,717 undergraduate students, 38% full-time, 55% women, 45% men

Undergraduates 2,521 full-time, 4,196 part-time. Students come from 23 states and territories; 4 other countries; 1% are from out of state; 5% Black or African American, non-Hispanic/Latino; 29% Hispanic/Latino; 1% Asian, non-Hispanic/Latino; 3% American Indian or Alaska Native, non-Hispanic/Latino; 6% Race/ethnicity unknown; 6% transferred in. *Retention:* 61% of full-time freshmen returned.

Freshmen *Admission:* 1,745 applied, 1,745 admitted, 1,745 enrolled.

Faculty *Total:* 427, 26% full-time. *Student/faculty ratio:* 19:1.

Majors Accounting technology and bookkeeping; animation, interactive technology, video graphics and special effects; autobody/collision and repair technology; automobile/automotive mechanics technology; business administration and management; business automation/technology/data entry; communications technology; computer and information sciences; cooking and related culinary arts; cosmetology; criminal justice/law enforcement administration; dental assisting; dental hygiene; early childhood education; electrical, electronic and communications engineering technology; electromechanical and instrumentation and maintenance technologies related; emergency medical technology (EMT paramedic); engineering technology; fire science/firefighting; general studies; liberal arts and sciences and humanities related; liberal arts and sciences/liberal studies; library and archives assisting; machine shop technology; manufacturing engineering technology; medical office management; occupational therapist assistant; physical therapy technology; polysomnography; psychiatric/mental health services technology; radiologic technology/science; registered nursing/registered nurse; respiratory care therapy; science technologies related; solar energy technology; web page, digital/multimedia and information resources design; welding technology.

Academics *Calendar:* semesters. *Degree:* certificates and associate. *Special study options:* academic remediation for entering students, accelerated degree program, advanced placement credit, cooperative education, distance learning, double majors, English as a second language, honors programs, independent study, internships, part-time degree program, services for LD students, summer session for credit.

Library The Library with 38,719 titles, 8,586 serial subscriptions, 15,870 audiovisual materials, an OPAC.

Student Life *Housing:* college housing not available. *Activities and Organizations:* drama/theater group, choral group, Phi Theta Kappa, Welding Club, Culinary Arts Club, Performing Arts Club, Art Club. *Campus security:* 24-hour emergency response devices and patrols, late-night transport/escort service. *Student services:* personal/psychological counseling.

Applying *Options:* electronic application, early admission, deferred entrance. *Application deadlines:* rolling (freshmen), rolling (out-of-state freshmen), rolling (transfers). *Notification:* continuous until 9/1 (freshmen), continuous until 9/1 (out-of-state freshmen), continuous until 9/1 (transfers).

Freshman Application Contact Ms. Barbara Benedict, Assistant Director of Admissions and Records, Pueblo Community College, 900 West Orman Avenue, Pueblo, CO 81004. *Phone:* 719-549-3039. *Toll-free phone:* 888-642-6017. *Fax:* 719-549-3012. *E-mail:* barbara.benedict@pueblocc.edu.

Website: http://www.pueblocc.edu/.

Red Rocks Community College
Lakewood, Colorado

- **State-supported** 2-year, founded 1969, part of Colorado Community College and Occupational Education System
- **Urban** 141-acre campus with easy access to Denver
- **Coed**

Undergraduates 2,854 full-time, 6,174 part-time. Students come from 27 other countries; 6% are from out of state; 2% Black or African American, non-Hispanic/Latino; 13% Hispanic/Latino; 2% Asian, non-Hispanic/Latino; 0.3% Native Hawaiian or other Pacific Islander, non-Hispanic/Latino; 1% American Indian or Alaska Native, non-Hispanic/Latino; 3% Two or more races, non-Hispanic/Latino; 7% Race/ethnicity unknown; 1% international; 22% transferred in.

Faculty *Student/faculty ratio:* 23:1.

Academics *Calendar:* semesters. *Degree:* certificates and associate. *Special study options:* academic remediation for entering students, adult/continuing education programs, cooperative education, distance learning, English as a second language, honors programs, off-campus study, part-time degree program, services for LD students, study abroad, summer session for credit. *ROTC:* Army (c), Air Force (c).

Student Life *Campus security:* 24-hour emergency response devices and patrols.

Costs (2013–14) *Tuition:* state resident $3585 full-time, $120 per credit hour part-time; nonresident $14,709 full-time, $490 per credit hour part-time. Full-time tuition and fees vary according to program and reciprocity agreements. Part-time tuition and fees vary according to program and reciprocity agreements. *Required fees:* $286 full-time, $9 per credit hour part-time, $32 per term part-time. *Payment plans:* installment, deferred payment.

Financial Aid Of all full-time matriculated undergraduates who enrolled in 2012, 21 Federal Work-Study jobs (averaging $5000). 95 state and other part-time jobs (averaging $5000).

Applying *Options:* electronic application, early admission.

Freshman Application Contact Admissions Office, Red Rocks Community College, 13300 West 6th Avenue, Lakewood, CO 80228-1255. *Phone:* 303-914-6360. *Fax:* 303-914-6919. *E-mail:* admissions@rrcc.edu.

Website: http://www.rrcc.edu/.

Redstone College–Denver
Broomfield, Colorado

Freshman Application Contact Redstone College–Denver, 10851 West 120th Avenue, Broomfield, CO 80021. *Phone:* 303-466-7383. *Toll-free phone:* 877-801-1025.

Website: http://www.redstone.edu/.

Trinidad State Junior College
Trinidad, Colorado

Freshman Application Contact Dr. Sandra Veltri, Vice President of Student/Academic Affairs, Trinidad State Junior College, 600 Prospect Street, Trinidad, CO 81082. *Phone:* 719-846-5559. *Toll-free phone:* 800-621-8752. *Fax:* 719-846-5620. *E-mail:* sandy.veltri@trinidadstate.edu.

Website: http://www.trinidadstate.edu/.

CONNECTICUT

Asnuntuck Community College
Enfield, Connecticut

Freshman Application Contact Timothy St. James, Director of Admissions, Asnuntuck Community College, 170 Elm Street, Enfield, CT 06082-3800. *Phone:* 860-253-3087. *Fax:* 860-253-3014. *E-mail:* tstjames@acc.commnet.edu.

Website: http://www.acc.commnet.edu/.

Capital Community College
Hartford, Connecticut

Freshman Application Contact Ms. Jackie Phillips, Director of the Welcome and Advising Center, Capital Community College, 950 Main Street, Hartford, CT 06103. *Phone:* 860-906-5078. *Toll-free phone:* 800-894-6126. *E-mail:* jphillips@ccc.commnet.edu.

Website: http://www.ccc.commnet.edu/.

Gateway Community College

New Haven, Connecticut

Freshman Application Contact Ms. Kim Shea, Director of Admissions, Gateway Community College, New Haven, CT 06511. *Phone:* 203-789-7043. *Toll-free phone:* 800-390-7723. *Fax:* 203-285-2018. *E-mail:* gateway_ctc@commnet.edu.

Website: http://www.gwcc.commnet.edu/.

Goodwin College

East Hartford, Connecticut

- **Independent** primarily 2-year, founded 1999
- **Suburban** 660-acre campus with easy access to Hartford
- **Coed,** 3,388 undergraduate students, 18% full-time, 83% women, 17% men

Undergraduates 593 full-time, 2,795 part-time. Students come from 11 states and territories; 4 other countries; 3% are from out of state; 23% Black or African American, non-Hispanic/Latino; 19% Hispanic/Latino; 2% Asian, non-Hispanic/Latino; 0.1% Native Hawaiian or other Pacific Islander, non-Hispanic/Latino; 0.4% American Indian or Alaska Native, non-Hispanic/Latino; 2% Two or more races, non-Hispanic/Latino; 0.1% Race/ethnicity unknown; 0.1% international; 21% transferred in. *Retention:* 54% of full-time freshmen returned.

Freshmen *Admission:* 626 applied, 250 enrolled.

Faculty *Total:* 293, 28% full-time, 20% with terminal degrees. *Student/faculty ratio:* 10:1.

Majors Business administration and management; business/commerce; child-care and support services management; child development; criminal justice/law enforcement administration; criminal justice/safety; dental hygiene; environmental studies; family systems; health services/allied health/health sciences; histologic technician; homeland security; homeland security, law enforcement, firefighting and protective services related; human services; liberal arts and sciences/liberal studies; logistics, materials, and supply chain management; medical/clinical assistant; medical insurance coding; medical insurance/medical billing; nonprofit management; occupational therapist assistant; office management; operations management; opticianry; organizational behavior; quality control technology; registered nursing/registered nurse; respiratory care therapy.

Academics *Calendar:* semesters. *Degrees:* certificates, associate, and bachelor's. *Special study options:* academic remediation for entering students, adult/continuing education programs, advanced placement credit, distance learning, double majors, English as a second language, internships, off-campus study, part-time degree program, services for LD students, summer session for credit.

Library Hoffman Family Library with 9,352 titles, 267 serial subscriptions, 843 audiovisual materials, an OPAC.

Student Life *Housing:* college housing not available. *Activities and Organizations:* choral group. *Campus security:* 24-hour emergency response devices, late-night transport/escort service, evening security patrolman. *Student services:* personal/psychological counseling.

Athletics *Intramural sports:* basketball M, football M/W, soccer M/W, softball M/W.

Costs (2013–14) *Tuition:* $18,900 full-time, $590 per credit hour part-time. Full-time tuition and fees vary according to course load and program. Part-time tuition and fees vary according to course load and program. *Required fees:* $500 full-time. *Payment plan:* installment. *Waivers:* employees or children of employees.

Financial Aid Of all full-time matriculated undergraduates who enrolled in 2011, 76 Federal Work-Study jobs (averaging $2878). *Average percent of need met:* 47%. *Average financial aid package:* $16,041. *Average need-based gift aid:* $12,269. *Average non-need-based aid:* $11,687.

Applying *Options:* electronic application, early admission, deferred entrance. *Application fee:* $50. *Required:* essay or personal statement, high school transcript, minimum 2.0 GPA, medical exam. *Recommended:* 2 letters of recommendation, interview. *Application deadlines:* rolling (freshmen), rolling (transfers), 6/1 (early action). *Early decision deadline:* 3/1. *Notification:* continuous (freshmen), continuous (transfers), 3/15 (early decision), 6/15 (early action).

Freshman Application Contact Mr. Nicholas Lentino, Assistant Vice President for Admissions, Goodwin College, One Riverside Drive, East Hartford, CT 06118. *Phone:* 860-727-6765. *Toll-free phone:* 800-889-3282. *Fax:* 860-291-9550. *E-mail:* nlentino@goodwin.edu.

Website: http://www.goodwin.edu/.

Housatonic Community College

Bridgeport, Connecticut

- **State-supported** 2-year, founded 1965, part of Connecticut Community Colleges and State Universities Board of Regents
- **Urban** 4-acre campus with easy access to New York City
- **Coed,** 5,813 undergraduate students

Undergraduates 30% Black or African American, non-Hispanic/Latino; 27% Hispanic/Latino; 2% Asian, non-Hispanic/Latino; 0.1% Native Hawaiian or other Pacific Islander, non-Hispanic/Latino; 1% American Indian or Alaska Native, non-Hispanic/Latino; 1% Two or more races, non-Hispanic/Latino; 2% Race/ethnicity unknown.

Faculty *Total:* 377, 18% full-time. *Student/faculty ratio:* 16:1.

Majors Accounting; administrative assistant and secretarial science; art; avionics maintenance technology; business administration and management; child development; clinical/medical laboratory technology; commercial and advertising art; computer typography and composition equipment operation; criminal justice/law enforcement administration; data processing and data processing technology; environmental studies; humanities; human services; journalism; liberal arts and sciences/liberal studies; mathematics; mental health counseling; physical therapy; pre-engineering; public administration; registered nursing/registered nurse; social sciences; substance abuse/addiction counseling.

Academics *Calendar:* semesters. *Degree:* certificates and associate. *Special study options:* academic remediation for entering students, adult/continuing education programs, advanced placement credit, cooperative education, distance learning, double majors, English as a second language, honors programs, independent study, internships, part-time degree program, services for LD students, summer session for credit. *ROTC:* Army (c). *Unusual degree programs:* nursing with Bridgeport Hospital.

Library Housatonic Community College Library with 30,000 titles, 300 serial subscriptions, an OPAC, a Web page.

Student Life *Housing:* college housing not available. *Activities and Organizations:* drama/theater group, student-run newspaper, Student Senate, Association of Latin American Students, Community Action Network, Drama Club. *Campus security:* 24-hour emergency response devices, late-night transport/escort service. *Student services:* health clinic, personal/psychological counseling, women's center.

Costs (2014–15) *Tuition:* state resident $3786 full-time, $140 per credit hour part-time; nonresident $11,318 full-time, $420 per credit hour part-time. *Required fees:* $406 full-time. *Payment plan:* installment. *Waivers:* senior citizens and employees or children of employees.

Financial Aid Of all full-time matriculated undergraduates who enrolled in 2012, 70 Federal Work-Study jobs (averaging $2850).

Applying *Options:* electronic application, deferred entrance. *Application fee:* $20. *Required:* high school transcript. *Required for some:* interview. *Application deadlines:* rolling (freshmen), rolling (transfers). *Notification:* continuous (freshmen), continuous (transfers).

Freshman Application Contact Ms. Delores Y. Curtis, Director of Admissions, Housatonic Community College, 900 Lafayette Boulevard, Bridgeport, CT 06604-4704. *Phone:* 203-332-5102.

Website: http://www.hctc.commnet.edu/.

Manchester Community College

Manchester, Connecticut

- **State-supported** 2-year, founded 1963, part of Connecticut Community–Technical College System
- **Small-town** campus
- **Coed,** 7,571 undergraduate students, 36% full-time, 53% women, 47% men

Undergraduates 2,713 full-time, 4,858 part-time. 17% Black or African American, non-Hispanic/Latino; 17% Hispanic/Latino; 4% Asian, non-Hispanic/Latino; 0.1% Native Hawaiian or other Pacific Islander, non-Hispanic/Latino; 0.1% American Indian or Alaska Native, non-Hispanic/Latino; 2% Two or more races, non-Hispanic/Latino; 5% Race/ethnicity unknown; 0.3% international; 14% transferred in. *Retention:* 61% of full-time freshmen returned.

Freshmen *Admission:* 2,989 applied, 2,980 admitted, 1,616 enrolled.

Faculty *Total:* 494, 21% full-time. *Student/faculty ratio:* 18:1.

Majors Accounting; administrative assistant and secretarial science; business administration and management; clinical/medical laboratory technology; commercial and advertising art; criminal justice/law enforcement administration; dramatic/theater arts; engineering science; fine/studio arts; general studies; hotel/motel administration; human services; industrial engineering; industrial technology; information science/studies; journalism; kindergarten/preschool education; legal administrative assistant/secretary; legal assistant/paralegal; liberal arts and sciences/liberal studies; management information systems; marketing/marketing management; medical administrative assistant and medical secretary; music; occupational therapist assistant; physical therapy technology; respiratory care therapy; social work; speech communication and rhetoric; surgical technology; teacher assistant/aide.

Academics *Calendar:* semesters. *Degree:* certificates and associate. *Special study options:* adult/continuing education programs, part-time degree program.

Student Life *Housing:* college housing not available.

Athletics Member NJCAA. *Intercollegiate sports:* baseball M, basketball M/W, soccer M/W, softball W.

Costs (2014–15) *Tuition:* state resident $3786 full-time; nonresident $11,318 full-time. *Required fees:* $426 full-time. *Payment plan:* installment. *Waivers:* senior citizens and employees or children of employees.

Financial Aid Of all full-time matriculated undergraduates who enrolled in 2013, 1,872 applied for aid, 1,538 were judged to have need. *Financial aid deadline:* 8/13.

Applying *Options:* electronic application. *Application fee:* $20. *Required:* high school transcript. *Application deadlines:* rolling (freshmen), rolling (transfers). *Notification:* continuous (freshmen), continuous (transfers).

Freshman Application Contact Director of Admissions, Manchester Community College, PO Box 1046, Manchester, CT 06045-1046. *Phone:* 860-512-3210. *Fax:* 860-512-3221.

Website: http://www.mcc.commnet.edu/.

Middlesex Community College

Middletown, Connecticut

Freshman Application Contact Mensimah Shabazz, Director of Admissions, Middlesex Community College, Middletown, CT 06457-4889. *Phone:* 860-343-5742. *Fax:* 860-344-3055. *E-mail:* mshabazz@mxcc.commnet.edu.

Website: http://www.mxcc.commnet.edu/.

Naugatuck Valley Community College

Waterbury, Connecticut

Freshman Application Contact Ms. Lucretia Sveda, Director of Enrollment Services, Naugatuck Valley Community College, Waterbury, CT 06708. *Phone:* 203-575-8016. *Fax:* 203-596-8766. *E-mail:* lsveda@nvcc.commnet.edu.

Website: http://www.nvcc.commnet.edu/.

Northwestern Connecticut Community College

Winsted, Connecticut

- **State-supported** 2-year, founded 1965, part of Connecticut State Colleges and Universities (CSCU)
- **Small-town** 5-acre campus with easy access to Hartford
- **Coed,** 1,549 undergraduate students, 30% full-time, 65% women, 35% men

Undergraduates 457 full-time, 1,092 part-time. Students come from 3 states and territories; 0.5% are from out of state; 9% transferred in. *Retention:* 55% of full-time freshmen returned.

Freshmen *Admission:* 260 enrolled.

Majors Accounting; administrative assistant and secretarial science; art; behavioral sciences; biology/biological sciences; business administration and management; child development; commercial and advertising art; communications technology; computer engineering technology; computer graphics; computer programming; computer science; criminal justice/law enforcement administration; criminal justice/police science; electrical, electronic and communications engineering technology; engineering; English; health professions related; human services; information science/studies; kindergarten/preschool education; legal assistant/paralegal; liberal arts and sciences/liberal studies; mathematics; medical/clinical assistant; parks, recreation and leisure; parks, recreation and leisure facilities management; physical sciences; pre-engineering; sign language interpretation and translation; social sciences; substance abuse/addiction counseling; therapeutic recreation; veterinary/animal health technology.

Academics *Calendar:* semesters. *Degree:* certificates and associate. *Special study options:* academic remediation for entering students, distance learning, English as a second language, independent study, internships, part-time degree program, services for LD students, summer session for credit.

Library Northwestern Connecticut Community–Technical College Learning Center with an OPAC.

Student Life *Housing:* college housing not available. *Activities and Organizations:* student-run newspaper. *Campus security:* evening security patrols.

Costs (2014–15) *Tuition:* state resident $3432 full-time; nonresident $10,296 full-time. *Required fees:* $434 full-time. *Waivers:* senior citizens and employees or children of employees.

Applying *Options:* deferred entrance. *Application fee:* $20. *Application deadlines:* rolling (freshmen), rolling (transfers). *Notification:* continuous (freshmen), continuous (transfers).

Freshman Application Contact Admissions Office, Northwestern Connecticut Community College, Park Place East, Winsted, CT 06098-1798. *Phone:* 860-738-6330. *Fax:* 860-738-6437. *E-mail:* admissions@nwcc.commnet.edu.

Website: http://www.nwcc.commnet.edu/.

Norwalk Community College

Norwalk, Connecticut

- **State-supported** 2-year, founded 1961, part of Connecticut Community–Technical College System
- **Suburban** 30-acre campus with easy access to New York City
- **Coed,** 6,556 undergraduate students, 33% full-time, 58% women, 42% men

Undergraduates 2,180 full-time, 4,376 part-time. 1% are from out of state; 17% Black or African American, non-Hispanic/Latino; 32% Hispanic/Latino; 5% Asian, non-Hispanic/Latino; 0.2% Native Hawaiian or other Pacific Islander, non-Hispanic/Latino; 0.2% American Indian or Alaska Native, non-Hispanic/Latino; 1% Two or more races, non-Hispanic/Latino; 6% Race/ethnicity unknown; 2% international.

Freshmen *Admission:* 1,792 applied, 1,214 admitted, 981 enrolled.

Faculty *Total:* 428, 24% full-time. *Student/faculty ratio:* 17:1.

Majors Accounting; administrative assistant and secretarial science; architectural engineering technology; art; business administration and management; commercial and advertising art; computer and information systems security; computer systems networking and telecommunications; construction engineering technology; criminal justice/law enforcement administration; early childhood education; engineering science; finance; fine/studio arts; fire science/firefighting; general studies; graphic design; hotel/motel administration; human services; information science/studies; information technology; interior design; kinesiology and exercise science; legal assistant/paralegal; liberal arts and sciences/liberal studies; marketing/marketing management; medical office management; parks, recreation and leisure; psychology; registered nursing/registered nurse; respiratory care therapy; restaurant/food services management; speech communication and rhetoric; web page, digital/multimedia and information resources design.

Academics *Calendar:* semesters. *Degree:* certificates and associate. *Special study options:* academic remediation for entering students, advanced placement credit, cooperative education, distance learning, English as a second language, independent study, internships, part-time degree program, services for LD students, summer session for credit.

Library Everett I. L. Baker Library with 174,780 titles, 120 serial subscriptions, 15,574 audiovisual materials, an OPAC, a Web page.

Student Life *Housing:* college housing not available. *Activities and Organizations:* drama/theater group, student-run newspaper, choral group, Student World Assembly, Accounting Club, Literature Club, Art Club, Phi Theta Kappa. *Campus security:* late-night transport/escort service, all buildings are secured each evening; there are foot patrols and vehicle patrols by security from 7 am to 11pm. *Student services:* personal/psychological counseling, women's center.

Costs (2014–15) *Tuition:* state resident $3360 full-time; nonresident $10,829 full-time. *Required fees:* $426 full-time. *Payment plan:* installment. *Waivers:* senior citizens and employees or children of employees.

Financial Aid Of all full-time matriculated undergraduates who enrolled in 2012, 53 Federal Work-Study jobs (averaging $2800). 20 state and other part-time jobs (averaging $2800).

Applying *Options:* electronic application, deferred entrance. *Application fee:* $20. *Required:* high school transcript, 4 math courses, 3 science courses, 2 labs; immunization form. *Application deadlines:* rolling (freshmen), rolling (transfers). *Notification:* continuous (freshmen), continuous (transfers).

Freshman Application Contact Mr. Curtis Antrum, Admissions Counselor, Norwalk Community College, 188 Richards Avenue, Norwalk, CT 06854-1655. *Phone:* 203-857-7060. *Fax:* 203-857-3335. *E-mail:* admissions@ncc.commnet.edu.

Website: http://www.ncc.commnet.edu/.

Quinebaug Valley Community College

Danielson, Connecticut

Freshman Application Contact Dr. Toni Moumouris, Director of Admissions, Quinebaug Valley Community College, 742 Upper Maple Street, Danielson, CT 06239. *Phone:* 860-774-1130 Ext. 318. *Fax:* 860-774-7768. *E-mail:* qu_isd@commnet.edu.

Website: http://www.qvcc.commnet.edu/.

St. Vincent's College
Bridgeport, Connecticut

Freshman Application Contact Mr. Joseph Marrone, Director of Admissions and Recruitment Marketing, St. Vincent's College, 2800 Main Street, Bridgeport, CT 06606-4292. *Phone:* 203-576-5515. *Toll-free phone:* 800-873-1013. *Fax:* 203-576-5893. *E-mail:* jmarrone@stvincentscollege.edu. *Website:* http://www.stvincentscollege.edu/.

Three Rivers Community College
Norwich, Connecticut

- **State-supported** 2-year, founded 1963, part of Connecticut State Colleges & Universities (ConnSCU)
- **Suburban** 40-acre campus with easy access to Hartford
- **Coed,** 4,749 undergraduate students, 34% full-time, 59% women, 41% men

Undergraduates 1,609 full-time, 3,140 part-time. Students come from 3 states and territories; 1% are from out of state; 8% Black or African American, non-Hispanic/Latino; 15% Hispanic/Latino; 4% Asian, non-Hispanic/Latino; 0.3% Native Hawaiian or other Pacific Islander, non-Hispanic/Latino; 0.7% American Indian or Alaska Native, non-Hispanic/Latino; 3% Two or more races, non-Hispanic/Latino; 4% Race/ethnicity unknown; 0.1% international; 8% transferred in.

Freshmen *Admission:* 938 enrolled.

Faculty *Total:* 285, 29% full-time. *Student/faculty ratio:* 17:1.

Majors Accounting; administrative assistant and secretarial science; architectural engineering technology; avionics maintenance technology; business administration and management; civil engineering technology; computer engineering technology; computer programming; consumer merchandising/retailing management; corrections; criminal justice/law enforcement administration; data processing and data processing technology; drafting and design technology; dramatic/theater arts; electrical, electronic and communications engineering technology; engineering; engineering science; engineering technology; environmental engineering technology; fire science/firefighting; hospitality administration; hotel/motel administration; human services; hydrology and water resources science; industrial technology; kindergarten/preschool education; laser and optical technology; legal administrative assistant/secretary; liberal arts and sciences/liberal studies; marketing/marketing management; mechanical engineering/mechanical technology; nuclear/nuclear power technology; pre-engineering; professional, technical, business, and scientific writing; public administration; registered nursing/registered nurse; special products marketing; substance abuse/addiction counseling; tourism and travel services management.

Academics *Calendar:* semesters. *Degrees:* certificates and associate (engineering technology programs are offered on the Thames Valley Campus; liberal arts, transfer and career programs are offered on the Mohegan Campus). *Special study options:* adult/continuing education programs, part-time degree program.

Library Three Rivers Community College Learning Resource Center plus 1 other with an OPAC.

Student Life *Housing:* college housing not available. *Activities and Organizations:* student-run newspaper. *Campus security:* 24-hour emergency response devices, late-night transport/escort service, 14-hour patrols by trained security personnel.

Athletics *Intramural sports:* baseball M(c)/W(c), golf M(c)/W(c).

Costs (2013–14) *Tuition:* state resident $3360 full-time, $140 per credit hour part-time; nonresident $10,080 full-time, $420 per credit hour part-time. Full-time tuition and fees vary according to course load and reciprocity agreements. Part-time tuition and fees vary according to course load and reciprocity agreements. *Required fees:* $426 full-time, $76 per credit hour part-time. *Payment plan:* installment. *Waivers:* senior citizens and employees or children of employees.

Financial Aid Of all full-time matriculated undergraduates who enrolled in 2010, 1,135 applied for aid, 967 were judged to have need, 266 had their need fully met. *Average percent of need met:* 48%. *Average financial aid package:* $2631. *Average need-based loan:* $3308. *Average need-based gift aid:* $2409.

Applying *Options:* electronic application, early admission, deferred entrance. *Recommended:* high school transcript. *Application deadlines:* rolling (freshmen), rolling (transfers). *Notification:* continuous (freshmen), continuous (transfers).

Freshman Application Contact Ms. Aida Garcia, Admissions and Recruitment Counselor, Three Rivers Community College, 574 New London Turnpike, Norwich, CT 06360. *Phone:* 860-215-9244. *Fax:* 860-215-9902. *E-mail:* admissions@trcc.commnet.edu. *Website:* http://www.trcc.commnet.edu/.

Tunxis Community College
Farmington, Connecticut

- **State-supported** 2-year, founded 1969, part of Connecticut State Colleges and Universities (ConnSCU), Board of Regents for Higher Education
- **Suburban** 12-acre campus with easy access to Hartford
- **Coed,** 4,590 undergraduate students, 37% full-time, 57% women, 43% men

Undergraduates 1,688 full-time, 2,902 part-time. Students come from 6 states and territories; 2% are from out of state; 6% Black or African American, non-Hispanic/Latino; 15% Hispanic/Latino; 4% Asian, non-Hispanic/Latino; 0.3% American Indian or Alaska Native, non-Hispanic/Latino; 5% Race/ethnicity unknown. *Retention:* 61% of full-time freshmen returned.

Freshmen *Admission:* 803 enrolled.

Faculty *Total:* 239, 28% full-time, 12% with terminal degrees. *Student/faculty ratio:* 19:1.

Majors Accounting; administrative assistant and secretarial science; art; business administration and management; commercial and advertising art; corrections; criminal justice/law enforcement administration; data processing and data processing technology; dental hygiene; design and applied arts related; engineering; engineering technology; fashion merchandising; forensic science and technology; human services; information science/studies; kindergarten/preschool education; legal administrative assistant/secretary; liberal arts and sciences/liberal studies; marketing/marketing management; medical administrative assistant and medical secretary; physical therapy; substance abuse/addiction counseling.

Academics *Calendar:* semesters. *Degree:* certificates and associate. *Special study options:* academic remediation for entering students, adult/continuing education programs, cooperative education, distance learning, double majors, English as a second language, honors programs, independent study, internships, part-time degree program, services for LD students, summer session for credit.

Library Tunxis Community College Library with 33,866 titles, 285 serial subscriptions, an OPAC.

Student Life *Housing:* college housing not available. *Activities and Organizations:* drama/theater group, student-run newspaper, Phi Theta Kappa, Student American Dental Hygiene Association (SADHA), Human Services Club, student newspaper, Criminal Justice Club. *Campus security:* 24-hour emergency response devices.

Costs (2013–14) *Tuition:* state resident $3360 full-time, $140 per credit hour part-time; nonresident $10,080 full-time, $420 per credit hour part-time. *Required fees:* $446 full-time, $114 per term part-time, $332 per term part-time. *Payment plan:* installment. *Waivers:* senior citizens and employees or children of employees.

Applying *Options:* deferred entrance. *Application fee:* $20. *Required:* high school transcript. *Application deadlines:* rolling (freshmen), rolling (transfers).

Freshman Application Contact Ms. Allison McCarthy, Interim Director of Admissions, Tunxis Community College, 271 Scott Swamp Road, Farmington, CT 06032. *Phone:* 860-255-3550. *Fax:* 860-255-3559. *E-mail:* pmccluskey@tunxis.edu. *Website:* http://www.tunxis.edu/.

DELAWARE

Delaware College of Art and Design
Wilmington, Delaware

Freshman Application Contact Ms. Allison Gullo, Delaware College of Art and Design, 600 North Market Street, Wilmington, DE 19801. *Phone:* 302-622-8867 Ext. 111. *Fax:* 302-622-8870. *E-mail:* agullo@dcad.edu. *Website:* http://www.dcad.edu/.

Delaware Technical & Community College, Jack F. Owens Campus
Georgetown, Delaware

- **State-supported** 2-year, founded 1967, part of Delaware Technical and Community College System
- **Small-town** campus
- **Coed,** 4,429 undergraduate students, 45% full-time, 62% women, 38% men

Undergraduates 1,981 full-time, 2,448 part-time. 19% Black or African American, non-Hispanic/Latino; 7% Hispanic/Latino; 2% Asian, non-Hispanic/Latino; 0.1% Native Hawaiian or other Pacific Islander, non-Hispanic/Latino; 0.6% American Indian or Alaska Native, non-

Hispanic/Latino; 2% Two or more races, non-Hispanic/Latino; 0.8% Race/ethnicity unknown; 3% international. *Retention:* 55% of full-time freshmen returned.

Freshmen *Admission:* 1,717 applied, 1,717 admitted, 879 enrolled.

Majors Accounting; aeronautical/aerospace engineering technology; agricultural business and management; agricultural production; applied horticulture/horticulture operations; architectural engineering technology; automobile/automotive mechanics technology; biology/biological sciences; biology/biotechnology laboratory technician; business automation/technology/data entry; business/commerce; civil engineering technology; clinical/medical laboratory assistant; computer and information sciences; computer technology/computer systems technology; construction management; criminal justice/law enforcement administration; criminal justice/police science; customer service support/call center/teleservice operation; diagnostic medical sonography and ultrasound technology; drafting and design technology; early childhood education; e-commerce; education (multiple levels); electrical, electronic and communications engineering technology; elementary education; emergency medical technology (EMT paramedic); energy management and systems technology; entrepreneurship; heating, air conditioning, ventilation and refrigeration maintenance technology; human services; kindergarten/preschool education; legal administrative assistant/secretary; licensed practical/vocational nurse training; management information systems; marketing/marketing management; mathematics teacher education; mechanical drafting and CAD/CADD; medical/clinical assistant; middle school education; nuclear engineering technology; occupational therapist assistant; office management; physical therapy technology; poultry science; radiologic technology/science; registered nursing/registered nurse; respiratory therapy technician; surveying technology; turf and turfgrass management; veterinary/animal health technology; water quality and wastewater treatment management and recycling technology.

Academics *Calendar:* semesters. *Degree:* certificates, diplomas, and associate. *Special study options:* part-time degree program.

Library Stephen J. Betze Library.

Student Life *Housing:* college housing not available. *Campus security:* 24-hour emergency response devices, late-night transport/escort service.

Athletics Member NJCAA. *Intercollegiate sports:* baseball M(s), golf M, softball W(s). *Intramural sports:* football M/W.

Financial Aid Of all full-time matriculated undergraduates who enrolled in 2012, 250 Federal Work-Study jobs (averaging $2000).

Applying *Options:* electronic application, early admission, deferred entrance. *Application fee:* $10. *Required for some:* high school transcript.

Freshman Application Contact Ms. Claire McDonald, Admissions Counselor, Delaware Technical & Community College, Jack F. Owens Campus, PO Box 610, Georgetown, DE 19947. *Phone:* 302-856-5400. *Fax:* 302-856-9461.

Website: http://www.dtcc.edu/.

Delaware Technical & Community College, Stanton/Wilmington Campus
Newark, Delaware

- **State-supported** 2-year, founded 1968, part of Delaware Technical and Community College System
- **Urban** campus
- **Coed,** 7,035 undergraduate students, 37% full-time, 58% women, 42% men

Undergraduates 2,616 full-time, 4,419 part-time. 28% Black or African American, non-Hispanic/Latino; 10% Hispanic/Latino; 4% Asian, non-Hispanic/Latino; 0.2% Native Hawaiian or other Pacific Islander, non-Hispanic/Latino; 0.4% American Indian or Alaska Native, non-Hispanic/Latino; 2% Two or more races, non-Hispanic/Latino; 2% Race/ethnicity unknown; 2% international. *Retention:* 52% of full-time freshmen returned.

Freshmen *Admission:* 3,826 applied, 3,826 admitted, 1,291 enrolled.

Majors Accounting; agricultural business and management; architectural engineering technology; automobile/automotive mechanics technology; biology/biological sciences; biology/biotechnology laboratory technician; business administration and management; business automation/technology/data entry; business/commerce; CAD/CADD drafting/design technology; cardiovascular technology; chemical technology; civil drafting and CAD/CADD; computer and information sciences; computer engineering technology; computer systems networking and telecommunications; construction management; criminal justice/law enforcement administration; criminal justice/police science; culinary arts; customer service management; customer service support/call center/teleservice operation; dental hygiene; diagnostic medical sonography and ultrasound technology; drafting and design technology; early childhood education; education (multiple levels); electrical, electronic and communications engineering technology; electrocardiograph technology; elementary education; emergency care attendant (EMT ambulance); emergency medical technology

(EMT paramedic); energy management and systems technology; engineering/industrial management; fire prevention and safety technology; fire science/firefighting; fire services administration; heating, ventilation, air conditioning and refrigeration engineering technology; histologic technology/histotechnologist; hotel/motel administration; human services; kindergarten/preschool education; kinesiology and exercise science; management information systems; management science; manufacturing engineering technology; marketing/marketing management; mathematics teacher education; mechanical engineering/mechanical technology; medical/clinical assistant; middle school education; nuclear engineering technology; nuclear medical technology; occupational therapist assistant; office management; operations research; physical therapy technology; radiologic technology/science; registered nursing/registered nurse; respiratory therapy technician; restaurant, culinary, and catering management; science technologies related; substance abuse/addiction counseling; surveying technology.

Academics *Calendar:* semesters. *Degree:* certificates, diplomas, and associate. *Special study options:* part-time degree program.

Library Stanton Campus Library and John Eugene Derrickson Memorial Library.

Student Life *Housing:* college housing not available. *Campus security:* 24-hour emergency response devices, late-night transport/escort service.

Athletics Member NJCAA. *Intercollegiate sports:* basketball M(s)/W(s), soccer M(s), softball W(s). *Intramural sports:* basketball M/W, football M/W, softball W, volleyball M/W.

Applying *Options:* electronic application, early admission, deferred entrance. *Application fee:* $10. *Required for some:* high school transcript. *Application deadlines:* rolling (freshmen), rolling (transfers). *Notification:* continuous (freshmen), continuous (transfers).

Freshman Application Contact Ms. Rebecca Bailey, Admissions Coordinator, Wilmington, Delaware Technical & Community College, Stanton/Wilmington Campus, 333 Shipley Street, Wilmington, DE 19713. *Phone:* 302-571-5343. *Fax:* 302-577-2548.

Website: http://www.dtcc.edu/.

Delaware Technical & Community College, Terry Campus
Dover, Delaware

- **State-supported** 2-year, founded 1972, part of Delaware Technical and Community College System
- **Small-town** campus
- **Coed,** 3,032 undergraduate students, 48% full-time, 63% women, 37% men

Undergraduates 1,445 full-time, 1,587 part-time. 28% Black or African American, non-Hispanic/Latino; 6% Hispanic/Latino; 3% Asian, non-Hispanic/Latino; 0.2% Native Hawaiian or other Pacific Islander, non-Hispanic/Latino; 0.5% American Indian or Alaska Native, non-Hispanic/Latino; 2% Two or more races, non-Hispanic/Latino; 2% Race/ethnicity unknown; 0.8% international. *Retention:* 50% of full-time freshmen returned.

Freshmen *Admission:* 1,569 applied, 1,569 admitted, 658 enrolled.

Majors Accounting; agricultural business and management; architectural engineering technology; bilingual and multilingual education; biomedical technology; business administration and management; business automation/technology/data entry; business/commerce; civil engineering technology; commercial and advertising art; computer and information sciences; computer engineering technology; computer systems networking and telecommunications; computer technology/computer systems technology; construction management; criminal justice/law enforcement administration; criminal justice/police science; culinary arts; digital communication and media/multimedia; drafting and design technology; early childhood education; e-commerce; education (multiple levels); electrical, electronic and communications engineering technology; electromechanical technology; elementary education; emergency medical technology (EMT paramedic); energy management and systems technology; entrepreneurship; hotel/motel administration; human resources management; human services; interior design; kindergarten/preschool education; legal administrative assistant/secretary; management information systems; marketing/marketing management; mathematics teacher education; medical/clinical assistant; middle school education; office management; photography; registered nursing/registered nurse; substance abuse/addiction counseling.

Academics *Calendar:* semesters. *Degree:* certificates, diplomas, and associate. *Special study options:* part-time degree program.

Student Life *Housing:* college housing not available. *Campus security:* 24-hour emergency response devices, late-night transport/escort service.

Athletics Member NJCAA. *Intercollegiate sports:* lacrosse M(s), soccer M(s)/W(s), softball W(s).

Financial Aid Of all full-time matriculated undergraduates who enrolled in 2012, 50 Federal Work-Study jobs (averaging $1500).

Applying *Options:* electronic application, early admission, deferred entrance. *Application fee:* $10. *Required for some:* high school transcript.

Freshman Application Contact Mrs. Maria Harris, Admissions Officer, Delaware Technical & Community College, Terry Campus, 100 Campus Drive, Dover, DE 19904. *Phone:* 302-857-1020. *Fax:* 302-857-1296. *E-mail:* terry-info@dtcc.edu.
Website: http://www.dtcc.edu/.

FLORIDA

Anthem College–Orlando
Orlando, Florida

Freshman Application Contact Admissions Office, Anthem College–Orlando, 3710 Maguire Boulevard, Orlando, FL 32803. *Toll-free phone:* 855-824-0055.
Website: http://anthem.edu/orlando-florida/.

Broward College
Fort Lauderdale, Florida

- **State-supported** primarily 2-year, founded 1960, part of Florida College System
- **Urban** campus with easy access to Miami
- **Coed,** 43,715 undergraduate students, 30% full-time, 59% women, 41% men

Undergraduates 13,327 full-time, 30,388 part-time. Students come from 143 other countries; 35% Black or African American, non-Hispanic/Latino; 34% Hispanic/Latino; 3% Asian, non-Hispanic/Latino; 0.2% Native Hawaiian or other Pacific Islander, non-Hispanic/Latino; 0.2% American Indian or Alaska Native, non-Hispanic/Latino; 2% Two or more races, non-Hispanic/Latino; 4% Race/ethnicity unknown; 3% international; 3% transferred in.

Freshmen *Admission:* 6,611 enrolled.

Faculty *Student/faculty ratio:* 30:1.

Majors Accounting; accounting technology and bookkeeping; actuarial science; advertising; aeronautical/aerospace engineering technology; African American/Black studies; airline pilot and flight crew; air traffic control; anthropology; applied mathematics; architecture; art; art history, criticism and conservation; art teacher education; astronomy; audiology and speech-language pathology; automobile/automotive mechanics technology; aviation/airway management; biochemistry; biology/biological sciences; biology teacher education; biomedical technology; botany/plant biology; building construction technology; business administration and management; chemical engineering; chemistry; chemistry teacher education; city/urban, community and regional planning; civil engineering; computer and information sciences; computer engineering; computer programming; computer systems analysis; criminal justice/law enforcement administration; dance; data modeling/warehousing and database administration; dental hygiene; diagnostic medical sonography and ultrasound technology; dietetics; dramatic/theater arts; early childhood education; ecology; economics; electrical and electronics engineering; elementary education; emergency medical technology (EMT paramedic); engineering; engineering science; English; English/language arts teacher education; entomology; environmental science; finance; fire science/firefighting; food science; foreign language teacher education; forensic science and technology; forest/forest resources management; French; geography; geology/earth science; German; golf course operation and grounds management; graphic design; health information/medical records administration; health services administration; health teacher education; history; horticultural science; hospitality administration; humanities; human nutrition; human resources management; information science/studies; information technology; insurance; interior design; international business/trade/commerce; international relations and affairs; Italian; Jewish/Judaic studies; journalism; kinesiology and exercise science; Latin American studies; legal administrative assistant/secretary; legal assistant/paralegal; legal studies; liberal arts and sciences/liberal studies; management information systems; management science; manufacturing engineering; marine biology and biological oceanography; marketing/marketing management; mass communication/media; mathematics; mathematics teacher education; mechanical engineering; mechanical engineering technologies related; medical office assistant; medical radiologic technology; music; music teacher education; natural resource recreation and tourism; network and system administration; nuclear engineering; nuclear medical technology; nutrition sciences; ocean engineering; opticianry; parks, recreation and leisure facilities management; pharmacy; philosophy; physical education teaching and coaching; physical therapy; physics; physics teacher education; playwriting and screenwriting; political science and government; Portuguese; pre-chiropractic; premedical studies; pre-occupational therapy; pre-optometry; pre-physical therapy; pre-veterinary studies; psychology;

public administration; public relations, advertising, and applied communication; radio and television; real estate; registered nursing/registered nurse; religious studies; respiratory care therapy; restaurant, culinary, and catering management; restaurant/food services management; sales and marketing/marketing and distribution teacher education; science teacher education; social psychology; social sciences; social studies teacher education; social work; sociology; Spanish; special education; special education–individuals with emotional disturbances; special education–individuals with intellectual disabilities; special education–individuals with specific learning disabilities; special education–individuals with vision impairments; statistics; systems engineering; theater design and technology; therapeutic recreation; tourism and travel services management; trade and industrial teacher education; women's studies; zoology/animal biology.

Academics *Calendar:* trimesters. *Degrees:* certificates, diplomas, associate, and bachelor's. *Special study options:* academic remediation for entering students, accelerated degree program, adult/continuing education programs, advanced placement credit, cooperative education, distance learning, English as a second language, honors programs, part-time degree program, services for LD students, student-designed majors, study abroad, summer session for credit. *ROTC:* Army (b).

Library South Regional/Broward Community College Library with an OPAC.

Student Life *Housing:* college housing not available. *Activities and Organizations:* drama/theater group, student-run newspaper, choral group. *Campus security:* 24-hour emergency response devices and patrols, late-night transport/escort service. *Student services:* personal/psychological counseling, women's center.

Athletics Member NJCAA. *Intercollegiate sports:* baseball M, basketball M/W, softball W, tennis W, volleyball W.

Financial Aid *Financial aid deadline:* 7/1.

Applying *Options:* electronic application, early admission, deferred entrance. *Application fee:* $35. *Required for some:* high school transcript.

Freshman Application Contact Mr. Willie J. Alexander, Associate Vice President for Student Affairs/College Registrar, Broward College, 225 East Las Olas Boulevard, Fort Lauderdale, FL 33301. *Phone:* 954-201-7471. *Fax:* 954-201-7466. *E-mail:* walexand@broward.edu.
Website: http://www.broward.edu/.

Brown Mackie College–Miami
Miramar, Florida

- **Proprietary** primarily 2-year, part of Education Management Corporation
- **Coed**

Majors Biomedical technology; business administration and management; computer support specialist; corrections and criminal justice related; criminal justice/law enforcement administration; early childhood education; health/health-care administration; information technology; legal assistant/paralegal; registered nursing/registered nurse.

Academics *Degrees:* diplomas, associate, and bachelor's.

Freshman Application Contact Brown Mackie College–Miami, 3700 Lakeside Drive, Miramar, FL 33027. *Phone:* 305-341-6600. *Toll-free phone:* 866-505-0335.
Website: http://www.brownmackie.edu/miami/.

See display on next page and page 406 for the College Close-Up.

Cambridge Institute of Allied Health and Technology
Delray Beach, Florida

Admissions Office Contact Cambridge Institute of Allied Health and Technology, 5150 Linton Boulevard, Suite 340, Delray Beach, FL 33484.
Website: http://www.cambridgehealth.edu/.

Central Florida Institute
Palm Harbor, Florida

Director of Admissions Carol Bruno, Director of Admissions, Central Florida Institute, 30522 US Highway 19 North, Suite 300, Palm Harbor, FL 34684. *Phone:* 727-786-4707. *Toll-free phone:* 888-831-8303.
Website: http://www.cfinstitute.com/.

Chipola College
Marianna, Florida

- **State-supported** primarily 2-year, founded 1947
- **Rural** 105-acre campus
- **Coed,** 2,189 undergraduate students, 43% full-time, 63% women, 37% men

Undergraduates 952 full-time, 1,237 part-time. Students come from 7 states and territories; 6 other countries; 8% are from out of state; 16% Black or

African American, non-Hispanic/Latino; 4% Hispanic/Latino; 0.6% Asian, non-Hispanic/Latino; 0.5% American Indian or Alaska Native, non-Hispanic/Latino; 2% Two or more races, non-Hispanic/Latino; 0.3% Race/ethnicity unknown; 7% transferred in.

Freshmen *Admission:* 595 applied, 471 admitted, 197 enrolled. *Average high school GPA:* 2.5. *Test scores:* SAT critical reading scores over 500: 16%; SAT math scores over 500: 36%; ACT scores over 18: 81%; SAT critical reading scores over 600: 4%; SAT math scores over 600: 12%; ACT scores over 24: 25%; ACT scores over 30: 3%.

Faculty *Total:* 127, 31% full-time, 13% with terminal degrees. *Student/faculty ratio:* 24:1.

Majors Accounting; agriculture; agronomy and crop science; art; biological and physical sciences; business administration and management; clinical laboratory science/medical technology; computer and information sciences related; computer science; education; finance; liberal arts and sciences/liberal studies; mass communication/media; mathematics teacher education; pre-engineering; registered nursing/registered nurse; science teacher education; secondary education; social work.

Academics *Calendar:* semesters. *Degrees:* certificates, associate, and bachelor's. *Special study options:* academic remediation for entering students, adult/continuing education programs, advanced placement credit, distance learning, honors programs, independent study, part-time degree program, services for LD students, summer session for credit.

Library Chipola Library with 37,740 titles, 226 serial subscriptions.

Student Life *Housing:* college housing not available. *Activities and Organizations:* drama/theater group, student-run newspaper, choral group, Drama/Theater Group. *Campus security:* night security personnel.

Athletics Member NJCAA. *Intercollegiate sports:* baseball M(s), basketball M(s)/W(s), softball W(s).

Costs (2013–14) *Tuition:* state resident $3060 full-time, $102 per semester hour part-time; nonresident $8891 full-time, $296 per semester hour part-time. Full-time tuition and fees vary according to degree level. Part-time tuition and fees vary according to degree level. *Required fees:* $40 full-time.

Applying *Options:* early admission. *Required:* high school transcript. *Application deadlines:* rolling (freshmen), rolling (transfers). *Notification:* continuous (freshmen), continuous (transfers).

Freshman Application Contact Mrs. Kathy L. Rehberg, Registrar, Chipola College, 3094 Indian Circle, Marianna, FL 32446-3065. *Phone:* 850-718-2233. *Fax:* 850-718-2287. *E-mail:* rehbergk@chipola.edu. *Website:* http://www.chipola.edu/.

City College
Almonte Springs, Florida

Director of Admissions Ms. Kimberly Bowden, Director of Admissions, City College, 177 Montgomery Road, Almonte Springs, FL 32714. *Phone:* 352-335-4000. *Fax:* 352-335-4303. *E-mail:* kbowden@citycollege.edu. *Website:* http://www.citycollege.edu/.

City College
Fort Lauderdale, Florida

Freshman Application Contact City College, 2000 West Commercial Boulevard, Suite 200, Fort Lauderdale, FL 33309. *Phone:* 954-492-5353. *Toll-free phone:* 866-314-5681. *Website:* http://www.citycollege.edu/.

City College
Gainesville, Florida

Freshman Application Contact Admissions Office, City College, 7001 Northwest 4th Boulevard, Gainesville, FL 32607. *Phone:* 352-335-4000. *Website:* http://www.citycollege.edu/.

City College
Miami, Florida

Freshman Application Contact Admissions Office, City College, 9300 South Dadeland Boulevard, Suite PH, Miami, FL 33156. *Phone:* 305-666-9242. *Fax:* 305-666-9243. *Website:* http://www.citycollege.edu/.

College of Business and Technology
Miami, Florida

Freshman Application Contact Ms. Ivis Delgado, Admissions Representative, College of Business and Technology, 8230 West Flagler Street, Miami, FL 33144. *Phone:* 305-273-4499 Ext. 2204. *Toll-free phone:* 866-626-8842. *Fax:* 305-485-4411. *E-mail:* admissions@cbt.edu. *Website:* http://www.cbt.edu/.

College of Business and Technology–Flagler Campus

Miami, Florida

Admissions Office Contact College of Business and Technology–Flagler Campus, 8230 W. Flagler Street, Miami, FL 33144.
Website: http://www.cbt.edu/.

College of Business and Technology–Hialeah Campus

Hialeah, Florida

Admissions Office Contact College of Business and Technology–Hialeah Campus, 935 West 49 Street, # 203, Hialeah, FL 33012.
Website: http://www.cbt.edu/.

College of Central Florida

Ocala, Florida

- **State and locally supported** primarily 2-year, founded 1957, part of Florida Community College System
- **Small-town** 139-acre campus
- **Endowment** $55.8 million
- **Coed,** 8,114 undergraduate students, 34% full-time, 63% women, 37% men

Undergraduates 2,790 full-time, 5,324 part-time. Students come from 2 states and territories; 24 other countries; 13% Black or African American, non-Hispanic/Latino; 11% Hispanic/Latino; 2% Asian, non-Hispanic/Latino; 0.1% Native Hawaiian or other Pacific Islander, non-Hispanic/Latino; 0.3% American Indian or Alaska Native, non-Hispanic/Latino; 12% Race/ethnicity unknown; 1% international; 4% transferred in.

Freshmen *Admission:* 6,111 applied, 3,370 admitted, 1,071 enrolled. *Test scores:* SAT critical reading scores over 500: 42%; SAT math scores over 500: 39%; SAT writing scores over 500: 42%; ACT scores over 18: 77%; SAT math scores over 600: 8%; ACT scores over 24: 29%; ACT scores over 30: 5%.

Faculty *Total:* 279, 45% full-time, 22% with terminal degrees. *Student/faculty ratio:* 26:1.

Majors Accounting technology and bookkeeping; automobile/automotive mechanics technology; business/commerce; drafting and design technology; early childhood education; emergency medical technology (EMT paramedic); fire science/firefighting; health information/medical records technology; human services; information technology; landscaping and groundskeeping; liberal arts and sciences/liberal studies; marketing/marketing management; office management; parks, recreation and leisure; physical therapy technology; registered nursing/registered nurse; restaurant, culinary, and catering management; veterinary/animal health technology.

Academics *Calendar:* semesters. *Degrees:* certificates, diplomas, associate, and bachelor's. *Special study options:* academic remediation for entering students, adult/continuing education programs, advanced placement credit, cooperative education, distance learning, English as a second language, freshman honors college, honors programs, independent study, internships, part-time degree program, services for LD students, summer session for credit.

Library Clifford B. Stearns Learning Resources Center plus 1 other with 143,478 titles, 39,817 serial subscriptions, 6,373 audiovisual materials, an OPAC, a Web page.

Student Life *Housing:* college housing not available. *Activities and Organizations:* drama/theater group, student-run newspaper, choral group, Inspirational Choir, Model United nations, Performing Arts, Phi Theta Kappa (PTK), Student Nurses Association (SNA). *Campus security:* 24-hour emergency response devices and patrols, student patrols, late-night transport/escort service. *Student services:* personal/psychological counseling.

Athletics Member NJCAA. *Intercollegiate sports:* baseball M(s), basketball M(s)/W(s), softball W(s), volleyball W(s).

Standardized Tests *Recommended:* SAT (for admission), ACT (for admission), SAT or ACT (for admission), SAT and SAT Subject Tests or ACT (for admission), SAT Subject Tests (for admission).

Costs (2014–15) *Tuition:* state resident $2388 full-time, $80 per credit part-time; nonresident $9552 full-time, $318 per credit part-time. Full-time tuition and fees vary according to course level, degree level, program, and student level. Part-time tuition and fees vary according to course level, degree level, program, and student level. *Required fees:* $765 full-time. *Payment plan:* deferred payment. *Waivers:* employees or children of employees.

Financial Aid Of all full-time matriculated undergraduates who enrolled in 2012, 85 Federal Work-Study jobs (averaging $1505).

Applying *Options:* electronic application, early admission. *Application fee:* $30. *Required:* high school transcript. *Application deadlines:* rolling (freshmen), rolling (transfers). *Notification:* continuous (freshmen), continuous (transfers).

Freshman Application Contact Ms. Devona Sewell, Registrar, Admission and Records, College of Central Florida, 3001 SW College Road, Ocala, FL 34474. *Phone:* 352-237-2111 Ext. 1398. *Fax:* 352-873-5882. *E-mail:* sewelld@cf.edu.
Website: http://www.cf.edu/.

Concorde Career Institute

Jacksonville, Florida

Admissions Office Contact Concorde Career Institute, 7259 Salisbury Road, Jacksonville, FL 32256.
Website: http://www.concorde.edu/.

Concorde Career Institute

Miramar, Florida

Admissions Office Contact Concorde Career Institute, 10933 Marks Way, Miramar, FL 33025.
Website: http://www.concorde.edu/.

Concorde Career Institute

Orlando, Florida

Admissions Office Contact Concorde Career Institute, 3444 McCrory Place, Orlando, FL 32803.
Website: http://www.concorde.edu/.

Concorde Career Institute

Tampa, Florida

Admissions Office Contact Concorde Career Institute, 4202 West Spruce Street, Tampa, FL 33607-4127.
Website: http://www.concorde.edu/.

Dade Medical College

Miami, Florida

Admissions Office Contact Dade Medical College, 3721-1 NW 7th Street, Miami, FL 33126.
Website: http://www.dademedical.edu/.

Daytona College

Ormond Beach, Florida

Admissions Office Contact Daytona College, 469 South Nova Road, Ormond Beach, FL 32174-8445.
Website: http://www.daytonacollege.edu/.

Daytona State College

Daytona Beach, Florida

- **State-supported** primarily 2-year, founded 1958, part of Florida Community College System
- **Suburban** 100-acre campus with easy access to Orlando
- **Endowment** $5.7 million
- **Coed,** 15,708 undergraduate students, 41% full-time, 60% women, 40% men

Undergraduates 6,429 full-time, 9,279 part-time. Students come from 130 other countries; 3% are from out of state; 13% Black or African American, non-Hispanic/Latino; 11% Hispanic/Latino; 2% Asian, non-Hispanic/Latino; 0.1% Native Hawaiian or other Pacific Islander, non-Hispanic/Latino; 0.5% American Indian or Alaska Native, non-Hispanic/Latino; 1% Two or more races, non-Hispanic/Latino; 0.9% Race/ethnicity unknown; 6% transferred in.

Freshmen *Admission:* 2,228 admitted, 1,769 enrolled.

Faculty *Total:* 881, 36% full-time, 18% with terminal degrees. *Student/faculty ratio:* 20:1.

Majors Accounting; administrative assistant and secretarial science; architectural engineering technology; automobile/automotive mechanics technology; biology teacher education; business administration and management; child development; communications technology; computer and information sciences related; computer engineering; computer engineering related; computer graphics; computer/information technology services administration related; computer programming; computer programming (specific applications); computer science; computer systems networking and telecommunications; computer technology/computer systems technology; criminal justice/law enforcement administration; criminal justice/police science; culinary arts; dental hygiene; drafting and design technology; electrical, electronic and communications engineering technology; elementary education; emergency medical technology (EMT paramedic); engineering; fire science/firefighting; health information/medical records administration;

hospitality administration; hotel/motel administration; human services; industrial radiologic technology; industrial technology; information technology; interior design; kindergarten/preschool education; legal assistant/paralegal; machine shop technology; mathematics teacher education; medical administrative assistant and medical secretary; occupational therapist assistant; photographic and film/video technology; physical therapy; plastics and polymer engineering technology; radio and television; registered nursing/registered nurse; respiratory care therapy; robotics technology; secondary education; special education–early childhood; tourism and travel services management.

Academics *Calendar:* semesters. *Degrees:* certificates, diplomas, associate, bachelor's, and postbachelor's certificates. *Special study options:* academic remediation for entering students, adult/continuing education programs, advanced placement credit, cooperative education, distance learning, double majors, English as a second language, external degree program, freshman honors college, honors programs, independent study, internships, off-campus study, part-time degree program, services for LD students, study abroad, summer session for credit. *ROTC:* Army (c), Air Force (c).

Library Mary Karl Memorial Learning Resources Center plus 1 other with 88,050 titles, 334 serial subscriptions, 6,036 audiovisual materials, an OPAC, a Web page.

Student Life *Housing:* college housing not available. *Activities and Organizations:* drama/theater group, student-run newspaper, choral group, Rotaract, Student Government Association, Student Occupational Therapy Club, Massage Therapy Club, Student Paralegal Club, national fraternities, national sororities. *Campus security:* 24-hour emergency response devices and patrols, late-night transport/escort service. *Student services:* personal/psychological counseling, women's center.

Athletics Member NJCAA. *Intercollegiate sports:* baseball M(s), basketball M(s)/W(s), golf W(s), softball W(s), volleyball W(s). *Intramural sports:* basketball M/W, cheerleading M/W, football M/W, golf M/W, racquetball M/W, soccer M/W, table tennis M/W, tennis M/W, volleyball M/W.

Costs (2013–14) *Tuition:* state resident $1940 full-time, $970 per year part-time; nonresident $7621 full-time, $3810 per year part-time. Full-time tuition and fees vary according to course load and degree level. Part-time tuition and fees vary according to course load and degree level. *Required fees:* $747 full-time, $388 per year part-time. *Payment plan:* installment.

Financial Aid Of all full-time matriculated undergraduates who enrolled in 2012, 5,549 were judged to have need, 298 had their need fully met. 155 Federal Work-Study jobs (averaging $2238). In 2012, 7 non-need-based awards were made. *Average need-based loan:* $1708. *Average need-based gift aid:* $1333. *Average non-need-based aid:* $770.

Applying *Options:* electronic application, early admission, deferred entrance. *Required:* high school transcript. *Application deadlines:* rolling (freshmen), rolling (transfers). *Notification:* continuous (freshmen), continuous (transfers).

Freshman Application Contact Dr. Karen Sanders, Director of Admissions and Recruitment, Daytona State College, 1200 International Speedway Boulevard, Daytona Beach, FL 32114. *Phone:* 386-506-3050. *E-mail:* sanderk@daytonastate.edu.

Website: http://www.daytonastate.edu/.

Eastern Florida State College
Cocoa, Florida

- **State-supported** primarily 2-year, founded 1960, part of Florida Community College System
- **Suburban** 100-acre campus with easy access to Orlando
- **Coed,** 16,711 undergraduate students, 35% full-time, 58% women, 42% men

Undergraduates 5,929 full-time, 10,782 part-time. Students come from 67 other countries; 11% Black or African American, non-Hispanic/Latino; 10% Hispanic/Latino; 2% Asian, non-Hispanic/Latino; 0.3% Native Hawaiian or other Pacific Islander, non-Hispanic/Latino; 0.6% American Indian or Alaska Native, non-Hispanic/Latino; 3% Two or more races, non-Hispanic/Latino; 1% Race/ethnicity unknown; 0.7% international.

Freshmen *Admission:* 6,438 applied, 6,438 admitted, 2,501 enrolled.

Faculty *Total:* 1,008, 24% full-time. *Student/faculty ratio:* 23:1.

Majors Aeronautics/aviation/aerospace science and technology; art; business administration and management; chemical technology; clinical/medical laboratory technology; computer programming; computer systems networking and telecommunications; criminal justice/law enforcement administration; dance; dental assisting; dental hygiene; digital communication and media/multimedia; drafting and design technology; dramatic/theater arts; early childhood education; emergency medical technology (EMT paramedic); engineering technology; fire science/firefighting; graphic communications related; information technology; legal assistant/paralegal; medical radiologic technology; music; office management; registered nursing/registered nurse; veterinary/animal health technology.

Academics *Calendar:* semesters. *Degrees:* certificates, associate, and bachelor's. *Special study options:* academic remediation for entering students, accelerated degree program, adult/continuing education programs, advanced placement credit, cooperative education, distance learning, double majors, English as a second language, external degree program, honors programs, independent study, internships, part-time degree program, services for LD students, study abroad, summer session for credit. *ROTC:* Army (b), Air Force (b).

Library UCF Library with 213,873 titles, 904 serial subscriptions, an OPAC, a Web page.

Student Life *Housing:* college housing not available. *Activities and Organizations:* drama/theater group, student-run newspaper, television station, choral group, Phi Theta Kappa, The Green Team, African-American Student Union, Student Government Association, Cosmetology in Action. *Campus security:* 24-hour emergency response devices and patrols. *Student services:* women's center.

Athletics Member NJCAA. *Intercollegiate sports:* baseball M(s), basketball M(s)/W(s), golf M(s), softball W(s), volleyball W(s).

Financial Aid Of all full-time matriculated undergraduates who enrolled in 2012, 200 Federal Work-Study jobs (averaging $2244). 200 state and other part-time jobs (averaging $2000).

Applying *Options:* electronic application, early admission. *Application fee:* $30. *Required:* high school transcript. *Application deadlines:* rolling (freshmen), rolling (transfers). *Notification:* continuous (freshmen), continuous (transfers).

Freshman Application Contact Ms. Stephanie Burnette, Registrar, Eastern Florida State College, 1519 Clearlake Road, Cocoa, FL 32922-6597. *Phone:* 321-433-7271. *Fax:* 321-433-7172. *E-mail:* cocoaadmissions@ brevardcc.edu.

Website: http://www.easternflorida.edu/.

Edison State College
Fort Myers, Florida

Freshman Application Contact Lauren Willison, Admissions Specialist, Edison State College, 8099 College Parkway, Fort Myers, FL 33919. *Phone:* 239-489-9257. *Toll-free phone:* 800-749-2ECC. *E-mail:* Lauren.Willison@ edison.edu.

Website: http://www.edison.edu/.

Everest Institute
Miami, Florida

Director of Admissions Director of Admissions, Everest Institute, 111 Northwest 183rd Street, Second Floor, Miami, FL 33169. *Phone:* 305-949-9500. *Toll-free phone:* 888-741-4270.

Website: http://www.everest.edu/.

Everest Institute
Miami, Florida

Freshman Application Contact Director of Admissions, Everest Institute, 9020 Southwest 137th Avenue, Miami, FL 33186. *Phone:* 305-386-9900. *Toll-free phone:* 888-741-4270. *Fax:* 305-388-1740.

Website: http://www.everest.edu/.

Everest University
Orange Park, Florida

Freshman Application Contact Admissions Office, Everest University, 805 Wells Road, Orange Park, FL 32073. *Phone:* 904-264-9122.

Website: http://www.everest.edu/.

Florida Career College
Miami, Florida

Director of Admissions Mr. David Knobel, President, Florida Career College, 1321 Southwest 107 Avenue, Suite 201B, Miami, FL 33174. *Phone:* 305-553-6065. *Toll-free phone:* 888-852-7272.

Website: http://www.careercollege.edu/.

Florida College of Natural Health
Bradenton, Florida

Freshman Application Contact Admissions Office, Florida College of Natural Health, 616 67th Street Circle East, Bradenton, FL 34208. *Phone:* 941-744-1244. *Toll-free phone:* 800-966-7117. *Fax:* 941-744-1242.

Website: http://www.fcnh.com/.

Florida College of Natural Health
Maitland, Florida

Freshman Application Contact Admissions Office, Florida College of Natural Health, 2600 Lake Lucien Drive, Suite 140, Maitland, FL 32751. *Phone:* 407-261-0319. *Toll-free phone:* 800-393-7337. *Website:* http://www.fcnh.com/.

Florida College of Natural Health
Miami, Florida

Director of Admissions Admissions Coordinator, Florida College of Natural Health, 7925 Northwest 12th Street, Suite 201, Miami, FL 33126. *Phone:* 305-597-9599. *Toll-free phone:* 800-599-9599. *Fax:* 305-597-9110. *Website:* http://www.fcnh.com/.

Florida College of Natural Health
Pompano Beach, Florida

Freshman Application Contact Admissions Office, Florida College of Natural Health, 2001 West Sample Road, Suite 100, Pompano Beach, FL 33064. *Phone:* 954-975-6400. *Toll-free phone:* 800-541-9299. *Website:* http://www.fcnh.com/.

Florida Gateway College
Lake City, Florida

- **State-supported** primarily 2-year, founded 1962, part of Florida Community College System
- **Small-town** 132-acre campus with easy access to Jacksonville
- **Coed,** 3,057 undergraduate students, 31% full-time, 65% women, 35% men

Undergraduates 951 full-time, 2,106 part-time. Students come from 2 states and territories; 11% Black or African American, non-Hispanic/Latino; 4% Hispanic/Latino; 0.8% Asian, non-Hispanic/Latino; 0.6% American Indian or Alaska Native, non-Hispanic/Latino; 0.6% Two or more races, non-Hispanic/Latino; 1% Race/ethnicity unknown; 4% transferred in.
Freshmen *Admission:* 518 enrolled.
Faculty *Total:* 179, 38% full-time, 8% with terminal degrees. *Student/faculty ratio:* 16:1.
Majors Computer and information sciences; computer programming; corrections; criminal justice/law enforcement administration; early childhood education; emergency medical technology (EMT paramedic); engineering technology; graphic design; health information/medical records administration; health services administration; information technology; landscaping and groundskeeping; liberal arts and sciences/liberal studies; logistics, materials, and supply chain management; natural resources/conservation; office management; physical therapy technology; registered nursing/registered nurse; turf and turfgrass management; veterinary/animal health technology.
Academics *Calendar:* semesters. *Degrees:* certificates, diplomas, associate, and bachelor's. *Special study options:* academic remediation for entering students, accelerated degree program, adult/continuing education programs, advanced placement credit, cooperative education, distance learning, double majors, English as a second language, independent study, internships, off-campus study, part-time degree program, services for LD students, summer session for credit.
Library Wilson S. Rivers Library and Media Center with 101,800 titles, 150 serial subscriptions, an OPAC, a Web page.
Student Life *Housing:* college housing not available. *Activities and Organizations:* drama/theater group, choral group, Anime Club, Art Club, FGC Board Game Club, Gay Straight Alliance, Rotaract. *Campus security:* 24-hour emergency response devices and patrols. *Student services:* personal/psychological counseling.
Costs (2013–14) *Tuition:* state resident $2368 full-time, $103 per credit hour part-time; nonresident $11,747 full-time, $392 per credit hour part-time. Full-time tuition and fees vary according to course level, course load, degree level, program, and reciprocity agreements. Part-time tuition and fees vary according to course level, course load, degree level, program, and reciprocity agreements. *Required fees:* $731 full-time, $24 per credit hour part-time. *Payment plan:* deferred payment. *Waivers:* employees or children of employees.
Applying *Required for some:* high school transcript. *Application deadlines:* 8/6 (freshmen), 8/6 (transfers). *Notification:* continuous (freshmen), continuous (transfers).
Freshman Application Contact Admissions, Florida Gateway College, 149 SE College Place, Lake City, FL 32025-8703. *Phone:* 386-755-4236. *E-mail:* admissions@fgc.edu.
Website: http://www.fgc.edu/.

Florida Keys Community College
Key West, Florida

Director of Admissions Ms. Cheryl A. Malsheimer, Director of Admissions and Records, Florida Keys Community College, 5901 College Road, Key West, FL 33040-4397. *Phone:* 305-296-9081 Ext. 201. *Website:* http://www.fkcc.edu/.

The Florida School of Traditional Midwifery
Gainseville, Florida

Freshman Application Contact Admissions Office, The Florida School of Traditional Midwifery, 810 East University Avenue, 2nd Floor, Gainesville, FL 32601. *Phone:* 352-338-0766. *Fax:* 352-338-2013. *E-mail:* info@midwiferyschool.org.
Website: http://www.midwiferyschool.org/.

Florida State College at Jacksonville
Jacksonville, Florida

- **State-supported** primarily 2-year, founded 1963, part of Florida College System
- **Urban** 825-acre campus
- **Endowment** $28.8 million
- **Coed,** 28,134 undergraduate students, 33% full-time, 59% women, 41% men

Undergraduates 9,217 full-time, 18,917 part-time. 26% Black or African American, non-Hispanic/Latino; 6% Hispanic/Latino; 4% Asian, non-Hispanic/Latino; 0.5% Native Hawaiian or other Pacific Islander, non-Hispanic/Latino; 0.4% American Indian or Alaska Native, non-Hispanic/Latino; 2% Two or more races, non-Hispanic/Latino; 13% Race/ethnicity unknown; 0.7% international; 9% transferred in.
Freshmen *Admission:* 7,160 applied, 7,160 admitted, 3,866 enrolled.
Faculty *Total:* 1,194, 33% full-time, 22% with terminal degrees. *Student/faculty ratio:* 26:1.
Majors Accounting; administrative assistant and secretarial science; aircraft powerplant technology; airframe mechanics and aircraft maintenance technology; airline pilot and flight crew; architectural drafting and CAD/CADD; architectural engineering technology; autobody/collision and repair technology; automobile/automotive mechanics technology; aviation/airway management; banking and financial support services; biomedical technology; business administration and management; business administration, management and operations related; child-care and support services management; child-care provision; civil engineering technology; commercial and advertising art; computer and information sciences; computer and information sciences and support services related; computer and information sciences related; computer and information systems security; computer engineering technology; computer graphics; computer hardware engineering; computer/information technology services administration related; computer programming; computer programming related; computer programming (specific applications); computer programming (vendor/product certification); computer software and media applications related; computer software engineering; computer systems analysis; computer systems networking and telecommunications; construction engineering technology; criminal justice/law enforcement administration; criminal justice/police science; culinary arts; data entry/microcomputer applications; data entry/microcomputer applications related; data modeling/warehousing and database administration; dental hygiene; design and visual communications; diagnostic medical sonography and ultrasound technology; dietetics; dietitian assistant; drafting and design technology; early childhood education; electrical, electronic and communications engineering technology; emergency medical technology (EMT paramedic); engineering technology; fashion merchandising; fire prevention and safety technology; fire science/firefighting; fire services administration; food service systems administration; health information/medical records administration; homeland security, law enforcement, firefighting and protective services related; hospitality administration; hospitality and recreation marketing; hotel/motel administration; human services; information science/studies; information technology; instrumentation technology; insurance; interior design; legal assistant/paralegal; liberal arts and sciences/liberal studies; machine shop technology; marketing/marketing management; masonry; medical office management; medical radiologic technology; network and system administration; nuclear/nuclear power technology; office management; office occupations and clerical services; physical therapy technology; printmaking; real estate; registered nursing/registered nurse; respiratory care therapy; retailing; sign language interpretation and translation; substance abuse/addiction counseling; theater design and technology; tourism and travel services marketing; visual and performing arts related; water quality and wastewater treatment management and recycling technology; web/multimedia

management and webmaster; web page, digital/multimedia and information resources design; word processing.

Academics *Calendar:* semesters. *Degrees:* certificates, diplomas, associate, and bachelor's. *Special study options:* academic remediation for entering students, accelerated degree program, adult/continuing education programs, advanced placement credit, cooperative education, distance learning, double majors, English as a second language, honors programs, independent study, internships, off-campus study, part-time degree program, services for LD students, study abroad, summer session for credit. *ROTC:* Navy (c).

Library Florida State College at Jacksonville Library and Learning Commons plus 7 others with 211,361 titles, 3,299 serial subscriptions, 21,541 audiovisual materials, an OPAC, a Web page.

Student Life *Activities and Organizations:* drama/theater group, student-run newspaper, radio and television station, choral group, Phi Theta Kappa, Forensic Team, Brain Bowl Team, International Student Association, DramaWorks. *Campus security:* 24-hour emergency response devices and patrols, late-night transport/escort service. *Student services:* personal/psychological counseling, women's center.

Athletics Member NJCAA. *Intercollegiate sports:* baseball M(s), basketball M(s)/W(s), softball W(s), tennis W(s), volleyball W(s). *Intramural sports:* badminton M/W, basketball M/W, bowling M/W, football M/W, golf M/W, soccer M/W, softball M/W, table tennis M/W, tennis M/W, volleyball M/W.

Applying *Options:* electronic application, early admission, deferred entrance. *Application fee:* $25. *Required:* high school transcript. *Application deadlines:* rolling (freshmen), rolling (out-of-state freshmen), rolling (transfers).

Freshman Application Contact Dr. Peter Biegel, AVP, Enrollment Management, Florida State College at Jacksonville, 501 West State Street, Jacksonville, FL 32202. *Phone:* 904-632-3131. *Toll-free phone:* 888-873-1145. *Fax:* 904-632-5105. *E-mail:* pbiegel@fscj.edu.
Website: http://www.fscj.edu/.

Florida Technical College
DeLand, Florida

Freshman Application Contact Mr. Bill Atkinson, Director, Florida Technical College, 1199 South Woodland Boulevard, 3rd Floor, DeLand, FL 32720. *Phone:* 386-734-3303. *Fax:* 386-734-5150.
Website: http://www.ftccollege.edu/.

Florida Technical College
Orlando, Florida

Director of Admissions Ms. Jeanette E. Muschlitz, Director of Admissions, Florida Technical College, 12900 Challenger Parkway, Orlando, FL 32826. *Phone:* 407-678-5600.
Website: http://www.ftccollege.edu/.

Fortis College
Largo, Florida

Admissions Office Contact Fortis College, 6565 Ulmerton Road, Largo, FL 33771.
Website: http://www.fortis.edu/.

Fortis College
Winter Park, Florida

Freshman Application Contact Admissions Office, Fortis College, 1573 West Fairbanks Avenue, Suite 100, Winter Park, FL 32789. *Phone:* 407-843-3984. *Toll-free phone:* 855-4-FORTIS. *Fax:* 407-843-9828.
Website: http://www.fortis.edu/.

Fortis Institute
Fort Lauderdale, Florida

Admissions Office Contact Fortis Institute, 4850 W. Oakland Park Boulevard, Suite 200, Fort Lauderdale, FL 33313.
Website: http://www.fortis.edu/.

Fortis Institute
Palm Springs, Florida

Director of Admissions Campus Director, Fortis Institute, 1630 South Congress Avenue, Palm Springs, FL 33461. *Phone:* 561-304-3466. *Toll-free phone:* 877-606-3382. *Fax:* 561-304-3471.
Website: http://www.fortis.edu/.

Golf Academy of America
Apopka, Florida

Admissions Office Contact Golf Academy of America, 510 South Hunt Club Boulevard, Apopka, FL 32703.
Website: http://www.golfacademy.edu/.

Gulf Coast State College
Panama City, Florida

Freshman Application Contact Mrs. Jackie Kuczenski, Administrative Secretary of Admissions, Gulf Coast State College, 5230 West U.S. Highway 98, Panama City, FL 32401. *Phone:* 850-769-1551 Ext. 4892. *Fax:* 850-913-3308. *E-mail:* jkuczenski@gulfcoast.edu.
Website: http://www.gulfcoast.edu/.

Hillsborough Community College
Tampa, Florida

- **State-supported** 2-year, founded 1968, part of Florida College System
- **Urban** campus with easy access to Tampa, Clearwater, St. Petersburg
- **Coed**, 26,590 undergraduate students, 43% full-time, 57% women, 43% men

Undergraduates 11,532 full-time, 15,058 part-time. Students come from 131 other countries; 0.8% are from out of state; 17% Black or African American, non-Hispanic/Latino; 25% Hispanic/Latino; 3% Asian, non-Hispanic/Latino; 0.2% Native Hawaiian or other Pacific Islander, non-Hispanic/Latino; 0.5% American Indian or Alaska Native, non-Hispanic/Latino; 2% Two or more races, non-Hispanic/Latino; 12% Race/ethnicity unknown; 3% international; 26% transferred in.

Freshmen *Admission:* 4,977 enrolled.

Faculty *Total:* 1,782, 22% full-time, 12% with terminal degrees. *Student/faculty ratio:* 22:1.

Majors Accounting technology and bookkeeping; aquaculture; architectural engineering technology; biology/biotechnology laboratory technician; business administration and management; child-care and support services management; cinematography and film/video production; computer/information technology services administration related; computer programming (specific applications); computer systems analysis; computer technology/computer systems technology; criminal justice/law enforcement administration; dental hygiene; diagnostic medical sonography and ultrasound technology; dietitian assistant; electrical, electronic and communications engineering technology; emergency medical technology (EMT paramedic); engineering technology; environmental control technologies related; executive assistant/executive secretary; fire prevention and safety technology; hospitality administration; legal assistant/paralegal; liberal arts and sciences/liberal studies; management information systems; management information systems and services related; medical radiologic technology; nuclear medical technology; operations management; opticianry; optometric technician; psychiatric/mental health services technology; registered nursing/registered nurse; respiratory care therapy; restaurant, culinary, and catering management; restaurant/food services management; special education–individuals with hearing impairments; veterinary/animal health technology.

Academics *Calendar:* semesters. *Degree:* certificates and associate. *Special study options:* academic remediation for entering students, advanced placement credit, cooperative education, distance learning, English as a second language, honors programs, independent study, internships, off-campus study, part-time degree program, services for LD students, study abroad, summer session for credit. *ROTC:* Army (c), Air Force (c).

Library Dale Mabry plus 5 others with an OPAC, a Web page.

Student Life *Housing Options:* Campus housing is provided by a third party. *Activities and Organizations:* drama/theater group, student-run newspaper, radio station, choral group. *Campus security:* 24-hour emergency response devices and patrols, late-night transport/escort service, emergency call boxes. *Student services:* personal/psychological counseling.

Athletics Member NJCAA. *Intercollegiate sports:* baseball M(s), basketball M(s)/W(s), softball W(s), tennis W(s), volleyball W(s).

Standardized Tests *Required:* Entrance exams are required for assessing student readiness for college level courses. Florida's Postsecondary Education Readiness Test (PERT) is the primary entrance exam used. Hillsborough Community College is an open-access institution (for admission).

Costs (2013–14) *Tuition:* state resident $2505 full-time, $104 per credit hour part-time; nonresident $9112 full-time, $380 per credit hour part-time. *Payment plan:* installment. *Waivers:* employees or children of employees.

Applying *Options:* electronic application, early admission. *Required:* high school transcript. *Application deadlines:* rolling (freshmen), rolling (out-of-state freshmen), rolling (transfers).

Freshman Application Contact Ms. Jennifer Williams, College Registrar, Hillsborough Community College, PO Box 31127, Tampa, FL 33631-3127. *Phone:* 813-259-6565. *E-mail:* jwilliams301@hccfl.edu.
Website: http://www.hccfl.edu/.

ITT Technical Institute
Bradenton, Florida

Freshman Application Contact Director of Recruitment, ITT Technical Institute, 8039 Cooper Creek Boulevard, Bradenton, FL 34201. *Phone:* 941-309-9200. *Toll-free phone:* 800-342-8684.
Website: http://www.itt-tech.edu/.

ITT Technical Institute
Fort Lauderdale, Florida

- **Proprietary** primarily 2-year, founded 1991, part of ITT Educational Services, Inc.
- **Suburban** campus
- **Coed**

Majors Computer programming (specific applications); construction management; cyber/computer forensics and counterterrorism; drafting and design technology; electrical, electronic and communications engineering technology; forensic science and technology; industrial technology; information technology project management; medical/clinical assistant; network and system administration; project management; registered nursing/registered nurse.
Academics *Calendar:* quarters. *Degrees:* associate and bachelor's.
Student Life *Housing:* college housing not available.
Freshman Application Contact Director of Recruitment, ITT Technical Institute, 3401 South University Drive, Fort Lauderdale, FL 33328-2021. *Phone:* 954-476-9300. *Toll-free phone:* 800-488-7797.
Website: http://www.itt-tech.edu/.

ITT Technical Institute
Fort Myers, Florida

- **Proprietary** primarily 2-year
- **Coed**

Majors Computer programming (specific applications); construction management; cyber/computer forensics and counterterrorism; drafting and design technology; electrical, electronic and communications engineering technology; forensic science and technology; industrial technology; information technology project management; legal assistant/paralegal; network and system administration; project management; registered nursing/registered nurse.
Academics *Degrees:* associate and bachelor's.
Freshman Application Contact Director of Recruitment, ITT Technical Institute, 13500 Powers Court, Suite 100, Fort Myers, FL 33912. *Phone:* 239-603-8700. *Toll-free phone:* 877-485-5313.
Website: http://www.itt-tech.edu/.

ITT Technical Institute
Jacksonville, Florida

- **Proprietary** primarily 2-year, founded 1991, part of ITT Educational Services, Inc.
- **Urban** campus
- **Coed**

Majors Computer programming (specific applications); construction management; cyber/computer forensics and counterterrorism; drafting and design technology; electrical, electronic and communications engineering technology; forensic science and technology; graphic communications; industrial technology; information technology project management; medical/clinical assistant; network and system administration; project management; registered nursing/registered nurse.
Academics *Calendar:* quarters. *Degrees:* associate and bachelor's.
Student Life *Housing:* college housing not available.
Financial Aid Of all full-time matriculated undergraduates who enrolled in 2012, 5 Federal Work-Study jobs.
Freshman Application Contact Director of Recruitment, ITT Technical Institute, 7011 A.C. Skinner Parkway, Suite 140, Jacksonville, FL 32256. *Phone:* 904-573-9100. *Toll-free phone:* 800-318-1264.
Website: http://www.itt-tech.edu/.

ITT Technical Institute
Lake Mary, Florida

- **Proprietary** primarily 2-year, founded 1989, part of ITT Educational Services, Inc.
- **Suburban** campus
- **Coed**

Majors Computer programming (specific applications); construction management; cyber/computer forensics and counterterrorism; drafting and design technology; electrical, electronic and communications engineering technology; forensic science and technology; health information/medical records technology; information technology project management; medical/clinical assistant; network and system administration; project management; registered nursing/registered nurse.
Academics *Calendar:* quarters. *Degrees:* associate and bachelor's.
Freshman Application Contact Director of Recruitment, ITT Technical Institute, 1400 South International Parkway, Lake Mary, FL 32746. *Phone:* 407-936-0600. *Toll-free phone:* 866-489-8441.
Website: http://www.itt-tech.edu/.

ITT Technical Institute
Miami, Florida

- **Proprietary** primarily 2-year, founded 1996, part of ITT Educational Services, Inc.
- **Coed**

Majors Business administration and management; computer programming (specific applications); construction management; cyber/computer forensics and counterterrorism; drafting and design technology; electrical, electronic and communications engineering technology; forensic science and technology; industrial technology; information technology project management; medical/clinical assistant; network and system administration; project management; registered nursing/registered nurse.
Academics *Calendar:* quarters. *Degrees:* associate and bachelor's.
Student Life *Housing:* college housing not available.
Freshman Application Contact Director of Recruitment, ITT Technical Institute, 7955 NW 12th Street, Suite 119, Miami, FL 33126. *Phone:* 305-477-3080.
Website: http://www.itt-tech.edu/.

ITT Technical Institute
Orlando, Florida

- **Proprietary** primarily 2-year, part of ITT Educational Services, Inc.
- **Coed**

Majors Computer programming (specific applications); construction management; drafting and design technology; electrical, electronic and communications engineering technology; forensic science and technology; industrial technology; information technology project management; network and system administration; project management; registered nursing/registered nurse.
Academics *Calendar:* quarters. *Degrees:* associate and bachelor's.
Freshman Application Contact Director of Recruitment, ITT Technical Institute, 8301 Southpark Circle, Suite 100, Orlando, FL 32819. *Phone:* 407-371-6000. *Toll-free phone:* 877-201-4367.
Website: http://www.itt-tech.edu/.

ITT Technical Institute
Pensacola, Florida

- **Proprietary** 2-year
- **Coed**

Majors Construction management; cyber/computer forensics and counterterrorism; drafting and design technology; electrical, electronic and communications engineering technology; information technology project management; network and system administration; project management.
Freshman Application Contact Director of Recruiting, ITT Technical Institute, 6913 North 9th Avenue, Pensacola, FL 32504. *Phone:* 850-483-5700. *Toll-free phone:* 877-290-8248.
Website: http://www.itt-tech.edu/.

ITT Technical Institute
St. Petersburg, Florida

- **Proprietary** primarily 2-year, part of ITT Educational Services, Inc.
- **Coed**

Majors Computer programming (specific applications); construction management; cyber/computer forensics and counterterrorism; drafting and design technology; electrical, electronic and communications engineering technology; forensic science and technology; industrial technology; information technology project management; medical/clinical assistant; network and system administration; project management; registered nursing/registered nurse.
Academics *Degrees:* associate and bachelor's.
Student Life *Housing:* college housing not available.
Freshman Application Contact Director of Recruitment, ITT Technical Institute, 877 Executive Center Drive W., Suite 100, St. Petersburg, FL 33702. *Phone:* 727-209-4700. *Toll-free phone:* 866-488-5084.
Website: http://www.itt-tech.edu/.

ITT Technical Institute

Tallahassee, Florida

- **Proprietary** primarily 2-year
- **Coed**

Majors Business administration and management; construction management; cyber/computer forensics and counterterrorism; drafting and design technology; electrical, electronic and communications engineering technology; forensic science and technology; graphic communications; information technology project management; network and system administration; project management; registered nursing/registered nurse.

Academics *Degrees:* associate and bachelor's.

Freshman Application Contact Director of Recruitment, ITT Technical Institute, 2639 North Monroe Street, Building A, Suite 100, Tallahassee, FL 32303. *Phone:* 850-422-6300. *Toll-free phone:* 877-230-3559.

Website: http://www.itt-tech.edu/.

ITT Technical Institute

Tampa, Florida

- **Proprietary** primarily 2-year, founded 1981, part of ITT Educational Services, Inc.
- **Suburban** campus
- **Coed**

Majors Computer programming (specific applications); construction management; cyber/computer forensics and counterterrorism; drafting and design technology; forensic science and technology; health information/medical records technology; industrial technology; information technology project management; medical/clinical assistant; network and system administration; project management; registered nursing/registered nurse.

Academics *Calendar:* quarters. *Degrees:* associate and bachelor's.

Student Life *Housing:* college housing not available.

Freshman Application Contact Director of Recruitment, ITT Technical Institute, 4809 Memorial Highway, Tampa, FL 33634-7151. *Phone:* 813-885-2244. *Toll-free phone:* 800-825-2831.

Website: http://www.itt-tech.edu/.

Kaplan College, Jacksonville Campus

Jacksonville, Florida

Freshman Application Contact Director of Admissions, Kaplan College, Jacksonville Campus, 7450 Beach Boulevard, Jacksonville, FL 32216. *Phone:* 904-855-2405.

Website: http://jacksonville.kaplancollege.com/.

Key College

Dania Beach, Florida

Director of Admissions Mr. Ronald H. Dooley, President and Director of Admissions, Key College, 225 East Dania Beach Boulevard, Dania Beach, FL 33004. *Phone:* 954-581-2223 Ext. 23. *Toll-free phone:* 800-581-8292.

Website: http://www.keycollege.edu/.

Lake-Sumter State College

Leesburg, Florida

Freshman Application Contact Ms. Bonnie Yanick, Enrollment Specialist, Lake-Sumter State College, 9501 U.S. Highway 441, Leesburg, FL 34788-8751. *Phone:* 352-365-3561. *Fax:* 352-365-3553. *E-mail:* admissinquiry@lscc.edu.

Website: http://www.lssc.edu/.

Le Cordon Bleu College of Culinary Arts in Miami

Miramar, Florida

Freshman Application Contact Admissions Office, Le Cordon Bleu College of Culinary Arts in Miami, 3221 Enterprise Way, Miramar, FL 33025. *Phone:* 954-628-4000. *Toll-free phone:* 888-569-3222.

Website: http://www.chefs.edu/Miami/.

Le Cordon Bleu College of Culinary Arts in Orlando

Orlando, Florida

Admissions Office Contact Le Cordon Bleu College of Culinary Arts in Orlando, 8511 Commodity Circle, Suite 100, Orlando, FL 32819. *Toll-free phone:* 888-793-3222.

Website: http://www.chefs.edu/Orlando/.

Lincoln College of Technology

West Palm Beach, Florida

Director of Admissions Mr. Kevin Cassidy, Director of Admissions, Lincoln College of Technology, 2410 Metrocentre Boulevard, West Palm Beach, FL 33407. *Phone:* 561-842-8324 Ext. 117. *Fax:* 561-842-9503.

Website: http://www.lincolnedu.com/.

Lincoln Technical Institute

Fern Park, Florida

Admissions Office Contact Lincoln Technical Institute, 7275 Estapona Circle, Fern Park, FL 32730.

Website: http://www.lincolnedu.com/.

Meridian College

Sarasota, Florida

Admissions Office Contact Meridian College, 7020 Professional Parkway East, Sarasota, FL 34240.

Website: http://www.meridian.edu/.

Miami Dade College

Miami, Florida

- **State and locally supported** primarily 2-year, founded 1960, part of Florida College System
- **Urban** campus
- **Endowment** $130.2 million
- **Coed,** 66,298 undergraduate students, 40% full-time, 58% women, 42% men

Undergraduates 26,579 full-time, 39,719 part-time. Students come from 187 other countries; 1% are from out of state; 16% Black or African American, non-Hispanic/Latino; 67% Hispanic/Latino; 1% Asian, non-Hispanic/Latino; 0.1% Native Hawaiian or other Pacific Islander, non-Hispanic/Latino; 0.1% American Indian or Alaska Native, non-Hispanic/Latino; 0.3% Two or more races, non-Hispanic/Latino; 3% Race/ethnicity unknown; 6% international; 2% transferred in.

Freshmen *Admission:* 22,955 applied, 22,955 admitted, 12,642 enrolled.

Faculty *Total:* 2,593, 29% full-time, 21% with terminal degrees. *Student/faculty ratio:* 30:1.

Majors Accounting technology and bookkeeping; administrative assistant and secretarial science; aeronautics/aviation/aerospace science and technology; agriculture; airline pilot and flight crew; air traffic control; American studies; anthropology; architectural drafting and CAD/CADD; architectural engineering technology; art; Asian studies; audiology and speech-language pathology; aviation/airway management; behavioral sciences; biology/biological sciences; biology teacher education; biomedical technology; biotechnology; business administration and management; business administration, management and operations related; chemistry; chemistry teacher education; child development; cinematography and film/video production; civil engineering technology; clinical/medical laboratory technology; commercial and advertising art; comparative literature; computer engineering technology; computer graphics; computer programming; computer science; computer software technology; computer technology/computer systems technology; construction engineering technology; cooking and related culinary arts; court reporting; criminal justice/law enforcement administration; criminal justice/police science; culinary arts; dance; dental hygiene; diagnostic medical sonography and ultrasound technology; dietetics; dietetic technology; drafting and design technology; dramatic/theater arts; economics; education; education related; electrical and electronic engineering technologies related; electrical, electronic and communications engineering technology; elementary education; emergency medical technology (EMT paramedic); engineering; engineering related; engineering technology; English; environmental engineering technology; finance; fire science/firefighting; food science; forestry; French; funeral service and mortuary science; general studies; geology/earth science; German; health information/medical records administration; health/medical preparatory programs related; health professions related; health services/allied health/health sciences; heating, air conditioning, ventilation and refrigeration maintenance technology; heating, ventilation, air conditioning and refrigeration engineering technology; histologic technician; history; homeland security, law enforcement, firefighting and protective services related; horticultural science; hospitality administration; humanities; human services; industrial technology; information science/studies; information technology; interior design; international relations and affairs; Italian; journalism; kindergarten/preschool education; landscaping and groundskeeping; Latin American studies; legal administrative assistant/secretary; legal assistant/paralegal; logistics, materials, and supply chain management; management information systems; marketing/marketing management; mass communication/media; mathematics; mathematics teacher education;

medical/clinical assistant; middle school education; music; music performance; music teacher education; natural sciences; nonprofit management; nuclear medical technology; ophthalmic technology; ornamental horticulture; parks, recreation and leisure; philosophy; photographic and film/video technology; photography; physical education teaching and coaching; physical sciences; physical therapy technology; physics; physics teacher education; plant nursery management; political science and government; Portuguese; pre-engineering; psychology; public administration; radio and television; radio and television broadcasting technology; radiologic technology/science; recording arts technology; registered nursing/registered nurse; respiratory care therapy; respiratory therapy technician; science teacher education; sign language interpretation and translation; social sciences; social work; sociology; Spanish; special education; substance abuse/addiction counseling; teacher assistant/aide; telecommunications technology; tourism and travel services management.

Academics *Calendar:* 16-16-6-6. *Degrees:* certificates, associate, bachelor's, and postbachelor's certificates. *Special study options:* academic remediation for entering students, accelerated degree program, adult/continuing education programs, advanced placement credit, cooperative education, distance learning, English as a second language, freshman honors college, honors programs, independent study, internships, off-campus study, part-time degree program, services for LD students, study abroad, summer session for credit. *ROTC:* Army (b), Air Force (b).

Library Miami Dade College Learning Resources plus 9 others with 374,172 titles, 733 serial subscriptions, 32,190 audiovisual materials, an OPAC, a Web page.

Student Life *Housing:* college housing not available. *Activities and Organizations:* drama/theater group, student-run newspaper, radio and television station, choral group, Student Government Association, Phi Theta Kappa, Phi Beta Lambda (Business), Future Educators of America Professional, Kappa Delta Pi Honor Society (Education), national fraternities. *Campus security:* 24-hour emergency response devices and patrols, late-night transport/escort service, Emergency Mass Notification System (EMNS), campus sirens and public address systems, In Case of Crisis smart phone application. *Student services:* health clinic, personal/psychological counseling.

Athletics Member NCAA, NJCAA. All NCAA Division I. *Intercollegiate sports:* baseball M(s), basketball M(s)/W(s), softball W(s), volleyball W(s).

Costs (2013–14) *Tuition:* state resident $2483 full-time, $83 per credit hour part-time; nonresident $9933 full-time, $331 per credit hour part-time. Full-time tuition and fees vary according to course load, degree level, and program. Part-time tuition and fees vary according to course load, degree level, and program. *Required fees:* $943 full-time, $31 per credit hour part-time. *Waivers:* employees or children of employees.

Financial Aid Of all full-time matriculated undergraduates who enrolled in 2012, 800 Federal Work-Study jobs (averaging $5000). 125 state and other part-time jobs (averaging $5000).

Applying *Options:* electronic application, early admission. *Application fee:* $30. *Required:* high school transcript. *Required for some:* Some programs such as Honors College and Medical programs have additional admissions requirements. *Application deadlines:* rolling (freshmen), rolling (out-of-state freshmen), rolling (transfers). *Notification:* continuous (freshmen), continuous (out-of-state freshmen), continuous (transfers).

Freshman Application Contact Mrs. Dulce Beltran, College Registrar, Miami Dade College, 11011 SW 104th Street, Miami, FL 33176. *Phone:* 305-237-2206. *Fax:* 305-237-2532. *E-mail:* dbeltran@mdc.edu. *Website:* http://www.mdc.edu/.

North Florida Community College

Madison, Florida

Freshman Application Contact Mr. Bobby Scott, North Florida Community College, 325 Northwest Turner Davis Drive, Madison, FL 32340. *Phone:* 850-973-9450. *Toll-free phone:* 866-937-6322. *Fax:* 850-973-1697. *Website:* http://www.nfcc.edu/.

Northwest Florida State College

Niceville, Florida

- **State and locally supported** primarily 2-year, founded 1963, part of Florida College System
- **Small-town** 264-acre campus
- **Endowment** $28.6 million
- **Coed,** 6,938 undergraduate students, 40% full-time, 59% women, 41% men

Undergraduates 2,758 full-time, 4,180 part-time. Students come from 12 states and territories; 4% are from out of state; 9% Black or African American, non-Hispanic/Latino; 7% Hispanic/Latino; 3% Asian, non-Hispanic/Latino; 0.4% Native Hawaiian or other Pacific Islander, non-Hispanic/Latino; 0.5% American Indian or Alaska Native, non-Hispanic/Latino; 3% Two or more races, non-Hispanic/Latino; 3% Race/ethnicity unknown; 0.5% international; 7% transferred in.

Freshmen *Admission:* 955 enrolled.

Faculty *Total:* 266, 38% full-time. *Student/faculty ratio:* 26:1.

Majors Accounting related; accounting technology and bookkeeping; architectural engineering technology; business administration and management; business, management, and marketing related; child-care provision; commercial and advertising art; computer/information technology services administration related; computer programming (specific applications); computer systems analysis; computer technology/computer systems technology; criminal justice/law enforcement administration; criminal justice/police science; dental assisting; drafting and design technology; electrical, electronic and communications engineering technology; elementary education; emergency medical technology (EMT paramedic); entrepreneurship; executive assistant/executive secretary; health/health-care administration; health information/medical records technology; legal assistant/paralegal; liberal arts and sciences/liberal studies; management information systems; manufacturing engineering technology; marketing/marketing management; mathematics teacher education; medical radiologic technology; merchandising, sales, and marketing operations related (general); music related; occupational safety and health technology; office management; operations management; public administration; purchasing, procurement/acquisitions and contracts management; registered nursing/registered nurse; science teacher education; selling skills and sales; surgical technology; visual and performing arts related; welding technology.

Academics *Calendar:* semesters plus summer sessions. *Degrees:* certificates, associate, and bachelor's. *Special study options:* academic remediation for entering students, accelerated degree program, adult/continuing education programs, advanced placement credit, distance learning, English as a second language, independent study, internships, part-time degree program, services for LD students, study abroad, summer session for credit. *ROTC:* Army (b).

Library Northwest Florida State College Learning Resources Center with 106,383 titles, 399 serial subscriptions, 10,219 audiovisual materials, an OPAC, a Web page.

Student Life *Housing:* college housing not available. *Activities and Organizations:* drama/theater group, choral group, Student Nurses Association, Ambassadors, Pre-Professional Educators Association, Campus Christian Fellowship, Film Club. *Campus security:* 24-hour patrols. *Student services:* women's center.

Athletics Member NJCAA. *Intercollegiate sports:* baseball M(s), basketball M(s)/W(s), cheerleading M/W, softball W(s).

Standardized Tests *Required for some:* ACT, SAT I, ACT ASSET, MAPS, or PERT are used for placement not admission.

Costs (2014–15) *Tuition:* state resident $2313 full-time, $77 per credit part-time; nonresident $9252 full-time, $308 per credit part-time. Full-time tuition and fees vary according to course level, degree level, program, and reciprocity agreements. Part-time tuition and fees vary according to course level, degree level, program, and reciprocity agreements. *Required fees:* $691 full-time, $23 per credit part-time. *Payment plans:* tuition prepayment, deferred payment. *Waivers:* minority students, senior citizens, and employees or children of employees.

Applying *Options:* electronic application. *Required:* high school transcript. *Application deadlines:* rolling (freshmen), rolling (out-of-state freshmen), rolling (transfers). *Notification:* continuous (freshmen), continuous (out-of-state freshmen), continuous (transfers).

Freshman Application Contact Ms. Karen Cooper, Director of Admissions, Northwest Florida State College, 100 College Boulevard, Niceville, FL 32578. *Phone:* 850-729-4901. *Fax:* 850-729-5206. *E-mail:* cooperk@nwfsc.edu. *Website:* http://www.nwfsc.edu/.

Pasco-Hernando State College

New Port Richey, Florida

- **State-supported** 2-year, founded 1972, part of Florida College System
- **Suburban** 142-acre campus with easy access to Tampa
- **Coed,** 10,206 undergraduate students, 39% full-time, 61% women, 39% men

Undergraduates 4,004 full-time, 6,202 part-time. 4% Black or African American, non-Hispanic/Latino; 14% Hispanic/Latino; 2% Asian, non-Hispanic/Latino; 0.2% Native Hawaiian or other Pacific Islander, non-Hispanic/Latino; 0.4% American Indian or Alaska Native, non-Hispanic/Latino; 3% Two or more races, non-Hispanic/Latino; 2% Race/ethnicity unknown; 0.2% international.

Freshmen *Admission:* 1,811 enrolled.

Faculty *Total:* 377, 33% full-time, 18% with terminal degrees. *Student/faculty ratio:* 26:1.

Majors Business administration and management; computer programming related; computer programming (specific applications); computer systems networking and telecommunications; computer technology/computer systems technology; criminal justice/law enforcement administration; dental hygiene;

drafting and design technology; e-commerce; emergency medical technology (EMT paramedic); human services; information technology; legal assistant/paralegal; liberal arts and sciences/liberal studies; marketing/marketing management; radiologic technology/science; registered nursing/registered nurse; web page, digital/multimedia and information resources design.

Academics *Calendar:* semesters. *Degree:* certificates, diplomas, and associate. *Special study options:* academic remediation for entering students, accelerated degree program, adult/continuing education programs, advanced placement credit, cooperative education, distance learning, double majors, honors programs, independent study, internships, off-campus study, part-time degree program, services for LD students, summer session for credit. *ROTC:* Army (c).

Library Alric Pottberg Library plus 5 others with an OPAC, a Web page.

Student Life *Housing:* college housing not available. *Activities and Organizations:* drama/theater group, choral group, Student Government Association, Phi Theta Kappa, Phi Beta Lambda, Human Services, Legal Eagles. *Campus security:* late-night transport/escort service. *Student services:* personal/psychological counseling.

Athletics Member NJCAA. *Intercollegiate sports:* baseball M(s), basketball M(s), cross-country running W(s), softball W(s), volleyball W(s). *Intramural sports:* cheerleading M/W.

Standardized Tests *Recommended:* SAT and SAT Subject Tests or ACT (for admission), PERT.

Costs (2014–15) *Tuition:* state resident $103 per credit hour part-time; nonresident $393 per credit hour part-time. Full-time tuition and fees vary according to program. Part-time tuition and fees vary according to program. *Payment plan:* installment.

Financial Aid Of all full-time matriculated undergraduates who enrolled in 2012, 83 Federal Work-Study jobs (averaging $3201).

Applying *Options:* electronic application. *Application fee:* $25. *Required:* high school transcript. *Application deadlines:* rolling (freshmen), rolling (out-of-state freshmen), rolling (transfers). *Notification:* continuous (freshmen), continuous (out-of-state freshmen), continuous (transfers).

Freshman Application Contact Ms. Estela Carrion, Director of Admissions and Student Records, Pasco-Hernando State College, 10230 Ridge Road, New Port Richey, FL 34654-5199. *Phone:* 727-816-3261. *Toll-free phone:* 877-TRY-PHCC. *Fax:* 727-816-3389. *E-mail:* carrioe@phsc.edu. *Website:* http://www.phcc.edu/.

Pensacola State College
Pensacola, Florida

- **State-supported** primarily 2-year, founded 1948, part of Florida College System
- **Urban** 130-acre campus
- **Coed,** 11,235 undergraduate students, 40% full-time, 60% women, 40% men

Undergraduates 4,467 full-time, 6,768 part-time. Students come from 19 states and territories; 1% are from out of state; 14% Black or African American, non-Hispanic/Latino; 5% Hispanic/Latino; 3% Asian, non-Hispanic/Latino; 0.4% Native Hawaiian or other Pacific Islander, non-Hispanic/Latino; 0.9% American Indian or Alaska Native, non-Hispanic/Latino; 5% Two or more races, non-Hispanic/Latino; 1% Race/ethnicity unknown; 0.2% international; 6% transferred in.

Freshmen *Admission:* 1,784 enrolled.

Faculty *Total:* 638, 29% full-time, 5% with terminal degrees. *Student/faculty ratio:* 25:1.

Majors Accounting; administrative assistant and secretarial science; agricultural business and management; agriculture; art; art teacher education; biochemistry; biology/biological sciences; botany/plant biology; building/property maintenance; business administration and management; business administration, management and operations related; business/commerce; chemical technology; chemistry; child-care and support services management; child-care provision; commercial and advertising art; communications technology; computer and information sciences; computer and information sciences related; computer engineering; computer programming; computer programming (specific applications); computer science; computer systems analysis; construction engineering technology; consumer services and advocacy; cooking and related culinary arts; criminal justice/law enforcement administration; cyber/computer forensics and counterterrorism; dental hygiene; diagnostic medical sonography and ultrasound technology; dietetics; drafting and design technology; dramatic/theater arts; early childhood education; education; electrical, electronic and communications engineering technology; elementary education; emergency medical technology (EMT paramedic); engineering; engineering technology; English; executive assistant/executive secretary; fire prevention and safety technology; fire science/firefighting; food service systems administration; foods, nutrition, and wellness; geology/earth science; graphic design; hazardous materials management and waste technology; health/health-

care administration; health information/medical records administration; health information/medical records technology; history; hospitality administration; information science/studies; journalism; landscaping and groundskeeping; legal administrative assistant/secretary; legal assistant/paralegal; liberal arts and sciences/liberal studies; management information systems; management information systems and services related; management science; manufacturing engineering technology; mathematics; medical radiologic technology; music; music teacher education; natural resources management and policy; nursing science; office management; operations management; ornamental horticulture; pharmacy technician; philosophy; photography; physical therapy technology; physics; pre-dentistry studies; pre-law studies; premedical studies; prenursing studies; pre-pharmacy studies; pre-veterinary studies; psychology; registered nursing/registered nurse; religious studies; restaurant, culinary, and catering management; sociology; special education; veterinary/animal health technology; zoology/animal biology.

Academics *Calendar:* semesters. *Degrees:* certificates, diplomas, associate, and bachelor's. *Special study options:* academic remediation for entering students, adult/continuing education programs, advanced placement credit, cooperative education, distance learning, double majors, English as a second language, external degree program, honors programs, independent study, part-time degree program, services for LD students, summer session for credit. *ROTC:* Army (b).

Library Edward M. Chadbourne Library plus 4 others with 116,312 titles, 93 serial subscriptions, 7,702 audiovisual materials, an OPAC, a Web page.

Student Life *Housing:* college housing not available. *Activities and Organizations:* drama/theater group, student-run newspaper, choral group. *Campus security:* 24-hour emergency response devices and patrols, late-night transport/escort service. *Student services:* health clinic, personal/psychological counseling, women's center.

Athletics Member NJCAA. *Intercollegiate sports:* baseball M(s), basketball M(s)/W(s), softball W(s), volleyball W. *Intramural sports:* archery M/W, badminton M/W, basketball M/W, bowling M/W, cross-country running M/W, gymnastics M/W, racquetball M/W, sailing M/W, swimming and diving M/W, tennis M/W, track and field M/W, volleyball M/W, weight lifting M/W, wrestling M.

Financial Aid Of all full-time matriculated undergraduates who enrolled in 2012, 120 Federal Work-Study jobs (averaging $3000).

Applying *Options:* electronic application, early admission. *Application fee:* $30. *Required:* high school transcript. *Application deadlines:* 8/30 (freshmen), 8/30 (transfers). *Notification:* continuous until 8/30 (freshmen), continuous until 8/30 (transfers).

Freshman Application Contact Dean Kathy Dutremble, Enrollment Services, Pensacola State College, 1000 College Blvd, Pensacola, FL 32504. *Phone:* 850-484-2076. *Fax:* 850-484-1020. *E-mail:* kdutremble@pensacolastate.edu. *Website:* http://www.pensacolastate.edu/.

Remington College–Orlando Campus
Heathrow, Florida

Admissions Office Contact Remington College–Orlando Campus, 500 International Parkway, Heathrow, FL 32746. *Toll-free phone:* 800-560-6192. *Website:* http://www.remingtoncollege.edu/.

Remington College–Tampa Campus
Tampa, Florida

Freshman Application Contact Remington College–Tampa Campus, 6302 E. Dr. Martin Luther King, Jr. Boulevard, Suite 400, Tampa, FL 33619. *Phone:* 813-932-0701. *Toll-free phone:* 800-560-6192. *Website:* http://www.remingtoncollege.edu/.

St. Johns River State College
Palatka, Florida

Director of Admissions Dean of Admissions and Records, St. Johns River State College, 5001 Saint Johns Avenue, Palatka, FL 32177-3897. *Phone:* 386-312-4032. *Fax:* 386-312-4289. *Website:* http://www.sjrstate.edu/.

Sanford-Brown College
Tampa, Florida

Admissions Office Contact Sanford-Brown College, 3725 West Grace Street, Tampa, FL 33607. *Toll-free phone:* 888-315-6111. *Website:* http://www.sanfordbrown.edu/Tampa.

Sanford-Brown Institute
Fort Lauderdale, Florida

Director of Admissions Scott Nelowet, Sanford-Brown Institute, 1201 West Cypress Creek Road, Fort Lauderdale, FL 33309. *Phone:* 904-363-6221. *Toll-*

free phone: 888-742-0333. *Fax:* 904-363-6824. *E-mail:* snelowet@sbjacksonville.com.
Website: http://www.sanfordbrown.edu/Fort-Lauderdale.

Sanford-Brown Institute
Jacksonville, Florida

Freshman Application Contact Denise Neal, Assistant Director of Admissions, Sanford-Brown Institute, 10255 Fortune Parkway, Suite 501. *Phone:* 904-380-2912. *Toll-free phone:* 888-577-5333. *Fax:* 904-363-6824. *E-mail:* dneal@sbjacksonville.com.
Website: http://www.sanfordbrown.edu/Jacksonville.

Seminole State College of Florida
Sanford, Florida

- **State and locally supported** primarily 2-year, founded 1966
- **Small-town** 200-acre campus with easy access to Orlando
- **Endowment** $10.9 million
- **Coed,** 18,427 undergraduate students, 37% full-time, 57% women, 43% men

Undergraduates 6,885 full-time, 11,542 part-time. Students come from 88 other countries; 0.5% are from out of state; 17% Black or African American, non-Hispanic/Latino; 23% Hispanic/Latino; 3% Asian, non-Hispanic/Latino; 0.2% Native Hawaiian or other Pacific Islander, non-Hispanic/Latino; 0.3% American Indian or Alaska Native, non-Hispanic/Latino; 3% Two or more races, non-Hispanic/Latino; 1% Race/ethnicity unknown; 2% international; 6% transferred in.
Freshmen *Admission:* 12,664 applied, 12,664 admitted, 2,774 enrolled.
Faculty *Total:* 783, 30% full-time, 16% with terminal degrees. *Student/faculty ratio:* 27:1.
Majors Accounting; administrative assistant and secretarial science; architectural engineering technology; automobile/automotive mechanics technology; banking and financial support services; building/construction finishing, management, and inspection related; business administration and management; child development; civil engineering technology; computer and information sciences and support services related; computer and information sciences related; computer and information systems security; computer engineering related; computer engineering technology; computer graphics; computer hardware engineering; computer/information technology services administration related; computer programming; computer programming related; computer programming (specific applications); computer programming (vendor/product certification); computer software and media applications related; computer software engineering; computer systems networking and telecommunications; construction engineering technology; criminal justice/law enforcement administration; data entry/microcomputer applications; data entry/microcomputer applications related; data modeling/warehousing and database administration; data processing and data processing technology; drafting and design technology; electrical, electronic and communications engineering technology; emergency medical technology (EMT paramedic); finance; fire science/firefighting; industrial technology; information science/studies; information technology; interior design; legal assistant/paralegal; liberal arts and sciences/liberal studies; marketing/marketing management; network and system administration; physical therapy; registered nursing/registered nurse; respiratory care therapy; telecommunications technology; web/multimedia management and webmaster; web page, digital/multimedia and information resources design; word processing.
Academics *Calendar:* semesters. *Degrees:* certificates, diplomas, associate, and bachelor's. *Special study options:* academic remediation for entering students, accelerated degree program, adult/continuing education programs, advanced placement credit, cooperative education, distance learning, double majors, English as a second language, external degree program, honors programs, independent study, internships, part-time degree program, services for LD students, study abroad, summer session for credit. *ROTC:* Army (b).
Library Seminole State College Library - SLM plus 8 others with 110,348 titles, 320 serial subscriptions, 7,045 audiovisual materials, an OPAC, a Web page.
Student Life *Housing:* college housing not available. *Activities and Organizations:* drama/theater group, student-run newspaper, choral group, Phi Beta Lambda, Phi Theta Kappa, Student Government Association, Sigma Phi Gamma, Hispanic Student Association. *Campus security:* 24-hour emergency response devices and patrols. *Student services:* personal/psychological counseling.
Athletics Member NJCAA. *Intercollegiate sports:* baseball M(s), golf W(s), softball W(s).
Standardized Tests *Recommended:* SAT (for admission), ACT (for admission), SAT or ACT (for admission), SAT and SAT Subject Tests or ACT (for admission), SAT Subject Tests (for admission), CPT, PERT.
Costs (2014–15) *Tuition:* state resident $3131 full-time, $104 per credit hour part-time; nonresident $11,456 full-time, $382 per credit hour part-time. Full-

time tuition and fees vary according to degree level and program. Part-time tuition and fees vary according to degree level and program. *Payment plan:* deferred payment. *Waivers:* senior citizens and employees or children of employees.
Applying *Options:* electronic application, early admission, deferred entrance. *Required:* high school transcript, minimum 2.0 GPA. *Application deadlines:* rolling (freshmen), rolling (transfers). *Notification:* continuous (freshmen), continuous (transfers).
Freshman Application Contact Ms. Pamela Mennechey, Associate Vice President - Student Recruitment and Enrollment, Seminole State College of Florida, Sanford, FL 32773-6199. *Phone:* 407-708-2050. *Fax:* 407-708-2395. *E-mail:* admissions@scc-fl.edu.
Website: http://www.seminolestate.edu/.

Southeastern College–Greenacres
Greenacres, Florida

Freshman Application Contact Admissions Office, Southeastern College–Greenacres, 6812 Forest Hill Boulevard, Suite D-1, Greenacres, FL 33413.
Website: http://www.sec.edu/.

Southeastern College-Jacksonville
Jacksonville, Florida

Admissions Office Contact Southeastern College-Jacksonville, 6700 Southpoint Parkway, Suite 400, Jacksonville, FL 3216.
Website: http://www.sec.edu/.

Southeastern College–Miami Lakes
Miami Lakes, Florida

Freshman Application Contact Admissions Office, Southeastern College–Miami Lakes, 17395 NW 59th Avenue, Miami Lakes, FL 33015.
Website: http://www.sec.edu/.

Southeastern College–St. Petersburg
St. Petersburg, Florida

Admissions Office Contact Southeastern College–St. Petersburg, 11208 Blue Heron Boulevard, Suite A, St. Petersburg, FL 33716.
Website: http://www.sec.edu/.

Southern Technical College
Orlando, Florida

Admissions Office Contact Southern Technical College, 1485 Florida Mall Avenue, Orlando, FL 32809. *Toll-free phone:* 407-438-6005.
Website: http://www.southerntech.edu/.

South Florida State College
Avon Park, Florida

- **State-supported** primarily 2-year, founded 1965, part of Florida State College System
- **Rural** 228-acre campus with easy access to Tampa-St. Petersburg, Orlando
- **Endowment** $5.0 million
- **Coed,** 2,699 undergraduate students, 36% full-time, 62% women, 38% men

Undergraduates 970 full-time, 1,729 part-time. 3% are from out of state; 10% Black or African American, non-Hispanic/Latino; 29% Hispanic/Latino; 2% Asian, non-Hispanic/Latino; 0.4% Native Hawaiian or other Pacific Islander, non-Hispanic/Latino; 0.1% American Indian or Alaska Native, non-Hispanic/Latino; 1% Two or more races, non-Hispanic/Latino; 2% Race/ethnicity unknown; 1% international; 0.9% transferred in.
Freshmen *Admission:* 736 applied, 736 admitted, 568 enrolled. *Average high school GPA:* 3.03.
Faculty *Total:* 145, 45% full-time, 18% with terminal degrees. *Student/faculty ratio:* 16:1.
Majors Accounting; accounting technology and bookkeeping; actuarial science; advertising; aerospace, aeronautical and astronautical/space engineering; agribusiness; agricultural economics; agricultural engineering; agricultural teacher education; agriculture; American studies; animal sciences; anthropology; applied mathematics; architecture; art; art history, criticism and conservation; art teacher education; astronomy; atmospheric sciences and meteorology; audiology and speech-language pathology; banking and financial support services; biochemistry; biological and physical sciences; biology/biological sciences; biomedical technology; botany/plant biology; business administration and management; business administration, management and operations related; business/commerce; business/managerial economics; business teacher education; chemical engineering; chemistry;

chemistry related; city/urban, community and regional planning; civil engineering; civil engineering technology; clinical laboratory science/medical technology; computer and information sciences; computer engineering; computer engineering technology; computer programming; construction engineering technology; criminal justice/law enforcement administration; criminal justice/safety; dental hygiene; dietetics; dramatic/theater arts; early childhood education; economics; electrical and electronics engineering; electrical, electronic and communications engineering technology; elementary education; emergency medical technology (EMT paramedic); engineering; engineering science; engineering technology; English; English/language arts teacher education; entomology; environmental/environmental health engineering; environmental science; family and consumer sciences/home economics teacher education; finance; fine/studio arts; fire prevention and safety technology; food science; foreign languages and literatures; foreign language teacher education; forensic science and technology; forestry; French; general studies; geography; geology/earth science; gerontology; graphic design; health/health-care administration; health information/medical records administration; health services/allied health/health sciences; health teacher education; history; horticultural science; hospitality administration; humanities; human resources management; industrial engineering; information science/studies; insurance; international business/trade/commerce; international relations and affairs; jazz/jazz studies; journalism; kinesiology and exercise science; landscaping and groundskeeping; legal assistant/paralegal; liberal arts and sciences and humanities related; liberal arts and sciences/liberal studies; linguistics; management information systems; management science; marine biology and biological oceanography; marketing/marketing management; materials engineering; mathematics; mathematics teacher education; mechanical engineering; medical microbiology and bacteriology; medical radiologic technology; middle school education; multi/interdisciplinary studies related; music; music history, literature, and theory; music performance; music teacher education; music theory and composition; music therapy; nuclear engineering; nursing education; occupational therapy; ocean engineering; office management; parks, recreation and leisure facilities management; pharmacy; philosophy; philosophy and religious studies related; physics; physics related; plant sciences; political science and government; pre-pharmacy studies; psychology; public administration; public relations/image management; radio and television; real estate; registered nursing/registered nurse; religious studies; respiratory care therapy; rhetoric and composition; science teacher education; secondary education; social psychology; social sciences; social science teacher education; social work; sociology; soil science and agronomy; Spanish; special education; special education–individuals with emotional disturbances; special education–individuals with intellectual disabilities; special education–individuals with specific learning disabilities; special education–individuals with vision impairments; speech communication and rhetoric; statistics; surveying technology; systems engineering; trade and industrial teacher education; transportation/mobility management; vocational rehabilitation counseling; water, wetlands, and marine resources management; zoology/animal biology.

Academics *Calendar:* semesters. *Degrees:* certificates, diplomas, associate, and bachelor's. *Special study options:* academic remediation for entering students, adult/continuing education programs, advanced placement credit, cooperative education, distance learning, English as a second language, internships, part-time degree program, services for LD students, summer session for credit.

Library Learning Resource Center with 154,239 titles, 68 serial subscriptions, 883 audiovisual materials, an OPAC, a Web page.

Student Life *Housing Options:* Campus housing is provided by a third party. *Activities and Organizations:* drama/theater group, student-run newspaper, choral group, Phi Theta Kappa, Phi Beta Lambda, Performing Arts Club, Anime & Gaming Club, Basketball Club. *Campus security:* 24-hour emergency response devices and patrols, late-night transport/escort service. *Student services:* personal/psychological counseling.

Athletics Member NJCAA. *Intercollegiate sports:* baseball M(s), cheerleading M/W, softball W(s), volleyball W(s). *Intramural sports:* basketball M(c)/W(c), soccer M(c)/W(c).

Costs (2014–15) *One-time required fee:* $15. *Tuition:* state resident $2505 full-time, $105 per credit hour part-time; nonresident $9463 full-time, $394 per credit hour part-time. Full-time tuition and fees vary according to degree level. Part-time tuition and fees vary according to degree level. *Room and board:* $5821; room only: $1500. *Payment plan:* installment. *Waivers:* employees or children of employees.

Applying *Options:* electronic application, early admission, deferred entrance. *Application fee:* $15. *Required:* high school transcript. *Application deadline:* rolling (freshmen). *Notification:* continuous (freshmen).

Freshman Application Contact Ms. Lynn Hintz, Admissions Director, South Florida State College, 600 West College Drive, Avon Park, FL 33825. *Phone:* 863-453-6661.

Website: http://www.southflorida.edu/.

Southwest Florida College
Tampa, Florida

Director of Admissions Admissions, Southwest Florida College, 3910 Riga Boulevard, Tampa, FL 33619. *Phone:* 813-630-4401. *Toll-free phone:* 877-493-5147.

Website: http://www.swfc.edu/.

Stenotype Institute of Jacksonville
Jacksonville, Florida

Admissions Office Contact Stenotype Institute of Jacksonville, 3563 Phillips Highway, Building E, Suite 501, Jacksonville, FL 32207. *Toll-free phone:* 800-273-5090.

Website: http://www.stenotype.edu/.

Tallahassee Community College
Tallahassee, Florida

- **State and locally supported** 2-year, founded 1966, part of Florida College System
- **Suburban** 214-acre campus
- **Endowment** $8.9 million
- **Coed,** 13,661 undergraduate students, 46% full-time, 53% women, 47% men

Undergraduates 6,344 full-time, 7,317 part-time. Students come from 88 other countries; 2% are from out of state; 33% Black or African American, non-Hispanic/Latino; 10% Hispanic/Latino; 1% Asian, non-Hispanic/Latino; 0.1% Native Hawaiian or other Pacific Islander, non-Hispanic/Latino; 0.2% American Indian or Alaska Native, non-Hispanic/Latino; 3% Two or more races, non-Hispanic/Latino; 3% Race/ethnicity unknown; 1% international; 22% transferred in.

Freshmen *Admission:* 5,166 applied, 5,166 admitted, 2,379 enrolled.

Faculty *Total:* 613, 32% full-time, 22% with terminal degrees. *Student/faculty ratio:* 26:1.

Majors Accounting technology and bookkeeping; CAD/CADD drafting/design technology; commercial and advertising art; computer graphics; computer programming; computer programming (specific applications); computer systems networking and telecommunications; construction engineering technology; corrections; criminal justice/law enforcement administration; criminal justice/police science; dental assisting; dental hygiene; diagnostic medical sonography and ultrasound technology; drafting and design technology; early childhood education; emergency medical technology (EMT paramedic); entrepreneurship; environmental science; fire science/firefighting; health information/medical records technology; homeland security related; information technology; legal assistant/paralegal; liberal arts and sciences/liberal studies; manufacturing engineering technology; masonry; medical radiologic technology; nursing assistant/aide and patient care assistant/aide; office management; pharmacy technician; physical fitness technician; registered nursing/registered nurse; respiratory care therapy; security and loss prevention; surgical technology; web page, digital/multimedia and information resources design; welding technology.

Academics *Calendar:* semesters. *Degree:* certificates and associate. *Special study options:* academic remediation for entering students, accelerated degree program, adult/continuing education programs, advanced placement credit, distance learning, English as a second language, external degree program, honors programs, independent study, off-campus study, part-time degree program, services for LD students, study abroad, summer session for credit. *ROTC:* Army (c), Navy (c), Air Force (c).

Library Tallahassee Community College Library with 97,919 titles, 28,985 serial subscriptions, 7,965 audiovisual materials, an OPAC.

Student Life *Housing:* college housing not available. *Activities and Organizations:* drama/theater group, student-run newspaper, choral group, Student Government Association, International Student Organization, Phi Theta Kappa, Model United Nations, Honors Council. *Campus security:* 24-hour emergency response devices and patrols, late-night transport/escort service. *Student services:* personal/psychological counseling.

Athletics Member NJCAA. *Intercollegiate sports:* baseball M(s), basketball M(s)/W(s), softball W(s). *Intramural sports:* basketball M/W, football M/W, soccer M/W, softball M/W, volleyball M/W.

Costs (2013–14) *Tuition:* state resident $2570 full-time, $99 per credit hour part-time; nonresident $9776 full-time, $376 per credit hour part-time. Full-time tuition and fees vary according to course load. Part-time tuition and fees vary according to course load. *Payment plan:* installment. *Waivers:* employees or children of employees.

Financial Aid Of all full-time matriculated undergraduates who enrolled in 2012, 4,685 applied for aid, 3,586 were judged to have need. *Average financial aid package:* $13,716. *Average need-based gift aid:* $13,898.

Applying *Options:* electronic application, early admission, deferred entrance. *Required:* high school transcript. *Application deadlines:* 8/1 (freshmen), 8/1 (transfers).

Freshman Application Contact Student Success Center, Tallahassee Community College, 444 Appleyard Drive, Tallahassee, FL 32304-2895. *Phone:* 850-201-8555. *E-mail:* admissions@tcc.fl.edu. *Website:* http://www.tcc.fl.edu/.

Virginia College in Jacksonville
Jacksonville, Florida

Admissions Office Contact Virginia College in Jacksonville, 5940 Beach Boulevard, Jacksonville, FL 32207. *Website:* http://www.vc.edu/.

Virginia College in Pensacola
Pensacola, Florida

Admissions Office Contact Virginia College in Pensacola, 19 West Garden Street, Pensacola, FL 32502. *Website:* http://www.vc.edu/.

WyoTech Daytona
Ormond Beach, Florida

Admissions Office Contact WyoTech Daytona, 470 Destination Daytona Lane, Ormond Beach, FL 32174. *Toll-free phone:* 800-881-2AMI. *Website:* http://www.wyotech.edu/.

GEORGIA

Albany Technical College
Albany, Georgia

- **State-supported** 2-year, founded 1961, part of Technical College System of Georgia
- **Coed,** 3,894 undergraduate students, 54% full-time, 60% women, 40% men

Undergraduates 2,091 full-time, 1,803 part-time. 0.4% are from out of state; 125% Black or African American, non-Hispanic/Latino; 2% Hispanic/Latino; 0.4% Asian, non-Hispanic/Latino; 0.4% Native Hawaiian or other Pacific Islander, non-Hispanic/Latino; 1% Two or more races, non-Hispanic/Latino. *Retention:* 55% of full-time freshmen returned.

Freshmen *Admission:* 790 enrolled.

Majors Accounting; adult development and aging; child development; computer and information sciences; corrections and criminal justice related; culinary arts; drafting and design technology; electrical and electronic engineering technologies related; forest technology; hotel/motel administration; human development and family studies related; industrial technology; manufacturing engineering technology; marketing/marketing management; medical radiologic technology; pharmacy technician; tourism and travel services management.

Academics *Calendar:* quarters. *Degree:* certificates, diplomas, and associate. *Special study options:* distance learning.

Library Albany Technical College Library and Media Center.

Student Life *Housing:* college housing not available.

Applying *Options:* early admission. *Application fee:* $23. *Required:* high school transcript.

Freshman Application Contact Albany Technical College, 1704 South Slappey Boulevard, Albany, GA 31701. *Phone:* 229-430-3520. *Toll-free phone:* 877-261-3113. *Website:* http://www.albanytech.edu/.

Altamaha Technical College
Jesup, Georgia

- **State-supported** 2-year, part of Technical College System of Georgia
- **Coed,** 1,244 undergraduate students, 29% full-time, 54% women, 46% men

Undergraduates 356 full-time, 888 part-time. 27% Black or African American, non-Hispanic/Latino; 5% Hispanic/Latino; 2% Asian, non-Hispanic/Latino; 0.4% Native Hawaiian or other Pacific Islander, non-Hispanic/Latino; 0.7% American Indian or Alaska Native, non-Hispanic/Latino; 0.4% Two or more races, non-Hispanic/Latino; 1% Race/ethnicity unknown; 0.4% international. *Retention:* 61% of full-time freshmen returned.

Freshmen *Admission:* 270 enrolled.

Majors Administrative assistant and secretarial science; child development; computer programming; computer systems networking and telecommunications; criminal justice/safety; information science/studies; machine tool technology; manufacturing engineering technology; marketing/marketing management.

Academics *Calendar:* quarters. *Degree:* certificates, diplomas, and associate. *Special study options:* distance learning.

Student Life *Housing:* college housing not available.

Applying *Options:* early admission. *Application fee:* $24. *Required:* high school transcript.

Freshman Application Contact Altamaha Technical College, 1777 West Cherry Street, Jesup, GA 31545. *Phone:* 912-427-1958. *Toll-free phone:* 800-645-8284. *Website:* http://www.altamahatech.edu/.

Andrew College
Cuthbert, Georgia

Freshman Application Contact Ms. Bridget Kurkowski, Director of Admission, Andrew College, 413 College Street, Cuthbert, GA 39840. *Phone:* 229-732-5986. *Toll-free phone:* 800-664-9250. *Fax:* 229-732-2176. *E-mail:* admissions@andrewcollege.edu. *Website:* http://www.andrewcollege.edu/.

Anthem College–Atlanta
Atlanta, Georgia

Director of Admissions Frank Webster, Office Manager, Anthem College–Atlanta, 2450 Piedmont Road NE, Atlanta, GA 30324. *Phone:* 770-988-9877. *Toll-free phone:* 855-268-4360. *Fax:* 770-988-8824. *E-mail:* ckusema@hightechschools.com. *Website:* http://anthem.edu/atlanta-georgia/.

Athens Technical College
Athens, Georgia

- **State-supported** 2-year, founded 1958, part of Technical College System of Georgia
- **Suburban** campus
- **Coed,** 4,563 undergraduate students, 28% full-time, 65% women, 35% men

Undergraduates 1,281 full-time, 3,282 part-time. 0.3% are from out of state; 22% Black or African American, non-Hispanic/Latino; 5% Hispanic/Latino; 1% Asian, non-Hispanic/Latino; 0.2% Native Hawaiian or other Pacific Islander, non-Hispanic/Latino; 0.1% American Indian or Alaska Native, non-Hispanic/Latino; 1% Two or more races, non-Hispanic/Latino; 8% Race/ethnicity unknown; 0.6% international. *Retention:* 59% of full-time freshmen returned.

Freshmen *Admission:* 898 enrolled.

Majors Accounting; administrative assistant and secretarial science; biology/biotechnology laboratory technician; child development; clinical laboratory science/medical technology; communications technology; computer programming; computer systems networking and telecommunications; criminal justice/law enforcement administration; dental assisting; dental hygiene; diagnostic medical sonography and ultrasound technology; electrical, electronic and communications engineering technology; emergency medical technology (EMT paramedic); hotel/motel administration; information science/studies; legal assistant/paralegal; licensed practical/vocational nurse training; logistics, materials, and supply chain management; marketing/marketing management; medical radiologic technology; physical therapy; registered nursing/registered nurse; respiratory care therapy; surgical technology; tourism and travel services management; veterinary/animal health technology.

Academics *Calendar:* quarters. *Degree:* certificates, diplomas, and associate. *Special study options:* distance learning.

Student Life *Housing:* college housing not available.

Financial Aid Of all full-time matriculated undergraduates who enrolled in 2012, 34 Federal Work-Study jobs (averaging $3090).

Applying *Options:* early admission. *Application fee:* $20. *Required:* high school transcript.

Freshman Application Contact Athens Technical College, 800 US Highway 29 North, Athens, GA 30601-1500. *Phone:* 706-355-5008. *Website:* http://www.athenstech.edu/.

Atlanta Metropolitan State College
Atlanta, Georgia

Freshman Application Contact Ms. Audrey Reid, Director, Office of Admissions, Atlanta Metropolitan State College, 1630 Metropolitan Parkway,

SW, Atlanta, GA 30310-4498. *Phone:* 404-756-4004. *Fax:* 404-756-4407. *E-mail:* admissions@atlm.edu.
Website: http://www.atlm.edu/.

Atlanta Technical College
Atlanta, Georgia

- **State-supported** 2-year, founded 1945, part of Technical College System of Georgia
- **Coed,** 4,859 undergraduate students, 36% full-time, 60% women, 40% men

Undergraduates 1,763 full-time, 3,096 part-time. 0.6% are from out of state; 90% Black or African American, non-Hispanic/Latino; 2% Hispanic/Latino; 4% Asian, non-Hispanic/Latino; 0.1% Native Hawaiian or other Pacific Islander, non-Hispanic/Latino; 0.4% American Indian or Alaska Native, non-Hispanic/Latino; 1% Two or more races, non-Hispanic/Latino; 0.1% Race/ethnicity unknown. *Retention:* 54% of full-time freshmen returned.
Freshmen *Admission:* 975 enrolled.
Majors Accounting; child development; computer programming; culinary arts; dental hygiene; health information/medical records technology; hotel/motel administration; information technology; legal assistant/paralegal; marketing/marketing management; tourism and travel services management.
Academics *Calendar:* quarters. *Degree:* certificates, diplomas, and associate. *Special study options:* distance learning, study abroad.
Student Life *Housing:* college housing not available.
Applying *Options:* early admission. *Application fee:* $20. *Required:* high school transcript.
Freshman Application Contact Atlanta Technical College, 1560 Metropolitan Parkway, SW, Atlanta, GA 30310. *Phone:* 404-225-4455. *Website:* http://www.atlantatech.edu/.

Augusta Technical College
Augusta, Georgia

- **State-supported** 2-year, founded 1961, part of Technical College System of Georgia
- **Urban** campus
- **Coed,** 4,379 undergraduate students, 40% full-time, 57% women, 43% men

Undergraduates 1,762 full-time, 2,617 part-time. 5% are from out of state; 45% Black or African American, non-Hispanic/Latino; 3% Hispanic/Latino; 0.6% Asian, non-Hispanic/Latino; 0.1% Native Hawaiian or other Pacific Islander, non-Hispanic/Latino; 0.4% American Indian or Alaska Native, non-Hispanic/Latino; 3% Two or more races, non-Hispanic/Latino; 4% Race/ethnicity unknown; 0.1% international. *Retention:* 56% of full-time freshmen returned.
Freshmen *Admission:* 823 enrolled.
Majors Accounting; administrative assistant and secretarial science; biotechnology; business administration and management; cardiovascular technology; child development; computer programming; computer systems networking and telecommunications; criminal justice/safety; culinary arts; e-commerce; electrical, electronic and communications engineering technology; emergency medical technology (EMT paramedic); fire science/firefighting; information science/studies; marketing/marketing management; mechanical engineering/mechanical technology; medical radiologic technology; occupational therapist assistant; parks, recreation and leisure facilities management; pharmacy technician; respiratory care therapy; respiratory therapy technician; surgical technology.
Academics *Calendar:* quarters. *Degree:* certificates, diplomas, and associate. *Special study options:* distance learning.
Library Information Technology Center.
Student Life *Housing:* college housing not available.
Applying *Options:* early admission. *Application fee:* $20. *Required:* high school transcript.
Freshman Application Contact Augusta Technical College, 3200 Augusta Tech Drive, Augusta, GA 30906. *Phone:* 706-771-4150.
Website: http://www.augustatech.edu/.

Bainbridge State College
Bainbridge, Georgia

- **State-supported** 2-year, founded 1972, part of University System of Georgia
- **Small-town** 160-acre campus
- **Coed,** 2,705 undergraduate students, 43% full-time, 72% women, 28% men

Undergraduates 1,150 full-time, 1,555 part-time. Students come from 4 states and territories; 3% are from out of state; 55% Black or African American, non-Hispanic/Latino; 3% Hispanic/Latino; 0.4% Asian, non-Hispanic/Latino; 0.1%

American Indian or Alaska Native, non-Hispanic/Latino; 0.8% Two or more races, non-Hispanic/Latino; 2% Race/ethnicity unknown.
Freshmen *Admission:* 1,085 applied, 651 admitted.
Faculty *Total:* 176, 40% full-time, 17% with terminal degrees.
Majors Accounting; administrative assistant and secretarial science; agriculture; art; biology/biological sciences; business administration and management; business teacher education; chemistry; criminal justice/law enforcement administration; data processing and data processing technology; drafting and design technology; dramatic/theater arts; education; electrical, electronic and communications engineering technology; elementary education; English; family and consumer sciences/human sciences; forestry; health teacher education; history; information science/studies; journalism; kindergarten/preschool education; liberal arts and sciences/liberal studies; licensed practical/vocational nurse training; marketing/marketing management; mathematics; political science and government; psychology; registered nursing/registered nurse; rhetoric and composition; sociology; welding technology.
Academics *Calendar:* semesters. *Degree:* certificates and associate. *Special study options:* academic remediation for entering students, advanced placement credit, distance learning, double majors, honors programs, independent study, part-time degree program, services for LD students, study abroad, summer session for credit.
Library Bainbridge State College Library with 46,234 titles, 83 serial subscriptions, 4,144 audiovisual materials, an OPAC.
Student Life *Housing:* college housing not available. *Activities and Organizations:* drama/theater group, choral group, Canoe Club, BANS, LPN Club, Honors, Student Government Association. *Campus security:* 24-hour patrols. *Student services:* personal/psychological counseling.
Athletics *Intramural sports:* table tennis M/W, volleyball M/W.
Standardized Tests *Required for some:* SAT or ACT (for admission), ACT COMPASS.
Costs (2013–14) *Tuition:* state resident $2077 full-time, $87 per credit hour part-time; nonresident $7858 full-time, $327 per credit hour part-time. Full-time tuition and fees vary according to course load. Part-time tuition and fees vary according to course load. *Required fees:* $888 full-time, $444 per term part-time. *Waivers:* senior citizens and employees or children of employees.
Applying *Options:* electronic application, early admission. *Required for some:* high school transcript, minimum 1.8 GPA, 3 letters of recommendation, interview, immunizations/waivers, medical records and criminal background. *Application deadlines:* rolling (freshmen), rolling (transfers). *Notification:* continuous (freshmen), continuous (transfers).
Freshman Application Contact Ms. Melanie Cleveland, Director of Admission, Bainbridge State College, 2500 East Shotwell Street, Bainbridge, GA 39819. *Phone:* 229-248-2504. *Toll-free phone:* 866-825-1715 (in-state); 888-825-1715 (out-of-state). *Fax:* 229-248-2525. *E-mail:* melanie.cleveland@bainbridge.edu.
Website: http://www.bainbridge.edu/.

Brown Mackie College–Atlanta
Atlanta, Georgia

- **Proprietary** 2-year, part of Education Management Corporation
- **Urban** campus
- **Coed**

Majors Business/commerce; corrections and criminal justice related; early childhood education; legal assistant/paralegal; medical/clinical assistant; medical office management; occupational therapist assistant; pharmacy technician.
Academics *Degree:* certificates and associate.
Freshman Application Contact Brown Mackie College–Atlanta, 4370 Peachtree Road, NE, Atlanta, GA 30319. *Phone:* 404-799-4500.
Website: http://www.brownmackie.edu/atlanta/.

See display on next page and page 380 for the College Close-Up.

Central Georgia Technical College
Warner Robins, Georgia

- **State-supported** 2-year, founded 1966, part of Technical College System of Georgia
- **Suburban** campus
- **Coed,** 7,796 undergraduate students, 41% full-time, 61% women, 39% men

Undergraduates 3,191 full-time, 4,605 part-time. 2% are from out of state; 53% Black or African American, non-Hispanic/Latino; 2% Hispanic/Latino; 0.8% Asian, non-Hispanic/Latino; 0.3% American Indian or Alaska Native, non-Hispanic/Latino; 1% Two or more races, non-Hispanic/Latino; 1% Race/ethnicity unknown; 0.1% international.
Freshmen *Admission:* 1,855 enrolled.
Majors Accounting; administrative assistant and secretarial science; adult development and aging; banking and financial support services; business

administration and management; cabinetmaking and millwork; cardiovascular technology; carpentry; child-care and support services management; child development; clinical/medical laboratory technology; computer programming; computer systems networking and telecommunications; criminal justice/safety; dental hygiene; drafting and design technology; e-commerce; electrical, electronic and communications engineering technology; hotel/motel administration; industrial technology; information science/studies; legal assistant/paralegal; marketing/marketing management; medical radiologic technology; tourism and travel services management; veterinary/animal health technology; web page, digital/multimedia and information resources design.

Academics *Calendar:* quarters. *Degree:* certificates, diplomas, and associate. *Special study options:* distance learning.

Student Life *Housing:* college housing not available.

Financial Aid Of all full-time matriculated undergraduates who enrolled in 2012, 175 Federal Work-Study jobs (averaging $2000). *Financial aid deadline:* 9/1.

Applying *Options:* early admission. *Application fee:* $15. *Required:* high school transcript.

Freshman Application Contact Central Georgia Technical College, 80 Cohen Walker Drive, Warner Robins, GA 31088. *Phone:* 770-531-6332. *Toll-free phone:* 866-430-0135.

Website: http://www.centralgatech.edu/.

Chattahoochee Technical College
Marietta, Georgia

- **State-supported** 2-year, founded 1961, part of Technical College System of Georgia
- **Suburban** campus
- **Coed,** 10,470 undergraduate students, 33% full-time, 56% women, 44% men

Undergraduates 3,434 full-time, 7,036 part-time. 0.2% are from out of state; 29% Black or African American, non-Hispanic/Latino; 10% Hispanic/Latino; 1% Asian, non-Hispanic/Latino; 0.2% Native Hawaiian or other Pacific Islander, non-Hispanic/Latino; 0.8% American Indian or Alaska Native, non-Hispanic/Latino; 2% Two or more races, non-Hispanic/Latino; 0.6% Race/ethnicity unknown; 0.7% international. *Retention:* 50% of full-time freshmen returned.

Freshmen *Admission:* 2,176 enrolled.

Majors Accounting; administrative assistant and secretarial science; automobile/automotive mechanics technology; biomedical technology; business administration and management; child development; civil

engineering technology; computer and information systems security; computer programming; computer systems networking and telecommunications; criminal justice/safety; culinary arts; drafting and design technology; electrical, electronic and communications engineering technology; fire science/firefighting; horticultural science; information science/studies; logistics, materials, and supply chain management; marketing/marketing management; medical radiologic technology; parks, recreation and leisure facilities management; web page, digital/multimedia and information resources design.

Academics *Calendar:* quarters. *Degree:* certificates, diplomas, and associate. *Special study options:* distance learning.

Student Life *Housing:* college housing not available.

Financial Aid Of all full-time matriculated undergraduates who enrolled in 2012, 40 Federal Work-Study jobs (averaging $2500).

Applying *Options:* early admission. *Application fee:* $15. *Required:* high school transcript.

Freshman Application Contact Chattahoochee Technical College, 980 South Cobb Drive, SE, Marietta, GA 30060. *Phone:* 770-757-3408.

Website: http://www.chattahoocheetech.edu/.

Columbus Technical College
Columbus, Georgia

- **State-supported** 2-year, founded 1961, part of Technical College System of Georgia
- **Urban** campus
- **Coed,** 3,739 undergraduate students, 38% full-time, 64% women, 36% men

Undergraduates 1,426 full-time, 2,313 part-time. 15% are from out of state; 53% Black or African American, non-Hispanic/Latino; 4% Hispanic/Latino; 0.6% Asian, non-Hispanic/Latino; 0.4% Native Hawaiian or other Pacific Islander, non-Hispanic/Latino; 0.9% American Indian or Alaska Native, non-Hispanic/Latino; 2% Two or more races, non-Hispanic/Latino; 1% Race/ethnicity unknown; 0.1% international. *Retention:* 46% of full-time freshmen returned.

Freshmen *Admission:* 676 enrolled.

Majors Accounting; administrative assistant and secretarial science; automobile/automotive mechanics technology; child development; computer engineering related; computer systems networking and telecommunications; dental hygiene; diagnostic medical sonography and ultrasound technology; drafting and design technology; electrical, electronic and communications engineering technology; emergency medical technology (EMT paramedic);

health information/medical records technology; horticultural science; industrial technology; information science/studies; machine tool technology; mechanical engineering/mechanical technology; medical office management; medical radiologic technology; pharmacy technician; registered nursing/registered nurse; respiratory therapy technician; surgical technology; web page, digital/multimedia and information resources design.

Academics *Calendar:* quarters. *Degree:* certificates, diplomas, and associate. *Special study options:* distance learning.

Library Columbus Technical College Library.

Student Life *Housing:* college housing not available.

Financial Aid Of all full-time matriculated undergraduates who enrolled in 2012, 6 Federal Work-Study jobs (averaging $2000).

Applying *Options:* early admission. *Application fee:* $25. *Required:* high school transcript.

Freshman Application Contact Columbus Technical College, 928 Manchester Expressway, Columbus, GA 31904-6572. *Phone:* 706-649-1901. *Website:* http://www.columbustech.edu/.

Darton State College
Albany, Georgia

- **State-supported** primarily 2-year, founded 1965, part of University System of Georgia
- **Urban** 185-acre campus
- **Endowment** $978,169
- **Coed,** 6,396 undergraduate students, 49% full-time, 70% women, 30% men

Undergraduates 3,137 full-time, 3,259 part-time. Students come from 46 other countries; 7% are from out of state; 45% Black or African American, non-Hispanic/Latino; 2% Hispanic/Latino; 0.9% Asian, non-Hispanic/Latino; 0.2% Native Hawaiian or other Pacific Islander, non-Hispanic/Latino; 0.4% American Indian or Alaska Native, non-Hispanic/Latino; 0.3% Two or more races, non-Hispanic/Latino; 0.6% Race/ethnicity unknown; 1% international; 15% transferred in. *Retention:* 53% of full-time freshmen returned.

Freshmen *Admission:* 1,251 enrolled. *Average high school GPA:* 2.73. *Test scores:* SAT critical reading scores over 500: 25%; SAT math scores over 500: 23%; SAT writing scores over 500: 17%; ACT scores over 18: 42%; SAT critical reading scores over 600: 6%; SAT math scores over 600: 4%; SAT writing scores over 600: 3%; ACT scores over 24: 5%; SAT critical reading scores over 700: 1%.

Faculty *Total:* 282, 43% full-time. *Student/faculty ratio:* 21:1.

Majors Accounting; agriculture; anthropology; art; art teacher education; behavioral aspects of health; biological and biomedical sciences related; biology/biological sciences; business administration and management; business teacher education; cardiovascular technology; chemistry; clinical laboratory science/medical technology; computer and information sciences; computer and information sciences and support services related; computer science; criminal justice/law enforcement administration; dance; dental hygiene; diagnostic medical sonography and ultrasound technology; drama and dance teacher education; dramatic/theater arts; economics; emergency medical technology (EMT paramedic); engineering technology; English; English/language arts teacher education; environmental studies; foreign languages and literatures; forensic science and technology; forestry; general studies; geography; health and physical education/fitness; health information/medical records administration; health information/medical records technology; health/medical preparatory programs related; histologic technician; history; history teacher education; journalism; mathematics; mathematics teacher education; middle school education; music; music teacher education; nuclear medical technology; occupational therapist assistant; philosophy; physical therapy technology; physics; political science and government; pre-dentistry studies; pre-engineering; pre-law studies; premedical studies; pre-pharmacy studies; pre-veterinary studies; psychology; registered nursing/registered nurse; respiratory care therapy; science teacher education; social work; sociology; special education; speech teacher education; trade and industrial teacher education.

Academics *Calendar:* semesters. *Degrees:* certificates, associate, bachelor's, and postbachelor's certificates. *Special study options:* academic remediation for entering students, accelerated degree program, adult/continuing education programs, advanced placement credit, cooperative education, distance learning, double majors, English as a second language, honors programs, independent study, off-campus study, part-time degree program, services for LD students, summer session for credit. *ROTC:* Army (c).

Library Weatherbee Learning Resources Center with 101,612 titles, 125 serial subscriptions, 5,182 audiovisual materials, an OPAC, a Web page.

Student Life *Housing Options:* coed. Campus housing is provided by a third party. *Activities and Organizations:* drama/theater group, choral group, Cultural Exchange Club, Democratic, Independent, & Republican Team (D.I.R.T.), Human Services Club, Outdoor Adventure Club (OAC), Music Club. *Campus security:* 24-hour emergency response devices and patrols,

student patrols, late-night transport/escort service, controlled dormitory access. *Student services:* health clinic, personal/psychological counseling.

Athletics Member NJCAA. *Intercollegiate sports:* baseball M(s), basketball W(s), cross-country running M(s)/W(s), golf M(s), soccer M(s)/W(s), softball W(s), swimming and diving M(s)/W(s), wrestling M. *Intramural sports:* badminton M/W, basketball M/W, bowling M/W, football M, racquetball M/W, table tennis M, volleyball M/W.

Standardized Tests *Required:* non-traditional students must take the COMPASS test (for admission). *Required for some:* SAT or ACT (for admission), SAT Subject Tests (for admission). *Recommended:* SAT or ACT (for admission), SAT Subject Tests (for admission).

Costs (2014–15) *Tuition:* state resident $2660 full-time, $89 per credit hour part-time; nonresident $9822 full-time, $335 per credit hour part-time. *Required fees:* $992 full-time, $587 per term part-time. *Room and board:* $9340. Room and board charges vary according to board plan and housing facility. *Waivers:* senior citizens and employees or children of employees.

Financial Aid Of all full-time matriculated undergraduates who enrolled in 2012, 60 Federal Work-Study jobs.

Applying *Options:* electronic application, deferred entrance. *Application fee:* $20. *Required:* minimum 2.0 GPA, proof of immunization. *Required for some:* high school transcript. *Application deadlines:* 7/20 (freshmen), 7/20 (transfers). *Notification:* continuous until 7/27 (freshmen), continuous until 7/27 (transfers).

Freshman Application Contact Darton State College, 2400 Gillionville Road, Albany, GA 31707-3098. *Phone:* 229-430-6740. *Toll-free phone:* 866-775-1214. *Website:* http://www.darton.edu/.

East Georgia State College
Swainsboro, Georgia

Freshman Application Contact East Georgia State College, 131 College Circle, Swainsboro, GA 30401-2699. *Phone:* 478-289-2017. *Website:* http://www.ega.edu/.

Emory University, Oxford College
Oxford, Georgia

Freshman Application Contact Emory University, Oxford College, 100 Hamill Street, PO Box 1328, Oxford, GA 30054. *Phone:* 770-784-8328. *Toll-free phone:* 800-723-8328. *Website:* http://oxford.emory.edu/.

Georgia Highlands College
Rome, Georgia

- **State-supported** primarily 2-year, founded 1970, part of University System of Georgia
- **Suburban** 226-acre campus with easy access to Atlanta
- **Endowment** $33,299
- **Coed,** 5,487 undergraduate students, 52% full-time, 62% women, 38% men

Undergraduates 2,840 full-time, 2,647 part-time. Students come from 4 states and territories; 50 other countries; 1% are from out of state; 17% Black or African American, non-Hispanic/Latino; 9% Hispanic/Latino; 2% Asian, non-Hispanic/Latino; 0.1% Native Hawaiian or other Pacific Islander, non-Hispanic/Latino; 0.3% American Indian or Alaska Native, non-Hispanic/Latino; 2% Two or more races, non-Hispanic/Latino; 0.7% Race/ethnicity unknown; 9% transferred in. *Retention:* 46% of full-time freshmen returned.

Freshmen *Admission:* 2,280 applied, 1,346 admitted, 1,196 enrolled. *Average high school GPA:* 2.9.

Faculty *Total:* 248, 50% full-time, 20% with terminal degrees. *Student/faculty ratio:* 22:1.

Majors Agriculture; art; biological and physical sciences; business administration and management; chemistry; clinical laboratory science/medical technology; communication and journalism related; computer and information sciences; criminal justice/police science; criminal justice/safety; dental hygiene; economics; education related; English; foreign languages and literatures; general studies; geology/earth science; health information/medical records administration; history; human services; journalism; liberal arts and sciences/liberal studies; marketing/marketing management; mathematics and statistics related; philosophy; physician assistant; physics; political science and government; pre-occupational therapy; pre-pharmacy studies; pre-physical therapy; psychology; registered nursing/registered nurse; respiratory therapy technician; secondary education; sociology.

Academics *Calendar:* semesters. *Degrees:* associate and bachelor's. *Special study options:* academic remediation for entering students, advanced placement credit, cooperative education, distance learning, double majors, honors programs, independent study, part-time degree program, services for LD students, study abroad, summer session for credit.

Library Georgia Highlands College Library - Floyd Campus plus 1 other with 64,239 titles, 82 serial subscriptions, 14,672 audiovisual materials, an OPAC, a Web page.

Student Life *Housing:* college housing not available. *Activities and Organizations:* drama/theater group, student-run newspaper, Highlands Association of Nursing Students, Green Highlands, Black Awareness Society, Political Science Association, Phi Theta Kappa. *Campus security:* 24-hour emergency response devices and patrols, emergency phone/email alert system. *Student services:* personal/psychological counseling.

Athletics Member NJCAA. *Intercollegiate sports:* baseball M(s)/W(s), basketball M(s)/W(s), softball M(s)/W(s). *Intramural sports:* basketball M/W, cheerleading M/W, football M/W, golf M/W, skiing (downhill) M/W, table tennis M/W, tennis M/W, ultimate Frisbee M/W, volleyball M/W, weight lifting M/W.

Standardized Tests *Required:* COMPASS Testing (for admission).

Costs (2014–15) *Tuition:* state resident $2596 full-time, $87 per hour part-time; nonresident $9822 full-time, $327 per hour part-time. Full-time tuition and fees vary according to course load. Part-time tuition and fees vary according to course load. *Required fees:* $934 full-time, $467 per term part-time. *Waivers:* senior citizens and employees or children of employees.

Financial Aid Of all full-time matriculated undergraduates who enrolled in 2012, 50 Federal Work-Study jobs (averaging $3500).

Applying *Options:* electronic application, deferred entrance. *Application fee:* $20. *Required:* high school transcript, minimum 2.0 GPA. *Required for some:* Additional requirements for Nursing. *Application deadlines:* rolling (freshmen), rolling (out-of-state freshmen), rolling (transfers). *Notification:* continuous (freshmen), continuous (out-of-state freshmen), continuous (transfers).

Freshman Application Contact Sandra Davis, Director of Admissions, Georgia Highlands College, 3175 Cedartown Highway, Rome, GA 30161. *Phone:* 706-295-6339. *Toll-free phone:* 800-332-2406. *Fax:* 706-295-6341. *E-mail:* sdavis@highlands.edu.
Website: http://www.highlands.edu/.

Georgia Military College

Milledgeville, Georgia

- **State and locally supported** 2-year, founded 1879, part of Georgia Independent College Association (GICA)
- **Small-town** campus
- **Endowment** $12.8 million
- **Coed,** 7,069 undergraduate students, 54% full-time, 54% women, 46% men

Undergraduates 3,788 full-time, 3,281 part-time. Students come from 18 states and territories; 11 other countries; 1% are from out of state; 40% Black or African American, non-Hispanic/Latino; 0.4% Hispanic/Latino; 2% Asian, non-Hispanic/Latino; 1% American Indian or Alaska Native, non-Hispanic/Latino; 16% Race/ethnicity unknown; 0.2% international; 12% transferred in; 4% live on campus. *Retention:* 46% of full-time freshmen returned.

Freshmen *Admission:* 3,228 enrolled.

Faculty *Total:* 472. *Student/faculty ratio:* 15:1.

Majors Army ROTC/military science; biology/biological sciences; business administration and management; criminal justice/law enforcement administration; early childhood education; education; general studies; health services/allied health/health sciences; health teacher education; history; homeland security, law enforcement, firefighting and protective services related; human development and family studies; information technology; international relations and affairs; legal assistant/paralegal; logistics, materials, and supply chain management; mass communication/media; prenursing studies; psychology; public health education and promotion; secondary education; social sciences.

Academics *Calendar:* quarters. *Degree:* associate. *Special study options:* academic remediation for entering students, advanced placement credit, cooperative education, distance learning, double majors, independent study, off-campus study, part-time degree program, services for LD students, student-designed majors, study abroad, summer session for credit. *ROTC:* Army (b).

Library Sibley Cone Library plus 1 other with 76,000 titles, 25,000 serial subscriptions, 7,500 audiovisual materials, an OPAC, a Web page.

Student Life *Housing:* on-campus residence required through sophomore year. *Options:* coed. Campus housing is university owned. *Activities and Organizations:* drama/theater group, student-run newspaper, choral group, Student Government Association, Alpha Phi Omega National Service Fraternity, Phi Theta Kappa, Drama Club, Biology Club. *Campus security:* 24-hour emergency response devices and patrols, controlled dormitory access. *Student services:* health clinic.

Athletics Member NJCAA. *Intercollegiate sports:* cheerleading M/W, cross-country running M/W, football M(s), golf M, riflery M(s)/W(s), soccer M(s)/W(s), softball W(s). *Intramural sports:* soccer M/W, softball M/W.

Costs (2014–15) *Tuition:* state resident $4980 full-time, $121 per credit hour part-time; nonresident $4980 full-time, $121 per credit hour part-time. Full-time tuition and fees vary according to course load and location. Part-time tuition and fees vary according to course load and location. *Required fees:* $469 full-time, $22 per credit hour part-time, $25 per term part-time. *Room and board:* $7050. Room and board charges vary according to location. *Waivers:* senior citizens and employees or children of employees.

Financial Aid Of all full-time matriculated undergraduates who enrolled in 2012, 6,554 applied for aid, 6,132 were judged to have need, 282 had their need fully met. 121 Federal Work-Study jobs (averaging $1614). In 2012, 61 non-need-based awards were made. *Average percent of need met:* 47%. *Average financial aid package:* $9567. *Average need-based loan:* $3189. *Average need-based gift aid:* $4626. *Average non-need-based aid:* $2226.

Applying *Options:* electronic application, early admission, deferred entrance. *Application fee:* $35. *Required for some:* essay or personal statement, high school transcript, interview. *Application deadlines:* rolling (freshmen), rolling (out-of-state freshmen), rolling (transfers).

Freshman Application Contact Georgia Military College, 201 East Greene Street, Old Capitol Building, Milledgeville, GA 31061-3398. *Phone:* 478-387-4948. *Toll-free phone:* 800-342-0413.
Website: http://www.gmc.cc.ga.us/.

Georgia Northwestern Technical College

Rome, Georgia

- **State-supported** 2-year, founded 1962, part of Technical College System of Georgia
- **Coed,** 6,051 undergraduate students, 35% full-time, 66% women, 34% men

Undergraduates 2,135 full-time, 3,916 part-time. 0.5% are from out of state; 10% Black or African American, non-Hispanic/Latino; 8% Hispanic/Latino; 0.6% Asian, non-Hispanic/Latino; 0.0% Native Hawaiian or other Pacific Islander, non-Hispanic/Latino; 0.3% American Indian or Alaska Native, non-Hispanic/Latino; 2% Two or more races, non-Hispanic/Latino; 0.1% international. *Retention:* 51% of full-time freshmen returned.

Freshmen *Admission:* 1,154 enrolled.

Majors Accounting; child development; computer programming; criminal justice/safety; environmental engineering technology; fire science/firefighting; information science/studies; legal assistant/paralegal; marketing/marketing management; medical office management; respiratory therapy technician; surgical technology; web page, digital/multimedia and information resources design.

Academics *Calendar:* quarters. *Degree:* certificates, diplomas, and associate. *Special study options:* distance learning.

Student Life *Housing:* college housing not available.

Applying *Options:* early admission. *Application fee:* $15. *Required:* high school transcript.

Freshman Application Contact Georgia Northwestern Technical College, One Maurice Culberson Drive, Rome, GA 30161. *Phone:* 706-295-6933. *Toll-free phone:* 866-983-GNTC.
Website: http://www.gntc.edu/.

Georgia Perimeter College

Decatur, Georgia

Freshman Application Contact Georgia Perimeter College, 3251 Panthersville Road, Decatur, GA 30034-3897. *Phone:* 678-891-3250. *Toll-free phone:* 888-696-2780.
Website: http://www.gpc.edu/.

Georgia Piedmont Technical College

Clarkston, Georgia

- **State-supported** 2-year, founded 1961, part of Technical College System of Georgia
- **Suburban** campus
- **Coed,** 4,431 undergraduate students, 33% full-time, 59% women, 41% men

Undergraduates 1,470 full-time, 2,961 part-time. 79% Black or African American, non-Hispanic/Latino; 2% Hispanic/Latino; 2% Asian, non-Hispanic/Latino; 0.2% Native Hawaiian or other Pacific Islander, non-Hispanic/Latino; 0.3% American Indian or Alaska Native, non-Hispanic/Latino; 2% Two or more races, non-Hispanic/Latino; 0.5% Race/ethnicity unknown; 2% international. *Retention:* 55% of full-time freshmen returned.

Freshmen *Admission:* 696 enrolled.

Majors Accounting; administrative assistant and secretarial science; automobile/automotive mechanics technology; business/commerce;

clinical/medical laboratory technology; computer engineering technology; computer programming; computer systems networking and telecommunications; criminal justice/safety; drafting and design technology; electrical, electronic and communications engineering technology; electromechanical technology; engineering technology; heating, ventilation, air conditioning and refrigeration engineering technology; industrial technology; information science/studies; instrumentation technology; legal administrative assistant/secretary; legal assistant/paralegal; machine tool technology; marketing/marketing management; medical/clinical assistant; operations management; ophthalmic laboratory technology; opticianry; surgical technology; telecommunications technology.

Academics *Calendar:* quarters. *Degree:* certificates, diplomas, and associate. *Special study options:* distance learning.

Student Life *Housing:* college housing not available.

Financial Aid Of all full-time matriculated undergraduates who enrolled in 2010, 7,200 applied for aid, 7,100 were judged to have need. 145 Federal Work-Study jobs (averaging $4000). *Average financial aid package:* $4500. *Average need-based gift aid:* $4500.

Applying *Options:* early admission. *Application fee:* $25. *Required:* high school transcript.

Freshman Application Contact Georgia Piedmont Technical College, 495 North Indian Creek Drive, Clarkston, GA 30021-2397. *Phone:* 404-297-9522 Ext. 1229.

Website: http://www.gptc.edu/.

Gordon State College
Barnesville, Georgia

- **State-supported** primarily 2-year, founded 1852, part of University System of Georgia
- **Small-town** 125-acre campus with easy access to Atlanta
- **Endowment** $7.8 million
- **Coed,** 4,189 undergraduate students

Undergraduates Students come from 9 states and territories; 1 other country; 0.1% are from out of state.

Freshmen *Admission:* 2,981 applied, 1,350 admitted.

Faculty *Total:* 206, 55% full-time. *Student/faculty ratio:* 23:1.

Majors Art; astronomy; biological and biomedical sciences related; biology teacher education; business administration and management; chemistry; communication; computer science; criminal justice/safety; dental services and allied professions related; dramatic/theater arts; early childhood education; elementary education; English; English as a second/foreign language (teaching); English/language arts teacher education; environmental science; foreign languages and literatures; forestry; general studies; health and physical education/fitness; health/medical preparatory programs related; history; history teacher education; information technology; liberal arts and sciences/liberal studies; mathematics; mathematics teacher education; middle school education; music; physics; political science and government; pre-engineering; pre-occupational therapy; pre-pharmacy studies; pre-physical therapy; psychology; radiologic technology/science; registered nursing/registered nurse; secondary education; social work; sociology.

Academics *Calendar:* semesters. *Degrees:* certificates, associate, and bachelor's. *Special study options:* academic remediation for entering students, accelerated degree program, adult/continuing education programs, advanced placement credit, cooperative education, honors programs, internships, off-campus study, part-time degree program, study abroad, summer session for credit.

Library Hightower Library with 150,062 titles, 55,588 serial subscriptions, 4,785 audiovisual materials, an OPAC, a Web page.

Student Life *Housing:* on-campus residence required for freshman year. *Options:* coed. Campus housing is university owned. Freshman applicants given priority for college housing. *Activities and Organizations:* drama/theater group, student-run newspaper, choral group, Campus Activity Board, Student Government Association, Earth wind fire (Science Club), Student African American Brotherhood (SAAB), Swazi Step Team. *Campus security:* 24-hour emergency response devices and patrols, student patrols, late-night transport/escort service, controlled dormitory access, RA's and RDs (housing) and Parking Patrol (Public Safety). *Student services:* health clinic, personal/psychological counseling.

Athletics Member NJCAA. *Intercollegiate sports:* baseball M, basketball M, soccer M/W, softball W, track and field M/W.

Standardized Tests *Required for some:* SAT and SAT Subject Tests or ACT (for admission).

Costs (2014–15) *Tuition:* state resident $3073 full-time; nonresident $9207 full-time. *Required fees:* $1074 full-time. *Room and board:* $9772; room only: $4410.

Financial Aid Of all full-time matriculated undergraduates who enrolled in 2012, 75 Federal Work-Study jobs (averaging $1850).

Applying *Options:* electronic application, early admission, deferred entrance. *Application fee:* $30. *Required:* high school transcript. *Application deadlines:* rolling (freshmen), rolling (transfers).

Freshman Application Contact Gordon State College, 419 College Drive, Barnesville, GA 30204-1762. *Phone:* 678-359-5021. *Toll-free phone:* 800-282-6504.

Website: http://www.gordonstate.edu/.

Gupton-Jones College of Funeral Service
Decatur, Georgia

Freshman Application Contact Ms. Beverly Wheaton, Registrar, Gupton-Jones College of Funeral Service, 5141 Snapfinger Woods Drive, Decatur, GA 30035-4022. *Phone:* 770-593-2257. *Toll-free phone:* 800-848-5352.

Website: http://www.gupton-jones.edu/.

Gwinnett Technical College
Lawrenceville, Georgia

- **State-supported** 2-year, founded 1984, part of Technical College System of Georgia
- **Suburban** campus
- **Coed,** 7,180 undergraduate students, 32% full-time, 61% women, 39% men

Undergraduates 2,282 full-time, 4,898 part-time. 0.6% are from out of state; 34% Black or African American, non-Hispanic/Latino; 12% Hispanic/Latino; 7% Asian, non-Hispanic/Latino; 0.1% Native Hawaiian or other Pacific Islander, non-Hispanic/Latino; 0.1% American Indian or Alaska Native, non-Hispanic/Latino; 2% Two or more races, non-Hispanic/Latino; 6% Race/ethnicity unknown; 0.3% international. *Retention:* 55% of full-time freshmen returned.

Freshmen *Admission:* 1,021 enrolled.

Majors Accounting; administrative assistant and secretarial science; automobile/automotive mechanics technology; building/construction finishing, management, and inspection related; business administration and management; computer programming; computer science; computer systems networking and telecommunications; drafting and design technology; electrical, electronic and communications engineering technology; emergency medical technology (EMT paramedic); horticultural science; hotel/motel administration; information science/studies; interior design; machine tool technology; management information systems; marketing/marketing management; medical/clinical assistant; medical radiologic technology; ornamental horticulture; photography; physical therapy; physical therapy technology; respiratory care therapy; tourism and travel services management; veterinary/animal health technology.

Academics *Calendar:* quarters. *Degree:* certificates, diplomas, and associate. *Special study options:* distance learning.

Library Gwinnett Technical Institute Media Center.

Student Life *Housing:* college housing not available.

Financial Aid Of all full-time matriculated undergraduates who enrolled in 2012, 20 Federal Work-Study jobs (averaging $2100).

Applying *Options:* early admission. *Application fee:* $20. *Required:* high school transcript.

Freshman Application Contact Gwinnett Technical College, 5150 Sugarloaf Parkway, Lawrenceville, GA 30043-5702. *Phone:* 678-762-7580 Ext. 434.

Website: http://www.gwinnetttech.edu/.

Interactive College of Technology
Chamblee, Georgia

Freshman Application Contact Director of Admissions, Interactive College of Technology, 5303 New Peachtree Road, Chamblee, GA 30341. *Phone:* 770-216-2960. *Toll-free phone:* 800-447-2011. *Fax:* 770-216-2988.

Website: http://ict.edu/.

ITT Technical Institute
Atlanta, Georgia

- **Proprietary** primarily 2-year, part of ITT Educational Services, Inc.
- **Coed**

Majors Business administration and management; construction management; cyber/computer forensics and counterterrorism; drafting and design technology; electrical, electronic and communications engineering technology; forensic science and technology; graphic communications; information technology project management; legal assistant/paralegal; network and system administration; project management.

Academics *Degrees:* associate and bachelor's.

Student Life *Housing:* college housing not available.

Freshman Application Contact Director of Recruitment, ITT Technical Institute, 485 Oak Place, Suite 800, Atlanta, GA 30349. *Phone:* 404-765-4600. *Toll-free phone:* 877-488-6102 (in-state); 877-788-6102 (out-of-state). *Website:* http://www.itt-tech.edu/.

ITT Technical Institute

Duluth, Georgia

- **Proprietary** primarily 2-year, founded 2003, part of ITT Educational Services, Inc.
- **Coed**

Majors Business administration and management; computer software technology; construction management; cyber/computer forensics and counterterrorism; design and visual communications; drafting and design technology; electrical, electronic and communications engineering technology; forensic science and technology; graphic communications; information technology project management; legal assistant/paralegal; network and system administration; project management.

Academics *Calendar:* quarters. *Degrees:* associate and bachelor's.

Student Life *Housing:* college housing not available.

Freshman Application Contact Director of Recruitment, ITT Technical Institute, 10700 Abbotts Bridge Road, Duluth, GA 30097. *Phone:* 678-957-8510. *Toll-free phone:* 866-489-8818. *Website:* http://www.itt-tech.edu/.

ITT Technical Institute

Kennesaw, Georgia

- **Proprietary** primarily 2-year, founded 2004, part of ITT Educational Services, Inc.
- **Coed**

Majors Business administration and management; construction management; cyber/computer forensics and counterterrorism; drafting and design technology; electrical, electronic and communications engineering technology; forensic science and technology; game and interactive media design; graphic communications; information technology project management; legal assistant/paralegal; network and system administration; project management.

Academics *Calendar:* quarters. *Degrees:* associate and bachelor's.

Freshman Application Contact Director of Recruitment, ITT Technical Institute, 2065 ITT Tech Way NW, Kennesaw, GA 30144. *Phone:* 770-426-2300. *Toll-free phone:* 877-231-6415 (in-state); 800-231-6415 (out-of-state). *Website:* http://www.itt-tech.edu/.

Lanier Technical College

Oakwood, Georgia

- **State-supported** 2-year, founded 1964, part of Technical College System of Georgia
- **Coed,** 3,579 undergraduate students, 29% full-time, 62% women, 38% men

Undergraduates 1,042 full-time, 2,537 part-time. 0.1% are from out of state; 10% Black or African American, non-Hispanic/Latino; 11% Hispanic/Latino; 2% Asian, non-Hispanic/Latino; 0.2% Native Hawaiian or other Pacific Islander, non-Hispanic/Latino; 0.4% American Indian or Alaska Native, non-Hispanic/Latino; 0.7% Two or more races, non-Hispanic/Latino; 0.2% Race/ethnicity unknown; 0.2% international. *Retention:* 62% of full-time freshmen returned.

Freshmen *Admission:* 898 enrolled.

Majors Accounting; administrative assistant and secretarial science; banking and financial support services; child development; computer and information systems security; computer programming; computer science; computer systems networking and telecommunications; criminal justice/safety; drafting and design technology; electrical, electronic and communications engineering technology; fire science/firefighting; health professions related; industrial technology; information science/studies; interior design; marketing/marketing management; medical radiologic technology; occupational safety and health technology; surgical technology; web page, digital/multimedia and information resources design.

Academics *Calendar:* quarters. *Degree:* certificates, diplomas, and associate. *Special study options:* distance learning.

Student Life *Housing:* college housing not available.

Applying *Options:* early admission. *Application fee:* $15. *Required:* high school transcript.

Freshman Application Contact Lanier Technical College, 2990 Landrum Education Drive, PO Box 58, Oakwood, GA 30566. *Phone:* 770-531-6332. *Website:* http://www.laniertech.edu/.

Le Cordon Bleu College of Culinary Arts in Atlanta

Tucker, Georgia

Freshman Application Contact Admissions Office, Le Cordon Bleu College of Culinary Arts in Atlanta, 1957 Lakeside Parkway, Tucker, GA 30084. *Toll-free phone:* 888-549-8222. *Website:* http://www.chefs.edu/Atlanta/.

Miller-Motte Technical College

Augusta, Georgia

Admissions Office Contact Miller-Motte Technical College, 621 NW Frontage Road, Augusta, GA 30907. *Toll-free phone:* 866-297-0267. *Website:* http://www.miller-motte.edu/.

Miller-Motte Technical College

Macon, Georgia

Admissions Office Contact Miller-Motte Technical College, 175 Tom Hill Sr. Boulevard, Macon, GA 31210. *Toll-free phone:* 866-297-0267. *Website:* http://www.miller-motte.edu/.

Moultrie Technical College

Moultrie, Georgia

- **State-supported** 2-year, founded 1964, part of Technical College System of Georgia
- **Coed,** 2,058 undergraduate students, 38% full-time, 62% women, 38% men

Undergraduates 789 full-time, 1,269 part-time. 35% Black or African American, non-Hispanic/Latino; 6% Hispanic/Latino; 0.1% Asian, non-Hispanic/Latino; 0.1% American Indian or Alaska Native, non-Hispanic/Latino; 0.1% Two or more races, non-Hispanic/Latino; 1% Race/ethnicity unknown; 0.1% international. *Retention:* 55% of full-time freshmen returned.

Freshmen *Admission:* 345 enrolled.

Majors Accounting; administrative assistant and secretarial science; child development; civil engineering technology; computer systems networking and telecommunications; criminal justice/safety; electrical, electronic and communications engineering technology; information science/studies; marketing/marketing management; web page, digital/multimedia and information resources design.

Academics *Calendar:* quarters. *Degree:* certificates, diplomas, and associate. *Special study options:* distance learning.

Student Life *Housing:* college housing not available.

Applying *Options:* early admission. *Application fee:* $20. *Required:* high school transcript.

Freshman Application Contact Moultrie Technical College, 800 Veterans Parkway North, Moultrie, GA 31788. *Phone:* 229-528-4581. *Website:* http://www.moultrietech.edu/.

North Georgia Technical College

Clarkesville, Georgia

- **State-supported** 2-year, founded 1943, part of Technical College System of Georgia
- **Coed,** 2,441 undergraduate students, 42% full-time, 58% women, 42% men

Undergraduates 1,027 full-time, 1,414 part-time. 2% are from out of state; 7% Black or African American, non-Hispanic/Latino; 3% Hispanic/Latino; 0.7% Asian, non-Hispanic/Latino; 0.2% American Indian or Alaska Native, non-Hispanic/Latino; 1% Two or more races, non-Hispanic/Latino; 0.5% Race/ethnicity unknown; 0.2% international. *Retention:* 50% of full-time freshmen returned.

Freshmen *Admission:* 675 enrolled.

Majors Administrative assistant and secretarial science; computer systems networking and telecommunications; criminal justice/safety; culinary arts; heating, ventilation, air conditioning and refrigeration engineering technology; horticultural science; industrial technology; parks, recreation and leisure facilities management; turf and turfgrass management; web page, digital/multimedia and information resources design.

Academics *Calendar:* quarters. *Degree:* certificates, diplomas, and associate. *Special study options:* distance learning.

Student Life *Housing Options:* coed.

Applying *Options:* early admission. *Application fee:* $15. *Required:* high school transcript.

Freshman Application Contact North Georgia Technical College, 1500 Georgia Highway 197, North, PO Box 65, Clarkesville, GA 30523. *Phone:* 706-754-7724.

Website: http://www.northgatech.edu/.

Oconee Fall Line Technical College
Sandersville, Georgia

- **State-supported** 2-year, part of Technical College System of Georgia
- **Coed**, 1,869 undergraduate students, 30% full-time, 56% women, 44% men

Undergraduates 554 full-time, 1,315 part-time. 45% Black or African American, non-Hispanic/Latino; 1% Hispanic/Latino; 0.6% Asian, non-Hispanic/Latino; 0.1% Native Hawaiian or other Pacific Islander, non-Hispanic/Latino; 0.2% American Indian or Alaska Native, non-Hispanic/Latino; 0.8% Two or more races, non-Hispanic/Latino; 0.3% Race/ethnicity unknown; 0.1% international. *Retention:* 44% of full-time freshmen returned.

Freshmen *Admission:* 336 enrolled.

Majors Accounting; administrative assistant and secretarial science; child development; computer systems networking and telecommunications; information science/studies.

Academics *Calendar:* quarters. *Degree:* certificates, diplomas, and associate. *Special study options:* distance learning.

Student Life *Housing:* college housing not available.

Applying *Options:* early admission. *Application fee:* $20. *Required:* high school transcript.

Freshman Application Contact Oconee Fall Line Technical College, 1189 Deepstep Road, Sandersville, GA 31082. *Phone:* 478-553-2050. *Toll-free phone:* 877-399-8324.

Website: http://www.oftc.edu/.

Ogeechee Technical College
Statesboro, Georgia

- **State-supported** 2-year, founded 1989, part of Technical College System of Georgia
- **Small-town** campus
- **Coed**, 2,216 undergraduate students, 39% full-time, 69% women, 31% men

Undergraduates 854 full-time, 1,362 part-time. 0.9% are from out of state; 40% Black or African American, non-Hispanic/Latino; 2% Hispanic/Latino; 0.8% Asian, non-Hispanic/Latino; 0.2% American Indian or Alaska Native, non-Hispanic/Latino; 1% Two or more races, non-Hispanic/Latino. *Retention:* 60% of full-time freshmen returned.

Freshmen *Admission:* 350 enrolled.

Majors Accounting; administrative assistant and secretarial science; agribusiness; automobile/automotive mechanics technology; banking and financial support services; child development; computer systems networking and telecommunications; construction trades; culinary arts; dental hygiene; forest technology; funeral service and mortuary science; health information/medical records technology; hotel/motel administration; information science/studies; interior design; legal assistant/paralegal; marketing/marketing management; opticianry; tourism and travel services management; veterinary/animal health technology; water quality and wastewater treatment management and recycling technology; wildlife, fish and wildlands science and management; wood science and wood products/pulp and paper technology.

Academics *Calendar:* quarters. *Degree:* certificates, diplomas, and associate. *Special study options:* distance learning.

Student Life *Housing:* college housing not available.

Applying *Options:* early admission. *Application fee:* $25. *Required:* high school transcript.

Freshman Application Contact Ogeechee Technical College, One Joe Kennedy Boulevard, Statesboro, GA 30458. *Phone:* 912-871-1600. *Toll-free phone:* 800-646-1316.

Website: http://www.ogeecheetech.edu/.

Okefenokee Technical College
Waycross, Georgia

- **State-supported** 2-year, part of Technical College System of Georgia
- **Small-town** campus
- **Coed,** 1,180 undergraduate students, 32% full-time, 65% women, 35% men

Undergraduates 382 full-time, 798 part-time. 21% Black or African American, non-Hispanic/Latino; 2% Hispanic/Latino; 0.6% Asian, non-Hispanic/Latino; 0.1% Native Hawaiian or other Pacific Islander, non-Hispanic/Latino; 0.8% American Indian or Alaska Native, non-Hispanic/Latino; 1% Two or more races, non-Hispanic/Latino; 0.2% Race/ethnicity unknown; 0.5% international. *Retention:* 51% of full-time freshmen returned.

Freshmen *Admission:* 272 enrolled.

Majors Administrative assistant and secretarial science; child development; clinical/medical laboratory technology; computer systems networking and telecommunications; computer technology/computer systems technology; criminal justice/police science; forest technology; information science/studies; occupational safety and health technology; respiratory therapy technician; surgical technology.

Academics *Calendar:* quarters. *Degree:* certificates, diplomas, and associate. *Special study options:* distance learning.

Student Life *Housing:* college housing not available.

Applying *Options:* early admission. *Application fee:* $20. *Required:* high school transcript.

Freshman Application Contact Okefenokee Technical College, 1701 Carswell Avenue, Waycross, GA 31503. *Phone:* 912-338-5251. *Toll-free phone:* 877-ED-AT-OTC.

Website: http://www.okefenokeetech.edu/.

SAE Institute Atlanta
Atlanta, Georgia

Admissions Office Contact SAE Institute Atlanta, 215 Peachtree Street, Suite 300, Atlanta, GA 30303.

Website: http://atlanta.sae.edu/.

Savannah Technical College
Savannah, Georgia

- **State-supported** 2-year, founded 1929, part of Technical College System of Georgia
- **Urban** campus
- **Coed,** 4,784 undergraduate students, 37% full-time, 62% women, 38% men

Undergraduates 1,749 full-time, 3,035 part-time. 1% are from out of state; 46% Black or African American, non-Hispanic/Latino; 6% Hispanic/Latino; 2% Asian, non-Hispanic/Latino; 0.2% Native Hawaiian or other Pacific Islander, non-Hispanic/Latino; 0.3% American Indian or Alaska Native, non-Hispanic/Latino; 2% Two or more races, non-Hispanic/Latino; 0.4% Race/ethnicity unknown; 0.6% international. *Retention:* 54% of full-time freshmen returned.

Freshmen *Admission:* 900 enrolled.

Majors Accounting; administrative assistant and secretarial science; automobile/automotive mechanics technology; child development; computer systems networking and telecommunications; criminal justice/safety; culinary arts; electrical, electronic and communications engineering technology; fire science/firefighting; heating, ventilation, air conditioning and refrigeration engineering technology; hotel/motel administration; industrial technology; information technology; marketing/marketing management; surgical technology; tourism and travel services management.

Academics *Calendar:* quarters. *Degree:* certificates, diplomas, and associate. *Special study options:* distance learning.

Student Life *Housing:* college housing not available.

Applying *Options:* early admission. *Application fee:* $20. *Required:* high school transcript.

Freshman Application Contact Savannah Technical College, 5717 White Bluff Road, Savannah, GA 31405. *Phone:* 912-443-5711. *Toll-free phone:* 800-769-6362.

Website: http://www.savannahtech.edu/.

Southeastern Technical College
Vidalia, Georgia

- **State-supported** 2-year, founded 1989, part of Technical College System of Georgia
- **Coed,** 1,533 undergraduate students, 29% full-time, 73% women, 27% men

Undergraduates 442 full-time, 1,091 part-time. 0.3% are from out of state; 32% Black or African American, non-Hispanic/Latino; 4% Hispanic/Latino; 0.7% Asian, non-Hispanic/Latino; 0.1% American Indian or Alaska Native, non-Hispanic/Latino; 0.4% Two or more races, non-Hispanic/Latino; 0.1% Race/ethnicity unknown. *Retention:* 60% of full-time freshmen returned.

Freshmen *Admission:* 287 enrolled.

Majors Accounting; administrative assistant and secretarial science; child development; computer systems networking and telecommunications; criminal justice/safety; dental hygiene; design and visual communications; electrical, electronic and communications engineering technology; information science/studies; marketing/marketing management; medical radiologic technology; respiratory therapy technician; web page, digital/multimedia and information resources design.

Academics *Calendar:* quarters. *Degree:* certificates, diplomas, and associate. *Special study options:* distance learning.

Student Life *Housing:* college housing not available.

Applying *Options:* early admission. *Application fee:* $20. *Required:* high school transcript.

Freshman Application Contact Southeastern Technical College, 3001 East First Street, Vidalia, GA 30474. *Phone:* 912-538-3121.

Website: http://www.southeasterntech.edu/.

Southern Crescent Technical College
Griffin, Georgia

- **State-supported** 2-year, founded 1965, part of Technical College System of Georgia
- **Small-town** campus
- **Coed,** 5,177 undergraduate students, 41% full-time, 65% women, 35% men

Undergraduates 2,142 full-time, 3,035 part-time. 0.1% are from out of state; 43% Black or African American, non-Hispanic/Latino; 3% Hispanic/Latino; 1% Asian, non-Hispanic/Latino; 0.1% Native Hawaiian or other Pacific Islander, non-Hispanic/Latino; 0.3% American Indian or Alaska Native, non-Hispanic/Latino; 1% Two or more races, non-Hispanic/Latino; 0.5% Race/ethnicity unknown; 0.3% international. *Retention:* 48% of full-time freshmen returned.

Freshmen *Admission:* 1,006 enrolled.

Majors Accounting; administrative assistant and secretarial science; automobile/automotive mechanics technology; business administration and management; child development; computer and information systems security; computer programming; computer systems networking and telecommunications; criminal justice/safety; drafting and design technology; electrical, electronic and communications engineering technology; emergency medical technology (EMT paramedic); heating, ventilation, air conditioning and refrigeration engineering technology; horticultural science; industrial technology; legal assistant/paralegal; manufacturing engineering technology; marketing/marketing management; medical radiologic technology; pharmacy technician; respiratory therapy technician; surgical technology; web page, digital/multimedia and information resources design.

Academics *Calendar:* quarters. *Degree:* certificates, diplomas, and associate. *Special study options:* distance learning.

Library Griffin Technical College Library.

Applying *Options:* early admission. *Application fee:* $15. *Required:* high school transcript.

Freshman Application Contact Southern Crescent Technical College, 501 Varsity Road, Griffin, GA 30223. *Phone:* 770-646-6160.

Website: http://www.sctech.edu/.

South Georgia State College
Douglas, Georgia

- **State-supported** primarily 2-year, founded 1906, part of University System of Georgia
- **Small-town** 340-acre campus
- **Endowment** $286,240
- **Coed,** 2,579 undergraduate students, 73% full-time, 61% women, 39% men

Undergraduates 1,877 full-time, 702 part-time. Students come from 17 states and territories; 2 other countries; 5% are from out of state; 32% Black or African American, non-Hispanic/Latino; 4% Hispanic/Latino; 0.8% Asian, non-Hispanic/Latino; 0.1% Native Hawaiian or other Pacific Islander, non-Hispanic/Latino; 0.4% American Indian or Alaska Native, non-Hispanic/Latino; 0.7% Two or more races, non-Hispanic/Latino; 0.2% international; 5% transferred in; 13% live on campus.

Freshmen *Admission:* 974 enrolled.

Faculty *Total:* 115, 53% full-time. *Student/faculty ratio:* 27:1.

Majors Biology/biological sciences; business administration and management; chemistry; communication; computer science; criminal justice/law enforcement administration; dramatic/theater arts; education (multiple levels); English; foreign languages and literatures; general studies; health/medical preparatory programs related; history; journalism; kinesiology and exercise science; logistics, materials, and supply chain management; mathematics; parks, recreation and leisure; philosophy; physics; political science and government; psychology; registered nursing/registered nurse; sociology.

Academics *Calendar:* semesters. *Degrees:* associate and bachelor's. *Special study options:* academic remediation for entering students, adult/continuing education programs, advanced placement credit, distance learning, double majors, part-time degree program, services for LD students, study abroad, summer session for credit.

Library William S. Smith Library plus 1 other with an OPAC, a Web page.

Student Life *Housing:* on-campus residence required for freshman year. *Options:* men-only, women-only. Campus housing is university owned. Freshman applicants given priority for college housing. *Activities and Organizations:* drama/theater group, student-run newspaper, choral group, Intramural Sports, Cultural Exchange Club, Georgia Association of Nursing Students, Student Government Association, Phi Theta Kappa Honors Society. *Campus security:* 24-hour emergency response devices and patrols, controlled dormitory access. *Student services:* personal/psychological counseling.

Athletics Member NJCAA. *Intercollegiate sports:* baseball M(s), basketball M(s), cross-country running M(s)/W(s), soccer W(s), softball W(s), swimming and diving M(s)/W(s). *Intramural sports:* basketball M/W, football M/W, table tennis M/W, ultimate Frisbee M/W, volleyball M/W.

Costs (2013–14) *Tuition:* state resident $2596 full-time, $87 per credit hour part-time; nonresident $9822 full-time, $327 per credit hour part-time. Full-time tuition and fees vary according to course load and location. Part-time tuition and fees vary according to course load and location. *Required fees:* $1030 full-time, $515 per term part-time. *Room and board:* $8000; room only: $4600. Room and board charges vary according to board plan and location. *Waivers:* senior citizens and employees or children of employees.

Applying *Options:* electronic application, early admission, deferred entrance. *Application fee:* $20. *Required:* high school transcript. *Application deadlines:* rolling (freshmen), rolling (transfers). *Notification:* continuous (freshmen), continuous (transfers).

Freshman Application Contact South Georgia State College, 100 West College Park Drive, Douglas, GA 31533-5098. *Phone:* 912-260-4409. *Toll-free phone:* 800-342-6364.

Website: http://www.sgc.edu/.

South Georgia Technical College
Americus, Georgia

- **State-supported** 2-year, founded 1948, part of Technical College System of Georgia
- **Coed,** 1,828 undergraduate students, 53% full-time, 50% women, 50% men

Undergraduates 976 full-time, 852 part-time. 4% are from out of state; 57% Black or African American, non-Hispanic/Latino; 2% Hispanic/Latino; 0.5% Asian, non-Hispanic/Latino; 0.1% American Indian or Alaska Native, non-Hispanic/Latino; 0.1% Two or more races, non-Hispanic/Latino; 0.3% Race/ethnicity unknown; 0.1% international. *Retention:* 60% of full-time freshmen returned.

Freshmen *Admission:* 524 enrolled.

Majors Accounting; administrative assistant and secretarial science; child development; computer systems networking and telecommunications; criminal justice/safety; culinary arts; drafting and design technology; electrical, electronic and communications engineering technology; heating, ventilation, air conditioning and refrigeration engineering technology; horticultural science; industrial technology; information science/studies; legal assistant/paralegal; manufacturing engineering technology; marketing/marketing management.

Academics *Calendar:* quarters. *Degree:* certificates, diplomas, and associate. *Special study options:* distance learning.

Applying *Options:* early admission. *Application fee:* $20. *Required:* high school transcript.

Freshman Application Contact South Georgia Technical College, 900 South Georgia Tech Parkway, Americus, GA 31709. *Phone:* 229-931-2299.

Website: http://www.southgatech.edu/.

Southwest Georgia Technical College
Thomasville, Georgia

- **State-supported** 2-year, founded 1963, part of Technical College System of Georgia
- **Coed,** 1,546 undergraduate students, 29% full-time, 67% women, 33% men

Undergraduates 443 full-time, 1,103 part-time. 4% are from out of state; 31% Black or African American, non-Hispanic/Latino; 1% Hispanic/Latino; 0.9% Asian, non-Hispanic/Latino; 0.8% American Indian or Alaska Native, non-Hispanic/Latino; 1% Two or more races, non-Hispanic/Latino; 0.2% Race/ethnicity unknown; 0.1% international. *Retention:* 58% of full-time freshmen returned.

Freshmen *Admission:* 226 enrolled.

Majors Accounting; administrative assistant and secretarial science; agricultural mechanization; child development; computer systems networking and telecommunications; criminal justice/safety; information science/studies; medical radiologic technology; registered nursing/registered nurse; respiratory care therapy; surgical technology.

Academics *Calendar:* quarters. *Degree:* certificates, diplomas, and associate. *Special study options:* distance learning.

Student Life *Housing:* college housing not available.
Applying *Options:* electronic application, early admission. *Application fee:* $20. *Required:* high school transcript.
Freshman Application Contact Southwest Georgia Technical College, 15689 US 19 North, Thomasville, GA 31792. *Phone:* 229-225-5089.
Website: http://www.southwestgatech.edu/.

Virginia College
Columbus, Georgia

Admissions Office Contact Virginia College, 5601 Veterans Parkway, Columbus, GA 31904.
Website: http://www.vc.edu/.

Virginia College
Savannah, Georgia

Admissions Office Contact Virginia College, 14045 Abercorn Street, Suite 1503, Savannah, GA 31419.
Website: http://www.vc.edu/.

Virginia College in Augusta
Augusta, Georgia

Admissions Office Contact Virginia College in Augusta, 2807 Wylds Road Extension, Suite B, Augusta, GA 30909.
Website: http://www.vc.edu/.

Virginia College in Macon
Macon, Georgia

Admissions Office Contact Virginia College in Macon, 1901 Paul Walsh Drive, Macon, GA 31206.
Website: http://www.vc.edu/.

West Georgia Technical College
Waco, Georgia

- **State-supported** 2-year, founded 1966, part of Technical College System of Georgia
- **Coed,** 6,915 undergraduate students, 32% full-time, 65% women, 35% men

Undergraduates 2,223 full-time, 4,692 part-time. 3% are from out of state; 32% Black or African American, non-Hispanic/Latino; 3% Hispanic/Latino; 0.9% Asian, non-Hispanic/Latino; 0.1% Native Hawaiian or other Pacific Islander, non-Hispanic/Latino; 0.4% American Indian or Alaska Native, non-Hispanic/Latino; 0.6% Two or more races, non-Hispanic/Latino; 2% Race/ethnicity unknown; 0.2% international. *Retention:* 55% of full-time freshmen returned.
Freshmen *Admission:* 1,602 enrolled.
Majors Accounting; administrative assistant and secretarial science; automobile/automotive mechanics technology; child development; computer systems networking and telecommunications; criminal justice/safety; electrical, electronic and communications engineering technology; fire science/firefighting; health information/medical records technology; industrial technology; information science/studies; marketing/marketing management; medical radiologic technology; pharmacy technician; plastics and polymer engineering technology; social work; web page, digital/multimedia and information resources design.
Academics *Calendar:* quarters. *Degree:* certificates, diplomas, and associate. *Special study options:* distance learning.
Student Life *Housing:* college housing not available.
Financial Aid Of all full-time matriculated undergraduates who enrolled in 2012, 68 Federal Work-Study jobs (averaging $800).
Applying *Options:* early admission. *Application fee:* $25. *Required:* high school transcript.
Freshman Application Contact West Georgia Technical College, 176 Murphy Campus Boulevard, Waco, GA 30182. *Phone:* 770-537-5719.
Website: http://www.westgatech.edu/.

Wiregrass Georgia Technical College
Valdosta, Georgia

- **State-supported** 2-year, founded 1963, part of Technical College System of Georgia
- **Suburban** campus
- **Coed,** 3,966 undergraduate students, 35% full-time, 65% women, 35% men

Undergraduates 1,386 full-time, 2,580 part-time. 1% are from out of state; 33% Black or African American, non-Hispanic/Latino; 3% Hispanic/Latino; 0.5% Asian, non-Hispanic/Latino; 0.1% Native Hawaiian or other Pacific Islander, non-Hispanic/Latino; 0.2% American Indian or Alaska Native, non-Hispanic/Latino; 0.9% Two or more races, non-Hispanic/Latino; 0.2% Race/ethnicity unknown; 0.1% international. *Retention:* 51% of full-time freshmen returned.
Freshmen *Admission:* 686 enrolled.
Majors Accounting; administrative assistant and secretarial science; banking and financial support services; child development; computer and information systems security; computer programming; computer systems networking and telecommunications; criminal justice/safety; drafting and design technology; e-commerce; fire science/firefighting; machine tool technology; marketing/marketing management; medical radiologic technology; web page, digital/multimedia and information resources design.
Academics *Calendar:* quarters. *Degree:* certificates, diplomas, and associate. *Special study options:* distance learning.
Student Life *Housing:* college housing not available.
Applying *Options:* early admission. *Application fee:* $15. *Required:* high school transcript.
Freshman Application Contact Wiregrass Georgia Technical College, 4089 Val Tech Road, Valdosta, GA 31602. *Phone:* 229-468-2278.
Website: http://www.wiregrass.edu/.

GUAM

Guam Community College
Barrigada, Guam

Freshman Application Contact Mr. Patrick L. Clymer, Registrar, Guam Community College, PO Box 23069, Sesame Street, Barrigada, GU 96921. *Phone:* 671-735-5561. *Fax:* 671-735-5531. *E-mail:* patrick.clymer@guamcc.edu.
Website: http://www.guamcc.net/.

HAWAII

Hawaii Community College
Hilo, Hawaii

Director of Admissions Mrs. Tammy M. Tanaka, Admissions Specialist, Hawaii Community College, 200 West Kawili Street, Hilo, HI 96720-4091. *Phone:* 808-974-7661.
Website: http://www.hawcc.hawaii.edu/.

Hawaii Tokai International College
Honolulu, Hawaii

- **Independent** 2-year, founded 1992, part of Tokai University Educational System (Japan)
- **Urban** campus
- **Endowment** $1.3 million
- **Coed**

Undergraduates 64 full-time. Students come from 2 states and territories; 3 other countries; 25% Race/ethnicity unknown; 75% international; 60% live on campus. *Retention:* 93% of full-time freshmen returned.
Academics *Calendar:* quarters. *Degree:* certificates, diplomas, and associate. *Special study options:* English as a second language, part-time degree program, study abroad, summer session for credit.
Student Life *Campus security:* 24-hour patrols.
Standardized Tests *Required for some:* TOEFL score of 450 PBT for international students.
Costs (2013–14) *Comprehensive fee:* $19,590 includes full-time tuition ($10,950), mandatory fees ($480), and room and board ($8160). Part-time tuition: $450 per credit. *Room and board:* Room and board charges vary according to board plan.
Applying *Options:* electronic application, deferred entrance. *Application fee:* $50. *Required:* essay or personal statement, high school transcript, minimum 2.5 GPA. *Required for some:* interview. *Recommended:* 1 letter of recommendation.
Freshman Application Contact Mrs. Jaelee Heupel, Director, Student Services, Hawaii Tokai International College, 2241 Kapiolani Boulevard, Honolulu, HI 96826. *Phone:* 808-983-4187. *Fax:* 808-983-4173. *E-mail:* studentservices@tokai.edu.
Website: http://www.hawaiitokai.edu/.

Heald College–Honolulu

Honolulu, Hawaii

Freshman Application Contact Director of Admissions, Heald College–Honolulu, 1500 Kapiolani Boulevard, Honolulu, HI 96814. *Phone:* 808-955-1500. *Toll-free phone:* 800-88-HEALD. *Fax:* 808-955-6964. *E-mail:* honoluluinfo@heald.edu.

Website: http://www.heald.edu/.

Honolulu Community College

Honolulu, Hawaii

- **State-supported** 2-year, founded 1920, part of University of Hawaii System
- **Urban** 20-acre campus
- **Coed,** 4,368 undergraduate students, 37% full-time, 41% women, 59% men

Undergraduates 1,632 full-time, 2,736 part-time. Students come from 26 states and territories; 12 other countries; 2% are from out of state; 2% Black or African American, non-Hispanic/Latino; 9% Hispanic/Latino; 42% Asian, non-Hispanic/Latino; 9% Native Hawaiian or other Pacific Islander, non-Hispanic/Latino; 0.2% American Indian or Alaska Native, non-Hispanic/Latino; 28% Two or more races, non-Hispanic/Latino; 0.7% Race/ethnicity unknown; 1% international; 10% transferred in. *Retention:* 61% of full-time freshmen returned.

Freshmen *Admission:* 670 enrolled.

Faculty *Total:* 216, 61% full-time. *Student/faculty ratio:* 16:1.

Majors Architectural engineering technology; automobile/automotive mechanics technology; avionics maintenance technology; carpentry; commercial and advertising art; community organization and advocacy; cosmetology; criminal justice/police science; drafting and design technology; electrical, electronic and communications engineering technology; engineering technology; fashion/apparel design; fire science/firefighting; food technology and processing; heating, air conditioning, ventilation and refrigeration maintenance technology; human services; kindergarten/preschool education; liberal arts and sciences/liberal studies; marine maintenance and ship repair technology; occupational safety and health technology; welding technology.

Academics *Calendar:* semesters. *Degree:* certificates and associate. *Special study options:* academic remediation for entering students, accelerated degree program, advanced placement credit, cooperative education, distance learning, English as a second language, internships, part-time degree program, services for LD students, student-designed majors, summer session for credit. *ROTC:* Army (c), Air Force (c).

Library Honolulu Community College Library plus 1 other with 54,902 titles, 1,280 serial subscriptions, 858 audiovisual materials, an OPAC, a Web page.

Student Life *Housing:* college housing not available. *Activities and Organizations:* student-run newspaper, Phi Theta Kappa, Hui 'Oiwi, Fashion Society. *Campus security:* 24-hour emergency response devices. *Student services:* health clinic, personal/psychological counseling.

Standardized Tests *Required for some:* TOEFL required for international applicants.

Costs (2014–15) *Tuition:* state resident $2766 full-time, $114 per credit part-time; nonresident $7584 full-time, $316 per credit part-time. *Required fees:* $30 full-time, $1 per credit part-time, $10 per term part-time.

Financial Aid Of all full-time matriculated undergraduates who enrolled in 2012, 30 Federal Work-Study jobs (averaging $1600).

Applying *Options:* early admission. *Application deadlines:* 8/15 (freshmen), 8/15 (transfers). *Notification:* continuous until 8/15 (freshmen), continuous until 8/15 (transfers).

Freshman Application Contact Admissions Office, Honolulu Community College, 874 Dillingham Boulevard, Honolulu, HI 96817. *Phone:* 808-845-9129. *E-mail:* honcc@hawaii.edu.

Website: http://www.honolulu.hawaii.edu/.

Kapiolani Community College

Honolulu, Hawaii

Freshman Application Contact Kapiolani Community College, 4303 Diamond Head Road, Honolulu, HI 96816-4421. *Phone:* 808-734-9555.

Website: http://www.kapiolani.hawaii.edu/.

Kauai Community College

Lihue, Hawaii

Freshman Application Contact Mr. Leighton Oride, Admissions Officer and Registrar, Kauai Community College, 3-1901 Kaumualii Highway, Lihue, HI 96766. *Phone:* 808-245-8225. *Fax:* 808-245-8297. *E-mail:* arkauai@hawaii.edu.

Website: http://kauai.hawaii.edu/.

Leeward Community College

Pearl City, Hawaii

Freshman Application Contact Ms. Anna Donald, Office Assistant, Leeward Community College, 96-045 Ala Ike, Pearl City, HI 96782-3393. *Phone:* 808-455-0642.

Website: http://www.lcc.hawaii.edu/.

Remington College–Honolulu Campus

Honolulu, Hawaii

Director of Admissions Louis LaMair, Director of Recruitment, Remington College–Honolulu Campus, 1111 Bishop Street, Suite 400, Honolulu, HI 96813. *Phone:* 808-942-1000. *Fax:* 808-533-3064. *E-mail:* louis.lamair@remingtoncollege.edu.

Website: http://www.remingtoncollege.edu/.

University of Hawaii Maui College

Kahului, Hawaii

- **State-supported** primarily 2-year, founded 1967, part of University of Hawaii System
- **Rural** 77-acre campus
- **Coed,** 4,071 undergraduate students, 36% full-time, 64% women, 36% men

Undergraduates 1,446 full-time, 2,625 part-time. 1% live on campus.

Freshmen *Admission:* 735 enrolled.

Faculty *Total:* 117, 99% full-time.

Majors Accounting; administrative assistant and secretarial science; agricultural mechanization; automobile/automotive mechanics technology; business administration and management; carpentry; construction engineering technology; criminal justice/law enforcement administration; fashion/apparel design; food technology and processing; horticultural science; hotel/motel administration; human services; liberal arts and sciences/liberal studies; marketing/marketing management; registered nursing/registered nurse; welding technology.

Academics *Calendar:* semesters. *Degrees:* certificates, associate, and bachelor's. *Special study options:* academic remediation for entering students, adult/continuing education programs, cooperative education, English as a second language, external degree program, part-time degree program, services for LD students, summer session for credit.

Library Maui Community College Library plus 1 other with 49,812 titles, 631 serial subscriptions, 1,333 audiovisual materials, an OPAC, a Web page.

Student Life *Housing Options:* coed. *Activities and Organizations:* student-run newspaper. *Campus security:* 24-hour emergency response devices and patrols. *Student services:* health clinic, personal/psychological counseling.

Athletics *Intramural sports:* basketball M/W, table tennis M/W, tennis M/W, volleyball M/W.

Costs (2014–15) *Tuition:* state resident $114 full-time; nonresident $316 full-time.

Financial Aid Of all full-time matriculated undergraduates who enrolled in 2012, 40 Federal Work-Study jobs (averaging $4000).

Applying *Options:* electronic application, early admission. *Application fee:* $25. *Required for some:* high school transcript. *Application deadlines:* rolling (freshmen), rolling (transfers).

Freshman Application Contact Mr. Stephen Kameda, Director of Admissions and Records, University of Hawaii Maui College, 310 Kaahumanu Avenue, Kahului, HI 96732. *Phone:* 808-984-3267. *Toll-free phone:* 800-479-6692. *Fax:* 808-984-3872. *E-mail:* skameda@hawaii.edu.

Website: http://maui.hawaii.edu/.

Windward Community College

Kaneohe, Hawaii

Director of Admissions Geri Imai, Registrar, Windward Community College, 45-720 Keaahala Road, Kaneohe, HI 96744-3528. *Phone:* 808-235-7430. *E-mail:* gerii@hawaii.edu.

Website: http://www.wcc.hawaii.edu/.

IDAHO

Brown Mackie College–Boise
Boise, Idaho

- **Proprietary** primarily 2-year, part of Education Management Corporation
- **Coed**

Majors Business administration and management; business/commerce; corrections and criminal justice related; drafting and design technology; information technology; legal assistant/paralegal; occupational therapist assistant; veterinary/animal health technology.

Academics *Degrees:* diplomas, associate, and bachelor's.

Freshman Application Contact Brown Mackie College–Boise, 9050 West Overland Road, Suite 100, Boise, ID 83709. *Phone:* 208-321-8800.

Website: http://www.brownmackie.edu/boise/.

See display below and page 384 for the College Close-Up.

Carrington College–Boise
Boise, Idaho

- **Proprietary** 2-year, founded 1980, part of Carrington Colleges Group, Inc.
- **Coed,** 552 undergraduate students, 90% full-time, 84% women, 16% men

Undergraduates 496 full-time, 56 part-time. 9% are from out of state; 2% Black or African American, non-Hispanic/Latino; 11% Hispanic/Latino; 2% Asian, non-Hispanic/Latino; 0.9% Native Hawaiian or other Pacific Islander, non-Hispanic/Latino; 1% American Indian or Alaska Native, non-Hispanic/Latino; 3% Two or more races, non-Hispanic/Latino; 0.4% Race/ethnicity unknown; 21% transferred in.

Freshmen *Admission:* 49 enrolled.

Faculty *Total:* 46, 41% full-time. *Student/faculty ratio:* 18:1.

Majors Dental assisting; dental hygiene; massage therapy; medical/clinical assistant; medical insurance/medical billing; medical office management; pharmacy technician; physical therapy technology; registered nursing/registered nurse.

Academics *Calendar:* semesters. *Degree:* certificates and associate.

Library an OPAC.

Student Life *Housing:* college housing not available.

Costs (2014–15) *Tuition:* $54,125 per degree program part-time. Total costs vary by program. Tuition provided is for largest program (Dental Hygiene).

Applying *Required:* essay or personal statement, high school transcript, interview, Entrance test administered by Carrington College.

Freshman Application Contact Carrington College–Boise, 1122 North Liberty Street, Boise, ID 83704.

Website: http://carrington.edu/.

College of Southern Idaho
Twin Falls, Idaho

- **State and locally supported** 2-year, founded 1964
- **Small-town** 287-acre campus
- **Coed,** 8,330 undergraduate students, 33% full-time, 64% women, 36% men

Undergraduates 2,730 full-time, 5,600 part-time. 4% are from out of state; 1% Black or African American, non-Hispanic/Latino; 20% Hispanic/Latino; 0.6% Asian, non-Hispanic/Latino; 0.6% Native Hawaiian or other Pacific Islander, non-Hispanic/Latino; 0.9% American Indian or Alaska Native, non-Hispanic/Latino; 2% Two or more races, non-Hispanic/Latino; 2% Race/ethnicity unknown; 1% international; 4% live on campus.

Freshmen *Admission:* 1,145 enrolled.

Faculty *Total:* 344, 46% full-time. *Student/faculty ratio:* 21:1.

Majors Accounting; administrative assistant and secretarial science; agricultural business and management; agricultural business and management related; agriculture; American Sign Language (ASL); animal sciences; anthropology; applied horticulture/horticulture operations; aquaculture; art; autobody/collision and repair technology; automobile/automotive mechanics technology; bilingual and multilingual education; biology/biological sciences; building/construction finishing, management, and inspection related; business administration and management; cabinetmaking and millwork; chemistry; child-care and support services management; clinical laboratory science/medical technology; commercial and advertising art; computer science; computer systems networking and telecommunications; criminal justice/law enforcement administration; culinary arts; dental assisting; diesel mechanics technology; drafting and design technology; dramatic/theater arts; education; elementary education; emergency medical technology (EMT paramedic); engineering; English; entrepreneurship; equestrian studies; foreign languages and literatures; forestry; geography; geology/earth science; history; hotel/motel administration; human services; hydrology and water resources science; liberal arts and sciences/liberal studies; library and information science; licensed practical/vocational nurse training;

Degrees in Business or Information Technology can be applied virtually anywhere.

BrownMackie.edu

ONE COURSE A MONTH℠

manufacturing engineering technology; mathematics; medical radiologic technology; music; photography; physical education teaching and coaching; physics; political science and government; pre-law studies; pre-pharmacy studies; psychiatric/mental health services technology; psychology; public health education and promotion; real estate; registered nursing/registered nurse; social sciences; sociology; speech communication and rhetoric; surgical technology; teacher assistant/aide; veterinary/animal health technology; water quality and wastewater treatment management and recycling technology; web page, digital/multimedia and information resources design; welding technology.

Academics *Calendar:* semesters. *Degree:* certificates and associate. *Special study options:* academic remediation for entering students, adult/continuing education programs, advanced placement credit, cooperative education, distance learning, English as a second language, honors programs, independent study, internships, part-time degree program, services for LD students, summer session for credit.

Library College of Southern Idaho Library with an OPAC, a Web page.

Student Life *Housing Options:* men-only, women-only. Campus housing is university owned. *Activities and Organizations:* drama/theater group, student-run newspaper, radio station, choral group, BPA, Delta Epsilon Chi, Chi Alpha (Christian Group), Vet Tech Club, Equine Club. *Campus security:* 24-hour emergency response devices and patrols, controlled dormitory access. *Student services:* health clinic, personal/psychological counseling, women's center, legal services.

Athletics Member NJCAA. *Intercollegiate sports:* baseball M(s), basketball M(s)/W(s), cheerleading M(s)/W(s), equestrian sports M(s)(c)/W(s)(c), softball W(s), volleyball M/W(s). *Intramural sports:* badminton M/W, basketball M/W, football M/W, racquetball M/W, rock climbing M/W, soccer M/W, softball M/W, tennis M/W, ultimate Frisbee M/W, volleyball M/W.

Costs (2014–15) *Tuition:* area resident $2760 full-time, $115 per credit hour part-time; state resident $3760 full-time, $165 per credit hour part-time; nonresident $6720 full-time, $280 per credit hour part-time. Full-time tuition and fees vary according to course load. Part-time tuition and fees vary according to course load. *Room and board:* Room and board charges vary according to board plan. *Payment plan:* installment. *Waivers:* senior citizens and employees or children of employees.

Financial Aid Of all full-time matriculated undergraduates who enrolled in 2012, 250 Federal Work-Study jobs (averaging $2000). 100 state and other part-time jobs (averaging $2000).

Applying *Required:* high school transcript. *Required for some:* interview.

Freshman Application Contact Director of Admissions, Registration, and Records, College of Southern Idaho, PO Box 1238, Twin Falls, ID 83303-1238. *Phone:* 208-732-6232. *Toll-free phone:* 800-680-0274. *Fax:* 208-736-3014.

Website: http://www.csi.edu/.

College of Western Idaho

Nampa, Idaho

- **State-supported** 2-year, founded 2007
- **Rural** campus with easy access to Boise
- **Coed,** 9,204 undergraduate students

Undergraduates 2% Black or African American, non-Hispanic/Latino; 14% Hispanic/Latino; 1% Asian, non-Hispanic/Latino; 0.7% Native Hawaiian or other Pacific Islander, non-Hispanic/Latino; 1% American Indian or Alaska Native, non-Hispanic/Latino; 2% Two or more races, non-Hispanic/Latino; 13% Race/ethnicity unknown.

Faculty *Total:* 408, 31% full-time. *Student/faculty ratio:* 22:1.

Majors Administrative assistant and secretarial science; agriculture; anthropology; autobody/collision and repair technology; automobile/automotive mechanics technology; baking and pastry arts; biology/biological sciences; biomedical sciences; business, management, and marketing related; communication; computer support specialist; criminal justice/police science; culinary arts; dental assisting; drafting and design technology; early childhood education; elementary education; English; fire systems technology; geography; geology/earth science; heavy equipment maintenance technology; history; horticultural science; liberal arts and sciences/liberal studies; machine tool technology; marketing/marketing management; medical administrative assistant and medical secretary; network and system administration; nursing practice; physical education teaching and coaching; political science and government; psychology; small engine mechanics and repair technology; sociology; surgical technology; web page, digital/multimedia and information resources design; wildland/forest firefighting and investigation.

Academics *Calendar:* semesters. *Degree:* certificates and associate. *Special study options:* academic remediation for entering students, advanced placement credit, cooperative education, English as a second language, honors

programs, internships, part-time degree program, services for LD students, summer session for credit.

Student Life *Housing:* college housing not available. *Activities and Organizations:* student-run newspaper.

Standardized Tests *Recommended:* SAT or ACT (for admission), Compass.

Costs (2014–15) *Tuition:* area resident $1632 full-time, $136 per credit part-time; state resident $2132 full-time, $186 per credit part-time; nonresident $3600 full-time, $300 per credit part-time. Full-time tuition and fees vary according to course load. Part-time tuition and fees vary according to course load. *Payment plan:* installment. *Waivers:* senior citizens and employees or children of employees.

Applying *Options:* electronic application. *Application fee:* $25. *Required:* high school transcript. *Application deadlines:* rolling (freshmen), rolling (out-of-state freshmen), rolling (transfers).

Freshman Application Contact College of Western Idaho, 6056 Birch Lane, Nampa, ID 83687.

Website: http://cwidaho.cc/.

Eastern Idaho Technical College

Idaho Falls, Idaho

- **State-supported** 2-year, founded 1970
- **Small-town** 40-acre campus
- **Endowment** $789,503
- **Coed,** 756 undergraduate students, 43% full-time, 60% women, 40% men

Undergraduates 325 full-time, 431 part-time. Students come from 3 states and territories; 0.3% Black or African American, non-Hispanic/Latino; 18% Hispanic/Latino; 1% Asian, non-Hispanic/Latino; 1% Native Hawaiian or other Pacific Islander, non-Hispanic/Latino; 1% American Indian or Alaska Native, non-Hispanic/Latino; 0.4% Two or more races, non-Hispanic/Latino; 2% Race/ethnicity unknown; 0.6% international.

Freshmen *Admission:* 126 applied, 84 admitted, 82 enrolled.

Faculty *Student/faculty ratio:* 8:1.

Majors Accounting; administrative assistant and secretarial science; automobile/automotive mechanics technology; computer systems networking and telecommunications; diesel mechanics technology; fire science/firefighting; legal assistant/paralegal; marketing/marketing management; medical/clinical assistant; registered nursing/registered nurse; surgical technology; welding technology.

Academics *Calendar:* semesters. *Degree:* certificates and associate. *Special study options:* academic remediation for entering students, adult/continuing education programs, advanced placement credit, English as a second language, part-time degree program, services for LD students, summer session for credit.

Library Richard and Lila Jordan Library plus 1 other with 20,000 titles, 120 serial subscriptions, 150 audiovisual materials, an OPAC.

Student Life *Housing:* college housing not available. *Campus security:* 24-hour patrols. *Student services:* personal/psychological counseling.

Standardized Tests *Required for some:* COMPASS, SAT, ACT, ASSET, or CPT.

Financial Aid Of all full-time matriculated undergraduates who enrolled in 2012, 37 Federal Work-Study jobs (averaging $1176). 11 state and other part-time jobs (averaging $1619).

Applying *Options:* electronic application, deferred entrance. *Application fee:* $10. *Required:* high school transcript, interview. *Required for some:* essay or personal statement. *Application deadline:* rolling (freshmen).

Freshman Application Contact Jessica Dixon, Career Placement and Recruiting Coordinator, Eastern Idaho Technical College, 1600 South 25th East, Idaho Falls, ID 83404. *Phone:* 208-524-3000 Ext. 3337. *Toll-free phone:* 800-662-0261. *Fax:* 208-524-0429. *E-mail:* Jessica.dixon@my.eitc.edu.

Website: http://www.eitc.edu/.

ITT Technical Institute

Boise, Idaho

- **Proprietary** primarily 2-year, founded 1906, part of ITT Educational Services, Inc.
- **Urban** campus
- **Coed**

Majors Computer programming (specific applications); construction management; cyber/computer forensics and counterterrorism; drafting and design technology; electrical, electronic and communications engineering technology; forensic science and technology; industrial technology; information technology project management; network and system administration; project management; registered nursing/registered nurse.

Academics *Calendar:* quarters. *Degrees:* associate and bachelor's.

Student Life *Housing:* college housing not available.

Financial Aid Of all full-time matriculated undergraduates who enrolled in 2012, 9 Federal Work-Study jobs (averaging $5500).

Freshman Application Contact Director of Recruitment, ITT Technical Institute, 12302 West Explorer Drive, Boise, ID 83713. *Phone:* 208-322-8844. *Toll-free phone:* 800-666-4888.

Website: http://www.itt-tech.edu/.

North Idaho College

Coeur d'Alene, Idaho

Freshman Application Contact North Idaho College, 1000 West Garden Avenue, Coeur d Alene, ID 83814-2199. *Phone:* 208-769-3303. *Toll-free phone:* 877-404-4536 Ext. 3311. *E-mail:* admit@nic.edu.

Website: http://www.nic.edu/.

ILLINOIS

Black Hawk College

Moline, Illinois

Freshman Application Contact Ms. Vashti Berry, College Recruiter, Black Hawk College, 6600-34th Avenue, Moline, IL 61265. *Phone:* 309-796-5341. *Toll-free phone:* 800-334-1311. *E-mail:* berryv@bhc.edu.

Website: http://www.bhc.edu/.

Carl Sandburg College

Galesburg, Illinois

Director of Admissions Ms. Carol Kreider, Dean of Student Support Services, Carl Sandburg College, 2400 Tom L. Wilson Boulevard, Galesburg, IL 61401-9576. *Phone:* 309-341-5234.

Website: http://www.sandburg.edu/.

City Colleges of Chicago, Harold Washington College

Chicago, Illinois

Freshman Application Contact Admissions Office, City Colleges of Chicago, Harold Washington College, 30 East Lake Street, Chicago, IL 60601-2449. *Phone:* 312-553-6010.

Website: http://hwashington.ccc.edu/.

City Colleges of Chicago, Harry S. Truman College

Chicago, Illinois

Freshman Application Contact City Colleges of Chicago, Harry S. Truman College, 1145 West Wilson Avenue, Chicago, IL 60640-5616. *Phone:* 773-907-4000 Ext. 1112.

Website: http://www.trumancollege.edu/.

City Colleges of Chicago, Kennedy-King College

Chicago, Illinois

Freshman Application Contact Admissions Office, City Colleges of Chicago, Kennedy-King College, 6301 South Halstead Street, Chicago, IL 60621. *Phone:* 773-602-5062. *Fax:* 773-602-5055.

Website: http://kennedyking.ccc.edu/.

City Colleges of Chicago, Malcolm X College

Chicago, Illinois

Freshman Application Contact Ms. Kimberly Hollingsworth, Dean of Student Services, City Colleges of Chicago, Malcolm X College, 1900 West Van Buren Street, Chicago, IL 60612-3145. *Phone:* 312-850-7120. *Fax:* 312-850-7119. *E-mail:* khollingsworth@ccc.edu.

Website: http://malcolmx.ccc.edu/.

City Colleges of Chicago, Olive-Harvey College

Chicago, Illinois

Freshman Application Contact City Colleges of Chicago, Olive-Harvey College, 10001 South Woodlawn Avenue, Chicago, IL 60628-1645. *Phone:* 773-291-6362.

Website: http://oliveharvey.ccc.edu/.

City Colleges of Chicago, Richard J. Daley College

Chicago, Illinois

Freshman Application Contact City Colleges of Chicago, Richard J. Daley College, 7500 South Pulaski Road, Chicago, IL 60652-1242. *Phone:* 773-838-7606.

Website: http://daley.ccc.edu/.

City Colleges of Chicago, Wilbur Wright College

Chicago, Illinois

Freshman Application Contact Ms. Amy Aiello, Assistant Dean of Student Services, City Colleges of Chicago, Wilbur Wright College, Chicago, IL 60634. *Phone:* 773-481-8207. *Fax:* 773-481-8185. *E-mail:* aaiello@ccc.edu.

Website: http://wright.ccc.edu/.

College of DuPage

Glen Ellyn, Illinois

Freshman Application Contact College of DuPage, IL. *E-mail:* admissions@cod.edu.

Website: http://www.cod.edu/.

College of Lake County

Grayslake, Illinois

- **District-supported** 2-year, founded 1967, part of Illinois Community College Board
- **Suburban** 226-acre campus with easy access to Chicago, Milwaukee
- **Coed**

Undergraduates 4,945 full-time, 12,632 part-time. Students come from 42 other countries; 1% are from out of state; 9% Black or African American, non-Hispanic/Latino; 29% Hispanic/Latino; 5% Asian, non-Hispanic/Latino; 0.1% Native Hawaiian or other Pacific Islander, non-Hispanic/Latino; 0.2% American Indian or Alaska Native, non-Hispanic/Latino; 1% Two or more races, non-Hispanic/Latino; 7% Race/ethnicity unknown.

Faculty *Student/faculty ratio:* 17:1.

Academics *Calendar:* semesters. *Degree:* certificates and associate. *Special study options:* academic remediation for entering students, adult/continuing education programs, advanced placement credit, cooperative education, distance learning, double majors, English as a second language, honors programs, independent study, internships, off-campus study, part-time degree program, services for LD students, student-designed majors, study abroad, summer session for credit.

Student Life *Campus security:* 24-hour emergency response devices and patrols, late-night transport/escort service.

Athletics Member NJCAA.

Costs (2013–14) *Tuition:* area resident $2790 full-time, $93 per credit hour part-time; state resident $7200 full-time, $240 per credit hour part-time; nonresident $9705 full-time, $324 per credit hour part-time. *Required fees:* $570 full-time, $19 per credit hour part-time.

Financial Aid Of all full-time matriculated undergraduates who enrolled in 2012, 98 Federal Work-Study jobs (averaging $1311).

Applying *Options:* electronic application, early admission, deferred entrance. *Required for some:* high school transcript, interview.

Freshman Application Contact Director, Student Recruitment, College of Lake County, Grayslake, IL 60030-1198. *Phone:* 847-543-2383. *Fax:* 847-543-3061.

Website: http://www.clcillinois.edu/.

Danville Area Community College
Danville, Illinois

- **State and locally supported** 2-year, founded 1946, part of Illinois Community College Board
- **Small-town** 50-acre campus
- **Coed,** 4,031 undergraduate students, 29% full-time, 55% women, 45% men

Undergraduates 1,175 full-time, 2,856 part-time. 13% Black or African American, non-Hispanic/Latino; 4% Hispanic/Latino; 1% Asian, non-Hispanic/Latino; 0.2% Native Hawaiian or other Pacific Islander, non-Hispanic/Latino; 0.3% American Indian or Alaska Native, non-Hispanic/Latino; 8% Race/ethnicity unknown; 3% transferred in.

Freshmen *Admission:* 653 enrolled.

Faculty *Total:* 177, 38% full-time, 7% with terminal degrees.

Majors Accounting technology and bookkeeping; agricultural business and management; automobile/automotive mechanics technology; business automation/technology/data entry; CAD/CADD drafting/design technology; child-care provision; computer programming (specific applications); computer systems networking and telecommunications; corrections; criminal justice/police science; electrician; energy management and systems technology; engineering; executive assistant/executive secretary; fire science/firefighting; floriculture/floristry management; general studies; health information/medical records technology; industrial electronics technology; industrial mechanics and maintenance technology; juvenile corrections; landscaping and groundskeeping; liberal arts and sciences/liberal studies; manufacturing engineering technology; medical administrative assistant and medical secretary; radiologic technology/science; registered nursing/registered nurse; selling skills and sales; teacher assistant/aide; turf and turfgrass management.

Academics *Calendar:* semesters. *Degree:* certificates and associate. *Special study options:* academic remediation for entering students, adult/continuing education programs, advanced placement credit, cooperative education, distance learning, double majors, English as a second language, independent study, internships, part-time degree program, services for LD students, summer session for credit.

Library Library with 50,000 titles, 2,487 audiovisual materials, an OPAC.

Student Life *Housing:* college housing not available. *Activities and Organizations:* drama/theater group, choral group. *Campus security:* 24-hour emergency response devices and patrols. *Student services:* personal/psychological counseling.

Athletics Member NJCAA. *Intercollegiate sports:* baseball M(s), basketball M(s)/W(s), cheerleading W, cross-country running M(s)/W(s), softball W(s).

Costs (2013–14) *Tuition:* area resident $3240 full-time, $108 per credit hour part-time; state resident $5700 full-time, $190 per credit hour part-time; nonresident $5700 full-time, $190 per credit hour part-time. Full-time tuition and fees vary according to program. Part-time tuition and fees vary according to program. *Required fees:* $360 full-time, $12 per credit hour part-time. *Payment plan:* installment. *Waivers:* senior citizens and employees or children of employees.

Financial Aid Of all full-time matriculated undergraduates who enrolled in 2011, 60 Federal Work-Study jobs (averaging $3000). 100 state and other part-time jobs (averaging $3000).

Applying *Options:* early admission, deferred entrance. *Required:* high school transcript. *Application deadlines:* rolling (freshmen), rolling (transfers).

Freshman Application Contact Danville Area Community College, 2000 East Main Street, Danville, IL 61832-5199. *Phone:* 217-443-8803. *Website:* http://www.dacc.edu/.

Elgin Community College
Elgin, Illinois

- **State and locally supported** 2-year, founded 1949, part of Illinois Community College Board
- **Suburban** 145-acre campus with easy access to Chicago
- **Coed,** 11,285 undergraduate students, 33% full-time, 55% women, 45% men

Undergraduates 3,780 full-time, 7,505 part-time. Students come from 4 states and territories; 15 other countries; 0.2% are from out of state; 5% Black or African American, non-Hispanic/Latino; 37% Hispanic/Latino; 6% Asian, non-Hispanic/Latino; 0.1% Native Hawaiian or other Pacific Islander, non-Hispanic/Latino; 0.2% American Indian or Alaska Native, non-Hispanic/Latino; 2% Two or more races, non-Hispanic/Latino; 3% Race/ethnicity unknown; 0.4% international; 4% transferred in. *Retention:* 77% of full-time freshmen returned.

Freshmen *Admission:* 1,357 enrolled.

Faculty *Total:* 598, 22% full-time, 13% with terminal degrees. *Student/faculty ratio:* 23:1.

Majors Accounting; administrative assistant and secretarial science; animation, interactive technology, video graphics and special effects; automobile/automotive mechanics technology; baking and pastry arts; biological and physical sciences; biology/biotechnology laboratory technician; business administration and management; CAD/CADD drafting/design technology; clinical/medical laboratory technology; computer and information systems security; criminal justice/police science; culinary arts; data entry/microcomputer applications; design and visual communications; engineering; entrepreneurship; executive assistant/executive secretary; fine/studio arts; fire science/firefighting; graphic design; health and physical education/fitness; heating, air conditioning, ventilation and refrigeration maintenance technology; industrial mechanics and maintenance technology; legal assistant/paralegal; liberal arts and sciences/liberal studies; machine tool technology; marketing/marketing management; music; physical therapy technology; radiologic technology/science; registered nursing/registered nurse; restaurant, culinary, and catering management; retailing; social work.

Academics *Calendar:* semesters. *Degree:* certificates, diplomas, and associate. *Special study options:* academic remediation for entering students, accelerated degree program, advanced placement credit, cooperative education, distance learning, double majors, English as a second language, honors programs, independent study, internships, off-campus study, part-time degree program, services for LD students, study abroad, summer session for credit.

Library Renner Learning Resource Center with an OPAC, a Web page.

Student Life *Housing:* college housing not available. *Activities and Organizations:* drama/theater group, student-run newspaper, choral group, Phi Theta Kappa Honor Society, Organization of Latin American Students, Asian Filipino Club, Amnesty International, student government. *Campus security:* grounds are patrolled Sunday-Saturday 7am-11pm during the academic year. *Student services:* personal/psychological counseling, legal services.

Athletics Member NJCAA. *Intercollegiate sports:* baseball M(s), basketball M(s)/W(s), cross-country running M(s)/W(s), golf M(s), soccer M(s)/W(s), softball W(s), tennis M(s)/W(s), volleyball W(s).

Applying *Options:* electronic application. *Required for some:* high school transcript, some academic programs have additional departmental admission requirements that students must meet. *Application deadlines:* rolling (freshmen), rolling (transfers). *Notification:* continuous (freshmen), continuous (transfers).

Freshman Application Contact Admissions, Recruitment, and Student Life, Elgin Community College, 1700 Spartan Drive, Elgin, IL 60123. *Phone:* 847-214-7414. *E-mail:* admissions@elgin.edu. *Website:* http://www.elgin.edu/.

Fox College
Bedford Park, Illinois

- **Private** 2-year, founded 1932
- **Suburban** campus
- **Coed,** 400 undergraduate students
- 65% of applicants were admitted

Freshmen *Admission:* 977 applied, 634 admitted.

Majors Accounting technology and bookkeeping; administrative assistant and secretarial science; graphic design; medical/clinical assistant; physical therapy technology; veterinary/animal health technology.

Academics *Degree:* diplomas and associate. *Special study options:* accelerated degree program, internships.

Student Life *Housing:* college housing not available.

Freshman Application Contact Admissions Office, Fox College, 6640 South Cicero, Bedford Park, IL 60638. *Phone:* 708-444-4500. *Website:* http://www.foxcollege.edu/.

Gem City College
Quincy, Illinois

Director of Admissions Admissions Director, Gem City College, PO Box 179, Quincy, IL 62301. *Phone:* 217-222-0391. *Website:* http://www.gemcitycollege.com/.

Harper College
Palatine, Illinois

- **State and locally supported** 2-year, founded 1965, part of Illinois Community College Board
- **Suburban** 200-acre campus with easy access to Chicago
- **Endowment** $4.0 million
- **Coed,** 14,827 undergraduate students, 37% full-time, 55% women, 45% men

Undergraduates 5,534 full-time, 9,293 part-time. Students come from 9 states and territories; 1% are from out of state; 5% Black or African American, non-Hispanic/Latino; 21% Hispanic/Latino; 10% Asian, non-Hispanic/Latino; 0.2% American Indian or Alaska Native, non-Hispanic/Latino; 6% Race/ethnicity unknown; 4% transferred in. *Retention:* 67% of full-time freshmen returned.

Freshmen *Admission:* 3,739 applied, 3,739 admitted, 2,183 enrolled. *Test scores:* ACT scores over 18: 73%; ACT scores over 24: 22%; ACT scores over 30: 3%.

Faculty *Total:* 827, 25% full-time. *Student/faculty ratio:* 19:1.

Majors Accounting; administrative assistant and secretarial science; architectural drafting and CAD/CADD; architectural engineering technology; art; banking and financial support services; biology/biological sciences; business administration and management; cardiovascular technology; chemistry; child-care provision; computer and information sciences; computer programming; computer programming (specific applications); computer science; criminal justice/law enforcement administration; cyber/computer forensics and counterterrorism; dental hygiene; diagnostic medical sonography and ultrasound technology; dietetics; dietetic technology; early childhood education; electrical, electronic and communications engineering technology; elementary education; emergency medical technology (EMT paramedic); engineering; English; environmental studies; fashion and fabric consulting; fashion/apparel design; fashion merchandising; finance; fine/studio arts; fire science/firefighting; food service systems administration; health teacher education; heating, air conditioning, ventilation and refrigeration maintenance technology; history; homeland security; hospitality administration; humanities; human services; interior design; international business/trade/commerce; legal administrative assistant/secretary; legal assistant/paralegal; liberal arts and sciences/liberal studies; marketing/marketing management; mathematics; medical administrative assistant and medical secretary; medical/clinical assistant; music; nanotechnology; philosophy; physical education teaching and coaching; physical sciences; psychology; public relations, advertising, and applied communication related; radiologic technology/science; registered nursing/registered nurse; sales, distribution, and marketing operations; small business administration; sociology and anthropology; speech communication and rhetoric; theater/theater arts management; web page, digital/multimedia and information resources design.

Academics *Calendar:* semesters. *Degree:* certificates and associate. *Special study options:* academic remediation for entering students, accelerated degree program, adult/continuing education programs, advanced placement credit, cooperative education, distance learning, English as a second language, honors programs, independent study, internships, part-time degree program, services for LD students, study abroad, summer session for credit.

Library Harper College Library with 128,068 titles, 242 serial subscriptions, 17,540 audiovisual materials, an OPAC, a Web page.

Student Life *Housing:* college housing not available. *Activities and Organizations:* drama/theater group, student-run newspaper, radio station, choral group, Student Radio Station, Program Board, Student Senate, Nursing Club, Phi Theta Kappa. *Campus security:* 24-hour emergency response devices and patrols, late-night transport/escort service. *Student services:* health clinic, personal/psychological counseling, women's center, legal services.

Athletics Member NJCAA. *Intercollegiate sports:* baseball M, basketball M/W, cross-country running M/W, soccer M/W, softball W, track and field M/W, volleyball W, wrestling M. *Intramural sports:* baseball M, basketball M, football M, racquetball M/W, softball M/W, table tennis M/W, tennis M/W, volleyball M/W.

Costs (2014–15) *Tuition:* area resident $3308 full-time, $110 per credit hour part-time; state resident $11,018 full-time, $367 per credit hour part-time; nonresident $13,283 full-time, $443 per credit hour part-time. Full-time tuition and fees vary according to course load and program. Part-time tuition and fees vary according to course load and program. No tuition increase for student's term of enrollment. *Payment plans:* installment, deferred payment. *Waivers:* senior citizens and employees or children of employees.

Financial Aid Of all full-time matriculated undergraduates who enrolled in 2012, 85 Federal Work-Study jobs (averaging $1210).

Applying *Options:* electronic application, early admission, deferred entrance. *Application fee:* $25. *Required:* high school transcript. *Application deadlines:* rolling (freshmen), rolling (transfers). *Notification:* continuous (freshmen), continuous (transfers).

Freshman Application Contact Admissions Office, Harper College, 1200 West Algonquin Road, Palatine, IL 60067. *Phone:* 847-925-6700. *Fax:* 847-925-6044. *E-mail:* admissions@harpercollege.edu.

Website: http://goforward.harpercollege.edu/.

Heartland Community College

Normal, Illinois

Freshman Application Contact Ms. Candace Brownlee, Director of Student Recruitment, Heartland Community College, 1500 West Raab Road, Normal, IL 61761. *Phone:* 309-268-8041. *Fax:* 309-268-7992. *E-mail:* candace.brownlee@heartland.edu.

Website: http://www.heartland.edu/.

Highland Community College

Freeport, Illinois

- **State and locally supported** 2-year, founded 1962, part of Illinois Community College Board
- **Rural** 240-acre campus
- **Coed**, 2,031 undergraduate students, 52% full-time, 61% women, 39% men

Undergraduates 1,050 full-time, 981 part-time. 3% are from out of state; 10% Black or African American, non-Hispanic/Latino; 3% Hispanic/Latino; 0.9% Asian, non-Hispanic/Latino; 2% American Indian or Alaska Native, non-Hispanic/Latino; 3% Two or more races, non-Hispanic/Latino; 2% Race/ethnicity unknown; 4% transferred in.

Freshmen *Admission:* 723 applied, 723 admitted, 423 enrolled.

Faculty *Total:* 147, 31% full-time, 5% with terminal degrees. *Student/faculty ratio:* 17:1.

Majors Accounting; agricultural business and management; autobody/collision and repair technology; automobile/automotive mechanics technology; biological and physical sciences; child-care provision; early childhood education; emergency medical technology (EMT paramedic); engineering; general studies; graphic design; health information/medical records technology; heavy equipment maintenance technology; horse husbandry/equine science and management; industrial technology; information technology; liberal arts and sciences/liberal studies; mathematics teacher education; medical/clinical assistant; registered nursing/registered nurse; special education; teacher assistant/aide.

Academics *Calendar:* semesters. *Degree:* certificates and associate. *Special study options:* academic remediation for entering students, adult/continuing education programs, advanced placement credit, cooperative education, distance learning, English as a second language, external degree program, honors programs, independent study, internships, part-time degree program, services for LD students, student-designed majors, summer session for credit.

Library Clarence Mitchell Libarary with 1.0 million titles, 90 serial subscriptions, 6,181 audiovisual materials, an OPAC, a Web page.

Student Life *Housing:* college housing not available. *Activities and Organizations:* drama/theater group, student-run newspaper, radio station, choral group, Phi Theta Kappa, Royal Scots, Prairie Wind, intramurals, Collegiate Choir. *Campus security:* 24-hour emergency response devices and patrols. *Student services:* personal/psychological counseling.

Athletics Member NJCAA. *Intercollegiate sports:* baseball M(s), basketball M(s)/W(s), bowling M(s)/W(s), golf M(s)/W(s), softball W(s), volleyball W(s). *Intramural sports:* basketball M/W, volleyball M/W.

Costs (2013–14) *Tuition:* area resident $3450 full-time, $115 per credit hour part-time; state resident $5100 full-time, $170 per credit hour part-time; nonresident $5790 full-time, $193 per credit hour part-time. Full-time tuition and fees vary according to program and reciprocity agreements. Part-time tuition and fees vary according to program and reciprocity agreements. *Required fees:* $510 full-time, $16 per credit hour part-time, $15 per term part-time. *Payment plans:* installment, deferred payment. *Waivers:* minority students, senior citizens, and employees or children of employees.

Financial Aid Of all full-time matriculated undergraduates who enrolled in 2012, 849 applied for aid, 768 were judged to have need. 44 Federal Work-Study jobs (averaging $1880). In 2012, 25 non-need-based awards were made. *Average percent of need met:* 41%. *Average financial aid package:* $6524. *Average need-based loan:* $3219. *Average need-based gift aid:* $6042. *Average non-need-based aid:* $3609.

Applying *Options:* electronic application, early admission, deferred entrance. *Required for some:* high school transcript, 1 letter of recommendation. *Recommended:* high school transcript. *Application deadlines:* rolling (freshmen), rolling (transfers).

Freshman Application Contact Mr. Jeremy Bradt, Director, Enrollment and Records, Highland Community College, 2998 West Pearl City Road, Freeport, IL 61032. *Phone:* 815-235-6121 Ext. 3500. *Fax:* 815-235-6130. *E-mail:* jeremy.bradt@highland.edu.

Website: http://www.highland.edu/.

Illinois Central College

East Peoria, Illinois

- **State and locally supported** 2-year, founded 1967, part of Illinois Community College Board
- **Suburban** 430-acre campus
- **Coed**

Undergraduates 4,123 full-time, 7,002 part-time. Students come from 4 other countries; 1% are from out of state; 12% Black or African American, non-Hispanic/Latino; 4% Hispanic/Latino; 2% Asian, non-Hispanic/Latino; 0.1% Native Hawaiian or other Pacific Islander, non-Hispanic/Latino; 0.3% American Indian or Alaska Native, non-Hispanic/Latino; 3% Two or more races, non-Hispanic/Latino; 4% Race/ethnicity unknown; 2% transferred in. *Retention:* 59% of full-time freshmen returned.

Faculty *Student/faculty ratio:* 18:1.
Academics *Calendar:* semesters. *Degree:* certificates and associate. *Special study options:* academic remediation for entering students, adult/continuing education programs, advanced placement credit, English as a second language, honors programs, independent study, internships, part-time degree program, services for LD students, summer session for credit.
Student Life *Campus security:* 24-hour emergency response devices and patrols, late-night transport/escort service.
Athletics Member NJCAA.
Costs (2013–14) *Tuition:* area resident $2760 full-time, $115 per credit hour part-time; state resident $6120 full-time, $255 per credit hour part-time; nonresident $6120 full-time, $255 per credit hour part-time. Full-time tuition and fees vary according to course load. Part-time tuition and fees vary according to course load. *Room and board:* Room and board charges vary according to housing facility.
Financial Aid Of all full-time matriculated undergraduates who enrolled in 2011, 6,521 applied for aid, 5,525 were judged to have need.
Applying *Options:* electronic application, early admission. *Required:* high school transcript.
Freshman Application Contact Angela Dreessen, Illinois Central College, East Peoria, IL. *Phone:* 309-694-5353.
Website: http://www.icc.edu/.

Illinois Eastern Community Colleges, Frontier Community College
Fairfield, Illinois

- **State and locally supported** 2-year, founded 1976, part of Illinois Eastern Community College System
- **Rural** 8-acre campus
- **Coed,** 2,194 undergraduate students, 10% full-time, 65% women, 35% men

Undergraduates 226 full-time, 1,968 part-time. 1% are from out of state; 0.4% Black or African American, non-Hispanic/Latino; 0.8% Hispanic/Latino; 0.3% Asian, non-Hispanic/Latino; 0.2% American Indian or Alaska Native, non-Hispanic/Latino; 0.1% Race/ethnicity unknown.
Freshmen *Admission:* 96 enrolled.
Faculty *Total:* 203, 3% full-time. *Student/faculty ratio:* 21:1.
Majors Automobile/automotive mechanics technology; biological and physical sciences; business automation/technology/data entry; construction trades; corrections; emergency care attendant (EMT ambulance); engineering; executive assistant/executive secretary; fire science/firefighting; general studies; health information/medical records technology; liberal arts and sciences/liberal studies; quality control technology; registered nursing/registered nurse.
Academics *Calendar:* semesters. *Degree:* certificates and associate. *Special study options:* academic remediation for entering students, adult/continuing education programs, advanced placement credit, cooperative education, distance learning, double majors, English as a second language, external degree program, independent study, part-time degree program, services for LD students, student-designed majors, summer session for credit.
Library Learning Resource Center plus 1 other with 15,318 titles, 919 audiovisual materials.
Student Life *Housing:* college housing not available.
Costs (2014–15) *Tuition:* area resident $2464 full-time, $77 per semester hour part-time; state resident $8383 full-time, $262 per semester hour part-time; nonresident $10,321 full-time, $323 per semester hour part-time. *Required fees:* $490 full-time, $15 per semester hour part-time, $5 per term part-time. *Payment plan:* installment. *Waivers:* senior citizens and employees or children of employees.
Applying *Options:* early admission, deferred entrance. *Required:* high school transcript. *Application deadlines:* rolling (freshmen), rolling (transfers). *Notification:* continuous (freshmen), continuous (transfers).
Freshman Application Contact Ms. Mary Johnston, Coordinator of Registration and Records, Illinois Eastern Community Colleges, Frontier Community College, Frontier Drive, Fairfield, IL 62837. *Phone:* 618-842-3711 Ext. 4111. *Fax:* 618-842-6340. *E-mail:* johnstonm@iecc.edu.
Website: http://www.iecc.edu/fcc/.

Illinois Eastern Community Colleges, Lincoln Trail College
Robinson, Illinois

- **State and locally supported** 2-year, founded 1969, part of Illinois Eastern Community College System
- **Rural** 120-acre campus
- **Coed,** 972 undergraduate students, 43% full-time, 58% women, 42% men

Undergraduates 421 full-time, 551 part-time. 3% are from out of state; 2% Black or African American, non-Hispanic/Latino; 0.9% Hispanic/Latino; 2%

Asian, non-Hispanic/Latino; 0.1% American Indian or Alaska Native, non-Hispanic/Latino; 0.1% Race/ethnicity unknown.
Freshmen *Admission:* 174 enrolled.
Faculty *Total:* 82, 21% full-time. *Student/faculty ratio:* 17:1.
Majors Biological and physical sciences; business automation/technology/data entry; computer systems networking and telecommunications; construction trades; corrections; general studies; health information/medical records administration; liberal arts and sciences/liberal studies; mechanical engineering/mechanical technology; quality control technology; teacher assistant/aide; telecommunications technology.
Academics *Calendar:* semesters. *Degree:* certificates and associate. *Special study options:* academic remediation for entering students, adult/continuing education programs, advanced placement credit, cooperative education, distance learning, double majors, English as a second language, external degree program, independent study, internships, part-time degree program, services for LD students, student-designed majors, summer session for credit.
Library Eagleton Learning Resource Center plus 1 other with 15,393 titles, 622 audiovisual materials.
Student Life *Housing:* college housing not available. *Activities and Organizations:* drama/theater group, choral group, national fraternities.
Athletics Member NJCAA. *Intercollegiate sports:* baseball M(s), basketball M(s)/W(s), softball W(s). *Intramural sports:* baseball M, basketball M, softball W.
Costs (2014–15) *Tuition:* area resident $2464 full-time, $77 per semester hour part-time; state resident $8383 full-time, $262 per semester hour part-time; nonresident $10,321 full-time, $323 per semester hour part-time. *Required fees:* $490 full-time, $15 per semester hour part-time, $5 per term part-time. *Payment plan:* installment. *Waivers:* senior citizens and employees or children of employees.
Applying *Options:* early admission, deferred entrance. *Required:* high school transcript. *Application deadlines:* rolling (freshmen), rolling (transfers). *Notification:* continuous (freshmen), continuous (transfers).
Freshman Application Contact Ms. Becky Mikeworth, Director of Admissions, Illinois Eastern Community Colleges, Lincoln Trail College, 11220 State Highway 1, Robinson, IL 62454. *Phone:* 618-544-8657 Ext. 1137. *Fax:* 618-544-7423. *E-mail:* mikeworthb@iecc.edu.
Website: http://www.iecc.edu/ltc/.

Illinois Eastern Community Colleges, Olney Central College
Olney, Illinois

- **State and locally supported** 2-year, founded 1962, part of Illinois Eastern Community College System
- **Rural** 128-acre campus
- **Coed,** 1,470 undergraduate students, 46% full-time, 65% women, 35% men

Undergraduates 680 full-time, 790 part-time. 2% are from out of state; 1% Black or African American, non-Hispanic/Latino; 1% Hispanic/Latino; 1% Asian, non-Hispanic/Latino; 0.1% Native Hawaiian or other Pacific Islander, non-Hispanic/Latino; 0.2% American Indian or Alaska Native, non-Hispanic/Latino; 0.1% Race/ethnicity unknown.
Freshmen *Admission:* 238 enrolled.
Faculty *Total:* 110, 42% full-time. *Student/faculty ratio:* 15:1.
Majors Accounting; autobody/collision and repair technology; automobile/automotive mechanics technology; biological and physical sciences; business administration and management; business automation/technology/data entry; engineering; general studies; human resources management; industrial mechanics and maintenance technology; information technology; liberal arts and sciences/liberal studies; medical administrative assistant and medical secretary; medical radiologic technology; registered nursing/registered nurse.
Academics *Calendar:* semesters. *Degree:* certificates and associate. *Special study options:* academic remediation for entering students, adult/continuing education programs, advanced placement credit, cooperative education, distance learning, double majors, English as a second language, external degree program, independent study, internships, part-time degree program, services for LD students, student-designed majors, summer session for credit.
Library Anderson Learning Resources Center plus 1 other with 21,990 titles, 907 audiovisual materials.
Student Life *Housing:* college housing not available. *Activities and Organizations:* drama/theater group, student-run newspaper, choral group.
Athletics Member NJCAA. *Intercollegiate sports:* baseball M(s), basketball M(s)/W(s), softball W(s). *Intramural sports:* baseball M, basketball M/W, softball W.
Costs (2014–15) *Tuition:* area resident $2464 full-time, $77 per semester hour part-time; state resident $8383 full-time, $262 per semester hour part-time; nonresident $10,321 full-time, $323 per semester hour part-time. *Required fees:* $490 full-time, $15 per semester hour part-time, $5 per term part-time.

Payment plan: installment. *Waivers:* senior citizens and employees or children of employees.

Applying *Options:* early admission, deferred entrance. *Required:* high school transcript. *Application deadlines:* rolling (freshmen), rolling (transfers). *Notification:* continuous (freshmen), continuous (transfers).

Freshman Application Contact Ms. Chris Webber, Assistant Dean for Student Services, Illinois Eastern Community Colleges, Olney Central College, 305 North West Street, Olney, IL 62450. *Phone:* 618-395-7777 Ext. 2005. *Fax:* 618-392-5212. *E-mail:* webberc@iecc.edu.

Website: http://www.iecc.edu/occ/.

Illinois Eastern Community Colleges, Wabash Valley College

Mount Carmel, Illinois

- **State and locally supported** 2-year, founded 1960, part of Illinois Eastern Community College System
- **Rural** 40-acre campus
- **Coed,** 4,512 undergraduate students, 12% full-time, 35% women, 65% men

Undergraduates 554 full-time, 3,958 part-time. 5% are from out of state; 4% Black or African American, non-Hispanic/Latino; 1% Hispanic/Latino; 0.9% Asian, non-Hispanic/Latino; 0.1% Native Hawaiian or other Pacific Islander, non-Hispanic/Latino; 0.2% American Indian or Alaska Native, non-Hispanic/Latino; 0.1% international.

Freshmen *Admission:* 364 enrolled.

Faculty *Total:* 126, 27% full-time.

Majors Agricultural business and management; agricultural production; biological and physical sciences; business administration and management; business automation/technology/data entry; child development; diesel mechanics technology; energy management and systems technology; engineering; executive assistant/executive secretary; general studies; industrial technology; legal assistant/paralegal; liberal arts and sciences/liberal studies; machine tool technology; manufacturing engineering technology; mining technology; radio and television; social work.

Academics *Calendar:* semesters. *Degree:* certificates and associate. *Special study options:* academic remediation for entering students, adult/continuing education programs, advanced placement credit, cooperative education, distance learning, double majors, English as a second language, external degree program, independent study, internships, part-time degree program, services for LD students, student-designed majors, summer session for credit.

Library Bauer Media Center plus 1 other with 33,749 titles, 1,545 audiovisual materials.

Student Life *Housing:* college housing not available. *Activities and Organizations:* drama/theater group, student-run newspaper, radio and television station, choral group.

Athletics Member NJCAA. *Intercollegiate sports:* baseball M(s), basketball M(s)/W(s), softball W(s). *Intramural sports:* baseball M, basketball M/W, softball W.

Costs (2014–15) *Tuition:* area resident $3464 full-time, $77 per semester hour part-time; state resident $8383 full-time, $262 per semester hour part-time; nonresident $10,321 full-time, $323 per semester hour part-time. *Required fees:* $490 full-time, $15 per semester hour part-time, $5 per term part-time. *Payment plan:* installment. *Waivers:* senior citizens and employees or children of employees.

Applying *Options:* early admission, deferred entrance. *Required:* high school transcript. *Application deadlines:* rolling (freshmen), rolling (transfers). *Notification:* continuous (freshmen), continuous (transfers).

Freshman Application Contact Mrs. Diana Spear, Assistant Dean for Student Services, Illinois Eastern Community Colleges, Wabash Valley College, 2200 College Drive, Mt. Carmel, IL 62863. *Phone:* 618-262-8641 Ext. 3101. *Fax:* 618-262-8641. *E-mail:* speard@iecc.edu.

Website: http://www.iecc.edu/wvc/.

Illinois Valley Community College

Oglesby, Illinois

Freshman Application Contact Mr. Mark Grzybowski, Director of Admissions and Records, Illinois Valley Community College, Oglesby, IL 61348. *Phone:* 815-224-0437. *Fax:* 815-224-3033. *E-mail:* mark_grzybowski@ivcc.edu.

Website: http://www.ivcc.edu/.

ITT Technical Institute

Arlington Heights, Illinois

- **Proprietary** primarily 2-year, founded 1986, part of ITT Educational Services, Inc.
- **Suburban** campus
- **Coed**

Majors Business administration and management; construction management; cyber/computer forensics and counterterrorism; drafting and design technology; electrical, electronic and communications engineering technology; forensic science and technology; graphic communications; information technology project management; network and system administration; project management.

Academics *Calendar:* quarters. *Degrees:* associate and bachelor's.

Student Life *Housing:* college housing not available.

Freshman Application Contact Director of Recruitment, ITT Technical Institute, 3800 N. Wilke Road, Arlington Heights, IL 60004. *Phone:* 847-454-1800.

Website: http://www.itt-tech.edu/.

ITT Technical Institute

Oak Brook, Illinois

- **Proprietary** primarily 2-year, founded 1998, part of ITT Educational Services, Inc.
- **Coed**

Majors Business administration and management; construction management; cyber/computer forensics and counterterrorism; drafting and design technology; electrical, electronic and communications engineering technology; forensic science and technology; information technology project management; network and system administration; project management.

Academics *Calendar:* quarters. *Degrees:* associate and bachelor's.

Student Life *Housing:* college housing not available.

Freshman Application Contact Director of Recruitment, ITT Technical Institute, 800 Jorie Boulevard, Suite 100, Oak Brook, IL 60523. *Phone:* 630-472-7000. *Toll-free phone:* 877-488-0001.

Website: http://www.itt-tech.edu/.

ITT Technical Institute

Orland Park, Illinois

- **Proprietary** primarily 2-year, founded 1993, part of ITT Educational Services, Inc.
- **Suburban** campus
- **Coed**

Majors Business administration and management; construction management; cyber/computer forensics and counterterrorism; electrical, electronic and communications engineering technology; forensic science and technology; information technology project management; network and system administration; project management; registered nursing/registered nurse; system, networking, and LAN/WAN management.

Academics *Calendar:* quarters. *Degrees:* associate and bachelor's.

Student Life *Housing:* college housing not available.

Financial Aid Of all full-time matriculated undergraduates who enrolled in 2012, 6 Federal Work-Study jobs (averaging $4000).

Freshman Application Contact Director of Recruitment, ITT Technical Institute, 11551 184th Place, Orland Park, IL 60467. *Phone:* 708-326-3200.

Website: http://www.itt-tech.edu/.

John A. Logan College

Carterville, Illinois

Director of Admissions Mr. Terry Crain, Dean of Student Services, John A. Logan College, 700 Logan College Road, Carterville, IL 62918-9900. *Phone:* 618-985-3741 Ext. 8382. *Fax:* 618-985-4433. *E-mail:* terrycrain@jalc.edu.

Website: http://www.jalc.edu/.

John Wood Community College

Quincy, Illinois

Freshman Application Contact Mr. Lee Wibbell, Director of Admissions, John Wood Community College, Quincy, IL 62305-8736. *Phone:* 217-641-4339. *Fax:* 217-224-4208. *E-mail:* admissions@jwcc.edu.

Website: http://www.jwcc.edu/.

Joliet Junior College

Joliet, Illinois

Freshman Application Contact Ms. Jennifer Kloberdanz, Director of Admissions and Recruitment, Joliet Junior College, 1215 Houbolt Road, Joliet, IL 60431. *Phone:* 815-729-9020 Ext. 2414. *E-mail:* admission@jjc.edu. *Website:* http://www.jjc.edu/.

Kankakee Community College

Kankakee, Illinois

- **State and locally supported** 2-year, founded 1966, part of Illinois Community College Board
- **Small-town** 178-acre campus with easy access to Chicago
- **Endowment** $5.3 million
- **Coed,** 3,825 undergraduate students, 42% full-time, 62% women, 38% men

Undergraduates 1,599 full-time, 2,226 part-time. Students come from 8 states and territories; 10 other countries; 1% are from out of state; 14% Black or African American, non-Hispanic/Latino; 8% Hispanic/Latino; 0.8% Asian, non-Hispanic/Latino; 0.1% Native Hawaiian or other Pacific Islander, non-Hispanic/Latino; 0.6% American Indian or Alaska Native, non-Hispanic/Latino; 0.4% Two or more races, non-Hispanic/Latino; 2% Race/ethnicity unknown; 0.1% international; 25% transferred in. *Retention:* 69% of full-time freshmen returned.

Freshmen *Admission:* 1,734 applied, 383 enrolled. *Average high school GPA:* 3.14.

Faculty *Total:* 282, 26% full-time, 5% with terminal degrees. *Student/faculty ratio:* 15:1.

Majors Administrative assistant and secretarial science; agriculture; applied horticulture/horticulture operations; art; automobile/automotive mechanics technology; biology/biological sciences; business administration and management; chemistry; clinical/medical laboratory technology; construction management; criminal justice/law enforcement administration; criminal justice/police science; desktop publishing and digital imaging design; drafting and design technology; early childhood education; education; elementary education; emergency medical technology (EMT paramedic); engineering; English; general studies; heating, air conditioning, ventilation and refrigeration maintenance technology; history; industrial electronics technology; legal assistant/paralegal; mathematics; mathematics teacher education; medical/clinical assistant; medical office assistant; physical therapy technology; physics; political science and government; psychology; radiologic technology/science; registered nursing/registered nurse; respiratory care therapy; secondary education; sociology; special education; teacher assistant/aide; visual and performing arts; welding technology.

Academics *Calendar:* semesters. *Degrees:* certificates, diplomas, and associate (also offers continuing education program with significant enrollment not reflected in profile). *Special study options:* academic remediation for entering students, advanced placement credit, distance learning, English as a second language, honors programs, independent study, internships, off-campus study, part-time degree program, services for LD students, student-designed majors, study abroad, summer session for credit. *ROTC:* Army (c).

Library Kankakee Community College Learning Resource Center with 35,308 titles, 120 serial subscriptions, 2,299 audiovisual materials, an OPAC, a Web page.

Student Life *Housing:* college housing not available. *Activities and Organizations:* drama/theater group, Phi Theta Kappa, Hort, Student Nursing, Gay Straight Alliance, Student Advisory Council. *Campus security:* 24-hour patrols, late-night transport/escort service.

Athletics Member NJCAA. *Intercollegiate sports:* baseball M(s), basketball M(s)/W(s), soccer M(s), softball W(s), volleyball W(s).

Costs (2014–15) *Tuition:* area resident $2688 full-time; state resident $6165 full-time; nonresident $12,837 full-time. *Required fees:* $312 full-time. *Payment plan:* installment. *Waivers:* senior citizens and employees or children of employees.

Financial Aid Of all full-time matriculated undergraduates who enrolled in 2012, 70 Federal Work-Study jobs (averaging $1100). *Financial aid deadline:* 10/1.

Applying *Options:* electronic application, early admission. *Required:* high school transcript. *Application deadlines:* rolling (freshmen), rolling (out-of-state freshmen), rolling (transfers). *Notification:* continuous (freshmen), continuous (out-of-state freshmen), continuous (transfers).

Freshman Application Contact Mrs. Oshunda Carpenter-Williams, Kankakee Community College, 100 College Drive, Kankakee, IL 60901. *Phone:* 815-802-8513. *Fax:* 815-802-8521. *E-mail:* ocarpenterwilliams@kcc.edu.

Website: http://www.kcc.edu/.

Kaskaskia College

Centralia, Illinois

- **State and locally supported** 2-year, founded 1966, part of Illinois Community College Board
- **Rural** 195-acre campus with easy access to St. Louis
- **Endowment** $6.7 million
- **Coed,** 5,258 undergraduate students, 37% full-time, 59% women, 41% men

Undergraduates 1,952 full-time, 3,306 part-time. Students come from 3 states and territories; 2 other countries; 1% are from out of state; 9% Black or African American, non-Hispanic/Latino; 2% Hispanic/Latino; 0.5% Asian, non-Hispanic/Latino; 0.6% American Indian or Alaska Native, non-Hispanic/Latino; 2% Two or more races, non-Hispanic/Latino; 0.3% Race/ethnicity unknown; 0.2% international; 2% transferred in.

Freshmen *Admission:* 257 applied, 257 admitted, 356 enrolled.

Faculty *Total:* 252, 30% full-time, 7% with terminal degrees. *Student/faculty ratio:* 21:1.

Majors Accounting; agriculture; animal sciences; applied horticulture/horticulture operations; architectural drafting and CAD/CADD; autobody/collision and repair technology; automobile/automotive mechanics technology; biological and physical sciences; business automation/technology/data entry; business/commerce; carpentry; child-care provision; clinical/medical laboratory technology; construction management; cosmetology; criminal justice/law enforcement administration; culinary arts; electrical, electronic and communications engineering technology; emergency medical technology (EMT paramedic); engineering; executive assistant/executive secretary; general studies; health information/medical records technology; industrial mechanics and maintenance technology; information science/studies; juvenile corrections; liberal arts and sciences/liberal studies; mathematics teacher education; music; network and system administration; occupational therapist assistant; physical therapy technology; radiologic technology/science; registered nursing/registered nurse; respiratory care therapy; robotics technology; teacher assistant/aide; veterinary/animal health technology; web/multimedia management and webmaster; welding technology.

Academics *Calendar:* semesters. *Degree:* certificates and associate. *Special study options:* academic remediation for entering students, accelerated degree program, adult/continuing education programs, cooperative education, distance learning, double majors, English as a second language, honors programs, independent study, internships, off-campus study, part-time degree program, services for LD students, study abroad, summer session for credit. *ROTC:* Army (c).

Library Kaskaskia College Library with 17,387 titles, 58 serial subscriptions, 491 audiovisual materials, an OPAC, a Web page.

Student Life *Housing:* college housing not available. *Activities and Organizations:* drama/theater group, student-run newspaper, choral group, Student Nurse Organization, Phi Theta Kappa Organization, Agriculture Club, Student Practical Nurses, B.A.S.I.C. Club. *Campus security:* 24-hour emergency response devices and patrols, late-night transport/escort service. *Student services:* personal/psychological counseling.

Athletics Member NJCAA. *Intercollegiate sports:* baseball M(s), basketball M(s)/W(s), cheerleading M(s)/W(s), cross-country running M(s)/W(s), golf M(s)/W(s), soccer W(s), softball W(s), tennis M(s), volleyball W(s).

Standardized Tests *Recommended:* ACT (for admission).

Costs (2014–15) *Tuition:* area resident $3360 full-time, $105 per contact hour part-time; state resident $6144 full-time, $192 per credit hour part-time; nonresident $12,896 full-time, $403 per credit hour part-time. Full-time tuition and fees vary according to program. Part-time tuition and fees vary according to program. *Required fees:* $480 full-time, $15 per credit hour part-time. *Payment plan:* installment. *Waivers:* senior citizens and employees or children of employees.

Financial Aid Of all full-time matriculated undergraduates who enrolled in 2012, 1,165 applied for aid, 923 were judged to have need, 242 had their need fully met. 59 Federal Work-Study jobs (averaging $2961). 75 state and other part-time jobs (averaging $3884). In 2012, 40 non-need-based awards were made. *Average percent of need met:* 46%. *Average financial aid package:* $4508. *Average need-based gift aid:* $4413. *Average non-need-based aid:* $3807.

Applying *Options:* electronic application, early admission, deferred entrance. *Required:* high school transcript. *Required for some:* interview. *Application deadlines:* rolling (freshmen), rolling (transfers). *Notification:* continuous (freshmen), continuous (transfers).

Freshman Application Contact Jan Ripperda, Manager of Records and Registration, Kaskaskia College, 27210 College Road, Centralia, IL 62801. *Phone:* 618-545-3041. *Toll-free phone:* 800-642-0859. *Fax:* 618-532-1990. *E-mail:* jripperda@kaskaskia.edu.

Website: http://www.kaskaskia.edu/.

Kishwaukee College
Malta, Illinois

Freshman Application Contact Ms. Sally Misciasci, Admission Analyst, Kishwaukee College, 21193 Malta Road, Malta, IL 60150. *Phone:* 815-825-2086 Ext. 400.
Website: http://www.kishwaukeecollege.edu/.

Lake Land College
Mattoon, Illinois

- **State and locally supported** 2-year, founded 1966, part of Illinois Community College Board
- **Rural** 308-acre campus
- **Endowment** $2.7 million
- **Coed,** 6,351 undergraduate students, 44% full-time, 52% women, 48% men

Undergraduates 2,809 full-time, 3,542 part-time. 1% are from out of state; 0.6% transferred in. *Retention:* 89% of full-time freshmen returned.
Freshmen *Admission:* 1,101 enrolled.
Faculty *Total:* 191, 61% full-time, 5% with terminal degrees. *Student/faculty ratio:* 21:1.
Majors Accounting technology and bookkeeping; administrative assistant and secretarial science; agricultural business and management; agricultural mechanization; agricultural production; architectural engineering technology; automobile/automotive mechanics technology; biological and physical sciences; business administration and management; child-care and support services management; civil engineering technology; computer programming (specific applications); computer systems networking and telecommunications; corrections; criminal justice/police science; dental hygiene; desktop publishing and digital imaging design; drafting and design technology; electrical, electronic and communications engineering technology; electromechanical technology; executive assistant/executive secretary; general studies; graphic and printing equipment operation/production; human services; industrial technology; information technology; legal administrative assistant/secretary; liberal arts and sciences/liberal studies; marketing/marketing management; medical administrative assistant and medical secretary; office management; physical therapy technology; printing press operation; radio and television; registered nursing/registered nurse; social work; telecommunications technology.
Academics *Calendar:* semesters. *Degree:* certificates and associate. *Special study options:* academic remediation for entering students, accelerated degree program, adult/continuing education programs, cooperative education, distance learning, English as a second language, external degree program, honors programs, internships, part-time degree program, services for LD students, summer session for credit.
Library Virgil H. Judge Learning Resource Center with 28,000 titles, 225 serial subscriptions, 1,939 audiovisual materials, an OPAC.
Student Life *Housing:* college housing not available. *Activities and Organizations:* student-run newspaper, radio station, choral group, Agriculture Production and Management Club, Cosmetology Club, Agriculture Transfer Club, Phi Theta Kappa, Civil Engineering Technology Club. *Campus security:* 24-hour patrols. *Student services:* personal/psychological counseling.
Athletics Member NJCAA. *Intercollegiate sports:* baseball M(s), basketball M(s)/W(s), cheerleading W, softball W(s), tennis M(s)/W, volleyball W(s). *Intramural sports:* basketball M/W, bowling M/W, golf M/W, soccer M/W, softball M/W, volleyball M/W.
Standardized Tests *Recommended:* ACT (for admission).
Costs (2014–15) *Tuition:* area resident $2775 full-time; state resident $6599 full-time; nonresident $12,400 full-time. *Required fees:* $684 full-time.
Financial Aid Of all full-time matriculated undergraduates who enrolled in 2012, 120 Federal Work-Study jobs (averaging $1400).
Applying *Options:* electronic application, early admission. *Recommended:* high school transcript. *Application deadlines:* rolling (freshmen), rolling (transfers). *Notification:* continuous (freshmen), continuous (transfers).
Freshman Application Contact Mr. Jon VanDyke, Dean of Admission Services, Lake Land College, Mattoon, IL 61938-9366. *Phone:* 217-234-5378. *E-mail:* admissions@lakeland.cc.il.us.
Website: http://www.lakelandcollege.edu/.

Le Cordon Bleu College of Culinary Arts in Chicago
Chicago, Illinois

Freshman Application Contact Mr. Matthew Verratti, Vice President of Admissions and Marketing, Le Cordon Bleu College of Culinary Arts in Chicago, 361 West Chestnut, Chicago, IL 60610. *Phone:* 312-873-2064. *Toll-free phone:* 888-295-7222. *Fax:* 312-798-2903. *E-mail:* mverratti@chicnet.org.
Website: http://www.chefs.edu/chicago/.

Lewis and Clark Community College
Godfrey, Illinois

Freshman Application Contact Lewis and Clark Community College, 5800 Godfrey Road, Godfrey, IL 62035-2466. *Phone:* 618-468-5100. *Toll-free phone:* 800-YES-LCCC.
Website: http://www.lc.edu/.

Lincoln College
Lincoln, Illinois

Director of Admissions Gretchen Bree, Director of Admissions, Lincoln College, 300 Keokuk Street, Lincoln, IL 62656-1699. *Phone:* 217-732-3155 Ext. 256. *Toll-free phone:* 800-569-0558. *E-mail:* gbree@lincolncollege.edu.
Website: http://www.lincolncollege.edu/.

Lincoln Land Community College
Springfield, Illinois

- **District-supported** 2-year, founded 1967, part of Illinois Community College Board
- **Suburban** 441-acre campus
- **Endowment** $3.5 million
- **Coed,** 7,020 undergraduate students, 43% full-time, 58% women, 42% men

Undergraduates 2,985 full-time, 4,035 part-time. Students come from 4 states and territories; 11% Black or African American, non-Hispanic/Latino; 2% Hispanic/Latino; 1% Asian, non-Hispanic/Latino; 0.1% Native Hawaiian or other Pacific Islander, non-Hispanic/Latino; 0.3% American Indian or Alaska Native, non-Hispanic/Latino; 0.6% Two or more races, non-Hispanic/Latino; 3% Race/ethnicity unknown; 3% transferred in. *Retention:* 56% of full-time freshmen returned.
Freshmen *Admission:* 1,418 enrolled. *Test scores:* ACT scores over 18: 57%; ACT scores over 24: 8%; ACT scores over 30: 1%.
Faculty *Total:* 371, 35% full-time, 12% with terminal degrees. *Student/faculty ratio:* 21:1.
Majors Accounting; administrative assistant and secretarial science; agricultural production; airframe mechanics and aircraft maintenance technology; architectural drafting and CAD/CADD; autobody/collision and repair technology; automobile/automotive mechanics technology; aviation/airway management; biological and physical sciences; building/property maintenance; business automation/technology/data entry; business/commerce; child-care provision; computer programming; computer programming (specific applications); computer systems networking and telecommunications; construction engineering technology; criminal justice/police science; culinary arts; early childhood education; electrical, electronic and communications engineering technology; electroneurodiagnostic/electroencephalographic technology; emergency medical technology (EMT paramedic); engineering; fine/studio arts; fire science/firefighting; general studies; graphic design; hospitality administration; industrial electronics technology; industrial technology; landscaping and groundskeeping; legal administrative assistant/secretary; liberal arts and sciences/liberal studies; music; occupational therapist assistant; radiologic technology/science; registered nursing/registered nurse; respiratory care therapy; special education; surgical technology; teacher assistant/aide.
Academics *Calendar:* semesters. *Degree:* certificates and associate. *Special study options:* academic remediation for entering students, accelerated degree program, adult/continuing education programs, advanced placement credit, distance learning, English as a second language, external degree program, honors programs, independent study, internships, off-campus study, part-time degree program, services for LD students, study abroad, summer session for credit.
Library Learning Resource Center with 97,192 titles, 1,111 serial subscriptions, 2,191 audiovisual materials, an OPAC, a Web page.
Student Life *Housing:* college housing not available. *Activities and Organizations:* drama/theater group, student-run newspaper, choral group, Student Government Association, Epicurean Club, Environmental Club, Chemistry Club, Agricultural Club. *Campus security:* 24-hour emergency response devices and patrols, late-night transport/escort service. *Student services:* health clinic, personal/psychological counseling.
Athletics Member NJCAA. *Intercollegiate sports:* baseball M(s), basketball M(s)/W(s), soccer M(s), softball W(s), volleyball W(s).
Costs (2013–14) *Tuition:* area resident $2376 full-time, $99 per credit hour part-time; state resident $4752 full-time, $198 per credit hour part-time; nonresident $7128 full-time, $297 per credit hour part-time. Full-time tuition and fees vary according to program. Part-time tuition and fees vary according to program. *Required fees:* $264 full-time, $11 per credit hour part-time. *Payment plans:* installment, deferred payment. *Waivers:* senior citizens and employees or children of employees.

Applying *Options:* electronic application, early admission, deferred entrance. *Recommended:* high school transcript. *Application deadlines:* rolling (freshmen), rolling (transfers). *Notification:* continuous (freshmen), continuous (transfers).

Freshman Application Contact Mr. Ron Gregoire, Executive Director of Admissions and Records, Lincoln Land Community College, 5250 Shepherd Road, PO Box 19256, Springfield, IL 62794-9256. *Phone:* 217-786-2243. *Toll-free phone:* 800-727-4161. *Fax:* 217-786-2492. *E-mail:* ron.gregoire@llcc.edu.

Website: http://www.llcc.edu/.

MacCormac College

Chicago, Illinois

Director of Admissions Mr. David Grassi, Director of Admissions, MacCormac College, 506 South Wabash Avenue, Chicago, IL 60605-1667. *Phone:* 312-922-1884 Ext. 102.

Website: http://www.maccormac.edu/.

McHenry County College

Crystal Lake, Illinois

- **State and locally supported** 2-year, founded 1967, part of Illinois Community College Board
- **Suburban** 168-acre campus with easy access to Chicago
- **Coed,** 6,976 undergraduate students, 37% full-time, 54% women, 46% men

Undergraduates 2,611 full-time, 4,365 part-time. 1% are from out of state; 2% Black or African American, non-Hispanic/Latino; 12% Hispanic/Latino; 2% Asian, non-Hispanic/Latino; 0.1% Native Hawaiian or other Pacific Islander, non-Hispanic/Latino; 0.3% American Indian or Alaska Native, non-Hispanic/Latino; 2% Two or more races, non-Hispanic/Latino; 6% Race/ethnicity unknown; 0.3% international.

Freshmen *Admission:* 2,630 applied, 2,630 admitted, 762 enrolled. *Average high school GPA:* 2.25.

Faculty *Total:* 400, 24% full-time. *Student/faculty ratio:* 21:1.

Majors Accounting; administrative assistant and secretarial science; animation, interactive technology, video graphics and special effects; applied horticulture/horticulture operations; biological and physical sciences; business administration and management; child-care provision; commercial photography; computer systems networking and telecommunications; construction management; criminal justice/police science; emergency medical technology (EMT paramedic); engineering; fine/studio arts; fire science/firefighting; general studies; health and physical education/fitness; information technology; liberal arts and sciences/liberal studies; music; occupational therapist assistant; operations management; registered nursing/registered nurse; restaurant, culinary, and catering management; robotics technology; selling skills and sales; special education.

Academics *Calendar:* semesters. *Degree:* certificates and associate. *Special study options:* academic remediation for entering students, accelerated degree program, adult/continuing education programs, advanced placement credit, cooperative education, distance learning, English as a second language, honors programs, independent study, internships, part-time degree program, services for LD students, study abroad, summer session for credit.

Library McHenry County College Library with 60,000 titles, 125 serial subscriptions, 5,042 audiovisual materials, an OPAC, a Web page.

Student Life *Housing:* college housing not available. *Activities and Organizations:* drama/theater group, student-run newspaper, radio station, choral group, Phi Theta Kappa, Student Senate, Equality Club, Writer's Block, Latinos Unidos. *Campus security:* 24-hour emergency response devices and patrols, late-night transport/escort service. *Student services:* personal/psychological counseling.

Athletics Member NJCAA. *Intercollegiate sports:* baseball M(s), basketball M(s)/W(s), soccer M(s), softball W(s), tennis M(s)/W(s), volleyball W(s).

Costs (2013–14) *Tuition:* area resident $2790 full-time, $93 per credit hour part-time; state resident $9040 full-time, $301 per credit hour part-time; nonresident $11,136 full-time, $371 per credit hour part-time. Full-time tuition and fees vary according to course load. Part-time tuition and fees vary according to course load. *Required fees:* $284 full-time, $9 per credit hour part-time, $7 per credit hour part-time. *Payment plan:* installment. *Waivers:* senior citizens and employees or children of employees.

Financial Aid Of all full-time matriculated undergraduates who enrolled in 2012, 200 Federal Work-Study jobs (averaging $3700). 130 state and other part-time jobs (averaging $2000).

Applying *Options:* electronic application, early admission, deferred entrance. *Application fee:* $15. *Recommended:* high school transcript. *Application deadlines:* rolling (freshmen), rolling (out-of-state freshmen), rolling (transfers). *Notification:* continuous (freshmen), continuous (out-of-state freshmen), continuous (transfers).

Freshman Application Contact Anne Weaver, New Student Enrollment Specialist, McHenry County College, 8900 US Highway 14, Crystal Lake, IL 60012-2761. *Phone:* 815-455-7782. *E-mail:* admissions@mchenry.edu.

Website: http://www.mchenry.edu/.

Moraine Valley Community College

Palos Hills, Illinois

- **State and locally supported** 2-year, founded 1967, part of Illinois Community College Board
- **Suburban** 294-acre campus with easy access to Chicago
- **Endowment** $13.4 million
- **Coed,** 16,106 undergraduate students, 42% full-time, 52% women, 48% men

Undergraduates 6,764 full-time, 9,342 part-time. Students come from 3 states and territories; 43 other countries; 10% Black or African American, non-Hispanic/Latino; 20% Hispanic/Latino; 2% Asian, non-Hispanic/Latino; 0.3% American Indian or Alaska Native, non-Hispanic/Latino; 1% Two or more races, non-Hispanic/Latino; 9% Race/ethnicity unknown; 1% international; 8% transferred in. *Retention:* 69% of full-time freshmen returned.

Freshmen *Admission:* 2,180 enrolled. *Test scores:* ACT scores over 18: 70%; ACT scores over 24: 17%; ACT scores over 30: 1%.

Faculty *Total:* 795, 26% full-time, 10% with terminal degrees. *Student/faculty ratio:* 25:1.

Majors Administrative assistant and secretarial science; automobile/automotive mechanics technology; baking and pastry arts; biological and physical sciences; business administration and management; business/commerce; child-care provision; computer and information systems security; computer graphics; criminal justice/police science; emergency medical technology (EMT paramedic); fire prevention and safety technology; fire science/firefighting; graphic design; health information/medical records technology; heating, air conditioning, ventilation and refrigeration maintenance technology; hospitality administration; human resources management; industrial electronics technology; instrumentation technology; liberal arts and sciences/liberal studies; management information systems; mathematics teacher education; mechanical engineering/mechanical technology; movement and mind-body therapies and education related; music; parks, recreation and leisure facilities management; radiologic technology/science; registered nursing/registered nurse; respiratory care therapy; restaurant, culinary, and catering management; retailing; science teacher education; small business administration; special education; substance abuse/addiction counseling; surveying technology; system, networking, and LAN/WAN management; teacher assistant/aide; tourism and travel services management; visual and performing arts; web/multimedia management and webmaster.

Academics *Calendar:* semesters. *Degree:* certificates and associate. *Special study options:* academic remediation for entering students, accelerated degree program, adult/continuing education programs, advanced placement credit, cooperative education, distance learning, double majors, English as a second language, honors programs, independent study, internships, off-campus study, part-time degree program, services for LD students, study abroad, summer session for credit.

Library Library with 70,878 titles, 412 serial subscriptions, 8,076 audiovisual materials, an OPAC, a Web page.

Student Life *Housing:* college housing not available. *Activities and Organizations:* drama/theater group, student-run newspaper, choral group, student newspaper, Speech Team, Alliance of Latin American Students, Phi Theta Kappa, Arab Student Union. *Campus security:* 24-hour emergency response devices and patrols, late-night transport/escort service, safety and security programs. *Student services:* personal/psychological counseling, women's center.

Athletics Member NJCAA. *Intercollegiate sports:* baseball M(s), basketball M(s)/W(s), cross-country running M(s)/W(s), golf M(s), soccer M(s)/W(s), softball W(s), tennis M(s)/W(s), volleyball W(s). *Intramural sports:* basketball M/W, football M, soccer M/W, volleyball M/W.

Costs (2014–15) *Tuition:* area resident $3420 full-time, $114 per credit hour part-time; state resident $8040 full-time, $275 per credit hour part-time; nonresident $9360 full-time, $321 per credit hour part-time. *Required fees:* $516 full-time, $17 part-time, $3 part-time. *Payment plan:* installment. *Waivers:* senior citizens and employees or children of employees.

Financial Aid Of all full-time matriculated undergraduates who enrolled in 2012, 68 Federal Work-Study jobs (averaging $1774). 274 state and other part-time jobs (averaging $2420).

Applying *Options:* electronic application, early admission, deferred entrance. *Recommended:* high school transcript. *Application deadlines:* rolling (freshmen), rolling (transfers). *Notification:* continuous (freshmen), continuous (transfers).

Freshman Application Contact Ms. Claudia Roselli, Director, Admissions and Recruitment, Moraine Valley Community College, 9000 West College Parkway, Palos Hills, IL 60465-0937. *Phone:* 708-974-5357. *Fax:* 708-974-0681. *E-mail:* roselli@morainevalley.edu.
Website: http://www.morainevalley.edu/.

Morrison Institute of Technology
Morrison, Illinois

Freshman Application Contact Mrs. Tammy Pruis, Admission Secretary, Morrison Institute of Technology, 701 Portland Avenue, Morrison, IL 61270. *Phone:* 815-772-7218. *Fax:* 815-772-7584. *E-mail:* admissions@ morrison.tec.il.us.
Website: http://www.morrisontech.edu/.

Morton College
Cicero, Illinois

Freshman Application Contact Morton College, 3801 South Central Avenue, Cicero, IL 60804-4398. *Phone:* 708-656-8000 Ext. 401.
Website: http://www.morton.edu/.

Northwestern College
Rosemont, Illinois

Freshman Application Contact Northwestern College, 9700 West Higgins Road, Suite 750, Rosemont, IL 60018. *Phone:* 773-481-3730. *Toll-free phone:* 888-205-2283.
Website: http://www.northwesterncollege.edu/.

Oakton Community College
Des Plaines, Illinois

- **District-supported** 2-year, founded 1969, part of Illinois Community College Board
- **Suburban** 193-acre campus with easy access to Chicago
- **Coed,** 10,016 undergraduate students

Majors Accounting technology and bookkeeping; administrative assistant and secretarial science; architectural drafting and CAD/CADD; automobile/automotive mechanics technology; banking and financial support services; biological and physical sciences; building/construction finishing, management, and inspection related; child-care provision; clinical/medical laboratory technology; computer programming; criminal justice/police science; electrical, electronic and communications engineering technology; engineering; fire science/firefighting; graphic design; health information/medical records administration; heating, ventilation, air conditioning and refrigeration engineering technology; information technology; liberal arts and sciences/liberal studies; manufacturing engineering technology; marketing/marketing management; mechanical engineering/mechanical technology; music; operations management; physical therapy technology; real estate; registered nursing/registered nurse; sales, distribution, and marketing operations; social work; substance abuse/addiction counseling.
Academics *Calendar:* semesters. *Degree:* certificates and associate. *Special study options:* academic remediation for entering students, adult/continuing education programs, advanced placement credit, distance learning, English as a second language, honors programs, independent study, part-time degree program, services for LD students, study abroad, summer session for credit.
Library Oakton Community College Library plus 1 other with 92,000 titles, 586 serial subscriptions, 10,500 audiovisual materials, an OPAC, a Web page.
Student Life *Housing:* college housing not available. *Activities and Organizations:* drama/theater group, student-run newspaper, choral group. *Campus security:* 24-hour emergency response devices and patrols, student patrols, late-night transport/escort service. *Student services:* health clinic, personal/psychological counseling.
Athletics Member NJCAA. *Intercollegiate sports:* baseball M, basketball M/W, cross-country running M/W, soccer M/W, softball W, tennis M/W, track and field M/W, volleyball W. *Intramural sports:* basketball M/W, cheerleading W, soccer M, table tennis M/W, volleyball M/W.
Costs (2013–14) *Tuition:* area resident $2288 full-time, $95 per semester hour part-time; state resident $6909 full-time, $288 per semester hour part-time; nonresident $8881 full-time, $370 per semester hour part-time. *Required fees:* $167 full-time.
Applying *Options:* electronic application. *Application fee:* $25. *Required for some:* interview. *Recommended:* high school transcript. *Application deadlines:* rolling (freshmen), rolling (transfers). *Notification:* continuous (freshmen), continuous (transfers).
Freshman Application Contact Mr. Danielle Nightingale, Admissions Specialist, Oakton Community College, 1600 East Golf Road, Des Plaines, IL

60016-1268. *Phone:* 847-635-1913. *Fax:* 847-635-1890. *E-mail:* dcohen@ oakton.edu.
Website: http://www.oakton.edu/.

Parkland College
Champaign, Illinois

- **District-supported** 2-year, founded 1967, part of Illinois Community College Board
- **Suburban** 233-acre campus
- **Coed**

Undergraduates 3,432 full-time, 5,936 part-time. 1% are from out of state; 16% Black or African American, non-Hispanic/Latino; 4% Hispanic/Latino; 3% Asian, non-Hispanic/Latino; 0.1% Native Hawaiian or other Pacific Islander, non-Hispanic/Latino; 0.5% American Indian or Alaska Native, non-Hispanic/Latino; 0.1% Two or more races, non-Hispanic/Latino; 19% Race/ethnicity unknown; 1% international; 4% transferred in.
Academics *Calendar:* semesters. *Degree:* certificates and associate. *Special study options:* academic remediation for entering students, accelerated degree program, adult/continuing education programs, advanced placement credit, cooperative education, distance learning, double majors, English as a second language, honors programs, independent study, internships, off-campus study, part-time degree program, services for LD students, student-designed majors, study abroad, summer session for credit. *ROTC:* Army (c), Navy (c), Air Force (c).
Student Life *Campus security:* 24-hour emergency response devices and patrols, late-night transport/escort service.
Athletics Member NJCAA.
Standardized Tests *Required for some:* ACT (for admission).
Costs (2013–14) *Tuition:* area resident $3270 full-time, $109 per credit hour part-time; state resident $8550 full-time, $285 per credit hour part-time; nonresident $13,050 full-time, $435 per credit hour part-time. *Required fees:* $255 full-time, $9 per credit hour part-time.
Financial Aid Of all full-time matriculated undergraduates who enrolled in 2012, 2,412 applied for aid, 2,116 were judged to have need, 139 had their need fully met. 89 Federal Work-Study jobs (averaging $2086). In 2012, 16. *Average percent of need met:* 54. *Average financial aid package:* $6593. *Average need-based loan:* $3187. *Average need-based gift aid:* $4866. *Average non-need-based aid:* $344.
Applying *Options:* deferred entrance. *Recommended:* high school transcript.
Freshman Application Contact Admissions Representative, Parkland College, Champaign, IL 61821-1899. *Phone:* 217-351-2482. *Toll-free phone:* 800-346-8089. *Fax:* 217-351-2640.
Website: http://www.parkland.edu/.

Prairie State College
Chicago Heights, Illinois

Freshman Application Contact Jaime Miller, Director of Admissions, Prairie State College, 202 South Halsted Street, Chicago Heights, IL 60411. *Phone:* 708-709-3513. *E-mail:* jmmiller@prairiestate.edu.
Website: http://www.prairiestate.edu/.

Rend Lake College
Ina, Illinois

- **State-supported** 2-year, founded 1967, part of Illinois Community College Board
- **Rural** 350-acre campus
- **Coed,** 2,714 undergraduate students, 54% full-time, 57% women, 43% men

Undergraduates 1,479 full-time, 1,235 part-time. 2% Black or African American, non-Hispanic/Latino; 0.5% Hispanic/Latino; 0.1% Asian, non-Hispanic/Latino; 0.3% Native Hawaiian or other Pacific Islander, non-Hispanic/Latino; 0.5% American Indian or Alaska Native, non-Hispanic/Latino; 0.1% Race/ethnicity unknown.
Freshmen *Admission:* 417 enrolled.
Faculty *Student/faculty ratio:* 25:1.
Majors Agricultural mechanics and equipment technology; agricultural mechanization; agricultural production; applied horticulture/horticulture operations; architectural drafting and CAD/CADD; automobile/automotive mechanics technology; biological and physical sciences; child-care provision; clinical/medical laboratory technology; computer technology/computer systems technology; criminal justice/police science; culinary arts; drafting and design technology; e-commerce; electrical, electronic and communications engineering technology; electrician; emergency medical technology (EMT paramedic); engineering; fine/studio arts; graphic design; health information/medical records technology; heavy equipment maintenance technology; industrial mechanics and maintenance technology; liberal arts and sciences/liberal studies; medical staff services technology; occupational therapist assistant; plant sciences; special education.

Academics *Calendar:* semesters. *Degree:* certificates and associate. *Special study options:* academic remediation for entering students, adult/continuing education programs, advanced placement credit, cooperative education, distance learning, double majors, English as a second language, honors programs, independent study, internships, off-campus study, part-time degree program, services for LD students, summer session for credit.

Library Learning Resource Center with 35,426 titles, 265 serial subscriptions, 3,770 audiovisual materials, an OPAC, a Web page.

Student Life *Housing:* college housing not available. *Activities and Organizations:* drama/theater group, student-run newspaper, choral group. *Campus security:* 24-hour emergency response devices and patrols, late-night transport/escort service.

Athletics Member NJCAA. *Intercollegiate sports:* baseball M(s), basketball M(s)/W(s), cross-country running M(s), golf M(s)/W(s), softball W(s), tennis W(s), track and field M/W, volleyball W(s).

Costs (2014–15) *Tuition:* area resident $2850 full-time, $95 per hour part-time; state resident $4455 full-time, $149 per hour part-time; nonresident $4500 full-time, $150 per hour part-time. Full-time tuition and fees vary according to course load, program, and reciprocity agreements. Part-time tuition and fees vary according to course load, program, and reciprocity agreements. *Required fees:* $90 full-time, $3 per hour part-time. *Payment plan:* installment. *Waivers:* senior citizens and employees or children of employees.

Financial Aid Of all full-time matriculated undergraduates who enrolled in 2012, 133 Federal Work-Study jobs (averaging $1000). 174 state and other part-time jobs (averaging $940).

Applying *Options:* electronic application, deferred entrance. *Required:* high school transcript. *Application deadlines:* 8/18 (freshmen), 8/18 (transfers).

Freshman Application Contact Mr. Jason Swann, Dean of Admissions and Enrollment Management, Rend Lake College, 468 North Ken Gray Parkway, Ina, IL 62846-9801. *Phone:* 618-437-5321 Ext. 1265. *Toll-free phone:* 800-369-5321. *Fax:* 618-437-5677. *E-mail:* swannj@rlc.edu. *Website:* http://www.rlc.edu/.

Richland Community College
Decatur, Illinois

Freshman Application Contact Ms. JoAnn Wirey, Director of Admissions and Records, Richland Community College, Decatur, IL 62521. *Phone:* 217-875-7200 Ext. 284. *Fax:* 217-875-7783. *E-mail:* jwirey@richland.edu. *Website:* http://www.richland.edu/.

Rockford Career College
Rockford, Illinois

Director of Admissions Ms. Barbara Holliman, Director of Admissions, Rockford Career College, 1130 South Alpine Road, Suite 100, Rockford, IL 61108. *Phone:* 815-965-8616 Ext. 16. *Website:* http://www.rockfordcareercollege.edu/.

Rock Valley College
Rockford, Illinois

- District-supported 2-year, founded 1964, part of Illinois Community College Board
- Suburban 217-acre campus with easy access to Chicago
- Coed, 8,849 undergraduate students, 49% full-time, 57% women, 43% men

Undergraduates 4,308 full-time, 4,541 part-time. Students come from 2 states and territories; 3 other countries; 2% are from out of state; 10% Black or African American, non-Hispanic/Latino; 9% Hispanic/Latino; 1% Asian, non-Hispanic/Latino; 0.1% Native Hawaiian or other Pacific Islander, non-Hispanic/Latino; 0.3% American Indian or Alaska Native, non-Hispanic/Latino; 2% Two or more races, non-Hispanic/Latino; 0.7% Race/ethnicity unknown; 0.2% international. *Retention:* 66% of full-time freshmen returned.

Freshmen *Admission:* 1,429 enrolled.

Faculty *Total:* 424, 37% full-time, 69% with terminal degrees. *Student/faculty ratio:* 24:1.

Majors Accounting; administrative assistant and secretarial science; automobile/automotive mechanics technology; avionics maintenance technology; business administration and management; child development; computer engineering technology; computer science; computer systems networking and telecommunications; construction engineering technology; criminal justice/law enforcement administration; dental hygiene; drafting/design engineering technologies related; electrical, electronic and communications engineering technology; electrician; energy management and systems technology; fire science/firefighting; graphic and printing equipment operation/production; human services; industrial and product design; industrial technology; liberal arts and sciences/liberal studies; marketing/marketing management; pre-engineering; quality control technology; registered

nursing/registered nurse; respiratory care therapy; sheet metal technology; sport and fitness administration/management; surgical technology; tool and die technology; welding technology.

Academics *Calendar:* semesters. *Degree:* certificates and associate. *Special study options:* academic remediation for entering students, adult/continuing education programs, advanced placement credit, cooperative education, distance learning, English as a second language, honors programs, independent study, internships, part-time degree program, services for LD students, student-designed majors, study abroad, summer session for credit.

Library Educational Resource Center with 67,168 titles, an OPAC, a Web page.

Student Life *Housing:* college housing not available. *Activities and Organizations:* drama/theater group, student-run newspaper, choral group, Black Student Alliance, Phi Theta Kappa, Adults on Campus, Inter-Varsity Club, Christian Fellowship. *Campus security:* 24-hour emergency response devices and patrols, late-night transport/escort service. *Student services:* personal/psychological counseling.

Athletics Member NJCAA. *Intercollegiate sports:* baseball M, basketball M/W, golf M, soccer M/W, softball W, squash W, tennis M/W, volleyball W. *Intramural sports:* skiing (downhill) M/W.

Costs (2014–15) *Tuition:* state resident $7650 full-time, $264 per credit part-time; nonresident $14,220 full-time, $456 per credit part-time. Full-time tuition and fees vary according to course load. Part-time tuition and fees vary according to course load. *Required fees:* $314 full-time. *Payment plans:* installment, deferred payment. *Waivers:* employees or children of employees.

Financial Aid Of all full-time matriculated undergraduates who enrolled in 2012, 120 Federal Work-Study jobs (averaging $1800).

Applying *Required:* high school transcript. *Application deadlines:* 8/29 (freshmen), 8/29 (transfers). *Notification:* continuous (freshmen), continuous (transfers).

Freshman Application Contact Mr. Patrick Peyer, Director, Student Retention and Success, Rock Valley College, 3301 North Mulford Rd, Rockford, IL 61008. *Phone:* 815-921-4103. *Toll-free phone:* 800-973-7821. *E-mail:* p.peyer@rockvalleycollege.edu. *Website:* http://www.rockvalleycollege.edu/.

Sauk Valley Community College
Dixon, Illinois

- District-supported 2-year, founded 1965, part of Illinois Community College Board
- Rural 165-acre campus
- Endowment $2.0 million
- Coed, 2,220 undergraduate students, 45% full-time, 60% women, 40% men

Undergraduates 998 full-time, 1,222 part-time. 4% Black or African American, non-Hispanic/Latino; 8% Hispanic/Latino; 0.7% Asian, non-Hispanic/Latino; 0.2% Native Hawaiian or other Pacific Islander, non-Hispanic/Latino; 0.3% American Indian or Alaska Native, non-Hispanic/Latino; 0.1% Two or more races, non-Hispanic/Latino; 2% Race/ethnicity unknown. *Retention:* 59% of full-time freshmen returned.

Freshmen *Admission:* 585 applied, 585 admitted, 471 enrolled.

Faculty *Total:* 145, 30% full-time, 11% with terminal degrees. *Student/faculty ratio:* 21:1.

Majors Accounting; administrative assistant and secretarial science; agricultural business and management; agriculture; art; athletic training; biology/biological sciences; business administration and management; chemistry; communication; computer and information sciences related; corrections; criminal justice/law enforcement administration; criminal justice/police science; dramatic/theater arts; early childhood education; economics; education; electrical, electronic and communications engineering technology; elementary education; English; fire science/firefighting; foreign languages related; heating, air conditioning, ventilation and refrigeration maintenance technology; history; legal administrative assistant/secretary; management science; marketing/marketing management; mathematics; medical office assistant; music; occupational therapy; physical education teaching and coaching; physics; political science and government; premedical studies; pre-physical therapy; psychology; radiologic technology/science; registered nursing/registered nurse; secondary education; social work; sociology; special education; speech communication and rhetoric.

Academics *Calendar:* semesters. *Degree:* certificates and associate. *Special study options:* academic remediation for entering students, accelerated degree program, adult/continuing education programs, cooperative education, distance learning, English as a second language, honors programs, independent study, internships, off-campus study, part-time degree program, services for LD students, summer session for credit.

Library Learning Resource Center plus 1 other with 59,000 titles, 95 serial subscriptions, 6,293 audiovisual materials, an OPAC, a Web page.

Student Life *Housing:* college housing not available. *Activities and Organizations:* drama/theater group, student-run newspaper, choral group, Phi

Theta Kappa, Criminal Justice Club, Health Careers Club, Association of Latin American Students. *Campus security:* 24-hour emergency response devices and patrols, late-night transport/escort service. *Student services:* personal/psychological counseling.

Athletics Member NJCAA. *Intercollegiate sports:* baseball M(s), basketball M(s)/W(s), cross-country running M(s)/W(s), softball W(s), tennis M(s)/W(s). *Intramural sports:* basketball M/W.

Standardized Tests *Recommended:* ACT (for admission).

Costs (2014–15) *Tuition:* area resident $2884 full-time, $103 per credit part-time; state resident $7224 full-time, $258 per credit part-time; nonresident $8008 full-time, $286 per credit part-time. Full-time tuition and fees vary according to course load and program. Part-time tuition and fees vary according to course load and program. *Required fees:* $150 full-time, $5 per credit part-time. *Room and board:* Room and board charges vary according to housing facility. *Payment plan:* deferred payment. *Waivers:* senior citizens and employees or children of employees.

Financial Aid Of all full-time matriculated undergraduates who enrolled in 2013, 804 applied for aid, 546 were judged to have need, 1 had their need fully met. *Average percent of need met:* 35%. *Average financial aid package:* $5206. *Average need-based loan:* $3025. *Average need-based gift aid:* $4465.

Applying *Options:* electronic application, early admission, deferred entrance. *Recommended:* high school transcript. *Application deadlines:* rolling (freshmen), rolling (transfers). *Notification:* continuous (freshmen), continuous (transfers).

Freshman Application Contact Sauk Valley Community College, 173 Illinois Route 2, Dixon, IL 61021. *Phone:* 815-288-5511 Ext. 378.

Website: http://www.svcc.edu/.

Shawnee Community College

Ullin, Illinois

- **State and locally supported** 2-year, founded 1967, part of Illinois Community College Board
- **Rural** 163-acre campus
- **Coed,** 1,579 undergraduate students, 55% full-time, 61% women, 39% men

Undergraduates 867 full-time, 712 part-time. Students come from 5 states and territories; 2 other countries; 2% are from out of state; 16% Black or African American, non-Hispanic/Latino; 2% Hispanic/Latino; 0.2% Asian, non-Hispanic/Latino; 0.5% American Indian or Alaska Native, non-Hispanic/Latino; 0.4% Race/ethnicity unknown; 7% transferred in. *Retention:* 39% of full-time freshmen returned.

Freshmen *Admission:* 123 applied, 123 admitted, 123 enrolled. *Test scores:* ACT scores over 18: 63%; ACT scores over 24: 16%; ACT scores over 30: 1%.

Faculty *Total:* 169, 24% full-time, 4% with terminal degrees. *Student/faculty ratio:* 13:1.

Majors Accounting; administrative assistant and secretarial science; agricultural business and management; agriculture; agronomy and crop science; animal sciences; automobile/automotive mechanics technology; biological and physical sciences; business administration and management; business automation/technology/data entry; child development; clinical/medical laboratory technology; computer graphics; computer systems networking and telecommunications; cosmetology; criminal justice/police science; electrical, electronic and communications engineering technology; health information/medical records technology; horticultural science; human services; information science/studies; legal administrative assistant/secretary; liberal arts and sciences/liberal studies; medical administrative assistant and medical secretary; occupational therapist assistant; registered nursing/registered nurse; social work; substance abuse/addiction counseling; veterinary/animal health technology; welding technology; wildlife, fish and wildlands science and management.

Academics *Calendar:* semesters. *Degree:* certificates, diplomas, and associate. *Special study options:* academic remediation for entering students, accelerated degree program, adult/continuing education programs, advanced placement credit, cooperative education, distance learning, double majors, English as a second language, external degree program, independent study, internships, off-campus study, part-time degree program, services for LD students, summer session for credit.

Library Shawnee Community College Library with 46,313 titles, 148 serial subscriptions, 1,842 audiovisual materials, an OPAC, a Web page.

Student Life *Housing:* college housing not available. *Activities and Organizations:* drama/theater group, choral group, Phi Theta Kappa, Phi Beta Lambda, Music Club, Student Senate, Future Teachers Organization. *Campus security:* 24-hour patrols. *Student services:* personal/psychological counseling.

Athletics Member NJCAA. *Intercollegiate sports:* baseball M(s), basketball M(s)/W(s), softball W(s). *Intramural sports:* weight lifting M/W.

Standardized Tests *Required for some:* ACT (for admission). *Recommended:* ACT (for admission).

Costs (2014–15) *Tuition:* area resident $2280 full-time; state resident $3504 full-time; nonresident $3816 full-time. *Payment plans:* installment, deferred payment. *Waivers:* senior citizens and employees or children of employees.

Financial Aid Of all full-time matriculated undergraduates who enrolled in 2012, 60 Federal Work-Study jobs (averaging $2000). 50 state and other part-time jobs (averaging $2000).

Applying *Options:* electronic application, early admission, deferred entrance. *Required:* high school transcript. *Application deadlines:* rolling (freshmen), rolling (out-of-state freshmen), rolling (transfers). *Notification:* continuous (freshmen), continuous (out-of-state freshmen), continuous (transfers).

Freshman Application Contact Mrs. Erin King, Recruiter/Advisor, Shawnee Community College, 8364 Shawnee College Road, Ullin, IL 62992. *Phone:* 618-634-3200. *Toll-free phone:* 800-481-2242. *Fax:* 618-634-3300. *E-mail:* erink@shawneecc.edu.

Website: http://www.shawneecc.edu/.

Solex College

Wheeling, Illinois

Freshman Application Contact Solex College, 350 East Dundee Road, Wheeling, IL 60090.

Website: http://www.solex.edu/.

Southeastern Illinois College

Harrisburg, Illinois

Freshman Application Contact Dr. David Nudo, Director of Counseling, Southeastern Illinois College, 3575 College Road, Harrisburg, IL 62946-4925, *Phone:* 618-252-5400 Ext. 2430. *Toll-free phone:* 866-338-2742.

Website: http://www.sic.edu/.

South Suburban College

South Holland, Illinois

- **State and locally supported** 2-year, founded 1927, part of Illinois Community College Board
- **Suburban** campus with easy access to Chicago
- **Coed,** 5,508 undergraduate students, 38% full-time, 43% women, 57% men

Undergraduates 2,076 full-time, 3,432 part-time. 6% are from out of state; 65% Black or African American, non-Hispanic/Latino; 12% Hispanic/Latino; 0.3% Asian, non-Hispanic/Latino; 1% American Indian or Alaska Native, non-Hispanic/Latino; 2% Two or more races, non-Hispanic/Latino; 0.4% Race/ethnicity unknown; 0.2% international. *Retention:* 15% of full-time freshmen returned.

Freshmen *Admission:* 873 applied, 873 admitted. *Average high school GPA:* 2.33.

Faculty *Total:* 474, 22% full-time. *Student/faculty ratio:* 20:1.

Majors Accounting; accounting technology and bookkeeping; architectural drafting and CAD/CADD; biological and physical sciences; building/home/construction inspection; CAD/CADD drafting/design technology; child-care provision; construction engineering technology; court reporting; criminal justice/safety; electrical, electronic and communications engineering technology; executive assistant/executive secretary; fine/studio arts; information technology; kinesiology and exercise science; legal assistant/paralegal; liberal arts and sciences/liberal studies; nursing administration; occupational therapist assistant; office management; radiologic technology/science; small business administration; social work.

Academics *Calendar:* semesters. *Degree:* certificates and associate. *Special study options:* academic remediation for entering students, adult/continuing education programs, advanced placement credit, cooperative education, distance learning, English as a second language, honors programs, internships, off-campus study, part-time degree program, services for LD students, study abroad, summer session for credit.

Library South Suburban College Library with 25,011 titles, 55 serial subscriptions, an OPAC, a Web page.

Student Life *Housing:* college housing not available. *Activities and Organizations:* drama/theater group, choral group. *Campus security:* 24-hour emergency response devices and patrols.

Athletics Member NJCAA. *Intercollegiate sports:* baseball M, basketball M/W, soccer M/W, softball W, volleyball W.

Costs (2014–15) *Tuition:* area resident $3600 full-time; state resident $9540 full-time; nonresident $11,190 full-time. Full-time tuition and fees vary according to course load and reciprocity agreements. Part-time tuition and fees vary according to course load and reciprocity agreements. *Required fees:* $533 full-time. *Payment plan:* installment. *Waivers:* senior citizens and employees or children of employees.

Applying *Options:* early admission, deferred entrance. *Required:* high school transcript. *Required for some:* essay or personal statement. *Recommended:* essay or personal statement, minimum 2.0 GPA. *Application deadlines:*

rolling (freshmen), rolling (transfers). *Notification:* continuous (freshmen), continuous (transfers).

Freshman Application Contact Ms. Tiffane Jones, Admissions, South Suburban College, 15800 South State Street, South Holland, IL 60473. *Phone:* 708-596-2000 Ext. 2158. *E-mail:* admissionsquestions@ssc.edu. *Website:* http://www.ssc.edu/.

Southwestern Illinois College
Belleville, Illinois

- **District-supported** 2-year, founded 1946, part of Illinois Community College Board
- **Suburban** 341-acre campus with easy access to St. Louis
- **Endowment** $5.2 million
- **Coed,** 11,331 undergraduate students, 43% full-time, 56% women, 44% men

Undergraduates 4,878 full-time, 6,453 part-time. Students come from 12 states and territories; 1% are from out of state; 24% Black or African American, non-Hispanic/Latino; 4% Hispanic/Latino; 2% Asian, non-Hispanic/Latino; 0.4% Native Hawaiian or other Pacific Islander, non-Hispanic/Latino; 0.6% American Indian or Alaska Native, non-Hispanic/Latino; 4% Race/ethnicity unknown; 5% transferred in.
Freshmen *Admission:* 1,447 applied, 1,447 admitted, 1,447 enrolled.
Faculty *Total:* 728, 21% full-time, 30% with terminal degrees. *Student/faculty ratio:* 19:1.
Majors Accounting; administrative assistant and secretarial science; airframe mechanics and aircraft maintenance technology; airline pilot and flight crew; applied horticulture/horticulture operations; autobody/collision and repair technology; aviation/airway management; biological and physical sciences; carpentry; child-care provision; clinical/medical laboratory technology; computer and information sciences; computer/information technology services administration related; computer programming; concrete finishing; construction trades; criminal justice/law enforcement administration; data modeling/warehousing and database administration; desktop publishing and digital imaging design; electrical and power transmission installation; electrical, electronic and communications engineering technology; electrician; emergency medical technology (EMT paramedic); fine/studio arts; fire science/firefighting; general studies; health information/medical records technology; heating, air conditioning, ventilation and refrigeration maintenance technology; industrial mechanics and maintenance technology; information technology; ironworking; legal administrative assistant/secretary; legal assistant/paralegal; liberal arts and sciences/liberal studies; machine tool technology; manufacturing engineering technology; masonry; massage therapy; mathematics teacher education; mechanical drafting and CAD/CADD; medical/clinical assistant; medical office assistant; music; music teacher education; network and system administration; painting and wall covering; physical therapy technology; pipefitting and sprinkler fitting; radiologic technology/science; registered nursing/registered nurse; respiratory care therapy; restaurant, culinary, and catering management; selling skills and sales; sheet metal technology; sign language interpretation and translation; small business administration; social work; teacher assistant/aide; web/multimedia management and webmaster; welding technology.
Academics *Calendar:* semesters. *Degree:* certificates, diplomas, and associate. *Special study options:* academic remediation for entering students, accelerated degree program, adult/continuing education programs, advanced placement credit, cooperative education, distance learning, double majors, English as a second language, internships, off-campus study, part-time degree program, services for LD students, study abroad, summer session for credit. *ROTC:* Army (c), Air Force (c).
Library Southwestern Illinois College Library with 85,265 titles, 60 serial subscriptions, 6,902 audiovisual materials, an OPAC, a Web page.
Student Life *Housing:* college housing not available. *Activities and Organizations:* drama/theater group, student-run newspaper, choral group, College Activities Board, Phi Theta Kappa, Student Nurses Association, Horticulture Club, Data Processing Management Association. *Campus security:* 24-hour emergency response devices and patrols, late-night transport/escort service. *Student services:* personal/psychological counseling.
Athletics Member NJCAA. *Intercollegiate sports:* baseball M(s), basketball M(s)/W(s), soccer M(s)/W(s), softball W(s), volleyball W(s).
Standardized Tests *Required for some:* ACT (for admission), ACT ASSET or ACT COMPASS.
Financial Aid Of all full-time matriculated undergraduates who enrolled in 2012, 170 Federal Work-Study jobs (averaging $1537). 179 state and other part-time jobs (averaging $1004).
Applying *Options:* electronic application, early admission, deferred entrance. *Required:* high school transcript. *Application deadlines:* rolling (freshmen), rolling (out-of-state freshmen), rolling (transfers).
Freshman Application Contact Michelle Birk, Dean of Enrollment Services, Southwestern Illinois College, 2500 Carlyle Ave, Belleville, IL 62221. *Phone:*

618-235-2700 Ext. 5400. *Toll-free phone:* 866-942-SWIC. *Fax:* 618-222-9768. *E-mail:* michelle.birk@swic.edu. *Website:* http://www.swic.edu/.

Spoon River College
Canton, Illinois

- **State-supported** 2-year, founded 1959, part of Illinois Community College Board
- **Rural** 160-acre campus
- **Endowment** $1.5 million
- **Coed,** 1,784 undergraduate students, 40% full-time, 58% women, 42% men

Undergraduates 713 full-time, 1,071 part-time. 6% Black or African American, non-Hispanic/Latino; 2% Hispanic/Latino; 0.9% Asian, non-Hispanic/Latino; 0.4% American Indian or Alaska Native, non-Hispanic/Latino; 0.2% Two or more races, non-Hispanic/Latino; 0.1% Race/ethnicity unknown; 0.1% international; 12% transferred in. *Retention:* 58% of full-time freshmen returned.
Freshmen *Admission:* 215 applied, 894 admitted, 485 enrolled. *Test scores:* ACT scores over 18: 67%; ACT scores over 24: 18%; ACT scores over 30: 2%.
Faculty *Total:* 104, 34% full-time. *Student/faculty ratio:* 17:1.
Majors Accounting; administrative assistant and secretarial science; agricultural business and management; agricultural mechanics and equipment technology; agricultural mechanization; agricultural teacher education; art; biological and physical sciences; biology/biological sciences; botany/plant biology; business administration and management; business teacher education; chemistry; child development; computer and information systems security; computer programming (specific applications); criminal justice/law enforcement administration; criminal justice/police science; dramatic/theater arts; education; electrical, electronic and communications engineering technology; English; finance; general studies; graphic design; health professions related; history; industrial technology; information science/studies; kindergarten/preschool education; legal administrative assistant/secretary; liberal arts and sciences/liberal studies; mass communication/media; mathematics; medical administrative assistant and medical secretary; physical education teaching and coaching; physical sciences; physics; political science and government; pre-engineering; psychology; registered nursing/registered nurse; rhetoric and composition; social sciences; sociology; truck and bus driver/commercial vehicle operation/instruction; web page, digital/multimedia and information resources design.
Academics *Calendar:* semesters. *Degree:* certificates and associate. *Special study options:* academic remediation for entering students, accelerated degree program, adult/continuing education programs, advanced placement credit, distance learning, English as a second language, freshman honors college, honors programs, internships, part-time degree program, services for LD students, summer session for credit. *ROTC:* Army (b).
Library Library/Learning Resource Center with 74,252 titles, 121 serial subscriptions, 2,285 audiovisual materials, an OPAC, a Web page.
Student Life *Housing:* college housing not available. *Activities and Organizations:* drama/theater group, student-run newspaper, Student Government Association, PEEPS, Intramural Athletics, Habitat for Humanity, Drama Club. *Campus security:* 24-hour emergency response devices, Night Patrol by trained security personnel. *Student services:* personal/psychological counseling.
Athletics Member NJCAA. *Intercollegiate sports:* baseball M(s), cross-country running M(s)/W(s), softball W(s), track and field M(s)/W(s).
Costs (2014–15) *Tuition:* area resident $4050 full-time, $135 per semester hour part-time; state resident $8640 full-time, $288 per semester hour part-time; nonresident $9720 full-time, $324 per semester hour part-time. Full-time tuition and fees vary according to course load and program. Part-time tuition and fees vary according to course load and program. *Required fees:* $600 full-time, $20 per semester hour part-time. *Payment plan:* deferred payment. *Waivers:* senior citizens and employees or children of employees.
Applying *Options:* electronic application, early admission, deferred entrance. *Required:* high school transcript. *Application deadlines:* rolling (freshmen), rolling (transfers). *Notification:* continuous (freshmen), continuous (transfers).
Freshman Application Contact Ms. Missy Wilkinson, Dean of Student Services, Spoon River College, 23235 North County 22, Canton, IL 61520-9801. *Phone:* 309-649-6305. *Toll-free phone:* 800-334-7337. *Fax:* 309-649-6235. *E-mail:* info@spoonrivercollege.edu. *Website:* http://www.src.edu/.

Taylor Business Institute
Chicago, Illinois

Director of Admissions Mr. Rashed Jahangir, Taylor Business Institute, 318 West Adams, Chicago, IL 60606. *Website:* http://www.tbiil.edu/.

Tribeca Flashpoint Media Arts Academy
Chicago, Illinois

Admissions Office Contact Tribeca Flashpoint Media Arts Academy, 28 North Clark Street, Chicago, IL 60602.
Website: http://www.tfa.edu/.

Triton College
River Grove, Illinois

Freshman Application Contact Ms. Mary-Rita Moore, Dean of Admissions, Triton College, 2000 Fifth Avenue, River Grove, IL 60171. *Phone:* 708-456-0300 Ext. 3679. *Fax:* 708-583-3162. *E-mail:* mpatrice@triton.edu.
Website: http://www.triton.edu/.

Vatterott College
Fairview Heights, Illinois

Admissions Office Contact Vatterott College, 110 Commerce Lane, Fairview Heights, IL 62208. *Toll-free phone:* 888-202-2636.
Website: http://www.vatterott.edu/.

Vet Tech Institute at Fox College
Tinley Park, Illinois

- **Private** 2-year, founded 2006
- **Suburban** campus
- **Coed,** 153 undergraduate students
- 60% of applicants were admitted

Freshmen *Admission:* 495 applied, 296 admitted.
Majors Veterinary/animal health technology.
Academics *Degree:* associate. *Special study options:* accelerated degree program, internships.
Student Life *Housing:* college housing not available.
Freshman Application Contact Admissions Office, Vet Tech Institute at Fox College, 18020 South Oak Park Avenue, Tinley Park, IL 60477. *Phone:* 888-884-3694. *Toll-free phone:* 888-884-3694.
Website: http://chicago.vettechinstitute.edu/.

Waubonsee Community College
Sugar Grove, Illinois

- **District-supported** 2-year, founded 1966, part of Illinois Community College Board
- **Small-town** 243-acre campus with easy access to Chicago
- **Coed,** 10,721 undergraduate students, 32% full-time, 56% women, 44% men

Undergraduates 3,469 full-time, 7,252 part-time. 7% Black or African American, non-Hispanic/Latino; 33% Hispanic/Latino; 3% Asian, non-Hispanic/Latino; 0.1% Native Hawaiian or other Pacific Islander, non-Hispanic/Latino; 0.1% American Indian or Alaska Native, non-Hispanic/Latino; 2% Two or more races, non-Hispanic/Latino; 3% Race/ethnicity unknown.
Freshmen *Admission:* 2,431 applied, 2,431 admitted, 1,475 enrolled.
Majors Accounting; autobody/collision and repair technology; automobile/automotive mechanics technology; biological and physical sciences; business administration and management; business automation/technology/data entry; CAD/CADD drafting/design technology; child-care provision; community health services counseling; computer programming; construction management; criminal justice/police science; electrical, electronic and communications engineering technology; electrician; emergency care attendant (EMT ambulance); engineering; executive assistant/executive secretary; fine/studio arts; fire science/firefighting; general studies; graphic design; health and physical education/fitness; health information/medical records technology; heating, air conditioning, ventilation and refrigeration maintenance technology; human resources management; liberal arts and sciences/liberal studies; library and archives assisting; manufacturing engineering technology; music; radio and television broadcasting technology; registered nursing/registered nurse; science technologies; sign language interpretation and translation; small business administration; social work; surveying technology; teacher assistant/aide; web page, digital/multimedia and information resources design; welding technology.
Academics *Calendar:* semesters. *Degree:* certificates and associate. *Special study options:* academic remediation for entering students, accelerated degree program, advanced placement credit, distance learning, English as a second language, honors programs, independent study, internships, off-campus study, part-time degree program, services for LD students, study abroad, summer session for credit. *ROTC:* Army (c).
Library Todd Library plus 3 others with 81,282 titles, 384 serial subscriptions, 3,248 audiovisual materials, an OPAC, a Web page.

Student Life *Housing:* college housing not available. *Activities and Organizations:* drama/theater group, choral group. *Campus security:* 24-hour emergency response devices and patrols, late-night transport/escort service.
Athletics Member NJCAA. *Intercollegiate sports:* baseball M, basketball M(s)/W(s), cheerleading M/W, cross-country running M(s)/W(s), golf M(s), soccer M(s)/W(s), softball W(s), tennis M(s)/W(s), volleyball W(s), wrestling M. *Intramural sports:* basketball M/W, table tennis M/W, volleyball M/W.
Costs (2014–15) *Tuition:* area resident $3120 full-time, $104 per credit hour part-time; state resident $8217 full-time, $274 per credit hour part-time; nonresident $8903 full-time, $297 per credit hour part-time. Full-time tuition and fees vary according to reciprocity agreements. Part-time tuition and fees vary according to reciprocity agreements. *Required fees:* $240 full-time, $8 per credit hour part-time. *Payment plan:* installment. *Waivers:* senior citizens and employees or children of employees.
Financial Aid Of all full-time matriculated undergraduates who enrolled in 2012, 23 Federal Work-Study jobs (averaging $2000).
Applying *Options:* electronic application. *Application deadlines:* rolling (freshmen), rolling (transfers). *Notification:* continuous (freshmen), continuous (transfers).
Freshman Application Contact Joy Sanders, Admissions Manager, Waubonsee Community College, Route 47 at Waubonsee Drive, Sugar Grove, IL 60554. *Phone:* 630-466-7900 Ext. 5756. *Fax:* 630-466-6663. *E-mail:* admissions@waubonsee.edu.
Website: http://www.waubonsee.edu/.

Worsham College of Mortuary Science
Wheeling, Illinois

Director of Admissions President, Worsham College of Mortuary Science, 495 Northgate Parkway, Wheeling, IL 60090-2646. *Phone:* 847-808-8444.
Website: http://www.worshamcollege.com/.

INDIANA

Ancilla College
Donaldson, Indiana

- **Independent Roman Catholic** 2-year, founded 1937
- **Rural** 63-acre campus with easy access to Chicago
- **Endowment** $4.0 million
- **Coed,** 424 undergraduate students, 67% full-time, 57% women, 43% men

Undergraduates 284 full-time, 140 part-time. Students come from 9 states and territories; 3 other countries; 5% are from out of state; 10% Black or African American, non-Hispanic/Latino; 7% Hispanic/Latino; 0.5% American Indian or Alaska Native, non-Hispanic/Latino; 0.8% Two or more races, non-Hispanic/Latino; 0.8% international; 8% transferred in. *Retention:* 57% of full-time freshmen returned.
Freshmen *Admission:* 689 applied, 428 admitted, 151 enrolled. *Average high school GPA:* 2.51. *Test scores:* SAT critical reading scores over 500: 15%; SAT math scores over 500: 24%; SAT critical reading scores over 600: 3%; SAT math scores over 600: 4%; SAT critical reading scores over 700: 1%; SAT math scores over 700: 1%.
Faculty *Total:* 41, 59% full-time, 27% with terminal degrees. *Student/faculty ratio:* 14:1.
Majors Behavioral sciences; biological and physical sciences; business administration and management; criminal justice/safety; early childhood education; elementary education; general studies; health and physical education related; health services/allied health/health sciences; history; logistics, materials, and supply chain management; mass communication/media; registered nursing/registered nurse; secondary education.
Academics *Calendar:* semesters. *Degree:* certificates and associate. *Special study options:* academic remediation for entering students, adult/continuing education programs, advanced placement credit, cooperative education, distance learning, double majors, independent study, internships, part-time degree program, services for LD students, student-designed majors, summer session for credit.
Library Ball Library with 28,262 titles, 66 serial subscriptions, 90 audiovisual materials, an OPAC, a Web page.
Student Life *Housing:* college housing not available. *Activities and Organizations:* Student Government Association, Student Nursing Organization, Ancilla Student Ambassadors, Phi Theta Kappa. *Campus security:* 24-hour patrols, late-night transport/escort service. *Student services:* personal/psychological counseling.
Athletics Member NJCAA. *Intercollegiate sports:* baseball M(s), basketball M(s)/W(s), cheerleading M(s)/W(s), golf M(s), soccer M(s), softball W(s), volleyball W(s).
Standardized Tests *Recommended:* SAT or ACT (for admission).

Costs (2014–15) *Tuition:* $13,500 full-time, $450 per credit part-time. Full-time tuition and fees vary according to course load and program. Part-time tuition and fees vary according to course load and program. *Required fees:* $230 full-time. *Payment plan:* installment. *Waivers:* employees or children of employees.

Financial Aid Of all full-time matriculated undergraduates who enrolled in 2013, 270 applied for aid, 248 were judged to have need. 12 Federal Work-Study jobs (averaging $2634). *Average need-based loan:* $1823. *Average need-based gift aid:* $1132. *Financial aid deadline:* 2/28.

Applying *Options:* electronic application. *Required:* high school transcript. *Application deadlines:* rolling (freshmen), rolling (out-of-state freshmen), rolling (transfers).

Freshman Application Contact Mrs. Sarah Lawrence, Assistant Director of Admissions, Ancilla College, 9601 Union Road, Donaldson, IN 46513. *Phone:* 574-936-8898 Ext. 396. *Toll-free phone:* 866-ANCILLA. *Fax:* 574-935-1773. *E-mail:* admissions@ancilla.edu.

Website: http://www.ancilla.edu/.

Brown Mackie College–Fort Wayne

Fort Wayne, Indiana

- **Proprietary** primarily 2-year, part of Education Management Corporation
- **Coed**

Majors Biomedical technology; business administration and management; business/commerce; criminal justice/safety; health/health-care administration; heating, air conditioning, ventilation and refrigeration maintenance technology; occupational therapist assistant; physical therapy technology; registered nursing/registered nurse; veterinary/animal health technology.

Academics *Calendar:* quarters. *Degrees:* certificates, associate, and bachelor's.

Freshman Application Contact Brown Mackie College–Fort Wayne, 3000 East Coliseum Boulevard, Fort Wayne, IN 46805. *Phone:* 260-484-4400. *Toll-free phone:* 866-433-2289.

Website: http://www.brownmackie.edu/fortwayne/.

See display below and page 392 for the College Close-Up.

Brown Mackie College–Indianapolis

Indianapolis, Indiana

- **Proprietary** primarily 2-year, part of Education Management Corporation
- **Coed**

Majors Accounting technology and bookkeeping; biomedical technology; business administration and management; business/commerce; corrections and criminal justice related; criminal justice/safety; health/health-care administration; legal assistant/paralegal; occupational therapist assistant.

Academics *Degrees:* certificates, diplomas, associate, and bachelor's.

Freshman Application Contact Brown Mackie College–Indianapolis, 1200 North Meridian Street, Suite 100, Indianapolis, IN 46204. *Phone:* 317-554-8300. *Toll-free phone:* 866-255-0279.

Website: http://www.brownmackie.edu/indianapolis/.

See display below and page 398 for the College Close-Up.

Brown Mackie College–Merrillville

Merrillville, Indiana

- **Proprietary** primarily 2-year, founded 1890, part of Education Management Corporation
- **Small-town** campus
- **Coed**

Majors Business administration and management; business/commerce; corrections and criminal justice related; criminal justice/safety; legal assistant/paralegal; occupational therapist assistant; registered nursing/registered nurse; surgical technology.

Academics *Calendar:* quarters. *Degrees:* certificates, associate, and bachelor's.

Freshman Application Contact Brown Mackie College–Merrillville, 1000 East 80th Place, Suite 205S, Merrillville, IN 46410. *Phone:* 219-769-3321. *Toll-free phone:* 800-258-3321.

Website: http://www.brownmackie.edu/merrillville/.

See display below and page 404 for the College Close-Up.

Programs that live up to your passion

Veterinary Technology

❦ BROWN MACKIE COLLEGE℠

BrownMackie.edu

ONE COURSE A MONTH℠

Brown Mackie College–South Bend

South Bend, Indiana

- **Proprietary** primarily 2-year, founded 1882, part of Education Management Corporation
- **Urban** campus
- **Coed, primarily women**

Majors Business administration and management; business/commerce; computer and information sciences and support services related; health/health-care administration; occupational therapist assistant; physical therapy technology; registered nursing/registered nurse; veterinary/animal health technology.

Academics *Calendar:* quarters. *Degrees:* certificates, diplomas, associate, and bachelor's.

Freshman Application Contact Brown Mackie College–South Bend, 3454 Douglas Road, South Bend, IN 46635. *Phone:* 574-237-0774. *Toll-free phone:* 800-743-2447.

Website: http://www.brownmackie.edu/southbend/.

See display below and page 424 for the College Close-Up.

College of Court Reporting

Hobart, Indiana

Freshman Application Contact Ms. Nicky Rodriquez, Director of Admissions, College of Court Reporting, 111 West Tenth Street, Suite 111, Hobart, IN 46342. *Phone:* 219-942-1459 Ext. 222. *Toll-free phone:* 866-294-3974. *Fax:* 219-942-1631. *E-mail:* nrodriquez@ccr.edu.

Website: http://www.ccr.edu/.

International Business College

Indianapolis, Indiana

- **Private** 2-year, founded 1889
- **Suburban** campus
- **Coed,** 403 undergraduate students
- 70% of applicants were admitted

Freshmen *Admission:* 1,012 applied, 707 admitted.

Majors Accounting technology and bookkeeping; administrative assistant and secretarial science; computer programming; computer systems networking and telecommunications; dental assisting; graphic design; hotel/motel administration; legal administrative assistant/secretary; legal assistant/paralegal; medical/clinical assistant; veterinary/animal health technology.

Academics *Calendar:* semesters. *Degree:* diplomas and associate. *Special study options:* accelerated degree program, internships.

Freshman Application Contact Admissions Office, International Business College, 7205 Shadeland Station, Indianapolis, IN 46256. *Phone:* 317-813-2300. *Toll-free phone:* 800-589-6500.

Website: http://www.ibcindianapolis.edu/.

ITT Technical Institute

Fort Wayne, Indiana

- **Proprietary** primarily 2-year, founded 1967, part of ITT Educational Services, Inc.
- **Coed**

Majors Automation engineer technology; business administration and management; computer programming (specific applications); construction management; cyber/computer forensics and counterterrorism; drafting and design technology; electrical, electronic and communications engineering technology; game and interactive media design; industrial technology; information technology project management; network and system administration; project management; registered nursing/registered nurse.

Academics *Calendar:* quarters. *Degrees:* associate and bachelor's.

Student Life *Housing:* college housing not available.

Freshman Application Contact Director of Recruitment, ITT Technical Institute, 2810 Dupont Commerce Court, Fort Wayne, IN 46825. *Phone:* 260-497-6200. *Toll-free phone:* 800-866-4488.

Website: http://www.itt-tech.edu/.

ITT Technical Institute

Merrillville, Indiana

- **Proprietary** primarily 2-year
- **Coed**

Majors Computer programming (specific applications); construction management; cyber/computer forensics and counterterrorism; drafting and design technology; electrical, electronic and communications engineering technology; forensic science and technology; information technology project management; network and system administration; project management; registered nursing/registered nurse.

Academics *Degrees:* associate and bachelor's.
Freshman Application Contact Director of Recruitment, ITT Technical Institute, 8488 Georgia Street, Merrillville, IN 46410. *Phone:* 219-738-6100. *Toll-free phone:* 877-418-8134.
Website: http://www.itt-tech.edu/.

ITT Technical Institute
Newburgh, Indiana

- **Proprietary** primarily 2-year, founded 1966, part of ITT Educational Services, Inc.
- **Coed**

Majors Business administration and management; computer programming (specific applications); construction management; cyber/computer forensics and counterterrorism; drafting and design technology; electrical, electronic and communications engineering technology; forensic science and technology; industrial technology; information technology project management; legal assistant/paralegal; network and system administration; project management; registered nursing/registered nurse.
Academics *Calendar:* quarters. *Degrees:* associate and bachelor's.
Student Life *Housing:* college housing not available.
Freshman Application Contact Director of Recruitment, ITT Technical Institute, 10999 Stahl Road, Newburgh, IN 47630-7430. *Phone:* 812-858-1600. *Toll-free phone:* 800-832-4488.
Website: http://www.itt-tech.edu/.

Ivy Tech Community College–Bloomington
Bloomington, Indiana

- **State-supported** 2-year, founded 2001, part of Ivy Tech Community College System
- **Coed,** 6,477 undergraduate students, 39% full-time, 62% women, 38% men

Undergraduates 2,503 full-time, 3,974 part-time. 1% are from out of state; 3% Black or African American, non-Hispanic/Latino; 2% Hispanic/Latino; 3% Asian, non-Hispanic/Latino; 0.3% American Indian or Alaska Native, non-Hispanic/Latino; 2% Two or more races, non-Hispanic/Latino; 21% Race/ethnicity unknown; 5% transferred in. *Retention:* 51% of full-time freshmen returned.
Freshmen *Admission:* 2,141 applied, 2,141 admitted, 874 enrolled.
Faculty *Total:* 409, 21% full-time. *Student/faculty ratio:* 20:1.
Majors Accounting technology and bookkeeping; building/property maintenance; business administration and management; business automation/technology/data entry; cabinetmaking and millwork; child-care and support services management; computer and information sciences; criminal justice/safety; early childhood education; electrical, electronic and communications engineering technology; electrician; emergency medical technology (EMT paramedic); executive assistant/executive secretary; general studies; heating, air conditioning, ventilation and refrigeration maintenance technology; human services; industrial technology; legal assistant/paralegal; liberal arts and sciences/liberal studies; library and archives assisting; machine tool technology; mechanic and repair technologies related; mechanics and repair; pipefitting and sprinkler fitting; psychiatric/mental health services technology; registered nursing/registered nurse; tool and die technology.
Academics *Calendar:* semesters. *Degree:* certificates and associate. *Special study options:* academic remediation for entering students, adult/continuing education programs, advanced placement credit, distance learning, external degree program, internships, part-time degree program, services for LD students, summer session for credit.
Library 5,516 titles, 97 serial subscriptions, 1,281 audiovisual materials, an OPAC, a Web page.
Student Life *Activities and Organizations:* student government, Phi Theta Kappa. *Campus security:* late-night transport/escort service.
Costs (2014–15) *Tuition:* state resident $3935 full-time, $132 per credit hour part-time; nonresident $7812 full-time, $260 per credit hour part-time. *Required fees:* $120 full-time, $60 per term part-time. *Payment plans:* installment, deferred payment. *Waivers:* senior citizens and employees or children of employees.
Financial Aid Of all full-time matriculated undergraduates who enrolled in 2012, 51 Federal Work-Study jobs (averaging $3259).
Applying *Options:* electronic application, deferred entrance. *Required:* high school transcript. *Required for some:* interview. *Application deadlines:* rolling (freshmen), rolling (transfers). *Notification:* continuous (freshmen), continuous (transfers).
Freshman Application Contact Mr. Neil Frederick, Assistant Director of Admissions, Ivy Tech Community College–Bloomington, 200 Daniels Way, Bloomington, IN 47404. *Phone:* 812-330-6026. *Toll-free phone:* 888-IVY-LINE. *Fax:* 812-332-8147. *E-mail:* nfrederi@ivytech.edu.
Website: http://www.ivytech.edu/.

Ivy Tech Community College–Central Indiana
Indianapolis, Indiana

- **State-supported** 2-year, founded 1963, part of Ivy Tech Community College System
- **Urban** 10-acre campus
- **Coed,** 21,978 undergraduate students, 32% full-time, 56% women, 44% men

Undergraduates 7,034 full-time, 14,944 part-time. 5% are from out of state; 27% Black or African American, non-Hispanic/Latino; 5% Hispanic/Latino; 2% Asian, non-Hispanic/Latino; 0.3% American Indian or Alaska Native, non-Hispanic/Latino; 3% Two or more races, non-Hispanic/Latino; 4% Race/ethnicity unknown; 5% transferred in. *Retention:* 48% of full-time freshmen returned.
Freshmen *Admission:* 3,568 enrolled.
Faculty *Total:* 946, 20% full-time. *Student/faculty ratio:* 27:1.
Majors Accounting technology and bookkeeping; automobile/automotive mechanics technology; biotechnology; building/property maintenance; business administration and management; business automation/technology/data entry; cabinetmaking and millwork; carpentry; child-care and support services management; child development; computer and information sciences; criminal justice/safety; design and visual communications; drafting and design technology; early childhood education; electrical, electronic and communications engineering technology; electrician; executive assistant/executive secretary; general studies; heating, air conditioning, ventilation and refrigeration maintenance technology; hospitality administration related; human services; industrial production technologies related; industrial technology; legal assistant/paralegal; liberal arts and sciences/liberal studies; machine shop technology; machine tool technology; masonry; mechanics and repair; medical/clinical assistant; medical radiologic technology; occupational safety and health technology; occupational therapist assistant; painting and wall covering; pipefitting and sprinkler fitting; psychiatric/mental health services technology; registered nursing/registered nurse; respiratory care therapy; sheet metal technology; surgical technology; tool and die technology.
Academics *Calendar:* semesters. *Degree:* certificates and associate. *Special study options:* academic remediation for entering students, adult/continuing education programs, advanced placement credit, cooperative education, distance learning, English as a second language, internships, off-campus study, part-time degree program, services for LD students, summer session for credit.
Library 20,247 titles, 138 serial subscriptions, 2,135 audiovisual materials, an OPAC, a Web page.
Student Life *Housing:* college housing not available. *Activities and Organizations:* student-run newspaper, student government, Phi Theta Kappa, Human Services Club, Administrative Office Assistants Club, Radiology Club. *Campus security:* 24-hour emergency response devices and patrols, late-night transport/escort service. *Student services:* personal/psychological counseling.
Athletics *Intramural sports:* baseball M, basketball M/W, cheerleading W, golf M/W, softball W, volleyball M/W.
Costs (2014–15) *Tuition:* state resident $3935 full-time, $132 per credit hour part-time; nonresident $7812 full-time, $260 per credit hour part-time. *Required fees:* $120 full-time, $60 per term part-time. *Payment plans:* installment, deferred payment. *Waivers:* senior citizens and employees or children of employees.
Financial Aid Of all full-time matriculated undergraduates who enrolled in 2012, 92 Federal Work-Study jobs (averaging $3766).
Applying *Options:* electronic application, early admission, deferred entrance. *Required:* high school transcript. *Required for some:* interview. *Application deadlines:* rolling (freshmen), rolling (transfers). *Notification:* continuous (freshmen), continuous (transfers).
Freshman Application Contact Ms. Tracy Funk, Director of Admissions, Ivy Tech Community College–Central Indiana, 50 West Fall Creek Parkway North Drive, Indianapolis, IN 46208-4777. *Phone:* 317-921-4371. *Toll-free phone:* 888-IVYLINE. *Fax:* 317-917-5919. *E-mail:* tfunk@ivytech.edu.
Website: http://www.ivytech.edu/.

Ivy Tech Community College–Columbus
Columbus, Indiana

- **State-supported** 2-year, founded 1963, part of Ivy Tech Community College System
- **Small-town** campus with easy access to Indianapolis
- **Coed,** 4,578 undergraduate students, 28% full-time, 63% women, 37% men

Undergraduates 1,283 full-time, 3,295 part-time. 1% are from out of state; 2% Black or African American, non-Hispanic/Latino; 2% Hispanic/Latino; 0.8% Asian, non-Hispanic/Latino; 0.4% American Indian or Alaska Native, non-Hispanic/Latino; 1% Two or more races, non-Hispanic/Latino; 21%

Race/ethnicity unknown; 4% transferred in. *Retention:* 52% of full-time freshmen returned.

Freshmen *Admission:* 677 enrolled.

Faculty *Total:* 283, 19% full-time. *Student/faculty ratio:* 18:1.

Majors Accounting technology and bookkeeping; automobile/automotive mechanics technology; building/property maintenance; business administration and management; business automation/technology/data entry; cabinetmaking and millwork; child-care and support services management; computer and information sciences; design and visual communications; drafting and design technology; early childhood education; electrical and power transmission installation; electrical, electronic and communications engineering technology; executive assistant/executive secretary; general studies; heating, air conditioning, ventilation and refrigeration maintenance technology; human services; industrial technology; legal assistant/paralegal; liberal arts and sciences/liberal studies; library and archives assisting; machine tool technology; masonry; mechanic and repair technologies related; mechanics and repair; medical/clinical assistant; medical radiologic technology; pipefitting and sprinkler fitting; psychiatric/mental health services technology; robotics technology; surgical technology; tool and die technology.

Academics *Calendar:* semesters. *Degree:* certificates and associate. *Special study options:* academic remediation for entering students, adult/continuing education programs, advanced placement credit, distance learning, internships, part-time degree program, services for LD students, summer session for credit.

Library 7,855 titles, 13,382 serial subscriptions, 989 audiovisual materials, an OPAC, a Web page.

Student Life *Housing:* college housing not available. *Activities and Organizations:* student government, Phi Theta Kappa, LPN Club. *Campus security:* late-night transport/escort service, trained evening security personnel, escort service.

Costs (2014–15) *Tuition:* state resident $3935 full-time, $132 per credit hour part-time; nonresident $7812 full-time, $260 per credit hour part-time. *Required fees:* $120 full-time, $60 per term part-time. *Payment plans:* installment, deferred payment. *Waivers:* senior citizens and employees or children of employees.

Financial Aid Of all full-time matriculated undergraduates who enrolled in 2012, 26 Federal Work-Study jobs (averaging $1694).

Applying *Options:* electronic application, early admission, deferred entrance. *Required:* high school transcript. *Required for some:* interview. *Application deadlines:* rolling (freshmen), rolling (transfers). *Notification:* continuous (freshmen), continuous (transfers).

Freshman Application Contact Alisa Deck, Director of Admissions, Ivy Tech Community College–Columbus, 4475 Central Avenue, Columbus, IN 47203-1868. *Phone:* 812-374-5129. *Toll-free phone:* 888-IVY-LINE. *Fax:* 812-372-0331. *E-mail:* adeck@ivytech.edu. *Website:* http://www.ivytech.edu/.

Ivy Tech Community College–East Central

Muncie, Indiana

- **State-supported** 2-year, founded 1968, part of Ivy Tech Community College System
- **Suburban** 15-acre campus with easy access to Indianapolis
- **Coed,** 7,466 undergraduate students, 44% full-time, 63% women, 37% men

Undergraduates 3,294 full-time, 4,172 part-time. 8% Black or African American, non-Hispanic/Latino; 2% Hispanic/Latino; 0.6% Asian, non-Hispanic/Latino; 0.5% American Indian or Alaska Native, non-Hispanic/Latino; 3% Two or more races, non-Hispanic/Latino; 7% Race/ethnicity unknown; 5% transferred in. *Retention:* 46% of full-time freshmen returned.

Freshmen *Admission:* 1,409 enrolled.

Faculty *Total:* 566, 20% full-time. *Student/faculty ratio:* 18:1.

Majors Accounting technology and bookkeeping; automobile/automotive mechanics technology; building/property maintenance; business administration and management; business automation/technology/data entry; cabinetmaking and millwork; carpentry; child-care and support services management; computer and information sciences; construction trades; construction trades related; criminal justice/safety; early childhood education; electrical, electronic and communications engineering technology; electrician; executive assistant/executive secretary; general studies; heating, air conditioning, ventilation and refrigeration maintenance technology; hospitality administration; hospitality administration related; human services; industrial mechanics and maintenance technology; industrial production technologies related; industrial technology; legal assistant/paralegal; liberal arts and sciences/liberal studies; library and archives assisting; machine tool technology; masonry; medical/clinical assistant; medical radiologic technology; painting and wall covering; physical therapy technology;

pipefitting and sprinkler fitting; psychiatric/mental health services technology; registered nursing/registered nurse; surgical technology; tool and die technology.

Academics *Calendar:* semesters. *Degree:* certificates and associate. *Special study options:* academic remediation for entering students, adult/continuing education programs, advanced placement credit, distance learning, internships, part-time degree program, services for LD students.

Library 5,779 titles, 145 serial subscriptions, 6,266 audiovisual materials, an OPAC, a Web page.

Student Life *Housing:* college housing not available. *Activities and Organizations:* Business Professionals of America, Skills USA - VICA, student government, Phi Theta Kappa, Human Services Club.

Costs (2014–15) *Tuition:* state resident $3935 full-time, $132 per credit hour part-time; nonresident $7812 full-time, $260 per credit hour part-time. *Required fees:* $120 full-time, $60 per term part-time. *Payment plans:* installment, deferred payment. *Waivers:* senior citizens and employees or children of employees.

Financial Aid Of all full-time matriculated undergraduates who enrolled in 2012, 65 Federal Work-Study jobs (averaging $2666).

Applying *Options:* electronic application, early admission, deferred entrance. *Required:* high school transcript. *Required for some:* interview. *Application deadlines:* rolling (freshmen), rolling (transfers). *Notification:* continuous (freshmen), continuous (transfers).

Freshman Application Contact Ms. Mary Lewellen, Ivy Tech Community College–East Central, 4301 South Cowan Road, Muncie, IN 47302-9448. *Phone:* 765-289-2291 Ext. 1391. *Toll-free phone:* 888-IVY-LINE. *Fax:* 765-289-2292. *E-mail:* mlewelle@ivytech.edu. *Website:* http://www.ivytech.edu/.

Ivy Tech Community College–Kokomo

Kokomo, Indiana

- **State-supported** 2-year, founded 1968, part of Ivy Tech Community College System
- **Small-town** 20-acre campus with easy access to Indianapolis
- **Coed,** 3,948 undergraduate students, 40% full-time, 63% women, 37% men

Undergraduates 1,587 full-time, 2,361 part-time. 6% Black or African American, non-Hispanic/Latino; 3% Hispanic/Latino; 0.6% Asian, non-Hispanic/Latino; 0.7% American Indian or Alaska Native, non-Hispanic/Latino; 2% Two or more races, non-Hispanic/Latino; 3% Race/ethnicity unknown; 4% transferred in. *Retention:* 49% of full-time freshmen returned.

Freshmen *Admission:* 645 enrolled.

Faculty *Total:* 329, 23% full-time. *Student/faculty ratio:* 15:1.

Majors Accounting technology and bookkeeping; automobile/automotive mechanics technology; building/property maintenance; business administration and management; business automation/technology/data entry; cabinetmaking and millwork; child-care and support services management; computer and information sciences; construction trades related; criminal justice/safety; drafting and design technology; early childhood education; electrical, electronic and communications engineering technology; electrician; emergency medical technology (EMT paramedic); executive assistant/executive secretary; general studies; heating, air conditioning, ventilation and refrigeration maintenance technology; human services; industrial technology; legal assistant/paralegal; liberal arts and sciences/liberal studies; library and archives assisting; machine tool technology; mechanic and repair technologies related; mechanics and repair; medical/clinical assistant; pipefitting and sprinkler fitting; psychiatric/mental health services technology; surgical technology; tool and die technology.

Academics *Calendar:* semesters. *Degree:* certificates and associate. *Special study options:* academic remediation for entering students, adult/continuing education programs, advanced placement credit, distance learning, internships, part-time degree program, services for LD students, summer session for credit.

Library 5,177 titles, 99 serial subscriptions, 772 audiovisual materials, an OPAC, a Web page.

Student Life *Housing:* college housing not available. *Activities and Organizations:* student-run newspaper, student government, Collegiate Secretaries International, Licensed Practical Nursing Club, Phi Theta Kappa. *Campus security:* 24-hour emergency response devices, late-night transport/escort service. *Student services:* personal/psychological counseling.

Costs (2014–15) *Tuition:* state resident $3935 full-time, $132 per credit hour part-time; nonresident $7812 full-time, $260 per credit hour part-time. *Required fees:* $120 full-time.

Financial Aid Of all full-time matriculated undergraduates who enrolled in 2012, 45 Federal Work-Study jobs (averaging $1829).

Applying *Options:* electronic application, early admission. *Required:* high school transcript. *Required for some:* interview. *Application deadlines:*

rolling (freshmen), rolling (transfers). *Notification:* continuous (freshmen), continuous (transfers).

Freshman Application Contact Mr. Mike Federspill, Director of Admissions, Ivy Tech Community College–Kokomo, 1815 East Morgan Street, Kokomo, IN 46903-1373. *Phone:* 765-459-0561 Ext. 233. *Toll-free phone:* 888-IVY-LINE. *Fax:* 765-454-5111. *E-mail:* mfedersp@ivytech.edu. *Website:* http://www.ivytech.edu/.

Ivy Tech Community College–Lafayette
Lafayette, Indiana

- **State-supported** 2-year, founded 1968, part of Ivy Tech Community College System
- **Suburban** campus with easy access to Indianapolis
- **Coed,** 6,398 undergraduate students, 44% full-time, 54% women, 46% men

Undergraduates 2,792 full-time, 3,606 part-time. 4% are from out of state; 4% Black or African American, non-Hispanic/Latino; 6% Hispanic/Latino; 2% Asian, non-Hispanic/Latino; 0.5% American Indian or Alaska Native, non-Hispanic/Latino; 2% Two or more races, non-Hispanic/Latino; 9% Race/ethnicity unknown; 5% transferred in. *Retention:* 55% of full-time freshmen returned.

Freshmen *Admission:* 1,088 enrolled.

Faculty *Total:* 439, 22% full-time. *Student/faculty ratio:* 19:1.

Majors Accounting; accounting technology and bookkeeping; automobile/automotive mechanics technology; biotechnology; building/property maintenance; business administration and management; business automation/technology/data entry; cabinetmaking and millwork; carpentry; child-care and support services management; computer and information sciences; drafting and design technology; early childhood education; electrical, electronic and communications engineering technology; electrician; executive assistant/executive secretary; general studies; heating, air conditioning, ventilation and refrigeration maintenance technology; human services; industrial production technologies related; industrial technology; ironworking; legal assistant/paralegal; liberal arts and sciences/liberal studies; library and archives assisting; lineworker; machine tool technology; masonry; mechanic and repair technologies related; mechanics and repair; medical/clinical assistant; painting and wall covering; pipefitting and sprinkler fitting; psychiatric/mental health services technology; quality control and safety technologies related; quality control technology; registered nursing/registered nurse; respiratory care therapy; robotics technology; sheet metal technology; surgical technology; tool and die technology.

Academics *Calendar:* semesters. *Degree:* certificates and associate. *Special study options:* academic remediation for entering students, advanced placement credit, distance learning, internships, part-time degree program, services for LD students, summer session for credit.

Library 8,043 titles, 200 serial subscriptions, 2,234 audiovisual materials, an OPAC, a Web page.

Student Life *Housing:* college housing not available. *Activities and Organizations:* student-run newspaper, student government, Phi Theta Kappa, LPN Club, Accounting Club, Student Computer Technology Association. *Student services:* personal/psychological counseling.

Costs (2014–15) *Tuition:* state resident $3935 full-time, $132 per credit hour part-time; nonresident $7812 full-time, $260 per credit hour part-time. *Required fees:* $120 full-time.

Financial Aid Of all full-time matriculated undergraduates who enrolled in 2012, 65 Federal Work-Study jobs (averaging $2222). 1 state and other part-time job (averaging $2436).

Applying *Options:* electronic application. *Required:* high school transcript. *Required for some:* interview. *Application deadlines:* rolling (freshmen), rolling (transfers). *Notification:* continuous (freshmen), continuous (transfers).

Freshman Application Contact Mr. Ivan Hernanadez, Director of Admissions, Ivy Tech Community College–Lafayette, 3101 South Creasy Lane, PO Box 6299, Lafayette, IN 47903. *Phone:* 765-269-5116. *Toll-free phone:* 888-IVY-LINE. *Fax:* 765-772-9293. *E-mail:* ihernand@ivytech.edu. *Website:* http://www.ivytech.edu/.

Ivy Tech Community College–North Central
South Bend, Indiana

- **State-supported** 2-year, founded 1968, part of Ivy Tech Community College System
- **Suburban** 4-acre campus
- **Coed,** 7,182 undergraduate students, 29% full-time, 61% women, 39% men

Undergraduates 2,059 full-time, 5,123 part-time. 4% are from out of state; 17% Black or African American, non-Hispanic/Latino; 9% Hispanic/Latino; 1% Asian, non-Hispanic/Latino; 0.4% American Indian or Alaska Native, non-Hispanic/Latino; 3% Two or more races, non-Hispanic/Latino; 4%

Race/ethnicity unknown; 0.1% international; 5% transferred in. *Retention:* 47% of full-time freshmen returned.

Freshmen *Admission:* 1,198 enrolled.

Faculty *Total:* 415, 26% full-time. *Student/faculty ratio:* 18:1.

Majors Accounting technology and bookkeeping; automobile/automotive mechanics technology; biotechnology; building/property maintenance; business administration and management; business automation/technology/data entry; cabinetmaking and millwork; carpentry; child-care and support services management; clinical/medical laboratory technology; computer and information sciences; criminal justice/safety; design and visual communications; early childhood education; educational/instructional technology; electrical, electronic and communications engineering technology; electrician; emergency medical technology (EMT paramedic); executive assistant/executive secretary; general studies; heating, air conditioning, ventilation and refrigeration maintenance technology; hospitality administration; human services; industrial production technologies related; industrial technology; interior design; ironworking; legal assistant/paralegal; liberal arts and sciences/liberal studies; library and archives assisting; machine tool technology; masonry; mechanic and repair technologies related; mechanics and repair; medical/clinical assistant; painting and wall covering; pipefitting and sprinkler fitting; registered nursing/registered nurse; robotics technology; sheet metal technology; telecommunications technology; tool and die technology.

Academics *Calendar:* semesters. *Degree:* certificates and associate. *Special study options:* academic remediation for entering students, adult/continuing education programs, advanced placement credit, distance learning, English as a second language, internships, off-campus study, part-time degree program, services for LD students, summer session for credit.

Library 6,246 titles, 90 serial subscriptions, 689 audiovisual materials, an OPAC, a Web page.

Student Life *Housing:* college housing not available. *Activities and Organizations:* Phi Theta Kappa, student government, LPN Club. *Campus security:* 24-hour emergency response devices and patrols, late-night transport/escort service, security during open hours. *Student services:* personal/psychological counseling, women's center.

Costs (2014–15) *Tuition:* state resident $3935 full-time, $131 per credit part-time; nonresident $7812 full-time, $260 per credit part-time. *Required fees:* $120 full-time.

Financial Aid Of all full-time matriculated undergraduates who enrolled in 2012, 100 Federal Work-Study jobs (averaging $1538).

Applying *Options:* electronic application, early admission, deferred entrance. *Required:* high school transcript. *Required for some:* interview. *Application deadlines:* rolling (freshmen), rolling (transfers). *Notification:* continuous (freshmen), continuous (transfers).

Freshman Application Contact Ms. Janice Austin, Director of Admissions, Ivy Tech Community College–North Central, 220 Dean Johnson Boulevard, South Bend, IN 46601-3415. *Phone:* 574-289-7001 Ext. 5326. *Toll-free phone:* 888-IVY-LINE. *Fax:* 574-236-7177. *E-mail:* jaustin@ivytech.edu. *Website:* http://www.ivytech.edu/.

Ivy Tech Community College–Northeast
Fort Wayne, Indiana

- **State-supported** 2-year, founded 1969, part of Ivy Tech Community College System
- **Urban** 22-acre campus
- **Coed,** 9,102 undergraduate students, 35% full-time, 57% women, 43% men

Undergraduates 3,177 full-time, 5,925 part-time. 6% are from out of state; 15% Black or African American, non-Hispanic/Latino; 5% Hispanic/Latino; 2% Asian, non-Hispanic/Latino; 0.5% American Indian or Alaska Native, non-Hispanic/Latino; 3% Two or more races, non-Hispanic/Latino; 3% Race/ethnicity unknown; 6% transferred in. *Retention:* 45% of full-time freshmen returned.

Freshmen *Admission:* 1,547 enrolled.

Faculty *Total:* 541, 25% full-time. *Student/faculty ratio:* 19:1.

Majors Accounting technology and bookkeeping; automobile/automotive mechanics technology; building/property maintenance; business administration and management; business automation/technology/data entry; cabinetmaking and millwork; child-care and support services management; computer and information sciences; construction trades; construction trades related; drafting and design technology; early childhood education; electrical, electronic and communications engineering technology; electrician; executive assistant/executive secretary; general studies; heating, air conditioning, ventilation and refrigeration maintenance technology; hospitality administration; hospitality administration related; human services; industrial production technologies related; industrial technology; ironworking; legal assistant/paralegal; liberal arts and sciences/liberal studies; library and archives assisting; machine tool technology; masonry; massage therapy; mechanics and repair; medical/clinical assistant; occupational safety and health technology; painting and wall covering; pipefitting and sprinkler fitting; psychiatric/mental health services technology; respiratory care therapy; robotics technology; sheet metal technology; tool and die technology.

Academics *Calendar:* semesters. *Degree:* certificates and associate. *Special study options:* adult/continuing education programs, advanced placement credit, distance learning, English as a second language, internships, part-time degree program, services for LD students, summer session for credit.

Library 18,389 titles, 110 serial subscriptions, 3,397 audiovisual materials, an OPAC, a Web page.

Student Life *Housing:* college housing not available. *Activities and Organizations:* student-run newspaper, student government, LPN Club, Phi Theta Kappa. *Campus security:* 24-hour emergency response devices and patrols, late-night transport/escort service.

Costs (2014–15) *Tuition:* state resident $3935 full-time, $132 per credit hour part-time; nonresident $7812 full-time, $260 per credit hour part-time. *Required fees:* $120 full-time.

Financial Aid Of all full-time matriculated undergraduates who enrolled in 2012, 40 Federal Work-Study jobs (averaging $4041).

Applying *Options:* early admission. *Required:* high school transcript. *Required for some:* interview. *Application deadlines:* rolling (freshmen), rolling (transfers). *Notification:* continuous (freshmen), continuous (transfers).

Freshman Application Contact Robyn Boss, Director of Admissions, Ivy Tech Community College–Northeast, 3800 North Anthony Boulevard, Ft. Wayne, IN 46805-1489. *Phone:* 260-480-4211. *Toll-free phone:* 888-IVY-LINE. *Fax:* 260-480-2053. *E-mail:* rboss1@ivytech.edu. *Website:* http://www.ivytech.edu/.

Ivy Tech Community College–Northwest
Gary, Indiana

- **State-supported** 2-year, founded 1963, part of Ivy Tech Community College System
- **Urban** 13-acre campus with easy access to Chicago
- **Coed**, 9,942 undergraduate students, 35% full-time, 58% women, 42% men

Undergraduates 3,431 full-time, 6,511 part-time. 3% are from out of state; 24% Black or African American, non-Hispanic/Latino; 10% Hispanic/Latino; 0.6% Asian, non-Hispanic/Latino; 0.4% American Indian or Alaska Native, non-Hispanic/Latino; 3% Two or more races, non-Hispanic/Latino; 8% Race/ethnicity unknown; 6% transferred in. *Retention:* 44% of full-time freshmen returned.

Freshmen *Admission:* 1,653 enrolled.

Faculty *Total:* 536, 24% full-time. *Student/faculty ratio:* 21:1.

Majors Accounting technology and bookkeeping; automobile/automotive mechanics technology; building/construction finishing, management, and inspection related; building/property maintenance; business administration and management; business automation/technology/data entry; cabinetmaking and millwork; carpentry; child-care and support services management; computer and information sciences; construction trades; criminal justice/safety; drafting and design technology; early childhood education; electrical, electronic and communications engineering technology; electrician; executive assistant/executive secretary; funeral service and mortuary science; general studies; heating, air conditioning, ventilation and refrigeration maintenance technology; hospitality administration; human services; industrial technology; ironworking; legal assistant/paralegal; liberal arts and sciences/liberal studies; library and archives assisting; machine tool technology; masonry; mechanic and repair technologies related; mechanics and repair; medical/clinical assistant; occupational safety and health technology; painting and wall covering; pipefitting and sprinkler fitting; psychiatric/mental health services technology; registered nursing/registered nurse; respiratory care therapy; sheet metal technology; surgical technology; telecommunications technology; tool and die technology.

Academics *Calendar:* semesters. *Degree:* certificates and associate. *Special study options:* academic remediation for entering students, adult/continuing education programs, advanced placement credit, distance learning, internships, part-time degree program, services for LD students, summer session for credit.

Library 13,805 titles, 160 serial subscriptions, 4,295 audiovisual materials, an OPAC, a Web page.

Student Life *Housing:* college housing not available. *Activities and Organizations:* Phi Theta Kappa, LPN Club, Computer Club, student government, Business Club. *Campus security:* 24-hour emergency response devices, late-night transport/escort service.

Costs (2014–15) *Tuition:* state resident $3935 full-time, $131 per credit part-time; nonresident $7812 full-time, $260 per credit part-time. *Required fees:* $120 full-time. *Waivers:* senior citizens and employees or children of employees.

Financial Aid Of all full-time matriculated undergraduates who enrolled in 2012, 74 Federal Work-Study jobs (averaging $2131).

Applying *Options:* electronic application, deferred entrance. *Required:* high school transcript. *Required for some:* interview. *Application deadlines:*

rolling (freshmen), rolling (transfers). *Notification:* continuous (freshmen), continuous (transfers).

Freshman Application Contact Ms. Twilla Lewis, Associate Dean of Student Affairs, Ivy Tech Community College–Northwest, 1440 East 35th Avenue, Gary, IN 46409-499. *Phone:* 219-981-1111 Ext. 2273. *Toll-free phone:* 888-IVY-LINE. *Fax:* 219-981-4415. *E-mail:* tlewis@ivytech.edu. *Website:* http://www.ivytech.edu/.

Ivy Tech Community College–Richmond
Richmond, Indiana

- **State-supported** 2-year, founded 1963, part of Ivy Tech Community College System
- **Small-town** 23-acre campus with easy access to Indianapolis
- **Coed**, 3,095 undergraduate students, 34% full-time, 66% women, 34% men

Undergraduates 1,042 full-time, 2,053 part-time. 8% are from out of state; 10% Black or African American, non-Hispanic/Latino; 1% Hispanic/Latino; 0.6% American Indian or Alaska Native, non-Hispanic/Latino; 2% Two or more races, non-Hispanic/Latino; 2% Race/ethnicity unknown; 3% transferred in. *Retention:* 46% of full-time freshmen returned.

Freshmen *Admission:* 541 enrolled.

Faculty *Total:* 198, 20% full-time. *Student/faculty ratio:* 19:1.

Majors Accounting technology and bookkeeping; automobile/automotive mechanics technology; building/property maintenance; business administration and management; business automation/technology/data entry; cabinetmaking and millwork; child-care and support services management; computer and information sciences; construction trades; construction trades related; early childhood education; electrical, electronic and communications engineering technology; electrician; executive assistant/executive secretary; general studies; heating, air conditioning, ventilation and refrigeration maintenance technology; human services; industrial production technologies related; industrial technology; legal assistant/paralegal; liberal arts and sciences/liberal studies; library and archives assisting; machine tool technology; mechanics and repair; medical/clinical assistant; pipefitting and sprinkler fitting; psychiatric/mental health services technology; registered nursing/registered nurse; robotics technology; tool and die technology.

Academics *Calendar:* semesters. *Degree:* certificates and associate. *Special study options:* academic remediation for entering students, adult/continuing education programs, advanced placement credit, distance learning, independent study, internships, off-campus study, part-time degree program, services for LD students, summer session for credit.

Student Life *Housing:* college housing not available. *Activities and Organizations:* student-run newspaper, student government, Phi Theta Kappa, LPN Club, CATS 2000, Business Professionals of America. *Campus security:* 24-hour emergency response devices, late-night transport/escort service. *Student services:* personal/psychological counseling.

Athletics *Intramural sports:* softball M/W.

Costs (2014–15) *Tuition:* state resident $3935 full-time, $132 per credit hour part-time; nonresident $7812 full-time, $260 per credit hour part-time. *Required fees:* $120 full-time.

Financial Aid Of all full-time matriculated undergraduates who enrolled in 2012, 14 Federal Work-Study jobs (averaging $3106). 1 state and other part-time job (averaging $3380).

Applying *Options:* electronic application, early admission. *Required:* high school transcript. *Required for some:* interview. *Application deadlines:* rolling (freshmen), rolling (transfers). *Notification:* continuous (freshmen), continuous (transfers).

Freshman Application Contact Christine Seger, Director of Admissions, Ivy Tech Community College–Richmond, 2325 Chester Boulevard, Richmond, IN 47374-1298. *Phone:* 765-966-2656 Ext. 1212. *Toll-free phone:* 888-IVY-LINE. *Fax:* 765-962-8741. *E-mail:* crethlake@ivytech.edu. *Website:* http://www.ivytech.edu/richmond/.

Ivy Tech Community College–Southeast
Madison, Indiana

- **State-supported** 2-year, founded 1963, part of Ivy Tech Community College System
- **Small-town** 5-acre campus with easy access to Louisville
- **Coed**, 2,881 undergraduate students, 34% full-time, 66% women, 34% men

Undergraduates 977 full-time, 1,904 part-time. 6% are from out of state; 0.8% Black or African American, non-Hispanic/Latino; 0.9% Hispanic/Latino; 0.3% Asian, non-Hispanic/Latino; 0.2% American Indian or Alaska Native, non-Hispanic/Latino; 1% Two or more races, non-Hispanic/Latino; 15% Race/ethnicity unknown; 4% transferred in. *Retention:* 55% of full-time freshmen returned.

Freshmen *Admission:* 479 enrolled.

Faculty *Total:* 226, 22% full-time. *Student/faculty ratio:* 15:1.

Majors Accounting technology and bookkeeping; business administration and management; business automation/technology/data entry; child-care and support services management; computer and information sciences; early childhood education; electrical, electronic and communications engineering technology; executive assistant/executive secretary; general studies; human services; industrial technology; legal assistant/paralegal; liberal arts and sciences/liberal studies; library and archives assisting; licensed practical/vocational nurse training; medical/clinical assistant; psychiatric/mental health services technology; registered nursing/registered nurse.

Academics *Calendar:* semesters. *Degree:* certificates and associate. *Special study options:* academic remediation for entering students, advanced placement credit, distance learning, internships, part-time degree program, services for LD students, summer session for credit.

Library 9,027 titles, 14,299 serial subscriptions, 1,341 audiovisual materials, an OPAC, a Web page.

Student Life *Housing:* college housing not available. *Activities and Organizations:* student government, Phi Theta Kappa, LPN Club. *Campus security:* 24-hour emergency response devices.

Costs (2014–15) *Tuition:* state resident $3935 full-time, $132 per credit hour part-time; nonresident $7812 full-time, $260 per credit hour part-time. *Required fees:* $120 full-time, $60 per term part-time.

Financial Aid Of all full-time matriculated undergraduates who enrolled in 2012, 26 Federal Work-Study jobs (averaging $1696).

Applying *Options:* electronic application. *Required:* high school transcript. *Required for some:* interview. *Application deadlines:* rolling (freshmen), rolling (transfers). *Notification:* continuous (freshmen), continuous (transfers).

Freshman Application Contact Ms. Cindy Hutcherson, Assistant Director of Admission/Career Counselor, Ivy Tech Community College–Southeast, 590 Ivy Tech Drive, Madison, IN 47250-1881. *Phone:* 812-265-2580 Ext. 4142. *Toll-free phone:* 888-IVY-LINE. *Fax:* 812-265-4028. *E-mail:* chutcher@ivytech.edu.
Website: http://www.ivytech.edu/.

Ivy Tech Community College–Southern Indiana

Sellersburg, Indiana

- **State-supported** 2-year, founded 1968, part of Ivy Tech Community College System
- **Small-town** 63-acre campus with easy access to Louisville
- **Coed**, 4,892 undergraduate students, 26% full-time, 55% women, 45% men

Undergraduates 1,285 full-time, 3,607 part-time. 8% are from out of state; 7% Black or African American, non-Hispanic/Latino; 2% Hispanic/Latino; 0.7% Asian, non-Hispanic/Latino; 0.5% American Indian or Alaska Native, non-Hispanic/Latino; 2% Two or more races, non-Hispanic/Latino; 11% Race/ethnicity unknown; 6% transferred in. *Retention:* 48% of full-time freshmen returned.

Freshmen *Admission:* 907 enrolled.

Faculty *Total:* 275, 21% full-time. *Student/faculty ratio:* 19:1.

Majors Accounting technology and bookkeeping; automobile/automotive mechanics technology; building/property maintenance; business administration and management; business automation/technology/data entry; cabinetmaking and millwork; carpentry; child-care and support services management; computer and information sciences; design and visual communications; early childhood education; electrical, electronic and communications engineering technology; electrician; executive assistant/executive secretary; general studies; heating, air conditioning, ventilation and refrigeration maintenance technology; human services; industrial technology; legal assistant/paralegal; liberal arts and sciences/liberal studies; library and archives assisting; machine tool technology; masonry; mechanics and repair; medical/clinical assistant; pipefitting and sprinkler fitting; psychiatric/mental health services technology; registered nursing/registered nurse; respiratory care therapy; sheet metal technology; tool and die technology.

Academics *Calendar:* semesters. *Degree:* certificates and associate. *Special study options:* academic remediation for entering students, adult/continuing education programs, advanced placement credit, cooperative education, distance learning, internships, part-time degree program, services for LD students, summer session for credit.

Library 7,634 titles, 66 serial subscriptions, 648 audiovisual materials, an OPAC, a Web page.

Student Life *Housing:* college housing not available. *Activities and Organizations:* Phi Theta Kappa, Practical Nursing Club, Medical Assistant Club, Accounting Club, student government. *Campus security:* late-night transport/escort service.

Costs (2014–15) *Tuition:* state resident $3935 full-time, $132 per credit hour part-time; nonresident $7812 full-time, $260 per credit hour part-time. *Required fees:* $120 full-time, $60 per term part-time.

Financial Aid Of all full-time matriculated undergraduates who enrolled in 2012, 20 Federal Work-Study jobs (averaging $5007). 1 state and other part-time job (averaging $6080).

Applying *Options:* electronic application, early admission, deferred entrance. *Required:* high school transcript. *Required for some:* interview. *Application deadlines:* rolling (freshmen), rolling (transfers). *Notification:* continuous (freshmen), continuous (transfers).

Freshman Application Contact Ben Harris, Director of Admissions, Ivy Tech Community College–Southern Indiana, 8204 Highway 311, Sellersburg, IN 47172-1897. *Phone:* 812-246-3301 Ext. 4137. *Toll-free phone:* 888-IVY-LINE. *Fax:* 812-246-9905. *E-mail:* bharris88@ivytech.edu.
Website: http://www.ivytech.edu/.

Ivy Tech Community College–Southwest

Evansville, Indiana

- **State-supported** 2-year, founded 1963, part of Ivy Tech Community College System
- **Suburban** 15-acre campus
- **Coed**, 5,475 undergraduate students, 33% full-time, 54% women, 46% men

Undergraduates 1,827 full-time, 3,648 part-time. 6% are from out of state; 10% Black or African American, non-Hispanic/Latino; 1% Hispanic/Latino; 0.4% Asian, non-Hispanic/Latino; 0.3% American Indian or Alaska Native, non-Hispanic/Latino; 2% Two or more races, non-Hispanic/Latino; 7% Race/ethnicity unknown; 5% transferred in. *Retention:* 48% of full-time freshmen returned.

Freshmen *Admission:* 857 enrolled.

Faculty *Total:* 344, 25% full-time. *Student/faculty ratio:* 18:1.

Majors Accounting technology and bookkeeping; automobile/automotive mechanics technology; boilermaking; building/property maintenance; business administration and management; business automation/technology/data entry; cabinetmaking and millwork; carpentry; child-care and support services management; computer and information sciences; construction/heavy equipment/earthmoving equipment operation; criminal justice/safety; design and visual communications; early childhood education; electrical, electronic and communications engineering technology; electrician; emergency medical technology (EMT paramedic); executive assistant/executive secretary; general studies; graphic design; heating, air conditioning, ventilation and refrigeration maintenance technology; human services; industrial production technologies related; industrial technology; interior design; ironworking; legal assistant/paralegal; liberal arts and sciences/liberal studies; library and archives assisting; machine tool technology; masonry; mechanic and repair technologies related; mechanics and repair; medical/clinical assistant; painting and wall covering; pipefitting and sprinkler fitting; psychiatric/mental health services technology; registered nursing/registered nurse; robotics technology; sheet metal technology; surgical technology; tool and die technology.

Academics *Calendar:* semesters. *Degree:* certificates and associate. *Special study options:* academic remediation for entering students, advanced placement credit, cooperative education, distance learning, independent study, internships, part-time degree program, services for LD students, summer session for credit.

Library 7,082 titles, 107 serial subscriptions, 1,755 audiovisual materials, an OPAC, a Web page.

Student Life *Housing:* college housing not available. *Activities and Organizations:* student government, Phi Theta Kappa, LPN Club, National Association of Industrial Technology, Design Club. *Campus security:* late-night transport/escort service.

Costs (2014–15) *Tuition:* state resident $3934 full-time, $132 per credit hour part-time; nonresident $7812 full-time, $260 per credit hour part-time. *Required fees:* $120 full-time, $60 per term part-time.

Financial Aid Of all full-time matriculated undergraduates who enrolled in 2012, 65 Federal Work-Study jobs (averaging $2264).

Applying *Options:* electronic application, early admission, deferred entrance. *Required:* high school transcript. *Required for some:* interview. *Application deadlines:* rolling (freshmen), rolling (transfers). *Notification:* continuous (freshmen), continuous (transfers).

Freshman Application Contact Ms. Denise Johnson-Kincade, Director of Admissions, Ivy Tech Community College–Southwest, 3501 First Avenue, Evansville, IN 47710-3398. *Phone:* 812-429-1430. *Toll-free phone:* 888-IVY-LINE. *Fax:* 812-429-9878. *E-mail:* ajohnson@ivytech.edu.
Website: http://www.ivytech.edu/.

Ivy Tech Community College–Wabash Valley

Terre Haute, Indiana

- **State-supported** 2-year, founded 1966, part of Ivy Tech Community College System
- **Suburban** 55-acre campus with easy access to Indianapolis
- **Coed,** 5,364 undergraduate students, 36% full-time, 55% women, 45% men

Undergraduates 1,921 full-time, 3,443 part-time. 5% are from out of state; 4% Black or African American, non-Hispanic/Latino; 0.9% Hispanic/Latino; 0.7% Asian, non-Hispanic/Latino; 0.4% American Indian or Alaska Native, non-Hispanic/Latino; 2% Two or more races, non-Hispanic/Latino; 4% Race/ethnicity unknown; 3% transferred in. *Retention:* 48% of full-time freshmen returned.

Freshmen *Admission:* 578 enrolled.

Faculty *Total:* 287, 34% full-time. *Student/faculty ratio:* 19:1.

Majors Accounting technology and bookkeeping; airframe mechanics and aircraft maintenance technology; allied health diagnostic, intervention, and treatment professions related; automobile/automotive mechanics technology; building/property maintenance; business administration and management; cabinetmaking and millwork; carpentry; child-care and support services management; clinical/medical laboratory technology; computer and information sciences; construction/heavy equipment/earthmoving equipment operation; criminal justice/safety; design and visual communications; early childhood education; electrical, electronic and communications engineering technology; electrician; emergency medical technology (EMT paramedic); executive assistant/executive secretary; general studies; heating, air conditioning, ventilation and refrigeration maintenance technology; human services; industrial production technologies related; industrial technology; ironworking; legal assistant/paralegal; liberal arts and sciences/liberal studies; library and archives assisting; machine tool technology; masonry; mechanics and repair; medical/clinical assistant; medical radiologic technology; occupational safety and health technology; office management; painting and wall covering; pipefitting and sprinkler fitting; psychiatric/mental health services technology; quality control and safety technologies related; registered nursing/registered nurse; robotics technology; sheet metal technology; surgical technology; tool and die technology.

Academics *Calendar:* semesters. *Degree:* certificates and associate. *Special study options:* academic remediation for entering students, adult/continuing education programs, advanced placement credit, distance learning, internships, part-time degree program, services for LD students, summer session for credit.

Library 4,403 titles, 77 serial subscriptions, 406 audiovisual materials, an OPAC, a Web page.

Student Life *Housing:* college housing not available. *Activities and Organizations:* student government, Phi Theta Kappa, LPN Club, National Association of Industrial Technology. *Campus security:* 24-hour emergency response devices. *Student services:* personal/psychological counseling, women's center.

Athletics *Intramural sports:* basketball M/W, volleyball M/W.

Costs (2014–15) *Tuition:* state resident $3935 full-time, $132 per credit hour part-time; nonresident $7812 full-time, $260 per credit hour part-time. *Required fees:* $120 full-time.

Financial Aid Of all full-time matriculated undergraduates who enrolled in 2012, 51 Federal Work-Study jobs (averaging $2110). 1 state and other part-time job (averaging $2963).

Applying *Options:* electronic application, early admission, deferred entrance. *Required:* high school transcript. *Required for some:* interview. *Application deadlines:* rolling (freshmen), rolling (transfers). *Notification:* continuous (freshmen), continuous (transfers).

Freshman Application Contact Mr. Michael Fisher, Director of Admissions, Ivy Tech Community College–Wabash Valley, 7999 U.S. Highway 41 South, Terre Haute, IN 47802-4898. *Phone:* 812-298-2300. *Toll-free phone:* 888-IVY-LINE. *Fax:* 812-298-2291. *E-mail:* mfisher@ivytech.edu.

Website: http://www.ivytech.edu/.

Kaplan College, Hammond Campus

Hammond, Indiana

Freshman Application Contact Kaplan College, Hammond Campus, 7833 Indianapolis Boulevard, Hammond, IN 46324. *Phone:* 219-844-0100. *Toll-free phone:* 800-935-1857.

Website: http://hammond.kaplancollege.com/.

Kaplan College, Southeast Indianapolis Campus

Indianapolis, Indiana

Freshman Application Contact Director of Admissions, Kaplan College, Southeast Indianapolis Campus, 4200 South East Street, Indianapolis, IN 46227. *Phone:* 317-782-0315.

Website: http://www.seindianapolis.kaplancollege.com/.

Lincoln College of Technology

Indianapolis, Indiana

Director of Admissions Ms. Cindy Ryan, Director of Admissions, Lincoln College of Technology, 7225 Winton Drive, Building 128, Indianapolis, IN 46268. *Phone:* 317-632-5553.

Website: http://www.lincolnedu.com/.

MedTech College

Ft. Wayne, Indiana

Admissions Office Contact MedTech College, 7230 Engle Road, Ft. Wayne, IN 46804.

Website: http://www.medtechcollege.edu/.

MedTech College

Greenwood, Indiana

Admissions Office Contact MedTech College, 1500 American Way, Greenwood, IN 46143.

Website: http://www.medtechcollege.edu/.

Mid-America College of Funeral Service

Jeffersonville, Indiana

Freshman Application Contact Mr. Richard Nelson, Dean of Students, Mid-America College of Funeral Service, 3111 Hamburg Pike, Jeffersonville, IN 47130-9630. *Phone:* 812-288-8878. *Toll-free phone:* 800-221-6158. *Fax:* 812-288-5942. *E-mail:* macfs@mindspring.com.

Website: http://www.mid-america.edu/.

Vet Tech Institute at International Business College

Fort Wayne, Indiana

- **Private** 2-year, founded 2005
- **Suburban** campus
- **Coed,** 128 undergraduate students
- 51% of applicants were admitted

Freshmen *Admission:* 306 applied, 155 admitted.

Majors Veterinary/animal health technology.

Academics *Degree:* associate. *Special study options:* accelerated degree program, internships.

Freshman Application Contact Admissions Office, Vet Tech Institute at International Business College, 5699 Coventry Lane, Fort Wayne, IN 46804. *Phone:* 800-589-6363. *Toll-free phone:* 800-589-6363.

Website: http://ftwayne.vettechinstitute.edu/.

Vet Tech Institute at International Business College

Indianapolis, Indiana

- **Private** 2-year, founded 2007
- **Suburban** campus
- **Coed,** 124 undergraduate students
- 52% of applicants were admitted

Freshmen *Admission:* 463 applied, 239 admitted.

Majors Veterinary/animal health technology.

Academics *Degree:* associate. *Special study options:* accelerated degree program, internships.

Freshman Application Contact Admissions Office, Vet Tech Institute at International Business College, 7205 Shadeland Station, Indianapolis, IN 46256. *Phone:* 800-589-6500. *Toll-free phone:* 877-835-7297.

Website: http://indianapolis.vettechinstitute.edu/.

Vincennes University
Vincennes, Indiana

- **State-supported** primarily 2-year, founded 1801
- **Small-town** 160-acre campus
- **Coed,** 18,383 undergraduate students, 33% full-time, 44% women, 56% men

Undergraduates 6,049 full-time, 12,334 part-time. 12% Black or African American, non-Hispanic/Latino; 3% Hispanic/Latino; 0.6% Asian, non-Hispanic/Latino; 0.2% Native Hawaiian or other Pacific Islander, non-Hispanic/Latino; 0.2% American Indian or Alaska Native, non-Hispanic/Latino; 2% Two or more races, non-Hispanic/Latino; 12% Race/ethnicity unknown; 0.4% international.

Freshmen *Admission:* 5,680 applied, 4,294 admitted, 3,039 enrolled.

Majors Accounting technology and bookkeeping; administrative assistant and secretarial science; agricultural business and management; agricultural engineering; agriculture; aircraft powerplant technology; airline pilot and flight crew; American Sign Language (ASL); anthropology; applied horticulture/horticulture operations; architectural drafting and CAD/CADD; art; art teacher education; art therapy; autobody/collision and repair technology; automobile/automotive mechanics technology; behavioral sciences; biochemistry; biological and biomedical sciences related; biological and physical sciences; biology/biological sciences; biotechnology; building/home/construction inspection; business administration and management; business/commerce; chemistry; chemistry related; chemistry teacher education; child-care and support services management; child-care provision; civil engineering; commercial and advertising art; communications technology; computer and information sciences; computer/information technology services administration related; computer programming; computer science; computer systems networking and telecommunications; construction trades; corrections; corrections and criminal justice related; cosmetology; criminal justice/police science; culinary arts; design and applied arts related; diesel mechanics technology; dietetics; dramatic/theater arts; early childhood education; economics; education; electrical, electronic and communications engineering technology; elementary education; emergency medical technology (EMT paramedic); engineering technology; English; English/language arts teacher education; family and consumer sciences/home economics teacher education; family and consumer sciences/human sciences; fashion merchandising; finance; fire science/firefighting; food science; foreign languages and literatures; foreign languages related; funeral service and mortuary science; geology/earth science; graphic and printing equipment operation/production; health and physical education/fitness; health information/medical records technology; history; hospitality administration; hotel/motel administration; industrial technology; journalism; legal assistant/paralegal; liberal arts and sciences/liberal studies; manufacturing engineering technology; marketing/marketing management; massage therapy; mathematics; mathematics teacher education; mechanical drafting and CAD/CADD; mechanical engineering/mechanical technology; medical radiologic technology; music; music teacher education; natural resources/conservation; nuclear medical technology; ophthalmic and optometric support services and allied professions related; parks, recreation and leisure; pharmacy technician; philosophy; photojournalism; physical education teaching and coaching; physical sciences; physical therapy technology; political science and government; pre-dentistry studies; premedical studies; pre-pharmacy studies; pre-veterinary studies; psychology; public relations/image management; radio and television broadcasting technology; recording arts technology; registered nursing/registered nurse; restaurant, culinary, and catering management; robotics technology; science teacher education; secondary education; securities services administration; security and loss prevention; sheet metal technology; social work; sociology; special education; sport and fitness administration/management; surgical technology; surveying technology; teacher assistant/aide; theater design and technology; tool and die technology; web/multimedia management and webmaster; woodworking.

Academics *Calendar:* semesters. *Degrees:* certificates, associate, and bachelor's. *Special study options:* academic remediation for entering students, accelerated degree program, adult/continuing education programs, advanced placement credit, distance learning, double majors, English as a second language, external degree program, freshman honors college, honors programs, independent study, internships, off-campus study, part-time degree program, services for LD students, student-designed majors, summer session for credit. *ROTC:* Army (b), Air Force (c).

Library Shake Learning Resource Center.

Student Life *Housing:* on-campus residence required for freshman year. *Options:* coed, men-only, women-only, special housing for students with disabilities. Campus housing is university owned. Freshman campus housing is guaranteed. *Activities and Organizations:* drama/theater group, student-run newspaper, radio and television station, choral group, national fraternities, national sororities. *Campus security:* 24-hour emergency response devices and patrols, student patrols, late-night transport/escort service, controlled dormitory access, surveillance cameras. *Student services:* health clinic, personal/psychological counseling.

Athletics Member NJCAA. *Intercollegiate sports:* baseball M, basketball M/W, bowling M, cross-country running M/W, golf M, tennis M, track and field M/W, volleyball W.

Costs (2013–14) *Tuition:* state resident $5020 full-time, $2143 per year part-time; nonresident $11,868 full-time, $4882 per term part-time. Full-time tuition and fees vary according to course level, course load, location, program, reciprocity agreements, and student level. Part-time tuition and fees vary according to course level, course load, location, program, reciprocity agreements, and student level. *Room and board:* $8478. Room and board charges vary according to board plan, gender, and housing facility. *Payment plan:* installment. *Waivers:* senior citizens and employees or children of employees.

Financial Aid Of all full-time matriculated undergraduates who enrolled in 2012, 220 Federal Work-Study jobs (averaging $1072).

Applying *Options:* electronic application, early admission, deferred entrance. *Application fee:* $20. *Required:* high school transcript. *Required for some:* interview. *Application deadlines:* rolling (freshmen), rolling (transfers). *Notification:* continuous until 8/1 (freshmen), continuous (transfers).

Freshman Application Contact Vincennes University, 1002 North First Street, Vincennes, IN 47591-5202. *Phone:* 812-888-4313. *Toll-free phone:* 800-742-9198.

Website: http://www.vinu.edu/.

IOWA

Brown Mackie College–Quad Cities
Bettendorf, Iowa

- **Proprietary** 2-year, part of Education Management Corporation
- **Coed**

Majors Business administration and management; computer support specialist; criminal justice/safety; medical office management; occupational therapist assistant.

Academics *Degree:* diplomas and associate.

Freshman Application Contact Brown Mackie College–Quad Cities, 2119 East Kimberly Road, Bettendorf, IA 52722. *Phone:* 563-344-1500. *Toll-free phone:* 888-420-1652.

Website: http://www.brownmackie.edu/quad-cities/.

See display on next page and page 416 for the College Close-Up.

Clinton Community College
Clinton, Iowa

Freshman Application Contact Mr. Gary Mohr, Executive Director of Enrollment Management and Marketing, Clinton Community College, 1000 Lincoln Boulevard, Clinton, IA 52732-6299. *Phone:* 563-336-3322. *Toll-free phone:* 800-462-3255. *Fax:* 563-336-3350. *E-mail:* gmohr@eicc.edu.

Website: http://www.eicc.edu/ccc/.

Des Moines Area Community College
Ankeny, Iowa

Freshman Application Contact Mr. Michael Lentsch, Director of Enrollment Management, Des Moines Area Community College, 2006 South Ankeny Boulevard, Ankeny, IA 50021-8995. *Phone:* 515-964-6216. *Toll-free phone:* 800-362-2127. *Fax:* 515-964-6391. *E-mail:* mjleutsch@dmacc.edu.

Website: http://www.dmacc.edu/.

Ellsworth Community College
Iowa Falls, Iowa

Director of Admissions Mrs. Nancy Walters, Registrar, Ellsworth Community College, 1100 College Avenue, Iowa Falls, IA 50126-1199. *Phone:* 641-648-4611. *Toll-free phone:* 800-ECC-9235.

Website: http://www.iavalley.cc.ia.us/ecc/.

Hawkeye Community College
Waterloo, Iowa

- **State and locally supported** 2-year, founded 1966
- **Rural** 320-acre campus
- **Endowment** $2.0 million
- **Coed,** 5,803 undergraduate students, 53% full-time, 57% women, 43% men

Undergraduates 3,066 full-time, 2,737 part-time. 1% are from out of state; 7% Black or African American, non-Hispanic/Latino; 2% Hispanic/Latino;

0.7% Asian, non-Hispanic/Latino; 0.1% Native Hawaiian or other Pacific Islander, non-Hispanic/Latino; 0.3% American Indian or Alaska Native, non-Hispanic/Latino; 1% Two or more races, non-Hispanic/Latino; 0.2% international; 32% transferred in.

Freshmen *Admission:* 4,905 applied, 3,756 admitted, 1,122 enrolled. *Test scores:* ACT scores over 18: 53%; ACT scores over 24: 15%.

Faculty *Total:* 344, 35% full-time, 9% with terminal degrees. *Student/faculty ratio:* 21:1.

Majors Accounting; agricultural/farm supplies retailing and wholesaling; agricultural power machinery operation; animal/livestock husbandry and production; applied horticulture/horticulture operations; autobody/collision and repair technology; automobile/automotive mechanics technology; carpentry; child-care provision; civil engineering technology; clinical/medical laboratory technology; commercial photography; computer/information technology services administration related; computer systems networking and telecommunications; criminal justice/police science; dental hygiene; diesel mechanics technology; digital communication and media/multimedia; electrical, electronic and communications engineering technology; energy management and systems technology; executive assistant/executive secretary; graphic communications; human resources management; interior design; liberal arts and sciences/liberal studies; machine tool technology; manufacturing engineering technology; medical administrative assistant and medical secretary; multi/interdisciplinary studies related; natural resources management and policy; occupational therapist assistant; physical therapy technology; registered nursing/registered nurse; respiratory care therapy; sales, distribution, and marketing operations; web page, digital/multimedia and information resources design.

Academics *Calendar:* semesters. *Degree:* certificates, diplomas, and associate. *Special study options:* academic remediation for entering students, accelerated degree program, adult/continuing education programs, advanced placement credit, cooperative education, distance learning, English as a second language, external degree program, part-time degree program, services for LD students, study abroad, summer session for credit. *ROTC:* Army (c).

Library Hawkeye Community College Library with 63,279 titles, 246 serial subscriptions, 1,869 audiovisual materials, an OPAC, a Web page.

Student Life *Housing:* college housing not available. *Activities and Organizations:* Student Senate, Phi Theta Kappa, Student Ambassadors, Chorus, Natural Resources. *Campus security:* 24-hour patrols. *Student services:* health clinic, personal/psychological counseling, women's center.

Athletics *Intramural sports:* badminton M/W, basketball M/W, bowling M/W, cross-country running M/W, golf M/W, soccer M/W, table tennis M/W, volleyball M/W.

Standardized Tests *Required:* COMPASS or the equivalent from ACT or accredited college course(s) (for admission). *Required for some:* ACT (for admission).

Applying *Options:* electronic application, deferred entrance. *Required:* high school transcript. *Application deadlines:* rolling (freshmen), rolling (out-of-state freshmen), rolling (transfers). *Notification:* continuous (freshmen), continuous (out-of-state freshmen), continuous (transfers).

Freshman Application Contact Ms. Holly Grimm-See, Associate Director, Admissions and Recruitment, Hawkeye Community College, PO Box 8015, Waterloo, IA 50704-8015. *Phone:* 319-296-4277. *Toll-free phone:* 800-670-4769. *Fax:* 319-296-2505. *E-mail:* holly.grimm-see@hawkeyecollege.edu. *Website:* http://www.hawkeyecollege.edu/.

Indian Hills Community College
Ottumwa, Iowa

Freshman Application Contact Mrs. Jane Sapp, Admissions Officer, Indian Hills Community College, 525 Grandview Avenue, Building #1, Ottumwa, IA 52501-1398. *Phone:* 641-683-5155. *Toll-free phone:* 800-726-2585. *Website:* http://www.ihcc.cc.ia.us/.

Iowa Central Community College
Fort Dodge, Iowa

Freshman Application Contact Mrs. Deb Bahls, Coordinator of Admissions, Iowa Central Community College, 330 Avenue M, Fort Dodge, IA 50501-5798. *Phone:* 515-576-0099 Ext. 2402. *Toll-free phone:* 800-362-2793. *Fax:* 515-576-7724. *E-mail:* bahls@iowacentral.com. *Website:* http://www.iccc.cc.ia.us/.

Iowa Lakes Community College
Estherville, Iowa

- **State and locally supported** 2-year, founded 1967, part of Iowa Community College System
- **Small-town** 20-acre campus
- **Endowment** $6.5 million
- **Coed,** 2,574 undergraduate students, 52% full-time, 55% women, 45% men

Undergraduates 1,343 full-time, 1,231 part-time. Students come from 8 other countries; 4% Black or African American, non-Hispanic/Latino; 4% Hispanic/Latino; 1% Asian, non-Hispanic/Latino; 0.3% Native Hawaiian or

other Pacific Islander, non-Hispanic/Latino; 0.5% American Indian or Alaska Native, non-Hispanic/Latino; 0.5% Two or more races, non-Hispanic/Latino; 2% Race/ethnicity unknown; 0.9% international; 37% live on campus. *Retention:* 54% of full-time freshmen returned.

Freshmen *Admission:* 1,425 applied, 1,318 admitted, 428 enrolled.

Faculty *Total:* 177, 51% full-time. *Student/faculty ratio:* 18:1.

Majors Accounting; accounting technology and bookkeeping; administrative assistant and secretarial science; agribusiness; agricultural business and management; agricultural business and management related; agricultural business technology; agricultural economics; agricultural/farm supplies retailing and wholesaling; agricultural mechanics and equipment technology; agricultural mechanization; agricultural power machinery operation; agricultural production; agricultural production related; agricultural teacher education; agriculture; agronomy and crop science; airline pilot and flight crew; animal/livestock husbandry and production; animal sciences; art; art history, criticism and conservation; art teacher education; astronomy; athletic training; autobody/collision and repair technology; automobile/automotive mechanics technology; aviation/airway management; behavioral sciences; biological and physical sciences; biology/biological sciences; botany/plant biology; broadcast journalism; business administration and management; business automation/technology/data entry; business machine repair; business teacher education; carpentry; ceramic arts and ceramics; chemistry; child-care provision; child development; commercial and advertising art; communication and journalism related; comparative literature; computer and information sciences related; computer graphics; computer/information technology services administration related; computer programming; computer science; computer software technology; computer systems networking and telecommunications; construction engineering technology; construction management; construction trades; consumer merchandising/retailing management; cooking and related culinary arts; corrections; criminal justice/law enforcement administration; criminal justice/police science; crop production; culinary arts related; data entry/microcomputer applications; data processing and data processing technology; design and applied arts related; desktop publishing and digital imaging design; developmental and child psychology; drawing; early childhood education; ecology; economics; education; electrical, electronic and communications engineering technology; electrical/electronics equipment installation and repair; elementary education; emergency care attendant (EMT ambulance); energy management and systems technology; engineering; engineering technology; English; environmental design/architecture; environmental education; environmental engineering technology; environmental studies; family and consumer sciences/human sciences; farm and ranch management; fashion merchandising; finance; fine/studio arts; fishing and fisheries sciences and management; flight instruction; food preparation; foods and nutrition related; food service and dining room management; foreign languages and literatures; forestry; general studies; geology/earth science; graphic and printing equipment operation/production; graphic communications; graphic design; health and physical education/fitness; health/health-care administration; heating, air conditioning, ventilation and refrigeration maintenance technology; heating, ventilation, air conditioning and refrigeration engineering technology; history; hospitality administration; hotel/motel administration; humanities; human resources management and services related; hydrology and water resources science; information technology; institutional food workers; jazz/jazz studies; journalism; keyboard instruments; kindergarten/preschool education; landscaping and groundskeeping; legal administrative assistant/secretary; legal assistant/paralegal; legal studies; liberal arts and sciences and humanities related; liberal arts and sciences/liberal studies; marine maintenance and ship repair technology; marketing/marketing management; massage therapy; mass communication/media; mathematics; medical administrative assistant and medical secretary; medical/clinical assistant; medical office assistant; medical office computer specialist; medical reception; medical transcription; meeting and event planning; merchandising, sales, and marketing operations related (general); motorcycle maintenance and repair technology; music; music teacher education; natural resources/conservation; natural sciences; office management; office occupations and clerical services; parks, recreation and leisure; percussion instruments; pharmacy; philosophy; photography; physical education teaching and coaching; physical sciences; political science and government; pre-dentistry studies; pre-engineering; pre-law studies; premedical studies; prenursing studies; pre-pharmacy studies; pre-veterinary studies; printing press operation; psychology; radio and television; radio and television broadcasting technology; real estate; receptionist; registered nursing/registered nurse; rehabilitation and therapeutic professions related; restaurant, culinary, and catering management; restaurant/food services management; retailing; rhetoric and composition; sales, distribution, and marketing operations; science teacher education; selling skills and sales; small business administration; small engine mechanics and repair technology; social sciences; social work; sociology; soil science and agronomy; Spanish; sport and fitness administration/management; surgical technology; system,

networking, and LAN/WAN management; technology/industrial arts teacher education; trade and industrial teacher education; turf and turfgrass management; voice and opera; water, wetlands, and marine resources management; welding technology; wildlife biology; wildlife, fish and wildlands science and management; woodwind instruments; word processing.
Academics *Calendar:* semesters. *Degree:* certificates, diplomas, and associate. *Special study options:* academic remediation for entering students, accelerated degree program, adult/continuing education programs, advanced placement credit, cooperative education, distance learning, English as a second language, honors programs, independent study, internships, part-time degree program, services for LD students, summer session for credit.
Library Iowa Lakes Community College Library plus 2 others with 25,305 titles, 3,651 serial subscriptions, 1,175 audiovisual materials, an OPAC.
Student Life *Housing Options:* coed, special housing for students with disabilities. Campus housing is university owned. Freshman campus housing is guaranteed. *Activities and Organizations:* drama/theater group, student-run radio and television station, choral group, music, Criminal Justice, nursing clubs, Environmental Studies, Business. *Campus security:* 24-hour emergency response devices, student patrols.
Athletics Member NJCAA. *Intercollegiate sports:* baseball M(s), basketball M(s)/W(s), cheerleading W(s), cross-country running M(s)/W(s), golf M(s)/W(s), soccer M(s)/W(s), softball W(s), swimming and diving M(s)/W(s), volleyball W(s), wrestling M(s). *Intramural sports:* basketball M/W, football M/W, golf M/W, racquetball M/W, skiing (cross-country) M/W, skiing (downhill) M/W, soccer M/W, softball M/W, swimming and diving M/W, table tennis M/W, tennis M/W, ultimate Frisbee M/W, volleyball M/W, weight lifting M/W, wrestling M.
Applying *Options:* electronic application. *Required for some:* interview. *Application deadlines:* rolling (freshmen), rolling (out-of-state freshmen), rolling (transfers).
Freshman Application Contact Ms. Anne Stansbury Johnson, Director of Admission, Iowa Lakes Community College, 3200 College Drive, Emmetsburg, IA 50536. *Phone:* 712-852-3554 Ext. 5254. *Toll-free phone:* 800-521-5054. *Fax:* 712-852-2152. *E-mail:* info@iowalakes.edu.
Website: http://www.iowalakes.edu/.

Iowa Western Community College
Council Bluffs, Iowa

Freshman Application Contact Ms. Tori Christie, Director of Admissions, Iowa Western Community College, 2700 College Road, Box 4-C, Council Bluffs, IA 51502. *Phone:* 712-325-3288. *Toll-free phone:* 800-432-5852. *E-mail:* admissions@iwcc.edu.
Website: http://www.iwcc.edu/.

ITT Technical Institute
Cedar Rapids, Iowa

Freshman Application Contact Director of Recruitment, ITT Technical Institute, 3735 Queen Court SW, Cedar Rapids, IA 52404. *Phone:* 319-297-3400. *Toll-free phone:* 877-320-4625.
Website: http://www.itt-tech.edu/.

ITT Technical Institute
Clive, Iowa

- **Proprietary** primarily 2-year, part of ITT Educational Services, Inc.
- **Coed**

Majors Business administration and management; computer programming (specific applications); construction management; cyber/computer forensics and counterterrorism; drafting and design technology; electrical, electronic and communications engineering technology; forensic science and technology; industrial technology; information technology project management; network and system administration; project management.
Academics *Degrees:* associate and bachelor's.
Student Life *Housing:* college housing not available.
Freshman Application Contact Director of Recruitment, ITT Technical Institute, 1860 Northwest 118th Street, Suite 110, Clive, IA 50325. *Phone:* 515-327-5500. *Toll-free phone:* 877-526-7312.
Website: http://www.itt-tech.edu/.

Kaplan University, Cedar Falls
Cedar Falls, Iowa

Freshman Application Contact Kaplan University, Cedar Falls, 7009 Nordic Drive, Cedar Falls, IA 50613. *Phone:* 319-277-0220. *Toll-free phone:* 866-527-5268 (in-state); 800-527-5268 (out-of-state).
Website: http://www.cedarfalls.kaplanuniversity.edu/.

Kaplan University, Cedar Rapids
Cedar Rapids, Iowa

Freshman Application Contact Kaplan University, Cedar Rapids, 3165 Edgewood Parkway, SW, Cedar Rapids, IA 52404. *Phone:* 319-363-0481. *Toll-free phone:* 866-527-5268 (in-state); 800-527-5268 (out-of-state). *Website:* http://www.cedarrapids.kaplanuniversity.edu/.

Kaplan University, Des Moines
Urbandale, Iowa

Freshman Application Contact Kaplan University, Des Moines, 4655 121st Street, Urbandale, IA 50323. *Phone:* 515-727-2100. *Toll-free phone:* 866-527-5268 (in-state); 800-527-5268 (out-of-state). *Website:* http://www.desmoines.kaplanuniversity.edu/.

Kirkwood Community College
Cedar Rapids, Iowa

Freshman Application Contact Kirkwood Community College, PO Box 2068, Cedar Rapids, IA 52406-2068. *Phone:* 319-398-5517. *Toll-free phone:* 800-332-2055. *Website:* http://www.kirkwood.edu/.

Marshalltown Community College
Marshalltown, Iowa

Freshman Application Contact Ms. Deana Inman, Director of Admissions, Marshalltown Community College, 3700 South Center Street, Marshalltown, IA 50158-4760. *Phone:* 641-752-7106. *Toll-free phone:* 866-622-4748. *Fax:* 641-752-8149. *Website:* http://www.marshalltowncommunitycollege.com/.

Muscatine Community College
Muscatine, Iowa

Freshman Application Contact Gary Mohr, Executive Director of Enrollment Management and Marketing, Muscatine Community College, 152 Colorado Street, Muscatine, IA 52761-5396. *Phone:* 563-336-3322. *Toll-free phone:* 800-351-4669. *Fax:* 563-336-3350. *E-mail:* gmohr@eicc.edu. *Website:* http://www.eicc.edu/general/muscatine/.

Northeast Iowa Community College
Calmar, Iowa

- **State and locally supported** 2-year, founded 1966, part of Iowa Area Community Colleges System
- **Rural** 210-acre campus
- **Coed,** 5,201 undergraduate students, 36% full-time, 60% women, 40% men

Undergraduates 1,856 full-time, 3,345 part-time. 14% are from out of state; 4% Black or African American, non-Hispanic/Latino; 2% Hispanic/Latino; 0.6% Asian, non-Hispanic/Latino; 0.2% Native Hawaiian or other Pacific Islander, non-Hispanic/Latino; 0.3% American Indian or Alaska Native, non-Hispanic/Latino; 0.7% Two or more races, non-Hispanic/Latino; 4% Race/ethnicity unknown; 0.2% international; 5% transferred in. *Retention:* 62% of full-time freshmen returned.

Freshmen *Admission:* 1,243 applied, 1,002 admitted, 770 enrolled.

Faculty *Total:* 348, 31% full-time, 7% with terminal degrees. *Student/faculty ratio:* 16:1.

Majors Accounting; administrative assistant and secretarial science; agribusiness; agricultural and food products processing; agricultural power machinery operation; agricultural production; automobile/automotive mechanics technology; business administration and management; business automation/technology/data entry; clinical/medical laboratory technology; computer programming (specific applications); construction trades; cosmetology; crop production; dairy husbandry and production; desktop publishing and digital imaging design; electrical, electronic and communications engineering technology; electrician; emergency medical technology (EMT paramedic); energy management and systems technology; fire science/firefighting; health information/medical records technology; liberal arts and sciences/liberal studies; plumbing technology; radiologic technology/science; registered nursing/registered nurse; respiratory care therapy; sales, distribution, and marketing operations; social work.

Academics *Calendar:* semesters. *Degree:* certificates, diplomas, and associate. *Special study options:* academic remediation for entering students, adult/continuing education programs, advanced placement credit, cooperative education, distance learning, double majors, external degree program, honors programs, internships, off-campus study, part-time degree program, services for LD students, summer session for credit.

Library Wilder Resource Center & Burton Payne Library plus 2 others with an OPAC, a Web page.

Student Life *Housing:* college housing not available. *Activities and Organizations:* student-run newspaper, choral group, national fraternities, national sororities. *Campus security:* security personnel on weeknights. *Student services:* personal/psychological counseling.

Athletics *Intramural sports:* basketball M/W, bowling M/W, football M, golf M/W, skiing (downhill) M/W, softball M/W, volleyball M/W.

Costs (2014–15) *Tuition:* state resident $150 per credit hour part-time; nonresident $150 per credit hour part-time.

Applying *Options:* electronic application. *Recommended:* high school transcript. *Application deadlines:* rolling (freshmen), rolling (out-of-state freshmen), rolling (transfers). *Notification:* continuous (freshmen), continuous (out-of-state freshmen), continuous (transfers).

Freshman Application Contact Ms. Brynn McConnell, Admissions Representative, Northeast Iowa Community College, Calmar, IA 52132. *Phone:* 563-562-3263 Ext. 307. *Toll-free phone:* 800-728-CALMAR. *Fax:* 563-562-4369. *E-mail:* mcconnellb@nicc.edu. *Website:* http://www.nicc.edu/.

North Iowa Area Community College
Mason City, Iowa

- **State and locally supported** 2-year, founded 1918, part of Iowa Community College System
- **Rural** 500-acre campus
- **Coed,** 3,207 undergraduate students, 49% full-time, 56% women, 44% men

Undergraduates 1,565 full-time, 1,642 part-time. 3% Black or African American, non-Hispanic/Latino; 5% Hispanic/Latino; 1% Asian, non-Hispanic/Latino; 0.3% American Indian or Alaska Native, non-Hispanic/Latino; 1% Two or more races, non-Hispanic/Latino; 0.3% Race/ethnicity unknown; 1% international.

Freshmen *Admission:* 1,744 applied, 1,744 admitted, 654 enrolled. *Test scores:* SAT critical reading scores over 500: 29%; SAT writing scores over 500: 14%; ACT scores over 18: 20%; SAT critical reading scores over 600: 14%; ACT scores over 24: 1%.

Faculty *Total:* 221, 36% full-time, 7% with terminal degrees. *Student/faculty ratio:* 25:1.

Majors Accounting; accounting technology and bookkeeping; administrative assistant and secretarial science; agricultural economics; agricultural/farm supplies retailing and wholesaling; agricultural production; automobile/automotive mechanics technology; business administration and management; carpentry; clinical/medical laboratory technology; computer systems networking and telecommunications; criminal justice/police science; desktop publishing and digital imaging design; early childhood education; electrical, electronic and communications engineering technology; emergency medical technology (EMT paramedic); entrepreneurship; fire prevention and safety technology; health and medical administrative services related; heating, air conditioning, ventilation and refrigeration maintenance technology; hospitality administration; insurance; legal administrative assistant/secretary; liberal arts and sciences/liberal studies; licensed practical/vocational nurse training; manufacturing engineering technology; mechanical drafting and CAD/CADD; medical administrative assistant and medical secretary; medical/clinical assistant; multi/interdisciplinary studies related; network and system administration; nursing assistant/aide and patient care assistant/aide; physical education teaching and coaching; physical therapy technology; registered nursing/registered nurse; sales, distribution, and marketing operations; sport and fitness administration/management; tool and die technology; web page, digital/multimedia and information resources design; welding technology.

Academics *Calendar:* semesters. *Degree:* certificates, diplomas, and associate. *Special study options:* academic remediation for entering students, advanced placement credit, cooperative education, distance learning, English as a second language, honors programs, internships, part-time degree program, services for LD students, student-designed majors, study abroad, summer session for credit.

Library an OPAC, a Web page.

Student Life *Housing Options:* coed. Campus housing is university owned. *Activities and Organizations:* drama/theater group, student-run newspaper, choral group, Ski Club, intramurals, Student Senate, Education Club, Sport Shooting Club. *Campus security:* 24-hour emergency response devices. *Student services:* health clinic, personal/psychological counseling.

Athletics Member NJCAA. *Intercollegiate sports:* baseball M(s), basketball M(s)/W(s), cross-country running M(s)/W(s), golf M(s)/W(s), soccer M(s), softball W(s), track and field M(s)/W(s), volleyball W(s), wrestling M(s). *Intramural sports:* cheerleading W.

Costs (2013–14) *Tuition:* state resident $3833 full-time; nonresident $5749 full-time. Full-time tuition and fees vary according to course load. Part-time tuition and fees vary according to course load. *Required fees:* $780 full-time.

Room and board: $5619. Room and board charges vary according to housing facility. *Payment plan:* installment. *Waivers:* senior citizens and employees or children of employees.

Financial Aid Of all full-time matriculated undergraduates who enrolled in 2012, 125 Federal Work-Study jobs (averaging $2000). 4 state and other part-time jobs (averaging $2000).

Applying *Options:* electronic application. *Application deadlines:* rolling (freshmen), rolling (transfers). *Notification:* continuous (freshmen), continuous (transfers).

Freshman Application Contact Ms. Rachel McGuire, Director of Admissions, North Iowa Area Community College, 500 College Drive, Mason City, IA 50401. *Phone:* 641-422-4104. *Toll-free phone:* 888-GO NIACC Ext. 4245. *Fax:* 641-422-4385. *E-mail:* request@niacc.edu. *Website:* http://www.niacc.edu/.

Northwest Iowa Community College
Sheldon, Iowa

Director of Admissions Ms. Lisa Story, Director of Enrollment Management, Northwest Iowa Community College, 603 West Park Street, Sheldon, IA 51201-1046. *Phone:* 712-324-5061 Ext. 115. *Toll-free phone:* 800-352-4907. *E-mail:* lstory@nwicc.edu. *Website:* http://www.nwicc.edu/.

St. Luke's College
Sioux City, Iowa

- **Independent** primarily 2-year, founded 1967, part of UnityPoint Health - St. Luke's (formerly St. Luke's Regional Medical Center and Iowa Health System)
- **Rural** 3-acre campus with easy access to Omaha
- **Endowment** $1.0 million
- **Coed,** 187 undergraduate students, 75% full-time, 85% women, 15% men

Undergraduates 141 full-time, 46 part-time. Students come from 16 states and territories; 1 other country; 30% are from out of state; 2% Black or African American, non-Hispanic/Latino; 6% Hispanic/Latino; 3% Asian, non-Hispanic/Latino; 0.5% Native Hawaiian or other Pacific Islander, non-Hispanic/Latino; 0.5% American Indian or Alaska Native, non-Hispanic/Latino; 1% Two or more races, non-Hispanic/Latino; 8% transferred in. *Retention:* 92% of full-time freshmen returned.

Freshmen *Admission:* 31 applied, 9 admitted, 1 enrolled. *Average high school GPA:* 3.41.

Faculty *Total:* 36, 58% full-time, 11% with terminal degrees. *Student/faculty ratio:* 5:1.

Majors Radiologic technology/science; registered nursing/registered nurse; respiratory care therapy.

Academics *Calendar:* semesters. *Degrees:* certificates, associate, and bachelor's. *Special study options:* advanced placement credit, cooperative education, summer session for credit.

Library St. Luke's College with 2,710 titles, 91 serial subscriptions, 249 audiovisual materials, an OPAC, a Web page.

Student Life *Housing:* college housing not available. *Campus security:* 24-hour emergency response devices and patrols, late-night transport/escort service. *Student services:* health clinic, personal/psychological counseling.

Standardized Tests *Required:* SAT or ACT (for admission).

Costs (2014–15) *Tuition:* $17,460 full-time, $485 per credit part-time. Full-time tuition and fees vary according to course load, degree level, and program. Part-time tuition and fees vary according to course load, degree level, and program. *Required fees:* $1270 full-time, $1270 per year part-time. *Payment plans:* installment, deferred payment.

Financial Aid Of all full-time matriculated undergraduates who enrolled in 2013, 84 applied for aid, 84 were judged to have need, 25 had their need fully met. 2 Federal Work-Study jobs (averaging $1375). 5 state and other part-time jobs (averaging $1456). *Average percent of need met:* 75%. *Average financial aid package:* $6230. *Average need-based loan:* $5967. *Average need-based gift aid:* $7680. *Average indebtedness upon graduation:* $13,597.

Applying *Options:* electronic application. *Application fee:* $50. *Required:* essay or personal statement, high school transcript, minimum 2.5 GPA, interview. *Application deadline:* 8/1 (freshmen). *Notification:* continuous (transfers).

Freshman Application Contact Ms. Sherry McCarthy, Admissions Coordinator, St. Luke's College, 2720 Stone Park Boulevard, Sioux City, IA 51104. *Phone:* 712-279-3149. *Toll-free phone:* 800-352-4660 Ext. 3149. *Fax:* 712-233-8017. *E-mail:* mccartsj@stlukes.org. *Website:* http://stlukescollege.edu/.

Scott Community College
Bettendorf, Iowa

Freshman Application Contact Mr. Gary Mohr, Executive Director of Enrollment Management and Marketing, Scott Community College, 500

Belmont Road, Bettendorf, IA 52722-6804. *Phone:* 563-336-3322. *Toll-free phone:* 800-895-0811. *Fax:* 563-336-3350. *E-mail:* gmohr@eicc.edu. *Website:* http://www.eicc.edu/scc/.

Southeastern Community College
West Burlington, Iowa

- **State and locally supported** 2-year, founded 1968, part of Iowa Department of Education Division of Community Colleges
- **Small-town** 160-acre campus
- **Coed,** 3,225 undergraduate students, 50% full-time, 60% women, 40% men

Undergraduates 1,611 full-time, 1,614 part-time. 14% are from out of state; 4% Black or African American, non-Hispanic/Latino; 4% Hispanic/Latino; 1% Asian, non-Hispanic/Latino; 0.2% Native Hawaiian or other Pacific Islander, non-Hispanic/Latino; 0.8% American Indian or Alaska Native, non-Hispanic/Latino; 3% Two or more races, non-Hispanic/Latino; 2% Race/ethnicity unknown; 1% international; 2% transferred in; 4% live on campus.

Freshmen *Admission:* 618 applied, 416 admitted, 381 enrolled. *Average high school GPA:* 2.75. *Test scores:* ACT scores over 18: 62%; ACT scores over 24: 17%; ACT scores over 30: 3%.

Faculty *Total:* 162, 46% full-time, 4% with terminal degrees. *Student/faculty ratio:* 18:1.

Majors Accounting; administrative assistant and secretarial science; agricultural business and management; agronomy and crop science; artificial intelligence; automobile/automotive mechanics technology; biomedical technology; business administration and management; child development; computer programming; construction engineering technology; cosmetology; criminal justice/law enforcement administration; drafting and design technology; electrical, electronic and communications engineering technology; emergency medical technology (EMT paramedic); engineering related; industrial radiologic technology; information science/studies; liberal arts and sciences/liberal studies; licensed practical/vocational nurse training; machine tool technology; mechanical engineering/mechanical technology; medical/clinical assistant; registered nursing/registered nurse; respiratory care therapy; substance abuse/addiction counseling; trade and industrial teacher education; welding technology.

Academics *Calendar:* semesters. *Degree:* certificates, diplomas, and associate. *Special study options:* adult/continuing education programs, part-time degree program.

Library Yohe Memorial Library.

Student Life *Housing Options:* coed, men-only, special housing for students with disabilities. Campus housing is university owned. *Campus security:* controlled dormitory access, night patrols by trained security personnel.

Athletics Member NJCAA. *Intercollegiate sports:* baseball M(s), basketball M(s), softball W(s), volleyball W(s). *Intramural sports:* basketball M, bowling M/W, softball M/W, volleyball M/W, weight lifting M/W.

Costs (2014–15) *Tuition:* state resident $4500 full-time, $150 per credit hour part-time; nonresident $4650 full-time, $155 per credit hour part-time. Full-time tuition and fees vary according to course load, program, and reciprocity agreements. Part-time tuition and fees vary according to course load, program, and reciprocity agreements. *Required fees:* $48 full-time. *Room and board:* $5820. Room and board charges vary according to board plan and housing facility. *Payment plan:* installment. *Waivers:* employees or children of employees.

Financial Aid Of all full-time matriculated undergraduates who enrolled in 2012, 1,244 applied for aid, 1,047 were judged to have need. In 2012, 42 non-need-based awards were made. *Average financial aid package:* $8116. *Average need-based loan:* $3169. *Average need-based gift aid:* $4517. *Average non-need-based aid:* $2398.

Applying *Options:* early admission, deferred entrance.

Freshman Application Contact Ms. Stacy White, Admissions, Southeastern Community College, 1500 West Agency Road, West Burlington, IA 52655-0180. *Phone:* 319-752-2731 Ext. 8137. *Toll-free phone:* 866-722-4692. *E-mail:* admoff@scciowa.edu. *Website:* http://www.scciowa.edu/.

Southwestern Community College
Creston, Iowa

Freshman Application Contact Ms. Lisa Carstens, Admissions Coordinator, Southwestern Community College, 1501 West Townline Street, Creston, IA 50801. *Phone:* 641-782-7081 Ext. 453. *Toll-free phone:* 800-247-4023. *Fax:* 641-782-3312. *E-mail:* carstens@swcciowa.edu. *Website:* http://www.swcciowa.edu/.

Vatterott College
Des Moines, Iowa

Freshman Application Contact Mr. Henry Franken, Co-Director, Vatterott College, 7000 Fleur Drive, Suite 290, Des Moines, IA 50321. *Phone:* 515-309-9000. *Toll-free phone:* 888-553-6627. *Fax:* 515-309-0366. *Website:* http://www.vatterott.edu/.

Western Iowa Tech Community College
Sioux City, Iowa

- **State-supported** 2-year, founded 1966, part of Iowa Department of Education Division of Community Colleges
- **Suburban** 143-acre campus
- **Endowment** $1.0 million
- **Coed**

Undergraduates 2,685 full-time, 3,740 part-time. Students come from 25 states and territories; 4 other countries; 18% are from out of state; 4% Black or African American, non-Hispanic/Latino; 12% Hispanic/Latino; 2% Asian, non-Hispanic/Latino; 0.2% Native Hawaiian or other Pacific Islander, non-Hispanic/Latino; 3% American Indian or Alaska Native, non-Hispanic/Latino; 0.5% Two or more races, non-Hispanic/Latino; 8% Race/ethnicity unknown; 0.1% international; 20% transferred in; 5% live on campus. *Retention:* 41% of full-time freshmen returned.

Faculty *Student/faculty ratio:* 22:1.

Academics *Calendar:* semesters. *Degree:* certificates, diplomas, and associate. *Special study options:* academic remediation for entering students, accelerated degree program, advanced placement credit, cooperative education, distance learning, double majors, English as a second language, honors programs, independent study, internships, off-campus study, part-time degree program, services for LD students, student-designed majors, study abroad, summer session for credit.

Student Life *Campus security:* 24-hour emergency response devices and patrols, controlled dormitory access.

Standardized Tests *Recommended:* ACT (for admission), SAT or ACT (for admission).

Costs (2013–14) *Tuition:* state resident $3072 full-time, $128 per credit hour part-time; nonresident $3192 full-time, $133 per credit hour part-time. Full-time tuition and fees vary according to class time and program. Part-time tuition and fees vary according to class time and program. *Required fees:* $372 full-time, $16 per credit hour part-time. *Room and board:* Room and board charges vary according to housing facility.

Financial Aid Of all full-time matriculated undergraduates who enrolled in 2012, 148 Federal Work-Study jobs (averaging $1000). 2 state and other part-time jobs (averaging $2500).

Applying *Options:* electronic application, early admission, deferred entrance. *Recommended:* high school transcript.

Freshman Application Contact Lora VanderZwaag, Director of Admissions, Western Iowa Tech Community College, 4647 Stone Avenue, PO Box 5199, Sioux City, IA 51102-5199. *Phone:* 712-274-6400. *Toll-free phone:* 800-352-4649 Ext. 6403. *Fax:* 712-274-6441. *Website:* http://www.witcc.edu/.

KANSAS

Allen Community College
Iola, Kansas

- **State and locally supported** 2-year, founded 1923, part of Kansas State Board of Regents
- **Small-town** 88-acre campus
- **Coed,** 2,852 undergraduate students

Undergraduates 6% Black or African American, non-Hispanic/Latino; 6% Hispanic/Latino; 1% Asian, non-Hispanic/Latino; 1% American Indian or Alaska Native, non-Hispanic/Latino; 0.2% Race/ethnicity unknown.

Faculty *Student/faculty ratio:* 22:1.

Majors Accounting; administrative assistant and secretarial science; agricultural production; architecture; art; athletic training; banking and financial support services; biology/biological sciences; business administration and management; business/commerce; business teacher education; chemistry; child development; computer science; computer systems networking and telecommunications; criminal justice/law enforcement administration; data processing and data processing technology; drafting and design technology; dramatic/theater arts; economics; electrical and electronics engineering; electrical, electronic and communications engineering technology; elementary education; emergency medical technology (EMT paramedic); engineering; engineering technology; equestrian studies; family and consumer

sciences/human sciences; farm and ranch management; forestry; funeral service and mortuary science; general studies; geography; health aide; health and physical education/fitness; history; home health aide/home attendant; hospital and health-care facilities administration; humanities; industrial technology; information science/studies; journalism; language interpretation and translation; library and information science; mathematics; music; nuclear/nuclear power technology; nursing assistant/aide and patient care assistant/aide; parks, recreation and leisure facilities management; philosophy; physical therapy; physics; political science and government; pre-dentistry studies; pre-law studies; premedical studies; pre-pharmacy studies; pre-veterinary studies; psychology; religious studies; rhetoric and composition; secondary education; social work; sociology; technology/industrial arts teacher education; writing.

Academics *Calendar:* semesters. *Degree:* certificates and associate. *Special study options:* academic remediation for entering students, adult/continuing education programs, cooperative education, distance learning, English as a second language, independent study, internships, part-time degree program, services for LD students, student-designed majors, summer session for credit.

Library Learning Resource Center plus 1 other with 49,416 titles, 159 serial subscriptions, an OPAC.

Student Life *Housing Options:* coed, men-only, women-only. Campus housing is university owned. *Activities and Organizations:* drama/theater group, student-run newspaper, choral group, intramurals, Student Senate, Biology Club, Theatre, Phi Theta Kappa. *Student services:* personal/psychological counseling.

Athletics Member NJCAA. *Intercollegiate sports:* baseball M(s), basketball M(s)/W(s), cheerleading M(s)/W(s), cross-country running M(s)/W(s), golf M(s), soccer M(s)/W(s), softball W(s), track and field M(s)/W(s), volleyball W(s). *Intramural sports:* basketball M/W, football M/W, soccer M/W, softball M/W, table tennis M/W, tennis M/W, volleyball M/W.

Costs (2014–15) *Tuition:* state resident $912 full-time; nonresident $912 full-time. *Required fees:* $576 full-time. *Room and board:* $4500.

Financial Aid Of all full-time matriculated undergraduates who enrolled in 2008, 510 applied for aid, 411 were judged to have need, 384 had their need fully met. 40 Federal Work-Study jobs (averaging $2600). 112 state and other part-time jobs (averaging $2600). In 2008, 22 non-need-based awards were made. *Average percent of need met:* 80%. *Average financial aid package:* $4738. *Average need-based loan:* $2482. *Average need-based gift aid:* $3257. *Average non-need-based aid:* $1241.

Applying *Options:* electronic application, early admission, deferred entrance. *Required:* high school transcript. *Application deadlines:* 8/24 (freshmen), 8/24 (transfers). *Notification:* continuous (freshmen), continuous (transfers).

Freshman Application Contact Rebecca Bilderback, Director of Admissions, Allen Community College, 1801 North Cottonwood, Iola, KS 66749. *Phone:* 620-365-5116 Ext. 267. *Fax:* 620-365-7406. *E-mail:* bilderback@allencc.edu. *Website:* http://www.allencc.edu/.

Barton County Community College
Great Bend, Kansas

- **State and locally supported** 2-year, founded 1969, part of Kansas Board of Regents
- **Rural** 140-acre campus
- **Coed**

Undergraduates 8% live on campus.

Faculty *Student/faculty ratio:* 23:1.

Academics *Calendar:* semesters. *Degree:* certificates and associate. *Special study options:* academic remediation for entering students, accelerated degree program, adult/continuing education programs, advanced placement credit, cooperative education, distance learning, double majors, English as a second language, external degree program, honors programs, independent study, internships, part-time degree program, services for LD students, summer session for credit. *ROTC:* Army (b).

Student Life *Campus security:* 24-hour emergency response devices and patrols.

Athletics Member NJCAA.

Costs (2013–14) *Tuition:* state resident $1770 full-time, $59 per credit hour part-time; nonresident $2700 full-time, $90 per credit hour part-time. Full-time tuition and fees vary according to course load. Part-time tuition and fees vary according to course load. *Required fees:* $960 full-time, $32 per credit hour part-time. *Room and board:* $5173. Room and board charges vary according to board plan. *Payment plans:* installment, deferred payment.

Applying *Options:* electronic application, early admission. *Recommended:* high school transcript.

Freshman Application Contact Ms. Tana Cooper, Director of Admissions and Promotions, Barton County Community College, 245 Northeast 30th Road, Great Bend, KS 67530. *Phone:* 620-792-9241. *Toll-free phone:* 800-722-6842. *Fax:* 620-786-1160. *E-mail:* admissions@bartonccc.edu. *Website:* http://www.bartonccc.edu/.

Brown Mackie College–Kansas City

Lenexa, Kansas

- **Proprietary** primarily 2-year, founded 1892, part of Education Management Corporation
- **Suburban** campus
- **Coed**

Majors Biomedical technology; business administration and management; business/commerce; corrections and criminal justice related; drafting and design technology; health/health-care administration; occupational therapist assistant; registered nursing/registered nurse; surgical technology; veterinary/animal health technology; welding technology.

Academics *Calendar:* quarters. *Degrees:* certificates, diplomas, associate, and bachelor's.

Freshman Application Contact Brown Mackie College–Kansas City, 9705 Lenexa Drive, Lenexa, KS 66215. *Phone:* 913-768-1900. *Toll-free phone:* 800-635-9101.

Website: http://www.brownmackie.edu/kansascity/.

See display below and page 400 for the College Close-Up.

Brown Mackie College–Salina

Salina, Kansas

- **Proprietary** primarily 2-year, founded 1892, part of Education Management Corporation
- **Small-town** campus
- **Coed**

Majors Business administration and management; business/commerce; corrections and criminal justice related; health/health-care administration; medical/clinical assistant; occupational therapist assistant; registered nursing/registered nurse; surgical technology; veterinary/animal health technology; welding technology.

Academics *Calendar:* modular. *Degrees:* certificates, diplomas, associate, and bachelor's.

Freshman Application Contact Brown Mackie College–Salina, 2106 South 9th Street, Salina, KS 67401-2810. *Phone:* 785-825-5422. *Toll-free phone:* 800-365-0433.

Website: http://www.brownmackie.edu/salina/.

See display below and page 420 for the College Close-Up.

Butler Community College

El Dorado, Kansas

Freshman Application Contact Mr. Glenn Lygrisse, Interim Director of Enrollment Management, Butler Community College, 901 South Haverhill Road, El Dorado, KS 67042. *Phone:* 316-321-2222. *Fax:* 316-322-3109. *E-mail:* admissions@butlercc.edu.

Website: http://www.butlercc.edu/.

Cloud County Community College

Concordia, Kansas

- **State and locally supported** 2-year, founded 1965, part of Kansas Community College System
- **Rural** 35-acre campus
- **Coed,** 2,318 undergraduate students, 38% full-time, 62% women, 38% men

Undergraduates 883 full-time, 1,435 part-time. Students come from 15 states and territories; 12 other countries; 8% are from out of state; 8% Black or African American, non-Hispanic/Latino; 7% Hispanic/Latino; 2% Asian, non-Hispanic/Latino; 0.3% American Indian or Alaska Native, non-Hispanic/Latino; 3% Two or more races, non-Hispanic/Latino; 2% Race/ethnicity unknown; 0.9% international; 8% transferred in. *Retention:* 55% of full-time freshmen returned.

Freshmen *Admission:* 406 enrolled.

Faculty *Total:* 306, 19% full-time. *Student/faculty ratio:* 20:1.

Majors Administrative assistant and secretarial science; agricultural business and management; agricultural/farm supplies retailing and wholesaling; business administration and management; business, management, and marketing related; child-care and support services management; child development; criminal justice/police science; graphic design; journalism; legal assistant/paralegal; liberal arts and sciences/liberal studies; mechanic and repair technologies related; office occupations and clerical services; radio and television broadcasting technology; registered nursing/registered nurse; system, networking, and LAN/WAN management; teacher assistant/aide; tourism and travel services management; web page, digital/multimedia and information resources design.

Academics *Calendar:* semesters. *Degree:* certificates, diplomas, and associate. *Special study options:* academic remediation for entering students, adult/continuing education programs, advanced placement credit, cooperative education, distance learning, internships, part-time degree program, services for LD students, summer session for credit.

Library 18,010 titles, 142 serial subscriptions.

Student Life *Activities and Organizations:* drama/theater group, student-run newspaper, radio station, choral group. *Campus security:* 24-hour emergency response devices. *Student services:* health clinic.

Athletics Member NJCAA. *Intercollegiate sports:* baseball M(s), basketball M(s)/W(s), cross-country running M(s)/W(s), soccer M(s)/W(s), softball W(s), tennis M(s)/W(s), track and field M(s)/W(s), volleyball W(s). *Intramural sports:* baseball M, basketball M/W, softball W, volleyball M/W.

Financial Aid Of all full-time matriculated undergraduates who enrolled in 2012, 122 Federal Work-Study jobs (averaging $800).

Applying *Options:* early admission, deferred entrance. *Required:* high school transcript. *Application deadlines:* 9/11 (freshmen), 9/11 (transfers). *Notification:* continuous (freshmen), continuous (transfers).

Freshman Application Contact Cloud County Community College, 2221 Campus Drive, PO Box 1002, Concordia, KS 66901-1002. *Phone:* 785-243-1435 Ext. 214. *Toll-free phone:* 800-729-5101.

Website: http://www.cloud.edu/.

Coffeyville Community College

Coffeyville, Kansas

Freshman Application Contact Stacia Meek, Admissions Counselor/Marketing Event Coordinator, Coffeyville Community College, 400 West 11th Street, Coffeyville, KS 67337-5063. *Phone:* 620-252-7100. *Toll-free phone:* 877-51-RAVEN. *E-mail:* staciam@coffeyville.edu.

Website: http://www.coffeyville.edu/.

Colby Community College

Colby, Kansas

- **State and locally supported** 2-year, founded 1964, part of Kansas State Board of Education
- **Small-town** 80-acre campus
- **Endowment** $3.4 million
- **Coed**

Undergraduates 723 full-time, 728 part-time. Students come from 15 states and territories; 5 other countries; 30% are from out of state; 7% Black or African American, non-Hispanic/Latino; 7% Hispanic/Latino; 2% Asian, non-Hispanic/Latino; 0.5% Native Hawaiian or other Pacific Islander, non-Hispanic/Latino; 0.6% American Indian or Alaska Native, non-Hispanic/Latino; 5% international; 6% transferred in; 30% live on campus.

Faculty *Student/faculty ratio:* 11:1.

Academics *Calendar:* semesters. *Degree:* certificates, diplomas, and associate. *Special study options:* academic remediation for entering students, adult/continuing education programs, advanced placement credit, cooperative education, distance learning, double majors, honors programs, internships, part-time degree program, services for LD students, student-designed majors, summer session for credit.

Student Life *Campus security:* 24-hour emergency response devices and patrols.

Athletics Member NJCAA.

Standardized Tests *Required:* COMPASS or ASSET (for admission). *Recommended:* SAT or ACT (for admission).

Costs (2013–14) *Tuition:* state resident $1920 full-time, $60 per credit part-time; nonresident $3648 full-time, $114 per credit part-time. Full-time tuition and fees vary according to course load and program. Part-time tuition and fees vary according to course load and program. *Required fees:* $1140 full-time, $38 per credit part-time, $38 per credit part-time. *Room and board:* $6090. Room and board charges vary according to board plan and housing facility.

Financial Aid Of all full-time matriculated undergraduates who enrolled in 2011, 737 applied for aid, 615 were judged to have need, 88 had their need fully met. In 2011, 73. *Average percent of need met:* 73. *Average financial aid package:* $6385. *Average need-based loan:* $2439. *Average need-based gift aid:* $4685. *Average non-need-based aid:* $1633.

Applying *Options:* electronic application, early admission, deferred entrance. *Required:* high school transcript. *Required for some:* interview.

Freshman Application Contact Ms. Nikol Nolan, Admissions Director, Colby Community College, Colby, KS 67701-4099. *Phone:* 785-462-3984 Ext. 5496. *Toll-free phone:* 888-634-9350. *Fax:* 785-460-4691. *E-mail:* admissions@colbycc.edu.

Website: http://www.colbycc.edu/.

Cowley County Community College and Area Vocational–Technical School

Arkansas City, Kansas

- **State and locally supported** 2-year, founded 1922, part of Kansas State Board of Education
- **Small-town** 19-acre campus
- **Endowment** $4.7 million
- **Coed**

Undergraduates 2,328 full-time, 2,000 part-time. 10% are from out of state; 12% live on campus. *Retention:* 58% of full-time freshmen returned.

Faculty *Student/faculty ratio:* 26:1.

Academics *Calendar:* semesters. *Degree:* certificates, diplomas, and associate. *Special study options:* academic remediation for entering students, accelerated degree program, adult/continuing education programs, advanced placement credit, cooperative education, distance learning, external degree program, independent study, off-campus study, part-time degree program, services for LD students, summer session for credit.

Student Life *Campus security:* 24-hour emergency response devices and patrols, student patrols, late-night transport/escort service, controlled dormitory access, residence hall entrances are locked at night.

Athletics Member NJCAA.

Standardized Tests *Recommended:* ACT (for admission).

Costs (2013–14) *Tuition:* area resident $1568 full-time, $49 per credit hour part-time; state resident $1888 full-time, $59 per credit hour part-time; nonresident $3392 full-time, $106 per credit hour part-time. *Required fees:* $864 full-time, $27 per credit hour part-time. *Room and board:* $4525. Room and board charges vary according to board plan.

Financial Aid Of all full-time matriculated undergraduates who enrolled in 2012, 2,204 applied for aid, 2,023 were judged to have need. 88 Federal Work-Study jobs (averaging $1191). 135 state and other part-time jobs (averaging $888). *Average financial aid package:* $3508. *Average need-based loan:* $3554. *Average need-based gift aid:* $4554.

Applying *Options:* electronic application, early admission. *Required:* high school transcript.

Freshman Application Contact Ms. Lory West, Director of Admissions, Cowley County Community College and Area Vocational–Technical School, PO Box 1147, Arkansas City, KS 67005. *Phone:* 620-441-5594. *Toll-free phone:* 800-593-CCCC. *Fax:* 620-441-5350. *E-mail:* admissions@cowley.edu.

Website: http://www.cowley.edu/.

Dodge City Community College

Dodge City, Kansas

Freshman Application Contact Dodge City Community College, 2501 North 14th Avenue, Dodge City, KS 67801-2399. *Phone:* 620-225-1321.

Website: http://www.dc3.edu/.

Donnelly College

Kansas City, Kansas

- **Independent Roman Catholic** primarily 2-year, founded 1949
- **Urban** 4-acre campus
- **Endowment** $47.9 million
- **Coed,** 419 undergraduate students, 53% full-time, 70% women, 30% men

Undergraduates 220 full-time, 199 part-time. Students come from 2 states and territories; 32 other countries; 26% are from out of state; 28% Black or African American, non-Hispanic/Latino; 42% Hispanic/Latino; 8% Asian, non-Hispanic/Latino; 1% American Indian or Alaska Native, non-Hispanic/Latino; 3% Two or more races, non-Hispanic/Latino; 7% international; 5% transferred in; 4% live on campus. *Retention:* 52% of full-time freshmen returned.

Freshmen *Admission:* 116 applied, 116 admitted, 135 enrolled.

Faculty *Total:* 55, 33% full-time, 11% with terminal degrees. *Student/faculty ratio:* 11:1.

Majors Computer and information systems security; elementary education; liberal arts and sciences/liberal studies; nonprofit management.

Academics *Calendar:* semesters. *Degrees:* certificates, associate, and bachelor's. *Special study options:* academic remediation for entering students, advanced placement credit, distance learning, double majors, English as a second language, external degree program, independent study, internships, part-time degree program, services for LD students, summer session for credit.

Library Trant Memorial Library plus 1 other with 18,432 titles, 8 serial subscriptions, 229 audiovisual materials, an OPAC, a Web page.

Student Life *Housing Options:* men-only, women-only. Campus housing is university owned and is provided by a third party. *Activities and Organizations:* Organization of Student Leadership, Student Ambassadors, Healthy Student Task Force, Men's Soccer Club, Women's Soccer Club.

Campus security: 24-hour emergency response devices. *Student services:* personal/psychological counseling.

Standardized Tests *Recommended:* ACT (for admission).

Costs (2014–15) *Comprehensive fee:* $12,244 includes full-time tuition ($5920), mandatory fees ($100), and room and board ($6224). Full-time tuition and fees vary according to course level and course load. Part-time tuition and fees vary according to course level. *Room and board:* Room and board charges vary according to housing facility. *Payment plan:* installment. *Waivers:* employees or children of employees.

Applying *Options:* electronic application, early admission, deferred entrance. *Recommended:* high school transcript. *Application deadlines:* rolling (freshmen), rolling (transfers).

Freshman Application Contact Mr. Edward Marquez, Director of Admissions, Donnelly College, 608 North 18th Street, Kansas City, KS 66102. *Phone:* 913-621-8713. *Fax:* 913-621-8719. *E-mail:* admissions@donnelly.edu.

Website: http://www.donnelly.edu/.

Flint Hills Technical College
Emporia, Kansas

Freshman Application Contact Admissions Office, Flint Hills Technical College, 3301 West 18th Avenue, Emporia, KS 66801. *Phone:* 620-341-1325. *Toll-free phone:* 800-711-6947.

Website: http://www.fhtc.edu/.

Fort Scott Community College
Fort Scott, Kansas

Director of Admissions Mrs. Mert Barrows, Director of Admissions, Fort Scott Community College, 2108 South Horton, Fort Scott, KS 66701. *Phone:* 620-223-2700 Ext. 353. *Toll-free phone:* 800-874-3722.

Website: http://www.fortscott.edu/.

Garden City Community College
Garden City, Kansas

- **County-supported** 2-year, founded 1919, part of Kansas Board of Regents
- **Rural** 63-acre campus
- **Endowment** $5.9 million
- **Coed,** 1,997 undergraduate students, 54% full-time, 54% women, 46% men

Undergraduates 1,069 full-time, 928 part-time. Students come from 5 other countries; 17% are from out of state; 7% Black or African American, non-Hispanic/Latino; 38% Hispanic/Latino; 3% Asian, non-Hispanic/Latino; 0.1% Native Hawaiian or other Pacific Islander, non-Hispanic/Latino; 0.7% American Indian or Alaska Native, non-Hispanic/Latino; 2% Race/ethnicity unknown; 0.3% international; 3% transferred in.

Freshmen *Admission:* 558 applied, 558 admitted, 507 enrolled. *Average high school GPA:* 3.07.

Faculty *Total:* 62.

Majors Administrative assistant and secretarial science; agricultural and food products processing; agricultural mechanization; agricultural production; architecture related; automobile/automotive mechanics technology; biology/biological sciences; business administration and management; computer science; computer systems networking and telecommunications; cosmetology; criminal justice/police science; drafting and design technology; education; emergency medical technology (EMT paramedic); engineering; English; family and consumer sciences/human sciences; fire science/firefighting; general studies; health and physical education related; health services/allied health/health sciences; humanities; liberal arts and sciences/liberal studies; manufacturing engineering technology; mathematics; physical sciences; pre-law studies; premedical studies; prenursing studies; pre-pharmacy studies; pre-veterinary studies; psychology; registered nursing/registered nurse; retailing; social sciences; social work; speech communication and rhetoric; substance abuse/addiction counseling; visual and performing arts; welding technology; zoology/animal biology.

Academics *Calendar:* semesters. *Degree:* certificates and associate. *Special study options:* academic remediation for entering students, adult/continuing education programs, advanced placement credit, distance learning, English as a second language, external degree program, part-time degree program, services for LD students, student-designed majors, summer session for credit.

Library Saffell Library with 15,984 titles, 31 serial subscriptions, 428 audiovisual materials, an OPAC, a Web page.

Student Life *Housing Options:* coed. Campus housing is university owned. *Activities and Organizations:* drama/theater group, student-run newspaper, choral group, HALO (Hispanic Student Leadership Organization), GC3 Media, Criminal Justice/Tau Epsilon Lambda, SGA (Student Government Association), PTK (Phi Theta Kappa). *Campus security:* 24-hour emergency response devices and patrols, student patrols, late-night transport/escort

service, controlled dormitory access. *Student services:* health clinic, personal/psychological counseling.

Athletics Member NJCAA. *Intercollegiate sports:* baseball M(s), basketball M(s)/W(s), cheerleading M(s)/W(s), cross-country running M(s)/W(s), football M(s), golf M(s), soccer W(s), softball W(s), track and field M(s)/W(s), volleyball W(s). *Intramural sports:* basketball M/W, bowling M/W, football M/W, racquetball M/W, riflery M/W, soccer M/W, softball M/W, table tennis M/W, tennis M/W, track and field M/W, ultimate Frisbee M/W, volleyball M/W.

Standardized Tests *Required:* ACT COMPASS (for admission). *Recommended:* ACT (for admission).

Costs (2014–15) *Tuition:* state resident $1760 full-time, $55 per credit hour part-time; nonresident $2368 full-time, $74 per credit hour part-time. Full-time tuition and fees vary according to course load. Part-time tuition and fees vary according to course load. *Required fees:* $960 full-time, $30 per credit hour part-time. *Room and board:* $4950. Room and board charges vary according to board plan and housing facility. *Payment plan:* installment. *Waivers:* senior citizens and employees or children of employees.

Financial Aid Of all full-time matriculated undergraduates who enrolled in 2012, 90 Federal Work-Study jobs (averaging $1000). 100 state and other part-time jobs (averaging $900).

Applying *Required:* high school transcript. *Application deadlines:* rolling (freshmen), rolling (transfers).

Freshman Application Contact Office of Admissions, Garden City Community College, 801 Campus Drive, Garden City, KS 67846. *Phone:* 620-276-9531. *Toll-free phone:* 800-658-1696. *Fax:* 620-276-9650. *E-mail:* admissions@gcccks.edu.

Website: http://www.gcccks.edu/.

Hesston College
Hesston, Kansas

Freshman Application Contact Joel Kauffman, Vice President of Admissions, Hesston College, Hesston, KS 67062. *Phone:* 620-327-8222. *Toll-free phone:* 800-995-2757. *Fax:* 620-327-8300. *E-mail:* admissions@hesston.edu.

Website: http://www.hesston.edu/.

Highland Community College
Highland, Kansas

Director of Admissions Ms. Cheryl Rasmussen, Vice President of Student Services, Highland Community College, 606 West Main Street, Highland, KS 66035. *Phone:* 785-442-6020. *Fax:* 785-442-6106.

Website: http://www.highlandcc.edu/.

Hutchinson Community College and Area Vocational School
Hutchinson, Kansas

- **State and locally supported** 2-year, founded 1928, part of Kansas Board of Regents
- **Small-town** 47-acre campus with easy access to Wichita
- **Coed,** 6,126 undergraduate students, 39% full-time, 54% women, 46% men

Undergraduates 2,374 full-time, 3,752 part-time. Students come from 9 other countries; 8% are from out of state; 5% Black or African American, non-Hispanic/Latino; 8% Hispanic/Latino; 0.8% Asian, non-Hispanic/Latino; 0.1% Native Hawaiian or other Pacific Islander, non-Hispanic/Latino; 1% American Indian or Alaska Native, non-Hispanic/Latino; 2% Two or more races, non-Hispanic/Latino; 7% Race/ethnicity unknown; 0.4% international; 7% transferred in; 8% live on campus. *Retention:* 45% of full-time freshmen returned.

Freshmen *Admission:* 2,995 applied, 2,995 admitted, 1,161 enrolled. *Average high school GPA:* 3.1. *Test scores:* ACT scores over 18: 75%; ACT scores over 24: 20%; ACT scores over 30: 1%.

Faculty *Total:* 474, 24% full-time, 4% with terminal degrees. *Student/faculty ratio:* 15:1.

Majors Administrative assistant and secretarial science; agricultural mechanics and equipment technology; agriculture; architectural drafting and CAD/CADD; autobody/collision and repair technology; automobile/automotive mechanics technology; biology/biological sciences; biology/biotechnology laboratory technician; business and personal/financial services marketing; business/commerce; carpentry; child-care and support services management; clinical/medical laboratory technology; communications technology; computer and information sciences; computer systems analysis; computer systems networking and telecommunications; criminal justice/police science; design and visual communications; drafting and design technology; drama and dance teacher education; education; electrical, electronic and communications engineering technology;

electrical/electronics equipment installation and repair; emergency medical technology (EMT paramedic); engineering; English; family and consumer sciences/human sciences; farm and ranch management; fire science/firefighting; foreign languages and literatures; health information/medical records technology; legal assistant/paralegal; liberal arts and sciences/liberal studies; machine tool technology; manufacturing engineering technology; mathematics; mechanical drafting and CAD/CADD; medical radiologic technology; natural resources management and policy; pharmacy technician; physical sciences; physical therapy technology; psychology; radio and television broadcasting technology; registered nursing/registered nurse; respiratory therapy technician; retailing; social sciences; speech communication and rhetoric; sport and fitness administration/management; surgical technology; visual and performing arts; web page, digital/multimedia and information resources design; welding technology.

Academics *Calendar:* semesters. *Degree:* certificates and associate. *Special study options:* academic remediation for entering students, adult/continuing education programs, advanced placement credit, cooperative education, distance learning, double majors, English as a second language, honors programs, independent study, internships, part-time degree program, services for LD students, student-designed majors, summer session for credit.

Library John F. Kennedy Library plus 1 other with 40,725 titles, 125 serial subscriptions, 2,282 audiovisual materials, an OPAC, a Web page.

Student Life *Housing Options:* men-only, women-only. Campus housing is university owned. *Activities and Organizations:* drama/theater group, student-run newspaper, choral group, Circle K, Student Fire Fighter Association, RESET (non-denominational religious group), DragonLAN, Block & Bridle Club. *Campus security:* 24-hour emergency response devices and patrols, student patrols, late-night transport/escort service, controlled dormitory access. *Student services:* health clinic, personal/psychological counseling.

Athletics Member NJCAA. *Intercollegiate sports:* baseball M(s), basketball M(s)/W(s), cheerleading M(s)/W(s), cross-country running M(s)/W(s), football M(s), golf M(s), soccer W(s), softball W(s), track and field M(s)/W(s), volleyball W(s). *Intramural sports:* badminton M/W, basketball M/W, football M/W, soccer M/W, table tennis M/W, tennis M/W, track and field M/W, volleyball M/W.

Costs (2014–15) *Tuition:* area resident $2112 full-time, $66 per credit hour part-time; state resident $2432 full-time, $76 per credit hour part-time; nonresident $3424 full-time, $107 per credit hour part-time. *Required fees:* $608 full-time, $19 per credit hour part-time. *Room and board:* $5361. Room and board charges vary according to board plan and housing facility. *Payment plan:* installment. *Waivers:* employees or children of employees.

Applying *Options:* electronic application, early admission, deferred entrance. *Required for some:* high school transcript, interview, Copy of GED certificate required from GED completers. *Application deadlines:* rolling (freshmen), rolling (out-of-state freshmen), rolling (transfers). *Notification:* continuous (freshmen), continuous (out-of-state freshmen), continuous (transfers).

Freshman Application Contact Mr. Corbin Strobel, Director of Admissions, Hutchinson Community College and Area Vocational School, 1300 North Plum, Hutchinson, KS 67501. *Phone:* 620-665-3536. *Toll-free phone:* 888-GO-HUTCH. *Fax:* 620-665-3301. *E-mail:* strobelc@hutchcc.edu. *Website:* http://www.hutchcc.edu/.

Independence Community College
Independence, Kansas

- **State-supported** 2-year, founded 1925, part of Kansas Board of Regents
- **Rural** 68-acre campus
- **Coed,** 1,031 undergraduate students, 56% full-time, 55% women, 45% men

Undergraduates 575 full-time, 456 part-time. Students come from 23 states and territories; 25 other countries; 30% are from out of state; 10% Black or African American, non-Hispanic/Latino; 4% Hispanic/Latino; 0.3% Asian, non-Hispanic/Latino; 0.6% Native Hawaiian or other Pacific Islander, non-Hispanic/Latino; 2% American Indian or Alaska Native, non-Hispanic/Latino; 3% Two or more races, non-Hispanic/Latino; 1% Race/ethnicity unknown; 2% international; 7% transferred in. *Retention:* 40% of full-time freshmen returned.

Freshmen *Admission:* 310 enrolled.

Faculty *Total:* 86, 35% full-time, 6% with terminal degrees. *Student/faculty ratio:* 11:1.

Majors Accounting; administrative assistant and secretarial science; architectural engineering technology; art; athletic training; biology/biological sciences; business administration and management; child-care and support services management; computer and information sciences; computer programming; computer science; computer systems networking and telecommunications; cosmetology; drafting and design technology; dramatic/theater arts; education; English; entrepreneurship; foreign languages and literatures; history; liberal arts and sciences/liberal studies; mathematics; music; physical sciences; small business administration; social sciences;

speech communication and rhetoric; veterinary/animal health technology; web page, digital/multimedia and information resources design.

Academics *Calendar:* semesters. *Degree:* certificates and associate. *Special study options:* academic remediation for entering students, advanced placement credit, cooperative education, distance learning, part-time degree program, services for LD students, summer session for credit.

Library Independence Community College Library plus 1 other with a Web page.

Student Life *Housing:* college housing not available. *Options:* coed. Campus housing is university owned and is provided by a third party. Freshman campus housing is guaranteed. *Activities and Organizations:* drama/theater group, choral group, marching band, Phi Theta Kappa, Ambassadors, International Student Organization. *Campus security:* controlled dormitory access, night patrol.

Athletics Member NJCAA. *Intercollegiate sports:* baseball M(s), basketball M(s)/W(s), football M(s), volleyball W(s). *Intramural sports:* cheerleading M/W.

Costs (2014–15) *Tuition:* area resident $1188 full-time; state resident $1270 full-time; nonresident $2590 full-time. *Required fees:* $1254 full-time. *Room and board:* $4700. *Payment plan:* installment. *Waivers:* senior citizens and employees or children of employees.

Financial Aid Of all full-time matriculated undergraduates who enrolled in 2012, 85 Federal Work-Study jobs (averaging $900).

Applying *Required:* high school transcript. *Required for some:* essay or personal statement, minimum 2.5 GPA, 2 letters of recommendation, interview.

Freshman Application Contact Ms. Brittany Thornton, Admissions Coordinator, Independence Community College, PO Box 708, 1057 W. College Avenue, Independence, KS 67301. *Phone:* 620-332-5495. *Toll-free phone:* 800-842-6063. *Fax:* 620-331-0946. *E-mail:* bthornton@indycc.edu. *Website:* http://www.indycc.edu/.

Johnson County Community College
Overland Park, Kansas

Director of Admissions Dr. Charles J. Carlsen, President, Johnson County Community College, 12345 College Boulevard, Overland Park, KS 66210-1299. *Phone:* 913-469-8500 Ext. 3806. *Website:* http://www.johnco.cc.ks.us/.

Kansas City Kansas Community College
Kansas City, Kansas

Freshman Application Contact Dr. Denise McDowell, Dean of Enrollment Management/Registrar, Kansas City Kansas Community College, Admissions Office, 7250 State Avenue, Kansas City, KS 66112. *Phone:* 913-288-7694. *Fax:* 913-288-7648. *E-mail:* dmcdowell@kckcc.edu. *Website:* http://www.kckcc.edu/.

Labette Community College
Parsons, Kansas

Freshman Application Contact Ms. Tammy Fuentez, Director of Admission, Labette Community College, 200 South 14th Street, Parsons, KS 67357-4299. *Phone:* 620-421-6700. *Toll-free phone:* 888-522-3883. *Fax:* 620-421-0180. *Website:* http://www.labette.edu/.

Manhattan Area Technical College
Manhattan, Kansas

- **State and locally supported** 2-year, founded 1965
- **Rural** 18-acre campus
- **Coed,** 825 undergraduate students, 60% full-time, 57% women, 43% men

Undergraduates 491 full-time, 334 part-time. Students come from 11 states and territories; 1% are from out of state; 8% Black or African American, non-Hispanic/Latino; 6% Hispanic/Latino; 2% Asian, non-Hispanic/Latino; 0.8% Native Hawaiian or other Pacific Islander, non-Hispanic/Latino; 0.6% American Indian or Alaska Native, non-Hispanic/Latino; 2% Two or more races, non-Hispanic/Latino; 1% Race/ethnicity unknown; 14% transferred in. *Retention:* 80% of full-time freshmen returned.

Freshmen *Admission:* 235 admitted, 235 enrolled. *Test scores:* ACT scores over 18: 72%; ACT scores over 24: 17%; ACT scores over 30: 2%.

Faculty *Total:* 73, 40% full-time, 4% with terminal degrees. *Student/faculty ratio:* 14:1.

Majors Accounting technology and bookkeeping; administrative assistant and secretarial science; autobody/collision and repair technology; automobile/automotive mechanics technology; biology/biotechnology laboratory technician; building/construction finishing, management, and inspection related; building/property maintenance; CAD/CADD drafting/design technology; carpentry; clinical/medical laboratory technology; computer systems networking and telecommunications; computer technology/computer systems technology; drafting and design technology; electrical and power transmission installation; electrical and power transmission installation related; heating, air conditioning, ventilation and refrigeration maintenance technology; heating, ventilation, air conditioning and refrigeration engineering technology; licensed practical/vocational nurse training; management information systems; medical office assistant; multi/interdisciplinary studies related; network and system administration; registered nursing/registered nurse; welding technology.

Academics *Calendar:* semesters. *Degree:* certificates and associate. *Special study options:* academic remediation for entering students, adult/continuing education programs, advanced placement credit, cooperative education, distance learning, double majors, honors programs, internships, part-time degree program, services for LD students, student-designed majors, summer session for credit.

Library MATC Library with an OPAC.

Student Life *Housing:* college housing not available. *Campus security:* late-night transport/escort service, Evening Security Guards.

Standardized Tests *Required:* If students do not have SAT or ACT scores, then students do COMPASS Testing to guide placement into Math and English courses (for admission).

Applying *Options:* electronic application. *Application fee:* $40. *Required:* high school transcript. *Required for some:* essay or personal statement, 3 letters of recommendation, interview, Admission to pre-allied health programs have specific criteria for admission. Electric Power and Distribution requires a Class A CDL. *Application deadlines:* rolling (freshmen), rolling (out-of-state freshmen), rolling (transfers).

Freshman Application Contact Ms. Nicole Bollig, Director of Admissions, Manhattan Area Technical College, 3136 Dickens Ave., Manhattan, KS 66503. *Phone:* 785-587-2800. *Toll-free phone:* 800-352-7575. *Fax:* 913-587-2804. *E-mail:* NicoleBollig@ManhattanTech.edu. *Website:* http://www.manhattantech.edu/.

National American University

Overland Park, Kansas

Freshman Application Contact Admissions Office, National American University, 10310 Mastin Street, Overland Park, KS 66212. *Website:* http://www.national.edu/.

Neosho County Community College

Chanute, Kansas

Freshman Application Contact Ms. Lisa Last, Dean of Student Development, Neosho County Community College, 800 West 14th Street, Chanute, KS 66720. *Phone:* 620-431-2820 Ext. 213. *Toll-free phone:* 800-729-6222. *Fax:* 620-431-0082. *E-mail:* llast@neosho.edu. *Website:* http://www.neosho.edu/.

North Central Kansas Technical College

Beloit, Kansas

Freshman Application Contact Ms. Judy Heidrick, Director of Admissions, North Central Kansas Technical College, PO Box 507, 3033 US Highway 24, Beloit, KS 67420. *Toll-free phone:* 800-658-4655. *E-mail:* jheidrick@ncktc.tec.ks.us. *Website:* http://www.ncktc.edu/.

Northwest Kansas Technical College

Goodland, Kansas

Admissions Office Contact Northwest Kansas Technical College, PO Box 668, 1209 Harrison Street, Goodland, KS 67735. *Toll-free phone:* 800-316-4127. *Website:* http://www.nwktc.edu/.

Pratt Community College

Pratt, Kansas

Freshman Application Contact Ms. Theresa Ziehr, Office Assistant, Student Services, Pratt Community College, 348 Northeast State Road 61, Pratt, KS 67124. *Phone:* 620-450-2217. *Toll-free phone:* 800-794-3091. *Fax:* 620-672-5288. *E-mail:* theresaz@prattcc.edu. *Website:* http://www.prattcc.edu/.

Seward County Community College and Area Technical School

Liberal, Kansas

Director of Admissions Dr. Gerald Harris, Dean of Student Services, Seward County Community College and Area Technical School, PO Box 1137, Liberal, KS 67905-1137. *Phone:* 620-624-1951 Ext. 617. *Toll-free phone:* 800-373-9951. *Website:* http://www.sccc.edu/.

Wichita Area Technical College

Wichita, Kansas

- **District-supported** 2-year, founded 1963
- **Urban** campus
- **Endowment** $1.1 million
- **Coed,** 2,936 undergraduate students, 37% full-time, 54% women, 46% men

Undergraduates 1,087 full-time, 1,849 part-time. Students come from 11 states and territories; 1% are from out of state; 16% Black or African American, non-Hispanic/Latino; 10% Hispanic/Latino; 4% Asian, non-Hispanic/Latino; 0.3% Native Hawaiian or other Pacific Islander, non-Hispanic/Latino; 2% American Indian or Alaska Native, non-Hispanic/Latino; 4% Two or more races, non-Hispanic/Latino; 8% Race/ethnicity unknown; 0.1% international; 3% transferred in. *Retention:* 58% of full-time freshmen returned.

Freshmen *Admission:* 380 enrolled.

Faculty *Total:* 167, 32% full-time. *Student/faculty ratio:* 19:1.

Majors Aeronautical/aerospace engineering technology; airframe mechanics and aircraft maintenance technology; autobody/collision and repair technology; automobile/automotive mechanics technology; avionics maintenance technology; business administration and management; clinical/medical laboratory technology; criminal justice/police science; dental assisting; drafting and design technology; entrepreneurship; health and medical administrative services related; heating, air conditioning, ventilation and refrigeration maintenance technology; industrial mechanics and maintenance technology; industrial radiologic technology; interior design; machine tool technology; mechanical drafting and CAD/CADD; mechanical engineering/mechanical technology; medical/clinical assistant; office occupations and clerical services; plastics and polymer engineering technology; precision production related; robotics technology; surgical technology; welding technology.

Academics *Calendar:* semesters. *Degree:* certificates, diplomas, and associate. *Special study options:* academic remediation for entering students, distance learning, internships, part-time degree program, services for LD students, summer session for credit.

Library WATC Library with 123,986 titles, 15,050 serial subscriptions, 373 audiovisual materials, an OPAC, a Web page.

Student Life *Housing:* college housing not available. *Activities and Organizations:* SkillsUSA, Shooting Club. *Campus security:* 24-hour emergency response devices and patrols, late-night transport/escort service.

Standardized Tests *Required for some:* WorkKeys, COMPASS and TEAS.

Costs (2013–14) *Tuition:* state resident $5510 full-time, $121 per credit hour part-time; nonresident $6918 full-time, $146 per credit hour part-time. Full-time tuition and fees vary according to course load, location, and program. Part-time tuition and fees vary according to course load, location, and program. *Required fees:* $1532 full-time, $29 per credit hour part-time, $10 per term part-time. *Payment plan:* installment. *Waivers:* employees or children of employees.

Applying *Required for some:* high school transcript.

Freshman Application Contact Mr. Andy McFayden, Director, Admissions, Wichita Area Technical College, 4004 N. Webb Road, Suite 100, Wichita, KS 67226 . *Phone:* 316-677-9400. *Fax:* 316-677-9555. *E-mail:* info@watc.edu. *Website:* http://www.watc.edu/.

Wright Career College

Overland Park, Kansas

- **Proprietary** primarily 2-year
- **Suburban** 5-acre campus with easy access to Kansas City
- **Coed,** 71 undergraduate students, 100% full-time, 83% women, 17% men

Undergraduates 71 full-time. Students come from 3 states and territories; 61% are from out of state; 51% Black or African American, non-Hispanic/Latino; 3% Hispanic/Latino; 1% Two or more races, non-Hispanic/Latino; 1% transferred in.

Freshmen *Admission:* 43 applied, 43 admitted, 39 enrolled.

Majors Accounting; business administration and management; computer installation and repair technology; computer programming; computer systems networking and telecommunications; computer technology/computer systems technology; entrepreneurial and small business related; health and physical education related; health/health-care administration; medical/clinical assistant; medical insurance coding; surgical technology; veterinary/animal health technology.

Academics *Degrees:* associate and bachelor's. *Special study options:* adult/continuing education programs, distance learning, internships, off-campus study.

Student Life *Housing:* college housing not available.

Applying *Application deadlines:* rolling (freshmen), rolling (out-of-state freshmen), rolling (transfers), rolling (early action). *Early decision deadline:* rolling (for plan 1), rolling (for plan 2). *Notification:* continuous (freshmen), continuous (out-of-state freshmen), continuous (transfers), rolling (early decision plan 1), rolling (early decision plan 2), rolling (early action).

Freshman Application Contact Wright Career College, 10700 Metcalf Avenue, Overland Park, KS 66210. *Phone:* 913-385-7700. *E-mail:* info@wrightcc.edu.

Website: http://www.wrightcc.edu/.

Wright Career College
Wichita, Kansas

- **Proprietary** primarily 2-year, founded 2011
- **Suburban** campus with easy access to Wichita
- **Coed,** 362 undergraduate students, 35% full-time, 71% women, 29% men

Undergraduates 127 full-time, 235 part-time. Students come from 1 other state; 48% Black or African American, non-Hispanic/Latino; 6% Hispanic/Latino; 0.8% Asian, non-Hispanic/Latino; 4% Two or more races, non-Hispanic/Latino; 0.6% Race/ethnicity unknown; 0.8% transferred in. *Retention:* 1% of full-time freshmen returned.

Freshmen *Admission:* 355 applied, 355 admitted, 165 enrolled.

Majors Business administration and management; computer installation and repair technology; computer programming; computer systems networking and telecommunications; computer technology/computer systems technology; entrepreneurial and small business related; health and physical education related; health/health-care administration; surgical technology.

Academics *Degrees:* diplomas, associate, and bachelor's. *Special study options:* adult/continuing education programs, distance learning, internships, off-campus study.

Student Life *Housing:* college housing not available.

Applying *Application deadlines:* rolling (freshmen), rolling (out-of-state freshmen), rolling (transfers), rolling (early action). *Early decision deadline:* rolling (for plan 1), rolling (for plan 2). *Notification:* continuous (freshmen), continuous (out-of-state freshmen), continuous (transfers), rolling (early decision plan 1), rolling (early decision plan 2), rolling (early action).

Freshman Application Contact Wright Career College, 7700 East Kellogg, Wichita, KS 67207. *Phone:* 316-927-7700. *Toll-free phone:* 800-555-4003. *E-mail:* info@wrightcc.edu.

Website: http://www.wrightcc.edu/.

KENTUCKY

Ashland Community and Technical College
Ashland, Kentucky

Freshman Application Contact Ashland Community and Technical College, 1400 College Drive, Ashland, KY 41101-3683. *Phone:* 606-326-2008. *Toll-free phone:* 800-928-4256.

Website: http://www.ashland.kctcs.edu/.

ATA College
Louisville, Kentucky

Freshman Application Contact Admissions Office, ATA College, 10180 Linn Station Road, Suite A200, Louisville, KY 40223. *Phone:* 502-371-8330. *Fax:* 502-371-8598.

Website: http://www.ata.edu/.

Beckfield College
Florence, Kentucky

Freshman Application Contact Mrs. Leah Boerger, Director of Admissions, Beckfield College, 16 Spiral Drive, Florence, KY 41042. *Phone:* 859-371-9393. *E-mail:* lboerger@beckfield.edu.

Website: http://www.beckfield.edu/.

Big Sandy Community and Technical College
Prestonsburg, Kentucky

Director of Admissions Jimmy Wright, Director of Admissions, Big Sandy Community and Technical College, One Bert T. Combs Drive, Prestonsburg, KY 41653-1815. *Phone:* 606-886-3863. *Toll-free phone:* 888-641-4132. *E-mail:* jimmy.wright@kctcs.edu.

Website: http://www.bigsandy.kctcs.edu/.

Bluegrass Community and Technical College
Lexington, Kentucky

Freshman Application Contact Mrs. Shelbie Hugle, Director of Admission Services, Bluegrass Community and Technical College, 470 Cooper Drive, Lexington, KY 40506. *Phone:* 859-246-6216. *Toll-free phone:* 800-744-4872 (in-state); 866-744-4872 (out-of-state). *E-mail:* shelbie.hugle@kctcs.edu.

Website: http://www.bluegrass.kctcs.edu/.

Brown Mackie College–Hopkinsville
Hopkinsville, Kentucky

- **Proprietary** 2-year, part of Education Management Corporation
- **Small-town** campus
- **Coed**

Majors Business/commerce; criminal justice/safety; medical office management; occupational therapist assistant.

Academics *Calendar:* quarters. *Degree:* diplomas and associate.

Freshman Application Contact Brown Mackie College–Hopkinsville, 4001 Fort Cambell Boulevard, Hopkinsville, KY 42240. *Phone:* 270-886-1302. *Toll-free phone:* 800-359-4753.

Website: http://www.brownmackie.edu/Hopkinsville/.

See display on next page and page 396 for the College Close-Up.

Brown Mackie College–Louisville
Louisville, Kentucky

- **Proprietary** primarily 2-year, founded 1972, part of Education Management Corporation
- **Suburban** campus
- **Coed**

Majors Biomedical technology; business administration and management; business/commerce; computer systems networking and telecommunications; criminal justice/law enforcement administration; electrical/electronics maintenance and repair technology related; health/health-care administration; legal assistant/paralegal; occupational therapist assistant; veterinary/animal health technology.

Academics *Calendar:* quarters. *Degrees:* certificates, diplomas, associate, and bachelor's.

Freshman Application Contact Brown Mackie College–Louisville, 3605 Fern Valley Road, Louisville, KY 40219. *Phone:* 502-968-7191. *Toll-free phone:* 800-999-7387.

Website: http://www.brownmackie.edu/louisville/.

See display on next page and page 402 for the College Close-Up.

Brown Mackie College–Northern Kentucky
Fort Mitchell, Kentucky

- **Proprietary** primarily 2-year, founded 1927, part of Education Management Corporation
- **Suburban** campus
- **Coed**

Majors Accounting technology and bookkeeping; business administration and management; corrections and criminal justice related; criminal justice/law enforcement administration; data entry/microcomputer applications; emergency medical technology (EMT paramedic); health/health-care administration; information technology; occupational therapist assistant; registered nursing/registered nurse.

Academics *Calendar:* quarters. *Degrees:* diplomas, associate, and bachelor's.

Freshman Application Contact Brown Mackie College–Northern Kentucky, 309 Buttermilk Pike, Fort Mitchell, KY 41017-2191. *Phone:* 859-341-5627. *Toll-free phone:* 800-888-1445.

Website: http://www.brownmackie.edu/northernkentucky/.

See display on next page and page 410 for the College Close-Up.

Daymar College
Bellevue, Kentucky

Freshman Application Contact Cathy Baird, Director of Admissions, Daymar College, 119 Fairfield Avenue, Bellevue, KY 41073. *Phone:* 859-291-0800. *Toll-free phone:* 877-258-7796. *Fax:* 859-491-7500.

Website: http://www.daymarcollege.edu/.

Daymar College

Bowling Green, Kentucky

Freshman Application Contact Mrs. Traci Henderson, Admissions Director, Daymar College, 2421 Fitzgerald Industrial Drive, Bowling Green, KY 42101. *Phone:* 270-843-6750. *Toll-free phone:* 877-258-7796. *E-mail:* thenderson@daymarcollege.edu.
Website: http://www.daymarcollege.edu/.

Daymar College

Louisville, Kentucky

Director of Admissions Mr. Patrick Carney, Director of Admissions, Daymar College, 4112 Fern Valley Road, Louisville, KY 40219. *Toll-free phone:* 877-258-7796.
Website: http://www.daymarcollege.edu/.

Daymar College

Madisonville, Kentucky

Admissions Office Contact Daymar College, 1105 National Mine Drive, Madisonville, KY 42431. *Toll-free phone:* 877-258-7796.
Website: http://www.daymarcollege.edu/.

Daymar College

Owensboro, Kentucky

Freshman Application Contact Ms. Vickie McDougal, Director of Admissions, Daymar College, 3361 Buckland Square, Owensboro, KY 42301. *Phone:* 270-926-4040. *Toll-free phone:* 877-258-7796. *Fax:* 270-685-4090. *E-mail:* info@daymarcollege.edu.
Website: http://www.daymarcollege.edu/.

Daymar College

Paducah, Kentucky

Freshman Application Contact Daymar College, 509 South 30th Street, Paducah, KY 42001. *Phone:* 270-444-9950. *Toll-free phone:* 877-258-7796.
Website: http://www.daymarcollege.edu/.

Elizabethtown Community and Technical College

Elizabethtown, Kentucky

- **State-supported** 2-year, founded 1966, part of Kentucky Community and Technical College System
- **Small-town** 80-acre campus
- **Endowment** $879,000
- **Coed**

Undergraduates 3,221 full-time, 4,365 part-time. Students come from 28 states and territories; 2 other countries; 1% are from out of state; 8% Black or African American, non-Hispanic/Latino; 4% Hispanic/Latino; 0.9% Asian, non-Hispanic/Latino; 0.3% Native Hawaiian or other Pacific Islander, non-Hispanic/Latino; 0.4% American Indian or Alaska Native, non-Hispanic/Latino; 2% Two or more races, non-Hispanic/Latino; 2% Race/ethnicity unknown; 5% transferred in. *Retention:* 56% of full-time freshmen returned.

Faculty *Student/faculty ratio:* 23:1.

Academics *Calendar:* semesters. *Degree:* certificates, diplomas, and associate. *Special study options:* academic remediation for entering students, advanced placement credit, cooperative education, distance learning, internships, off-campus study, part-time degree program, services for LD students, summer session for credit.

Student Life *Campus security:* late-night transport/escort service.

Standardized Tests *Recommended:* ACT (for admission).

Applying *Options:* electronic application. *Required for some:* high school transcript.

Freshman Application Contact Elizabethtown Community and Technical College, 620 College Street Road, Elizabethtown, KY 42701. *Phone:* 270-706-8800. *Toll-free phone:* 877-246-2322.

Website: http://www.elizabethtown.kctcs.edu/.

Gateway Community and Technical College

Florence, Kentucky

- **State-supported** 2-year, founded 1961, part of Kentucky Community and Technical College System
- **Suburban** campus with easy access to Cincinnati
- **Coed,** 4,789 undergraduate students, 31% full-time, 52% women, 48% men

Undergraduates 1,467 full-time, 3,322 part-time. 10% Black or African American, non-Hispanic/Latino; 3% Hispanic/Latino; 0.6% Asian, non-Hispanic/Latino; 0.2% Native Hawaiian or other Pacific Islander, non-Hispanic/Latino; 0.2% American Indian or Alaska Native, non-Hispanic/Latino; 2% Two or more races, non-Hispanic/Latino; 2% Race/ethnicity unknown.

Freshmen *Admission:* 1,661 applied, 1,163 admitted, 413 enrolled.

Faculty *Total:* 322, 28% full-time. *Student/faculty ratio:* 15:1.

Majors Business administration and management; CAD/CADD drafting/design technology; computer and information sciences; criminal justice/law enforcement administration; early childhood education; educational/instructional technology; engineering technology; fire science/firefighting; general studies; health professions related; industrial technology; manufacturing engineering technology; office occupations and clerical services; registered nursing/registered nurse; teacher assistant/aide.

Academics *Calendar:* semesters. *Degree:* certificates, diplomas, and associate. *Special study options:* academic remediation for entering students, cooperative education, distance learning, internships, part-time degree program, services for LD students, summer session for credit.

Library Main Library plus 3 others.

Student Life *Housing:* college housing not available. *Activities and Organizations:* National Technical Honor Society, Student Government Association, Speech Team, American Criminal Justice Association, Phi Theta Kappa. *Student services:* personal/psychological counseling.

Standardized Tests *Required:* ACT or ACT COMPASS (for admission).

Applying *Options:* electronic application, early admission, deferred entrance. *Required:* high school transcript. *Application deadlines:* rolling (freshmen), rolling (out-of-state freshmen), rolling (transfers). *Notification:* continuous (freshmen), continuous (out-of-state freshmen), continuous (transfers).

Freshman Application Contact Gateway Community and Technical College, 500 Technology Way, Florence, KY 41042. *Phone:* 859-441-4500. *E-mail:* andre.washington@kctcs.edu.

Website: http://www.gateway.kctcs.edu/.

Hazard Community and Technical College

Hazard, Kentucky

Freshman Application Contact Director of Admissions, Hazard Community and Technical College, 1 Community College Drive, Hazard, KY 41701-2403. *Phone:* 606-487-3102. *Toll-free phone:* 800-246-7521.

Website: http://www.hazard.kctcs.edu/.

Henderson Community College

Henderson, Kentucky

Freshman Application Contact Ms. Teresa Hamiton, Admissions Counselor, Henderson Community College, 2660 South Green Street, Henderson, KY 42420-4623. *Phone:* 270-827-1867 Ext. 354. *Toll-free phone:* 800-696-9958. *Website:* http://www.henderson.kctcs.edu/.

Hopkinsville Community College

Hopkinsville, Kentucky

- **State-supported** 2-year, founded 1965, part of Kentucky Community and Technical College System
- **Small-town** 69-acre campus with easy access to Nashville
- **Coed,** 3,609 undergraduate students, 45% full-time, 66% women, 34% men

Undergraduates 1,627 full-time, 1,982 part-time. 24% Black or African American, non-Hispanic/Latino; 7% Hispanic/Latino; 1% Asian, non-Hispanic/Latino; 0.5% Native Hawaiian or other Pacific Islander, non-Hispanic/Latino; 0.5% American Indian or Alaska Native, non-Hispanic/Latino; 3% Two or more races, non-Hispanic/Latino; 1% Race/ethnicity unknown; 0.1% international; 7% transferred in. *Retention:* 52% of full-time freshmen returned.

Freshmen *Admission:* 1,627 applied, 1,627 admitted, 650 enrolled.

Faculty *Total:* 145, 47% full-time. *Student/faculty ratio:* 23:1.

Majors Administrative assistant and secretarial science; agricultural production; animal/livestock husbandry and production; business administration and management; child-care and support services management; child-care provision; computer and information sciences; criminal justice/law enforcement administration; criminal justice/police science; early childhood education; electrical, electronic and communications engineering technology; engineering technology; executive assistant/executive secretary; human services; industrial technology; liberal arts and sciences/liberal studies; multi/interdisciplinary studies related; registered nursing/registered nurse; social work; teacher assistant/aide.

Academics *Calendar:* semesters. *Degree:* certificates, diplomas, and associate. *Special study options:* academic remediation for entering students, advanced placement credit, cooperative education, distance learning, honors programs, independent study, part-time degree program, services for LD students, summer session for credit.

Library Learning Resource Center with an OPAC, a Web page.

Student Life *Housing:* college housing not available. *Activities and Organizations:* student-run newspaper, Ag Tech, Amateur Radio, Ballroom Dance, Baptist Campus Ministries, Black Men United. *Campus security:* 24-hour emergency response devices, late-night transport/escort service, security provided by trained security personnel during hours of normal operation.

Athletics *Intramural sports:* basketball M, football M, golf M, table tennis M/W, volleyball M/W.

Costs (2013–14) *Tuition:* state resident $4320 full-time, $144 per credit hour part-time; nonresident $15,120 full-time, $504 per credit hour part-time. Full-time tuition and fees vary according to reciprocity agreements. Part-time tuition and fees vary according to reciprocity agreements. *Payment plan:* installment. *Waivers:* senior citizens and employees or children of employees.

Financial Aid Of all full-time matriculated undergraduates who enrolled in 2012, 30 Federal Work-Study jobs (averaging $1500). *Financial aid deadline:* 6/30.

Applying *Options:* electronic application, deferred entrance. *Recommended:* high school transcript. *Application deadlines:* rolling (freshmen), rolling (out-of-state freshmen), rolling (transfers). *Notification:* continuous (freshmen), continuous (out-of-state freshmen), continuous (transfers).

Freshman Application Contact Ms. Janet Level, Student Records, Hopkinsville Community College, Room 135, English Education Center, 202 Bastogne Avenue, Fort Campbell, KY. *Phone:* 270-707-3918. *Toll-free phone:* 866-534-2224. *Fax:* 270-707-3973. *E-mail:* janet.level@kctcs.edu. *Website:* http://hopkinsville.kctcs.edu/.

ITT Technical Institute

Louisville, Kentucky

- **Proprietary** primarily 2-year, founded 1993, part of ITT Educational Services, Inc.
- **Suburban** campus
- **Coed**

Majors Business administration and management; computer programming (specific applications); construction management; cyber/computer forensics and counterterrorism; drafting and design technology; electrical, electronic and communications engineering technology; game and interactive media design; information technology project management; medical/clinical assistant; network and system administration; project management; registered nursing/registered nurse.

Academics *Calendar:* quarters. *Degrees:* associate and bachelor's.

Student Life *Housing:* college housing not available.

Freshman Application Contact Director of Recruitment, ITT Technical Institute, 9500 Ormsby Station Road, Suite 100, Louisville, KY 40223. *Phone:* 502-327-7424. *Toll-free phone:* 888-790-7427.

Website: http://www.itt-tech.edu/.

Jefferson Community and Technical College

Louisville, Kentucky

Freshman Application Contact Ms. Melanie Vaughan-Cooke, Admissions Coordinator, Jefferson Community and Technical College, Louisville, KY 40202. *Phone:* 502-213-4000. *Fax:* 502-213-2540.

Website: http://www.jefferson.kctcs.edu/.

Madisonville Community College

Madisonville, Kentucky

Director of Admissions Mr. Jay Parent, Registrar, Madisonville Community College, 2000 College Drive, Madisonville, KY 42431-9185. *Phone:* 270-821-2250.

Website: http://www.madcc.kctcs.edu/.

Maysville Community and Technical College

Maysville, Kentucky

Director of Admissions Ms. Patee Massie, Registrar, Maysville Community and Technical College, 1755 US 68, Maysville, KY 41056. *Phone:* 606-759-7141. *Fax:* 606-759-5818. *E-mail:* ccsmayrg@ukcc.uky.edu.
Website: http://www.maysville.kctcs.edu/.

Maysville Community and Technical College

Morehead, Kentucky

Director of Admissions Patee Massie, Registrar, Maysville Community and Technical College, 609 Viking Drive, Morehead, KY 40351. *Phone:* 606-759-7141 Ext. 66184.
Website: http://www.maysville.kctcs.edu/.

MedTech College

Lexington, Kentucky

Admissions Office Contact MedTech College, 1648 McGrathiana Parkway, Suite 200, Lexington, KY 40511.
Website: http://www.medtechcollege.edu/.

National College

Danville, Kentucky

Director of Admissions James McGuire, Campus Director, National College, 115 East Lexington Avenue, Danville, KY 40422. *Phone:* 859-236-6991. *Toll-free phone:* 888-9-JOBREADY.
Website: http://www.national-college.edu/.

National College

Florence, Kentucky

Director of Admissions Mr. Terry Kovacs, Campus Director, National College, 7627 Ewing Boulevard, Florence, KY 41042. *Phone:* 859-525-6510. *Toll-free phone:* 888-9-JOBREADY.
Website: http://www.national-college.edu/.

National College

Lexington, Kentucky

Director of Admissions Kim Thomasson, Campus Director, National College, 2376 Sir Barton Way, Lexington, KY 40509. *Phone:* 859-253-0621. *Toll-free phone:* 888-9-JOBREADY.
Website: http://www.national-college.edu/.

National College

Louisville, Kentucky

Director of Admissions Vincent C. Tinebra, Campus Director, National College, 4205 Dixie Highway, Louisville, KY 40216. *Phone:* 502-447-7634. *Toll-free phone:* 888-9-JOBREADY.
Website: http://www.national-college.edu/.

National College

Pikeville, Kentucky

Director of Admissions Tammy Riley, Campus Director, National College, 50 National College Boulevard, Pikeville, KY 41501. *Phone:* 606-478-7200. *Toll-free phone:* 888-9-JOBREADY.
Website: http://www.national-college.edu/.

National College

Richmond, Kentucky

Director of Admissions Ms. Keeley Gadd, Campus Director, National College, 125 South Killarney Lane, Richmond, KY 40475. *Phone:* 859-623-8956. *Toll-free phone:* 888-9-JOBREADY.
Website: http://www.national-college.edu/.

Owensboro Community and Technical College

Owensboro, Kentucky

- **State-supported** 2-year, founded 1986, part of Kentucky Community and Technical College System
- **Suburban** 102-acre campus
- **Coed,** 4,297 undergraduate students, 43% full-time, 58% women, 42% men

Undergraduates 1,850 full-time, 2,447 part-time. Students come from 8 states and territories; 3% are from out of state; 4% Black or African American, non-Hispanic/Latino; 1% Hispanic/Latino; 0.7% Asian, non-Hispanic/Latino; 0.1% American Indian or Alaska Native, non-Hispanic/Latino; 2% Two or more races, non-Hispanic/Latino; 2% Race/ethnicity unknown. *Retention:* 38% of full-time freshmen returned.
Freshmen *Admission:* 706 enrolled.
Faculty *Total:* 249, 38% full-time, 5% with terminal degrees. *Student/faculty ratio:* 21:1.
Majors Agricultural production; applied horticulture/horticulture operations; biology/biotechnology laboratory technician; business administration and management; child-care provision; computer and information sciences; construction trades; emergency medical technology (EMT paramedic); engineering technology; executive assistant/executive secretary; fire science/firefighting; human services; liberal arts and sciences/liberal studies; mechanics and repair; medical administrative assistant and medical secretary; medical radiologic technology; precision production trades; registered nursing/registered nurse; surgical technology; teacher assistant/aide; veterinary/animal health technology.
Academics *Calendar:* semesters. *Degree:* certificates, diplomas, and associate. *Special study options:* academic remediation for entering students, adult/continuing education programs, advanced placement credit, cooperative education, distance learning, double majors, English as a second language, external degree program, honors programs, independent study, off-campus study, part-time degree program, services for LD students, student-designed majors, study abroad, summer session for credit.
Library Learning Resource Center with 86,065 titles, 1,750 audiovisual materials, an OPAC, a Web page.
Student Life *Housing:* college housing not available. *Activities and Organizations:* drama/theater group, choral group, Student Government Association. *Campus security:* 24-hour emergency response devices, late-night transport/escort service.
Standardized Tests *Recommended:* SAT or ACT (for admission).
Costs (2013–14) *Tuition:* state resident $4320 full-time, $144 per credit hour part-time; nonresident $15,120 full-time, $504 per credit hour part-time. Full-time tuition and fees vary according to reciprocity agreements. Part-time tuition and fees vary according to reciprocity agreements. *Payment plan:* installment. *Waivers:* senior citizens and employees or children of employees.
Financial Aid Of all full-time matriculated undergraduates who enrolled in 2013, 50 Federal Work-Study jobs (averaging $5120). *Financial aid deadline:* 4/1.
Applying *Options:* electronic application. *Required:* high school transcript. *Application deadlines:* rolling (freshmen), rolling (transfers). *Notification:* continuous (freshmen), continuous (transfers).
Freshman Application Contact Ms. Barbara Tipmore, Admissions Counselor, Owensboro Community and Technical College, 4800 New Hartford Road, Owensboro, KY 42303. *Phone:* 270-686-4530. *Toll-free phone:* 866-755-6282. *E-mail:* barb.tipmore@kctcs.edu.
Website: http://www.octc.kctcs.edu/.

Somerset Community College

Somerset, Kentucky

- **State-supported** 2-year, founded 1965, part of Kentucky Community and Technical College System
- **Small-town** 70-acre campus
- **Coed,** 7,878 undergraduate students

Undergraduates *Retention:* 60% of full-time freshmen returned.
Freshmen *Admission:* 1,282 applied, 1,282 admitted.
Faculty *Total:* 340, 54% full-time. *Student/faculty ratio:* 23:1.
Majors Aircraft powerplant technology; business administration and management; child-care provision; clinical/medical laboratory assistant; computer and information sciences; criminal justice/law enforcement administration; engineering technology; executive assistant/executive secretary; industrial mechanics and maintenance technology; liberal arts and sciences/liberal studies; medical administrative assistant and medical secretary; medical radiologic technology; multi/interdisciplinary studies related; physical therapy technology; registered nursing/registered nurse; respiratory care therapy; surgical technology; teacher assistant/aide.

Academics *Calendar:* semesters. *Degree:* certificates, diplomas, and associate. *Special study options:* academic remediation for entering students, adult/continuing education programs, advanced placement credit, distance learning, part-time degree program, summer session for credit. ·

Library Somerset Community College Library.

Student Life *Housing:* college housing not available.

Costs (2013–14) *Tuition:* state resident $4320 full-time, $144 per credit hour part-time; nonresident $15,120 full-time, $504 per credit hour part-time. Full-time tuition and fees vary according to course load. Part-time tuition and fees vary according to course load. *Payment plan:* installment. *Waivers:* senior citizens and employees or children of employees.

Applying *Options:* electronic application, early admission. *Required:* high school transcript. *Application deadlines:* 8/14 (freshmen), 8/14 (transfers). *Notification:* continuous (freshmen), continuous (transfers).

Freshman Application Contact Director of Admission, Somerset Community College, 808 Monticello Street, Somerset, KY 42501-2973. *Phone:* 606-451-6630. *Toll-free phone:* 877-629-9722. *E-mail:* somerset-admissions@kctcs.edu.

Website: http://www.somerset.kctcs.edu/.

Southcentral Kentucky Community and Technical College

Bowling Green, Kentucky

Director of Admissions Mark Garrett, Chief Student Affairs Officer, Southcentral Kentucky Community and Technical College, 1845 Loop Drive, Bowling Green, KY 42101. *Phone:* 270-901-1114. *Toll-free phone:* 800-790-0990.

Website: http://www.bowlinggreen.kctcs.edu/.

Southeast Kentucky Community and Technical College

Cumberland, Kentucky

Freshman Application Contact Southeast Kentucky Community and Technical College, 700 College Road, Cumberland, KY 40823-1099. *Phone:* 606-589-2145 Ext. 13018. *Toll-free phone:* 888-274-SECC. ·

Website: http://www.southeast.kctcs.edu/.

Spencerian College

Louisville, Kentucky

- **Proprietary** 2-year, founded 1892
- **Urban** 10-acre campus
- **Coed,** 532 undergraduate students, 57% full-time, 86% women, 14% men

Undergraduates 301 full-time, 231 part-time. 23% Black or African American, non-Hispanic/Latino; 3% Hispanic/Latino; 0.4% Asian, non-Hispanic/Latino; 0.4% Native Hawaiian or other Pacific Islander, non-Hispanic/Latino; 0.2% American Indian or Alaska Native, non-Hispanic/Latino; 9% Two or more races, non-Hispanic/Latino; 2% Race/ethnicity unknown; 1% live on campus.

Freshmen *Admission:* 124 enrolled.

Majors Accounting technology and bookkeeping; cardiovascular technology; clinical/medical laboratory technology; massage therapy; medical insurance coding; medical insurance/medical billing; office management; radiologic technology/science; registered nursing/registered nurse; respiratory care therapy; surgical technology.

Academics *Calendar:* quarters. *Degree:* certificates, diplomas, and associate. *Special study options:* distance learning, summer session for credit.

Library Spencerian College Learning Resource Center with 1,585 titles, 300 audiovisual materials, an OPAC, a Web page.

Student Life *Housing Options:* coed. Campus housing is university owned. ·

Costs (2013–14) *Comprehensive fee:* $25,895 includes full-time tuition ($16,320), mandatory fees ($1310), and room and board ($8265). Full-time tuition and fees vary according to class time and program. Part-time tuition: $272 per credit hour. Part-time tuition and fees vary according to class time and program. *Required fees:* $50 per course part-time. *Room and board:* college room only: $5535. Room and board charges vary according to housing facility. *Waivers:* employees or children of employees.

Financial Aid Of all full-time matriculated undergraduates who enrolled in 2012, 637 applied for aid, 573 were judged to have need. In 2012, 307 non-need-based awards were made. *Average need-based loan:* $3508. *Average need-based gift aid:* $1982. *Average non-need-based aid:* $652.

Applying *Application fee:* $50. *Required:* high school transcript. *Required for some:* essay or personal statement, interview, Some medical programs have

specific selective admission criteria. *Notification:* continuous (freshmen), continuous (out-of-state freshmen), continuous (transfers).

Freshman Application Contact Spencerian College, 4627 Dixie Highway, Louisville, KY 40216. *Phone:* 502-447-1000 Ext. 7808. *Toll-free phone:* 800-264-1799.

Website: http://www.spencerian.edu/.

Spencerian College–Lexington

Lexington, Kentucky

- **Proprietary** 2-year, founded 1997, part of Sullivan University System
- **Urban** campus with easy access to Louisville
- **Coed,** 160 undergraduate students, 78% full-time, 50% women, 50% men

Undergraduates 125 full-time, 35 part-time.

Freshmen *Average high school GPA:* 2.5.

Faculty *Total:* 38, 63% full-time. *Student/faculty ratio:* 4:1.

Majors Biomedical technology; CAD/CADD drafting/design technology; clinical/medical laboratory technology; computer and information systems security; computer engineering technology; computer graphics; electrical and electronic engineering technologies related; electrical, electronic and communications engineering technology; massage therapy; medical insurance coding; medical office management; radiologic technology/science.

Academics *Calendar:* quarters. *Degree:* certificates, diplomas, and associate. *Special study options:* academic remediation for entering students, cooperative education, independent study, part-time degree program, services for LD students, summer session for credit.

Library Spencerian College Library with 450 titles, 30 serial subscriptions, 25 audiovisual materials.

Student Life *Housing Options:* men-only, women-only. Campus housing is leased by the school. *Activities and Organizations:* student-run newspaper. *Campus security:* 24-hour emergency response devices.

Standardized Tests *Required for some:* ASSET.

Costs (2014–15) *One-time required fee:* $50. *Tuition:* $14,374 full-time, $320 per credit hour part-time. Full-time tuition and fees vary according to class time, course load, program, and student level. Part-time tuition and fees vary according to class time, course load, program, and student level. *Required fees:* $1500 full-time, $1500 per year part-time. *Room only:* $5535. *Payment plans:* tuition prepayment, installment, deferred payment. *Waivers:* employees or children of employees.

Applying *Application fee:* $90. *Required:* high school transcript, interview. *Application deadline:* rolling (freshmen).

Freshman Application Contact Spencerian College–Lexington, 1575 Winchester Road, Lexington, KY 40505. *Phone:* 859-223-9608 Ext. 5430. *Toll-free phone:* 800-456-3253.

Website: http://www.spencerian.edu/.

Sullivan College of Technology and Design

Louisville, Kentucky

- **Proprietary** primarily 2-year, founded 1961, part of The Sullivan University System, Inc.
- **Suburban** 10-acre campus with easy access to Louisville
- **Coed,** 457 undergraduate students, 69% full-time, 32% women, 68% men

Undergraduates 316 full-time, 144 part-time. Students come from 3 states and territories; 8% are from out of state; 12% Black or African American, non-Hispanic/Latino; 5% Hispanic/Latino; 1% Asian, non-Hispanic/Latino; 0.2% Native Hawaiian or other Pacific Islander, non-Hispanic/Latino; 0.2% American Indian or Alaska Native, non-Hispanic/Latino; 8% Two or more races, non-Hispanic/Latino; 0.2% Race/ethnicity unknown; 6% transferred in; 8% live on campus.

Freshmen *Admission:* 57 enrolled.

Faculty *Total:* 61, 46% full-time. *Student/faculty ratio:* 10:1.

Majors Animation, interactive technology, video graphics and special effects; architectural drafting and CAD/CADD; architectural engineering technology; architecture related; artificial intelligence; CAD/CADD drafting/design technology; civil drafting and CAD/CADD; computer and information sciences; computer and information sciences and support services related; computer and information systems security; computer engineering technology; computer graphics; computer hardware engineering; computer hardware technology; computer installation and repair technology; computer programming (vendor/product certification); computer systems networking and telecommunications; computer technology/computer systems technology; desktop publishing and digital imaging design; digital communication and media/multimedia; drafting and design technology; drafting/design engineering technologies related; electrical and electronic engineering technologies related; electrical, electronic and communications engineering technology; electrical/electronics equipment installation and repair; electrical/electronics maintenance and repair technology related; electromechanical and instrumentation and maintenance technologies related;

engineering technologies and engineering related; engineering technology; graphic and printing equipment operation/production; graphic communications; graphic communications related; graphic design; heating, ventilation, air conditioning and refrigeration engineering technology; housing and human environments; industrial electronics technology; industrial mechanics and maintenance technology; information technology; interior design; manufacturing engineering technology; mechanical drafting and CAD/CADD; mechanical engineering/mechanical technology; network and system administration; robotics technology; web page, digital/multimedia and information resources design.

Academics *Calendar:* quarters. *Degrees:* associate and bachelor's. *Special study options:* academic remediation for entering students, accelerated degree program, adult/continuing education programs, advanced placement credit, double majors, independent study, internships, part-time degree program, services for LD students, summer session for credit.

Library Sullivan College of Technology and Design Library plus 1 other with 17,000 titles, 66 serial subscriptions, 370 audiovisual materials, an OPAC, a Web page.

Student Life *Housing Options:* coed. Campus housing is university owned and leased by the school. Freshman applicants given priority for college housing. *Activities and Organizations:* ASID, IIDA, ADDA, MAKE Club, Skills USA. *Campus security:* late-night transport/escort service, controlled dormitory access, telephone alarm device during hours school is open; patrols by trained security personnel while classes are in session.

Standardized Tests *Required:* ASSET or ACT or SAT Language and Math scores in place of ASSET results (for admission). *Recommended:* SAT or ACT (for admission).

Costs (2014–15) *Comprehensive fee:* $28,447 includes full-time tuition ($17,592), mandatory fees ($1735), and room and board ($9120). Full-time tuition and fees vary according to course load, degree level, and program. Part-time tuition and fees vary according to course load, degree level, and program. No tuition increase for student's term of enrollment. *Room and board:* Room and board charges vary according to board plan and housing facility. *Payment plan:* installment. *Waivers:* employees or children of employees.

Applying *Options:* electronic application, deferred entrance. *Application fee:* $50. *Required:* high school transcript, interview, ASSET Exam or ACT/SAT Scores. *Application deadlines:* rolling (freshmen), rolling (out-of-state freshmen), rolling (transfers). *Notification:* continuous (freshmen), continuous (out-of-state freshmen), continuous (transfers).

Freshman Application Contact Ms. Heather Wilson, Director of Admissions, Sullivan College of Technology and Design, 3901 Atkinson Square Drive, Louisville, KY 40218. *Phone:* 502-456-6509 Ext. 8220. *Toll-free phone:* 800-884-6528. *Fax:* 502-456-2341. *E-mail:* hwilson@sctd.edu. *Website:* http://www.sctd.edu/.

West Kentucky Community and Technical College
Paducah, Kentucky

- **State-supported** 2-year, founded 1932, part of Kentucky Community and Technical College System
- **Small-town** 117-acre campus
- **Coed,** 4,668 undergraduate students, 51% full-time, 63% women, 37% men

Undergraduates 2,364 full-time, 2,304 part-time. Students come from 22 states and territories; 6% are from out of state; 9% Black or African American, non-Hispanic/Latino; 2% Hispanic/Latino; 0.6% Asian, non-Hispanic/Latino; 0.3% American Indian or Alaska Native, non-Hispanic/Latino; 1% Two or more races, non-Hispanic/Latino; 1% Race/ethnicity unknown; 0.1% international. *Retention:* 61% of full-time freshmen returned.

Freshmen *Admission:* 872 enrolled.

Majors Accounting; business administration and management; computer and information sciences; court reporting; criminal justice/law enforcement administration; culinary arts; diagnostic medical sonography and ultrasound technology; electrician; fire science/firefighting; machine shop technology; physical therapy technology; registered nursing/registered nurse; respiratory care therapy; surgical technology.

Academics *Calendar:* semesters. *Degree:* certificates, diplomas, and associate. *Special study options:* academic remediation for entering students, adult/continuing education programs, cooperative education, distance learning, English as a second language, honors programs, independent study, internships, part-time degree program, study abroad.

Library WKCTC Matheson Library with 74,676 titles, 155 serial subscriptions, 5,043 audiovisual materials, an OPAC, a Web page.

Student Life *Housing:* college housing not available. *Activities and Organizations:* drama/theater group, choral group. *Campus security:* late-night transport/escort service, 14-hour patrols by trained security personnel.

Athletics *Intramural sports:* basketball M.

Standardized Tests *Required:* SAT or ACT (for admission). *Recommended:* ACT (for admission).

Financial Aid Of all full-time matriculated undergraduates who enrolled in 2012, 50 Federal Work-Study jobs (averaging $1650).

Applying *Options:* early admission. *Required for some:* high school transcript. *Application deadlines:* rolling (freshmen), rolling (transfers).

Freshman Application Contact Ms. Debbie Smith, Admissions Counselor, West Kentucky Community and Technical College, 4810 Alben Barkley Drive, Paducah, KY 42001. *Phone:* 270-554-3266. *E-mail:* Debbie.Smith@kctcs.edu. *Website:* http://www.westkentucky.kctcs.edu/.

LOUISIANA

Baton Rouge Community College
Baton Rouge, Louisiana

Director of Admissions Nancy Clay, Interim Executive Director for Enrollment Services, Baton Rouge Community College, 201 Community College Drive, Baton Rouge, LA 70806. *Phone:* 225-216-8700. *Toll-free phone:* 800-601-4558. *Website:* http://www.mybrcc.edu/.

Baton Rouge School of Computers
Baton Rouge, Louisiana

Freshman Application Contact Admissions Office, Baton Rouge School of Computers, 10425 Plaza Americana, Baton Rouge, LA 70816. *Phone:* 225-923-2524. *Toll-free phone:* 888-920-BRSC. *Fax:* 225-923-2979. *E-mail:* admissions@brsc.net. *Website:* http://www.brsc.edu/.

Blue Cliff College–Lafayette
Lafayette, Louisiana

Freshman Application Contact Admissions Office, Blue Cliff College–Lafayette, 100 Asma Boulevard, Suite 350, Lafayette, LA 70508-3862. *Toll-free phone:* 800-514-2609. *Website:* http://www.bluecliffcollege.com/.

Blue Cliff College–Shreveport
Shreveport, Louisiana

Freshman Application Contact Blue Cliff College–Shreveport, 8731 Park Plaza Drive, Shreveport, LA 71105. *Toll-free phone:* 800-516-6597. *Website:* http://www.bluecliffcollege.com/.

Bossier Parish Community College
Bossier City, Louisiana

- **State-supported** 2-year, founded 1967, part of Louisiana Community and Technical College System
- **Urban** 64-acre campus
- **Coed,** 8,512 undergraduate students, 60% full-time, 64% women, 36% men

Undergraduates 5,116 full-time, 3,396 part-time. 2% are from out of state; 41% Black or African American, non-Hispanic/Latino; 10% Hispanic/Latino; 0.6% Asian, non-Hispanic/Latino; 0.1% Native Hawaiian or other Pacific Islander, non-Hispanic/Latino; 0.8% American Indian or Alaska Native, non-Hispanic/Latino; 1% Two or more races, non-Hispanic/Latino; 3% Race/ethnicity unknown; 0.1% international; 2% transferred in. *Retention:* 51% of full-time freshmen returned.

Freshmen *Admission:* 4,102 applied, 4,052 admitted, 1,530 enrolled.

Faculty *Total:* 328, 41% full-time, 48% with terminal degrees.

Majors Administrative assistant and secretarial science; business/commerce; construction engineering; criminal justice/safety; culinary arts; drafting and design technology; dramatic/theater arts; education; educational/instructional technology; emergency medical technology (EMT paramedic); foods, nutrition, and wellness; general studies; industrial mechanics and maintenance technology; information science/studies; liberal arts and sciences/liberal studies; medical/clinical assistant; music; pharmacy technician; physical therapy; recording arts technology; respiratory care therapy.

Academics *Calendar:* semesters. *Degree:* certificates, diplomas, and associate. *Special study options:* academic remediation for entering students, adult/continuing education programs, advanced placement credit, distance learning, double majors, part-time degree program, services for LD students, summer session for credit.

Library Bossier Parish Community College Library with 29,600 titles, 384 serial subscriptions, an OPAC.

Student Life *Housing:* college housing not available. *Activities and Organizations:* drama/theater group, student-run newspaper, choral group. *Campus security:* student patrols. *Student services:* personal/psychological counseling.

Athletics Member NJCAA. *Intercollegiate sports:* baseball M(s), basketball M(s), soccer W, softball W(s). *Intramural sports:* badminton M/W, bowling M/W, football M, racquetball M, softball M, table tennis M/W, volleyball M/W.

Costs (2013–14) *Tuition:* state resident $2656 full-time, $165 per credit hour part-time; nonresident $6205 full-time, $313 per credit hour part-time. Full-time tuition and fees vary according to course load, location, and program. Part-time tuition and fees vary according to course load, location, and program. *Required fees:* $636 full-time. *Payment plan:* deferred payment. *Waivers:* employees or children of employees.

Financial Aid Of all full-time matriculated undergraduates who enrolled in 2011, 3,624 applied for aid, 3,317 were judged to have need, 87 had their need fully met. In 2011, 1 non-need-based awards were made. *Average percent of need met:* 35%. *Average financial aid package:* $11,694. *Average need-based loan:* $3165. *Average need-based gift aid:* $2544. *Average non-need-based aid:* $500.

Applying *Options:* early admission. *Application fee:* $15. *Required:* high school transcript. *Application deadlines:* 8/10 (freshmen), 8/10 (transfers). **Freshman Application Contact** Ms. Ann Jampole, Director of Admissions, Bossier Parish Community College, 6220 East Texas Street, Bossier City, LA 71111. *Phone:* 318-678-6166. *Fax:* 318-742-8664. *Website:* http://www.bpcc.edu/.

Camelot College
Baton Rouge, Louisiana

Freshman Application Contact Camelot College, 2618 Wooddale Boulevard, Suite A, Baton Rouge, LA 70805. *Phone:* 225-928-3005. *Toll-free phone:* 800-470-3320.
Website: http://www.camelotcollege.com/.

Cameron College
New Orleans, Louisiana

Admissions Office Contact Cameron College, 2740 Canal Street, New Orleans, LA 70119.
Website: http://www.cameroncollege.com/.

Career Technical College
Monroe, Louisiana

- **Proprietary** 2-year, founded 1985, part of Delta Career Education Corporation
- **Small-town** campus with easy access to Shreveport
- **Coed,** 576 undergraduate students, 78% full-time, 81% women, 19% men

Undergraduates 452 full-time, 124 part-time. Students come from 2 states and territories; 1% are from out of state; 71% Black or African American, non-Hispanic/Latino; 0.7% Hispanic/Latino; 0.2% Asian, non-Hispanic/Latino; 0.3% American Indian or Alaska Native, non-Hispanic/Latino; 2% Two or more races, non-Hispanic/Latino; 0.2% Race/ethnicity unknown. *Retention:* 90% of full-time freshmen returned.

Freshmen *Admission:* 576 enrolled.

Faculty *Total:* 35, 54% full-time. *Student/faculty ratio:* 20:1.

Majors Administrative assistant and secretarial science; business administration and management; computer and information sciences and support services related; corrections and criminal justice related; legal administrative assistant/secretary; management science; massage therapy; medical/clinical assistant; medical office management; radiologic technology/science; respiratory therapy technician; surgical technology.

Academics *Calendar:* quarters. *Degree:* diplomas and associate. *Special study options:* academic remediation for entering students, adult/continuing education programs, advanced placement credit, cooperative education, double majors, independent study, internships.

Library Library & Information Resources Network.

Student Life *Housing:* college housing not available. *Activities and Organizations:* Medical Assisting Club, Surgical Technology Club, Criminal Justice Club, Rad Tech Club, Management/Information Processing Club. *Campus security:* 24-hour emergency response devices, late-night transport/escort service, evening security guard.

Standardized Tests *Required:* SLE-Wonderlic Scholastic Level Exam; Math Proficiency Exam; English Proficiency Exam (for admission).

Costs (2013–14) *One-time required fee:* $120. *Tuition:* $11,376 full-time. Full-time tuition and fees vary according to course load and program. Part-time tuition and fees vary according to course load and program. No tuition increase for student's term of enrollment. *Required fees:* $1368 full-time. *Payment plans:* tuition prepayment, installment. *Waivers:* employees or children of employees.

Applying *Options:* deferred entrance. *Application fee:* $40. *Required:* high school transcript, interview. *Application deadlines:* rolling (freshmen), rolling (out-of-state freshmen), rolling (transfers). *Notification:* continuous (freshmen), continuous (out-of-state freshmen), continuous (transfers). **Freshman Application Contact** Mrs. Susan Boudreaux, Admissions Office, Career Technical College, 2319 Louisville Avenue, Monroe, LA 71201. *Phone:* 318-323-2889. *Toll-free phone:* 800-923-1947. *Fax:* 318-324-9883. *E-mail:* susan.boudreaux@careertc.edu.
Website: http://www.careertc.edu/.

Central Louisiana Technical College
Alexandria, Louisiana

Director of Admissions Ms. Janice Bolden, Vice Chancellor of Student Services, Enrollment Management and College Registrar, Central Louisiana Technical College, 4311 South MacArthur Drive, Alexandria, LA 71302. *Phone:* 800-351-7611.
Website: http://www.cltcc.edu/.

Delgado Community College
New Orleans, Louisiana

Freshman Application Contact Ms. Gwen Boute, Director of Admissions, Delgado Community College, 615 City Park Avenue, New Orleans, LA 70119. *Phone:* 504-671-5010. *Fax:* 504-483-1895. *E-mail:* enroll@dcc.edu. *Website:* http://www.dcc.edu/.

Delta College of Arts and Technology
Baton Rouge, Louisiana

Freshman Application Contact Ms. Beulah Laverghe-Brown, Admissions Director, Delta College of Arts and Technology, 7380 Exchange Place, Baton Rouge, LA 70806-3851. *Phone:* 225-928-7770. *Fax:* 225-927-9096. *E-mail:* bbrown@deltacollege.com.
Website: http://www.deltacollege.com/.

Delta School of Business & Technology
Lake Charles, Louisiana

Freshman Application Contact Jeffery Tibodeaux, Director of Admissions, Delta School of Business & Technology, 517 Broad Street, Lake Charles, LA 70601. *Phone:* 337-439-5765.
Website: http://www.deltatech.edu/.

Fletcher Technical Community College
Schriever, Louisiana

Director of Admissions Admissions Office, Fletcher Technical Community College, 1407 Highway 311, Schriever, LA 70395. *Phone:* 985-857-3659. *Website:* http://www.fletcher.edu/.

Fortis College
Baton Rouge, Louisiana

Director of Admissions Ms. Sheri Kirley, Associate Director of Admissions, Fortis College, 9255 Interline Avenue, Baton Rouge, LA 70809. *Phone:* 225-248-1015.
Website: http://www.fortis.edu/.

ITI Technical College
Baton Rouge, Louisiana

- **Proprietary** 2-year, founded 1973
- **Suburban** 10-acre campus
- **Coed,** 585 undergraduate students, 100% full-time, 15% women, 85% men

Undergraduates 585 full-time. Students come from 3 states and territories; 1% are from out of state; 38% Black or African American, non-Hispanic/Latino; 2% Hispanic/Latino; 0.7% Asian, non-Hispanic/Latino; 0.9% American Indian or Alaska Native, non-Hispanic/Latino; 0.7% Two or more races, non-Hispanic/Latino. *Retention:* 81% of full-time freshmen returned.

Freshmen *Admission:* 174 applied, 172 admitted, 142 enrolled.

Faculty *Total:* 51, 47% full-time, 49% with terminal degrees. *Student/faculty ratio:* 15:1.

Majors Computer technology/computer systems technology; drafting and design technology; electrical, electronic and communications engineering technology; information science/studies; information technology; instrumentation technology; manufacturing engineering technology; office occupations and clerical services.

Academics *Calendar:* continuous. *Degree:* certificates and associate. *Special study options:* internships.

Library ITI Technical College Library with 1,260 titles.

Student Life *Housing:* college housing not available. *Campus security:* electronic alarm devices are activated during non-business hours and security cameras monitor campus 24 hours.

Applying *Required:* high school transcript, interview.

Freshman Application Contact Mr. Shawn Norris, Admissions Director, ITI Technical College, 13944 Airline Highway, Baton Rouge, LA 70817. *Phone:* 225-752-4230 Ext. 261. *Toll-free phone:* 888-211-7165. *Fax:* 225-756-0903. *E-mail:* snorris@iticollege.edu.

Website: http://www.iticollege.edu/.

ITT Technical Institute

Baton Rouge, Louisiana

- **Proprietary** primarily 2-year
- **Coed**

Majors Business administration and management; computer programming (specific applications); computer systems networking and telecommunications; construction management; cyber/computer forensics and counterterrorism; drafting and design technology; electrical, electronic and communications engineering technology; forensic science and technology; graphic communications; information technology project management; legal assistant/paralegal; network and system administration; project management.

Academics *Degrees:* associate and bachelor's.

Student Life *Housing:* college housing not available.

Freshman Application Contact Director of Recruitment, ITT Technical Institute, 14111 Airline Highway, Suite 101, Baton Rouge, LA 70817. *Phone:* 225-754-5800. *Toll-free phone:* 800-295-8485.

Website: http://www.itt-tech.edu/.

ITT Technical Institute

St. Rose, Louisiana

- **Proprietary** primarily 2-year, founded 1998, part of ITT Educational Services, Inc.
- **Coed**

Majors Business administration and management; computer programming (specific applications); construction management; cyber/computer forensics and counterterrorism; drafting and design technology; electrical, electronic and communications engineering technology; forensic science and technology; game and interactive media design; graphic communications; industrial technology; information technology project management; network and system administration; project management.

Academics *Calendar:* quarters. *Degrees:* associate and bachelor's.

Student Life *Housing:* college housing not available.

Freshman Application Contact Director of Recruitment, ITT Technical Institute, 140 James Drive East, St. Rose, LA 70087. *Phone:* 504-463-0338. *Toll-free phone:* 866-463-0338.

Website: http://www.itt-tech.edu/.

Louisiana Culinary Institute

Baton Rouge, Louisiana

Admissions Office Contact Louisiana Culinary Institute, 10550 Airline Highway, Baton Rouge, LA 70816. *Toll-free phone:* 877-533-3198.

Website: http://www.louisianaculinary.com/.

Louisiana Delta Community College

Monroe, Louisiana

Admissions Office Contact Louisiana Delta Community College, 7500 Millhaven Road, Monroe, LA 71203. *Toll-free phone:* 866-500-LDCC.

Website: http://www.ladelta.edu/.

Louisiana State University at Eunice

Eunice, Louisiana

Freshman Application Contact Ms. Gracie Guillory, Director of Financial Aid, Louisiana State University at Eunice, PO Box 1129, Eunice, LA 70535-1129. *Phone:* 337-550-1282. *Toll-free phone:* 888-367-5783.

Website: http://www.lsue.edu/.

Northshore Technical Community College

Bogalusa, Louisiana

Director of Admissions Admissions Office, Northshore Technical Community College, 1710 Sullivan Drive, Bogalusa, LA 70427. *Phone:* 985-732-6640.

Website: http://www.northshorecollege.edu/.

Northwest Louisiana Technical College

Minden, Louisiana

Director of Admissions Ms. Helen Deville, Admissions Office, Northwest Louisiana Technical College, 9500 Industrial Drive, Minden, LA 71055. *Phone:* 318-371-3035. *Toll-free phone:* 800-529-1387. *Fax:* 318-371-3155. *Website:* http://www.nwltc.edu/.

Nunez Community College

Chalmette, Louisiana

- **State-supported** 2-year, founded 1992, part of Louisiana Community and Technical College System
- **Suburban** 20-acre campus with easy access to New Orleans
- **Endowment** $1.2 million
- **Coed,** 2,506 undergraduate students, 37% full-time, 66% women, 34% men

Undergraduates 918 full-time, 1,588 part-time. Students come from 2 states and territories. *Retention:* 70% of full-time freshmen returned.

Freshmen *Admission:* 296 enrolled. *Average high school GPA:* 2.26.

Faculty *Total:* 82, 46% full-time. *Student/faculty ratio:* 29:1.

Majors Child-care provision; education; general studies; industrial technology; kindergarten/preschool education; legal assistant/paralegal.

Academics *Calendar:* semesters. *Degree:* certificates, diplomas, and associate. *Special study options:* academic remediation for entering students, adult/continuing education programs, advanced placement credit, cooperative education, distance learning, double majors, independent study, internships, off-campus study, part-time degree program, services for LD students, student-designed majors, summer session for credit.

Library Nunez Community College Library with 72,500 titles, 2,500 serial subscriptions, 3,128 audiovisual materials, an OPAC, a Web page.

Student Life *Housing:* college housing not available. *Activities and Organizations:* Nunez Environmental Team. *Campus security:* 24-hour emergency response devices, late-night transport/escort service, security cameras. *Student services:* health clinic, personal/psychological counseling.

Athletics *Intramural sports:* basketball M, football M/W.

Standardized Tests *Recommended:* ACT (for admission).

Costs (2013–14) *Tuition:* state resident $3256 full-time; nonresident $6446 full-time. Full-time tuition and fees vary according to course load and location. Part-time tuition and fees vary according to course load and location. *Required fees:* $1200 full-time. *Payment plan:* installment. *Waivers:* senior citizens and employees or children of employees.

Financial Aid Of all full-time matriculated undergraduates who enrolled in 2012, 70 Federal Work-Study jobs (averaging $1452).

Applying *Options:* electronic application, early admission, deferred entrance. *Application fee:* $10. *Required for some:* high school transcript. *Application deadlines:* rolling (freshmen), rolling (transfers).

Freshman Application Contact Mrs. Becky Maillet, Nunez Community College, 3710 Paris Road, Chalmette, LA 70043. *Phone:* 504-278-6477. *E-mail:* bmaillet@nunez.edu.

Website: http://www.nunez.edu/.

Remington College–Baton Rouge Campus

Baton Rouge, Louisiana

Director of Admissions Monica Butler-Johnson, Director of Recruitment, Remington College–Baton Rouge Campus, 10551 Coursey Boulevard, Baton Rouge, LA 70816. *Phone:* 225-236-3200. *Fax:* 225-922-3250. *E-mail:* monica.johnson@remingtoncollege.edu.

Website: http://www.remingtoncollege.edu/.

Remington College–Lafayette Campus

Lafayette, Louisiana

Freshman Application Contact Remington College–Lafayette Campus, 303 Rue Louis XIV, Lafayette, LA 70508. *Phone:* 337-981-4010. *Toll-free phone:* 800-560-6192.

Website: http://www.remingtoncollege.edu/.

Remington College–Shreveport

Shreveport, Louisiana

Freshman Application Contact Marc Wright, Remington College–Shreveport, 2106 Bert Kouns Industrial Loop, Shreveport, LA 71118. *Phone:* 318-671-4000.

Website: http://www.remingtoncollege.edu/.

River Parishes Community College

Sorrento, Louisiana

Director of Admissions Ms. Allison Dauzat, Dean of Students and Enrollment Management, River Parishes Community College, 7384 John Leblanc Boulevard, Sorrento, LA 70778. *Phone:* 225-675-8270. *Fax:* 225-675-5478. *E-mail:* adauzat@rpcc.cc.la.us. *Website:* http://www.rpcc.edu/.

South Central Louisiana Technical College

Morgan City, Louisiana

Director of Admissions Ms. Melanie Henry, Admissions Office, South Central Louisiana Technical College, 900 Youngs Road, Morgan City, LA 70380. *Phone:* 504-380-2436. *Fax:* 504-380-2440. *Website:* http://www.scl.edu/.

Southern University at Shreveport

Shreveport, Louisiana

- **State-supported** 2-year, founded 1964, part of Southern University System
- **Urban** 103-acre campus
- **Endowment** $619,644
- **Coed,** 3,018 undergraduate students, 70% full-time, 71% women, 29% men

Undergraduates 2,121 full-time, 897 part-time. Students come from 5 states and territories; 45% are from out of state; 89% Black or African American, non-Hispanic/Latino; 0.5% Hispanic/Latino; 0.6% Asian, non-Hispanic/Latino; 0.1% Native Hawaiian or other Pacific Islander, non-Hispanic/Latino; 0.2% American Indian or Alaska Native, non-Hispanic/Latino; 0.4% Two or more races, non-Hispanic/Latino; 0.2% Race/ethnicity unknown; 0.5% international; 7% transferred in; 7% live on campus. *Retention:* 43% of full-time freshmen returned.
Freshmen *Admission:* 405 enrolled. *Average high school GPA:* 2. *Test scores:* ACT scores over 18: 8%.
Faculty *Total:* 200, 41% full-time, 10% with terminal degrees. *Student/faculty ratio:* 20:1.
Majors Accounting; accounting technology and bookkeeping; avionics maintenance technology; banking and financial support services; biology/biological sciences; business/commerce; cardiovascular technology; chemistry; clinical/medical laboratory technology; computer science; criminal justice/law enforcement administration; dental hygiene; electrical, electronic and communications engineering technology; general studies; health information/medical records administration; health information/medical records technology; hospitality administration; hotel/motel administration; human services; kindergarten/preschool education; legal assistant/paralegal; liberal arts and sciences and humanities related; mathematics; mechanical engineering/mechanical technology; medical radiologic technology; mental health counseling; physical therapy technology; public administration; radiologic technology/science; registered nursing/registered nurse; respiratory care therapy; robotics technology; sociology; surgical technology; teacher assistant/aide; tourism and travel services management.
Academics *Calendar:* semesters. *Degree:* certificates and associate. *Special study options:* academic remediation for entering students, accelerated degree program, adult/continuing education programs, advanced placement credit, cooperative education, distance learning, honors programs, internships, off-campus study, part-time degree program, student-designed majors, summer session for credit. *ROTC:* Army (c).
Library Library/Learning Resources Center plus 1 other with 380 serial subscriptions, 24,016 audiovisual materials, an OPAC.
Student Life *Housing Options:* coed. Campus housing is provided by a third party. *Activities and Organizations:* drama/theater group, student-run newspaper, choral group, Afro-American Society, SUSLA Gospel Choir, Student Center Board, Allied Health, Engineering Club. *Campus security:* 24-hour patrols, controlled dormitory access. *Student services:* personal/psychological counseling.
Athletics Member NJCAA. *Intercollegiate sports:* basketball M(s)/W(s). *Intramural sports:* basketball M/W, cheerleading M/W.
Standardized Tests *Required for some:* SAT or ACT (for admission). *Recommended:* ACT (for admission).
Costs (2014–15) *Tuition:* state resident $4497 full-time; nonresident $6116 full-time. Full-time tuition and fees vary according to course load, location, and program. Part-time tuition and fees vary according to course load, location, and program. *Room and board:* $10,270; room only: $7920. Room and board charges vary according to board plan. *Payment plans:* installment, deferred payment.

Applying *Required:* high school transcript.
Freshman Application Contact Ms. Danielle Anderson, Admissions Advisor, Southern University at Shreveport, 3050 Martin Luther King Jr. Drive, Shreveport, LA 71107. *Phone:* 318-670-9211. *Toll-free phone:* 800-458-1472. *Fax:* 318-670-6483. *E-mail:* danderson@susla.edu. *Website:* http://www.susla.edu/.

South Louisiana Community College

Lafayette, Louisiana

- **State-supported** 2-year, part of Louisiana College and Technical College System
- **Small-town** campus
- **Coed,** 7,563 undergraduate students, 43% full-time, 54% women, 46% men

Undergraduates 3,234 full-time, 4,329 part-time. Students come from 14 states and territories; 17 other countries; 1% are from out of state; 33% Black or African American, non-Hispanic/Latino; 2% Hispanic/Latino; 2% Asian, non-Hispanic/Latino; 0.4% American Indian or Alaska Native, non-Hispanic/Latino; 1% Two or more races, non-Hispanic/Latino; 7% Race/ethnicity unknown; 0.2% international; 7% transferred in. *Retention:* 51% of full-time freshmen returned.
Freshmen *Admission:* 1,921 enrolled.
Faculty *Total:* 257, 52% full-time. *Student/faculty ratio:* 26:1.
Majors Administrative assistant and secretarial science; aircraft powerplant technology; autobody/collision and repair technology; automobile/automotive mechanics technology; business/commerce; carpentry; clinical/medical laboratory technology; computer systems networking and telecommunications; criminal justice/safety; culinary arts; desktop publishing and digital imaging design; diesel mechanics technology; direct entry midwifery; drafting and design technology; education; electrician; emergency medical technology (EMT paramedic); energy management and systems technology; general studies; heating, air conditioning, ventilation and refrigeration maintenance technology; industrial electronics technology; industrial mechanics and maintenance technology; industrial radiologic technology; industrial technology; licensed practical/vocational nurse training; machine tool technology; registered nursing/registered nurse; surgical technology; surveying technology; web page, digital/multimedia and information resources design; welding technology.
Academics *Calendar:* semesters. *Degree:* certificates, diplomas, and associate. *Special study options:* academic remediation for entering students, advanced placement credit, distance learning, double majors, English as a second language, independent study, internships, services for LD students, summer session for credit.
Student Life *Housing:* college housing not available.
Standardized Tests *Required:* ACT (for admission).
Costs (2014–15) *Tuition:* state resident $3450 full-time, $150 per credit part-time; nonresident $6415 full-time, $280 per credit part-time. Full-time tuition and fees vary according to program. Part-time tuition and fees vary according to program. *Payment plan:* installment. *Waivers:* employees or children of employees.
Applying *Options:* electronic application. *Required:* high school transcript.
Freshman Application Contact Mme. Chris Stutes, Director of Admissions, South Louisiana Community College, 1101 Bertrand Drive, Lafayette, LA 70506. *Phone:* 337-521-8953. *E-mail:* chris.stutes@solacc.edu. *Website:* http://www.solacc.edu/.

Sowela Technical Community College

Lake Charles, Louisiana

- **State-supported** 2-year, founded 1938, part of Louisiana Community Technical College System
- **Urban** 77-acre campus
- **Coed,** 3,225 undergraduate students, 53% full-time, 42% women, 58% men
- **100%** of applicants were admitted

Undergraduates 1,702 full-time, 1,523 part-time. Students come from 13 states and territories; 2 other countries; 0.4% are from out of state; 26% Black or African American, non-Hispanic/Latino; 2% Hispanic/Latino; 0.7% Asian, non-Hispanic/Latino; 0.1% Native Hawaiian or other Pacific Islander, non-Hispanic/Latino; 0.7% American Indian or Alaska Native, non-Hispanic/Latino; 2% Two or more races, non-Hispanic/Latino; 4% Race/ethnicity unknown; 0.1% international. *Retention:* 46% of full-time freshmen returned.
Freshmen *Admission:* 1,842 applied, 1,838 admitted, 761 enrolled. *Average high school GPA:* 2.2.
Faculty *Total:* 128, 55% full-time. *Student/faculty ratio:* 25:1.
Majors Computer programming; computer systems networking and telecommunications; drafting and design technology; electrician; general studies; instrumentation technology; plumbing technology.

Academics *Calendar:* semesters. *Degree:* certificates, diplomas, and associate. *Special study options:* academic remediation for entering students, adult/continuing education programs, distance learning, double majors, part-time degree program, services for LD students, summer session for credit.
Library Library & Learning Resource Center (LLRC) plus 1 other with 30,522 titles, 45,000 serial subscriptions, 386 audiovisual materials, an OPAC, a Web page.
Student Life *Housing:* college housing not available. *Activities and Organizations:* SkillsUSA, Student Government Association (SGA), Gamerz, Criminal Justice, LRA. *Campus security:* Security guard on duty. *Student services:* personal/psychological counseling.
Standardized Tests *Required:* For Placement Purposes Only: Compass, Asset, ACT (for admission).
Costs (2014–15) *Tuition:* area resident $3320 full-time; state resident $1320 full-time, $111 per credit part-time; nonresident $6594 full-time, $220 per credit part-time. *Required fees:* $735 full-time, $24 per credit part-time, $15 per term part-time. *Room and board:* $8921. *Payment plan:* deferred payment. *Waivers:* employees or children of employees.
Applying *Options:* electronic application, early admission. *Required:* high school transcript, Compass Test, Asset or ACT for placement purposes, Proof of Immunization, Proof of Selective Service Status, College Transcript if applicable Note: High School transcript required for all AAS and Practical Nursing Programs. *Application deadlines:* 8/23 (freshmen), 8/23 (out-of-state freshmen), 12/28 (transfers). *Notification:* continuous (freshmen), continuous (out-of-state freshmen), continuous (transfers).
Freshman Application Contact Office of Admissions, Sowela Technical Community College, 3820 Senator J. Bennett Johnston Ave., Lake Charles, LA 70616. *Phone:* 337-421-6540. *Fax:* 337-491-2663.
Website: http://www.sowela.edu/.

Virginia College
Bossier City, Louisiana

Admissions Office Contact Virginia College, 2950 East Texas Street, Suite C, Bossier City, LA 71111.
Website: http://www.vc.edu/.

Virginia College in Baton Rouge
Baton Rouge, Louisiana

Admissions Office Contact Virginia College in Baton Rouge, 9501 Cortana Place, Baton Rouge, LA 70815.
Website: http://www.vc.edu/.

MAINE

Beal College
Bangor, Maine

- **Proprietary** 2-year, founded 1891
- **Small-town** 4-acre campus
- **Coed,** 464 undergraduate students, 78% full-time, 66% women, 34% men

Undergraduates 363 full-time, 101 part-time. Students come from 1 other state; 0.9% Black or African American, non-Hispanic/Latino; 1% Hispanic/Latino; 0.6% Asian, non-Hispanic/Latino; 0.2% Native Hawaiian or other Pacific Islander, non-Hispanic/Latino; 2% American Indian or Alaska Native, non-Hispanic/Latino; 4% Race/ethnicity unknown; 10% transferred in. *Retention:* 60% of full-time freshmen returned.
Freshmen *Admission:* 93 enrolled.
Faculty *Total:* 40, 20% full-time, 3% with terminal degrees. *Student/faculty ratio:* 30:1.
Majors Accounting; administrative assistant and secretarial science; business administration and management; criminal justice/law enforcement administration; health information/medical records technology; human resources management; human services; medical/clinical assistant; medical office assistant; substance abuse/addiction counseling; welding technology.
Academics *Calendar:* modular. *Degree:* certificates, diplomas, and associate. *Special study options:* accelerated degree program, adult/continuing education programs, advanced placement credit, internships, part-time degree program, summer session for credit.
Library Beal College Library with 9,351 titles, 76 serial subscriptions, a Web page.
Student Life *Housing:* college housing not available. *Activities and Organizations:* student-run newspaper.
Costs (2014–15) *Tuition:* $6240 full-time, $208 per credit part-time. Full-time tuition and fees vary according to course load and program. Part-time tuition and fees vary according to course load and program. *Payment plan:* installment.

Applying *Options:* deferred entrance. *Application fee:* $30. *Required:* essay or personal statement, high school transcript, 1 letter of recommendation, interview, Entrance exam; immunizations. *Application deadlines:* rolling (freshmen), rolling (transfers).
Freshman Application Contact Sue Borden, Admissions Assistant, Beal College, 99 Farm Road, Bangor, ME 04401. *Phone:* 207-947-4591. *Toll-free phone:* 800-660-7351. *Fax:* 207-947-0208. *E-mail:* admissions@bealcollege.edu.
Website: http://www.bealcollege.edu/.

Central Maine Community College
Auburn, Maine

- **State-supported** 2-year, founded 1964, part of Maine Community College System
- **Small-town** 135-acre campus
- **Endowment** $530,000
- **Coed,** 3,109 undergraduate students, 47% full-time, 53% women, 47% men

Undergraduates 1,447 full-time, 1,662 part-time. Students come from 13 states and territories; 3 other countries; 3% are from out of state; 4% Black or African American, non-Hispanic/Latino; 2% Hispanic/Latino; 1% Asian, non-Hispanic/Latino; 0.2% Native Hawaiian or other Pacific Islander, non-Hispanic/Latino; 0.8% American Indian or Alaska Native, non-Hispanic/Latino; 2% Two or more races, non-Hispanic/Latino; 7% Race/ethnicity unknown; 0.2% international; 14% transferred in; 8% live on campus.
Freshmen *Admission:* 1,929 applied, 782 admitted, 600 enrolled. *Test scores:* SAT critical reading scores over 500: 22%; SAT math scores over 500: 24%; SAT writing scores over 500: 17%; SAT critical reading scores over 600: 4%; SAT math scores over 600: 3%; SAT writing scores over 600: 2%; SAT critical reading scores over 700: 1%.
Faculty *Total:* 385, 15% full-time, 0.8% with terminal degrees. *Student/faculty ratio:* 17:1.
Majors Accounting; accounting technology and bookkeeping; administrative assistant and secretarial science; architectural engineering technology; automobile/automotive mechanics technology; building construction technology; business administration and management; child development; civil engineering technology; computer installation and repair technology; construction trades related; criminal justice/law enforcement administration; criminal justice/safety; early childhood education; electromechanical technology; graphic and printing equipment operation/production; graphic communications; human services; liberal arts and sciences/liberal studies; licensed practical/vocational nurse training; machine tool technology; medical/clinical assistant; multi/interdisciplinary studies related; network and system administration; registered nursing/registered nurse.
Academics *Calendar:* semesters. *Degree:* certificates, diplomas, and associate. *Special study options:* academic remediation for entering students, accelerated degree program, adult/continuing education programs, advanced placement credit, cooperative education, distance learning, English as a second language, independent study, internships, part-time degree program, services for LD students, summer session for credit.
Library Central Maine Community College Library with 15,914 titles, 200 serial subscriptions, 2 audiovisual materials, an OPAC, a Web page.
Student Life *Housing Options:* coed, men-only, women-only. Campus housing is university owned. Freshman applicants given priority for college housing. *Activities and Organizations:* drama/theater group. *Campus security:* 24-hour emergency response devices, student patrols, controlled dormitory access, night patrols by police.
Athletics Member USCAA. *Intercollegiate sports:* baseball M, basketball M/W, golf M/W, lacrosse M/W, soccer M/W, softball W. *Intramural sports:* volleyball M/W.
Standardized Tests *Recommended:* SAT (for admission), SAT and SAT Subject Tests or ACT (for admission), SAT Subject Tests (for admission).
Costs (2014–15) *Tuition:* state resident $2640 full-time, $1320 per year part-time; nonresident $5280 full-time, $2640 per year part-time. Full-time tuition and fees vary according to course load and program. Part-time tuition and fees vary according to course load and program. *Required fees:* $1034 full-time, $33 per credit part-time, $199 per term part-time. *Room and board:* $8916; room only: $4150. Room and board charges vary according to housing facility. *Payment plan:* installment. *Waivers:* employees or children of employees.
Financial Aid Of all full-time matriculated undergraduates who enrolled in 2012, 89 Federal Work-Study jobs (averaging $1200). *Financial aid deadline:* 8/1.
Applying *Options:* electronic application, deferred entrance. *Application fee:* $20. *Required:* high school transcript. *Recommended:* essay or personal statement. *Application deadlines:* rolling (freshmen), rolling (transfers). *Notification:* continuous (freshmen), continuous (transfers).
Freshman Application Contact Ms. Joan Nichols, Admissions Assistant, Central Maine Community College, 1250 Turner Street, Auburn, ME 04210.

Phone: 207-755-5273. *Toll-free phone:* 800-891-2002. *Fax:* 207-755-5493. *E-mail:* enroll@cmcc.edu.

Website: http://www.cmcc.edu/.

Central Maine Medical Center College of Nursing and Health Professions

Lewiston, Maine

- **Independent** 2-year, founded 1891
- **Urban** campus
- **Coed,** 227 undergraduate students, 27% full-time, 89% women, 11% men

Undergraduates 61 full-time, 166 part-time. Students come from 2 states and territories; 2% are from out of state; 3% Black or African American, non-Hispanic/Latino; 1% Hispanic/Latino; 0.9% Asian, non-Hispanic/Latino; 0.4% Native Hawaiian or other Pacific Islander, non-Hispanic/Latino; 2% live on campus.

Freshmen *Admission:* 2 enrolled.

Faculty *Total:* 19, 84% full-time. *Student/faculty ratio:* 10:1.

Majors Nuclear medical technology; radiologic technology/science; registered nursing/registered nurse.

Academics *Calendar:* semesters. *Degree:* associate. *Special study options:* advanced placement credit, off-campus study, services for LD students, summer session for credit.

Library Gerrish True Health Sciences Library plus 1 other with 1,975 titles, 339 serial subscriptions, an OPAC, a Web page.

Student Life *Housing Options:* coed. Campus housing is university owned. *Activities and Organizations:* Student Communication Council, student government, Student Nurses Association. *Campus security:* 24-hour emergency response devices and patrols, late-night transport/escort service, controlled dormitory access. *Student services:* health clinic, personal/psychological counseling.

Standardized Tests *Required:* SAT or ACT (for admission), ACCUPLACER Entrance Exam (for admission).

Costs (2014–15) *Tuition:* $7665 full-time. *Waivers:* employees or children of employees.

Financial Aid Of all full-time matriculated undergraduates who enrolled in 2010, 5 applied for aid, 4 were judged to have need. *Average financial aid package:* $17,200. *Average need-based loan:* $4000. *Average need-based gift aid:* $7700.

Applying *Application fee:* $40. *Required:* essay or personal statement, high school transcript, Entrance exam, SAT or ACT, high school or college level algebra, second math, biology, chemistry, high school transcript or GED. *Application deadline:* 1/15 (freshmen). *Notification:* 3/15 (freshmen).

Freshman Application Contact Ms. Dagmar Jenison, Assistant Registrar, Central Maine Medical Center College of Nursing and Health Professions, 70 Middle Street, Lewiston, ME 04240. *Phone:* 207-795-2843. *Fax:* 207-795-2849. *E-mail:* jenisod@cmhc.org.

Website: http://www.cmmccollege.edu/.

Eastern Maine Community College

Bangor, Maine

Freshman Application Contact Mr. W. Gregory Swett, Director of Admissions, Eastern Maine Community College, 354 Hogan Road, Bangor, ME 04401. *Phone:* 207-974-4680. *Toll-free phone:* 800-286-9357. *Fax:* 207-974-4683. *E-mail:* admissions@emcc.edu.

Website: http://www.emcc.edu/.

Kaplan University

Lewiston, Maine

Freshman Application Contact Kaplan University, 475 Lisbon Street, Lewiston, ME 04240. *Phone:* 207-333-3300. *Toll-free phone:* 866-527-5268 (in-state); 800-527-5268 (out-of-state).

Website: http://lewiston.kaplanuniversity.edu/.

Kaplan University

South Portland, Maine

Freshman Application Contact Kaplan University, 265 Western Avenue, South Portland, ME 04106. *Phone:* 207-774-6126. *Toll-free phone:* 866-527-5268 (in-state); 800-527-5268 (out-of-state).

Website: http://portland.kaplanuniversity.edu/.

Kennebec Valley Community College

Fairfield, Maine

- **State-supported** 2-year, founded 1970, part of Maine Community College System
- **Small-town** 61-acre campus
- **Coed**

Undergraduates 714 full-time, 1,756 part-time. Students come from 9 states and territories; 1% are from out of state; 0.7% Black or African American, non-Hispanic/Latino; 1% Hispanic/Latino; 0.7% Asian, non-Hispanic/Latino; 0.6% American Indian or Alaska Native, non-Hispanic/Latino; 0.3% Two or more races, non-Hispanic/Latino; 10% Race/ethnicity unknown; 0.1% international; 8% transferred in.

Academics *Calendar:* semesters. *Degree:* certificates, diplomas, and associate. *Special study options:* academic remediation for entering students, accelerated degree program, adult/continuing education programs, advanced placement credit, distance learning, external degree program, independent study, internships, part-time degree program, services for LD students, summer session for credit.

Student Life *Campus security:* evening security patrol.

Standardized Tests *Required for some:* HESI nursing exam, HOBET for Allied Health programs, ACCUPLACER. *Recommended:* SAT or ACT (for admission).

Costs (2013–14) *One-time required fee:* $30. *Tuition:* state resident $2640 full-time, $88 per credit hour part-time; nonresident $5280 full-time, $176 per credit hour part-time. *Required fees:* $606 full-time, $3 per credit hour part-time.

Financial Aid Of all full-time matriculated undergraduates who enrolled in 2012, 974 applied for aid, 881 were judged to have need, 32 had their need fully met. In 2012, 5. *Average percent of need met:* 52. *Average financial aid package:* $6220. *Average need-based loan:* $3110. *Average need-based gift aid:* $4611. *Average non-need-based aid:* $1103.

Applying *Options:* electronic application, deferred entrance. *Application fee:* $20. *Required:* essay or personal statement, high school transcript. *Required for some:* interview.

Freshman Application Contact Mr. Jim Bourgoin, Director of Admissions, Kennebec Valley Community College, Fairfield, ME 04937-1367. *Phone:* 207-453-5035. *Toll-free phone:* 800-528-5882. *Fax:* 207-453-5011. *E-mail:* admissions@kvcc.me.edu.

Website: http://www.kvcc.me.edu/.

Northern Maine Community College

Presque Isle, Maine

Freshman Application Contact Ms. Nancy Gagnon, Admissions Secretary, Northern Maine Community College, 33 Edgemont Drive, Presque Isle, ME 04769-2016. *Phone:* 207-768-2785. *Toll-free phone:* 800-535-6682. *Fax:* 207-768-2848. *E-mail:* ngagnon@nmcc.edu.

Website: http://www.nmcc.edu/.

Southern Maine Community College

South Portland, Maine

- **State-supported** 2-year, founded 1946, part of Maine Community College System
- **Urban** 80-acre campus
- **Coed,** 7,131 undergraduate students, 42% full-time, 48% women, 52% men

Undergraduates 3,019 full-time, 4,112 part-time. 4% Black or African American, non-Hispanic/Latino; 2% Hispanic/Latino; 2% Asian, non-Hispanic/Latino; 0.1% Native Hawaiian or other Pacific Islander, non-Hispanic/Latino; 0.7% American Indian or Alaska Native, non-Hispanic/Latino; 2% Two or more races, non-Hispanic/Latino; 6% Race/ethnicity unknown; 0.5% international; 8% transferred in; 5% live on campus. *Retention:* 53% of full-time freshmen returned.

Freshmen *Admission:* 1,383 enrolled.

Faculty *Total:* 482, 23% full-time. *Student/faculty ratio:* 20:1.

Majors Agroecology and sustainable agriculture; automobile/automotive mechanics technology; biotechnology; business administration and management; cardiovascular technology; computer engineering technology; computer science; culinary arts; dietetic technology; digital communication and media/multimedia; drafting and design technology; early childhood education; electrical, electronic and communications engineering technology; emergency medical technology (EMT paramedic); fire science/firefighting; health information/medical records technology; heating, air conditioning, ventilation and refrigeration maintenance technology; liberal arts and sciences and humanities related; machine tool technology; marine biology and biological oceanography; materials engineering; medical/clinical assistant; medical radiologic technology; plumbing technology; pre-engineering;

radiologic technology/science; registered nursing/registered nurse; respiratory care therapy; surgical technology.

Academics *Calendar:* semesters. *Degree:* certificates and associate. *Special study options:* academic remediation for entering students, advanced placement credit, distance learning, double majors, English as a second language, honors programs, independent study, internships, off-campus study, part-time degree program, services for LD students, study abroad, summer session for credit.

Library Southern Maine Community College Library with an OPAC, a Web page.

Student Life *Housing Options:* coed. Campus housing is university owned. *Activities and Organizations:* drama/theater group, student-run newspaper, choral group, Student Senate. *Campus security:* 24-hour emergency response devices and patrols, student patrols, late-night transport/escort service, controlled dormitory access. *Student services:* personal/psychological counseling.

Athletics Member USCAA. *Intercollegiate sports:* baseball M, basketball M/W, golf M/W, soccer M/W, softball W. *Intramural sports:* cheerleading M(c)/W, cross-country running M(c)/W(c), ice hockey M(c), rock climbing M(c)/W(c), soccer M/W, volleyball M/W.

Standardized Tests *Recommended:* SAT or ACT (for admission), ACCUPLACER.

Costs (2013–14) *One-time required fee:* $20. *Tuition:* state resident $2112 full-time, $88 per credit hour part-time; nonresident $4224 full-time, $176 per credit hour part-time. Full-time tuition and fees vary according to course load. Part-time tuition and fees vary according to course load. *Required fees:* $628 full-time, $24 per credit hour part-time, $25 per term part-time. *Room and board:* $8140; room only: $5040. *Payment plan:* installment. *Waivers:* senior citizens and employees or children of employees.

Financial Aid Of all full-time matriculated undergraduates who enrolled in 2012, 130 Federal Work-Study jobs (averaging $1500).

Applying *Options:* electronic application. *Application fee:* $20. *Required:* high school transcript or proof of high school graduation. *Application deadlines:* rolling (freshmen), rolling (out-of-state freshmen), rolling (transfers). *Notification:* continuous (freshmen), continuous (out-of-state freshmen), continuous (transfers).

Freshman Application Contact Amy Lee, Director of Enrollment Services, Southern Maine Community College, 2 Fort Road, South, Portland, ME 04106. *Phone:* 207-741-5800. *Toll-free phone:* 877-282-2182. *Fax:* 207-741-5760. *E-mail:* alee@smccme.edu.
Website: http://www.smccme.edu/.

Washington County Community College
Calais, Maine

Director of Admissions Mr. Kent Lyons, Admissions Counselor, Washington County Community College, One College Drive, Calais, ME 04619. *Phone:* 207-454-1000. *Toll-free phone:* 800-210-6932.
Website: http://www.wccc.me.edu/.

York County Community College
Wells, Maine

- **State-supported** 2-year, founded 1994, part of Maine Community College System
- **Small-town** 84-acre campus with easy access to Boston
- **Endowment** $553,788
- **Coed,** 1,583 undergraduate students, 40% full-time, 66% women, 34% men

Undergraduates 634 full-time, 949 part-time. Students come from 13 states and territories; 3% are from out of state; 0.8% Black or African American, non-Hispanic/Latino; 2% Hispanic/Latino; 1% Asian, non-Hispanic/Latino; 0.8% American Indian or Alaska Native, non-Hispanic/Latino; 2% Two or more races, non-Hispanic/Latino; 8% Race/ethnicity unknown; 0.5% international; 17% transferred in. *Retention:* 63% of full-time freshmen returned.

Freshmen *Admission:* 651 applied, 325 admitted, 287 enrolled.

Faculty *Total:* 136, 13% full-time, 9% with terminal degrees. *Student/faculty ratio:* 15:1.

Majors Accounting; architectural drafting and CAD/CADD; business administration and management; child development; construction trades related; criminal justice/safety; culinary arts; design and visual communications; education; health information/medical records technology; health services/allied health/health sciences; liberal arts and sciences and humanities related; machine tool technology; management information systems; medical/clinical assistant; multi/interdisciplinary studies related; social work.

Academics *Calendar:* semesters. *Degree:* certificates and associate. *Special study options:* academic remediation for entering students, adult/continuing education programs, advanced placement credit, cooperative education, distance learning, internships, off-campus study, part-time degree program, services for LD students, summer session for credit.

Library Library and Learning Resource Center plus 1 other with 14,385 titles, 10 serial subscriptions, 1,628 audiovisual materials, an OPAC, a Web page.

Student Life *Housing:* college housing not available. *Activities and Organizations:* Student Senate, Phi Theta Kappa. *Campus security:* 24-hour emergency response devices, late-night transport/escort service.

Athletics *Intramural sports:* basketball M/W, bowling M/W, cross-country running M/W, football M/W, ice hockey M/W, skiing (downhill) M/W, soccer M/W, softball M/W, ultimate Frisbee M/W, volleyball M/W.

Costs (2014–15) *Tuition:* state resident $2640 full-time, $88 per credit part-time; nonresident $5280 full-time, $176 per credit part-time. *Required fees:* $606 full-time. *Payment plan:* installment. *Waivers:* employees or children of employees.

Financial Aid Of all full-time matriculated undergraduates who enrolled in 2012, 600 applied for aid, 497 were judged to have need, 19 had their need fully met. 26 Federal Work-Study jobs (averaging $1554). In 2012, 27 non-need-based awards were made. *Average percent of need met:* 41%. *Average financial aid package:* $5942. *Average need-based loan:* $2899. *Average need-based gift aid:* $4752. *Average non-need-based aid:* $1385.

Applying *Options:* electronic application. *Required:* high school transcript, interview. *Application deadlines:* rolling (freshmen), rolling (transfers).

Freshman Application Contact Fred Quistgard, Director of Admissions, York County Community College, 112 College Drive, Wells, ME 04090. *Phone:* 207-216-4406 Ext. 311. *Toll-free phone:* 800-580-3820. *Fax:* 207-641-0837.
Website: http://www.yccc.edu/.

MARSHALL ISLANDS

College of the Marshall Islands
Majuro, Marshall Islands, Marshall Islands

Freshman Application Contact Ms. Rosita Capelle, Director of Admissions and Records, College of the Marshall Islands, PO Box 1258, Majuro, MH 96960, Marshall Islands. *Phone:* 692-625-6823. *Fax:* 692-625-7203. *E-mail:* cmiadmissions@cmi.edu.
Website: http://www.cmi.edu/.

MARYLAND

Allegany College of Maryland
Cumberland, Maryland

Freshman Application Contact Ms. Cathy Nolan, Director of Admissions and Registration, Allegany College of Maryland, Cumberland, MD 21502. *Phone:* 301-784-5000 Ext. 5202. *Fax:* 301-784-5220. *E-mail:* cnolan@allegany.edu.
Website: http://www.allegany.edu/.

Anne Arundel Community College
Arnold, Maryland

- **State and locally supported** 2-year, founded 1961
- **Suburban** 230-acre campus with easy access to Baltimore and Washington, DC
- **Coed**

Undergraduates 5,098 full-time, 12,552 part-time. 18% Black or African American, non-Hispanic/Latino; 5% Hispanic/Latino; 4% Asian, non-Hispanic/Latino; 0.3% Native Hawaiian or other Pacific Islander, non-Hispanic/Latino; 0.5% American Indian or Alaska Native, non-Hispanic/Latino; 2% Two or more races, non-Hispanic/Latino; 8% Race/ethnicity unknown; 0.8% international.

Faculty *Student/faculty ratio:* 16:1.

Academics *Calendar:* semesters. *Degree:* certificates and associate. *Special study options:* academic remediation for entering students, accelerated degree program, adult/continuing education programs, advanced placement credit, cooperative education, distance learning, English as a second language, freshman honors college, honors programs, independent study, internships, part-time degree program, services for LD students, summer session for credit. *ROTC:* Army (c), Air Force (c).

Student Life *Campus security:* 24-hour emergency response devices and patrols, student patrols, late-night transport/escort service.

Athletics Member NJCAA.

Financial Aid Of all full-time matriculated undergraduates who enrolled in 2012, 104 Federal Work-Study jobs (averaging $1900). 55 state and other part-time jobs (averaging $1740).

Applying *Options:* electronic application, early admission, deferred entrance.

Freshman Application Contact Mr. Thomas McGinn, Director of Enrollment Development and Admissions, Anne Arundel Community College, 101 College Parkway, Arnold, MD 21012-1895. *Phone:* 410-777-2240. *Fax:* 410-777-2246. *E-mail:* 4info@aacc.edu.

Website: http://www.aacc.edu/.

Baltimore City Community College

Baltimore, Maryland

Freshman Application Contact Baltimore City Community College, 2901 Liberty Heights Avenue, Baltimore, MD 21215-7893. *Phone:* 410-462-8311. *Toll-free phone:* 888-203-1261.

Website: http://www.bccc.edu/.

Carroll Community College

Westminster, Maryland

- **State and locally supported** 2-year, founded 1993, part of Maryland Higher Education Commission
- **Suburban** 80-acre campus with easy access to Baltimore
- **Endowment** $4.2 million
- **Coed,** 3,794 undergraduate students, 38% full-time, 61% women, 39% men

Undergraduates 1,437 full-time, 2,357 part-time. Students come from 7 states and territories; 16 other countries; 2% are from out of state; 3% Black or African American, non-Hispanic/Latino; 3% Hispanic/Latino; 1% Asian, non-Hispanic/Latino; 0.1% Native Hawaiian or other Pacific Islander, non-Hispanic/Latino; 0.3% American Indian or Alaska Native, non-Hispanic/Latino; 2% Two or more races, non-Hispanic/Latino; 2% Race/ethnicity unknown; 0.2% international; 7% transferred in.

Freshmen *Admission:* 733 applied, 733 admitted, 733 enrolled.

Faculty *Total:* 271, 29% full-time, 5% with terminal degrees. *Student/faculty ratio:* 16:1.

Majors Accounting technology and bookkeeping; administrative assistant and secretarial science; architectural drafting and CAD/CADD; art; business administration and management; chemistry teacher education; child-care and support services management; computer engineering; computer graphics; criminal justice/police science; early childhood education; education; electrical and electronics engineering; elementary education; emergency medical technology (EMT paramedic); English/language arts teacher education; forensic science and technology; general studies; health information/medical records technology; health professions related; kinesiology and exercise science; legal studies; liberal arts and sciences/liberal studies; licensed practical/vocational nurse training; management information systems; mathematics teacher education; multi/interdisciplinary studies related; music; physical therapy technology; psychology; registered nursing/registered nurse; Spanish language teacher education; theater design and technology.

Academics *Calendar:* semesters plus winter session. *Degree:* certificates and associate. *Special study options:* academic remediation for entering students, advanced placement credit, distance learning, English as a second language, honors programs, independent study, internships, part-time degree program, services for LD students, summer session for credit.

Library Carroll Community College Library with 151,001 titles, 177 serial subscriptions, 3,426 audiovisual materials, an OPAC, a Web page.

Student Life *Housing:* college housing not available. *Activities and Organizations:* drama/theater group, Student Government Organization, S.T.E.M. Club, Campus Activities Board, Service Learning Club, Academic Communities (Creativity, Education, Great Ideas, Health and Wellness). *Campus security:* 24-hour emergency response devices, late-night transport/escort service.

Costs (2013–14) *Tuition:* area resident $4128 full-time, $138 per credit hour part-time; state resident $6000 full-time, $200 per credit hour part-time; nonresident $8376 full-time, $279 per credit hour part-time. *Payment plan:* deferred payment. *Waivers:* senior citizens and employees or children of employees.

Financial Aid Of all full-time matriculated undergraduates who enrolled in 2012, 29 Federal Work-Study jobs (averaging $2187).

Applying *Options:* electronic application. *Required:* high school transcript. *Application deadlines:* rolling (freshmen), rolling (out-of-state freshmen), rolling (transfers). *Notification:* continuous (freshmen), continuous (out-of-state freshmen), continuous (transfers).

Freshman Application Contact Ms. Candace Edwards, Director of Admissions, Carroll Community College, 1601 Washington Road, Westminster, MD 21157. *Phone:* 410-386-8405. *Toll-free phone:* 888-221-9748. *Fax:* 410-386-8446. *E-mail:* cedwards@carrollcc.edu. *Website:* http://www.carrollcc.edu/.

Cecil College

North East, Maryland

- **County-supported** 2-year, founded 1968
- **Small-town** 159-acre campus with easy access to Baltimore
- **Coed,** 2,527 undergraduate students, 33% full-time, 62% women, 38% men

Undergraduates 845 full-time, 1,682 part-time. Students come from 8 states and territories; 15 other countries; 12% are from out of state; 9% Black or African American, non-Hispanic/Latino; 4% Hispanic/Latino; 1% Asian, non-Hispanic/Latino; 0.6% American Indian or Alaska Native, non-Hispanic/Latino; 3% Two or more races, non-Hispanic/Latino; 0.2% Race/ethnicity unknown; 0.2% international; 4% transferred in. *Retention:* 59% of full-time freshmen returned.

Freshmen *Admission:* 657 applied, 657 admitted, 492 enrolled.

Faculty *Total:* 290, 17% full-time, 6% with terminal degrees. *Student/faculty ratio:* 12:1.

Majors Administrative assistant and secretarial science; aeronautics/aviation/aerospace science and technology; air traffic control; animation, interactive technology, video graphics and special effects; applied horticulture/horticulture operations; biology/biological sciences; biotechnology; business administration and management; business/commerce; business/corporate communications; chemistry; child-care and support services management; commercial photography; criminal justice/police science; design and visual communications; drawing; education; electrical, electronic and communications engineering technology; elementary education; emergency medical technology (EMT paramedic); English/language arts teacher education; financial planning and services; fine/studio arts; fire science/firefighting; general studies; health services/allied health/health sciences; horse husbandry/equine science and management; human resources management; liberal arts and sciences/liberal studies; logistics, materials, and supply chain management; management information systems; marketing/marketing management; mathematics; office management; photography; physics; purchasing, procurement/acquisitions and contracts management; registered nursing/registered nurse; secondary education; transportation and materials moving related; transportation/mobility management; web page, digital/multimedia and information resources design.

Academics *Calendar:* semesters. *Degree:* certificates and associate. *Special study options:* academic remediation for entering students, accelerated degree program, adult/continuing education programs, advanced placement credit, cooperative education, distance learning, double majors, English as a second language, independent study, internships, off-campus study, part-time degree program, services for LD students, summer session for credit.

Library Cecil County Veterans Memorial Library with 65,908 titles, 35 serial subscriptions, 808 audiovisual materials, an OPAC, a Web page.

Student Life *Housing:* college housing not available. *Activities and Organizations:* drama/theater group, student government, Non-traditional Student Organization, Student Nurses Association, national fraternities. *Campus security:* 24-hour emergency response devices, late-night transport/escort service. *Student services:* personal/psychological counseling, women's center.

Athletics Member NJCAA. *Intercollegiate sports:* baseball M(s), basketball M(s)/W(s), cheerleading W, soccer M(s)/W(s), softball W(s), tennis W(s), volleyball W(s).

Costs (2013–14) *Tuition:* area resident $2850 full-time, $95 per credit hour part-time; state resident $5550 full-time, $185 per credit hour part-time; nonresident $6900 full-time, $230 per credit hour part-time. *Required fees:* $315 full-time. *Payment plan:* deferred payment. *Waivers:* senior citizens and employees or children of employees.

Applying *Options:* electronic application, early admission, deferred entrance. *Required:* high school transcript. *Application deadlines:* rolling (freshmen), rolling (out-of-state freshmen), rolling (transfers). *Notification:* continuous (freshmen), continuous (out-of-state freshmen), continuous (transfers).

Freshman Application Contact Dr. Diane Lane, Cecil College, One Seahawk Drive, North East, MD 21901-1999. *Phone:* 410-287-1002. *Fax:* 410-287-1001. *E-mail:* dlane@cecil.edu.

Website: http://www.cecil.edu/.

Chesapeake College

Wye Mills, Maryland

Freshman Application Contact Randy Holliday, Director of Student Recruitment and Outreach, Chesapeake College, PO Box 8, Wye Mills, MD 21679-0008. *Phone:* 410-822-5400. *Fax:* 410-827-5875. *E-mail:* rholliday@chesapeake.edu.

Website: http://www.chesapeake.edu/.

College of Southern Maryland
La Plata, Maryland

- **State and locally supported** 2-year, founded 1958
- **Rural** 175-acre campus with easy access to Washington, DC
- **Coed,** 8,781 undergraduate students, 38% full-time, 61% women, 39% men

Undergraduates 3,317 full-time, 5,464 part-time. 25% Black or African American, non-Hispanic/Latino; 6% Hispanic/Latino; 3% Asian, non-Hispanic/Latino; 0.4% Native Hawaiian or other Pacific Islander, non-Hispanic/Latino; 0.6% American Indian or Alaska Native, non-Hispanic/Latino; 5% Two or more races, non-Hispanic/Latino; 2% Race/ethnicity unknown; 0.4% international; 6% transferred in.
Freshmen *Admission:* 2,105 enrolled.
Faculty *Total:* 529, 24% full-time, 12% with terminal degrees. *Student/faculty ratio:* 20:1.
Majors Accounting; accounting technology and bookkeeping; building/construction finishing, management, and inspection related; business administration and management; business/commerce; child-care and support services management; clinical/medical laboratory technology; computer and information sciences; computer programming; criminal justice/law enforcement administration; early childhood education; education; electrician; elementary education; emergency medical technology (EMT paramedic); engineering; engineering technologies and engineering related; environmental engineering technology; fire science/firefighting; health and physical education related; hospitality administration; information technology; legal assistant/paralegal; liberal arts and sciences and humanities related; liberal arts and sciences/liberal studies; licensed practical/vocational nurse training; lineworker; massage therapy; mental and social health services and allied professions related; multi/interdisciplinary studies related; physical therapy technology; registered nursing/registered nurse.
Academics *Calendar:* semesters. *Degree:* certificates and associate. *Special study options:* academic remediation for entering students, accelerated degree program, adult/continuing education programs, advanced placement credit, cooperative education, distance learning, honors programs, independent study, part-time degree program, services for LD students, study abroad, summer session for credit.
Library College of Southern Maryland Library with an OPAC, a Web page.
Student Life *Housing:* college housing not available. *Activities and Organizations:* drama/theater group, student-run newspaper, television station, choral group, Spanish Club, Nursing Student Association, Science Club, Black Student Union, BACCHUS. *Campus security:* 24-hour emergency response devices and patrols. *Student services:* personal/psychological counseling.
Athletics Member NJCAA. *Intercollegiate sports:* baseball M, basketball M/W, golf M/W, soccer M/W, softball W, tennis M/W, volleyball W.
Costs (2014–15) *Tuition:* area resident $3390 full-time, $113 per credit hour part-time; state resident $5850 full-time, $195 per credit hour part-time; nonresident $7560 full-time, $252 per credit hour part-time. Full-time tuition and fees vary according to course load. Part-time tuition and fees vary according to course load. *Required fees:* $780 full-time. *Payment plan:* deferred payment. *Waivers:* senior citizens and employees or children of employees.
Financial Aid Of all full-time matriculated undergraduates who enrolled in 2013, 2,067 applied for aid, 1,496 were judged to have need, 10 had their need fully met. In 2013, 12 non-need-based awards were made. *Average percent of need met:* 35%. *Average financial aid package:* $5727. *Average need-based loan:* $3115. *Average need-based gift aid:* $5347. *Average non-need-based aid:* $1090.
Applying *Options:* electronic application, early admission, deferred entrance. *Recommended:* high school transcript. *Application deadlines:* rolling (freshmen), rolling (transfers). *Notification:* continuous (freshmen), continuous (transfers).
Freshman Application Contact Information Center Coordinator, College of Southern Maryland, PO Box 910, La Plata, MD 20646-0910. *Phone:* 301-934-7520 Ext. 7765. *Toll-free phone:* 800-933-9177. *Fax:* 301-934-7698. *E-mail:* info@csmd.edu.
Website: http://www.csmd.edu/.

The Community College of Baltimore County
Baltimore, Maryland

- **County-supported** 2-year, founded 1957
- **Suburban** 350-acre campus
- **Coed,** 24,275 undergraduate students, 33% full-time, 61% women, 39% men

Undergraduates 7,984 full-time, 16,291 part-time. 39% Black or African American, non-Hispanic/Latino; 4% Hispanic/Latino; 5% Asian, non-Hispanic/Latino; 0.2% Native Hawaiian or other Pacific Islander, non-Hispanic/Latino; 0.3% American Indian or Alaska Native, non-Hispanic/Latino; 3% Two or more races, non-Hispanic/Latino; 0.8% Race/ethnicity unknown; 4% international.
Freshmen *Admission:* 4,941 enrolled.
Faculty *Total:* 1,386, 32% full-time, 8% with terminal degrees.
Majors Accounting technology and bookkeeping; administrative assistant and secretarial science; aeronautics/aviation/aerospace science and technology; applied horticulture/horticulture operations; architectural drafting and CAD/CADD; automobile/automotive mechanics technology; biological and physical sciences; building/construction finishing, management, and inspection related; building/construction site management; business administration and management; business/commerce; chemistry teacher education; child-care and support services management; clinical/medical laboratory technology; commercial and advertising art; computer and information sciences; computer and information systems security; computer systems networking and telecommunications; criminal justice/police science; dental hygiene; early childhood education; education; elementary education; emergency medical technology (EMT paramedic); engineering; engineering technologies and engineering related; funeral service and mortuary science; geography; heating, ventilation, air conditioning and refrigeration engineering technology; hotel/motel administration; hydraulics and fluid power technology; legal assistant/paralegal; liberal arts and sciences and humanities related; liberal arts and sciences/liberal studies; management information systems; massage therapy; mathematics teacher education; medical administrative assistant and medical secretary; medical informatics; medical radiologic technology; occupational safety and health technology; occupational therapy; parks, recreation and leisure; parks, recreation, leisure, and fitness studies related; physics teacher education; psychiatric/mental health services technology; registered nursing/registered nurse; respiratory care therapy; sign language interpretation and translation; Spanish language teacher education; substance abuse/addiction counseling; surveying technology; veterinary/animal health technology; visual and performing arts.
Academics *Calendar:* semesters. *Degree:* certificates and associate. *Special study options:* academic remediation for entering students, advanced placement credit, cooperative education, distance learning, English as a second language, honors programs, independent study, internships, off-campus study, services for LD students, study abroad, summer session for credit.
Student Life *Housing:* college housing not available. *Campus security:* 24-hour emergency response devices and patrols, late-night transport/escort service.
Athletics Member NJCAA. *Intercollegiate sports:* baseball M(s), basketball M(s)/W(s), cross-country running W(s), lacrosse M(s)/W(s), soccer M(s)/W(s), softball W(s), track and field W(s), volleyball W(s).
Standardized Tests *Recommended:* SAT or ACT (for admission).
Costs (2013–14) *Tuition:* area resident $3270 full-time, $109 per credit part-time; state resident $6240 full-time, $208 per credit part-time; nonresident $9360 full-time, $312 per credit part-time. Full-time tuition and fees vary according to course load. Part-time tuition and fees vary according to course load. *Required fees:* $807 full-time. *Payment plan:* installment. *Waivers:* employees or children of employees.
Applying *Options:* electronic application. *Required:* high school transcript. *Application deadlines:* rolling (freshmen), rolling (out-of-state freshmen), rolling (transfers).
Freshman Application Contact Ms. Diane Drake, Director of Admissions, The Community College of Baltimore County, 7201 Rossville Boulevard, Baltimore, MD 21237-3899. *Phone:* 443-840-4392. *E-mail:* ddrake@ccbcmd.edu.
Website: http://www.ccbcmd.edu/.

Frederick Community College
Frederick, Maryland

Freshman Application Contact Ms. Lisa A. Freel, Director of Admissions, Frederick Community College, 7932 Opossumtown Pike, Frederick, MD 21702. *Phone:* 301-846-2468. *Fax:* 301-624-2799. *E-mail:* admissions@frederick.edu.
Website: http://www.frederick.edu/.

Garrett College
McHenry, Maryland

- **State and locally supported** 2-year, founded 1966
- **Rural** 62-acre campus
- **Coed,** 769 undergraduate students, 78% full-time, 48% women, 52% men

Undergraduates 597 full-time, 172 part-time. Students come from 12 other countries; 22% are from out of state; 22% Black or African American, non-Hispanic/Latino; 3% Hispanic/Latino; 0.5% Native Hawaiian or other Pacific Islander, non-Hispanic/Latino; 0.3% American Indian or Alaska Native, non-Hispanic/Latino; 2% Two or more races, non-Hispanic/Latino; 1% Race/ethnicity unknown; 0.8% international; 5% transferred in; 22% live on campus.

Freshmen *Admission:* 1,508 applied, 1,311 admitted, 219 enrolled. *Average high school GPA:* 2.42. *Test scores:* SAT critical reading scores over 500: 33%; SAT math scores over 500: 36%; SAT writing scores over 500: 25%; ACT scores over 18: 50%; SAT critical reading scores over 600: 10%; SAT math scores over 600: 13%; SAT writing scores over 600: 5%; ACT scores over 24: 7%.

Faculty *Total:* 84, 27% full-time. *Student/faculty ratio:* 15:1.

Majors Business administration and management; business automation/technology/data entry; business/commerce; corrections; early childhood education; education; electrical and electronics engineering; elementary education; liberal arts and sciences and humanities related; liberal arts and sciences/liberal studies; management information systems; sport and fitness administration/management; wildlife, fish and wildlands science and management.

Academics *Calendar:* semesters. *Degree:* certificates and associate. *Special study options:* academic remediation for entering students, adult/continuing education programs, advanced placement credit, cooperative education, distance learning, double majors, external degree program, honors programs, independent study, internships, part-time degree program, services for LD students, summer session for credit.

Library Learning Resource Center with 53,293 titles, 63 serial subscriptions, 2,975 audiovisual materials, an OPAC, a Web page.

Student Life *Housing Options:* coed, special housing for students with disabilities. Campus housing is university owned and leased by the school. *Activities and Organizations:* drama/theater group, SGA, Theatre Club. *Campus security:* 24-hour emergency response devices and patrols, controlled dormitory access. *Student services:* health clinic, personal/psychological counseling.

Athletics Member NJCAA. *Intercollegiate sports:* baseball M(s), basketball M(s)/W(s), cross-country running M/W, golf M/W, softball W, volleyball W. *Intramural sports:* basketball M/W, football M/W, rock climbing M/W, ultimate Frisbee M/W.

Standardized Tests *Recommended:* SAT or ACT (for admission).

Costs (2013–14) *Tuition:* area resident $2632 full-time, $94 per credit hour part-time; state resident $6048 full-time, $216 per credit hour part-time; nonresident $7140 full-time, $255 per credit hour part-time. Full-time tuition and fees vary according to reciprocity agreements. Part-time tuition and fees vary according to reciprocity agreements. *Required fees:* $758 full-time, $26 per credit hour part-time, $15 per semester part-time. *Room and board:* $7400; room only: $5400. Room and board charges vary according to board plan and housing facility. *Payment plans:* installment, deferred payment. *Waivers:* senior citizens.

Financial Aid Of all full-time matriculated undergraduates who enrolled in 2013, 461 applied for aid, 403 were judged to have need, 43 had their need fully met. In 2013, 53 non-need-based awards were made. *Average percent of need met:* 57%. *Average financial aid package:* $7788. *Average need-based loan:* $3096. *Average need-based gift aid:* $5122. *Average non-need-based aid:* $3220.

Applying *Options:* early admission, deferred entrance. *Required:* high school transcript. *Application deadlines:* rolling (freshmen), rolling (out-of-state freshmen), rolling (transfers). *Notification:* continuous (freshmen), continuous (out-of-state freshmen), continuous (transfers).

Freshman Application Contact Mrs. Rachelle Davis, Director of Admissions, Garrett College, 687 Mosser Road, McHenry, MD 21541. *Phone:* 301-387-3044. *Toll-free phone:* 866-55-GARRETT. *E-mail:* admissions@garrettcollege.edu.
Website: http://www.garrettcollege.edu/.

Hagerstown Community College
Hagerstown, Maryland

- **State and locally supported** 2-year, founded 1946
- **Suburban** 319-acre campus with easy access to Baltimore and Washington, DC
- **Coed,** 4,903 undergraduate students, 25% full-time, 62% women, 38% men

Undergraduates 1,231 full-time, 3,672 part-time. Students come from 14 states and territories; 20% are from out of state; 10% Black or African American, non-Hispanic/Latino; 4% Hispanic/Latino; 2% Asian, non-Hispanic/Latino; 0.2% Native Hawaiian or other Pacific Islander, non-Hispanic/Latino; 0.3% American Indian or Alaska Native, non-Hispanic/Latino; 3% Two or more races, non-Hispanic/Latino; 2% Race/ethnicity unknown; 0.5% international; 8% transferred in.

Freshmen *Admission:* 950 enrolled.

Faculty *Total:* 265, 31% full-time, 6% with terminal degrees. *Student/faculty ratio:* 17:1.

Majors Accounting technology and bookkeeping; animation, interactive technology, video graphics and special effects; biology/biotechnology laboratory technician; business administration and management; business/commerce; child-care and support services management; commercial

and advertising art; computer and information sciences; computer and information systems security; criminal justice/police science; dental hygiene; early childhood education; education; elementary education; emergency medical technology (EMT paramedic); engineering; engineering technologies and engineering related; English/language arts teacher education; industrial technology; instrumentation technology; liberal arts and sciences and humanities related; liberal arts and sciences/liberal studies; management information systems; mechanical engineering/mechanical technology; medical radiologic technology; psychiatric/mental health services technology; registered nursing/registered nurse; transportation/mobility management; web page, digital/multimedia and information resources design.

Academics *Calendar:* semesters. *Degree:* certificates and associate. *Special study options:* academic remediation for entering students, accelerated degree program, adult/continuing education programs, advanced placement credit, cooperative education, distance learning, English as a second language, honors programs, independent study, internships, off-campus study, part-time degree program, services for LD students, summer session for credit.

Library William Brish Library with an OPAC, a Web page.

Student Life *Activities and Organizations:* drama/theater group, student-run newspaper, choral group, Phi Theta Kappa, Robinwood Players Theater Club, Association of Nursing Students, Radiography Club, Art and Design Club. *Campus security:* 24-hour patrols, student patrols. *Student services:* personal/psychological counseling.

Athletics Member NJCAA. *Intercollegiate sports:* baseball M(s), basketball M(s)/W(s), cross-country running M(s)/W(s), golf M/W, soccer M(s)/W, softball W(s), track and field M(s)/W(s), volleyball W(s). *Intramural sports:* cheerleading M/W, golf M/W, lacrosse M/W, table tennis M/W, tennis M/W.

Costs (2013–14) *Tuition:* area resident $2568 full-time, $107 per credit hour part-time; state resident $4032 full-time, $168 per credit hour part-time; nonresident $5280 full-time, $220 per credit hour part-time. Full-time tuition and fees vary according to course load. Part-time tuition and fees vary according to course load and reciprocity agreements. *Required fees:* $418 full-time, $13 per credit hour part-time. *Payment plan:* installment. *Waivers:* senior citizens and employees or children of employees.

Applying *Options:* electronic application, early admission, deferred entrance. *Required for some:* high school transcript, selective admissions for RN, LPN, EMT, and radiography programs. *Application deadlines:* rolling (freshmen), rolling (out-of-state freshmen), rolling (transfers). *Notification:* continuous (freshmen), continuous (out-of-state freshmen), continuous (transfers).

Freshman Application Contact Assistant Director, Admissions, Records and Registration, Hagerstown Community College, 11400 Robinwood Drive, Hagerstown, MD 21742-6514. *Phone:* 240-500-2338. *Fax:* 301-791-9165. *E-mail:* admissions@hagerstowncc.edu.
Website: http://www.hagerstowncc.edu/.

Harford Community College
Bel Air, Maryland

- **State and locally supported** 2-year, founded 1957
- **Small-town** 331-acre campus with easy access to Baltimore
- **Coed,** 7,039 undergraduate students, 37% full-time, 58% women, 42% men

Undergraduates 2,601 full-time, 4,438 part-time. 14% Black or African American, non-Hispanic/Latino; 4% Hispanic/Latino; 2% Asian, non-Hispanic/Latino; 0.2% Native Hawaiian or other Pacific Islander, non-Hispanic/Latino; 0.3% American Indian or Alaska Native, non-Hispanic/Latino; 3% Two or more races, non-Hispanic/Latino; 0.8% Race/ethnicity unknown; 0.5% international.

Freshmen *Admission:* 1,567 enrolled. *Test scores:* SAT critical reading scores over 500: 74%; SAT math scores over 500: 66%; SAT critical reading scores over 600: 18%; SAT math scores over 600: 17%; SAT critical reading scores over 700: 2%; SAT math scores over 700: 3%.

Faculty *Total:* 364, 29% full-time, 13% with terminal degrees. *Student/faculty ratio:* 21:1.

Majors Accounting; accounting technology and bookkeeping; advertising; agricultural business and management; anthropology; biology/biological sciences; business administration and management; business/commerce; CAD/CADD drafting/design technology; chemistry; chemistry teacher education; computer and information sciences; computer and information systems security; computer science; criminal justice/police science; design and visual communications; digital arts; early childhood education; economics; education; electroneurodiagnostic/electroencephalographic technology; elementary education; engineering; engineering technology; English; English/language arts teacher education; entrepreneurship; environmental science; environmental studies; equestrian studies; fine/studio arts; general studies; golf course operation and grounds management; graphic design; history; human resources management; interior design; landscaping and groundskeeping; legal assistant/paralegal; legal studies; liberal arts and sciences/liberal studies; licensed practical/vocational nurse training; marketing/marketing management; mass communication/media; mathematics;

mathematics teacher education; medical/clinical assistant; medical office assistant; multi/interdisciplinary studies related; music; philosophy; photography; physics; physics teacher education; political science and government; psychology; registered nursing/registered nurse; science technologies; secondary education; social work; sociology; Spanish language teacher education; theater design and technology; turf and turfgrass management; visual and performing arts.

Academics *Calendar:* semesters. *Degree:* certificates, diplomas, and associate. *Special study options:* academic remediation for entering students, adult/continuing education programs, advanced placement credit, cooperative education, distance learning, double majors, English as a second language, honors programs, independent study, internships, part-time degree program, services for LD students, student-designed majors, study abroad, summer session for credit.

Library Harford Community College Library with 52,069 titles, 129 serial subscriptions, 4,224 audiovisual materials, an OPAC, a Web page.

Student Life *Activities and Organizations:* drama/theater group, student-run newspaper, radio station, choral group, Student Government Association, Phi Theta Kappa, Student Nurses Association, Actor's Guild, Paralegal Club. *Campus security:* 24-hour patrols, late-night transport/escort service. *Student services:* personal/psychological counseling.

Athletics Member NJCAA. *Intercollegiate sports:* baseball M(s), basketball M(s)/W(s), cross-country running M(s)/W(s), golf M(s), lacrosse M(s)/W(s), soccer M(s)/W(s), softball W(s), tennis M(s)/W(s), volleyball W(s). *Intramural sports:* badminton M/W, basketball M/W, cheerleading M(c)/W(c), football M/W, soccer M/W, softball M/W, swimming and diving M/W, tennis M/W, volleyball M/W.

Costs (2013–14) *Tuition:* area resident $2760 full-time, $92 per credit hour part-time; state resident $5370 full-time, $179 per credit hour part-time; nonresident $7980 full-time, $266 per credit hour part-time. *Required fees:* $481 full-time, $16 per credit hour part-time. *Payment plan:* installment. *Waivers:* senior citizens and employees or children of employees.

Financial Aid Of all full-time matriculated undergraduates who enrolled in 2012, 1,532 applied for aid, 1,220 were judged to have need. 49 Federal Work-Study jobs (averaging $2716).

Applying *Options:* electronic application. *Application deadlines:* rolling (freshmen), rolling (transfers). *Notification:* continuous (transfers).

Freshman Application Contact Jennifer Starkey, Enrollment Services Associate - Admissions, Harford Community College, 401 Thomas Run Road, Bel Air, MD 21015-1698. *Phone:* 443-412-2311. *Fax:* 443-412-2169. *E-mail:* jestarkey@harford.edu.
Website: http://www.harford.edu/.

Howard Community College
Columbia, Maryland

- **State and locally supported** 2-year, founded 1966
- **Suburban** 122-acre campus with easy access to Baltimore and Washington, DC
- **Coed,** 10,223 undergraduate students, 36% full-time, 56% women, 44% men

Undergraduates 3,693 full-time, 6,532 part-time. Students come from 5 states and territories; 111 other countries; 0.4% are from out of state; 27% Black or African American, non-Hispanic/Latino; 8% Hispanic/Latino; 11% Asian, non-Hispanic/Latino; 0.3% Native Hawaiian or other Pacific Islander, non-Hispanic/Latino; 0.3% American Indian or Alaska Native, non-Hispanic/Latino; 4% Two or more races, non-Hispanic/Latino; 2% Race/ethnicity unknown; 5% international.

Freshmen *Admission:* 1,819 enrolled.

Faculty *Total:* 925, 20% full-time, 17% with terminal degrees. *Student/faculty ratio:* 15:1.

Majors Accounting; architecture; art; biological and physical sciences; biomedical technology; biotechnology; business administration and management; cardiovascular technology; child development; clinical laboratory science/medical technology; computer and information sciences related; computer graphics; computer/information technology services administration related; computer science; computer systems networking and telecommunications; criminal justice/law enforcement administration; design and applied arts related; diagnostic medical sonography and ultrasound technology; dramatic/theater arts; electrical, electronic and communications engineering technology; elementary education; emergency medical technology (EMT paramedic); engineering; environmental studies; financial planning and services; general studies; health teacher education; information science/studies; information technology; kindergarten/preschool education; legal administrative assistant/secretary; liberal arts and sciences/liberal studies; licensed practical/vocational nurse training; medical administrative assistant and medical secretary; music; nuclear medical technology; office management; photography; physical sciences; physical therapy technology; pre-dentistry studies; premedical studies; pre-pharmacy studies; pre-veterinary studies; psychology; registered nursing/registered nurse; secondary education; social

sciences; sport and fitness administration/management; substance abuse/addiction counseling; telecommunications technology; theater design and technology.

Academics *Calendar:* semesters. *Degree:* certificates and associate. *Special study options:* academic remediation for entering students, adult/continuing education programs, advanced placement credit, cooperative education, distance learning, double majors, English as a second language, external degree program, freshman honors college, honors programs, off-campus study, part-time degree program, services for LD students, study abroad, summer session for credit.

Library Howard Community College Library with 45,707 titles, 39,910 serial subscriptions, 2,636 audiovisual materials, an OPAC, a Web page.

Student Life *Housing:* college housing not available. *Activities and Organizations:* drama/theater group, student-run newspaper, radio station, choral group, Phi Theta Kappa, Nursing Club, Black Leadership Organization, student newspaper, Student Government Association. *Campus security:* 24-hour emergency response devices and patrols, late-night transport/escort service. *Student services:* personal/psychological counseling.

Athletics Member NJCAA. *Intercollegiate sports:* basketball M/W, cross-country running M/W, lacrosse M/W, soccer M/W, track and field M/W, volleyball W. *Intramural sports:* basketball M/W.

Standardized Tests *Required for some:* SAT or ACT (for admission).

Costs (2013–14) *Tuition:* area resident $3750 full-time, $125 per credit hour part-time; state resident $6240 full-time, $208 per credit hour part-time; nonresident $7590 full-time, $253 per credit hour part-time. *Required fees:* $628 full-time, $21 per credit hour part-time. *Payment plan:* installment. *Waivers:* senior citizens and employees or children of employees.

Financial Aid Of all full-time matriculated undergraduates who enrolled in 2013, 571 applied for aid, 477 were judged to have need. In 2013, 31 non-need-based awards were made. *Average percent of need met:* 22%. *Average financial aid package:* $3871. *Average need-based loan:* $2525. *Average need-based gift aid:* $4032. *Average non-need-based aid:* $1288.

Applying *Options:* electronic application, early admission, deferred entrance. *Application fee:* $25. *Required for some:* essay or personal statement, high school transcript, 2 letters of recommendation. *Application deadlines:* rolling (freshmen), rolling (out-of-state freshmen), rolling (transfers). *Notification:* continuous (freshmen), continuous (out-of-state freshmen), continuous (transfers).

Freshman Application Contact Ms. Christine Palmer, Assistant Director of Admissions, Howard Community College, 10901 Little Patuxent Parkway, Columbia, MD 21044-3197. *Phone:* 443-518-4599. *Fax:* 443-518-4711. *E-mail:* admissions@howardcc.edu.
Website: http://www.howardcc.edu/.

ITT Technical Institute
Owings Mills, Maryland

- **Proprietary** primarily 2-year, founded 2005
- **Coed**

Majors Construction management; cyber/computer forensics and counterterrorism; drafting and design technology; electrical, electronic and communications engineering technology; game and interactive media design; graphic communications; information technology project management; network and system administration; project management.

Academics *Calendar:* quarters. *Degrees:* associate and bachelor's.

Student Life *Housing:* college housing not available.

Freshman Application Contact Director of Recruitment, ITT Technical Institute, 11301 Red Run Boulevard, Owings Mills, MD 21117. *Phone:* 443-394-7115. *Toll-free phone:* 877-411-6782.
Website: http://www.itt-tech.edu/.

Kaplan University, Hagerstown Campus
Hagerstown, Maryland

Freshman Application Contact Kaplan University, Hagerstown Campus, 18618 Crestwood Drive, Hagerstown, MD 21742-2797. *Phone:* 301-739-2680 Ext. 217. *Toll-free phone:* 866-527-5268 (in-state); 800-527-5268 (out-of-state).
Website: http://www.ku-hagerstown.com/.

Montgomery College
Rockville, Maryland

- **State and locally supported** 2-year, founded 1946
- **Suburban** 333-acre campus with easy access to Washington, DC
- **Endowment** $19.5 million
- **Coed,** 26,155 undergraduate students, 35% full-time, 53% women, 47% men

Undergraduates 9,240 full-time, 16,915 part-time. Students come from 27 states and territories; 164 other countries; 3% are from out of state; 26% Black or African American, non-Hispanic/Latino; 21% Hispanic/Latino; 12% Asian, non-Hispanic/Latino; 0.3% Native Hawaiian or other Pacific Islander, non-Hispanic/Latino; 0.3% American Indian or Alaska Native, non-Hispanic/Latino; 2% Two or more races, non-Hispanic/Latino; 0.2% Race/ethnicity unknown; 9% international; 6% transferred in.

Freshmen *Admission:* 10,706 applied, 10,706 admitted, 4,210 enrolled.

Faculty *Total:* 1,348, 40% full-time, 30% with terminal degrees. *Student/faculty ratio:* 18:1.

Majors Accounting technology and bookkeeping; American Sign Language (ASL); animation, interactive technology, video graphics and special effects; applied horticulture/horticulture operations; architectural drafting and CAD/CADD; art; automobile/automotive mechanics technology; biology/biotechnology laboratory technician; building/construction finishing, management, and inspection related; business/commerce; chemistry teacher education; child-care provision; commercial and advertising art; commercial photography; communications technologies and support services related; computer and information sciences; computer and information systems security; computer technology/computer systems technology; criminal justice/police science; crisis/emergency/disaster management; data entry/microcomputer applications; diagnostic medical sonography and ultrasound technology; early childhood education; elementary education; engineering; English/language arts teacher education; fire prevention and safety technology; geography; health information/medical records technology; hotel/motel administration; interior design; legal assistant/paralegal; liberal arts and sciences and humanities related; liberal arts and sciences/liberal studies; mathematics teacher education; medical radiologic technology; physical therapy technology; physics teacher education; psychiatric/mental health services technology; registered nursing/registered nurse; Spanish language teacher education; speech communication and rhetoric; surgical technology; web page, digital/multimedia and information resources design.

Academics *Calendar:* semesters. *Degree:* certificates and associate. *Special study options:* academic remediation for entering students, adult/continuing education programs, advanced placement credit, cooperative education, distance learning, double majors, English as a second language, external degree program, honors programs, independent study, internships, off-campus study, part-time degree program, services for LD students, study abroad, summer session for credit. *ROTC:* Air Force (c).

Library Montgomery College Library plus 4 others with 504,068 titles, 54,103 serial subscriptions, 32,832 audiovisual materials, an OPAC, a Web page.

Student Life *Activities and Organizations:* drama/theater group, student-run newspaper, choral group, Math Club, International Club, Anime Society Club, Animation & Video Game Club, Soccer, basketball, Rugby, Cricket, Tennis, Lacrosse and Swim Clubs. *Campus security:* 24-hour emergency response devices and patrols, late-night transport/escort service. *Student services:* personal/psychological counseling, women's center.

Athletics Member NJCAA. *Intercollegiate sports:* baseball M, basketball M/W, soccer M/W, softball W, tennis M/W, track and field M/W, volleyball W. *Intramural sports:* baseball M, basketball M/W, cheerleading W, cross-country running M, soccer M/W, softball W, tennis M/W, track and field M/W, volleyball W.

Costs (2013–14) *Tuition:* area resident $2688 full-time, $112 per credit hour part-time; state resident $5496 full-time, $229 per credit hour part-time; nonresident $7536 full-time, $314 per credit hour part-time. Full-time tuition and fees vary according to course load. Part-time tuition and fees vary according to course load. *Required fees:* $874 full-time, $36 per credit hour part-time. *Payment plans:* installment, deferred payment. *Waivers:* senior citizens and employees or children of employees.

Financial Aid Of all full-time matriculated undergraduates who enrolled in 2012, 27,000 applied for aid, 20,000 were judged to have need. In 2012, 1382 non-need-based awards were made. *Average percent of need met:* 75%. *Average financial aid package:* $8500. *Average need-based loan:* $4000. *Average need-based gift aid:* $5500. *Average non-need-based aid:* $1400.

Applying *Options:* electronic application, early admission, deferred entrance. *Application fee:* $25. *Recommended:* high school transcript. *Application deadlines:* rolling (freshmen), rolling (out-of-state freshmen), rolling (transfers). *Notification:* continuous (freshmen), continuous (out-of-state freshmen), continuous (transfers).

Freshman Application Contact Montgomery College, 51 Mannakee Street, Rockville, MD 20850. *Phone:* 240-567-5036. *Website:* http://www.montgomerycollege.edu/.

Prince George's Community College
Largo, Maryland

Freshman Application Contact Ms. Vera Bagley, Director of Admissions and Records, Prince George's Community College, 301 Largo Road, Largo, MD 20774-2199. *Phone:* 301-322-0801. *Fax:* 301-322-0119. *E-mail:* enrollmentservices@pgcc.edu. *Website:* http://www.pgcc.edu/.

TESST College of Technology
Baltimore, Maryland

Freshman Application Contact TESST College of Technology, 1520 South Caton Avenue, Baltimore, MD 21227. *Phone:* 410-644-6400. *Toll-free phone:* 800-935-1857. *Website:* http://www.baltimore.tesst.com/.

TESST College of Technology
Beltsville, Maryland

Freshman Application Contact TESST College of Technology, 4600 Powder Mill Road, Beltsville, MD 20705. *Phone:* 301-937-8448. *Toll-free phone:* 800-935-1857. *Website:* http://www.beltsville.tesst.com/.

TESST College of Technology
Towson, Maryland

Freshman Application Contact TESST College of Technology, 803 Glen Eagles Court, Towson, MD 21286. *Phone:* 410-296-5350. *Toll-free phone:* 800-935-1857. *Website:* http://www.towson.tesst.com/.

Wor-Wic Community College
Salisbury, Maryland

- **State and locally supported** 2-year, founded 1976
- **Small-town** 202-acre campus
- **Endowment** $10.6 million
- **Coed,** 3,419 undergraduate students, 32% full-time, 63% women, 37% men

Undergraduates 1,091 full-time, 2,328 part-time. Students come from 14 states and territories; 3% are from out of state; 23% Black or African American, non-Hispanic/Latino; 3% Hispanic/Latino; 1% Asian, non-Hispanic/Latino; 0.1% Native Hawaiian or other Pacific Islander, non-Hispanic/Latino; 0.4% American Indian or Alaska Native, non-Hispanic/Latino; 3% Two or more races, non-Hispanic/Latino; 1% Race/ethnicity unknown; 0.3% international; 7% transferred in.

Freshmen *Admission:* 1,197 applied, 1,197 admitted, 678 enrolled.

Faculty *Total:* 185, 38% full-time, 13% with terminal degrees. *Student/faculty ratio:* 17:1.

Majors Accounting technology and bookkeeping; administrative assistant and secretarial science; biological and physical sciences; business administration and management; business/commerce; child-care and support services management; computer and information sciences; computer systems analysis; criminal justice/police science; early childhood education; education; electrical, electronic and communications engineering technology; elementary education; emergency medical technology (EMT paramedic); engineering technologies and engineering related; environmental engineering technology; hospitality administration; liberal arts and sciences and humanities related; liberal arts and sciences/liberal studies; medical radiologic technology; occupational therapist assistant; registered nursing/registered nurse; substance abuse/addiction counseling.

Academics *Calendar:* semesters. *Degree:* certificates and associate. *Special study options:* academic remediation for entering students, accelerated degree program, adult/continuing education programs, advanced placement credit, distance learning, double majors, English as a second language, honors programs, independent study, internships, part-time degree program, services for LD students, summer session for credit.

Library Patricia M. Hazel Media Center plus 2 others with 74 serial subscriptions, a Web page.

Student Life *Housing:* college housing not available. *Activities and Organizations:* drama/theater group, choral group, PTK, Anime, Role-Playing and Gaming Association, Criminal Justice Club, Nursing Student Organization. *Campus security:* 24-hour emergency response devices, late-night transport/escort service, patrols by trained security personnel 9 am to midnight. *Student services:* personal/psychological counseling.

Standardized Tests *Required for some:* ACT (for admission).

Costs (2014–15) *Tuition:* area resident $3000 full-time, $100 per credit part-time; state resident $6720 full-time, $224 per credit part-time; nonresident $8280 full-time, $276 per credit part-time. *Required fees:* $360 full-time, $12 per credit part-time. *Payment plan:* installment. *Waivers:* senior citizens and employees or children of employees.

Applying *Options:* early admission. *Recommended:* high school transcript. *Application deadlines:* rolling (freshmen), rolling (transfers).

Freshman Application Contact Mr. Richard Webster, Director of Admissions, Wor-Wic Community College, 32000 Campus Drive, Salisbury, MD 21804. *Phone:* 410-334-2895. *Fax:* 410-334-2954. *E-mail:* admissions@worwic.edu. *Website:* http://www.worwic.edu/.

MASSACHUSETTS

Bay State College
Boston, Massachusetts

- **Independent** primarily 2-year, founded 1946
- **Urban** campus
- **Coed,** 1,098 undergraduate students

Undergraduates 13% are from out of state; 26% live on campus. *Retention:* 76% of full-time freshmen returned.

Freshmen *Admission:* 1,988 applied, 1,045 admitted.

Faculty *Student/faculty ratio:* 20:1.

Majors Accounting; adult health nursing; animation, interactive technology, video graphics and special effects; business administration and management; business automation/technology/data entry; criminal justice/safety; education; fashion merchandising; medical/clinical assistant; medical office management; merchandising, sales, and marketing operations related (specialized); physical therapy technology; tourism and travel services marketing.

Academics *Calendar:* semesters. *Degrees:* certificates, diplomas, associate, and bachelor's. *Special study options:* academic remediation for entering students, accelerated degree program, adult/continuing education programs, advanced placement credit, cooperative education, distance learning, English as a second language, independent study, internships, part-time degree program, study abroad, summer session for credit.

Library Bay State College Library with 6,000 titles, 80 serial subscriptions, an OPAC.

Student Life *Housing Options:* coed, women-only. Campus housing is provided by a third party. *Activities and Organizations:* student-run radio station. *Campus security:* late-night transport/escort service, controlled dormitory access, 14-hour patrols by trained security personnel. *Student services:* personal/psychological counseling.

Standardized Tests *Recommended:* SAT or ACT (for admission).

Costs (2014–15) *Comprehensive fee:* $36,580 includes full-time tuition ($24,780) and room and board ($11,800). Full-time tuition and fees vary according to class time, location, and program. Part-time tuition: $826 per credit. Part-time tuition and fees vary according to class time, location, and program. *Payment plan:* installment.

Financial Aid Of all full-time matriculated undergraduates who enrolled in 2012, 20 Federal Work-Study jobs (averaging $2600).

Applying *Options:* electronic application, early admission. *Required:* high school transcript, minimum 2.3 GPA. *Recommended:* interview. *Application deadlines:* rolling (freshmen), rolling (transfers).

Freshman Application Contact Kimberly Odusami, Director of Admissions, Bay State College, 122 Commonwealth Avenue, Boston, MA 02116. *Phone:* 617-217-9186. *Toll-free phone:* 800-81-LEARN. *E-mail:* admissions@baystate.edu.

Website: http://www.baystate.edu/.

See display below and page 374 for the College Close-Up.

Benjamin Franklin Institute of Technology
Boston, Massachusetts

- **Independent** primarily 2-year, founded 1908
- **Urban** 3-acre campus
- **Coed,** 470 undergraduate students, 88% full-time, 10% women, 90% men

Undergraduates 412 full-time, 58 part-time. 6% are from out of state; 32% Black or African American, non-Hispanic/Latino; 23% Hispanic/Latino; 8% Asian, non-Hispanic/Latino; 0.4% American Indian or Alaska Native, non-Hispanic/Latino; 4% Two or more races, non-Hispanic/Latino; 6% Race/ethnicity unknown; 1% international; 12% transferred in; 8% live on campus.

Freshmen *Admission:* 662 applied, 409 admitted, 185 enrolled. *Average high school GPA:* 2.18. *Test scores:* SAT critical reading scores over 500: 16%; SAT math scores over 500: 20%; SAT writing scores over 500: 4%.

Faculty *Total:* 62, 56% full-time, 10% with terminal degrees. *Student/faculty ratio:* 10:1.

Majors Architectural drafting and CAD/CADD; architectural engineering technology; automobile/automotive mechanics technology; automotive engineering technology; bioengineering and biomedical engineering; biomedical technology; computer engineering technology; computer science; computer technology/computer systems technology; drafting and design technology; electrical and electronic engineering technologies related; electrical and power transmission installation; electrical, electronic and communications engineering technology; engineering technology; mechanical engineering/mechanical technology; opticianry.

Academics *Calendar:* semesters. *Degrees:* certificates, associate, and bachelor's. *Special study options:* academic remediation for entering students, adult/continuing education programs, advanced placement credit, cooperative

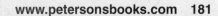

education, English as a second language, internships, off-campus study, part-time degree program, services for LD students, summer session for credit.

Library Lufkin Memorial Library with an OPAC.

Student Life *Housing Options:* coed. Campus housing is provided by a third party. Freshman campus housing is guaranteed. *Activities and Organizations:* Phi Theta Kappa, Student Government and Leadership, yearbook and video club, Green Technology Club, Women's Forum. *Campus security:* 24-hour emergency response devices. *Student services:* personal/psychological counseling.

Athletics Member NJCAA. *Intercollegiate sports:* soccer M. *Intramural sports:* basketball M/W, table tennis M/W.

Standardized Tests *Recommended:* SAT or ACT (for admission).

Costs (2013–14) *Tuition:* $16,950 full-time, $707 per credit hour part-time. Full-time tuition and fees vary according to course load, degree level, and program. Part-time tuition and fees vary according to course load, degree level, and program. *Room only:* $10,900. Room and board charges vary according to housing facility. *Payment plan:* installment. *Waivers:* employees or children of employees.

Financial Aid Of all full-time matriculated undergraduates who enrolled in 2009, 470 applied for aid, 430 were judged to have need, 12 had their need fully met. 22 Federal Work-Study jobs (averaging $1635). In 2009, 3 non-need-based awards were made. *Average percent of need met:* 41%. *Average financial aid package:* $5094. *Average need-based loan:* $1979. *Average need-based gift aid:* $3239. *Average non-need-based aid:* $917.

Applying *Options:* electronic application, deferred entrance. *Application fee:* $25. *Required:* high school transcript. *Recommended:* essay or personal statement, minimum 2.0 GPA, interview.

Freshman Application Contact Ms. Brittainy Johnson, Associate Director of Admissions, Benjamin Franklin Institute of Technology, Boston, MA 02116. *Phone:* 617-423-4630 Ext. 122. *Toll-free phone:* 877-400-BFIT. *Fax:* 617-482-3706. *E-mail:* bjohnson@bfit.edu.

Website: http://www.bfit.edu/.

Berkshire Community College

Pittsfield, Massachusetts

- **State-supported** 2-year, founded 1960, part of Massachusetts Public Higher Education System
- **Rural** 180-acre campus with easy access to Hartford, CT and Albany, NY
- **Endowment** $8.7 million
- **Coed,** 2,400 undergraduate students, 34% full-time, 62% women, 38% men

Undergraduates 821 full-time, 1,579 part-time. Students come from 5 states and territories; 4 other countries; 2% are from out of state; 7% Black or African American, non-Hispanic/Latino; 6% Hispanic/Latino; 2% Asian, non-Hispanic/Latino; 0.1% Native Hawaiian or other Pacific Islander, non-Hispanic/Latino; 0.3% American Indian or Alaska Native, non-Hispanic/Latino; 2% Two or more races, non-Hispanic/Latino; 3% Race/ethnicity unknown; 0.3% international; 42% transferred in. *Retention:* 48% of full-time freshmen returned.

Freshmen *Admission:* 573 applied, 469 admitted, 469 enrolled. *Average high school GPA:* 2.69.

Faculty *Total:* 231, 23% full-time. *Student/faculty ratio:* 15:1.

Majors Business administration and management; business automation/technology/data entry; business/commerce; community organization and advocacy; computer and information sciences; criminal justice/safety; electrical, electronic and communications engineering technology; engineering; environmental studies; fire science/firefighting; health professions related; hospitality administration; human services; international/global studies; liberal arts and sciences/liberal studies; medical insurance coding; physical therapy technology; registered nursing/registered nurse; respiratory care therapy; visual and performing arts.

Academics *Calendar:* semesters. *Degree:* certificates and associate. *Special study options:* academic remediation for entering students, accelerated degree program, adult/continuing education programs, advanced placement credit, cooperative education, distance learning, double majors, English as a second language, honors programs, independent study, internships, off-campus study, part-time degree program, services for LD students, summer session for credit.

Library Jonathan Edwards Library plus 1 other with 76,988 titles, 211 serial subscriptions, an OPAC, a Web page.

Student Life *Housing:* college housing not available. *Activities and Organizations:* drama/theater group, student-run newspaper, choral group, Mass PIRG, Student Nurse Organization, Student Senate, Diversity Club, LPN Organization. *Campus security:* 24-hour emergency response devices and patrols, late-night transport/escort service. *Student services:* personal/psychological counseling.

Costs (2013–14) *One-time required fee:* $35. *Tuition:* state resident $624 full-time, $26 per credit hour part-time; nonresident $6240 full-time, $260 per credit hour part-time. Full-time tuition and fees vary according to class time, course load, program, and reciprocity agreements. Part-time tuition and fees

vary according to class time, course load, program, and reciprocity agreements. *Required fees:* $4980 full-time, $166 per credit hour part-time. *Payment plan:* installment. *Waivers:* senior citizens and employees or children of employees.

Financial Aid Of all full-time matriculated undergraduates who enrolled in 2012, 1,751 applied for aid, 1,590 were judged to have need. 191 Federal Work-Study jobs (averaging $867). 21 state and other part-time jobs (averaging $502). In 2012, 142 non-need-based awards were made. *Average financial aid package:* $5655. *Average need-based loan:* $1857. *Average need-based gift aid:* $4431. *Average non-need-based aid:* $1149.

Applying *Options:* deferred entrance. *Application fee:* $10. *Required:* high school transcript. *Recommended:* interview. *Application deadlines:* rolling (freshmen), rolling (out-of-state freshmen), rolling (transfers). *Notification:* continuous (freshmen), continuous (out-of-state freshmen), continuous (transfers).

Freshman Application Contact Ms. Tina Schettini, Enrollment Services, Berkshire Community College, 1350 West Street, Pittsfield, MA 01201-5786. *Phone:* 413-236-1635. *Toll-free phone:* 800-816-1233. *Fax:* 413-496-9511. *E-mail:* tschetti@berkshirecc.edu.

Website: http://www.berkshirecc.edu/.

Bristol Community College

Fall River, Massachusetts

- **State-supported** 2-year, founded 1965, part of Massachusetts Community College System
- **Urban** 105-acre campus with easy access to Boston
- **Endowment** $4.4 million
- **Coed,** 9,335 undergraduate students, 47% full-time, 61% women, 39% men

Undergraduates 4,429 full-time, 4,906 part-time. Students come from 13 other countries; 6% are from out of state; 7% Black or African American, non-Hispanic/Latino; 8% Hispanic/Latino; 2% Asian, non-Hispanic/Latino; 0.1% Native Hawaiian or other Pacific Islander, non-Hispanic/Latino; 0.4% American Indian or Alaska Native, non-Hispanic/Latino; 4% Two or more races, non-Hispanic/Latino; 3% Race/ethnicity unknown; 0.1% international.

Freshmen *Admission:* 5,133 applied, 1,995 admitted, 2,158 enrolled.

Faculty *Total:* 686, 19% full-time, 79% with terminal degrees. *Student/faculty ratio:* 19:1.

Majors Accounting; American Sign Language (ASL); banking and financial support services; business administration and management; business/commerce; business, management, and marketing related; business operations support and secretarial services related; child-care and support services management; civil engineering related; clinical/medical laboratory technology; computer and information sciences; computer and information sciences related; computer programming; computer science; computer systems analysis; cosmetology and personal grooming arts related; criminal justice/safety; culinary arts related; data processing and data processing technology; dental hygiene; design and visual communications; dramatic/theater arts and stagecraft related; electromechanical technology; engineering; engineering related; engineering science; engineering technologies and engineering related; entrepreneurship; environmental engineering technology; environmental/environmental health engineering; environmental studies; finance and financial management services related; fine/studio arts; fire prevention and safety technology; fire science/firefighting; general studies; graphic design; humanities; information science/studies; intermedia/multimedia; kindergarten/preschool education; legal assistant/paralegal; legal professions and studies related; liberal arts and sciences/liberal studies; manufacturing engineering; marketing/marketing management; mathematics and statistics related; mechanical engineering; medical administrative assistant and medical secretary; occupational therapist assistant; real estate; receptionist; registered nursing/registered nurse; social sciences; social work; speech communication and rhetoric; structural engineering; water quality and wastewater treatment management and recycling technology; water resources engineering.

Academics *Calendar:* semesters. *Degree:* certificates and associate. *Special study options:* academic remediation for entering students, accelerated degree program, adult/continuing education programs, advanced placement credit, cooperative education, distance learning, English as a second language, honors programs, independent study, internships, off-campus study, part-time degree program, services for LD students, student-designed majors, summer session for credit.

Library Learning Resources Center with 79,532 titles, 256 serial subscriptions, 18,757 audiovisual materials, an OPAC, a Web page.

Student Life *Housing:* college housing not available. *Activities and Organizations:* drama/theater group, student-run newspaper, International Club, Dental Hygiene, Criminal Justice Society, Occupational Therapy Assistant, Portuguese Club. *Campus security:* 24-hour emergency response devices and patrols, late-night transport/escort service. *Student services:* health clinic, personal/psychological counseling, women's center.

Athletics Member NJCAA. *Intramural sports:* basketball M/W, soccer M/W, tennis M/W.

Costs (2014–15) *Tuition:* state resident $720 full-time, $24 per credit part-time; nonresident $6900 full-time, $230 per credit part-time. Full-time tuition and fees vary according to course load. Part-time tuition and fees vary according to course load. *Required fees:* $4484 full-time. *Payment plan:* installment. *Waivers:* senior citizens and employees or children of employees.

Financial Aid Of all full-time matriculated undergraduates who enrolled in 2012, 205 Federal Work-Study jobs (averaging $1627). 65 state and other part-time jobs (averaging $1478).

Applying *Options:* electronic application, deferred entrance. *Application fee:* $10. *Required:* high school transcript. *Notification:* continuous (freshmen), continuous (transfers).

Freshman Application Contact Ms. Shilo Henriques, Dean of Admissions, Bristol Community College, 777 Elsbree Street, Fall River, MA 02720. *Phone:* 508-678-2811 Ext. 2947. *Fax:* 508-730-3265. *E-mail:* Shilo.Henriques@bristolcc.edu.

Website: http://www.bristolcc.edu/.

Bunker Hill Community College

Boston, Massachusetts

- **State-supported** 2-year, founded 1973
- **Urban** 21-acre campus
- **Coed,** 14,023 undergraduate students, 33% full-time, 57% women, 43% men

Undergraduates 4,651 full-time, 9,372 part-time. 26% Black or African American, non-Hispanic/Latino; 21% Hispanic/Latino; 11% Asian, non-Hispanic/Latino; 0.2% Native Hawaiian or other Pacific Islander, non-Hispanic/Latino; 0.4% American Indian or Alaska Native, non-Hispanic/Latino; 1% Two or more races, non-Hispanic/Latino; 9% Race/ethnicity unknown; 4% international; 8% transferred in.

Freshmen *Admission:* 3,334 applied, 3,237 admitted, 2,216 enrolled.

Faculty *Total:* 784, 19% full-time. *Student/faculty ratio:* 20:1.

Majors Accounting; art; bioengineering and biomedical engineering; biology/biological sciences; biotechnology; business administration and management; business administration, management and operations related; business operations support and secretarial services related; cardiovascular technology; chemistry; clinical/medical laboratory technology; computer and information sciences and support services related; computer and information systems security; computer/information technology services administration related; computer programming; computer programming (specific applications); computer science; computer systems networking and telecommunications; criminal justice/law enforcement administration; criminal justice/police science; culinary arts; data entry/microcomputer applications; design and visual communications; diagnostic medical sonography and ultrasound technology; dramatic/theater arts; early childhood education; education; electrical/electronics maintenance and repair technology related; engineering; English; entrepreneurship; finance; fire prevention and safety technology; foreign languages and literatures; general studies; health information/medical records administration; history; hospitality administration; hospitality administration related; hotel/motel administration; human services; international business/trade/commerce; legal assistant/paralegal; mass communication/media; mathematics; medical administrative assistant and medical secretary; medical radiologic technology; music; operations management; physics; psychology; registered nursing/registered nurse; respiratory therapy technician; sociology; speech communication and rhetoric; tourism and travel services management; web page, digital/multimedia and information resources design.

Academics *Calendar:* semesters. *Degree:* certificates and associate. *Special study options:* academic remediation for entering students, accelerated degree program, advanced placement credit, cooperative education, distance learning, English as a second language, external degree program, honors programs, independent study, internships, part-time degree program, services for LD students, study abroad, summer session for credit.

Library Bunker Hill Community College Library with 45,933 titles, 218 serial subscriptions, 19,312 audiovisual materials, an OPAC, a Web page.

Student Life *Housing:* college housing not available. *Activities and Organizations:* drama/theater group, student-run radio station, choral group, Alpha Kappa Mu Honor Society, Asian-Pacific Students Association, African Students Club, Latinos Unidos Club, Haitian Students Club. *Campus security:* 24-hour emergency response devices and patrols, late-night transport/escort service. *Student services:* health clinic, personal/psychological counseling.

Athletics Member NJCAA. *Intercollegiate sports:* baseball M, basketball M/W, golf M/W, soccer M/W, softball M/W, volleyball M/W. *Intramural sports:* basketball M/W, soccer M/W, volleyball W.

Costs (2013–14) *Tuition:* state resident $576 full-time, $24 per credit hour part-time; nonresident $5520 full-time, $230 per credit hour part-time. Full-

time tuition and fees vary according to course load, program, and reciprocity agreements. Part-time tuition and fees vary according to course load, program, and reciprocity agreements. *Required fees:* $2808 full-time, $117 per credit hour part-time. *Payment plan:* installment. *Waivers:* minority students, senior citizens, and employees or children of employees.

Financial Aid Of all full-time matriculated undergraduates who enrolled in 2010, 135 Federal Work-Study jobs (averaging $2376).

Applying *Application fee:* $10. *Application deadlines:* rolling (freshmen), rolling (transfers). *Notification:* continuous (freshmen), continuous (transfers).

Freshman Application Contact Admissions and Enrollment Services, Bunker Hill Community College, MA. *Phone:* 617-228-3398. *E-mail:* admissions@bhcc.mass.edu.

Website: http://www.bhcc.mass.edu/.

Cape Cod Community College

West Barnstable, Massachusetts

Freshman Application Contact Director of Admissions, Cape Cod Community College, 2240 Iyannough Road, West Barnstable, MA 02668-1599. *Phone:* 508-362-2131 Ext. 4311. *Toll-free phone:* 877-846-3672. *Fax:* 508-375-4089. *E-mail:* admiss@capecod.edu.

Website: http://www.capecod.edu/.

Dean College

Franklin, Massachusetts

- **Independent** primarily 2-year, founded 1865
- **Small-town** 100-acre campus with easy access to Boston, Providence
- **Coed,** 1,300 undergraduate students, 83% full-time, 47% women, 53% men

Undergraduates 1,076 full-time, 224 part-time. 55% are from out of state; 16% Black or African American, non-Hispanic/Latino; 6% Hispanic/Latino; 1% Asian, non-Hispanic/Latino; 0.2% Native Hawaiian or other Pacific Islander, non-Hispanic/Latino; 0.5% American Indian or Alaska Native, non-Hispanic/Latino; 3% Two or more races, non-Hispanic/Latino; 17% Race/ethnicity unknown; 12% international; 2% transferred in; 89% live on campus.

Freshmen *Admission:* 2,594 applied, 1,773 admitted, 528 enrolled. *Average high school GPA:* 2.37. *Test scores:* SAT critical reading scores over 500: 19%; SAT math scores over 500: 17%; SAT writing scores over 500: 15%; ACT scores over 18: 43%; SAT critical reading scores over 600: 3%; SAT math scores over 600: 2%; SAT writing scores over 600: 3%; ACT scores over 24: 7%; SAT critical reading scores over 700: 1%; SAT writing scores over 700: 1%.

Faculty *Total:* 138, 22% full-time, 29% with terminal degrees. *Student/faculty ratio:* 16:1.

Majors Athletic training; business administration and management; criminal justice/law enforcement administration; criminal justice/police science; dance; dramatic/theater arts; early childhood education; fine and studio arts management; liberal arts and sciences/liberal studies; mathematics and computer science; physical education teaching and coaching; speech communication and rhetoric; sport and fitness administration/management.

Academics *Calendar:* semesters. *Degrees:* certificates, diplomas, associate, and bachelor's. *Special study options:* academic remediation for entering students, accelerated degree program, adult/continuing education programs, advanced placement credit, English as a second language, freshman honors college, honors programs, independent study, internships, off-campus study, part-time degree program, services for LD students, student-designed majors, summer session for credit.

Library E. Ross Anderson Library.

Student Life *Housing:* on-campus residence required through sophomore year. *Options:* coed, men-only, women-only, special housing for students with disabilities. Campus housing is university owned. Freshman campus housing is guaranteed. *Activities and Organizations:* drama/theater group, student-run radio station, choral group, Emerging Leaders, College Success Staff, Student Ambassadors, student government, Phi Theta Kappa. *Campus security:* 24-hour emergency response devices and patrols, late-night transport/escort service, controlled dormitory access. *Student services:* health clinic, personal/psychological counseling.

Athletics Member NJCAA. *Intercollegiate sports:* baseball M(s), basketball M(s)/W(s), football M(s), golf M, lacrosse M(s)/W(s), soccer M(s)/W(s), softball W(s), volleyball W(s). *Intramural sports:* basketball M, football M, golf M, lacrosse M, skiing (cross-country) M/W, skiing (downhill) M/W, tennis M/W, volleyball M/W.

Standardized Tests *Required:* SAT or ACT (for admission).

Costs (2014–15) *Comprehensive fee:* $47,790 includes full-time tuition ($33,230), mandatory fees ($300), and room and board ($14,260). *Room and board:* college room only: $9010.

Applying *Options:* electronic application, early action, deferred entrance. *Application fee:* $35. *Required:* essay or personal statement, high school transcript. *Recommended:* minimum 2.0 GPA, interview.

Freshman Application Contact Mr. James Fowler, Dean College, 99 Main Street, Franklin, MA 02038. *Phone:* 508-541-1547. *Toll-free phone:* 877-TRY-DEAN. *Fax:* 508-541-8726. *E-mail:* jfowler@dean.edu.

Website: http://www.dean.edu/.

FINE Mortuary College, LLC
Norwood, Massachusetts

Freshman Application Contact Dean Marsha Wise, Admissions Office, FINE Mortuary College, LLC, 150 Kerry Place, Norwood, MA 02062. *Phone:* 781-762-1211. *Fax:* 781-762-7177. *E-mail:* mwise@fine-ne.com.

Website: http://www.fine-ne.com/.

Greenfield Community College
Greenfield, Massachusetts

- **State-supported** 2-year, founded 1962, part of Commonwealth of Massachusetts Department of Higher Education
- **Small-town** 120-acre campus
- **Coed,** 2,243 undergraduate students, 36% full-time, 60% women, 40% men

Undergraduates 815 full-time, 1,428 part-time. Students come from 14 states and territories; 11 other countries; 9% are from out of state; 3% Black or African American, non-Hispanic/Latino; 6% Hispanic/Latino; 3% Asian, non-Hispanic/Latino; 0.1% Native Hawaiian or other Pacific Islander, non-Hispanic/Latino; 0.4% American Indian or Alaska Native, non-Hispanic/Latino; 3% Two or more races, non-Hispanic/Latino; 3% Race/ethnicity unknown; 11% transferred in. *Retention:* 60% of full-time freshmen returned.

Freshmen *Admission:* 377 enrolled.

Faculty *Total:* 185, 34% full-time. *Student/faculty ratio:* 13:1.

Majors Accounting technology and bookkeeping; acting; administrative assistant and secretarial science; American studies; art; business administration and management; business/commerce; community health services counseling; computer and information sciences; computer and information sciences and support services related; criminal justice/police science; crop production; dance; early childhood education; economics; education; engineering science; English; environmental science; film/video and photographic arts related; fine/studio arts; fire prevention and safety technology; food science; health professions related; hospitality administration; international relations and affairs; liberal arts and sciences/liberal studies; music performance; natural resources/conservation related; registered nursing/registered nurse; sales, distribution, and marketing operations; social sciences; social sciences related; women's studies.

Academics *Calendar:* semesters. *Degree:* certificates and associate. *Special study options:* academic remediation for entering students, adult/continuing education programs, advanced placement credit, cooperative education, distance learning, double majors, English as a second language, independent study, internships, part-time degree program, services for LD students, summer session for credit.

Library Greenfield Community College Library with 69,974 titles, 106 serial subscriptions, 1,158 audiovisual materials, an OPAC, a Web page.

Student Life *Housing:* college housing not available. *Activities and Organizations:* drama/theater group, choral group, Student Senate, Art Club, Permaculture Club, VetNet, International Students Club. *Campus security:* 24-hour emergency response devices and patrols, late-night transport/escort service. *Student services:* personal/psychological counseling, women's center, legal services.

Standardized Tests *Required for some:* Psychological Corporation Practical Nursing Entrance Examination.

Costs (2013–14) *Tuition:* state resident $4838 full-time, $26 per credit part-time; nonresident $10,958 full-time, $281 per credit part-time. Full-time tuition and fees vary according to class time, course load, and program. Part-time tuition and fees vary according to class time, course load, and program. *Required fees:* $171 per credit part-time, $61 per term part-time. *Payment plan:* installment. *Waivers:* senior citizens and employees or children of employees.

Applying *Options:* electronic application. *Required for some:* high school transcript, interview. *Application deadlines:* rolling (freshmen), rolling (transfers).

Freshman Application Contact Ms. Colleen Kucinski, Assistant Director of Admission, Greenfield Community College, 1 College Drive, Greenfield, MA 01301-9739. *Phone:* 413-775-1000. *Fax:* 413-773-5129. *E-mail:* admission@gcc.mass.edu.

Website: http://www.gcc.mass.edu/.

Holyoke Community College
Holyoke, Massachusetts

- **State-supported** 2-year, founded 1946, part of Massachusetts Public Higher Education System
- **Small-town** 135-acre campus
- **Endowment** $10.0 million
- **Coed,** 6,688 undergraduate students, 48% full-time, 60% women, 40% men

Undergraduates 3,240 full-time, 3,448 part-time. Students come from 16 states and territories; 1% are from out of state; 7% transferred in.

Freshmen *Admission:* 1,532 admitted, 1,532 enrolled.

Faculty *Total:* 508, 25% full-time, 22% with terminal degrees. *Student/faculty ratio:* 18:1.

Majors Accounting technology and bookkeeping; administrative assistant and secretarial science; art; business administration and management; child-care and support services management; computer programming (specific applications); criminal justice/safety; engineering; environmental control technologies related; geography; health and physical education/fitness; hospitality administration related; liberal arts and sciences and humanities related; liberal arts and sciences/liberal studies; medical radiologic technology; music; opticianry; registered nursing/registered nurse; retailing; social work; sport and fitness administration/management; veterinary/animal health technology.

Academics *Calendar:* semesters. *Degree:* certificates and associate. *Special study options:* academic remediation for entering students, adult/continuing education programs, advanced placement credit, cooperative education, distance learning, double majors, English as a second language, external degree program, honors programs, independent study, internships, off-campus study, part-time degree program, services for LD students, student-designed majors, study abroad, summer session for credit. *ROTC:* Army (c), Air Force (c).

Library Holyoke Community College Library plus 1 other with 100,357 titles, 49,591 serial subscriptions, 21,975 audiovisual materials, an OPAC, a Web page.

Student Life *Housing:* college housing not available. *Activities and Organizations:* drama/theater group, student-run newspaper, radio station, Drama Club, Japanese Anime Club, Student Senate, LISA Club, STRIVE. *Campus security:* 24-hour emergency response devices and patrols, late-night transport/escort service. *Student services:* health clinic, personal/psychological counseling, women's center.

Athletics Member NJCAA. *Intercollegiate sports:* baseball M, basketball M/W, cross-country running M/W, golf M/W, soccer M/W, softball W, volleyball W.

Costs (2013–14) *One-time required fee:* $60. *Tuition:* state resident $576 full-time, $141 per credit hour part-time; nonresident $5520 full-time, $347 per credit hour part-time. Full-time tuition and fees vary according to course load. Part-time tuition and fees vary according to course load. *Required fees:* $2998 full-time, $95 per term part-time. *Payment plan:* installment. *Waivers:* senior citizens and employees or children of employees.

Applying *Options:* electronic application, early admission, deferred entrance. *Required:* high school transcript. *Recommended:* interview. *Application deadlines:* rolling (freshmen), rolling (transfers). *Notification:* continuous (freshmen), continuous (transfers).

Freshman Application Contact Ms. Marcia Rosbury-Henne, Director of Admissions and Transfer Affairs, Holyoke Community College, Admission Office, Holyoke, MA 01040. *Phone:* 413-552-2321. *Fax:* 413-552-2045. *E-mail:* admissions@hcc.edu.

Website: http://www.hcc.edu/.

ITT Technical Institute
Norwood, Massachusetts

- **Proprietary** primarily 2-year, founded 1990, part of ITT Educational Services, Inc.
- **Suburban** campus
- **Coed**

Majors CAD/CADD drafting/design technology; computer and information systems security; computer engineering technology; computer software and media applications related; computer systems networking and telecommunications; electrical, electronic and communications engineering technology; game and interactive media design; web/multimedia management and webmaster.

Academics *Calendar:* quarters. *Degrees:* associate and bachelor's.

Student Life *Housing:* college housing not available.

Freshman Application Contact Director of Recruitment, ITT Technical Institute, 333 Providence Highway, Norwood, MA 02062. *Phone:* 781-278-7200. *Toll-free phone:* 800-879-8324.

Website: http://www.itt-tech.edu/.

ITT Technical Institute
Wilmington, Massachusetts

- **Proprietary** primarily 2-year, founded 2000, part of ITT Educational Services, Inc.
- **Coed**

Majors CAD/CADD drafting/design technology; computer and information systems security; computer engineering technology; computer software and media applications related; computer systems networking and telecommunications; digital communication and media/multimedia; electrical, electronic and communications engineering technology; game and interactive media design; web/multimedia management and webmaster.

Academics *Calendar:* quarters. *Degrees:* associate and bachelor's.

Student Life *Housing:* college housing not available.

Freshman Application Contact Director of Recruitment, ITT Technical Institute, 200 Ballardvale Street, Suite 200, Wilmington, MA 01887. *Phone:* 978-658-2636. *Toll-free phone:* 800-430-5097.

Website: http://www.itt-tech.edu/.

Labouré College
Boston, Massachusetts

Director of Admissions Ms. Gina M. Morrissette, Director of Admissions, Labouré College, 2120 Dorchester Avenue, Boston, MA 02124-5698. *Phone:* 617-296-8300.

Website: http://www.laboure.edu/.

Marian Court College
Swampscott, Massachusetts

Director of Admissions Bryan Boppert, Director of Admissions, Marian Court College, 35 Little's Point Road, Swampscott, MA 01907-2840. *Phone:* 781-309-5230. *Fax:* 781-309-5286.

Website: http://www.mariancourt.edu/.

Massachusetts Bay Community College
Wellesley Hills, Massachusetts

- **State-supported** 2-year, founded 1961
- **Suburban** 84-acre campus with easy access to Boston
- **Coed,** 5,377 undergraduate students, 36% full-time, 54% women, 46% men

Undergraduates 1,961 full-time, 3,416 part-time. Students come from 12 states and territories; 100 other countries; 2% are from out of state; 18% Black or African American, non-Hispanic/Latino; 16% Hispanic/Latino; 4% Asian, non-Hispanic/Latino; 0.1% Native Hawaiian or other Pacific Islander, non-Hispanic/Latino; 0.7% American Indian or Alaska Native, non-Hispanic/Latino; 8% Race/ethnicity unknown; 2% international; 7% transferred in. *Retention:* 60% of full-time freshmen returned.

Freshmen *Admission:* 2,132 applied, 2,132 admitted, 1,219 enrolled.

Faculty *Total:* 346, 25% full-time. *Student/faculty ratio:* 18:1.

Majors Accounting; automotive engineering technology; biological and physical sciences; biology/biotechnology laboratory technician; business administration and management; business/commerce; chemical technology; child-care and support services management; computer and information sciences; computer engineering technology; computer science; criminal justice/law enforcement administration; drafting and design technology; engineering technology; environmental engineering technology; forensic science and technology; general studies; hospitality administration; human services; information science/studies; international relations and affairs; legal assistant/paralegal; liberal arts and sciences/liberal studies; mechanical engineering/mechanical technology; medical radiologic technology; physical therapy technology; registered nursing/registered nurse; respiratory care therapy; social sciences; speech communication and rhetoric.

Academics *Calendar:* semesters. *Degree:* certificates and associate. *Special study options:* academic remediation for entering students, adult/continuing education programs, advanced placement credit, cooperative education, distance learning, honors programs, internships, part-time degree program, services for LD students, summer session for credit.

Library Perkins Library with 51,429 titles, 280 serial subscriptions, 4,780 audiovisual materials, an OPAC, a Web page.

Student Life *Housing:* college housing not available. *Activities and Organizations:* drama/theater group, student-run newspaper, Student Government Association, Latino Student Organization, New World Society Club, Mass Bay Players, Student Occupational Therapy Association. *Campus security:* 24-hour emergency response devices and patrols. *Student services:* health clinic, personal/psychological counseling.

Athletics Member NJCAA. *Intercollegiate sports:* baseball M, basketball M/W, cross-country running M/W, golf M/W, soccer M/W, softball W, tennis M/W, volleyball W. *Intramural sports:* ice hockey M, soccer M/W.

Costs (2013–14) *Tuition:* state resident $576 full-time, $24 per credit part-time; nonresident $5520 full-time, $230 per credit part-time. Full-time tuition and fees vary according to program and reciprocity agreements. Part-time tuition and fees vary according to program and reciprocity agreements. *Required fees:* $3680 full-time, $130 per credit part-time, $20 per term part-time. *Payment plan:* installment. *Waivers:* senior citizens and employees or children of employees.

Financial Aid Of all full-time matriculated undergraduates who enrolled in 2012, 59 Federal Work-Study jobs (averaging $1840).

Applying *Options:* electronic application, deferred entrance. *Application fee:* $20. *Application deadlines:* rolling (freshmen), rolling (transfers). *Notification:* continuous (freshmen), continuous (transfers).

Freshman Application Contact Ms. Donna Raposa, Director of Admissions, Massachusetts Bay Community College, 50 Oakland Street, Wellesley Hills, MA 02481. *Phone:* 781-239-2500. *Fax:* 781-239-1047. *E-mail:* info@massbay.edu.

Website: http://www.massbay.edu/.

Massasoit Community College
Brockton, Massachusetts

Freshman Application Contact Michelle Hughes, Director of Admissions, Massasoit Community College, 1 Massasoit Boulevard, Brockton, MA 02302-3996. *Phone:* 508-588-9100. *Toll-free phone:* 800-CAREERS.

Website: http://www.massasoit.mass.edu/.

Middlesex Community College
Bedford, Massachusetts

- **State-supported** 2-year, founded 1970, part of Massachusetts Public Higher Education System
- **Suburban** 200-acre campus with easy access to Boston
- **Coed**

Academics *Calendar:* semesters. *Degree:* certificates and associate. *Special study options:* academic remediation for entering students, accelerated degree program, adult/continuing education programs, advanced placement credit, cooperative education, distance learning, English as a second language, honors programs, independent study, internships, off-campus study, part-time degree program, services for LD students, study abroad, summer session for credit. *ROTC:* Air Force (c).

Student Life *Campus security:* 24-hour emergency response devices and patrols.

Standardized Tests *Required for some:* CPT.

Costs (2013–14) *Tuition:* state resident $4224 full-time; nonresident $9168 full-time. Full-time tuition and fees vary according to course load and reciprocity agreements. Part-time tuition and fees vary according to course load and reciprocity agreements. *Required fees:* $50 full-time.

Financial Aid Of all full-time matriculated undergraduates who enrolled in 2012, 68 Federal Work-Study jobs (averaging $2200).

Applying *Options:* electronic application, early admission. *Required for some:* essay or personal statement, high school transcript, 3 letters of recommendation, interview.

Freshman Application Contact Middlesex Community College, Springs Road, Bedford, MA 01730-1655. *Phone:* 978-656-3207. *Toll-free phone:* 800-818-3434.

Website: http://www.middlesex.mass.edu/.

Mount Wachusett Community College
Gardner, Massachusetts

- **State-supported** 2-year, founded 1963, part of Massachusetts Public Higher Education System
- **Small-town** 270-acre campus with easy access to Boston
- **Endowment** $3.5 million
- **Coed,** 4,734 undergraduate students, 42% full-time, 65% women, 35% men

Undergraduates 2,000 full-time, 2,734 part-time. Students come from 14 states and territories; 4% are from out of state; 7% Black or African American, non-Hispanic/Latino; 14% Hispanic/Latino; 2% Asian, non-Hispanic/Latino; 0.1% Native Hawaiian or other Pacific Islander, non-Hispanic/Latino; 0.5% American Indian or Alaska Native, non-Hispanic/Latino; 3% Two or more races, non-Hispanic/Latino; 3% Race/ethnicity unknown; 0.7% international; 7% transferred in.

Freshmen *Admission:* 1,952 applied, 1,895 admitted, 915 enrolled.

Faculty *Total:* 392, 19% full-time, 12% with terminal degrees. *Student/faculty ratio:* 16:1.

Majors Allied health and medical assisting services related; alternative and complementary medical support services related; art; automobile/automotive mechanics technology; biotechnology; business/commerce; child-care and support services management; child development; clinical/medical laboratory technology; computer and information sciences; computer graphics;

corrections; criminal justice/law enforcement administration; criminal justice/safety; dental hygiene; energy management and systems technology; environmental studies; fire prevention and safety technology; general studies; health information/medical records administration; human services; legal assistant/paralegal; liberal arts and sciences/liberal studies; medical/clinical assistant; physical therapy technology; plastics and polymer engineering technology; radio and television broadcasting technology; registered nursing/registered nurse; web page, digital/multimedia and information resources design.

Academics *Calendar:* semesters. *Degree:* certificates, diplomas, and associate. *Special study options:* academic remediation for entering students, accelerated degree program, adult/continuing education programs, advanced placement credit, cooperative education, distance learning, double majors, English as a second language, honors programs, independent study, internships, part-time degree program, services for LD students, study abroad, summer session for credit.

Library LaChance Library with 41,792 titles, 50 serial subscriptions, 747 audiovisual materials, an OPAC, a Web page.

Student Life *Housing:* college housing not available. *Activities and Organizations:* drama/theater group, student-run newspaper, television station, Art Club, Dental Hygienist Club, Math Club, Student Government Association, Student Nurses Association. *Campus security:* 24-hour emergency response devices and patrols. *Student services:* health clinic, personal/psychological counseling.

Athletics *Intramural sports:* badminton M/W, basketball M/W, football M/W, soccer M/W, softball M/W, table tennis M/W, volleyball M/W, water polo M/W.

Standardized Tests *Recommended:* SAT (for admission), ACT (for admission), SAT or ACT (for admission), SAT and SAT Subject Tests or ACT (for admission), SAT Subject Tests (for admission).

Costs (2013–14) *Tuition:* state resident $4900 full-time, $25 per credit hour part-time; nonresident $9820 full-time, $230 per credit hour part-time. Full-time tuition and fees vary according to program and reciprocity agreements. Part-time tuition and fees vary according to program and reciprocity agreements. *Required fees:* $340 full-time, $165 per credit hour part-time, $170 per term part-time. *Payment plan:* installment. *Waivers:* senior citizens and employees or children of employees.

Financial Aid Of all full-time matriculated undergraduates who enrolled in 2012, 47 Federal Work-Study jobs (averaging $2228).

Applying *Options:* electronic application, early admission. *Required:* high school transcript. *Required for some:* 2 letters of recommendation. *Recommended:* interview. *Application deadlines:* rolling (freshmen), rolling (transfers). *Notification:* continuous (freshmen), continuous (transfers).

Freshman Application Contact Mr. John Walsh, Interim Director of Admissions, Mount Wachusett Community College, 444 Green Street, Gardner, MA 01440-1000. *Phone:* 978-632-6600 Ext. 110. *Fax:* 978-630-9554. *E-mail:* admissions@mwcc.mass.edu. *Website:* http://www.mwcc.mass.edu/.

Northern Essex Community College
Haverhill, Massachusetts

- **State-supported** 2-year, founded 1960
- **Suburban** 106-acre campus with easy access to Boston
- **Endowment** $3.3 million
- **Coed,** 7,352 undergraduate students, 33% full-time, 62% women, 38% men

Undergraduates 2,438 full-time, 4,914 part-time. Students come from 8 states and territories; 16% are from out of state; 4% Black or African American, non-Hispanic/Latino; 35% Hispanic/Latino; 1% Asian, non-Hispanic/Latino; 0.5% Native Hawaiian or other Pacific Islander, non-Hispanic/Latino; 0.1% American Indian or Alaska Native, non-Hispanic/Latino; 1% Two or more races, non-Hispanic/Latino; 3% Race/ethnicity unknown; 0.7% international; 6% transferred in. *Retention:* 62% of full-time freshmen returned.

Freshmen *Admission:* 3,000 applied, 2,800 admitted, 1,518 enrolled.

Faculty *Total:* 657, 16% full-time. *Student/faculty ratio:* 22:1.

Majors Accounting; administrative assistant and secretarial science; biological and physical sciences; business administration and management; business teacher education; civil engineering technology; commercial and advertising art; computer and information sciences; computer engineering technology; computer graphics; computer programming; computer programming related; computer programming (specific applications); computer science; computer systems networking and telecommunications; computer typography and composition equipment operation; criminal justice/law enforcement administration; dance; data processing and data processing technology; dental assisting; dramatic/theater arts; education; electrical, electronic and communications engineering technology; elementary education; engineering science; finance; general studies; health information/medical records administration; history; hotel/motel administration; human services; industrial radiologic technology; international relations and affairs; journalism; kindergarten/preschool education; legal assistant/paralegal; liberal arts and sciences/liberal studies; machine tool technology; marketing/marketing management; materials science; medical administrative assistant and medical secretary; medical transcription; mental health counseling; music; parks, recreation and leisure; physical education teaching and coaching; political science and government; radiologic technology/science; real estate; registered nursing/registered nurse; respiratory care therapy; respiratory therapy technician; sign language interpretation and translation; telecommunications technology; tourism and travel services management; web/multimedia management and webmaster; web page, digital/multimedia and information resources design; women's studies.

Academics *Calendar:* semesters. *Degree:* certificates and associate. *Special study options:* academic remediation for entering students, adult/continuing education programs, advanced placement credit, cooperative education, distance learning, double majors, English as a second language, freshman honors college, honors programs, independent study, internships, off-campus study, part-time degree program, services for LD students, study abroad, summer session for credit. *ROTC:* Air Force (c).

Library Bentley Library with 61,120 titles, 598 serial subscriptions, an OPAC.

Student Life *Housing:* college housing not available. *Activities and Organizations:* drama/theater group, student-run newspaper. *Campus security:* 24-hour emergency response devices and patrols. *Student services:* health clinic, personal/psychological counseling, women's center.

Athletics Member NJCAA. *Intercollegiate sports:* baseball M, basketball M/W, cross-country running M/W, volleyball M/W. *Intramural sports:* basketball M/W, cross-country running M/W, football M/W, golf M/W, racquetball M/W, skiing (cross-country) M/W, skiing (downhill) M/W, weight lifting M/W.

Standardized Tests *Required:* Psychological Corporation Aptitude Test for Practical Nursing (for admission).

Costs (2013–14) *Tuition:* state resident $600 full-time, $25 per credit hour part-time; nonresident $6384 full-time, $266 per credit hour part-time. Full-time tuition and fees vary according to reciprocity agreements. Part-time tuition and fees vary according to reciprocity agreements. *Required fees:* $3288 full-time, $162 per credit hour part-time. *Payment plan:* installment. *Waivers:* employees or children of employees.

Financial Aid Of all full-time matriculated undergraduates who enrolled in 2012, 74 Federal Work-Study jobs (averaging $1759).

Applying *Options:* early admission. *Application fee:* $25. *Required:* high school transcript. *Application deadlines:* rolling (freshmen), rolling (transfers). *Notification:* continuous (freshmen), continuous (transfers).

Freshman Application Contact Ms. Laurie Dimitrov, Director of Admissions, Northern Essex Community College, Haverhill, MA 01830. *Phone:* 978-556-3616. *Fax:* 978-556-3155. *Website:* http://www.necc.mass.edu/.

North Shore Community College
Danvers, Massachusetts

- **State-supported** 2-year, founded 1965
- **Suburban** campus with easy access to Boston
- **Endowment** $5.5 million
- **Coed,** 7,750 undergraduate students, 39% full-time, 60% women, 40% men

Undergraduates 3,018 full-time, 4,732 part-time. Students come from 9 states and territories; 8 other countries; 2% are from out of state; 9% Black or African American, non-Hispanic/Latino; 21% Hispanic/Latino; 4% Asian, non-Hispanic/Latino; 0.1% Native Hawaiian or other Pacific Islander, non-Hispanic/Latino; 0.2% American Indian or Alaska Native, non-Hispanic/Latino; 2% Two or more races, non-Hispanic/Latino; 3% Race/ethnicity unknown; 0.1% international; 8% transferred in.

Freshmen *Admission:* 4,696 applied, 3,891 admitted, 1,489 enrolled.

Faculty *Total:* 486, 28% full-time, 18% with terminal degrees. *Student/faculty ratio:* 17:1.

Majors Accounting; administrative assistant and secretarial science; airline pilot and flight crew; biology/biotechnology laboratory technician; business administration and management; child development; computer and information sciences related; computer engineering technology; computer graphics; computer programming; computer programming (specific applications); computer science; criminal justice/law enforcement administration; culinary arts; data entry/microcomputer applications; engineering science; fire science/firefighting; foods, nutrition, and wellness; gerontology; health professions related; hospitality administration; information science/studies; interdisciplinary studies; kindergarten/preschool education; legal administrative assistant/secretary; legal assistant/paralegal; liberal arts and sciences/liberal studies; marketing/marketing management; medical administrative assistant and medical secretary; medical radiologic technology; mental health counseling; occupational therapy; physical therapy technology; pre-engineering; registered nursing/registered nurse; respiratory care therapy; substance abuse/addiction counseling; tourism and travel services management; veterinary/animal health technology; web page, digital/multimedia and information resources design.

Academics *Calendar:* semesters. *Degree:* certificates and associate. *Special study options:* academic remediation for entering students, accelerated degree program, adult/continuing education programs, advanced placement credit, cooperative education, distance learning, English as a second language, honors programs, independent study, internships, part-time degree program, services for LD students, summer session for credit.

Library Learning Resource Center plus 2 others with 68,035 titles, 257 serial subscriptions, 4,213 audiovisual materials, an OPAC, a Web page.

Student Life *Housing:* college housing not available. *Activities and Organizations:* drama/theater group, student-run newspaper, Program Council, student government, performing arts, student newspaper, Phi Theta Kappa, national fraternities. *Campus security:* 24-hour emergency response devices and patrols, late-night transport/escort service. *Student services:* health clinic, personal/psychological counseling, women's center.

Athletics *Intramural sports:* basketball M/W, soccer M/W.

Costs (2013–14) *Tuition:* state resident $750 full-time, $25 per credit hour part-time; nonresident $7710 full-time, $257 per credit hour part-time. *Required fees:* $4320 full-time, $144 per credit hour part-time. *Payment plan:* installment. *Waivers:* senior citizens and employees or children of employees.

Financial Aid Of all full-time matriculated undergraduates who enrolled in 2009, 1,658 applied for aid, 1,438 were judged to have need, 23 had their need fully met. 123 Federal Work-Study jobs (averaging $1359). In 2009, 11 non-need-based awards were made. *Average percent of need met:* 18%. *Average financial aid package:* $6856. *Average need-based loan:* $1639. *Average need-based gift aid:* $2522. *Average non-need-based aid:* $614.

Applying *Options:* electronic application, early admission, deferred entrance. *Required for some:* essay or personal statement, high school transcript, interview. *Application deadlines:* rolling (freshmen), rolling (transfers). *Notification:* continuous (freshmen), continuous (transfers).

Freshman Application Contact Mrs. Lisa Barrett, Academic Counselor, North Shore Community College, Danvers, MA 01923. *Phone:* 978-762-4000 Ext. 6225. *Fax:* 978-762-4015. *E-mail:* lbarrett@northshore.edu. *Website:* http://www.northshore.edu/.

Quincy College
Quincy, Massachusetts

Freshman Application Contact Paula Smith, Dean, Enrollment Services, Quincy College, 34 Coddington Street, Quincy, MA 02169-4522. *Phone:* 617-984-1700. *Toll-free phone:* 800-698-1700. *Fax:* 617-984-1779. *E-mail:* psmith@quincycollege.edu. *Website:* http://www.quincycollege.edu/.

Quinsigamond Community College
Worcester, Massachusetts

- **State-supported** 2-year, founded 1963, part of Massachusetts System of Higher Education
- **Urban** 57-acre campus with easy access to Boston
- **Endowment** $408,167
- **Coed,** 8,583 undergraduate students, 40% full-time, 57% women, 43% men

Undergraduates 3,441 full-time, 5,142 part-time. Students come from 24 states and territories; 25 other countries; 1% are from out of state; 12% Black or African American, non-Hispanic/Latino; 16% Hispanic/Latino; 4% Asian, non-Hispanic/Latino; 0.2% Native Hawaiian or other Pacific Islander, non-Hispanic/Latino; 0.4% American Indian or Alaska Native, non-Hispanic/Latino; 2% Two or more races, non-Hispanic/Latino; 6% Race/ethnicity unknown; 0.2% international.

Freshmen *Admission:* 3,823 applied, 2,354 admitted, 1,856 enrolled.

Faculty *Total:* 628, 21% full-time, 15% with terminal degrees. *Student/faculty ratio:* 20:1.

Majors Alternative and complementary medicine related; American Sign Language (ASL); automobile/automotive mechanics technology; bioengineering and biomedical engineering; biotechnology; business administration and management; business/commerce; computer and information systems security; computer engineering technology; computer graphics; computer programming (specific applications); computer science; computer systems analysis; criminal justice/police science; data modeling/warehousing and database administration; dental hygiene; dental services and allied professions related; electrical, electronic and communications engineering technology; electromechanical technology; elementary education; emergency medical technology (EMT paramedic); energy management and systems technology; engineering technologies and engineering related; executive assistant/executive secretary; fire services administration; general studies; health services/allied health/health sciences; hospitality administration; human services; kindergarten/preschool education; liberal arts and sciences/liberal studies; manufacturing engineering technology; medical administrative assistant and medical secretary;

occupational therapy; pre-pharmacy studies; radiologic technology/science; registered nursing/registered nurse; respiratory care therapy; restaurant/food services management; telecommunications technology; trade and industrial teacher education; web page, digital/multimedia and information resources design.

Academics *Calendar:* semesters. *Degree:* certificates and associate. *Special study options:* academic remediation for entering students, accelerated degree program, advanced placement credit, cooperative education, distance learning, double majors, English as a second language, honors programs, independent study, internships, off-campus study, part-time degree program, services for LD students, summer session for credit. *ROTC:* Army (c).

Library Alden Library with 95,000 titles, 110 serial subscriptions, 1,500 audiovisual materials, an OPAC, a Web page.

Student Life *Housing:* college housing not available. *Activities and Organizations:* drama/theater group, student-run newspaper, Phi Theta Kappa, academic-related clubs, Student Senate, Chess Club, Business Club. *Campus security:* 24-hour emergency response devices and patrols, late-night transport/escort service. *Student services:* personal/psychological counseling.

Athletics Member NJCAA. *Intercollegiate sports:* baseball M, basketball M/W, softball W. *Intramural sports:* basketball M/W, soccer M/W, ultimate Frisbee M/W, volleyball M/W.

Costs (2013–14) *Tuition:* state resident $576 full-time, $24 per credit part-time; nonresident $5520 full-time, $230 per credit part-time. Full-time tuition and fees vary according to course load and program. Part-time tuition and fees vary according to course load and program. *Required fees:* $4518 full-time, $157 per credit part-time, $280 per term part-time. *Payment plan:* installment. *Waivers:* senior citizens and employees or children of employees.

Applying *Options:* electronic application. *Application fee:* $20. *Required:* high school transcript. *Required for some:* interview. *Application deadlines:* rolling (freshmen), rolling (out-of-state freshmen), rolling (transfers). *Notification:* continuous (freshmen), continuous (out-of-state freshmen), continuous (transfers).

Freshman Application Contact Quinsigamond Community College, 670 West Boylston Street, Worcester, MA 01606-2092. *Phone:* 508-854-4260. *Website:* http://www.qcc.edu/.

Roxbury Community College
Roxbury Crossing, Massachusetts

Director of Admissions Mr. Michael Walker, Director, Admissions, Roxbury Community College, 1234 Columbus Avenue, Roxbury Crossing, MA 02120-3400. *Phone:* 617-541-5310. *Website:* http://www.rcc.mass.edu/.

Salter College
Chicopee, Massachusetts

Admissions Office Contact Salter College, 645 Shawinigan Drive, Chicopee, MA 01020. *Website:* http://www.saltercollege.com/.

Springfield Technical Community College
Springfield, Massachusetts

- **State-supported** 2-year, founded 1967
- **Urban** 34-acre campus
- **Coed,** 6,792 undergraduate students, 47% full-time, 58% women, 42% men

Undergraduates 3,212 full-time, 3,580 part-time. Students come from 10 states and territories; 3% are from out of state; 15% Black or African American, non-Hispanic/Latino; 26% Hispanic/Latino; 3% Asian, non-Hispanic/Latino; 0.5% American Indian or Alaska Native, non-Hispanic/Latino; 2% Two or more races, non-Hispanic/Latino; 2% Race/ethnicity unknown; 0.8% international; 7% transferred in.

Freshmen *Admission:* 3,328 applied, 2,884 admitted, 1,491 enrolled.

Faculty *Total:* 492, 30% full-time. *Student/faculty ratio:* 17:1.

Majors Accounting; administrative assistant and secretarial science; animation, interactive technology, video graphics and special effects; automotive engineering technology; biology/biological sciences; biotechnology; building/construction finishing, management, and inspection related; business administration and management; business/commerce; chemistry; civil engineering technology; clinical/medical laboratory technology; commercial and advertising art; commercial photography; computer and information systems security; computer engineering technology; computer programming (specific applications); computer science; criminal justice/police science; dental hygiene; diagnostic medical sonography and ultrasound technology; early childhood education; electrical, electronic and communications engineering technology; electromechanical technology; elementary education; engineering; finance; fine/studio arts; fire prevention and safety technology; general studies; heating, ventilation, air conditioning and refrigeration engineering technology; landscaping and groundskeeping; laser and optical technology; liberal arts and sciences/liberal studies; marketing/marketing management; massage therapy; mathematics; mechanical engineering/mechanical technology; medical administrative assistant and medical secretary; medical/clinical assistant; medical insurance coding; occupational therapist assistant; physical therapy technology; physics; premedical studies; radio and television broadcasting technology; radiologic technology/science; recording arts technology; registered nursing/registered nurse; respiratory care therapy; secondary education; small business administration; sport and fitness administration/management; surgical technology; telecommunications technology.

Academics *Calendar:* semesters. *Degree:* certificates and associate. *Special study options:* academic remediation for entering students, adult/continuing education programs, advanced placement credit, cooperative education, distance learning, English as a second language, honors programs, independent study, internships, off-campus study, part-time degree program, services for LD students, summer session for credit.

Library Springfield Technical Community College Library with 53,009 titles, 239 serial subscriptions, 9,435 audiovisual materials, an OPAC, a Web page.

Student Life *Housing:* college housing not available. *Activities and Organizations:* Phi Theta Kappa, Campus Civitian Club, Tech Times (student newspaper), Dental Hygiene Club, Landscape Design Club. *Campus security:* 24-hour emergency response devices and patrols, late-night transport/escort service. *Student services:* health clinic, personal/psychological counseling.

Athletics Member NJCAA. *Intercollegiate sports:* basketball M/W, golf M, soccer M/W, wrestling M. *Intramural sports:* basketball M/W, cross-country running M/W, golf M/W, skiing (cross-country) M/W, volleyball M/W, weight lifting M/W.

Standardized Tests *Required for some:* SAT (for admission).

Costs (2014–15) *Tuition:* state resident $750 full-time, $25 per credit part-time; nonresident $7260 full-time, $242 per credit part-time. Full-time tuition and fees vary according to course load and reciprocity agreements. Part-time tuition and fees vary according to course load and reciprocity agreements. No tuition increase for student's term of enrollment. *Required fees:* $4356 full-time, $138 per credit part-time, $108 per term part-time. *Payment plan:* installment. *Waivers:* senior citizens and employees or children of employees.

Financial Aid Of all full-time matriculated undergraduates who enrolled in 2012, 124 Federal Work-Study jobs (averaging $2400).

Applying *Options:* electronic application. *Application fee:* $10. *Required:* high school transcript. *Required for some:* interview. *Application deadlines:* rolling (freshmen), rolling (transfers).

Freshman Application Contact Mr. Ray Blair, Dean of Student Affairs, Springfield Technical Community College, Springfield, MA 01105. *Phone:* 413-781-7822 Ext. 4868. *E-mail:* rblair@stcc.edu. *Website:* http://www.stcc.edu/.

Urban College of Boston
Boston, Massachusetts

Director of Admissions Dr. Henry J. Johnson, Director of Enrollment Services/Registrar, Urban College of Boston, 178 Tremont Street, Boston, MA 02111. *Phone:* 617-348-6353. *Website:* http://www.urbancollege.edu/.

MICHIGAN

Alpena Community College
Alpena, Michigan

- **State and locally supported** 2-year, founded 1952
- **Small-town** 700-acre campus
- **Endowment** $3.3 million
- **Coed**

Undergraduates Students come from 4 states and territories; 2% live on campus. *Retention:* 55% of full-time freshmen returned.

Faculty *Student/faculty ratio:* 17:1.

Academics *Calendar:* semesters. *Degree:* certificates and associate. *Special study options:* academic remediation for entering students, advanced placement credit, distance learning, double majors, internships, part-time degree program, services for LD students, summer session for credit.

Student Life *Campus security:* 24-hour emergency response devices.

Athletics Member NJCAA.

Costs (2013–14) *Tuition:* area resident $3180 full-time, $106 per contact hour part-time; state resident $3660 full-time, $122 per contact hour part-time; nonresident $3660 full-time, $122 per contact hour part-time. *Required fees:* $600 full-time, $16 per hour part-time, $30 per term part-time. *Room and board:* $3500.

Financial Aid Of all full-time matriculated undergraduates who enrolled in 2013, 90 Federal Work-Study jobs (averaging $1200). 20 state and other part-time jobs (averaging $800).

Applying *Options:* electronic application, early admission, deferred entrance. *Recommended:* high school transcript.

Freshman Application Contact Mr. Mike Kollien, Director of Admissions, Alpena Community College, 665 Johnson, Alpena, MI 49707. *Phone:* 989-358-7339. *Toll-free phone:* 888-468-6222. *Fax:* 989-358-7540. *E-mail:* kollienm@alpenacc.edu. *Website:* http://www.alpenacc.edu/.

Bay de Noc Community College
Escanaba, Michigan

Freshman Application Contact Bay de Noc Community College, 2001 North Lincoln Road, Escanaba, MI 49829-2511. *Phone:* 906-786-5802 Ext. 1276. *Toll-free phone:* 800-221-2001. *Website:* http://www.baycollege.edu/.

Bay Mills Community College
Brimley, Michigan

Freshman Application Contact Ms. Elaine Lehre, Admissions Officer, Bay Mills Community College, 12214 West Lakeshore Drive, Brimley, MI 49715. *Phone:* 906-248-3354. *Toll-free phone:* 800-844-BMCC. *Fax:* 906-248-3351. *Website:* http://www.bmcc.edu/.

Delta College
University Center, Michigan

- **District-supported** 2-year, founded 1961
- **Rural** 640-acre campus
- **Endowment** $15.2 million
- **Coed,** 10,273 undergraduate students, 38% full-time, 55% women, 45% men

Undergraduates 3,881 full-time, 6,392 part-time. Students come from 3 states and territories; 4 other countries; 9% Black or African American, non-Hispanic/Latino; 6% Hispanic/Latino; 0.8% Asian, non-Hispanic/Latino; 0.5% American Indian or Alaska Native, non-Hispanic/Latino; 2% Two or more races, non-Hispanic/Latino; 1% Race/ethnicity unknown; 0.2% international; 3% transferred in.

Freshmen *Admission:* 6,701 applied, 6,701 admitted, 1,497 enrolled.

Faculty *Total:* 571, 38% full-time. *Student/faculty ratio:* 16:1.

Majors Accounting technology and bookkeeping; administrative assistant and secretarial science; architectural engineering technology; automobile/automotive mechanics technology; building/construction finishing, management, and inspection related; building/property maintenance; business administration and management; carpentry; chemical technology; child-care provision; computer and information sciences related; computer and information systems security; computer installation and repair technology; computer programming; computer software and media applications related; computer systems networking and telecommunications; construction engineering technology; corrections; criminal justice/police science; dental assisting; dental hygiene; diagnostic medical sonography and ultrasound technology; electrical and power transmission installation; electrician; energy management and systems technology; environmental engineering technology; fine/studio arts; fire prevention and safety technology; fire science/firefighting; fire services administration; general studies; heating, air conditioning, ventilation and refrigeration maintenance technology; industrial mechanics and maintenance technology; international/global studies; journalism; legal assistant/paralegal; liberal arts and sciences/liberal studies; machine shop technology; manufacturing engineering technology; marketing/marketing management; mechanical engineering/mechanical technology; medical administrative assistant and medical secretary; medical radiologic technology; merchandising; physical therapy technology; pipefitting and sprinkler fitting; plumbing technology; precision metal working related; precision production related; radio and television; registered nursing/registered nurse; respiratory care therapy; retailing; salon/beauty salon management; security and loss prevention; sheet metal technology; small business administration; sport and fitness administration/management; surgical technology; technology/industrial arts teacher education; tool and die technology; water quality and wastewater treatment management and recycling technology; web/multimedia management and webmaster; welding technology.

Academics *Calendar:* semesters. *Degree:* certificates and associate. *Special study options:* academic remediation for entering students, adult/continuing education programs, advanced placement credit, cooperative education, distance learning, double majors, freshman honors college, honors programs, independent study, internships, off-campus study, part-time degree program, services for LD students, study abroad, summer session for credit.

Library Library Learning Information Center plus 1 other with 110,985 titles, 200 serial subscriptions, 4,500 audiovisual materials, an OPAC, a Web page.

Student Life *Housing:* college housing not available. *Activities and Organizations:* drama/theater group, student-run newspaper, Intramural Activities, Student Senate, Phi Theta Kappa, Inter-Varsity Christian Fellowship, DECA. *Campus security:* 24-hour emergency response devices, student patrols, late-night transport/escort service. *Student services:* personal/psychological counseling.

Athletics Member NJCAA. *Intercollegiate sports:* baseball M(s), basketball M(s)/W(s), golf M, soccer W(s), softball W(s). *Intramural sports:* basketball M/W, football M/W.

Costs (2014–15) *Tuition:* area resident $2384 full-time, $92 per credit part-time; state resident $3819 full-time, $147 per credit part-time; nonresident $7387 full-time, $284 per credit part-time. Full-time tuition and fees vary according to course load. Part-time tuition and fees vary according to course load. *Required fees:* $40 per term part-time. *Payment plan:* installment. *Waivers:* senior citizens and employees or children of employees.

Financial Aid Of all full-time matriculated undergraduates who enrolled in 2012, 115 Federal Work-Study jobs (averaging $2307). 67 state and other part-time jobs (averaging $2214).

Applying *Options:* electronic application, early admission, deferred entrance. *Required for some:* essay or personal statement. *Recommended:* high school transcript. *Application deadlines:* rolling (freshmen), rolling (transfers).

Freshman Application Contact Mrs. Terri Gould, Interim Director of Admissions, Delta College, 1961 Delta Road, University Center, MI 48710. *Phone:* 989-686-9081. *Fax:* 989-667-2202. *E-mail:* admit@delta.edu. *Website:* http://www.delta.edu/.

Glen Oaks Community College
Centreville, Michigan

- **State and locally supported** 2-year, founded 1965
- **Rural** 300-acre campus
- **Coed,** 1,221 undergraduate students, 43% full-time, 61% women, 39% men

Undergraduates 531 full-time, 690 part-time. 6% Black or African American, non-Hispanic/Latino; 6% Hispanic/Latino; 1% Asian, non-Hispanic/Latino; 0.4% American Indian or Alaska Native, non-Hispanic/Latino; 3% Race/ethnicity unknown; 0.1% international; 4% transferred in.

Freshmen *Admission:* 173 enrolled.

Faculty *Student/faculty ratio:* 16:1.

Majors Business administration and management; business, management, and marketing related; child-care and support services management; general studies; health professions related; mechanical engineering technologies related; registered nursing/registered nurse.

Academics *Calendar:* semesters. *Degree:* certificates and associate. *Special study options:* academic remediation for entering students, advanced placement credit, distance learning, internships, part-time degree program, services for LD students, summer session for credit.

Library E. J. Shaheen Library with 37,087 titles, 347 serial subscriptions, an OPAC.

Student Life *Housing:* college housing not available. *Campus security:* 24-hour emergency response devices. *Student services:* personal/psychological counseling.

Athletics Member NJCAA. *Intercollegiate sports:* baseball M(s), basketball M(s)/W(s), golf M(s), softball W(s), track and field M/W. *Intramural sports:* baseball M, basketball M/W.

Financial Aid Of all full-time matriculated undergraduates who enrolled in 2012, 70 Federal Work-Study jobs (averaging $1100). 38 state and other part-time jobs (averaging $1200).

Applying *Options:* electronic application. *Required:* high school transcript. *Application deadlines:* rolling (freshmen), rolling (transfers).

Freshman Application Contact Ms. Beverly M. Andrews, Director of Admissions/Registrar, Glen Oaks Community College, 62249 Shimmel Road, Centreville, MI 49032-9719. *Phone:* 269-294-4249. *Toll-free phone:* 888-994-7818. *Fax:* 269-467-4114. *E-mail:* thowden@glenoaks.edu. *Website:* http://www.glenoaks.edu/.

Gogebic Community College
Ironwood, Michigan

- **State and locally supported** 2-year, founded 1932, part of Michigan Department of Education
- **Small-town** 195-acre campus
- **Coed,** 1,199 undergraduate students, 54% full-time, 57% women, 43% men

Undergraduates 647 full-time, 552 part-time. Students come from 5 states and territories; 1 other country; 1% Black or African American, non-Hispanic/Latino; 0.8% Hispanic/Latino; 0.8% Asian, non-Hispanic/Latino; 6% American Indian or Alaska Native, non-Hispanic/Latino; 5% Race/ethnicity unknown; 0.1% international.

Freshmen *Admission:* 293 enrolled.

Majors Accounting; accounting and computer science; automobile/automotive mechanics technology; business administration and management; business/commerce; computer and information sciences; construction engineering technology; criminal justice/law enforcement administration; drafting and design technology; early childhood education; education; elementary education; graphic communications; information technology; parks, recreation and leisure facilities management; psychology; registered nursing/registered nurse; secondary education; social work.

Academics *Calendar:* semesters. *Degree:* certificates and associate. *Special study options:* academic remediation for entering students, adult/continuing education programs, advanced placement credit, cooperative education, distance learning, honors programs, internships, part-time degree program, services for LD students, study abroad, summer session for credit.

Library Alex D. Chisholm Learning Resources Center with 22,000 titles, 220 serial subscriptions, an OPAC, a Web page.

Student Life *Housing Options:* coed. *Activities and Organizations:* drama/theater group, choral group, Chieftain Student Newspaper, Phi Theta Kappa, Student Senate, Alcohol and Drug Prevention Team (ADAPT), Intramural sports. *Campus security:* controlled dormitory access. *Student services:* personal/psychological counseling.

Athletics Member NJCAA. *Intercollegiate sports:* basketball M(s)/W(s), cross-country running M/W, skiing (cross-country) M/W, volleyball W. *Intramural sports:* basketball M/W, bowling M/W, football M/W, golf M/W, skiing (downhill) M/W, softball M/W, track and field M/W, volleyball M/W.

Costs (2013–14) *Tuition:* area resident $3162 full-time, $102 per credit hour part-time; state resident $4340 full-time, $140 per credit hour part-time; nonresident $5301 full-time, $171 per credit hour part-time. Full-time tuition and fees vary according to course load and reciprocity agreements. Part-time tuition and fees vary according to course load and reciprocity agreements. *Required fees:* $952 full-time, $10 per credit hour part-time. *Room and board:* $6704; room only: $4004. *Payment plan:* installment. *Waivers:* senior citizens and employees or children of employees.

Financial Aid Of all full-time matriculated undergraduates who enrolled in 2012, 75 Federal Work-Study jobs (averaging $1800). 50 state and other part-time jobs (averaging $1800).

Applying *Options:* electronic application, early admission, deferred entrance. *Application fee:* $10. *Required:* high school transcript. *Application deadlines:* rolling (freshmen), 8/15 (out-of-state freshmen), 8/15 (transfers). *Notification:* continuous (freshmen).

Freshman Application Contact Ms. Kim Zeckovich, Director of Admissions, Marketing, and Public Relations, Gogebic Community College, E4946 Jackson Road, Ironwood, MI 49938. *Phone:* 906-932-4231 Ext. 347. *Toll-free phone:* 800-682-5910. *Fax:* 906-932-2339. *E-mail:* jeanneg@gogebic.edu. *Website:* http://www.gogebic.edu/.

Grand Rapids Community College
Grand Rapids, Michigan

- **District-supported** 2-year, founded 1914, part of Michigan Department of Education
- **Urban** 35-acre campus
- **Endowment** $34.2 million
- **Coed,** 16,590 undergraduate students, 34% full-time, 52% women, 48% men

Undergraduates 5,669 full-time, 10,921 part-time. Students come from 9 states and territories; 23 other countries; 1% are from out of state; 11% Black or African American, non-Hispanic/Latino; 8% Hispanic/Latino; 3% Asian, non-Hispanic/Latino; 0.7% American Indian or Alaska Native, non-Hispanic/Latino; 0.8% Two or more races, non-Hispanic/Latino; 6% Race/ethnicity unknown; 0.1% international; 6% transferred in. *Retention:* 55% of full-time freshmen returned.

Freshmen *Admission:* 10,217 applied, 3,529 enrolled. *Average high school GPA:* 2.8. *Test scores:* ACT scores over 18: 72%; ACT scores over 24: 19%; ACT scores over 30: 1%.

Faculty *Total:* 847, 30% full-time, 10% with terminal degrees. *Student/faculty ratio:* 22:1.

Majors Architectural engineering technology; architecture; art; automobile/automotive mechanics technology; business administration and management; chemistry; child-care and support services management; computer programming; corrections; criminal justice/law enforcement administration; criminal justice/police science; culinary arts; dental hygiene; drafting and design technology; electrical, electronic and communications engineering technology; engineering; English; fashion merchandising; foreign languages and literatures; forestry; geology/earth science; heating, air conditioning, ventilation and refrigeration maintenance technology; industrial technology; liberal arts and sciences/liberal studies; library and information science; licensed practical/vocational nurse training; mass communication/media; medical administrative assistant and medical secretary; music; plastics and polymer engineering technology; quality control technology; registered nursing/registered nurse; welding technology.

Academics *Calendar:* semesters. *Degree:* certificates and associate. *Special study options:* academic remediation for entering students, adult/continuing education programs, advanced placement credit, cooperative education, distance learning, English as a second language, honors programs, independent study, internships, off-campus study, part-time degree program, services for LD students, study abroad, summer session for credit.

Library Arthur Andrews Memorial Library with 161,263 titles, 33,064 serial subscriptions, 3,200 audiovisual materials, an OPAC, a Web page.

Student Life *Housing:* college housing not available. *Activities and Organizations:* drama/theater group, student-run newspaper, choral group, Student Congress, Phi Theta Kappa, Hispanic Student Organization, Student Gamers Association, Foreign Affairs Club. *Campus security:* 24-hour emergency response devices, late-night transport/escort service. *Student services:* personal/psychological counseling.

Athletics Member NJCAA. *Intercollegiate sports:* baseball M(s), basketball M(s)/W(s), cross-country running M/W, golf M(s), softball W(s), volleyball W(s).

Standardized Tests *Recommended:* SAT or ACT (for admission).

Costs (2013–14) *Tuition:* area resident $3090 full-time, $103 per contact hour part-time; state resident $6645 full-time, $222 per contact hour part-time; nonresident $9855 full-time, $329 per contact hour part-time. Full-time tuition and fees vary according to course load. Part-time tuition and fees vary according to course load. *Required fees:* $459 full-time, $6 per contact hour part-time, $147 per term part-time. *Payment plan:* installment. *Waivers:* employees or children of employees.

Financial Aid Of all full-time matriculated undergraduates who enrolled in 2008, 6,142 applied for aid, 4,896 were judged to have need, 1,012 had their need fully met. In 2008, 96 non-need-based awards were made. *Average financial aid package:* $4850. *Average need-based loan:* $2764. *Average need-based gift aid:* $3984. *Average non-need-based aid:* $1051.

Applying *Options:* electronic application, early admission, deferred entrance. *Required:* high school transcript. *Application deadline:* 8/30 (freshmen). *Notification:* continuous (freshmen), continuous (transfers).

Freshman Application Contact Ms. Diane Patrick, Director of Admissions, Grand Rapids Community College, Grand Rapids, MI 49503-3201. *Phone:* 616-234-4100. *Fax:* 616-234-4005. *E-mail:* dpatrick@grcc.edu.

Website: http://www.grcc.edu/.

Henry Ford Community College

Dearborn, Michigan

Freshman Application Contact Admissions Office, Henry Ford Community College, 5101 Evergreen Road, Dearborn, MI 48128-1495. *Phone:* 313-845-6403. *Toll-free phone:* 800-585-HFCC. *Fax:* 313-845-6464. *E-mail:* enroll@hfcc.edu.

Website: http://www.hfcc.edu/.

ITT Technical Institute

Canton, Michigan

- **Proprietary** primarily 2-year, founded 2002, part of ITT Educational Services, Inc.
- **Coed**

Majors Business administration and management; computer programming (specific applications); construction management; cyber/computer forensics and counterterrorism; drafting and design technology; electrical, electronic and communications engineering technology; forensic science and technology; graphic communications; industrial technology; information technology project management; medical/clinical assistant; network and system administration; project management; registered nursing/registered nurse.

Academics *Calendar:* quarters. *Degrees:* associate and bachelor's.

Student Life *Housing:* college housing not available.

Freshman Application Contact Director of Recruitment, ITT Technical Institute, 1905 South Haggerty Road, Canton, MI 48188-2025. *Phone:* 784-397-7800. *Toll-free phone:* 800-247-4477.

Website: http://www.itt-tech.edu/.

ITT Technical Institute

Dearborn, Michigan

- **Proprietary** primarily 2-year, part of ITT Educational Services, Inc.
- **Coed**

Majors Business administration and management; computer programming (specific applications); construction management; cyber/computer forensics and counterterrorism; drafting and design technology; electrical, electronic and communications engineering technology; forensic science and technology; graphic communications; industrial technology; information technology project management; network and system administration; project management.

Academics *Calendar:* quarters. *Degrees:* associate and bachelor's.

Freshman Application Contact Director of Recruitment, ITT Technical Institute, 19855 W. Outer Drive, Suite L10W, Dearborn, MI 48124. *Phone:* 313-278-5208. *Toll-free phone:* 800-605-0801.

Website: http://www.itt-tech.edu/.

ITT Technical Institute

Swartz Creek, Michigan

- **Proprietary** primarily 2-year, founded 2005, part of ITT Educational Services, Inc.
- **Coed**

Majors Business administration and management; computer programming (specific applications); construction management; cyber/computer forensics and counterterrorism; drafting and design technology; electrical, electronic and communications engineering technology; forensic science and technology; graphic communications; industrial technology; information technology project management; network and system administration; project management.

Academics *Calendar:* quarters. *Degrees:* associate and bachelor's.

Freshman Application Contact Director of Recruitment, ITT Technical Institute, 6359 Miller Road, Swartz Creek, MI 48473. *Phone:* 810-628-2500. *Toll-free phone:* 800-514-6564.

Website: http://www.itt-tech.edu/.

ITT Technical Institute

Troy, Michigan

- **Proprietary** primarily 2-year, founded 1987, part of ITT Educational Services, Inc.
- **Coed**

Majors Business administration and management; computer programming (specific applications); construction management; cyber/computer forensics and counterterrorism; drafting and design technology; electrical, electronic and communications engineering technology; forensic science and technology; game and interactive media design; graphic communications; industrial technology; information technology project management; network and system administration; project management.

Academics *Calendar:* quarters. *Degrees:* associate and bachelor's.

Student Life *Housing:* college housing not available.

Freshman Application Contact Director of Recruitment, ITT Technical Institute, 1522 East Big Beaver Road, Troy, MI 48083-1905. *Phone:* 248-524-1800. *Toll-free phone:* 800-832-6817.

Website: http://www.itt-tech.edu/.

ITT Technical Institute

Wyoming, Michigan

- **Proprietary** primarily 2-year, part of ITT Educational Services, Inc.
- **Coed**

Majors Business administration and management; computer programming (specific applications); construction management; cyber/computer forensics and counterterrorism; drafting and design technology; electrical, electronic and communications engineering technology; forensic science and technology; graphic communications; industrial technology; information technology project management; legal assistant/paralegal; network and system administration; project management.

Academics *Calendar:* quarters. *Degrees:* associate and bachelor's.

Student Life *Housing:* college housing not available.

Freshman Application Contact Director of Recruitment, ITT Technical Institute, 1980 Metro Court SW, Wyoming, MI 49519. *Phone:* 616-406-1200. *Toll-free phone:* 800-632-4676.

Website: http://www.itt-tech.edu/.

Jackson College

Jackson, Michigan

- **County-supported** 2-year, founded 1928
- **Suburban** 580-acre campus with easy access to Detroit
- **Coed,** 5,665 undergraduate students, 42% full-time, 62% women, 38% men

Undergraduates 2,389 full-time, 3,276 part-time. 2% are from out of state; 17% Black or African American, non-Hispanic/Latino; 9% Hispanic/Latino; 4% Two or more races, non-Hispanic/Latino; 8% Race/ethnicity unknown. *Retention:* 57% of full-time freshmen returned.

Freshmen *Admission:* 1,219 enrolled.

Faculty *Total:* 407, 21% full-time. *Student/faculty ratio:* 18:1.

Majors Accounting and finance; administrative assistant and secretarial science; airline pilot and flight crew; automobile/automotive mechanics technology; business administration and management; computer and information sciences and support services related; construction trades related; corrections; criminal justice/law enforcement administration; data processing and data processing technology; diagnostic medical sonography and ultrasound technology; early childhood education; electrical, electronic and communications engineering technology; emergency medical technology (EMT paramedic); executive assistant/executive secretary; general studies; graphic design; heating, ventilation, air conditioning and refrigeration engineering technology; liberal arts and sciences/liberal studies; licensed practical/vocational nurse training; marketing/marketing management; medical/clinical assistant; medical insurance/medical billing; medical radiologic technology; medical transcription; registered nursing/registered nurse.

Academics *Calendar:* semesters. *Degree:* certificates and associate. *Special study options:* academic remediation for entering students, accelerated degree program, adult/continuing education programs, advanced placement credit, cooperative education, distance learning, double majors, English as a second language, freshman honors college, honors programs, independent study, internships, part-time degree program, services for LD students, summer session for credit.

Library Atkinson Learning Resources Center.

Student Life *Housing Options:* coed. Campus housing is university owned. *Activities and Organizations:* drama/theater group, choral group. *Campus security:* 24-hour emergency response devices and patrols, student patrols, late-night transport/escort service, controlled dormitory access. *Student services:* health clinic.

Athletics Member NJCAA. *Intercollegiate sports:* baseball M(s), basketball M(s)/W(s), cross-country running M(s)/W(s), golf M(s)/W(s), soccer M(s)/W(s), softball W(s), volleyball W(s).

Applying *Options:* electronic application. *Required:* Minimum ACT of 16 is required for housing admission. *Required for some:* minimum #### GPA.

Freshman Application Contact Mr. Daniel Vainner, Registrar, Jackson College, 2111 Emmons Road, Jackson, MI 49201. *Phone:* 517-796-8425. *Toll-free phone:* 888-522-7344. *Fax:* 517-796-8446. *E-mail:* admissions@jccmi.edu.
Website: http://www.jccmi.edu/.

Kalamazoo Valley Community College
Kalamazoo, Michigan

Freshman Application Contact Kalamazoo Valley Community College, PO Box 4070, Kalamazoo, MI 49003-4070. *Phone:* 269-488-4207.
Website: http://www.kvcc.edu/.

Kellogg Community College
Battle Creek, Michigan

Freshman Application Contact Ms. Denise Newman, Director of Enrollment Services, Kellogg Community College, 450 North Avenue, Battle Creek, MI 49017. *Phone:* 269-965-3931 Ext. 2620. *Fax:* 269-965-4133. *E-mail:* harriss@kellogg.edu.
Website: http://www.kellogg.edu/.

Keweenaw Bay Ojibwa Community College
Baraga, Michigan

Freshman Application Contact Megan Shanahan, Admissions Officer, Keweenaw Bay Ojibwa Community College, 111 Beartown Road, Baraga, MI 49908. *Phone:* 909-353-4600. *E-mail:* megan@kbocc.org.
Website: http://www.kbocc.org/.

Kirtland Community College
Roscommon, Michigan

- **District-supported** 2-year, founded 1966
- **Rural** 180-acre campus
- **Coed,** 1,805 undergraduate students, 38% full-time, 63% women, 37% men

Undergraduates 694 full-time, 1,111 part-time. Students come from 4 states and territories; 3 other countries; 0.7% Black or African American, non-Hispanic/Latino; 1% Hispanic/Latino; 0.4% Asian, non-Hispanic/Latino; 0.1% Native Hawaiian or other Pacific Islander, non-Hispanic/Latino; 1% American Indian or Alaska Native, non-Hispanic/Latino; 1% Two or more races, non-Hispanic/Latino; 5% Race/ethnicity unknown; 0.3% international.

Freshmen *Admission:* 494 applied, 494 admitted, 271 enrolled. *Test scores:* ACT scores over 18: 70%; ACT scores over 24: 11%; ACT scores over 30: 2%.

Faculty *Total:* 116, 28% full-time. *Student/faculty ratio:* 18:1.

Majors Administrative assistant and secretarial science; animation, interactive technology, video graphics and special effects; art; automobile/automotive mechanics technology; business administration and management; cardiovascular technology; commercial photography; computer systems

analysis; corrections; corrections administration; cosmetology; criminal justice/law enforcement administration; criminal justice/police science; electrical, electronic and communications engineering technology; electromechanical technology; emergency medical technology (EMT paramedic); general studies; graphic design; health information/medical records technology; heating, air conditioning, ventilation and refrigeration maintenance technology; industrial and product design; information science/studies; legal administrative assistant/secretary; liberal arts and sciences/liberal studies; licensed practical/vocational nurse training; management information systems; medical administrative assistant and medical secretary; medical/clinical assistant; pharmacy technician; registered nursing/registered nurse; robotics technology; surgical technology; teacher assistant/aide; web/multimedia management and webmaster; welding technology.

Academics *Calendar:* semesters. *Degree:* certificates and associate. *Special study options:* academic remediation for entering students, adult/continuing education programs, advanced placement credit, cooperative education, distance learning, English as a second language, honors programs, independent study, internships, part-time degree program, services for LD students, summer session for credit.

Library Kirtland Community College Library with 33,000 titles, 320 serial subscriptions, an OPAC.

Student Life *Housing:* college housing not available. *Campus security:* 24-hour emergency response devices, student patrols, late-night transport/escort service, campus warning siren, uniformed armed police officers, RAVE alert system (text, email, voice).

Athletics Member NJCAA. *Intercollegiate sports:* basketball M(s)/W(s), cross-country running M(s)/W(s), golf M(s)/W(s).

Standardized Tests *Recommended:* ACT (for admission).

Costs (2013–14) *Tuition:* area resident $2880 full-time, $96 per contact hour part-time; state resident $4020 full-time, $134 per contact hour part-time; nonresident $6630 full-time, $221 per contact hour part-time. *Required fees:* $475 full-time, $16 per contact hour part-time, $35 per term part-time. *Payment plan:* installment. *Waivers:* minority students, senior citizens, and employees or children of employees.

Financial Aid Of all full-time matriculated undergraduates who enrolled in 2012, 50 Federal Work-Study jobs (averaging $1253). 28 state and other part-time jobs (averaging $1647).

Applying *Options:* electronic application. *Application deadlines:* rolling (freshmen), rolling (transfers). *Notification:* continuous until 8/22 (freshmen), continuous until 8/22 (transfers).

Freshman Application Contact Ms. Michelle Vyskocil, Dean of Student Services, Kirtland Community College, 10775 North Saint Helen Road, Roscommon, MI 48653. *Phone:* 989-275-5000 Ext. 248. *Fax:* 989-275-6789. *E-mail:* registrar@kirtland.edu.
Website: http://www.kirtland.edu/.

Lake Michigan College
Benton Harbor, Michigan

- **District-supported** 2-year, founded 1946, part of Michigan Department of Education
- **Small-town** 260-acre campus
- **Endowment** $6.4 million
- **Coed**

Undergraduates 1,508 full-time, 3,040 part-time. Students come from 5 states and territories; 50 other countries; 2% are from out of state; 21% Black or African American, non-Hispanic/Latino; 6% Hispanic/Latino; 1% Asian, non-Hispanic/Latino; 0.4% Native Hawaiian or other Pacific Islander, non-Hispanic/Latino; 0.8% American Indian or Alaska Native, non-Hispanic/Latino; 2% Two or more races, non-Hispanic/Latino; 5% Race/ethnicity unknown; 6% transferred in. *Retention:* 42% of full-time freshmen returned.

Faculty *Student/faculty ratio:* 17:1.

Academics *Calendar:* semesters. *Degree:* certificates and associate. *Special study options:* academic remediation for entering students, adult/continuing education programs, cooperative education, distance learning, English as a second language, honors programs, independent study, off-campus study, part-time degree program, services for LD students, student-designed majors, summer session for credit.

Student Life *Campus security:* 24-hour emergency response devices, contracted campus security force.

Athletics Member NJCAA.

Costs (2013–14) *Tuition:* area resident $2610 full-time, $87 per contact hour part-time; state resident $4035 full-time, $135 per contact hour part-time; nonresident $5385 full-time, $180 per contact hour part-time. *Required fees:* $1260 full-time, $42 per contact hour part-time. *Payment plans:* installment, deferred payment.

Applying *Options:* electronic application. *Required:* high school transcript. *Required for some:* interview.

Freshman Application Contact Mr. Louis Thomas, Lead Admissions Specialist, Lake Michigan College, 2755 East Napier Avenue, Benton Harbor, MI 49022-1899. *Phone:* 269-927-6584. *Toll-free phone:* 800-252-1LMC. *Fax:* 269-927-6718. *E-mail:* thomas@lakemichigancollege.edu. *Website:* http://www.lakemichigancollege.edu/.

Lansing Community College
Lansing, Michigan

- **State and locally supported** 2-year, founded 1957, part of Michigan Department of Education
- **Urban** 28-acre campus
- **Endowment** $7.3 million
- **Coed,** 17,562 undergraduate students, 38% full-time, 55% women, 45% men

Undergraduates 6,587 full-time, 10,975 part-time. Students come from 17 states and territories; 37 other countries; 1% are from out of state; 12% Black or African American, non-Hispanic/Latino; 2% Hispanic/Latino; 3% Asian, non-Hispanic/Latino; 0.3% Native Hawaiian or other Pacific Islander, non-Hispanic/Latino; 0.7% American Indian or Alaska Native, non-Hispanic/Latino; 3% Two or more races, non-Hispanic/Latino; 10% Race/ethnicity unknown; 0.6% international.

Freshmen *Admission:* 3,386 enrolled.

Faculty *Total:* 1,898, 11% full-time. *Student/faculty ratio:* 13:1.

Majors Accounting related; accounting technology and bookkeeping; administrative assistant and secretarial science; African American/Black studies; agricultural business and management; aircraft powerplant technology; airframe mechanics and aircraft maintenance technology; airline pilot and flight crew; American studies; animation, interactive technology, video graphics and special effects; anthropology; architectural engineering technology; architectural technology; art; art history, criticism and conservation; autobody/collision and repair technology; automobile/automotive mechanics technology; avionics maintenance technology; banking and financial support services; biology/biological sciences; biotechnology; business administration and management; business/commerce; carpentry; chemical technology; chemistry; child-care provision; cinematography and film/video production; civil engineering technology; community organization and advocacy; computer and information sciences; computer programming (specific applications); computer systems networking and telecommunications; computer technology/computer systems technology; construction/heavy equipment/earthmoving equipment operation; construction management; corrections; criminal justice/police science; customer service support/call center/teleservice operation; data modeling/warehousing and database administration; dental hygiene; diagnostic medical sonography and ultrasound technology; dramatic/theater arts; e-commerce; economics; electrical and power transmission installation; electrician; electromechanical technology; elementary education; emergency medical technology (EMT paramedic); energy management and systems technology; engineering; engineering physics/applied physics; English; environmental engineering technology; fashion merchandising; fine/studio arts; fire science/firefighting; foreign languages and literatures; French; geography; Germanic languages; graphic design; health and physical education/fitness; heating, air conditioning, ventilation and refrigeration maintenance technology; higher education/higher education administration; histologic technician; history; hotel/motel administration; humanities; human resources management; industrial production technologies related; interior design; international business/trade/commerce; international relations and affairs; Japanese; juvenile corrections; legal assistant/paralegal; liberal arts and sciences/liberal studies; licensed practical/vocational nurse training; machine tool technology; magnetic resonance imaging (MRI) technology; management information systems; mathematics; mechanical drafting and CAD/CADD; music; music performance; office management; philosophy; photography; political science and government; premedical studies; psychology; radio and television broadcasting technology; radiologic technology/science; real estate; registered nursing/registered nurse; religious studies; sales, distribution, and marketing operations; secondary education; selling skills and sales; sign language interpretation and translation; social sciences; sociology; Spanish; speech communication and rhetoric; surgical technology; surveying technology; teacher assistant/aide; theater design and technology; tourism and travel services management; veterinary/animal health technology; web page, digital/multimedia and information resources design; welding technology.

Academics *Calendar:* semesters. *Degree:* certificates and associate. *Special study options:* academic remediation for entering students, adult/continuing education programs, advanced placement credit, cooperative education, distance learning, double majors, English as a second language, external degree program, honors programs, independent study, internships, part-time degree program, services for LD students, study abroad, summer session for credit. *ROTC:* Army (c), Air Force (c).

Library Lansing Community College Library with 340,420 titles, 164 serial subscriptions, 7,455 audiovisual materials, an OPAC, a Web page.

Student Life *Housing:* college housing not available. *Activities and Organizations:* drama/theater group, student-run newspaper, choral group, American Marketing Association, Phi Theta Kappa, Future Teachers' Club, Health Career Related Clubs (Dental Hygiene, Nurses), Gay-Straight Alliance, national fraternities, national sororities. *Campus security:* 24-hour emergency response devices and patrols, student patrols, late-night transport/escort service. *Student services:* personal/psychological counseling, women's center.

Athletics Member NJCAA. *Intercollegiate sports:* baseball M(s), basketball M(s)/W(s), cross-country running M(s)/W(s), softball W(s), track and field M/W, volleyball W(s).

Costs (2013–14) *Tuition:* area resident $2490 full-time, $83 per credit hour part-time; state resident $4980 full-time, $166 per credit hour part-time; nonresident $7470 full-time, $249 per credit hour part-time. *Required fees:* $230 full-time, $6 per credit hour part-time, $25 per credit hour part-time. *Payment plan:* installment. *Waivers:* senior citizens and employees or children of employees.

Financial Aid Of all full-time matriculated undergraduates who enrolled in 2012, 125 Federal Work-Study jobs (averaging $2636). 122 state and other part-time jobs (averaging $2563).

Applying *Options:* electronic application, early admission, deferred entrance. *Required for some:* essay or personal statement, high school transcript, 2 letters of recommendation, interview, Special requirements for health, aviation, music, police academy, and fire academy program admissions. *Application deadlines:* 8/7 (freshmen), 8/7 (transfers).

Freshman Application Contact Ms. Tammy Grossbauer, Director of Admissions/Registrar, Lansing Community College, 1121 - Enrollment Services, PO BOX 40010, Lansing, MI 48901. *Phone:* 517-483-1200. *Toll-free phone:* 800-644-4LCC. *Fax:* 517-483-1170. *E-mail:* grossbt@lcc.edu. *Website:* http://www.lcc.edu/.

Macomb Community College
Warren, Michigan

- **District-supported** 2-year, founded 1954, part of Michigan Public Community College System
- **Suburban** 384-acre campus with easy access to Detroit
- **Endowment** $17.3 million
- **Coed,** 23,446 undergraduate students, 32% full-time, 53% women, 47% men

Undergraduates 7,508 full-time, 15,938 part-time. Students come from 4 states and territories; 11% Black or African American, non-Hispanic/Latino; 2% Hispanic/Latino; 4% Asian, non-Hispanic/Latino; 0.1% Native Hawaiian or other Pacific Islander, non-Hispanic/Latino; 0.6% American Indian or Alaska Native, non-Hispanic/Latino; 1% Two or more races, non-Hispanic/Latino; 10% Race/ethnicity unknown; 2% international. *Retention:* 56% of full-time freshmen returned.

Freshmen *Admission:* 1,475 enrolled.

Faculty *Total:* 1,083, 21% full-time, 10% with terminal degrees. *Student/faculty ratio:* 27:1.

Majors Accounting; administrative assistant and secretarial science; agriculture; architectural drafting and CAD/CADD; automobile/automotive mechanics technology; automotive engineering technology; biology/biological sciences; business administration and management; business automation/technology/data entry; business/commerce; cabinetmaking and millwork; chemistry; child-care and support services management; civil engineering technology; commercial and advertising art; computer programming; computer programming (specific applications); construction engineering technology; criminal justice/law enforcement administration; criminal justice/police science; culinary arts; drafting and design technology; drafting/design engineering technologies related; electrical, electronic and communications engineering technology; electrical/electronics equipment installation and repair; electromechanical technology; emergency medical technology (EMT paramedic); energy management and systems technology; engineering related; finance; fire prevention and safety technology; forensic science and technology; general studies; graphic and printing equipment operation/production; heating, air conditioning, ventilation and refrigeration maintenance technology; heating, ventilation, air conditioning and refrigeration engineering technology; industrial mechanics and maintenance technology; industrial technology; international/global studies; legal assistant/paralegal; legal studies; liberal arts and sciences/liberal studies; machine tool technology; manufacturing engineering technology; marketing/marketing management; mathematics; mechanical drafting and CAD/CADD; mechanical engineering/mechanical technology; mechanic and repair technologies related; medical/clinical assistant; mental health counseling; metallurgical technology; music performance; occupational therapist assistant; operations management; physical therapy technology; plastics and polymer engineering technology; plumbing technology; pre-engineering; quality control and safety technologies related; quality control technology; registered nursing/registered nurse; respiratory care therapy; robotics technology; sheet metal technology; social psychology; speech communication and rhetoric; surgical technology; surveying technology; tool and die technology; veterinary/animal health technology; welding technology. **Academics** *Calendar:* semesters. *Degree:* certificates and associate. *Special study options:* academic remediation for entering students, adult/continuing education programs, advanced placement credit, cooperative education, English as a second language, honors programs, internships, off-campus study, part-time degree program, services for LD students, student-designed majors, summer session for credit.

Library Library of South Campus, Library of Center Campus with 159,226 titles, 4,240 serial subscriptions, an OPAC.

Student Life *Housing:* college housing not available. *Activities and Organizations:* drama/theater group, Phi Beta Kappa, Adventure Unlimited, Alpha Rho Rho, SADD. *Campus security:* 24-hour emergency response devices and patrols, late-night transport/escort service, security phones in parking lots, surveillance cameras. *Student services:* health clinic, personal/psychological counseling.

Athletics Member NJCAA. *Intercollegiate sports:* baseball M(s), basketball M(s), cross-country running M(s)/W(s), soccer M(s), softball W(s), track and field M(s)/W(s), volleyball W(s). *Intramural sports:* baseball M, basketball M, bowling M/W, cross-country running M/W, football M/W, skiing (cross-country) M/W, skiing (downhill) M/W, volleyball M/W.

Applying *Options:* early admission, deferred entrance. *Application deadlines:* rolling (freshmen), rolling (transfers).

Freshman Application Contact Mr. Brian Bouwman, Coordinator of Admissions and Transfer Credit, Macomb Community College, G312, 14500 East 12 Mile Road, Warren, MI 48088-3896. *Phone:* 586-445-7246. *Toll-free phone:* 866-MACOMB1. *Fax:* 586-445-7140. *E-mail:* stevensr@macomb.edu. *Website:* http://www.macomb.edu/.

Mid Michigan Community College
Harrison, Michigan

Freshman Application Contact Jennifer Casebeer, Admissions Specialist, Mid Michigan Community College, 1375 South Clare Avenue, Harrison, MI 48625-9447. *Phone:* 989-386-6661. *E-mail:* apply@midmich.edu. *Website:* http://www.midmich.edu/.

Monroe County Community College
Monroe, Michigan

- **County-supported** 2-year, founded 1964, part of Michigan Department of Education
- **Small-town** 150-acre campus with easy access to Detroit, Toledo
- **Coed**

Undergraduates Students come from 3 other countries; 4% are from out of state.

Freshmen *Admission:* 1,700 applied, 1,698 admitted. *Average high school GPA:* 2.5.

Faculty *Total:* 196, 28% full-time.

Majors Accounting; administrative assistant and secretarial science; architectural engineering technology; art; biology/biological sciences; business administration and management; child development; clinical laboratory science/medical technology; computer and information sciences related; computer engineering technology; computer graphics; computer programming (specific applications); criminal justice/police science; criminal justice/safety; culinary arts; data processing and data processing technology; drafting and design technology; electrical, electronic and communications engineering technology; elementary education; English; finance; funeral service and mortuary science; industrial technology; information technology; journalism; legal administrative assistant/secretary; liberal arts and sciences/liberal studies; marketing/marketing management; mass communication/media; mathematics; medical administrative assistant and medical secretary; physical therapy; pre-engineering; psychology; registered nursing/registered nurse; respiratory care therapy; rhetoric and composition; social work; web/multimedia management and webmaster; web page, digital/multimedia and information resources design; welding technology; word processing.

Academics *Calendar:* semesters. *Degree:* certificates and associate. *Special study options:* academic remediation for entering students, advanced placement credit, distance learning, independent study, part-time degree program, services for LD students, summer session for credit.

Library Campbell Learning Resource Center with 47,352 titles, 321 serial subscriptions, an OPAC.

Student Life *Housing:* college housing not available. *Activities and Organizations:* drama/theater group, student-run newspaper, choral group, student government, Society of Auto Engineers, Oasis, Nursing Students Organization. *Campus security:* police patrols during open hours.

Athletics *Intramural sports:* soccer M/W, volleyball M/W.

Standardized Tests *Required:* ACT, ACT COMPASS (for admission). *Required for some:* ACT (for admission). *Recommended:* ACT (for admission).

Costs (2013–14) *Tuition:* area resident $2496 full-time, $104 per contact hour part-time; state resident $4080 full-time, $170 per contact hour part-time; nonresident $4512 full-time, $188 per contact hour part-time. Full-time tuition and fees vary according to reciprocity agreements. Part-time tuition and fees vary according to reciprocity agreements. *Required fees:* $204 full-time, $35 per term part-time. *Payment plan:* installment. *Waivers:* senior citizens and employees or children of employees.

Applying *Options:* early admission, deferred entrance. *Required:* high school transcript, Baseline cut scores on ACT or COMPASS. *Application deadline:* rolling (transfers). *Notification:* continuous (freshmen), continuous (transfers).

Freshman Application Contact Mr. Mark V. Hall, Director of Admissions and Guidance Services, Monroe County Community College, 1555 South Raisinville Road, Monroe, MI 48161. *Phone:* 734-384-4261. *Toll-free phone:* 877-YES-MCCC. *Fax:* 734-242-9711. *E-mail:* mhall@monroeccc.edu. *Website:* http://www.monroeccc.edu/.

Montcalm Community College
Sidney, Michigan

- **State and locally supported** 2-year, founded 1965, part of Michigan Department of Education
- **Rural** 240-acre campus with easy access to Grand Rapids
- **Endowment** $4.7 million
- **Coed**

Undergraduates 680 full-time, 1,331 part-time. 0.2% Black or African American, non-Hispanic/Latino; 2% Hispanic/Latino; 0.2% Asian, non-Hispanic/Latino; 0.2% American Indian or Alaska Native, non-Hispanic/Latino; 1% Two or more races, non-Hispanic/Latino; 28% Race/ethnicity unknown; 19% transferred in.

Academics *Calendar:* semesters. *Degree:* certificates and associate. *Special study options:* academic remediation for entering students, adult/continuing education programs, advanced placement credit, cooperative education, distance learning, double majors, independent study, internships, off-campus study, part-time degree program, services for LD students, study abroad, summer session for credit.

Costs (2013–14) *Tuition:* area resident $2730 full-time, $91 per credit hour part-time; state resident $5130 full-time, $171 per credit hour part-time; nonresident $7620 full-time, $254 per credit hour part-time. Full-time tuition and fees vary according to course load. Part-time tuition and fees vary according to course load. *Required fees:* $420 full-time, $14 per credit hour part-time.

Financial Aid *Average indebtedness upon graduation:* $2600.

Applying *Options:* electronic application, early admission, deferred entrance. *Recommended:* high school transcript.

Freshman Application Contact Ms. Debra Alexander, Associate Dean of Student Services, Montcalm Community College, 2800 College Drive, SW, Sidney, MI 48885. *Phone:* 989-328-1276. *Toll-free phone:* 877-328-2111. *E-mail:* admissions@montcalm.edu. *Website:* http://www.montcalm.edu/.

Mott Community College
Flint, Michigan

- **District-supported** 2-year, founded 1923, part of Michigan Workforce Programs/Postsecondary Services/Community College Services
- **Urban** 32-acre campus with easy access to Detroit
- **Endowment** $37.5 million
- **Coed**, 9,683 undergraduate students, 30% full-time, 58% women, 42% men

Undergraduates 2,903 full-time, 6,780 part-time. 20% Black or African American, non-Hispanic/Latino; 4% Hispanic/Latino; 0.5% Asian, non-Hispanic/Latino; 0.1% Native Hawaiian or other Pacific Islander, non-Hispanic/Latino; 1% American Indian or Alaska Native, non-Hispanic/Latino; 3% Two or more races, non-Hispanic/Latino; 7% Race/ethnicity unknown; 1% international; 2% transferred in.

Freshmen *Admission:* 741 enrolled.

Faculty *Total:* 509, 28% full-time, 12% with terminal degrees. *Student/faculty ratio:* 20:1.

Majors Accounting technology and bookkeeping; administrative assistant and secretarial science; architectural engineering technology; automobile/automotive mechanics technology; baking and pastry arts; biology/biological sciences; business administration and management; business/commerce; child-care provision; cinematography and film/video production; communications technology; community health services counseling; computer programming; computer programming (specific applications); computer systems networking and telecommunications; criminal justice/police science; culinary arts; dental assisting; dental hygiene; drafting and design technology; early childhood education; electrical, electronic and communications engineering technology; emergency medical technology (EMT paramedic); engineering technologies and engineering related; entrepreneurship; fire prevention and safety technology; food service systems administration; general studies; graphic design; health information/medical records technology; heating, ventilation, air conditioning and refrigeration engineering technology; histologic technician; liberal arts and sciences/liberal studies; marketing/marketing management; mechanical engineering/mechanical technology; medical informatics; medical radiologic technology; music technology; occupational therapist assistant; photography; physical therapy technology; precision production related; registered nursing/registered nurse; respiratory care therapy; salon/beauty salon management; sign language interpretation and translation; visual and performing arts; web page, digital/multimedia and information resources design.

Academics *Calendar:* semesters. *Degree:* certificates and associate. *Special study options:* academic remediation for entering students, accelerated degree program, adult/continuing education programs, advanced placement credit, cooperative education, distance learning, double majors, English as a second language, honors programs, independent study, internships, part-time degree program, services for LD students, summer session for credit.

Library Charles Stewart Mott Library with 70,089 titles, 160 serial subscriptions, an OPAC, a Web page.

Student Life *Housing:* college housing not available. *Activities and Organizations:* student-run newspaper, choral group, Otaku Club, L.E.A.R.N, Respiratory Care Student Society, Student Nurses Association, Transitions Cosmetology. *Campus security:* 24-hour emergency response devices and patrols, student patrols, late-night transport/escort service. *Student services:* health clinic, personal/psychological counseling.

Athletics Member NJCAA. *Intercollegiate sports:* baseball M(s), basketball M(s)/W(s), cross-country running M(s)/W(s), golf M(s), softball W(s), volleyball W(s). *Intramural sports:* cheerleading W(c).

Costs (2014–15) *Tuition:* area resident $2940 full-time, $123 per contact hour part-time; state resident $4271 full-time, $178 per contact hour part-time; nonresident $6085 full-time, $254 per contact hour part-time. Full-time tuition and fees vary according to course load. Part-time tuition and fees vary according to course load. *Required fees:* $617 full-time, $16 per contact hour part-time, $123 per term part-time. *Payment plan:* installment. *Waivers:* senior citizens and employees or children of employees.

Financial Aid Of all full-time matriculated undergraduates who enrolled in 2011, 16,668 applied for aid, 15,858 were judged to have need, 810 had their need fully met. 7,449 Federal Work-Study jobs (averaging $6303). In 2011, 95 non-need-based awards were made. *Average percent of need met:* 79%. *Average financial aid package:* $21,292. *Average need-based loan:* $3019. *Average need-based gift aid:* $3471. *Average non-need-based aid:* $2356.

Applying *Options:* electronic application, early admission, deferred entrance. *Required:* high school transcript. *Application deadline:* 8/31 (freshmen). *Notification:* continuous (transfers).

Freshman Application Contact Ms. Regina Broomfield, Supervisor of Admissions Operations, Mott Community College, 1401 East Court Street, Flint, MI 48503. *Phone:* 810-762-0358. *Toll-free phone:* 800-852-8614. *Fax:* 810-232-9442. *E-mail:* regina.broomfield@mcc.edu. *Website:* http://www.mcc.edu/.

Muskegon Community College
Muskegon, Michigan

Freshman Application Contact Ms. Darlene Peklar, Enrollment Generalist, Muskegon Community College, 221 South Quarterline Road, Muskegon, MI 49442-1493. *Phone:* 231-777-0366. *Toll-free phone:* 866-711-4622. *E-mail:* Dalene.Peklar@muskegoncc.edu. *Website:* http://www.muskegoncc.edu/.

North Central Michigan College
Petoskey, Michigan

Director of Admissions Ms. Julieanne Tobin, Director of Enrollment Management, North Central Michigan College, 1515 Howard Street, Petoskey, MI 49770-8717. *Phone:* 231-439-6511. *Toll-free phone:* 888-298-6605. *E-mail:* jtobin@ncmich.edu. *Website:* http://www.ncmich.edu/.

Northwestern Michigan College
Traverse City, Michigan

Freshman Application Contact Mr. James Bensley, Coordinator of Admissions, Northwestern Michigan College, 1701 East Front Street, Traverse City, MI 49686-3061. *Phone:* 231-995-1034. *Toll-free phone:* 800-748-0566. *Fax:* 616-955-1339. *E-mail:* welcome@nmc.edu. *Website:* http://www.nmc.edu/.

Oakland Community College
Bloomfield Hills, Michigan

- **State and locally supported** 2-year, founded 1964
- **Suburban** 540-acre campus with easy access to Detroit
- **Endowment** $1.2 million
- **Coed**, 26,405 undergraduate students, 31% full-time, 57% women, 43% men

Undergraduates 8,058 full-time, 18,347 part-time. Students come from 11 states and territories; 47 other countries; 0.1% are from out of state; 30% Black or African American, non-Hispanic/Latino; 3% Hispanic/Latino; 2% Asian, non-Hispanic/Latino; 0.1% Native Hawaiian or other Pacific Islander, non-Hispanic/Latino; 0.5% American Indian or Alaska Native, non-Hispanic/Latino; 2% Two or more races, non-Hispanic/Latino; 3% Race/ethnicity unknown; 4% international; 5% transferred in. *Retention:* 48% of full-time freshmen returned.

Freshmen *Admission:* 7,672 applied, 7,672 admitted, 2,412 enrolled.

Faculty *Total:* 1,458, 17% full-time. *Student/faculty ratio:* 22:1.

Majors Accounting and business/management; accounting technology and bookkeeping; architectural engineering technology; art; automobile/automotive mechanics technology; biotechnology; business administration and management; business automation/technology/data entry; carpentry; ceramic arts and ceramics; child-care and support services management; community health services counseling; computer and information sciences and support services related; computer and information systems security; computer/information technology services administration related; computer programming; computer support specialist; computer systems analysis; construction management; corrections; cosmetology; court reporting; criminalistics and criminal science; criminal justice/law enforcement administration; criminal justice/police science; culinary arts; dental hygiene; diagnostic medical sonography and ultrasound technology; drafting and design technology; dramatic/theater arts and stagecraft related; electrical, electronic and communications engineering technology; electrician; electromechanical technology; emergency medical technology (EMT paramedic); entrepreneurship; film/cinema/video studies; fire science/firefighting; general studies; graphic design; health/health-care administration; heating, ventilation, air conditioning and refrigeration engineering technology; histologic technology/histotechnologist; hotel/motel administration; industrial technology; interior design; international/global studies; kinesiology and exercise science; landscaping and groundskeeping; legal assistant/paralegal; liberal arts and sciences and humanities related; liberal arts and sciences/liberal studies; library and archives assisting; manufacturing engineering technology; massage therapy; materials engineering; mechanical drafting and CAD/CADD; medical/clinical assistant; medical radiologic technology; medical transcription; music performance; music theory and composition; nanotechnology; nuclear medical technology; occupational therapist assistant; office management; pharmacy technician; photography; physical therapy technology; pipefitting and sprinkler fitting; precision metal working related; radio and television broadcasting technology; registered nursing/registered nurse; respiratory care therapy; restaurant/food services management; robotics technology; salon/beauty salon management; science technologies related; sign language interpretation and translation; surgical technology; veterinary/animal health technology; voice and opera; welding technology.

Academics *Calendar:* semesters. *Degree:* certificates and associate. *Special study options:* academic remediation for entering students, adult/continuing education programs, advanced placement credit, cooperative education, distance learning, English as a second language, independent study, internships, off-campus study, part-time degree program, services for LD students, study abroad, summer session for credit.

Library Main Library plus 5 others with 260,016 titles, 1,652 serial subscriptions, 9,219 audiovisual materials, an OPAC, a Web page.

Student Life *Housing:* college housing not available. *Activities and Organizations:* drama/theater group, choral group, Phi Theta Kappa, Gamers Guild, BELIEVERS, Criminal Justice Student Organization, student government. *Campus security:* 24-hour emergency response devices, late-night transport/escort service. *Student services:* personal/psychological counseling, women's center.

Athletics Member NJCAA. *Intercollegiate sports:* basketball M(s)/W(s), cross-country running M(s)/W(s), golf M(s), softball W(s), volleyball W(s).

Costs (2013–14) *Tuition:* area resident $2292 full-time, $76 per credit hour part-time; state resident $4173 full-time, $139 per credit hour part-time; nonresident $5855 full-time, $195 per credit hour part-time. Full-time tuition and fees vary according to course load and reciprocity agreements. Part-time tuition and fees vary according to course load and reciprocity agreements. *Required fees:* $70 full-time, $35 per term part-time. *Waivers:* senior citizens and employees or children of employees.

Financial Aid Of all full-time matriculated undergraduates who enrolled in 2013, 3,517 applied for aid, 3,077 were judged to have need, 4 had their need fully met. 9 Federal Work-Study jobs (averaging $5061). In 2013, 53 non-need-based awards were made. *Average percent of need met:* 42%. *Average financial aid package:* $4484. *Average need-based loan:* $1471. *Average need-based gift aid:* $4834. *Average non-need-based aid:* $1779.

Applying *Options:* electronic application, deferred entrance. *Application deadlines:* rolling (freshmen), rolling (transfers). *Notification:* continuous (freshmen), continuous (transfers).

Freshman Application Contact Stephan M. Linden, Registrar, Oakland Community College, 2480 Opdyke Road, Bloomfield Hills, MI 48304-2266. *Phone:* 248-341-2192. *Fax:* 248-341-2099. *E-mail:* smlinden@oaklandcc.edu.
Website: http://www.oaklandcc.edu/.

Saginaw Chippewa Tribal College
Mount Pleasant, Michigan

- **Independent** 2-year, founded 1998
- **Coed,** 127 undergraduate students, 36% full-time, 65% women, 35% men

Undergraduates 46 full-time, 81 part-time.

Freshmen *Admission:* 18 applied, 18 admitted, 27 enrolled.

Faculty *Total:* 18, 33% full-time, 17% with terminal degrees. *Student/faculty ratio:* 9:1.

Majors American Indian/Native American studies; business/commerce; liberal arts and sciences/liberal studies.

Academics *Calendar:* semesters. *Degree:* associate.

Costs (2013–14) *Tuition:* $1560 full-time, $60 per credit hour part-time. Full-time tuition and fees vary according to class time, course level, course load, degree level, location, program, and student level. Part-time tuition and fees vary according to class time, course level, course load, degree level, location, program, and student level. *Required fees:* $650 full-time, $25 per credit hour part-time. *Payment plans:* installment, deferred payment.

Applying *Required:* high school transcript.

Freshman Application Contact Ms. Amanda Flaugher, Admissions Officer/Registrar/Financial Aid, Saginaw Chippewa Tribal College, 2274 Enterprise Drive, Mount Pleasant, MI 48858. *Phone:* 989-775-4123. *Fax:* 989-775-4528. *E-mail:* flaugher.amanda@sagchip.org.
Website: http://www.sagchip.edu/.

St. Clair County Community College
Port Huron, Michigan

- **State and locally supported** 2-year, founded 1923, part of Michigan Department of Education
- **Small-town** 25-acre campus with easy access to Detroit
- **Coed,** 4,324 undergraduate students, 41% full-time, 59% women, 41% men

Undergraduates 1,763 full-time, 2,561 part-time. 3% Black or African American, non-Hispanic/Latino; 4% Hispanic/Latino; 0.4% Asian, non-Hispanic/Latino; 0.1% Native Hawaiian or other Pacific Islander, non-Hispanic/Latino; 0.9% American Indian or Alaska Native, non-Hispanic/Latino; 1% Two or more races, non-Hispanic/Latino; 3% Race/ethnicity unknown; 0.2% international; 22% transferred in. *Retention:* 59% of full-time freshmen returned.

Freshmen *Admission:* 757 enrolled.

Faculty *Total:* 249, 29% full-time. *Student/faculty ratio:* 19:1.

Majors Accounting technology and bookkeeping; architectural engineering technology; business/commerce; commercial and advertising art; computer programming; criminal justice/police science; data processing and data processing technology; electrical, electronic and communications engineering technology; energy management and systems technology; engineering; executive assistant/executive secretary; health information/medical records technology; industrial production technologies related; kindergarten/preschool education; liberal arts and sciences/liberal studies; marketing/marketing management; massage therapy; mechanical drafting and CAD/CADD; medical administrative assistant and medical secretary; medical/clinical assistant; office management; robotics technology; teacher assistant/aide; transportation and materials moving related; web/multimedia management and webmaster; welding technology.

Academics *Calendar:* semesters. *Degree:* certificates and associate. *Special study options:* academic remediation for entering students, adult/continuing education programs, advanced placement credit, cooperative education, distance learning, honors programs, independent study, part-time degree program, summer session for credit.

Library Library plus 1 other with an OPAC, a Web page.

Student Life *Housing:* college housing not available. *Activities and Organizations:* drama/theater group, student-run newspaper, radio station, Phi Theta Kappa, Zombie Defense Council, Marketing and Management Club, Gay-Straight Alliance, Criminal Justice Club. *Campus security:* 24-hour emergency response devices, late-night transport/escort service, patrols by security until 10 pm. *Student services:* personal/psychological counseling.

Athletics Member NJCAA. *Intercollegiate sports:* baseball M(s), basketball M(s)/W(s), golf M, softball W(s), volleyball W(s).

Costs (2013–14) *Tuition:* area resident $2889 full-time, $96 per contact hour part-time; state resident $5346 full-time, $187 per contact hour part-time; nonresident $7641 full-time, $272 per contact hour part-time. Full-time tuition and fees vary according to course load and location. Part-time tuition and fees vary according to course load and location. *Required fees:* $120 full-time, $11 per contact hour part-time. *Payment plan:* deferred payment. *Waivers:* senior citizens and employees or children of employees.

Applying *Options:* electronic application, early admission. *Required:* high school transcript. *Application deadlines:* rolling (freshmen), · rolling (transfers).

Freshman Application Contact St. Clair County Community College, 323 Erie Street, PO Box 5015, Port Huron, MI 48061-5015. *Phone:* 810-989-5501. *Toll-free phone:* 800-553-2427.
Website: http://www.sc4.edu/.

Schoolcraft College
Livonia, Michigan

- **District-supported** 2-year, founded 1961, part of Michigan Department of Education
- **Suburban** 183-acre campus with easy access to Detroit
- **Coed,** 12,384 undergraduate students, 35% full-time, 55% women, 45% men

Undergraduates 4,385 full-time, 7,999 part-time. 15% Black or African American, non-Hispanic/Latino; 3% Hispanic/Latino; 3% Asian, non-Hispanic/Latino; 0.2% Native Hawaiian or other Pacific Islander, non-Hispanic/Latino; 0.7% American Indian or Alaska Native, non-Hispanic/Latino; 2% Two or more races, non-Hispanic/Latino; 8% Race/ethnicity unknown; 1% international; 23% transferred in. *Retention:* 58% of full-time freshmen returned.

Freshmen *Admission:* 1,876 enrolled.

Faculty *Total:* 514, 18% full-time. *Student/faculty ratio:* 28:1.

Majors Accounting technology and bookkeeping; administrative assistant and secretarial science; baking and pastry arts; biomedical technology; business administration and management; business automation/technology/data entry; business/commerce; child development; computer graphics; computer installation and repair technology; computer programming; computer programming (specific applications); computer systems networking and telecommunications; criminal justice/police science; culinary arts; drafting and design technology; education; electrical, electronic and communications engineering technology; electrical/electronics equipment installation and repair; emergency medical technology (EMT paramedic); engineering; environmental engineering technology; executive assistant/executive secretary; fine arts related; fire science/firefighting; general studies; health information/medical records technology; health services/allied health/health sciences; homeland security, law enforcement, firefighting and protective services related; licensed practical/vocational nurse training; manufacturing engineering technology; marketing/marketing management; massage therapy; medical insurance/medical billing; medical office assistant; medical transcription; metallurgical technology; nursing assistant/aide and patient care assistant/aide; phlebotomy technology; pre-pharmacy studies; radio and television broadcasting technology; recording arts technology; registered nursing/registered nurse; salon/beauty salon management; sculpture; small business administration; web page, digital/multimedia and information resources design; welding technology.

Academics *Calendar:* semesters. *Degree:* certificates and associate. *Special study options:* academic remediation for entering students, adult/continuing education programs, advanced placement credit, distance learning, English as a second language, honors programs, independent study, internships, part-time degree program, services for LD students, study abroad, summer session for credit.

Library Bradner Library with an OPAC.

Student Life *Housing:* college housing not available. *Activities and Organizations:* drama/theater group, student-run newspaper, choral group, Phi Theta Kappa, The Schoolcraft Connection Newspaper, Student Activities Board, Project Playhem Gaming Club, Otaku Anime Japanese Animation Club. *Campus security:* 24-hour emergency response devices and patrols, late-night transport/escort service. *Student services:* health clinic, personal/psychological counseling, women's center, legal services.

Athletics Member NJCAA. *Intercollegiate sports:* basketball M(s)/W(s), cross-country running M/W, golf M, soccer M(s)/W(s), volleyball W(s).

Costs (2013–14) *Tuition:* area resident $2700 full-time, $90 per credit hour part-time; state resident $3930 full-time, $131 per credit hour part-time; nonresident $5850 full-time, $195 per credit hour part-time. *Required fees:* $440 full-time, $12 per credit hour part-time, $40 per term part-time. *Payment plans:* installment, deferred payment. *Waivers:* senior citizens and employees or children of employees.

Financial Aid Of all full-time matriculated undergraduates who enrolled in 2012, 42 Federal Work-Study jobs (averaging $1722).

Applying *Options:* electronic application, early admission, deferred entrance. *Required for some:* high school transcript. *Recommended:* high school transcript. *Application deadlines:* rolling (freshmen), rolling (transfers).

Freshman Application Contact Ms. Nicole Wilson-Fennell, Registrar, Schoolcraft College, 18600 Haggerty Road, Livonia, MI 48152-2696. *Phone:* 734-462-4683. *Fax:* 734-462-4553. *E-mail:* gotoSC@schoolcraft.edu. *Website:* http://www.schoolcraft.edu/.

Southwestern Michigan College
Dowagiac, Michigan

- **State and locally supported** 2-year, founded 1964
- **Rural** 240-acre campus
- **Coed,** 2,801 undergraduate students, 50% full-time, 59% women, 41% men

Undergraduates 1,409 full-time, 1,392 part-time. Students come from 14 states and territories; 8 other countries; 13% are from out of state; 12% Black or African American, non-Hispanic/Latino; 5% Hispanic/Latino; 0.7% Asian, non-Hispanic/Latino; 0.8% American Indian or Alaska Native, non-Hispanic/Latino; 6% Two or more races, non-Hispanic/Latino; 3% Race/ethnicity unknown; 0.4% international; 30% transferred in; 14% live on campus. *Retention:* 56% of full-time freshmen returned.

Freshmen *Admission:* 2,277 applied, 2,254 admitted, 765 enrolled.

Faculty *Total:* 176, 30% full-time, 21% with terminal degrees. *Student/faculty ratio:* 20:1.

Majors Accounting technology and bookkeeping; automation engineer technology; automobile/automotive mechanics technology; business administration and management; carpentry; computer programming; computer support specialist; computer systems networking and telecommunications; criminal justice/safety; early childhood education; engineering technology; executive assistant/executive secretary; fire science/firefighting; general studies; graphic design; health information/medical records technology; industrial mechanics and maintenance technology; industrial production technologies related; liberal arts and sciences/liberal studies; machine tool technology; medical/clinical assistant; meeting and event planning; prenursing studies; professional, technical, business, and scientific writing; registered nursing/registered nurse; social work; teacher assistant/aide.

Academics *Calendar:* semesters. *Degree:* certificates and associate. *Special study options:* academic remediation for entering students, accelerated degree program, adult/continuing education programs, advanced placement credit, cooperative education, distance learning, double majors, English as a second language, independent study, internships, part-time degree program, services for LD students, summer session for credit.

Library Fred L. Mathews Library with 29,687 titles, 14,968 serial subscriptions, 3,482 audiovisual materials, an OPAC, a Web page.

Student Life *Housing Options:* coed. Campus housing is university owned. *Activities and Organizations:* drama/theater group, choral group, Dionysus Drama Club, Rock Climbing Club, SMC Community of Veterans, Alpha Kappa Omega, STEM Club. *Campus security:* 24-hour emergency response devices and patrols, controlled dormitory access, day and evening police patrols.

Athletics *Intramural sports:* basketball M/W, football M/W, golf M/W, rock climbing M/W, soccer M/W, softball M/W, tennis M/W, volleyball M/W.

Costs (2013–14) *Tuition:* area resident $2847 full-time, $110 per contact hour part-time; state resident $3679 full-time, $142 per contact hour part-time; nonresident $4004 full-time, $154 per contact hour part-time. *Required fees:* $1086 full-time, $42 per contact hour part-time. *Room and board:* $7840; room only: $5650. *Payment plan:* installment. *Waivers:* employees or children of employees.

Financial Aid Of all full-time matriculated undergraduates who enrolled in 2012, 125 Federal Work-Study jobs (averaging $1000). 75 state and other part-time jobs (averaging $1000).

Applying *Options:* electronic application, deferred entrance. *Required:* high school transcript. *Required for some:* interview. *Application deadlines:* rolling (freshmen), rolling (transfers). *Notification:* continuous (freshmen), continuous (transfers).

Freshman Application Contact Ms. Angela Palsak, Executive Director of Student Services, Southwestern Michigan College, Dowagiac, MI 49047. *Phone:* 269-782-1000 Ext. 1310. *Toll-free phone:* 800-456-8675. *Fax:* 269-782-1331. *E-mail:* apalsak@swmich.edu. *Website:* http://www.swmich.edu/.

Washtenaw Community College
Ann Arbor, Michigan

Freshman Application Contact Washtenaw Community College, 4800 East Huron River Drive, PO Box D-1, Ann Arbor, MI 48106. *Phone:* 734-973-3315. *Website:* http://www.wccnet.edu/.

Wayne County Community College District
Detroit, Michigan

- **State and locally supported** 2-year, founded 1967
- **Urban** campus
- **Coed,** 18,119 undergraduate students, 21% full-time, 67% women, 33% men

Undergraduates 3,862 full-time, 14,257 part-time. 74% Black or African American, non-Hispanic/Latino; 2% Hispanic/Latino; 1% Asian, non-Hispanic/Latino; 0.1% Native Hawaiian or other Pacific Islander, non-Hispanic/Latino; 0.5% American Indian or Alaska Native, non-Hispanic/Latino; 0.2% Two or more races, non-Hispanic/Latino; 8% Race/ethnicity unknown; 0.2% international; 14% transferred in.

Freshmen *Admission:* 3,613 enrolled.

Faculty *Total:* 907, 8% full-time. *Student/faculty ratio:* 24:1.

Majors Accounting technology and bookkeeping; aircraft powerplant technology; airframe mechanics and aircraft maintenance technology; automobile/automotive mechanics technology; biomedical technology; building/property maintenance; business administration and management; CAD/CADD drafting/design technology; child-care and support services management; computer programming; corrections; criminal justice/police science; dental hygiene; digital communication and media/multimedia; e-commerce; electrical and electronic engineering technologies related; electrical, electronic and communications engineering technology; electromechanical technology; elementary education; emergency medical technology (EMT paramedic); engineering; fire prevention and safety technology; food service systems administration; heating, air conditioning, ventilation and refrigeration maintenance technology; legal assistant/paralegal; liberal arts and sciences/liberal studies; machine tool technology; manufacturing engineering technology; mortuary science and embalming; office management; pharmacy technician; premedical studies; registered nursing/registered nurse; social work; surgical technology; veterinary/animal health technology; welding technology.

Academics *Calendar:* semesters. *Degree:* certificates and associate. *Special study options:* academic remediation for entering students, adult/continuing education programs, advanced placement credit, cooperative education, distance learning, double majors, English as a second language, honors programs, internships, part-time degree program, services for LD students, study abroad, summer session for credit.

Library Learning Resource Center plus 5 others with an OPAC, a Web page.

Student Life *Housing:* college housing not available. *Campus security:* 24-hour emergency response devices.

Athletics Member NJCAA. *Intercollegiate sports:* basketball M/W.

Financial Aid Of all full-time matriculated undergraduates who enrolled in 2012, 239 Federal Work-Study jobs (averaging $2360). 147 state and other part-time jobs (averaging $1200).

Applying *Options:* electronic application, early admission, deferred entrance. *Required:* high school transcript. *Application deadlines:* rolling (freshmen), rolling (transfers).

Freshman Application Contact Mr. Adrian Phillips, District Associate Vice Chancellor of Student Services, Wayne County Community College District, 801 West Fort Street, Detroit, MI 48226-9975. *Phone:* 313-496-2820. *Fax:* 313-962-1643. *E-mail:* aphilli1@wcccd.edu. *Website:* http://www.wcccd.edu/.

West Shore Community College
Scottville, Michigan

Freshman Application Contact Wendy Fought, Director of Admissions, West Shore Community College, PO Box 277, 3000 North Stiles Road, Scottville, MI 49454-0277. *Phone:* 231-843-5503. *Fax:* 231-845-3944. *E-mail:* admissions@westshore.edu. *Website:* http://www.westshore.edu/.

MICRONESIA

College of Micronesia–FSM
Kolonia Pohnpei, Federated States of Micronesia, Micronesia

Freshman Application Contact Rita Hinga, Student Services Specialist, College of Micronesia–FSM, PO Box 159, Kolonia Pohnpei, FM 96941-0159, Micronesia. *Phone:* 691-320-3795 Ext. 15. *E-mail:* rhinga@comfsm.fm. *Website:* http://www.comfsm.fm/.

MINNESOTA

Alexandria Technical and Community College

Alexandria, Minnesota

- **State-supported** 2-year, founded 1961, part of Minnesota State Colleges and Universities System
- **Small-town** 98-acre campus
- **Coed,** 2,630 undergraduate students, 56% full-time, 49% women, 51% men

Undergraduates 1,478 full-time, 1,152 part-time. Students come from 15 states and territories; 1 other country; 4% are from out of state; 2% Black or African American, non-Hispanic/Latino; 1% Hispanic/Latino; 0.6% Asian, non-Hispanic/Latino; 0.1% Native Hawaiian or other Pacific Islander, non-Hispanic/Latino; 1% American Indian or Alaska Native, non-Hispanic/Latino; 4% Race/ethnicity unknown.

Faculty *Total:* 101, 66% full-time, 4% with terminal degrees. *Student/faculty ratio:* 21:1.

Majors Accounting; automation engineer technology; business administration and management; child development; clinical/medical laboratory technology; commercial and advertising art; computer systems networking and telecommunications; criminal justice/police science; diesel mechanics technology; fashion merchandising; human services; industrial mechanics and maintenance technology; information science/studies; interior design; legal administrative assistant/secretary; legal assistant/paralegal; liberal arts and sciences/liberal studies; marketing/marketing management; mechanical drafting and CAD/CADD; medical administrative assistant and medical secretary; multi/interdisciplinary studies related; physical fitness technician; pre-engineering; registered nursing/registered nurse; sales, distribution, and marketing operations; speech-language pathology assistant.

Academics *Calendar:* semesters. *Degree:* certificates, diplomas, and associate. *Special study options:* academic remediation for entering students, advanced placement credit, distance learning, double majors, independent study, internships, part-time degree program, services for LD students, student-designed majors, summer session for credit.

Library Learning Resource Center with 23,886 titles, 1,995 serial subscriptions, 1,378 audiovisual materials, an OPAC, a Web page.

Student Life *Housing:* college housing not available. *Activities and Organizations:* choral group, Skills USA, Business Professionals of America, Delta Epsilon Chi, Student Senate, Phi Theta Kappa. *Campus security:* student patrols, late-night transport/escort service, security cameras inside and outside. *Student services:* personal/psychological counseling.

Athletics *Intramural sports:* basketball M/W, football M/W, softball M/W, volleyball M/W.

Costs (2014–15) *Tuition:* state resident $4817 full-time, $161 per credit part-time; nonresident $4817 full-time, $161 per credit part-time. *Required fees:* $569 full-time, $19 part-time. *Room and board:* $5200. *Payment plan:* deferred payment. *Waivers:* senior citizens and employees or children of employees.

Financial Aid Of all full-time matriculated undergraduates who enrolled in 2012, 94 Federal Work-Study jobs (averaging $1871).

Applying *Options:* electronic application, early admission, deferred entrance. *Application fee:* $20. *Required:* high school transcript. *Required for some:* interview. *Recommended:* interview. *Application deadlines:* rolling (freshmen), rolling (out-of-state freshmen), rolling (transfers). *Notification:* continuous (freshmen), continuous (out-of-state freshmen), continuous (transfers).

Freshman Application Contact Janet Dropik, Admissions Receptionist, Alexandria Technical and Community College, 1601 Jefferson Street, Alexandria, MN 56308. *Phone:* 320-762-4520. *Toll-free phone:* 888-234-1222. *Fax:* 320-762-4603. *E-mail:* admissionsrep@alextech.edu. *Website:* http://www.alextech.edu/.

Anoka-Ramsey Community College

Coon Rapids, Minnesota

- **State-supported** 2-year, founded 1965, part of Minnesota State Colleges and Universities System
- **Suburban** 100-acre campus with easy access to Minneapolis-St. Paul
- **Coed,** 7,807 undergraduate students

Undergraduates 5% are from out of state; 8% Black or African American, non-Hispanic/Latino; 5% Hispanic/Latino; 4% Asian, non-Hispanic/Latino; 0.1% Native Hawaiian or other Pacific Islander, non-Hispanic/Latino; 0.5% American Indian or Alaska Native, non-Hispanic/Latino; 4% Two or more races, non-Hispanic/Latino; 2% Race/ethnicity unknown; 0.4% international. *Retention:* 51% of full-time freshmen returned.

Freshmen *Admission:* 2,667 applied, 1,661 admitted.

Faculty *Total:* 219, 47% full-time. *Student/faculty ratio:* 31:1.

Majors Accounting; accounting technology and bookkeeping; bioengineering and biomedical engineering; biology/biological sciences; biomedical technology; business administration and management; business/commerce; community health and preventive medicine; computer science; computer systems networking and telecommunications; creative writing; dramatic/theater arts; environmental science; fine/studio arts; health services/allied health/health sciences; holistic health; human resources management; liberal arts and sciences/liberal studies; multi/interdisciplinary studies related; music; physical therapy technology; pre-engineering; registered nursing/registered nurse; sales, distribution, and marketing operations.

Academics *Calendar:* semesters. *Degree:* certificates and associate. *Special study options:* academic remediation for entering students, accelerated degree program, advanced placement credit, cooperative education, distance learning, double majors, honors programs, independent study, internships, off-campus study, part-time degree program, services for LD students, study abroad, summer session for credit. *ROTC:* Air Force (c).

Library Coon Rapids Campus Library with 43,156 titles, 113 serial subscriptions, 1,952 audiovisual materials, an OPAC, a Web page.

Student Life *Housing:* college housing not available. *Activities and Organizations:* drama/theater group, student-run newspaper, choral group, student government, Phi Theta Kappa, Multicultural Club, CRU (Campus Christian group), Rampage (student newspaper). *Campus security:* 24-hour emergency response devices, late-night transport/escort service. *Student services:* personal/psychological counseling.

Athletics Member NJCAA. *Intercollegiate sports:* baseball M, basketball M/W, soccer M/W, softball W, volleyball W. *Intramural sports:* badminton M/W, basketball M/W, bowling M/W, football M/W, golf M/W, ice hockey M/W, soccer M/W, softball M/W, tennis M/W, volleyball M/W.

Costs (2013–14) *Tuition:* state resident $4349 full-time, $145 per credit hour part-time; nonresident $4349 full-time, $145 per credit hour part-time. Full-time tuition and fees vary according to course load and program. Part-time tuition and fees vary according to course load and program. *Required fees:* $651 full-time, $22 per credit part-time. *Payment plans:* installment, deferred payment. *Waivers:* senior citizens and employees or children of employees.

Financial Aid Of all full-time matriculated undergraduates who enrolled in 2012, 2,375 applied for aid, 2,281 were judged to have need, 1,655 had their need fully met. In 2012, 15 non-need-based awards were made. *Average percent of need met:* 94%. *Average financial aid package:* $4852. *Average need-based loan:* $1925. *Average need-based gift aid:* $2262. *Average non-need-based aid:* $795.

Applying *Options:* electronic application, early admission, deferred entrance. *Required for some:* high school transcript. *Application deadlines:* rolling (freshmen), rolling (out-of-state freshmen), rolling (transfers). *Notification:* continuous (freshmen), continuous (out-of-state freshmen), continuous (transfers).

Freshman Application Contact Admissions Department, Anoka-Ramsey Community College, 11200 Mississippi Boulevard NW, Coon Rapids, MN 55433-3470. *Phone:* 763-433-1300. *Fax:* 763-433-1521. *E-mail:* admissions@anokaramsey.edu. *Website:* http://www.anokaramsey.edu/.

Anoka-Ramsey Community College, Cambridge Campus

Cambridge, Minnesota

- **State-supported** 2-year, founded 1965, part of Minnesota State Colleges and Universities System
- **Small-town** campus
- **Coed,** 2,313 undergraduate students

Undergraduates 3% are from out of state; 2% Black or African American, non-Hispanic/Latino; 3% Hispanic/Latino; 2% Asian, non-Hispanic/Latino; 0.1% Native Hawaiian or other Pacific Islander, non-Hispanic/Latino; 0.4% American Indian or Alaska Native, non-Hispanic/Latino; 3% Two or more races, non-Hispanic/Latino; 0.9% Race/ethnicity unknown. *Retention:* 47% of full-time freshmen returned.

Freshmen *Admission:* 768 applied, 389 admitted.

Faculty *Total:* 55, 49% full-time.

Majors Accounting; accounting technology and bookkeeping; bioengineering and biomedical engineering; biology/biological sciences; biomedical technology; business administration and management; business/commerce; community health and preventive medicine; computer science; computer systems networking and telecommunications; creative writing; dramatic/theater arts; environmental science; fine/studio arts; health services/allied health/health sciences; holistic health; human resources management; liberal arts and sciences/liberal studies; multi/interdisciplinary studies related; music; pre-engineering; registered nursing/registered nurse; sales, distribution, and marketing operations.

Academics *Calendar:* semesters. *Degree:* certificates and associate. *Special study options:* academic remediation for entering students, accelerated degree program, advanced placement credit, cooperative education, distance learning, double majors, honors programs, independent study, internships, off-campus study, part-time degree program, services for LD students, study abroad, summer session for credit. *ROTC:* Air Force (c).

Library Cambridge Campus Library with 17,103 titles, 131 serial subscriptions, 1,602 audiovisual materials, an OPAC, a Web page.

Student Life *Housing:* college housing not available. *Activities and Organizations:* drama/theater group, student-run newspaper, choral group. *Campus security:* 24-hour emergency response devices, late-night transport/escort service. *Student services:* personal/psychological counseling.

Athletics Member NJCAA. *Intercollegiate sports:* baseball M, basketball M/W, soccer M/W, softball W, volleyball W. *Intramural sports:* bowling M/W, golf M/W, volleyball M/W.

Costs (2013–14) *Tuition:* state resident $4349 full-time, $145 per credit hour part-time; nonresident $4349 full-time, $145 per credit hour part-time. Full-time tuition and fees vary according to course load and program. Part-time tuition and fees vary according to course load and program. *Required fees:* $651 full-time, $22 per credit hour part-time. *Payment plans:* installment, deferred payment. *Waivers:* senior citizens and employees or children of employees.

Applying *Options:* electronic application, early admission, deferred entrance. *Required for some:* high school transcript. *Application deadlines:* rolling (freshmen), rolling (out-of-state freshmen), rolling (transfers). *Notification:* continuous (freshmen), continuous (out-of-state freshmen), continuous (transfers).

Freshman Application Contact Admissions Department, Anoka-Ramsey Community College, Cambridge Campus, 300 Spirit River Drive South, Cambridge, MN 55008-5704. *Phone:* 763-433-1300. *Toll-free phone:* 866-433-5590. *Fax:* 763-433-1841. *E-mail:* admissions@anokaramsey.edu.
Website: http://www.anokaramsey.edu/.

Anoka Technical College
Anoka, Minnesota

- **State-supported** 2-year, founded 1967, part of Minnesota State Colleges and Universities System
- **Small-town** campus with easy access to Minneapolis-St. Paul
- **Coed,** 2,152 undergraduate students

Undergraduates 2% are from out of state; 8% Black or African American, non-Hispanic/Latino; 4% Hispanic/Latino; 3% Asian, non-Hispanic/Latino; 0.1% Native Hawaiian or other Pacific Islander, non-Hispanic/Latino; 0.7% American Indian or Alaska Native, non-Hispanic/Latino; 3% Two or more races, non-Hispanic/Latino; 1% Race/ethnicity unknown; 0.1% international. *Retention:* 50% of full-time freshmen returned.

Freshmen *Admission:* 830 applied, 614 admitted.

Faculty *Total:* 98, 56% full-time. *Student/faculty ratio:* 20:1.

Majors Accounting; administrative assistant and secretarial science; architectural drafting and CAD/CADD; automobile/automotive mechanics technology; aviation/airway management; computer numerically controlled (CNC) machinist technology; computer technology/computer systems technology; court reporting; developmental services worker; electrical, electronic and communications engineering technology; golf course operation and grounds management; health information/medical records technology; landscaping and groundskeeping; legal administrative assistant/secretary; licensed practical/vocational nurse training; mechanical drafting and CAD/CADD; medical administrative assistant and medical secretary; medical/clinical assistant; occupational therapist assistant; office management; surgical technology; welding technology.

Academics *Calendar:* semesters. *Degree:* certificates, diplomas, and associate. *Special study options:* academic remediation for entering students, advanced placement credit, cooperative education, distance learning, double majors, English as a second language, internships, part-time degree program, services for LD students.

Student Life *Housing:* college housing not available. *Campus security:* late-night transport/escort service. *Student services:* personal/psychological counseling.

Costs (2013–14) *Tuition:* state resident $5567 full-time, $167 per credit part-time; nonresident $5567 full-time, $167 per credit part-time. Full-time tuition and fees vary according to program and reciprocity agreements. Part-time tuition and fees vary according to program and reciprocity agreements. *Required fees:* $557 full-time, $19 per credit part-time. *Payment plan:* installment. *Waivers:* senior citizens and employees or children of employees.

Applying *Options:* electronic application, deferred entrance. *Required:* high school transcript. *Required for some:* interview.

Freshman Application Contact Anoka Technical College, 1355 West Highway 10, Anoka, MN 55303. *Phone:* 763-576-4784.
Website: http://www.anokatech.edu/.

Anthem College–St. Louis Park
St. Louis Park, Minnesota

Freshman Application Contact Admissions Office, Anthem College–St. Louis Park, 5100 Gamble Drive, St. Louis Park, MN 55416. *Toll-free phone:* 855-331-7769.
Website: http://anthem.edu/minneapolis-minnesota/.

Central Lakes College
Brainerd, Minnesota

Freshman Application Contact Ms. Rose Tretter, Central Lakes College, 501 West College Drive, Brainerd, MN 56401-3904. *Phone:* 218-855-8036. *Toll-free phone:* 800-933-0346. *Fax:* 218-855-8220. *E-mail:* cdaniels@clcmn.edu. *Website:* http://www.clcmn.edu/.

Century College
White Bear Lake, Minnesota

- **State-supported** 2-year, founded 1970, part of Minnesota State Colleges and Universities System
- **Suburban** 170-acre campus with easy access to Minneapolis-St. Paul
- **Coed,** 10,009 undergraduate students, 40% full-time, 55% women, 45% men

Undergraduates 3,975 full-time, 6,034 part-time. Students come from 46 other countries; 6% are from out of state; 11% Black or African American, non-Hispanic/Latino; 6% Hispanic/Latino; 17% Asian, non-Hispanic/Latino; 0.2% Native Hawaiian or other Pacific Islander, non-Hispanic/Latino; 0.5% American Indian or Alaska Native, non-Hispanic/Latino; 5% Two or more races, non-Hispanic/Latino; 0.5% Race/ethnicity unknown; 1% international; 45% transferred in.

Freshmen *Admission:* 3,289 applied, 3,289 admitted, 1,336 enrolled.

Faculty *Total:* 378, 52% full-time. *Student/faculty ratio:* 23:1.

Majors Accounting; administrative assistant and secretarial science; building/property maintenance; business administration and management; CAD/CADD drafting/design technology; computer and information systems security; computer science; computer systems networking and telecommunications; computer technology/computer systems technology; cosmetology; criminalistics and criminal science; criminal justice/police science; criminal justice/safety; dental assisting; dental hygiene; digital communication and media/multimedia; e-commerce; education; emergency medical technology (EMT paramedic); energy management and systems technology; fine/studio arts; greenhouse management; health services/allied health/health sciences; heating, air conditioning, ventilation and refrigeration maintenance technology; homeland security, law enforcement, firefighting and protective services related; horticultural science; human services; information science/studies; interior design; landscaping and groundskeeping; language interpretation and translation; liberal arts and sciences/liberal studies; marketing/marketing management; medical administrative assistant and medical secretary; multi/interdisciplinary studies related; music; orthotics/prosthetics; pre-engineering; radiologic technology/science; registered nursing/registered nurse; substance abuse/addiction counseling; teacher assistant/aide.

Academics *Calendar:* semesters. *Degree:* certificates, diplomas, and associate. *Special study options:* academic remediation for entering students, advanced placement credit, distance learning, double majors, English as a second language, honors programs, internships, part-time degree program, services for LD students, student-designed majors, summer session for credit. *ROTC:* Air Force (c).

Library Century College Library plus 1 other with 138,524 titles, 290 serial subscriptions, 17,228 audiovisual materials, an OPAC.

Student Life *Housing:* college housing not available. *Activities and Organizations:* drama/theater group, student-run newspaper, choral group, Asian Student Association, Intercultural Club, Student Senate, Phi Theta Kappa, Planning Activities Committee. *Campus security:* late-night transport/escort service, day patrols. *Student services:* health clinic, personal/psychological counseling.

Athletics Member NJCAA. *Intercollegiate sports:* baseball M, soccer M/W, softball W. *Intramural sports:* badminton M/W, basketball M/W, bowling M/W, football M/W, golf M/W, ice hockey M/W, soccer M/W, softball M/W, table tennis M/W, volleyball M/W.

Costs (2013–14) *Tuition:* state resident $4818 full-time, $161 per semester hour part-time; nonresident $4818 full-time, $161 per credit hour part-time. Full-time tuition and fees vary according to class time, program, and reciprocity agreements. Part-time tuition and fees vary according to class time, program, and reciprocity agreements. *Required fees:* $539 full-time, $18 per semester hour part-time. *Payment plan:* installment. *Waivers:* senior citizens and employees or children of employees.

Financial Aid Of all full-time matriculated undergraduates who enrolled in 2012, 81 Federal Work-Study jobs (averaging $2763). 85 state and other part-time jobs (averaging $2646).

Applying *Options:* electronic application, deferred entrance. *Application fee:* $20. *Required:* high school transcript. *Application deadlines:* rolling (freshmen), rolling (transfers).
Freshman Application Contact Ms. Christine Paulos, Admissions Director, Century College, 3300 Century Avenue North, White Bear Lake, MN 55110. *Phone:* 651-779-2619. *Toll-free phone:* 800-228-1978. *Fax:* 651-773-1796. *E-mail:* admissions@century.edu.
Website: http://www.century.edu/.

Dakota County Technical College
Rosemount, Minnesota

Freshman Application Contact Mr. Patrick Lair, Admissions Director, Dakota County Technical College, 1300 East 145th Street, Rosemount, MN 55068. *Phone:* 651-423-8399. *Toll-free phone:* 877-YES-DCTC. *Fax:* 651-423-8775. *E-mail:* admissions@dctc.mnscu.edu.
Website: http://www.dctc.edu/.

Duluth Business University
Duluth, Minnesota

Freshman Application Contact Mr. Mark Traux, Director of Admissions, Duluth Business University, 4724 Mike Colalillo Drive, Duluth, MN 55807. *Phone:* 218-722-4000. *Toll-free phone:* 800-777-8406. *Fax:* 218-628-2127. *E-mail:* markt@dbumn.edu.
Website: http://www.dbumn.edu/.

Dunwoody College of Technology
Minneapolis, Minnesota

- **Independent** primarily 2-year, founded 1914
- **Urban** 12-acre campus with easy access to Minneapolis
- **Endowment** $19.9 million
- **Coed, primarily men,** 1,071 undergraduate students, 80% full-time, 12% women, 88% men

Undergraduates 855 full-time, 216 part-time. 3% are from out of state; 6% Black or African American, non-Hispanic/Latino; 2% Hispanic/Latino; 4% Asian, non-Hispanic/Latino; 0.1% Native Hawaiian or other Pacific Islander, non-Hispanic/Latino; 0.8% American Indian or Alaska Native, non-Hispanic/Latino; 4% Two or more races, non-Hispanic/Latino; 11% Race/ethnicity unknown. *Retention:* 100% of full-time freshmen returned.
Freshmen *Admission:* 770 applied, 520 admitted, 168 enrolled. *Average high school GPA:* 2.45.
Faculty *Total:* 143, 55% full-time, 8% with terminal degrees. *Student/faculty ratio:* 9:1.
Majors Architectural drafting and CAD/CADD; architectural technology; autobody/collision and repair technology; automobile/automotive mechanics technology; building/construction site management; business administration and management; CAD/CADD drafting/design technology; computer science; computer systems networking and telecommunications; construction management; desktop publishing and digital imaging design; electrical, electronic and communications engineering technology; electrical/electronics drafting and CAD/CADD; electrician; graphic design; heating, air conditioning, ventilation and refrigeration maintenance technology; heating, ventilation, air conditioning and refrigeration engineering technology; industrial technology; interior design; medical radiologic technology; printing press operation; robotics technology; tool and die technology; web page, digital/multimedia and information resources design; welding technology.
Academics *Calendar:* quarters. *Degrees:* diplomas, associate, and bachelor's. *Special study options:* academic remediation for entering students, distance learning, independent study, internships, study abroad, summer session for credit.
Library Learning Resource Center with 8,000 titles, 115 serial subscriptions, 250 audiovisual materials, an OPAC, a Web page.
Student Life *Housing:* college housing not available. *Activities and Organizations:* Phi Theta Kappa, Historic Green. *Campus security:* 24-hour emergency response devices, late-night transport/escort service. *Student services:* personal/psychological counseling, women's center.
Standardized Tests *Recommended:* SAT or ACT (for admission).
Costs (2014–15) *Tuition:* $17,760 full-time. *Required fees:* $1495 full-time. *Payment plans:* installment, deferred payment.
Financial Aid Of all full-time matriculated undergraduates who enrolled in 2012, 950 applied for aid, 863 were judged to have need, 34 had their need fully met. *Average percent of need met:* 39%. *Average financial aid package:* $8130. *Average need-based loan:* $3799. *Average need-based gift aid:* $5415. *Average non-need-based aid:* $2000. *Average indebtedness upon graduation:* $9423.
Applying *Options:* electronic application. *Application fee:* $50. *Required:* essay or personal statement, high school transcript, minimum 2.5 GPA, interview. *Required for some:* minimum 3.0 GPA, . *Application deadlines:* rolling (freshmen), rolling (out-of-state freshmen), rolling (transfers).

Notification: continuous (freshmen), continuous (out-of-state freshmen), continuous (transfers).
Freshman Application Contact Bonney Bielen, Director of Admissions and Student Services, Dunwoody College of Technology, 818 Dunwoody Boulevard, Minneapolis, MN 55403. *Phone:* 612-374-5800. *Toll-free phone:* 800-292-4625.
Website: http://www.dunwoody.edu/.

Fond du Lac Tribal and Community College
Cloquet, Minnesota

Freshman Application Contact Kathie Jubie, Admissions Representative, Fond du Lac Tribal and Community College, 2101 14th Street, Cloquet, MN 55720. *Phone:* 218-879-0808. *Toll-free phone:* 800-657-3712. *E-mail:* admissions@fdltcc.edu.
Website: http://www.fdltcc.edu/.

Hennepin Technical College
Brooklyn Park, Minnesota

Freshman Application Contact Hennepin Technical College, 9000 Brooklyn Boulevard, Brooklyn Park, MN 55445. *Phone:* 763-488-2415. *Toll-free phone:* 800-345-4655 (in-state); 800-645-4655 (out-of-state).
Website: http://www.hennepintech.edu/.

Herzing University
Minneapolis, Minnesota

Freshman Application Contact Ms. Shelly Larson, Director of Admissions, Herzing University, 5700 West Broadway, Minneapolis, MN 55428. *Phone:* 763-231-3155. *Toll-free phone:* 800-596-0724. *Fax:* 763-535-9205. *E-mail:* info@mpls.herzing.edu.
Website: http://www.herzing.edu/minneapolis.

Hibbing Community College
Hibbing, Minnesota

Freshman Application Contact Admissions, Hibbing Community College, 1515 East 25th Street, Hibbing, MN 55746. *Phone:* 218-262-7200. *Toll-free phone:* 800-224-4HCC. *Fax:* 218-262-6717. *E-mail:* admissions@hibbing.edu.
Website: http://www.hcc.mnscu.edu/.

The Institute of Production and Recording
Minneapolis, Minnesota

- **Proprietary** 2-year, part of Globe Education Network (GEN) which is composed of Globe University, Minnesota School of Business, Broadview University, The Institute of Production and Recording and Minnesota School of Cosmetology
- **Urban** 4-acre campus with easy access to Minneapolis-St. Paul
- **Coed,** 242 undergraduate students, 63% full-time, 10% women, 90% men

Undergraduates 153 full-time, 89 part-time. Students come from 20 states and territories; 24% are from out of state; 10% Black or African American, non-Hispanic/Latino; 5% Hispanic/Latino; 2% Asian, non-Hispanic/Latino; 0.4% Native Hawaiian or other Pacific Islander, non-Hispanic/Latino; 0.4% American Indian or Alaska Native, non-Hispanic/Latino; 5% Two or more races, non-Hispanic/Latino; 3% Race/ethnicity unknown; 0.4% international; 15% transferred in.
Freshmen *Admission:* 45 enrolled.
Faculty *Total:* 40, 38% full-time.
Majors Music management; recording arts technology.
Academics *Degree:* associate. *Special study options:* academic remediation for entering students, accelerated degree program, adult/continuing education programs, advanced placement credit, independent study, internships, part-time degree program, services for LD students, summer session for credit.
Library Institute of Production and Recording Campus Library with an OPAC, a Web page.
Student Life *Housing:* college housing not available. *Campus security:* 24-hour emergency response devices.
Standardized Tests *Required:* ACCUPLACER is required of most applicants unless documentation of a minimum ACT composite score of 21 or documentation of a minimum composite score of 1485 on the SAT is presented (for admission).
Applying *Options:* electronic application. *Application fee:* $50. *Required:* high school transcript, interview, Certification of high school graduation or GED. *Application deadlines:* rolling (freshmen), rolling (out-of-state

freshmen), rolling (transfers). *Notification:* continuous (freshmen), continuous (out-of-state freshmen), continuous (transfers).

Freshman Application Contact The Institute of Production and Recording, 300 North 1st Avenue, Suite 500, Minneapolis, MN 55401.
Website: http://www.ipr.edu/.

Inver Hills Community College
Inver Grove Heights, Minnesota

Freshman Application Contact Mr. Casey Carmody, Admissions Representative, Inver Hills Community College, 2500 East 80th Street, Inver Grove Heights, MN 55076-3224. *Phone:* 651-450-3589. *Fax:* 651-450-3677.
E-mail: admissions@inverhills.edu.
Website: http://www.inverhills.edu/.

Itasca Community College
Grand Rapids, Minnesota

Freshman Application Contact Ms. Candace Perry, Director of Enrollment Services, Itasca Community College, Grand Rapids, MN 55744. *Phone:* 218-322-2340. *Toll-free phone:* 800-996-6422. *Fax:* 218-327-4350. *E-mail:* iccinfo@itascacc.edu.
Website: http://www.itascacc.edu/.

ITT Technical Institute
Brooklyn Center, Minnesota

- **Proprietary** primarily 2-year, part of ITT Educational Services, Inc.
- **Coed**

Majors Business administration and management; construction management; cyber/computer forensics and counterterrorism; drafting and design technology; electrical, electronic and communications engineering technology; information technology project management; network and system administration; project management.

Academics *Calendar:* quarters. *Degrees:* associate and bachelor's.

Freshman Application Contact Director of Recruitment, ITT Technical Institute, 6120 Earle Brown Drive, Suite 100, Brooklyn Center, MN 55430. *Phone:* 763-549-5900. *Toll-free phone:* 800-216-8883.
Website: http://www.itt-tech.edu/.

ITT Technical Institute
Eden Prairie, Minnesota

- **Proprietary** primarily 2-year, founded 2003, part of ITT Educational Services, Inc.
- **Coed**

Majors Business administration and management; construction management; cyber/computer forensics and counterterrorism; drafting and design technology; electrical, electronic and communications engineering technology; forensic science and technology; game and interactive media design; information technology project management; network and system administration; project management.

Academics *Calendar:* quarters. *Degrees:* associate and bachelor's.

Freshman Application Contact Director of Recruitment, ITT Technical Institute, 7905 Golden Triangle Drive, Eden Prairie, MN 55344. *Phone:* 952-914-5300. *Toll-free phone:* 888-488-9646.
Website: http://www.itt-tech.edu/.

Lake Superior College
Duluth, Minnesota

- **State-supported** 2-year, founded 1995, part of Minnesota State Colleges and Universities System
- **Urban** 105-acre campus
- **Coed,** 5,050 undergraduate students, 42% full-time, 58% women, 42% men

Undergraduates 2,108 full-time, 2,942 part-time. Students come from 28 states and territories; 6 other countries; 15% are from out of state; 4% Black or African American, non-Hispanic/Latino; 3% Hispanic/Latino; 1% Asian, non-Hispanic/Latino; 0.1% Native Hawaiian or other Pacific Islander, non-Hispanic/Latino; 2% American Indian or Alaska Native, non-Hispanic/Latino; 4% Two or more races, non-Hispanic/Latino; 1% Race/ethnicity unknown; 0.1% international; 39% transferred in.

Freshmen *Admission:* 1,062 applied, 1,062 admitted, 700 enrolled.

Faculty *Total:* 251, 39% full-time, 6% with terminal degrees. *Student/faculty ratio:* 21:1.

Majors Accounting; airline pilot and flight crew; architectural drafting and CAD/CADD; automobile/automotive mechanics technology; building construction technology; business administration and management; business automation/technology/data entry; CAD/CADD drafting/design technology; civil engineering technology; clinical/medical laboratory technology;

computer numerically controlled (CNC) machinist technology; computer technology/computer systems technology; dental hygiene; electrical, electronic and communications engineering technology; electrician; fine/studio arts; fire prevention and safety technology; health services/allied health/health sciences; legal administrative assistant/secretary; legal assistant/paralegal; liberal arts and sciences/liberal studies; management information systems; mechanical drafting and CAD/CADD; medical administrative assistant and medical secretary; multi/interdisciplinary studies related; network and system administration; office management; physical therapy technology; radiologic technology/science; registered nursing/registered nurse; respiratory care therapy; sheet metal technology; surgical technology; web page, digital/multimedia and information resources design.

Academics *Calendar:* semesters. *Degree:* certificates, diplomas, and associate. *Special study options:* academic remediation for entering students, advanced placement credit, distance learning, double majors, independent study, internships, part-time degree program, services for LD students, study abroad, summer session for credit.

Library Harold P. Erickson Library with an OPAC, a Web page.

Student Life *Housing:* college housing not available. *Activities and Organizations:* choral group. *Campus security:* late-night transport/escort service. *Student services:* personal/psychological counseling.

Financial Aid Of all full-time matriculated undergraduates who enrolled in 2012, 67 Federal Work-Study jobs (averaging $2720). 111 state and other part-time jobs (averaging $2720).

Applying *Options:* electronic application. *Application fee:* $20. *Required:* transcripts from high school, GED, or HSED and official transcripts from all previous post-secondary institutions attended. *Required for some:* high school transcript. *Application deadlines:* rolling (freshmen), rolling (transfers). *Notification:* continuous (freshmen), continuous (transfers).

Freshman Application Contact Ms. Melissa Leno, Director of Admissions, Lake Superior College, 2101 Trinity Road, Duluth, MN 55811. *Phone:* 218-733-5903. *Toll-free phone:* 800-432-2884. *E-mail:* enroll@lsc.edu.
Website: http://www.lsc.edu/.

Le Cordon Bleu College of Culinary Arts in Minneapolis/St. Paul
Mendota Heights, Minnesota

Freshman Application Contact Admissions Office, Le Cordon Bleu College of Culinary Arts in Minneapolis/St. Paul, 1315 Mendota Heights Road, Mendota Heights, MN 55120. *Phone:* 651-675-4700. *Toll-free phone:* 888-348-5222.
Website: http://www.chefs.edu/Minneapolis-St-Paul/.

Leech Lake Tribal College
Cass Lake, Minnesota

Freshman Application Contact Ms. Shelly Braford, Recruiter, Leech Lake Tribal College, PO Box 180, 6945 Littlewolf Road NW, Cass Lake, MN 56633. *Phone:* 218-335-4200 Ext. 4270. *Fax:* 218-335-4217. *E-mail:* shelly.braford@lltc.edu.
Website: http://www.lltc.edu/.

Mesabi Range Community and Technical College
Virginia, Minnesota

- **State-supported** 2-year, founded 1918, part of Minnesota State Colleges and Universities System
- **Small-town** 30-acre campus
- **Coed,** 1,451 undergraduate students, 61% full-time, 45% women, 55% men

Undergraduates 878 full-time, 573 part-time. Students come from 6 states and territories; 2 other countries; 4% are from out of state; 7% Black or African American, non-Hispanic/Latino; 0.5% Hispanic/Latino; 1% Asian, non-Hispanic/Latino; 4% American Indian or Alaska Native, non-Hispanic/Latino; 10% Race/ethnicity unknown; 10% live on campus.

Faculty *Total:* 109. *Student/faculty ratio:* 24:1.

Majors Administrative assistant and secretarial science; business/commerce; computer graphics; computer/information technology services administration related; computer programming related; computer programming (specific applications); computer software and media applications related; computer systems networking and telecommunications; electrical/electronics equipment installation and repair; human services; information technology; instrumentation technology; liberal arts and sciences/liberal studies; pre-engineering; substance abuse/addiction counseling; web page, digital/multimedia and information resources design.

Academics *Calendar:* semesters. *Degree:* certificates, diplomas, and associate. *Special study options:* academic remediation for entering students, adult/continuing education programs, advanced placement credit, cooperative education, distance learning, independent study, internships, off-campus study, part-time degree program, services for LD students, student-designed majors, study abroad, summer session for credit.

Library Mesabi Library with 23,000 titles, 167 serial subscriptions.

Student Life *Housing Options:* coed. Campus housing is provided by a third party. *Activities and Organizations:* drama/theater group, student-run newspaper, choral group, Student Senate, Human Services Club, Career Program Clubs, Student Life Club, Diversity Club. *Campus security:* late-night transport/escort service. *Student services:* personal/psychological counseling.

Athletics Member NJCAA. *Intercollegiate sports:* baseball M, basketball M/W, football M, golf M/W, softball W, volleyball W. *Intramural sports:* badminton M/W, basketball M/W, bowling M/W, field hockey M/W, football M/W, golf M/W, ice hockey M/W, skiing (cross-country) M/W, skiing (downhill) M/W, tennis M/W, volleyball M/W.

Costs (2014–15) *Tuition:* state resident $4729 full-time, $158 per credit part-time; nonresident $5911 full-time, $197 per credit part-time. Full-time tuition and fees vary according to reciprocity agreements. Part-time tuition and fees vary according to reciprocity agreements. *Required fees:* $564 full-time, $19 per credit part-time, $19 per credit part-time. *Room and board:* room only: $3936.

Financial Aid Of all full-time matriculated undergraduates who enrolled in 2011, 168 Federal Work-Study jobs (averaging $1227). 82 state and other part-time jobs (averaging $1380).

Applying *Options:* electronic application, early admission, deferred entrance. *Required:* high school transcript. *Application deadlines:* rolling (freshmen), rolling (transfers). *Notification:* continuous (freshmen), continuous (transfers).

Freshman Application Contact Ms. Brenda Kochevar, Enrollment Services Director, Mesabi Range Community and Technical College, Virginia, MN 55792. *Phone:* 218-749-0314. *Toll-free phone:* 800-657-3860. *Fax:* 218-749-0318. *E-mail:* b.kochevar@mr.mnscu.edu.

Website: http://www.mesabirange.edu/.

Minneapolis Business College

Roseville, Minnesota

- **Private** 2-year, founded 1874
- **Suburban** campus with easy access to Minneapolis-St. Paul
- **Coed,** 267 undergraduate students
- 86% of applicants were admitted

Freshmen *Admission:* 509 applied, 439 admitted.

Majors Accounting technology and bookkeeping; administrative assistant and secretarial science; computer programming; computer systems networking and telecommunications; graphic design; hotel/motel administration; legal administrative assistant/secretary; legal assistant/paralegal; medical/clinical assistant.

Academics *Degree:* diplomas and associate. *Special study options:* accelerated degree program, internships.

Freshman Application Contact Admissions Office, Minneapolis Business College, 1711 West County Road B, Roseville, MN 55113. *Phone:* 651-636-7406. *Toll-free phone:* 800-279-5200.

Website: http://www.minneapolisbusinesscollege.edu/.

Minneapolis Community and Technical College

Minneapolis, Minnesota

- **State-supported** 2-year, founded 1965, part of Minnesota State Colleges and Universities System
- **Urban** 22-acre campus
- **Coed,** 9,718 undergraduate students, 35% full-time, 53% women, 47% men

Undergraduates 3,413 full-time, 6,305 part-time. 13% transferred in.

Freshmen *Admission:* 636 enrolled.

Faculty *Total:* 397, 45% full-time, 20% with terminal degrees. *Student/faculty ratio:* 27:1.

Majors Accounting; accounting technology and bookkeeping; administrative assistant and secretarial science; air traffic control; allied health diagnostic, intervention, and treatment professions related; animation, interactive technology, video graphics and special effects; biology/biological sciences; biotechnology; business administration and management; business automation/technology/data entry; chemistry; child-care and support services management; child development; cinematography and film/video production; commercial photography; community organization and advocacy; computer and information systems security; computer programming; computer systems networking and telecommunications; criminal justice/police science; criminal justice/safety; culinary arts; dental assisting; design and visual communications; digital communication and media/multimedia; dramatic/theater arts; education; education (multiple levels); electroneurodiagnostic/electroencephalographic technology; fine/studio arts;

heating, air conditioning, ventilation and refrigeration maintenance technology; human services; liberal arts and sciences/liberal studies; library and archives assisting; mathematics; network and system administration; philosophy; photographic and film/video technology; playwriting and screenwriting; polysomnography; public administration; recording arts technology; registered nursing/registered nurse; restaurant/food services management; substance abuse/addiction counseling; web page, digital/multimedia and information resources design.

Academics *Calendar:* semesters. *Degree:* certificates, diplomas, and associate. *Special study options:* academic remediation for entering students, accelerated degree program, adult/continuing education programs, advanced placement credit, distance learning, English as a second language, honors programs, independent study, internships, off-campus study, part-time degree program, services for LD students, study abroad, summer session for credit.

Library Minneapolis Community and Technical College Library plus 1 other.

Student Life *Housing:* college housing not available. *Activities and Organizations:* drama/theater group, student-run newspaper, choral group, Student Senate, College Choirs, Student African American Brotherhood /B2B, Science Club, Phi Theta Kappa. *Campus security:* 24-hour emergency response devices and patrols, late-night transport/escort service. *Student services:* health clinic, personal/psychological counseling, women's center, legal services.

Athletics *Intramural sports:* basketball M/W, soccer M/W, tennis M/W, volleyball M/W.

Costs (2014–15) *Tuition:* state resident $4658 full-time; nonresident $4658 full-time. Full-time tuition and fees vary according to course load and program. Part-time tuition and fees vary according to course load and program. *Required fees:* $685 full-time. *Waivers:* employees or children of employees.

Applying *Options:* electronic application, early admission, deferred entrance. *Application fee:* $20. *Required:* high school transcript. *Application deadlines:* rolling (freshmen), rolling (transfers). *Notification:* continuous (freshmen), continuous (transfers).

Freshman Application Contact Minneapolis Community and Technical College, 1501 Hennepin Avenue, Minneapolis, MN 55403. *Phone:* 612-659-6200. *Toll-free phone:* 800-247-0911. *E-mail:* admissions.office@minneapolis.edu.

Website: http://www.minneapolis.edu/.

Minneapolis Media Institute

Edina, Minnesota

Admissions Office Contact Minneapolis Media Institute, 4100 West 76th Street, Edina, MN 55435. *Toll-free phone:* 800-236-4997.

Website: http://www.mediainstitute.edu/.

Minnesota School of Business–Brooklyn Center

Brooklyn Center, Minnesota

- **Proprietary** primarily 2-year, founded 1989, part of Globe Education Network (GEN) which is composed of Globe University, Minnesota School of Business, Broadview University, The Institute of Production and Recording and Minnesota School of Cosmetology
- **Suburban** 4-acre campus with easy access to Minneapolis-St. Paul
- **Coed,** 169 undergraduate students, 59% full-time, 66% women, 34% men

Undergraduates 100 full-time, 69 part-time. Students come from 3 states and territories; 2% are from out of state; 28% Black or African American, non-Hispanic/Latino; 4% Hispanic/Latino; 15% Asian, non-Hispanic/Latino; 2% American Indian or Alaska Native, non-Hispanic/Latino; 3% Two or more races, non-Hispanic/Latino; 18% Race/ethnicity unknown; 18% transferred in.

Freshmen *Admission:* 12 enrolled.

Faculty *Total:* 16, 44% full-time.

Majors Accounting; business administration and management; computer programming (specific applications); computer systems networking and telecommunications; criminal justice/law enforcement administration; health/health-care administration; information technology; legal assistant/paralegal; marketing/marketing management; medical administrative assistant and medical secretary; medical/clinical assistant.

Academics *Calendar:* quarters. *Degrees:* certificates, diplomas, associate, and bachelor's. *Special study options:* academic remediation for entering students, accelerated degree program, adult/continuing education programs, advanced placement credit, independent study, internships, part-time degree program, services for LD students, summer session for credit.

Library Brooklyn Center Campus Library with an OPAC, a Web page.

Student Life *Housing:* college housing not available. *Campus security:* 24-hour emergency response devices.

Standardized Tests *Required:* ACCUPLACER is required of most applicants unless documentation of a minimum ACT composite score of 21 or documentation of a minimum composite score of 1485 on the SAT is presented (for admission).

Applying *Options:* electronic application. *Application fee:* $50. *Required:* interview, Certification of high school graduation or GED. *Application deadlines:* rolling (freshmen), rolling (out-of-state freshmen), rolling (transfers). *Notification:* continuous (freshmen), continuous (out-of-state freshmen), continuous (transfers).

Freshman Application Contact Minnesota School of Business–Brooklyn Center, 5910 Shingle Creek Parkway, Brooklyn Center, MN 55430.
Website: http://www.msbcollege.edu/.

Minnesota School of Business–Plymouth
Plymouth, Minnesota

- **Proprietary** primarily 2-year, founded 2002, part of Globe Education Network (GEN) which is composed of Globe University, Minnesota School of Business, Broadview University, The Institute of Production and Recording and Minnesota School of Cosmetology
- **Suburban** 7-acre campus with easy access to Minneapolis-St. Paul
- **Coed,** 190 undergraduate students, 56% full-time, 75% women, 25% men

Undergraduates 107 full-time, 83 part-time. Students come from 2 states and territories; 0.5% are from out of state; 5% Black or African American, non-Hispanic/Latino; 3% Hispanic/Latino; 2% Asian, non-Hispanic/Latino; 0.5% Native Hawaiian or other Pacific Islander, non-Hispanic/Latino; 1% American Indian or Alaska Native, non-Hispanic/Latino; 4% Two or more races, non-Hispanic/Latino; 8% Race/ethnicity unknown; 15% transferred in.

Freshmen *Admission:* 17 enrolled.

Faculty *Total:* 36, 19% full-time.

Majors Accounting; business administration and management; computer programming (specific applications); computer systems networking and telecommunications; financial forensics and fraud investigation; health/health-care administration; information technology; marketing/marketing management; massage therapy; physical fitness technician; veterinary/animal health technology.

Academics *Calendar:* quarters. *Degrees:* certificates, diplomas, associate, and bachelor's. *Special study options:* academic remediation for entering students, accelerated degree program, adult/continuing education programs, advanced placement credit, independent study, internships, part-time degree program, services for LD students, summer session for credit.

Library Plymouth Campus Library with an OPAC, a Web page.

Student Life *Housing:* college housing not available. *Campus security:* 24-hour emergency response devices.

Standardized Tests *Required:* ACCUPLACER is required of most applicants unless documentation of a minimum ACT composite score of 21 or documentation of a minimum composite score of 1485 on the SAT is presented (for admission).

Applying *Options:* electronic application. *Application fee:* $50. *Required:* interview, Certification of high school graduation or GED. *Application deadlines:* rolling (freshmen), rolling (out-of-state freshmen), rolling (transfers). *Notification:* continuous (freshmen), continuous (out-of-state freshmen), continuous (transfers).

Freshman Application Contact Minnesota School of Business–Plymouth, 1455 Country Road 101 North, Plymouth, MN 55447.
Website: http://www.msbcollege.edu/.

Minnesota State College–Southeast Technical
Winona, Minnesota

- **State-supported** 2-year, founded 1992, part of Minnesota State Colleges and Universities System
- **Small-town** 132-acre campus with easy access to Minneapolis-St. Paul
- **Coed,** 2,184 undergraduate students, 52% full-time, 59% women, 41% men

Undergraduates 1,143 full-time, 1,041 part-time. 28% are from out of state; 4% Black or African American, non-Hispanic/Latino; 3% Hispanic/Latino; 2% Asian, non-Hispanic/Latino; 0.1% Native Hawaiian or other Pacific Islander, non-Hispanic/Latino; 0.4% American Indian or Alaska Native, non-Hispanic/Latino; 3% Two or more races, non-Hispanic/Latino; 0.1% Race/ethnicity unknown; 0.3% international; 12% transferred in. *Retention:* 40% of full-time freshmen returned.

Freshmen *Admission:* 705 admitted, 300 enrolled. *Average high school GPA:* 2.57.

Faculty *Total:* 130, 62% full-time. *Student/faculty ratio:* 15:1.

Majors Accounting; accounting technology and bookkeeping; administrative assistant and secretarial science; autobody/collision and repair technology; biomedical technology; business administration and management; CAD/CADD drafting/design technology; carpentry; computer programming; computer systems networking and telecommunications; computer technology/computer systems technology; cosmetology; criminal justice/safety; early childhood education; electrical, electronic and communications engineering technology; heating, air conditioning, ventilation and refrigeration maintenance technology; industrial mechanics and maintenance technology; legal administrative assistant/secretary; massage therapy; medical administrative assistant and medical secretary; multi/interdisciplinary studies related; radiologic technology/science; registered nursing/registered nurse; retailing; sales, distribution, and marketing operations; selling skills and sales; web page, digital/multimedia and information resources design.

Academics *Calendar:* semesters. *Degree:* certificates, diplomas, and associate. *Special study options:* distance learning, double majors, internships.

Library Learning Resource Center.

Student Life *Activities and Organizations:* student-run newspaper. *Campus security:* 24-hour emergency response devices, late-night transport/escort service.

Costs (2014–15) *Tuition:* state resident $5019 full-time, $167 per credit part-time; nonresident $5019 full-time, $167 per credit part-time. *Required fees:* $667 full-time, $22 per credit part-time.

Financial Aid Of all full-time matriculated undergraduates who enrolled in 2012, 1,089 applied for aid, 1,003 were judged to have need, 24 had their need fully met. 47 Federal Work-Study jobs (averaging $3081). 26 state and other part-time jobs (averaging $4145). In 2012, 28 non-need-based awards were made. *Average percent of need met:* 39%. *Average financial aid package:* $7111. *Average need-based loan:* $3496. *Average need-based gift aid:* $4740. *Average non-need-based aid:* $2351.

Applying *Options:* electronic application. *Application fee:* $20. *Required:* high school transcript. *Recommended:* interview. *Application deadlines:* rolling (freshmen), rolling (out-of-state freshmen), rolling (transfers). *Notification:* continuous (freshmen), continuous (out-of-state freshmen), continuous (transfers).

Freshman Application Contact Admissions, SE Technical, Minnesota State College–Southeast Technical, 1250 Homer Road, PO Box 409, Winona, MN 55987. *Phone:* 877-853-8324. *Toll-free phone:* 800-372-8164. *Fax:* 507-453-2715. *E-mail:* enrollmentservices@southeastmn.edu.
Website: http://www.southeastmn.edu/.

Minnesota State Community and Technical College
Fergus Falls, Minnesota

Freshman Application Contact Ms. Carrie Brimhall, Dean of Enrollment Management, Minnesota State Community and Technical College, Fergus Falls, MN 56537-1009. *Phone:* 218-736-1528. *Toll-free phone:* 877-450-3322. *E-mail:* carrie.brimhall@minnesota.edu.
Website: http://www.minnesota.edu/.

Minnesota State Community and Technical College–Detroit Lakes
Detroit Lakes, Minnesota

Director of Admissions Mr. Dale Westley, Enrollment Manager, Minnesota State Community and Technical College–Detroit Lakes, 900 Highway 34, E, Detroit Lakes, MN 56501. *Phone:* 218-846-3777. *Toll-free phone:* 800-492-4836.
Website: http://www.minnesota.edu/.

Minnesota State Community and Technical College–Moorhead
Moorhead, Minnesota

Director of Admissions Laurie McKeever, Enrollment Manager, Minnesota State Community and Technical College–Moorhead, 1900 28th Avenue, South, Moorhead, MN 56560. *Phone:* 218-299-6583. *Toll-free phone:* 800-426-5603. *Fax:* 218-299-6810.
Website: http://www.minnesota.edu/.

Minnesota State Community and Technical College–Wadena
Wadena, Minnesota

Director of Admissions Mr. Paul Drange, Enrollment Manager, Minnesota State Community and Technical College–Wadena, 405 Colfax Avenue, SW, PO Box 566, Wadena, MN 56482. *Phone:* 218-631-7818. *Toll-free phone:* 800-247-2007.
Website: http://www.minnesota.edu/.

Minnesota West Community and Technical College

Pipestone, Minnesota

- **State-supported** 2-year, founded 1967, part of Minnesota State Colleges and Universities System
- **Rural** campus
- **Coed**

Undergraduates 1,316 full-time, 2,151 part-time. Students come from 3 other countries; 11% are from out of state; 4% Black or African American, non-Hispanic/Latino; 5% Hispanic/Latino; 2% Asian, non-Hispanic/Latino; 0.1% Native Hawaiian or other Pacific Islander, non-Hispanic/Latino; 1% American Indian or Alaska Native, non-Hispanic/Latino; 2% Two or more races, non-Hispanic/Latino; 5% Race/ethnicity unknown; 0.2% international; 0.8% transferred in. *Retention:* 54% of full-time freshmen returned.

Faculty *Student/faculty ratio:* 13:1.

Academics *Calendar:* semesters. *Degrees:* certificates, diplomas, and associate (profile contains information from Canby, Granite Falls, Jackson, and Worthington campuses). *Special study options:* academic remediation for entering students, advanced placement credit, cooperative education, distance learning, double majors, external degree program, honors programs, independent study, internships, part-time degree program, services for LD students, summer session for credit.

Athletics Member NJCAA.

Standardized Tests *Required:* ACCUPLACER (for admission).

Costs (2013–14) *Tuition:* state resident $172 per credit part-time. Full-time tuition and fees vary according to course load, program, and reciprocity agreements. Part-time tuition and fees vary according to course load, program, and reciprocity agreements. *Required fees:* $17 per credit hour part-time. *Room and board:* Room and board charges vary according to location.

Financial Aid Of all full-time matriculated undergraduates who enrolled in 2012, 3,160 applied for aid.

Applying *Options:* electronic application. *Application fee:* $20. *Required:* high school transcript.

Freshman Application Contact Ms. Crystal Strouth, College Registrar, Minnesota West Community and Technical College, 1450 Collegeway, Worthington, MN 56187. *Phone:* 507-372-3451. *Toll-free phone:* 800-658-2330. *Fax:* 507-372-5803. *E-mail:* crystal.strouth@mnwest.edu.

Website: http://www.mnwest.edu/.

National American University

Bloomington, Minnesota

Freshman Application Contact Ms. Jennifer Michaelson, Admissions Assistant, National American University, 321 Kansas City Street, Rapid City, SD 57201. *Phone:* 605-394-4827. *Toll-free phone:* 866-628-6387. *E-mail:* jmichaelson@national.edu.

Website: http://www.national.edu/.

National American University

Brooklyn Center, Minnesota

Freshman Application Contact Admissions Office, National American University, 6200 Shingle Creek Parkway, Suite 130, Brooklyn Center, MN 55430.

Website: http://www.national.edu/.

Normandale Community College

Bloomington, Minnesota

- **State-supported** 2-year, founded 1968, part of Minnesota State Colleges and Universities System
- **Suburban** 90-acre campus with easy access to Minneapolis-St. Paul
- **Coed**, 9,296 undergraduate students, 43% full-time, 55% women, 45% men

Undergraduates 4,012 full-time, 5,284 part-time. *Retention:* 50% of full-time freshmen returned.

Freshmen *Admission:* 2,590 applied, 1,243 admitted, 2,040 enrolled. *Average high school GPA:* 3.09.

Faculty *Total:* 358, 54% full-time.

Majors Computer science; computer technology/computer systems technology; creative writing; criminal justice/police science; criminal justice/safety; dental hygiene; dietetic technology; dramatic/theater arts; elementary education; fine/studio arts; food science; hospitality administration; liberal arts and sciences/liberal studies; management information systems; manufacturing engineering technology;

marketing/marketing management; medical office computer specialist; multi/interdisciplinary studies related; music; pre-engineering; registered nursing/registered nurse; special education; theater design and technology.

Academics *Calendar:* semesters. *Degree:* certificates and associate. *Special study options:* academic remediation for entering students, adult/continuing education programs, advanced placement credit, cooperative education, distance learning, English as a second language, external degree program, independent study, internships, off-campus study, part-time degree program, services for LD students, student-designed majors, study abroad, summer session for credit.

Library Library plus 1 other with 93,000 titles, 600 serial subscriptions, 40,000 audiovisual materials, an OPAC, a Web page.

Student Life *Housing:* college housing not available. *Activities and Organizations:* drama/theater group, student-run newspaper, choral group, Program Board (NPB), Student Senate, Phi Theta Kappa, Inter-Varsity Christian Fellowship, Latino Student Club. *Campus security:* 24-hour emergency response devices, student patrols, late-night transport/escort service. *Student services:* personal/psychological counseling.

Athletics *Intramural sports:* archery M/W, badminton M/W, basketball M/W, ice hockey M/W, soccer M/W, softball M/W, table tennis M/W, tennis M/W, volleyball M/W, weight lifting M/W.

Costs (2014–15) *Tuition:* state resident $4845 full-time, $161 per credit part-time; nonresident $4845 full-time, $161 per credit part-time. Full-time tuition and fees vary according to program and reciprocity agreements. Part-time tuition and fees vary according to program and reciprocity agreements. *Required fees:* $850 full-time, $28 per credit part-time, $28 per credit part-time. *Payment plan:* installment. *Waivers:* senior citizens and employees or children of employees.

Applying *Options:* electronic application, deferred entrance. *Application fee:* $20. *Required for some:* high school transcript, GED is also accepted for admission. *Application deadlines:* 8/11 (freshmen), 8/11 (transfers). *Notification:* 8/11 (freshmen), 8/11 (transfers).

Freshman Application Contact Admissions Office, Normandale Community College, Normandale Community College, 9700 France Avenue South, Bloomington, MN 55431. *Phone:* 952-358-8201. *Toll-free phone:* 800-481-5412. *Fax:* 952-358-8230. *E-mail:* information@normandale.edu.

Website: http://www.normandale.edu/.

North Hennepin Community College

Brooklyn Park, Minnesota

- **State-supported** 2-year, founded 1966, part of Minnesota State Colleges and Universities System
- **Suburban** 80-acre campus
- **Endowment** $697,321
- **Coed**

Undergraduates 2,260 full-time, 5,397 part-time. Students come from 18 states and territories; 47 other countries; 0.3% are from out of state; 20% Black or African American, non-Hispanic/Latino; 5% Hispanic/Latino; 11% Asian, non-Hispanic/Latino; 0.4% American Indian or Alaska Native, non-Hispanic/Latino; 5% Two or more races, non-Hispanic/Latino; 2% Race/ethnicity unknown; 1% international; 14% transferred in. *Retention:* 56% of full-time freshmen returned.

Faculty *Student/faculty ratio:* 31:1.

Academics *Calendar:* semesters. *Degree:* certificates and associate. *Special study options:* academic remediation for entering students, accelerated degree program, adult/continuing education programs, advanced placement credit, distance learning, double majors, English as a second language, external degree program, honors programs, independent study, internships, off-campus study, part-time degree program, services for LD students, student-designed majors, study abroad, summer session for credit. *ROTC:* Army (c), Navy (c), Air Force (c).

Student Life *Campus security:* 24-hour emergency response devices, student patrols, late-night transport/escort service.

Costs (2013–14) *Tuition:* state resident $4952 full-time, $206 per credit part-time; nonresident $4952 full-time, $21 per credit part-time. Full-time tuition and fees vary according to course load, location, and program. Part-time tuition and fees vary according to course load, location, and program. *Required fees:* $495 full-time.

Applying *Options:* electronic application, early admission, deferred entrance. *Application fee:* $20. *Recommended:* high school transcript.

Freshman Application Contact Ms. Alison Leintz, Admissions Specialist, North Hennepin Community College, 7411 85th Ave N., Brooklyn Park, MN 55445. *Phone:* 763-424-0722. *Toll-free phone:* 800-818-0395. *Fax:* 763-424-0929. *E-mail:* aleintz@nhcc.edu.

Website: http://www.nhcc.edu/.

Northland Community and Technical College–Thief River Falls & East Grand Forks

Thief River Falls, Minnesota

Freshman Application Contact Mr. Eugene Klinke, Director of Enrollment Management and Multicultural Services, Northland Community and Technical College–Thief River Falls & East Grand Forks, 1101 Highway One East, Thief River Falls, MN 56701. *Phone:* 218-683-8554. *Toll-free phone:* 800-959-6282. *Fax:* 218-683-8980. *E-mail:* eugene.klinke@northlandcollege.edu. *Website:* http://www.northlandcollege.edu/.

Northwest Technical College

Bemidji, Minnesota

- **State-supported** 2-year, founded 1993, part of Minnesota State Colleges and Universities System
- **Small-town** campus
- **Coed,** 1,203 undergraduate students, 36% full-time, 69% women, 31% men

Undergraduates 436 full-time, 767 part-time. 12% are from out of state; 2% Black or African American, non-Hispanic/Latino; 2% Hispanic/Latino; 1% Asian, non-Hispanic/Latino; 0.1% Native Hawaiian or other Pacific Islander, non-Hispanic/Latino; 9% American Indian or Alaska Native, non-Hispanic/Latino; 6% Two or more races, non-Hispanic/Latino; 0.5% Race/ethnicity unknown; 12% transferred in; 2% live on campus. *Retention:* 46% of full-time freshmen returned.
Freshmen *Admission:* 126 enrolled.
Faculty *Total:* 47, 64% full-time. *Student/faculty ratio:* 19:1.
Majors Accounting; administrative assistant and secretarial science; automobile/automotive mechanics technology; business administration and management; child-care and support services management; computer systems networking and telecommunications; dental assisting; energy management and systems technology; engine machinist; industrial safety technology; industrial technology; licensed practical/vocational nurse training; manufacturing engineering technology; medical administrative assistant and medical secretary; registered nursing/registered nurse; sales, distribution, and marketing operations.
Academics *Calendar:* semesters. *Degree:* certificates, diplomas, and associate. *Special study options:* part-time degree program.
Library Northwest Technical College Learning Enrichment Center.
Student Life *Housing Options:* coed, special housing for students with disabilities. Campus housing is provided by a third party.
Costs (2013–14) *Tuition:* state resident $5190 full-time, $173 per credit hour part-time; nonresident $5190 full-time, $173 per credit hour part-time. Full-time tuition and fees vary according to program. Part-time tuition and fees vary according to program. *Required fees:* $292 full-time, $10 per credit hour part-time. *Room and board:* $7256; room only: $4554. Room and board charges vary according to board plan and housing facility. *Payment plan:* installment. *Waivers:* senior citizens and employees or children of employees.
Applying *Options:* electronic application. *Application fee:* $20. *Required:* high school transcript. *Application deadlines:* rolling (freshmen), rolling (transfers). *Notification:* continuous (freshmen), continuous (transfers).
Freshman Application Contact Ms. Kari Kantack-Miller, Diversity and Enrollment Representative, Northwest Technical College, 905 Grant Avenue, Southeast, Bemidji, MN 56601. *Phone:* 218-333-6645. *Toll-free phone:* 800-942-8324. *Fax:* 218-333-6694. *E-mail:* kari.kantack@ntcmn.edu. *Website:* http://www.ntcmn.edu/.

Pine Technical College

Pine City, Minnesota

Freshman Application Contact Pine Technical College, 900 4th Street SE, Pine City, MN 55063. *Phone:* 320-629-5100. *Toll-free phone:* 800-521-7463. *Website:* http://www.pinetech.edu/.

Rainy River Community College

International Falls, Minnesota

- **State-supported** 2-year, founded 1967, part of Minnesota State Colleges and Universities System
- **Small-town** 80-acre campus
- **Coed,** 304 undergraduate students, 78% full-time, 61% women, 39% men

Undergraduates 236 full-time, 68 part-time. 16% Black or African American, non-Hispanic/Latino; 3% Hispanic/Latino; 1% Asian, non-Hispanic/Latino; 5% American Indian or Alaska Native, non-Hispanic/Latino; 10% international.
Freshmen *Admission:* 66 enrolled.
Faculty *Total:* 25, 40% full-time. *Student/faculty ratio:* 15:1.

Majors Administrative assistant and secretarial science; biological and physical sciences; business administration and management; liberal arts and sciences/liberal studies; pre-engineering.
Academics *Calendar:* semesters. *Degree:* certificates, diplomas, and associate. *Special study options:* academic remediation for entering students, adult/continuing education programs, advanced placement credit, cooperative education, honors programs, independent study, internships, part-time degree program, services for LD students, summer session for credit.
Library Rainy River Community College Library with 20,000 titles, an OPAC.
Student Life *Housing Options:* special housing for students with disabilities. Campus housing is university owned. *Activities and Organizations:* drama/theater group, Anishinaabe Student Coalition, Student Senate, Black Student Association. *Campus security:* 24-hour emergency response devices, late-night transport/escort service, controlled dormitory access. *Student services:* personal/psychological counseling.
Athletics Member NJCAA. *Intercollegiate sports:* basketball M/W, ice hockey W, softball W, volleyball W. *Intramural sports:* archery M/W, badminton M/W, baseball M, bowling M/W, cheerleading M/W, cross-country running M/W, ice hockey M, skiing (cross-country) M/W, skiing (downhill) M/W, swimming and diving M/W, table tennis M/W, tennis M/W, volleyball M/W, weight lifting M/W.
Costs (2013–14) *Tuition:* state resident $4729 full-time; nonresident $5911 full-time. Full-time tuition and fees vary according to program and reciprocity agreements. Part-time tuition and fees vary according to program and reciprocity agreements. *Required fees:* $594 full-time. *Room and board:* room only: $2950. Room and board charges vary according to housing facility. *Payment plan:* installment. *Waivers:* employees or children of employees.
Applying *Options:* electronic application, early admission, deferred entrance. *Application fee:* $20. *Recommended:* high school transcript. *Application deadlines:* rolling (freshmen), rolling (out-of-state freshmen), rolling (transfers). *Notification:* continuous (freshmen), continuous (out-of-state freshmen), continuous (transfers).
Freshman Application Contact Ms. Berta Hagen, Registrar, Rainy River Community College, 1501 Highway 71, International Falls, MN 56649. *Phone:* 218-285-2207. *Toll-free phone:* 800-456-3996. *Fax:* 218-285-2314. *E-mail:* berta.hagen@rainyriver.edu. *Website:* http://www.rrcc.mnscu.edu/.

Ridgewater College

Willmar, Minnesota

Freshman Application Contact Ms. Linda Barron, Admissions Assistant, Ridgewater College, PO Box 1097, Willmar, MN 56201-1097. *Phone:* 320-222-5976. *Toll-free phone:* 800-722-1151. *E-mail:* linda.barron@ridgewater.edu. *Website:* http://www.ridgewater.edu/.

Riverland Community College

Austin, Minnesota

Freshman Application Contact Ms. Renee Njos, Admission Secretary, Riverland Community College, Austin, MN 55912. *Phone:* 507-433-0820. *Toll-free phone:* 800-247-5039. *Fax:* 507-433-0515. *E-mail:* admissions@riverland.edu. *Website:* http://www.riverland.edu/.

Rochester Community and Technical College

Rochester, Minnesota

Director of Admissions Mr. Troy Tynsky, Director of Admissions, Rochester Community and Technical College, 851 30th Avenue, SE, Rochester, MN 55904-4999. *Phone:* 507-280-3509. *Website:* http://www.rctc.edu/.

St. Cloud Technical & Community College

St. Cloud, Minnesota

- **State-supported** 2-year, founded 1948, part of Minnesota State Colleges and Universities System
- **Urban** 35-acre campus with easy access to Minneapolis-St. Paul
- **Coed**

Undergraduates 2,230 full-time, 2,521 part-time. Students come from 7 states and territories; 1 other country; 3% are from out of state; 6% Black or African American, non-Hispanic/Latino; 3% Hispanic/Latino; 1% Asian, non-Hispanic/Latino; 0.5% American Indian or Alaska Native, non-Hispanic/Latino; 4% Two or more races, non-Hispanic/Latino; 1%

Race/ethnicity unknown; 0.3% international; 37% transferred in. *Retention:* 49% of full-time freshmen returned.

Faculty *Student/faculty ratio:* 22:1.

Academics *Calendar:* semesters. *Degree:* certificates, diplomas, and associate. *Special study options:* academic remediation for entering students, adult/continuing education programs, advanced placement credit, cooperative education, distance learning, English as a second language, independent study, internships, part-time degree program, services for LD students, summer session for credit.

Student Life *Campus security:* late-night transport/escort service.

Athletics Member NJCAA.

Costs (2013–14) *Tuition:* state resident $4767 full-time, $159 per credit part-time; nonresident $4767 full-time, $159 per credit part-time. Full-time tuition and fees vary according to location and program. Part-time tuition and fees vary according to course load, location, and program. *Required fees:* $534 full-time, $18 per credit part-time.

Applying *Options:* electronic application, early admission, deferred entrance. *Application fee:* $20. *Required:* high school transcript. *Required for some:* essay or personal statement, interview.

Freshman Application Contact Ms. Jodi Elness, Admissions Office, St. Cloud Technical & Community College, 1540 Northway Drive, St. Cloud, MN 56303. *Phone:* 320-308-5089. *Toll-free phone:* 800-222-1009. *Fax:* 320-308-5981. *E-mail:* jelness@sctcc.edu.
Website: http://www.sctcc.edu/.

Saint Paul College–A Community & Technical College
St. Paul, Minnesota

Freshman Application Contact Ms. Sarah Carrico, Saint Paul College–A Community & Technical College, 235 Marshall Avenue, Saint Paul, MN 55102. *Phone:* 651-846-1424. *Toll-free phone:* 800-227-6029. *Fax:* 651-846-1703. *E-mail:* admissions@saintpaul.edu.
Website: http://www.saintpaul.edu/.

Sanford-Brown College
Mendota Heights, Minnesota

Freshman Application Contact Mr. Mark Fredrichs, Registrar, Sanford-Brown College, 1440 Northland Drive, Mendota Heights, MN 55120. *Phone:* 651-905-3400. *Toll-free phone:* 855-502-7016. *Fax:* 651-905-3550.
Website: http://www.sanfordbrown.edu/Mendota-Heights.

South Central College
North Mankato, Minnesota

Freshman Application Contact Ms. Beverly Herda, Director of Admissions, South Central College, 1920 Lee Boulevard, North Mankato, MN 56003. *Phone:* 507-389-7334. *Fax:* 507-388-9951.
Website: http://southcentral.edu/.

Vermilion Community College
Ely, Minnesota

Freshman Application Contact Mr. Todd Heiman, Director of Enrollment Services, Vermilion Community College, 1900 East Camp Street, Ely, MN 55731-1996. *Phone:* 218-365-7224. *Toll-free phone:* 800-657-3608.
Website: http://www.vcc.edu/.

MISSISSIPPI

Antonelli College
Hattiesburg, Mississippi

Freshman Application Contact Mrs. Karen Gautreau, Director, Antonelli College, 1500 North 31st Avenue, Hattiesburg, MS 39401. *Phone:* 601-583-4100. *Fax:* 601-583-0839. *E-mail:* admissionsh@antonellicollege.edu.
Website: http://www.antonellicollege.edu/.

Antonelli College
Jackson, Mississippi

Freshman Application Contact Antonelli College, 2323 Lakeland Drive, Jackson, MS 39232. *Phone:* 601-362-9991.
Website: http://www.antonellicollege.edu/.

Coahoma Community College
Clarksdale, Mississippi

Freshman Application Contact Mrs. Wanda Holmes, Director of Admissions and Records, Coahoma Community College, Clarksdale, MS 38614-9799. *Phone:* 662-621-4205. *Toll-free phone:* 866-470-1CCC.
Website: http://www.ccc.cc.ms.us/.

Copiah-Lincoln Community College
Wesson, Mississippi

- **State and locally supported** 2-year, founded 1928, part of Mississippi Community College Board
- **Rural** 525-acre campus with easy access to Jackson
- **Endowment** $2.5 million
- **Coed**, 3,157 undergraduate students, 79% full-time, 63% women, 37% men

Undergraduates 2,509 full-time, 648 part-time. Students come from 6 states and territories; 1% are from out of state; 42% Black or African American, non-Hispanic/Latino; 1% Hispanic/Latino; 0.3% Asian, non-Hispanic/Latino; 0.3% American Indian or Alaska Native, non-Hispanic/Latino; 0.2% Two or more races, non-Hispanic/Latino; 1% Race/ethnicity unknown; 6% transferred in; 30% live on campus.

Freshmen *Admission:* 692 enrolled.

Faculty *Total:* 138.

Majors Accounting; agribusiness; agricultural business and management; agricultural business and management related; agricultural economics; agricultural/farm supplies retailing and wholesaling; agriculture; architecture; art teacher education; biological and physical sciences; biology/biological sciences; business administration and management; chemistry; child development; civil engineering technology; clinical/medical laboratory technology; computer programming; cosmetology; criminal justice/police science; data processing and data processing technology; drafting and design technology; economics; education; electrical, electronic and communications engineering technology; elementary education; engineering; English; family and consumer sciences/home economics teacher education; farm and ranch management; food technology and processing; forestry; health teacher education; history; industrial radiologic technology; journalism; liberal arts and sciences/liberal studies; library and information science; music teacher education; physical education teaching and coaching; registered nursing/registered nurse; special products marketing; trade and industrial teacher education.

Academics *Calendar:* semesters. *Degree:* certificates and associate. *Special study options:* academic remediation for entering students, adult/continuing education programs, advanced placement credit, honors programs, part-time degree program, student-designed majors, summer session for credit.

Library Oswalt Memorial Library with 34,357 titles, 166 serial subscriptions.

Student Life *Housing Options:* Campus housing is university owned. *Activities and Organizations:* drama/theater group, student-run newspaper, radio station, choral group, marching band. *Campus security:* 24-hour patrols. *Student services:* health clinic, personal/psychological counseling.

Athletics Member NJCAA. *Intercollegiate sports:* baseball M(s), basketball M(s)/W(s), football M(s), golf M/W, softball W, tennis M/W, track and field M. *Intramural sports:* basketball M/W, football M, golf M/W, tennis M/W, volleyball M/W.

Costs (2014–15) *Tuition:* state resident $2350 full-time; nonresident $4350 full-time. *Room and board:* Room and board charges vary according to board plan and housing facility. *Waivers:* senior citizens and employees or children of employees.

Financial Aid Of all full-time matriculated undergraduates who enrolled in 2012, 125 Federal Work-Study jobs (averaging $1000).

Applying *Options:* early admission. *Required:* high school transcript. *Application deadlines:* rolling (freshmen), rolling (transfers).

Freshman Application Contact Ms. Gay Langham, Student Records Manager, Copiah-Lincoln Community College, PO Box 649, Wesson, MS 39191-0457. *Phone:* 601-643-8307. *E-mail:* gay.langham@colin.edu.
Website: http://www.colin.edu/.

East Central Community College
Decatur, Mississippi

Director of Admissions Ms. Donna Luke, Director of Admissions, Records, and Research, East Central Community College, PO Box 129, Decatur, MS 39327-0129. *Phone:* 601-635-2111 Ext. 206. *Toll-free phone:* 877-462-3222.
Website: http://www.eccc.edu/.

East Mississippi Community College

Scooba, Mississippi

Director of Admissions Ms. Melinda Sciple, Admissions Officer, East Mississippi Community College, PO Box 158, Scooba, MS 39358-0158. *Phone:* 662-476-5041.

Website: http://www.eastms.edu/.

Hinds Community College

Raymond, Mississippi

- **State and locally supported** 2-year, founded 1917, part of Mississippi Community College Board

- **Small-town** 671-acre campus

- **Coed,** 11,893 undergraduate students, 71% full-time, 63% women, 37% men

Undergraduates 8,468 full-time, 3,425 part-time. Students come from 24 states and territories; 14 other countries; 4% are from out of state; 57% Black or African American, non-Hispanic/Latino; 1% Hispanic/Latino; 0.7% Asian, non-Hispanic/Latino; 0.4% American Indian or Alaska Native, non-Hispanic/Latino; 1% Two or more races, non-Hispanic/Latino; 2% Race/ethnicity unknown; 8% transferred in; 12% live on campus. *Retention:* 52% of full-time freshmen returned.

Freshmen *Admission:* 2,942 enrolled. *Test scores:* ACT scores over 18: 44%; ACT scores over 24: 6%.

Faculty *Total:* 745, 54% full-time. *Student/faculty ratio:* 19:1.

Majors Accounting; accounting technology and bookkeeping; administrative assistant and secretarial science; aeronautics/aviation/aerospace science and technology; agribusiness; agricultural mechanization related; agriculture; airframe mechanics and aircraft maintenance technology; applied horticulture/horticultural business services related; architecture; art; aviation/airway management; banking and financial support services; biology/biological sciences; business automation/technology/data entry; business/commerce; business teacher education; carpentry; chemistry; childcare provision; clinical laboratory science/medical technology; clinical/medical laboratory technology; computer and information sciences; computer and information systems security; computer installation and repair technology; computer programming; computer systems networking and telecommunications; construction engineering technology; cooking and related culinary arts; corrections and criminal justice related; court reporting; criminal justice/safety; dance; dental assisting; dental hygiene; diagnostic medical sonography and ultrasound technology; diesel mechanics technology; digital communication and media/multimedia; drafting and design technology; dramatic/theater arts; electrical, electronic and communications engineering technology; electrical/electronics equipment installation and repair; electrician; elementary education; emergency medical technology (EMT paramedic); engineering; English; family and consumer sciences/human sciences; fashion merchandising; floriculture/floristry management; forestry; game and interactive media design; general studies; geographic information science and cartography; geology/earth science; graphic and printing equipment operation/production; graphic design; health and medical administrative services related; health information/medical records administration; health information/medical records technology; health professions related; heating, air conditioning, ventilation and refrigeration maintenance technology; history; hospitality administration; housing and human environments related; institutional food workers; insurance; journalism; landscape architecture; landscaping and groundskeeping; legal assistant/paralegal; machine tool technology; marketing/marketing management; masonry; mathematics; medical/clinical assistant; music; nursing administration; occupational therapy; photographic and film/video technology; physical education teaching and coaching; physical sciences; physical therapy; physical therapy technology; plumbing technology; political science and government; pre-dentistry studies; pre-law studies; premedical studies; prenursing studies; pre-pharmacy studies; pre-veterinary studies; psychology; radio and television; radio and television broadcasting technology; radiologic technology/science; real estate; registered nursing/registered nurse; respiratory care therapy; secondary education; sign language interpretation and translation; social sciences; sociology; speech communication and rhetoric; surgical technology; technology/industrial arts teacher education; telecommunications technology; tourism and travel services management; turf and turfgrass management; veterinary/animal health technology; welding technology.

Academics *Calendar:* semesters. *Degrees:* certificates, diplomas, and associate (reported data includes Raymond, Jackson Academic and Technical Center, Jackson Nursing-Allied Health Center, Rankin, Utica, and Vicksburg campus locations). *Special study options:* academic remediation for entering students, accelerated degree program, adult/continuing education programs, advanced placement credit, cooperative education, distance learning, double majors, freshman honors college, honors programs, independent study, internships, part-time degree program, services for LD students, study abroad, summer session for credit. *ROTC:* Army (c).

Library McLendon Library plus 5 others with an OPAC.

Student Life *Housing Options:* coed, men-only, women-only. Campus housing is university owned. *Activities and Organizations:* drama/theater group, student-run newspaper, choral group, marching band. *Campus security:* 24-hour emergency response devices and patrols, late-night transport/escort service, controlled dormitory access. *Student services:* personal/psychological counseling, legal services.

Athletics Member NJCAA. *Intercollegiate sports:* baseball M(s), basketball M(s)/W(s), cheerleading M(s)/W(s), football M(s), golf M(s), soccer M(s)/W(s), softball W(s), tennis M(s)/W(s), track and field M(s)/W(s). *Intramural sports:* basketball M/W, bowling M/W, cross-country running M/W, football M/W, golf M/W, softball M/W, swimming and diving M/W, tennis M/W, ultimate Frisbee M/W, volleyball M/W.

Standardized Tests *Required for some:* SAT and SAT Subject Tests or ACT (for admission).

Costs (2013–14) *Tuition:* state resident $2160 full-time, $100 per semester hour part-time; nonresident $4760 full-time, $200 per semester hour part-time. Part-time tuition and fees vary according to course load. *Required fees:* $100 full-time, $50 per term part-time. *Room and board:* $3900. Room and board charges vary according to board plan and housing facility. *Payment plan:* installment. *Waivers:* senior citizens and employees or children of employees.

Financial Aid Of all full-time matriculated undergraduates who enrolled in 2012, 300 Federal Work-Study jobs (averaging $1250). 200 state and other part-time jobs (averaging $1000).

Applying *Required:* high school transcript.

Freshman Application Contact Hinds Community College, PO Box 1100, Raymond, MS 39154-1100. *Phone:* 601-857-3280. *Toll-free phone:* 800-HINDSCC.

Website: http://www.hindscc.edu/.

Holmes Community College

Goodman, Mississippi

Director of Admissions Dr. Lynn Wright, Dean of Admissions and Records, Holmes Community College, PO Box 369, Goodman, MS 39079-0369. *Phone:* 601-472-2312 Ext. 1023. *Toll-free phone:* 800-HOLMES-4.

Website: http://www.holmescc.edu/.

Itawamba Community College

Fulton, Mississippi

Freshman Application Contact Mr. Larry Boggs, Director of Student Recruitment and Scholarships, Itawamba Community College, 602 West Hill Street, Fulton, MS 38843. *Phone:* 601-862-8252. *E-mail:* laboggs@iccms.edu.

Website: http://www.iccms.edu/.

Jones County Junior College

Ellisville, Mississippi

Director of Admissions Mrs. Dianne Speed, Director of Admissions and Records, Jones County Junior College, 900 South Court Street, Ellisville, MS 39437-3901. *Phone:* 601-477-4025.

Website: http://www.jcjc.edu/.

Meridian Community College

Meridian, Mississippi

Freshman Application Contact Ms. Angela Payne, Director of Admissions, Meridian Community College, 910 Highway 19 North, Meridian, MS 39307. *Phone:* 601-484-8357. *Toll-free phone:* 800-MCC-THE-1. *E-mail:* apayne@meridiancc.edu.

Website: http://www.meridiancc.edu/.

Miller-Motte Technical College

Gulfport, Mississippi

Admissions Office Contact Miller-Motte Technical College, 12121 Highway 49 North, Gulfport, MS 39503. *Toll-free phone:* 866-297-0267.

Website: http://www.miller-motte.edu/.

Mississippi Delta Community College
Moorhead, Mississippi

- **District-supported** 2-year, founded 1926, part of Mississippi State Board for Community and Junior Colleges
- **Small-town** 425-acre campus
- **Coed,** 2,950 undergraduate students, 78% full-time, 63% women, 37% men

Undergraduates 2,305 full-time, 645 part-time. Students come from 6 states and territories; 64% Black or African American, non-Hispanic/Latino; 0.9% Hispanic/Latino; 0.8% Asian, non-Hispanic/Latino; 0.8% Race/ethnicity unknown; 25% live on campus. *Retention:* 58% of full-time freshmen returned.
Freshmen *Admission:* 909 applied, 909 admitted, 738 enrolled. *Test scores:* ACT scores over 18: 31%; ACT scores over 24: 3%.
Faculty *Total:* 208, 54% full-time, 8% with terminal degrees. *Student/faculty ratio:* 18:1.
Majors Accounting; administrative assistant and secretarial science; advertising; agricultural business and management; agricultural economics; American studies; architectural engineering technology; art teacher education; behavioral sciences; biology/biological sciences; business machine repair; civil engineering technology; clinical/medical laboratory technology; computer engineering technology; criminal justice/law enforcement administration; dental hygiene; design and applied arts related; developmental and child psychology; dramatic/theater arts; economics; education; electrical, electronic and communications engineering technology; elementary education; English; family and consumer sciences/human sciences; geography; graphic and printing equipment operation/production; health information/medical records administration; health teacher education; history; horticultural science; liberal arts and sciences/liberal studies; management information systems; masonry; mathematics; medical office computer specialist; medical radiologic technology; music; music teacher education; physical education teaching and coaching; political science and government; registered nursing/registered nurse; science teacher education; social work.
Academics *Calendar:* semesters. *Degree:* certificates, diplomas, and associate. *Special study options:* academic remediation for entering students, adult/continuing education programs, advanced placement credit, part-time degree program, summer session for credit.
Library Stanny Sanders Library with 33,020 titles, 250 serial subscriptions, an OPAC.
Student Life *Housing Options:* men-only, women-only. Campus housing is university owned. *Activities and Organizations:* choral group, marching band, Phi Theta Kappa, Skills USA, Phi Beta Lambda, Student Government Association, Nursing Club. *Campus security:* 24-hour emergency response devices and patrols, late-night transport/escort service, controlled dormitory access. *Student services:* personal/psychological counseling.
Athletics Member NJCAA. *Intercollegiate sports:* baseball M(s), basketball M(s)/W(s), football M(s), softball W(s). *Intramural sports:* basketball M/W, football M/W, softball M/W, table tennis M/W, volleyball M/W.
Standardized Tests *Required for some:* ACT (for admission).
Costs (2014–15) *Tuition:* state resident $2490 full-time, $125 per credit hour part-time; nonresident $4098 full-time, $125 per credit hour part-time. Full-time tuition and fees vary according to course load and location. Part-time tuition and fees vary according to course load and location. *Required fees:* $30 full-time. *Room and board:* $2740; room only: $940. Room and board charges vary according to board plan. *Payment plan:* installment. *Waivers:* employees or children of employees.
Financial Aid Of all full-time matriculated undergraduates who enrolled in 2012, 100 Federal Work-Study jobs (averaging $1400). 100 state and other part-time jobs (averaging $1400).
Applying *Options:* deferred entrance. *Required:* high school transcript. *Application deadlines:* 7/27 (freshmen), rolling (out-of-state freshmen), 7/27 (transfers). *Notification:* continuous (freshmen), continuous (out-of-state freshmen), continuous (transfers).
Freshman Application Contact Mississippi Delta Community College, PO Box 668, Highway 3 and Cherry Street, Moorhead, MS 38761-0668. *Phone:* 662-246-6302.
Website: http://www.msdelta.edu/.

Mississippi Gulf Coast Community College
Perkinston, Mississippi

- **District-supported** 2-year, founded 1911
- **Small-town** 600-acre campus with easy access to New Orleans
- **Coed,** 10,074 undergraduate students, 69% full-time, 60% women, 40% men

Undergraduates 6,935 full-time, 3,139 part-time. Students come from 15 states and territories; 4% are from out of state; 24% Black or African American, non-Hispanic/Latino; 3% Hispanic/Latino; 3% Asian, non-Hispanic/Latino; 0.1% Native Hawaiian or other Pacific Islander, non-Hispanic/Latino; 0.5% American Indian or Alaska Native, non-Hispanic/Latino; 2% Two or more races, non-Hispanic/Latino; 3% Race/ethnicity unknown; 7% live on campus. *Retention:* 62% of full-time freshmen returned.
Freshmen *Admission:* 2,919 enrolled.
Faculty *Total:* 488, 59% full-time. *Student/faculty ratio:* 24:1.
Majors Accounting; administrative assistant and secretarial science; advertising; agricultural business and management; art; art teacher education; automobile/automotive mechanics technology; biological and physical sciences; business administration and management; business teacher education; chemical engineering; clinical/medical laboratory technology; computer and information sciences related; computer engineering technology; computer graphics; computer programming related; computer science; computer systems networking and telecommunications; court reporting; criminal justice/law enforcement administration; criminal justice/police science; data entry/microcomputer applications; data entry/microcomputer applications related; drafting and design technology; education; electrical, electronic and communications engineering technology; elementary education; emergency medical technology (EMT paramedic); fashion merchandising; finance; horticultural science; hotel/motel administration; human services; industrial radiologic technology; information technology; kindergarten/preschool education; legal assistant/paralegal; liberal arts and sciences/liberal studies; marketing/marketing management; ornamental horticulture; pre-engineering; registered nursing/registered nurse; respiratory care therapy; welding technology; word processing.
Academics *Calendar:* semesters. *Degree:* certificates, diplomas, and associate. *Special study options:* academic remediation for entering students, adult/continuing education programs, advanced placement credit, cooperative education, distance learning, English as a second language, honors programs, independent study, internships, part-time degree program, study abroad, summer session for credit.
Library Main Library plus 3 others with 100,472 titles, 922 serial subscriptions, an OPAC.
Student Life *Housing Options:* men-only, women-only. Campus housing is university owned. *Activities and Organizations:* drama/theater group, student-run newspaper, choral group, marching band, Student Government Association, Students in Free Enterprise (SIFE), Reflections. *Campus security:* 24-hour emergency response devices and patrols. *Student services:* personal/psychological counseling, women's center.
Athletics Member NJCAA. *Intercollegiate sports:* baseball M(s), basketball M(s)/W(s), football M(s), golf M(s), soccer M(s)/W(s), softball W(s), tennis M(s)/W(s), track and field M(s). *Intramural sports:* basketball M/W, football M, soccer M/W, softball M/W, volleyball M/W.
Costs (2014–15) *Tuition:* state resident $1150 full-time, $115 per semester hour part-time; nonresident $2073 full-time. *Required fees:* $86 full-time. *Room and board:* $1785. *Payment plan:* installment.
Applying *Required:* high school transcript.
Freshman Application Contact Mrs. Nichol Green, Director of Admissions, Mississippi Gulf Coast Community College, PO Box 548, Perkinston, MS 39573. *Phone:* 601-928-6264. *Fax:* 601-928-6345.
Website: http://www.mgccc.edu/.

Northeast Mississippi Community College
Booneville, Mississippi

Freshman Application Contact Office of Enrollment Services, Northeast Mississippi Community College, 101 Cunningham Boulevard, Booneville, MS 38829. *Phone:* 662-720-7239. *Toll-free phone:* 800-555-2154. *E-mail:* admitme@nemcc.edu.
Website: http://www.nemcc.edu/.

Northwest Mississippi Community College
Senatobia, Mississippi

- **State and locally supported** 2-year, founded 1927, part of Mississippi State Board for Community and Junior Colleges
- **Rural** 75-acre campus with easy access to Memphis
- **Coed,** 6,300 undergraduate students

Freshmen *Admission:* 2,000 applied, 2,000 admitted.
Faculty *Total:* 200. *Student/faculty ratio:* 20:1.
Majors Accounting; agricultural business and management; agricultural economics; agricultural mechanization; agriculture; animal sciences; art; business administration and management; civil engineering technology; commercial and advertising art; computer and information sciences; computer programming; computer programming (specific applications); court reporting;

dairy science; data processing and data processing technology; drafting and design technology; education; electrical, electronic and communications engineering technology; elementary education; family and consumer sciences/home economics teacher education; fashion merchandising; foods, nutrition, and wellness; heating, air conditioning, ventilation and refrigeration maintenance technology; heating, ventilation, air conditioning and refrigeration engineering technology; hotel/motel administration; journalism; legal assistant/paralegal; liberal arts and sciences/liberal studies; licensed practical/vocational nurse training; machine tool technology; mathematics teacher education; medical administrative assistant and medical secretary; music teacher education; office management; physical education teaching and coaching; plant sciences; poultry science; radio and television; radio and television broadcasting technology; registered nursing/registered nurse; respiratory care therapy; sales and marketing/marketing and distribution teacher education; science teacher education; social science teacher education; social studies teacher education; speech teacher education; telecommunications technology.

Academics *Calendar:* semesters. *Degree:* associate. *Special study options:* academic remediation for entering students, adult/continuing education programs, honors programs, part-time degree program, services for LD students, summer session for credit. *ROTC:* Air Force (b).

Library R. C. Pugh Library with 38,000 titles, 325 serial subscriptions.

Student Life *Activities and Organizations:* drama/theater group, student-run newspaper, radio station, choral group, marching band. *Campus security:* 24-hour emergency response devices, late-night transport/escort service, controlled dormitory access. *Student services:* health clinic.

Athletics Member NJCAA. *Intercollegiate sports:* baseball M, basketball M(s)/W(s), equestrian sports M(s)/W(s), football M(s), golf M, softball W(s), tennis M(s)/W(s). *Intramural sports:* basketball M/W, football M.

Applying *Options:* early admission, deferred entrance. *Required:* high school transcript. *Application deadlines:* 9/7 (freshmen), 9/7 (transfers). *Notification:* continuous (freshmen), continuous (transfers).

Freshman Application Contact Northwest Mississippi Community College, 4975 Highway 51 North, Senatobia, MS 38668-1701. *Phone:* 662-562-3222.

Website: http://www.northwestms.edu/.

Pearl River Community College
Poplarville, Mississippi

Freshman Application Contact Mr. J. Dow Ford, Director of Admissions, Pearl River Community College, 101 Highway 11 North, Poplarville, MS 39470. *Phone:* 601-403-1000. *E-mail:* dford@prcc.edu.

Website: http://www.prcc.edu/.

Southwest Mississippi Community College
Summit, Mississippi

Freshman Application Contact Mr. Matthew Calhoun, Vice President of Admissions and Records, Southwest Mississippi Community College, 1156 College Drive, Summit, MS 39666. *Phone:* 601-276-2001. *Fax:* 601-276-3888. *E-mail:* mattc@smcc.edu.

Website: http://www.smcc.cc.ms.us/.

Virginia College in Jackson
Jackson, Mississippi

Director of Admissions Director of Admissions, Virginia College in Jackson, 5841 Ridgewood Road, Jackson, MS 39211. *Phone:* 601-977-0960.

Website: http://www.vc.edu/.

MISSOURI

American Business & Technology University
Saint Joseph, Missouri

Director of Admissions Richard Lingle, Lead Admission Coordinator, American Business & Technology University, 2300 Frederick Avenue, Saint Joseph, MO 64506. *Phone:* 800-908-9329 Ext. 13. *Toll-free phone:* 800-908-9329. *E-mail:* ricahrd@acot.edu.

Website: http://www.abtu.edu/.

Anthem College–Fenton
Fenton, Missouri

Admissions Office Contact Anthem College–Fenton, 645 Gravois Bluffs Boulevard, Fenton, MO 63026.
Website: http://anthem.edu/fenton-missouri/.

Anthem College–Kansas City
Kansas City, Missouri

Freshman Application Contact Admissions Office, Anthem College–Kansas City, 9001 State Line Road, Kansas City, MO 64114. *Phone:* 816-444-4300. *Toll-free phone:* 855-464-2684. *Fax:* 816-444-4494.
Website: http://anthem.edu/kansas-city-missouri/.

Anthem College–Maryland Heights
Maryland Heights, Missouri

Freshman Application Contact Mr. Brad Coleman, Admissions Office, Anthem College–Maryland Heights, 13723 Riverport Drive, Maryland Heights, MO 63043. *Phone:* 314-595-3400. *Toll-free phone:* 855-526-8436. *Fax:* 314-739-5133.
Website: http://anthem.edu/maryland-heights-missouri/.

Brown Mackie College–St. Louis
Fenton, Missouri

- **Proprietary** primarily 2-year, part of Education Management Corporation
- **Coed**

Majors Biomedical technology; business administration and management; business/commerce; corrections and criminal justice related; health/health-care administration; information technology; medical office management; occupational therapist assistant; veterinary/animal health technology.
Academics *Degrees:* diplomas, associate, and bachelor's.
Freshman Application Contact Brown Mackie College–St. Louis, #2 Soccer Park Road, Fenton, MO 63026. *Phone:* 636-651-3290.
Website: http://www.brownmackie.edu/st-louis/.

See display on next page and page 418 for the College Close-Up.

Bryan University
Columbia, Missouri

Admissions Office Contact Bryan University, 3215 LeMone Industrial Boulevard, Columbia, MO 65201. *Toll-free phone:* 855-566-0650.
Website: http://www.bryanu.edu/.

Bryan University
Springfield, Missouri

Admissions Office Contact Bryan University, 4255 Nature Center Way, Springfield, MO 65804.

Concorde Career College
Kansas City, Missouri

Freshman Application Contact Deborah Crow, Director, Concorde Career College, 3239 Broadway, Kansas City, MO 64111-2407. *Phone:* 816-531-5223. *Fax:* 816-756-3231. *E-mail:* dcrow@concorde.edu.
Website: http://www.concorde.edu/.

Cottey College
Nevada, Missouri

- **Independent** primarily 2-year, founded 1884
- **Small-town** 51-acre campus
- **Endowment** $95,497
- **Women only,** 284 undergraduate students, 100% full-time

Undergraduates 284 full-time. Students come from 40 states and territories; 21 other countries; 80% are from out of state; 4% Black or African American, non-Hispanic/Latino; 11% Hispanic/Latino; 0.4% Asian, non-Hispanic/Latino; 0.4% Native Hawaiian or other Pacific Islander, non-Hispanic/Latino; 1% American Indian or Alaska Native, non-Hispanic/Latino; 3% Two or more races, non-Hispanic/Latino; 10% international; 0.7% transferred in; 98% live on campus. *Retention:* 79% of full-time freshmen returned.
Freshmen *Admission:* 135 enrolled. *Average high school GPA:* 3.47. *Test scores:* SAT critical reading scores over 500: 75%; SAT math scores over 500: 55%; ACT scores over 18: 92%; SAT critical reading scores over 600: 33%; SAT math scores over 600: 10%; ACT scores over 24: 44%; SAT critical reading scores over 700: 4%; ACT scores over 30: 4%.

Faculty *Total:* 44, 82% full-time, 80% with terminal degrees. *Student/faculty ratio:* 8:1.

Majors Liberal arts and sciences/liberal studies.

Academics *Calendar:* semesters. *Degrees:* associate and bachelor's. *Special study options:* advanced placement credit, distance learning, independent study, internships, part-time degree program, services for LD students, study abroad.

Library Blanche Skiff Ross Memorial Library plus 1 other with 54,200 titles, 246 serial subscriptions, an OPAC.

Student Life *Housing Options:* women-only. Campus housing is university owned. *Activities and Organizations:* drama/theater group, student-run newspaper, choral group, International Friendship Circle, Cottey Intramural Association, Ozarks Explorers Club, Inter-Varsity Club, Golden Keys. *Campus security:* 24-hour emergency response devices and patrols, late-night transport/escort service, controlled dormitory access. *Student services:* health clinic, personal/psychological counseling.

Athletics Member NJCAA. *Intercollegiate sports:* basketball W(s), softball W(s), volleyball W(s). *Intramural sports:* swimming and diving W, tennis W.

Standardized Tests *Required:* SAT or ACT (for admission).

Costs (2014–15) *Comprehensive fee:* $26,050 includes full-time tuition ($18,000), mandatory fees ($800), and room and board ($7250). Part-time tuition: $125 per hour. *Room and board:* college room only: $4000. Room and board charges vary according to housing facility. *Payment plan:* installment.

Financial Aid Of all full-time matriculated undergraduates who enrolled in 2012, 245 applied for aid, 205 were judged to have need, 53 had their need fully met. 24 Federal Work-Study jobs (averaging $1934). 170 state and other part-time jobs (averaging $1941). In 2012, 84 non-need-based awards were made. *Average percent of need met:* 85%. *Average financial aid package:* $17,575. *Average need-based loan:* $3258. *Average need-based gift aid:* $13,940. *Average non-need-based aid:* $9983. *Average indebtedness upon graduation:* $12,148.

Applying *Required:* essay or personal statement, high school transcript, 1 letter of recommendation. *Recommended:* minimum 2.6 GPA, interview.

Freshman Application Contact Ms. Judi Steege, Director of Admission, Cottey College, 1000 West Austin Boulevard, Nevada, MO 64772. *Phone:* 417-667-8181. *Toll-free phone:* 888-526-8839. *Fax:* 417-667-8103. *E-mail:* enrollmgt@cottey.edu.

Website: http://www.cottey.edu/.

Court Reporting Institute of St. Louis
Clayton, Missouri

Freshman Application Contact Admissions Office, Court Reporting Institute of St. Louis, 7730 Carondelet Avenue, Suite 400, Clayton, MO 63105. *Phone:* 713-996-8300. *Toll-free phone:* 888-208-6780.
Website: http://www.cri.edu/st-louis-court-reporting-school.asp.

Crowder College
Neosho, Missouri

- **State and locally supported** 2-year, founded 1963, part of Missouri Coordinating Board for Higher Education
- **Rural** 608-acre campus
- **Coed,** 5,845 undergraduate students, 44% full-time, 64% women, 36% men

Undergraduates 2,561 full-time, 3,284 part-time. 1% Black or African American, non-Hispanic/Latino; 7% Hispanic/Latino; 1% Asian, non-Hispanic/Latino; 0.3% Native Hawaiian or other Pacific Islander, non-Hispanic/Latino; 2% American Indian or Alaska Native, non-Hispanic/Latino; 2% Two or more races, non-Hispanic/Latino; 1% Race/ethnicity unknown; 0.8% international; 5% transferred in; 10% live on campus.

Freshmen *Admission:* 1,286 enrolled.

Faculty *Total:* 494, 19% full-time, 8% with terminal degrees. *Student/faculty ratio:* 12:1.

Majors Administrative assistant and secretarial science; agribusiness; agricultural mechanization; agriculture; art; autobody/collision and repair technology; automobile/automotive mechanics technology; biology/biological sciences; business administration and management; business automation/technology/data entry; computer systems analysis; computer systems networking and telecommunications; construction engineering technology; construction trades; drafting and design technology; dramatic/theater arts; education; electrical, electronic and communications engineering technology; elementary education; emergency medical technology (EMT paramedic); energy management and systems technology; environmental engineering technology; executive assistant/executive secretary; farm and ranch management; fire science/firefighting; general studies; health information/medical records technology; industrial technology; legal administrative assistant/secretary; liberal arts and sciences/liberal studies; manufacturing engineering technology; mass communication/media; mathematics; mathematics and computer science; medical administrative assistant and medical secretary; music; occupational therapist assistant;

physical education teaching and coaching; physical sciences; pre-engineering; psychology; public relations/image management; registered nursing/registered nurse; solar energy technology; veterinary/animal health technology; welding technology.

Academics *Calendar:* semesters. *Degree:* certificates and associate. *Special study options:* academic remediation for entering students, adult/continuing education programs, advanced placement credit, cooperative education, English as a second language, freshman honors college, honors programs, independent study, part-time degree program, student-designed majors, study abroad, summer session for credit.

Library Bill & Margot Lee Library with 183,354 titles, 132 serial subscriptions, 6,558 audiovisual materials, a Web page.

Student Life *Housing Options:* men-only, women-only. Campus housing is university owned. *Activities and Organizations:* drama/theater group, student-run newspaper, choral group, Phi Theta Kappa, Students in Free Enterprise (SIFE), Baptist Student Union, Student Senate, Student Ambassadors. *Campus security:* 24-hour patrols.

Athletics Member NJCAA. *Intercollegiate sports:* baseball M(s), basketball W(s), soccer M(s).

Costs (2013–14) *Tuition:* area resident $1872 full-time, $78 per credit hour part-time; state resident $2568 full-time, $107 per credit hour part-time; nonresident $2568 full-time, $107 per credit hour part-time. Full-time tuition and fees vary according to program. Part-time tuition and fees vary according to program. *Required fees:* $288 full-time, $12 per credit hour part-time. *Room and board:* $2334; room only: $1034. Room and board charges vary according to board plan. *Payment plan:* installment. *Waivers:* senior citizens and employees or children of employees.

Financial Aid Of all full-time matriculated undergraduates who enrolled in 2012, 150 Federal Work-Study jobs (averaging $1000).

Applying *Application fee:* $25. *Required:* high school transcript. *Application deadlines:* rolling (freshmen), rolling (transfers). *Notification:* continuous (freshmen).

Freshman Application Contact Mr. Jim Riggs, Admissions Coordinator, Crowder College, Neosho, MO 64850. *Phone:* 417-451-3223 Ext. 5466. *Toll-free phone:* 866-238-7788. *Fax:* 417-455-5731. *E-mail:* jimriggs@crowder.edu.
Website: http://www.crowder.edu/.

Culinary Institute of St. Louis at Hickey College
St. Louis, Missouri

- **Private** 2-year, founded 2009
- **Suburban** campus
- **Coed**, 91 undergraduate students
- 81% of applicants were admitted

Freshmen *Admission:* 185 applied, 149 admitted.
Majors Cooking and related culinary arts.
Academics *Degree:* associate.
Freshman Application Contact Admissions Office, Culinary Institute of St. Louis at Hickey College, 2700 North Lindbergh Boulevard, St. Louis, MO 63114. *Phone:* 314-434-2212.
Website: http://www.ci-stl.com/.

East Central College
Union, Missouri

- **District-supported** 2-year, founded 1959
- **Rural** 207-acre campus with easy access to St. Louis
- **Endowment** $2.8 million
- **Coed**, 3,900 undergraduate students, 47% full-time, 62% women, 38% men

Undergraduates 1,852 full-time, 2,048 part-time. Students come from 3 states and territories; 0.1% are from out of state; 0.6% Black or African American, non-Hispanic/Latino; 1% Hispanic/Latino; 0.4% Asian, non-Hispanic/Latino; 0.2% Native Hawaiian or other Pacific Islander, non-Hispanic/Latino; 0.3% American Indian or Alaska Native, non-Hispanic/Latino; 0.1% Two or more races, non-Hispanic/Latino; 1% Race/ethnicity unknown; 6% transferred in.
Freshmen *Admission:* 773 admitted, 773 enrolled.
Faculty *Total:* 233, 29% full-time, 10% with terminal degrees. *Student/faculty ratio:* 20:1.
Majors Accounting technology and bookkeeping; administrative assistant and secretarial science; automobile/automotive mechanics technology; biology/biotechnology laboratory technician; business/commerce; chemical technology; child-care and support services management; commercial and advertising art; computer systems networking and telecommunications; construction trades; construction trades related; culinary arts; drafting and design technology; education; emergency medical technology (EMT paramedic); engineering; fine/studio arts; fire science/firefighting; general

studies; health information/medical records technology; heating, air conditioning, ventilation and refrigeration maintenance technology; heavy/industrial equipment maintenance technologies related; machine tool technology; management information systems; medical/clinical assistant; medical radiologic technology; occupational therapist assistant; precision production related; registered nursing/registered nurse; respiratory care therapy; technical teacher education; welding technology.

Academics *Calendar:* semesters. *Degree:* certificates and associate. *Special study options:* academic remediation for entering students, adult/continuing education programs, advanced placement credit, distance learning, English as a second language, honors programs, independent study, internships, off-campus study, part-time degree program, services for LD students, study abroad, summer session for credit.

Library East Central College Library with 175,042 titles, 142 serial subscriptions, 3,422 audiovisual materials, an OPAC, a Web page.

Student Life *Housing:* college housing not available. *Activities and Organizations:* drama/theater group, student-run newspaper, choral group, AHERO Club, Art Club, Phi Theta Kappa, R&R Club, Student Government Association. *Campus security:* 24-hour emergency response devices, late-night transport/escort service. *Student services:* personal/psychological counseling.

Athletics Member NJCAA. *Intercollegiate sports:* soccer M(s), softball W(s), volleyball W(s).

Costs (2014–15) *Tuition:* area resident $1800 full-time, $75 per credit hour part-time; state resident $2544 full-time, $106 per credit hour part-time; nonresident $3840 full-time, $160 per credit hour part-time. Full-time tuition and fees vary according to program. Part-time tuition and fees vary according to program. *Required fees:* $456 full-time, $19 per credit hour part-time. *Payment plans:* installment, deferred payment. *Waivers:* senior citizens and employees or children of employees.

Applying *Options:* early admission, deferred entrance. *Required:* high school transcript. *Application deadlines:* rolling (freshmen), rolling (transfers).
Freshman Application Contact Mr. Nathaniel Mitchell, Director, Admissions, East Central College, 1964 Prairie Dell Road, Union, MO 63084. *Phone:* 636-584-6552. *E-mail:* nemitche@eastcentral.edu.
Website: http://www.eastcentral.edu/.

Everest College
Springfield, Missouri

Freshman Application Contact Admissions Office, Everest College, 1010 West Sunshine, Springfield, MO 65807-2488. *Phone:* 417-864-7220. *Toll-free phone:* 888-741-4270. *Fax:* 417-864-5697.
Website: http://www.everest.edu/.

Heritage College
Kansas City, Missouri

Freshman Application Contact Admissions Office, Heritage College, 1200 East 104th Street, Suite 300, Kansas City, MO 64131. *Phone:* 816-942-5474. *Toll-free phone:* 888-334-7339. *E-mail:* info@heritage-education.com.
Website: http://www.heritage-education.com/.

IHM Academy of EMS
St. Louis, Missouri

Freshman Application Contact Admissions Director, IHM Academy of EMS, 2500 Abbott Place, St. Louis, MO 63143. *Phone:* 314-768-1234. *Fax:* 314-768-1595. *E-mail:* info@ihmhealthstudies.edu.
Website: http://www.ihmacademyofems.net/.

ITT Technical Institute
Arnold, Missouri

- **Proprietary** primarily 2-year, founded 1997, part of ITT Educational Services, Inc.
- **Coed**

Majors Business administration and management; computer programming (specific applications); construction management; cyber/computer forensics and counterterrorism; drafting and design technology; electrical, electronic and communications engineering technology; forensic science and technology; game and interactive media design; graphic communications; industrial technology; information technology project management; network and system administration; project management.
Academics *Calendar:* quarters. *Degrees:* associate and bachelor's.
Student Life *Housing:* college housing not available.
Freshman Application Contact Director of Recruitment, ITT Technical Institute, 1930 Meyer Drury Drive, Arnold, MO 63010. *Phone:* 636-464-6600. *Toll-free phone:* 888-488-1082.
Website: http://www.itt-tech.edu/.

ITT Technical Institute

Earth City, Missouri

- **Proprietary** primarily 2-year, founded 1936, part of ITT Educational Services, Inc.
- **Suburban** campus
- **Coed**

Majors Business administration and management; computer programming (specific applications); construction management; cyber/computer forensics and counterterrorism; drafting and design technology; electrical, electronic and communications engineering technology; forensic science and technology; graphic communications; industrial technology; information technology project management; network and system administration; project management; registered nursing/registered nurse.

Academics *Calendar:* quarters. *Degrees:* associate and bachelor's.

Student Life *Housing:* college housing not available.

Freshman Application Contact Director of Recruitment, ITT Technical Institute, 3640 Corporate Trail Drive, Earth City, MO 63045. *Phone:* 314-298-7800. *Toll-free phone:* 800-235-5488.

Website: http://www.itt-tech.edu/.

ITT Technical Institute

Kansas City, Missouri

- **Proprietary** primarily 2-year, founded 2004, part of ITT Educational Services, Inc.
- **Coed**

Majors Business administration and management; computer programming (specific applications); construction management; cyber/computer forensics and counterterrorism; drafting and design technology; electrical, electronic and communications engineering technology; forensic science and technology; graphic communications; industrial technology; information technology project management; network and system administration; project management.

Academics *Calendar:* quarters. *Degrees:* associate and bachelor's.

Freshman Application Contact Director of Recruitment, ITT Technical Institute, 9150 East 41st Terrace, Kansas City, MO 64133. *Phone:* 816-276-1400. *Toll-free phone:* 877-488-1442.

Website: http://www.itt-tech.edu/.

Jefferson College

Hillsboro, Missouri

- **District-supported** 2-year, founded 1963
- **Rural** 455-acre campus with easy access to St. Louis
- **Endowment** $684,672
- **Coed,** 5,194 undergraduate students, 52% full-time, 59% women, 41% men

Undergraduates 2,715 full-time, 2,479 part-time. 12% are from out of state; 2% Black or African American, non-Hispanic/Latino; 0.4% Hispanic/Latino; 0.8% Asian, non-Hispanic/Latino; 0.1% Native Hawaiian or other Pacific Islander, non-Hispanic/Latino; 0.5% American Indian or Alaska Native, non-Hispanic/Latino; 5% Race/ethnicity unknown; 0.3% international.

Freshmen *Admission:* 1,134 enrolled.

Faculty *Total:* 367, 26% full-time, 10% with terminal degrees.

Majors Administrative assistant and secretarial science; automobile/automotive mechanics technology; business administration and management; business/commerce; child-care and support services management; computer systems networking and telecommunications; criminal justice/law enforcement administration; criminal justice/police science; culinary arts; education (specific levels and methods) related; electrical, electronic and communications engineering technology; emergency medical technology (EMT paramedic); engineering; fire prevention and safety technology; heating, air conditioning, ventilation and refrigeration maintenance technology; information technology; legal administrative assistant/secretary; liberal arts and sciences/liberal studies; licensed practical/vocational nurse training; machine tool technology; manufacturing engineering technology; medical administrative assistant and medical secretary; precision production related; registered nursing/registered nurse; veterinary/animal health technology; welding technology.

Academics *Calendar:* semesters. *Degree:* certificates, diplomas, and associate. *Special study options:* academic remediation for entering students, adult/continuing education programs, advanced placement credit, distance learning, English as a second language, freshman honors college, honors programs, internships, off-campus study, part-time degree program, services for LD students, summer session for credit.

Library Jefferson College Library plus 1 other with 73,443 titles, 21,509 serial subscriptions, 2,805 audiovisual materials, an OPAC, a Web page.

Student Life *Housing Options:* coed. Campus housing is university owned. *Activities and Organizations:* drama/theater group, student-run newspaper, television station, choral group, Student Senate, Nursing associations, Baptist Student Unit, Phi Theta Kappa, National Technical Honors Society, national sororities. *Campus security:* 24-hour patrols. *Student services:* personal/psychological counseling.

Athletics Member NJCAA. *Intercollegiate sports:* baseball M(s), basketball W(s), cheerleading M(s)/W(s), soccer M(s), softball W(s), volleyball W(s).

Costs (2014–15) *One-time required fee:* $25. *Tuition:* area resident $2850 full-time; state resident $4290 full-time; nonresident $5700 full-time. Full-time tuition and fees vary according to program. Part-time tuition and fees vary according to program. *Required fees:* $90 full-time. *Room and board:* $5121; room only: $3240. Room and board charges vary according to housing facility. *Payment plan:* installment. *Waivers:* senior citizens and employees or children of employees.

Financial Aid Of all full-time matriculated undergraduates who enrolled in 2013, 2,642 applied for aid, 2,079 were judged to have need, 82 had their need fully met. 95 Federal Work-Study jobs (averaging $1350). 166 state and other part-time jobs (averaging $1287). In 2013, 148 non-need-based awards were made. *Average percent of need met:* 58%. *Average financial aid package:* $5017. *Average need-based loan:* $2893. *Average need-based gift aid:* $2564. *Average non-need-based aid:* $1659.

Applying *Options:* electronic application, early admission. *Application fee:* $25. *Required:* high school transcript. *Application deadlines:* rolling (freshmen), rolling (transfers).

Freshman Application Contact Ms. Kim Harvey, Director of Student Records and Admissions Services, Jefferson College, 1000 Viking Drive, Hillsboro, MO 63050-2441. *Phone:* 636-481-3217 Ext. 3217. *Fax:* 636-789-5103. *E-mail:* admissions@jeffco.edu.

Website: http://www.jeffco.edu/.

Linn State Technical College

Linn, Missouri

Freshman Application Contact Linn State Technical College, One Technology Drive, Linn, MO 65051-9606. *Phone:* 573-897-5196. *Toll-free phone:* 800-743-TECH.

Website: http://www.linnstate.edu/.

Metro Business College

Cape Girardeau, Missouri

Director of Admissions Ms. Kyla Evans, Admissions Director, Metro Business College, 1732 North Kingshighway, Cape Girardeau, MO 63701. *Phone:* 573-334-9181. *Toll-free phone:* 888-206-4545. *Fax:* 573-334-0617.

Website: http://www.metrobusinesscollege.edu/.

Metro Business College

Jefferson City, Missouri

- **Proprietary** 2-year, founded 1979
- **Suburban** campus
- **Coed,** 142 undergraduate students, 80% full-time, 85% women, 15% men

Undergraduates 113 full-time, 29 part-time. Students come from 1 other state; 18% Black or African American, non-Hispanic/Latino; 2% Asian, non-Hispanic/Latino; 0.7% American Indian or Alaska Native, non-Hispanic/Latino; 4% Race/ethnicity unknown; 4% transferred in.

Freshmen *Admission:* 14 enrolled.

Faculty *Total:* 14, 64% full-time, 14% with terminal degrees. *Student/faculty ratio:* 11:1.

Majors Computer and information sciences related; medical administrative assistant and medical secretary.

Academics *Calendar:* quarters. *Degree:* certificates, diplomas, and associate. *Special study options:* academic remediation for entering students, adult/continuing education programs, advanced placement credit, independent study, internships, part-time degree program, services for LD students, summer session for credit.

Student Life *Housing:* college housing not available. *Activities and Organizations:* student-run newspaper, Student Council. *Student services:* personal/psychological counseling.

Standardized Tests *Required:* Wonderlic aptitude test (for admission).

Costs (2014–15) *Tuition:* $10,200 full-time, $1278 per term part-time. Full-time tuition and fees vary according to program. Part-time tuition and fees vary according to program. *Required fees:* $125 full-time. *Payment plans:* tuition prepayment, installment, deferred payment. *Waivers:* senior citizens and employees or children of employees.

Applying *Required:* essay or personal statement, high school transcript, interview.

Freshman Application Contact Ms. Cheri Chockley, Campus Director, Metro Business College, 210 El Mercado Plaza, Jefferson City, MO 65109. *Phone:* 573-635-6600. *Toll-free phone:* 888-206-4545. *Fax:* 573-635-6999. *E-mail:* cheri@metrobusinesscollege.edu.

Website: http://www.metrobusinesscollege.edu/.

Metro Business College

Rolla, Missouri

Freshman Application Contact Admissions Office, Metro Business College, 1202 East Highway 72, Rolla, MO 65401. *Phone:* 573-364-8464. *Toll-free phone:* 888-206-4545. *Fax:* 573-364-8077. *E-mail:* inforolla@metrobusinesscollege.edu.
Website: http://www.metrobusinesscollege.edu/.

Metropolitan Community College–Kansas City

Lee's Summit, Missouri

- **State and locally supported** 2-year, founded 1969, part of Metropolitan Community Colleges System
- **Suburban** 420-acre campus with easy access to Kansas City
- **Endowment** $4.5 million
- **Coed,** 19,234 undergraduate students, 40% full-time, 57% women, 43% men

Undergraduates 7,734 full-time, 11,500 part-time. Students come from 19 states and territories; 74 other countries; 1% are from out of state; 17% Black or African American, non-Hispanic/Latino; 9% Hispanic/Latino; 3% Asian, non-Hispanic/Latino; 0.3% Native Hawaiian or other Pacific Islander, non-Hispanic/Latino; 0.3% American Indian or Alaska Native, non-Hispanic/Latino; 6% Two or more races, non-Hispanic/Latino; 0.7% Race/ethnicity unknown; 4% transferred in. *Retention:* 52% of full-time freshmen returned.
Freshmen *Admission:* 4,160 applied, 4,160 admitted, 4,183 enrolled.
Faculty *Total:* 904, 24% full-time, 8% with terminal degrees. *Student/faculty ratio:* 26:1.
Majors Automobile/automotive mechanics technology; biology/biological sciences; building/construction site management; business administration and management; chemistry; child-care provision; commercial and advertising art; computer and information sciences related; computer graphics; computer programming; computer science; computer typography and composition equipment operation; corrections; criminal justice/law enforcement administration; criminal justice/police science; drafting and design technology; electrical, electronic and communications engineering technology; emergency medical technology (EMT paramedic); engineering; family and consumer sciences/human sciences; fashion/apparel design; fashion merchandising; fire science/firefighting; glazier; health information/medical records administration; heavy equipment maintenance technology; human services; information science/studies; information technology; legal administrative assistant/secretary; liberal arts and sciences/liberal studies; machine shop technology; marketing/marketing management; masonry; medical administrative assistant and medical secretary; network and system administration; occupational therapy; physical therapy; pre-engineering; quality control technology; registered nursing/registered nurse; respiratory care therapy; special products marketing; system, networking, and LAN/WAN management; web/multimedia management and webmaster; web page, digital/multimedia and information resources design.
Academics *Calendar:* semesters. *Degree:* certificates and associate. *Special study options:* academic remediation for entering students, accelerated degree program, adult/continuing education programs, advanced placement credit, cooperative education, distance learning, English as a second language, honors programs, independent study, internships, off-campus study, part-time degree program, services for LD students, summer session for credit.
Library College Library with 10,098 titles, 288 serial subscriptions, 103 audiovisual materials, an OPAC.
Student Life *Housing:* college housing not available. *Activities and Organizations:* drama/theater group, student-run newspaper, choral group, student newspaper, student government, Phi Theta Kappa, Metropolitan Chorale of KC, Student Ambassadors, national fraternities. *Campus security:* 24-hour emergency response devices and patrols, late-night transport/escort service. *Student services:* personal/psychological counseling.
Athletics Member NJCAA. *Intercollegiate sports:* baseball M(s), basketball M(s)/W(s), cross-country running W(s), soccer M(s)/W(s), softball W(s), volleyball W(s).
Standardized Tests *Recommended:* ACT (for admission), Placement Testing for first-time freshman.
Costs (2013–14) *One-time required fee:* $30. *Tuition:* area resident $2610 full-time, $87 per credit hour part-time; state resident $5010 full-time, $167 per credit hour part-time; nonresident $6630 full-time, $221 per credit hour part-time. Full-time tuition and fees vary according to class time, course load, location, and program. Part-time tuition and fees vary according to class time, course load, location, and program. *Required fees:* $150 full-time, $5 per credit hour part-time, $10 per term part-time. *Payment plan:* installment. *Waivers:* senior citizens and employees or children of employees.

Applying *Options:* electronic application, early admission, deferred entrance. *Application deadlines:* rolling (freshmen), rolling (transfers). *Notification:* continuous (freshmen), continuous (transfers).
Freshman Application Contact Dr. Tuesday Stanley, Vice Chancellor of Student Development and Enrollment Services, Metropolitan Community College–Kansas City, 3200 Broadway, Kansas City, MO 64111-2429. *Phone:* 816-604-1253. *E-mail:* tuesday.stanley@mcckc.edu.
Website: http://www.mcckc.edu/.

Midwest Institute

Fenton, Missouri

Freshman Application Contact Admissions Office, Midwest Institute, 964 S. Highway Drive, Fenton, MO 63026. *Toll-free phone:* 800-695-5550.
Website: http://www.midwestinstitute.com/.

Midwest Institute

St. Louis, Missouri

Freshman Application Contact Admissions Office, Midwest Institute, 4260 Shoreline Drive, St. Louis, MO 63045. *Phone:* 314-344-4440. *Toll-free phone:* 800-695-5550. *Fax:* 314-344-0495.
Website: http://www.midwestinstitute.com/.

Mineral Area College

Park Hills, Missouri

- **District-supported** 2-year, founded 1922, part of Missouri Coordinating Board for Higher Education
- **Rural** 240-acre campus with easy access to St. Louis
- **Coed,** 4,508 undergraduate students, 64% full-time, 57% women, 43% men

Undergraduates 2,869 full-time, 1,639 part-time. Students come from 14 states and territories; 2 other countries; 1% are from out of state; 2% Black or African American, non-Hispanic/Latino; 1% Hispanic/Latino; 0.4% Asian, non-Hispanic/Latino; 0.1% Native Hawaiian or other Pacific Islander, non-Hispanic/Latino; 0.6% American Indian or Alaska Native, non-Hispanic/Latino; 5% Race/ethnicity unknown; 0.1% international; 4% transferred in. *Retention:* 68% of full-time freshmen returned.
Freshmen *Admission:* 840 enrolled.
Faculty *Total:* 316, 23% full-time. *Student/faculty ratio:* 14:1.
Majors Administrative assistant and secretarial science; agribusiness; applied horticulture/horticulture operations; autobody/collision and repair technology; automobile/automotive mechanics technology; business/commerce; carpentry; child-care provision; civil engineering technology; computer programming; criminal justice/police science; culinary arts; drafting and design technology; electrical, electronic and communications engineering technology; emergency medical technology (EMT paramedic); engineering technology; fire science/firefighting; general studies; graphic and printing equipment operation/production; health professions related; heating, ventilation, air conditioning and refrigeration engineering technology; heavy/industrial equipment maintenance technologies related; industrial technology; liberal arts and sciences/liberal studies; machine tool technology; operations management; precision production related; precision production trades; radio and television broadcasting technology; registered nursing/registered nurse; respiratory therapy technician; system, networking, and LAN/WAN management; technical teacher education.
Academics *Calendar:* semesters. *Degree:* certificates and associate. *Special study options:* academic remediation for entering students, advanced placement credit, distance learning, honors programs, internships, off-campus study, part-time degree program, services for LD students, summer session for credit.
Library C. H. Cozen Learning Resource Center with 32,228 titles, 214 serial subscriptions, 4,859 audiovisual materials, an OPAC, a Web page.
Student Life *Housing Options:* coed. Campus housing is university owned. *Activities and Organizations:* drama/theater group, choral group. *Campus security:* 24-hour patrols. *Student services:* personal/psychological counseling.
Athletics Member NJCAA. *Intercollegiate sports:* baseball M(s), basketball M(s)/W(s), golf M, softball W(s), volleyball W(s).
Costs (2014–15) *Tuition:* area resident $2820 full-time, $94 per semester hour part-time; state resident $3780 full-time, $126 per semester hour part-time; nonresident $4950 full-time, $165 per semester hour part-time. *Room and board:* room only: $3612. Room and board charges vary according to board plan and housing facility. *Payment plan:* installment. *Waivers:* senior citizens and employees or children of employees.
Financial Aid Of all full-time matriculated undergraduates who enrolled in 2012, 65 Federal Work-Study jobs (averaging $3708).

Applying *Options:* electronic application, early admission. *Application fee:* $15. *Required:* high school transcript. *Application deadlines:* rolling (freshmen), rolling (transfers). *Notification:* continuous (freshmen).

Freshman Application Contact Pam Reeder, Registrar, Mineral Area College, PO Box 1000, Park Hills, MO 63601-1000. *Phone:* 573-518-2204. *Fax:* 573-518-2166. *E-mail:* preeder@mineralarea.edu. *Website:* http://www.mineralarea.edu/.

Missouri College
Brentwood, Missouri

Director of Admissions Mr. Doug Brinker, Admissions Director, Missouri College, 1405 South Hanley Road, Brentwood, MO 63117. *Phone:* 314-821-7700. *Toll-free phone:* 800-216-6732. *Fax:* 314-821-0891. *Website:* http://www.missouricollege.edu/.

Missouri State University–West Plains
West Plains, Missouri

- **State-supported** 2-year, founded 1963, part of Missouri State University
- **Small-town** 20-acre campus
- **Endowment** $6.4 million
- **Coed,** 2,123 undergraduate students, 62% full-time, 57% women, 43% men

Undergraduates 1,310 full-time, 813 part-time. Students come from 27 states and territories; 3 other countries; 4% are from out of state; 2% Black or African American, non-Hispanic/Latino; 2% Hispanic/Latino; 1% Asian, non-Hispanic/Latino; 1% American Indian or Alaska Native, non-Hispanic/Latino; 4% Race/ethnicity unknown; 0.6% international; 5% transferred in; 4% live on campus. *Retention:* 47% of full-time freshmen returned.

Freshmen *Admission:* 1,330 applied, 795 admitted, 627 enrolled. *Average high school GPA:* 3.16. *Test scores:* ACT scores over 18: 71%; ACT scores over 24: 16%; ACT scores over 30: 1%.

Faculty *Total:* 116, 32% full-time, 9% with terminal degrees. *Student/faculty ratio:* 25:1.

Majors Accounting; agriculture; business administration and management; business/commerce; child-care and support services management; computer and information sciences related; computer graphics; computer programming (specific applications); criminal justice/law enforcement administration; criminal justice/police science; engineering; entrepreneurship; food science; general studies; horticultural science; industrial technology; information technology; legal assistant/paralegal; management information systems and services related; registered nursing/registered nurse; respiratory therapy technician.

Academics *Calendar:* semesters. *Degree:* certificates and associate. *Special study options:* academic remediation for entering students, adult/continuing education programs, advanced placement credit, cooperative education, distance learning, honors programs, internships, off-campus study, part-time degree program, services for LD students, study abroad, summer session for credit.

Library Garnett Library with 40,385 titles, 160 serial subscriptions, 1,458 audiovisual materials, an OPAC, a Web page.

Student Life *Housing Options:* men-only, women-only. Campus housing is university owned. *Activities and Organizations:* Student Government Association, Chi Alpha, Adult Students in Higher Education, Lambda Lambda Lambda, Programming Board. *Campus security:* access only with key. *Student services:* personal/psychological counseling, legal services.

Athletics Member NJCAA. *Intercollegiate sports:* basketball M(s), volleyball W(s).

Costs (2014–15) *Tuition:* state resident $3720 full-time; nonresident $6958 full-time. Full-time tuition and fees vary according to course load, location, and program. Part-time tuition and fees vary according to course load and location. *Required fees:* $294 full-time. *Room and board:* $5480. Room and board charges vary according to board plan. *Payment plan:* deferred payment. *Waivers:* senior citizens and employees or children of employees.

Financial Aid Of all full-time matriculated undergraduates who enrolled in 2012, 63 Federal Work-Study jobs (averaging $2000).

Applying *Options:* electronic application. *Application fee:* $15. *Required for some:* high school transcript. *Application deadlines:* 8/20 (freshmen), 8/20 (out-of-state freshmen), 8/20 (transfers). *Notification:* continuous (freshmen), continuous (out-of-state freshmen), continuous (transfers).

Freshman Application Contact Ms. Melissa Jett, Coordinator of Admissions, Missouri State University–West Plains, 128 Garfield, West Plains, MO 65775. *Phone:* 417-255-7955. *Toll-free phone:* 888-466-7897. *Fax:* 417-255-7959. *E-mail:* melissajett@missouristate.edu. *Website:* http://wp.missouristate.edu/.

Moberly Area Community College
Moberly, Missouri

Freshman Application Contact Dr. James Grant, Dean of Student Services, Moberly Area Community College, Moberly, MO 65270-1304. *Phone:* 660-263-4110 Ext. 235. *Toll-free phone:* 800-622-2070. *Fax:* 660-263-2406. *E-mail:* info@macc.edu. *Website:* http://www.macc.edu/.

North Central Missouri College
Trenton, Missouri

Freshman Application Contact Megan Goodin, Admissions Assistant, North Central Missouri College, Trenton, MO 64683. *Phone:* 660-359-3948 Ext. 1410. *E-mail:* megoodin@mail.ncmissouri.edu. *Website:* http://www.ncmissouri.edu/.

Ozarks Technical Community College
Springfield, Missouri

- **District-supported** 2-year, founded 1990, part of Missouri Coordinating Board for Higher Education
- **Urban** campus
- **Endowment** $1.7 million
- **Coed,** 14,798 undergraduate students, 48% full-time, 58% women, 42% men

Undergraduates 7,049 full-time, 7,749 part-time. 2% are from out of state; 2% Black or African American, non-Hispanic/Latino; 2% Hispanic/Latino; 1% Asian, non-Hispanic/Latino; 0.8% American Indian or Alaska Native, non-Hispanic/Latino; 26% Race/ethnicity unknown.

Faculty *Total:* 667, 28% full-time. *Student/faculty ratio:* 25:1.

Majors Accounting; administrative assistant and secretarial science; autobody/collision and repair technology; automobile/automotive mechanics technology; business administration and management; business machine repair; computer systems networking and telecommunications; construction engineering technology; culinary arts; diesel mechanics technology; electrical, electronic and communications engineering technology; emergency medical technology (EMT paramedic); fire science/firefighting; graphic and printing equipment operation/production; health information/medical records technology; heating, air conditioning, ventilation and refrigeration maintenance technology; heavy equipment maintenance technology; hotel/motel administration; industrial technology; information science/studies; instrumentation technology; kindergarten/preschool education; liberal arts and sciences/liberal studies; machine tool technology; management information systems; mechanical drafting and CAD/CADD; occupational therapist assistant; occupational therapy; physical sciences; physical therapy technology; radio and television broadcasting technology; respiratory care therapy; turf and turfgrass management; welding technology.

Academics *Calendar:* semesters. *Degree:* certificates, diplomas, and associate. *Special study options:* academic remediation for entering students, adult/continuing education programs, cooperative education, distance learning, double majors, English as a second language, honors programs, internships, off-campus study, part-time degree program, services for LD students, summer session for credit.

Library Library plus 1 other with 6,000 titles, 190 serial subscriptions, an OPAC, a Web page.

Student Life *Housing:* college housing not available. *Activities and Organizations:* student-run newspaper, Phi Theta Kappa. *Campus security:* 24-hour emergency response devices. *Student services:* personal/psychological counseling.

Costs (2014–15) *Tuition:* area resident $2208 full-time, $92 per credit hour part-time; state resident $3120 full-time, $130 per credit hour part-time; nonresident $4104 full-time, $171 per credit hour part-time. *Required fees:* $500 full-time, $19 per credit hour part-time, $45 per term part-time. *Payment plans:* installment, deferred payment. *Waivers:* employees or children of employees.

Financial Aid Of all full-time matriculated undergraduates who enrolled in 2012, 201 Federal Work-Study jobs.

Applying *Options:* electronic application. *Required:* high school transcript. *Application deadlines:* rolling (freshmen), rolling (out-of-state freshmen), rolling (transfers). *Notification:* continuous (freshmen), continuous (out-of-state freshmen), continuous (transfers).

Freshman Application Contact Ozarks Technical Community College, 1001 E. Chestnut Expressway, Springfield, MO 65802. *Website:* http://www.otc.edu/.

Pinnacle Career Institute
Kansas City, Missouri

Director of Admissions Ms. Ruth Matous, Director of Admissions, Pinnacle Career Institute, 1001 East 101st Terrace, Suite 325, Kansas City, MO 64131. *Phone:* 816-331-5700 Ext. 212. *Toll-free phone:* 877-241-3097. *Website:* http://www.pcitraining.edu/.

Ranken Technical College
St. Louis, Missouri

Director of Admissions Ms. Elizabeth Keserauskis, Director of Admissions, Ranken Technical College, 4431 Finney Avenue, St. Louis, MO 63113. *Phone:* 314-371-0233 Ext. 4811. *Toll-free phone:* 866-4-RANKEN. *Website:* http://www.ranken.edu/.

Saint Charles Community College
Cottleville, Missouri

Freshman Application Contact Ms. Kathy Brockgreitens-Gober, Director of Admissions/Registrar/Financial Assistance, Saint Charles Community College, 4601 Mid Rivers Mall Drive, Cottleville, MO 63376-0975. *Phone:* 636-922-8229. *Fax:* 636-922-8236. *E-mail:* regist@stchas.edu. *Website:* http://www.stchas.edu/.

St. Louis College of Health Careers
Fenton, Missouri

Admissions Office Contact St. Louis College of Health Careers, 1297 North Highway Drive, Fenton, MO 63026. *Website:* http://www.slchc.com/.

St. Louis College of Health Careers
St. Louis, Missouri

Freshman Application Contact Admissions Office, St. Louis College of Health Careers, 909 South Taylor Avenue, St. Louis, MO 63110-1511. *Phone:* 314-652-0300. *Toll-free phone:* 888-789-4820. *Fax:* 314-652-4825. *Website:* http://www.slchc.com/.

St. Louis Community College
St. Louis, Missouri

- **Public** 2-year, part of St. Louis Community College System
- **Suburban** campus with easy access to St. Louis
- **Coed,** 24,005 undergraduate students, 42% full-time, 59% women, 41% men

Undergraduates 9,968 full-time, 14,037 part-time. Students come from 25 states and territories; 118 other countries; 2% are from out of state; 38% Black or African American, non-Hispanic/Latino; 3% Hispanic/Latino; 3% Asian, non-Hispanic/Latino; 0.2% Native Hawaiian or other Pacific Islander, non-Hispanic/Latino; 0.3% American Indian or Alaska Native, non-Hispanic/Latino; 3% Two or more races, non-Hispanic/Latino; 1% Race/ethnicity unknown; 0.7% international; 8% transferred in. *Retention:* 42% of full-time freshmen returned.

Freshmen *Admission:* 4,007 enrolled.

Academics *Degree:* certificates and associate. *Special study options:* academic remediation for entering students, accelerated degree program, adult/continuing education programs, advanced placement credit, distance learning, English as a second language, honors programs, independent study, internships, part-time degree program, services for LD students, study abroad, summer session for credit.

Library an OPAC, a Web page.

Student Life *Housing:* college housing not available. *Activities and Organizations:* drama/theater group, student-run newspaper. *Campus security:* 24-hour emergency response devices, late-night transport/escort service. *Student services:* personal/psychological counseling.

Athletics Member NJCAA. *Intercollegiate sports:* baseball M(s), basketball M(s)/W(s), soccer M(s)/W(s), softball W(s), volleyball W(s).

Standardized Tests *Recommended:* SAT or ACT (for admission).

Costs (2014–15) *Tuition:* area resident $2940 full-time, $89 per credit part-time; state resident $4320 full-time, $135 per credit part-time; nonresident $5970 full-time, $190 per credit part-time. Full-time tuition and fees vary according to course load. Part-time tuition and fees vary according to course load. *Payment plan:* installment. *Waivers:* senior citizens and employees or children of employees.

Applying *Options:* electronic application. *Required for some:* high school transcript, interview. *Application deadlines:* rolling (freshmen), rolling (out-of-state freshmen), rolling (transfers). *Notification:* continuous (freshmen), continuous (out-of-state freshmen), continuous (transfers).

Freshman Application Contact St. Louis Community College, 300 South Broadway, St. Louis, MO 63102. *Website:* http://www.stlcc.edu/.

Southeast Missouri Hospital College of Nursing and Health Sciences
Cape Girardeau, Missouri

Freshman Application Contact Southeast Missouri Hospital College of Nursing and Health Sciences, 2001 William Street, Cape Girardeau, MO 63701. *Phone:* 573-334-6825 Ext. 12. *Website:* http://www.sehcollege.edu/.

State Fair Community College
Sedalia, Missouri

- **District-supported** 2-year, founded 1966, part of Missouri Coordinating Board for Higher Education
- **Small-town** 128-acre campus
- **Endowment** $10.1 million
- **Coed,** 5,185 undergraduate students, 53% full-time, 64% women, 36% men

Undergraduates 2,744 full-time, 2,441 part-time. Students come from 8 states and territories; 4% Black or African American, non-Hispanic/Latino; 2% Hispanic/Latino; 0.8% Asian, non-Hispanic/Latino; 0.2% Native Hawaiian or other Pacific Islander, non-Hispanic/Latino; 0.6% American Indian or Alaska Native, non-Hispanic/Latino; 3% Two or more races, non-Hispanic/Latino; 5% Race/ethnicity unknown; 7% transferred in. *Retention:* 60% of full-time freshmen returned.

Freshmen *Admission:* 1,257 admitted, 1,257 enrolled.

Faculty *Total:* 398, 18% full-time. *Student/faculty ratio:* 9:1.

Majors Accounting; accounting and computer science; agribusiness; applied horticulture/horticulture operations; automobile/automotive mechanics technology; building/construction site management; business administration and management; CAD/CADD drafting/design technology; child-care and support services management; computer programming (specific applications); computer systems networking and telecommunications; criminal justice/police science; dental hygiene; education (specific subject areas) related; health information/medical records technology; liberal arts and sciences/liberal studies; machine tool technology; manufacturing engineering technology; marine maintenance and ship repair technology; mechanic and repair technologies related; medical administrative assistant and medical secretary; occupational therapist assistant; physical therapy technology; radiologic technology/science; registered nursing/registered nurse; special products marketing; teacher assistant/aide; technical teacher education; web page, digital/multimedia and information resources design.

Academics *Calendar:* semesters. *Degree:* certificates and associate. *Special study options:* academic remediation for entering students, adult/continuing education programs, advanced placement credit, distance learning, English as a second language, internships, off-campus study, part-time degree program, services for LD students, summer session for credit. *ROTC:* Army (b), Navy (b), Air Force (b).

Library Donald C. Proctor Library with 41,258 titles, 10,227 serial subscriptions, 1,633 audiovisual materials, an OPAC, a Web page.

Student Life *Housing Options:* coed. Campus housing is university owned. *Activities and Organizations:* drama/theater group, choral group. *Campus security:* 24-hour emergency response devices, controlled dormitory access, Campus Safety Officer on campus M-Th from 11 am - 10 pm, security during evening class hours.

Athletics Member NJCAA. *Intercollegiate sports:* basketball M(s)/W(s).

Costs (2014–15) *Tuition:* area resident $2940 full-time, $98 per credit part-time; state resident $4110 full-time, $131 per credit part-time; nonresident $5940 full-time, $196 per credit part-time. *Required fees:* $98 per credit part-time. *Room and board:* $3448. Room and board charges vary according to location.

Financial Aid Of all full-time matriculated undergraduates who enrolled in 2013, 87 Federal Work-Study jobs (averaging $1148).

Applying *Options:* electronic application. *Application fee:* $25. *Required:* high school transcript. *Application deadlines:* rolling (freshmen), rolling (transfers).

Freshman Application Contact State Fair Community College, 3201 West 16th Street, Sedalia, MO 65301-2199. *Phone:* 660-596-7221. *Toll-free phone:* 877-311-7322. *Website:* http://www.sfccmo.edu/.

Three Rivers Community College
Poplar Bluff, Missouri

Freshman Application Contact Ms. Marcia Fields, Director of Admissions and Recruiting, Three Rivers Community College, Poplar Bluff, MO 63901. *Phone:* 573-840-9675. *Toll-free phone:* 877-TRY-TRCC. *E-mail:* trytrcc@trcc.edu.
Website: http://www.trcc.edu/.

Vatterott College
Berkeley, Missouri

Director of Admissions Ann Farajallah, Director of Admissions, Vatterott College, 8580 Evans Avenue, Berkeley, MO 63134. *Phone:* 314-264-1020. *Toll-free phone:* 888-553-6627.
Website: http://www.vatterott.edu/.

Vatterott College
Kansas City, Missouri

Admissions Office Contact Vatterott College, 4131 N. Corrington Avenue, Kansas City, MO 64117. *Toll-free phone:* 888-553-6627.
Website: http://www.vatterott.edu/.

Vatterott College
St. Charles, Missouri

Director of Admissions Gertrude Bogan-Jones, Director of Admissions, Vatterott College, 3550 West Clay Street, St. Charles, MO 63301. *Phone:* 636-978-7488. *Toll-free phone:* 888-553-6627. *Fax:* 636-978-5121. *E-mail:* ofallon@vatterott-college.edu.
Website: http://www.vatterott.edu/.

Vatterott College
St. Joseph, Missouri

Director of Admissions Director of Admissions, Vatterott College, 3708 Belt Highway, St. Joseph, MO 64506. *Phone:* 816-364-5399. *Toll-free phone:* 888-553-6627. *Fax:* 816-364-1593.
Website: http://www.vatterott.edu/.

Vatterott College
Springfield, Missouri

Freshman Application Contact Mr. Scott Lester, Director of Admissions, Vatterott College, 3850 South Campbell Avenue, Springfield, MO 65807. *Phone:* 417-831-8116. *Toll-free phone:* 888-553-6627. *Fax:* 417-831-5099. *E-mail:* springfield@vatterott-college.edu.
Website: http://www.vatterott.edu/.

Vatterott College
Sunset Hills, Missouri

Director of Admissions Director of Admission, Vatterott College, 12900 Maurer Industrial Drive, Sunset Hills, MO 63127. *Phone:* 314-843-4200. *Toll-free phone:* 888-553-6627. *Fax:* 314-843-1709.
Website: http://www.vatterott.edu/.

Vet Tech Institute at Hickey College
St. Louis, Missouri

- **Private** 2-year, founded 2007
- **Suburban** campus
- **Coed,** 126 undergraduate students
- 62% of applicants were admitted

Freshmen *Admission:* 441 applied, 275 admitted.
Majors Veterinary/animal health technology.
Academics *Degree:* associate. *Special study options:* accelerated degree program, internships.
Freshman Application Contact Admissions Office, Vet Tech Institute at Hickey College, 2780 North Lindbergh Boulevard, St. Louis, MO 63114. *Phone:* 888-884-1459. *Toll-free phone:* 888-884-1459.
Website: http://stlouis.vettechinstitute.edu/.

Wentworth Military Academy and College
Lexington, Missouri

Freshman Application Contact Capt. Mike Bellis, College Admissions Director, Wentworth Military Academy and College, 1880 Washington Avenue, Lexington, MO 64067. *Phone:* 660-259-2221 Ext. 1351. *Fax:* 660-259-2677. *E-mail:* admissions@wma.edu.
Website: http://www.wma.edu/.

MONTANA

Aaniiih Nakoda College
Harlem, Montana

Director of Admissions Ms. Dixie Brockie, Registrar and Admissions Officer, Aaniiih Nakoda College, PO Box 159, Harlem, MT 59526-0159. *Phone:* 406-353-2607 Ext. 233. *Fax:* 406-353-2898. *E-mail:* dbrockie@mail.fbcc.edu.
Website: http://www.ancollege.edu/.

Blackfeet Community College
Browning, Montana

Freshman Application Contact Ms. Deana M. McNabb, Registrar and Admissions Officer, Blackfeet Community College, PO Box 819, Browning, MT 59417-0819. *Phone:* 406-338-5421. *Toll-free phone:* 800-549-7457. *Fax:* 406-338-3272.
Website: http://www.bfcc.edu/.

Chief Dull Knife College
Lame Deer, Montana

Freshman Application Contact Director of Admissions, Chief Dull Knife College, PO Box 98, 1 College Drive, Lame Deer, MT 59043-0098. *Phone:* 406-477-6215.
Website: http://www.cdkc.edu/.

Dawson Community College
Glendive, Montana

Freshman Application Contact Dawson Community College, 300 College Drive, PO Box 421, Glendive, MT 59330-0421. *Phone:* 406-377-3396 Ext. 410. *Toll-free phone:* 800-821-8320.
Website: http://www.dawson.edu/.

Flathead Valley Community College
Kalispell, Montana

- **State and locally supported** 2-year, founded 1967, part of Montana University System
- **Small-town** 209-acre campus
- **Endowment** $6.5 million
- **Coed,** 2,216 undergraduate students, 49% full-time, 61% women, 39% men

Undergraduates 1,082 full-time, 1,134 part-time. Students come from 18 states and territories; 3% are from out of state; 0.3% Black or African American, non-Hispanic/Latino; 2% Hispanic/Latino; 0.9% Asian, non-Hispanic/Latino; 0.3% Native Hawaiian or other Pacific Islander, non-Hispanic/Latino; 3% American Indian or Alaska Native, non-Hispanic/Latino; 13% Race/ethnicity unknown; 0.1% international; 8% transferred in; 1% live on campus. *Retention:* 52% of full-time freshmen returned.
Freshmen *Admission:* 368 enrolled.
Faculty *Total:* 206, 26% full-time, 12% with terminal degrees. *Student/faculty ratio:* 16:1.
Majors Accounting; administrative assistant and secretarial science; business administration and management; carpentry; child-care and support services management; computer/information technology services administration related; criminal justice/law enforcement administration; crisis/emergency/disaster management; culinary arts; electrician; emergency medical technology (EMT paramedic); hospitality and recreation marketing; human services; liberal arts and sciences/liberal studies; licensed practical/vocational nurse training; medical administrative assistant and medical secretary; medical/clinical assistant; medical insurance coding; medical radiologic technology; metal and jewelry arts; registered nursing/registered nurse; small business administration; substance abuse/addiction counseling; surgical technology; surveying technology; web/multimedia management and webmaster; welding technology; wildlife, fish and wildlands science and management.
Academics *Calendar:* semesters. *Degree:* certificates and associate. *Special study options:* academic remediation for entering students, adult/continuing education programs, advanced placement credit, cooperative education, distance learning, double majors, English as a second language, honors programs, independent study, internships, part-time degree program, services for LD students, study abroad, summer session for credit.

Library Flathead Valley Community College Library with 35,000 titles, 125 serial subscriptions, 514 audiovisual materials, an OPAC, a Web page.

Student Life *Housing Options:* coed. Campus housing is leased by the school. *Activities and Organizations:* drama/theater group, student-run newspaper, choral group, Forestry Club, Phi Theta Kappa. *Student services:* health clinic, personal/psychological counseling.

Athletics *Intramural sports:* basketball M/W, bowling M/W, cross-country running M/W, softball M/W, table tennis M/W, ultimate Frisbee M/W, volleyball M/W.

Standardized Tests *Required:* COMPASS Placement Test (for admission). *Recommended:* ACT (for admission).

Costs (2014–15) *Tuition:* area resident $2761 full-time, $99 per credit hour part-time; state resident $4133 full-time, $148 per credit hour part-time; nonresident $9901 full-time, $354 per credit hour part-time. Full-time tuition and fees vary according to course load. Part-time tuition and fees vary according to course load. *Required fees:* $1076 full-time, $38 part-time. *Payment plans:* installment, deferred payment. *Waivers:* senior citizens and employees or children of employees.

Applying *Options:* electronic application, early admission, deferred entrance. *Required:* high school transcript. *Application deadlines:* rolling (freshmen), rolling (transfers).

Freshman Application Contact Ms. Marlene C. Stoltz, Admissions/Graduation Coordinator, Flathead Valley Community College, 777 Grandview Drive, Kalispell, MT 59901-2622. *Phone:* 406-756-3846. *Toll-free phone:* 800-313-3822. *E-mail:* mstoltz@fvcc.cc.mt.us. *Website:* http://www.fvcc.edu/.

Fort Peck Community College
Poplar, Montana

Director of Admissions Mr. Robert McAnally, Vice President for Student Services, Fort Peck Community College, PO Box 398, Poplar, MT 59255-0398. *Phone:* 406-768-6329. *Website:* http://www.fpcc.edu/.

Great Falls College Montana State University
Great Falls, Montana

- **State-supported** 2-year, founded 1969, part of Montana University System
- **Small-town** 40-acre campus
- **Coed,** 1,875 undergraduate students, 48% full-time, 72% women, 28% men

Undergraduates 892 full-time, 983 part-time. Students come from 27 states and territories; 1 other country; 3% are from out of state; 1% Black or African American, non-Hispanic/Latino; 4% Hispanic/Latino; 1% Asian, non-Hispanic/Latino; 0.2% Native Hawaiian or other Pacific Islander, non-Hispanic/Latino; 7% American Indian or Alaska Native, non-Hispanic/Latino; 5% Two or more races, non-Hispanic/Latino; 1% Race/ethnicity unknown; 9% transferred in.

Freshmen *Admission:* 397 applied, 381 admitted, 284 enrolled.

Faculty *Total:* 141, 33% full-time, 13% with terminal degrees. *Student/faculty ratio:* 16:1.

Majors Accounting technology and bookkeeping; business administration and management; computer systems networking and telecommunications; dental hygiene; emergency medical technology (EMT paramedic); entrepreneurship; graphic design; health information/medical records technology; information technology; liberal arts and sciences and humanities related; licensed practical/vocational nurse training; medical/clinical assistant; medical insurance/medical billing; medical transcription; physical therapy technology; radiologic technology/science; respiratory care therapy; surgical technology; web page, digital/multimedia and information resources design; welding technology.

Academics *Calendar:* semesters. *Degree:* certificates and associate. *Special study options:* academic remediation for entering students, advanced placement credit, distance learning, double majors, independent study, internships, off-campus study, part-time degree program, services for LD students, summer session for credit.

Library Weaver Library with 50,470 titles, 50,274 serial subscriptions, 1,294 audiovisual materials, an OPAC, a Web page.

Student Life *Activities and Organizations:* The Associated Students of Great Falls College Montana State University, Native American Students, Veteran's Club. *Campus security:* 24-hour emergency response devices.

Costs (2013–14) *Tuition:* state resident $2496 full-time, $104 per credit part-time; nonresident $8748 full-time, $364 per credit part-time. Full-time tuition and fees vary according to course load and program. Part-time tuition and fees vary according to course load and program. *Required fees:* $589 full-time, $25 per credit part-time. *Payment plan:* deferred payment. *Waivers:* minority students, senior citizens, and employees or children of employees.

Financial Aid Of all full-time matriculated undergraduates who enrolled in 2011, 878 applied for aid, 792 were judged to have need, 22 had their need fully met. 39 Federal Work-Study jobs (averaging $2000). 37 state and other part-time jobs (averaging $2000). In 2011, 1 non-need-based awards were made. *Average percent of need met:* 66%. *Average financial aid package:* $9018. *Average need-based loan:* $3031. *Average need-based gift aid:* $5330. *Average non-need-based aid:* $250. *Average indebtedness upon graduation:* $16,557.

Applying *Options:* early admission. *Application fee:* $30. *Required:* high school transcript, proof of immunization. *Application deadlines:* rolling (freshmen), rolling (out-of-state freshmen), rolling (transfers). *Notification:* continuous (freshmen), continuous (out-of-state freshmen), continuous (transfers).

Freshman Application Contact Ms. Brittany Budeski, Admissions, Great Falls College Montana State University, 2100 16th Avenue South, Great Falls, MT 59405. *Phone:* 406-771-4300. *Toll-free phone:* 800-446-2698. *Fax:* 406-771-4329. *E-mail:* brittany.budeski@gfcmsu.edu. *Website:* http://www.gfcmsu.edu/.

Helena College University of Montana
Helena, Montana

- **State-supported** 2-year, founded 1939, part of Montana University System
- **Small-town** campus
- **Endowment** $75,877
- **Coed,** 1,430 undergraduate students, 47% full-time, 58% women, 42% men

Undergraduates 670 full-time, 760 part-time. Students come from 12 states and territories; 0.6% Black or African American, non-Hispanic/Latino; 2% Hispanic/Latino; 1% Asian, non-Hispanic/Latino; 4% American Indian or Alaska Native, non-Hispanic/Latino; 1% Two or more races, non-Hispanic/Latino; 6% Race/ethnicity unknown; 7% transferred in. *Retention:* 53% of full-time freshmen returned.

Freshmen *Admission:* 669 applied, 582 admitted, 271 enrolled.

Faculty *Total:* 155, 26% full-time. *Student/faculty ratio:* 12:1.

Majors Accounting; airframe mechanics and aircraft maintenance technology; automobile/automotive mechanics technology; computer numerically controlled (CNC) machinist technology; computer programming; construction engineering technology; fire science/firefighting; general studies; legal administrative assistant/secretary; licensed practical/vocational nurse training; medical office assistant; metal fabricator; office occupations and clerical services; registered nursing/registered nurse; small business administration; water resources engineering; welding technology.

Academics *Calendar:* semesters. *Degree:* certificates and associate. *Special study options:* academic remediation for entering students, adult/continuing education programs, advanced placement credit, distance learning, double majors, internships, part-time degree program, services for LD students, study abroad, summer session for credit.

Library Helena College with 528,158 titles, 59,206 serial subscriptions, an OPAC, a Web page.

Student Life *Housing:* college housing not available. *Activities and Organizations:* Student Government Association, Phi Theta Kappa, College Christian Fellowship, Aviation Club, Future Machinists of America. *Campus security:* late-night transport/escort service. *Student services:* personal/psychological counseling.

Financial Aid Of all full-time matriculated undergraduates who enrolled in 2008, 445 applied for aid, 334 were judged to have need. 42 Federal Work-Study jobs (averaging $1549). 22 state and other part-time jobs (averaging $1476). In 2008, 37 non-need-based awards were made. *Average financial aid package:* $6368. *Average need-based loan:* $3428. *Average need-based gift aid:* $3111. *Average non-need-based aid:* $1769. *Average indebtedness upon graduation:* $14,068.

Applying *Options:* electronic application, early admission, deferred entrance. *Application fee:* $30. *Required for some:* high school transcript. *Application deadlines:* rolling (freshmen), rolling (transfers).

Freshman Application Contact Mr. Ryan Loomis, Admissions Representative/Recruiter, Helena College University of Montana, 1115 North Roberts Street, Helena, MT 59601. *Phone:* 406-447-6904. *Toll-free phone:* 800-241-4882. *Website:* http://www.umhelena.edu/.

Little Big Horn College
Crow Agency, Montana

Freshman Application Contact Ms. Ann Bullis, Dean of Student Services, Little Big Horn College, Box 370, 1 Forest Lane, Crow Agency, MT 59022-0370. *Phone:* 406-638-2228 Ext. 50. *Website:* http://www.lbhc.edu/.

Miles Community College
Miles City, Montana

- **State and locally supported** 2-year, founded 1939, part of Montana University System
- **Small-town** 8-acre campus
- **Coed**

Undergraduates 280 full-time, 161 part-time. Students come from 24 states and territories; 4 other countries; 14% are from out of state; 2% Black or African American, non-Hispanic/Latino; 2% Hispanic/Latino; 1% Asian, non-Hispanic/Latino; 4% American Indian or Alaska Native, non-Hispanic/Latino; 0.7% Two or more races, non-Hispanic/Latino; 2% international; 11% transferred in; 32% live on campus.

Faculty *Student/faculty ratio:* 10:1.

Academics *Calendar:* semesters. *Degree:* certificates and associate. *Special study options:* academic remediation for entering students, accelerated degree program, adult/continuing education programs, advanced placement credit, cooperative education, distance learning, double majors, English as a second language, honors programs, independent study, internships, part-time degree program, services for LD students, summer session for credit.

Student Life *Campus security:* 24-hour emergency response devices, Manual dormitory entrances locked all the time, only accessible with key.

Athletics Member NJCAA.

Costs (2013–14) *Tuition:* area resident $2430 full-time; state resident $3450 full-time; nonresident $6300 full-time. Full-time tuition and fees vary according to course load, program, and reciprocity agreements. Part-time tuition and fees vary according to course load, program, and reciprocity agreements. *Required fees:* $1380 full-time. *Room and board:* $4930; room only: $2510. Room and board charges vary according to board plan and housing facility.

Financial Aid Of all full-time matriculated undergraduates who enrolled in 2012, 25 Federal Work-Study jobs (averaging $1400). 22 state and other part-time jobs (averaging $1300).

Applying *Options:* electronic application, early admission, deferred entrance. *Application fee:* $30. *Required:* high school transcript.

Freshman Application Contact Mr. Haley Anderson, Admissions Representative, Miles Community College, 2715 Dickinson Street, Miles City, MT 59301. *Phone:* 406-874-6178. *Toll-free phone:* 800-541-9281. *E-mail:* andersonh@milescc.edu.

Website: http://www.milescc.edu/.

Salish Kootenai College
Pablo, Montana

Freshman Application Contact Ms. Jackie Moran, Admissions Officer, Salish Kootenai College, PO Box 70, Pablo, MT 59855-0117. *Phone:* 406-275-4866. *Fax:* 406-275-4810. *E-mail:* jackie_moran@skc.edu.

Website: http://www.skc.edu/.

Stone Child College
Box Elder, Montana

Director of Admissions Mr. Ted Whitford, Director of Admissions/Registrar, Stone Child College, RR1, Box 1082, Box Elder, MT 59521. *Phone:* 406-395-4313 Ext. 110. *E-mail:* uanet337@quest.ocsc.montana.edu.

Website: http://www.stonechild.edu/.

NEBRASKA

Central Community College–Columbus Campus
Columbus, Nebraska

Freshman Application Contact Ms. Erica Leffler, Admissions/Recruiting Coordinator, Central Community College–Columbus Campus, PO Box 1027, Columbus, NE 68602-1027. *Phone:* 402-562-1296. *Toll-free phone:* 877-CCC-0780. *Fax:* 402-562-1201. *E-mail:* eleffler@ccneb.edu.

Website: http://www.cccneb.edu/.

Central Community College–Grand Island Campus
Grand Island, Nebraska

Freshman Application Contact Michelle Lubken, Admissions Director, Central Community College–Grand Island Campus, PO Box 4903, Grand Island, NE 68802-4903. *Phone:* 308-398-7406 Ext. 406. *Toll-free phone:* 877-CCC-0780. *Fax:* 308-398-7398. *E-mail:* mlubken@ccneb.edu.

Website: http://www.cccneb.edu/.

Central Community College–Hastings Campus
Hastings, Nebraska

Freshman Application Contact Mr. Robert Glenn, Admissions and Recruiting Director, Central Community College–Hastings Campus, PO Box 1024, East Highway 6, Hastings, NE 68902-1024. *Phone:* 402-461-2428. *Toll-free phone:* 877-CCC-0780. *E-mail:* rglenn@ccneb.edu.

Website: http://www.cccneb.edu/.

ITT Technical Institute
Omaha, Nebraska

- **Proprietary** primarily 2-year, founded 1991, part of ITT Educational Services, Inc.
- **Urban** campus
- **Coed**

Majors Business administration and management; construction management; cyber/computer forensics and counterterrorism; drafting and design technology; electrical, electronic and communications engineering technology; forensic science and technology; game and interactive media design; graphic communications; information technology project management; network and system administration; project management; registered nursing/registered nurse.

Academics *Calendar:* quarters. *Degrees:* associate and bachelor's.

Student Life *Housing:* college housing not available.

Freshman Application Contact Director of Recruitment, ITT Technical Institute, 1120 North 103rd Plaza, Suite 200, Omaha, NE 68114. *Phone:* 402-331-2900. *Toll-free phone:* 800-677-9260.

Website: http://www.itt-tech.edu/.

Kaplan University, Lincoln
Lincoln, Nebraska

Freshman Application Contact Kaplan University, Lincoln, 1821 K Street, Lincoln, NE 68501-2826. *Phone:* 402-474-5315. *Toll-free phone:* 866-527-5268 (in-state); 800-527-5268 (out-of-state).

Website: http://www.lincoln.kaplanuniversity.edu/.

Kaplan University, Omaha
Omaha, Nebraska

Freshman Application Contact Kaplan University, Omaha, 5425 North 103rd Street, Omaha, NE 68134. *Phone:* 402-572-8500. *Toll-free phone:* 866-527-5268 (in-state); 800-527-5268 (out-of-state).

Website: http://www.omaha.kaplanuniversity.edu/.

Little Priest Tribal College
Winnebago, Nebraska

- **Independent** 2-year, founded 1996
- **Rural** 10-acre campus with easy access to Sioux City
- **Endowment** $1.5 million
- **Coed**

Undergraduates 80 full-time, 42 part-time. Students come from 10 states and territories; 10% are from out of state; 93% American Indian or Alaska Native, non-Hispanic/Latino.

Faculty *Student/faculty ratio:* 6:1.

Academics *Degree:* associate.

Student Life *Campus security:* 24-hour emergency response devices.

Costs (2013–14) *Tuition:* state resident $2400 full-time, $100 per credit hour part-time; nonresident $2400 full-time, $100 per credit hour part-time. *Required fees:* $176 full-time, $88 per term part-time.

Financial Aid Of all full-time matriculated undergraduates who enrolled in 2012, 8 Federal Work-Study jobs (averaging $750).

Applying *Options:* electronic application, early admission. *Application fee:* $10. *Required:* high school transcript.

Freshman Application Contact Little Priest Tribal College, PO Box 270, Winnebago, NE 68071. *Phone:* 402-878-2380 Ext. 112.

Website: http://www.littlepriest.edu/.

Metropolitan Community College
Omaha, Nebraska

Freshman Application Contact Ms. Maria Vazquez, Associate Vice President for Student Affairs, Metropolitan Community College, PO Box 3777, Omaha,

NE 69103-0777. *Phone:* 402-457-2430. *Toll-free phone:* 800-228-9553. *Fax:* 402-457-2238. *E-mail:* mvazquez@mccneb.edu. *Website:* http://www.mccneb.edu/.

Mid-Plains Community College
North Platte, Nebraska

- **District-supported** 2-year, founded 1973
- **Small-town** campus
- **Endowment** $5.2 million
- **Coed,** 2,491 undergraduate students, 39% full-time, 61% women, 39% men

Undergraduates 960 full-time, 1,531 part-time. Students come from 13 other countries; 12% are from out of state; 4% Black or African American, non-Hispanic/Latino; 8% Hispanic/Latino; 0.8% Asian, non-Hispanic/Latino; 0.2% Native Hawaiian or other Pacific Islander, non-Hispanic/Latino; 0.6% American Indian or Alaska Native, non-Hispanic/Latino; 2% Two or more races, non-Hispanic/Latino; 3% Race/ethnicity unknown; 1% international; 3% transferred in; 8% live on campus.

Freshmen *Admission:* 480 applied, 480 admitted, 480 enrolled. *Average high school GPA:* 2.87.

Faculty *Total:* 326, 20% full-time, 2% with terminal degrees. *Student/faculty ratio:* 12:1.

Majors Administrative assistant and secretarial science; autobody/collision and repair technology; automobile/automotive mechanics technology; building/construction finishing, management, and inspection related; business administration and management; clinical/medical laboratory technology; commercial and advertising art; computer and information sciences; construction engineering technology; dental assisting; diesel mechanics technology; fire science/firefighting; heating, air conditioning, ventilation and refrigeration maintenance technology; liberal arts and sciences/liberal studies; licensed practical/vocational nurse training; registered nursing/registered nurse; transportation and materials moving related; welding technology.

Academics *Calendar:* semesters. *Degree:* certificates, diplomas, and associate. *Special study options:* academic remediation for entering students, accelerated degree program, adult/continuing education programs, advanced placement credit, cooperative education, distance learning, double majors, English as a second language, external degree program, independent study, internships, part-time degree program, services for LD students, summer session for credit.

Library McDonald-Belton Learning Resource Center (LRC) plus 1 other with 45,403 titles, 86 serial subscriptions, 1,822 audiovisual materials, an OPAC, a Web page.

Student Life *Housing Options:* coed, special housing for students with disabilities. Campus housing is university owned. *Activities and Organizations:* drama/theater group, student-run newspaper, choral group, Student Senate, Phi Theta Kappa, Phi Beta Lambda, Intercollegiate Athletics, MPCC Student Nurses Association, national fraternities, national sororities. *Campus security:* controlled dormitory access, patrols by trained security personnel.

Athletics Member NJCAA. *Intercollegiate sports:* baseball M(s), basketball M(s)/W(s), golf M(s), softball W(s), volleyball W(s). *Intramural sports:* baseball M, basketball M/W, softball W, volleyball W.

Standardized Tests *Required for some:* COMPASS. *Recommended:* ACT (for admission).

Costs (2013–14) *Tuition:* state resident $2310 full-time, $77 per credit hour part-time; nonresident $3000 full-time, $100 per credit hour part-time. Full-time tuition and fees vary according to reciprocity agreements. Part-time tuition and fees vary according to reciprocity agreements. *Required fees:* $450 full-time, $15 per credit hour part-time. *Room and board:* $5460. Room and board charges vary according to board plan, housing facility, and location. *Payment plan:* installment. *Waivers:* senior citizens and employees or children of employees.

Financial Aid Of all full-time matriculated undergraduates who enrolled in 2012, 1,106 applied for aid, 899 were judged to have need, 180 had their need fully met. 53 Federal Work-Study jobs (averaging $809). In 2012, 101 non-need-based awards were made. *Average percent of need met:* 71%. *Average financial aid package:* $5762. *Average need-based loan:* $2529. *Average need-based gift aid:* $4277. *Average non-need-based aid:* $1100. *Average indebtedness upon graduation:* $10,011.

Applying *Options:* electronic application, deferred entrance. *Required:* high school transcript. *Required for some:* 2 letters of recommendation, interview. *Application deadlines:* rolling (freshmen), rolling (out-of-state freshmen), rolling (transfers). *Notification:* continuous (freshmen), continuous (out-of-state freshmen), continuous (transfers).

Freshman Application Contact Mr. Michael Driskell, Area Recruiter, Mid-Plains Community College, 1101 Halligan Dr, North Platte, NE 69101.

Phone: 308-535-3709. *Toll-free phone:* 800-658-4308 (in-state); 800-658-4348 (out-of-state). *Fax:* 308-534-5767. *E-mail:* driskellm@mpcc.edu. *Website:* http://www.mpcc.edu/.

Myotherapy Institute
Lincoln, Nebraska

Freshman Application Contact Admissions Office, Myotherapy Institute, 6020 South 58th Street, Lincoln, NE 68516. *Phone:* 402-421-7410. *Website:* http://www.myotherapy.edu/.

Nebraska College of Technical Agriculture
Curtis, Nebraska

Freshman Application Contact Kevin Martin, Assistant Admissions Coordinator, Nebraska College of Technical Agriculture, 404 East 7th Street, Curtis, NE 69025. *Phone:* 308-367-4124. *Toll-free phone:* 800-3CURTIS. *Website:* http://www.ncta.unl.edu/.

Nebraska Indian Community College
Macy, Nebraska

Director of Admissions Ms. Theresa Henry, Admission Counselor, Nebraska Indian Community College, PO Box 428, Macy, NE 68039-0428. *Phone:* 402-837-5078. *Website:* http://www.thenicc.edu/.

Northeast Community College
Norfolk, Nebraska

Freshman Application Contact Maureen Baker, Dean of Students, Northeast Community College, 801 East Benjamin Avenue, PO Box 469, Norfolk, NE 68702-0469. *Phone:* 402-844-7258. *Toll-free phone:* 800-348-9033 Ext. 7260. *Fax:* 402-844-7403. *E-mail:* admission@northeast.edu. *Website:* http://www.northeast.edu/.

Omaha School of Massage and Healthcare of Herzing University
Omaha, Nebraska

Admissions Office Contact Omaha School of Massage and Healthcare of Herzing University, 9748 Park Drive, Omaha, NE 68127. *Website:* http://www.osmhc.com/.

Southeast Community College, Beatrice Campus
Beatrice, Nebraska

Freshman Application Contact Admissions Office, Southeast Community College, Beatrice Campus, 4771 West Scott Road, Beatrice, NE 68310. *Phone:* 402-228-3468. *Toll-free phone:* 800-233-5027. *Fax:* 402-228-2218. *Website:* http://www.southeast.edu/.

Southeast Community College, Lincoln Campus
Lincoln, Nebraska

Freshman Application Contact Admissions Office, Southeast Community College, Lincoln Campus, 8800 O Street, Lincoln, NE 68520-1299. *Phone:* 402-471-3333. *Toll-free phone:* 800-642-4075. *Fax:* 402-437-2404. *Website:* http://www.southeast.edu/.

Southeast Community College, Milford Campus
Milford, Nebraska

Freshman Application Contact Admissions Office, Southeast Community College, Milford Campus, 600 State Street, Milford, NE 68405. *Phone:* 402-761-2131. *Toll-free phone:* 800-933-7223. *Fax:* 402-761-2324. *Website:* http://www.southeast.edu/.

Universal College of Healing Arts
Omaha, Nebraska

Admissions Office Contact Universal College of Healing Arts, 8702 North 30th Street, Omaha, NE 68112-1810. *Website:* http://www.ucha.edu/.

Vatterott College
Omaha, Nebraska

Freshman Application Contact Admissions Office, Vatterott College, 11818 I Street, Omaha, NE 68137. *Phone:* 402-891-9411. *Toll-free phone:* 888-553-6627. *Fax:* 402-891-9413.
Website: http://www.vatterott.edu/.

Western Nebraska Community College
Sidney, Nebraska

Director of Admissions Mr. Troy Archuleta, Admissions and Recruitment Director, Western Nebraska Community College, 371 College Drive, Sidney, NE 69162. *Phone:* 308-635-6015. *Toll-free phone:* 800-222-9682. *E-mail:* rhovey@wncc.net.
Website: http://www.wncc.net/.

Wright Career College
Omaha, Nebraska

- **Proprietary** primarily 2-year, founded 2011
- **Suburban** campus with easy access to Omaha
- **Coed,** 306 undergraduate students, 31% full-time, 80% women, 20% men

Undergraduates 96 full-time, 210 part-time. Students come from 3 states and territories; 3% are from out of state; 72% Black or African American, non-Hispanic/Latino; 3% Hispanic/Latino; 0.3% Asian, non-Hispanic/Latino; 1% American Indian or Alaska Native, non-Hispanic/Latino; 2% Two or more races, non-Hispanic/Latino; 0.7% Race/ethnicity unknown; 2% transferred in. *Retention:* 1% of full-time freshmen returned.
Freshmen *Admission:* 306 applied, 306 admitted, 127 enrolled.
Majors Accounting; business administration and management; computer installation and repair technology; computer programming; computer systems networking and telecommunications; computer technology/computer systems technology; entrepreneurial and small business related; health and physical education related; health/health-care administration; medical/clinical assistant.
Academics *Degrees:* diplomas, associate, and bachelor's. *Special study options:* adult/continuing education programs, distance learning, internships, off-campus study.
Student Life *Housing:* college housing not available.
Applying *Application deadlines:* rolling (freshmen), rolling (out-of-state freshmen), rolling (transfers). *Early decision deadline:* rolling (for plan 1), rolling (for plan 2). *Notification:* continuous (freshmen), continuous (out-of-state freshmen), continuous (transfers), rolling (early decision plan 1), rolling (early decision plan 2).
Freshman Application Contact Wright Career College, 3000 S. 84th Street, Omaha, NE 68124. *Phone:* 402-514-2500. *Toll-free phone:* 800-555-4003. *E-mail:* info@wrightcc.edu.
Website: http://www.wrightcc.edu/.

NEVADA

Anthem College–Las Vegas
Las Vegas, Nevada

Freshman Application Contact Admissions Office, Anthem College–Las Vegas, 2320 South Rancho Drive, Las Vegas, NV 89102. *Phone:* 702-385-6700. *Toll-free phone:* 855-331-7762.
Website: http://anthem.edu/las-vegas-nevada/.

Career College of Northern Nevada
Sparks, Nevada

Freshman Application Contact Ms. Laura Goldhammer, Director of Admissions, Career College of Northern Nevada, 1421 Pullman Drive, Sparks, NV 89434. *Phone:* 775-856-2266 Ext. 11. *Fax:* 775-856-0935. *E-mail:* lgoldhammer@ccnn4u.com.
Website: http://www.ccnn.edu/.

Carrington College–Las Vegas
Las Vegas, Nevada

- **Proprietary** 2-year, part of Carrington Colleges Group, Inc.
- **Coed,** 255 undergraduate students, 88% full-time, 63% women, 37% men

Undergraduates 224 full-time, 31 part-time. 3% are from out of state; 19% Black or African American, non-Hispanic/Latino; 13% Hispanic/Latino; 16% Asian, non-Hispanic/Latino; 6% Native Hawaiian or other Pacific Islander, non-Hispanic/Latino; 0.4% American Indian or Alaska Native, non-Hispanic/Latino; 4% Two or more races, non-Hispanic/Latino; 2% Race/ethnicity unknown; 24% transferred in.
Freshmen *Admission:* 28 enrolled.
Faculty *Total:* 17, 53% full-time. *Student/faculty ratio:* 20:1.
Majors Physical therapy technology; respiratory therapy technician.
Academics *Degree:* certificates and associate.
Student Life *Housing:* college housing not available.
Applying *Required:* essay or personal statement, high school transcript, interview, Entrance test administered by Carrington College.
Freshman Application Contact Carrington College–Las Vegas, 5740 South Eastern Avenue, Las Vegas, NV 89119.
Website: http://carrington.edu/.

Carrington College–Reno
Reno, Nevada

- **Proprietary** 2-year, part of Carrington Colleges Group, Inc.
- **Coed,** 333 undergraduate students, 76% full-time, 83% women, 17% men

Undergraduates 254 full-time, 79 part-time. 8% are from out of state; 0.6% Black or African American, non-Hispanic/Latino; 16% Hispanic/Latino; 3% Asian, non-Hispanic/Latino; 2% Native Hawaiian or other Pacific Islander, non-Hispanic/Latino; 0.6% American Indian or Alaska Native, non-Hispanic/Latino; 2% Two or more races, non-Hispanic/Latino; 1% Race/ethnicity unknown; 14% transferred in.
Freshmen *Admission:* 9 enrolled.
Faculty *Total:* 31, 42% full-time. *Student/faculty ratio:* 15:1.
Majors Registered nursing/registered nurse.
Academics *Degree:* certificates and associate.
Student Life *Housing:* college housing not available.
Applying *Required:* essay or personal statement, high school transcript, interview, Entrance test administered by Carrington College.
Freshman Application Contact Carrington College–Reno, 5580 Kietzke Lane, Reno, NV 89511. *Phone:* 775-335-2900.
Website: http://carrington.edu/.

College of Southern Nevada
North Las Vegas, Nevada

Freshman Application Contact Admissions and Records, College of Southern Nevada, 3200 East Cheyenne Avenue, North Las Vegas, NV 89030-4296. *Phone:* 702-651-4060.
Website: http://www.csn.edu/.

Everest College
Henderson, Nevada

Admissions Office Contact Everest College, 170 North Stephanie Street, 1st Floor, Henderson, NV 89074. *Toll-free phone:* 888-741-4270.
Website: http://www.everest.edu/.

Great Basin College
Elko, Nevada

- **State-supported** primarily 2-year, founded 1967, part of University and Community College System of Nevada
- **Small-town** 45-acre campus
- **Coed,** 3,185 undergraduate students

Undergraduates Students come from 13 states and territories; 3% Black or African American, non-Hispanic/Latino; 13% Hispanic/Latino; 2% Asian, non-Hispanic/Latino; 0.4% Native Hawaiian or other Pacific Islander, non-Hispanic/Latino; 3% American Indian or Alaska Native, non-Hispanic/Latino; 2% Two or more races, non-Hispanic/Latino; 5% Race/ethnicity unknown; 0.2% international; 5% live on campus.
Faculty *Total:* 190, 32% full-time. *Student/faculty ratio:* 16:1.
Majors Anthropology; art; business administration and management; business/commerce; chemistry; criminal justice/safety; data processing and data processing technology; diesel mechanics technology; electrical, electronic and communications engineering technology; elementary education; English; geology/earth science; history; industrial technology; interdisciplinary studies; kindergarten/preschool education; management science; mathematics; natural resources management and policy related; office management; operations management; physics; psychology; registered nursing/registered nurse; secondary education; social sciences; social work; sociology; surveying technology; welding technology.
Academics *Calendar:* semesters. *Degrees:* certificates, associate, bachelor's, and postbachelor's certificates. *Special study options:* academic remediation for entering students, accelerated degree program, adult/continuing education programs, cooperative education, distance learning, double majors, English as a second language, external degree program, independent study, off-campus study, part-time degree program, services for LD students, summer session for credit.

Library Learning Resource Center with 113,341 titles, 142 serial subscriptions, 1,852 audiovisual materials, an OPAC.

Student Life *Housing Options:* coed, special housing for students with disabilities. Campus housing is university owned. *Activities and Organizations:* Student Nurses Organization, Housing Central, Skills USA, Agriculture Student Organization, Colleges Against Cancer. *Campus security:* late-night transport/escort service, evening patrols by trained security personnel. *Student services:* personal/psychological counseling.

Athletics *Intramural sports:* rock climbing M/W, volleyball M/W, weight lifting M/W.

Financial Aid Of all full-time matriculated undergraduates who enrolled in 2012, 35 Federal Work-Study jobs (averaging $1000). 50 state and other part-time jobs (averaging $1800).

Applying *Options:* electronic application, early admission, deferred entrance. *Application fee:* $10. *Application deadlines:* rolling (freshmen), rolling (out-of-state freshmen), rolling (transfers). *Notification:* continuous (freshmen), continuous (out-of-state freshmen), continuous (transfers).

Freshman Application Contact Ms. Jan King, Director of Admissions and Registrar, Great Basin College, 1500 College Parkway, Elko, NV 89801-3348. *Phone:* 775-753-2102.

Website: http://www.gbcnv.edu/.

ITT Technical Institute

Henderson, Nevada

- **Proprietary** primarily 2-year, founded 1997, part of ITT Educational Services, Inc.
- **Coed**

Majors Business administration and management; computer programming (specific applications); construction management; cyber/computer forensics and counterterrorism; drafting and design technology; electrical, electronic and communications engineering technology; forensic science and technology; game and interactive media design; graphic communications; information technology project management; network and system administration; project management.

Academics *Degrees:* associate and bachelor's.

Student Life *Housing:* college housing not available.

Financial Aid Of all full-time matriculated undergraduates who enrolled in 2012, 6 Federal Work-Study jobs (averaging $5000).

Freshman Application Contact Director of Recruitment, ITT Technical Institute, 168 North Gibson Road, Henderson, NV 89014. *Phone:* 702-558-5404. *Toll-free phone:* 800-488-8459.

Website: http://www.itt-tech.edu/.

ITT Technical Institute

North Las Vegas, Nevada

- **Proprietary** primarily 2-year, part of ITT Educational Services, Inc.
- **Coed**

Majors Business administration and management; construction management; cyber/computer forensics and counterterrorism; drafting and design technology; electrical, electronic and communications engineering technology; forensic science and technology; game and interactive media design; information technology project management; network and system administration; project management.

Academics *Calendar:* quarters. *Degrees:* associate and bachelor's.

Freshman Application Contact Director of Recruitment, ITT Technical Institute, 3825 W. Cheyenne Avenue, Suite 600, North Las Vegas, NV 89032. *Phone:* 702-240-0967. *Toll-free phone:* 877-832-8442.

Website: http://www.itt-tech.edu/.

Kaplan College, Las Vegas Campus

Las Vegas, Nevada

Freshman Application Contact Admissions Office, Kaplan College, Las Vegas Campus, 3535 West Sahara Avenue, Las Vegas, NV 89102. *Phone:* 702-368-2338. *Toll-free phone:* 800-935-1857.

Website: http://las-vegas.kaplancollege.com/.

Le Cordon Bleu College of Culinary Arts in Las Vegas

Las Vegas, Nevada

Freshman Application Contact Admissions Office, Le Cordon Bleu College of Culinary Arts in Las Vegas, 1451 Center Crossing Road, Las Vegas, NV 89144. *Toll-free phone:* 888-551-8222.

Website: http://www.chefs.edu/Las-Vegas/.

Pima Medical Institute

Las Vegas, Nevada

Freshman Application Contact Admissions Office, Pima Medical Institute, 3333 East Flamingo Road, Las Vegas, NV 89121. *Phone:* 702-458-9650 Ext. 202. *Toll-free phone:* 800-477-PIMA.

Website: http://www.pmi.edu/.

Truckee Meadows Community College

Reno, Nevada

- **State-supported** 2-year, founded 1971, part of Nevada System of Higher Education
- **Suburban** 63-acre campus
- **Endowment** $11.2 million
- **Coed**, 11,204 undergraduate students, 26% full-time, 55% women, 45% men

Undergraduates 2,905 full-time, 8,299 part-time. Students come from 20 states and territories; 6% are from out of state; 2% Black or African American, non-Hispanic/Latino; 23% Hispanic/Latino; 5% Asian, non-Hispanic/Latino; 0.2% Native Hawaiian or other Pacific Islander, non-Hispanic/Latino; 1% American Indian or Alaska Native, non-Hispanic/Latino; 3% Two or more races, non-Hispanic/Latino; 2% Race/ethnicity unknown; 0.5% international; 5% transferred in. *Retention:* 65% of full-time freshmen returned.

Freshmen *Admission:* 1,903 applied, 1,903 admitted, 1,504 enrolled.

Faculty *Total:* 563, 29% full-time. *Student/faculty ratio:* 21:1.

Majors Administrative assistant and secretarial science; anthropology; architecture; automobile/automotive mechanics technology; biology/biological sciences; building construction technology; business administration and management; chemistry; civil engineering; computer programming; construction management; criminal justice/law enforcement administration; culinary arts; dance; dental hygiene; diesel mechanics technology; dietetics; dietetic technology; drafting and design technology; dramatic/theater arts; early childhood education; elementary education; engineering; English; entrepreneurship; environmental science; fine/studio arts; fire science/firefighting; general studies; geological and earth sciences/geosciences related; heating, ventilation, air conditioning and refrigeration engineering technology; history; landscape architecture; legal assistant/paralegal; logistics, materials, and supply chain management; manufacturing engineering technology; mathematics; mental health counseling; music; network and system administration; philosophy; physics; psychology; radiologic technology/science; registered nursing/registered nurse; special education; special education–elementary school; substance abuse/addiction counseling; veterinary/animal health technology; web/multimedia management and webmaster; welding technology.

Academics *Calendar:* semesters. *Degree:* certificates and associate. *Special study options:* academic remediation for entering students, accelerated degree program, adult/continuing education programs, advanced placement credit, cooperative education, distance learning, double majors, English as a second language, independent study, internships, part-time degree program, services for LD students, summer session for credit. *ROTC:* Army (c).

Library Elizabeth Sturm Library with an OPAC, a Web page.

Student Life *Housing:* college housing not available. *Activities and Organizations:* drama/theater group, student-run newspaper, Entrepreneurship Club, International Club, Phi Theta Kappa, Student Government Association, Student Media and Broadcasting Club. *Campus security:* 24-hour emergency response devices and patrols, late-night transport/escort service. *Student services:* personal/psychological counseling.

Costs (2013–14) *Tuition:* state resident $2535 full-time, $85 per credit hour part-time; nonresident $9180 full-time, $178 per credit hour part-time. Full-time tuition and fees vary according to course load and program. Part-time tuition and fees vary according to course load and program. *Required fees:* $165 full-time, $6 per credit hour part-time. *Payment plan:* installment. *Waivers:* employees or children of employees.

Financial Aid Of all full-time matriculated undergraduates who enrolled in 2012, 126 Federal Work-Study jobs (averaging $5000). 368 state and other part-time jobs (averaging $5000).

Applying *Options:* electronic application, early admission. *Application fee:* $10. *Application deadlines:* 8/9 (freshmen), 8/9 (out-of-state freshmen), 8/9 (transfers).

Freshman Application Contact Truckee Meadows Community College, 7000 Dandini Boulevard, Reno, NV 89512-3901. *Phone:* 775-673-7240.

Website: http://www.tmcc.edu/.

Western Nevada College
Carson City, Nevada

- **State-supported** primarily 2-year, founded 1971, part of Nevada System of Higher Education
- **Small-town** 200-acre campus
- **Coed,** 3,976 undergraduate students, 28% full-time, 59% women, 41% men

Undergraduates 1,129 full-time, 2,847 part-time. 5% are from out of state; 1% Black or African American, non-Hispanic/Latino; 17% Hispanic/Latino; 2% Asian, non-Hispanic/Latino; 0.7% Native Hawaiian or other Pacific Islander, non-Hispanic/Latino; 3% American Indian or Alaska Native, non-Hispanic/Latino; 3% Two or more races, non-Hispanic/Latino; 5% Race/ethnicity unknown; 7% transferred in.

Freshmen *Admission:* 1,674 applied, 1,674 admitted, 694 enrolled.

Faculty *Total:* 267, 16% full-time, 14% with terminal degrees. *Student/faculty ratio:* 18:1.

Majors Accounting; automobile/automotive mechanics technology; biology/biological sciences; business/commerce; child-care and support services management; clinical/medical laboratory technology; computer and information sciences; computer programming; construction management; corrections; criminal justice/law enforcement administration; criminal justice/police science; drafting and design technology; electrical and power transmission installation; electrical, electronic and communications engineering technology; engineering; environmental studies; fire prevention and safety technology; general studies; industrial technology; liberal arts and sciences/liberal studies; machine tool technology; management information systems; mathematics; physical sciences; registered nursing/registered nurse; welding technology.

Academics *Calendar:* semesters. *Degrees:* certificates, associate, and bachelor's. *Special study options:* academic remediation for entering students, adult/continuing education programs, advanced placement credit, cooperative education, distance learning, double majors, English as a second language, honors programs, independent study, internships, part-time degree program, services for LD students, summer session for credit.

Library Western Nevada Community College Library and Media Services with an OPAC, a Web page.

Student Life *Housing:* college housing not available. *Activities and Organizations:* drama/theater group, choral group, Wildcat Productions, Lone Mountain Writers, Art Club, ASL Club, Latino Student Club. *Campus security:* late-night transport/escort service. *Student services:* personal/psychological counseling.

Athletics *Intercollegiate sports:* baseball M, softball W.

Standardized Tests *Recommended:* SAT or ACT (for admission).

Costs (2013–14) *Tuition:* state resident $2265 full-time, $85 per credit hour part-time; nonresident $8910 full-time, $178 per credit hour part-time. Full-time tuition and fees vary according to course level and reciprocity agreements. Part-time tuition and fees vary according to course level and reciprocity agreements. *Required fees:* $435 full-time, $6 per credit hour part-time. *Payment plan:* deferred payment. *Waivers:* employees or children of employees.

Financial Aid Of all full-time matriculated undergraduates who enrolled in 2012, 922 applied for aid, 835 were judged to have need, 70 had their need fully met. In 2012, 11 non-need-based awards were made. *Average percent of need met:* 44%. *Average financial aid package:* $6417. *Average need-based loan:* $3749. *Average need-based gift aid:* $1043. *Average non-need-based aid:* $1043.

Applying *Options:* early admission. *Application fee:* $15. *Required for some:* high school transcript. *Application deadlines:* rolling (freshmen), rolling (transfers).

Freshman Application Contact Admissions and Records, Western Nevada College, 2201 West College Parkway, Carson City, NV 89703. *Phone:* 775-445-2377. *Fax:* 775-445-3147. *E-mail:* wncc_aro@wncc.edu.

Website: http://www.wnc.edu/.

NEW HAMPSHIRE

Great Bay Community College
Portsmouth, New Hampshire

Freshman Application Contact Matt Thornton, Admissions Coordinator, Great Bay Community College, 320 Corporate Drive, Portsmouth, NH 03801. *Phone:* 603-427-7605. *Toll-free phone:* 800-522-1194. *E-mail:* askgreatbay@ccsnh.edu.

Website: http://www.greatbay.edu/.

Lakes Region Community College
Laconia, New Hampshire

- **State-supported** 2-year, part of Community College System of New Hampshire
- **Small-town** campus
- **Coed,** 1,179 undergraduate students, 42% full-time, 54% women, 46% men

Undergraduates 490 full-time, 689 part-time. Students come from 2 other countries; 3% are from out of state; 0.5% Black or African American, non-Hispanic/Latino; 1% Hispanic/Latino; 0.5% Asian, non-Hispanic/Latino; 0.1% Native Hawaiian or other Pacific Islander, non-Hispanic/Latino; 0.5% American Indian or Alaska Native, non-Hispanic/Latino; 0.9% Two or more races, non-Hispanic/Latino; 22% Race/ethnicity unknown.

Freshmen *Admission:* 311 enrolled.

Faculty *Student/faculty ratio:* 9:1.

Majors Accounting; animation, interactive technology, video graphics and special effects; automobile/automotive mechanics technology; business automation/technology/data entry; business/commerce; computer and information sciences; culinary arts; early childhood education; education; electrical/electronics equipment installation and repair; energy management and systems technology; fine/studio arts; fire prevention and safety technology; fire science/firefighting; general studies; gerontology; graphic and printing equipment operation/production; hospitality administration; human services; liberal arts and sciences/liberal studies; marine maintenance and ship repair technology; registered nursing/registered nurse; restaurant/food services management.

Academics *Degree:* associate. *Special study options:* academic remediation for entering students, adult/continuing education programs, cooperative education, distance learning, double majors, independent study, internships, part-time degree program, services for LD students, summer session for credit.

Library Hugh Bennett Library plus 1 other.

Student Life *Housing:* college housing not available. *Campus security:* 24-hour emergency response devices.

Costs (2014–15) *Tuition:* state resident $6800 full-time; nonresident $10,200 full-time. *Payment plan:* installment. *Waivers:* employees or children of employees.

Applying *Options:* electronic application, deferred entrance. *Application fee:* $20. *Required:* high school transcript. *Notification:* continuous (freshmen), continuous (out-of-state freshmen), continuous (transfers).

Freshman Application Contact Kathy Plummer, Admissions, Lakes Region Community College, Lakes Region Community College, Admissions Office 379 Belmont Road, Laconia, NH 03246. *Phone:* 603-524-3207 Ext. 6410. *Toll-free phone:* 800-357-2992. *E-mail:* lrccinfo@ccsnh.edu.

Website: http://www.lrcc.edu/.

Manchester Community College
Manchester, New Hampshire

Freshman Application Contact Ms. Jacquie Poirier, Coordinator of Admissions, Manchester Community College, 1066 Front Street, Manchester, NH 03102-8518. *Phone:* 603-668-6706 Ext. 283. *Toll-free phone:* 800-924-3445. *E-mail:* jpoirier@nhctc.edu.

Website: http://www.mccnh.edu/.

Mount Washington College
Manchester, New Hampshire

Freshman Application Contact Mount Washington College, 3 Sundial Avenue, Manchester, NH 03103. *Phone:* 603-668-6660. *Toll-free phone:* 888-971-2190.

Website: http://www.mountwashington.edu/.

Mount Washington College
Nashua, New Hampshire

Freshman Application Contact Mount Washington College, 410 Amherst Street, Nashua, NH 03063. *Phone:* 603-883-0404. *Toll-free phone:* 888-971-2190.

Website: http://www.mountwashington.edu/.

Mount Washington College
Salem, New Hampshire

Freshman Application Contact Mount Washington College, 11 Manor Parkway, Salem, NH 03079. *Phone:* 603-898-3480. *Toll-free phone:* 888-971-2190.

Website: http://www.mountwashington.edu/.

Nashua Community College
Nashua, New Hampshire

Freshman Application Contact Ms. Patricia Goodman, Vice President of Student Services, Nashua Community College, Nashua, NH 03063. *Phone:* 603-882-6923 Ext. 1529. *Fax:* 603-882-8690. *E-mail:* pgoodman@ccsnh.edu.
Website: http://www.nashuacc.edu/.

NHTI, Concord's Community College
Concord, New Hampshire

- **State-supported** 2-year, founded 1964, part of Community College System of New Hampshire
- **Small-town** 225-acre campus with easy access to Boston
- **Coed**

Undergraduates 23% live on campus.
Faculty *Student/faculty ratio:* 15:1.
Academics *Calendar:* semesters. *Degree:* certificates, diplomas, and associate. *Special study options:* academic remediation for entering students, adult/continuing education programs, advanced placement credit, distance learning, double majors, English as a second language, external degree program, part-time degree program, services for LD students, summer session for credit.
Student Life *Campus security:* 24-hour emergency response devices and patrols, late-night transport/escort service, controlled dormitory access, cameras in vital locations.
Standardized Tests *Required for some:* National League of Nursing Exam. *Recommended:* SAT or ACT (for admission).
Applying *Options:* electronic application. *Application fee:* $20. *Required:* high school transcript. *Required for some:* essay or personal statement, interview. *Recommended:* minimum 2.0 GPA.
Freshman Application Contact Mr. Francis P. Meyer, Director of Admissions, NHTI, Concord's Community College, 31 College Drive, Concord, NH 03301-7412. *Phone:* 603-271-6484 Ext. 2459. *Toll-free phone:* 800-247-0179. *E-mail:* fmeyer@ccsnh.edu.
Website: http://www.nhti.edu/.

River Valley Community College
Claremont, New Hampshire

- **State-supported** 2-year, part of Community College System of NH
- **Rural** campus
- **Coed,** 982 undergraduate students, 36% full-time, 71% women, 29% men
- **76%** of applicants were admitted

Undergraduates 351 full-time, 631 part-time. 6% are from out of state; 1% Black or African American, non-Hispanic/Latino; 2% Hispanic/Latino; 2% Asian, non-Hispanic/Latino; 4% American Indian or Alaska Native, non-Hispanic/Latino; 0.5% Two or more races, non-Hispanic/Latino; 9% Race/ethnicity unknown.
Freshmen *Admission:* 335 applied, 254 admitted, 155 enrolled.
Faculty *Total:* 113, 24% full-time, 4% with terminal degrees.
Majors Accounting; business administration and management; clinical/medical laboratory technology; computer science; computer systems networking and telecommunications; criminal justice/law enforcement administration; early childhood education; general studies; human services; liberal arts and sciences/liberal studies; management information systems; occupational therapist assistant; physical therapy technology; registered nursing/registered nurse; respiratory care therapy; web/multimedia management and webmaster.
Academics *Degree:* certificates, diplomas, and associate. *Special study options:* academic remediation for entering students, distance learning, double majors, independent study, part-time degree program, services for LD students, summer session for credit.
Library Charles Puksta Library plus 1 other with an OPAC.
Student Life *Housing:* college housing not available. *Activities and Organizations:* Student Senate. *Campus security:* 24-hour emergency response devices, security personnel on campus during open hours of operation - 6:30 am to 10 pm.
Financial Aid Of all full-time matriculated undergraduates who enrolled in 2012, 22 Federal Work-Study jobs (averaging $1000).
Applying *Options:* electronic application. *Application fee:* $20. *Required:* high school transcript. *Required for some:* 2 letters of recommendation, interview, program specific requirements.
Freshman Application Contact River Valley Community College, 1 College Place, Claremont, NH 03743. *Phone:* 603-542-7744 Ext. 5322. *Toll-free phone:* 800-837-0658.
Website: http://www.rivervalley.edu/.

St. Joseph School of Nursing
Nashua, New Hampshire

Admissions Office Contact St. Joseph School of Nursing, 5 Woodward Avenue, Nashua, NH 03060.
Website: http://www.sjhacademiccenter.org/.

White Mountains Community College
Berlin, New Hampshire

Freshman Application Contact Ms. Jamie Rivard, Program Assistant, White Mountains Community College, 2020 Riverside Drive, Berlin, NH 03570. *Phone:* 603-752-1113 Ext. 3000. *Toll-free phone:* 800-445-4525. *Fax:* 603-752-6335. *E-mail:* jrivard@ccsnh.edu.
Website: http://www.wmcc.edu/.

NEW JERSEY

Assumption College for Sisters
Mendham, New Jersey

Freshman Application Contact Sr. Gerardine Tantsits, Academic Dean/Registrar, Assumption College for Sisters, 350 Bernardsville Road, Mendham, NJ 07945-2923. *Phone:* 973-543-6528 Ext. 228. *Fax:* 973-543-1738. *E-mail:* deanregistrar@acs350.org.
Website: http://www.acs350.org/.

Atlantic Cape Community College
Mays Landing, New Jersey

Freshman Application Contact Mrs. Linda McLeod, Assistant Director, Admissions and College Recruitment, Atlantic Cape Community College, 5100 Black Horse Pike, Mays Landing, NJ 08330-2699. *Phone:* 609-343-5009. *Fax:* 609-343-4921. *E-mail:* accadmit@atlantic.edu.
Website: http://www.atlantic.edu/.

Bergen Community College
Paramus, New Jersey

Freshman Application Contact Admissions Office, Bergen Community College, 400 Paramus Road, Paramus, NJ 07652-1595. *Phone:* 201-447-7195. *E-mail:* admsoffice@bergen.edu.
Website: http://www.bergen.edu/.

Brookdale Community College
Lincroft, New Jersey

Director of Admissions Ms. Kim Toomey, Registrar, Brookdale Community College, 765 Newman Springs Road, Lincroft, NJ 07738-1597. *Phone:* 732-224-2268.
Website: http://www.brookdalecc.edu/.

Burlington County College
Pemberton, New Jersey

- **County-supported** 2-year, founded 1966
- **Suburban** 225-acre campus with easy access to Philadelphia
- **Coed**

Undergraduates 5,129 full-time, 4,942 part-time. Students come from 17 states and territories; 1% are from out of state; 19% Black or African American, non-Hispanic/Latino; 9% Hispanic/Latino; 3% Asian, non-Hispanic/Latino; 0.2% Native Hawaiian or other Pacific Islander, non-Hispanic/Latino; 0.2% American Indian or Alaska Native, non-Hispanic/Latino; 3% Two or more races, non-Hispanic/Latino; 7% Race/ethnicity unknown; 2% international; 7% transferred in. *Retention:* 60% of full-time freshmen returned.
Faculty *Student/faculty ratio:* 26:1.
Academics *Calendar:* semesters plus 2 summer terms. *Degree:* certificates and associate. *Special study options:* academic remediation for entering students, accelerated degree program, adult/continuing education programs, advanced placement credit, cooperative education, distance learning, double majors, English as a second language, honors programs, independent study, internships, part-time degree program, services for LD students, study abroad, summer session for credit.
Student Life *Campus security:* 24-hour emergency response devices and patrols, late-night transport/escort service, electronic entrances to buildings and rooms, surveillance cameras.
Athletics Member NJCAA.

Costs (2013–14) *Tuition:* area resident $2760 full-time, $92 per credit hour part-time; state resident $3240 full-time, $108 per credit hour part-time; nonresident $5190 full-time, $173 per credit hour part-time. Full-time tuition and fees vary according to course load and program. Part-time tuition and fees vary according to course load and program. *Required fees:* $855 full-time, $92 per credit hour part-time. *Payment plans:* installment, deferred payment.
Financial Aid Of all full-time matriculated undergraduates who enrolled in 2012, 100 Federal Work-Study jobs (averaging $1200). 100 state and other part-time jobs (averaging $2000).
Applying *Options:* electronic application, early admission, deferred entrance. *Application fee:* $20. *Recommended:* high school transcript.
Freshman Application Contact Burlington County College, 601 Pemberton Browns Mills Road, Pemberton, NJ 08068. *Phone:* 609-894-9311 Ext. 1200. *Website:* http://www.bcc.edu/.

Camden County College
Blackwood, New Jersey

Freshman Application Contact Donald Delaney, Outreach Coordinator, School and Community Academic Programs, Camden County College, PO Box 200, Blackwood, NJ 08012-0200. *Phone:* 856-227-7200 Ext. 4371. *Fax:* 856-374-4916. *E-mail:* ddelaney@camdencc.edu.
Website: http://www.camdencc.edu/.

County College of Morris
Randolph, New Jersey

- **County-supported** 2-year, founded 1966
- **Suburban** 218-acre campus with easy access to New York City
- **Coed,** 8,447 undergraduate students, 54% full-time, 49% women, 51% men

Undergraduates 4,549 full-time, 3,898 part-time. Students come from 3 states and territories; 5% Black or African American, non-Hispanic/Latino; 18% Hispanic/Latino; 5% Asian, non-Hispanic/Latino; 0.1% Native Hawaiian or other Pacific Islander, non-Hispanic/Latino; 0.3% American Indian or Alaska Native, non-Hispanic/Latino; 2% Two or more races, non-Hispanic/Latino; 9% Race/ethnicity unknown; 2% international.
Freshmen *Admission:* 4,361 applied, 4,085 admitted.
Faculty *Total:* 540, 30% full-time. *Student/faculty ratio:* 20:1.
Majors Administrative assistant and secretarial science; agricultural business and management; airline pilot and flight crew; biology/biotechnology laboratory technician; business administration and management; business, management, and marketing related; chemical technology; criminal justice/police science; design and applied arts related; electrical, electronic and communications engineering technology; engineering science; fine/studio arts; fire prevention and safety technology; graphic design; hospitality and recreation marketing; kindergarten/preschool education; kinesiology and exercise science; liberal arts and sciences/liberal studies; management information systems; mechanical engineering/mechanical technology; multi/interdisciplinary studies related; music; photography; public administration; radiologic technology/science; registered nursing/registered nurse; respiratory care therapy; telecommunications technology; veterinary/animal health technology; web page, digital/multimedia and information resources design.
Academics *Calendar:* semesters. *Degree:* certificates and associate. *Special study options:* academic remediation for entering students, accelerated degree program, advanced placement credit, cooperative education, distance learning, double majors, English as a second language, independent study, internships, services for LD students, study abroad, summer session for credit.
Library Learning Resource Center plus 1 other.
Student Life *Housing:* college housing not available. *Activities and Organizations:* drama/theater group, student-run newspaper, choral group, Phi Theta Kappa Honor Society, EOF Student Alliance, Student Nurses Association, New Social Engine, Volunteer Club. *Campus security:* 24-hour emergency response devices and patrols, late-night transport/escort service. *Student services:* health clinic, personal/psychological counseling, women's center.
Athletics Member NJCAA. *Intercollegiate sports:* baseball M(s), basketball M(s)/W(s), golf M, ice hockey M(s), lacrosse M, soccer M/W(s), softball W(s), volleyball W. *Intramural sports:* badminton M, basketball M/W, bowling M/W, soccer M/W, table tennis M/W, tennis M/W, volleyball M/W.
Costs (2014–15) *Tuition:* area resident $3540 full-time, $118 per credit hour part-time; state resident $7080 full-time, $236 per credit hour part-time; nonresident $10,080 full-time, $336 per credit hour part-time. Full-time tuition and fees vary according to course load, location, and program. Part-time tuition and fees vary according to course load, location, and program. *Required fees:* $790 full-time, $20 per credit hour part-time, $19 per course part-time. *Waivers:* senior citizens and employees or children of employees.
Financial Aid Of all full-time matriculated undergraduates who enrolled in 2012, 588 Federal Work-Study jobs (averaging $1947).

Applying *Options:* electronic application. *Application fee:* $30. *Required:* high school transcript. *Application deadlines:* rolling (freshmen), rolling (out-of-state freshmen), rolling (transfers). *Notification:* continuous (freshmen), continuous (out-of-state freshmen), continuous (transfers).
Freshman Application Contact County College of Morris, 214 Center Grove Road, Randolph, NJ 07869-2086. *Phone:* 973-328-5100.
Website: http://www.ccm.edu/.

Cumberland County College
Vineland, New Jersey

- **State and locally supported** 2-year, founded 1963, part of New Jersey Commission on Higher Education
- **Small-town** 100-acre campus with easy access to Philadelphia
- **Coed,** 3,919 undergraduate students, 60% full-time, 62% women, 38% men

Undergraduates 2,335 full-time, 1,584 part-time. *Retention:* 61% of full-time freshmen returned.
Faculty *Total:* 296, 16% full-time. *Student/faculty ratio:* 13:1.
Majors Accounting; administrative assistant and secretarial science; aeronautical/aerospace engineering technology; building/construction finishing, management, and inspection related; business administration and management; computer and information sciences; computer systems networking and telecommunications; criminal justice/police science; education; fine/studio arts; health and medical administrative services related; horticultural science; industrial technology; legal assistant/paralegal; liberal arts and sciences/liberal studies; medical radiologic technology; ornamental horticulture; registered nursing/registered nurse; respiratory care therapy; social work.
Academics *Calendar:* semesters. *Degree:* certificates and associate. *Special study options:* academic remediation for entering students, advanced placement credit, cooperative education, distance learning, double majors, English as a second language, honors programs, independent study, part-time degree program, services for LD students, summer session for credit.
Library Cumberland County College Library with 51,000 titles, 213 serial subscriptions, 480 audiovisual materials, an OPAC, a Web page.
Student Life *Housing:* college housing not available. *Activities and Organizations:* drama/theater group, student-run newspaper, television station, choral group. *Campus security:* 24-hour emergency response devices, late-night transport/escort service. *Student services:* personal/psychological counseling.
Athletics Member NJCAA. *Intercollegiate sports:* baseball M, basketball M/W, cross-country running M/W, softball W, track and field M. *Intramural sports:* fencing M/W, soccer M.
Costs (2013–14) *Tuition:* area resident $3300 full-time, $110 per credit hour part-time; state resident $3600 full-time, $120 per credit hour part-time; nonresident $13,200 full-time, $440 per credit hour part-time. *Required fees:* $900 full-time, $30 per credit hour part-time. *Payment plan:* installment. *Waivers:* employees or children of employees.
Financial Aid Of all full-time matriculated undergraduates who enrolled in 2012, 100 Federal Work-Study jobs (averaging $500). 100 state and other part-time jobs (averaging $600).
Applying *Options:* electronic application, early admission, deferred entrance. *Required:* high school transcript. *Application deadlines:* rolling (freshmen), rolling (transfers). *Notification:* continuous (freshmen), continuous (transfers).
Freshman Application Contact Ms. Anne Daly-Eimer, Director of Admissions and Registration, Cumberland County College, PO Box 1500, College Drive, Vineland, NJ 08362. *Phone:* 856-691-8986.
Website: http://www.cccnj.edu/.

Eastern International College
Belleville, New Jersey

Admissions Office Contact Eastern International College, 251 Washington Avenue, Belleville, NJ 07109.
Website: http://www.eicollege.edu/.

Essex County College
Newark, New Jersey

- **County-supported** 2-year, founded 1966, part of New Jersey Commission on Higher Education
- **Urban** 22-acre campus with easy access to New York City
- **Coed**

Undergraduates 6,569 full-time, 5,410 part-time. Students come from 9 states and territories; 49 other countries; 1% are from out of state; 48% Black or African American, non-Hispanic/Latino; 24% Hispanic/Latino; 4% Asian, non-Hispanic/Latino; 0.1% Native Hawaiian or other Pacific Islander, non-Hispanic/Latino; 0.2% American Indian or Alaska Native, non-Hispanic/Latino; 0.5% Two or more races, non-Hispanic/Latino; 6%

Race/ethnicity unknown; 8% international; 2% transferred in. *Retention:* 50% of full-time freshmen returned.

Faculty *Student/faculty ratio:* 29:1.

Academics *Calendar:* semesters. *Degree:* certificates and associate. *Special study options:* academic remediation for entering students, accelerated degree program, adult/continuing education programs, advanced placement credit, cooperative education, distance learning, double majors, English as a second language, independent study, internships, off-campus study, part-time degree program, services for LD students, summer session for credit. *ROTC:* Army (c).

Student Life *Campus security:* 24-hour emergency response devices and patrols.

Athletics Member NJCAA.

Financial Aid Of all full-time matriculated undergraduates who enrolled in 2009, 256 Federal Work-Study jobs (averaging $2488).

Applying *Options:* electronic application, deferred entrance. *Application fee:* $25. *Required:* high school transcript.

Freshman Application Contact Ms. Marva Mack, Director of Admissions, Essex County College, 303 University Avenue, Newark, NJ 07102. *Phone:* 973-877-3119. *Fax:* 973-623-6449.

Website: http://www.essex.edu/.

Gloucester County College

Sewell, New Jersey

Freshman Application Contact Ms. Judy Atkinson, Registrar/Admissions, Gloucester County College, 1400 Tanyard Road, Sewell, NJ 08080. *Phone:* 856-415-2209. *E-mail:* jatkinso@gccnj.edu.

Website: http://www.gccnj.edu/.

Hudson County Community College

Jersey City, New Jersey

- **State and locally supported** 2-year, founded 1974
- **Urban** campus with easy access to New York City
- **Coed,** 9,036 undergraduate students, 67% full-time, 59% women, 41% men

Undergraduates 6,066 full-time, 2,970 part-time. Students come from 4 states and territories; 0.5% are from out of state; 15% Black or African American, non-Hispanic/Latino; 56% Hispanic/Latino; 7% Asian, non-Hispanic/Latino; 0.7% Native Hawaiian or other Pacific Islander, non-Hispanic/Latino; 0.3% American Indian or Alaska Native, non-Hispanic/Latino; 1% Two or more races, non-Hispanic/Latino; 9% Race/ethnicity unknown; 0.4% international; 0.1% transferred in. *Retention:* 52% of full-time freshmen returned.

Freshmen *Admission:* 4,296 applied, 4,296 admitted, 2,582 enrolled.

Faculty *Total:* 661, 13% full-time.

Majors Biological and physical sciences; business administration and management; computer and information sciences; criminal justice/police science; culinary arts; electrical, electronic and communications engineering technology; emergency medical technology (EMT paramedic); engineering science; fine/studio arts; health information/medical records technology; health services/allied health/health sciences; legal assistant/paralegal; liberal arts and sciences/liberal studies; medical/clinical assistant; registered nursing/registered nurse; respiratory care therapy; social work.

Academics *Calendar:* semesters. *Degree:* certificates and associate. *Special study options:* academic remediation for entering students, advanced placement credit, distance learning, double majors, English as a second language, honors programs, independent study, internships, part-time degree program, services for LD students, summer session for credit.

Library Hudson County Community College Library.

Student Life *Housing:* college housing not available. *Activities and Organizations:* drama/theater group, student-run newspaper. *Campus security:* 24-hour emergency response devices. *Student services:* personal/psychological counseling.

Costs (2013–14) *Tuition:* $113 per credit hour part-time; state resident $225 per credit hour part-time; nonresident $338 per credit hour part-time. Full-time tuition and fees vary according to program. Part-time tuition and fees vary according to program. *Required fees:* $39 per credit hour part-time, $20 per term part-time. *Payment plan:* installment. *Waivers:* senior citizens and employees or children of employees.

Financial Aid Of all full-time matriculated undergraduates who enrolled in 2012, 102 Federal Work-Study jobs (averaging $3000).

Applying *Options:* electronic application. *Application fee:* $20. *Application deadlines:* 9/1 (freshmen), 9/1 (transfers). *Notification:* continuous until 9/1 (freshmen), continuous until 9/1 (transfers).

Freshman Application Contact Hudson County Community College, 70 Sip Avenue, Jersey City, NJ 07306. *Phone:* 201-360-4131.

Website: http://www.hccc.edu/.

ITT Technical Institute

Marlton, New Jersey

- **Proprietary** 2-year
- **Coed**

Majors CAD/CADD drafting/design technology; computer engineering technology; computer systems networking and telecommunications.

Academics *Degree:* associate.

Freshman Application Contact Director of Recruitment, ITT Technical Institute, 9000 Lincoln Drive East, Suite 100, Marlton, NJ 08053. *Phone:* 856-396-3500. *Toll-free phone:* 877-209-5410.

Website: http://www.itt-tech.edu/.

Mercer County Community College

Trenton, New Jersey

- **State and locally supported** 2-year, founded 1966
- **Suburban** 292-acre campus with easy access to New York City, Philadelphia
- **Coed,** 8,501 undergraduate students, 36% full-time, 52% women, 48% men

Undergraduates 3,093 full-time, 5,408 part-time. Students come from 5 states and territories; 91 other countries; 7% are from out of state; 33% Black or African American, non-Hispanic/Latino; 13% Hispanic/Latino; 4% Asian, non-Hispanic/Latino; 0.2% Native Hawaiian or other Pacific Islander, non-Hispanic/Latino; 0.5% American Indian or Alaska Native, non-Hispanic/Latino; 10% Race/ethnicity unknown; 4% international; 4% transferred in. *Retention:* 68% of full-time freshmen returned.

Freshmen *Admission:* 2,151 enrolled.

Faculty *Total:* 797, 15% full-time. *Student/faculty ratio:* 15:1.

Majors Accounting; administrative assistant and secretarial science; airline flight attendant; airline pilot and flight crew; architectural engineering technology; art; art history, criticism and conservation; automotive engineering technology; aviation/airway management; biology/biological sciences; biology/biotechnology laboratory technician; business administration and management; ceramic arts and ceramics; chemistry; civil engineering technology; clinical/medical laboratory technology; commercial and advertising art; community organization and advocacy; computer graphics; computer science; computer systems networking and telecommunications; corrections; criminal justice/police science; culinary arts; dance; dramatic/theater arts; electrical, electronic and communications engineering technology; engineering science; fire science/firefighting; funeral service and mortuary science; health professions related; heating, ventilation, air conditioning and refrigeration engineering technology; hotel/motel administration; humanities; legal assistant/paralegal; liberal arts and sciences/liberal studies; management information systems; mass communication/media; mathematics; medical radiologic technology; music; ornamental horticulture; photography; physical therapy technology; physics; plant sciences; radio and television broadcasting technology; registered nursing/registered nurse; respiratory care therapy; sculpture; teacher assistant/aide.

Academics *Calendar:* semesters. *Degree:* certificates and associate. *Special study options:* academic remediation for entering students, accelerated degree program, adult/continuing education programs, advanced placement credit, cooperative education, distance learning, double majors, English as a second language, external degree program, independent study, internships, part-time degree program, services for LD students, student-designed majors, summer session for credit. *ROTC:* Army (c), Air Force (c).

Library Mercer County Community College Library plus 1 other with 57,317 titles, 8,934 audiovisual materials, an OPAC, a Web page.

Student Life *Housing:* college housing not available. *Activities and Organizations:* drama/theater group, student-run newspaper, radio station, choral group, Student Government Association, student radio station, African-American Student Organization, Student Activities Board, Phi Theta Kappa. *Campus security:* 24-hour emergency response devices and patrols. *Student services:* personal/psychological counseling.

Athletics Member NJCAA. *Intercollegiate sports:* baseball M, basketball M(s)/W(s), golf M/W, soccer M(s)/W(s), softball W, tennis M/W, track and field M/W. *Intramural sports:* basketball M/W, skiing (downhill) M/W, softball M/W, volleyball M/W.

Costs (2014–15) *Tuition:* area resident $3528 full-time, $114 per credit part-time; state resident $4644 full-time, $162 per credit part-time; nonresident $6732 full-time, $249 per credit part-time. Full-time tuition and fees vary according to program and reciprocity agreements. Part-time tuition and fees vary according to program and reciprocity agreements. *Required fees:* $756 full-time, $32 per credit part-time. *Payment plan:* installment. *Waivers:* senior citizens and employees or children of employees.

Financial Aid Of all full-time matriculated undergraduates who enrolled in 2012, 100 Federal Work-Study jobs (averaging $1500). 12 state and other part-time jobs (averaging $1500).

Applying *Options:* electronic application, deferred entrance. *Required:* high school transcript. *Recommended:* interview. *Application deadlines:* rolling (freshmen), rolling (transfers). *Notification:* continuous (freshmen), continuous (transfers).

Freshman Application Contact Dr. L. Campbell, Dean for Student and Academic Services, Mercer County Community College, 1200 Old Trenton Road, PO Box B, Trenton, NJ 08690-1004. *Phone:* 609-586-4800 Ext. 3222. *Toll-free phone:* 800-392-MCCC. *Fax:* 609-586-6944. *E-mail:* admiss@ mccc.edu.

Website: http://www.mccc.edu/.

Middlesex County College

Edison, New Jersey

- **County-supported** 2-year, founded 1964
- **Suburban** 200-acre campus with easy access to New York City
- **Coed,** 12,611 undergraduate students

Undergraduates 11% Black or African American, non-Hispanic/Latino; 27% Hispanic/Latino; 11% Asian, non-Hispanic/Latino; 1% Native Hawaiian or other Pacific Islander, non-Hispanic/Latino; 0.3% American Indian or Alaska Native, non-Hispanic/Latino; 2% Two or more races, non-Hispanic/Latino; 12% Race/ethnicity unknown; 2% international. *Retention:* 64% of full-time freshmen returned.

Faculty *Student/faculty ratio:* 20:1.

Majors Accounting; administrative assistant and secretarial science; automotive engineering technology; biology/biotechnology laboratory technician; biotechnology; business administration and management; civil engineering technology; clinical/medical laboratory technology; communications technologies and support services related; computer and information sciences; criminal justice/police science; dental hygiene; dietitian assistant; electrical, electronic and communications engineering technology; energy management and systems technology; engineering science; engineering technologies and engineering related; environmental control technologies related; fire prevention and safety technology; geology/earth science; graphic communications related; health professions related; health services/allied health/health sciences; hotel/motel administration; industrial production technologies related; legal assistant/paralegal; liberal arts and sciences/liberal studies; marketing/marketing management; mechanical engineering/mechanical technology; mechanical engineering technologies related; medical radiologic technology; merchandising, sales, and marketing operations related (specialized); physical sciences; registered nursing/registered nurse; rehabilitation and therapeutic professions related; respiratory care therapy; small business administration; surveying technology; teacher assistant/aide; visual and performing arts.

Academics *Calendar:* semesters. *Degree:* certificates and associate. *Special study options:* academic remediation for entering students, adult/continuing education programs, advanced placement credit, cooperative education, distance learning, English as a second language, independent study, internships, off-campus study, part-time degree program, services for LD students, study abroad, summer session for credit. *ROTC:* Army (c).

Library Middlesex County College Library plus 1 other with an OPAC, a Web page.

Student Life *Housing:* college housing not available. *Activities and Organizations:* drama/theater group, student-run newspaper, radio station, choral group. *Campus security:* 24-hour emergency response devices and patrols. *Student services:* health clinic, personal/psychological counseling.

Athletics Member NJCAA. *Intercollegiate sports:* baseball M, basketball M/W, cross-country running M/W, soccer M/W, softball W, track and field M/W, wrestling M.

Costs (2014–15) *Tuition:* $104 per credit part-time; state resident $208 per credit part-time; nonresident $208 per credit part-time. *Required fees:* $35 per credit part-time. *Waivers:* employees or children of employees.

Financial Aid Of all full-time matriculated undergraduates who enrolled in 2012, 69 Federal Work-Study jobs (averaging $3350).

Applying *Options:* early admission, deferred entrance. *Application fee:* $25. *Required:* high school transcript. *Application deadlines:* rolling (freshmen), rolling (transfers). *Notification:* continuous (freshmen), continuous (transfers).

Freshman Application Contact Middlesex County College, 2600 Woodbridge Avenue, PO Box 3050, Edison, NJ 08818-3050. *Phone:* 732-906-3130.

Website: http://www.middlesexcc.edu/.

Ocean County College

Toms River, New Jersey

- **County-supported** 2-year, founded 1964, part of New Jersey Higher Education
- **Suburban** 275-acre campus with easy access to Philadelphia
- **Coed,** 9,477 undergraduate students, 54% full-time, 55% women, 45% men

Undergraduates 5,138 full-time, 4,339 part-time. Students come from 22 states and territories; 6 other countries; 0.4% are from out of state; 6% Black or African American, non-Hispanic/Latino; 10% Hispanic/Latino; 2% Asian, non-Hispanic/Latino; 0.2% Native Hawaiian or other Pacific Islander, non-Hispanic/Latino; 0.6% American Indian or Alaska Native, non-Hispanic/Latino; 5% Race/ethnicity unknown; 0.7% international; 4% transferred in. *Retention:* 73% of full-time freshmen returned.

Freshmen *Admission:* 3,843 applied, 3,843 admitted, 2,216 enrolled.

Faculty *Total:* 504, 20% full-time, 26% with terminal degrees. *Student/faculty ratio:* 29:1.

Majors Administrative assistant and secretarial science; broadcast journalism; business administration and management; business/commerce; communications technologies and support services related; computer and information sciences; criminal justice/police science; dental hygiene; engineering; engineering technologies and engineering related; environmental science; fire prevention and safety technology; general studies; homeland security, law enforcement, firefighting and protective services related; human services; liberal arts and sciences/liberal studies; occupational therapist assistant; registered nursing/registered nurse; sign language interpretation and translation.

Academics *Calendar:* semesters. *Degree:* certificates, diplomas, and associate. *Special study options:* academic remediation for entering students, accelerated degree program, adult/continuing education programs, advanced placement credit, cooperative education, distance learning, English as a second language, honors programs, independent study, internships, part-time degree program, services for LD students, study abroad, summer session for credit.

Library Ocean County College Library with 68,344 titles, 239 serial subscriptions, 2,535 audiovisual materials, an OPAC, a Web page.

Student Life *Housing:* college housing not available. *Activities and Organizations:* drama/theater group, student-run newspaper, radio and television station, choral group, Student Activities Board, student government, OCC Vikings Cheerleaders, Speech and Theater Club, Veterans' Club. *Campus security:* 24-hour emergency response devices and patrols, late-night transport/escort service, security cameras in hallways and parking lots. *Student services:* personal/psychological counseling.

Athletics Member NJCAA. *Intercollegiate sports:* baseball M, basketball M/W, cross-country running M/W, golf M/W, soccer M/W, softball W, swimming and diving M/W, tennis M/W. *Intramural sports:* basketball M/W, cheerleading M(c)/W(c), ice hockey M, sailing M(c)/W(c), soccer M/W, softball W, volleyball M/W.

Standardized Tests *Required for some:* ACCUPLACER is required for degree seeking students. Waiver may be obtained by meeting institution's minimum ACT or SAT scores, or English and math transfer credits.

Costs (2014–15) *Tuition:* $104 per credit part-time; state resident $133 per credit part-time; nonresident $215 per credit part-time. Full-time tuition and fees vary according to program. Part-time tuition and fees vary according to program. *Required fees:* $30 part-time, $20 part-time. *Payment plan:* installment. *Waivers:* senior citizens and employees or children of employees.

Financial Aid Of all full-time matriculated undergraduates who enrolled in 2012, 76 Federal Work-Study jobs (averaging $1300). 45 state and other part-time jobs (averaging $850).

Applying *Options:* electronic application. *Required for some:* high school transcript, Accuplacer testing required for degree seeking students not meeting minimum ACT or SAT institutional requirements. Selective admissions for nursing students. *Application deadlines:* rolling (freshmen), rolling (out-of-state freshmen), rolling (transfers). *Notification:* continuous (freshmen), continuous (out-of-state freshmen), continuous (transfers).

Freshman Application Contact Ms. Elizabeth Clements, Registrar, Ocean County College, College Drive, PO Box 2001, Toms River, NJ 08754-2001. *Phone:* 732-255-0400 Ext. 2377. *E-mail:* eclements@ocean.edu.

Website: http://www.ocean.edu/.

Passaic County Community College

Paterson, New Jersey

Freshman Application Contact Mr. Patrick Noonan, Director of Admissions, Passaic County Community College, One College Boulevard, Paterson, NJ 07505-1179. *Phone:* 973-684-6304.

Website: http://www.pccc.cc.nj.us/.

Raritan Valley Community College
Branchburg, New Jersey

- **State and locally supported** 2-year, founded 1965
- **Suburban** 225-acre campus with easy access to New York City, Philadelphia
- **Coed,** 8,405 undergraduate students, 43% full-time, 52% women, 48% men

Undergraduates 3,600 full-time, 4,805 part-time. Students come from 10 states and territories; 1% are from out of state; 10% Black or African American, non-Hispanic/Latino; 16% Hispanic/Latino; 7% Asian, non-Hispanic/Latino; 0.3% Native Hawaiian or other Pacific Islander, non-Hispanic/Latino; 0.2% American Indian or Alaska Native, non-Hispanic/Latino; 2% Two or more races, non-Hispanic/Latino; 8% Race/ethnicity unknown; 2% international; 6% transferred in. *Retention:* 71% of full-time freshmen returned.

Freshmen *Admission:* 1,578 enrolled.

Faculty *Total:* 495, 24% full-time. *Student/faculty ratio:* 21:1.

Majors Accounting related; accounting technology and bookkeeping; administrative assistant and secretarial science; animation, interactive technology, video graphics and special effects; automotive engineering technology; biotechnology; business administration and management; business/commerce; chemical technology; child-care provision; cinematography and film/video production; communication and media related; computer and information sciences and support services related; computer programming (vendor/product certification); computer systems networking and telecommunications; construction engineering technology; corrections; criminal justice/law enforcement administration; criminal justice/police science; critical incident response/special police operations; dance; dental assisting; dental hygiene; design and applied arts related; diesel mechanics technology; digital communication and media/multimedia; engineering science; engineering technologies and engineering related; English; financial planning and services; fine/studio arts; health and physical education/fitness; health information/medical records technology; health services/allied health/health sciences; heating, ventilation, air conditioning and refrigeration engineering technology; information technology; interior design; international business/trade/commerce; kindergarten/preschool education; kinesiology and exercise science; legal assistant/paralegal; liberal arts and sciences/liberal studies; lineworker; management information systems; manufacturing engineering technology; marketing/marketing management; medical/clinical assistant; meeting and event planning; multi/interdisciplinary studies related; music; optician; optometric technician; registered nursing/registered nurse; respiratory care therapy; restaurant, culinary, and catering management; small business administration; web page, digital/multimedia and information resources design.

Academics *Calendar:* semesters. *Degree:* certificates and associate. *Special study options:* academic remediation for entering students, adult/continuing education programs, advanced placement credit, cooperative education, distance learning, double majors, English as a second language, honors programs, independent study, internships, off-campus study, part-time degree program, services for LD students, summer session for credit. *ROTC:* Army (c), Air Force (c).

Library Evelyn S. Field Library with 149,823 titles, 27,000 serial subscriptions, 3,109 audiovisual materials, an OPAC, a Web page.

Student Life *Housing:* college housing not available. *Activities and Organizations:* drama/theater group, student-run radio station, choral group, Phi Theta Kappa, Orgullo Latino, Student Nurses Association, Business Club/SIFE, Environmental club. *Campus security:* 24-hour emergency response devices and patrols, late-night transport/escort service, 24-hour outdoor and indoor surveillance cameras; 24-hr mobile patrols; 24-hr communication center. *Student services:* personal/psychological counseling.

Athletics Member NJCAA. *Intercollegiate sports:* baseball M(s), basketball M(s)/W(s), golf M/W, soccer M/W, softball W(s). *Intramural sports:* basketball M/W, volleyball M/W.

Costs (2013–14) *Tuition:* area resident $3000 full-time, $125 per credit hour part-time; state resident $3480 full-time, $145 per credit hour part-time; nonresident $3480 full-time, $145 per credit hour part-time. *Required fees:* $742 full-time, $22 per credit hour part-time, $82 per semester part-time. *Payment plan:* installment. *Waivers:* employees or children of employees.

Financial Aid Of all full-time matriculated undergraduates who enrolled in 2012, 12 Federal Work-Study jobs (averaging $2500).

Applying *Required:* high school transcript.

Freshman Application Contact Mr. Daniel Palubniak, Registrar, Enrollment Services, Raritan Valley Community College, 118 Lamington Road, Branchburg, NJ 08876-1265. *Phone:* 908-526-1200 Ext. 8206. *Fax:* 908-704-3442. *E-mail:* dpalubni@raritanval.edu.
Website: http://www.raritanval.edu/.

Salem Community College
Carneys Point, New Jersey

Freshman Application Contact Lynn Fishlock, Director of Enrollment and Transfer Services, Salem Community College, 460 Hollywood Avenue, Carneys Point, NJ 08069. *Phone:* 856-351-2701. *Fax:* 856-299-9193. *E-mail:* info@salemcc.edu.
Website: http://www.salemcc.edu/.

Sussex County Community College
Newton, New Jersey

- **State and locally supported** 2-year, founded 1981, part of New Jersey Commission on Higher Education
- **Small-town** 160-acre campus with easy access to New York City
- **Coed,** 3,732 undergraduate students, 55% full-time, 56% women, 44% men

Undergraduates 2,059 full-time, 1,673 part-time. Students come from 3 states and territories; 12% are from out of state; 2% Black or African American, non-Hispanic/Latino; 9% Hispanic/Latino; 1% Asian, non-Hispanic/Latino; 0.2% American Indian or Alaska Native, non-Hispanic/Latino; 1% Two or more races, non-Hispanic/Latino; 0.7% Race/ethnicity unknown; 0.5% international; 5% transferred in. *Retention:* 66% of full-time freshmen returned.

Freshmen *Admission:* 739 enrolled.

Faculty *Total:* 276, 16% full-time, 13% with terminal degrees. *Student/faculty ratio:* 21:1.

Majors Accounting; automotive engineering technology; biological and physical sciences; broadcast journalism; business administration and management; commercial and advertising art; computer and information sciences; corrections and criminal justice related; English; environmental studies; fine/studio arts; fire protection related; health professions related; human services; journalism; legal assistant/paralegal; liberal arts and sciences/liberal studies.

Academics *Calendar:* 4-1-4. *Degree:* certificates and associate. *Special study options:* academic remediation for entering students, advanced placement credit, distance learning, double majors, English as a second language, internships, part-time degree program, services for LD students, summer session for credit.

Library Sussex County Community College Library with 34,346 titles, 266 serial subscriptions, 602 audiovisual materials, an OPAC, a Web page.

Student Life *Housing:* college housing not available. *Activities and Organizations:* drama/theater group, student-run newspaper, choral group, Student Government Association, The College Hill (newspaper), Human Services Club, Arts Club, Returning Adult Support Group. *Campus security:* late-night transport/escort service, trained security personnel. *Student services:* personal/psychological counseling, women's center.

Athletics Member NJCAA. *Intercollegiate sports:* baseball M, basketball M/W, soccer M/W, softball W.

Financial Aid Of all full-time matriculated undergraduates who enrolled in 2012, 29 Federal Work-Study jobs (averaging $1500).

Applying *Options:* electronic application. *Application fee:* $25. *Application deadlines:* rolling (freshmen), rolling (transfers). *Notification:* continuous (freshmen), continuous (transfers).

Freshman Application Contact Mr. Todd Poltersdorf, Director of Admissions, Sussex County Community College, 1 College Hill Road, Newton, NJ 07860. *Phone:* 973-300-2253. *E-mail:* tpoltersdorf@sussex.edu.
Website: http://www.sussex.edu/.

Union County College
Cranford, New Jersey

- **State and locally supported** 2-year, founded 1933, part of New Jersey Commission on Higher Education
- **Urban** 49-acre campus with easy access to New York City
- **Endowment** $9.0 million
- **Coed**

Undergraduates 5,886 full-time, 6,260 part-time. Students come from 10 states and territories; 77 other countries; 3% are from out of state; 27% Black or African American, non-Hispanic/Latino; 31% Hispanic/Latino; 4% Asian, non-Hispanic/Latino; 0.4% Native Hawaiian or other Pacific Islander, non-Hispanic/Latino; 0.5% American Indian or Alaska Native, non-Hispanic/Latino; 0.4% Two or more races, non-Hispanic/Latino; 12% Race/ethnicity unknown; 3% international; 2% transferred in. *Retention:* 60% of full-time freshmen returned.

Faculty *Student/faculty ratio:* 27:1.

Academics *Calendar:* semesters. *Degree:* certificates, diplomas, and associate. *Special study options:* academic remediation for entering students, accelerated degree program, adult/continuing education programs, advanced placement credit, distance learning, English as a second language, honors programs, independent study, internships, off-campus study, part-time degree program, services for LD students, student-designed majors, summer session for credit. *ROTC:* Air Force (c).

Student Life *Campus security:* 24-hour emergency response devices and patrols, late-night transport/escort service.

Athletics Member NJCAA.

Costs (2013–14) *Tuition:* area resident $4080 full-time, $122 per credit part-time; state resident $8160 full-time, $244 per credit part-time; nonresident $8160 full-time, $244 per quarter hour part-time. Full-time tuition and fees vary according to course load. Part-time tuition and fees vary according to course load. *Required fees:* $918 full-time, $38 per credit part-time.

Financial Aid Of all full-time matriculated undergraduates who enrolled in 2012, 150 Federal Work-Study jobs (averaging $1700).

Applying *Options:* electronic application, early admission, deferred entrance. *Required:* high school transcript. *Required for some:* interview.

Freshman Application Contact Ms. Nina Hernandez, Director of Admissions, Records, and Registration, Union County College, Cranford, NJ 07016. *Phone:* 908-709-7127. *Fax:* 908-709-7125. *E-mail:* hernandez@ucc.edu.

Website: http://www.ucc.edu/.

Warren County Community College

Washington, New Jersey

Freshman Application Contact Shannon Horwath, Associate Director of Admissions, Warren County Community College, 475 Route 57 West, Washington, NJ 07882-9605. *Phone:* 908-835-2300. *E-mail:* shorwath@warren.edu.

Website: http://www.warren.edu/.

NEW MEXICO

Brown Mackie College–Albuquerque

Albuquerque, New Mexico

- **Proprietary** primarily 2-year, part of Education Management Corporation
- **Coed**

Majors Architectural drafting and CAD/CADD; business administration and management; computer support specialist; corrections and criminal justice

related; criminal justice/safety; legal assistant/paralegal; medical office management; occupational therapist assistant; pharmacy technician; registered nursing/registered nurse; surgical technology; veterinary/animal health technology.

Academics *Degrees:* diplomas, associate, and bachelor's.

Freshman Application Contact Brown Mackie College–Albuquerque, 10500 Copper Avenue NE, Albuquerque, NM 87123. *Phone:* 505-559-5200. *Toll-free phone:* 877-271-3488.

Website: http://www.brownmackie.edu/albuquerque/.

See display below and page 378 for the College Close-Up.

Carrington College–Albuquerque

Albuquerque, New Mexico

- **Proprietary** 2-year, part of Carrington Colleges Group, Inc.
- **Coed,** 647 undergraduate students, 84% full-time, 85% women, 15% men

Undergraduates 545 full-time, 102 part-time. 2% are from out of state; 3% Black or African American, non-Hispanic/Latino; 52% Hispanic/Latino; 2% Asian, non-Hispanic/Latino; 0.2% Native Hawaiian or other Pacific Islander, non-Hispanic/Latino; 16% American Indian or Alaska Native, non-Hispanic/Latino; 2% Two or more races, non-Hispanic/Latino; 2% Race/ethnicity unknown; 16% transferred in.

Freshmen *Admission:* 50 enrolled.

Faculty *Total:* 52, 21% full-time. *Student/faculty ratio:* 24:1.

Majors Medical office management; physical therapy technology; registered nursing/registered nurse.

Academics *Degree:* certificates and associate.

Costs (2014–15) *Tuition:* $54,125 per degree program part-time. Total costs vary by program. Tuition provided is for largest program (Dental Hygiene).

Applying *Required:* essay or personal statement, high school transcript, interview, Entrance test administered by Carrington College.

Freshman Application Contact Carrington College–Albuquerque, 1001 Menaul Boulevard NE, Albuquerque, NM 87107.

Website: http://carrington.edu/.

Central New Mexico Community College
Albuquerque, New Mexico

- **State-supported** 2-year, founded 1965
- **Urban** 312-acre campus
- **Endowment** $1.6 million
- **Coed**

Undergraduates 9,324 full-time, 18,999 part-time. Students come from 29 states and territories; 0.4% are from out of state; 3% Black or African American, non-Hispanic/Latino; 45% Hispanic/Latino; 2% Asian, non-Hispanic/Latino; 0.3% Native Hawaiian or other Pacific Islander, non-Hispanic/Latino; 7% American Indian or Alaska Native, non-Hispanic/Latino; 2% Two or more races, non-Hispanic/Latino; 4% Race/ethnicity unknown; 3% international; 5% transferred in. *Retention:* 58% of full-time freshmen returned.

Faculty *Student/faculty ratio:* 28:1.

Academics *Calendar:* trimesters. *Degree:* certificates and associate. *Special study options:* academic remediation for entering students, adult/continuing education programs, advanced placement credit, cooperative education, distance learning, English as a second language, honors programs, independent study, internships, part-time degree program, services for LD students, summer session for credit. *ROTC:* Army (c), Navy (c), Air Force (c).

Student Life *Campus security:* 24-hour emergency response devices and patrols, late-night transport/escort service.

Costs (2013–14) *Tuition:* state resident $1188 full-time, $50 per credit hour part-time; nonresident $6660 full-time, $50 per credit hour part-time. *Required fees:* $176 full-time, $4 per credit hour part-time, $40 per term part-time.

Applying *Options:* electronic application.

Freshman Application Contact Mother Supr. Glenn Damiani, Sr. Director, Enrollment Services, Central New Mexico Community College, Albuquerque, NM 87106. *Phone:* 505-224-3223.

Website: http://www.cnm.edu/.

Clovis Community College
Clovis, New Mexico

Freshman Application Contact Ms. Rosie Corrie, Director of Admissions and Records/Registrar, Clovis Community College, Clovis, NM 88101-8381. *Phone:* 575-769-4962. *Toll-free phone:* 800-769-1409. *Fax:* 575-769-4190. *E-mail:* admissions@clovis.edu.

Website: http://www.clovis.edu/.

Doña Ana Community College
Las Cruces, New Mexico

Freshman Application Contact Mrs. Ricci Montes, Admissions Advisor, Doña Ana Community College, MSC-3DA, Box 30001, 3400 South Espina Street, Las Cruces, NM 88003-8001. *Phone:* 575-527-7683. *Toll-free phone:* 800-903-7503. *Fax:* 575-527-7515.

Website: http://dabcc-www.nmsu.edu/.

Eastern New Mexico University–Roswell
Roswell, New Mexico

Freshman Application Contact Eastern New Mexico University–Roswell, PO Box 6000, Roswell, NM 88202-6000. *Phone:* 505-624-7142. *Toll-free phone:* 800-243-6687 (in-state); 800-624-7000 (out-of-state).

Website: http://www.roswell.enmu.edu/.

ITT Technical Institute
Albuquerque, New Mexico

- **Proprietary** primarily 2-year, founded 1989, part of ITT Educational Services, Inc.
- **Coed**

Majors Computer programming (specific applications); computer software technology; construction management; cyber/computer forensics and counterterrorism; drafting and design technology; electrical, electronic and communications engineering technology; forensic science and technology; graphic communications; health information/medical records technology; information technology project management; network and system administration; project management; registered nursing/registered nurse.

Academics *Calendar:* quarters. *Degrees:* associate and bachelor's.

Student Life *Housing:* college housing not available.

Freshman Application Contact Director of Recruitment, ITT Technical Institute, 5100 Masthead Street, NE, Albuquerque, NM 87109-4366. *Phone:* 505-828-1114. *Toll-free phone:* 800-636-1114.

Website: http://www.itt-tech.edu/.

Luna Community College
Las Vegas, New Mexico

Freshman Application Contact Ms. Henrietta Griego, Director of Admissions, Recruitment, and Retention, Luna Community College, PO Box 1510, Las Vegas, NM 87701. *Phone:* 505-454-2020. *Toll-free phone:* 800-588-7232 (in-state); 800-5888-7232 (out-of-state). *Fax:* 505-454-2588. *E-mail:* hgriego@luna.cc.nm.us.

Website: http://www.luna.edu/.

Mesalands Community College
Tucumcari, New Mexico

Director of Admissions Mr. Ken Brashear, Director of Enrollment Management, Mesalands Community College, 911 South Tenth Street, Tucumcari, NM 88401. *Phone:* 505-461-4413.

Website: http://www.mesalands.edu/.

National American University
Albuquerque, New Mexico

Freshman Application Contact Admissions Office, National American University, 10131 Coors Boulevard NW, Suite I-01, Albuquerque, NM 87114.

Website: http://www.national.edu/.

Navajo Technical University
Crownpoint, New Mexico

Director of Admissions Director of Admission, Navajo Technical University, PO Box 849, Crownpoint, NM 87313. *Phone:* 505-786-4100.

Website: http://www.navajotech.edu/.

New Mexico Junior College
Hobbs, New Mexico

Director of Admissions Mr. Robert Bensing, Dean of Enrollment Management, New Mexico Junior College, 5317 Lovington Highway, Hobbs, NM 88240-9123. *Phone:* 505-392-5092. *Toll-free phone:* 800-657-6260.

Website: http://www.nmjc.edu/.

New Mexico Military Institute
Roswell, New Mexico

Freshman Application Contact New Mexico Military Institute, Roswell, NM 88201-5173. *Phone:* 505-624-8050. *Toll-free phone:* 800-421-5376. *Fax:* 505-624-8058. *E-mail:* admissions@nmmi.edu.

Website: http://www.nmmi.edu/.

New Mexico State University–Alamogordo
Alamogordo, New Mexico

- **State-supported** 2-year, founded 1958, part of New Mexico State University System
- **Small-town** 540-acre campus
- **Endowment** $147,086
- **Coed,** 3,371 undergraduate students, 30% full-time, 64% women, 36% men

Undergraduates 1,005 full-time, 2,366 part-time. Students come from 26 states and territories; 15% are from out of state; 4% Black or African American, non-Hispanic/Latino; 38% Hispanic/Latino; 2% Asian, non-Hispanic/Latino; 0.1% Native Hawaiian or other Pacific Islander, non-Hispanic/Latino; 3% American Indian or Alaska Native, non-Hispanic/Latino; 1% Two or more races, non-Hispanic/Latino; 6% Race/ethnicity unknown; 2% international; 6% transferred in. *Retention:* 50% of full-time freshmen returned.

Freshmen *Admission:* 449 applied, 355 admitted, 331 enrolled. *Average high school GPA:* 2.73.

Faculty *Total:* 158, 34% full-time, 9% with terminal degrees. *Student/faculty ratio:* 20:1.

Majors Administrative assistant and secretarial science; animation, interactive technology, video graphics and special effects; automobile/automotive mechanics technology; biomedical technology; business/commerce; computer programming; criminal justice/safety; early childhood education; education; electrical, electronic and communications engineering technology; electrician; ethnic, cultural minority, gender, and group studies related; fine/studio arts; general studies; graphic design; human services; information technology; legal assistant/paralegal; office occupations and clerical services; pre-engineering.

Academics *Calendar:* semesters. *Degree:* certificates and associate. *Special study options:* academic remediation for entering students, adult/continuing education programs, advanced placement credit, distance learning, double

majors, independent study, internships, off-campus study, part-time degree program, services for LD students, study abroad, summer session for credit.
Library David H. Townsend Library with 50,000 titles, 350 serial subscriptions, an OPAC, a Web page.
Student Life *Housing:* college housing not available. *Activities and Organizations:* drama/theater group, choral group, Student Nurse Association, Student Media Solutions, Social Science Club, League of United Latin American Citizens - Young Adult, Student Veterans of America-Alamogordo. *Campus security:* 24-hour emergency response devices.
Costs (2013–14) *Tuition:* area resident $1824 full-time, $76 per credit hour part-time; state resident $2184 full-time, $91 per credit hour part-time; nonresident $5064 full-time, $211 per credit hour part-time. Full-time tuition and fees vary according to course load. *Required fees:* $96 full-time, $4 per credit hour part-time. *Payment plans:* installment, deferred payment. *Waivers:* senior citizens and employees or children of employees.
Financial Aid Of all full-time matriculated undergraduates who enrolled in 2012, 10 Federal Work-Study jobs (averaging $3300). 60 state and other part-time jobs (averaging $3300). *Financial aid deadline:* 5/1.
Applying *Options:* electronic application, early admission, deferred entrance. *Application fee:* $20. *Required:* high school transcript, minimum 2.0 GPA. *Application deadlines:* rolling (freshmen), rolling (out-of-state freshmen), rolling (transfers). *Notification:* continuous (freshmen), continuous (out-of-state freshmen), continuous (transfers).
Freshman Application Contact Ms. Elma Hernandez, Coordinator of Admissions and Records, New Mexico State University–Alamogordo, 2400 North Scenic Drive, Alamogordo, NM 88311-0477. *Phone:* 575-439-3700. *E-mail:* advisor@nmsua.nmsu.edu.
Website: http://nmsua.edu/.

New Mexico State University–Carlsbad
Carlsbad, New Mexico

Freshman Application Contact Ms. Everal Shannon, Records Specialist, New Mexico State University–Carlsbad, 1500 University Drive, Carlsbad, NM 88220. *Phone:* 575-234-9222. *Fax:* 575-885-4951. *E-mail:* eshannon@nmsu.edu.
Website: http://www.cavern.nmsu.edu/.

New Mexico State University–Grants
Grants, New Mexico

Director of Admissions Ms. Irene Lutz, Campus Student Services Officer, New Mexico State University–Grants, 1500 3rd Street, Grants, NM 87020-2025. *Phone:* 505-287-7981.
Website: http://grants.nmsu.edu/.

Northern New Mexico College
Española, New Mexico

Freshman Application Contact Mr. Mike L. Costello, Registrar, Northern New Mexico College, 921 Paseo de Oñate, Española, NM 87532. *Phone:* 505-747-2193. *Fax:* 505-747-2191. *E-mail:* dms@nnmc.edu.
Website: http://www.nnmc.edu/.

Pima Medical Institute
Albuquerque, New Mexico

Freshman Application Contact Admissions Office, Pima Medical Institute, 4400 Cutler Avenue NE, Albuquerque, NM 87110. *Phone:* 505-881-1234. *Toll-free phone:* 800-477-PIMA (in-state); 888-477-PIMA (out-of-state). *Fax:* 505-881-5329.
Website: http://www.pmi.edu/.

Pima Medical Institute
Albuquerque, New Mexico

Freshman Application Contact Pima Medical Institute, RMTS 32, 8601 Golf Course Road, NW, Albuquerque, NM 87114. *Phone:* 505-816-0556.
Website: http://www.pmi.edu/.

San Juan College
Farmington, New Mexico

- **State-supported** 2-year, founded 1958, part of New Mexico Higher Education Department
- **Small-town** 698-acre campus
- **Endowment** $12.2 million
- **Coed,** 8,491 undergraduate students, 29% full-time, 61% women, 39% men

Undergraduates 2,494 full-time, 5,997 part-time. Students come from 28 other countries; 24% are from out of state; 1% Black or African American,

non-Hispanic/Latino; 15% Hispanic/Latino; 0.6% Asian, non-Hispanic/Latino; 0.2% Native Hawaiian or other Pacific Islander, non-Hispanic/Latino; 30% American Indian or Alaska Native, non-Hispanic/Latino; 1% Two or more races, non-Hispanic/Latino; 4% Race/ethnicity unknown; 0.9% international; 4% transferred in. *Retention:* 50% of full-time freshmen returned.

Freshmen *Admission:* 4,082 applied, 4,082 admitted, 919 enrolled.
Faculty *Total:* 419, 40% full-time. *Student/faculty ratio:* 19:1.

Majors Accounting technology and bookkeeping; American Indian/Native American studies; autobody/collision and repair technology; automobile/automotive mechanics technology; biology/biological sciences; business administration and management; carpentry; chemistry; child-care provision; clinical/medical laboratory technology; commercial and advertising art; cosmetology; criminal justice/police science; data processing and data processing technology; dental hygiene; diesel mechanics technology; drafting and design technology; electrical, electronic and communications engineering technology; elementary education; emergency medical technology (EMT paramedic); engineering; fire science/firefighting; general studies; geology/earth science; health and physical education/fitness; health information/medical records technology; industrial mechanics and maintenance technology; industrial technology; instrumentation technology; landscaping and groundskeeping; legal assistant/paralegal; liberal arts and sciences/liberal studies; machine shop technology; mathematics; occupational safety and health technology; occupational therapist assistant; parks, recreation and leisure; physical sciences; physical therapy technology; physics; premedical studies; psychology; registered nursing/registered nurse; respiratory care therapy; secondary education; social work; solar energy technology; special education; surgical technology; theater design and technology; veterinary/animal health technology; welding technology.

Academics *Calendar:* semesters. *Degree:* certificates, diplomas, and associate. *Special study options:* academic remediation for entering students, adult/continuing education programs, advanced placement credit, cooperative education, distance learning, double majors, English as a second language, freshman honors college, honors programs, independent study, internships, part-time degree program, services for LD students, summer session for credit.

Library San Juan College Library with 110,218 titles, 267 serial subscriptions, 5,262 audiovisual materials, an OPAC, a Web page.

Student Life *Housing:* college housing not available. *Activities and Organizations:* drama/theater group, student-run newspaper, choral group, AGAVE, SJC National Society of Leadership and Success, Psychology/PSI Beta, Associated Students of San Juan College, American Indian Science and Leadership Society (AISES), national fraternities, national sororities. *Campus security:* 24-hour emergency response devices and patrols, late-night transport/escort service. *Student services:* personal/psychological counseling.

Athletics *Intramural sports:* badminton M/W, basketball M/W, cross-country running M/W, football M/W, golf M/W, rock climbing M/W, skiing (cross-country) M/W, skiing (downhill) M/W, soccer M/W, softball M/W, table tennis M/W, ultimate Frisbee M/W, volleyball M/W, weight lifting M/W.

Costs (2014–15) *Tuition:* state resident $984 full-time, $41 per credit hour part-time; nonresident $2520 full-time, $105 per credit hour part-time. Full-time tuition and fees vary according to reciprocity agreements. *Required fees:* $354 full-time, $15 per credit hour part-time. *Payment plans:* tuition prepayment, installment. *Waivers:* senior citizens and employees or children of employees.

Financial Aid Of all full-time matriculated undergraduates who enrolled in 2012, 150 Federal Work-Study jobs (averaging $2500). 175 state and other part-time jobs (averaging $2500).

Applying *Options:* electronic application, early admission, deferred entrance. *Application fee:* $10. *Required:* high school transcript. *Application deadlines:* rolling (freshmen), rolling (transfers). *Notification:* continuous (freshmen), continuous (transfers).

Freshman Application Contact Mr. Milo McMinn, Enrollment Services Coordinator, San Juan College, 4601 College Blvd, Farmington, NM 87402. *Phone:* 505-566-3532. *Fax:* 505-566-3500. *E-mail:* calcotea@sanjuancollege.edu.

Website: http://www.sanjuancollege.edu/.

Santa Fe Community College
Santa Fe, New Mexico

Freshman Application Contact Ms. Rebecca Estrada, Director of Recruitment, Santa Fe Community College, 6401 Richards Ave, Santa Fe, NM 87508. *Phone:* 505-428-1604. *Fax:* 505-428-1468. *E-mail:* rebecca.estrada@sfcc.edu.
Website: http://www.sfcc.edu/.

Southwestern Indian Polytechnic Institute

Albuquerque, New Mexico

- **Federally supported** 2-year, founded 1971
- **Suburban** 144-acre campus
- **Coed,** 480 undergraduate students, 85% full-time, 53% women, 47% men

Undergraduates 406 full-time, 74 part-time. Students come from 21 states and territories; 60% live on campus.

Freshmen *Admission:* 247 applied, 136 admitted, 158 enrolled. *Average high school GPA:* 2.11.

Faculty *Total:* 48, 29% full-time, 21% with terminal degrees. *Student/faculty ratio:* 15:1.

Majors Accounting technology and bookkeeping; business administration and management; business/commerce; early childhood education; engineering; geographic information science and cartography; institutional food workers; instrumentation technology; liberal arts and sciences/liberal studies; natural resources and conservation related; opticianry; system, networking, and LAN/WAN management.

Academics *Calendar:* trimesters. *Degree:* certificates and associate. *Special study options:* academic remediation for entering students, advanced placement credit, cooperative education, distance learning, double majors, internships, part-time degree program, services for LD students, summer session for credit.

Library Southwester Indian Polytechnic Institute Library with 27,000 titles, 715 serial subscriptions.

Student Life *Housing Options:* men-only, women-only. Campus housing is university owned. *Activities and Organizations:* Dance club, Student Senate, rodeo club, Natural Resources, Pow-wow club. *Campus security:* 24-hour emergency response devices and patrols, late-night transport/escort service. *Student services:* personal/psychological counseling.

Athletics *Intramural sports:* basketball M/W, softball M/W, volleyball M/W.

Costs (2013–14) *Tuition:* state resident $675 full-time, $150 per term part-time; nonresident $675 full-time, $150 per term part-time. *Room and board:* $165. *Payment plan:* deferred payment.

Financial Aid Of all full-time matriculated undergraduates who enrolled in 2010, 351 applied for aid, 351 were judged to have need, 23 had their need fully met. 14 Federal Work-Study jobs (averaging $661). 36 state and other part-time jobs (averaging $726). *Average percent of need met:* 27%. *Average financial aid package:* $2943. *Average need-based gift aid:* $2878.

Applying *Required:* high school transcript, Certificate of Indian Blood. *Application deadlines:* 7/30 (freshmen), 7/30 (transfers). *Notification:* continuous (freshmen).

Freshman Application Contact Southwestern Indian Polytechnic Institute, 9169 Coors, NW, Box 10146, Albuquerque, NM 87184-0146. *Phone:* 505-346-2324. *Toll-free phone:* 800-586-7474. *Website:* http://www.sipi.edu/.

University of New Mexico–Gallup

Gallup, New Mexico

Director of Admissions Ms. Pearl A. Morris, Admissions Representative, University of New Mexico–Gallup, 200 College Road, Gallup, NM 87301-5603. *Phone:* 505-863-7576. *Website:* http://www.gallup.unm.edu/.

University of New Mexico–Los Alamos Branch

Los Alamos, New Mexico

- **State-supported** 2-year, founded 1980, part of New Mexico Commission on Higher Education
- **Small-town** 5-acre campus
- **Coed,** 744 undergraduate students, 26% full-time, 57% women, 43% men

Undergraduates 191 full-time, 553 part-time. 1% are from out of state; 1% Black or African American, non-Hispanic/Latino; 43% Hispanic/Latino; 3% Asian, non-Hispanic/Latino; 0.4% Native Hawaiian or other Pacific Islander, non-Hispanic/Latino; 5% American Indian or Alaska Native, non-Hispanic/Latino; 2% Two or more races, non-Hispanic/Latino; 3% Race/ethnicity unknown; 3% transferred in. *Retention:* 57% of full-time freshmen returned.

Freshmen *Admission:* 76 enrolled.

Faculty *Total:* 88, 5% full-time, 34% with terminal degrees. *Student/faculty ratio:* 9:1.

Majors Accounting; administrative assistant and secretarial science; biological and physical sciences; business administration and management; computer engineering technology; computer programming; computer science; design and applied arts related; early childhood education; electrical, electronic and communications engineering technology; engineering; environmental

studies; fine/studio arts; general studies; liberal arts and sciences/liberal studies; physical sciences; pre-engineering; sales, distribution, and marketing operations.

Academics *Calendar:* semesters. *Degree:* certificates and associate. *Special study options:* academic remediation for entering students, adult/continuing education programs, advanced placement credit, cooperative education, distance learning, double majors, English as a second language, internships, off-campus study, part-time degree program, services for LD students, summer session for credit.

Library University of New University of New Mexico - Los Alamos Library with 129,731 titles, 165,075 serial subscriptions, 790 audiovisual materials, an OPAC, a Web page.

Student Life *Housing Options:* Campus housing is university owned.

Standardized Tests *Recommended:* SAT or ACT (for admission).

Costs (2014–15) *Tuition:* state resident $1536 full-time, $64 per credit part-time; nonresident $4776 full-time, $199 per credit part-time. *Required fees:* $108 full-time, $5 per credit part-time. *Payment plan:* deferred payment.

Financial Aid Of all full-time matriculated undergraduates who enrolled in 2012, 15 Federal Work-Study jobs (averaging $5000). 10 state and other part-time jobs (averaging $7000).

Applying *Required:* high school transcript.

Freshman Application Contact Mrs. Irene K. Martinez, Enrollment Representative, University of New Mexico–Los Alamos Branch, 4000 University Drive, Los Alamos, NM 87544-2233. *Phone:* 505-662-0332. *E-mail:* L65130@unm.edu. *Website:* http://www.la.unm.edu/.

University of New Mexico–Taos

Taos, New Mexico

Director of Admissions Vickie Alvarez, Student Enrollment Associate, University of New Mexico–Taos, 115 Civic Plaza Drive, Taos, NM 87571. *Phone:* 575-737-6425. *E-mail:* valvarez@unm.edu. *Website:* http://taos.unm.edu/.

University of New Mexico–Valencia Campus

Los Lunas, New Mexico

Director of Admissions Richard M. Hulett, Director of Admissions and Recruitment, University of New Mexico–Valencia Campus, 280 La Entrada, Los Lunas, NM 87031-7633. *Phone:* 505-277-2446. *E-mail:* mhulett@unm.edu. *Website:* http://www.unm.edu/~unmvc/.

NEW YORK

Adirondack Community College

Queensbury, New York

- **State and locally supported** 2-year, founded 1960, part of State University of New York System
- **Small-town** 141-acre campus
- **Endowment** $2.9 million
- **Coed**

Undergraduates 2,263 full-time, 1,724 part-time. Students come from 10 states and territories; 9 other countries; 0.6% are from out of state; 1% Black or African American, non-Hispanic/Latino; 2% Hispanic/Latino; 0.5% Asian, non-Hispanic/Latino; 0.3% American Indian or Alaska Native, non-Hispanic/Latino; 1% Two or more races, non-Hispanic/Latino; 2% Race/ethnicity unknown; 0.4% international; 5% transferred in. *Retention:* 59% of full-time freshmen returned.

Faculty *Student/faculty ratio:* 14:1.

Academics *Calendar:* semesters. *Degree:* certificates and associate. *Special study options:* academic remediation for entering students, accelerated degree program, adult/continuing education programs, advanced placement credit, cooperative education, distance learning, double majors, independent study, internships, part-time degree program, services for LD students, study abroad, summer session for credit.

Student Life *Campus security:* late-night transport/escort service, patrols by trained security personnel 8 am to 10 pm.

Athletics Member NJCAA.

Costs (2013–14) *One-time required fee:* $75. *Tuition:* state resident $3774 full-time, $158 per credit hour part-time; nonresident $7548 full-time, $315 per credit hour part-time. Full-time tuition and fees vary according to course load and program. Part-time tuition and fees vary according to course load and program. *Required fees:* $402 full-time, $14 per credit hour part-time, $3 per term part-time. *Room and board:* $9850; room only: $6750.

Financial Aid Of all full-time matriculated undergraduates who enrolled in 2012, 98 Federal Work-Study jobs (averaging $462).

Applying *Options:* electronic application. *Application fee:* $35.

Freshman Application Contact Office of Admissions, Adirondack Community College, 640 Bay Road, Queensbury, NY 12804. *Phone:* 518-743-2264. *Toll-free phone:* 888-SUNY-ADK. *Fax:* 518-743-2200. *Website:* http://www.sunyacc.edu/.

American Academy McAllister Institute of Funeral Service

New York, New York

Freshman Application Contact Mr. Norman Provost, Registrar, American Academy McAllister Institute of Funeral Service, 450 West 56th Street, New York, NY 10019-3602. *Phone:* 212-757-1190. *Toll-free phone:* 866-932-2264.

Website: http://www.funeraleducation.org/.

American Academy of Dramatic Arts–New York

New York, New York

- **Independent** 2-year, founded 1884
- **Urban** campus
- **Endowment** $6.0 million
- **Coed**

Undergraduates 258 full-time. Students come from 34 states and territories; 20 other countries; 86% are from out of state; 8% Black or African American, non-Hispanic/Latino; 7% Hispanic/Latino; 2% Asian, non-Hispanic/Latino; 38% international; 40% live on campus.

Faculty *Student/faculty ratio:* 9:1.

Academics *Calendar:* continuous. *Degree:* certificates and associate. *Special study options:* academic remediation for entering students, honors programs.

Student Life *Campus security:* 24-hour emergency response devices and patrols, controlled dormitory access, trained security guard during hours of operation and campus housing.

Costs (2013–14) *Tuition:* $29,900 full-time. *Required fees:* $750 full-time. *Room only:* Room and board charges vary according to housing facility.

Financial Aid Of all full-time matriculated undergraduates who enrolled in 2012, 240 applied for aid, 231 were judged to have need. 50 Federal Work-Study jobs (averaging $900). 50 state and other part-time jobs (averaging $2000). In 2012, 59. *Average percent of need met:* 67. *Average financial aid package:* $18,150. *Average need-based loan:* $4500. *Average need-based gift aid:* $7000. *Average non-need-based aid:* $7000. *Average indebtedness upon graduation:* $15,000. *Financial aid deadline:* 5/15.

Applying *Options:* electronic application, deferred entrance. *Application fee:* $50. *Required:* essay or personal statement, high school transcript, minimum 2.0 GPA, 2 letters of recommendation, interview, audition.

Freshman Application Contact Steven Hong, Director of Admissions, American Academy of Dramatic Arts–New York, 120 Madison Avenue, New York, NY 10016. *Phone:* 323-464-2777 Ext. 103. *Toll-free phone:* 800-463-8990. *E-mail:* shong@aada.edu.

Website: http://www.aada.org/.

The Art Institute of New York City

New York, New York

- **Proprietary** 2-year, founded 1980, part of Education Management Corporation
- **Urban** campus
- **Coed**

Majors Fashion/apparel design; graphic design; web page, digital/multimedia and information resources design.

Academics *Calendar:* quarters. *Degree:* associate.

Freshman Application Contact The Art Institute of New York City, 218-232 West 40th Street, New York, NY 10018. *Phone:* 212-226-5500. *Toll-free phone:* 800-654-2433.

Website: http://www.artinstitutes.edu/newyork/.

ASA College

Brooklyn, New York

Freshman Application Contact Admissions Office, ASA College, 81 Willoughby Street, Brooklyn, NY 11201. *Phone:* 718-522-9073. *Toll-free phone:* 877-679-8772.

Website: http://www.asa.edu/.

The Belanger School of Nursing

Schenectady, New York

- **Independent** 2-year, founded 1906
- **Urban** campus
- **Coed, primarily women,** 124 undergraduate students, 30% full-time, 83% women, 17% men

Undergraduates 37 full-time, 87 part-time. Students come from 3 states and territories; 12% Black or African American, non-Hispanic/Latino; 6% Hispanic/Latino; 5% Asian, non-Hispanic/Latino; 2% American Indian or Alaska Native, non-Hispanic/Latino; 0.8% Two or more races, non-Hispanic/Latino.

Freshmen *Admission:* 2 enrolled. *Average high school GPA:* 3.2.

Faculty *Student/faculty ratio:* 6:1.

Majors Registered nursing/registered nurse.

Academics *Degree:* associate.

Student Life *Housing:* college housing not available.

Standardized Tests *Recommended:* SAT or ACT (for admission).

Costs (2014–15) *Tuition:* $8357 full-time, $7511 per year part-time. *Required fees:* $962 full-time, $962 per year part-time.

Applying *Required:* essay or personal statement, high school transcript, minimum 3.0 GPA, 2 letters of recommendation.

Freshman Application Contact Carolyn Lansing, Student Services Manager, The Belanger School of Nursing, 65 McClellan Street, Schenectady, NY 12304. *Phone:* 518-831-8810. *Fax:* 518-243-4470. *E-mail:* lansingc@ellismedicine.org.

Website: http://www.ellismedicine.org/school-of-nursing/.

Berkeley College–Westchester Campus

White Plains, New York

Freshman Application Contact Director of Admissions, Berkeley College–Westchester Campus, White Plains, NY 10601. *Phone:* 914-694-1122. *Toll-free phone:* 800-446-5400. *Fax:* 914-328-9469. *E-mail:* info@berkeleycollege.edu.

Website: http://www.berkeleycollege.edu/.

Borough of Manhattan Community College of the City University of New York

New York, New York

- **State and locally supported** 2-year, founded 1963, part of City University of New York System
- **Urban** 5-acre campus
- **Coed,** 24,186 undergraduate students, 66% full-time, 57% women, 43% men

Undergraduates 15,889 full-time, 8,297 part-time. 1% are from out of state; 30% Black or African American, non-Hispanic/Latino; 40% Hispanic/Latino; 13% Asian, non-Hispanic/Latino; 0.2% American Indian or Alaska Native, non-Hispanic/Latino; 7% international; 4% transferred in.

Freshmen *Admission:* 25,285 applied, 25,043 admitted, 5,403 enrolled. *Test scores:* SAT critical reading scores over 500: 9%; SAT math scores over 500: 10%; SAT critical reading scores over 600: 1%; SAT math scores over 600: 2%.

Faculty *Total:* 2,639, 45% full-time.

Majors Accounting technology and bookkeeping; administrative assistant and secretarial science; biotechnology; business administration and management; community organization and advocacy; computer and information sciences; computer science; computer systems networking and telecommunications; criminal justice/police science; criminal justice/safety; emergency medical technology (EMT paramedic); engineering; English; forensic science and technology; health information/medical records technology; liberal arts and sciences/liberal studies; mathematics; physical sciences; radio and television broadcasting technology; registered nursing/registered nurse; respiratory therapy technician; small business administration; teacher assistant/aide; visual and performing arts; web page, digital/multimedia and information resources design.

Academics *Calendar:* semesters. *Degree:* certificates and associate. *Special study options:* academic remediation for entering students, adult/continuing education programs, advanced placement credit, cooperative education, distance learning, English as a second language, honors programs, independent study, internships, off-campus study, part-time degree program, services for LD students, study abroad, summer session for credit.

Library A. Philip Randolph Library with 342,000 titles, 250 serial subscriptions, 2,374 audiovisual materials, an OPAC, a Web page.

Student Life *Housing:* college housing not available. *Activities and Organizations:* drama/theater group, student-run newspaper, choral group, Chinese Culture Association, Chinese Cultural Studies Society, Math Club,

African Students Association, Student Nurses Association. *Campus security:* 24-hour patrols. *Student services:* health clinic, personal/psychological counseling, women's center.

Athletics Member NJCAA. *Intercollegiate sports:* baseball M, basketball M/W, soccer M/W, swimming and diving M/W, volleyball W.

Standardized Tests *Recommended:* SAT or ACT (for admission).

Costs (2013–14) *Tuition:* $180 per credit hour part-time; state resident $4200 full-time; nonresident $8400 full-time, $280 per credit hour part-time. Full-time tuition and fees vary according to course load. Part-time tuition and fees vary according to course load. *Required fees:* $318 full-time, $174 per year part-time. *Payment plans:* installment, deferred payment. *Waivers:* senior citizens and employees or children of employees.

Applying *Options:* electronic application, deferred entrance. *Application fee:* $65. *Required:* high school transcript. *Application deadlines:* rolling (freshmen), rolling (transfers). *Notification:* continuous (freshmen), continuous (transfers).

Freshman Application Contact Dr. Eugenio Barrios, Director of Enrollment Management, Borough of Manhattan Community College of the City University of New York, 199 Chambers Street, Room S-310, New York, NY 10007. *Phone:* 212-220-1265. *Toll-free phone:* 866-583-5729 (in-state); 866-593-5729 (out-of-state). *Fax:* 212-220-2366. *E-mail:* admissions@bmcc.cuny.edu.
Website: http://www.bmcc.cuny.edu/.

Bramson ORT College

Forest Hills, New York

Freshman Application Contact Admissions Office, Bramson ORT College, 69-30 Austin Street, Forest Hills, NY 11375-4239. *Phone:* 718-261-5800. *Fax:* 718-575-5119. *E-mail:* admissions@bramsonort.edu.
Website: http://www.bramsonort.edu/.

Bronx Community College of the City University of New York

Bronx, New York

- **State and locally supported** 2-year, founded 1959, part of City University of New York System
- **Urban** 50-acre campus with easy access to New York City
- **Endowment** $469,572
- **Coed,** 11,368 undergraduate students, 58% full-time, 57% women, 43% men

Undergraduates 6,598 full-time, 4,770 part-time. Students come from 119 other countries; 8% are from out of state; 9% transferred in. *Retention:* 65% of full-time freshmen returned.

Freshmen *Admission:* 1,842 enrolled.

Faculty *Total:* 406, 75% full-time. *Student/faculty ratio:* 26:1.

Majors Accounting; administrative assistant and secretarial science; African American/Black studies; art; biology/biological sciences; business administration and management; business teacher education; chemistry; child development; clinical/medical laboratory technology; computer science; data processing and data processing technology; electrical, electronic and communications engineering technology; history; human services; international relations and affairs; legal assistant/paralegal; liberal arts and sciences/liberal studies; marketing/marketing management; mathematics; medical administrative assistant and medical secretary; music; nuclear medical technology; ornamental horticulture; pre-engineering; psychology; registered nursing/registered nurse.

Academics *Calendar:* semesters. *Degree:* certificates and associate. *Special study options:* academic remediation for entering students, accelerated degree program, adult/continuing education programs, advanced placement credit, cooperative education, distance learning, double majors, English as a second language, honors programs, independent study, internships, off-campus study, part-time degree program, services for LD students, study abroad, summer session for credit.

Library Library & Gerald S. Lieblich Learning Resources Center with 75,000 titles, 800 serial subscriptions, 4,501 audiovisual materials, an OPAC, a Web page.

Student Life *Activities and Organizations:* drama/theater group, student-run newspaper, choral group, Muslim Students Association, Top Models Club, Anime/Manga Gaming Club, Business Club, Media Technology and Film Society. *Campus security:* 24-hour emergency response devices and patrols, late-night transport/escort service, A free shuttle bus service provides evening students with transportation from campus to several subway and bus lines between 5pm-11pm. *Student services:* health clinic, personal/psychological counseling.

Athletics Member NJCAA. *Intercollegiate sports:* baseball M, basketball M, cross-country running M/W, soccer M, track and field M/W, volleyball W. *Intramural sports:* basketball M, soccer M, volleyball M/W.

Standardized Tests *Recommended:* SAT or ACT (for admission).

Applying *Options:* early admission. *Application fee:* $65. *Required:* high school transcript, copy of accredited high school diploma or GED scores. *Application deadlines:* 7/1 (freshmen), 7/1 (transfers). *Notification:* 8/15 (freshmen), 8/15 (transfers).

Freshman Application Contact Ms. Patricia A. Ramos, Admissions Officer, Bronx Community College of the City University of New York, 2155 University Avenue, Bronx, NY 10453. *Phone:* 718-289-5888. *E-mail:* admission@bcc.cuny.edu.
Website: http://www.bcc.cuny.edu/.

Broome Community College

Binghamton, New York

Freshman Application Contact Ms. Jenae Norris, Director of Admissions, Broome Community College, PO Box 1017, Upper Front Street, Binghamton, NY 13902. *Phone:* 607-778-5001. *Fax:* 607-778-5394. *E-mail:* admissions@sunybroome.edu.
Website: http://www.sunybroome.edu/.

Bryant & Stratton College - Albany Campus

Albany, New York

Freshman Application Contact Mr. Robert Ferrell, Director of Admissions, Bryant & Stratton College - Albany Campus, 1259 Central Avenue, Albany, NY 12205. *Phone:* 518-437-1802 Ext. 205. *Fax:* 518-437-1048.
Website: http://www.bryantstratton.edu/.

Bryant & Stratton College - Amherst Campus

Clarence, New York

Freshman Application Contact Mr. Brian K. Dioguardi, Director of Admissions, Bryant & Stratton College - Amherst Campus, Audubon Business Center, 40 Hazelwood Drive, Amherst, NY 14228. *Phone:* 716-691-0012. *Fax:* 716-691-0012. *E-mail:* bkdioguardi@bryantstratton.edu.
Website: http://www.bryantstratton.edu/.

Bryant & Stratton College - Buffalo Campus

Buffalo, New York

Freshman Application Contact Mr. Philip J. Struebel, Director of Admissions, Bryant & Stratton College - Buffalo Campus, 465 Main Street, Suite 400, Buffalo, NY 14203. *Phone:* 716-884-9120. *Fax:* 716-884-0091. *E-mail:* pjstruebel@bryantstratton.edu.
Website: http://www.bryantstratton.edu/.

Bryant & Stratton College - Greece Campus

Rochester, New York

Freshman Application Contact Bryant & Stratton College - Greece Campus, 150 Bellwood Drive, Rochester, NY 14606. *Phone:* 585-720-0660.
Website: http://www.bryantstratton.edu/.

Bryant & Stratton College - Henrietta Campus

Rochester, New York

Freshman Application Contact Bryant & Stratton College - Henrietta Campus, 1225 Jefferson Road, Rochester, NY 14623-3136. *Phone:* 585-292-5627 Ext. 101.
Website: http://www.bryantstratton.edu/.

Bryant & Stratton College - North Campus

Liverpool, New York

Freshman Application Contact Ms. Heather Macnik, Director of Admissions, Bryant & Stratton College - North Campus, 8687 Carling Road, Liverpool, NY 13090-1315. *Phone:* 315-652-6500.
Website: http://www.bryantstratton.edu/.

Bryant & Stratton College - Southtowns Campus

Orchard Park, New York

Freshman Application Contact Bryant & Stratton College - Southtowns Campus, 200 Redtail, Orchard Park, NY 14127. *Phone:* 716-677-9500. *Website:* http://www.bryantstratton.edu/.

Bryant & Stratton College - Syracuse Campus

Syracuse, New York

Freshman Application Contact Ms. Dawn Rajkowski, Director of High School Enrollments, Bryant & Stratton College - Syracuse Campus, 953 James Street, Syracuse, NY 13203-2502. *Phone:* 315-472-6603 Ext. 248. *Fax:* 315-474-4383.
Website: http://www.bryantstratton.edu/.

Business Informatics Center, Inc.

Valley Stream, New York

Freshman Application Contact Admissions Office, Business Informatics Center, Inc., 134 South Central Avenue, Valley Stream, NY 11580-5431. *Phone:* 516-561-0050. *Fax:* 516-561-0074. *E-mail:* info@thecollegeforbusiness.com.
Website: http://www.thecollegeforbusiness.com/.

Cayuga County Community College

Auburn, New York

- **State and locally supported** 2-year, founded 1953, part of State University of New York System
- **Small-town** 50-acre campus with easy access to Rochester, Syracuse
- **Endowment** $6.3 million
- **Coed,** 4,619 undergraduate students, 49% full-time, 62% women, 38% men

Undergraduates 2,252 full-time, 2,385 part-time. 6% Black or African American, non-Hispanic/Latino; 4% Hispanic/Latino; 0.4% Asian, non-Hispanic/Latino; 0.6% American Indian or Alaska Native, non-Hispanic/Latino; 3% Two or more races, non-Hispanic/Latino; 6% Race/ethnicity unknown; 7% transferred in. *Retention:* 56% of full-time freshmen returned.
Freshmen *Admission:* 2,588 applied, 1,821 admitted, 693 enrolled.
Faculty *Total:* 252, 21% full-time. *Student/faculty ratio:* 22:1.
Majors Accounting technology and bookkeeping; art; business administration and management; child-care and support services management; communication and journalism related; communications systems installation and repair technology; computer and information sciences; computer and information sciences and support services related; corrections; criminal justice/police science; drafting and design technology; education (multiple levels); electrical, electronic and communications engineering technology; fine/studio arts; game and interactive media design; general studies; geography; graphic design; humanities; information science/studies; liberal arts and sciences/liberal studies; literature related; mathematics related; mechanical engineering; mechanical engineering/mechanical technology; music related; psychology related; radio, television, and digital communication related; registered nursing/registered nurse; science technologies related; sport and fitness administration/management; telecommunications technology; wine steward/sommelier; writing.
Academics *Calendar:* semesters. *Degree:* certificates and associate. *Special study options:* academic remediation for entering students, accelerated degree program, adult/continuing education programs, advanced placement credit, cooperative education, distance learning, double majors, honors programs, independent study, internships, off-campus study, part-time degree program, services for LD students, study abroad, summer session for credit. *ROTC:* Air Force (c).
Library Norman F. Bourke Memorial Library plus 2 others with 92,156 titles, 187 serial subscriptions, 5,240 audiovisual materials, an OPAC, a Web page.
Student Life *Housing Options:* coed. Campus housing is provided by a third party. *Activities and Organizations:* drama/theater group, student-run newspaper, radio and television station, choral group, Student Activity Board, Student government, Criminal Justice Club, Tutor Club, Early Childhood Club. *Campus security:* security from 8 am to 9 pm. *Student services:* health clinic.
Athletics Member NJCAA. *Intercollegiate sports:* basketball M/W, bowling M/W, golf M/W, lacrosse M, soccer M/W, softball W, volleyball W. *Intramural sports:* basketball M/W, skiing (downhill) M/W, volleyball M/W.

Standardized Tests *Required for some:* SAT or ACT (for admission).
Costs (2014–15) *Tuition:* state resident $2045 full-time; nonresident $4090 full-time. *Required fees:* $206 full-time.
Financial Aid Of all full-time matriculated undergraduates who enrolled in 2012, 150 Federal Work-Study jobs (averaging $2000). 200 state and other part-time jobs (averaging $1000).
Applying *Options:* electronic application, deferred entrance. *Required:* high school transcript. *Required for some:* interview. *Application deadlines:* rolling (freshmen), rolling (transfers). *Notification:* continuous (freshmen), continuous (transfers).
Freshman Application Contact Cayuga County Community College, 197 Franklin Street, Auburn, NY 13021-3099. *Phone:* 315-255-1743 Ext. 2244. *Toll-free phone:* 866-598-8883.
Website: http://www.cayuga-cc.edu/.

Clinton Community College

Plattsburgh, New York

- **State and locally supported** 2-year, founded 1969, part of State University of New York System
- **Small-town** 100-acre campus
- **Coed,** 1,997 undergraduate students, 54% full-time, 52% women, 48% men

Undergraduates 1,087 full-time, 910 part-time. Students come from 10 states and territories; 18 other countries; 3% are from out of state; 7% Black or African American, non-Hispanic/Latino; 2% Hispanic/Latino; 2% Asian, non-Hispanic/Latino; 0.3% Native Hawaiian or other Pacific Islander, non-Hispanic/Latino; 0.6% American Indian or Alaska Native, non-Hispanic/Latino; 4% Race/ethnicity unknown; 10% live on campus. *Retention:* 53% of full-time freshmen returned.
Faculty *Total:* 130, 39% full-time. *Student/faculty ratio:* 16:1.
Majors Accounting; biological and physical sciences; business administration and management; community organization and advocacy; computer/information technology services administration related; consumer merchandising/retailing management; criminal justice/law enforcement administration; criminal justice/police science; electrical, electronic and communications engineering technology; energy management and systems technology; engineering technologies and engineering related; humanities; industrial technology; liberal arts and sciences/liberal studies; physical education teaching and coaching; registered nursing/registered nurse; social sciences.
Academics *Calendar:* semesters. *Degree:* certificates and associate. *Special study options:* academic remediation for entering students, adult/continuing education programs, advanced placement credit, cooperative education, distance learning, English as a second language, external degree program, independent study, internships, off-campus study, part-time degree program, services for LD students, student-designed majors, summer session for credit.
Library Clinton Community College Learning Resource Center plus 1 other with 40,665 titles, 59,765 serial subscriptions, 1,687 audiovisual materials, an OPAC, a Web page.
Student Life *Housing Options:* coed, special housing for students with disabilities. Campus housing is provided by a third party. Freshman campus housing is guaranteed. *Activities and Organizations:* drama/theater group, student-run newspaper, choral group, Athletics, Future Human Services Professionals, PTK (Honor Society), Drama Club, Criminal Justice Club. *Campus security:* 24-hour emergency response devices and patrols, late-night transport/escort service, controlled dormitory access. *Student services:* health clinic, personal/psychological counseling.
Athletics Member NJCAA. *Intercollegiate sports:* baseball M, basketball M/W, soccer M/W, softball W. *Intramural sports:* volleyball M/W.
Costs (2014–15) *Tuition:* state resident $3960 full-time, $366 per hour part-time; nonresident $8800 full-time, $366 per hour part-time. Full-time tuition and fees vary according to program. Part-time tuition and fees vary according to program. *Required fees:* $395 full-time, $6 per hour part-time, $27 per year part-time. *Room and board:* $8490; room only: $4700. Room and board charges vary according to board plan.
Financial Aid Of all full-time matriculated undergraduates who enrolled in 2012, 45 Federal Work-Study jobs (averaging $1260).
Applying *Options:* electronic application, deferred entrance. *Required:* high school transcript. *Required for some:* essay or personal statement, 3 letters of recommendation, interview. *Application deadlines:* 8/26 (freshmen), 9/3 (transfers). *Notification:* continuous (freshmen), continuous (out-of-state freshmen), continuous (transfers).
Freshman Application Contact Clinton Community College, 136 Clinton Point Drive, Plattsburgh, NY 12901-9573. *Phone:* 518-562-4100. *Toll-free phone:* 800-552-1160.
Website: http://clintoncc.suny.edu/.

Cochran School of Nursing
Yonkers, New York

Freshman Application Contact Cochran School of Nursing, 967 North Broadway, Yonkers, NY 10701. *Phone:* 914-964-4606.
Website: http://www.cochranschoolofnursing.us/.

The College of Westchester
White Plains, New York

Freshman Application Contact Mr. Dale T. Smith, Vice President, The College of Westchester, 325 Central Avenue, PO Box 710, White Plains, NY 10602. *Phone:* 914-948-4442 Ext. 311. *Toll-free phone:* 800-660-7093. *Fax:* 914-948-5441. *E-mail:* admissions@cw.edu.
Website: http://www.cw.edu/.

Columbia-Greene Community College
Hudson, New York

- **State and locally supported** 2-year, founded 1969, part of State University of New York System
- **Rural** 143-acre campus
- **Coed,** 2,112 undergraduate students, 46% full-time, 63% women, 37% men

Undergraduates 964 full-time, 1,148 part-time. Students come from 4 states and territories; 2 other countries; 0.1% are from out of state; 7% Black or African American, non-Hispanic/Latino; 7% Hispanic/Latino; 2% Asian, non-Hispanic/Latino; 0.1% Native Hawaiian or other Pacific Islander, non-Hispanic/Latino; 0.2% American Indian or Alaska Native, non-Hispanic/Latino; 2% Two or more races, non-Hispanic/Latino; 0.3% Race/ethnicity unknown; 6% transferred in.
Freshmen *Admission:* 403 enrolled.
Faculty *Total:* 176, 26% full-time, 5% with terminal degrees. *Student/faculty ratio:* 19:1.
Majors Accounting technology and bookkeeping; administrative assistant and secretarial science; art; automobile/automotive mechanics technology; biology teacher education; business administration and management; community organization and advocacy; computer and information sciences; computer and information sciences and support services related; criminal justice/law enforcement administration; criminal justice/safety; entrepreneurship; humanities; information science/studies; kindergarten/preschool education; liberal arts and sciences and humanities related; liberal arts and sciences/liberal studies; medical office management; registered nursing/registered nurse; rehabilitation and therapeutic professions related; teacher assistant/aide.
Academics *Calendar:* semesters. *Degree:* certificates and associate. *Special study options:* academic remediation for entering students, adult/continuing education programs, advanced placement credit, distance learning, double majors, honors programs, independent study, internships, part-time degree program, services for LD students, summer session for credit.
Library CGCC Library with an OPAC, a Web page.
Student Life *Housing:* college housing not available. *Activities and Organizations:* drama/theater group, student-run radio station, Criminal Justice Club, Human Services Club, Psychology Club, Student Senate, Animal Avocates. *Campus security:* 24-hour patrols, late-night transport/escort service.
Athletics Member NCAA, NJCAA. All NCAA Division III. *Intercollegiate sports:* baseball M, basketball M, bowling M/W, golf M/W, softball W.
Costs (2013–14) *Tuition:* state resident $3960 full-time, $165 per semester hour part-time; nonresident $7920 full-time, $330 per semester hour part-time. Full-time tuition and fees vary according to course load, location, and program. Part-time tuition and fees vary according to course load, location, and program. *Required fees:* $330 full-time. *Payment plan:* installment. *Waivers:* senior citizens and employees or children of employees.
Applying *Required:* high school transcript. *Required for some:* interview.
Freshman Application Contact Josh Horn, Director of Admissions, Columbia-Greene Community College, 4400 Route 23, Hudson, NY 12534-0327. *Phone:* 518-828-4181 Ext. 3370. *E-mail:* josh.horn@sunycgcc.edu.
Website: http://www.sunycgcc.edu/.

Corning Community College
Corning, New York

- **State and locally supported** 2-year, founded 1956, part of State University of New York System
- **Rural** 500-acre campus
- **Endowment** $535,490
- **Coed**

Undergraduates 2,298 full-time, 2,659 part-time. Students come from 7 states and territories; 19 other countries; 5% are from out of state; 4% Black or African American, non-Hispanic/Latino; 5% Hispanic/Latino; 0.9% Asian, non-Hispanic/Latino; 0.3% American Indian or Alaska Native, non-Hispanic/Latino; 2% Two or more races, non-Hispanic/Latino; 10% Race/ethnicity unknown; 0.1% international; 4% transferred in. *Retention:* 56% of full-time freshmen returned.
Faculty *Student/faculty ratio:* 22:1.
Academics *Calendar:* semesters. *Degree:* certificates and associate. *Special study options:* academic remediation for entering students, accelerated degree program, adult/continuing education programs, advanced placement credit, cooperative education, distance learning, double majors, English as a second language, honors programs, independent study, internships, off-campus study, part-time degree program, services for LD students, student-designed majors, study abroad, summer session for credit.
Student Life *Campus security:* 24-hour emergency response devices and patrols, late-night transport/escort service, controlled dormitory access.
Athletics Member NJCAA.
Costs (2013–14) *Tuition:* state resident $3950 full-time, $165 per credit hour part-time; nonresident $7900 full-time, $330 per credit hour part-time. Part-time tuition and fees vary according to course load. *Required fees:* $442 full-time, $9 per credit hour part-time. *Room and board:* $4250.
Financial Aid Of all full-time matriculated undergraduates who enrolled in 2012, 264 Federal Work-Study jobs (averaging $1128).
Applying *Options:* electronic application, early admission. *Application fee:* $25. *Required:* high school transcript. *Required for some:* interview.
Freshman Application Contact Corning Community College, One Academic Drive, Corning, NY 14830-3297. *Phone:* 607-962-9427. *Toll-free phone:* 800-358-7171.
Website: http://www.corning-cc.edu/.

Crouse Hospital School of Nursing
Syracuse, New York

Freshman Application Contact Ms. Amy Graham, Enrollment Management Supervisor, Crouse Hospital School of Nursing, 736 Irving Avenue, Syracuse, NY 13210. *Phone:* 315-470-7481. *Fax:* 315-470-7925. *E-mail:* amygraham@crouse.org.
Website: http://www.crouse.org/nursing/.

Dorothea Hopfer School of Nursing at The Mount Vernon Hospital
Mount Vernon, New York

Director of Admissions Sandra Farrior, Coordinator of Student Services, Dorothea Hopfer School of Nursing at The Mount Vernon Hospital, 53 Valentine Street, Mount Vernon, NY 10550. *Phone:* 914-361-6472. *E-mail:* hopferadmissions@sshsw.org.
Website: http://www.montefiorehealthsystem.org/landing.cfm?id=19.

Dutchess Community College
Poughkeepsie, New York

- **State and locally supported** 2-year, founded 1957, part of State University of New York System
- **Suburban** 130-acre campus with easy access to New York City
- **Coed,** 10,232 undergraduate students, 48% full-time, 54% women, 46% men

Undergraduates 4,893 full-time, 5,339 part-time. 10% Black or African American, non-Hispanic/Latino; 16% Hispanic/Latino; 3% Asian, non-Hispanic/Latino; 0.1% Native Hawaiian or other Pacific Islander, non-Hispanic/Latino; 0.2% American Indian or Alaska Native, non-Hispanic/Latino; 3% Two or more races, non-Hispanic/Latino; 2% Race/ethnicity unknown; 1% international; 3% transferred in; 5% live on campus.
Freshmen *Admission:* 2,114 enrolled. *Average high school GPA:* 2.5.
Faculty *Total:* 555, 23% full-time, 5% with terminal degrees.
Majors Accounting; accounting technology and bookkeeping; airline pilot and flight crew; architectural engineering technology; art; aviation/airway management; business administration and management; child-care and support services management; clinical/medical laboratory technology; commercial and advertising art; communications systems installation and repair technology; community health services counseling; computer/information technology services administration related; computer science; construction trades related; criminal justice/police science; electrical, electronic and communications engineering technology; emergency medical technology (EMT paramedic); engineering; fire services administration; general studies; humanities; human services; information science/studies; legal assistant/paralegal; liberal arts and sciences and humanities related; liberal arts and sciences/liberal studies; physical education teaching and coaching; registered nursing/registered nurse; speech communication and rhetoric; visual and performing arts.
Academics *Calendar:* semesters. *Degree:* certificates and associate. *Special study options:* academic remediation for entering students, adult/continuing

education programs, advanced placement credit, distance learning, English as a second language, freshman honors college, honors programs, internships, off-campus study, part-time degree program, services for LD students, summer session for credit.

Library Dutchess Library plus 1 other with 200,688 titles, 202 serial subscriptions, 2,453 audiovisual materials, an OPAC, a Web page.

Student Life *Housing Options:* coed. Campus housing is university owned. *Activities and Organizations:* drama/theater group, student-run newspaper, radio station, choral group, Rap, Poetry & Music, Outdoor Adventure, Gamers Guild, Masquers Guild, Christian Fellowship. *Campus security:* 24-hour emergency response devices and patrols, late-night transport/escort service. *Student services:* health clinic, personal/psychological counseling.

Athletics Member NJCAA. *Intercollegiate sports:* baseball M, basketball M/W, cross-country running M/W, soccer M, softball W, volleyball W.

Costs (2013–14) *Tuition:* state resident $3200 full-time, $133 per hour part-time; nonresident $6400 full-time, $266 per hour part-time. *Required fees:* $435 full-time, $10 per hour part-time, $19 per term part-time. *Room and board:* $9330. Room and board charges vary according to board plan. *Payment plan:* installment. *Waivers:* senior citizens and employees or children of employees.

Applying *Options:* early admission, deferred entrance. *Required:* high school transcript. *Application deadlines:* rolling (freshmen), rolling (transfers). *Notification:* continuous (freshmen), continuous (transfers).

Freshman Application Contact Dutchess Community College, 53 Pendell Road, Poughkeepsie, NY 12601-1595. *Phone:* 845-431-8010. *Website:* http://www.sunydutchess.edu/.

Elmira Business Institute
Elmira, New York

- **Private** 2-year, founded 1858
- **Urban** campus
- **Coed, primarily women,** 98 undergraduate students, 76% full-time, 83% women, 17% men

Undergraduates 74 full-time, 24 part-time.

Freshmen *Admission:* 22 enrolled.

Faculty *Student/faculty ratio:* 9:1.

Majors Accounting; administrative assistant and secretarial science; medical/clinical assistant; medical insurance coding.

Academics *Calendar:* semesters. *Degree:* certificates and associate. *Special study options:* academic remediation for entering students, advanced placement credit, internships, part-time degree program.

Library Elmira Business Institute Library plus 1 other.

Student Life *Housing:* college housing not available. *Campus security:* 24-hour emergency response devices.

Costs (2014–15) *Tuition:* Full-time tuition and fees vary according to program. Part-time tuition and fees vary according to program. No tuition increase for student's term of enrollment. *Payment plan:* installment.

Financial Aid Of all full-time matriculated undergraduates who enrolled in 2011, 316 applied for aid, 306 were judged to have need. *Average percent of need met:* 85%. *Average financial aid package:* $30,450. *Average need-based loan:* $3500. *Average need-based gift aid:* $18,950. *Average indebtedness upon graduation:* $14,000.

Applying *Options:* electronic application. *Required:* high school transcript, interview. *Required for some:* essay or personal statement. *Application deadline:* rolling (freshmen).

Freshman Application Contact Ms. Lindsay Dull, Director of Student services, Elmira Business Institute, Elmira, NY 14901. *Phone:* 607-733-7177. *Toll-free phone:* 800-843-1812. *E-mail:* info@ebi-college.com. *Website:* http://www.ebi-college.com/.

Erie Community College
Buffalo, New York

- **State and locally supported** 2-year, founded 1971, part of State University of New York System
- **Urban** 1-acre campus
- **Coed,** 3,281 undergraduate students, 75% full-time, 60% women, 40% men

Undergraduates 2,445 full-time, 836 part-time. Students come from 22 states and territories; 9 other countries; 1% are from out of state; 33% Black or African American, non-Hispanic/Latino; 11% Hispanic/Latino; 2% Asian, non-Hispanic/Latino; 0.1% Native Hawaiian or other Pacific Islander, non-Hispanic/Latino; 0.7% American Indian or Alaska Native, non-Hispanic/Latino; 4% Two or more races, non-Hispanic/Latino; 3% Race/ethnicity unknown; 6% international; 6% transferred in.

Freshmen *Admission:* 2,975 applied, 2,122 admitted, 804 enrolled. *Test scores:* SAT critical reading scores over 500: 41%; SAT critical reading scores over 600: 9%; SAT critical reading scores over 700: 2%.

Faculty *Student/faculty ratio:* 18:1.

Majors Building/property maintenance; business administration and management; child-care and support services management; community health services counseling; criminal justice/police science; culinary arts; elementary education; humanities; legal assistant/paralegal; liberal arts and sciences/liberal studies; medical radiologic technology; physical education teaching and coaching; public administration and social service professions related; registered nursing/registered nurse; substance abuse/addiction counseling.

Academics *Calendar:* semesters. *Degree:* certificates, diplomas, and associate. *Special study options:* academic remediation for entering students, adult/continuing education programs, advanced placement credit, cooperative education, distance learning, double majors, English as a second language, honors programs, independent study, internships, part-time degree program, services for LD students, student-designed majors, study abroad, summer session for credit. *ROTC:* Army (c).

Library Leon E. Butler Library with 23,840 titles, 94 serial subscriptions, 1,810 audiovisual materials, an OPAC, a Web page.

Student Life *Housing:* college housing not available. *Campus security:* 24-hour emergency response devices and patrols, late-night transport/escort service. *Student services:* health clinic, personal/psychological counseling, women's center.

Athletics Member NJCAA. *Intercollegiate sports:* baseball M, basketball M/W, bowling M/W, cheerleading W, football M, ice hockey M, lacrosse W, soccer M/W, softball W, swimming and diving M/W, volleyball W.

Costs (2013–14) *One-time required fee:* $75. *Tuition:* area resident $3995 full-time, $167 per credit hour part-time; state resident $7990 full-time, $334 per credit hour part-time; nonresident $7990 full-time, $334 per credit hour part-time. *Required fees:* $600 full-time, $15 per credit hour part-time, $70 per term part-time. *Payment plan:* installment. *Waivers:* senior citizens and employees or children of employees.

Applying *Options:* electronic application. *Application fee:* $25. *Required:* high school transcript. *Required for some:* interview. *Application deadlines:* rolling (freshmen), rolling (transfers). *Notification:* continuous (freshmen), continuous (transfers).

Freshman Application Contact Erie Community College, 121 Ellicott Street, Buffalo, NY 14203-2698. *Phone:* 716-851-1155. *Fax:* 716-270-2821. *Website:* http://www.ecc.edu/.

Erie Community College, North Campus
Williamsville, New York

- **State and locally supported** 2-year, founded 1946, part of State University of New York System
- **Suburban** 120-acre campus with easy access to Buffalo
- **Coed,** 6,466 undergraduate students, 65% full-time, 49% women, 51% men

Undergraduates 4,228 full-time, 2,238 part-time. Students come from 23 states and territories; 20 other countries; 0.7% are from out of state; 14% Black or African American, non-Hispanic/Latino; 6% Hispanic/Latino; 2% Asian, non-Hispanic/Latino; 0.5% American Indian or Alaska Native, non-Hispanic/Latino; 3% Two or more races, non-Hispanic/Latino; 4% Race/ethnicity unknown; 4% international; 8% transferred in.

Freshmen *Admission:* 5,004 applied, 3,759 admitted, 1,349 enrolled. *Test scores:* SAT critical reading scores over 500: 84%; SAT math scores over 500: 86%; SAT critical reading scores over 600: 13%; SAT math scores over 600: 17%; SAT critical reading scores over 700: 1%; SAT math scores over 700: 2%.

Faculty *Student/faculty ratio:* 18:1.

Majors Business administration and management; civil engineering technology; clinical/medical laboratory technology; computer and information sciences; construction management; criminal justice/police science; culinary arts; dental hygiene; dietitian assistant; electrical, electronic and communications engineering technology; engineering; environmental science; geological and earth sciences/geosciences related; health information/medical records technology; humanities; industrial technology; information technology; liberal arts and sciences/liberal studies; mechanical engineering/mechanical technology; medical office management; occupational therapist assistant; office management; opticianry; physical education teaching and coaching; registered nursing/registered nurse; respiratory care therapy; restaurant, culinary, and catering management.

Academics *Calendar:* semesters plus summer sessions, winter intersession. *Degree:* certificates, diplomas, and associate. *Special study options:* academic remediation for entering students, adult/continuing education programs, advanced placement credit, cooperative education, distance learning, double majors, English as a second language, honors programs, independent study, internships, part-time degree program, services for LD students, student-designed majors, study abroad, summer session for credit. *ROTC:* Army (c).

Library Richard R. Dry Memorial Library with 51,056 titles, 193 serial subscriptions, 3,972 audiovisual materials, an OPAC, a Web page.

Student Life *Housing:* college housing not available. *Campus security:* 24-hour emergency response devices and patrols, late-night transport/escort service. *Student services:* health clinic, personal/psychological counseling, women's center.

Athletics Member NJCAA. *Intercollegiate sports:* baseball M, basketball M/W, bowling M/W, cheerleading W, football M, ice hockey M, lacrosse W, soccer M/W, softball W, swimming and diving M/W, volleyball W.

Costs (2013–14) *One-time required fee:* $75. *Tuition:* area resident $3995 full-time, $167 per credit hour part-time; state resident $7990 full-time, $334 per credit hour part-time; nonresident $7990 full-time, $334 per credit hour part-time. *Required fees:* $600 full-time, $15 per credit hour part-time, $70 per term part-time. *Payment plan:* installment. *Waivers:* senior citizens and employees or children of employees.

Applying *Options:* electronic application. *Application fee:* $25. *Required:* high school transcript. *Required for some:* interview. *Application deadlines:* rolling (freshmen), rolling (transfers). *Notification:* continuous (freshmen), continuous (transfers).

Freshman Application Contact Erie Community College, North Campus, 6205 Main Street, Williamsville, NY 14221-7095. *Phone:* 716-851-1455. *Fax:* 716-270-2961.

Website: http://www.ecc.edu/.

Erie Community College, South Campus
Orchard Park, New York

- **State and locally supported** 2-year, founded 1974, part of State University of New York System
- **Suburban** 110-acre campus with easy access to Buffalo
- **Coed,** 3,902 undergraduate students, 61% full-time, 44% women, 56% men

Undergraduates 2,366 full-time, 1,536 part-time. Students come from 16 states and territories; 4 other countries; 1% are from out of state; 6% Black or African American, non-Hispanic/Latino; 5% Hispanic/Latino; 0.8% Asian, non-Hispanic/Latino; 0.9% American Indian or Alaska Native, non-Hispanic/Latino; 2% Two or more races, non-Hispanic/Latino; 4% Race/ethnicity unknown; 1% international; 5% transferred in.

Freshmen *Admission:* 2,138 applied, 1,749 admitted, 815 enrolled. *Test scores:* SAT critical reading scores over 500: 90%; SAT math scores over 500: 93%; SAT critical reading scores over 600: 20%; SAT math scores over 600: 14%; SAT critical reading scores over 700: 2%; SAT math scores over 700: 1%.

Faculty *Student/faculty ratio:* 18:1.

Majors Architectural engineering technology; autobody/collision and repair technology; automobile/automotive mechanics technology; business administration and management; CAD/CADD drafting/design technology; communications systems installation and repair technology; computer technology/computer systems technology; criminal justice/police science; dental laboratory technology; emergency medical technology (EMT paramedic); fire services administration; graphic and printing equipment operation/production; humanities; information technology; liberal arts and sciences/liberal studies; office management; physical education teaching and coaching; speech communication and rhetoric; telecommunications technology.

Academics *Calendar:* semesters plus summer sessions, winter intersession. *Degree:* certificates, diplomas, and associate. *Special study options:* academic remediation for entering students, adult/continuing education programs, advanced placement credit, cooperative education, distance learning, double majors, English as a second language, honors programs, independent study, internships, part-time degree program, services for LD students, student-designed majors, study abroad, summer session for credit. *ROTC:* Army (c).

Library 37,459 titles, 186 serial subscriptions, 1,518 audiovisual materials, an OPAC, a Web page.

Student Life *Housing:* college housing not available. *Campus security:* 24-hour emergency response devices and patrols, late-night transport/escort service. *Student services:* health clinic, personal/psychological counseling, women's center.

Athletics Member NJCAA. *Intercollegiate sports:* baseball M, basketball M/W, bowling M/W, cheerleading W, football M, ice hockey M, lacrosse W, soccer M/W, softball W, swimming and diving M/W, volleyball W.

Costs (2013–14) *One-time required fee:* $75. *Tuition:* area resident $3995 full-time, $167 per credit hour part-time; state resident $7990 full-time, $334 per credit hour part-time; nonresident $7990 full-time, $334 per credit hour part-time. *Required fees:* $600 full-time, $15 per credit hour part-time, $70 per term part-time. *Payment plan:* installment. *Waivers:* senior citizens and employees or children of employees.

Applying *Options:* electronic application. *Application fee:* $25. *Required:* high school transcript. *Required for some:* interview. *Application deadlines:* rolling (freshmen), rolling (transfers). *Notification:* continuous (freshmen), continuous (transfers).

Freshman Application Contact Erie Community College, South Campus, 4041 Southwestern Boulevard, Orchard Park, NY 14127-2199. *Phone:* 716-851-1655. *Fax:* 716-851-1687.

Website: http://www.ecc.edu/.

Eugenio María de Hostos Community College of the City University of New York
Bronx, New York

Freshman Application Contact Mr. Roland Velez, Director of Admissions, Eugenio María de Hostos Community College of the City University of New York, 120 149th Street, Bronx, NY 10451. *Phone:* 718-319-7968. *Fax:* 718-319-7919. *E-mail:* admissions@hostos.cuny.edu.

Website: http://www.hostos.cuny.edu/.

Everest Institute
Rochester, New York

Freshman Application Contact Deanna Pfluke, Director of Admissions, Everest Institute, 1630 Portland Avenue, Rochester, NY 14621. *Phone:* 585-266-0430. *Toll-free phone:* 888-741-4270. *Fax:* 585-266-8243.

Website: http://www.everest.edu/campus/rochester/.

Fashion Institute of Technology
New York, New York

- **State and locally supported** comprehensive, founded 1944, part of State University of New York System
- **Urban** 5-acre campus with easy access to New York City
- **Coed, primarily women,** 9,566 undergraduate students, 76% full-time, 85% women, 15% men

Undergraduates 7,257 full-time, 2,309 part-time. 41% are from out of state; 9% Black or African American, non-Hispanic/Latino; 16% Hispanic/Latino; 10% Asian, non-Hispanic/Latino; 0.3% Native Hawaiian or other Pacific Islander, non-Hispanic/Latino; 0.1% American Indian or Alaska Native, non-Hispanic/Latino; 3% Two or more races, non-Hispanic/Latino; 2% Race/ethnicity unknown; 13% international; 10% transferred in; 22% live on campus. *Retention:* 88% of full-time freshmen returned.

Freshmen *Admission:* 4,567 applied, 2,044 admitted, 1,304 enrolled. *Average high school GPA:* 3.4.

Faculty *Total:* 943, 25% full-time. *Student/faculty ratio:* 17:1.

Majors Advertising; animation, interactive technology, video graphics and special effects; apparel and textile manufacturing; cinematography and film/video production; commercial and advertising art; commercial photography; entrepreneurial and small business related; fashion/apparel design; fashion merchandising; fashion modeling; fine and studio arts management; fine/studio arts; graphic design; illustration; industrial and product design; interior design; international marketing; marketing research; merchandising, sales, and marketing operations related (specialized); metal and jewelry arts; special products marketing.

Academics *Calendar:* semesters. *Degrees:* certificates, associate, bachelor's, and master's. *Special study options:* academic remediation for entering students, adult/continuing education programs, advanced placement credit, distance learning, English as a second language, honors programs, independent study, internships, part-time degree program, services for LD students, study abroad, summer session for credit.

Library Gladys Marcus Library.

Student Life *Housing Options:* coed, women-only, special housing for students with disabilities. Campus housing is university owned. Freshman applicants given priority for college housing. *Activities and Organizations:* drama/theater group, student-run newspaper, radio and television station, choral group, Asian Student Network, Fashion Show Club, Black Student Union, Phi Theta Kappa, Gospel Choir. *Campus security:* 24-hour emergency response devices and patrols, late-night transport/escort service, controlled dormitory access. *Student services:* health clinic, personal/psychological counseling.

Athletics Member NJCAA. *Intercollegiate sports:* cross-country running M/W, soccer W, swimming and diving M/W, table tennis M/W, tennis W, track and field M/W, volleyball W. *Intramural sports:* archery M(c)/W(c).

Standardized Tests *Recommended:* SAT or ACT (for admission).

Costs (2013–14) *Tuition:* state resident $4425 full-time, $184 per credit hour part-time; nonresident $16,370 full-time, $553 per credit hour part-time. Full-time tuition and fees vary according to degree level. Part-time tuition and fees vary according to degree level. *Required fees:* $680 full-time, $9 per credit hour part-time, $200 per term part-time. *Room and board:* $12,818. Room and board charges vary according to board plan and housing facility. *Payment* *plan:* installment. *Waivers:* senior citizens and employees or children of employees.

Financial Aid Of all full-time matriculated undergraduates who enrolled in 2012, 4,447 applied for aid, 3,644 were judged to have need, 1,312 had their need fully met. In 2012, 84 non-need-based awards were made. *Average percent of need met:* 70%. *Average financial aid package:* $11,605. *Average need-based loan:* $3470. *Average need-based gift aid:* $5551. *Average non-need-based aid:* $497. *Average indebtedness upon graduation:* $26,205.

Applying *Options:* electronic application. *Application fee:* $50. *Required:* essay or personal statement, high school transcript. *Required for some:* portfolio for art and design programs. *Application deadlines:* 1/1 (freshmen), 1/1 (transfers). *Notification:* 4/1 (freshmen), 4/1 (transfers).

Freshman Application Contact Ms. Laura Arbogast, Director of Admissions and Strategic Recruitment, Fashion Institute of Technology, Seventh Avenue at 27th Street, New York, NY 10001-5992. *E-mail:* fitinfo@fitnyc.edu. *Website:* http://www.fitnyc.edu/.

See display below and page 430 for the College Close-Up.

Finger Lakes Community College
Canandaigua, New York

- **State and locally supported** 2-year, founded 1965, part of State University of New York System
- **Small-town** 300-acre campus with easy access to Rochester
- **Coed,** 6,389 undergraduate students, 53% full-time, 58% women, 42% men

Undergraduates 3,404 full-time, 2,985 part-time. Students come from 14 states and territories; 2 other countries; 0.1% are from out of state; 7% Black or African American, non-Hispanic/Latino; 4% Hispanic/Latino; 0.5% Asian, non-Hispanic/Latino; 0.1% Native Hawaiian or other Pacific Islander, non-Hispanic/Latino; 0.5% American Indian or Alaska Native, non-Hispanic/Latino; 2% Two or more races, non-Hispanic/Latino; 6% Race/ethnicity unknown; 0.1% international; 5% transferred in.

Freshmen *Admission:* 4,369 admitted, 1,449 enrolled.

Faculty *Total:* 398, 29% full-time. *Student/faculty ratio:* 22:1.

Majors Accounting; administrative assistant and secretarial science; animation, interactive technology, video graphics and special effects; architectural engineering technology; biological and physical sciences; biology/biological sciences; biology/biotechnology laboratory technician; business administration and management; chemistry; commercial and advertising art; computer and information sciences; computer science; criminal justice/law enforcement administration; criminal justice/police science; culinary arts; data processing and data processing technology; digital communication and media/multimedia; drafting and design technology; dramatic/theater arts; early childhood education; e-commerce; emergency medical technology (EMT paramedic); engineering science; environmental studies; fine/studio arts; fishing and fisheries sciences and management; hotel/motel administration; humanities; human services; instrumentation technology; kindergarten/preschool education; legal assistant/paralegal; liberal arts and sciences/liberal studies; marketing/marketing management; mass communication/media; mathematics; mechanical engineering/mechanical technology; music; natural resources/conservation; natural resources law enforcement and protective services; natural resources management and policy; natural resources management and policy related; ornamental horticulture; physical education teaching and coaching; physics; political science and government; pre-engineering; psychology; recording arts technology; registered nursing/registered nurse; resort management; social sciences; sociology; sports studies; substance abuse/addiction counseling; tourism and travel services management; viticulture and enology.

Academics *Calendar:* semesters. *Degree:* certificates and associate. *Special study options:* academic remediation for entering students, accelerated degree program, advanced placement credit, distance learning, honors programs, internships, off-campus study, part-time degree program, services for LD students, study abroad, summer session for credit. *ROTC:* Air Force (c).

Library Charles Meder Library with 75,610 titles, 464 serial subscriptions, an OPAC.

Student Life *Housing Options:* Campus housing is provided by a third party. *Activities and Organizations:* drama/theater group, student-run radio station, choral group. *Campus security:* 24-hour emergency response devices and patrols, late-night transport/escort service. *Student services:* health clinic, personal/psychological counseling, legal services.

Athletics Member NJCAA. *Intercollegiate sports:* baseball M, basketball M/W, cross-country running M/W, lacrosse M, soccer M/W, softball W, track and field M/W, volleyball W. *Intramural sports:* basketball M/W, tennis M/W, volleyball M/W.

Financial Aid Of all full-time matriculated undergraduates who enrolled in 2011, 200 Federal Work-Study jobs (averaging $2200). 100 state and other part-time jobs (averaging $2200).

Applying *Options:* electronic application, early admission, deferred entrance. *Application fee:* $20. *Required:* high school transcript. *Application deadlines:* 8/22 (freshmen), 8/22 (transfers).

Freshman Application Contact Ms. Bonnie B. Ritts, Director of Admissions, Finger Lakes Community College, 3325 Marvin Sands Drive, Canandaigua,

NY 14424-8395. *Phone:* 585-785-1278. *Fax:* 585-785- 1734. *E-mail:* admissions@flcc.edu.
Website: http://www.flcc.edu/.

Fiorello H. LaGuardia Community College of the City University of New York

Long Island City, New York

- **State and locally supported** 2-year, founded 1970, part of City University of New York System
- **Urban** 10-acre campus with easy access to New York City
- **Coed,** 19,586 undergraduate students, 53% full-time, 58% women, 42% men

Undergraduates 10,455 full-time, 9,131 part-time. Students come from 15 states and territories; 160 other countries; 2% are from out of state; 21% Black or African American, non-Hispanic/Latino; 40% Hispanic/Latino; 17% Asian, non-Hispanic/Latino; 0.2% American Indian or Alaska Native, non-Hispanic/Latino; 9% international; 9% transferred in.

Freshmen *Admission:* 18,418 applied, 18,267 admitted, 3,043 enrolled.

Faculty *Total:* 1,135, 29% full-time, 27% with terminal degrees. *Student/faculty ratio:* 23:1.

Majors Accounting technology and bookkeeping; administrative assistant and secretarial science; adult development and aging; biology/biological sciences; business administration and management; civil engineering; commercial photography; computer and information sciences and support services related; computer installation and repair technology; computer programming; computer science; computer systems networking and telecommunications; criminal justice/safety; data entry/microcomputer applications; dietetic technology; digital arts; dramatic/theater arts; electrical and electronics engineering; emergency medical technology (EMT paramedic); English; environmental science; fine/studio arts; funeral service and mortuary science; industrial and product design; legal assistant/paralegal; liberal arts and sciences/liberal studies; licensed practical/vocational nurse training; mechanical engineering; medical radiologic technology; occupational therapist assistant; philosophy; physical therapy technology; psychiatric/mental health services technology; psychology; recording arts technology; registered nursing/registered nurse; restaurant/food services management; Spanish; speech communication and rhetoric; teacher assistant/aide; tourism and travel services management; veterinary/animal health technology; visual and performing arts.

Academics *Calendar:* enhanced semester. *Degree:* certificates and associate. *Special study options:* academic remediation for entering students, accelerated degree program, adult/continuing education programs, advanced placement credit, cooperative education, distance learning, double majors, English as a second language, honors programs, independent study, internships, off-campus study, part-time degree program, services for LD students, student-designed majors, study abroad, summer session for credit.

Library Fiorello H. LaGuardia Community College Library Media Resources Center plus 1 other with 384,946 titles, 532 serial subscriptions, 3,630 audiovisual materials, an OPAC, a Web page.

Student Life *Housing:* college housing not available. *Activities and Organizations:* drama/theater group, student-run newspaper, radio station, Bangladesh Student Association, Christian Club, Chinese Club, Web Radio, Black Student Union. *Campus security:* 24-hour emergency response devices and patrols, late-night transport/escort service. *Student services:* health clinic, personal/psychological counseling, women's center, legal services.

Athletics *Intercollegiate sports:* basketball M/W. *Intramural sports:* basketball M/W, bowling M/W, soccer M/W, softball M/W, swimming and diving M/W, table tennis M/W, volleyball M/W.

Costs (2014–15) *Tuition:* state resident $4200 full-time, $165 per credit part-time; nonresident $8400 full-time, $260 per credit part-time. *Required fees:* $366 full-time, $86 part-time.

Financial Aid Of all full-time matriculated undergraduates who enrolled in 2012, 7,961 applied for aid, 7,741 were judged to have need, 286 had their need fully met. 352 Federal Work-Study jobs (averaging $1175). *Average percent of need met:* 45%. *Average financial aid package:* $5523. *Average need-based gift aid:* $5818.

Applying *Options:* electronic application, early admission, deferred entrance. *Application fee:* $65. *Required:* high school transcript. *Application deadlines:* rolling (freshmen), rolling (transfers). *Notification:* continuous (freshmen), continuous (transfers).

Freshman Application Contact Ms. LaVora Desvigne, Director of Admissions, Fiorello H. LaGuardia Community College of the City University of New York, RM-147, 31-10 Thomson Avenue, Long Island City, NY 11101. *Phone:* 718-482-5114. *Fax:* 718-482-5112. *E-mail:* admissions@lagcc.cuny.edu.
Website: http://www.lagcc.cuny.edu/.

Fulton-Montgomery Community College

Johnstown, New York

Freshman Application Contact Fulton-Montgomery Community College, 2805 State Highway 67, Johnstown, NY 12095-3790. *Phone:* 518-762-4651 Ext. 8301.
Website: http://www.fmcc.suny.edu/.

Genesee Community College

Batavia, New York

- **State and locally supported** 2-year, founded 1966, part of State University of New York System
- **Small-town** 256-acre campus with easy access to Buffalo, Rochester
- **Endowment** $3.6 million
- **Coed,** 7,087 undergraduate students, 47% full-time, 64% women, 36% men

Undergraduates 3,326 full-time, 3,761 part-time. Students come from 26 states and territories; 15 other countries; 2% are from out of state; 9% Black or African American, non-Hispanic/Latino; 4% Hispanic/Latino; 0.5% Asian, non-Hispanic/Latino; 1% American Indian or Alaska Native, non-Hispanic/Latino; 1% Two or more races, non-Hispanic/Latino; 4% Race/ethnicity unknown; 3% international; 6% transferred in.

Freshmen *Admission:* 3,233 applied, 2,654 admitted, 1,153 enrolled.

Faculty *Total:* 349, 26% full-time, 6% with terminal degrees. *Student/faculty ratio:* 18:1.

Majors Accounting; administrative assistant and secretarial science; biology/biological sciences; biology/biotechnology laboratory technician; biotechnology; business administration and management; business administration, management and operations related; business, management, and marketing related; business operations support and secretarial services related; chemistry; civil drafting and CAD/CADD; clinical/medical laboratory technology; computer and information sciences related; computer graphics; computer installation and repair technology; computer programming related; computer science; computer software and media applications related; computer support specialist; computer systems networking and telecommunications; corrections and criminal justice related; criminal justice/law enforcement administration; criminal justice/police science; criminal justice/safety; criminology; digital arts; drafting and design technology; drafting/design engineering technologies related; dramatic/theater arts; dramatic/theater arts and stagecraft related; e-commerce; education; education (multiple levels); education related; elementary education; engineering; engineering science; entrepreneurship; environmental studies; fashion/apparel design; fashion merchandising; fine/studio arts; foreign languages related; general studies; gerontology; graphic design; health and physical education/fitness; health and physical education related; health professions related; hospitality administration; hotel/motel administration; humanities; human services; information science/studies; kindergarten/preschool education; legal assistant/paralegal; liberal arts and sciences and humanities related; liberal arts and sciences/liberal studies; marketing/marketing management; mass communication/media; mathematics; mathematics related; medical administrative assistant and medical secretary; network and system administration; nursing practice; parks, recreation, leisure, and fitness studies related; physical education teaching and coaching; physical therapy; physical therapy technology; polysomnography; psychology; psychology related; radio and television; radio and television broadcasting technology; radio, television, and digital communication related; registered nursing, nursing administration, nursing research and clinical nursing related; registered nursing/registered nurse; respiratory care therapy; social sciences; social sciences related; social work; social work related; sports studies; substance abuse/addiction counseling; teacher assistant/aide; theater design and technology; theater/theater arts management; tourism and travel services management; tourism promotion; veterinary/animal health technology; web page, digital/multimedia and information resources design.

Academics *Calendar:* semesters. *Degree:* certificates and associate. *Special study options:* academic remediation for entering students, adult/continuing education programs, advanced placement credit, cooperative education, distance learning, double majors, English as a second language, honors programs, independent study, internships, part-time degree program, services for LD students, study abroad, summer session for credit.

Library Alfred C. OConnell Library with 82,603 titles, 44,519 serial subscriptions, 6,756 audiovisual materials, an OPAC, a Web page.

Student Life *Housing Options:* special housing for students with disabilities. Campus housing is university owned. *Activities and Organizations:* drama/theater group, student-run newspaper, radio station, choral group, Cougarettes Dance Team, Honor Society, Multi Cultural Communications Club, Christian Students United, Theater Group. *Campus security:* 24-hour emergency response devices and patrols, student patrols, late-night transport/escort service, controlled dormitory access. *Student services:* health clinic, personal/psychological counseling.

Athletics Member NJCAA. *Intercollegiate sports:* baseball M(s), basketball M(s)/W(s), cheerleading M/W, golf M/W, lacrosse M(s)/W, soccer M/W, softball W, swimming and diving M/W, volleyball W(s). *Intramural sports:* badminton M/W, basketball M/W, soccer M/W, tennis M/W, track and field M/W, volleyball M/W, water polo M/W.

Standardized Tests *Recommended:* ACT (for admission).

Costs (2014–15) *Tuition:* state resident $150 per credit hour part-time; nonresident $175 per credit hour part-time. Full-time tuition and fees vary according to course load. Part-time tuition and fees vary according to course load. *Required fees:* $2 per credit hour part-time, $42 per term part-time. *Room and board:* Room and board charges vary according to board plan and housing facility. *Payment plan:* installment. *Waivers:* senior citizens and employees or children of employees.

Financial Aid Of all full-time matriculated undergraduates who enrolled in 2012, 2,812 applied for aid, 2,615 were judged to have need, 1,015 had their need fully met. 166 Federal Work-Study jobs (averaging $948). 88 state and other part-time jobs (averaging $1804). *Average percent of need met:* 77%. *Average financial aid package:* $4545. *Average need-based loan:* $3445. *Average need-based gift aid:* $3125. *Average indebtedness upon graduation:* $8978.

Applying *Options:* electronic application. *Required:* high school transcript. *Required for some:* 1 letter of recommendation. *Application deadlines:* rolling (freshmen), rolling (out-of-state freshmen), rolling (transfers). *Notification:* continuous (freshmen), continuous (out-of-state freshmen), continuous (transfers).

Freshman Application Contact Mrs. Tanya Lane-Martin, Director of Admissions, Genesee Community College, Batavia, NY 14020. *Phone:* 585-343-0055 Ext. 6413. *Toll-free phone:* 800-CALL GCC. *Fax:* 585-345-6892. *E-mail:* tmlanemartin@genesee.edu.
Website: http://www.genesee.edu/.

Helene Fuld College of Nursing of North General Hospital
New York, New York

Freshman Application Contact Helene Fuld College of Nursing of North General Hospital, 24 East 120th Street, New York, NY 10035. *Phone:* 212-616-7271.
Website: http://www.helenefuld.edu/.

Herkimer County Community College
Herkimer, New York

- **State and locally supported** 2-year, founded 1966, part of State University of New York System
- **Small-town** 500-acre campus with easy access to Syracuse
- **Endowment** $2.8 million
- **Coed,** 3,223 undergraduate students, 65% full-time, 62% women, 38% men

Undergraduates 2,089 full-time, 1,134 part-time. Students come from 13 other countries; 3% are from out of state; 12% Black or African American, non-Hispanic/Latino; 5% Hispanic/Latino; 0.7% Asian, non-Hispanic/Latino; 0.7% American Indian or Alaska Native, non-Hispanic/Latino; 1% Two or more races, non-Hispanic/Latino; 11% Race/ethnicity unknown; 3% international; 6% transferred in; 19% live on campus.

Freshmen *Admission:* 722 enrolled. *Average high school GPA:* 2.52.

Faculty *Total:* 172, 38% full-time. *Student/faculty ratio:* 19:1.

Majors Accounting technology and bookkeeping; art; broadcast journalism; business administration and management; child-care and support services management; community organization and advocacy; computer and information sciences; computer and information sciences and support services related; corrections; criminal justice/law enforcement administration; emergency medical technology (EMT paramedic); entrepreneurship; fashion merchandising; forensic science and technology; general studies; health and physical education related; health professions related; humanities; human resources management; international business/trade/commerce; legal administrative assistant/secretary; legal assistant/paralegal; liberal arts and sciences/liberal studies; merchandising, sales, and marketing operations related (general); parks, recreation and leisure facilities management; photographic and film/video technology; physical therapy; tourism and travel services marketing; visual and performing arts.

Academics *Calendar:* semesters. *Degree:* certificates and associate. *Special study options:* academic remediation for entering students, adult/continuing education programs, advanced placement credit, distance learning, English as a second language, honors programs, independent study, internships, part-time degree program, services for LD students, summer session for credit. *ROTC:* Army (c).

Library Herkimer County Community College Library with 70,000 titles, 220 serial subscriptions, an OPAC.

Student Life *Housing Options:* coed. *Activities and Organizations:* drama/theater group, choral group, Phi Theta Kappa, Campus Christian Fellowship, International Students Association, Physical Therapy Assistants Club, Criminal Justice. *Campus security:* 24-hour emergency response devices and patrols. *Student services:* personal/psychological counseling.

Athletics Member NJCAA. *Intercollegiate sports:* baseball M, basketball M/W, cross-country running M/W, field hockey W, lacrosse M/W, soccer M/W, softball W, swimming and diving M/W, tennis M/W, track and field M/W, volleyball W. *Intramural sports:* badminton M/W, baseball M, basketball M/W, bowling M/W, lacrosse M/W, soccer M/W, softball M/W, swimming and diving M/W, tennis M/W, volleyball M/W.

Costs (2014–15) *Tuition:* state resident $3840 full-time, $129 per credit part-time; nonresident $5900 full-time, $233 per credit part-time. *Required fees:* $620 full-time. *Room and board:* $8400. Room and board charges vary according to board plan and housing facility. *Payment plan:* installment. *Waivers:* employees or children of employees.

Financial Aid Of all full-time matriculated undergraduates who enrolled in 2012, 150 Federal Work-Study jobs (averaging $700).

Applying *Required:* high school transcript.

Freshman Application Contact Herkimer County Community College, 100 Reservoir Road, Herkimer, NY 13350. *Phone:* 315-866-0300 Ext. 8278. *Toll-free phone:* 888-464-4222 Ext. 8278.
Website: http://www.herkimer.edu/.

Hudson Valley Community College
Troy, New York

Freshman Application Contact Ms. Marie Claire Bauer, Director of Admissions, Hudson Valley Community College, 80 Vandenburgh Avenue, Troy, NY 12180-6096. *Phone:* 518-629-7309. *Toll-free phone:* 877-325-HVCC.
Website: http://www.hvcc.edu/.

Institute of Design and Construction
Brooklyn, New York

- **Independent** 2-year, founded 1947
- **Urban** campus
- **Coed,** 103 undergraduate students, 42% full-time, 15% women, 85% men

Undergraduates 43 full-time, 60 part-time. Students come from 3 states and territories; 2 other countries; 42% Black or African American, non-Hispanic/Latino; 25% Hispanic/Latino; 9% Asian, non-Hispanic/Latino; 2% international; 10% transferred in. *Retention:* 47% of full-time freshmen returned.

Freshmen *Admission:* 14 applied, 14 admitted, 10 enrolled.

Faculty *Total:* 21, 62% with terminal degrees. *Student/faculty ratio:* 9:1.

Majors Architectural engineering technology; construction engineering technology; drafting and design technology; interior architecture.

Academics *Calendar:* semesters. *Degree:* associate. *Special study options:* academic remediation for entering students, adult/continuing education programs, advanced placement credit, cooperative education, part-time degree program, services for LD students, summer session for credit.

Library Vito P. Battista Library plus 1 other with 1,682 titles, 22 serial subscriptions, 12 audiovisual materials, an OPAC.

Student Life *Housing:* college housing not available. *Campus security:* 24-hour emergency response devices. *Student services:* personal/psychological counseling.

Costs (2014–15) *One-time required fee:* $30. *Tuition:* $8160 full-time, $340 per credit part-time. Full-time tuition and fees vary according to course load. Part-time tuition and fees vary according to course load. *Required fees:* $280 full-time, $140 per term part-time. *Payment plan:* installment. *Waivers:* employees or children of employees.

Applying *Options:* electronic application, deferred entrance. *Application fee:* $30. *Required:* high school transcript. *Recommended:* interview. *Application deadlines:* rolling (freshmen), rolling (transfers). *Notification:* continuous until 9/6 (freshmen), 9/6 (transfers).

Freshman Application Contact Mr. Marquise Martin, Director of Admissions, Institute of Design and Construction, 141 Willoughby Street, Brooklyn, NV 11201. *Phone:* 718-855-3661. *Fax:* 718-852-5889. *E-mail:* mmartin@idc.edu.
Website: http://www.idc.edu/.

Island Drafting and Technical Institute
Amityville, New York

- **Proprietary** 2-year, founded 1957
- **Suburban** campus with easy access to New York City
- **Coed, primarily men,** 116 undergraduate students, 100% full-time, 14% women, 86% men

Undergraduates 116 full-time. Students come from 1 other state; 18% Black or African American, non-Hispanic/Latino; 21% Hispanic/Latino; 0.9% Asian, non-Hispanic/Latino; 0.9% Two or more races, non-Hispanic/Latino. *Retention:* 80% of full-time freshmen returned.

Freshmen *Admission:* 53 applied, 40 admitted, 45 enrolled. *Average high school GPA:* 2.5.

Faculty *Total:* 11, 45% full-time. *Student/faculty ratio:* 15:1.

Majors Architectural drafting and CAD/CADD; computer and information sciences and support services related; computer and information systems security; computer systems networking and telecommunications; computer technology/computer systems technology; electrical, electronic and communications engineering technology; mechanical drafting and CAD/CADD; network and system administration.

Academics *Calendar:* semesters. *Degree:* certificates, diplomas, and associate. *Special study options:* accelerated degree program, adult/continuing education programs, summer session for credit.

Student Life *Housing:* college housing not available.

Costs (2014–15) *Tuition:* $15,300 full-time. No tuition increase for student's term of enrollment. *Required fees:* $350 full-time. *Payment plan:* installment.

Applying *Options:* early admission. *Application fee:* $25. *Required:* interview. *Recommended:* high school transcript. *Notification:* continuous (freshmen).

Freshman Application Contact Larry Basile, Island Drafting and Technical Institute, Island Drafting and Technical Institute, 128 Broadway, Amityville, NY 11701. *Phone:* 631-691-8733 Ext. 114. *Fax:* 631-691-8738. *E-mail:* info@idti.edu.

Website: http://www.idti.edu/.

ITT Technical Institute
Albany, New York

- **Proprietary** 2-year, founded 1998, part of ITT Educational Services, Inc.
- **Coed**

Majors Computer systems networking and telecommunications; design and visual communications; drafting and design technology; electrical, electronic and communications engineering technology; network and system administration.

Academics *Calendar:* quarters. *Degree:* associate.

Student Life *Housing:* college housing not available.

Freshman Application Contact Director of Recruitment, ITT Technical Institute, 13 Airline Drive, Albany, NY 12205. *Phone:* 518-452-9300. *Toll-free phone:* 800-489-1191.

Website: http://www.itt-tech.edu/.

ITT Technical Institute
Getzville, New York

- **Proprietary** 2-year, part of ITT Educational Services, Inc.
- **Coed**

Majors Computer engineering technology; computer software and media applications related; computer systems networking and telecommunications; design and visual communications; drafting and design technology; electrical, electronic and communications engineering technology; forensic science and technology; graphic communications; network and system administration.

Academics *Degree:* associate.

Student Life *Housing:* college housing not available.

Freshman Application Contact Director of Recruitment, ITT Technical Institute, 2295 Millersport Highway, Getzville, NY 14068. *Phone:* 716-689-2200. *Toll-free phone:* 800-469-7593.

Website: http://www.itt-tech.edu/.

ITT Technical Institute
Liverpool, New York

- **Proprietary** 2-year, founded 1998, part of ITT Educational Services, Inc.
- **Coed**

Majors Computer systems networking and telecommunications; design and visual communications; drafting and design technology; electrical, electronic and communications engineering technology; graphic communications; network and system administration.

Academics *Calendar:* semesters. *Degree:* associate.

Student Life *Housing:* college housing not available.

Freshman Application Contact Director of Recruitment, ITT Technical Institute, 235 Greenfield Parkway, Liverpool, NY 13088. *Phone:* 315-461-8000. *Toll-free phone:* 877-488-0011.

Website: http://www.itt-tech.edu/.

Jamestown Business College
Jamestown, New York

- **Proprietary** primarily 2-year, founded 1886
- **Small-town** 1-acre campus
- **Coed,** 294 undergraduate students, 98% full-time, 73% women, 27% men

Undergraduates 288 full-time, 6 part-time. Students come from 2 states and territories; 11% are from out of state; 2% Black or African American, non-Hispanic/Latino; 3% Hispanic/Latino; 0.7% Asian, non-Hispanic/Latino; 0.3% Native Hawaiian or other Pacific Islander, non-Hispanic/Latino; 2% American Indian or Alaska Native, non-Hispanic/Latino; 2% Two or more races, non-Hispanic/Latino; 2% Race/ethnicity unknown; 10% transferred in.

Freshmen *Admission:* 98 applied, 91 admitted, 65 enrolled.

Faculty *Total:* 25, 24% full-time, 8% with terminal degrees. *Student/faculty ratio:* 23:1.

Majors Administrative assistant and secretarial science; business administration and management; medical/clinical assistant; office management.

Academics *Calendar:* quarters. *Degrees:* certificates, associate, and bachelor's. *Special study options:* advanced placement credit, double majors, off-campus study, part-time degree program, summer session for credit.

Library James Prendergast Library with 279,270 titles, 372 serial subscriptions, an OPAC, a Web page.

Student Life *Housing:* college housing not available. *Campus security:* 24-hour emergency response devices.

Athletics *Intramural sports:* basketball M(c)/W(c), racquetball M(c)/W(c), softball M(c)/W(c), swimming and diving M(c)/W(c), table tennis M(c)/W(c), tennis M(c)/W(c), volleyball M(c)/W(c), weight lifting M(c)/W(c).

Costs (2013–14) *One-time required fee:* $25. *Tuition:* $10,800 full-time, $300 per credit hour part-time. Full-time tuition and fees vary according to course load. Part-time tuition and fees vary according to course load. *Required fees:* $900 full-time, $150 per term part-time. *Waivers:* employees or children of employees.

Financial Aid Of all full-time matriculated undergraduates who enrolled in 2011, 311 applied for aid, 311 were judged to have need. *Average need-based loan:* $6049. *Average need-based gift aid:* $8254.

Applying *Application fee:* $25. *Required:* essay or personal statement, high school transcript, interview. *Application deadlines:* rolling (freshmen), rolling (transfers).

Freshman Application Contact Mrs. Brenda Salemme, Director of Admissions and Placement, Jamestown Business College, 7 Fairmount Avenue, Box 429, Jamestown, NY 14702-0429. *Phone:* 716-664-5100. *Fax:* 716-664-3144. *E-mail:* brendasalemme@jamestownbusinesscollege.edu. *Website:* http://www.jamestownbusinesscollege.edu/.

Jamestown Community College
Jamestown, New York

- **State and locally supported** 2-year, founded 1950, part of State University of New York System
- **Small-town** 107-acre campus
- **Endowment** $11.4 million
- **Coed,** 3,600 undergraduate students, 74% full-time, 59% women, 41% men

Undergraduates 2,656 full-time, 944 part-time. Students come from 13 states and territories; 13 other countries; 9% are from out of state; 4% Black or African American, non-Hispanic/Latino; 7% Hispanic/Latino; 0.4% Asian, non-Hispanic/Latino; 0.1% Native Hawaiian or other Pacific Islander, non-Hispanic/Latino; 1% American Indian or Alaska Native, non-Hispanic/Latino; 3% Two or more races, non-Hispanic/Latino; 1% Race/ethnicity unknown; 0.7% international; 7% transferred in; 9% live on campus.

Freshmen *Admission:* 2,036 applied, 1,990 admitted, 1,039 enrolled. *Average high school GPA:* 3.22.

Faculty *Total:* 382, 23% full-time. *Student/faculty ratio:* 17:1.

Majors Accounting technology and bookkeeping; administrative assistant and secretarial science; avionics maintenance technology; biology/biological sciences; biology/biotechnology laboratory technician; business administration and management; commercial and advertising art; computer programming; criminal justice/police science; data processing and data processing technology; early childhood education; electrical, electronic and communications engineering technology; elementary education; engineering; fine/studio arts; fire prevention and safety technology; health information/medical records technology; humanities; human services; information technology; kindergarten/preschool education; liberal arts and sciences and humanities related; liberal arts and sciences/liberal studies; mechanical engineering/mechanical technology; music; occupational therapist assistant; physical education teaching and coaching; registered nursing/registered nurse; speech communication and rhetoric; welding technology.

Academics *Calendar:* semesters. *Degree:* certificates and associate. *Special study options:* academic remediation for entering students, adult/continuing education programs, advanced placement credit, distance learning, honors programs, independent study, internships, off-campus study, part-time degree program, services for LD students, study abroad, summer session for credit.

Library Hultquist Library plus 1 other with 89,159 titles, 345 serial subscriptions, 7,773 audiovisual materials, an OPAC, a Web page.

Student Life *Housing Options:* coed. Campus housing is university owned. *Activities and Organizations:* drama/theater group, student-run radio station, choral group, Nursing Club, InterVarsity Christian Fellowship, Anime Club, Earth Awareness, Campus Activities Board. *Campus security:* 24-hour emergency response devices, controlled dormitory access. *Student services:* health clinic, personal/psychological counseling.

Athletics Member NJCAA. *Intercollegiate sports:* baseball M, basketball M/W, golf M/W, soccer M/W, softball W, swimming and diving M/W, volleyball W, wrestling M. *Intramural sports:* basketball M/W, bowling M/W, cross-country running M/W, softball M/W, volleyball M/W.

Costs (2013–14) *Tuition:* state resident $4220 full-time, $176 per credit hour part-time; nonresident $8440 full-time, $352 per credit hour part-time. Full-time tuition and fees vary according to course load and program. Part-time tuition and fees vary according to course load and program. *Required fees:* $503 full-time. *Room and board:* $10,030; room only: $6930. Room and board charges vary according to board plan. *Payment plan:* installment. *Waivers:* employees or children of employees.

Financial Aid Of all full-time matriculated undergraduates who enrolled in 2012, 85 Federal Work-Study jobs (averaging $1500). 85 state and other part-time jobs (averaging $1300).

Applying *Options:* electronic application, deferred entrance. *Required:* high school transcript. *Required for some:* standardized test scores used for placement, GEDs accepted. TOEFL (or equivalent) for international students. *Application deadlines:* rolling (freshmen), rolling (out-of-state freshmen), rolling (transfers). *Notification:* continuous (freshmen), continuous (out-of-state freshmen), continuous (transfers).

Freshman Application Contact Ms. Wendy Present, Director of Admissions and Recruitment, Jamestown Community College, 525 Falconer Street, PO Box 20, Jamestown, NY 14702-0020. *Phone:* 716-338-1001. *Toll-free phone:* 800-388-8557. *Fax:* 716-338-1450. *E-mail:* admissions@mail.sunyjcc.edu. *Website:* http://www.sunyjcc.edu/.

Jefferson Community College
Watertown, New York

- **State and locally supported** 2-year, founded 1961, part of State University of New York System
- **Small-town** 90-acre campus with easy access to Syracuse
- **Coed,** 4,127 undergraduate students, 55% full-time, 61% women, 39% men

Undergraduates 2,250 full-time, 1,877 part-time. 7% Black or African American, non-Hispanic/Latino; 2% Hispanic/Latino; 1% Asian, non-Hispanic/Latino; 0.5% Native Hawaiian or other Pacific Islander, non-Hispanic/Latino; 1% American Indian or Alaska Native, non-Hispanic/Latino; 8% Two or more races, non-Hispanic/Latino; 3% Race/ethnicity unknown.

Freshmen *Admission:* 832 enrolled.

Faculty *Total:* 220, 36% full-time. *Student/faculty ratio:* 19:1.

Majors Accounting; accounting technology and bookkeeping; administrative assistant and secretarial science; animal/livestock husbandry and production; business administration and management; child-care and support services management; child development; community organization and advocacy; computer and information sciences; computer and information sciences and support services related; computer/information technology services administration related; computer science; computer technology/computer systems technology; criminal justice/law enforcement administration; early childhood education; emergency medical technology (EMT paramedic); engineering; engineering science; fire prevention and safety technology; fire services administration; forest technology; hospitality administration; humanities; human services; information science/studies; legal assistant/paralegal; liberal arts and sciences/liberal studies; mathematics; mechanical engineering technologies related; medical administrative assistant and medical secretary; office management; office occupations and clerical services; registered nursing/registered nurse; sport and fitness administration/management; teacher assistant/aide; tourism promotion.

Academics *Calendar:* semesters. *Degree:* certificates and associate. *Special study options:* academic remediation for entering students, advanced placement credit, cooperative education, distance learning, double majors, honors programs, independent study, internships, part-time degree program, services for LD students, student-designed majors, summer session for credit.

Library Melvil Dewey Library with 180,832 titles, 134 serial subscriptions, 5,736 audiovisual materials, an OPAC, a Web page.

Student Life *Housing:* college housing not available. *Activities and Organizations:* student-run newspaper. *Campus security:* 24-hour emergency

response devices and patrols. *Student services:* health clinic, personal/psychological counseling.

Athletics Member NJCAA. *Intercollegiate sports:* baseball M, basketball M/W, lacrosse M/W, soccer M/W, softball W, volleyball W.

Standardized Tests *Recommended:* SAT or ACT (for admission).

Costs (2013–14) *Tuition:* state resident $3864 full-time, $161 per credit hour part-time; nonresident $5832 full-time, $243 per credit hour part-time. Full-time tuition and fees vary according to course load, location, and program. Part-time tuition and fees vary according to course load, location, and program. *Required fees:* $533 full-time. *Payment plan:* installment. *Waivers:* senior citizens and employees or children of employees.

Financial Aid Of all full-time matriculated undergraduates who enrolled in 2009, 1,748 applied for aid. 98 Federal Work-Study jobs (averaging $1093).

Applying *Options:* electronic application, early admission, deferred entrance. *Required:* high school transcript. *Required for some:* interview. *Application deadlines:* 9/6 (freshmen), rolling (transfers). *Notification:* continuous (freshmen), continuous (transfers).

Freshman Application Contact Ms. Rosanne N. Weir, Director of Admissions, Jefferson Community College, 1220 Coffeen Street, Watertown, NY 13601. *Phone:* 315-786-2277. *Toll-free phone:* 888-435-6522. *Fax:* 315-786-2459. *E-mail:* admissions@sunyjefferson.edu. *Website:* http://www.sunyjefferson.edu/.

Kingsborough Community College of the City University of New York
Brooklyn, New York

- **State and locally supported** 2-year, founded 1963, part of City University of New York System
- **Urban** 72-acre campus with easy access to New York City
- **Coed,** 18,794 undergraduate students, 57% full-time, 57% women, 43% men

Undergraduates 10,735 full-time, 8,059 part-time. Students come from 10 states and territories; 136 other countries; 1% are from out of state; 26% Black or African American, non-Hispanic/Latino; 18% Hispanic/Latino; 13% Asian, non-Hispanic/Latino; 0.5% Native Hawaiian or other Pacific Islander, non-Hispanic/Latino; 0.7% American Indian or Alaska Native, non-Hispanic/Latino; 13% Race/ethnicity unknown; 3% international; 9% transferred in. *Retention:* 67% of full-time freshmen returned.

Freshmen *Admission:* 2,651 enrolled. *Average high school GPA:* 2.7.

Majors Accounting; administrative assistant and secretarial science; art; biology/biological sciences; broadcast journalism; business administration and management; chemistry; commercial and advertising art; community health services counseling; computer and information sciences; computer science; cooking and related culinary arts; criminal justice/law enforcement administration; data processing and data processing technology; design and applied arts related; dramatic/theater arts; early childhood education; education; elementary education; engineering science; fashion merchandising; health and physical education related; human services; journalism; labor and industrial relations; liberal arts and sciences/liberal studies; marine maintenance and ship repair technology; marketing/marketing management; mathematics; mental health counseling; music; parks, recreation and leisure; physical therapy; physical therapy technology; physics; psychiatric/mental health services technology; registered nursing/registered nurse; sport and fitness administration/management; teacher assistant/aide; tourism and travel services management.

Academics *Calendar:* semesters. *Degree:* associate. *Special study options:* academic remediation for entering students, adult/continuing education programs, advanced placement credit, distance learning, English as a second language, honors programs, independent study, internships, off-campus study, part-time degree program, services for LD students, summer session for credit.

Library Robert J. Kibbee Library with 198,343 titles, 335 serial subscriptions, 2,145 audiovisual materials, an OPAC.

Student Life *Housing:* college housing not available. *Activities and Organizations:* drama/theater group, student-run newspaper, radio station, choral group, Peer Advisors, Caribbean Club, DECA. *Campus security:* 24-hour emergency response devices and patrols. *Student services:* health clinic, personal/psychological counseling, women's center.

Athletics Member NJCAA. *Intercollegiate sports:* baseball M, basketball M/W, soccer M, softball W, tennis M/W, track and field M/W, volleyball W. *Intramural sports:* baseball M, basketball M/W, soccer M, softball W, tennis M/W, track and field M/W, volleyball W.

Costs (2014–15) *Tuition:* state resident $4850 full-time, $195 per credit part-time; nonresident $9000 full-time, $300 per credit part-time. *Required fees:* $350 full-time, $92 per term part-time. *Payment plan:* installment. *Waivers:* senior citizens.

Applying *Application fee:* $65. *Required:* high school transcript. *Application deadlines:* 8/15 (freshmen), rolling (transfers).

Freshman Application Contact Mr. Robert Ingenito, Director of Admissions Information Center, Kingsborough Community College of the City University of New York, 2001 Oriental Boulevard, Brooklyn, NY 11235. *Phone:* 718-368-4600. *Fax:* 718-368-5356. *E-mail:* info@kbcc.cuny.edu. *Website:* http://www.kbcc.cuny.edu/.

Long Island Business Institute
Flushing, New York

- **Proprietary** 2-year, founded 1968
- **Urban** campus with easy access to New York City
- **Coed, primarily women,** 443 undergraduate students, 74% full-time, 74% women, 26% men

Undergraduates 330 full-time, 113 part-time. Students come from 2 states and territories; 28 other countries; 1% are from out of state; 15% Black or African American, non-Hispanic/Latino; 22% Hispanic/Latino; 38% Asian, non-Hispanic/Latino; 0.2% Two or more races, non-Hispanic/Latino; 0.2% Race/ethnicity unknown; 5% international; 5% transferred in.

Freshmen *Admission:* 100 applied, 89 admitted, 86 enrolled.

Faculty *Total:* 95, 18% full-time, 2% with terminal degrees. *Student/faculty ratio:* 10:1.

Majors Accounting; business administration and management; business, management, and marketing related; court reporting; homeland security; hospitality administration related; medical office management.

Academics *Calendar:* semesters. *Degrees:* certificates and associate (information provided for Commack and Flushing campuses). *Special study options:* academic remediation for entering students, adult/continuing education programs, advanced placement credit, cooperative education, English as a second language, honors programs, independent study, part-time degree program, summer session for credit.

Library Flushing Main Campus Library, Commack Campus Library with 7,314 titles, 77 serial subscriptions, 1,209 audiovisual materials, an OPAC, a Web page.

Student Life *Housing:* college housing not available. *Activities and Organizations:* Small Business Club, Web Design Club, Investment Club, Court Reporting Alumni Association. *Campus security:* 24-hour emergency response devices.

Standardized Tests *Required:* COMPASS, CELSA (for admission).

Costs (2014–15) *Tuition:* $13,299 full-time, $375 per credit part-time. *Required fees:* $1350 full-time, $450 per term part-time. *Payment plans:* installment, deferred payment.

Applying *Required:* essay or personal statement, high school transcript, interview. *Application deadlines:* rolling (freshmen), rolling (transfers).

Freshman Application Contact Mr. Sam Wanigasinghe, Associate Director of Admissions, Long Island Business Institute, 136-18 39th Avenue, Flushing, NY 11354. *Phone:* 718-939-5100. *Fax:* 718-939-9235. *E-mail:* samw@libi.edu.

Website: http://www.libi.edu/.

Memorial Hospital School of Nursing
Albany, New York

Freshman Application Contact Admissions Office, Memorial Hospital School of Nursing, 600 Northern Boulevard, Albany, NY 12204.

Website: http://www.nehealth.com/son/.

Mildred Elley–New York City
New York, New York

Admissions Office Contact Mildred Elley–New York City, 25 Broadway, 16th Floor, New York, NY 10004-1010.

Website: http://www.mildred-elley.edu/.

Mildred Elley School
Albany, New York

Director of Admissions Mr. Michael Cahalan, Enrollment Manager, Mildred Elley School, 855 Central Avenue, Albany, NY 12206. *Phone:* 518-786-3171 Ext. 227. *Toll-free phone:* 800-622-6327.

Website: http://www.mildred-elley.edu/.

Mohawk Valley Community College
Utica, New York

- **State and locally supported** 2-year, founded 1946, part of State University of New York System
- **Suburban** 80-acre campus
- **Endowment** $4.3 million
- **Coed,** 7,419 undergraduate students, 62% full-time, 53% women, 47% men

Undergraduates 4,616 full-time, 2,803 part-time. Students come from 17 states and territories; 20 other countries; 0.3% are from out of state; 8% Black or African American, non-Hispanic/Latino; 7% Hispanic/Latino; 4% Asian, non-Hispanic/Latino; 0.1% Native Hawaiian or other Pacific Islander, non-Hispanic/Latino; 0.7% American Indian or Alaska Native, non-Hispanic/Latino; 2% Two or more races, non-Hispanic/Latino; 0.1% Race/ethnicity unknown; 1% international; 5% transferred in; 7% live on campus.

Freshmen *Admission:* 3,456 applied, 3,452 admitted, 1,566 enrolled. *Average high school GPA:* 2.75.

Faculty *Total:* 475, 30% full-time, 11% with terminal degrees. *Student/faculty ratio:* 22:1.

Majors Accounting technology and bookkeeping; administrative assistant and secretarial science; advertising; airframe mechanics and aircraft maintenance technology; art; banking and financial support services; building/property maintenance; business administration and management; CAD/CADD drafting/design technology; chemical technology; civil engineering technology; commercial and advertising art; commercial photography; communications systems installation and repair technology; computer and information sciences; computer and information sciences and support services related; computer and information systems security; computer programming; criminal justice/law enforcement administration; design and applied arts related; dietetic technology; electrical and electronic engineering technologies related; electrical, electronic and communications engineering technology; electrical/electronics maintenance and repair technology related; emergency care attendant (EMT ambulance); engineering; engineering-related technologies; fire services administration; general studies; heating, air conditioning, ventilation and refrigeration maintenance technology; hotel/motel administration; humanities; human services; liberal arts and sciences and humanities related; manufacturing engineering technology; mechanical engineering/mechanical technology; mechanical engineering technologies related; medical/clinical assistant; medical radiologic technology; parks, recreation and leisure facilities management; registered nursing/registered nurse; respiratory care therapy; restaurant, culinary, and catering management; sign language interpretation and translation; substance abuse/addiction counseling; surveying technology; web page, digital/multimedia and information resources design; welding technology.

Academics *Calendar:* semesters. *Degree:* certificates and associate. *Special study options:* academic remediation for entering students, advanced placement credit, distance learning, double majors, English as a second language, honors programs, independent study, internships, off-campus study, part-time degree program, services for LD students, student-designed majors, summer session for credit. *ROTC:* Army (c), Air Force (c).

Library Mohawk Valley Community College Library plus 1 other with 127,754 titles, 71,110 serial subscriptions, 7,036 audiovisual materials, an OPAC, a Web page.

Student Life *Housing Options:* coed, men-only, women-only, special housing for students with disabilities. Campus housing is provided by a third party. Freshman applicants given priority for college housing. *Activities and Organizations:* drama/theater group, student-run newspaper, Student Congress, Student Nurses Organization (SNO), Photography Club, Recreation Club, Phi Theta Kappa. *Campus security:* 24-hour emergency response devices and patrols, late-night transport/escort service, controlled dormitory access. *Student services:* health clinic, personal/psychological counseling.

Athletics Member NJCAA. *Intercollegiate sports:* baseball M, basketball M/W, bowling M/W, cross-country running M/W, golf M/W, ice hockey M, lacrosse M/W, soccer M/W, softball W, tennis M/W, track and field M/W, volleyball W. *Intramural sports:* badminton M/W, basketball M/W, soccer M/W, tennis M/W, volleyball M/W.

Costs (2013–14) *Tuition:* state resident $3710 full-time, $150 per credit hour part-time; nonresident $7420 full-time, $300 per credit hour part-time. *Required fees:* $578 full-time, $9 per credit hour part-time, $52 per term part-time. *Room and board:* $9430; room only: $5680. Room and board charges vary according to board plan. *Payment plans:* installment, deferred payment. *Waivers:* senior citizens and employees or children of employees.

Financial Aid Of all full-time matriculated undergraduates who enrolled in 2012, 229 Federal Work-Study jobs (averaging $1750).

Applying *Options:* electronic application, deferred entrance. *Required for some:* high school transcript. *Recommended:* interview. *Application deadlines:* rolling (freshmen), rolling (out-of-state freshmen), rolling (transfers). *Notification:* continuous (freshmen), continuous (out-of-state freshmen), continuous (transfers).

Freshman Application Contact Ms. Michelle Collea, Data Processing Clerk, Admissions, Mohawk Valley Community College, Utica, NY 13501. *Phone:* 315-792-5640. *Toll-free phone:* 800-SEE-MVCC. *Fax:* 315-792-5527. *E-mail:* mcollea@mvcc.edu.

Website: http://www.mvcc.edu/.

Monroe Community College

Rochester, New York

- **State and locally supported** 2-year, founded 1961, part of State University of New York System
- **Suburban** 314-acre campus with easy access to Buffalo
- **Coed,** 16,458 undergraduate students, 62% full-time, 54% women, 46% men

Undergraduates 10,260 full-time, 6,198 part-time. 19% Black or African American, non-Hispanic/Latino; 8% Hispanic/Latino; 4% Asian, non-Hispanic/Latino; 0.1% Native Hawaiian or other Pacific Islander, non-Hispanic/Latino; 0.3% American Indian or Alaska Native, non-Hispanic/Latino; 4% Two or more races, non-Hispanic/Latino; 0.5% Race/ethnicity unknown; 0.8% international; 7% transferred in. *Retention:* 53% of full-time freshmen returned.

Freshmen *Admission:* 3,794 enrolled. *Test scores:* SAT critical reading scores over 500: 35%; SAT math scores over 500: 41%; SAT writing scores over 500: 26%; ACT scores over 18: 81%; SAT critical reading scores over 600: 7%; SAT math scores over 600: 9%; SAT writing scores over 600: 4%; ACT scores over 24: 26%; SAT critical reading scores over 700: 1%; SAT math scores over 700: 1%; ACT scores over 30: 2%.

Faculty *Total:* 909, 35% full-time, 10% with terminal degrees. *Student/faculty ratio:* 24:1.

Majors Accounting; administrative assistant and secretarial science; art; automobile/automotive mechanics technology; behavioral sciences; biological and physical sciences; biology/biological sciences; biology/biotechnology laboratory technician; business administration and management; chemical engineering; chemistry; civil engineering technology; commercial and advertising art; computer and information sciences and support services related; computer and information sciences related; computer engineering related; computer engineering technology; computer science; construction engineering technology; consumer merchandising/retailing management; corrections; criminal justice/law enforcement administration; criminal justice/police science; data processing and data processing technology; dental hygiene; electrical, electronic and communications engineering technology; engineering science; environmental studies; family and consumer sciences/human sciences; fashion/apparel design; fashion merchandising; fire science/firefighting; food technology and processing; forestry; graphic and printing equipment operation/production; health information/medical records administration; heating, air conditioning, ventilation and refrigeration maintenance technology; history; hotel/motel administration; human services; industrial radiologic technology; industrial technology; information science/studies; information technology; instrumentation technology; interior design; international business/trade/commerce; landscape architecture; laser and optical technology; legal administrative assistant/secretary; liberal arts and sciences/liberal studies; marketing/marketing management; mass communication/media; mathematics; mechanical engineering/mechanical technology; music; parks, recreation and leisure; physical education teaching and coaching; physics; political science and government; pre-pharmacy studies; quality control technology; registered nursing/registered nurse; social sciences; special products marketing; telecommunications technology; tourism and travel services management.

Academics *Calendar:* semesters. *Degree:* certificates and associate. *Special study options:* academic remediation for entering students, accelerated degree program, adult/continuing education programs, advanced placement credit, cooperative education, English as a second language, honors programs, internships, off-campus study, part-time degree program, services for LD students, summer session for credit. *ROTC:* Army (c), Air Force (c).

Library LeRoy V. Good Library plus 1 other with 110,748 titles, 745 serial subscriptions, 4,100 audiovisual materials, an OPAC.

Student Life *Housing Options:* Campus housing is university owned. *Activities and Organizations:* drama/theater group, student-run newspaper, radio station, choral group, student newspaper, Phi Theta Kappa, student government. *Campus security:* 24-hour emergency response devices, late-night transport/escort service. *Student services:* health clinic, personal/psychological counseling.

Athletics Member NJCAA. *Intercollegiate sports:* baseball M(s), basketball M(s)/W(s), golf M, ice hockey M(s), lacrosse M(s), soccer M(s)/W(s), softball W, swimming and diving M(s)/W(s), tennis M/W, volleyball W. *Intramural sports:* archery M/W, basketball M/W, bowling M/W, cheerleading W, cross-country running M/W, football M, lacrosse W, racquetball M/W, rugby M, skiing (cross-country) M/W, soccer M/W, softball M/W, swimming and diving M/W, tennis M/W, volleyball M/W.

Costs (2014–15) *Tuition:* state resident $3240 full-time, $135 per credit hour part-time; nonresident $6480 full-time, $270 per credit hour part-time. Full-time tuition and fees vary according to program. Part-time tuition and fees vary according to course load and program. *Required fees:* $282 full-time. *Room and board:* $5970. Room and board charges vary according to housing facility. *Payment plan:* installment. *Waivers:* senior citizens and employees or children of employees.

Applying *Options:* electronic application, early admission. *Application fee:* $20. *Required:* high school transcript. *Application deadlines:* rolling (freshmen), rolling (transfers). *Notification:* continuous (freshmen), continuous (transfers).

Freshman Application Contact Ms. Christine Casalinuovo-Adams, Director of Admissions, Monroe Community College, 1000 East Henrietta Road, Rochester, NY 14623. *Phone:* 585-292-2222. *Fax:* 585-292-3860. *E-mail:* admissions@monroecc.edu.

Website: http://www.monroecc.edu/.

Nassau Community College

Garden City, New York

- **State and locally supported** 2-year, founded 1959, part of State University of New York System
- **Suburban** 225-acre campus with easy access to New York City
- **Coed,** 23,034 undergraduate students, 60% full-time, 50% women, 50% men

Undergraduates 13,927 full-time, 9,107 part-time. Students come from 19 states and territories; 69 other countries; 0.3% are from out of state; 24% Black or African American, non-Hispanic/Latino; 21% Hispanic/Latino; 6% Asian, non-Hispanic/Latino; 0.4% Native Hawaiian or other Pacific Islander, non-Hispanic/Latino; 0.3% American Indian or Alaska Native, non-Hispanic/Latino; 6% Race/ethnicity unknown; 1% international; 6% transferred in. *Retention:* 32% of full-time freshmen returned.

Freshmen *Admission:* 5,997 applied, 5,681 admitted, 4,762 enrolled. *Average high school GPA:* 2.51.

Faculty *Total:* 1,422, 35% full-time, 28% with terminal degrees. *Student/faculty ratio:* 21:1.

Majors Accounting; accounting technology and bookkeeping; administrative assistant and secretarial science; African American/Black studies; art; business administration and management; civil engineering technology; clinical/medical laboratory technology; commercial and advertising art; computer and information sciences; computer and information sciences related; computer graphics; computer science; computer systems networking and telecommunications; criminal justice/law enforcement administration; criminal justice/safety; dance; data processing and data processing technology; design and visual communications; dramatic/theater arts; engineering; entrepreneurship; fashion/apparel design; fashion merchandising; funeral service and mortuary science; general studies; hotel/motel administration; instrumentation technology; insurance; interior design; kindergarten/preschool education; legal administrative assistant/secretary; legal assistant/paralegal; liberal arts and sciences/liberal studies; management information systems; marketing/marketing management; mass communication/media; mathematics; medical administrative assistant and medical secretary; medical radiologic technology; music performance; photography; physical therapy technology; real estate; registered nursing/registered nurse; rehabilitation and therapeutic professions related; respiratory care therapy; retailing; speech communication and rhetoric; surgical technology; theater design and technology; transportation and materials moving related; visual and performing arts.

Academics *Calendar:* semesters. *Degree:* certificates and associate. *Special study options:* academic remediation for entering students, adult/continuing education programs, advanced placement credit, cooperative education, distance learning, English as a second language, honors programs, internships, off-campus study, part-time degree program, services for LD students, summer session for credit.

Library A. Holly Patterson Library with 186,782 titles, 401 serial subscriptions, 18,903 audiovisual materials, an OPAC, a Web page.

Student Life *Housing:* college housing not available. *Activities and Organizations:* drama/theater group, student-run newspaper, radio station, choral group, Muslim Student Association, Make a Difference Club, Interact Club, Political Science Club, Investment Club. *Campus security:* 24-hour emergency response devices and patrols, late-night transport/escort service. *Student services:* personal/psychological counseling, women's center.

Athletics Member NJCAA. *Intercollegiate sports:* baseball M, basketball M/W, bowling M/W, cheerleading M/W, cross-country running M/W, football M, golf M/W, lacrosse M/W, soccer M/W, softball W, tennis M/W, track and field M/W, volleyball W, wrestling M. *Intramural sports:* badminton M/W, baseball M, basketball M/W, racquetball M/W, soccer M/W, softball M/W, swimming and diving M/W, table tennis M/W, tennis M/W, volleyball M/W.

Standardized Tests *Recommended:* SAT or ACT (for admission).

Costs (2013–14) *Tuition:* area resident $4088 full-time, $171 per credit hour part-time; state resident $8176 full-time, $342 per credit hour part-time; nonresident $8176 full-time, $342 per credit hour part-time. *Required fees:* $520 full-time. *Payment plan:* installment.

Financial Aid Of all full-time matriculated undergraduates who enrolled in 2012, 400 Federal Work-Study jobs (averaging $3000).

Applying *Options:* electronic application, deferred entrance. *Application fee:* $40. *Required:* high school transcript. *Required for some:* minimum 3.0 GPA, interview. *Recommended:* minimum 2.0 GPA. *Application deadlines:* 8/7 (freshmen), 8/7 (transfers). *Notification:* continuous (freshmen), continuous (transfers).

Freshman Application Contact Mr. Craig Wright, Vice President of Enrollment Management, Nassau Community College, Garden City, NY 11530. *Phone:* 516-572-7345. *E-mail:* admissions@sunynassau.edu. *Website:* http://www.ncc.edu/.

New York Career Institute
New York, New York

- **Proprietary** 2-year, founded 1942
- **Urban** campus
- **Coed, primarily women,** 702 undergraduate students, 66% full-time, 90% women, 10% men

Undergraduates 461 full-time, 241 part-time. 25% Black or African American, non-Hispanic/Latino; 17% Hispanic/Latino; 2% Asian, non-Hispanic/Latino; 0.7% American Indian or Alaska Native, non-Hispanic/Latino; 3% Two or more races, non-Hispanic/Latino; 19% Race/ethnicity unknown.

Faculty *Total:* 42, 21% full-time.

Majors Court reporting; legal assistant/paralegal; medical office assistant.

Academics *Calendar:* trimesters (semesters for evening division). *Degree:* certificates and associate. *Special study options:* academic remediation for entering students, advanced placement credit, internships, part-time degree program, summer session for credit.

Library 5,010 titles, 23 serial subscriptions.

Student Life *Housing:* college housing not available.

Costs (2014–15) *Tuition:* $13,350 full-time, $420 per credit hour part-time. Full-time tuition and fees vary according to class time. Part-time tuition and fees vary according to class time. *Required fees:* $150 full-time, $50 per term part-time. *Payment plan:* installment.

Applying *Options:* electronic application. *Application fee:* $50. *Required:* high school transcript, interview. *Application deadlines:* 9/7 (freshmen), 9/7 (transfers). *Notification:* continuous (freshmen), continuous (transfers).

Freshman Application Contact Mr. Larry Stieglitz, Director of Admissions, New York Career Institute, 11 Park Place, New York, NY 10007. *Phone:* 212-962-0002 Ext. 115. *Fax:* 212-385-7574. *E-mail:* lstieglitz@nyci.edu. *Website:* http://www.nyci.com/.

Niagara County Community College
Sanborn, New York

- **State and locally supported** 2-year, founded 1962, part of State University of New York System
- **Rural** 287-acre campus with easy access to Buffalo
- **Endowment** $4.5 million
- **Coed,** 6,648 undergraduate students, 63% full-time, 57% women, 43% men

Undergraduates 4,164 full-time, 2,484 part-time. Students come from 17 states and territories; 3 other countries; 1% are from out of state; 9% Black or African American, non-Hispanic/Latino; 2% Hispanic/Latino; 1% Asian, non-Hispanic/Latino; 1% American Indian or Alaska Native, non-Hispanic/Latino; 9% Race/ethnicity unknown; 7% transferred in; 4% live on campus.

Freshmen *Admission:* 3,084 applied, 2,427 admitted, 1,501 enrolled. *Average high school GPA:* 2.48.

Faculty *Total:* 376, 29% full-time, 13% with terminal degrees. *Student/faculty ratio:* 17:1.

Majors Accounting; administrative assistant and secretarial science; animal sciences; baking and pastry arts; biological and physical sciences; business administration and management; business, management, and marketing related; chemical technology; computer science; consumer merchandising/retailing management; criminal justice/law enforcement administration; culinary arts; design and applied arts related; drafting and design technology; drafting/design engineering technologies related; dramatic/theater arts; elementary education; fine/studio arts; general studies; hospitality administration; humanities; human services; information science/studies; liberal arts and sciences/liberal studies; massage therapy; mass communication/media; mathematics; medical/clinical assistant; medical radiologic technology; music; natural resources/conservation; occupational health and industrial hygiene; parks, recreation and leisure; physical education teaching and coaching; physical therapy technology; registered nursing/registered nurse; social sciences; sport and fitness administration/management; surgical technology; tourism and travel services management; web page, digital/multimedia and information resources design; wine steward/sommelier.

Academics *Calendar:* semesters. *Degree:* certificates and associate. *Special study options:* academic remediation for entering students, adult/continuing education programs, advanced placement credit, cooperative education, distance learning, double majors, honors programs, independent study, internships, off-campus study, part-time degree program, services for LD

students, student-designed majors, study abroad, summer session for credit. *ROTC:* Army (c).

Library Henrietta G. Lewis Library with 89,168 titles, 341 serial subscriptions, 6,193 audiovisual materials, an OPAC, a Web page.

Student Life *Housing Options:* coed. Campus housing is provided by a third party. *Activities and Organizations:* drama/theater group, student-run newspaper, radio station, choral group, student radio station, Student Nurses Association, Phi Theta Kappa, Alpha Beta Gamma, Physical Education Club. *Campus security:* 24-hour emergency response devices and patrols, student patrols, late-night transport/escort service. *Student services:* health clinic, personal/psychological counseling.

Athletics Member NJCAA. *Intercollegiate sports:* baseball M, basketball M(s)/W(s), golf M/W, lacrosse M/W, soccer M/W, softball W, volleyball W, wrestling M(s). *Intramural sports:* basketball M/W, racquetball M/W, soccer M/W, swimming and diving M/W, tennis M/W.

Costs (2013–14) *Tuition:* state resident $3792 full-time, $158 per credit hour part-time; nonresident $9480 full-time, $395 per credit hour part-time. Full-time tuition and fees vary according to course load and program. Part-time tuition and fees vary according to course load and program. *Required fees:* $372 full-time. *Room and board:* $10,660; room only: $8160. Room and board charges vary according to housing facility. *Payment plan:* installment. *Waivers:* senior citizens and employees or children of employees.

Financial Aid Of all full-time matriculated undergraduates who enrolled in 2012, 6,045 applied for aid, 6,045 were judged to have need. 92 Federal Work-Study jobs (averaging $1630). 114 state and other part-time jobs (averaging $343). *Average percent of need met:* 72%. *Average financial aid package:* $5286. *Average need-based loan:* $3746. *Average need-based gift aid:* $916.

Applying *Options:* electronic application, early admission. *Required:* high school transcript. *Required for some:* minimum 2.0 GPA. *Notification:* continuous until 8/31 (freshmen), continuous until 8/31 (transfers).

Freshman Application Contact Ms. Kathy Saunders, Director of Enrollment Services, Niagara County Community College, 3111 Saunders Settlement Road, Sanborn, NY 14132. *Phone:* 716-614-6200. *Fax:* 716-614-6820. *E-mail:* admissions@niagaracc.suny.edu. *Website:* http://www.niagaracc.suny.edu/.

North Country Community College
Saranac Lake, New York

Freshman Application Contact Enrollment Management Assistant, North Country Community College, 23 Santanoni Avenue, PO Box 89, Saranac Lake, NY 12983-0089. *Phone:* 518-891-2915 Ext. 686. *Toll-free phone:* 800-TRY-NCCC (in-state); 888-TRY-NCCC (out-of-state). *Fax:* 518-891-0898. *E-mail:* info@nccc.edu. *Website:* http://www.nccc.edu/.

Onondaga Community College
Syracuse, New York

- **State and locally supported** 2-year, founded 1962, part of State University of New York System
- **Suburban** 280-acre campus
- **Endowment** $9.1 million
- **Coed,** 12,841 undergraduate students, 51% full-time, 52% women, 48% men

Undergraduates 6,540 full-time, 6,301 part-time. Students come from 22 states and territories; 23 other countries; 6% are from out of state; 11% Black or African American, non-Hispanic/Latino; 4% Hispanic/Latino; 2% Asian, non-Hispanic/Latino; 0.1% Native Hawaiian or other Pacific Islander, non-Hispanic/Latino; 1% American Indian or Alaska Native, non-Hispanic/Latino; 2% Two or more races, non-Hispanic/Latino; 21% Race/ethnicity unknown; 0.5% international; 49% transferred in; 6% live on campus.

Freshmen *Admission:* 7,500 applied, 5,487 admitted, 2,476 enrolled.

Faculty *Total:* 695, 26% full-time. *Student/faculty ratio:* 25:1.

Majors Accounting; accounting technology and bookkeeping; architectural engineering technology; architectural technology; art; automobile/automotive mechanics technology; business administration and management; business/commerce; computer engineering technology; computer science; computer systems networking and telecommunications; construction engineering technology; criminal justice/law enforcement administration; criminal justice/police science; design and applied arts related; education (multiple levels); electrical and electronic engineering technologies related; electrical, electronic and communications engineering technology; engineering science; environmental engineering technology; fire prevention and safety technology; general studies; health information/medical records technology; health professions related; homeland security, law enforcement, firefighting and protective services related; hospitality administration; humanities; interior design; liberal arts and sciences and humanities related; mechanical engineering/mechanical technology; music; parks, recreation and leisure; photography; physical therapy technology; public administration and social service professions related; radio and television; registered nursing/registered nurse; respiratory care therapy; speech communication and rhetoric.

Academics *Calendar:* semesters. *Degree:* certificates, diplomas, and associate. *Special study options:* academic remediation for entering students, accelerated degree program, adult/continuing education programs, advanced placement credit, cooperative education, distance learning, double majors, English as a second language, external degree program, honors programs, internships, part-time degree program, services for LD students, study abroad, summer session for credit. *ROTC:* Air Force (c).

Library Sidney B. Coulter Library with 123,729 titles, 268 serial subscriptions, 15,353 audiovisual materials, an OPAC, a Web page.

Student Life *Housing Options:* coed. Campus housing is provided by a third party. *Activities and Organizations:* drama/theater group, student-run newspaper, radio station, choral group. *Campus security:* 24-hour emergency response devices and patrols, controlled dormitory access. *Student services:* personal/psychological counseling.

Athletics Member NJCAA. *Intercollegiate sports:* baseball M, basketball M/W, cross-country running M/W, lacrosse M/W, soccer M/W, softball W, tennis M/W, volleyball W. *Intramural sports:* badminton M/W, basketball M/W, golf M/W, skiing (downhill) M/W, swimming and diving M/W, table tennis M/W, tennis M/W, volleyball M/W.

Costs (2014–15) *Tuition:* state resident $4172 full-time; nonresident $8344 full-time. Full-time tuition and fees vary according to program. Part-time tuition and fees vary according to course load and program. *Required fees:* $584 full-time. *Room and board:* room only: $6270. Room and board charges vary according to board plan. *Payment plan:* installment. *Waivers:* senior citizens and employees or children of employees.

Financial Aid Of all full-time matriculated undergraduates who enrolled in 2012, 5,793 applied for aid, 5,218 were judged to have need, 252 had their need fully met. *Average percent of need met:* 55%. *Average financial aid package:* $6595. *Average need-based loan:* $2977. *Average need-based gift aid:* $5221.

Applying *Options:* electronic application. *Required:* high school transcript, some programs require specific prerequisite courses and/or tests to be admitted directly to the program; an alternate program is offered. *Required for some:* minimum 2.0 GPA, interview. *Notification:* continuous (freshmen), continuous (transfers).

Freshman Application Contact Mrs. Katherine Perry, Director of Admissions, Onondaga Community College, 4585 West Seneca Turnpike, Syracuse, NY 13215. *Phone:* 315-488-2602. *Fax:* 315-488-2107. *E-mail:* admissions@sunyocc.edu.

Website: http://www.sunyocc.edu/.

Orange County Community College
Middletown, New York

Freshman Application Contact Michael Roe, Director of Admissions and Recruitment, Orange County Community College, 115 South Street, Middletown, NY 10940. *Phone:* 845-341-4205. *Fax:* 845-343-1228. *E-mail:* apply@sunyorange.edu.

Website: http://www.sunyorange.edu/.

Phillips Beth Israel School of Nursing
New York, New York

Freshman Application Contact Mrs. Bernice Pass-Stern, Assistant Dean, Phillips Beth Israel School of Nursing, 776 Sixth Avenue, 4th Floor, New York, NY 10010-6354. *Phone:* 212-614-6176. *Fax:* 212-614-6109. *E-mail:* bstern@chpnet.org.

Website: http://www.futurenursebi.org/.

Plaza College
Jackson Heights, New York

Freshman Application Contact Dean Rose Ann Black, Dean of Administration, Plaza College, 74-09 37th Avenue, Jackson Heights, NY 11372. *Phone:* 718-779-1430. *E-mail:* info@plazacollege.edu.

Website: http://www.plazacollege.edu/.

Queensborough Community College of the City University of New York
Bayside, New York

Freshman Application Contact Ms. Ann Tullio, Director of Registration, Queensborough Community College of the City University of New York, 222-05 56th Avenue, Bayside, NY 11364. *Phone:* 718-631-6307. *Fax:* 718-281-5189.

Website: http://www.qcc.cuny.edu/.

Rockland Community College
Suffern, New York

Freshman Application Contact Rockland Community College, 145 College Road, Suffern, NY 10901-3699. *Phone:* 845-574-4237. *Toll-free phone:* 800-722-7666.

Website: http://www.sunyrockland.edu/.

St. Elizabeth College of Nursing
Utica, New York

- **Independent** 2-year, founded 1904
- **Small-town** 1-acre campus with easy access to Syracuse
- **Coed,** 159 undergraduate students, 45% full-time, 86% women, 14% men
- 32% of applicants were admitted

Undergraduates 72 full-time, 87 part-time. Students come from 1 other state; 2% Black or African American, non-Hispanic/Latino; 2% Hispanic/Latino; 1% Asian, non-Hispanic/Latino; 3% Two or more races, non-Hispanic/Latino; 1% international; 51% transferred in. *Retention:* 75% of full-time freshmen returned.

Freshmen *Admission:* 19 applied, 6 admitted, 3 enrolled.

Faculty *Total:* 18, 72% full-time. *Student/faculty ratio:* 7:1.

Majors Registered nursing/registered nurse.

Academics *Calendar:* semesters. *Degree:* associate. *Special study options:* academic remediation for entering students, advanced placement credit, off-campus study, part-time degree program, services for LD students.

Student Life *Housing:* college housing not available. *Campus security:* 24-hour emergency response devices and patrols. *Student services:* health clinic, personal/psychological counseling.

Standardized Tests *Required:* SAT or ACT (for admission).

Applying *Options:* electronic application. *Application fee:* $65. *Required:* high school transcript, 2 letters of recommendation. *Recommended:* minimum 3.0 GPA. *Application deadline:* rolling (freshmen). *Notification:* continuous (freshmen).

Freshman Application Contact Donna Ernst, Director of Recruitment, St. Elizabeth College of Nursing, 2215 Genesee Street, Utica, NY 13501. *Phone:* 315-798-8189. *E-mail:* dernst@secon.edu.

Website: http://www.secon.edu/.

St. Joseph's College of Nursing
Syracuse, New York

Freshman Application Contact Ms. Felicia Corp, Recruiter, St. Joseph's College of Nursing, 206 Prospect Avenue, Syracuse, NY 13203. *Phone:* 315-448-5040. *Fax:* 315-448-5745. *E-mail:* collegeofnursing@sjhsyr.org.

Website: http://www.sjhsyr.org/nursing/.

St. Paul's School of Nursing
Rego Park, New York

Director of Admissions Nancy Wolinski, Chairperson of Admissions, St. Paul's School of Nursing, 97-77 Queens Boulevard, Rego Park, NY 11374. *Phone:* 718-357-0500 Ext. 131. *E-mail:* nwolinski@svcmcny.org.

Website: http://www.stpaulsschoolofnursing.com/.

St. Paul's School of Nursing
Staten Island, New York

Admissions Office Contact St. Paul's School of Nursing, Corporate Commons Two, 2 Teleport Drive, Suite 203, Staten Island, NY 10311.

Website: http://www.stpaulsschoolofnursing.com/.

Samaritan Hospital School of Nursing
Troy, New York

Director of Admissions Ms. Jennifer Marrone, Student Services Coordinator, Samaritan Hospital School of Nursing, 2215 Burdett Avenue, Troy, NY 12180. *Phone:* 518-271-3734. *Fax:* 518-271-3303. *E-mail:* marronej@nehealth.com.

Website: http://www.nehealth.com/.

SBI Campus—an affiliate of Sanford-Brown
Melville, New York

Director of Admissions Ms. Cynthia Gamache, Director of Admissions, SBI Campus–an affiliate of Sanford-Brown, 320 South Service Road, Melville, NY 11747-3785. *Phone:* 631-370-3307.

Website: http://www.sbmelville.edu/.

Schenectady County Community College

Schenectady, New York

Freshman Application Contact Mr. David Sampson, Director of Admissions, Schenectady County Community College, 78 Washington Avenue, Schenectady, NY 12305-2294. *Phone:* 518-381-1370. *E-mail:* sampsodg@gw.sunysccc.edu.

Website: http://www.sunysccc.edu/.

State University of New York College of Technology at Alfred

Alfred, New York

- **State-supported** primarily 2-year, founded 1908, part of The State University of New York System
- **Rural** 1084-acre campus with easy access to Rochester, Buffalo
- **Endowment** $4.1 million
- **Coed**, 3,549 undergraduate students, 91% full-time, 40% women, 60% men

Undergraduates 3,216 full-time, 333 part-time. Students come from 19 other countries; 7% are from out of state; 9% Black or African American, non-Hispanic/Latino; 6% Hispanic/Latino; 2% Asian, non-Hispanic/Latino; 0.1% Native Hawaiian or other Pacific Islander, non-Hispanic/Latino; 0.2% American Indian or Alaska Native, non-Hispanic/Latino; 2% Two or more races, non-Hispanic/Latino; 4% Race/ethnicity unknown; 7% transferred in; 68% live on campus. *Retention:* 81% of full-time freshmen returned.

Freshmen *Admission:* 5,761 applied, 3,165 admitted, 1,101 enrolled. *Average high school GPA:* 2.9.

Faculty *Total:* 226, 73% full-time, 17% with terminal degrees. *Student/faculty ratio:* 18:1.

Majors Accounting technology and bookkeeping; agribusiness; agriculture; agroecology and sustainable agriculture; agronomy and crop science; animal sciences; architectural engineering technology; autobody/collision and repair technology; automotive engineering technology; baking and pastry arts; banking and financial support services; biology/biological sciences; business, management, and marketing related; CAD/CADD drafting/design technology; carpentry; community organization and advocacy; computer and information sciences; computer and information sciences and support services related; computer and information systems security; computer engineering technology; computer hardware technology; computer science; computer systems networking and telecommunications; construction engineering technology; construction trades related; cooking and related culinary arts; court reporting; culinary arts related; dairy science; data processing and data processing technology; design and applied arts related; diesel mechanics technology; digital arts; digital communication and media/multimedia; electrical, electronic and communications engineering technology; electrical/electronics equipment installation and repair; electrician; electromechanical technology; engineering; engineering technologies and engineering related; entrepreneurial and small business related; entrepreneurship; environmental science; finance; finance and financial management services related; financial planning and services; forensic science and technology; health information/medical records technology; heating, air conditioning, ventilation and refrigeration maintenance technology; heating, ventilation, air conditioning and refrigeration engineering technology; heavy equipment maintenance technology; humanities; human resources management; human services; industrial technology; information technology; interior architecture; interior design; liberal arts and sciences/liberal studies; machine tool technology; manufacturing engineering technology; marketing/marketing management; masonry; mechanical drafting and CAD/CADD; mechanical engineering/mechanical technology; merchandising, sales, and marketing operations related (general); network and system administration; plumbing technology; registered nursing/registered nurse; robotics technology; secondary education; sport and fitness administration/management; surveying technology; system, networking, and LAN/WAN management; urban forestry; vehicle maintenance and repair technologies related; veterinary/animal health technology; web/multimedia management and webmaster; welding technology.

Academics *Calendar:* semesters. *Degrees:* certificates, associate, and bachelor's. *Special study options:* academic remediation for entering students, adult/continuing education programs, advanced placement credit, cooperative education, distance learning, double majors, English as a second language, honors programs, independent study, internships, off-campus study, part-time degree program, services for LD students, student-designed majors, study abroad, summer session for credit. *ROTC:* Army (c).

Library Walter C. Hinkle Memorial Library plus 1 other with 61,639 titles, 68,689 serial subscriptions, 4,478 audiovisual materials, an OPAC, a Web page.

Student Life *Housing Options:* coed, men-only, women-only, special housing for students with disabilities. Campus housing is university owned. Freshman campus housing is guaranteed. *Activities and Organizations:* drama/theater group, student-run newspaper, radio station, choral group, Outdoor Recreation Club, International Club, Intramural sports, Pioneer Woodsmen Team, Black Student Union. *Campus security:* 24-hour emergency response devices and patrols, late-night transport/escort service, controlled dormitory access, residence hall entrance guards. *Student services:* health clinic, personal/psychological counseling.

Athletics Member NCAA, USCAA. All Division III. *Intercollegiate sports:* baseball M, basketball M(s)/W(s), cross-country running M/W, equestrian sports M/W, football M(s), lacrosse M(s), soccer M/W, softball W, swimming and diving M/W, track and field M/W, volleyball W, wrestling M. *Intramural sports:* basketball M/W, football M(c), golf M/W, ice hockey M(c)/W(c), lacrosse M(c)/W(c), rock climbing M/W, soccer M/W, softball M/W, swimming and diving M(c)/W(c), tennis M/W, ultimate Frisbee M/W, volleyball M/W.

Standardized Tests *Required for some:* SAT or ACT (for admission). *Recommended:* SAT or ACT (for admission).

Costs (2014–15) *One-time required fee:* $100. *Tuition:* state resident $5870 full-time, $245 per credit hour part-time; nonresident $9740 full-time, $406 per credit hour part-time. Full-time tuition and fees vary according to course load and degree level. Part-time tuition and fees vary according to course load and degree level. *Required fees:* $1424 full-time, $58 per credit hour part-time, $10 per credit hour part-time. *Room and board:* $11,580; room only: $6880. Room and board charges vary according to board plan and housing facility. *Payment plan:* installment. *Waivers:* employees or children of employees.

Financial Aid Of all full-time matriculated undergraduates who enrolled in 2013, 2,971 applied for aid, 2,652 were judged to have need, 219 had their need fully met. 238 Federal Work-Study jobs (averaging $1119). In 2013, 117 non-need-based awards were made. *Average percent of need met:* 60%. *Average financial aid package:* $10,914. *Average need-based loan:* $4266. *Average need-based gift aid:* $6616. *Average non-need-based aid:* $5275. *Average indebtedness upon graduation:* $27,970.

Applying *Options:* electronic application. *Application fee:* $50. *Required:* high school transcript, minimum 2.0 GPA. *Recommended:* essay or personal statement, interview. *Application deadlines:* rolling (freshmen), rolling (out-of-state freshmen), rolling (transfers). *Notification:* continuous (freshmen), continuous (out-of-state freshmen), continuous (transfers).

Freshman Application Contact Mrs. Goodrich Deborah, Associate Vice President for Enrollment Management, State University of New York College of Technology at Alfred, Huntington Administration Building, 10 Upper College Drive, Alfred, NY 14802. *Phone:* 607-587-3945. *Toll-free phone:* 800-4-ALFRED. *Fax:* 607-587-4299. *E-mail:* admissions@alfredstate.edu. *Website:* http://www.alfredstate.edu/.

Stella and Charles Guttman Community College

New York, New York

Admissions Office Contact Stella and Charles Guttman Community College, 50 West 40th Street, New York, NY 10018.

Website: http://guttman.cuny.edu/.

Suffolk County Community College

Selden, New York

Freshman Application Contact Suffolk County Community College, 533 College Road, Selden, NY 11784-2899. *Phone:* 631-451-4000.

Website: http://www.sunysuffolk.edu/.

Sullivan County Community College

Loch Sheldrake, New York

- **State and locally supported** 2-year, founded 1962, part of State University of New York System
- **Rural** 405-acre campus
- **Endowment** $1.0 million
- **Coed**, 1,585 undergraduate students, 64% full-time, 55% women, 45% men

Undergraduates 1,019 full-time, 566 part-time. Students come from 10 states and territories; 5 other countries; 2% are from out of state; 19% Black or African American, non-Hispanic/Latino; 17% Hispanic/Latino; 2% Asian, non-Hispanic/Latino; 0.1% Native Hawaiian or other Pacific Islander, non-Hispanic/Latino; 0.4% American Indian or Alaska Native, non-Hispanic/Latino; 21% Race/ethnicity unknown; 0.3% international; 8% transferred in; 22% live on campus.

Freshmen *Admission:* 2,453 applied, 2,185 admitted, 391 enrolled.

Faculty *Total:* 119, 41% full-time, 16% with terminal degrees. *Student/faculty ratio:* 19:1.

Majors Accounting; administrative assistant and secretarial science; baking and pastry arts; business administration and management; commercial and advertising art; computer graphics; computer programming (specific applications); construction engineering technology; consumer merchandising/retailing management; criminal justice/police science; crisis/emergency/disaster management; culinary arts; data entry/microcomputer applications; electrical, electronic and communications engineering technology; elementary education; environmental studies; fire prevention and safety technology; forensic science and technology; hospitality administration; human services; information science/studies; kindergarten/preschool education; legal assistant/paralegal; liberal arts and sciences/liberal studies; marketing/marketing management; mathematics; medical/clinical assistant; parks, recreation and leisure; photography; psychology; radio and television; radio, television, and digital communication related; registered nursing/registered nurse; respiratory care therapy; science technologies related; sport and fitness administration/management; tourism and travel services management.

Academics *Calendar:* 4-1-4. *Degree:* certificates and associate. *Special study options:* academic remediation for entering students, adult/continuing education programs, advanced placement credit, distance learning, double majors, honors programs, independent study, internships, off-campus study, part-time degree program, services for LD students, summer session for credit.

Library Hermann Memorial Library plus 1 other with 131,870 titles, 126 serial subscriptions, 8,857 audiovisual materials, an OPAC, a Web page.

Student Life *Housing Options:* coed. Campus housing is provided by a third party. Freshman applicants given priority for college housing. *Activities and Organizations:* student-run newspaper, radio station, Science Alliance, Black Student Union, Gay Straight Alliance, Dance Club, Honor Society. *Campus security:* 24-hour emergency response devices and patrols, student patrols, controlled dormitory access. *Student services:* health clinic, personal/psychological counseling, legal services.

Athletics Member NJCAA. *Intercollegiate sports:* basketball M/W, cross-country running M/W, softball W, volleyball M/W, wrestling M. *Intramural sports:* basketball M/W, bowling M/W, cross-country running M/W, football M, golf M/W, racquetball M/W, skiing (downhill) M/W, soccer M/W, softball M/W, table tennis M/W, tennis M/W, volleyball M/W, weight lifting M/W.

Costs (2014–15) *Tuition:* state resident $4474 full-time, $174 per credit hour part-time; nonresident $8948 full-time, $230 per credit hour part-time. Full-time tuition and fees vary according to program. Part-time tuition and fees vary according to program. *Required fees:* $642 full-time, $67 per credit hour part-time. *Room and board:* $9552; room only: $5800. Room and board charges vary according to board plan and housing facility. *Payment plans:* installment, deferred payment. *Waivers:* senior citizens and employees or children of employees.

Financial Aid Of all full-time matriculated undergraduates who enrolled in 2012, 1,214 applied for aid, 1,112 were judged to have need, 1,112 had their need fully met. 72 Federal Work-Study jobs (averaging $850). 23 state and other part-time jobs (averaging $1009). *Average percent of need met:* 100%. *Average financial aid package:* $5747. *Average need-based loan:* $2853. *Average need-based gift aid:* $5747.

Applying *Options:* electronic application, early admission, deferred entrance. *Required:* high school transcript. *Application deadlines:* rolling (freshmen), rolling (out-of-state freshmen), rolling (transfers). *Notification:* continuous (freshmen), continuous (out-of-state freshmen), continuous (transfers).

Freshman Application Contact Ms. Sari Rosenheck, Director of Admissions and Registration Services, Sullivan County Community College, 112 College Road, Loch Sheldrake, NY 12759. *Phone:* 845-434-5750 Ext. 4200. *Toll-free phone:* 800-577-5243. *Fax:* 845-434-4806. *E-mail:* sarir@sunysullivan.edu. *Website:* http://www.sullivan.suny.edu/.

TCI–The College of Technology
New York, New York
- **Proprietary** 2-year, founded 1909
- **Urban** campus
- **Coed,** 3,020 undergraduate students, 87% full-time, 38% women, 62% men

Undergraduates 2,640 full-time, 380 part-time. 42% Black or African American, non-Hispanic/Latino; 34% Hispanic/Latino; 3% Asian, non-Hispanic/Latino; 0.1% Native Hawaiian or other Pacific Islander, non-Hispanic/Latino; 0.6% Two or more races, non-Hispanic/Latino; 14% Race/ethnicity unknown; 0.6% international.

Faculty *Student/faculty ratio:* 24:1.

Majors Accounting technology and bookkeeping; automobile/automotive mechanics technology; building/property maintenance; business administration and management; computer software technology; computer systems networking and telecommunications; digital communication and media/multimedia; health information/medical records technology; heating,

ventilation, air conditioning and refrigeration engineering technology; human services; legal assistant/paralegal; optometric technician; securities services administration.

Academics *Calendar:* semesters. *Degree:* certificates and associate. *Special study options:* academic remediation for entering students, adult/continuing education programs, advanced placement credit, distance learning, English as a second language, part-time degree program, summer session for credit.

Library Technical Career Institutes Library with an OPAC.

Student Life *Housing:* college housing not available. *Campus security:* 24-hour patrols. *Student services:* personal/psychological counseling.

Applying *Options:* deferred entrance. *Required:* essay or personal statement, high school transcript, interview. *Application deadlines:* rolling (freshmen), rolling (transfers). *Notification:* continuous (freshmen), continuous (transfers).

Freshman Application Contact TCI–The College of Technology, 320 West 31st Street, New York, NY 10001-2705. *Phone:* 212-594-4000. *Toll-free phone:* 800-878-8246. *Website:* http://www.tcicollege.edu/.

Tompkins Cortland Community College
Dryden, New York
- **State and locally supported** 2-year, founded 1968, part of State University of New York System
- **Rural** 300-acre campus with easy access to Syracuse
- **Coed,** 5,450 undergraduate students, 49% full-time, 56% women, 44% men

Undergraduates 2,686 full-time, 2,764 part-time. Students come from 24 states and territories; 29 other countries; 2% are from out of state; 12% Black or African American, non-Hispanic/Latino; 10% Hispanic/Latino; 1% Asian, non-Hispanic/Latino; 0.1% Native Hawaiian or other Pacific Islander, non-Hispanic/Latino; 0.4% American Indian or Alaska Native, non-Hispanic/Latino; 3% Two or more . races, non-Hispanic/Latino; 0.2% Race/ethnicity unknown; 2% international; 35% transferred in.

Freshmen *Admission:* 1,006 enrolled.

Faculty *Total:* 317, 21% full-time, 15% with terminal degrees. *Student/faculty ratio:* 20:1.

Majors Accounting technology and bookkeeping; administrative assistant and secretarial science; biotechnology; business administration and management; business, management, and marketing related; child-care and support services management; commercial and advertising art; community organization and advocacy; computer and information sciences; computer and information sciences and support services related; construction trades related; creative writing; criminal justice/law enforcement administration; early childhood education; electrical, electronic and communications engineering technology; engineering; forensic science and technology; hotel/motel administration; humanities; information science/studies; international business/trade/commerce; international/global studies; kindergarten/preschool education; legal assistant/paralegal; liberal arts and sciences/liberal studies; natural resources/conservation; parks, recreation and leisure facilities management; parks, recreation, leisure, and fitness studies related; photography; radio and television broadcasting technology; registered nursing/registered nurse; speech communication and rhetoric; sport and fitness administration/management; substance abuse/addiction counseling; web/multimedia management and webmaster.

Academics *Calendar:* semesters. *Degree:* certificates and associate. *Special study options:* academic remediation for entering students, adult/continuing education programs, advanced placement credit, cooperative education, distance learning, double majors, English as a second language, freshman honors college, honors programs, independent study, internships, off-campus study, part-time degree program, services for LD students, study abroad, summer session for credit.

Library Gerald A. Barry Memorial Library plus 1 other with 65,386 titles, 200 serial subscriptions, 3,445 audiovisual materials, an OPAC, a Web page.

Student Life *Housing Options:* coed. Campus housing is provided by a third party. *Activities and Organizations:* drama/theater group, College Entertainment Board, Sport Management Club, Nursing Club, Media Club, Writer's Guild. *Campus security:* 24-hour patrols, late-night transport/escort service, controlled dormitory access, armed peace officers. *Student services:* health clinic, personal/psychological counseling.

Athletics Member NJCAA. *Intercollegiate sports:* baseball M, basketball M/W, golf M/W, lacrosse M, soccer M/W, softball W, volleyball W. *Intramural sports:* archery M/W, badminton M/W, basketball M/W, bowling M/W, football M/W, golf M/W, lacrosse M/W, racquetball M/W, skiing (cross-country) M/W, skiing (downhill) M/W, soccer M/W, softball M/W, squash M/W, swimming and diving M/W, table tennis M/W, tennis M/W, ultimate Frisbee M/W, volleyball M/W, water polo M/W, weight lifting M/W, wrestling M/W.

Costs (2013–14) *Tuition:* state resident $4300 full-time, $152 per credit hour part-time; nonresident $8900 full-time, $314 per credit hour part-time. Part-time tuition and fees vary according to course load. *Required fees:* $785 full-time, $27 per credit hour part-time, $12 per term part-time. *Room and board:* $9800. Room and board charges vary according to board plan and housing facility. *Payment plans:* installment, deferred payment. *Waivers:* employees or children of employees.

Financial Aid Of all full-time matriculated undergraduates who enrolled in 2012, 150 Federal Work-Study jobs (averaging $1000). 150 state and other part-time jobs (averaging $1000).

Applying *Options:* electronic application, early admission, deferred entrance. *Application fee:* $15. *Required:* high school transcript. *Required for some:* essay or personal statement, interview. *Application deadlines:* rolling (freshmen), rolling (out-of-state freshmen), rolling (transfers). *Notification:* continuous (freshmen), continuous (out-of-state freshmen), continuous (transfers).

Freshman Application Contact Mr. Sandy Drumluk, Director of Admissions, Tompkins Cortland Community College, 170 North Street, PO Box 139, Dryden, NY 13053-0139. *Phone:* 607-844-6580. *Toll-free phone:* 888-567-8211. *Fax:* 607-844-6538. *E-mail:* admissions@tc3.edu. *Website:* http://www.TC3.edu/.

Trocaire College
Buffalo, New York

Freshman Application Contact Mrs. Theresa Horner, Director of Records, Trocaire College, 360 Choate Avenue, Buffalo, NY 14220-2094. *Phone:* 716-827-2459. *Fax:* 716-828-6107. *E-mail:* info@trocaire.edu. *Website:* http://www.trocaire.edu/.

Ulster County Community College
Stone Ridge, New York

Freshman Application Contact Admissions Office, Ulster County Community College, 491 Cottekill Road, Stone Ridge, NY 12484. *Phone:* 845-687-5022. *Toll-free phone:* 800-724-0833. *E-mail:* admissionsoffice@sunyulster.edu. *Website:* http://www.sunyulster.edu/.

Utica School of Commerce
Utica, New York

Freshman Application Contact Senior Admissions Coordinator, Utica School of Commerce, 201 Bleecker Street, Utica, NY 13501-2280. *Phone:* 315-733-2300. *Toll-free phone:* 800-321-4USC. *Fax:* 315-733-9281. *Website:* http://www.uscny.edu/.

Westchester Community College
Valhalla, New York

- **State and locally supported** 2-year, founded 1946, part of State University of New York System
- **Suburban** 218-acre campus with easy access to New York City
- **Coed,** 13,781 undergraduate students, 55% full-time, 52% women, 48% men

Undergraduates 7,640 full-time, 6,141 part-time. Students come from 14 states and territories; 108 other countries; 0.4% are from out of state; 22% Black or African American, non-Hispanic/Latino; 29% Hispanic/Latino; 4% Asian, non-Hispanic/Latino; 0.2% Native Hawaiian or other Pacific Islander, non-Hispanic/Latino; 0.6% American Indian or Alaska Native, non-Hispanic/Latino; 2% Two or more races, non-Hispanic/Latino; 7% Race/ethnicity unknown; 6% transferred in.

Freshmen *Admission:* 5,190 applied, 5,045 admitted, 2,512 enrolled.

Faculty *Total:* 1,086, 15% full-time.

Majors Accounting; administrative assistant and secretarial science; apparel and textile manufacturing; business administration and management; child development; civil engineering technology; clinical laboratory science/medical technology; clinical/medical laboratory technology; community organization and advocacy; computer and information sciences; computer and information sciences and support services related; computer and information sciences related; computer and information systems security; computer science; computer systems networking and telecommunications; consumer merchandising/retailing management; corrections; culinary arts; dance; data processing and data processing technology; design and applied arts related; dietetics; education (multiple levels); electrical, electronic and communications engineering technology; emergency medical technology (EMT paramedic); energy management and systems technology; engineering science; engineering technology; environmental control technologies related; environmental science; environmental studies; film/video and photographic arts related; finance; fine/studio arts; food technology and processing; humanities; information science/studies; international business/trade/commerce; journalism; legal assistant/paralegal; liberal arts and sciences/liberal studies; marketing/marketing management; mass communication/media; mechanical engineering/mechanical technology; public

administration; registered nursing/registered nurse; respiratory care therapy; social sciences; substance abuse/addiction counseling; veterinary/animal health technology.

Academics *Calendar:* semesters. *Degree:* certificates and associate. *Special study options:* academic remediation for entering students, adult/continuing education programs, advanced placement credit, cooperative education, distance learning, double majors, English as a second language, honors programs, independent study, internships, off-campus study, part-time degree program, services for LD students, student-designed majors, study abroad, summer session for credit.

Library Harold L. Drimmer Library plus 1 other with 225,843 titles, 179 serial subscriptions, 4,930 audiovisual materials, an OPAC, a Web page.

Student Life *Housing:* college housing not available. *Activities and Organizations:* drama/theater group, student-run newspaper, radio station, choral group, Deca Fashion Retail, Future Educators, Respiratory Club, Black Student Union, Diversity Action. *Campus security:* 24-hour emergency response devices and patrols, late-night transport/escort service. *Student services:* health clinic, personal/psychological counseling, women's center.

Athletics Member NJCAA. *Intercollegiate sports:* baseball M, basketball M/W, bowling M/W, golf M, soccer M, softball W, volleyball W. *Intramural sports:* badminton M/W, basketball M/W, softball M/W, swimming and diving M/W, tennis M/W, volleyball M/W, weight lifting M/W.

Costs (2014–15) *Tuition:* state resident $4280 full-time, $179 per credit part-time; nonresident $11,770 full-time, $493 per credit part-time. Full-time tuition and fees vary according to location. Part-time tuition and fees vary according to location. *Required fees:* $443 full-time, $102 per term part-time. *Payment plan:* installment.

Financial Aid Of all full-time matriculated undergraduates who enrolled in 2012, 200 Federal Work-Study jobs (averaging $1000).

Applying *Options:* early admission. *Application fee:* $35. *Required:* high school transcript. *Recommended:* interview. *Application deadlines:* rolling (freshmen), rolling (transfers). *Notification:* continuous until 2/2 (freshmen), continuous (transfers).

Freshman Application Contact Ms. Gloria Leon, Director of Admissions, Westchester Community College, 75 Grasslands Road, Administration Building, Valhalla, NY 10595-1698. *Phone:* 914-606-6735. *Fax:* 914-606-6540. *E-mail:* admissions@sunywcc.edu. *Website:* http://www.sunywcc.edu/.

Wood Tobe–Coburn School
New York, New York

- **Private** 2-year, founded 1879
- **Urban** campus
- **Coed,** 523 undergraduate students
- **88%** of applicants were admitted

Freshmen *Admission:* 953 applied, 835 admitted.

Majors Accounting technology and bookkeeping; administrative assistant and secretarial science; computer programming; computer systems networking and telecommunications; fashion/apparel design; graphic design; hotel/motel administration; medical/clinical assistant; retailing.

Academics *Calendar:* semesters. *Degree:* diplomas and associate. *Special study options:* accelerated degree program, internships.

Student Life *Housing:* college housing not available.

Freshman Application Contact Admissions Office, Wood Tobe–Coburn School, 8 East 40th Street, New York, NY 10016. *Phone:* 212-686-9040. *Toll-free phone:* 800-394-9663. *Website:* http://www.woodtobecoburn.edu/.

NORTH CAROLINA

Alamance Community College
Graham, North Carolina

- **State-supported** 2-year, founded 1959, part of North Carolina Community College System
- **Small-town** 48-acre campus
- **Endowment** $2.9 million
- **Coed,** 4,648 undergraduate students, 47% full-time, 63% women, 37% men

Undergraduates 2,184 full-time, 2,464 part-time. Students come from 7 states and territories; 3 other countries; 1% are from out of state; 21% Black or African American, non-Hispanic/Latino; 9% Hispanic/Latino; 1% Asian, non-Hispanic/Latino; 0.8% American Indian or Alaska Native, non-Hispanic/Latino; 2% Two or more races, non-Hispanic/Latino; 1% Race/ethnicity unknown; 0.5% international; 27% transferred in.

Freshmen *Admission:* 587 applied, 587 admitted, 587 enrolled.

Faculty *Total:* 435, 26% full-time, 3% with terminal degrees. *Student/faculty ratio:* 12:1.

Majors Accounting technology and bookkeeping; animal sciences; applied horticulture/horticulture operations; automobile/automotive mechanics technology; banking and financial support services; biotechnology; business administration and management; carpentry; clinical/medical laboratory technology; commercial and advertising art; criminal justice/safety; culinary arts; electrical, electronic and communications engineering technology; executive assistant/executive secretary; heating, ventilation, air conditioning and refrigeration engineering technology; information science/studies; kindergarten/preschool education; legal administrative assistant/secretary; liberal arts and sciences/liberal studies; machine tool technology; mechanical engineering/mechanical technology; medical administrative assistant and medical secretary; medical/clinical assistant; office occupations and clerical services; registered nursing/registered nurse; retailing; teacher assistant/aide; welding technology.

Academics *Calendar:* semesters. *Degree:* certificates, diplomas, and associate. *Special study options:* academic remediation for entering students, adult/continuing education programs, cooperative education, distance learning, double majors, English as a second language, independent study, off-campus study, part-time degree program, services for LD students, summer session for credit.

Library Learning Resources Center with 22,114 titles, 185 serial subscriptions, an OPAC, a Web page.

Student Life *Housing:* college housing not available. *Campus security:* 24-hour emergency response devices and patrols, student patrols, late-night transport/escort service. *Student services:* personal/psychological counseling.

Athletics *Intramural sports:* basketball M/W, bowling M/W, tennis M/W, volleyball M/W.

Costs (2013–14) *Tuition:* state resident $2144 full-time; nonresident $7905 full-time. Full-time tuition and fees vary according to course load. Part-time tuition and fees vary according to course load. *Required fees:* $30 full-time. *Waivers:* senior citizens.

Financial Aid Of all full-time matriculated undergraduates who enrolled in 2010, 4,000 applied for aid, 3,000 were judged to have need. 200 Federal Work-Study jobs. *Average percent of need met:* 30%. *Average financial aid package:* $4500. *Average need-based gift aid:* $4500. *Average indebtedness upon graduation:* $2500.

Applying *Options:* electronic application. *Required:* high school transcript. *Application deadlines:* rolling (freshmen), rolling (transfers). *Notification:* continuous (freshmen), continuous (transfers).

Freshman Application Contact Ms. Elizabeth Brehler, Director for Enrollment Management, Alamance Community College, Graham, NC 27253-8000. *Phone:* 336-506-4120. *Fax:* 336-506-4264. *E-mail:* brehlere@alamancecc.edu.
Website: http://www.alamancecc.edu/.

Asheville-Buncombe Technical Community College
Asheville, North Carolina

Freshman Application Contact Asheville-Buncombe Technical Community College, 340 Victoria Road, Asheville, NC 28801-4897. *Phone:* 828-254-1921 Ext. 7520.
Website: http://www.abtech.edu/.

Beaufort County Community College
Washington, North Carolina

- **State-supported** 2-year, founded 1967, part of North Carolina Community College System
- **Rural** 67-acre campus
- **Coed**

Undergraduates 32% Black or African American, non-Hispanic/Latino; 2% Hispanic/Latino; 0.2% Asian, non-Hispanic/Latino; 0.6% American Indian or Alaska Native, non-Hispanic/Latino; 3% Race/ethnicity unknown.

Academics *Calendar:* semesters. *Degree:* certificates, diplomas, and associate. *Special study options:* academic remediation for entering students, advanced placement credit, cooperative education, distance learning, English as a second language, part-time degree program, services for LD students, summer session for credit.

Student Life *Campus security:* 24-hour emergency response devices and patrols, late-night transport/escort service.

Standardized Tests *Required:* ACCUPLACER, COMPASS, ASSET (for admission). *Recommended:* SAT or ACT (for admission).

Applying *Options:* electronic application. *Required for some:* high school transcript.

Freshman Application Contact Mr. Gary Burbage, Director of Admissions, Beaufort County Community College, PO Box 1069, 5337 US Highway 264 East, Washington, NC 27889-1069. *Phone:* 252-940-6233. *Fax:* 252-940-6393. *E-mail:* garyb@beaufortccc.edu.
Website: http://www.beaufortccc.edu/.

Bladen Community College
Dublin, North Carolina

Freshman Application Contact Ms. Andrea Fisher, Enrollment Specialist, Bladen Community College, PO Box 266, Dublin, NC 28332. *Phone:* 910-879-5593. *Fax:* 910-879-5564. *E-mail:* acarterfisher@bladencc.edu.
Website: http://www.bladen.cc.nc.us/.

Blue Ridge Community College
Flat Rock, North Carolina

Freshman Application Contact Blue Ridge Community College, 180 West Campus Drive, Flat Rock, NC 28731. *Phone:* 828-694-1810.
Website: http://www.blueridge.edu/.

Brunswick Community College
Supply, North Carolina

Freshman Application Contact Admissions Counselor, Brunswick Community College, 50 College Road, PO Box 30, Supply, NC 28462-0030. *Phone:* 910-755-7300. *Toll-free phone:* 800-754-1050. *Fax:* 910-754-9609. *E-mail:* admissions@brunswickcc.edu.
Website: http://www.brunswickcc.edu/.

Caldwell Community College and Technical Institute
Hudson, North Carolina

Freshman Application Contact Carolyn Woodard, Director of Enrollment Management Services, Caldwell Community College and Technical Institute, 2855 Hickory Boulevard, Hudson, NC 28638. *Phone:* 828-726-2703. *Fax:* 828-726-2709. *E-mail:* cwoodard@cccti.edu.
Website: http://www.cccti.edu/.

Cape Fear Community College
Wilmington, North Carolina

- **State-supported** 2-year, founded 1959, part of North Carolina Community College System
- **Urban** 150-acre campus
- **Endowment** $6.2 million
- **Coed**, 9,246 undergraduate students, 49% full-time, 54% women, 46% men

Undergraduates 4,507 full-time, 4,739 part-time. Students come from 49 other countries; 6% are from out of state; 15% Black or African American, non-Hispanic/Latino; 5% Hispanic/Latino; 0.9% Asian, non-Hispanic/Latino; 0.2% Native Hawaiian or other Pacific Islander, non-Hispanic/Latino; 0.9% American Indian or Alaska Native, non-Hispanic/Latino; 2% Two or more races, non-Hispanic/Latino; 3% Race/ethnicity unknown; 0.1% international; 9% transferred in.

Freshmen *Admission:* 3,341 applied, 1,840 admitted, 1,589 enrolled.

Faculty *Total:* 729, 40% full-time. *Student/faculty ratio:* 14:1.

Majors Accounting technology and bookkeeping; architectural engineering technology; automobile/automotive mechanics technology; building/property maintenance; business administration and management; chemical technology; cinematography and film/video production; computer systems networking and telecommunications; computer technology/computer systems technology; criminal justice/police science; culinary arts; dental hygiene; diagnostic medical sonography and ultrasound technology; early childhood education; electrical, electronic and communications engineering technology; electrical/electronics equipment installation and repair; electromechanical and instrumentation and maintenance technologies related; executive assistant/executive secretary; fire prevention and safety technology; hotel/motel administration; instrumentation technology; interior design; landscaping and groundskeeping; language interpretation and translation; liberal arts and sciences/liberal studies; machine shop technology; marine maintenance and ship repair technology; mechanical engineering/mechanical technology; medical office management; medical radiologic technology; nuclear/nuclear power technology; occupational therapist assistant; oceanography (chemical and physical); registered nursing/registered nurse; surgical technology.

Academics *Calendar:* semesters. *Degree:* certificates, diplomas, and associate. *Special study options:* academic remediation for entering students, adult/continuing education programs, advanced placement credit, cooperative education, distance learning, double majors, English as a second language, independent study, off-campus study, part-time degree program, services for LD students, summer session for credit.

Library Cape Fear Community College Library with 85,351 titles, 16,375 audiovisual materials, an OPAC, a Web page.

Student Life *Housing:* college housing not available. *Activities and Organizations:* student-run newspaper, choral group, Nursing Club, Dental Hygiene Club, Pineapple Guild, Phi Theta Kappa, Occupational Therapy. *Campus security:* 24-hour emergency response devices and patrols, late-night transport/escort service, armed police officer. *Student services:* personal/psychological counseling.

Athletics Member NJCAA. *Intercollegiate sports:* basketball M/W, cheerleading M/W, golf M, soccer M/W, volleyball W. *Intramural sports:* basketball M/W, table tennis M/W.

Costs (2014–15) *Tuition:* state resident $2288 full-time; nonresident $8432 full-time. Full-time tuition and fees vary according to course load. Part-time tuition and fees vary according to course load. *Required fees:* $137 full-time. *Payment plan:* installment.

Financial Aid Of all full-time matriculated undergraduates who enrolled in 2012, 150 Federal Work-Study jobs (averaging $1687).

Applying *Options:* electronic application, early admission. *Required for some:* high school transcript, interview, placement testing. *Application deadlines:* 8/16 (freshmen), rolling (transfers). *Notification:* continuous (freshmen), continuous (transfers).

Freshman Application Contact Ms. Linda Kasyan, Director of Enrollment Management, Cape Fear Community College, 411 North Front Street, Wilmington, NC 28401-3993. *Phone:* 910-362-7054. *Toll-free phone:* 877-799-2322. *Fax:* 910-362-7080. *E-mail:* admissions@cfcc.edu.
Website: http://www.cfcc.edu/.

Carolinas College of Health Sciences
Charlotte, North Carolina

- **Public** 2-year, founded 1990
- **Urban** 3-acre campus with easy access to Charlotte
- **Endowment** $1.8 million
- **Coed,** 438 undergraduate students, 13% full-time, 86% women, 14% men

Undergraduates 58 full-time, 380 part-time. Students come from 4 states and territories; 6% are from out of state; 9% Black or African American, non-Hispanic/Latino; 4% Hispanic/Latino; 2% Asian, non-Hispanic/Latino; 0.7% Native Hawaiian or other Pacific Islander, non-Hispanic/Latino; 0.5% American Indian or Alaska Native, non-Hispanic/Latino; 3% Two or more races, non-Hispanic/Latino; 3% Race/ethnicity unknown.

Freshmen *Admission:* 14 enrolled. *Average high school GPA:* 3.5.

Faculty *Total:* 71, 37% full-time. *Student/faculty ratio:* 11:1.

Majors Medical radiologic technology; radiologic technology/science; registered nursing/registered nurse.

Academics *Calendar:* semesters. *Degree:* certificates, diplomas, and associate. *Special study options:* advanced placement credit, distance learning, double majors, honors programs, independent study, services for LD students, summer session for credit.

Library AHEC Library with 9,810 titles, 503 serial subscriptions, an OPAC, a Web page.

Student Life *Housing Options:* Campus housing is provided by a third party. *Campus security:* 24-hour emergency response devices and patrols, late-night transport/escort service. *Student services:* health clinic, personal/psychological counseling.

Standardized Tests *Required for some:* SAT or ACT (for admission).

Costs (2014–15) *Tuition:* state resident $13,311 full-time; nonresident $13,311 full-time. Full-time tuition and fees vary according to course load and program. Part-time tuition and fees vary according to course load and program. *Required fees:* $1220 full-time. *Waivers:* employees or children of employees.

Financial Aid Of all full-time matriculated undergraduates who enrolled in 2012, 8 Federal Work-Study jobs (averaging $2087).

Applying *Options:* electronic application. *Application fee:* $50. *Required:* minimum 2.5 GPA. *Required for some:* high school transcript, 1 letter of recommendation, interview, SAT or ACT scores.

Freshman Application Contact Ms. Laura Holland, Admissions Representative, Carolinas College of Health Sciences, 1200 Blythe Boulevard, Charlotte, NC 28203. *Phone:* 704-355-5583. *Fax:* 704-355-9336. *E-mail:* Laura.Holland@CarolinasCollege.edu.
Website: http://www.carolinascollege.edu/.

Carteret Community College
Morehead City, North Carolina

Freshman Application Contact Ms. Margie Ward, Admissions Officer, Carteret Community College, 3505 Arendell Street, Morehead City, NC 28557-2989. *Phone:* 252-222-6155. *Fax:* 252-222-6265. *E-mail:* admissions@carteret.edu.
Website: http://www.carteret.edu/.

Catawba Valley Community College
Hickory, North Carolina

- **State and locally supported** 2-year, founded 1960, part of North Carolina Community College System
- **Small-town** 50-acre campus with easy access to Charlotte
- **Endowment** $1.3 million
- **Coed,** 4,561 undergraduate students, 39% full-time, 59% women, 41% men

Undergraduates 1,779 full-time, 2,782 part-time. Students come from 4 states and territories; 9% Black or African American, non-Hispanic/Latino; 8% Hispanic/Latino; 7% Asian, non-Hispanic/Latino; 0.8% American Indian or Alaska Native, non-Hispanic/Latino; 0.9% Two or more races, non-Hispanic/Latino; 2% Race/ethnicity unknown; 23% transferred in.

Freshmen *Admission:* 1,939 applied, 1,303 admitted, 928 enrolled. *Average high school GPA:* 3.11.

Faculty *Total:* 422, 37% full-time. *Student/faculty ratio:* 10:1.

Majors Accounting technology and bookkeeping; applied horticulture/horticulture operations; architectural engineering technology; automobile/automotive mechanics technology; business administration and management; commercial and advertising art; computer engineering technology; computer programming; computer systems networking and telecommunications; criminal justice/safety; cyber/computer forensics and counterterrorism; dental hygiene; early childhood education; electrical, electronic and communications engineering technology; electromechanical and instrumentation and maintenance technologies related; electroneurodiagnostic/electroencephalographic technology; emergency medical technology (EMT paramedic); fire prevention and safety technology; forensic science and technology; general studies; health information/medical records technology; information science/studies; information technology; liberal arts and sciences/liberal studies; machine shop technology; mechanical engineering/mechanical technology; medical office management; medical radiologic technology; office management; photographic and film/video technology; polysomnography; registered nursing/registered nurse; respiratory care therapy; turf and turfgrass management.

Academics *Calendar:* semesters. *Degree:* certificates, diplomas, and associate. *Special study options:* academic remediation for entering students, adult/continuing education programs, advanced placement credit, cooperative education, distance learning, double majors, English as a second language, independent study, part-time degree program, services for LD students, student-designed majors, summer session for credit.

Library Learning Resource Center with 29,315 titles, 1,250 serial subscriptions, 1,000 audiovisual materials, an OPAC, a Web page.

Student Life *Housing:* college housing not available. *Activities and Organizations:* drama/theater group, choral group, Skills USA, Campus Crusade for Christ, Emerging Entrepreneurs, Circle K, Phi Theta Kappa. *Campus security:* 24-hour patrols. *Student services:* personal/psychological counseling.

Athletics Member NJCAA. *Intercollegiate sports:* baseball M, basketball M/W, cheerleading M/W, volleyball W.

Standardized Tests *Required:* COMPASS test series (for admission).

Costs (2014–15) *Tuition:* state resident $1815 full-time, $72 per credit part-time; nonresident $6423 full-time, $264 per credit hour part-time. Part-time tuition and fees vary according to course load. *Required fees:* $99 full-time, $5 per credit hour part-time, $17 per term part-time. *Payment plan:* installment.

Applying *Options:* electronic application. *Required:* high school transcript. *Required for some:* 1 letter of recommendation. *Application deadlines:* rolling (freshmen), rolling (out-of-state freshmen), rolling (transfers). *Notification:* continuous (freshmen), continuous (out-of-state freshmen), continuous (transfers).

Freshman Application Contact Catawba Valley Community College, 2550 Highway 70 SE, Hickory, NC 28602-9699. *Phone:* 828-327-7000 Ext. 4618.
Website: http://www.cvcc.edu/.

Central Carolina Community College
Sanford, North Carolina

- **State and locally supported** 2-year, founded 1962, part of North Carolina Community College System
- **Small-town** 41-acre campus with easy access to Raleigh, NC; Fayetteville, NC
- **Endowment** $3.0 million
- **Coed,** 4,900 undergraduate students, 44% full-time, 66% women, 34% men

Undergraduates 2,138 full-time, 2,762 part-time. 6% are from out of state; 23% Black or African American, non-Hispanic/Latino; 9% Hispanic/Latino; 0.7% Asian, non-Hispanic/Latino; 0.1% Native Hawaiian or other Pacific Islander, non-Hispanic/Latino; 0.8% American Indian or Alaska Native, non-Hispanic/Latino; 1% Two or more races, non-Hispanic/Latino; 0.5% Race/ethnicity unknown; 0.4% international.

Freshmen *Admission:* 736 applied, 736 admitted, 1,130 enrolled.

Faculty *Total:* 1,050, 35% full-time.

Majors Accounting; administrative assistant and secretarial science; automobile/automotive mechanics technology; business administration and management; computer/information technology services administration related; computer programming; computer programming (specific applications); computer systems networking and telecommunications; criminal justice/law enforcement administration; drafting and design technology; electrical, electronic and communications engineering technology; information science/studies; information technology; instrumentation technology; kindergarten/preschool education; laser and optical technology; legal administrative assistant/secretary; legal assistant/paralegal; liberal arts and sciences/liberal studies; marketing/marketing management; medical administrative assistant and medical secretary; medical/clinical assistant; operations management; quality control technology; radio and television; registered nursing/registered nurse; social work; telecommunications technology; veterinary/animal health technology.

Academics *Calendar:* semesters. *Degree:* certificates, diplomas, and associate. *Special study options:* academic remediation for entering students, adult/continuing education programs, advanced placement credit, distance learning, double majors, English as a second language, independent study, internships, part-time degree program, services for LD students, summer session for credit.

Library Library/Learning Resources Center plus 2 others with 50,479 titles, 240 serial subscriptions, 5,946 audiovisual materials, an OPAC, a Web page.

Student Life *Housing:* college housing not available. *Activities and Organizations:* student-run radio and television station. *Campus security:* 24-hour emergency response devices and patrols, student patrols, patrols by trained security personnel during operating hours. *Student services:* personal/psychological counseling.

Athletics Member NJCAA. *Intercollegiate sports:* basketball M/W, golf M, volleyball W.

Standardized Tests *Required for some:* Our college accepts SAT, ACT, Compass, Asset, and Accuplacer test scores within the last five years. *Recommended:* SAT or ACT (for admission).

Costs (2014–15) *Tuition:* state resident $2288 full-time; nonresident $8432 full-time. Full-time tuition and fees vary according to course load. Part-time tuition and fees vary according to course load. *Payment plan:* installment.

Financial Aid Of all full-time matriculated undergraduates who enrolled in 2012, 70 Federal Work-Study jobs (averaging $1361). *Financial aid deadline:* 5/4.

Applying *Options:* electronic application, early admission, deferred entrance. *Required:* high school transcript. *Application deadlines:* rolling (freshmen), rolling (out-of-state freshmen), rolling (transfers). *Notification:* continuous (freshmen), continuous (out-of-state freshmen), continuous (transfers).

Freshman Application Contact Mrs. Jamie Tyson Childress, Dean of Enrollment/Registrar, Central Carolina Community College, 1105 Kelly Drive, Sanford, NC 27330-9000. *Phone:* 919-718-7239. *Toll-free phone:* 800-682-8353. *Fax:* 919-718-7380.

Website: http://www.cccc.edu/.

Central Piedmont Community College
Charlotte, North Carolina

Freshman Application Contact Ms. Linda McComb, Associate Dean, Central Piedmont Community College, PO Box 35009, Charlotte, NC 28235-5009. *Phone:* 704-330-6784. *Fax:* 704-330-6136.

Website: http://www.cpcc.edu/.

Cleveland Community College
Shelby, North Carolina

- **State-supported** 2-year, founded 1965, part of North Carolina Community College System
- **Small-town** 43-acre campus with easy access to Charlotte
- **Coed,** 3,371 undergraduate students, 35% full-time, 62% women, 38% men

Undergraduates 1,175 full-time, 2,196 part-time. 22% Black or African American, non-Hispanic/Latino; 3% Hispanic/Latino; 0.5% Asian, non-Hispanic/Latino; 0.4% American Indian or Alaska Native, non-Hispanic/Latino; 1% Two or more races, non-Hispanic/Latino; 1% Race/ethnicity unknown; 0.8% international.

Freshmen *Admission:* 833 enrolled.

Faculty *Total:* 308, 25% full-time. *Student/faculty ratio:* 11:1.

Majors Accounting; banking and financial support services; biology/biotechnology laboratory technician; business administration and management; computer and information systems security; computer systems networking and telecommunications; criminal justice/safety; early childhood education; electrical, electronic and communications engineering technology; electrician; elementary education; emergency medical technology (EMT

paramedic); entrepreneurship; fire prevention and safety technology; general studies; information science/studies; information technology; language interpretation and translation; legal administrative assistant/secretary; liberal arts and sciences and humanities related; liberal arts and sciences/liberal studies; marketing/marketing management; mechanical drafting and CAD/CADD; medical/clinical assistant; medical office management; office management; operations management; pre-engineering; prenursing studies; radio and television broadcasting technology; radiologic technology/science; registered nursing/registered nurse.

Academics *Calendar:* semesters. *Degree:* certificates, diplomas, and associate. *Special study options:* academic remediation for entering students, adult/continuing education programs, advanced placement credit, cooperative education, distance learning, double majors, English as a second language, independent study, off-campus study, part-time degree program, summer session for credit.

Library Jim & Patsy Rose Library with an OPAC, a Web page.

Student Life *Housing:* college housing not available. *Activities and Organizations:* drama/theater group, student-run television station. *Campus security:* security personnel during open hours. *Student services:* personal/psychological counseling.

Costs (2013–14) *Tuition:* state resident $2208 full-time, $69 per credit hour part-time; nonresident $8352 full-time, $261 per credit hour part-time. Full-time tuition and fees vary according to course load. Part-time tuition and fees vary according to course load. *Required fees:* $94 full-time.

Financial Aid Of all full-time matriculated undergraduates who enrolled in 2012, 20 Federal Work-Study jobs.

Applying *Options:* electronic application, deferred entrance. *Required:* high school transcript. *Application deadlines:* rolling (freshmen), rolling (transfers). *Notification:* continuous (freshmen), continuous (transfers).

Freshman Application Contact Cleveland Community College, 137 South Post Road, Shelby, NC 28152. *Phone:* 704-669-4139.

Website: http://www.clevelandcc.edu/.

Coastal Carolina Community College
Jacksonville, North Carolina

Freshman Application Contact Ms. Heather Calihan, Counseling Coordinator, Coastal Carolina Community College, Jacksonville, NC 28546. *Phone:* 910-938-6241. *Fax:* 910-455-2767. *E-mail:* calihanh@coastal.cc.nc.us.

Website: http://www.coastalcarolina.edu/.

College of The Albemarle
Elizabeth City, North Carolina

Freshman Application Contact Mr. Kenny Krentz, Director of Admissions and International Students, College of The Albemarle, PO Box 2327, Elizabeth City, NC 27906-2327. *Phone:* 252-335-0821. *Fax:* 252-335-2011. *E-mail:* kkrentz@albemarle.edu.

Website: http://www.albemarle.edu/.

Craven Community College
New Bern, North Carolina

Freshman Application Contact Ms. Millicent Fulford, Recruiter, Craven Community College, 800 College Court, New Bern, NC 28562-4984. *Phone:* 252-638-7232.

Website: http://www.cravencc.edu/.

Davidson County Community College
Lexington, North Carolina

Freshman Application Contact Davidson County Community College, PO Box 1287, Lexington, NC 27293-1287. *Phone:* 336-249-8186 Ext. 6715. *Fax:* 336-224-0240. *E-mail:* admissions@davidsonccc.edu.

Website: http://www.davidsonccc.edu/.

Durham Technical Community College
Durham, North Carolina

Director of Admissions Ms. Penny Augustine, Director of Admissions and Testing, Durham Technical Community College, 1637 Lawson Street, Durham, NC 27703-5023. *Phone:* 919-686-3619.

Website: http://www.durhamtech.edu/.

ECPI University
Charlotte, North Carolina

Admissions Office Contact ECPI University, 4800 Airport Center Parkway, Charlotte, NC 28208. *Toll-free phone:* 866-708-6167.

Website: http://www.ecpi.edu/.

ECPI University
Greensboro, North Carolina

Admissions Office Contact ECPI University, 7802 Airport Center Drive, Greensboro, NC 27409. *Toll-free phone:* 866-708-6170.
Website: http://www.ecpi.edu/.

Edgecombe Community College
Tarboro, North Carolina

Freshman Application Contact Ms. Jackie Heath, Admissions Officer, Edgecombe Community College, 2009 West Wilson Street, Tarboro, NC 27886-9399. *Phone:* 252-823-5166 Ext. 254.
Website: http://www.edgecombe.edu/.

Fayetteville Technical Community College
Fayetteville, North Carolina

- **State-supported** 2-year, founded 1961, part of North Carolina Community College System
- **Suburban** 209-acre campus with easy access to Raleigh
- **Endowment** $39,050
- **Coed**, 12,383 undergraduate students, 41% full-time, 59% women, 41% men

Undergraduates 5,117 full-time, 7,266 part-time. Students come from 38 other countries; 19% are from out of state; 45% Black or African American, non-Hispanic/Latino; 9% Hispanic/Latino; 1% Asian, non-Hispanic/Latino; 0.4% Native Hawaiian or other Pacific Islander, non-Hispanic/Latino; 3% American Indian or Alaska Native, non-Hispanic/Latino; 4% Two or more races, non-Hispanic/Latino; 2% Race/ethnicity unknown; 0.7% international; 21% transferred in.
Freshmen *Admission:* 3,905 applied, 3,905 admitted, 1,961 enrolled. *Average high school GPA:* 2.55. *Test scores:* SAT critical reading scores over 500: 66%; SAT math scores over 500: 43%; SAT writing scores over 500: 47%; ACT scores over 18: 100%; SAT critical reading scores over 600: 13%; SAT math scores over 600: 8%; SAT writing scores over 600: 14%; ACT scores over 24: 25%; SAT critical reading scores over 700: 4%.
Faculty *Total:* 492, 54% full-time, 8% with terminal degrees. *Student/faculty ratio:* 22:1.
Majors Accounting; applied horticulture/horticulture operations; architectural engineering technology; automobile/automotive mechanics technology; banking and financial support services; building/construction finishing, management, and inspection related; business administration and management; civil engineering technology; commercial and advertising art; computer and information systems security; computer programming; computer systems networking and telecommunications; corrections and criminal justice related; criminal justice/safety; crisis/emergency/disaster management; culinary arts; dental hygiene; early childhood education; electrical, electronic and communications engineering technology; electrician; elementary education; emergency medical technology (EMT paramedic); fire prevention and safety technology; forensic science and technology; funeral service and mortuary science; game and interactive media design; health and physical education related; heating, air conditioning, ventilation and refrigeration maintenance technology; hotel, motel, and restaurant management; human resources management; information science/studies; information technology; legal assistant/paralegal; liberal arts and sciences and humanities related; liberal arts and sciences/liberal studies; machine shop technology; marketing/marketing management; medical office management; nuclear medical technology; office management; operations management; pharmacy technician; physical therapy technology; public administration; radiologic technology/science; registered nursing/registered nurse; respiratory care therapy; speech-language pathology assistant; surgical technology.
Academics *Calendar:* semesters. *Degree:* certificates, diplomas, and associate. *Special study options:* academic remediation for entering students, accelerated degree program, adult/continuing education programs, advanced placement credit, cooperative education, distance learning, double majors, English as a second language, independent study, internships, off-campus study, part-time degree program, services for LD students, summer session for credit.
Library Paul H. Thompson Library plus 1 other with 66,745 titles, 136 serial subscriptions, 582 audiovisual materials, an OPAC, a Web page.
Student Life *Housing:* college housing not available. *Activities and Organizations:* Parents for Higher Education, Intercultural Club, Phi Beta Lambda, Association of Nursing Students, African-American Heritage Club. *Campus security:* 24-hour emergency response devices and patrols, late-night transport/escort service, campus-wide emergency notification system. *Student services:* personal/psychological counseling.
Athletics *Intramural sports:* basketball M/W, football M/W, soccer M/W, softball M/W, volleyball M/W.

Standardized Tests *Required:* ACCUPLACER is required or ACT and SAT scores in lieu of ACCUPLACER if the scores are no more than 5 years old or ASSET and COMPASS scores are also accepted if they are no more than 3 years old. Pilot testing use of High School GPA/coursework (for admission).
Costs (2013–14) *One-time required fee:* $25. *Tuition:* state resident $2288 full-time, $72 per credit hour part-time; nonresident $8432 full-time, $264 per credit hour part-time. Full-time tuition and fees vary according to course load. Part-time tuition and fees vary according to course load. *Required fees:* $90 full-time, $45 per term part-time. *Payment plan:* installment. *Waivers:* employees or children of employees.
Financial Aid Of all full-time matriculated undergraduates who enrolled in 2012, 75 Federal Work-Study jobs (averaging $2000). *Financial aid deadline:* 6/1.
Applying *Options:* electronic application, deferred entrance. *Required for some:* essay or personal statement, high school transcript, interview. *Application deadlines:* rolling (freshmen), rolling (out-of-state freshmen), rolling (transfers). *Notification:* continuous (freshmen), continuous (out-of-state freshmen), continuous (transfers).
Freshman Application Contact Ms. Evelyn Bryant, Assistant Registrar/Curriculum, Fayetteville Technical Community College, 2201 Hull Road, P.O. Box 35236, Fayetteville, NC 28303. *Phone:* 910-678-8271. *Fax:* 910-678-0085. *E-mail:* bryante@faytechcc.edu.
Website: http://www.faytechcc.edu/.

Forsyth Technical Community College
Winston-Salem, North Carolina

- **State-supported** 2-year, founded 1964, part of North Carolina Community College System
- **Suburban** 38-acre campus
- **Coed**

Undergraduates 4,639 full-time, 5,302 part-time. 1% are from out of state; 26% transferred in.
Faculty *Student/faculty ratio:* 17:1.
Academics *Calendar:* semesters. *Degree:* certificates, diplomas, and associate. *Special study options:* academic remediation for entering students, adult/continuing education programs, advanced placement credit, cooperative education, distance learning, double majors, English as a second language, independent study, internships, off-campus study, part-time degree program, services for LD students, summer session for credit.
Student Life *Campus security:* 24-hour emergency response devices and patrols, late-night transport/escort service.
Standardized Tests *Required:* COMPASS (for admission).
Financial Aid Of all full-time matriculated undergraduates who enrolled in 2012, 42 Federal Work-Study jobs (averaging $2083).
Applying *Required:* high school transcript.
Freshman Application Contact Admissions Office, Forsyth Technical Community College, 2100 Silas Creek Parkway, Winston-Salem, NC 27103-5197. *Phone:* 336-734-7556. *E-mail:* admissions@forsythtech.edu.
Website: http://www.forsythtech.edu/.

Gaston College
Dallas, North Carolina

Freshman Application Contact Terry Basier, Director of Enrollment Management and Admissions, Gaston College, 201 Highway 321 South, Dallas, NC 28034. *Phone:* 704-922-6214. *Fax:* 704-922-6443.
Website: http://www.gaston.edu/.

Guilford Technical Community College
Jamestown, North Carolina

- **State and locally supported** 2-year, founded 1958, part of North Carolina Community College System
- **Urban** 158-acre campus with easy access to Raleigh, Charlotte, Greensboro
- **Coed**

Undergraduates 7,903 full-time, 6,890 part-time. Students come from 10 states and territories; 98 other countries; 0.1% are from out of state; 46% Black or African American, non-Hispanic/Latino; 5% Hispanic/Latino; 3% Asian, non-Hispanic/Latino; 0.1% Native Hawaiian or other Pacific Islander, non-Hispanic/Latino; 0.8% American Indian or Alaska Native, non-Hispanic/Latino; 1% Two or more races, non-Hispanic/Latino; 3% Race/ethnicity unknown; 0.7% international; 9% transferred in. *Retention:* 52% of full-time freshmen returned.
Faculty *Student/faculty ratio:* 24:1.
Academics *Calendar:* semesters. *Degree:* certificates, diplomas, and associate. *Special study options:* academic remediation for entering students, adult/continuing education programs, advanced placement credit, cooperative education, distance learning, double majors, English as a second language, external degree program, independent study, internships, off-campus study,

part-time degree program, services for LD students, student-designed majors, summer session for credit. *ROTC:* Army (c), Air Force (c).

Student Life *Campus security:* 24-hour emergency response devices and patrols, late-night transport/escort service.

Athletics Member NJCAA.

Costs (2013–14) *Tuition:* state resident $1656 full-time, $69 per credit hour part-time; nonresident $6264 full-time, $261 per credit hour part-time. Full-time tuition and fees vary according to course load and program. Part-time tuition and fees vary according to course load and program. *Required fees:* $167 full-time, $49 per term part-time.

Applying *Options:* electronic application, early admission, deferred entrance. *Required for some:* high school transcript, interview.

Freshman Application Contact Guilford Technical Community College, PO Box 309, Jamestown, NC 27282-0309. *Phone:* 336-334-4822 Ext. 50125. *Website:* http://www.gtcc.edu/.

Halifax Community College
Weldon, North Carolina

- **State and locally supported** 2-year, founded 1967, part of North Carolina Community College System
- **Rural** 109-acre campus
- **Endowment** $1.0 million
- **Coed,** 1,510 undergraduate students, 57% full-time, 66% women, 34% men

Undergraduates 859 full-time, 651 part-time. 0.5% are from out of state; 56% Black or African American, non-Hispanic/Latino; 1% Hispanic/Latino; 0.1% Asian, non-Hispanic/Latino; 2% American Indian or Alaska Native, non-Hispanic/Latino; 1% Two or more races, non-Hispanic/Latino; 0.9% Race/ethnicity unknown; 0.8% international. *Retention:* 51% of full-time freshmen returned.

Freshmen *Admission:* 462 applied, 297 admitted.

Faculty *Total:* 101, 60% full-time. *Student/faculty ratio:* 12:1.

Majors Accounting; business administration and management; clinical/medical laboratory technology; clinical/medical social work; commercial and advertising art; computer systems networking and telecommunications; criminal justice/police science; dental hygiene; early childhood education; health professions related; information technology; legal assistant/paralegal; medical administrative assistant and medical secretary; office management; registered nursing/registered nurse.

Academics *Calendar:* semesters. *Degree:* certificates, diplomas, and associate. *Special study options:* academic remediation for entering students, cooperative education, distance learning, double majors, part-time degree program, services for LD students, summer session for credit.

Library Learning Resources Center with 32,611 titles, 103 serial subscriptions, 1,944 audiovisual materials, an OPAC, a Web page.

Student Life *Housing:* college housing not available. *Campus security:* 12-hour patrols by trained security personnel. *Student services:* health clinic.

Costs (2014–15) *Tuition:* state resident $1716 full-time, $72 per credit hour part-time; nonresident $6324 full-time, $263 per credit hour part-time. Full-time tuition and fees vary according to program. Part-time tuition and fees vary according to program. *Required fees:* $117 full-time. *Payment plan:* installment.

Applying *Options:* deferred entrance. *Required:* high school transcript. *Application deadlines:* rolling (freshmen), rolling (transfers). *Notification:* continuous (freshmen), continuous (transfers).

Freshman Application Contact Halifax Community College, PO Drawer 809, Weldon, NC 27890-0809. *Phone:* 252-536-7220. *Website:* http://www.halifaxcc.edu/.

Harrison College
Morrisville, North Carolina

- **Proprietary** 2-year, founded 2011, part of Harrison College
- **Suburban** campus with easy access to Raleigh
- **Coed,** 200 undergraduate students, 80% full-time, 49% women, 51% men

Undergraduates 159 full-time, 41 part-time. 48% Black or African American, non-Hispanic/Latino; 7% Hispanic/Latino; 0.5% Asian, non-Hispanic/Latino; 3% Two or more races, non-Hispanic/Latino; 2% Race/ethnicity unknown.

Freshmen *Admission:* 49 applied, 49 admitted, 20 enrolled.

Faculty *Total:* 14, 36% full-time. *Student/faculty ratio:* 14:1.

Majors Baking and pastry arts; cooking and related culinary arts.

Academics *Degree:* associate. *Special study options:* adult/continuing education programs, advanced placement credit, cooperative education, distance learning, double majors, internships, off-campus study, part-time degree program, summer session for credit.

Library North Carolina Learning Resource Center.

Student Life *Housing:* college housing not available.

Standardized Tests *Required:* Wonderlic Scholastic Level Exam (SLE) (for admission).

Applying *Options:* electronic application. *Required:* high school transcript, interview. *Application deadlines:* rolling (freshmen), rolling (out-of-state freshmen), rolling (transfers). *Notification:* continuous (freshmen), continuous (out-of-state freshmen), continuous (transfers).

Freshman Application Contact Mr. Jason Howanec, Vice President of Enrollment, Harrison College, 500 N. Meridian St., Indianapolis, IN 46204. *Phone:* 800-919-2500. *E-mail:* Admissions@harrison.edu. *Website:* http://www.harrison.edu/.

Haywood Community College
Clyde, North Carolina

Director of Admissions Ms. Debbie Rowland, Coordinator of Admissions, Haywood Community College, 185 Freedlander Drive, Clyde, NC 28721-9453. *Phone:* 828-627-4505. *Toll-free phone:* 866-GOTOHCC. *Website:* http://www.haywood.edu/.

Isothermal Community College
Spindale, North Carolina

Freshman Application Contact Ms. Vickie Searcy, Enrollment Management Office, Isothermal Community College, PO Box 804, Spindale, NC 28160-0804. *Phone:* 828-286-3636 Ext. 251. *Fax:* 828-286-8109. *E-mail:* vsearcy@isothermal.edu. *Website:* http://www.isothermal.edu/.

ITT Technical Institute
Cary, North Carolina

- **Proprietary** primarily 2-year, part of ITT Educational Services, Inc.
- **Coed**

Majors Construction management; cyber/computer forensics and counterterrorism; drafting and design technology; electrical, electronic and communications engineering technology; forensic science and technology; information technology project management; network and system administration; project management.

Academics *Degrees:* associate and bachelor's.

Student Life *Housing:* college housing not available.

Freshman Application Contact Director of Recruitment, ITT Technical Institute, 5520 Dillard Drive, Suite 100, Cary, NC 27518. *Phone:* 919-233-2520. *Toll-free phone:* 877-203-5533. *Website:* http://www.itt-tech.edu/.

ITT Technical Institute
Charlotte, North Carolina

- **Proprietary** primarily 2-year
- **Coed**

Majors Business administration and management; construction management; cyber/computer forensics and counterterrorism; drafting and design technology; electrical, electronic and communications engineering technology; forensic science and technology; information technology project management; network and system administration; project management.

Academics *Degrees:* associate and bachelor's.

Student Life *Housing:* college housing not available.

Freshman Application Contact Director of Recruitment, ITT Technical Institute, 4135 Southstream Boulevard, Suite 200, Charlotte, NC 28217. *Phone:* 704-423-3100. *Toll-free phone:* 800-488-0173. *Website:* http://www.itt-tech.edu/.

ITT Technical Institute
High Point, North Carolina

- **Proprietary** primarily 2-year, founded 2007, part of ITT Educational Services, Inc.
- **Coed**

Majors Construction management; cyber/computer forensics and counterterrorism; drafting and design technology; electrical, electronic and communications engineering technology; forensic science and technology; graphic communications; information technology project management; network and system administration; project management; registered nursing/registered nurse.

Academics *Calendar:* quarters. *Degrees:* associate and bachelor's.

Student Life *Housing:* college housing not available.

Freshman Application Contact Director of Recruitment, ITT Technical Institute, 4050 Piedmont Parkway, Suite 110, High Point, NC 27265. *Phone:* 336-819-5900. *Toll-free phone:* 877-536-5231. *Website:* http://www.itt-tech.edu/.

James Sprunt Community College
Kenansville, North Carolina

- **State-supported** 2-year, founded 1964, part of North Carolina Community College System
- **Rural** 51-acre campus
- **Endowment** $1.2 million
- **Coed,** 1,291 undergraduate students, 54% full-time, 71% women, 29% men

Undergraduates 697 full-time, 594 part-time. Students come from 8 states and territories; 1% are from out of state; 41% Black or African American, non-Hispanic/Latino; 12% Hispanic/Latino; 0.2% Asian, non-Hispanic/Latino; 0.2% Native Hawaiian or other Pacific Islander, non-Hispanic/Latino; 0.4% American Indian or Alaska Native, non-Hispanic/Latino; 0.9% Two or more races, non-Hispanic/Latino; 0.1% Race/ethnicity unknown; 17% transferred in. *Retention:* 83% of full-time freshmen returned.

Freshmen *Admission:* 700 applied, 700 admitted, 182 enrolled.

Faculty *Total:* 75, 59% full-time, 7% with terminal degrees. *Student/faculty ratio:* 16:1.

Majors Accounting; agribusiness; animal sciences; business administration and management; child development; commercial and advertising art; criminal justice/safety; early childhood education; elementary education; general studies; information technology; institutional food workers; liberal arts and sciences and humanities related; liberal arts and sciences/liberal studies; medical/clinical assistant; registered nursing/registered nurse; viticulture and enology.

Academics *Calendar:* semesters. *Degree:* certificates, diplomas, and associate. *Special study options:* academic remediation for entering students, accelerated degree program, advanced placement credit, cooperative education, distance learning, double majors, English as a second language, independent study, internships, part-time degree program, services for LD students, summer session for credit.

Library James Sprunt Community College Library with 25,268 titles, 92 serial subscriptions, 200 audiovisual materials, an OPAC, a Web page.

Student Life *Housing:* college housing not available. *Activities and Organizations:* student-run newspaper, Student Nurses Association, Art Club, Alumni Association, National Technical-Vocational Honor Society, Phi Theta Kappa, national sororities. *Campus security:* day, evening and Saturday trained security personnel. *Student services:* personal/psychological counseling.

Athletics *Intercollegiate sports:* softball M/W, volleyball M/W.

Costs (2014–15) *Tuition:* state resident $2288 full-time, $72 per credit part-time; nonresident $8132 full-time, $264 per credit part-time. Full-time tuition and fees vary according to course load. Part-time tuition and fees vary according to course load. *Required fees:* $70 full-time, $35 per term part-time.

Financial Aid Of all full-time matriculated undergraduates who enrolled in 2012, 35 Federal Work-Study jobs (averaging $1057).

Applying *Options:* electronic application. *Required:* high school transcript. *Application deadlines:* rolling (freshmen), rolling (out-of-state freshmen), rolling (transfers). *Notification:* continuous (freshmen), continuous (out-of-state freshmen), continuous (transfers).

Freshman Application Contact Ms. Lea Matthews, Admissions Specialist, James Sprunt Community College, Highway 11 South, 133 James Sprunt Drive, Kenansville, NC 28349. *Phone:* 910-296-6078. *Fax:* 910-296-1222. *E-mail:* lmatthews@jamessprunt.edu.
Website: http://www.jamessprunt.edu/.

Johnston Community College
Smithfield, North Carolina

- **State-supported** 2-year, founded 1969, part of North Carolina Community College System
- **Rural** 100-acre campus
- **Coed,** 4,235 undergraduate students, 52% full-time, 66% women, 34% men

Undergraduates 2,187 full-time, 2,048 part-time. 20% Black or African American, non-Hispanic/Latino; 10% Hispanic/Latino; 0.4% Asian, non-Hispanic/Latino; 0.2% Native Hawaiian or other Pacific Islander, non-Hispanic/Latino; 0.6% American Indian or Alaska Native, non-Hispanic/Latino; 0.9% Two or more races, non-Hispanic/Latino; 5% Race/ethnicity unknown; 1% international.

Freshmen *Admission:* 1,252 applied, 773 admitted, 738 enrolled.

Faculty *Total:* 414, 34% full-time. *Student/faculty ratio:* 17:1.

Majors Accounting; administrative assistant and secretarial science; business administration and management; criminal justice/police science; diesel mechanics technology; early childhood education; heating, air conditioning, ventilation and refrigeration maintenance technology; legal assistant/paralegal; liberal arts and sciences/liberal studies; medical/clinical assistant; medical office management; office management; registered nursing/registered nurse.

Academics *Calendar:* semesters. *Degree:* certificates, diplomas, and associate. *Special study options:* academic remediation for entering students, adult/continuing education programs, advanced placement credit, cooperative education, distance learning, double majors, honors programs, independent study, part-time degree program, services for LD students, summer session for credit.

Library Johnston Community College Library plus 1 other with 35,722 titles, 103 serial subscriptions, 9,409 audiovisual materials, an OPAC, a Web page.

Student Life *Housing:* college housing not available. *Activities and Organizations:* choral group. *Campus security:* 24-hour patrols. *Student services:* personal/psychological counseling.

Athletics Member NJCAA. *Intercollegiate sports:* golf M/W.

Standardized Tests *Required:* ACCUPLACER (for admission). *Recommended:* SAT or ACT (for admission).

Costs (2013–14) *Tuition:* state resident $2288 full-time, $72 per credit hour part-time; nonresident $8432 full-time, $264 per credit hour part-time. *Required fees:* $97 full-time.

Financial Aid Of all full-time matriculated undergraduates who enrolled in 2012, 35 Federal Work-Study jobs (averaging $1853).

Applying *Options:* electronic application. *Required:* high school transcript, interview. *Application deadlines:* rolling (freshmen), rolling (transfers). *Notification:* continuous (freshmen), continuous (transfers).

Freshman Application Contact Dr. Pamela J. Harrell, Vice President of Student Services, Johnston Community College, Smithfield, NC 27577-2350. *Phone:* 919-209-2048. *Fax:* 919-989-7862. *E-mail:* pjharrell@johnstoncc.edu.
Website: http://www.johnstoncc.edu/.

Kaplan College, Charlotte Campus
Charlotte, North Carolina

Freshman Application Contact Director of Admissions, Kaplan College, Charlotte Campus, 6070 East Independence Boulevard, Charlotte, NC 28212. *Phone:* 704-567-3700.
Website: http://charlotte.kaplancollege.com/.

King's College
Charlotte, North Carolina

- **Private** 2-year, founded 1901
- **Suburban** campus
- **Coed,** 501 undergraduate students
- 78% of applicants were admitted

Freshmen *Admission:* 1,024 applied, 801 admitted.

Majors Accounting technology and bookkeeping; administrative assistant and secretarial science; computer programming; computer systems networking and telecommunications; graphic design; hotel/motel administration; legal administrative assistant/secretary; legal assistant/paralegal; medical/clinical assistant.

Academics *Calendar:* quarters. *Degree:* diplomas and associate. *Special study options:* accelerated degree program, internships.

Freshman Application Contact Admissions Office, King's College, 322 Lamar Avenue, Charlotte, NC 28204-2436. *Phone:* 704-372-0266. *Toll-free phone:* 800-768-2255.
Website: http://www.kingscollegecharlotte.edu/.

Lenoir Community College
Kinston, North Carolina

- **State-supported** 2-year, founded 1960, part of North Carolina Community College System
- **Small-town** 86-acre campus
- **Coed,** 2,813 undergraduate students, 48% full-time, 59% women, 41% men

Undergraduates 1,343 full-time, 1,470 part-time. Students come from 1 other country; 1% are from out of state; 33% Black or African American, non-Hispanic/Latino; 8% Hispanic/Latino; 0.5% Asian, non-Hispanic/Latino; 0.1% Native Hawaiian or other Pacific Islander, non-Hispanic/Latino; 0.6% American Indian or Alaska Native, non-Hispanic/Latino; 0.9% Two or more races, non-Hispanic/Latino; 0.7% Race/ethnicity unknown; 0.1% international; 10% transferred in.

Freshmen *Admission:* 494 applied, 436 admitted, 540 enrolled.

Faculty *Total:* 345, 28% full-time. *Student/faculty ratio:* 15:1.

Majors Airline pilot and flight crew; art; aviation/airway management; avionics maintenance technology; business administration and management; computer programming; consumer merchandising/retailing management; cosmetology; criminal justice/law enforcement administration; criminal justice/police science; elementary education; finance; food technology and processing; graphic and printing equipment operation/production; horticultural science; industrial technology; liberal arts and sciences/liberal studies; marketing/marketing management; medical administrative assistant and medical secretary; medical/clinical assistant; ornamental horticulture; pre-engineering; registered nursing/registered nurse; trade and industrial teacher education; welding technology.

Academics *Calendar:* semesters. *Degree:* certificates, diplomas, and associate. *Special study options:* academic remediation for entering students, adult/continuing education programs, advanced placement credit, cooperative education, distance learning, double majors, English as a second language, independent study, part-time degree program, summer session for credit.

Library Learning Resources Center plus 1 other with 55,053 titles, 381 serial subscriptions.

Student Life *Housing:* college housing not available. *Activities and Organizations:* student-run newspaper, choral group, Student Government Association, Automotive Club, Electronics Club, Drafting Club, Cosmetology Club. *Campus security:* 24-hour emergency response devices and patrols, student patrols. *Student services:* personal/psychological counseling.

Athletics Member NJCAA. *Intercollegiate sports:* baseball M, basketball M/W, volleyball W.

Standardized Tests *Required for some:* Assessment and Placement Services for Community Colleges. *Recommended:* SAT or ACT (for admission).

Costs (2014–15) *Tuition:* state resident $2288 full-time, $72 per credit part-time; nonresident $8432 full-time, $264 per credit part-time. Full-time tuition and fees vary according to course load. Part-time tuition and fees vary according to course load. *Required fees:* $119 full-time, $14 per credit part-time. *Waivers:* senior citizens and employees or children of employees.

Applying *Options:* electronic application, early admission. *Required:* high school transcript. *Application deadlines:* rolling (freshmen), rolling (transfers). *Notification:* continuous (freshmen), continuous (transfers).

Freshman Application Contact Mrs. Kim Hill, Enrollment Management Coordinator, Lenoir Community College, PO Box188, Kinston, NB 28502-0188. *Phone:* 252-527-6223 Ext. 301. *Fax:* 252-233-6895. *E-mail:* krhill01@lenoircc.edu.
Website: http://www.lenoircc.edu/.

Living Arts College
Raleigh, North Carolina

- **Proprietary** primarily 2-year, founded 1992
- **Suburban** campus with easy access to Raleigh
- **Coed,** 578 undergraduate students, 100% full-time, 57% women, 43% men

Undergraduates 578 full-time. Students come from 8 states and territories; 1 other country; 1% are from out of state; 48% Black or African American, non-Hispanic/Latino; 5% Hispanic/Latino; 0.9% Asian, non-Hispanic/Latino; 0.7% American Indian or Alaska Native, non-Hispanic/Latino; 2% Two or more races, non-Hispanic/Latino; 3% Race/ethnicity unknown; 35% live on campus. *Retention:* 69% of full-time freshmen returned.

Freshmen *Admission:* 95 applied, 95 admitted, 95 enrolled.

Faculty *Total:* 53, 70% full-time, 19% with terminal degrees. *Student/faculty ratio:* 10:1.

Majors Animation, interactive technology, video graphics and special effects; cinematography and film/video production; interior design; photography; recording arts technology; web page, digital/multimedia and information resources design.

Academics *Calendar:* quarters. *Degree:* certificates, diplomas, and bachelor's. *Special study options:* cooperative education, summer session for credit.

Student Life *Housing Options:* Campus housing is university owned. Freshman applicants given priority for college housing. *Activities and Organizations:* MODIV - student council, Student Ambassadors, Firebreathers Animation Studio, NVTHS-National Vocational Technical Honor Society. *Campus security:* controlled dormitory access.

Standardized Tests *Required:* Wonderlic aptitude test (for admission).

Costs (2013–14) *One-time required fee:* $275. *Tuition:* $23,968 full-time. No tuition increase for student's term of enrollment. *Room only:* $7100.

Applying *Options:* electronic application, early admission, early decision, early action, deferred entrance. *Application fee:* $25. *Required:* essay or personal statement, high school transcript, interview, portfolio for selected program. *Application deadlines:* rolling (freshmen), rolling (out-of-state freshmen), rolling (early action). *Notification:* continuous (freshmen), continuous (out-of-state freshmen), rolling (early action).

Freshman Application Contact Julie Wenta, Director of Admissions, Living Arts College, 3000 Wakefield Crossing Drive, Raleigh, NC 27614. *Phone:* 919-488-5902. *Toll-free phone:* 800-288-7442. *Fax:* 919-488-8490. *E-mail:* jwenta@living-arts-college.edu.
Website: http://www.living-arts-college.edu/.

Louisburg College
Louisburg, North Carolina

Freshman Application Contact Mr. Stephanie Tolbert, Vice President for Enrollment Management, Louisburg College, 501 North Main Street,

Louisburg, NC 27549-2399. *Phone:* 919-497-3233. *Toll-free phone:* 800-775-0208. *Fax:* 919-496-1788. *E-mail:* admissions@louisburg.edu.
Website: http://www.louisburg.edu/.

Martin Community College
Williamston, North Carolina

Freshman Application Contact Martin Community College, 1161 Kehukee Park Road, Williamston, NC 27892. *Phone:* 252-792-1521 Ext. 243.
Website: http://www.martin.cc.nc.us/.

Mayland Community College
Spruce Pine, North Carolina

Director of Admissions Ms. Cathy Morrison, Director of Admissions, Mayland Community College, PO Box 547, Spruce Pine, NC 28777-0547. *Phone:* 828-765-7351 Ext. 224. *Toll-free phone:* 800-462-9526.
Website: http://www.mayland.edu/.

McDowell Technical Community College
Marion, North Carolina

Freshman Application Contact Mr. Rick L. Wilson, Director of Admissions, McDowell Technical Community College, 54 College Drive, Marion, NC 28752. *Phone:* 828-652-0632. *Fax:* 828-652-1014. *E-mail:* rickw@mcdowelltech.edu.
Website: http://www.mcdowelltech.edu/.

Miller-Motte College
Jacksonville, North Carolina

Admissions Office Contact Miller-Motte College, 1291 Hargett Street, Jacksonville, NC 28540. *Toll-free phone:* 866-297-0267.
Website: http://www.miller-motte.edu/.

Miller-Motte College
Wilmington, North Carolina

Freshman Application Contact Admissions Office, Miller-Motte College, 5000 Market Street, Wilmington, NC 28405. *Toll-free phone:* 800-784-2110.
Website: http://www.miller-motte.edu/.

Mitchell Community College
Statesville, North Carolina

- **State-supported** 2-year, founded 1852, part of North Carolina Community College System
- **Small-town** 8-acre campus with easy access to Charlotte
- **Endowment** $2.5 million
- **Coed,** 3,514 undergraduate students, 44% full-time, 64% women, 36% men

Undergraduates 1,532 full-time, 1,982 part-time. Students come from 27 states and territories; 15% Black or African American, non-Hispanic/Latino; 7% Hispanic/Latino; 2% Asian, non-Hispanic/Latino; 0.1% Native Hawaiian or other Pacific Islander, non-Hispanic/Latino; 0.7% American Indian or Alaska Native, non-Hispanic/Latino; 0.9% Two or more races, non-Hispanic/Latino; 2% Race/ethnicity unknown; 0.5% international; 3% transferred in. *Retention:* 46% of full-time freshmen returned.

Freshmen *Admission:* 580 enrolled.

Majors Accounting; business administration and management; child-care and support services management; computer programming; computer programming (specific applications); computer systems analysis; criminal justice/law enforcement administration; early childhood education; electrical, electronic and communications engineering technology; electrician; electromechanical and instrumentation and maintenance technologies related; elementary education; engineering/industrial management; executive assistant/executive secretary; general studies; health professions related; information science/studies; information technology; kindergarten/preschool education; liberal arts and sciences and humanities related; liberal arts and sciences/liberal studies; machine shop technology; manufacturing engineering; manufacturing engineering technology; mechanical drafting and CAD/CADD; mechanical engineering/mechanical technology; medical/clinical assistant; office management; operations management; registered nursing/registered nurse; special education–early childhood; teacher assistant/aide.

Academics *Calendar:* semesters. *Degree:* certificates, diplomas, and associate. *Special study options:* academic remediation for entering students, adult/continuing education programs, advanced placement credit, distance learning, English as a second language, part-time degree program, services for LD students, summer session for credit. *ROTC:* Army (c).

Library Main Library plus 1 other with 37,760 titles, 218 serial subscriptions, 2,225 audiovisual materials, an OPAC.

Student Life *Housing:* college housing not available. *Activities and Organizations:* choral group. *Campus security:* day and evening security guards. *Student services:* personal/psychological counseling.

Financial Aid Of all full-time matriculated undergraduates who enrolled in 2012, 30 Federal Work-Study jobs.

Applying *Required:* high school transcript. *Application deadlines:* rolling (freshmen), rolling (transfers). *Notification:* continuous (freshmen), continuous (transfers).

Freshman Application Contact Mr. Doug Rhoney, Counselor, Mitchell Community College, 500 West Broad, Statesville, NC 28677-5293. *Phone:* 704-878-3280.

Website: http://www.mitchellcc.edu/.

Montgomery Community College
Troy, North Carolina

- **State-supported** 2-year, founded 1967, part of North Carolina Community College System
- **Rural** 159-acre campus
- **Coed**

Undergraduates 381 full-time, 456 part-time. Students come from 10 states and territories; 1% are from out of state; 21% Black or African American, non-Hispanic/Latino; 7% Hispanic/Latino; 2% Asian, non-Hispanic/Latino; 0.4% American Indian or Alaska Native, non-Hispanic/Latino; 0.4% Two or more races, non-Hispanic/Latino; 0.1% international.

Academics *Calendar:* semesters. *Degree:* certificates, diplomas, and associate. *Special study options:* academic remediation for entering students, advanced placement credit, distance learning, English as a second language, part-time degree program, services for LD students, summer session for credit.

Student Life *Campus security:* 24-hour emergency response devices.

Costs (2013–14) *Tuition:* state resident $2208 full-time, $69 per credit part-time; nonresident $8352 full-time, $261 per credit part-time. Part-time tuition and fees vary according to course load. *Required fees:* $75 full-time, $75 per year part-time.

Financial Aid Of all full-time matriculated undergraduates who enrolled in 2012, 24 Federal Work-Study jobs (averaging $500).

Applying *Options:* electronic application, early admission, deferred entrance. *Required:* high school transcript.

Freshman Application Contact Montgomery Community College, 1011 Page Street, Troy, NC 27371. *Phone:* 910-576-6222 Ext. 240.

Website: http://www.montgomery.edu/.

Nash Community College
Rocky Mount, North Carolina

Freshman Application Contact Ms. Dorothy Gardner, Admissions Officer, Nash Community College, PO Box 7488, Rocky Mount, NC 27804. *Phone:* 252-451-8300. *E-mail:* dgardner@nashcc.edu.

Website: http://www.nashcc.edu/.

Pamlico Community College
Grantsboro, North Carolina

Director of Admissions Mr. Floyd H. Hardison, Admissions Counselor, Pamlico Community College, PO Box 185, Grantsboro, NC 28529-0185. *Phone:* 252-249-1851 Ext. 28.

Website: http://www.pamlico.cc.nc.us/.

Piedmont Community College
Roxboro, North Carolina

- **State-supported** 2-year, founded 1970, part of North Carolina Community College System
- **Small-town** 178-acre campus
- **Coed,** 1,591 undergraduate students, 44% full-time, 47% women, 53% men

Undergraduates 699 full-time, 892 part-time.

Faculty *Student/faculty ratio:* 11:1.

Majors Accounting; building/property maintenance; business administration and management; child-care and support services management; cinematography and film/video production; clinical/medical social work; computer programming (specific applications); computer systems networking and telecommunications; criminal justice/law enforcement administration; e-commerce; electrical and power transmission installation; electrician; electromechanical and instrumentation and maintenance technologies related; elementary education; general studies; graphic communications; health professions related; industrial technology; information technology; liberal arts and sciences and humanities related; liberal arts and sciences/liberal studies; medical administrative assistant and medical secretary; office management; registered nursing/registered nurse.

Academics *Calendar:* semesters. *Degree:* certificates, diplomas, and associate. *Special study options:* academic remediation for entering students, adult/continuing education programs, advanced placement credit, cooperative education, distance learning, double majors, English as a second language, off-campus study, part-time degree program, summer session for credit.

Library Learning Resource Center with 18,576 titles, 161 serial subscriptions.

Student Life *Housing:* college housing not available. *Activities and Organizations:* drama/theater group, choral group. *Campus security:* routine patrols by the local sheriff's department.

Athletics *Intramural sports:* volleyball M/W.

Costs (2014–15) *Tuition:* state resident $1716 full-time; nonresident $6324 full-time. Full-time tuition and fees vary according to course load. Part-time tuition and fees vary according to course load. *Required fees:* $115 full-time. *Payment plan:* installment.

Financial Aid Of all full-time matriculated undergraduates who enrolled in 2012, 30 Federal Work-Study jobs (averaging $1500).

Applying *Options:* electronic application, early admission, deferred entrance. *Required for some:* high school transcript. *Application deadlines:* rolling (freshmen), rolling (transfers). *Notification:* continuous until 9/29 (freshmen), continuous until 9/29 (transfers).

Freshman Application Contact Piedmont Community College, PO Box 1197, Roxboro, NC 27573-1197. *Phone:* 336-599-1181 Ext. 2115.

Website: http://www.piedmont.cc.nc.us/.

Pitt Community College
Greenville, North Carolina

- **State and locally supported** 2-year, founded 1961, part of North Carolina Community College System
- **Small-town** 294-acre campus
- **Coed,** 8,902 undergraduate students, 52% full-time, 60% women, 40% men

Undergraduates 4,670 full-time, 4,232 part-time. 28% Black or African American, non-Hispanic/Latino; 2% Hispanic/Latino; 0.5% Asian, non-Hispanic/Latino; 0.1% Native Hawaiian or other Pacific Islander, non-Hispanic/Latino; 0.3% American Indian or Alaska Native, non-Hispanic/Latino; 0.2% Two or more races, non-Hispanic/Latino; 39% Race/ethnicity unknown; 0.7% international. *Retention:* 68% of full-time freshmen returned.

Freshmen *Admission:* 1,481 enrolled.

Faculty *Total:* 391, 48% full-time.

Majors Accounting; allied health diagnostic, intervention, and treatment professions related; architectural engineering technology; automobile/automotive mechanics technology; biology/biotechnology laboratory technician; building/construction finishing, management, and inspection related; business administration and management; commercial and advertising art; computer and information systems security; computer programming (specific applications); computer systems networking and telecommunications; construction trades related; corrections and criminal justice related; criminal justice/police science; criminal justice/safety; diagnostic medical sonography and ultrasound technology; early childhood education; e-commerce; electrical, electronic and communications engineering technology; electrical/electronics maintenance and repair technology related; electrician; electromechanical and instrumentation and maintenance technologies related; elementary education; general studies; health information/medical records technology; health professions related; health services/allied health/health sciences; heating, air conditioning, ventilation and refrigeration maintenance technology; human resources management and services related; information science/studies; information technology; international business/trade/commerce; legal administrative assistant/secretary; legal assistant/paralegal; liberal arts and sciences and humanities related; liberal arts and sciences/liberal studies; logistics, materials, and supply chain management; machine shop technology; manufacturing engineering technology; marketing/marketing management; massage therapy; mechanical engineering/mechanical technology; medical/clinical assistant; medical office management; medical radiologic technology; nuclear medical technology; occupational therapist assistant; office management; operations management; radiologic technology/science; registered nursing/registered nurse; respiratory care therapy; substance abuse/addiction counseling; system, networking, and LAN/WAN management; welding technology.

Academics *Calendar:* semesters. *Degree:* certificates, diplomas, and associate. *Special study options:* academic remediation for entering students, adult/continuing education programs, advanced placement credit, cooperative education, distance learning, double majors, English as a second language, external degree program, independent study, internships, part-time degree program, services for LD students, summer session for credit. *ROTC:* Army (b).

Library Pitt Community College Library with 43,302 titles, 242 serial subscriptions, 4,166 audiovisual materials, an OPAC, a Web page.

Student Life *Housing:* college housing not available. *Activities and Organizations:* drama/theater group, choral group. *Campus security:* 24-hour patrols, student patrols, late-night transport/escort service. *Student services:* personal/psychological counseling.

Athletics Member NJCAA. *Intercollegiate sports:* baseball M(s), basketball M(s), golf M(s), softball W, volleyball W(s). *Intramural sports:* basketball M/W, softball W, volleyball M/W.

Costs (2013–14) *Tuition:* state resident $2288 full-time, $72 per credit hour part-time; nonresident $8432 full-time, $264 per credit hour part-time. Part-time tuition and fees vary according to course level. *Required fees:* $86 full-time, $43 per term part-time.

Financial Aid Of all full-time matriculated undergraduates who enrolled in 2012, 79 Federal Work-Study jobs (averaging $1772).

Applying *Options:* electronic application, deferred entrance. *Required:* high school transcript. *Application deadlines:* rolling (freshmen), rolling (transfers).

Freshman Application Contact Dr. Kimberly Williamson, Interim Coordinator of Counseling, Pitt Community College, PO Drawer 7007, Greenville, NC 27835-7007. *Phone:* 252-493-7217. *Fax:* 252-321-4612. *E-mail:* pittadm@pcc.pitt.cc.nc.us.
Website: http://www.pittcc.edu/.

Randolph Community College
Asheboro, North Carolina

- **State-supported** 2-year, founded 1962, part of North Carolina Community College System
- **Small-town** 40-acre campus with easy access to Greensboro, Winston-Salem, High Point
- **Endowment** $9.1 million
- **Coed**, 3,024 undergraduate students, 38% full-time, 64% women, 36% men

Undergraduates 1,155 full-time, 1,869 part-time. Students come from 4 states and territories; 13 other countries; 1% are from out of state; 9% Black or African American, non-Hispanic/Latino; 10% Hispanic/Latino; 1% Asian, non-Hispanic/Latino; 0.1% Native Hawaiian or other Pacific Islander, non-Hispanic/Latino; 0.9% American Indian or Alaska Native, non-Hispanic/Latino; 3% Two or more races, non-Hispanic/Latino; 0.2% Race/ethnicity unknown; 0.5% international; 23% transferred in. *Retention:* 68% of full-time freshmen returned.

Freshmen *Admission:* 2,920 applied, 2,920 admitted, 647 enrolled. *Average high school GPA:* 2.87.

Faculty *Total:* 284, 30% full-time. *Student/faculty ratio:* 12:1.

Majors Accounting; autobody/collision and repair technology; automobile/automotive mechanics technology; biology/biotechnology laboratory technician; business administration and management; commercial and advertising art; commercial photography; computer systems networking and telecommunications; cosmetology; criminal justice/safety; early childhood education; electrician; electromechanical and instrumentation and maintenance technologies related; funeral service and mortuary science; information technology; interior design; liberal arts and sciences and humanities related; liberal arts and sciences/liberal studies; logistics, materials, and supply chain management; machine shop technology; mechatronics, robotics, and automation engineering; medical/clinical assistant; medical office management; photographic and film/video technology; photojournalism; physical therapy technology; pre-engineering; prenursing studies; radiologic technology/science; registered nursing/registered nurse.

Academics *Calendar:* semesters. *Degree:* certificates, diplomas, and associate. *Special study options:* academic remediation for entering students, adult/continuing education programs, advanced placement credit, cooperative education, distance learning, double majors, English as a second language, independent study, internships, off-campus study, part-time degree program, services for LD students, summer session for credit. *ROTC:* Air Force (c).

Library R. Alton Cox Learning Resources Center with 22,000 titles, 2,000 audiovisual materials, an OPAC, a Web page.

Student Life *Housing:* college housing not available. *Activities and Organizations:* Student Government Association, Phi Theta Kappa, Student Nurse Association, Phi Beta Lambda, Campus Crusaders. *Campus security:* 24-hour emergency response devices, security officer during open hours. *Student services:* personal/psychological counseling.

Athletics *Intramural sports:* basketball M/W, football M/W, golf M/W, volleyball M/W.

Costs (2014–15) *Tuition:* state resident $2288 full-time, $72 per credit part-time; nonresident $8432 full-time, $264 per credit part-time. *Required fees:* $88 full-time, $3 per credit part-time. *Payment plan:* installment.

Applying *Options:* electronic application, deferred entrance. *Application deadlines:* rolling (freshmen), rolling (transfers). *Notification:* continuous (freshmen), continuous (transfers).

Freshman Application Contact Ms. Brandi F. Hagerman, Director of Enrollment Management/Registrar, Randolph Community College, 629 Industrial Park Avenue, Asheboro, NC 27205-7333. *Phone:* 336-633-0213. *Fax:* 336-629-9547. *E-mail:* bhagerman@randolph.edu. *Website:* http://www.randolph.edu/.

Richmond Community College
Hamlét, North Carolina

- **State-supported** 2-year, founded 1964, part of North Carolina Community College System
- **Rural** 163-acre campus
- **Coed**, 2,664 undergraduate students, 42% full-time, 67% women, 33% men

Undergraduates 1,112 full-time, 1,552 part-time. 0.5% are from out of state; 38% Black or African American, non-Hispanic/Latino; 2% Hispanic/Latino; 0.6% Asian, non-Hispanic/Latino; 9% American Indian or Alaska Native, non-Hispanic/Latino; 2% Two or more races, non-Hispanic/Latino; 6% Race/ethnicity unknown; 5% transferred in.

Freshmen *Admission:* 474 enrolled.

Faculty *Student/faculty ratio:* 17:1.

Majors Accounting; business administration and management; computer engineering technology; criminal justice/safety; early childhood education; electrical and power transmission installation; electrical, electronic and communications engineering technology; electromechanical and instrumentation and maintenance technologies related; electromechanical technology; elementary education; entrepreneurship; health information/medical records technology; health professions related; heating, air conditioning, ventilation and refrigeration maintenance technology; information technology; liberal arts and sciences/liberal studies; mechanical engineering/mechanical technology; medical/clinical assistant; medical office computer specialist; mental and social health services and allied professions related; office management; registered nursing/registered nurse; welding technology.

Academics *Calendar:* semesters. *Degree:* certificates, diplomas, and associate. *Special study options:* academic remediation for entering students, adult/continuing education programs, advanced placement credit, cooperative education, distance learning, double majors, English as a second language, independent study, internships, part-time degree program, student-designed majors, summer session for credit.

Library Richmond Community College Library with 30,088 titles, 236 serial subscriptions, an OPAC.

Student Life *Housing:* college housing not available. *Campus security:* 24-hour emergency response devices, security guard during operating hours. *Student services:* personal/psychological counseling.

Financial Aid Of all full-time matriculated undergraduates who enrolled in 2012, 35 Federal Work-Study jobs (averaging $2000).

Applying *Options:* electronic application, deferred entrance. *Required:* high school transcript. *Application deadlines:* rolling (freshmen), rolling (transfers). *Notification:* continuous until 8/1 (freshmen), continuous until 8/1 (transfers).

Freshman Application Contact Lori J. Graham, Registrar, Richmond Community College, P.O. Box 1189, 1042 W. Hamlet Ave., Hamlet, NC 28345. *Phone:* 910-410-1737. *Fax:* 910-582-7102. *E-mail:* ljgraham1273@richmondcc.edu.
Website: http://www.richmondcc.edu/.

Roanoke-Chowan Community College
Ahoskie, North Carolina

Director of Admissions Miss Sandra Copeland, Director, Counseling Services, Roanoke-Chowan Community College, 109 Community College Road, Ahoskie, NC 27910. *Phone:* 252-862-1225.
Website: http://www.roanokechowan.edu/.

Robeson Community College
Lumberton, North Carolina

- **State-supported** 2-year, founded 1965, part of North Carolina Community College System
- **Small-town** 78-acre campus
- **Coed**

Academics *Calendar:* semesters. *Degree:* associate. *Special study options:* academic remediation for entering students, cooperative education, distance learning, services for LD students.

Applying *Options:* electronic application, early admission. *Required:* high school transcript.

Freshman Application Contact Ms. Patricia Locklear, College Recruiter, Robeson Community College, PO Box 1420, Lumberton, NC 28359. *Phone:* 910-272-3356 Ext. 251. *Fax:* 910-618-5686. *E-mail:* plocklear@robeson.edu.
Website: http://www.robeson.cc.nc.us/.

Rockingham Community College

Wentworth, North Carolina

Freshman Application Contact Mr. Derrick Satterfield, Director of Enrollment Services, Rockingham Community College, PO Box 38, Wentworth, NC 27375-0038. *Phone:* 336-342-4261 Ext. 2114. *Fax:* 336-342-1809. *E-mail:* admissions@rockinghamcc.edu.
Website: http://www.rockinghamcc.edu/.

Rowan-Cabarrus Community College

Salisbury, North Carolina

Freshman Application Contact Mrs. Gail Cummins, Director of Admissions and Recruitment, Rowan-Cabarrus Community College, PO Box 1595, Salisbury, NC 28145-1595. *Phone:* 704-637-0760. *Fax:* 704-633-6804.
Website: http://www.rccc.edu/.

Sampson Community College

Clinton, North Carolina

Director of Admissions Mr. William R. Jordan, Director of Admissions, Sampson Community College, PO Box 318, 1801 Sunset Avenue, Highway 24 West, Clinton, NC 28329-0318. *Phone:* 910-592-8084 Ext. 2022.
Website: http://www.sampsoncc.edu/.

Sandhills Community College

Pinehurst, North Carolina

Freshman Application Contact Mr. Isai Robledo, Recruiter, Sandhills Community College, 3395 Airport Road, Pinehurst, NC 28374-8299. *Phone:* 910-246-5365. *Toll-free phone:* 800-338-3944. *Fax:* 910-695-3981. *E-mail:* robledoi@sandhills.edu.
Website: http://www.sandhills.edu/.

South College–Asheville

Asheville, North Carolina

Freshman Application Contact Director of Admissions, South College–Asheville, 1567 Patton Avenue, Asheville, NC 28806. *Phone:* 828-277-5521. *Fax:* 828-277-6151.
Website: http://www.southcollegenc.edu/.

Southeastern Community College

Whiteville, North Carolina

- **State-supported** 2-year, founded 1964, part of North Carolina Community College System
- **Rural** 106-acre campus
- **Coed,** 1,402 undergraduate students, 55% full-time, 66% women, 34% men

Undergraduates 766 full-time, 636 part-time. 0.8% are from out of state; 24% Black or African American, non-Hispanic/Latino; 3% Hispanic/Latino; 0.4% Asian, non-Hispanic/Latino; 7% American Indian or Alaska Native, non-Hispanic/Latino; 2% Race/ethnicity unknown. *Retention:* 48% of full-time freshmen returned.
Freshmen *Admission:* 890 applied, 890 admitted, 248 enrolled.
Faculty *Total:* 91, 82% full-time, 1% with terminal degrees. *Student/faculty ratio:* 20:1.
Majors Administrative assistant and secretarial science; art; biological and physical sciences; biotechnology; business administration and management; clinical/medical laboratory technology; computer engineering technology; cosmetology; criminal justice/law enforcement administration; electrical, electronic and communications engineering technology; environmental studies; forest technology; industrial technology; kindergarten/preschool education; liberal arts and sciences/liberal studies; music; parks, recreation and leisure; parks, recreation and leisure facilities management; registered nursing/registered nurse; teacher assistant/aide; welding technology.
Academics *Calendar:* semesters. *Degree:* certificates, diplomas, and associate. *Special study options:* academic remediation for entering students, adult/continuing education programs, advanced placement credit, cooperative education, distance learning, double majors, English as a second language, honors programs, independent study, internships, part-time degree program, services for LD students, summer session for credit.
Library Southeastern Community College Library with 50,297 titles, 192 serial subscriptions, an OPAC.
Student Life *Housing:* college housing not available. *Activities and Organizations:* drama/theater group, choral group, Student Government Association, Nursing Club, Environmental Club. *Campus security:* 24-hour emergency response devices. *Student services:* personal/psychological counseling.

Athletics Member NJCAA. *Intercollegiate sports:* baseball M(s), softball W, squash W, volleyball W(s).
Applying *Options:* electronic application, early admission, deferred entrance. *Required:* high school transcript. *Application deadlines:* rolling (freshmen), rolling (transfers).
Freshman Application Contact Ms. Sylvia McQueen, Registrar, Southeastern Community College, PO Box 151, Whiteville, NC 28472. *Phone:* 910-642-7141 Ext. 249. *Fax:* 910-642-5658.
Website: http://www.sccnc.edu/.

South Piedmont Community College

Polkton, North Carolina

- **State-supported** 2-year, founded 1962, part of North Carolina Community College System
- **Rural** 56-acre campus with easy access to Charlotte
- **Endowment** $27,818
- **Coed,** 2,773 undergraduate students

Undergraduates Students come from 3 states and territories; 1% are from out of state.
Freshmen *Admission:* 740 applied, 618 admitted.
Faculty *Total:* 106. *Student/faculty ratio:* 17:1.
Majors Accounting; allied health diagnostic, intervention, and treatment professions related; automobile/automotive mechanics technology; biotechnology; business administration and management; commercial and advertising art; criminal justice/safety; cyber/computer forensics and counterterrorism; diagnostic medical sonography and ultrasound technology; early childhood education; electrician; electromechanical and instrumentation and maintenance technologies related; electromechanical technology; elementary education; entrepreneurship; fire prevention and safety technology; game and interactive media design; general studies; heating, air conditioning, ventilation and refrigeration maintenance technology; information science/studies; information technology; legal assistant/paralegal; liberal arts and sciences/liberal studies; massage therapy; mechanical engineering/mechanical technology; medical/clinical assistant; medical office management; mental and social health services and allied professions related; registered nursing/registered nurse.
Academics *Calendar:* semesters. *Degree:* certificates, diplomas, and associate. *Special study options:* academic remediation for entering students, accelerated degree program, adult/continuing education programs, cooperative education, English as a second language, independent study, internships, off-campus study, part-time degree program, services for LD students, summer session for credit.
Library Martin Learning Resource Center with 18,917 titles, 170 serial subscriptions, an OPAC.
Student Life *Housing:* college housing not available. *Activities and Organizations:* choral group, Student Association, Phi Beta Lambda, Phi Theta Kappa, Social Services Club, Criminal Justice Club. *Campus security:* 24-hour emergency response devices and patrols, evening security. *Student services:* personal/psychological counseling, women's center.
Costs (2014–15) *Tuition:* state resident $2288 full-time, $72 per semester hour part-time; nonresident $8432 full-time, $264 per semester hour part-time. *Required fees:* $149 full-time, $3 per semester hour part-time, $27 per semester part-time.
Applying *Options:* electronic application, early admission, deferred entrance. *Required:* high school transcript. *Application deadlines:* rolling (freshmen), rolling (transfers). *Notification:* continuous (freshmen), continuous (transfers).
Freshman Application Contact Ms. Amanda Secrest, Assistant Director Admissions and Testing, South Piedmont Community College, P.O. Box 126, Polkton, NC 28135. *Phone:* 704-290-5847. *Toll-free phone:* 800-766-0319. *E-mail:* asecrest@spcc.edu.
Website: http://www.spcc.edu/.

Southwestern Community College

Sylva, North Carolina

- **State-supported** 2-year, founded 1964, part of North Carolina Community College System
- **Small-town** 77-acre campus
- **Coed,** 2,689 undergraduate students

Faculty *Student/faculty ratio:* 16:1.
Majors Accounting; administrative assistant and secretarial science; automobile/automotive mechanics technology; business administration and management; child development; clinical/medical laboratory technology; commercial and advertising art; computer engineering technology; cosmetology; criminal justice/police science; culinary arts; electrical, electronic and communications engineering technology; emergency medical technology (EMT paramedic); environmental studies; health information/medical records administration; health information/medical records technology; information science/studies; legal assistant/paralegal;

liberal arts and sciences/liberal studies; licensed practical/vocational nurse training; marketing/marketing management; massage therapy; medical radiologic technology; mental health counseling; parks, recreation, leisure, and fitness studies related; physical therapy; physical therapy technology; registered nursing/registered nurse; respiratory care therapy; substance abuse/addiction counseling; system, networking, and LAN/WAN management; trade and industrial teacher education.

Academics *Calendar:* semesters. *Degree:* certificates, diplomas, and associate. *Special study options:* academic remediation for entering students, adult/continuing education programs, advanced placement credit, cooperative education, distance learning, double majors, English as a second language, honors programs, independent study, off-campus study, part-time degree program, services for LD students, summer session for credit.

Library Southwestern Community College Library with an OPAC, a Web page.

Student Life *Housing:* college housing not available. *Campus security:* security during hours college is open. *Student services:* personal/psychological counseling.

Applying *Required:* high school transcript. *Required for some:* minimum 2.5 GPA, interview.

Freshman Application Contact Ms. Dominique Benson, Admissions Officer, Southwestern Community College, 447 College Dr, Sylva, NC 28779. *Phone:* 828-339-4217. *Toll-free phone:* 800-447-4091 (in-state); 800-447-7091 (out-of-state). *E-mail:* D_Benson@southwesternccc.edu.

Website: http://www.southwesternccc.edu/.

Stanly Community College

Albemarle, North Carolina

Freshman Application Contact Mrs. Denise B. Ross, Associate Dean, Admissions, Stanly Community College, 141 College Drive, Albemarle, NC 28001. *Phone:* 704-982-0121 Ext. 264. *Fax:* 704-982-0255. *E-mail:* dross7926@stanly.edu.

Website: http://www.stanly.edu/.

Surry Community College

Dobson, North Carolina

Freshman Application Contact Renita Hazelwood, Director of Admissions, Surry Community College, 630 South Main Street, Dobson, NC 27017. *Phone:* 336-386-3392. *Fax:* 336-386-3690. *E-mail:* hazelwoodr@surry.edu.

Website: http://www.surry.edu/.

Tri-County Community College

Murphy, North Carolina

- **State-supported** 2-year, founded 1964, part of North Carolina Community College System
- **Rural** 40-acre campus
- **Coed**

Faculty *Student/faculty ratio:* 21:1.

Academics *Calendar:* semesters. *Degree:* certificates, diplomas, and associate. *Special study options:* academic remediation for entering students, adult/continuing education programs, distance learning, double majors, internships, part-time degree program, study abroad, summer session for credit.

Standardized Tests *Recommended:* SAT and SAT Subject Tests or ACT (for admission).

Financial Aid Of all full-time matriculated undergraduates who enrolled in 2012, 11 Federal Work-Study jobs.

Applying *Options:* electronic application. *Required:* high school transcript.

Freshman Application Contact Dr. Jason Chambers, Director of Student Services and Admissions, Tri-County Community College, 21 Campus Circle, Murphy, NC 28906-7919. *Phone:* 828-837-6810. *Fax:* 828-837-3266. *E-mail:* jchambers@tricountyccc.edu.

Website: http://www.tricountyccc.edu/.

Vance-Granville Community College

Henderson, North Carolina

Freshman Application Contact Ms. Kathy Kutl, Admissions Officer, Vance-Granville Community College, PO Box 917, State Road 1126, Henderson, NC 27536. *Phone:* 252-492-2061 Ext. 3265. *Fax:* 252-430-0460.

Website: http://www.vgcc.edu/.

Wake Technical Community College

Raleigh, North Carolina

Director of Admissions Ms. Susan Bloomfield, Director of Admissions, Wake Technical Community College, 9101 Fayetteville Road, Raleigh, NC 27603-5696. *Phone:* 919-866-5452. *E-mail:* srbloomfield@waketech.edu.

Website: http://www.waketech.edu/.

Wayne Community College

Goldsboro, North Carolina

- **State and locally supported** 2-year, founded 1957, part of North Carolina Community College System
- **Small-town** 175-acre campus with easy access to Raleigh
- **Endowment** $92,408
- **Coed**, 3,837 undergraduate students, 47% full-time, 60% women, 40% men

Undergraduates 1,813 full-time, 2,024 part-time. 4% are from out of state; 27% Black or African American, non-Hispanic/Latino; 8% Hispanic/Latino; 2% Asian, non-Hispanic/Latino; 0.3% Native Hawaiian or other Pacific Islander, non-Hispanic/Latino; 0.6% American Indian or Alaska Native, non-Hispanic/Latino; 0.8% Two or more races, non-Hispanic/Latino; 2% Race/ethnicity unknown; 0.3% international; 26% transferred in.

Freshmen *Admission:* 2,328 applied, 1,335 admitted, 655 enrolled.

Faculty *Total:* 333, 42% full-time, 1% with terminal degrees. *Student/faculty ratio:* 20:1.

Majors Accounting; agribusiness; agroecology and sustainable agriculture; airframe mechanics and aircraft maintenance technology; animal/livestock husbandry and production; autobody/collision and repair technology; automobile/automotive mechanics technology; biology/biotechnology laboratory technician; business administration and management; criminal justice/police science; criminal justice/safety; crisis/emergency/disaster management; dental hygiene; early childhood education; electrical, electronic and communications engineering technology; electromechanical and instrumentation and maintenance technologies related; elementary education; energy management and systems technology; forensic science and technology; forest technology; game and interactive media design; information technology; liberal arts and sciences and humanities related; liberal arts and sciences/liberal studies; machine shop technology; mechanical engineering/mechanical technology; medical/clinical assistant; medical office management; mental and social health services and allied professions related; office management; operations management; registered nursing/registered nurse; turf and turfgrass management.

Academics *Calendar:* semesters. *Degree:* certificates, diplomas, and associate. *Special study options:* academic remediation for entering students, adult/continuing education programs, advanced placement credit, cooperative education, distance learning, double majors, English as a second language, external degree program, honors programs, part-time degree program, services for LD students, summer session for credit.

Library Dr. Clyde A. Erwin, Jr. Library with 32,548 titles, 53 serial subscriptions, 1,272 audiovisual materials, an OPAC, a Web page.

Student Life *Housing:* college housing not available. *Activities and Organizations:* choral group, Student Government Association, Phi Beta Lambda, Phi Theta Kappa, Criminal Justice, International. *Campus security:* 24-hour emergency response devices and patrols. *Student services:* personal/psychological counseling.

Athletics *Intramural sports:* football M/W.

Standardized Tests *Recommended:* SAT or ACT (for admission).

Costs (2014–15) *Tuition:* state resident $2288 full-time, $72 per credit part-time; nonresident $8432 full-time, $264 per credit part-time. Full-time tuition and fees vary according to course load. Part-time tuition and fees vary according to course load. *Required fees:* $92 full-time, $23 per term part-time. *Waivers:* senior citizens.

Financial Aid Of all full-time matriculated undergraduates who enrolled in 2012, 100 Federal Work-Study jobs (averaging $2000).

Applying *Options:* electronic application. *Required:* high school transcript, interview. *Application deadlines:* rolling (freshmen), rolling (out-of-state freshmen), rolling (transfers). *Notification:* continuous (freshmen), continuous (out-of-state freshmen), continuous (transfers).

Freshman Application Contact Mrs. Jennifer P Mayo, Associate Director of Admissions and Records, Wayne Community College, PO Box 8002, Goldsboro, NC 27533. *Phone:* 919-735-5151 Ext. 6721. *Fax:* 919-736-9425. *E-mail:* jbmayo@waynecc.edujbmayo@waynecc.edujbmayo@waynecc.edu.

Website: http://www.waynecc.edu/.

Western Piedmont Community College

Morganton, North Carolina

Freshman Application Contact Susan Williams, Director of Admissions, Western Piedmont Community College, 1001 Burkemont Avenue, Morganton,

NC 28655-4511. *Phone:* 828-438-6051. *Fax:* 828-438-6065. *E-mail:* swilliams@wpcc.edu.
Website: http://www.wpcc.edu/.

Wilkes Community College
Wilkesboro, North Carolina

Freshman Application Contact Mr. Mac Warren, Director of Admissions, Wilkes Community College, PO Box 120, Wilkesboro, NC 28697. *Phone:* 336-838-6141. *Fax:* 336-838-6547. *E-mail:* mac.warren@wilkescc.edu. *Website:* http://www.wilkescc.edu/.

Wilson Community College
Wilson, North Carolina

- **State-supported** 2-year, founded 1958, part of North Carolina Community College System
- **Small-town** 35-acre campus with easy access to Raleigh
- **Coed**

Undergraduates 897 full-time, 940 part-time. Students come from 3 states and territories; 45% Black or African American, non-Hispanic/Latino; 5% Hispanic/Latino; 0.7% Asian, non-Hispanic/Latino; 0.1% Native Hawaiian or other Pacific Islander, non-Hispanic/Latino; 0.9% American Indian or Alaska Native, non-Hispanic/Latino; 0.1% Two or more races, non-Hispanic/Latino; 2% Race/ethnicity unknown; 27% transferred in.
Faculty *Student/faculty ratio:* 12:1.
Academics *Calendar:* semesters. *Degree:* certificates, diplomas, and associate. *Special study options:* academic remediation for entering students, advanced placement credit, cooperative education, distance learning, double majors, English as a second language, independent study, internships, part-time degree program, services for LD students, summer session for credit.
Student Life *Campus security:* 11-hour patrols by trained security personnel; also have a certified sworn Law Enforcement Agency on campus.
Financial Aid Of all full-time matriculated undergraduates who enrolled in 2012, 65 Federal Work-Study jobs (averaging $1500).
Applying *Options:* electronic application, deferred entrance. *Required:* high school transcript.
Freshman Application Contact Mrs. Maegan Williams, Admissions Technician, Wilson Community College, Wilson, NC 27893-0305. *Phone:* 252-246-1275. *Fax:* 252-243-7148. *E-mail:* mwilliams@wilsoncc.edu. *Website:* http://www.wilsoncc.edu/.

NORTH DAKOTA

Bismarck State College
Bismarck, North Dakota

- **State-supported** primarily 2-year, founded 1939, part of North Dakota University System
- **Urban** 100-acre campus
- **Coed,** 4,062 undergraduate students, 58% full-time, 44% women, 56% men

Undergraduates 2,365 full-time, 1,697 part-time. Students come from 6 other countries; 25% are from out of state; 3% Black or African American, non-Hispanic/Latino; 3% Hispanic/Latino; 0.4% Asian, non-Hispanic/Latino; 0.1% Native Hawaiian or other Pacific Islander, non-Hispanic/Latino; 2% American Indian or Alaska Native, non-Hispanic/Latino; 2% Two or more races, non-Hispanic/Latino; 2% Race/ethnicity unknown; 0.3% international; 7% transferred in; 9% live on campus.
Freshmen *Admission:* 1,141 applied, 1,141 admitted, 907 enrolled. *Average high school GPA:* 3.02. *Test scores:* ACT scores over 18: 73%; ACT scores over 24: 19%; ACT scores over 30: 1%.
Faculty *Total:* 322, 39% full-time, 10% with terminal degrees. *Student/faculty ratio:* 15:1.
Majors Administrative assistant and secretarial science; agricultural business and management; autobody/collision and repair technology; automobile/automotive mechanics technology; building/home/construction inspection; business automation/technology/data entry; business/commerce; carpentry; clinical/medical laboratory technology; commercial and advertising art; computer systems networking and telecommunications; criminal justice/safety; electrical, electronic and communications engineering technology; emergency medical technology (EMT paramedic); engineering technology; environmental control technologies related; farm and ranch management; geographic information science and cartography; heating, air conditioning, ventilation and refrigeration maintenance technology; human services; industrial mechanics and maintenance technology; industrial production technologies related; industrial technology; instrumentation technology; legal administrative assistant/secretary; liberal arts and

sciences/liberal studies; licensed practical/vocational nurse training; lineworker; medical administrative assistant and medical secretary; multi/interdisciplinary studies related; nuclear engineering technology; operations management; public relations/image management; registered nursing/registered nurse; social work; surgical technology; surveying technology; water quality and wastewater treatment management and recycling technology; web page, digital/multimedia and information resources design; welding technology.
Academics *Calendar:* semesters. *Degrees:* certificates, diplomas, associate, and bachelor's. *Special study options:* academic remediation for entering students, adult/continuing education programs, advanced placement credit, cooperative education, distance learning, independent study, internships, part-time degree program, services for LD students, study abroad, summer session for credit.
Library Bismarck State College Library with an OPAC, a Web page.
Student Life *Housing Options:* coed, men-only, women-only, special housing for students with disabilities. Campus housing is university owned. *Activities and Organizations:* drama/theater group, student-run newspaper, radio station, choral group. *Campus security:* late-night transport/escort service, controlled dormitory access. *Student services:* health clinic.
Athletics Member NJCAA. *Intercollegiate sports:* baseball M(s), basketball M(s)/W(s), golf M(s)/W, soccer M/W, softball W(s), volleyball W(s). *Intramural sports:* baseball M/W, bowling M/W, football M/W, golf M/W, soccer M/W, softball M/W.
Standardized Tests *Required for some:* SAT or ACT (for admission).
Financial Aid Of all full-time matriculated undergraduates who enrolled in 2012, 1,806 applied for aid, 1,301 were judged to have need, 530 had their need fully met. 53 Federal Work-Study jobs (averaging $975). In 2012, 281 non-need-based awards were made. *Average percent of need met:* 52%. *Average financial aid package:* $10,330. *Average need-based loan:* $4428. *Average need-based gift aid:* $4329. *Average non-need-based aid:* $842. *Average indebtedness upon graduation:* $12,377.
Applying *Options:* electronic application, early admission. *Application fee:* $35. *Required:* high school transcript. *Required for some:* interview. *Application deadlines:* rolling (freshmen), rolling (out-of-state freshmen), 11/10 (transfers). *Notification:* continuous (freshmen), continuous (out-of-state freshmen), continuous (transfers).
Freshman Application Contact Karen Erickson, Director of Admissions and Enrollment Services, Bismarck State College, PO Box 5587, Bismarck, ND 58506. *Phone:* 701-224-5424. *Toll-free phone:* 800-445-5073. *Fax:* 701-224-5643. *E-mail:* karen.erickson@bismarckstate.edu. *Website:* http://www.bismarckstate.edu/.

Cankdeska Cikana Community College
Fort Totten, North Dakota

Director of Admissions Mr. Ermen Brown Jr., Registrar, Cankdeska Cikana Community College, PO Box 269, Fort Totten, ND 58335-0269. *Phone:* 701-766-1342. *Toll-free phone:* 888-783-1463. *Website:* http://www.littlehoop.edu/.

Dakota College at Bottineau
Bottineau, North Dakota

- **State-supported** 2-year, founded 1906, part of North Dakota University System
- **Rural** 35-acre campus
- **Coed,** 793 undergraduate students, 46% full-time, 51% women, 49% men

Undergraduates 367 full-time, 426 part-time. Students come from 3 other countries; 23% are from out of state; 10% Black or African American, non-Hispanic/Latino; 3% Hispanic/Latino; 0.4% Asian, non-Hispanic/Latino; 0.3% Native Hawaiian or other Pacific Islander, non-Hispanic/Latino; 2% American Indian or Alaska Native, non-Hispanic/Latino; 3% Two or more races, non-Hispanic/Latino; 17% Race/ethnicity unknown; 3% international.
Faculty *Total:* 88, 32% full-time, 6% with terminal degrees. *Student/faculty ratio:* 10:1.
Majors Accounting; accounting related; accounting technology and bookkeeping; administrative assistant and secretarial science; adult development and aging; advertising; agriculture; applied horticulture/horticultural business services related; applied horticulture/horticulture operations; biology/biological sciences; business administration and management; business automation/technology/data entry; chemistry; child-care and support services management; child-care provision; computer and information sciences; computer and information sciences and support services related; computer software and media applications related; computer technology/computer systems technology; crop production; education; entrepreneurial and small business related; environmental engineering technology; executive assistant/executive secretary; fishing and fisheries sciences and management; floriculture/floristry management; general studies; greenhouse management; health and physical education/fitness; health services/allied health/health sciences; history; horticultural science; hospitality

and recreation marketing; humanities; information science/studies; information technology; landscaping and groundskeeping; land use planning and management; liberal arts and sciences and humanities related; liberal arts and sciences/liberal studies; licensed practical/vocational nurse training; marketing/marketing management; marketing related; mathematics; medical administrative assistant and medical secretary; medical/clinical assistant; medical insurance coding; medical office assistant; natural resources/conservation; network and system administration; office management; office occupations and clerical services; ornamental horticulture; parks, recreation and leisure; parks, recreation and leisure facilities management; parks, recreation, leisure, and fitness studies related; photography; physical sciences; physical sciences related; premedical studies; prenursing studies; pre-veterinary studies; psychology; receptionist; registered nursing/registered nurse; science technologies related; small business administration; social sciences; teacher assistant/aide; urban forestry; wildlife, fish and wildlands science and management; zoology/animal biology.

Academics *Calendar:* semesters. *Degree:* certificates, diplomas, and associate. *Special study options:* academic remediation for entering students, advanced placement credit, cooperative education, distance learning, double majors, off-campus study, part-time degree program, services for LD students, summer session for credit.

Library Dakota College at Bottineau Library plus 1 other with 41,411 titles, 5,544 serial subscriptions, 1,339 audiovisual materials, an OPAC, a Web page.

Student Life *Housing:* on-campus residence required through sophomore year. *Options:* men-only, women-only. Campus housing is university owned. Freshman campus housing is guaranteed. *Activities and Organizations:* drama/theater group, Student Senate, Wildlife Club/Horticulture Club, Snowboarding Club, Phi Theta Kappa, Delta Epsilon Chi. *Campus security:* controlled dormitory access, security cameras. *Student services:* health clinic, personal/psychological counseling.

Athletics Member NJCAA. *Intercollegiate sports:* baseball M(s), basketball M(s)/W(s), football M, ice hockey M(s), softball W(s), volleyball W(s). *Intramural sports:* badminton M/W, basketball M/W, skiing (downhill) M/W, table tennis M/W, volleyball M/W.

Standardized Tests *Required:* SAT or ACT (for admission). *Recommended:* ACT (for admission).

Financial Aid Of all full-time matriculated undergraduates who enrolled in 2012, 290 applied for aid, 237 were judged to have need, 63 had their need fully met. 60 Federal Work-Study jobs (averaging $1500). In 2012, 33 non-need-based awards were made. *Average percent of need met:* 61%. *Average financial aid package:* $10,670. *Average need-based loan:* $4616. *Average need-based gift aid:* $4757. *Average non-need-based aid:* $664.

Applying *Options:* electronic application, early admission, deferred entrance. *Application fee:* $35. *Required:* high school transcript, immunization records, previous college official transcripts, ACT or SAT scores. *Application deadlines:* rolling (freshmen), rolling (out-of-state freshmen), rolling (transfers).

Freshman Application Contact Mrs. Luann Soland, Admissions Counselor, Dakota College at Bottineau, 105 Simrall Boulevard, Bottineau, ND 58318. *Phone:* 701-228-5487. *Toll-free phone:* 800-542-6866. *Fax:* 701-228-5499. *E-mail:* luann.soland@dakotacollege.edu. *Website:* http://www.dakotacollege.edu/.

Fort Berthold Community College
New Town, North Dakota

Freshman Application Contact Office of Admissions, Fort Berthold Community College, PO Box 490, 220 8th Avenue North, New Town, ND 58763-0490. *Phone:* 701-627-4738 Ext. 295. *Website:* http://www.fortbertholdcc.edu/.

Lake Region State College
Devils Lake, North Dakota

- **State-supported** 2-year, founded 1941, part of North Dakota University System
- **Small-town** 120-acre campus
- **Coed,** 1,898 undergraduate students, 26% full-time, 58% women, 42% men

Undergraduates 486 full-time, 1,412 part-time. Students come from 25 states and territories; 8 other countries; 12% are from out of state; 6% Black or African American, non-Hispanic/Latino; 3% Hispanic/Latino; 0.5% Asian, non-Hispanic/Latino; 5% American Indian or Alaska Native, non-Hispanic/Latino; 3% Two or more races, non-Hispanic/Latino; 2% Race/ethnicity unknown; 5% international; 5% transferred in; 10% live on campus. *Retention:* 52% of full-time freshmen returned.

Freshmen *Admission:* 278 applied, 268 admitted, 206 enrolled. *Test scores:* ACT scores over 18: 60%; ACT scores over 24: 10%; ACT scores over 30: 1%.

Faculty *Total:* 144, 31% full-time, 8% with terminal degrees. *Student/faculty ratio:* 13:1.

Majors Administrative assistant and secretarial science; agricultural business and management; automobile/automotive mechanics technology; business administration and management; child-care provision; criminal justice/police science; electrical and electronic engineering technologies related; electrical/electronics equipment installation and repair; language interpretation and translation; liberal arts and sciences/liberal studies; management information systems; merchandising, sales, and marketing operations related (general); physical fitness technician; registered nursing/registered nurse; speech-language pathology.

Academics *Calendar:* semesters. *Degree:* certificates, diplomas, and associate. *Special study options:* academic remediation for entering students, cooperative education, distance learning, double majors, English as a second language, honors programs, internships, part-time degree program, summer session for credit.

Library Paul Hoghaug Library with 40,000 titles, 92 serial subscriptions, 2,000 audiovisual materials, an OPAC.

Student Life *Housing Options:* coed, men-only, women-only. Campus housing is university owned. *Activities and Organizations:* drama/theater group, choral group, Student Senate, Phi Theta Kappa, Delta Epsilon Chi, Phi Theta Lambda, Student Nurse Organization. *Campus security:* 24-hour emergency response devices, controlled dormitory access. *Student services:* personal/psychological counseling.

Athletics Member NJCAA. *Intercollegiate sports:* basketball M(s)/W(s), golf M(s)/W(s), volleyball W(s). *Intramural sports:* basketball M/W, cheerleading M/W, golf M/W, volleyball M/W.

Standardized Tests *Required for some:* SAT or ACT (for admission), COMPASS Tests required for some.

Costs (2014–15) *Tuition:* state resident $3197 full-time, $133 per credit part-time; nonresident $3197 full-time, $133 per credit part-time. Full-time tuition and fees vary according to course load, location, and program. Part-time tuition and fees vary according to location and program. *Required fees:* $877 full-time, $29 per credit part-time. *Room and board:* $5055; room only: $2125. Room and board charges vary according to board plan and housing facility. *Payment plan:* installment. *Waivers:* minority students, senior citizens, and employees or children of employees.

Financial Aid Of all full-time matriculated undergraduates who enrolled in 2013, 379 applied for aid, 307 were judged to have need, 106 had their need fully met. In 2013, 182 non-need-based awards were made. *Average percent of need met:* 55%. *Average financial aid package:* $9946. *Average need-based loan:* $4615. *Average need-based gift aid:* $4415. *Average non-need-based aid:* $578. *Average indebtedness upon graduation:* $10,646.

Applying *Options:* electronic application. *Application fee:* $35. *Required:* Immunizations records and college transcripts. *Required for some:* high school transcript, interview. *Application deadlines:* rolling (freshmen), rolling (transfers). *Notification:* continuous (freshmen), continuous (transfers).

Freshman Application Contact Samantha Cordrey, Administrative Assistant, Admissions Office, Lake Region State College, 1801 College Drive North, Devils Lake, ND 58301. *Phone:* 701-662-1514. *Toll-free phone:* 800-443-1313. *Fax:* 701-662-1581. *E-mail:* samantha.cordrey@lrsc.edu. *Website:* http://www.lrsc.edu/.

North Dakota State College of Science
Wahpeton, North Dakota

- **State-supported** 2-year, founded 1903, part of North Dakota University System
- **Rural** 128-acre campus
- **Endowment** $12.9 million
- **Coed,** 3,168 undergraduate students, 54% full-time, 47% women, 53% men

Undergraduates 1,712 full-time, 1,456 part-time. Students come from 39 states and territories; 5 other countries; 40% are from out of state; 5% Black or African American, non-Hispanic/Latino; 1% Hispanic/Latino; 0.9% Asian, non-Hispanic/Latino; 1% American Indian or Alaska Native, non-Hispanic/Latino; 2% Two or more races, non-Hispanic/Latino; 1% Race/ethnicity unknown; 7% transferred in; 56% live on campus.

Freshmen *Admission:* 1,249 applied, 785 admitted, 796 enrolled. *Test scores:* ACT scores over 18: 61%; ACT scores over 24: 14%; ACT scores over 30: 1%.

Faculty *Total:* 299, 36% full-time, 8% with terminal degrees. *Student/faculty ratio:* 13:1.

Majors Agricultural business and management; agricultural mechanics and equipment technology; architectural engineering technology; autobody/collision and repair technology; automobile/automotive mechanics technology; biology/biotechnology laboratory technician; building construction technology; business administration and management; civil engineering technology; computer and information sciences; computer and information systems security; computer programming; computer systems networking and telecommunications; construction engineering technology; culinary arts; data entry/microcomputer applications; dental assisting; dental hygiene; diesel mechanics technology; e-commerce; electrical and electronic engineering technologies related; emergency medical technology (EMT paramedic); energy management and systems technology; health information/medical records technology; heating, air conditioning, ventilation and refrigeration maintenance technology; heating, ventilation, air conditioning and refrigeration engineering technology; liberal arts and sciences/liberal studies; licensed practical/vocational nurse training; machine tool technology; manufacturing engineering technology; medical insurance coding; multi/interdisciplinary studies related; nanotechnology; occupational therapist assistant; pharmacy technician; psychiatric/mental health services technology; registered nursing/registered nurse; small engine mechanics and repair technology; vehicle maintenance and repair technologies related; web page, digital/multimedia and information resources design; welding technology.

Academics *Calendar:* semesters. *Degree:* certificates, diplomas, and associate. *Special study options:* academic remediation for entering students, adult/continuing education programs, cooperative education, distance learning, double majors, English as a second language, independent study, internships, part-time degree program, services for LD students, student-designed majors, summer session for credit.

Library Mildred Johnson Library with 91,541 titles, 133 serial subscriptions, 2,855 audiovisual materials, an OPAC, a Web page.

Student Life *Housing:* on-campus residence required for freshman year. *Options:* coed, men-only, women-only, special housing for students with disabilities. Campus housing is university owned. Freshman campus housing is guaranteed. *Activities and Organizations:* drama/theater group, choral group, marching band, Skills USA, Welding Club, Dental Club, Diesel Club, CRU (Intervarsity Christian). *Campus security:* 24-hour emergency response devices and patrols, student patrols, late-night transport/escort service, controlled dormitory access. *Student services:* health clinic, personal/psychological counseling, legal services.

Athletics Member NJCAA. *Intercollegiate sports:* basketball M(s)/W(s), football M(s), softball W, volleyball W(s). *Intramural sports:* basketball M/W, football M, racquetball M/W, softball M/W, ultimate Frisbee M/W, volleyball M/W.

Costs (2013–14) *Tuition:* state resident $3710 full-time, $116 per credit hour part-time; nonresident $9905 full-time. Full-time tuition and fees vary according to location, program, and reciprocity agreements. Part-time tuition and fees vary according to location, program, and reciprocity agreements. *Required fees:* $615 full-time, $26 per credit hour part-time. *Room and board:* $5384. Room and board charges vary according to board plan and housing facility. *Payment plan:* installment. *Waivers:* minority students and employees or children of employees.

Financial Aid Of all full-time matriculated undergraduates who enrolled in 2012, 1,554 applied for aid, 1,258 were judged to have need, 463 had their need fully met. In 2012, 339 non-need-based awards were made. *Average percent of need met:* 65%. *Average financial aid package:* $11,942. *Average need-based loan:* $5595. *Average need-based gift aid:* $4329. *Average non-need-based aid:* $607. *Average indebtedness upon graduation:* $15,662. *Financial aid deadline:* 4/15.

Applying *Options:* electronic application, early admission. *Application fee:* $35. *Required:* high school transcript. *Application deadlines:* rolling (freshmen), rolling (out-of-state freshmen), rolling (transfers). *Notification:* continuous (freshmen), continuous (out-of-state freshmen), continuous (transfers).

Freshman Application Contact Ms. Barb Mund, Director of Admissions and Records, North Dakota State College of Science, 800 North 6th Street, Wahpeton, ND 58076. *Phone:* 701-671-2204. *Toll-free phone:* 800-342-4325. *Fax:* 701-671-2201. *E-mail:* Barb.Mund@ndscs.edu.

Website: http://www.ndscs.edu/.

Sitting Bull College

Fort Yates, North Dakota

Director of Admissions Ms. Melody Silk, Director of Registration and Admissions, Sitting Bull College, 1341 92nd Street, Fort Yates, ND 58538-9701. *Phone:* 701-854-3864. *Fax:* 701-854-3403. *E-mail:* melodys@sbcl.edu.

Website: http://www.sittingbull.edu/.

Turtle Mountain Community College

Belcourt, North Dakota

Director of Admissions Ms. Joni LaFontaine, Admissions/Records Officer, Turtle Mountain Community College, Box 340, Belcourt, ND 58316-0340. *Phone:* 701-477-5605 Ext. 217. *E-mail:* jlafontaine@tm.edu.

Website: http://www.turtle-mountain.cc.nd.us/.

United Tribes Technical College

Bismarck, North Dakota

Freshman Application Contact Ms. Vivian Gillette, Director of Admissions, United Tribes Technical College, Bismarck, ND 58504. *Phone:* 701-255-3285 Ext. 1334. *Fax:* 701-530-0640. *E-mail:* vgillette@uttc.edu.

Website: http://www.uttc.edu/.

Williston State College

Williston, North Dakota

- **State-supported** 2-year, founded 1957, part of North Dakota University System
- **Small-town** 80-acre campus
- **Coed,** 909 undergraduate students

Undergraduates Students come from 7 other countries; 24% are from out of state; 2% Black or African American, non-Hispanic/Latino; 5% Hispanic/Latino; 1% Asian, non-Hispanic/Latino; 0.1% Native Hawaiian or other Pacific Islander, non-Hispanic/Latino; 2% American Indian or Alaska Native, non-Hispanic/Latino; 4% Two or more races, non-Hispanic/Latino; 3% Race/ethnicity unknown; 4% international.

Freshmen *Admission:* 294 applied, 236 admitted.

Faculty *Total:* 33, 94% full-time, 6% with terminal degrees. *Student/faculty ratio:* 27:1.

Majors Accounting technology and bookkeeping; administrative assistant and secretarial science; agriculture; automobile/automotive mechanics technology; business administration, management and operations related; carpentry; computer and information sciences and support services related; data processing and data processing technology; diesel mechanics technology; entrepreneurial and small business related; health information/medical records technology; liberal arts and sciences/liberal studies; licensed practical/vocational nurse training; marketing/marketing management; massage therapy; medical administrative assistant and medical secretary; medical insurance coding; medical transcription; multi/interdisciplinary studies related; petroleum technology; physical therapy technology; psychiatric/mental health services technology; registered nursing/registered nurse; speech-language pathology; system, networking, and LAN/WAN management; welding technology.

Academics *Calendar:* semesters. *Degree:* certificates, diplomas, and associate. *Special study options:* academic remediation for entering students, advanced placement credit, cooperative education, distance learning, honors programs, independent study, off-campus study, part-time degree program, services for LD students, student-designed majors, study abroad, summer session for credit.

Library Williston State College Learning Commons with 18,950 titles, 26 serial subscriptions, 478 audiovisual materials, an OPAC, a Web page.

Student Life *Housing Options:* coed, special housing for students with disabilities. Campus housing is university owned. *Activities and Organizations:* drama/theater group, student-run newspaper, choral group, Phi Theta Kappa, Student Senate, Teton Activity Board, Biz-Tech, Student Nurses Organization, national sororities. *Campus security:* controlled dormitory access. *Student services:* personal/psychological counseling.

Athletics Member NJCAA. *Intercollegiate sports:* baseball M(s), basketball M(s)/W(s), ice hockey M(s), softball W(s), volleyball W(s). *Intramural sports:* basketball M/W, volleyball M/W.

Costs (2014–15) *One-time required fee:* $35. *Tuition:* state resident $2618 full-time, $101 per credit hour part-time; nonresident $2618 full-time, $101 per credit hour part-time. Full-time tuition and fees vary according to course load, location, and reciprocity agreements. Part-time tuition and fees vary according to course load, location, and reciprocity agreements. *Required fees:* $1006 full-time, $39 per credit hour part-time. *Room and board:* $7000; room only: $3700. Room and board charges vary according to board plan and housing facility. *Payment plan:* installment. *Waivers:* minority students and employees or children of employees.

Applying *Options:* electronic application. *Application fee:* $35. *Required:* high school transcript. *Application deadlines:* rolling (freshmen), rolling (out-of-state freshmen), rolling (transfers). *Notification:* continuous (freshmen), continuous (out-of-state freshmen), continuous (transfers).

Freshman Application Contact Ms. Brittney O'Neill, Enrollment Services Associate, Williston State College, 1410 University Avenue, Williston, ND 58801. *Phone:* 701-774-4202. *Toll-free phone:* 888-863-9455. *E-mail:* brittney.f.oneill@willistonstate.edu.

Website: http://www.willistonstate.edu/.

NORTHERN MARIANA ISLANDS

Northern Marianas College

Saipan, Northern Mariana Islands

Freshman Application Contact Ms. Leilani M. Basa-Alam, Admission Specialist, Northern Marianas College, PO Box 501250, Saipan, MP 96950-1250. *Phone:* 670-234-3690 Ext. 1539. *Fax:* 670-235-4967. *E-mail:* leilanib@nmcnet.edu.

Website: http://www.nmcnet.edu/.

OHIO

Akron Institute of Herzing University

Akron, Ohio

Admissions Office Contact Akron Institute of Herzing University, 1600 South Arlington Street, Suite 100, Akron, OH 44306. *Toll-free phone:* 800-311-0512.

Website: http://www.akroninstitute.com/.

Antonelli College

Cincinnati, Ohio

Freshman Application Contact Antonelli College, 124 East Seventh Street, Cincinnati, OH 45202. *Phone:* 513-241-4338. *Toll-free phone:* 877-500-4304.

Website: http://www.antonellicollege.edu/.

The Art Institute of Cincinnati

Cincinnati, Ohio

- **Independent** primarily 2-year, founded 1976
- **Urban** 3-acre campus with easy access to Cincinnati
- **Coed,** 35 undergraduate students, 86% full-time, 57% women, 43% men
- 80% of applicants were admitted

Undergraduates 30 full-time, 5 part-time. Students come from 3 states and territories; 23% are from out of state; 20% Black or African American, non-Hispanic/Latino. *Retention:* 75% of full-time freshmen returned.

Freshmen *Admission:* 56 applied, 45 admitted, 10 enrolled. *Average high school GPA:* 3.2.

Faculty *Total:* 11, 36% full-time, 18% with terminal degrees. *Student/faculty ratio:* 5:1.

Majors Computer graphics.

Academics *Degrees:* associate and bachelor's. *Special study options:* academic remediation for entering students, accelerated degree program, advanced placement credit, cooperative education, part-time degree program, services for LD students, summer session for credit.

Library The Art Institute of Cincinnati Library plus 1 other with 3,000 titles, 10 serial subscriptions, 75 audiovisual materials, an OPAC, a Web page.

Student Life *Housing:* college housing not available. *Activities and Organizations:* AIGA Student Chapter. *Campus security:* 24-hour emergency response devices, SMS. *Student services:* personal/psychological counseling.

Standardized Tests *Recommended:* SAT or ACT (for admission).

Costs (2014–15) *Tuition:* $23,001 full-time, $479 per credit part-time. Full-time tuition and fees vary according to student level. Part-time tuition and fees vary according to class time, course load, and student level. No tuition increase for student's term of enrollment. *Required fees:* $1800 full-time. *Payment plan:* installment. *Waivers:* employees or children of employees.

Applying *Options:* early admission, early decision. *Application fee:* $100. *Required:* essay or personal statement, high school transcript, interview. *Recommended:* minimum 2.0 GPA, ACT or SAT. Placement testing is offered. *Application deadlines:* rolling (freshmen), rolling (out-of-state freshmen), rolling (transfers), rolling (early action). *Early decision deadline:* rolling (for plan 1), rolling (for plan 2). *Notification:* continuous (freshmen), continuous (out-of-state freshmen), continuous (transfers), rolling (early decision plan 1), rolling (early decision plan 2), rolling (early action).

Freshman Application Contact The Art Institute of Cincinnati, 1171 East Kemper Road, Cincinnati, OH 45246. *Phone:* 513-751-1206.

Website: http://www.aic-arts.edu/.

ATS Institute of Technology

Highland Heights, Ohio

Freshman Application Contact Admissions Office, ATS Institute of Technology, 325 Alpha Park, Highland Heights, OH 44143. *Phone:* 440-449-1700 Ext. 103. *E-mail:* info@atsinstitute.edu.

Website: http://www.atsinstitute.edu/cleveland/.

Belmont College

St. Clairsville, Ohio

Director of Admissions Michael Sterling, Director of Recruitment, Belmont College, 120 Fox Shannon Place, St. Clairsville, OH 43950-9735. *Phone:* 740-695-9500 Ext. 1563. *Toll-free phone:* 800-423-1188. *E-mail:* msterling@btc.edu.

Website: http://www.belmontcollege.edu/.

Bowling Green State University-Firelands College

Huron, Ohio

- **State-supported** primarily 2-year, founded 1968, part of Bowling Green State University System
- **Rural** 216-acre campus with easy access to Cleveland, Toledo
- **Endowment** $3.0 million
- **Coed,** 2,441 undergraduate students, 51% full-time, 65% women, 35% men

Undergraduates 1,236 full-time, 1,205 part-time. Students come from 2 states and territories; 6% Black or African American, non-Hispanic/Latino; 5% Hispanic/Latino; 0.5% Asian, non-Hispanic/Latino; 0.1% Native Hawaiian or other Pacific Islander, non-Hispanic/Latino; 0.5% American Indian or Alaska Native, non-Hispanic/Latino; 3% Two or more races, non-Hispanic/Latino; 4% Race/ethnicity unknown; 0.1% international; 6% transferred in. *Retention:* 55% of full-time freshmen returned.

Freshmen *Admission:* 930 applied, 638 admitted, 408 enrolled. *Average high school GPA:* 2.8.

Faculty *Total:* 135, 41% full-time, 33% with terminal degrees. *Student/faculty ratio:* 20:1.

Majors Allied health and medical assisting services related; business administration and management; communications technologies and support services related; computer and information sciences and support services related; computer engineering technology; computer systems networking and telecommunications; criminal justice/safety; design and visual communications; diagnostic medical sonography and ultrasound technology; education; electrical, electronic and communications engineering technology; electromechanical technology; health information/medical records administration; health professions related; human services; industrial technology; interdisciplinary studies; liberal arts and sciences/liberal studies; management information systems and services related; manufacturing engineering technology; mechanical engineering/mechanical technology; medical radiologic technology; registered nursing/registered nurse; respiratory care therapy; social work.

Academics *Calendar:* semesters. *Degrees:* certificates, associate, and bachelor's (also offers some upper-level and graduate courses). *Special study options:* academic remediation for entering students, adult/continuing education programs, advanced placement credit, cooperative education, distance learning, double majors, honors programs, independent study, internships, part-time degree program, services for LD students, student-designed majors, study abroad, summer session for credit. *ROTC:* Army (c), Air Force (c).

Library BGSU Firelands College Library with 61,019 titles, 223 serial subscriptions, 1,958 audiovisual materials, an OPAC, a Web page.

Student Life *Housing:* college housing not available. *Activities and Organizations:* drama/theater group, Humanity Organized for Peace through Education- H.O.P.E, Science and Environment Club, Speech Activities Organization - Theatre, Visual Communication Technology Organization, intramurals. *Campus security:* 24-hour emergency response devices, late-night transport/escort service, patrols by trained security personnel.

Athletics *Intramural sports:* basketball M/W, bowling M/W, football M, table tennis M/W, volleyball M/W.

Costs (2013–14) *Tuition:* state resident $4706 full-time, $196 per credit hour part-time; nonresident $12,014 full-time, $501 per credit hour part-time. Full-time tuition and fees vary according to location. Part-time tuition and fees vary according to location. *Required fees:* $240 full-time, $9 per credit hour part-time, $120 per term part-time. *Payment plan:* installment. *Waivers:* employees or children of employees.

Applying *Options:* electronic application, early admission, deferred entrance. *Application fee:* $45. *Required:* high school transcript. *Application deadlines:*

8/6 (freshmen), 8/6 (transfers). *Notification:* continuous (freshmen), continuous (transfers).

Freshman Application Contact Debralee Divers, Director of Admissions and Financial Aid, Bowling Green State University-Firelands College, One University Drive, Huron, OH 44839-9791. *Phone:* 419-433-5560. *Toll-free phone:* 800-322-4787. *Fax:* 419-372-0604. *E-mail:* divers@bgsu.edu. *Website:* http://www.firelands.bgsu.edu/.

Bradford School
Columbus, Ohio

- **Private** 2-year, founded 1911
- **Suburban** campus
- **Coed, primarily women,** 541 undergraduate students

Majors Cooking and related culinary arts; graphic design; medical/clinical assistant; physical therapy technology; veterinary/animal health technology.

Academics *Calendar:* semesters. *Degree:* diplomas and associate.

Freshman Application Contact Admissions Office, Bradford School, 2469 Stelzer Road, Columbus, OH 43219. *Phone:* 614-416-6200. *Toll-free phone:* 800-678-7981.

Website: http://www.bradfordschoolcolumbus.edu/.

Brown Mackie College–Akron
Akron, Ohio

- **Proprietary** primarily 2-year, founded 1968, part of Education Management Corporation
- **Suburban** campus
- **Coed**

Majors Business administration and management; business/commerce; medical office management; occupational therapist assistant; veterinary/animal health technology.

Academics *Calendar:* quarters. *Degrees:* diplomas, associate, and bachelor's.

Freshman Application Contact Brown Mackie College–Akron, 755 White Pond Drive, Suite 101, Akron, OH 44320. *Phone:* 330-869-3600.

Website: http://www.brownmackie.edu/akron/.

See display on next page and page 376 for the College Close-Up.

Brown Mackie College–Cincinnati
Cincinnati, Ohio

- **Proprietary** primarily 2-year, founded 1927, part of Education Management Corporation
- **Suburban** campus
- **Coed**

Majors Biomedical technology; business administration and management; computer and information sciences and support services related; criminal justice/law enforcement administration; criminal justice/safety; early childhood education; health/health-care administration; medical office management; pharmacy technician; surgical technology; veterinary/animal health technology.

Academics *Calendar:* quarters. *Degrees:* diplomas, associate, and bachelor's.

Freshman Application Contact Brown Mackie College–Cincinnati, 1011 Glendale-Milford Road, Cincinnati, OH 45215. *Phone:* 513-771-2424. *Toll-free phone:* 800-888-1445.

Website: http://www.brownmackie.edu/cincinnati/.

See display on next page and page 386 for the College Close-Up.

Brown Mackie College–Findlay
Findlay, Ohio

- **Proprietary** primarily 2-year, founded 1929, part of Education Management Corporation
- **Rural** campus
- **Coed**

Majors Business administration and management; criminal justice/law enforcement administration; criminal justice/safety; health/health-care administration; occupational therapist assistant; pharmacy technician; registered nursing/registered nurse; surgical technology; veterinary/animal health technology.

Academics *Calendar:* continuous. *Degrees:* diplomas, associate, and bachelor's.

Freshman Application Contact Brown Mackie College–Findlay, 1700 Fostoria Avenue, Suite 100, Findlay, OH 45840. *Phone:* 419-423-2211. *Toll-free phone:* 800-842-3687.

Website: http://www.brownmackie.edu/findlay/.

See display on next page and page 390 for the College Close-Up.

Brown Mackie College–North Canton
Canton, Ohio

- **Proprietary** primarily 2-year, founded 1929, part of Education Management Corporation
- **Suburban** campus
- **Coed**

Majors Business administration and management; computer and information sciences and support services related; health/health-care administration; legal assistant/paralegal; registered nursing/registered nurse; surgical technology; veterinary/animal health technology.

Academics *Calendar:* quarters. *Degrees:* diplomas, associate, and bachelor's.

Freshman Application Contact Brown Mackie College–North Canton, 4300 Munson Street NW, Canton, OH 44718-3674. *Phone:* 330-494-1214. *Website:* http://www.brownmackie.edu/northcanton/.

See display on next page and page 408 for the College Close-Up.

Bryant & Stratton College - Eastlake Campus
Eastlake, Ohio

Freshman Application Contact Ms. Melanie Pettit, Director of Admissions, Bryant & Stratton College - Eastlake Campus, 35350 Curtis Boulevard, Eastlake, OH 44095. *Phone:* 440-510-1112.
Website: http://www.bryantstratton.edu/.

Bryant & Stratton College - Parma Campus
Parma, Ohio

Freshman Application Contact Bryant & Stratton College - Parma Campus, 12955 Snow Road, Parma, OH 44130-1013. *Phone:* 216-265-3151. *Toll-free phone:* 866-948-0571.
Website: http://www.bryantstratton.edu/.

Central Ohio Technical College
Newark, Ohio

- **State-supported** 2-year, founded 1971, part of Ohio Board of Regents
- **Small-town** 155-acre campus with easy access to Columbus
- **Endowment** $2.5 million
- **Coed,** 3,648 undergraduate students, 27% full-time, 70% women, 30% men

Undergraduates 995 full-time, 2,653 part-time. 1% are from out of state; 11% Black or African American, non-Hispanic/Latino; 2% Hispanic/Latino; 0.5% Asian, non-Hispanic/Latino; 0.2% Native Hawaiian or other Pacific Islander, non-Hispanic/Latino; 0.4% American Indian or Alaska Native, non-Hispanic/Latino; 3% Two or more races, non-Hispanic/Latino; 4% Race/ethnicity unknown; 11% transferred in. *Retention:* 43% of full-time freshmen returned.

Freshmen *Admission:* 602 enrolled.

Faculty *Total:* 255, 24% full-time. *Student/faculty ratio:* 15:1.

Majors Accounting; advertising; architectural drafting and CAD/CADD; business administration and management; CAD/CADD drafting/design technology; civil drafting and CAD/CADD; civil engineering technology; computer graphics; computer programming; computer support specialist; criminal justice/law enforcement administration; criminal justice/police science; culinary arts; diagnostic medical sonography and ultrasound technology; early childhood education; electrical, electronic and communications engineering technology; emergency medical technology (EMT paramedic); fire science/firefighting; forensic science and technology; human services; liberal arts and sciences/liberal studies; licensed practical/vocational nurse training; manufacturing engineering technology; mechanical engineering/mechanical technology; medical radiologic technology; registered nursing/registered nurse; surgical technology; web page, digital/multimedia and information resources design.

Academics *Calendar:* quarters. *Degree:* certificates and associate. *Special study options:* academic remediation for entering students, accelerated degree program, adult/continuing education programs, advanced placement credit, cooperative education, distance learning, double majors, internships, off-campus study, part-time degree program, services for LD students, summer session for credit.

Library Newark Campus Library with 45,000 titles, 500 serial subscriptions, an OPAC, a Web page.

Student Life *Housing:* college housing not available. *Activities and Organizations:* drama/theater group, choral group, Student Nurses Organization, Phi Theta Kappa, Forensic Science Club, Campus Chorus, Student Senate. *Campus security:* 24-hour emergency response devices and patrols, student patrols, late-night transport/escort service. *Student services:* personal/psychological counseling.

Athletics *Intercollegiate sports:* baseball M, basketball M/W, softball W, volleyball M/W. *Intramural sports:* baseball M, basketball M/W, cheerleading M/W, football M, skiing (downhill) M/W, softball W, volleyball M/W, weight lifting M/W.

Costs (2014–15) *Tuition:* state resident $4296 full-time, $179 per semester hour part-time; nonresident $7056 full-time, $294 per semester hour part-time. *Payment plan:* installment. *Waivers:* senior citizens and employees or children of employees.

Financial Aid Of all full-time matriculated undergraduates who enrolled in 2012, 43 Federal Work-Study jobs (averaging $4000).

Applying *Options:* electronic application, early admission, deferred entrance. *Application fee:* $20. *Required:* high school transcript. *Application deadlines:* rolling (freshmen), rolling (transfers).

Freshman Application Contact Teri Holder, Interim Director of Gateway Operations, Central Ohio Technical College, 1179 University Drive, Newark, OH 43055-1767. *Phone:* 740-366-9222. *Toll-free phone:* 800-9NEWARK. *Fax:* 740-366-5047.

Website: http://www.cotc.edu/.

Chatfield College

St. Martin, Ohio

Freshman Application Contact Chatfield College, 20918 State Route 251, St. Martin, OH 45118-9705. *Phone:* 513-875-3344 Ext. 137.

Website: http://www.chatfield.edu/.

The Christ College of Nursing and Health Sciences

Cincinnati, Ohio

Freshman Application Contact Mr. Bradley Jackson, Admissions, The Christ College of Nursing and Health Sciences, 2139 Auburn Avenue, Cincinnati, OH 45219. *Phone:* 513-585-0016. *E-mail:* bradley.jackson@thechristcollege.edu.

Website: http://www.thechristcollege.edu/.

Cincinnati State Technical and Community College

Cincinnati, Ohio

- **State-supported** 2-year, founded 1966, part of Ohio Board of Regents
- **Urban** 46-acre campus
- **Coed,** 11,167 undergraduate students, 37% full-time, 49% women, 51% men

Undergraduates 4,157 full-time, 7,010 part-time. Students come from 15 states and territories; 96 other countries; 10% are from out of state; 30% Black or African American, non-Hispanic/Latino; 2% Hispanic/Latino; 1% Asian, non-Hispanic/Latino; 0.1% Native Hawaiian or other Pacific Islander, non-Hispanic/Latino; 0.4% American Indian or Alaska Native, non-Hispanic/Latino; 2% Two or more races, non-Hispanic/Latino; 5% Race/ethnicity unknown; 1% international.

Freshmen *Admission:* 2,112 enrolled.

Faculty *Total:* 732, 30% full-time. *Student/faculty ratio:* 16:1.

Majors Accounting; administrative assistant and secretarial science; aeronautical/aerospace engineering technology; allied health and medical assisting services related; applied horticulture/horticultural business services related; architectural engineering technology; audiovisual communications technologies related; automobile/automotive mechanics technology; automotive engineering technology; baking and pastry arts; biology/biological sciences; biomedical technology; business administration and management; business administration, management and operations related; chemical technology; civil engineering technology; clinical/medical laboratory technology; commercial and advertising art; computer and information sciences; computer engineering technology; computer programming (specific applications); computer support specialist; computer systems analysis; crisis/emergency/disaster management; culinary arts; desktop publishing and digital imaging design; diagnostic medical sonography and ultrasound technology; dietetics; early childhood education; electrical, electronic and communications engineering technology; electromechanical technology; emergency medical technology (EMT paramedic); energy management and systems technology; engineering technologies and engineering related; entrepreneurship; environmental control technologies related; environmental engineering technology; executive assistant/executive secretary; financial planning and services; fire science/firefighting; general studies; health information/medical records technology; hospitality administration; industrial technology; information technology project management; landscaping and groundskeeping; liberal arts and sciences/liberal studies; marketing/marketing

management; mechanical engineering/mechanical technology; medical office assistant; multi/interdisciplinary studies related; network and system administration; nuclear medical technology; occupational safety and health technology; occupational therapist assistant; parks, recreation, leisure, and fitness studies related; plastics and polymer engineering technology; real estate; registered nursing/registered nurse; restaurant, culinary, and catering management; sign language interpretation and translation; surgical technology; turf and turfgrass management.

Academics *Calendar:* 5 ten-week terms. *Degree:* certificates and associate. *Special study options:* academic remediation for entering students, advanced placement credit, cooperative education, distance learning, double majors, English as a second language, honors programs, independent study, internships, off-campus study, part-time degree program, services for LD students, student-designed majors, summer session for credit. *ROTC:* Army (c).

Library Johnnie Mae Berry Library plus 1 other with 31,413 titles, 124 serial subscriptions, 6,169 audiovisual materials, an OPAC, a Web page.

Student Life *Housing:* college housing not available. *Activities and Organizations:* Student government, Nursing Student Association, Phi Theta Kappa, American Society of Civil Engineers, Respiratory care club. *Campus security:* 24-hour emergency response devices and patrols, late-night transport/escort service. *Student services:* personal/psychological counseling.

Athletics Member NJCAA. *Intercollegiate sports:* basketball M(s)/W(s), golf M/W, soccer M(s)/W(s), volleyball W.

Costs (2013–14) *One-time required fee:* $15. *Tuition:* state resident $5320 full-time, $145 per credit hour part-time; nonresident $10,462 full-time, $291 per credit hour part-time. *Required fees:* $612 full-time, $9 per credit hour part-time, $47 per term part-time. *Payment plan:* installment. *Waivers:* senior citizens and employees or children of employees.

Financial Aid Of all full-time matriculated undergraduates who enrolled in 2012, 100 Federal Work-Study jobs (averaging $3500).

Applying *Options:* electronic application, deferred entrance. *Required:* high school transcript. *Application deadlines:* rolling (freshmen), rolling (out-of-state freshmen), rolling (transfers). *Notification:* continuous (freshmen), continuous (out-of-state freshmen), continuous (transfers).

Freshman Application Contact Ms. Gabriele Boeckermann, Director of Admission, Cincinnati State Technical and Community College, Office of Admissions, 3520 Central Parkway, Cincinnati, OH 45223-2690. *Phone:* 513-569-1550. *Toll-free phone:* 877-569-0115. *Fax:* 513-569-1562. *E-mail:* adm@cincinnatistate.edu.
Website: http://www.cincinnatistate.edu/.

Clark State Community College

Springfield, Ohio

- **State-supported** 2-year, founded 1962, part of Ohio Board of Regents
- **Suburban** 60-acre campus with easy access to Columbus, Dayton
- **Endowment** $9.2 million
- **Coed,** 5,653 undergraduate students, 30% full-time, 65% women, 35% men

Undergraduates 1,693 full-time, 3,960 part-time. Students come from 8 states and territories; 11 other countries; 0.5% are from out of state; 19% Black or African American, non-Hispanic/Latino; 1% Hispanic/Latino; 0.9% Asian, non-Hispanic/Latino; 0.2% Native Hawaiian or other Pacific Islander, non-Hispanic/Latino; 0.5% American Indian or Alaska Native, non-Hispanic/Latino; 5% Race/ethnicity unknown; 0.7% international; 15% transferred in. *Retention:* 39% of full-time freshmen returned.

Freshmen *Admission:* 3,638 applied, 3,638 admitted, 783 enrolled.

Faculty *Total:* 472, 17% full-time, 5% with terminal degrees. *Student/faculty ratio:* 14:1.

Majors Accounting; administrative assistant and secretarial science; agricultural business and management; agricultural mechanization; agriculture; applied horticulture/horticulture operations; business administration and management; business, management, and marketing related; business operations support and secretarial services related; civil engineering technology; clinical/medical laboratory technology; commercial and advertising art; computer and information sciences and support services related; computer and information systems security; computer programming; computer programming related; computer systems networking and telecommunications; corrections; court reporting; criminal justice/law enforcement administration; criminal justice/police science; diesel mechanics technology; digital arts; drafting and design technology; dramatic/theater arts; early childhood education; electrical, electronic and communications engineering technology; emergency medical technology (EMT paramedic); engineering related; engineering technologies and engineering related; geographic information science and cartography; health services/allied health/health sciences; heating, ventilation, air conditioning and refrigeration engineering technology; horticultural science; human resources management;

human services; industrial technology; information science/studies; information technology; insurance; kindergarten/preschool education; kinesiology and exercise science; landscaping and groundskeeping; legal assistant/paralegal; liberal arts and sciences/liberal studies; library and archives assisting; licensed practical/vocational nurse training; logistics, materials, and supply chain management; marketing/marketing management; mechanical engineering/mechanical technology; medical administrative assistant and medical secretary; medical/clinical assistant; physical therapy; physical therapy technology; registered nursing/registered nurse; social work.

Academics *Calendar:* quarters. *Degree:* certificates and associate. *Special study options:* academic remediation for entering students, adult/continuing education programs, advanced placement credit, cooperative education, distance learning, double majors, honors programs, independent study, internships, off-campus study, part-time degree program, services for LD students, summer session for credit. *ROTC:* Army (c).

Library Clark State Community College Library with 26,000 titles, 3,000 audiovisual materials, an OPAC, a Web page.

Student Life *Housing:* college housing not available. *Activities and Organizations:* drama/theater group, choral group, Student Senate, Gay Straight Alliance, Student Theatre Guild, Chi Alpha, Creative Writers Club. *Campus security:* late-night transport/escort service. *Student services:* health clinic, personal/psychological counseling.

Athletics Member NJCAA. *Intercollegiate sports:* baseball M, basketball M/W, softball W, volleyball W. *Intramural sports:* baseball M, basketball M/W, tennis M/W, volleyball M/W.

Applying *Options:* electronic application. *Application fee:* $15. *Required:* high school transcript. *Application deadlines:* rolling (freshmen), rolling (out-of-state freshmen), rolling (transfers). *Notification:* continuous (freshmen), continuous (out-of-state freshmen), continuous (transfers).

Freshman Application Contact Admissions Office, Clark State Community College, PO Box 570, Springfield, OH 45501-0570. *Phone:* 937-328-3858. *Fax:* 937-328-6133. *E-mail:* admissions@clarkstate.edu.
Website: http://www.clarkstate.edu/.

Cleveland Institute of Electronics

Cleveland, Ohio

- **Proprietary** 2-year, founded 1934
- **Coed, primarily men,** 1,477 undergraduate students

Undergraduates Students come from 52 states and territories; 70 other countries; 97% are from out of state.

Faculty *Total:* 7, 43% full-time, 14% with terminal degrees.

Majors Computer/information technology services administration related; computer software engineering; electrical, electronic and communications engineering technology.

Academics *Calendar:* continuous. *Degrees:* diplomas and associate (offers only external degree programs conducted through home study). *Special study options:* accelerated degree program, adult/continuing education programs, distance learning, external degree program, independent study, part-time degree program.

Library 5,000 titles, 38 serial subscriptions.

Costs (2013–14) *Tuition:* $2075 per term part-time. No tuition increase for student's term of enrollment. *Payment plans:* tuition prepayment, installment.

Applying *Options:* electronic application, early admission. *Required:* high school transcript. *Application deadlines:* rolling (freshmen), rolling (out-of-state freshmen), rolling (transfers). *Notification:* continuous (freshmen), continuous (out-of-state freshmen), continuous (transfers).

Freshman Application Contact Mr. Scott Katzenmeyer, Registrar, Cleveland Institute of Electronics, Cleveland, OH 44114. *Phone:* 216-781-9400. *Toll-free phone:* 800-243-6446. *Fax:* 216-781-0331. *E-mail:* instruct@cie-wc.edu.
Website: http://www.cie-wc.edu/.

Columbus Culinary Institute at Bradford School

Columbus, Ohio

- **Private** 2-year, founded 2006
- **Suburban** campus
- **Coed,** 150 undergraduate students
- **54%** of applicants were admitted

Freshmen *Admission:* 681 applied, 368 admitted.

Majors Cooking and related culinary arts.

Academics *Calendar:* semesters. *Degree:* associate.

Freshman Application Contact Admissions Office, Columbus Culinary Institute at Bradford School, 2435 Stelzer Road, Columbus, OH 43219. *Phone:* 614-944-4200. *Toll-free phone:* 877-506-5006.
Website: http://www.columbusculinary.com/.

Columbus State Community College
Columbus, Ohio

- **State-supported** 2-year, founded 1963, part of Ohio Board of Regents
- **Urban** 75-acre campus
- **Endowment** $3.9 million
- **Coed**, 25,249 undergraduate students, 35% full-time, 54% women, 46% men

Undergraduates 8,817 full-time, 16,432 part-time. Students come from 50 other countries; 2% are from out of state; 20% Black or African American, non-Hispanic/Latino; 4% Hispanic/Latino; 3% Asian, non-Hispanic/Latino; 0.1% Native Hawaiian or other Pacific Islander, non-Hispanic/Latino; 0.3% American Indian or Alaska Native, non-Hispanic/Latino; 3% Two or more races, non-Hispanic/Latino; 5% Race/ethnicity unknown; 1% international; 24% transferred in. *Retention:* 50% of full-time freshmen returned.

Freshmen *Admission:* 13,066 applied, 11,859 admitted, 2,950 enrolled.

Majors Accounting technology and bookkeeping; administrative assistant and secretarial science; adult development and aging; aeronautical/aerospace engineering technology; architectural engineering technology; automotive engineering technology; business administration and management; business, management, and marketing related; clinical laboratory science/medical technology; clinical/medical laboratory assistant; communications technologies and support services related; computer and information sciences; computer engineering technology; computer programming; computer programming (specific applications); construction engineering technology; criminal justice/police science; culinary arts; dental hygiene; dental laboratory technology; electrical and electronic engineering technologies related; electrical, electronic and communications engineering technology; electromechanical technology; emergency medical technology (EMT paramedic); engineering technologies and engineering related; entrepreneurship; environmental control technologies related; finance and financial management services related; fire science/firefighting; graphic and printing equipment operation/production; health and physical education related; health information/medical records administration; health information/medical records technology; heating, air conditioning, ventilation and refrigeration maintenance technology; hospitality administration; hospitality administration related; human development and family studies related; human resources management; human resources management and services related; legal assistant/paralegal; liberal arts and sciences/liberal studies; logistics, materials, and supply chain management; marketing/marketing management; marketing related; mechanical engineering/mechanical technology; medical/clinical assistant; medical radiologic technology; mental and social health services and allied professions related; multi/interdisciplinary studies related; nuclear medical technology; parks, recreation, leisure, and fitness studies related; purchasing, procurement/acquisitions and contracts management; quality control technology; real estate; registered nursing/registered nurse; rehabilitation and therapeutic professions related; respiratory care therapy; sign language interpretation and translation; sport and fitness administration/management; surgical technology; tourism and travel services management; veterinary/animal health technology.

Academics *Calendar:* quarters. *Degree:* certificates and associate. *Special study options:* academic remediation for entering students, adult/continuing education programs, advanced placement credit, cooperative education, distance learning, double majors, English as a second language, honors programs, independent study, internships, off-campus study, part-time degree program, services for LD students, student-designed majors, study abroad, summer session for credit. *ROTC:* Army (b), Air Force (c). *Unusual degree programs:* 3-2 business administration with Franklin University.

Library Columbus State Library plus 1 other with 38,192 titles, 106,237 serial subscriptions, 6,220 audiovisual materials, an OPAC, a Web page.

Student Life *Housing:* college housing not available. *Activities and Organizations:* choral group, Phi Theta Kappa, Student Nurses Association, Student American Dental Hygiene Association, Athletic Club, Landscaping Association. *Campus security:* 24-hour emergency response devices and patrols, late-night transport/escort service. *Student services:* health clinic, personal/psychological counseling.

Athletics Member NJCAA. *Intercollegiate sports:* basketball M(s)/W(s), cross-country running M(s)/W(s), golf M(s)/W(s), track and field M/W, volleyball W(s). *Intramural sports:* badminton M/W, basketball M/W, soccer M/W, table tennis M/W, ultimate Frisbee M/W, volleyball M/W, weight lifting M/W.

Standardized Tests *Recommended:* ACT (for admission), Applicants can utilize ACT scores for course placement purposes and as part of determining their eligibility for Post Secondary Enrollment Options Program. TOEFL scores are utilized for admission of international applicants.

Costs (2014–15) *One-time required fee:* $50. *Tuition:* state resident $3808 full-time; nonresident $8430 full-time.

Financial Aid Of all full-time matriculated undergraduates who enrolled in 2012, 133 Federal Work-Study jobs (averaging $1500).

Applying *Options:* electronic application, early admission, deferred entrance. *Application fee:* $50. *Required for some:* essay or personal statement, high school transcript, minimum 3.0 GPA, 1 letter of recommendation, interview, Some special population applicants (e.g. Post Secondary Enrollment Options, International, Immigrant, Criminal Background) must submit additional documentation as part of their admission process. *Recommended:* high school transcript. *Application deadlines:* 8/19 (freshmen), 8/19 (out-of-state freshmen), 8/19 (transfers). *Notification:* continuous (freshmen), continuous (out-of-state freshmen), continuous (transfers).

Freshman Application Contact Ms. Tari Blaney, Director of Admissions, Columbus State Community College, 550 East Spring Street, Columbus, OH 43215. *Phone:* 614-287-2669. *Toll-free phone:* 800-621-6407 Ext. 2669. *Fax:* 614-287-6019. *E-mail:* tblaney@cscc.edu. *Website:* http://www.cscc.edu/.

Cuyahoga Community College
Cleveland, Ohio

- **State and locally supported** 2-year, founded 1963
- **Urban** campus
- **Endowment** $22.5 million
- **Coed**

Undergraduates 10,590 full-time, 19,475 part-time. Students come from 27 other countries; 1% are from out of state; 28% Black or African American, non-Hispanic/Latino; 5% Hispanic/Latino; 2% Asian, non-Hispanic/Latino; 0.9% American Indian or Alaska Native, non-Hispanic/Latino; 0.2% Two or more races, non-Hispanic/Latino; 16% Race/ethnicity unknown; 1% international; 5% transferred in. *Retention:* 48% of full-time freshmen returned.

Faculty *Student/faculty ratio:* 18:1.

Academics *Calendar:* semesters. *Degree:* certificates and associate. *Special study options:* adult/continuing education programs, advanced placement credit, cooperative education, distance learning, English as a second language, external degree program, independent study, part-time degree program, services for LD students, summer session for credit.

Student Life *Campus security:* 24-hour emergency response devices and patrols, late-night transport/escort service.

Athletics Member NJCAA.

Costs (2013–14) *Tuition:* area resident $2936 full-time, $98 per credit part-time; state resident $3753 full-time, $125 per credit part-time; nonresident $7268 full-time, $242 per credit part-time.

Financial Aid Of all full-time matriculated undergraduates who enrolled in 2012, 802 Federal Work-Study jobs (averaging $3300).

Applying *Options:* early admission, deferred entrance. *Required for some:* high school transcript.

Freshman Application Contact Mr. Kevin McDaniel, Director of Admissions and Records, Cuyahoga Community College, Cleveland, OH 44115. *Phone:* 216-987-4030. *Toll-free phone:* 800-954-8742. *Fax:* 216-696-2567. *Website:* http://www.tri-c.edu/.

Davis College
Toledo, Ohio

- **Proprietary** 2-year, founded 1858
- **Urban** 1-acre campus with easy access to Detroit
- **Coed**, 218 undergraduate students, 24% full-time, 80% women, 20% men

Undergraduates 53 full-time, 165 part-time. Students come from 2 states and territories; 42% Black or African American, non-Hispanic/Latino; 5% Hispanic/Latino; 0.5% American Indian or Alaska Native, non-Hispanic/Latino; 0.5% Two or more races, non-Hispanic/Latino; 1% Race/ethnicity unknown.

Freshmen *Admission:* 27 applied, 27 admitted, 25 enrolled.

Faculty *Total:* 25, 24% full-time. *Student/faculty ratio:* 9:1.

Majors Accounting; accounting related; administrative assistant and secretarial science; business administration and management; business operations support and secretarial services related; computer systems networking and telecommunications; early childhood education; fashion merchandising; graphic design; hotel, motel, and restaurant management; information technology; insurance; interior design; marketing/marketing management; marketing related; medical administrative assistant and medical secretary; medical/clinical assistant; medical insurance coding; retail management; web page, digital/multimedia and information resources design.

Academics *Calendar:* quarters. *Degree:* diplomas and associate. *Special study options:* academic remediation for entering students, adult/continuing education programs, advanced placement credit, distance learning, internships, part-time degree program, summer session for credit.

Library Davis College Resource Center with 3,400 titles, 45 serial subscriptions, 191 audiovisual materials, an OPAC.

Student Life *Housing:* college housing not available. *Campus security:* 24-hour emergency response devices, security cameras for parking lot. *Student services:* personal/psychological counseling.

Standardized Tests *Required:* CPAt (for admission).

Costs (2014–15) *Tuition:* $12,600 full-time, $350 per credit part-time. *Required fees:* $1050 full-time, $350 per credit part-time, $350 per term part-time. *Waivers:* employees or children of employees.

Financial Aid Of all full-time matriculated undergraduates who enrolled in 2012, 10 Federal Work-Study jobs (averaging $3500).

Applying *Options:* electronic application, early admission, deferred entrance. *Application fee:* $30. *Required:* high school transcript, interview. *Application deadlines:* rolling (freshmen), rolling (transfers). *Notification:* continuous (freshmen), continuous (transfers).

Freshman Application Contact Ms. Dana Stern, Davis College, 4747 Monroe Street, Toledo, OH 43623-4307. *Phone:* 419-473-2700. *Toll-free phone:* 800-477-7021. *Fax:* 419-473-2472. *E-mail:* dstern@daviscollege.edu. *Website:* http://daviscollege.edu/.

Daymar College
Chillicothe, Ohio

Freshman Application Contact Admissions Office, Daymar College, 1410 Industrial Drive, Chillicothe, OH 45601. *Phone:* 740-774-6300. *Toll-free phone:* 877-258-7796. *Fax:* 740-774-6317. *Website:* http://www.daymarcollege.edu/.

Daymar College
Jackson, Ohio

Freshman Application Contact Admissions Office, Daymar College, 980 East Main Street, Jackson, OH 45640. *Phone:* 740-286-1554. *Toll-free phone:* 877-258-7796. *Fax:* 740-774-6317. *Website:* http://www.daymarcollege.edu/.

Daymar College
Lancaster, Ohio

Freshman Application Contact Holly Hankinson, Admissions Office, Daymar College, 1579 Victor Road, NW, Lancaster, OH 43130. *Phone:* 740-687-6126. *Toll-free phone:* 877-258-7796. *E-mail:* hhankinson@daymarcollege.edu. *Website:* http://www.daymarcollege.edu/.

Daymar College
New Boston, Ohio

Freshman Application Contact Mike Bell, Admissions Representative, Daymar College, 3879 Rhodes Avenue, New Boston, OH 45662. *Phone:* 740-456-4124. *Toll-free phone:* 877-258-7796. *Website:* http://www.daymarcollege.edu/.

Eastern Gateway Community College
Steubenville, Ohio

- **State and locally supported** 2-year, founded 1966, part of Ohio Board of Regents
- **Small-town** 83-acre campus with easy access to Pittsburgh
- **Endowment** $339,277
- **Coed,** 2,929 undergraduate students, 48% full-time, 64% women, 36% men

Undergraduates 1,414 full-time, 1,515 part-time.

Freshmen *Admission:* 1,724 applied, 1,724 admitted, 629 enrolled.

Faculty *Total:* 187, 25% full-time. *Student/faculty ratio:* 16:1.

Majors Accounting; administrative assistant and secretarial science; business administration and management; child-care and support services management; computer engineering related; corrections; criminal justice/police science; data processing and data processing technology; dental assisting; drafting and design technology; electrical, electronic and communications engineering technology; emergency medical technology (EMT paramedic); industrial radiologic technology; industrial technology; legal administrative assistant/secretary; licensed practical/vocational nurse training; mechanical engineering/mechanical technology; medical administrative assistant and medical secretary; medical/clinical assistant; real estate; respiratory care therapy.

Academics *Calendar:* semesters. *Degree:* certificates and associate. *Special study options:* academic remediation for entering students, accelerated degree program, adult/continuing education programs, cooperative education, distance learning, double majors, off-campus study, part-time degree program, services for LD students, summer session for credit.

Library Eastern Gateway Community College Library with an OPAC.

Student Life *Housing:* college housing not available. *Activities and Organizations:* Student Senate, Phi Theta Kappa. *Campus security:* 24-hour emergency response devices, day and evening security.

Athletics *Intramural sports:* football M/W, softball M/W.

Standardized Tests *Required for some:* SAT or ACT (for admission).

Financial Aid Of all full-time matriculated undergraduates who enrolled in 2012, 30 Federal Work-Study jobs (averaging $1500).

Applying *Options:* electronic application, early admission, deferred entrance. *Application fee:* $20. *Required for some:* high school transcript. *Notification:* continuous (freshmen), continuous (out-of-state freshmen), continuous (transfers).

Freshman Application Contact Mrs. Marlana Featner, Director of Admissions-Jefferson Campus, Eastern Gateway Community College, 4000 Sunset Boulevard, Steubenville, OH 43952. *Phone:* 740-264-5591 Ext. 1642. *Toll-free phone:* 800-68-COLLEGE. *Fax:* 740-266-2944. *E-mail:* mfeatner@egcc.edu. *Website:* http://www.egcc.edu/.

Edison Community College
Piqua, Ohio

- **State-supported** 2-year, founded 1973, part of Ohio Board of Regents' University System of Ohio
- **Small-town** 130-acre campus with easy access to Dayton, Columbus, Cincinnati
- **Endowment** $1.7 million
- **Coed,** 2,993 undergraduate students, 29% full-time, 64% women, 36% men

Undergraduates 877 full-time, 2,116 part-time. Students come from 3 states and territories; 3 other countries; 1% are from out of state; 4% Black or African American, non-Hispanic/Latino; 1% Hispanic/Latino; 1% Asian, non-Hispanic/Latino; 0.5% American Indian or Alaska Native, non-Hispanic/Latino; 1% Two or more races, non-Hispanic/Latino; 5% Race/ethnicity unknown; 0.1% international; 5% transferred in. *Retention:* 51% of full-time freshmen returned.

Freshmen *Admission:* 597 applied, 593 admitted, 439 enrolled. *Average high school GPA:* 2.88. *Test scores:* ACT scores over 18: 79%; ACT scores over 24: 23%; ACT scores over 30: 2%.

Faculty *Total:* 202, 25% full-time, 12% with terminal degrees. *Student/faculty ratio:* 16:1.

Majors Accounting; art; biology/biological sciences; business administration and management; child development; clinical/medical laboratory technology; computer and information sciences; computer and information systems security; computer programming; computer systems networking and telecommunications; criminal justice/police science; dramatic/theater arts; economics; education; electrical, electronic and communications engineering technology; electromechanical technology; English; executive assistant/executive secretary; geology/earth science; health/medical preparatory programs related; history; human resources management; industrial technology; legal assistant/paralegal; liberal arts and sciences/liberal studies; logistics, materials, and supply chain management; manufacturing engineering technology; marketing/marketing management; mathematics; mechanical drafting and CAD/CADD; mechanical engineering/mechanical technology; medical administrative assistant and medical secretary; medical/clinical assistant; medium/heavy vehicle and truck technology; philosophy and religious studies related; physical therapy technology; prenursing studies; psychology; registered nursing/registered nurse; social work; speech communication and rhetoric.

Academics *Calendar:* semesters. *Degrees:* certificates, associate, and postbachelor's certificates. *Special study options:* academic remediation for entering students, accelerated degree program, adult/continuing education programs, advanced placement credit, distance learning, double majors, English as a second language, honors programs, independent study, internships, off-campus study, part-time degree program, services for LD students, student-designed majors, summer session for credit.

Library Edison Community College Library with 27,433 titles, 75,282 serial subscriptions, 2,608 audiovisual materials, an OPAC, a Web page.

Student Life *Housing:* college housing not available. *Activities and Organizations:* drama/theater group, Campus Crusade for Christ, Student Ambassadors, Edison Stagelight Players, Writers Club, Edison Photo Society. *Campus security:* late-night transport/escort service, 18-hour patrols by trained security personnel. *Student services:* health clinic, personal/psychological counseling.

Athletics Member NJCAA. *Intercollegiate sports:* basketball M(s)/W(s), volleyball W(s). *Intramural sports:* baseball M(c).

Standardized Tests *Required:* ACT COMPASS (for admission).

Costs (2013–14) *One-time required fee:* $20. *Tuition:* state resident $4149 full-time, $138 per credit hour part-time; nonresident $7658 full-time, $255 per credit hour part-time. Full-time tuition and fees vary according to program and reciprocity agreements. Part-time tuition and fees vary according to program and reciprocity agreements. *Required fees:* $15 full-time. *Payment plans:* installment, deferred payment. *Waivers:* senior citizens and employees or children of employees.

Financial Aid Of all full-time matriculated undergraduates who enrolled in 2012, 42 Federal Work-Study jobs (averaging $3000).

Applying *Options:* electronic application. *Application fee:* $20. *Required:* high school transcript. *Application deadlines:* rolling (freshmen), rolling (out-of-state freshmen), rolling (transfers).

Freshman Application Contact Ms. Stacey Bean, Enrollment Manager, Edison Community College, 1973 Edison Drive, Piqua, OH 45356. *Phone:* 937-778-7844. *Toll-free phone:* 800-922-3722. *Fax:* 937-778-4692. *E-mail:* sbean@edisonohio.edu. *Website:* http://www.edisonohio.edu/.

ETI Technical College of Niles
Niles, Ohio

Freshman Application Contact Ms. Diane Marsteller, Director of Admissions, ETI Technical College of Niles, 2076 Youngstown-Warren Road, Niles, OH 44446-4398. *Phone:* 330-652-9919 Ext. 16. *Fax:* 330-652-4399. *E-mail:* dianemarsteller@eticollege.edu. *Website:* http://eticollege.edu/.

Fortis College
Centerville, Ohio

Freshman Application Contact Fortis College, 555 East Alex Bell Road, Centerville, OH 45459. *Phone:* 937-433-3410. *Toll-free phone:* 855-4-FORTIS. *Website:* http://www.fortis.edu/.

Fortis College
Cuyahoga Falls, Ohio

Freshman Application Contact Admissions Office, Fortis College, 2545 Bailey Road, Cuyahoga Falls, OH 44221. *Phone:* 330-923-9959. *Fax:* 330-923-0886. *Website:* http://www.fortis.edu/.

Fortis College
Ravenna, Ohio

Freshman Application Contact Admissions Office, Fortis College, 653 Enterprise Parkway, Ravenna, OH 44266. *Toll-free phone:* 855-4-FORTIS. *Website:* http://www.fortis.edu/.

Gallipolis Career College
Gallipolis, Ohio

Freshman Application Contact Mr. Jack Henson, Director of Admissions, Gallipolis Career College, 1176 Jackson Pike, Suite 312, Gallipolis, OH 45631. *Phone:* 740-446-4367. *Toll-free phone:* 800-214-0452. *Fax:* 740-446-4124. *E-mail:* admissions@gallipoliscareercollege.com. *Website:* http://www.gallipoliscareercollege.com/.

Good Samaritan College of Nursing and Health Science
Cincinnati, Ohio

Freshman Application Contact Admissions Office, Good Samaritan College of Nursing and Health Science, 375 Dixmyth Avenue, Cincinnati, OH 45220. *Phone:* 513-862-2743. *Fax:* 513-862-3572. *Website:* http://www.gscollege.edu/.

Herzing University
Toledo, Ohio

Admissions Office Contact Herzing University, 5212 Hill Avenue, Toledo, OH 43615. *Toll-free phone:* 800-596-0724. *Website:* http://www.herzing.edu/toledo.

Hocking College
Nelsonville, Ohio

- **State-supported** 2-year, founded 1968, part of Ohio Board of Regents
- **Rural** 1600-acre campus with easy access to Columbus
- **Endowment** $4.8 million
- **Coed,** 4,094 undergraduate students, 74% full-time, 51% women, 49% men

Undergraduates 3,012 full-time, 1,082 part-time. Students come from 25 states and territories; 17 other countries; 3% are from out of state; 4% Black or

African American, non-Hispanic/Latino; 2% Hispanic/Latino; 0.5% Asian, non-Hispanic/Latino; 0.5% American Indian or Alaska Native, non-Hispanic/Latino; 3% Two or more races, non-Hispanic/Latino; 2% Race/ethnicity unknown; 2% international; 9% live on campus. *Retention:* 44% of full-time freshmen returned.

Freshmen *Admission:* 2,270 applied, 2,270 admitted.

Faculty *Total:* 281, 62% full-time. *Student/faculty ratio:* 16:1.

Majors Accounting; business administration and management; ceramic sciences and engineering; child development; computer engineering technology; computer programming; computer science; corrections; criminal justice/law enforcement administration; criminal justice/police science; culinary arts; dietetics; drafting and design technology; ecology; electrical, electronic and communications engineering technology; emergency medical technology (EMT paramedic); equestrian studies; fire science/firefighting; fishing and fisheries sciences and management; food science; forestry; forest technology; health information/medical records administration; hospitality administration; hotel/motel administration; industrial technology; land use planning and management; licensed practical/vocational nurse training; marketing/marketing management; medical administrative assistant and medical secretary; medical/clinical assistant; natural resources/conservation; natural resources management and policy; natural resources management and policy related; ophthalmic laboratory technology; physical therapy technology; registered nursing/registered nurse; tourism and travel services management; wildlife, fish and wildlands science and management.

Academics *Calendar:* quarters. *Degree:* certificates, diplomas, and associate. *Special study options:* academic remediation for entering students, accelerated degree program, adult/continuing education programs, advanced placement credit, cooperative education, distance learning, double majors, English as a second language, internships, part-time degree program, services for LD students, student-designed majors, summer session for credit. *ROTC:* Army (c).

Library Hocking College Learning Resources Center plus 1 other with 17,583 titles, 157 serial subscriptions, 2,810 audiovisual materials, an OPAC, a Web page.

Student Life *Housing Options:* coed. Campus housing is university owned and is provided by a third party. *Activities and Organizations:* drama/theater group, choral group, Phi Theta Kappa, Recycling Club, Kappa Beta Delta (Business Honor Society), Alpha Beta Gamma, Native American Club. *Campus security:* 24-hour emergency response devices and patrols, student patrols, late-night transport/escort service, controlled dormitory access. *Student services:* personal/psychological counseling.

Athletics *Intramural sports:* archery M/W, basketball M/W, cross-country running M/W, football M/W, golf M/W, soccer M/W, softball M/W, tennis M/W, volleyball M/W, weight lifting M/W.

Costs (2014–15) *Tuition:* state resident $4390 full-time, $183 per credit hour part-time; nonresident $8780 full-time, $366 per credit hour part-time. Full-time tuition and fees vary according to course load and program. Part-time tuition and fees vary according to program. *Room and board:* $6560. Room and board charges vary according to board plan and housing facility. *Payment plan:* installment. *Waivers:* senior citizens and employees or children of employees.

Financial Aid Of all full-time matriculated undergraduates who enrolled in 2012, 125 Federal Work-Study jobs (averaging $1700). 225 state and other part-time jobs (averaging $1700).

Applying *Options:* electronic application. *Application fee:* $15. *Required:* high school transcript. *Application deadlines:* rolling (freshmen), rolling (out-of-state freshmen), rolling (transfers). *Notification:* continuous (freshmen), continuous (out-of-state freshmen), continuous (transfers).

Freshman Application Contact Hocking College, 3301 Hocking Parkway, Nelsonville, OH 45764-9588. *Phone:* 740-753-3591 Ext. 2803. *Toll-free phone:* 877-462-5464. *Website:* http://www.hocking.edu/.

Hondros College
Westerville, Ohio

Director of Admissions Ms. Carol Thomas, Operations Manager, Hondros College, 4140 Executive Parkway, Westerville, OH 43081-3855. *Phone:* 614-508-7244. *Toll-free phone:* 888-HONDROS. *Website:* http://www.hondros.edu/.

International College of Broadcasting
Dayton, Ohio

- **Private** 2-year, founded 1968
- **Urban** 1-acre campus with easy access to Dayton
- **Coed,** 88 undergraduate students

Faculty *Total:* 16, 25% full-time, 6% with terminal degrees.

Majors Recording arts technology.

Academics *Calendar:* semesters. *Degree:* diplomas and associate. *Special study options:* academic remediation for entering students, internships, services for LD students.
Student Life *Housing:* college housing not available. *Activities and Organizations:* student-run radio station.
Standardized Tests *Required:* Wonderlic aptitude test (for admission).
Costs (2014–15) *Tuition:* $30,485 full-time. No tuition increase for student's term of enrollment. *Payment plans:* tuition prepayment, installment.
Applying *Options:* early admission. *Application fee:* $100. *Required:* high school transcript, interview, passing Wonderlic Test.
Freshman Application Contact International College of Broadcasting, 6 South Smithville Road, Dayton, OH 45431-1833. *Phone:* 937-258-8251. *Toll-free phone:* 800-517-7284.
Website: http://www.icb.edu/.

ITT Technical Institute
Akron, Ohio
- **Proprietary** primarily 2-year
- **Coed**

Majors Business administration and management; computer programming (specific applications); construction management; cyber/computer forensics and counterterrorism; drafting and design technology; electrical, electronic and communications engineering technology; forensic science and technology; graphic communications; industrial technology; information technology project management; medical/clinical assistant; network and system administration; project management; registered nursing/registered nurse.
Academics *Degrees:* associate and bachelor's.
Freshman Application Contact Director of Recruitment, ITT Technical Institute, 3428 West Market Street, Akron, OH 44333. *Phone:* 330-865-8600. *Toll-free phone:* 877-818-0154.
Website: http://www.itt-tech.edu/.

ITT Technical Institute
Columbus, Ohio
- **Proprietary** primarily 2-year, part of ITT Educational Services, Inc.
- **Coed**

Majors Business administration and management; computer programming (specific applications); construction management; cyber/computer forensics and counterterrorism; drafting and design technology; electrical, electronic and communications engineering technology; forensic science and technology; industrial technology; information technology project management; legal assistant/paralegal; network and system administration; project management.
Academics *Calendar:* quarters. *Degrees:* associate and bachelor's.
Freshman Application Contact Director of Recruitment, ITT Technical Institute, 4717 Hilton Corporate Drive, Columbus, OH 43232. *Phone:* 614-868-2000. *Toll-free phone:* 877-233-8864.
Website: http://www.itt-tech.edu/.

ITT Technical Institute
Dayton, Ohio
- **Proprietary** primarily 2-year, founded 1935, part of ITT Educational Services, Inc.
- **Suburban** campus
- **Coed**

Majors Business administration and management; computer programming (specific applications); construction management; cyber/computer forensics and counterterrorism; drafting and design technology; electrical, electronic and communications engineering technology; forensic science and technology; graphic communications; industrial technology; information technology project management; medical/clinical assistant; network and system administration; project management; registered nursing/registered nurse.
Academics *Calendar:* quarters. *Degrees:* associate and bachelor's.
Student Life *Housing:* college housing not available.
Freshman Application Contact Director of Recruitment, ITT Technical Institute, 3325 Stop 8 Road, Dayton, OH 45414-3425. *Phone:* 937-264-7700. *Toll-free phone:* 800-568-3241.
Website: http://www.itt-tech.edu/.

ITT Technical Institute
Hilliard, Ohio
- **Proprietary** primarily 2-year, founded 2003, part of ITT Educational Services, Inc.
- **Coed**

Majors Business administration and management; computer and information systems security; computer programming (specific applications); construction management; cyber/computer forensics and counterterrorism; drafting and design technology; electrical, electronic and communications engineering

technology; forensic science and technology; graphic communications; industrial technology; information technology project management; medical/clinical assistant; network and system administration; project management; registered nursing/registered nurse.
Academics *Calendar:* quarters. *Degrees:* associate and bachelor's.
Freshman Application Contact Director of Recruitment, ITT Technical Institute, 3781 Park Mill Run Drive, Hilliard, OH 43026. *Phone:* 614-771-4888. *Toll-free phone:* 888-483-4888.
Website: http://www.itt-tech.edu/.

ITT Technical Institute
Maumee, Ohio
- **Proprietary** primarily 2-year
- **Coed**

Majors Business administration and management; computer programming (specific applications); construction management; cyber/computer forensics and counterterrorism; drafting and design technology; electrical, electronic and communications engineering technology; forensic science and technology; graphic communications; industrial technology; information technology project management; network and system administration; project management.
Academics *Degrees:* associate and bachelor's.
Student Life *Housing:* college housing not available.
Freshman Application Contact Director of Recruitment, ITT Technical Institute, 1656 Henthorne Drive, Suite B, Maumee, OH 43537. *Phone:* 419-861-6500. *Toll-free phone:* 877-205-4639.
Website: http://www.itt-tech.edu/.

ITT Technical Institute
Norwood, Ohio
- **Proprietary** primarily 2-year, founded 1995, part of ITT Educational Services, Inc.
- **Coed**

Majors Business administration and management; computer programming (specific applications); construction management; cyber/computer forensics and counterterrorism; drafting and design technology; electrical, electronic and communications engineering technology; forensic science and technology; industrial technology; information technology project management; medical/clinical assistant; network and system administration; project management; registered nursing/registered nurse.
Academics *Calendar:* quarters. *Degrees:* associate and bachelor's.
Student Life *Housing:* college housing not available.
Freshman Application Contact Director of Recruitment, ITT Technical Institute, 4750 Wesley Avenue, Norwood, OH 45212. *Phone:* 513-531-8300. *Toll-free phone:* 800-314-8324.
Website: http://www.itt-tech.edu/.

ITT Technical Institute
Strongsville, Ohio
- **Proprietary** primarily 2-year, founded 1994, part of ITT Educational Services, Inc.
- **Coed**

Majors Business administration and management; computer programming (specific applications); computer software technology; construction management; cyber/computer forensics and counterterrorism; drafting and design technology; electrical, electronic and communications engineering technology; forensic science and technology; industrial technology; information technology project management; medical/clinical assistant; network and system administration; project management; registered nursing/registered nurse.
Academics *Calendar:* quarters. *Degrees:* associate and bachelor's.
Student Life *Housing:* college housing not available.
Freshman Application Contact Director of Recruitment, ITT Technical Institute, 14955 Sprague Road, Strongsville, OH 44136. *Phone:* 440-234-9091. *Toll-free phone:* 800-331-1488.
Website: http://www.itt-tech.edu/.

ITT Technical Institute
Warrensville Heights, Ohio
- **Proprietary** primarily 2-year, founded 2005
- **Coed**

Majors Business administration and management; computer programming (specific applications); construction management; cyber/computer forensics and counterterrorism; drafting and design technology; electrical, electronic and communications engineering technology; forensic science and technology; graphic communications; industrial technology; information technology project management; medical/clinical assistant; network and system administration; project management; registered nursing/registered nurse.

Academics *Calendar:* quarters. *Degrees:* associate and bachelor's.
Student Life *Housing:* college housing not available.
Freshman Application Contact Director of Recruitment, ITT Technical Institute, 24865 Emery Road, Warrensville Heights, OH 44128. *Phone:* 216-896-6500. *Toll-free phone:* 800-741-3494.
Website: http://www.itt-tech.edu/.

ITT Technical Institute
Youngstown, Ohio

- **Proprietary** primarily 2-year, founded 1967, part of ITT Educational Services, Inc.
- **Suburban** campus
- **Coed**

Majors Business administration and management; computer programming (specific applications); construction management; cyber/computer forensics and counterterrorism; drafting and design technology; electrical, electronic and communications engineering technology; forensic science and technology; graphic communications; industrial technology; information technology project management; medical/clinical assistant; network and system administration; project management; registered nursing/registered nurse.
Academics *Calendar:* quarters. *Degrees:* associate and bachelor's.
Student Life *Housing:* college housing not available.
Financial Aid Of all full-time matriculated undergraduates who enrolled in 2012, 5 Federal Work-Study jobs (averaging $3979).
Freshman Application Contact Director of Recruitment, ITT Technical Institute, 1030 North Meridian Road, Youngstown, OH 44509-4098. *Phone:* 330-270-1600. *Toll-free phone:* 800-832-5001.
Website: http://www.itt-tech.edu/.

James A. Rhodes State College
Lima, Ohio

- **State-supported** 2-year, founded 1971
- **Small-town** 565-acre campus
- **Endowment** $1.7 million
- **Coed**

Undergraduates 1,548 full-time, 2,335 part-time. Students come from 4 states and territories; 1% are from out of state; 8% Black or African American, non-Hispanic/Latino; 2% Hispanic/Latino; 0.6% Asian, non-Hispanic/Latino; 0.1% Native Hawaiian or other Pacific Islander, non-Hispanic/Latino; 0.4% American Indian or Alaska Native, non-Hispanic/Latino; 0.1% Two or more races, non-Hispanic/Latino; 0.9% Race/ethnicity unknown; 7% transferred in. *Retention:* 55% of full-time freshmen returned.
Faculty *Student/faculty ratio:* 15:1.
Academics *Calendar:* quarters. *Degree:* certificates and associate. *Special study options:* academic remediation for entering students, adult/continuing education programs, advanced placement credit, cooperative education, distance learning, independent study, internships, off-campus study, part-time degree program, services for LD students, student-designed majors, summer session for credit.
Student Life *Campus security:* 24-hour emergency response devices and patrols, student patrols, late-night transport/escort service.
Financial Aid Of all full-time matriculated undergraduates who enrolled in 2012, 110 Federal Work-Study jobs (averaging $1000).
Applying *Options:* electronic application, early admission, deferred entrance. *Application fee:* $25. *Required:* high school transcript.
Freshman Application Contact Traci Cox, Director, Office of Admissions, James A. Rhodes State College, http://www.rhodesstate.edu/Admissions/Apply%20Now.aspx, Lima, OH 45804-3597. *Phone:* 419-995-8040.
E-mail: cox.t@rhodesstate.edu.
Website: http://www.rhodesstate.edu/.

Kaplan Career Institute, Cleveland Campus
Brooklyn, Ohio

Freshman Application Contact Admissions Office, Kaplan Career Institute, Cleveland Campus, 8720 Brookpark Road, Brooklyn, OH 44129. *Toll-free phone:* 800-935-1857.
Website: http://cleveland.kaplancareerinstitute.com/.

Kaplan College, Dayton Campus
Dayton, Ohio

Freshman Application Contact Kaplan College, Dayton Campus, 2800 East River Road, Dayton, OH 45439. *Phone:* 937-294-6155. *Toll-free phone:* 800-935-1857.
Website: http://dayton.kaplancollege.com/.

Kent State University at Ashtabula
Ashtabula, Ohio

- **State-supported** primarily 2-year, founded 1958, part of Kent State University System
- **Small-town** 120-acre campus with easy access to Cleveland
- **Coed,** 2,339 undergraduate students, 53% full-time, 67% women, 33% men

Undergraduates 1,228 full-time, 1,111 part-time. 4% Black or African American, non-Hispanic/Latino; 3% Hispanic/Latino; 0.8% Asian, non-Hispanic/Latino; 0.1% Native Hawaiian or other Pacific Islander, non-Hispanic/Latino; 0.7% American Indian or Alaska Native, non-Hispanic/Latino; 2% Two or more races, non-Hispanic/Latino; 2% Race/ethnicity unknown; 0.4% international; 15% transferred in. *Retention:* 50% of full-time freshmen returned.
Freshmen *Admission:* 372 applied, 368 admitted, 224 enrolled. *Average high school GPA:* 2.82. *Test scores:* SAT critical reading scores over 500: 63%; SAT math scores over 500: 75%; ACT scores over 18: 70%; SAT critical reading scores over 600: 50%; SAT math scores over 600: 63%; ACT scores over 24: 15%; SAT critical reading scores over 700: 13%; SAT math scores over 700: 38%.
Faculty *Total:* 111, 45% full-time. *Student/faculty ratio:* 23:1.
Majors Accounting; accounting technology and bookkeeping; administrative assistant and secretarial science; aerospace, aeronautical and astronautical/space engineering; biological and biomedical sciences related; business administration and management; business/commerce; computer programming (specific applications); criminal justice/safety; electrical and electronic engineering technologies related; English; general studies; health and medical administrative services related; health/medical preparatory programs related; hospitality administration; liberal arts and sciences and humanities related; medical radiologic technology; occupational therapist assistant; physical therapy technology; psychology; registered nursing/registered nurse; respiratory care therapy; sociology; speech communication and rhetoric; viticulture and enology.
Academics *Calendar:* semesters. *Degrees:* certificates, associate, and bachelor's (also offers some upper-level and graduate courses). *Special study options:* academic remediation for entering students, advanced placement credit, distance learning, double majors, independent study, internships, part-time degree program, services for LD students, student-designed majors, study abroad, summer session for credit. *ROTC:* Army (c), Air Force (c).
Library Kent State at Ashtabula Library with 51,884 titles, 225 serial subscriptions, 640 audiovisual materials, an OPAC, a Web page.
Student Life *Housing:* college housing not available. *Activities and Organizations:* student government, student veterans association, Student Nurses Association, Student Occupational Therapy Association (SOTA), Media Club. *Campus security:* 24-hour emergency response devices.
Standardized Tests *Required for some:* SAT or ACT (for admission). *Recommended:* SAT or ACT (for admission).
Costs (2013–14) *Tuition:* state resident $5554 full-time, $253 per credit hour part-time; nonresident $13,514 full-time, $615 per credit hour part-time. Full-time tuition and fees vary according to course level and course load. Part-time tuition and fees vary according to course level and course load. *Payment plan:* installment. *Waivers:* senior citizens and employees or children of employees.
Financial Aid Of all full-time matriculated undergraduates who enrolled in 2013, 751 applied for aid, 711 were judged to have need, 23 had their need fully met. In 2013, 23 non-need-based awards were made. *Average percent of need met:* 41%. *Average financial aid package:* $7622. *Average need-based loan:* $3870. *Average need-based gift aid:* $4622. *Average non-need-based aid:* $804.
Applying *Options:* electronic application, deferred entrance. *Application fee:* $30. *Required:* high school transcript. *Application deadlines:* rolling (freshmen), rolling (transfers). *Notification:* continuous (freshmen), continuous (transfers).
Freshman Application Contact Kent State University at Ashtabula, 3300 Lake Road West, Ashtabula, OH 44004-2299. *Phone:* 440-964-4217.
Website: http://www.ashtabula.kent.edu/.

Kent State University at East Liverpool
East Liverpool, Ohio

- **State-supported** primarily 2-year, founded 1967, part of Kent State University System
- **Small-town** 4-acre campus with easy access to Pittsburgh
- **Coed,** 1,671 undergraduate students, 53% full-time, 70% women, 30% men

Undergraduates 884 full-time, 787 part-time. Students come from 8 states and territories; 2 other countries; 5% are from out of state; 5% Black or African American, non-Hispanic/Latino; 2% Hispanic/Latino; 1% Asian, non-Hispanic/Latino; 0.1% Native Hawaiian or other Pacific Islander, non-Hispanic/Latino; 0.3% American Indian or Alaska Native, non-

Hispanic/Latino; 2% Two or more races, non-Hispanic/Latino; 3% Race/ethnicity unknown; 0.3% international; 4% transferred in. *Retention:* 60% of full-time freshmen returned.

Freshmen *Admission:* 167 applied, 159 admitted, 122 enrolled. *Average high school GPA:* 2.96. *Test scores:* ACT scores over 18: 54%; ACT scores over 24: 11%.

Faculty *Total:* 70, 39% full-time. *Student/faculty ratio:* 28:1.

Majors Accounting technology and bookkeeping; biological and biomedical sciences related; business/commerce; computer programming (specific applications); criminal justice/safety; English; general studies; legal assistant/paralegal; liberal arts and sciences and humanities related; occupational therapist assistant; physical therapy technology; psychology; registered nursing/registered nurse; speech communication and rhetoric.

Academics *Calendar:* semesters. *Degrees:* certificates, associate, bachelor's, and master's (also offers some upper-level and graduate courses). *Special study options:* academic remediation for entering students, accelerated degree program, adult/continuing education programs, advanced placement credit, distance learning, double majors, freshman honors college, honors programs, independent study, internships, part-time degree program, services for LD students, student-designed majors, study abroad, summer session for credit. *ROTC:* Army (c), Air Force (c).

Library Blair Memorial Library with 31,320 titles, 135 serial subscriptions, an OPAC, a Web page.

Student Life *Housing:* college housing not available. *Activities and Organizations:* student-run newspaper, student government, Student Nurses Association, Environmental Club, Occupational Therapist Assistant Club, Physical Therapist Assistant Club. *Campus security:* student patrols, late-night transport/escort service.

Standardized Tests *Required for some:* SAT or ACT (for admission). *Recommended:* SAT or ACT (for admission).

Costs (2013–14) *Tuition:* state resident $5554 full-time, $253 per credit hour part-time; nonresident $13,514 full-time, $615 per credit hour part-time. Full-time tuition and fees vary according to course level and course load. Part-time tuition and fees vary according to course level and course load. *Payment plan:* installment. *Waivers:* senior citizens and employees or children of employees.

Financial Aid Of all full-time matriculated undergraduates who enrolled in 2013, 348 applied for aid, 334 were judged to have need, 9 had their need fully met. *Average percent of need met:* 43%. *Average financial aid package:* $7997. *Average need-based loan:* $3871. *Average need-based gift aid:* $4854.

Applying *Options:* electronic application, deferred entrance. *Application fee:* $30. *Required:* high school transcript. *Application deadlines:* rolling (freshmen), rolling (transfers). *Notification:* continuous (freshmen), continuous (transfers).

Freshman Application Contact Kent State University at East Liverpool, OH. *Phone:* 330-385-3805.
Website: http://www.eliv.kent.edu/.

Kent State University at Salem
Salem, Ohio

- **State-supported** primarily 2-year, founded 1966, part of Kent State University System
- **Rural** 98-acre campus
- **Coed,** 1,844 undergraduate students, 67% full-time, 71% women, 29% men

Undergraduates 1,228 full-time, 616 part-time. Students come from 11 states and territories; 4 other countries; 2% are from out of state; 3% Black or African American, non-Hispanic/Latino; 2% Hispanic/Latino; 0.7% Asian, non-Hispanic/Latino; 0.1% Native Hawaiian or other Pacific Islander, non-Hispanic/Latino; 0.5% American Indian or Alaska Native, non-Hispanic/Latino; 1% Two or more races, non-Hispanic/Latino; 3% Race/ethnicity unknown; 0.2% international; 7% transferred in. *Retention:* 56% of full-time freshmen returned.

Freshmen *Admission:* 370 applied, 366 admitted, 205 enrolled. *Average high school GPA:* 3.01. *Test scores:* SAT critical reading scores over 500: 100%; SAT writing scores over 500: 67%; ACT scores over 18: 71%; ACT scores over 24: 14%.

Faculty *Total:* 135, 33% full-time. *Student/faculty ratio:* 19:1.

Majors Accounting technology and bookkeeping; administrative assistant and secretarial science; applied horticulture/horticulture operations; biological and biomedical sciences related; business administration and management; business/commerce; computer programming (specific applications); criminal justice/safety; early childhood education; education related; English; general studies; health and medical administrative services related; human development and family studies; insurance; liberal arts and sciences and humanities related; liberal arts and sciences/liberal studies; medical radiologic technology; psychology; registered nursing/registered nurse; speech communication and rhetoric.

Academics *Calendar:* semesters. *Degrees:* certificates, associate, and bachelor's (also offers some upper-level and graduate courses). *Special study*

options: academic remediation for entering students, accelerated degree program, adult/continuing education programs, advanced placement credit, cooperative education, distance learning, double majors, freshman honors college, honors programs, independent study, internships, part-time degree program, services for LD students, student-designed majors, study abroad, summer session for credit. *ROTC:* Army (c), Air Force (c).

Library Kent State Salem Library with 19,000 titles, 163 serial subscriptions, 158 audiovisual materials, an OPAC, a Web page.

Student Life *Housing:* college housing not available. *Activities and Organizations:* choral group, Criminal Justice Club, Human Services Technology Club, Radiologic Technology Club, Student Government Organization, Students for Professional Nursing. *Campus security:* 24-hour emergency response devices, late-night transport/escort service. *Student services:* personal/psychological counseling.

Athletics *Intramural sports:* basketball M/W, skiing (downhill) M/W, table tennis M/W, tennis M/W, volleyball M/W.

Standardized Tests *Required for some:* SAT or ACT (for admission). *Recommended:* SAT or ACT (for admission).

Costs (2013–14) *Tuition:* state resident $5554 full-time, $253 per credit hour part-time; nonresident $13,514 full-time, $615 per credit hour part-time. Full-time tuition and fees vary according to course level and course load. Part-time tuition and fees vary according to course level and course load. *Payment plan:* installment. *Waivers:* senior citizens and employees or children of employees.

Financial Aid Of all full-time matriculated undergraduates who enrolled in 2013, 755 applied for aid, 686 were judged to have need, 28 had their need fully met. In 2013, 6 non-need-based awards were made. *Average percent of need met:* 44%. *Average financial aid package:* $7446. *Average need-based loan:* $3906. *Average need-based gift aid:* $4621. *Average non-need-based aid:* $1399.

Applying *Options:* electronic application, deferred entrance. *Application fee:* $30. *Required:* high school transcript. *Required for some:* essay or personal statement. *Application deadlines:* rolling (freshmen), rolling (out-of-state freshmen), rolling (transfers). *Notification:* continuous (freshmen), continuous (out-of-state freshmen), continuous (transfers).

Freshman Application Contact Kent State University at Salem, 2491 State Route 45 South, Salem, OH 44460-9412. *Phone:* 330-382-7415. *Website:* http://www.salem.kent.edu/.

Kent State University at Trumbull
Warren, Ohio

- **State-supported** primarily 2-year, founded 1954, part of Kent State University System
- **Suburban** 200-acre campus with easy access to Cleveland
- **Coed,** 3,061 undergraduate students, 61% full-time, 63% women, 37% men

Undergraduates 1,857 full-time, 1,204 part-time. Students come from 16 states and territories; 3 other countries; 2% are from out of state; 9% Black or African American, non-Hispanic/Latino; 3% Hispanic/Latino; 0.6% Asian, non-Hispanic/Latino; 0.1% American Indian or Alaska Native, non-Hispanic/Latino; 2% Two or more races, non-Hispanic/Latino; 3% Race/ethnicity unknown; 0.4% international; 6% transferred in. *Retention:* 55% of full-time freshmen returned.

Freshmen *Admission:* 495 applied, 494 admitted, 371 enrolled. *Average high school GPA:* 280. *Test scores:* SAT critical reading scores over 500: 100%; SAT math scores over 500: 100%; SAT writing scores over 500: 50%; ACT scores over 18: 65%; SAT math scores over 600: 50%; SAT writing scores over 600: 50%; ACT scores over 24: 11%.

Faculty *Total:* 117, 50% full-time. *Student/faculty ratio:* 29:1.

Majors Accounting technology and bookkeeping; administrative assistant and secretarial science; biological and biomedical sciences related; business administration and management; business/commerce; computer/information technology services administration related; computer programming (specific applications); criminal justice/safety; electrical and electronic engineering technologies related; electrical, electronic and communications engineering technology; emergency medical technology (EMT paramedic); English; environmental engineering technology; general studies; health/health-care administration; industrial production technologies related; industrial technology; legal assistant/paralegal; liberal arts and sciences and humanities related; liberal arts and sciences/liberal studies; mechanical engineering/mechanical technology; nursing science; psychology; registered nursing/registered nurse; speech communication and rhetoric; urban forestry.

Academics *Calendar:* semesters. *Degrees:* certificates, associate, and bachelor's (also offers some upper-level and graduate courses). *Special study options:* academic remediation for entering students, adult/continuing education programs, advanced placement credit, distance learning, double majors, freshman honors college, honors programs, independent study, internships, part-time degree program, services for LD students, student-designed majors, study abroad, summer session for credit. *ROTC:* Army (c), Air Force (c).

Library Trumbull Campus Library with 65,951 titles, 759 serial subscriptions, an OPAC, a Web page.

Student Life *Housing:* college housing not available. *Activities and Organizations:* drama/theater group, National Student Nurses Association, Spot On Improv Group, ENACTUS, GLOW (Gay, Lesbian, or Whatever), If These Hands Could Talk - ASL. *Campus security:* 24-hour emergency response devices, late-night transport/escort service, patrols by trained security personnel during open hours. *Student services:* personal/psychological counseling.

Standardized Tests *Required for some:* SAT or ACT (for admission). *Recommended:* SAT or ACT (for admission).

Costs (2013–14) *Tuition:* state resident $5554 full-time, $253 per credit hour part-time; nonresident $13,514 full-time, $615 per credit hour part-time. Full-time tuition and fees vary according to course level and course load. Part-time tuition and fees vary according to course level and course load. *Payment plan:* installment. *Waivers:* senior citizens and employees or children of employees.

Financial Aid Of all full-time matriculated undergraduates who enrolled in 2013, 1,027 applied for aid, 968 were judged to have need, 25 had their need fully met. In 2013, 10 non-need-based awards were made. *Average percent of need met:* 42%. *Average financial aid package:* $7646. *Average need-based loan:* $3851. *Average need-based gift aid:* $4841. *Average non-need-based aid:* $1250.

Applying *Options:* electronic application, deferred entrance. *Application fee:* $30. *Required:* high school transcript. *Application deadlines:* rolling (freshmen), rolling (out-of-state freshmen), rolling (transfers). *Notification:* continuous (freshmen), continuous (out-of-state freshmen), continuous (transfers).

Freshman Application Contact Kent State University at Trumbull, Warren, OH 44483. *Phone:* 330-675-8935. *Website:* http://www.trumbull.kent.edu/.

Kent State University at Tuscarawas
New Philadelphia, Ohio

- **State-supported** primarily 2-year, founded 1962, part of Kent State University System
- **Small-town** 172-acre campus with easy access to Cleveland
- **Coed,** 2,375 undergraduate students, 57% full-time, 57% women, 43% men

Undergraduates 1,347 full-time, 1,028 part-time. 0.9% are from out of state; 2% Black or African American, non-Hispanic/Latino; 1% Hispanic/Latino; 0.5% Asian, non-Hispanic/Latino; 0.1% Native Hawaiian or other Pacific Islander, non-Hispanic/Latino; 0.2% American Indian or Alaska Native, non-Hispanic/Latino; 1% Two or more races, non-Hispanic/Latino; 3% Race/ethnicity unknown; 0.1% international; 4% transferred in. *Retention:* 63% of full-time freshmen returned.

Freshmen *Admission:* 470 applied, 430 admitted, 329 enrolled. *Average high school GPA:* 2.97. *Test scores:* SAT critical reading scores over 500: 75%; SAT math scores over 500: 100%; SAT writing scores over 500: 75%; ACT scores over 18: 80%; SAT critical reading scores over 600: 25%; SAT math scores over 600: 25%; SAT writing scores over 600: 50%; ACT scores over 24: 18%; SAT critical reading scores over 700: 25%; SAT math scores over 700: 25%.

Faculty *Total:* 129, 41% full-time. *Student/faculty ratio:* 22:1.

Majors Accounting; accounting technology and bookkeeping; administrative assistant and secretarial science; biological and biomedical sciences related; business administration and management; business/commerce; CAD/CADD drafting/design technology; computer programming (specific applications); criminal justice/police science; criminal justice/safety; early childhood education; education related; electrical and electronic engineering technologies related; engineering technologies and engineering related; engineering technology; English; general studies; industrial technology; liberal arts and sciences and humanities related; liberal arts and sciences/liberal studies; mechanical engineering/mechanical technology; psychology; registered nursing/registered nurse; speech communication and rhetoric; veterinary/animal health technology.

Academics *Calendar:* semesters. *Degrees:* certificates, associate, and bachelor's (also offers some upper-level and graduate courses). *Special study options:* academic remediation for entering students, accelerated degree program, adult/continuing education programs, advanced placement credit, distance learning, double majors, freshman honors college, honors programs, independent study, internships, part-time degree program, services for LD students, student-designed majors, study abroad, summer session for credit. *ROTC:* Army (c), Air Force (c).

Library Tuscarawas Campus Library with 63,880 titles, 208 serial subscriptions, 1,179 audiovisual materials, an OPAC, a Web page.

Student Life *Housing:* college housing not available. *Activities and Organizations:* drama/theater group, choral group, Society of Manufacturing Engineers, IEEE, Animation Imagineers, Justice Studies Club, Student Activities Council. *Campus security:* 24-hour emergency response devices.

Athletics *Intramural sports:* basketball M/W, volleyball M/W.

Standardized Tests *Required for some:* SAT or ACT (for admission). *Recommended:* SAT or ACT (for admission).

Costs (2013–14) *Tuition:* state resident $5554 full-time, $253 per credit hour part-time; nonresident $13,514 full-time, $615 per credit hour part-time. Full-time tuition and fees vary according to course level and course load. Part-time tuition and fees vary according to course level and course load. *Payment plan:* installment. *Waivers:* senior citizens and employees or children of employees.

Financial Aid Of all full-time matriculated undergraduates who enrolled in 2013, 871 applied for aid, 808 were judged to have need, 38 had their need fully met. In 2013, 27 non-need-based awards were made. *Average percent of need met:* 44%. *Average financial aid package:* $7691. *Average need-based loan:* $3891. *Average need-based gift aid:* $4234. *Average non-need-based aid:* $1098.

Applying *Options:* electronic application, deferred entrance. *Application fee:* $30. *Required:* high school transcript. *Application deadlines:* rolling (freshmen), rolling (out-of-state freshmen), rolling (transfers). *Notification:* continuous (freshmen), continuous (out-of-state freshmen), continuous (transfers).

Freshman Application Contact Kent State University at Tuscarawas, Kent State University at Tuscarawas, 330 University Drive Northeast, New Philadelphia, OH 44663-9403. *Phone:* 330-339-3391 Ext. 47425. *Fax:* 330-339-3321. *E-mail:* info@tusc.kent.edu. *Website:* http://www.tusc.kent.edu/.

Lakeland Community College
Kirtland, Ohio

- **State and locally supported** 2-year, founded 1967, part of Ohio Board of Regents
- **Suburban** 380-acre campus with easy access to Cleveland
- **Endowment** $355,124
- **Coed,** 8,839 undergraduate students, 36% full-time, 59% women, 41% men

Undergraduates 3,171 full-time, 5,668 part-time. 15% Black or African American, non-Hispanic/Latino; 3% Hispanic/Latino; 1% Asian, non-Hispanic/Latino; 0.2% Native Hawaiian or other Pacific Islander, non-Hispanic/Latino; 0.4% American Indian or Alaska Native, non-Hispanic/Latino; 1% Two or more races, non-Hispanic/Latino; 5% Race/ethnicity unknown; 0.2% international; 6% transferred in. *Retention:* 47% of full-time freshmen returned.

Freshmen *Admission:* 1,232 enrolled.

Faculty *Total:* 565, 21% full-time. *Student/faculty ratio:* 19:1.

Majors Accounting; administrative assistant and secretarial science; biotechnology; business administration and management; child-care provision; civil engineering technology; clinical/medical laboratory technology; commercial and advertising art; computer engineering technology; computer programming (specific applications); computer systems analysis; computer systems networking and telecommunications; computer technology/computer systems technology; corrections; criminal justice/police science; dental hygiene; electrical, electronic and communications engineering technology; energy management and systems technology; fire prevention and safety technology; health professions related; homeland security, law enforcement, firefighting and protective services related; hospitality administration; instrumentation technology; legal assistant/paralegal; liberal arts and sciences/liberal studies; management information systems; marketing/marketing management; mechanical engineering/mechanical technology; medical radiologic technology; nuclear medical technology; ophthalmic technology; quality control technology; registered nursing/registered nurse; respiratory care therapy; restaurant, culinary, and catering management; sign language interpretation and translation; social work; surgical technology; tourism and travel services management.

Academics *Calendar:* semesters. *Degree:* certificates and associate. *Special study options:* academic remediation for entering students, adult/continuing education programs, advanced placement credit, cooperative education, distance learning, English as a second language, external degree program, independent study, internships, off-campus study, part-time degree program, services for LD students, study abroad, summer session for credit.

Library Lakeland Community College Library with 65,814 titles, 248 serial subscriptions, 4,212 audiovisual materials, an OPAC, a Web page.

Student Life *Housing:* college housing not available. *Activities and Organizations:* drama/theater group, student-run newspaper, radio station, choral group, Campus Activities Board, Lakeland Student Government, Lakeland Signers, Gamer's Guild. *Campus security:* 24-hour emergency response devices and patrols, student patrols, late-night transport/escort service. *Student services:* health clinic, personal/psychological counseling, women's center.

Athletics Member NJCAA. *Intercollegiate sports:* baseball M(s), basketball M(s)/W(s), golf M(s), soccer M(s), softball W(s), volleyball W(s).

Standardized Tests *Required:* Compass test is required (for admission).

Costs (2013–14) *Tuition:* area resident $3188 full-time, $106 per credit hour part-time; state resident $4037 full-time, $135 per credit hour part-time; nonresident $8877 full-time, $296 per credit hour part-time. Full-time tuition and fees vary according to course load. Part-time tuition and fees vary according to course load. *Required fees:* $14 per term part-time. *Payment plan:* installment. *Waivers:* senior citizens and employees or children of employees.

Financial Aid Of all full-time matriculated undergraduates who enrolled in 2012, 3,429 applied for aid, 2,958 were judged to have need, 468 had their need fully met. 64 Federal Work-Study jobs (averaging $2840). *Average percent of need met:* 56%. *Average financial aid package:* $7026. *Average need-based loan:* $3232. *Average need-based gift aid:* $5251.

Applying *Options:* electronic application, early admission, deferred entrance. *Application fee:* $15. *Required:* high school transcript. *Application deadlines:* 9/1 (freshmen), 9/1 (transfers). *Notification:* continuous until 9/1 (freshmen), continuous until 9/1 (transfers).

Freshman Application Contact Lakeland Community College, 7700 Clocktower Drive, Kirtland, OH 44094-5198. *Phone:* 440-525-7230. *Toll-free phone:* 800-589-8520.
Website: http://www.lakeland.cc.oh.us/.

Lorain County Community College
Elyria, Ohio

- **State and locally supported** 2-year, founded 1963, part of Ohio Board of Regents
- **Suburban** 280-acre campus with easy access to Cleveland
- **Endowment** $21.7 million
- **Coed,** 12,280 undergraduate students, 28% full-time, 64% women, 36% men

Undergraduates 3,393 full-time, 8,887 part-time. Students come from 17 states and territories; 28 other countries; 1% are from out of state; 10% Black or African American, non-Hispanic/Latino; 6% Hispanic/Latino; 1% Asian, non-Hispanic/Latino; 0.1% Native Hawaiian or other Pacific Islander, non-Hispanic/Latino; 0.5% American Indian or Alaska Native, non-Hispanic/Latino; 5% Two or more races, non-Hispanic/Latino; 1% Race/ethnicity unknown; 0.9% international. *Retention:* 58% of full-time freshmen returned.

Freshmen *Admission:* 2,221 applied, 2,221 admitted, 1,933 enrolled.
Faculty *Total:* 726, 18% full-time. *Student/faculty ratio:* 20:1.

Majors Accounting; administrative assistant and secretarial science; art; artificial intelligence; athletic training; biological and physical sciences; biology/biological sciences; business administration and management; chemistry; civil engineering technology; clinical/medical laboratory technology; computer and information sciences related; computer engineering technology; computer programming; computer programming related; computer programming (specific applications); computer programming (vendor/product certification); computer science; computer systems networking and telecommunications; computer technology/computer systems technology; consumer merchandising/retailing management; corrections; cosmetology; cosmetology and personal grooming arts related; criminal justice/police science; data entry/microcomputer applications; data entry/microcomputer applications related; diagnostic medical sonography and ultrasound technology; drafting and design technology; drafting/design engineering technologies related; dramatic/theater arts; education; electrical, electronic and communications engineering technology; elementary education; engineering; engineering technology; finance; fire science/firefighting; history; human services; industrial radiologic technology; industrial technology; information science/studies; information technology; journalism; kindergarten/preschool education; liberal arts and sciences/liberal studies; machine tool technology; marketing/marketing management; mass communication/media; mathematics; music; nuclear medical technology; pharmacy; physical education teaching and coaching; physical therapy technology; physics; plastics and polymer engineering technology; political science and government; pre-engineering; psychology; quality control technology; real estate; registered nursing/registered nurse; social sciences; social work; sociology; sport and fitness administration/management; surgical technology; tourism and travel services management; urban studies/affairs; word processing.

Academics *Calendar:* semesters. *Degree:* certificates and associate. *Special study options:* academic remediation for entering students, adult/continuing education programs, advanced placement credit, cooperative education, distance learning, double majors, English as a second language, external degree program, honors programs, independent study, internships, part-time degree program, services for LD students, student-designed majors, summer session for credit.

Library Learning Resource Center with 198,984 titles, 3,289 audiovisual materials, an OPAC.

Student Life *Housing:* college housing not available. *Activities and Organizations:* drama/theater group, student-run newspaper, radio station,

choral group, Phi Beta Kappa, Black Progressives, Hispanic Club, national fraternities, national sororities. *Campus security:* 24-hour emergency response devices and patrols, late-night transport/escort service. *Student services:* health clinic, personal/psychological counseling, women's center, legal services.

Athletics *Intramural sports:* archery M/W, basketball M/W, softball M/W, volleyball M/W, weight lifting M/W, wrestling M.

Costs (2013–14) *Tuition:* area resident $2977 full-time, $115 per credit hour part-time; state resident $3558 full-time, $137 per credit hour part-time; nonresident $7059 full-time, $272 per credit hour part-time. *Payment plans:* installment, deferred payment. *Waivers:* senior citizens and employees or children of employees.

Applying *Options:* early admission, deferred entrance. *Required for some:* high school transcript. *Application deadlines:* rolling (freshmen), rolling (transfers). *Notification:* continuous (freshmen), continuous (transfers).

Freshman Application Contact Lorain County Community College, 1005 Abbe Road, North, Elyria, OH 44035. *Phone:* 440-366-7622. *Toll-free phone:* 800-995-5222 Ext. 4032.
Website: http://www.lorainccc.edu/.

Marion Technical College
Marion, Ohio

- **State-supported** 2-year, founded 1971, part of University System of Ohio
- **Small-town** 180-acre campus with easy access to Columbus
- **Coed**

Undergraduates 5% Black or African American, non-Hispanic/Latino; 1% Hispanic/Latino; 0.5% Asian, non-Hispanic/Latino; 0.2% American Indian or Alaska Native, non-Hispanic/Latino; 2% Race/ethnicity unknown. *Retention:* 57% of full-time freshmen returned.

Faculty *Student/faculty ratio:* 18:1.

Academics *Calendar:* quarters. *Degree:* certificates and associate. *Special study options:* academic remediation for entering students, accelerated degree program, adult/continuing education programs, advanced placement credit, cooperative education, distance learning, double majors, independent study, internships, off-campus study, part-time degree program, services for LD students, student-designed majors, summer session for credit.

Standardized Tests *Required:* COMPASS or ACT (for admission). *Required for some:* ACT (for admission).

Costs (2013–14) *Tuition:* state resident $4282 full-time, $166 per semester hour part-time; nonresident $6200 full-time, $246 per semester hour part-time. Full-time tuition and fees vary according to course load, program, and reciprocity agreements. Part-time tuition and fees vary according to course load, program, and reciprocity agreements. *Required fees:* $250 full-time.

Financial Aid Of all full-time matriculated undergraduates who enrolled in 2012, 28 Federal Work-Study jobs (averaging $1200). 45 state and other part-time jobs (averaging $1000).

Applying *Options:* electronic application, early admission, deferred entrance. *Application fee:* $20. *Required:* high school transcript. *Required for some:* minimum 2.5 GPA, some programs are Limited Enrollment Programs with specific admission criteria. *Recommended:* interview.

Freshman Application Contact Mr. Joel Liles, Dean of Enrollment Services, Marion Technical College, 1467 Mount Vernon Avenue, Marion, OH 43302. *Phone:* 740-389-4636 Ext. 249. *Fax:* 740-389-6136. *E-mail:* enroll@ mtc.edu.
Website: http://www.mtc.edu/.

Miami-Jacobs Career College
Columbus, Ohio

Admissions Office Contact Miami-Jacobs Career College, 150 E. Gay Street, Columbus, OH 43215.
Website: http://www.miamijacobs.edu/.

Miami-Jacobs Career College
Dayton, Ohio

Director of Admissions Mary Percell, Vice President of Information Services, Miami-Jacobs Career College, 110 N. Patterson Boulevard, Dayton, OH 45402. *Phone:* 937-461-5174 Ext. 118.
Website: http://www.miamijacobs.edu/.

Miami-Jacobs Career College
Independence, Ohio

Freshman Application Contact Director of Admissions, Miami-Jacobs Career College, 6400 Rockside Road, Independence, OH 44131. *Phone:* 216-861-3222. *Toll-free phone:* 866-324-0142. *Fax:* 216-861-4517.
Website: http://www.miamijacobs.edu/.

Miami University–Middletown Campus
Middletown, Ohio

Freshman Application Contact Diane Cantonwine, Assistant Director of Admission and Financial Aid, Miami University–Middletown Campus, 4200 East University Boulevard, Middletown, OH 45042-3497. *Phone:* 513-727-3346. *Toll-free phone:* 866-426-4643. *Fax:* 513-727-3223. *E-mail:* cantondm@muohio.edu.
Website: http://www.mid.muohio.edu/.

National College
Canton, Ohio

Admissions Office Contact National College, 4736 Dressler Road NW, Canton, OH 44718.
Website: http://www.national-college.edu/.

National College
Youngstown, Ohio

Admissions Office Contact National College, 3487 Belmont Avenue, Youngstown, OH 44505.
Website: http://www.national-college.edu/.

National College of Business and Technology
Stow, Ohio

Admissions Office Contact National College of Business and Technology, 3855 Fishcreek Road, Stow, OH 44224.
Website: http://www.national-college.edu/.

North Central State College
Mansfield, Ohio

Freshman Application Contact Ms. Nikia L. Fletcher, Director of Admissions, North Central State College, 2441 Kenwood Circle, PO Box 698, Mansfield, OH 44901-0698. *Phone:* 419-755-4813. *Toll-free phone:* 888-755-4899. *E-mail:* nfletcher@ncstatecollege.edu.
Website: http://www.ncstatecollege.edu/.

Northwest State Community College
Archbold, Ohio

- **State-supported** 2-year, founded 1968, part of Ohio Board of Regents
- **Rural** 80-acre campus with easy access to Toledo
- **Coed**

Undergraduates 881 full-time, 3,363 part-time. Students come from 9 states and territories; 6 other countries; 0.2% are from out of state; 2% Black or African American, non-Hispanic/Latino; 6% Hispanic/Latino; 0.5% Asian, non-Hispanic/Latino; 0.2% American Indian or Alaska Native, non-Hispanic/Latino; 0.8% Two or more races, non-Hispanic/Latino; 16% Race/ethnicity unknown; 2% transferred in. *Retention:* 53% of full-time freshmen returned.
Faculty *Student/faculty ratio:* 15:1.
Academics *Calendar:* semesters. *Degree:* certificates and associate. *Special study options:* academic remediation for entering students, adult/continuing education programs, advanced placement credit, cooperative education, distance learning, double majors, external degree program, independent study, internships, off-campus study, part-time degree program, services for LD students, student-designed majors, summer session for credit.
Student Life *Campus security:* 24-hour emergency response devices, security patrols.
Costs (2013–14) *Tuition:* state resident $3504 full-time, $146 per credit part-time; nonresident $6864 full-time, $286 per credit part-time. Full-time tuition and fees vary according to course load. Part-time tuition and fees vary according to course load. *Required fees:* $70 full-time, $146 per credit part-time, $35 per term part-time.
Financial Aid Of all full-time matriculated undergraduates who enrolled in 2012, 43 Federal Work-Study jobs (averaging $1077).
Applying *Options:* electronic application, early admission, deferred entrance. *Application fee:* $20. *Required:* high school transcript.
Freshman Application Contact Mr. Dennis Giacomino, Director of Admissions, Northwest State Community College, 22600 State Route 34, Archbold, OH 43502. *Phone:* 419-267-1356. *Fax:* 419-267-3688. *E-mail:* admissions@northweststate.edu.
Website: http://www.northweststate.edu/.

Ohio Business College
Hilliard, Ohio

- **Proprietary** 2-year
- **Suburban** campus
- **Coed**

Academics *Degree:* diplomas and associate.
Freshman Application Contact Ohio Business College, 4525 Trueman Boulevard, Hilliard, OH 43026. *Toll-free phone:* 800-954-4274.
Website: http://www.ohiobusinesscollege.edu/.

Ohio Business College
Sandusky, Ohio

Freshman Application Contact Ohio Business College, 5202 Timber Commons Drive, Sandusky, OH 44870. *Phone:* 419-627-8345. *Toll-free phone:* 888-627-8345.
Website: http://www.ohiobusinesscollege.edu/.

Ohio Business College
Sheffield Village, Ohio

Director of Admissions Mr. Jim Unger, Admissions Director, Ohio Business College, 5095 Waterford Drive, Sheffield Village, OH 44035. *Toll-free phone:* 888-514-3126.
Website: http://www.ohiobusinesscollege.edu/.

Ohio College of Massotherapy
Akron, Ohio

Director of Admissions Mr. John Atkins, Director of Admissions and Marketing, Ohio College of Massotherapy, 225 Heritage Woods Drive, Akron, OH 44321. *Phone:* 330-665-1084 Ext. 11. *Toll-free phone:* 888-888-4325. *E-mail:* johna@ocm.edu.
Website: http://www.ocm.edu/.

The Ohio State University Agricultural Technical Institute
Wooster, Ohio

- **State-supported** 2-year, founded 1971, part of The Ohio State University System
- **Small-town** 1942-acre campus with easy access to Cleveland, Columbus, Akron, Canton
- **Endowment** $2.2 million
- **Coed,** 694 undergraduate students, 100% full-time, 47% women, 53% men

Undergraduates 694 full-time. Students come from 11 states and territories; 2% are from out of state; 5% transferred in. *Retention:* 64% of full-time freshmen returned.
Freshmen *Admission:* 651 applied, 555 admitted, 337 enrolled. *Test scores:* ACT scores over 18: 57%; ACT scores over 24: 11%.
Faculty *Total:* 70, 47% full-time, 33% with terminal degrees. *Student/faculty ratio:* 17:1.
Majors Agribusiness; agricultural business and management; agricultural business technology; agricultural communication/journalism; agricultural economics; agricultural mechanization; agricultural power machinery operation; agricultural teacher education; agronomy and crop science; animal/livestock husbandry and production; animal sciences; biology/biotechnology laboratory technician; building/construction site management; clinical/medical laboratory technology; construction engineering technology; construction management; crop production; dairy husbandry and production; dairy science; environmental science; equestrian studies; floriculture/floristry management; greenhouse management; heavy equipment maintenance technology; horse husbandry/equine science and management; horticultural science; hydraulics and fluid power technology; industrial technology; landscaping and groundskeeping; livestock management; natural resources management and policy; natural resources management and policy related; plant nursery management; soil science and agronomy; turf and turfgrass management.
Academics *Calendar:* quarters. *Degree:* certificates, diplomas, and associate. *Special study options:* academic remediation for entering students, accelerated degree program, adult/continuing education programs, advanced placement credit, cooperative education, distance learning, double majors, independent study, internships, off-campus study, part-time degree program, services for LD students, student-designed majors, study abroad, summer session for credit. *ROTC:* Army (c), Navy (c), Air Force (c).
Library Agricultural Technical Institute Library plus 1 other with 9,000 titles, 260 serial subscriptions, 100 audiovisual materials, an OPAC, a Web page.

Student Life *Housing:* on-campus residence required for freshman year. *Options:* coed, special housing for students with disabilities. Campus housing is university owned. *Activities and Organizations:* Hoof-n-Hide Club, Collegiate FFA, Campus Crusade for Christ, Phi Theta Kappa, Community Council. *Campus security:* 24-hour emergency response devices and patrols, controlled dormitory access. *Student services:* personal/psychological counseling.

Athletics *Intramural sports:* badminton M/W, basketball M/W, bowling M/W, football M/W, racquetball M/W, soccer M/W, softball M/W, volleyball M/W.

Standardized Tests *Required for some:* SAT or ACT (for admission).

Costs (2013–14) *Tuition:* state resident $7104 full-time, $296 per credit hour part-time; nonresident $22,824 full-time, $951 per credit hour part-time. Full-time tuition and fees vary according to course load. Part-time tuition and fees vary according to course load. *Room and board:* $10,370; room only: $6020.

Financial Aid Of all full-time matriculated undergraduates who enrolled in 2010, 540 applied for aid, 474 were judged to have need, 25 had their need fully met. 64 Federal Work-Study jobs (averaging $2000). In 2010, 24 non-need-based awards were made. *Average percent of need met:* 44%. *Average financial aid package:* $6859. *Average need-based loan:* $3826. *Average need-based gift aid:* $4241. *Average non-need-based aid:* $2107.

Applying *Options:* electronic application. *Application fee:* $60. *Required:* high school transcript. *Application deadlines:* 6/1 (freshmen), 6/1 (out-of-state freshmen), 6/1 (transfers). *Notification:* continuous (freshmen).

Freshman Application Contact Ms. Julia Morris, Admissions Counselor, The Ohio State University Agricultural Technical Institute, 1328 Dover Road, Wooster, OH 44691. *Phone:* 330-287-1327. *Toll-free phone:* 800-647-8283 Ext. 1327. *Fax:* 330-287-1333. *E-mail:* morris.878@osu.edu. *Website:* http://www.ati.osu.edu/.

Ohio Technical College
Cleveland, Ohio

Director of Admissions Mr. Marc Brenner, President, Ohio Technical College, 1374 East 51st Street, Cleveland, OH 44103. *Phone:* 216-881-1700. *Toll-free phone:* 800-322-7000. *Fax:* 216-881-9145. *E-mail:* ohioauto@aol.com. *Website:* http://www.ohiotechnicalcollege.com/.

Ohio Valley College of Technology
East Liverpool, Ohio

Freshman Application Contact Mr. Scott S. Rogers, Director, Ohio Valley College of Technology, 16808 St. Clair Avenue, PO Box 7000, East Liverpool, OH 43920. *Phone:* 330-385-1070. *Website:* http://www.ovct.edu/.

Owens Community College
Toledo, Ohio

- **State-supported** 2-year, founded 1966
- **Suburban** 420-acre campus with easy access to Detroit
- **Endowment** $1.6 million
- **Coed,** 14,674 undergraduate students, 35% full-time, 51% women, 49% men

Undergraduates 5,064 full-time, 9,610 part-time. 3% are from out of state; 13% Black or African American, non-Hispanic/Latino; 6% Hispanic/Latino; 0.9% Asian, non-Hispanic/Latino; 0.1% Native Hawaiian or other Pacific Islander, non-Hispanic/Latino; 0.4% American Indian or Alaska Native, non-Hispanic/Latino; 2% Two or more races, non-Hispanic/Latino; 3% Race/ethnicity unknown; 1% international; 0.6% transferred in.

Freshmen *Admission:* 10,148 applied, 10,148 admitted, 2,200 enrolled. *Average high school GPA:* 2.56. *Test scores:* SAT critical reading scores over 500: 5%; SAT math scores over 500: 42%; SAT writing scores over 500: 16%; ACT scores over 18: 58%; ACT scores over 24: 8%.

Faculty *Total:* 1,420, 14% full-time, 11% with terminal degrees. *Student/faculty ratio:* 11:1.

Majors Accounting technology and bookkeeping; agricultural mechanization; architectural drafting and CAD/CADD; architectural engineering technology; automotive engineering technology; biomedical technology; business/commerce; commercial and advertising art; commercial photography; computer and information systems security; computer engineering technology; computer programming (specific applications); construction engineering technology; criminal justice/law enforcement administration; criminal justice/police science; dental hygiene; diagnostic medical sonography and ultrasound technology; dietetics; early childhood education; electrical, electronic and communications engineering technology; energy management and systems technology; environmental engineering technology; executive assistant/executive secretary; fire prevention and safety technology; fire science/firefighting; general studies; golf course operation and grounds management; health/health-care administration; health information/medical records technology; industrial and product design; industrial technology;

information technology; international business/trade/commerce; landscaping and groundskeeping; magnetic resonance imaging (MRI) technology; manufacturing engineering technology; massage therapy; medical administrative assistant and medical secretary; medical/health management and clinical assistant; medical radiologic technology; music technology; nuclear medical technology; occupational therapist assistant; office management; operations management; physical therapy technology; quality control technology; registered nursing/registered nurse; restaurant/food services management; sales, distribution, and marketing operations; surgical technology; tool and die technology; welding technology.

Academics *Calendar:* semesters. *Degree:* certificates and associate. *Special study options:* academic remediation for entering students, accelerated degree program, adult/continuing education programs, advanced placement credit, cooperative education, distance learning, double majors, English as a second language, honors programs, independent study, internships, part-time degree program, services for LD students, study abroad, summer session for credit.

Library Owens Community College Library plus 1 other with 151,796 titles, 18,453 serial subscriptions, 8,856 audiovisual materials, an OPAC, a Web page.

Student Life *Housing:* college housing not available. *Activities and Organizations:* drama/theater group, student-run newspaper, choral group, Gay Straight Alliance, Photography Club, Commercial Arts Club, Martial Arts Club, Institute of Management Accountants. *Campus security:* 24-hour emergency response devices and patrols, student patrols, classroom doors that lock from the inside; campus alert system. *Student services:* personal/psychological counseling.

Athletics Member NJCAA. *Intercollegiate sports:* baseball M(s), basketball M(s)/W(s), golf M(s)/W(s), soccer M(s)/W(s), softball W(s), volleyball W(s). *Intramural sports:* basketball M/W, bowling M/W, football M, golf M/W, softball M/W, table tennis M/W, tennis M/W, volleyball M/W, weight lifting M.

Costs (2013–14) *Tuition:* state resident $4189 full-time, $150 per credit hour part-time; nonresident $7944 full-time, $284 per credit hour part-time. Full-time tuition and fees vary according to course load and reciprocity agreements. Part-time tuition and fees vary according to course load and reciprocity agreements. *Required fees:* $454 full-time, $16 per credit hour part-time, $10 per term part-time. *Payment plans:* installment, deferred payment. *Waivers:* senior citizens and employees or children of employees.

Financial Aid Of all full-time matriculated undergraduates who enrolled in 2012, 5,071 applied for aid, 4,575 were judged to have need, 240 had their need fully met. In 2012, 201 non-need-based awards were made. *Average percent of need met:* 59%. *Average financial aid package:* $7384. *Average need-based loan:* $7881. *Average need-based gift aid:* $4955. *Average non-need-based aid:* $1056.

Applying *Options:* electronic application, early admission, deferred entrance. *Application fee:* $20. *Required for some:* high school transcript, minimum 2.0 GPA, interview, Health Technology, Peace Officer Academy, and Early Childhood Education programs require high school transcripts and test scores for admission. *Recommended:* high school transcript. *Application deadlines:* rolling (freshmen), rolling (out-of-state freshmen), rolling (transfers). *Notification:* continuous (freshmen), continuous (out-of-state freshmen), continuous (transfers).

Freshman Application Contact Ms. Meghan L Schmidbauer, Director, Admissions, Owens Community College, P.O. Box 10000, Toledo, OH 43699. *Phone:* 567-661-2155. *Toll-free phone:* 800-GO-OWENS. *Fax:* 567-661-7734. *E-mail:* meghan_schmidbauer@owens.edu. *Website:* http://www.owens.edu/.

Professional Skills Institute
Toledo, Ohio

Director of Admissions Ms. Hope Finch, Director of Marketing, Professional Skills Institute, 1505 Holland Road, Maumee, Toledo, OH 43537. *Phone:* 419-531-9610. *Website:* http://www.proskills.com/.

Remington College–Cleveland Campus
Cleveland, Ohio

Director of Admissions Director of Recruitment, Remington College–Cleveland Campus, 14445 Broadway Avenue, Cleveland, OH 44125. *Phone:* 216-475-7520. *Fax:* 216-475-6055. *Website:* http://www.remingtoncollege.edu/.

Rosedale Bible College
Irwin, Ohio

Director of Admissions Mr. John Showalter, Director of Enrollment Services, Rosedale Bible College, 2270 Rosedale Road, Irwin, OH 43029-9501. *Phone:* 740-857-1311. *Fax:* 740-857-1577. *E-mail:* pweber@rosedale.edu. *Website:* http://www.rosedale.edu/.

School of Advertising Art
Kettering, Ohio

Freshman Application Contact Ms. Abigail Heaney, Admissions, School of Advertising Art, 1725 East David Road, Kettering, OH 45440. *Phone:* 937-294-0592. *Toll-free phone:* 877-300-9866. *Fax:* 937-294-5869. *E-mail:* Abbie@saa.edu.
Website: http://www.saa.edu/.

Sinclair Community College
Dayton, Ohio

Freshman Application Contact Ms. Sara Smith, Director and Systems Manager, Outreach Services, Sinclair Community College, 444 West Third Street, Dayton, OH 45402-1460. *Phone:* 937-512-3060. *Toll-free phone:* 800-315-3000. *Fax:* 937-512-2393. *E-mail:* ssmith@sinclair.edu.
Website: http://www.sinclair.edu/.

Southern State Community College
Hillsboro, Ohio

- **State-supported** 2-year, founded 1975
- **Rural** 60-acre campus
- **Endowment** $1.9 million
- **Coed,** 2,431 undergraduate students, 48% full-time, 67% women, 33% men

Undergraduates 1,175 full-time, 1,256 part-time. Students come from 2 states and territories; 2% Black or African American, non-Hispanic/Latino; 0.7% Hispanic/Latino; 0.5% Asian, non-Hispanic/Latino; 0.1% Native Hawaiian or other Pacific Islander, non-Hispanic/Latino; 0.3% American Indian or Alaska Native, non-Hispanic/Latino; 1% Two or more races, non-Hispanic/Latino; 2% Race/ethnicity unknown.

Freshmen *Admission:* 405 applied, 405 admitted, 405 enrolled.

Faculty *Total:* 179, 32% full-time, 13% with terminal degrees. *Student/faculty ratio:* 16:1.

Majors Accounting technology and bookkeeping; administrative assistant and secretarial science; agricultural production; agriculture; business administration and management; business/commerce; CAD/CADD drafting/design technology; computer programming; computer programming (specific applications); computer systems analysis; computer technology/computer systems technology; corrections; criminal justice/law enforcement administration; criminal justice/police science; drafting and design technology; early childhood education; electrical, electronic and communications engineering technology; electromechanical technology; emergency medical technology (EMT paramedic); entrepreneurship; executive assistant/executive secretary; human services; kindergarten/preschool education; liberal arts and sciences/liberal studies; medical/clinical assistant; registered nursing/registered nurse; respiratory care therapy; substance abuse/addiction counseling; teacher assistant/aide.

Academics *Calendar:* quarters. *Degree:* certificates and associate. *Special study options:* academic remediation for entering students, advanced placement credit, cooperative education, distance learning, double majors, independent study, internships, off-campus study, part-time degree program, services for LD students, student-designed majors, summer session for credit.

Library Library plus 4 others with 83,421 titles, 271 serial subscriptions, 12,035 audiovisual materials, an OPAC, a Web page.

Student Life *Housing:* college housing not available. *Activities and Organizations:* drama/theater group, choral group, Student Government Association, Drama Club. *Student services:* personal/psychological counseling.

Athletics Member USCAA. *Intercollegiate sports:* basketball M(s)/W(s), soccer M(s), softball W(s), volleyball W(s).

Costs (2013–14) *Tuition:* state resident $4132 full-time, $158 per semester hour part-time; nonresident $7752 full-time, $299 per semester hour part-time. Full-time tuition and fees vary according to course load and reciprocity agreements. Part-time tuition and fees vary according to course load and reciprocity agreements. *Payment plan:* deferred payment. *Waivers:* senior citizens and employees or children of employees.

Financial Aid Of all full-time matriculated undergraduates who enrolled in 2011, 3,082 applied for aid, 3,082 were judged to have need, 2,537 had their need fully met. 61 Federal Work-Study jobs (averaging $2030). In 2011, 754 non-need-based awards were made. *Average percent of need met:* 92%. *Average financial aid package:* $4570. *Average need-based loan:* $2247. *Average need-based gift aid:* $3560. *Average non-need-based aid:* $1675.

Applying *Options:* electronic application, early admission, deferred entrance. *Recommended:* high school transcript. *Application deadlines:* rolling (freshmen), rolling (transfers). *Notification:* continuous (freshmen), continuous (transfers).

Freshman Application Contact Ms. Wendy Johnson, Director of Admissions, Southern State Community College, Hillsboro, OH 45133.

Phone: 937-393-3431 Ext. 2720. *Toll-free phone:* 800-628-7722. *Fax:* 937-393-6682. *E-mail:* wjohnson@sscc.edu.
Website: http://www.sscc.edu/.

Stark State College
North Canton, Ohio

- **State-related** 2-year, founded 1970, part of University System of Ohio
- **Suburban** 34-acre campus with easy access to Cleveland
- **Endowment** $4.6 million
- **Coed,** 15,450 undergraduate students, 29% full-time, 60% women, 40% men

Undergraduates 4,469 full-time, 10,981 part-time. Students come from 15 states and territories; 6 other countries; 0.8% are from out of state; 20% Black or African American, non-Hispanic/Latino; 0.9% Hispanic/Latino; 0.9% Asian, non-Hispanic/Latino; 0.1% Native Hawaiian or other Pacific Islander, non-Hispanic/Latino; 0.4% American Indian or Alaska Native, non-Hispanic/Latino; 3% Two or more races, non-Hispanic/Latino; 7% Race/ethnicity unknown; 7% transferred in. *Retention:* 46% of full-time freshmen returned.

Freshmen *Admission:* 2,839 enrolled. *Test scores:* ACT scores over 18: 48%; ACT scores over 24: 6%; ACT scores over 30: 1%.

Faculty *Total:* 730, 27% full-time. *Student/faculty ratio:* 21:1.

Majors Accounting; administrative assistant and secretarial science; architectural engineering technology; automobile/automotive mechanics technology; biomedical technology; business administration and management; child development; civil engineering technology; clinical/medical laboratory technology; computer and information sciences and support services related; computer and information sciences related; computer engineering related; computer hardware engineering; computer/information technology services administration related; computer programming; computer programming related; computer programming (specific applications); computer programming (vendor/product certification); computer software and media applications related; computer software engineering; computer systems networking and telecommunications; consumer merchandising/retailing management; court reporting; data entry/microcomputer applications; data entry/microcomputer applications related; dental hygiene; drafting and design technology; environmental studies; finance; fire science/firefighting; food technology and processing; health information/medical records administration; human services; industrial technology; information technology; international business/trade/commerce; legal administrative assistant/secretary; marketing/marketing management; mechanical engineering/mechanical technology; medical/clinical assistant; occupational therapy; operations management; physical therapy; registered nursing/registered nurse; respiratory care therapy; surveying technology; web/multimedia management and webmaster; web page, digital/multimedia and information resources design; word processing.

Academics *Calendar:* semesters. *Degree:* certificates and associate. *Special study options:* academic remediation for entering students, adult/continuing education programs, cooperative education, distance learning, double majors, external degree program, independent study, off-campus study, part-time degree program, services for LD students, student-designed majors, summer session for credit.

Library Learning Resource Center plus 1 other with 82,728 titles, 23,331 serial subscriptions, an OPAC, a Web page.

Student Life *Housing:* college housing not available. *Activities and Organizations:* student-run newspaper, Phi Theta Kappa, Business Student Club, Institute of Management Accountants, Stark State College Association of Medical Assistants, Student Health Information Management Association, national fraternities, national sororities. *Campus security:* late-night transport/escort service, patrols by trained security personnel at anytime the campus is open. *Student services:* personal/psychological counseling.

Standardized Tests *Recommended:* SAT or ACT (for admission).

Costs (2014–15) *Tuition:* state resident $2796 full-time, $117 per credit hour part-time; nonresident $4980 full-time, $208 per credit hour part-time. Full-time tuition and fees vary according to course load and program. Part-time tuition and fees vary according to program. *Required fees:* $890 full-time, $34 per credit hour part-time, $30 per term part-time. *Payment plan:* installment. *Waivers:* senior citizens and employees or children of employees.

Financial Aid Of all full-time matriculated undergraduates who enrolled in 2012, 194 Federal Work-Study jobs (averaging $2383).

Applying *Required:* high school transcript.

Freshman Application Contact Cheri Rice, Vice President, Student Services and Enrollment Management, Stark State College, 6200 Frank Road NE, Canton, OH 44720. *Phone:* 330-494-6170 Ext. 4344. *Toll-free phone:* 800-797-8275. *E-mail:* info@starkstate.edu.
Website: http://www.starkstate.edu/.

Stautzenberger College
Brecksville, Ohio

Admissions Office Contact Stautzenberger College, 8001 Katherine Boulevard, Brecksville, OH 44141. *Toll-free phone:* 800-437-2997. *Website:* http://www.sctoday.edu/.

Stautzenberger College
Maumee, Ohio

Director of Admissions Ms. Karen Fitzgerald, Director of Admissions and Marketing, Stautzenberger College, 1796 Indian Wood Circle, Maumee, OH 43537. *Phone:* 419-866-0261. *Toll-free phone:* 800-552-5099. *Fax:* 419-867-9821. *E-mail:* klfitzgerald@stautzenberger.com. *Website:* http://www.sctoday.edu/maumee/.

Terra State Community College
Fremont, Ohio

- **State-supported** 2-year, founded 1968, part of Ohio Board of Regents
- **Small-town** 100-acre campus with easy access to Toledo
- **Coed**

Undergraduates 1,252 full-time, 1,920 part-time. 5% Black or African American, non-Hispanic/Latino; 7% Hispanic/Latino; 0.5% Asian, non-Hispanic/Latino; 0.3% American Indian or Alaska Native, non-Hispanic/Latino; 0.9% Two or more races, non-Hispanic/Latino; 3% Race/ethnicity unknown; 0.2% international.
Faculty *Student/faculty ratio:* 20:1.
Academics *Calendar:* semesters. *Degree:* certificates, diplomas, and associate. *Special study options:* academic remediation for entering students, adult/continuing education programs, advanced placement credit, cooperative education, distance learning, double majors, independent study, internships, off-campus study, part-time degree program, services for LD students, student-designed majors, summer session for credit.
Student Life *Campus security:* 24-hour emergency response devices.
Costs (2013–14) *Tuition:* state resident $3127 full-time, $130 per semester hour part-time; nonresident $5109 full-time, $213 per semester hour part-time. *Required fees:* $347 full-time, $14 per semester hour part-time, $10 per term part-time.
Financial Aid Of all full-time matriculated undergraduates who enrolled in 2012, 57 Federal Work-Study jobs (averaging $1450).
Applying *Options:* electronic application, early admission, deferred entrance. *Required:* high school transcript.
Freshman Application Contact Ms. Kristen Taylor, Director of Admissions and Enrollment Services, Terra State Community College, 2830 Napoleon Road, Fremont, OH 43420. *Phone:* 419-559-2154. *Toll-free phone:* 866-AT-TERRA. *Fax:* 419-559-2352. *E-mail:* ktaylor01@terra.edu. *Website:* http://www.terra.edu/.

Trumbull Business College
Warren, Ohio

Director of Admissions Admissions Office, Trumbull Business College, 3200 Ridge Road, Warren, OH 44484. *Phone:* 330-369-6792. *Toll-free phone:* 888-766-1598. *E-mail:* admissions@tbc-trumbullbusiness.com. *Website:* http://www.tbc-trumbullbusiness.com/.

The University of Akron–Wayne College
Orrville, Ohio

- **State-supported** primarily 2-year, founded 1972, part of The University of Akron
- **Rural** 157-acre campus
- **Coed,** 2,353 undergraduate students, 47% full-time, 59% women, 41% men

Undergraduates 1,109 full-time, 1,244 part-time. Students come from 2 states and territories; 2 other countries; 3% Black or African American, non-Hispanic/Latino; 1% Hispanic/Latino; 0.6% Asian, non-Hispanic/Latino; 0.1% Native Hawaiian or other Pacific Islander, non-Hispanic/Latino; 0.3% American Indian or Alaska Native, non-Hispanic/Latino; 2% Two or more races, non-Hispanic/Latino; 4% Race/ethnicity unknown; 2% transferred in. *Retention:* 55% of full-time freshmen returned.
Freshmen *Admission:* 1,053 applied, 806 admitted, 343 enrolled. *Average high school GPA:* 3.01. *Test scores:* ACT scores over 18: 76%; ACT scores over 24: 18%; ACT scores over 30: 1%.
Faculty *Total:* 186, 13% full-time, 23% with terminal degrees. *Student/faculty ratio:* 20:1.
Majors Administrative assistant and secretarial science; business administration and management; general studies; liberal arts and sciences/liberal studies; medical office management; office management; social work; teacher assistant/aide.

Academics *Calendar:* semesters. *Degrees:* certificates, associate, and bachelor's. *Special study options:* academic remediation for entering students, adult/continuing education programs, advanced placement credit, cooperative education, distance learning, double majors, honors programs, independent study, internships, off-campus study, part-time degree program, services for LD students, summer session for credit. *ROTC:* Army (c), Air Force (c).
Library Wayne College Library with 16,974 titles, 94 serial subscriptions, 1,257 audiovisual materials, an OPAC, a Web page.
Student Life *Housing:* college housing not available. *Activities and Organizations:* Associated Student Government (ASG), Campus Crusade for Christ (CRU), Waynessence, Nursing Club, Adult Learner Student Organization (ALSO). *Campus security:* 24-hour emergency response devices, late-night transport/escort service. *Student services:* personal/psychological counseling.
Athletics *Intercollegiate sports:* basketball M/W, cheerleading W, golf M, volleyball W. *Intramural sports:* basketball M/W, golf M, volleyball M/W.
Standardized Tests *Required for some:* SAT or ACT (for admission), ACT COMPASS. *Recommended:* SAT or ACT (for admission), ACT COMPASS.
Financial Aid Of all full-time matriculated undergraduates who enrolled in 2012, 8 Federal Work-Study jobs (averaging $2200).
Applying *Options:* electronic application, early admission, deferred entrance. *Application fee:* $40. *Required for some:* high school transcript. *Application deadlines:* 8/13 (freshmen), 8/13 (transfers). *Notification:* continuous (freshmen), continuous (transfers).
Freshman Application Contact Ms. Alicia Broadus, Student Services Counselor, The University of Akron–Wayne College, Orrville, OH 44667. *Phone:* 800-221-8308 Ext. 8901. *Toll-free phone:* 800-221-8308. *Fax:* 330-684-8989. *E-mail:* wayneadmissions@uakron.edu. *Website:* http://www.wayne.uakron.edu/.

University of Cincinnati Blue Ash
Cincinnati, Ohio

Freshman Application Contact Leigh Schlegal, Admission Counselor, University of Cincinnati Blue Ash, 9555 Plainfield Road, Cincinnati, OH 45236-1007. *Phone:* 513-745-5783. *Fax:* 513-745-5768. *Website:* http://www.ucblueash.edu/.

University of Cincinnati Clermont College
Batavia, Ohio

Freshman Application Contact Mrs. Jamie Adkins, Records Management Officer, University of Cincinnati Clermont College, 4200 Clermont College Drive, Batavia, OH 45103. *Phone:* 513-732-5294. *Fax:* 513-732-5303. *E-mail:* jamie.adkins@uc.edu. *Website:* http://www.ucclermont.edu/.

Vatterott College
Broadview Heights, Ohio

Director of Admissions Mr. Jack Chalk, Director of Admissions, Vatterott College, 5025 East Royalton Road, Broadview Heights, OH 44147. *Phone:* 440-526-1660. *Toll-free phone:* 888-553-6627. *Website:* http://www.vatterott.edu/.

Vet Tech Institute at Bradford School
Columbus, Ohio

- **Private** 2-year, founded 2005
- **Suburban** campus
- **Coed,** 156 undergraduate students
- **30%** of applicants were admitted

Freshmen *Admission:* 552 applied, 165 admitted.
Majors Veterinary/animal health technology.
Academics *Degree:* associate. *Special study options:* accelerated degree program, internships.
Freshman Application Contact Admissions Office, Vet Tech Institute at Bradford School, 2469 Stelzer Road, Columbus, OH 43219. *Phone:* 800-678-7981. *Toll-free phone:* 800-678-7981. *Website:* http://columbus.vettechinstitute.edu/.

Virginia Marti College of Art and Design
Lakewood, Ohio

Freshman Application Contact Virginia Marti College of Art and Design, 11724 Detroit Avenue, PO Box 580, Lakewood, OH 44107-3002. *Phone:* 216-221-8584 Ext. 106. *Website:* http://www.vmcad.edu/.

Washington State Community College
Marietta, Ohio

Freshman Application Contact Ms. Rebecca Peroni, Director of Admissions, Washington State Community College, 110 Coligate Drive, Marietta, OH 45750. *Phone:* 740-374-8716. *Fax:* 740-376-0257. *E-mail:* rperoni@wscc.edu.
Website: http://www.wscc.edu/.

Wright State University, Lake Campus
Celina, Ohio

Freshman Application Contact Sandra Gilbert, Student Services Officer, Wright State University, Lake Campus, 7600 State Route 703, Celina, OH 45822-2921. *Phone:* 419-586-0324. *Toll-free phone:* 800-237-1477. *Fax:* 419-586-0358.
Website: http://www.wright.edu/lake/.

Zane State College
Zanesville, Ohio

Director of Admissions Mr. Paul Young, Director of Admissions, Zane State College, 1555 Newark Road, Zanesville, OH 43701-2626. *Phone:* 740-454-2501 Ext. 1225. *Toll-free phone:* 800-686-8324. *E-mail:* pyoung@zanestate.edu.
Website: http://www.zanestate.edu/.

OKLAHOMA

Brown Mackie College–Oklahoma City
Oklahoma City, Oklahoma

- **Proprietary** primarily 2-year, part of Education Management Corporation
- **Coed**

Majors Biomedical technology; business administration and management; business/commerce; health/health-care administration; legal assistant/paralegal; medical/clinical assistant; medical office management; occupational therapist assistant; registered nursing/registered nurse.

Academics *Degrees:* associate and bachelor's.
Freshman Application Contact Brown Mackie College–Oklahoma City, 7101 Northwest Expressway, Suite 800, Oklahoma City, OK 73132. *Phone:* 405-621-8000. *Toll-free phone:* 888-229-3280.
Website: http://www.brownmackie.edu/oklahoma-city/.

See display below and page 412 for the College Close-Up.

Brown Mackie College–Tulsa
Tulsa, Oklahoma

- **Proprietary** primarily 2-year, part of Education Management Corporation
- **Coed**

Majors Business administration and management; business/commerce; corrections and criminal justice related; health/health-care administration; information technology; medical/clinical assistant; occupational therapist assistant; registered nursing/registered nurse; surgical technology.
Academics *Degrees:* diplomas, associate, and bachelor's.
Freshman Application Contact Brown Mackie College–Tulsa, 4608 South Garnett, Suite 110, Tulsa, OK 74146. *Phone:* 918-628-3700. *Toll-free phone:* 888-794-8411.
Website: http://www.brownmackie.edu/tulsa/.

See display below and page 428 for the College Close-Up.

Carl Albert State College
Poteau, Oklahoma

- **State-supported** 2-year, founded 1934, part of Oklahoma State Regents for Higher Education
- **Small-town** 78-acre campus
- **Endowment** $5.7 million
- **Coed,** 2,460 undergraduate students, 56% full-time, 66% women, 34% men

Undergraduates 1,373 full-time, 1,087 part-time. Students come from 16 states and territories; 9 other countries; 12% live on campus.
Freshmen *Admission:* 733 applied, 733 admitted, 605 enrolled.
Faculty *Total:* 154, 33% full-time, 2% with terminal degrees. *Student/faculty ratio:* 16:1.
Majors Biology/biological sciences; business administration and management; business/commerce; child development; computer and information sciences; elementary education; engineering; engineering

technologies and engineering related; English; film/cinema/video studies; fine arts related; foods, nutrition, and wellness; health professions related; health services/allied health/health sciences; hotel/motel administration; journalism; management information systems; mathematics; music related; physical education teaching and coaching; physical sciences; physical therapy technology; pre-law studies; radiologic technology/science; registered nursing/registered nurse; rhetoric and composition; secondary education; social sciences; telecommunications technology.

Academics *Calendar:* semesters. *Degree:* certificates and associate. *Special study options:* academic remediation for entering students, adult/continuing education programs, cooperative education, part-time degree program.

Library Joe E. White Library with 27,200 titles, 1,350 serial subscriptions, an OPAC.

Student Life *Housing Options:* men-only, women-only. Campus housing is university owned. *Activities and Organizations:* drama/theater group, student-run newspaper, radio station, choral group, Student Government Association, Phi Theta Kappa, Baptist Student Union, BACCHUS, Student Physical Therapist Assistant Association. *Campus security:* security guards. *Student services:* health clinic, personal/psychological counseling.

Athletics Member NJCAA. *Intercollegiate sports:* baseball M, basketball M(s)/W(s), softball M. *Intramural sports:* tennis M/W, volleyball M/W, weight lifting M.

Costs (2013–14) *Tuition:* state resident $1234 full-time, $94 per credit hour part-time; nonresident $2643 full-time, $194 per credit hour part-time. *Required fees:* $868 full-time, $450 per term part-time. *Room and board:* $1930; room only: $1650. Room and board charges vary according to board plan. *Waivers:* employees or children of employees.

Financial Aid Of all full-time matriculated undergraduates who enrolled in 2012, 112 Federal Work-Study jobs (averaging $2100).

Applying *Required:* high school transcript. *Application deadlines:* 8/13 (freshmen), 8/15 (transfers). *Notification:* continuous (freshmen), continuous (transfers).

Freshman Application Contact Admission Clerk, Carl Albert State College, 1507 South McKenna, Poteau, OK 74953-5208. *Phone:* 918-647-1300. *Fax:* 918-647-1306.

Website: http://www.carlalbert.edu/.

Clary Sage College

Tulsa, Oklahoma

- **Proprietary** 2-year, part of Dental Directions, Inc.
- **Urban** 6-acre campus with easy access to Tulsa
- **Coed, primarily women,** 228 undergraduate students, 100% full-time, 96% women, 4% men

Undergraduates 228 full-time. Students come from 3 states and territories; 1% are from out of state; 15% Black or African American, non-Hispanic/Latino; 7% Hispanic/Latino; 4% Asian, non-Hispanic/Latino; 12% American Indian or Alaska Native, non-Hispanic/Latino; 1% Two or more races, non-Hispanic/Latino; 4% Race/ethnicity unknown.

Freshmen *Admission:* 14 enrolled.

Faculty *Total:* 23, 100% full-time. *Student/faculty ratio:* 9:1.

Majors Cosmetology; fashion/apparel design; interior design.

Academics *Degree:* diplomas and associate. *Special study options:* adult/continuing education programs, distance learning, internships, part-time degree program.

Student Life *Housing:* college housing not available. *Activities and Organizations:* Student Ambassadors. *Campus security:* security guard during hours of operation. *Student services:* personal/psychological counseling.

Costs (2013–14) *Tuition:* $20,730 full-time. Full-time tuition and fees vary according to class time, course level, course load, degree level, location, program, reciprocity agreements, and student level. Part-time tuition and fees vary according to class time, course level, location, reciprocity agreements, and student level. *Required fees:* $3566 full-time. *Payment plans:* tuition prepayment, installment. *Waivers:* employees or children of employees.

Applying *Options:* electronic application. *Application fee:* $100. *Required:* essay or personal statement, high school transcript, interview. *Application deadlines:* rolling (freshmen), rolling (out-of-state freshmen), rolling (transfers). *Notification:* continuous (freshmen), continuous (out-of-state freshmen), continuous (transfers).

Freshman Application Contact Ms. Teresa Knox, Chief Executive Officer, Clary Sage College, 3131 South Sheridan, Tulsa, OK 74145. *Phone:* 918-610-0027 Ext. 2005. *E-mail:* tknox@communitycarecollege.edu.

Website: http://www.clarysagecollege.com/.

Community Care College

Tulsa, Oklahoma

- **Proprietary** 2-year, founded 1995, part of Dental Directions, Inc.
- **Urban** 6-acre campus
- **Coed, primarily women,** 942 undergraduate students, 100% full-time, 91% women, 9% men

Undergraduates 942 full-time. Students come from 17 states and territories; 13% are from out of state; 12% Black or African American, non-Hispanic/Latino; 4% Hispanic/Latino; 3% Asian, non-Hispanic/Latino; 9% American Indian or Alaska Native, non-Hispanic/Latino; 1% Two or more races, non-Hispanic/Latino; 8% Race/ethnicity unknown.

Freshmen *Admission:* 227 enrolled.

Faculty *Total:* 27, 100% full-time. *Student/faculty ratio:* 27:1.

Majors Business administration, management and operations related; dental assisting; early childhood education; health and physical education/fitness; health/health-care administration; legal assistant/paralegal; massage therapy; medical/clinical assistant; medical insurance coding; pharmacy technician; surgical technology; veterinary/animal health technology.

Academics *Calendar:* continuous. *Degree:* diplomas and associate. *Special study options:* adult/continuing education programs, distance learning, independent study, internships, services for LD students.

Student Life *Housing:* college housing not available. *Activities and Organizations:* Student Ambassadors. *Campus security:* campus security personnel are available during school hours.

Costs (2014–15) *Tuition:* $21,826 full-time. Full-time tuition and fees vary according to class time, course level, course load, degree level, location, program, and reciprocity agreements. Part-time tuition and fees vary according to class time, course level, location, and reciprocity agreements. *Required fees:* $2689 full-time. *Payment plans:* tuition prepayment, installment. *Waivers:* employees or children of employees.

Applying *Options:* electronic application. *Application fee:* $100. *Required:* essay or personal statement, high school transcript, interview. *Required for some:* 1 letter of recommendation. *Application deadlines:* rolling (freshmen), rolling (out-of-state freshmen). *Notification:* continuous (freshmen), continuous (out-of-state freshmen).

Freshman Application Contact Ms. Teresa L. Knox, Chief Executive Officer, Community Care College, 4242 South Sheridan, Tulsa, OK 74145. *Phone:* 918-610-0027 Ext. 2005. *Fax:* 918-610-0029. *E-mail:* tknox@communitycarecollege.edu.

Website: http://www.communitycarecollege.edu/.

Connors State College

Warner, Oklahoma

Freshman Application Contact Ms. Sonya Baker, Registrar, Connors State College, Route 1 Box 1000, Warner, OK 74469-9700. *Phone:* 918-463-6233.

Website: http://www.connorsstate.edu/.

Eastern Oklahoma State College

Wilburton, Oklahoma

Freshman Application Contact Ms. Leah McLaughlin, Director of Admissions, Eastern Oklahoma State College, 1301 West Main, Wilburton, OK 74578-4999. *Phone:* 918-465-1811. *Toll-free phone:* 855-534-3672. *Fax:* 918-465-2431. *E-mail:* lmiller@eosc.edu.

Website: http://www.eosc.edu/.

Heritage College

Oklahoma City, Oklahoma

Freshman Application Contact Admissions Office, Heritage College, 7202 I-35 Services Road, Suite 7118, Oklahoma City, OK 73149. *Phone:* 405-631-3399. *Toll-free phone:* 888-334-7339. *E-mail:* info@heritage-education.com.

Website: http://www.heritage-education.com/.

ITT Technical Institute

Tulsa, Oklahoma

- **Proprietary** primarily 2-year, founded 2005
- **Coed**

Majors Business administration and management; computer programming (specific applications); construction management; cyber/computer forensics and counterterrorism; drafting and design technology; electrical, electronic and communications engineering technology; forensic science and technology; graphic communications; industrial technology; information technology project management; medical/clinical assistant; network and system administration; project management; registered nursing/registered nurse.

Academics *Calendar:* quarters. *Degrees:* associate and bachelor's.

Student Life *Housing:* college housing not available.

Freshman Application Contact Director of Recruitment, ITT Technical Institute, 4500 South 129th East Avenue, Suite 152, Tulsa, OK 74134. *Phone:* 918-615-3900. *Toll-free phone:* 800-514-6535. *Website:* http://www.itt-tech.edu/.

Murray State College
Tishomingo, Oklahoma

Freshman Application Contact Murray State College, One Murray Campus, Tishomingo, OK 73460-3130. *Phone:* 580-371-2371 Ext. 171. *Website:* http://www.mscok.edu/.

Northeastern Oklahoma Agricultural and Mechanical College
Miami, Oklahoma

Freshman Application Contact Amy Ishmael, Vice President for Enrollment Management, Northeastern Oklahoma Agricultural and Mechanical College, 200 I Street, NE, Miami, OK 74354-6434. *Phone:* 918-540-6212. *Toll-free phone:* 800-464-6636. *Fax:* 918-540-6946. *E-mail:* neoadmission@neo.edu. *Website:* http://www.neo.edu/.

Northern Oklahoma College
Tonkawa, Oklahoma

Freshman Application Contact Ms. Sheri Snyder, Director of College Relations, Northern Oklahoma College, 1220 East Grand Avenue, PO Box 310, Tonkawa, OK 74653-0310. *Phone:* 580-628-6290. *Website:* http://www.noc.edu/.

Oklahoma City Community College
Oklahoma City, Oklahoma

- **State-supported** 2-year, founded 1969, part of Oklahoma State Regents for Higher Education
- **Urban** 143-acre campus with easy access to Oklahoma City
- **Endowment** $296,574
- **Coed,** 13,026 undergraduate students, 35% full-time, 59% women, 41% men

Undergraduates 4,554 full-time, 8,472 part-time. Students come from 23 states and territories; 41 other countries; 4% are from out of state; 10% Black or African American, non-Hispanic/Latino; 12% Hispanic/Latino; 5% Asian, non-Hispanic/Latino; 0.4% Native Hawaiian or other Pacific Islander, non-Hispanic/Latino; 5% American Indian or Alaska Native, non-Hispanic/Latino; 3% Two or more races, non-Hispanic/Latino; 7% Race/ethnicity unknown; 3% international.

Freshmen *Admission:* 4,958 applied, 4,958 admitted, 1,956 enrolled. *Test scores:* ACT scores over 18: 76%; ACT scores over 24: 22%; ACT scores over 30: 2%.

Faculty *Total:* 475, 32% full-time, 14% with terminal degrees. *Student/faculty ratio:* 28:1.

Majors Accounting; administrative assistant and secretarial science; airframe mechanics and aircraft maintenance technology; American government and politics; animation, interactive technology, video graphics and special effects; architectural drafting and CAD/CADD; art; automobile/automotive mechanics technology; automotive engineering technology; banking and financial support services; biology/biological sciences; biotechnology; broadcast journalism; business administration and management; business/commerce; chemistry; child development; cinematography and film/video production; commercial and advertising art; computer engineering technology; computer science; computer systems analysis; computer systems networking and telecommunications; cyber/electronic operations and warfare; design and applied arts related; design and visual communications; diagnostic medical sonography and ultrasound technology; diesel mechanics technology; digital communication and media/multimedia; drafting and design technology; dramatic/theater arts; electrical, electronic and communications engineering technology; elementary education; emergency medical technology (EMT paramedic); engineering technologies and engineering related; finance; fine/studio arts; foreign languages and literatures; game and interactive media design; general studies; geographic information science and cartography; graphic communications; health information/medical records administration; history; humanities; legal administrative assistant/secretary; liberal arts and sciences/liberal studies; literature; management information systems; manufacturing engineering technology; mass communication/media; mathematics; medical/clinical assistant; multi/interdisciplinary studies related; music; occupational therapy; orthotics/prosthetics; philosophy; photographic and film/video technology; physical therapy; physics; political science and government; pre-engineering; psychology; public relations, advertising, and applied communication; registered nursing/registered nurse; respiratory care

therapy; sociology; speech-language pathology assistant; surgical technology; system, networking, and LAN/WAN management; web/multimedia management and webmaster.

Academics *Calendar:* semesters. *Degree:* certificates and associate. *Special study options:* academic remediation for entering students, accelerated degree program, advanced placement credit, cooperative education, distance learning, double majors, English as a second language, honors programs, independent study, internships, part-time degree program, services for LD students, student-designed majors, summer session for credit.

Library Keith Leftwich Memorial Library with 99,907 titles, 25,104 serial subscriptions, 46,990 audiovisual materials, an OPAC, a Web page.

Student Life *Housing:* college housing not available. *Activities and Organizations:* drama/theater group, student-run newspaper, choral group, Health Professions Association, Black Student Association, Nursing Student Association, Hispanic Organization Promoting Education (H.O.P.E). *Campus security:* 24-hour emergency response devices and patrols, late-night transport/escort service. *Student services:* personal/psychological counseling.

Athletics *Intramural sports:* basketball M/W, bowling M/W, football M/W, rock climbing M/W, soccer M(c)/W(c), table tennis M/W, ultimate Frisbee M/W, volleyball M/W, weight lifting M/W.

Standardized Tests *Required for some:* ACT (for admission). *Recommended:* ACT (for admission), SAT or ACT (for admission).

Costs (2014–15) *One-time required fee:* $25. *Tuition:* state resident $2337 full-time, $78 per credit part-time; nonresident $7127 full-time, $238 per credit part-time. Full-time tuition and fees vary according to class time and course level. Part-time tuition and fees vary according to class time and course level. *Required fees:* $764 full-time, $25 per contact hour part-time. *Payment plan:* installment. *Waivers:* senior citizens and employees or children of employees.

Financial Aid Of all full-time matriculated undergraduates who enrolled in 2012, 4,062 applied for aid, 3,608 were judged to have need, 1,576 had their need fully met. 315 Federal Work-Study jobs (averaging $4800). 240 state and other part-time jobs (averaging $2502). In 2012, 321 non-need-based awards were made. *Average percent of need met:* 70%. *Average financial aid package:* $7351. *Average need-based loan:* $2801. *Average need-based gift aid:* $4769. *Average non-need-based aid:* $589.

Applying *Options:* electronic application. *Application fee:* $25. *Required:* Proof of English Proficiency, All college and university transcripts. *Required for some:* high school transcript. *Application deadlines:* rolling (freshmen), rolling (out-of-state freshmen), rolling (transfers). *Notification:* continuous (freshmen), continuous (out-of-state freshmen), continuous (transfers).

Freshman Application Contact Mr. Jon Horinek, Director of Recruitment and Admissions, Oklahoma City Community College, 7777 South May Avenue, Oklahoma City, OK 73159. *Phone:* 405-682-7743. *Fax:* 405-682-7817. *E-mail:* jhorinek@occc.edu. *Website:* http://www.occc.edu/.

Oklahoma State University Institute of Technology
Okmulgee, Oklahoma

- **State-supported** primarily 2-year, founded 1946, part of Oklahoma State University
- **Small-town** 160-acre campus with easy access to Tulsa
- **Endowment** $6.9 million
- **Coed,** 2,877 undergraduate students, 72% full-time, 36% women, 64% men

Undergraduates 2,074 full-time, 803 part-time. Students come from 27 states and territories; 22 other countries; 12% are from out of state; 5% Black or African American, non-Hispanic/Latino; 5% Hispanic/Latino; 0.7% Asian, non-Hispanic/Latino; 0.1% Native Hawaiian or other Pacific Islander, non-Hispanic/Latino; 19% American Indian or Alaska Native, non-Hispanic/Latino; 9% Two or more races, non-Hispanic/Latino; 4% Race/ethnicity unknown; 1% international; 9% transferred in; 29% live on campus. *Retention:* 57% of full-time freshmen returned.

Freshmen *Admission:* 2,026 applied, 1,090 admitted, 711 enrolled. *Average high school GPA:* 2.9. *Test scores:* ACT scores over 18: 56%; ACT scores over 24: 7%.

Faculty *Total:* 167, 73% full-time, 4% with terminal degrees. *Student/faculty ratio:* 17:1.

Majors Construction engineering technology; heating, air conditioning, ventilation and refrigeration maintenance technology; photography.

Academics *Calendar:* trimesters. *Degrees:* associate and bachelor's. *Special study options:* academic remediation for entering students, adult/continuing education programs, advanced placement credit, distance learning, double majors, independent study, internships, part-time degree program, services for LD students, summer session for credit.

Library Oklahoma State University Institute of Technology Library with 17,469 titles, 186 serial subscriptions, 1,404 audiovisual materials, an OPAC, a Web page.

Student Life *Housing:* on-campus residence required for freshman year. *Options:* coed, men-only. Campus housing is university owned. Freshman campus housing is guaranteed. *Activities and Organizations:* Phi Theta Kappa, Future Art Directors Club, Air Conditioning and Refrigeration Club, Future Chefs Association Club, Instrumentation, Society and Automation Club. *Campus security:* 24-hour emergency response devices and patrols, late-night transport/escort service, controlled dormitory access. *Student services:* health clinic, personal/psychological counseling.

Athletics *Intramural sports:* basketball M/W, football M/W, racquetball M/W, soccer M/W, softball M/W, table tennis M/W, volleyball M/W.

Standardized Tests *Required for some:* SAT or ACT (for admission). *Recommended:* ACT (for admission).

Costs (2014–15) *Tuition:* state resident $3315 full-time, $111 per credit hour part-time; nonresident $8925 full-time, $298 per credit hour part-time. Full-time tuition and fees vary according to course level, location, program, and student level. Part-time tuition and fees vary according to course level, location, program, and student level. *Required fees:* $1080 full-time, $36 per credit hour part-time, $36 per credit hour part-time. *Room and board:* $5800. Room and board charges vary according to board plan and housing facility. *Payment plan:* installment. *Waivers:* senior citizens and employees or children of employees.

Applying *Options:* deferred entrance. *Required:* high school transcript. *Application deadlines:* rolling (freshmen), rolling (out-of-state freshmen), rolling (transfers).

Freshman Application Contact Crystal Bowles, Registrar, Oklahoma State University Institute of Technology, 1801 E 4th St, Okmulgee, OK 74447. *Phone:* 918-293-5274. *Toll-free phone:* 800-722-4471. *Fax:* 918-293-4643. *E-mail:* crystal.bowles@okstate.edu. *Website:* http://www.osuit.edu/.

Oklahoma State University, Oklahoma City

Oklahoma City, Oklahoma

- **State-supported** primarily 2-year, founded 1961, part of Oklahoma State University
- **Urban** 110-acre campus
- **Coed,** 6,996 undergraduate students, 32% full-time, 60% women, 40% men

Undergraduates 2,251 full-time, 4,745 part-time. Students come from 21 states and territories; 3% are from out of state; 16% Black or African American, non-Hispanic/Latino; 9% Hispanic/Latino; 2% Asian, non-Hispanic/Latino; 4% American Indian or Alaska Native, non-Hispanic/Latino; 8% Two or more races, non-Hispanic/Latino; 3% Race/ethnicity unknown; 11% transferred in. *Retention:* 40% of full-time freshmen returned.

Freshmen *Admission:* 988 applied, 988 admitted, 988 enrolled.

Faculty *Total:* 436, 19% full-time. *Student/faculty ratio:* 16:1.

Majors Accounting; American Sign Language (ASL); architectural engineering technology; art; building/home/construction inspection; business administration and management; civil engineering technology; construction engineering technology; construction management; construction trades; criminal justice/police science; drafting and design technology; early childhood education; economics; electrical and power transmission installation; electrical, electronic and communications engineering technology; electrocardiograph technology; emergency medical technology (EMT paramedic); engineering technology; fire prevention and safety technology; fire science/firefighting; general studies; health/health-care administration; history; horticultural science; humanities; human services; illustration; information science/studies; information technology; language interpretation and translation; occupational safety and health technology; physics; pre-engineering; prenursing studies; professional, technical, business, and scientific writing; psychology; public administration and social service professions related; radiologic technology/science; registered nursing/registered nurse; sign language interpretation and translation; substance abuse/addiction counseling; surveying technology; turf and turfgrass management; veterinary/animal health technology; web page, digital/multimedia and information resources design.

Academics *Calendar:* semesters. *Degrees:* certificates, associate, and bachelor's. *Special study options:* academic remediation for entering students, advanced placement credit, cooperative education, distance learning, double majors, honors programs, independent study, part-time degree program, services for LD students, study abroad, summer session for credit.

Library Oklahoma State University-Oklahoma City Campus Library with 15,000 titles, 300 serial subscriptions, an OPAC, a Web page.

Student Life *Housing:* college housing not available. *Activities and Organizations:* Student Government Association, Go Green, Wind Energy Student Association, Hispanic Student Association, OSU-OKC Chapter of the OK Student Nurse Association. *Campus security:* 24-hour patrols, late-night transport/escort service.

Applying *Options:* electronic application, early admission. *Required:* high school transcript. *Application deadlines:* rolling (freshmen), rolling (transfers). *Notification:* continuous (freshmen), continuous (transfers).

Freshman Application Contact Mr. Kyle Williams, Director, Enrollment Management, Oklahoma State University, Oklahoma City, 900 North Portland Avenue, AD202, Oklahoma City, OK 73107. *Phone:* 405-945-9152. *Toll-free phone:* 800-560-4099. *E-mail:* wilkylw@osuokc.edu. *Website:* http://www.osuokc.edu/.

Oklahoma Technical College

Tulsa, Oklahoma

- **Proprietary** 2-year, part of Dental Directions, Inc.
- **Urban** 9-acre campus with easy access to Tulsa
- **Coed,** 84 undergraduate students, 100% full-time, 12% women, 88% men

Undergraduates 84 full-time. Students come from 2 states and territories; 2% are from out of state; 26% Black or African American, non-Hispanic/Latino; 7% Hispanic/Latino; 0.7% Asian, non-Hispanic/Latino; 12% American Indian or Alaska Native, non-Hispanic/Latino; 0.4% Two or more races, non-Hispanic/Latino; 4% Race/ethnicity unknown.

Freshmen *Admission:* 6 enrolled.

Faculty *Total:* 10, 80% full-time. *Student/faculty ratio:* 9:1.

Majors Automobile/automotive mechanics technology; barbering; diesel mechanics technology; heating, ventilation, air conditioning and refrigeration engineering technology; welding technology.

Academics *Degree:* diplomas and associate. *Special study options:* adult/continuing education programs, distance learning, internships, services for LD students.

Student Life *Housing:* college housing not available. *Activities and Organizations:* Student Ambassadors. *Campus security:* Campus security is available during school hours. *Student services:* personal/psychological counseling.

Costs (2014–15) *Tuition:* $28,434 full-time. Full-time tuition and fees vary according to class time, course level, course load, degree level, location, program, and student level. Part-time tuition and fees vary according to class time and degree level. *Required fees:* $3860 full-time. *Payment plans:* tuition prepayment, installment. *Waivers:* employees or children of employees.

Applying *Options:* electronic application. *Application fee:* $100. *Required:* essay or personal statement, high school transcript, interview. *Application deadlines:* rolling (freshmen), rolling (out-of-state freshmen), rolling (transfers). *Notification:* continuous (freshmen), continuous (out-of-state freshmen), continuous (transfers).

Freshman Application Contact Ms. Teresa L. Knox, Chief Executive Officer, Oklahoma Technical College, 4242 South Sheridan, Tulsa, OK 74145. *Phone:* 918-610-0027 Ext. 2005. *Fax:* 918-610-0029. *E-mail:* tknox@communitycarecollege.edu. *Website:* http://www.oklahomatechnicalcollege.com/.

Platt College

Moore, Oklahoma

Admissions Office Contact Platt College, 201 North Eastern Avenue, Moore, OK 73160. *Website:* http://www.plattcolleges.edu/.

Platt College

Oklahoma City, Oklahoma

Freshman Application Contact Ms. Kim Lamb, Director of Admissions, Platt College, 309 South Ann Arbor, Oklahoma City, OK 73128. *Phone:* 405-946-7799. *Fax:* 405-943-2150. *E-mail:* klamb@plattcollege.org. *Website:* http://www.plattcolleges.edu/.

Platt College

Tulsa, Oklahoma

Director of Admissions Mrs. Susan Rone, Director, Platt College, 3801 South Sheridan Road, Tulsa, OK 74145-111. *Phone:* 918-663-9000. *Fax:* 918-622-1240. *E-mail:* susanr@plattcollege.org. *Website:* http://www.plattcolleges.edu/.

Redlands Community College

El Reno, Oklahoma

- **State-supported** 2-year, founded 1938, part of Oklahoma State Regents for Higher Education
- **Suburban** 55-acre campus with easy access to Oklahoma City
- **Coed**

Undergraduates 915 full-time, 1,645 part-time. 97% are from out of state; 6% Black or African American, non-Hispanic/Latino; 5% Hispanic/Latino; 1% Asian, non-Hispanic/Latino; 0.1% Native Hawaiian or other Pacific Islander, non-Hispanic/Latino; 14% American Indian or Alaska Native, non-Hispanic/Latino; 5% Two or more races, non-Hispanic/Latino; 3% Race/ethnicity unknown; 9% transferred in; 10% live on campus. *Retention:* 41% of full-time freshmen returned.

Faculty *Student/faculty ratio:* 24:1.

Academics *Calendar:* semesters. *Degree:* certificates and associate. *Special study options:* academic remediation for entering students, accelerated degree program, adult/continuing education programs, advanced placement credit, cooperative education, distance learning, double majors, external degree program, honors programs, internships, part-time degree program, services for LD students, summer session for credit.

Student Life *Campus security:* 24-hour patrols.

Athletics Member NJCAA.

Standardized Tests *Recommended:* SAT or ACT (for admission).

Costs (2013–14) *Tuition:* state resident $3495 full-time, $117 per credit hour part-time; nonresident $5745 full-time, $192 per credit hour part-time. Full-time tuition and fees vary according to location, program, and reciprocity agreements. Part-time tuition and fees vary according to location, program, and reciprocity agreements. *Room and board:* room only: $5724. Room and board charges vary according to board plan and housing facility.

Financial Aid Of all full-time matriculated undergraduates who enrolled in 2012, 25 Federal Work-Study jobs (averaging $2000). 70 state and other part-time jobs (averaging $2000).

Applying *Options:* electronic application, early admission, deferred entrance. *Application fee:* $25. *Required:* high school transcript.

Freshman Application Contact Redlands Community College, 1300 South Country Club Road, El Reno, OK 73036-5304. *Phone:* 405-262-2552 Ext. 1263. *Toll-free phone:* 866-415-6367.

Website: http://www.redlandscc.edu/.

Rose State College
Midwest City, Oklahoma

Freshman Application Contact Ms. Mechelle Aitson-Roessler, Registrar and Director of Admissions, Rose State College, 6420 Southeast 15th Street, Midwest City, OK 73110-2799. *Phone:* 405-733-7308. *Toll-free phone:* 866-621-0987. *Fax:* 405-736-0203. *E-mail:* maitson@ms.rose.cc.ok.us.

Website: http://www.rose.edu/.

Seminole State College
Seminole, Oklahoma

- **State-supported** 2-year, founded 1931, part of Oklahoma State Regents for Higher Education
- **Small-town** 40-acre campus with easy access to Oklahoma City
- **Endowment** $1.3 million
- **Coed,** 2,123 undergraduate students, 56% full-time, 62% women, 38% men

Undergraduates 1,191 full-time, 932 part-time. Students come from 13 states and territories; 12 other countries; 3% are from out of state; 6% Black or African American, non-Hispanic/Latino; 3% Hispanic/Latino; 0.5% Asian, non-Hispanic/Latino; 0.2% Native Hawaiian or other Pacific Islander, non-Hispanic/Latino; 24% American Indian or Alaska Native, non-Hispanic/Latino; 2% international; 5% transferred in; 8% live on campus.

Freshmen *Admission:* 572 applied, 572 admitted, 518 enrolled. *Test scores:* ACT scores over 18: 77%; ACT scores over 24: 18%; ACT scores over 30: 1%.

Faculty *Total:* 91, 48% full-time, 7% with terminal degrees. *Student/faculty ratio:* 25:1.

Majors Accounting; art; behavioral sciences; biological and biomedical sciences related; biology/biological sciences; business administration and management; business/commerce; child development; clinical/medical laboratory technology; computer science; criminal justice/law enforcement administration; criminal justice/police science; elementary education; engineering; English; fine arts related; general studies; humanities; industrial production technologies related; liberal arts and sciences/liberal studies; management information systems and services related; mathematics; physical education teaching and coaching; physical sciences; pre-engineering; psychology related; registered nursing/registered nurse; social sciences.

Academics *Calendar:* semesters. *Degree:* diplomas and associate. *Special study options:* academic remediation for entering students, adult/continuing education programs, advanced placement credit, cooperative education, distance learning, double majors, honors programs, independent study, off-campus study, part-time degree program, services for LD students, student-designed majors, study abroad, summer session for credit.

Library Boren Library plus 1 other with 27,507 titles, 200 serial subscriptions, 651 audiovisual materials, an OPAC, a Web page.

Student Life *Housing Options:* coed. Campus housing is university owned. *Activities and Organizations:* student-run newspaper, Student Government Association, Native American Student Association, Psi Beta Honor Society, Student Nurses Association, Phi Theta Kappa. *Campus security:* 24-hour

emergency response devices and patrols, student patrols, late-night transport/escort service, controlled dormitory access. *Student services:* personal/psychological counseling.

Athletics Member NJCAA. *Intercollegiate sports:* baseball M(s), basketball M(s)/W(s), cheerleading W(s), golf M(s)/W(s), softball W(s), tennis M(s)/W(s), volleyball W(s).

Standardized Tests *Recommended:* ACT (for admission).

Costs (2014–15) *One-time required fee:* $15. *Tuition:* state resident $2325 full-time, $78 per credit hour part-time; nonresident $7125 full-time, $238 per credit hour part-time. *Required fees:* $1175 full-time, $39 per credit hour part-time. *Room and board:* $6500; room only: $3770. *Payment plans:* installment, deferred payment. *Waivers:* senior citizens and employees or children of employees.

Financial Aid Of all full-time matriculated undergraduates who enrolled in 2011, 17 Federal Work-Study jobs (averaging $3447).

Applying *Options:* early admission, deferred entrance. *Application fee:* $15. *Required:* high school transcript. *Application deadlines:* rolling (freshmen), rolling (transfers). *Notification:* continuous (freshmen), continuous (transfers).

Freshman Application Contact Mr. Charles Morton, Director of Admissions, Seminole State College, PO Box 351, 2701 Boren Boulevard, Seminole, OK 74818-0351. *Phone:* 405-382-9249. *Fax:* 405-382-9524. *E-mail:* c.morton@sscok.edu.

Website: http://www.sscok.edu/.

Southwestern Oklahoma State University at Sayre
Sayre, Oklahoma

Freshman Application Contact Ms. Kim Seymour, Registrar, Southwestern Oklahoma State University at Sayre, 409 East Mississippi Avenue, Sayre, OK 73662. *Phone:* 580-928-5533 Ext. 101. *Fax:* 580-928-1140. *E-mail:* kim.seymour@swosu.edu.

Website: http://www.swosu.edu/sayre/.

Spartan College of Aeronautics and Technology
Tulsa, Oklahoma

Freshman Application Contact Mr. Mark Fowler, Vice President of Student Records and Finance, Spartan College of Aeronautics and Technology, 8820 East Pine Street, PO Box 582833, Tulsa, OK 74158-2833. *Phone:* 918-836-6886. *Toll-free phone:* 800-331-1204 (in-state); 800-331-124 (out-of-state).

Website: http://www.spartan.edu/.

Tulsa Community College
Tulsa, Oklahoma

- **State-supported** 2-year, founded 1968, part of Oklahoma State Regents for Higher Education
- **Urban** 160-acre campus
- **Coed,** 17,876 undergraduate students, 36% full-time, 60% women, 40% men

Undergraduates 6,390 full-time, 11,486 part-time. 1% are from out of state; 10% Black or African American, non-Hispanic/Latino; 8% Hispanic/Latino; 4% Asian, non-Hispanic/Latino; 0.1% Native Hawaiian or other Pacific Islander, non-Hispanic/Latino; 8% American Indian or Alaska Native, non-Hispanic/Latino; 7% Two or more races, non-Hispanic/Latino; 2% Race/ethnicity unknown; 2% international; 3% transferred in.

Freshmen *Admission:* 3,871 enrolled. *Average high school GPA:* 2.94. *Test scores:* ACT scores over 18: 76%; ACT scores over 24: 21%; ACT scores over 30: 1%.

Faculty *Total:* 1,025, 30% full-time, 6% with terminal degrees. *Student/faculty ratio:* 19:1.

Majors Accounting technology and bookkeeping; administrative assistant and secretarial science; aeronautical/aerospace engineering technology; applied horticulture/horticulture operations; banking and financial support services; biology/biological sciences; biomedical technology; biotechnology; business administration and management; business/commerce; business, management, and marketing related; business teacher education; CAD/CADD drafting/design technology; chemical technology; child development; civil engineering; clinical/medical laboratory technology; computer/information technology services administration related; computer installation and repair technology; computer programming (specific applications); computer science; criminal justice/police science; dental assisting; dental hygiene; desktop publishing and digital imaging design; drafting and design technology; dramatic/theater arts; education; electrical, electronic and communications engineering technology; electromechanical and instrumentation and maintenance technologies related; emergency medical technology (EMT paramedic); engineering; engineering technologies and engineering related; engineering technology; environmental science; family and consumer sciences/human sciences; finance; fine arts related; fire prevention and safety technology; fire services administration; foreign languages and literatures; general studies; graphic and printing equipment operation/production; health information/medical records administration; health information/medical records technology; health professions related; heating, air conditioning, ventilation and refrigeration maintenance technology; hospital and health-care facilities administration; hotel/motel administration; humanities; human resources management; industrial technology; interior architecture; interior design; international business/trade/commerce; journalism; legal administrative assistant/secretary; management information systems and services related; marketing/marketing management; mass communication/media; mathematics; mechanical drafting and CAD/CADD; mechanical engineering/mechanical technology; medical administrative assistant and medical secretary; medical/clinical assistant; medical radiologic technology; music; nutrition sciences; occupational safety and health technology; occupational therapy; petroleum technology; physical sciences; physical therapy; pre-pharmacy studies; quality control technology; real estate; registered nursing/registered nurse; respiratory care therapy; sign language interpretation and translation; social sciences; social work; sport and fitness administration/management; surgical technology; surveying technology; theater design and technology; tourism and travel services management; veterinary/animal health technology.

Academics *Calendar:* semesters. *Degree:* certificates and associate. *Special study options:* academic remediation for entering students, accelerated degree program, adult/continuing education programs, advanced placement credit, cooperative education, distance learning, English as a second language, external degree program, freshman honors college, honors programs, independent study, internships, off-campus study, part-time degree program, services for LD students, student-designed majors, summer session for credit.

Library Learning Resource Center with an OPAC, a Web page.

Student Life *Housing:* college housing not available. *Activities and Organizations:* drama/theater group, student-run newspaper. *Campus security:* 24-hour emergency response devices and patrols, student patrols, late-night transport/escort service. *Student services:* health clinic, personal/psychological counseling, women's center.

Athletics *Intramural sports:* basketball M/W, bowling M/W, cross-country running M/W, football M/W, golf M/W, racquetball M/W, soccer M/W, tennis M/W, track and field M/W, volleyball M/W.

Costs (2014–15) *Tuition:* state resident $2362 full-time, $79 per credit hour part-time; nonresident $7914 full-time, $264 per credit hour part-time. *Required fees:* $894 full-time. *Payment plan:* installment. *Waivers:* senior citizens and employees or children of employees.

Financial Aid Of all full-time matriculated undergraduates who enrolled in 2013, 4,059 applied for aid, 3,427 were judged to have need, 506 had their need fully met. In 2013, 970 non-need-based awards were made. *Average percent of need met:* 26%. *Average financial aid package:* $4057. *Average need-based loan:* $1797. *Average need-based gift aid:* $1530. *Average non-need-based aid:* $733.

Applying *Options:* early admission. *Application fee:* $20. *Required:* high school transcript. *Application deadlines:* rolling (freshmen), rolling (transfers).

Freshman Application Contact Ms. Leanne Brewer, Director of Admissions and Records, Tulsa Community College, 6111 East Skelly Drive, Tulsa, OK 74135. *Phone:* 918-595-7811. *Fax:* 918-595-7910. *E-mail:* lbrewer@tulsacc.edu.
Website: http://www.tulsacc.edu/.

Tulsa Welding School
Tulsa, Oklahoma

Freshman Application Contact Mrs. Debbie Renee Burke, Vice President/Executive Director, Tulsa Welding School, 2545 East 11th Street, Tulsa, OK 74104. *Phone:* 918-587-6789 Ext. 2258. *Toll-free phone:* 888-765-5555. *Fax:* 918-295-6812. *E-mail:* dburke@twsweld.com.
Website: http://www.weldingschool.com/.

Vatterott College
Tulsa, Oklahoma

Freshman Application Contact Mr. Terry Queeno, Campus Director, Vatterott College, 4343 South 118th East Avenue, Suite A, Tulsa, OK 74146. *Phone:* 918-836-6656. *Toll-free phone:* 888-553-6627. *Fax:* 918-836-9698. *E-mail:* tulsa@vatterott-college.edu.
Website: http://www.vatterott.edu/.

Vatterott College
Warr Acres, Oklahoma

Freshman Application Contact Mr. Mark Hybers, Director of Admissions, Vatterott College, Oklahoma City, OK 73127. *Phone:* 405-945-0088 Ext. 4416. *Toll-free phone:* 888-553-6627. *Fax:* 405-945-0788. *E-mail:* mark.hybers@vatterott-college.edu.
Website: http://www.vatterott.edu/.

Virginia College
Tulsa, Oklahoma

Admissions Office Contact Virginia College, 5124 South Peoria Avenue, Tulsa, OK 74105.
Website: http://www.vc.edu/.

Western Oklahoma State College
Altus, Oklahoma

- **State-supported** 2-year, founded 1926, part of Oklahoma State Regents for Higher Education
- **Rural** 142-acre campus
- **Endowment** $5.4 million
- **Coed,** 1,690 undergraduate students, 40% full-time, 57% women, 43% men

Undergraduates 675 full-time, 1,015 part-time. Students come from 6 other countries; 12% are from out of state; 10% Black or African American, non-Hispanic/Latino; 16% Hispanic/Latino; 0.9% Asian, non-Hispanic/Latino; 0.2% Native Hawaiian or other Pacific Islander, non-Hispanic/Latino; 2% American Indian or Alaska Native, non-Hispanic/Latino; 8% Two or more races, non-Hispanic/Latino; 9% Race/ethnicity unknown; 1% international; 48% transferred in; 6% live on campus. *Retention:* 49% of full-time freshmen returned.

Freshmen *Admission:* 615 applied, 615 admitted, 344 enrolled. *Average high school GPA:* 3.22.

Faculty *Total:* 71, 52% full-time, 6% with terminal degrees. *Student/faculty ratio:* 19:1.

Majors Accounting technology and bookkeeping; aviation/airway management; child development; computer/information technology services administration related; criminal justice/police science; fire protection related; liberal arts and sciences/liberal studies; mechanics and repair; medical radiologic technology; registered nursing/registered nurse.

Academics *Calendar:* semesters. *Degree:* certificates and associate. *Special study options:* academic remediation for entering students, adult/continuing education programs, advanced placement credit, distance learning, English as a second language, honors programs, independent study, off-campus study, part-time degree program, services for LD students, student-designed majors, summer session for credit.

Library Learning Resources Center with 33,000 titles, 1,000 serial subscriptions, an OPAC, a Web page.

Student Life *Housing Options:* coed. Campus housing is university owned. *Activities and Organizations:* drama/theater group, choral group, Baptist Student Union, Phi Theta Kappa, Student Senate, Behavioral Science Club, Aggie Club. *Campus security:* 24-hour emergency response devices, Trained security personnel 8:00 AM - 10:00 PM M-F. *Student services:* personal/psychological counseling.

Athletics Member NJCAA. *Intercollegiate sports:* baseball M(s), basketball M(s)/W(s), equestrian sports M(s)/W(s), softball W(s). *Intramural sports:* golf M/W, volleyball M/W.

Standardized Tests *Required for some:* ACT (for admission).

Costs (2014–15) *Tuition:* state resident $2118 full-time, $71 per credit part-time; nonresident $6473 full-time, $216 per credit part-time. *Required fees:* $1013 full-time, $34 per credit part-time. *Room and board:* $1900. *Payment plan:* installment. *Waivers:* employees or children of employees.

Financial Aid Of all full-time matriculated undergraduates who enrolled in 2012, 56 Federal Work-Study jobs (averaging $2700).

Applying *Options:* electronic application, early admission. *Application fee:* $15. *Required:* high school transcript. *Application deadlines:* rolling (freshmen), rolling (transfers). *Notification:* continuous (freshmen), continuous (transfers).

Freshman Application Contact Dean Chad E. Wiginton, Dean of Student Support Services, Western Oklahoma State College, 2801 North Main, Altus, OK 73521. *Phone:* 580-477-7918. *Fax:* 580-477-7716. *E-mail:* chad.wiginton@wosc.edu.
Website: http://www.wosc.edu/.

Wright Career College
Oklahoma City, Oklahoma

- **Proprietary** primarily 2-year
- **Suburban** campus with easy access to Oklahoma City
- **Coed,** 254 undergraduate students, 71% full-time, 74% women, 26% men

Undergraduates 180 full-time, 74 part-time. Students come from 2 states and territories; 44% Black or African American, non-Hispanic/Latino; 9% Hispanic/Latino; 0.8% Asian, non-Hispanic/Latino; 0.4% Native Hawaiian or other Pacific Islander, non-Hispanic/Latino; 4% American Indian or Alaska

Native, non-Hispanic/Latino; 2% Two or more races, non-Hispanic/Latino; 1% Race/ethnicity unknown; 2% transferred in. *Retention:* 2% of full-time freshmen returned.

Freshmen *Admission:* 254 applied, 254 admitted, 115 enrolled.

Majors Business administration and management; computer installation and repair technology; computer programming; computer systems networking and telecommunications; computer technology/computer systems technology; entrepreneurial and small business related; health and physical education related; health/health-care administration; surgical technology.

Academics *Degrees:* diplomas, associate, and bachelor's. *Special study options:* adult/continuing education programs, distance learning, internships, off-campus study.

Student Life *Housing:* college housing not available.

Applying *Application deadlines:* rolling (freshmen), rolling (out-of-state freshmen), rolling (transfers). *Early decision deadline:* rolling (for plan 1), rolling (for plan 2). *Notification:* continuous (freshmen), continuous (out-of-state freshmen), continuous (transfers), rolling (early decision plan 1), rolling (early decision plan 2).

Freshman Application Contact Wright Career College, 2219 W I-240 Service Road, Suite #124, Oklahoma City, OK 73159. *Phone:* 405-681-2300. *Toll-free phone:* 800-555-4003. *E-mail:* info@wrightcc.edu.

Website: http://www.wrightcc.edu/.

Wright Career College

Tulsa, Oklahoma

- **Proprietary** primarily 2-year
- **Suburban** campus with easy access to Tulsa
- **Coed,** 309 undergraduate students, 36% full-time, 71% women, 29% men

Undergraduates 110 full-time, 199 part-time. Students come from 3 states and territories; 45% Black or African American, non-Hispanic/Latino; 2% Hispanic/Latino; 0.6% Native Hawaiian or other Pacific Islander, non-Hispanic/Latino; 6% American Indian or Alaska Native, non-Hispanic/Latino; 5% Two or more races, non-Hispanic/Latino; 0.3% Race/ethnicity unknown; 1% transferred in.

Freshmen *Admission:* 308 applied, 308 admitted, 111 enrolled.

Majors Business administration and management; computer installation and repair technology; computer programming; computer systems networking and telecommunications; computer technology/computer systems technology; entrepreneurial and small business related; health and physical education related; health/health-care administration; surgical technology.

Academics *Degrees:* diplomas, associate, and bachelor's. *Special study options:* distance learning, internships, off-campus study.

Student Life *Housing:* college housing not available.

Applying *Application deadlines:* rolling (freshmen), rolling (out-of-state freshmen), rolling (transfers). *Early decision deadline:* rolling (for plan 1), rolling (for plan 2). *Notification:* continuous (freshmen), continuous (out-of-state freshmen), continuous (transfers), rolling (early decision plan 1), rolling (early decision plan 2).

Freshman Application Contact Wright Career College, 4908 S Sheridan, Tulsa, OK 74145. *Phone:* 918-628-7700. *Toll-free phone:* 800-555-4003. *E-mail:* info@wrightcc.edu.

Website: http://www.wrightcc.edu/.

OREGON

American College of Healthcare Sciences

Portland, Oregon

Freshman Application Contact Admissions Office, American College of Healthcare Sciences, 5940 SW Hood Avenue, Portland, OR 97239. *Phone:* 503-244-0726. *Toll-free phone:* 800-487-8839. *Fax:* 503-244-0727. *E-mail:* achs@achs.edu.

Website: http://www.achs.edu/.

Blue Mountain Community College

Pendleton, Oregon

Director of Admissions Ms. Theresa Bosworth, Director of Admissions, Blue Mountain Community College, 2411 Northwest Carden Avenue, PO Box 100, Pendleton, OR 97801-1000. *Phone:* 541-278-5774. *E-mail:* tbosworth@bluecc.edu.

Website: http://www.bluecc.edu/.

Central Oregon Community College

Bend, Oregon

- **District-supported** 2-year, founded 1949, part of Oregon Community College Association
- **Small-town** 193-acre campus
- **Endowment** $10.0 million
- **Coed,** 6,760 undergraduate students, 44% full-time, 56% women, 44% men

Undergraduates 2,977 full-time, 3,783 part-time. Students come from 28 states and territories; 4% are from out of state; 0.7% Black or African American, non-Hispanic/Latino; 8% Hispanic/Latino; 1% Asian, non-Hispanic/Latino; 0.5% Native Hawaiian or other Pacific Islander, non-Hispanic/Latino; 2% American Indian or Alaska Native, non-Hispanic/Latino; 2% Two or more races, non-Hispanic/Latino; 10% Race/ethnicity unknown; 10% transferred in; 1% live on campus. *Retention:* 53% of full-time freshmen returned.

Freshmen *Admission:* 1,569 applied, 1,569 admitted, 691 enrolled.

Faculty *Total:* 254, 47% full-time, 17% with terminal degrees. *Student/faculty ratio:* 26:1.

Majors Accounting; administrative assistant and secretarial science; airline pilot and flight crew; art; automobile/automotive mechanics technology; biological and physical sciences; biology/biological sciences; business administration and management; CAD/CADD drafting/design technology; child-care and support services management; computer and information sciences related; computer science; computer systems networking and telecommunications; cooking and related culinary arts; customer service management; dental assisting; dietetics; drafting and design technology; early childhood education; education; electrical, electronic and communications engineering technology; emergency medical technology (EMT paramedic); engineering; fire science/firefighting; fishing and fisheries sciences and management; foreign languages and literatures; forestry; forest technology; health and physical education/fitness; health information/medical records technology; hotel/motel administration; humanities; industrial technology; kinesiology and exercise science; liberal arts and sciences/liberal studies; licensed practical/vocational nurse training; management information systems; manufacturing engineering technology; marketing/marketing management; massage therapy; mathematics; medical/clinical assistant; natural resources/conservation; physical sciences; physical therapy; polymer/plastics engineering; pre-law studies; premedical studies; pre-pharmacy studies; radiologic technology/science; registered nursing/registered nurse; retailing; social sciences; speech communication and rhetoric; sport and fitness administration/management; substance abuse/addiction counseling.

Academics *Calendar:* quarters. *Degree:* certificates and associate. *Special study options:* academic remediation for entering students, cooperative education, distance learning, double majors, English as a second language, independent study, internships, part-time degree program, student-designed majors, study abroad, summer session for credit. *ROTC:* Army (c).

Library COCC Library plus 1 other with 76,421 titles, 329 serial subscriptions, 3,570 audiovisual materials, an OPAC, a Web page.

Student Life *Housing Options:* coed. Campus housing is university owned. *Activities and Organizations:* drama/theater group, student-run newspaper, choral group, club sports, student newspaper, Criminal Justice Club, Aviation Club. *Campus security:* 24-hour emergency response devices and patrols, late-night transport/escort service. *Student services:* personal/psychological counseling.

Athletics *Intercollegiate sports:* golf M/W. *Intramural sports:* baseball M, basketball M/W, cross-country running M/W, football M, skiing (cross-country) M/W, skiing (downhill) M/W, soccer M/W, track and field M/W, volleyball M/W, weight lifting M/W.

Financial Aid Of all full-time matriculated undergraduates who enrolled in 2012, 725 Federal Work-Study jobs (averaging $2130).

Applying *Options:* electronic application. *Application fee:* $25. *Application deadlines:* rolling (freshmen), rolling (transfers). *Notification:* continuous (freshmen), continuous (transfers).

Freshman Application Contact Central Oregon Community College, 2600 Northwest College Way, Bend, OR 97701-5998. *Phone:* 541-383-7500. *Website:* http://www.cocc.edu/.

Chemeketa Community College

Salem, Oregon

- **State and locally supported** 2-year, founded 1955
- **Urban** 72-acre campus with easy access to Portland
- **Endowment** $3.7 million
- **Coed**

Undergraduates 6,225 full-time, 6,146 part-time. Students come from 21 states and territories; 20 other countries; 5% are from out of state; 1% Black or African American, non-Hispanic/Latino; 18% Hispanic/Latino; 2% Asian, non-Hispanic/Latino; 0.8% Native Hawaiian or other Pacific Islander, non-

Hispanic/Latino; 2% American Indian or Alaska Native, non-Hispanic/Latino; 4% Two or more races, non-Hispanic/Latino; 4% Race/ethnicity unknown; 0.6% international; 1% transferred in. *Retention:* 61% of full-time freshmen returned.

Faculty *Student/faculty ratio:* 26:1.

Academics *Calendar:* quarters. *Degree:* certificates, diplomas, and associate. *Special study options:* academic remediation for entering students, adult/continuing education programs, advanced placement credit, cooperative education, distance learning, double majors, English as a second language, independent study, internships, part-time degree program, services for LD students, study abroad, summer session for credit.

Student Life *Campus security:* 24-hour emergency response devices and patrols, late-night transport/escort service.

Costs (2013–14) *Tuition:* state resident $3690 full-time, $82 per quarter hour part-time; nonresident $10,980 full-time, $244 per quarter hour part-time. *Required fees:* $640 full-time, $14 per quarter hour part-time. *Payment plans:* installment, deferred payment.

Applying *Required for some:* high school transcript, interview.

Freshman Application Contact Admissions Office, Chemeketa Community College, Chemeketa Community College, PO Box 14009. *Phone:* 503-399-5001. *E-mail:* admissions@chemeketa.edu.

Website: http://www.chemeketa.edu/.

Clackamas Community College

Oregon City, Oregon

Freshman Application Contact Ms. Tara Sprehe, Registrar, Clackamas Community College, 19600 South Molalla Avenue, Oregon City, OR 97045. *Phone:* 503-657-6958 Ext. 2742. *Fax:* 503-650-6654. *E-mail:* pattyw@clackamas.edu.

Website: http://www.clackamas.edu/.

Clatsop Community College

Astoria, Oregon

- **County-supported** 2-year, founded 1958
- **Small-town** 20-acre campus
- **Coed,** 1,071 undergraduate students, 42% full-time, 57% women, 43% men

Undergraduates 455 full-time, 616 part-time. Students come from 5 states and territories; 12% are from out of state; 0.6% Black or African American, non-Hispanic/Latino; 12% Hispanic/Latino; 1% Asian, non-Hispanic/Latino; 0.2% Native Hawaiian or other Pacific Islander, non-Hispanic/Latino; 2% American Indian or Alaska Native, non-Hispanic/Latino; 2% Two or more races, non-Hispanic/Latino; 8% Race/ethnicity unknown; 5% transferred in.

Freshmen *Admission:* 340 applied, 277 admitted, 124 enrolled.

Faculty *Total:* 99, 27% full-time. *Student/faculty ratio:* 13:1.

Majors Accounting; business administration and management; fire science/firefighting; liberal arts and sciences/liberal studies; registered nursing/registered nurse.

Academics *Calendar:* quarters. *Degree:* certificates and associate. *Special study options:* academic remediation for entering students, adult/continuing education programs, advanced placement credit, cooperative education, distance learning, English as a second language, freshman honors college, honors programs, independent study, internships, part-time degree program, services for LD students, summer session for credit.

Library Dora Badollet Library with 48,517 titles, 180 serial subscriptions, 5,000 audiovisual materials, an OPAC, a Web page.

Student Life *Housing:* college housing not available. *Activities and Organizations:* student-run newspaper. *Campus security:* 24-hour emergency response devices, late-night transport/escort service. *Student services:* personal/psychological counseling.

Costs (2014–15) *One-time required fee:* $90. *Tuition:* state resident $3978 full-time, $98 per credit part-time; nonresident $7956 full-time, $196 per credit part-time. Full-time tuition and fees vary according to reciprocity agreements. Part-time tuition and fees vary according to reciprocity agreements. *Required fees:* $10 per credit part-time, $30 per term part-time. *Payment plan:* deferred payment. *Waivers:* senior citizens and employees or children of employees.

Financial Aid Of all full-time matriculated undergraduates who enrolled in 2012, 220 Federal Work-Study jobs (averaging $2175).

Applying *Options:* electronic application. *Application fee:* $15. *Recommended:* high school transcript. *Application deadlines:* rolling (freshmen), rolling (transfers). *Notification:* continuous (freshmen), continuous (transfers).

Freshman Application Contact Ms. Monica Van Steenberg, Recruiting Coordinator, Clatsop Community College, 1651 Lexington Avenue, Astoria, OR 97103. *Phone:* 503-338-2417. *Toll-free phone:* 855-252-8767. *Fax:* 503-325-5738. *E-mail:* admissions@clatsopcc.edu.

Website: http://www.clatsopcc.edu/.

Columbia Gorge Community College

The Dalles, Oregon

- **State-supported** 2-year, founded 1977
- **Small-town** 78-acre campus
- **Coed,** 1,245 undergraduate students, 44% full-time, 62% women, 38% men

Undergraduates 542 full-time, 703 part-time. Students come from 24 states and territories; 1% are from out of state; 0.6% Black or African American, non-Hispanic/Latino; 7% Hispanic/Latino; 0.8% Asian, non-Hispanic/Latino; 0.1% Native Hawaiian or other Pacific Islander, non-Hispanic/Latino; 5% American Indian or Alaska Native, non-Hispanic/Latino; 0.3% Two or more races, non-Hispanic/Latino; 17% Race/ethnicity unknown. *Retention:* 21% of full-time freshmen returned.

Freshmen *Admission:* 210 enrolled.

Faculty *Total:* 125, 14% full-time.

Majors Accounting; administrative assistant and secretarial science; business administration and management; child-care and support services management; electrical, electronic and communications engineering technology; general studies; liberal arts and sciences/liberal studies; management information systems; registered nursing/registered nurse.

Academics *Calendar:* quarters. *Degree:* certificates, diplomas, and associate. *Special study options:* academic remediation for entering students, cooperative education, distance learning, English as a second language, honors programs, independent study, part-time degree program, services for LD students, summer session for credit.

Library Columbia Gorge Community College Library with 92,328 titles, 48 serial subscriptions, 2,342 audiovisual materials, an OPAC, a Web page.

Student Life *Housing:* college housing not available. *Activities and Organizations:* Nursing Club, Delta Club, Japanese Culture Club, Environmental Club. *Campus security:* 24-hour emergency response devices.

Costs (2013–14) *Tuition:* state resident $3030 full-time, $89 per credit hour part-time; nonresident $6750 full-time, $225 per credit hour part-time. *Required fees:* $360 full-time. *Waivers:* senior citizens and employees or children of employees.

Applying *Options:* electronic application.

Freshman Application Contact Columbia Gorge Community College, 400 East Scenic Drive, The Dalles, OR 97058. *Phone:* 541-506-6025.

Website: http://www.cgcc.cc.or.us/.

Concorde Career College

Portland, Oregon

Admissions Office Contact Concorde Career College, 1425 NE Irving Street, Suite 300, Portland, OR 97232.

Website: http://www.concorde.edu/.

Everest College

Portland, Oregon

Freshman Application Contact Admissions Office, Everest College, 425 Southwest Washington Street, Portland, OR 97204. *Phone:* 503-222-3225. *Toll-free phone:* 888-741-4270. *Fax:* 503-228-6926.

Website: http://www.everest.edu/.

Heald College–Portland

Portland, Oregon

Freshman Application Contact Director of Admissions, Heald College–Portland, 6035 NE 78th Court, Portland, OR 97218. *Phone:* 503-229-0492. *Toll-free phone:* 800-88-HEALD. *Fax:* 503-229-0498. *E-mail:* portlandinfo@heald.edu.

Website: http://www.heald.edu/.

ITT Technical Institute

Portland, Oregon

- **Proprietary** primarily 2-year, founded 1971, part of ITT Educational Services, Inc.
- **Urban** campus
- **Coed**

Majors Automation engineer technology; business administration and management; computer programming (specific applications); computer software technology; construction management; cyber/computer forensics and counterterrorism; drafting and design technology; electrical, electronic and communications engineering technology; forensic science and technology; graphic communications; information technology project management; network and system administration; project management; registered nursing/registered nurse.

Academics *Calendar:* quarters. *Degrees:* associate and bachelor's.

Student Life *Housing:* college housing not available.

Financial Aid Of all full-time matriculated undergraduates who enrolled in 2012, 15 Federal Work-Study jobs (averaging $5000).

Freshman Application Contact Director of Recruitment, ITT Technical Institute, 9500 Northeast Cascades Parkway, Portland, OR 97220. *Phone:* 503-255-6500. *Toll-free phone:* 800-234-5488. *Website:* http://www.itt-tech.edu/.

Klamath Community College

Klamath Falls, Oregon

- **State-supported** 2-year, founded 1996
- **Small-town** 58-acre campus
- **Endowment** $129,870
- **Coed**

Undergraduates 385 full-time, 763 part-time. Students come from 2 states and territories; 0.1% are from out of state; 1% Black or African American, non-Hispanic/Latino; 13% Hispanic/Latino; 0.6% Asian, non-Hispanic/Latino; 0.2% Native Hawaiian or other Pacific Islander, non-Hispanic/Latino; 6% American Indian or Alaska Native, non-Hispanic/Latino; 0.7% Two or more races, non-Hispanic/Latino; 5% Race/ethnicity unknown; 14% transferred in. *Retention:* 58% of full-time freshmen returned.

Faculty *Student/faculty ratio:* 14:1.

Academics *Calendar:* quarters. *Degree:* certificates and associate. *Special study options:* academic remediation for entering students, advanced placement credit, cooperative education, distance learning, double majors, English as a second language, independent study, internships, services for LD students, student-designed majors, summer session for credit.

Student Life *Campus security:* 24-hour emergency response devices.

Costs (2013–14) *Tuition:* state resident $2988 full-time, $83 per credit part-time; nonresident $5796 full-time, $161 per credit part-time. No tuition increase for student's term of enrollment. *Required fees:* $12 full-time, $12 per credit part-time.

Applying *Options:* electronic application. *Required:* high school transcript.

Freshman Application Contact Tammi Garlock, Retention Coordinator, Klamath Community College, 7390 So. 6th St., Klamath Falls, OR 97603. *Phone:* 541-882-3521. *Fax:* 541-885-7758. *E-mail:* garlock@klamathcc.edu. *Website:* http://www.klamathcc.edu/.

Lane Community College

Eugene, Oregon

- **State and locally supported** 2-year, founded 1964
- **Suburban** 240-acre campus
- **Coed,** 11,002 undergraduate students, 45% full-time, 51% women, 49% men

Undergraduates 4,996 full-time, 6,006 part-time. 2% Black or African American, non-Hispanic/Latino; 9% Hispanic/Latino; 1% Asian, non-Hispanic/Latino; 0.6% Native Hawaiian or other Pacific Islander, non-Hispanic/Latino; 2% American Indian or Alaska Native, non-Hispanic/Latino; 5% Two or more races, non-Hispanic/Latino; 11% Race/ethnicity unknown; 0.7% international.

Freshmen *Admission:* 9,805 enrolled.

Majors Accounting technology and bookkeeping; administrative assistant and secretarial science; airframe mechanics and aircraft maintenance technology; airline pilot and flight crew; animation, interactive technology, video graphics and special effects; autobody/collision and repair technology; automobile/automotive mechanics technology; business/commerce; child-care provision; commercial and advertising art; community organization and advocacy; computer programming; computer systems networking and telecommunications; construction engineering technology; criminal justice/law enforcement administration; dental hygiene; diesel mechanics technology; drafting and design technology; e-commerce; electrical, electronic and communications engineering technology; emergency medical technology (EMT paramedic); energy management and systems technology; general studies; hotel/motel administration; legal administrative assistant/secretary; liberal arts and sciences/liberal studies; management information systems; manufacturing engineering technology; mechanical drafting and CAD/CADD; office management; registered nursing/registered nurse; respiratory care therapy; restaurant, culinary, and catering management; sport and fitness administration/management; welding technology.

Academics *Calendar:* quarters. *Degree:* certificates and associate. *Special study options:* academic remediation for entering students, adult/continuing education programs, advanced placement credit, English as a second language, internships, part-time degree program, services for LD students, summer session for credit.

Library Lane Community College Library plus 1 other with 67,051 titles, 513 serial subscriptions, an OPAC, a Web page.

Student Life *Housing:* college housing not available. *Activities and Organizations:* drama/theater group, student-run newspaper, radio and television station, choral group. *Campus security:* 24-hour emergency

response devices and patrols, student patrols, late-night transport/escort service. *Student services:* health clinic, personal/psychological counseling, women's center, legal services.

Athletics *Intercollegiate sports:* baseball M(s), basketball M(s)/W(s), cross-country running M(s)/W(s), soccer W, track and field M(s)/W(s). *Intramural sports:* badminton M/W, basketball M/W, bowling M/W, football M/W, golf M/W, skiing (cross-country) M/W, skiing (downhill) M/W, soccer M/W, softball M/W, tennis M/W, volleyball M, weight lifting M/W.

Financial Aid Of all full-time matriculated undergraduates who enrolled in 2012, 400 Federal Work-Study jobs (averaging $3600).

Applying *Options:* early admission. *Application deadlines:* rolling (freshmen), rolling (transfers). *Notification:* continuous (freshmen), continuous (transfers).

Freshman Application Contact Lane Community College, 4000 East 30th Avenue, Eugene, OR 97405-0640. *Phone:* 541-747-4501 Ext. 2686. *Website:* http://www.lanecc.edu/.

Le Cordon Bleu College of Culinary Arts in Portland

Portland, Oregon

Admissions Office Contact Le Cordon Bleu College of Culinary Arts in Portland, 600 SW 10th Avenue, Suite 500, Portland, OR 97205. *Toll-free phone:* 888-891-6222. *Website:* http://www.chefs.edu/Portland/.

Linn-Benton Community College

Albany, Oregon

- **State and locally supported** 2-year, founded 1966
- **Small-town** 104-acre campus
- **Coed,** 5,617 undergraduate students, 46% full-time, 52% women, 48% men

Undergraduates 2,604 full-time, 3,013 part-time. 3% are from out of state; 1% Black or African American, non-Hispanic/Latino; 8% Hispanic/Latino; 2% Asian, non-Hispanic/Latino; 0.5% Native Hawaiian or other Pacific Islander, non-Hispanic/Latino; 2% American Indian or Alaska Native, non-Hispanic/Latino; 3% Two or more races, non-Hispanic/Latino; 4% Race/ethnicity unknown; 2% international; 10% transferred in. *Retention:* 55% of full-time freshmen returned.

Freshmen *Admission:* 3,282 applied, 3,268 admitted, 1,398 enrolled.

Majors Accounting technology and bookkeeping; administrative assistant and secretarial science; agricultural business and management; agriculture; animal sciences; art; automobile/automotive mechanics technology; biological and physical sciences; biology/biological sciences; business administration and management; chemistry; commercial and advertising art; computer and information sciences; criminal justice/safety; culinary arts; culinary arts related; diesel mechanics technology; drafting and design technology; dramatic/theater arts; economics; elementary education; engineering; English; family and consumer sciences/human sciences; foreign languages and literatures; horse husbandry/equine science and management; legal administrative assistant/secretary; liberal arts and sciences/liberal studies; machine tool technology; mathematics; medical administrative assistant and medical secretary; medical/clinical assistant; metallurgical technology; network and system administration; physical education teaching and coaching; physics; pre-engineering; professional, technical, business, and scientific writing; registered nursing/registered nurse; restaurant, culinary, and catering management; rhetoric and composition; teacher assistant/aide; water quality and wastewater treatment management and recycling technology; welding technology.

Academics *Calendar:* quarters. *Degree:* certificates and associate. *Special study options:* academic remediation for entering students, advanced placement credit, cooperative education, distance learning, English as a second language, independent study, internships, part-time degree program, services for LD students, student-designed majors, study abroad, summer session for credit. *ROTC:* Army (c), Navy (c), Air Force (c).

Library Linn-Benton Community College Library with 42,561 titles, 91 serial subscriptions, 8,758 audiovisual materials, an OPAC, a Web page.

Student Life *Housing:* college housing not available. *Activities and Organizations:* drama/theater group, student-run newspaper, choral group, EBOP Club, Multicultural Club, Campus Family Co-op, Horticulture Club, Collegiate Secretary Club. *Campus security:* 24-hour emergency response devices and patrols, student patrols, late-night transport/escort service. *Student services:* personal/psychological counseling.

Athletics *Intercollegiate sports:* basketball M(s), volleyball W(s). *Intramural sports:* basketball M/W, tennis M/W, ultimate Frisbee M/W, volleyball M/W.

Costs (2014–15) *Tuition:* state resident $4221 full-time, $94 per credit part-time; nonresident $9171 full-time, $204 per credit part-time. Full-time tuition and fees vary according to program. Part-time tuition and fees vary according to program. *Payment plan:* deferred payment. *Waivers:* employees or children of employees.

Financial Aid Of all full-time matriculated undergraduates who enrolled in 2012, 290 Federal Work-Study jobs (averaging $1800).

Applying *Options:* electronic application, deferred entrance. *Application fee:* $30. *Application deadlines:* rolling (freshmen), rolling (transfers).

Freshman Application Contact Ms. Kim Sullivan, Outreach Coordinator, Linn-Benton Community College, 6500 Pacific Boulevard, SW, Albany, OR 97321. *Phone:* 541-917-4847. *Fax:* 541-917-4838. *E-mail:* admissions@linnbenton.edu.
Website: http://www.linnbenton.edu/.

Mt. Hood Community College
Gresham, Oregon

Director of Admissions Dr. Craig Kolins, Associate Vice President of Enrollment Services, Mt. Hood Community College, 26000 Southeast Stark Street, Gresham, OR 97030-3300. *Phone:* 503-491-7265.
Website: http://www.mhcc.edu/.

Oregon Coast Community College
Newport, Oregon

- **Public** 2-year, founded 1987
- **Small-town** 24-acre campus
- **Coed,** 540 undergraduate students, 29% full-time, 63% women, 37% men

Undergraduates 159 full-time, 381 part-time. 1% are from out of state; 1% Black or African American, non-Hispanic/Latino; 6% Hispanic/Latino; 1% Asian, non-Hispanic/Latino; 0.2% Native Hawaiian or other Pacific Islander, non-Hispanic/Latino; 3% American Indian or Alaska Native, non-Hispanic/Latino; 5% Two or more races, non-Hispanic/Latino; 14% Race/ethnicity unknown; 17% transferred in. *Retention:* 40% of full-time freshmen returned.

Freshmen *Admission:* 169 applied, 169 admitted, 122 enrolled.

Faculty *Total:* 59, 17% full-time, 17% with terminal degrees. *Student/faculty ratio:* 11:1.

Majors Criminal justice/safety; general studies; liberal arts and sciences/liberal studies; marine biology and biological oceanography; registered nursing/registered nurse.

Academics *Calendar:* quarters. *Degree:* certificates and associate. *Special study options:* academic remediation for entering students, cooperative education, distance learning, English as a second language, honors programs, internships, part-time degree program, services for LD students, summer session for credit.

Library Oregon Coast Community College Library with 114,948 titles, 44 serial subscriptions, 2,723 audiovisual materials, an OPAC, a Web page.

Student Life *Housing:* college housing not available. *Activities and Organizations:* Psych club, Triangle club, Writing club, ASG. *Campus security:* 24-hour emergency response devices.

Standardized Tests *Required for some:* nursing entrance exam.

Costs (2013–14) *Tuition:* state resident $3564 full-time, $99 per credit part-time; nonresident $7704 full-time, $214 per credit part-time. Full-time tuition and fees vary according to course load and program. Part-time tuition and fees vary according to course load and program. *Required fees:* $252 full-time, $7 per credit part-time. *Payment plan:* deferred payment. *Waivers:* employees or children of employees.

Applying *Required for some:* essay or personal statement, 2 letters of recommendation, interview.

Freshman Application Contact Student Services, Oregon Coast Community College, 400 SE College Way, Newport, OR 97366. *Phone:* 541-265-2283. *Fax:* 541-265-3820. *E-mail:* webinfo@occc.cc.or.us.
Website: http://www.oregoncoastcc.org.

Portland Community College
Portland, Oregon

Freshman Application Contact PCC Admissions and Registration Office, Portland Community College, PO Box 19000, Portland, OR 97280. *Phone:* 503-977-8888. *Toll-free phone:* 866-922-1010.
Website: http://www.pcc.edu/.

Rogue Community College
Grants Pass, Oregon

- **State and locally supported** 2-year, founded 1970
- **Rural** 84-acre campus
- **Endowment** $6.8 million
- **Coed,** 5,530 undergraduate students, 43% full-time, 57% women, 43% men

Undergraduates 2,392 full-time, 3,138 part-time. Students come from 26 states and territories; 6 other countries; 3% are from out of state; 1% Black or African American, non-Hispanic/Latino; 13% Hispanic/Latino; 2% Asian, non-Hispanic/Latino; 0.5% Native Hawaiian or other Pacific Islander, non-Hispanic/Latino; 2% American Indian or Alaska Native, non-Hispanic/Latino; 3% Two or more races, non-Hispanic/Latino; 5% Race/ethnicity unknown; 0.1% international; 68% transferred in.

Freshmen *Admission:* 816 enrolled.

Faculty *Total:* 472, 17% full-time. *Student/faculty ratio:* 15:1.

Majors Accounting technology and bookkeeping; automobile/automotive mechanics technology; business administration and management; business/commerce; child-care and support services management; computer and information sciences; computer software technology; construction engineering technology; construction trades; criminal justice/police science; diesel mechanics technology; electrical and power transmission installation; electrical, electronic and communications engineering technology; emergency medical technology (EMT paramedic); fire prevention and safety technology; general studies; liberal arts and sciences/liberal studies; manufacturing engineering technology; marketing/marketing management; mechanics and repair; medical office computer specialist; registered nursing/registered nurse; social work; visual and performing arts; welding technology.

Academics *Calendar:* quarters. *Degree:* certificates and associate. *Special study options:* academic remediation for entering students, adult/continuing education programs, advanced placement credit, cooperative education, distance learning, double majors, English as a second language, independent study, internships, part-time degree program, services for LD students, study abroad, summer session for credit.

Library Rogue Community College Library with 33,000 titles, 275 serial subscriptions, an OPAC.

Student Life *Activities and Organizations:* drama/theater group, student-run newspaper, choral group. *Campus security:* 24-hour emergency response devices and patrols, late-night transport/escort service. *Student services:* personal/psychological counseling.

Athletics *Intramural sports:* badminton M/W, basketball M/W, soccer M/W, softball M/W, volleyball M/W.

Costs (2013–14) *Tuition:* state resident $3276 full-time, $91 per credit hour part-time; nonresident $3996 full-time, $111 per credit hour part-time. *Required fees:* $549 full-time, $4 per credit hour part-time, $135 per term part-time. *Payment plan:* installment. *Waivers:* employees or children of employees.

Financial Aid Of all full-time matriculated undergraduates who enrolled in 2013, 1,837 applied for aid, 1,628 were judged to have need, 50 had their need fully met. 64 Federal Work-Study jobs (averaging $3213). In 2013, 33 non-need-based awards were made. *Average percent of need met:* 73%. *Average financial aid package:* $9135. *Average need-based loan:* $3513. *Average need-based gift aid:* $5616. *Average non-need-based aid:* $1222.

Applying *Options:* electronic application, early admission. *Application deadlines:* rolling (freshmen), rolling (out-of-state freshmen), rolling (transfers).

Freshman Application Contact Ms. Claudia Sullivan, Director of Enrollment Services, Rogue Community College, 3345 Redwood Highway, Grants Pass, OR 97527-9291. *Phone:* 541-956-7176. *Fax:* 541-471-3585. *E-mail:* csullivan@roguecc.edu.
Website: http://www.roguecc.edu/.

Southwestern Oregon Community College
Coos Bay, Oregon

Freshman Application Contact Miss Lela Wells, Southwestern Oregon Community College, Student First Stop, 1988 Newmark Avenue, Coos Bay, OR 97420. *Phone:* 541-888-7611. *Toll-free phone:* 800-962-2838. *E-mail:* lwells@socc.edu.
Website: http://www.socc.edu/.

Sumner College
Portland, Oregon

Admissions Office Contact Sumner College, 8909 SW Barbur Boulevard, Suite 100, Portland, OR 97219.
Website: http://www.sumnercollege.edu/.

Tillamook Bay Community College
Tillamook, Oregon

Freshman Application Contact Lori Gates, Tillamook Bay Community College, 4301 Third Street, Tillamook, OR 97141. *Phone:* 503-842-8222. *Fax:* 503-842-2214. *E-mail:* gates@tillamookbay.cc.
Website: http://www.tbcc.cc.or.us/.

Treasure Valley Community College

Ontario, Oregon

- **State and locally supported** 2-year, founded 1962
- **Rural** 95-acre campus with easy access to Boise, Idaho
- **Coed,** 2,443 undergraduate students, 50% full-time, 60% women, 40% men

Undergraduates 1,212 full-time, 1,231 part-time. Students come from 14 states and territories; 2 other countries; 68% are from out of state; 2% Black or African American, non-Hispanic/Latino; 20% Hispanic/Latino; 1% Asian, non-Hispanic/Latino; 1% American Indian or Alaska Native, non-Hispanic/Latino; 18% Race/ethnicity unknown; 15% transferred in; 6% live on campus.

Freshmen *Admission:* 633 enrolled.

Faculty *Total:* 135, 39% full-time. *Student/faculty ratio:* 21:1.

Majors Agricultural business and management; agricultural economics; agriculture; agronomy and crop science; airline pilot and flight crew; animal sciences; art; athletic training; bilingual and multilingual education; biology/biological sciences; business/commerce; carpentry; chemistry; computer and information sciences; computer science; criminal justice/police science; criminal justice/safety; dental hygiene; drafting and design technology; early childhood education; elementary education; emergency medical technology (EMT paramedic); English; farm and ranch management; fire prevention and safety technology; fire science/firefighting; foreign languages and literatures; forestry; general studies; geology/earth science; health/medical preparatory programs related; history; horticultural science; legal administrative assistant/secretary; management information systems; mathematics; medical administrative assistant and medical secretary; medical radiologic technology; music; natural resources/conservation; office management; physical education teaching and coaching; physical therapy; physics; political science and government; pre-dentistry studies; pre-engineering; pre-law studies; premedical studies; prenursing studies; pre-pharmacy studies; pre-veterinary studies; psychology; range science and management; registered nursing/registered nurse; secondary education; social sciences; social work; soil science and agronomy; solar energy technology; speech communication and rhetoric; welding technology; wildlife, fish and wildlands science and management.

Academics *Calendar:* quarters. *Degree:* certificates and associate. *Special study options:* academic remediation for entering students, accelerated degree program, adult/continuing education programs, advanced placement credit, cooperative education, distance learning, English as a second language, honors programs, independent study, internships, part-time degree program, services for LD students, summer session for credit.

Library Treasure Valley Community College Library with 26,537 titles, 82 serial subscriptions, 2,134 audiovisual materials, an OPAC, a Web page.

Student Life *Housing Options:* coed. Campus housing is university owned. *Activities and Organizations:* choral group, Phi Theta Kappa, Natural Resources, International Business Club, Circle K International (Service Organization), Ag Ambassadors. *Campus security:* 24-hour emergency response devices, late-night transport/escort service, controlled dormitory access, Emergency response phone and computer notifications.

Athletics *Intercollegiate sports:* baseball M(s), basketball M(s)/W(s), cross-country running M(s)/W(s), soccer M(s)/W(s), softball W(s), tennis M(s)/W(s), track and field M(s)/W(s), volleyball W(s). *Intramural sports:* basketball M/W, bowling M/W, softball M/W, table tennis M/W, ultimate Frisbee M/W, volleyball M/W.

Financial Aid Of all full-time matriculated undergraduates who enrolled in 2012, 90 Federal Work-Study jobs (averaging $1500).

Applying *Options:* electronic application, early admission, deferred entrance. *Application deadlines:* rolling (freshmen), rolling (out-of-state freshmen), rolling (transfers). *Notification:* continuous (freshmen), continuous (out-of-state freshmen), continuous (transfers).

Freshman Application Contact Christina Coyne, Office of Admissions and Student Services, Treasure Valley Community College, 650 College Boulevard, Ontario, OR 97914. *Phone:* 541-881-5822. *E-mail:* ccoyne@tvcc.cc.

Website: http://www.tvcc.cc/.

Umpqua Community College

Roseburg, Oregon

- **State and locally supported** 2-year, founded 1964
- **Rural** 100-acre campus
- **Endowment** $4.5 million
- **Coed,** 2,114 undergraduate students, 43% full-time, 58% women, 42% men

Undergraduates 899 full-time, 1,215 part-time. Students come from 11 states and territories; 1% Black or African American, non-Hispanic/Latino; 6% Hispanic/Latino; 1% Asian, non-Hispanic/Latino; 0.2% Native Hawaiian or other Pacific Islander, non-Hispanic/Latino; 2% American Indian or Alaska Native, non-Hispanic/Latino; 4% Two or more races, non-Hispanic/Latino; 3% Race/ethnicity unknown; 14% transferred in. *Retention:* 47% of full-time freshmen returned.

Freshmen *Admission:* 145 applied, 145 admitted, 145 enrolled.

Faculty *Total:* 209, 31% full-time. *Student/faculty ratio:* 19:1.

Majors Accounting; administrative assistant and secretarial science; agriculture; anthropology; art; art history, criticism and conservation; art teacher education; automobile/automotive mechanics technology; behavioral sciences; biological and physical sciences; biology/biological sciences; business administration and management; chemistry; child development; civil engineering technology; computer engineering technology; computer science; cosmetology; criminal justice/law enforcement administration; desktop publishing and digital imaging design; dramatic/theater arts; economics; education; electrical, electronic and communications engineering technology; elementary education; emergency medical technology (EMT paramedic); engineering; English; fire science/firefighting; forestry; health teacher education; history; humanities; human resources management; journalism; kindergarten/preschool education; legal administrative assistant/secretary; liberal arts and sciences/liberal studies; marketing/marketing management; mathematics; medical administrative assistant and medical secretary; music; music teacher education; natural sciences; physical education teaching and coaching; physical sciences; political science and government; pre-engineering; psychology; registered nursing/registered nurse; social sciences; social work; sociology.

Academics *Calendar:* quarters. *Degree:* certificates and associate. *Special study options:* academic remediation for entering students, accelerated degree program, adult/continuing education programs, advanced placement credit, cooperative education, distance learning, English as a second language, honors programs, independent study, internships, part-time degree program, services for LD students, study abroad, summer session for credit.

Library Umpqua Community College Library with 41,000 titles, 350 serial subscriptions, an OPAC, a Web page.

Student Life *Housing:* college housing not available. *Activities and Organizations:* drama/theater group, student-run newspaper, choral group, Phi Theta Kappa, Computer Club, Phi Beta Lambda, Nursing Club, Umpqua Accounting Associates. *Campus security:* 24-hour emergency response devices and patrols. *Student services:* personal/psychological counseling.

Athletics *Intercollegiate sports:* basketball M(s)/W(s), volleyball W(s). *Intramural sports:* basketball M/W.

Costs (2014–15) *Tuition:* state resident $4163 full-time; nonresident $9428 full-time. *Required fees:* $302 full-time. *Waivers:* employees or children of employees.

Financial Aid Of all full-time matriculated undergraduates who enrolled in 2012, 120 Federal Work-Study jobs (averaging $3000).

Applying *Options:* electronic application, early admission, deferred entrance. *Application fee:* $25. *Recommended:* high school transcript. *Application deadlines:* rolling (freshmen), rolling (transfers).

Freshman Application Contact Admissions Office, Umpqua Community College, PO Box 967, Roseburg, OR 97470-0226. *Phone:* 541-440-7743. *Fax:* 541-440-4612.

Website: http://www.umpqua.edu/.

PENNSYLVANIA

Antonelli Institute

Erdenheim, Pennsylvania

- **Proprietary** 2-year, founded 1938
- **Suburban** 15-acre campus with easy access to Philadelphia
- **Coed,** 176 undergraduate students
- **90%** of applicants were admitted

Freshmen *Admission:* 249 applied, 224 admitted.

Majors Graphic design; photography.

Academics *Calendar:* semesters. *Degree:* associate.

Financial Aid Of all full-time matriculated undergraduates who enrolled in 2012, 5 Federal Work-Study jobs (averaging $2000).

Freshman Application Contact Admissions Office, Antonelli Institute, 300 Montgomery Avenue, Erdenheim, PA 19038. *Phone:* 800-722-7871. *Toll-free phone:* 800-722-7871.

Website: http://www.antonelli.edu/.

Berks Technical Institute

Wyomissing, Pennsylvania

Freshman Application Contact Mr. Allan Brussolo, Academic Dean, Berks Technical Institute, 2205 Ridgewood Road, Wyomissing, PA 19610-1168.

Phone: 610-372-1722. *Toll-free phone:* 866-591-8384. *Fax:* 610-376-4684. *E-mail:* abrussolo@berks.edu. *Website:* http://www.berks.edu/.

Bidwell Training Center
Pittsburgh, Pennsylvania

Freshman Application Contact Admissions Office, Bidwell Training Center, 1815 Metropolitan Street, Pittsburgh, PA 15233. *Phone:* 412-322-1773. *Toll-free phone:* 800-516-1800. *E-mail:* admissions@mcg-btc.org. *Website:* http://www.bidwell-training.org/.

Bradford School
Pittsburgh, Pennsylvania

- **Private** 2-year, founded 1968
- **Urban** campus
- **Coed,** 387 undergraduate students
- 86% of applicants were admitted

Freshmen *Admission:* 839 applied, 725 admitted.

Majors Accounting technology and bookkeeping; administrative assistant and secretarial science; computer programming; computer systems networking and telecommunications; dental assisting; graphic design; hotel/motel administration; legal administrative assistant/secretary; legal assistant/paralegal; medical/clinical assistant; retailing.

Academics *Degree:* diplomas and associate.

Freshman Application Contact Admissions Office, Bradford School, 125 West Station Square Drive, Pittsburgh, PA 15219. *Phone:* 412-391-6710. *Toll-free phone:* 800-391-6810. *Website:* http://www.bradfordpittsburgh.edu/.

Bucks County Community College
Newtown, Pennsylvania

- **County-supported** 2-year, founded 1964
- **Suburban** 200-acre campus with easy access to Philadelphia
- **Endowment** $5.5 million
- **Coed,** 9,880 undergraduate students, 33% full-time, 55% women, 45% men

Undergraduates 3,260 full-time, 6,620 part-time. Students come from 12 states and territories; 1% are from out of state; 5% Black or African American, non-Hispanic/Latino; 5% Hispanic/Latino; 2% Asian, non-Hispanic/Latino; 0.1% Native Hawaiian or other Pacific Islander, non-Hispanic/Latino; 0.9% American Indian or Alaska Native, non-Hispanic/Latino; 2% Two or more races, non-Hispanic/Latino; 22% Race/ethnicity unknown; 0.3% international; 74% transferred in. *Retention:* 65% of full-time freshmen returned.

Freshmen *Admission:* 4,960 applied, 4,813 admitted, 2,345 enrolled.

Faculty *Total:* 575, 27% full-time, 27% with terminal degrees. *Student/faculty ratio:* 21:1.

Majors Accounting technology and bookkeeping; American studies; baking and pastry arts; biology/biotechnology laboratory technician; biology teacher education; biotechnology; building/home/construction inspection; business administration and management; business/commerce; business, management, and marketing related; cabinetmaking and millwork; chemical technology; chemistry teacher education; child-care provision; cinematography and film/video production; commercial and advertising art; commercial photography; computer and information sciences; computer programming (specific applications); computer systems networking and telecommunications; corrections; criminal justice/law enforcement administration; criminal justice/safety; crisis/emergency/disaster management; culinary arts; dramatic/theater arts; early childhood education; education; engineering technology; environmental science; fire prevention and safety technology; food service systems administration; health professions related; history teacher education; human development and family studies; humanities; industrial technology; information science/studies; journalism; legal professions and studies related; liberal arts and sciences and humanities related; liberal arts and sciences/liberal studies; mathematics; mathematics teacher education; medical/clinical assistant; medical insurance coding; multi/interdisciplinary studies related; music; network and system administration; neuroscience; physical education teaching and coaching; precision production trades; psychology; registered nursing/registered nurse; retailing; speech communication and rhetoric; sport and fitness administration/management; tourism and travel services management; visual and performing arts; web page, digital/multimedia and information resources design; women's studies.

Academics *Calendar:* semesters. *Degree:* certificates and associate. *Special study options:* academic remediation for entering students, adult/continuing education programs, advanced placement credit, cooperative education, distance learning, English as a second language, external degree program, independent study, internships, part-time degree program, services for LD students, student-designed majors, summer session for credit.

Library Bucks County Community College Library with 131,156 titles, 268 serial subscriptions, 1,828 audiovisual materials, an OPAC, a Web page.

Student Life *Housing:* college housing not available. *Activities and Organizations:* drama/theater group, student-run newspaper, radio and television station, choral group, Phi Theta Kappa, Inter-Varsity Christian Fellowship, Drama Club, Habitat for Humanity, Future Teachers Organization. *Campus security:* 24-hour emergency response devices and patrols, late-night transport/escort service. *Student services:* personal/psychological counseling, women's center.

Athletics Member NJCAA. *Intercollegiate sports:* baseball M, basketball M/W, equestrian sports M/W, golf M, soccer M/W, tennis M/W, volleyball W. *Intramural sports:* basketball M/W, soccer M/W, tennis M/W, ultimate Frisbee M/W, volleyball W.

Costs (2013–14) *Tuition:* area resident $3690 full-time, $123 per credit hour part-time; state resident $7380 full-time, $246 per credit hour part-time; nonresident $11,070 full-time, $369 per credit hour part-time. Full-time tuition and fees vary according to program. Part-time tuition and fees vary according to program. *Required fees:* $1130 full-time, $61 per credit hour part-time. *Payment plans:* installment, deferred payment. *Waivers:* senior citizens and employees or children of employees.

Applying *Options:* electronic application, early admission. *Required:* high school transcript. *Required for some:* essay or personal statement, interview.

Freshman Application Contact Ms. Marlene Barlow, Director of Admissions, Bucks County Community College, Newtown, PA 18940. *Phone:* 215-968-8137. *Fax:* 215-968-8110. *E-mail:* marlene.barlow@bucks.edu. *Website:* http://www.bucks.edu/.

Butler County Community College
Butler, Pennsylvania

- **County-supported** 2-year, founded 1965
- **Rural** 300-acre campus with easy access to Pittsburgh
- **Coed,** 3,686 undergraduate students, 44% full-time, 59% women, 41% men

Undergraduates 1,615 full-time, 2,071 part-time. 1% are from out of state; 3% Black or African American, non-Hispanic/Latino; 1% Hispanic/Latino; 0.6% Asian, non-Hispanic/Latino; 0.3% American Indian or Alaska Native, non-Hispanic/Latino; 1% Two or more races, non-Hispanic/Latino; 9% Race/ethnicity unknown; 0.1% international.

Faculty *Total:* 359, 18% full-time. *Student/faculty ratio:* 18:1.

Majors Administrative assistant and secretarial science; architectural drafting and CAD/CADD; biology/biological sciences; business administration and management; business/commerce; business, management, and marketing related; CAD/CADD drafting/design technology; civil engineering technology; computer and information sciences; computer and information systems security; computer programming (specific applications); computer technology/computer systems technology; cooking and related culinary arts; corrections; cosmetology; criminal justice/law enforcement administration; criminal justice/police science; digital communication and media/multimedia; education; electrical, electronic and communications engineering technology; elementary education; engineering; English; fine arts related; fire science/firefighting; food service systems administration; food technology and processing; general studies; health and medical administrative services related; health/health-care administration; heating, air conditioning, ventilation and refrigeration maintenance technology; homeland security; homeland security, law enforcement, firefighting and protective services related; hospitality administration related; human resources management; instrumentation technology; kindergarten/preschool education; legal administrative assistant/secretary; machine shop technology; machine tool technology; manufacturing engineering technology; massage therapy; mathematics; mechanical drafting and CAD/CADD; medical insurance coding; medical office assistant; network and system administration; office occupations and clerical services; organizational communication; parks, recreation and leisure facilities management; photography; physical sciences; physical therapy technology; precision production trades; psychology; radiologic technology/science; registered nursing/registered nurse; robotics technology; selling skills and sales; social work related; sport and fitness administration/management; web page, digital/multimedia and information resources design.

Academics *Calendar:* semesters. *Degree:* certificates, diplomas, and associate. *Special study options:* academic remediation for entering students, adult/continuing education programs, advanced placement credit, cooperative education, distance learning, English as a second language, internships, part-time degree program, services for LD students, summer session for credit.

Library John A. Beck, Jr. Library with 70,000 titles, 305 serial subscriptions.

Student Life *Housing:* college housing not available. *Activities and Organizations:* student-run newspaper. *Campus security:* 24-hour emergency response devices, late-night transport/escort service. *Student services:* personal/psychological counseling.

Athletics Member NJCAA. *Intercollegiate sports:* baseball M, basketball M, golf M/W, softball W, volleyball W. *Intramural sports:* basketball M/W, table tennis M/W, volleyball M/W.

Financial Aid Of all full-time matriculated undergraduates who enrolled in 2012, 65 Federal Work-Study jobs (averaging $1545).

Applying *Options:* electronic application. *Application fee:* $25. *Required:* high school transcript. *Required for some:* interview. *Application deadlines:* 8/15 (freshmen), 8/15 (transfers). *Notification:* continuous until 8/15 (freshmen), continuous until 8/15 (transfers).

Freshman Application Contact Ms. Patricia Bajuszik, Director of Admissions, Butler County Community College, College Drive, PO Box 1205, Butler, PA 16003-1203. *Phone:* 724-287-8711 Ext. 344. *Toll-free phone:* 888-826-2829. *Fax:* 724-287-4961. *E-mail:* pattie.bajuszik@bc3.edu. *Website:* http://www.bc3.edu/.

Cambria-Rowe Business College
Indiana, Pennsylvania

- **Proprietary** 2-year, founded 1959
- **Small-town** 1-acre campus
- **Coed,** 105 undergraduate students, 100% full-time, 80% women, 20% men
- 78% of applicants were admitted

Undergraduates 105 full-time. 2% Black or African American, non-Hispanic/Latino; 4% Two or more races, non-Hispanic/Latino.

Freshmen *Admission:* 65 applied, 51 admitted, 28 enrolled.

Faculty *Total:* 8, 100% full-time, 38% with terminal degrees. *Student/faculty ratio:* 13:1.

Majors Accounting; administrative assistant and secretarial science; business administration and management; computer and information sciences and support services related; computer technology/computer systems technology; legal administrative assistant/secretary; medical office assistant.

Academics *Calendar:* quarters. *Degree:* diplomas and associate.

Library LIRN.

Student Life *Housing:* college housing not available.

Costs (2014–15) *Comprehensive fee:* $21,692 includes full-time tuition ($13,000), mandatory fees ($1330), and room and board ($7362). Full-time tuition and fees vary according to course load. Part-time tuition and fees vary according to course load. *Room and board:* Room and board charges vary according to housing facility and location. *Payment plan:* installment. *Waivers:* employees or children of employees.

Freshman Application Contact Mrs. Stacey Bell-Leger, Representative at Indiana Campus, Cambria-Rowe Business College, 422 South 13th Street, Indiana, PA 15701. *Phone:* 724-463-0222. *Toll-free phone:* 800-NEW-CAREER. *Fax:* 724-463-7246. *E-mail:* sbell-leger@crbc.net. *Website:* http://www.crbc.net/.

Cambria-Rowe Business College
Johnstown, Pennsylvania

- **Proprietary** 2-year, founded 1891
- **Small-town** campus with easy access to Pittsburgh
- **Coed, primarily women,** 142 undergraduate students, 99% full-time, 85% women, 15% men

Undergraduates 141 full-time, 1 part-time. 9% Black or African American, non-Hispanic/Latino; 0.7% American Indian or Alaska Native, non-Hispanic/Latino; 2% Two or more races, non-Hispanic/Latino. *Retention:* 50% of full-time freshmen returned.

Freshmen *Admission:* 80 applied, 72 admitted, 42 enrolled.

Faculty *Total:* 10, 100% full-time. *Student/faculty ratio:* 13:1.

Majors Accounting; administrative assistant and secretarial science; business administration and management; computer support specialist; computer technology/computer systems technology; health services/allied health/health sciences; legal administrative assistant/secretary; management information systems; management science; medical administrative assistant and medical secretary.

Academics *Calendar:* quarters. *Degree:* associate. *Special study options:* accelerated degree program, advanced placement credit, part-time degree program, summer session for credit.

Student Life *Housing:* college housing not available.

Costs (2014–15) *Comprehensive fee:* $21,642 includes full-time tuition ($12,950), mandatory fees ($1330), and room and board ($7362). Full-time tuition and fees vary according to course load. Part-time tuition and fees vary according to course load. *Required fees:* $1330 per degree program part-time. *Room and board:* Room and board charges vary according to housing facility and location. *Payment plan:* installment. *Waivers:* employees or children of employees.

Financial Aid *Financial aid deadline:* 8/1.

Applying *Options:* electronic application, early admission. *Application fee:* $15. *Required:* high school transcript, entrance exam. *Recommended:*

interview. *Application deadline:* rolling (freshmen). *Notification:* continuous (freshmen).

Freshman Application Contact Mrs. Riley McDonald, Admissions Representative, Cambria-Rowe Business College, 221 Central Avenue, Johnstown, PA 15902-2494. *Phone:* 814-536-5168. *Toll-free phone:* 800-NEWCAREER. *Fax:* 814-536-5160. *E-mail:* admissions@crbc.net. *Website:* http://www.crbc.net/.

Career Training Academy
Monroeville, Pennsylvania

Freshman Application Contact Career Training Academy, 4314 Old William Penn Highway, Suite 103, Monroeville, PA 15146. *Phone:* 412-372-3900. *Toll-free phone:* 866-673-7773. *Website:* http://www.careerta.edu/.

Career Training Academy
New Kensington, Pennsylvania

Freshman Application Contact Career Training Academy, 950 Fifth Avenue, New Kensington, PA 15068-6301. *Phone:* 724-337-1000. *Toll-free phone:* 866-673-7773. *Website:* http://www.careerta.edu/.

Career Training Academy
Pittsburgh, Pennsylvania

- **Proprietary** 2-year
- **Suburban** campus with easy access to Pittsburgh
- **Coed**

Undergraduates 70 full-time. Students come from 1 other state; 33% Black or African American, non-Hispanic/Latino; 4% Hispanic/Latino; 1% Native Hawaiian or other Pacific Islander, non-Hispanic/Latino.

Faculty *Student/faculty ratio:* 9:1.

Academics *Calendar:* continuous. *Degree:* diplomas and associate. *Special study options:* academic remediation for entering students, advanced placement credit, cooperative education, internships, services for LD students.

Student Life *Campus security:* 24-hour emergency response devices, late-night transport/escort service.

Costs (2013–14) *Tuition:* $12,218 full-time. Full-time tuition and fees vary according to program. No tuition increase for student's term of enrollment. *Payment plans:* tuition prepayment, installment.

Applying *Application fee:* $30. *Required:* essay or personal statement, high school transcript, minimum 1.5 GPA, interview.

Freshman Application Contact Jaimie Vignone, Career Training Academy, 1500 Northway Mall, Suite 200, Pittsburgh, PA 15237. *Phone:* 412-367-4000. *Toll-free phone:* 866-673-7773. *Fax:* 412-369-7223. *E-mail:* admission3@careerta.edu. *Website:* http://www.careerta.edu/.

Commonwealth Technical Institute
Johnstown, Pennsylvania

- **State-supported** 2-year
- **Suburban** 12-acre campus
- **Coed,** 208 undergraduate students, 100% full-time, 36% women, 64% men

Undergraduates 208 full-time. 1% are from out of state. *Retention:* 64% of full-time freshmen returned.

Freshmen *Admission:* 32 enrolled.

Faculty *Total:* 27, 100% full-time. *Student/faculty ratio:* 15:1.

Majors Architectural drafting and CAD/CADD; computer technology/computer systems technology; culinary arts; dental laboratory technology; mechanical drafting and CAD/CADD; medical office assistant.

Academics *Calendar:* trimesters. *Degree:* diplomas and associate. *Special study options:* academic remediation for entering students, advanced placement credit, services for LD students.

Library Commonwealth Technical Institute at the Hiram G. Andrews Center Library with 5,000 titles, 55 serial subscriptions, 470 audiovisual materials.

Student Life *Housing Options:* men-only, women-only, special housing for students with disabilities. Campus housing is university owned. *Activities and Organizations:* drama/theater group, choral group. *Campus security:* 24-hour patrols, controlled dormitory access. *Student services:* health clinic, personal/psychological counseling.

Costs (2014–15) *Tuition:* state resident $11,224 full-time. *Room and board:* $4758. *Payment plan:* installment.

Financial Aid Of all full-time matriculated undergraduates who enrolled in 2011, 403 applied for aid, 259 were judged to have need. 35 Federal Work-Study jobs (averaging $1000). *Average percent of need met:* 30%. *Average financial aid package:* $2500. *Average need-based gift aid:* $2500.

Applying *Required for some:* high school transcript. *Recommended:* high school transcript. *Application deadline:* rolling (freshmen). *Notification:* continuous (freshmen).

Freshman Application Contact Mr. Jason Gies, Admissions Supervisor, Commonwealth Technical Institute, Commonwealth Technical Institute @ Hiram G. Andrews Center, 727 Goucher Street, Johnstown, PA 15905. *Phone:* 814-255-8200 Ext. 0564. *Toll-free phone:* 800-762-4211. *Fax:* 814-255-8283. *E-mail:* rhalza@state.pa.us.
Website: http://www.portal.state.pa.us/portal/server.pt/community/commonwealth_technical_institute/10361.

Community College of Allegheny County
Pittsburgh, Pennsylvania

- **County-supported** 2-year, founded 1966
- **Urban** 242-acre campus
- **Coed,** 18,207 undergraduate students, 35% full-time, 57% women, 43% men

Undergraduates 6,309 full-time, 11,898 part-time. 2% are from out of state.
Freshmen *Admission:* 3,931 enrolled.

Majors Accounting technology and bookkeeping; administrative assistant and secretarial science; airline pilot and flight crew; applied horticulture/horticulture operations; architectural drafting and CAD/CADD; art; athletic training; automotive engineering technology; aviation/airway management; banking and financial support services; biology/biological sciences; building/property maintenance; business administration and management; business automation/technology/data entry; business machine repair; carpentry; chemical technology; chemistry; child-care provision; child development; civil drafting and CAD/CADD; civil engineering technology; clinical/medical laboratory technology; commercial and advertising art; communications technologies and support services related; community health services counseling; computer engineering technology; computer systems networking and telecommunications; computer technology/computer systems technology; construction engineering technology; construction trades related; corrections; cosmetology and personal grooming arts related; court reporting; criminal justice/police science; culinary arts; diagnostic medical sonography and ultrasound technology; dietitian assistant; drafting and design technology; drafting/design engineering technologies related; dramatic/theater arts; education (specific levels and methods) related; education (specific subject areas) related; electrical, electronic and communications engineering technology; electroneurodiagnostic/electroencephalographic technology; energy management and systems technology; engineering technologies and engineering related; English; entrepreneurship; environmental engineering technology; fire prevention and safety technology; food service systems administration; foreign languages and literatures; general studies; greenhouse management; health and physical education/fitness; health information/medical records technology; health professions related; health unit coordinator/ward clerk; heating, air conditioning, ventilation and refrigeration maintenance technology; hotel/motel administration; housing and human environments related; human development and family studies related; humanities; human resources management; industrial technology; insurance; journalism; landscaping and groundskeeping; legal administrative assistant/secretary; legal assistant/paralegal; liberal arts and sciences/liberal studies; licensed practical/vocational nurse training; machine shop technology; management information systems; marketing/marketing management; mathematics; mechanical drafting and CAD/CADD; medical administrative assistant and medical secretary; medical/clinical assistant; medical radiologic technology; music; nuclear medical technology; nursing assistant/aide and patient care assistant/aide; occupational therapist assistant; office management; ornamental horticulture; perioperative/operating room and surgical nursing; pharmacy technician; physical therapy technology; physics; plant nursery management; psychiatric/mental health services technology; psychology; quality control technology; real estate; registered nursing/registered nurse; respiratory care therapy; restaurant, culinary, and catering management; retailing; robotics technology; science technologies related; sheet metal technology; sign language interpretation and translation; social sciences; social work; sociology; solar energy technology; substance abuse/addiction counseling; surgical technology; therapeutic recreation; tourism promotion; turf and turfgrass management; visual and performing arts related; welding technology.

Academics *Calendar:* semesters. *Degree:* certificates, diplomas, and associate. *Special study options:* part-time degree program.
Library Community College of Allegheny County Library.
Student Life *Housing:* college housing not available. *Campus security:* 24-hour emergency response devices and patrols, late-night transport/escort service.
Athletics Member NJCAA. *Intercollegiate sports:* baseball M, basketball M/W, bowling M/W, golf M/W, ice hockey M, softball W, table tennis M/W, tennis M/W, volleyball W. *Intramural sports:* badminton M/W, basketball M/W, bowling M/W, cross-country running M/W, football M, golf M/W, lacrosse M, racquetball M/W, softball M/W, table tennis M/W, tennis M/W, volleyball M/W, weight lifting M/W.

Costs (2013–14) *Tuition:* area resident $2993 full-time, $100 per credit part-time; state resident $5985 full-time, $200 per credit part-time; nonresident $8978 full-time, $299 per credit part-time. Full-time tuition and fees vary according to program. Part-time tuition and fees vary according to program. *Required fees:* $548 full-time, $27 per credit part-time, $20 per course part-time. *Payment plan:* installment. *Waivers:* senior citizens and employees or children of employees.

Applying *Options:* early decision, early action. *Recommended:* high school transcript.
Freshman Application Contact Admissions Office, Community College of Allegheny County, 808 Ridge Avenue, Pittsburgh, PA 15212. *Phone:* 412-237-2511.
Website: http://www.ccac.edu/.

Community College of Beaver County
Monaca, Pennsylvania

- **State-supported** 2-year, founded 1966
- **Small-town** 75-acre campus with easy access to Pittsburgh
- **Coed**

Undergraduates 2% are from out of state.
Faculty *Student/faculty ratio:* 16:1.
Academics *Calendar:* semesters. *Degree:* certificates, diplomas, and associate. *Special study options:* academic remediation for entering students, adult/continuing education programs, advanced placement credit, cooperative education, distance learning, double majors, independent study, internships, off-campus study, part-time degree program, services for LD students, summer session for credit.
Student Life *Campus security:* 24-hour emergency response devices and patrols, late-night transport/escort service.
Athletics Member NJCAA.
Applying *Options:* early admission. *Required:* interview. *Recommended:* high school transcript.
Freshman Application Contact Enrollment Management, Community College of Beaver County, One Campus Drive, Monaca, PA 15061-2588. *Phone:* 724-480-3500. *Toll-free phone:* 800-335-0222. *E-mail:* admissions@ccbc.edu.
Website: http://www.ccbc.edu/.

Community College of Philadelphia
Philadelphia, Pennsylvania

- **State and locally supported** 2-year, founded 1964
- **Urban** 14-acre campus
- **Coed,** 39,500 undergraduate students

Undergraduates Students come from 50 other countries.
Faculty *Total:* 1,109, 39% full-time.
Majors Accounting; architectural engineering technology; art; automobile/automotive mechanics technology; business administration and management; chemical technology; clinical/medical laboratory technology; computer science; construction engineering technology; criminal justice/law enforcement administration; culinary arts; dental hygiene; drafting and design technology; education; engineering; engineering technology; facilities planning and management; finance; fire science/firefighting; forensic science and technology; health information/medical records administration; health professions related; hotel/motel administration; human services; kindergarten/preschool education; liberal arts and sciences/liberal studies; medical administrative assistant and medical secretary; medical radiologic technology; mental health counseling; music; occupational therapist assistant; photography; pre-engineering; psychology; recording arts technology; registered nursing/registered nurse; respiratory care therapy; sign language interpretation and translation.
Academics *Calendar:* semesters. *Degree:* certificates, diplomas, and associate. *Special study options:* academic remediation for entering students, accelerated degree program, adult/continuing education programs, advanced placement credit, cooperative education, distance learning, English as a second language, external degree program, honors programs, independent study, internships, off-campus study, part-time degree program, services for LD students, student-designed majors, study abroad, summer session for credit. *ROTC:* Army (c).
Library Main Campus Library plus 2 others with 110,000 titles, 420 serial subscriptions, an OPAC, a Web page.
Student Life *Housing:* college housing not available. *Activities and Organizations:* drama/theater group, student-run newspaper, choral group, Philadelphia L.E.A.D.S, Phi Theta Kappa, Student Government Association, Vanguard Student Newspaper, Fundraising Club. *Campus security:* 24-hour emergency response devices and patrols, phone/alert systems in

classrooms/buildings. *Student services:* personal/psychological counseling, women's center.

Athletics *Intercollegiate sports:* baseball M, basketball M/W, cheerleading M/W, cross-country running M/W, soccer M, tennis M/W, track and field M/W, volleyball M/W. *Intramural sports:* basketball M/W, soccer M/W, tennis M/W, track and field M/W, volleyball M/W.

Costs (2013–14) *Tuition:* area resident $5100 full-time, $153 per credit hour part-time; state resident $9070 full-time, $306 per credit hour part-time; nonresident $13,040 full-time, $459 per credit hour part-time. Full-time tuition and fees vary according to program. Part-time tuition and fees vary according to program. *Payment plan:* installment. *Waivers:* senior citizens and employees or children of employees.

Applying *Options:* electronic application, early admission, deferred entrance. *Application fee:* $20. *Required for some:* high school transcript, allied health and nursing programs have specific entry requirements. *Application deadlines:* rolling (freshmen), rolling (transfers). *Notification:* continuous (freshmen), continuous (transfers).

Freshman Application Contact Community College of Philadelphia, 1700 Spring Garden Street, Philadelphia, PA 19130-3991. *Phone:* 215-751-8010. *Website:* http://www.ccp.edu/.

Consolidated School of Business
Lancaster, Pennsylvania

Freshman Application Contact Ms. Libby Paul, Admissions Representative, Consolidated School of Business, 2124 Ambassador Circle, Lancaster, PA 17603. *Phone:* 717-394-6211. *Toll-free phone:* 800-541-8298. *Fax:* 717-394-6213. *E-mail:* lpaul@csb.edu. *Website:* http://www.csb.edu/.

Consolidated School of Business
York, Pennsylvania

Freshman Application Contact Ms. Sandra Swanger, Admissions Representative, Consolidated School of Business, 1605 Clugston Road, York, PA 17404. *Phone:* 717-764-9550. *Toll-free phone:* 800-520-0691. *Fax:* 717-764-9469. *E-mail:* sswanger@csb.edu. *Website:* http://www.csb.edu/.

Dean Institute of Technology
Pittsburgh, Pennsylvania

Director of Admissions Mr. Richard D. Ali, Admissions Director, Dean Institute of Technology, 1501 West Liberty Avenue, Pittsburgh, PA 15226-1103. *Phone:* 412-531-4433. *Website:* http://www.deantech.edu/.

Delaware County Community College
Media, Pennsylvania

Freshman Application Contact Ms. Hope Diehl, Director of Admissions and Enrollment Services, Delaware County Community College, 901 South Media Line Road, Media, PA 19063-1094. *Phone:* 610-359-5050. *Fax:* 610-723-1530. *E-mail:* admiss@dccc.edu. *Website:* http://www.dccc.edu/.

Douglas Education Center
Monessen, Pennsylvania

Freshman Application Contact Ms. Sherry Lee Walters, Director of Enrollment Services, Douglas Education Center, 130 Seventh Street, Monessen, PA 15062. *Phone:* 724-684-3684 Ext. 2181. *Toll-free phone:* 800-413-6013. *Website:* http://www.dec.edu/.

DuBois Business College
DuBois, Pennsylvania

Director of Admissions Terry Khoury, Director of Admissions, DuBois Business College, 1 Beaver Drive, DuBois, PA 15801-2401. *Phone:* 814-371-6920. *Toll-free phone:* 800-692-6213. *Fax:* 814-371-3947. *E-mail:* dotylj@dbcollege.com. *Website:* http://www.dbcollege.com/.

Erie Business Center, Main
Erie, Pennsylvania

Freshman Application Contact Erie Business Center, Main, 246 West Ninth Street, Erie, PA 16501-1392. *Phone:* 814-456-7504. *Toll-free phone:* 800-352-3743. *Website:* http://www.eriebc.edu/.

Erie Business Center, South
New Castle, Pennsylvania

Freshman Application Contact Erie Business Center, South, 170 Cascade Galleria, New Castle, PA 16101-3950. *Phone:* 724-658-9066. *Toll-free phone:* 800-722-6227. *E-mail:* admissions@eriebcs.com. *Website:* http://www.eriebc.edu/newcastle/.

Erie Institute of Technology
Erie, Pennsylvania

Freshman Application Contact Erie Institute of Technology, 940 Millcreek Mall, Erie, PA 16565. *Phone:* 814-868-9900. *Toll-free phone:* 866-868-3743. *Website:* http://www.erieit.edu/.

Everest Institute
Pittsburgh, Pennsylvania

Director of Admissions Director of Admissions, Everest Institute, 100 Forbes Avenue, Suite 1200, Pittsburgh, PA 15222. *Phone:* 412-261-4520. *Toll-free phone:* 888-741-4270. *Fax:* 412-261-4546. *Website:* http://www.everest.edu/.

Fortis Institute
Erie, Pennsylvania

Director of Admissions Guy M. Euliano, President, Fortis Institute, 5757 West 26th Street, Erie, PA 16506. *Phone:* 814-838-7673. *Fax:* 814-838-8642. *E-mail:* geuliano@tsbi.org. *Website:* http://www.fortis.edu/.

Fortis Institute
Forty Fort, Pennsylvania

Freshman Application Contact Admissions Office, Fortis Institute, 166 Slocum Street, Forty Fort, PA 18704. *Phone:* 570-288-8400. *Website:* http://www.fortis.edu/.

Harcum College
Bryn Mawr, Pennsylvania

Freshman Application Contact Office of Enrollment Management, Harcum College, 750 Montgomery Avenue, Bryn Mawr, PA 19010-3476. *Phone:* 610-526-6050. *E-mail:* enroll@harcum.edu. *Website:* http://www.harcum.edu/.

Harrisburg Area Community College
Harrisburg, Pennsylvania

- **State and locally supported** 2-year, founded 1964
- **Urban** 212-acre campus
- **Coed,** 20,780 undergraduate students, 31% full-time, 63% women, 37% men

Undergraduates 6,506 full-time, 14,274 part-time. 1% are from out of state; 13% Black or African American, non-Hispanic/Latino; 10% Hispanic/Latino; 3% Asian, non-Hispanic/Latino; 0.2% Native Hawaiian or other Pacific Islander, non-Hispanic/Latino; 0.4% American Indian or Alaska Native, non-Hispanic/Latino; 2% Two or more races, non-Hispanic/Latino; 1% Race/ethnicity unknown; 2% international; 6% transferred in.

Freshmen *Admission:* 9,624 applied, 9,579 admitted, 2,051 enrolled.

Faculty *Total:* 1,085, 31% full-time, 60% with terminal degrees. *Student/faculty ratio:* 19:1.

Majors Accounting and business/management; accounting technology and bookkeeping; administrative assistant and secretarial science; agribusiness; architectural engineering technology; architecture; art; automobile/automotive mechanics technology; banking and financial support services; biology/biological sciences; building/home/construction inspection; business administration and management; business/commerce; cabinetmaking and millwork; cardiovascular technology; chemistry; civil engineering technology; clinical/medical laboratory technology; computer and information sciences; computer and information systems security; computer installation and repair technology; computer science; computer systems networking and telecommunications; construction engineering technology; construction trades; court reporting; crafts, folk art and artisanry; criminalistics and criminal science; criminal justice/law enforcement administration; criminal justice/police science; culinary arts; dental hygiene; design and visual communications; diagnostic medical sonography and ultrasound technology; dietetics; dramatic/theater arts; early childhood education; electrical, electronic and communications engineering technology; electrician; emergency medical technology (EMT paramedic); energy management and systems technology; engineering; engineering technologies and engineering related; environmental science; environmental studies; fire science/firefighting; food service systems administration; general studies; geographic information science and cartography; graphic design; health/health-care administration; health services administration; heating, air conditioning, ventilation and refrigeration maintenance technology; hospitality administration; hotel/motel administration; human services; international relations and affairs; landscaping and groundskeeping; legal assistant/paralegal; lineworker; management information systems and services related; mass communication/media; mathematics; mechanical engineering/mechanical technology; mechatronics, robotics, and automation engineering; medical/clinical assistant; music management; nuclear medical technology; philosophy; photography; physical sciences; psychology; radiologic technology/science; real estate; registered nursing/registered nurse; respiratory care therapy; sales, distribution, and marketing operations; secondary education; small business administration; social sciences; social work; surgical technology; tourism and travel services management; visual and performing arts; viticulture and enology; web page, digital/multimedia and information resources design.

Academics *Calendar:* semesters. *Degree:* certificates, diplomas, and associate. *Special study options:* academic remediation for entering students, adult/continuing education programs, advanced placement credit, distance learning, double majors, English as a second language, honors programs, independent study, internships, part-time degree program, services for LD students, student-designed majors, study abroad, summer session for credit. *ROTC:* Army (b).

Library McCormick Library with an OPAC, a Web page.

Student Life *Housing:* college housing not available. *Activities and Organizations:* drama/theater group, student-run newspaper, Student Government Association, Phi Theta Kappa, African American Student Association, Mosiaco Club, Fourth Estate. *Campus security:* 24-hour emergency response devices and patrols, late-night transport/escort service.

Athletics *Intercollegiate sports:* basketball M/W, soccer M, tennis M/W. *Intramural sports:* basketball M/W, soccer M/W, swimming and diving M/W, tennis M/W, volleyball M/W.

Costs (2013–14) *Tuition:* area resident $4275 full-time, $143 per credit hour part-time; state resident $6030 full-time, $201 per credit hour part-time; nonresident $9045 full-time, $302 per credit hour part-time. Full-time tuition and fees vary according to program. Part-time tuition and fees vary according to program. *Required fees:* $1170 full-time, $39 per credit hour part-time. *Payment plan:* installment. *Waivers:* employees or children of employees.

Financial Aid Of all full-time matriculated undergraduates who enrolled in 2013, 3,286 applied for aid.

Applying *Options:* electronic application, early admission, deferred entrance. *Application fee:* $35. *Required for some:* high school transcript, 1 letter of recommendation, interview.

Freshman Application Contact Mrs. Vanita L. Cowan, Administrative Clerk, Admissions, Harrisburg Area Community College, Harrisburg, PA 17110. *Phone:* 717-780-2694. *Toll-free phone:* 800-ABC-HACC. *Fax:* 717-231-7674. *E-mail:* admit@hacc.edu. *Website:* http://www.hacc.edu/.

Hussian School of Art
Philadelphia, Pennsylvania

Freshman Application Contact Director of Admissions, Hussian School of Art, The Bourse, Suite 300, 111 South Independence Mall East, Philadelphia, PA 19106. *Phone:* 215-574-9600. *Fax:* 215-574-9800. *E-mail:* info@hussianart.edu. *Website:* http://www.hussianart.edu/.

ITT Technical Institute
Dunmore, Pennsylvania

- **Proprietary** 2-year, part of ITT Educational Services, Inc.
- **Coed**

Majors CAD/CADD drafting/design technology; computer engineering technology; computer systems networking and telecommunications; criminal justice/law enforcement administration; design and visual communications.
Academics *Calendar:* quarters. *Degree:* diplomas and associate.
Freshman Application Contact Director of Recruitment, ITT Technical Institute, 1000 Meade Street, Dunmore, PA 18512. *Phone:* 570-330-0600. *Toll-free phone:* 800-774-9791.
Website: http://www.itt-tech.edu/.

ITT Technical Institute
Harrisburg, Pennsylvania

- **Proprietary** 2-year, part of ITT Educational Services, Inc.
- **Coed**

Majors CAD/CADD drafting/design technology; computer engineering technology; computer software and media applications related; computer systems networking and telecommunications; criminal justice/law enforcement administration; design and visual communications; digital communication and media/multimedia.
Academics *Degree:* diplomas and associate.
Freshman Application Contact Director of Recruitment, ITT Technical Institute, 449 Eisenhower Boulevard, Suite 100, Harrisburg, PA 17111. *Phone:* 717-565-1700. *Toll-free phone:* 800-847-4756.
Website: http://www.itt-tech.edu/.

ITT Technical Institute
Levittown, Pennsylvania

- **Proprietary** 2-year, founded 2000, part of ITT Educational Services, Inc.
- **Coed**

Majors CAD/CADD drafting/design technology; computer engineering technology; computer systems networking and telecommunications; criminal justice/law enforcement administration; design and visual communications.
Academics *Calendar:* quarters. *Degree:* diplomas and associate.
Student Life *Housing:* college housing not available.
Freshman Application Contact Director of Recruitment, ITT Technical Institute, 311 Veterans Highway, Levittown, PA 19056. *Phone:* 215-702-6300. *Toll-free phone:* 866-488-8324.
Website: http://www.itt-tech.edu/.

ITT Technical Institute
Philadelphia, Pennsylvania

- **Proprietary** 2-year
- **Coed**

Majors CAD/CADD drafting/design technology; computer engineering technology; computer systems networking and telecommunications.
Freshman Application Contact Director of Recruiting, ITT Technical Institute, 105 South 7th Street, Philadelphia, PA 19106. *Phone:* 215-413-4300.
Website: http://www.itt-tech.edu/.

ITT Technical Institute
Pittsburgh, Pennsylvania

- **Proprietary** 2-year, part of ITT Educational Services, Inc.
- **Coed**

Majors CAD/CADD drafting/design technology; computer engineering technology; computer software and media applications related; computer systems networking and telecommunications; criminal justice/law enforcement administration; design and visual communications.
Academics *Calendar:* quarters. *Degree:* diplomas and associate.
Student Life *Housing:* college housing not available.
Freshman Application Contact Director of Recruitment, ITT Technical Institute, 5460 Campbells Run Road, Pittsburgh, PA 15205. *Phone:* 412-446-2900. *Toll-free phone:* 800-353-8324.
Website: http://www.itt-tech.edu/.

ITT Technical Institute
Plymouth Meeting, Pennsylvania

- **Proprietary** 2-year, founded 2002, part of ITT Educational Services, Inc.
- **Coed**

Majors CAD/CADD drafting/design technology; computer engineering technology; computer systems networking and telecommunications; criminal justice/law enforcement administration; design and visual communications.
Academics *Calendar:* quarters. *Degree:* diplomas and associate.
Freshman Application Contact Director of Recruitment, ITT Technical Institute, 220 West Germantown Pike, Suite 100, Plymouth Meeting, PA 19462. *Phone:* 610-832-3400. *Toll-free phone:* 866-902-8324.
Website: http://www.itt-tech.edu/.

ITT Technical Institute
Tarentum, Pennsylvania

- **Proprietary** 2-year, part of ITT Educational Services, Inc.
- **Coed**

Majors CAD/CADD drafting/design technology; computer engineering technology; computer systems networking and telecommunications; criminal justice/law enforcement administration; design and visual communications.
Academics *Calendar:* quarters. *Degree:* diplomas and associate.
Student Life *Housing:* college housing not available.
Freshman Application Contact Director of Recruitment, ITT Technical Institute, 100 Pittsburgh Mills Circle, Suite 100, Tarentum, PA 15084. *Phone:* 724-274-1400. *Toll-free phone:* 800-488-0121.
Website: http://www.itt-tech.edu/.

JNA Institute of Culinary Arts
Philadelphia, Pennsylvania

- **Proprietary** 2-year, founded 1988
- **Urban** campus with easy access to Philadelphia
- **Coed**

Undergraduates 65 full-time. 57% Black or African American, non-Hispanic/Latino; 26% Hispanic/Latino; 3% Asian, non-Hispanic/Latino.
Academics *Calendar:* continuous. *Degree:* associate.
Freshman Application Contact Admissions Office, JNA Institute of Culinary Arts, 1212 South Broad Street, Philadelphia, PA 19146.
Website: http://www.culinaryarts.com/.

Johnson College
Scranton, Pennsylvania

Freshman Application Contact Ms. Melissa Ide, Director of Enrollment Management, Johnson College, 3427 North Main Avenue, Scranton, PA 18508. *Phone:* 570-702-8910. *Toll-free phone:* 800-2WE-WORK. *Fax:* 570-348-2181. *E-mail:* admit@johnson.edu.
Website: http://www.johnson.edu/.

Kaplan Career Institute, Broomall Campus
Broomall, Pennsylvania

Freshman Application Contact Kaplan Career Institute, Broomall Campus, 1991 Sproul Road, Suite 42, Broomall, PA 19008. *Phone:* 610-353-3300. *Toll-free phone:* 800-935-1857.
Website: http://broomall.kaplancareerinstitute.com/.

Kaplan Career Institute, Franklin Mills Campus
Philadelphia, Pennsylvania

Freshman Application Contact Kaplan Career Institute, Franklin Mills Campus, 177 Franklin Mills Boulevard, Philadelphia, PA 19154. *Phone:* 215-612-6600. *Toll-free phone:* 800-935-1857.
Website: http://franklin-mills.kaplancareerinstitute.com/.

Kaplan Career Institute, Harrisburg Campus
Harrisburg, Pennsylvania

Freshman Application Contact Kaplan Career Institute, Harrisburg Campus, 5650 Derry Street, Harrisburg, PA 17111-3518. *Phone:* 717-558-1300. *Toll-free phone:* 800-935-1857.
Website: http://harrisburg.kaplancareerinstitute.com/.

Kaplan Career Institute, Philadelphia Campus
Philadelphia, Pennsylvania

Freshman Application Contact Admissions Director, Kaplan Career Institute, Philadelphia Campus, 3010 Market Street, Philadelphia, PA 19104. *Toll-free phone:* 800-935-1857.
Website: http://philadelphia.kaplancareerinstitute.com/.

Kaplan Career Institute, Pittsburgh Campus
Pittsburgh, Pennsylvania

Freshman Application Contact Kaplan Career Institute, Pittsburgh Campus, 933 Penn Avenue, Pittsburgh, PA 15222. *Phone:* 412-261-2647. *Toll-free phone:* 800-935-1857.
Website: http://pittsburgh.kaplancareerinstitute.com/.

Keystone Technical Institute
Harrisburg, Pennsylvania

Freshman Application Contact Tom Bogush, Director of Admissions, Keystone Technical Institute, 2301 Academy Drive, Harrisburg, PA 17112. *Phone:* 717-545-4747. *Toll-free phone:* 800-400-3322. *Fax:* 717-901-9090. *E-mail:* info@acadcampus.com.
Website: http://www.kti.edu/.

Lackawanna College
Scranton, Pennsylvania

Freshman Application Contact Ms. Stacey Muchal, Associate Director of Admissions, Lackawanna College, 501 Vine Street, Scranton, PA 18509. *Phone:* 570-961-7868. *Toll-free phone:* 877-346-3552. *Fax:* 570-961-7843. *E-mail:* muchals@lackawanna.edu.
Website: http://www.lackawanna.edu/.

Lansdale School of Business
North Wales, Pennsylvania

Director of Admissions Ms. Marianne H. Johnson, Director of Admissions, Lansdale School of Business, 201 Church Road, North Wales, PA 19454-4148. *Phone:* 215-699-5700 Ext. 112. *Toll-free phone:* 800-219-0486. *Fax:* 215-699-8770. *E-mail:* mjohnson@lsb.edu.
Website: http://www.lsb.edu/.

Laurel Business Institute
Uniontown, Pennsylvania

Freshman Application Contact Mrs. Lisa Dolan, Laurel Business Institute, 11 East Penn Street, PO Box 877, Uniontown, PA 15401. *Phone:* 724-439-4900 Ext. 158. *Fax:* 724-439-3607. *E-mail:* ldolan@laurel.edu.
Website: http://www.laurel.edu/lbi/.

Laurel Technical Institute
Sharon, Pennsylvania

Freshman Application Contact Irene Lewis, Laurel Technical Institute, 335 Boyd Drive, Sharon, PA 16146. *Phone:* 724-983-0700. *Fax:* 724-983-8355. *E-mail:* info@biop.edu.
Website: http://www.laurel.edu/lti/.

Lehigh Carbon Community College
Schnecksville, Pennsylvania

- **State and locally supported** 2-year, founded 1967
- **Suburban** 254-acre campus with easy access to Philadelphia
- **Endowment** $2.7 million
- **Coed,** 7,128 undergraduate students, 36% full-time, 60% women, 40% men

Undergraduates 2,544 full-time, 4,584 part-time. Students come from 10 states and territories; 12 other countries; 0.3% are from out of state; 6% Black or African American, non-Hispanic/Latino; 17% Hispanic/Latino; 2% Asian, non-Hispanic/Latino; 0.2% American Indian or Alaska Native, non-Hispanic/Latino; 3% Two or more races, non-Hispanic/Latino; 7% Race/ethnicity unknown; 0.2% international; 55% transferred in.
Freshmen *Admission:* 4,607 applied, 4,607 admitted, 1,423 enrolled.
Faculty *Total:* 445, 20% full-time, 4% with terminal degrees. *Student/faculty ratio:* 20:1.
Majors Accounting technology and bookkeeping; aeronautics/aviation/aerospace science and technology; airline pilot and flight crew; animation, interactive technology, video graphics and special effects; art; biology/biological sciences; biotechnology; building/construction site management; business administration and management; business/commerce; chemical technology; chemistry; computer and information sciences; computer and information systems security; computer programming; computer programming (specific applications); computer systems networking and telecommunications; construction trades; criminal justice/law enforcement administration; criminal justice/safety; drafting and design technology; early childhood education; education; electrical, electronic and communications engineering technology; engineering; environmental science; fashion/apparel design; game and interactive media design; general studies; geographic information science and cartography; graphic design; health information/medical records technology; heating, air conditioning, ventilation and refrigeration maintenance technology; humanities; human resources management; human services; industrial electronics technology; interior design; legal assistant/paralegal; liberal arts and sciences/liberal studies; manufacturing engineering technology; mathematics; mechanical engineering/mechanical technology; medical/clinical assistant; nanotechnology; occupational therapist assistant; physical sciences; physical therapy technology; psychology; public administration; radio and television broadcasting technology; recording arts technology; registered nursing/registered nurse; resort management; social work; special education; speech communication and rhetoric; sport and fitness administration/management; teacher assistant/aide; veterinary/animal health technology; web page, digital/multimedia and information resources design.
Academics *Calendar:* semesters. *Degree:* certificates, diplomas, and associate. *Special study options:* academic remediation for entering students, advanced placement credit, cooperative education, distance learning, English

as a second language, external degree program, honors programs, independent study, internships, part-time degree program, services for LD students, summer session for credit. *ROTC:* Army (c).

Library Rothrock Library with 95,816 titles, 317 serial subscriptions, 5,608 audiovisual materials, an OPAC, a Web page.

Student Life *Housing:* college housing not available. *Activities and Organizations:* drama/theater group, choral group, Phi Theta Kappa, Criminal Justice/Justice Society, Psychology Club, Student Government Association, Teacher Education Student Association (TESA). *Campus security:* 24-hour emergency response devices. *Student services:* personal/psychological counseling.

Athletics Member NJCAA. *Intercollegiate sports:* baseball M, basketball M/W, golf M/W, soccer M, softball W, volleyball W. *Intramural sports:* basketball M/W, golf M/W, table tennis M/W, volleyball M/W.

Standardized Tests *Required for some:* TEAS (for those applying to Nursing Program).

Costs (2014–15) *Tuition:* area resident $3000 full-time, $100 per credit part-time; state resident $6270 full-time, $209 per credit part-time; nonresident $9540 full-time, $318 per credit part-time. *Required fees:* $510 full-time, $27 per credit part-time. *Payment plan:* installment. *Waivers:* senior citizens and employees or children of employees.

Applying *Options:* electronic application. *Required for some:* essay or personal statement, high school transcript, interview. *Application deadlines:* rolling (freshmen), rolling (out-of-state freshmen), rolling (transfers). *Notification:* continuous (freshmen), continuous (out-of-state freshmen), continuous (transfers).

Freshman Application Contact Mr. Louis Hegyes, Director of Recruitment/Admissions, Lehigh Carbon Community College, 4525 Education Park Drive, Schnecksville, PA 18078. *Phone:* 610-799-1575. *Fax:* 610-799-1527. *E-mail:* admissions@lccc.edu.
Website: http://www.lccc.edu/.

Lincoln Technical Institute
Allentown, Pennsylvania

Freshman Application Contact Admissions Office, Lincoln Technical Institute, 5151 Tilghman Street, Allentown, PA 18104-3298. *Phone:* 610-398-5301.
Website: http://www.lincolnedu.com/.

Lincoln Technical Institute
Philadelphia, Pennsylvania

Director of Admissions Mr. James Kuntz, Executive Director, Lincoln Technical Institute, 9191 Torresdale Avenue, Philadelphia, PA 19136-1595. *Phone:* 215-335-0800. *Fax:* 215-335-1443. *E-mail:* jkuntz@lincolntech.com. *Website:* http://www.lincolnedu.com/.

Luzerne County Community College
Nanticoke, Pennsylvania

- **County-supported** 2-year, founded 1966
- **Suburban** 122-acre campus with easy access to Philadelphia
- **Coed,** 6,411 undergraduate students, 49% full-time, 60% women, 40% men

Undergraduates 3,172 full-time, 3,239 part-time. 0.2% are from out of state; 4% Black or African American, non-Hispanic/Latino; 10% Hispanic/Latino; 1% Asian, non-Hispanic/Latino; 0.2% Native Hawaiian or other Pacific Islander, non-Hispanic/Latino; 0.1% American Indian or Alaska Native, non-Hispanic/Latino; 1% Two or more races, non-Hispanic/Latino; 7% Race/ethnicity unknown. *Retention:* 59% of full-time freshmen returned.

Freshmen *Admission:* 2,238 applied, 2,238 admitted, 1,497 enrolled.

Faculty *Total:* 459, 24% full-time. *Student/faculty ratio:* 17:1.

Majors Accounting; administrative assistant and secretarial science; airline pilot and flight crew; architectural engineering; architectural engineering technology; automobile/automotive mechanics technology; aviation/airway management; baking and pastry arts; banking and financial support services; biological and physical sciences; building/property maintenance; business administration and management; child-care provision; commercial and advertising art; commercial photography; computer and information sciences; computer and information sciences related; computer graphics; computer programming related; computer science; computer systems networking and telecommunications; computer technology/computer systems technology; court reporting; criminal justice/law enforcement administration; culinary arts; data entry/microcomputer applications; data processing and data processing technology; dental assisting; dental hygiene; drafting and design technology; drafting/design engineering technologies related; drawing; early childhood education; education; electrical, electronic and communications engineering technology; electrician; emergency medical technology (EMT paramedic); engineering technology; executive assistant/executive secretary; fire science/firefighting; food technology and processing; funeral service and

mortuary science; general studies; graphic and printing equipment operation/production; graphic design; health and physical education/fitness; health/health-care administration; heating, air conditioning, ventilation and refrigeration maintenance technology; horticultural science; hospitality and recreation marketing; hotel/motel administration; humanities; human services; industrial and product design; international business/trade/commerce; journalism; legal assistant/paralegal; liberal arts and sciences and humanities related; liberal arts and sciences/liberal studies; mathematics; medical administrative assistant and medical secretary; painting; photography; physical education teaching and coaching; plumbing technology; pre-pharmacy studies; radio and television broadcasting technology; real estate; registered nursing/registered nurse; respiratory care therapy; social sciences; surgical technology; tourism and travel services management; tourism and travel services marketing.

Academics *Calendar:* semesters. *Degree:* certificates, diplomas, and associate. *Special study options:* academic remediation for entering students, accelerated degree program, advanced placement credit, distance learning, external degree program, internships, part-time degree program, services for LD students, summer session for credit. *ROTC:* Air Force (c).

Library Learning Resources Center with an OPAC, a Web page.

Student Life *Housing:* college housing not available. *Activities and Organizations:* student-run newspaper, radio and television station, student government, Circle K, Nursing Forum, Science Club, SADAH. *Campus security:* 24-hour patrols.

Athletics Member NJCAA. *Intercollegiate sports:* baseball M, basketball M/W, cross-country running M/W, golf M/W, soccer M/W, softball W, volleyball W. *Intramural sports:* badminton M/W, basketball M/W, bowling M/W, softball M/W, tennis M/W, volleyball M/W.

Costs (2013–14) *Tuition:* area resident $3300 full-time, $110 per credit hour part-time; state resident $6600 full-time, $220 per credit hour part-time; nonresident $9900 full-time, $330 per credit hour part-time. Full-time tuition and fees vary according to course load. Part-time tuition and fees vary according to course load. *Required fees:* $840 full-time, $28 per credit hour part-time. *Payment plan:* installment. *Waivers:* senior citizens and employees or children of employees.

Applying *Options:* early admission, deferred entrance. *Recommended:* high school transcript.

Freshman Application Contact Mr. Francis Curry, Director of Admissions, Luzerne County Community College, 1333 South Prospect Street, Nanticoke, PA 18634-9804. *Phone:* 570-740-0337. *Toll-free phone:* 800-377-5222 Ext. 7337. *Fax:* 570-740-0238. *E-mail:* admissions@luzerne.edu. *Website:* http://www.luzerne.edu/.

Manor College
Jenkintown, Pennsylvania

- **Independent Byzantine Catholic** 2-year, founded 1947
- **Small-town** 35-acre campus with easy access to Philadelphia
- **Coed**

Undergraduates 616 full-time, 310 part-time. Students come from 4 states and territories; 2% are from out of state; 28% Black or African American, non-Hispanic/Latino; 6% Hispanic/Latino; 3% Asian, non-Hispanic/Latino; 0.1% Native Hawaiian or other Pacific Islander, non-Hispanic/Latino; 1% Two or more races, non-Hispanic/Latino; 14% Race/ethnicity unknown; 0.1% international.

Faculty *Student/faculty ratio:* 10:1.

Academics *Calendar:* semesters. *Degrees:* certificates, diplomas, associate, and postbachelor's certificates. *Special study options:* academic remediation for entering students, adult/continuing education programs, advanced placement credit, distance learning, double majors, English as a second language, honors programs, independent study, internships, part-time degree program, summer session for credit.

Student Life *Campus security:* 24-hour emergency response devices and patrols.

Athletics Member NJCAA.

Standardized Tests *Required:* SAT or ACT (for admission).

Costs (2013–14) *Comprehensive fee:* $22,120 includes full-time tuition ($14,650), mandatory fees ($600), and room and board ($6870). Full-time tuition and fees vary according to course load and program. Part-time tuition: $349 per credit hour. Part-time tuition and fees vary according to course load and program. *Required fees:* $100 per term part-time.

Financial Aid Of all full-time matriculated undergraduates who enrolled in 2009, 35 Federal Work-Study jobs (averaging $3000). 10 state and other part-time jobs (averaging $3600).

Applying *Options:* electronic application, deferred entrance. *Application fee:* $25. *Required:* high school transcript, interview.

Freshman Application Contact Manor College, 700 Fox Chase Road, Jenkintown, PA 19046. *Phone:* 215-884-2216.
Website: http://www.manor.edu/.

McCann School of Business & Technology

Pottsville, Pennsylvania

- **Proprietary** 2-year, founded 1897
- **Small-town** campus
- **Coed**

Academics *Calendar:* quarters. *Degree:* certificates, diplomas, and associate. *Special study options:* advanced placement credit, cooperative education, double majors, internships, part-time degree program, services for LD students, summer session for credit.

Student Life *Campus security:* controlled dormitory access.

Standardized Tests *Required:* Wonderlic aptitude test (for admission).

Applying *Options:* electronic application. *Application fee:* $40. *Required:* high school transcript, minimum 2.0 GPA, interview, GED or High School Attestation form.

Freshman Application Contact Mrs. Amelia Hopkins, Director, Pottsville Campus, McCann School of Business & Technology, 2650 Woodglen Rd., Pottsville, PA 17901. *Phone:* 570-622-7622. *Fax:* 570-622-7770. *Website:* http://www.mccannschool.com/.

Mercyhurst North East

North East, Pennsylvania

Director of Admissions Travis Lindahl, Director of Admissions, Mercyhurst North East, 16 West Division Street, North East, PA 16428. *Phone:* 814-725-6217. *Toll-free phone:* 866-846-6042. *Fax:* 814-725-6251. *E-mail:* neadmiss@mercyhurst.edu. *Website:* http://northeast.mercyhurst.edu/.

Metropolitan Career Center Computer Technology Institute

Philadelphia, Pennsylvania

Freshman Application Contact Admissions Office, Metropolitan Career Center Computer Technology Institute, 100 South Broad Street, Suite 830, Philadelphia, PA 19110. *Phone:* 215-568-7861. *Website:* http://www.careersinit.org/.

Montgomery County Community College

Blue Bell, Pennsylvania

- **County-supported** 2-year, founded 1964
- **Suburban** 186-acre campus with easy access to Philadelphia
- **Coed,** 13,122 undergraduate students, 35% full-time, 56% women, 44% men

Undergraduates 4,567 full-time, 8,555 part-time. Students come from 11 states and territories; 105 other countries; 0.4% are from out of state; 15% Black or African American, non-Hispanic/Latino; 6% Hispanic/Latino; 6% Asian, non-Hispanic/Latino; 0.2% Native Hawaiian or other Pacific Islander, non-Hispanic/Latino; 0.3% American Indian or Alaska Native, non-Hispanic/Latino; 2% Two or more races, non-Hispanic/Latino; 8% Race/ethnicity unknown; 2% international; 3% transferred in. *Retention:* 62% of full-time freshmen returned.

Freshmen *Admission:* 13,137 applied, 13,137 admitted, 3,243 enrolled.

Faculty *Total:* 769, 24% full-time. *Student/faculty ratio:* 19:1.

Majors Accounting; accounting technology and bookkeeping; administrative assistant and secretarial science; architectural drafting and CAD/CADD; art; automobile/automotive mechanics technology; baking and pastry arts; biology/biological sciences; biotechnology; business administration and management; business/commerce; business/corporate communications; CAD/CADD drafting/design technology; child-care and support services management; clinical/medical laboratory technology; commercial and advertising art; communications technologies and support services related; computer and information sciences; computer programming; computer systems networking and telecommunications; criminal justice/police science; culinary arts; dental hygiene; electrical, electronic and communications engineering technology; electromechanical technology; elementary education; engineering science; engineering technologies and engineering related; environmental science; fire prevention and safety technology; health and physical education/fitness; hospitality and recreation marketing; humanities; information science/studies; liberal arts and sciences/liberal studies; management information systems and services related; mathematics; mechanical drafting and CAD/CADD; mechanical engineering/mechanical technology; medical/clinical assistant; medical radiologic technology; network and system administration; physical education teaching and coaching; physical sciences; psychiatric/mental health services technology; psychology; radiologic technology/science; radio, television, and digital communication related; real estate; recording arts technology; registered nursing/registered

nurse; sales, distribution, and marketing operations; secondary education; social sciences; speech communication and rhetoric; surgical technology; teacher assistant/aide; tourism and travel services marketing; web/multimedia management and webmaster.

Academics *Calendar:* semesters. *Degree:* certificates and associate. *Special study options:* academic remediation for entering students, accelerated degree program, adult/continuing education programs, advanced placement credit, cooperative education, distance learning, English as a second language, honors programs, independent study, internships, part-time degree program, services for LD students, student-designed majors, study abroad, summer session for credit.

Library The Brendlinger Library/Branch Library Pottstown Campus with 86,001 titles, 348 serial subscriptions, 13,533 audiovisual materials, an OPAC, a Web page.

Student Life *Housing:* college housing not available. *Activities and Organizations:* drama/theater group, student-run newspaper, radio and television station, choral group, student government, Thrive (Christian Fellowship), radio station, Drama Club, African - American Student League. *Campus security:* 24-hour emergency response devices and patrols, late-night transport/escort service, bicycle patrol. *Student services:* health clinic, personal/psychological counseling.

Athletics Member NJCAA. *Intercollegiate sports:* baseball M, basketball M/W, soccer M/W, softball W, volleyball W. *Intramural sports:* badminton M/W, basketball M/W, bowling M/W, cross-country running M/W, football M, racquetball M/W, soccer M/W, table tennis M/W, tennis M/W, volleyball M/W, weight lifting M/W.

Costs (2013–14) *Tuition:* area resident $3750 full-time, $125 per credit part-time; state resident $7800 full-time, $250 per credit part-time; nonresident $11,850 full-time, $375 per credit part-time. *Required fees:* $840 full-time, $28 per credit part-time. *Payment plan:* deferred payment. *Waivers:* senior citizens and employees or children of employees.

Financial Aid Of all full-time matriculated undergraduates who enrolled in 2012, 60 Federal Work-Study jobs (averaging $2500).

Applying *Options:* electronic application, early admission, deferred entrance. *Application fee:* $25. *Required:* high school transcript. *Required for some:* interview. *Application deadline:* rolling (transfers). *Notification:* continuous (freshmen), continuous (transfers).

Freshman Application Contact Montgomery County Community College, Blue Bell, PA 19422. *Phone:* 215-641-6551. *Fax:* 215-619-7188. *E-mail:* admrec@admin.mc3.edu. *Website:* http://www.mc3.edu/.

New Castle School of Trades

New Castle, Pennsylvania

Freshman Application Contact Mr. James Catheline, Admissions Director, New Castle School of Trades, 4117 Pulaski Road, New Castle, PA 16101. *Phone:* 724-964-8811. *Toll-free phone:* 800-837-8299. *Website:* http://www.ncstrades.com/.

Northampton Community College

Bethlehem, Pennsylvania

- **State and locally supported** 2-year, founded 1967
- **Suburban** 165-acre campus with easy access to Philadelphia
- **Endowment** $34.1 million
- **Coed,** 10,666 undergraduate students, 44% full-time, 59% women, 41% men

Undergraduates 4,679 full-time, 5,987 part-time. Students come from 20 states and territories; 46 other countries; 1% are from out of state; 11% Black or African American, non-Hispanic/Latino; 19% Hispanic/Latino; 2% Asian, non-Hispanic/Latino; 0.2% Native Hawaiian or other Pacific Islander, non-Hispanic/Latino; 0.3% American Indian or Alaska Native, non-Hispanic/Latino; 2% Two or more races, non-Hispanic/Latino; 2% Race/ethnicity unknown; 1% international; 8% transferred in; 3% live on campus.

Freshmen *Admission:* 4,722 applied, 4,722 admitted, 2,158 enrolled.

Faculty *Total:* 703, 17% full-time, 19% with terminal degrees. *Student/faculty ratio:* 21:1.

Majors Accounting technology and bookkeeping; acting; administrative assistant and secretarial science; architectural engineering technology; athletic training; automobile/automotive mechanics technology; biology/biological sciences; biotechnology; business administration and management; business/commerce; CAD/CADD drafting/design technology; chemistry; computer and information systems security; computer installation and repair technology; computer programming; computer science; computer systems networking and telecommunications; construction management; criminal justice/safety; culinary arts; dental hygiene; diagnostic medical sonography and ultrasound technology; early childhood education; electrical, electronic and communications engineering technology; electrician; electromechanical technology; engineering; environmental science; fine/studio arts; fire science/firefighting; fire services administration; funeral service and mortuary science; general studies; graphic design; heating, air conditioning, ventilation and refrigeration maintenance technology; hotel/motel administration; industrial electronics technology; interior design; journalism; legal administrative assistant/secretary; legal assistant/paralegal; liberal arts and sciences and humanities related; liberal arts and sciences/liberal studies; marketing/marketing management; mathematics; medical administrative assistant and medical secretary; meeting and event planning; middle school education; physics; quality control technology; radio and television broadcasting technology; radiologic technology/science; registered nursing/registered nurse; restaurant/food services management; secondary education; social work; speech communication and rhetoric; sport and fitness administration/management; teacher assistant/aide; veterinary/animal health technology; web page, digital/multimedia and information resources design.

Academics *Calendar:* semesters. *Degree:* certificates, diplomas, and associate. *Special study options:* academic remediation for entering students, adult/continuing education programs, advanced placement credit, distance learning, English as a second language, honors programs, independent study, internships, off-campus study, part-time degree program, services for LD students, student-designed majors, study abroad, summer session for credit.

Library Paul & Harriett Mack Library with 113,375 titles, 195 serial subscriptions, 18,678 audiovisual materials, an OPAC, a Web page.

Student Life *Housing Options:* coed. Campus housing is university owned. *Activities and Organizations:* drama/theater group, student-run newspaper, radio station, choral group, Phi Theta Kappa, Student Senate, College and Hospital Association of Radiologic Technologies Students (CHARTS), American Dental Hygiene Association (ADHA), International Student Organization. *Campus security:* 24-hour emergency response devices and patrols, controlled dormitory access. *Student services:* health clinic, personal/psychological counseling.

Athletics Member NJCAA. *Intercollegiate sports:* baseball M, basketball M/W, cross-country running M/W, golf M, lacrosse M, soccer M/W, softball W, volleyball W. *Intramural sports:* basketball M/W, cheerleading M(c)/W(c), soccer M/W, volleyball M/W.

Costs (2013–14) *Tuition:* area resident $2640 full-time, $88 per credit hour part-time; state resident $5280 full-time, $176 per credit hour part-time; nonresident $7920 full-time, $264 per credit hour part-time. Full-time tuition and fees vary according to course load. Part-time tuition and fees vary according to course load. *Required fees:* $1050 full-time, $35 per credit hour part-time. *Room and board:* $7948; room only: $4556. Room and board charges vary according to board plan and housing facility. *Payment plan:* installment. *Waivers:* senior citizens and employees or children of employees.

Financial Aid Of all full-time matriculated undergraduates who enrolled in 2013, 211 Federal Work-Study jobs (averaging $2400). 98 state and other part-time jobs (averaging $2000).

Applying *Options:* electronic application, deferred entrance. *Application fee:* $25. *Required for some:* high school transcript, minimum 2.5 GPA, interview, interview for rad and veterinary. *Recommended:* high school transcript. *Application deadlines:* rolling (freshmen), rolling (out-of-state freshmen), rolling (transfers). *Notification:* continuous (freshmen), continuous (out-of-state freshmen), continuous (transfers).

Freshman Application Contact Mr. James McCarthy, Director of Admissions, Northampton Community College, 3835 Green Pond Road, Bethlehem, PA 18020-7599. *Phone:* 610-861-5506. *Fax:* 610-861-5551. *E-mail:* jrmccarthy@northampton.edu.

Website: http://www.northampton.edu/.

Orleans Technical Institute

Philadelphia, Pennsylvania

Freshman Application Contact Mrs. Dorothy Stinson, Admissions Secretary, Orleans Technical Institute, 2770 Red Lion Road, Philadelphia, PA 19114. *Phone:* 215-728-4700. *Fax:* 215-745-1689. *E-mail:* stinsd@jevs.org.

Website: http://www.orleanstech.edu/.

Penn Commercial Business and Technical School

Washington, Pennsylvania

Director of Admissions Mr. Michael John Joyce, Director of Admissions, Penn Commercial Business and Technical School, 242 Oak Spring Road, Washington, PA 15301. *Phone:* 724-222-5330 Ext. 1. *Toll-free phone:* 888-309-7484. *E-mail:* mjoyce@penn-commercial.com.

Website: http://www.penncommercial.net/.

Pennco Tech

Bristol, Pennsylvania

Freshman Application Contact Pennco Tech, 3815 Otter Street, Bristol, PA 19007-3696. *Phone:* 215-785-0111. *Toll-free phone:* 800-575-9399. *Website:* http://www.penncotech.com/.

Penn State Beaver

Monaca, Pennsylvania

- **State-related** primarily 2-year, founded 1964, part of Pennsylvania State University
- **Small-town** campus
- **Coed,** 703 undergraduate students, 89% full-time, 39% women, 61% men

Undergraduates 626 full-time, 77 part-time. 9% are from out of state; 12% Black or African American, non-Hispanic/Latino; 5% Hispanic/Latino; 3% Asian, non-Hispanic/Latino; 0.2% American Indian or Alaska Native, non-Hispanic/Latino; 3% Two or more races, non-Hispanic/Latino; 2% Race/ethnicity unknown; 3% international; 5% transferred in; 23% live on campus. *Retention:* 68% of full-time freshmen returned.

Freshmen *Admission:* 750 applied, 636 admitted, 241 enrolled. *Average high school GPA:* 3.01. *Test scores:* SAT critical reading scores over 500: 37%; SAT math scores over 500: 47%; SAT writing scores over 500: 32%; ACT scores over 18: 71%; SAT critical reading scores over 600: 8%; SAT math scores over 600: 21%; SAT writing scores over 600: 5%; ACT scores over 24: 7%; SAT critical reading scores over 700: 1%; SAT math scores over 700: 3%.

Faculty *Total:* 56, 57% full-time, 39% with terminal degrees. *Student/faculty ratio:* 16:1.

Majors Accounting; acting; actuarial science; adult and continuing education administration; advertising; aerospace, aeronautical and astronautical/space engineering; African American/Black studies; agribusiness; agricultural and extension education; agricultural business and management related; agricultural engineering; agricultural mechanization; agriculture; agronomy and crop science; animal sciences; animal sciences related; anthropology; applied economics; archeology; architectural engineering; art; art history, criticism and conservation; art teacher education; Asian studies (East); astronomy; atmospheric sciences and meteorology; biochemistry; bioengineering and biomedical engineering; biological and biomedical sciences related; biological and physical sciences; biology/biological sciences; biology/biotechnology laboratory technician; business administration and management; business/commerce; business/managerial economics; chemical engineering; chemistry; civil engineering; classics and classical languages; communication and journalism related; communication sciences and disorders; comparative literature; computer and information sciences; computer engineering; criminal justice/law enforcement administration; economics; electrical and electronics engineering; elementary education; engineering science; English; environmental/environmental health engineering; film/cinema/video studies; finance; food science; foreign language teacher education; forest sciences and biology; forest technology; French; geography; geological and earth sciences/geosciences related; geology/earth science; German; graphic design; health/health-care administration; history; horticultural science; hospitality administration related; human development and family studies; human nutrition; industrial engineering; information science/studies; international relations and affairs; Italian; Japanese; Jewish/Judaic studies; journalism; kinesiology and exercise science; labor and industrial relations; landscaping and groundskeeping; Latin American studies; liberal arts and sciences/liberal studies; logistics, materials, and supply chain management; management information systems; marketing/marketing management; materials science; mathematics; mechanical engineering; medical microbiology and bacteriology; medieval and Renaissance studies; mining and mineral engineering; music; natural resources and conservation related; natural resources/conservation; nuclear engineering; organizational behavior; parks, recreation and leisure facilities management; petroleum engineering; philosophy; physics; political science and government; premedical studies; psychology; registered nursing/registered nurse; rehabilitation and therapeutic professions related; religious studies; Russian; secondary education; sociology; soil science and agronomy; Spanish; special education; speech communication and rhetoric; statistics; theater design and technology; toxicology; turf and turfgrass management; visual and performing arts; women's studies.

Academics *Calendar:* semesters. *Degrees:* certificates, bachelor's, and postbachelor's certificates. *Special study options:* adult/continuing education programs.

Student Life *Housing Options:* coed, special housing for students with disabilities. Campus housing is university owned. Freshman campus housing is guaranteed.

Athletics Member NJCAA. *Intercollegiate sports:* baseball M, basketball M, softball M/W, volleyball W. *Intramural sports:* basketball M/W, cheerleading M(c)/W(c), cross-country running M/W, football M, golf M/W, soccer M/W, softball M/W, table tennis M/W.

Standardized Tests *Required:* SAT or ACT (for admission).

Costs (2013–14) *Tuition:* state resident $12,474 full-time, $504 per credit hour part-time; nonresident $19,030 full-time, $793 per credit hour part-time. Full-time tuition and fees vary according to course level, degree level, location, program, and student level. Part-time tuition and fees vary according to course level, course load, degree level, location, program, and student level. *Required fees:* $876 full-time. *Room and board:* $9690; room only: $4910. Room and board charges vary according to board plan, housing facility, and location. *Payment plans:* installment, deferred payment. *Waivers:* employees or children of employees.

Financial Aid Of all full-time matriculated undergraduates who enrolled in 2012, 546 applied for aid, 464 were judged to have need, 23 had their need fully met. In 2012, 47 non-need-based awards were made. *Average percent of need met:* 63%. *Average financial aid package:* $10,632. *Average need-based loan:* $4038. *Average need-based gift aid:* $6560. *Average non-need-based aid:* $2055. *Average indebtedness upon graduation:* $35,430.

Applying *Options:* electronic application, early admission, deferred entrance. *Application fee:* $50. *Required:* high school transcript. *Required for some:* interview. *Recommended:* essay or personal statement. *Application deadlines:* rolling (freshmen), rolling (transfers). *Notification:* continuous (freshmen), continuous (transfers).

Freshman Application Contact Admissions Office, Penn State Beaver, 100 University Drive, Monaca, PA 15061. *Phone:* 724-773-3800. *Fax:* 724-773-3658. *E-mail:* br-admissions@psu.edu.

Website: http://www.br.psu.edu/.

Penn State Brandywine
Media, Pennsylvania

- **State-related** primarily 2-year, founded 1966, part of Pennsylvania State University
- **Small-town** campus
- **Coed,** 1,492 undergraduate students, 84% full-time, 43% women, 57% men

Undergraduates 1,253 full-time, 239 part-time. 5% are from out of state; 14% Black or African American, non-Hispanic/Latino; 5% Hispanic/Latino; 9% Asian, non-Hispanic/Latino; 0.2% Native Hawaiian or other Pacific Islander, non-Hispanic/Latino; 0.1% American Indian or Alaska Native, non-Hispanic/Latino; 2% Two or more races, non-Hispanic/Latino; 3% Race/ethnicity unknown; 0.6% international; 4% transferred in. *Retention:* 74% of full-time freshmen returned.

Freshmen *Admission:* 1,069 applied, 867 admitted, 333 enrolled. *Average high school GPA:* 3.02. *Test scores:* SAT critical reading scores over 500: 48%; SAT math scores over 500: 56%; SAT writing scores over 500: 41%; ACT scores over 18: 80%; SAT critical reading scores over 600: 13%; SAT math scores over 600: 16%; SAT writing scores over 600: 11%; ACT scores over 24: 20%; SAT critical reading scores over 700: 2%; SAT math scores over 700: 3%; SAT writing scores over 700: 2%; ACT scores over 30: 10%.

Faculty *Total:* 135, 45% full-time, 51% with terminal degrees. *Student/faculty ratio:* 16:1.

Majors Accounting; acting; actuarial science; adult and continuing education administration; advertising; aerospace, aeronautical and astronautical/space engineering; African American/Black studies; agribusiness; agricultural and extension education; agricultural business and management related; agricultural engineering; agricultural mechanization; agriculture; agronomy and crop science; American studies; animal sciences; animal sciences related; anthropology; applied economics; archeology; architectural engineering; art; art history, criticism and conservation; art teacher education; Asian studies (East); astronomy; atmospheric sciences and meteorology; biochemistry; bioengineering and biomedical engineering; biological and biomedical sciences related; biological and physical sciences; biology/biological sciences; biology/biotechnology laboratory technician; business administration and management; business/commerce; business/managerial economics; chemical engineering; chemistry; civil engineering; classics and classical languages; communication and journalism related; communication sciences and disorders; comparative literature; computer and information sciences; computer engineering; criminal justice/law enforcement administration; economics; electrical and electronics engineering; electrical, electronic and communications engineering technology; elementary education; engineering science; English; environmental/environmental health engineering; film/cinema/video studies; finance; food science; foreign language teacher education; forest sciences and biology; forest technology; French; geography; geological and earth sciences/geosciences related; geology/earth science; German; graphic design; health/health-care administration; history; horticultural science; hospitality administration related; human development and family studies; human nutrition; industrial engineering; information science/studies; international relations and affairs; Italian; Japanese; Jewish/Judaic studies; journalism; kinesiology and exercise science; labor and industrial relations; landscape architecture; landscaping and groundskeeping; Latin American studies; liberal arts and sciences/liberal studies; logistics,

materials, and supply chain management; management information systems; marketing/marketing management; materials science; mathematics; mechanical engineering; medical microbiology and bacteriology; medieval and Renaissance studies; mining and mineral engineering; music; natural resources and conservation related; natural resources/conservation; nuclear engineering; organizational behavior; parks, recreation and leisure facilities management; petroleum engineering; philosophy; physics; political science and government; premedical studies; psychology; registered nursing/registered nurse; rehabilitation and therapeutic professions related; religious studies; Russian; secondary education; sociology; soil science and agronomy; Spanish; special education; speech communication and rhetoric; statistics; theater design and technology; turf and turfgrass management; visual and performing arts; women's studies.

Academics *Calendar:* semesters. *Degrees:* certificates, associate, and bachelor's. *Special study options:* adult/continuing education programs. *ROTC:* Army (c), Air Force (c).

Student Life *Housing:* college housing not available. *Campus security:* late-night transport/escort service, part-time trained security personnel.

Athletics Member NJCAA. *Intercollegiate sports:* baseball M, basketball M/W, soccer M/W, tennis M/W, volleyball W. *Intramural sports:* basketball M/W, cheerleading M(c)/W(c), golf M/W, ice hockey M(c)/W(c), lacrosse M/W, soccer M/W, softball W(c), tennis M/W, volleyball M(c)/W.

Standardized Tests *Required:* SAT or ACT (for admission).

Costs (2013–14) *Tuition:* state resident $12,474 full-time, $504 per credit hour part-time; nonresident $19,030 full-time, $793 per credit hour part-time. Full-time tuition and fees vary according to course level, degree level, location, program, and student level. Part-time tuition and fees vary according to course level, course load, degree level, location, program, and student level. *Required fees:* $882 full-time. *Payment plans:* installment, deferred payment. *Waivers:* employees or children of employees.

Financial Aid Of all full-time matriculated undergraduates who enrolled in 2012, 1,045 applied for aid, 818 were judged to have need, 33 had their need fully met. In 2012, 116 non-need-based awards were made. *Average percent of need met:* 61%. *Average financial aid package:* $9993. *Average need-based loan:* $3970. *Average need-based gift aid:* $6690. *Average non-need-based aid:* $1991. *Average indebtedness upon graduation:* $35,430.

Applying *Options:* electronic application, early admission, deferred entrance. *Application fee:* $50. *Required:* high school transcript. *Required for some:* interview. *Recommended:* essay or personal statement. *Application deadlines:* rolling (freshmen), rolling (transfers). *Notification:* continuous (freshmen), continuous (transfers).

Freshman Application Contact Admissions Office, Penn State Brandywine, 25 Yearsley Mill Road, Media, PA 19063-5596. *Phone:* 610-892-1200. *Fax:* 610-892-1320. *E-mail:* bwadmissions@psu.edu.

Website: http://www.brandywine.psu.edu/.

Penn State DuBois
DuBois, Pennsylvania

- **State-related** primarily 2-year, founded 1935, part of Pennsylvania State University
- **Small-town** campus
- **Coed,** 704 undergraduate students, 79% full-time, 48% women, 52% men

Undergraduates 557 full-time, 147 part-time. 2% are from out of state; 2% Black or African American, non-Hispanic/Latino; 2% Hispanic/Latino; 1% Asian, non-Hispanic/Latino; 0.3% American Indian or Alaska Native, non-Hispanic/Latino; 0.7% Two or more races, non-Hispanic/Latino; 1% Race/ethnicity unknown; 1% international; 4% transferred in. *Retention:* 77% of full-time freshmen returned.

Freshmen *Admission:* 407 applied, 353 admitted, 191 enrolled. *Average high school GPA:* 3.09. *Test scores:* SAT critical reading scores over 500: 39%; SAT math scores over 500: 44%; SAT writing scores over 500: 21%; ACT scores over 18: 67%; SAT critical reading scores over 600: 4%; SAT math scores over 600: 7%; SAT writing scores over 600: 4%; ACT scores over 24: 33%.

Faculty *Total:* 59, 76% full-time, 54% with terminal degrees. *Student/faculty ratio:* 12:1.

Majors Accounting; acting; actuarial science; adult and continuing education administration; advertising; aerospace, aeronautical and astronautical/space engineering; African American/Black studies; agribusiness; agricultural and extension education; agricultural business and management related; agricultural engineering; agricultural mechanization; agriculture; agronomy and crop science; animal sciences; animal sciences related; anthropology; applied economics; archeology; architectural engineering; art; art history, criticism and conservation; art teacher education; Asian studies (East); astronomy; atmospheric sciences and meteorology; biochemistry; bioengineering and biomedical engineering; biological and biomedical sciences related; biological and physical sciences; biology/biological sciences; biology/biotechnology laboratory technician; biomedical technology; business administration and management; business/commerce; business/managerial economics; chemical engineering; chemistry; civil engineering; classics and classical languages; clinical/medical laboratory technology; communication and journalism related; communication sciences and disorders; comparative literature; computer and information sciences; computer engineering; criminal justice/law enforcement administration; economics; electrical and electronics engineering; electrical, electronic and communications engineering technology; elementary education; engineering science; English; environmental/environmental health engineering; film/cinema/video studies; finance; food science; foreign language teacher education; forest sciences and biology; forest technology; French; geography; geological and earth sciences/geosciences related; geology/earth science; German; graphic design; health/health-care administration; history; horticultural science; hospitality administration related; human development and family studies; human nutrition; industrial engineering; information science/studies; international business/trade/commerce; international relations and affairs; Italian; Japanese; Jewish/Judaic studies; journalism; kinesiology and exercise science; labor and industrial relations; landscaping and groundskeeping; Latin American studies; liberal arts and sciences/liberal studies; management information systems; marketing/marketing management; materials science; mathematics; mechanical engineering; mechanical engineering/mechanical technology; medical microbiology and bacteriology; medieval and Renaissance studies; metallurgical technology; mining and mineral engineering; music; natural resources and conservation related; natural resources/conservation; nuclear engineering; occupational therapist assistant; organizational behavior; parks, recreation and leisure facilities management; petroleum engineering; philosophy; physical therapy technology; physics; political science and government; premedical studies; psychology; registered nursing/registered nurse; rehabilitation and therapeutic professions related; religious studies; Russian; secondary education; sociology; soil science and agronomy; Spanish; special education; speech communication and rhetoric; statistics; telecommunications technology; theater design and technology; toxicology; turf and turfgrass management; visual and performing arts; wildlife, fish and wildlands science and management; women's studies.

Academics *Calendar:* semesters. *Degrees:* certificates, associate, and bachelor's. *Special study options:* adult/continuing education programs.

Student Life *Housing:* college housing not available.

Athletics Member NJCAA. *Intercollegiate sports:* basketball M, cross-country running M/W, golf M/W, volleyball W. *Intramural sports:* basketball M/W, football M, soccer M/W, table tennis M/W, volleyball M/W.

Standardized Tests *Required:* SAT or ACT (for admission).

Costs (2013–14) *Tuition:* state resident $12,474 full-time, $504 per credit hour part-time; nonresident $19,030 full-time, $793 per credit hour part-time. Full-time tuition and fees vary according to course level, degree level, location, program, and student level. Part-time tuition and fees vary according to course level, course load, degree level, location, program, and student level. *Required fees:* $770 full-time. *Payment plans:* installment, deferred payment. *Waivers:* employees or children of employees.

Financial Aid Of all full-time matriculated undergraduates who enrolled in 2012, 480 applied for aid, 432 were judged to have need, 19 had their need fully met. In 2012, 16 non-need-based awards were made. *Average percent of need met:* 62%. *Average financial aid package:* $11,134. *Average need-based loan:* $3913. *Average need-based gift aid:* $6108. *Average non-need-based aid:* $1709. *Average indebtedness upon graduation:* $35,430.

Applying *Options:* electronic application, early admission, deferred entrance. *Application fee:* $50. *Required:* high school transcript. *Required for some:* interview. *Recommended:* essay or personal statement. *Application deadlines:* rolling (freshmen), rolling (transfers). *Notification:* continuous (freshmen), continuous (transfers).

Freshman Application Contact Admissions Office, Penn State DuBois, College Place, DuBois, PA 15801-3199. *Phone:* 814-375-4720. *Toll-free phone:* 800-346-7627. *Fax:* 814-375-4784. *E-mail:* duboisinfo@psi.edu. *Website:* http://www.ds.psu.edu/.

Penn State Fayette, The Eberly Campus
Uniontown, Pennsylvania

- **State-related** primarily 2-year, founded 1934, part of Pennsylvania State University
- **Small-town** campus
- **Coed,** 846 undergraduate students, 77% full-time, 56% women, 44% men

Undergraduates 653 full-time, 193 part-time. 5% are from out of state; 4% Black or African American, non-Hispanic/Latino; 2% Hispanic/Latino; 0.7% Asian, non-Hispanic/Latino; 0.1% American Indian or Alaska Native, non-Hispanic/Latino; 2% Two or more races, non-Hispanic/Latino; 1% Race/ethnicity unknown; 3% international; 6% transferred in. *Retention:* 74% of full-time freshmen returned.

Freshmen *Admission:* 514 applied, 433 admitted, 202 enrolled. *Average high school GPA:* 3.21. *Test scores:* SAT critical reading scores over 500: 39%; SAT math scores over 500: 40%; SAT writing scores over 500: 29%; ACT

scores over 18: 70%; SAT critical reading scores over 600: 6%; SAT math scores over 600: 11%; SAT writing scores over 600: 5%; ACT scores over 24: 60%; SAT critical reading scores over 700: 1%; SAT math scores over 700: 2%.

Faculty *Total:* 87, 60% full-time, 36% with terminal degrees. *Student/faculty ratio:* 11:1.

Majors Accounting; acting; actuarial science; adult and continuing education administration; advertising; aerospace, aeronautical and astronautical/space engineering; African American/Black studies; agribusiness; agricultural and extension education; agricultural business and management related; agricultural engineering; agricultural mechanization; agriculture; agronomy and crop science; animal sciences; animal sciences related; anthropology; applied economics; archeology; architectural engineering; architectural engineering technology; art; art history, criticism and conservation; art teacher education; Asian studies (East); astronomy; atmospheric sciences and meteorology; biochemistry; bioengineering and biomedical engineering; biological and biomedical sciences related; biological and physical sciences; biology/biological sciences; biology/biotechnology laboratory technician; biomedical technology; business administration and management; business/commerce; business/managerial economics; chemical engineering; chemistry; civil engineering; classics and classical languages; communication and journalism related; communication sciences and disorders; comparative literature; computer and information sciences; computer engineering; criminal justice/law enforcement administration; criminal justice/safety; economics; electrical and electronics engineering; electrical, electronic and communications engineering technology; elementary education; engineering science; English; environmental/environmental health engineering; film/cinema/video studies; finance; food science; foreign language teacher education; forest sciences and biology; forest technology; French; geography; geological and earth sciences/geosciences related; geology/earth science; German; graphic design; health/health-care administration; history; horticultural science; hospitality administration related; human development and family studies; human nutrition; industrial engineering; information science/studies; international relations and affairs; Italian; Japanese; Jewish/Judaic studies; journalism; kinesiology and exercise science; labor and industrial relations; landscaping and groundskeeping; Latin American studies; liberal arts and sciences/liberal studies; logistics, materials, and supply chain management; management information systems; manufacturing engineering; marketing/marketing management; materials science; mathematics; mechanical engineering; medical microbiology and bacteriology; medieval and Renaissance studies; metallurgical technology; mining and mineral engineering; natural resources and conservation related; natural resources/conservation; nuclear engineering; organizational behavior; parks, recreation and leisure facilities management; petroleum engineering; philosophy; physics; political science and government; premedical studies; psychology; registered nursing/registered nurse; rehabilitation and therapeutic professions related; religious studies; Russian; secondary education; sociology; soil science and agronomy; Spanish; special education; speech communication and rhetoric; statistics; telecommunications technology; theater design and technology; toxicology; turf and turfgrass management; visual and performing arts; women's studies.

Academics *Calendar:* semesters. *Degrees:* certificates, associate, and bachelor's. *Special study options:* adult/continuing education programs. *ROTC:* Army (b).

Student Life *Housing:* college housing not available. *Campus security:* student patrols, 8-hour patrols by trained security personnel.

Athletics Member NJCAA. *Intercollegiate sports:* baseball M, basketball M, softball W, volleyball W. *Intramural sports:* badminton M/W, basketball M/W, cheerleading M(c)/W(c), equestrian sports M(c)/W(c), football M/W, golf M(c)/W(c), softball M/W, tennis M/W, volleyball M/W, weight lifting M/W.

Standardized Tests *Required:* SAT or ACT (for admission).

Costs (2013–14) *Tuition:* state resident $12,474 full-time, $504 per credit hour part-time; nonresident $19,030 full-time, $793 per credit hour part-time. Full-time tuition and fees vary according to course level, degree level, location, program, and student level. Part-time tuition and fees vary according to course level, course load, degree level, location, program, and student level. *Required fees:* $826 full-time. *Payment plans:* installment, deferred payment. *Waivers:* employees or children of employees.

Financial Aid Of all full-time matriculated undergraduates who enrolled in 2012, 610 applied for aid, 554 were judged to have need, 23 had their need fully met. In 2012, 44 non-need-based awards were made. *Average percent of need met:* 61%. *Average financial aid package:* $10,566. *Average need-based loan:* $3930. *Average need-based gift aid:* $6572. *Average non-need-based aid:* $2029. *Average indebtedness upon graduation:* $35,430.

Applying *Options:* electronic application, early admission, deferred entrance. *Application fee:* $50. *Required:* high school transcript. *Required for some:* interview. *Recommended:* essay or personal statement. *Application deadlines:*

rolling (freshmen), rolling (transfers). *Notification:* continuous (freshmen), continuous (transfers).
Freshman Application Contact Admissions Office, Penn State Fayette, The Eberly Campus, 1 University Drive, PO Box 519, Uniontown, PA 15401-0519. *Phone:* 724-430-4130. *Toll-free phone:* 877-568-4130. *Fax:* 724-430-4175. *E-mail:* feadm@psu.edu.
Website: http://www.fe.psu.edu/.

Penn State Greater Allegheny
McKeesport, Pennsylvania

- **State-related** primarily 2-year, founded 1947, part of Pennsylvania State University
- **Small-town** campus
- **Coed,** 623 undergraduate students, 90% full-time, 46% women, 54% men

Undergraduates 562 full-time, 61 part-time. 11% are from out of state; 19% Black or African American, non-Hispanic/Latino; 5% Hispanic/Latino; 2% Asian, non-Hispanic/Latino; 0.2% Native Hawaiian or other Pacific Islander, non-Hispanic/Latino; 4% Two or more races, non-Hispanic/Latino; 1% Race/ethnicity unknown; 8% international; 6% transferred in; 26% live on campus. *Retention:* 71% of full-time freshmen returned.
Freshmen *Admission:* 776 applied, 594 admitted, 193 enrolled. *Average high school GPA:* 3.05. *Test scores:* SAT critical reading scores over 500: 37%; SAT math scores over 500: 31%; SAT writing scores over 500: 28%; ACT scores over 18: 75%; SAT critical reading scores over 600: 8%; SAT math scores over 600: 11%; SAT writing scores over 600: 6%; ACT scores over 24: 25%; SAT critical reading scores over 700: 1%; SAT math scores over 700: 4%; SAT writing scores over 700: 2%; ACT scores over 30: 13%.
Faculty *Total:* 69, 52% full-time, 41% with terminal degrees. *Student/faculty ratio:* 12:1.
Majors Accounting; acting; actuarial science; adult and continuing education administration; advertising; aerospace, aeronautical and astronautical/space engineering; African American/Black studies; agribusiness; agricultural and extension education; agricultural business and management related; agricultural engineering; agricultural mechanization; agriculture; agronomy and crop science; animal sciences; animal sciences related; anthropology; applied economics; archeology; architectural engineering; art; art history, criticism and conservation; art teacher education; Asian studies (East); astronomy; atmospheric sciences and meteorology; biochemistry; bioengineering and biomedical engineering; biological and biomedical sciences related; biological and physical sciences; biology/biological sciences; biology/biotechnology laboratory technician; business administration and management; business/commerce; business/managerial economics; chemical engineering; chemistry; civil engineering; classics and classical languages; communication and journalism related; communication sciences and disorders; comparative literature; computer and information sciences; computer engineering; criminal justice/law enforcement administration; economics; electrical and electronics engineering; elementary education; engineering science; English; environmental/environmental health engineering; film/cinema/video studies; finance; food science; foreign language teacher education; forest sciences and biology; forest technology; French; geography; geological and earth sciences/geosciences related; geology/earth science; German; graphic design; health/health-care administration; history; horticultural science; hospitality administration related; human development and family studies; human nutrition; industrial engineering; information science/studies; international relations and affairs; Italian; Japanese; Jewish/Judaic studies; journalism; kinesiology and exercise science; labor and industrial relations; landscaping and groundskeeping; Latin American studies; liberal arts and sciences/liberal studies; logistics, materials, and supply chain management; management information systems; manufacturing engineering; marketing/marketing management; materials science; mathematics; mechanical engineering; medical microbiology and bacteriology; medieval and Renaissance studies; mining and mineral engineering; music; natural resources and conservation related; natural resources/conservation; nuclear engineering; organizational behavior; parks, recreation and leisure facilities management; petroleum engineering; philosophy; physics; political science and government; premedical studies; psychology; registered nursing/registered nurse; rehabilitation and therapeutic professions related; religious studies; Russian; secondary education; sociology; soil science and agronomy; Spanish; special education; speech communication and rhetoric; statistics; theater design and technology; toxicology; turf and turfgrass management; visual and performing arts; women's studies.
Academics *Calendar:* semesters. *Degrees:* certificates, associate, bachelor's, and master's. *Special study options:* adult/continuing education programs.
Student Life *Housing Options:* coed, special housing for students with disabilities. Campus housing is university owned. Freshman campus housing is guaranteed. *Campus security:* 24-hour patrols, controlled dormitory access.
Athletics Member NJCAA. *Intercollegiate sports:* baseball M, basketball M, softball W, volleyball W. *Intramural sports:* basketball M/W, cheerleading M(c)/W(c), football M/W, ice hockey M(c), racquetball M/W, skiing (cross-country) M(c)/W(c), skiing (downhill) M(c)/W(c), soccer M(c)/W(c), softball M/W, tennis M/W, volleyball M/W.
Standardized Tests *Required:* SAT or ACT (for admission).
Costs (2013–14) *Tuition:* state resident $12,474 full-time, $504 per credit hour part-time; nonresident $19,030 full-time, $793 per credit hour part-time. Full-time tuition and fees vary according to course level, degree level, location, program, and student level. Part-time tuition and fees vary according to course level, course load, degree level, location, program, and student level. *Required fees:* $882 full-time. *Room and board:* $9690; room only: $4910. Room and board charges vary according to board plan, housing facility, and location. *Payment plans:* installment, deferred payment. *Waivers:* employees or children of employees.
Financial Aid Of all full-time matriculated undergraduates who enrolled in 2012, 493 applied for aid, 443 were judged to have need, 20 had their need fully met. In 2012, 37 non-need-based awards were made. *Average percent of need met:* 66%. *Average financial aid package:* $12,674. *Average need-based loan:* $3993. *Average need-based gift aid:* $7240. *Average non-need-based aid:* $2958. *Average indebtedness upon graduation:* $35,430.
Applying *Options:* electronic application, early admission, deferred entrance. *Application fee:* $50. *Required:* high school transcript. *Required for some:* interview. *Recommended:* essay or personal statement. *Application deadlines:* rolling (freshmen), rolling (transfers). *Notification:* continuous (freshmen), continuous (transfers).
Freshman Application Contact Admissions Office, Penn State Greater Allegheny, 4000 University Drive, McKeesport, PA 15132-7698. *Phone:* 412-675-9010. *Fax:* 412-675-9046. *E-mail:* psuga@psu.edu.
Website: http://www.ga.psu.edu/.

Penn State Hazleton
Hazleton, Pennsylvania

- **State-related** primarily 2-year, founded 1934, part of Pennsylvania State University
- **Small-town** campus
- **Coed,** 951 undergraduate students, 93% full-time, 48% women, 52% men

Undergraduates 881 full-time, 70 part-time. 25% are from out of state; 16% Black or African American, non-Hispanic/Latino; 15% Hispanic/Latino; 3% Asian, non-Hispanic/Latino; 0.3% Native Hawaiian or other Pacific Islander, non-Hispanic/Latino; 0.1% American Indian or Alaska Native, non-Hispanic/Latino; 3% Two or more races, non-Hispanic/Latino; 2% Race/ethnicity unknown; 2% international; 3% transferred in; 48% live on campus. *Retention:* 76% of full-time freshmen returned.
Freshmen *Admission:* 939 applied, 786 admitted, 363 enrolled. *Average high school GPA:* 2.99. *Test scores:* SAT critical reading scores over 500: 33%; SAT math scores over 500: 35%; SAT writing scores over 500: 29%; ACT scores over 18: 92%; SAT critical reading scores over 600: 6%; SAT math scores over 600: 8%; SAT writing scores over 600: 5%; ACT scores over 24: 35%.
Faculty *Total:* 72, 75% full-time, 50% with terminal degrees. *Student/faculty ratio:* 15:1.
Majors Accounting; acting; actuarial science; adult and continuing education administration; advertising; aerospace, aeronautical and astronautical/space engineering; African American/Black studies; agribusiness; agricultural and extension education; agricultural business and management related; agricultural engineering; agricultural mechanization; agriculture; agronomy and crop science; animal sciences; animal sciences related; anthropology; applied economics; archeology; architectural engineering; art; art history, criticism and conservation; art teacher education; Asian studies (East); astronomy; atmospheric sciences and meteorology; biochemistry; bioengineering and biomedical engineering; biological and biomedical sciences related; biological and physical sciences; biology/biological sciences; biology/biotechnology laboratory technician; biomedical technology; business administration and management; business/commerce; business/managerial economics; chemical engineering; chemistry; civil engineering; classics and classical languages; clinical/medical laboratory technology; communication and journalism related; communication sciences and disorders; comparative literature; computer and information sciences; computer engineering; criminal justice/law enforcement administration; economics; electrical and electronics engineering; electrical, electronic and communications engineering technology; elementary education; engineering science; English; environmental/environmental health engineering; film/cinema/video studies; finance; food science; forest sciences and biology; forest technology; French; geography; geological and earth sciences/geosciences related; geology/earth science; German; graphic design; health/health-care administration; history; horticultural science; hospitality administration related; human development and family studies; human nutrition; industrial engineering; information science/studies; international relations and affairs; Italian; Japanese; Jewish/Judaic studies; journalism; kinesiology and exercise science; labor and industrial relations; landscaping and groundskeeping; Latin American studies; liberal arts and sciences/liberal studies; logistics, materials, and supply chain

management; management information systems; manufacturing engineering; marketing/marketing management; materials science; mathematics; mechanical engineering; mechanical engineering/mechanical technology; medical microbiology and bacteriology; medieval and Renaissance studies; metallurgical technology; mining and mineral engineering; music; natural resources and conservation related; natural resources/conservation; nuclear engineering; organizational behavior; parks, recreation and leisure facilities management; petroleum engineering; philosophy; physical therapy technology; physics; political science and government; premedical studies; psychology; registered nursing/registered nurse; rehabilitation and therapeutic professions related; religious studies; Russian; secondary education; sociology; soil science and agronomy; Spanish; special education; speech communication and rhetoric; statistics; telecommunications technology; theater design and technology; toxicology; turf and turfgrass management; visual and performing arts; women's studies.

Academics *Calendar:* semesters. *Degrees:* certificates, associate, and bachelor's. *Special study options:* adult/continuing education programs. *ROTC:* Army (b), Air Force (c).

Student Life *Housing Options:* coed. Campus housing is university owned. Freshman campus housing is guaranteed. *Campus security:* 24-hour patrols, late-night transport/escort service, controlled dormitory access.

Athletics Member NJCAA. *Intercollegiate sports:* baseball M, basketball M/W, cheerleading M/W, soccer M, softball W(s), tennis M/W, volleyball M/W. *Intramural sports:* basketball M/W, skiing (downhill) M(c)/W(c), soccer M/W, volleyball M/W.

Standardized Tests *Required:* SAT or ACT (for admission).

Costs (2013–14) *Tuition:* state resident $12,474 full-time, $504 per credit hour part-time; nonresident $19,030 full-time, $793 per credit hour part-time. Full-time tuition and fees vary according to course level, degree level, location, program, and student level. Part-time tuition and fees vary according to course level, course load, degree level, location, program, and student level. *Required fees:* $826 full-time. *Room and board:* $9690; room only: $4910. Room and board charges vary according to board plan, housing facility, and location. *Payment plans:* installment, deferred payment. *Waivers:* employees or children of employees.

Financial Aid Of all full-time matriculated undergraduates who enrolled in 2012, 881 applied for aid, 796 were judged to have need, 16 had their need fully met. In 2012, 68 non-need-based awards were made. *Average percent of need met:* 61%. *Average financial aid package:* $10,315. *Average need-based loan:* $3821. *Average need-based gift aid:* $6785. *Average non-need-based aid:* $2939. *Average indebtedness upon graduation:* $35,430.

Applying *Options:* electronic application, early admission, deferred entrance. *Application fee:* $50. *Required:* high school transcript. *Required for some:* interview. *Recommended:* essay or personal statement. *Application deadlines:* rolling (freshmen), rolling (transfers). *Notification:* continuous (freshmen), continuous (transfers).

Freshman Application Contact Admissions Office, Penn State Hazleton, Hazleton, PA 18201-1291. *Phone:* 570-450-3142. *Toll-free phone:* 800-279-8495. *Fax:* 570-450-3182. *E-mail:* admissions-hn@psu.edu. *Website:* http://www.hn.psu.edu/.

Penn State Lehigh Valley
Fogelsville, Pennsylvania

- **State-related** primarily 2-year, founded 1912, part of Pennsylvania State University
- **Rural** campus
- **Coed,** 889 undergraduate students, 81% full-time, 43% women, 57% men

Undergraduates 719 full-time, 170 part-time. 5% are from out of state; 4% Black or African American, non-Hispanic/Latino; 16% Hispanic/Latino; 10% Asian, non-Hispanic/Latino; 0.3% Native Hawaiian or other Pacific Islander, non-Hispanic/Latino; 2% Two or more races, non-Hispanic/Latino; 2% Race/ethnicity unknown; 0.8% international; 9% transferred in. *Retention:* 81% of full-time freshmen returned.

Freshmen *Admission:* 860 applied, 741 admitted, 233 enrolled. *Average high school GPA:* 3. *Test scores:* SAT critical reading scores over 500: 45%; SAT math scores over 500: 52%; SAT writing scores over 500: 37%; ACT scores over 18: 100%; SAT critical reading scores over 600: 12%; SAT math scores over 600: 17%; SAT writing scores over 600: 10%; SAT math scores over 700: 2%.

Faculty *Total:* 86, 48% full-time, 44% with terminal degrees. *Student/faculty ratio:* 14:1.

Majors Accounting; acting; actuarial science; adult and continuing education administration; advertising; aerospace, aeronautical and astronautical/space engineering; African American/Black studies; agribusiness; agricultural and extension education; agricultural business and management related; agricultural engineering; agricultural mechanization; agriculture; American studies; animal sciences; animal sciences related; anthropology; applied economics; archeology; architectural engineering; art; art history, criticism and conservation; art teacher education; Asian studies (East); astronomy;

atmospheric sciences and meteorology; biochemistry; bioengineering and biomedical engineering; biological and biomedical sciences related; biological and physical sciences; biology/biological sciences; biology/biotechnology laboratory technician; business/commerce; business/managerial economics; chemical engineering; chemistry; civil engineering; classics and classical languages; communication and journalism related; communication sciences and disorders; comparative literature; computer and information sciences; computer engineering; criminal justice/law enforcement administration; economics; electrical and electronics engineering; elementary education; engineering science; English; environmental/environmental health engineering; film/cinema/video studies; finance; food science; foreign languages and literatures; forest sciences and biology; forest technology; French; geography; geological and earth sciences/geosciences related; geology/earth science; German; graphic design; health/health-care administration; history; horticultural science; hospitality administration related; human development and family studies; human nutrition; industrial engineering; information science/studies; international business/trade/commerce; international relations and affairs; Italian; Japanese; Jewish/Judaic studies; journalism; kinesiology and exercise science; labor and industrial relations; landscape architecture; landscaping and groundskeeping; Latin American studies; liberal arts and sciences/liberal studies; logistics, materials, and supply chain management; management information systems; management sciences and quantitative methods related; marketing/marketing management; materials science; mathematics; mechanical engineering; medical microbiology and bacteriology; medieval and Renaissance studies; mining and mineral engineering; natural resources and conservation related; natural resources/conservation; nuclear engineering; organizational behavior; parks, recreation and leisure facilities management; petroleum engineering; philosophy; physics; political science and government; premedical studies; professional, technical, business, and scientific writing; psychology; registered nursing/registered nurse; rehabilitation and therapeutic professions related; religious studies; Russian; secondary education; sociology; soil science and agronomy; Spanish; special education; speech communication and rhetoric; statistics; theater design and technology; turf and turfgrass management; visual and performing arts; women's studies.

Academics *Calendar:* semesters. *Degrees:* certificates, associate, bachelor's, and postbachelor's certificates (enrollment figures include students enrolled at The Graduate School at Penn State who are taking courses at this location). *Special study options:* adult/continuing education programs. *ROTC:* Army (c).

Student Life *Housing:* college housing not available.

Athletics Member NJCAA. *Intercollegiate sports:* baseball M, basketball M/W, bowling M(c)/W(c), cheerleading M/W, cross-country running M/W, football M(c), golf M(c)/W(c), ice hockey M(c)/W(c), skiing (downhill) M(c)/W(c), soccer M(c)/W, tennis M/W, volleyball M(c)/W. *Intramural sports:* badminton M/W, basketball M/W, football M/W, golf M/W, soccer M/W, volleyball M/W.

Standardized Tests *Required:* SAT or ACT (for admission).

Costs (2013–14) *Tuition:* state resident $12,474 full-time, $504 per credit hour part-time; nonresident $19,030 full-time, $793 per credit hour part-time. Full-time tuition and fees vary according to course level, degree level, location, program, and student level. Part-time tuition and fees vary according to course level, course load, degree level, location, program, and student level. *Required fees:* $876 full-time. *Payment plans:* installment, deferred payment. *Waivers:* employees or children of employees.

Financial Aid Of all full-time matriculated undergraduates who enrolled in 2012, 588 applied for aid, 486 were judged to have need, 9 had their need fully met. In 2012, 47 non-need-based awards were made. *Average percent of need met:* 59%. *Average financial aid package:* $9985. *Average need-based loan:* $4109. *Average need-based gift aid:* $6861. *Average non-need-based aid:* $1901. *Average indebtedness upon graduation:* $35,430.

Applying *Options:* electronic application, early admission, deferred entrance. *Application fee:* $50. *Required:* high school transcript. *Application deadlines:* rolling (freshmen), rolling (transfers). *Notification:* continuous (freshmen), continuous (transfers).

Freshman Application Contact Admissions Office, Penn State Lehigh Valley, 2809 Saucon Valley Road, Fogelsville, PA 18051-9999. *Phone:* 610-285-5000. *Fax:* 610-285-5220. *E-mail:* admissions-lv@psu.edu. *Website:* http://www.lv.psu.edu/.

Penn State Mont Alto
Mont Alto, Pennsylvania

- **State-related** primarily 2-year, founded 1929, part of Pennsylvania State University
- **Small-town** campus
- **Coed,** 1,022 undergraduate students, 72% full-time, 60% women, 40% men

Undergraduates 737 full-time, 285 part-time. 16% are from out of state; 11% Black or African American, non-Hispanic/Latino; 4% Hispanic/Latino; 1% Asian, non-Hispanic/Latino; 0.1% Native Hawaiian or other Pacific Islander, non-Hispanic/Latino; 3% Two or more races, non-Hispanic/Latino; 1% Race/ethnicity unknown; 0.3% international; 4% transferred in; 27% live on campus. *Retention:* 74% of full-time freshmen returned.

Freshmen *Admission:* 808 applied, 654 admitted, 321 enrolled. *Average high school GPA:* 3.05. *Test scores:* SAT critical reading scores over 500: 36%; SAT math scores over 500: 41%; SAT writing scores over 500: 30%; ACT scores over 18: 64%; SAT critical reading scores over 600: 10%; SAT math scores over 600: 12%; SAT writing scores over 600: 5%; ACT scores over 24: 18%; SAT math scores over 700: 1%.

Faculty *Total:* 103, 55% full-time, 37% with terminal degrees. *Student/faculty ratio:* 12:1.

Majors Accounting; acting; actuarial science; adult and continuing education administration; advertising; aerospace, aeronautical and astronautical/space engineering; African American/Black studies; agribusiness; agricultural and extension education; agricultural business and management related; agricultural engineering; agricultural mechanization; agriculture; agronomy and crop science; animal sciences; animal sciences related; anthropology; applied economics; archeology; architectural engineering; art; art history, criticism and conservation; art teacher education; Asian studies (East); astronomy; atmospheric sciences and meteorology; biochemistry; bioengineering and biomedical engineering; biological and biomedical sciences related; biological and physical sciences; biology/biological sciences; biology/biotechnology laboratory technician; business administration and management; business/commerce; business/managerial economics; chemical engineering; chemistry; civil engineering; classics and classical languages; communication and journalism related; communication sciences and disorders; comparative literature; computer and information sciences; computer engineering; criminal justice/law enforcement administration; economics; electrical and electronics engineering; elementary education; engineering science; English; environmental/environmental health engineering; film/cinema/video studies; finance; food science; foreign language teacher education; forest sciences and biology; forest technology; French; geography; geological and earth sciences/geosciences related; geology/earth science; German; graphic design; health/health-care administration; history; horticultural science; hospitality administration related; human development and family studies; human nutrition; industrial engineering; information science/studies; international relations and affairs; Italian; Japanese; Jewish/Judaic studies; journalism; kinesiology and exercise science; labor and industrial relations; landscaping and groundskeeping; Latin American studies; liberal arts and sciences/liberal studies; management information systems; marketing/marketing management; materials science; mathematics; mechanical engineering; medical microbiology and bacteriology; medieval and Renaissance studies; mining and mineral engineering; music; natural resources and conservation related; natural resources/conservation; nuclear engineering; occupational therapist assistant; occupational therapy; organizational behavior; parks, recreation and leisure facilities management; petroleum engineering; philosophy; physical therapy technology; physics; political science and government; premedical studies; psychology; registered nursing/registered nurse; rehabilitation and therapeutic professions related; religious studies; Russian; secondary education; sociology; soil science and agronomy; Spanish; special education; speech communication and rhetoric; statistics; theater design and technology; toxicology; turf and turfgrass management; visual and performing arts; women's studies.

Academics *Calendar:* semesters. *Degrees:* certificates, associate, and bachelor's. *Special study options:* adult/continuing education programs. *ROTC:* Army (c).

Student Life *Housing Options:* coed, special housing for students with disabilities. Campus housing is university owned. Freshman campus housing is guaranteed. *Campus security:* 24-hour patrols, controlled dormitory access.

Athletics Member NJCAA. *Intercollegiate sports:* basketball M/W, cheerleading M/W, cross-country running M/W, golf M/W, soccer M/W, softball W, tennis M/W, volleyball W. *Intramural sports:* badminton M/W, basketball M/W, cheerleading M(c)/W(c), racquetball M/W, soccer M/W, softball W, volleyball M/W.

Standardized Tests *Required:* SAT or ACT (for admission).

Costs (2013–14) *Tuition:* state resident $12,474 full-time, $504 per credit hour part-time; nonresident $19,030 full-time, $793 per credit hour part-time. Full-time tuition and fees vary according to course level, degree level, location, program, and student level. Part-time tuition and fees vary according to course level, course load, degree level, location, program, and student level. *Required fees:* $882 full-time. *Room and board:* $9690; room only: $4910. Room and board charges vary according to board plan, housing facility, and location. *Payment plans:* installment, deferred payment. *Waivers:* employees or children of employees.

Financial Aid Of all full-time matriculated undergraduates who enrolled in 2012, 730 applied for aid, 650 were judged to have need, 37 had their need fully met. In 2012, 42 non-need-based awards were made. *Average percent of need met:* 61%. *Average financial aid package:* $11,013. *Average need-based loan:* $4020. *Average need-based gift aid:* $6302. *Average non-need-based aid:* $3053. *Average indebtedness upon graduation:* $35,430.

Applying *Options:* electronic application, early admission, deferred entrance. *Application fee:* $50. *Required:* high school transcript. *Required for some:* interview. *Recommended:* essay or personal statement. *Application deadlines:* rolling (freshmen), rolling (transfers). *Notification:* continuous (freshmen), continuous (transfers).

Freshman Application Contact Admissions Office, Penn State Mont Alto, 1 Campus Drive, Mont Alto, PA 17237-9703. *Phone:* 717-749-6130. *Toll-free phone:* 800-392-6173. *Fax:* 717-749-6132. *E-mail:* psuma@psu.edu. *Website:* http://www.ma.psu.edu/.

Penn State New Kensington
New Kensington, Pennsylvania

- **State-related** primarily 2-year, founded 1958, part of Pennsylvania State University
- **Small-town** campus
- **Coed,** 680 undergraduate students, 77% full-time, 42% women, 58% men

Undergraduates 524 full-time, 156 part-time. 3% are from out of state; 4% Black or African American, non-Hispanic/Latino; 1% Hispanic/Latino; 2% Asian, non-Hispanic/Latino; 0.2% Native Hawaiian or other Pacific Islander, non-Hispanic/Latino; 1% Two or more races, non-Hispanic/Latino; 0.8% Race/ethnicity unknown; 2% international; 8% transferred in. *Retention:* 71% of full-time freshmen returned.

Freshmen *Admission:* 457 applied, 362 admitted, 168 enrolled. *Average high school GPA:* 3.16. *Test scores:* SAT critical reading scores over 500: 47%; SAT math scores over 500: 58%; SAT writing scores over 500: 32%; ACT scores over 18: 100%; SAT critical reading scores over 600: 10%; SAT math scores over 600: 21%; SAT writing scores over 600: 3%; ACT scores over 24: 75%; SAT math scores over 700: 1%; ACT scores over 30: 25%.

Faculty *Total:* 61, 59% full-time, 46% with terminal degrees. *Student/faculty ratio:* 13:1.

Majors Accounting; acting; actuarial science; adult and continuing education administration; advertising; aerospace, aeronautical and astronautical/space engineering; African American/Black studies; agribusiness; agricultural and extension education; agricultural business and management related; agricultural engineering; agricultural mechanization; agriculture; agronomy and crop science; animal sciences; animal sciences related; anthropology; applied economics; archeology; architectural engineering; art; art history, criticism and conservation; art teacher education; Asian studies (East); astronomy; atmospheric sciences and meteorology; biochemistry; bioengineering and biomedical engineering; biological and biomedical sciences related; biological and physical sciences; biology/biological sciences; biology/biotechnology laboratory technician; biomedical technology; business administration and management; business/commerce; business/managerial economics; chemical engineering; chemistry; civil engineering; classics and classical languages; communication and journalism related; communication sciences and disorders; comparative literature; computer and information sciences; computer engineering; computer engineering technology; criminal justice/law enforcement administration; economics; electrical and electronics engineering; electrical, electronic and communications engineering technology; elementary education; engineering science; English; environmental/environmental health engineering; film/cinema/video studies; finance; food science; forest sciences and biology; forest technology; French; geography; geological and earth sciences/geosciences related; geology/earth science; German; graphic design; health/health-care administration; history; horticultural science; hospitality administration related; human development and family studies; human nutrition; industrial engineering; information science/studies; international relations and affairs; Italian; Japanese; Jewish/Judaic studies; journalism; kinesiology and exercise science; labor and industrial relations; landscaping and groundskeeping; Latin American studies; liberal arts and sciences/liberal studies; logistics, materials, and supply chain management; management information systems; marketing/marketing management; materials science; mathematics; mechanical engineering; mechanical engineering/mechanical technology; medical microbiology and bacteriology; medical radiologic technology; medieval and Renaissance studies; metallurgical technology; mining and mineral engineering; music; natural resources and conservation related; natural resources/conservation; nuclear engineering; organizational behavior; parks, recreation and leisure facilities management; petroleum engineering; philosophy; physics; political science and government; premedical studies; psychology; registered nursing/registered nurse; rehabilitation and therapeutic professions related; religious studies; Russian; secondary education; sociology; soil science and agronomy; Spanish; special education; speech communication and rhetoric; statistics; telecommunications technology; theater design and technology; toxicology; turf and turfgrass management; visual and performing arts; women's studies.

Academics *Calendar:* semesters. *Degrees:* certificates, associate, bachelor's, and master's. *Special study options:* adult/continuing education programs, external degree program. *ROTC:* Air Force (c).

Student Life *Campus security:* part-time trained security personnel.

Athletics Member NJCAA. *Intercollegiate sports:* baseball M, basketball M/W, cheerleading M/W, golf M/W, softball W, volleyball W. *Intramural sports:* badminton M/W, basketball M/W, bowling M/W, cheerleading M(c)/W(c), football M/W, ice hockey M(c)/W(c), racquetball M/W, skiing (downhill) M(c)/W(c), soccer M/W, softball W, volleyball M/W.

Standardized Tests *Required:* SAT or ACT (for admission).

Costs (2013–14) *Tuition:* state resident $504 per credit part-time; nonresident $793 per credit part-time. Full-time tuition and fees vary according to course level, degree level, location, program, and student level. Part-time tuition and fees vary according to course level, course load, degree level, location, program, and student level. *Payment plans:* installment, deferred payment. *Waivers:* employees or children of employees.

Financial Aid Of all full-time matriculated undergraduates who enrolled in 2012, 492 applied for aid, 423 were judged to have need, 25 had their need fully met. In 2012, 38 non-need-based awards were made. *Average percent of need met:* 62%. *Average financial aid package:* $9664. *Average need-based loan:* $4073. *Average need-based gift aid:* $5709. *Average non-need-based aid:* $2470. *Average indebtedness upon graduation:* $35,430.

Applying *Options:* electronic application, early admission, deferred entrance. *Application fee:* $50. *Required:* high school transcript. *Required for some:* interview. *Recommended:* essay or personal statement. *Application deadlines:* rolling (freshmen), rolling (transfers). *Notification:* continuous (freshmen), continuous (transfers).

Freshman Application Contact Admissions Office, Penn State New Kensington, 3550 Seventh Street Road, New Kensington, PA 15068. *Phone:* 724-334-5466. *Toll-free phone:* 888-968-7297. *Fax:* 724-334-6111. *E-mail:* nkadmissions@psu.edu.

Website: http://www.nk.psu.edu/.

Penn State Schuylkill
Schuylkill Haven, Pennsylvania

- **State-related** primarily 2-year, founded 1934, part of Pennsylvania State University
- **Small-town** campus
- **Coed,** 837 undergraduate students, 79% full-time, 61% women, 39% men

Undergraduates 658 full-time, 179 part-time. 13% are from out of state; 22% Black or African American, non-Hispanic/Latino; 6% Hispanic/Latino; 2% Asian, non-Hispanic/Latino; 0.1% Native Hawaiian or other Pacific Islander, non-Hispanic/Latino; 0.3% American Indian or Alaska Native, non-Hispanic/Latino; 2% Two or more races, non-Hispanic/Latino; 3% Race/ethnicity unknown; 2% international; 6% transferred in; 31% live on campus. *Retention:* 71% of full-time freshmen returned.

Freshmen *Admission:* 723 applied, 522 admitted, 260 enrolled. *Average high school GPA:* 2.76. *Test scores:* SAT critical reading scores over 500: 23%; SAT math scores over 500: 30%; SAT writing scores over 500: 18%; ACT scores over 18: 63%; SAT critical reading scores over 600: 4%; SAT math scores over 600: 9%; SAT writing scores over 600: 4%; ACT scores over 24: 13%; SAT math scores over 700: 2%; ACT scores over 30: 13%.

Faculty *Total:* 67, 58% full-time, 51% with terminal degrees. *Student/faculty ratio:* 15:1.

Majors Accounting; acting; actuarial science; adult and continuing education administration; advertising; aerospace, aeronautical and astronautical/space engineering; African American/Black studies; agribusiness; agricultural and extension education; agricultural business and management related; agricultural engineering; agricultural mechanization; agriculture; American studies; animal sciences; animal sciences related; anthropology; applied economics; archeology; architectural engineering; art; art history, criticism and conservation; art teacher education; Asian studies (East); astronomy; atmospheric sciences and meteorology; biochemistry; bioengineering and biomedical engineering; biological and biomedical sciences related; biological and physical sciences; biology/biological sciences; biology/biotechnology laboratory technician; biomedical technology; business/commerce; business/managerial economics; chemical engineering; chemistry; civil engineering; classics and classical languages; clinical/medical laboratory technology; communication and journalism related; communication sciences and disorders; comparative literature; computer and information sciences; computer engineering; criminal justice/law enforcement administration; criminal justice/safety; economics; electrical and electronics engineering; electrical, electronic and communications engineering technology; elementary education; engineering science; English; environmental/environmental health engineering; film/cinema/video studies; finance; food science; forest sciences and biology; forest technology; French; geography; geological and earth sciences/geosciences related; geology/earth science; German; graphic design; health/health-care administration; history; horticultural science; hospitality administration related; human development and family studies; human nutrition; industrial engineering; information science/studies; international business/trade/commerce; international relations and affairs; Italian; Japanese; Jewish/Judaic studies; journalism; kinesiology and exercise science; labor and industrial relations; landscape architecture; landscaping and groundskeeping;

Latin American studies; liberal arts and sciences/liberal studies; logistics, materials, and supply chain management; management information systems; management sciences and quantitative methods related; marketing/marketing management; materials science; mathematics; mechanical engineering; medical microbiology and bacteriology; medical radiologic technology; medieval and Renaissance studies; metallurgical technology; mining and mineral engineering; natural resources and conservation related; natural resources/conservation; nuclear engineering; organizational behavior; parks, recreation and leisure facilities management; petroleum engineering; philosophy; physics; political science and government; premedical studies; psychology; registered nursing/registered nurse; rehabilitation and therapeutic professions related; religious studies; Russian; secondary education; sociology; soil science and agronomy; Spanish; special education; speech communication and rhetoric; statistics; telecommunications technology; theater design and technology; turf and turfgrass management; visual and performing arts; women's studies.

Academics *Calendar:* semesters. *Degrees:* certificates, associate, and bachelor's (bachelor's degree programs completed at the Harrisburg campus). *Special study options:* adult/continuing education programs, external degree program.

Student Life *Housing Options:* special housing for students with disabilities. *Campus security:* 24-hour patrols, controlled dormitory access.

Athletics Member NJCAA. *Intercollegiate sports:* basketball M, cross-country running M/W, golf M, soccer M, softball W, volleyball W. *Intramural sports:* basketball M/W, football M, soccer M/W, softball M/W, table tennis M/W, volleyball M/W.

Standardized Tests *Required:* SAT or ACT (for admission).

Financial Aid Of all full-time matriculated undergraduates who enrolled in 2012, 636 applied for aid, 586 were judged to have need, 15 had their need fully met. In 2012, 17 non-need-based awards were made. *Average percent of need met:* 63%. *Average financial aid package:* $11,497. *Average need-based loan:* $4077. *Average need-based gift aid:* $6889. *Average non-need-based aid:* $2121. *Average indebtedness upon graduation:* $35,430.

Applying *Options:* electronic application, early admission, deferred entrance. *Application fee:* $50. *Required:* high school transcript. *Application deadlines:* rolling (freshmen), rolling (transfers). *Notification:* continuous (freshmen), continuous (transfers).

Freshman Application Contact Admissions Office, Penn State Schuylkill, 200 University Drive, Schuylkill Haven, PA 17972-2208. *Phone:* 570-385-6252. *Fax:* 570-385-6272. *E-mail:* sl-admissions@psu.edu.

Website: http://www.sl.psu.edu/.

Penn State Wilkes-Barre
Lehman, Pennsylvania

- **State-related** primarily 2-year, founded 1916, part of Pennsylvania State University
- **Rural** campus
- **Coed,** 606 undergraduate students, 86% full-time, 27% women, 73% men

Undergraduates 519 full-time, 87 part-time. 6% are from out of state; 4% Black or African American, non-Hispanic/Latino; 6% Hispanic/Latino; 0.7% Asian, non-Hispanic/Latino; 0.2% Native Hawaiian or other Pacific Islander, non-Hispanic/Latino; 2% Two or more races, non-Hispanic/Latino; 1% Race/ethnicity unknown; 0.7% international; 5% transferred in. *Retention:* 81% of full-time freshmen returned.

Freshmen *Admission:* 451 applied, 400 admitted, 168 enrolled. *Average high school GPA:* 3.05. *Test scores:* SAT critical reading scores over 500: 46%; SAT math scores over 500: 58%; SAT writing scores over 500: 32%; ACT scores over 18: 83%; SAT critical reading scores over 600: 9%; SAT math scores over 600: 17%; SAT writing scores over 600: 4%; ACT scores over 24: 33%; SAT math scores over 700: 1%; SAT writing scores over 700: 1%.

Faculty *Total:* 51, 67% full-time, 51% with terminal degrees. *Student/faculty ratio:* 14:1.

Majors Accounting; acting; actuarial science; adult and continuing education administration; advertising; aerospace, aeronautical and astronautical/space engineering; African American/Black studies; agribusiness; agricultural and extension education; agricultural business and management related; agricultural engineering; agricultural mechanization; agriculture; agronomy and crop science; animal sciences; animal sciences related; anthropology; applied economics; archeology; architectural engineering; art; art history, criticism and conservation; art teacher education; astronomy; atmospheric sciences and meteorology; biochemistry; bioengineering and biomedical engineering; biological and biomedical sciences related; biological and physical sciences; biology/biological sciences; biology/biotechnology laboratory technician; business administration and management; business/commerce; business/managerial economics; chemical engineering; chemistry; civil engineering; classics and classical languages; communication and journalism related; communication sciences and disorders; comparative literature; computer and information sciences; computer engineering; criminal justice/law enforcement administration; criminal justice/safety; economics;

electrical and electronics engineering; electrical, electronic and communications engineering technology; elementary education; engineering science; English; environmental/environmental health engineering; film/cinema/video studies; finance; food science; forest sciences and biology; forest technology; French; geography; geological and earth sciences/geosciences related; geology/earth science; German; graphic design; health/health-care administration; history; horticultural science; hospitality administration related; human development and family studies; human nutrition; industrial engineering; information science/studies; international relations and affairs; Italian; Japanese; Jewish/Judaic studies; journalism; kinesiology and exercise science; labor and industrial relations; landscape architecture; landscaping and groundskeeping; Latin American studies; liberal arts and sciences/liberal studies; management information systems; manufacturing engineering; marketing/marketing management; materials science; mathematics; mechanical engineering; medical microbiology and bacteriology; medieval and Renaissance studies; metallurgical technology; mining and mineral engineering; music; natural resources and conservation related; natural resources/conservation; nuclear engineering; organizational behavior; parks, recreation and leisure facilities management; petroleum engineering; philosophy; physics; political science and government; premedical studies; psychology; registered nursing/registered nurse; rehabilitation and therapeutic professions related; religious studies; Russian; secondary education; sociology; soil science and agronomy; Spanish; special education; speech communication and rhetoric; statistics; surveying technology; telecommunications technology; theater design and technology; toxicology; turf and turfgrass management; visual and performing arts; women's studies.

Academics *Calendar:* semesters. *Degrees:* certificates, associate, bachelor's, and postbachelor's certificates (enrollment figures include students enrolled at The Graduate School at Penn State who are taking courses at this location). *Special study options:* adult/continuing education programs. *ROTC:* Army (c), Air Force (c).

Student Life *Housing:* college housing not available.

Athletics Member NJCAA. *Intercollegiate sports:* baseball M, basketball M, cross-country running M/W, golf M/W, soccer M/W, volleyball W. *Intramural sports:* basketball M/W, bowling M(c)/W(c), cheerleading M(c)/W(c), football M, racquetball M/W, softball W, volleyball M(c)/W.

Standardized Tests *Required:* SAT or ACT (for admission).

Costs (2013–14) *Tuition:* state resident $12,474 full-time, $504 per credit hour part-time; nonresident $19,030 full-time, $793 per credit hour part-time. Full-time tuition and fees vary according to course level, degree level, location, program, and student level. Part-time tuition and fees vary according to course level, course load, degree level, location, program, and student level. *Required fees:* $764 full-time. *Payment plans:* installment, deferred payment. *Waivers:* employees or children of employees.

Financial Aid Of all full-time matriculated undergraduates who enrolled in 2012, 484 applied for aid, 399 were judged to have need, 9 had their need fully met. In 2012, 36 non-need-based awards were made. *Average percent of need met:* 63%. *Average financial aid package:* $10,091. *Average need-based loan:* $4071. *Average need-based gift aid:* $6346. *Average non-need-based aid:* $2766. *Average indebtedness upon graduation:* $35,430.

Applying *Options:* electronic application, early admission, deferred entrance. *Application fee:* $50. *Required:* high school transcript. *Required for some:* interview. *Recommended:* essay or personal statement. *Application deadlines:* rolling (freshmen), rolling (transfers). *Notification:* continuous (freshmen), continuous (transfers).

Freshman Application Contact Admissions Office, Penn State Wilkes-Barre, PO PSU, Lehman, PA 18627-0217. *Phone:* 570-675-9238. *Fax:* 570-675-9113. *E-mail:* wbadmissions@psu.edu. *Website:* http://www.wb.psu.edu/.

Penn State Worthington Scranton

Dunmore, Pennsylvania

- **State-related** primarily 2-year, founded 1923, part of Pennsylvania State University
- **Small-town** campus
- **Coed,** 1,178 undergraduate students, 80% full-time, 55% women, 45% men

Undergraduates 943 full-time, 235 part-time. 2% are from out of state; 3% Black or African American, non-Hispanic/Latino; 5% Hispanic/Latino; 5% Asian, non-Hispanic/Latino; 0.1% Native Hawaiian or other Pacific Islander, non-Hispanic/Latino; 0.1% American Indian or Alaska Native, non-Hispanic/Latino; 2% Two or more races, non-Hispanic/Latino; 2% Race/ethnicity unknown; 0.7% international; 6% transferred in. *Retention:* 65% of full-time freshmen returned.

Freshmen *Admission:* 690 applied, 554 admitted, 257 enrolled. *Average high school GPA:* 2.93. *Test scores:* SAT critical reading scores over 500: 36%; SAT math scores over 500: 36%; SAT writing scores over 500: 34%; ACT scores over 18: 100%; SAT critical reading scores over 600: 9%; SAT math scores over 600: 7%; SAT writing scores over 600: 8%; ACT scores over 24: 33%; SAT critical reading scores over 700: 1%; ACT scores over 30: 17%.

Faculty *Total:* 97, 52% full-time, 40% with terminal degrees. *Student/faculty ratio:* 16:1.

Majors Accounting; acting; actuarial science; adult and continuing education administration; advertising; aerospace, aeronautical and astronautical/space engineering; African American/Black studies; agribusiness; agricultural and extension education; agricultural business and management related; agricultural engineering; agricultural mechanization; agriculture; agronomy and crop science; American studies; animal sciences; animal sciences related; anthropology; applied economics; archeology; architectural engineering; architectural engineering technology; art; art history, criticism and conservation; art teacher education; Asian studies (East); astronomy; atmospheric sciences and meteorology; biochemistry; bioengineering and biomedical engineering; biological and biomedical sciences related; biological and physical sciences; biology/biological sciences; biology/biotechnology laboratory technician; business administration and management; business/commerce; business/managerial economics; chemical engineering; chemistry; civil engineering; classics and classical languages; communication and journalism related; communication sciences and disorders; comparative literature; computer and information sciences; computer engineering; criminal justice/law enforcement administration; economics; electrical and electronics engineering; electrical, electronic and communications engineering technology; elementary education; engineering science; English; environmental/environmental health engineering; film/cinema/video studies; finance; food science; foreign language teacher education; forest sciences and biology; forest technology; French; geography; geological and earth sciences/geosciences related; geology/earth science; German; graphic design; health/health-care administration; history; horticultural science; hospitality administration related; human development and family studies; human nutrition; industrial engineering; information science/studies; international relations and affairs; Italian; Japanese; Jewish/Judaic studies; journalism; kinesiology and exercise science; labor and industrial relations; landscaping and groundskeeping; Latin American studies; liberal arts and sciences/liberal studies; management information systems; marketing/marketing management; materials science; mathematics; mechanical engineering; medical microbiology and bacteriology; medieval and Renaissance studies; mining and mineral engineering; music; natural resources and conservation related; natural resources/conservation; nuclear engineering; organizational behavior; parks, recreation and leisure facilities management; petroleum engineering; philosophy; physics; political science and government; premedical studies; psychology; registered nursing/registered nurse; rehabilitation and therapeutic professions related; religious studies; Russian; secondary education; sociology; soil science and agronomy; Spanish; special education; speech communication and rhetoric; statistics; theater design and technology; turf and turfgrass management; visual and performing arts; women's studies.

Academics *Calendar:* semesters. *Degrees:* certificates, associate, and bachelor's. *Special study options:* adult/continuing education programs. *ROTC:* Army (c), Air Force (c).

Student Life *Housing:* college housing not available. *Options:* coed.

Athletics Member NJCAA. *Intercollegiate sports:* baseball M, basketball M/W, cheerleading M/W, cross-country running M/W, soccer M, softball W, volleyball W. *Intramural sports:* basketball M/W, bowling M(c)/W(c), skiing (downhill) M(c)/W(c), soccer M/W, softball M/W, volleyball M/W(c), weight lifting M(c)/W(c).

Standardized Tests *Required:* SAT or ACT (for admission).

Costs (2013–14) *Tuition:* state resident $12,474 full-time, $504 per credit hour part-time; nonresident $19,030 full-time, $793 per credit hour part-time. Full-time tuition and fees vary according to course level, degree level, location, program, and student level. Part-time tuition and fees vary according to course level, course load, degree level, location, program, and student level. *Required fees:* $756 full-time. *Payment plans:* installment, deferred payment. *Waivers:* employees or children of employees.

Financial Aid Of all full-time matriculated undergraduates who enrolled in 2012, 861 applied for aid, 764 were judged to have need, 27 had their need fully met. In 2012, 31 non-need-based awards were made. *Average percent of need met:* 59%. *Average financial aid package:* $9736. *Average need-based loan:* $3959. *Average need-based gift aid:* $6445. *Average non-need-based aid:* $2447. *Average indebtedness upon graduation:* $35,430.

Applying *Options:* electronic application, early admission, deferred entrance. *Application fee:* $50. *Required:* high school transcript. *Required for some:* interview. *Recommended:* essay or personal statement. *Application deadlines:* rolling (freshmen), rolling (transfers). *Notification:* continuous (freshmen), continuous (transfers).

Freshman Application Contact Admissions Office, Penn State Worthington Scranton, 120 Ridge View Drive, Dunmore, PA 18512-1699. *Phone:* 570-963-2500. *Fax:* 570-963-2524. *E-mail:* wsadmissions@psu.edu. *Website:* http://www.sn.psu.edu/.

Penn State York

York, Pennsylvania

- **State-related** primarily 2-year, founded 1926, part of Pennsylvania State University
- **Suburban** campus
- **Coed,** 1,141 undergraduate students, 72% full-time, 44% women, 56% men

Undergraduates 822 full-time, 319 part-time. 8% are from out of state; 8% Black or African American, non-Hispanic/Latino; 7% Hispanic/Latino; 6% Asian, non-Hispanic/Latino; 0.2% American Indian or Alaska Native, non-Hispanic/Latino; 2% Two or more races, non-Hispanic/Latino; 2% Race/ethnicity unknown; 7% international; 4% transferred in. *Retention:* 76% of full-time freshmen returned.

Freshmen *Admission:* 1,154 applied, 944 admitted, 292 enrolled. *Average high school GPA:* 3.07. *Test scores:* SAT critical reading scores over 500: 44%; SAT math scores over 500: 59%; SAT writing scores over 500: 43%; ACT scores over 18: 73%; SAT critical reading scores over 600: 12%; SAT math scores over 600: 25%; SAT writing scores over 600: 10%; ACT scores over 24: 20%; SAT critical reading scores over 700: 1%; SAT math scores over 700: 6%; SAT writing scores over 700: 2%.

Faculty *Total:* 97, 52% full-time, 53% with terminal degrees. *Student/faculty ratio:* 15:1.

Majors Accounting; acting; actuarial science; adult and continuing education administration; advertising; aerospace, aeronautical and astronautical/space engineering; African American/Black studies; agribusiness; agricultural and extension education; agricultural business and management related; agricultural engineering; agricultural mechanization; agriculture; agronomy and crop science; American studies; animal sciences; animal sciences related; anthropology; applied economics; archeology; architectural engineering; art; art history, criticism and conservation; art teacher education; Asian studies (East); astronomy; atmospheric sciences and meteorology; biochemistry; bioengineering and biomedical engineering; biological and biomedical sciences related; biological and physical sciences; biology/biological sciences; biology/biotechnology laboratory technician; biomedical technology; business administration and management; business/commerce; business/managerial economics; chemical engineering; chemistry; civil engineering; classics and classical languages; communication and journalism related; communication sciences and disorders; comparative literature; computer and information sciences; computer engineering; criminal justice/law enforcement administration; economics; electrical and electronics engineering; electrical, electronic and communications engineering technology; elementary education; engineering science; English; environmental/environmental health engineering; film/cinema/video studies; finance; food science; foreign language teacher education; forest sciences and biology; forest technology; French; geography; geological and earth sciences/geosciences related; geology/earth science; German; graphic design; health/health-care administration; history; horticultural science; hospitality administration related; human development and family studies; human nutrition; industrial engineering; industrial technology; information science/studies; international relations and affairs; Italian; Japanese; Jewish/Judaic studies; journalism; kinesiology and exercise science; labor and industrial relations; landscaping and groundskeeping; Latin American studies; liberal arts and sciences/liberal studies; logistics, materials, and supply chain management; management information systems; manufacturing engineering; marketing/marketing management; materials science; mathematics; mechanical engineering; mechanical engineering/mechanical technology; medical microbiology and bacteriology; medieval and Renaissance studies; metallurgical technology; mining and mineral engineering; music; natural resources and conservation related; natural resources/conservation; nuclear engineering; organizational behavior; parks, recreation and leisure facilities management; petroleum engineering; philosophy; physics; political science and government; premedical studies; psychology; registered nursing/registered nurse; rehabilitation and therapeutic professions related; religious studies; Russian; secondary education; sociology; soil science and agronomy; Spanish; special education; speech communication and rhetoric; statistics; telecommunications technology; theater design and technology; toxicology; turf and turfgrass management; visual and performing arts; women's studies.

Academics *Calendar:* semesters. *Degrees:* certificates, associate, bachelor's, and master's (also offers up to 2 years of most bachelor's degree programs offered at University Park campus). *Special study options:* adult/continuing education programs.

Student Life *Housing:* college housing not available.

Athletics Member NJCAA.

Standardized Tests *Required:* SAT or ACT (for admission).

Costs (2013–14) *Tuition:* state resident $12,474 full-time, $504 per credit hour part-time; nonresident $19,030 full-time, $793 per credit hour part-time. Full-time tuition and fees vary according to course level, degree level, location, program, and student level. Part-time tuition and fees vary according to course level, course load, degree level, location, program, and student level. *Required fees:* $764 full-time. *Payment plans:* installment, deferred payment. *Waivers:* employees or children of employees.

Financial Aid Of all full-time matriculated undergraduates who enrolled in 2012, 660 applied for aid, 535 were judged to have need, 35 had their need fully met. In 2012, 76 non-need-based awards were made. *Average percent of need met:* 61%. *Average financial aid package:* $10,183. *Average need-based loan:* $3893. *Average need-based gift aid:* $6435. *Average non-need-based aid:* $2275. *Average indebtedness upon graduation:* $35,430.

Applying *Options:* electronic application, early admission, deferred entrance. *Application fee:* $50. *Required:* high school transcript. *Required for some:* interview. *Recommended:* essay or personal statement. *Application deadlines:* rolling (freshmen), rolling (transfers). *Notification:* continuous (freshmen), continuous (transfers).

Freshman Application Contact Admissions Office, Penn State York, 1031 Edgecomb Avenue, York, PA 17403. *Phone:* 717-771-4040. *Toll-free phone:* 800-778-6227. *Fax:* 717-771-4005. *E-mail:* ykadmission@psu.edu. *Website:* http://www.yk.psu.edu/.

Pennsylvania College of Health Sciences

Lancaster, Pennsylvania

- **Independent** primarily 2-year, founded 1903
- **Urban** campus with easy access to Harrisburg
- **Endowment** $1.1 million
- **Coed, primarily women,** 1,429 undergraduate students, 36% full-time, 86% women, 14% men

Undergraduates 520 full-time, 909 part-time. Students come from 8 states and territories; 2% are from out of state; 4% Black or African American, non-Hispanic/Latino; 5% Hispanic/Latino; 3% Asian, non-Hispanic/Latino; 0.3% Native Hawaiian or other Pacific Islander, non-Hispanic/Latino; 0.1% American Indian or Alaska Native, non-Hispanic/Latino; 0.2% Two or more races, non-Hispanic/Latino; 3% Race/ethnicity unknown; 18% transferred in. *Retention:* 88% of full-time freshmen returned.

Freshmen *Admission:* 423 applied, 220 admitted, 155 enrolled. *Test scores:* SAT critical reading scores over 500: 41%; SAT math scores over 500: 44%; SAT critical reading scores over 600: 6%; SAT math scores over 600: 7%; SAT critical reading scores over 700: 2%.

Faculty *Total:* 168, 38% full-time. *Student/faculty ratio:* 8:1.

Majors Cardiovascular technology; diagnostic medical sonography and ultrasound technology; electrocardiograph technology; health/health-care administration; health services/allied health/health sciences; medical radiologic technology; nuclear medical technology; radiologic technology/science; registered nursing/registered nurse; respiratory care therapy; surgical technology.

Academics *Degrees:* certificates, associate, and bachelor's. *Special study options:* accelerated degree program, adult/continuing education programs, advanced placement credit, distance learning, part-time degree program, services for LD students, summer session for credit.

Library Health Sciences Library with 60,590 titles, 17,719 serial subscriptions, 112 audiovisual materials, an OPAC, a Web page.

Student Life *Housing:* college housing not available. *Activities and Organizations:* Student Government Association, Soccer Club, Distance Running. *Campus security:* 24-hour emergency response devices and patrols, late-night transport/escort service. *Student services:* health clinic, personal/psychological counseling.

Athletics *Intramural sports:* cross-country running M(c)/W(c), soccer M(c)/W(c).

Standardized Tests *Required for some:* SAT or ACT (for admission).

Costs (2014–15) *Tuition:* $13,560 full-time, $452 per credit part-time. Full-time tuition and fees vary according to program. Part-time tuition and fees vary according to program. *Required fees:* $825 full-time. *Payment plans:* installment, deferred payment. *Waivers:* employees or children of employees.

Applying *Options:* electronic application, deferred entrance. *Application fee:* $35. *Required:* minimum 3.0 GPA, 2 letters of recommendation, Official GED transcript may be substituted in lieu of high school transcript. SAT or ACT scores required if graduated from high school within last 2 years. Official transcripts of all institutions attended. *Required for some:* essay or personal statement, high school transcript. *Application deadline:* 2/1 (freshmen). *Notification:* continuous (freshmen).

Freshman Application Contact Admissions Office, Pennsylvania College of Health Sciences, 410 Lime Street, Lancaster, PA 17602. *Phone:* 800-622-5443. *Toll-free phone:* 800-622-5443. *E-mail:* admission@pacollege.edu. *Website:* http://www.pacollege.edu/.

Pennsylvania Highlands Community College
Johnstown, Pennsylvania

- **State and locally supported** 2-year, founded 1994
- **Small-town** campus
- **Coed,** 2,506 undergraduate students, 39% full-time, 58% women, 42% men

Undergraduates 984 full-time, 1,522 part-time. 4% Black or African American, non-Hispanic/Latino; 0.2% Hispanic/Latino; 0.6% Asian, non-Hispanic/Latino; 0.3% American Indian or Alaska Native, non-Hispanic/Latino; 7% Race/ethnicity unknown. *Retention:* 57% of full-time freshmen returned.
Faculty *Total:* 135, 17% full-time. *Student/faculty ratio:* 17:1.
Majors Accounting; accounting technology and bookkeeping; computer and information sciences; general studies; human services.
Academics *Calendar:* semesters. *Degree:* certificates, diplomas, and associate. *Special study options:* academic remediation for entering students, adult/continuing education programs, advanced placement credit, cooperative education, distance learning, honors programs, independent study, internships, part-time degree program, services for LD students, summer session for credit.
Library Pennsylvania Highlands Community College Main Library plus 1 other with an OPAC, a Web page.
Student Life *Housing:* college housing not available.
Athletics Member NJCAA. *Intercollegiate sports:* basketball M, volleyball W.
Financial Aid Of all full-time matriculated undergraduates who enrolled in 2012, 25 Federal Work-Study jobs (averaging $2500).
Applying *Options:* electronic application. *Application fee:* $20. *Required:* high school transcript.
Freshman Application Contact Mr. Jeff Maul, Admissions Officer, Pennsylvania Highlands Community College, 101 Community College Way, Johnstown, PA 15904. *Phone:* 814-262-6431. *E-mail:* jmaul@pennhighlands.edu.
Website: http://www.pennhighlands.edu/.

Pennsylvania Institute of Technology
Media, Pennsylvania

- **Independent** 2-year, founded 1953
- **Small-town** 12-acre campus with easy access to Philadelphia
- **Coed,** 743 undergraduate students, 64% full-time, 76% women, 24% men

Undergraduates 474 full-time, 269 part-time. 63% Black or African American, non-Hispanic/Latino; 6% Hispanic/Latino; 2% Asian, non-Hispanic/Latino; 0.3% American Indian or Alaska Native, non-Hispanic/Latino; 2% Two or more races, non-Hispanic/Latino; 13% Race/ethnicity unknown. *Retention:* 53% of full-time freshmen returned.
Freshmen *Admission:* 375 enrolled.
Faculty *Total:* 80, 30% full-time. *Student/faculty ratio:* 13:1.
Majors Allied health and medical assisting services related; business administration and management; electrical, electronic and communications engineering technology; engineering technology; medical office management; pharmacy technician; physical therapy technology.
Academics *Calendar:* semesters. *Degree:* certificates and associate. *Special study options:* academic remediation for entering students, adult/continuing education programs, advanced placement credit, cooperative education, part-time degree program, summer session for credit.
Library Pennsylvania Institute of Technology Library/Learning Resource Center with 16,500 titles, 217 serial subscriptions, an OPAC, a Web page.
Student Life *Housing:* college housing not available. *Campus security:* 24-hour emergency response devices. *Student services:* personal/psychological counseling.
Athletics *Intramural sports:* basketball M/W.
Costs (2014–15) *Tuition:* $11,250 full-time, $375 per credit part-time. Full-time tuition and fees vary according to program. Part-time tuition and fees vary according to course load and program. *Required fees:* $1500 full-time, $50 per credit part-time.
Financial Aid Of all full-time matriculated undergraduates who enrolled in 2012, 15 Federal Work-Study jobs (averaging $1025). *Financial aid deadline:* 8/1.
Applying *Options:* electronic application, deferred entrance. *Application fee:* $25. *Required:* high school transcript, interview. *Required for some:* 2 letters of recommendation. *Recommended:* essay or personal statement. *Application deadlines:* 9/19 (freshmen), 9/19 (transfers). *Notification:* continuous until 9/19 (freshmen), continuous until 9/19 (transfers).
Freshman Application Contact Mr. John DeTurris, Director of Admissions, Pennsylvania Institute of Technology, 800 Manchester Avenue, Media, PA 19063-4036. *Phone:* 610-892-1543. *Toll-free phone:* 800-422-0025. *Fax:* 610-892-1510. *E-mail:* info@pit.edu.
Website: http://www.pit.edu/.

Pennsylvania School of Business
Allentown, Pennsylvania

Freshman Application Contact Mr. Bill Barber, Director, Pennsylvania School of Business, 406 West Hamilton Street, Allentown, PA 18101. *Phone:* 610-841-3333. *Fax:* 610-841-3334. *E-mail:* wbarber@pennschoolofbusiness.edu.
Website: http://www.psb.edu/.

Pittsburgh Institute of Aeronautics
Pittsburgh, Pennsylvania

Freshman Application Contact Steven J. Sabold, Director of Admissions, Pittsburgh Institute of Aeronautics, PO Box 10897, Pittsburgh, PA 15236-0897. *Phone:* 412-346-2100. *Toll-free phone:* 800-444-1440. *Fax:* 412-466-5013. *E-mail:* admissions@pia.edu.
Website: http://www.pia.edu/.

Pittsburgh Institute of Mortuary Science, Incorporated
Pittsburgh, Pennsylvania

Freshman Application Contact Ms. Karen Rocco, Registrar, Pittsburgh Institute of Mortuary Science, Incorporated, 5808 Baum Boulevard, Pittsburgh, PA 15206-3706. *Phone:* 412-362-8500 Ext. 105. *Fax:* 412-362-1684. *E-mail:* pims5808@aol.com.
Website: http://www.pims.edu/.

Pittsburgh Technical Institute
Oakdale, Pennsylvania

- **Proprietary** 2-year, founded 1946
- **Suburban** 180-acre campus with easy access to Pittsburgh
- **Coed,** 1,841 undergraduate students, 100% full-time, 43% women, 57% men
- **84% of applicants were admitted**

Undergraduates 1,841 full-time. Students come from 22 states and territories; 19% are from out of state; 11% Black or African American, non-Hispanic/Latino; 1% Hispanic/Latino; 0.9% Asian, non-Hispanic/Latino; 0.2% Native Hawaiian or other Pacific Islander, non-Hispanic/Latino; 0.1% American Indian or Alaska Native, non-Hispanic/Latino; 5% Two or more races, non-Hispanic/Latino; 12% Race/ethnicity unknown; 14% transferred in; 40% live on campus.
Freshmen *Admission:* 2,114 applied, 1,777 admitted, 719 enrolled. *Average high school GPA:* 3.33.
Faculty *Total:* 117, 62% full-time. *Student/faculty ratio:* 25:1.
Majors Business administration and management; computer graphics; computer programming; computer technology/computer systems technology; cooking and related culinary arts; drafting and design technology; electrical, electronic and communications engineering technology; electrical/electronics equipment installation and repair; homeland security, law enforcement, firefighting and protective services related; hotel/motel administration; medical/health management and clinical assistant; medical office assistant; registered nursing/registered nurse; surgical technology; web page, digital/multimedia and information resources design.
Academics *Calendar:* quarters. *Degree:* certificates and associate. *Special study options:* academic remediation for entering students, advanced placement credit, cooperative education, distance learning, double majors, internships, services for LD students.
Library Library Resource Center with 10,039 titles, 155 serial subscriptions, 2,272 audiovisual materials, an OPAC.
Student Life *Housing Options:* coed. Campus housing is university owned and leased by the school. Freshman campus housing is guaranteed. *Activities and Organizations:* drama/theater group, American Society of Travel Agents (ASTA), MEDICS Club, Alpha Beta Gamma (ABG), Drama Club, Direct Connect. *Campus security:* 24-hour emergency response devices and patrols, controlled dormitory access. *Student services:* personal/psychological counseling.
Athletics *Intramural sports:* basketball M/W, soccer M/W, softball M/W, ultimate Frisbee M/W, volleyball M/W.
Costs (2014–15) *Comprehensive fee:* $25,011 includes full-time tuition ($16,416) and room and board ($8595). Full-time tuition and fees vary according to course load and program. No tuition increase for student's term of enrollment. *Room and board:* college room only: $6100. Room and board charges vary according to housing facility. *Payment plans:* installment, deferred payment. *Waivers:* children of alumni and employees or children of employees.
Applying *Options:* electronic application, deferred entrance. *Required:* high school transcript. *Required for some:* essay or personal statement, certain programs require a criminal background check; some programs require

applicants to be in top 50-80% of class; Practical Nursing certificate and Associate Degree in Nursing require entrance exam. *Recommended:* interview. *Application deadlines:* rolling (freshmen), rolling (out-of-state freshmen), rolling (transfers), 11/15 (early action). *Notification:* continuous (freshmen), continuous (out-of-state freshmen), continuous (transfers).
Freshman Application Contact Ms. Nancy Goodlin, Admissions Office Assistant, Pittsburgh Technical Institute, 1111 McKee Road, Oakdale, PA 15071. *Phone:* 412-809-5100. *Toll-free phone:* 800-784-9675. *Fax:* 412-809-5351. *E-mail:* goodlin.nancy@pti.edu.
Website: http://www.pti.edu/.

Prism Career Institute
Upper Darby, Pennsylvania

Director of Admissions Ms. Dina Gentile, Director, Prism Career Institute, 6800 Market Street, Upper Darby, PA 19082. *Phone:* 610-789-6700. *Toll-free phone:* 800-571-2213. *Fax:* 610-789-5208. *E-mail:* dgentile@pjaschool.com.
Website: http://www.prismcareerinstitute.edu/.

Reading Area Community College
Reading, Pennsylvania

- **County-supported** 2-year, founded 1971
- **Urban** 14-acre campus with easy access to Philadelphia
- **Endowment** $8.6 million
- **Coed,** 4,538 undergraduate students, 22% full-time, 63% women, 37% men

Undergraduates 976 full-time, 3,562 part-time. 0.5% are from out of state; 13% Black or African American, non-Hispanic/Latino; 28% Hispanic/Latino; 2% Asian, non-Hispanic/Latino; 0.1% Native Hawaiian or other Pacific Islander, non-Hispanic/Latino; 0.3% American Indian or Alaska Native, non-Hispanic/Latino; 2% Two or more races, non-Hispanic/Latino; 1% Race/ethnicity unknown.
Freshmen *Admission:* 963 enrolled.
Faculty *Total:* 253, 25% full-time. *Student/faculty ratio:* 17:1.
Majors Accounting; accounting technology and bookkeeping; art; business administration and management; child-care and support services management; child-care provision; child development; clinical/medical laboratory technology; communication and media related; computer and information sciences; computer technology/computer systems technology; criminal justice/police science; elementary education; food preparation; general studies; health information/medical records technology; health professions related; health services/allied health/health sciences; human services; industrial mechanics and maintenance technology; interdisciplinary studies; liberal arts and sciences/liberal studies; licensed practical/vocational nurse training; machine tool technology; medical administrative assistant and medical secretary; medical transcription; occupational therapist assistant; physical sciences; physical therapy technology; psychology; registered nursing/registered nurse; respiratory care therapy; restaurant, culinary, and catering management; science technologies related; secondary education; social sciences; social work; substance abuse/addiction counseling; web page, digital/multimedia and information resources design.
Academics *Calendar:* quarters. *Degree:* certificates, diplomas, and associate. *Special study options:* academic remediation for entering students, adult/continuing education programs, cooperative education, distance learning, English as a second language, external degree program, honors programs, internships, part-time degree program, services for LD students, summer session for credit.
Library Yocum Library with 52,143 titles, 150 serial subscriptions, 12,758 audiovisual materials, an OPAC, a Web page.
Student Life *Housing:* college housing not available. *Activities and Organizations:* student-run newspaper. *Campus security:* 24-hour emergency response devices and patrols. *Student services:* personal/psychological counseling.
Standardized Tests *Required for some:* TOEFL. *Recommended:* SAT (for admission), ACT (for admission).
Costs (2014–15) *Tuition:* area resident $3510 full-time, $117 per credit part-time; state resident $7020 full-time, $234 per credit part-time; nonresident $10,530 full-time, $351 per credit part-time. Full-time tuition and fees vary according to course load and program. Part-time tuition and fees vary according to course load and program. *Required fees:* $1440 full-time, $48 per credit part-time. *Payment plan:* installment. *Waivers:* senior citizens and employees or children of employees.
Financial Aid Of all full-time matriculated undergraduates who enrolled in 2012, 80 Federal Work-Study jobs (averaging $5400). 20 state and other part-time jobs (averaging $3300).
Applying *Options:* electronic application, early admission. *Required for some:* essay or personal statement, high school transcript, 1 letter of recommendation, interview, background/criminal check, physical exam, proof of insurance: For selective admissions programs. *Recommended:* high school

transcript. *Application deadlines:* rolling (freshmen), rolling (out-of-state freshmen), rolling (transfers).
Freshman Application Contact Reading Area Community College, PO Box 1706, Reading, PA 19603-1706. *Phone:* 610-607-6224.
Website: http://www.racc.edu/.

The Restaurant School at Walnut Hill College
Philadelphia, Pennsylvania

Freshman Application Contact Miss Toni Morelli, Director of Admissions, The Restaurant School at Walnut Hill College, 4207 Walnut Street, Philadelphia, PA 19104-3518. *Phone:* 267-295-2353. *Fax:* 215-222-4219. *E-mail:* tmorelli@walnuthillcollege.edu.
Website: http://www.walnuthillcollege.edu/.

Rosedale Technical Institute
Pittsburgh, Pennsylvania

Freshman Application Contact Ms. Debbie Bier, Director of Admissions, Rosedale Technical Institute, 215 Beecham Drive, Suite 2, Pittsburgh, PA 15205-9791. *Phone:* 412-521-6200. *Toll-free phone:* 800-521-6262. *Fax:* 412-521-2520. *E-mail:* admissions@rosedaletech.org.
Website: http://www.rosedaletech.org/.

South Hills School of Business & Technology
Altoona, Pennsylvania

Freshman Application Contact Ms. Holly J. Emerick, Director of Admissions, South Hills School of Business & Technology, 508 58th Street, Altoona, PA 16602. *Phone:* 814-944-6134. *Fax:* 814-944-4684. *E-mail:* hemerick@southhills.edu.
Website: http://www.southhills.edu/.

South Hills School of Business & Technology
State College, Pennsylvania

Freshman Application Contact Ms. Diane M. Brown, Director of Admissions, South Hills School of Business & Technology, 480 Waupelani Drive, State College, PA 16801-4516. *Phone:* 814-234-7755 Ext. 2020. *Toll-free phone:* 888-282-7427. *Fax:* 814-234-0926. *E-mail:* admissions@southhills.edu.
Website: http://www.southhills.edu/.

Thaddeus Stevens College of Technology
Lancaster, Pennsylvania

Director of Admissions Ms. Erin Kate Nelsen, Director of Enrollment, Thaddeus Stevens College of Technology, 750 East King Street, Lancaster, PA 17602-3198. *Phone:* 717-299-7772. *Toll-free phone:* 800-842-3832.
Website: http://www.stevenscollege.edu/.

Triangle Tech–Greensburg School
Greensburg, Pennsylvania

Freshman Application Contact Mr. John Mazzarese, Vice President of Admissions, Triangle Tech–Greensburg School, 222 East Pittsburgh Street, Greensburg, PA 15601. *Phone:* 412-359-1000. *Toll-free phone:* 800-874-8324.
Website: http://www.triangle-tech.edu/.

Triangle Tech Inc–Bethlehem
Bethlehem, Pennsylvania

Freshman Application Contact Triangle Tech Inc–Bethlehem, Lehigh Valley Industrial Park IV, 31 South Commerce Way, Bethlehem, PA 18017.
Website: http://www.triangle-tech.edu/.

Triangle Tech, Inc.–DuBois School
DuBois, Pennsylvania

Freshman Application Contact Terry Kucic, Director of Admissions, Triangle Tech, Inc.–DuBois School, PO Box 551, DuBois, PA 15801. *Phone:* 814-371-2090. *Toll-free phone:* 800-874-8324. *Fax:* 814-371-9227. *E-mail:* tkucic@triangle-tech.com.
Website: http://www.triangle-tech.edu/.

Triangle Tech, Inc.–Erie School
Erie, Pennsylvania

Freshman Application Contact Admissions Representative, Triangle Tech, Inc.–Erie School, 2000 Liberty Street, Erie, PA 16502-2594. *Phone:* 814-453-6016. *Toll-free phone:* 800-874-8324 (in-state); 800-TRI-TECH (out-of-state). *Website:* http://www.triangle-tech.edu/.

Triangle Tech, Inc.–Pittsburgh School
Pittsburgh, Pennsylvania

- **Proprietary** 2-year, founded 1944, part of Triangle Tech Group, Inc.
- **Urban** 5-acre campus
- **Coed, primarily men,** 103 undergraduate students, 100% full-time, 2% women, 98% men

Undergraduates 103 full-time. Students come from 3 states and territories; 2% are from out of state; 29% Black or African American, non-Hispanic/Latino; 1% Hispanic/Latino; 0.2% Native Hawaiian or other Pacific Islander, non-Hispanic/Latino; 2% Two or more races, non-Hispanic/Latino; 1% transferred in. *Retention:* 78% of full-time freshmen returned.
Freshmen *Admission:* 103 enrolled.
Faculty *Student/faculty ratio:* 12:1.
Majors Architectural drafting and CAD/CADD; carpentry; educational/instructional technology; electrician; heating, air conditioning, ventilation and refrigeration maintenance technology; mechanical drafting and CAD/CADD.
Academics *Calendar:* semesters. *Degree:* associate. *Special study options:* academic remediation for entering students.
Student Life *Housing:* college housing not available. *Campus security:* 16-hour patrols by trained security personnel.
Financial Aid Of all full-time matriculated undergraduates who enrolled in 2012, 16 Federal Work-Study jobs (averaging $1500). *Financial aid deadline:* 7/1.
Applying *Required:* high school transcript, minimum 2.0 GPA, interview. *Application deadlines:* rolling (freshmen), rolling (transfers).
Freshman Application Contact Director of Admissions, Triangle Tech, Inc.–Pittsburgh School, 1940 Perrysville Avenue, Pittsburgh, PA 15214-3897. *Phone:* 412-359-1000. *Toll-free phone:* 800-874-8324. *Fax:* 412-359-1012. *E-mail:* info@triangle-tech.edu. *Website:* http://www.triangle-tech.edu/.

Triangle Tech, Inc.–Sunbury School
Sunbury, Pennsylvania

Freshman Application Contact Triangle Tech, Inc.–Sunbury School, 191 Performance Road, Sunbury, PA 17801. *Phone:* 412-359-1000. *Website:* http://www.triangle-tech.edu/.

University of Pittsburgh at Titusville
Titusville, Pennsylvania

- **State-related** 2-year, founded 1963, part of University of Pittsburgh System
- **Small-town** 10-acre campus
- **Endowment** $850,000
- **Coed**

Undergraduates 313 full-time, 75 part-time. Students come from 15 states and territories; 8% are from out of state; 14% Black or African American, non-Hispanic/Latino; 4% Hispanic/Latino; 2% Asian, non-Hispanic/Latino; 2% Two or more races, non-Hispanic/Latino; 2% Race/ethnicity unknown; 4% transferred in; 42% live on campus.
Faculty *Student/faculty ratio:* 15:1.
Academics *Calendar:* semesters. *Degree:* associate. *Special study options:* academic remediation for entering students, advanced placement credit, distance learning, internships, part-time degree program, study abroad, summer session for credit.
Student Life *Campus security:* 24-hour emergency response devices and patrols, late-night transport/escort service, controlled dormitory access.
Athletics Member NJCAA.
Standardized Tests *Required:* SAT or ACT (for admission).
Costs (2013–14) *Tuition:* state resident $10,544 full-time, $439 per credit hour part-time; nonresident $19,918 full-time, $829 per credit hour part-time. Full-time tuition and fees vary according to program. Part-time tuition and fees vary according to program. *Required fees:* $780 full-time. *Room and board:* $9964; room only: $5156. Room and board charges vary according to board plan.
Financial Aid Of all full-time matriculated undergraduates who enrolled in 2009, 429 applied for aid, 408 were judged to have need, 23 had their need fully met. In 2009, 10. *Average percent of need met:* 80. *Average financial aid package:* $15,305. *Average need-based loan:* $9451. *Average need-based gift aid:* $1992. *Average non-need-based aid:* $39,059.

Applying *Required:* high school transcript, minimum 2.0 GPA. *Required for some:* essay or personal statement, 3 letters of recommendation. *Recommended:* interview.
Freshman Application Contact Mr. Robert J. Wyant, Director of Admissions, University of Pittsburgh at Titusville, 504 E Main St, Titusville, PA 16354. *Phone:* 814-827-4457. *Toll-free phone:* 888-878-0462. *Fax:* 814-827-4519. *E-mail:* wyant@pitt.edu. *Website:* http://www.upt.pitt.edu/.

Valley Forge Military College
Wayne, Pennsylvania

Freshman Application Contact Maj. Greg Potts, Dean of Enrollment Management, Valley Forge Military College, 1001 Eagle Road, Wayne, PA 19087-3695. *Phone:* 610-989-1300. *Toll-free phone:* 800-234-8362. *Fax:* 610-688-1545. *E-mail:* admissions@vfmac.edu. *Website:* http://www.vfmac.edu/.

Vet Tech Institute
Pittsburgh, Pennsylvania

- **Private** 2-year, founded 1958
- **Urban** campus
- **Coed,** 337 undergraduate students
- **64%** of applicants were admitted

Freshmen *Admission:* 533 applied, 342 admitted.
Majors Veterinary/animal health technology.
Academics *Calendar:* quarters. *Degree:* associate. *Special study options:* accelerated degree program, internships, summer session for credit.
Freshman Application Contact Admissions Office, Vet Tech Institute, 125 7th Street, Pittsburgh, PA 15222-3400. *Phone:* 412-391-7021. *Toll-free phone:* 800-570-0693. *Website:* http://pittsburgh.vettechinstitute.edu/.

Westmoreland County Community College
Youngwood, Pennsylvania

- **County-supported** 2-year, founded 1970
- **Rural** 85-acre campus with easy access to Pittsburgh
- **Endowment** $509,521
- **Coed,** 6,104 undergraduate students, 49% full-time, 64% women, 36% men

Undergraduates 2,967 full-time, 3,137 part-time. Students come from 3 states and territories; 0.2% are from out of state; 4% Black or African American, non-Hispanic/Latino; 1% Hispanic/Latino; 0.7% Asian, non-Hispanic/Latino; 0.1% Native Hawaiian or other Pacific Islander, non-Hispanic/Latino; 0.1% American Indian or Alaska Native, non-Hispanic/Latino; 2% Two or more races, non-Hispanic/Latino; 3% transferred in. *Retention:* 59% of full-time freshmen returned.
Freshmen *Admission:* 2,532 applied, 2,532 admitted, 1,512 enrolled.
Faculty *Total:* 524, 17% full-time. *Student/faculty ratio:* 17:1.
Majors Accounting technology and bookkeeping; administrative assistant and secretarial science; applied horticulture/horticulture operations; architectural drafting and CAD/CADD; baking and pastry arts; banking and financial support services; biology/biotechnology laboratory technician; business administration and management; business/commerce; casino management; chemical technology; child-care provision; clinical laboratory science/medical technology; clinical/medical laboratory assistant; communications systems installation and repair technology; computer and information systems security; computer numerically controlled (CNC) machinist technology; computer programming; computer programming (specific applications); computer support specialist; computer systems networking and telecommunications; corrections; criminal justice/police science; criminal justice/safety; culinary arts; data entry/microcomputer applications; data processing and data processing technology; dental assisting; dental hygiene; diagnostic medical sonography and ultrasound technology; dietetic technology; early childhood education; electrical and power transmission installation; electrical, electronic and communications engineering technology; family and community services; fire prevention and safety technology; floriculture/floristry management; food service and dining room management; graphic design; health and medical administrative services related; heating, air conditioning, ventilation and refrigeration maintenance technology; homeland security, law enforcement, firefighting and protective services related; hotel/motel administration; human resources management; industrial mechanics and maintenance technology; industrial technology; legal assistant/paralegal; liberal arts and sciences/liberal studies; library and information science; licensed practical/vocational nurse training; logistics, materials, and supply chain management; machine tool technology; manufacturing engineering technology; mechanical drafting and CAD/CADD; mechanical engineering/mechanical technology; mechatronics,

robotics, and automation engineering; medical/clinical assistant; medical office assistant; phlebotomy technology; physical science technologies related; pre-engineering; radio and television broadcasting technology; radiologic technology/science; real estate; registered nursing/registered nurse; restaurant, culinary, and catering management; sales, distribution, and marketing operations; special education–elementary school; tourism and travel services management; turf and turfgrass management; web page, digital/multimedia and information resources design; welding technology.

Academics *Calendar:* semesters. *Degree:* certificates, diplomas, and associate. *Special study options:* academic remediation for entering students, adult/continuing education programs, advanced placement credit, cooperative education, distance learning, double majors, English as a second language, honors programs, independent study, internships, off-campus study, part-time degree program, services for LD students, summer session for credit.

Library Westmoreland County Community College Learning Resources Center with 64,000 titles, 250 serial subscriptions, 3,500 audiovisual materials, an OPAC, a Web page.

Student Life *Housing:* college housing not available. *Activities and Organizations:* drama/theater group, choral group, Phi Theta Kappa, Sigma Alpha Pi Leadership Society, Criminal Justice Fraternity, Gay Straight Alliance, SADAA/SADHA. *Campus security:* 24-hour emergency response devices and patrols, late-night transport/escort service. *Student services:* personal/psychological counseling.

Athletics Member NJCAA. *Intercollegiate sports:* baseball M, basketball M/W, bowling M/W, cross-country running M/W, golf M/W, soccer M/W, softball W, volleyball W. *Intramural sports:* basketball M/W, bowling M/W, golf M/W, skiing (downhill) M/W, volleyball M/W, weight lifting M/W.

Costs (2013–14) *One-time required fee:* $25. *Tuition:* area resident $2790 full-time, $93 per credit part-time; state resident $5580 full-time, $186 per credit part-time; nonresident $8370 full-time, $279 per credit part-time. Full-time tuition and fees vary according to course load. Part-time tuition and fees vary according to course load. *Required fees:* $630 full-time, $21 per credit part-time. *Payment plans:* installment, deferred payment. *Waivers:* senior citizens and employees or children of employees.

Applying *Options:* electronic application, early admission. *Application fee:* $25. *Application deadlines:* rolling (freshmen), rolling (out-of-state freshmen), rolling (transfers). *Notification:* continuous (freshmen), continuous (out-of-state freshmen), continuous (transfers).

Freshman Application Contact Mr. James Pirlo, Admissions Coordinator, Westmoreland County Community College, 145 Pavillon Lane, Youngwood, PA 15697. *Phone:* 724-925-6953. *Toll-free phone:* 800-262-2103. *Fax:* 724-925-4292. *E-mail:* admission@wccc.edu.
Website: http://www.wccc.edu/.

The Williamson Free School of Mechanical Trades
Media, Pennsylvania

- **Independent** 2-year, founded 1888
- **Small-town** 222-acre campus with easy access to Philadelphia
- **Men only,** 270 undergraduate students, 100% full-time

Undergraduates 270 full-time. Students come from 7 states and territories; 15% are from out of state; 100% live on campus.

Freshmen *Admission:* 351 applied, 101 admitted, 100 enrolled. *Average high school GPA:* 2.5.

Faculty *Total:* 29. *Student/faculty ratio:* 12:1.

Majors Carpentry; construction engineering technology; electrical, electronic and communications engineering technology; energy management and systems technology; horticultural science; landscaping and groundskeeping; machine tool technology; turf and turfgrass management.

Academics *Calendar:* semesters. *Degree:* diplomas and associate. *Special study options:* academic remediation for entering students, independent study, off-campus study.

Library Shrigley Library plus 3 others with 1,600 titles, 70 serial subscriptions.

Student Life *Housing Options:* men-only. Freshman campus housing is guaranteed. *Activities and Organizations:* student-run newspaper, choral group, Campus Crusade for Christ, Skills USA. *Campus security:* Evening patrols; Gate security. *Student services:* health clinic, personal/psychological counseling.

Athletics Member NJCAA. *Intercollegiate sports:* baseball M, basketball M, cross-country running M, football M, lacrosse M, soccer M, tennis M, wrestling M. *Intramural sports:* archery M, basketball M, table tennis M, volleyball M, weight lifting M.

Standardized Tests *Required:* Armed Services Vocational Aptitude Battery (for admission).

Financial Aid *Financial aid deadline:* 2/28.

Applying *Required:* essay or personal statement, high school transcript, minimum 2.0 GPA, interview, Average performance or better on the Armed Services Vocational Aptitude Battery (ASVAB). *Application deadline:* 2/28 (freshmen).

Freshman Application Contact Mr. Jay Merillat, Dean of Admissions, The Williamson Free School of Mechanical Trades, 106 South New Middletown Road, Media, PA 19063. *Phone:* 610-566-1776 Ext. 235. *E-mail:* jmerillat@williamson.edu.
Website: http://www.williamson.edu/.

WyoTech Blairsville
Blairsville, Pennsylvania

Freshman Application Contact Mr. Tim Smyers, WyoTech Blairsville, 500 Innovation Drive, Blairsville, PA 15717. *Phone:* 724-459-2311. *Toll-free phone:* 888-577-7559. *Fax:* 724-459-6499. *E-mail:* tsmyers@wyotech.edu.
Website: http://www.wyotech.edu/.

Yorktowne Business Institute
York, Pennsylvania

Director of Admissions Director of Admissions, Yorktowne Business Institute, West Seventh Avenue, York, PA 17404. *Phone:* 717-846-5000. *Toll-free phone:* 800-840-1004.
Website: http://www.ybi.edu/.

YTI Career Institute–Altoona
Altoona, Pennsylvania

Admissions Office Contact YTI Career Institute–Altoona, 2900 Fairway Drive, Altoona, PA 16602.
Website: http://www.yti.edu/.

YTI Career Institute–Capital Region
Mechanicsburg, Pennsylvania

Admissions Office Contact YTI Career Institute–Capital Region, 401 East Winding Hill Road, Mechanicsburg, PA 17055.
Website: http://www.yti.edu/.

YTI Career Institute–York
York, Pennsylvania

Freshman Application Contact YTI Career Institute–York, 1405 Williams Road, York, PA 17402-9017. *Phone:* 717-757-1100 Ext. 318. *Toll-free phone:* 800-557-6335.
Website: http://www.yti.edu/.

PUERTO RICO

The Center of Cinematography, Arts and Television
Bayamon, Puerto Rico

Admissions Office Contact The Center of Cinematography, Arts and Television, 51 Dr. Veve Street, Degetau Street Corner, Bayamon, PR 00960.
Website: http://ccatmiami.com/.

Centro de Estudios Multidisciplinarios
Rio Piedras, Puerto Rico

Director of Admissions Admissions Department, Centro de Estudios Multidisciplinarios, Calle 13 #1206, Ext. San Agustin, Rio Piedras, PR 00926. *Phone:* 787-765-4210 Ext. 115. *Toll-free phone:* 877-779-CDEM.
Website: http://www.cempr.edu/.

EDIC College
Caguas, Puerto Rico

Admissions Office Contact EDIC College, Calle 8, Equina 5 Urb., Box 9120, Caguas, PR 00726.
Website: http://www.ediccollege.edu/.

Huertas Junior College
Caguas, Puerto Rico

Director of Admissions Mrs. Barbara Hassim López, Director of Admissions, Huertas Junior College, PO Box 8429, Caguas, PR 00726. *Phone:* 787-743-1242. *Fax:* 787-743-0203. *E-mail:* huertas@huertas.org.
Website: http://www.huertas.edu/.

Humacao Community College

Humacao, Puerto Rico

Director of Admissions Ms. Xiomara Sanchez, Director of Admissions, Humacao Community College, PO Box 9139, Humacao, PR 00792. *Phone:* 787-852-2525.
Website: http://www.hccpr.edu/.

ICPR Junior College–Hato Rey Campus

Hato Rey, Puerto Rico

Freshman Application Contact Admissions Office, ICPR Junior College–Hato Rey Campus, 558 Munoz Rivera Avenue, PO Box 190304, Hato Rey, PR 00919-0304. *Phone:* 787-753-6335.
Website: http://www.icprjc.edu/.

RHODE ISLAND

Community College of Rhode Island

Warwick, Rhode Island

- **State-supported** 2-year, founded 1964
- **Urban** 205-acre campus with easy access to Boston
- **Coed**, 17,699 undergraduate students, 31% full-time, 59% women, 41% men

Undergraduates 5,459 full-time, 12,240 part-time. Students come from 21 states and territories; 4% are from out of state; 10% Black or African American, non-Hispanic/Latino; 18% Hispanic/Latino; 3% Asian, non-Hispanic/Latino; 0.6% American Indian or Alaska Native, non-Hispanic/Latino; 3% Two or more races, non-Hispanic/Latino; 4% Race/ethnicity unknown; 0.1% international.
Freshmen *Admission:* 7,094 applied, 7,053 admitted, 3,376 enrolled.
Faculty *Total:* 915, 36% full-time. *Student/faculty ratio:* 18:1.
Majors Accounting; administrative assistant and secretarial science; adult development and aging; art; banking and financial support services; biological and physical sciences; business administration and management; business/commerce; chemical technology; clinical/medical laboratory technology; computer and information sciences; computer engineering technology; computer programming (specific applications); computer support specialist; computer systems networking and telecommunications; criminal justice/police science; crisis/emergency/disaster management; customer service management; dental hygiene; diagnostic medical sonography and ultrasound technology; dramatic/theater arts; electromechanical technology; engineering; fire science/firefighting; general studies; histologic technician; jazz/jazz studies; kindergarten/preschool education; legal administrative assistant/secretary; legal assistant/paralegal; liberal arts and sciences/liberal studies; licensed practical/vocational nurse training; marketing/marketing management; massage therapy; medical administrative assistant and medical secretary; mental health counseling; music; occupational therapist assistant; opticianry; physical therapy technology; radiologic technology/science; registered nursing/registered nurse; respiratory care therapy; social work; special education; substance abuse/addiction counseling; surveying engineering; web/multimedia management and webmaster.
Academics *Calendar:* semesters. *Degree:* certificates, diplomas, and associate. *Special study options:* academic remediation for entering students, adult/continuing education programs, advanced placement credit, cooperative education, distance learning, double majors, English as a second language, external degree program, honors programs, independent study, internships, off-campus study, part-time degree program, services for LD students, study abroad, summer session for credit. *ROTC:* Army (c).
Library Community College of Rhode Island Learning Resources Center plus 3 others with an OPAC, a Web page.
Student Life *Housing:* college housing not available. *Activities and Organizations:* drama/theater group, student-run newspaper, choral group, Distributive Education Clubs of America, Theater group - Players, Skills USA, Phi Theta Kappa, student government. *Campus security:* 24-hour emergency response devices and patrols. *Student services:* health clinic, personal/psychological counseling.
Athletics Member NJCAA. *Intercollegiate sports:* baseball M(s), basketball M(s)/W(s), golf M/W, soccer M(s)/W(s), softball W(s), tennis M/W, track and field M/W, volleyball W(s). *Intramural sports:* basketball M/W, volleyball M/W.
Costs (2013–14) *Tuition:* state resident $3624 full-time, $165 per credit hour part-time; nonresident $10,256 full-time, $490 per semester hour part-time. Full-time tuition and fees vary according to program. Part-time tuition and fees vary according to course load and program. *Required fees:* $326 full-time, $12 per credit hour part-time; $30 per term part-time. *Payment plans:* installment,

deferred payment. *Waivers:* senior citizens and employees or children of employees.
Financial Aid Of all full-time matriculated undergraduates who enrolled in 2012, 500 Federal Work-Study jobs (averaging $2500).
Applying *Options:* deferred entrance. *Application fee:* $20. *Application deadlines:* rolling (freshmen), rolling (transfers). *Notification:* continuous (freshmen).
Freshman Application Contact Community College of Rhode Island, Flanagan Campus, 1762 Louisquisset Pike, Lincoln, RI 02865-4585. *Phone:* 401-333-7490. *Fax:* 401-333-7122. *E-mail:* webadmission@ccri.edu.
Website: http://www.ccri.edu/.

SOUTH CAROLINA

Aiken Technical College

Aiken, South Carolina

Freshman Application Contact Ms. Lisa Sommers, Aiken Technical College, PO Drawer 696, Aiken, SC 29802. *Phone:* 803-593-9231 Ext. 1584. *Fax:* 803-593-6526. *E-mail:* sommersl@atc.edu.
Website: http://www.atc.edu/.

Brown Mackie College–Greenville

Greenville, South Carolina

- **Proprietary** primarily 2-year, part of Education Management Corporation
- **Coed**

Majors Business administration and management; corrections and criminal justice related; health/health-care administration; information technology; legal assistant/paralegal; medical office management; occupational therapist assistant; registered nursing/registered nurse; surgical technology.
Academics *Degrees:* certificates, associate, and bachelor's.
Freshman Application Contact Brown Mackie College–Greenville, Two Liberty Square, 75 Beattie Place, Suite 100, Greenville, SC 29601. *Phone:* 864-239-5300. *Toll-free phone:* 877-479-8465.
Website: http://www.brownmackie.edu/greenville/.

See display on next page and page 394 for the College Close-Up.

Central Carolina Technical College

Sumter, South Carolina

Freshman Application Contact Ms. Barbara Wright, Director of Admissions and Counseling, Central Carolina Technical College, 506 North Guignard Drive, Sumter, SC 29150. *Phone:* 803-778-6695. *Toll-free phone:* 800-221-8711. *Fax:* 803-778-6696. *E-mail:* wrightb@cctech.edu.
Website: http://www.cctech.edu/.

Clinton Junior College

Rock Hill, South Carolina

Director of Admissions Robert M. Copeland, Vice President for Student Affairs, Clinton Junior College, PO Box 968, 1029 Crawford Road, Rock Hill, SC 29730. *Phone:* 803-327-7402. *Toll-free phone:* 877-837-9645. *Fax:* 803-327-3261. *E-mail:* rcopeland@clintonjrcollege.org.
Website: http://www.clintonjuniorcollege.edu/.

Denmark Technical College

Denmark, South Carolina

- **State-supported** 2-year, founded 1948, part of South Carolina State Board for Technical and Comprehensive Education
- **Rural** 53-acre campus
- **Coed**

Undergraduates 1,821 full-time, 182 part-time. 3% are from out of state; 96% Black or African American, non-Hispanic/Latino; 0.2% Hispanic/Latino; 0.0% American Indian or Alaska Native, non-Hispanic/Latino; 0.1% Race/ethnicity unknown; 2% transferred in. *Retention:* 54% of full-time freshmen returned.
Faculty *Student/faculty ratio:* 21:1.
Academics *Calendar:* semesters. *Degree:* certificates, diplomas, and associate. *Special study options:* academic remediation for entering students, adult/continuing education programs, advanced placement credit, cooperative education, distance learning, independent study, internships, off-campus study, part-time degree program, summer session for credit.
Student Life *Campus security:* 24-hour patrols, late-night transport/escort service, 24-hour emergency contact line/alarm devices.
Athletics Member NJCAA.

Standardized Tests *Required:* ACT, ASSET, COMPASS, and TEAS (Nursing) (for admission). *Recommended:* SAT or ACT (for admission).

Costs (2013–14) *Tuition:* state resident $2662 full-time; nonresident $5014 full-time. *Room and board:* $3566; room only: $1762.

Financial Aid Of all full-time matriculated undergraduates who enrolled in 2012, 250 Federal Work-Study jobs (averaging $2000).

Applying *Options:* electronic application, early admission, deferred entrance. *Application fee:* $10. *Required:* high school transcript. *Required for some:* essay or personal statement. *Recommended:* SLED Check, TEAS Testing, Drug Test, PPD Test (all requirement for LPN).

Freshman Application Contact Ms. Kara Troy, Administrative Specialist II, Denmark Technical College, PO Box 327, 1126 Solomon Blatt Boulevard, Denmark, SC 29042. *Phone:* 803-793-5180. *Fax:* 803-793-5942. *E-mail:* troyk@denmarktech.edu.
Website: http://www.denmarktech.edu/.

ECPI University
Columbia, South Carolina

Admissions Office Contact ECPI University, 250 Berryhill Road, #300, Columbia, SC 29210. *Toll-free phone:* 866-708-6168.
Website: http://www.ecpi.edu/.

ECPI University
Greenville, South Carolina

Admissions Office Contact ECPI University, 1001 Keys Drive, #100, Greenville, SC 29615. *Toll-free phone:* 866-708-6171.
Website: http://www.ecpi.edu/.

ECPI University
North Charleston, South Carolina

Admissions Office Contact ECPI University, 7410 Northside Drive, Suite 100, North Charleston, SC 29420. *Toll-free phone:* 866-708-6166.
Website: http://www.ecpi.edu/.

Florence-Darlington Technical College
Florence, South Carolina

Director of Admissions Shelley Fortin, Vice President for Enrollment Management and Student Services, Florence-Darlington Technical College, 2715 West Lucas Street, PO Box 100548, Florence, SC 29501-0548. *Phone:* 843-661-8111 Ext. 117. *Toll-free phone:* 800-228-5745. *E-mail:* shelley.fortin@fdtc.edu.
Website: http://www.fdtc.edu/.

Forrest College
Anderson, South Carolina

- **Proprietary** 2-year, founded 1946
- **Rural** 3-acre campus
- **Coed**

Undergraduates 86 full-time, 34 part-time. Students come from 2 states and territories; 1% are from out of state.

Faculty *Student/faculty ratio:* 6:1.

Academics *Calendar:* quarters. *Degree:* certificates, diplomas, and associate. *Special study options:* advanced placement credit, cooperative education, double majors, independent study, internships, part-time degree program, summer session for credit.

Student Life *Campus security:* 24-hour emergency response devices, late-night transport/escort service.

Standardized Tests *Required:* Gates-McGinnity (for admission).

Costs (2013–14) *Tuition:* $8820 full-time, $245 per credit part-time. *Required fees:* $375 full-time.

Financial Aid Of all full-time matriculated undergraduates who enrolled in 2012, 135 applied for aid, 135 were judged to have need.

Applying *Required:* essay or personal statement, high school transcript, minimum 2.0 GPA, interview. *Recommended:* minimum 2.5 GPA.

Freshman Application Contact Ms. Janie Turmon, Admissions and Placement Coordinator/Representative, Forrest College, 601 East River Street, Anderson, SC 29624. *Phone:* 864-225-7653 Ext. 210. *Fax:* 864-261-7471. *E-mail:* janieturmon@forrestcollege.com.
Website: http://www.forrestcollege.edu/.

Golf Academy of America
Myrtle Beach, South Carolina

Admissions Office Contact Golf Academy of America, 3268 Waccamaw Boulevard, Myrtle Beach, SC 29579.
Website: http://www.golfacademy.edu/.

Greenville Technical College
Greenville, South Carolina

- **State-supported** 2-year, founded 1962, part of South Carolina State Board for Technical and Comprehensive Education
- **Urban** 604-acre campus
- **Coed,** 13,448 undergraduate students, 41% full-time, 58% women, 42% men

Undergraduates 5,452 full-time, 7,996 part-time. Students come from 65 other countries; 2% are from out of state; 24% Black or African American, non-Hispanic/Latino; 7% Hispanic/Latino; 1% Asian, non-Hispanic/Latino; 0.1% Native Hawaiian or other Pacific Islander, non-Hispanic/Latino; 0.5% American Indian or Alaska Native, non-Hispanic/Latino; 2% Two or more races, non-Hispanic/Latino; 4% Race/ethnicity unknown; 0.3% international; 4% transferred in.

Freshmen *Admission:* 7,485 applied, 4,152 admitted, 2,275 enrolled.

Faculty *Total:* 783, 45% full-time. *Student/faculty ratio:* 16:1.

Majors Accounting; administrative assistant and secretarial science; architectural engineering technology; automobile/automotive mechanics technology; biotechnology; business administration and management; child-care and support services management; clinical/medical laboratory technology; construction engineering technology; criminal justice/safety; culinary arts; data processing and data processing technology; dental hygiene; diagnostic medical sonography and ultrasound technology; electrical, electronic and communications engineering technology; electromechanical and instrumentation and maintenance technologies related; emergency medical technology (EMT paramedic); fire science/firefighting; geographic information science and cartography; health information/medical records technology; industrial mechanics and maintenance technology; institutional food workers; legal assistant/paralegal; liberal arts and sciences/liberal studies; machine tool technology; mechanical drafting and CAD/CADD; mechanical engineering/mechanical technology; mechanic and repair technologies related; medical radiologic technology; multi/interdisciplinary studies related; occupational therapist assistant; physical therapy technology; purchasing, procurement/acquisitions and contracts management; registered nursing/registered nurse; respiratory care therapy; sales, distribution, and marketing operations; social work; technical teacher education.

Academics *Calendar:* semesters. *Degree:* certificates, diplomas, and associate. *Special study options:* academic remediation for entering students, advanced placement credit, cooperative education, distance learning, double majors, English as a second language, honors programs, independent study, internships, part-time degree program, services for LD students, summer session for credit.

Library Verne Smith Library/Technical Resource Center plus 4 others with 109,337 titles, 171 serial subscriptions, 2,370 audiovisual materials, an OPAC, a Web page.

Student Life *Housing:* college housing not available. *Activities and Organizations:* Phi Theta Kappa, AAMLI, Cosmetology Club, Engineering Club, SGA/SAT Club. *Campus security:* 24-hour emergency response devices and patrols, late-night transport/escort service.

Athletics *Intramural sports:* badminton M(c)/W(c), basketball M(c)/W(c), football M(c)/W(c), soccer M(c)/W(c), softball M(c)/W(c), tennis M(c)/W(c), volleyball M(c)/W(c).

Standardized Tests *Recommended:* SAT, ACT ASSET, or ACT COMPASS.

Financial Aid Of all full-time matriculated undergraduates who enrolled in 2011, 97 Federal Work-Study jobs (averaging $3856).

Applying *Options:* electronic application, early admission, deferred entrance. *Application fee:* $35. *Required:* high school transcript. *Application deadlines:* rolling (freshmen), rolling (transfers). *Notification:* continuous until 8/18 (freshmen), continuous until 8/18 (transfers).

Freshman Application Contact Greenville Technical College, PO Box 5616, Greenville, SC 29606-5616. *Phone:* 864-250-8287. *Toll-free phone:* 800-992-1183 (in-state); 800-723-0673 (out-of-state).

Website: http://www.gvltec.edu/.

Horry-Georgetown Technical College
Conway, South Carolina

- **State and locally supported** 2-year, founded 1966, part of South Carolina State Board for Technical and Comprehensive Education
- **Small-town** campus
- **Coed**

Undergraduates 2,936 full-time, 4,762 part-time. 23% Black or African American, non-Hispanic/Latino; 3% Hispanic/Latino; 0.9% Asian, non-Hispanic/Latino; 0.2% Native Hawaiian or other Pacific Islander, non-Hispanic/Latino; 0.5% American Indian or Alaska Native, non-Hispanic/Latino; 1% Two or more races, non-Hispanic/Latino; 2% Race/ethnicity unknown; 0.2% international. *Retention:* 54% of full-time freshmen returned.

Faculty *Student/faculty ratio:* 16:1.

Academics *Calendar:* semesters. *Degree:* certificates, diplomas, and associate. *Special study options:* academic remediation for entering students, adult/continuing education programs, advanced placement credit, cooperative education, internships, part-time degree program, services for LD students, summer session for credit.

Applying *Options:* early admission. *Application fee:* $25. *Required for some:* high school transcript.

Freshman Application Contact Mr. George Swindoll, Vice President for Enrollment, Development, and Registration, Horry-Georgetown Technical College, 2050 Highway 502 East, PO Box 261966, Conway, SC 29528-6066. *Phone:* 843-349-5277. *Fax:* 843-349-7501. *E-mail:* george.swindoll@hgtc.edu.

Website: http://www.hgtc.edu/.

ITT Technical Institute
Columbia, South Carolina

- **Proprietary** primarily 2-year, part of ITT Educational Services, Inc.
- **Coed**

Majors Construction management; cyber/computer forensics and counterterrorism; drafting and design technology; electrical, electronic and communications engineering technology; forensic science and technology; graphic communications; information technology project management; network and system administration; project management.

Academics *Degrees:* associate and bachelor's.

Student Life *Housing:* college housing not available.

Freshman Application Contact Director of Recruitment, ITT Technical Institute, 1628 Browning Road, Suite 180, Columbia, SC 29210. *Phone:* 803-216-6000. *Toll-free phone:* 800-242-5158.

Website: http://www.itt-tech.edu/.

ITT Technical Institute
Greenville, South Carolina

- **Proprietary** primarily 2-year, founded 1992, part of ITT Educational Services, Inc.
- **Coed**

Majors Construction management; cyber/computer forensics and counterterrorism; drafting and design technology; electrical, electronic and communications engineering technology; forensic science and technology; information technology project management; network and system administration; project management.

Academics *Calendar:* quarters. *Degrees:* associate and bachelor's.

Student Life *Housing:* college housing not available.

Financial Aid Of all full-time matriculated undergraduates who enrolled in 2012, 3 Federal Work-Study jobs.

Freshman Application Contact Director of Recruitment, ITT Technical Institute, 6 Independence Pointe, Greenville, SC 29615. *Phone:* 864-288-0777. *Toll-free phone:* 800-932-4488.

Website: http://www.itt-tech.edu/.

ITT Technical Institute
Myrtle Beach, South Carolina

- **Proprietary** primarily 2-year, part of ITT Educational Services, Inc.
- **Coed**

Majors Construction management; cyber/computer forensics and counterterrorism; drafting and design technology; electrical, electronic and communications engineering technology; information technology project management; legal assistant/paralegal; network and system administration; project management.

Academics *Calendar:* quarters. *Degrees:* associate and bachelor's.

Freshman Application Contact Director of Recruitment, ITT Technical Institute, 9654 N. Kings Highway, Suite 101, Myrtle Beach, SC 29572. *Phone:* 843-497-7820. *Toll-free phone:* 877-316-7054.

Website: http://www.itt-tech.edu/.

ITT Technical Institute
North Charleston, South Carolina

- **Proprietary** primarily 2-year, part of ITT Educational Services, Inc.
- **Coed**

Majors Construction management; cyber/computer forensics and counterterrorism; drafting and design technology; electrical, electronic and communications engineering technology; information technology project management; network and system administration; project management.

Academics *Calendar:* quarters. *Degrees:* associate and bachelor's.

Freshman Application Contact Director of Recruitment, ITT Technical Institute, 2431 W. Aviation Avenue, North Charleston, SC 29406. *Phone:* 843-745-5700. *Toll-free phone:* 877-291-0900.

Website: http://www.itt-tech.edu/.

Midlands Technical College
Columbia, South Carolina

Freshman Application Contact Ms. Sylvia Littlejohn, Director of Admissions, Midlands Technical College, PO Box 2408, Columbia, SC 29202. *Phone:* 803-738-8324. *Toll-free phone:* 800-922-8038. *Fax:* 803-790-7524. *E-mail:* admissions@midlandstech.edu.
Website: http://www.midlandstech.edu/.

Miller-Motte Technical College
Charleston, South Carolina

Freshman Application Contact Ms. Elaine Cue, Campus President, Miller-Motte Technical College, 8085 Rivers Avenue, Suite E, Charleston, SC 29406. *Phone:* 843-574-0101. *Toll-free phone:* 800-923-4162. *Fax:* 843-266-3424. *E-mail:* juliasc@miller-mott.net.
Website: http://www.miller-motte.edu/.

Miller-Motte Technical College
Conway, South Carolina

Admissions Office Contact Miller-Motte Technical College, 2451 Highway 501 East, Conway, SC 29526. *Toll-free phone:* 866-297-0267.
Website: http://www.miller-motte.edu/.

Northeastern Technical College
Cheraw, South Carolina

- **State and locally supported** 2-year, founded 1967, part of South Carolina State Board for Technical and Comprehensive Education
- **Rural** 59-acre campus
- **Endowment** $31,355
- **Coed,** 976 undergraduate students, 46% full-time, 72% women, 28% men

Undergraduates 446 full-time, 530 part-time. Students come from 3 states and territories; 1% are from out of state; 3% transferred in.
Freshmen *Admission:* 468 applied, 468 admitted, 249 enrolled.
Faculty *Student/faculty ratio:* 25:1.
Majors Accounting; administrative assistant and secretarial science; business administration and management; computer programming; computer science; data processing and data processing technology; drafting/design engineering technologies related; electrical, electronic and communications engineering technology; liberal arts and sciences/liberal studies; machine tool technology; marketing/marketing management; registered nursing/registered nurse.
Academics *Calendar:* semesters. *Degree:* certificates, diplomas, and associate. *Special study options:* academic remediation for entering students, adult/continuing education programs, advanced placement credit, distance learning, independent study, part-time degree program, study abroad.
Library Northeastern Technical College Library with 24,129 titles, 1,113 audiovisual materials, an OPAC, a Web page.
Student Life *Housing:* college housing not available. *Activities and Organizations:* Student Government Association, Alpha Beta Delta. *Campus security:* 24-hour emergency response devices. *Student services:* personal/psychological counseling.
Standardized Tests *Required:* COMPASS (for admission). *Required for some:* SAT (for admission).
Financial Aid Of all full-time matriculated undergraduates who enrolled in 2012, 26 Federal Work-Study jobs (averaging $2800).
Applying *Options:* electronic application, early admission. *Application fee:* $25. *Required:* high school transcript, interview. *Application deadlines:* 8/4 (freshmen), rolling (transfers). *Notification:* continuous (freshmen).
Freshman Application Contact Mrs. Mary K. Newton, Dean of Students, Northeastern Technical College, 1201 Chesterfield Highway, Cheraw, SC 29520-1007. *Phone:* 843-921-6935. *Toll-free phone:* 800-921-7399. *Fax:* 843-921-1476. *E-mail:* mpace@netc.edu.
Website: http://www.netc.edu/.

Orangeburg-Calhoun Technical College
Orangeburg, South Carolina

Freshman Application Contact Mr. Dana Rickards, Director of Recruitment, Orangeburg-Calhoun Technical College, 3250 St Matthews Road, NE, Orangeburg, SC 29118-8299. *Phone:* 803-535-1219. *Toll-free phone:* 800-813-6519.
Website: http://www.octech.edu/.

Piedmont Technical College
Greenwood, South Carolina

Director of Admissions Mr. Steve Coleman, Director of Admissions, Piedmont Technical College, 620 North Emerald Road, PO Box 1467, Greenwood, SC 29648-1467. *Phone:* 864-941-8603. *Toll-free phone:* 800-868-5528.
Website: http://www.ptc.edu/.

Spartanburg Community College
Spartanburg, South Carolina

- **State-supported** 2-year, founded 1961, part of South Carolina State Board for Technical and Comprehensive Education
- **Suburban** 104-acre campus with easy access to Charlotte
- **Coed,** 5,864 undergraduate students, 48% full-time, 59% women, 41% men

Undergraduates 2,789 full-time, 3,075 part-time. Students come from 14 states and territories; 3 other countries; 2% are from out of state; 23% Black or African American, non-Hispanic/Latino; 5% Hispanic/Latino; 3% Asian, non-Hispanic/Latino; 0.1% Native Hawaiian or other Pacific Islander, non-Hispanic/Latino; 0.5% American Indian or Alaska Native, non-Hispanic/Latino; 2% Two or more races, non-Hispanic/Latino; 2% Race/ethnicity unknown; 8% transferred in. *Retention:* 58% of full-time freshmen returned.
Freshmen *Admission:* 1,251 enrolled.
Faculty *Total:* 371, 30% full-time. *Student/faculty ratio:* 16:1.
Majors Accounting; administrative assistant and secretarial science; applied horticulture/horticulture operations; automobile/automotive mechanics technology; business administration and management; clinical/medical laboratory technology; data processing and data processing technology; electrical, electronic and communications engineering technology; heating, air conditioning, ventilation and refrigeration maintenance technology; industrial electronics technology; liberal arts and sciences/liberal studies; machine tool technology; manufacturing engineering technology; mechanical engineering/mechanical technology; medical radiologic technology; multi/interdisciplinary studies related; radiation protection/health physics technology; registered nursing/registered nurse; respiratory care therapy.
Academics *Calendar:* semesters condensed semesters plus summer sessions. *Degree:* certificates, diplomas, and associate. *Special study options:* academic remediation for entering students, adult/continuing education programs, advanced placement credit, cooperative education, distance learning, English as a second language, part-time degree program, services for LD students, summer session for credit.
Library Spartanburg Community College Library with 40,078 titles, 295 serial subscriptions, an OPAC, a Web page.
Student Life *Activities and Organizations:* drama/theater group, student-run newspaper. *Campus security:* 24-hour emergency response devices and patrols. *Student services:* personal/psychological counseling, women's center.
Standardized Tests *Required for some:* SAT or ACT (for admission).
Financial Aid Of all full-time matriculated undergraduates who enrolled in 2012, 47 Federal Work-Study jobs (averaging $3212).
Applying *Options:* electronic application, early admission. *Application fee:* $25. *Required:* high school transcript, high school diploma, GED or equivalent. *Recommended:* interview. *Application deadlines:* rolling (freshmen), rolling (transfers). *Notification:* continuous (freshmen), continuous (transfers).
Freshman Application Contact Sabrina Sims, Admissions Counselor, Spartanburg Community College, PO Box 4386, Spartanburg, SC 29305. *Phone:* 864-592-4816. *Toll-free phone:* 866-591-3700. *Fax:* 864-592-4564. *E-mail:* admissions@stcsc.edu.
Website: http://www.sccsc.edu/.

Spartanburg Methodist College
Spartanburg, South Carolina

- **Independent Methodist** 2-year, founded 1911
- **Suburban** 110-acre campus with easy access to Charlotte
- **Endowment** $19.4 million
- **Coed,** 818 undergraduate students, 98% full-time, 48% women, 52% men

Undergraduates 799 full-time, 19 part-time. Students come from 7 states and territories; 4 other countries; 6% are from out of state; 28% Black or African American, non-Hispanic/Latino; 5% Hispanic/Latino; 0.2% Asian, non-Hispanic/Latino; 0.4% American Indian or Alaska Native, non-Hispanic/Latino; 1% Two or more races, non-Hispanic/Latino; 1% international; 6% transferred in; 65% live on campus.
Freshmen *Admission:* 1,389 applied, 469 admitted, 469 enrolled. *Average high school GPA:* 3.35. *Test scores:* SAT critical reading scores over 500: 151%; SAT math scores over 500: 157%; SAT writing scores over 500: 60%; ACT scores over 18: 137%; SAT critical reading scores over 600: 42%; SAT math scores over 600: 30%; SAT writing scores over 600: 6%; ACT scores over 24: 18%; SAT math scores over 700: 7%; SAT writing scores over 700: 1%; ACT scores over 30: 1%.
Faculty *Total:* 49, 57% full-time, 53% with terminal degrees. *Student/faculty ratio:* 20:1.

Majors Business/commerce; criminal justice/law enforcement administration; liberal arts and sciences/liberal studies; religious studies related; visual and performing arts.

Academics *Calendar:* semesters. *Degree:* associate. *Special study options:* academic remediation for entering students, advanced placement credit, English as a second language, honors programs, independent study, part-time degree program, services for LD students, summer session for credit.

Library Marie Blair Burgess Learning Resource Center plus 1 other with 75,000 titles, 5,000 serial subscriptions, 3,150 audiovisual materials, an OPAC, a Web page.

Student Life *Housing Options:* coed, men-only, women-only. Campus housing is university owned. Freshman campus housing is guaranteed. *Activities and Organizations:* drama/theater group, student-run newspaper, choral group, College Christian Movement, Alpha Phi Omega, Campus Union, Fellowship of Christian Athletes, Kappa Sigma Alpha. *Campus security:* 24-hour emergency response devices and patrols, student patrols, late-night transport/escort service, controlled dormitory access. *Student services:* health clinic, personal/psychological counseling.

Athletics Member NJCAA. *Intercollegiate sports:* baseball M(s), basketball M(s)/W(s), cross-country running M(s)/W(s), golf M(s)/W(s), soccer M(s)/W(s), softball W(s), tennis M(s)/W(s), volleyball W(s), wrestling M(s). *Intramural sports:* basketball M/W, cheerleading M/W, football M/W, softball M/W, table tennis M/W, volleyball M/W.

Standardized Tests *Required:* SAT or ACT (for admission).

Costs (2013–14) *One-time required fee:* $175. *Comprehensive fee:* $24,021 includes full-time tuition ($14,882), mandatory fees ($903), and room and board ($8236). Full-time tuition and fees vary according to course load. Part-time tuition: $402 per semester hour. Part-time tuition and fees vary according to course load. *Payment plan:* installment. *Waivers:* employees or children of employees.

Financial Aid Of all full-time matriculated undergraduates who enrolled in 2012, 80 Federal Work-Study jobs (averaging $1600). 90 state and other part-time jobs (averaging $1600). *Financial aid deadline:* 8/30.

Applying *Options:* electronic application, deferred entrance. *Application fee:* $20. *Required:* essay or personal statement, high school transcript, minimum 2.0 GPA, high school rank considered along with other criteria. *Required for some:* interview. *Recommended:* interview. *Application deadlines:* rolling (freshmen), rolling (transfers). *Notification:* continuous (freshmen), continuous (transfers).

Freshman Application Contact Daniel L. Philbeck, Vice President for Enrollment Management, Spartanburg Methodist College, 1000 Powell Mill Road, Spartanburg, SC 29301-5899. *Phone:* 864-587-4223. *Toll-free phone:* 800-772-7286. *Fax:* 864-587-4355. *E-mail:* admiss@smcsc.edu. *Website:* http://www.smcsc.edu/.

Technical College of the Lowcountry
Beaufort, South Carolina

- **State-supported** 2-year, founded 1972, part of South Carolina Technical and Comprehensive Education System
- **Small-town** 12-acre campus
- **Coed,** 2,427 undergraduate students

Undergraduates 6% are from out of state; 36% Black or African American, non-Hispanic/Latino; 6% Hispanic/Latino; 1% Asian, non-Hispanic/Latino; 0.4% American Indian or Alaska Native, non-Hispanic/Latino; 1% Two or more races, non-Hispanic/Latino; 4% Race/ethnicity unknown; 0.1% international.

Faculty *Student/faculty ratio:* 15:1.

Majors Administrative assistant and secretarial science; business/commerce; child-care provision; civil engineering technology; construction engineering technology; data processing and data processing technology; early childhood education; education; emergency medical technology (EMT paramedic); fire services administration; golf course operation and grounds management; hospitality administration; industrial electronics technology; legal assistant/paralegal; liberal arts and sciences and humanities related; liberal arts and sciences/liberal studies; medical radiologic technology; physical therapy technology; registered nursing/registered nurse.

Academics *Calendar:* semesters. *Degree:* certificates, diplomas, and associate. *Special study options:* academic remediation for entering students, adult/continuing education programs, advanced placement credit, distance learning, part-time degree program, summer session for credit.

Student Life *Housing:* college housing not available. *Campus security:* security during class hours.

Standardized Tests *Required:* ACT ASSET (for admission). *Recommended:* SAT and SAT Subject Tests or ACT (for admission).

Financial Aid Of all full-time matriculated undergraduates who enrolled in 2012, 56 Federal Work-Study jobs (averaging $1700).

Applying *Options:* early admission, deferred entrance. *Application fee:* $25. *Application deadlines:* rolling (freshmen), rolling (transfers).

Freshman Application Contact Rhonda Cole, Admissions Services Manager, Technical College of the Lowcountry, 921 Ribaut Road, PO Box 1288, Beaufort, SC 29901-1288. *Phone:* 843-525-8229. *Fax:* 843-525-8285. *E-mail:* rcole@tcl.edu. *Website:* http://www.tcl.edu/.

Tri-County Technical College
Pendleton, South Carolina

Director of Admissions Renae Frazier, Director, Recruitment and Admissions, Tri-County Technical College, PO Box 587, 7900 Highway 76, Pendleton, SC 29670-0587. *Phone:* 864-646-1550. *Fax:* 864-646-1890. *E-mail:* infocent@tctc.edu. *Website:* http://www.tctc.edu/.

Trident Technical College
Charleston, South Carolina

- **State and locally supported** 2-year, founded 1964, part of South Carolina State Board for Technical and Comprehensive Education
- **Urban** campus
- **Coed,** 17,489 undergraduate students, 43% full-time, 60% women, 40% men

Undergraduates 7,521 full-time, 9,968 part-time. Students come from 71 other countries; 3% are from out of state; 34% Black or African American, non-Hispanic/Latino; 4% Hispanic/Latino; 2% Asian, non-Hispanic/Latino; 0.3% Native Hawaiian or other Pacific Islander, non-Hispanic/Latino; 0.7% American Indian or Alaska Native, non-Hispanic/Latino; 2% Two or more races, non-Hispanic/Latino; 2% Race/ethnicity unknown; 7% transferred in.

Freshmen *Admission:* 2,768 admitted, 2,768 enrolled.

Faculty *Total:* 899, 38% full-time. *Student/faculty ratio:* 21:1.

Majors Accounting; administrative assistant and secretarial science; airframe mechanics and aircraft maintenance technology; automobile/automotive mechanics technology; biological and physical sciences; business administration and management; child-care provision; civil engineering technology; clinical/medical laboratory technology; commercial and advertising art; computer engineering technology; computer graphics; computer/information technology services administration related; computer programming (specific applications); computer systems networking and telecommunications; criminal justice/law enforcement administration; culinary arts; dental hygiene; electrical, electronic and communications engineering technology; engineering technology; horticultural science; hotel/motel administration; human services; industrial technology; legal assistant/paralegal; legal studies; liberal arts and sciences/liberal studies; machine tool technology; marketing/marketing management; mechanical engineering/mechanical technology; medical administrative assistant and medical secretary; occupational therapy; physical therapy; registered nursing/registered nurse; respiratory care therapy; telecommunications technology; veterinary/animal health technology; web/multimedia management and webmaster; web page, digital/multimedia and information resources design.

Academics *Calendar:* semesters. *Degree:* certificates, diplomas, and associate. *Special study options:* academic remediation for entering students, advanced placement credit, cooperative education, distance learning, double majors, English as a second language, internships, off-campus study, part-time degree program, services for LD students, study abroad, summer session for credit.

Library Learning Resource Center plus 2 others with 107,671 titles, 280 serial subscriptions, 5,042 audiovisual materials, an OPAC, a Web page.

Student Life *Housing:* college housing not available. *Activities and Organizations:* drama/theater group, student-run newspaper, radio station, Phi Theta Kappa, Lex Artis Paralegal Society, Hospitality and Culinary Student Association, Partnership for Change in Communities and Families, Society of Student Leaders. *Campus security:* 24-hour emergency response devices and patrols, late-night transport/escort service. *Student services:* personal/psychological counseling.

Costs (2013–14) *Tuition:* area resident $3834 full-time, $153 per credit hour part-time; state resident $4236 full-time, $170 per credit hour part-time; nonresident $7122 full-time, $290 per credit hour part-time. Full-time tuition and fees vary according to course load. *Required fees:* $100 full-time. *Payment plan:* installment. *Waivers:* senior citizens.

Applying *Options:* electronic application, early admission. *Application fee:* $30. *Required for some:* high school transcript. *Application deadlines:* 8/6 (freshmen), 8/6 (transfers). *Notification:* continuous (freshmen), continuous (transfers).

Freshman Application Contact Ms. Clara Martin, Admissions Director, Trident Technical College, Charleston, SC 29423-8067. *Phone:* 843-574-6326. *Fax:* 843-574-6109. *E-mail:* Clara.Martin@tridenttech.edu. *Website:* http://www.tridenttech.edu/.

University of South Carolina Lancaster
Lancaster, South Carolina

Freshman Application Contact Susan Vinson, Admissions Counselor, University of South Carolina Lancaster, PO Box 889, Lancaster, SC 29721. *Phone:* 803-313-7000. *Fax:* 803-313-7116. *E-mail:* vinsons@mailbox.sc.edu. *Website:* http://usclancaster.sc.edu/.

University of South Carolina Salkehatchie
Allendale, South Carolina

- **State-supported** 2-year, founded 1965, part of University of South Carolina System
- **Rural** 95-acre campus
- **Coed**

Undergraduates 4% are from out of state. *Retention:* 45% of full-time freshmen returned.
Faculty *Student/faculty ratio:* 16:1.
Academics *Calendar:* semesters. *Degree:* associate. *Special study options:* academic remediation for entering students, adult/continuing education programs, advanced placement credit, distance learning, part-time degree program, summer session for credit.
Student Life *Campus security:* 24-hour emergency response devices.
Athletics Member NJCAA.
Standardized Tests *Required:* SAT or ACT (for admission).
Applying *Options:* electronic application. *Application fee:* $40. *Required:* high school transcript, minimum 2.0 GPA.
Freshman Application Contact Ms. Carmen Brown, Admissions Coordinator, University of South Carolina Salkehatchie, PO Box 617, Allendale, SC 29810. *Phone:* 803-584-3446. *Toll-free phone:* 800-922-5500. *Fax:* 803-584-3884. *E-mail:* cdbrown@mailbox.sc.edu. *Website:* http://uscsalkehatchie.sc.edu/.

University of South Carolina Sumter
Sumter, South Carolina

Freshman Application Contact Mr. Keith Britton, Director of Admissions, University of South Carolina Sumter, 200 Miller Road, Sumter, SC 29150-2498. *Phone:* 803-938-3882. *Fax:* 803-938-3901. *E-mail:* kbritton@usc.sumter.edu. *Website:* http://www.uscsumter.edu/.

University of South Carolina Union
Union, South Carolina

- **State-supported** 2-year, founded 1965, part of University of South Carolina System
- **Small-town** campus with easy access to Charlotte
- **Coed**

Undergraduates 250 full-time, 250 part-time.
Faculty *Student/faculty ratio:* 14:1.
Academics *Calendar:* semesters. *Degree:* associate. *Special study options:* part-time degree program.
Standardized Tests *Required:* SAT or ACT (for admission).
Financial Aid Of all full-time matriculated undergraduates who enrolled in 2012, 16 Federal Work-Study jobs (averaging $3400).
Applying *Application fee:* $40. *Required:* high school transcript.
Freshman Application Contact Mr. Michael B. Greer, Director of Enrollment Services, University of South Carolina Union, PO Drawer 729, Union, SC 29379-0729. *Phone:* 864-429-8728. *E-mail:* tyoung@gwm.sc.edu. *Website:* http://uscunion.sc.edu/.

Virginia College
Florence, South Carolina

Admissions Office Contact Virginia College, 2400 David H. McLeod Boulevard, Florence, SC 29501. *Website:* http://www.vc.edu/.

Virginia College in Charleston
North Charleston, South Carolina

Admissions Office Contact Virginia College in Charleston, 6185 Rivers Avenue, North Charleston, SC 29406. *Website:* http://www.vc.edu/.

Virginia College in Columbia
Columbia, South Carolina

Admissions Office Contact Virginia College in Columbia, 7201 Two Notch Road, Suite 1000, Columbia, SC 29223. *Website:* http://www.vc.edu/.

Virginia College in Greenville
Greenville, South Carolina

Admissions Office Contact Virginia College in Greenville, 78 Global Drive, Suite 200, Greenville, SC 29607. *Website:* http://www.vc.edu/.

Virginia College in Spartanburg
Spartanburg, South Carolina

Admissions Office Contact Virginia College in Spartanburg, 8150 Warren H. Abernathy Highway, Spartanburg, SC 29301. *Website:* http://www.vc.edu/.

Williamsburg Technical College
Kingstree, South Carolina

Freshman Application Contact Williamsburg Technical College, 601 Martin Luther King, Jr Avenue, Kingstree, SC 29556-4197. *Phone:* 843-355-4162. *Toll-free phone:* 800-768-2021. *Website:* http://www.wiltech.edu/.

York Technical College
Rock Hill, South Carolina

Freshman Application Contact Mr. Kenny Aldridge, Admissions Department Manager, York Technical College, Rock Hill, SC 29730. *Phone:* 803-327-8008. *Toll-free phone:* 800-922-8324. *Fax:* 803-981-7237. *E-mail:* kaldridge@yorktech.com. *Website:* http://www.yorktech.com/.

SOUTH DAKOTA

Kilian Community College
Sioux Falls, South Dakota

- **Independent** 2-year, founded 1977
- **Urban** 2-acre campus
- **Coed**, 253 undergraduate students, 13% full-time, 73% women, 27% men

Undergraduates 34 full-time, 219 part-time. Students come from 3 states and territories; 2% are from out of state; 13% Black or African American, non-Hispanic/Latino; 1% Hispanic/Latino; 0.4% Asian, non-Hispanic/Latino; 7% American Indian or Alaska Native, non-Hispanic/Latino; 25% Race/ethnicity unknown; 15% transferred in. *Retention:* 33% of full-time freshmen returned.
Freshmen *Admission:* 33 enrolled.
Faculty *Total:* 34, 15% full-time, 18% with terminal degrees. *Student/faculty ratio:* 8:1.
Majors Accounting; American Indian/Native American studies; business administration and management; counseling psychology; criminal justice/law enforcement administration; education; environmental studies; financial planning and services; history; information technology; liberal arts and sciences/liberal studies; medical office management; psychology; social work; sociology; substance abuse/addiction counseling.
Academics *Calendar:* trimesters. *Degree:* certificates and associate. *Special study options:* academic remediation for entering students, advanced placement credit, double majors, English as a second language, independent study, part-time degree program, services for LD students, summer session for credit.
Library Sioux Falls Public Library with 78,000 titles, 395 serial subscriptions, an OPAC, a Web page.
Student Life *Housing:* college housing not available. *Activities and Organizations:* Phi Theta Kappa. *Campus security:* late-night transport/escort service. *Student services:* personal/psychological counseling.
Financial Aid Of all full-time matriculated undergraduates who enrolled in 2011, 31 applied for aid, 31 were judged to have need. 26 Federal Work-Study jobs (averaging $1500). *Average percent of need met:* 61%. *Average financial aid package:* $9000. *Average need-based loan:* $4500. *Average need-based gift aid:* $4500.

Applying *Options:* electronic application, deferred entrance. *Application fee:* $25. *Required:* high school transcript. *Application deadlines:* rolling (freshmen), rolling (out-of-state freshmen), rolling (transfers).
Freshman Application Contact Ms. Mary Klockman, Director of Admissions, Kilian Community College, 300 East 6th Street, Sioux Falls, SD 57103. *Phone:* 605-221-3100. *Toll-free phone:* 800-888-1147. *Fax:* 605-336-2606. *E-mail:* info@killian.edu.
Website: http://www.kilian.edu/.

Lake Area Technical Institute
Watertown, South Dakota

- **State-supported** 2-year, founded 1964
- **Small-town** 40-acre campus
- **Coed**, 1,600 undergraduate students

Undergraduates 1% Black or African American, non-Hispanic/Latino; 1% Hispanic/Latino; 2% American Indian or Alaska Native, non-Hispanic/Latino. *Retention:* 81% of full-time freshmen returned.
Freshmen *Admission:* 1,689 applied, 1,020 admitted.
Faculty *Total:* 97, 98% full-time. *Student/faculty ratio:* 16:1.
Majors Agricultural business and management; agricultural production; aircraft powerplant technology; autobody/collision and repair technology; automobile/automotive mechanics technology; banking and financial support services; biology/biotechnology laboratory technician; carpentry; clinical/medical laboratory technology; computer programming; computer science; construction engineering technology; dental assisting; diesel mechanics technology; drafting and design technology; electrical, electronic and communications engineering technology; electrical/electronics equipment installation and repair; electromechanical technology; emergency medical technology (EMT paramedic); engineering technology; environmental science; human services; licensed practical/vocational nurse training; machine tool technology; manufacturing engineering technology; marketing/marketing management; medical/clinical assistant; occupational therapist assistant; physical therapy technology; robotics technology; sales, distribution, and marketing operations; small business administration; welding technology.
Academics *Calendar:* semesters. *Degree:* diplomas and associate. *Special study options:* academic remediation for entering students, distance learning, internships, services for LD students.
Library Leonard H. Timmerman Library plus 1 other with 5,000 titles, 128 serial subscriptions.
Student Life *Housing:* college housing not available.
Athletics *Intramural sports:* basketball M/W, softball M/W, volleyball M/W.
Standardized Tests *Required:* ACT (for admission).
Applying *Options:* electronic application. *Application fee:* $20. *Required:* high school transcript. *Required for some:* essay or personal statement, 3 letters of recommendation, interview.
Freshman Application Contact Lake Area Technical Institute, 1201 Arrow Ave, Watertown, SD 57201. *Phone:* 605-882-5284. *Toll-free phone:* 800-657-4344.
Website: http://www.lakeareatech.edu/.

Mitchell Technical Institute
Mitchell, South Dakota

- **State-supported** 2-year, founded 1968, part of South Dakota Board of Education
- **Rural** 90-acre campus
- **Coed**, 1,221 undergraduate students, 77% full-time, 35% women, 65% men

Undergraduates 937 full-time, 284 part-time. 7% are from out of state; 0.3% Black or African American, non-Hispanic/Latino; 0.3% Hispanic/Latino; 0.1% Native Hawaiian or other Pacific Islander, non-Hispanic/Latino; 4% American Indian or Alaska Native, non-Hispanic/Latino; 1% Two or more races, non-Hispanic/Latino; 0.2% Race/ethnicity unknown; 6% transferred in. *Retention:* 76% of full-time freshmen returned.
Freshmen *Admission:* 714 applied, 564 admitted, 405 enrolled. *Average high school GPA:* 2.64. *Test scores:* ACT scores over 18: 73%; ACT scores over 24: 12%.
Faculty *Total:* 88, 85% full-time, 1% with terminal degrees. *Student/faculty ratio:* 13:1.
Majors Accounting and business/management; agricultural mechanics and equipment technology; agricultural production; automation engineer technology; building construction technology; building/property maintenance; business automation/technology/data entry; clinical/medical laboratory technology; computer support specialist; construction trades related; culinary arts; electrician; energy management and systems technology; geographic information science and cartography; heating, air conditioning, ventilation and refrigeration maintenance technology; lineworker; medical/clinical assistant; medical office assistant; medical radiologic technology; network and system administration; radiologic technology/science; radio, television, and digital communication related; small engine mechanics and repair technology; speech-language pathology assistant; telecommunications technology; welding engineering technology.
Academics *Calendar:* semesters. *Degree:* certificates, diplomas, and associate. *Special study options:* academic remediation for entering students, advanced placement credit, cooperative education, distance learning, internships, part-time degree program, services for LD students, summer session for credit.
Library Instructional Services Center with an OPAC.
Student Life *Housing Options:* Campus housing is provided by a third party. *Activities and Organizations:* Student Representative Board, Skills USA, Post-Secondary Agricultural Students, Rodeo Club, Student Veterans Organization. *Student services:* personal/psychological counseling.
Athletics *Intercollegiate sports:* equestrian sports M/W. *Intramural sports:* basketball M/W, bowling M/W, riflery M/W, softball M/W, volleyball M/W.
Standardized Tests *Required for some:* SAT or ACT (for admission). *Recommended:* SAT or ACT (for admission).
Costs (2013–14) *Tuition:* state resident $3120 full-time, $104 per credit hour part-time; nonresident $3120 full-time, $104 per credit hour part-time. Full-time tuition and fees vary according to course load and program. Part-time tuition and fees vary according to course load and program. *Required fees:* $2292 full-time, $76 per credit hour part-time. *Payment plan:* installment. *Waivers:* employees or children of employees.
Financial Aid Of all full-time matriculated undergraduates who enrolled in 2013, 830 applied for aid, 696 were judged to have need, 65 had their need fully met. *Average percent of need met:* 53%. *Average financial aid package:* $6497. *Average need-based loan:* $3684. *Average need-based gift aid:* $4675. *Average indebtedness upon graduation:* $6438.
Applying *Options:* electronic application. *Required:* high school transcript. *Required for some:* essay or personal statement, interview. *Recommended:* minimum 2.0 GPA. *Application deadlines:* rolling (freshmen), rolling (out-of-state freshmen), rolling (transfers). *Notification:* continuous (freshmen), continuous (out-of-state freshmen), continuous (transfers).
Freshman Application Contact Mr. Clayton Deuter, Director of Admissions, Mitchell Technical Institute, 1800 East Spruce Street, Mitchell, SD 57301. *Phone:* 605-995-3025. *Toll-free phone:* 800-684-1969. *Fax:* 605-995-3067. *E-mail:* clayton.deuter@mitchelltech.edu.
Website: http://www.mitchelltech.edu/.

National American University
Ellsworth AFB, South Dakota

Freshman Application Contact Admissions Office, National American University, 1000 Ellsworth Street, Suite 2400B, Ellsworth AFB, SD 57706. *Website:* http://www.national.edu/.

Sisseton-Wahpeton College
Sisseton, South Dakota

Freshman Application Contact Sisseton-Wahpeton College, Old Agency Box 689, Sisseton, SD 57262. *Phone:* 605-698-3966 Ext. 1180. *Website:* http://www.swc.tc/.

Southeast Technical Institute
Sioux Falls, South Dakota

- **State-supported** 2-year, founded 1968
- **Urban** 138-acre campus
- **Endowment** $768,716
- **Coed**, 2,467 undergraduate students, 68% full-time, 52% women, 48% men

Undergraduates 1,683 full-time, 784 part-time. Students come from 11 states and territories; 8% are from out of state; 3% Black or African American, non-Hispanic/Latino; 3% Hispanic/Latino; 0.8% Asian, non-Hispanic/Latino; 0.1% Native Hawaiian or other Pacific Islander, non-Hispanic/Latino; 2% American Indian or Alaska Native, non-Hispanic/Latino; 2% Two or more races, non-Hispanic/Latino; 5% Race/ethnicity unknown; 14% transferred in; 2% live on campus. *Retention:* 56% of full-time freshmen returned.
Freshmen *Admission:* 2,887 applied, 1,202 admitted, 565 enrolled. *Average high school GPA:* 2.7.
Faculty *Total:* 201, 44% full-time, 3% with terminal degrees. *Student/faculty ratio:* 18:1.
Majors Accounting; animation, interactive technology, video graphics and special effects; applied horticulture/horticulture operations; architectural engineering technology; autobody/collision and repair technology; automobile/automotive mechanics technology; banking and financial support services; biomedical technology; building/construction finishing, management, and inspection related; business administration and management; cardiovascular technology; child-care and support services management; child-care provision; civil engineering technology; clinical/medical laboratory science and allied professions related; clinical/medical laboratory technology;

commercial and advertising art; computer and information sciences and support services related; computer and information systems security; computer/information technology services administration related; computer installation and repair technology; computer programming; computer programming related; computer software engineering; computer systems networking and telecommunications; computer technology/computer systems technology; construction engineering technology; criminal justice/police science; desktop publishing and digital imaging design; diagnostic medical sonography and ultrasound technology; diesel mechanics technology; electrical, electronic and communications engineering technology; electrical/electronics equipment installation and repair; electromechanical technology; electroneurodiagnostic/electroencephalographic technology; finance; health unit coordinator/ward clerk; heating, air conditioning, ventilation and refrigeration maintenance technology; horticultural science; industrial technology; licensed practical/vocational nurse training; marketing/marketing management; mechanical engineering/mechanical technology; medical insurance coding; merchandising, sales, and marketing operations related (general); nuclear medical technology; office occupations and clerical services; plumbing technology; registered nursing/registered nurse; surgical technology; surveying technology; turf and turfgrass management; welding technology.

Academics *Calendar:* semesters. *Degree:* certificates, diplomas, and associate. *Special study options:* academic remediation for entering students, advanced placement credit, distance learning, double majors, independent study, internships, part-time degree program, services for LD students, summer session for credit.

Library Southeast Library with 10,643 titles, 158 serial subscriptions, an OPAC, a Web page.

Student Life *Housing Options:* coed. Campus housing is provided by a third party. *Activities and Organizations:* VICA (Vocational Industrial Clubs of America), American Landscape Contractors Association. *Campus security:* 24-hour patrols, late-night transport/escort service, controlled dormitory access. *Student services:* personal/psychological counseling.

Athletics *Intramural sports:* basketball M/W, bowling M/W, volleyball M/W.

Standardized Tests *Recommended:* ACT (for admission).

Costs (2014–15) *Tuition:* state resident $3120 full-time, $104 per credit part-time; nonresident $3120 full-time, $104 per credit part-time. Full-time tuition and fees vary according to program. Part-time tuition and fees vary according to program. *Required fees:* $2730 full-time, $91 per credit part-time. *Room and board:* $2730; room only: $4650. *Payment plan:* installment.

Financial Aid Of all full-time matriculated undergraduates who enrolled in 2012, 35 Federal Work-Study jobs (averaging $2550).

Applying *Options:* electronic application. *Required:* high school transcript, minimum 2.2 GPA. *Required for some:* interview, background check and drug testing for certain programs. *Application deadlines:* rolling (freshmen), rolling (out-of-state freshmen), rolling (transfers). *Notification:* continuous (freshmen), continuous (out-of-state freshmen), continuous (transfers).

Freshman Application Contact Mr. Scott Dorman, Recruiter, Southeast Technical Institute, Sioux Falls, SD 57107. *Phone:* 605-367-4458. *Toll-free phone:* 800-247-0789. *Fax:* 605-367-8305. *E-mail:* scott.dorman@southeasttech.edu.

Website: http://www.southeasttech.edu/.

Western Dakota Technical Institute

Rapid City, South Dakota

- **State-supported** 2-year, founded 1968
- **Small-town** 5-acre campus
- **Coed,** 1,088 undergraduate students, 73% full-time, 48% women, 52% men

Undergraduates 795 full-time, 293 part-time. Students come from 17 states and territories; 3% are from out of state; 3% Black or African American, non-Hispanic/Latino; 5% Hispanic/Latino; 1% Asian, non-Hispanic/Latino; 0.4% Native Hawaiian or other Pacific Islander, non-Hispanic/Latino; 15% American Indian or Alaska Native, non-Hispanic/Latino; 0.3% Two or more races, non-Hispanic/Latino; 0.1% Race/ethnicity unknown; 30% transferred in. *Retention:* 50% of full-time freshmen returned.

Freshmen *Admission:* 1,458 applied, 861 admitted, 261 enrolled. *Average high school GPA:* 3.42. *Test scores:* ACT scores over 18: 56%; ACT scores over 24: 14%; ACT scores over 30: 3%.

Faculty *Total:* 123, 37% full-time. *Student/faculty ratio:* 18:1.

Majors Accounting; autobody/collision and repair technology; business administration and management; computer systems networking and telecommunications; criminal justice/police science; drafting and design technology; electrician; emergency medical technology (EMT paramedic); environmental control technologies related; fire science/firefighting; heating, air conditioning, ventilation and refrigeration maintenance technology; legal assistant/paralegal; library and archives assisting; medical/clinical assistant;

medical transcription; pharmacy technician; precision metal working related; surgical technology; vehicle maintenance and repair technologies related.

Academics *Calendar:* semesters. *Degree:* certificates, diplomas, and associate. *Special study options:* academic remediation for entering students, advanced placement credit, distance learning, independent study, internships, part-time degree program, services for LD students, summer session for credit.

Library Western Dakota Technical Institute Library with 3,823 titles, 68 serial subscriptions, 529 audiovisual materials, an OPAC, a Web page.

Student Life *Housing:* college housing not available. *Campus security:* 24-hour video surveillance.

Standardized Tests *Recommended:* SAT or ACT (for admission).

Costs (2014–15) *One-time required fee:* $250. *Tuition:* state resident $3744 full-time, $104 per credit hour part-time; nonresident $3744 full-time, $104 per credit hour part-time. Full-time tuition and fees vary according to course load and program. Part-time tuition and fees vary according to course load. *Required fees:* $2959 full-time, $79 per credit hour part-time. *Payment plans:* installment, deferred payment. *Waivers:* employees or children of employees.

Financial Aid Of all full-time matriculated undergraduates who enrolled in 2012, 85 Federal Work-Study jobs (averaging $1400).

Applying *Options:* electronic application. *Application fee:* $20. *Required:* high school transcript, Placement test. *Required for some:* essay or personal statement, 3 letters of recommendation, interview. *Recommended:* minimum 2.0 GPA. *Application deadlines:* 8/1 (freshmen), 8/1 (transfers). *Notification:* continuous until 8/15 (freshmen), continuous until 8/15 (transfers).

Freshman Application Contact Jill Elder, Admissions Coordinator, Western Dakota Technical Institute, 800 Mickelson Drive, Rapid City, SD 57703. *Phone:* 605-718-2411. *Toll-free phone:* 800-544-8765. *Fax:* 605-394-2204. *E-mail:* jill.elder@wdt.edu.

Website: http://www.wdt.edu/.

TENNESSEE

Anthem Career College

Memphis, Tennessee

Freshman Application Contact Admissions Office, Anthem Career College, 5865 Shelby Oaks Circle, Suite 100, Memphis, TN 38134. *Toll-free phone:* 866-381-5623.

Website: http://www.anthem.edu/memphis-tennessee/.

Anthem Career College–Nashville

Nashville, Tennessee

Freshman Application Contact Admissions Office, Anthem Career College–Nashville, 560 Royal Parkway, Nashville, TN 37214. *Phone:* 615-902-9705. *Toll-free phone:* 866-381-5791.

Website: http://anthem.edu/nashville-tennessee/.

Chattanooga College–Medical, Dental and Technical Careers

Chattanooga, Tennessee

- **Proprietary** 2-year
- **Urban** campus
- **Coed,** 330 undergraduate students

Majors Electrical, electronic and communications engineering technology.

Academics *Degree:* associate.

Costs (2013–14) *One-time required fee:* $25. *Tuition:* $9515 full-time. Full-time tuition and fees vary according to degree level and program. No tuition increase for student's term of enrollment. *Required fees:* $2600 full-time. *Payment plans:* installment, deferred payment.

Applying *Application fee:* $25.

Freshman Application Contact Chattanooga College–Medical, Dental and Technical Careers, 248 Northgate Mall Drive, Suite 130, Chattanooga, TN 37415. *Phone:* 423-305-7781. *Toll-free phone:* 877-313-2373.

Website: http://www.chattanoogacollege.edu/.

Chattanooga State Community College

Chattanooga, Tennessee

Freshman Application Contact Brad McCormick, Director of Admissions and Records, Chattanooga State Community College, 4501 Amnicola Highway, Chattanooga, TN 37406. *Phone:* 423-697-4401 Ext. 3264. *Toll-free phone:* 866-547-3733. *Fax:* 423-697-4709. *E-mail:* brad.mccormick@chattanoogastate.edu.

Website: http://www.chattanoogastate.edu/.

Cleveland State Community College
Cleveland, Tennessee

- **State-supported** 2-year, founded 1967, part of Tennessee Board of Regents
- **Suburban** 83-acre campus
- **Endowment** $5.2 million
- **Coed,** 3,790 undergraduate students, 50% full-time, 60% women, 40% men

Undergraduates 1,885 full-time, 1,905 part-time. Students come from 8 states and territories; 1 other country; 1% are from out of state; 6% Black or African American, non-Hispanic/Latino; 3% Hispanic/Latino; 1% Asian, non-Hispanic/Latino; 0.4% American Indian or Alaska Native, non-Hispanic/Latino; 1% Two or more races, non-Hispanic/Latino; 4% Race/ethnicity unknown; 0.1% international; 13% transferred in.

Freshmen *Admission:* 1,425 applied, 777 admitted, 777 enrolled. *Average high school GPA:* 3.08. *Test scores:* ACT scores over 18: 68%; ACT scores over 24: 9%.

Faculty *Total:* 188, 38% full-time, 19% with terminal degrees. *Student/faculty ratio:* 23:1.

Majors Administrative assistant and secretarial science; business administration and management; child development; community organization and advocacy; criminal justice/police science; general studies; industrial technology; kindergarten/preschool education; liberal arts and sciences and humanities related; liberal arts and sciences/liberal studies; public administration and social service professions related; registered nursing/registered nurse; science technologies related.

Academics *Calendar:* semesters. *Degree:* certificates and associate. *Special study options:* academic remediation for entering students, adult/continuing education programs, advanced placement credit, cooperative education, distance learning, double majors, external degree program, honors programs, independent study, internships, off-campus study, part-time degree program, services for LD students, summer session for credit.

Library Cleveland State Community College Library with 153,456 titles, 1,137 serial subscriptions, 8,142 audiovisual materials, an OPAC, a Web page.

Student Life *Housing:* college housing not available. *Activities and Organizations:* student-run newspaper, choral group, Human Services/Social Work, Computer Aided Design, Phi Theta Kappa, Student Nursing Association, Early Childhood Education. *Campus security:* 24-hour emergency response devices and patrols. *Student services:* personal/psychological counseling.

Athletics Member NJCAA. *Intercollegiate sports:* baseball M(s), basketball M(s)/W(s), softball W(s). *Intramural sports:* archery M/W, basketball M/W, bowling M/W, cheerleading M(c)/W(c), softball W, table tennis M/W, volleyball M/W.

Costs (2013–14) *Tuition:* state resident $3504 full-time, $139 per credit hour part-time; nonresident $14,446 full-time, $574 per credit hour part-time. Full-time tuition and fees vary according to course load. *Required fees:* $269 full-time, $14 per credit hour part-time, $22 per term part-time. *Payment plan:* deferred payment. *Waivers:* senior citizens and employees or children of employees.

Financial Aid Of all full-time matriculated undergraduates who enrolled in 2012, 52 Federal Work-Study jobs (averaging $1025).

Applying *Options:* electronic application, early admission, deferred entrance. *Application fee:* $20. *Required:* high school transcript. *Application deadlines:* rolling (freshmen), rolling (transfers). *Notification:* continuous (freshmen), continuous (transfers).

Freshman Application Contact Mrs. Suzanne Bayne, Assistant Director of Admissions and Recruitment, Cleveland State Community College, P O Box 3570, Cleveland, TN 37320-3570. *Phone:* 423-472-7141 Ext. 743. *Toll-free phone:* 800-604-2722. *Fax:* 423-614-8711. *E-mail:* SBayne@clevelandstatecc.edu.
Website: http://www.clevelandstatecc.edu/.

Columbia State Community College
Columbia, Tennessee

Freshman Application Contact Mr. Joey Scruggs, Coordinator of Recruitment, Columbia State Community College, PO Box 1315, Columbia, TN 38402-1315. *Phone:* 931-540-2540. *E-mail:* scruggs@coscc.cc.tn.us.
Website: http://www.columbiastate.edu/.

Concorde Career College
Memphis, Tennessee

Freshman Application Contact Dee Vickers, Director, Concorde Career College, 5100 Poplar Avenue, Suite 132, Memphis, TN 38137. *Phone:* 901-761-9494. *Fax:* 901-761-3293. *E-mail:* dvickers@concorde.edu.
Website: http://www.concorde.edu/.

Daymar Institute
Nashville, Tennessee

Director of Admissions Admissions Office, Daymar Institute, 340 Plus Park Boulevard, Nashville, TN 37217. *Phone:* 615-361-7555. *Fax:* 615-367-2736. *Website:* http://www.daymarinstitute.edu/.

Dyersburg State Community College
Dyersburg, Tennessee

- **State-supported** 2-year, founded 1969, part of Tennessee Board of Regents
- **Small-town** 115-acre campus with easy access to Memphis
- **Endowment** $3.8 million
- **Coed,** 3,258 undergraduate students, 40% full-time, 66% women, 34% men

Undergraduates 1,292 full-time, 1,966 part-time. Students come from 9 states and territories; 1 other country; 18% Black or African American, non-Hispanic/Latino; 2% Hispanic/Latino; 0.7% Asian, non-Hispanic/Latino; 0.4% American Indian or Alaska Native, non-Hispanic/Latino; 1% Two or more races, non-Hispanic/Latino; 1% Race/ethnicity unknown; 5% transferred in. *Retention:* 51% of full-time freshmen returned.

Freshmen *Admission:* 652 enrolled. *Average high school GPA:* 2.8. *Test scores:* ACT scores over 18: 61%; ACT scores over 24: 10%; ACT scores over 30: 1%.

Faculty *Total:* 183, 31% full-time. *Student/faculty ratio:* 20:1.

Majors Agriculture; automation engineer technology; business administration and management; child development; computer and information systems security; criminal justice/police science; criminal justice/safety; education; emergency medical technology (EMT paramedic); general studies; health information/medical records technology; health services/allied health/health sciences; industrial electronics technology; industrial mechanics and maintenance technology; information science/studies; liberal arts and sciences/liberal studies; medical informatics; music performance; registered nursing/registered nurse; web page, digital/multimedia and information resources design.

Academics *Calendar:* semesters. *Degree:* certificates and associate. *Special study options:* academic remediation for entering students, adult/continuing education programs, advanced placement credit, cooperative education, distance learning, double majors, honors programs, independent study, part-time degree program, services for LD students, summer session for credit.

Library Learning Resource Center with 65,685 titles, 25 serial subscriptions, 542 audiovisual materials, an OPAC, a Web page.

Student Life *Housing:* college housing not available. *Activities and Organizations:* drama/theater group, choral group, Psychology Club, Phi Theta Kappa, student government, Media Club, Criminal Justice Association. *Campus security:* 24-hour emergency response devices and patrols. *Student services:* personal/psychological counseling.

Athletics Member NJCAA. *Intercollegiate sports:* baseball M(s), basketball M(s)/W(s), cheerleading W(s), softball W(s). *Intramural sports:* basketball M/W, soccer M/W, table tennis M/W, ultimate Frisbee M/W, volleyball M/W.

Standardized Tests *Required:* An official copy of ACT scores is required for all first-time degree-seeking students under the age of 21. ACT scores may be used only if the ACT scores are no older than three years. Official SAT scores may be accepted in lieu of ACT scores. The ACT Compass is required by student who are over 21.

Costs (2013–14) *One-time required fee:* $10. *Tuition:* state resident $3336 full-time, $139 per credit hour part-time; nonresident $13,776 full-time, $574 per credit hour part-time. Full-time tuition and fees vary according to course load. Part-time tuition and fees vary according to course load. *Required fees:* $291 full-time, $146 per term part-time. *Payment plan:* deferred payment. *Waivers:* senior citizens and employees or children of employees.

Financial Aid Of all full-time matriculated undergraduates who enrolled in 2012, 40 Federal Work-Study jobs (averaging $2117). 113 state and other part-time jobs (averaging $1424).

Applying *Required:* high school transcript.

Freshman Application Contact Ms. Josh Caviness, Admissions Counselor, Dyersburg State Community College, Dyersburg, TN 38024. *Phone:* 731-286-3324. *Fax:* 731-286-3325. *E-mail:* jcaviness@dscc.edu.
Website: http://www.dscc.edu/.

Fortis Institute
Cookeville, Tennessee

Director of Admissions Ms. Sharon Mellott, Director of Admissions, Fortis Institute, 1025 Highway 111, Cookeville, TN 38501. *Phone:* 931-526-3660. *Toll-free phone:* 855-4-FORTIS.
Website: http://www.fortis.edu/.

Fountainhead College of Technology
Knoxville, Tennessee

- **Proprietary** primarily 2-year, founded 1947
- **Suburban** 2-acre campus
- **Coed**

Undergraduates 230 full-time. *Retention:* 82% of full-time freshmen returned.

Faculty *Student/faculty ratio:* 9:1.

Academics *Calendar:* semesters. *Degrees:* associate and bachelor's. *Special study options:* accelerated degree program, distance learning, double majors, summer session for credit.

Student Life *Campus security:* 24-hour emergency response devices.

Standardized Tests *Required for some:* SAT or ACT (for admission).

Applying *Required:* high school transcript, interview.

Freshman Application Contact Mr. Joel B Southern, Director of Admissions, Fountainhead College of Technology, 10208 Technology Drive, Knoxville, TN 37932. *Phone:* 865-688-9422. *Toll-free phone:* 888-218-7335. *Fax:* 865-688-2419. *E-mail:* joel.southern@fountainheadcollege.edu.

Website: http://www.fountainheadcollege.edu/.

ITT Technical Institute
Chattanooga, Tennessee

- **Proprietary** primarily 2-year, part of ITT Educational Services, Inc.
- **Coed**

Majors Business administration and management; computer programming (specific applications); construction management; cyber/computer forensics and counterterrorism; drafting and design technology; electrical, electronic and communications engineering technology; forensic science and technology; industrial technology; information technology project management; network and system administration; project management.

Academics *Degrees:* associate and bachelor's.

Student Life *Housing:* college housing not available.

Freshman Application Contact Director of Recruitment, ITT Technical Institute, 5600 Brainerd Road, Suite G-1, Chattanooga, TN 37411. *Phone:* 423-510-6800. *Toll-free phone:* 877-474-8312.

Website: http://www.itt-tech.edu/.

ITT Technical Institute
Cordova, Tennessee

- **Proprietary** primarily 2-year, founded 1994, part of ITT Educational Services, Inc.
- **Suburban** campus
- **Coed**

Majors Business administration and management; computer programming (specific applications); construction management; cyber/computer forensics and counterterrorism; drafting and design technology; electrical, electronic and communications engineering technology; forensic science and technology; graphic communications; industrial technology; information technology project management; network and system administration; project management.

Academics *Calendar:* quarters. *Degrees:* associate and bachelor's.

Student Life *Housing:* college housing not available.

Freshman Application Contact Director of Recruitment, ITT Technical Institute, 7260 Goodlett Farms Parkway, Cordova, TN 38016. *Phone:* 901-381-0200. *Toll-free phone:* 866-444-5141.

Website: http://www.itt-tech.edu/.

ITT Technical Institute
Johnson City, Tennessee

- **Proprietary** primarily 2-year
- **Coed**

Majors Business administration and management; computer programming (specific applications); construction management; cyber/computer forensics and counterterrorism; drafting and design technology; electrical, electronic and communications engineering technology; forensic science and technology; industrial technology; information technology project management; legal assistant/paralegal; network and system administration; project management.

Academics *Degrees:* associate and bachelor's.

Freshman Application Contact Director of Recruitment, ITT Technical Institute, 4721 Lake Park Drive, Suite 100, Johnson City, TN 37615. *Phone:* 423-952-4400. *Toll-free phone:* 877-301-9691.

Website: http://www.itt-tech.edu/.

ITT Technical Institute
Knoxville, Tennessee

- **Proprietary** primarily 2-year, founded 1988, part of ITT Educational Services, Inc.
- **Suburban** campus
- **Coed**

Majors Business administration and management; computer programming (specific applications); construction management; cyber/computer forensics and counterterrorism; drafting and design technology; electrical, electronic and communications engineering technology; forensic science and technology; game and interactive media design; graphic communications; industrial technology; information technology project management; network and system administration; project management.

Academics *Calendar:* quarters. *Degrees:* associate and bachelor's.

Student Life *Housing:* college housing not available.

Freshman Application Contact Director of Recruitment, ITT Technical Institute, 9123 Executive Park Drive, Knoxville, TN 37923. *Phone:* 865-342-2300. *Toll-free phone:* 800-671-2801.

Website: http://www.itt-tech.edu/.

ITT Technical Institute
Nashville, Tennessee

- **Proprietary** primarily 2-year, founded 1984, part of ITT Educational Services, Inc.
- **Urban** campus
- **Coed**

Majors Business administration and management; computer programming (specific applications); construction management; cyber/computer forensics and counterterrorism; drafting and design technology; electrical, electronic and communications engineering technology; forensic science and technology; game and interactive media design; graphic communications; industrial technology; information technology project management; network and system administration; project management; registered nursing/registered nurse.

Academics *Calendar:* quarters. *Degrees:* associate and bachelor's.

Student Life *Housing:* college housing not available.

Freshman Application Contact Director of Recruitment, ITT Technical Institute, 2845 Elm Hill Pike, Nashville, TN 37214. *Phone:* 615-889-8700. *Toll-free phone:* 800-331-8386.

Website: http://www.itt-tech.edu/.

Jackson State Community College
Jackson, Tennessee

- **State-supported** 2-year, founded 1967, part of Tennessee Board of Regents
- **Suburban** 100-acre campus with easy access to Memphis
- **Coed,** 4,585 undergraduate students

Faculty *Total:* 288, 32% full-time. *Student/faculty ratio:* 18:1.

Majors Agriculture; business administration and management; clinical/medical laboratory technology; computer science; education; general studies; industrial technology; liberal arts and sciences/liberal studies; management information systems; medical radiologic technology; physical therapy technology; registered nursing/registered nurse; science technologies related.

Academics *Calendar:* semesters. *Degree:* certificates, diplomas, and associate. *Special study options:* academic remediation for entering students, accelerated degree program, adult/continuing education programs, advanced placement credit, cooperative education, distance learning, external degree program, honors programs, independent study, internships, off-campus study, part-time degree program, services for LD students, study abroad, summer session for credit. *ROTC:* Army (b).

Library Jackson State Community College Library with 58,104 titles, 82 serial subscriptions, 1,686 audiovisual materials, an OPAC, a Web page.

Student Life *Housing:* college housing not available. *Activities and Organizations:* choral group, Spanish Club, Gay/Straight Alliance, Art Club, H2O Wellness, Biology Club. *Campus security:* 24-hour patrols, late-night transport/escort service, field camera surveillance. *Student services:* personal/psychological counseling.

Athletics Member NJCAA. *Intercollegiate sports:* baseball M(s), basketball M(s)/W(s), softball W(s).

Standardized Tests *Required:* SAT or ACT (for admission), COMPASS (for admission). *Recommended:* ACT (for admission).

Financial Aid Of all full-time matriculated undergraduates who enrolled in 2012, 30 Federal Work-Study jobs (averaging $3000). 10 state and other part-time jobs (averaging $3000).

Applying *Options:* electronic application. *Application fee:* $10. *Required for some:* high school transcript. *Application deadlines:* 8/23 (freshmen), 8/23

(out-of-state freshmen), rolling (transfers). *Notification:* continuous (freshmen), continuous (out-of-state freshmen), continuous (transfers).
Freshman Application Contact Ms. Andrea Winchester, Director of High School Initiatives, Jackson State Community College, 2046 North Parkway, Jackson, TN 38301-3797. *Phone:* 731-424-3520 Ext. 50484. *Toll-free phone:* 800-355-5722. *Fax:* 731-425-9559. *E-mail:* awinchester@jscc.edu.
Website: http://www.jscc.edu/.

John A. Gupton College
Nashville, Tennessee

- **Independent** 2-year, founded 1946
- **Urban** 1-acre campus with easy access to Nashville
- **Endowment** $60,000
- **Coed,** 122 undergraduate students, 59% full-time, 53% women, 47% men

Undergraduates 72 full-time, 50 part-time. Students come from 8 states and territories; 10% are from out of state; 24% Black or African American, non-Hispanic/Latino; 0.8% Asian, non-Hispanic/Latino; 0.8% American Indian or Alaska Native, non-Hispanic/Latino; 51% transferred in; 11% live on campus.
Freshmen *Admission:* 64 applied, 44 admitted, 23 enrolled.
Faculty *Total:* 13, 15% full-time. *Student/faculty ratio:* 8:1.
Majors Funeral service and mortuary science.
Academics *Calendar:* semesters. *Degree:* certificates, diplomas, and associate. *Special study options:* part-time degree program.
Library Memorial Library with 4,000 titles, 54 serial subscriptions, a Web page.
Student Life *Housing Options:* coed. Campus housing is university owned. *Campus security:* controlled dormitory access, day patrols.
Standardized Tests *Required:* ACT (for admission).
Costs (2014–15) *Tuition:* $9440 full-time, $295 per semester hour part-time. Full-time tuition and fees vary according to course load. Part-time tuition and fees vary according to course load. *Required fees:* $70 full-time. *Room only:* $3600. *Payment plan:* installment.
Financial Aid *Financial aid deadline:* 6/1.
Applying *Options:* deferred entrance. *Application fee:* $50. *Required:* essay or personal statement, high school transcript, 2 letters of recommendation. *Application deadlines:* rolling (freshmen), rolling (transfers).
Freshman Application Contact John A. Gupton College, 1616 Church Street, Nashville, TN 37203-2920. *Phone:* 615-327-3927.
Website: http://www.guptoncollege.edu/.

Kaplan Career Institute, Nashville Campus
Nashville, Tennessee

Freshman Application Contact Kaplan Career Institute, Nashville Campus, 750 Envious Lane, Nashville, TN 37217. *Phone:* 615-269-9900. *Toll-free phone:* 800-935-1857.
Website: http://nashville.kaplancareerinstitute.com/.

L'Ecole Culinaire
Cordova, Tennessee

Admissions Office Contact L'Ecole Culinaire, 1245 N. Germantown Parkway, Cordova, TN 38016.
Website: http://www.lecole.edu/memphis/.

Lincoln College of Technology
Nashville, Tennessee

Freshman Application Contact Ms. Peggie Werrbach, Director of Admissions, Lincoln College of Technology, 1524 Gallatin Road, Nashville, TN 37206. *Phone:* 615-226-3990 Ext. 8465. *Toll-free phone:* 800-228-6232. *Fax:* 615-262-8466. *E-mail:* wpruitt@nadcedu.com.
Website: http://www.lincolnedu.com/campus/nashville-tn.

Miller-Motte Technical College
Chattanooga, Tennessee

Admissions Office Contact Miller-Motte Technical College, 6020 Shallowford Road, Suite 100, Chattanooga, TN 37421.
Website: http://www.miller-motte.edu/.

Miller-Motte Technical College
Clarksville, Tennessee

Director of Admissions Nicholas Deshazor, Director of Admissions, Miller-Motte Technical College, 1820 Business Park Drive, Clarksville, TN 37040. *Phone:* 800-558-0071. *E-mail:* lisateague@hotmail.com.
Website: http://www.miller-motte.edu/.

Miller-Motte Technical College
Madison, Tennessee

Admissions Office Contact Miller-Motte Technical College, 1515 Gallatin Pike North, Madison, TN 37115.
Website: http://www.miller-motte.edu/.

Motlow State Community College
Tullahoma, Tennessee

- **State-supported** 2-year, founded 1969, part of Tennessee Board of Regents
- **Rural** 187-acre campus with easy access to Nashville
- **Endowment** $5.0 million
- **Coed,** 4,732 undergraduate students, 38% full-time, 61% women, 39% men

Undergraduates 1,775 full-time, 2,957 part-time. Students come from 17 states and territories; 24 other countries; 1% are from out of state; 10% Black or African American, non-Hispanic/Latino; 3% Hispanic/Latino; 2% Asian, non-Hispanic/Latino; 0.3% American Indian or Alaska Native, non-Hispanic/Latino; 2% Two or more races, non-Hispanic/Latino; 2% Race/ethnicity unknown; 0.3% international; 7% transferred in.
Freshmen *Admission:* 5,066 applied, 2,141 admitted, 1,106 enrolled.
Faculty *Total:* 268, 34% full-time, 12% with terminal degrees.
Majors Business administration and management; education; electromechanical technology; general studies; liberal arts and sciences/liberal studies; registered nursing/registered nurse; special education–early childhood; web page, digital/multimedia and information resources design.
Academics *Calendar:* semesters. *Degree:* certificates and associate. *Special study options:* academic remediation for entering students, accelerated degree program, adult/continuing education programs, advanced placement credit, cooperative education, distance learning, double majors, honors programs, independent study, part-time degree program, services for LD students, study abroad, summer session for credit.
Library Clayton-Glass Library with 235,121 titles, 100 serial subscriptions, 4,379 audiovisual materials, an OPAC, a Web page.
Student Life *Housing:* college housing not available. *Activities and Organizations:* drama/theater group, choral group, PTK Club, Communication Club, Student Government Association, Art Club, Baptist Student Union. *Campus security:* 24-hour patrols, late-night transport/escort service. *Student services:* personal/psychological counseling.
Athletics Member NJCAA. *Intercollegiate sports:* baseball M(s), basketball M(s)/W(s), softball W(s). *Intramural sports:* badminton M/W, basketball M/W, bowling M/W, golf M/W, tennis M/W, volleyball M/W.
Costs (2014–15) *Tuition:* state resident $3612 full-time; nonresident $14,052 full-time. *Payment plans:* installment, deferred payment. *Waivers:* senior citizens and employees or children of employees.
Financial Aid Of all full-time matriculated undergraduates who enrolled in 2012, 1,766 applied for aid, 1,438 were judged to have need, 78 had their need fully met. 28 Federal Work-Study jobs (averaging $2220). In 2012, 213 non-need-based awards were made. *Average percent of need met:* 56%. *Average financial aid package:* $5257. *Average need-based loan:* $2513. *Average need-based gift aid:* $4294. *Average non-need-based aid:* $3087.
Applying *Options:* electronic application, early admission, deferred entrance. *Application fee:* $10. *Required:* high school transcript. *Application deadlines:* 8/13 (freshmen), 8/13 (transfers). *Notification:* continuous (freshmen), continuous (transfers).
Freshman Application Contact Ms. Sheri Mason, Assistant Director of Student Services, Motlow State Community College, Lynchburg, TN 37352-8500. *Phone:* 931-393-1764. *Toll-free phone:* 800-654-4877. *Fax:* 931-393-1681. *E-mail:* smason@mscc.edu.
Website: http://www.mscc.edu/.

Nashville State Community College
Nashville, Tennessee

Freshman Application Contact Mr. Beth Mahan, Coordinator of Recruitment, Nashville State Community College, 120 White Bridge Road, Nashville, TN 37209-4515. *Phone:* 615-353-3214. *Toll-free phone:* 800-272-7363. *E-mail:* beth.mahan@nscc.edu.
Website: http://www.nscc.edu/.

National College
Bristol, Tennessee

Freshman Application Contact National College, 1328 Highway 11 West, Bristol, TN 37620. *Phone:* 423-878-4440. *Toll-free phone:* 888-9-JOBREADY.
Website: http://www.national-college.edu/.

National College
Knoxville, Tennessee

Director of Admissions Frank Alvey, Campus Director, National College, 8415 Kingston Pike, Knoxville, TN 37919. *Phone:* 865-539-2011. *Toll-free phone:* 888-9-JOBREADY. *Fax:* 865-539-2049.
Website: http://www.national-college.edu/.

National College of Business and Technology
Nashville, Tennessee

Director of Admissions Jerry Lafferty, Campus Director, National College of Business and Technology, 1638 Bell Road, Nashville, TN 37211. *Phone:* 615-333-3344. *Toll-free phone:* 888-9-JOBREADY.
Website: http://www.national-college.edu/.

North Central Institute
Clarksville, Tennessee

Freshman Application Contact Dale Wood, Director of Admissions, North Central Institute, 168 Jack Miller Boulevard, Clarksville, TN 37042. *Phone:* 931-431-9700. *Toll-free phone:* 800-603-4116. *Fax:* 931-431-9771. *E-mail:* admissions@nci.edu.
Website: http://www.nci.edu/.

Northeast State Community College
Blountville, Tennessee

Freshman Application Contact Dr. Jon P. Harr, Vice President for Student Affairs, Northeast State Community College, PO Box 246, Blountville, TN 37617. *Phone:* 423-323-0231. *Toll-free phone:* 800-836-7822. *Fax:* 423-323-0240. *E-mail:* jpharr@northeaststate.edu.
Website: http://www.northeaststate.edu/.

Nossi College of Art
Nashville, Tennessee

- **Independent** primarily 2-year
- **Urban** 10-acre campus with easy access to Nashville
- **Coed,** 279 undergraduate students, 100% full-time, 54% women, 46% men

Undergraduates 279 full-time. Students come from 1 other country; 9% are from out of state; 24% Black or African American, non-Hispanic/Latino; 4% Hispanic/Latino; 1% Asian, non-Hispanic/Latino; 1% Two or more races, non-Hispanic/Latino; 0.4% Race/ethnicity unknown; 0.4% international; 18% transferred in. *Retention:* 72% of full-time freshmen returned.
Freshmen *Admission:* 83 enrolled.
Faculty *Total:* 21, 24% full-time. *Student/faculty ratio:* 10:1.
Majors Commercial and advertising art; commercial photography; film/video and photographic arts related; graphic design; illustration.
Academics *Calendar:* semesters. *Degrees:* associate and bachelor's. *Special study options:* independent study, internships, off-campus study, part-time degree program.
Library Learning Resource Center with an OPAC.
Student Life *Housing:* college housing not available. *Activities and Organizations:* national fraternities. *Campus security:* campus has a gated entrance, all doors are kept locked.
Costs (2014–15) *One-time required fee:* $200. *Tuition:* $10,200 full-time. Full-time tuition and fees vary according to degree level. Part-time tuition and fees vary according to degree level. No tuition increase for student's term of enrollment. *Payment plan:* installment.
Applying *Options:* electronic application, early admission. *Application fee:* $100. *Required:* essay or personal statement, high school transcript, interview, portfolio of work for Associate or Bachelor of Graphic Art and Design program and the Bachelor of Illustration program. *Application deadlines:* rolling (freshmen), rolling (out-of-state freshmen). *Notification:* continuous (freshmen), continuous (out-of-state freshmen).
Freshman Application Contact Ms. Mary Alexander, Admissions Director, Nossi College of Art, 590 Cheron Road, Madison, TN 37115. *Phone:* 615-514-2787 (ARTS). *Toll-free phone:* 888-986-ARTS. *Fax:* 615-514-2788. *E-mail:* admissions@nossi.edu.
Website: http://www.nossi.edu/.

Pellissippi State Community College
Knoxville, Tennessee

Freshman Application Contact Director of Admissions and Records, Pellissippi State Community College, PO Box 22990, Knoxville, TN 37933-0990. *Phone:* 865-694-6400. *Fax:* 865-539-7217.
Website: http://www.pstcc.edu/.

Remington College–Memphis Campus
Memphis, Tennessee

Director of Admissions Randal Hayes, Director of Recruitment, Remington College–Memphis Campus, 2710 Nonconnah Boulevard, Memphis, TN 38132. *Phone:* 901-345-1000. *Fax:* 901-396-8310. *E-mail:* randal.hayes@remingtoncollege.edu.
Website: http://www.remingtoncollege.edu/.

Remington College–Nashville Campus
Nashville, Tennessee

Director of Admissions Mr. Frank Vivelo, Campus President, Remington College–Nashville Campus, 441 Donelson Pike, Suite 150, Nashville, TN 37214. *Phone:* 615-889-5520. *Fax:* 615-889-5528. *E-mail:* frank.vivelo@remingtoncollege.edu.
Website: http://www.remingtoncollege.edu/.

Roane State Community College
Harriman, Tennessee

- **State-supported** 2-year, founded 1971, part of Tennessee Board of Regents
- **Small-town** 104-acre campus with easy access to Knoxville
- **Endowment** $9.0 million
- **Coed,** 6,214 undergraduate students, 41% full-time, 66% women, 34% men

Undergraduates 2,535 full-time, 3,679 part-time. Students come from 13 states and territories; 9 other countries; 1% are from out of state; 3% Black or African American, non-Hispanic/Latino; 3% Hispanic/Latino; 0.6% Asian, non-Hispanic/Latino; 0.3% American Indian or Alaska Native, non-Hispanic/Latino; 3% Two or more races, non-Hispanic/Latino; 1% Race/ethnicity unknown; 0.4% international; 5% transferred in. *Retention:* 62% of full-time freshmen returned.
Freshmen *Admission:* 2,389 applied, 2,386 admitted, 1,187 enrolled. *Average high school GPA:* 3.19. *Test scores:* ACT scores over 18: 69%; ACT scores over 24: 11%.
Faculty *Total:* 378, 33% full-time. *Student/faculty ratio:* 19:1.
Majors Accounting; administrative assistant and secretarial science; art; art teacher education; biology/biological sciences; business administration and management; business teacher education; chemistry; clinical/medical laboratory technology; computer engineering technology; computer science; corrections; criminal justice/law enforcement administration; criminal justice/police science; dental hygiene; early childhood education; education; elementary education; emergency medical technology (EMT paramedic); engineering; environmental health; general studies; health information/medical records administration; industrial radiologic technology; information technology; kindergarten/preschool education; laser and optical technology; legal administrative assistant/secretary; liberal arts and sciences/liberal studies; mathematics; medical administrative assistant and medical secretary; music teacher education; occupational therapy; pharmacy technician; physical education teaching and coaching; physical sciences; physical therapy; pre-engineering; registered nursing/registered nurse; respiratory care therapy; social sciences; technology/industrial arts teacher education.
Academics *Calendar:* semesters. *Degree:* certificates and associate. *Special study options:* academic remediation for entering students, accelerated degree program, advanced placement credit, cooperative education, distance learning, double majors, honors programs, independent study, internships, off-campus study, services for LD students, study abroad, summer session for credit. *ROTC:* Army (c), Air Force (c).
Library Roane State Community College Library plus 3 others with 316,114 titles, 3,030 audiovisual materials, an OPAC, a Web page.
Student Life *Housing:* college housing not available. *Activities and Organizations:* drama/theater group, choral group, Baptist Student Union, American Chemical Society, Physical Therapy Student Association, Student Artists At Roane State (S.T.A.R.S.), Phi Theta Kappa. *Campus security:* 24-hour patrols. *Student services:* personal/psychological counseling.
Athletics Member NJCAA. *Intercollegiate sports:* baseball M(s), basketball M(s)/W(s), softball W(s). *Intramural sports:* basketball M/W, football M, golf M, soccer M, softball M/W, volleyball M/W, weight lifting M.
Financial Aid Of all full-time matriculated undergraduates who enrolled in 2012, 2,858 applied for aid, 2,499 were judged to have need, 220 had their need fully met. 64 Federal Work-Study jobs (averaging $1676). In 2012, 106 non-need-based awards were made. *Average percent of need met:* 56%. *Average financial aid package:* $7104. *Average need-based loan:* $3393. *Average need-based gift aid:* $6219. *Average non-need-based aid:* $5952.
Applying *Options:* electronic application, early admission, deferred entrance. *Application fee:* $20. *Required:* high school transcript. *Application deadlines:*

rolling (freshmen), rolling (transfers). *Notification:* continuous (freshmen), continuous (transfers).

Freshman Application Contact Admissions Office, Roane State Community College, 276 Patton Lane, Harriman, TN 37748. *Phone:* 865-882-4523. *Toll-free phone:* 866-462-7722 Ext. 4554. *E-mail:* admissionsrecords@roanestate.edu.

Website: http://www.roanestate.edu/.

Southwest Tennessee Community College
Memphis, Tennessee

Freshman Application Contact Ms. Cindy Meziere, Assistant Director of Recruiting, Southwest Tennessee Community College, PO Box 780, Memphis, TN 38103-0780. *Phone:* 901-333-4195. *Toll-free phone:* 877-717-STCC. *Fax:* 901-333-4473. *E-mail:* cmeziere@southwest.tn.edu.

Website: http://www.southwest.tn.edu/.

Vatterott College
Memphis, Tennessee

Admissions Office Contact Vatterott College, 2655 Dividend Drive, Memphis, TN 38132. *Toll-free phone:* 888-553-6627.

Website: http://www.vatterott.edu/.

Virginia College
Knoxville, Tennessee

Admissions Office Contact Virginia College, 5003 North Broadway Street, Knoxville, TN 37918.

Website: http://www.vc.edu/.

Virginia College School of Business and Health at Chattanooga
Chattanooga, Tennessee

Admissions Office Contact Virginia College School of Business and Health at Chattanooga, 721 Eastgate Loop Road, Chattanooga, TN 37411.

Website: http://www.vc.edu/site/campus.cfm?campus=chattanooga.

Volunteer State Community College
Gallatin, Tennessee

- **State-supported** 2-year, founded 1970, part of Tennessee Board of Regents
- **Suburban** 110-acre campus with easy access to Nashville
- **Endowment** $3.5 million
- **Coed,** 8,153 undergraduate students, 42% full-time, 61% women, 39% men

Undergraduates 3,447 full-time, 4,706 part-time. Students come from 13 states and territories; 12 other countries; 1% are from out of state; 8% Black or African American, non-Hispanic/Latino; 3% Hispanic/Latino; 1% Asian, non-Hispanic/Latino; 0.1% Native Hawaiian or other Pacific Islander, non-Hispanic/Latino; 0.3% American Indian or Alaska Native, non-Hispanic/Latino; 2% Two or more races, non-Hispanic/Latino; 3% Race/ethnicity unknown; 0.5% international; 7% transferred in.

Freshmen *Admission:* 2,058 applied, 2,058 admitted, 1,476 enrolled. *Average high school GPA:* 2.94. *Test scores:* ACT scores over 18: 65%; ACT scores over 24: 11%.

Faculty *Total:* 366, 43% full-time, 15% with terminal degrees. *Student/faculty ratio:* 22:1.

Majors Business administration and management; child development; clinical/medical laboratory technology; criminal justice/police science; education; fire science/firefighting; general studies; health information/medical records technology; health professions related; legal assistant/paralegal; liberal arts and sciences/liberal studies; medical radiologic technology; ophthalmic technology; physical therapy technology; respiratory care therapy; science technologies related; veterinary/animal health technology; web page, digital/multimedia and information resources design.

Academics *Calendar:* semesters. *Degree:* certificates and associate. *Special study options:* academic remediation for entering students, accelerated degree program, adult/continuing education programs, advanced placement credit, cooperative education, distance learning, double majors, English as a second language, honors programs, independent study, internships, part-time degree program, services for LD students, study abroad, summer session for credit.

Library Thigpen Library with 193,000 titles, 155 serial subscriptions, 2,052 audiovisual materials, an OPAC, a Web page.

Student Life *Housing:* college housing not available. *Activities and Organizations:* drama/theater group, student-run newspaper, radio station, choral group, Gamma Beta Phi, Returning Woman's Organization, Phi Theta

Kappa, Student Government Association, The Settler. *Campus security:* 24-hour emergency response devices and patrols, late-night transport/escort service. *Student services:* personal/psychological counseling.

Athletics Member NJCAA. *Intercollegiate sports:* baseball M(s), basketball M(s)/W(s), softball W(s). *Intramural sports:* bowling M/W, soccer M/W.

Standardized Tests *Required for some:* SAT or ACT (for admission).

Costs (2014–15) *Tuition:* state resident $3336 full-time, $139 per credit part-time; nonresident $13,776 full-time, $574 per credit part-time. Full-time tuition and fees vary according to course load. Part-time tuition and fees vary according to course load. *Required fees:* $23 per credit part-time. *Payment plan:* deferred payment. *Waivers:* senior citizens and employees or children of employees.

Financial Aid Of all full-time matriculated undergraduates who enrolled in 2013, 3,105 applied for aid, 2,435 were judged to have need, 117 had their need fully met. 47 Federal Work-Study jobs (averaging $1732). In 2013, 66 non-need-based awards were made. *Average percent of need met:* 45%. *Average financial aid package:* $5629. *Average need-based loan:* $2764. *Average need-based gift aid:* $4452. *Average non-need-based aid:* $1856.

Applying *Options:* electronic application, early admission, deferred entrance. *Application fee:* $20. *Required:* high school transcript. *Required for some:* minimum 2.0 GPA, interview. *Application deadlines:* 8/25 (freshmen), 8/25 (transfers). *Notification:* continuous (freshmen), continuous (transfers).

Freshman Application Contact Mr. Tim Amyx, Director of Admissions, Volunteer State Community College, 1480 Nashville Pike, Gallatin, TN 37066-3188. *Phone:* 615-452-8600 Ext. 3614. *Toll-free phone:* 888-335-8722. *Fax:* 615-230-4875. *E-mail:* admissions@volstate.edu.

Website: http://www.volstate.edu/.

Walters State Community College
Morristown, Tennessee

- **State-supported** 2-year, founded 1970, part of Tennessee Board of Regents
- **Small-town** 100-acre campus
- **Endowment** $10.8 million
- **Coed,** 6,265 undergraduate students, 51% full-time, 61% women, 39% men

Undergraduates 3,171 full-time, 3,094 part-time. Students come from 13 states and territories; 5 other countries; 1% are from out of state; 2% Black or African American, non-Hispanic/Latino; 2% Hispanic/Latino; 0.6% Asian, non-Hispanic/Latino; 0.2% American Indian or Alaska Native, non-Hispanic/Latino; 2% Two or more races, non-Hispanic/Latino; 0.1% Race/ethnicity unknown; 0.5% international; 3% transferred in. *Retention:* 58% of full-time freshmen returned.

Freshmen *Admission:* 1,366 applied, 1,366 admitted, 1,363 enrolled. *Average high school GPA:* 3.28. *Test scores:* SAT math scores over 500: 40%; ACT scores over 18: 67%; SAT math scores over 600: 10%; ACT scores over 24: 13%; ACT scores over 30: 1%.

Faculty *Total:* 383, 42% full-time, 21% with terminal degrees. *Student/faculty ratio:* 19:1.

Majors Business administration and management; child development; computer and information sciences; criminal justice/police science; criminal justice/safety; data processing and data processing technology; education; energy management and systems technology; general studies; health information/medical records technology; industrial technology; liberal arts and sciences/liberal studies; music performance; occupational therapist assistant; ornamental horticulture; physical therapy technology; registered nursing/registered nurse; respiratory care therapy; surgical technology; web page, digital/multimedia and information resources design.

Academics *Calendar:* semesters. *Degree:* certificates and associate. *Special study options:* academic remediation for entering students, accelerated degree program, advanced placement credit, cooperative education, distance learning, English as a second language, freshman honors college, honors programs, independent study, internships, off-campus study, part-time degree program, services for LD students, student-designed majors, study abroad, summer session for credit. *ROTC:* Army (c), Navy (c), Air Force (c).

Library Walters State Library with 192,037 titles, 135 serial subscriptions, 4,599 audiovisual materials, an OPAC, a Web page.

Student Life *Housing:* college housing not available. *Activities and Organizations:* drama/theater group, choral group, Baptist Collegiate Ministry, Phi Theta Kappa, Debate Club, Student Government Association, Service Learners Club. *Campus security:* 24-hour emergency response devices and patrols, late-night transport/escort service, Security Cameras. *Student services:* health clinic, personal/psychological counseling.

Athletics Member NJCAA. *Intercollegiate sports:* baseball M(s), basketball M(s)/W(s), golf M(s), softball W(s), volleyball W(s). *Intramural sports:* baseball M, basketball M/W.

Standardized Tests *Required:* SAT or ACT (for admission).

Costs (2014–15) *Tuition:* state resident $3336 full-time, $139 per credit hour part-time; nonresident $13,776 full-time, $574 per credit hour part-time. Full-time tuition and fees vary according to course load. Part-time tuition and fees vary according to course load. *Required fees:* $279 full-time, $16 per credit hour part-time, $15 per term part-time. *Payment plan:* deferred payment. *Waivers:* senior citizens and employees or children of employees.

Applying *Options:* electronic application, early admission. *Required:* high school transcript. *Application deadlines:* rolling (freshmen), rolling (transfers). *Notification:* continuous (freshmen), continuous (transfers).

Freshman Application Contact Mr. Michael Campbell, Assistant Vice President for Student Affairs, Walters State Community College, 500 South Davy Crockett Parkway, Morristown, TN 37813-6899. *Phone:* 423-585-2682. *Toll-free phone:* 800-225-4770. *Fax:* 423-585-6876. *E-mail:* mike.campbell@ws.edu.

Website: http://www.ws.edu/.

West Tennessee Business College

Jackson, Tennessee

Admissions Office Contact West Tennessee Business College, 1186 Highway 45 Bypass, Jackson, TN 38343.

Website: http://www.wtbc.edu/.

TEXAS

Alvin Community College

Alvin, Texas

- **State and locally supported** 2-year, founded 1949
- **Suburban** 114-acre campus with easy access to Houston
- **Coed,** 5,794 undergraduate students, 27% full-time, 54% women, 46% men

Undergraduates 1,560 full-time, 4,234 part-time. 10% Black or African American, non-Hispanic/Latino; 4% Hispanic/Latino; 5% Asian, non-Hispanic/Latino; 0.3% Native Hawaiian or other Pacific Islander, non-Hispanic/Latino; 2% American Indian or Alaska Native, non-Hispanic/Latino; 1% Race/ethnicity unknown.

Freshmen *Admission:* 1,097 enrolled.

Faculty *Total:* 262, 37% full-time. *Student/faculty ratio:* 17:1.

Majors Accounting; administrative assistant and secretarial science; aeronautics/aviation/aerospace science and technology; art; biology/biological sciences; business administration and management; chemical technology; child development; computer engineering technology; computer programming; corrections; court reporting; criminal justice/police science; drafting and design technology; dramatic/theater arts; electrical, electronic and communications engineering technology; emergency medical technology (EMT paramedic); legal administrative assistant/secretary; legal assistant/paralegal; legal studies; liberal arts and sciences/liberal studies; marketing/marketing management; mathematics; medical administrative assistant and medical secretary; mental health counseling; music; physical education teaching and coaching; physical sciences; radio and television; registered nursing/registered nurse; respiratory care therapy; substance abuse/addiction counseling; voice and opera.

Academics *Calendar:* semesters. *Degree:* certificates, diplomas, and associate. *Special study options:* academic remediation for entering students, accelerated degree program, adult/continuing education programs, advanced placement credit, distance learning, double majors, English as a second language, honors programs, independent study, internships, part-time degree program, services for LD students, student-designed majors, study abroad, summer session for credit.

Library Alvin Community College Library with an OPAC, a Web page.

Student Life *Housing:* college housing not available. *Activities and Organizations:* student-run radio station. *Campus security:* 24-hour patrols, late-night transport/escort service. *Student services:* personal/psychological counseling.

Athletics Member NJCAA. *Intercollegiate sports:* baseball M(s), softball W(s). *Intramural sports:* soccer M(c)/W(c).

Costs (2013–14) *Tuition:* area resident $1510 full-time, $44 per credit hour part-time; state resident $2566 full-time, $88 per credit hour part-time; nonresident $3670 full-time, $134 per credit hour part-time. Full-time tuition and fees vary according to program. Part-time tuition and fees vary according to program. *Required fees:* $454 full-time, $227 per term part-time. *Payment plan:* installment.

Financial Aid Of all full-time matriculated undergraduates who enrolled in 2013, 27 Federal Work-Study jobs (averaging $3100). 4 state and other part-time jobs (averaging $2773).

Applying *Options:* electronic application. *Required for some:* high school transcript. *Application deadlines:* rolling (freshmen), rolling (transfers).

Freshman Application Contact Alvin Community College, 3110 Mustang Road, Alvin, TX 77511-4898. *Phone:* 281-756-3531.

Website: http://www.alvincollege.edu/.

Amarillo College

Amarillo, Texas

- **State and locally supported** 2-year, founded 1929
- **Urban** 1542-acre campus
- **Endowment** $33.6 million
- **Coed,** 11,530 undergraduate students

Undergraduates 5% Black or African American, non-Hispanic/Latino; 34% Hispanic/Latino; 3% Asian, non-Hispanic/Latino; 1% American Indian or Alaska Native, non-Hispanic/Latino; 1% Race/ethnicity unknown. *Retention:* 52% of full-time freshmen returned.

Faculty *Total:* 425, 52% full-time.

Majors Accounting; administrative assistant and secretarial science; airframe mechanics and aircraft maintenance technology; architectural engineering technology; art; automobile/automotive mechanics technology; behavioral sciences; biblical studies; biology/biological sciences; broadcast journalism; business administration and management; business teacher education; chemical technology; chemistry; child development; clinical laboratory science/medical technology; commercial and advertising art; computer engineering technology; computer programming; computer science; computer systems analysis; corrections; criminal justice/law enforcement administration; criminal justice/police science; dental hygiene; drafting and design technology; dramatic/theater arts; electrical, electronic and communications engineering technology; elementary education; emergency medical technology (EMT paramedic); engineering; English; environmental health; fine/studio arts; fire science/firefighting; funeral service and mortuary science; general studies; geology/earth science; health information/medical records administration; heating, air conditioning, ventilation and refrigeration maintenance technology; heavy equipment maintenance technology; history; industrial radiologic technology; information science/studies; instrumentation technology; interior design; journalism; laser and optical technology; legal administrative assistant/secretary; liberal arts and sciences/liberal studies; licensed practical/vocational nurse training; machine tool technology; mass communication/media; mathematics; medical administrative assistant and medical secretary; modern languages; music; music teacher education; natural sciences; nuclear medical technology; occupational therapy; photography; physical education teaching and coaching; physical sciences; physical therapy; physics; pre-engineering; pre-pharmacy studies; psychology; public relations/image management; radio and television; radiologic technology/science; real estate; registered nursing/registered nurse; religious studies; respiratory care therapy; rhetoric and composition; social sciences; social work; substance abuse/addiction counseling; telecommunications technology; tourism and travel services management; visual and performing arts.

Academics *Calendar:* semesters. *Degree:* certificates and associate. *Special study options:* academic remediation for entering students, adult/continuing education programs, advanced placement credit, cooperative education, distance learning, English as a second language, freshman honors college, honors programs, part-time degree program, services for LD students, summer session for credit.

Library Lynn Library Learning Center plus 2 others with 59,964 titles, 24,020 serial subscriptions, an OPAC, a Web page.

Student Life *Housing:* college housing not available. *Activities and Organizations:* drama/theater group, student-run newspaper, radio station, choral group, Student Government Association, College Republicans. *Campus security:* 24-hour emergency response devices, late-night transport/escort service, Campus police patrol Monday through Saturday, 0700 to 2300.

Athletics *Intramural sports:* basketball M/W, soccer M/W, softball M/W, tennis M/W, volleyball M/W.

Costs (2013–14) *Tuition:* area resident $1914 full-time, $80 per semester hour part-time; state resident $2898 full-time, $121 per semester hour part-time; nonresident $4362 full-time, $182 per semester hour part-time. Full-time tuition and fees vary according to course load. Part-time tuition and fees vary according to course load. *Payment plan:* installment. *Waivers:* senior citizens and employees or children of employees.

Financial Aid Of all full-time matriculated undergraduates who enrolled in 2012, 100 Federal Work-Study jobs (averaging $3000).

Applying *Options:* early admission, deferred entrance. *Required:* high school transcript. *Notification:* continuous (freshmen), continuous (transfers).

Freshman Application Contact Amarillo College, PO Box 447, Amarillo, TX 79178-0001. *Phone:* 806-371-5000. *Toll-free phone:* 800-227-8784. *Fax:* 806-371-5497. *E-mail:* askac@actx.edu.

Website: http://www.actx.edu/.

Anamarc College

El Paso, Texas

Admissions Office Contact Anamarc College, 8720 Gateway East Boulevard, El Paso, TX 79936.
Website: http://www.anamarc.edu/.

Angelina College

Lufkin, Texas

Freshman Application Contact Angelina College, PO Box 1768, Lufkin, TX 75902-1768. *Phone:* 936-633-5213.
Website: http://www.angelina.cc.tx.us/.

Austin Community College

Austin, Texas

- **State and locally supported** 2-year, founded 1972
- **Urban** campus with easy access to Austin
- **Endowment** $4.6 million
- **Coed,** 41,627 undergraduate students, 23% full-time, 56% women, 44% men

Undergraduates 9,476 full-time, 32,151 part-time. Students come from 111 other countries; 2% are from out of state; 8% Black or African American, non-Hispanic/Latino; 29% Hispanic/Latino; 5% Asian, non-Hispanic/Latino; 0.2% Native Hawaiian or other Pacific Islander, non-Hispanic/Latino; 0.8% American Indian or Alaska Native, non-Hispanic/Latino; 2% Two or more races, non-Hispanic/Latino; 6% Race/ethnicity unknown; 3% international.
Faculty *Total:* 1,881, 29% full-time, 22% with terminal degrees. *Student/faculty ratio:* 20:1.
Majors Accounting technology and bookkeeping; administrative assistant and secretarial science; animation, interactive technology, video graphics and special effects; anthropology; art; automobile/automotive mechanics technology; banking and financial support services; biology/biological sciences; biology/biotechnology laboratory technician; business administration and management; business/commerce; carpentry; chemistry; child development; clinical/medical laboratory technology; commercial and advertising art; commercial photography; computer and information sciences; computer programming; computer systems networking and telecommunications; corrections; creative writing; criminal justice/police science; culinary arts; dance; dental hygiene; diagnostic medical sonography and ultrasound technology; drafting and design technology; dramatic/theater arts; early childhood education; economics; electrical, electronic and communications engineering technology; emergency medical technology (EMT paramedic); engineering; environmental engineering technology; fire prevention and safety technology; foreign languages and literatures; French; general studies; geographic information science and cartography; geography; geology/earth science; German; health and physical education/fitness; health information/medical records technology; health teacher education; heating, ventilation, air conditioning and refrigeration engineering technology; history; hospitality administration; human services; international business/trade/commerce; Japanese; journalism; Latin; legal assistant/paralegal; marketing/marketing management; mathematics; middle school education; music; music management; occupational therapist assistant; philosophy; physical sciences; physical therapy technology; physics; political science and government; pre-dentistry studies; premedical studies; pre-pharmacy studies; pre-veterinary studies; professional, technical, business, and scientific writing; psychology; radio and television; radiologic technology/science; real estate; registered nursing/registered nurse; rhetoric and composition; Russian; secondary education; sign language interpretation and translation; social work; sociology; Spanish; substance abuse/addiction counseling; surgical technology; surveying technology; therapeutic recreation; watchmaking and jewelrymaking; welding technology; writing.
Academics *Calendar:* semesters. *Degrees:* certificates, associate, and postbachelor's certificates. *Special study options:* academic remediation for entering students, accelerated degree program, adult/continuing education programs, advanced placement credit, cooperative education, distance learning, English as a second language, honors programs, independent study, internships, part-time degree program, services for LD students, summer session for credit. *ROTC:* Army (c), Air Force (c).
Library Main Library plus 8 others with 205,043 titles, 51,789 serial subscriptions, 12,503 audiovisual materials, an OPAC, a Web page.
Student Life *Housing:* college housing not available. *Activities and Organizations:* student-run newspaper, Intramurals, Student Government Association (SGA), Phi Theta Kappa (PTK), Center for Student Political Studies (CSPS), Circle K International (CKI). *Campus security:* 24-hour emergency response devices and patrols, late-night transport/escort service. *Student services:* personal/psychological counseling.
Athletics *Intramural sports:* basketball M/W, soccer M/W, volleyball W.
Costs (2013–14) *Tuition:* area resident $2010 full-time, $67 per credit hour part-time; state resident $7380 full-time, $246 per credit hour part-time;

nonresident $9390 full-time, $313 per credit hour part-time. Full-time tuition and fees vary according to course load. Part-time tuition and fees vary according to course load. *Required fees:* $480 full-time, $16 per credit hour part-time. *Payment plan:* installment. *Waivers:* senior citizens and employees or children of employees.
Financial Aid Of all full-time matriculated undergraduates who enrolled in 2013, 5,437 applied for aid, 4,649 were judged to have need. 317 Federal Work-Study jobs (averaging $3635). 40 state and other part-time jobs (averaging $3713). *Average need-based loan:* $3051. *Average need-based gift aid:* $2993.
Applying *Options:* electronic application. *Required:* high school transcript. *Application deadlines:* rolling (freshmen), rolling (transfers).
Freshman Application Contact Ms. Linda Kluck, Director, Admissions and Records, Austin Community College, 5930 Middle Fiskville Road, Austin, TX 78752. *Phone:* 512-223-7503. *Fax:* 512-223-7665. *E-mail:* admission@austincc.edu.
Website: http://www.austincc.edu/.

Blinn College

Brenham, Texas

Freshman Application Contact Mrs. Stephanie Wehring, Coordinator, Recruitment and Admissions, Blinn College, 902 College Avenue, Brenham, TX 77833-4049. *Phone:* 979-830-4152. *Fax:* 979-830-4110. *E-mail:* recruit@blinn.edu.
Website: http://www.blinn.edu/.

Brazosport College

Lake Jackson, Texas

Freshman Application Contact Brazosport College, 500 College Drive, Lake Jackson, TX 77566-3199. *Phone:* 979-230-3020.
Website: http://www.brazosport.edu/.

Brookhaven College

Farmers Branch, Texas

- **County-supported** 2-year, founded 1978, part of Dallas County Community College District System
- **Suburban** 200-acre campus with easy access to Dallas-Fort Worth
- **Coed,** 12,319 undergraduate students, 19% full-time, 58% women, 42% men

Undergraduates 2,342 full-time, 9,977 part-time. Students come from 29 states and territories; 14 other countries; 0.2% are from out of state; 19% Black or African American, non-Hispanic/Latino; 35% Hispanic/Latino; 10% Asian, non-Hispanic/Latino; 0.1% Native Hawaiian or other Pacific Islander, non-Hispanic/Latino; 0.4% American Indian or Alaska Native, non-Hispanic/Latino; 0.8% Two or more races, non-Hispanic/Latino; 3% Race/ethnicity unknown; 0.3% international; 8% transferred in.
Freshmen *Admission:* 1,511 enrolled.
Faculty *Total:* 568, 33% full-time. *Student/faculty ratio:* 21:1.
Majors Accounting; automobile/automotive mechanics technology; business administration and management; business/commerce; child development; computer engineering technology; computer programming; computer technology/computer systems technology; criminal justice/law enforcement administration; design and visual communications; e-commerce; education (multiple levels); emergency medical technology (EMT paramedic); executive assistant/executive secretary; general studies; geographic information science and cartography; graphic design; humanities; information science/studies; liberal arts and sciences/liberal studies; marketing/marketing management; music; office management; radiologic technology/science; registered nursing/registered nurse; secondary education; speech communication and rhetoric.
Academics *Calendar:* semesters. *Degree:* certificates and associate. *Special study options:* academic remediation for entering students, adult/continuing education programs, advanced placement credit, cooperative education, distance learning, English as a second language, honors programs, independent study, internships, off-campus study, part-time degree program, services for LD students, student-designed majors, study abroad, summer session for credit.
Library Brookhaven College Learning Resources Center plus 1 other with an OPAC, a Web page.
Student Life *Housing:* college housing not available. *Activities and Organizations:* drama/theater group, student-run newspaper, choral group. *Campus security:* 24-hour emergency response devices and patrols, late-night transport/escort service. *Student services:* health clinic, personal/psychological counseling.
Athletics Member NJCAA. *Intercollegiate sports:* baseball M, basketball M, soccer W, volleyball W. *Intramural sports:* weight lifting M/W.
Standardized Tests *Required:* State Developed test scores or an approved test for Reading, Writing and Math course placement. Test scores used for

placement, not admission, purposes. Certain programs require specific tests (for admission).

Costs (2014–15) *Tuition:* area resident $1560 full-time, $52 per credit part-time; state resident $2910 full-time, $97 per credit part-time; nonresident $4590 full-time, $153 per credit part-time. *Payment plan:* installment. *Waivers:* senior citizens and employees or children of employees.

Applying *Options:* electronic application, early admission, deferred entrance. *Required:* high school transcript. *Required for some:* Admission to the nursing program is based on a point system consisting of three parts: (1) HESI score, (2) GPA of prerequisite courses, and (3) completion of support courses. *Application deadlines:* rolling (freshmen), rolling (transfers).

Freshman Application Contact Admissions Office, Brookhaven College, 3939 Valley View Lane, Farmers Branch, TX 75244-4997. *Phone:* 972-860-4883. *Fax:* 972-860-4886. *E-mail:* bhcAdmissions@dcccd.edu.

Website: http://www.brookhavencollege.edu/.

Brown Mackie College–Dallas/Ft. Worth
Bedford, Texas

- **Proprietary** 4-year
- **Coed**

Majors Biomedical technology; business administration and management; business/commerce; computer support specialist; criminal justice/safety; graphic design; health/health-care administration; medical office management; occupational therapist assistant; registered nursing/registered nurse; surgical technology.

Academics *Degrees:* diplomas, associate, and bachelor's.

Freshman Application Contact Brown Mackie College–Dallas/Ft. Worth, 2200 North Highway 121, Suite 250, Bedford, TX 76021. *Phone:* 817-799-0500.

Website: http://www.brownmackie.edu/dallas/.

See display below and page 388 for the College Close-Up.

Brown Mackie College–San Antonio
San Antonio, Texas

- **Proprietary** 4-year, part of Education Management Corporation
- **Coed**

Majors Business administration and management; business/commerce; computer support specialist; criminal justice/safety; health/health-care administration; legal assistant/paralegal; medical office management; pharmacy technician; registered nursing/registered nurse; surgical technology.

Academics *Degrees:* diplomas, associate, and bachelor's.

Freshman Application Contact Brown Mackie College–San Antonio, 4715 Fredericksburg Road, Suite 100, San Antonio, TX 78229. *Phone:* 210-428-2210. *Toll-free phone:* 877-460-1714.

Website: http://www.brownmackie.edu/san-antonio.

See display below and page 422 for the College Close-Up.

Cedar Valley College
Lancaster, Texas

Freshman Application Contact Admissions Office, Cedar Valley College, Lancaster, TX 75134-3799. *Phone:* 972-860-8206. *Fax:* 972-860-8207.

Website: http://www.cedarvalleycollege.edu/.

Center for Advanced Legal Studies
Houston, Texas

Freshman Application Contact Mr. James Scheffer, Center for Advanced Legal Studies, 3910 Kirby, Suite 200, Houston, TX 77098. *Phone:* 713-529-2778. *Toll-free phone:* 800-446-6931. *Fax:* 713-523-2715. *E-mail:* james.scheffer@paralegal.edu.

Website: http://www.paralegal.edu/.

Central Texas College
Killeen, Texas

Freshman Application Contact Admissions Office, Central Texas College, PO Box 1800, Killeen, TX 76540-1800. *Phone:* 254-526-1696. *Toll-free phone:* 800-223-4760 (in-state); 800-792-3348 (out-of-state). *Fax:* 254-526-1545. *E-mail:* admrec@ctcd.edu.

Website: http://www.ctcd.edu/.

Cisco College
Cisco, Texas

Freshman Application Contact Mr. Olin O. Odom III, Dean of Admission/Registrar, Cisco College, 101 College Heights, Cisco, TX 76437-9321. *Phone:* 254-442-2567 Ext. 5130. *E-mail:* oodom@cjc.edu.

Website: http://www.cisco.edu/.

Clarendon College
Clarendon, Texas

Freshman Application Contact Ms. Martha Smith, Admissions Director, Clarendon College, PO Box 968, Clarendon, TX 79226. *Phone:* 806-874-3571 Ext. 106. *Toll-free phone:* 800-687-9737. *Fax:* 806-874-3201. *E-mail:* martha.smith@clarendoncollege.edu. *Website:* http://www.clarendoncollege.edu/.

Coastal Bend College
Beeville, Texas

Freshman Application Contact Ms. Alicia Ulloa, Director of Admissions/Registrar, Coastal Bend College, Beeville, TX 78102-2197. *Phone:* 361-354-2245. *Toll-free phone:* 866-722-2838 (in-state); 866-262-2838 (out-of-state). *Fax:* 361-354-2254. *E-mail:* register@coastalbend.edu. *Website:* http://www.coastalbend.edu/.

The College of Health Care Professions
Houston, Texas

Freshman Application Contact Admissions Office, The College of Health Care Professions, 240 Northwest Mall Boulevard, Houston, TX 77092. *Phone:* 713-425-3100. *Toll-free phone:* 800-487-6728. *Fax:* 713-425-3193. *Website:* http://www.chcp.edu/.

College of the Mainland
Texas City, Texas

- **State and locally supported** 2-year, founded 1967
- **Suburban** 128-acre campus with easy access to Houston
- **Coed,** 4,188 undergraduate students, 27% full-time, 58% women, 42% men

Undergraduates 1,121 full-time, 3,067 part-time. Students come from 3 states and territories; 16% Black or African American, non-Hispanic/Latino; 27% Hispanic/Latino; 3% Asian, non-Hispanic/Latino; 0.2% Native Hawaiian or other Pacific Islander, non-Hispanic/Latino; 0.4% American Indian or Alaska Native, non-Hispanic/Latino; 0.5% Two or more races, non-Hispanic/Latino; 5% transferred in. *Retention:* 54% of full-time freshmen returned.
Freshmen *Admission:* 1,781 applied, 838 admitted, 561 enrolled. *Average high school GPA:* 2.85.
Faculty *Total:* 270, 40% full-time. *Student/faculty ratio:* 15:1.
Majors Business/commerce; CAD/CADD drafting/design technology; chemical technology; child development; computer and information sciences; cosmetology, barber/styling, and nail instruction; criminal justice/safety; dramatic/theater arts; early childhood education; fine/studio arts; fire prevention and safety technology; general studies; health information/medical records technology; mathematics; middle school education; music; natural sciences; occupational safety and health technology; pharmacy technician; registered nursing/registered nurse; secondary education; web page, digital/multimedia and information resources design.
Academics *Calendar:* semesters. *Degree:* certificates, diplomas, and associate. *Special study options:* academic remediation for entering students, adult/continuing education programs, cooperative education, distance learning, English as a second language, honors programs, internships, part-time degree program, services for LD students, summer session for credit. *ROTC:* Air Force (c).
Library COM Library plus 1 other with 126,021 titles, 24,840 serial subscriptions, 117,909 audiovisual materials, an OPAC, a Web page.
Student Life *Housing:* college housing not available. *Activities and Organizations:* Process Technology Club, Geology Club, Veterans' Club, Biology Club, Phi Theta Kappa. *Campus security:* 24-hour emergency response devices and patrols, student patrols, late-night transport/escort service, Vehicular assistance - lock outs, jump starts. *Student services:* personal/psychological counseling.
Athletics *Intercollegiate sports:* basketball M(c), soccer M(c), volleyball W(c). *Intramural sports:* basketball M/W, football M/W, soccer M/W, table tennis M/W, volleyball M/W.
Standardized Tests *Recommended:* SAT or ACT (for admission).
Costs (2014–15) *Tuition:* area resident $1494 full-time, $540 per year part-time; state resident $2454 full-time, $1020 per year part-time; nonresident $3174 full-time, $1380 per year part-time. Full-time tuition and fees vary according to course load and program. Part-time tuition and fees vary according to course load and program. *Required fees:* $414 full-time, $390 per year part-time. *Payment plan:* installment. *Waivers:* employees or children of employees.
Financial Aid Of all full-time matriculated undergraduates who enrolled in 2012, 93 Federal Work-Study jobs (averaging $1203). 88 state and other part-time jobs (averaging $1069).
Applying *Options:* electronic application, early admission, deferred entrance. *Required for some:* high school transcript. *Application deadlines:* rolling

(freshmen), rolling (transfers). *Notification:* continuous (freshmen), continuous (transfers).
Freshman Application Contact Mr. Martin Perez, Director of Admissions/International Affairs, College of the Mainland, 1200 Amburn Road, Texas City, TX 77591. *Phone:* 409-933-8653. *Toll-free phone:* 888-258-8859 Ext. 8264. *E-mail:* mperez@com.edu. *Website:* http://www.com.edu/.

Collin County Community College District
McKinney, Texas

- **State and locally supported** 2-year, founded 1985
- **Suburban** 333-acre campus with easy access to Dallas-Fort Worth
- **Endowment** $4.6 million
- **Coed,** 27,972 undergraduate students, 34% full-time, 56% women, 44% men

Undergraduates 9,544 full-time, 18,428 part-time. Students come from 48 states and territories; 109 other countries; 12% Black or African American, non-Hispanic/Latino; 18% Hispanic/Latino; 8% Asian, non-Hispanic/Latino; 0.3% Native Hawaiian or other Pacific Islander, non-Hispanic/Latino; 0.5% American Indian or Alaska Native, non-Hispanic/Latino; 3% Two or more races, non-Hispanic/Latino; 0.8% Race/ethnicity unknown; 3% international; 7% transferred in. *Retention:* 68% of full-time freshmen returned.
Freshmen *Admission:* 4,839 applied, 4,839 admitted, 4,831 enrolled.
Faculty *Total:* 1,177, 32% full-time, 21% with terminal degrees. *Student/faculty ratio:* 24:1.
Majors Administrative assistant and secretarial science; baking and pastry arts; biology/biotechnology laboratory technician; business administration and management; business/commerce; child-care provision; child development; commercial and advertising art; computer and information sciences; computer and information systems security; computer science; criminal justice/police science; culinary arts; dental hygiene; drafting and design technology; early childhood education; electrical, electronic and communications engineering technology; electroneurodiagnostic/electroencephalographic technology; emergency medical technology (EMT paramedic); engineering; engineering technology; fire prevention and safety technology; fire science/firefighting; game and interactive media design; geographic information science and cartography; graphic design; health information/medical records technology; hospitality administration; illustration; integrated circuit design; interior design; legal assistant/paralegal; liberal arts and sciences/liberal studies; medical insurance coding; middle school education; music; music management; network and system administration; real estate; registered nursing/registered nurse; respiratory care therapy; retail management; secondary education; sign language interpretation and translation; speech communication and rhetoric; surgical technology; system, networking, and LAN/WAN management; telecommunications technology; web page, digital/multimedia and information resources design.
Academics *Calendar:* semesters. *Degree:* certificates and associate. *Special study options:* academic remediation for entering students, adult/continuing education programs, advanced placement credit, cooperative education, distance learning, English as a second language, honors programs, internships, part-time degree program, services for LD students, summer session for credit. *ROTC:* Air Force (c).
Library Spring Creek Library, Preston Ridge Library, Central Park Library plus 3 others with 262,770 titles, 861 serial subscriptions, 36,862 audiovisual materials, an OPAC, a Web page.
Student Life *Housing:* college housing not available. *Activities and Organizations:* drama/theater group, choral group, student government, Phi Theta Kappa, Baptist Student Ministry, National Society of Leadership Success, Political Science Club. *Campus security:* 24-hour emergency response devices and patrols, late-night transport/escort service. *Student services:* personal/psychological counseling.
Athletics Member NJCAA. *Intercollegiate sports:* basketball M(s)/W(s), tennis M(s)/W(s).
Costs (2014–15) *Tuition:* $38 per credit hour part-time; state resident $75 per credit hour part-time; nonresident $135 per credit hour part-time. *Payment plan:* installment. *Waivers:* senior citizens.
Financial Aid Of all full-time matriculated undergraduates who enrolled in 2012, 5,068 applied for aid, 4,677 were judged to have need, 23 had their need fully met. In 2012, 156 non-need-based awards were made. *Average percent of need met:* 46%. *Average financial aid package:* $5884. *Average need-based loan:* $3205. *Average need-based gift aid:* $4362. *Average non-need-based aid:* $714.
Applying *Options:* electronic application. *Required:* high school transcript. *Application deadlines:* rolling (freshmen), rolling (out-of-state freshmen), rolling (transfers). *Notification:* continuous (freshmen), continuous (out-of-state freshmen), continuous (transfers).
Freshman Application Contact Mr. Todd Fields, Registrar/Director of Admissions, Collin County Community College District, 2800 E. Spring Creek

Pkwy., Plano, TX 75074. *Phone:* 972-881-5174. *Fax:* 972-881-5175. *E-mail:* tfields@collin.edu.
Website: http://www.collin.edu/.

Commonwealth Institute of Funeral Service
Houston, Texas

Freshman Application Contact Ms. Patricia Moreno, Registrar, Commonwealth Institute of Funeral Service, 415 Barren Springs Drive, Houston, TX 77090. *Phone:* 281-873-0262. *Toll-free phone:* 800-628-1580. *Fax:* 281-873-5232. *E-mail:* p.moreno@commonwealth.edu.
Website: http://www.commonwealth.edu/.

Computer Career Center
El Paso, Texas

Director of Admissions Ms. Sarah Hernandez, Registrar, Computer Career Center, 6101 Montana Avenue, El Paso, TX 79925. *Phone:* 915-779-8031. *Toll-free phone:* 866-442-4197.
Website: http://www.vistacollege.edu/.

Concorde Career College
Dallas, Texas

Admissions Office Contact Concorde Career College, 12606 Greenville Avenue, Suite 130, Dallas, TX 75243.
Website: http://www.concorde.edu/.

Concorde Career College
San Antonio, Texas

Admissions Office Contact Concorde Career College, 4803 NW Loop 410, San Antonio, TX 78229.
Website: http://www.concorde.edu/.

Concorde Career Institute
Arlington, Texas

Admissions Office Contact Concorde Career Institute, 600 East Lamar Boulevard, Suite 200, Arlington, TX 76011.
Website: http://www.concorde.edu/.

Court Reporting Institute of Dallas
Dallas, Texas

Director of Admissions Ms. Debra Smith-Armstrong, Director of Admissions, Court Reporting Institute of Dallas, 1341 West Mockingbird Lane, Suite 200E, Dallas, TX 75247. *Phone:* 214-350-9722 Ext. 227. *Toll-free phone:* 877-841-3557 (in-state); 888-841-3557 (out-of-state).
Website: http://www.crid.com/.

Culinary Institute LeNotre
Houston, Texas

- **Proprietary** 2-year
- **Urban** campus with easy access to Houston
- **Coed,** 403 undergraduate students, 62% full-time, 55% women, 45% men

Undergraduates 248 full-time, 155 part-time. Students come from 6 states and territories; 3 other countries; 6% are from out of state; 22% Black or African American, non-Hispanic/Latino; 40% Hispanic/Latino; 2% Asian, non-Hispanic/Latino; 0.2% Native Hawaiian or other Pacific Islander, non-Hispanic/Latino; 0.5% Two or more races, non-Hispanic/Latino; 1% Race/ethnicity unknown.
Faculty *Total:* 27, 44% full-time. *Student/faculty ratio:* 12:1.
Majors Baking and pastry arts; culinary arts; restaurant, culinary, and catering management.
Academics *Degree:* diplomas and associate. *Special study options:* academic remediation for entering students, adult/continuing education programs, cooperative education, internships, part-time degree program, study abroad.
Library Learning Resource Center with an OPAC.
Student Life *Housing:* college housing not available. *Campus security:* late-night transport/escort service.
Applying *Application fee:* $50. *Required:* essay or personal statement, high school transcript, minimum 2.0 GPA, interview.
Freshman Application Contact Admissions Office, Culinary Institute LeNotre, 7070 Allensby, Houston, TX 77022-4322. *Phone:* 713-358-5070. *Toll-free phone:* 888-LENOTRE.
Website: http://www.culinaryinstitute.edu/.

Dallas Institute of Funeral Service
Dallas, Texas

Freshman Application Contact Director of Admissions, Dallas Institute of Funeral Service, 3909 South Buckner Boulevard, Dallas, TX 75227. *Phone:* 214-388-5466. *Toll-free phone:* 800-235-5444. *Fax:* 214-388-0316. *E-mail:* difs@dallasinstitute.edu.
Website: http://www.dallasinstitute.edu/.

Del Mar College
Corpus Christi, Texas

Freshman Application Contact Ms. Frances P. Jordan, Director of Admissions and Registrar, Del Mar College, 101 Baldwin, Corpus Christi, TX 78404. *Phone:* 361-698-1255. *Toll-free phone:* 800-652-3357. *Fax:* 361-698-1595. *E-mail:* fjordan@delmar.edu.
Website: http://www.delmar.edu/.

Eastfield College
Mesquite, Texas

Freshman Application Contact Ms. Glynis Miller, Director of Admissions/Registrar, Eastfield College, 3737 Motley Drive, Mesquite, TX 75150-2099. *Phone:* 972-860-7010. *Fax:* 972-860-8306. *E-mail:* efc@dcccd.edu.
Website: http://www.efc.dcccd.edu/.

El Centro College
Dallas, Texas

- **County-supported** 2-year, founded 1966, part of Dallas County Community College District System
- **Urban** 2-acre campus
- **Coed**

Undergraduates 2,314 full-time, 7,787 part-time. Students come from 49 other countries; 1% are from out of state; 19% Black or African American, non-Hispanic/Latino; 38% Hispanic/Latino; 3% Asian, non-Hispanic/Latino; 0.0% Native Hawaiian or other Pacific Islander, non-Hispanic/Latino; 0.3% American Indian or Alaska Native, non-Hispanic/Latino; 24% Two or more races, non-Hispanic/Latino; 2% Race/ethnicity unknown; 0.3% international; 74% transferred in. *Retention:* 39% of full-time freshmen returned.
Faculty *Student/faculty ratio:* 19:1.
Academics *Calendar:* semesters. *Degree:* certificates and associate. *Special study options:* academic remediation for entering students, adult/continuing education programs, advanced placement credit, cooperative education, distance learning, double majors, English as a second language, freshman honors college, honors programs, internships, part-time degree program, services for LD students, summer session for credit. *ROTC:* Army (c).
Student Life *Campus security:* 24-hour emergency response devices and patrols, late-night transport/escort service, e-mail and text message alerts.
Costs (2013–14) *Tuition:* area resident $1248 full-time, $52 per credit hour part-time; state resident $2328 full-time, $97 per credit hour part-time; nonresident $3672 full-time, $153 per credit hour part-time. Full-time tuition and fees vary according to program. Part-time tuition and fees vary according to program. *Payment plans:* installment, deferred payment.
Applying *Options:* electronic application, early admission. *Required for some:* high school transcript, 1 letter of recommendation.
Freshman Application Contact Ms. Rebecca Garza, Director of Admissions and Registrar, El Centro College, Dallas, TX 75202. *Phone:* 214-860-2618. *Fax:* 214-860-2233. *E-mail:* rgarza@dcccd.edu.
Website: http://www.elcentrocollege.edu/.

El Paso Community College
El Paso, Texas

Freshman Application Contact Daryle Hendry, Director of Admissions, El Paso Community College, PO Box 20500, El Paso, TX 79998-0500. *Phone:* 915-831-2580. *E-mail:* daryleh@epcc.edu.
Website: http://www.epcc.edu/.

Everest College
Arlington, Texas

Freshman Application Contact Admissions Office, Everest College, 300 Six Flags Drive, Suite 200, Arlington, TX 76011. *Phone:* 817-652-7790. *Toll-free phone:* 888-741-4270. *Fax:* 817-649-6033.
Website: http://www.everest.edu/.

Everest College
Dallas, Texas

Freshman Application Contact Admissions Office, Everest College, 6080 North Central Expressway, Dallas, TX 75206. *Phone:* 214-234-4850. *Toll-free phone:* 888-741-4270. *Fax:* 214-696-6208.
Website: http://www.everest.edu/.

Everest College
Fort Worth, Texas

Freshman Application Contact Admissions Office, Everest College, 5237 North Riverside Drive, Suite 100, Fort Worth, TX 76137. *Phone:* 817-838-3000. *Toll-free phone:* 888-741-4270. *Fax:* 817-838-2040.
Website: http://www.everest.edu/.

Frank Phillips College
Borger, Texas

- **State and locally supported** 2-year, founded 1948
- **Small-town** 60-acre campus
- **Endowment** $1.3 million
- **Coed,** 1,148 undergraduate students, 44% full-time, 53% women, 47% men

Undergraduates 501 full-time, 647 part-time. Students come from 15 states and territories; 6 other countries; 10% are from out of state; 5% Black or African American, non-Hispanic/Latino; 17% Hispanic/Latino; 0.8% Asian, non-Hispanic/Latino; 0.2% Native Hawaiian or other Pacific Islander, non-Hispanic/Latino; 3% American Indian or Alaska Native, non-Hispanic/Latino; 5% Race/ethnicity unknown; 0.2% international; 7% transferred in; 20% live on campus. *Retention:* 41% of full-time freshmen returned.
Freshmen *Admission:* 156 enrolled.
Faculty *Total:* 75, 47% full-time, 8% with terminal degrees. *Student/faculty ratio:* 16:1.
Majors Accounting; agricultural business and management; animal/livestock husbandry and production; biology/biological sciences; business administration and management; business/commerce; chemistry; elementary education; English; farm and ranch management; general studies; history; industrial technology; liberal arts and sciences/liberal studies; mathematics; physics; psychology; secondary education; sociology; visual and performing arts.
Academics *Calendar:* semesters. *Degree:* certificates and associate. *Special study options:* academic remediation for entering students, accelerated degree program, adult/continuing education programs, advanced placement credit, cooperative education, distance learning, honors programs, internships, part-time degree program, services for LD students, summer session for credit.
Library James W. Dillard Library with 42,700 titles, 14,360 serial subscriptions, 1,175 audiovisual materials, an OPAC.
Student Life *Housing Options:* coed, men-only, women-only. Campus housing is university owned. *Activities and Organizations:* choral group. *Campus security:* 24-hour emergency response devices and patrols, controlled dormitory access. *Student services:* personal/psychological counseling.
Athletics Member NJCAA. *Intercollegiate sports:* baseball M(s), basketball M(s)/W(s), softball W(s), volleyball W(s). *Intramural sports:* basketball M/W, cheerleading M/W, racquetball M/W, volleyball M/W.
Financial Aid Of all full-time matriculated undergraduates who enrolled in 2012, 24 Federal Work-Study jobs (averaging $5200). 6 state and other part-time jobs (averaging $4800). *Financial aid deadline:* 8/31.
Applying *Options:* electronic application, early admission, deferred entrance. *Required:* high school transcript. *Application deadline:* 8/25 (freshmen). *Notification:* continuous until 8/25 (freshmen).
Freshman Application Contact Ms. Michele Stevens, Director of Enrollment Management, Frank Phillips College, PO Box 5118, Borger, TX 79008-5118. *Phone:* 806-457-4200 Ext. 707. *Fax:* 806-457-4225. *E-mail:* mstevens@fpctx.edu.
Website: http://www.fpctx.edu/.

Galveston College
Galveston, Texas

- **State and locally supported** 2-year, founded 1967
- **Urban** 11-acre campus with easy access to Houston
- **Coed,** 2,131 undergraduate students, 27% full-time, 57% women, 43% men

Undergraduates 577 full-time, 1,554 part-time. 17% Black or African American, non-Hispanic/Latino; 30% Hispanic/Latino; 3% Asian, non-Hispanic/Latino; 0.2% Native Hawaiian or other Pacific Islander, non-Hispanic/Latino; 0.3% American Indian or Alaska Native, non-Hispanic/Latino; 0.3% Two or more races, non-Hispanic/Latino; 4% Race/ethnicity unknown; 0.7% international; 13% transferred in. *Retention:* 52% of full-time freshmen returned.

Freshmen *Admission:* 305 enrolled.
Faculty *Total:* 118, 43% full-time, 4% with terminal degrees. *Student/faculty ratio:* 15:1.
Majors Administrative assistant and secretarial science; behavioral sciences; biological and physical sciences; business administration and management; computer science; criminal justice/safety; culinary arts; data entry/microcomputer applications; dramatic/theater arts; education; electromechanical technology; emergency medical technology (EMT paramedic); English; general studies; heating, air conditioning, ventilation and refrigeration maintenance technology; history; humanities; information technology; liberal arts and sciences/liberal studies; mathematics; medical administrative assistant and medical secretary; medical radiologic technology; music; natural sciences; nuclear medical technology; physical education teaching and coaching; radiologic technology/science; registered nursing/registered nurse; social sciences; social work; welding technology; word processing.
Academics *Calendar:* semesters. *Degree:* certificates and associate. *Special study options:* adult/continuing education programs, advanced placement credit, cooperative education, distance learning, internships, off-campus study, part-time degree program, services for LD students, summer session for credit.
Library David Glenn Hunt Memorial Library with 45,193 titles, 4,000 serial subscriptions, 1,500 audiovisual materials, an OPAC, a Web page.
Student Life *Housing Options:* Campus housing is university owned. *Activities and Organizations:* choral group, student government, Phi Theta Kappa, Student Nurses Association, ATTC, Hispanic Student Organization. *Campus security:* 24-hour emergency response devices and patrols, late-night transport/escort service. *Student services:* personal/psychological counseling.
Athletics Member NJCAA. *Intercollegiate sports:* baseball M(s), softball W(s). *Intramural sports:* basketball M/W, bowling M/W.
Costs (2014–15) *Tuition:* area resident $1110 full-time; state resident $1470 full-time; nonresident $3360 full-time. *Required fees:* $790 full-time.
Financial Aid Of all full-time matriculated undergraduates who enrolled in 2012, 36 Federal Work-Study jobs (averaging $2000).
Applying *Required for some:* high school transcript. *Application deadlines:* rolling (freshmen), rolling (transfers). *Notification:* continuous (freshmen), continuous (transfers).
Freshman Application Contact Galveston College, 4015 Avenue Q, Galveston, TX 77550-7496. *Phone:* 409-944-1216.
Website: http://www.gc.edu/.

Golf Academy of America
Farmers Branch, Texas

Admissions Office Contact Golf Academy of America, 1861 Valley View Lane, Suite 100, Farmers Branch, TX 75234. *Toll-free phone:* 800-342-7342.
Website: http://www.golfacademy.edu/.

Grayson College
Denison, Texas

- **State and locally supported** 2-year, founded 1964
- **Rural** 500-acre campus with easy access to Dallas-Fort Worth
- **Endowment** $8.7 million
- **Coed,** 5,014 undergraduate students, 42% full-time, 60% women, 40% men

Undergraduates 2,101 full-time, 2,913 part-time. Students come from 14 states and territories; 18 other countries; 5% are from out of state; 7% Black or African American, non-Hispanic/Latino; 12% Hispanic/Latino; 1% Asian, non-Hispanic/Latino; 0.2% Native Hawaiian or other Pacific Islander, non-Hispanic/Latino; 2% American Indian or Alaska Native, non-Hispanic/Latino; 4% Two or more races, non-Hispanic/Latino; 0.4% Race/ethnicity unknown; 2% international; 12% transferred in; 17% live on campus. *Retention:* 53% of full-time freshmen returned.
Freshmen *Admission:* 936 admitted, 936 enrolled. *Average high school GPA:* 2.87.
Faculty *Total:* 240, 44% full-time. *Student/faculty ratio:* 26:1.
Majors Accounting; art; autobody/collision and repair technology; biology/biological sciences; business administration and management; business automation/technology/data entry; chemistry; clinical/medical laboratory technology; computer programming; computer technology/computer systems technology; cooking and related culinary arts; criminal justice/safety; data processing and data processing technology; dental assisting; drafting and design technology; dramatic/theater arts; early childhood education; electrical, electronic and communications engineering technology; electrician; elementary education; emergency medical technology (EMT paramedic); engineering; English; food science; forensic science and technology; geology/earth science; heating, air conditioning, ventilation and refrigeration maintenance technology; industrial mechanics and maintenance technology; kindergarten/preschool education; liberal arts and sciences/liberal studies; machine tool technology; mathematics; middle school education; music; physical education teaching and coaching; physics; psychology;

radiologic technology/science; registered nursing/registered nurse; secondary education; sociology; Spanish; substance abuse/addiction counseling; viticulture and enology; welding technology.

Academics *Calendar:* semesters. *Degree:* certificates, diplomas, and associate. *Special study options:* academic remediation for entering students, adult/continuing education programs, advanced placement credit, distance learning, English as a second language, freshman honors college, honors programs, part-time degree program, summer session for credit.

Library Grayson College Library plus 1 other with 51,984 titles, 30 serial subscriptions, 2,130 audiovisual materials, an OPAC.

Student Life *Housing Options:* coed. Campus housing is university owned. *Activities and Organizations:* drama/theater group, student-run newspaper, choral group, Graduate Nursing Student Association, Vocational Nursing Student Association, Phi Theta Kappa, Dental Assisting Club, TIPS/Culinary student club. *Campus security:* 24-hour emergency response devices and patrols, student patrols, late-night transport/escort service, controlled dormitory access.

Athletics Member NJCAA. *Intercollegiate sports:* baseball M(s), softball W(s).

Costs (2014–15) *Tuition:* area resident $1176 full-time, $49 per credit hour part-time; state resident $2088 full-time, $102 per credit hour part-time; nonresident $3192 full-time, $148 per credit hour part-time. Full-time tuition and fees vary according to course load. Part-time tuition and fees vary according to course load. *Required fees:* $360 full-time, $15 per credit hour part-time, $12 per term part-time. *Room and board:* $5020. *Payment plan:* installment. *Waivers:* employees or children of employees.

Applying *Options:* electronic application, early admission, deferred entrance. *Application deadline:* 8/31 (freshmen). *Notification:* continuous (freshmen), continuous (transfers).

Freshman Application Contact Charles Leslie, Enrollment Advisor, Grayson College, 6101 Grayson Drive, Denison, TX 75020. *Phone:* 903-415-2532. *Fax:* 903-463-5284. *E-mail:* lesliec@grayson.edu. *Website:* http://www.grayson.edu/.

Hallmark College of Technology
San Antonio, Texas

- **Independent** primarily 2-year, founded 1969
- **Suburban** 2-acre campus with easy access to San Antonio
- **Coed,** 356 undergraduate students, 100% full-time, 55% women, 45% men

Undergraduates 356 full-time. Students come from 1 other state; 15% Black or African American, non-Hispanic/Latino; 55% Hispanic/Latino; 0.6% Asian, non-Hispanic/Latino; 0.3% Native Hawaiian or other Pacific Islander, non-Hispanic/Latino; 4% Two or more races, non-Hispanic/Latino; 1% Race/ethnicity unknown.

Freshmen *Admission:* 356 enrolled.

Faculty *Total:* 43, 47% full-time, 7% with terminal degrees. *Student/faculty ratio:* 8:1.

Majors Aviation/airway management; business administration and management; business administration, management and operations related; business automation/technology/data entry; computer systems networking and telecommunications; data processing and data processing technology; electrical, electronic and communications engineering technology; information technology; medical administrative assistant and medical secretary; medical/clinical assistant; medical insurance coding; registered nursing/registered nurse; system, networking, and LAN/WAN management.

Academics *Calendar:* continuous. *Degrees:* certificates, associate, bachelor's, and master's. *Special study options:* academic remediation for entering students, accelerated degree program, advanced placement credit, distance learning, internships.

Library Randall K. Williams Virtual Library (Virtual Library) plus 1 other with 140,000 titles, a Web page.

Student Life *Housing:* college housing not available. *Activities and Organizations:* Alpha Beta Kappa Honor Society. *Campus security:* 24-hour emergency response devices and patrols.

Standardized Tests *Required:* Wonderlic aptitude test, SAT/ACT is used for entrance to some degree programs (for admission). *Required for some:* SAT or ACT (for admission), SAT and SAT Subject Tests or ACT (for admission), SAT Subject Tests (for admission).

Costs (2013–14) *Tuition:* Full-time tuition and fees vary according to course load, degree level, location, and program. No tuition increase for student's term of enrollment. Tuition is charged by program: Accounting Certificate, Healthcare Information Specialist Certificate, Medical Assistant Certificate, AAS Medical Assistant and MBA Global Management are charged $330 per credit. The following programs are charged $440 per credit: AS Business Administration, AAS Information Systems Administration, AAS IT Cisco, AAS IT Microsoft, AAS Nursing, BS Aviation Maintenance Management, BS Business Administration, BS Business Management and BS Information Systems. Tuition includes books/supplies except for the MBA. Registration fee

is $110 for all programs but AAS Nursing and it is $25. *Payment plans:* tuition prepayment, installment. *Waivers:* employees or children of employees.

Applying *Application fee:* $60. *Required:* high school transcript, interview, tour, admission requirements differ depending on program of enrollment. *Required for some:* essay or personal statement, . *Application deadlines:* rolling (freshmen), rolling (transfers). *Notification:* continuous (freshmen), continuous (transfers).

Freshman Application Contact Sal Ross, Vice President of Admissions, Hallmark College of Technology, 10401 IH-10 West, San Antonio, TX 78230. *Phone:* 210-690-9000 Ext. 214. *Fax:* 210-697-8225. *E-mail:* slross@hallmarkcollege.edu. *Website:* http://www.hallmarkcollege.edu/.

Hallmark Institute of Aeronautics
San Antonio, Texas

- **Private** 2-year
- **Urban** 2-acre campus with easy access to San Antonio
- **Coed,** 227 undergraduate students, 100% full-time, 7% women, 93% men

Undergraduates 227 full-time. Students come from 1 other state; 10% Black or African American, non-Hispanic/Latino; 49% Hispanic/Latino; 1% Asian, non-Hispanic/Latino; 0.4% Native Hawaiian or other Pacific Islander, non-Hispanic/Latino; 3% Two or more races, non-Hispanic/Latino; 0.4% Race/ethnicity unknown; 2% transferred in; 1% live on campus.

Freshmen *Admission:* 193 enrolled.

Faculty *Total:* 17, 100% full-time. *Student/faculty ratio:* 17:1.

Majors Aircraft powerplant technology; airframe mechanics and aircraft maintenance technology.

Academics *Calendar:* continuous. *Degree:* diplomas and associate. *Special study options:* academic remediation for entering students.

Library (Virtual Library) plus 1 other with 140,000 titles, a Web page.

Student Life *Housing Options:* Campus housing is leased by the school. *Activities and Organizations:* Alpha Beta Kappa National Honor Society. *Campus security:* 24-hour emergency response devices and patrols.

Costs (2014–15) *One-time required fee:* $150. *Tuition:* $0 full-time. Full-time tuition and fees vary according to degree level, location, and program. No tuition increase for student's term of enrollment. *Payment plans:* tuition prepayment, installment. *Waivers:* employees or children of employees.

Applying *Application fee:* $110. *Required:* high school transcript, interview, assessment, tour, background check. *Application deadlines:* rolling (freshmen), rolling (transfers). *Notification:* continuous (freshmen), continuous (transfers).

Freshman Application Contact Hallmark Institute of Aeronautics, 8901 Wetmore Road, San Antonio, TX 78216. *Phone:* 210-690-9000 Ext. 214. *Website:* http://www.hallmarkcollege.edu/programs/school-of-aeronautics/.

Hill College
Hillsboro, Texas

Freshman Application Contact Ms. Diane Harvey, Director of Admissions/Registrar, Hill College, 112 Lamar Drive, Hillsboro, TX 76645. *Phone:* 254-582-2555. *Fax:* 254-582-7591. *E-mail:* diharvey@hill-college.cc.tx.us. *Website:* http://www.hillcollege.edu/.

Houston Community College System
Houston, Texas

- **State and locally supported** 2-year, founded 1971
- **Urban** campus
- **Coed,** 57,978 undergraduate students, 31% full-time, 58% women, 42% men

Undergraduates 17,728 full-time, 40,250 part-time. 7% are from out of state; 31% Black or African American, non-Hispanic/Latino; 32% Hispanic/Latino; 9% Asian, non-Hispanic/Latino; 0.2% Native Hawaiian or other Pacific Islander, non-Hispanic/Latino; 0.2% American Indian or Alaska Native, non-Hispanic/Latino; 1% Two or more races, non-Hispanic/Latino; 2% Race/ethnicity unknown; 9% international; 8% transferred in.

Freshmen *Admission:* 8,621 enrolled.

Majors Accounting; animation, interactive technology, video graphics and special effects; applied horticulture/horticulture operations; automobile/automotive mechanics technology; banking and financial support services; biology/biotechnology laboratory technician; business administration and management; business automation/technology/data entry; business/corporate communications; cardiovascular technology; chemical technology; child development; cinematography and film/video production; clinical/medical laboratory science and allied professions related; clinical/medical laboratory technology; commercial photography; computer engineering technology; computer programming; computer programming (specific applications); computer systems networking and telecommunications; construction engineering technology; cosmetology; court reporting; criminal justice/police science; culinary arts; desktop publishing and digital imaging design; drafting and design technology; emergency medical technology (EMT paramedic); fashion/apparel design; fashion merchandising; fire prevention and safety technology; geographic information science and cartography; graphic and printing equipment operation/production; health and physical education/fitness; health information/medical records technology; histologic technician; hotel/motel administration; instrumentation technology; interior design; international business/trade/commerce; legal assistant/paralegal; logistics, materials, and supply chain management; manufacturing engineering technology; marketing/marketing management; music management; music performance; music theory and composition; network and system administration; nuclear medical technology; occupational therapist assistant; physical therapy technology; psychiatric/mental health services technology; public administration; radio and television broadcasting technology; radiologic technology/science; real estate; registered nursing/registered nurse; respiratory care therapy; sign language interpretation and translation; tourism and travel services management; turf and turfgrass management.

Academics *Calendar:* semesters. *Degree:* certificates and associate. *Special study options:* adult/continuing education programs, part-time degree program. *ROTC:* Army (c), Air Force (c).

Student Life *Housing:* college housing not available. *Activities and Organizations:* drama/theater group, student-run newspaper, television station. *Campus security:* 24-hour emergency response devices and patrols, late-night transport/escort service. *Student services:* personal/psychological counseling.

Costs (2013–14) *Tuition:* area resident $1630 full-time; state resident $3358 full-time; nonresident $3754 full-time. *Payment plan:* installment. *Waivers:* employees or children of employees.

Applying *Required for some:* high school transcript, interview. *Application deadlines:* rolling (freshmen), rolling (transfers). *Notification:* continuous (transfers).

Freshman Application Contact Ms. Mary Lemburg, Registrar, Houston Community College System, 3100 Main Street, PO Box 667517, Houston, TX 77266-7517. *Phone:* 713-718-2000. *Toll-free phone:* 877-422-6111. *Fax:* 713-718-2111. *E-mail:* student.info@hccs.edu. *Website:* http://www.hccs.edu/.

Howard College
Big Spring, Texas

Freshman Application Contact Ms. TaNeal Richardson, Assistant Registrar, Howard College, 1001 Birdwell Lane, Big Spring, TX 79720-3702. *Phone:* 432-264-5105. *Toll-free phone:* 866-HC-HAWKS. *Fax:* 432-264-5604. *E-mail:* trichardson@howardcollege.edu. *Website:* http://www.howardcollege.edu/.

ITT Technical Institute
Arlington, Texas

- **Proprietary** primarily 2-year, founded 1982, part of ITT Educational Services, Inc.
- **Suburban** campus
- **Coed**

Majors Accounting; business administration and management; computer programming (specific applications); construction management; cyber/computer forensics and counterterrorism; drafting and design technology; electrical, electronic and communications engineering technology; information technology project management; legal assistant/paralegal; network and system administration; project management.

Academics *Calendar:* quarters. *Degrees:* associate and bachelor's.

Student Life *Housing:* college housing not available.

Freshman Application Contact Director of Recruitment, ITT Technical Institute, 551 Ryan Plaza Drive, Arlington, TX 76011. *Phone:* 817-794-5100. *Toll-free phone:* 888-288-4950. *Website:* http://www.itt-tech.edu/.

ITT Technical Institute
Austin, Texas

- **Proprietary** primarily 2-year, founded 1985, part of ITT Educational Services, Inc.
- **Urban** campus
- **Coed**

Majors Accounting; business administration and management; computer programming (specific applications); construction management; cyber/computer forensics and counterterrorism; drafting and design technology; electrical, electronic and communications engineering technology; information technology project management; legal assistant/paralegal; network and system administration; project management.

Academics *Calendar:* quarters. *Degrees:* associate and bachelor's.

Student Life *Housing:* college housing not available.

Financial Aid Of all full-time matriculated undergraduates who enrolled in 2012, 1 Federal Work-Study job.

Freshman Application Contact Director of Recruitment, ITT Technical Institute, 6330 East Highway 290, Suite 150, Austin, TX 78723-1061. *Phone:* 512-467-6800. *Toll-free phone:* 800-431-0677. *Website:* http://www.itt-tech.edu/.

ITT Technical Institute
DeSoto, Texas

- **Proprietary** primarily 2-year
- **Coed**

Majors Accounting; business administration and management; computer programming (specific applications); construction management; cyber/computer forensics and counterterrorism; drafting and design technology; electrical, electronic and communications engineering technology; industrial technology; information technology project management; legal assistant/paralegal; network and system administration; project management.

Academics *Degrees:* associate and bachelor's.

Freshman Application Contact Director of Recruitment, ITT Technical Institute, 921 West Belt Line Road, Suite 181, DeSoto, TX 75115. *Phone:* 972-274-8600. *Toll-free phone:* 877-854-5728. *Website:* http://www.itt-tech.edu/.

ITT Technical Institute
Houston, Texas

- **Proprietary** primarily 2-year, founded 1985, part of ITT Educational Services, Inc.
- **Suburban** campus
- **Coed**

Majors Accounting; business administration and management; computer programming (specific applications); construction management; cyber/computer forensics and counterterrorism; drafting and design technology; electrical, electronic and communications engineering technology; industrial technology; information technology project management; legal assistant/paralegal; network and system administration; project management.

Academics *Calendar:* quarters. *Degrees:* associate and bachelor's.

Student Life *Housing:* college housing not available.

Freshman Application Contact Director of Recruitment, ITT Technical Institute, 15651 North Freeway, Houston, TX 77090. *Phone:* 281-873-0512. *Toll-free phone:* 800-879-6486. *Website:* http://www.itt-tech.edu/.

ITT Technical Institute
Houston, Texas

- **Proprietary** primarily 2-year, founded 1983, part of ITT Educational Services, Inc.
- **Urban** campus
- **Coed**

Majors Accounting; business administration and management; computer programming (specific applications); construction management; cyber/computer forensics and counterterrorism; drafting and design technology; electrical, electronic and communications engineering technology; information technology project management; network and system administration; project management.

Academics *Calendar:* quarters. *Degrees:* associate and bachelor's.

Student Life *Housing:* college housing not available.

Freshman Application Contact Director of Recruitment, ITT Technical Institute, 2950 South Gessner, Houston, TX 77063-3751. *Phone:* 713-952-2294. *Toll-free phone:* 800-235-4787. *Website:* http://www.itt-tech.edu/.

ITT Technical Institute
Richardson, Texas

- **Proprietary** primarily 2-year, founded 1989, part of ITT Educational Services, Inc.
- **Suburban** campus
- **Coed**

Majors Accounting technology and bookkeeping; business administration and management; computer programming (specific applications); construction management; cyber/computer forensics and counterterrorism; drafting and design technology; electrical, electronic and communications engineering technology; information technology project management; legal assistant/paralegal; medical/clinical assistant; network and system administration; project management; registered nursing/registered nurse.

Academics *Calendar:* quarters. *Degrees:* associate and bachelor's.

Student Life *Housing:* college housing not available.

Financial Aid Of all full-time matriculated undergraduates who enrolled in 2012, 5 Federal Work-Study jobs (averaging $5000).

Freshman Application Contact Director of Recruitment, ITT Technical Institute, 2101 Waterview Parkway, Richardson, TX 75080. *Phone:* 972-690-9100. *Toll-free phone:* 888-488-5761.
Website: http://www.itt-tech.edu/.

ITT Technical Institute
San Antonio, Texas

- **Proprietary** primarily 2-year
- **Coed**

Majors Accounting; computer programming (specific applications); construction management; cyber/computer forensics and counterterrorism; drafting and design technology; electrical, electronic and communications engineering technology; information technology project management; network and system administration; project management.

Academics *Degrees:* associate and bachelor's.

Freshman Application Contact Director of Recruiting, ITT Technical Institute, 2895 NE Loop 410, San Antonio, TX 78218. *Phone:* 210-651-8500. *Toll-free phone:* 877-400-8894.
Website: http://www.itt-tech.edu/.

ITT Technical Institute
San Antonio, Texas

- **Proprietary** primarily 2-year, founded 1988, part of ITT Educational Services, Inc.
- **Urban** campus
- **Coed**

Majors Accounting; business administration and management; computer programming (specific applications); construction management; cyber/computer forensics and counterterrorism; drafting and design technology; electrical, electronic and communications engineering technology; information technology project management; legal assistant/paralegal; network and system administration; project management.

Academics *Calendar:* quarters. *Degrees:* associate and bachelor's.

Student Life *Housing:* college housing not available.

Freshman Application Contact Director of Recruitment, ITT Technical Institute, 5700 Northwest Parkway, San Antonio, TX 78249-3303. *Phone:* 210-694-4612. *Toll-free phone:* 800-880-0570.
Website: http://www.itt-tech.edu/.

ITT Technical Institute
Waco, Texas

- **Proprietary** primarily 2-year, part of ITT Educational Services, Inc.
- **Coed**

Majors Accounting; business administration and management; computer programming (specific applications); construction management; cyber/computer forensics and counterterrorism; drafting and design technology; electrical, electronic and communications engineering technology; information technology project management; legal assistant/paralegal; network and system administration; project management.

Academics *Calendar:* quarters. *Degrees:* associate and bachelor's.

Freshman Application Contact Director of Recruitment, ITT Technical Institute, 3700 S. Jack Kultgen Expressway, Suite 100, Waco, TX 76706. *Phone:* 254-523-3940. *Toll-free phone:* 877-201-7143.
Website: http://www.itt-tech.edu/.

ITT Technical Institute
Webster, Texas

- **Proprietary** primarily 2-year, founded 1995, part of ITT Educational Services, Inc.
- **Coed**

Majors Accounting; business administration and management; computer programming (specific applications); construction management; cyber/computer forensics and counterterrorism; drafting and design technology; electrical, electronic and communications engineering technology; graphic communications; information technology project management; legal assistant/paralegal; network and system administration; project management.

Academics *Calendar:* quarters. *Degrees:* associate and bachelor's.

Student Life *Housing:* college housing not available.

Freshman Application Contact Director of Recruitment, ITT Technical Institute, 1001 Magnolia Avenue, Webster, TX 77598. *Phone:* 281-316-4700. *Toll-free phone:* 888-488-9347.
Website: http://www.itt-tech.edu/.

Jacksonville College
Jacksonville, Texas

Freshman Application Contact Danny Morris, Director of Admissions, Jacksonville College, 105 B.J. Albritton Drive, Jacksonville, TX 75766. *Phone:* 903-589-7110. *Toll-free phone:* 800-256-8522. *E-mail:* admissions@jacksonville-college.org.
Website: http://www.jacksonville-college.edu/.

Kaplan College, Arlington Campus
Arlington, Texas

Freshman Application Contact Kaplan College, Arlington Campus, 2241 South Watson Road, Arlington, TX 76010. *Phone:* 866-249-2074. *Toll-free phone:* 800-935-1857.
Website: http://arlington.kaplancollege.com/.

Kaplan College, Beaumont Campus
Beaumont, Texas

Freshman Application Contact Admissions Office, Kaplan College, Beaumont Campus, 6115 Eastex Freeway, Beaumont, TX 77706. *Phone:* 409-833-2722. *Toll-free phone:* 800-935-1857.
Website: http://beaumont.kaplancollege.com/.

Kaplan College, Brownsville Campus
Brownsville, Texas

Freshman Application Contact Director of Admissions, Kaplan College, Brownsville Campus, 1900 North Expressway, Suite O, Brownsville, TX 78521. *Phone:* 956-547-8200.
Website: http://brownsville.kaplancollege.com/.

Kaplan College, Corpus Christi Campus
Corpus Christi, Texas

Freshman Application Contact Admissions Director, Kaplan College, Corpus Christi Campus, 1620 South Padre Island Drive, Suite 600, Corpus Christi, TX 78416. *Phone:* 361-852-2900.
Website: http://corpus-christi.kaplancollege.com/.

Kaplan College, Dallas Campus
Dallas, Texas

Freshman Application Contact Kaplan College, Dallas Campus, 12005 Ford Road, Suite 100, Dallas, TX 75234. *Phone:* 972-385-1446. *Toll-free phone:* 800-935-1857.
Website: http://dallas.kaplancollege.com/.

Kaplan College, El Paso Campus
El Paso, Texas

Freshman Application Contact Director of Admissions, Kaplan College, El Paso Campus, 8360 Burnham Road, Suite 100, El Paso, TX 79907.
Website: http://el-paso.kaplancollege.com/.

Kaplan College, Fort Worth Campus
Fort Worth, Texas

Freshman Application Contact Director of Admissions, Kaplan College, Fort Worth Campus, 2001 Beach Street, Suite 201, Fort Worth, TX 76103. *Phone:* 817-413-2000.
Website: http://fort-worth.kaplancollege.com/.

Kaplan College, Laredo Campus
Laredo, Texas

Freshman Application Contact Admissions Office, Kaplan College, Laredo Campus, 6410 McPherson Road, Laredo, TX 78041. *Phone:* 956-717-5909. *Toll-free phone:* 800-935-1857.
Website: http://laredo.kaplancollege.com/.

Kaplan College, Lubbock Campus
Lubbock, Texas

Freshman Application Contact Admissions Office, Kaplan College, Lubbock Campus, 1421 Ninth Street, Lubbock, TX 79401. *Phone:* 806-765-7051. *Toll-free phone:* 800-935-1857.
Website: http://lubbock.kaplancollege.com/.

Kaplan College, McAllen Campus
McAllen, Texas

Admissions Office Contact Kaplan College, McAllen Campus, 1500 South Jackson Road, McAllen, TX 78503. *Toll-free phone:* 800-935-1857.
Website: http://mcallen.kaplancollege.com/.

Kaplan College, San Antonio Campus
San Antonio, Texas

Freshman Application Contact Admissions Office, Kaplan College, San Antonio Campus, 6441 NW Loop 410, San Antonio, TX 78238. *Phone:* 210-308-8584. *Toll-free phone:* 800-935-1857.
Website: http://wsan-antonio.kaplancollege.com/.

Kaplan College, San Antonio–San Pedro Area Campus
San Antonio, Texas

Freshman Application Contact Director of Admissions, Kaplan College, San Antonio–San Pedro Area Campus, 7142 San Pedro Avenue, Suite 100, San Antonio, TX 78216. *Toll-free phone:* 800-935-1857.
Website: http://nsan-antonio.kaplancollege.com/.

KD Studio
Dallas, Texas

Freshman Application Contact Mr. T. A. Taylor, Director of Education, KD Studio, 2600 Stemmons Freeway, Suite 117, Dallas, TX 75207. *Phone:* 214-638-0484. *Toll-free phone:* 877-278-2283. *Fax:* 214-630-5140. *E-mail:* tataylor@kdstudio.com.
Website: http://www.kdstudio.com/.

Kilgore College
Kilgore, Texas

- **State and locally supported** 2-year, founded 1935
- **Small-town** 35-acre campus with easy access to Dallas-Fort Worth
- **Coed,** 5,867 undergraduate students, 45% full-time, 61% women, 39% men

Undergraduates 2,623 full-time, 3,244 part-time. Students come from 21 states and territories; 25 other countries; 1% are from out of state; 20% Black or African American, non-Hispanic/Latino; 14% Hispanic/Latino; 0.7% Asian, non-Hispanic/Latino; 0.1% Native Hawaiian or other Pacific Islander, non-Hispanic/Latino; 0.4% American Indian or Alaska Native, non-Hispanic/Latino; 2% Two or more races, non-Hispanic/Latino; 0.9% Race/ethnicity unknown; 0.6% international; 6% transferred in; 7% live on campus. *Retention:* 51% of full-time freshmen returned.
Freshmen *Admission:* 1,197 enrolled.
Faculty *Total:* 295, 49% full-time, 8% with terminal degrees. *Student/faculty ratio:* 19:1.
Majors Accounting technology and bookkeeping; aerospace, aeronautical and astronautical/space engineering; agriculture; architecture; art; autobody/collision and repair technology; automobile/automotive mechanics technology; biological and physical sciences; business administration and management; business/commerce; chemical engineering; chemistry; child-care and support services management; child-care provision; civil engineering; commercial and advertising art; commercial photography; computer and information sciences; computer programming; computer systems networking and telecommunications; criminal justice/law enforcement administration; dance; diesel mechanics technology; drafting and design technology; dramatic/theater arts; electrical, electronic and communications engineering technology; elementary education; emergency medical technology (EMT paramedic); English; executive assistant/executive secretary; forestry; general studies; geology/earth science; health teacher education; heating, air conditioning, ventilation and refrigeration maintenance technology; journalism; legal assistant/paralegal; management information systems; mathematics; mechanical engineering; medical radiologic technology; metallurgical technology; music; occupational safety and health technology; operations management; petroleum engineering; physical education teaching and coaching; physical therapy; physical therapy technology; physics; pre-dentistry studies; pre-law studies; premedical studies; pre-pharmacy studies; pre-veterinary studies; psychology; radiologic technology/science; registered nursing/registered nurse; religious studies; social sciences; surgical technology; welding technology.
Academics *Calendar:* semesters. *Degree:* certificates and associate. *Special study options:* academic remediation for entering students, adult/continuing education programs, advanced placement credit, cooperative education,

distance learning, English as a second language, internships, part-time degree program, services for LD students, student-designed majors, summer session for credit.
Library Randolph C. Watson Library plus 1 other with 65,000 titles, 6,679 serial subscriptions, 13,351 audiovisual materials, an OPAC, a Web page.
Student Life *Housing Options:* coed, men-only, women-only. Campus housing is university owned. *Activities and Organizations:* drama/theater group, student-run newspaper, choral group, marching band. *Campus security:* 24-hour emergency response devices and patrols. *Student services:* personal/psychological counseling.
Athletics Member NJCAA. *Intercollegiate sports:* basketball M(s)/W(s), cheerleading M(s)/W(s), football M(s), softball W. *Intramural sports:* basketball M/W, football M/W, racquetball M/W, tennis M/W, volleyball M/W.
Costs (2013–14) *Tuition:* area resident $696 full-time, $29 per semester hour part-time; state resident $2304 full-time, $96 per semester hour part-time; nonresident $3456 full-time, $144 per semester hour part-time. *Required fees:* $672 full-time. *Room and board:* $4270. Room and board charges vary according to board plan and housing facility. *Payment plan:* installment. *Waivers:* senior citizens and employees or children of employees.
Financial Aid Of all full-time matriculated undergraduates who enrolled in 2012, 80 Federal Work-Study jobs (averaging $2500). *Financial aid deadline:* 6/1.
Applying *Options:* electronic application, early admission. *Required:* high school transcript. *Required for some:* interview. *Application deadlines:* rolling (freshmen), rolling (out-of-state freshmen), rolling (transfers).
Freshman Application Contact Kilgore College, 1100 Broadway Boulevard, Kilgore, TX 75662-3299. *Phone:* 903-983-8200. *E-mail:* register@kilgore.cc.tx.us.
Website: http://www.kilgore.edu/.

Lamar Institute of Technology
Beaumont, Texas

Freshman Application Contact Admissions Office, Lamar Institute of Technology, 855 East Lavaca, Beaumont, TX 77705. *Phone:* 409-880-8354. *Toll-free phone:* 800-950-6989.
Website: http://www.lit.edu/.

Lamar State College–Orange
Orange, Texas

- **State-supported** 2-year, founded 1969, part of Texas State University System
- **Small-town** 21-acre campus
- **Coed,** 2,426 undergraduate students, 41% full-time, 69% women, 31% men

Undergraduates 992 full-time, 1,434 part-time. 16% Black or African American, non-Hispanic/Latino; 6% Hispanic/Latino; 2% Asian, non-Hispanic/Latino; 0.5% American Indian or Alaska Native, non-Hispanic/Latino. *Retention:* 47% of full-time freshmen returned.
Freshmen *Admission:* 434 enrolled.
Faculty *Total:* 96, 52% full-time, 13% with terminal degrees. *Student/faculty ratio:* 19:1.
Majors Accounting; administrative assistant and secretarial science; architectural engineering technology; business administration and management; clinical/medical laboratory technology; comparative literature; computer science; data processing and data processing technology; environmental studies; information science/studies; liberal arts and sciences/liberal studies; mass communication/media; mathematics; real estate; registered nursing/registered nurse; social sciences.
Academics *Calendar:* semesters. *Degree:* certificates and associate. *Special study options:* academic remediation for entering students, distance learning, double majors, internships, part-time degree program, summer session for credit.
Library Lamar State College-Orange Library plus 1 other with 71,092 titles, 1,306 serial subscriptions, 288 audiovisual materials, an OPAC.
Student Life *Housing:* college housing not available. *Campus security:* 24-hour emergency response devices, late-night transport/escort service.
Athletics *Intramural sports:* archery M, basketball M/W, volleyball M/W, weight lifting M/W.
Costs (2013–14) *Tuition:* state resident $2544 full-time, $106 per credit hour part-time; nonresident $11,040 full-time, $460 per credit hour part-time. *Required fees:* $952 full-time, $65 per credit hour part-time. *Payment plan:* installment.
Financial Aid Of all full-time matriculated undergraduates who enrolled in 2012, 20 Federal Work-Study jobs (averaging $3000). 2 state and other part-time jobs (averaging $2000).

Applying *Required:* high school transcript. *Application deadlines:* rolling (freshmen), rolling (transfers). *Notification:* continuous (freshmen), continuous (transfers).

Freshman Application Contact Kerry Olson, Director of Admissions and Financial Aid, Lamar State College–Orange, 410 Front Street, Orange, TX 77632. *Phone:* 409-882-3362. *Fax:* 409-882-3374.
Website: http://www.lsco.edu/.

Lamar State College–Port Arthur
Port Arthur, Texas

Freshman Application Contact Ms. Connie Nicholas, Registrar, Lamar State College–Port Arthur, PO Box 310, Port Arthur, TX 77641-0310. *Phone:* 409-984-6165. *Toll-free phone:* 800-477-5872. *Fax:* 409-984-6025. *E-mail:* nichoca@lamarpa.edu.
Website: http://www.lamarpa.edu/.

Laredo Community College
Laredo, Texas

Freshman Application Contact Ms. Josie Soliz, Admissions Records Supervisor, Laredo Community College, Laredo, TX 78040-4395. *Phone:* 956-721-5177. *Fax:* 956-721-5493.
Website: http://www.laredo.edu/.

Le Cordon Bleu College of Culinary Arts in Austin
Austin, Texas

Director of Admissions Paula Paulette, Vice President of Marketing and Admissions, Le Cordon Bleu College of Culinary Arts in Austin, 3110 Esperanza Crossing, Suite 100, Austin, TX 78758. *Phone:* 512-837-2665. *Toll-free phone:* 888-559-7222. *E-mail:* ppaulette@txca.com.
Website: http://www.chefs.edu/Austin/.

Lee College
Baytown, Texas

Director of Admissions Ms. Becki Griffith, Registrar, Lee College, PO Box 818, Baytown, TX 77522-0818. *Phone:* 281-425-6399. *E-mail:* bgriffit@lee.edu.
Website: http://www.lee.edu/.

Lone Star College–CyFair
Cypress, Texas

- **State and locally supported** 2-year, founded 2002, part of Lone Star College System
- **Suburban** campus with easy access to Houston
- **Coed,** 19,544 undergraduate students, 32% full-time, 57% women, 43% men

Undergraduates 6,344 full-time, 13,200 part-time. Students come from 64 other countries; 15% Black or African American, non-Hispanic/Latino; 40% Hispanic/Latino; 10% Asian, non-Hispanic/Latino; 0.3% American Indian or Alaska Native, non-Hispanic/Latino; 3% Two or more races, non-Hispanic/Latino; 4% Race/ethnicity unknown; 6% transferred in.
Freshmen *Admission:* 3,141 applied, 3,141 admitted, 3,141 enrolled.
Faculty *Total:* 1,033, 18% full-time, 16% with terminal degrees. *Student/faculty ratio:* 19:1.
Majors Accounting; animation, interactive technology, video graphics and special effects; business administration and management; computer and information sciences; computer science; criminal justice/law enforcement administration; dance; design and visual communications; diagnostic medical sonography and ultrasound technology; economics; education; electrical, electronic and communications engineering technology; emergency medical technology (EMT paramedic); fire science/firefighting; health information/medical records technology; industrial technology; information technology; logistics, materials, and supply chain management; marketing/marketing management; medical radiologic technology; music; office occupations and clerical services; radiation protection/health physics technology; registered nursing/registered nurse; speech communication and rhetoric; welding technology.
Academics *Calendar:* semesters. *Degree:* certificates, diplomas, and associate. *Special study options:* academic remediation for entering students, accelerated degree program, adult/continuing education programs, advanced placement credit, cooperative education, distance learning, double majors, English as a second language, honors programs, independent study, internships, part-time degree program, services for LD students, study abroad, summer session for credit.
Library LSC-CyFair Library with an OPAC, a Web page.

Student Life *Housing:* college housing not available. *Activities and Organizations:* drama/theater group, choral group. *Campus security:* 24-hour emergency response devices and patrols, late-night transport/escort service. *Student services:* personal/psychological counseling.
Costs (2014–15) *Tuition:* area resident $960 full-time, $480 per year part-time; state resident $2640 full-time, $1320 per year part-time; nonresident $3000 full-time, $1500 per year part-time. Full-time tuition and fees vary according to program. Part-time tuition and fees vary according to program. *Required fees:* $448 full-time, $192 per year part-time, $64 per year part-time. *Payment plan:* installment.
Applying *Options:* electronic application, early admission.
Freshman Application Contact Admissions Office, Lone Star College–CyFair, 9191 Barker Cypress Road, Cypress, TX 77433-1383. *Phone:* 281-290-3200. *E-mail:* cfc.info@lonestar.edu.
Website: http://www.lonestar.edu/cyfair.

Lone Star College–Kingwood
Kingwood, Texas

- **State and locally supported** 2-year, founded 1984, part of Lone Star College System
- **Suburban** 264-acre campus with easy access to Houston
- **Coed,** 11,943 undergraduate students, 35% full-time, 64% women, 36% men

Undergraduates 4,170 full-time, 7,773 part-time. Students come from 42 other countries; 15% Black or African American, non-Hispanic/Latino; 27% Hispanic/Latino; 4% Asian, non-Hispanic/Latino; 0.4% American Indian or Alaska Native, non-Hispanic/Latino; 3% Two or more races, non-Hispanic/Latino; 4% Race/ethnicity unknown; 6% transferred in.
Freshmen *Admission:* 1,555 applied, 1,555 admitted, 1,555 enrolled.
Faculty *Total:* 675, 18% full-time, 13% with terminal degrees. *Student/faculty ratio:* 18:1.
Majors Accounting; administrative assistant and secretarial science; business administration and management; computer and information sciences; computer science; cosmetology; criminal justice/law enforcement administration; dental hygiene; design and visual communications; education; information science/studies; interior design; marketing/marketing management; music; occupational therapy; registered nursing/registered nurse; respiratory care therapy.
Academics *Calendar:* semesters. *Degree:* certificates and associate. *Special study options:* academic remediation for entering students, accelerated degree program, adult/continuing education programs, advanced placement credit, cooperative education, distance learning, double majors, English as a second language, honors programs, independent study, internships, part-time degree program, services for LD students, study abroad, summer session for credit.
Library LSC-Kingwood Library with an OPAC, a Web page.
Student Life *Housing:* college housing not available. *Activities and Organizations:* drama/theater group, student-run television station, choral group. *Campus security:* 24-hour emergency response devices and patrols, late-night transport/escort service. *Student services:* personal/psychological counseling.
Athletics *Intramural sports:* baseball M.
Costs (2014–15) *Tuition:* area resident $960 full-time, $480 per year part-time; state resident $2640 full-time, $1320 per year part-time; nonresident $3000 full-time, $1500 per year part-time. *Required fees:* $448 full-time, $192 per year part-time, $64 per year part-time.
Financial Aid Of all full-time matriculated undergraduates who enrolled in 2009, 28 Federal Work-Study jobs, 6 state and other part-time jobs. *Financial aid deadline:* 4/1.
Applying *Options:* electronic application, early admission. *Application deadlines:* rolling (freshmen), rolling (transfers).
Freshman Application Contact Admissions Office, Lone Star College–Kingwood, 20000 Kingwood Drive, Kingwood, TX 77339. *Phone:* 281-312-1525. *Fax:* 281-312-1477. *E-mail:* kingwoodadvising@lonestar.edu.
Website: http://www.lonestar.edu/kingwood.htm.

Lone Star College–Montgomery
Conroe, Texas

- **State and locally supported** 2-year, founded 1995, part of Lone Star College System
- **Suburban** campus with easy access to Houston
- **Coed,** 12,758 undergraduate students, 34% full-time, 61% women, 39% men

Undergraduates 4,394 full-time, 8,364 part-time. Students come from 63 other countries; 11% Black or African American, non-Hispanic/Latino; 25% Hispanic/Latino; 4% Asian, non-Hispanic/Latino; 0.4% American Indian or Alaska Native, non-Hispanic/Latino; 3% Two or more races, non-Hispanic/Latino; 3% Race/ethnicity unknown; 6% transferred in.
Freshmen *Admission:* 1,941 applied, 1,941 admitted, 1,941 enrolled.

Faculty *Total:* 665, 22% full-time, 16% with terminal degrees. *Student/faculty ratio:* 19:1.

Majors Accounting and business/management; automobile/automotive mechanics technology; biology/biotechnology laboratory technician; business administration and management; computer science; criminal justice/law enforcement administration; education; fire science/firefighting; human services; information technology; music; physical therapy technology; registered nursing/registered nurse.

Academics *Calendar:* semesters. *Degree:* certificates and associate. *Special study options:* academic remediation for entering students, adult/continuing education programs, advanced placement credit, cooperative education, distance learning, double majors, English as a second language, honors programs, independent study, internships, part-time degree program, services for LD students, study abroad, summer session for credit.

Library LSC-Montgomery Library with an OPAC, a Web page.

Student Life *Housing:* college housing not available. *Activities and Organizations:* drama/theater group, student-run newspaper, choral group, Campus Crusade for Christ, Criminal Justice Club, Phi Theta Kappa, Latino-American Student Association, African-American Cultural Awareness. *Campus security:* 24-hour emergency response devices and patrols, late-night transport/escort service. *Student services:* personal/psychological counseling.

Costs (2014–15) *Tuition:* area resident $960 full-time, $480 per year part-time; state resident $2640 full-time, $1320 per year part-time; nonresident $3000 full-time, $1500 per year part-time. *Required fees:* $448 full-time, $192 per year part-time, $64 per year part-time.

Financial Aid Of all full-time matriculated undergraduates who enrolled in 2012, 25 Federal Work-Study jobs (averaging $2500). 4 state and other part-time jobs.

Applying *Options:* electronic application, early admission. *Application deadlines:* rolling (freshmen), rolling (transfers).

Freshman Application Contact Lone Star College–Montgomery, 3200 College Park Drive, Conroe, TX 77384. *Phone:* 936-273-7236.

Website: http://www.lonestar.edu/montgomery.

Lone Star College–North Harris

Houston, Texas

- **State and locally supported** 2-year, founded 1972, part of Lone Star College System
- **Suburban** campus with easy access to Houston
- **Coed,** 17,217 undergraduate students, 32% full-time, 62% women, 38% men

Undergraduates 5,541 full-time, 11,676 part-time. Students come from 50 other countries; 31% Black or African American, non-Hispanic/Latino; 37% Hispanic/Latino; 5% Asian, non-Hispanic/Latino; 0.2% American Indian or Alaska Native, non-Hispanic/Latino; 3% Two or more races, non-Hispanic/Latino; 5% Race/ethnicity unknown; 6% transferred in.

Freshmen *Admission:* 2,777 applied, 2,777 admitted, 2,777 enrolled.

Faculty *Total:* 1,058, 20% full-time, 11% with terminal degrees. *Student/faculty ratio:* 16:1.

Majors Accounting; automobile/automotive mechanics technology; business administration and management; computer science; cosmetology; criminal justice/law enforcement administration; design and visual communications; drafting and design technology; education; emergency medical technology (EMT paramedic); health information/medical records technology; heating, air conditioning, ventilation and refrigeration maintenance technology; music; pharmacy technician; registered nursing/registered nurse; welding technology.

Academics *Calendar:* semesters. *Degree:* certificates and associate. *Special study options:* academic remediation for entering students, adult/continuing education programs, advanced placement credit, cooperative education, distance learning, double majors, English as a second language, honors programs, independent study, internships, part-time degree program, services for LD students, study abroad, summer session for credit.

Library LSC-North Harris Library with an OPAC, a Web page.

Student Life *Activities and Organizations:* drama/theater group, student-run newspaper, choral group, Student Government Association, Phi Theta Kappa, Ambassadors, honors student organizations, Soccer Club. *Campus security:* 24-hour emergency response devices and patrols, late-night transport/escort service. *Student services:* personal/psychological counseling, women's center.

Athletics *Intramural sports:* badminton M/W, baseball M/W, basketball M/W, bowling M/W, football M/W, golf M/W, gymnastics M/W, racquetball M/W, soccer M/W, softball M/W, table tennis M/W, tennis M/W, track and field M/W, volleyball M/W, weight lifting M/W.

Costs (2014–15) *Tuition:* area resident $960 full-time, $480 per year part-time; state resident $2640 full-time, $1320 per year part-time; nonresident $3000 full-time, $1500 per year part-time. *Required fees:* $448 full-time, $192 per year part-time, $64 per year part-time.

Applying *Options:* electronic application, early admission. *Application deadlines:* rolling (freshmen), rolling (transfers).

Freshman Application Contact Admissions Office, Lone Star College–North Harris, 2700 W. W. Thorne Drive, Houston, TX 77073-3499. *Phone:* 281-618-5410. *E-mail:* nhcounselor@lonestar.edu.

Website: http://www.lonestar.edu/northharris.

Lone Star College–Tomball

Tomball, Texas

- **State and locally supported** 2-year, founded 1988, part of Lone Star College System
- **Suburban** campus with easy access to Houston
- **Coed,** 8,862 undergraduate students, 33% full-time, 63% women, 37% men

Undergraduates 2,907 full-time, 5,955 part-time. Students come from 43 other countries; 14% Black or African American, non-Hispanic/Latino; 24% Hispanic/Latino; 5% Asian, non-Hispanic/Latino; 0.4% American Indian or Alaska Native, non-Hispanic/Latino; 3% Two or more races, non-Hispanic/Latino; 4% Race/ethnicity unknown; 6% transferred in.

Freshmen *Admission:* 1,242 applied, 1,242 admitted, 1,242 enrolled.

Faculty *Total:* 368, 27% full-time, 15% with terminal degrees. *Student/faculty ratio:* 24:1.

Majors Accounting; administrative assistant and secretarial science; animation, interactive technology, video graphics and special effects; business administration and management; computer programming; computer science; criminal justice/law enforcement administration; education; electrical, electronic and communications engineering technology; music; registered nursing/registered nurse; system, networking, and LAN/WAN management; veterinary/animal health technology.

Academics *Calendar:* semesters. *Degree:* certificates and associate. *Special study options:* academic remediation for entering students, adult/continuing education programs, advanced placement credit, cooperative education, distance learning, double majors, English as a second language, honors programs, independent study, internships, part-time degree program, services for LD students, study abroad, summer session for credit.

Library LSC-Tomball Community Library with an OPAC, a Web page.

Student Life *Housing:* college housing not available. *Activities and Organizations:* drama/theater group, student-run newspaper, choral group, Phi Theta Kappa, Occupational Therapy OTA, Veterinary Technicians Student Organization, STARS, Student Nurses Association. *Campus security:* 24-hour emergency response devices and patrols, late-night transport/escort service, trained security personnel during open hours. *Student services:* personal/psychological counseling.

Costs (2014–15) *Tuition:* area resident $960 full-time, $480 per year part-time; state resident $2640 full-time, $1320 per year part-time; nonresident $3000 full-time, $1500 per year part-time. Full-time tuition and fees vary according to program. Part-time tuition and fees vary according to program. *Required fees:* $448 full-time, $192 per year part-time, $64 per year part-time.

Financial Aid Of all full-time matriculated undergraduates who enrolled in 2012, 34 Federal Work-Study jobs (averaging $3000).

Applying *Options:* electronic application, early admission. *Application deadlines:* rolling (freshmen), rolling (transfers).

Freshman Application Contact Admissions Office, Lone Star College–Tomball, 30555 Tomball Parkway, Tomball, TX 77375-4036. *Phone:* 281-351-3310. *E-mail:* tcinfo@lonestar.edu.

Website: http://www.lonestar.edu/tomball.

Lone Star College–University Park

Houston, Texas

- **State and locally supported** 2-year, founded 2010, part of Lone Star College System
- **Suburban** campus with easy access to Houston
- **Coed,** 7,297 undergraduate students, 32% full-time, 58% women, 42% men

Undergraduates 2,340 full-time, 4,957 part-time. Students come from 47 other countries; 16% Black or African American, non-Hispanic/Latino; 32% Hispanic/Latino; 10% Asian, non-Hispanic/Latino; 0.3% American Indian or Alaska Native, non-Hispanic/Latino; 3% Two or more races, non-Hispanic/Latino; 6% Race/ethnicity unknown; 5% transferred in.

Freshmen *Admission:* 1,063 enrolled.

Faculty *Total:* 291, 14% full-time, 11% with terminal degrees. *Student/faculty ratio:* 25:1.

Majors Accounting; business administration and management; criminal justice/law enforcement administration; speech communication and rhetoric.

Academics *Degree:* certificates and associate. *Special study options:* academic remediation for entering students, advanced placement credit, cooperative education, distance learning, English as a second language, honors programs, independent study, internships, off-campus study, part-time degree program, services for LD students, study abroad, summer session for credit.

Student Life *Housing:* college housing not available. *Campus security:* 24-hour emergency response devices and patrols, late-night transport/escort service.

Costs (2014–15) *Tuition:* area resident $960 full-time, $480 per year part-time; state resident $2640 full-time, $1320 per year part-time; nonresident $3000 full-time, $1500 per year part-time. *Required fees:* $448 full-time, $224 per year part-time. *Payment plan:* installment. *Waivers:* senior citizens.

Applying *Recommended:* high school transcript.

Freshman Application Contact Lone Star College–University Park, 20515 SH 249, Houston, TX 77070-2607.

Website: http://www.lonestar.edu/universitypark.

McLennan Community College
Waco, Texas

Freshman Application Contact Dr. Vivian G. Jefferson, Director, Admissions and Recruitment, McLennan Community College, 1400 College Drive, Waco, TX 76708. *Phone:* 254-299-8689. *Fax:* 254-299-8694. *E-mail:* vjefferson@mclennan.edu.

Website: http://www.mclennan.edu/.

Mountain View College
Dallas, Texas

- **State and locally supported** 2-year, founded 1970, part of Dallas County Community College District System
- **Urban** 200-acre campus
- **Coed,** 9,068 undergraduate students, 23% full-time, 58% women, 42% men

Undergraduates 2,066 full-time, 7,002 part-time. Students come from 12 states and territories; 26% Black or African American, non-Hispanic/Latino; 53% Hispanic/Latino; 4% Asian, non-Hispanic/Latino; 0.3% American Indian or Alaska Native, non-Hispanic/Latino; 0.5% Two or more races, non-Hispanic/Latino; 3% Race/ethnicity unknown; 0.3% international; 18% transferred in. *Retention:* 57% of full-time freshmen returned.

Freshmen *Admission:* 2,500 applied, 2,500 admitted, 1,476 enrolled.

Faculty *Total:* 386, 22% full-time. *Student/faculty ratio:* 28:1.

Majors Accounting; business administration and management; computer systems networking and telecommunications; criminal justice/safety; drafting and design technology; education; electrical, electronic and communications engineering technology; liberal arts and sciences/liberal studies; music; speech communication and rhetoric; welding technology.

Academics *Calendar:* semesters. *Degree:* certificates and associate. *Special study options:* academic remediation for entering students, adult/continuing education programs, advanced placement credit, cooperative education, distance learning, double majors, English as a second language, external degree program, freshman honors college, honors programs, independent study, internships, part-time degree program, services for LD students, summer session for credit.

Student Life *Housing:* college housing not available. *Activities and Organizations:* drama/theater group, choral group. *Campus security:* 24-hour patrols, late-night transport/escort service. *Student services:* health clinic, personal/psychological counseling.

Athletics Member NJCAA. *Intercollegiate sports:* baseball M, basketball M/W, soccer M/W, volleyball W.

Costs (2014–15) *Tuition:* $52 per credit hour part-time; state resident $97 per credit hour part-time; nonresident $153 per credit hour part-time.

Financial Aid Of all full-time matriculated undergraduates who enrolled in 2012, 145 Federal Work-Study jobs (averaging $2700).

Applying *Options:* electronic application, early admission, deferred entrance. *Required:* high school transcript. *Application deadlines:* rolling (freshmen), rolling (transfers). *Notification:* continuous (freshmen), continuous (transfers).

Freshman Application Contact Ms. Glenda Hall, Director of Admissions, Mountain View College, 4849 West Illinois Avenue, Dallas, TX 75211-6599. *Phone:* 214-860-8666. *Fax:* 214-860-8570. *E-mail:* ghall@dcccd.edu.

Website: http://www.mountainviewcollege.edu/.

Navarro College
Corsicana, Texas

Freshman Application Contact David Edwards, Registrar, Navarro College, 3200 West 7th Avenue, Corsicana, TX 75110-4899. *Phone:* 903-875-7348. *Toll-free phone:* 800-NAVARRO (in-state); 800-628-2776 (out-of-state). *Fax:* 903-875-7353. *E-mail:* david.edwards@navarrocollege.edu.

Website: http://www.navarrocollege.edu/.

North Central Texas College
Gainesville, Texas

Freshman Application Contact Melinda Carroll, Director of Admissions/Registrar, North Central Texas College, 1525 West California, Gainesville, TX 76240-4699. *Phone:* 940-668-7731. *Fax:* 940-668-7075. *E-mail:* mcarroll@nctc.edu.

Website: http://www.nctc.edu/.

Northeast Texas Community College
Mount Pleasant, Texas

- **State and locally supported** 2-year, founded 1985
- **Rural** 175-acre campus
- **Coed,** 3,282 undergraduate students, 34% full-time, 62% women, 38% men

Undergraduates 1,104 full-time, 2,178 part-time. Students come from 19 states and territories; 4 other countries; 2% are from out of state; 13% Black or African American, non-Hispanic/Latino; 24% Hispanic/Latino; 0.4% Asian, non-Hispanic/Latino; 0.1% Native Hawaiian or other Pacific Islander, non-Hispanic/Latino; 0.2% American Indian or Alaska Native, non-Hispanic/Latino; 3% Two or more races, non-Hispanic/Latino; 2% Race/ethnicity unknown; 1% international. *Retention:* 50% of full-time freshmen returned.

Freshmen *Admission:* 806 enrolled.

Faculty *Total:* 178, 43% full-time. *Student/faculty ratio:* 17:1.

Majors Accounting; accounting and business/management; agricultural business and management; agroecology and sustainable agriculture; art; autobody/collision and repair technology; automobile/automotive mechanics technology; biology/biological sciences; biomedical sciences; business administration and management; chemistry; civil engineering; clinical/medical laboratory technology; communication; computer and information sciences; computer systems networking and telecommunications; corrections; cosmetology; criminal justice/law enforcement administration; criminal justice/police science; culinary arts; data entry/microcomputer applications; dental hygiene; dramatic/theater arts; education (multiple levels); electrical and electronics engineering; emergency medical technology (EMT paramedic); English; environmental science; executive assistant/executive secretary; health and physical education/fitness; history; industrial engineering; industrial technology; legal administrative assistant/secretary; liberal arts and sciences/liberal studies; mathematics; mechanical engineering; medical administrative assistant and medical secretary; medical/clinical assistant; music; physical therapy technology; physics; political science and government; psychology; registered nursing/registered nurse; social work; sociology; Spanish; welding technology.

Academics *Calendar:* semesters. *Degree:* certificates and associate. *Special study options:* academic remediation for entering students, adult/continuing education programs, advanced placement credit, cooperative education, distance learning, honors programs, independent study, part-time degree program, services for LD students, summer session for credit.

Library Learning Resource Center with 35,000 titles, 200 serial subscriptions, 4 audiovisual materials, an OPAC, a Web page.

Student Life *Housing Options:* Campus housing is university owned. *Activities and Organizations:* drama/theater group, student-run newspaper, choral group, Phi Theta Kappa, Student Government Association. *Campus security:* 24-hour patrols.

Athletics Member NJCAA. *Intercollegiate sports:* baseball M(s), equestrian sports M(s)/W(s), soccer M(s)/W(s), softball W(s). *Intramural sports:* basketball M/W, table tennis M/W, tennis M/W, volleyball M/W.

Costs (2013–14) *One-time required fee:* $10. *Tuition:* area resident $816 full-time, $34 per credit hour part-time; state resident $2040 full-time, $85 per credit hour part-time; nonresident $3154 full-time, $131 per credit hour part-time. Full-time tuition and fees vary according to program. Part-time tuition and fees vary according to program. *Required fees:* $959 full-time, $39 per credit hour part-time, $23 per credit hour part-time. *Room and board:* $5850. Room and board charges vary according to housing facility. *Payment plan:* installment. *Waivers:* senior citizens and employees or children of employees.

Financial Aid Of all full-time matriculated undergraduates who enrolled in 2009, 98 Federal Work-Study jobs (averaging $1600). 13 state and other part-time jobs (averaging $1600).

Applying *Options:* electronic application, early admission. *Required:* high school transcript. *Application deadlines:* rolling (freshmen), rolling (out-of-state freshmen), rolling (transfers).

Freshman Application Contact Linda Bond, Admissions Specialist, Northeast Texas Community College, PO Box 1307, Mount Pleasant, TX 75456-1307. *Phone:* 903-434-8140. *Toll-free phone:* 800-870-0142. *E-mail:* lbond@ntcc.edu.

Website: http://www.ntcc.edu/.

North Lake College
Irving, Texas

Freshman Application Contact Admissions/Registration Office (A405), North Lake College, 5001 North MacArthur Boulevard, Irving, TX 75038. *Phone:* 972-273-3183.
Website: http://www.northlakecollege.edu/.

Northwest Vista College
San Antonio, Texas

Freshman Application Contact Dr. Elaine Lang, Interim Director of Enrollment Management, Northwest Vista College, 3535 North Ellison Drive, San Antonio, TX 78251. *Phone:* 210-348-2016. *E-mail:* elang@accd.edu.
Website: http://www.alamo.edu/nvc/.

Odessa College
Odessa, Texas

Freshman Application Contact Ms. Tracy Hilliard, Associate Director, Admissions, Odessa College, 201 West University Avenue, Odessa, TX 79764. *Phone:* 432-335-6816. *Fax:* 432-335-6303. *E-mail:* thilliard@odessa.edu.
Website: http://www.odessa.edu/.

Palo Alto College
San Antonio, Texas

Freshman Application Contact Ms. Rachel Montejano, Director of Enrollment Management, Palo Alto College, 1400 West Villaret Boulevard, San Antonio, TX 78224. *Phone:* 210-921-5279. *Fax:* 210-921-5310. *E-mail:* pacar@accd.edu.
Website: http://www.alamo.edu/pac/.

Panola College
Carthage, Texas

- **State and locally supported** 2-year, founded 1947
- **Small-town** 35-acre campus
- **Endowment** $2.4 million
- **Coed,** 2,699 undergraduate students, 49% full-time, 65% women, 35% men

Undergraduates 1,327 full-time, 1,372 part-time. Students come from 18 states and territories; 12 other countries; 8% are from out of state; 22% Black or African American, non-Hispanic/Latino; 10% Hispanic/Latino; 0.3% Asian, non-Hispanic/Latino; 0.5% American Indian or Alaska Native, non-Hispanic/Latino; 0.5% Two or more races, non-Hispanic/Latino; 1% Race/ethnicity unknown; 2% international; 28% transferred in; 9% live on campus. *Retention:* 44% of full-time freshmen returned.
Freshmen *Admission:* 455 admitted, 447 enrolled.
Faculty *Total:* 140, 49% full-time, 5% with terminal degrees. *Student/faculty ratio:* 19:1.
Majors Administrative assistant and secretarial science; clinical/medical laboratory technology; early childhood education; education; general studies; health information/medical records technology; industrial technology; information science/studies; information technology; medical/clinical assistant; middle school education; occupational therapist assistant; petroleum technology; registered nursing/registered nurse.
Academics *Calendar:* semesters. *Degree:* certificates and associate. *Special study options:* academic remediation for entering students, advanced placement credit, cooperative education, distance learning, English as a second language, part-time degree program, services for LD students, summer session for credit.
Library M. P. Baker Library with 163,500 titles, 37,885 serial subscriptions, 4,397 audiovisual materials, an OPAC, a Web page.
Student Life *Housing Options:* coed. Campus housing is university owned. *Activities and Organizations:* drama/theater group, student-run newspaper, choral group, Student Government Organization, Student Occupational Therapy Assistant Club, Baptist Student Ministries, Texas Nursing Student Association, Phi Theta Kappa. *Campus security:* controlled dormitory access.
Athletics Member NCAA, NJCAA. *Intercollegiate sports:* baseball M(s), basketball M(s)/W(s), volleyball W(s). *Intramural sports:* basketball M/W, football M/W, racquetball M/W, table tennis M/W, volleyball M/W, weight lifting M/W.
Costs (2013–14) *Tuition:* area resident $750 full-time, $70 per semester hour part-time; state resident $2040 full-time, $113 per semester hour part-time; nonresident $2940 full-time, $143 per semester hour part-time. Full-time tuition and fees vary according to reciprocity agreements. Part-time tuition and fees vary according to reciprocity agreements. *Required fees:* $1350 full-time. *Room and board:* $4400. Room and board charges vary according to housing facility. *Payment plan:* deferred payment. *Waivers:* employees or children of employees.

Applying *Options:* electronic application, early admission. *Required for some:* high school transcript. *Recommended:* high school transcript. *Application deadlines:* rolling (freshmen), rolling (out-of-state freshmen), rolling (transfers). *Notification:* continuous (freshmen), continuous (out-of-state freshmen), continuous (transfers).
Freshman Application Contact Mr. Jeremy Dorman, Registrar/Director of Admissions, Panola College, 1109 West Panola Street, Carthage, TX 75633-2397. *Phone:* 903-693-2009. *Fax:* 903-693-2031. *E-mail:* bsimpson@panola.edu.
Website: http://www.panola.edu/.

Paris Junior College
Paris, Texas

- **State and locally supported** 2-year, founded 1924
- **Rural** 54-acre campus with easy access to Dallas-Fort Worth
- **Endowment** $17.9 million
- **Coed,** 5,301 undergraduate students, 47% full-time, 59% women, 41% men

Undergraduates 2,470 full-time, 2,831 part-time. Students come from 26 states and territories; 4 other countries; 3% are from out of state; 11% Black or African American, non-Hispanic/Latino; 12% Hispanic/Latino; 0.9% Asian, non-Hispanic/Latino; 2% American Indian or Alaska Native, non-Hispanic/Latino; 0.7% Two or more races, non-Hispanic/Latino; 0.3% international; 6% transferred in; 4% live on campus. *Retention:* 49% of full-time freshmen returned.
Freshmen *Admission:* 1,066 applied, 1,066 admitted, 1,221 enrolled.
Faculty *Total:* 257, 36% full-time, 7% with terminal degrees. *Student/faculty ratio:* 22:1.
Majors Accounting; agricultural mechanization; agriculture; art; biological and physical sciences; biology/biological sciences; business administration and management; business automation/technology/data entry; business/commerce; business teacher education; chemistry; computer and information sciences; computer engineering technology; computer typography and composition equipment operation; cosmetology; criminal justice/safety; criminology; drafting and design technology; dramatic/theater arts; early childhood education; education; education (multiple levels); electrical, electronic and communications engineering technology; electromechanical technology; elementary education; emergency medical technology (EMT paramedic); engineering; English; foreign languages and literatures; general studies; health and physical education/fitness; health information/medical records technology; health services/allied health/health sciences; heating, air conditioning, ventilation and refrigeration maintenance technology; history; information science/studies; journalism; liberal arts and sciences/liberal studies; mathematics; medical insurance coding; metal and jewelry arts; music; nursing administration; physical sciences; physics; political science and government; pre-law studies; premedical studies; prenursing studies; pre-pharmacy studies; psychology; radiologic technology/science; registered nursing/registered nurse; rhetoric and composition; secondary education; social sciences; social work; sociology; surgical technology; system, networking, and LAN/WAN management; watchmaking and jewelrymaking; welding technology.
Academics *Calendar:* semesters. *Degree:* certificates, diplomas, and associate. *Special study options:* academic remediation for entering students, adult/continuing education programs, advanced placement credit, cooperative education, distance learning, English as a second language, part-time degree program, services for LD students, summer session for credit.
Library Mike Rheudasil Learning Center with 38,150 titles, 404 serial subscriptions, an OPAC.
Student Life *Housing Options:* men-only, women-only. Campus housing is university owned. *Activities and Organizations:* drama/theater group, student-run newspaper, choral group, Student Government Organization, Blends Club for all ethic groups. *Campus security:* 24-hour emergency response devices and patrols, late-night transport/escort service, controlled dormitory access. *Student services:* personal/psychological counseling.
Athletics Member NJCAA. *Intercollegiate sports:* baseball M(s), basketball M(s)/W(s), golf M(s), soccer M(s)/W(s), softball W(s), volleyball W(s). *Intramural sports:* badminton M/W, basketball M, football M, table tennis M/W, tennis M/W, volleyball M/W.
Costs (2013–14) *Tuition:* area resident $1740 full-time, $50 per credit hour part-time; state resident $2670 full-time, $81 per credit hour part-time; nonresident $4080 full-time, $128 per credit hour part-time. Full-time tuition and fees vary according to class time, course level, course load, location, and program. Part-time tuition and fees vary according to class time, course level, course load, location, and program. *Required fees:* $240 full-time. *Room and board:* $4208. Room and board charges vary according to board plan and housing facility. *Payment plan:* installment. *Waivers:* senior citizens and employees or children of employees.
Financial Aid Of all full-time matriculated undergraduates who enrolled in 2012, 60 Federal Work-Study jobs (averaging $3800).

Applying *Options:* electronic application, early admission. *Required:* high school transcript. *Application deadlines:* rolling (freshmen), rolling (out-of-state freshmen), rolling (transfers). *Notification:* continuous (freshmen), continuous (out-of-state freshmen), continuous (transfers).

Freshman Application Contact Paris Junior College, 2400 Clarksville Street, Paris, TX 75460-6298. *Phone:* 903-782-0211. *Toll-free phone:* 800-232-5804.

Website: http://www.parisjc.edu/.

Pima Medical Institute

Houston, Texas

Freshman Application Contact Christopher Luebke, Corporate Director of Admissions, Pima Medical Institute, 2160 South Power Road, Mesa, AZ 85209. *Phone:* 480-610-6063. *E-mail:* cluebke@pmi.edu.

Website: http://www.pmi.edu/.

Ranger College

Ranger, Texas

Freshman Application Contact Dr. Jim Davis, Dean of Students, Ranger College, 1100 College Circle, Ranger, TX 76470. *Phone:* 254-647-3234 Ext. 110.

Website: http://www.rangercollege.edu/.

Remington College–Dallas Campus

Garland, Texas

Director of Admissions Ms. Shonda Wisenhunt, Remington College–Dallas Campus, 1800 Eastgate Drive, Garland, TX 75041. *Phone:* 972-686-7878. *Fax:* 972-686-5116. *E-mail:* shonda.wisenhunt@remingtoncollege.edu.

Website: http://www.remingtoncollege.edu/.

Remington College–Fort Worth Campus

Fort Worth, Texas

Director of Admissions Marcia Kline, Director of Recruitment, Remington College–Fort Worth Campus, 300 East Loop 820, Fort Worth, TX 76112. *Phone:* 817-451-0017. *Toll-free phone:* 800-560-6192. *Fax:* 817-496-1257. *E-mail:* marcia.kline@remingtoncollege.edu.

Website: http://www.remingtoncollege.edu/.

Remington College–Houston Campus

Houston, Texas

Director of Admissions Kevin Wilkinson, Director of Recruitment, Remington College–Houston Campus, 3110 Hayes Road, Suite 380, Houston, TX 77082. *Phone:* 281-899-1240. *Fax:* 281-597-8466. *E-mail:* kevin.wilkinson@remingtoncollege.edu.

Website: http://www.remingtoncollege.edu/.

Remington College–Houston Southeast

Webster, Texas

Director of Admissions Lori Minor, Director of Recruitment, Remington College–Houston Southeast, 20985 Interstate 45 South, Webster, TX 77598. *Phone:* 281-554-1700. *Fax:* 281-554-1765. *E-mail:* lori.minor@remingtoncollege.edu.

Website: http://www.remingtoncollege.edu/.

Remington College–North Houston Campus

Houston, Texas

Director of Admissions Edmund Flores, Director of Recruitment, Remington College–North Houston Campus, 11310 Greens Crossing Boulevard, Suite 300, Houston, TX 77067. *Phone:* 281-885-4450. *Fax:* 281-875-9964. *E-mail:* edmund.flores@remingtoncollege.edu.

Website: http://www.remingtoncollege.edu/.

Richland College

Dallas, Texas

Freshman Application Contact Ms. Carol McKinney, Department Assistant, Richland College, 12800 Abrams Road, Dallas, TX 75243-2199. *Phone:* 972-238-6100.

Website: http://www.rlc.dcccd.edu/.

St. Philip's College

San Antonio, Texas

- **District-supported** 2-year, founded 1898, part of Alamo Community College District
- **Urban** 68-acre campus with easy access to San Antonio
- **Coed**

Undergraduates 2,232 full-time, 8,478 part-time. Students come from 11 other countries; 1% are from out of state; 13% Black or African American, non-Hispanic/Latino; 50% Hispanic/Latino; 2% Asian, non-Hispanic/Latino; 0.4% American Indian or Alaska Native, non-Hispanic/Latino; 2% Two or more races, non-Hispanic/Latino; 0.3% international; 10% transferred in.

Faculty *Student/faculty ratio:* 15:1.

Academics *Calendar:* semesters. *Degree:* certificates, diplomas, and associate. *Special study options:* academic remediation for entering students, adult/continuing education programs, advanced placement credit, cooperative education, distance learning, double majors, English as a second language, honors programs, independent study, internships, off-campus study, part-time degree program, services for LD students, study abroad, summer session for credit. *ROTC:* Army (c).

Student Life *Campus security:* 24-hour emergency response devices and patrols, late-night transport/escort service.

Costs (2013–14) *Tuition:* area resident $2008 full-time, $80 per credit hour part-time; state resident $5470 full-time, $195 per credit hour part-time; nonresident $10,660 full-time, $368 per credit hour part-time. Full-time tuition and fees vary according to course load and program. Part-time tuition and fees vary according to course load and program. *Required fees:* $30 full-time, $1 per credit hour part-time.

Applying *Options:* electronic application, early admission. *Required:* high school transcript.

Freshman Application Contact Ms. Penelope Velasco, Associate Director, Residency and Reports, St. Philip's College, 1801 Martin Luther King Drive, San Antonio, TX 78203-2098. *Phone:* 210-486-2283. *Fax:* 210-486-2103. *E-mail:* pvelasco@alamo.edu.

Website: http://www.alamo.edu/spc/.

San Antonio College

San Antonio, Texas

Director of Admissions Mr. J. Martin Ortega, Director of Admissions and Records, San Antonio College, 1300 San Pedro Avenue, San Antonio, TX 78212-4299. *Phone:* 210-733-2582.

Website: http://www.alamo.edu/sac/.

San Jacinto College District

Pasadena, Texas

- **State and locally supported** 2-year, founded 1961
- **Suburban** 445-acre campus with easy access to Houston
- **Endowment** $3.9 million
- **Coed,** 28,385 undergraduate students, 27% full-time, 56% women, 44% men

Undergraduates 7,656 full-time, 20,729 part-time. Students come from 76 other countries; 1% are from out of state; 10% Black or African American, non-Hispanic/Latino; 46% Hispanic/Latino; 5% Asian, non-Hispanic/Latino; 0.2% Native Hawaiian or other Pacific Islander, non-Hispanic/Latino; 0.2% American Indian or Alaska Native, non-Hispanic/Latino; 2% Two or more races, non-Hispanic/Latino; 5% Race/ethnicity unknown; 2% international; 5% transferred in.

Freshmen *Admission:* 12,310 applied, 12,310 admitted, 5,576 enrolled. *Test scores:* SAT critical reading scores over 500: 38%; SAT math scores over 500: 38%; ACT scores over 18: 100%; SAT critical reading scores over 600: 6%; SAT math scores over 600: 4%; ACT scores over 24: 75%; SAT critical reading scores over 700: 2%; SAT math scores over 700: 2%; ACT scores over 30: 6%.

Faculty *Total:* 1,342, 40% full-time, 8% with terminal degrees. *Student/faculty ratio:* 18:1.

Majors Accounting; administrative assistant and secretarial science; agribusiness; agriculture; airline pilot and flight crew; art; autobody/collision and repair technology; automobile/automotive mechanics technology; aviation/airway management; baking and pastry arts; behavioral sciences; biology/biological sciences; biotechnology; business administration and management; business automation/technology/data entry; business/commerce; chemical process technology; chemical technology; chemistry; child development; clinical laboratory science/medical technology; clinical/medical laboratory technology; commercial and advertising art; computer and information sciences; construction engineering technology; cosmetology; cosmetology, barber/styling, and nail instruction; criminal justice/police science; culinary arts; dance; design and visual communications; diagnostic medical sonography and ultrasound technology; diesel mechanics technology;

digital communication and media/multimedia; drafting and design technology; dramatic/theater arts; education (multiple levels); electrical and power transmission installation; electrical, electronic and communications engineering technology; elementary education; emergency medical technology (EMT paramedic); engineering; engineering mechanics; English; environmental science; film/cinema/video studies; fire prevention and safety technology; fire science/firefighting; food preparation; food service systems administration; foreign languages and literatures; general studies; geology/earth science; health and physical education/fitness; health information/medical records technology; heating, air conditioning, ventilation and refrigeration maintenance technology; Hispanic-American, Puerto Rican, and Mexican-American/Chicano studies; history; institutional food workers; instrumentation technology; interior design; international business/trade/commerce; journalism; kindergarten/preschool education; legal assistant/paralegal; licensed practical/vocational nurse training; management information systems; marine science/merchant marine officer; mathematics; medical administrative assistant and medical secretary; mental health counseling; middle school education; multi/interdisciplinary studies related; music; occupational safety and health technology; optometric technician; philosophy; physical sciences; physical therapy technology; physics; political science and government; psychology; radio and television broadcasting technology; radiologic technology/science; real estate; registered nursing/registered nurse; respiratory care therapy; restaurant, culinary, and catering management; rhetoric and composition; science teacher education; secondary education; social sciences; sociology; speech communication and rhetoric; surgical technology; welding technology.

Academics *Calendar:* semesters. *Degree:* certificates and associate. *Special study options:* academic remediation for entering students, accelerated degree program, adult/continuing education programs, advanced placement credit, cooperative education, distance learning, double majors, English as a second language, honors programs, part-time degree program, services for LD students, student-designed majors, study abroad, summer session for credit. *ROTC:* Army (c), Air Force (c).

Library Lee Davis Library (C), Edwin E. Lehr (N), and Parker Williams (S) with an OPAC, a Web page.

Student Life *Housing:* college housing not available. *Activities and Organizations:* drama/theater group, student-run newspaper, choral group, Phi Theta Kappa honor society, Nurses Association, Student Government Association, ABG Radiography, Texas Student Education Association. *Campus security:* 24-hour emergency response devices and patrols, late-night transport/escort service.

Athletics Member NJCAA. *Intercollegiate sports:* baseball M(s), basketball M(s)/W(s), soccer M(s), softball W(s), volleyball W(s). *Intramural sports:* basketball M/W, football M/W, golf M/W, soccer M/W, softball M/W, table tennis M/W, weight lifting M/W.

Costs (2014–15) *Tuition:* area resident $1570 full-time, $43 per credit part-time; state resident $2800 full-time, $84 per credit part-time; nonresident $4300 full-time, $134 per credit part-time. Full-time tuition and fees vary according to course load. Part-time tuition and fees vary according to course load. *Required fees:* $280 full-time. *Payment plan:* installment. *Waivers:* senior citizens.

Applying *Options:* electronic application, early admission. *Required:* high school transcript. *Required for some:* interview. *Application deadlines:* rolling (freshmen), rolling (out-of-state freshmen), rolling (transfers). *Notification:* continuous (freshmen), continuous (out-of-state freshmen), continuous (transfers).

Freshman Application Contact San Jacinto College District, 4624 Fairmont Parkway, Pasadena, TX 77504-3323. *Phone:* 281-998-6150.
Website: http://www.sanjac.edu/.

South Plains College

Levelland, Texas

- **State and locally supported** 2-year, founded 1958
- **Small-town** 177-acre campus
- **Endowment** $3.0 million
- **Coed,** 9,444 undergraduate students, 46% full-time, 54% women, 46% men

Undergraduates 4,382 full-time, 5,062 part-time. Students come from 21 states and territories; 8 other countries; 4% are from out of state; 6% Black or African American, non-Hispanic/Latino; 38% Hispanic/Latino; 2% Asian, non-Hispanic/Latino; 0.3% Native Hawaiian or other Pacific Islander, non-Hispanic/Latino; 3% American Indian or Alaska Native, non-Hispanic/Latino; 0.7% international; 10% transferred in; 10% live on campus. *Retention:* 45% of full-time freshmen returned.

Freshmen *Admission:* 3,189 applied, 3,189 admitted, 1,384 enrolled.
Faculty *Total:* 454, 60% full-time. *Student/faculty ratio:* 20:1.
Majors Accounting; administrative assistant and secretarial science; advertising; agricultural economics; agriculture; agronomy and crop science;

art; automobile/automotive mechanics technology; biological and physical sciences; biology/biological sciences; business administration and management; carpentry; chemistry; child development; commercial and advertising art; computer engineering technology; computer programming; computer science; consumer merchandising/retailing management; cosmetology; criminal justice/law enforcement administration; criminal justice/police science; data processing and data processing technology; developmental and child psychology; dietetics; drafting and design technology; education; electrical, electronic and communications engineering technology; engineering; fashion merchandising; fire science/firefighting; health/health-care administration; health information/medical records administration; heating, air conditioning, ventilation and refrigeration maintenance technology; industrial radiologic technology; journalism; legal administrative assistant/secretary; liberal arts and sciences/liberal studies; licensed practical/vocational nurse training; machine tool technology; marketing/marketing management; mass communication/media; medical administrative assistant and medical secretary; mental health counseling; music; petroleum technology; physical education teaching and coaching; physical therapy; pre-engineering; real estate; recording arts technology; registered nursing/registered nurse; respiratory care therapy; social work; special products marketing; surgical technology; telecommunications technology; welding technology.

Academics *Calendar:* semesters. *Degree:* certificates and associate. *Special study options:* academic remediation for entering students, accelerated degree program, adult/continuing education programs, advanced placement credit, distance learning, double majors, internships, off-campus study, part-time degree program, services for LD students, study abroad, summer session for credit. *ROTC:* Army (c), Air Force (c).

Library South Plains College Library plus 1 other with 70,000 titles, 310 serial subscriptions, an OPAC.

Student Life *Housing:* on-campus residence required through sophomore year. *Options:* men-only, women-only. Campus housing is university owned. Freshman applicants given priority for college housing. *Activities and Organizations:* drama/theater group, student-run newspaper, radio and television station, choral group, student government, Phi Beta Kappa, Bleacher Bums, Law Enforcement Association. *Campus security:* 24-hour emergency response devices and patrols, controlled dormitory access. *Student services:* health clinic.

Athletics Member NJCAA. *Intercollegiate sports:* basketball M(s)/W(s), cross-country running M(s)/W(s), equestrian sports M(s)/W(s), track and field M(s)/W(s). *Intramural sports:* basketball M/W, cross-country running M/W, football M/W, golf M/W, racquetball M/W, softball M/W, table tennis M/W, tennis M/W, volleyball M/W.

Standardized Tests *Recommended:* ACT (for admission), SAT Subject Tests (for admission).

Costs (2013–14) *Tuition:* area resident $864 full-time, $36 per hour part-time; state resident $1329 full-time, $48 per hour part-time; nonresident $1776 full-time, $64 per hour part-time. *Required fees:* $1250 full-time. *Room and board:* $3100. *Payment plan:* installment.

Financial Aid Of all full-time matriculated undergraduates who enrolled in 2012, 80 Federal Work-Study jobs (averaging $2000). 22 state and other part-time jobs (averaging $2000).

Applying *Options:* electronic application, early admission. *Required:* high school transcript. *Application deadlines:* rolling (freshmen), rolling (out-of-state freshmen), rolling (transfers). *Notification:* continuous (freshmen), continuous (out-of-state freshmen), continuous (transfers).

Freshman Application Contact Mrs. Andrea Rangel, Dean of Admissions and Records, South Plains College, 1401 College Avenue, Levelland, TX 78336. *Phone:* 806-894-9611 Ext. 2370. *Fax:* 806-897-3167. *E-mail:* arangel@southplainscollege.edu.
Website: http://www.southplainscollege.edu/.

South Texas College

McAllen, Texas

Freshman Application Contact Mr. Matthew Hebbard, Director of Enrollment Services and Registrar, South Texas College, 3201 West Pecan, McAllen, TX 78501. *Phone:* 956-872-2147. *Toll-free phone:* 800-742-7822. *E-mail:* mshebbar@southtexascollege.edu.
Website: http://www.southtexascollege.edu/.

Southwest Institute of Technology

Austin, Texas

Freshman Application Contact Director of Admissions, Southwest Institute of Technology, 5424 Highway 290 West, Suite 200, Austin, TX 78735-8800. *Phone:* 512-892-2640. *Fax:* 512-892-1045.
Website: http://www.swse.net/.

Southwest Texas Junior College

Uvalde, Texas

Director of Admissions Dr. Blaine C. Bennett, Dean of Admissions and Student Services, Southwest Texas Junior College, 2401 Garner Field Road, Uvalde, TX 78801-6297. *Phone:* 830-278-4401 Ext. 7284. *Website:* http://www.swtjc.edu/.

Tarrant County College District

Fort Worth, Texas

- **County-supported** 2-year, founded 1967
- **Urban** 667-acre campus with easy access to Dallas-Fort Worth
- **Endowment** $5.8 million
- **Coed,** 50,439 undergraduate students, 35% full-time, 59% women, 41% men

Undergraduates 17,466 full-time, 32,973 part-time. 19% Black or African American, non-Hispanic/Latino; 26% Hispanic/Latino; 6% Asian, non-Hispanic/Latino; 0.2% Native Hawaiian or other Pacific Islander, non-Hispanic/Latino; 0.5% American Indian or Alaska Native, non-Hispanic/Latino; 1% Two or more races, non-Hispanic/Latino; 0.9% Race/ethnicity unknown; 0.8% international.

Freshmen *Admission:* 9,021 applied, 9,021 admitted, 9,021 enrolled.

Faculty *Total:* 1,870, 35% full-time. *Student/faculty ratio:* 29:1.

Majors Accounting; administrative assistant and secretarial science; architectural engineering technology; automobile/automotive mechanics technology; avionics maintenance technology; business administration and management; clinical laboratory science/medical technology; clinical/medical laboratory technology; computer programming; computer science; construction engineering technology; consumer merchandising/retailing management; criminal justice/law enforcement administration; dental hygiene; developmental and child psychology; dietetics; drafting and design technology; educational/instructional technology; electrical, electronic and communications engineering technology; electromechanical technology; emergency medical technology (EMT paramedic); fashion merchandising; fire science/firefighting; food technology and processing; graphic and printing equipment operation/production; health information/medical records administration; heating, air conditioning, ventilation and refrigeration maintenance technology; horticultural science; industrial radiologic technology; legal assistant/paralegal; liberal arts and sciences/liberal studies; machine tool technology; marketing/marketing management; mechanical engineering/mechanical technology; mental health counseling; physical therapy; quality control technology; registered nursing/registered nurse; respiratory care therapy; sign language interpretation and translation; surgical technology; welding technology.

Academics *Calendar:* semesters. *Degree:* certificates and associate. *Special study options:* academic remediation for entering students, adult/continuing education programs, advanced placement credit, distance learning, English as a second language, honors programs, part-time degree program, services for LD students, summer session for credit. *ROTC:* Army (c), Air Force (c).

Library 197,352 titles, 1,649 serial subscriptions, 18,833 audiovisual materials, an OPAC, a Web page.

Student Life *Housing:* college housing not available. *Activities and Organizations:* drama/theater group, student-run newspaper, choral group. *Campus security:* 24-hour emergency response devices and patrols, late-night transport/escort service. *Student services:* health clinic, personal/psychological counseling.

Athletics *Intramural sports:* football M, golf M, sailing M/W, table tennis M, tennis M/W, volleyball M/W.

Costs (2014–15) *Tuition:* area resident $1320 full-time, $55 per credit hour part-time; state resident $2064 full-time, $86 per credit hour part-time; nonresident $4920 full-time, $205 per credit hour part-time. Full-time tuition and fees vary according to course load and program. Part-time tuition and fees vary according to course load and program. *Payment plans:* installment, deferred payment. *Waivers:* senior citizens and employees or children of employees.

Financial Aid Of all full-time matriculated undergraduates who enrolled in 2012, 12,659 applied for aid, 10,824 were judged to have need. 41 Federal Work-Study jobs (averaging $1883). 17 state and other part-time jobs (averaging $2226). In 2012, 362 non-need-based awards were made. *Average need-based loan:* $3029. *Average need-based gift aid:* $4138. *Average non-need-based aid:* $1339.

Applying *Options:* electronic application. *Application deadlines:* rolling (freshmen), rolling (transfers).

Freshman Application Contact Mr. Vikas Rajpurohit, Assistant Director of Admissions Services, Tarrant County College District, 300 Trinity Campus Circle, Fort Worth, TX 76102-6599. *Phone:* 817-515-1581. *E-mail:* vikas.rajpurohit@tccd.edu. *Website:* http://www.tccd.edu/.

Temple College

Temple, Texas

- **District-supported** 2-year, founded 1926
- **Suburban** 106-acre campus with easy access to Austin
- **Endowment** $638,964
- **Coed,** 5,506 undergraduate students, 33% full-time, 65% women, 35% men

Undergraduates 1,821 full-time, 3,685 part-time. Students come from 24 states and territories; 6 other countries; 2% are from out of state; 20% Black or African American, non-Hispanic/Latino; 21% Hispanic/Latino; 2% Asian, non-Hispanic/Latino; 0.2% Native Hawaiian or other Pacific Islander, non-Hispanic/Latino;* 0.7% American Indian or Alaska Native, non-Hispanic/Latino; 3% Race/ethnicity unknown; 0.1% international; 6% transferred in.

Freshmen *Admission:* 671 enrolled.

Faculty *Total:* 289, 43% full-time, 15% with terminal degrees. *Student/faculty ratio:* 25:1.

Majors Administrative assistant and secretarial science; art; biology/biotechnology laboratory technician; business administration and management; computer and information sciences; computer programming; computer science; criminal justice/law enforcement administration; criminal justice/police science; data processing and data processing technology; dental hygiene; diagnostic medical sonography and ultrasound technology; drafting and design technology; emergency medical technology (EMT paramedic); liberal arts and sciences/liberal studies; licensed practical/vocational nurse training; registered nursing/registered nurse; respiratory care therapy; system, networking, and LAN/WAN management; web/multimedia management and webmaster.

Academics *Calendar:* semesters. *Degree:* certificates and associate. *Special study options:* academic remediation for entering students, adult/continuing education programs, advanced placement credit, cooperative education, distance learning, English as a second language, internships, off-campus study, part-time degree program, services for LD students, study abroad, summer session for credit.

Library Hubert Dawson Library with 58,907 titles, 271 serial subscriptions, 2,900 audiovisual materials, an OPAC, a Web page.

Student Life *Housing Options:* coed, special housing for students with disabilities. Campus housing is provided by a third party. *Activities and Organizations:* drama/theater group, choral group, Baptist Student Ministries, student government, Phi Theta Kappa, Delta Epsilon Chi, Nursing Student Organization. *Campus security:* 24-hour emergency response devices and patrols.

Athletics Member NJCAA. *Intercollegiate sports:* baseball M(s), basketball M(s)/W(s), softball W(s), tennis M(s)/W(s), volleyball W(s).

Costs (2013–14) *Tuition:* area resident $2640 full-time, $88 per semester hour part-time; state resident $4620 full-time, $154 per semester hour part-time; nonresident $7020 full-time, $330 per semester hour part-time. Full-time tuition and fees vary according to course load and program. Part-time tuition and fees vary according to course load and program. *Required fees:* $150 full-time, $24 per course part-time, $48 per term part-time. *Room and board:* $7696. *Payment plan:* installment. *Waivers:* employees or children of employees.

Financial Aid Of all full-time matriculated undergraduates who enrolled in 2009, 116 Federal Work-Study jobs (averaging $2007). 67 state and other part-time jobs (averaging $1119).

Applying *Options:* electronic application, early admission. *Required:* high school transcript. *Application deadlines:* rolling (freshmen), rolling (transfers).

Freshman Application Contact Ms. Carey Rose, Director of Admissions and Records, Temple College, 2600 South First Street, Temple, TX 76504. *Phone:* 254-298-8303. *Toll-free phone:* 800-460-4636. *E-mail:* carey.rose@templejc.edu. *Website:* http://www.templejc.edu/.

Texarkana College

Texarkana, Texas

- **State and locally supported** 2-year, founded 1927
- **Urban** 90-acre campus
- **Coed,** 4,111 undergraduate students, 39% full-time, 63% women, 37% men

Undergraduates 1,587 full-time, 2,524 part-time. Students come from 7 states and territories; 27% are from out of state; 23% Black or African American, non-Hispanic/Latino; 5% Hispanic/Latino; 1% Asian, non-Hispanic/Latino; 0.8% American Indian or Alaska Native, non-Hispanic/Latino; 3% Two or more races, non-Hispanic/Latino; 3% Race/ethnicity unknown; 1% live on campus.

Faculty *Total:* 172, 53% full-time. *Student/faculty ratio:* 21:1.

Majors Administrative assistant and secretarial science; agriculture; art; automobile/automotive mechanics technology; biology/biological sciences; business administration and management; business/commerce; chemistry; child-care and support services management; child development; computer and information sciences; cosmetology; criminal justice/law enforcement administration; criminal justice/safety; culinary arts; diesel mechanics technology; drafting and design technology; dramatic/theater arts; electrical, electronic and communications engineering technology; emergency medical technology (EMT paramedic); engineering; foreign languages and literatures; health aide; heating, air conditioning, ventilation and refrigeration maintenance technology; history; humanities; industrial mechanics and maintenance technology; journalism; liberal arts and sciences/liberal studies; licensed practical/vocational nurse training; marketing/marketing management; mathematics; music; pharmacy technician; physics; political science and government; real estate; registered nursing/registered nurse; social sciences; substance abuse/addiction counseling; welding technology.

Academics *Calendar:* semesters. *Degree:* certificates and associate. *Special study options:* academic remediation for entering students, adult/continuing education programs, advanced placement credit, cooperative education, honors programs, part-time degree program, services for LD students, summer session for credit.

Library Palmer Memorial Library with 46,700 titles, 646 serial subscriptions.

Student Life *Housing Options:* coed. Campus housing is university owned. *Activities and Organizations:* drama/theater group, student-run newspaper, radio station, choral group, Black Student Association, Earth Club, Culinary Arts Club, Cultural Awareness Student Association, Cosmetology Club. *Campus security:* 24-hour patrols. *Student services:* personal/psychological counseling.

Athletics Member NJCAA. *Intramural sports:* basketball M/W, football M/W, racquetball M/W, soccer M/W, tennis M/W, volleyball M/W.

Financial Aid Of all full-time matriculated undergraduates who enrolled in 2012, 30 Federal Work-Study jobs (averaging $3090).

Applying *Options:* electronic application, early admission, deferred entrance. *Required:* high school transcript. *Recommended:* Interview recommended for nursing program. Must have meningitis vaccine before student can start. *Application deadlines:* rolling (freshmen), rolling (transfers).

Freshman Application Contact Mr. Lee Williams, Director of Admissions, Texarkana College, 2500 North Robison Road, Texarkana, TX 75599-0001. *Phone:* 903-823-3016. *Fax:* 903-823-3451. *E-mail:* lee.williams@texarkanacollege.edu. *Website:* http://www.texarkanacollege.edu/.

Texas School of Business, Friendswood Campus

Friendswood, Texas

Freshman Application Contact Admissions Office, Texas School of Business, Friendswood Campus, 3208 Farm to Market Road 528, Friendswood, TX 77546. *Website:* http://www.friendswood.tsb.edu/.

Texas School of Business, Houston North Campus

Houston, Texas

Freshman Application Contact Admissions Office, Texas School of Business, Houston North Campus, 711 East Airtex Drive, Houston, TX 77073. *Phone:* 281-443-8900. *Website:* http://www.north.tsb.edu/.

Texas Southmost College

Brownsville, Texas

Freshman Application Contact New Student Relations, Texas Southmost College, 80 Fort Brown, Brownsville, TX 78520-4991. *Phone:* 956-882-8860. *Toll-free phone:* 877-882-8721. *Fax:* 956-882-8959. *Website:* http://www.utb.edu/.

Texas State Technical College Harlingen

Harlingen, Texas

- **State-supported** 2-year, founded 1967, part of Texas State Technical College System
- **Small-town** 125-acre campus
- **Coed**

Undergraduates 2,361 full-time, 3,148 part-time. Students come from 18 states and territories; 2 other countries; 0.4% are from out of state; 0.7% Black or African American, non-Hispanic/Latino; 88% Hispanic/Latino; 0.6% Asian, non-Hispanic/Latino; 0.1% Native Hawaiian or other Pacific Islander, non-Hispanic/Latino; 0.1% American Indian or Alaska Native, non-

Hispanic/Latino; 1% Two or more races, non-Hispanic/Latino; 1% Race/ethnicity unknown; 0.1% international; 6% transferred in; 5% live on campus.

Faculty *Student/faculty ratio:* 19:1.

Academics *Calendar:* semesters. *Degree:* certificates and associate. *Special study options:* academic remediation for entering students, adult/continuing education programs, cooperative education, distance learning, double majors, English as a second language, internships, part-time degree program, services for LD students, summer session for credit.

Student Life *Campus security:* 24-hour emergency response devices and patrols, late-night transport/escort service, night watchman for housing area.

Financial Aid Of all full-time matriculated undergraduates who enrolled in 2012, 850 applied for aid, 827 were judged to have need, 568 had their need fully met. 144 Federal Work-Study jobs (averaging $2159). 31 state and other part-time jobs (averaging $3689). In 2012, 1. *Average percent of need met:* 85. *Average financial aid package:* $6056. *Average need-based gift aid:* $5497. *Average non-need-based aid:* $2500.

Applying *Options:* electronic application, early admission, deferred entrance. *Required:* high school transcript.

Freshman Application Contact Texas State Technical College Harlingen, 1902 North Loop 499, Harlingen, TX 78550-3697. *Phone:* 956-364-4100. *Toll-free phone:* 800-852-8784. *Website:* http://www.harlingen.tstc.edu/.

Texas State Technical College–Marshall

Marshall, Texas

Director of Admissions Pat Robbins, Registrar, Texas State Technical College–Marshall, 2650 East End Boulevard South, Marshall, TX 75671. *Phone:* 903-935-1010. *Toll-free phone:* 888-382-8782. *Fax:* 903-923-3282. *E-mail:* Pat.Robbins@marshall.tstc.edu. *Website:* http://www.marshall.tstc.edu/.

Texas State Technical College Waco

Waco, Texas

- **State-supported** 2-year, founded 1965, part of Texas State Technical College System
- **Suburban** 200-acre campus
- **Coed**, 7,269 undergraduate students, 74% full-time, 21% women, 79% men

Undergraduates 5,357 full-time, 1,912 part-time. 1% are from out of state; 14% Black or African American, non-Hispanic/Latino; 20% Hispanic/Latino; 0.9% Asian, non-Hispanic/Latino; 0.2% Native Hawaiian or other Pacific Islander, non-Hispanic/Latino; 0.5% American Indian or Alaska Native, non-Hispanic/Latino; 0.2% Two or more races, non-Hispanic/Latino; 4% Race/ethnicity unknown; 0.1% international; 16% transferred in. *Retention:* 48% of full-time freshmen returned.

Freshmen *Admission:* 819 applied, 819 admitted, 819 enrolled.

Faculty *Total:* 283, 89% full-time, 3% with terminal degrees. *Student/faculty ratio:* 17:1.

Majors Aircraft powerplant technology; airframe mechanics and aircraft maintenance technology; airline pilot and flight crew; air traffic control; autobody/collision and repair technology; automobile/automotive mechanics technology; avionics maintenance technology; biomedical technology; chemical technology; computer and information systems security; computer programming; computer technology/computer systems technology; construction trades; culinary arts; diesel mechanics technology; drafting and design technology; educational/instructional technology; electrical, electronic and communications engineering technology; electromechanical technology; environmental engineering technology; game and interactive media design; graphic design; heating, ventilation, air conditioning and refrigeration engineering technology; instrumentation technology; laser and optical technology; manufacturing engineering technology; mechanical engineering/mechanical technology; network and system administration; nuclear/nuclear power technology; occupational safety and health technology; robotics technology; solar energy technology; surveying technology; system, networking, and LAN/WAN management; telecommunications technology; turf and turfgrass management; viticulture and enology; web page, digital/multimedia and information resources design.

Academics *Calendar:* trimesters. *Degree:* certificates and associate. *Special study options:* academic remediation for entering students, adult/continuing education programs, cooperative education, distance learning, internships, part-time degree program, services for LD students, summer session for credit.

Library Texas State Technical College-Waco Campus Library with 52,296 titles, 235,477 serial subscriptions, 5,335 audiovisual materials, an OPAC, a Web page.

Student Life *Housing:* on-campus residence required for freshman year. *Options:* coed, men-only, women-only, special housing for students with disabilities. Campus housing is university owned. *Activities and Organizations:* Student Ambassador Association, SkillsUSA, Student

Leadership Council, Phi Theta Kappa, Hispanic Student Association. *Campus security:* 24-hour emergency response devices and patrols, late-night transport/escort service, controlled dormitory access. *Student services:* health clinic, personal/psychological counseling, women's center.

Athletics *Intramural sports:* basketball M/W, football M, golf M/W, racquetball M/W, softball M/W, volleyball M/W, weight lifting M.

Standardized Tests *Required:* Texas Success Initiative assessment (for admission).

Costs (2013–14) *Tuition:* state resident $2238 full-time, $93 per credit hour part-time; nonresident $6096 full-time, $254 per credit hour part-time. Full-time tuition and fees vary according to course load. Part-time tuition and fees vary according to course load. *Required fees:* $1104 full-time, $1104 per year part-time. *Room and board:* room only: $2440. Room and board charges vary according to board plan, housing facility, and location. *Payment plan:* installment. *Waivers:* employees or children of employees.

Applying *Options:* electronic application, early admission. *Required:* high school transcript. *Required for some:* interview. *Application deadlines:* rolling (freshmen), rolling (transfers). *Notification:* continuous (freshmen), continuous (transfers).

Freshman Application Contact Ms. Mary Daniel, Registrar/Director of Admission and Records, Texas State Technical College Waco, 3801 Campus Drive, Waco, TX 76705. *Phone:* 254-867-3363. *Toll-free phone:* 800-792-8784 Ext. 2362. *E-mail:* mary.daniel@tstc.edu.
Website: http://waco.tstc.edu/.

Texas State Technical College West Texas

Sweetwater, Texas

Freshman Application Contact Ms. Maria Aguirre-Acuna, Texas State Technical College West Texas, 300 Homer K Taylor Drive, Sweetwater, TX 79556-4108. *Phone:* 325-235-7349. *Toll-free phone:* 800-592-8784. *Fax:* 325-235-7443. *E-mail:* maria.aquirre@sweetwater.tstc.edu.
Website: http://www.westtexas.tstc.edu/.

Trinity Valley Community College

Athens, Texas

- **State and locally supported** 2-year, founded 1946
- **Rural** 65-acre campus with easy access to Dallas-Fort Worth
- **Coed,** 5,172 undergraduate students, 52% full-time, 62% women, 52% men

Undergraduates 2,685 full-time, 3,194 part-time. Students come from 28 states and territories; 15 other countries; 1% are from out of state; 17% Black or African American, non-Hispanic/Latino; 7% Hispanic/Latino; 0.4% Asian, non-Hispanic/Latino; 0.4% American Indian or Alaska Native, non-Hispanic/Latino; 11% Two or more races, non-Hispanic/Latino; 2% Race/ethnicity unknown; 0.3% international; 14% live on campus.

Freshmen *Admission:* 1,320 enrolled.

Faculty *Total:* 277, 56% full-time, 3% with terminal degrees. *Student/faculty ratio:* 16:1.

Majors Accounting; agricultural teacher education; animal sciences; art; automobile/automotive mechanics technology; biology/biological sciences; business administration and management; business teacher education; chemistry; child development; commercial photography; computer science; corrections; cosmetology; criminal justice/law enforcement administration; criminal justice/police science; dance; data processing and data processing technology; developmental and child psychology; drafting and design technology; dramatic/theater arts; education; elementary education; emergency medical technology (EMT paramedic); English; farm and ranch management; fashion merchandising; finance; geology/earth science; heating, air conditioning, ventilation and refrigeration maintenance technology; history; horticultural science; insurance; journalism; kindergarten/preschool education; legal administrative assistant/secretary; liberal arts and sciences/liberal studies; licensed practical/vocational nurse training; marketing/marketing management; mathematics; music; physical education teaching and coaching; physical sciences; political science and government; pre-engineering; psychology; range science and management; real estate; registered nursing/registered nurse; religious studies; rhetoric and composition; sociology; Spanish; surgical technology; welding technology.

Academics *Calendar:* semesters. *Degree:* certificates, diplomas, and associate. *Special study options:* academic remediation for entering students, adult/continuing education programs, advanced placement credit, cooperative education, distance learning, double majors, English as a second language, honors programs, independent study, internships, part-time degree program, services for LD students, summer session for credit.

Library Ginger Murchison Learning Resource Center plus 3 others with 62,045 titles, 655 serial subscriptions, 4,530 audiovisual materials, an OPAC, a Web page.

Student Life *Housing Options:* coed, men-only, women-only. Campus housing is university owned. *Activities and Organizations:* drama/theater group, student-run newspaper, choral group, marching band, Student Senate, Phi Theta Kappa, Delta Epsilon Chi. *Campus security:* 24-hour emergency response devices and patrols, controlled dormitory access. *Student services:* personal/psychological counseling.

Athletics Member NJCAA. *Intercollegiate sports:* basketball M(s)/W(s), cheerleading M(s)/W(s), football M(s), softball W(s), volleyball W(s). *Intramural sports:* baseball M/W, basketball M/W, football M, table tennis M/W, volleyball M/W.

Costs (2014–15) *Tuition:* area resident $2160 full-time, $30 per semester hour part-time; state resident $3600 full-time, $78 per semester hour part-time; nonresident $4440 full-time, $106 per semester hour part-time. Full-time tuition and fees vary according to course load. Part-time tuition and fees vary according to course load. *Required fees:* $42 per semester hour part-time. *Room and board:* $8880. Room and board charges vary according to board plan. *Payment plan:* installment. *Waivers:* employees or children of employees.

Financial Aid Of all full-time matriculated undergraduates who enrolled in 2012, 80 Federal Work-Study jobs (averaging $1544). 40 state and other part-time jobs (averaging $1544).

Applying *Options:* electronic application, early admission. *Required:* high school transcript. *Application deadlines:* rolling (freshmen), rolling (transfers). *Notification:* continuous (freshmen), continuous (transfers).

Freshman Application Contact Dr. Colette Hilliard, Dean of Enrollment Management and Registrar, Trinity Valley Community College, 100 Cardinal Drive, Athens, TX 75751. *Phone:* 903-675-6209 Ext. 209.
Website: http://www.tvcc.edu/.

Tyler Junior College

Tyler, Texas

- **State and locally supported** 2-year, founded 1926
- **Suburban** 85-acre campus
- **Coed,** 11,308 undergraduate students, 55% full-time, 58% women, 42% men

Undergraduates 6,200 full-time, 5,108 part-time. Students come from 39 other countries; 2% are from out of state; 22% Black or African American, non-Hispanic/Latino; 14% Hispanic/Latino; 2% Asian, non-Hispanic/Latino; 0.1% Native Hawaiian or other Pacific Islander, non-Hispanic/Latino; 0.6% American Indian or Alaska Native, non-Hispanic/Latino; 2% Two or more races, non-Hispanic/Latino; 1% Race/ethnicity unknown; 0.7% international; 7% transferred in; 8% live on campus. *Retention:* 48% of full-time freshmen returned.

Freshmen *Admission:* 2,452 applied, 2,452 admitted, 2,958 enrolled.

Faculty *Total:* 505, 58% full-time, 15% with terminal degrees. *Student/faculty ratio:* 22:1.

Majors Accounting; administrative assistant and secretarial science; art; automobile/automotive mechanics technology; behavioral sciences; biology/biological sciences; business administration and management; chemistry; child development; clinical/medical laboratory technology; commercial and advertising art; computer and information sciences; computer and information sciences related; computer engineering technology; computer graphics; computer programming related; computer science; computer systems networking and telecommunications; criminal justice/law enforcement administration; criminal justice/police science; dance; data entry/microcomputer applications; dental hygiene; dramatic/theater arts; economics; emergency medical technology (EMT paramedic); engineering; environmental science; family and consumer sciences/human sciences; fire science/firefighting; geology/earth science; health/health-care administration; health information/medical records technology; industrial radiologic technology; information technology; legal administrative assistant/secretary; liberal arts and sciences/liberal studies; licensed practical/vocational nurse training; mathematics; medical administrative assistant and medical secretary; modern languages; optometric technician; photography; physical education teaching and coaching; physics; political science and government; psychology; registered nursing/registered nurse; respiratory care therapy; sign language interpretation and translation; social sciences; speech communication and rhetoric; substance abuse/addiction counseling; surgical technology; surveying technology; welding technology.

Academics *Calendar:* semesters. *Degree:* certificates, diplomas, and associate. *Special study options:* academic remediation for entering students, accelerated degree program, adult/continuing education programs, advanced placement credit, distance learning, English as a second language, freshman honors college, honors programs, part-time degree program, services for LD students, summer session for credit.

Library Vaughn Library and Learning Resource Center with an OPAC.

Student Life *Housing Options:* coed, men-only, women-only. Campus housing is university owned. *Activities and Organizations:* drama/theater group, student-run newspaper, choral group, marching band, student government, religious affiliation clubs, Phi Theta Kappa, national fraternities, national sororities. *Campus security:* 24-hour emergency response devices and patrols, controlled dormitory access. *Student services:* health clinic, personal/psychological counseling.

Athletics Member NJCAA. *Intercollegiate sports:* baseball M, basketball M(s)/W(s), football M(s), golf M/W, soccer M(s)/W(s), tennis M(s)/W(s), volleyball W(s). *Intramural sports:* basketball M/W, racquetball M/W, volleyball M/W, weight lifting M/W.

Costs (2014–15) *Tuition:* area resident $900 full-time, $30 per credit hour part-time; state resident $2310 full-time, $77 per credit hour part-time; nonresident $2910 full-time, $97 per credit hour part-time. *Required fees:* $1452 full-time. *Room and board:* $7200. Room and board charges vary according to housing facility. *Payment plan:* installment. *Waivers:* employees or children of employees.

Financial Aid Of all full-time matriculated undergraduates who enrolled in 2012, 4,750 applied for aid, 4,214 were judged to have need, 61 had their need fully met. In 2012, 793 non-need-based awards were made. *Average percent of need met:* 63%. *Average financial aid package:* $3714. *Average need-based loan:* $1299. *Average need-based gift aid:* $2426. *Average non-need-based aid:* $804.

Applying *Options:* electronic application, early admission. *Required:* high school transcript. *Application deadlines:* rolling (freshmen), rolling (transfers). *Notification:* continuous (freshmen), continuous (transfers).

Freshman Application Contact Ms. Janna Chancey, Director of Enrollment Management, Tyler Junior College, PO Box 9020, Tyler, TX 75711-9020. *Phone:* 903-510-3325. *Toll-free phone:* 800-687-5680. *E-mail:* jcha@tjc.edu. *Website:* http://www.tjc.edu/.

Universal Technical Institute
Houston, Texas

Director of Admissions Director of Admissions, Universal Technical Institute, 721 Lockhaven Drive, Houston, TX 77073-5598. *Phone:* 281-443-6262. *Toll-free phone:* 800-510-5072. *Fax:* 281-443-0610. *Website:* http://www.uti.edu/.

Vernon College
Vernon, Texas

Director of Admissions Mr. Joe Hite, Dean of Admissions/Registrar, Vernon College, 4400 College Drive, Vernon, TX 76384-4092. *Phone:* 940-552-6291 Ext. 2204. *Website:* http://www.vernoncollege.edu/.

Vet Tech Institute of Houston
Houston, Texas

- **Private** 2-year, founded 1958
- **Suburban** campus
- **Coed,** 256 undergraduate students
- 62% of applicants were admitted

Freshmen *Admission:* 553 applied, 344 admitted.
Majors Veterinary/animal health technology.
Academics *Degree:* associate. *Special study options:* accelerated degree program, internships.
Student Life *Housing:* college housing not available.
Freshman Application Contact Admissions Office, Vet Tech Institute of Houston, 4669 Southwest Freeway, Suite 100, Houston, TX 77027. *Phone:* 800-275-2736. *Toll-free phone:* 800-275-2736. *Website:* http://houston.vettechinstitute.edu/.

Victoria College
Victoria, Texas

- **County-supported** 2-year, founded 1925
- **Urban** 80-acre campus
- **Endowment** $2.3 million
- **Coed,** 4,419 undergraduate students, 31% full-time, 66% women, 34% men

Undergraduates 1,385 full-time, 3,034 part-time. Students come from 14 states and territories; 14 other countries; 0.4% are from out of state; 5% Black or African American, non-Hispanic/Latino; 42% Hispanic/Latino; 2% Asian, non-Hispanic/Latino; 0.1% Native Hawaiian or other Pacific Islander, non-Hispanic/Latino; 0.4% American Indian or Alaska Native, non-Hispanic/Latino; 1% Two or more races, non-Hispanic/Latino; 0.5% Race/ethnicity unknown; 59% transferred in.
Freshmen *Admission:* 1,885 applied, 1,885 admitted, 680 enrolled.
Faculty *Total:* 250, 38% full-time. *Student/faculty ratio:* 17:1.
Majors Accounting; administrative assistant and secretarial science; business administration and management; clinical/medical laboratory technology; computer programming; computer systems networking and telecommunications; criminal justice/police science; drafting and design technology; electrical, electronic and communications engineering technology; emergency medical technology (EMT paramedic); industrial technology; information science/studies; legal assistant/paralegal; liberal arts and sciences/liberal studies; registered nursing/registered nurse; respiratory care therapy.

Academics *Calendar:* semesters. *Degree:* certificates and associate. *Special study options:* academic remediation for entering students, adult/continuing education programs, distance learning, off-campus study, part-time degree program, services for LD students, summer session for credit.
Library Victoria College Library with 150,000 titles, 1,500 serial subscriptions.
Student Life *Housing:* college housing not available. *Activities and Organizations:* drama/theater group, choral group, Student Senate. *Campus security:* 24-hour emergency response devices. *Student services:* personal/psychological counseling.
Athletics *Intramural sports:* basketball M/W, tennis M/W, volleyball W.
Costs (2013–14) *Tuition:* area resident $1380 full-time, $46 per credit hour part-time; state resident $2790 full-time, $93 per credit hour part-time; nonresident $3390 full-time, $113 per credit hour part-time. *Required fees:* $37 per credit hour part-time. *Payment plan:* installment. *Waivers:* employees or children of employees.
Applying *Options:* electronic application. *Required:* high school transcript. *Application deadlines:* rolling (freshmen), rolling (transfers).
Freshman Application Contact Missy Klimitchek, Registrar, Victoria College, 2200 E Red River, Victoria, TX 77901. *Phone:* 361-573-3291 Ext. 6407. *Toll-free phone:* 877-843-4369. *Fax:* 361-582-2525. *E-mail:* registrar@victoriacollege.eduregistrar@victoriacollege.eduregistrar@victoriacollege.edu. *Website:* http://www.victoriacollege.edu/.

Virginia College in Austin
Austin, Texas

Admissions Office Contact Virginia College in Austin, 6301 East Highway 290, Austin, TX 78723. *Website:* http://www.vc.edu/.

Wade College
Dallas, Texas

Freshman Application Contact Wade College, INFOMart, 1950 Stemmons Freeway, Suite 4080, LB 562, Dallas, TX 75207. *Phone:* 214-637-3530. *Toll-free phone:* 800-624-4850. *Website:* http://www.wadecollege.edu/.

Weatherford College
Weatherford, Texas

Freshman Application Contact Mr. Ralph Willingham, Director of Admissions, Weatherford College, 225 College Park Drive, Weatherford, TX 76086-5699. *Phone:* 817-598-6248. *Toll-free phone:* 800-287-5471. *Fax:* 817-598-6205. *E-mail:* willingham@wc.edu. *Website:* http://www.wc.edu/.

Western Technical College
El Paso, Texas

Freshman Application Contact Laura Pena, Director of Admissions, Western Technical College, 9451 Diana, El Paso, TX 79930-2610. *Phone:* 915-566-9621. *Toll-free phone:* 800-201-9232. *E-mail:* lpena@westerntech.edu. *Website:* http://www.westerntech.edu/.

Western Technical College
El Paso, Texas

Freshman Application Contact Mr. Bill Terrell, Chief Admissions Officer, Western Technical College, 9624 Plaza Circle, El Paso, TX 79927. *Phone:* 915-532-3737 Ext. 117. *Fax:* 915-532-6946. *E-mail:* bterrell@wtc-ep.edu. *Website:* http://www.westerntech.edu/.

Western Texas College
Snyder, Texas

- **State and locally supported** 2-year, founded 1969
- **Small-town** 165-acre campus
- **Coed,** 2,473 undergraduate students, 28% full-time, 50% women, 50% men

Undergraduates 702 full-time, 1,771 part-time. Students come from 22 other countries; 5% are from out of state. *Retention:* 50% of full-time freshmen returned.
Freshmen *Admission:* 1,511 enrolled.

Faculty *Total:* 82, 55% full-time, 9% with terminal degrees. *Student/faculty ratio:* 21:1.

Majors Accounting; administrative assistant and secretarial science; agricultural teacher education; agriculture; art; art teacher education; automobile/automotive mechanics technology; business administration and management; computer engineering technology; computer science; corrections; criminal justice/law enforcement administration; criminal justice/police science; education; journalism; landscape architecture; liberal arts and sciences/liberal studies; licensed practical/vocational nurse training; marketing/marketing management; mass communication/media; parks, recreation and leisure facilities management; welding technology.

Academics *Calendar:* semesters. *Degree:* certificates and associate. *Special study options:* academic remediation for entering students, adult/continuing education programs, advanced placement credit, internships, part-time degree program, services for LD students, student-designed majors, summer session for credit.

Library Western Texas College Resource Center with an OPAC, a Web page.

Student Life *Housing:* on-campus residence required for freshman year. *Options:* coed. Campus housing is university owned. *Activities and Organizations:* drama/theater group, student-run newspaper, radio station, choral group. *Campus security:* 24-hour emergency response devices and patrols. *Student services:* personal/psychological counseling.

Athletics Member NJCAA. *Intercollegiate sports:* baseball M, basketball M/W, cross-country running M/W, golf M/W, soccer M/W, softball W, track and field M/W, volleyball W. *Intramural sports:* basketball M/W, bowling M/W, football M, racquetball M/W, soccer M, softball M/W, swimming and diving M/W, tennis M/W, volleyball M/W, weight lifting M/W.

Costs (2014–15) *Tuition:* area resident $2370 full-time; state resident $3240 full-time; nonresident $4350 full-time. *Required fees:* $400 full-time. *Room and board:* $2550.

Financial Aid Of all full-time matriculated undergraduates who enrolled in 2012, 19 Federal Work-Study jobs (averaging $1600).

Applying *Options:* early admission, deferred entrance. *Required:* high school transcript. *Application deadlines:* rolling (freshmen), rolling (transfers). *Notification:* continuous (freshmen), continuous (transfers).

Freshman Application Contact Western Texas College, 6200 College Avenue, Snyder, TX 79549. *Phone:* 325-573-8511 Ext. 204. *Toll-free phone:* 888-GO-TO-WTC.

Website: http://www.wtc.edu/.

Wharton County Junior College

Wharton, Texas

Freshman Application Contact Mr. Albert Barnes, Dean of Admissions and Registration, Wharton County Junior College, 911 Boling Highway, Wharton, TX 77488-3298. *Phone:* 979-532-6381. *E-mail:* albertb@wcjc.edu.

Website: http://www.wcjc.edu/.

UTAH

AmeriTech College

Draper, Utah

Admissions Office Contact AmeriTech College, 12257 South Business Park Drive, Suite 108, Draper, UT 84020-6545.

Website: http://www.ameritech.edu/.

Everest College

West Valley City, Utah

Director of Admissions Director of Admissions, Everest College, 3280 West 3500 South, West Valley City, UT 84119. *Phone:* 801-840-4800. *Toll-free phone:* 888-741-4270. *Fax:* 801-969-0828.

Website: http://www.everest.edu/.

ITT Technical Institute

Murray, Utah

- **Proprietary** primarily 2-year, founded 1984, part of ITT Educational Services, Inc.
- **Suburban** campus
- **Coed**

Majors Accounting; business administration and management; computer programming (specific applications); construction management;

cyber/computer forensics and counterterrorism; drafting and design technology; electrical, electronic and communications engineering technology; forensic science and technology; graphic communications; industrial technology; information technology project management; network and system administration; project management.

Academics *Calendar:* quarters. *Degrees:* associate and bachelor's.

Student Life *Housing:* college housing not available.

Freshman Application Contact Director of Recruitment, ITT Technical Institute, 920 West Levoy Drive, Murray, UT 84123-2500. *Phone:* 801-263-3313. *Toll-free phone:* 800-365-2136.

Website: http://www.itt-tech.edu/.

LDS Business College

Salt Lake City, Utah

- **Independent** 2-year, founded 1886, affiliated with The Church of Jesus Christ of Latter-day Saints, part of Latter-day Saints Church Educational System
- **Urban** 2-acre campus with easy access to Salt Lake City
- **Coed**, 2,191 undergraduate students, 73% full-time, 47% women, 53% men

Undergraduates 1,589 full-time, 602 part-time. Students come from 60 other countries; 45% are from out of state; 0.2% Black or African American, non-Hispanic/Latino; 11% Hispanic/Latino; 1% Asian, non-Hispanic/Latino; 2% Native Hawaiian or other Pacific Islander, non-Hispanic/Latino; 0.5% American Indian or Alaska Native, non-Hispanic/Latino; 4% Two or more races, non-Hispanic/Latino; 3% Race/ethnicity unknown; 13% international; 34% transferred in. *Retention:* 48% of full-time freshmen returned.

Freshmen *Admission:* 878 applied, 820 admitted, 604 enrolled.

Faculty *Total:* 142, 10% full-time, 66% with terminal degrees. *Student/faculty ratio:* 25:1.

Majors Accounting; accounting and business/management; accounting technology and bookkeeping; administrative assistant and secretarial science; business administration and management; entrepreneurship; health information/medical records administration; information technology; interior design; liberal arts and sciences/liberal studies; medical administrative assistant and medical secretary; medical/clinical assistant; medical office assistant; system, networking, and LAN/WAN management; web page, digital/multimedia and information resources design.

Academics *Calendar:* semesters. *Degree:* certificates and associate. *Special study options:* academic remediation for entering students, adult/continuing education programs, advanced placement credit, internships, part-time degree program, services for LD students, summer session for credit. *ROTC:* Army (c), Air Force (c).

Library LDS Business College Library with 115,920 titles, 121 serial subscriptions, 1,128 audiovisual materials, an OPAC, a Web page.

Student Life *Housing:* college housing not available. *Activities and Organizations:* drama/theater group, choral group. *Campus security:* 24-hour emergency response devices and patrols.

Standardized Tests *Recommended:* SAT or ACT (for admission).

Costs (2014–15) *Tuition:* $3060 full-time, $128 per credit part-time. Full-time tuition and fees vary according to course load. Part-time tuition and fees vary according to course load. *Payment plan:* deferred payment. *Waivers:* employees or children of employees.

Applying *Options:* electronic application, deferred entrance. *Application fee:* $35. *Required:* essay or personal statement, high school transcript, interview. *Application deadlines:* rolling (freshmen), rolling (out-of-state freshmen), rolling (transfers). *Notification:* continuous (freshmen), continuous (out-of-state freshmen), continuous (transfers).

Freshman Application Contact Miss Dawn Fellows, Assistant Director of Admissions, LDS Business College, 95 North 300 West, Salt Lake City, UT 84101-3500. *Phone:* 801-524-8146. *Toll-free phone:* 800-999-5767. *Fax:* 801-524-1900. *E-mail:* DFellows@ldsbc.edu.

Website: http://www.ldsbc.edu/.

Provo College

Provo, Utah

Director of Admissions Mr. Gordon Peters, College Director, Provo College, 1450 West 820 North, Provo, UT 84601. *Phone:* 801-375-1861. *Toll-free phone:* 877-777-5886. *Fax:* 801-375-9728. *E-mail:* gordonp@provocollege.org.

Website: http://www.provocollege.edu/.

Salt Lake Community College

Salt Lake City, Utah

- **State-supported** 2-year, founded 1948, part of Utah System of Higher Education
- **Urban** 114-acre campus with easy access to Salt Lake City
- **Endowment** $826,231
- **Coed,** 31,137 undergraduate students, 28% full-time, 52% women, 48% men

Undergraduates 8,634 full-time, 22,503 part-time. 2% Black or African American, non-Hispanic/Latino; 14% Hispanic/Latino; 4% Asian, non-Hispanic/Latino; 1% Native Hawaiian or other Pacific Islander, non-Hispanic/Latino; 0.8% American Indian or Alaska Native, non-Hispanic/Latino; 2% Two or more races, non-Hispanic/Latino; 9% Race/ethnicity unknown; 1% international; 4% transferred in.

Freshmen *Admission:* 2,928 applied, 2,928 admitted, 2,928 enrolled.

Faculty *Total:* 1,483, 23% full-time. *Student/faculty ratio:* 21:1.

Majors Accounting technology and bookkeeping; airline pilot and flight crew; architectural engineering technology; autobody/collision and repair technology; avionics maintenance technology; biology/biological sciences; biology/biotechnology laboratory technician; building/construction finishing, management, and inspection related; business administration and management; chemistry; clinical/medical laboratory technology; computer and information sciences; computer science; cosmetology; criminal justice/law enforcement administration; culinary arts; dental hygiene; design and visual communications; diesel mechanics technology; drafting and design technology; economics; electrical, electronic and communications engineering technology; engineering; engineering technology; English; entrepreneurship; environmental engineering technology; finance; general studies; geology/earth science; graphic design; health professions related; heating, air conditioning, ventilation and refrigeration maintenance technology; history; human development and family studies; humanities; industrial radiologic technology; information science/studies; information technology; instrumentation technology; international/global studies; international relations and affairs; kinesiology and exercise science; legal assistant/paralegal; marketing/marketing management; mass communication/media; medical/clinical assistant; medical radiologic technology; music; occupational therapist assistant; photographic and film/video technology; physical sciences; physical therapy technology; physics; political science and government; psychology; public health related; quality control technology; radio and television broadcasting technology; registered nursing/registered nurse; sign language interpretation and translation; social work; sociology; speech communication and rhetoric; sport and fitness administration/management; surveying technology; teacher assistant/aide; telecommunications technology; welding technology.

Academics *Calendar:* semesters. *Degree:* certificates, diplomas, and associate. *Special study options:* academic remediation for entering students, advanced placement credit, cooperative education, distance learning, double majors, English as a second language, internships, part-time degree program, services for LD students, student-designed majors, study abroad, summer session for credit. *ROTC:* Army (c), Air Force (c).

Library Markosian Library plus 2 others with 152,537 titles, 21,736 serial subscriptions, 20,645 audiovisual materials, an OPAC, a Web page.

Student Life *Housing:* college housing not available. *Activities and Organizations:* drama/theater group, student-run newspaper, radio and television station, choral group, marching band. *Campus security:* 24-hour emergency response devices and patrols, late-night transport/escort service. *Student services:* health clinic, personal/psychological counseling.

Athletics Member NJCAA. *Intercollegiate sports:* baseball M(s), basketball M(s)/W(s), cheerleading M(s)/W(s), soccer M(c)/W(c), softball W(s), volleyball W(s).

Costs (2013–14) *Tuition:* state resident $2924 full-time, $122 per credit hour part-time; nonresident $10,176 full-time, $424 per credit hour part-time. *Required fees:* $418 full-time. *Payment plan:* installment. *Waivers:* senior citizens and employees or children of employees.

Financial Aid Of all full-time matriculated undergraduates who enrolled in 2012, 132 Federal Work-Study jobs (averaging $2567).

Applying *Options:* electronic application, early admission. *Application fee:* $40. *Application deadlines:* rolling (freshmen), rolling (transfers).

Freshman Application Contact Ms. Kathy Thompson, Salt Lake Community College, Salt Lake City, UT 84130. *Phone:* 801-957-4485. *E-mail:* kathy.thompson@slcc.edu.

Website: http://www.slcc.edu/.

Snow College

Ephraim, Utah

- **State-supported** 2-year, founded 1888, part of Utah System of Higher Education
- **Rural** 50-acre campus
- **Endowment** $6.2 million
- **Coed,** 4,605 undergraduate students, 61% full-time, 56% women, 44% men

Undergraduates 2,813 full-time, 1,792 part-time. Students come from 24 other countries; 6% are from out of state; 1% Black or African American, non-Hispanic/Latino; 4% Hispanic/Latino; 0.7% Asian, non-Hispanic/Latino; 2% Native Hawaiian or other Pacific Islander, non-Hispanic/Latino; 2% American Indian or Alaska Native, non-Hispanic/Latino; 1% Two or more races, non-Hispanic/Latino; 1% Race/ethnicity unknown; 3% international; 2% transferred in; 20% live on campus. *Retention:* 34% of full-time freshmen returned.

Freshmen *Admission:* 3,008 applied, 3,008 admitted, 1,403 enrolled. *Average high school GPA:* 3.3.

Faculty *Total:* 252, 46% full-time, 6% with terminal degrees. *Student/faculty ratio:* 21:1.

Majors Accounting; administrative assistant and secretarial science; agricultural business and management; agriculture; animal sciences; art; automobile/automotive mechanics technology; biology/biological sciences; botany/plant biology; building/construction finishing, management, and inspection related; business administration and management; business teacher education; chemistry; child development; computer science; construction engineering technology; criminal justice/law enforcement administration; dance; dramatic/theater arts; economics; education; elementary education; family and community services; family and consumer sciences/human sciences; farm and ranch management; foods, nutrition, and wellness; forestry; French; geography; geology/earth science; history; humanities; industrial mechanics and maintenance technology; information science/studies; Japanese; kindergarten/preschool education; liberal arts and sciences/liberal studies; mass communication/media; mathematics; music; music history, literature, and theory; music teacher education; natural resources and conservation related; philosophy; physical education teaching and coaching; physical sciences; physics; political science and government; pre-engineering; range science and management; registered nursing/registered nurse; science teacher education; sociology; soil science and agronomy; Spanish; zoology/animal biology.

Academics *Calendar:* semesters. *Degree:* certificates, diplomas, and associate. *Special study options:* academic remediation for entering students, adult/continuing education programs, advanced placement credit, cooperative education, distance learning, English as a second language, external degree program, honors programs, independent study, part-time degree program, services for LD students, summer session for credit.

Library Eccles Library with 51,352 titles, 201 serial subscriptions, 6,676 audiovisual materials, an OPAC, a Web page.

Student Life *Housing Options:* coed, men-only, women-only, special housing for students with disabilities. Campus housing is university owned. *Activities and Organizations:* drama/theater group, student-run newspaper, radio and television station, choral group, Phi Beta Lambda, Latter Day Saints Student Association, International Student Society, BAAD Club (Alcohol and Drug Prevention), Dead Cats Society (Life Science Club). *Campus security:* 24-hour emergency response devices and patrols, student patrols, late-night transport/escort service, controlled dormitory access. *Student services:* personal/psychological counseling.

Athletics Member NJCAA. *Intercollegiate sports:* basketball M(s)/W(s), football M(s), softball W(s), volleyball W(s). *Intramural sports:* badminton M/W, basketball M/W, bowling M/W, football M/W, golf M/W, lacrosse M/W, racquetball M/W, rugby M, soccer M/W, softball M/W, tennis M/W, ultimate Frisbee M/W, volleyball M/W, water polo M/W, wrestling M.

Standardized Tests *Recommended:* SAT or ACT (for admission).

Costs (2014–15) *Tuition:* state resident $2830 full-time, $153 per credit part-time; nonresident $10,332 full-time, $561 per credit part-time. Full-time tuition and fees vary according to degree level. *Required fees:* $390 full-time. *Room and board:* room only $3500. Room and board charges vary according to board plan, housing facility, and location. *Waivers:* children of alumni and employees or children of employees.

Financial Aid *Average financial aid package:* $2351. *Average need-based loan:* $2903. *Average need-based gift aid:* $2395.

Applying *Options:* electronic application, early admission. *Application fee:* $30. *Required:* high school transcript. *Application deadlines:* 6/15 (freshmen), 6/1 (transfers). *Notification:* continuous (freshmen), continuous (transfers).

Freshman Application Contact Ms. Lorie Parry, Admissions Advisor, Snow College, 150 East College Avenue, Ephraim, UT 84627. *Phone:* 435-283-7144. *Fax:* 435-283-7157. *E-mail:* snowcollege@snow.edu.

Website: http://www.snow.edu/.

Vista College
Clearfield, Utah

Admissions Office Contact Vista College, 775 South 2000 East, Clearfield, UT 84015.
Website: http://www.vistacollege.edu/.

VERMONT

Community College of Vermont
Montpelier, Vermont

- **State-supported** 2-year, founded 1970, part of Vermont State Colleges System
- **Rural** campus
- **Coed,** 6,619 undergraduate students, 15% full-time, 69% women, 31% men

Undergraduates 995 full-time, 5,624 part-time. Students come from 22 states and territories; 4% are from out of state; 2% Black or African American, non-Hispanic/Latino; 3% Hispanic/Latino; 2% Asian, non-Hispanic/Latino; 0.2% Native Hawaiian or other Pacific Islander, non-Hispanic/Latino; 1% American Indian or Alaska Native, non-Hispanic/Latino; 4% Two or more races, non-Hispanic/Latino; 4% Race/ethnicity unknown. *Retention:* 57% of full-time freshmen returned.

Freshmen *Admission:* 1,695 applied, 1,008 admitted.

Faculty *Total:* 735, 11% with terminal degrees. *Student/faculty ratio:* 13:1.

Majors Accounting; administrative assistant and secretarial science; art; business administration and management; CAD/CADD drafting/design technology; child development; community organization and advocacy; computer and information sciences; computer science; computer systems networking and telecommunications; criminal justice/law enforcement administration; data entry/microcomputer applications; developmental and child psychology; digital communication and media/multimedia; early childhood education; education; environmental science; graphic design; hospitality administration; human services; industrial technology; information technology; liberal arts and sciences/liberal studies; medical/clinical assistant; social sciences; teacher assistant/aide.

Academics *Calendar:* semesters. *Degree:* certificates and associate. *Special study options:* academic remediation for entering students, accelerated degree program, adult/continuing education programs, advanced placement credit, cooperative education, distance learning, double majors, English as a second language, external degree program, independent study, internships, part-time degree program, services for LD students, student-designed majors, study abroad, summer session for credit.

Library Hartness Library plus 1 other with 59,000 titles, 36,500 serial subscriptions, 6,200 audiovisual materials, an OPAC, a Web page.

Student Life *Housing:* college housing not available.

Standardized Tests *Required for some:* ACCUPLACER assessments are required for degree seeking applicants and some continuing education applicants. SAT/ACT scores as well as college transcripts may be used to waive the ACCUPLACER. *Recommended:* SAT or ACT (for admission).

Costs (2013–14) *Tuition:* state resident $6960 full-time, $232 per credit hour part-time; nonresident $13,920 full-time, $464 per credit hour part-time. *Required fees:* $130 full-time, $65 per term part-time. *Payment plan:* installment. *Waivers:* senior citizens and employees or children of employees.

Financial Aid Of all full-time matriculated undergraduates who enrolled in 2012, 55 Federal Work-Study jobs (averaging $2400).

Applying *Options:* electronic application. *Application deadlines:* rolling (freshmen), rolling (out-of-state freshmen), rolling (transfers). *Notification:* continuous (freshmen), continuous (out-of-state freshmen), continuous (transfers).

Freshman Application Contact Community College of Vermont, 660 Elm Street, Montpelier, VT 05602. *Phone:* 802-654-0505. *Toll-free phone:* 800-CCV-6686.
Website: http://www.ccv.edu/.

Landmark College
Putney, Vermont

- **Independent** primarily 2-year, founded 1983
- **Small-town** 125-acre campus
- **Endowment** $16.2 million
- **Coed,** 487 undergraduate students, 99% full-time, 27% women, 73% men

Undergraduates 484 full-time, 3 part-time. Students come from 44 states and territories; 10 other countries; 95% are from out of state; 6% Black or African American, non-Hispanic/Latino; 3% Hispanic/Latino; 2% Asian, non-Hispanic/Latino; 3% Two or more races, non-Hispanic/Latino; 15%

Race/ethnicity unknown; 2% international; 21% transferred in; 95% live on campus. *Retention:* 68% of full-time freshmen returned.

Freshmen *Admission:* 266 applied, 230 admitted, 133 enrolled.

Faculty *Total:* 78, 100% full-time, 13% with terminal degrees. *Student/faculty ratio:* 6:1.

Majors Biology/biological sciences; business administration and management; business/commerce; computer science; general studies; liberal arts and sciences/liberal studies.

Academics *Calendar:* semesters. *Degrees:* associate and bachelor's. *Special study options:* academic remediation for entering students, advanced placement credit, distance learning, internships, services for LD students, study abroad, summer session for credit.

Library Landmark College Library with 140 titles, 115 serial subscriptions, 1,500 audiovisual materials, an OPAC, a Web page.

Student Life *Housing:* on-campus residence required for freshman year. *Options:* coed, special housing for students with disabilities. Campus housing is university owned. Freshman campus housing is guaranteed. *Activities and Organizations:* drama/theater group, student-run newspaper, radio station, choral group, Student Government Association, Campus Activities Board, Phi Theta Kappa Honor Society, Equestrian Club, PBL Business Club. *Campus security:* 24-hour emergency response devices and patrols, late-night transport/escort service, controlled dormitory access. *Student services:* health clinic, personal/psychological counseling, women's center.

Athletics *Intercollegiate sports:* baseball M(c), basketball M(c)/W(c), cross-country running M(c)/W(c), equestrian sports M/W, rock climbing M(c)/W(c), soccer M/W, softball W(c). *Intramural sports:* badminton M(c)/W(c), basketball M(c)/W(c), fencing M(c)/W(c), skiing (cross-country) M(c)/W(c), tennis M(c)/W(c), volleyball M(c)/W(c), weight lifting M(c)/W(c).

Standardized Tests *Required:* Cognitive and achievement tests such as the Wechsler Adult Intelligence Scale III and the Nelson Denny Reading Test are required (for admission).

Costs (2013–14) *Comprehensive fee:* $59,930 includes full-time tuition ($49,500), mandatory fees ($130), and room and board ($10,300). *Room and board:* college room only: $5300. Room and board charges vary according to board plan and housing facility. *Payment plan:* installment. *Waivers:* employees or children of employees.

Financial Aid Of all full-time matriculated undergraduates who enrolled in 2010, 341 applied for aid, 243 were judged to have need, 3 had their need fully met. 85 Federal Work-Study jobs (averaging $1000). 3 state and other part-time jobs (averaging $1000). In 2010, 18 non-need-based awards were made. *Average percent of need met:* 45%. *Average financial aid package:* $26,000. *Average need-based loan:* $4500. *Average need-based gift aid:* $21,000. *Average non-need-based aid:* $7800. *Average indebtedness upon graduation:* $6100.

Applying *Options:* electronic application, early action, deferred entrance. *Application fee:* $75. *Required:* essay or personal statement, high school transcript, diagnosis of LD and/or ADHD and cognitive testing. *Recommended:* 2 letters of recommendation, interview. *Application deadlines:* rolling (freshmen), rolling (transfers), 12/1 (early action). *Notification:* continuous (freshmen), continuous (transfers), 1/5 (early action).

Freshman Application Contact Admissions Main Desk, Landmark College, Landmark College Admissions, River Road South, Putney, VT 05346. *Phone:* 802-387-6718. *Fax:* 802-387-6868. *E-mail:* admissions@landmark.edu.
Website: http://www.landmark.edu/.

New England Culinary Institute
Montpelier, Vermont

- **Proprietary** primarily 2-year, founded 1980
- **Small-town** campus
- **Coed,** 425 undergraduate students, 100% full-time, 44% women, 56% men

Undergraduates 425 full-time. Students come from 46 states and territories; 6 other countries; 79% are from out of state; 2% Black or African American, non-Hispanic/Latino; 5% Hispanic/Latino; 1% Asian, non-Hispanic/Latino; 0.7% Native Hawaiian or other Pacific Islander, non-Hispanic/Latino; 2% Two or more races, non-Hispanic/Latino; 10% Race/ethnicity unknown; 3% international; 80% live on campus. *Retention:* 65% of full-time freshmen returned.

Freshmen *Admission:* 249 applied, 224 admitted.

Faculty *Total:* 42, 57% full-time. *Student/faculty ratio:* 10:1.

Majors Baking and pastry arts; culinary arts; restaurant, culinary, and catering management.

Academics *Calendar:* quarters. *Degrees:* certificates, associate, and bachelor's. *Special study options:* academic remediation for entering students, accelerated degree program, advanced placement credit, cooperative education, distance learning, honors programs, internships, services for LD students.

Library New England Culinary Institute Library with 4,075 titles, 32 serial subscriptions, 325 audiovisual materials, an OPAC, a Web page.

Student Life *Housing:* on-campus residence required for freshman year. *Options:* coed, men-only, women-only. Campus housing is leased by the school. Freshman applicants given priority for college housing. *Activities and Organizations:* American Culinary Federation, Slow Food, Student Council, Special Guest Lecture Series, Student Ambassadors (Leadership Program). *Campus security:* 24-hour emergency response devices, student patrols.

Standardized Tests *Recommended:* SAT or ACT (for admission).

Costs (2014–15) *Comprehensive fee:* $36,990 includes full-time tuition ($26,250), mandatory fees ($2740), and room and board ($8000). Full-time tuition and fees vary according to course load, degree level, program, reciprocity agreements, and student level. Part-time tuition: $7500 per term. Part-time tuition and fees vary according to course load, degree level, program, reciprocity agreements, and student level. *Required fees:* $5625 per term part-time, $200 per term part-time. *Room and board:* college room only: $5600. Room and board charges vary according to housing facility. *Payment plan:* installment. *Waivers:* employees or children of employees.

Financial Aid Of all full-time matriculated undergraduates who enrolled in 2012, 320 Federal Work-Study jobs (averaging $1000).

Applying *Options:* electronic application, early admission, deferred entrance. *Required:* high school transcript. *Required for some:* interview. *Recommended:* essay or personal statement, 2 letters of recommendation, culinary experience. *Application deadline:* rolling (freshmen).

Freshman Application Contact Dwight A Cross, Director of Admissions, New England Culinary Institute, 56 College Street, Montpelier, VT 05602-3115. *Phone:* 802-225-3211. *Toll-free phone:* 877-223-6324. *Fax:* 802-225-3280. *E-mail:* admissions@neci.edu. *Website:* http://www.neci.edu/.

VIRGINIA

Advanced Technology Institute
Virginia Beach, Virginia

Freshman Application Contact Admissions Office, Advanced Technology Institute, 5700 Southern Boulevard, Suite 100, Virginia Beach, VA 23462. *Phone:* 757-490-1241. *Toll-free phone:* 888-468-1093. *Website:* http://www.auto.edu/.

American National University
Charlottesville, Virginia

Director of Admissions Kimberly Moore, Campus Director, American National University, 3926 Seminole Trail, Charlottesville, VA 22911. *Phone:* 434-295-0136. *Toll-free phone:* 888-9-JOBREADY. *Fax:* 434-979-8061. *Website:* http://www.national-college.edu/.

American National University
Danville, Virginia

Freshman Application Contact Admissions Office, American National University, 336 Old Riverside Drive, Danville, VA 24541. *Phone:* 434-793-6822. *Toll-free phone:* 888-9-JOBREADY. *Website:* http://www.national-college.edu/.

American National University
Harrisonburg, Virginia

Director of Admissions Jack Evey, Campus Director, American National University, 1515 Country Club Road, Harrisonburg, VA 22802. *Phone:* 540-432-0943. *Toll-free phone:* 888-9-JOBREADY. *Website:* http://www.national-college.edu/.

American National University
Lynchburg, Virginia

Freshman Application Contact Admissions Representative, American National University, 104 Candlewood Court, Lynchburg, VA 24502-2653. *Phone:* 804-239-3500. *Toll-free phone:* 888-9-JOBREADY. *Website:* http://www.national-college.edu/.

American National University
Martinsville, Virginia

Director of Admissions Mr. John Scott, Campus Director, American National University, 905 Memorial Boulevard North, Martinsville, VA 24112. *Phone:* 276-632-5621. *Toll-free phone:* 888-9-JOBREADY. *Website:* http://www.national-college.edu/.

American National University
Salem, Virginia

Freshman Application Contact Director of Admissions, American National University, 1813 East Main Street, Salem, VA 24153. *Phone:* 540-986-1800. *Toll-free phone:* 888-9-JOBREADY. *Fax:* 540-444-4198. *Website:* http://www.national-college.edu/.

Blue Ridge Community College
Weyers Cave, Virginia

Freshman Application Contact Blue Ridge Community College, PO Box 80, Weyers Cave, VA 24486-0080. *Phone:* 540-453-2217. *Toll-free phone:* 888-750-2722. *Website:* http://www.brcc.edu/.

Bryant & Stratton College - Richmond Campus
Richmond, Virginia

Freshman Application Contact Mr. David K. Mayle, Director of Admissions, Bryant & Stratton College - Richmond Campus, 8141 Hull Street Road, Richmond, VA 23235-6411. *Phone:* 804-745-2444. *Fax:* 804-745-6884. *E-mail:* tlawson@bryanstratton.edu. *Website:* http://www.bryantstratton.edu/.

Bryant & Stratton College - Virginia Beach
Virginia Beach, Virginia

Freshman Application Contact Bryant & Stratton College - Virginia Beach, 301 Centre Pointe Drive, Virginia Beach, VA 23462-4417. *Phone:* 757-499-7900 Ext. 173. *Website:* http://www.bryantstratton.edu/.

Central Virginia Community College
Lynchburg, Virginia

- **State-supported** 2-year, founded 1966, part of Virginia Community College System
- **Suburban** 104-acre campus
- **Coed,** 4,767 undergraduate students

Undergraduates 15% Black or African American, non-Hispanic/Latino; 3% Hispanic/Latino; 2% Asian, non-Hispanic/Latino; 0.1% Native Hawaiian or other Pacific Islander, non-Hispanic/Latino; 0.4% American Indian or Alaska Native, non-Hispanic/Latino; 4% Two or more races, non-Hispanic/Latino; 0.9% Race/ethnicity unknown; 0.3% international.

Freshmen *Admission:* 2,127 applied, 2,126 admitted.

Faculty *Student/faculty ratio:* 18:1.

Majors Accounting related; business administration and management; business/commerce; business operations support and secretarial services related; computer and information sciences; criminal justice/law enforcement administration; culinary arts; design and visual communications; education; emergency medical technology (EMT paramedic); engineering; engineering technology; industrial technology; liberal arts and sciences/liberal studies; management science; medical/clinical assistant; radiologic technology/science; respiratory care therapy; science technologies.

Academics *Calendar:* semesters. *Degree:* certificates, diplomas, and associate. *Special study options:* academic remediation for entering students, advanced placement credit, cooperative education, distance learning, independent study, internships, part-time degree program, services for LD students, summer session for credit.

Library Bedford Learning Resources Center with an OPAC, a Web page.

Student Life *Housing:* college housing not available. *Activities and Organizations:* drama/theater group. *Campus security:* 24-hour emergency response devices.

Athletics Member NJCAA. *Intercollegiate sports:* baseball M.

Costs (2014–15) *Tuition:* state resident $4080 full-time, $136 per credit hour part-time; nonresident $9738 full-time, $325 per credit hour part-time. *Payment plan:* installment.

Financial Aid Of all full-time matriculated undergraduates who enrolled in 2012, 65 Federal Work-Study jobs (averaging $2700).

Applying *Options:* electronic application, early admission, deferred entrance. *Application deadlines:* rolling (freshmen), rolling (transfers). *Notification:* continuous (freshmen), continuous (transfers).

Freshman Application Contact Admissions Office, Central Virginia Community College, 3506 Wards Road, Lynchburg, VA 24502. *Phone:* 434-832-7633. *Toll-free phone:* 800-562-3060. *Fax:* 434-832-7793. *Website:* http://www.cvcc.vccs.edu/.

Centura College
Chesapeake, Virginia

Director of Admissions Director of Admissions, Centura College, 932 Ventures Way, Chesapeake, VA 23320. *Phone:* 757-549-2121. *Toll-free phone:* 877-575-5627. *Fax:* 575-549-1196.
Website: http://www.centuracollege.edu/.

Centura College
Newport News, Virginia

Director of Admissions Victoria Whitehead, Director of Admissions, Centura College, 616 Denbigh Boulevard, Newport News, VA 23608. *Phone:* 757-874-2121. *Toll-free phone:* 877-575-5627. *Fax:* 757-874-3857. *E-mail:* admdircpen@centura.edu.
Website: http://www.centuracollege.edu/.

Centura College
Norfolk, Virginia

Director of Admissions Director of Admissions, Centura College, 7020 North Military Highway, Norfolk, VA 23518. *Phone:* 757-853-2121. *Toll-free phone:* 877-575-5627. *Fax:* 757-852-9017.
Website: http://www.centuracollege.edu/.

Centura College
North Chesterfield, Virginia

Freshman Application Contact Admissions Office, Centura College, 7914 Midlothian Turnpike, North Chesterfield, VA 23235-5230. *Phone:* 804-330-0111. *Toll-free phone:* 877-575-5627. *Fax:* 804-330-3809.
Website: http://www.centuracollege.edu/.

Centura College
Virginia Beach, Virginia

Freshman Application Contact Admissions Office, Centura College, 2697 Dean Drive, Suite 100, Virginia Beach, VA 23452. *Phone:* 757-340-2121. *Toll-free phone:* 877-575-5627. *Fax:* 757-340-9704.
Website: http://www.centuracollege.edu/.

Dabney S. Lancaster Community College
Clifton Forge, Virginia

- **State-supported** 2-year, founded 1964, part of Virginia Community College System
- **Rural** 117-acre campus
- **Endowment** $3.3 million
- **Coed,** 1,284 undergraduate students, 24% full-time, 55% women, 45% men

Undergraduates 314 full-time, 970 part-time. Students come from 4 states and territories; 2% are from out of state; 5% Black or African American, non-Hispanic/Latino; 2% Hispanic/Latino; 0.1% Asian, non-Hispanic/Latino; 0.8% American Indian or Alaska Native, non-Hispanic/Latino; 2% Two or more races, non-Hispanic/Latino; 32% transferred in.
Freshmen *Admission:* 174 enrolled.
Faculty *Total:* 97, 24% full-time. *Student/faculty ratio:* 16:1.
Majors Administrative assistant and secretarial science; biological and physical sciences; business administration and management; computer programming; criminal justice/law enforcement administration; data processing and data processing technology; drafting and design technology; drafting/design engineering technologies related; education; electrical, electronic and communications engineering technology; forest technology; information science/studies; legal administrative assistant/secretary; liberal arts and sciences/liberal studies; medical administrative assistant and medical secretary; registered nursing/registered nurse; wood science and wood products/pulp and paper technology.
Academics *Calendar:* semesters. *Degree:* certificates, diplomas, and associate. *Special study options:* academic remediation for entering students, adult/continuing education programs, advanced placement credit, cooperative education, distance learning, honors programs, independent study, internships, part-time degree program, services for LD students, study abroad, summer session for credit.
Library DSLCC Library plus 1 other with 34,397 titles, 853 serial subscriptions, 1,260 audiovisual materials, an OPAC.
Student Life *Housing:* college housing not available. *Campus security:* 24-hour emergency response devices. *Student services:* personal/psychological counseling.
Athletics *Intercollegiate sports:* basketball M. *Intramural sports:* basketball M/W, bowling M/W, skiing (downhill) M/W, volleyball M/W.

Standardized Tests *Required for some:* SAT (for admission), ACT (for admission), SAT or ACT (for admission), SAT and SAT Subject Tests or ACT (for admission), SAT Subject Tests (for admission), Virginia Placement Test.
Costs (2014–15) *Tuition:* state resident $3180 full-time, $133 per credit part-time; nonresident $7850 full-time, $327 per credit part-time. *Required fees:* $240 full-time, $10 per credit hour part-time. *Payment plan:* installment. *Waivers:* senior citizens.
Applying *Recommended:* high school transcript, interview.
Freshman Application Contact Mrs. Lorrie Wilhelm Ferguson, Registrar, Dabney S. Lancaster Community College, Backels Hall, Clifton Forge, VA 24422. *Phone:* 540-863-2823. *Toll-free phone:* 877-73-DSLCC. *Fax:* 540-863-2915. *E-mail:* lwferguson@dslcc.edu.
Website: http://www.dslcc.edu/.

Danville Community College
Danville, Virginia

Freshman Application Contact Cathy Pulliam, Coordinator of Student Recruitment and Enrollment, Danville Community College, 1008 South Main Street, Danville, VA 24541-4088. *Phone:* 434-797-8538. *Toll-free phone:* 800-560-4291. *E-mail:* cpulliam@dcc.vccs.edu.
Website: http://www.dcc.vccs.edu/.

Eastern Shore Community College
Melfa, Virginia

- **State-supported** 2-year, founded 1971, part of Virginia Community College System (VCCS)
- **Rural** 117-acre campus with easy access to Hampton Roads/Virginia Beach, Norfolk
- **Coed,** 857 undergraduate students, 31% full-time, 67% women, 33% men

Undergraduates 264 full-time, 593 part-time.
Faculty *Total:* 87, 20% full-time. *Student/faculty ratio:* 13:1.
Majors Administrative assistant and secretarial science; biological and physical sciences; business administration and management; computer and information sciences and support services related; computer/information technology services administration related; education; electrical, electronic and communications engineering technology; liberal arts and sciences/liberal studies; registered nursing/registered nurse.
Academics *Calendar:* semesters. *Degree:* certificates and associate. *Special study options:* academic remediation for entering students, adult/continuing education programs, distance learning, internships, off-campus study, part-time degree program, services for LD students, summer session for credit.
Library Learning Resources Center plus 1 other with 25,000 titles, 102 serial subscriptions, an OPAC, a Web page.
Student Life *Housing:* college housing not available. *Activities and Organizations:* All Christians Together in Service (ACTS), Phi Theta Kappa, Phi Beta Lambda, The Electronics Club, SNAP Photography Club. *Campus security:* security guards, day and night during classes when the college is in session.
Standardized Tests *Required:* The Virginia Community College System (VCCS) has a placement test designed for and utilized by all schools in its system (for admission).
Financial Aid Of all full-time matriculated undergraduates who enrolled in 2012, 11 Federal Work-Study jobs.
Applying *Options:* electronic application. *Required:* high school transcript, high school diploma or GED. *Application deadlines:* rolling (freshmen), rolling (transfers). *Notification:* continuous (freshmen), continuous (transfers).
Freshman Application Contact P. Bryan Smith, Dean of Student Services, Eastern Shore Community College, 29300 Lankford Highway, Melfa, VA 23410. *Phone:* 757-789-1732. *Toll-free phone:* 877-871-8455. *Fax:* 757-789-1737. *E-mail:* bsmith@es.vccs.edu.
Website: http://www.es.vccs.edu/.

ECPI University
Richmond, Virginia

Freshman Application Contact Director, ECPI University, 800 Moorefield Park Drive, Richmond, VA 23236. *Phone:* 804-330-5533. *Toll-free phone:* 800-986-1200. *Fax:* 804-330-5577. *E-mail:* agerard@ecpi.edu.
Website: http://www.ecpi.edu/.

Fortis College
Norfolk, Virginia

Admissions Office Contact Fortis College, 6300 Center Drive, Suite 100, Norfolk, VA 23502.
Website: http://www.fortis.edu/.

Fortis College
Richmond, Virginia

Admissions Office Contact Fortis College, 2000 Westmoreland Street, Suite A, Richmond, VA 23230.
Website: http://www.fortis.edu/.

Germanna Community College
Locust Grove, Virginia

Freshman Application Contact Ms. Rita Dunston, Registrar, Germanna Community College, 10000 Germanna Point Drive, Fredericksburg, VA 22408. *Phone:* 540-891-3020. *Fax:* 540-891-3092.
Website: http://www.germanna.edu/.

ITT Technical Institute
Chantilly, Virginia

- **Proprietary** primarily 2-year, founded 2002, part of ITT Educational Services, Inc.
- **Coed**

Majors Business administration and management; computer programming (specific applications); construction management; cyber/computer forensics and counterterrorism; drafting and design technology; electrical, electronic and communications engineering technology; forensic science and technology; graphic communications; industrial technology; information technology project management; medical/clinical assistant; network and system administration; project management.
Academics *Calendar:* quarters. *Degrees:* associate and bachelor's.
Student Life *Housing:* college housing not available.
Freshman Application Contact Director of Recruitment, ITT Technical Institute, 14420 Albemarle Point Place, Suite 100, Chantilly, VA 20151. *Phone:* 703-263-2541. *Toll-free phone:* 888-895-8324.
Website: http://www.itt-tech.edu/.

ITT Technical Institute
Norfolk, Virginia

- **Proprietary** primarily 2-year, founded 1988, part of ITT Educational Services, Inc.
- **Suburban** campus
- **Coed**

Majors Business administration and management; computer programming (specific applications); construction management; cyber/computer forensics and counterterrorism; drafting and design technology; electrical, electronic and communications engineering technology; forensic science and technology; game and interactive media design; graphic communications; industrial technology; information technology project management; medical/clinical assistant; network and system administration; project management; registered nursing/registered nurse.
Academics *Calendar:* quarters. *Degrees:* associate and bachelor's.
Student Life *Housing:* college housing not available.
Financial Aid Of all full-time matriculated undergraduates who enrolled in 2012, 3 Federal Work-Study jobs (averaging $5000).
Freshman Application Contact Director of Recruitment, ITT Technical Institute, 5425 Robin Hood Road, Norfolk, VA 23513. *Phone:* 757-466-1260. *Toll-free phone:* 888-253-8324.
Website: http://www.itt-tech.edu/.

ITT Technical Institute
Richmond, Virginia

- **Proprietary** primarily 2-year, founded 1999, part of ITT Educational Services, Inc.
- **Coed**

Majors Business administration and management; computer programming (specific applications); construction management; cyber/computer forensics and counterterrorism; drafting and design technology; electrical, electronic and communications engineering technology; forensic science and technology; graphic communications; industrial technology; information technology project management; medical/clinical assistant; network and system administration; project management.
Academics *Calendar:* quarters. *Degrees:* associate and bachelor's.
Student Life *Housing:* college housing not available.
Freshman Application Contact Director of Recruitment, ITT Technical Institute, 300 Gateway Centre Parkway, Richmond, VA 23235. *Phone:* 804-330-4992. *Toll-free phone:* 888-330-4888.
Website: http://www.itt-tech.edu/.

ITT Technical Institute
Salem, Virginia

- **Proprietary** primarily 2-year
- **Coed**

Majors Business administration and management; computer programming (specific applications); construction management; cyber/computer forensics and counterterrorism; drafting and design technology; electrical, electronic and communications engineering technology; forensic science and technology; industrial technology; information technology project management; medical/clinical assistant; network and system administration; project management; registered nursing/registered nurse.
Academics *Degrees:* associate and bachelor's.
Freshman Application Contact Director of Recruitment, ITT Technical Institute, 2159 Apperson Drive, Salem, VA 24153. *Phone:* 540-989-2500. *Toll-free phone:* 877-208-6132.
Website: http://www.itt-tech.edu/.

ITT Technical Institute
Springfield, Virginia

- **Proprietary** primarily 2-year, founded 2002, part of ITT Educational Services, Inc.
- **Coed**

Majors Business administration and management; computer programming (specific applications); construction management; cyber/computer forensics and counterterrorism; drafting and design technology; electrical, electronic and communications engineering technology; forensic science and technology; industrial technology; information technology project management; medical/clinical assistant; network and system administration; project management.
Academics *Calendar:* quarters. *Degrees:* associate and bachelor's.
Student Life *Housing:* college housing not available.
Freshman Application Contact Director of Recruitment, ITT Technical Institute, 7300 Boston Boulevard, Springfield, VA 22153. *Phone:* 703-440-9535. *Toll-free phone:* 866-817-8324.
Website: http://www.itt-tech.edu/.

John Tyler Community College
Chester, Virginia

- **State-supported** 2-year, founded 1967, part of Virginia Community College System
- **Suburban** 160-acre campus with easy access to Richmond
- **Coed,** 10,157 undergraduate students, 27% full-time, 57% women, 43% men

Undergraduates 2,697 full-time, 7,460 part-time. 25% Black or African American, non-Hispanic/Latino; 4% Hispanic/Latino; 4% Asian, non-Hispanic/Latino; 0.5% American Indian or Alaska Native, non-Hispanic/Latino; 1% Race/ethnicity unknown. *Retention:* 58% of full-time freshmen returned.
Freshmen *Admission:* 1,429 enrolled.
Faculty *Total:* 558, 22% full-time. *Student/faculty ratio:* 20:1.
Majors Accounting related; architectural technology; business administration and management; business administration, management and operations related; business/commerce; child-care provision; computer and information sciences; criminal justice/law enforcement administration; engineering; funeral service and mortuary science; general studies; humanities; human services; industrial electronics technology; industrial technology; information technology; liberal arts and sciences/liberal studies; management information systems; mechanical engineering technologies related; mental and social health services and allied professions related; registered nursing/registered nurse; visual and performing arts related.
Academics *Calendar:* semesters. *Degree:* certificates and associate. *Special study options:* academic remediation for entering students, adult/continuing education programs, advanced placement credit, distance learning, external degree program, honors programs, off-campus study, part-time degree program, services for LD students, study abroad, summer session for credit. *ROTC:* Army (c).
Library John Tyler Community College Learning Resource and Technology Center with 52,000 titles, 10,150 serial subscriptions, 1,335 audiovisual materials, an OPAC, a Web page.
Student Life *Housing:* college housing not available. *Activities and Organizations:* drama/theater group, choral group, Phi Theta Kappa -TauRho, Phi Theta Kappa - BOO, Art Club, Elements of Life Club, Funeral Services Club. *Campus security:* 24-hour emergency response devices and patrols.
Costs (2013–14) *Tuition:* state resident $3120 full-time, $130 per credit hour part-time; nonresident $7790 full-time, $325 per credit hour part-time. Full-time tuition and fees vary according to course load. Part-time tuition and fees

vary according to course load. *Required fees:* $70 full-time, $35 per term part-time. *Payment plan:* installment. *Waivers:* senior citizens.

Financial Aid Of all full-time matriculated undergraduates who enrolled in 2012, 60 Federal Work-Study jobs (averaging $2437).

Applying *Options:* early admission, deferred entrance. *Recommended:* high school transcript. *Application deadline:* rolling (freshmen). *Notification:* continuous (freshmen).

Freshman Application Contact Ms. Joy James, Director of Admission, John Tyler Community College, 13101 Jefferson Davis Highway, Chester, VA 23831. *Phone:* 804-706-5214. *Toll-free phone:* 800-552-3490. *Fax:* 804-796-4362.

Website: http://www.jtcc.edu/.

J. Sargeant Reynolds Community College
Richmond, Virginia

- **State-supported** 2-year, founded 1972, part of Virginia Community College System
- **Suburban** 207-acre campus with easy access to Richmond
- **Coed**, 12,469 undergraduate students, 29% full-time, 61% women, 39% men

Undergraduates 3,583 full-time, 8,886 part-time. Students come from 26 states and territories; 18 other countries; 1% are from out of state; 37% Black or African American, non-Hispanic/Latino; 2% Hispanic/Latino; 4% Asian, non-Hispanic/Latino; 0.2% Native Hawaiian or other Pacific Islander, non-Hispanic/Latino; 0.5% American Indian or Alaska Native, non-Hispanic/Latino; 5% Two or more races, non-Hispanic/Latino; 1% Race/ethnicity unknown; 11% transferred in.

Freshmen *Admission:* 1,919 enrolled.

Faculty *Total:* 711, 21% full-time. *Student/faculty ratio:* 19:1.

Majors Accounting related; allied health and medical assisting services related; applied horticulture/horticulture operations; architectural and building sciences; automobile/automotive mechanics technology; baking and pastry arts; biological and physical sciences; building/construction site management; business administration and management; business administration, management and operations related; business operations support and secretarial services related; CAD/CADD drafting/design technology; child-care provision; civil engineering; civil engineering technology; clinical/medical laboratory technology; computer and information sciences; computer/information technology services administration related; computer programming; computer science; computer systems networking and telecommunications; consumer merchandising/retailing management; cooking and related culinary arts; criminal justice/law enforcement administration; dental assisting; dental laboratory technology; diesel mechanics technology; emergency care attendant (EMT ambulance); emergency medical technology (EMT paramedic); engineering; fire science/firefighting; floriculture/floristry management; food preparation; health information/medical records technology; hospitality administration; hospitality administration related; hotel/motel administration; industrial electronics technology; legal assistant/paralegal; liberal arts and sciences and humanities related; licensed practical/vocational nurse training; mathematics; mental and social health services and allied professions related; opticianry; pharmacy technician; real estate; registered nursing/registered nurse; respiratory care therapy; restaurant/food services management; sign language interpretation and translation; small business administration; social sciences; substance abuse/addiction counseling; web page, digital/multimedia and information resources design; welding technology.

Academics *Calendar:* semesters. *Degree:* certificates and associate. *Special study options:* academic remediation for entering students, adult/continuing education programs, advanced placement credit, distance learning, double majors, English as a second language, independent study, internships, off-campus study, part-time degree program, services for LD students, summer session for credit.

Library J. Sargeant Reynolds Community College Library plus 2 others with 130,000 titles, 50,000 serial subscriptions, 3,000 audiovisual materials, an OPAC, a Web page.

Student Life *Housing:* college housing not available. *Campus security:* 24-hour emergency response devices and patrols, late-night transport/escort service, security during open hours. *Student services:* personal/psychological counseling.

Costs (2014–15) *Tuition:* state resident $3194 full-time, $126 per credit part-time; nonresident $7685 full-time, $320 per credit part-time. Full-time tuition and fees vary according to course load and program. Part-time tuition and fees vary according to course load and program. *Required fees:* $384 full-time, $16 per credit part-time. *Payment plan:* installment. *Waivers:* senior citizens.

Financial Aid Of all full-time matriculated undergraduates who enrolled in 2009, 14,628 applied for aid, 11,184 were judged to have need. 64 Federal Work-Study jobs (averaging $2600). In 2009, 121 non-need-based awards were made. *Average percent of need met:* 49%. *Average financial aid*

package: $6950. *Average need-based loan:* $2792. *Average need-based gift aid:* $3400. *Average non-need-based aid:* $891. *Average indebtedness upon graduation:* $3891.

Applying *Options:* electronic application. *Required:* high school transcript. *Required for some:* interview, Interviews with some departments; A few require criminal background checks and/or drug screening; At least one has minimal physical standards. *Application deadlines:* rolling (freshmen), rolling (transfers). *Notification:* continuous (freshmen), continuous (transfers).

Freshman Application Contact Ms. Karen Pettis-Walden, Director of Admissions and Records, J. Sargeant Reynolds Community College, PO Box 85622, Richmond, VA 23285-5622. *Phone:* 804-523-5029. *Fax:* 804-371-3650. *E-mail:* kpettis-walden@reynolds.edu.

Website: http://www.reynolds.edu/.

Lord Fairfax Community College
Middletown, Virginia

Freshman Application Contact Karen Bucher, Director of Enrollment Management, Lord Fairfax Community College, 173 Skirmisher Lane, Middletown, VA 22645. *Phone:* 540-868-7132. *Toll-free phone:* 800-906-LFCC. *Fax:* 540-868-7005. *E-mail:* kbucher@lfcc.edu.

Website: http://www.lfcc.edu/.

Miller-Motte Technical College
Lynchburg, Virginia

Director of Admissions Ms. Betty J. Dierstein, Director, Miller-Motte Technical College, 1011 Creekside Lane, Lynchburg, VA 24502. *Phone:* 434-239-5222. *Fax:* 434-239-1069. *E-mail:* bjdierstein@miller-mott.com.

Website: http://www.miller-motte.edu/.

Miller-Motte Technical College
Roanoke, Virginia

Admissions Office Contact Miller-Motte Technical College, 4444 Electric Road, Roanoke, VA 24018.

Website: http://www.miller-motte.edu/.

Mountain Empire Community College
Big Stone Gap, Virginia

- **State-supported** 2-year, founded 1972, part of Virginia Community College System
- **Rural** campus
- **Coed,** 2,924 undergraduate students, 45% full-time, 59% women, 41% men

Undergraduates 1,310 full-time, 1,614 part-time. Students come from 9 states and territories; 4% are from out of state; 2% Black or African American, non-Hispanic/Latino; 0.4% Hispanic/Latino; 0.2% Asian, non-Hispanic/Latino; 0.3% American Indian or Alaska Native, non-Hispanic/Latino; 0.3% Race/ethnicity unknown. *Retention:* 61% of full-time freshmen returned.

Faculty *Total:* 160, 28% full-time.

Majors Accounting related; business administration, management and operations related; business operations support and secretarial services related; CAD/CADD drafting/design technology; corrections; criminal justice/law enforcement administration; electrical, electronic and communications engineering technology; emergency medical technology (EMT paramedic); environmental control technologies related; industrial production technologies related; industrial technology; legal assistant/paralegal; liberal arts and sciences/liberal studies; natural resources/conservation; registered nursing/registered nurse; respiratory care therapy.

Academics *Calendar:* semesters. *Degree:* certificates and associate. *Special study options:* academic remediation for entering students, adult/continuing education programs, advanced placement credit, cooperative education, distance learning, double majors, external degree program, independent study, internships, part-time degree program, student-designed majors, summer session for credit.

Library Wampler Library with 44,136 titles, 148 serial subscriptions, an OPAC, a Web page.

Student Life *Housing:* college housing not available. *Activities and Organizations:* drama/theater group, Phi Theta Kappa, Healing Hands, Rho Nu (SNAV), Students in Free Enterprise (SIFE), Merits. *Campus security:* 24-hour emergency response devices and patrols. *Student services:* personal/psychological counseling.

Athletics *Intramural sports:* basketball M/W, football M/W, volleyball M/W.

Financial Aid Of all full-time matriculated undergraduates who enrolled in 2012, 150 Federal Work-Study jobs (averaging $1200). 30 state and other part-time jobs (averaging $650).

Applying *Options:* electronic application, early admission, deferred entrance. *Required:* high school transcript. *Required for some:* minimum 2.0 GPA.

Application deadlines: rolling (freshmen), rolling (transfers). *Notification:* continuous (freshmen), continuous (transfers).
Freshman Application Contact Mountain Empire Community College, 3441 Mountain Empire Road, Big Stone Gap, VA 24219. *Phone:* 276-523-2400 Ext. 219.
Website: http://www.mecc.edu/.

New River Community College
Dublin, Virginia

Freshman Application Contact Ms. Margaret G. Taylor, Director of Student Services, New River Community College, PO Box 1127, Dublin, VA 24084-1127. *Phone:* 540-674-3600. *Toll-free phone:* 866-462-6722. *Fax:* 540-674-3644. *E-mail:* nrtaylm@nr.edu.
Website: http://www.nr.edu/.

Northern Virginia Community College
Annandale, Virginia

Director of Admissions Dr. Max L. Bassett, Dean of Academic and Student Services, Northern Virginia Community College, 4001 Wakefield Chapel Road, Annandale, VA 22003-3796. *Phone:* 703-323-3195.
Website: http://www.nvcc.edu/.

Patrick Henry Community College
Martinsville, Virginia

- **State-supported** 2-year, founded 1962, part of Virginia Community College System
- **Rural** 137-acre campus with easy access to Greensboro, NC
- **Endowment** $10.6 million
- **Coed,** 3,163 undergraduate students, 47% full-time, 60% women, 40% men

Undergraduates 1,486 full-time, 1,677 part-time. Students come from 6 states and territories; 1% are from out of state; 24% Black or African American, non-Hispanic/Latino; 4% Hispanic/Latino; 0.5% Asian, non-Hispanic/Latino; 0.3% American Indian or Alaska Native, non-Hispanic/Latino; 2% Two or more races, non-Hispanic/Latino; 0.1% Race/ethnicity unknown; 0.3% international. *Retention:* 59% of full-time freshmen returned.
Faculty *Total:* 237, 23% full-time. *Student/faculty ratio:* 18:1.
Majors Accounting; administrative assistant and secretarial science; agricultural business and management; automobile/automotive mechanics technology; biological and physical sciences; business administration and management; criminal justice/law enforcement administration; emergency medical technology (EMT paramedic); engineering technology; industrial electronics technology; industrial technology; information technology; legal assistant/paralegal; liberal arts and sciences/liberal studies; medical office assistant; registered nursing/registered nurse; teacher assistant/aide.
Academics *Calendar:* semesters. *Degree:* certificates and associate. *Special study options:* academic remediation for entering students, adult/continuing education programs, advanced placement credit, cooperative education, distance learning, independent study, internships, part-time degree program, services for LD students, summer session for credit.
Library Lester Library with 31,282 titles, 126 serial subscriptions, 2,147 audiovisual materials, an OPAC, a Web page.
Student Life *Housing:* college housing not available. *Activities and Organizations:* drama/theater group, Student Government Association, Student Support Services, Phi Theta Kappa, Gospel Choir, Black Student Association. *Campus security:* 24-hour emergency response devices and patrols, late-night transport/escort service. *Student services:* personal/psychological counseling.
Athletics Member NJCAA. *Intercollegiate sports:* baseball M, basketball M/W, cheerleading W, golf M/W, soccer M/W, softball W. *Intramural sports:* basketball M/W, tennis M/W, volleyball M/W.
Costs (2013–14) *Tuition:* state resident $3675 full-time, $123 per credit hour part-time; nonresident $10,133 full-time, $317 per credit hour part-time. Full-time tuition and fees vary according to course load. Part-time tuition and fees vary according to course load. *Required fees:* $225 full-time, $8 per credit hour part-time. *Payment plans:* installment, deferred payment. *Waivers:* senior citizens.
Financial Aid Of all full-time matriculated undergraduates who enrolled in 2012, 41 Federal Work-Study jobs (averaging $2000).
Applying *Options:* electronic application, early admission. *Required:* high school transcript. *Application deadlines:* rolling (freshmen), rolling (transfers). *Notification:* continuous (freshmen), continuous (transfers).
Freshman Application Contact Mr. Travis Tisdale, Coordinator, Admissions and Records, Patrick Henry Community College, 645 Patriot Avenue, Martinsville, VA 24112. *Phone:* 276-656-0311. *Toll-free phone:* 800-232-7997. *Fax:* 276-656-0352.
Website: http://www.ph.vccs.edu/.

Paul D. Camp Community College
Franklin, Virginia

- **State-supported** 2-year, founded 1971, part of Virginia Community College System
- **Small-town** 99-acre campus
- **Endowment** $500,000
- **Coed**

Undergraduates 426 full-time, 1,153 part-time. Students come from 2 states and territories; 2 other countries; 0.5% are from out of state; 38% Black or African American, non-Hispanic/Latino; 4% Race/ethnicity unknown. *Retention:* 66% of full-time freshmen returned.
Faculty *Student/faculty ratio:* 16:1.
Academics *Calendar:* semesters. *Degree:* certificates and associate. *Special study options:* academic remediation for entering students, adult/continuing education programs, advanced placement credit, cooperative education, distance learning, honors programs, independent study, internships, off-campus study, part-time degree program, summer session for credit.
Student Life *Campus security:* late-night transport/escort service.
Costs (2013–14) *Tuition:* state resident $3965 full-time, $122 per credit part-time; nonresident $9803 full-time, $298 per credit part-time. *Required fees:* $10 per credit part-time.
Financial Aid Of all full-time matriculated undergraduates who enrolled in 2012, 30 Federal Work-Study jobs (averaging $2000).
Applying *Options:* electronic application, deferred entrance. *Required:* high school transcript.
Freshman Application Contact Mrs. Trina Jones, Dean Student Services, Paul D. Camp Community College, PO Box 737, 100 N College Drive, Franklin, VA 23851. *Phone:* 757-569-6720. *E-mail:* tjones@pdc.edu.
Website: http://www.pdc.edu/.

Piedmont Virginia Community College
Charlottesville, Virginia

- **State-supported** 2-year, founded 1972, part of Virginia Community College System
- **Suburban** 114-acre campus with easy access to Richmond
- **Coed,** 5,630 undergraduate students, 21% full-time, 59% women, 41% men

Undergraduates 1,208 full-time, 4,422 part-time. Students come from 15 states and territories; 13% Black or African American, non-Hispanic/Latino; 5% Hispanic/Latino; 4% Asian, non-Hispanic/Latino; 0.2% Native Hawaiian or other Pacific Islander, non-Hispanic/Latino; 0.3% American Indian or Alaska Native, non-Hispanic/Latino; 4% Two or more races, non-Hispanic/Latino; 1% Race/ethnicity unknown; 0.5% international; 6% transferred in.
Freshmen *Admission:* 765 enrolled.
Faculty *Total:* 78. *Student/faculty ratio:* 16:1.
Majors Biological and physical sciences; business administration and management; computer and information sciences and support services related; computer programming; computer science; criminal justice/police science; culinary arts; diagnostic medical sonography and ultrasound technology; education; emergency medical technology (EMT paramedic); engineering; general studies; liberal arts and sciences/liberal studies; marketing/marketing management; radiologic technology/science; registered nursing/registered nurse; visual and performing arts.
Academics *Calendar:* semesters. *Degree:* certificates and associate. *Special study options:* academic remediation for entering students, adult/continuing education programs, advanced placement credit, cooperative education, distance learning, English as a second language, honors programs, independent study, internships, part-time degree program, services for LD students, summer session for credit. *ROTC:* Army (c).
Library Jessup Library with 38,799 titles, 53 serial subscriptions, 1,143 audiovisual materials, an OPAC, a Web page.
Student Life *Housing:* college housing not available. *Activities and Organizations:* drama/theater group, student-run newspaper, choral group. *Campus security:* 24-hour emergency response devices and patrols, late-night transport/escort service.
Athletics *Intramural sports:* basketball M/W, golf M/W, soccer M/W, table tennis M/W, tennis M/W, ultimate Frisbee M/W, volleyball M/W, weight lifting M/W.
Costs (2014–15) *Tuition:* state resident $3995 full-time, $123 per credit hour part-time; nonresident $8973 full-time, $299 per credit hour part-time. Full-time tuition and fees vary according to course load. Part-time tuition and fees vary according to course load. *Required fees:* $335 full-time, $11 per credit hour part-time. *Payment plan:* installment. *Waivers:* senior citizens and employees or children of employees.
Financial Aid Of all full-time matriculated undergraduates who enrolled in 2012, 50 Federal Work-Study jobs.

Applying *Options:* electronic application, early admission, deferred entrance. *Required for some:* high school transcript, Admission to programs in Nursing, Practical Nursing, Radiography, Sonography, Surgical Technology, Emergency Medical Services, Health Information Management, and Patient Admissions Coordination is competitive and/or requires completion of specific prerequisites. *Application deadlines:* rolling (freshmen), rolling (transfers). *Notification:* continuous (freshmen), continuous (transfers).
Freshman Application Contact Ms. Mary Lee Walsh, Dean of Student Services, Piedmont Virginia Community College, 501 College Drive, Charlottesville, VA 22902-7589. *Phone:* 434-961-6540. *Fax:* 434-961-5425. *E-mail:* mwalsh@pvcc.edu.
Website: http://www.pvcc.edu/.

Rappahannock Community College
Glenns, Virginia

- **State and locally supported** 2-year, founded 1970, part of Virginia Community College System
- **Rural** campus
- **Coed**, 3,555 undergraduate students, 23% full-time, 62% women, 38% men

Undergraduates 832 full-time, 2,723 part-time.
Majors Accounting; administrative assistant and secretarial science; biological and physical sciences; business administration and management; business administration, management and operations related; criminal justice/law enforcement administration; criminal justice/police science; engineering technology; information science/studies; liberal arts and sciences/liberal studies; registered nursing/registered nurse.
Academics *Calendar:* semesters. *Degree:* certificates and associate. *Special study options:* academic remediation for entering students, adult/continuing education programs, distance learning, honors programs, internships, off-campus study, part-time degree program, services for LD students, summer session for credit.
Library an OPAC, a Web page.
Student Life *Student services:* personal/psychological counseling.
Athletics *Intercollegiate sports:* softball W.
Costs (2013–14) *Tuition:* state resident $3675 full-time, $123 per credit hour part-time; nonresident $8973 full-time, $299 per credit hour part-time. Full-time tuition and fees vary according to course load. Part-time tuition and fees vary according to course load. *Required fees:* $381 full-time, $13 per credit hour part-time. *Payment plan:* deferred payment.
Financial Aid Of all full-time matriculated undergraduates who enrolled in 2012, 40 Federal Work-Study jobs (averaging $1015).
Applying *Options:* electronic application, early admission. *Application deadlines:* rolling (freshmen), rolling (transfers). *Notification:* continuous (freshmen), continuous (transfers).
Freshman Application Contact Ms. Felicia Packett, Admissions and Records Officer, Rappahannock Community College, 12745 College Drive, Glenns, VA 23149-0287. *Phone:* 804-758-6740. *Toll-free phone:* 800-836-9381.
Website: http://www.rappahannock.edu/.

Richard Bland College of The College of William and Mary
Petersburg, Virginia

Freshman Application Contact Office of Admissions, Richard Bland College of The College of William and Mary, 11301 Johnson Road, Petersburg, VA 23805-7100. *Phone:* 804-862-6249.
Website: http://www.rbc.edu/.

Southside Virginia Community College
Alberta, Virginia

Freshman Application Contact Mr. Brent Richey, Dean of Enrollment Management, Southside Virginia Community College, 109 Campus Drive, Alberta, VA 23821. *Phone:* 434-949-1012. *Fax:* 434-949-7863. *E-mail:* rhina.jones@sv.vccs.edu.
Website: http://www.southside.edu/.

Southwest Virginia Community College
Richlands, Virginia

- **State-supported** 2-year, founded 1968, part of Virginia Community College System
- **Rural** 100-acre campus
- **Endowment** $11.0 million
- **Coed**, 2,766 undergraduate students, 42% full-time, 60% women, 40% men

Undergraduates 1,159 full-time, 1,607 part-time. Students come from 4 states and territories; 2% are from out of state; 3% Black or African American, non-Hispanic/Latino; 0.8% Hispanic/Latino; 0.8% Asian, non-Hispanic/Latino; 0.1% Native Hawaiian or other Pacific Islander, non-Hispanic/Latino; 0.4% American Indian or Alaska Native, non-Hispanic/Latino; 0.6% Two or more races, non-Hispanic/Latino; 0.3% Race/ethnicity unknown; 0.1% international; 19% transferred in. *Retention:* 57% of full-time freshmen returned.
Freshmen *Admission:* 504 enrolled.
Faculty *Total:* 226, 22% full-time. *Student/faculty ratio:* 16:1.
Majors Accounting related; business administration, management and operations related; business operations support and secretarial services related; child-care provision; computer and information sciences; criminal justice/law enforcement administration; electrical, electronic and communications engineering technology; emergency medical technology (EMT paramedic); liberal arts and sciences/liberal studies; mental and social health services and allied professions related; radiologic technology/science; registered nursing/registered nurse.
Academics *Calendar:* semesters. *Degree:* certificates, diplomas, and associate. *Special study options:* academic remediation for entering students, accelerated degree program, adult/continuing education programs, advanced placement credit, distance learning, double majors, honors programs, internships, off-campus study, part-time degree program, summer session for credit.
Library Southwest Virginia Community College Library with 111,000 titles, 950 serial subscriptions, 1,000 audiovisual materials, an OPAC, a Web page.
Student Life *Housing:* college housing not available. *Activities and Organizations:* choral group, Phi Theta Kappa, Phi Beta Lambda, Intervoice, Helping Minds Club, Project ACHEIVE. *Campus security:* 24-hour emergency response devices and patrols, student patrols, heavily saturated camera system. *Student services:* personal/psychological counseling.
Standardized Tests *Required:* VCCS Math and English Assessments (for admission).
Costs (2013–14) *Tuition:* state resident $3336 full-time, $130 per credit hour part-time; nonresident $8438 full-time, $352 per credit hour part-time. Full-time tuition and fees vary according to reciprocity agreements. Part-time tuition and fees vary according to reciprocity agreements. No tuition increase for student's term of enrollment. *Required fees:* $216 full-time, $9 per credit hour part-time. *Payment plan:* tuition prepayment.
Financial Aid Of all full-time matriculated undergraduates who enrolled in 2012, 150 Federal Work-Study jobs (averaging $1140).
Applying *Options:* electronic application, early admission, deferred entrance. *Required:* high school transcript, interview. *Application deadlines:* rolling (freshmen), rolling (transfers).
Freshman Application Contact Ms. Dionne Cook, Admissions Counselor, Southwest Virginia Community College, Box SVCC, Richlands, VA 24641. *Phone:* 276-964-7301. *Toll-free phone:* 800-822-7822. *Fax:* 276-964-7716. *E-mail:* dionne.cook@sw.edu.
Website: http://www.sw.edu/.

Thomas Nelson Community College
Hampton, Virginia

- **State-supported** 2-year, founded 1968, part of Virginia Community College System
- **Suburban** 85-acre campus with easy access to Virginia Beach
- **Coed**

Undergraduates 3,689 full-time, 7,253 part-time.
Faculty *Student/faculty ratio:* 22:1.
Academics *Calendar:* semesters. *Degree:* certificates, diplomas, and associate. *Special study options:* academic remediation for entering students, accelerated degree program, adult/continuing education programs, advanced placement credit, cooperative education, distance learning, English as a second language, honors programs, internships, off-campus study, part-time degree program, services for LD students, summer session for credit.
Student Life *Campus security:* 24-hour emergency response devices and patrols, late-night transport/escort service.
Costs (2013–14) *Tuition:* state resident $3705 full-time, $124 per credit hour part-time; nonresident $9003 full-time, $300 per credit hour part-time. *Required fees:* $276 full-time, $8 per credit hour part-time, $25 per term part-time.
Financial Aid Of all full-time matriculated undergraduates who enrolled in 2012, 62 Federal Work-Study jobs (averaging $4800).
Applying *Options:* electronic application, early admission, deferred entrance. *Required for some:* interview. *Recommended:* high school transcript.
Freshman Application Contact Ms. Geraldine Newson, Sr. Admission Specialist, Thomas Nelson Community College, PO Box 9407, Hampton, VA 23670-0407. *Phone:* 757-825-2800. *Fax:* 757-825-2763. *E-mail:* admissions@tncc.edu.
Website: http://www.tncc.edu/.

Tidewater Community College
Norfolk, Virginia

Freshman Application Contact Kellie Sorey PhD, Registrar, Tidewater Community College, Norfolk, VA 23510. *Phone:* 757-822-1900. *E-mail:* CentralRecords@tcc.edu.
Website: http://www.tcc.edu/.

Virginia College in Richmond
Richmond, Virginia

Admissions Office Contact Virginia College in Richmond, 7200 Midlothian Turnpike, Richmond, VA 23225.
Website: http://www.vc.edu/.

Virginia Highlands Community College
Abingdon, Virginia

Freshman Application Contact Karen Cheers, Acting Director of Admissions, Records, and Financial Aid, Virginia Highlands Community College, PO Box 828, 100 VHCC Drive Abingdon, Abingdon, VA 24212. *Phone:* 276-739-2490. *Toll-free phone:* 877-207-6115. *E-mail:* kcheers@vhcc.edu.
Website: http://www.vhcc.edu/.

Virginia Western Community College
Roanoke, Virginia

- **State-supported** 2-year, founded 1966, part of Virginia Community College System
- **Suburban** 70-acre campus
- **Endowment** $3.0 million
- **Coed,** 8,652 undergraduate students, 17% full-time, 55% women, 45% men

Undergraduates 1,477 full-time, 7,175 part-time. Students come from 9 states and territories; 54 other countries; 2% are from out of state; 12% Black or African American, non-Hispanic/Latino; 3% Hispanic/Latino; 0.4% Asian, non-Hispanic/Latino; 0.3% American Indian or Alaska Native, non-Hispanic/Latino; 3% Two or more races, non-Hispanic/Latino; 0.7% Race/ethnicity unknown; 0.6% international; 4% transferred in. *Retention:* 55% of full-time freshmen returned.
Freshmen *Admission:* 2,464 enrolled.
Faculty *Total:* 432, 22% full-time. *Student/faculty ratio:* 19:1.
Majors Accounting; administrative assistant and secretarial science; art; automobile/automotive mechanics technology; biological and physical sciences; business administration and management; child development; civil engineering technology; commercial and advertising art; computer science; criminal justice/law enforcement administration; data processing and data processing technology; dental hygiene; education; electrical, electronic and communications engineering technology; engineering; industrial radiologic technology; kindergarten/preschool education; liberal arts and sciences/liberal studies; mechanical engineering/mechanical technology; mental health counseling; pre-engineering; radio and television; radiologic technology/science; registered nursing/registered nurse.
Academics *Calendar:* semesters. *Degree:* certificates and associate. *Special study options:* academic remediation for entering students, advanced placement credit, cooperative education, distance learning, double majors, English as a second language, honors programs, independent study, internships, part-time degree program, services for LD students, summer session for credit.
Library Brown Library with an OPAC, a Web page.
Student Life *Housing:* college housing not available. *Activities and Organizations:* drama/theater group, student-run newspaper. *Campus security:* 24-hour emergency response devices and patrols, late-night transport/escort service. *Student services:* personal/psychological counseling.
Athletics *Intramural sports:* basketball M/W, soccer M, volleyball W.
Costs (2014–15) *Tuition:* state resident $3422 full-time, $143 per credit part-time; nonresident $8093 full-time, $337 per credit part-time. *Waivers:* employees or children of employees.
Applying *Options:* electronic application, early admission, deferred entrance. *Required for some:* high school transcript. *Recommended:* high school transcript. *Application deadlines:* rolling (freshmen), rolling (transfers). *Notification:* continuous (freshmen), continuous (transfers).
Freshman Application Contact Admissions Office, Virginia Western Community College, PO Box 14007, Roanoke, VA 24038. *Phone:* 540-857-7231.
Website: http://www.virginiawestern.edu/.

Wytheville Community College
Wytheville, Virginia

- **State-supported** 2-year, founded 1967, part of Virginia Community College System
- **Rural** 141-acre campus
- **Coed,** 3,468 undergraduate students, 35% full-time, 64% women, 36% men

Undergraduates 1,209 full-time, 2,259 part-time. 8% Black or African American, non-Hispanic/Latino; 1% Hispanic/Latino; 1% Asian, non-Hispanic/Latino; 0.3% American Indian or Alaska Native, non-Hispanic/Latino; 3% Two or more races, non-Hispanic/Latino; 0.1% Race/ethnicity unknown. *Retention:* 55% of full-time freshmen returned.
Faculty *Total:* 163, 28% full-time. *Student/faculty ratio:* 17:1.
Majors Accounting; administrative assistant and secretarial science; biological and physical sciences; business administration and management; civil engineering technology; clinical/medical laboratory technology; corrections; criminal justice/law enforcement administration; criminal justice/police science; dental hygiene; drafting and design technology; education; electrical, electronic and communications engineering technology; information science/studies; liberal arts and sciences/liberal studies; machine tool technology; mass communication/media; mechanical engineering/mechanical technology; medical administrative assistant and medical secretary; physical therapy; registered nursing/registered nurse.
Academics *Calendar:* semesters. *Degree:* certificates, diplomas, and associate. *Special study options:* academic remediation for entering students, adult/continuing education programs, advanced placement credit, distance learning, external degree program, independent study, part-time degree program, services for LD students, summer session for credit.
Library Wytheville Community College Library.
Student Life *Housing:* college housing not available. *Activities and Organizations:* drama/theater group, student-run newspaper. *Campus security:* 24-hour emergency response devices and patrols.
Athletics Member NJCAA. *Intercollegiate sports:* basketball M, volleyball W. *Intramural sports:* golf M/W.
Costs (2013–14) *Tuition:* state resident $3675 full-time, $123 per credit part-time; nonresident $8973 full-time, $299 per credit part-time. *Required fees:* $315 full-time, $11 per credit part-time.
Financial Aid Of all full-time matriculated undergraduates who enrolled in 2012, 125 Federal Work-Study jobs (averaging $2592).
Applying *Options:* early admission. *Required:* high school transcript. *Required for some:* interview. *Application deadlines:* rolling (freshmen), rolling (transfers). *Notification:* continuous (freshmen), continuous (transfers).
Freshman Application Contact Wytheville Community College, 1000 East Main Street, Wytheville, VA 24382-3308. *Phone:* 276-223-4701. *Toll-free phone:* 800-468-1195.
Website: http://www.wcc.vccs.edu/.

WASHINGTON

Bates Technical College
Tacoma, Washington

Director of Admissions Director of Admissions, Bates Technical College, 1101 South Yakima Avenue, Tacoma, WA 98405-4895. *Phone:* 253-680-7000. *E-mail:* registration@bates.ctc.edu.
Website: http://www.bates.ctc.edu/.

Bellevue College
Bellevue, Washington

Freshman Application Contact Morenika Jacobs, Associate Dean of Enrollment Services, Bellevue College, 3000 Landerholm Circle, SE, Bellevue, WA 98007-6484. *Phone:* 425-564-2205. *Fax:* 425-564-4065.
Website: http://www.bcc.ctc.edu/.

Bellingham Technical College
Bellingham, Washington

- **State-supported** 2-year, founded 1957, part of Washington State Board for Community and Technical Colleges (SBCTC)
- **Suburban** 21-acre campus with easy access to Vancouver BC Canada
- **Coed,** 2,864 undergraduate students

Faculty *Total:* 189, 67% full-time. *Student/faculty ratio:* 24:1.
Majors Accounting technology and bookkeeping; autobody/collision and repair technology; automobile/automotive mechanics technology; building/property maintenance; civil engineering technology; communications systems installation and repair technology; computer systems networking and

telecommunications; culinary arts; data entry/microcomputer applications; diesel mechanics technology; electrician; executive assistant/executive secretary; fishing and fisheries sciences and management; heating, air conditioning, ventilation and refrigeration maintenance technology; heavy/industrial equipment maintenance technologies related; industrial mechanics and maintenance technology; instrumentation technology; legal assistant/paralegal; machine tool technology; marketing/marketing management; medical radiologic technology; registered nursing/registered nurse; surgical technology; surveying technology; welding technology.

Academics *Degree:* certificates and associate. *Special study options:* academic remediation for entering students, distance learning, English as a second language, internships, part-time degree program, services for LD students, summer session for credit.

Library Information Technology Resource Center with an OPAC, a Web page.

Student Life *Housing:* college housing not available. *Student services:* personal/psychological counseling.

Standardized Tests *Required:* ACCUPLACER entrance exam or waiver (for admission).

Applying *Options:* early admission, deferred entrance. *Required for some:* high school transcript, some programs have prerequisites. *Application deadlines:* rolling (freshmen), rolling (out-of-state freshmen), rolling (transfers).

Freshman Application Contact Bellingham Technical College, 3028 Lindbergh Avenue, Bellingham, WA 98225. *Phone:* 360-752-8324.

Website: http://www.btc.ctc.edu/.

Big Bend Community College
Moses Lake, Washington

- **State-supported** 2-year, founded 1962
- **Small-town** 159-acre campus
- **Coed,** 1,840 undergraduate students, 71% full-time, 57% women, 43% men

Undergraduates 1,311 full-time, 529 part-time. 2% Black or African American, non-Hispanic/Latino; 32% Hispanic/Latino; 1% Asian, non-Hispanic/Latino; 0.7% American Indian or Alaska Native, non-Hispanic/Latino; 2% Two or more races, non-Hispanic/Latino; 2% Race/ethnicity unknown; 0.2% international; 5% live on campus.

Freshmen *Admission:* 261 enrolled.

Faculty *Student/faculty ratio:* 21:1.

Majors Accounting technology and bookkeeping; agricultural production; airline pilot and flight crew; automobile/automotive mechanics technology; avionics maintenance technology; computer support specialist; computer systems networking and telecommunications; early childhood education; industrial electronics technology; industrial mechanics and maintenance technology; liberal arts and sciences/liberal studies; licensed practical/vocational nurse training; medical/clinical assistant; medical office management; network and system administration; office management; registered nursing/registered nurse; welding technology.

Academics *Calendar:* quarters. *Degree:* certificates and associate. *Special study options:* academic remediation for entering students, advanced placement credit, cooperative education, distance learning, English as a second language, part-time degree program, services for LD students, summer session for credit.

Library Big Bend Community College Library with 42,647 titles, 115 serial subscriptions, 4,124 audiovisual materials, an OPAC, a Web page.

Student Life *Housing Options:* coed. Campus housing is university owned. *Activities and Organizations:* choral group. *Campus security:* 24-hour emergency response devices, student patrols, late-night transport/escort service, controlled dormitory access, daytime security on campus during the week, student security in dorms four evenings a week, Enhanced Campus Notification System. *Student services:* personal/psychological counseling.

Athletics *Intercollegiate sports:* baseball M, basketball M/W, softball W, volleyball W.

Costs (2013–14) *One-time required fee:* $30. *Tuition:* state resident $4150 full-time, $112 per credit hour part-time; nonresident $4550 full-time, $125 per credit hour part-time. Full-time tuition and fees vary according to course load and program. Part-time tuition and fees vary according to course load and program. *Required fees:* $150 full-time, $5 per credit hour part-time. *Room and board:* $7140. *Payment plan:* installment. *Waivers:* senior citizens.

Applying *Options:* electronic application, early admission, deferred entrance. *Application fee:* $30. *Required for some:* high school transcript. *Application deadlines:* rolling (freshmen), rolling (transfers). *Notification:* continuous (freshmen), continuous (transfers).

Freshman Application Contact Candis Lacher, Associate Vice President of Student Services, Big Bend Community College, 7662 Chanute Street, Moses Lake, WA 98837. *Phone:* 509-793-2061. *Toll-free phone:* 877-745-1212. *Fax:* 509-793-6243. *E-mail:* admissions@bigbend.edu. *Website:* http://www.bigbend.edu/.

Carrington College–Spokane
Spokane, Washington

- **Proprietary** 2-year, founded 1976, part of Carrington Colleges Group, Inc.
- **Coed,** 538 undergraduate students, 100% full-time, 83% women, 17% men

Undergraduates 538 full-time. 18% are from out of state; 4% Black or African American, non-Hispanic/Latino; 8% Hispanic/Latino; 1% Asian, non-Hispanic/Latino; 0.4% Native Hawaiian or other Pacific Islander, non-Hispanic/Latino; 3% American Indian or Alaska Native, non-Hispanic/Latino; 3% Two or more races, non-Hispanic/Latino; 1% Race/ethnicity unknown; 15% transferred in.

Freshmen *Admission:* 71 enrolled.

Faculty *Total:* 29, 34% full-time. *Student/faculty ratio:* 33:1.

Majors Medical administrative assistant and medical secretary; medical office management; medical radiologic technology.

Academics *Degree:* certificates and associate.

Student Life *Housing:* college housing not available.

Applying *Required:* essay or personal statement, high school transcript, interview, Entrance test administered by Carrington College.

Freshman Application Contact Carrington College–Spokane, 10102 East Knox Avenue, Suite 200, Spokane, WA 99206.

Website: http://carrington.edu/.

Cascadia Community College
Bothell, Washington

- **State-supported** 2-year, founded 1999
- **Suburban** 128-acre campus
- **Coed,** 2,670 undergraduate students, 40% full-time, 48% women, 52% men

Undergraduates 1,060 full-time, 1,610 part-time. 3% Black or African American, non-Hispanic/Latino; 9% Hispanic/Latino; 11% Asian, non-Hispanic/Latino; 1% American Indian or Alaska Native, non-Hispanic/Latino; 3% Two or more races, non-Hispanic/Latino; 11% Race/ethnicity unknown; 4% international.

Freshmen *Admission:* 393 enrolled.

Faculty *Total:* 131, 29% full-time. *Student/faculty ratio:* 23:1.

Majors Liberal arts and sciences and humanities related; liberal arts and sciences/liberal studies; science technologies related.

Academics *Calendar:* quarters. *Degree:* certificates and associate. *Special study options:* academic remediation for entering students, accelerated degree program, adult/continuing education programs, advanced placement credit, cooperative education, distance learning, double majors, English as a second language, independent study, internships, off-campus study, part-time degree program, services for LD students, study abroad, summer session for credit.

Library UWB/CCC Campus Library with 73,749 titles, 850 serial subscriptions, 6,100 audiovisual materials, an OPAC, a Web page.

Student Life *Housing:* college housing not available. *Activities and Organizations:* drama/theater group, student-run newspaper. *Campus security:* 24-hour emergency response devices, late-night transport/escort service.

Costs (2014–15) *One-time required fee:* $30. *Tuition:* state resident $4020 full-time; nonresident $4818 full-time. Full-time tuition and fees vary according to course load and program. Part-time tuition and fees vary according to course load and program. *Required fees:* $270 full-time. *Waivers:* senior citizens and employees or children of employees.

Applying *Options:* electronic application. *Application deadlines:* rolling (freshmen), rolling (out-of-state freshmen), rolling (transfers). *Notification:* continuous (freshmen), continuous (out-of-state freshmen), continuous (transfers).

Freshman Application Contact Ms. Erin Blakeney, Dean for Student Success, Cascadia Community College, 18345 Campus Way, NE, Bothell, WA 98011. *Phone:* 425-352-8000. *Fax:* 425-352-8137. *E-mail:* admissions@cascadia.edu.

Website: http://www.cascadia.edu/.

Centralia College
Centralia, Washington

Freshman Application Contact Admissions Office, Centralia College, Centralia, WA 98531. *Phone:* 360-736-9391 Ext. 221. *Fax:* 360-330-7503. *E-mail:* admissions@centralia.edu.

Website: http://www.centralia.edu/.

Clark College

Vancouver, Washington

- **State-supported** 2-year, founded 1933, part of Washington State Board for Community and Technical Colleges
- **Urban** 101-acre campus with easy access to Portland
- **Coed,** 11,462 undergraduate students, 49% full-time, 57% women, 43% men

Undergraduates 5,636 full-time, 5,826 part-time. 3% are from out of state; 2% Black or African American, non-Hispanic/Latino; 8% Hispanic/Latino; 4% Asian, non-Hispanic/Latino; 0.1% Native Hawaiian or other Pacific Islander, non-Hispanic/Latino; 0.7% American Indian or Alaska Native, non-Hispanic/Latino; 8% Two or more races, non-Hispanic/Latino; 6% Race/ethnicity unknown; 0.6% international; 4% transferred in.

Freshmen *Admission:* 1,810 applied, 1,810 admitted, 1,284 enrolled.

Faculty *Total:* 660, 31% full-time, 14% with terminal degrees. *Student/faculty ratio:* 21:1.

Majors Accounting technology and bookkeeping; applied horticulture/horticulture operations; automobile/automotive mechanics technology; baking and pastry arts; business administration and management; business automation/technology/data entry; computer programming; computer systems networking and telecommunications; construction engineering technology; culinary arts; data entry/microcomputer applications; dental hygiene; diesel mechanics technology; early childhood education; electrical, electronic and communications engineering technology; emergency medical technology (EMT paramedic); executive assistant/executive secretary; graphic communications; human resources management; landscaping and groundskeeping; legal administrative assistant/secretary; legal assistant/paralegal; liberal arts and sciences/liberal studies; machine tool technology; manufacturing engineering technology; medical administrative assistant and medical secretary; medical/clinical assistant; radiologic technology/science; registered nursing/registered nurse; retailing; selling skills and sales; sport and fitness administration/management; substance abuse/addiction counseling; surveying technology; telecommunications technology; web/multimedia management and webmaster; welding technology.

Academics *Calendar:* quarters. *Degree:* certificates, diplomas, and associate. *Special study options:* adult/continuing education programs, part-time degree program. *ROTC:* Army (c), Air Force (c).

Library Lewis D. Cannell Library.

Student Life *Housing:* college housing not available. *Campus security:* 24-hour patrols, late-night transport/escort service, security staff during hours of operation.

Athletics *Intercollegiate sports:* baseball M, basketball M(s)/W(s), cross-country running M(s)/W(s), fencing M(c)/W(c), soccer M(s)/W(s), softball W, track and field M(s)/W(s), volleyball W(s). *Intramural sports:* basketball M/W, fencing M/W, soccer M/W, softball M/W, volleyball M/W.

Costs (2013–14) *Tuition:* area resident $4154 full-time, $110 per credit hour part-time; state resident $4544 full-time, $123 per credit hour part-time; nonresident $9389 full-time, $282 per credit hour part-time. Full-time tuition and fees vary according to course load and reciprocity agreements. Part-time tuition and fees vary according to course load and reciprocity agreements. *Payment plan:* installment. *Waivers:* senior citizens and employees or children of employees.

Applying *Options:* electronic application, early admission, deferred entrance. *Application fee:* $20.

Freshman Application Contact Ms. Sheryl Anderson, Director of Admissions, Clark College, Vancouver, WA 98663. *Phone:* 360-992-2308. *Fax:* 360-992-2867. *E-mail:* admissions@clark.edu. ·

Website: http://www.clark.edu/.

Clover Park Technical College

Lakewood, Washington

Director of Admissions Ms. Judy Richardson, Registrar, Clover Park Technical College, 4500 Steilacoom Boulevard, SW, Lakewood, WA 98499. *Phone:* 253-589-5570.

Website: http://www.cptc.edu/.

Columbia Basin College

Pasco, Washington

Freshman Application Contact Admissions Department, Columbia Basin College, 2600 North 20th Avenue, Pasco, WA 99301-3397. *Phone:* 509-542-4524. *Fax:* 509-544-2023. *E-mail:* admissions@columbiabasin.edu.

Website: http://www.columbiabasin.edu/.

Edmonds Community College

Lynnwood, Washington

Freshman Application Contact Ms. Nancy Froemming, Enrollment Services Office Manager, Edmonds Community College, 20000 68th Avenue West, Lynwood, WA 98036-5999. *Phone:* 425-640-1853. *Fax:* 425-640-1159. *E-mail:* nanci.froemming@edcc.edu.

Website: http://www.edcc.edu/.

Everest College

Vancouver, Washington

Director of Admissions Ms. Renee Schiffhauer, Director of Admissions, Everest College, 120 Northeast 136th Avenue, Suite 130, Vancouver, WA 98684. *Phone:* 360-254-3282. *Toll-free phone:* 888-741-4270. *Fax:* 360-254-3035. *E-mail:* rschiffhauer@cci.edu.

Website: http://www.everest.edu/.

Everett Community College

Everett, Washington

Freshman Application Contact Ms. Linda Baca, Entry Services Manager, Everett Community College, 2000 Tower Street, Everett, WA 98201-1327. *Phone:* 425-388-9219. *Fax:* 425-388-9173. *E-mail:* admissions@everettcc.edu.

Website: http://www.everettcc.edu/.

Grays Harbor College

Aberdeen, Washington

- **State-supported** 2-year, founded 1930, part of Washington State Board for Community and Technical Colleges
- **Small-town** 125-acre campus
- **Endowment** $8.6 million
- **Coed,** 1,966 undergraduate students, 67% full-time, 50% women, 50% men

Undergraduates 1,312 full-time, 654 part-time. Students come from 1 other state; 4% Black or African American, non-Hispanic/Latino; 8% Hispanic/Latino; 2% Asian, non-Hispanic/Latino; 0.5% Native Hawaiian or other Pacific Islander, non-Hispanic/Latino; 3% American Indian or Alaska Native, non-Hispanic/Latino; 6% Two or more races, non-Hispanic/Latino; 2% Race/ethnicity unknown; 0.2% international; 23% transferred in. *Retention:* 57% of full-time freshmen returned.

Freshmen *Admission:* 52 enrolled.

Faculty *Total:* 134, 52% full-time, 100% with terminal degrees. *Student/faculty ratio:* 19:1.

Majors Accounting technology and bookkeeping; automobile/automotive mechanics technology; business administration and management; carpentry; child-care and support services management; criminal justice/police science; diesel mechanics technology; general studies; human services; industrial technology; information science/studies; liberal arts and sciences/liberal studies; natural resources/conservation; office management; registered nursing/registered nurse; welding technology.

Academics *Calendar:* quarters. *Degree:* certificates, diplomas, and associate. *Special study options:* academic remediation for entering students, accelerated degree program, adult/continuing education programs, advanced placement credit, cooperative education, distance learning, double majors, English as a second language, external degree program, honors programs, independent study, internships, part-time degree program, services for LD students, study abroad, summer session for credit.

Library Spellman Library with 40,000 titles, 240 serial subscriptions, an OPAC, a Web page.

Student Life *Housing:* college housing not available. *Activities and Organizations:* drama/theater group, student-run newspaper, choral group, Phi Theta Kappa, TYEE, Student Nurses Association, Human Services Student Association, Student Council. *Campus security:* 24-hour emergency response devices, late-night transport/escort service. *Student services:* personal/psychological counseling, women's center.

Athletics *Intercollegiate sports:* baseball M(s), basketball M(s)/W(s), golf M(s)/W(s), soccer W, softball W(s), volleyball W.

Financial Aid Of all full-time matriculated undergraduates who enrolled in 2012, 1,458 applied for aid, 1,415 were judged to have need. 58 Federal Work-Study jobs (averaging $1315). 132 state and other part-time jobs (averaging $2089). *Average financial aid package:* $5932. *Average need-based gift aid:* $6094.

Applying *Options:* electronic application, early admission. *Recommended:* high school transcript. *Application deadlines:* rolling (freshmen), 9/1 (transfers). *Notification:* continuous (freshmen), continuous (transfers).
Freshman Application Contact Ms. Brenda Dell, Admissions Officer, Grays Harbor College, 1620 Edward P. Smith Drive, Aberdeen, WA 98520. *Phone:* 360-532-4216. *Toll-free phone:* 800-562-4830.
Website: http://www.ghc.edu/.

Green River Community College
Auburn, Washington

Freshman Application Contact Ms. Peggy Morgan, Program Support Supervisor, Green River Community College, 12401 Southeast 320th Street, Auburn, WA 98092-3699. *Phone:* 253-833-9111. *Fax:* 253-288-3454.
Website: http://www.greenriver.edu/.

Highline Community College
Des Moines, Washington

Freshman Application Contact Ms. Michelle Kuwasaki, Director of Admissions, Highline Community College, 2400 South 240th Street, Des Moines, WA 98198-9800. *Phone:* 206-878-3710 Ext. 9800.
Website: http://www.highline.edu/.

ITT Technical Institute
Everett, Washington

- **Proprietary** primarily 2-year, part of ITT Educational Services, Inc.
- **Coed**

Majors Business administration and management; construction management; cyber/computer forensics and counterterrorism; drafting and design technology; electrical, electronic and communications engineering technology; forensic science and technology; game and interactive media design; graphic communications; information technology project management; network and system administration; project management.
Academics *Degrees:* associate and bachelor's.
Freshman Application Contact Director of Recruitment, ITT Technical Institute, 1615 75th Street SW, Everett, WA 98203. *Phone:* 425-583-0200.
Toll-free phone: 800-272-3791.
Website: http://www.itt-tech.edu/.

ITT Technical Institute
Seattle, Washington

- **Proprietary** primarily 2-year, founded 1932, part of ITT Educational Services, Inc.
- **Urban** campus
- **Coed**

Majors Business administration and management; computer programming (specific applications); construction management; cyber/computer forensics and counterterrorism; drafting and design technology; electrical, electronic and communications engineering technology; forensic science and technology; graphic communications; industrial technology; information technology project management; network and system administration; project management.
Academics *Calendar:* quarters. *Degrees:* associate and bachelor's.
Student Life *Housing:* college housing not available.
Freshman Application Contact Director of Recruitment, ITT Technical Institute, 12720 Gateway Drive, Suite 100, Seattle, WA 98168-3333. *Phone:* 206-244-3300. *Toll-free phone:* 800-422-2029.
Website: http://www.itt-tech.edu/.

ITT Technical Institute
Spokane Valley, Washington

- **Proprietary** primarily 2-year, founded 1985, part of ITT Educational Services, Inc.
- **Suburban** campus
- **Coed**

Majors Business administration and management; computer programming (specific applications); construction management; cyber/computer forensics and counterterrorism; drafting and design technology; electrical, electronic and communications engineering technology; forensic science and technology; game and interactive media design; graphic communications; industrial technology; information technology project management; network and system administration; project management.
Academics *Calendar:* quarters. *Degrees:* associate and bachelor's.
Student Life *Housing:* college housing not available.
Freshman Application Contact Director of Recruitment, ITT Technical Institute, 13518 East Indiana Avenue, Spokane Valley, WA 99216. *Phone:* 509-926-2900. *Toll-free phone:* 800-777-8324.
Website: http://www.itt-tech.edu/.

Lake Washington Institute of Technology
Kirkland, Washington

Freshman Application Contact Shawn Miller, Registrar Enrollment Services, Lake Washington Institute of Technology, 11605 132nd Avenue NE, Kirkland, WA 98034-8506. *Phone:* 425-739-8104. *E-mail:* info@lwtech.edu.
Website: http://www.lwtech.edu/.

Lower Columbia College
Longview, Washington

- **State-supported** 2-year, founded 1934, part of Washington State Board for Community and Technical Colleges
- **Rural** 39-acre campus with easy access to Portland
- **Endowment** $13.6 million
- **Coed**, 3,199 undergraduate students, 55% full-time, 61% women, 39% men

Undergraduates 1,773 full-time, 1,426 part-time. Students come from 7 states and territories; 3 other countries; 7% are from out of state; 12% transferred in.
Freshmen *Admission:* 179 enrolled.
Faculty *Total:* 195, 31% full-time. *Student/faculty ratio:* 18:1.
Majors Accounting; accounting technology and bookkeeping; administrative assistant and secretarial science; automobile/automotive mechanics technology; business administration and management; criminal justice/law enforcement administration; data entry/microcomputer applications; diesel mechanics technology; early childhood education; fire science/firefighting; industrial mechanics and maintenance technology; instrumentation technology; legal administrative assistant/secretary; liberal arts and sciences/liberal studies; machine tool technology; medical administrative assistant and medical secretary; medical/clinical assistant; registered nursing/registered nurse; substance abuse/addiction counseling; welding technology.
Academics *Calendar:* quarters. *Degree:* certificates, diplomas, and associate. *Special study options:* academic remediation for entering students, adult/continuing education programs, advanced placement credit, cooperative education, distance learning, English as a second language, external degree program, independent study, internships, part-time degree program, services for LD students, student-designed majors, summer session for credit.
Library Alan Thompson Library plus 1 other with 28,005 titles, 57 serial subscriptions, 4,355 audiovisual materials, an OPAC, a Web page.
Student Life *Housing:* college housing not available. *Activities and Organizations:* drama/theater group, choral group, Phi Theta Kappa, Electric Vehicle Club, Multicultural Club, Global Medical Brigade, Sustainability Club. *Campus security:* 24-hour emergency response devices and patrols. *Student services:* personal/psychological counseling.
Athletics *Intercollegiate sports:* baseball M(s), basketball M(s)/W(s), soccer W(s), softball W(s), volleyball W(s).
Costs (2013–14) *One-time required fee:* $30. *Tuition:* state resident $4279 full-time, $115 per credit part-time; nonresident $4818 full-time, $129 per credit part-time. Full-time tuition and fees vary according to course load and reciprocity agreements. Part-time tuition and fees vary according to course load and reciprocity agreements. *Required fees:* $264 full-time, $7 per credit part-time. *Payment plan:* deferred payment. *Waivers:* senior citizens and employees or children of employees.
Financial Aid Of all full-time matriculated undergraduates who enrolled in 2012, 440 Federal Work-Study jobs (averaging $708). 447 state and other part-time jobs (averaging $2415).
Applying *Options:* electronic application. *Application fee:* $30. *Recommended:* high school transcript. *Application deadlines:* rolling (freshmen), rolling (transfers). *Notification:* continuous (freshmen).
Freshman Application Contact Ms. Karla Rivers, Acting Registrar, Lower Columbia College, 1600 Maple Street, Longview, WA 98632. *Phone:* 360-442-2373. *Toll-free phone:* 866-900-2311. *Fax:* 360-442-2379. *E-mail:* registration@lowercolumbia.edu.
Website: http://www.lowercolumbia.edu/.

North Seattle Community College
Seattle, Washington

Freshman Application Contact Ms. Betsy Abts, Registrar, North Seattle Community College, Seattle, WA 98103-3599. *Phone:* 206-934-3663. *Fax:* 206-934-3671. *E-mail:* arrc@seattlecolleges.edu.
Website: http://www.northseattle.edu/.

Northwest Indian College
Bellingham, Washington

Freshman Application Contact Office of Admissions, Northwest Indian College, 2522 Kwina Road, Bellingham, WA 98226. *Phone:* 360-676-2772.

Toll-free phone: 866-676-2772. *Fax:* 360-392-4333. *E-mail:* admissions@nwic.edu.
Website: http://www.nwic.edu/.

Northwest School of Wooden Boatbuilding
Port Hadlock, Washington

Director of Admissions Student Services Coordinator, Northwest School of Wooden Boatbuilding, 42 North Water Street, Port Hadlock, WA 98339. *Phone:* 360-385-4948. *Fax:* 360-385-5089. *E-mail:* info@nwboatschool.org. *Website:* http://www.nwboatschool.org/.

Olympic College
Bremerton, Washington

- **State-supported** primarily 2-year, founded 1946, part of Washington State Board for Community and Technical Colleges
- **Suburban** 33-acre campus with easy access to Seattle by ferry 30 miles, Tacoma by hwy 35 miles
- **Coed,** 7,951 undergraduate students

Undergraduates 5% Black or African American, non-Hispanic/Latino; 7% Hispanic/Latino; 9% Asian, non-Hispanic/Latino; 2% American Indian or Alaska Native, non-Hispanic/Latino; 1% international.
Freshmen *Admission:* 3,286 applied, 3,286 admitted.
Faculty *Total:* 450, 26% full-time.
Majors Accounting technology and bookkeeping; administrative assistant and secretarial science; business administration and management; computer systems networking and telecommunications; cosmetology; culinary arts; drafting and design technology; early childhood education; electrical, electronic and communications engineering technology; industrial technology; legal administrative assistant/secretary; medical/clinical assistant; organizational leadership; physical therapy technology; registered nursing/registered nurse; substance abuse/addiction counseling; welding technology.
Academics *Calendar:* quarters. *Degrees:* certificates, diplomas, associate, and bachelor's. *Special study options:* academic remediation for entering students, adult/continuing education programs, advanced placement credit, cooperative education, distance learning, English as a second language, honors programs, independent study, internships, off-campus study, part-time degree program, services for LD students, summer session for credit.
Library Haselwood Library with an OPAC, a Web page.
Student Life *Housing:* college housing not available. *Options:* coed. Campus housing is university owned. *Activities and Organizations:* drama/theater group, student-run newspaper, choral group, Phi Theta Kappa, International Student Club, Environmental Outreach, Armed Services, ASL. *Campus security:* 24-hour emergency response devices and patrols, student patrols, late-night transport/escort service. *Student services:* personal/psychological counseling.
Athletics *Intercollegiate sports:* baseball M(s), basketball M(s)/W(s), cross-country running M/W, golf M(s)/W(s), soccer M(s)/W(s), softball W(s), track and field M/W, volleyball W(s). *Intramural sports:* basketball M/W, table tennis M/W, volleyball M/W.
Costs (2013–14) *Tuition:* state resident $4000 full-time, $107 per credit part-time; nonresident $4465 full-time, $120 per credit part-time. Full-time tuition and fees vary according to course load and degree level. Part-time tuition and fees vary according to course load and degree level. *Required fees:* $195 full-time. *Payment plan:* installment. *Waivers:* senior citizens and employees or children of employees.
Financial Aid Of all full-time matriculated undergraduates who enrolled in 2012, 105 Federal Work-Study jobs (averaging $2380). 31 state and other part-time jobs (averaging $2880).
Applying *Options:* electronic application. *Required for some:* high school transcript. *Application deadlines:* rolling (freshmen), rolling (out-of-state freshmen), rolling (transfers).
Freshman Application Contact Ms. Jennifer Fyllingness, Director of Admissions, Outreach and International Student Services, Olympic College, 1600 Chester Avenue, Bremerton, WA 98337-1699. *Phone:* 360-475-7128. *Toll-free phone:* 800-259-6718. *Fax:* 360-475-7202. *E-mail:* jfyllingness@olympic.edu.
Website: http://www.olympic.edu/.

Peninsula College
Port Angeles, Washington

Freshman Application Contact Ms. Pauline Marvin, Peninsula College, 1502 East Lauridsen Boulevard, Port Angeles, WA 98362. *Phone:* 360-417-6596. *Toll-free phone:* 877-452-9277. *Fax:* 360-457-8100. *E-mail:* admissions@pencol.edu.
Website: http://www.pc.ctc.edu/.

Pierce College at Puyallup
Puyallup, Washington

- **State-supported** 2-year, founded 1967, part of Washington State Board for Community and Technical Colleges
- **Suburban** 140-acre campus with easy access to Seattle
- **Coed**

Undergraduates Students come from 12 other countries.
Academics *Calendar:* quarters. *Degree:* certificates, diplomas, and associate. *Special study options:* academic remediation for entering students, adult/continuing education programs, advanced placement credit, cooperative education, distance learning, English as a second language, independent study, internships, off-campus study, part-time degree program, services for LD students, study abroad, summer session for credit. *ROTC:* Army (c).
Student Life *Campus security:* 24-hour emergency response devices and patrols, late-night transport/escort service.
Financial Aid Of all full-time matriculated undergraduates who enrolled in 2012, 18 Federal Work-Study jobs (averaging $1889). 55 state and other part-time jobs (averaging $3058).
Applying *Options:* electronic application, early admission.
Freshman Application Contact Pierce College at Puyallup, 1601 39th Avenue Southeast, Puyallup, WA 98374. *Phone:* 253-840-8400.
Website: http://www.pierce.ctc.edu/.

Pima Medical Institute
Renton, Washington

Freshman Application Contact Pima Medical Institute, 555 South Renton Village Place, Renton, WA 98057. *Phone:* 425-228-9600.
Website: http://www.pmi.edu/.

Pima Medical Institute
Seattle, Washington

Freshman Application Contact Admissions Office, Pima Medical Institute, 9709 Third Avenue NE, Suite 400, Seattle, WA 98115. *Phone:* 206-322-6100. *Toll-free phone:* 800-477-PIMA (in-state); 888-477-PIMA (out-of-state). *Website:* http://www.pmi.edu/.

Renton Technical College
Renton, Washington

Director of Admissions Robin Young, Vice President for Student Services, Renton Technical College, 3000 NE Fourth Street, Renton, WA 98056. *Phone:* 425-235-2463.
Website: http://www.rtc.edu/.

Seattle Central Community College
Seattle, Washington

Freshman Application Contact Admissions Office, Seattle Central Community College, 1701 Broadway, Seattle, WA 98122-2400. *Phone:* 206-587-5450.
Website: http://www.seattlecentral.edu/.

Shoreline Community College
Shoreline, Washington

- **State-supported** 2-year, founded 1964, part of Washington State Board for Community and Technical Colleges
- **Suburban** 80-acre campus
- **Coed,** 8,591 undergraduate students

Faculty *Total:* 415, 37% full-time. *Student/faculty ratio:* 21:1.
Majors Accounting; automobile/automotive mechanics technology; biology/biotechnology laboratory technician; business administration and management; chemical engineering; child development; cinematography and film/video production; civil engineering technology; clinical/medical laboratory technology; commercial and advertising art; computer and information sciences; computer graphics; consumer merchandising/retailing management; cosmetology; dental hygiene; dietetics; drafting and design technology; education; engineering technology; environmental engineering technology; graphic and printing equipment operation/production; health information/medical records administration; human development and family studies; industrial technology; international business/trade/commerce; kindergarten/preschool education; liberal arts and sciences/liberal studies; machine tool technology; marine biology and biological oceanography; marine maintenance and ship repair technology; marketing/marketing management; mechanical engineering/mechanical technology; medical administrative assistant and medical secretary; music; oceanography (chemical and physical); photography; pre-engineering; purchasing, procurement/acquisitions and

contracts management; recording arts technology; registered nursing/registered nurse; teacher assistant/aide.

Academics *Calendar:* quarters. *Degree:* certificates, diplomas, and associate. *Special study options:* academic remediation for entering students, adult/continuing education programs, advanced placement credit, cooperative education, distance learning, English as a second language, independent study, internships, part-time degree program, services for LD students, study abroad, summer session for credit.

Library Ray W. Howard Library/Media Center with 79,554 titles, 1,735 serial subscriptions, an OPAC, a Web page.

Student Life *Housing:* college housing not available. *Campus security:* 24-hour emergency response devices and patrols. *Student services:* personal/psychological counseling, women's center.

Athletics *Intercollegiate sports:* archery M/W, baseball M(s), basketball M(s)/W(s), cross-country running M/W, soccer M(s)/W(s), softball W(s), tennis M(s)/W(s), volleyball W(s). *Intramural sports:* archery M/W, badminton M/W, basketball M/W, fencing M/W, gymnastics W, racquetball M/W, skiing (cross-country) M/W, skiing (downhill) M/W, softball M/W, swimming and diving M/W, volleyball M/W.

Standardized Tests *Recommended:* ACT ASSET or ACT COMPASS.

Applying *Options:* electronic application. *Required:* high school transcript. *Application deadlines:* rolling (freshmen), rolling (transfers).

Freshman Application Contact Shoreline Community College, 16101 Greenwood Avenue North, Shoreline, WA 98133-5696. *Phone:* 206-546-4613.

Website: http://www.shoreline.edu/.

Skagit Valley College
Mount Vernon, Washington

Freshman Application Contact Ms. Karen Marie Bade, Admissions and Recruitment Coordinator, Skagit Valley College, 2405 College Way, Mount Vernon, WA 98273-5899. *Phone:* 360-416-7620. *E-mail:* karenmarie.bade@skagit.edu.

Website: http://www.skagit.edu/.

South Puget Sound Community College
Olympia, Washington

- **State-supported** 2-year, founded 1970, part of Washington State Board for Community and Technical Colleges
- **Suburban** 102-acre campus with easy access to Seattle
- **Coed**

Undergraduates 2,693 full-time, 2,262 part-time. Students come from 16 states and territories; 27 other countries; 0.4% are from out of state; 2% Black or African American, non-Hispanic/Latino; 8% Hispanic/Latino; 5% Asian, non-Hispanic/Latino; 0.7% Native Hawaiian or other Pacific Islander, non-Hispanic/Latino; 1% American Indian or Alaska Native, non-Hispanic/Latino; 7% Two or more races, non-Hispanic/Latino; 11% Race/ethnicity unknown; 1% international; 33% transferred in. *Retention:* 59% of full-time freshmen returned.

Faculty *Student/faculty ratio:* 18:1.

Academics *Calendar:* quarters. *Degree:* certificates, diplomas, and associate. *Special study options:* academic remediation for entering students, adult/continuing education programs, advanced placement credit, cooperative education, distance learning, English as a second language, internships, part-time degree program, services for LD students, study abroad, summer session for credit. *ROTC:* Army (c).

Student Life *Campus security:* 24-hour emergency response devices and patrols, late-night transport/escort service.

Financial Aid Of all full-time matriculated undergraduates who enrolled in 2012, 42 Federal Work-Study jobs (averaging $3150). 14 state and other part-time jobs (averaging $4400). *Financial aid deadline:* 6/29.

Applying *Options:* electronic application, early admission, deferred entrance.

Freshman Application Contact Ms. Heidi Dearborn, South Puget Sound Community College, 2011 Mottman Road, SW, Olympia, WA 98512-6292. *Phone:* 360-754-7711 Ext. 5358. *E-mail:* hdearborn@spcc.edu.

Website: http://www.spscc.ctc.edu/.

South Seattle Community College
Seattle, Washington

Director of Admissions Ms. Kim Manderbach, Dean of Student Services/Registration, South Seattle Community College, 6000 16th Avenue, SW, Seattle, WA 98106-1499. *Phone:* 206-764-5378. *Fax:* 206-764-7947. *E-mail:* kimmanderb@sccd.ctc.edu.

Website: http://southseattle.edu/.

Spokane Community College
Spokane, Washington

Freshman Application Contact Ann Hightower-Chavez, Researcher, District Institutional Research, Spokane Community College, Spokane, WA 99217-5399. *Phone:* 509-434-5242. *Toll-free phone:* 800-248-5644. *Fax:* 509-434-5249. *E-mail:* mlee@ccs.spokane.edu.

Website: http://www.scc.spokane.edu/.

Spokane Falls Community College
Spokane, Washington

Freshman Application Contact Admissions Office, Spokane Falls Community College, Admissions MS 3011, 3410 West Fort George Wright Drive, Spokane, WA 99224. *Phone:* 509-533-3401. *Toll-free phone:* 888-509-7944. *Fax:* 509-533-3852.

Website: http://www.spokanefalls.edu/.

Tacoma Community College
Tacoma, Washington

Freshman Application Contact Enrollment Services, Tacoma Community College, 6501 South 19th Street, Tacoma, WA 98466. *Phone:* 253-566-5325. *Fax:* 253-566-6034.

Website: http://www.tacomacc.edu/.

Walla Walla Community College
Walla Walla, Washington

- **State-supported** 2-year, founded 1967, part of Washington State Board for Community and Technical Colleges
- **Small-town** 125-acre campus
- **Coed,** 5,109 undergraduate students, 58% full-time, 43% women, 57% men

Undergraduates 2,969 full-time, 2,140 part-time. Students come from 11 states and territories; 24% are from out of state; 4% Black or African American, non-Hispanic/Latino; 17% Hispanic/Latino; 1% Asian, non-Hispanic/Latino; 0.4% Native Hawaiian or other Pacific Islander, non-Hispanic/Latino; 1% American Indian or Alaska Native, non-Hispanic/Latino; 5% Two or more races, non-Hispanic/Latino; 5% Race/ethnicity unknown; 0.1% international; 15% transferred in. *Retention:* 67% of full-time freshmen returned.

Freshmen *Admission:* 491 enrolled.

Faculty *Total:* 313, 39% full-time. *Student/faculty ratio:* 20:1.

Majors Accounting technology and bookkeeping; administrative assistant and secretarial science; agricultural and domestic animal services related; agricultural business and management; agricultural business and management related; agricultural mechanization; agricultural mechanization related; agricultural production; autobody/collision and repair technology; automobile/automotive mechanics technology; biology/biological sciences; business administration and management; computer programming (vendor/product certification); computer systems networking and telecommunications; computer technology/computer systems technology; cosmetology; culinary arts; diesel mechanics technology; early childhood education; electrician; elementary education; engineering technology; fire science/firefighting; golf course operation and grounds management; heating, air conditioning, ventilation and refrigeration maintenance technology; legal administrative assistant/secretary; liberal arts and sciences/liberal studies; mathematics teacher education; medical administrative assistant and medical secretary; natural resources/conservation; natural resources/conservation related; registered nursing/registered nurse; turf and turfgrass management; viticulture and enology; web/multimedia management and webmaster; welding technology.

Academics *Calendar:* quarters. *Degree:* certificates, diplomas, and associate. *Special study options:* academic remediation for entering students, adult/continuing education programs, advanced placement credit, cooperative education, distance learning, external degree program, off-campus study, part-time degree program, summer session for credit.

Library Walla Walla Community College Library plus 1 other with 30,010 titles, 57 serial subscriptions, 19,000 audiovisual materials, an OPAC, a Web page.

Student Life *Housing:* college housing not available. *Activities and Organizations:* drama/theater group. *Campus security:* student patrols, late-night transport/escort service.

Athletics *Intercollegiate sports:* baseball M, basketball M/W, golf M/W, soccer M/W, softball W, volleyball W.

Costs (2014–15) *Tuition:* state resident $4376 full-time, $119 per credit part-time; nonresident $5675 full-time, $132 per credit part-time.

Financial Aid Of all full-time matriculated undergraduates who enrolled in 2012, 95 Federal Work-Study jobs (averaging $1600). 20 state and other part-time jobs (averaging $2000).

Applying *Options:* electronic application. *Required for some:* interview. *Recommended:* high school transcript. *Application deadlines:* rolling (freshmen), rolling (transfers).

Freshman Application Contact Walla Walla Community College, 500 Tausick Way, Walla Walla, WA 99362-9267. *Phone:* 509-522-2500. *Toll-free phone:* 877-992-9922.

Website: http://www.wwcc.edu/.

Wenatchee Valley College

Wenatchee, Washington

- **State and locally supported** 2-year, founded 1939, part of Washington State Board for Community and Technical Colleges
- **Rural** 56-acre campus
- **Coed,** 4,102 undergraduate students

Majors Accounting; accounting technology and bookkeeping; administrative assistant and secretarial science; agricultural production; athletic training; automobile/automotive mechanics technology; biology/biological sciences; business administration and management; casino management; chemistry; clinical/medical laboratory assistant; clinical/medical laboratory technology; computer systems networking and telecommunications; criminal justice/police science; design and applied arts related; early childhood education; economics; education; electrical/electronics equipment installation and repair; heating, air conditioning, ventilation and refrigeration maintenance technology; history; industrial electronics technology; kindergarten/preschool education; legal administrative assistant/secretary; liberal arts and sciences/liberal studies; licensed practical/vocational nurse training; mathematics; medical administrative assistant and medical secretary; medical/clinical assistant; music; music teacher education; natural resource recreation and tourism; office management; physical sciences; pre-engineering; radiologic technology/science; registered nursing/registered nurse; sociology; substance abuse/addiction counseling.

Academics *Calendar:* quarters. *Degree:* certificates, diplomas, and associate. *Special study options:* academic remediation for entering students, adult/continuing education programs, advanced placement credit, cooperative education, distance learning, English as a second language, external degree program, independent study, internships, part-time degree program, services for LD students, summer session for credit.

Library John Brown Library plus 1 other with an OPAC, a Web page.

Student Life *Housing Options:* coed. Campus housing is university owned. *Activities and Organizations:* drama/theater group, choral group. *Campus security:* 24-hour patrols, controlled dormitory access.

Athletics *Intercollegiate sports:* baseball M, basketball M(s)/W(s), soccer M/W, softball W(s), volleyball W(s). *Intramural sports:* basketball M/W, racquetball M/W, skiing (cross-country) M/W, skiing (downhill) M/W, tennis M/W, volleyball M/W, weight lifting M/W.

Applying *Options:* electronic application, early admission, deferred entrance. *Required for some:* high school transcript. *Application deadline:* rolling (freshmen).

Freshman Application Contact Escobedo, Wenatchee Valley College, 1300 Fifth Street, Wenatchee, WA 98801-1799. *Phone:* 509-682-6835 Ext. 2145.

Website: http://www.wvc.edu/.

Whatcom Community College

Bellingham, Washington

Freshman Application Contact Entry and Advising Center, Whatcom Community College, 237 West Kellogg Road, Bellingham, WA 98226-8003. *Phone:* 360-676-2170. *Fax:* 360-676-2171. *E-mail:* admit@whatcom.ctc.edu.

Website: http://www.whatcom.ctc.edu/.

Yakima Valley Community College

Yakima, Washington

Freshman Application Contact Denise Anderson, Registrar and Director for Enrollment Services, Yakima Valley Community College, PO Box 1647, Yakima, WA 98907-1647. *Phone:* 509-574-4702. *Fax:* 509-574-6879. *E-mail:* admis@yvcc.edu.

Website: http://www.yvcc.edu/.

WEST VIRGINIA

Blue Ridge Community and Technical College

Martinsburg, West Virginia

- **State-supported** 2-year, founded 1974, part of Community and Technical College System of West Virginia
- **Small-town** 46-acre campus
- **Coed,** 5,021 undergraduate students, 24% full-time, 66% women, 34% men

Undergraduates 1,191 full-time, 3,830 part-time. 5% are from out of state; 11% Black or African American, non-Hispanic/Latino; 4% Hispanic/Latino; 0.7% Asian, non-Hispanic/Latino; 0.1% Native Hawaiian or other Pacific Islander, non-Hispanic/Latino; 0.2% American Indian or Alaska Native, non-Hispanic/Latino; 3% Two or more races, non-Hispanic/Latino; 0.2% Race/ethnicity unknown; 6% transferred in. *Retention:* 51% of full-time freshmen returned.

Freshmen *Admission:* 865 applied, 705 admitted, 487 enrolled. *Average high school GPA:* 2.69. *Test scores:* SAT critical reading scores over 500: 45%; ACT scores over 18: 55%; SAT critical reading scores over 600: 10%; ACT scores over 24: 6%.

Faculty *Total:* 181, 34% full-time, 12% with terminal degrees. *Student/faculty ratio:* 23:1.

Majors Accounting; allied health and medical assisting services related; automation engineer technology; baking and pastry arts; business administration and management; business administration, management and operations related; clinical/medical laboratory technology; computer and information systems security; criminal justice/safety; culinary arts; data entry/microcomputer applications related; electrical and electronic engineering technologies related; emergency medical technology (EMT paramedic); general studies; information technology; legal assistant/paralegal; liberal arts and sciences/liberal studies; medical/clinical assistant; multi/interdisciplinary studies related; operations management; physical therapy technology; registered nursing/registered nurse; restaurant, culinary, and catering management; science technologies related; system, networking, and LAN/WAN management.

Academics *Degree:* certificates and associate. *Special study options:* academic remediation for entering students, accelerated degree program, adult/continuing education programs, advanced placement credit, double majors, English as a second language, independent study, internships, part-time degree program, services for LD students.

Library Martinsburg Public Library with 188,774 titles, 322 serial subscriptions, 17,081 audiovisual materials, an OPAC, a Web page.

Student Life *Housing:* college housing not available. *Activities and Organizations:* drama/theater group, Student Leadership Academy, Drama Club, Phi Theta Kappa, Skills USA, Student Nurses Association, national fraternities. *Campus security:* late-night transport/escort service. *Student services:* personal/psychological counseling.

Standardized Tests *Recommended:* SAT and SAT Subject Tests or ACT (for admission).

Applying *Options:* deferred entrance. *Application fee:* $25. *Required:* high school transcript. *Required for some:* interview.

Freshman Application Contact Brenda K. Neal, Director of Access, Blue Ridge Community and Technical College, 13650 Apple Harvest Drive, Martinsburg, WV 25403. *Phone:* 304-260-4380 Ext. 2109. *Fax:* 304-260-4376. *E-mail:* bneal@blueridgectc.edu.

Website: http://www.blueridgectc.edu/.

BridgeValley Community and Technical College

Montgomery, West Virginia

Director of Admissions Ms. Lisa Graham, Director of Admissions, BridgeValley Community and Technical College, 619 2nd Avenue, Montgomery, WV 25136. *Phone:* 304-442-3167.

Website: http://www.bridgevalley.edu/.

BridgeValley Community and Technical College

South Charleston, West Virginia

Freshman Application Contact Mr. Bryce Casto, Vice President, Student Affairs, BridgeValley Community and Technical College, 333 Sullivan Hall. *Phone:* 304-766-3140. *Fax:* 304-766-4158. *E-mail:* castosb@wvstateu.edu.

Website: http://www.bridgevalley.edu/.

Eastern West Virginia Community and Technical College

Moorefield, West Virginia

Freshman Application Contact Learner Support Services, Eastern West Virginia Community and Technical College, HC 65 Box 402, Moorefield, WV 26836. *Phone:* 304-434-8000. *Toll-free phone:* 877-982-2322. *Fax:* 304-434-7000. *E-mail:* askeast@eastern.wvnet.edu.
Website: http://www.eastern.wvnet.edu/.

Everest Institute

Cross Lanes, West Virginia

Freshman Application Contact Director of Admissions, Everest Institute, 5514 Big Tyler Road, Cross Lanes, WV 25313-1390. *Phone:* 304-776-6290. *Toll-free phone:* 888-741-4270. *Fax:* 304-776-6262.
Website: http://www.everest.edu/.

Huntington Junior College

Huntington, West Virginia

Director of Admissions Mr. James Garrett, Educational Services Director, Huntington Junior College, 900 Fifth Avenue, Huntington, WV 25701-2004. *Phone:* 304-697-7550. *Toll-free phone:* 800-344-4522.
Website: http://www.huntingtonjuniorcollege.com/.

ITT Technical Institute

Huntington, West Virginia

- **Proprietary** 2-year, part of ITT Educational Services, Inc.
- **Coed**

Majors Business administration and management; computer programming (specific applications); drafting and design technology; electrical, electronic and communications engineering technology; forensic science and technology; graphic communications; legal assistant/paralegal; network and system administration; registered nursing/registered nurse.

Academics *Calendar:* quarters. *Degree:* associate.

Freshman Application Contact Director of Recruitment, ITT Technical Institute, 5183 US Route 60, Building 1, Suite 40, Huntington, WV 25705. *Phone:* 304-733-8700. *Toll-free phone:* 800-224-4695.
Website: http://www.itt-tech.edu/.

Mountain State College

Parkersburg, West Virginia

- **Proprietary** 2-year, founded 1888
- **Small-town** campus
- **Coed,** 176 undergraduate students, 99% full-time, 92% women, 8% men

Undergraduates 174 full-time, 2 part-time. Students come from 2 states and territories; 3% transferred in. *Retention:* 70% of full-time freshmen returned.

Freshmen *Admission:* 28 enrolled.

Faculty *Total:* 11, 64% full-time, 36% with terminal degrees. *Student/faculty ratio:* 17:1.

Majors Accounting and business/management; administrative assistant and secretarial science; computer and information sciences; legal assistant/paralegal; medical/clinical assistant; medical transcription; substance abuse/addiction counseling.

Academics *Calendar:* quarters. *Degree:* diplomas and associate. *Special study options:* distance learning, double majors, honors programs, independent study, internships, part-time degree program.

Library Mountain State College Library with an OPAC.

Student Life *Housing:* college housing not available. *Student services:* personal/psychological counseling.

Standardized Tests *Required:* CPAt (for admission).

Costs (2013–14) *Tuition:* $8100 full-time, $2700 per term part-time. Full-time tuition and fees vary according to program. Part-time tuition and fees vary according to program. No tuition increase for student's term of enrollment. *Payment plan:* installment.

Applying *Required:* interview.

Freshman Application Contact Ms. Judith Sutton, President, Mountain State College, 1508 Spring Street, Parkersburg, WV 26101-3993. *Phone:* 304-485-5487. *Toll-free phone:* 800-841-0201. *Fax:* 304-485-3524. *E-mail:* jsutton@msc.edu.
Website: http://www.msc.edu/.

Mountwest Community & Technical College

Huntington, West Virginia

Freshman Application Contact Dr. Tammy Johnson, Admissions Director, Mountwest Community & Technical College, 1 John Marshall Drive, Huntington, WV 25755. *Phone:* 304-696-3160. *Toll-free phone:* 866-676-5533. *Fax:* 304-696-3135. *E-mail:* admissions@marshall.edu.
Website: http://www.mctc.edu/.

New River Community and Technical College

Beckley, West Virginia

Director of Admissions Dr. Allen B. Withers, Vice President, Student Services, New River Community and Technical College, 167 Dye Drive, Beckley, WV 25801. *Phone:* 304-929-5011. *E-mail:* awithers@newriver.edu.
Website: http://www.newriver.edu/.

Pierpont Community & Technical College

Fairmont, West Virginia

Freshman Application Contact Mr. Steve Leadman, Director of Admissions and Recruiting, Pierpont Community & Technical College, 1201 Locust Avenue, Fairmont, WV 26554. *Phone:* 304-367-4892. *Toll-free phone:* 800-641-5678. *Fax:* 304-367-4789.
Website: http://www.pierpont.edu/.

Potomac State College of West Virginia University

Keyser, West Virginia

- **State-supported** primarily 2-year, founded 1901, part of West Virginia Higher Education Policy Commission
- **Small-town** 18-acre campus
- **Coed,** 1,660 undergraduate students, 78% full-time, 54% women, 46% men

Undergraduates 1,289 full-time, 371 part-time. Students come from 25 states and territories; 4 other countries; 36% are from out of state; 16% Black or African American, non-Hispanic/Latino; 3% Hispanic/Latino; 0.2% Asian, non-Hispanic/Latino; 0.2% Native Hawaiian or other Pacific Islander, non-Hispanic/Latino; 0.4% American Indian or Alaska Native, non-Hispanic/Latino; 4% Two or more races, non-Hispanic/Latino; 0.6% Race/ethnicity unknown; 0.4% international; 3% transferred in; 38% live on campus. *Retention:* 45% of full-time freshmen returned.

Freshmen *Admission:* 3,149 applied, 1,064 admitted, 631 enrolled. *Average high school GPA:* 2.85. *Test scores:* SAT critical reading scores over 500: 17%; SAT math scores over 500: 19%; ACT scores over 18: 68%; SAT critical reading scores over 600: 2%; SAT math scores over 600: 4%; ACT scores over 24: 15%; ACT scores over 30: 1%.

Faculty *Total:* 88, 47% full-time, 13% with terminal degrees. *Student/faculty ratio:* 25:1.

Majors Accounting; administrative assistant and secretarial science; agricultural business and management; agricultural economics; agricultural mechanization; agricultural teacher education; agriculture; agriculture and agriculture operations related; agronomy and crop science; animal sciences; biological and physical sciences; biology/biological sciences; business administration and management; business/managerial economics; chemistry; civil engineering technology; computer and information sciences related; computer engineering technology; computer programming; computer programming (specific applications); computer science; computer systems networking and telecommunications; criminal justice/safety; data processing and data processing technology; economics; education; electrical, electronic and communications engineering technology; elementary education; engineering; English; forestry; forest technology; geology/earth science; history; horticultural science; hospitality administration; information technology; journalism; kindergarten/preschool education; liberal arts and sciences/liberal studies; mathematics; mechanical engineering/mechanical technology; medical administrative assistant and medical secretary; network and system administration; parks, recreation and leisure facilities management; physical education teaching and coaching; political science and government; pre-engineering; psychology; social work; sociology; wildlife, fish and wildlands science and management; wood science and wood products/pulp and paper technology.

Academics *Calendar:* semesters. *Degrees:* associate and bachelor's. *Special study options:* academic remediation for entering students, adult/continuing education programs, advanced placement credit, distance learning, double majors, honors programs, independent study, internships, part-time degree program, services for LD students, study abroad, summer session for credit.

Library Mary F. Shipper Library with 39,116 titles, 18,277 serial subscriptions, 244 audiovisual materials, an OPAC.

Student Life *Housing:* on-campus residence required through sophomore year. *Options:* coed. Campus housing is university owned. Freshman applicants given priority for college housing. *Activities and Organizations:* drama/theater group, student-run newspaper, choral group, Agriculture & Forestry Club, Black Student Alliance, Gamers & Geeks Club, Campus & Community Ministries. *Campus security:* 24-hour patrols, late-night transport/escort service, controlled dormitory access. *Student services:* health clinic, personal/psychological counseling.

Athletics Member NJCAA. *Intercollegiate sports:* baseball M(s), basketball M(s)/W(s), cross-country running M(s)/W(s), lacrosse M(s)/W(s), soccer M/W, softball W(s), volleyball W(s). *Intramural sports:* basketball M/W, football M/W, soccer M/W, softball M/W, table tennis M/W, ultimate Frisbee M/W, volleyball M/W.

Standardized Tests *Recommended:* SAT or ACT (for admission).

Costs (2013–14) *Tuition:* state resident $3336 full-time, $139 per credit hour part-time; nonresident $9288 full-time, $387 per credit hour part-time. Full-time tuition and fees vary according to degree level. Part-time tuition and fees vary according to course load and degree level. *Room and board:* $7858; room only: $4148. Room and board charges vary according to board plan and housing facility. *Payment plan:* installment. *Waivers:* senior citizens and employees or children of employees.

Financial Aid Of all full-time matriculated undergraduates who enrolled in 2012, 70 Federal Work-Study jobs (averaging $1300).

Applying *Options:* electronic application. *Required:* high school transcript. *Application deadlines:* rolling (freshmen), rolling (transfers).

Freshman Application Contact Ms. Beth Little, Director of Enrollment Services, Potomac State College of West Virginia University, 75 Arnold Street, Keyser, WV 26726. *Phone:* 304-788-6820. *Toll-free phone:* 800-262-7332 Ext. 6820. *Fax:* 304-788-6939. *E-mail:* go2psc@mail.wvu.edu.

Website: http://www.potomacstatecollege.edu/.

Southern West Virginia Community and Technical College

Mount Gay, West Virginia

Freshman Application Contact Mr. Roy Simmons, Registrar, Southern West Virginia Community and Technical College, PO Box 2900, Mt. Gay, WV 25637. *Phone:* 304-792-7160 Ext. 120. *Fax:* 304-792-7096. *E-mail:* admissions@southern.wvnet.edu.

Website: http://southernwv.edu/.

Valley College

Martinsburg, West Virginia

Freshman Application Contact Ms. Gail Kennedy, Admissions Director, Valley College, 287 Aikens Center, Martinsburg, WV 25404. *Phone:* 304-263-0878. *Fax:* 304-263-2413. *E-mail:* gkennedy@vct.edu.

Website: http://www.valley.edu/.

West Virginia Business College

Nutter Fort, West Virginia

Director of Admissions Robert Wright, Campus Director, West Virginia Business College, 116 Pennsylvania Avenue, Nutter Fort, WV 26301. *Phone:* 304-624-7695. *E-mail:* info@wvbc.edu.

Website: http://www.wvbc.edu/.

West Virginia Business College

Wheeling, West Virginia

Freshman Application Contact Ms. Karen D. Shaw, Director, West Virginia Business College, 1052 Main Street, Wheeling, WV 26003. *Phone:* 304-232-0361. *Fax:* 304-232-0363. *E-mail:* wvbcwheeling@stratuswave.net.

Website: http://www.wvbc.edu/.

West Virginia Junior College–Bridgeport

Bridgeport, West Virginia

- **Proprietary** 2-year, founded 1922, part of West Virginia Junior College-Charleston, WV; West Virginia Junior College-Morgantown, WV;

Pennsylvania Institute of Health & Technology-Uniontown, PA; Ohio Institute of Health & Technology, E. Liverpool, OH
- **Small-town** 3-acre campus with easy access to Pittsburgh
- **Coed,** 389 undergraduate students, 100% full-time, 85% women, 15% men

Undergraduates 389 full-time. Students come from 4 states and territories; 0.5% Black or African American, non-Hispanic/Latino; 10% transferred in. *Retention:* 80% of full-time freshmen returned.

Freshmen *Admission:* 389 enrolled. *Average high school GPA:* 2.5.

Faculty *Total:* 19, 42% full-time, 79% with terminal degrees. *Student/faculty ratio:* 15:1.

Majors Business administration and management; computer technology/computer systems technology; dental assisting; medical administrative assistant and medical secretary; medical/clinical assistant; medical insurance coding; pharmacy technician; web/multimedia management and webmaster.

Academics *Calendar:* quarters. *Degree:* diplomas and associate. *Special study options:* cooperative education, distance learning, independent study, internships, services for LD students, summer session for credit.

Library WVJC Resource Center plus 1 other with an OPAC.

Student Life *Housing:* college housing not available. *Activities and Organizations:* Medical Club, Business Club, Computer Club, Dental Assisting Club, Pharmacy Tech Club. *Campus security:* 24-hour emergency response devices.

Standardized Tests *Recommended:* SAT or ACT (for admission).

Financial Aid Of all full-time matriculated undergraduates who enrolled in 2012, 10 Federal Work-Study jobs.

Applying *Options:* electronic application. *Application fee:* $25. *Required:* essay or personal statement, minimum 2.5 GPA, interview, Applicants are required to meet with an Admissions Representative. *Required for some:* 1 letter of recommendation. *Recommended:* high school transcript. *Application deadline:* rolling (freshmen). *Notification:* continuous (freshmen).

Freshman Application Contact Mr. Adam Pratt, High School Admissions Coordinator, West Virginia Junior College–Bridgeport, 176 Thompson Drive, Bridgeport, WV 26330. *Phone:* 304-842-4007 Ext. 112. *Toll-free phone:* 800-470-5627. *Fax:* 304-842-8191. *E-mail:* apratt@wvjcinfo.net.

Website: http://www.wvjc.edu/.

West Virginia Junior College–Charleston

Charleston, West Virginia

Freshman Application Contact West Virginia Junior College–Charleston, 1000 Virginia Street East, Charleston, WV 25301-2817. *Phone:* 304-345-2820. *Toll-free phone:* 800-924-5208.

Website: http://www.wvjc.edu/.

West Virginia Junior College–Morgantown

Morgantown, West Virginia

Freshman Application Contact Admissions Office, West Virginia Junior College–Morgantown, 148 Willey Street, Morgantown, WV 26505-5521. *Phone:* 304-296-8282.

Website: http://www.wvjcmorgantown.edu/.

West Virginia Northern Community College

Wheeling, West Virginia

- **State-supported** 2-year, founded 1972
- **Small-town** campus with easy access to Pittsburgh
- **Endowment** $659,426
- **Coed**

Undergraduates 1,156 full-time, 1,349 part-time. Students come from 14 states and territories; 24% are from out of state; 5% Black or African American, non-Hispanic/Latino; 0.4% Hispanic/Latino; 0.4% Asian, non-Hispanic/Latino; 0.3% American Indian or Alaska Native, non-Hispanic/Latino; 2% Two or more races, non-Hispanic/Latino; 1% Race/ethnicity unknown; 12% transferred in.

Academics *Calendar:* semesters. *Degree:* certificates and associate. *Special study options:* academic remediation for entering students, accelerated degree program, adult/continuing education programs, advanced placement credit, cooperative education, distance learning, double majors, honors programs, internships, part-time degree program, services for LD students, student-designed majors, summer session for credit.

Student Life *Campus security:* police officer on staff during the day at Main Campus, security personnel during evening and during night classes.

Standardized Tests *Required for some:* Compass. *Recommended:* Compass.

Costs (2013–14) *Tuition:* state resident $2400 full-time, $100 per credit hour part-time; nonresident $7896 full-time, $329 per credit hour part-time. Full-time tuition and fees vary according to course load, location, program, reciprocity agreements, and student level. Part-time tuition and fees vary according to course load, location, program, reciprocity agreements, and student level. *Required fees:* $490 full-time, $15 per credit hour part-time, $65 per term part-time.
Applying *Options:* electronic application, early admission, deferred entrance. *Required for some:* high school transcript.
Freshman Application Contact Mrs. Janet Fike, Vice President of Student Services, West Virginia Northern Community College, 1704 Market Street, Wheeling, WV 26003. *Phone:* 304-214-8837. *E-mail:* jfike@northern.wvnet.edu.
Website: http://www.wvncc.edu/.

West Virginia University at Parkersburg
Parkersburg, West Virginia

Freshman Application Contact Christine Post, Associate Dean of Enrollment Management, West Virginia University at Parkersburg, 300 Campus Drive, Parkersburg, WV 26104. *Phone:* 304-424-8223 Ext. 223. *Toll-free phone:* 800-WVA-WVUP. *Fax:* 304-424-8332. *E-mail:* christine.post@mail.wvu.edu.
Website: http://www.wvup.edu/.

WISCONSIN

Anthem College–Brookfield
Brookfield, Wisconsin

Admissions Office Contact Anthem College–Brookfield, 440 S. Executive Drive, Suite 200, Brookfield, WI 53005.
Website: http://anthem.edu/milwaukee-wisconsin/.

Blackhawk Technical College
Janesville, Wisconsin

- **District-supported** 2-year, founded 1968, part of Wisconsin Technical College System
- **Small-town** 84-acre campus
- **Coed,** 2,522 undergraduate students, 40% full-time, 61% women, 39% men

Undergraduates 997 full-time, 1,525 part-time. Students come from 3 states and territories; 1% are from out of state; 9% Black or African American, non-Hispanic/Latino; 8% Hispanic/Latino; 0.8% Asian, non-Hispanic/Latino; 0.1% Native Hawaiian or other Pacific Islander, non-Hispanic/Latino; 0.4% American Indian or Alaska Native, non-Hispanic/Latino; 3% Two or more races, non-Hispanic/Latino; 2% Race/ethnicity unknown. *Retention:* 83% of full-time freshmen returned.
Freshmen *Admission:* 405 enrolled.
Faculty *Total:* 226, 47% full-time, 2% with terminal degrees. *Student/faculty ratio:* 10:1.
Majors Accounting; administrative assistant and secretarial science; business administration and management; clinical/medical laboratory technology; computer and information systems security; computer systems networking and telecommunications; criminal justice/police science; culinary arts; drafting/design engineering technologies related; early childhood education; electromechanical technology; fire prevention and safety technology; fire science/firefighting; heating, air conditioning, ventilation and refrigeration maintenance technology; heating, ventilation, air conditioning and refrigeration engineering technology; human resources management; industrial engineering; industrial technology; legal administrative assistant/secretary; marketing/marketing management; mechanical drafting and CAD/CADD; medical administrative assistant and medical secretary; medical radiologic technology; physical therapy; physical therapy technology; radiologic technology/science; registered nursing/registered nurse; restaurant, culinary, and catering management; web page, digital/multimedia and information resources design.
Academics *Calendar:* semesters. *Degree:* associate. *Special study options:* academic remediation for entering students, accelerated degree program, adult/continuing education programs, advanced placement credit, cooperative education, distance learning, English as a second language, independent study, internships, part-time degree program, services for LD students, student-designed majors, summer session for credit.
Library Blackhawk Technical College Library with 311,368 titles, 280 serial subscriptions, 6,130 audiovisual materials, an OPAC, a Web page.
Student Life *Housing:* college housing not available. *Activities and Organizations:* student-run newspaper, student government, Association of

Information Technology Professionals, Criminal Justice, Epicurean Club, Phi Theta Kappa Honor Society. *Campus security:* student patrols.
Costs (2013–14) *Tuition:* state resident $3666 full-time, $122 per credit hour part-time; nonresident $5499 full-time, $183 per credit hour part-time. Full-time tuition and fees vary according to course load. Part-time tuition and fees vary according to course load. *Required fees:* $478 full-time, $6 per credit hour part-time. *Payment plan:* deferred payment. *Waivers:* senior citizens.
Financial Aid Of all full-time matriculated undergraduates who enrolled in 2012, 33 Federal Work-Study jobs (averaging $1150).
Applying *Options:* electronic application. *Application fee:* $30. *Required:* high school transcript. *Application deadlines:* rolling (freshmen), rolling (transfers). *Notification:* continuous (freshmen), continuous (transfers).
Freshman Application Contact Blackhawk Technical College, PO Box 5009, Janesville, WI 53547-5009. *Phone:* 608-757-7713.
Website: http://www.blackhawk.edu/.

Bryant & Stratton College - Milwaukee Campus
Milwaukee, Wisconsin

Freshman Application Contact Mr. Dan Basile, Director of Admissions, Bryant & Stratton College - Milwaukee Campus, 310 West Wisconsin Avenue, Suite 500 East, Milwaukee, WI 53203-2214. *Phone:* 414-276-5200.
Website: http://www.bryantstratton.edu/.

Chippewa Valley Technical College
Eau Claire, Wisconsin

- **District-supported** 2-year, founded 1912, part of Wisconsin Technical College System
- **Suburban** 255-acre campus
- **Coed,** 5,617 undergraduate students, 44% full-time, 57% women, 43% men

Undergraduates 2,445 full-time, 3,172 part-time. 2% are from out of state; 1% Black or African American, non-Hispanic/Latino; 2% Hispanic/Latino; 4% Asian, non-Hispanic/Latino; 0.1% Native Hawaiian or other Pacific Islander, non-Hispanic/Latino; 0.5% American Indian or Alaska Native, non-Hispanic/Latino; 2% Two or more races, non-Hispanic/Latino; 7% Race/ethnicity unknown. *Retention:* 59% of full-time freshmen returned.
Freshmen *Admission:* 1,366 enrolled.
Faculty *Total:* 491, 46% full-time, 7% with terminal degrees. *Student/faculty ratio:* 14:1.
Majors Accounting; administrative assistant and secretarial science; agricultural business and management related; applied horticulture/horticultural business services related; business administration and management; civil engineering technology; clinical/medical laboratory technology; computer programming; computer systems networking and telecommunications; criminal justice/police science; dental hygiene; diagnostic medical sonography and ultrasound technology; early childhood education; electromechanical technology; emergency medical technology (EMT paramedic); health information/medical records technology; heating, ventilation, air conditioning and refrigeration engineering technology; human resources management; legal assistant/paralegal; liberal arts and sciences/liberal studies; marketing/marketing management; medical radiologic technology; multi/interdisciplinary studies related; nanotechnology; physical therapy technology; registered nursing/registered nurse; respiratory care therapy; substance abuse/addiction counseling.
Academics *Calendar:* semesters. *Degree:* certificates, diplomas, and associate. *Special study options:* academic remediation for entering students, accelerated degree program, adult/continuing education programs, advanced placement credit, cooperative education, distance learning, double majors, English as a second language, honors programs, independent study, internships, part-time degree program, services for LD students, student-designed majors, summer session for credit.
Library The Learning Center with an OPAC, a Web page.
Student Life *Housing:* college housing not available. *Activities and Organizations:* Collegiate DECA. *Campus security:* 24-hour emergency response devices, late-night transport/escort service, security cameras. *Student services:* health clinic, personal/psychological counseling.
Standardized Tests *Required:* COMPASS, ACCUPLACER (for admission). *Recommended:* ACT (for admission).
Financial Aid Of all full-time matriculated undergraduates who enrolled in 2012, 218 Federal Work-Study jobs (averaging $875).
Applying *Options:* electronic application, early admission, deferred entrance. *Application fee:* $30. *Required for some:* high school transcript. *Application deadlines:* rolling (freshmen), rolling (transfers). *Notification:* continuous (freshmen), continuous (transfers).
Freshman Application Contact Admissions Office, Chippewa Valley Technical College, 620 W. Clairemont Avenue, Eau Claire, WI 54701. *Phone:*

715-833-6200. *Toll-free phone:* 800-547-2882. *Fax:* 715-833-6470. *E-mail:* infocenter@cvtc.edu. *Website:* http://www.cvtc.edu/.

College of Menominee Nation
Keshena, Wisconsin

Director of Admissions Tessa James, Admissions Coordinator, College of Menominee Nation, PO Box 1179, Keshena, WI 54135. *Phone:* 715-799-5600 Ext. 3053. *Toll-free phone:* 800-567-2344. *E-mail:* tjames@menominee.edu. *Website:* http://www.menominee.edu/.

Fox Valley Technical College
Appleton, Wisconsin

- **State and locally supported** 2-year, founded 1967, part of Wisconsin Technical College System
- **Suburban** 100-acre campus
- **Endowment** $2.5 million
- **Coed,** 10,502 undergraduate students, 28% full-time, 49% women, 51% men

Undergraduates 2,902 full-time, 7,600 part-time. Students come from 14 states and territories; 25 other countries; 1% are from out of state; 2% Black or African American, non-Hispanic/Latino; 3% Hispanic/Latino; 4% Asian, non-Hispanic/Latino; 0.2% Native Hawaiian or other Pacific Islander, non-Hispanic/Latino; 1% American Indian or Alaska Native, non-Hispanic/Latino; 0.4% Two or more races, non-Hispanic/Latino; 6% Race/ethnicity unknown; 0.1% international.

Freshmen *Admission:* 1,774 applied, 1,493 admitted, 946 enrolled.

Faculty *Total:* 910, 36% full-time. *Student/faculty ratio:* 11:1.

Majors Accounting; administrative assistant and secretarial science; agricultural/farm supplies retailing and wholesaling; agricultural mechanization; airline pilot and flight crew; autobody/collision and repair technology; automation engineer technology; automobile/automotive mechanics technology; avionics maintenance technology; banking and financial support services; biology/biotechnology laboratory technician; building/construction site management; business administration and management; computer engineering technology; computer programming; computer support specialist; computer systems networking and telecommunications; court reporting; criminal justice/police science; culinary arts; dental hygiene; diesel mechanics technology; early childhood education; electrical and electronic engineering technologies related; electrical, electronic and communications engineering technology; electromechanical technology; emergency medical technology (EMT paramedic); energy management and systems technology; fire protection related; fire science/firefighting; forensic science and technology; graphic and printing equipment operation/production; graphic communications; health information/medical records technology; homeland security related; hospitality administration; human resources management; industrial safety technology; interior design; legal assistant/paralegal; logistics, materials, and supply chain management; manufacturing engineering technology; marketing/marketing management; mechanical drafting and CAD/CADD; meeting and event planning; multi/interdisciplinary studies related; natural resources/conservation; occupational therapist assistant; office management; professional, technical, business, and scientific writing; radio, television, and digital communication related; registered nursing/registered nurse; substance abuse/addiction counseling; web/multimedia management and webmaster; welding technology; wildland/forest firefighting and investigation.

Academics *Calendar:* semesters. *Degree:* certificates, diplomas, and associate. *Special study options:* academic remediation for entering students, accelerated degree program, advanced placement credit, cooperative education, distance learning, double majors, English as a second language, independent study, internships, off-campus study, part-time degree program, services for LD students, student-designed majors, study abroad, summer session for credit.

Library Student Success Center Library with 100,000 titles, 10,000 serial subscriptions, 1,000 audiovisual materials, an OPAC, a Web page.

Student Life *Housing:* college housing not available. *Activities and Organizations:* student-run newspaper, Student Government Association, Phi Theta Kappa, Culinary Arts, Machine Tool, Post Secondary Agribusiness. *Campus security:* 24-hour emergency response devices, late-night transport/escort service, Trained security personnel patrol during the colleges hours of operation. *Student services:* health clinic, personal/psychological counseling.

Athletics *Intercollegiate sports:* basketball M/W, volleyball W. *Intramural sports:* basketball M/W, football M/W, soccer M/W, softball M/W, table tennis M/W, volleyball M/W.

Costs (2013–14) *Tuition:* state resident $3666 full-time, $138 per credit part-time; nonresident $5499 full-time, $200 per credit part-time. *Required fees:* $486 full-time, $16 per credit part-time. *Payment plan:* installment.

Applying *Options:* electronic application, early admission, deferred entrance. *Application fee:* $30. *Required:* high school transcript. *Application deadlines:* rolling (freshmen), rolling (transfers).

Freshman Application Contact Admissions Center, Fox Valley Technical College, 1825 North Bluemound Drive, PO Box 2277, Appleton, WI 54912-2277. *Phone:* 920-735-5643. *Toll-free phone:* 800-735-3882. *Fax:* 920-735-2582. *Website:* http://www.fvtc.edu/.

Gateway Technical College
Kenosha, Wisconsin

- **State and locally supported** 2-year, founded 1911, part of Wisconsin Technical College System
- **Urban** 10-acre campus with easy access to Chicago, Milwaukee
- **Coed**

Undergraduates 1,717 full-time, 7,003 part-time. Students come from 7 states and territories; 2 other countries; 1% are from out of state; 15% Black or African American, non-Hispanic/Latino; 12% Hispanic/Latino; 1% Asian, non-Hispanic/Latino; 0.1% Native Hawaiian or other Pacific Islander, non-Hispanic/Latino; 0.5% American Indian or Alaska Native, non-Hispanic/Latino; 2% Two or more races, non-Hispanic/Latino; 0.9% Race/ethnicity unknown; 1% transferred in. *Retention:* 64% of full-time freshmen returned.

Faculty *Student/faculty ratio:* 16:1.

Academics *Calendar:* semesters. *Degree:* certificates, diplomas, and associate. *Special study options:* academic remediation for entering students, advanced placement credit, cooperative education, distance learning, double majors, English as a second language, independent study, internships, part-time degree program, services for LD students, student-designed majors, summer session for credit.

Student Life *Campus security:* 24-hour emergency response devices and patrols, late-night transport/escort service.

Applying *Options:* electronic application, early admission, deferred entrance. *Application fee:* $30. *Required:* high school transcript.

Freshman Application Contact Admissions, Gateway Technical College, 3520 30th Avenue, Kenosha, WI 53144-1690. *Phone:* 262-564-2300. *Fax:* 262-564-2301. *E-mail:* admissions@gtc.edu. *Website:* http://www.gtc.edu/.

ITT Technical Institute
Green Bay, Wisconsin

- **Proprietary** primarily 2-year, founded 2000, part of ITT Educational Services, Inc.
- **Coed**

Majors Business administration and management; computer programming (specific applications); computer software technology; construction management; cyber/computer forensics and counterterrorism; drafting and design technology; electrical, electronic and communications engineering technology; graphic communications; information technology project management; network and system administration; project management.

Academics *Calendar:* quarters. *Degrees:* associate and bachelor's.

Student Life *Housing:* college housing not available.

Freshman Application Contact Director of Recruitment, ITT Technical Institute, 470 Security Boulevard, Green Bay, WI 54313. *Phone:* 920-662-9000. *Toll-free phone:* 888-884-3626. *Website:* http://www.itt-tech.edu/.

ITT Technical Institute
Greenfield, Wisconsin

- **Proprietary** primarily 2-year, founded 1968, part of ITT Educational Services, Inc.
- **Suburban** campus
- **Coed**

Majors Business administration and management; computer programming (specific applications); construction management; cyber/computer forensics and counterterrorism; drafting and design technology; electrical, electronic and communications engineering technology; forensic science and technology; game and interactive media design; graphic communications; information technology project management; legal assistant/paralegal; network and system administration; project management.

Academics *Calendar:* quarters. *Degrees:* associate and bachelor's.

Student Life *Housing:* college housing not available.

Freshman Application Contact Director of Recruitment, ITT Technical Institute, 6300 West Layton Avenue, Greenfield, WI 53220-4612. *Phone:* 414-282-9494. *Website:* http://www.itt-tech.edu/.

ITT Technical Institute
Madison, Wisconsin

- **Proprietary** primarily 2-year, part of ITT Educational Services, Inc.
- **Coed**

Majors Business administration and management; computer programming (specific applications); construction management; cyber/computer forensics and counterterrorism; drafting and design technology; electrical, electronic and communications engineering technology; information technology project management; network and system administration; project management.

Academics *Degrees:* associate and bachelor's.

Freshman Application Contact Director of Recruitment, ITT Technical Institute, 2450 Rimrock Road, Suite 100, Madison, WI 53713. *Phone:* 608-288-6301. *Toll-free phone:* 877-628-5960.

Website: http://www.itt-tech.edu/.

Lac Courte Oreilles Ojibwa Community College
Hayward, Wisconsin

Freshman Application Contact Ms. Annette Wiggins, Registrar, Lac Courte Oreilles Ojibwa Community College, 13466 West Trepania Road, Hayward, WI 54843-2181. *Phone:* 715-634-4790 Ext. 104. *Toll-free phone:* 888-526-6221.

Website: http://www.lco.edu/.

Lakeshore Technical College
Cleveland, Wisconsin

Freshman Application Contact Lakeshore Technical College, 1290 North Avenue, Cleveland, WI 53015. *Phone:* 920-693-1339. *Toll-free phone:* 888-GO TO LTC. *Fax:* 920-693-3561.

Website: http://www.gotoltc.com/.

Madison Area Technical College
Madison, Wisconsin

Director of Admissions Ms. Maureen Menendez, Interim Admissions Administrator, Madison Area Technical College, 1701 Wright Street, Madison, WI 53704. *Phone:* 608-246-6212. *Toll-free phone:* 800-322-6282.

Website: http://madisoncollege.edu/.

Madison Media Institute
Madison, Wisconsin

Freshman Application Contact Mr. Chris K. Hutchings, President/Director, Madison Media Institute, 2702 Agriculture Drive, Madison, WI 53718. *Phone:* 608-237-8301. *Toll-free phone:* 800-236-4997.

Website: http://www.mediainstitute.edu/.

Mid-State Technical College
Wisconsin Rapids, Wisconsin

Freshman Application Contact Ms. Carole Prochnow, Admissions Assistant, Mid-State Technical College, 500 32nd Street North, Wisconsin Rapids, WI 54494-5599. *Phone:* 715-422-5444.

Website: http://www.mstc.edu/.

Milwaukee Area Technical College
Milwaukee, Wisconsin

Freshman Application Contact Sarah Adams, Director, Enrollment Services, Milwaukee Area Technical College, 700 West State Street, Milwaukee, WI 53233-1443. *Phone:* 414-297-6595. *Fax:* 414-297-7800. *E-mail:* adamss4@matc.edu.

Website: http://www.matc.edu/.

Moraine Park Technical College
Fond du Lac, Wisconsin

- **District-supported** 2-year, founded 1967, part of Wisconsin Technical College System
- **Small-town** 40-acre campus with easy access to Milwaukee
- **Coed,** 6,613 undergraduate students, 17% full-time, 59% women, 41% men

Undergraduates 1,112 full-time, 5,501 part-time. 2% Black or African American, non-Hispanic/Latino; 4% Hispanic/Latino; 1% Asian, non-Hispanic/Latino; 0.8% American Indian or Alaska Native, non-Hispanic/Latino; 0.2% Two or more races, non-Hispanic/Latino; 2% Race/ethnicity unknown.

Freshmen *Admission:* 341 enrolled.

Faculty *Total:* 275, 53% full-time. *Student/faculty ratio:* 15:1.

Majors Accounting; administrative assistant and secretarial science; automobile/automotive mechanics technology; business administration and management; chiropractic assistant; clinical/medical laboratory technology; computer programming related; computer support specialist; computer systems networking and telecommunications; corrections; court reporting; culinary arts; early childhood education; electrical and electronic engineering technologies related; electromechanical technology; emergency medical technology (EMT paramedic); graphic design; health information/medical records technology; heating, ventilation, air conditioning and refrigeration engineering technology; hotel/motel administration; human resources management; legal administrative assistant/secretary; legal assistant/paralegal; machine tool technology; marketing/marketing management; mechanical drafting and CAD/CADD; mechanical engineering technologies related; medical radiologic technology; multi/interdisciplinary studies related; office management; registered nursing/registered nurse; respiratory care therapy; structural engineering; substance abuse/addiction counseling; surgical technology; teacher assistant/aide; water quality and wastewater treatment management and recycling technology.

Academics *Calendar:* semesters. *Degree:* certificates, diplomas, and associate. *Special study options:* academic remediation for entering students, accelerated degree program, adult/continuing education programs, advanced placement credit, distance learning, double majors, English as a second language, external degree program, independent study, internships, part-time degree program, services for LD students, student-designed majors, study abroad, summer session for credit.

Library Moraine Park Technical College Library/Learning Resource Center with 33,510 titles, 97 serial subscriptions, 13,980 audiovisual materials, an OPAC, a Web page.

Student Life *Housing:* college housing not available. *Activities and Organizations:* Student Government, Student Nurses Association Club, Electrical Power Distribution Club, Electricity Club, Auto Technician Club. *Campus security:* late-night transport/escort service, Campus Security Services between 5-10 pm M-Th during the academic year. Services include night patrols. *Student services:* personal/psychological counseling.

Standardized Tests *Required:* ACT, ACCUPLACER OR COMPASS (for admission). *Required for some:* ACT (for admission).

Costs (2014–15) *Tuition:* state resident $3838 full-time, $128 per credit hour part-time; nonresident $5757 full-time, $192 per credit hour part-time. Full-time tuition and fees vary according to program. Part-time tuition and fees vary according to program. *Required fees:* $302 full-time, $10 per credit hour part-time. *Payment plans:* installment, deferred payment. *Waivers:* senior citizens.

Applying *Required:* high school transcript, interview, Placement test required for all; Criminal background ground check required for some. *Required for some:* interview.

Freshman Application Contact Ms. Karen Jarvis, Student Services, Moraine Park Technical College, 235 North National Avenue, Fond du Lac, WI 54935. *Phone:* 920-924-3200. *Toll-free phone:* 800-472-4554. *Fax:* 920-924-3421. *E-mail:* kjarvis@morainepark.edu.

Website: http://www.morainepark.edu/.

Nicolet Area Technical College
Rhinelander, Wisconsin

Freshman Application Contact Ms. Susan Kordula, Director of Admissions, Nicolet Area Technical College, PO Box 518, Rhinelander, WI 54501. *Phone:* 715-365-4451. *Toll-free phone:* 800-544-3039. *E-mail:* inquire@nicoletcollege.edu.

Website: http://www.nicoletcollege.edu/.

Northcentral Technical College
Wausau, Wisconsin

- **District-supported** 2-year, founded 1912, part of Wisconsin Technical College System
- **Rural** 96-acre campus
- **Coed,** 4,373 undergraduate students, 43% full-time, 61% women, 39% men

Undergraduates 1,896 full-time, 2,477 part-time. 0.8% Black or African American, non-Hispanic/Latino; 0.3% Hispanic/Latino; 5% Asian, non-Hispanic/Latino; 0.1% Native Hawaiian or other Pacific Islander, non-Hispanic/Latino; 1% American Indian or Alaska Native, non-Hispanic/Latino; 0.6% Two or more races, non-Hispanic/Latino; 19% Race/ethnicity unknown. *Retention:* 60% of full-time freshmen returned.

Freshmen *Admission:* 788 enrolled.

Faculty *Student/faculty ratio:* 23:1.

Majors Accounting; administrative assistant and secretarial science; architectural engineering technology; automobile/automotive mechanics technology; business administration and management; clinical/medical laboratory technology; computer and information sciences and support services related; computer systems analysis; computer systems networking and telecommunications; criminal justice/police science; dental hygiene; early childhood education; electromechanical technology; emergency medical technology (EMT paramedic); furniture design and manufacturing; general studies; graphic communications; manufacturing engineering technology; marketing/marketing management; mechanical drafting and CAD/CADD; medical insurance/medical billing; medical radiologic technology; mental and social health services and allied professions related; merchandising, sales, and marketing operations related (general); multi/interdisciplinary studies related; operations management; registered nursing/registered nurse; sign language interpretation and translation; teacher assistant/aide.

Academics *Calendar:* semesters. *Degree:* certificates, diplomas, and associate. *Special study options:* academic remediation for entering students, accelerated degree program, adult/continuing education programs, advanced placement credit, distance learning, double majors, English as a second language, independent study, internships, off-campus study, part-time degree program, services for LD students, student-designed majors, summer session for credit.

Library Northcentral Technical College, Wausau Campus Library plus 1 other with 30,000 titles, 400 serial subscriptions, an OPAC, a Web page.

Student Life *Housing Options:* Campus housing is provided by a third party. *Campus security:* 24-hour emergency response devices, student patrols, late-night transport/escort service. *Student services:* personal/psychological counseling, women's center.

Athletics *Intramural sports:* badminton M/W, basketball M/W, bowling M/W, racquetball M/W, softball M/W, table tennis M/W, tennis M/W, volleyball M/W.

Costs (2013–14) *Tuition:* state resident $4026 full-time; nonresident $5859 full-time. Full-time tuition and fees vary according to course level, course load, and program. Part-time tuition and fees vary according to course level, course load, and program. *Room and board:* Room and board charges vary according to board plan. *Payment plan:* deferred payment. *Waivers:* senior citizens.

Financial Aid Of all full-time matriculated undergraduates who enrolled in 2012, 366 Federal Work-Study jobs (averaging $2000).

Applying *Options:* electronic application, early admission, deferred entrance. *Application fee:* $30. *Required:* high school transcript. *Required for some:* interview. *Application deadlines:* rolling (freshmen), rolling (transfers). *Notification:* continuous (freshmen), continuous (transfers).

Freshman Application Contact Northcentral Technical College, 1000 West Campus Drive, Wausau, WI 54401-1899. *Phone:* 715-675-3331.

Website: http://www.ntc.edu/.

Northeast Wisconsin Technical College

Green Bay, Wisconsin

Freshman Application Contact Christine Lemerande, Program Enrollment Supervisor, Northeast Wisconsin Technical College, 2740 W Mason Street, PO Box 19042, Green Bay, WI 54307-9042. *Phone:* 920-498-5444. *Toll-free phone:* 888-385-6982. *Fax:* 920-498-6882.

Website: http://www.nwtc.edu/.

Southwest Wisconsin Technical College

Fennimore, Wisconsin

Freshman Application Contact Student Services, Southwest Wisconsin Technical College, 1800 Bronson Boulevard, Fennimore, WI 53809-9778. *Phone:* 608-822-2354. *Toll-free phone:* 800-362-3322. *Fax:* 608-822-6019. *E-mail:* student-services@swtc.edu.

Website: http://www.swtc.edu/.

University of Wisconsin–Baraboo/Sauk County

Baraboo, Wisconsin

Freshman Application Contact Ms. Jan Gerlach, Assistant Director of Student Services, University of Wisconsin–Baraboo/Sauk County, Baraboo, WI 53913-1015. *Phone:* 608-355-5270. *E-mail:* booinfo@uwc.edu.

Website: http://www.baraboo.uwc.edu/.

University of Wisconsin–Barron County

Rice Lake, Wisconsin

Freshman Application Contact Assistant Dean for Student Services, University of Wisconsin–Barron County, 1800 College Drive, Rice Lake, WI 54868-2497. *Phone:* 715-234-8024. *Fax:* 715-234-8024.

Website: http://www.barron.uwc.edu/.

University of Wisconsin–Fond du Lac

Fond du Lac, Wisconsin

Freshman Application Contact University of Wisconsin–Fond du Lac, 400 University Drive, Fond du Lac, WI 54935. *Phone:* 920-929-1122.

Website: http://www.fdl.uwc.edu/.

University of Wisconsin–Fox Valley

Menasha, Wisconsin

- **State-supported** 2-year, founded 1933, part of University of Wisconsin System
- **Urban** 33-acre campus
- **Coed,** 1,797 undergraduate students, 58% full-time, 52% women, 48% men

Undergraduates 1,037 full-time, 760 part-time. Students come from 3 states and territories; 4 other countries; 1% are from out of state. *Retention:* 60% of full-time freshmen returned.

Freshmen *Admission:* 1,166 enrolled. *Average high school GPA:* 2.5.

Faculty *Total:* 91, 34% full-time. *Student/faculty ratio:* 20:1.

Majors Liberal arts and sciences/liberal studies.

Academics *Calendar:* semesters. *Degree:* certificates and associate. *Special study options:* academic remediation for entering students, accelerated degree program, adult/continuing education programs, advanced placement credit, cooperative education, distance learning, honors programs, independent study, internships, off-campus study, part-time degree program, services for LD students, study abroad, summer session for credit.

Library UW Fox Library with 30,000 titles, 230 serial subscriptions, an OPAC, a Web page.

Student Life *Housing:* college housing not available. *Options:* Campus housing is provided by a third party. *Activities and Organizations:* drama/theater group, student-run newspaper, radio and television station, choral group, Business Club, Education Club, Earth Science Club, Computer Science Club, Political Science Club. *Campus security:* 24-hour emergency response devices, late-night transport/escort service. *Student services:* personal/psychological counseling.

Athletics Member NJCAA. *Intercollegiate sports:* basketball M/W, golf M/W, soccer M/W, tennis M/W, volleyball M/W. *Intramural sports:* baseball M(c), basketball M/W, volleyball M/W, wrestling M(c).

Standardized Tests *Required:* ACT (for admission).

Costs (2014–15) *Tuition:* state resident $2512 full-time, $209 per credit part-time; nonresident $6005 full-time, $500 per credit part-time. Full-time tuition and fees vary according to course load. Part-time tuition and fees vary according to course load. *Payment plan:* installment. *Waivers:* senior citizens.

Applying *Required:* essay or personal statement, high school transcript. *Required for some:* interview.

Freshman Application Contact University of Wisconsin–Fox Valley, 1478 Midway Road, Menasha, WI 54952. *Phone:* 920-832-2620.

Website: http://www.uwfox.uwc.edu/.

University of Wisconsin–Manitowoc

Manitowoc, Wisconsin

Freshman Application Contact Dr. Christopher Lewis, Assistant Campus Dean for Student Services, University of Wisconsin–Manitowoc, 705 Viebahn Street, Manitowoc, WI 54220-6699. *Phone:* 920-683-4707. *Fax:* 920-683-4776. *E-mail:* christopher.lewis@uwc.edu.

Website: http://www.manitowoc.uwc.edu/.

University of Wisconsin–Marathon County

Wausau, Wisconsin

Freshman Application Contact Dr. Nolan Beck, Director of Student Services, University of Wisconsin–Marathon County, 518 South Seventh Avenue, Wausau, WI 54401-5396. *Phone:* 715-261-6238. *Toll-free phone:* 888-367-8962. *Fax:* 715-848-3568.

Website: http://www.uwmc.uwc.edu/.

University of Wisconsin–Marinette

Marinette, Wisconsin

Freshman Application Contact Ms. Cynthia M. Bailey, Assistant Campus Dean for Student Services, University of Wisconsin–Marinette, 750 West Bay Shore, Marinette, WI 54143-4299. *Phone:* 715-735-4301. *E-mail:* cynthia.bailey@uwc.edu.

Website: http://www.marinette.uwc.edu/.

University of Wisconsin–Marshfield/Wood County
Marshfield, Wisconsin

Freshman Application Contact Brittany Lueth, Director of Student Services, University of Wisconsin–Marshfield/Wood County, 2000 West 5th Street, Marshfield, WI 54449. *Phone:* 715-389-6500. *Fax:* 715-384-1718.
Website: http://marshfield.uwc.edu/.

University of Wisconsin–Richland
Richland Center, Wisconsin

- **State-supported** 2-year, founded 1967, part of University of Wisconsin System
- **Rural** 135-acre campus
- **Coed**

Undergraduates 291 full-time, 228 part-time. 4% Black or African American, non-Hispanic/Latino; 0.6% Hispanic/Latino; 1% Asian, non-Hispanic/Latino; 0.4% American Indian or Alaska Native, non-Hispanic/Latino; 0.6% Race/ethnicity unknown. *Retention:* 58% of full-time freshmen returned.
Faculty *Student/faculty ratio:* 17:1.
Academics *Calendar:* semesters. *Degree:* associate. *Special study options:* academic remediation for entering students, adult/continuing education programs, advanced placement credit, distance learning, external degree program, independent study, off-campus study, part-time degree program, services for LD students, study abroad, summer session for credit.
Standardized Tests *Required:* SAT or ACT (for admission). *Recommended:* ACT (for admission).
Applying *Options:* electronic application. *Application fee:* $44. *Required:* high school transcript. *Required for some:* interview.
Freshman Application Contact Mr. John D. Poole, Assistant Campus Dean, University of Wisconsin–Richland, 1200 Highway 14 West, Richland Center, WI 53581. *Phone:* 608-647-8422. *Fax:* 608-647-2275. *E-mail:* john.poole@uwc.edu.
Website: http://richland.uwc.edu/.

University of Wisconsin–Rock County
Janesville, Wisconsin

Freshman Application Contact University of Wisconsin–Rock County, 2909 Kellogg Avenue, Janesville, WI 53546-5699. *Phone:* 608-758-6523. *Toll-free phone:* 888-INFO-UWC.
Website: http://rock.uwc.edu/.

University of Wisconsin–Sheboygan
Sheboygan, Wisconsin

- **State-supported** 2-year, founded 1933, part of University of Wisconsin System
- **Small-town** 75-acre campus with easy access to Milwaukee
- **Coed,** 747 undergraduate students, 46% full-time, 53% women, 47% men

Undergraduates 342 full-time, 405 part-time.
Freshmen *Admission:* 317 applied, 317 admitted.
Faculty *Student/faculty ratio:* 18:1.
Majors Liberal arts and sciences/liberal studies.
Academics *Calendar:* semesters. *Degree:* associate. *Special study options:* academic remediation for entering students, adult/continuing education programs, advanced placement credit, distance learning, English as a second language, independent study, off-campus study, part-time degree program, services for LD students, study abroad, summer session for credit.
Library University Library - Open for use by all Sheboygan County residents with an OPAC.
Student Life *Housing:* college housing not available. *Activities and Organizations:* drama/theater group, student-run newspaper, choral group, Student Government Association (SGA), English Club, University Theatre, Intramural Athletics, Southeast Asian Club (SEAC). *Campus security:* 24-hour patrols by city police. *Student services:* personal/psychological counseling.
Athletics *Intercollegiate sports:* basketball M, golf M/W, soccer M/W, tennis M/W, volleyball W. *Intramural sports:* basketball M/W, football M/W, ultimate Frisbee M/W, volleyball M/W.
Standardized Tests *Required:* SAT or ACT (for admission).
Costs (2014–15) *Tuition:* state resident $5096 full-time, $212 per credit part-time; nonresident $12,080 full-time, $503 per credit part-time. Full-time tuition and fees vary according to course load. Part-time tuition and fees vary according to course load.
Applying *Options:* electronic application. *Application fee:* $44. *Required:* essay or personal statement, high school transcript. *Required for some:* ACT Scores required for students under age 22. *Application deadlines:* rolling

(freshmen), rolling (transfers). *Notification:* continuous (freshmen), continuous (transfers).
Freshman Application Contact Ms. Elisa Waltz, High School Relations and Recruitment Coordinator, University of Wisconsin–Sheboygan, One University Drive, Sheboygan, WI 53081. *Phone:* 920-459-5956. *Fax:* 920-459-6602. *E-mail:* elisa.waltz@uwc.edu.
Website: http://www.sheboygan.uwc.edu/.

University of Wisconsin–Washington County
West Bend, Wisconsin

Freshman Application Contact Mr. Dan Cebrario, Associate Director of Student Services, University of Wisconsin–Washington County, Student Services Office, 400 University Drive, West Bend, WI 53095. *Phone:* 262-335-5201. *Fax:* 262-335-5220. *E-mail:* dan.cibrario@uwc.edu.
Website: http://www.washington.uwc.edu/.

University of Wisconsin–Waukesha
Waukesha, Wisconsin

- **State-supported** primarily 2-year, founded 1966, part of University of Wisconsin System
- **Suburban** 86-acre campus with easy access to Milwaukee
- **Coed,** 2,155 undergraduate students, 47% full-time, 47% women, 53% men

Undergraduates 1,014 full-time, 1,141 part-time. Students come from 6 states and territories; 1 other country; 1% are from out of state; 4% Black or African American, non-Hispanic/Latino; 3% Hispanic/Latino; 2% Asian, non-Hispanic/Latino; 0.6% Native Hawaiian or other Pacific Islander, non-Hispanic/Latino; 0.2% American Indian or Alaska Native, non-Hispanic/Latino; 0.1% Race/ethnicity unknown; 6% transferred in.
Freshmen *Admission:* 1,446 applied, 706 admitted, 1,323 enrolled.
Faculty *Total:* 91, 59% full-time, 89% with terminal degrees. *Student/faculty ratio:* 23:1.
Majors Liberal arts and sciences/liberal studies.
Academics *Calendar:* semesters. *Degrees:* associate and bachelor's. *Special study options:* academic remediation for entering students, accelerated degree program, advanced placement credit, distance learning, honors programs, internships, off-campus study, part-time degree program, services for LD students, study abroad, summer session for credit.
Library University of Wisconsin-Waukesha Library plus 1 other with 68,600 titles, 1,825 serial subscriptions, 5,121 audiovisual materials, a Web page.
Student Life *Housing:* college housing not available. *Activities and Organizations:* drama/theater group, student-run newspaper, choral group, Student Government, Student Activities Committee, Campus Crusade, Phi Theta Kappa, Circle K. *Campus security:* late-night transport/escort service, part-time patrols by trained security personnel. *Student services:* personal/psychological counseling.
Athletics Member NJCAA. *Intercollegiate sports:* basketball M/W, golf M/W, soccer M/W, tennis M/W, volleyball W. *Intramural sports:* basketball M, bowling M/W, cheerleading W, football M/W, skiing (downhill) M/W, table tennis M/W, volleyball M(c).
Standardized Tests *Required:* SAT or ACT (for admission).
Costs (2014–15) *Tuition:* state resident $5091 full-time, $215 per credit part-time; nonresident $12,072 full-time, $506 per credit part-time. Full-time tuition and fees vary according to course load. Part-time tuition and fees vary according to course load. *Required fees:* $230 full-time. *Payment plan:* installment.
Applying *Options:* electronic application, early admission, deferred entrance. *Application fee:* $44. *Required:* high school transcript. *Required for some:* interview. *Recommended:* essay or personal statement, admission interview may be recommended. *Application deadline:* rolling (freshmen). *Notification:* continuous (freshmen).
Freshman Application Contact Ms. Deb Kusick, Sr. Admission Specialist, University of Wisconsin–Waukesha, 1500 North University Drive, Waukesha, WI 53188-2799. *Phone:* 262-521-5040. *Fax:* 262-521-5530. *E-mail:* deborah.kusick@uwc.edu.
Website: http://www.waukesha.uwc.edu/.

Waukesha County Technical College
Pewaukee, Wisconsin

- **State and locally supported** 2-year, founded 1923, part of Wisconsin Technical College System
- **Suburban** 137-acre campus with easy access to Milwaukee
- **Coed,** 8,799 undergraduate students, 22% full-time, 48% women, 52% men

Undergraduates 1,905 full-time, 6,894 part-time. 9% Black or African American, non-Hispanic/Latino; 7% Hispanic/Latino; 2% Asian, non-

366 Peterson's Two-Year Colleges 2015

Hispanic/Latino; 0.1% Native Hawaiian or other Pacific Islander, non-Hispanic/Latino; 0.8% American Indian or Alaska Native, non-Hispanic/Latino; 2% Two or more races, non-Hispanic/Latino; 1% Race/ethnicity unknown.

Freshmen *Admission:* 518 enrolled.

Faculty *Total:* 857, 22% full-time. *Student/faculty ratio:* 18:1.

Majors Accounting; administrative assistant and secretarial science; architectural drafting and CAD/CADD; autobody/collision and repair technology; automobile/automotive mechanics technology; baking and pastry arts; business administration and management; business administration, management and operations related; computer and information sciences and support services related; computer programming; computer support specialist; computer systems networking and telecommunications; criminal justice/police science; dental hygiene; digital arts; early childhood education; electrical, electronic and communications engineering technology; electromechanical and instrumentation and maintenance technologies related; emergency medical technology (EMT paramedic); fire prevention and safety technology; graphic communications; graphic design; health information/medical records technology; hotel, motel, and restaurant management; human resources management; interior design; international marketing; marketing/marketing management; mechanical drafting and CAD/CADD; medical radiologic technology; mental and social health services and allied professions related; metal fabricator; multi/interdisciplinary studies related; operations management; physical therapy technology; real estate; registered nursing/registered nurse; restaurant, culinary, and catering management; surgical technology; teacher assistant/aide.

Academics *Calendar:* semesters. *Degree:* certificates, diplomas, and associate. *Special study options:* academic remediation for entering students, accelerated degree program, adult/continuing education programs, advanced placement credit, cooperative education, distance learning, English as a second language, part-time degree program, services for LD students, student-designed majors, summer session for credit.

Student Life *Housing:* college housing not available. *Campus security:* patrols by police officers 8 am to 10 pm.

Costs (2013–14) *Tuition:* state resident $3666 full-time, $122 per credit hour part-time; nonresident $5499 full-time, $183 per credit hour part-time. Full-time tuition and fees vary according to program. Part-time tuition and fees vary according to program. *Required fees:* $219 full-time, $7 per credit hour part-time. *Payment plans:* installment, deferred payment. *Waivers:* senior citizens.

Financial Aid Of all full-time matriculated undergraduates who enrolled in 2012, 67 Federal Work-Study jobs (averaging $2157). 180 state and other part-time jobs (averaging $3423).

Applying *Options:* electronic application. *Application fee:* $30. *Required:* high school transcript. *Required for some:* interview. *Application deadlines:* rolling (freshmen), rolling (transfers).

Freshman Application Contact Waukesha County Technical College, 800 Main Street, Pewaukee, WI 53072-4601. *Phone:* 262-691-5464.

Website: http://www.wctc.edu/.

Western Technical College
La Crosse, Wisconsin

Freshman Application Contact Ms. Jane Wells, Manager of Admissions, Registration, and Records, Western Technical College, PO Box 908, La Crosse, WI 54602-0908. *Phone:* 608-785-9158. *Toll-free phone:* 800-322-9982. *Fax:* 608-785-9094. *E-mail:* mildes@wwtc.edu. *Website:* http://www.westerntc.edu/.

Wisconsin Indianhead Technical College
Shell Lake, Wisconsin

- **District-supported** 2-year, founded 1912, part of Wisconsin Technical College System
- **Urban** 118-acre campus
- **Endowment** $3.1 million
- **Coed,** 3,418 undergraduate students, 43% full-time, 60% women, 40% men

Undergraduates 1,469 full-time, 1,949 part-time. Students come from 8 states and territories; 8% are from out of state; 0.7% Black or African American, non-Hispanic/Latino; 0.5% Hispanic/Latino; 0.7% Asian, non-Hispanic/Latino; 2% American Indian or Alaska Native, non-Hispanic/Latino; 2% Two or more races, non-Hispanic/Latino; 1% Race/ethnicity unknown.

Freshmen *Admission:* 549 enrolled.

Faculty *Total:* 740, 23% full-time. *Student/faculty ratio:* 17:1.

Majors Accounting; administrative assistant and secretarial science; architectural engineering technology; business administration and management; child-care and support services management; computer and information sciences; computer installation and repair technology; computer support specialist; computer systems networking and telecommunications; corrections and criminal justice related; court reporting; criminal justice/police science; early childhood education; emergency medical technology (EMT

paramedic); energy management and systems technology; finance; mental and social health services and allied professions related; multi/interdisciplinary studies related; occupational therapist assistant; operations management; web page, digital/multimedia and information resources design.

Academics *Calendar:* semesters. *Degree:* certificates, diplomas, and associate.

Student Life *Housing:* college housing not available. *Student services:* health clinic.

Costs (2013–14) *Tuition:* state resident $3666 full-time, $122 per credit part-time; nonresident $5499 full-time, $183 per credit part-time. Full-time tuition and fees vary according to course load, location, program, and reciprocity agreements. Part-time tuition and fees vary according to course load, location, program, and reciprocity agreements. *Required fees:* $378 full-time, $122 per credit part-time. *Payment plans:* installment, deferred payment.

Applying *Options:* electronic application. *Application fee:* $30. *Application deadline:* rolling (freshmen).

Freshman Application Contact Mr. Steve Bitzer, Vice President, Student Affairs and Campus Administrator, Wisconsin Indianhead Technical College, 2100 Beaser Avenue, Ashland, WI 54806. *Phone:* 715-468-2815 Ext. 3149. *Toll-free phone:* 800-243-9482. *Fax:* 715-468-2819. *E-mail:* Steve.Bitzer@witc.edu. *Website:* http://www.witc.edu/.

WYOMING

Casper College
Casper, Wyoming

- **State and locally supported** 2-year, founded 1945
- **Small-town** 200-acre campus
- **Coed,** 4,179 undergraduate students, 47% full-time, 58% women, 42% men

Undergraduates 1,958 full-time, 2,221 part-time. Students come from 15 other countries; 10% are from out of state; 1% Black or African American, non-Hispanic/Latino; 5% Hispanic/Latino; 0.8% Asian, non-Hispanic/Latino; 0.3% Native Hawaiian or other Pacific Islander, non-Hispanic/Latino; 0.5% American Indian or Alaska Native, non-Hispanic/Latino; 1% Two or more races, non-Hispanic/Latino; 3% Race/ethnicity unknown; 0.8% international; 5% transferred in; 10% live on campus. *Retention:* 55% of full-time freshmen returned.

Freshmen *Admission:* 1,322 applied, 1,322 admitted, 686 enrolled. *Average high school GPA:* 3.1. *Test scores:* ACT scores over 18: 75%; ACT scores over 24: 25%; ACT scores over 30: 1%.

Faculty *Total:* 260, 58% full-time, 22% with terminal degrees. *Student/faculty ratio:* 14:1.

Majors Accounting; accounting technology and bookkeeping; acting; administrative assistant and secretarial science; agricultural business and management; agriculture; airline pilot and flight crew; animal sciences; anthropology; art; art teacher education; athletic training; autobody/collision and repair technology; automobile/automotive mechanics technology; biology/biological sciences; business administration and management; business automation/technology/data entry; chemistry; clinical laboratory science/medical technology; computer and information systems security; computer programming; construction management; construction trades; criminal justice/law enforcement administration; crisis/emergency/disaster management; dance; diesel mechanics technology; drafting and design technology; economics; electrical, electronic and communications engineering technology; elementary education; emergency medical technology (EMT paramedic); energy management and systems technology; engineering; English; entrepreneurship; environmental science; fine/studio arts; fire science/firefighting; foreign languages and literatures; forensic science and technology; general studies; geographic information science and cartography; geology/earth science; graphic design; health services/allied health/health sciences; history; hospitality administration; industrial mechanics and maintenance technology; international relations and affairs; journalism; kindergarten/preschool education; legal assistant/paralegal; liberal arts and sciences/liberal studies; machine tool technology; manufacturing engineering technology; marketing/marketing management; mass communication/media; mathematics; mining technology; museum studies; music; musical theater; music performance; music teacher education; nutrition sciences; occupational therapist assistant; pharmacy technician; photography; physical education teaching and coaching; physics; political science and government; pre-dentistry studies; pre-law studies; premedical studies; pre-occupational therapy; pre-optometry; pre-pharmacy studies; pre-physical therapy; pre-veterinary studies; psychology; radiologic technology/science; range science and management; registered nursing/registered nurse; respiratory care therapy; retailing; robotics technology; social studies teacher education; social work;

sociology; speech communication and rhetoric; statistics related; substance abuse/addiction counseling; technology/industrial arts teacher education; theater design and technology; water quality and wastewater treatment management and recycling technology; web/multimedia management and webmaster; web page, digital/multimedia and information resources design; welding technology; wildlife, fish and wildlands science and management; women's studies.

Academics *Calendar:* semesters. *Degree:* certificates and associate. *Special study options:* academic remediation for entering students, accelerated degree program, advanced placement credit, cooperative education, distance learning, English as a second language, honors programs, independent study, internships, off-campus study, part-time degree program, services for LD students, summer session for credit.

Library Goodstein Foundation Library with 128,000 titles, 385 serial subscriptions, an OPAC, a Web page.

Student Life *Housing Options:* coed. Campus housing is university owned. *Activities and Organizations:* drama/theater group, student-run newspaper, choral group, Student Senate, Student Activities Board, Agriculture Club, Theater Club, Phi Theta Kappa. *Campus security:* 24-hour patrols, late-night transport/escort service. *Student services:* health clinic, personal/psychological counseling.

Athletics Member NJCAA. *Intercollegiate sports:* basketball M(s)/W(s), equestrian sports M/W, volleyball W(s). *Intramural sports:* basketball M/W, bowling M/W, football M/W, golf M/W, racquetball M/W, soccer M/W, softball M/W, tennis M/W.

Costs (2013–14) *Tuition:* state resident $1896 full-time, $79 per credit hour part-time; nonresident $5688 full-time, $237 per credit hour part-time. Part-time tuition and fees vary according to course load. *Required fees:* $552 full-time, $23 per credit hour part-time. *Room and board:* $5820. Room and board charges vary according to board plan and housing facility. *Payment plan:* deferred payment. *Waivers:* senior citizens and employees or children of employees.

Financial Aid Of all full-time matriculated undergraduates who enrolled in 2012, 80 Federal Work-Study jobs (averaging $2000).

Applying *Options:* electronic application, early admission. *Required:* high school transcript. *Application deadlines:* 8/15 (freshmen), 8/15 (transfers). *Notification:* continuous until 8/15 (freshmen), continuous until 8/15 (transfers).

Freshman Application Contact Mrs. Kyla Foltz, Director of Admissions Services, Casper College, 125 College Drive, Casper, WY 82601. *Phone:* 307-268-2111. *Toll-free phone:* 800-442-2963. *Fax:* 307-268-2611. *E-mail:* kfoltz@caspercollege.edu.
Website: http://www.caspercollege.edu/.

Central Wyoming College
Riverton, Wyoming

- **State and locally supported** 2-year, founded 1966, part of Wyoming Community College Commission
- **Small-town** 200-acre campus
- **Endowment** $14.9 million
- **Coed,** 2,265 undergraduate students, 37% full-time, 54% women, 46% men

Undergraduates 833 full-time, 1,432 part-time. Students come from 6 other countries; 13% are from out of state; 1% Black or African American, non-Hispanic/Latino; 9% Hispanic/Latino; 0.6% Asian, non-Hispanic/Latino; 0.4% Native Hawaiian or other Pacific Islander, non-Hispanic/Latino; 12% American Indian or Alaska Native, non-Hispanic/Latino; 3% Two or more races, non-Hispanic/Latino; 2% Race/ethnicity unknown; 0.4% international; 5% transferred in; 7% live on campus. *Retention:* 47% of full-time freshmen returned.

Freshmen *Admission:* 609 applied, 609 admitted, 269 enrolled. *Average high school GPA:* 2.96. *Test scores:* SAT critical reading scores over 500: 50%; SAT math scores over 500: 33%; SAT critical reading scores over 600: 6%.

Faculty *Total:* 229, 35% full-time, 32% with terminal degrees. *Student/faculty ratio:* 10:1.

Majors Accounting; accounting technology and bookkeeping; acting; administrative assistant and secretarial science; agricultural business and management; American Indian/Native American studies; area studies related; art; athletic training; automobile/automotive mechanics technology; biology/biological sciences; building/property maintenance; business administration and management; business/commerce; carpentry; child-care and support services management; commercial photography; computer science; computer technology/computer systems technology; criminal justice/law enforcement administration; culinary arts; customer service support/call center/teleservice operation; dramatic/theater arts; early childhood education; elementary education; engineering; English; entrepreneurship; environmental/environmental health engineering; environmental science; equestrian studies; fire science/firefighting; general studies; geology/earth science; graphic design; health services/allied health/health sciences;

homeland security, law enforcement, firefighting and protective services related; hotel/motel administration; international/global studies; mathematics; medical office assistant; music; occupational safety and health technology; parks, recreation and leisure; parks, recreation and leisure facilities management; physical sciences; pre-law studies; psychology; radio and television; range science and management; registered nursing/registered nurse; rehabilitation and therapeutic professions related; secondary education; social sciences; teacher assistant/aide; theater design and technology; welding technology.

Academics *Calendar:* semesters. *Degree:* certificates, diplomas, and associate. *Special study options:* academic remediation for entering students, adult/continuing education programs, advanced placement credit, cooperative education, distance learning, double majors, English as a second language, honors programs, independent study, off-campus study, part-time degree program, services for LD students, summer session for credit.

Library Central Wyoming College Library with 54,974 titles, 2,940 serial subscriptions, 1,450 audiovisual materials, an OPAC, a Web page.

Student Life *Housing Options:* coed. Campus housing is university owned. *Activities and Organizations:* drama/theater group, student-run radio and television station, choral group, Multi-Cultural Club, La Vida Nueva Club, Fellowship of College Christians, Quality Leaders, Science Club. *Campus security:* 24-hour emergency response devices, late-night transport/escort service, controlled dormitory access. *Student services:* personal/psychological counseling.

Athletics Member NJCAA. *Intercollegiate sports:* basketball M(s)/W(s), equestrian sports M(s)/W(s), volleyball W(s). *Intramural sports:* badminton M/W, basketball M/W, football M/W, rock climbing M/W, skiing (cross-country) M/W, skiing (downhill) M/W, soccer M/W, softball M/W, swimming and diving M/W, table tennis M/W, tennis M/W, ultimate Frisbee M/W, volleyball M/W, weight lifting M/W.

Costs (2014–15) *Tuition:* state resident $1992 full-time, $83 per credit part-time; nonresident $5976 full-time, $249 per credit part-time. Full-time tuition and fees vary according to course load, program, and reciprocity agreements. Part-time tuition and fees vary according to course load, program, and reciprocity agreements. *Required fees:* $888 full-time, $37 per credit part-time. *Room and board:* $5105; room only: $2505. Room and board charges vary according to board plan and housing facility. *Payment plans:* installment, deferred payment. *Waivers:* senior citizens and employees or children of employees.

Financial Aid Of all full-time matriculated undergraduates who enrolled in 2012, 488 applied for aid, 390 were judged to have need. 37 Federal Work-Study jobs (averaging $2323). *Financial aid deadline:* 6/30.

Applying *Options:* electronic application, early admission, deferred entrance. *Recommended:* high school transcript. *Application deadlines:* rolling (freshmen), rolling (out-of-state freshmen), rolling (transfers).

Freshman Application Contact Mrs. Deborah Lively, Admissions Assistant, Central Wyoming College, 2660 Peck Avenue, Riverton, WY 82501-2273. *Phone:* 307-855-2061. *Toll-free phone:* 800-735-8418. *Fax:* 307-855-2065. *E-mail:* admit@cwc.edu.
Website: http://www.cwc.edu/.

Eastern Wyoming College
Torrington, Wyoming

- **State and locally supported** 2-year, founded 1948, part of Wyoming Community College Commission
- **Rural** 40-acre campus
- **Coed,** 1,876 undergraduate students, 36% full-time, 58% women, 42% men

Undergraduates 680 full-time, 1,196 part-time. 1% Black or African American, non-Hispanic/Latino; 6% Hispanic/Latino; 0.4% Asian, non-Hispanic/Latino; 0.3% Native Hawaiian or other Pacific Islander, non-Hispanic/Latino; 1% American Indian or Alaska Native, non-Hispanic/Latino; 0.6% Two or more races, non-Hispanic/Latino; 2% Race/ethnicity unknown.

Freshmen *Admission:* 262 enrolled.

Faculty *Total:* 76, 58% full-time. *Student/faculty ratio:* 19:1.

Majors Accounting; administrative assistant and secretarial science; agribusiness; agricultural teacher education; art; biology/biological sciences; business administration and management; business teacher education; computer systems networking and telecommunications; corrections administration; cosmetology; criminal justice/law enforcement administration; criminal justice/police science; criminal justice/safety; early childhood education; economics; elementary education; English; environmental biology; farm and ranch management; foreign languages and literatures; general studies; health/medical preparatory programs related; liberal arts and sciences/liberal studies; mathematics; mathematics teacher education; music; music teacher education; office management; physical education teaching and coaching; pre-dentistry studies; premedical studies; pre-pharmacy studies; pre-veterinary studies; psychology; range science and management; secondary education; social sciences; speech communication and rhetoric; statistics;

veterinary/animal health technology; welding technology; wildlife, fish and wildlands science and management.

Academics *Calendar:* semesters. *Degree:* certificates, diplomas, and associate. *Special study options:* academic remediation for entering students, accelerated degree program, advanced placement credit, distance learning, English as a second language, independent study, internships, part-time degree program, services for LD students, student-designed majors, summer session for credit.

Library Eastern Wyoming College Library plus 1 other with an OPAC, a Web page.

Student Life *Housing Options:* coed, men-only, women-only. Campus housing is university owned. *Activities and Organizations:* drama/theater group, student-run newspaper, choral group, Criminal Justice Club, Veterinary Technology Club, Student Senate, Music Club, Rodeo Club. *Campus security:* 24-hour emergency response devices, controlled dormitory access. *Student services:* personal/psychological counseling.

Athletics Member NJCAA. *Intercollegiate sports:* basketball M/W, equestrian sports M/W, golf M, volleyball W.

Costs (2014–15) *Tuition:* state resident $1992 full-time, $83 per contact hour part-time; nonresident $5976 full-time, $249 per contact hour part-time. Full-time tuition and fees vary according to location. Part-time tuition and fees vary according to location. *Required fees:* $576 full-time, $24 per credit hour part-time. *Room and board:* $6200; room only: $3166. Room and board charges vary according to housing facility. *Payment plan:* installment. *Waivers:* senior citizens and employees or children of employees.

Applying *Recommended:* high school transcript.

Freshman Application Contact Dr. Rex Cogdill, Vice President for Students Services, Eastern Wyoming College, 3200 West C Street, Torrington, WY 82240. *Phone:* 307-532-8257. *Toll-free phone:* 866-327-8996. *Fax:* 307-532-8222. *E-mail:* rex.cogdill@ewc.wy.edu. *Website:* http://www.ewc.wy.edu/.

Laramie County Community College
Cheyenne, Wyoming

- **District-supported** 2-year, founded 1968, part of Wyoming Community College Commission
- **Small-town** 271-acre campus
- **Coed,** 4,632 undergraduate students, 43% full-time, 60% women, 40% men

Undergraduates 1,982 full-time, 2,650 part-time. Students come from 17 other countries; 23% are from out of state; 3% Black or African American, non-Hispanic/Latino; 10% Hispanic/Latino; 1% Asian, non-Hispanic/Latino; 0.2% Native Hawaiian or other Pacific Islander, non-Hispanic/Latino; 1% American Indian or Alaska Native, non-Hispanic/Latino; 0.3% Two or more races, non-Hispanic/Latino; 3% Race/ethnicity unknown; 0.6% international; 15% transferred in; 8% live on campus.

Freshmen *Admission:* 1,582 applied, 1,582 admitted, 420 enrolled. *Average high school GPA:* 2.91. *Test scores:* ACT scores over 18: 70%; ACT scores over 24: 14%.

Faculty *Total:* 680, 17% full-time, 3% with terminal degrees. *Student/faculty ratio:* 15:1.

Majors Accounting; agribusiness; agricultural business technology; agricultural production; agriculture; anthropology; art; autobody/collision and repair technology; automobile/automotive mechanics technology; biological and physical sciences; biology/biological sciences; business administration and management; business/commerce; chemistry; computer programming; computer science; corrections; criminal justice/law enforcement administration; dental hygiene; diagnostic medical sonography and ultrasound technology; diesel mechanics technology; digital communication and media/multimedia; drafting and design technology; early childhood education; economics; education; emergency medical technology (EMT paramedic); energy management and systems technology; engineering; English; entrepreneurship; equestrian studies; fire science/firefighting; general studies; heating, air conditioning, ventilation and refrigeration maintenance technology; history; homeland security, law enforcement, firefighting and protective services related; humanities; human services; kinesiology and exercise science; legal assistant/paralegal; mass communication/media; mathematics; mechanic and repair technologies related; medical insurance coding; music; physical education teaching and coaching; physical therapy technology; political science and government; pre-law studies; pre-pharmacy studies; psychology; public administration; radiologic technology/science; registered nursing/registered nurse; religious studies; social sciences; sociology; Spanish; speech communication and rhetoric; surgical technology; wildlife, fish and wildlands science and management.

Academics *Calendar:* semesters. *Degree:* certificates and associate. *Special study options:* academic remediation for entering students, adult/continuing education programs, advanced placement credit, cooperative education, distance learning, double majors, English as a second language, honors programs, independent study, internships, off-campus study, part-time degree

program, services for LD students, summer session for credit. *ROTC:* Army (c), Air Force (c).

Library Ludden Library plus 1 other with 56,943 titles, 170 serial subscriptions, 5,886 audiovisual materials, an OPAC, a Web page.

Student Life *Housing Options:* coed. Campus housing is university owned. *Activities and Organizations:* drama/theater group, student-run newspaper, choral group, Student Government Association, Phi Theta Kappa, Block and Bridle, Student Nursing Club, Skills USA. *Campus security:* 24-hour emergency response devices and patrols, late-night transport/escort service, controlled dormitory access. *Student services:* health clinic, personal/psychological counseling.

Athletics Member NJCAA. *Intercollegiate sports:* basketball M(s), cheerleading M(s)/W(s), equestrian sports M(s)/W(s), soccer M(s)/W(s), volleyball W(s). *Intramural sports:* basketball M/W, equestrian sports M/W, racquetball M/W, rock climbing M/W, skiing (cross-country) M/W, soccer M/W, softball M/W, table tennis M/W, ultimate Frisbee M/W, volleyball M/W.

Costs (2014–15) *Tuition:* state resident $2736 full-time, $79 per credit part-time; nonresident $6528 full-time, $237 per credit part-time. Part-time tuition and fees vary according to course load. *Required fees:* $840 full-time, $35 per credit part-time. *Room and board:* $7826; room only: $4648. Room and board charges vary according to housing facility. *Payment plan:* installment. *Waivers:* senior citizens and employees or children of employees.

Applying *Options:* electronic application, deferred entrance. *Required for some:* high school transcript, interview. *Application deadlines:* rolling (freshmen), rolling (out-of-state freshmen), rolling (transfers). *Notification:* continuous (freshmen), continuous (out-of-state freshmen), continuous (transfers).

Freshman Application Contact Ms. Holly Bruegman, Director of Admissions, Laramie County Community College, 1400 East College Drive, Cheyenne, WY 82007. *Phone:* 307-778-1117. *Toll-free phone:* 800-522-2993 Ext. 1357. *Fax:* 307-778-1360. *E-mail:* learnmore@lccc.wy.edu. *Website:* http://www.lccc.wy.edu/.

Northwest College
Powell, Wyoming

- **State and locally supported** 2-year, founded 1946, part of Wyoming Community College System
- **Rural** 132-acre campus
- **Coed,** 1,881 undergraduate students, 57% full-time, 59% women, 41% men

Undergraduates 1,078 full-time, 803 part-time. Students come from 29 other countries; 24% are from out of state; 0.5% Black or African American, non-Hispanic/Latino; 8% Hispanic/Latino; 0.2% Asian, non-Hispanic/Latino; 0.1% Native Hawaiian or other Pacific Islander, non-Hispanic/Latino; 0.8% American Indian or Alaska Native, non-Hispanic/Latino; 2% Two or more races, non-Hispanic/Latino; 4% international. *Retention:* 54% of full-time freshmen returned.

Freshmen *Admission:* 401 enrolled.

Faculty *Total:* 151, 52% full-time. *Student/faculty ratio:* 13:1.

Majors Accounting; administrative assistant and secretarial science; aeronautics/aviation/aerospace science and technology; agribusiness; agricultural communication/journalism; agricultural production; agricultural teacher education; animal sciences; anthropology; archeology; art; athletic training; biology/biological sciences; broadcast journalism; business administration and management; business/commerce; CAD/CADD drafting/design technology; chemistry; cinematography and film/video production; commercial and advertising art; commercial photography; criminal justice/law enforcement administration; crop production; desktop publishing and digital imaging design; electrician; elementary education; engineering; English; equestrian studies; farm and ranch management; French; general studies; graphic and printing equipment operation/production; health and physical education/fitness; health/medical preparatory programs related; health services/allied health/health sciences; history; international relations and affairs; journalism; kindergarten/preschool education; liberal arts and sciences/liberal studies; mathematics; music; natural resources management and policy; parks, recreation and leisure; physics; playwriting and screenwriting; political science and government; pre-pharmacy studies; psychology; radio and television; radio, television, and digital communication related; range science and management; registered nursing/registered nurse; secondary education; social sciences; sociology; Spanish; speech communication and rhetoric; veterinary/animal health technology; visual and performing arts related; welding technology.

Academics *Calendar:* semesters. *Degree:* certificates and associate. *Special study options:* academic remediation for entering students, adult/continuing education programs, advanced placement credit, cooperative education, distance learning, double majors, English as a second language, external degree program, independent study, internships, off-campus study, part-time degree program, services for LD students, study abroad, summer session for credit.

Library John Taggart Hinckley Library with an OPAC, a Web page.

Student Life *Housing:* on-campus residence required for freshman year. *Options:* coed, women-only, special housing for students with disabilities. Campus housing is university owned. Freshman campus housing is guaranteed. *Activities and Organizations:* drama/theater group, student-run newspaper, radio and television station, choral group. *Campus security:* 24-hour emergency response devices and patrols, late-night transport/escort service, controlled dormitory access. *Student services:* health clinic, personal/psychological counseling.

Athletics Member NJCAA. *Intercollegiate sports:* basketball M(s)/W(s), equestrian sports M(s)/W(s), soccer M(s)/W(s), volleyball W(s), wrestling M(s). *Intramural sports:* basketball M/W, football M/W, golf M/W, softball M/W, tennis M/W, ultimate Frisbee M/W, volleyball M/W.

Standardized Tests *Recommended:* SAT or ACT (for admission), ACT COMPASS.

Costs (2014–15) *Tuition:* state resident $1992 full-time, $83 per credit part-time; nonresident $5976 full-time, $249 per credit part-time. Full-time tuition and fees vary according to course load, location, and program. Part-time tuition and fees vary according to course load, location, and program. *Required fees:* $772 full-time, $26 per credit part-time. *Room and board:* $5640; room only: $2820. Room and board charges vary according to board plan and housing facility. *Payment plan:* installment. *Waivers:* children of alumni, senior citizens, and employees or children of employees.

Financial Aid Of all full-time matriculated undergraduates who enrolled in 2012, 115 Federal Work-Study jobs (averaging $2700). 215 state and other part-time jobs (averaging $2700).

Applying *Options:* electronic application. *Required:* high school transcript. *Required for some:* minimum 2.0 GPA. *Recommended:* minimum 2.0 GPA. *Application deadlines:* rolling (freshmen), rolling (out-of-state freshmen), rolling (transfers). *Notification:* continuous (freshmen), continuous (out-of-state freshmen), continuous (transfers).

Freshman Application Contact Mr. West Hernandez, Admissions Manager, Northwest College, 231 West 6th Street, Orendorff Building 1, Powell, WY 82435-1898. *Phone:* 307-754-6103. *Toll-free phone:* 800-560-4692. *Fax:* 307-754-6249. *E-mail:* west.hernandez@northwestcollege.edu.
Website: http://www.northwestcollege.edu/.

Sheridan College
Sheridan, Wyoming

- **State and locally supported** 2-year, founded 1948, part of Wyoming Community College Commission
- **Small-town** 124-acre campus
- **Endowment** $26.2 million
- **Coed,** 4,437 undergraduate students, 32% full-time, 49% women, 51% men

Undergraduates 1,441 full-time, 2,996 part-time. Students come from 6 other countries; 20% are from out of state; 1% Black or African American, non-Hispanic/Latino; 6% Hispanic/Latino; 0.5% Asian, non-Hispanic/Latino; 0.1% Native Hawaiian or other Pacific Islander, non-Hispanic/Latino; 1% American Indian or Alaska Native, non-Hispanic/Latino; 2% Two or more races, non-Hispanic/Latino; 0.7% international; 3% transferred in; 10% live on campus.

Freshmen *Admission:* 531 enrolled.

Faculty *Total:* 211, 49% full-time, 12% with terminal degrees. *Student/faculty ratio:* 17:1.

Majors Agricultural business and management; agriculture; agriculture and agriculture operations related; animal sciences; art; biological and physical sciences; biology/biological sciences; building construction technology; business/commerce; CAD/CADD drafting/design technology; computer and information sciences; computer and information systems security; criminal justice/safety; culinary arts; dental hygiene; diesel mechanics technology; dramatic/theater arts; early childhood education; electrical and electronic engineering technologies related; elementary education; engineering; English; environmental engineering technology; general studies; health and physical education/fitness; health services/allied health/health sciences; history; horticultural science; hospitality administration; information science/studies; kinesiology and exercise science; machine tool technology; massage therapy; mathematics; mining technology; multi/interdisciplinary studies related; music; precision production related; psychology; range science and management; registered nursing/registered nurse; secondary education; social sciences; surveying technology; teacher assistant/aide; turf and turfgrass management; web/multimedia management and webmaster; welding technology.

Academics *Calendar:* semesters. *Degree:* certificates and associate. *Special study options:* academic remediation for entering students, accelerated degree program, advanced placement credit, cooperative education, distance learning, double majors, English as a second language, independent study, internships, off-campus study, part-time degree program, services for LD students, summer session for credit.

Library Griffith Memorial Library plus 1 other with 53,828 titles, 93 serial subscriptions, 5,029 audiovisual materials, an OPAC, a Web page.

Student Life *Housing Options:* coed. Campus housing is university owned and leased by the school. *Activities and Organizations:* drama/theater group, student-run television station, choral group, National Society of Leadership and Success, Student Senate, Baptist Collegiate Ministries, Nursing Club, Dental Hygiene Club. *Campus security:* 24-hour emergency response devices, student patrols, controlled dormitory access, night patrols by certified officers. *Student services:* personal/psychological counseling.

Athletics Member NJCAA. *Intercollegiate sports:* basketball M(s)/W(s), cross-country running M(s)/W(s), equestrian sports M(s)/W(s), volleyball W(s). *Intramural sports:* basketball M/W, bowling M/W, football M/W, softball M/W, table tennis M/W, tennis M/W, ultimate Frisbee M/W, volleyball M/W.

Costs (2014–15) *Tuition:* state resident $1992 full-time, $83 per credit part-time; nonresident $5976 full-time, $249 per credit part-time. Full-time tuition and fees vary according to course load, location, and reciprocity agreements. Part-time tuition and fees vary according to location and reciprocity agreements. *Required fees:* $900 full-time, $30 per hour part-time. *Room and board:* $6050. Room and board charges vary according to board plan, housing facility, and location. *Payment plan:* installment. *Waivers:* senior citizens and employees or children of employees.

Applying *Options:* electronic application, early admission, deferred entrance. *Required for some:* high school transcript. *Recommended:* high school transcript. *Application deadlines:* rolling (freshmen), rolling (out-of-state freshmen), rolling (transfers). *Notification:* continuous (freshmen), continuous (out-of-state freshmen), continuous (transfers).

Freshman Application Contact Mr. Matt Adams, Admissions Coordinator, Sheridan College, PO Box 1500, Sheridan, WY 82801-1500. *Phone:* 307-674-6446 Ext. 2005. *Toll-free phone:* 800-913-9139 Ext. 2002. *Fax:* 307-674-3373. *E-mail:* madams@sheridan.edu.
Website: http://www.sheridan.edu/.

Western Wyoming Community College
Rock Springs, Wyoming

- **State and locally supported** 2-year, founded 1959
- **Small-town** 342-acre campus
- **Endowment** $9.3 million
- **Coed,** 3,621 undergraduate students, 34% full-time, 53% women, 47% men

Undergraduates 1,222 full-time, 2,399 part-time. 29% live on campus.

Freshmen *Test scores:* ACT scores over 18: 50%; ACT scores over 24: 17%.

Faculty *Total:* 218, 33% full-time. *Student/faculty ratio:* 18:1.

Majors Accounting; administrative assistant and secretarial science; anthropology; archeology; art; automobile/automotive mechanics technology; biological and physical sciences; biology/biological sciences; business administration and management; chemistry; computer and information sciences; computer programming (specific applications); computer science; criminal justice/law enforcement administration; criminology; dance; data entry/microcomputer applications; data processing and data processing technology; diesel mechanics technology; dramatic/theater arts; early childhood education; economics; education; education (multiple levels); electrical, electronic and communications engineering technology; electrical/electronics equipment installation and repair; electrician; elementary education; engineering technology; English; environmental science; forestry; general studies; geology/earth science; health/medical preparatory programs related; health services/allied health/health sciences; heavy equipment maintenance technology; history; humanities; human services; industrial electronics technology; industrial mechanics and maintenance technology; information science/studies; information technology; instrumentation technology; international relations and affairs; journalism; kinesiology and exercise science; legal administrative assistant/secretary; liberal arts and sciences/liberal studies; licensed practical/vocational nurse training; marketing/marketing management; mathematics; mechanics and repair; medical administrative assistant and medical secretary; medical/clinical assistant; medical office assistant; medical office computer specialist; mining technology; music; nursing assistant/aide and patient care assistant/aide; photography; political science and government; pre-dentistry studies; pre-engineering; pre-law studies; premedical studies; prenursing studies; pre-pharmacy studies; pre-veterinary studies; psychology; secondary education; social sciences; social work; sociology; Spanish; speech communication and rhetoric; theater design and technology; visual and performing arts; web/multimedia management and webmaster; web page, digital/multimedia and information resources design; welding technology; wildlife, fish and wildlands science and management; word processing.

Academics *Calendar:* semesters. *Degree:* certificates, diplomas, and associate. *Special study options:* academic remediation for entering students, adult/continuing education programs, advanced placement credit, cooperative education, distance learning, double majors, English as a second language, honors programs, independent study, internships, part-time degree program, services for LD students, summer session for credit.

Library Hay Library with 146,229 titles, 14,072 serial subscriptions, 4,467 audiovisual materials, an OPAC, a Web page.

Student Life *Housing Options:* coed, special housing for students with disabilities. Campus housing is university owned. *Activities and Organizations:* drama/theater group, student-run newspaper, radio station, choral group, marching band, Phi Theta Kappa, Students Without Borders (international club), Residence Hall Association, Associated Student Government, LDSSA. *Campus security:* 24-hour emergency response devices and patrols, late-night transport/escort service, controlled dormitory access, patrols by trained security personnel from 4 pm to 8 am, 24-hour patrols on weekends and holidays. *Student services:* personal/psychological counseling.

Athletics Member NJCAA. *Intercollegiate sports:* basketball M(s)/W(s), cheerleading M(s)/W(s), soccer M(s)(c)/W(s)(c), volleyball W(s), wrestling M(s). *Intramural sports:* badminton M/W, basketball M/W, bowling M/W, football M/W, rock climbing M/W, skiing (downhill) M/W, soccer M/W, softball M/W, table tennis M/W, tennis M/W, ultimate Frisbee M/W, volleyball M/W, water polo M/W.

Standardized Tests *Recommended:* SAT or ACT (for admission).

Financial Aid Of all full-time matriculated undergraduates who enrolled in 2012, 20 Federal Work-Study jobs (averaging $1500).

Applying *Options:* electronic application, early admission, deferred entrance. *Required:* high school transcript. *Application deadlines:* rolling (freshmen), rolling (transfers).

Freshman Application Contact Director of Admissions, Western Wyoming Community College, PO Box 428, Rock Springs, WY 82902-0428. *Phone:* 307-382-1647. *Toll-free phone:* 800-226-1181. *Fax:* 307-382-1636. *E-mail:* admissions@wwcc.wy.edu.

Website: http://www.wwcc.wy.edu/.

WyoTech Laramie
Laramie, Wyoming

Director of Admissions Director of Admissions, WyoTech Laramie, 4373 North Third Street, Laramie, WY 82072-9519. *Phone:* 307-742-3776. *Toll-free phone:* 888-577-7559. *Fax:* 307-721-4854.

Website: http://www.wyotech.edu/.

CANADA

Southern Alberta Institute of Technology
Calgary, Alberta, Canada

Freshman Application Contact Southern Alberta Institute of Technology, 1301 16th Avenue NW, Calgary, AB T2M 0L4, Canada. *Phone:* 403-284-8857. *Toll-free phone:* 877-284-SAIT.

Website: http://www.sait.ca/.

INTERNATIONAL

MEXICO

Westhill University
Sante Fe, Mexico

Freshman Application Contact Admissions, Westhill University, 56 Domingo Garcia Ramos, Zona Escolar, Prados de la Montana I, 05610 Sante Fe, Cuajimalpa, Mexico. *Phone:* 52-55 5292-1121. *Toll-free phone:* 877-403-4535. *E-mail:* admissions@westhill.edu.mx.

Website: http://www.westhill.edu.mx/.

PALAU

Palau Community College
Koror, Palau

Freshman Application Contact Ms. Dahlia Katosang, Director of Admissions and Financial Aid, Palau Community College, PO Box 9, Koror, PW 96940-0009. *Phone:* 680-488-2471 Ext. 233. *Fax:* 680-488-4468. *E-mail:* dahliapcc@palaunet.com.

Website: http://www.palau.edu/.

College
Close-Ups

BAY STATE COLLEGE
BOSTON, MASSACHUSETTS

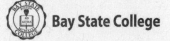

The College and Its Mission

Founded in 1946, Bay State College is a private, independent, coeducational institution located in Boston's historic Back Bay. Since its founding, Bay State College has been preparing graduates for outstanding careers and continued education.

Bay State College is a small, private college focused on passionate students who want to turn their interests into a rewarding career. The College offers associate and bachelor's degrees in a number of rewarding fields. Everyone at Bay State—from admissions counselors and professors to the career services team—helps to assist, guide, and advise students, from the moment they apply and throughout their careers. Located in Boston's Back Bay, the College offers the city of Boston as a campus, small classes, and one-on-one attention. For students seeking a career in one of the professions offered by Bay State, a degree program at the College could be a strong first step on their career path.

The College offers associate degrees and bachelor's degrees. The educational experience offered through the variety of programs prepares students to excel in the careers of their choice. Personalized attention is the cornerstone of a Bay State College education. Through the transformative power of its core values of quality, respect, and support, Bay State College has been able to assist students with setting and achieving goals that prepare them for careers and continued education.

Recognizing that one of the most important aspects of college is life outside the classroom, the Office of Student Affairs seeks to provide services from orientation through graduation and beyond. Special events throughout the year include a fashion show and a host of events produced by the Entertainment Management Association. Students also enjoy professional sports teams such as the Boston Celtics and Boston Red Sox.

Bay State College's campus experience can be whatever the student chooses it to be. It's not the typical college campus—its residence halls are actually brownstones along Boston's trendy Commonwealth Avenue and Bay State's quad could be Boston Common, the banks of the Charles River by the Esplanade, or Copley Square. That's the advantage of being located in Boston's Back Bay, which is also the safest neighborhood in the city. Students can relax at a favorite coffee shop, bike along the Charles River, ice skate on the Frog Pond, check out the city's nightlife, or take in a ball game at Fenway Park.

Bay State College is accredited by the New England Association of Schools and Colleges and is authorized to award the Associate in Science, Associate in Applied Science, and three Bachelor of Science degrees by the Commonwealth of Massachusetts. Bay State is a member of several professional educational associations. Its medical assisting program is accredited by the Accrediting Bureau of Health Education Schools (ABHES). The physical therapist assistant program is accredited by the Commission on Accreditation in Physical Therapy Education (CAPTE) of the American Physical Therapy Association (APTA).

Academic Programs

Bay State College operates on a semester calendar. The fall semester runs from early September to late December. The spring semester runs from late January until mid-May. A satellite campus is located in Taunton, Massachusetts.

Bachelor's degrees are offered in criminal justice, entertainment management, fashion merchandising, information technology, and management.

Associate degrees are offered in business administration, criminal justice, entertainment management (with a concentration in audio production), fashion design, fashion merchandising, health studies, information technology, marketing, medical assisting, nursing, physical therapist assistant studies, retail business management, and hospitality management.

Bay State College also offers courses on-ground and online to working adults in its Evening and Online Division. The courses are offered in eight-week sessions and allow more flexibility for students who must balance work and family commitments while pursuing their education.

Bay State College reviews, enhances, and adds new programs to help graduates remain industry-current in their respective fields.

Off-Campus Programs

Many students cite Bay State's internship program as a turning point for them. Bay State internships allow students to gain hands-on experience and spend time working in their chosen fields. These valuable opportunities can give students an advantage when they apply for positions after they have completed school.

Bay State's Boston location allows the College to offer internships at many well-known companies and organizations. Students are able to apply what they've learned in the classroom and do meaningful work in their field of study. In addition, they build working relationships with people in their chosen profession. For more information on internships, prospective students may contact Tom Corrigan, Director of Career Services, at 617-217-9000.

Costs

Tuition charges are assessed on a per-credit-hour basis and vary depending upon program of study. This provides students with maximum flexibility based on individual financial and academic needs, making a Bay State College education more accommodating and affordable. Rates quoted below by program were for the 2013–14 academic year. Charges are not prorated unless noted. Program flow sheets may require more or less than 30 credits per academic year.

Medical assisting, and health studies: $749 per credit, $22,470 (30 credits). Business, criminal justice, fashion merchandising, fashion design, entertainment management, and hospitality management: $826 per credit, $24,780 (30 credits).Nursing and physical therapy assistant: $849 per credit, $25,470 (30 credits).

Evening students pay $340 per credit. Room and board were $11,800 per year, the student services fee was $400 (for day students only), and the student activity fee was $50. The cost of books and additional fees vary by major. A residence hall security deposit of $300 and a technology fee of $300 are required of all resident students.

The fall tuition payment due date is July 1; the spring tuition payment is due December 1.

Financial Aid

Each student works with a personal advocate to thoroughly explain financial options and guide them through the financial aid application process. Many options are available: aid, grants and scholarships, federal programs, and private loans. Bay State College's Financial Aid Department and tuition planners can help students determine what aid may apply. Approximately 85 percent of students receive some form of financial assistance. Bay State College requires a completed Free Application for Federal Student Aid (FAFSA) form and signed federal tax forms. The College's institutional financial aid priority deadline is March 15. Financial aid is granted on a rolling basis.

Faculty

There are 72 faculty members, many holding advanced degrees and several holding doctoral degrees. The student-faculty ratio is 20:1.

Student Body Profile

There are approximately 1,200 students in degree programs in both the day and evening divisions.

Student Activities

Bay State College students participate in a multitude of activities offered by the College through existing student organizations. Students also have the opportunity to create clubs and organizations that meet their interests. Existing organizations include the Student Government Association, Entertainment Management Association, Justice Society, and the Criminal Justice Society. Students produce an annual talent show as well as an annual fashion show that showcases student work from the College's fashion design program. An annual literary magazine also features the work of students throughout the College.

Facilities and Resources

Advisement/Counseling: Trained staff members assist students in selecting courses and programs of study. A counseling center is available to provide mental and physical health referrals to all students in need of such services. Referral networks are extensive, within a wide range of geographic areas, and provide access to a variety of public and private health agencies.

Specialized Services: The Office of Academic Development at Bay State College is designed to meet and support the various academic needs of the student body and serve as a resource for supplemental instruction, academic plans, learning accommodations, and other types of support. The Office of Academic Development operates on the belief that all students can achieve success in their courses by accessing support services and creating individual academic plans.

The Center for Learning and Academic Success (CLAS) at Bay State College is a key component available to help students achieve academic success. Students come to CLAS to get support in specific subject areas as well as study skills such as note-taking, reading comprehension, writing research papers, time management, and coping with exam anxiety. They utilize CLAS to develop study plans and strategies that positively impact their grades in all subjects. Students can also take advantage of the tutoring and seminars CLAS offers. CLAS's goal is to ensure that students are provided with exceptional academic support in all areas of study.

Career Planning/Placement: For many college students, the transition from student life to professional life is filled with questions and uncharted realities. Bay State College's Career Services Department offers students their own personal career advancement team. The department can help students learn to write a resume and cover letter, use social networks, practice interviewing skills, find the right job opportunity, and learn other career-related functions. Students even receive a Professionalism Grade, which lets future employers know they have what it takes to start contributing on day one. The Career Services Department at is determined to see each student succeed and offers valuable instruction that will serve students throughout their professional careers.

Library and Audiovisual Services: The library is staffed with trained librarians who are available to guide students in their research process. The library's resources include 7,500 books, eighty-five periodical subscriptions, and a dramatically increased reach through its online library resource databases that include ProQuest, InfoTrac, and LexisNexis. In addition, the library provides computer access and study space for students. The library catalog and databases are accessible from any Internet-ready terminal.

First-Year Experience: The First-Year Experience (FYE) is a 1-credit course that is required of all first-year students and takes place during the first three days that students are on campus. FYE combines social activities with an academic syllabus that is designed to ease the transition into the college experience. Through FYE, students have the opportunity to connect with their academic advisers as well as with other students in their academic programs. At the conclusion of FYE, students are on the road to mapping out their personal action plan for success. The plan, designed by students, guided by academic advisers, and revisited each semester, helps students set, monitor, and achieve academic and life goals. It also builds the preparation for lifelong accomplishment.

Location

Located in the historic city of Boston, Massachusetts, and surrounded by dozens of colleges and universities, Bay State College is an ideal setting in which to pursue a college degree. Tree-lined streets around the school are mirrored in the skyscrapers of the Back Bay. The College is located within walking distance of several major league sport franchises, concert halls, museums, the Freedom Trail, Boston Symphony Hall, the Boston Public Library, and the Boston Public Garden. World-class shopping and major cultural and sporting events help make college life a memorable experience.

The College is accessible by the MBTA and commuter rail and bus, and it is near Boston Logan International Airport.

Admission Requirements

Applicants must be a high school graduate, a current high school student working toward graduation, or a recipient of a GED certificate. The Office of Admissions requires that applicants to the associate degree programs have a minimum of a 2.0 GPA (on a 4.0 scale); if available, applicants may submit SAT and/or ACT scores. Applicants to bachelor's degree programs must have a minimum 2.3 GPA (on a 4.0 scale) and must also submit SAT or ACT scores. International applicants must also submit high school transcripts translated to English with an explanation of the grading system, financial documentation, and a minimum TOEFL score of 500 on the paper-based exam or 173 on the computer-based exam if English is not their native language.

The physical therapist assistant studies and nursing programs require a minimum 2.7 GPA (on a 4.0 scale) and the Evening Division has different or additional admission requirements. For more information about these programs, interested students should visit the website at http://www.baystate.edu.

A personal interview is required for all prospective students—parents are encouraged to attend. Applicants must receive the recommendation of a Bay State College Admissions Officer.

Application and Information

Applications are accepted on a rolling basis. Students are responsible for arranging for their official high school transcripts, test scores, and letters of recommendation to be submitted to Bay State College.

The Bay State College Admissions Office notifies applicants of a decision within one week of receipt of the transcript and other required documents. There is a $100 nonrefundable tuition deposit required upon acceptance to ensure a place in the class; the deposit is credited toward the tuition fee. Deposits are due within thirty days of acceptance. Once a student is accepted, a Bay State College representative creates a personalized financial plan that provides payment options for a Bay State College education.

Applications should be submitted to:

Admissions Office
Bay State College
122 Commonwealth Avenue
Boston, Massachusetts 02116
Phone: 800-81-LEARN (53276)
Fax: 617-249-0400 (eFax)
E-mail: admissions@baystate.edu
Website: http://www.baystate.edu
http://www.facebook.com/baystatecollege
http://twitter.com/baystatecollege

Giving students access is an essential part of a Bay State College education. Students have access to a community of support, experiential learning, faculty with real-world experience, and a dynamic location in the heart of the city.

BROWN MACKIE COLLEGE — AKRON

AKRON, OHIO

The College and Its Mission

Brown Mackie College — Akron (Brown Mackie College) is one of over twenty-five locations in the Brown Mackie College system of schools (www.brownmackie.edu), which is dedicated to providing educational programs that prepare students to pursue entry-level positions in a competitive, rapidly changing workplace. Brown Mackie College schools offer bachelor's degree, associate degree, diploma, and certificate programs in health sciences, business, information technology, legal studies, and design to thousands of students in the Midwest, Southeast, Southwest, and Western United States.

Brown Mackie College was founded in Cincinnati, Ohio, in February 1927, as a traditional business college. In March 1980, the college added a branch campus in Akron, Ohio. The college outgrew this space and relocated to its current address in January 2007.

Brown Mackie College — Akron is accredited by the Accrediting Council for Independent Colleges and Schools to award associate degrees and diplomas. The Accrediting Council for Independent Colleges and Schools is listed as a nationally recognized accrediting agency by the United States Department of Education and is recognized by the Council for Higher Education Accreditation. ACICS can be contacted at 750 First Street NE, Suite 980, Washington, D.C. 20002; phone: 202-336-6780.

Brown Mackie College — Akron is licensed by the Ohio State Board of Career Colleges and Schools, 30 East Broad Street, 24th Floor, Suite 2481, Columbus, Ohio 43215-3138; phone: 614-466-2752. Ohio registration #03-09-1685T.

The occupational therapy assistant program is accredited by the Accreditation Council for Occupational Therapy Education (ACOTE) of the American Occupational Therapy Association (AOTA), located at 4720 Montgomery Lane, P.O. Box 31220, Bethesda, Maryland 20824-1220; phone: 301-652-AOTA. Graduates of the program will be eligible to sit for the national certification examination for the occupational therapy assistant administered by the National Board for Certification in Occupational Therapy (NBCOT). After successful completion of this exam, the individual will be a Certified Occupational Therapy Assistant (COTA). In addition, most states require licensure in order to practice; however, state licenses are usually based on the results of the NBCOT Certification Examination. Note that a felony conviction may affect a graduate's ability to sit for the NBCOT certification examination or attain state licensure.

The veterinary technology program at Brown Mackie College — Akron has provisional programmatic accreditation granted by the American Veterinary Medical Association (AVMA) through the Committee on Veterinary Technician Education and Activities (CVTEA), 1931 North Meacham Road, Suite 100, Schaumburg, Illinois 60173; phone: 800-248-2862; www.avma.org.

Academic Programs

Brown Mackie College — Akron provides higher education to traditional and nontraditional students through associate degree and diploma programs that can assist them in enhancing their career opportunities, broadening their perspectives through appropriate general education courses, thinking independently and critically, and improving problem-solving abilities.

Each college quarter comprises twelve weeks. Associate degree programs require a minimum of eight quarters to complete. Programs are offered on a year-round basis, providing students with the ability to work uninterrupted toward their degree. Brown Mackie College offers all programs in a unique One Course

a Month format. This schedule allows students to focus studies on only one course for four weeks and has proven convenient for students with multiple obligations such as jobs and family.

Associate Degree Programs: The Associate of Applied Business degree is awarded in business management.

The Associate of Applied Science degree is awarded in health care administration, occupational therapy assistant, and veterinary technology.

Diploma Programs: Brown Mackie College offers diploma programs in general business, medical assistant, and practical nursing.

The American Medical Technologists (AMT), which offers the certification for Registered Medical Assistant (RMA), accepts the accreditation of Brown Mackie College — Akron. Students will qualify to take the Registered Medical Assistant certification examination upon graduating the Brown Mackie College — Akron medical assistant programs. Information on application procedures can be found at http://americanmedtech.org/SchoolsStudents/CertificationProcess.aspx.

Brown Mackie College — Akron does not guarantee third-party certification. Outside agencies control the requirements for certifications and are subject to change without notice to Brown Mackie College.

Program availability and degree offerings are subject to change.

Costs

Tuition for the 2013–14 academic year was $314 per credit hour and $20 per credit hour for general fees. Tuition for the practical nursing program was $381 per credit hour and $30 per credit hour for general fees. Tuition for the occupational therapy assistant program was $381 per credit hour and $20 per credit hour for general fees. The cost of textbooks, if applicable, and other instructional materials varies by program.

Financial Aid

The College maintains a full-time staff of financial aid professionals to assist qualified students in obtaining the financial assistance they require to meet their education expenses. Financial aid is available to those students who qualify.

Available resources may include federal grants and loans, state aid, student loans from private lenders, and federal work-study opportunities, both on and off College premises. Federal assistance programs are administered through the U.S. Department of Education, Office of Student Financial Assistance. Any U.S. citizen, national, or person in the United States for other than temporary reasons who is enrolled or accepted for enrollment may apply for these programs. Most forms of financial assistance are available for each July 1–June 30 award period.

Every student considering application for financial aid should request a copy of the current Student Guide, published by the U.S. Department of Education. This important document may be obtained in the Student Financial Services Office and will assist persons in understanding eligibility requirements, the application process, deadlines, and the various forms of grants and loans available.

Details on school-specific loans and scholarships are available on the school's website (http://www.brownmackie.edu/Akron) or prospective students can contact the school's Student Financial Services Department; phone: 330-869-3600; e-mail: bmcakadm@brownmackie.edu.

Faculty

There are 20 full-time and 39 part-time faculty members. The student-faculty ratio is 14:1.

Facilities and Resources

Brown Mackie College provides media presentation rooms for special instructional needs, a library that provides instructional resources and academic support for both faculty members and students, and qualified and experienced faculty members who are committed to the academic and technical preparation of their students. Brown Mackie College is nonresidential; students who are unable to commute daily from their homes may request assistance from the Office of Admissions in locating off-campus housing. The college is accessible by public transportation and provides ample parking, available at no charge.

Brown Mackie College — Akron is fully committed to using eTextbooks and computer tablets in the classroom. Utilizing these tablets to access expanded course material, students are able to increase their acumen for using this technology and further enhance their educational experience. Students have the ability to directly download their eTextbooks to their tablet, eliminating the need to carry heavy, physical textbooks and reducing the overall cost of supplies.

The College is a nonresidential, smoke-free institution.

Location

Brown Mackie College — Akron is located at 755 White Pond Drive in Akron, Ohio.

Admission Requirements

Each applicant for admission is assigned an assistant director of admissions who directs the applicant through the steps of the process; provides information on curriculum, policies, procedures, and services; and assists the applicant in setting necessary appointments and interviews.

To be considered for admission to Brown Mackie College, a candidate must be a high school graduate or hold a General Education Development (GED) certificate. As part of the admission process, applicants must sign a document attesting to graduation or completion and containing the information to obtain verification of such. Official high school transcripts or official documentation of high school graduation equivalency must be obtained within the first financial aid payment period or the student will be withdrawn from the institution following established guidelines for withdrawn students noted in the catalog. Title IV aid will not be dispersed until verification of graduation or completion has been received by the College.

Where applicable, students seeking entry into the College with a high school diploma completed in a foreign country must provide an original U.S.–equivalency evaluation from an evaluating agency that is a member of the National Association of Credential Evaluation Services (NACES, http://www.naces.org/) or the Association of International Credential Evaluators, Inc. (AICES, http://www.aice-eval.org/). The cost of evaluating the foreign transcript is borne by the applicant.

Admission to the College is based upon the applicant meeting the school's admissions requirements, a review of the applicant's previous educational records, and a review of the applicant's career interests. It is the responsibility of the applicant to ensure that the College receives all required documentation

Prior to admission, students are given an assessment of academic skills, commonly referred to as the academic readiness evaluation. Though the results of this assessment do not determine eligibility for admission, they provide the College with a means of determining the need for academic support through transitional studies courses and academic advisement, as well as a means by which the College can evaluate the effectiveness of its educational programs.

An applicant must obtain a minimum score of 60 in writing and 51 in mathematics on the COMPASS student academic readiness assessment. If a student does not achieve these scores, he/she will be enrolled in the appropriate transitional studies course(s).

In addition to the general admission requirements above, some programs have additional requirements specific to the program. For information on those requirements, and other school-specific requirements, visit the school's website (http://www.brownmackie.edu/Akron) or contact the school's admissions department; phone: 330-869-3600; e-mail: bmcakadm@brownmackie.edu.

Application and Information

Applicants must complete and submit an application form along with documentation of graduation from an accredited high school or state-approved secondary education curriculum or official documentation of high school graduation equivalency.

See BMCprograms.info for program duration, tuition, fees and other costs, median debt, federal salary data, alumni success, programmatic accreditation, and other important information.

Brown Mackie College — Akron is one of over 25 school locations of the Brown Mackie College system of schools. Programs, credential levels, technology, and scheduling options are subject to change. ©2014 Brown Mackie College.

For additional information, prospective students should contact:

Senior Director of Admissions
Brown Mackie College — Akron
755 White Pond Drive, Suite 101
Akron, Ohio 44320
Phone: 330-869-3600
Fax: 330-869-3650
E-mail: bmcakadm@brownmackie.edu
Website: http://www.brownmackie.edu/Akron

BROWN MACKIE COLLEGE — ALBUQUERQUE

ALBUQUERQUE, NEW MEXICO

BROWN MACKIE COLLEGE®
ALBUQUERQUE

The College and Its Mission

Brown Mackie College — Albuquerque (Brown Mackie College) is one of over twenty-five locations in the Brown Mackie College system of schools (www.brownmackie.edu), which is dedicated to providing educational programs that prepare students to pursue entry-level positions in a competitive, rapidly changing workplace. Brown Mackie College schools offer bachelor's degree, associate degree, diploma, and certificate programs in health sciences, business, information technology, legal studies, and design to thousands of students in the Midwest, Southeast, Southwest, and Western United States.

Brown Mackie College was originally founded and approved by the Board of Trustees of Kansas Wesleyan College in Salina, Kansas on July 30, 1892. In 1938, the college was incorporated as the Brown Mackie School of Business under the ownership of Perry E. Brown and A.B. Mackie, former instructors at Kansas Wesleyan University in Salina, Kansas. Their last names formed the name of Brown Mackie. By January 1975, with improvements in curricula and higher degree-granting status, the Brown Mackie School of Business became Brown Mackie College.

Brown Mackie College — Albuquerque is accredited by the Accrediting Council for Independent Colleges and Schools to award associate degrees and diplomas. The Accrediting Council for Independent Colleges and Schools is listed as a nationally recognized accrediting agency by the United States Department of Education and is recognized by the Council for Higher Education Accreditation. ACICS can be contacted at 750 First Street NE, Suite 980, Washington, D.C. 20002; phone: 202-336-6780.

Brown Mackie College — Albuquerque is licensed by the New Mexico Higher Education Department, 2048 Galisteo Street, Santa Fe, New Mexico 87505-2100; phone: 505-476-8400.

The occupational therapy assistant program is accredited by the Accreditation Council for Occupational Therapy Education (ACOTE) of the American Occupational Therapy Association (AOTA), 4720 Montgomery Lane, P.O. Box 31220, Bethesda, Maryland 20824-1220; phone: 301-652-AOTA. Graduates of the program will be eligible to sit for the national certification examination for the occupational therapy assistant administered by the National Board for Certification in Occupational Therapy (NBCOT). After successful completion of this exam, the individual will be a Certified Occupational Therapy Assistant (COTA). In addition, most states require licensure in order to practice; however, state licenses are usually based on the results of the NBCOT Certification Examination. Note that a felony conviction may affect a graduate's ability to sit for the NBCOT certification examination or attain state licensure.

The Brown Mackie College — Albuquerque Associate of Applied Science in surgical technology program is accredited by the Accrediting Bureau of Health Education Schools, ABHES.

The Brown Mackie College — Albuquerque Associate of Applied Science in surgical technology program is accredited by the Commission on Accreditation of Allied Health Education Programs (www.caahep.org) upon the recommendation of the Accreditation Review Committee on Education in Surgical Technology.

The veterinary technology program at Brown Mackie College — Albuquerque has provisional programmatic accreditation granted by the American Veterinary Medical Association (AVMA) through the Committee on Veterinary Technician Education and Activities (CVTEA), 1931 North Meacham Road, Suite 100, Schaumburg, Illinois 60173; phone: 800-248-2862; www.avma.org.

Academic Programs

Brown Mackie College — Albuquerque provides higher education to traditional and nontraditional students through associate degree and diploma programs that assist in enhancing their career opportunities, broadening their perspectives through appropriate general education courses, thinking independently and critically, and improving problem-solving abilities. The college strives to develop within its students the desire for lifelong and continued education.

Each college quarter comprises twelve weeks. Associate degree programs require a minimum of eight quarters to complete. Programs are offered on a year-round basis, providing students with the ability to work uninterrupted toward completion of their programs. The college offers all programs in a unique One Course a Month format. This allows students to focus studies on only one course for four weeks. This schedule has proven convenient for students with multiple obligations such as jobs and family.

Associate Degree Programs: The Associate of Applied Science degree is awarded in architectural design and drafting technology, business management, criminal justice, health care administration, information technology, nursing, occupational therapy assistant, paralegal, pharmacy technology, surgical technology, and veterinary technology.

Diploma Programs: Brown Mackie College — Albuquerque offers diploma programs in accounting, business, criminal justice, and medical assistant.

The American Medical Technologists (AMT), which offers the certification for Registered Medical Assistant (RMA), accepts the accreditation of Brown Mackie College — Albuquerque. Students will qualify to take the Registered Medical Assistant certification examination upon graduating the Brown Mackie College — Albuquerque medical assisting and medical assistant programs. Graduates of the 48-credit-hour medical assistant program are not qualified to take the AMT/RMA exam. Information on application procedures can be found at http://americanmedtech.org/SchoolsStudents/CertificationProcess.aspx. Note that a felony conviction may affect a graduate's ability to sit for the RMA exam.

Brown Mackie College does not guarantee third-party certification/licensing exams. Outside agencies control the requirements for certification/licensing and are subject to change without notification to the College.

Program availability and degree offerings are subject to change.

Costs

Tuition in the 2013–14 academic year for all bachelor's and associate degrees and certificates was $324 per credit hour; fees were $25 per credit hour. Tuition for the occupational therapy assistant program was $355 per credit hour; fees were $25 per credit hour. Tuition for the surgical technology program was $339 per credit hour; fees were $25 per credit hour. Tuition for the nursing program was $390 per credit hour; fees were $30 per credit hour. The cost of textbooks, if applicable, and other instructional materials varies by program.

Financial Aid

The College maintains a full-time staff of financial aid professionals to assist qualified students in obtaining the financial assistance they require to meet their education expenses. Financial aid is available to those students who qualify.

Available resources may include federal grants and loans, state aid, student loans from private lenders, and federal work-study opportunities, both on and off College premises. Federal assistance programs are administered through the U.S. Department of Education, Office of Student Financial Assistance. Any U.S. citizen, national, or person in the United States for other than temporary reasons who is enrolled or accepted for enrollment may apply for these programs. Most forms of financial assistance are available for each July 1–June 30 award period.

Every student considering application for financial aid should request a copy of the current Student Guide, published by the U.S. Department of Education. This important document may be obtained in the Student Financial Services Office and will assist persons in understanding eligibility requirements, the application process, deadlines, and the various forms of grants and loans available.

Details on school-specific loans and scholarships are available online (http://www.brownmackie.edu/Albuquerque) or by contacting the school's Student Financial Services Department at 505-559-5200; e-mail: bmcalbadm@edmc.edu.

Faculty

Experienced faculty members provide academic support and are committed to the academic and technical preparation of their students. The college has both full-time and part-time instructors, with a student-faculty ratio of 15:1.

Facilities and Resources

A modern facility, Brown Mackie College — Albuquerque comprises more than 38,000 square feet. The college is equipped with multiple computer labs, housing over 150 computers. High-speed access to the Internet and other online resources are available to students and faculty. Multimedia classrooms are outfitted with overhead projectors, VCR/DVD players, and computers.

Brown Mackie College — Albuquerque is fully committed to using eTextbooks and computer tablets in the classroom. Utilizing these tablets to access expanded course material, students are able to increase their acumen for using this technology and further enhance their educational experience. Students have the ability to directly download their eTextbooks to their tablet, eliminating the need to carry heavy, physical textbooks and reducing the overall cost of supplies.

Brown Mackie College is nonresidential; public transportation and ample parking at no cost are available. The campus is a smoke-free facility.

Location

Brown Mackie College — Albuquerque is conveniently located at 10500 Copper Avenue NE, in Albuquerque, New Mexico.

Admission Requirements

Each applicant for admission is assigned an assistant director of admissions who directs the applicant through the steps of the process; provide information on curriculum, policies, procedures, and services; and assists the applicant in setting necessary appointments and interviews.

To be considered for admission to Brown Mackie College, a candidate must be a high school graduate or hold a General Education Development (GED) certificate. As part of the admission process applicants must sign a document attesting to graduation or completion and containing the information to obtain verification of such. Official high school transcripts or official documentation of high school graduation equivalency must be obtained within the first financial aid payment period or the student will be withdrawn from the institution following established guidelines for withdrawn students noted in the catalog. Title IV aid will not be dispersed until verification of graduation or completion has been received by the College.

Where applicable, students seeking entry into the College with a high school diploma completed in a foreign country must provide an original U.S.–equivalency evaluation from an evaluating agency which is a member of the National Association of Credential Evaluation Services (NACES, http://www.naces.org/) or the Association of International Credential Evaluators, Inc. (AICES, http://www.aice-eval.org/). The cost of evaluating the foreign transcript is borne by the applicant.

Admission to the College is based upon the applicant meeting the school's admission requirements, a review of the applicant's previous educational records, and a review of the applicant's career interests. It is the responsibility of the applicant to ensure that the College receives all required documentation

Prior to admission, students are given an assessment of academic skills, commonly referred to as the academic readiness evaluation. Though the results of this assessment do not determine eligibility for admission, they provide the College with a means of determining the need for academic support through transitional studies courses and academic advisement, as well as a means by which the College can evaluate the effectiveness of its educational programs.

An applicant must obtain a minimum score of 60 in writing and 51 in mathematics on the COMPASS student academic readiness assessment. If a student does not achieve these scores, he/she will be enrolled in the appropriate transitional studies course(s).

In addition to the general admission requirements above, some programs have additional requirements specific to the program. For information on those requirements, and other school-specific requirements, please visit the school's website (http://www.brownmackie.edu/Albuquerque) or contact the school's Admissions department at 505-559-5200; e-mail: bmcalbadm@edmc.edu.

Application and Information

Applicants must complete and submit an application form, along with documentation of graduation from an accredited high school or state-approved secondary education curriculum or official documentation of high school graduation equivalency.

See BMCprograms.info for program duration, tuition, fees and other costs, median debt, federal salary data, alumni success, programmatic accreditation and other important information.

Brown Mackie College — Albuquerque is one of over 25 school locations of the Brown Mackie College system of schools. Programs, credential levels, technology, and scheduling options are subject to change. ©2014 Brown Mackie College.

For additional information, prospective students should contact:

Director of Admissions
Brown Mackie College — Albuquerque
10500 Copper Avenue NE, Suite C
Albuquerque, New Mexico 87123
Phone: 505-559-5200
      877-271-3488 (toll-free)
Fax: 505-559-5222
E-mail: bmcalbadm@edmc.edu
Website: http://www.brownmackie.edu/Albuquerque

BROWN MACKIE COLLEGE — ATLANTA
ATLANTA, GEORGIA

The College and Its Mission

Brown Mackie College — Atlanta (Brown Mackie College) is one of over twenty-five locations in the Brown Mackie College system of schools (http://www.brownmackie.edu), which is dedicated to providing educational programs that prepare students to pursue entry-level positions in a competitive, rapidly changing workplace. Brown Mackie College schools offer bachelor degree, associate degree, certificate, and diploma programs in health sciences, business, information technology, legal studies, and design to thousands of students in the Midwest, Southeast, Southwest, and Western United States.

Brown Mackie College — Atlanta is accredited by the Accrediting Council for Independent Colleges and Schools (ACICS) to award associate degrees and diplomas. The Accrediting Council for Independent Colleges and Schools is listed as a nationally recognized accrediting agency by the United States Department of Education and is recognized by the Council for Higher Education Accreditation. ACICS can be contacted at 750 First Street NE, Suite 980, Washington, D.C. 20002; phone: 202-336-6780.

The occupational therapy assistant program is accredited by the Accreditation Council for Occupational Therapy Education (ACOTE) of the American Occupational Therapy Association (AOTA), located at 4720 Montgomery Lane, Suite 200, Bethesda, Maryland 20814-3449; phone: 301-652-AOTA. Graduates of the program will be eligible to sit for the national certification examination for the occupational therapy assistant administered by the National Board for Certification in Occupational Therapy (NBCOT). After successful completion of this exam, the individual will be a Certified Occupational Therapy Assistant (COTA). In addition, most states require licensure in order to practice; however, state licenses are usually based on the results of the NBCOT Certification Examination. Note that a felony conviction may affect a graduate's ability to sit for the NBCOT certification examination or attain state licensure.

Academic Programs

Brown Mackie College — Atlanta provides higher education to traditional and nontraditional students through associate degree and diploma programs that can assist students in enhancing their career opportunities, broadening their perspectives through appropriate general education courses, thinking independently and critically, and improving problem-solving abilities. Brown Mackie College strives to develop within its students the desire for lifelong and continued education.

Each College quarter comprises twelve weeks. Associate degree programs require a minimum of eight quarters to complete. Programs are offered on a year-round basis, providing students with the ability to work uninterrupted toward their degrees. Brown Mackie College offers all programs in a unique One Course a Month format. This schedule allows students to focus studies on only one course for four weeks and has proven convenient for students with multiple obligations such as jobs and family.

Associate Degree Programs: The Associate of Applied Business degree is awarded in accounting technology, business management, criminal justice, and paralegal. The Associate of Applied Science degree is awarded in early childhood education, health care administration, medical assisting, occupational therapy assistant, and pharmacy technology.

Diploma Programs: Brown Mackie College — Atlanta also offers diploma programs in bookkeeping specialist, criminal justice specialist, general business, and medical assistant.

The American Medical Technologists (AMT), which offers the certification for Registered Medical Assistant (RMA), accepts the accreditation of Brown Mackie College — Atlanta. Students will qualify to take the RMA certification examination upon graduating the Brown Mackie College — Atlanta medical assisting and medical assistant programs. Graduates of the 48 credit-hour medical assistant program are not qualified to take the AMT/RMA exam. Information on application procedures can be found at http://americanmedtech.org/SchoolsStudents/CertificationProcess.aspx.

Brown Mackie College — Atlanta does not guarantee third-party certification. Outside agencies control the requirements for certifications and are subject to change without notice to Brown Mackie College.

Program availability and degree offerings are subject to change.

Costs

Tuition for the 2013–14 academic year was $366 per credit hour and $20 per credit hour for general fees. Tuition for the occupational therapy assistant program was $381 per credit hour and $20 per credit hour for general fees. The cost of textbooks, if applicable, and other instructional materials varies by program.

Financial Aid

The College maintains a full-time staff of financial aid professionals to assist qualified students in obtaining the financial assistance they require to meet their education expenses. Financial aid is available to those students who qualify.

Available resources may include federal grants and loans, state aid, student loans from private lenders, and federal work-study opportunities, both on and off College premises. Federal assistance programs are administered through the U.S. Department of Education, Office of Student Financial Assistance. Any U.S. citizen, national, or person in the United States for other than temporary reasons who is enrolled or accepted for enrollment may apply for these programs. Most forms of financial assistance are available for each July 1–June 30 award period.

Every student considering application for financial aid should request a copy of the current Student Guide, published by the U.S. Department of Education. This important document may be obtained in the Student Financial Services Office and will assist persons in understanding eligibility requirements, the application process, deadlines, and the various forms of grants and loans available.

Details on school-specific loans and scholarships are available on the school's website (http://www.brownmackie.edu/Atlanta) or prospective students can contact the school's Student Financial

Services Department; phone: 404-799-4500; e-mail: bmcatadm@brownmackie.edu.

Faculty

There are 4 full-time and 5 part-time faculty members. The average student-faculty ratio is 19:1. Each student has a faculty and student adviser.

Facilities and Resources

Brown Mackie College — Atlanta comprises administrative offices, faculty and student lounges, a reception area, and spacious classrooms and laboratories. Instructional equipment includes personal computers, LANs, printers, and transcribers. The library provides support for the academic programs through volumes covering a broad range of subjects, as well as through Internet access. Vehicle parking is provided for both students and staff members.

Brown Mackie College — Atlanta is fully committed to using eTextbooks and computer tablets in the classroom. Utilizing these tablets to access expanded course material, students are able to increase their acumen for using this technology and further enhance their educational experience. Students have the ability to directly download their eTextbooks to their tablet, eliminating the need to carry heavy, physical textbooks and reducing the overall cost of supplies.

Brown Mackie College is a nonresidential, smoke-free institution.

Location

Brown Mackie College — Atlanta is located at 4370 Peachtree Road NE in Atlanta, Georgia, which is easily accessible from I-285 and the MARTA Brookhaven rail station.

Admission Requirements

Each applicant for admission is assigned an assistant director of admissions who directs the applicant through the steps of the admissions process; provides information on curriculum, policies, procedures, and services; and assists the applicant in setting necessary appointments and interviews.

To be considered for admission to Brown Mackie College, a candidate must be a high school graduate or hold a General Education Development (GED) certificate. As part of the admission process, applicants must sign a document attesting to graduation or completion and containing the information to obtain verification of such. Official high school transcripts or official documentation of high school graduation equivalency must be obtained within the first financial aid payment period or the student will be withdrawn from the institution following established guidelines for withdrawn students noted in the catalog. Title IV aid will not be dispersed until verification of graduation or completion has been received by the College.

Where applicable, students seeking entry into the College with a high school diploma completed in a foreign country must provide an original U.S.–equivalency evaluation from an evaluating agency that is a member of the National Association of Credential Evaluation Services (NACES, http://www.naces.org/) or the Association of International Credential Evaluators, Inc. (AICES, http://www.aice-eval.org/). The cost of evaluating the foreign transcript is borne by the applicant.

Admission to the College is based upon the applicant meeting the school's admissions requirements, a review of the applicant's previous educational records, and a review of the applicant's career interests. It is the responsibility of the applicant to ensure that the College receives all required documentation

Prior to admission, students are given an assessment of academic skills, commonly referred to as the academic readiness evaluation. Though the results of this assessment do not determine eligibility for admission, they provide the College with a means of determining the need for academic support through transitional studies courses and academic advisement, as well as a means by which the College can evaluate the effectiveness of its educational programs.

An applicant must obtain a minimum score of 60 in writing and 51 in mathematics on the COMPASS student academic readiness assessment. If a student does not achieve these scores, he/she will be enrolled in the appropriate transitional studies course(s).

In addition to the general admission requirements above, some programs have additional requirements specific to the program. For information on those, and other school-specific requirements, visit the school's website (http://www.brownmackie.edu/Atlanta) or contact the school's admissions department; phone: 404-799-4500; e-mail: bmcatadm@brownmackie.edu.

Application and Information

Applicants must complete and submit an application form along with documentation of graduation from an accredited high school or state-approved secondary education curriculum or official documentation of high school graduation equivalency.

See BMCprograms.info for program duration, tuition, fees and other costs, median debt, federal salary data, alumni success, programmatic accreditation, and other important information.

Brown Mackie College—Atlanta is one of over 25 school locations of the Brown Mackie College system of schools. Programs, credential levels, technology, and scheduling options are subject to change. ©2014 Brown Mackie College.

For additional information, prospective students should contact:

Senior Director of Admissions
Brown Mackie College — Atlanta
4370 Peachtree Road NE
Atlanta, Georgia 30319
Phone: 404-799-4500
          877-479-8419 (toll-free)
Fax: 404-799-4522
E-mail: bmcatadm@brownmackie.edu
Website: http://www.brownmackie.edu/Atlanta

BROWN MACKIE COLLEGE — BIRMINGHAM
BIRMINGHAM, ALABAMA

The College and Its Mission

Brown Mackie College — Birmingham (Brown Mackie College) is one of over twenty-five locations in the Brown Mackie College system of schools (www.brownmackie.edu), which is dedicated to providing educational programs that prepare students to pursue entry-level positions in a competitive, rapidly changing workplace. Brown Mackie College schools offer bachelor's degree, associate degree, diploma, and certificate programs in health sciences, business, information technology, legal studies, and design to thousands of students in the Midwest, Southeast, Southwest, and Western United States.

Brown Mackie College was originally founded and approved by the Board of Trustees of Kansas Wesleyan College in Salina, Kansas on July 30, 1892. In 1938, the College was incorporated as the Brown Mackie School of Business under the ownership of Perry E. Brown and A.B. Mackie, former instructors at Kansas Wesleyan University in Salina, Kansas. Their last names formed the name of Brown Mackie. By January 1975, with improvements in curricula and higher degree-granting status, the Brown Mackie School of Business became Brown Mackie College.

Brown Mackie College — Birmingham is accredited by the Accrediting Council for Independent Colleges and Schools to award associate degrees and diplomas. The Accrediting Council for Independent Colleges and Schools is listed as a nationally recognized accrediting agency by the United States Department of Education and is recognized by the Council for Higher Education Accreditation. ACICS can be contacted at 750 First Street NE, Suite 980, Washington, D.C. 20002; phone: 202-336-6780.

The occupational therapy assistant program is accredited by the Accreditation Council for Occupational Therapy Education (ACOTE) of the American Occupational Therapy Association (AOTA), located at 4720 Montgomery Lane, P.O. Box 31220, Bethesda, Maryland 20824-1220; phone: 301-652-AOTA. Graduates of the program will be eligible to sit for the national certification examination for the occupational therapy assistant administered by the National Board for Certification in Occupational Therapy (NBCOT). After successful completion of this exam, the individual will be a Certified Occupational Therapy Assistant (COTA). In addition, most states require licensure in order to practice; however, state licenses are usually based on the results of the NBCOT Certification Examination. Note that a felony conviction may affect a graduate's ability to sit for the NBCOT certification examination or attain state licensure.

The Brown Mackie College — Birmingham Associate of Science in surgical technology program is accredited by the Accrediting Bureau of Health Education Schools, AHBES.

Academic Programs

Brown Mackie College — Birmingham provides higher education to traditional and nontraditional students through associate degree and diploma programs that assist in enhancing their career opportunities, broadening their perspectives through appropriate general education courses, thinking independently and critically, and improving problem-solving abilities. The college strives to develop within its students the desire for lifelong and continued education.

Each college quarter comprises twelve weeks. Associate degree programs require a minimum of eight quarters to complete. Programs are offered on a year-round basis, providing students with the ability to work uninterrupted toward completion of their programs. The college offers all programs in a unique One Course a Month format. This allows students to focus studies on only one course for four weeks. This schedule has proven convenient for students with multiple obligations such as jobs and family.

Associate Degree Programs: The Associate of Science degree is awarded in architectural design and drafting technology, biomedical equipment technology, business management, graphic design, health care administration, information technology, paralegal, and surgical technology.

The Associate of Applied Science degree is awarded in occupational therapy assistant.

Diploma Programs: The college offers diploma programs in dental assistant, general business, medical assistant, and medical insurance specialist.

The American Medical Technologists (AMT), which offers the certification for Registered Medical Assistant (RMA), accepts the accreditation of Brown Mackie College — Birmingham. Students will qualify to take the Registered Medical Assistant certification examination upon graduating the Brown Mackie College — Birmingham medical assistant program. Graduates of the 48-credit-hour medical assistant program are not qualified to take the AMT/RMA exam. Information on application procedures can be found at http://americanmedtech.org/SchoolsStudents/CertificationProcess.aspx.

Brown Mackie College does not guarantee third-party certification/licensing exams. Outside agencies control the requirements for certification/licensing and are subject to change without notification to the college.

Program availability and degree offerings are subject to change.

Costs

Tuition in the 2013–14 academic year for most bachelor's and associate degrees and certificates was $315 per credit hour; fees were $20 per credit hour. Tuition for the surgical technology program was $350 per credit hour; fees were $20 per credit hour. Tuition for the occupational therapy assistant program was $381 per credit hour; fees were $20 per credit hour. The cost of textbooks, if applicable, and other instructional materials varies by program.

Financial Aid

The College maintains a full-time staff of financial aid professionals to assist qualified students in obtaining the financial assistance they require to meet their education expenses. Financial aid is available to those students who qualify.

Available resources may include federal grants and loans, state aid, student loans from private lenders, and federal work-study opportunities, both on and off College premises. Federal assistance programs are administered through the U.S. Department of Education, Office of Student Financial Assistance. Any U.S. citizen, national, or person in the United States for other than temporary reasons who is enrolled or accepted for enrollment may apply for these programs. Most forms of financial assistance are available for each July 1–June 30 award period.

Every student considering application for financial aid should request a copy of the current Student Guide, published by the U.S. Department of Education. This important document may be obtained in the Student Financial Services Office and will assist persons in understanding eligibility requirements, the application process, deadlines, and the various forms of grants and loans available.

Details on school-specific loans and scholarships are available on the school's website (http://www.brownmackie.edu/Birmingham) or prospective students can contact the school's Student Financial Services Department at 205-909-1500; e-mail: bmbiradm@ brownmackie.edu.

Faculty

Experienced faculty members provide academic support and are committed to the academic and technical preparation of their students. The college has both full-time and part-time instructors, with a student-faculty ratio of 15:1.

Facilities and Resources

A modern facility, Brown Mackie College offers approximately 35,000 square feet of classroom, computer and allied health labs, library, and office space. The college is equipped with multiple computer labs, housing over 100 computers. High-speed access to the Internet and other online resources are available to students and faculty. Multimedia classrooms are outfitted with overhead projectors, VCR/DVD players, and computers.

An expansion of the facility to 44,000 square feet was completed in May 2013, providing ten new classrooms, five of which are computer labs, as well as additional administrative space.

Brown Mackie College — Birmingham is fully committed to using eTextbooks and computer tablets in the classroom. Utilizing these tablets to access expanded course material, students are able to increase their acumen for using this technology and further enhance their educational experience. Students have the ability to directly download their eTextbooks to their tablet, eliminating the need to carry heavy, physical textbooks and reducing the overall cost of supplies.

Brown Mackie College is nonresidential; public transportation and ample parking at no cost are available. The campus is a smoke-free facility.

Location

Brown Mackie College — Birmingham is conveniently located at 105 Vulcan Road, in Birmingham, Alabama.

Admission Requirements

Each applicant for admission is assigned an assistant director of admissions who directs the applicant through the steps of the process; provides information on curriculum, policies, procedures, and services; and assists the applicant in setting necessary appointments and interviews.

To be considered for admission to Brown Mackie College, a candidate must be a high school graduate or hold a General Education Development (GED) certificate. As part of the admission process applicants must sign a document attesting to graduation or completion and containing the information to obtain verification of such. Official high school transcripts or official documentation of high school graduation equivalency must be obtained within the first financial aid payment period or the student will be withdrawn from the institution following established guidelines for withdrawn students noted in the catalog. Title IV aid will not be dispersed until verification of graduation or completion has been received by the College.

Where applicable, students seeking entry into the College with a high school diploma completed in a foreign country must provide an original U.S.–equivalency evaluation from an evaluating agency which is a member of the National Association of Credential Evaluation Services (NACES, http://www.naces.org/) or the Association of International Credential Evaluators, Inc. (AICES, http://www.aice-eval.org/). The cost of evaluating the foreign transcript is borne by the applicant.

Admission to the College is based upon the applicant meeting the school's admissions requirements, a review of the applicant's previous educational records, and a review of the applicant's career interests. It is the responsibility of the applicant to ensure that the College receives all required documentation

Prior to admission, students are given an assessment of academic skills, commonly referred to as the academic readiness evaluation. Though the results of this assessment do not determine eligibility for admission, they provide the College with a means of determining the need for academic support through transitional studies courses and academic advisement, as well as a means by which the College can evaluate the effectiveness of its educational programs.

An applicant must obtain a minimum score of 60 in writing and 51 in mathematics on the COMPASS student academic readiness assessment. If a student does not achieve these scores, he/she will be enrolled in the appropriate transitional studies course(s).

In addition to the general admission requirements above, some programs have additional requirements specific to the program. Information on those requirements and other school-specific requirements can be found on the school's website (http://www. brownmackie.edu/Birmingham) or by contacting the school's Admissions department at 205-909-1500; e-mail: bmbiradm@ brownmackie.edu.

Application and Information

Applicants must complete and submit an application form, along with documentation of graduation from an accredited high school or state-approved secondary education curriculum or official documentation of high school graduation equivalency.

See BMCprograms.info for program duration, tuition, fees and other costs, median debt, federal salary data, alumni success, programmatic accreditation, and other important information.

Brown Mackie College — Birmingham is one of over 25 school locations of the Brown Mackie College system of schools. Programs, credential levels, technology, and scheduling options are subject to change. ©2014 Brown Mackie College.

For additional information, prospective students should contact:

Director of Admissions
Brown Mackie College — Birmingham
105 Vulcan Road, Suite 100
Birmingham, Alabama 35209
Phone: 205-909-1500
      888-299-4699 (toll-free)
Fax: 205-909-1588
E-mail: bmbirmadm@brownmackie.edu
Website: http://www.brownmackie.edu/Birmingham

BROWN MACKIE COLLEGE — BOISE

BOISE, IDAHO

BROWN
MACKIE
COLLEGE®

BOISE

The College and Its Mission

Brown Mackie College — Boise (Brown Mackie College) is one of over twenty-five locations in the Brown Mackie College system of schools (www.brownmackie.edu), which is dedicated to providing educational programs that prepare students to pursue entry-level positions in a competitive, rapidly changing workplace. Brown Mackie College schools offer bachelor's degree, associate degree, diploma, and certificate programs in health sciences, business, information technology, legal studies, and design to thousands of students in the Midwest, Southeast, Southwest, and Western United States.

Brown Mackie College — Boise is accredited by the Accrediting Council for Independent Colleges and Schools to award associate degrees and diplomas. The Accrediting Council for Independent Colleges and Schools is listed as a nationally recognized accrediting agency by the United States Department of Education and is recognized by the Council for Higher Education Accreditation. ACICS can be contacted at 750 First Street NE, Suite 980, Washington, D.C. 20002; phone: 202-336-6780.

Brown Mackie College — Boise is registered with the State Board of Education in accordance with Section 33-2403, Idaho Code.

The occupational therapy assistant program is accredited by the Accreditation Council for Occupational Therapy Education (ACOTE) of the American Occupational Therapy Association (AOTA), located at 4720 Montgomery Lane, P.O. Box 31220, Bethesda, Maryland 20824-1220; phone: 301-652-AOTA. Graduates of the program will be eligible to sit for the national certification examination for the occupational therapy assistant administered by the National Board for Certification in Occupational Therapy (NBCOT). After successful completion of this exam, the individual will be a Certified Occupational Therapy Assistant (COTA). In addition, most states require licensure in order to practice; however, state licenses are usually based on the results of the NBCOT Certification Examination. Note that a felony conviction may affect a graduate's ability to sit for the NBCOT certification examination or attain state licensure.

The veterinary technology program at Brown Mackie College — Boise has provisional programmatic accreditation granted by the American Veterinary Medical Association (AVMA) through the Committee on Veterinary Technician Education and Activities (CVTEA), 1931 North Meacham Road, Suite 100, Schaumburg, Illinois 60173; phone: 800-248-2862; www.avma.org.

Academic Programs

Brown Mackie College — Boise provides higher education to traditional and nontraditional students through associate degree, and diploma programs that assist in enhancing their career opportunities, broadening their perspectives through appropriate general education courses, thinking independently and critically, and improving problem-solving abilities.

Each college quarter comprises twelve weeks. Associate degree programs require a minimum of eight quarters to complete. Programs are offered on a year-round basis, providing students with the opportunity to work uninterrupted toward completion of their programs. The college offers all programs in a unique One Course a Month format. This allows students to focus studies on only one course for four weeks. This schedule has proven convenient for students with multiple obligations such as jobs and family.

Associate Degree Programs: The Associate of Science degree is awarded in architectural design and drafting technology, business management, criminal justice, information technology, paralegal, and veterinary technology.

The Associate of Applied Science degree is awarded in occupational therapy assistant.

Diploma Programs: Diploma programs are offered in general business and medical assistant.

The American Medical Technologists (AMT), which offers the certification for Registered Medical Assistant (RMA), accepts the accreditation of Brown Mackie College — Boise. Students will qualify to take the Registered Medical Assistant certification examination upon graduating the Brown Mackie College — Boise medical assistant program. Graduates of the 48-credit-hour medical assistant program are not qualified to take the AMT/RMA exam. Information on application procedures can be found at: http://americanmedtech.org/SchoolsStudents/CertificationProcess.aspx.

Brown Mackie College does not guarantee third-party certification/licensing exams. Outside agencies control the requirements for certification/licensing and are subject to change without notification to the College.

Program availability and degree offerings are subject to change.

Costs

Tuition for programs in the 2013–14 academic year was $324 per credit hour, with a general fee of $20 per credit hour applied to instructional costs for activities and services. Tuition for the occupational therapy assistant courses was $381 per credit hour with a $20 per credit fee applied to instructional costs for activities and services. Tuition for the surgical technology courses was $360 per credit hour with a $20 per credit fee applied to instructional costs for activities and services. The cost of textbooks and other instructional materials varies by program

Financial Aid

The College maintains a full-time staff of financial aid professionals to assist qualified students in obtaining the financial assistance they require to meet their education expenses. Financial aid is available to those students who qualify.

Available resources may include federal grants and loans, state aid, student loans from private lenders, and federal work-study opportunities, both on and off College premises. Federal assistance programs are administered through the U.S. Department of Education, Office of Student Financial Assistance. Any U.S. citizen, national, or person in the United States for other than temporary reasons who is enrolled or accepted for enrollment may apply for these programs. Most forms of financial assistance are available for each July 1–June 30 award period.

Every student considering application for financial aid should request a copy of the current Student Guide, published by the U.S. Department of Education. This important document may be obtained in the Student Financial Services Office and will assist persons in understanding eligibility requirements, the application process, deadlines, and the various forms of grants and loans available.

For details on school-specific loans and scholarships, visit the school's website or contact the school's Student Financial

Services Department; phone: 208-321-8800; e-mail: bmcbsadm@brownmackie.edu; website: http://www.brownmackie.edu/Boise.

Faculty

There are 14 full-time and 34 part-time faculty members at the college. The average student-faculty ratio is 15:1. Each student is assigned to a program department chair as an advisor.

Facilities and Resources

Opened in 2008, this modern facility offers more than 40,000 square feet of tastefully decorated classrooms, laboratories, and office space designed to specifications of the Brown Mackie College for its business, medical, and technical programs. Instructional equipment is comparable to current technology used in business and industry. Modern classrooms for special instructional needs offer multimedia capabilities with surround sound and overhead projectors accessible through computer or DVD. Internet access and instructional resources are available at the college's library. Experienced faculty members provide academic support and are committed to the academic and technical preparation of their students.

Brown Mackie College — Boise is fully committed to using eTextbooks and computer tablets in the classroom. Utilizing these tablets to access expanded course material, students are able to increase their acumen for using this technology and further enhance their educational experience. Students have the ability to directly download their eTextbooks to their tablet, eliminating the need to carry heavy, physical textbooks and reducing the overall cost of supplies.

The campus is nonresidential; public transportation and ample parking at no cost are available.

Location

Brown Mackie College — Boise is conveniently located at 9050 West Overland Road in Boise, Idaho.

Admission Requirements

Each applicant for admission is assigned an assistant director of admissions who directs the applicant through the steps of the process; provides information on curriculum, policies, procedures, and services; and assists the applicant in setting necessary appointments and interviews.

To be considered for admission to Brown Mackie College, a candidate must be a high school graduate or hold a General Education Development (GED) certificate. As part of the admission process applicants must sign a document attesting to graduation or completion and containing the information to obtain verification of such. Official high school transcripts or official documentation of high school graduation equivalency must be obtained within the first financial aid payment period or the student will be withdrawn from the institution following established guidelines for withdrawn students noted in the catalog. Title IV aid will not be dispersed until verification of graduation or completion has been received by the College.

Where applicable, students seeking entry into the College with a high school diploma completed in a foreign country must provide an original U.S.–equivalency evaluation from an evaluating agency which is a member of the National Association of Credential Evaluation Services (NACES, http://www.naces.org/) or the Association of International Credential Evaluators, Inc. (AICES, http://www.aice-eval.org/). The cost of evaluating the foreign transcript is borne by the applicant.

Admission to the College is based upon the applicant meeting the school's admissions requirements, a review of the applicant's previous educational records, and a review of the applicant's career interests. It is the responsibility of the applicant to ensure that the College receives all required documentation.

Prior to admission, students are given an assessment of academic skills, commonly referred to as the academic readiness evaluation. Though the results of this assessment do not determine eligibility for admission, they provide the College with a means of determining the need for academic support through transitional studies courses and academic advisement, as well as a means by which the College can evaluate the effectiveness of its educational programs.

An applicant must obtain a minimum score of 60 in writing and 51 in mathematics on the COMPASS student academic readiness assessment. If a student does not achieve these scores, he/she will be enrolled in the appropriate transitional studies course(s).

In addition to the general admission requirements above, some programs have additional requirements specific to the program. For information on those requirements, and other school-specific requirements, please visit the school's website or contact the school's Admissions department; phone: 208-321-8800; e-mail: bmcbsadm@brownmackie.edu; website: http://www.brownmackie.edu/Boise.

Application and Information

Applicants must complete and submit an application form, along with documentation of graduation from an accredited high school or state-approved secondary education curriculum or official documentation of high school graduation equivalency.

See BMCprograms.info for program duration, tuition, fees and other costs, median debt, federal salary data, alumni success, programmatic accreditation, and other important information.

Brown Mackie College — Boise is one of over 25 school locations of the Brown Mackie College system of schools. Programs, credential levels, technology, and scheduling options are subject to change. ©2014 Brown Mackie College.

For additional information, prospective students should contact:

Director of Admissions
Brown Mackie College — Boise
9050 West Overland Road
Suite 100
Boise, Idaho 83709
Phone: 208-321-8800
          888-810-9286 (toll-free)
Fax: 208-375-3249
E-mail: bmcbsadm@brownmackie.edu
Website: http://www.brownmackie.edu/Boise

BROWN MACKIE COLLEGE — CINCINNATI
CINCINNATI, OHIO

The College and Its Mission

Brown Mackie College — Cincinnati (Brown Mackie College) is one of over twenty-five locations in the Brown Mackie College system of schools (www.brownmackie.edu), which is dedicated to providing educational programs that prepare students to pursue entry-level positions in a competitive, rapidly changing workplace. Brown Mackie College schools offer bachelor's degree, associate degree, diploma, and certificate programs in health sciences, business, information technology, legal studies, and design to thousands of students in the Midwest, Southeast, Southwest, and Western United States.

Brown Mackie College — Cincinnati was founded in February 1927 as Southern Ohio Business College. In 1978, the College's main location was relocated from downtown Cincinnati to the Bond Hill–Roselawn area and in 1995 to its current location at 1011 Glendale-Milford Road in the community of Woodlawn.

Brown Mackie College — Cincinnati is accredited by the Accrediting Council for Independent Colleges and Schools to award associate degrees, diplomas, and certificates. The Accrediting Council for Independent Colleges and Schools is listed as a nationally recognized accrediting agency by the United States Department of Education and is recognized by the Council for Higher Education Accreditation. ACICS can be contacted at 750 First Street NE, Suite 980, Washington, D.C. 20002; phone: 202-336-6780.

The Brown Mackie College — Cincinnati Associate of Applied Science degree in surgical technology is accredited by the Commission on Accreditation of Allied Health Education Programs (www.caahep.org), upon the recommendation of the Accreditation Review Committee on Education in Surgical Technology.

The veterinary technology program at Brown Mackie College — Cincinnati has provisional programmatic accreditation granted by the American Veterinary Medical Association (AVMA) through the Committee on Veterinary Technician Education and Activities (CVTEA), 1931 North Meacham Road, Suite 100, Schaumburg, Illinois 60173; phone: 800-248-2862; website: www.avma.org.

The practical nursing diploma program complies with the Ohio Board of Nursing guidelines as set forth in the Ohio Administrative Code, Chapter 4723-5. The program is administered at the following locations: Brown Mackie College — Cincinnati, Brown Mackie College — Findlay, Brown Mackie College — Akron, and Brown Mackie College — North Canton, and all operate under the same approval. The Ohio Board of Nursing is located at 17 South High Street, Suite 400, Columbus, Ohio 43215-3413; phone: 614-466-3947.

Brown Mackie College — Cincinnati is licensed by the Ohio State Board of Career Colleges and Schools, 30 East Broad Street, 24th Floor, Suite 2481, Columbus, Ohio 43215-3138; phone: 614-466-2752. Ohio registration #03-09-1686T.

Brown Mackie College — Cincinnati is regulated by the Board for Proprietary Education Indiana Commission for Higher Education, 101 West Ohio Street, Suite 670, Indianapolis, Indiana 46204; phone: 317-464-4400.

Academic Programs

Brown Mackie — Cincinnati provides higher education to traditional and nontraditional students through associate degrees, diploma, and certificate programs that can assist them in enhancing their career opportunities, broadening their perspectives through appropriate general education courses, thinking independently and critically, and improving problem-solving abilities. The College strives to develop within its students the desire for lifelong and continued education.

Each College quarter comprises twelve weeks. Associate degree programs require a minimum of eight quarters to complete. Programs are offered on a year-round basis, providing students with the ability to work uninterrupted toward their degrees. The College offers all programs in a unique One Course a Month format. This schedule allows students to focus studies on only one course for four weeks and has proven convenient for students with multiple obligations such as jobs and family.

Associate Degree Programs: The Associate of Applied Business degree is awarded in accounting technology, business management, computer networking and applications, criminal justice, information technology, and paralegal.

The Associate of Applied Business degree is awarded in business management, computer networking and applications, and criminal justice.

The Associate of Applied Science degree is awarded in biomedical equipment technology, early childhood education, health care administration, pharmacy technology, surgical technology, and veterinary technology.

Diploma Programs: Diploma programs are offered in medical assistant and practical nursing.

Brown Mackie College — Cincinnati does not guarantee third-party certification. Outside agencies control the requirements for certifications and are subject to change without notice to Brown Mackie College.

Program availability and degree offerings are subject to change.

Costs

Tuition for the 2013–14 academic year was $314 per credit hour and $20 per credit hour for general fees. Tuition for the practical nursing program was $381 per credit hour and $30 per credit hour for general fees. Tuition for the surgical technology program was $360 per credit hour and $20 per credit hour for general fees. Tuition for the computer networking and computer networking and applications program was $314 per credit hour and $25 per credit hour for general fees. The cost of textbooks, if applicable, and other instructional materials varies by program.

Financial Aid

The College maintains a full-time staff of financial aid professionals to assist qualified students in obtaining the financial assistance they require to meet their education expenses. Financial aid is available to those students who qualify.

Available resources may include federal grants and loans, state aid, student loans from private lenders, and federal work-study opportunities, both on and off College premises. Federal assistance programs are administered through the U.S. Department of Education, Office of Student Financial Assistance. Any U.S. citizen, national, or person in the United States for other than temporary reasons who is enrolled or accepted for enrollment may apply for these programs. Most forms of financial assistance are available for each July 1–June 30 award period.

Every student considering application for financial aid should request a copy of the current Student Guide, published by the U.S. Department of Education. This important document may

be obtained in the Student Financial Services Office and will assist persons in understanding eligibility requirements, the application process, deadlines, and the various forms of grants and loans available.

For details on school-specific loans and scholarships, students should visit the school's website or contact the school's Student Financial Services Department; phone: 513-771-2424; e-mail: bmcciadm@brownmackie.edu; http://www.brownmackie.edu/Cincinnati.

Faculty

There are 20 full-time and 90 part-time faculty members. The average student-faculty ratio is 20:1. Each student has a faculty and student adviser.

Facilities and Resources

Brown Mackie College — Cincinnati consists of more than 57,000 square feet of classroom, laboratory, and office space at the main campus and more than 28,000 square feet at the learning site. Both sites are designed to specifications of Brown Mackie College for its business, computer, medical, and creative programs.

Brown Mackie College — Cincinnati is fully committed to using eTextbooks and computer tablets in the classroom. Utilizing these tablets to access expanded course material, students are able to increase their acumen for using this technology and further enhance their educational experience. Students have the ability to directly download their eTextbooks to their tablet, eliminating the need to carry heavy, physical textbooks and reducing the overall cost of supplies.

Location

Brown Mackie College — Cincinnati is located in the Woodlawn section of Cincinnati, Ohio. The College is accessible by public transportation and provides parking at no cost. For added convenience, the College also holds classes at the Norwood Learning Site at 4805 Montgomery Road in Norwood, Ohio.

Admission Requirements

Each applicant for admission is assigned an assistant director of admissions who directs the applicant through the steps of the process; provides information on curriculum, policies, procedures, and services; and assists the applicant in setting necessary appointments and interviews.

To be considered for admission to Brown Mackie College, a candidate must be a high school graduate or hold a General Education Development (GED) certificate. As part of the admission process applicants must sign a document attesting to graduation or completion and containing the information to obtain verification of such. Official high school transcripts or official documentation of high school graduation equivalency must be obtained within the first financial aid payment period or the student will be withdrawn from the institution following established guidelines for withdrawn students noted in the catalog. Title IV aid will not be dispersed until verification of graduation or completion has been received by the College.

Where applicable, students seeking entry into the College with a high school diploma completed in a foreign country must provide an original U.S.–equivalency evaluation from an evaluating agency which is a member of the National Association of Credential Evaluation Services (NACES, http://www.naces.org/) or the Association of International Credential Evaluators,

Inc. (AICES, http://www.aice-eval.org/). The cost of evaluating the foreign transcript is borne by the applicant.

Admission to the College is based upon the applicant meeting the school's admission requirements, a review of the applicant's previous educational records, and a review of the applicant's career interests. It is the responsibility of the applicant to ensure that the College receives all required documentation

Prior to admission, students are given an assessment of academic skills, commonly referred to as the academic readiness evaluation. Though the results of this assessment do not determine eligibility for admission, they provide the College with a means of determining the need for academic support through transitional studies courses and academic advisement, as well as a means by which the College can evaluate the effectiveness of its educational programs.

An applicant must obtain a minimum score of 60 in writing and 51 in mathematics on the COMPASS student academic readiness assessment. If a student does not achieve these scores, he/she will be enrolled in the appropriate transitional studies course(s).

In addition to the general admission requirements above, some programs have additional requirements specific to the program. For information on those requirements, and other school-specific requirements, students should visit the school's website (http://www.brownmackie.edu/Cincinnati) or contact the school's admissions department: phone: 513-771-2424; e-mail: bmcciadm@brownmackie.edu.

Application and Information

Applicants must complete and submit an application form, along with documentation of graduation from an accredited high school or state-approved secondary education curriculum or official documentation of high school graduation equivalency.

See BMCprograms.info for program duration, tuition, fees and other costs, median debt, federal salary data, alumni success, programmatic accreditation, and other important info.

Brown Mackie College — Cincinnati is one of over 25 school locations of the Brown Mackie College system of schools. Programs, credential levels, technology, and scheduling options are subject to change. ©2014 Brown Mackie College.

For additional information, prospective students should contact:

Senior Director of Admissions
Brown Mackie College — Cincinnati
1011 Glendale-Milford Road
Cincinnati, Ohio 45215
Phone: 513-771-2424
          800-888-1445 (toll-free)
Fax: 513-771-3413
E-mail: bmcciadm@brownmackie.edu
Website: http://www.brownmackie.edu/Cincinnati

BROWN MACKIE COLLEGE — DALLAS/FORT WORTH

BEDFORD, TEXAS

BROWN
MACKIE
COLLEGE®
DALLAS/
FT. WORTH

The College and Its Mission

Brown Mackie College — Dallas/Fort Worth (Brown Mackie College) is one of over twenty-five locations in the Brown Mackie College system of schools (www.brownmackie.edu), which is dedicated to providing educational programs that prepare students to pursue entry-level positions in a competitive, rapidly changing workplace. The Brown Mackie College family of schools offers bachelor's degree, associate degree, diploma, and certificate programs in health sciences, business, information technology, legal studies, and design to thousands of students in the Midwest, Southeast, Southwest, and Western United States.

Brown Mackie College — Dallas/Fort Worth is accredited by the Accrediting Council for Independent Colleges and Schools to award associate degrees and diplomas. The Accrediting Council for Independent Colleges and Schools is listed as a nationally recognized accrediting agency by the United States Department of Education and is recognized by the Council for Higher Education Accreditation. ACICS can be contacted at 750 First Street NE, Suite 980, Washington, D.C. 20002; phone: 202-336-6780.

Brown Mackie College — Dallas/Fort Worth is approved and regulated by the Texas Workforce Commission, Career Schools and Colleges, Austin, Texas.

Brown Mackie College — Dallas/Fort Worth holds a Certificate of Authorization acknowledging exemption from the Texas Higher Education Coordinating Board Regulations.

Academic Programs

Brown Mackie College — Dallas/Fort Worth provides higher education to traditional and nontraditional students through associate degree and diploma programs that assist them in enhancing their career opportunities, broadening their perspectives through appropriate general education courses, thinking independently and critically, and improving problem-solving abilities. The College strives to develop within its students the desire for lifelong and continued education.

Each College quarter comprises ten to twelve weeks. Associate degree programs require a minimum of eight quarters to complete. Programs are offered on a year-round basis, providing students with the ability to work uninterrupted toward their degrees. The College offers all programs in a unique One Course a Month format. This allows students to focus studies on only one course for four weeks. This schedule has proven convenient for students with multiple obligations such as jobs and family.

Associate Degree Programs: The Associate of Science degree is awarded in biomedical equipment technology, business management, computer networking, graphic design, health care administration, information technology, occupational therapy assistant, and surgical technology.

Diploma Programs: Brown Mackie College offers medical assistant and paralegal assistant diploma programs.

The American Medical Technologists (AMT), which offers the certification for Registered Medical Assistant (RMA), accepts the accreditation of Brown Mackie College — Dallas/Fort Worth. Students will qualify to take the Registered Medical Assistant certification examination upon graduating the Brown Mackie College — Dallas/Fort Worth medical assistant program. Graduates of the 48-credit-hour medical assistant program are not qualified to take the AMT/RMA exam. Information on application procedures can be found at: http://americanmedtech. org/SchoolsStudents/CertificationProcess.aspx.

Brown Mackie College does not guarantee third-party certification/licensing exams. Outside agencies control the requirements for certification/licensing and are subject to change without notification to the College.

Program availability and degree offerings are subject to change.

Costs

Tuition for the 2013–14 academic year was $324 per credit hour and general fees were $20 per credit hour, with some exceptions. The surgical technology tuition was $371 per credit hour and general fees were $20 per credit hour. The occupational assistant tuition was $392 per credit hour and general fees were $20 per credit hour. The cost of textbooks, if applicable, and other instructional materials varies by program.

Financial Aid

The College maintains a full-time staff of financial aid professionals to assist qualified students in obtaining the financial assistance they require to meet their education expenses. Financial aid is available to those students who qualify.

Available resources may include federal grants and loans, state aid, student loans from private lenders, and federal work-study opportunities, both on and off College premises. Federal assistance programs are administered through the U.S. Department of Education, Office of Student Financial Assistance. Any U.S. citizen, national, or person in the United States for other than temporary reasons who is enrolled or accepted for enrollment may apply for these programs. Most forms of financial assistance are available for each July 1– June 30 award period.

Every student considering application for financial aid should request a copy of the current Student Guide, published by the U.S. Department of Education. This important document may be obtained in the Student Financial Services Office and will assist persons in understanding eligibility requirements, the application process, deadlines, and the various forms of grants and loans available.

For details on school-specific loans and scholarships, students should visit the school's website or contact the school's Student Financial Services Department; phone: 817-799-0500; e-mail: bmdaladm@brownmackie.edu; website: http://www. brownmackie.edu/Dallas.

Faculty

There are 4 full-time and 20 part-time adjunct instructors at the College. The average student-faculty ratio is 14:1. Each student is able to meet and speak with the director of their program.

Academic Facilities

Brown Mackie College — Dallas/Fort Worth offers media presentation rooms for special instructional needs and a library that provides instructional resources and academic support for both faculty members and students.

Brown Mackie College — Dallas/Fort Worth is fully committed to using eTextbooks and computer tablets in the classroom. Utilizing these tablets to access expanded course material, students are able to increase their acumen for using this technology and further enhance their educational experience. Students have the ability to directly download their eTextbooks to their tablet, eliminating the need to carry heavy, physical textbooks and reducing the overall cost of supplies.

Brown Mackie College — Dallas/Fort Worth is nonresidential; ample parking is available at no cost. The campus is a smoke-free facility.

Location

Brown Mackie College — Dallas/Fort Worth is conveniently located at 2200 North Highway 121, Suite 250, Bedford, Texas.

Admission Requirements

Each applicant for admission is assigned an assistant director of admissions who directs the applicant through the steps of the admissions process; provides information on curriculum, policies, procedures, and services; and assists the applicant in setting necessary appointments and interviews.

To be considered for admission to Brown Mackie College, a candidate must be a high school graduate or hold a General Education Development (GED) certificate. As part of the admissions process applicants must sign a document attesting to graduation or completion and containing the information to obtain verification of such. Official high school transcripts or official documentation of high school graduation equivalency must be obtained within the first financial aid payment period or the student will be withdrawn from the institution following established guidelines for withdrawn students noted in the catalog. Title IV aid will not be dispersed until verification of graduation or completion has been received by the College.

Where applicable, students seeking entry into the College with a high school diploma completed in a foreign country must provide an original U.S.–equivalency evaluation from an evaluating agency which is a member of the National Association of Credential Evaluation Services (NACES, http://www.naces.org/) or the Association of International Credential Evaluators, Inc. (AICES, http://www.aice-eval.org/). The cost of evaluating the foreign transcript is borne by the applicant.

Admission to the College is based upon the applicant meeting the school's admission requirements, a review of the applicant's previous educational records, and a review of the applicant's career interests. It is the responsibility of the applicant to ensure that the College receives all required documentation.

Prior to admission, students are given an assessment of academic skills, commonly referred to as the academic readiness evaluation. Though the results of this assessment do not determine eligibility for admission, they provide the College with a means of determining the need for academic support through transitional studies courses and academic advisement, as well as a means by which the College can evaluate the effectiveness of its educational programs.

An applicant must obtain a minimum score of 60 in writing and 51 in mathematics on the COMPASS student academic readiness assessment. If a student does not achieve these scores, he/she will be enrolled in the appropriate transitional studies course(s).

In addition to the general admission requirements above, some programs have additional requirements specific to the program. For information on those and other school-specific requirements, students should visit the school's website or contact the school's admissions department; phone: 817-799-0500; e-mail: bmdaladm@brownmackie.edu; website: http://www.brownmackie.edu/Dallas.

Application and Information

Applicants must complete and submit an application form, along with documentation of graduation from an accredited high school or state-approved secondary education curriculum or official documentation of high school graduation equivalency.

See BMCprograms.info for program duration, tuition, fees and other costs, median debt, federal salary data, alumni success, programmatic accreditation, and other important info.

Brown Mackie College — Dallas/Fort Worth is one of over 25 school locations of the Brown Mackie College system of schools. Programs, credential levels, technology, and scheduling options are subject to change. ©2014 Brown Mackie College.

For additional information, prospective students should contact:

Director of Admissions
Brown Mackie College — Dallas/Fort Worth
2200 North Highway 121, Suite 250
Bedford, Texas 76021
Phone: 817-799-0500
      888-299-4799 (toll-free)
Fax: 817-799-0515
E-mail: bmdaladm@brownmackie.edu
Website: http://www.brownmackie.edu/Dallas

BROWN MACKIE COLLEGE — FINDLAY

FINDLAY, OHIO

The College and Its Mission

Brown Mackie — Findlay (Brown Mackie College) is one of over twenty-five locations in the Brown Mackie College system of schools (www.brownmackie.edu), which is dedicated to providing educational programs that prepare students to pursue entry-level positions in a competitive, rapidly changing workplace. The Brown Mackie College family of schools offers bachelor's degree, associate degree, diploma, and certificate programs in health sciences, business, information technology, legal studies, and design to thousands of students in the Midwest, Southeast, Southwest, and Western United States.

Brown Mackie College — Findlay was founded in 1926 by William H. Stautzenberger to provide solid business education at a reasonable cost. In 1960, the college was acquired by George R. Hawes, who served as its president until 1969. The college changed its name from Southern Ohio College–Findlay in 2001 to AEC Southern Ohio College; it was changed again to Brown Mackie College — Findlay in November 2004.

Brown Mackie College — Findlay is accredited by the Accrediting Council for Independent Colleges and Schools to award associate degrees and diplomas. The Accrediting Council for Independent Colleges and Schools is listed as a nationally recognized accrediting agency by the United States Department of Education and is recognized by the Council for Higher Education Accreditation. ACICS can be contacted at 750 First Street NE, Suite 980, Washington, D.C. 20002; phone: 202-336-6780.

The occupational therapy assistant program is accredited by the Accreditation Council for Occupational Therapy Education (ACOTE) of the American Occupational Therapy Association (AOTA), located at 4720 Montgomery Lane, P.O. Box 31220, Bethesda, Maryland 20824-1220; phone: 301-652-AOTA. Graduates of the program will be eligible to sit for the national certification examination for the occupational therapy assistant administered by the National Board for Certification in Occupational Therapy (NBCOT). After successful completion of this exam, the individual will be a Certified Occupational Therapy Assistant (COTA). In addition, most states require licensure in order to practice; however, state licenses are usually based on the results of the NBCOT Certification Examination. Note that a felony conviction may affect a graduate's ability to sit for the NBCOT certification examination or attain state licensure.

The Brown Mackie College — Findlay Associate of Applied Science in surgical technology program is accredited by the Commission on Accreditation of Allied Health Education Programs (www.caahep.org) upon the recommendation of the Accreditation Review Committee on Education in Surgical Technology.

The Brown Mackie College — Findlay Associate of Applied Science in surgical technology program is accredited by the Accrediting Bureau of Health Education Schools, ABHES.

The veterinary technology program at Brown Mackie College — Findlay has provisional programmatic accreditation granted by the American Veterinary Medical Association (AVMA) through the Committee on Veterinary Technician Education and Activities (CVTEA), 1931 North Meacham Road, Suite 100, Schaumburg, Illinois 60173; phone; 800-248-2862; www.avma.org.

Brown Mackie College — Findlay is licensed by the Ohio State Board of Career Colleges and Schools, 30 East Broad Street, 24th Floor, Suite 2481, Columbus, Ohio 43215-3138; phone: 614-466-2752. Ohio registration #03-09-1687T.

Academic Programs

Brown Mackie College — Findlay provides higher education to traditional and nontraditional students through associate degree and diploma programs that can assist them in enhancing their career opportunities, broadening their perspectives through appropriate general education courses, thinking independently and critically, and improving problem-solving abilities. The College strives to develop within its students the desire for lifelong and continued education.

Each College quarter comprises twelve weeks. Associate degree programs require a minimum of eight quarters to complete. Programs are offered on a year-round basis, providing students with the ability to work uninterrupted toward completion of their programs. The College offers all programs in a unique One Course a Month format. This schedule allows students to focus studies on only one course for four weeks and has proven convenient for students with multiple obligations such as jobs and family.

Associate Degree Programs: The Associate of Applied Business degree is awarded in business management and criminal justice.

The Associate of Applied Science degree is awarded in nursing, occupational therapy assistant, pharmacy technology, surgical technology, and veterinary technology.

Diploma Programs: In addition to the associate degree programs, the College offers diploma programs in dental assistant, medical assistant, and practical nursing.

The American Medical Technologists (AMT), which offers the certification for Registered Medical Assistant (RMA), accepts the accreditation of Brown Mackie College — Findlay. Students will qualify to take the Registered Medical Assistant certification examination upon graduating the Brown Mackie College — Findlay medical assistant program. Graduates of the 48-credit-hour medical assistant program are not qualified to take the AMT/RMA exam.

Brown Mackie College does not guarantee third-party certification/licensing exams. Outside agencies control the requirements for certification/licensing and are subject to change without notification to the College.

Program availability and degree offerings are subject to change.

Costs

Tuition for programs in the 2013–14 academic year was $314 per credit hour, with a general fee of $20 per credit hour. Tuition for the practical nursing diploma and nursing associate degree programs was $381 per credit hour, with a general fee of $30 per credit hour. Tuition for the occupational therapy assistant program was $381 per credit hour, with a general fee of $20 per credit hour. Tuition for the surgical technology program was $360 per credit hour, with a general fee of $20 per credit hour. The length of the program determines total cost. The cost of textbooks, if applicable, and other instructional materials varies by program.

Financial Aid

The College maintains a full-time staff of financial aid professionals to assist qualified students in obtaining the financial assistance they require to meet their education expenses. Financial aid is available to those students who qualify.

Available resources may include federal grants and loans, state aid, student loans from private lenders, and federal work-study opportunities, both on and off College premises. Federal assistance programs are administered through the U.S. Department of

Education, Office of Student Financial Assistance. Any U.S. citizen, national, or person in the United States for other than temporary reasons who is enrolled or accepted for enrollment may apply for these programs. Most forms of financial assistance are available for each July 1–June 30 award period.

Every student considering application for financial aid should request a copy of the current Student Guide, published by the U.S. Department of Education. This important document may be obtained in the Student Financial Services Office and will assist persons in understanding eligibility requirements, the application process, deadlines, and the various forms of grants and loans available.

For details on school-specific loans and scholarships, students can visit the school's website or contact the school's Student Financial Services Department; phone: 419-423-2211; e-mail: bmcfiadm@brownmackie.edu; website: http://www.brownmackie.edu/Findlay.

Faculty

There are 27 full-time and 90 part-time adjunct instructors at the College. The average student-faculty ratio is 14:1. Each student is assigned a faculty adviser.

Academic Facilities

Brown Mackie College — Findlay is a nonresidential, smoke-free institution. Although the College does not offer residential housing, students who are unable to commute daily from their homes may request assistance from the Admissions Office in locating housing. Ample parking is available at no additional cost.

Brown Mackie College — Findlay is fully committed to using eTextbooks and computer tablets in the classroom. Utilizing these tablets to access expanded course material, students are able to increase their acumen for using this technology and further enhance their educational experience. Students have the ability to directly download their eTextbooks to their tablet, eliminating the need to carry heavy, physical textbooks and reducing the overall cost of supplies.

Location

Located at 1700 Fostoria Avenue, Suite 100, in Findlay, Ohio, the College is easily accessible from Interstate 75.

Admission Requirements

Each applicant for admission is assigned an assistant director of admissions who directs the applicant through the steps of the admissions process; provides information on curriculum, policies, procedures, and services; and assists the applicant in setting necessary appointments and interviews.

To be considered for admission to Brown Mackie College, a candidate must be a high school graduate or hold a General Education Development (GED) certificate. As part of the admission process applicants must sign a document attesting to graduation or completion and containing the information to obtain verification of such. Official high school transcripts or official documentation of high school graduation equivalency must be obtained within the first financial aid payment period or the student will be withdrawn from the institution, following established guidelines for withdrawn students noted in the catalog. Title IV aid will not be dispersed until verification of graduation or completion has been received by the College.

Where applicable, students seeking entry into the College with a high school diploma completed in a foreign country must provide an original U.S.–equivalency evaluation from an evaluating agency which is a member of the National Association of Credential Evaluation Services (NACES, http://www.naces.org/) or the Association of International Credential Evaluators, Inc. (AICES, http://www.aice-eval.org/). The cost of evaluating the foreign transcript is borne by the applicant.

Admission to the College is based upon the applicant meeting the school's admissions requirements, a review of the applicant's previous educational records, and a review of the applicant's career interests. It is the responsibility of the applicant to ensure that the College receives all required documentation.

Prior to admission, students are given an assessment of academic skills, commonly referred to as the academic readiness evaluation. Though the results of this assessment do not determine eligibility for admission, they provide the College with a means of determining the need for academic support through transitional studies courses and academic advisement, as well as a means by which the College can evaluate the effectiveness of its educational programs.

An applicant must obtain a minimum score of 60 in writing and 51 in mathematics on the COMPASS student academic readiness assessment. If a student does not achieve these scores, he/she will be enrolled in the appropriate transitional studies course(s).

In addition to the general admission requirements above, some programs have additional requirements specific to the program. For information on those requirements, and other school-specific requirements, students should visit the school's website or contact the school's admissions department; phone: 419-423-2211; e-mail: bmcfiadm@brownmackie.edu; website: http://www.brownmackie.edu/Findlay.

Application and Information

Applicants must complete and submit an application form, along with documentation of graduation from an accredited high school or state-approved secondary education curriculum or official documentation of high school graduation equivalency.

See BMCprograms.info for program duration, tuition, fees and other costs, median debt, federal salary data, alumni success, programmatic accreditation, and other important info.

Brown Mackie College — Findlay is one of over 25 school locations of the Brown Mackie College system of schools. Programs, credential levels, technology, and scheduling options are subject to change. ©2014 Brown Mackie College.

For additional information, prospective students should contact:

Director of Admissions
Brown Mackie College — Findlay
1700 Fostoria Avenue, Suite 100
Findlay, Ohio 45840
Phone: 419-423-2211
  800-842-3687 (toll-free)
Fax: 419-423-0725
E-mail: bmcfiadm@brownmackie.edu
Web site: http://www.brownmackie.edu/Findlay

BROWN MACKIE COLLEGE — FORT WAYNE

FORT WAYNE, INDIANA

BROWN MACKIE COLLEGE®
FORT WAYNE

The College and Its Mission

Brown Mackie College — Fort Wayne (Brown Mackie College) is one of over twenty-five locations in the Brown Mackie College system of schools (www.brownmackie.edu), which is dedicated to providing educational programs that prepare students to pursue entry-level positions in a competitive, rapidly changing workplace. Brown Mackie College schools offer bachelor degree, associate degree, diploma, and certificate programs in health sciences, business, information technology, legal studies, and design to thousands of students in the Midwest, Southeast, Southwest, and Western United States.

Brown Mackie College — Fort Wayne is one of the oldest institutions of its kind in the country and the oldest in the state of Indiana. Established in 1882 as the South Bend Commercial College, the school later changed its name to Michiana College. In 1930, the College was incorporated under the laws of the state of Indiana and was authorized to confer associate degrees and certificates in business. In 1992, the College in South Bend added a branch location in Fort Wayne, Indiana. In 2004, Michiana College changed its name to Brown Mackie College — Fort Wayne.

Brown Mackie College — Fort Wayne is accredited by the Accrediting Council for Independent Colleges and Schools to award associate degrees, diplomas, and certificates. The Accrediting Council for Independent Colleges and Schools is listed as a nationally recognized accrediting agency by the United States Department of Education and is recognized by the Council for Higher Education Accreditation. ACICS can be contacted at 750 First Street NE, Suite 980, Washington, D.C. 20002; phone: 202-336-6780.

The occupational therapy assistant program is accredited by the Accreditation Council for Occupational Therapy Education (ACOTE) of the American Occupational Therapy Association (AOTA), located at 4720 Montgomery Lane, P.O. Box 31220, Bethesda, Maryland 20824-1220; phone: 301-652-AOTA. Graduates of the program will be eligible to sit for the national certification examination for the occupational therapy assistant administered by the National Board for Certification in Occupational Therapy (NBCOT). After successful completion of this exam, the individual will be a Certified Occupational Therapy Assistant (COTA). In addition, most states require licensure in order to practice; however, state licenses are usually based on the results of the NBCOT Certification Examination. Note that a felony conviction may affect a graduate's ability to sit for the NBCOT certification examination or attain state licensure.

The Associate of Applied Science in physical therapist assistant program at Brown Mackie College — Fort Wayne is accredited by the Commission on Accreditation in Physical Therapy Education (CAPTE), 1111 North Fairfax Street, Alexandria, Virginia 22314; phone: 703-706-3245; e-mail: accreditation@apta.org; www. capteonline.org.

The veterinary technology program at Brown Mackie College — Fort Wayne has provisional programmatic accreditation granted by the American Veterinary Medical Association (AVMA) through the Committee on Veterinary Technician Education and Activities (CVTEA), 1931 North Meacham Road, Suite 100, Schaumburg, Illinois 60173; phone: 800-248-2862; www.avma.org.

Brown Mackie College — Fort Wayne is authorized by the Indiana Board for Proprietary Education, 101 West Ohio Street, Suite 670, Indianapolis, Indiana 46204-1984; phone: 317-464-4400, Ext. 138 or 141.

Academic Programs

Brown Mackie College — Fort Wayne provides higher education to traditional and nontraditional students through associate degree, diploma, and certificate programs that assist them in enhancing their career opportunities, broadening their perspectives through appropriate general education courses, thinking independently and critically, and improving problem-solving abilities. The College strives to develop within its students the desire for lifelong and continued education.

Each college quarter comprises twelve weeks. Associate degree programs require a minimum of eight quarters to complete. Programs are offered on a year-round basis, providing students with the ability to work uninterrupted toward their degrees. The College offers all programs in a unique One Course a Month format. This allows students to focus studies on only one course for four weeks. This schedule has proven convenient for students with multiple obligations such as jobs and family.

Associate Degree Programs: The Associate of Science degree is awarded in business management, and health care administration.

The Associate of Applied Science degree is awarded in biomedical equipment technology, nursing, occupational therapy assistant, physical therapist assistant, and veterinary technology.

Diploma Program: Brown Mackie College — Fort Wayne offers diploma programs in general business and medical assistant.

Certificate Programs: The College offers certificate programs in bookkeeping specialist, criminal justice, fitness trainer, general business, medical assistant, and paralegal assistant.

The American Medical Technologists (AMT), which offers the certification for Registered Medical Assistant (RMA), accepts the accreditation of Brown Mackie College — Fort Wayne. Students will qualify to take the Registered Medical Assistant certification examination upon graduating the Brown Mackie College — Fort Wayne medical assistant program. Graduates of the 48-credit-hour medical assistant program are not qualified to take the AMT/RMA exam. Information on application procedures can be found at http://americanmedtech.org/SchoolsStudents/CertificationProcess.aspx.

Brown Mackie College does not guarantee third-party certification/licensing exams. Outside agencies control the requirements for certification/licensing and are subject to change without notification to the College.

Program availability and degree offerings are subject to change.

Costs

Tuition in the 2013–14 academic year was $314 per credit hour with fees of $20 per credit hour for all programs except nursing, occupational therapy assistant studies, and physical therapist assistant studies. Costs for textbooks, if applicable, and other instructional materials vary by program. For the nursing program, tuition was $410 per credit hour; fees were $30 per credit hour. Textbook expenses are estimated at $400 for the first term, $600 for the second term, and $100 for the third, fourth, and fifth terms. For certain courses in the occupational therapy assistant studies and physical therapist assistant studies programs, tuition was $381 per credit hour; fees were $20 per credit hour.

Financial Aid

The College maintains a full-time staff of financial aid professionals to assist qualified students in obtaining the financial assistance they require to meet their education expenses. Financial aid is available to those students who qualify.

Available resources may include federal grants and loans, state aid, student loans from private lenders, and federal work-study opportunities, both on and off College premises. Federal assistance programs are administered through the U.S. Department of Education, Office of Student Financial Assistance. Any U.S. citizen, national, or person in the United States for other than temporary reasons who is enrolled or accepted for enrollment may apply for these programs. Most forms of financial assistance are available for each July 1–June 30 award period.

Every student considering application for financial aid should request a copy of the current Student Guide, published by the U.S. Department of Education. This important document may be obtained in the Student Financial Services Office and will assist persons in understanding eligibility requirements, the application process, deadlines, and the various forms of grants and loans available.

For details on school-specific loans and scholarships, students can visit the school's website at http://www.brownmackie.edu/FortWayne or contact the school's Student Financial Services Department: phone: 260-484-4400; e-mail: bmcfwadm@brownmackie.edu.

Faculty

The College has 18 full-time and 50 part-time instructors, with a student-faculty ratio of 15:1. Each student is assigned a faculty adviser.

Facilities and Resources

In 2005, the campus relocated to a 75,000-square-foot facility at 3000 East Coliseum Boulevard. Record enrollment allowed the institution to triple in size in less than one year. The three-story building offers a modern, professional environment for study. Ten classrooms are outfitted as "classrooms of the future," with an instructor workstation, full multimedia capabilities, a surround sound system, and projection screen that can be accessed by computer, DVD, or VHS equipment. The Brown Mackie College — Fort Wayne facility includes a criminal justice lab, surgical technology labs, medical labs, computer labs, and occupational and physical therapy labs, as well as a library and bookstore. The labs provide students with hands-on opportunities to apply knowledge and skills learned in the classroom. Students are welcome to use the labs when those facilities are not in use for scheduled classes.

Brown Mackie College — Fort Wayne is fully committed to using eTextbooks and computer tablets in the classroom. Utilizing these tablets to access expanded course material, students are able to increase their acumen for using this technology and further enhance their educational experience. Students have the ability to directly download their eTextbooks to their tablet, eliminating the need to carry heavy, physical textbooks and reducing the overall cost of supplies.

The College is nonresidential; public transportation and ample parking at no cost are available. The campus is a smoke-free facility.

Location

Brown Mackie College — Fort Wayne is located at 3000 East Coliseum Boulevard in Fort Wayne, Indiana.

Admission Requirements

Each applicant for admission is assigned an assistant director of admissions who directs the applicant through the steps of the admissions process; provides information on curriculum, policies, procedures, and services; and assists the applicant in setting necessary appointments and interviews.

To be considered for admission to Brown Mackie College, a candidate must be a high school graduate or hold a General Education Development (GED) certificate. As part of the admission process applicants must sign a document attesting to graduation or completion and containing the information to obtain verification of such. Official high school transcripts or official documentation of high school graduation equivalency must be obtained within the first financial aid payment period or the student will be withdrawn from the institution following established guidelines for withdrawn students noted in the catalog. Title IV aid will not be dispersed until verification of graduation or completion has been received by the College.

Where applicable, students seeking entry into the College with a high school diploma completed in a foreign country must provide an original U.S.–equivalency evaluation from an evaluating agency which is a member of the National Association of Credential Evaluation Services (NACES, http://www.naces.org/) or the Association of International Credential Evaluators, Inc. (AICES, http://www.aice-eval.org/). The cost of evaluating the foreign transcript is borne by the applicant.

Admission to the College is based upon the applicant meeting the school's admissions requirements, a review of the applicant's previous educational records, and a review of the applicant's career interests. It is the responsibility of the applicant to ensure that the College receives all required documentation.

Prior to admission, students are given an assessment of academic skills, commonly referred to as the academic readiness evaluation. Though the results of this assessment do not determine eligibility for admission, they provide the College with a means of determining the need for academic support through transitional studies courses and academic advisement, as well as a means by which the College can evaluate the effectiveness of its educational programs.

An applicant must obtain a minimum score of 60 in writing and 51 in mathematics on the COMPASS student academic readiness assessment. If a student does not achieve these scores, he/she will be enrolled in the appropriate transitional studies course(s).

In addition to the general admission requirements above, some programs have additional requirements specific to the program. For information on those requirements, and other school-specific requirements, students should visit the school's website or contact the school's Admissions Department; phone: 260-484-4400; e-mail: bmcfwadm@brownmackie.edu; website: http://www.brownmackie.edu/FortWayne.

Application and Information

Applicants must complete and submit an application form, along with documentation of graduation from an accredited high school or state-approved secondary education curriculum or official documentation of high school graduation equivalency.

See BMCprograms.info for program duration, tuition, fees and other costs, median debt, federal salary data, alumni success, programmatic accreditation, and other important info.

Brown Mackie College — Fort Wayne is one of over 25 school locations of the Brown Mackie College system of schools. Programs, credential levels, technology, and scheduling options are subject to change. ©2014 Brown Mackie College.

For additional information, prospective students should contact:

Director of Admissions
Brown Mackie College — Fort Wayne
3000 East Coliseum Boulevard
Fort Wayne, Indiana 46805
Phone: 260-484-4400
　　　866-433-2289 (toll-free)
Fax: 260-484-2678
E-mail: bmcfwaadm@brownmackie.edu
Website: http://www.brownmackie.edu/FortWayne

BROWN MACKIE COLLEGE — GREENVILLE

GREENVILLE, SOUTH CAROLINA

The College and Its Mission

Brown Mackie College — Greenville (Brown Mackie College) is one of over twenty-five locations in the Brown Mackie College system of schools (www.brownmackie.edu), which is dedicated to providing educational programs that prepare students to pursue entry-level positions in a competitive, rapidly changing workplace. Brown Mackie College schools offer bachelor's degree, associate degree, diploma, and certificate programs in health sciences, business, information technology, and legal studies to thousands of students in the Midwest, Southeast, Southwest, and Western United States.

Brown Mackie College was originally founded and approved by the Board of Trustees of Kansas Wesleyan College in Salina, Kansas on July 30, 1892. In 1938, the College was incorporated as The Brown Mackie School of Business under the ownership of Perry E. Brown and A.B. Mackie, former instructors at Kansas Wesleyan University in Salina, Kansas. Their last names formed the name of Brown Mackie. By January 1975, with improvements in curricula and higher degree-granting status, The Brown Mackie School of Business became Brown Mackie College.

Brown Mackie College — Greenville is accredited by the Accrediting Council for Independent Colleges and Schools to award associate degrees and certificates. The Accrediting Council for Independent Colleges and Schools is listed as a nationally recognized accrediting agency by the United States Department of Education and is recognized by the Council for Higher Education Accreditation. ACICS can be contacted at 750 First Street NE, Suite 980, Washington, D.C. 20002; phone: 202-336-6780.

Brown Mackie College — Greenville is licensed by the South Carolina Commission on Higher Education, 1122 Lady Street, Suite 300, Columbia, South Carolina 29201; phone: 803-737-2260. Licensure indicates only that minimum standards have been met; it is not equal to or synonymous with accreditation by an accrediting agency recognized by the U.S. Department of Education.

The occupational therapy assistant program is accredited by the Accreditation Council for Occupational Therapy Education (ACOTE) of the American Occupational Therapy Association (AOTA), located at 4720 Montgomery Lane, P.O. Box 31220, Bethesda, Maryland 20824-1220; phone: 301-652-AOTA. Graduates of the program will be eligible to sit for the national certification examination for the occupational therapy assistant administered by the National Board for Certification in Occupational Therapy (NBCOT). After successful completion of this exam, the individual will be a Certified Occupational Therapy Assistant (COTA). In addition, most states require licensure in order to practice; however, state licenses are usually based on the results of the NBCOT Certification Examination. Note that a felony conviction may affect a graduate's ability to sit for the NBCOT certification examination or attain state licensure.

The surgical technology program is accredited by the Accrediting Bureau of Health Education Schools and by the Commission on Accreditation of Allied Health Education Programs (www.caahep.org) upon the recommendation of the Accreditation Review Committee on Education in Surgical Technology.

The Associate of Applied Science in nursing program holds initial approval status from the South Carolina Board of Nursing, which is a type of approval granted to new programs that have demonstrated the ability or meet the standards of the Board (South Carolina Code of Regulations Chapter 91-5). The South Carolina Board of Nursing is located at Synergy Business Park, Suite 202, Kingstree Building, 110 Centerview Drive, Columbia, South Carolina 29210; phone: 803-896-4550.

Academic Programs

Brown Mackie College — Greenville provides higher education to traditional and nontraditional students through associate degree and certificate programs that assist in enhancing their career opportunities, broadening their perspectives through appropriate general education courses, thinking independently and critically, and improving problem-solving abilities. The College strives to develop within its students the desire for lifelong and continued education.

Each College quarter comprises twelve weeks. Associate degree programs require a minimum of eight quarters to complete. Programs are offered on a year-round basis, providing students with the ability to work uninterrupted toward completion of their degrees. The College offers all programs in a unique One Course a Month format. This allows students to focus studies on only one course for four weeks. This schedule has proven convenient for students with multiple obligations such as jobs and family.

Associate Degree Programs: The Associate of Applied Science degree is awarded in accounting technology, business management, criminal justice, health care administration, information technology, nursing, occupational therapy assistant, paralegal, and surgical technology.

Certificate Programs: The certificate is awarded in business, criminal justice, and medical assistant.

The American Medical Technologists (AMT), which offers the certification for Registered Medical Assistant (RMA), accepts the accreditation of Brown Mackie College — Greenville. Students will qualify to take the Registered Medical Assistant certification examination upon graduating the Brown Mackie College—Greenville medical assistant programs. Graduates of the 48-credit-hour medical assistant program are not qualified to take the AMT/RMA exam. Information on application procedures can be found at http://americanmedtech.org/SchoolsStudents/CertificaitonProcess.aspx.

Brown Mackie College does not guarantee third-party certification/licensing exams. Outside agencies control the requirements for certification/licensing and are subject to change without notification to the College.

Program availability and degree offerings are subject to change.

Costs

Tuition in the 2013–14 academic year for most bachelor's and associate degrees and certificates was $314 per credit hour; fees were $20 per credit hour. Tuition for the nursing program was $410 per credit hour; fees were $30 per credit hour. Tuition for the occupational therapy assistant program was $381 per credit hour; fees were $20 per credit hour. Tuition for the surgical technology program was $360 per credit hour; fees were $20 per credit hour. The cost of textbooks, if applicable, and other instructional expenses vary by program.

Financial Aid

The College maintains a full-time staff of financial aid professionals to assist qualified students in obtaining the financial assistance they require to meet their education expenses. Financial aid is available to those students who qualify.

Available resources may include federal grants and loans, state aid, student loans from private lenders, and federal work-study opportunities, both on and off College premises. Federal assistance programs are administered through the U.S. Department of Education, Office of Student Financial Assistance. Any U.S. citizen, national, or person in the United States for other than temporary reasons who is enrolled or accepted for enrollment may apply for these programs. Most forms of financial assistance are available for each July 1–June 30 award period.

Every student considering application for financial aid should request a copy of the current Student Guide, published by the U.S. Department of Education. This important document may be obtained in the Student Financial Services Office and will assist persons in understanding eligibility requirements, the application process, deadlines, and the various forms of grants and loans available.

For details on school-specific loans and scholarships, visit the school's website or contact the school's Student Financial Services Department; phone: 864-239-5300; e-mail: bmcgrweb@ brownmackie.edu; http://www.brownmackie.edu/Greenville.

Faculty

Experienced faculty members provide academic support and are committed to the academic and technical preparation of their students. The College has 9 full-time and 30 part-time instructors, with a student-faculty ratio of 24:1. Each student is assigned a faculty adviser.

Facilities and Resources

A modern facility, Brown Mackie College — Greenville offers nearly 50,000 square feet. The College is equipped with multiple computer labs housing over 100 computers. High-speed access to the Internet and other online resources are available for students and faculty. Multimedia classrooms are outfitted with overhead projectors, VCR/ DVD players, and computers.

Brown Mackie College — Greenville is fully committed to using eTextbooks and computer tablets in the classroom. Utilizing these tablets to access expanded course material, students are able to increase their acumen for using this technology and further enhance their educational experience. Students have the ability to directly download their eTextbooks to their tablet, eliminating the need to carry heavy, physical textbooks and reducing the overall cost of supplies.

Brown Mackie College is nonresidential; public transportation and ample parking at no cost are available. The College is a smoke-free facility.

Location

Brown Mackie College — Greenville is conveniently located at Two Liberty Square, 75 Beattie Place, Suite 100, in Greenville, South Carolina.

Admission Requirements

Each applicant for admission is assigned an assistant director of admissions who directs the applicant through the steps of the admissions process; provides information on curriculum, policies, procedures, and services; and assists the applicant in setting necessary appointments and interviews.

To be considered for admission to Brown Mackie College, a candidate must be a high school graduate or hold a General Education Development (GED) certificate. As part of the admissions process applicants must sign a document attesting to graduation or completion and containing the information to obtain verification of such. Official high school transcripts or official documentation of high school graduation equivalency must be obtained within the first financial aid payment period or the student will be withdrawn from the institution following established guidelines for withdrawn students noted in the catalog. Title IV aid will not be dispersed until verification of graduation or completion has been received by the College.

Where applicable, students seeking entry into the College with a high school diploma completed in a foreign country must provide an original U.S.–equivalency evaluation from an evaluating agency which is a member of the National Association of Credential Evaluation Services (NACES, http://www.naces.org/) or the Association of International Credential Evaluators, Inc. (AICES, http://www.aice-eval.org/). The cost of evaluating the foreign transcript is borne by the applicant.

Admission to the College is based upon the applicant meeting the school's admission requirements, a review of the applicant's previous educational records, and a review of the applicant's career interests. It is the responsibility of the applicant to ensure that the College receives all required documentation.

Prior to admission, students are given an assessment of academic skills, commonly referred to as the academic readiness evaluation. Though the results of this assessment do not determine eligibility for admission, they provide the College with a means of determining the need for academic support through transitional studies courses and academic advisement, as well as a means by which the College can evaluate the effectiveness of its educational programs.

An applicant must obtain a minimum score of 60 in writing and 51 in mathematics on the COMPASS student academic readiness assessment. If a student does not achieve these scores, he/she will be enrolled in the appropriate transitional studies course(s).

In addition to the general admission requirements above, some programs have additional requirements specific to the program. For information on those requirements, and other school-specific requirements, please visit the school's website or contact the school's admissions department; phone: 864-239-5300; e-mail: bmcgrweb@ brownmackie.edu; http://www.brownmackie.edu/Greenville.

Application and Information

Applicants must complete and submit an application form along with documentation of graduation from an accredited high school or state-approved secondary education curriculum or official documentation of high school graduation equivalency.

See BMCprograms.info for program duration, tuition, fees and other costs, median debt, federal salary data, alumni success, programmatic accreditation, and other important info.

Brown Mackie College — Greenville is one of over 25 school locations of the Brown Mackie College system of schools. Programs, credential levels, technology, and scheduling options are subject to change. ©2014 Brown Mackie College.

For additional information, prospective students should contact:

Director of Admissions
Brown Mackie College — Greenville
Two Liberty Square
75 Beattie Place, Suite 100
Greenville, South Carolina 29601
Phone: 864-239-5300
      877-479-8465 (toll-free)
Fax: 864-232-4094
E-mail: bmcgrweb@brownmackie.edu
Website: http://www.brownmackie.edu/greenville

BROWN MACKIE COLLEGE — HOPKINSVILLE

HOPKINSVILLE, KENTUCKY

The College and Its Mission

Brown Mackie College — Hopkinsville (Brown Mackie College) is one of over twenty-five locations in the Brown Mackie College system of schools (www.brownmackie.edu), which is dedicated to providing educational programs that prepare students to pursue entry-level positions in a competitive, rapidly changing workplace. Brown Mackie College schools offer bachelor degree, associate degree, certificate, and diploma programs in health sciences, business, information technology, legal studies, and design to thousands of students in the Midwest, Southeast, Southwest, and Western United States.

Brown Mackie College — Hopkinsville is accredited by the Accrediting Council for Independent Colleges and Schools (ACICS) to award associate degrees and diplomas. ACICS is listed as a nationally recognized accrediting agency by the United States Department of Education and is recognized by the Council for Higher Education Accreditation. ACICS can be contacted at 750 First Street NE, Suite 980, Washington, D.C. 20002; phone: 202-336-6780.

The Associate of Applied Science in occupational therapy assistant program is accredited by the Accreditation Council for Occupational Therapy Education (ACOTE) of the American Occupational Therapy Association (AOTA), located at 4720 Montgomery Lane, Suite 200, Bethesda, Maryland, 20814-3449; phone 301-652-AOTA. Graduates of the program will be eligible to sit for the national certification examination for the occupational therapy assistant administered by the National Board for Certification in Occupational Therapy (NBCOT). After successful completion of this exam, the individual will be a Certified Occupational Therapy Assistant (COTA). In addition, most states require licensure in order to practice; however, state licenses are usually based on the results of the NBCOT Certification Examination. Note that a felony conviction may affect a graduate's ability to sit for the NBCOT certification examination or attain state licensure.

Brown Mackie College — Hopkinsville is licensed by the Kentucky State Board for Proprietary Education and is authorized for operation as a postsecondary educational institution by the Tennessee Higher Education Commission (www.state.tn.us/thec).

Academic Programs

Brown Mackie College — Hopkinsville provides higher education to traditional and nontraditional students through associate degree and diploma programs that can assist them in enhancing their career opportunities, broadening their perspectives through appropriate general education courses, thinking independently and critically, and improving problem-solving abilities.

Each College quarter comprises at least twelve weeks. Programs are offered on a year-round basis, providing students with the ability to work uninterrupted toward their degrees. Brown Mackie College offers all programs in a unique One Course a Month format. This schedule allows students to focus studies on only one course for four weeks and has proven convenient for students with multiple obligations such as jobs and family.

Associate Degree Programs: Associate degree programs require a minimum of eight quarters to complete. The Associate of Applied Business degree is awarded in business management and criminal justice.

The Associate of Applied Science degree is awarded in health care administration and occupational therapy assistant.

Diploma Programs: Brown Mackie College also offers diploma programs in general business, medical assistant, and medical insurance specialist.

The American Medical Technologists (AMT), which offers the certification for Registered Medical Assistant (RMA), accepts the accreditation of Brown Mackie College — Hopkinsville. Students will qualify to take the RMA certification examination upon graduating the Brown Mackie College — Hopkinsville medical assistant program. Graduates of the 48 credit-hour medical assistant program are not qualified to take the AMT/RMA exam. Information on application procedures can be found at http://americanmedtech.org/SchoolsStudents/CertificationProcess.aspx.

Brown Mackie College — Hopkinsville does not guarantee third-party certification. Outside agencies control the requirements for certifications and are subject to change without notice to Brown Mackie College.

Program availability and degree offerings are subject to change.

Costs

Tuition for the 2013–14 academic year was $314 per credit hour with a general fee of $20 per credit hour. Tuition for the occupational therapy assistant program was $381 per credit hour, with a general fee of $20 per credit hour. The cost of textbooks, if applicable, and other instructional materials varied by program.

Financial Aid

The College maintains a full-time staff of financial aid professionals to assist qualified students in obtaining the financial assistance they require to meet their education expenses. Financial aid is available to those students who qualify.

Available resources may include federal grants and loans, state aid, student loans from private lenders, and federal work-study opportunities, both on and off College premises. Federal assistance programs are administered through the U.S. Department of Education, Office of Student Financial Assistance. Any U.S. citizen, national, or person in the United States for other than temporary reasons who is enrolled or accepted for enrollment may apply for these programs. Most forms of financial assistance are available for each July 1–June 30 award period.

Every student considering application for financial aid should request a copy of the current Student Guide, published by the U.S. Department of Education. This important document may be obtained in the Student Financial Services Office and will assist persons in understanding eligibility requirements, the application process, deadlines, and the various forms of grants and loans available.

Details on school-specific loans and scholarships are available on the school's website (http://www.brownmackie.edu/Hopkinsville) or prospective students can contact the school's

Student Financial Services Department; phone: 270-886-1302; e-mail: bmchoadm@brownmackie.edu.

Faculty

There is 1 full-time and approximately 15 adjunct instructors. The student-faculty ratio is 12:1.

Facilities and Resources

Brown Mackie College — Hopkinsville occupies a spacious building that has been specifically designed to provide a comfortable and effective environment for learning. The facility comprises approximately 17,100 square feet, including sixteen classrooms, two medical laboratories, an academic resource center, administrative and faculty offices, a bookstore, and a student lounge. Computer equipment for hands-on learning includes six networked laboratories. Medical equipment includes monocular and binocular microscopes, electrocardiograph, autoclave, centrifuge, and other equipment appropriate to hands-on laboratory and clinical instruction.

Brown Mackie College — Hopkinsville is fully committed to using eTextbooks and computer tablets in the classroom. Utilizing these tablets to access expanded course material, students will be able to increase their acumen for using this technology and further enhance their educational experience. Students have the ability to directly download their eTextbooks to their tablet, eliminating the need to carry heavy, physical textbooks and reducing the overall cost of supplies.

Convenient parking is available to all students. Brown Mackie College is a nonresidential, smoke-free institution.

Location

Brown Mackie College — Hopkinsville is conveniently located at 4001 Fort Campbell Boulevard in Hopkinsville, Kentucky.

Admission Requirements

Each applicant for admission is assigned an assistant director of admissions who directs the applicant through the steps of the admissions process; provides information on curriculum, policies, procedures, and services; and assists the applicant in setting necessary appointments and interviews.

To be considered for admission to Brown Mackie College, a candidate must be a high school graduate or hold a General Education Development (GED) certificate. As part of the admissions process, applicants must sign a document attesting to graduation or completion and containing the information to obtain verification of such. Official high school transcripts or official documentation of high school graduation equivalency must be obtained within the first financial aid payment period or the student will be withdrawn from the institution following established guidelines for withdrawn students noted in the catalog. Title IV aid will not be dispersed until verification of graduation or completion has been received by the College.

Where applicable, students seeking entry into the College with a high school diploma completed in a foreign country must provide an original U.S.–equivalency evaluation from an evaluating agency that is a member of the National Association of Credential Evaluation Services (NACES, http://www.naces.org/) or the Association of International Credential Evaluators, Inc. (AICES, http://www.aice-eval.org/). The cost of evaluating the foreign transcript is borne by the applicant.

Admission to the College is based upon the applicant meeting the school's admission requirements, a review of the applicant's previous educational records, and a review of the applicant's career interests. It is the responsibility of the applicant to ensure that the College receives all required documentation

Prior to admission, students are given an assessment of academic skills, commonly referred to as the academic readiness evaluation. Though the results of this assessment do not determine eligibility for admission, they provide the College with a means of determining the need for academic support through transitional studies courses and academic advisement, as well as a means by which the College can evaluate the effectiveness of its educational programs.

An applicant must obtain a minimum score of 60 in writing and 51 in mathematics on the COMPASS student academic readiness assessment. If a student does not achieve these scores, he/she will be enrolled in the appropriate transitional studies course(s).

In addition to the general admission requirements above, some programs have additional requirements specific to the program. For information on those, and other school-specific requirements, visit the school's website (http://www.brownmackie.edu/Hopkinsville) or contact the school's Admissions department; phone: 270-886-1302; e-mail: bmchoadm@brownmackie.edu.

Application and Information

Applicants must complete and submit an application form along with documentation of graduation from an accredited high school or state-approved secondary education curriculum or official documentation of high school graduation equivalency.

See BMCprograms.info for program duration, tuition, fees and other costs, median debt, federal salary data, alumni success, programmatic accreditation, and other important information.

Brown Mackie College—Hopkinsville is one of over 25 school locations of the Brown Mackie College system of schools. Programs, credential levels, technology, and scheduling options are subject to change. ©2014 Brown Mackie College.

For additional information, prospective students should contact:

Senior Director of Admissions
Brown Mackie College — Hopkinsville
4001 Fort Campbell Boulevard
Hopkinsville, Kentucky 42240
Phone: 270-886-1302
      800-359-4753 (toll-free)
Fax: 270-886-3544
E-mail: bmchoadm@brownmackie.edu
Website: http://www.brownmackie.edu/Hopkinsville

BROWN MACKIE COLLEGE — INDIANAPOLIS

INDIANAPOLIS, INDIANA

The College and Its Mission

Brown Mackie College — Indianapolis (Brown Mackie College) is one of over twenty-five locations in the Brown Mackie College system of schools (http://www.brownmackie.edu), which is dedicated to providing educational programs that prepare students to pursue entry-level positions in a competitive, rapidly changing workplace. The Brown Mackie College schools offer bachelor's degree, associate degree, diploma, and certificate programs in health sciences, business, information technology, legal studies, and design to thousands of students in the Midwest, Southeast, Southwest, and Western United States.

Brown Mackie College — Indianapolis was founded in 2007 as a branch of Brown Mackie College — Findlay, Ohio.

Brown Mackie College — Indianapolis is accredited by the Accrediting Council for Independent Colleges and Schools to award associate degrees, diplomas, and certificates. The Accrediting Council for Independent Colleges and Schools is listed as a nationally recognized accrediting agency by the United States Department of Education and is recognized by the Council for Higher Education Accreditation. ACICS can be contacted at 750 First Street NE, Suite 980, Washington, D.C. 20002; phone: 202-336-6780.

The occupational therapy assistant program is accredited by the Accreditation Council for Occupational Therapy Education (ACOTE) of the American Occupational Therapy Association (AOTA), located at 4720 Montgomery Lane, P.O. Box 31220, Bethesda, Maryland 20824-1220; phone: 301-652-AOTA. Graduates of the program will be eligible to sit for the national certification examination for the occupational therapy assistant administered by the National Board for Certification in Occupational Therapy (NBCOT). After successful completion of this exam, the individual will be a Certified Occupational Therapy Assistant (COTA). In addition, most states require licensure in order to practice; however, state licenses are usually based on the results of the NBCOT Certification Examination. Note that a felony conviction may affect a graduate's ability to sit for the NBCOT certification examination or attain state licensure.

Brown Mackie College — Indianapolis is authorized by the Indiana Board for Proprietary Education, 101 West Ohio Street, Suite 670, Indianapolis, Indiana 46204-1984; phone: 317-464-4400 Ext. 138, 141. Indiana advertising code: AC0078.

Academic Programs

Brown Mackie College — Indianapolis provides higher education to traditional and nontraditional students through associate degree, diploma, and certificate programs that assist them in enhancing their career opportunities, broadening their perspectives through appropriate general education courses, thinking independently and critically, and improving problem-solving abilities. The College strives to develop within its students the desire for lifelong and continued education.

Each College quarter comprises twelve weeks. Associate degree programs require a minimum of eight quarters to complete. Programs are offered on a year-round basis, providing students with the ability to work uninterrupted toward their degrees. The College offers all programs in a unique One Course a Month format. This allows students to focus studies on only one course for four weeks. This schedule has proven convenient for students with multiple obligations such as jobs and family.

Associate Degree Programs: The Associate of Science degree is awarded in business management, criminal justice, health care administration, and medical assisting. The Associate of Applied Science degree is awarded in occupational therapy assistant.

Diploma Program: The College offers a diploma program in practical nursing.

Certificate Programs: The College offers certificate programs in biomedical equipment technician, medical assistant, and medical insurance specialist.

The American Medical Technologists (AMT), which offers the certification for Registered Medical Assistant (RMA), accepts the accreditation of Brown Mackie College — Indianapolis. Students will qualify to take the Registered Medical Assistant certification examination upon graduating the Brown Mackie College — Indianapolis medical assistant program. Graduates of the 48-credit-hour medical assistant program are not qualified to take the AMT/RMA exam. Information on application procedures can be found at http://americanmedtech.org/SchoolsStudents/CertificationProcess.aspx.

Brown Mackie College — Indianapolis does not guarantee third-party certification. Outside agencies control the requirements for certifications and are subject to change without notice to Brown Mackie College.

Program availability and degree offerings are subject to change.

Costs

Tuition for most programs in the 2013–14 academic year was $332 per credit hour with a general fee of $20 per credit hour. Tuition for the practical nursing diploma program was $381 per credit hour with a general fee of $30 per credit hour applied to instructional costs for activities and services. For the occupational therapy assistant program, the tuition was $381 per credit hour with a general fee of $20 per credit hour.

Financial Aid

The College maintains a full-time staff of financial aid professionals to assist qualified students in obtaining the financial assistance they require to meet their education expenses. Financial aid is available to those students who qualify.

Available resources may include federal grants and loans, state aid, student loans from private lenders, and federal work-study opportunities, both on and off College premises. Federal assistance programs are administered through the U.S. Department of Education, Office of Student Financial Assistance. Any U.S. citizen, national, or person in the United States for other than temporary reasons who is enrolled or accepted for enrollment may apply for these programs. Most forms of financial assistance are available for each July 1–June 30 award period.

Every student considering application for financial aid should request a copy of the current Student Guide, published by the U.S. Department of Education. This important document may be obtained in the Student Financial Services Office and will assist persons in understanding eligibility requirements, the application process, deadlines, and the various forms of grants and loans available.

For details on school-specific loans and scholarships, visit the school's website (http://www.brownmackie.edu/Indianapolis) or contact the school's Student Financial Services Department, phone: 317-554-8300; e-mail: bmcindweb@brownmackie.edu.

Faculty

The College has 18 full-time instructors, 70 adjunct instructors, and 16 lab assistants, with a student-faculty ratio of 12:1. Faculty members provide tutoring and additional academic services to students as needed.

Facilities and Resources

Opened in January 2008, this modern facility offers more than 22,000 square feet of tastefully decorated classrooms, laboratories, and office space designed to the specifications of the College for its business, health-care, and technical programs. The Circle Centre Mall branch learning site boasts 25,000 square feet with 20 lecture rooms, computer labs, 2 medical labs, college store, and more. Instructional equipment is comparable to current technology used in business and industry today. Modern classrooms for special instructional needs offer multimedia capabilities with surround sound and overhead projectors accessible through computer, DVD, or VHS. Internet access and instructional resources are available at the College's library. Experienced faculty members provide academic support and are committed to the academic and technical preparation of their students.

Brown Mackie College — Indianapolis is fully committed to using eTextbooks and computer tablets in the classroom. Utilizing these tablets to access expanded course material, students are able to increase their acumen for using this technology and further enhance their educational experience. Students have the ability to directly download their eTextbooks to their tablet, eliminating the need to carry heavy, physical textbooks and reducing the overall cost of supplies.

Brown Mackie College — Indianapolis is nonresidential; public transportation and ample parking are available at no additional cost.

Location

Brown Mackie College — Indianapolis is conveniently located at 1200 North Meridian Street in Indianapolis, Indiana. The College has a generous parking area and is easily accessible by public transportation.

In November 2011, the College opened an innovative branch learning site on Level 4 of Circle Centre Mall located at 49 West Maryland Street in the heart of downtown Indianapolis. Daily shuttle service is provided to and from the main college.

Admission Requirements

Each applicant for admission is assigned an assistant director of admissions who directs the applicant through the steps of the admissions process; provides information on curriculum, policies, procedures, and services; and assists the applicant in setting necessary appointments and interviews.

To be considered for admission to Brown Mackie College, a candidate must be a high school graduate or hold a General Education Development (GED) certificate. As part of the admission process applicants must sign a document attesting to graduation or completion and containing the information to obtain verification of such. Official high school transcripts or official documentation of high school graduation equivalency must be obtained within the first financial aid payment period or the student will be withdrawn from the institution following established guidelines for withdrawn students noted in the catalog. Title IV aid will not be dispersed until verification of graduation or completion has been received by the College.

Where applicable, students seeking entry into the College with a high school diploma completed in a foreign country must provide an original U.S.–equivalency evaluation from an evaluating agency which is a member of the National Association of Credential Evaluation Services (NACES, http://www.naces.org/) or the Association of International Credential Evaluators, Inc. (AICES, http://www.aice-eval.org/). The cost of evaluating the foreign transcript is borne by the applicant.

Admission to the College is based upon the applicant meeting the school's admission requirements, a review of the applicant's previous educational records, and a review of the applicant's career interests. It is the responsibility of the applicant to ensure that the College receives all required documentation.

Prior to admission, students are given an assessment of academic skills, commonly referred to as the academic readiness evaluation. Though the results of this assessment do not determine eligibility for admission, they provide the College with a means of determining the need for academic support through transitional studies courses and academic advisement, as well as a means by which the College can evaluate the effectiveness of its educational programs.

An applicant must obtain a minimum score of 60 in writing and 51 in mathematics on the COMPASS student academic readiness assessment. If a student does not achieve these scores, he/she will be enrolled in the appropriate transitional studies course(s).

In addition to the general admission requirements above, some programs have additional requirements specific to the program. For information on those requirements, and other school-specific requirements, please visit the school's website or contact the school's admissions department: phone: 317-554-8300; e-mail: bmcindweb@brownmackie.edu; website: http://www.brownmackie.edu/Indianapolis.

Application and Information

Applicants must complete and submit an application form, along with documentation of graduation from an accredited high school or state-approved secondary education curriculum or official documentation of high school graduation equivalency.

See BMCprograms.info for program duration, tuition, fees and other costs, median debt, federal salary data, alumni success, programmatic accreditation, and other important info.

Brown Mackie College — Indianapolis is one of over 25 school locations of the Brown Mackie College system of schools. Programs, credential levels, technology, and scheduling options are subject to change. ©2014 Brown Mackie College.

For additional information, prospective students should contact:

Director of Admissions
Brown Mackie College — Indianapolis
1200 North Meridian Street, Suite 100
Indianapolis, Indiana 46204
Phone: 317-554-8300
      866-255-0279 (toll-free)
Fax: 317-632-4557
E-mail: bmcindweb@brownmackie.edu
Website: http://www.brownmackie.edu/Indianapolis

BROWN MACKIE COLLEGE — KANSAS CITY

LENEXA, KANSAS

The College and Its Mission

Brown Mackie College — Kansas City (Brown Mackie College) is one of over twenty-five locations in the Brown Mackie College system of schools (www.brownmackie.edu), which is dedicated to providing educational programs that prepare students to pursue entry-level positions in a competitive, rapidly changing workplace. Brown Mackie College schools offer bachelor degree, associate degree, certificate, and diploma programs in health sciences, business, information technology, legal studies, and design to thousands of students in the Midwest, Southeast, Southwest, and Western United States.

The College was founded in Salina, Kansas, in July 1892 as the Kansas Wesleyan School of Business. In 1938, the College was incorporated as the Brown Mackie School of Business under the ownership of former Kansas Wesleyan instructors Perry E. Brown and A. B. Mackie. It became Brown Mackie College in January 1975.

Brown Mackie College in Lenexa, Kansas is a branch of Brown Mackie College in Salina, Kansas, which is accredited by the Higher Learning Commission and is a member of the North Central Association (NCA), 230 South LaSalle Street, Suite 7-500, Chicago, Illinois 60604-1413; phone: 800-621-7440 (toll free); www.ncahlc.org.

Brown Mackie College in Lenexa, Kansas is approved and authorized to grant the Associate of Applied Science (AAS) degree by the Kansas Board of Regents, 1000 Southwest Jackson Street, Suite 520, Topeka, Kansas 66612-1368.

The occupational therapy assistant program is accredited by the Accreditation Council for Occupational Therapy Education (ACOTE) of the American Occupational Therapy Association (AOTA), 4720 Montgomery Lane, Suite 200, Bethesda, Maryland 20814-3449; phone: 301-652-AOTA. Graduates of the program will be eligible to sit for the national certification examination for the occupational therapy assistant administered by the National Board for Certification in Occupational Therapy (NBCOT). After successful completion of this exam, the individual will be a Certified Occupational Therapy Assistant (COTA). In addition, most states require licensure in order to practice; however, state licenses are usually based on the results of the NBCOT Certification Examination. Note that a felony conviction may affect a graduate's ability to sit for the NBCOT certification examination or attain state licensure.

The veterinary technology program at Brown Mackie College — Kansas City has provisional programmatic accreditation granted by the American Veterinary Medical Association (AVMA) through the Committee on Veterinary Technician Education and Activities (CVTEA), 1931 North Meacham Road, Suite 100, Schaumburg, Illinois 60173; phone: 800-248-2862; website: www.avma.org.

Academic Programs

Brown Mackie College — Kansas City provides higher education to traditional and nontraditional students through associate degree, diploma, and certificate programs that can assist them in enhancing their career opportunities, broadening their perspectives through appropriate general education courses, thinking independently and critically, and improving problem-solving abilities. Brown Mackie College strives to develop within its students the desire for lifelong and continued education.

In most programs, students can participate in day or evening classes, which begin every month. Programs are offered on a year-round basis, providing students with the ability to work uninterrupted toward completion of their programs. Brown Mackie College offers all programs in a unique One Course a Month format. This schedule allows students to focus studies on only one course for four weeks and has proven convenient for students with multiple obligations such as jobs and family.

Associate Degree Programs: The Associate of Applied Science degree is awarded in architectural design and drafting technology, biomedical equipment technology, business management, criminal justice, health care administration, nursing, occupational therapy assistant, surgical technology, and veterinary technology.

Diploma Programs: Brown Mackie College — Kansas City also offers diploma programs in architectural drafting specialist, criminal justice specialist, general business, and medical assistant.

Certificate Program: A certificate program is offered in practical nursing.

The American Medical Technologists (AMT), which offers the certification for Registered Medical Assistant (RMA), accepts the accreditation of Brown Mackie College — Kansas City. Students will qualify to take the Registered Medical Assistant certification examination upon graduating the Brown Mackie College — Kansas City medical assisting and medical assistant programs. Graduates of the 48 credit-hour medical assistant program are not qualified to take the AMT/RMA exam. Information on application procedures can be found at http://americanmedtech.org/SchoolsStudents/CertificationProcess.aspx.

Brown Mackie College does not guarantee third-party certification/licensing exams. Outside agencies control the requirements for certification/licensing and are subject to change without notification to the College.

Program availability and degree offerings are subject to change.

Costs

Tuition for most programs in the 2013–14 academic year was $314 per credit hour and $20 per credit hour for general fees. Tuition for nursing programs was $381 per credit hour with general fees of $30 per credit hour. Tuition for the occupational therapy assistant program was $381 per credit hour with fees of $20 per credit hour. Tuition for the surgical technology program was $360 per credit hour with fees of $20 per credit hour. The cost of textbooks, if applicable, and other instructional materials varies by program.

Financial Aid

The College maintains a full-time staff of financial aid professionals to assist qualified students in obtaining the financial assistance they require to meet their education expenses. Financial aid is available to those students who qualify.

Available resources may include federal grants and loans, state aid, student loans from private lenders, and federal work-study opportunities, both on and off College premises. Federal assistance programs are administered through the U.S. Department of Education, Office of Student Financial Assistance. Any U.S. citizen, national, or person in the United States for other than temporary reasons who is enrolled or accepted for enrollment may apply for these programs. Most forms of financial assistance are available for each July 1–June 30 award period.

Every student considering application for financial aid should request a copy of the current Student Guide, published by the U.S. Department of Education. This important document may

be obtained in the Student Financial Services Office and will assist persons in understanding eligibility requirements, the application process, deadlines, and the various forms of grants and loans available.

For details on school-specific loans and scholarships, visit the school's website or contact the school's Student Financial Services Department; phone: 913-768-1900; e-mail: bmcleweb@brownmackie.edu; http://www.brownmackie.edu/KansasCity.

Faculty

There are 18 full-time faculty members and 29 adjunct faculty members. The average class student-instructor ratio is 14:1.

Facilities and Resources

In addition to classrooms and computer labs, Brown Mackie College — Kansas City maintains a library of curriculum-related resources, technical and general education materials, academic and professional periodicals, and audiovisual resources. Internet access also is available for research. The College has a bookstore that stocks texts, courseware, and other educational supplies required for courses and a variety of personal, recreational, and gift items, including apparel, supplies, and general merchandise incorporating the Brown Mackie College logo. Hours are posted at the bookstore entrance.

Brown Mackie College — Kansas City is fully committed to using eTextbooks and computer tablets in the classroom. Utilizing these tablets to access expanded course material, students are able to increase their acumen for using this technology and further enhance their educational experience. Students have the ability to directly download their eTextbooks to their tablet, eliminating the need to carry heavy, physical textbooks and reducing the overall cost of supplies.

Location

Brown Mackie College — Kansas City is located at 9705 Lenexa Drive in Lenexa, Kansas, just off Interstate 35 at 95th Street in Johnson County. The Olathe course site is located at 450 North Rogers Road, Suite 175, in Olathe, Kansas, just off Interstate 35 and Santa Fe Street in Johnson County.

Admission Requirements

Each applicant for admission is assigned an assistant director of admissions who directs the applicant through the steps of the admissions process; provides information on curriculum, policies, procedures, and services; and assists the applicant in setting necessary appointments and interviews.

To be considered for admission to Brown Mackie College, a candidate must be a high school graduate or hold a General Education Development (GED) certificate. As part of the admission process applicants must sign a document attesting to graduation or completion and containing the information to obtain verification of such. Official high school transcripts or official documentation of high school graduation equivalency must be obtained within the first financial aid payment period or the student will be withdrawn from the institution following established guidelines for withdrawn students noted in the catalog. Title IV aid will not be dispersed until verification of graduation or completion has been received by the College.

Where applicable, students seeking entry into the College with a high school diploma completed in a foreign country must provide an original U.S.–equivalency evaluation from an evaluating agency which is a member of the National Association of Credential Evaluation Services (NACES, http://www.naces.org/) or the Association of International Credential Evaluators, Inc.

(AICES, http://www.aice-eval.org/). The cost of evaluating the foreign transcript is borne by the applicant.

Admission to the College is based upon the applicant meeting the school's admission requirements, a review of the applicant's previous educational records, and a review of the applicant's career interests. It is the responsibility of the applicant to ensure that the College receives all required documentation.

Prior to admission, students are given an assessment of academic skills, commonly referred to as the academic readiness evaluation. Though the results of this assessment do not determine eligibility for admission, they provide the College with a means of determining the need for academic support through transitional studies courses and academic advisement, as well as a means by which the College can evaluate the effectiveness of its educational programs.

An applicant must obtain a minimum score of 60 in writing and 51 in mathematics on the COMPASS student academic readiness assessment. If a student does not achieve these scores, he/she will be enrolled in the appropriate transitional studies course(s).

In addition to the general admission requirements above, some programs have additional requirements specific to the program. For information on those requirements, and other school-specific requirements, please visit the school's website or contact the school's Admissions department; phone: 913-768-1900; e-mail: bmcleweb@brownmackie.edu; http://www.brownmackie.edu/KansasCity.

Application and Information

Applicants must complete and submit an application form, along with documentation of graduation from an accredited high school or state-approved secondary education curriculum or official documentation of high school graduation equivalency.

See BMCprograms.info for program duration, tuition, fees and other costs, median debt, federal salary data, alumni success, programmatic accreditation, and other important information.

Brown Mackie College — Kansas City is one of over 25 school locations of the Brown Mackie College system of schools. Programs, credential levels, technology, and scheduling options are subject to change. ©2014 Brown Mackie College.

For additional information, prospective students should contact:

Director of Admissions
Brown Mackie College — Kansas City
9705 Lenexa Drive
Lenexa, Kansas 66215
Phone: 913-768-1900
　　　800-635-9101 (toll-free)
Fax: 913-495-9555
E-mail: bmcleweb@brownmackie.edu
Website: http://www.brownmackie.edu/KansasCity

BROWN MACKIE COLLEGE — LOUISVILLE
LOUISVILLE, KENTUCKY

The College and Its Mission

Brown Mackie College — Louisville (Brown Mackie College) is one of over twenty-five locations in the Brown Mackie College system of schools (www.brownmackie.edu), which is dedicated to providing educational programs that prepare students to pursue entry-level positions in a competitive, rapidly changing workplace. Brown Mackie College schools offer bachelor degree, associate degree, diploma, and certificate programs in health sciences, business, information technology, legal studies, and design to thousands of students in the Midwest, Southeast, Southwest, and Western United States.

Brown Mackie College — Louisville opened in 1972 as RETS Institute of Technology. The first RETS school was founded in 1935 in Detroit in response to the rapid growth of radio broadcasting and the need for qualified radio technicians. The RETS Institute changed its name to Brown Mackie College — Louisville in 2004.

Brown Mackie College — Louisville is accredited by the Accrediting Council for Independent Colleges and Schools to award associate degrees, diplomas, and certificates. The Accrediting Council for Independent Colleges and Schools is listed as a nationally recognized accrediting agency by the United States Department of Education. Its accreditation of degree-granting institutions is recognized by the Council for Higher Education Accreditation. ACICS can be contacted at 750 First Street NE, Suite 980, Washington, D.C. 20002; phone: 202-336-6780.

Brown Mackie College — Louisville is licensed by the Kentucky Council on Postsecondary Education, located at 1024 Capital Center Drive, Suite 320, Frankfort, Kentucky 40601.

Brown Mackie College — Louisville is authorized by the Indiana Board for Proprietary Education, 101 West Ohio Street, Suite 670, Indianapolis, Indiana 46204-1984; phone: 317-464-4400 Ext. 138, 141.

The Brown Mackie College — Louisville veterinary technology program has probationary programmatic accreditation granted by the American Veterinary Medical Association (AVMA) through the Committee on Veterinary Technician Education and Activities (CVTEA).

The occupational therapy assistant program is accredited by the Accreditation Council for Occupational Therapy Education (ACOTE) of the American Occupational Therapy Association (AOTA), located at 4720 Montgomery Lane, P.O. Box 31220, Bethesda, Maryland 20824-1220; phone: 301-652-AOTA. Graduates of the program will be eligible to sit for the national certification examination for the occupational therapy assistant administered by the National Board for Certification in Occupational Therapy (NBCOT). After successful completion of this exam, the individual will be a Certified Occupational Therapy Assistant (COTA). In addition, most states require licensure in order to practice; however, state licenses are usually based on the results of the NBCOT Certification Examination. Note that a felony conviction may affect a graduate's ability to sit for the NBCOT certification examination or attain state licensure.

Academic Programs

Brown Mackie College — Louisville provides higher education to traditional and nontraditional students through associate degree, and diploma programs that assist in enhancing their career opportunities, broadening their perspectives through appropriate general education courses, thinking independently and critically, and improving problem-solving abilities.

Each College quarter comprises twelve weeks. Associate degree programs require a minimum of eight quarters to complete. Programs are offered on a year-round basis, providing students with the ability to work uninterrupted toward completion of their programs. The College offers all programs in a unique One Course a Month format. This allows students to focus studies on only one course for four weeks. This schedule has proven convenient for students with multiple obligations such as jobs and family.

Associate Degree Programs: The Associate of Applied Business degree is awarded in business management, computer networking and applications, criminal justice, and paralegal.

The Associate of Applied Science degree is awarded in biomedical equipment technology, electronics, health care administration, occupational therapy assistant, and veterinary technology.

Diploma Program: The College offers diploma programs in medical assistant and practical nursing.

Certificate Program: The College offers a certificate program in computer networking.

The American Medical Technologists (AMT), which offers the certification for Registered Medical Assistant (RMA), accepts the accreditation of Brown Mackie College — Louisville. Students will qualify to take the Registered Medical Assistant certification examination upon graduating the Brown Mackie College — Louisville medical assistant program. Information on application procedures can be found at http://americanmedtech.org/SchoolsStudents/CertificationProcess.aspx.

Brown Mackie College — Louisville does not guarantee third-party certification. Outside agencies control the requirements for certifications and are subject to change without notice to Brown Mackie College.

Program availability and degree offerings are subject to change.

Costs

Tuition for most programs in the 2013–14 academic year was $314 per credit hour, and the general fees were $20 per credit hour. The practical nursing diploma program was $381 per credit hour, and the general fees were $30 per credit hour. The occupational therapy program was $381 per credit hour, and the general fees were $20 per credit hour. The computer networking certificate program was $314 per credit hour, and the general fees were $25 per credit hour. The length of the program determines total cost. The cost of textbooks, if applicable, and other instructional materials varies by program.

Financial Aid

The College maintains a full-time staff of financial aid professionals to assist qualified students in obtaining the financial assistance they require to meet their education expenses. Financial aid is available to those students who qualify.

Available resources may include federal grants and loans, state aid, student loans from private lenders, and federal work-study opportunities, both on and off College premises. Federal assistance programs are administered through the U.S. Department of Education, Office of Student Financial Assistance. Any U.S. citizen, national, or person in the United States for other than temporary reasons who is enrolled or accepted for enrollment may apply for these programs. Most forms of financial assistance are available for each July 1–June 30 award period.

Every student considering application for financial aid should request a copy of the current Student Guide, published by the U.S. Department of Education. This important document may

be obtained in the Student Financial Services Office and will assist persons in understanding eligibility requirements, the application process, deadlines, and the various forms of grants and loans available.

For details on school-specific loans and scholarships, visit the school's website or contact the school's Student Financial Services Department; phone: 502-968-7191; e-mail: bmcloadm@brownmackie.edu; http://www.brownmackie.edu/Louisville.

Faculty

There are 32 full-time and over 100 part-time faculty members at the College. The average student-faculty ratio is 20:1.

Facilities and Resources

Brown Mackie College — Louisville has more than 69,000 square feet of multipurpose classrooms, including networked computer laboratories, electronics laboratories, veterinary technology labs, medical labs, nursing labs, a resource center, and offices for administrative personnel as well as for student services such as admissions, student financial services, and career-services assistance. In 2009, 6,000 square feet were added to the Louisville location. Included in this build-out was an occupational therapy lab, a criminal justice lab, additional classrooms, and faculty space. In 2010, an additional 25,000 square feet opened at this location. This build-out included a biomedical equipment lab, additional classrooms, a career services center, and additional faculty/administration space.

Brown Mackie College — Louisville is fully committed to using eTextbooks and computer tablets in the classroom. Utilizing these tablets to access expanded course material, students are able to increase their acumen for using this technology and further enhance their educational experience. Students have the ability to directly download their eTextbooks to their tablet, eliminating the need to carry heavy, physical textbooks and reducing the overall cost of supplies.

Brown Mackie College — Louisville is nonresidential; ample parking at no cost is available. Brown Mackie College is a smoke-free facility.

Location

Brown Mackie College — Louisville is conveniently located at 3605 Fern Valley Road in Louisville, Kentucky. The College is easily accessible by public transportation.

Admission Requirements

Each applicant for admission is assigned an assistant director of admissions who directs the applicant through the steps of the admissions process; provides information on curriculum, policies, procedures, and services; and assists the applicant in setting necessary appointments and interviews.

To be considered for admission to Brown Mackie College, a candidate must be a high school graduate or hold a General Education Development (GED) certificate. As part of the admissions process applicants must sign a document attesting to graduation or completion and containing the information to obtain verification of such. Official high school transcripts or official documentation of high school graduation equivalency must be obtained within the first financial aid payment period or the student will be withdrawn from the institution following established guidelines for withdrawn students noted in the catalog. Title IV aid will not be dispersed until verification of graduation or completion has been received by the College.

Where applicable, students seeking entry into the College with a high school diploma completed in a foreign country must provide an original U.S.–equivalency evaluation from an evaluating agency which is a member of the National Association of Credential Evaluation Services (NACES, http://www.naces.org/) or the Association of International Credential Evaluators, Inc.

(AICES, http://www.aice-eval.org/). The cost of evaluating the foreign transcript is borne by the applicant.

Admission to the College is based upon the applicant meeting the school's admission requirements, a review of the applicant's previous educational records, and a review of the applicant's career interests. It is the responsibility of the applicant to ensure that the College receives all required documentation

Prior to admission, students are given an assessment of academic skills, commonly referred to as the academic readiness evaluation. Though the results of this assessment do not determine eligibility for admission, they provide the College with a means of determining the need for academic support through transitional studies courses and academic advisement, as well as a means by which the College can evaluate the effectiveness of its educational programs.

An applicant must obtain a minimum score of 60 in writing and 51 in mathematics on the COMPASS student academic readiness assessment. If a student does not achieve these scores, he/she will be enrolled in the appropriate transitional studies course(s).

In addition to the general admission requirements above, some programs have additional requirements specific to the program. For information on those requirements, and other school-specific requirements, contact the school's admissions department: phone: 502-968-7191; e-mail: bmcloadm@brownmackie.edu; or visit the school's website: http://www.brownmackie.edu/Louisville.

Application and Information

Applicants must complete and submit an application form along with documentation of graduation from an accredited high school or completion of state-approved secondary education curriculum or official documentation of high school graduation equivalency.

See BMCprograms.info for program duration, tuition, fees and other costs, median debt, federal salary data, alumni success, programmatic accreditation, and other important information.

Brown Mackie College — Louisville is one of over 25 school locations of the Brown Mackie College system of schools. Programs, credential levels, technology, and scheduling options are subject to change. ©2014 Brown Mackie College.

For additional information, prospective students should contact:

Director of Admissions
Brown Mackie College — Louisville
3605 Fern Valley Road
Louisville, Kentucky 40219
Phone: 502-968-7191
    800-999-7387 (toll-free)
Fax: 502-357-9956
E-mail: bmcloadm@brownmackie.edu
Website: http://www.brownmackie.edu/Louisville

BROWN MACKIE COLLEGE — MERRILLVILLE
MERRILLVILLE, INDIANA

The College and Its Mission

Brown Mackie College — Merrillville (Brown Mackie College) is one of over twenty-five locations in the Brown Mackie College system of schools (www.brownmackie.edu), which is dedicated to providing educational programs that prepare students to pursue entry-level positions in a competitive, rapidly changing workplace. Brown Mackie College schools offer bachelor's degree, associate degree, diploma, and certificate programs in health sciences, business, information technology, legal studies, and design to thousands of students in the Midwest, Southeast, Southwest, and Western United States.

Founded in 1890 by A. N. Hirons as LaPorte Business College in LaPorte, Indiana, the institution later became known as Commonwealth Business College. In 1919, ownership was transferred to Grace and J. J. Moore, who successfully operated the College under the name of Reese School of Business for several decades. In 1975, the College came under the ownership of Steven C. Smith as Commonwealth Business College. A second location, now known as Brown Mackie College — Merrillville, was opened in 1984 in Merrillville, Indiana.

Brown Mackie College — Merrillville is accredited by the Accrediting Council for Independent Colleges and Schools to award associate degrees, diplomas, and certificates. The Accrediting Council for Independent Colleges and Schools is listed as a nationally recognized accrediting agency by the United States Department of Education and is recognized by the Council for Higher Education Accreditation. ACICS can be contacted at 750 First Street NE, Suite 980, Washington, D.C. 20002; phone: 202-336-6780.

Brown Mackie College — Merrillville is regulated by the Board for Proprietary Education Indiana Commission for Higher Education, 101 West Ohio Street, Suite 670, Indianapolis, Indiana 46204; phone: 317-464-4400.

The Brown Mackie College — Merrillville Associate of Science in surgical technology is accredited by the Commission on Accreditation of Allied Health Education Programs (www.caahep.org) upon the recommendation of the Accreditation Review Committee on Education in Surgical Technology.

The Associate of Applied Science in occupational therapy assistant program is accredited by the Accreditation Council for Occupational Therapy Education (ACOTE) of the American Occupational Therapy Association (AOTA), 4720 Montgomery Lane, Suite 200, Bethesda, Maryland 20814-3449; phone: 301-652-AOTA. Graduates of the program will be eligible to sit for the national certification examination for the occupational therapy assistant administered by the National Board for Certification in Occupational Therapy (NBCOT). After successful completion of this exam, the individual will be a Certified Occupational Therapy Assistant (COTA). In addition, most states require licensure in order to practice; however, state licenses are usually based on the results of the NBCOT Certification Examination. Note that a felony conviction may affect a graduate's ability to sit for the NBCOT certification examination or attain state licensure.

Academic Programs

Brown Mackie College — Merrillville provides higher education to traditional and nontraditional students through associate degree, diploma, and certificate programs that assist in enhancing their career opportunities, broadening their perspectives through appropriate general education courses, thinking independently and critically, and improving problem-solving abilities. The College strives to develop within its students the desire for lifelong and continued education.

Each College quarter comprises ten to twelve weeks. Associate degree programs require a minimum of eight quarters to complete. Programs are offered on a year-round basis, providing students with the ability to work uninterrupted toward completion of their programs. The College offers all programs in a unique One Course a Month format. This allows students to focus on only one course for four weeks. This schedule has proven convenient for students with multiple obligations such as jobs and family.

Associate Degree Programs: The Associate of Science degree is awarded in business management, criminal justice, paralegal, and surgical technology.

The Associate of Applied Science degree is awarded in occupational therapy assistant.

Certificate Programs: The College offers certificate programs in general business, medical assistant, and paralegal assistant.

The American Medical Technologists (AMT), which offers the certification for Registered Medical Assistant (RMA), accepts the accreditation of Brown Mackie College — Merrillville. Students will qualify to take the RMA certification examination upon graduating the Brown Mackie College — Merrillville medical assistant program. Graduates of the 48 credit-hour medical assistant program are not qualified to take the AMT/RMA exam. Information on application procedures can be found at http://americanmedtech.org/SchoolsStudents/CertificationProcess.aspx.

Brown Mackie College — Merrillville does not guarantee third-party certification. Outside agencies control the requirements for certifications and are subject to change without notice to Brown Mackie College.

Program availability and degree offerings are subject to change.

Costs

Tuition for most programs in the 2013–14 academic year was $314 per credit hour and fees were $20 per credit hour, with some exceptions. For the surgical technology program, tuition was $360 per credit hour and fees were $20 per credit hour. For the occupational therapy assistant program, tuition was $381 per credit hour and fees were $20 per credit hour. The length of the program determines total cost. Textbook fees, if applicable, vary according to program.

Financial Aid

The College maintains a full-time staff of financial aid professionals to assist qualified students in obtaining the financial assistance they require to meet their education expenses. Financial aid is available to those students who qualify.

Available resources may include federal grants and loans, state aid, student loans from private lenders, and federal work-study opportunities, both on and off College premises. Federal assistance programs are administered through the U.S. Department of Education, Office of Student Financial Assistance. Any U.S. citizen, national, or person in the United States for other than temporary reasons who is enrolled or accepted for enrollment may apply for these programs. Most forms of financial assistance are available for each July 1–June 30 award period.

Every student considering application for financial aid should request a copy of the current Student Guide, published by the U.S. Department of Education. This important document may be obtained in the Student Financial Services Office and will assist persons in understanding eligibility requirements, the application process, deadlines, and the various forms of grants and loans available.

For details on school-specific loans and scholarships, visit the school's website or contact the school's Student Financial

Services Department; phone: 219-769-3321; e-mail: bmcmeadm@brownmackie.edu; http://www.brownmackie.edu/ Merrillville.

Faculty

There are approximately 16 full-time and 25 part-time faculty members at the College, practitioners in their fields of expertise. The average student-faculty ratio is 17:1.

Facilities and Resources

Occupying 29,000 square feet, Brown Mackie College — Merrillville was opened to students in October 1998 in the Twin Towers complex of Merrillville and comprises several instructional rooms, including five computer labs with networked computers and four medical laboratories. The administrative offices, College library, and student lounge are all easily accessible to students. The College bookstore stocks texts, courseware, and other educational supplies required for courses at the College. Students also find a variety of personal, recreational, and gift items, including apparel, supplies, and general merchandise incorporating the College logo. Hours are posted at the bookstore entrance.

Brown Mackie College — Merrillville is fully committed to using eTextbooks and computer tablets in the classroom. Utilizing these tablets to access expanded course material, students are able to increase their acumen for using this technology and further enhance their educational experience. Students have the ability to directly download their eTextbooks to their tablet, eliminating the need to carry heavy, physical textbooks and reducing the overall cost of supplies.

The College is a nonresidential, smoke-free institution.

Location

Brown Mackie College — Merrillville is conveniently located in northwest Indiana at 1000 East 80th Place, Merrillville, in the Twin Towers business complex just west of the intersection of U.S. Route 30 and Interstate 65. A spacious parking lot provides ample parking at no additional charge.

Admission Requirements

Each applicant for admission is assigned an assistant director of admissions who directs the applicant through the steps of the admissions process; provides information on curriculum, policies, procedures, and services; and assists the applicant in setting necessary appointments and interviews.

To be considered for admission to Brown Mackie College, a candidate must be a high school graduate or hold a General Education Development (GED) certificate. As part of the admissions process applicants must sign a document attesting to graduation or completion and containing the information to obtain verification of such. Official high school transcripts or official documentation of high school graduation equivalency must be obtained within the first financial aid payment period or the student will be withdrawn from the institution following established guidelines for withdrawn students noted in the catalog. Title IV aid will not be dispersed until verification of graduation or completion has been received by the College.

Where applicable, students seeking entry into the College with a high school diploma completed in a foreign country must provide an original U.S.–equivalency evaluation from an evaluating agency which is a member of the National Association of Credential Evaluation Services (NACES, http://www.naces.org/) or the Association of International Credential Evaluators, Inc. (AICES, http://www.aice-eval.org/). The cost of evaluating the foreign transcript is borne by the applicant.

Admission to the College is based upon the applicant meeting the school's admission requirements, a review of the applicant's previous educational records, and a review of the applicant's career interests. It is the responsibility of the applicant to ensure that the College receives all required documentation

Prior to admission, students are given an assessment of academic skills, commonly referred to as the academic readiness evaluation. Though the results of this assessment do not determine eligibility for admission, they provide the College with a means of determining the need for academic support through transitional studies courses and academic advisement, as well as a means by which the College can evaluate the effectiveness of its educational programs.

An applicant must obtain a minimum score of 60 in writing and 51 in mathematics on the COMPASS student academic readiness assessment. If a student does not achieve these scores, he/she will be enrolled in the appropriate transitional studies course(s).

In addition to the general admission requirements above, some programs have additional requirements specific to the program. For information on those, and other school-specific requirements, please visit the school's website or contact the school's Admissions department; phone: 219-769-3321; e-mail: bmcmeadm@brownmackie.edu; http://www.brownmackie.edu/Merrillville.

Application and Information

Applicants must complete and submit an application form along with documentation of graduation from an accredited high school or completion of state-approved secondary education curriculum or provide official documentation of high school graduation equivalency.

See BMCprograms.info for program duration, tuition, fees and other costs, median debt, federal salary data, alumni success, programmatic accreditation, and other important information.

Brown Mackie College — Merrillville is one of over 25 school locations of the Brown Mackie College system of schools. Programs, credential levels, technology, and scheduling options are subject to change. ©2014 Brown Mackie College.

For additional information, prospective students should contact:

Brown Mackie College — Merrillville
1000 East 80th Place, Suite 205M
Merrillville, Indiana 46410
Phone: 219-769-3321
    800-258-3321 (toll-free)
Fax: 219-738-1076
E-mail: bmcmeadm@brownmackie.edu
Website: http://www.brownmackie.edu/Merrillville

BROWN MACKIE COLLEGE — MIAMI
MIRAMAR, FLORIDA

BROWN
MACKIE
COLLEGE®
MIAMI

The College and Its Mission

Brown Mackie College — Miami (Brown Mackie College) is one of over twenty-five locations in the Brown Mackie College system of schools (www.brownmackie.edu), which is dedicated to providing educational programs that prepare students to pursue entry-level positions in a competitive, rapidly changing workplace. Brown Mackie College schools offer bachelor's degree, associate degree, diploma, and certificate programs in health sciences, business, information technology, legal studies, criminal justice, early childhood education, and design to thousands of students in the Midwest, Southeast, Southwest, and Western United States.

Brown Mackie College — Miami is accredited by the Accrediting Council for Independent Colleges and Schools to award associate degrees and diplomas. The Accrediting Council for Independent Colleges and Schools is listed as a nationally recognized accrediting agency by the United States Department of Education and is recognized by the Council for Higher Education Accreditation. ACICS can be contacted at 750 First Street NE, Suite 980, Washington, D.C. 20002; phone: 202-336-6780.

Brown Mackie College — Miami is licensed by the Commission for Independent Education, Florida Department of Education. Additional information regarding this institution may be obtained by contacting the Commission at 325 West Gaines Street, Suite 1414, Tallahassee, Florida 32399-0400; phone: 888-224-6684 (toll-free). Licensed by the Commission for Independent Education, license no. 3206.

The Brown Mackie College – Miami location is approved by the Florida Board of Nursing to offer the Associate of Science in nursing; 4052 Bald Cypress Way, Bin C-02; Tallahassee, Florida 32399-3252; phone: 850-488-0595; http://www.doh.state.fl.us/mqa/nursing/index.html.

Academic Programs

Brown Mackie College — Miami provides higher education to traditional and nontraditional students through associate degree and diploma programs that assist them in enhancing their career opportunities, broadening their perspectives through appropriate general education courses, thinking independently and critically, and improving problem-solving abilities. The College strives to develop within its students the desire for lifelong and continued education.

Each College quarter comprises twelve weeks. Associate degree programs require a minimum of eight quarters to complete. Programs are offered on a year-round basis, providing students with the ability to work uninterrupted toward their degrees. The College offers all programs in a unique One Course a Month format. This allows students to focus studies on only one course for four weeks. This schedule has proven convenient for students with multiple obligations such as jobs and family.

Associate Degree Programs: The Associate of Science degree is awarded in biomedical equipment technology, business management, criminal justice, early childhood education, health care administration, information technology, nursing, and paralegal.

Diploma Program: The College offers diploma programs in criminal justice specialist, medical assistant, and medical insurance specialist.

The American Medical Technologists (AMT), which offers the certification for Registered Medical Assistant (RMA), accepts the accreditation of Brown Mackie College — Miami. Students will qualify to take the RMA certification examination upon graduating the Brown Mackie College — Miami medical assistant program. Information on application procedures can be found at http://americanmedtech.org/SchoolsStudents/CertificationProcess.aspx.

Brown Mackie College — Miami does not guarantee third-party certification. Outside agencies control the requirements for certifications and are subject to change without notice to Brown Mackie College.

Program availability and degree offerings are subject to change.

Costs

Tuition in the 2013–14 academic year for most programs was $391 per credit hour; fees were $20 per credit hour. For the nursing associate degree program, tuition was $410 per credit hour; fees were $30 per credit hour. Textbooks, if applicable, and other instructional materials vary by program.

Financial Aid

The College maintains a full-time staff of financial aid professionals to assist qualified students in obtaining the financial assistance they require to meet their education expenses. Financial aid is available to those students who qualify.

Available resources may include federal grants and loans, state aid, student loans from private lenders, and federal work-study opportunities, both on and off College premises. Federal assistance programs are administered through the U.S. Department of Education, Office of Student Financial Assistance. Any U.S. citizen, national, or person in the United States for other than temporary reasons who is enrolled or accepted for enrollment may apply for these programs. Most forms of financial assistance are available for each July 1–June 30 award period.

Every student considering application for financial aid should request a copy of the current Student Guide, published by the U.S. Department of Education. This important document may be obtained in the Student Financial Services Office and will assist persons in understanding eligibility requirements, the application process, deadlines, and the various forms of grants and loans available.

For details on school-specific loans and scholarships, visit the school's website or contact the school's Student Financial Services Department; phone: 330-869-3600; e-mail: bmcmiweb@brownmackie.edu; http://www.brownmackie.edu/Miami.

Faculty

There are 15 full-time and more than 70 adjunct faculty members at the College. The average student-faculty ratio is 15:1.

Facilities and Resources

Brown Mackie College — Miami main campus is conveniently located at 3700 Lakeside Drive, Miramar, Florida. The College occupies more than 40,000 square feet on the first, second, and third floors of the Space Coast building, which is located in central Miramar.

The two nursing labs, as well as multiple computer classrooms, offer students a modern and professional environment for study. A medical assisting lab is used to instruct clinical medical skills. The College offers a computer networking lab as well as biomedical equipment technology lab for hands-on use and repair of equipment. The facility offers an equipped criminal justice lab including a crime scene and computers with facial recognition software. Each student has access to the technology, tools, and facilities needed to complete projects in each subject area. Students are welcome to use the labs when they are not being used for scheduled classes.

The College features a comfortable student lounge as well as a College store offering retail items including iPad accessories, kits specific to programs of study, and college apparel. The onsite library offers multimedia resources including laptop and iPad stations, power towers for convenient connectivity, books, and electronic resources specific to all academic programs offered.

The College offers an additional academic location in downtown Miami on the fifth and sixth floors of the Bayfront Plaza building. This location offers a number of computer classrooms as well as a criminal justice lab with a crime scene and facial recognition software. The downtown location also has an on-site library including laptop and iPad stations, books, and a wealth of electronic resources specific to all academic programs offered. Course delivery at both Brown Mackie College – Miami locations includes on-ground as well as blended courses.

Brown Mackie College — Miami is fully committed to using eTextbooks and computer tablets in the classroom. Utilizing these tablets to access expanded course material, students are able to increase their acumen for using this technology and further enhance their educational experience. Students have the ability to directly download their eTextbooks to their tablet, eliminating the need to carry heavy, physical textbooks and reducing the overall cost of supplies.

The College is a nonresidential, smoke-free institution.

Location

Brown Mackie College — Miami has its main campus in Miramar, Florida in Broward County. Here, the College occupies space on the first, second, and third floors within the newly renovated Space Coast Building. Brown Mackie College — Miami maintains a presence in the downtown Miami area through an additional location on the fifth and sixth floors of the Bayfront Plaza Building at 100 South Biscayne Boulevard, Miami. Both locations provide access to several transportation options including private shuttle, Metro Mover City Bus, and Florida's regional Tri-Rail system. Ample parking is also available at no cost to students.

Admission Requirements

Each applicant for admission is assigned an assistant director of admissions who directs the applicant through the steps of the admissions process; provides information on curriculum, policies, procedures, and services; and assists the applicant in setting necessary appointments and interviews.

To be considered for admission to Brown Mackie College, a candidate must be a high school graduate or hold a General Education Development (GED) certificate. As part of the admissions process applicants must sign a document attesting to graduation or completion and containing the information to obtain verification of such. Official high school transcripts or official documentation of high school graduation equivalency must be obtained within the first financial aid payment period or the student will be withdrawn from the institution following established guidelines for withdrawn students noted in the catalog. Title IV aid will not be dispersed until verification of graduation or completion has been received by the College.

Where applicable, students seeking entry into the College with a high school diploma completed in a foreign country must provide an original U.S.–equivalency evaluation from an evaluating agency which is a member of the National Association of Credential Evaluation Services (NACES, http://www.naces.org/) or the Association of International Credential Evaluators, Inc. (AICES, http://www.aice-eval.org/). The cost of evaluating the foreign transcript is borne by the applicant.

Admission to the College is based upon the applicant meeting the school's admission requirements, a review of the applicant's previous educational records, and a review of the applicant's career interests. It is the responsibility of the applicant to ensure that the College receives all required documentation.

Prior to admission, students are given an assessment of academic skills, commonly referred to as the academic readiness evaluation. Though the results of this assessment do not determine eligibility for admission, they provide the College with a means of determining the need for academic support through transitional studies courses and academic advisement, as well as a means by which the College can evaluate the effectiveness of its educational programs.

An applicant must obtain a minimum score of 60 in writing and 51 in mathematics on the COMPASS student academic readiness assessment. If a student does not achieve these scores, he/she will be enrolled in the appropriate transitional studies course(s).

In addition to the general admission requirements above, some programs have additional requirements specific to the program. For information on those, and other school-specific requirements, please visit the school's website or contact the school's Admissions department; phone: 330-869-3600; e-mail: bmcmiweb@brownmackie.edu; http://www.brownmackie.edu/Miami.

Application and Information

Applicants must complete and submit an application form, along with documentation of graduation from an accredited high school or state-approved secondary education curriculum or official documentation of high school graduation equivalency.

Specific details regarding program duration, tuition, fees and other costs, median debt, federal salary data, alumni success, programmatic accreditation, and other important information is available online at BMCprograms.info.

Brown Mackie College — Miami is one of over 25 school locations of the Brown Mackie College system of schools. Programs, credential levels, technology, and scheduling options are subject to change. ©2014 Brown Mackie College.

For additional information, prospective students should contact:

Director of Admissions
Brown Mackie College — Miami
3700 Lakeside Drive
Miramar, Florida 33027-3264
Phone: 305-341-6600
        866-505-0335 (toll-free)
Fax: 305-373-8814
E-mail: bmcmiweb@brownmackie.edu
Website: http://www.brownmackie.edu/Miami

BROWN MACKIE COLLEGE — NORTH CANTON

CANTON, OHIO

BROWN MACKIE COLLEGE®
NORTH CANTON

The College and Its Mission

Brown Mackie College — North Canton (Brown Mackie College) one of over twenty-five locations in the Brown Mackie College system of schools (www.brownmackie.edu), which is dedicated to providing educational programs that prepare students to pursue entry-level positions in a competitive, rapidly changing workplace. Brown Mackie College schools offer bachelor's degree, associate degree, diploma, and certificate programs in health sciences, business, information technology, legal studies, and design to thousands of students in the Midwest, Southeast, Southwest, and Western United States.

The College opened in the 1980s as the National Electronics Institute. In 2002, the Southern Ohio College took ownership. The following year it became part of the Brown Mackie College family of schools.

Brown Mackie College — North Canton is accredited by the Accrediting Council for Independent Colleges and Schools to award associate degrees and diplomas. The Accrediting Council for Independent Colleges and Schools is listed as a nationally recognized accrediting agency by the United States Department of Education and is recognized by the Council for Higher Education Accreditation. ACICS can be contacted at 750 First Street NE, Suite 980, Washington, D.C. 20002; phone: 202-336-6780.

Brown Mackie College — North Canton is licensed by the Ohio State Board of Career Colleges and Schools, 30 East Broad Street, 24th Floor, Suite 2481, Columbus, Ohio 43215-3138; phone: 614-466-2752. Ohio registration #03-09-1688T.

The Associate of Science in medical assisting program is accredited by the Accrediting Bureau of Health Education Schools.

The Associate of Science in surgical technology is accredited by the Commission on Accreditation of Allied Health Education Programs (www.caahep.org) upon the recommendation of the Accreditation Review Committee on Education in Surgical Technology. The Commission on Accreditation of Allied Health Education Programs can be contacted at 1361 Park Street, Clearwater, Florida 33756; phone: 727-210-2350.

The Brown Mackie College — North Canton Associate of Applied Science in surgical technology program is accredited by the Accrediting Bureau of Health Education Schools, ABHES.

The veterinary technology program at Brown Mackie College — North Canton has provisional programmatic accreditation granted by the American Veterinary Medical Association (AVMA) through the Committee on Veterinary Technician Education and Activities (CVTEA), 1931 North Meacham Road, Suite 100, Schaumburg, Illinois 60173; phone: 800-248-2862; www.avma.org.

Academic Programs

Brown Mackie College — North Canton provides higher education to traditional and nontraditional students through associate degree and diploma programs that can assist students in enhancing their career opportunities, broadening their perspectives through appropriate general education courses, thinking independently and critically, and improving problem-solving abilities. The College strives to develop within its students the desire for lifelong and continued education.

Each College quarter comprises twelve weeks. Associate degree programs require a minimum of eight quarters to complete.

Programs are offered on a year-round basis, providing students with the ability to work uninterrupted toward their degrees. The College offers all programs in a unique One Course a Month format. This schedule allows students to focus studies on only one course for four weeks and has proven convenient for students with multiple obligations such as jobs and family.

Associate Degree Programs: The Associate of Applied Business degree is awarded in accounting technology, business management, criminal justice, and paralegal.

The Associate of Applied Science degree is awarded in health care administration, surgical technology, and veterinary technology.

Diploma Programs: The College also offers diploma programs in medical assistant and practical nursing.

The American Medical Technologists (AMT), which offers the certification for Registered Medical Assistant (RMA), accepts the accreditation of Brown Mackie College — North Canton. Students will qualify to take the Registered Medical Assistant certification examination upon graduating the Brown Mackie College — North Canton medical assistant program. Graduates of the 48-credit-hour medical assistant program are not qualified to take the AMT/RMA exam. Information on application procedures can be found at http://americanmedtech. org/SchoolsStudents/CertificationProcess.aspx.

Brown Mackie College — North Canton does not guarantee third-party certification. Outside agencies control the requirements for certifications and are subject to change without notice to Brown Mackie College.

Program availability and degree offerings are subject to change.

Costs

Tuition for the 2013–14 academic year was $314 per credit hour and $20 per credit hour for general fees. The tuition for the surgical technology program was $360 per credit hour and $20 per credit hour for general fees. The tuition for the practical nursing program was $381 per credit hour and $30 per credit hour for general fees. The cost of textbooks, if applicable, and other instructional materials varies by program.

Financial Aid

The College maintains a full-time staff of financial aid professionals to assist qualified students in obtaining the financial assistance they require to meet their education expenses. Financial aid is available to those students who qualify.

Available resources may include federal grants and loans, state aid, student loans from private lenders, and federal work-study opportunities, both on and off College premises. Federal assistance programs are administered through the U.S. Department of Education, Office of Student Financial Assistance. Any U.S. citizen, national, or person in the United States for other than temporary reasons who is enrolled or accepted for enrollment may apply for these programs. Most forms of financial assistance are available for each July 1– June 30 award period.

Every student considering application for financial aid should request a copy of the current Student Guide, published by the U.S. Department of Education. This important document may be obtained in the Student Financial Services Office and will assist persons in understanding eligibility requirements, the application process, deadlines, and the various forms of grants and loans available.

For details on school-specific loans and scholarships, visit the school's website or contact the school's Student Financial Services Department; phone: 330-494-1214; e-mail: bmcncadm@ brownmackie.edu; http://www.brownmackie.edu/North-Canton.

Faculty

There are approximately 35 full-time and approximately 45 part-time faculty members. The average student-faculty ratio is approximately 14:1. Each student has a faculty and student adviser.

Facilities and Resources

The College comprises administrative offices, faculty and student lounges, a reception area, and spacious classrooms and laboratories. Instructional equipment includes personal computers, LANs, printers, and LCD projectors. The library provides support for the academic programs through volumes covering a broad range of subjects, as well as through Internet access. Vehicle parking is provided for both students and staff members.

Brown Mackie College —North Canton is fully committed to using eTextbooks and computer tablets in the classroom. Utilizing these tablets to access expanded course material, students are able to increase their acumen for using this technology and further enhance their educational experience. Students have the ability to directly download their eTextbooks to their tablet, eliminating the need to carry heavy, physical textbooks and reducing the overall cost of supplies.

Location

Brown Mackie College—North Canton is located at 4300 Munson Street, NW in Canton, Ohio. The school is easily accessible from I-77 and Route 687 and by the SARTA bus line.

Admission Requirements

Each applicant for admission is assigned an assistant director of admissions who directs the applicant through the steps of the admissions process; provides information on curriculum, policies, procedures, and services; and assists the applicant in setting necessary appointments and interviews.

To be considered for admission to Brown Mackie College, a candidate must be a high school graduate or hold a General Education Development (GED) certificate. As part of the admissions process applicants must sign a document attesting to graduation or completion and containing the information to obtain verification of such. Official high school transcripts or official documentation of high school graduation equivalency must be obtained within the first financial aid payment period or the student will be withdrawn from the institution following established guidelines for withdrawn students noted in the catalog. Title IV aid will not be dispersed until verification of graduation or completion has been received by the College.

Where applicable, students seeking entry into the College with a high school diploma completed in a foreign country must provide an original U.S.–equivalency evaluation from an evaluating agency which is a member of the National Association of Credential Evaluation Services (NACES, http://www.naces.org/) or the Association of International Credential Evaluators, Inc. (AICES, http://www.aice-eval.org/). The cost of evaluating the foreign transcript is borne by the applicant.

Admission to the College is based upon the applicant meeting the school's admissions requirements, a review of the applicant's previous educational records, and a review of the applicant's career interests. It is the responsibility of the applicant to ensure that the College receives all required documentation.

Prior to admission, students are given an assessment of academic skills, commonly referred to as the academic readiness evaluation. Though the results of this assessment do not determine eligibility for admission, they provide the College with a means of determining the need for academic support through transitional studies courses and academic advisement, as well as a means by which the College can evaluate the effectiveness of its educational programs.

An applicant must obtain a minimum score of 60 in writing and 51 in mathematics on the COMPASS student academic readiness assessment. If a student does not achieve these scores, he/she will be enrolled in the appropriate transitional studies course(s).

In addition to the general admission requirements above, some programs have additional requirements specific to the program. For information on those, and other school-specific requirements, please visit the school's website or contact the school's Admissions department; phone: 330-494-1214; e-mail: bmcncadm@brownmackie.edu; http://www.brownmackie.edu/North-Canton.

Application and Information

Applicants must complete and submit an application form, along with documentation of graduation from an accredited high school or state-approved secondary education curriculum or official documentation of high school graduation equivalency.

Specific details regarding program duration, tuition, fees and other costs, median debt, federal salary data, alumni success, programmatic accreditation, and other important information is available online at BMCprograms.info.

Brown Mackie College — North Canton is one of over 25 school locations of the Brown Mackie College system of schools. Programs, credential levels, technology, and scheduling options are subject to change. ©2014 Brown Mackie College.

For additional information, prospective students should contact:
Director of Admissions
Brown Mackie College — North Canton
4300 Munson Street NW
Canton, Ohio 44718-3674
Phone: 330-494-1214
Fax: 330-494-8112
E-mail: bmcncadm@brownmackie.edu
Website: http://www.brownmackie.edu/North-Canton

BROWN MACKIE COLLEGE — NORTHERN KENTUCKY
FORT MITCHELL, KENTUCKY

The College and Its Mission

Brown Mackie College — Northern Kentucky (Brown Mackie College) is one of over twenty-five locations in the Brown Mackie College system of schools (www.brownmackie.edu), which is dedicated to providing educational programs that prepare students to pursue entry-level positions in a competitive, rapidly changing workplace. The Brown Mackie College schools offer bachelor's degree, associate degree, diploma, and certificate programs in health sciences, business, information technology, legal studies, and design to thousands of students in the Midwest, Southeast, Southwest, and Western United States.

The College was founded in Cincinnati, Ohio, in February 1927 as a traditional business college. In May 1981, the College opened a branch location in northern Kentucky, which moved in 1986 to its current location in Fort Mitchell.

Brown Mackie College — Northern Kentucky is accredited by the Accrediting Council for Independent Colleges and Schools to award associate degrees and diplomas. The Accrediting Council for Independent Colleges and Schools is listed as a nationally recognized accrediting agency by the United States Department of Education and is recognized by the Council for Higher Education Accreditation. ACICS can be contacted at 750 First Street NE, Suite 980, Washington, D.C. 20002; phone: 202-336-6780.

Brown Mackie College — Northern Kentucky is authorized by the Indiana Board for Proprietary Education, 101 West Ohio Street, Suite 670, Indianapolis, Indiana 46204-1984; phone: 317-464-4400 Ext. 138, 141.

Brown Mackie College — Northern Kentucky is licensed by the Kentucky Council on Postsecondary Education, located at 1024 Capital Center Drive, Suite 320, Frankfort, Kentucky 40601.

Brown Mackie College — Northern Kentucky is licensed by the Ohio State Board of Career Colleges and Schools, located at 30 East Broad Street, 24th Floor, Suite 2481, Columbus, Ohio 43215-3138; phone: 614-466-2752. Ohio registration # 06-03-1781T.

The occupational therapy assistant program is accredited by the Accreditation Council for Occupational Therapy Education (ACOTE) of the American Occupational Therapy Association (AOTA), located at 4720 Montgomery Lane, P.O. Box 31220, Bethesda, Maryland 20824-1220; phone: 301-652-AOTA. Graduates of the program will be eligible to sit for the national certification examination for the occupational therapy assistant administered by the National Board for Certification in Occupational Therapy (NBCOT). After successful completion of this exam, the individual will be a Certified Occupational Therapy Assistant (COTA). In addition, most states require licensure in order to practice; however, state licenses are usually based on the results of the NBCOT Certification Examination. Note that a felony conviction may affect a graduate's ability to sit for the NBCOT certification examination or attain state licensure.

The surgical technology program is accredited by the Commission on Accreditation of Allied Health Education Programs (www.caahep.org) upon the recommendation of the Accreditation Review Council on Education in Surgical Technology and Surgical Assisting (ARC/STSA).

The Kentucky Board of Nursing has granted conditional approval status for the prelicensure of the practical nursing diploma program at Brown Mackie College — Northern Kentucky. A factor in the decision was based on the graduates' first-time NCLEX pass rate of 91 percent.

Academic Programs

Brown Mackie College — Northern Kentucky provides higher education to traditional and nontraditional students through associate degree, and diploma programs that assist them in enhancing their career opportunities, broadening their perspectives through appropriate general education courses, thinking independently and critically, and improving problem-solving abilities. The College strives to develop within its students the desire for lifelong and continued education.

Each College quarter comprises ten to twelve weeks. Associate degree programs require a minimum of eight quarters to complete. Programs are offered on a year-round basis, providing students with the ability to work uninterrupted toward their degrees. The College offers all programs in a unique One Course a Month format. This allows students to focus studies on only one course for four weeks. This schedule has proven convenient for students with multiple obligations such as jobs and family.

Associate Degree Programs: The Associate of Applied Business degree is awarded in business management, criminal justice, health care administration, and information technology.

The Associate of Applied Science degree is awarded in occupational therapy assistant.

Diploma Programs: The College offers diploma programs in business, dental assistant, medical assistant, and practical nursing.

The American Medical Technologists (AMT), which offers the certification for Registered Medical Assistant (RMA), accepts the accreditation of Brown Mackie College — Northern Kentucky. Students will qualify to take the RMA certification examination upon graduating the Brown Mackie College — Northern Kentucky medical assisting and medical assistant programs. Graduates of the 48 credit-hour medical assistant program are not qualified to take the AMT/RMA exam. Information on application procedures can be found at http://americanmedtech.org/SchoolsStudents/CertificationProcess.aspx.

Brown Mackie College — Northern Kentucky does not guarantee third-party certification. Outside agencies control the requirements for certifications and are subject to change without notice to Brown Mackie College.

Program availability and degree offerings are subject to change.

Costs

Tuition for the 2013–14 academic year was $314 per credit hour and general fees were $20 per credit hour, with some exceptions. The practical nursing program tuition was $381 per credit hour and general fees were $30 per credit hour. Tuition for the occupational therapy assistant program was $381 per credit hour and general fees were $20 per credit hour. The cost of textbooks, if applicable, and other instructional materials varies by program.

Financial Aid

The College maintains a full-time staff of financial aid professionals to assist qualified students in obtaining the financial assistance they require to meet their education expenses. Financial aid is available to those students who qualify.

Available resources may include federal grants and loans, state aid, student loans from private lenders, and federal work-study opportunities, both on and off College premises. Federal assistance programs are administered through the U.S. Department of Education, Office of Student Financial Assistance. Any U.S. citizen, national, or person in the United States for other than temporary reasons who is enrolled or accepted for enrollment may apply for these programs. Most forms of financial assistance are available for each July 1–June 30 award period.

Every student considering application for financial aid should request a copy of the current Student Guide, published by the U.S. Department of Education. This important document may be obtained in the Student Financial Services Office and will assist persons in understanding eligibility requirements, the application process, deadlines, and the various forms of grants and loans available.

For details on school-specific loans and scholarships, prospective students should visit the school's website or contact the school's Student Financial Services Department; phone: 859-341-5627; e-mail: bmcfmweb@brownmackie.edu; http://www.brownmackie.edu/NorthernKentucky.

Faculty

There are 12 full-time and 30 adjunct faculty members. The student-faculty ratio is 12:1.

Facilities and Resources

Brown Mackie College offers media presentation rooms for special instructional needs and a library that provides instructional resources and academic support for both faculty members and students.

Brown Mackie College — Northern Kentucky is fully committed to using eTextbooks and computer tablets in the classroom. Utilizing these tablets to access expanded course material, students are able to increase their acumen for using this technology and further enhance their educational experience. Students have the ability to directly download their eTextbooks to their tablet, eliminating the need to carry heavy, physical textbooks and reducing the overall cost of supplies.

The College is nonresidential; public transportation and ample parking at no cost are available. The campus is a smoke-free facility.

Location

Brown Mackie College — Northern Kentucky is conveniently located at 309 Buttermilk Pike in Fort Mitchell, Kentucky.

Admission Requirements

Each applicant for admission is assigned an assistant director of admissions who directs the applicant through the steps of the admissions process; provides information on curriculum, policies, procedures, and services; and assists the applicant in setting necessary appointments and interviews.

To be considered for admission to Brown Mackie College, a candidate must be a high school graduate or hold a General Education Development (GED) Certificate. As part of the admissions process applicants must sign a document attesting to graduation or completion and containing the information to obtain verification of such. Official high school transcripts or official documentation of high school graduation equivalency must be obtained within the first financial aid payment period or the student will be withdrawn from the institution following established guidelines for withdrawn students noted in the catalog. Title IV aid will not be dispersed until verification of graduation or completion has been received by the College.

Where applicable, students seeking entry into the College with a high school diploma completed in a foreign country must provide an original U.S.–equivalency evaluation from an evaluating agency which is a member of the National Association of Credential Evaluation Services (NACES, http://www.naces.org/) or the Association of International Credential Evaluators, Inc. (AICES, http://www.aice-eval.org/). The cost of evaluating the foreign transcript is borne by the applicant.

Admission to the College is based upon the applicant meeting the school's admissions requirements, a review of the applicant's previous educational records, and a review of the applicant's career interests. It is the responsibility of the applicant to ensure that the College receives all required documentation.

Prior to admission, students are given an assessment of academic skills, commonly referred to as the academic readiness evaluation. Though the results of this assessment do not determine eligibility for admission, they provide the College with a means of determining the need for academic support through transitional studies courses and academic advisement, as well as a means by which the College can evaluate the effectiveness of its educational programs.

An applicant must obtain a minimum score of 60 in writing and 51 in mathematics on the COMPASS student academic readiness assessment. If a student does not achieve these scores, he/she will be enrolled in the appropriate transitional studies course(s).

In addition to the general admissions requirements above, some programs have additional requirements specific to the program. For information on those, and other school-specific requirements, please contact the school's admissions department: phone: 859-341-5627; e-mail: bmcfmweb@brownmackie.edu; or visit the school's website at http://www.brownmackie.edu/NorthernKentucky.

Application and Information

Applicants must complete and submit an application form, along with documentation of graduation from an accredited high school or state-approved secondary education curriculum or official documentation of high school graduation equivalency.

See bmcprograms.info for program duration; tuition, fees, and other costs; median debt; federal salary data; alumni success; and other important information.

Brown Mackie College — Northern Kentucky is one of over 25 school locations of the Brown Mackie College system of schools. Programs, credential levels, technology, and scheduling options are subject to change. ©2014 Brown Mackie College.

For additional information, prospective students should contact:
Director of Admissions
Brown Mackie College — Northern Kentucky
309 Buttermilk Pike
Fort Mitchell, Kentucky 41017
Phone: 859-341-5627
    800-888-1445 (toll-free)
Fax: 859-341-6483
E-mail: bmcfmweb@brownmackie.edu
Website: http://www.brownmackie.edu/NorthernKentucky

BROWN MACKIE COLLEGE — OKLAHOMA CITY

OKLAHOMA CITY, OKLAHOMA

BROWN MACKIE COLLEGE®
OKLAHOMA CITY

The College and Its Mission

Brown Mackie College — Oklahoma City (Brown Mackie College) is one of over twenty-five locations in the Brown Mackie College system of schools (www.brownmackie.edu), which is dedicated to providing educational programs that prepare students to pursue entry-level positions in a competitive, rapidly changing workplace. Brown Mackie College schools offer bachelor's degree, associate degree, certificate, and diploma programs in health sciences, business, information technology, legal studies, and design to thousands of students in the Midwest, Southeast, Southwest, and Western United States.

Brown Mackie College — Oklahoma City is a branch campus of Brown Mackie College — Salina which is accredited by the Higher Learning Commission and a member of the North Central Association, 230 South LaSalle Street, Suite 7-500, Chicago, Illinois 60604-1413; phone: 800-621-7440 (toll-free); www.ncahlc.org.

This institution has been granted authority to operate in Oklahoma by the Oklahoma State Regents for Higher Education (OSRHE), 655 Research Parkway, Suite 200, Oklahoma City, Oklahoma 73101; phone: 405-225-9100.

The Associate of Applied Science in occupational therapy assistant program has applied for accreditation to the Accreditation Council for Occupational Therapy Education (ACOTE) of the American Occupational Therapy Association (AOTA), located at 4720 Montgomery Lane, Suite 200, Bethesda, Maryland 20814-3449; phone: 301-652-AOTA. Graduates of the program will be eligible to sit for the national certification examination for the occupational therapy assistant administered by the National Board for Certification in Occupational Therapy (NBCOT). After successful completion of this exam, the individual will be a Certified Occupational Therapy Assistant (COTA). In addition, most states require licensure in order to practice; however, state licenses are usually based on the results of the NBCOT Certification Examination. Note that a felony conviction may affect a graduate's ability to sit for the NBCOT certification examination or attain state licensure.

Academic Programs

Brown Mackie College — Oklahoma City provides higher education to traditional and nontraditional students through associate degree programs that can assist students in enhancing their career opportunities, broadening their perspectives through appropriate general education courses, thinking independently and critically, and improving problem-solving abilities. Brown Mackie College strives to develop within its students the desire for lifelong and continued education.

Each College quarter comprises twelve weeks. Associate degree programs require a minimum of eight quarters to complete. Programs are offered on a year-round basis, providing students with the ability to work uninterrupted toward their degrees. Brown Mackie College offers all programs in a unique One Course a Month format. This schedule allows students to focus studies on only one course for four weeks and has proven convenient for students with multiple obligations such as jobs and family.

Associate Degree Programs: The Associate of Applied Science degree is awarded in biomedical equipment technology, business management, health care administration, medical assisting, nursing, occupational therapy assistant, and paralegal.

The American Medical Technologists (AMT), which offers the certification for Registered Medical Assistant (RMA), accepts the accreditation of Brown Mackie College — Oklahoma City. Students will qualify to take the Registered Medical Assistant certification examination upon graduating the Brown Mackie College — Oklahoma City medical assisting program. Information on application procedures can be found online at http://americanmedtech.org/SchoolsStudents/CertificationProcess.aspx.

Brown Mackie College does not guarantee third-party certification/licensing exams. Outside agencies control the requirements for certification/licensing and are subject to change without notification to the College.

Program availability and degree offerings are subject to change.

Costs

Tuition for the 2013–14 academic year was $314 per credit hour, and $20 per credit hour for general fees. Tuition for the occupational therapy assistant program was $381 per credit hour, and $20 per credit hour for general fees. Tuition for the nursing program was $381 per credit hour, and $30 per credit hour for general fees. The cost of textbooks, if applicable, and other instructional materials varies by program.

Financial Aid

The College maintains a full-time staff of financial aid professionals to assist qualified students in obtaining the financial assistance they require to meet their education expenses. Financial aid is available to those students who qualify.

Available resources may include federal grants and loans, state aid, student loans from private lenders, and federal work-study opportunities, both on and off College premises. Federal assistance programs are administered through the U.S. Department of Education, Office of Student Financial Assistance. Any U.S. citizen, national, or person in the United States for other than temporary reasons who is enrolled or accepted for enrollment may apply for these programs. Most forms of financial assistance are available for each July 1–June 30 award period.

Every student considering application for financial aid should request a copy of the current Student Guide, published by the U.S. Department of Education. This important document may be obtained in the Student Financial Services Office and will assist persons in understanding eligibility requirements, the application process, deadlines, and the various forms of grants and loans available.

For details on school-specific loans and scholarships, visit the school's website or contact the school's Student Financial Services Department; phone: 405-621-8000; e-mail: bmokcadm@brownmackie.edu; http://www.brownmackie.edu/Oklahoma-City.

Faculty

Brown Mackie College — Oklahoma City has 11 full-time and 30 regular adjunct faculty members, with an average student-faculty ratio of 15:1.

Facilities and Resources

Brown Mackie College — Oklahoma City comprises administrative offices, faculty and student lounges, a reception area, and spacious classrooms and laboratories. Instructional equipment includes personal computers, LANs, printers, and transcribers. The library provides support for the academic programs through volumes covering a broad range of subjects, as well as through Internet access. Vehicle parking is provided for both students and staff members.

Brown Mackie College — Oklahoma City is fully committed to using eTextbooks and computer tablets in the classroom. Utilizing these tablets to access expanded course material, students are able to increase their acumen for using this technology and further enhance their educational experience. Students have the ability to directly download their eTextbooks to their tablet, eliminating the need to carry heavy, physical textbooks and reducing the overall cost of supplies.

The College is nonresidential; public transportation and ample parking at no cost are available. The school is a smoke-free facility.

Location

Brown Mackie College — Oklahoma City is located at 7101 Northwest Expressway, Suite 800, in Oklahoma City, Oklahoma.

Admission Requirements

Each applicant for admission is assigned an assistant director of admissions who directs the applicant through the steps of the admissions process; provides information on curriculum, policies, procedures, and services; and assists the applicant in setting necessary appointments and interviews.

To be considered for admission to Brown Mackie College, a candidate must be a high school graduate or hold a General Education Development (GED) certificate. As part of the admissions process applicants must sign a document attesting to graduation or completion and containing the information to obtain verification of such. Official high school transcripts or official documentation of high school graduation equivalency must be obtained within the first financial aid payment period or the student will be withdrawn from the institution following established guidelines for withdrawn students noted in the catalog. Title IV aid will not be dispersed until verification of graduation or completion has been received by the College.

Where applicable, students seeking entry into the College with a high school diploma completed in a foreign country must provide an original U.S.–equivalency evaluation from an evaluating agency which is a member of the National Association of Credential Evaluation Services (NACES, http://www.naces.org/) or the Association of International Credential Evaluators, Inc. (AICES, http://www.aice-eval.org/). The cost of evaluating the foreign transcript is borne by the applicant.

Admission to the College is based upon the applicant meeting the school's admission requirements, a review of the applicant's previous educational records, and a review of the applicant's career interests. It is the responsibility of the applicant to ensure that the College receives all required documentation.

Prior to admission, students are given an assessment of academic skills, commonly referred to as the academic readiness evaluation. Though the results of this assessment do not determine eligibility for admission, they provide the College with a means of determining the need for academic support through transitional studies courses and academic advisement, as well as a means by which the College can evaluate the effectiveness of its educational programs.

An applicant must obtain a minimum score of 60 in writing and 51 in mathematics on the COMPASS student academic readiness assessment. If a student does not achieve these scores, he/she will be enrolled in the appropriate transitional studies course(s).

In addition to the general admission requirements above, some programs have additional requirements specific to the program. For information on those, and other school-specific requirements, please visit the school's website or contact the school's admissions department; phone: 405-621-8000; e-mail: bmokcadm@brownmackie.edu; http://www.brownmackie.edu/Oklahoma-City.

Application and Information

Applicants must complete and submit an application form along with documentation of graduation from an accredited high school or state-approved secondary education curriculum, or applicants must provide official documentation of high school graduation equivalency.

Specific details regarding program duration; tuition, fees, and other costs; median debt; federal salary data; alumni success; programmatic accreditation; and other important information is available at BMCprograms.info.

Brown Mackie College—Oklahoma City is one of over 25 school locations of the Brown Mackie College system of schools. Programs, credential levels, technology, and scheduling options are subject to change. ©2014 Brown Mackie College.

For additional information, prospective students should contact:

Director of Admissions
Brown Mackie College — Oklahoma City
7101 Northwest Expressway, Suite 800
Oklahoma City, Oklahoma 73132
Phone: 405-621-8000
      888-229-3280 (toll-free)
Fax: 405-621-8055
E-mail: bmokcadm@brownmackie.edu
Website: http://www.brownmackie.edu/Oklahoma-City

BROWN MACKIE COLLEGE — PHOENIX
PHOENIX, ARIZONA

BROWN
MACKIE
COLLEGE®
PHOENIX

The College and Its Mission

Brown Mackie College — Phoenix (Brown Mackie College) is one of over twenty-five locations in the Brown Mackie College system of schools (www.brownmackie.edu), which is dedicated to providing educational programs that prepare students to pursue entry-level positions in a competitive, rapidly changing workplace. The Brown Mackie College schools offer bachelor's degree, associate degree, diploma, and certificate programs in health sciences, business, information technology, legal studies, and design to thousands of students in the Midwest, Southeast, Southwest, and Western United States.

Brown Mackie College — Phoenix was founded in 2009 as a branch of Brown Mackie College — Tucson, Arizona.

Brown Mackie College — Phoenix is accredited by the Accrediting Council for Independent Colleges and Schools to award associate degrees and diplomas. The Accrediting Council for Independent Colleges and Schools is listed as a nationally recognized accrediting agency by the United States Department of Education and is recognized by the Council for Higher Education Accreditation. ACICS can be contacted at 750 First Street NE, Suite 980, Washington, D.C. 20002; phone: 202-336-6780.

Brown Mackie College — Phoenix is authorized by the Arizona State Board for Private Postsecondary Education, 1400 West Washington Street, Room 2560, Phoenix, Arizona 85007; phone: 602-542-5709; http://azppse.state.az.us.

The occupational therapy assistant program is accredited by the Accreditation Council for Occupational Therapy Education (ACOTE) of the American Occupational Therapy Association (AOTA), located at 4720 Montgomery Lane, Suite 200, Bethesda, Maryland 20814-3449; phone: 301-652-AOTA. Graduates of the program will be eligible to sit for the national certification examination for the occupational therapy assistant administered by the National Board for Certification in Occupational Therapy (NBCOT). After successful completion of this exam, the individual will be a Certified Occupational Therapy Assistant (COTA). In addition, most states require licensure in order to practice; however, state licenses are usually based on the results of the NBCOT Certification Examination. Note that a felony conviction may affect a graduate's ability to sit for the NBCOT certification examination or attain state licensure.

The Brown Mackie College — Phoenix Associate of Science in surgical technology program is accredited by the Accrediting Bureau of Health Education Schools, ABHES.

Academic Programs

Brown Mackie College provides higher education to traditional and nontraditional students through associate degree and diploma programs that assist in enhancing their career opportunities, broadening their perspectives through appropriate general education courses, thinking independently and critically, and improving problem-solving abilities. The College strives to develop within its students the desire for lifelong and continued education.

Each College quarter comprises twelve weeks. Associate degree programs require a minimum of eight quarters to complete. Programs are offered on a year-round basis, providing students with the ability to work uninterrupted toward completion of their programs. The College offers all programs in a unique One Course a Month format. This allows students to focus studies on only one course for four weeks. This schedule has proven convenient for students with multiple obligations such as jobs and family.

Associate Degree Programs: The Associate of Science degree is awarded in business management, criminal justice, health care administration, paralegal, and surgical technology.

The Associate of Applied Science degree is awarded in biomedical equipment technology, nursing, and occupational therapy assistant.

Diploma Programs: Brown Mackie College — Phoenix offers diploma programs in biomedical equipment technician, bookkeeping specialist, general business, and medical assistant.

The American Medical Technologists (AMT), which offers the certification for Registered Medical Assistant (RMA), accepts the accreditation of Brown Mackie College — Phoenix. Students will qualify to take the RMA certification examination upon graduating the Brown Mackie College — Phoenix medical assisting and medical assistant programs. Graduates of the 48 credit-hour medical assistant program are not qualified to take the AMT/RMA exam. Information on application procedures can be found at http://americanmedtech.org/SchoolsStudents/CertificationProcess.aspx.

Brown Mackie College — Phoenix does not guarantee third-party certification. Outside agencies control the requirements for certifications and are subject to change without notice to Brown Mackie College.

Program availability and degree offerings are subject to change.

Costs

Tuition for programs in the 2013–14 academic year was $314 per credit hour, with a $20 per credit hour general fee applied to instructional costs for activities and services. For the surgical technology program, the tuition was $360 per credit hour with a $20 per credit hour general fee applied to instructional costs for activities. For the occupational therapy assistant program, the tuition was $381 per credit hour with a $20 per credit hour general fee applied to instructional costs for activities. For the nursing program, the tuition was $410 per credit hour with a $30 per credit hour general fee applied to instructional costs for activities. Textbooks, if applicable, and other instructional materials vary by program.

Financial Aid

The College maintains a full-time staff of financial aid professionals to assist qualified students in obtaining the financial assistance they require to meet their education expenses. Financial aid is available to those students who qualify.

Available resources may include federal grants and loans, state aid, student loans from private lenders, and federal work-study opportunities, both on and off College premises. Federal assistance programs are administered through the U.S. Department of Education, Office of Student Financial Assistance. Any U.S. citizen, national, or person in the United States for other than temporary reasons who is enrolled or accepted for enrollment may apply for these programs. Most forms of financial assistance are available for each July 1–June 30 award period.

Every student considering application for financial aid should request a copy of the current Student Guide, published by the U.S. Department of Education. This important document may be obtained in the Student Financial Services Office and will assist persons in understanding eligibility requirements, the application process, deadlines, and the various forms of grants and loans available.

For details on school-specific loans and scholarships, visit the school's website or contact the school's Student Financial

Services Department; phone: 602-337-3044; e-mail: bmcpxweb@brownmackie.edu; http://www.brownmackie.edu/Phoenix.

Faculty

Experienced faculty members provide academic support and are committed to the academic and technical preparation of their students. The College has both full- and part-time faculty members. The average student-faculty ratio is 14:1. Each student is assigned a program director as an adviser.

Facilities and Resources

Brown Mackie College — Phoenix has a variety of classrooms including computer labs housing the latest technology in the industry. High-speed access to the Internet and other online resources are available for students and faculty. Multimedia classrooms provide a learning environment equipped with overhead projectors, TVs, DVD/VCR players, computers, and sound systems.

Brown Mackie College — Phoenix is fully committed to using eTextbooks and computer tablets in the classroom. Utilizing these tablets to access expanded course material, students are able to increase their acumen for using this technology and further enhance their educational experience. Students have the ability to directly download their eTextbooks to their tablet, eliminating the need to carry heavy, physical textbooks and reducing the overall cost of supplies.

The College has a generous parking area and is easily accessible by public transportation. The College is a nonresidential, smoke-free institution.

Location

Brown Mackie College — Phoenix is conveniently located at 13430 North Black Canyon Highway, Suite 190, in Phoenix, Arizona.

Admission Requirements

Each applicant for admission is assigned an assistant director of admissions who directs the applicant through the steps of the admissions process; provides information on curriculum, policies, procedures, and services; and assists the applicant in setting necessary appointments and interviews.

To be considered for admission to Brown Mackie College, a candidate must be a high school graduate or hold a General Education Development (GED) certificate. As part of the admissions process applicants must sign a document attesting to graduation or completion and containing the information to obtain verification of such. Official high school transcripts or official documentation of high school graduation equivalency must be obtained within the first financial aid payment period or the student will be withdrawn from the institution following established guidelines for withdrawn students noted in the catalog. Title IV aid will not be dispersed until verification of graduation or completion has been received by the College.

Where applicable, students seeking entry into the College with a high school diploma completed in a foreign country must provide an original U.S.–equivalency evaluation from an evaluating agency which is a member of the National Association of Credential Evaluation Services (NACES, http://www.naces.org/) or the Association of International Credential Evaluators, Inc. (AICES, http://www.aice-eval.org/). The cost of evaluating the foreign transcript is borne by the applicant.

Admission to the College is based upon the applicant meeting the school's admission requirements, a review of the applicant's previous educational records, and a review of the applicant's career interests. It is the responsibility of the applicant to ensure that the College receives all required documentation.

Prior to admission, students are given an assessment of academic skills, commonly referred to as the academic readiness evaluation. Though the results of this assessment do not determine eligibility for admission, they provide the College with a means of determining the need for academic support through transitional studies courses and academic advisement, as well as a means by which the College can evaluate the effectiveness of its educational programs.

An applicant must obtain a minimum score of 60 in writing and 51 in mathematics on the COMPASS student academic readiness assessment. If a student does not achieve these scores, he/she will be enrolled in the appropriate transitional studies course(s).

In addition to the general admission requirements above, some programs have additional requirements specific to the program. For information on those, and other school-specific requirements, please visit the school's website or contact the school's admissions department; phone: 602-337-3044; e-mail: bmcpxweb@brownmackie.edu; http://www.brownmackie.edu/Phoenix.

Application and Information

Applicants must complete and submit an application form, along with documentation of graduation from an accredited high school or state-approved secondary education curriculum or official documentation of high school graduation equivalency.

See BMCprograms.info for program duration; tuition, fees, and other costs; median debt; federal salary data; alumni success; programmatic accreditation; and other important information.

Brown Mackie College — Phoenix is one of over 25 school locations of the Brown Mackie College system of schools. Programs, credential levels, technology, and scheduling options are subject to change. ©2014 Brown Mackie College.

For additional information, prospective students should contact:

Director of Admissions
Brown Mackie College — Phoenix
13430 North Black Canyon Highway, Suite 190
Phoenix, Arizona 85029
Phone: 602-337-3044
      866-824-4793 (toll-free)
Fax: 480-375-2450
E-mail: bmcpxweb@brownmackie.edu
Website: http://www.brownmackie.edu/Phoenix

BROWN MACKIE COLLEGE — QUAD CITIES
BETTENDORF, IOWA

The College and Its Mission

Brown Mackie College — Quad Cities (Brown Mackie College) is one of over twenty-five locations in the Brown Mackie College system of schools (www.brownmackie.edu), which is dedicated to providing educational programs that prepare students to pursue entry-level positions in a competitive, rapidly changing workplace. Brown Mackie College schools offer bachelor's degree, associate degree, certificate, and diploma programs in health sciences, business, information technology, legal studies, and design to thousands of students in the Midwest, Southeast, Southwest, and Western United States.

Founded in 1890 by A. N. Hirons as LaPorte Business College in LaPorte, Indiana, the institution later became known as Commonwealth Business College. In 1919, ownership was transferred to Grace and J. J. Moore, who successfully operated the College for almost thirty years. Following World War II, Harley and Stephanie Reese operated the College under the name of Reese School of Business for several decades.

In 1975, the College came under the ownership of Steven C. Smith as Commonwealth Business College. A second location, now known as Brown Mackie College — Merrillville, was opened in 1984 in Merrillville, Indiana, and a third location was opened a year later in Davenport, Iowa. In 1987, the Davenport site relocated to Moline, Illinois. In September 2003, the College changed ownership again and the name was changed to Brown Mackie College — Moline in November 2004. In 2010, the College moved to its current location in Bettendorf, Iowa, and changed its name to Brown Mackie College — Quad Cities.

Brown Mackie College — Quad Cities is accredited by the Accrediting Council for Independent Colleges and Schools (ACICS) to award associate degrees and diplomas. ACICS is listed as a nationally recognized accrediting agency by the United States Department of Education and is recognized by the Council for Higher Education Accreditation. ACICS can be contacted at 750 First Street NE, Suite 980, Washington, D.C. 20002; phone: 202-336-6780.

The occupational therapy assistant program is accredited by the Accreditation Council for Occupational Therapy Education (ACOTE) of the American Occupational Therapy Association (AOTA), located at 4720 Montgomery Lane, Suite 200, Bethesda, Maryland 20814-3449; phone: 301-652-AOTA. Graduates of the program will be eligible to sit for the national certification examination for the occupational therapy assistant administered by the National Board for Certification in Occupational Therapy (NBCOT). After successful completion of this exam, the individual will be a Certified Occupational Therapy Assistant (COTA). In addition, most states require licensure in order to practice; however, state licenses are usually based on the results of the NBCOT Certification Examination. Note that a felony conviction may affect a graduate's ability to sit for the NBCOT certification examination or attain state licensure.

Brown Mackie College — Quad Cities is approved and registered by the Iowa College Student Aid Commission (ICSAC) under the authority of Chapters 261 and 261B of the Iowa Code. ICSCA can be contacted at 200 10th Street, fourth floor, Des Moines, Iowa 50309-3609; phone: 877-272-4456 (toll-free); www.iowacollegeaid.gov.

Academic Programs

Brown Mackie College — Quad Cities provides higher education to traditional and nontraditional students through associate degree and diploma programs that can assist them in enhancing their career opportunities, broadening their perspectives through appropriate general education courses, thinking independently and critically, and improving problem-solving abilities. The College strives to develop within its students the desire for lifelong and continued education.

Each College quarter comprises twelve weeks. Programs are offered on a year-round basis, providing students with the ability to work uninterrupted toward the completion of their programs. Brown Mackie College offers all programs in a unique One Course a Month format. This schedule allows students to focus studies on only one course for four weeks and has proven convenient for students with multiple obligations such as jobs and family.

Associate Degree Programs: The Associate of Applied Science degree is awarded in business management, criminal justice, health care administration, information technology, occupational therapy assistant, and paralegal.

Diploma Programs: Brown Mackie College — Quad Cities offers a diploma program for medical assistant.

The American Medical Technologists (AMT), which offers the certification for Registered Medical Assistant (RMA), accepts the accreditation of Brown Mackie College — Quad Cities. Students will qualify to take the RMA certification examination upon graduating the Brown Mackie College — Quad Cities medical assistant program. Graduates of the 48 credit-hour medical assistant program are not qualified to take the AMT/RMA exam. Information on application procedures can be found at http://americanmedtech.org/SchoolsStudents/CertificationProcess.aspx.

Brown Mackie College — Quad Cities does not guarantee third-party certification. Outside agencies control the requirements for certifications and are subject to change without notice to Brown Mackie College.

Program availability and degree offerings are subject to change.

Costs

Tuition for the 2013–14 academic year was $314 per credit hour and $20 per credit hour for general fees. Tuition for the occupational therapy assistant program was $381 per credit hour and $20 per credit hour for general fees. Textbook costs, if applicable, vary by program.

Financial Aid

The College maintains a full-time staff of financial aid professionals to assist qualified students in obtaining the financial assistance they require to meet their education expenses. Financial aid is available to those students who qualify.

Available resources may include federal grants and loans, state aid, student loans from private lenders, and federal work-study opportunities, both on and off College premises. Federal assistance programs are administered through the U.S. Department of Education, Office of Student Financial Assistance. Any U.S. citizen, national, or person in the United States for other than temporary reasons who is enrolled or accepted for enrollment may apply for these programs. Most forms of financial assistance are available for each July 1–June 30 award period.

Every student considering application for financial aid should request a copy of the current Student Guide, published by the

U.S. Department of Education. This important document may be obtained in the Student Financial Services Office and will assist persons in understanding eligibility requirements, the application process, deadlines, and the various forms of grants and loans available.

Details on school-specific loans and scholarships are available on the school's website (http://www.brownmackie.edu/Quad-Cities) or prospective students can contact the school's Student Financial Services Department; phone: 563-344-1500; e-mail: bmcmoadm@brownmackie.edu.

Faculty

Brown Mackie College — Quad Cities has 5 full-time and 43 regular adjunct faculty members, with an average student-faculty ratio of 12:1.

Facilities and Resources

Brown Mackie College — Quad Cities maintains a library of curriculum-related resources. Technical and general education materials, academic and professional periodicals, and audiovisual resources are available to both students and faculty members. Students have borrowing privileges at several local libraries. Internet access is available for research.

Brown Mackie College — Quad Cities is fully committed to using eTextbooks and computer tablets in the classroom. Utilizing these tablets to access expanded course material, students are able to increase their acumen for using this technology and further enhance their educational experience. Students have the ability to directly download their eTextbooks to their tablet, eliminating the need to carry heavy, physical textbooks and reducing the overall cost of supplies.

The College is a nonresidential, smoke-free institution.

Location

Brown Mackie College — Quad Cities is located at 2119 East Kimberly Road in Bettendorf, Iowa. The College is easily accessible by public transportation, and ample parking is available at no cost.

Admission Requirements

Each applicant for admission is assigned an assistant director of admissions who directs the applicant through the steps of the admissions process; provides information on curriculum, policies, procedures, and services; and assists the applicant in setting necessary appointments and interviews.

To be considered for admission to Brown Mackie College, a candidate must be a high school graduate or hold a General Education Development (GED) certificate. As part of the admissions process, applicants must sign a document attesting to graduation or completion and containing the information to obtain verification of such. Official high school transcripts or official documentation of high school graduation equivalency must be obtained within the first financial aid payment period or the student will be withdrawn from the institution following established guidelines for withdrawn students noted in the catalog. Title IV aid will not be dispersed until verification of graduation or completion has been received by the College.

Where applicable, students seeking entry into the College with a high school diploma completed in a foreign country must provide an original U.S.–equivalency evaluation from an evaluating agency that is a member of the National Association of Credential Evaluation Services (NACES, http://www.naces.org/) or the Association of International Credential Evaluators, Inc. (AICES, http://www.aice-eval.org/). The cost of evaluating the foreign transcript is borne by the applicant.

Admission to the College is based upon the applicant meeting the school's admission requirements, a review of the applicant's previous educational records, and a review of the applicant's career interests. It is the responsibility of the applicant to ensure that the College receives all required documentation

Prior to admission, students are given an assessment of academic skills, commonly referred to as the academic readiness evaluation. Though the results of this assessment do not determine eligibility for admission, they provide the College with a means of determining the need for academic support through transitional studies courses and academic advisement, as well as a means by which the College can evaluate the effectiveness of its educational programs.

An applicant must obtain a minimum score of 60 in writing and 51 in mathematics on the COMPASS student academic readiness assessment. If a student does not achieve these scores, he/she will be enrolled in the appropriate transitional studies course(s).

In addition to the general admission requirements above, some programs have additional requirements specific to the program. For information on those, and other school-specific requirements, visit the school's website (http://www.brownmackie.edu/Quad-Cities) or contact the school's admissions department; phone: 563-344-1500; e-mail: bmcmoadm@brownmackie.edu.

Application and Information

Applicants must complete and submit an application form along with documentation of graduation from an accredited high school or state-approved secondary education curriculum or official documentation of high school graduation equivalency.

See BMCprograms.info for program duration, tuition, fees and other costs, median debt, federal salary data, alumni success, programmatic accreditation, and other important information.

Brown Mackie College—Quad Cities is one of over 25 school locations of the Brown Mackie College system of schools. Programs, credential levels, technology, and scheduling options are subject to change. ©2014 Brown Mackie College.

For further information, prospective students should contact:

Director of Admissions
Brown Mackie College — Quad Cities
2119 East Kimberly Road
Bettendorf, Iowa 52722
Phone: 563-344-1500
         888-420-1652 (toll-free)
Fax: 563-344-1501
E-mail: bmcmoadm@brownmackie.edu
Website: http://www.brownmackie.edu/Quad-Cities

BROWN MACKIE COLLEGE — ST. LOUIS
FENTON, MISSOURI

BROWN
MACKIE
COLLEGE®
ST. LOUIS

The College and Its Mission

Brown Mackie College — St. Louis (Brown Mackie College) is one of over twenty-five locations in the Brown Mackie College system of schools (www.brownmackie.edu), which is dedicated to providing educational programs that prepare students to pursue entry-level positions in a competitive, rapidly changing workplace. The Brown Mackie College schools offer bachelor's degree, associate degree, diploma, and certificate programs in health sciences, business, information technology, legal studies, and design to thousands of students in the Midwest, Southeast, Southwest, and Western United States.

Brown Mackie College was originally founded and approved by the Board of Trustees of Kansas Wesleyan College in Salina, Kansas on July 30, 1892. In 1938, the College was incorporated as The Brown Mackie School of Business under the ownership of Perry E. Brown and A. B. Mackie, former instructors at Kansas Wesleyan University in Salina, Kansas. Their last names formed the name of Brown Mackie. By January 1975, with improvements in curricula and higher degree-granting status, The Brown Mackie School of Business became Brown Mackie College.

Brown Mackie College — St. Louis is accredited by the Accrediting Council for Independent Colleges and Schools to award associate degrees and certificates. The Accrediting Council for Independent Colleges and Schools is listed as a nationally recognized accrediting agency by the United States Department of Education and is recognized by the Council for Higher Education Accreditation. ACICS can be contacted at 750 First Street NE, Suite 980, Washington, D.C. 20002; phone: 202-336-6780.

The Associate of Applied Science in occupational therapy assistant program is accredited by the Accreditation Council for Occupational Therapy Education (ACOTE) of the American Occupational Therapy Association (AOTA), located at 4720 Montgomery Lane, Suite 200, Bethesda, Maryland 20814-3449; phone: 301-652-AOTA. Graduates of the program will be eligible to sit for the national certification examination for the occupational therapy assistant administered by the National Board for Certification in Occupational Therapy (NBCOT). After successful completion of this exam, the individual will be a Certified Occupational Therapy Assistant (COTA). In addition, most states require licensure in order to practice; however, state licenses are usually based on the results of the NBCOT Certification Examination. Note that a felony conviction may affect a graduate's ability to sit for the NBCOT certification examination or attain state licensure.

The Brown Mackie College — St. Louis Associate of Applied Science in surgical technology program is accredited by the Accrediting Bureau of Health Education Schools, ABHES.

The Brown Mackie College — St. Louis Associate of Applied Science in surgical technology program is accredited by the Commission on Accreditation of Allied Health Education Programs (www.caahep.org) upon the recommendation of the Accreditation Review Committee on Education in Surgical Technology.

The veterinary technology program at Brown Mackie College — St. Louis has provisional programmatic accreditation granted by the American Veterinary Medical Association (AVMA) through the Committee on Veterinary Technician Education and Activities (CVTEA), 1931 North Meacham Road, Suite 100, Schaumburg, Illinois 60173; phone: 800-248-2862; www.avma.org.

Academic Programs

Brown Mackie College — St. Louis provides higher education to traditional and nontraditional students through associate degree programs that assist in enhancing their career opportunities, broadening their perspectives through appropriate general education courses, thinking independently and critically, and improving problem-solving abilities. The College strives to develop within its students the desire for lifelong and continued education.

Each College quarter comprises twelve weeks. Associate degree programs require a minimum of eight quarters to complete. Programs are offered on a year-round basis, providing students with the ability to work uninterrupted toward completion of their programs. The College offers all programs in a unique One Course a Month format. This allows students to focus studies on only one course for four weeks. This schedule has proven convenient for students with multiple obligations such as jobs and family.

Associate Degree Programs: The Associate of Applied Science degree is awarded in biomedical equipment technology, business management, criminal justice, health care administration, information technology, nursing, occupational therapy assistant, surgical technology, and veterinary technology.

Certificate Programs: The College offers certificate programs in biomedical equipment technician, business, and medical assistant.

The American Medical Technologists (AMT), which offers the certification for Registered Medical Assistant (RMA), accepts the accreditation of Brown Mackie College — St. Louis. Students will qualify to take the RMA certification examination upon graduating the Brown Mackie College — St. Louis medical assistant program. Graduates of the 48 credit-hour medical assistant program are not qualified to take the AMT/RMA exam. Information on application procedures can be found at http://americanmedtech.org/SchoolsStudents/CertificationProcess.aspx.

Brown Mackie College — St. Louis does not guarantee third party certification. Outside agencies control the requirements for certifications and are subject to change without notice to Brown Mackie College.

Program availability and degree offerings are subject to change.

Costs

Tuition in the 2013–14 academic year for most associate degree and diploma programs was $288 per credit hour; fees were $20 per credit hour. Tuition for the surgical technology program was $339 per credit hour; fees were $20 per credit hour. Tuition for the nursing program was $410 per credit hour; fees were $30 per credit hour. Tuition for the occupational therapy assistant program was $355 per credit hour; fees were $20 per credit hour. The cost of textbooks, if applicable, and other instructional materials varies by program.

Financial Aid

The College maintains a full-time staff of financial aid professionals to assist qualified students in obtaining the financial assistance they require to meet their education expenses. Financial aid is available to those students who qualify.

Available resources may include federal grants and loans, state aid, student loans from private lenders, and federal work-study opportunities, both on and off College premises. Federal assistance programs are administered through the U.S. Department of Education, Office of Student Financial Assistance. Any U.S. citizen, national, or person in the United States for other than temporary reasons who is enrolled or accepted for enrollment may apply for these programs. Most forms of financial assistance are available for each July 1–June 30 award period.

Every student considering application for financial aid should request a copy of the current Student Guide, published by the U.S. Department of Education. This important document may be obtained in the Student Financial Services Office and will assist persons in understanding eligibility requirements, the application process, deadlines, and the various forms of grants and loans available.

For details on school-specific loans and scholarships, visit the school's website or contact the school's Student Financial Services Department; phone: 636-651-3290; e-mail: _bmcstlweb@brownmackie.edu; http://www.brownmackie.edu/StLouis.

Faculty

Experienced faculty members provide academic support and are committed to the academic and technical preparation of their students. The College has 12 full-time and 23 part-time instructors, with a student-faculty ratio of 20:1.

Facilities and Resources

A modern facility, Brown Mackie College — St. Louis offers more than 30,000 square feet. The College is equipped with multiple computer labs, housing over 100 computers. High-speed access to the Internet and other online resources are available for students and faculty. Multimedia classrooms are outfitted with overhead projectors, VCR/DVD players, and computers.

Brown Mackie College — St. Louis is fully committed to using eTextbooks and computer tablets in the classroom. Utilizing these tablets to access expanded course material, students are able to increase their acumen for using this technology and further enhance their educational experience. Students have the ability to directly download their eTextbooks to their tablet, eliminating the need to carry heavy, physical textbooks and reducing the overall cost of supplies.

Brown Mackie College — St. Louis is nonresidential and is a smoke-free facility.

Location

Brown Mackie College — St. Louis is conveniently located at #2 Soccer Park Road in Fenton, Missouri. The College has a generous parking area available to students and staff.

Admission Requirements

Each applicant for admission is assigned an assistant director of admissions who directs the applicant through the steps of the admissions process; provides information on curriculum, policies, procedures, and services; and assists the applicant in setting necessary appointments and interviews.

To be considered for admission to Brown Mackie College, a candidate must be a high school graduate or hold a General Education Development (GED) certificate. As part of the admissions process applicants must sign a document attesting to graduation or completion and containing the information to obtain verification of such. Official high school transcripts or official documentation of high school graduation equivalency must be obtained within the first financial aid payment period or the student will be withdrawn from the institution following established guidelines for withdrawn students noted in the catalog. Title IV aid will not be dispersed until verification of graduation or completion has been received by the College.

Where applicable, students seeking entry into the College with a high school diploma completed in a foreign country must provide an original U.S.–equivalency evaluation from an evaluating agency which is a member of the National Association of Credential Evaluation Services (NACES, http://www.naces.org/) or the Association of International Credential Evaluators, Inc. (AICES, http://www.aice-eval.org/). The cost of evaluating the foreign transcript is borne by the applicant.

Admission to the College is based upon the applicant meeting the school's admission requirements, a review of the applicant's previous educational records, and a review of the applicant's career interests. It is the responsibility of the applicant to ensure that the College receives all required documentation.

Prior to admission, students are given an assessment of academic skills, commonly referred to as the academic readiness evaluation. Though the results of this assessment do not determine eligibility for admission, they provide the College with a means of determining the need for academic support through transitional studies courses and academic advisement, as well as a means by which the College can evaluate the effectiveness of its educational programs.

An applicant must obtain a minimum score of 60 in writing and 51 in mathematics on the COMPASS student academic readiness assessment. If a student does not achieve these scores, he/she will be enrolled in the appropriate transitional studies course(s).

In addition to the general admission requirements above, some programs have additional requirements specific to the program. For information on those, and other school-specific requirements, please visit the school's website or contact the school's admissions department; phone: 636-651-3290; e-mail: _bmcstlweb@brownmackie.edu; http://www.brownmackie.edu/StLouis.

Application and Information

Applicants must complete and submit an application form, along with documentation of graduation from an accredited high school or state-approved secondary education curriculum or official documentation of high school graduation equivalency.

Specific details regarding program duration; tuition, fees and other costs; median debt; federal salary data; alumni success; programmatic accreditation; and other important information are available online at BMCprograms.info.

Brown Mackie College — St. Louis is one of over 25 school locations of the Brown Mackie College system of schools. Programs, credential levels, technology, and scheduling options are subject to change. ©2014 Brown Mackie College.

For additional information, prospective students should contact:

Director of Admissions
Brown Mackie College — St. Louis
#2 Soccer Park Road
Fenton, Missouri 63026
Phone: 636-651-3290
        888-874-4375 (toll-free)
Fax: 636-651-3349
E-mail: _bmcstlweb@brownmackie.edu
Website: http://www.brownmackie.edu/StLouis

BROWN MACKIE COLLEGE — SALINA

SALINA, KANSAS

BROWN
MACKIE
COLLEGE®
SALINA

The College and Its Mission

Brown Mackie College — Salina (Brown Mackie College) is one of over twenty-five locations in the Brown Mackie College system of schools (www.brownmackie.edu), which is dedicated to providing educational programs that prepare students to pursue entry-level positions in a competitive, rapidly changing workplace. Brown Mackie College schools offer bachelor's degree, associate degree, certificate, and diploma programs in health sciences, business, information technology, legal studies, and design to thousands of students in the Midwest, Southeast, Southwest, and Western United States.

The College was originally founded in July 1892 as the Kansas Wesleyan School of Business. In 1938, the College was incorporated as the Brown Mackie School of Business under the ownership of former Kansas Wesleyan instructors Perry E. Brown and A. B. Mackie; it became Brown Mackie College in January 1975.

Brown Mackie College — Salina is accredited by the Higher Learning Commission and is a member of the North Central Association (NCA), 230 South LaSalle Street, Suite 7-500, Chicago, Illinois 60604-1413; phone 800-621-7440 (toll-free); www.ncahlc.org.

Brown Mackie College — Salina is approved and authorized to grant the Associate of Applied Science (A.A.S.) and Associate of General Studies (A.G.D.) degrees by the Kansas Board of Regents, 1000 Southwest Jackson Street, Suite 520, Topeka, Kansas 66612-1368.

The Associate of Applied Science in occupational therapy assistant program is accredited by the Accreditation Council for Occupational Therapy Education (ACOTE) of the American Occupational Therapy Association (AOTA), located at 4720 Montgomery Lane, Suite 200, Bethesda, Maryland 20814-3449; phone: 301-652-AOTA. Graduates of the program will be eligible to sit for the national certification examination for the occupational therapy assistant administered by the National Board for Certification in Occupational Therapy (NBCOT). After successful completion of this exam, the individual will be a Certified Occupational Therapy Assistant (COTA). In addition, most states require licensure in order to practice; however, state licenses are usually based on the results of the NBCOT Certification Examination. Note that a felony conviction may affect a graduate's ability to sit for the NBCOT certification examination or attain state licensure.

The veterinary technology program at Brown Mackie College — Salina has provisional programmatic accreditation granted by the American Veterinary Medical Association (AVMA) through the Committee on Veterinary Technician Education and Activities (CVTEA), 1931 North Meacham Road, Suite 100, Schaumburg, Illinois 60173; phone: 800-248-2862; www.avma.org.

Academic Programs

Brown Mackie College — Salina provides higher education to traditional and nontraditional students through associate degree, diploma, and certificate programs that can assist them in enhancing their career opportunities, broadening their perspectives through appropriate general education courses, thinking independently and critically, and improving problem-solving abilities. The College strives to develop within its students the desire for lifelong and continued education.

In most programs, students can participate in day or evening classes, which begin every month. Programs are offered on a year-round basis, providing students with the ability to work uninterrupted toward completion of their programs. Brown Mackie College offers all programs in a unique One Course a Month format. This schedule allows students to focus studies on only one course for four weeks and has proven convenient for students with multiple obligations such as jobs and family.

Associate Degree Programs: The Associate of Applied Science degree is awarded in business management, construction trades—welding, criminal justice, health care administration, medical assisting, nursing, occupational therapy assistant, and veterinary technology.

An Associate of General Studies degree is awarded in operational management. This program of study creates a greater level of flexibility for students who may be unsure of their career choice, who want a more generalized education, or who want to transfer to a baccalaureate program.

Diploma Programs: Brown Mackie College — Salina also offers diploma programs in general business, and medical assistant.

Certificate Programs: A certificate program is offered in practical nursing.

The American Medical Technologists (AMT), which offers the certification for Registered Medical Assistant (RMA), accepts the accreditation of Brown Mackie College — Salina. Students will qualify to take the RMA certification examination upon graduating the Brown Mackie College — Salina medical assisting and medical assistant programs. Graduates of the 48 credit-hour medical assistant program are not qualified to take the AMT/RMA exam. Information on application procedures can be found at: http://americanmedtech.org/SchoolsStudents/CertificationProcess.aspx.

Brown Mackie College does not guarantee third-party certification/licensing exams. Outside agencies control the requirements for certification/licensing and are subject to change without notification to the College.

Program availability and degree offerings are subject to change.

Costs

Tuition for the 2013–14 academic year was $314 per credit hour and general fees were $20 per credit hour. Tuition for the nursing programs was $381 per credit hour and general fees were $30 per credit hour. Tuition for the occupational therapy assistant program was $381 per credit hour and general fees were $20 per credit hour. The cost of textbooks, if applicable, and other instructional materials varies by program.

Financial Aid

The College maintains a full-time staff of financial aid professionals to assist qualified students in obtaining the financial assistance they require to meet their education expenses. Financial aid is available to those students who qualify.

Available resources may include federal grants and loans, state aid, student loans from private lenders, and federal work-study opportunities, both on and off College premises. Federal assistance programs are administered through the U.S. Department of Education, Office of Student Financial Assistance. Any U.S. citizen, national, or person in the United States for other than temporary reasons who is enrolled or accepted for enrollment may apply for these programs. Most forms of financial assistance are available for each July 1–June 30 award period.

Every student considering application for financial aid should request a copy of the current Student Guide, published by the U.S. Department of Education. This important document may be obtained in the Student Financial Services Office and will assist persons in understanding eligibility requirements, the application process, deadlines, and the various forms of grants and loans available.

For details on school-specific loans and scholarships, visit the school's website or contact the school's Student Financial Services Department; phone: 785-825-5422; e-mail: bmcsaadm@brownmackie.edu; http://www.brownmackie.edu/Salina.

Faculty

There are 21 full-time and 19 adjunct faculty members. The average student-instructor ratio is 15:1.

Facilities and Resources

In addition to classrooms and computer labs, Brown Mackie College — Salina maintains a library of curriculum-related resources, technical and general education materials, academic and professional periodicals, and audiovisual resources. Internet access is also available for research. The College has a bookstore that stocks texts, courseware, and other educational supplies that are required for courses and a variety of personal, recreational, and gift items, including apparel, supplies, and general merchandise incorporating the Brown Mackie College logo. Hours are posted at the bookstore entrance.

Brown Mackie College — Salina is fully committed to using eTextbooks and computer tablets in the classroom. Utilizing these tablets to access expanded course material, students are able to increase their acumen for using this technology and further enhance their educational experience. Students have the ability to directly download their eTextbooks to their tablet, eliminating the need to carry heavy, physical textbooks and reducing the overall cost of supplies.

Location

Brown Mackie College — Salina is located at 2106 South Ninth Street in Salina, Kansas. The Salina course location is located at 2525 South Ohio Street in Salina, Kansas.

Admission Requirements

Each applicant for admission is assigned an assistant director of admissions who directs the applicant through the steps of the admissions process; provides information on curriculum, policies, procedures, and services; and assists the applicant in setting necessary appointments and interviews.

To be considered for admission to Brown Mackie College, a candidate must be a high school graduate or hold a General Education Development (GED) certificate. As part of the admissions process applicants must sign a document attesting to graduation or completion and containing the information to obtain verification of such. Official high school transcripts or official documentation of high school graduation equivalency must be obtained within the first financial aid payment period or the student will be withdrawn from the institution following established guidelines for withdrawn students noted in the catalog. Title IV aid will not be dispersed until verification of graduation or completion has been received by the College.

Where applicable, students seeking entry into the College with a high school diploma completed in a foreign country must provide an original U.S.–equivalency evaluation from an evaluating agency which is a member of the National Association of Credential Evaluation Services (NACES, http://www.naces.org/) or the Association of International Credential Evaluators, Inc. (AICES, http://www.aice-eval.org/). The cost of evaluating the foreign transcript is borne by the applicant.

Admission to the College is based upon the applicant meeting the school's admission requirements, a review of the applicant's previous educational records, and a review of the applicant's career interests. It is the responsibility of the applicant to ensure that the College receives all required documentation.

Prior to admission, students are given an assessment of academic skills, commonly referred to as the academic readiness evaluation. Though the results of this assessment do not determine eligibility for admission, they provide the College with a means of determining the need for academic support through transitional studies courses and academic advisement, as well as a means by which the College can evaluate the effectiveness of its educational programs.

An applicant must obtain a minimum score of 60 in writing and 51 in mathematics on the COMPASS student academic readiness assessment. If a student does not achieve these scores, he/she will be enrolled in the appropriate transitional studies course(s).

In addition to the general admission requirements above, some programs have additional requirements specific to the program. For information on those, and other school-specific requirements, please visit the school's website or contact the school's Admissions department; phone: 785-825-5422; e-mail: bmcsaadm@brownmackie.edu; http://www.brownmackie.edu/Salina.

Application and Information

Applicants must complete and submit an application form, along with documentation of graduation from an accredited high school or state-approved secondary education curriculum or official documentation of high school graduation equivalency.

Specific details regarding program duration; tuition, fees, and other costs; median debt; federal salary data; alumni success; programmatic accreditation; and other important information is available online at BMCprograms.info.

Brown Mackie College—Salina is one of over 25 school locations of the Brown Mackie College system of schools. Programs, credential levels, technology, and scheduling options are subject to change. ©2014 Brown Mackie College.

For additional information, prospective students should contact:

Senior Director of Admissions
Brown Mackie College — Salina
2106 South Ninth Street
Salina, Kansas 67401
Phone: 785-825-5422
    800-365-0433 (toll-free)
Fax: 785-827-7623
E-mail: bmcsaadm@brownmackie.edu
Website: http://www.brownmackie.edu/Salina)

BROWN MACKIE COLLEGE — SAN ANTONIO

SAN ANTONIO, TEXAS

The College and Its Mission

Brown Mackie College — San Antonio (Brown Mackie College) is one of over twenty-five locations in the Brown Mackie College system of schools (www.brownmackie.edu), which is dedicated to providing educational programs that prepare students to pursue entry-level positions in a competitive, rapidly changing workplace. The Brown Mackie College schools offer bachelor's degree, associate degree, diploma, and certificate programs in health sciences, business, information technology, legal studies, and design to thousands of students in the Midwest, Southeast, Southwest, and Western United States.

Brown Mackie College was originally founded and approved by the Board of Trustees of Kansas Wesleyan College in Salina, Kansas on July 30, 1892. In 1938, the College was incorporated as the Brown Mackie School of Business under the ownership of Perry E. Brown and A. B. Mackie, former instructors at Kansas Wesleyan University in Salina, Kansas. Their last names formed the name of Brown Mackie. By January 1975, with improvements in curricula and higher degree-granting status, the Brown Mackie School of Business became Brown Mackie College.

Brown Mackie College — San Antonio is accredited by the Accrediting Council for Independent Colleges and Schools to award associate degrees and diplomas. The Accrediting Council for Independent Colleges and Schools is listed as a nationally recognized accrediting agency by the United States Department of Education and is recognized by the Council for Higher Education Accreditation. ACICS can be contacted at 750 First Street NE, Suite 980, Washington, D.C. 20002; phone: 202-336-6780.

Brown Mackie College — San Antonio is approved and regulated by the Texas Workforce Commission, Career School and Colleges, Austin, Texas.

Brown Mackie College — San Antonio holds a Certificate of Authorization acknowledging exemption from Texas Higher Education Coordinating Board regulations.

The Brown Mackie College — San Antonio Associate of Science in surgical technology program is accredited by the Accrediting Bureau of Health Education Schools, ABHES.

Academic Programs

Brown Mackie College — San Antonio provides higher education to traditional and nontraditional students through associate degree programs that assist in enhancing their career opportunities, broadening their perspectives through appropriate general education courses, thinking independently and critically, and improving problem-solving abilities. The College strives to develop within its students the desire for lifelong and continued education.

Each College quarter comprises twelve weeks. Associate degree programs require a minimum of eight quarters to complete. Programs are offered on a year-round basis, providing students with the ability to work uninterrupted toward completion of their programs. The College offers all programs in a unique One Course a Month format. This allows students to focus studies on only one course for four weeks. This schedule has proven convenient for students with multiple obligations such as jobs and family.

Associate Degree Programs: The Associate of Science degree is awarded in business management, criminal justice, health care administration, information technology, paralegal, pharmacy technology, and surgical technology.

Diploma Programs: Brown Mackie College — San Antonio offers a diploma program in medical assistant.

The American Medical Technologists (AMT), which offers the certification for Registered Medical Assistant (RMA), accepts the accreditation of Brown Mackie College — San Antonio. Students will qualify to take the RMA certification examination upon graduating the Brown Mackie College — San Antonio medical assisting and medical assistant programs. Information on application procedures can be found at http://americanmedtech.org/SchoolsStudents/CertificationProcess.aspx.

Brown Mackie College — San Antonio does not guarantee third-party certification. Outside agencies control the requirements for certifications and are subject to change without notice to Brown Mackie College.

Program availability and degree offerings are subject to change.

Costs

Tuition in the 2013–14 academic year for most of the associate degree and diploma programs was $324 per credit hour; fees were $20 per credit hour. Tuition for the surgical technology program was $360 per credit hour; fees were $20 per credit hour. The cost of textbooks, if applicable, and other instructional materials varies by program.

Financial Aid

The College maintains a full-time staff of financial aid professionals to assist qualified students in obtaining the financial assistance they require to meet their education expenses. Financial aid is available to those students who qualify.

Available resources may include federal grants and loans, state aid, student loans from private lenders, and federal work-study opportunities, both on and off College premises. Federal assistance programs are administered through the U.S. Department of Education, Office of Student Financial Assistance. Any U.S. citizen, national, or person in the United States for other than temporary reasons who is enrolled or accepted for enrollment may apply for these programs. Most forms of financial assistance are available for each July 1–June 30 award period.

Every student considering application for financial aid should request a copy of the current Student Guide, published by the U.S. Department of Education. This important document may be obtained in the Student Financial Services Office and will assist persons in understanding eligibility requirements, the application process, deadlines, and the various forms of grants and loans available.

For details on school-specific loans and scholarships, visit the school's website or contact the school's Student Financial Services Department; phone: 210-428-2210; e-mail: bmsanweb@brownmackie.edu; http://www.brownmackie.edu/SanAntonio.

Faculty

Experienced faculty members provide academic support and are committed to the academic and technical preparation of their students. Brown Mackie College — San Antonio has both full-time and part-time instructors, with a student-faculty ratio of 15:1.

Facilities and Resources

A modern facility, Brown Mackie College — San Antonio offers more than 35,000 square feet. The College is equipped with multiple computer labs, housing over 100 computers. High-speed access to the Internet and other online resources are available to students and faculty. Multimedia classrooms are outfitted with overhead projectors, VCR/DVD players, and computers.

Brown Mackie College — San Antonio is fully committed to using eTextbooks and computer tablets in the classroom. Utilizing these tablets to access expanded course material, students are able to increase their acumen for using this technology and further enhance their educational experience. Students have the ability to directly download their eTextbooks to their tablet, eliminating the need to carry heavy, physical textbooks and reducing the overall cost of supplies.

The College is nonresidential; public transportation and ample parking at no cost are available. The College has a generous parking area and is easily accessible by public transportation. The campus is a smoke-free facility.

Location

Brown Mackie College — San Antonio is conveniently located at 4715 Fredericksburg Road in San Antonio, Texas.

Admission Requirements

Each applicant for admission is assigned an assistant director of admissions who directs the applicant through the steps of the admissions process; provides information on curriculum, policies, procedures, and services; and assists the applicant in setting necessary appointments and interviews.

To be considered for admission to Brown Mackie College, a candidate must be a high school graduate or hold a General Education Development (GED) certificate. As part of the admissions process applicants must sign a document attesting to graduation or completion and containing the information to obtain verification of such. Official high school transcripts or official documentation of high school graduation equivalency must be obtained within the first financial aid payment period or the student will be withdrawn from the institution following established guidelines for withdrawn students noted in the catalog. Title IV aid will not be dispersed until verification of graduation or completion has been received by the College.

Where applicable, students seeking entry into the College with a high school diploma completed in a foreign country must provide an original U.S.–equivalency evaluation from an evaluating agency which is a member of the National Association of Credential Evaluation Services (NACES, http://www.naces.org/) or the Association of International Credential Evaluators, Inc. (AICES, http://www.aice-eval.org/). The cost of evaluating the foreign transcript is borne by the applicant.

Admission to the College is based upon the applicant meeting the school's admission requirements, a review of the applicant's previous educational records, and a review of the applicant's career interests. It is the responsibility of the applicant to ensure that the College receives all required documentation.

Prior to admission, students are given an assessment of academic skills, commonly referred to as the academic readiness evaluation. Though the results of this assessment do not determine eligibility for admission, they provide the College with a means of determining the need for academic support through transitional studies courses and academic advisement, as well as a means by which the College can evaluate the effectiveness of its educational programs.

An applicant must obtain a minimum score of 60 in writing and 51 in mathematics on the COMPASS student academic readiness assessment. If a student does not achieve these scores, he/she will be enrolled in the appropriate transitional studies course(s).

In addition to the general admission requirements above, some programs have additional requirements specific to the program. For information on those, and other school-specific requirements, please visit the school's website or contact the school's admissions department; phone: 210-428-2210; e-mail: _bmsanweb@brownmackie.edu; http://www.brownmackie.edu/SanAntonio.

Application and Information

Applicants must complete and submit an application form, along with documentation of graduation from an accredited high school or state-approved secondary education curriculum or official documentation of high school graduation equivalency.

Specific details regarding program duration; tuition, fees, and other costs; median debt; federal salary data; alumni success; programmatic accreditation; and other important information is available online at BMCprograms.info.

Brown Mackie College — San Antonio is one of over 25 school locations of the Brown Mackie College system of schools. Programs, credential levels, technology, and scheduling options are subject to change. ©2014 Brown Mackie College.

For additional information, prospective students should contact:

Director of Admissions
Brown Mackie College — San Antonio
4715 Fredericksburg Road, Suite 100
San Antonio, Texas 78229
Phone: 210-428-2210
          877-460-1714 (toll-free)
Fax: 210-428-2265
E-mail: _bmsanweb@brownmackie.edu
Website: http://www.brownmackie.edu/SanAntonio

BROWN MACKIE COLLEGE — SOUTH BEND

SOUTH BEND, INDIANA

The College and Its Mission

Brown Mackie College — South Bend (Brown Mackie College) is one of over twenty-five locations in the Brown Mackie College system of schools (www.brownmackie.edu), which is dedicated to providing educational programs that prepare students to pursue entry-level positions in a competitive, rapidly changing workplace. The Brown Mackie College schools offer bachelor's degree, associate degree, diploma, and certificate programs in health sciences, business, information technology, legal studies, and design to thousands of students in the Midwest, Southeast, Southwest, and Western United States.

Brown Mackie College — South Bend is one of the oldest institutions of its kind in the country and the oldest in the state of Indiana. Established in 1882 as the South Bend Commercial College, the school later changed its name to Michiana College. In 1930, the school was incorporated under the laws of the state of Indiana and was authorized to confer associate degrees and certificates in business. The College relocated to East Jefferson Boulevard in 1987. In September 2009, Brown Mackie College — South Bend officially opened a new 46,000-square-foot facility at 3454 Douglas Road in South Bend, Indiana.

Brown Mackie College — South Bend is accredited by the Accrediting Council for Independent Colleges and Schools to award associate degrees, diplomas, and certificates. The Accrediting Council for Independent Colleges and Schools is listed as a nationally recognized accrediting agency by the United States Department of Education and is recognized by the Council for Higher Education Accreditation. ACICS can be contacted at 750 First Street NE, Suite 980, Washington, D.C. 20002; phone: 202-336-6780.

Brown Mackie College — South Bend is authorized by the Indiana Board for Proprietary Education, 101 West Ohio Street, Suite 670, Indianapolis, Indiana 46204-1984; phone: 317-464-4400 Ext. 138, 141.

The Brown Mackie College — South Bend practical nursing diploma program is accredited by the Indiana State Board of Nursing, located at 402 West Washington Street, Room W066, Indianapolis, Indiana 46204; phone: 317-234-2043.

The occupational therapy assistant program is accredited by the Accreditation Council for Occupational Therapy Education (ACOTE) of the American Occupational Therapy Association (AOTA), located at 4720 Montgomery Lane, P.O. Box 31220, Bethesda, Maryland 20824-1220; phone: 301-652-AOTA. Graduates of the program will be eligible to sit for the national certification examination for the occupational therapy assistant administered by the National Board for Certification in Occupational Therapy (NBCOT). After successful completion of this exam, the individual will be a Certified Occupational Therapy Assistant (COTA). In addition, most states require licensure in order to practice; however, state licenses are usually based on the results of the NBCOT Certification Examination. Note that a felony conviction may affect a graduate's ability to sit for the NBCOT certification examination or attain state licensure.

The physical therapist assistant program at Brown Mackie College — South Bend is accredited by the Commission on Accreditation in Physical Therapy Education (CAPTE) 1111 North Fairfax Street, Alexandria, Virginia 22314; 703-706-3245; e-mail: accreditation@apta.org; www.capteonline.org.

The veterinary technology program at Brown Mackie College — South Bend has provisional programmatic accreditation granted by the American Veterinary Medical Association (AVMA) through the Committee on Veterinary Technician Education and Activities (CVTEA), 1931 North Meacham Road, Suite 100, Schaumburg, Illinois 60173; phone: 800-248-2862; www.avma.org.

Academic Programs

Brown Mackie College — South Bend provides higher education to traditional and nontraditional students through associate degrees, diploma, and certificate programs that assist in enhancing their career opportunities, broadening their perspectives through appropriate general education courses, thinking independently and critically, and improving problem-solving abilities.

Each College quarter comprises twelve weeks. Associate degree programs require a minimum of eight quarters to complete. Programs are offered on a year-round basis, providing students with the ability to work uninterrupted toward completion of their programs. The College offers all programs in a unique One Course a Month format. This allows students to focus studies on only one course for four weeks. This schedule has proven convenient for students with multiple obligations such as jobs and family.

Associate Degree Programs: The Associate of Science degree is awarded in business management and veterinary technology.

The Associate of Applied Science degree is awarded in occupational therapy assistant and physical therapist assistant.

Diploma Program: The College offers a diploma program in practical nursing.

Certificate Programs: The College offers a certificate program in medical assistant.

The American Medical Technologists (AMT), which offers the certification for Registered Medical Assistant (RMA), accepts the accreditation of Brown Mackie College — South Bend. Students will qualify to take the RMA certification examination upon graduating the Brown Mackie College — South Bend medical assistant program. Graduates of the 48 credit-hour medical assistant program are not qualified to take the AMT/RMA exam. Information on application procedures can be found at: http://americanmedtech.org/SchoolsStudents/CertificationProcess.aspx.

Brown Mackie College — South Bend does not guarantee third-party certification. Outside agencies control the requirements for certifications and are subject to change without notice to Brown Mackie College.

Program availability and degree offerings are subject to change.

Costs

Tuition for programs in the 2013–14 academic year was $314 per credit hour, with a general fee of $20 per credit hour applied to instructional costs for activities and services. Tuition for the practical nursing program was $381 per credit hour, with a general fee of $30 per credit hour applied to instructional costs for activities and services. Tuition for the physical therapist assistant program was $381 per credit hour with a general fee of $20 per credit hour. Tuition for the occupational therapy assistant program was $381 per credit hour with a general fee of $20 per credit hour. Textbooks, if applicable, and other instructional materials vary by program.

Financial Aid

The College maintains a full-time staff of financial aid. Applicants must complete and submit an application form, along with documentation of graduation from an accredited high school or state-approved secondary education curriculum or official documentation of high school graduation equivalency.

Specific details regarding program duration; tuition, fees, and other costs; median debt; federal salary data; alumni success; programmatic accreditation; and other important information are available at BMCprograms.info.

Brown Mackie College — South Bend is one of over 25 school locations of the Brown Mackie College system of schools. Programs, credential levels, technology, and scheduling options are subject to change. ©2014 Brown Mackie College

professionals to assist qualified students in obtaining the financial assistance they require to meet their education expenses. Financial aid is available to those students who qualify.

Available resources may include federal grants and loans, state aid, student loans from private lenders, and federal work-study opportunities, both on and off College premises. Federal assistance programs are administered through the U.S. Department of Education, Office of Student Financial Assistance. Any U.S. citizen, national, or person in the United States for other than temporary reasons who is enrolled or accepted for enrollment may apply for these programs. Most forms of financial assistance are available for each July 1–June 30 award period.

Every student considering application for financial aid should request a copy of the current Student Guide, published by the U.S. Department of Education. This important document may be obtained in the Student Financial Services Office and will assist persons in understanding eligibility requirements, the application process, deadlines, and the various forms of grants and loans available.

For details on school-specific loans and scholarships, visit the school's website or contact the school's Student Financial Services Department; phone: 574-237-0774; e-mail: bmcsbadm@brownmackie. edu; http://www.brownmackie.edu/SouthBend.

Faculty

There are 17 full-time and 45 part-time faculty members at the College. The average student-faculty ratio is 11:1. Each student is assigned a program director as an adviser.

Facilities and Resources

Brown Mackie College — South Bend's new location has a generous parking area and is easily accessible by public transportation. The College's smoke-free, three-story 46,000 square foot building offers a modern, professional environment for study. The facility offers "classrooms of the future," with instructor workstations and full multimedia capabilities that include surround sound and projection screens that can be accessed by computer, DVD, and VHS machines. The new facility includes medical, computer, and occupational and physical therapy labs, as well as a library and bookstore. The labs provide students with hands-on opportunities to apply knowledge and skills learned in the classroom. The veterinary technology lab is 2,600 square feet and includes surgery areas, treatment areas, and kennels.

Brown Mackie College — South Bend is fully committed to using eTextbooks and computer tablets in the classroom. Utilizing these tablets to access expanded course material, students are able to increase their acumen for using this technology and further enhance their educational experience. Students have the ability to directly download their eTextbooks to their tablet, eliminating the need to carry heavy, physical textbooks and reducing the overall cost of supplies.

The College has a generous parking area and is also easily accessible by public transportation. The College is a nonresidential, smoke-free institution.

Location

Brown Mackie College — South Bend is conveniently located at 3454 Douglas Road in South Bend, Indiana.

Admission Requirements

Each applicant for admission is assigned an assistant director of admissions who directs the applicant through the steps of the admissions process; provides information on curriculum, policies, procedures, and services; and assists the applicant in setting necessary appointments and interviews.

To be considered for admission to Brown Mackie College, a candidate must be a high school graduate or hold a General Education Development (GED) certificate. As part of the admissions process applicants must sign a document attesting to graduation or completion and containing the information to obtain verification of such. Official high school transcripts or official documentation of high school graduation equivalency must be obtained within the first financial aid payment period or the student will be withdrawn from the institution following established guidelines for withdrawn students noted in the catalog. Title IV aid will not be dispersed until verification of graduation or completion has been received by the College.

Where applicable, students seeking entry into the College with a high school diploma completed in a foreign country must provide an original U.S.–equivalency evaluation from an evaluating agency which is a member of the National Association of Credential Evaluation Services (NACES, http://www.naces.org/) or the Association of International Credential Evaluators, Inc. (AICES, http://www.aice-eval.org/). The cost of evaluating the foreign transcript is borne by the applicant.

Admission to the College is based upon the applicant meeting the school's admission requirements, a review of the applicant's previous educational records, and a review of the applicant's career interests. It is the responsibility of the applicant to ensure that the College receives all required documentation.

Prior to admission, students are given an assessment of academic skills, commonly referred to as the academic readiness evaluation.

Though the results of this assessment do not determine eligibility for admission, they provide the College with a means of determining the need for academic support through transitional studies courses and academic advisement, as well as a means by which the College can evaluate the effectiveness of its educational programs.

An applicant must obtain a minimum score of 60 in writing and 51 in mathematics on the COMPASS student academic readiness assessment. If a student does not achieve these scores, he/she will be enrolled in the appropriate transitional studies course(s).

In addition to the general admission requirements above, some programs have additional requirements specific to the program. For information on those, and other school-specific requirements, please visit the school's website or contact the school's Admissions department; phone: 574-237-0774; e-mail: bmcsbadm@brownmackie. edu; http://www.brownmackie.edu/SouthBend.

Application and Information

Applicants must complete and submit an application form, along with documentation of graduation from an accredited high school or state-approved secondary education curriculum or official documentation of high school graduation equivalency.

Specific details regarding program duration; tuition, fees, and other costs; median debt; federal salary data; alumni success; programmatic accreditation; and other important information are available at BMCprograms.info.

Brown Mackie College — South Bend is one of over 25 school locations of the Brown Mackie College system of schools. Programs, credential levels, technology, and scheduling options are subject to change. ©2014 Brown Mackie College.

For additional information, prospective students should contact:

Director of Admissions
Brown Mackie College — South Bend
3454 Douglas Road
South Bend, Indiana 46635
Phone: 574-237-0774
      800-743-2447 (toll-free)
Fax: 574-237-3585
E-mail: bmcsbadm@brownmackie.edu
Website: http://www.brownmackie.edu/SouthBend)

BROWN MACKIE COLLEGE — TUCSON
TUCSON, ARIZONA

The College and Its Mission

Brown Mackie College — Tucson (Brown Mackie College) is one of over twenty-five locations in the Brown Mackie College system of schools (www.brownmackie.edu), which is dedicated to providing educational programs that prepare students to pursue entry-level positions in a competitive, rapidly changing workplace. Brown Mackie College schools offer bachelor's degree, associate degree, diploma, and certificate programs in health sciences, business, information technology, legal studies, and design to thousands of students in the Midwest, Southeast, Southwest, and Western United States.

Brown Mackie College was originally founded and approved by the Board of Trustees of Kansas Wesleyan College in Salina, Kansas on July 30, 1892. In 1938, the College was incorporated as The Brown Mackie School of Business under the ownership of Perry E. Brown and A. B. Mackie, former instructors at Kansas Wesleyan University in Salina, Kansas. Their last names formed the name of Brown Mackie. By January 1975, with improvements in curricula and higher degree-granting status, The Brown Mackie School of Business became Brown Mackie College.

Brown Mackie College entered the Arizona market in 2007 when it purchased a school that had been previously established in the Tucson area. That school had an established history in the community and was converted into what is now known as Brown Mackie College — Tucson. The historical timeline of Brown Mackie College — Tucson started in 1972 when Rockland West Corporation first formed a partnership with Lamson Business College. At that time the school was a career college that offered only short-term programs focusing on computer training and secretarial skills. In 1994 the College became accredited as a junior college and began offering associate degrees in academic subjects. The mission was then modified to include the goal of instilling in graduates an appreciation for lifelong learning through the general education courses that became a part of every program.

In 1996 the College applied for and received status as a senior college by the Accrediting Commission of Independent Colleges and Schools. This gave the school the ability to offer course work leading to a Bachelor of Science degree in business administration. Since then the program offerings for associate degrees have expanded.

In 1986, the College moved from 5001 East Speedway to the 4585 East Speedway location where it remains today. In 2008, two of the College's three buildings were remodeled which resulted in updated classrooms; networked computer laboratories; new medical, surgical technology, and forensics laboratories; a larger library and offices for student services such as academics, admissions, and student financial services; and a full-service college store. In 2009, the third building was remodeled and provides newer classrooms and a new career services department.

Brown Mackie College — Tucson is accredited by the Accrediting Council for Independent Colleges and Schools to award associate degrees and diplomas. The Accrediting Council for Independent Colleges and Schools is listed as a nationally recognized accrediting agency by the United States Department of Education and is recognized by the Council for Higher Education Accreditation. ACICS can be contacted at 750 First Street NE, Suite 980, Washington, D.C. 20002; phone: 202-336-6780.

Brown Mackie College — Tucson is authorized by the Arizona State Board for Private Post-secondary Education, 1400 West Washington Street, Room 2560, Phoenix, Arizona 85007; phone: 602-542-5709; http://azppse.state.az.us.

The Associate of Science in surgical technology program is accredited by the Accrediting Bureau of Health Education Schools.

The Associate of Applied Science in occupational therapy assistant program is accredited by the Accreditation Council for Occupational Therapy Education (ACOTE) of the American Occupational Therapy Association (AOTA), located at 4720 Montgomery Lane, Suite 200, Bethesda, Maryland 20814-3449; phone: 301-652-AOTA. Graduates of the program will be eligible to sit for the national certification examination for the occupational therapy assistant administered by the National Board for Certification in Occupational Therapy (NBCOT). After successful completion of this exam, the individual will be a Certified Occupational Therapy Assistant (COTA). In addition, most states require licensure in order to practice; however, state licenses are usually based on the results of the NBCOT Certification Examination. Note that a felony conviction may affect a graduate's ability to sit for the NBCOT certification examination or attain state licensure.

Academic Programs

Brown Mackie College — Tucson provides higher education to traditional and nontraditional students through associate degree and diploma programs that assist in enhancing their career opportunities, broadening their perspectives through appropriate general education courses, thinking independently and critically, and improving problem-solving abilities. The College strives to develop within its students the desire for lifelong and continued education.

Each College quarter comprises twelve weeks. Associate degree programs require a minimum of eight quarters to complete. Programs are offered on a year-round basis, providing students with the ability to work uninterrupted toward their degrees. The College offers all programs in a unique One Course a Month format. This allows students to focus studies on only one course for four weeks. This schedule has proven convenient for students with multiple obligations such as jobs and family.

Associate Degree Programs: The Associate of Science degree is awarded in accounting technology, business management, computer networking and security, criminal justice, graphic design, health care administration, and surgical technology.

The Associate of Applied Science degree is awarded in biomedical equipment technology and occupational therapy assistant.

Diploma Program: A diploma is awarded in medical assistant and practical nursing.

The American Medical Technologists (AMT), which offers the certification for Registered Medical Assistant (RMA), accepts the accreditation of Brown Mackie College — Tucson. Students will qualify to take the RMA certification examination upon graduating the Brown Mackie College — Tucson medical assisting and medical assistant programs. Graduates of the 48 credit-hour medical assistant program are not qualified to take the AMT/RMA exam. Information on application procedures can be found at: http://americanmedtech.org/SchoolsStudents/CertificationProcess.aspx.

Brown Mackie College — Tucson does not guarantee third-party certification. Outside agencies control the requirements for certifications and are subject to change without notice to Brown Mackie College.

Program availability and degree offerings are subject to change.

Costs

Tuition in the 2013–14 academic year for most associate and diploma programs was $344 per credit hour; fees were $20 per credit hour. Tuition for the surgical technology program was $360 per credit hour; fees were $20 per credit hour. Tuition for the occupational therapy assistant program was $381 per credit hour; fees were $20 per credit hour. Tuition for the practical nursing program was $381 per credit hour; fees were $30 per credit hour. Textbooks, if applicable, and other instructional expenses vary by program.

Financial Aid

The College maintains a full-time staff of financial aid professionals to assist qualified students in obtaining the financial assistance they require to meet their education expenses. Financial aid is available to those students who qualify.

Available resources may include federal grants and loans, state aid, student loans from private lenders, and federal work-study opportunities, both on and off College premises. Federal assistance programs are administered through the U.S. Department of Education, Office of Student Financial Assistance. Any U.S. citizen, national, or person in the United States for other than temporary reasons who is enrolled or accepted for enrollment may apply for these programs. Most forms of financial assistance are available for each July 1–June 30 award period.

Every student considering application for financial aid should request a copy of the current Student Guide, published by the U.S. Department of Education. This important document may be obtained in the Student Financial Services Office and will assist persons in understanding eligibility requirements, the application process, deadlines, and the various forms of grants and loans available.

For details on school-specific loans and scholarships, visit the school's website or contact the school's Student Financial Services Department; phone: 520-319-3300; e-mail: _bmctuweb@ brownmackie.edu; http://www.brownmackie.edu/Tucson.

Faculty

Experienced faculty members provide academic support and are committed to the academic and technical preparation of their students. The College has 15 full-time and 35 part-time instructors, with a student-faculty ratio of 13:1. Each student is assigned a faculty adviser.

Facilities and Resources

A modern facility, Brown Mackie College — Tucson offers more than 31,000 square feet. The College is equipped with multiple computer labs housing over 200 computers. High-speed access to the Internet and other online resources are available for students and faculty. Multimedia classrooms are outfitted with overhead projectors, VCR/ DVD players, and computers. The College is nonresidential; public transportation and parking at no cost are available.

Brown Mackie College — Tucson is fully committed to using eTextbooks and computer tablets in the classroom. Utilizing these tablets to access expanded course material, students are able to increase their acumen for using this technology and further enhance their educational experience. Students have the ability to directly download their eTextbooks to their tablet, eliminating the need to carry heavy, physical textbooks and reducing the overall cost of supplies.

The College has a generous parking area and is also easily accessible by public transportation.

Location

Brown Mackie College — Tucson is conveniently located at 4585 East Speedway Boulevard in Tucson, Arizona.

Admission Requirements

Each applicant for admission is assigned an assistant director of admissions who directs the applicant through the steps of the admissions process; provides information on curriculum, policies, procedures, and services; and assists the applicant in setting necessary appointments and interviews.

To be considered for admission to Brown Mackie College, a candidate must be a high school graduate or hold a General Education Development (GED) certificate. As part of the admissions process applicants must sign a document attesting to graduation or completion and containing the information to obtain verification of such. Official high school transcripts or official documentation of high school graduation equivalency must be obtained within the first financial aid payment period or the student will be withdrawn from the institution following established guidelines for withdrawn students noted in the catalog. Title IV aid will not be dispersed until verification of graduation or completion has been received by the College.

Where applicable, students seeking entry into the College with a high school diploma completed in a foreign country must provide an original U.S.–equivalency evaluation from an evaluating agency which is a member of the National Association of Credential Evaluation Services (NACES, http://www.naces.org/) or the Association of International Credential Evaluators, Inc. (AICES, http://www.aice-eval.org/). The cost of evaluating the foreign transcript is borne by the applicant.

Admission to the College is based upon the applicant meeting the school's admission requirements, a review of the applicant's previous educational records, and a review of the applicant's career interests. It is the responsibility of the applicant to ensure that the College receives all required documentation.

Prior to admission, students are given an assessment of academic skills, commonly referred to as the academic readiness evaluation. Though the results of this assessment do not determine eligibility for admission, they provide the College with a means of determining the need for academic support through transitional studies courses and academic advisement, as well as a means by which the College can evaluate the effectiveness of its educational programs.

An applicant must obtain a minimum score of 60 in writing and 51 in mathematics on the COMPASS student academic readiness assessment. If a student does not achieve these scores, he/she will be enrolled in the appropriate transitional studies course(s).

In addition to the general admission requirements above, some programs have additional requirements specific to the program. For information on those, and other school-specific requirements, please visit the school's website or contact the school's admissions department; phone: 520-319-3300; e-mail: _bmctuweb@ brownmackie.edu; http://www.brownmackie.edu/Tucson.

Application and Information

Applicants must complete and submit an application form, along with documentation of graduation from an accredited high school or state-approved secondary education curriculum or official documentation of high school graduation equivalency.

Specific details regarding program duration; tuition, fees, and other costs; median debt; federal salary data; alumni success; programmatic accreditation; and other important information are available at BMCprograms.info.

Brown Mackie College — Tucson is one of over 25 school locations of the Brown Mackie College system of schools. Programs, credential levels, technology, and scheduling options are subject to change. ©2014 Brown Mackie College.

For additional information, prospective students should contact:

Senior Director of Admissions
Brown Mackie College — Tucson
4585 East Speedway Boulevard, Suite 204
Tucson, Arizona 85712
Phone: 520-319-3300
Fax: 520-319-3495
E-mail: _bmctuweb@brownmackie.edu
Website: http://www.brownmackie.edu/Tucson

BROWN MACKIE COLLEGE — TULSA

TULSA, OKLAHOMA

The College and Its Mission

Brown Mackie College — Tulsa (Brown Mackie College) is one of over twenty-five locations in the Brown Mackie College system of schools (www.brownmackie.edu), which is dedicated to providing educational programs that prepare students to pursue entry-level positions in a competitive, rapidly changing workplace. Brown Mackie College schools offer bachelor's degree, associate degree, diploma, and certificate programs in health sciences, business, information technology, legal studies, and design to thousands of students in the Midwest, Southeast, Southwest, and Western United States.

Brown Mackie College — Tulsa was founded in 2008 as a branch of Brown Mackie College — South Bend, Indiana.

Brown Mackie College — Tulsa is accredited by the Accrediting Council for Independent Colleges and Schools to award associate degrees and diplomas. The Accrediting Council for Independent Colleges and Schools is listed as a nationally recognized accrediting agency by the United States Department of Education and is recognized by the Council for Higher Education Accreditation. ACICS can be contacted at 750 First Street NE, Suite 980, Washington, D.C. 20002; phone: 202-336-6780.

This institution is licensed by the Oklahoma Board of Private Vocational Schools (OBPVS), 3700 North Classen Boulevard, Suite 250, Oklahoma City, Oklahoma 73118; phone: 405-528-3370.

This institution has been granted authority to operate in Oklahoma by the Oklahoma State Regents for Higher Education (OSRHE), 655 Research Parkway, Suite 200, Oklahoma City, Oklahoma 73101; phone: 405-225-9100; www.okhighered.org.

The occupational therapy assistant program is accredited by the Accreditation Council for Occupational Therapy Education (ACOTE) of the American Occupational Therapy Association (AOTA), located at 4720 Montgomery Lane, Suite 200, Bethesda, Maryland 20814-3449; phone: 301-652-AOTA. Graduates of the program will be eligible to sit for the national certification examination for the occupational therapy assistant administered by the National Board for Certification in Occupational Therapy (NBCOT). After successful completion of this exam, the individual will be a Certified Occupational Therapy Assistant (COTA). In addition, most states require licensure in order to practice; however, state licenses are usually based on the results of the NBCOT Certification Examination. Note that a felony conviction may affect a graduate's ability to sit for the NBCOT certification examination or attain state licensure.

The Brown Mackie College — Tulsa Associate of Applied Science in surgical technology program is accredited by the Accrediting Bureau of Health Education Schools, ABHES.

The Brown Mackie College — Tulsa Associate of Applied Science in surgical technology program is accredited by the Commission on Accreditation of Allied Health Education Programs (www.caahep.org) upon the recommendation of the Accreditation Review Committee on Education in Surgical Technology.

Academic Programs

Brown Mackie College — Tulsa provides higher education to traditional and nontraditional students through associate degree and diploma programs that assist in enhancing their career opportunities, broadening their perspectives through appropriate general education courses, thinking independently and critically, and improving problem-solving abilities. The College strives to develop within its students the desire for lifelong and continued education.

Each College quarter comprises twelve weeks. Associate degree programs require a minimum of eight quarters to complete. Programs are offered on a year-round basis, providing students with the ability to work uninterrupted toward completion of their programs. The College offers all programs in a unique One Course a Month format. This allows students to focus on only one course for four weeks. This schedule has proven convenient for students with multiple obligations such as jobs and family.

Associate Degree Programs: The Associate of Applied Science degree is awarded in accounting technology, business management, criminal justice, health care administration, information technology, medical assisting, nursing, occupational therapy assistant, and surgical technology.

Diploma Programs: Diploma programs are offered in accounting, business, criminal justice, and medical assistant.

The American Medical Technologists (AMT), which offers the certification for Registered Medical Assistant (RMA), accepts the accreditation of Brown Mackie College — Tulsa. Students will qualify to take the RMA certification examination upon graduating the Brown Mackie College — Tulsa medical assisting and medical assistant programs. Graduates of the 48 credit-hour medical assistant program are not qualified to take the AMT/RMA exam. Information on application procedures can be found at: http://americanmedtech.org/SchoolsStudents/CertificationProcess.aspx.

Brown Mackie College — Tulsa does not guarantee third-party certification. Outside agencies control the requirements for certifications and are subject to change without notice to Brown Mackie College.

Program availability and degree offerings are subject to change.

Costs

Tuition for programs in the 2013–14 academic year was $314 per credit hour, with a general fee of $20 per credit hour applied to instructional costs for activities and services. Tuition for the occupational therapy program was $381 per credit hour with a general fee of $20 per credit hour applied to instructional costs for activities. Tuition for the surgical technology program was $360 per credit hour with a general fee of $20 per credit hour applied to instructional costs for activities. Tuition for the nursing program was $410 per credit hour with a general fee of $30 per credit hour applied to instructional costs for activities. Textbooks, if applicable, and other instructional materials vary by program.

Financial Aid

The College maintains a full-time staff of financial aid professionals to assist qualified students in obtaining the financial assistance they require to meet their education expenses. Financial aid is available to those students who qualify.

Available resources may include federal grants and loans, state aid, student loans from private lenders, and federal work-study opportunities, both on and off College premises. Federal assistance programs are administered through the U.S. Department of Education, Office of Student Financial Assistance. Any U.S. citizen, national, or person in the United States for other than temporary reasons who is enrolled or accepted for enrollment may apply for these programs. Most forms of financial assistance are available for each July 1–June 30 award period.

Every student considering application for financial aid should request a copy of the current Student Guide, published by the U.S. Department of Education. This important document may be obtained in the Student Financial Services Office and will assist persons in understanding eligibility requirements, the application process, deadlines, and the various forms of grants and loans available.

For details on school-specific loans and scholarships, visit the school's website or contact the school's Student Financial Services Department; phone: 918-628-3700; e-mail: _bmctladm@brownmackie.edu; http://www.brownmackie.edu/Tulsa.

Faculty

There are 11 full-time and 30 adjunct faculty members. The student-faculty ratio is 15:1.

Facilities and Resources

Opened in 2008, this modern facility offers more than 25,000 square feet of tastefully decorated classrooms, laboratories, and office space designed to specifications of Brown Mackie College for its business, medical, and technical programs. Instructional equipment is comparable to current technology used in business and industry today. Modern classrooms for special instructional needs offer multimedia capabilities with surround sound and overhead projectors accessible through computer and DVD. Internet access and instructional resources are available at the College's library. Experienced faculty members provide academic support and are committed to the academic and technical preparation of their students.

Brown Mackie College — Tulsa is fully committed to using eTextbooks and computer tablets in the classroom. Utilizing these tablets to access expanded course material, students are able to increase their acumen for using this technology and further enhance their educational experience. Students have the ability to directly download their eTextbooks to their tablet, eliminating the need to carry heavy, physical textbooks and reducing the overall cost of supplies.

The College is nonresidential; public transportation and ample parking at no cost are available.

Location

Brown Mackie College — Tulsa is conveniently located at 4608 South Garnett Road, Suite 110 in Tulsa, Oklahoma.

Admission Requirements

Each applicant for admission is assigned an assistant director of admissions who directs the applicant through the steps of the admissions process; provides information on curriculum, policies, procedures, and services; and assists the applicant in setting necessary appointments and interviews.

To be considered for admission to Brown Mackie College, a candidate must be a high school graduate or hold a General Education Development (GED) certificate. As part of the admissions process applicants must sign a document attesting to graduation or completion and containing the information to obtain verification of such. Official high school transcripts or official documentation of high school graduation equivalency must be obtained within the first financial aid payment period or the student will be withdrawn from the institution following established guidelines for withdrawn students noted in the catalog. Title IV aid will not be dispersed until verification of graduation or completion has been received by the College.

Where applicable, students seeking entry into the College with a high school diploma completed in a foreign country must provide an original U.S.–equivalency evaluation from an evaluating agency which is a member of the National Association of Credential Evaluation Services (NACES, http://www.naces.org/) or the Association of International Credential Evaluators, Inc. (AICES, http://www.aice-eval.org/). The cost of evaluating the foreign transcript is borne by the applicant.

Admission to the College is based upon the applicant meeting the school's admission requirements, a review of the applicant's previous educational records, and a review of the applicant's career interests. It is the responsibility of the applicant to ensure that the College receives all required documentation.

Prior to admission, students are given an assessment of academic skills, commonly referred to as the academic readiness evaluation. Though the results of this assessment do not determine eligibility for admission, they provide the College with a means of determining the need for academic support through transitional studies courses and academic advisement, as well as a means by which the College can evaluate the effectiveness of its educational programs.

An applicant must obtain a minimum score of 60 in writing and 51 in mathematics on the COMPASS student academic readiness assessment. If a student does not achieve these scores, he/she will be enrolled in the appropriate transitional studies course(s).

In addition to the general admission requirements above, some programs have additional requirements specific to the program. For information on those, and other school-specific requirements, please contact the school's Admissions department: phone: 918-628-3700; e-mail: _bmctladm@brownmackie.edu; or visit the school's website at http://www.brownmackie.edu/Tulsa.

Application and Information

Applicants must complete and submit an application form, along with documentation of graduation from an accredited high school or state-approved secondary education curriculum or official documentation of high school graduation equivalency.

Specific details regarding program duration, tuition, fees, and other costs; median debt; federal salary data; alumni success; programmatic accreditation; and other important information are available at BMCprograms.info.

Brown Mackie College — Tulsa is one of over 25 school locations of the Brown Mackie College system of schools. Programs, credential levels, technology, and scheduling options are subject to change. ©2014 Brown Mackie College.

For additional information, prospective students should contact:

Senior Director of Admissions
Brown Mackie College — Tulsa
4608 South Garnett Road, Suite 110
Tulsa, Oklahoma 74146
Phone: 918-628-3700
      888-794-8411 (toll-free)
Fax: 918-828-9083
E-mail: _bmctladm@brownmackie.edu
Website: http://www.brownmackie.edu/Tulsa

FASHION INSTITUTE OF TECHNOLOGY
State University of New York
NEW YORK, NEW YORK

The College and Its Mission

The Fashion Institute of Technology (FIT) is New York's celebrated urban college for creative and business talent. A State University of New York (SUNY) college of art, design, business, and technology, FIT is a dynamic mix of innovative achievers, original thinkers, and industry pioneers. FIT balances a real-world-based curriculum and hands-on instruction with a rigorous liberal arts foundation. The college marries design and business and supports individual creativity in a collaborative environment. It offers a complete college experience with a vibrant student and residential life.

With an extraordinary location at the center of New York City—world capital of the arts, business, and media—FIT maintains close ties with the design, fashion, advertising, communications, and international commerce industries. Academic departments consult with advisory boards of noted experts to ensure that the curricula and classroom technology reflect current industry practices. The college's faculty of successful professionals brings experience to the classroom, while field trips, guest lectures, and sponsored competitions introduce students to the opportunities and challenges of their disciplines.

FIT's mission is to produce well-rounded graduates—doers and thinkers who raise the professional bar to become the next generation of business pacesetters and creative icons.

FIT's four residence halls house 2,300 students in fully furnished traditional or apartment-style accommodations. Various dining options and meal plans are available. Residential counselors and student staff members live in the residence halls, helping students adjust to college life and New York City.

FIT is accredited by the Middle States Commission on Higher Education, the National Association of Schools of Art and Design, and the Council for Interior Design Accreditation.

Academic Programs

FIT serves approximately 10,000 full-time, part-time, and evening/weekend students from the metropolitan area, New York State, across the country, and around the world, offering nearly fifty programs leading to the A.A.S., B.F.A., B.S., M.A., M.F.A., and M.P.S. degrees. Each undergraduate program includes a core of traditional liberal arts courses, providing students with a global perspective, critical-thinking skills, and the ability to communicate effectively. All degree programs are designed to prepare students for creative and business careers and to provide them with the prerequisite studies to go on to baccalaureate, master's, or doctoral degrees, if they wish.

All students complete a two-year A.A.S. program in their major area and the liberal arts. They may then choose to go on to a related, two-year B.F.A. or B.S. program or begin their careers with their A.A.S. degree, which qualifies them for entry-level positions.

Associate Degree Programs: For the A.A.S. degree, FIT offers ten majors through the School of Art and Design, four through the Jay and Patty Baker School of Business and Technology, and one through the School of Liberal Arts. The A.A.S. programs are accessories design*, advertising and marketing communications*, communication design foundation*, fashion design*, fashion merchandising management* (with an online option), filmmaking, fine arts, illustration, interior design, jewelry design*, menswear, photography, production management: fashion and related industries, textile development and marketing*, and textile/surface design*. Programs with an asterisk (*) are also available in a one-year format for students with sufficient transferable credits.

Bachelor's Degree Programs: Many A.A.S. graduates choose to pursue a related, two-year baccalaureate program at the college. FIT offers twenty-six baccalaureate programs—fourteen B.F.A. programs through the School of Art and Design, ten B.S. programs through the Baker School of Business and Technology, and two B.S. programs through the School of Liberal Arts. The B.F.A. programs are accessories design, advertising design, computer animation and interactive media, fabric styling, fashion design (with specializations

in children's wear, intimate apparel, knitwear, special occasion, and sportswear), fine arts, graphic design, illustration, interior design, packaging design, photography and the digital image, textile/surface design, toy design, and visual presentation and exhibition design. The B.S. programs are advertising and marketing communications, art history and museum professions, cosmetics and fragrance marketing, direct and interactive marketing, entrepreneurship for the fashion and design industries, fashion merchandising management, film and media, home products development, international trade and marketing for the fashion industries, production management: fashion and related industries, technical design, and textile development and marketing.

Liberal Arts Minors: The School of Liberal Arts offers FIT students the opportunity to minor in a variety of liberal arts areas in two forms: traditional subject-based minors and interdisciplinary minors unique to the FIT liberal arts curriculum. Selected minors include dance and performing arts, economics, English literature, ethics and sustainability, international politics, Asian studies, and psychology.

Evening/Weekend Programs: To meet the needs of nontraditional students, FIT offers nine degree programs through evening/weekend study: advertising and marketing communications (A.A.S. and B.S.), communication design foundation (A.A.S.), fashion design (A.A.S.), fashion merchandising management (A.A.S. and B.S.), graphic design (B.F.A.), illustration (B.F.A.), and international trade and marketing for the fashion industries (B.S.). In addition, FIT's School of Continuing and Professional Studies provides evening and weekend credit and noncredit classes to students and working professionals interested in pursuing a degree or certificate or furthering their knowledge of a particular industry, while balancing the demands of career or family.

Honors Program: The Presidential Scholars honors program, available to academically exceptional students in all majors, offers special courses, projects, colloquia, and off-campus activities that broaden horizons and stimulate discourse. Presidential Scholars receive priority course registration and an annual merit stipend.

Internships: Internships are a required element of most programs and are available to all matriculated students. Nearly one third of FIT student interns are offered employment on completion of their internships; past sponsors include American Eagle Outfitters, Bloomingdale's, Calvin Klein, Estée Lauder, Fairchild Publications, MTV, and Saatchi & Saatchi.

Precollege Programs: Precollege programs (Saturday Live, Sunday Live, and Summer Live) are available to middle and high school students during the fall, spring, and summer. More than 100 courses provide the chance to learn in an innovative environment, develop art and design portfolios, explore the business and technological sides of many creative careers, and discover natural talents and abilities.

Off-Campus Programs

The study-abroad experience lets students immerse themselves in diverse cultures and prepares them to live and work in a global community. FIT has two campuses in Italy—one in Milan, one in Florence—where students study fashion design or fashion merchandising management and gain firsthand experience in the dynamics of European fashion. FIT also offers study-abroad options in countries like Australia, China, England, France, and Mexico. Students can study abroad during the winter or summer sessions, for a semester, or for a full academic year.

Costs

As a SUNY college, FIT offers affordable tuition for both New York State residents and nonresidents. The 2013–14 associate-level tuition per semester for in-state residents was $2,212; for nonresidents, $6,637. Baccalaureate-level tuition per semester was $3,034 for in-state residents and $8,185 for nonresidents. Per-semester housing costs were $6,314–$6,504 for traditional residence hall accommodations with mandatory meal plan and

$5,911–$9,846 for apartment-style accommodations. Meal plans ranged from $1,693 to $2,169 per semester. Textbook costs and other nominal fees, such as locker rental or laboratory use, vary per program. All costs are subject to change.

Financial Aid

FIT offers scholarships, grants, loans, and work-study employment for students with financial need. Overall, two-thirds of full-time, matriculated undergraduate students who complete the federal financial aid application process receive some type of assistance through loans and/or grants. The college directly administers its own institutional grants and scholarships, which are provided by the FIT Foundation.

College-administered funding includes Federal Pell Grants, Federal Perkins Loans, Federal Supplemental Educational Opportunity Grants, Federal Work-Study, and the Federal Family Educational Loan Program, which includes student and parent loans. New York State residents who meet eligibility guidelines may also receive Tuition Assistance Program (TAP) and/or Educational Opportunity Program (EOP) grants. Financial aid applicants must file the Free Application for Federal Student Aid (FAFSA) and should also apply to all available outside sources of aid. Additional documentation may be requested by the Financial Aid Office. Applications for financial aid should be completed prior to February 15 for fall admission or November 1 for spring admission.

Faculty

FIT's faculty is drawn from top professionals in academia, art, design, communications, and business, providing a curriculum rich in real-world experience and traditional educational values. Student-instructor interaction is encouraged, with a maximum class size of 25, and courses are structured to foster participation, independent thinking, and self-expression.

Student Body Profile

Fall 2013 enrollment was 9,755 with 8,242 students enrolled in degree programs. Forty-four percent of degree-seeking students are enrolled in the School of Art and Design; 52 percent are in the Baker School of Business and Technology. The average age of full-time degree seekers is 23. Forty percent of FIT's students are New York City residents, 23 percent are New York State (non–New York City) residents, and 37 percent are out-of-state residents or international students. The ethnic/racial makeup of the student body is approximately 10 percent Asian; 9 percent black; 16 percent Hispanic; 3 percent multiracial; 1 percent Native Hawaiian, Pacific Islander, American Indian, or Alaskan; and 46 percent white. There are 1,212 international students.

Student Activities

Participation in campus life is encouraged, and the college is home to more than sixty student organizations, societies, athletic teams, major-related groups, and special-interest clubs. Each organization is open to all students who have paid their activity fee.

Student Government: The Student Council, the governing body of the Student Association, grants all students the privileges and responsibilities of citizens in a self-governing college community. Faculty committees often include student representatives, and the president of the student government sits on FIT's Board of Trustees.

Athletics: FIT has intercollegiate teams in cross-country, half marathon, track and field, table tennis, tennis, women's soccer, swimming and diving, and women's volleyball. Athletics and Recreation offers a full array of group fitness classes, including aerobics, dance, spin, and yoga at no extra cost. Students can also work out on their own in a 5,000-square-foot fitness center. Open gym activities allow students to participate in both team and individual sports.

Events: Concerts, dances, field trips, films, flea markets, and other events are planned by the FIT Student Association and Programming Board and various clubs. Student-run publications include a campus newspaper, a literary and art magazine, and the FIT yearbook.

Facilities and Resources

FIT's campus provides its students with classrooms, laboratories, and studios that reflect the most advanced educational and industry practices. The Fred P. Pomerantz Art and Design Center houses drawing, painting, photography, printmaking, and sculpture studios; display and exhibition design rooms; a model-making workshop; and a graphics printing service bureau. The Peter G. Scotese Computer-Aided Design and Communications Center provides the latest technology in computer graphics, design, photography, and animation. Other cutting-edge facilities include a professionally equipped fragrance-development laboratory—the only one of its kind on a U.S. college campus—cutting and sewing labs, a design/research lighting laboratory, knitting lab, broadcasting studio, multimedia foreign languages laboratory, and forty-six computer labs containing Mac and PC workstations.

The Museum at FIT, New York City's only museum dedicated to fashion, contains one of the most important collections of fashion and textiles in the world. The museum, which is accredited by the American Alliance of Museums, operates year-round, and its exhibitions are free and open to the public. The Gladys Marcus Library provides more than 300,000 volumes of print, nonprint, and electronic materials. The periodicals collection includes over 500 current subscriptions, with a specialization in international design and trade publications; online resources include more than 90 searchable databases.

The David Dubinsky Student Center offers student lounges, a game room, a student radio station, the Style Shop (a student-run boutique), a full-service dining hall and Starbucks, student government and club offices, disability services, comprehensive health services and a counseling center, two gyms, a state-of-the-art fitness center, and a dance studio.

Location

Occupying an entire block in Manhattan's Chelsea neighborhood, FIT makes extensive use of the city's creative, commercial, and cultural resources, providing students with unrivaled internship opportunities and professional connections. A wide range of cultural and entertainment options are available within a short walk of the campus, as is convenient access to several subway and bus lines and the city's major rail and bus transportation hubs.

Admission Requirements

Applicants for admission must be either candidates for or recipients of a high school diploma or a General Educational Development (GED) certificate. Admission is based on strength and performance in college-preparatory coursework and the student essay. A portfolio evaluation is required for art and design majors. Specific portfolio requirements are explained on FIT's website. SAT and ACT scores are required for placement in math and English classes and they are required for students applying to the Presidential Scholars honors program. International applicants whose native language is not English must submit scores from TOEFL, PTE, or IELTS examinations.

Transfer students must submit official transcripts for admission and credit evaluation. Students may qualify for the one-year A.A.S. option if they hold a bachelor's degree or if they have a minimum of 30 transferable college credits, including 24 credits equivalent to FIT's liberal arts requirements.

Students seeking admission to a B.F.A. or B.S. program must hold an A.A.S. degree from FIT or an equivalent college degree and must meet the prerequisites for the specific major. Further requirements may include an interview with a departmental committee, review of academic standing, and portfolio review for applicants to B.F.A. programs. Any student who applies for baccalaureate-level transfer to FIT from a four-year program must have completed a minimum of 60 credits, including the requisite art or technical courses and the liberal arts requirements.

Application and Information

Students wishing to visit FIT are encouraged to attend a group information session and take a tour of FIT's campus. The visit schedule is available online at fitnyc.edu/visitfit. A virtual tour of the campus can be found at fitnyc.edu/virtualtour. Candidates may apply online at fitnyc.edu/admissions. More information is available by contacting:

Admissions
Fashion Institute of Technology
227 West 27 Street, Room C139
New York, New York 10001-5992
Phone: 212-217-3760
        800-GO-TO-FIT (toll-free)
E-mail: fitinfo@fitnyc.edu
Website: http://www.fitnyc.edu
        http://www.facebook.com/FashionInstituteofTechnology

FIDM/FASHION INSTITUTE OF DESIGN & MERCHANDISING

LOS ANGELES, CALIFORNIA

The Institute and Its Mission

FIDM/Fashion Institute of Design & Merchandising provides a dynamic and exciting community of learning in the fashion, graphics, interior design, digital media, and entertainment industries. Students can launch into one of thousands of exciting careers in as little as two years. FIDM offers two-year and four-year degree programs—Associate of Arts (A.A.), A.A. professional designation, A.A. advanced study, and Bachelor of Science (B.S.).

FIDM offers a highly focused education that prepares students for the professional world. Students can choose from twenty specialized creative business and design majors.

Established in 1969, FIDM is a private college that enrolls more than 7,500 students a year and has graduated nearly 50,000 students. Graduates receive membership in the Alumni Association, which keeps them well connected while providing up-to-the-minute alumni news and information. FIDM alumni chapters can be found in thirty-five locations around the United States, Europe, and Asia.

Career planning and job placement are among the most important services offered by the college. Career assistance includes job search techniques, preparation for employment interviews, resume preparation, virtual portfolios, and job adjustment assistance. FIDM's full-time Career Center department and advisers partner one-on-one with current students and graduates to help them move forward on their career path, within their chosen major. Employers post over 19,000 jobs a year on FIDM's alumni job search site, which is available 24/7 exclusively to FIDM students and graduates. FIDM career advisers connect students to internships and directly to professionals in the industry. FIDM also offers job fairs, open portfolio days, and networking days to allow students to meet alumni and industry leaders face-to-face. Because of the college's long-standing industry relationships, many firms come to FIDM first to recruit its students. Over 90 percent of FIDM graduates in all majors are successfully employed in their field of study within six months of graduation. Some of FIDM's successful graduates include celebrity designers Nick Verreos, Monique Lhuillier, and the co-founder of Juicy Couture, as well as Hollywood costume designer Marlene Stewart.

FIDM's ethnically and culturally diverse student body is one of the factors that attracts students. The current population includes students from more than thirty different countries. The Student Activities Department plans and coordinates social activities, cultural events, and community projects. Student organizations include the ASID student chapter, Cross-Cultural Student Alliance, American Association of Textile Chemists and Colorists, Phi Theta Kappa honor society, and the Alumni Association. The students also produce *FIDM MODE*, the student magazine that promotes awareness about the design industry, current events, and FIDM student life.

FIDM is accredited by the Accrediting Commission for Community and Junior and Senior Colleges of the Western Association of Schools and Colleges (WASC) and the National Association of Schools of Art and Design (NASAD).

Academic Programs

FIDM offers Associate of Arts (A.A.) degree programs, Bachelor's degree programs, Advanced Study programs, and Professional Designation programs. There are 22 specialized creative business and design majors to choose from.

Students can choose from the following Associate of Arts degrees: Apparel Industry Management, Beauty Industry Merchandising & Marketing, Digital Media, Fashion Design, Fashion Knitwear Design, Graphic Design, Interior Design, Jewelry Design, Merchandise Marketing, Merchandising Product Development, Textile Design, and Visual Communications. All of these programs offer the highly specialized curriculum of a specific major combined with a core general education/liberal arts foundation.

Many FIDM A.A. graduates take their skills to the next level through FIDM's B.S. in Business Management program as well. Only FIDM graduates from A.A. majors are eligible to apply to the Bachelor's program, which is offered at the Los Angeles and San Francisco campuses and available online. Students from all FIDM majors study and collaborate on business projects and take courses in accounting, human resource management, international finance, ethics, leadership, and more, giving them extensive knowledge of managing a business and the creative edge that is a growing necessity in the corporate world. FIDM's unique industry partnerships offer exciting opportunities for students through internships, job fairs events, and informative guest speakers that include companies such as Forever 21, JCPenney, Mattel, NBC Universal, Oakley, Smashbox, and Stila.

Students from other regionally accredited college programs have the opportunity to complement their previous college education by enrolling in FIDM's Professional Designation programs. Students can determine which credits will transfer and receive a personalized schedule toward completion of their professional designation program by consulting with FIDM admissions advisers. FIDM offers professional designation programs in Apparel Industry Management, Beauty Industry Management, Digital Media, Fashion Design, Fashion Knitwear Design, Graphic Design, Interior Design, International Manufacturing and Product Development, Jewelry Design, Textile Design, and Visual Communications. For more information about FIDM transfer programs, students can visit http://fidm.edu/go/admissionstransfer.

FIDM operates on a four-quarter academic calendar. New students may begin their studies at the start of any quarter throughout the year. Detailed information about FIDM majors and curriculum is also available online at http://fidm.edu/en/Majors/.

Department chairs and trained Advisors assist students in selecting the correct sequence of courses to complete degree requirements. The counseling department provides personal guidance and referral to outside counseling services and matches peer tutors to specific students' needs. Individual Development and Education Assistance (IDEA) Centers at each campus provide students with additional educational assistance in the areas of writing, mathematics, computer competency, study skills, research skills, and reading comprehension.

FIDM's eLearning program, which includes the B.S. in Business Management and some classes in other majors, ensures that a student's educational experience can take place anywhere. The online courses are designed to replicate the experience of classes on campus. Students in the eLearning program are granted the same high-quality education as students on campus and have immediate access to valuable campus resources, including the FIDM Library, career advisers, and instructors.

Off-Campus Programs

Internships are available within each major. Paid and volunteer positions provide work experience for students to gain practical application of classroom skills.

FIDM provides the opportunity for students to participate in academic study tours in Europe, Asia, and New York. These tours are specifically designed to broaden and enhance the specialized education offered at FIDM. Participants may earn academic credit under faculty-supervised directed studies. Exchange programs are also available with Esmod, Paris; Instituto Artictico dell' Abbigliamento Marangoni, Milan; Accademia Internazionale d'Alta Mode e d'Arte del Costume Koefia, Rome; St. Martins School of Art, London; College of Distributive Trades, London; and Janette Klein Design School, Mexico City.

Costs

For the 2014–15 academic year, tuition, fees, books, and most supplies start at $30,085, depending on the selected major. First-year application fees range from $225 for California residents to $525 for international students.

Financial Aid

There are several sources of financial funding available to the student, including federal financial aid and education loan programs, California state aid programs, institutional loan programs, and FIDM awards and scholarships. The FIDM Student Financial Services Office and FIDM admissions advisors work one-on-one with students and parents to help them find funding for their FIDM education. More information on FIDM scholarships and financial aid can be found at http://fidm.edu/go/fidmscholarships.

Faculty

FIDM faculty members are selected as specialists in their fields, working professionals with impressive resumes and invaluable industry connections. They bring daily exposure from their industry into the classroom for the benefit of the students. In pursuit of the best faculty members, consideration is given to both academic excellence and practical experience.

Facilities and Resources

FIDM's award-winning campuses feature design studios with computer labs and innovative study spaces, spacious classrooms, imaginative common areas, and state-of-the-industry technology. Computer labs support and enhance the educational programs of the Institute. Specialized labs offer computerized cutting and marking; graphic, interior, and textile design; word processing; and database management.

The FIDM Library goes beyond traditional sources of information. It houses a print and electronic collection of over 2.5 million titles that encompass all subject areas, with an emphasis on fashion, interior design, retailing, and costume. The library subscribes to over 160 international and national periodicals, offering the latest information on art, design, graphics, fashion, beauty, business, and current trends. The FIDM Library also features an international video library, subscriptions to major predictive services, interior design workrooms, textile samples, a trimmings/findings collection, and access to the Internet.

The FIDM Museum & Galleries' permanent and study collections contain more than 12,000 garments from the eighteenth century to present day, including film and theater costumes. One of the largest collections in the United States, it features top designer holdings including Chanel, Yves Saint Laurent, Dior, and Lacroix. The collection also includes items from the California Historical Society (First Families), the Hollywood Collection, and the Rudi Gernreich Collection.

Location

FIDM's main campus is in the heart of downtown Los Angeles near the famed California Market Center and Fashion District. There are additional California campuses in San Francisco, San Diego, and Orange County. A virtual tour of the campuses and their locations is available at http://fidm.edu/en/Visit+FIDM/Launch+Virtual+Tour.

FIDM Los Angeles is nestled at the center of an incredibly vibrant apparel and entertainment hub, surrounded by the fashion, entertainment, jewelry, and financial districts. It is situated next to beautiful Grand Hope Park, a tree-filled oasis amid the hustle and bustle of downtown Los Angeles. Newly renovated by acclaimed architect Clive Wilkinson, FIDM San Francisco stands in the heart of historic Union Square. The country's third-largest shopping area and stimulating atmosphere combined with the industry-based staff and faculty make this campus as incredible as the city in which it is located.

The FIDM Orange County campus is a dynamic visual experience with ultramodern lofts, an indoor/outdoor student lounge, eye-popping colors, and a one-of-a-kind audiovisual igloo. Also designed by world-renowned architect Clive Wilkinson, this campus has received several prestigious architectural awards and has been featured in numerous national magazines.

FIDM San Diego's gorgeous campus overlooks PETCO Park and is near the historic Gaslamp district and the San Diego harbor. FIDM's newest campus is sophisticated, stylish, and tech savvy, reflecting the importance of California's fastest-growing city and its appeal to the global industry.

Admission Requirements

Students are accepted into one of FIDM's specialized Associate of Arts degree programs which offer 16–25 challenging courses per major. Associate of Arts programs are designed for high school graduates or applicants with strong GED scores. These programs offer the highly specialized curriculum of a specific major, as well as a traditional liberal arts/ general studies foundation. Official transcripts from high school/secondary schools and all colleges/universities attended are needed to apply. International students must send transcripts accompanied by official English translations. Three recommendations from teachers, counselors, or employers are also required for admission. FIDM provides a reference request form on its website in the Admissions section under "How To Apply." All references must be sealed and mailed to the school when applying. An admissions essay portion and portfolio/entrance project requirement, which is specific to the student's selected major, are also available on the website's Admissions section under "How To Apply."

For more information on the application process, prospective students can go to www.fidm.edu.

Application and Information

FIDM/Fashion Institute of Design & Merchandising
919 South Grand Avenue
Los Angeles, California 90015
United States
Phone: 800-624-1200 (toll-free)
Fax: 213-624-4799
Website: http://www.fidm.edu
        http://www.facebook.com/home.php/#!/FIDMCollege
        http://twitter.com/#!/FIDM

FIDM Los Angeles (exterior campus)

Indexes

2013–14 Changes in Institutions

Following is an alphabetical listing of institutions that have recently closed, merged with other institutions, or changed their name or status. In the case of a name change, the former name appears first, followed by the new name.

American College of Technology (Saint Joseph, MO): *name changed to American Business & Technology University.*

Anthem Institute–Las Vegas (Las Vegas, NV): *name changed to Anthem College–Las Vegas.*

Applied Professional Training, Inc. (Carlsbad, CA): *name changed to APT College.*

The Art Institute of Ohio–Cincinnati (Cincinnati, OH): *now classified as 4-year college.*

The Art Institute of Seattle (Seattle, WA): *now classified as 4-year college.*

The Art Institute of York–Pennsylvania (York, PA): *now classified as 4-year college.*

ASA The College For Excellence (Brooklyn, NY): *name changed to ASA College.*

ATI Career Training Center (Fort Lauderdale, FL): *closed.*

ATI College of Health (Miami, FL): *closed.*

ATI Technical Training Center (Dallas, TX): *closed.*

Aviation Institute of Maintenance–Chesapeake (Chesapeake, VA): *no longer offers undergraduate degrees.*

Aviation Institute of Maintenance–Indianapolis (Indianapolis, IN): *no longer offers undergraduate degrees.*

Aviation Institute of Maintenance–Kansas City (Kansas City, MO): *no longer offers undergraduate degrees.*

Aviation Institute of Maintenance–Manassas (Manassas, VA): *no longer offers undergraduate degrees.*

Bainbridge College (Bainbridge, GA): *name changed to Bainbridge State College.*

Benedictine University at Springfield (Springfield, IL): *now classified as 4-year college.*

Boulder College of Massage Therapy (Boulder, CO): *closed.*

Bowling Green Technical College (Bowling Green, KY): *name changed to Southcentral Kentucky Community and Technical College.*

Brevard Community College (Cocoa, FL): *name changed to Eastern Florida State College.*

Bridgemont Community & Technical College (Montgomery, WV): *name changed to BridgeValley Community and Technical College.*

Brown College (Mendota Heights, MN): *name changed to Sanford-Brown College.*

California Culinary Academy (San Francisco, CA): *name changed to Le Cordon Bleu College of Culinary Arts in San Francisco.*

Capital Area Technical College–Baton Rouge Campus (Baton Rouge, LA): *merged into Baton Rouge Community College (Baton Rouge, LA).*

Carrington College of California–Antioch (Antioch, CA): *closed.*

Carrington College of California–Citrus Heights (Citrus Heights, CA): *name changed to Carrington College California–Citrus Heights.*

Carrington College of California–Emeryville (Emeryville, CA): *closed.*

Carrington College of California–Sacramento (Sacramento, CA): *name changed to Carrington College California–Sacramento.*

Carrington College–Portland (Portland, OR): *closed.*

Centura College (Richmond, VA): *closed.*

Centura Institute (Orlando, FL): *no longer offers undergraduate degrees.*

The College of Office Technology (Chicago, IL): *closed.*

Copiah-Lincoln Community College–Natchez Campus (Natchez, MS): *merged into a single entry for Copiah-Lincoln Community College (Wesson, MS) by request from the institution.*

Court Reporting Institute of Houston (Houston, TX): *name changed to Court Reporting Institute of St. Louis (school moved from Houston to St. Louis).*

ECPI College of Technology (Charlotte, NC): *name changed to ECPI University.*

ECPI College of Technology (Greensboro, NC): *name changed to ECPI University.*

ECPI College of Technology (Columbia, SC): *name changed to ECPI University.*

ECPI College of Technology (Greenville, SC): *name changed to ECPI University.*

ECPI College of Technology (North Charleston, SC): *name changed to ECPI University.*

ECPI College of Technology (Richmond, VA): *name changed to ECPI University.*

Elaine P. Nunez Community College (Chalmette, LA): *name changed to Nunez Community College.*

Ellis School of Nursing (Schenectady, NY): *name changed to The Belanger School of Nursing.*

Everest College (Arlington, VA): *closed.*

Everest Institute (Fort Lauderdale, FL): *closed.*

Everest Institute (Hialeah, FL): *closed.*

Fortis College (Tampa, FL): *closed and merged into Fortis College (Largo, FL).*

Grayson County College (Denison, TX): *name changed to Grayson College.*

Hesser College, Concord (Concord, NH): *closed.*

Hesser College, Manchester (Manchester, NH): *name changed to Mount Washington College.*

Hesser College, Nashua (Nashua, NH): *name changed to Mount Washington College.*

Hesser College, Portsmouth (Portsmouth, NH): *closed.*

Hesser College, Salem (Salem, NH): *name changed to Mount Washington College.*

Instituto Comercial de Puerto Rico Junior College (San Juan, PR): *name changed to ICPR Junior College–Hato Rey Campus.*

Kanawha Valley Community and Technical College (South Charleston, WV): *name changed to BridgeValley Community and Technical College.*

Kaplan University, Council Bluffs (Council Bluffs, IA): *closed.*

Lancaster General College of Nursing & Health Sciences (Lancaster, PA): *name changed to Pennsylvania College of Health Sciences.*

Laurel Technical Institute (Meadville, PA): *merged into a single entry for Laurel Technical Institute (Sharon, PA) by request from the institution.*

Le Cordon Bleu College of Culinary Arts (Saint Paul, MN): *name changed to Le Cordon Bleu College of Culinary Arts in Minneapolis/ St. Paul.*

Le Cordon Bleu College of Culinary Arts, Atlanta (Tucker, GA): *name changed to Le Cordon Bleu College of Culinary Arts in Atlanta.*

Le Cordon Bleu College of Culinary Arts, Las Vegas (Las Vegas, NV): *name changed to Le Cordon Bleu College of Culinary Arts in Las Vegas.*

Le Cordon Bleu College of Culinary Arts, Miami (Miramar, FL): *name changed to Le Cordon Bleu College of Culinary Arts in Miami.*

Le Cordon Bleu Institute of Culinary Arts in Pittsburgh (Pittsburgh, PA): *closed.*

Lincoln College of New England (Suffield, CT): *closed.*

Lincoln College of Technology (Florence, KY): *closed.*

Lincoln College of Technology (Cincinnati, OH): *closed.*

Lincoln College of Technology (Dayton, OH): *closed.*

Long Island College Hospital School of Nursing (Brooklyn, NY): *closed.*

MedVance Institute (Palm Springs, FL): *name changed to Fortis Institute.*

Middle Georgia Technical College (Warner Robbins, GA): *merged into Central Georgia Technical College (Warner Robins, GA).*

Minnesota School of Business–Richfield (Richfield, MN): *now classified as 4-year college.*

Minnesota School of Business–St. Cloud (Waite Park, MN): *now classified as 4-year college.*

Minnesota School of Business–Shakopee (Shakopee, MN): *now classified as 4-year college.*

National College (Stow, OH): *name changed to National College of Business and Technology.*

National College (Charlottesville, VA): *name changed to American National University.*

National College (Danville, VA): *name changed to American National University.*

National College (Harrisonburg, VA): *name changed to American National University.*

National College (Lynchburg, VA): *name changed to American National University.*

National College (Martinsville, VA): *name changed to American National University.*

National College (Salem, VA): *name changed to American National University.*

National College of Business and Technology (Bristol, TN): *name changed to National College.*

National College of Business and Technology (Knoxville, TN): *name changed to National College.*

Navajo Technical College (Crownpoint, NM): *name changed to Navajo Technical University.*

Newport Business Institute (Lower Burrell, PA): *closed.*

Newport Business Institute (Williamsport, PA): *closed.*

Northeast Louisiana Technical College–Northeast Campus (Winnsboro, LA): *merged into Louisiana Delta Community College (Monroe, LA).*

Northshore Technical Community College–Florida Parishes Campus (Greensburg, LA): *merged into a single entry for Northshore Technical Community College (Bogalusa, LA).*

Northwest Technical Institute (Eagan, MN): *merged into a single entry for Globe University–Woodbury (Woodbury, MN) by request from the institution.*

Oakbridge Academy of Arts (Lower Burrell, PA): *closed.*

Oconee Fall Line Technical College–North Campus (Sandersville, GA): *name changed to Oconee Fall Line Technical College.*

Oconee Fall Line Technical College–South Campus (Dublin, GA): *merged into a single entry for Oconee Fall Line Technical College (Sandersville, GA) by request from the institution.*

Olean Business Institute (Olean, NY): *closed.*

Omaha School of Massage Therapy and Healthcare of Herzing University (Omaha, NE): *name changed to Omaha School of Massage and Healthcare of Herzing University.*

Pace Institute (Reading, PA): *closing and acquired by Baker College System.*

Pasco-Hernando Community College (New Port Richey, FL): *name changed to Pasco-Hernando State College.*

Ramírez College of Business and Technology (San Juan, PR): *closed.*

Rasmussen College Aurora (Aurora, IL): *now classified as 4-year college.*

Rasmussen College Bismarck (Bismarck, ND): *now classified as 4-year college.*

Rasmussen College Bloomington (Bloomington, MN): *now classified as 4-year college.*

Rasmussen College Brooklyn Park (Brooklyn Park, MN): *now classified as 4-year college.*

Rasmussen College Eagan (Eagan, MN): *now classified as 4-year college.*

Rasmussen College Fargo (Fargo, ND): *now classified as 4-year college.*

Rasmussen College Fort Myers (Fort Myers, FL): *now classified as 4-year college.*

Rasmussen College Green Bay (Green Bay, WI): *now classified as 4-year college.*

Rasmussen College Lake Elmo/Woodbury (Lake Elmo, MN): *now classified as 4-year college.*

Rasmussen College Mankato (Mankato, MN): *now classified as 4-year college.*

Rasmussen College Moorhead (Moorhead, MN): *now classified as 4-year college.*

Rasmussen College New Port Richey (New Port Richey, FL): *now classified as 4-year college.*

Rasmussen College Ocala (Ocala, FL): *now classified as 4-year college.*

Rasmussen College Rockford (Rockford, IL): *now classified as 4-year college.*

Rasmussen College St. Cloud (St. Cloud, MN): *now classified as 4-year college.*

Remington College–Cleveland West Campus (North Olmstead, OH): *closed.*

St. Louis Community College at Florissant Valley (St. Louis, MO): *merged into a single entry for St. Louis Community College (St. Louis, MO) by request from the institution.*

St. Louis Community College at Forest Park (St. Louis, MO): *merged into a single entry for St. Louis Community College (St. Louis, MO) by request from the institution.*

St. Louis Community College at Meramec (Kirkwood, MO): *merged into a single entry for St. Louis Community College (St. Louis, MO) by request from the institution.*

Sanford-Brown Institute (Tampa, FL): *name changed to Sanford-Brown College.*

Sanford-Brown Institute–Pittsburgh (Pittsburgh, PA): *closed.*

School of Urban Missions (Oakland, CA): *name changed to SUM Bible College & Theological Seminary.*

Simmons Institute of Funeral Service (Syracuse, NY): *closed.*

South Central Louisiana Technical College–Young Memorial Campus (Morgan City, LA): *name changed to South Central Louisiana Technical College.*

Southern Technical College (Auburndale, FL): *merged into a single entry for Southern Technical College (Orlando, FL).*

South Georgia State College (Waycross, GA): *merged into a single entry for South Georgia State College (Douglas, GA) by request from the institution.*

State University of New York College of Environmental Science and Forestry, Ranger School (Wanakena, NY): *merged into a single entry for State University of New York College of Environmental Science and Forestry (Syracuse, NY) by request from the institution.*

The University of Montana–Helena College of Technology (Helena, MT): *name changed to Helena College University of Montana.*

Valley College of Technology (Martinsburg, WV): *name changed to Valley College.*

Vincennes University Jasper Campus (Jasper, IN): *merged into a single entry for Vincennes University (Vincennes, IN) by request from the institution.*

WyoTech Sacramento (West Sacramento, CA): *closed.*

Associate Degree Programs at Two-Year Colleges

ACCOUNTING

Albany Tech Coll (GA)
Alexandria Tech and Comm Coll (MN)
Allen Comm Coll (KS)
Alvin Comm Coll (TX)
Amarillo Coll (TX)
American Samoa Comm Coll (AS)
Anoka-Ramsey Comm Coll (MN)
Anoka-Ramsey Comm Coll, Cambridge Campus (MN)
Anoka Tech Coll (MN)
Arizona Western Coll (AZ)
Athens Tech Coll (GA)
Atlanta Tech Coll (GA)
Augusta Tech Coll (GA)
Bainbridge State Coll (GA)
Bay State Coll (MA)
Beal Coll (ME)
Berkeley City Coll (CA)
Blackhawk Tech Coll (WI)
Blue Ridge Comm and Tech Coll (WV)
Bristol Comm Coll (MA)
Bronx Comm Coll of the City U of New York (NY)
Brookhaven Coll (TX)
Broward Coll (FL)
Bunker Hill Comm Coll (MA)
Butte Coll (CA)
Cambria-Rowe Business Coll, Indiana (PA)
Cambria-Rowe Business Coll, Johnstown (PA)
Casper Coll (WY)
Central Carolina Comm Coll (NC)
Central Georgia Tech Coll (GA)
Central Maine Comm Coll (ME)
Central Ohio Tech Coll (OH)
Central Oregon Comm Coll (OR)
Central Wyoming Coll (WY)
Century Coll (MN)
Chandler-Gilbert Comm Coll (AZ)
Chattahoochee Tech Coll (GA)
Chipola Coll (FL)
Chippewa Valley Tech Coll (WI)
Cincinnati State Tech and Comm Coll (OH)
Clark State Comm Coll (OH)
Clatsop Comm Coll (OR)
Cleveland Comm Coll (NC)
Clinton Comm Coll (NY)
Coll of Southern Idaho (ID)
Coll of Southern Maryland (MD)
Coll of the Ouachitas (AR)
Colorado Northwestern Comm Coll (CO)
Columbia Gorge Comm Coll (OR)
Columbus Tech Coll (GA)
Comm Coll of Philadelphia (PA)
Comm Coll of Rhode Island (RI)
Comm Coll of Vermont (VT)
Copiah-Lincoln Comm Coll (MS)
Cumberland County Coll (NJ)
Dakota Coll at Bottineau (ND)
Darton State Coll (GA)
Davis Coll (OH)
Daytona State Coll (FL)
De Anza Coll (CA)
Delaware Tech & Comm Coll, Jack F. Owens Campus (DE)
Delaware Tech & Comm Coll, Stanton/Wilmington Campus (DE)
Delaware Tech & Comm Coll, Terry Campus (DE)
Dutchess Comm Coll (NY)
Eastern Gateway Comm Coll (OH)
Eastern Idaho Tech Coll (ID)
Eastern Wyoming Coll (WY)

Edison Comm Coll (OH)
Elgin Comm Coll (IL)
Elmira Business Inst (NY)
Fayetteville Tech Comm Coll (NC)
Finger Lakes Comm Coll (NY)
Flathead Valley Comm Coll (MT)
Florida State Coll at Jacksonville (FL)
Fox Valley Tech Coll (WI)
Frank Phillips Coll (TX)
Genesee Comm Coll (NY)
Georgia Northwestern Tech Coll (GA)
Georgia Piedmont Tech Coll (GA)
Gogebic Comm Coll (MI)
Golden West Coll (CA)
Grayson Coll (TX)
Greenville Tech Coll (SC)
Gwinnett Tech Coll (GA)
Halifax Comm Coll (NC)
Harford Comm Coll (MD)
Harper Coll (IL)
Hawkeye Comm Coll (IA)
Helena Coll U of Montana (MT)
Highland Comm Coll (IL)
Hinds Comm Coll (MS)
Hocking Coll (OH)
Housatonic Comm Coll (CT)
Houston Comm Coll System (TX)
Howard Comm Coll (MD)
Illinois Eastern Comm Colls, Olney Central College (IL)
Imperial Valley Coll (CA)
Independence Comm Coll (KS)
Iowa Lakes Comm Coll (IA)
ITT Tech Inst, Arlington (TX)
ITT Tech Inst, Austin (TX)
ITT Tech Inst, DeSoto (TX)
ITT Tech Inst, Houston (TX)
ITT Tech Inst, Houston (TX)
ITT Tech Inst, San Antonio (TX)
ITT Tech Inst, San Antonio (TX)
ITT Tech Inst, Waco (TX)
ITT Tech Inst, Webster (TX)
ITT Tech Inst (UT)
Ivy Tech Comm Coll–Lafayette (IN)
James Sprunt Comm Coll (NC)
Jefferson Comm Coll (NY)
Johnston Comm Coll (NC)
Kaskaskia Coll (IL)
Kent State U at Ashtabula (OH)
Kent State U at Tuscarawas (OH)
Kilian Comm Coll (SD)
Kingsborough Comm Coll of the City U of New York (NY)
Lakeland Comm Coll (OH)
Lakes Region Comm Coll (NH)
Lake Superior Coll (MN)
Lake Tahoe Comm Coll (CA)
Lamar Comm Coll (CO)
Lamar State Coll–Orange (TX)
Lanier Tech Coll (GA)
Laramie County Comm Coll (WY)
LDS Business Coll (UT)
Lincoln Land Comm Coll (IL)
Lone Star Coll–CyFair (TX)
Lone Star Coll–Kingwood (TX)
Lone Star Coll–North Harris (TX)
Lone Star Coll–Tomball (TX)
Lone Star Coll–U Park (TX)
Long Island Business Inst (NY)
Lorain County Comm Coll (OH)
Los Angeles Mission Coll (CA)
Lower Columbia Coll (WA)
Luzerne County Comm Coll (PA)
Macomb Comm Coll (MI)
Manchester Comm Coll (CT)
Massachusetts Bay Comm Coll (MA)
McHenry County Coll (IL)

Mercer County Comm Coll (NJ)
Mesa Comm Coll (AZ)
Middlesex County Coll (NJ)
Minneapolis Comm and Tech Coll (MN)
Minnesota School of Business–Brooklyn Center (MN)
Minnesota School of Business–Plymouth (MN)
Minnesota State Coll–Southeast Tech (MN)
Mississippi Delta Comm Coll (MS)
Mississippi Gulf Coast Comm Coll (MS)
Missouri State U–West Plains (MO)
Mitchell Comm Coll (NC)
Mohave Comm Coll (AZ)
Monroe Comm Coll (NY)
Monroe County Comm Coll (MI)
Montgomery County Comm Coll (PA)
Moraine Park Tech Coll (WI)
Moultrie Tech Coll (GA)
Mountain View Coll (TX)
Mt. San Antonio Coll (CA)
Nassau Comm Coll (NY)
Niagara County Comm Coll (NY)
Northcentral Tech Coll (WI)
Northeastern Jr Coll (CO)
Northeastern Tech Coll (SC)
Northeast Iowa Comm Coll (IA)
Northeast Texas Comm Coll (TX)
Northern Essex Comm Coll (MA)
North Iowa Area Comm Coll (IA)
North Shore Comm Coll (MA)
NorthWest Arkansas Comm Coll (AR)
Northwest Coll (WY)
Northwestern Connecticut Comm Coll (CT)
Northwest Mississippi Comm Coll (MS)
Northwest Tech Coll (MN)
Norwalk Comm Coll (CT)
Oconee Fall Line Tech Coll (GA)
Ogeechee Tech Coll (GA)
Oklahoma City Comm Coll (OK)
Oklahoma State U, Oklahoma City (OK)
Onondaga Comm Coll (NY)
Orange Coast Coll (CA)
Ozarks Tech Comm Coll (MO)
Palomar Coll (CA)
Paris Jr Coll (TX)
Pasadena City Coll (CA)
Patrick Henry Comm Coll (VA)
Pennsylvania Highlands Comm Coll (PA)
Pensacola State Coll (FL)
Phoenix Coll (AZ)
Piedmont Comm Coll (NC)
Pima Comm Coll (AZ)
Pitt Comm Coll (NC)
Potomac State Coll of West Virginia U (WV)
Randolph Comm Coll (NC)
Rappahannock Comm Coll (VA)
Reading Area Comm Coll (PA)
Richmond Comm Coll (NC)
River Valley Comm Coll (NH)
Roane State Comm Coll (TN)
Rock Valley Coll (IL)
San Diego City Coll (CA)
San Jacinto Coll District (TX)
Santa Monica Coll (CA)
Sauk Valley Comm Coll (IL)
Savannah Tech Coll (GA)
Scottsdale Comm Coll (AZ)
Seminole State Coll (OK)
Seminole State Coll of Florida (FL)

Shawnee Comm Coll (IL)
Shoreline Comm Coll (WA)
Snow Coll (UT)
Southeastern Comm Coll (IA)
Southeastern Tech Coll (GA)
Southeast Tech Inst (SD)
Southern Crescent Tech Coll (GA)
Southern U at Shreveport (LA)
South Florida State Coll (FL)
South Georgia Tech Coll (GA)
South Piedmont Comm Coll (NC)
South Plains Coll (TX)
South Suburban Coll (IL)
Southwestern Comm Coll (NC)
Southwestern Illinois Coll (IL)
Southwest Georgia Tech Coll (GA)
Spartanburg Comm Coll (SC)
Spoon River Coll (IL)
Springfield Tech Comm Coll (MA)
Stark State Coll (OH)
State Fair Comm Coll (MO)
Sullivan County Comm Coll (NY)
Sussex County Comm Coll (NJ)
Tarrant County Coll District (TX)
Three Rivers Comm Coll (CT)
Trident Tech Coll (SC)
Trinity Valley Comm Coll (TX)
Tunxis Comm Coll (CT)
Tyler Jr Coll (TX)
Umpqua Comm Coll (OR)
U of Hawaii Maui Coll (HI)
U of New Mexico–Los Alamos Branch (NM)
Victoria Coll (TX)
Virginia Western Comm Coll (VA)
Waubonsee Comm Coll (IL)
Waukesha County Tech Coll (WI)
Wayne Comm Coll (NC)
Wenatchee Valley Coll (WA)
Westchester Comm Coll (NY)
Western Dakota Tech Inst (SD)
Western Nevada Coll (NV)
Western Texas Coll (TX)
Western Wyoming Comm Coll (WY)
West Georgia Tech Coll (GA)
West Kentucky Comm and Tech Coll (KY)
Wiregrass Georgia Tech Coll (GA)
Wisconsin Indianhead Tech Coll (WI)
Wright Career Coll, Overland Park (KS)
Wright Career Coll (NE)
Wytheville Comm Coll (VA)
York County Comm Coll (ME)

ACCOUNTING AND BUSINESS/MANAGEMENT
Berkeley City Coll (CA)
Harrisburg Area Comm Coll (PA)
LDS Business Coll (UT)
Lone Star Coll–Montgomery (TX)
Mitchell Tech Inst (SD)
Mountain State Coll (WV)
Northeast Texas Comm Coll (TX)
Oakland Comm Coll (MI)

ACCOUNTING AND COMPUTER SCIENCE
Gogebic Comm Coll (MI)
State Fair Comm Coll (MO)

ACCOUNTING AND FINANCE
Jackson Coll (MI)

ACCOUNTING RELATED
Central Virginia Comm Coll (VA)
Dakota Coll at Bottineau (ND)
Davis Coll (OH)
John Tyler Comm Coll (VA)

J. Sargeant Reynolds Comm Coll (VA)
Lansing Comm Coll (MI)
Mountain Empire Comm Coll (VA)
Northwest Florida State Coll (FL)
Raritan Valley Comm Coll (NJ)
Southwest Virginia Comm Coll (VA)

ACCOUNTING TECHNOLOGY AND BOOKKEEPING
Alamance Comm Coll (NC)
Anoka-Ramsey Comm Coll (MN)
Anoka-Ramsey Comm Coll, Cambridge Campus (MN)
Arapahoe Comm Coll (CO)
Austin Comm Coll (TX)
Barstow Comm Coll (CA)
Bellingham Tech Coll (WA)
Big Bend Comm Coll (WA)
Bishop State Comm Coll (AL)
Borough of Manhattan Comm Coll of the City U of New York (NY)
Bradford School (PA)
Broward Coll (FL)
Brown Mackie Coll–Indianapolis (IN)
Bucks County Comm Coll (PA)
Ca&nnada Coll (CA)
Cape Fear Comm Coll (NC)
Carrington Coll California–Citrus Heights (CA)
Carrington Coll California–Pleasant Hill (CA)
Carrington Coll California–San Jose (CA)
Carrington Coll California–San Leandro (CA)
Carroll Comm Coll (MD)
Casper Coll (WY)
Catawba Valley Comm Coll (NC)
Cayuga County Comm Coll (NY)
Central Maine Comm Coll (ME)
Central Wyoming Coll (WY)
Chandler-Gilbert Comm Coll (AZ)
Clark Coll (WA)
Coconino Comm Coll (AZ)
Coll of Central Florida (FL)
Coll of Marin (CA)
Coll of Southern Maryland (MD)
Coll of the Canyons (CA)
Columbia-Greene Comm Coll (NY)
Columbus State Comm Coll (OH)
Comm Coll of Allegheny County (PA)
The Comm Coll of Baltimore County (MD)
Cosumnes River Coll, Sacramento (CA)
Dakota Coll at Bottineau (ND)
Danville Area Comm Coll (IL)
Delta Coll (MI)
Dutchess Comm Coll (NY)
East Central Coll (MO)
Fiorello H. LaGuardia Comm Coll of the City U of New York (NY)
Fox Coll (IL)
Fullerton Coll (CA)
Gadsden State Comm Coll (AL)
Gavilan Coll (CA)
Glendale Comm Coll (AZ)
Grays Harbor Coll (WA)
Great Falls Coll Montana State U (MT)
Greenfield Comm Coll (MA)
Hagerstown Comm Coll (MD)
Harford Comm Coll (MD)
Harrisburg Area Comm Coll (PA)
Herkimer County Comm Coll (NY)
Hillsborough Comm Coll (FL)
Hinds Comm Coll (MS)
Holyoke Comm Coll (MA)

Ilisagvik Coll (AK)
Inst of Business & Medical Careers (CO)
International Business Coll, Indianapolis (IN)
Iowa Lakes Comm Coll (IA)
ITT Tech Inst, Richardson (TX)
Ivy Tech Comm Coll–Bloomington (IN)
Ivy Tech Comm Coll–Central Indiana (IN)
Ivy Tech Comm Coll–Columbus (IN)
Ivy Tech Comm Coll–East Central (IN)
Ivy Tech Comm Coll–Kokomo (IN)
Ivy Tech Comm Coll–Lafayette (IN)
Ivy Tech Comm Coll–North Central (IN)
Ivy Tech Comm Coll–Northeast (IN)
Ivy Tech Comm Coll–Northwest (IN)
Ivy Tech Comm Coll–Richmond (IN)
Ivy Tech Comm Coll–Southeast (IN)
Ivy Tech Comm Coll–Southern Indiana (IN)
Ivy Tech Comm Coll–Southwest (IN)
Ivy Tech Comm Coll–Wabash Valley (IN)
Jamestown Comm Coll (NY)
Jefferson Comm Coll (NY)
Jefferson State Comm Coll (AL)
Kent State U at Ashtabula (OH)
Kent State U at East Liverpool (OH)
Kent State U at Salem (OH)
Kent State U at Trumbull (OH)
Kent State U at Tuscarawas (OH)
Kilgore Coll (TX)
King's Coll (NC)
Lake Land Coll (IL)
Lane Comm Coll (OR)
Lansing Comm Coll (MI)
Lawson State Comm Coll (AL)
LDS Business Coll (UT)
Lehigh Carbon Comm Coll (PA)
Linn-Benton Comm Coll (OR)
Lower Columbia Coll (WA)
Manhattan Area Tech Coll (KS)
Miami Dade Coll (FL)
Minneapolis Business Coll (MN)
Minneapolis Comm and Tech Coll (MN)
Minnesota State Coll–Southeast Tech (MN)
MiraCosta Coll (CA)
Mohawk Valley Comm Coll (NY)
Montgomery Coll (MD)
Montgomery County Comm Coll (PA)
Mott Comm Coll (MI)
Nassau Comm Coll (NY)
Northampton Comm Coll (PA)
North Iowa Area Comm Coll (IA)
Northwest Florida State Coll (FL)
Oakland Comm Coll (MI)
Oakton Comm Coll (IL)
Olympic Coll (WA)
Onondaga Comm Coll (NY)
Owens Comm Coll, Toledo (OH)
Pasadena City Coll (CA)
Pennsylvania Highlands Comm Coll (PA)
Pueblo Comm Coll (CO)
Raritan Valley Comm Coll (NJ)
Reading Area Comm Coll (PA)
Rogue Comm Coll (OR)
St. Clair County Comm Coll (MI)
Salt Lake Comm Coll (UT)
San Juan Coll (NM)
Schoolcraft Coll (MI)
Southern State Comm Coll (OH)
Southern U at Shreveport (LA)
South Florida State Coll (FL)
South Suburban Coll (IL)
Southwestern Indian Polytechnic Inst (NM)
Southwestern Michigan Coll (MI)
Spencerian Coll (KY)
State U of New York Coll of Technology at Alfred (NY)
Tallahassee Comm Coll (FL)
TCI–The Coll of Technology (NY)
Tompkins Cortland Comm Coll (NY)
Tulsa Comm Coll (OK)
Vincennes U (IN)
Walla Walla Comm Coll (WA)
Wayne County Comm Coll District (MI)
Wenatchee Valley Coll (WA)
Western Oklahoma State Coll (OK)
Westmoreland County Comm Coll (PA)
Williston State Coll (ND)

Wood Tobe–Coburn School (NY)
Wor-Wic Comm Coll (MD)

ACTING
Casper Coll (WY)
Central Wyoming Coll (WY)
Greenfield Comm Coll (MA)
Northampton Comm Coll (PA)

ACTUARIAL SCIENCE
Broward Coll (FL)
South Florida State Coll (FL)

ADMINISTRATIVE ASSISTANT AND SECRETARIAL SCIENCE
Allen Comm Coll (KS)
Altamaha Tech Coll (GA)
Alvin Comm Coll (TX)
Amarillo Coll (TX)
Anoka Tech Coll (MN)
Antelope Valley Coll (CA)
Athens Tech Coll (GA)
Augusta Tech Coll (GA)
Austin Comm Coll (TX)
Bainbridge State Coll (GA)
Beal Coll (ME)
Bevill State Comm Coll (AL)
Bishop State Comm Coll (AL)
Bismarck State Coll (ND)
Blackhawk Tech Coll (WI)
Borough of Manhattan Comm Coll of the City U of New York (NY)
Bossier Parish Comm Coll (LA)
Bradford School (PA)
Bronx Comm Coll of the City U of New York (NY)
Butler County Comm Coll (PA)
Butte Coll (CA)
Cambria-Rowe Business Coll, Indiana (PA)
Cambria-Rowe Business Coll, Johnstown (PA)
Ca&nnada Coll (CA)
Career Tech Coll, Monroe (LA)
Carroll Comm Coll (MD)
Casper Coll (WY)
Cecil Coll (MD)
Central Carolina Comm Coll (NC)
Central Georgia Tech Coll (GA)
Central Maine Comm Coll (ME)
Central Oregon Comm Coll (OR)
Central Wyoming Coll (WY)
Century Coll (MN)
Chattahoochee Tech Coll (GA)
Chippewa Valley Tech Coll (WI)
Cincinnati State Tech and Comm Coll (OH)
Clark State Comm Coll (OH)
Cleveland State Comm Coll (TN)
Cloud County Comm Coll (KS)
Cochise Coll, Sierra Vista (AZ)
Coll of Southern Idaho (ID)
Coll of the Canyons (CA)
Coll of the Ouachitas (AR)
Coll of Western Idaho (ID)
Collin County Comm Coll District (TX)
Columbia Coll (CA)
Columbia Gorge Comm Coll (OR)
Columbia-Greene Comm Coll (NY)
Columbus State Comm Coll (OH)
Columbus Tech Coll (GA)
Comm Coll of Allegheny County (PA)
The Comm Coll of Baltimore County (MD)
Comm Coll of Rhode Island (RI)
Comm Coll of Vermont (VT)
Cosumnes River Coll, Sacramento (CA)
County Coll of Morris (NJ)
Crowder Coll (MO)
Cumberland County Coll (NJ)
Dabney S. Lancaster Comm Coll (VA)
Dakota Coll at Bottineau (ND)
Davis Coll (OH)
Daytona State Coll (FL)
De Anza Coll (CA)
Delta Coll (MI)
East Central Coll (MO)
Eastern Gateway Comm Coll (OH)
Eastern Idaho Tech Coll (ID)
Eastern Shore Comm Coll (VA)
Eastern Wyoming Coll (WY)
Elgin Comm Coll (IL)
Elmira Business Inst (NY)
Feather River Coll (CA)
Finger Lakes Comm Coll (NY)
Fiorello H. LaGuardia Comm Coll of the City U of New York (NY)

Flathead Valley Comm Coll (MT)
Florida State Coll at Jacksonville (FL)
Fox Coll (IL)
Fox Valley Tech Coll (WI)
Fullerton Coll (CA)
Gadsden State Comm Coll (AL)
Galveston Coll (TX)
Garden City Comm Coll (KS)
Gavilan Coll (CA)
Genesee Comm Coll (NY)
Georgia Piedmont Tech Coll (GA)
Glendale Comm Coll (AZ)
Golden West Coll (CA)
Greenfield Comm Coll (MA)
Greenville Tech Coll (SC)
Gwinnett Tech Coll (GA)
Harper Coll (IL)
Harrisburg Area Comm Coll (PA)
Hinds Comm Coll (MS)
Holyoke Comm Coll (MA)
Hopkinsville Comm Coll (KY)
Housatonic Comm Coll (CT)
Hutchinson Comm Coll and Area Vocational School (KS)
Imperial Valley Coll (CA)
Independence Comm Coll (KS)
International Business Coll, Indianapolis (IN)
Iowa Lakes Comm Coll (IA)
Jackson Coll (MI)
Jamestown Business Coll (NY)
Jamestown Comm Coll (NY)
Jefferson Coll (MO)
Jefferson Comm Coll (NY)
Jefferson State Comm Coll (AL)
Johnston Comm Coll (NC)
Kankakee Comm Coll (IL)
Kent State U at Ashtabula (OH)
Kent State U at Salem (OH)
Kent State U at Trumbull (OH)
Kent State U at Tuscarawas (OH)
Kingsborough Comm Coll of the City U of New York (NY)
King's Coll (NC)
Kirtland Comm Coll (MI)
Lake Land Coll (IL)
Lakeland Comm Coll (OH)
Lake Region State Coll (ND)
Lake Tahoe Comm Coll (CA)
Lamar State Coll–Orange (TX)
Lane Comm Coll (OR)
Lanier Tech Coll (GA)
Lansing Comm Coll (MI)
Lawson State Comm Coll (AL)
LDS Business Coll (UT)
Lincoln Land Comm Coll (IL)
Linn-Benton Comm Coll (OR)
Lone Star Coll–Kingwood (TX)
Lone Star Coll–Tomball (TX)
Lorain County Comm Coll (OH)
Los Angeles Mission Coll (CA)
Lower Columbia Coll (WA)
Lurleen B. Wallace Comm Coll (AL)
Luzerne County Comm Coll (PA)
Macomb Comm Coll (MI)
Manchester Comm Coll (CT)
Manhattan Area Tech Coll (KS)
McHenry County Coll (IL)
Mercer County Comm Coll (NJ)
Mesabi Range Comm and Tech Coll (MN)
Mesa Comm Coll (AZ)
Miami Dade Coll (FL)
Middlesex County Coll (NJ)
Mid-Plains Comm Coll, North Platte (NE)
Mineral Area Coll (MO)
Minneapolis Business Coll (MN)
Minneapolis Comm and Tech Coll (MN)
Minnesota State Coll–Southeast Tech (MN)
MiraCosta Coll (CA)
Mississippi Delta Comm Coll (MS)
Mississippi Gulf Coast Comm Coll (MS)
Mohawk Valley Comm Coll (NY)
Monroe Comm Coll (NY)
Monroe County Comm Coll (MI)
Montgomery County Comm Coll (PA)
Moraine Park Tech Coll (WI)
Moraine Valley Comm Coll (IL)
Mott Comm Coll (MI)
Moultrie Tech Coll (GA)
Mountain State Coll (WV)
Mt. San Antonio Coll (CA)
Mt. San Jacinto Coll (CA)
Nassau Comm Coll (NY)

New Mexico State U–Alamogordo (NM)
Niagara County Comm Coll (NY)
Northampton Comm Coll (PA)
Northcentral Tech Coll (WI)
Northeastern Tech Coll (SC)
Northeast Iowa Comm Coll (IA)
Northern Essex Comm Coll (MA)
North Georgia Tech Coll (GA)
North Iowa Area Comm Coll (IA)
North Shore Comm Coll (MA)
Northwest Coll (WY)
Northwestern Connecticut Comm Coll (CT)
Northwest-Shoals Comm Coll (AL)
Northwest Tech Coll (MN)
Norwalk Comm Coll (CT)
Oakton Comm Coll (IL)
Ocean County Coll (NJ)
Oconee Fall Line Tech Coll (GA)
Ogeechee Tech Coll (GA)
Okefenokee Tech Coll (GA)
Oklahoma City Comm Coll (OK)
Olympic Coll (WA)
Orange Coast Coll (CA)
Otero Jr Coll (CO)
Oxnard Coll (CA)
Ozarks Tech Comm Coll (MO)
Palomar Coll (CA)
Panola Coll (TX)
Pasadena City Coll (CA)
Patrick Henry Comm Coll (VA)
Pensacola State Coll (FL)
Phoenix Coll (AZ)
Pima Comm Coll (AZ)
Potomac State Coll of West Virginia U (WV)
Rainy River Comm Coll (MN)
Rappahannock Comm Coll (VA)
Raritan Valley Comm Coll (NJ)
Reid State Tech Coll (AL)
Roane State Comm Coll (TN)
Rock Valley Coll (IL)
San Diego City Coll (CA)
San Jacinto Coll District (TX)
Santa Monica Coll (CA)
Sauk Valley Comm Coll (IL)
Savannah Tech Coll (GA)
Schoolcraft Coll (MI)
Scottsdale Comm Coll (AZ)
Seminole State Coll of Florida (FL)
Shawnee Comm Coll (IL)
Shelton State Comm Coll (AL)
Snow Coll (UT)
Southeastern Comm Coll (IA)
Southeastern Comm Coll (NC)
Southeastern Tech Coll (GA)
Southern Crescent Tech Coll (GA)
Southern State Comm Coll (OH)
South Georgia Tech Coll (GA)
South Louisiana Comm Coll (LA)
South Plains Coll (TX)
Southwestern Comm Coll (NC)
Southwestern Illinois Coll (IL)
Southwest Georgia Tech Coll (GA)
Spartanburg Comm Coll (SC)
Spoon River Coll (IL)
Springfield Tech Comm Coll (MA)
Stark State Coll (OH)
Sullivan County Comm Coll (NY)
Tarrant County Coll District (TX)
Tech Coll of the Lowcountry (SC)
Temple Coll (TX)
Texarkana Coll (TX)
Three Rivers Comm Coll (CT)
Tompkins Cortland Comm Coll (NY)
Trident Tech Coll (SC)
Truckee Meadows Comm Coll (NV)
Tulsa Comm Coll (OK)
Tunxis Comm Coll (CT)
Tyler Jr Coll (TX)
Umpqua Comm Coll (OR)
The U of Akron–Wayne Coll (OH)
U of Hawaii Maui Coll (HI)
U of New Mexico–Los Alamos Branch (NM)
Victoria Coll (TX)
Victor Valley Coll (CA)
Vincennes U (IN)
Virginia Western Comm Coll (VA)
Walla Walla Comm Coll (WA)
Waukesha County Tech Coll (WI)
Wenatchee Valley Coll (WA)
Westchester Comm Coll (NY)
Western Texas Coll (TX)
Western Wyoming Comm Coll (WY)
West Georgia Tech Coll (GA)
Westmoreland County Comm Coll (PA)
Williston State Coll (ND)

Wiregrass Georgia Tech Coll (GA)
Wisconsin Indianhead Tech Coll (WI)
Wood Tobe–Coburn School (NY)
Wor-Wic Comm Coll (MD)
Wytheville Comm Coll (VA)

ADULT AND CONTINUING EDUCATION
Cochise Coll, Sierra Vista (AZ)

ADULT DEVELOPMENT AND AGING
Albany Tech Coll (GA)
Central Georgia Tech Coll (GA)
Columbus State Comm Coll (OH)
Comm Coll of Rhode Island (RI)
Dakota Coll at Bottineau (ND)
Fiorello H. LaGuardia Comm Coll of the City U of New York (NY)
MiraCosta Coll (CA)
Mt. San Jacinto Coll (CA)

ADULT HEALTH NURSING
Bay State Coll (MA)

ADVERTISING
Broward Coll (FL)
Central Ohio Tech Coll (OH)
Dakota Coll at Bottineau (ND)
Fashion Inst of Technology (NY)
Harford Comm Coll (MD)
Mississippi Delta Comm Coll (MS)
Mississippi Gulf Coast Comm Coll (MS)
Mohawk Valley Comm Coll (NY)
Mt. San Antonio Coll (CA)
Palomar Coll (CA)
South Florida State Coll (FL)
South Plains Coll (TX)

AERONAUTICAL/AEROSPACE ENGINEERING TECHNOLOGY
Broward Coll (FL)
Cincinnati State Tech and Comm Coll (OH)
Columbus State Comm Coll (OH)
Cumberland County Coll (NJ)
Delaware Tech & Comm Coll, Jack F. Owens Campus (DE)
Tulsa Comm Coll (OK)
Wichita Area Tech Coll (KS)

AERONAUTICS/AVIATION/ AEROSPACE SCIENCE AND TECHNOLOGY
Alvin Comm Coll (TX)
Cecil Coll (MD)
The Comm Coll of Baltimore County (MD)
Cossatot Comm Coll of the U of Arkansas (AR)
Eastern Florida State Coll (FL)
Hinds Comm Coll (MS)
Lehigh Carbon Comm Coll (PA)
Miami Dade Coll (FL)
Northwest Coll (WY)
Orange Coast Coll (CA)

AEROSPACE, AERONAUTICAL AND ASTRONAUTICAL/SPACE ENGINEERING
Kent State U at Ashtabula (OH)
Kilgore Coll (TX)
South Florida State Coll (FL)

AESTHETICIAN/ESTHETICIAN AND SKIN CARE
Inst of Business & Medical Careers (CO)

AFRICAN AMERICAN/BLACK STUDIES
Bronx Comm Coll of the City U of New York (NY)
Broward Coll (FL)
Lansing Comm Coll (MI)
Nassau Comm Coll (NY)
San Diego City Coll (CA)

AGRIBUSINESS
Butte Coll (CA)
Coll of the Desert (CA)
Copiah-Lincoln Comm Coll (MS)
Cosumnes River Coll, Sacramento (CA)
Crowder Coll (MO)
Eastern Wyoming Coll (WY)
Harrisburg Area Comm Coll (PA)
Hinds Comm Coll (MS)
Iowa Lakes Comm Coll (IA)
James Sprunt Comm Coll (NC)

Laramie County Comm Coll (WY)
Mineral Area Coll (MO)
MiraCosta Coll (CA)
Northeast Iowa Comm Coll (IA)
Northwest Coll (WY)
Ogeechee Tech Coll (GA)
The Ohio State U Ag Tech Inst (OH)
San Jacinto Coll District (TX)
South Florida State Coll (FL)
State Fair Comm Coll (MO)
State U of New York Coll of
    Technology at Alfred (NY)
Wayne Comm Coll (NC)

AGRICULTURAL AND DOMESTIC ANIMAL SERVICES RELATED
Walla Walla Comm Coll (WA)

AGRICULTURAL AND FOOD PRODUCTS PROCESSING
Garden City Comm Coll (KS)
Northeast Iowa Comm Coll (IA)

AGRICULTURAL BUSINESS AND MANAGEMENT
Alabama Southern Comm Coll (AL)
American Samoa Comm Coll (AS)
Arizona Western Coll (AZ)
Bismarck State Coll (ND)
Casper Coll (WY)
Central Wyoming Coll (WY)
Clark State Comm Coll (OH)
Cloud County Comm Coll (KS)
Cochise Coll, Sierra Vista (AZ)
Coll of Southern Idaho (ID)
Copiah-Lincoln Comm Coll (MS)
Cossatot Comm Coll of the U of
    Arkansas (AR)
County Coll of Morris (NJ)
Danville Area Comm Coll (IL)
Delaware Tech & Comm Coll, Jack F.
    Owens Campus (DE)
Delaware Tech & Comm Coll,
    Stanton/Wilmington Campus (DE)
Delaware Tech & Comm Coll, Terry
    Campus (DE)
Frank Phillips Coll (TX)
Harford Comm Coll (MD)
Highland Comm Coll (IL)
Illinois Eastern Comm Colls, Wabash
    Valley College (IL)
Imperial Valley Coll (CA)
Iowa Lakes Comm Coll (IA)
Lake Area Tech Inst (SD)
Lake Land Coll (IL)
Lake Region State Coll (ND)
Lamar Comm Coll (CO)
Lansing Comm Coll (MI)
Linn-Benton Comm Coll (OR)
Mesa Comm Coll (AZ)
Mississippi Delta Comm Coll (MS)
Mississippi Gulf Coast Comm Coll
    (MS)
Mt. San Antonio Coll (CA)
North Dakota State Coll of Science
    (ND)
Northeastern Jr Coll (CO)
Northeast Texas Comm Coll (TX)
Northwest Mississippi Comm Coll
    (MS)
The Ohio State U Ag Tech Inst (OH)
Otero Jr Coll (CO)
Patrick Henry Comm Coll (VA)
Pensacola State Coll (FL)
Potomac State Coll of West Virginia
    U (WV)
Santa Rosa Jr Coll (CA)
Sauk Valley Comm Coll (IL)
Shawnee Comm Coll (IL)
Sheridan Coll (WY)
Snow Coll (UT)
Southeastern Comm Coll (IA)
Spoon River Coll (IL)
Treasure Valley Comm Coll (OR)
Vincennes U (IN)
Walla Walla Comm Coll (WA)

AGRICULTURAL BUSINESS AND MANAGEMENT RELATED
Chippewa Valley Tech Coll (WI)
Coll of Southern Idaho (ID)
Copiah-Lincoln Comm Coll (MS)
Iowa Lakes Comm Coll (IA)
Penn State Beaver (PA)
Penn State Brandywine (PA)
Penn State DuBois (PA)
Penn State Fayette, The Eberly
    Campus (PA)
Penn State Greater Allegheny (PA)
Penn State Hazleton (PA)
Penn State Lehigh Valley (PA)

Penn State Mont Alto (PA)
Penn State New Kensington (PA)
Penn State Schuylkill (PA)
Penn State Wilkes-Barre (PA)
Penn State Worthington Scranton
    (PA)
Penn State York (PA)
Walla Walla Comm Coll (WA)

AGRICULTURAL BUSINESS TECHNOLOGY
Iowa Lakes Comm Coll (IA)
Laramie County Comm Coll (WY)
The Ohio State U Ag Tech Inst (OH)

AGRICULTURAL COMMUNICATION/ JOURNALISM
Northwest Coll (WY)
The Ohio State U Ag Tech Inst (OH)
Santa Rosa Jr Coll (CA)

AGRICULTURAL ECONOMICS
Copiah-Lincoln Comm Coll (MS)
Iowa Lakes Comm Coll (IA)
Mississippi Delta Comm Coll (MS)
Northeastern Jr Coll (CO)
North Iowa Area Comm Coll (IA)
Northwest Mississippi Comm Coll
    (MS)
The Ohio State U Ag Tech Inst (OH)
Potomac State Coll of West Virginia
    U (WV)
South Florida State Coll (FL)
South Plains Coll (TX)
Treasure Valley Comm Coll (OR)

AGRICULTURAL ENGINEERING
South Florida State Coll (FL)
Vincennes U (IN)

AGRICULTURAL/FARM SUPPLIES RETAILING AND WHOLESALING
Cloud County Comm Coll (KS)
Copiah-Lincoln Comm Coll (MS)
Fox Valley Tech Coll (WI)
Hawkeye Comm Coll (IA)
Iowa Lakes Comm Coll (IA)
North Iowa Area Comm Coll (IA)

AGRICULTURAL MECHANICS AND EQUIPMENT TECHNOLOGY
Butte Coll (CA)
Hutchinson Comm Coll and Area
    Vocational School (KS)
Iowa Lakes Comm Coll (IA)
Mitchell Tech Inst (SD)
North Dakota State Coll of Science
    (ND)
Rend Lake Coll (IL)
Spoon River Coll (IL)

AGRICULTURAL MECHANIZATION
Clark State Comm Coll (OH)
Crowder Coll (MO)
Fox Valley Tech Coll (WI)
Garden City Comm Coll (KS)
Imperial Valley Coll (CA)
Iowa Lakes Comm Coll (IA)
Lake Land Coll (IL)
Mesa Comm Coll (AZ)
Northeastern Jr Coll (CO)
Northwest Mississippi Comm Coll
    (MS)
The Ohio State U Ag Tech Inst (OH)
Owens Comm Coll, Toledo (OH)
Paris Jr Coll (TX)
Potomac State Coll of West Virginia
    U (WV)
Rend Lake Coll (IL)
Southwest Georgia Tech Coll (GA)
Spoon River Coll (IL)
U of Hawaii Maui Coll (HI)
Walla Walla Comm Coll (WA)

AGRICULTURAL MECHANIZATION RELATED
Hinds Comm Coll (MS)
Walla Walla Comm Coll (WA)

AGRICULTURAL POWER MACHINERY OPERATION
Hawkeye Comm Coll (IA)
Iowa Lakes Comm Coll (IA)
Northeast Iowa Comm Coll (IA)
The Ohio State U Ag Tech Inst (OH)

AGRICULTURAL PRODUCTION
Allen Comm Coll (KS)

Big Bend Comm Coll (WA)
Delaware Tech & Comm Coll, Jack F.
    Owens Campus (DE)
Garden City Comm Coll (KS)
Hopkinsville Comm Coll (KY)
Illinois Eastern Comm Colls, Wabash
    Valley College (IL)
Iowa Lakes Comm Coll (IA)
Lake Area Tech Inst (SD)
Lake Land Coll (IL)
Laramie County Comm Coll (WY)
Lincoln Land Comm Coll (IL)
Mitchell Tech Inst (SD)
Northeast Iowa Comm Coll (IA)
North Iowa Area Comm Coll (IA)
Northwest Coll (WY)
Owensboro Comm and Tech Coll
    (KY)
Rend Lake Coll (IL)
Southern State Comm Coll (OH)
Walla Walla Comm Coll (WA)
Wenatchee Valley Coll (WA)

AGRICULTURAL PRODUCTION RELATED
Iowa Lakes Comm Coll (IA)

AGRICULTURAL TEACHER EDUCATION
Eastern Wyoming Coll (WY)
Iowa Lakes Comm Coll (IA)
Northeastern Jr Coll (CO)
Northwest Coll (WY)
The Ohio State U Ag Tech Inst (OH)
Potomac State Coll of West Virginia
    U (WV)
South Florida State Coll (FL)
Spoon River Coll (IL)
Trinity Valley Comm Coll (TX)
Victor Valley Coll (CA)
Western Texas Coll (TX)

AGRICULTURE
Alabama Southern Comm Coll (AL)
American Samoa Comm Coll (AS)
Arizona Western Coll (AZ)
Bainbridge State Coll (GA)
Butte Coll (CA)
Casper Coll (WY)
Chipola Coll (FL)
Clark State Comm Coll (OH)
Coll of Southern Idaho (ID)
Coll of the Desert (CA)
Coll of Western Idaho (ID)
Copiah-Lincoln Comm Coll (MS)
Cosumnes River Coll, Sacramento
    (CA)
Crowder Coll (MO)
Dakota Coll at Bottineau (ND)
Darton State Coll (GA)
Dyersburg State Comm Coll (TN)
Feather River Coll (CA)
Georgia Highlands Coll (GA)
Hinds Comm Coll (MS)
Hutchinson Comm Coll and Area
    Vocational School (KS)
Imperial Valley Coll (CA)
Iowa Lakes Comm Coll (IA)
Jackson State Comm Coll (TN)
Kankakee Comm Coll (IL)
Kaskaskia Coll (IL)
Kilgore Coll (TX)
Lamar Comm Coll (CO)
Laramie County Comm Coll (WY)
Linn-Benton Comm Coll (OR)
Macomb Comm Coll (MI)
Miami Dade Coll (FL)
Missouri State U–West Plains (MO)
Mt. San Antonio Coll (CA)
Northeastern Jr Coll (CO)
Northwest Mississippi Comm Coll
    (MS)
Paris Jr Coll (TX)
Pensacola State Coll (FL)
Potomac State Coll of West Virginia
    U (WV)
San Jacinto Coll District (TX)
Sauk Valley Comm Coll (IL)
Shawnee Comm Coll (IL)
Sheridan Coll (WY)
Snow Coll (UT)
Southern State Comm Coll (OH)
South Florida State Coll (FL)
South Plains Coll (TX)
State U of New York Coll of
    Technology at Alfred (NY)
Texarkana Coll (TX)
Treasure Valley Comm Coll (OR)
Umpqua Comm Coll (OR)
Vincennes U (IN)
Western Texas Coll (TX)
Williston State Coll (ND)

AGRICULTURE AND AGRICULTURE OPERATIONS RELATED
Potomac State Coll of West Virginia
    U (WV)
Sheridan Coll (WY)

AGROECOLOGY AND SUSTAINABLE AGRICULTURE
Northeast Texas Comm Coll (TX)
Santa Rosa Jr Coll (CA)
Southern Maine Comm Coll (ME)
State U of New York Coll of
    Technology at Alfred (NY)
Wayne Comm Coll (NC)

AGRONOMY AND CROP SCIENCE
Chipola Coll (FL)
Iowa Lakes Comm Coll (IA)
Lamar Comm Coll (CO)
Mesa Comm Coll (AZ)
Northeastern Jr Coll (CO)
The Ohio State U Ag Tech Inst (OH)
Potomac State Coll of West Virginia
    U (WV)
Shawnee Comm Coll (IL)
Southeastern Comm Coll (IA)
South Plains Coll (TX)
State U of New York Coll of
    Technology at Alfred (NY)
Treasure Valley Comm Coll (OR)

AIR AND SPACE OPERATIONS TECHNOLOGY
Cochise Coll, Sierra Vista (AZ)

AIRCRAFT POWERPLANT TECHNOLOGY
Antelope Valley Coll (CA)
Colorado Northwestern Comm Coll
    (CO)
Florida State Coll at Jacksonville (FL)
Hallmark Inst of Aeronautics (TX)
Lake Area Tech Inst (SD)
Lansing Comm Coll (MI)
Somerset Comm Coll (KY)
South Louisiana Comm Coll (LA)
Texas State Tech Coll Waco (TX)
Vincennes U (IN)
Wayne County Comm Coll District
    (MI)

AIRFRAME MECHANICS AND AIRCRAFT MAINTENANCE TECHNOLOGY
Amarillo Coll (TX)
Antelope Valley Coll (CA)
Florida State Coll at Jacksonville (FL)
Gavilan Coll (CA)
Hallmark Inst of Aeronautics (TX)
Helena Coll U of Montana (MT)
Hinds Comm Coll (MS)
Ivy Tech Comm Coll–Wabash Valley
    (IN)
Lane Comm Coll (OR)
Lansing Comm Coll (MI)
Lincoln Land Comm Coll (IL)
Mohawk Valley Comm Coll (NY)
Mt. San Antonio Coll (CA)
Oklahoma City Comm Coll (OK)
Pima Comm Coll (AZ)
San Joaquin Valley Coll–Fresno
    Aviation Campus (CA)
Southwestern Illinois Coll (IL)
Texas State Tech Coll Waco (TX)
Trident Tech Coll (SC)
Wayne Comm Coll (NC)
Wayne County Comm Coll District
    (MI)
Wichita Area Tech Coll (KS)

AIRLINE FLIGHT ATTENDANT
Mercer County Comm Coll (NJ)

AIRLINE PILOT AND FLIGHT CREW
Big Bend Comm Coll (WA)
Broward Coll (FL)
Casper Coll (WY)
Central Oregon Comm Coll (OR)
Chandler-Gilbert Comm Coll (AZ)
Cochise Coll, Sierra Vista (AZ)
Colorado Northwestern Comm Coll
    (CO)
Comm Coll of Allegheny County (PA)
County Coll of Morris (NJ)
Dutchess Comm Coll (NY)
Florida State Coll at Jacksonville (FL)
Fox Valley Tech Coll (WI)
Iowa Lakes Comm Coll (IA)
Jackson Coll (MI)

Lake Superior Coll (MN)
Lane Comm Coll (OR)
Lansing Comm Coll (MI)
Lehigh Carbon Comm Coll (PA)
Lenoir Comm Coll (NC)
Luzerne County Comm Coll (PA)
Mercer County Comm Coll (NJ)
Miami Dade Coll (FL)
Mt. San Antonio Coll (CA)
North Shore Comm Coll (MA)
Orange Coast Coll (CA)
Palomar Coll (CA)
Salt Lake Comm Coll (UT)
San Jacinto Coll District (TX)
Southwestern Illinois Coll (IL)
Texas State Tech Coll Waco (TX)
Treasure Valley Comm Coll (OR)
Vincennes U (IN)

AIR TRAFFIC CONTROL
Broward Coll (FL)
Cecil Coll (MD)
Miami Dade Coll (FL)
Minneapolis Comm and Tech Coll
    (MN)
Mt. San Antonio Coll (CA)
Texas State Tech Coll Waco (TX)

AIR TRANSPORTATION RELATED
Cochise Coll, Sierra Vista (AZ)

ALLIED HEALTH AND MEDICAL ASSISTING SERVICES RELATED
Blue Ridge Comm and Tech Coll
    (WV)
Bowling Green State U-Firelands Coll
    (OH)
Carrington Coll California–San Jose
    (CA)
Cincinnati State Tech and Comm Coll
    (OH)
J. Sargeant Reynolds Comm Coll
    (VA)
Mount Wachusett Comm Coll (MA)
Pennsylvania Inst of Technology (PA)

ALLIED HEALTH DIAGNOSTIC, INTERVENTION, AND TREATMENT PROFESSIONS RELATED
Ivy Tech Comm Coll–Wabash Valley
    (IN)
Minneapolis Comm and Tech Coll
    (MN)
Pitt Comm Coll (NC)
South Piedmont Comm Coll (NC)

ALTERNATIVE AND COMPLEMENTARY MEDICAL SUPPORT SERVICES RELATED
Mount Wachusett Comm Coll (MA)

ALTERNATIVE AND COMPLEMENTARY MEDICINE RELATED
Quinsigamond Comm Coll (MA)

AMERICAN GOVERNMENT AND POLITICS
Oklahoma City Comm Coll (OK)

AMERICAN INDIAN/NATIVE AMERICAN STUDIES
Central Wyoming Coll (WY)
Ilisagvik Coll (AK)
Kilian Comm Coll (SD)
Pima Comm Coll (AZ)
Saginaw Chippewa Tribal Coll (MI)
San Juan Coll (NM)

AMERICAN SIGN LANGUAGE (ASL)
Berkeley City Coll (CA)
Bristol Comm Coll (MA)
Coll of Southern Idaho (ID)
Montgomery Coll (MD)
Oklahoma State U, Oklahoma City
    (OK)
Pima Comm Coll (AZ)
Quinsigamond Comm Coll (MA)
Santa Rosa Jr Coll (CA)
Vincennes U (IN)

AMERICAN STUDIES
Bucks County Comm Coll (PA)
Greenfield Comm Coll (MA)
Lansing Comm Coll (MI)
Miami Dade Coll (FL)
MiraCosta Coll (CA)
Mississippi Delta Comm Coll (MS)
South Florida State Coll (FL)

ANATOMY
Northeastern Jr Coll (CO)

ANIMAL/LIVESTOCK HUSBANDRY AND PRODUCTION
Frank Phillips Coll (TX)
Hawkeye Comm Coll (IA)
Hopkinsville Comm Coll (KY)
Iowa Lakes Comm Coll (IA)
Jefferson Comm Coll (NY)
The Ohio State U Ag Tech Inst (OH)
Wayne Comm Coll (NC)

ANIMAL SCIENCES
Alamance Comm Coll (NC)
Casper Coll (WY)
Coll of Southern Idaho (ID)
Iowa Lakes Comm Coll (IA)
James Sprunt Comm Coll (NC)
Kaskaskia Coll (IL)
Lamar Comm Coll (CO)
Linn-Benton Comm Coll (OR)
Mt. San Antonio Coll (CA)
Niagara County Comm Coll (NY)
Northeastern Jr Coll (CO)
Northwest Coll (WY)
Northwest Mississippi Comm Coll (MS)
The Ohio State U Ag Tech Inst (OH)
Potomac State Coll of West Virginia U (WV)
Santa Rosa Jr Coll (CA)
Shawnee Comm Coll (IL)
Sheridan Coll (WY)
Snow Coll (UT)
South Florida State Coll (FL)
State U of New York Coll of Technology at Alfred (NY)
Treasure Valley Comm Coll (OR)
Trinity Valley Comm Coll (TX)

ANIMAL TRAINING
Lamar Comm Coll (CO)

ANIMATION, INTERACTIVE TECHNOLOGY, VIDEO GRAPHICS AND SPECIAL EFFECTS
Austin Comm Coll (TX)
Bay State Coll (MA)
Ca&nnada Coll (CA)
Cecil Coll (MD)
Coll of Marin (CA)
Coll of the Canyons (CA)
Elgin Comm Coll (IL)
Finger Lakes Comm Coll (NY)
Hagerstown Comm Coll (MD)
Houston Comm Coll System (TX)
Kirtland Comm Coll (MI)
Lakes Region Comm Coll (NH)
Lane Comm Coll (OR)
Lansing Comm Coll (MI)
Lehigh Carbon Comm Coll (PA)
Lone Star Coll–CyFair (TX)
Lone Star Coll–Tomball (TX)
McHenry County Coll (IL)
Minneapolis Comm and Tech Coll (MN)
Montgomery Coll (MD)
New Mexico State U–Alamogordo (NM)
Oklahoma City Comm Coll (OK)
Palomar Coll (CA)
Pasadena City Coll (CA)
Pueblo Comm Coll (CO)
Raritan Valley Comm Coll (NJ)
Santa Monica Coll (CA)
Sessions Coll for Professional Design (AZ)
Southeast Tech Inst (SD)
Springfield Tech Comm Coll (MA)
Sullivan Coll of Technology and Design (KY)

ANTHROPOLOGY
Austin Comm Coll (TX)
Broward Coll (FL)
Ca&nnada Coll (CA)
Casper Coll (WY)
Coconino Comm Coll (AZ)
Coll of Southern Idaho (ID)
Coll of the Desert (CA)
Coll of Western Idaho (ID)
Copper Mountain Coll (CA)
Darton State Coll (GA)
Eastern Arizona Coll (AZ)
Fullerton Coll (CA)
Great Basin Coll (NV)
Harford Comm Coll (MD)

Imperial Valley Coll (CA)
Lansing Comm Coll (MI)
Laramie County Comm Coll (WY)
Miami Dade Coll (FL)
MiraCosta Coll (CA)
Northwest Coll (WY)
Orange Coast Coll (CA)
Oxnard Coll (CA)
Pasadena City Coll (CA)
Pima Comm Coll (AZ)
San Diego City Coll (CA)
Santa Monica Coll (CA)
Santa Rosa Jr Coll (CA)
South Florida State Coll (FL)
Truckee Meadows Comm Coll (NV)
Umpqua Comm Coll (OR)
Vincennes U (IN)
Western Wyoming Comm Coll (WY)

APPAREL AND ACCESSORIES MARKETING
FIDM/The Fashion Inst of Design & Merchandising, Los Angeles Campus (CA)
FIDM/The Fashion Inst of Design & Merchandising, San Diego Campus (CA)
FIDM/The Fashion Inst of Design & Merchandising, San Francisco Campus (CA)

APPAREL AND TEXTILE MANUFACTURING
Academy of Couture Art (CA)
Ca&nnada Coll (CA)
Fashion Inst of Technology (NY)
Westchester Comm Coll (NY)

APPAREL AND TEXTILE MARKETING MANAGEMENT
Fullerton Coll (CA)
Palomar Coll (CA)
Santa Monica Coll (CA)

APPAREL AND TEXTILES
Antelope Valley Coll (CA)
FIDM/The Fashion Inst of Design & Merchandising, Los Angeles Campus (CA)
FIDM/The Fashion Inst of Design & Merchandising, Orange County Campus (CA)
FIDM/The Fashion Inst of Design & Merchandising, San Francisco Campus (CA)
Fullerton Coll (CA)
Mt. San Antonio Coll (CA)

APPLIED HORTICULTURE/ HORTICULTURAL BUSINESS SERVICES RELATED
Chippewa Valley Tech Coll (WI)
Cincinnati State Tech and Comm Coll (OH)
Dakota Coll at Bottineau (ND)
Hinds Comm Coll (MS)

APPLIED HORTICULTURE/ HORTICULTURE OPERATIONS
Alamance Comm Coll (NC)
Catawba Valley Comm Coll (NC)
Cecil Coll (MD)
Clark Coll (WA)
Clark State Comm Coll (OH)
Coll of Southern Idaho (ID)
Coll of the Desert (CA)
Comm Coll of Allegheny County (PA)
The Comm Coll of Baltimore County (MD)
Dakota Coll at Bottineau (ND)
Delaware Tech & Comm Coll, Jack F. Owens Campus (DE)
Fayetteville Tech Comm Coll (NC)
Fullerton Coll (CA)
Hawkeye Comm Coll (IA)
Houston Comm Coll System (TX)
J. Sargeant Reynolds Comm Coll (VA)
Kankakee Comm Coll (IL)
Kaskaskia Coll (IL)
Kent State U at Salem (OH)
McHenry County Coll (IL)
Mineral Area Coll (MO)
Montgomery Coll (MD)
Owensboro Comm and Tech Coll (KY)
Rend Lake Coll (IL)
Southeast Tech Inst (SD)
Southwestern Illinois Coll (IL)
Spartanburg Comm Coll (SC)

State Fair Comm Coll (MO)
Tulsa Comm Coll (OK)
Vincennes U (IN)
Westmoreland County Comm Coll (PA)

APPLIED MATHEMATICS
Broward Coll (FL)
Northeastern Jr Coll (CO)
South Florida State Coll (FL)

AQUACULTURE
Coll of Southern Idaho (ID)
Hillsborough Comm Coll (FL)

ARCHEOLOGY
Ca&nnada Coll (CA)
Northwest Coll (WY)
Palomar Coll (CA)
Western Wyoming Comm Coll (WY)

ARCHITECTURAL AND BUILDING SCIENCES
J. Sargeant Reynolds Comm Coll (VA)

ARCHITECTURAL DRAFTING AND CAD/CADD
American Samoa Comm Coll (AS)
Anoka Tech Coll (MN)
Benjamin Franklin Inst of Technology (MA)
Brown Mackie Coll–Albuquerque (NM)
Butler County Comm Coll (PA)
Carrington Coll California–San Jose (CA)
Carroll Comm Coll (MD)
Central Ohio Tech Coll (OH)
Coconino Comm Coll (AZ)
Coll of the Canyons (CA)
Commonwealth Tech Inst (PA)
Comm Coll of Allegheny County (PA)
The Comm Coll of Baltimore County (MD)
Cosumnes River Coll, Sacramento (CA)
Dunwoody Coll of Technology (MN)
Florida State Coll at Jacksonville (FL)
Glendale Comm Coll (AZ)
Harper Coll (IL)
Hutchinson Comm Coll and Area Vocational School (KS)
Island Drafting and Tech Inst (NY)
Kaskaskia Coll (IL)
Lake Superior Coll (MN)
Lincoln Land Comm Coll (IL)
Macomb Comm Coll (MI)
Miami Dade Coll (FL)
Montgomery Coll (MD)
Montgomery County Comm Coll (PA)
Oakton Comm Coll (IL)
Oklahoma City Comm Coll (OK)
Owens Comm Coll, Toledo (OH)
Palomar Coll (CA)
Phoenix Coll (AZ)
Rend Lake Coll (IL)
South Suburban Coll (IL)
Sullivan Coll of Technology and Design (KY)
Triangle Tech, Inc.–Pittsburgh School (PA)
Vincennes U (IN)
Waukesha County Tech Coll (WI)
Westmoreland County Comm Coll (PA)
York County Comm Coll (ME)

ARCHITECTURAL ENGINEERING
Luzerne County Comm Coll (PA)

ARCHITECTURAL ENGINEERING TECHNOLOGY
Amarillo Coll (TX)
Arapahoe Comm Coll (CO)
Benjamin Franklin Inst of Technology (MA)
Cape Fear Comm Coll (NC)
Catawba Valley Comm Coll (NC)
Central Maine Comm Coll (ME)
Cincinnati State Tech and Comm Coll (OH)
Coconino Comm Coll (AZ)
Columbus State Comm Coll (OH)
Comm Coll of Philadelphia (PA)
Daytona State Coll (FL)
Delaware Tech & Comm Coll, Jack F. Owens Campus (DE)

Delaware Tech & Comm Coll, Stanton/Wilmington Campus (DE)
Delaware Tech & Comm Coll, Terry Campus (DE)
Delta Coll (MI)
Dutchess Comm Coll (NY)
Erie Comm Coll, South Campus (NY)
Fayetteville Tech Comm Coll (NC)
Finger Lakes Comm Coll (NY)
Florida State Coll at Jacksonville (FL)
Golden West Coll (CA)
Grand Rapids Comm Coll (MI)
Greenville Tech Coll (SC)
Harper Coll (IL)
Harrisburg Area Comm Coll (PA)
Hillsborough Comm Coll (FL)
Honolulu Comm Coll (HI)
Independence Comm Coll (KS)
Inst of Design and Construction (NY)
Lake Land Coll (IL)
Lamar State Coll–Orange (TX)
Lansing Comm Coll (MI)
Luzerne County Comm Coll (PA)
Mercer County Comm Coll (NJ)
Miami Dade Coll (FL)
Mississippi Delta Comm Coll (MS)
Monroe County Comm Coll (MI)
Mott Comm Coll (MI)
Mt. San Antonio Coll (CA)
Northampton Comm Coll (PA)
Northcentral Tech Coll (WI)
North Dakota State Coll of Science (ND)
Northwest Florida State Coll (FL)
Norwalk Comm Coll (CT)
Oakland Comm Coll (MI)
Oklahoma State U, Oklahoma City (OK)
Onondaga Comm Coll (NY)
Orange Coast Coll (CA)
Owens Comm Coll, Toledo (OH)
Penn State Fayette, The Eberly Campus (PA)
Penn State Worthington Scranton (PA)
Pitt Comm Coll (NC)
St. Clair County Comm Coll (MI)
Salt Lake Comm Coll (UT)
Seminole State Coll of Florida (FL)
Southeast Tech Inst (SD)
Stark State Coll (OH)
State U of New York Coll of Technology at Alfred (NY)
Sullivan Coll of Technology and Design (KY)
Tarrant County Coll District (TX)
Three Rivers Comm Coll (CT)
Wisconsin Indianhead Tech Coll (WI)

ARCHITECTURAL TECHNOLOGY
Arizona Western Coll (AZ)
Coconino Comm Coll (AZ)
Coll of Marin (CA)
Coll of the Desert (CA)
Cosumnes River Coll, Sacramento (CA)
Dunwoody Coll of Technology (MN)
Fullerton Coll (CA)
John Tyler Comm Coll (VA)
Lansing Comm Coll (MI)
MiraCosta Coll (CA)
Onondaga Comm Coll (NY)

ARCHITECTURE
Allen Comm Coll (KS)
Broward Coll (FL)
Copiah-Lincoln Comm Coll (MS)
Grand Rapids Comm Coll (MI)
Harrisburg Area Comm Coll (PA)
Hinds Comm Coll (MS)
Howard Comm Coll (MD)
Kilgore Coll (TX)
Pasadena City Coll (CA)
South Florida State Coll (FL)
Truckee Meadows Comm Coll (NV)

ARCHITECTURE RELATED
Garden City Comm Coll (KS)
Sullivan Coll of Technology and Design (KY)

AREA STUDIES RELATED
Ca&nnada Coll (CA)
Central Wyoming Coll (WY)
Coconino Comm Coll (AZ)
Fullerton Coll (CA)
MiraCosta Coll (CA)

ARMY ROTC/MILITARY SCIENCE
Georgia Military Coll (GA)

ART
Alabama Southern Comm Coll (AL)
Allen Comm Coll (KS)
Alvin Comm Coll (TX)
Amarillo Coll (TX)
American Samoa Comm Coll (AS)
Austin Comm Coll (TX)
Bainbridge State Coll (GA)
Berkeley City Coll (CA)
Bronx Comm Coll of the City U of New York (NY)
Broward Coll (FL)
Bunker Hill Comm Coll (MA)
Butte Coll (CA)
Ca&nnada Coll (CA)
Carroll Comm Coll (MD)
Casper Coll (WY)
Cayuga County Comm Coll (NY)
Central Oregon Comm Coll (OR)
Central Wyoming Coll (WY)
Chipola Coll (FL)
Cochise Coll, Sierra Vista (AZ)
Coll of Marin (CA)
Coll of Southern Idaho (ID)
Coll of the Canyons (CA)
Coll of the Desert (CA)
Columbia Coll (CA)
Columbia-Greene Comm Coll (NY)
Comm Coll of Allegheny County (PA)
Comm Coll of Philadelphia (PA)
Comm Coll of Rhode Island (RI)
Comm Coll of Vermont (VT)
Copper Mountain Coll (CA)
Cosumnes River Coll, Sacramento (CA)
Crowder Coll (MO)
Darton State Coll (GA)
De Anza Coll (CA)
Dutchess Comm Coll (NY)
Eastern Arizona Coll (AZ)
Eastern Florida State Coll (FL)
Eastern Wyoming Coll (WY)
Edison Comm Coll (OH)
Fullerton Coll (CA)
Gavilan Coll (CA)
Georgia Highlands Coll (GA)
Golden West Coll (CA)
Gordon State Coll (GA)
Grand Rapids Comm Coll (MI)
Grayson Coll (TX)
Great Basin Coll (NV)
Greenfield Comm Coll (MA)
Harper Coll (IL)
Harrisburg Area Comm Coll (PA)
Herkimer County Comm Coll (NY)
Hinds Comm Coll (MS)
Holyoke Comm Coll (MA)
Housatonic Comm Coll (CT)
Howard Comm Coll (MD)
Imperial Valley Coll (CA)
Independence Comm Coll (KS)
Iowa Lakes Comm Coll (IA)
Kankakee Comm Coll (IL)
Kilgore Coll (TX)
Kingsborough Comm Coll of the City U of New York (NY)
Kirtland Comm Coll (MI)
Lake Tahoe Comm Coll (CA)
Lansing Comm Coll (MI)
Laramie County Comm Coll (WY)
Lehigh Carbon Comm Coll (PA)
Lenoir Comm Coll (NC)
Linn-Benton Comm Coll (OR)
Lorain County Comm Coll (OH)
Mercer County Comm Coll (NJ)
Mesa Comm Coll (AZ)
Miami Dade Coll (FL)
MiraCosta Coll (CA)
Mississippi Gulf Coast Comm Coll (MS)
Mohave Comm Coll (AZ)
Mohawk Valley Comm Coll (NY)
Monroe Comm Coll (NY)
Monroe County Comm Coll (MI)
Montgomery Coll (MD)
Montgomery County Comm Coll (PA)
Mt. San Jacinto Coll (CA)
Mount Wachusett Comm Coll (MA)
Nassau Comm Coll (NY)
Northeastern Jr Coll (CO)
Northeast Texas Comm Coll (TX)
Northwest Coll (WY)
Northwestern Connecticut Comm Coll (CT)
Northwest Mississippi Comm Coll (MS)

Norwalk Comm Coll (CT)
Oakland Comm Coll (MI)
Oklahoma City Comm Coll (OK)
Oklahoma State U, Oklahoma City (OK)
Onondaga Comm Coll (NY)
Orange Coast Coll (CA)
Oxnard Coll (CA)
Palomar Coll (CA)
Paris Jr Coll (TX)
Pasadena City Coll (CA)
Pensacola State Coll (FL)
Phoenix Coll (AZ)
Reading Area Comm Coll (PA)
Roane State Comm Coll (TN)
San Diego City Coll (CA)
San Jacinto Coll District (TX)
Santa Monica Coll (CA)
Santa Rosa Jr Coll (CA)
Sauk Valley Comm Coll (IL)
Seminole State Coll (OK)
Sheridan Coll (WY)
Snow Coll (UT)
Southeastern Comm Coll (NC)
South Florida State Coll (FL)
South Plains Coll (TX)
Spoon River Coll (IL)
Temple Coll (TX)
Texarkana Coll (TX)
Treasure Valley Comm Coll (OR)
Trinity Valley Comm Coll (TX)
Tunxis Comm Coll (CT)
Tyler Jr Coll (TX)
Umpqua Comm Coll (OR)
Victor Valley Coll (CA)
Vincennes U (IN)
Virginia Western Comm Coll (VA)
Western Texas Coll (TX)
Western Wyoming Comm Coll (WY)

ART HISTORY, CRITICISM AND CONSERVATION
Broward Coll (FL)
De Anza Coll (CA)
Iowa Lakes Comm Coll (IA)
Lansing Comm Coll (MI)
Mercer County Comm Coll (NJ)
Santa Rosa Jr Coll (CA)
South Florida State Coll (FL)
Umpqua Comm Coll (OR)

ARTIFICIAL INTELLIGENCE
Lorain County Comm Coll (OH)
San Diego City Coll (CA)
Southeastern Comm Coll (IA)
Sullivan Coll of Technology and Design (KY)

ART TEACHER EDUCATION
Broward Coll (FL)
Casper Coll (WY)
Cochise Coll, Sierra Vista (AZ)
Copiah-Lincoln Comm Coll (MS)
Darton State Coll (GA)
Eastern Arizona Coll (AZ)
Iowa Lakes Comm Coll (IA)
Mississippi Delta Comm Coll (MS)
Mississippi Gulf Coast Comm Coll (MS)
Northeastern Jr Coll (CO)
Pensacola State Coll (FL)
Roane State Comm Coll (TN)
South Florida State Coll (FL)
Umpqua Comm Coll (OR)
Vincennes U (IN)
Western Texas Coll (TX)

ART THERAPY
Vincennes U (IN)

ASIAN STUDIES
Miami Dade Coll (FL)

ASTRONOMY
Broward Coll (FL)
Fullerton Coll (CA)
Gordon State Coll (GA)
Iowa Lakes Comm Coll (IA)
MiraCosta Coll (CA)
Palomar Coll (CA)
South Florida State Coll (FL)

ATHLETIC TRAINING
Allen Comm Coll (KS)
Casper Coll (WY)
Central Wyoming Coll (WY)
Coll of the Canyons (CA)
Comm Coll of Allegheny County (PA)
Dean Coll (MA)
Independence Comm Coll (KS)
Iowa Lakes Comm Coll (IA)
Lorain County Comm Coll (OH)

Northampton Comm Coll (PA)
Northwest Coll (WY)
Orange Coast Coll (CA)
Sauk Valley Comm Coll (IL)
Treasure Valley Comm Coll (OR)
Wenatchee Valley Coll (WA)

ATMOSPHERIC SCIENCES AND METEOROLOGY
South Florida State Coll (FL)

AUDIOLOGY AND SPEECH-LANGUAGE PATHOLOGY
Broward Coll (FL)
Miami Dade Coll (FL)
Pasadena City Coll (CA)
South Florida State Coll (FL)

AUDIOVISUAL COMMUNICATIONS TECHNOLOGIES RELATED
Cincinnati State Tech and Comm Coll (OH)

AUTOBODY/COLLISION AND REPAIR TECHNOLOGY
American Samoa Comm Coll (AS)
Antelope Valley Coll (CA)
Arkansas State U–Newport (AR)
Bellingham Tech Coll (WA)
Bismarck State Coll (ND)
Casper Coll (WY)
Coll of Marin (CA)
Coll of Southern Idaho (ID)
Coll of Western Idaho (ID)
Crowder Coll (MO)
Dunwoody Coll of Technology (MN)
Erie Comm Coll, South Campus (NY)
Florida State Coll at Jacksonville (FL)
Fox Valley Tech Coll (WI)
Grayson Coll (TX)
Hawkeye Comm Coll (IA)
Highland Comm Coll (IL)
Hutchinson Comm Coll and Area Vocational School (KS)
Illinois Eastern Comm Colls, Olney Central College (IL)
Iowa Lakes Comm Coll (IA)
Kaskaskia Coll (IL)
Kilgore Coll (TX)
Lake Area Tech Inst (SD)
Lane Comm Coll (OR)
Lansing Comm Coll (MI)
Laramie County Comm Coll (WY)
Lincoln Land Comm Coll (IL)
Manhattan Area Tech Coll (KS)
Mid-Plains Comm Coll, North Platte (NE)
Mineral Area Coll (MO)
Minnesota State Coll–Southeast Tech (MN)
North Dakota State Coll of Science (ND)
Northeast Texas Comm Coll (TX)
Oxnard Coll (CA)
Ozarks Tech Comm Coll (MO)
Palomar Coll (CA)
Pueblo Comm Coll (CO)
Randolph Comm Coll (NC)
Salt Lake Comm Coll (UT)
San Jacinto Coll District (TX)
San Juan Coll (NM)
Southeast Tech Inst (SD)
South Louisiana Comm Coll (LA)
Southwestern Illinois Coll (IL)
State U of New York Coll of Technology at Alfred (NY)
Texas State Tech Coll Waco (TX)
U of Arkansas Comm Coll at Morrilton (AR)
Vincennes U (IN)
Walla Walla Comm Coll (WA)
Waubonsee Comm Coll (IL)
Waukesha County Tech Coll (WI)
Wayne Comm Coll (NC)
Western Dakota Tech Inst (SD)
Wichita Area Tech Coll (KS)

AUTOMATION ENGINEER TECHNOLOGY
Alexandria Tech and Comm Coll (MN)
Blue Ridge Comm and Tech Coll (WV)
Dyersburg State Comm Coll (TN)
Fox Valley Tech Coll (WI)
Mitchell Tech Inst (SD)
Southwestern Michigan Coll (MI)

AUTOMOBILE/AUTOMOTIVE MECHANICS TECHNOLOGY
Alamance Comm Coll (NC)

Amarillo Coll (TX)
American Samoa Comm Coll (AS)
Anoka Tech Coll (MN)
Antelope Valley Coll (CA)
Arapahoe Comm Coll (CO)
Arkansas State U–Newport (AR)
Austin Comm Coll (TX)
Barstow Comm Coll (CA)
Bellingham Tech Coll (WA)
Benjamin Franklin Inst of Technology (MA)
Big Bend Comm Coll (WA)
Bismarck State Coll (ND)
Brookhaven Coll (TX)
Broward Coll (FL)
Butte Coll (CA)
Cape Fear Comm Coll (NC)
Casper Coll (WY)
Catawba Valley Comm Coll (NC)
Central Carolina Comm Coll (NC)
Central Maine Comm Coll (ME)
Central Oregon Comm Coll (OR)
Central Wyoming Coll (WY)
Chattahoochee Tech Coll (GA)
Cincinnati State Tech and Comm Coll (OH)
Clark Coll (WA)
Cochise Coll, Sierra Vista (AZ)
Coll of Central Florida (FL)
Coll of Marin (CA)
Coll of Southern Idaho (ID)
Coll of the Canyons (CA)
Coll of the Desert (CA)
Coll of the Ouachitas (AR)
Coll of Western Idaho (ID)
Columbia Coll (CA)
Columbia-Greene Comm Coll (NY)
Columbus Tech Coll (GA)
The Comm Coll of Baltimore County (MD)
Comm Coll of Philadelphia (PA)
Copper Mountain Coll (CA)
Cossatot Comm Coll of the U of Arkansas (AR)
Cosumnes River Coll, Sacramento (CA)
Crowder Coll (MO)
Danville Area Comm Coll (IL)
Daytona State Coll (FL)
De Anza Coll (CA)
Delaware Tech & Comm Coll, Jack F. Owens Campus (DE)
Delaware Tech & Comm Coll, Stanton/Wilmington Campus (DE)
Delta Coll (MI)
Dunwoody Coll of Technology (MN)
East Central Coll (MO)
Eastern Arizona Coll (AZ)
Eastern Idaho Tech Coll (ID)
Elgin Comm Coll (IL)
Erie Comm Coll, South Campus (NY)
Fayetteville Tech Comm Coll (NC)
Florida State Coll at Jacksonville (FL)
Fox Valley Tech Coll (WI)
Fullerton Coll (CA)
Garden City Comm Coll (KS)
Georgia Piedmont Tech Coll (GA)
Glendale Comm Coll (AZ)
Gogebic Comm Coll (MI)
Golden West Coll (CA)
Grand Rapids Comm Coll (MI)
Grays Harbor Coll (WA)
Greenville Tech Coll (SC)
Gwinnett Tech Coll (GA)
Harrisburg Area Comm Coll (PA)
Hawkeye Comm Coll (IA)
Helena Coll U of Montana (MT)
Highland Comm Coll (IL)
Honolulu Comm Coll (HI)
Houston Comm Coll System (TX)
Hutchinson Comm Coll and Area Vocational School (KS)
Illinois Eastern Comm Colls, Frontier Community College (IL)
Illinois Eastern Comm Colls, Olney Central College (IL)
Imperial Valley Coll (CA)
Iowa Lakes Comm Coll (IA)
Ivy Tech Comm Coll–Central Indiana (IN)
Ivy Tech Comm Coll–Columbus (IN)
Ivy Tech Comm Coll–East Central (IN)
Ivy Tech Comm Coll–Kokomo (IN)
Ivy Tech Comm Coll–Lafayette (IN)
Ivy Tech Comm Coll–North Central (IN)
Ivy Tech Comm Coll–Northeast (IN)
Ivy Tech Comm Coll–Northwest (IN)
Ivy Tech Comm Coll–Richmond (IN)

Ivy Tech Comm Coll–Southern Indiana (IN)
Ivy Tech Comm Coll–Southwest (IN)
Ivy Tech Comm Coll–Wabash Valley (IN)
Jackson Coll (MI)
Jefferson Coll (MO)
J. Sargeant Reynolds Comm Coll (VA)
Kankakee Comm Coll (IL)
Kaskaskia Coll (IL)
Kilgore Coll (TX)
Kirtland Comm Coll (MI)
Lake Area Tech Inst (SD)
Lake Land Coll (IL)
Lake Region State Coll (ND)
Lakes Region Comm Coll (NH)
Lake Superior Coll (MN)
Lane Comm Coll (OR)
Lansing Comm Coll (MI)
Laramie County Comm Coll (WY)
Lincoln Coll of Technology (CO)
Lincoln Land Comm Coll (IL)
Linn-Benton Comm Coll (OR)
Lone Star Coll–Montgomery (TX)
Lone Star Coll–North Harris (TX)
Lower Columbia Coll (WA)
Luzerne County Comm Coll (PA)
Macomb Comm Coll (MI)
Manhattan Area Tech Coll (KS)
Mesa Comm Coll (AZ)
Metropolitan Comm Coll–Kansas City (MO)
Mid-Plains Comm Coll, North Platte (NE)
Mineral Area Coll (MO)
MiraCosta Coll (CA)
Mississippi Gulf Coast Comm Coll (MS)
Mohave Comm Coll (AZ)
Monroe Comm Coll (NY)
Montgomery Coll (MD)
Montgomery County Comm Coll (PA)
Moraine Park Tech Coll (WI)
Moraine Valley Comm Coll (IL)
Mott Comm Coll (MI)
Mt. San Jacinto Coll (CA)
Mount Wachusett Comm Coll (MA)
New Mexico State U–Alamogordo (NM)
Northampton Comm Coll (PA)
Northcentral Tech Coll (WI)
North Dakota State Coll of Science (ND)
Northeastern Jr Coll (CO)
Northeast Iowa Comm Coll (IA)
Northeast Texas Comm Coll (TX)
North Iowa Area Comm Coll (IA)
Northwest Tech Coll (MN)
Oakland Comm Coll (MI)
Oakton Comm Coll (IL)
Ogeechee Tech Coll (GA)
Oklahoma City Comm Coll (OK)
Oklahoma Tech Coll (OK)
Onondaga Comm Coll (NY)
Otero Jr Coll (CO)
Oxnard Coll (CA)
Ozarks Tech Comm Coll (MO)
Palomar Coll (CA)
Pasadena City Coll (CA)
Patrick Henry Comm Coll (VA)
Pima Comm Coll (AZ)
Pitt Comm Coll (NC)
Pueblo Comm Coll (CO)
Quinsigamond Comm Coll (MA)
Randolph Comm Coll (NC)
Rend Lake Coll (IL)
Rock Valley Coll (IL)
Rogue Comm Coll (OR)
San Diego City Coll (CA)
San Jacinto Coll District (TX)
San Juan Coll (NM)
Santa Rosa Jr Coll (CA)
Savannah Tech Coll (GA)
Seminole State Coll of Florida (FL)
Shawnee Comm Coll (IL)
Shoreline Comm Coll (WA)
Snow Coll (UT)
Southeastern Comm Coll (IA)
Southeast Tech Inst (SD)
Southern Crescent Tech Coll (GA)
Southern Maine Comm Coll (ME)
South Louisiana Comm Coll (LA)
South Piedmont Comm Coll (NC)
South Plains Coll (TX)
Southwestern Comm Coll (NC)
Southwestern Michigan Coll (MI)
Spartanburg Comm Coll (SC)
Stark State Coll (OH)
State Fair Comm Coll (MO)
Tarrant County Coll District (TX)

TCI–The Coll of Technology (NY)
Texarkana Coll (TX)
Texas State Tech Coll Waco (TX)
Trident Tech Coll (SC)
Trinity Valley Comm Coll (TX)
Truckee Meadows Comm Coll (NV)
Tyler Jr Coll (TX)
Umpqua Comm Coll (OR)
U of Arkansas Comm Coll at Morrilton (AR)
U of Hawaii Maui Coll (HI)
Victor Valley Coll (CA)
Vincennes U (IN)
Virginia Western Comm Coll (VA)
Walla Walla Comm Coll (WA)
Waubonsee Comm Coll (IL)
Waukesha County Tech Coll (WI)
Wayne Comm Coll (NC)
Wayne County Comm Coll District (MI)
Wenatchee Valley Coll (WA)
Western Nevada Coll (NV)
Western Texas Coll (TX)
Western Wyoming Comm Coll (WY)
West Georgia Tech Coll (GA)
Wichita Area Tech Coll (KS)
Williston State Coll (ND)

AUTOMOTIVE ENGINEERING TECHNOLOGY
Benjamin Franklin Inst of Technology (MA)
Cincinnati State Tech and Comm Coll (OH)
Columbus State Comm Coll (OH)
Comm Coll of Allegheny County (PA)
Lawson State Comm Coll (AL)
Macomb Comm Coll (MI)
Massachusetts Bay Comm Coll (MA)
Mercer County Comm Coll (NJ)
Middlesex County Coll (NJ)
Oklahoma City Comm Coll (OK)
Owens Comm Coll, Toledo (OH)
Raritan Valley Comm Coll (NJ)
Springfield Tech Comm Coll (MA)
State U of New York Coll of Technology at Alfred (NY)
Sussex County Comm Coll (NJ)

AVIATION/AIRWAY MANAGEMENT
Anoka Tech Coll (MN)
Broward Coll (FL)
Comm Coll of Allegheny County (PA)
Dutchess Comm Coll (NY)
Florida State Coll at Jacksonville (FL)
Hinds Comm Coll (MS)
Iowa Lakes Comm Coll (IA)
Lenoir Comm Coll (NC)
Lincoln Land Comm Coll (IL)
Luzerne County Comm Coll (PA)
Mercer County Comm Coll (NJ)
Miami Dade Coll (FL)
Palomar Coll (CA)
San Jacinto Coll District (TX)
Southwestern Illinois Coll (IL)
Western Oklahoma State Coll (OK)

AVIONICS MAINTENANCE TECHNOLOGY
Antelope Valley Coll (CA)
Big Bend Comm Coll (WA)
Cochise Coll, Sierra Vista (AZ)
Fox Valley Tech Coll (WI)
Honolulu Comm Coll (HI)
Housatonic Comm Coll (CT)
Jamestown Comm Coll (NY)
Lansing Comm Coll (MI)
Lenoir Comm Coll (NC)
Mt. San Antonio Coll (CA)
Orange Coast Coll (CA)
Rock Valley Coll (IL)
Salt Lake Comm Coll (UT)
San Joaquin Valley Coll, Hanford (CA)
San Joaquin Valley Coll, Hesperia (CA)
San Joaquin Valley Coll, Temecula (CA)
Southern U at Shreveport (LA)
Tarrant County Coll District (TX)
Texas State Tech Coll Waco (TX)
Three Rivers Comm Coll (CT)
Wichita Area Tech Coll (KS)

BAKING AND PASTRY ARTS
Blue Ridge Comm and Tech Coll (WV)
Bucks County Comm Coll (PA)
Cincinnati State Tech and Comm Coll (OH)
Clark Coll (WA)

Coll of Western Idaho (ID)
Collin County Comm Coll District (TX)
Culinary Inst LeNotre (TX)
Elgin Comm Coll (IL)
Harrison Coll (NC)
J. Sargeant Reynolds Comm Coll (VA)
Luzerne County Comm Coll (PA)
Montgomery County Comm Coll (PA)
Moraine Valley Comm Coll (IL)
Mott Comm Coll (MI)
New England Culinary Inst (VT)
Niagara County Comm Coll (NY)
San Jacinto Coll District (TX)
Schoolcraft Coll (MI)
State U of New York Coll of Technology at Alfred (NY)
Sullivan County Comm Coll (NY)
Waukesha County Tech Coll (WI)
Westmoreland County Comm Coll (PA)

BANKING AND FINANCIAL SUPPORT SERVICES
Alamance Comm Coll (NC)
Allen Comm Coll (KS)
Arapahoe Comm Coll (CO)
Austin Comm Coll (TX)
Bristol Comm Coll (MA)
Central Georgia Tech Coll (GA)
Cleveland Comm Coll (NC)
Colorado Northwestern Comm Coll (CO)
Comm Coll of Allegheny County (PA)
Comm Coll of Rhode Island (RI)
Cosumnes River Coll, Sacramento (CA)
Fayetteville Tech Comm Coll (NC)
Florida State Coll at Jacksonville (FL)
Fox Valley Tech Coll (WI)
Harper Coll (IL)
Harrisburg Area Comm Coll (PA)
Hinds Comm Coll (MS)
Houston Comm Coll System (TX)
Lake Area Tech Inst (SD)
Lanier Tech Coll (GA)
Lansing Comm Coll (MI)
Luzerne County Comm Coll (PA)
Mohawk Valley Comm Coll (NY)
Oakton Comm Coll (IL)
Ogeechee Tech Coll (GA)
Oklahoma Comm Coll (OK)
Phoenix Coll (AZ)
Seminole State Coll of Florida (FL)
Southeast Tech Inst (SD)
Southern U at Shreveport (LA)
South Florida State Coll (FL)
State U of New York Coll of Technology at Alfred (NY)
Tulsa Comm Coll (OK)
Westmoreland County Comm Coll (PA)
Wiregrass Georgia Tech Coll (GA)

BARBERING
Oklahoma Tech Coll (OK)

BEHAVIORAL ASPECTS OF HEALTH
Darton State Coll (GA)

BEHAVIORAL SCIENCES
Amarillo Coll (TX)
Ancilla Coll (IN)
De Anza Coll (CA)
Galveston Coll (TX)
Glendale Comm Coll (AZ)
Imperial Valley Coll (CA)
Iowa Lakes Comm Coll (IA)
Miami Dade Coll (FL)
Mississippi Delta Comm Coll (MS)
Monroe Comm Coll (NY)
Northwestern Connecticut Comm Coll (CT)
Orange Coast Coll (CA)
San Diego City Coll (CA)
San Jacinto Coll District (TX)
Santa Rosa Jr Coll (CA)
Seminole State Coll (OK)
Tyler Jr Coll (TX)
Umpqua Comm Coll (OR)
Vincennes U (IN)

BIBLICAL STUDIES
Amarillo Coll (TX)

BILINGUAL AND MULTILINGUAL EDUCATION
Coll of Southern Idaho (ID)
Delaware Tech & Comm Coll, Terry Campus (DE)
Treasure Valley Comm Coll (OR)

BIOCHEMISTRY
Broward Coll (FL)
Pasadena City Coll (CA)
Pensacola State Coll (FL)
South Florida State Coll (FL)
Vincennes U (IN)

BIOENGINEERING AND BIOMEDICAL ENGINEERING
Anoka-Ramsey Comm Coll (MN)
Anoka-Ramsey Comm Coll, Cambridge Campus (MN)
Benjamin Franklin Inst of Technology (MA)
Bunker Hill Comm Coll (MA)
Quinsigamond Comm Coll (MA)

BIOLOGICAL AND BIOMEDICAL SCIENCES RELATED
Darton State Coll (GA)
Gordon State Coll (GA)
Seminole State Coll (OK)
Vincennes U (IN)

BIOLOGICAL AND PHYSICAL SCIENCES
Ancilla Coll (IN)
Barstow Comm Coll (CA)
Ca&nnada Coll (CA)
Central Oregon Comm Coll (OR)
Chipola Coll (FL)
Clinton Comm Coll (NY)
Coll of Marin (CA)
Coll of the Canyons (CA)
Coll of the Desert (CA)
Columbia Coll (CA)
The Comm Coll of Baltimore County (MD)
Comm Coll of Rhode Island (RI)
Copiah-Lincoln Comm Coll (MS)
Cosumnes River Coll, Sacramento (CA)
Dabney S. Lancaster Comm Coll (VA)
Eastern Shore Comm Coll (VA)
Elgin Comm Coll (IL)
Finger Lakes Comm Coll (NY)
Fullerton Coll (CA)
Galveston Coll (TX)
Gavilan Coll (CA)
Georgia Highlands Coll (GA)
Golden West Coll (CA)
Highland Comm Coll (IL)
Howard Comm Coll (MD)
Hudson County Comm Coll (NJ)
Illinois Eastern Comm Colls, Frontier Community College (IL)
Illinois Eastern Comm Colls, Lincoln Trail College (IL)
Illinois Eastern Comm Colls, Olney Central College (IL)
Illinois Eastern Comm Colls, Wabash Valley College (IL)
Imperial Valley Coll (CA)
Iowa Lakes Comm Coll (IA)
J. Sargeant Reynolds Comm Coll (VA)
Kaskaskia Coll (IL)
Kilgore Coll (TX)
Lake Land Coll (IL)
Lake Tahoe Comm Coll (CA)
Lamar Comm Coll (CO)
Laramie County Comm Coll (WY)
Lincoln Land Comm Coll (IL)
Linn-Benton Comm Coll (OR)
Lorain County Comm Coll (OH)
Luzerne County Comm Coll (PA)
Marion Military Inst (AL)
Massachusetts Bay Comm Coll (MA)
McHenry County Coll (IL)
MiraCosta Coll (CA)
Mississippi Gulf Coast Comm Coll (MS)
Monroe Comm Coll (NY)
Moraine Valley Comm Coll (IL)
Mt. San Antonio Coll (CA)
Mt. San Jacinto Coll (CA)
Niagara County Comm Coll (NY)
Northeastern Jr Coll (CO)
Northern Essex Comm Coll (MA)
Oakton Comm Coll (IL)
Otero Jr Coll (CO)

Palomar Coll (CA)
Paris Jr Coll (TX)
Pasadena City Coll (CA)
Patrick Henry Comm Coll (VA)
Penn State Beaver (PA)
Penn State DuBois (PA)
Penn State Fayette, The Eberly Campus (PA)
Penn State Greater Allegheny (PA)
Penn State New Kensington (PA)
Penn State Schuylkill (PA)
Piedmont Virginia Comm Coll (VA)
Potomac State Coll of West Virginia U (WV)
Rainy River Comm Coll (MN)
Rappahannock Comm Coll (VA)
Rend Lake Coll (IL)
Santa Monica Coll (CA)
Shawnee Comm Coll (IL)
Sheridan Coll (WY)
Southeastern Comm Coll (NC)
South Florida State Coll (FL)
South Plains Coll (TX)
South Suburban Coll (IL)
Southwestern Illinois Coll (IL)
Spoon River Coll (IL)
Sussex County Comm Coll (NJ)
Trident Tech Coll (SC)
Umpqua Comm Coll (OR)
U of New Mexico–Los Alamos Branch (NM)
Victor Valley Coll (CA)
Vincennes U (IN)
Virginia Western Comm Coll (VA)
Waubonsee Comm Coll (IL)
Western Wyoming Comm Coll (WY)
Wor-Wic Comm Coll (MD)
Wytheville Comm Coll (VA)

BIOLOGY/BIOLOGICAL SCIENCES
Alabama Southern Comm Coll (AL)
Allen Comm Coll (KS)
Alvin Comm Coll (TX)
Amarillo Coll (TX)
Anoka-Ramsey Comm Coll (MN)
Anoka-Ramsey Comm Coll, Cambridge Campus (MN)
Antelope Valley Coll (CA)
Arizona Western Coll (AZ)
Austin Comm Coll (TX)
Bainbridge State Coll (GA)
Bronx Comm Coll of the City U of New York (NY)
Broward Coll (FL)
Bunker Hill Comm Coll (MA)
Butler County Comm Coll (PA)
Butte Coll (CA)
Ca&nnada Coll (CA)
Carl Albert State Coll (OK)
Casper Coll (WY)
Cecil Coll (MD)
Central Oregon Comm Coll (OR)
Central Wyoming Coll (WY)
Cincinnati State Tech and Comm Coll (OH)
Cochise Coll, Sierra Vista (AZ)
Coll of Marin (CA)
Coll of Southern Idaho (ID)
Coll of the Desert (CA)
Coll of Western Idaho (ID)
Columbia Coll (CA)
Comm Coll of Allegheny County (PA)
Copiah-Lincoln Comm Coll (MS)
Crowder Coll (MO)
Dakota Coll at Bottineau (ND)
Darton State Coll (GA)
De Anza Coll (CA)
Delaware Tech & Comm Coll, Jack F. Owens Campus (DE)
Delaware Tech & Comm Coll, Stanton/Wilmington Campus (DE)
Eastern Arizona Coll (AZ)
Eastern Wyoming Coll (WY)
Edison Comm Coll (OH)
Feather River Coll (CA)
Finger Lakes Comm Coll (NY)
Fiorello H. LaGuardia Comm Coll of the City U of New York (NY)
Frank Phillips Coll (TX)
Fullerton Coll (CA)
Garden City Comm Coll (KS)
Gavilan Coll (CA)
Genesee Comm Coll (NY)
Georgia Military Coll (GA)
Golden West Coll (CA)
Grayson Coll (TX)
Harford Comm Coll (MD)
Harper Coll (IL)
Harrisburg Area Comm Coll (PA)

Hinds Comm Coll (MS)
Hutchinson Comm Coll and Area Vocational School (KS)
Independence Comm Coll (KS)
Iowa Lakes Comm Coll (IA)
Jamestown Comm Coll (NY)
Kankakee Comm Coll (IL)
Kingsborough Comm Coll of the City U of New York (NY)
Lamar Comm Coll (CO)
Landmark Coll (VT)
Lansing Comm Coll (MI)
Laramie County Comm Coll (WY)
Lehigh Carbon Comm Coll (PA)
Linn-Benton Comm Coll (OR)
Lorain County Comm Coll (OH)
Los Angeles Mission Coll (CA)
Macomb Comm Coll (MI)
Mercer County Comm Coll (NJ)
Mesa Comm Coll (AZ)
Metropolitan Comm Coll–Kansas City (MO)
Miami Dade Coll (FL)
Minneapolis Comm and Tech Coll (MN)
MiraCosta Coll (CA)
Mississippi Delta Comm Coll (MS)
Monroe Comm Coll (NY)
Monroe County Comm Coll (MI)
Montgomery County Comm Coll (PA)
Mott Comm Coll (MI)
Northampton Comm Coll (PA)
Northeastern Jr Coll (CO)
Northeast Texas Comm Coll (TX)
Northwest Coll (WY)
Northwestern Connecticut Comm Coll (CT)
Oklahoma City Comm Coll (OK)
Orange Coast Coll (CA)
Otero Jr Coll (CO)
Oxnard Coll (CA)
Palomar Coll (CA)
Paris Jr Coll (TX)
Pasadena City Coll (CA)
Pensacola State Coll (FL)
Potomac State Coll of West Virginia U (WV)
Roane State Comm Coll (TN)
Salt Lake Comm Coll (UT)
San Diego City Coll (CA)
San Jacinto Coll District (TX)
San Juan Coll (NM)
Santa Rosa Jr Coll (CA)
Sauk Valley Comm Coll (IL)
Seminole State Coll (OK)
Sheridan Coll (WY)
Snow Coll (UT)
Southern U at Shreveport (LA)
South Florida State Coll (FL)
South Georgia State Coll, Douglas (GA)
South Plains Coll (TX)
Spoon River Coll (IL)
Springfield Tech Comm Coll (MA)
State U of New York Coll of Technology at Alfred (NY)
Texarkana Coll (TX)
Treasure Valley Comm Coll (OR)
Trinity Valley Comm Coll (TX)
Truckee Meadows Comm Coll (NV)
Tulsa Comm Coll (OK)
Tyler Jr Coll (TX)
Umpqua Comm Coll (OR)
Victor Valley Coll (CA)
Vincennes U (IN)
Walla Walla Comm Coll (WA)
Wenatchee Valley Coll (WA)
Western Nevada Coll (NV)
Western Wyoming Comm Coll (WY)

BIOLOGY/BIOTECHNOLOGY LABORATORY TECHNICIAN
Athens Tech Coll (GA)
Austin Comm Coll (TX)
Berkeley City Coll (CA)
Bucks County Comm Coll (PA)
Carrington Coll California–San Jose (CA)
Cleveland Comm Coll (NC)
Collin County Comm Coll District (TX)
County Coll of Morris (NJ)
Delaware Tech & Comm Coll, Jack F. Owens Campus (DE)
Delaware Tech & Comm Coll, Stanton/Wilmington Campus (DE)
East Central Coll (MO)
Elgin Comm Coll (IL)
Finger Lakes Comm Coll (NY)
Fox Valley Tech Coll (WI)

Genesee Comm Coll (NY)
Hagerstown Comm Coll (MD)
Hillsborough Comm Coll (FL)
Houston Comm Coll System (TX)
Hutchinson Comm Coll and Area Vocational School (KS)
Jamestown Comm Coll (NY)
Lake Area Tech Inst (SD)
Lone Star Coll–Montgomery (TX)
Manhattan Area Tech Coll (KS)
Massachusetts Bay Comm Coll (MA)
Mercer County Comm Coll (NJ)
Middlesex County Coll (NJ)
Monroe Comm Coll (NY)
Montgomery Coll (MD)
North Dakota State Coll of Science (ND)
North Shore Comm Coll (MA)
The Ohio State U Ag Tech Inst (OH)
Owensboro Comm and Tech Coll (KY)
Pitt Comm Coll (NC)
Randolph Comm Coll (NC)
Salt Lake Comm Coll (UT)
Shoreline Comm Coll (WA)
Temple Coll (TX)
Wayne Comm Coll (NC)
Westmoreland County Comm Coll (PA)

BIOLOGY TEACHER EDUCATION
Bucks County Comm Coll (PA)
Columbia-Greene Comm Coll (NY)

BIOMEDICAL SCIENCES
Coll of Western Idaho (ID)
Northeast Texas Comm Coll (TX)

BIOMEDICAL TECHNOLOGY
Alabama Southern Comm Coll (AL)
Anoka-Ramsey Comm Coll (MN)
Anoka-Ramsey Comm Coll, Cambridge Campus (MN)
Benjamin Franklin Inst of Technology (MA)
Broward Coll (FL)
Brown Mackie Coll–Birmingham (AL)
Brown Mackie Coll–Cincinnati (OH)
Brown Mackie Coll–Dallas/Ft. Worth (TX)
Brown Mackie Coll–Fort Wayne (IN)
Brown Mackie Coll–Indianapolis (IN)
Brown Mackie Coll–Kansas City (KS)
Brown Mackie Coll–Louisville (KY)
Brown Mackie Coll–Miami (FL)
Brown Mackie Coll–Oklahoma City (OK)
Brown Mackie Coll–Phoenix (AZ)
Brown Mackie Coll–St. Louis (MO)
Brown Mackie Coll–Tucson (AZ)
Chattahoochee Tech Coll (GA)
Cincinnati State Tech and Comm Coll (OH)
Delaware Tech & Comm Coll, Terry Campus (DE)
Florida State Coll at Jacksonville (FL)
Fullerton Coll (CA)
Howard Comm Coll (MD)
Miami Dade Coll (FL)
Minnesota State Coll–Southeast Tech (MN)
MiraCosta Coll (CA)
New Mexico State U–Alamogordo (NM)
Owens Comm Coll, Toledo (OH)
Penn State DuBois (PA)
Penn State Fayette, The Eberly Campus (PA)
Penn State Hazleton (PA)
Penn State New Kensington (PA)
Penn State Schuylkill (PA)
Penn State York (PA)
Schoolcraft Coll (MI)
Southeastern Comm Coll (IA)
Southeast Tech Inst (SD)
South Florida State Coll (FL)
Spencerian Coll–Lexington (KY)
Stark State Coll (OH)
Texas State Tech Coll Waco (TX)
Tulsa Comm Coll (OK)
Wayne County Comm Coll District (MI)

BIOTECHNOLOGY
Alamance Comm Coll (NC)
Augusta Tech Coll (GA)
Borough of Manhattan Comm Coll of the City U of New York (NY)

Bucks County Comm Coll (PA)
Bunker Hill Comm Coll (MA)
Cecil Coll (MD)
Genesee Comm Coll (NY)
Glendale Comm Coll (AZ)
Greenville Tech Coll (SC)
Howard Comm Coll (MD)
Ivy Tech Comm Coll–Central Indiana (IN)
Ivy Tech Comm Coll–Lafayette (IN)
Ivy Tech Comm Coll–North Central (IN)
Lakeland Comm Coll (OH)
Lansing Comm Coll (MI)
Lehigh Carbon Comm Coll (PA)
Miami Dade Coll (FL)
Middlesex County Coll (NJ)
Minneapolis Comm and Tech Coll (MN)
Montgomery County Comm Coll (PA)
Mount Wachusett Comm Coll (MA)
Northampton Comm Coll (PA)
Oakland Comm Coll (MI)
Oklahoma City Comm Coll (OK)
Quinsigamond Comm Coll (MA)
Raritan Valley Comm Coll (NJ)
San Jacinto Coll District (TX)
Southeastern Comm Coll (NC)
Southern Maine Comm Coll (ME)
South Piedmont Comm Coll (NC)
Springfield Tech Comm Coll (MA)
Tompkins Cortland Comm Coll (NY)
Tulsa Comm Coll (OK)
Vincennes U (IN)

BOILERMAKING
Ivy Tech Comm Coll–Southwest (IN)

BOTANY/PLANT BIOLOGY
Broward Coll (FL)
Iowa Lakes Comm Coll (IA)
Pensacola State Coll (FL)
Snow Coll (UT)
South Florida State Coll (FL)
Spoon River Coll (IL)

BROADCAST JOURNALISM
Amarillo Coll (TX)
Cosumnes River Coll, Sacramento (CA)
Herkimer County Comm Coll (NY)
Iowa Lakes Comm Coll (IA)
Kingsborough Comm Coll of the City U of New York (NY)
Northwest Coll (WY)
Ocean County Coll (NJ)
Oklahoma City Comm Coll (OK)
Pasadena City Coll (CA)
Sussex County Comm Coll (NJ)

BUILDING/CONSTRUCTION FINISHING, MANAGEMENT, AND INSPECTION RELATED
Coll of Southern Idaho (ID)
Coll of Southern Maryland (MD)
The Comm Coll of Baltimore County (MD)
Cumberland County Coll (NJ)
Delta Coll (MI)
Fayetteville Tech Comm Coll (NC)
Gwinnett Tech Coll (GA)
Ivy Tech Comm Coll–Northwest (IN)
Lawson State Comm Coll (AL)
Manhattan Area Tech Coll (KS)
Mid-Plains Comm Coll, North Platte (NE)
Mohave Comm Coll (AZ)
Montgomery Coll (MD)
Mt. San Antonio Coll (CA)
Oakton Comm Coll (IL)
Pitt Comm Coll (NC)
Salt Lake Comm Coll (UT)
Seminole State Coll of Florida (FL)
Snow Coll (UT)
Southeast Tech Inst (SD)
Springfield Tech Comm Coll (MA)
Victor Valley Coll (CA)

BUILDING/CONSTRUCTION SITE MANAGEMENT
Coll of the Canyons (CA)
Coll of the Desert (CA)
The Comm Coll of Baltimore County (MD)
Cosumnes River Coll, Sacramento (CA)
Dunwoody Coll of Technology (MN)
Fox Valley Tech Coll (WI)
Fullerton Coll (CA)
J. Sargeant Reynolds Comm Coll (VA)
Lehigh Carbon Comm Coll (PA)

Metropolitan Comm Coll–Kansas City (MO)
The Ohio State U Ag Tech Inst (OH)
State Fair Comm Coll (MO)

BUILDING CONSTRUCTION TECHNOLOGY
Broward Coll (FL)
Central Maine Comm Coll (ME)
Cochise Coll, Sierra Vista (AZ)
Coconino Comm Coll (AZ)
Lake Superior Coll (MN)
Mitchell Tech Inst (SD)
North Dakota State Coll of Science (ND)
Sheridan Coll (WY)
Truckee Meadows Comm Coll (NV)

BUILDING/HOME/ CONSTRUCTION INSPECTION
Bismarck State Coll (ND)
Bucks County Comm Coll (PA)
Cosumnes River Coll, Sacramento (CA)
Fullerton Coll (CA)
Harrisburg Area Comm Coll (PA)
Oklahoma State U, Oklahoma City (OK)
Orange Coast Coll (CA)
Palomar Coll (CA)
Pasadena City Coll (CA)
Phoenix Coll (AZ)
South Suburban Coll (IL)
Vincennes U (IN)

BUILDING/PROPERTY MAINTENANCE
Bellingham Tech Coll (WA)
Cape Fear Comm Coll (NC)
Central Wyoming Coll (WY)
Century Coll (MN)
Comm Coll of Allegheny County (PA)
Delta Coll (MI)
Erie Comm Coll (NY)
Ivy Tech Comm Coll–Bloomington (IN)
Ivy Tech Comm Coll–Central Indiana (IN)
Ivy Tech Comm Coll–Columbus (IN)
Ivy Tech Comm Coll–East Central (IN)
Ivy Tech Comm Coll–Kokomo (IN)
Ivy Tech Comm Coll–Lafayette (IN)
Ivy Tech Comm Coll–North Central (IN)
Ivy Tech Comm Coll–Northeast (IN)
Ivy Tech Comm Coll–Northwest (IN)
Ivy Tech Comm Coll–Richmond (IN)
Ivy Tech Comm Coll–Southern Indiana (IN)
Ivy Tech Comm Coll–Southwest (IN)
Ivy Tech Comm Coll–Wabash Valley (IN)
Lincoln Land Comm Coll (IL)
Luzerne County Comm Coll (PA)
Manhattan Area Tech Coll (KS)
Mitchell Tech Inst (SD)
Mohawk Valley Comm Coll (NY)
Pensacola State Coll (FL)
Piedmont Comm Coll (NC)
Pima Comm Coll (AZ)
TCI–The Coll of Technology (NY)
Wayne County Comm Coll District (MI)

BUSINESS ADMINISTRATION AND MANAGEMENT
Alamance Comm Coll (NC)
Alexandria Tech and Comm Coll (MN)
Allen Comm Coll (KS)
Alvin Comm Coll (TX)
Amarillo Coll (TX)
American Samoa Comm Coll (AS)
Ancilla Coll (IN)
Anoka-Ramsey Comm Coll (MN)
Anoka-Ramsey Comm Coll, Cambridge Campus (MN)
Antelope Valley Coll (CA)
Arapahoe Comm Coll (CO)
Arizona Western Coll (AZ)
Augusta Tech Coll (GA)
Austin Comm Coll (TX)
Bainbridge State Coll (GA)
Barstow Comm Coll (CA)
Bay State Coll (MA)
Beal Coll (ME)
Berkeley City Coll (CA)
Berkshire Comm Coll (MA)
Blackhawk Tech Coll (WI)
Blue Ridge Comm and Tech Coll (WV)

Borough of Manhattan Comm Coll of the City U of New York (NY)
Bowling Green State U-Firelands Coll (OH)
Bristol Comm Coll (MA)
Bronx Comm Coll of the City U of New York (NY)
Brookhaven Coll (TX)
Broward Coll (FL)
Brown Mackie Coll–Albuquerque (NM)
Brown Mackie Coll–Birmingham (AL)
Brown Mackie Coll–Cincinnati (OH)
Brown Mackie Coll–Findlay (OH)
Brown Mackie Coll–Greenville (SC)
Brown Mackie Coll–Miami (FL)
Brown Mackie Coll–Northern Kentucky (KY)
Brown Mackie Coll–Phoenix (AZ)
Brown Mackie Coll–Quad Cities (IA)
Bucks County Comm Coll (PA)
Bunker Hill Comm Coll (MA)
Butler County Comm Coll (PA)
Butte Coll (CA)
Cambria-Rowe Business Coll, Indiana (PA)
Cambria-Rowe Business Coll, Johnstown (PA)
Ca&nnada Coll (CA)
Cape Fear Comm Coll (NC)
Career Tech Coll, Monroe (LA)
Carl Albert State Coll (OK)
Carrington Coll California–Citrus Heights (CA)
Carrington Coll California–Pleasant Hill (CA)
Carrington Coll California–San Jose (CA)
Carrington Coll California–San Leandro (CA)
Carroll Comm Coll (MD)
Casper Coll (WY)
Catawba Valley Comm Coll (NC)
Cayuga County Comm Coll (NY)
Cecil Coll (MD)
Central Carolina Comm Coll (NC)
Central Georgia Tech Coll (GA)
Central Maine Comm Coll (ME)
Central Ohio Tech Coll (OH)
Central Oregon Comm Coll (OR)
Central Virginia Comm Coll (VA)
Central Wyoming Coll (WY)
Century Coll (MN)
Chandler-Gilbert Comm Coll (AZ)
Chattahoochee Tech Coll (GA)
Chipola Coll (FL)
Chippewa Valley Tech Coll (WI)
Cincinnati State Tech and Comm Coll (OH)
Clark Coll (WA)
Clark State Comm Coll (OH)
Clatsop Comm Coll (OR)
Cleveland Comm Coll (NC)
Cleveland State Comm Coll (TN)
Clinton Comm Coll (NY)
Cloud County Comm Coll (KS)
Cochise Coll, Sierra Vista (AZ)
Coconino Comm Coll (AZ)
CollAmerica–Flagstaff (AZ)
Coll of Marin (CA)
Coll of Southern Idaho (ID)
Coll of Southern Maryland (MD)
Coll of the Canyons (CA)
Coll of the Desert (CA)
Coll of the Ouachitas (AR)
Collin County Comm Coll District (TX)
Columbia Coll (CA)
Columbia Gorge Comm Coll (OR)
Columbia-Greene Comm Coll (NY)
Columbus State Comm Coll (OH)
Comm Coll of Allegheny County (PA)
The Comm Coll of Baltimore County (MD)
Comm Coll of Philadelphia (PA)
Comm Coll of Rhode Island (RI)
Comm Coll of Vermont (VT)
Copiah-Lincoln Comm Coll (MS)
Copper Mountain Coll (CA)
Cossatot Comm Coll of the U of Arkansas (AR)
Cosumnes River Coll, Sacramento (CA)
County Coll of Morris (NJ)
Crowder Coll (MO)
Cumberland County Coll (NJ)
Dabney S. Lancaster Comm Coll (VA)
Dakota Coll at Bottineau (ND)
Darton State Coll (GA)
Davis Coll (OH)

Daytona State Coll (FL)
Dean Coll (MA)
De Anza Coll (CA)
Delaware Tech & Comm Coll, Stanton/Wilmington Campus (DE)
Delaware Tech & Comm Coll, Terry Campus (DE)
Delta Coll (MI)
Dutchess Comm Coll (NY)
Dyersburg State Comm Coll (TN)
Eastern Arizona Coll (AZ)
Eastern Florida State Coll (FL)
Eastern Gateway Comm Coll (OH)
Eastern Shore Comm Coll (VA)
Eastern Wyoming Coll (WY)
Edison Comm Coll (OH)
Elgin Comm Coll (IL)
Erie Comm Coll (NY)
Erie Comm Coll, North Campus (NY)
Erie Comm Coll, South Campus (NY)
Fayetteville Tech Comm Coll (NC)
Finger Lakes Comm Coll (NY)
Fiorello H. LaGuardia Comm Coll of the City U of New York (NY)
Flathead Valley Comm Coll (MT)
Florida State Coll at Jacksonville (FL)
Fox Valley Tech Coll (WI)
Frank Phillips Coll (TX)
Fullerton Coll (CA)
Galveston Coll (TX)
Garden City Comm Coll (KS)
Garrett Coll (MD)
Gateway Comm and Tech Coll (KY)
Gavilan Coll (CA)
Genesee Comm Coll (NY)
Georgia Highlands Coll (GA)
Georgia Military Coll (GA)
Glendale Comm Coll (AZ)
Glen Oaks Comm Coll (MI)
Gogebic Comm Coll (MI)
Golden West Coll (CA)
Goodwin Coll (CT)
Gordon State Coll (GA)
Grand Rapids Comm Coll (MI)
Grays Harbor Coll (WA)
Grayson Coll (TX)
Great Basin Coll (NV)
Great Falls Coll Montana State U (MT)
Greenfield Comm Coll (MA)
Greenville Tech Coll (SC)
Gwinnett Tech Coll (GA)
Hagerstown Comm Coll (MD)
Halifax Comm Coll (NC)
Hallmark Coll of Technology (TX)
Harford Comm Coll (MD)
Harper Coll (IL)
Harrisburg Area Comm Coll (PA)
Herkimer County Comm Coll (NY)
Hillsborough Comm Coll (FL)
Hocking Coll (OH)
Holyoke Comm Coll (MA)
Hopkinsville Comm Coll (KY)
Housatonic Comm Coll (CT)
Houston Comm Coll System (TX)
Howard Comm Coll (MD)
Hudson County Comm Coll (NJ)
Ilisagvik Coll (AK)
Illinois Eastern Comm Colls, Olney Central College (IL)
Illinois Eastern Comm Colls, Wabash Valley College (IL)
Imperial Valley Coll (CA)
Independence Comm Coll (KS)
Inst of Business & Medical Careers (CO)
Iowa Lakes Comm Coll (IA)
ITT Tech Inst, Bessemer (AL)
ITT Tech Inst, Madison (AL)
ITT Tech Inst, Mobile (AL)
ITT Tech Inst, Tucson (AZ)
ITT Tech Inst (AR)
ITT Tech Inst, Culver City (CA)
ITT Tech Inst, Lathrop (CA)
ITT Tech Inst, National City (CA)
ITT Tech Inst, Oakland (CA)
ITT Tech Inst, Orange (CA)
ITT Tech Inst, Oxnard (CA)
ITT Tech Inst, Rancho Cordova (CA)
ITT Tech Inst, San Bernardino (CA)
ITT Tech Inst, San Dimas (CA)
ITT Tech Inst, Sylmar (CA)
ITT Tech Inst, Torrance (CA)
ITT Tech Inst, Aurora (CO)
ITT Tech Inst, Westminster (CO)
ITT Tech Inst, Miami (FL)
ITT Tech Inst, Tallahassee (FL)
ITT Tech Inst, Atlanta (GA)
ITT Tech Inst, Duluth (GA)
ITT Tech Inst, Kennesaw (GA)
ITT Tech Inst, Arlington Heights (IL)

ITT Tech Inst, Oak Brook (IL)
ITT Tech Inst, Orland Park (IL)
ITT Tech Inst, Fort Wayne (IN)
ITT Tech Inst, Newburgh (IN)
ITT Tech Inst, Clive (IA)
ITT Tech Inst, Louisville (KY)
ITT Tech Inst, Baton Rouge (LA)
ITT Tech Inst, St. Rose (LA)
ITT Tech Inst, Canton (MI)
ITT Tech Inst, Dearborn (MI)
ITT Tech Inst, Swartz Creek (MI)
ITT Tech Inst, Troy (MI)
ITT Tech Inst, Wyoming (MI)
ITT Tech Inst, Brooklyn Center (MN)
ITT Tech Inst, Eden Prairie (MN)
ITT Tech Inst, Arnold (MO)
ITT Tech Inst , Earth City (MO)
ITT Tech Inst, Kansas City (MO)
ITT Tech Inst (NE)
ITT Tech Inst, Henderson (NV)
ITT Tech Inst, North Las Vegas (NV)
ITT Tech Inst, Charlotte (NC)
ITT Tech Inst, Akron (OH)
ITT Tech Inst, Columbus (OH)
ITT Tech Inst, Dayton (OH)
ITT Tech Inst, Hilliard (OH)
ITT Tech Inst, Maumee (OH)
ITT Tech Inst, Norwood (OH)
ITT Tech Inst, Strongsville (OH)
ITT Tech Inst, Warrensville Heights (OH)
ITT Tech Inst , Youngstown (OH)
ITT Tech Inst, Tulsa (OK)
ITT Tech Inst, Portland (OR)
ITT Tech Inst, Chattanooga (TN)
ITT Tech Inst, Cordova (TN)
ITT Tech Inst, Johnson City (TN)
ITT Tech Inst, Knoxville (TN)
ITT Tech Inst, Arlington (TX)
ITT Tech Inst, Austin (TX)
ITT Tech Inst, Houston (TX)
ITT Tech Inst, Houston (TX)
ITT Tech Inst, Richardson (TX)
ITT Tech Inst, San Antonio (TX)
ITT Tech Inst, Waco (TX)
ITT Tech Inst, Webster (TX)
ITT Tech Inst (UT)
ITT Tech Inst, Chantilly (VA)
ITT Tech Inst, Norfolk (VA)
ITT Tech Inst, Richmond (VA)
ITT Tech Inst, Salem (VA)
ITT Tech Inst, Springfield (VA)
ITT Tech Inst, Everett (WA)
ITT Tech Inst, Seattle (WA)
ITT Tech Inst, Spokane Valley (WA)
ITT Tech Inst (WV)
ITT Tech Inst, Green Bay (WI)
ITT Tech Inst , Greenfield (WI)
ITT Tech Inst, Madison (WI)
Ivy Tech Comm Coll–Bloomington (IN)
Ivy Tech Comm Coll–Central Indiana (IN)
Ivy Tech Comm Coll–Columbus (IN)
Ivy Tech Comm Coll–East Central (IN)
Ivy Tech Comm Coll–Kokomo (IN)
Ivy Tech Comm Coll–Lafayette (IN)
Ivy Tech Comm Coll–North Central (IN)
Ivy Tech Comm Coll–Northeast (IN)
Ivy Tech Comm Coll–Northwest (IN)
Ivy Tech Comm Coll–Richmond (IN)
Ivy Tech Comm Coll–Southeast (IN)
Ivy Tech Comm Coll–Southern Indiana (IN)
Ivy Tech Comm Coll–Southwest (IN)
Ivy Tech Comm Coll–Wabash Valley (IN)
Jackson Coll (MI)
Jackson State Comm Coll (TN)
James Sprunt Comm Coll (NC)
Jamestown Business Coll (NY)
Jamestown Comm Coll (NY)
Jefferson Coll (MO)
Jefferson Comm Coll (NY)
Johnston Comm Coll (NC)
John Tyler Comm Coll (VA)
J. Sargeant Reynolds Comm Coll (VA)
Kankakee Comm Coll (IL)
Kilgore Coll (TX)
Kilian Comm Coll (SD)
Kingsborough Comm Coll of the City U of New York (NY)
Kirtland Comm Coll (MI)
Lake Land Coll (IL)
Lakeland Comm Coll (OH)
Lake Region State Coll (ND)
Lake Superior Coll (MN)
Lake Tahoe Comm Coll (CA)

Lamar Comm Coll (CO)
Lamar State Coll–Orange (TX)
Landmark Coll (VT)
Lansing Comm Coll (MI)
Laramie County Comm Coll (WY)
Lawson State Comm Coll (AL)
LDS Business Coll (UT)
Lehigh Carbon Comm Coll (PA)
Lenoir Comm Coll (NC)
Linn-Benton Comm Coll (OR)
Lone Star Coll–CyFair (TX)
Lone Star Coll–Kingwood (TX)
Lone Star Coll–Montgomery (TX)
Lone Star Coll–North Harris (TX)
Lone Star Coll–Tomball (TX)
Lone Star Coll–U Park (TX)
Long Island Business Inst (NY)
Lorain County Comm Coll (OH)
Los Angeles Mission Coll (CA)
Lower Columbia Coll (WA)
Luzerne County Comm Coll (PA)
Macomb Comm Coll (MI)
Manchester Comm Coll (CT)
Massachusetts Bay Comm Coll (MA)
McHenry County Coll (IL)
Mercer County Comm Coll (NJ)
Mesa Comm Coll (AZ)
Metropolitan Comm Coll–Kansas City (MO)
Miami Dade Coll (FL)
Middlesex County Coll (NJ)
Mid-Plains Comm Coll, North Platte (NE)
Minneapolis Comm and Tech Coll (MN)
Minnesota School of Business–Brooklyn Center (MN)
Minnesota School of Business–Plymouth (MN)
Minnesota State Coll–Southeast Tech (MN)
MiraCosta Coll (CA)
Mississippi Gulf Coast Comm Coll (MS)
Missouri State U–West Plains (MO)
Mitchell Comm Coll (NC)
Mohave Comm Coll (AZ)
Mohawk Valley Comm Coll (NY)
Monroe Comm Coll (NY)
Monroe County Comm Coll (MI)
Montgomery County Comm Coll (PA)
Moraine Park Tech Coll (WI)
Moraine Valley Comm Coll (IL)
Motlow State Comm Coll (TN)
Mott Comm Coll (MI)
Mountain View Coll (TX)
Mt. San Antonio Coll (CA)
Mt. San Jacinto Coll (CA)
Nassau Comm Coll (NY)
Niagara County Comm Coll (NY)
Northampton Comm Coll (PA)
Northcentral Tech Coll (WI)
North Dakota State Coll of Science (ND)
Northeastern Jr Coll (CO)
Northeastern Tech Coll (SC)
Northeast Iowa Comm Coll (IA)
Northeast Texas Comm Coll (TX)
Northern Essex Comm Coll (MA)
North Iowa Area Comm Coll (IA)
North Shore Comm Coll (MA)
NorthWest Arkansas Comm Coll (AR)
Northwest Coll (WY)
Northwestern Connecticut Comm Coll (CT)
Northwest Florida State Coll (FL)
Northwest Mississippi Comm Coll (MS)
Northwest Tech Coll (MN)
Norwalk Comm Coll (CT)
Oakland Comm Coll (MI)
Ocean County Coll (NJ)
Oklahoma City Comm Coll (OK)
Oklahoma State U, Oklahoma City (OK)
Olympic Coll (WA)
Onondaga Comm Coll (NY)
Orange Coast Coll (CA)
Otero Jr Coll (CO)
Owensboro Comm and Tech Coll (KY)
Oxnard Coll (CA)
Ozarks Tech Comm Coll (MO)
Palomar Coll (CA)
Paris Jr Coll (TX)
Pasadena City Coll (CA)
Pasco-Hernando State Coll (FL)
Patrick Henry Comm Coll (VA)
Pennsylvania Inst of Technology (PA)

Pensacola State Coll (FL)
Phoenix Coll (AZ)
Piedmont Comm Coll (NC)
Piedmont Virginia Comm Coll (VA)
Pitt Comm Coll (NC)
Pittsburgh Tech Inst, Oakdale (PA)
Potomac State Coll of West Virginia U (WV)
Pueblo Comm Coll (CO)
Quinsigamond Comm Coll (MA)
Rainy River Comm Coll (MN)
Randolph Comm Coll (NC)
Rappahannock Comm Coll (VA)
Raritan Valley Comm Coll (NJ)
Reading Area Comm Coll (PA)
Richmond Comm Coll (NC)
River Valley Comm Coll (NH)
Roane State Comm Coll (TN)
Rock Valley Coll (IL)
Rogue Comm Coll (OR)
Salt Lake Comm Coll (UT)
San Diego City Coll (CA)
San Jacinto Coll District (TX)
San Joaquin Valley Coll, Bakersfield (CA)
San Joaquin Valley Coll, Hanford (CA)
San Joaquin Valley Coll, Temecula (CA)
San Joaquin Valley Coll–Online (CA)
San Juan Coll (NM)
Santa Monica Coll (CA)
Santa Rosa Jr Coll (CA)
Sauk Valley Comm Coll (IL)
Schoolcraft Coll (MI)
Scottsdale Comm Coll (AZ)
Seminole State Coll (OK)
Seminole State Coll of Florida (FL)
Shawnee Comm Coll (IL)
Shoreline Comm Coll (WA)
Snead State Comm Coll (AL)
Snow Coll (UT)
Somerset Comm Coll (KY)
Southeastern Comm Coll (IA)
Southeastern Comm Coll (NC)
Southeast Tech Inst (SD)
Southern Crescent Tech Coll (GA)
Southern Maine Comm Coll (ME)
Southern State Comm Coll (OH)
South Florida State Coll (FL)
South Georgia State Coll, Douglas (GA)
South Piedmont Comm Coll (NC)
South Plains Coll (TX)
Southwestern Comm Coll (NC)
Southwestern Indian Polytechnic Inst (NM)
Southwestern Michigan Coll (MI)
Spartanburg Comm Coll (SC)
Spoon River Coll (IL)
Springfield Tech Comm Coll (MA)
Stark State Coll (OH)
State Fair Comm Coll (MO)
Sullivan County Comm Coll (NY)
Sussex County Comm Coll (NJ)
Tarrant County Coll District (TX)
TCI–The Coll of Technology (NY)
Temple Coll (TX)
Texarkana Coll (TX)
Three Rivers Comm Coll (CT)
Tompkins Cortland Comm Coll (NY)
Trident Tech Coll (SC)
Trinity Valley Comm Coll (TX)
Truckee Meadows Comm Coll (NV)
Tulsa Comm Coll (OK)
Tunxis Comm Coll (CT)
Tyler Jr Coll (TX)
Umpqua Comm Coll (OR)
The U of Akron–Wayne Coll (OH)
U of New Mexico–Los Alamos Branch (NM)
Victoria Coll (TX)
Victor Valley Coll (CA)
Vincennes U (IN)
Virginia Western Comm Coll (VA)
Volunteer State Comm Coll (TN)
Walla Walla Comm Coll (WA)
Walters State Comm Coll (TN)
Waubonsee Comm Coll (IL)
Waukesha County Tech Coll (WI)
Wayne Comm Coll (NC)
Wayne County Comm Coll District (MI)
Wenatchee Valley Coll (WA)
Westchester Comm Coll (NY)
Western Dakota Tech Inst (SD)
Western Texas Coll (TX)
Western Wyoming Comm Coll (WY)
West Kentucky Comm and Tech Coll (KY)

Westmoreland County Comm Coll (PA)
West Virginia Jr Coll–Bridgeport (WV)
Wichita Area Tech Coll (KS)
Wisconsin Indianhead Tech Coll (WI)
Wor-Wic Comm Coll (MD)
Wright Career Coll, Overland Park (KS)
Wright Career Coll, Wichita (KS)
Wright Career Coll (NE)
Wright Career Coll, Oklahoma City (OK)
Wright Career Coll, Tulsa (OK)
Wytheville Comm Coll (VA)
York County Comm Coll (ME)

BUSINESS ADMINISTRATION, MANAGEMENT AND OPERATIONS RELATED

Berkeley City Coll (CA)
Blue Ridge Comm and Tech Coll (WV)
Bunker Hill Comm Coll (MA)
Chandler-Gilbert Comm Coll (AZ)
Cincinnati State Tech and Comm Coll (OH)
Comm Care Coll (OK)
Genesee Comm Coll (NY)
John Tyler Comm Coll (VA)
J. Sargeant Reynolds Comm Coll (VA)
Mountain Empire Comm Coll (VA)
Rappahannock Comm Coll (VA)
Southwest Virginia Comm Coll (VA)
Waukesha County Tech Coll (WI)
Williston State Coll (ND)

BUSINESS AND PERSONAL/FINANCIAL SERVICES MARKETING

Hutchinson Comm Coll and Area Vocational School (KS)

BUSINESS AUTOMATION/TECHNOLOGY/DATA ENTRY

Bay State Coll (MA)
Berkshire Comm Coll (MA)
Bismarck State Coll (ND)
Casper Coll (WY)
Clark Coll (WA)
Comm Coll of Allegheny County (PA)
Crowder Coll (MO)
Dakota Coll at Bottineau (ND)
Danville Area Comm Coll (IL)
Delaware Tech & Comm Coll, Jack F. Owens Campus (DE)
Delaware Tech & Comm Coll, Stanton/Wilmington Campus (DE)
Delaware Tech & Comm Coll, Terry Campus (DE)
Garrett Coll (MD)
Grayson Coll (TX)
Hallmark Coll of Technology (TX)
Hinds Comm Coll (MS)
Houston Comm Coll System (TX)
Illinois Eastern Comm Colls, Frontier Community College (IL)
Illinois Eastern Comm Colls, Lincoln Trail College (IL)
Illinois Eastern Comm Colls, Olney Central College (IL)
Illinois Eastern Comm Colls, Wabash Valley College (IL)
Iowa Lakes Comm Coll (IA)
Ivy Tech Comm Coll–Bloomington (IN)
Ivy Tech Comm Coll–Central Indiana (IN)
Ivy Tech Comm Coll–Columbus (IN)
Ivy Tech Comm Coll–East Central (IN)
Ivy Tech Comm Coll–Kokomo (IN)
Ivy Tech Comm Coll–Lafayette (IN)
Ivy Tech Comm Coll–North Central (IN)
Ivy Tech Comm Coll–Northeast (IN)
Ivy Tech Comm Coll–Northwest (IN)
Ivy Tech Comm Coll–Richmond (IN)
Ivy Tech Comm Coll–Southeast (IN)
Ivy Tech Comm Coll–Southern Indiana (IN)
Ivy Tech Comm Coll–Southwest (IN)
Kaskaskia Coll (IL)
Lakes Region Comm Coll (NH)
Lake Superior Coll (MN)
Lincoln Land Comm Coll (IL)
Macomb Comm Coll (MI)
Minneapolis Comm and Tech Coll (MN)

Mitchell Tech Inst (SD)
Northeast Iowa Comm Coll (IA)
Oakland Comm Coll (MI)
Paris Jr Coll (TX)
Pasadena City Coll (CA)
Pueblo Comm Coll (CO)
San Jacinto Coll District (TX)
Schoolcraft Coll (MI)
Shawnee Comm Coll (IL)
Waubonsee Comm Coll (IL)

BUSINESS/COMMERCE

Allen Comm Coll (KS)
Anoka-Ramsey Comm Coll (MN)
Anoka-Ramsey Comm Coll, Cambridge Campus (MN)
Antelope Valley Coll (CA)
Arizona Western Coll (AZ)
Arkansas State U–Newport (AR)
Austin Comm Coll (TX)
Barstow Comm Coll (CA)
Berkeley City Coll (CA)
Berkshire Comm Coll (MA)
Bismarck State Coll (ND)
Bossier Parish Comm Coll (LA)
Bristol Comm Coll (MA)
Brookhaven Coll (TX)
Brown Mackie Coll–Akron (OH)
Brown Mackie Coll–Atlanta (GA)
Brown Mackie Coll–Boise (ID)
Brown Mackie Coll–Dallas/Ft. Worth (TX)
Brown Mackie Coll–Fort Wayne (IN)
Brown Mackie Coll–Hopkinsville (KY)
Brown Mackie Coll–Indianapolis (IN)
Brown Mackie Coll–Kansas City (KS)
Brown Mackie Coll–Louisville (KY)
Brown Mackie Coll–Merrillville (IN)
Brown Mackie Coll–Oklahoma City (OK)
Brown Mackie Coll–St. Louis (MO)
Brown Mackie Coll–Salina (KS)
Brown Mackie Coll–San Antonio (TX)
Brown Mackie Coll–South Bend (IN)
Brown Mackie Coll–Tucson (AZ)
Brown Mackie Coll–Tulsa (OK)
Bucks County Comm Coll (PA)
Butler County Comm Coll (PA)
Carl Albert State Coll (OK)
Cecil Coll (MD)
Central Virginia Comm Coll (VA)
Central Wyoming Coll (WY)
Chandler-Gilbert Comm Coll (AZ)
Coconino Comm Coll (AZ)
Coll of Central Florida (FL)
Coll of Marin (CA)
Coll of Southern Maryland (MD)
Coll of the Desert (CA)
Coll of the Mainland (TX)
Collin County Comm Coll District (TX)
Columbia Coll (CA)
The Comm Coll of Baltimore County (MD)
Comm Coll of Rhode Island (RI)
Copper Mountain Coll (CA)
Cossatot Comm Coll of the U of Arkansas (AR)
Cosumnes River Coll, Sacramento (CA)
Delaware Tech & Comm Coll, Jack F. Owens Campus (DE)
Delaware Tech & Comm Coll, Stanton/Wilmington Campus (DE)
Delaware Tech & Comm Coll, Terry Campus (DE)
East Central Coll (MO)
Feather River Coll (CA)
Frank Phillips Coll (TX)
Garrett Coll (MD)
Gavilan Coll (CA)
Georgia Piedmont Tech Coll (GA)
Glendale Comm Coll (AZ)
Gogebic Comm Coll (MI)
Goodwin Coll (CT)
Great Basin Coll (NV)
Greenfield Comm Coll (MA)
Hagerstown Comm Coll (MD)
Harford Comm Coll (MD)
Harrisburg Area Comm Coll (PA)
Hinds Comm Coll (MS)
Hutchinson Comm Coll and Area Vocational School (KS)
Jefferson Coll (MO)
John Tyler Comm Coll (VA)
Kaskaskia Coll (IL)
Kent State U at Ashtabula (OH)
Kent State U at East Liverpool (OH)
Kent State U at Salem (OH)

Kent State U at Trumbull (OH)
Kent State U at Tuscarawas (OH)
Kilgore Coll (TX)
Lakes Region Comm Coll (NH)
Landmark Coll (VT)
Lane Comm Coll (OR)
Lansing Comm Coll (MI)
Laramie County Comm Coll (WY)
Lehigh Carbon Comm Coll (PA)
Lincoln Land Comm Coll (IL)
Macomb Comm Coll (MI)
Massachusetts Bay Comm Coll (MA)
Mesabi Range Comm and Tech Coll (MN)
Mineral Area Coll (MO)
Missouri State U–West Plains (MO)
Montgomery Coll (MD)
Montgomery County Comm Coll (PA)
Moraine Valley Comm Coll (IL)
Mott Comm Coll (MI)
Mount Wachusett Comm Coll (MA)
New Mexico State U–Alamogordo (NM)
Northampton Comm Coll (PA)
Northwest Coll (WY)
Ocean County Coll (NJ)
Oklahoma City Comm Coll (OK)
Onondaga Comm Coll (NY)
Owens Comm Coll, Toledo (OH)
Palomar Coll (CA)
Paris Jr Coll (TX)
Penn State Beaver (PA)
Penn State Brandywine (PA)
Penn State DuBois (PA)
Penn State Fayette, The Eberly Campus (PA)
Penn State Greater Allegheny (PA)
Penn State Hazleton (PA)
Penn State Lehigh Valley (PA)
Penn State Mont Alto (PA)
Penn State New Kensington (PA)
Penn State Schuylkill (PA)
Penn State Wilkes-Barre (PA)
Penn State Worthington Scranton (PA)
Penn State York (PA)
Pensacola State Coll (FL)
Phoenix Coll (AZ)
Pima Comm Coll (AZ)
Quinsigamond Comm Coll (MA)
Raritan Valley Comm Coll (NJ)
Rogue Comm Coll (OR)
Saginaw Chippewa Tribal Coll (MI)
St. Clair County Comm Coll (MI)
San Jacinto Coll District (TX)
San Joaquin Valley Coll, Visalia (CA)
Schoolcraft Coll (MI)
Seminole State Coll (OK)
Shelton State Comm Coll (AL)
Sheridan Coll (WY) .
Southern State Comm Coll (OH)
Southern U at Shreveport (LA)
South Florida State Coll (FL)
South Louisiana Comm Coll (LA)
Southwestern Indian Polytechnic Inst (NM)
Spartanburg Methodist Coll (SC)
Springfield Tech Comm Coll (MA)
Tech Coll of the Lowcountry (SC)
Texarkana Coll (TX)
Treasure Valley Comm Coll (OR)
Tulsa Comm Coll (OK)
U of Arkansas Comm Coll at Hope (AR)
U of Arkansas Comm Coll at Morrilton (AR)
Victor Valley Coll (CA)
Vincennes U (IN)
Western Nevada Coll (NV)
Westmoreland County Comm Coll (PA)
Wor-Wic Comm Coll (MD)

BUSINESS/CORPORATE COMMUNICATIONS

Cecil Coll (MD)
Houston Comm Coll System (TX)
Montgomery County Comm Coll (PA)

BUSINESS MACHINE REPAIR

Comm Coll of Allegheny County (PA)
De Anza Coll (CA)
Iowa Lakes Comm Coll (IA)
Mississippi Delta Comm Coll (MS)
Ozarks Tech Comm Coll (MO)

BUSINESS, MANAGEMENT, AND MARKETING RELATED

Berkeley City Coll (CA)
Bristol Comm Coll (MA)

Bucks County Comm Coll (PA)
Butler County Comm Coll (PA)
Chandler-Gilbert Comm Coll (AZ)
Clark State Comm Coll (OH)
Cloud County Comm Coll (KS)
Coll of Western Idaho (ID)
Columbus State Comm Coll (OH)
County Coll of Morris (NJ)
Eastern Arizona Coll (AZ)
Genesee Comm Coll (NY)
Glen Oaks Comm Coll (MI)
Long Island Business Inst (NY)
Niagara County Comm Coll (NY)
Northwest Florida State Coll (FL)
Tompkins Cortland Comm Coll (NY)
Tulsa Comm Coll (OK)

BUSINESS/MANAGERIAL ECONOMICS
Potomac State Coll of West Virginia U (WV)
South Florida State Coll (FL)

BUSINESS OPERATIONS SUPPORT AND SECRETARIAL SERVICES RELATED
Bristol Comm Coll (MA)
Bunker Hill Comm Coll (MA)
Central Virginia Comm Coll (VA)
Clark State Comm Coll (OH)
Davis Coll (OH)
Eastern Arizona Coll (AZ)
Genesee Comm Coll (NY)
J. Sargeant Reynolds Comm Coll (VA)
Mountain Empire Comm Coll (VA)
Southwest Virginia Comm Coll (VA)

BUSINESS TEACHER EDUCATION
Allen Comm Coll (KS)
Amarillo Coll (TX)
Bainbridge State Coll (GA)
Bronx Comm Coll of the City U of New York (NY)
Darton State Coll (GA)
Eastern Arizona Coll (AZ)
Eastern Wyoming Coll (WY)
Hinds Comm Coll (MS)
Iowa Lakes Comm Coll (IA)
Mississippi Gulf Coast Comm Coll (MS)
Mt. San Antonio Coll (CA)
Northeastern Jr Coll (CO)
Northern Essex Comm Coll (MA)
Paris Jr Coll (TX)
Rio Hondo Coll (CA)
Roane State Comm Coll (TN)
Snow Coll (UT)
South Florida State Coll (FL)
Spoon River Coll (IL)
Trinity Valley Comm Coll (TX)
Tulsa Comm Coll (OK)

CABINETMAKING AND MILLWORK
Bucks County Comm Coll (PA)
Central Georgia Tech Coll (GA)
Coll of Southern Idaho (ID)
Harrisburg Area Comm Coll (PA)
Ivy Tech Comm Coll–Bloomington (IN)
Ivy Tech Comm Coll–Central Indiana (IN)
Ivy Tech Comm Coll–Columbus (IN)
Ivy Tech Comm Coll–East Central (IN)
Ivy Tech Comm Coll–Kokomo (IN)
Ivy Tech Comm Coll–Lafayette (IN)
Ivy Tech Comm Coll–North Central (IN)
Ivy Tech Comm Coll–Northeast (IN)
Ivy Tech Comm Coll–Northwest (IN)
Ivy Tech Comm Coll–Richmond (IN)
Ivy Tech Comm Coll–Southern Indiana (IN)
Ivy Tech Comm Coll–Southwest (IN)
Ivy Tech Comm Coll–Wabash Valley (IN)
Macomb Comm Coll (MI)
Palomar Coll (CA)

CAD/CADD DRAFTING/DESIGN TECHNOLOGY
Butler County Comm Coll (PA)
Central Ohio Tech Coll (OH)
Central Oregon Comm Coll (OR)
Century Coll (MN)
Coll of the Mainland (TX)
Comm Coll of Vermont (VT)
Danville Area Comm Coll (IL)

Delaware Tech & Comm Coll, Stanton/Wilmington Campus (DE)
Dunwoody Coll of Technology (MN)
Elgin Comm Coll (IL)
Erie Comm Coll, South Campus (NY)
Gateway Comm and Tech Coll (KY)
Glendale Comm Coll (AZ)
Harford Comm Coll (MD)
ITT Tech Inst, Norwood (MA)
ITT Tech Inst, Wilmington (MA)
ITT Tech Inst (NJ)
ITT Tech Inst, Dunmore (PA)
ITT Tech Inst, Harrisburg (PA)
ITT Tech Inst, Levittown (PA)
ITT Tech Inst, Philadelphia (PA)
ITT Tech Inst, Pittsburgh (PA)
ITT Tech Inst, Plymouth Meeting (PA)
ITT Tech Inst, Tarentum (PA)
J. Sargeant Reynolds Comm Coll (VA)
Kent State U at Tuscarawas (OH)
Lake Superior Coll (MN)
Manhattan Area Tech Coll (KS)
Minnesota State Coll–Southeast Tech (MN)
Mohawk Valley Comm Coll (NY)
Montgomery County Comm Coll (PA)
Mountain Empire Comm Coll (VA)
Northampton Comm Coll (PA)
Northwest Coll (WY)
Pima Comm Coll (AZ)
Sheridan Coll (WY)
Southern State Comm Coll (OH)
South Suburban Coll (IL)
Spencerian Coll–Lexington (KY)
State Fair Comm Coll (MO)
State U of New York Coll of Technology at Alfred (NY)
Sullivan Coll of Technology and Design (KY)
Tallahassee Comm Coll (FL)
Tulsa Comm Coll (OK)
Waubonsee Comm Coll (IL)
Wayne County Comm Coll District (MI)

CARDIOVASCULAR TECHNOLOGY
Augusta Tech Coll (GA)
Bunker Hill Comm Coll (MA)
Central Georgia Tech Coll (GA)
Darton State Coll (GA)
Delaware Tech & Comm Coll, Stanton/Wilmington Campus (DE)
Harper Coll (IL)
Harrisburg Area Comm Coll (PA)
Houston Comm Coll System (TX)
Howard Comm Coll (MD)
Kirtland Comm Coll (MI)
Orange Coast Coll (CA)
Pennsylvania Coll of Health Sciences (PA)
Southeast Tech Inst (SD)
Southern Maine Comm Coll (ME)
Southern U at Shreveport (LA)
Spencerian Coll (KY)

CARPENTRY
Alamance Comm Coll (NC)
Arizona Western Coll (AZ)
Austin Comm Coll (TX)
Bismarck State Coll (ND)
Central Georgia Tech Coll (GA)
Central Wyoming Coll (WY)
Coconino Comm Coll (AZ)
Comm Coll of Allegheny County (PA)
Delta Coll (MI)
Flathead Valley Comm Coll (MT)
Fullerton Coll (CA)
Gavilan Coll (CA)
Grays Harbor Coll (WA)
Hawkeye Comm Coll (IA)
Hinds Comm Coll (MS)
Honolulu Comm Coll (HI)
Hutchinson Comm Coll and Area Vocational School (KS)
Iowa Lakes Comm Coll (IA)
Ivy Tech Comm Coll–Central Indiana (IN)
Ivy Tech Comm Coll–East Central (IN)
Ivy Tech Comm Coll–Lafayette (IN)
Ivy Tech Comm Coll–North Central (IN)
Ivy Tech Comm Coll–Northwest (IN)
Ivy Tech Comm Coll–Southern Indiana (IN)
Ivy Tech Comm Coll–Southwest (IN)
Ivy Tech Comm Coll–Wabash Valley (IN)
Kaskaskia Coll (IL)
Lake Area Tech Inst (SD)

Lansing Comm Coll (MI)
Manhattan Area Tech Coll (KS)
Mineral Area Coll (MO)
Minnesota State Coll–Southeast Tech (MN)
North Iowa Area Comm Coll (IA)
Oakland Comm Coll (MI)
Palomar Coll (CA)
San Diego City Coll (CA)
San Juan Coll (NM)
South Louisiana Comm Coll (LA)
South Plains Coll (TX)
Southwestern Illinois Coll (IL)
Southwestern Michigan Coll (MI)
State U of New York Coll of Technology at Alfred (NY)
Treasure Valley Comm Coll (OR)
Triangle Tech, Inc.–Pittsburgh School (PA)
U of Hawaii Maui Coll (HI)
The Williamson Free School of Mecha Trades (PA)
Williston State Coll (ND)

CASINO MANAGEMENT
Wenatchee Valley Coll (WA)
Westmoreland County Comm Coll (PA)

CERAMIC ARTS AND CERAMICS
Butte Coll (CA)
De Anza Coll (CA)
Iowa Lakes Comm Coll (IA)
Mercer County Comm Coll (NJ)
Oakland Comm Coll (MI)
Palomar Coll (CA)

CERAMIC SCIENCES AND ENGINEERING
Hocking Coll (OH)

CHEMICAL ENGINEERING
Broward Coll (FL)
Kilgore Coll (TX)
Mississippi Gulf Coast Comm Coll (MS)
Monroe Comm Coll (NY)
Shoreline Comm Coll (WA)
South Florida State Coll (FL)

CHEMICAL PROCESS TECHNOLOGY
San Jacinto Coll District (TX)

CHEMICAL TECHNOLOGY
Alvin Comm Coll (TX)
Amarillo Coll (TX)
Bucks County Comm Coll (PA)
Cape Fear Comm Coll (NC)
Cincinnati State Tech and Comm Coll (OH)
Coll of the Mainland (TX)
Comm Coll of Allegheny County (PA)
Comm Coll of Philadelphia (PA)
Comm Coll of Rhode Island (RI)
County Coll of Morris (NJ)
Delaware Tech & Comm Coll, Stanton/Wilmington Campus (DE)
Delta Coll (MI)
East Central Coll (MO)
Eastern Florida State Coll (FL)
Fullerton Coll (CA)
Houston Comm Coll System (TX)
Lansing Comm Coll (MI)
Lehigh Carbon Comm Coll (PA)
Massachusetts Bay Comm Coll (MA)
Mohawk Valley Comm Coll (NY)
Niagara County Comm Coll (NY)
Pensacola State Coll (FL)
Raritan Valley Comm Coll (NJ)
San Jacinto Coll District (TX)
Texas State Tech Coll Waco (TX)
Tulsa Comm Coll (OK)
Westmoreland County Comm Coll (PA)

CHEMISTRY
Alabama Southern Comm Coll (AL)
Allen Comm Coll (KS)
Amarillo Coll (TX)
Arizona Western Coll (AZ)
Austin Comm Coll (TX)
Bainbridge State Coll (GA)
Bronx Comm Coll of the City U of New York (NY)
Broward Coll (FL)
Bunker Hill Comm Coll (MA)
Butte Coll (CA)
Ca&nnada Coll (CA)
Casper Coll (WY)
Cecil Coll (MD)
Cochise Coll, Sierra Vista (AZ)

Coll of Marin (CA)
Coll of Southern Idaho (ID)
Coll of the Desert (CA)
Comm Coll of Allegheny County (PA)
Copiah-Lincoln Comm Coll (MS)
Cosumnes River Coll, Sacramento (CA)
Dakota Coll at Bottineau (ND)
Darton State Coll (GA)
Eastern Arizona Coll (AZ)
Finger Lakes Comm Coll (NY)
Frank Phillips Coll (TX)
Fullerton Coll (CA)
Genesee Comm Coll (NY)
Georgia Highlands Coll (GA)
Gordon State Coll (GA)
Grand Rapids Comm Coll (MI)
Grayson Coll (TX)
Great Basin Coll (NV)
Harford Comm Coll (MD)
Harper Coll (IL)
Harrisburg Area Comm Coll (PA)
Hinds Comm Coll (MS)
Iowa Lakes Comm Coll (IA)
Kankakee Comm Coll (IL)
Kilgore Coll (TX)
Kingsborough Comm Coll of the City U of New York (NY)
Lansing Comm Coll (MI)
Laramie County Comm Coll (WY)
Lehigh Carbon Comm Coll (PA)
Linn-Benton Comm Coll (OR)
Lorain County Comm Coll (OH)
Macomb Comm Coll (MI)
Mercer County Comm Coll (NJ)
Metropolitan Comm Coll–Kansas City (MO)
Miami Dade Coll (FL)
Minneapolis Comm and Tech Coll (MN)
MiraCosta Coll (CA)
Monroe Comm Coll (NY)
Northampton Comm Coll (PA)
Northeast Texas Comm Coll (TX)
Northwest Coll (WY)
Oklahoma City Comm Coll (OK)
Orange Coast Coll (CA)
Palomar Coll (CA)
Paris Jr Coll (TX)
Pasadena City Coll (CA)
Pensacola State Coll (FL)
Potomac State Coll of West Virginia U (WV)
Roane State Comm Coll (TN)
Salt Lake Comm Coll (UT)
San Jacinto Coll District (TX)
San Juan Coll (NM)
Santa Rosa Jr Coll (CA)
Sauk Valley Comm Coll (IL)
Snow Coll (UT)
Southern U at Shreveport (LA)
South Florida State Coll (FL)
South Georgia State Coll, Douglas (GA)
South Plains Coll (TX)
Spoon River Coll (IL)
Springfield Tech Comm Coll (MA)
Texarkana Coll (TX)
Treasure Valley Comm Coll (OR)
Trinity Valley Comm Coll (TX)
Truckee Meadows Comm Coll (NV)
Tyler Jr Coll (TX)
Umpqua Comm Coll (OR)
Vincennes U (IN)
Wenatchee Valley Coll (WA)
Western Wyoming Comm Coll (WY)

CHEMISTRY RELATED
South Florida State Coll (FL)
Vincennes U (IN)

CHEMISTRY TEACHER EDUCATION
Broward Coll (FL)
Bucks County Comm Coll (PA)
Carroll Comm Coll (MD)
The Comm Coll of Baltimore County (MD)
Harford Comm Coll (MD)
Montgomery Coll (MD)
Vincennes U (IN)

CHILD-CARE AND SUPPORT SERVICES MANAGEMENT
Antelope Valley Coll (CA)
Bevill State Comm Coll (AL)
Bishop State Comm Coll (AL)
Bristol Comm Coll (MA)
Carroll Comm Coll (MD)
Cayuga County Comm Coll (NY)
Cecil Coll (MD)
Central Georgia Tech Coll (GA)

Central Oregon Comm Coll (OR)
Central Wyoming Coll (WY)
Cloud County Comm Coll (KS)
Coll of Southern Idaho (ID)
Coll of Southern Maryland (MD)
Coll of the Desert (CA)
Coll of the Ouachitas (AR)
Columbia Gorge Comm Coll (OR)
The Comm Coll of Baltimore County (MD)
Cosumnes River Coll, Sacramento (CA)
Dakota Coll at Bottineau (ND)
Dutchess Comm Coll (NY)
East Central Coll (MO)
Eastern Gateway Comm Coll (OH)
Erie Comm Coll (NY)
Flathead Valley Comm Coll (MT)
Florida State Coll at Jacksonville (FL)
Gadsden State Comm Coll (AL)
Glen Oaks Comm Coll (MI)
Goodwin Coll (CT)
Grand Rapids Comm Coll (MI)
Grays Harbor Coll (WA)
Greenville Tech Coll (SC)
Hagerstown Comm Coll (MD)
Herkimer County Comm Coll (NY)
Hillsborough Comm Coll (FL)
Holyoke Comm Coll (MA)
Hopkinsville Comm Coll (KY)
Hutchinson Comm Coll and Area Vocational School (KS)
Independence Comm Coll (KS)
Ivy Tech Comm Coll–Bloomington (IN)
Ivy Tech Comm Coll–Central Indiana (IN)
Ivy Tech Comm Coll–Columbus (IN)
Ivy Tech Comm Coll–East Central (IN)
Ivy Tech Comm Coll–Kokomo (IN)
Ivy Tech Comm Coll–Lafayette (IN)
Ivy Tech Comm Coll–North Central (IN)
Ivy Tech Comm Coll–Northeast (IN)
Ivy Tech Comm Coll–Northwest (IN)
Ivy Tech Comm Coll–Richmond (IN)
Ivy Tech Comm Coll–Southeast (IN)
Ivy Tech Comm Coll–Southern Indiana (IN)
Ivy Tech Comm Coll–Southwest (IN)
Ivy Tech Comm Coll–Wabash Valley (IN)
Jefferson Coll (MO)
Jefferson Comm Coll (NY)
Jefferson State Comm Coll (AL)
Kilgore Coll (TX)
Lake Land Coll (IL)
Lawson State Comm Coll (AL)
Lurleen B. Wallace Comm Coll (AL)
Macomb Comm Coll (MI)
Massachusetts Bay Comm Coll (MA)
Minneapolis Comm and Tech Coll (MN)
MiraCosta Coll (CA)
Missouri State U–West Plains (MO)
Mitchell Comm Coll (NC)
Montgomery County Comm Coll (PA)
Mount Wachusett Comm Coll (MA)
Northwest-Shoals Comm Coll (AL)
Northwest Tech Coll (MN)
Oakland Comm Coll (MI)
Orange Coast Coll (CA)
Pensacola State Coll (FL)
Phoenix Coll (AZ)
Piedmont Comm Coll (NC)
Reading Area Comm Coll (PA)
Reid State Tech Coll (AL)
Rogue Comm Coll (OR)
Snead State Comm Coll (AL)
Southeast Tech Inst (SD)
State Fair Comm Coll (MO)
Texarkana Coll (TX)
Tompkins Cortland Comm Coll (NY)
U of Arkansas Comm Coll at Hope (AR)
Victor Valley Coll (CA)
Vincennes U (IN)
Wayne County Comm Coll District (MI)
Western Nevada Coll (NV)
Wisconsin Indianhead Tech Coll (WI)
Wor-Wic Comm Coll (MD)

CHILD-CARE PROVISION
Barstow Comm Coll (CA)
Bucks County Comm Coll (PA)
Ca&nnada Coll (CA)
Coll of Marin (CA)
Coll of the Canyons (CA)

Collin County Comm Coll District (TX)
Columbia Coll (CA)
Comm Coll of Allegheny County (PA)
Cosumnes River Coll, Sacramento (CA)
Dakota Coll at Bottineau (ND)
Danville Area Comm Coll (IL)
Delta Coll (MI)
Feather River Coll (CA)
Florida State Coll at Jacksonville (FL)
Fullerton Coll (CA)
Gavilan Coll (CA)
Harper Coll (IL)
Hawkeye Comm Coll (IA)
Highland Comm Coll (IL)
Hinds Comm Coll (MS)
Hopkinsville Comm Coll (KY)
Iowa Lakes Comm Coll (IA)
John Tyler Comm Coll (VA)
J. Sargeant Reynolds Comm Coll (VA)
Kaskaskia Coll (IL)
Kilgore Coll (TX)
Lakeland Comm Coll (OH)
Lake Region State Coll (ND)
Lane Comm Coll (OR)
Lansing Comm Coll (MI)
Lincoln Land Comm Coll (IL)
Luzerne County Comm Coll (PA)
McHenry County Coll (IL)
Metropolitan Comm Coll–Kansas City (MO)
Mineral Area Coll (MO)
MiraCosta Coll (CA)
Montgomery Coll (MD)
Moraine Valley Comm Coll (IL)
Mott Comm Coll (MI)
Northwest Florida State Coll (FL)
Nunez Comm Coll (LA)
Oakton Comm Coll (IL)
Orange Coast Coll (CA)
Owensboro Comm and Tech Coll (KY)
Pensacola State Coll (FL)
Raritan Valley Comm Coll (NJ)
Reading Area Comm Coll (PA)
Rend Lake Coll (IL)
San Juan Coll (NM)
Somerset Comm Coll (KY)
Southeast Tech Inst (SD)
South Suburban Coll (IL)
Southwestern Illinois Coll (IL)
Southwest Virginia Comm Coll (VA)
Tech Coll of the Lowcountry (SC)
Trident Tech Coll (SC)
Vincennes U (IN)
Waubonsee Comm Coll (IL)
Westmoreland County Comm Coll (PA)

CHILD DEVELOPMENT
Albany Tech Coll (GA)
Alexandria Tech and Comm Coll (MN)
Allen Comm Coll (KS)
Altamaha Tech Coll (GA)
Alvin Comm Coll (TX)
Amarillo Coll (TX)
Antelope Valley Coll (CA)
Athens Tech Coll (GA)
Atlanta Tech Coll (GA)
Augusta Tech Coll (GA)
Austin Comm Coll (TX)
Bronx Comm Coll of the City U of New York (NY)
Brookhaven Coll (TX)
Butte Coll (CA)
Carl Albert State Coll (OK)
Central Georgia Tech Coll (GA)
Central Maine Comm Coll (ME)
Chattahoochee Tech Coll (GA)
Cleveland State Comm Coll (TN)
Cloud County Comm Coll (KS)
Coll of the Mainland (TX)
Collin County Comm Coll District (TX)
Columbus Tech Coll (GA)
Comm Coll of Allegheny County (PA)
Comm Coll of Vermont (VT)
Copiah-Lincoln Comm Coll (MS)
Daytona State Coll (FL)
De Anza Coll (CA)
Dyersburg State Comm Coll (TN)
Edison Comm Coll (OH)
Georgia Northwestern Tech Coll (GA)
Goodwin Coll (CT)
Hocking Coll (OH)

Housatonic Comm Coll (CT)
Houston Comm Coll System (TX)
Howard Comm Coll (MD)
Illinois Eastern Comm Colls, Wabash Valley College (IL)
Iowa Lakes Comm Coll (IA)
Ivy Tech Comm Coll–Central Indiana (IN)
James Sprunt Comm Coll (NC)
Jefferson Comm Coll (NY)
Lanier Tech Coll (GA)
Mesa Comm Coll (AZ)
Miami Dade Coll (FL)
Minneapolis Comm and Tech Coll (MN)
Monroe County Comm Coll (MI)
Moultrie Tech Coll (GA)
Mt. San Antonio Coll (CA)
Mt. San Jacinto Coll (CA)
Mount Wachusett Comm Coll (MA)
North Shore Comm Coll (MA)
Northwestern Connecticut Comm Coll (CT)
Northwest-Shoals Comm Coll (AL)
Oconee Fall Line Tech Coll (GA)
Ogeechee Tech Coll (GA)
Okefenokee Tech Coll (GA)
Oklahoma City Comm Coll (OK)
Otero Jr Coll (CO)
Oxnard Coll (CA)
Palomar Coll (CA)
Pasadena City Coll (CA)
Reading Area Comm Coll (PA)
Rock Valley Coll (IL)
San Jacinto Coll District (TX)
Santa Monica Coll (CA)
Santa Rosa Jr Coll (CA)
Savannah Tech Coll (GA)
Schoolcraft Coll (MI)
Seminole State Coll (OK)
Seminole State Coll of Florida (FL)
Shawnee Comm Coll (IL)
Shoreline Comm Coll (WA)
Snow Coll (UT)
Southeastern Comm Coll (IA)
Southeastern Tech Coll (GA)
Southern Crescent Tech Coll (GA)
South Georgia Tech Coll (GA)
South Plains Coll (TX)
Southwestern Comm Coll (NC)
Southwest Georgia Tech Coll (GA)
Spoon River Coll (IL)
Stark State Coll (OH)
Texarkana Coll (TX)
Trinity Valley Comm Coll (TX)
Tulsa Comm Coll (OK)
Tyler Jr Coll (TX)
Umpqua Comm Coll (OR)
U of Arkansas Comm Coll at Morrilton (AR)
Victor Valley Coll (CA)
Virginia Western Comm Coll (VA)
Volunteer State Comm Coll (TN)
Walters State Comm Coll (TN)
Westchester Comm Coll (NY)
Western Oklahoma State Coll (OK)
West Georgia Tech Coll (GA)
Wiregrass Georgia Tech Coll (GA)
York County Comm Coll (ME)

CHIROPRACTIC ASSISTANT
Moraine Park Tech Coll (WI)

CINEMATOGRAPHY AND FILM/VIDEO PRODUCTION
Antelope Valley Coll (CA)
Bucks County Comm Coll (PA)
Cape Fear Comm Coll (NC)
Coll of Marin (CA)
Coll of the Canyons (CA)
Fashion Inst of Technology (NY)
Gavilan Coll (CA)
Glendale Comm Coll (AZ)
Hillsborough Comm Coll (FL)
Houston Comm Coll System (TX)
Lansing Comm Coll (MI)
Minneapolis Comm and Tech Coll (MN)
Mott Comm Coll (MI)
Northwest Coll (WY)
Oklahoma City Comm Coll (OK)
Orange Coast Coll (CA)
Pasadena City Coll (CA)
Piedmont Comm Coll (NC)
Pima Comm Coll (AZ)
Raritan Valley Comm Coll (NJ)
Shoreline Comm Coll (WA)

CITY/URBAN, COMMUNITY AND REGIONAL PLANNING
Broward Coll (FL)
South Florida State Coll (FL)

CIVIL DRAFTING AND CAD/CADD
Central Ohio Tech Coll (OH)
Comm Coll of Allegheny County (PA)
Delaware Tech & Comm Coll, Stanton/Wilmington Campus (DE)
Genesee Comm Coll (NY)
Sullivan Coll of Technology and Design (KY)

CIVIL ENGINEERING
American Samoa Comm Coll (AS)
Broward Coll (FL)
Fiorello H. LaGuardia Comm Coll of the City U of New York (NY)
J. Sargeant Reynolds Comm Coll (VA)
Kilgore Coll (TX)
Northeast Texas Comm Coll (TX)
South Florida State Coll (FL)
Truckee Meadows Comm Coll (NV)
Tulsa Comm Coll (OK)
Vincennes U (IN)

CIVIL ENGINEERING RELATED
Bristol Comm Coll (MA)

CIVIL ENGINEERING TECHNOLOGY
Arapahoe Comm Coll (CO)
Arizona Western Coll (AZ)
Bellingham Tech Coll (WA)
Bishop State Comm Coll (AL)
Butler County Comm Coll (PA)
Central Maine Comm Coll (ME)
Central Ohio Tech Coll (OH)
Chattahoochee Tech Coll (GA)
Chippewa Valley Tech Coll (WI)
Cincinnati State Tech and Comm Coll (OH)
Clark State Comm Coll (OH)
Comm Coll of Allegheny County (PA)
Copiah-Lincoln Comm Coll (MS)
Delaware Tech & Comm Coll, Jack F. Owens Campus (DE)
Delaware Tech & Comm Coll, Terry Campus (DE)
Eastern Arizona Coll (AZ)
Erie Comm Coll, North Campus (NY)
Fayetteville Tech Comm Coll (NC)
Florida State Coll at Jacksonville (FL)
Gadsden State Comm Coll (AL)
Harrisburg Area Comm Coll (PA)
Hawkeye Comm Coll (IA)
J. Sargeant Reynolds Comm Coll (VA)
Lake Land Coll (IL)
Lakeland Comm Coll (OH)
Lake Superior Coll (MN)
Lansing Comm Coll (MI)
Lorain County Comm Coll (OH)
Macomb Comm Coll (MI)
Mercer County Comm Coll (NJ)
Miami Dade Coll (FL)
Middlesex County Coll (NJ)
Mineral Area Coll (MO)
Mississippi Delta Comm Coll (MS)
Mohawk Valley Comm Coll (NY)
Monroe Comm Coll (NY)
Moultrie Tech Coll (GA)
Mt. San Antonio Coll (CA)
Nassau Comm Coll (NY)
North Dakota State Coll of Science (ND)
Northern Essex Comm Coll (MA)
Northwest Mississippi Comm Coll (MS)
Oklahoma State U, Oklahoma City (OK)
Phoenix Coll (AZ)
Potomac State Coll of West Virginia U (WV)
Santa Rosa Jr Coll (CA)
Seminole State Coll of Florida (FL)
Shoreline Comm Coll (WA)
Southeast Tech Inst (SD)
South Florida State Coll (FL)
Springfield Tech Comm Coll (MA)
Stark State Coll (OH)
Tech Coll of the Lowcountry (SC)
Three Rivers Comm Coll (CT)
Trident Tech Coll (SC)
Umpqua Comm Coll (OR)
Virginia Western Comm Coll (VA)

Westchester Comm Coll (NY)
Wytheville Comm Coll (VA)

CLASSICS AND CLASSICAL LANGUAGES
Pasadena City Coll (CA)

CLINICAL LABORATORY SCIENCE/MEDICAL TECHNOLOGY
Amarillo Coll (TX)
Athens Tech Coll (GA)
Casper Coll (WY)
Chipola Coll (FL)
Coll of Southern Idaho (ID)
Columbus State Comm Coll (OH)
Darton State Coll (GA)
Georgia Highlands Coll (GA)
Hinds Comm Coll (MS)
Howard Comm Coll (MD)
Monroe County Comm Coll (MI)
Northeastern Jr Coll (CO)
Orange Coast Coll (CA)
San Jacinto Coll District (TX)
South Florida State Coll (FL)
Tarrant County Coll District (TX)
Westchester Comm Coll (NY)
Westmoreland County Comm Coll (PA)

CLINICAL/MEDICAL LABORATORY ASSISTANT
Columbus State Comm Coll (OH)
Delaware Tech & Comm Coll, Jack F. Owens Campus (DE)
Pima Comm Coll (AZ)
Somerset Comm Coll (KY)
Wenatchee Valley Coll (WA)
Westmoreland County Comm Coll (PA)

CLINICAL/MEDICAL LABORATORY SCIENCE AND ALLIED PROFESSIONS RELATED
Houston Comm Coll System (TX)
Southeast Tech Inst (SD)

CLINICAL/MEDICAL LABORATORY TECHNOLOGY
Alamance Comm Coll (NC)
Alexandria Tech and Comm Coll (MN)
Arapahoe Comm Coll (CO)
Austin Comm Coll (TX)
Bismarck State Coll (ND)
Blackhawk Tech Coll (WI)
Blue Ridge Comm and Tech Coll (WV)
Bristol Comm Coll (MA)
Bronx Comm Coll of the City U of New York (NY)
Bunker Hill Comm Coll (MA)
Carrington Coll–Phoenix Westside (AZ)
Carrington Coll–Tucson (AZ)
Central Georgia Tech Coll (GA)
Chippewa Valley Tech Coll (WI)
Cincinnati State Tech and Comm Coll (OH)
Clark State Comm Coll (OH)
Coll of Southern Maryland (MD)
Comm Coll of Allegheny County (PA)
The Comm Coll of Baltimore County (MD)
Comm Coll of Philadelphia (PA)
Comm Coll of Rhode Island (RI)
Copiah-Lincoln Comm Coll (MS)
Dutchess Comm Coll (NY)
Eastern Florida State Coll (FL)
Edison Comm Coll (OH)
Elgin Comm Coll (IL)
Erie Comm Coll, North Campus (NY)
Gadsden State Comm Coll (AL)
Genesee Comm Coll (NY)
Georgia Piedmont Tech Coll (GA)
Grayson Coll (TX)
Greenville Tech Coll (SC)
Halifax Comm Coll (NC)
Harrisburg Area Comm Coll (PA)
Hawkeye Comm Coll (IA)
Hinds Comm Coll (MS)
Housatonic Comm Coll (CT)
Houston Comm Coll System (TX)
Hutchinson Comm Coll and Area Vocational School (KS)
Ivy Tech Comm Coll–North Central (IN)
Ivy Tech Comm Coll–Wabash Valley (IN)

Jackson State Comm Coll (TN)
Jefferson State Comm Coll (AL)
J. Sargeant Reynolds Comm Coll (VA)
Kankakee Comm Coll (IL)
Kaskaskia Coll (IL)
Lake Area Tech Inst (SD)
Lakeland Comm Coll (OH)
Lake Superior Coll (MN)
Lamar State Coll–Orange (TX)
Lorain County Comm Coll (OH)
Manchester Comm Coll (CT)
Manhattan Area Tech Coll (KS)
Mercer County Comm Coll (NJ)
Miami Dade Coll (FL)
Middlesex County Coll (NJ)
Mid-Plains Comm Coll, North Platte (NE)
Mississippi Delta Comm Coll (MS)
Mississippi Gulf Coast Comm Coll (MS)
Mitchell Tech Inst (SD)
Montgomery County Comm Coll (PA)
Moraine Park Tech Coll (WI)
Mount Wachusett Comm Coll (MA)
Nassau Comm Coll (NY)
Northcentral Tech Coll (WI)
Northeast Iowa Comm Coll (IA)
Northeast Texas Comm Coll (TX)
North Iowa Area Comm Coll (IA)
Oakton Comm Coll (IL)
The Ohio State U Ag Tech Inst (OH)
Okefenokee Tech Coll (GA)
Panola Coll (TX)
Penn State Hazleton (PA)
Penn State Schuylkill (PA)
Phoenix Coll (AZ)
Pima Comm Coll (AZ)
Reading Area Comm Coll (PA)
Rend Lake Coll (IL)
River Valley Comm Coll (NH)
Roane State Comm Coll (TN)
Salt Lake Comm Coll (UT)
San Jacinto Coll District (TX)
San Juan Coll (NM)
Seminole State Coll (OK)
Shawnee Comm Coll (IL)
Shoreline Comm Coll (WA)
Southeastern Comm Coll (NC)
Southeast Tech Inst (SD)
Southern U at Shreveport (LA)
South Louisiana Comm Coll (LA)
Southwestern Comm Coll (NC)
Southwestern Illinois Coll (IL)
Spartanburg Comm Coll (SC)
Spencerian Coll (KY)
Spencerian Coll–Lexington (KY)
Springfield Tech Comm Coll (MA)
Stark State Coll (OH)
Tarrant County Coll District (TX)
Trident Tech Coll (SC)
Tulsa Comm Coll (OK)
Tyler Jr Coll (TX)
Victoria Coll (TX)
Volunteer State Comm Coll (TN)
Wenatchee Valley Coll (WA)
Westchester Comm Coll (NY)
Western Nevada Coll (NV)
Wichita Area Tech Coll (KS)
Wytheville Comm Coll (VA)

CLINICAL/MEDICAL SOCIAL WORK
Halifax Comm Coll (NC)
Piedmont Comm Coll (NC)
Pima Comm Coll (AZ)

CLINICAL RESEARCH COORDINATOR
Pima Comm Coll (AZ)

COMMERCIAL AND ADVERTISING ART
Alamance Comm Coll (NC)
Alexandria Tech and Comm Coll (MN)
Amarillo Coll (TX)
Austin Comm Coll (TX)
Bismarck State Coll (ND)
Bucks County Comm Coll (PA)
Catawba Valley Comm Coll (NC)
Cincinnati State Tech and Comm Coll (OH)
Clark State Comm Coll (OH)
Coll of Southern Idaho (ID)
Collin County Comm Coll District (TX)
Comm Coll of Allegheny County (PA)
The Comm Coll of Baltimore County (MD)

De Anza Coll (CA)
Delaware Tech & Comm Coll, Terry Campus (DE)
Dutchess Comm Coll (NY)
East Central Coll (MO)
Eastern Arizona Coll (AZ)
Fashion Inst of Technology (NY)
Fayetteville Tech Comm Coll (NC)
FIDM/The Fashion Inst of Design & Merchandising, Los Angeles Campus (CA)
FIDM/The Fashion Inst of Design & Merchandising, Orange County Campus (CA)
FIDM/The Fashion Inst of Design & Merchandising, San Diego Campus (CA)
FIDM/The Fashion Inst of Design & Merchandising, San Francisco Campus (CA)
Finger Lakes Comm Coll (NY)
Florida State Coll at Jacksonville (FL)
Glendale Comm Coll (AZ)
Golden West Coll (CA)
Hagerstown Comm Coll (MD)
Halifax Comm Coll (NC)
Honolulu Comm Coll (HI)
Housatonic Comm Coll (CT)
Iowa Lakes Comm Coll (IA)
James Sprunt Comm Coll (NC)
Jamestown Comm Coll (NY)
Kilgore Coll (TX)
Kingsborough Comm Coll of the City U of New York (NY)
Lakeland Comm Coll (OH)
Lane Comm Coll (OR)
Linn-Benton Comm Coll (OR)
Luzerne County Comm Coll (PA)
Macomb Comm Coll (MI)
Manchester Comm Coll (CT)
Mercer County Comm Coll (NJ)
Metropolitan Comm Coll–Kansas City (MO)
Miami Dade Coll (FL)
Mid-Plains Comm Coll, North Platte (NE)
Mohawk Valley Comm Coll (NY)
Monroe Comm Coll (NY)
Montgomery Coll (MD)
Montgomery County Comm Coll (PA)
Mt. San Antonio Coll (CA)
Nassau Comm Coll (NY)
Northern Essex Comm Coll (MA)
NorthWest Arkansas Comm Coll (AR)
Northwest Coll (WY)
Northwestern Connecticut Comm Coll (CT)
Northwest Florida State Coll (FL)
Northwest Mississippi Comm Coll (MS)
Norwalk Comm Coll (CT)
Nossi Coll of Art (TN)
Oklahoma City Comm Coll (OK)
Orange Coast Coll (CA)
Owens Comm Coll, Toledo (OH)
Palomar Coll (CA)
Pensacola State Coll (FL)
Phoenix Coll (AZ)
Pitt Comm Coll (NC)
Randolph Comm Coll (NC)
St. Clair County Comm Coll (MI)
San Diego City Coll (CA)
San Jacinto Coll District (TX)
San Juan Coll (NM)
Shoreline Comm Coll (WA)
Southeast Tech Inst (SD)
South Piedmont Comm Coll (NC)
South Plains Coll (TX)
Southwestern Comm Coll (NC)
Springfield Tech Comm Coll (MA)
Sullivan County Comm Coll (NY)
Sussex County Comm Coll (NJ)
Tallahassee Comm Coll (FL)
Tompkins Cortland Comm Coll (NY)
Trident Tech Coll (SC)
Tunxis Comm Coll (CT)
Tyler Jr Coll (TX)
U of Arkansas Comm Coll at Morrilton (AR)
Vincennes U (IN)
Virginia Western Comm Coll (VA)

COMMERCIAL PHOTOGRAPHY
Austin Comm Coll (TX)
Bucks County Comm Coll (PA)
Cecil Coll (MD)
Central Wyoming Coll (WY)
Fashion Inst of Technology (NY)
Fiorello H. LaGuardia Comm Coll of the City U of New York (NY)

Hawkeye Comm Coll (IA)
Houston Comm Coll System (TX)
Kilgore Coll (TX)
Kirtland Comm Coll (MI)
Luzerne County Comm Coll (PA)
McHenry County Coll (IL)
Minneapolis Comm and Tech Coll (MN)
Mohawk Valley Comm Coll (NY)
Montgomery Coll (MD)
Northwest Coll (WY)
Nossi Coll of Art (TN)
Owens Comm Coll, Toledo (OH)
Palomar Coll (CA)
Phoenix Coll (AZ)
Randolph Comm Coll (NC)
Santa Monica Coll (CA)
Springfield Tech Comm Coll (MA)
Trinity Valley Comm Coll (TX)

COMMUNICATION
Coll of Western Idaho (ID)
Gordon State Coll (GA)
Northeast Texas Comm Coll (TX)
Santa Rosa Jr Coll (CA)
Sauk Valley Comm Coll (IL)
South Georgia State Coll, Douglas (GA)

COMMUNICATION AND JOURNALISM RELATED
Cayuga County Comm Coll (NY)
Gadsden State Comm Coll (AL)
Georgia Highlands Coll (GA)
Iowa Lakes Comm Coll (IA)

COMMUNICATION AND MEDIA RELATED
Raritan Valley Comm Coll (NJ)
Reading Area Comm Coll (PA)

COMMUNICATION SCIENCES AND DISORDERS
San Joaquin Valley Coll, Hesperia (CA)

COMMUNICATIONS SYSTEMS INSTALLATION AND REPAIR TECHNOLOGY
Bellingham Tech Coll (WA)
Cayuga County Comm Coll (NY)
Dutchess Comm Coll (NY)
Erie Comm Coll, South Campus (NY)
Mohawk Valley Comm Coll (NY)
Westmoreland County Comm Coll (PA)

COMMUNICATIONS TECHNOLOGIES AND SUPPORT SERVICES RELATED
Bowling Green State U-Firelands Coll (OH)
Columbus State Comm Coll (OH)
Comm Coll of Allegheny County (PA)
Middlesex County Coll (NJ)
Montgomery Coll (MD)
Montgomery County Comm Coll (PA)
Ocean County Coll (NJ)

COMMUNICATIONS TECHNOLOGY
Athens Tech Coll (GA)
Daytona State Coll (FL)
Hutchinson Comm Coll and Area Vocational School (KS)
ITT Tech Inst, Sylmar (CA)
Mott Comm Coll (MI)
Northwestern Connecticut Comm Coll (CT)
Orange Coast Coll (CA)
Pensacola State Coll (FL)
Pueblo Comm Coll (CO)
Vincennes U (IN)

COMMUNITY HEALTH AND PREVENTIVE MEDICINE
Anoka-Ramsey Comm Coll (MN)
Anoka-Ramsey Comm Coll, Cambridge Campus (MN)

COMMUNITY HEALTH SERVICES COUNSELING
Comm Coll of Allegheny County (PA)
Dutchess Comm Coll (NY)
Erie Comm Coll (NY)
Greenfield Comm Coll (MA)
Kingsborough Comm Coll of the City U of New York (NY)
Mott Comm Coll (MI)
Oakland Comm Coll (MI)
Santa Rosa Jr Coll (CA)
Waubonsee Comm Coll (IL)

COMMUNITY ORGANIZATION AND ADVOCACY
Berkshire Comm Coll (MA)
Borough of Manhattan Comm Coll of the City U of New York (NY)
Cleveland State Comm Coll (TN)
Clinton Comm Coll (NY)
Columbia-Greene Comm Coll (NY)
Comm Coll of Vermont (VT)
Herkimer County Comm Coll (NY)
Honolulu Comm Coll (HI)
Jefferson Comm Coll (NY)
Lane Comm Coll (OR)
Lansing Comm Coll (MI)
Mercer County Comm Coll (NJ)
Minneapolis Comm and Tech Coll (MN)
State U of New York Coll of Technology at Alfred (NY)
Tompkins Cortland Comm Coll (NY)
Westchester Comm Coll (NY)

COMPARATIVE LITERATURE
Iowa Lakes Comm Coll (IA)
Lamar State Coll–Orange (TX)
Miami Dade Coll (FL)
Otero Jr Coll (CO)

COMPUTER AND INFORMATION SCIENCES
Albany Tech Coll (GA)
Antelope Valley Coll (CA)
Arapahoe Comm Coll (CO)
Arizona Western Coll (AZ)
Austin Comm Coll (TX)
Berkeley City Coll (CA)
Berkshire Comm Coll (MA)
Bevill State Comm Coll (AL)
Bishop State Comm Coll (AL)
Borough of Manhattan Comm Coll of the City U of New York (NY)
Bristol Comm Coll (MA)
Broward Coll (FL)
Bucks County Comm Coll (PA)
Butler County Comm Coll (PA)
Carl Albert State Coll (OK)
Cayuga County Comm Coll (NY)
Central Virginia Comm Coll (VA)
Chandler-Gilbert Comm Coll (AZ)
Cincinnati State Tech and Comm Coll (OH)
Coll of Southern Maryland (MD)
Coll of the Mainland (TX)
Coll of the Ouachitas (AR)
Collin County Comm Coll District (TX)
Columbia-Greene Comm Coll (NY)
Columbus State Comm Coll (OH)
The Comm Coll of Baltimore County (MD)
Comm Coll of Rhode Island (RI)
Comm Coll of Vermont (VT)
Cumberland County Coll (NJ)
Dakota Coll at Bottineau (ND)
Darton State Coll (GA)
Delaware Tech & Comm Coll, Jack F. Owens Campus (DE)
Delaware Tech & Comm Coll, Stanton/Wilmington Campus (DE)
Delaware Tech & Comm Coll, Terry Campus (DE)
Edison Comm Coll (OH)
Erie Comm Coll, North Campus (NY)
Finger Lakes Comm Coll (NY)
Florida Gateway Coll (FL)
Florida State Coll at Jacksonville (FL)
Gadsden State Comm Coll (AL)
Gateway Comm and Tech Coll (KY)
Georgia Highlands Coll (GA)
Glendale Comm Coll (AZ)
Gogebic Comm Coll (MI)
Greenfield Comm Coll (MA)
Hagerstown Comm Coll (MD)
Harford Comm Coll (MD)
Harper Coll (IL)
Harrisburg Area Comm Coll (PA)
Herkimer County Comm Coll (NY)
Hinds Comm Coll (MS)
Hopkinsville Comm Coll (KY)
Hudson County Comm Coll (NJ)
Hutchinson Comm Coll and Area Vocational School (KS)
Independence Comm Coll (KS)
Ivy Tech Comm Coll–Bloomington (IN)
Ivy Tech Comm Coll–Central Indiana (IN)
Ivy Tech Comm Coll–Columbus (IN)
Ivy Tech Comm Coll–East Central (IN)
Ivy Tech Comm Coll–Kokomo (IN)
Ivy Tech Comm Coll–Lafayette (IN)

Ivy Tech Comm Coll–North Central (IN)
Ivy Tech Comm Coll–Northeast (IN)
Ivy Tech Comm Coll–Northwest (IN)
Ivy Tech Comm Coll–Richmond (IN)
Ivy Tech Comm Coll–Southeast (IN)
Ivy Tech Comm Coll–Southern Indiana (IN)
Ivy Tech Comm Coll–Southwest (IN)
Ivy Tech Comm Coll–Wabash Valley (IN)
Jefferson Comm Coll (NY)
Jefferson State Comm Coll (AL)
John Tyler Comm Coll (VA)
J. Sargeant Reynolds Comm Coll (VA)
Kilgore Coll (TX)
Kingsborough Comm Coll of the City U of New York (NY)
Lakes Region Comm Coll (NH)
Lansing Comm Coll (MI)
Lawson State Comm Coll (AL)
Lehigh Carbon Comm Coll (PA)
Linn-Benton Comm Coll (OR)
Lone Star Coll–CyFair (TX)
Lone Star Coll–Kingwood (TX)
Lurleen B. Wallace Comm Coll (AL)
Luzerne County Comm Coll (PA)
Massachusetts Bay Comm Coll (MA)
Middlesex County Coll (NJ)
Mid-Plains Comm Coll, North Platte (NE)
Mid-South Comm Coll (AR)
Mohawk Valley Comm Coll (NY)
Montgomery Coll (MD)
Montgomery County Comm Coll (PA)
Mountain State Coll (WV)
Mt. San Antonio Coll (CA)
Mount Wachusett Comm Coll (MA)
Nassau Comm Coll (NY)
North Dakota State Coll of Science (ND)
Northeast Texas Comm Coll (TX)
Northern Essex Comm Coll (MA)
Northwest Mississippi Comm Coll (MS)
Northwest-Shoals Comm Coll (AL)
Ocean County Coll (NJ)
Owensboro Comm and Tech Coll (KY)
Paris Jr Coll (TX)
Penn State Schuylkill (PA)
Pennsylvania Highlands Comm Coll (PA)
Pensacola State Coll (FL)
Phoenix Coll (AZ)
Pueblo Comm Coll (CO)
Reading Area Comm Coll (PA)
Reid State Tech Coll (AL)
Rogue Comm Coll (OR)
Salt Lake Comm Coll (UT)
San Jacinto Coll District (TX)
Sheridan Coll (WY)
Shoreline Comm Coll (WA)
Snead State Comm Coll (AL)
Somerset Comm Coll (KY)
South Florida State Coll (FL)
Southwestern Illinois Coll (IL)
Southwest Virginia Comm Coll (VA)
State U of New York Coll of Technology at Alfred (NY)
Sullivan Coll of Technology and Design (KY)
Sussex County Comm Coll (NJ)
Temple Coll (TX)
Texarkana Coll (TX)
Tompkins Cortland Comm Coll (NY)
Treasure Valley Comm Coll (OR)
Tyler Jr Coll (TX)
U of Arkansas Comm Coll at Hope (AR)
U of Arkansas Comm Coll at Morrilton (AR)
Victor Valley Coll (CA)
Vincennes U (IN)
Walters State Comm Coll (TN)
Westchester Comm Coll (NY)
Western Nevada Coll (NV)
Western Wyoming Comm Coll (WY)
West Kentucky Comm and Tech Coll (KY)
Wisconsin Indianhead Tech Coll (WI)
Wor-Wic Comm Coll (MD)

COMPUTER AND INFORMATION SCIENCES AND SUPPORT SERVICES RELATED
Arapahoe Comm Coll (CO)
Bowling Green State U-Firelands Coll (OH)
Brown Mackie Coll–Cincinnati (OH)

Brown Mackie Coll–North Canton (OH)
Brown Mackie Coll–South Bend (IN)
Brown Mackie Coll–Tucson (AZ)
Bunker Hill Comm Coll (MA)
Cambria-Rowe Business Coll, Indiana (PA)
Career Tech Coll, Monroe (LA)
Cayuga County Comm Coll (NY)
Chandler-Gilbert Comm Coll (AZ)
Clark State Comm Coll (OH)
Columbia-Greene Comm Coll (NY)
Dakota Coll at Bottineau (ND)
Darton State Coll (GA)
Eastern Shore Comm Coll (VA)
Fiorello H. LaGuardia Comm Coll of the City U of New York (NY)
Florida State Coll at Jacksonville (FL)
Greenfield Comm Coll (MA)
Herkimer County Comm Coll (NY)
Island Drafting and Tech Inst (NY)
Jackson Coll (MI)
Jefferson Comm Coll (NY)
Mohawk Valley Comm Coll (NY)
Monroe Comm Coll (NY)
Northcentral Tech Coll (WI)
Oakland Comm Coll (MI)
Piedmont Virginia Comm Coll (VA)
Raritan Valley Comm Coll (NJ)
San Joaquin Valley Coll, Visalia (CA)
Seminole State Coll of Florida (FL)
Southeast Tech Inst (SD)
Stark State Coll (OH)
Sullivan Coll of Technology and Design (KY)
Tompkins Cortland Comm Coll (NY)
Waukesha County Tech Coll (WI)
Westchester Comm Coll (NY)
Williston State Coll (ND)

COMPUTER AND INFORMATION SCIENCES RELATED
Berkeley City Coll (CA)
Bristol Comm Coll (MA)
Central Oregon Comm Coll (OR)
Chipola Coll (FL)
Daytona State Coll (FL)
Delta Coll (MI)
Florida State Coll at Jacksonville (FL)
Genesee Comm Coll (NY)
Howard Comm Coll (MD)
Iowa Lakes Comm Coll (IA)
Lorain County Comm Coll (OH)
Luzerne County Comm Coll (PA)
Metro Business Coll, Jefferson City (MO)
Metropolitan Comm Coll–Kansas City (MO)
Mississippi Gulf Coast Comm Coll (MS)
Missouri State U–West Plains (MO)
Mohave Comm Coll (AZ)
Monroe Comm Coll (NY)
Monroe County Comm Coll (MI)
Nassau Comm Coll (NY)
North Shore Comm Coll (MA)
Pensacola State Coll (FL)
Potomac State Coll of West Virginia U (WV)
Sauk Valley Comm Coll (IL)
Seminole State Coll of Florida (FL)
Stark State Coll (OH)
Tyler Jr Coll (TX)
Westchester Comm Coll (NY)

COMPUTER AND INFORMATION SYSTEMS SECURITY
Berkeley City Coll (CA)
Blackhawk Tech Coll (WI)
Blue Ridge Comm and Tech Coll (WV)
Bunker Hill Comm Coll (MA)
Butler County Comm Coll (PA)
Casper Coll (WY)
Century Coll (MN)
Chattahoochee Tech Coll (GA)
Clark State Comm Coll (OH)
Cleveland Comm Coll (NC)
Cochise Coll, Sierra Vista (AZ)
Collin County Comm Coll District (TX)
The Comm Coll of Baltimore County (MD)
Delta Coll (MI)
Dyersburg State Comm Coll (TN)
Edison Comm Coll (OH)
Elgin Comm Coll (IL)
Fayetteville Tech Comm Coll (NC)
Florida State Coll at Jacksonville (FL)
Glendale Comm Coll (AZ)

Hagerstown Comm Coll (MD)
Harford Comm Coll (MD)
Harrisburg Area Comm Coll (PA)
Hinds Comm Coll (MS)
Island Drafting and Tech Inst (NY)
Lanier Tech Coll (GA)
Lehigh Carbon Comm Coll (PA)
Minneapolis Comm and Tech Coll (MN)
Mohawk Valley Comm Coll (NY)
Montgomery Coll (MD)
Moraine Valley Comm Coll (IL)
Northampton Comm Coll (PA)
North Dakota State Coll of Science (ND)
Norwalk Comm Coll (CT)
Oakland Comm Coll (MI)
Owens Comm Coll, Toledo (OH)
Oxnard Coll (CA)
Pitt Comm Coll (NC)
Quinsigamond Comm Coll (MA)
Seminole State Coll of Florida (FL)
Sheridan Coll (WY)
Southeast Tech Inst (SD)
Southern Crescent Tech Coll (GA)
Spencerian Coll–Lexington (KY)
Spoon River Coll (IL)
Springfield Tech Comm Coll (MA)
Sullivan Coll of Technology and Design (KY)
Texas State Tech Coll Waco (TX)
Westchester Comm Coll (NY)
Westmoreland County Comm Coll (PA)
Wiregrass Georgia Tech Coll (GA)

COMPUTER ENGINEERING
Broward Coll (FL)
Carroll Comm Coll (MD)
Daytona State Coll (FL)
Pensacola State Coll (FL)
South Florida State Coll (FL)

COMPUTER ENGINEERING RELATED
Columbus Tech Coll (GA)
Daytona State Coll (FL)
Eastern Gateway Comm Coll (OH)
Monroe Comm Coll (NY)
Seminole State Coll of Florida (FL)
Stark State Coll (OH)

COMPUTER ENGINEERING TECHNOLOGY
Alvin Comm Coll (TX)
Amarillo Coll (TX)
Benjamin Franklin Inst of Technology (MA)
Bowling Green State U-Firelands Coll (OH)
Brookhaven Coll (TX)
Catawba Valley Comm Coll (NC)
Cincinnati State Tech and Comm Coll (OH)
Columbus State Comm Coll (OH)
Comm Coll of Allegheny County (PA)
Comm Coll of Rhode Island (RI)
Delaware Tech & Comm Coll, Stanton/Wilmington Campus (DE)
Delaware Tech & Comm Coll, Terry Campus (DE)
Florida State Coll at Jacksonville (FL)
Fox Valley Tech Coll (WI)
Georgia Piedmont Tech Coll (GA)
Hocking Coll (OH)
Houston Comm Coll System (TX)
ITT Tech Inst, Norwood (MA)
ITT Tech Inst, Wilmington (MA)
ITT Tech Inst (NJ)
ITT Tech Inst, Getzville (NY)
ITT Tech Inst, Dunmore (PA)
ITT Tech Inst, Harrisburg (PA)
ITT Tech Inst, Levittown (PA)
ITT Tech Inst, Philadelphia (PA)
ITT Tech Inst, Pittsburgh (PA)
ITT Tech Inst, Plymouth Meeting (PA)
ITT Tech Inst, Tarentum (PA)
Lakeland Comm Coll (OH)
Lorain County Comm Coll (OH)
Massachusetts Bay Comm Coll (MA)
Miami Dade Coll (FL)
Mississippi Delta Comm Coll (MS)
Mississippi Gulf Coast Comm Coll (MS)
Monroe Comm Coll (NY)
Monroe County Comm Coll (MI)
Mt. San Antonio Coll (CA)
Northeastern Jr Coll (CO)
Northern Essex Comm Coll (MA)
North Shore Comm Coll (MA)
Northwestern Connecticut Comm Coll (CT)
Oklahoma City Comm Coll (OK)
Onondaga Comm Coll (NY)
Orange Coast Coll (CA)
Owens Comm Coll, Toledo (OH)
Paris Jr Coll (TX)
Penn State New Kensington (PA)
Potomac State Coll of West Virginia U (WV)
Quinsigamond Comm Coll (MA)
Richmond Comm Coll (NC)
Roane State Comm Coll (TN)
Rock Valley Coll (IL)
San Diego City Coll (CA)
Seminole State Coll of Florida (FL)
Southeastern Comm Coll (NC)
Southern Maine Comm Coll (ME)
South Florida State Coll (FL)
South Plains Coll (TX)
Southwestern Comm Coll (NC)
Spencerian Coll–Lexington (KY)
Springfield Tech Comm Coll (MA)
State U of New York Coll of Technology at Alfred (NY)
Sullivan Coll of Technology and Design (KY)
Three Rivers Comm Coll (CT)
Trident Tech Coll (SC)
Tyler Jr Coll (TX)
Umpqua Comm Coll (OR)
U of New Mexico–Los Alamos Branch (NM)
Western Texas Coll (TX)

COMPUTER GRAPHICS
Antelope Valley Coll (CA)
Arizona Western Coll (AZ)
The Art Inst of Cincinnati (OH)
Berkeley City Coll (CA)
Carrington Coll California–San Jose (CA)
Carroll Comm Coll (MD)
Central Ohio Tech Coll (OH)
Coll of the Desert (CA)
Daytona State Coll (FL)
De Anza Coll (CA)
Florida State Coll at Jacksonville (FL)
Gavilan Coll (CA)
Genesee Comm Coll (NY)
Howard Comm Coll (MD)
Iowa Lakes Comm Coll (IA)
Luzerne County Comm Coll (PA)
Mercer County Comm Coll (NJ)
Mesabi Range Comm and Tech Coll (MN)
Metropolitan Comm Coll–Kansas City (MO)
Miami Dade Coll (FL)
Mississippi Gulf Coast Comm Coll (MS)
Missouri State U–West Plains (MO)
Monroe County Comm Coll (MI)
Moraine Valley Comm Coll (IL)
Mt. San Antonio Coll (CA)
Mount Wachusett Comm Coll (MA)
Nassau Comm Coll (NY)
Northern Essex Comm Coll (MA)
North Shore Comm Coll (MA)
Northwestern Connecticut Comm Coll (CT)
Orange Coast Coll (CA)
Phoenix Coll (AZ)
Pittsburgh Tech Inst, Oakdale (PA)
Quinsigamond Comm Coll (MA)
Schoolcraft Coll (MI)
Seminole State Coll of Florida (FL)
Shawnee Comm Coll (IL)
Shoreline Comm Coll (WA)
Spencerian Coll–Lexington (KY)
Sullivan Coll of Technology and Design (KY)
Sullivan County Comm Coll (NY)
Tallahassee Comm Coll (FL)
Trident Tech Coll (SC)
Tyler Jr Coll (TX)

COMPUTER HARDWARE ENGINEERING
Florida State Coll at Jacksonville (FL)
Seminole State Coll of Florida (FL)
Stark State Coll (OH)
Sullivan Coll of Technology and Design (KY)

COMPUTER HARDWARE TECHNOLOGY
State U of New York Coll of Technology at Alfred (NY)
Sullivan Coll of Technology and Design (KY)

COMPUTER/INFORMATION TECHNOLOGY SERVICES ADMINISTRATION RELATED
Bunker Hill Comm Coll (MA)
Central Carolina Comm Coll (NC)
Cleveland Inst of Electronics (OH)
Clinton Comm Coll (NY)
Daytona State Coll (FL)
Dutchess Comm Coll (NY)
Eastern Shore Comm Coll (VA)
Flathead Valley Comm Coll (MT)
Florida State Coll at Jacksonville (FL)
Hawkeye Comm Coll (IA)
Hillsborough Comm Coll (FL)
Howard Comm Coll (MD)
Iowa Lakes Comm Coll (IA)
Jefferson Comm Coll (NY)
J. Sargeant Reynolds Comm Coll (VA)
Kent State U at Trumbull (OH)
Mesabi Range Comm and Tech Coll (MN)
Northwest Florida State Coll (FL)
Oakland Comm Coll (MI)
Pasadena City Coll (CA)
Seminole State Coll of Florida (FL)
Southeast Tech Inst (SD)
Southwestern Illinois Coll (IL)
Stark State Coll (OH)
Trident Tech Coll (SC)
Tulsa Comm Coll (OK)
Vincennes U (IN)
Western Oklahoma State Coll (OK)

COMPUTER INSTALLATION AND REPAIR TECHNOLOGY
Central Maine Comm Coll (ME)
Delta Coll (MI)
Fiorello H. LaGuardia Comm Coll of the City U of New York (NY)
Genesee Comm Coll (NY)
Harrisburg Area Comm Coll (PA)
Hinds Comm Coll (MS)
Northampton Comm Coll (PA)
Palomar Coll (CA)
Schoolcraft Coll (MI)
Southeast Tech Inst (SD)
Sullivan Coll of Technology and Design (KY)
Tulsa Comm Coll (OK)
Wisconsin Indianhead Tech Coll (WI)
Wright Career Coll, Overland Park (KS)
Wright Career Coll, Wichita (KS)
Wright Career Coll (NE)
Wright Career Coll, Oklahoma City (OK)
Wright Career Coll, Tulsa (OK)

COMPUTER NUMERICALLY CONTROLLED (CNC) MACHINIST TECHNOLOGY
Anoka Tech Coll (MN)
Helena Coll U of Montana (MT)
Lake Superior Coll (MN)
Westmoreland County Comm Coll (PA)

COMPUTER PROGRAMMING
Altamaha Tech Coll (GA)
Alvin Comm Coll (TX)
Amarillo Coll (TX)
Antelope Valley Coll (CA)
Athens Tech Coll (GA)
Atlanta Tech Coll (GA)
Augusta Tech Coll (GA)
Austin Comm Coll (TX)
Bradford School (PA)
Bristol Comm Coll (MA)
Brookhaven Coll (TX)
Broward Coll (FL)
Bunker Hill Comm Coll (MA)
Casper Coll (WY)
Catawba Valley Comm Coll (NC)
Central Carolina Comm Coll (NC)
Central Georgia Tech Coll (GA)
Central Ohio Tech Coll (OH)
Chandler-Gilbert Comm Coll (AZ)
Chattahoochee Tech Coll (GA)
Chippewa Valley Tech Coll (WI)
Clark Coll (WA)
Clark State Comm Coll (OH)
Cochise Coll, Sierra Vista (AZ)
Coll of Southern Maryland (MD)
Columbus State Comm Coll (OH)
Copiah-Lincoln Comm Coll (MS)
Cosumnes River Coll, Sacramento (CA)
Dabney S. Lancaster Comm Coll (VA)
Daytona State Coll (FL)
De Anza Coll (CA)
Delta Coll (MI)
Eastern Florida State Coll (FL)
Edison Comm Coll (OH)
Fayetteville Tech Comm Coll (NC)
Fiorello H. LaGuardia Comm Coll of the City U of New York (NY)
Florida Gateway Coll (FL)
Florida State Coll at Jacksonville (FL)
Fox Valley Tech Coll (WI)
Gavilan Coll (CA)
Georgia Northwestern Tech Coll (GA)
Georgia Piedmont Tech Coll (GA)
Grand Rapids Comm Coll (MI)
Grayson Coll (TX)
Gwinnett Tech Coll (GA)
Harper Coll (IL)
Helena Coll U of Montana (MT)
Hinds Comm Coll (MS)
Hocking Coll (OH)
Houston Comm Coll System (TX)
Independence Comm Coll (KS)
International Business Coll, Indianapolis (IN)
Iowa Lakes Comm Coll (IA)
Jamestown Comm Coll (NY)
J. Sargeant Reynolds Comm Coll (VA)
Kilgore Coll (TX)
King's Coll (NC)
Lake Area Tech Inst (SD)
Lamar Comm Coll (CO)
Lane Comm Coll (OR)
Lanier Tech Coll (GA)
Laramie County Comm Coll (WY)
Lehigh Carbon Comm Coll (PA)
Lenoir Comm Coll (NC)
Lincoln Land Comm Coll (IL)
Lone Star Coll–Tomball (TX)
Lorain County Comm Coll (OH)
Los Angeles Mission Coll (CA)
Macomb Comm Coll (MI)
Metropolitan Comm Coll–Kansas City (MO)
Miami Dade Coll (FL)
Mineral Area Coll (MO)
Minneapolis Business Coll (MN)
Minneapolis Comm and Tech Coll (MN)
Minnesota State Coll–Southeast Tech (MN)
MiraCosta Coll (CA)
Mitchell Comm Coll (NC)
Mohawk Valley Comm Coll (NY)
Montgomery County Comm Coll (PA)
Mott Comm Coll (MI)
New Mexico State U–Alamogordo (NM)
Northampton Comm Coll (PA)
North Dakota State Coll of Science (ND)
Northeastern Tech Coll (SC)
Northern Essex Comm Coll (MA)
North Shore Comm Coll (MA)
NorthWest Arkansas Comm Coll (AR)
Northwestern Connecticut Comm Coll (CT)
Northwest Mississippi Comm Coll (MS)
Oakland Comm Coll (MI)
Oakton Comm Coll (IL)
Orange Coast Coll (CA)
Palomar Coll (CA)
Pensacola State Coll (FL)
Piedmont Virginia Comm Coll (VA)
Pittsburgh Tech Inst, Oakdale (PA)
Potomac State Coll of West Virginia U (WV)
St. Clair County Comm Coll (MI)
Santa Monica Coll (CA)
Schoolcraft Coll (MI)
Seminole State Coll of Florida (FL)
Southeastern Comm Coll (IA)
Southeast Tech Inst (SD)
Southern Crescent Tech Coll (GA)
Southern State Comm Coll (OH)
South Florida State Coll (FL)
South Plains Coll (TX)
Southwestern Illinois Coll (IL)
Southwestern Michigan Coll (MI)
Sowela Tech Comm Coll (LA)
Stark State Coll (OH)
Tallahassee Comm Coll (FL)
Tarrant County Coll District (TX)
Temple Coll (TX)
Texas State Tech Coll Waco (TX)
Three Rivers Comm Coll (CT)
Truckee Meadows Comm Coll (NV)
U of New Mexico–Los Alamos Branch (NM)
Victoria Coll (TX)
Vincennes U (IN)
Waubonsee Comm Coll (IL)
Waukesha County Tech Coll (WI)
Wayne County Comm Coll District (MI)
Western Nevada Coll (NV)
Westmoreland County Comm Coll (PA)
Wiregrass Georgia Tech Coll (GA)
Wood Tobe–Coburn School (NY)
Wright Career Coll, Overland Park (KS)
Wright Career Coll, Wichita (KS)
Wright Career Coll (NE)
Wright Career Coll, Oklahoma City (OK)
Wright Career Coll, Tulsa (OK)

COMPUTER PROGRAMMING RELATED
Clark State Comm Coll (OH)
Florida State Coll at Jacksonville (FL)
Genesee Comm Coll (NY)
Lorain County Comm Coll (OH)
Luzerne County Comm Coll (PA)
Mesabi Range Comm and Tech Coll (MN)
Mississippi Gulf Coast Comm Coll (MS)
Moraine Park Tech Coll (WI)
Northern Essex Comm Coll (MA)
Pasco-Hernando State Coll (FL)
Seminole State Coll of Florida (FL)
Southeast Tech Inst (SD)
Stark State Coll (OH)
Tyler Jr Coll (TX)

COMPUTER PROGRAMMING (SPECIFIC APPLICATIONS)
Bucks County Comm Coll (PA)
Bunker Hill Comm Coll (MA)
Butler County Comm Coll (PA)
Central Carolina Comm Coll (NC)
Cincinnati State Tech and Comm Coll (OH)
Columbus State Comm Coll (OH)
Comm Coll of Rhode Island (RI)
Danville Area Comm Coll (IL)
Daytona State Coll (FL)
Florida State Coll at Jacksonville (FL)
Harper Coll (IL)
Hillsborough Comm Coll (FL)
Holyoke Comm Coll (MA)
Houston Comm Coll System (TX)
ITT Tech Inst, Bessemer (AL)
ITT Tech Inst, Madison (AL)
ITT Tech Inst, Mobile (AL)
ITT Tech Inst, Tucson (AZ)
ITT Tech Inst, Culver City (CA)
ITT Tech Inst, Lathrop (CA)
ITT Tech Inst, National City (CA)
ITT Tech Inst, Oakland (CA)
ITT Tech Inst, Orange (CA)
ITT Tech Inst, Oxnard (CA)
ITT Tech Inst, Rancho Cordova (CA)
ITT Tech Inst, San Bernardino (CA)
ITT Tech Inst, San Dimas (CA)
ITT Tech Inst, Sylmar (CA)
ITT Tech Inst, Aurora (CO)
ITT Tech Inst, Westminster (CO)
ITT Tech Inst, Fort Lauderdale (FL)
ITT Tech Inst, Fort Myers (FL)
ITT Tech Inst, Jacksonville (FL)
ITT Tech Inst, Lake Mary (FL)
ITT Tech Inst, Miami (FL)
ITT Tech Inst, Orlando (FL)
ITT Tech Inst, St. Petersburg (FL)
ITT Tech Inst, Tampa (FL)
ITT Tech Inst (ID)
ITT Tech Inst, Fort Wayne (IN)
ITT Tech Inst, Merrillville (IN)
ITT Tech Inst, Newburgh (IN)
ITT Tech Inst, Clive (IA)
ITT Tech Inst, Louisville (KY)
ITT Tech Inst, Baton Rouge (LA)

ITT Tech Inst, St. Rose (LA)
ITT Tech Inst, Canton (MI)
ITT Tech Inst, Dearborn (MI)
ITT Tech Inst, Swartz Creek (MI)
ITT Tech Inst, Troy (MI)
ITT Tech Inst, Wyoming (MI)
ITT Tech Inst, Arnold (MO)
ITT Tech Inst , Earth City (MO)
ITT Tech Inst, Kansas City (MO)
ITT Tech Inst, Akron (OH)
ITT Tech Inst, Columbus (OH)
ITT Tech Inst, Dayton (OH)
ITT Tech Inst, Hilliard (OH)
ITT Tech Inst, Maumee (OH)
ITT Tech Inst, Norwood (OH)
ITT Tech Inst, Strongsville (OH)
ITT Tech Inst, Warrensville Heights (OH)
ITT Tech Inst , Youngstown (OH)
ITT Tech Inst, Tulsa (OK)
ITT Tech Inst, Portland (OR)
ITT Tech Inst, Chattanooga (TN)
ITT Tech Inst, Cordova (TN)
ITT Tech Inst, Johnson City (TN)
ITT Tech Inst, Knoxville (TN)
ITT Tech Inst, Nashville (TN)
ITT Tech Inst, DeSoto (TX)
ITT Tech Inst, Houston (TX)
ITT Tech Inst (UT)
ITT Tech Inst, Chantilly (VA)
ITT Tech Inst, Norfolk (VA)
ITT Tech Inst, Richmond (VA)
ITT Tech Inst, Salem (VA)
ITT Tech Inst, Springfield (VA)
ITT Tech Inst, Seattle (WA)
ITT Tech Inst, Spokane Valley (WA)
ITT Tech Inst (WV)
ITT Tech Inst, Green Bay (WI)
ITT Tech Inst , Greenfield (WI)
ITT Tech Inst, Madison (WI)
Kent State U at Ashtabula (OH)
Kent State U at East Liverpool (OH)
Kent State U at Salem (OH)
Kent State U at Trumbull (OH)
Kent State U at Tuscarawas (OH)
Lake Land Coll (IL)
Lakeland Comm Coll (OH)
Lansing Comm Coll (MI)
Lehigh Carbon Comm Coll (PA)
Lincoln Land Comm Coll (IL)
Lorain County Comm Coll (OH)
Macomb Comm Coll (MI)
Mesabi Range Comm and Tech Coll (MN)
Minnesota School of Business–Brooklyn Center (MN)
Minnesota School of Business–Plymouth (MN)
Missouri State U–West Plains (MO)
Mitchell Comm Coll (NC)
Mohave Comm Coll (AZ)
Monroe County Comm Coll (MI)
Mott Comm Coll (MI)
Northeast Iowa Comm Coll (IA)
Northern Essex Comm Coll (MA)
North Shore Comm Coll (MA)
Northwest Florida State Coll (FL)
Northwest Mississippi Comm Coll (MS)
Orange Coast Coll (CA)
Owens Comm Coll, Toledo (OH)
Pasco-Hernando State Coll (FL)
Pensacola State Coll (FL)
Piedmont Comm Coll (NC)
Pitt Comm Coll (NC)
Potomac State Coll of West Virginia U (WV)
Quinsigamond Comm Coll (MA)
Schoolcraft Coll (MI)
Seminole State Coll of Florida (FL)
Southern State Comm Coll (OH)
Spoon River Coll (IL)
Springfield Tech Comm Coll (MA)
Stark State Coll (OH)
State Fair Comm Coll (MO)
Sullivan County Comm Coll (NY)
Tallahassee Comm Coll (FL)
Trident Tech Coll (SC)
Tulsa Comm Coll (OK)
Victor Valley Coll (CA)
Western Wyoming Comm Coll (WY)
Westmoreland County Comm Coll (PA)

COMPUTER PROGRAMMING (VENDOR/PRODUCT CERTIFICATION)
Chandler-Gilbert Comm Coll (AZ)
Florida State Coll at Jacksonville (FL)
Lorain County Comm Coll (OH)
Raritan Valley Comm Coll (NJ)

Seminole State Coll of Florida (FL)
Stark State Coll (OH)
Sullivan Coll of Technology and Design (KY)
Walla Walla Comm Coll (WA)

COMPUTER SCIENCE
Alabama Southern Comm Coll (AL)
Allen Comm Coll (KS)
Amarillo Coll (TX)
Anoka-Ramsey Comm Coll (MN)
Anoka-Ramsey Comm Coll, Cambridge Campus (MN)
Benjamin Franklin Inst of Technology (MA)
Borough of Manhattan Comm Coll of the City U of New York (NY)
Bristol Comm Coll (MA)
Bronx Comm Coll of the City U of New York (NY)
Bunker Hill Comm Coll (MA)
Butte Coll (CA)
Ca&nnada Coll (CA)
Central Oregon Comm Coll (OR)
Central Wyoming Coll (WY)
Century Coll (MN)
Chipola Coll (FL)
Cochise Coll, Sierra Vista (AZ)
Coll of Marin (CA)
Coll of Southern Idaho (ID)
Coll of the Canyons (CA)
Coll of the Desert (CA)
Collin County Comm Coll District (TX)
Columbia Coll (CA)
Comm Coll of Philadelphia (PA)
Comm Coll of Vermont (VT)
Copper Mountain Coll (CA)
Cosumnes River Coll, Sacramento (CA)
Darton State Coll (GA)
Daytona State Coll (FL)
De Anza Coll (CA)
Dutchess Comm Coll (NY)
Finger Lakes Comm Coll (NY)
Fiorello H. LaGuardia Comm Coll of the City U of New York (NY)
Fullerton Coll (CA)
Galveston Coll (TX)
Garden City Comm Coll (KS)
Gavilan Coll (CA)
Genesee Comm Coll (NY)
Gordon State Coll (GA)
Gwinnett Tech Coll (GA)
Harford Comm Coll (MD)
Harper Coll (IL)
Harrisburg Area Comm Coll (PA)
Hocking Coll (OH)
Howard Comm Coll (MD)
Independence Comm Coll (KS)
Iowa Lakes Comm Coll (IA)
Jackson State Comm Coll (TN)
Jefferson Comm Coll (NY)
J. Sargeant Reynolds Comm Coll (VA)
Kingsborough Comm Coll of the City U of New York (NY)
Lake Area Tech Inst (SD)
Lake Tahoe Comm Coll (CA)
Lamar Comm Coll (CO)
Lamar State Coll–Orange (TX)
Landmark Coll (VT)
Lanier Tech Coll (GA)
Laramie County Comm Coll (WY)
Lone Star Coll–CyFair (TX)
Lone Star Coll–Kingwood (TX)
Lone Star Coll–Montgomery (TX)
Lone Star Coll–North Harris (TX)
Lone Star Coll–Tomball (TX)
Lorain County Comm Coll (OH)
Luzerne County Comm Coll (PA)
Massachusetts Bay Comm Coll (MA)
Mercer County Comm Coll (NJ)
Metropolitan Comm Coll–Kansas City (MO)
Miami Dade Coll (FL)
MiraCosta Coll (CA)
Mississippi Gulf Coast Comm Coll (MS)
Mohave Comm Coll (AZ)
Monroe Comm Coll (NY)
Mt. San Antonio Coll (CA)
Nassau Comm Coll (NY)
Niagara County Comm Coll (NY)
Normandale Comm Coll (MN)
Northampton Comm Coll (PA)
Northeastern Jr Coll (CO)
Northeastern Tech Coll (SC)
Northern Essex Comm Coll (MA)
North Shore Comm Coll (MA)

Northwestern Connecticut Comm Coll (CT)
Oklahoma City Comm Coll (OK)
Onondaga Comm Coll (NY)
Pasadena City Coll (CA)
Pensacola State Coll (FL)
Piedmont Virginia Comm Coll (VA)
Potomac State Coll of West Virginia U (WV)
Quinsigamond Comm Coll (MA)
River Valley Comm Coll (NH)
Roane State Comm Coll (TN)
Rock Valley Coll (IL)
Salt Lake Comm Coll (UT)
Santa Monica Coll (CA)
Santa Rosa Jr Coll (CA)
Seminole State Coll (OK)
Snow Coll (UT)
Southern Maine Comm Coll (ME)
Southern U at Shreveport (LA)
South Georgia State Coll, Douglas (GA)
South Plains Coll (TX)
Springfield Tech Comm Coll (MA)
State U of New York Coll of Technology at Alfred (NY)
Tarrant County Coll District (TX)
Temple Coll (TX)
Treasure Valley Comm Coll (OR)
Trinity Valley Comm Coll (TX)
Tulsa Comm Coll (OK)
Tyler Jr Coll (TX)
Umpqua Comm Coll (OR)
U of New Mexico–Los Alamos Branch (NM)
Victor Valley Coll (CA)
Vincennes U (IN)
Virginia Western Comm Coll (VA)
Westchester Comm Coll (NY)
Western Texas Coll (TX)
Western Wyoming Comm Coll (WY)

COMPUTER SOFTWARE AND MEDIA APPLICATIONS RELATED
Berkeley City Coll (CA)
Dakota Coll at Bottineau (ND)
Delta Coll (MI)
Florida State Coll at Jacksonville (FL)
Genesee Comm Coll (NY)
ITT Tech Inst, Norwood (MA)
ITT Tech Inst, Wilmington (MA)
ITT Tech Inst, Getzville (NY)
ITT Tech Inst, Harrisburg (PA)
ITT Tech Inst, Pittsburgh (PA)
Mesabi Range Comm and Tech Coll (MN)
Seminole State Coll of Florida (FL)
Stark State Coll (OH)

COMPUTER SOFTWARE ENGINEERING
Cleveland Inst of Electronics (OH)
Florida State Coll at Jacksonville (FL)
Seminole State Coll of Florida (FL)
Southeast Tech Inst (SD)
Stark State Coll (OH)

COMPUTER SOFTWARE TECHNOLOGY
Coconino Comm Coll (AZ)
Iowa Lakes Comm Coll (IA)
ITT Tech Inst, Bessemer (AL)
ITT Tech Inst, Madison (AL)
ITT Tech Inst, Duluth (GA)
ITT Tech Inst (NM)
ITT Tech Inst, Strongsville (OH)
ITT Tech Inst, Portland (OR)
ITT Tech Inst, Green Bay (WI)
Miami Dade Coll (FL)
Rogue Comm Coll (OR)
TCI–The Coll of Technology (NY)

COMPUTER SUPPORT SPECIALIST
Big Bend Comm Coll (WA)
Brown Mackie Coll–Albuquerque (NM)
Brown Mackie Coll–Birmingham (AL)
Brown Mackie Coll–Dallas/Ft. Worth (TX)
Brown Mackie Coll–Quad Cities (IA)
Brown Mackie Coll–San Antonio (TX)
Cambria-Rowe Business Coll, Johnstown (PA)
Central Ohio Tech Coll (OH)
Cincinnati State Tech and Comm Coll (OH)
Coll of Western Idaho (ID)
Comm Coll of Rhode Island (RI)
Fox Valley Tech Coll (WI)
Genesee Comm Coll (NY)

Inst of Business & Medical Careers (CO)
Mitchell Tech Inst (SD)
Moraine Park Tech Coll (WI)
Oakland Comm Coll (MI)
Southwestern Michigan Coll (MI)
Waukesha County Tech Coll (WI)
Westmoreland County Comm Coll (PA)
Wisconsin Indianhead Tech Coll (WI)

COMPUTER SYSTEMS ANALYSIS
Amarillo Coll (TX)
Bristol Comm Coll (MA)
Broward Coll (FL)
Chandler-Gilbert Comm Coll (AZ)
Cincinnati State Tech and Comm Coll (OH)
Crowder Coll (MO)
Florida State Coll at Jacksonville (FL)
Glendale Comm Coll (AZ)
Hillsborough Comm Coll (FL)
Hutchinson Comm Coll and Area Vocational School (KS)
Kirtland Comm Coll (MI)
Lakeland Comm Coll (OH)
Mitchell Comm Coll (NC)
Northcentral Tech Coll (WI)
Northwest Florida State Coll (FL)
Oakland Comm Coll (MI)
Oklahoma City Comm Coll (OK)
Pensacola State Coll (FL)
Phoenix Coll (AZ)
Pima Comm Coll (AZ)
Quinsigamond Comm Coll (MA)
Southern State Comm Coll (OH)
Wor-Wic Comm Coll (MD)

COMPUTER SYSTEMS NETWORKING AND TELECOMMUNICATIONS
Alexandria Tech and Comm Coll (MN)
Allen Comm Coll (KS)
Altamaha Tech Coll (GA)
Anoka-Ramsey Comm Coll (MN)
Anoka-Ramsey Comm Coll, Cambridge Campus (MN)
Athens Tech Coll (GA)
Augusta Tech Coll (GA)
Austin Comm Coll (TX)
Bellingham Tech Coll (WA)
Big Bend Comm Coll (WA)
Bismarck State Coll (ND)
Blackhawk Tech Coll (WI)
Borough of Manhattan Comm Coll of the City U of New York (NY)
Bowling Green State U-Firelands Coll (OH)
Bradford School (PA)
Brown Mackie Coll–Louisville (KY)
Bucks County Comm Coll (PA)
Bunker Hill Comm Coll (MA)
Ca&nnada Coll (CA)
Cape Fear Comm Coll (NC)
Catawba Valley Comm Coll (NC)
Central Carolina Comm Coll (NC)
Central Georgia Tech Coll (GA)
Central Oregon Comm Coll (OR)
Century Coll (MN)
Chandler-Gilbert Comm Coll (AZ)
Chattahoochee Tech Coll (GA)
Chippewa Valley Tech Coll (WI)
Clark Coll (WA)
Clark State Comm Coll (OH)
Cleveland Comm Coll (NC)
Cochise Coll, Sierra Vista (AZ)
CollAmerica–Flagstaff (AZ)
Coll of Marin (CA)
Coll of Southern Idaho (ID)
Coll of the Canyons (CA)
Columbus Tech Coll (GA)
Comm Coll of Allegheny County (PA)
The Comm Coll of Baltimore County (MD)
Comm Coll of Rhode Island (RI)
Comm Coll of Vermont (VT)
Cosumnes River Coll, Sacramento (CA)
Crowder Coll (MO)
Cumberland County Coll (NJ)
Danville Area Comm Coll (IL)
Davis Coll (OH)
Daytona State Coll (FL)
Delaware Tech & Comm Coll, Stanton/Wilmington Campus (DE)
Delaware Tech & Comm Coll, Terry Campus (DE)
Delta Coll (MI)
Dunwoody Coll of Technology (MN)
East Central Coll (MO)

Eastern Florida State Coll (FL)
Eastern Idaho Tech Coll (ID)
Eastern Wyoming Coll (WY)
Edison Comm Coll (OH)
Fayetteville Tech Comm Coll (NC)
Fiorello H. LaGuardia Comm Coll of the City U of New York (NY)
Florida State Coll at Jacksonville (FL)
Fox Valley Tech Coll (WI)
Garden City Comm Coll (KS)
Gavilan Coll (CA)
Genesee Comm Coll (NY)
Georgia Piedmont Tech Coll (GA)
Glendale Comm Coll (AZ)
Great Falls Coll Montana State U (MT)
Gwinnett Tech Coll (GA)
Halifax Comm Coll (NC)
Hallmark Coll of Technology (TX)
Harrisburg Area Comm Coll (PA)
Hawkeye Comm Coll (IA)
Hinds Comm Coll (MS)
Houston Comm Coll System (TX)
Howard Comm Coll (MD)
Hutchinson Comm Coll and Area Vocational School (KS)
Illinois Eastern Comm Colls, Lincoln Trail College (IL)
Independence Comm Coll (KS)
International Business Coll, Indianapolis (IN)
Iowa Lakes Comm Coll (IA)
Island Drafting and Tech Inst (NY)
ITT Tech Inst, Bessemer (AL)
ITT Tech Inst, Baton Rouge (LA)
ITT Tech Inst, Norwood (MA)
ITT Tech Inst, Wilmington (MA)
ITT Tech Inst (NJ)
ITT Tech Inst, Albany (NY)
ITT Tech Inst, Getzville (NY)
ITT Tech Inst, Liverpool (NY)
ITT Tech Inst, Dunmore (PA)
ITT Tech Inst, Harrisburg (PA)
ITT Tech Inst, Levittown (PA)
ITT Tech Inst, Philadelphia (PA)
ITT Tech Inst, Pittsburgh (PA)
ITT Tech Inst, Plymouth Meeting (PA)
ITT Tech Inst, Tarentum (PA)
Jefferson Coll (MO)
J. Sargeant Reynolds Comm Coll (VA)
Kilgore Coll (TX)
King's Coll (NC)
Lake Land Coll (IL)
Lakeland Comm Coll (OH)
Lane Comm Coll (OR)
Lanier Tech Coll (GA)
Lansing Comm Coll (MI)
Lehigh Carbon Comm Coll (PA)
Lincoln Land Comm Coll (IL)
Lorain County Comm Coll (OH)
Luzerne County Comm Coll (PA)
Manhattan Area Tech Coll (KS)
McHenry County Coll (IL)
Mercer County Comm Coll (NJ)
Mesabi Range Comm and Tech Coll (MN)
Minneapolis Business Coll (MN)
Minneapolis Comm and Tech Coll (MN)
Minnesota School of Business–Brooklyn Center (MN)
Minnesota School of Business–Plymouth (MN)
Minnesota State Coll–Southeast Tech (MN)
MiraCosta Coll (CA)
Mississippi Gulf Coast Comm Coll (MS)
Montgomery County Comm Coll (PA)
Moraine Park Tech Coll (WI)
Mott Comm Coll (MI)
Moultrie Tech Coll (GA)
Mountain View Coll (TX)
Nassau Comm Coll (NY)
Northampton Comm Coll (PA)
Northcentral Tech Coll (WI)
North Dakota State Coll of Science (ND)
Northeast Texas Comm Coll (TX)
Northern Essex Comm Coll (MA)
North Georgia Tech Coll (GA)
North Iowa Area Comm Coll (IA)
Northwest Tech Coll (MN)
Norwalk Comm Coll (CT)
Oconee Fall Line Tech Coll (GA)
Ogeechee Tech Coll (GA)
Okefenokee Tech Coll (GA)
Oklahoma City Comm Coll (OK)
Olympic Coll (WA)
Onondaga Comm Coll (NY)

Oxnard Coll (CA)
Ozarks Tech Comm Coll (MO)
Palomar Coll (CA)
Pasco-Hernando State Coll (FL)
Piedmont Comm Coll (NC)
Pima Comm Coll (AZ)
Pitt Comm Coll (NC)
Potomac State Coll of West Virginia U (WV)
Randolph Comm Coll (NC)
Raritan Valley Comm Coll (NJ)
River Valley Comm Coll (NH)
Rock Valley Coll (IL)
Savannah Tech Coll (GA)
Schoolcraft Coll (MI)
Seminole State Coll of Florida (FL)
Shawnee Comm Coll (IL)
Southeastern Tech Coll (GA)
Southeast Tech Inst (SD)
Southern Crescent Tech Coll (GA)
South Georgia Tech Coll (GA)
South Louisiana Comm Coll (LA)
Southwestern Michigan Coll (MI)
Southwest Georgia Tech Coll (GA)
Sowela Tech Comm Coll (LA)
Stark State Coll (OH)
State Fair Comm Coll (MO)
Sullivan Coll of Technology and Design (KY)
Tallahassee Comm Coll (FL)
TCI–The Coll of Technology (NY)
Trident Tech Coll (SC)
Tyler Jr Coll (TX)
Victoria Coll (TX)
Vincennes U (IN)
Walla Walla Comm Coll (WA)
Waukesha County Tech Coll (WI)
Wenatchee Valley Coll (WA)
Westchester Comm Coll (NY)
Western Dakota Tech Inst (SD)
West Georgia Tech Coll (GA)
Westmoreland County Comm Coll (PA)
Wiregrass Georgia Tech Coll (GA)
Wisconsin Indianhead Tech Coll (WI)
Wood Tobe–Coburn School (NY)
Wright Career Coll, Overland Park (KS)
Wright Career Coll, Wichita (KS)
Wright Career Coll (NE)
Wright Career Coll, Oklahoma City (OK)
Wright Career Coll, Tulsa (OK)

COMPUTER TECHNOLOGY/ COMPUTER SYSTEMS TECHNOLOGY
Anoka Tech Coll (MN)
Arkansas State U–Newport (AR)
Benjamin Franklin Inst of Technology (MA)
Brookhaven Coll (TX)
Butler County Comm Coll (PA)
Cambria-Rowe Business Coll, Indiana (PA)
Cambria-Rowe Business Coll, Johnstown (PA)
Cape Fear Comm Coll (NC)
Central Wyoming Coll (WY)
Century Coll (MN)
Coconino Comm Coll (AZ)
Commonwealth Tech Inst (PA)
Comm Coll of Allegheny County (PA)
Dakota Coll at Bottineau (ND)
Daytona State Coll (FL)
Delaware Tech & Comm Coll, Jack F. Owens Campus (DE)
Delaware Tech & Comm Coll, Terry Campus (DE)
Erie Comm Coll, South Campus (NY)
Grayson Coll (TX)
Hillsborough Comm Coll (FL)
Island Drafting and Tech Inst (NY)
ITI Tech Coll (LA)
Jefferson Comm Coll (NY)
Lakeland Comm Coll (OH)
Lake Superior Coll (MN)
Lansing Comm Coll (MI)
Lorain County Comm Coll (OH)
Luzerne County Comm Coll (PA)
Manhattan Area Tech Coll (KS)
Miami Dade Coll (FL)
Minnesota State Coll–Southeast Tech (MN)
Montgomery Coll (MD)
Normandale Comm Coll (MN)
Northwest Florida State Coll (FL)
Okefenokee Tech Coll (GA)
Pasadena City Coll (CA)

Pasco-Hernando State Coll (FL)
Pittsburgh Tech Inst, Oakdale (PA)
Reading Area Comm Coll (PA)
Rend Lake Coll (IL)
Southeast Tech Inst (SD)
Southern State Comm Coll (OH)
Sullivan Coll of Technology and Design (KY)
Texas State Tech Coll Waco (TX)
U of Arkansas Comm Coll at Morrilton (AR)
Walla Walla Comm Coll (WA)
West Virginia Jr Coll–Bridgeport (WV)

COMPUTER TYPOGRAPHY AND COMPOSITION EQUIPMENT OPERATION
Housatonic Comm Coll (CT)
Lamar Comm Coll (CO)
Metropolitan Comm Coll–Kansas City (MO)
Northern Essex Comm Coll (MA)
Orange Coast Coll (CA)
Paris Jr Coll (TX)

CONCRETE FINISHING
Southwestern Illinois Coll (IL)

CONSTRUCTION ENGINEERING
Bossier Parish Comm Coll (LA)

CONSTRUCTION ENGINEERING TECHNOLOGY
Antelope Valley Coll (CA)
Clark Coll (WA)
Columbus State Comm Coll (OH)
Comm Coll of Allegheny County (PA)
Comm Coll of Philadelphia (PA)
Crowder Coll (MO)
De Anza Coll (CA)
Delta Coll (MI)
Florida State Coll at Jacksonville (FL)
Gogebic Comm Coll (MI)
Greenville Tech Coll (SC)
Harrisburg Area Comm Coll (PA)
Helena Coll U of Montana (MT)
Hinds Comm Coll (MS)
Houston Comm Coll System (TX)
Inst of Design and Construction (NY)
Iowa Lakes Comm Coll (IA)
Jefferson State Comm Coll (AL)
Lake Area Tech Inst (SD)
Lane Comm Coll (OR)
Lincoln Land Comm Coll (IL)
Macomb Comm Coll (MI)
Miami Dade Coll (FL)
Mid-Plains Comm Coll, North Platte (NE)
Monroe Comm Coll (NY)
North Dakota State Coll of Science (ND)
Norwalk Comm Coll (CT)
The Ohio State U Ag Tech Inst (OH)
Oklahoma State U Inst of Technology (OK)
Oklahoma State U, Oklahoma City (OK)
Onondaga Comm Coll (NY)
Orange Coast Coll (CA)
Owens Comm Coll, Toledo (OH)
Ozarks Tech Comm Coll (MO)
Pensacola State Coll (FL)
Raritan Valley Comm Coll (NJ)
Rock Valley Coll (IL)
Rogue Comm Coll (OR)
San Jacinto Coll District (TX)
Seminole State Coll of Florida (FL)
Snow Coll (UT)
Southeastern Comm Coll (IA)
Southeast Tech Inst (SD)
South Florida State Coll (FL)
South Suburban Coll (IL)
State U of New York Coll of Technology at Alfred (NY)
Sullivan County Comm Coll (NY)
Tallahassee Comm Coll (FL)
Tarrant County Coll District (TX)
Tech Coll of the Lowcountry (SC)
U of Hawaii Maui Coll (HI)
Victor Valley Coll (CA)
The Williamson Free School of Mecha Trades (PA)

CONSTRUCTION/HEAVY EQUIPMENT/EARTHMOVING EQUIPMENT OPERATION
Ivy Tech Comm Coll–Southwest (IN)

Ivy Tech Comm Coll–Wabash Valley (IN)
Lansing Comm Coll (MI)

CONSTRUCTION MANAGEMENT
Casper Coll (WY)
Coconino Comm Coll (AZ)
Delaware Tech & Comm Coll, Jack F. Owens Campus (DE)
Delaware Tech & Comm Coll, Stanton/Wilmington Campus (DE)
Delaware Tech & Comm Coll, Terry Campus (DE)
Dunwoody Coll of Technology (MN)
Erie Comm Coll, North Campus (NY)
Iowa Lakes Comm Coll (IA)
Kankakee Comm Coll (IL)
Kaskaskia Coll (IL)
Lansing Comm Coll (MI)
McHenry County Coll (IL)
Northampton Comm Coll (PA)
Oakland Comm Coll (MI)
The Ohio State U Ag Tech Inst (OH)
Oklahoma State U, Oklahoma City (OK)
Phoenix Coll (AZ)
San Joaquin Valley Coll, Hanford (CA)
San Joaquin Valley Coll, Ontario (CA)
San Joaquin Valley Coll, Temecula (CA)
San Joaquin Valley Coll–Online (CA)
Truckee Meadows Comm Coll (NV)
Waubonsee Comm Coll (IL)

CONSTRUCTION TRADES
American Samoa Comm Coll (AS)
Casper Coll (WY)
Crowder Coll (MO)
East Central Coll (MO)
Harrisburg Area Comm Coll (PA)
Illinois Eastern Comm Colls, Frontier Community College (IL)
Illinois Eastern Comm Colls, Lincoln Trail College (IL)
Iowa Lakes Comm Coll (IA)
Ivy Tech Comm Coll–East Central (IN)
Ivy Tech Comm Coll–Northeast (IN)
Ivy Tech Comm Coll–Northwest (IN)
Ivy Tech Comm Coll–Richmond (IN)
Lamar Comm Coll (CO)
Lehigh Carbon Comm Coll (PA)
Northeast Iowa Comm Coll (IA)
Ogeechee Tech Coll (GA)
Oklahoma State U, Oklahoma City (OK)
Owensboro Comm and Tech Coll (KY)
Pasadena City Coll (CA)
Rogue Comm Coll (OR)
Southwestern Illinois Coll (IL)
Texas State Tech Coll Waco (TX)
Vincennes U (IN)

CONSTRUCTION TRADES RELATED
Arizona Western Coll (AZ)
Central Maine Comm Coll (ME)
Coconino Comm Coll (AZ)
Comm Coll of Allegheny County (PA)
Cosumnes River Coll, Sacramento (CA)
Dutchess Comm Coll (NY)
East Central Coll (MO)
Fullerton Coll (CA)
Ivy Tech Comm Coll–East Central (IN)
Ivy Tech Comm Coll–Kokomo (IN)
Ivy Tech Comm Coll–Northeast (IN)
Ivy Tech Comm Coll–Richmond (IN)
Jackson Coll (MI)
Mitchell Tech Inst (SD)
Pitt Comm Coll (NC)
State U of New York Coll of Technology at Alfred (NY)
Tompkins Cortland Comm Coll (NY)
York County Comm Coll (ME)

CONSUMER MERCHANDISING/ RETAILING MANAGEMENT
Clinton Comm Coll (NY)
FIDM/The Fashion Inst of Design & Merchandising, Los Angeles Campus (CA)
FIDM/The Fashion Inst of Design & Merchandising, Orange County Campus (CA)

FIDM/The Fashion Inst of Design & Merchandising, San Diego Campus (CA)
FIDM/The Fashion Inst of Design & Merchandising, San Francisco Campus (CA)
Golden West Coll (CA)
Iowa Lakes Comm Coll (IA)
J. Sargeant Reynolds Comm Coll (VA)
Lenoir Comm Coll (NC)
Lorain County Comm Coll (OH)
Monroe Comm Coll (NY)
Niagara County Comm Coll (NY)
Shoreline Comm Coll (WA)
South Plains Coll (TX)
Stark State Coll (OH)
Sullivan County Comm Coll (NY)
Tarrant County Coll District (TX)
Three Rivers Comm Coll (CT)
Westchester Comm Coll (NY)

CONSUMER SERVICES AND ADVOCACY
Pensacola State Coll (FL)
San Diego City Coll (CA)

COOKING AND RELATED CULINARY ARTS
Bradford School (OH)
Butler County Comm Coll (PA)
Central Oregon Comm Coll (OR)
Columbia Coll (CA)
Columbus Culinary Inst at Bradford School (OH)
Culinary Inst of St. Louis at Hickey Coll (MO)
Grayson Coll (TX)
Harrison Coll (NC)
Hinds Comm Coll (MS)
Iowa Lakes Comm Coll (IA)
J. Sargeant Reynolds Comm Coll (VA)
Kingsborough Comm Coll of the City U of New York (NY)
Miami Dade Coll (FL)
Palomar Coll (CA)
Pensacola State Coll (FL)
Pittsburgh Tech Inst, Oakdale (PA)
Pueblo Comm Coll (CO)
State U of New York Coll of Technology at Alfred (NY)

CORRECTIONS
Alvin Comm Coll (TX)
Amarillo Coll (TX)
Antelope Valley Coll (CA)
Austin Comm Coll (TX)
Bucks County Comm Coll (PA)
Butler County Comm Coll (PA)
Cayuga County Comm Coll (NY)
Clark State Comm Coll (OH)
Coconino Comm Coll (AZ)
Comm Coll of Allegheny County (PA)
Danville Area Comm Coll (IL)
De Anza Coll (CA)
Delta Coll (MI)
Eastern Gateway Comm Coll (OH)
Florida Gateway Coll (FL)
Garrett Coll (MD)
Gavilan Coll (CA)
Grand Rapids Comm Coll (MI)
Herkimer County Comm Coll (NY)
Hocking Coll (OH)
Illinois Eastern Comm Colls, Frontier Community College (IL)
Illinois Eastern Comm Colls, Lincoln Trail College (IL)
Iowa Lakes Comm Coll (IA)
Jackson Coll (MI)
Kirtland Comm Coll (MI)
Lake Land Coll (IL)
Lakeland Comm Coll (OH)
Lansing Comm Coll (MI)
Laramie County Comm Coll (WY)
Lorain County Comm Coll (OH)
Mercer County Comm Coll (NJ)
Metropolitan Comm Coll–Kansas City (MO)
Monroe Comm Coll (NY)
Moraine Park Tech Coll (WI)
Mountain Empire Comm Coll (VA)
Mt. San Antonio Coll (CA)
Mount Wachusett Comm Coll (MA)
Northeastern Jr Coll (CO)
Northeast Texas Comm Coll (TX)
Oakland Comm Coll (MI)
Raritan Valley Comm Coll (NJ)
Roane State Comm Coll (TN)

San Joaquin Valley Coll, Bakersfield (CA)
San Joaquin Valley Coll, Fresno (CA)
San Joaquin Valley Coll, Ontario (CA)
San Joaquin Valley Coll, Visalia (CA)
Sauk Valley Comm Coll (IL)
Southern State Comm Coll (OH)
Tallahassee Comm Coll (FL)
Three Rivers Comm Coll (CT)
Trinity Valley Comm Coll (TX)
Tunxis Comm Coll (CT)
Vincennes U (IN)
Wayne County Comm Coll District (MI)
Westchester Comm Coll (NY)
Western Nevada Coll (NV)
Western Texas Coll (TX)
Westmoreland County Comm Coll (PA)
Wytheville Comm Coll (VA)

CORRECTIONS ADMINISTRATION
Eastern Wyoming Coll (WY)
Kirtland Comm Coll (MI)

CORRECTIONS AND CRIMINAL JUSTICE RELATED
Albany Tech Coll (GA)
Brown Mackie Coll–Albuquerque (NM)
Brown Mackie Coll–Atlanta (GA)
Brown Mackie Coll–Boise (ID)
Brown Mackie Coll–Greenville (SC)
Brown Mackie Coll–Indianapolis (IN)
Brown Mackie Coll–Kansas City (KS)
Brown Mackie Coll–Merrillville (IN)
Brown Mackie Coll–Northern Kentucky (KY)
Brown Mackie Coll–Phoenix (AZ)
Brown Mackie Coll–St. Louis (MO)
Brown Mackie Coll–Salina (KS)
Brown Mackie Coll–Tucson (AZ)
Brown Mackie Coll–Tulsa (OK)
Career Tech Coll, Monroe (LA)
Coconino Comm Coll (AZ)
Fayetteville Tech Comm Coll (NC)
Genesee Comm Coll (NY)
Hinds Comm Coll (MS)
Pitt Comm Coll (NC)
Sussex County Comm Coll (NJ)
Wisconsin Indianhead Tech Coll (WI)

COSMETOLOGY
Barstow Comm Coll (CA)
Butler County Comm Coll (PA)
Butte Coll (CA)
Century Coll (MN)
Clary Sage Coll (OK)
Colorado Northwestern Comm Coll (CO)
Copiah-Lincoln Comm Coll (MS)
Eastern Arizona Coll (AZ)
Eastern Wyoming Coll (WY)
Fullerton Coll (CA)
Garden City Comm Coll (KS)
Gavilan Coll (CA)
Golden West Coll (CA)
Honolulu Comm Coll (HI)
Houston Comm Coll System (TX)
Independence Comm Coll (KS)
Kaskaskia Coll (IL)
Kirtland Comm Coll (MI)
Lamar Comm Coll (CO)
Lenoir Comm Coll (NC)
Lone Star Coll–Kingwood (TX)
Lone Star Coll–North Harris (TX)
Lorain County Comm Coll (OH)
Minnesota State Coll–Southeast Tech (MN)
MiraCosta Coll (CA)
Northeastern Jr Coll (CO)
Northeast Iowa Comm Coll (IA)
Northeast Texas Comm Coll (TX)
Oakland Comm Coll (MI)
Olympic Coll (WA)
Paris Jr Coll (TX)
Pasadena City Coll (CA)
Pueblo Comm Coll (CO)
Randolph Comm Coll (NC)
Salt Lake Comm Coll (UT)
San Diego City Coll (CA)
San Jacinto Coll District (TX)
San Juan Coll (NM)
Santa Monica Coll (CA)
Shawnee Comm Coll (IL)
Shoreline Comm Coll (WA)
Southeastern Comm Coll (IA)
Southeastern Comm Coll (NC)

South Plains Coll (TX)
Southwestern Comm Coll (NC)
Texarkana Coll (TX)
Trinity Valley Comm Coll (TX)
Umpqua Comm Coll (OR)
Vincennes U (IN)
Walla Walla Comm Coll (WA)

COSMETOLOGY AND PERSONAL GROOMING ARTS RELATED
Bristol Comm Coll (MA)
Comm Coll of Allegheny County (PA)
Lorain County Comm Coll (OH)

COSMETOLOGY, BARBER/ STYLING, AND NAIL INSTRUCTION
Coll of the Mainland (TX)
Inst of Business & Medical Careers (CO)
Pasadena City Coll (CA)
San Jacinto Coll District (TX)

COUNSELING PSYCHOLOGY
Kilian Comm Coll (SD)

COURT REPORTING
Alvin Comm Coll (TX)
Anoka Tech Coll (MN)
Clark State Comm Coll (OH)
Coll of Marin (CA)
Comm Coll of Allegheny County (PA)
Fox Valley Tech Coll (WI)
Gadsden State Comm Coll (AL)
Harrisburg Area Comm Coll (PA)
Hinds Comm Coll (MS)
Houston Comm Coll System (TX)
Long Island Business Inst (NY)
Luzerne County Comm Coll (PA)
Miami Dade Coll (FL)
Mississippi Gulf Coast Comm Coll (MS)
Moraine Park Tech Coll (WI)
New York Career Inst (NY)
Northwest Mississippi Comm Coll (MS)
Oakland Comm Coll (MI)
San Diego City Coll (CA)
South Suburban Coll (IL)
Stark State Coll (OH)
State U of New York Coll of Technology at Alfred (NY)
West Kentucky Comm and Tech Coll (KY)
Wisconsin Indianhead Tech Coll (WI)

CRAFTS, FOLK ART AND ARTISANRY
Harrisburg Area Comm Coll (PA)

CREATIVE WRITING
Anoka-Ramsey Comm Coll (MN)
Anoka-Ramsey Comm Coll, Cambridge Campus (MN)
Austin Comm Coll (TX)
Berkeley City Coll (CA)
Coll of the Desert (CA)
Normandale Comm Coll (MN)
Tompkins Cortland Comm Coll (NY)

CRIMINALISTICS AND CRIMINAL SCIENCE
Century Coll (MN)
Harrisburg Area Comm Coll (PA)
Oakland Comm Coll (MI)

CRIMINAL JUSTICE/LAW ENFORCEMENT ADMINISTRATION
Alabama Southern Comm Coll (AL)
Allen Comm Coll (KS)
Amarillo Coll (TX)
Antelope Valley Coll (CA)
Arapahoe Comm Coll (CO)
Arizona Western Coll (AZ)
Arkansas State U–Newport (AR)
Athens Tech Coll (GA)
Bainbridge State Coll (GA)
Beal Coll (ME)
Brookhaven Coll (TX)
Broward Coll (FL)
Brown Mackie Coll–Louisville (KY)
Brown Mackie Coll–Miami (FL)
Bucks County Comm Coll (PA)
Bunker Hill Comm Coll (MA)
Butler County Comm Coll (PA)
Casper Coll (WY)
Central Carolina Comm Coll (NC)
Central Maine Comm Coll (ME)
Central Ohio Tech Coll (OH)
Central Virginia Comm Coll (VA)
Central Wyoming Coll (WY)
Clark State Comm Coll (OH)
Clinton Comm Coll (NY)
Coconino Comm Coll (AZ)
Coll of Southern Idaho (ID)
Coll of Southern Maryland (MD)
Columbia-Greene Comm Coll (NY)
Comm Coll of Philadelphia (PA)
Comm Coll of Vermont (VT)
Cossatot Comm Coll of the U of Arkansas (AR)
Dabney S. Lancaster Comm Coll (VA)
Darton State Coll (GA)
Daytona State Coll (FL)
Dean Coll (MA)
De Anza Coll (CA)
Delaware Tech & Comm Coll, Jack F. Owens Campus (DE)
Delaware Tech & Comm Coll, Stanton/Wilmington Campus (DE)
Delaware Tech & Comm Coll, Terry Campus (DE)
Eastern Arizona Coll (AZ)
Eastern Florida State Coll (FL)
Eastern Wyoming Coll (WY)
Finger Lakes Comm Coll (NY)
Flathead Valley Comm Coll (MT)
Florida Gateway Coll (FL)
Florida State Coll at Jacksonville (FL)
Gateway Comm and Tech Coll (KY)
Genesee Comm Coll (NY)
Georgia Military Coll (GA)
Gogebic Comm Coll (MI)
Golden West Coll (CA)
Goodwin Coll (CT)
Grand Rapids Comm Coll (MI)
Harper Coll (IL)
Harrisburg Area Comm Coll (PA)
Herkimer County Comm Coll (NY)
Hillsborough Comm Coll (FL)
Hocking Coll (OH)
Hopkinsville Comm Coll (KY)
Housatonic Comm Coll (CT)
Howard Comm Coll (MD)
Imperial Valley Coll (CA)
Iowa Lakes Comm Coll (IA)
ITT Tech Inst, Dunmore (PA)
ITT Tech Inst, Harrisburg (PA)
ITT Tech Inst, Levittown (PA)
ITT Tech Inst, Pittsburgh (PA)
ITT Tech Inst, Plymouth Meeting (PA)
ITT Tech Inst, Tarentum (PA)
Jackson Coll (MI)
Jefferson Coll (MO)
Jefferson Comm Coll (NY)
John Tyler Comm Coll (VA)
J. Sargeant Reynolds Comm Coll (VA)
Kankakee Comm Coll (IL)
Kaskaskia Coll (IL)
Kilgore Coll (TX)
Kilian Comm Coll (SD)
Kingsborough Comm Coll of the City U of New York (NY)
Kirtland Comm Coll (MI)
Lake Tahoe Comm Coll (CA)
Lane Comm Coll (OR)
Laramie County Comm Coll (WY)
Lehigh Carbon Comm Coll (PA)
Lenoir Comm Coll (NC)
Lone Star Coll–CyFair (TX)
Lone Star Coll–Kingwood (TX)
Lone Star Coll–Montgomery (TX)
Lone Star Coll–North Harris (TX)
Lone Star Coll–Tomball (TX)
Lone Star Coll–U Park (TX)
Lower Columbia Coll (WA)
Luzerne County Comm Coll (PA)
Macomb Comm Coll (MI)
Manchester Comm Coll (CT)
Massachusetts Bay Comm Coll (MA)
Mesa Comm Coll (AZ)
Metropolitan Comm Coll–Kansas City (MO)
Miami Dade Coll (FL)
Minnesota School of Business–Brooklyn Center (MN)
Mississippi Delta Comm Coll (MS)
Mississippi Gulf Coast Comm Coll (MS)
Missouri State U–West Plains (MO)
Mitchell Comm Coll (NC)
Mohawk Valley Comm Coll (NY)
Monroe Comm Coll (NY)
Mountain Empire Comm Coll (VA)
Mount Wachusett Comm Coll (MA)
Nassau Comm Coll (NY)
Niagara County Comm Coll (NY)
Northeast Texas Comm Coll (TX)
Northern Essex Comm Coll (MA)
North Shore Comm Coll (MA)
NorthWest Arkansas Comm Coll (AR)
Northwest Coll (WY)
Northwestern Connecticut Comm Coll (CT)
Northwest Florida State Coll (FL)
Norwalk Comm Coll (CT)
Oakland Comm Coll (MI)
Onondaga Comm Coll (NY)
Owens Comm Coll, Toledo (OH)
Pasadena City Coll (CA)
Pasco-Hernando State Coll (FL)
Patrick Henry Comm Coll (VA)
Pensacola State Coll (FL)
Piedmont Comm Coll (NC)
Pueblo Comm Coll (CO)
Rappahannock Comm Coll (VA)
Raritan Valley Comm Coll (NJ)
Rio Hondo Coll (CA)
River Valley Comm Coll (NH)
Roane State Comm Coll (TN)
Rock Valley Coll (IL)
Salt Lake Comm Coll (UT)
San Joaquin Valley Coll, Hanford (CA)
San Joaquin Valley Coll, Hesperia (CA)
San Joaquin Valley Coll, Temecula (CA)
Santa Rosa Jr Coll (CA)
Sauk Valley Comm Coll (IL)
Scottsdale Comm Coll (AZ)
Seminole State Coll (OK)
Seminole State Coll of Florida (FL)
Snow Coll (UT)
Somerset Comm Coll (KY)
Southeastern Comm Coll (IA)
Southeastern Comm Coll (NC)
Southern State Comm Coll (OH)
Southern U at Shreveport (LA)
South Florida State Coll (FL)
South Georgia State Coll, Douglas (GA)
South Plains Coll (TX)
Southwestern Illinois Coll (IL)
Southwest Virginia Comm Coll (VA)
Spartanburg Methodist Coll (SC)
Spoon River Coll (IL)
Tallahassee Comm Coll (FL)
Tarrant County Coll District (TX)
Temple Coll (TX)
Texarkana Coll (TX)
Three Rivers Comm Coll (CT)
Tompkins Cortland Comm Coll (NY)
Trident Tech Coll (SC)
Trinity Valley Comm Coll (TX)
Truckee Meadows Comm Coll (NV)
Tunxis Comm Coll (CT)
Tyler Jr Coll (TX)
Umpqua Comm Coll (OR)
U of Arkansas Comm Coll at Morrilton (AR)
U of Hawaii Maui Coll (HI)
Virginia Western Comm Coll (VA)
Western Nevada Coll (NV)
Western Texas Coll (TX)
Western Wyoming Comm Coll (WY)
West Kentucky Comm and Tech Coll (KY)
Wytheville Comm Coll (VA)

CRIMINAL JUSTICE/POLICE SCIENCE
Alexandria Tech and Comm Coll (MN)
Alvin Comm Coll (TX)
Amarillo Coll (TX)
Antelope Valley Coll (CA)
Austin Comm Coll (TX)
Barstow Comm Coll (CA)
Blackhawk Tech Coll (WI)
Borough of Manhattan Comm Coll of the City U of New York (NY)
Bunker Hill Comm Coll (MA)
Butler County Comm Coll (PA)
Butte Coll (CA)
Cape Fear Comm Coll (NC)
Carrington Coll California–Pleasant Hill (CA)
Carroll Comm Coll (MD)
Cayuga County Comm Coll (NY)
Cecil Coll (MD)
Central Ohio Tech Coll (OH)
Century Coll (MN)
Chippewa Valley Tech Coll (WI)
Clark State Comm Coll (OH)
Cleveland State Comm Coll (TN)
Clinton Comm Coll (NY)
Cloud County Comm Coll (KS)
Cochise Coll, Sierra Vista (AZ)
Coll of Marin (CA)
Coll of the Canyons (CA)
Coll of the Desert (CA)
Coll of Western Idaho (ID)
Collin County Comm Coll District (TX)
Columbus State Comm Coll (OH)
Comm Coll of Allegheny County (PA)
The Comm Coll of Baltimore County (MD)
Comm Coll of Rhode Island (RI)
Copiah-Lincoln Comm Coll (MS)
Copper Mountain Coll (CA)
County Coll of Morris (NJ)
Cumberland County Coll (NJ)
Danville Area Comm Coll (IL)
Daytona State Coll (FL)
Dean Coll (MA)
De Anza Coll (CA)
Delaware Tech & Comm Coll, Jack F. Owens Campus (DE)
Delaware Tech & Comm Coll, Stanton/Wilmington Campus (DE)
Delaware Tech & Comm Coll, Terry Campus (DE)
Delta Coll (MI)
Dutchess Comm Coll (NY)
Dyersburg State Comm Coll (TN)
Eastern Arizona Coll (AZ)
Eastern Gateway Comm Coll (OH)
Eastern Wyoming Coll (WY)
Edison Comm Coll (OH)
Elgin Comm Coll (IL)
Erie Comm Coll (NY)
Erie Comm Coll, North Campus (NY)
Erie Comm Coll, South Campus (NY)
Feather River Coll (CA)
Finger Lakes Comm Coll (NY)
Florida State Coll at Jacksonville (FL)
Fox Valley Tech Coll (WI)
Fullerton Coll (CA)
Gadsden State Comm Coll (AL)
Garden City Comm Coll (KS)
Gavilan Coll (CA)
Genesee Comm Coll (NY)
Georgia Highlands Coll (GA)
Golden West Coll (CA)
Grand Rapids Comm Coll (MI)
Grays Harbor Coll (WA)
Greenfield Comm Coll (MA)
Hagerstown Comm Coll (MD)
Halifax Comm Coll (NC)
Harford Comm Coll (MD)
Harrisburg Area Comm Coll (PA)
Hawkeye Comm Coll (IA)
Hocking Coll (OH)
Honolulu Comm Coll (HI)
Hopkinsville Comm Coll (KY)
Houston Comm Coll System (TX)
Hudson County Comm Coll (NJ)
Hutchinson Comm Coll and Area Vocational School (KS)
Iowa Lakes Comm Coll (IA)
Jamestown Comm Coll (NY)
Jefferson Coll (MO)
Jefferson State Comm Coll (AL)
Johnston Comm Coll (NC)
Kankakee Comm Coll (IL)
Kent State U at Tuscarawas (OH)
Kirtland Comm Coll (MI)
Lake Land Coll (IL)
Lakeland Comm Coll (OH)
Lake Region State Coll (ND)
Lake Tahoe Comm Coll (CA)
Lansing Comm Coll (MI)
Lawson State Comm Coll (AL)
Lenoir Comm Coll (NC)
Lincoln Land Comm Coll (IL)
Lorain County Comm Coll (OH)
Los Angeles Mission Coll (CA)
Macomb Comm Coll (MI)
McHenry County Coll (IL)
Mercer County Comm Coll (NJ)
Metropolitan Comm Coll–Kansas City (MO)
Miami Dade Coll (FL)
Middlesex County Coll (NJ)
Mineral Area Coll (MO)
Minneapolis Comm and Tech Coll (MN)
MiraCosta Coll (CA)
Mississippi Gulf Coast Comm Coll (MS)
Missouri State U–West Plains (MO)
Mohave Comm Coll (AZ)
Monroe Comm Coll (NY)
Monroe County Comm Coll (MI)
Montgomery Coll (MD)
Montgomery County Comm Coll (PA)
Moraine Valley Comm Coll (IL)
Mott Comm Coll (MI)
Mt. San Antonio Coll (CA)
Mt. San Jacinto Coll (CA)
Normandale Comm Coll (MN)
Northcentral Tech Coll (WI)
Northeastern Jr Coll (CO)
Northeast Texas Comm Coll (TX)
North Iowa Area Comm Coll (IA)
Northwestern Connecticut Comm Coll (CT)
Northwest Florida State Coll (FL)
Northwest-Shoals Comm Coll (AL)
Oakland Comm Coll (MI)
Oakton Comm Coll (IL)
Ocean County Coll (NJ)
Okefenokee Tech Coll (GA)
Oklahoma State U, Oklahoma City (OK)
Onondaga Comm Coll (NY)
Owens Comm Coll, Toledo (OH)
Palomar Coll (CA)
Piedmont Virginia Comm Coll (VA)
Pima Comm Coll (AZ)
Pitt Comm Coll (NC)
Quinsigamond Comm Coll (MA)
Rappahannock Comm Coll (VA)
Raritan Valley Comm Coll (NJ)
Reading Area Comm Coll (PA)
Rend Lake Coll (IL)
Roane State Comm Coll (TN)
Rogue Comm Coll (OR)
St. Clair County Comm Coll (MI)
San Jacinto Coll District (TX)
San Juan Coll (NM)
Sauk Valley Comm Coll (IL)
Schoolcraft Coll (MI)
Seminole State Coll (OK)
Shawnee Comm Coll (IL)
Southeast Tech Inst (SD)
Southern State Comm Coll (OH)
South Plains Coll (TX)
Southwestern Comm Coll (NC)
Spoon River Coll (IL)
Springfield Tech Comm Coll (MA)
State Fair Comm Coll (MO)
Sullivan County Comm Coll (NY)
Tallahassee Comm Coll (FL)
Temple Coll (TX)
Treasure Valley Comm Coll (OR)
Trinity Valley Comm Coll (TX)
Tulsa Comm Coll (OK)
Tyler Jr Coll (TX)
Victoria Coll (TX)
Victor Valley Coll (CA)
Vincennes U (IN)
Volunteer State Comm Coll (TN)
Walters State Comm Coll (TN)
Waubonsee Comm Coll (IL)
Waukesha County Tech Coll (WI)
Wayne Comm Coll (NC)
Wayne County Comm Coll District (MI)
Wenatchee Valley Coll (WA)
Western Dakota Tech Inst (SD)
Western Nevada Coll (NV)
Western Oklahoma State Coll (OK)
Western Texas Coll (TX)
Westmoreland County Comm Coll (PA)
Wichita Area Tech Coll (KS)
Wisconsin Indianhead Tech Coll (WI)
Wor-Wic Comm Coll (MD)
Wytheville Comm Coll (VA)

CRIMINAL JUSTICE/SAFETY
Alamance Comm Coll (NC)
Altamaha Tech Coll (GA)
American Samoa Comm Coll (AS)
Ancilla Coll (IN)
Augusta Tech Coll (GA)
Bay State Coll (MA)
Berkshire Comm Coll (MA)
Bismarck State Coll (ND)
Blue Ridge Comm and Tech Coll (WV)
Borough of Manhattan Comm Coll of the City U of New York (NY)
Bossier Parish Comm Coll (LA)
Bowling Green State U-Firelands Coll (OH)
Bristol Comm Coll (MA)
Brown Mackie Coll–Cincinnati (OH)
Brown Mackie Coll–Findlay (OH)
Brown Mackie Coll–Hopkinsville (KY)
Brown Mackie Coll–Quad Cities (IA)
Brown Mackie Coll–San Antonio (TX)
Bucks County Comm Coll (PA)
Carrington Coll California–Citrus Heights (CA)
Carrington Coll California–Pleasant Hill (CA)

Carrington Coll California–San Jose (CA)
Catawba Valley Comm Coll (NC)
Central Georgia Tech Coll (GA)
Central Maine Comm Coll (ME)
Century Coll (MN)
Chandler-Gilbert Comm Coll (AZ)
Chattahoochee Tech Coll (GA)
Cleveland Comm Coll (NC)
Coll of the Mainland (TX)
Columbia-Greene Comm Coll (NY)
Cossatot Comm Coll of the U of Arkansas (AR)
Dyersburg State Comm Coll (TN)
Eastern Wyoming Coll (WY)
Fayetteville Tech Comm Coll (NC)
Fiorello H. LaGuardia Comm Coll of the City U of New York (NY)
Galveston Coll (TX)
Genesee Comm Coll (NY)
Georgia Highlands Coll (GA)
Georgia Northwestern Tech Coll (GA)
Georgia Piedmont Tech Coll (GA)
Glendale Comm Coll (AZ)
Gordon State Coll (GA)
Grayson Coll (TX)
Great Basin Coll (NV)
Greenville Tech Coll (SC)
Hinds Comm Coll (MS)
Holyoke Comm Coll (MA)
Ivy Tech Comm Coll–Bloomington (IN)
Ivy Tech Comm Coll–Central Indiana (IN)
Ivy Tech Comm Coll–East Central (IN)
Ivy Tech Comm Coll–Kokomo (IN)
Ivy Tech Comm Coll–North Central (IN)
Ivy Tech Comm Coll–Northwest (IN)
Ivy Tech Comm Coll–Southwest (IN)
Ivy Tech Comm Coll–Wabash Valley (IN)
James Sprunt Comm Coll (NC)
Kent State U at Ashtabula (OH)
Kent State U at East Liverpool (OH)
Kent State U at Salem (OH)
Kent State U at Trumbull (OH)
Kent State U at Tuscarawas (OH)
Lamar Comm Coll (CO)
Lanier Tech Coll (GA)
Lehigh Carbon Comm Coll (PA)
Linn-Benton Comm Coll (OR)
Minneapolis Comm and Tech Coll (MN)
Minnesota State Coll–Southeast Tech (MN)
Monroe Comm Coll (MI)
Moultrie Tech Coll (GA)
Mountain View Coll (TX)
Mount Wachusett Comm Coll (MA)
Nassau Comm Coll (NY)
New Mexico State U–Alamogordo (NM)
Normandale Comm Coll (MN)
Northampton Comm Coll (PA)
North Georgia Tech Coll (GA)
NorthWest Arkansas Comm Coll (AR)
Oregon Coast Comm Coll (OR)
Paris Jr Coll (TX)
Phoenix Coll (AZ)
Pima Comm Coll (AZ)
Pitt Comm Coll (NC)
Potomac State Coll of West Virginia U (WV)
Randolph Comm Coll (NC)
Richmond Comm Coll (NC)
Savannah Tech Coll (GA)
Sheridan Coll (WY)
Southeastern Tech Coll (GA)
Southern Crescent Tech Coll (GA)
South Florida State Coll (FL)
South Georgia Tech Coll (GA)
South Louisiana Comm Coll (LA)
South Piedmont Comm Coll (NC)
South Suburban Coll (IL)
Southwestern Michigan Coll (MI)
Southwest Georgia Tech Coll (GA)
Texarkana Coll (TX)
Treasure Valley Comm Coll (OR)
Walters State Comm Coll (TN)
Wayne Comm Coll (NC)
West Georgia Tech Coll (GA)
Westmoreland County Comm Coll (PA)
Wiregrass Georgia Tech Coll (GA)
York County Comm Coll (ME)

CRIMINOLOGY
Genesee Comm Coll (NY)
Paris Jr Coll (TX)
Western Wyoming Comm Coll (WY)

CRISIS/EMERGENCY/DISASTER MANAGEMENT
Bucks County Comm Coll (PA)
Casper Coll (WY)
Cincinnati State Tech and Comm Coll (OH)
Comm Coll of Rhode Island (RI)
Fayetteville Tech Comm Coll (NC)
Flathead Valley Comm Coll (MT)
Montgomery Coll (MD)
Sullivan County Comm Coll (NY)
Wayne Comm Coll (NC)

CRITICAL INCIDENT RESPONSE/SPECIAL POLICE OPERATIONS
Raritan Valley Comm Coll (NJ)

CROP PRODUCTION
Arizona Western Coll (AZ)
Coll of the Desert (CA)
Dakota Coll at Bottineau (ND)
Greenfield Comm Coll (MA)
Iowa Lakes Comm Coll (IA)
Northeast Iowa Comm Coll (IA)
Northwest Coll (WY)
The Ohio State U Ag Tech Inst (OH)

CULINARY ARTS
Alamance Comm Coll (NC)
Albany Tech Coll (GA)
Arizona Western Coll (AZ)
Atlanta Tech Coll (GA)
Augusta Tech Coll (GA)
Austin Comm Coll (TX)
Bellingham Tech Coll (WA)
Blackhawk Tech Coll (WI)
Blue Ridge Comm and Tech Coll (WV)
Bossier Parish Comm Coll (LA)
Bucks County Comm Coll (PA)
Bunker Hill Comm Coll (MA)
Cape Fear Comm Coll (NC)
Central Ohio Tech Coll (OH)
Central Virginia Comm Coll (VA)
Central Wyoming Coll (WY)
Chattahoochee Tech Coll (GA)
Cincinnati State Tech and Comm Coll (OH)
Clark Coll (WA)
Cochise Coll, Sierra Vista (AZ)
Coll of Southern Idaho (ID)
Coll of the Desert (CA)
Coll of Western Idaho (ID)
Collin County Comm Coll District (TX)
Columbus State Comm Coll (OH)
Commonwealth Tech Inst (PA)
Comm Coll of Allegheny County (PA)
Comm Coll of Philadelphia (PA)
Culinary Inst LeNotre (TX)
Daytona State Coll (FL)
Delaware Tech & Comm Coll, Stanton/Wilmington Campus (DE)
Delaware Tech & Comm Coll, Terry Campus (DE)
East Central Coll (MO)
Elgin Comm Coll (IL)
Erie Comm Coll (NY)
Erie Comm Coll, North Campus (NY)
Fayetteville Tech Comm Coll (NC)
Finger Lakes Comm Coll (NY)
Flathead Valley Comm Coll (MT)
Florida State Coll at Jacksonville (FL)
Fox Valley Tech Coll (WI)
Galveston Coll (TX)
Grand Rapids Comm Coll (MI)
Greenville Tech Coll (SC)
Harrisburg Area Comm Coll (PA)
Hocking Coll (OH)
Houston Comm Coll System (TX)
Hudson County Comm Coll (NJ)
Jefferson Coll (MO)
Kaskaskia Coll (IL)
Lakes Region Comm Coll (NH)
Lincoln Land Comm Coll (IL)
Linn-Benton Comm Coll (OR)
Los Angeles Mission Coll (CA)
Luzerne County Comm Coll (PA)
Macomb Comm Coll (MI)
Mercer County Comm Coll (NJ)
Miami Dade Coll (FL)
Mineral Area Coll (MO)

Minneapolis Comm and Tech Coll (MN)
Mitchell Tech Inst (SD)
Mohave Comm Coll (AZ)
Monroe County Comm Coll (MI)
Montgomery County Comm Coll (PA)
Moraine Park Tech Coll (WI)
Mott Comm Coll (MI)
New England Culinary Inst (VT)
Niagara County Comm Coll (NY)
Northampton Comm Coll (PA)
North Dakota State Coll of Science (ND)
Northeast Texas Comm Coll (TX)
North Georgia Tech Coll (GA)
North Shore Comm Coll (MA)
NorthWest Arkansas Comm Coll (AR)
Oakland Comm Coll (MI)
Ogeechee Tech Coll (GA)
Olympic Coll (WA)
Orange Coast Coll (CA)
Oxnard Coll (CA)
Ozarks Tech Comm Coll (MO)
Phoenix Coll (AZ)
Piedmont Virginia Comm Coll (VA)
Rend Lake Coll (IL)
Salt Lake Comm Coll (UT)
San Jacinto Coll District (TX)
Santa Rosa Jr Coll (CA)
Savannah Tech Coll (GA)
Schoolcraft Coll (MI)
Scottsdale Comm Coll (AZ)
Shelton State Comm Coll (AL)
Sheridan Coll (WY)
Southern Maine Comm Coll (ME)
South Georgia Tech Coll (GA)
South Louisiana Comm Coll (LA)
Southwestern Comm Coll (NC)
Sullivan County Comm Coll (NY)
Texarkana Coll (TX)
Texas State Tech Coll Waco (TX)
Trident Tech Coll (SC)
Truckee Meadows Comm Coll (NV)
Vincennes U (IN)
Walla Walla Comm Coll (WA)
Westchester Comm Coll (NY)
West Kentucky Comm and Tech Coll (KY)
Westmoreland County Comm Coll (PA)
York County Comm Coll (ME)

CULINARY ARTS RELATED
Bristol Comm Coll (MA)
Iowa Lakes Comm Coll (IA)
Linn-Benton Comm Coll (OR)
State U of New York Coll of Technology at Alfred (NY)

CUSTOMER SERVICE MANAGEMENT
Central Oregon Comm Coll (OR)
Comm Coll of Rhode Island (RI)
Delaware Tech & Comm Coll, Stanton/Wilmington Campus (DE)

CUSTOMER SERVICE SUPPORT/ CALL CENTER/TELESERVICE OPERATION
Central Wyoming Coll (WY)
Delaware Tech & Comm Coll, Jack F. Owens Campus (DE)
Delaware Tech & Comm Coll, Stanton/Wilmington Campus (DE)
Lansing Comm Coll (MI)

CYBER/COMPUTER FORENSICS AND COUNTERTERRORISM
Catawba Valley Comm Coll (NC)
Harper Coll (IL)
Pensacola State Coll (FL)
South Piedmont Comm Coll (NC)

CYBER/ELECTRONIC OPERATIONS AND WARFARE
Oklahoma City Comm Coll (OK)

DAIRY HUSBANDRY AND PRODUCTION
Northeast Iowa Comm Coll (IA)
The Ohio State U Ag Tech Inst (OH)

DAIRY SCIENCE
Mt. San Antonio Coll (CA)
Northwest Mississippi Comm Coll (MS)
The Ohio State U Ag Tech Inst (OH)
State U of New York Coll of Technology at Alfred (NY)

DANCE
Austin Comm Coll (TX)
Broward Coll (FL)
Casper Coll (WY)
Coll of Marin (CA)
Darton State Coll (GA)
Dean Coll (MA)
Eastern Florida State Coll (FL)
Fullerton Coll (CA)
Greenfield Comm Coll (MA)
Hinds Comm Coll (MS)
Kilgore Coll (TX)
Lone Star Coll–CyFair (TX)
Mercer County Comm Coll (NJ)
Miami Dade Coll (FL)
MiraCosta Coll (CA)
Mt. San Jacinto Coll (CA)
Nassau Comm Coll (NY)
Northern Essex Comm Coll (MA)
Orange Coast Coll (CA)
Palomar Coll (CA)
Pasadena City Coll (CA)
Raritan Valley Comm Coll (NJ)
San Jacinto Coll District (TX)
Santa Monica Coll (CA)
Santa Rosa Jr Coll (CA)
Snow Coll (UT)
Trinity Valley Comm Coll (TX)
Truckee Meadows Comm Coll (NV)
Tyler Jr Coll (TX)
Westchester Comm Coll (NY)
Western Wyoming Comm Coll (WY)

DATA ENTRY/ MICROCOMPUTER APPLICATIONS
Arizona Western Coll (AZ)
Bellingham Tech Coll (WA)
Brown Mackie Coll–Northern Kentucky (KY)
Bunker Hill Comm Coll (MA)
Chandler-Gilbert Comm Coll (AZ)
Clark Coll (WA)
Comm Coll of Vermont (VT)
Elgin Comm Coll (IL)
Fiorello H. LaGuardia Comm Coll of the City U of New York (NY)
Florida State Coll at Jacksonville (FL)
Galveston Coll (TX)
Gavilan Coll (CA)
Glendale Comm Coll (AZ)
Iowa Lakes Comm Coll (IA)
Lorain County Comm Coll (OH)
Lower Columbia Coll (WA)
Luzerne County Comm Coll (PA)
MiraCosta Coll (CA)
Mississippi Gulf Coast Comm Coll (MS)
Montgomery Coll (MD)
North Dakota State Coll of Science (ND)
Northeast Texas Comm Coll (TX)
North Shore Comm Coll (MA)
Santa Monica Coll (CA)
Seminole State Coll of Florida (FL)
Stark State Coll (OH)
Sullivan County Comm Coll (NY)
Tyler Jr Coll (TX)
Western Wyoming Comm Coll (WY)
Westmoreland County Comm Coll (PA)

DATA ENTRY/ MICROCOMPUTER APPLICATIONS RELATED
Berkeley City Coll (CA)
Blue Ridge Comm and Tech Coll (WV)
Butte Coll (CA)
Florida State Coll at Jacksonville (FL)
Lorain County Comm Coll (OH)
Mississippi Gulf Coast Comm Coll (MS)
Orange Coast Coll (CA)
Pasadena City Coll (CA)
Seminole State Coll of Florida (FL)
Stark State Coll (OH)

DATA MODELING/ WAREHOUSING AND DATABASE ADMINISTRATION
Broward Coll (FL)
Chandler-Gilbert Comm Coll (AZ)
Coll of Marin (CA)
Florida State Coll at Jacksonville (FL)
Lansing Comm Coll (MI)
Quinsigamond Comm Coll (MA)

Santa Monica Coll (CA)
Seminole State Coll of Florida (FL)
Southwestern Illinois Coll (IL)

DATA PROCESSING AND DATA PROCESSING TECHNOLOGY
Allen Comm Coll (KS)
Antelope Valley Coll (CA)
Bainbridge State Coll (GA)
Bristol Comm Coll (MA)
Bronx Comm Coll of the City U of New York (NY)
Copiah-Lincoln Comm Coll (MS)
Dabney S. Lancaster Comm Coll (VA)
Eastern Gateway Comm Coll (OH)
Finger Lakes Comm Coll (NY)
Grayson Coll (TX)
Great Basin Coll (NV)
Greenville Tech Coll (SC)
Hallmark Coll of Technology (TX)
Housatonic Comm Coll (CT)
Iowa Lakes Comm Coll (IA)
Jackson Coll (MI)
Jamestown Comm Coll (NY)
Kingsborough Comm Coll of the City U of New York (NY)
Lamar Comm Coll (CO)
Lamar State Coll–Orange (TX)
Luzerne County Comm Coll (PA)
Mesa Comm Coll (AZ)
Monroe Comm Coll (NY)
Monroe County Comm Coll (MI)
Mt. San Antonio Coll (CA)
Nassau Comm Coll (NY)
Northeastern Tech Coll (SC)
Northern Essex Comm Coll (MA)
NorthWest Arkansas Comm Coll (AR)
Northwest Mississippi Comm Coll (MS)
Orange Coast Coll (CA)
Otero Jr Coll (CO)
Potomac State Coll of West Virginia U (WV)
St. Clair County Comm Coll (MI)
San Diego City Coll (CA)
San Juan Coll (NM)
Seminole State Coll of Florida (FL)
South Plains Coll (TX)
Spartanburg Comm Coll (SC)
State U of New York Coll of Technology at Alfred (NY)
Tech Coll of the Lowcountry (SC)
Temple Coll (TX)
Three Rivers Comm Coll (CT)
Trinity Valley Comm Coll (TX)
Tunxis Comm Coll (CT)
Virginia Western Comm Coll (VA)
Walters State Comm Coll (TN)
Westchester Comm Coll (NY)
Western Wyoming Comm Coll (WY)
Westmoreland County Comm Coll (PA)
Williston State Coll (ND)

DENTAL ASSISTING
Athens Tech Coll (GA)
Bradford School (PA)
Carrington Coll–Boise (ID)
Carrington Coll California–Citrus Heights (CA)
Carrington Coll California–Pleasant Hill (CA)
Carrington Coll California–Sacramento (CA)
Carrington Coll California–San Jose (CA)
Carrington Coll California–San Leandro (CA)
Central Oregon Comm Coll (OR)
Century Coll (MN)
Coll of Marin (CA)
Coll of Southern Idaho (ID)
Coll of Western Idaho (ID)
Comm Care Coll (OK)
Delta Coll (MI)
Eastern Florida State Coll (FL)
Eastern Gateway Comm Coll (OH)
Grayson Coll (TX)
Hinds Comm Coll (MS)
Inst of Business & Medical Careers (CO)
International Business Coll, Indianapolis (IN)
J. Sargeant Reynolds Comm Coll (VA)
Lake Area Tech Inst (SD)
Luzerne County Comm Coll (PA)

Mid-Plains Comm Coll, North Platte (NE)
Minneapolis Comm and Tech Coll (MN)
Mohave Comm Coll (AZ)
Mott Comm Coll (MI)
North Dakota State Coll of Science (ND)
Northern Essex Comm Coll (MA)
Northwest Florida State Coll (FL)
Northwest Tech Coll (MN)
Palomar Coll (CA)
Pasadena City Coll (CA)
Phoenix Coll (AZ)
Pueblo Comm Coll (CO)
Raritan Valley Comm Coll (NJ)
Tallahassee Comm Coll (FL)
Tulsa Comm Coll (OK)
Westmoreland County Comm Coll (PA)
West Virginia Jr Coll–Bridgeport (WV)
Wichita Area Tech Coll (KS)

DENTAL HYGIENE
Amarillo Coll (TX)
Athens Tech Coll (GA)
Atlanta Tech Coll (GA)
Austin Comm Coll (TX)
Bristol Comm Coll (MA)
Broward Coll (FL)
Cape Fear Comm Coll (NC)
Carrington Coll–Boise (ID)
Carrington Coll California–Sacramento (CA)
Carrington Coll California–San Jose (CA)
Carrington Coll–Mesa (AZ)
Catawba Valley Comm Coll (NC)
Central Georgia Tech Coll (GA)
Century Coll (MN)
Chippewa Valley Tech Coll (WI)
Clark Coll (WA)
Collin County Comm Coll District (TX)
Colorado Northwestern Comm Coll (CO)
Columbus State Comm Coll (OH)
Columbus Tech Coll (GA)
The Comm Coll of Baltimore County (MD)
Comm Coll of Philadelphia (PA)
Comm Coll of Rhode Island (RI)
Darton State Coll (GA)
Daytona State Coll (FL)
Delaware Tech & Comm Coll, Stanton/Wilmington Campus (DE)
Delta Coll (MI)
Eastern Florida State Coll (FL)
Erie Comm Coll, North Campus (NY)
Fayetteville Tech Comm Coll (NC)
Florida State Coll at Jacksonville (FL)
Fox Valley Tech Coll (WI)
Georgia Highlands Coll (GA)
Goodwin Coll (CT)
Grand Rapids Comm Coll (MI)
Great Falls Coll Montana State U (MT)
Greenville Tech Coll (SC)
Hagerstown Comm Coll (MD)
Halifax Comm Coll (NC)
Harper Coll (IL)
Harrisburg Area Comm Coll (PA)
Hawkeye Comm Coll (IA)
Hillsborough Comm Coll (FL)
Hinds Comm Coll (MS)
Lake Land Coll (IL)
Lakeland Comm Coll (OH)
Lake Superior Coll (MN)
Lane Comm Coll (OR)
Lansing Comm Coll (MI)
Laramie County Comm Coll (WY)
Lone Star Coll–Kingwood (TX)
Luzerne County Comm Coll (PA)
Miami Dade Coll (FL)
Middlesex County Coll (NJ)
Mississippi Delta Comm Coll (MS)
Mohave Comm Coll (AZ)
Monroe Comm Coll (NY)
Montgomery County Comm Coll (PA)
Mott Comm Coll (MI)
Mount Wachusett Comm Coll (MA)
Normandale Comm Coll (MN)
Northampton Comm Coll (PA)
Northcentral Tech Coll (WI)
North Dakota State Coll of Science (ND)
Northeast Texas Comm Coll (TX)
Oakland Comm Coll (MI)
Ocean County Coll (NJ)
Ogeechee Tech Coll (GA)

Orange Coast Coll (CA)
Owens Comm Coll, Toledo (OH)
Oxnard Coll (CA)
Pasadena City Coll (CA)
Pasco-Hernando State Coll (FL)
Pensacola State Coll (FL)
Phoenix Coll (AZ)
Pima Comm Coll (AZ)
Pueblo Comm Coll (CO)
Quinsigamond Comm Coll (MA)
Raritan Valley Comm Coll (NJ)
Roane State Comm Coll (TN)
Rock Valley Coll (IL)
Salt Lake Comm Coll (UT)
San Joaquin Valley Coll, Hanford (CA)
San Joaquin Valley Coll, Hesperia (CA)
San Joaquin Valley Coll, Ontario (CA)
San Joaquin Valley Coll, Temecula (CA)
San Joaquin Valley Coll, Visalia (CA)
San Juan Coll (NM)
Santa Rosa Jr Coll (CA)
Sheridan Coll (WY)
Shoreline Comm Coll (WA)
Southeastern Tech Coll (GA)
Southern U at Shreveport (LA)
South Florida State Coll (FL)
Springfield Tech Comm Coll (MA)
Stark State Coll (OH)
State Fair Comm Coll (MO)
Tallahassee Comm Coll (FL)
Tarrant County Coll District (TX)
Temple Coll (TX)
Treasure Valley Comm Coll (OR)
Trident Tech Coll (SC)
Truckee Meadows Comm Coll (NV)
Tulsa Comm Coll (OK)
Tunxis Comm Coll (CT)
Tyler Jr Coll (TX)
Virginia Western Comm Coll (VA)
Waukesha County Tech Coll (WI)
Wayne Comm Coll (NC)
Wayne County Comm Coll District (MI)
Westmoreland County Comm Coll (PA)
Wytheville Comm Coll (VA)

DENTAL LABORATORY TECHNOLOGY
Columbus State Comm Coll (OH)
Commonwealth Tech Inst (PA)
Erie Comm Coll, South Campus (NY)
J. Sargeant Reynolds Comm Coll (VA)
Pasadena City Coll (CA)
Pima Comm Coll (AZ)

DENTAL SERVICES AND ALLIED PROFESSIONS RELATED
Gordon State Coll (GA)
Quinsigamond Comm Coll (MA)

DESIGN AND APPLIED ARTS RELATED
County Coll of Morris (NJ)
Howard Comm Coll (MD)
Iowa Lakes Comm Coll (IA)
Kingsborough Comm Coll of the City U of New York (NY)
Mississippi Delta Comm Coll (MS)
Mohawk Valley Comm Coll (NY)
Niagara County Comm Coll (NY)
Oklahoma City Comm Coll (OK)
Onondaga Comm Coll (NY)
Raritan Valley Comm Coll (NJ)
State U of New York Coll of Technology at Alfred (NY)
Tunxis Comm Coll (CT)
U of New Mexico–Los Alamos Branch (NM)
Vincennes U (IN)
Wenatchee Valley Coll (WA)
Westchester Comm Coll (NY)

DESIGN AND VISUAL COMMUNICATIONS
Bristol Comm Coll (MA)
Brookhaven Coll (TX)
Bunker Hill Comm Coll (MA)
Cecil Coll (MD)
Central Virginia Comm Coll (VA)
Coll of Marin (CA)
Elgin Comm Coll (IL)
FIDM/The Fashion Inst of Design & Merchandising, Los Angeles Campus (CA)
FIDM/The Fashion Inst of Design & Merchandising, San Diego Campus (CA)

FIDM/The Fashion Inst of Design & Merchandising, San Francisco Campus (CA)
Florida State Coll at Jacksonville (FL)
Harford Comm Coll (MD)
Harrisburg Area Comm Coll (PA)
Hutchinson Comm Coll and Area Vocational School (KS)
ITT Tech Inst, Duluth (GA)
ITT Tech Inst, Albany (NY)
ITT Tech Inst, Getzville (NY)
ITT Tech Inst, Liverpool (NY)
ITT Tech Inst, Dunmore (PA)
ITT Tech Inst, Harrisburg (PA)
ITT Tech Inst, Levittown (PA)
ITT Tech Inst, Pittsburgh (PA)
ITT Tech Inst, Plymouth Meeting (PA)
ITT Tech Inst, Tarentum (PA)
Ivy Tech Comm Coll–Central Indiana (IN)
Ivy Tech Comm Coll–Columbus (IN)
Ivy Tech Comm Coll–North Central (IN)
Ivy Tech Comm Coll–Southern Indiana (IN)
Ivy Tech Comm Coll–Southwest (IN)
Ivy Tech Comm Coll–Wabash Valley (IN)
Lone Star Coll–CyFair (TX)
Lone Star Coll–Kingwood (TX)
Lone Star Coll–North Harris (TX)
Minneapolis Comm and Tech Coll (MN)
Mt. San Jacinto Coll (CA)
Nassau Comm Coll (NY)
Oklahoma City Comm Coll (OK)
Palomar Coll (CA)
Pima Comm Coll (AZ)
Salt Lake Comm Coll (UT)
San Jacinto Coll District (TX)
Southeastern Tech Coll (GA)
York County Comm Coll (ME)

DESKTOP PUBLISHING AND DIGITAL IMAGING DESIGN
Cincinnati State Tech and Comm Coll (OH)
Coconino Comm Coll (AZ)
Dunwoody Coll of Technology (MN)
Gavilan Coll (CA)
Houston Comm Coll System (TX)
Iowa Lakes Comm Coll (IA)
Kankakee Comm Coll (IL)
Lake Land Coll (IL)
Northeast Iowa Comm Coll (IA)
North Iowa Area Comm Coll (IA)
Northwest Coll (WY)
Palomar Coll (CA)
Pasadena City Coll (CA)
Southeast Tech Inst (SD)
South Louisiana Comm Coll (LA)
Southwestern Illinois Coll (IL)
Sullivan Coll of Technology and Design (KY)
Tulsa Comm Coll (OK)
Umpqua Comm Coll (OR)

DEVELOPMENTAL AND CHILD PSYCHOLOGY
Comm Coll of Vermont (VT)
De Anza Coll (CA)
Iowa Lakes Comm Coll (IA)
Los Angeles Mission Coll (CA)
Mississippi Delta Comm Coll (MS)
San Diego City Coll (CA)
South Plains Coll (TX)
Tarrant County Coll District (TX)
Trinity Valley Comm Coll (TX)

DEVELOPMENTAL SERVICES WORKER
Anoka Tech Coll (MN)

DIAGNOSTIC MEDICAL SONOGRAPHY AND ULTRASOUND TECHNOLOGY
Athens Tech Coll (GA)
Austin Comm Coll (TX)
Bowling Green State U-Firelands Coll (OH)
Broward Coll (FL)
Bunker Hill Comm Coll (MA)
Cape Fear Comm Coll (NC)
Central Ohio Tech Coll (OH)
Chippewa Valley Tech Coll (WI)
Cincinnati State Tech and Comm Coll (OH)
Columbus Tech Coll (GA)
Comm Coll of Allegheny County (PA)
Comm Coll of Rhode Island (RI)
Darton State Coll (GA)

Delaware Tech & Comm Coll, Jack F. Owens Campus (DE)
Delaware Tech & Comm Coll, Stanton/Wilmington Campus (DE)
Delta Coll (MI)
Florida State Coll at Jacksonville (FL)
Greenville Tech Coll (SC)
Harper Coll (IL)
Harrisburg Area Comm Coll (PA)
Hillsborough Comm Coll (FL)
Hinds Comm Coll (MS)
Howard Comm Coll (MD)
Jackson Coll (MI)
Lansing Comm Coll (MI)
Laramie County Comm Coll (WY)
Lone Star Coll–CyFair (TX)
Lorain County Comm Coll (OH)
Lurleen B. Wallace Comm Coll (AL)
Miami Dade Coll (FL)
Montgomery Coll (MD)
Mt. San Jacinto Coll (CA)
Northampton Comm Coll (PA)
Oakland Comm Coll (MI)
Oklahoma City Comm Coll (OK)
Owens Comm Coll, Toledo (OH)
Pennsylvania Coll of Health Sciences (PA)
Pensacola State Coll (FL)
Piedmont Virginia Comm Coll (VA)
Pitt Comm Coll (NC)
San Jacinto Coll District (TX)
San Joaquin Valley Coll, Hanford (CA)
San Joaquin Valley Coll, Hesperia (CA)
San Joaquin Valley Coll, Temecula (CA)
Southeast Tech Inst (SD)
South Piedmont Comm Coll (NC)
Springfield Tech Comm Coll (MA)
Tallahassee Comm Coll (FL)
Temple Coll (TX)
West Kentucky Comm and Tech Coll (KY)
Westmoreland County Comm Coll (PA)

DIESEL MECHANICS TECHNOLOGY
Alexandria Tech and Comm Coll (MN)
Barstow Comm Coll (CA)
Bellingham Tech Coll (WA)
Casper Coll (WY)
Clark Coll (WA)
Clark State Comm Coll (OH)
Coll of Southern Idaho (ID)
Eastern Arizona Coll (AZ)
Eastern Idaho Tech Coll (ID)
Fox Valley Tech Coll (WI)
Grays Harbor Coll (WA)
Great Basin Coll (NV)
Hawkeye Comm Coll (IA)
Hinds Comm Coll (MS)
Illinois Eastern Comm Colls, Wabash Valley College (IL)
Johnston Comm Coll (NC)
J. Sargeant Reynolds Comm Coll (VA)
Kilgore Coll (TX)
Lake Area Tech Inst (SD)
Lane Comm Coll (OR)
Laramie County Comm Coll (WY)
Lincoln Coll of Technology (CO)
Linn-Benton Comm Coll (OR)
Lower Columbia Coll (WA)
Mid-Plains Comm Coll, North Platte (NE)
North Dakota State Coll of Science (ND)
Oklahoma City Comm Coll (OK)
Oklahoma Tech Coll (OK)
Ozarks Tech Comm Coll (MO)
Palomar Coll (CA)
Raritan Valley Comm Coll (NJ)
Rogue Comm Coll (OR)
Salt Lake Comm Coll (UT)
San Jacinto Coll District (TX)
San Juan Coll (NM)
Santa Rosa Jr Coll (CA)
Shelton State Comm Coll (AL)
Sheridan Coll (WY)
Southeast Tech Inst (SD)
South Louisiana Comm Coll (LA)
State U of New York Coll of Technology at Alfred (NY)
Texarkana Coll (TX)
Texas State Tech Coll Waco (TX)
Truckee Meadows Comm Coll (NV)
Vincennes U (IN)
Walla Walla Comm Coll (WA)

Western Wyoming Comm Coll (WY)
Williston State Coll (ND)

DIETETICS
Broward Coll (FL)
Central Oregon Comm Coll (OR)
Cincinnati State Tech and Comm Coll (OH)
Florida State Coll at Jacksonville (FL)
Harper Coll (IL)
Harrisburg Area Comm Coll (PA)
Hocking Coll (OH)
Miami Dade Coll (FL)
Orange Coast Coll (CA)
Owens Comm Coll, Toledo (OH)
Pensacola State Coll (FL)
Shoreline Comm Coll (WA)
South Florida State Coll (FL)
South Plains Coll (TX)
Tarrant County Coll District (TX)
Truckee Meadows Comm Coll (NV)
Vincennes U (IN)
Westchester Comm Coll (NY)

DIETETIC TECHNOLOGY
Chandler-Gilbert Comm Coll (AZ)
Coll of the Desert (CA)
Cosumnes River Coll, Sacramento (CA)
Fiorello H. LaGuardia Comm Coll of the City U of New York (NY)
Harper Coll (IL)
Miami Dade Coll (FL)
Mohawk Valley Comm Coll (NY)
Normandale Comm Coll (MN)
Santa Rosa Jr Coll (CA)
Southern Maine Comm Coll (ME)
Truckee Meadows Comm Coll (NV)
Westmoreland County Comm Coll (PA)

DIETITIAN ASSISTANT
Chandler-Gilbert Comm Coll (AZ)
Comm Coll of Allegheny County (PA)
Erie Comm Coll, North Campus (NY)
Florida State Coll at Jacksonville (FL)
Hillsborough Comm Coll (FL)
Middlesex County Coll (NJ)

DIGITAL ARTS
Clark State Comm Coll (OH)
Fiorello H. LaGuardia Comm Coll of the City U of New York (NY)
Genesee Comm Coll (NY)
Harford Comm Coll (MD)
Pima Comm Coll (AZ)
State U of New York Coll of Technology at Alfred (NY)
Waukesha County Tech Coll (WI)

DIGITAL COMMUNICATION AND MEDIA/MULTIMEDIA
Butler County Comm Coll (PA)
Butte Coll (CA)
Century Coll (MN)
Cochise Coll, Sierra Vista (AZ)
Comm Coll of Vermont (VT)
Delaware Tech & Comm Coll, Terry Campus (DE)
Eastern Florida State Coll (FL)
Finger Lakes Comm Coll (NY)
Hawkeye Comm Coll (IA)
Hinds Comm Coll (MS)
ITT Tech Inst, Wilmington (MA)
ITT Tech Inst, Harrisburg (PA)
Laramie County Comm Coll (WY)
Minneapolis Comm and Tech Coll (MN)
Mt. San Jacinto Coll (CA)
Oklahoma City Comm Coll (OK)
Palomar Coll (CA)
Pasadena City Coll (CA)
Pima Comm Coll (AZ)
Raritan Valley Comm Coll (NJ)
San Jacinto Coll District (TX)
Santa Monica Coll (CA)
Santa Rosa Jr Coll (CA)
Southern Maine Comm Coll (ME)
State U of New York Coll of Technology at Alfred (NY)
Sullivan Coll of Technology and Design (KY)
TCI–The Coll of Technology (NY)
Wayne County Comm Coll District (MI)

DIRECT ENTRY MIDWIFERY
South Louisiana Comm Coll (LA)

DRAFTING AND DESIGN TECHNOLOGY
Albany Tech Coll (GA)

Allen Comm Coll (KS)
Alvin Comm Coll (TX)
Amarillo Coll (TX)
Antelope Valley Coll (CA)
Austin Comm Coll (TX)
Bainbridge State Coll (GA)
Benjamin Franklin Inst of Technology (MA)
Bevill State Comm Coll (AL)
Bishop State Comm Coll (AL)
Bossier Parish Comm Coll (LA)
Brown Mackie Coll–Birmingham (AL)
Brown Mackie Coll–Boise (ID)
Brown Mackie Coll–Kansas City (KS)
Butte Coll (CA)
Carrington Coll California–San Jose (CA)
Casper Coll (WY)
Cayuga County Comm Coll (NY)
Central Carolina Comm Coll (NC)
Central Georgia Tech Coll (GA)
Central Oregon Comm Coll (OR)
Chattahoochee Tech Coll (GA)
Clark State Comm Coll (OH)
Coll of Central Florida (FL)
Coll of Southern Idaho (ID)
Coll of the Desert (CA)
Coll of Western Idaho (ID)
Collin County Comm Coll District (TX)
Columbus Tech Coll (GA)
Comm Coll of Allegheny County (PA)
Comm Coll of Philadelphia (PA)
Copiah-Lincoln Comm Coll (MS)
Crowder Coll (MO)
Dabney S. Lancaster Comm Coll (VA)
Daytona State Coll (FL)
Delaware Tech & Comm Coll, Jack F. Owens Campus (DE)
Delaware Tech & Comm Coll, Stanton/Wilmington Campus (DE)
Delaware Tech & Comm Coll, Terry Campus (DE)
East Central Coll (MO)
Eastern Arizona Coll (AZ)
Eastern Florida State Coll (FL)
Eastern Gateway Comm Coll (OH)
Finger Lakes Comm Coll (NY)
Florida State Coll at Jacksonville (FL)
Fullerton Coll (CA)
Gadsden State Comm Coll (AL)
Garden City Comm Coll (KS)
Gavilan Coll (CA)
Genesee Comm Coll (NY)
Georgia Piedmont Tech Coll (GA)
Gogebic Comm Coll (MI)
Golden West Coll (CA)
Grand Rapids Comm Coll (MI)
Grayson Coll (TX)
Gwinnett Tech Coll (GA)
Hinds Comm Coll (MS)
Hocking Coll (OH)
Honolulu Comm Coll (HI)
Houston Comm Coll System (TX)
Hutchinson Comm Coll and Area Vocational School (KS)
Independence Comm Coll (KS)
Inst of Design and Construction (NY)
ITI Tech Coll (LA)
ITT Tech Inst, Bessemer (AL)
ITT Tech Inst, Madison (AL)
ITT Tech Inst, Mobile (AL)
ITT Tech Inst, Tucson (AZ)
ITT Tech Inst (AR)
ITT Tech Inst, Culver City (CA)
ITT Tech Inst, Lathrop (CA)
ITT Tech Inst, National City (CA)
ITT Tech Inst, Oakland (CA)
ITT Tech Inst, Orange (CA)
ITT Tech Inst, Oxnard (CA)
ITT Tech Inst, Rancho Cordova (CA)
ITT Tech Inst, San Bernardino (CA)
ITT Tech Inst, San Dimas (CA)
ITT Tech Inst, Sylmar (CA)
ITT Tech Inst, Torrance (CA)
ITT Tech Inst, Aurora (CO)
ITT Tech Inst, Westminster (CO)
ITT Tech Inst, Fort Lauderdale (FL)
ITT Tech Inst, Fort Myers (FL)
ITT Tech Inst, Jacksonville (FL)
ITT Tech Inst, Lake Mary (FL)
ITT Tech Inst, Miami (FL)
ITT Tech Inst, Orlando (FL)
ITT Tech Inst, Pensacola (FL)
ITT Tech Inst, St. Petersburg (FL)
ITT Tech Inst, Tallahassee (FL)
ITT Tech Inst, Tampa (FL)
ITT Tech Inst, Atlanta (GA)
ITT Tech Inst, Duluth (GA)
ITT Tech Inst, Kennesaw (GA)
ITT Tech Inst (ID)
ITT Tech Inst, Arlington Heights (IL)
ITT Tech Inst, Oak Brook (IL)
ITT Tech Inst, Fort Wayne (IN)
ITT Tech Inst, Merrillville (IN)
ITT Tech Inst, Newburgh (IN)
ITT Tech Inst, Clive (IA)
ITT Tech Inst, Louisville (KY)
ITT Tech Inst, Baton Rouge (LA)
ITT Tech Inst, St. Rose (LA)
ITT Tech Inst, Owings Mills (MD)
ITT Tech Inst, Canton (MI)
ITT Tech Inst, Dearborn (MI)
ITT Tech Inst, Swartz Creek (MI)
ITT Tech Inst, Troy (MI)
ITT Tech Inst, Wyoming (MI)
ITT Tech Inst, Brooklyn Center (MN)
ITT Tech Inst, Eden Prairie (MN)
ITT Tech Inst, Arnold (MO)
ITT Tech Inst , Earth City (MO)
ITT Tech Inst, Kansas City (MO)
ITT Tech Inst (NE)
ITT Tech Inst, Henderson (NV)
ITT Tech Inst, North Las Vegas (NV)
ITT Tech Inst (NM)
ITT Tech Inst, Albany (NY)
ITT Tech Inst, Getzville (NY)
ITT Tech Inst, Liverpool (NY)
ITT Tech Inst, Cary (NC)
ITT Tech Inst, Charlotte (NC)
ITT Tech Inst, High Point (NC)
ITT Tech Inst, Akron (OH)
ITT Tech Inst, Columbus (OH)
ITT Tech Inst, Dayton (OH)
ITT Tech Inst, Hilliard (OH)
ITT Tech Inst, Maumee (OH)
ITT Tech Inst, Norwood (OH)
ITT Tech Inst, Strongsville (OH)
ITT Tech Inst, Warrensville Heights (OH)
ITT Tech Inst , Youngstown (OH)
ITT Tech Inst, Tulsa (OK)
ITT Tech Inst, Portland (OR)
ITT Tech Inst, Columbia (SC)
ITT Tech Inst, Greenville (SC)
ITT Tech Inst, Myrtle Beach (SC)
ITT Tech Inst, North Charleston (SC)
ITT Tech Inst, Chattanooga (TN)
ITT Tech Inst, Cordova (TN)
ITT Tech Inst, Johnson City (TN)
ITT Tech Inst, Knoxville (TN)
ITT Tech Inst, Nashville (TN)
ITT Tech Inst, Arlington (TX)
ITT Tech Inst, Austin (TX)
ITT Tech Inst, DeSoto (TX)
ITT Tech Inst, Houston (TX)
ITT Tech Inst, Houston (TX)
ITT Tech Inst, Richardson (TX)
ITT Tech Inst, San Antonio (TX)
ITT Tech Inst, San Antonio (TX)
ITT Tech Inst, Waco (TX)
ITT Tech Inst, Webster (TX)
ITT Tech Inst (UT)
ITT Tech Inst, Chantilly (VA)
ITT Tech Inst, Norfolk (VA)
ITT Tech Inst, Richmond (VA)
ITT Tech Inst, Salem (VA)
ITT Tech Inst, Springfield (VA)
ITT Tech Inst, Everett (WA)
ITT Tech Inst, Seattle (WA)
ITT Tech Inst, Spokane Valley (WA)
ITT Tech Inst (WV)
ITT Tech Inst, Green Bay (WI)
ITT Tech Inst , Greenfield (WI)
ITT Tech Inst, Madison (WI)
Ivy Tech Comm Coll–Central Indiana (IN)
Ivy Tech Comm Coll–Columbus (IN)
Ivy Tech Comm Coll–Kokomo (IN)
Ivy Tech Comm Coll–Lafayette (IN)
Ivy Tech Comm Coll–Northeast (IN)
Ivy Tech Comm Coll–Northwest (IN)
Kankakee Comm Coll (IL)
Kilgore Coll (TX)
Lake Area Tech Inst (SD)
Lake Land Coll (IL)
Lane Comm Coll (OR)
Lanier Tech Coll (GA)
Laramie County Comm Coll (WY)
Lawson State Comm Coll (AL)
Lehigh Carbon Comm Coll (PA)
Linn-Benton Comm Coll (OR)
Lone Star Coll–North Harris (TX)
Lorain County Comm Coll (OH)
Luzerne County Comm Coll (PA)
Macomb Comm Coll (MI)
Manhattan Area Tech Coll (KS)
Massachusetts Bay Comm Coll (MA)
Mesa Comm Coll (AZ)
Metropolitan Comm Coll–Kansas City (MO)
Miami Dade Coll (FL)
Mineral Area Coll (MO)
MiraCosta Coll (CA)
Mississippi Gulf Coast Comm Coll (MS)
Mohave Comm Coll (AZ)
Monroe County Comm Coll (MI)
Mott Comm Coll (MI)
Mountain View Coll (TX)
Mt. San Antonio Coll (CA)
Mt. San Jacinto Coll (CA)
Niagara County Comm Coll (NY)
NorthWest Arkansas Comm Coll (AR)
Northwest Florida State Coll (FL)
Northwest Mississippi Comm Coll (MS)
Northwest-Shoals Comm Coll (AL)
Oakland Comm Coll (MI)
Oklahoma City Comm Coll (OK)
Oklahoma State U, Oklahoma City (OK)
Olympic Coll (WA)
Orange Coast Coll (CA)
Palomar Coll (CA)
Paris Jr Coll (TX)
Pasadena City Coll (CA)
Pasco-Hernando State Coll (FL)
Pensacola State Coll (FL)
Pittsburgh Tech Inst, Oakdale (PA)
Rend Lake Coll (IL)
Salt Lake Comm Coll (UT)
San Diego City Coll (CA)
San Jacinto Coll District (TX)
San Juan Coll (NM)
Schoolcraft Coll (MI)
Seminole State Coll of Florida (FL)
Shelton State Comm Coll (AL)
Shoreline Comm Coll (WA)
Southeastern Comm Coll (IA)
Southern Crescent Tech Coll (GA)
Southern Maine Comm Coll (ME)
Southern State Comm Coll (OH)
South Georgia Tech Coll (GA)
South Louisiana Comm Coll (LA)
South Plains Coll (TX)
Sowela Tech Comm Coll (LA)
Stark State Coll (OH)
Sullivan Coll of Technology and Design (KY)
Tallahassee Comm Coll (FL)
Tarrant County Coll District (TX)
Temple Coll (TX)
Texarkana Coll (TX)
Texas State Tech Coll Waco (TX)
Three Rivers Comm Coll (CT)
Treasure Valley Comm Coll (OR)
Trinity Valley Comm Coll (TX)
Truckee Meadows Comm Coll (NV)
Tulsa Comm Coll (OK)
U of Arkansas Comm Coll at Morrilton (AR)
Victoria Coll (TX)
Western Dakota Tech Inst (SD)
Western Nevada Coll (NV)
Wichita Area Tech Coll (KS)
Wiregrass Georgia Tech Coll (GA)
Wytheville Comm Coll (VA)

DRAFTING/DESIGN ENGINEERING TECHNOLOGIES RELATED
Blackhawk Tech Coll (WI)
Comm Coll of Allegheny County (PA)
Dabney S. Lancaster Comm Coll (VA)
De Anza Coll (CA)
Genesee Comm Coll (NY)
Lorain County Comm Coll (OH)
Luzerne County Comm Coll (PA)
Macomb Comm Coll (MI)
Mt. San Antonio Coll (CA)
Niagara County Comm Coll (NY)
Northeastern Tech Coll (SC)
Rock Valley Coll (IL)
Sullivan Coll of Technology and Design (KY)

DRAMA AND DANCE TEACHER EDUCATION
Darton State Coll (GA)
Hutchinson Comm Coll and Area Vocational School (KS)

DRAMATIC/THEATER ARTS
Alabama Southern Comm Coll (AL)
Allen Comm Coll (KS)
Alvin Comm Coll (TX)
Amarillo Coll (TX)
Anoka-Ramsey Comm Coll (MN)
Anoka-Ramsey Comm Coll, Cambridge Campus (MN)
Arizona Western Coll (AZ)
Austin Comm Coll (TX)
Bainbridge State Coll (GA)
Bossier Parish Comm Coll (LA)
Broward Coll (FL)
Bucks County Comm Coll (PA)
Bunker Hill Comm Coll (MA)
Ca&nnada Coll (CA)
Central Wyoming Coll (WY)
Chandler-Gilbert Comm Coll (AZ)
Clark State Comm Coll (OH)
Cochise Coll, Sierra Vista (AZ)
Coll of Marin (CA)
Coll of Southern Idaho (ID)
Coll of the Canyons (CA)
Coll of the Desert (CA)
Coll of the Mainland (TX)
Comm Coll of Allegheny County (PA)
Comm Coll of Rhode Island (RI)
Cosumnes River Coll, Sacramento (CA)
Crowder Coll (MO)
Darton State Coll (GA)
Dean Coll (MA)
De Anza Coll (CA)
Eastern Arizona Coll (AZ)
Eastern Florida State Coll (FL)
Edison Comm Coll (OH)
Finger Lakes Comm Coll (NY)
Fiorello H. LaGuardia Comm Coll of the City U of New York (NY)
Fullerton Coll (CA)
Galveston Coll (TX)
Gavilan Coll (CA)
Genesee Comm Coll (NY)
Gordon State Coll (GA)
Grayson Coll (TX)
Harrisburg Area Comm Coll (PA)
Hinds Comm Coll (MS)
Howard Comm Coll (MD)
Independence Comm Coll (KS)
Kilgore Coll (TX)
Kingsborough Comm Coll of the City U of New York (NY)
Lake Tahoe Comm Coll (CA)
Lansing Comm Coll (MI)
Linn-Benton Comm Coll (OR)
Lorain County Comm Coll (OH)
Los Angeles Mission Coll (CA)
Manchester Comm Coll (CT)
Mercer County Comm Coll (NJ)
Miami Dade Coll (FL)
Minneapolis Comm and Tech Coll (MN)
MiraCosta Coll (CA)
Mississippi Delta Comm Coll (MS)
Mt. San Jacinto Coll (CA)
Nassau Comm Coll (NY)
Niagara County Comm Coll (NY)
Normandale Comm Coll (MN)
Northeastern Jr Coll (CO)
Northeast Texas Comm Coll (TX)
Northern Essex Comm Coll (MA)
Oklahoma City Comm Coll (OK)
Orange Coast Coll (CA)
Otero Jr Coll (CO)
Palomar Coll (CA)
Paris Jr Coll (TX)
Pasadena City Coll (CA)
Pensacola State Coll (FL)
Phoenix Coll (AZ)
San Diego City Coll (CA)
San Jacinto Coll District (TX)
Santa Monica Coll (CA)
Santa Rosa Jr Coll (CA)
Sauk Valley Comm Coll (IL)
Scottsdale Comm Coll (AZ)
Sheridan Coll (WY)
Snow Coll (UT)
South Florida State Coll (FL)
South Georgia State Coll, Douglas (GA)
Spoon River Coll (IL)
Texarkana Coll (TX)
Three Rivers Comm Coll (CT)
Trinity Valley Comm Coll (TX)
Truckee Meadows Comm Coll (NV)
Tulsa Comm Coll (OK)
Tyler Jr Coll (TX)
Umpqua Comm Coll (OR)
Victor Valley Coll (CA)
Vincennes U (IN)
Western Wyoming Comm Coll (WY)

DRAMATIC/THEATER ARTS AND STAGECRAFT RELATED
Bristol Comm Coll (MA)
Genesee Comm Coll (NY)
Oakland Comm Coll (MI)

DRAWING
Cecil Coll (MD)
Copper Mountain Coll (CA)
De Anza Coll (CA)
Iowa Lakes Comm Coll (IA)
Luzerne County Comm Coll (PA)
Northeastern Jr Coll (CO)
Palomar Coll (CA)

DRYWALL INSTALLATION
Palomar Coll (CA)

EARLY CHILDHOOD EDUCATION
Alabama Southern Comm Coll (AL)
Ancilla Coll (IN)
Arizona Western Coll (AZ)
Arkansas State U–Newport (AR)
Austin Comm Coll (TX)
Big Bend Comm Coll (WA)
Blackhawk Tech Coll (WI)
Broward Coll (FL)
Brown Mackie Coll–Atlanta (GA)
Brown Mackie Coll–Cincinnati (OH)
Brown Mackie Coll–Miami (FL)
Bucks County Comm Coll (PA)
Bunker Hill Comm Coll (MA)
Cape Fear Comm Coll (NC)
Carroll Comm Coll (MD)
Catawba Valley Comm Coll (NC)
Central Maine Comm Coll (ME)
Central Ohio Tech Coll (OH)
Central Oregon Comm Coll (OR)
Central Wyoming Coll (WY)
Chippewa Valley Tech Coll (WI)
Cincinnati State Tech and Comm Coll (OH)
Clark Coll (WA)
Clark State Comm Coll (OH)
Cleveland Comm Coll (NC)
Cochise Coll, Sierra Vista (AZ)
Coconino Comm Coll (AZ)
Coll of Central Florida (FL)
Coll of Southern Maryland (MD)
Coll of the Mainland (TX)
Coll of Western Idaho (ID)
Collin County Comm Coll District (TX)
Colorado Northwestern Comm Coll (CO)
Comm Care Coll (OK)
The Comm Coll of Baltimore County (MD)
Comm Coll of Vermont (VT)
Cossatot Comm Coll of the U of Arkansas (AR)
Davis Coll (OH)
Dean Coll (MA)
Delaware Tech & Comm Coll, Jack F. Owens Campus (DE)
Delaware Tech & Comm Coll, Stanton/Wilmington Campus (DE)
Delaware Tech & Comm Coll, Terry Campus (DE)
Eastern Arizona Coll (AZ)
Eastern Florida State Coll (FL)
Eastern Wyoming Coll (WY)
Fayetteville Tech Comm Coll (NC)
Finger Lakes Comm Coll (NY)
Florida Gateway Coll (FL)
Fox Valley Tech Coll (WI)
Garrett Coll (MD)
Gateway Comm and Tech Coll (KY)
Georgia Military Coll (GA)
Glendale Comm Coll (AZ)
Gogebic Comm Coll (MI)
Gordon State Coll (GA)
Grayson Coll (TX)
Greenfield Comm Coll (MA)
Hagerstown Comm Coll (MD)
Halifax Comm Coll (NC)
Harford Comm Coll (MD)
Harper Coll (IL)
Harrisburg Area Comm Coll (PA)
Highland Comm Coll (IL)
Hopkinsville Comm Coll (KY)
Iowa Lakes Comm Coll (IA)
Ivy Tech Comm Coll–Bloomington (IN)
Ivy Tech Comm Coll–Central Indiana (IN)
Ivy Tech Comm Coll–Columbus (IN)
Ivy Tech Comm Coll–East Central (IN)

Ivy Tech Comm Coll–Kokomo (IN)
Ivy Tech Comm Coll–Lafayette (IN)
Ivy Tech Comm Coll–North Central (IN)
Ivy Tech Comm Coll–Northeast (IN)
Ivy Tech Comm Coll–Northwest (IN)
Ivy Tech Comm Coll–Richmond (IN)
Ivy Tech Comm Coll–Southeast (IN)
Ivy Tech Comm Coll–Southern Indiana (IN)
Ivy Tech Comm Coll–Southwest (IN)
Ivy Tech Comm Coll–Wabash Valley (IN)
Jackson Coll (MI)
James Sprunt Comm Coll (NC)
Jamestown Comm Coll (NY)
Jefferson Comm Coll (NY)
Johnston Comm Coll (NC)
Kankakee Comm Coll (IL)
Kingsborough Comm Coll of the City U of New York (NY)
Lakes Region Comm Coll (NH)
Laramie County Comm Coll (WY)
Lehigh Carbon Comm Coll (PA)
Lincoln Land Comm Coll (IL)
Lower Columbia Coll (WA)
Luzerne County Comm Coll (PA)
Minnesota State Coll–Southeast Tech (MN)
Mitchell Comm Coll (NC)
Montgomery Coll (MD)
Moraine Park Tech Coll (WI)
Mott Comm Coll (MI)
New Mexico State U–Alamogordo (NM)
Northampton Comm Coll (PA)
Northcentral Tech Coll (WI)
North Iowa Area Comm Coll (IA)
NorthWest Arkansas Comm Coll (AR)
Norwalk Comm Coll (CT)
Oklahoma State U, Oklahoma City (OK)
Olympic Coll (WA)
Owens Comm Coll, Toledo (OH)
Panola Coll (TX)
Paris Jr Coll (TX)
Pensacola State Coll (FL)
Pima Comm Coll (AZ)
Pitt Comm Coll (NC)
Pueblo Comm Coll (CO)
Randolph Comm Coll (NC)
Richmond Comm Coll (NC)
River Valley Comm Coll (NH)
Roane State Comm Coll (TN)
Santa Rosa Jr Coll (CA)
Sauk Valley Comm Coll (IL)
Sheridan Coll (WY)
Southern Maine Comm Coll (ME)
Southern State Comm Coll (OH)
South Florida State Coll (FL)
South Piedmont Comm Coll (NC)
Southwestern Indian Polytechnic Inst (NM)
Southwestern Michigan Coll (MI)
Springfield Tech Comm Coll (MA)
Tallahassee Comm Coll (FL)
Tech Coll of the Lowcountry (SC)
Tompkins Cortland Comm Coll (NY)
Treasure Valley Comm Coll (OR)
Truckee Meadows Comm Coll (NV)
U of New Mexico–Los Alamos Branch (NM)
Vincennes U (IN)
Walla Walla Comm Coll (WA)
Waukesha County Tech Coll (WI)
Wayne Comm Coll (NC)
Wenatchee Valley Coll (WA)
Western Wyoming Comm Coll (WY)
Westmoreland County Comm Coll (PA)
Wisconsin Indianhead Tech Coll (WI)
Wor-Wic Comm Coll (MD)

ECOLOGY
Broward Coll (FL)
Hocking Coll (OH)
Iowa Lakes Comm Coll (IA)

E-COMMERCE
Augusta Tech Coll (GA)
Brookhaven Coll (TX)
Central Georgia Tech Coll (GA)
Century Coll (MN)
Delaware Tech & Comm Coll, Jack F. Owens Campus (DE)
Delaware Tech & Comm Coll, Terry Campus (DE)
Finger Lakes Comm Coll (NY)
Genesee Comm Coll (NY)
Lane Comm Coll (OR)
Lansing Comm Coll (MI)
North Dakota State Coll of Science (ND)
Palomar Coll (CA)
Pasco-Hernando State Coll (FL)
Piedmont Comm Coll (NC)
Pitt Comm Coll (NC)
Rend Lake Coll (IL)
Wayne County Comm Coll District (MI)
Wiregrass Georgia Tech Coll (GA)

ECONOMICS
Allen Comm Coll (KS)
Austin Comm Coll (TX)
Broward Coll (FL)
Ca&nnada Coll (CA)
Casper Coll (WY)
Cochise Coll, Sierra Vista (AZ)
Coll of the Desert (CA)
Copiah-Lincoln Comm Coll (MS)
Copper Mountain Coll (CA)
Darton State Coll (GA)
De Anza Coll (CA)
Eastern Wyoming Coll (WY)
Edison Comm Coll (OH)
Fullerton Coll (CA)
Georgia Highlands Coll (GA)
Greenfield Comm Coll (MA)
Harford Comm Coll (MD)
Iowa Lakes Comm Coll (IA)
Lansing Comm Coll (MI)
Laramie County Comm Coll (WY)
Linn-Benton Comm Coll (OR)
Lone Star Coll–CyFair (TX)
Miami Dade Coll (FL)
MiraCosta Coll (CA)
Mississippi Delta Comm Coll (MS)
Northeastern Jr Coll (CO)
Oklahoma State U, Oklahoma City (OK)
Orange Coast Coll (CA)
Oxnard Coll (CA)
Palomar Coll (CA)
Potomac State Coll of West Virginia U (WV)
Salt Lake Comm Coll (UT)
Santa Rosa Jr Coll (CA)
Sauk Valley Comm Coll (IL)
Snow Coll (UT)
South Florida State Coll (FL)
Tyler Jr Coll (TX)
Umpqua Comm Coll (OR)
Vincennes U (IN)
Wenatchee Valley Coll (WA)
Western Wyoming Comm Coll (WY)

EDUCATION
American Samoa Comm Coll (AS)
Bainbridge State Coll (GA)
Bay State Coll (MA)
Bossier Parish Comm Coll (LA)
Bowling Green State U-Firelands Coll (OH)
Bucks County Comm Coll (PA)
Bunker Hill Comm Coll (MA)
Butler County Comm Coll (PA)
Carroll Comm Coll (MD)
Cecil Coll (MD)
Central Oregon Comm Coll (OR)
Central Virginia Comm Coll (VA)
Century Coll (MN)
Chipola Coll (FL)
Coll of Southern Idaho (ID)
Coll of Southern Maryland (MD)
The Comm Coll of Baltimore County (MD)
Comm Coll of Philadelphia (PA)
Comm Coll of Vermont (VT)
Copiah-Lincoln Comm Coll (MS)
Crowder Coll (MO)
Cumberland County Coll (NJ)
Dabney S. Lancaster Comm Coll (VA)
Dakota Coll at Bottineau (ND)
Dyersburg State Comm Coll (TN)
East Central Coll (MO)
Eastern Shore Comm Coll (VA)
Edison Comm Coll (OH)
Galveston Coll (TX)
Garden City Comm Coll (KS)
Garrett Coll (MD)
Genesee Comm Coll (NY)
Georgia Military Coll (GA)
Gogebic Comm Coll (MI)
Greenfield Comm Coll (MA)
Hagerstown Comm Coll (MD)
Harford Comm Coll (MD)
Hutchinson Comm Coll and Area Vocational School (KS)
Independence Comm Coll (KS)
Iowa Lakes Comm Coll (IA)
Jackson State Comm Coll (TN)
Kankakee Comm Coll (IL)
Kilian Comm Coll (SD)
Kingsborough Comm Coll of the City U of New York (NY)
Lakes Region Comm Coll (NH)
Laramie County Comm Coll (WY)
Lehigh Carbon Comm Coll (PA)
Lone Star Coll–CyFair (TX)
Lone Star Coll–Kingwood (TX)
Lone Star Coll–Montgomery (TX)
Lone Star Coll–North Harris (TX)
Lone Star Coll–Tomball (TX)
Lorain County Comm Coll (OH)
Luzerne County Comm Coll (PA)
Miami Dade Coll (FL)
Minneapolis Comm and Tech Coll (MN)
Mississippi Delta Comm Coll (MS)
Mississippi Gulf Coast Comm Coll (MS)
Mohave Comm Coll (AZ)
Motlow State Comm Coll (TN)
Mountain View Coll (TX)
New Mexico State U–Alamogordo (NM)
Northeastern Jr Coll (CO)
Northern Essex Comm Coll (MA)
NorthWest Arkansas Comm Coll (AR)
Northwest Mississippi Comm Coll (MS)
Nunez Comm Coll (LA)
Panola Coll (TX)
Paris Jr Coll (TX)
Pensacola State Coll (FL)
Piedmont Virginia Comm Coll (VA)
Pima Comm Coll (AZ)
Potomac State Coll of West Virginia U (WV)
Roane State Comm Coll (TN)
Sauk Valley Comm Coll (IL)
Schoolcraft Coll (MI)
Shoreline Comm Coll (WA)
Snow Coll (UT)
South Louisiana Comm Coll (LA)
South Plains Coll (TX)
Spoon River Coll (IL)
Tech Coll of the Lowcountry (SC)
Trinity Valley Comm Coll (TX)
Tulsa Comm Coll (OK)
Umpqua Comm Coll (OR)
Vincennes U (IN)
Virginia Western Comm Coll (VA)
Volunteer State Comm Coll (TN)
Walters State Comm Coll (TN)
Wenatchee Valley Coll (WA)
Western Texas Coll (TX)
Western Wyoming Comm Coll (WY)
Wor-Wic Comm Coll (MD)
Wytheville Comm Coll (VA)
York County Comm Coll (ME)

EDUCATIONAL/ INSTRUCTIONAL TECHNOLOGY
Bossier Parish Comm Coll (LA)
Gateway Comm and Tech Coll (KY)
Ivy Tech Comm Coll–North Central (IN)
Tarrant County Coll District (TX)
Texas State Tech Coll Waco (TX)
Triangle Tech, Inc.–Pittsburgh School (PA)

EDUCATIONAL LEADERSHIP AND ADMINISTRATION
Glendale Comm Coll (AZ)

EDUCATION (MULTIPLE LEVELS)
Arkansas State U–Newport (AR)
Brookhaven Coll (TX)
Cayuga County Comm Coll (NY)
Delaware Tech & Comm Coll, Jack F. Owens Campus (DE)
Delaware Tech & Comm Coll, Stanton/Wilmington Campus (DE)
Delaware Tech & Comm Coll, Terry Campus (DE)
Genesee Comm Coll (NY)
Mid-South Comm Coll (AR)
Minneapolis Comm and Tech Coll (MN)
Northeast Texas Comm Coll (TX)
Onondaga Comm Coll (NY)
Paris Jr Coll (TX)
San Jacinto Coll District (TX)
South Georgia State Coll, Douglas (GA)
U of Arkansas Comm Coll at Hope (AR)
U of Arkansas Comm Coll at Morrilton (AR)
Westchester Comm Coll (NY)
Western Wyoming Comm Coll (WY)

EDUCATION RELATED
Genesee Comm Coll (NY)
Georgia Highlands Coll (GA)
Kent State U at Salem (OH)
Kent State U at Tuscarawas (OH)
Miami Dade Coll (FL)

EDUCATION (SPECIFIC LEVELS AND METHODS) RELATED
Comm Coll of Allegheny County (PA)
Jefferson Coll (MO)

EDUCATION (SPECIFIC SUBJECT AREAS) RELATED
Comm Coll of Allegheny County (PA)
State Fair Comm Coll (MO)

ELECTRICAL AND ELECTRONIC ENGINEERING TECHNOLOGIES RELATED
Albany Tech Coll (GA)
Benjamin Franklin Inst of Technology (MA)
Blue Ridge Comm and Tech Coll (WV)
Columbus State Comm Coll (OH)
Fox Valley Tech Coll (WI)
Kent State U at Ashtabula (OH)
Kent State U at Trumbull (OH)
Kent State U at Tuscarawas (OH)
Lake Region State Coll (ND)
Miami Dade Coll (FL)
Mohawk Valley Comm Coll (NY)
Moraine Park Tech Coll (WI)
North Dakota State Coll of Science (ND)
Onondaga Comm Coll (NY)
Pasadena City Coll (CA)
Sheridan Coll (WY)
Spencerian Coll–Lexington (KY)
Sullivan Coll of Technology and Design (KY)
Wayne County Comm Coll District (MI)

ELECTRICAL AND ELECTRONICS ENGINEERING
Allen Comm Coll (KS)
Broward Coll (FL)
Carroll Comm Coll (MD)
Fiorello H. LaGuardia Comm Coll of the City U of New York (NY)
Garrett Coll (MD)
Northeast Texas Comm Coll (TX)
Pasadena City Coll (CA)
South Florida State Coll (FL)

ELECTRICAL AND POWER TRANSMISSION INSTALLATION
Benjamin Franklin Inst of Technology (MA)
Delta Coll (MI)
Ivy Tech Comm Coll–Columbus (IN)
Lansing Comm Coll (MI)
Manhattan Area Tech Coll (KS)
Oklahoma State U, Oklahoma City (OK)
Orange Coast Coll (CA)
Piedmont Comm Coll (NC)
Richmond Comm Coll (NC)
Rogue Comm Coll (OR)
San Jacinto Coll District (TX)
Southwestern Illinois Coll (IL)
Western Nevada Coll (NV)
Westmoreland County Comm Coll (PA)

ELECTRICAL AND POWER TRANSMISSION INSTALLATION RELATED
Manhattan Area Tech Coll (KS)

ELECTRICAL, ELECTRONIC AND COMMUNICATIONS ENGINEERING TECHNOLOGY
Alamance Comm Coll (NC)
Allen Comm Coll (KS)
Alvin Comm Coll (TX)
Amarillo Coll (TX)
American Samoa Comm Coll (AS)
Anoka Tech Coll (MN)
Antelope Valley Coll (CA)
Arapahoe Comm Coll (CO)
Athens Tech Coll (GA)
Augusta Tech Coll (GA)
Austin Comm Coll (TX)
Bainbridge State Coll (GA)
Benjamin Franklin Inst of Technology (MA)
Berkshire Comm Coll (MA)
Bishop State Comm Coll (AL)
Bismarck State Coll (ND)
Bowling Green State U-Firelands Coll (OH)
Bronx Comm Coll of the City U of New York (NY)
Butler County Comm Coll (PA)
Cape Fear Comm Coll (NC)
Casper Coll (WY)
Catawba Valley Comm Coll (NC)
Cayuga County Comm Coll (NY)
Cecil Coll (MD)
Central Carolina Comm Coll (NC)
Central Georgia Tech Coll (GA)
Central Ohio Tech Coll (OH)
Central Oregon Comm Coll (OR)
Chattahoochee Tech Coll (GA)
Chattanooga Coll–Medical, Dental and Tech Careers (TN)
Cincinnati State Tech and Comm Coll (OH)
Clark Coll (WA)
Clark State Comm Coll (OH)
Cleveland Comm Coll (NC)
Cleveland Inst of Electronics (OH)
Clinton Comm Coll (NY)
Cochise Coll, Sierra Vista (AZ)
Coconino Comm Coll (AZ)
Collin County Comm Coll District (TX)
Columbia Gorge Comm Coll (OR)
Columbus State Comm Coll (OH)
Columbus Tech Coll (GA)
Comm Coll of Allegheny County (PA)
Copiah-Lincoln Comm Coll (MS)
County Coll of Morris (NJ)
Crowder Coll (MO)
Dabney S. Lancaster Comm Coll (VA)
Daytona State Coll (FL)
Delaware Tech & Comm Coll, Jack F. Owens Campus (DE)
Delaware Tech & Comm Coll, Stanton/Wilmington Campus (DE)
Delaware Tech & Comm Coll, Terry Campus (DE)
Dunwoody Coll of Technology (MN)
Dutchess Comm Coll (NY)
Eastern Gateway Comm Coll (OH)
Eastern Shore Comm Coll (VA)
Edison Comm Coll (OH)
Erie Comm Coll, North Campus (NY)
Fayetteville Tech Comm Coll (NC)
Florida State Coll at Jacksonville (FL)
Fox Valley Tech Coll (WI)
Gadsden State Comm Coll (AL)
Georgia Piedmont Tech Coll (GA)
Golden West Coll (CA)
Grand Rapids Comm Coll (MI)
Grayson Coll (TX)
Great Basin Coll (NV)
Greenville Tech Coll (SC)
Gwinnett Tech Coll (GA)
Hallmark Coll of Technology (TX)
Harper Coll (IL)
Harrisburg Area Comm Coll (PA)
Hawkeye Comm Coll (IA)
Hillsborough Comm Coll (FL)
Hinds Comm Coll (MS)
Hocking Coll (OH)
Honolulu Comm Coll (HI)
Hopkinsville Comm Coll (KY)
Howard Comm Coll (MD)
Hudson County Comm Coll (NJ)
Hutchinson Comm Coll and Area Vocational School (KS)
Iowa Lakes Comm Coll (IA)
Island Drafting and Tech Inst (NY)
ITI Tech Coll (LA)
ITT Tech Inst, Bessemer (AL)
ITT Tech Inst, Madison (AL)
ITT Tech Inst, Mobile (AL)
ITT Tech Inst, Tucson (AZ)
ITT Tech Inst (AR)
ITT Tech Inst, Culver City (CA)
ITT Tech Inst, Lathrop (CA)
ITT Tech Inst, National City (CA)
ITT Tech Inst, Oakland (CA)
ITT Tech Inst, Orange (CA)
ITT Tech Inst, Oxnard (CA)
ITT Tech Inst, Rancho Cordova (CA)
ITT Tech Inst, San Bernardino (CA)
ITT Tech Inst, San Dimas (CA)
ITT Tech Inst, Sylmar (CA)
ITT Tech Inst, Torrance (CA)
ITT Tech Inst, Aurora (CO)
ITT Tech Inst, Westminster (CO)
ITT Tech Inst, Fort Lauderdale (FL)

ITT Tech Inst, Fort Myers (FL)
ITT Tech Inst, Jacksonville (FL)
ITT Tech Inst, Lake Mary (FL)
ITT Tech Inst, Miami (FL)
ITT Tech Inst, Orlando (FL)
ITT Tech Inst, Pensacola (FL)
ITT Tech Inst, St. Petersburg (FL)
ITT Tech Inst, Tallahassee (FL)
ITT Tech Inst, Atlanta (GA)
ITT Tech Inst, Kennesaw (GA)
ITT Tech Inst (ID)
ITT Tech Inst, Arlington Heights (IL)
ITT Tech Inst, Oak Brook (IL)
ITT Tech Inst, Orland Park (IL)
ITT Tech Inst, Fort Wayne (IN)
ITT Tech Inst, Merrillville (IN)
ITT Tech Inst, Newburgh (IN)
ITT Tech Inst, Clive (IA)
ITT Tech Inst, Louisville (KY)
ITT Tech Inst, Baton Rouge (LA)
ITT Tech Inst, St. Rose (LA)
ITT Tech Inst, Owings Mills (MD)
ITT Tech Inst, Canton (MI)
ITT Tech Inst, Dearborn (MI)
ITT Tech Inst, Swartz Creek (MI)
ITT Tech Inst, Troy (MI)
ITT Tech Inst, Wyoming (MI)
ITT Tech Inst, Brooklyn Center (MN)
ITT Tech Inst, Eden Prairie (MN)
ITT Tech Inst, Arnold (MO)
ITT Tech Inst , Earth City (MO)
ITT Tech Inst, Kansas City (MO)
ITT Tech Inst (NE)
ITT Tech Inst, Henderson (NV)
ITT Tech Inst, North Las Vegas (NV)
ITT Tech Inst (NM)
ITT Tech Inst, Albany (NY)
ITT Tech Inst, Getzville (NY)
ITT Tech Inst, Liverpool (NY)
ITT Tech Inst, Cary (NC)
ITT Tech Inst, Charlotte (NC)
ITT Tech Inst, High Point (NC)
ITT Tech Inst, Akron (OH)
ITT Tech Inst, Columbus (OH)
ITT Tech Inst, Dayton (OH)
ITT Tech Inst, Hilliard (OH)
ITT Tech Inst, Maumee (OH)
ITT Tech Inst, Norwood (OH)
ITT Tech Inst, Strongsville (OH)
ITT Tech Inst, Warrensville Heights (OH)
ITT Tech Inst , Youngstown (OH)
ITT Tech Inst, Tulsa (OK)
ITT Tech Inst, Portland (OR)
ITT Tech Inst, Columbia (SC)
ITT Tech Inst, Greenville (SC)
ITT Tech Inst, Myrtle Beach (SC)
ITT Tech Inst, North Charleston (SC)
ITT Tech Inst, Chattanooga (TN)
ITT Tech Inst, Cordova (TN)
ITT Tech Inst, Johnson City (TN)
ITT Tech Inst, Knoxville (TN)
ITT Tech Inst, Nashville (TN)
ITT Tech Inst, Arlington (TX)
ITT Tech Inst, Austin (TX)
ITT Tech Inst, DeSoto (TX)
ITT Tech Inst, Houston (TX)
ITT Tech Inst, Houston (TX)
ITT Tech Inst, Richardson (TX)
ITT Tech Inst, San Antonio (TX)
ITT Tech Inst, San Antonio (TX)
ITT Tech Inst, Waco (TX)
ITT Tech Inst, Webster (TX)
ITT Tech Inst (UT)
ITT Tech Inst, Chantilly (VA)
ITT Tech Inst, Norfolk (VA)
ITT Tech Inst, Richmond (VA)
ITT Tech Inst, Salem (VA)
ITT Tech Inst, Springfield (VA)
ITT Tech Inst, Everett (WA)
ITT Tech Inst, Seattle (WA)
ITT Tech Inst, Spokane Valley (WA)
ITT Tech Inst (WV)
ITT Tech Inst, Green Bay (WI)
ITT Tech Inst , Greenfield (WI)
ITT Tech Inst, Madison (WI)
Ivy Tech Comm Coll–Bloomington (IN)
Ivy Tech Comm Coll–Central Indiana (IN)
Ivy Tech Comm Coll–Columbus (IN)
Ivy Tech Comm Coll–East Central (IN)
Ivy Tech Comm Coll–Kokomo (IN)
Ivy Tech Comm Coll–Lafayette (IN)
Ivy Tech Comm Coll–North Central (IN)
Ivy Tech Comm Coll–Northeast (IN)
Ivy Tech Comm Coll–Northwest (IN)
Ivy Tech Comm Coll–Richmond (IN)
Ivy Tech Comm Coll–Southeast (IN)
Ivy Tech Comm Coll–Southern Indiana (IN)
Ivy Tech Comm Coll–Southwest (IN)
Ivy Tech Comm Coll–Wabash Valley (IN)
Jackson Coll (MI)
Jamestown Comm Coll (NY)
Jefferson Coll (MO)
Kaskaskia Coll (IL)
Kent State U at Trumbull (OH)
Kilgore Coll (TX)
Kirtland Comm Coll (MI)
Lake Area Tech Inst (SD)
Lake Land Coll (IL)
Lakeland Comm Coll (OH)
Lake Superior Coll (MN)
Lane Comm Coll (OR)
Lanier Tech Coll (GA)
Lehigh Carbon Comm Coll (PA)
Lincoln Land Comm Coll (IL)
Lone Star Coll–CyFair (TX)
Lone Star Coll–Tomball (TX)
Lorain County Comm Coll (OH)
Luzerne County Comm Coll (PA)
Macomb Comm Coll (MI)
Mercer County Comm Coll (NJ)
Mesa Comm Coll (AZ)
Metropolitan Comm Coll–Kansas City (MO)
Miami Dade Coll (FL)
Middlesex County Coll (NJ)
Mineral Area Coll (MO)
Minnesota State Coll–Southeast Tech (MN)
Mississippi Delta Comm Coll (MS)
Mississippi Gulf Coast Comm Coll (MS)
Mitchell Comm Coll (NC)
Mohawk Valley Comm Coll (NY)
Monroe Comm Coll (NY)
Monroe County Comm Coll (MI)
Montgomery County Comm Coll (PA)
Mott Comm Coll (MI)
Moultrie Tech Coll (GA)
Mountain Empire Comm Coll (VA)
Mountain View Coll (TX)
Mt. San Antonio Coll (CA)
New Mexico State U–Alamogordo (NM)
Northampton Comm Coll (PA)
Northeastern Tech Coll (SC)
Northeast Iowa Comm Coll (IA)
Northern Essex Comm Coll (MA)
North Iowa Area Comm Coll (IA)
NorthWest Arkansas Comm Coll (AR)
Northwestern Connecticut Comm Coll (CT)
Northwest Florida State Coll (FL)
Northwest Mississippi Comm Coll (MS)
Oakland Comm Coll (MI)
Oakton Comm Coll (IL)
Oklahoma City Comm Coll (OK)
Oklahoma State U, Oklahoma City (OK)
Olympic Coll (WA)
Onondaga Comm Coll (NY)
Orange Coast Coll (CA)
Owens Comm Coll, Toledo (OH)
Ozarks Tech Comm Coll (MO)
Paris Jr Coll (TX)
Penn State Brandywine (PA)
Penn State DuBois (PA)
Penn State Fayette, The Eberly Campus (PA)
Penn State Hazleton (PA)
Penn State New Kensington (PA)
Penn State Schuylkill (PA)
Penn State Wilkes-Barre (PA)
Penn State Worthington Scranton (PA)
Penn State York (PA)
Pennsylvania Inst of Technology (PA)
Pensacola State Coll (FL)
Pitt Comm Coll (NC)
Pittsburgh Tech Inst, Oakdale (PA)
Potomac State Coll of West Virginia U (WV)
Pueblo Comm Coll (CO)
Quinsigamond Comm Coll (MA)
Reid State Tech Coll (AL)
Rend Lake Coll (IL)
Richmond Comm Coll (NC)
Rock Valley Coll (IL)
Rogue Comm Coll (OR)
St. Clair County Comm Coll (MI)
Salt Lake Comm Coll (UT)
San Diego City Coll (CA)
San Jacinto Coll District (TX)
San Juan Coll (NM)
Santa Rosa Jr Coll (CA)
Sauk Valley Comm Coll (IL)
Savannah Tech Coll (GA)
Schoolcraft Coll (MI)
Scottsdale Comm Coll (AZ)
Seminole State Coll of Florida (FL)
Shawnee Comm Coll (IL)
Shelton State Comm Coll (AL)
Southeastern Comm Coll (IA)
Southeastern Comm Coll (NC)
Southeastern Tech Coll (GA)
Southeast Tech Inst (SD)
Southern Crescent Tech Coll (GA)
Southern Maine Comm Coll (ME)
Southern State Comm Coll (OH)
Southern U at Shreveport (LA)
South Florida State Coll (FL)
South Georgia Tech Coll (GA)
South Plains Coll (TX)
South Suburban Coll (IL)
Southwestern Comm Coll (NC)
Southwestern Illinois Coll (IL)
Southwest Virginia Comm Coll (VA)
Spartanburg Comm Coll (SC)
Spencerian Coll–Lexington (KY)
Spoon River Coll (IL)
Springfield Tech Comm Coll (MA)
State U of New York Coll of Technology at Alfred (NY)
Sullivan Coll of Technology and Design (KY)
Sullivan County Comm Coll (NY)
Tarrant County Coll District (TX)
Texarkana Coll (TX)
Texas State Tech Coll Waco (TX)
Three Rivers Comm Coll (CT)
Tompkins Cortland Comm Coll (NY)
Trident Tech Coll (SC)
Tulsa Comm Coll (OK)
Umpqua Comm Coll (OR)
U of Arkansas Comm Coll at Hope (AR)
U of New Mexico–Los Alamos Branch (NM)
Victoria Coll (TX)
Victor Valley Coll (CA)
Vincennes U (IN)
Virginia Western Comm Coll (VA)
Waubonsee Comm Coll (IL)
Waukesha County Tech Coll (WI)
Wayne Comm Coll (NC)
Wayne County Comm Coll District (MI)
Westchester Comm Coll (NY)
Western Nevada Coll (NV)
Western Wyoming Comm Coll (WY)
West Georgia Tech Coll (GA)
Westmoreland County Comm Coll (PA)
The Williamson Free School of Mecha Trades (PA)
Wor-Wic Comm Coll (MD)
Wytheville Comm Coll (VA)

ELECTRICAL/ELECTRONICS DRAFTING AND CAD/CADD

Dunwoody Coll of Technology (MN)
Palomar Coll (CA)

ELECTRICAL/ELECTRONICS EQUIPMENT INSTALLATION AND REPAIR

Arizona Western Coll (AZ)
Barstow Comm Coll (CA)
Cape Fear Comm Coll (NC)
Fullerton Coll (CA)
Hinds Comm Coll (MS)
Hutchinson Comm Coll and Area Vocational School (KS)
Iowa Lakes Comm Coll (IA)
Lake Area Tech Inst (SD)
Lake Region State Coll (ND)
Lakes Region Comm Coll (NH)
Macomb Comm Coll (MI)
Mesabi Range Comm and Tech Coll (MN)
Orange Coast Coll (CA)
Palomar Coll (CA)
Pima Comm Coll (AZ)
Pittsburgh Tech Inst, Oakdale (PA)
Schoolcraft Coll (MI)
Southeast Tech Inst (SD)
State U of New York Coll of Technology at Alfred (NY)
Sullivan Coll of Technology and Design (KY)
Wenatchee Valley Coll (WA)
Western Wyoming Comm Coll (WY)

ELECTRICAL/ELECTRONICS MAINTENANCE AND REPAIR TECHNOLOGY RELATED

Brown Mackie Coll–Louisville (KY)
Bunker Hill Comm Coll (MA)
Mohawk Valley Comm Coll (NY)
Pima Comm Coll (AZ)
Pitt Comm Coll (NC)
Sullivan Coll of Technology and Design (KY)

ELECTRICIAN

Barstow Comm Coll (CA)
Bellingham Tech Coll (WA)
Bevill State Comm Coll (AL)
Cleveland Comm Coll (NC)
Coll of Southern Maryland (MD)
Danville Area Comm Coll (IL)
Delta Coll (MI)
Dunwoody Coll of Technology (MN)
Fayetteville Tech Comm Coll (NC)
Flathead Valley Comm Coll (MT)
Grayson Coll (TX)
Harrisburg Area Comm Coll (PA)
Hinds Comm Coll (MS)
Ivy Tech Comm Coll–Bloomington (IN)
Ivy Tech Comm Coll–Central Indiana (IN)
Ivy Tech Comm Coll–East Central (IN)
Ivy Tech Comm Coll–Kokomo (IN)
Ivy Tech Comm Coll–Lafayette (IN)
Ivy Tech Comm Coll–North Central (IN)
Ivy Tech Comm Coll–Northeast (IN)
Ivy Tech Comm Coll–Northwest (IN)
Ivy Tech Comm Coll–Richmond (IN)
Ivy Tech Comm Coll–Southern Indiana (IN)
Ivy Tech Comm Coll–Southwest (IN)
Ivy Tech Comm Coll–Wabash Valley (IN)
Lake Superior Coll (MN)
Lansing Comm Coll (MI)
Luzerne County Comm Coll (PA)
Mitchell Comm Coll (NC)
Mitchell Tech Inst (SD)
New Mexico State U–Alamogordo (NM)
Northampton Comm Coll (PA)
Northeast Iowa Comm Coll (IA)
Northwest Coll (WY)
Oakland Comm Coll (MI)
Palomar Coll (CA)
Piedmont Comm Coll (NC)
Pitt Comm Coll (NC)
Randolph Comm Coll (NC)
Rend Lake Coll (IL)
Rock Valley Coll (IL)
Shelton State Comm Coll (AL)
South Louisiana Comm Coll (LA)
South Piedmont Comm Coll (NC)
Southwestern Illinois Coll (IL)
Sowela Tech Comm Coll (LA)
State U of New York Coll of Technology at Alfred (NY)
Triangle Tech, Inc.–Pittsburgh School (PA)
Walla Walla Comm Coll (WA)
Waubonsee Comm Coll (IL)
Western Dakota Tech Inst (SD)
Western Wyoming Comm Coll (WY)
West Kentucky Comm and Tech Coll (KY)

ELECTROCARDIOGRAPH TECHNOLOGY

Delaware Tech & Comm Coll, Stanton/Wilmington Campus (DE)
Oklahoma State U, Oklahoma City (OK)
Pennsylvania Coll of Health Sciences (PA)

ELECTROMECHANICAL AND INSTRUMENTATION AND MAINTENANCE TECHNOLOGIES RELATED

Cape Fear Comm Coll (NC)
Catawba Valley Comm Coll (NC)
Greenville Tech Coll (SC)
Mitchell Comm Coll (NC)
Piedmont Comm Coll (NC)
Pitt Comm Coll (NC)
Pueblo Comm Coll (CO)
Randolph Comm Coll (NC)
Richmond Comm Coll (NC)
South Piedmont Comm Coll (NC)
Sullivan Coll of Technology and Design (KY)
Tulsa Comm Coll (OK)
Waukesha County Tech Coll (WI)
Wayne Comm Coll (NC)

ELECTROMECHANICAL TECHNOLOGY

Blackhawk Tech Coll (WI)
Bowling Green State U-Firelands Coll (OH)
Bristol Comm Coll (MA)
Central Maine Comm Coll (ME)
Chandler-Gilbert Comm Coll (AZ)
Chippewa Valley Tech Coll (WI)
Cincinnati State Tech and Comm Coll (OH)
Coll of the Ouachitas (AR)
Columbus State Comm Coll (OH)
Comm Coll of Rhode Island (RI)
Delaware Tech & Comm Coll, Terry Campus (DE)
Edison Comm Coll (OH)
Fox Valley Tech Coll (WI)
Galveston Coll (TX)
Georgia Piedmont Tech Coll (GA)
Kirtland Comm Coll (MI)
Lake Area Tech Inst (SD)
Lake Land Coll (IL)
Lansing Comm Coll (MI)
Macomb Comm Coll (MI)
Montgomery County Comm Coll (PA)
Moraine Park Tech Coll (WI)
Motlow State Comm Coll (TN)
Northampton Comm Coll (PA)
Northcentral Tech Coll (WI)
Oakland Comm Coll (MI)
Paris Jr Coll (TX)
Quinsigamond Comm Coll (MA)
Richmond Comm Coll (NC)
Southeast Tech Inst (SD)
Southern State Comm Coll (OH)
South Piedmont Comm Coll (NC)
Springfield Tech Comm Coll (MA)
State U of New York Coll of Technology at Alfred (NY)
Tarrant County Coll District (TX)
Texas State Tech Coll Waco (TX)
Wayne County Comm Coll District (MI)

ELECTRONEURODIAGNOSTIC/ ELECTROENCEPHALOGRAPHIC TECHNOLOGY

Catawba Valley Comm Coll (NC)
Collin County Comm Coll District (TX)
Comm Coll of Allegheny County (PA)
Harford Comm Coll (MD)
Lincoln Land Comm Coll (IL)
Minneapolis Comm and Tech Coll (MN)
Southeast Tech Inst (SD)

ELEMENTARY EDUCATION

Alabama Southern Comm Coll (AL)
Allen Comm Coll (KS)
Amarillo Coll (TX)
Ancilla Coll (IN)
Arizona Western Coll (AZ)
Bainbridge State Coll (GA)
Broward Coll (FL)
Butler County Comm Coll (PA)
Carl Albert State Coll (OK)
Carroll Comm Coll (MD)
Casper Coll (WY)
Cecil Coll (MD)
Central Wyoming Coll (WY)
Chandler-Gilbert Comm Coll (AZ)
Cleveland Comm Coll (NC)
Cochise Coll, Sierra Vista (AZ)
Coconino Comm Coll (AZ)
Coll of Southern Idaho (ID)
Coll of Southern Maryland (MD)
Coll of Western Idaho (ID)
The Comm Coll of Baltimore County (MD)
Copiah-Lincoln Comm Coll (MS)
Crowder Coll (MO)
Delaware Tech & Comm Coll, Jack F. Owens Campus (DE)
Delaware Tech & Comm Coll, Stanton/Wilmington Campus (DE)
Delaware Tech & Comm Coll, Terry Campus (DE)
Eastern Arizona Coll (AZ)
Eastern Wyoming Coll (WY)
Erie Comm Coll (NY)
Fayetteville Tech Comm Coll (NC)
Frank Phillips Coll (TX)

Garrett Coll (MD)
Genesee Comm Coll (NY)
Gogebic Comm Coll (MI)
Grayson Coll (TX)
Great Basin Coll (NV)
Hagerstown Comm Coll (MD)
Harford Comm Coll (MD)
Harper Coll (IL)
Hinds Comm Coll (MS)
Howard Comm Coll (MD)
Iowa Lakes Comm Coll (IA)
James Sprunt Comm Coll (NC)
Jamestown Comm Coll (NY)
Kankakee Comm Coll (IL)
Kilgore Coll (TX)
Kingsborough Comm Coll of the City U of New York (NY)
Lansing Comm Coll (MI)
Lenoir Comm Coll (NC)
Linn-Benton Comm Coll (OR)
Lorain County Comm Coll (OH)
Miami Dade Coll (FL)
Mississippi Delta Comm Coll (MS)
Mississippi Gulf Coast Comm Coll (MS)
Mitchell Comm Coll (NC)
Monroe County Comm Coll (MI)
Montgomery Coll (MD)
Montgomery County Comm Coll (PA)
Niagara County Comm Coll (NY)
Normandale Comm Coll (MN)
Northeastern Jr Coll (CO)
Northern Essex Comm Coll (MA)
Northwest Coll (WY)
Northwest Mississippi Comm Coll (MS)
Oklahoma City Comm Coll (OK)
Otero Jr Coll (CO)
Paris Jr Coll (TX)
Pensacola State Coll (FL)
Phoenix Coll (AZ)
Piedmont Comm Coll (NC)
Pima Comm Coll (AZ)
Pitt Comm Coll (NC)
Potomac State Coll of West Virginia U (WV)
Quinsigamond Comm Coll (MA)
Reading Area Comm Coll (PA)
Richmond Comm Coll (NC)
Roane State Comm Coll (TN)
San Jacinto Coll District (TX)
San Juan Coll (NM)
Sauk Valley Comm Coll (IL)
Seminole State Coll (OK)
Sheridan Coll (WY)
Snow Coll (UT)
South Florida State Coll (FL)
South Piedmont Comm Coll (NC)
Springfield Tech Comm Coll (MA)
Sullivan County Comm Coll (NY)
Treasure Valley Comm Coll (OR)
Trinity Valley Comm Coll (TX)
Truckee Meadows Comm Coll (NV)
Umpqua Comm Coll (OR)
Vincennes U (IN)
Walla Walla Comm Coll (WA)
Wayne Comm Coll (NC)
Wayne County Comm Coll District (MI)
Western Wyoming Comm Coll (WY)
Wor-Wic Comm Coll (MD)

EMERGENCY CARE ATTENDANT (EMT AMBULANCE)
Coconino Comm Coll (AZ)
Delaware Tech & Comm Coll, Stanton/Wilmington Campus (DE)
Illinois Eastern Comm Colls, Frontier Community College (IL)
Iowa Lakes Comm Coll (IA)
J. Sargeant Reynolds Comm Coll (VA)
Mohawk Valley Comm Coll (NY)
Waubonsee Comm Coll (IL)

EMERGENCY MEDICAL TECHNOLOGY (EMT PARAMEDIC)
Allen Comm Coll (KS)
Alvin Comm Coll (TX)
Amarillo Coll (TX)
Arapahoe Comm Coll (CO)
Arizona Western Coll (AZ)
Arkansas State U–Newport (AR)
Athens Tech Coll (GA)
Augusta Tech Coll (GA)
Austin Comm Coll (TX)
Barstow Comm Coll (CA)
Bevill State Comm Coll (AL)
Bishop State Comm Coll (AL)
Bismarck State Coll (ND)

Blue Ridge Comm and Tech Coll (WV)
Borough of Manhattan Comm Coll of the City U of New York (NY)
Bossier Parish Comm Coll (LA)
Brookhaven Coll (TX)
Broward Coll (FL)
Brown Mackie Coll–Northern Kentucky (KY)
Butte Coll (CA)
Carroll Comm Coll (MD)
Casper Coll (WY)
Catawba Valley Comm Coll (NC)
Cecil Coll (MD)
Central Ohio Tech Coll (OH)
Central Oregon Comm Coll (OR)
Central Virginia Comm Coll (VA)
Century Coll (MN)
Chippewa Valley Tech Coll (WI)
Cincinnati State Tech and Comm Coll (OH)
Clark Coll (WA)
Clark State Comm Coll (OH)
Cleveland Comm Coll (NC)
Cochise Coll, Sierra Vista (AZ)
Coll of Central Florida (FL)
Coll of Southern Idaho (ID)
Coll of Southern Maryland (MD)
Collin County Comm Coll District (TX)
Colorado Northwestern Comm Coll (CO)
Columbia Coll (CA)
Columbus State Comm Coll (OH)
Columbus Tech Coll (GA)
The Comm Coll of Baltimore County (MD)
Crowder Coll (MO)
Darton State Coll (GA)
Daytona State Coll (FL)
Delaware Tech & Comm Coll, Jack F. Owens Campus (DE)
Delaware Tech & Comm Coll, Stanton/Wilmington Campus (DE)
Delaware Tech & Comm Coll, Terry Campus (DE)
Dutchess Comm Coll (NY)
Dyersburg State Comm Coll (TN)
East Central Coll (MO)
Eastern Arizona Coll (AZ)
Eastern Florida State Coll (FL)
Eastern Gateway Comm Coll (OH)
Erie Comm Coll, South Campus (NY)
Fayetteville Tech Comm Coll (NC)
Finger Lakes Comm Coll (NY)
Fiorello H. LaGuardia Comm Coll of the City U of New York (NY)
Flathead Valley Comm Coll (MT)
Florida Gateway Coll (FL)
Florida State Coll at Jacksonville (FL)
Fox Valley Tech Coll (WI)
Gadsden State Comm Coll (AL)
Galveston Coll (TX)
Garden City Comm Coll (KS)
Glendale Comm Coll (AZ)
Grayson Coll (TX)
Great Falls Coll Montana State U (MT)
Greenville Tech Coll (SC)
Gwinnett Tech Coll (GA)
Hagerstown Comm Coll (MD)
Harper Coll (IL)
Harrisburg Area Comm Coll (PA)
Herkimer County Comm Coll (NY)
Highland Comm Coll (IL)
Hillsborough Comm Coll (FL)
Hinds Comm Coll (MS)
Hocking Coll (OH)
Houston Comm Coll System (TX)
Howard Comm Coll (MD)
Hudson County Comm Coll (NJ)
Hutchinson Comm Coll and Area Vocational School (KS)
Ivy Tech Comm Coll–Bloomington (IN)
Ivy Tech Comm Coll–Kokomo (IN)
Ivy Tech Comm Coll–North Central (IN)
Ivy Tech Comm Coll–Southwest (IN)
Ivy Tech Comm Coll–Wabash Valley (IN)
Jackson Coll (MI)
Jefferson Coll (MO)
Jefferson Comm Coll (NY)
Jefferson State Comm Coll (AL)
J. Sargeant Reynolds Comm Coll (VA)
Kankakee Comm Coll (IL)
Kaskaskia Coll (IL)
Kent State U at Trumbull (OH)
Kilgore Coll (TX)

Kirtland Comm Coll (MI)
Lake Area Tech Inst (SD)
Lamar Comm Coll (CO)
Lane Comm Coll (OR)
Lansing Comm Coll (MI)
Laramie County Comm Coll (WY)
Lincoln Land Comm Coll (IL)
Lone Star Coll–CyFair (TX)
Lone Star Coll–North Harris (TX)
Lurleen B. Wallace Comm Coll (AL)
Luzerne County Comm Coll (PA)
Macomb Comm Coll (MI)
McHenry County Coll (IL)
Metropolitan Comm Coll–Kansas City (MO)
Miami Dade Coll (FL)
Mineral Area Coll (MO)
Mississippi Gulf Coast Comm Coll (MS)
Mohave Comm Coll (AZ)
Moraine Park Tech Coll (WI)
Moraine Valley Comm Coll (IL)
Mott Comm Coll (MI)
Mountain Empire Comm Coll (VA)
Mt. San Antonio Coll (CA)
Northcentral Tech Coll (WI)
North Dakota State Coll of Science (ND)
Northeastern Jr Coll (CO)
Northeast Iowa Comm Coll (IA)
Northeast Texas Comm Coll (TX)
North Iowa Area Comm Coll (IA)
NorthWest Arkansas Comm Coll (AR)
Northwest Florida State Coll (FL)
Northwest-Shoals Comm Coll (AL)
Oakland Comm Coll (MI)
Oklahoma City Comm Coll (OK)
Oklahoma State U, Oklahoma City (OK)
Orange Coast Coll (CA)
Owensboro Comm and Tech Coll (KY)
Ozarks Tech Comm Coll (MO)
Palomar Coll (CA)
Paris Jr Coll (TX)
Pasco-Hernando State Coll (FL)
Patrick Henry Comm Coll (VA)
Pensacola State Coll (FL)
Phoenix Coll (AZ)
Piedmont Virginia Comm Coll (VA)
Pima Comm Coll (AZ)
Pueblo Comm Coll (CO)
Quinsigamond Comm Coll (MA)
Rend Lake Coll (IL)
Roane State Comm Coll (TN)
Rogue Comm Coll (OR)
San Diego City Coll (CA)
San Jacinto Coll District (TX)
San Juan Coll (NM)
Santa Rosa Jr Coll (CA)
Schoolcraft Coll (MI)
Scottsdale Comm Coll (AZ)
Seminole State Coll of Florida (FL)
Southeastern Comm Coll (IA)
Southern Crescent Tech Coll (GA)
Southern Maine Comm Coll (ME)
Southern State Comm Coll (OH)
South Florida State Coll (FL)
South Louisiana Comm Coll (LA)
Southwestern Comm Coll (NC)
Southwestern Illinois Coll (IL)
Southwest Virginia Comm Coll (VA)
Tallahassee Comm Coll (FL)
Tarrant County Coll District (TX)
Tech Coll of the Lowcountry (SC)
Temple Coll (TX)
Texarkana Coll (TX)
Treasure Valley Comm Coll (OR)
Trinity Valley Comm Coll (TX)
Tulsa Comm Coll (OK)
Tyler Jr Coll (TX)
Umpqua Comm Coll (OR)
U of Arkansas Comm Coll at Hope (AR)
Victoria Coll (TX)
Vincennes U (IN)
Waukesha County Tech Coll (WI)
Wayne County Comm Coll District (MI)
Westchester Comm Coll (NY)
Western Dakota Tech Inst (SD)
Wisconsin Indianhead Tech Coll (WI)
Wor-Wic Comm Coll (MD)

ENERGY MANAGEMENT AND SYSTEMS TECHNOLOGY
Casper Coll (WY)
Century Coll (MN)
Cincinnati State Tech and Comm Coll (OH)

Clinton Comm Coll (NY)
Comm Coll of Allegheny County (PA)
Crowder Coll (MO)
Danville Area Comm Coll (IL)
Delaware Tech & Comm Coll, Jack F. Owens Campus (DE)
Delaware Tech & Comm Coll, Stanton/Wilmington Campus (DE)
Delaware Tech & Comm Coll, Terry Campus (DE)
Delta Coll (MI)
Fox Valley Tech Coll (WI)
Harrisburg Area Comm Coll (PA)
Hawkeye Comm Coll (IA)
Illinois Eastern Comm Colls, Wabash Valley College (IL)
Iowa Lakes Comm Coll (IA)
Lakeland Comm Coll (OH)
Lakes Region Comm Coll (NH)
Lane Comm Coll (OR)
Lansing Comm Coll (MI)
Laramie County Comm Coll (WY)
Macomb Comm Coll (MI)
Middlesex County Coll (NJ)
Mitchell Tech Inst (SD)
Mount Wachusett Comm Coll (MA)
North Dakota State Coll of Science (ND)
Northeast Iowa Comm Coll (IA)
Northwest Tech Coll (MN)
Owens Comm Coll, Toledo (OH)
Quinsigamond Comm Coll (MA)
Rock Valley Coll (IL)
St. Clair County Comm Coll (MI)
South Louisiana Comm Coll (LA)
Walters State Comm Coll (TN)
Wayne Comm Coll (NC)
Westchester Comm Coll (NY)
The Williamson Free School of Mecha Trades (PA)
Wisconsin Indianhead Tech Coll (WI)

ENGINEERING
Allen Comm Coll (KS)
Amarillo Coll (TX)
Antelope Valley Coll (CA)
Arizona Western Coll (AZ)
Austin Comm Coll (TX)
Berkshire Comm Coll (MA)
Borough of Manhattan Comm Coll of the City U of New York (NY)
Bristol Comm Coll (MA)
Broward Coll (FL)
Bunker Hill Comm Coll (MA)
Butler County Comm Coll (PA)
Butte Coll (CA)
Ca&nnada Coll (CA)
Carl Albert State Coll (OK)
Casper Coll (WY)
Central Oregon Comm Coll (OR)
Central Virginia Comm Coll (VA)
Central Wyoming Coll (WY)
Cochise Coll, Sierra Vista (AZ)
Coll of Marin (CA)
Coll of Southern Idaho (ID)
Coll of Southern Maryland (MD)
Collin County Comm Coll District (TX)
The Comm Coll of Baltimore County (MD)
Comm Coll of Philadelphia (PA)
Comm Coll of Rhode Island (RI)
Copiah-Lincoln Comm Coll (MS)
Cosumnes River Coll, Sacramento (CA)
Danville Area Comm Coll (IL)
Daytona State Coll (FL)
De Anza Coll (CA)
Dutchess Comm Coll (NY)
East Central Coll (MO)
Elgin Comm Coll (IL)
Erie Comm Coll, North Campus (NY)
Fullerton Coll (CA)
Garden City Comm Coll (KS)
Gavilan Coll (CA)
Genesee Comm Coll (NY)
Grand Rapids Comm Coll (MI)
Grayson Coll (TX)
Hagerstown Comm Coll (MD)
Harford Comm Coll (MD)
Harper Coll (IL)
Harrisburg Area Comm Coll (PA)
Highland Comm Coll (IL)
Hinds Comm Coll (MS)
Holyoke Comm Coll (MA)
Howard Comm Coll (MD)
Hutchinson Comm Coll and Area Vocational School (KS)
Illinois Eastern Comm Colls, Frontier Community College (IL)

Illinois Eastern Comm Colls, Olney Central College (IL)
Illinois Eastern Comm Colls, Wabash Valley College (IL)
Iowa Lakes Comm Coll (IA)
Jamestown Comm Coll (NY)
Jefferson Coll (MO)
Jefferson Comm Coll (NY)
John Tyler Comm Coll (VA)
J. Sargeant Reynolds Comm Coll (VA)
Kankakee Comm Coll (IL)
Kaskaskia Coll (IL)
Lansing Comm Coll (MI)
Laramie County Comm Coll (WY)
Lehigh Carbon Comm Coll (PA)
Lincoln Land Comm Coll (IL)
Linn-Benton Comm Coll (OR)
Lorain County Comm Coll (OH)
Marion Military Inst (AL)
McHenry County Coll (IL)
Metropolitan Comm Coll–Kansas City (MO)
Miami Dade Coll (FL)
Missouri State U–West Plains (MO)
Mohawk Valley Comm Coll (NY)
Montgomery Coll (MD)
Nassau Comm Coll (NY)
Northampton Comm Coll (PA)
Northwest Coll (WY)
Northwestern Connecticut Comm Coll (CT)
Oakton Comm Coll (IL)
Ocean County Coll (NJ)
Orange Coast Coll (CA)
Palomar Coll (CA)
Paris Jr Coll (TX)
Pensacola State Coll (FL)
Piedmont Virginia Comm Coll (VA)
Potomac State Coll of West Virginia U (WV)
Rend Lake Coll (IL)
Roane State Comm Coll (TN)
St. Clair County Comm Coll (MI)
Salt Lake Comm Coll (UT)
San Jacinto Coll District (TX)
San Juan Coll (NM)
Santa Rosa Jr Coll (CA)
Schoolcraft Coll (MI)
Seminole State Coll (OK)
Sheridan Coll (WY)
South Florida State Coll (FL)
South Plains Coll (TX)
Southwestern Indian Polytechnic Inst (NM)
Springfield Tech Comm Coll (MA)
State U of New York Coll of Technology at Alfred (NY)
Texarkana Coll (TX)
Three Rivers Comm Coll (CT)
Tompkins Cortland Comm Coll (NY)
Truckee Meadows Comm Coll (NV)
Tulsa Comm Coll (OK)
Tunxis Comm Coll (CT)
Tyler Jr Coll (TX)
Umpqua Comm Coll (OR)
U of New Mexico–Los Alamos Branch (NM)
Virginia Western Comm Coll (VA)
Waubonsee Comm Coll (IL)
Wayne County Comm Coll District (MI)
Western Nevada Coll (NV)

ENGINEERING/INDUSTRIAL MANAGEMENT
Delaware Tech & Comm Coll, Stanton/Wilmington Campus (DE)
Mitchell Comm Coll (NC)

ENGINEERING MECHANICS
San Jacinto Coll District (TX)

ENGINEERING PHYSICS/ APPLIED PHYSICS
Lansing Comm Coll (MI)

ENGINEERING RELATED
Bristol Comm Coll (MA)
Clark State Comm Coll (OH)
Macomb Comm Coll (MI)
Miami Dade Coll (FL)
Southeastern Comm Coll (IA)

ENGINEERING-RELATED TECHNOLOGIES
Mohawk Valley Comm Coll (NY)

ENGINEERING SCIENCE
Bristol Comm Coll (MA)
Broward Coll (FL)
County Coll of Morris (NJ)

Finger Lakes Comm Coll (NY)
Genesee Comm Coll (NY)
Greenfield Comm Coll (MA)
Hudson County Comm Coll (NJ)
Jefferson Comm Coll (NY)
Kingsborough Comm Coll of the City
U of New York (NY)
Manchester Comm Coll (CT)
Mercer County Comm Coll (NJ)
Middlesex County Coll (NJ)
Monroe Comm Coll (NY)
Montgomery County Comm Coll (PA)
Northern Essex Comm Coll (MA)
North Shore Comm Coll (MA)
Norwalk Comm Coll (CT)
Onondaga Comm Coll (NY)
Raritan Valley Comm Coll (NJ)
South Florida State Coll (FL)
Three Rivers Comm Coll (CT)
Westchester Comm Coll (NY)

**ENGINEERING TECHNOLOGIES
AND ENGINEERING RELATED**
Bristol Comm Coll (MA)
Butte Coll (CA)
Carl Albert State Coll (OK)
Cincinnati State Tech and Comm
Coll (OH)
Clark State Comm Coll (OH)
Clinton Comm Coll (NY)
Coll of Southern Maryland (MD)
Columbus State Comm Coll (OH)
Comm Coll of Allegheny County (PA)
The Comm Coll of Baltimore County
(MD)
Hagerstown Comm Coll (MD)
Harrisburg Area Comm Coll (PA)
Kent State U at Tuscarawas (OH)
Middlesex County Coll (NJ)
Montgomery County Comm Coll (PA)
Mott Comm Coll (MI)
Ocean County Coll (NJ)
Oklahoma City Comm Coll (OK)
Quinsigamond Comm Coll (MA)
Raritan Valley Comm Coll (NJ)
State U of New York Coll of
Technology at Alfred (NY)
Sullivan Coll of Technology and
Design (KY)
Tulsa Comm Coll (OK)
Wor-Wic Comm Coll (MD)

ENGINEERING TECHNOLOGY
Allen Comm Coll (KS)
Antelope Valley Coll (CA)
Arapahoe Comm Coll (CO)
Benjamin Franklin Inst of Technology
(MA)
Bismarck State Coll (ND)
Bucks County Comm Coll (PA)
Central Virginia Comm Coll (VA)
Coll of Marin (CA)
Collin County Comm Coll District
(TX)
Comm Coll of Philadelphia (PA)
Darton State Coll (GA)
De Anza Coll (CA)
Eastern Florida State Coll (FL)
Florida Gateway Coll (FL)
Florida State Coll at Jacksonville
(FL)
Gateway Comm and Tech Coll (KY)
Georgia Piedmont Tech Coll (GA)
Glendale Comm Coll (AZ)
Golden West Coll (CA)
Harford Comm Coll (MD)
Hillsborough Comm Coll (FL)
Honolulu Comm Coll (HI)
Hopkinsville Comm Coll (KY)
Iowa Lakes Comm Coll (IA)
Jefferson State Comm Coll (AL)
Kent State U at Tuscarawas (OH)
Lake Area Tech Inst (SD)
Lorain County Comm Coll (OH)
Luzerne County Comm Coll (PA)
Massachusetts Bay Comm Coll (MA)
Mesa Comm Coll (AZ)
Miami Dade Coll (FL)
Mineral Area Coll (MO)
Mt. San Antonio Coll (CA)
Oklahoma State U, Oklahoma City
(OK)
Owensboro Comm and Tech Coll
(KY)
Pasadena City Coll (CA)
Patrick Henry Comm Coll (VA)
Pennsylvania Inst of Technology (PA)
Pensacola State Coll (FL)
Pueblo Comm Coll (CO)
Rappahannock Comm Coll (VA)

Salt Lake Comm Coll (UT)
San Diego City Coll (CA)
Shoreline Comm Coll (WA)
Snead State Comm Coll (AL)
Somerset Comm Coll (KY)
South Florida State Coll (FL)
Southwestern Michigan Coll (MI)
Sullivan Coll of Technology and
Design (KY)
Three Rivers Comm Coll (CT)
Trident Tech Coll (SC)
Tulsa Comm Coll (OK)
Tunxis Comm Coll (CT)
Vincennes U (IN)
Walla Walla Comm Coll (WA)
Westchester Comm Coll (NY)
Western Wyoming Comm Coll (WY)

ENGINE MACHINIST
Northwest Tech Coll (MN)

ENGLISH
Amarillo Coll (TX)
Arizona Western Coll (AZ)
Bainbridge State Coll (GA)
Berkeley City Coll (CA)
Borough of Manhattan Comm Coll of
the City U of New York (NY)
Broward Coll (FL)
Bunker Hill Comm Coll (MA)
Butler County Comm Coll (PA)
Ca&nnada Coll (CA)
Carl Albert State Coll (OK)
Casper Coll (WY)
Central Wyoming Coll (WY)
Cochise Coll, Sierra Vista (AZ)
Coll of Marin (CA)
Coll of Southern Idaho (ID)
Coll of the Canyons (CA)
Coll of the Desert (CA)
Coll of Western Idaho (ID)
Columbia Coll (CA)
Comm Coll of Allegheny County (PA)
Copiah-Lincoln Comm Coll (MS)
Copper Mountain Coll (CA)
Cosumnes River Coll, Sacramento
(CA)
Darton State Coll (GA)
De Anza Coll (CA)
Eastern Arizona Coll (AZ)
Eastern Wyoming Coll (WY)
Edison Comm Coll (OH)
Feather River Coll (CA)
Fiorello H. LaGuardia Comm Coll of
the City U of New York (NY)
Frank Phillips Coll (TX)
Fullerton Coll (CA)
Galveston Coll (TX)
Garden City Comm Coll (KS)
Gavilan Coll (CA)
Georgia Highlands Coll (GA)
Gordon State Coll (GA)
Grand Rapids Comm Coll (MI)
Grayson Coll (TX)
Great Basin Coll (NV)
Greenfield Comm Coll (MA)
Harford Comm Coll (MD)
Harper Coll (IL)
Hinds Comm Coll (MS)
Hutchinson Comm Coll and Area
Vocational School (KS)
Imperial Valley Coll (CA)
Independence Comm Coll (KS)
Iowa Lakes Comm Coll (IA)
Kankakee Comm Coll (IL)
Kilgore Coll (TX)
Lansing Comm Coll (MI)
Laramie County Comm Coll (WY)
Linn-Benton Comm Coll (OR)
Los Angeles Mission Coll (CA)
Miami Dade Coll (FL)
MiraCosta Coll (CA)
Mississippi Delta Comm Coll (MS)
Mohave Comm Coll (AZ)
Monroe County Comm Coll (MI)
Northeastern Jr Coll (CO)
Northeast Texas Comm Coll (TX)
Northwest Coll (WY)
Northwestern Connecticut Comm
Coll (CT)
Orange Coast Coll (CA)
Oxnard Coll (CA)
Palomar Coll (CA)
Paris Jr Coll (TX)
Pensacola State Coll (FL)
Potomac State Coll of West Virginia
U (WV)
Raritan Valley Comm Coll (NJ)
Salt Lake Comm Coll (UT)
San Diego City Coll (CA)

San Jacinto Coll District (TX)
Santa Rosa Jr Coll (CA)
Sauk Valley Comm Coll (IL)
Seminole State Coll (OK)
Sheridan Coll (WY)
South Florida State Coll (FL)
South Georgia State Coll, Douglas
(GA)
Spoon River Coll (IL)
Sussex County Comm Coll (NJ)
Treasure Valley Comm Coll (OR)
Trinity Valley Comm Coll (TX)
Truckee Meadows Comm Coll (NV)
Umpqua Comm Coll (OR)
Vincennes U (IN)
Western Wyoming Comm Coll (WY)

**ENGLISH AS A SECOND/
FOREIGN LANGUAGE
(TEACHING)**
Gordon State Coll (GA)

**ENGLISH LANGUAGE AND
LITERATURE RELATED**
Butte Coll (CA)
Mt. San Antonio Coll (CA)

**ENGLISH/LANGUAGE ARTS
TEACHER EDUCATION**
Broward Coll (FL)
Carroll Comm Coll (MD)
Cecil Coll (MD)
Darton State Coll (GA)
Hagerstown Comm Coll (MD)
Harford Comm Coll (MD)
Montgomery Coll (MD)
South Florida State Coll (FL)
Vincennes U (IN)

ENTOMOLOGY
Broward Coll (FL)
South Florida State Coll (FL)

**ENTREPRENEURIAL AND
SMALL BUSINESS RELATED**
Dakota Coll at Bottineau (ND)
State U of New York Coll of
Technology at Alfred (NY)
Williston State Coll (ND)
Wright Career Coll, Overland Park
(KS)
Wright Career Coll, Wichita (KS)
Wright Career Coll (NE)
Wright Career Coll, Oklahoma City
(OK)
Wright Career Coll, Tulsa (OK)

ENTREPRENEURSHIP
Bristol Comm Coll (MA)
Bunker Hill Comm Coll (MA)
Casper Coll (WY)
Central Wyoming Coll (WY)
Cincinnati State Tech and Comm
Coll (OH)
Cleveland Comm Coll (NC)
Coll of Southern Idaho (ID)
Columbia-Greene Comm Coll (NY)
Columbus State Comm Coll (OH)
Comm Coll of Allegheny County (PA)
Delaware Tech & Comm Coll, Jack F.
Owens Campus (DE)
Delaware Tech & Comm Coll, Terry
Campus (DE)
Eastern Arizona Coll (AZ)
Elgin Comm Coll (IL)
Genesee Comm Coll (NY)
Great Falls Coll Montana State U
(MT)
Harford Comm Coll (MD)
Herkimer County Comm Coll (NY)
Independence Comm Coll (KS)
Lamar Comm Coll (CO)
Laramie County Comm Coll (WY)
LDS Business Coll (UT)
Missouri State U–West Plains (MO)
Mott Comm Coll (MI)
Nassau Comm Coll (NY)
North Iowa Area Comm Coll (IA)
Northwest Florida State Coll (FL)
Oakland Comm Coll (MI)
Richmond Comm Coll (NC)
Salt Lake Comm Coll (UT)
Southern State Comm Coll (OH)
South Piedmont Comm Coll (NC)
State U of New York Coll of
Technology at Alfred (NY)
Tallahassee Comm Coll (FL)
Truckee Meadows Comm Coll (NV)
Wichita Area Tech Coll (KS)

ENVIRONMENTAL BIOLOGY
Eastern Arizona Coll (AZ)
Eastern Wyoming Coll (WY)

**ENVIRONMENTAL CONTROL
TECHNOLOGIES RELATED**
Bismarck State Coll (ND)
Cincinnati State Tech and Comm
Coll (OH)
Columbus State Comm Coll (OH)
Hillsborough Comm Coll (FL)
Holyoke Comm Coll (MA)
Middlesex County Coll (NJ)
Mountain Empire Comm Coll (VA)
Westchester Comm Coll (NY)
Western Dakota Tech Inst (SD)

**ENVIRONMENTAL DESIGN/
ARCHITECTURE**
Iowa Lakes Comm Coll (IA)
Scottsdale Comm Coll (AZ)

ENVIRONMENTAL EDUCATION
Iowa Lakes Comm Coll (IA)

**ENVIRONMENTAL
ENGINEERING TECHNOLOGY**
Austin Comm Coll (TX)
Bristol Comm Coll (MA)
Cincinnati State Tech and Comm
Coll (OH)
Coll of Southern Maryland (MD)
Comm Coll of Allegheny County (PA)
Crowder Coll (MO)
Dakota Coll at Bottineau (ND)
Delta Coll (MI)
Georgia Northwestern Tech Coll
(GA)
Iowa Lakes Comm Coll (IA)
Kent State U at Trumbull (OH)
Lansing Comm Coll (MI)
Massachusetts Bay Comm Coll (MA)
Miami Dade Coll (FL)
Northwest-Shoals Comm Coll (AL)
Onondaga Comm Coll (NY)
Owens Comm Coll, Toledo (OH)
Oxnard Coll (CA)
Salt Lake Comm Coll (UT)
San Diego City Coll (CA)
Schoolcraft Coll (MI)
Sheridan Coll (WY)
Shoreline Comm Coll (WA)
Texas State Tech Coll Waco (TX)
Three Rivers Comm Coll (CT)
Wor-Wic Comm Coll (MD)

**ENVIRONMENTAL/
ENVIRONMENTAL HEALTH
ENGINEERING**
Bristol Comm Coll (MA)
Central Wyoming Coll (WY)
South Florida State Coll (FL)

ENVIRONMENTAL HEALTH
Amarillo Coll (TX)
Roane State Comm Coll (TN)

ENVIRONMENTAL SCIENCE
Anoka-Ramsey Comm Coll (MN)
Anoka-Ramsey Comm Coll,
Cambridge Campus (MN)
Arizona Western Coll (AZ)
Broward Coll (FL)
Bucks County Comm Coll (PA)
Butte Coll (CA)
Casper Coll (WY)
Central Wyoming Coll (WY)
Coconino Comm Coll (AZ)
Coll of the Desert (CA)
Columbia Coll (CA)
Comm Coll of Vermont (VT)
Copper Mountain Coll (CA)
Erie Comm Coll, North Campus (NY)
Fiorello H. LaGuardia Comm Coll of
the City U of New York (NY)
Gordon State Coll (GA)
Greenfield Comm Coll (MA)
Harford Comm Coll (MD)
Harrisburg Area Comm Coll (PA)
Lake Area Tech Inst (SD)
Lehigh Carbon Comm Coll (PA)
MiraCosta Coll (CA)
Montgomery County Comm Coll (PA)
Northampton Comm Coll (PA)
Northeast Texas Comm Coll (TX)
NorthWest Arkansas Comm Coll
(AR)
Ocean County Coll (NJ)
The Ohio State U Ag Tech Inst (OH)
San Jacinto Coll District (TX)
South Florida State Coll (FL)

State U of New York Coll of
Technology at Alfred (NY)
Tallahassee Comm Coll (FL)
Truckee Meadows Comm Coll (NV)
Tulsa Comm Coll (OK)
Tyler Jr Coll (TX)
Westchester Comm Coll (NY)
Western Wyoming Comm Coll (WY)

ENVIRONMENTAL STUDIES
Berkshire Comm Coll (MA)
Bristol Comm Coll (MA)
Coll of the Desert (CA)
Cosumnes River Coll, Sacramento
(CA)
Darton State Coll (GA)
De Anza Coll (CA)
Feather River Coll (CA)
Finger Lakes Comm Coll (NY)
Fullerton Coll (CA)
Genesee Comm Coll (NY)
Goodwin Coll (CT)
Harford Comm Coll (MD)
Harper Coll (IL)
Harrisburg Area Comm Coll (PA)
Housatonic Comm Coll (CT)
Howard Comm Coll (MD)
Iowa Lakes Comm Coll (IA)
Kilian Comm Coll (SD)
Lamar State Coll–Orange (TX)
Monroe Comm Coll (NY)
Mount Wachusett Comm Coll (MA)
Oxnard Coll (CA)
Santa Rosa Jr Coll (CA)
Southeastern Comm Coll (NC)
Southwestern Comm Coll (NC)
Stark State Coll (OH)
Sullivan County Comm Coll (NY)
Sussex County Comm Coll (NJ)
U of New Mexico–Los Alamos
Branch (NM)
Westchester Comm Coll (NY)
Western Nevada Coll (NV)

EQUESTRIAN STUDIES
Allen Comm Coll (KS)
Central Wyoming Coll (WY)
Coll of Southern Idaho (ID)
Colorado Northwestern Comm Coll
(CO)
Feather River Coll (CA)
Harford Comm Coll (MD)
Hocking Coll (OH)
Lamar Comm Coll (CO)
Laramie County Comm Coll (WY)
Northeastern Jr Coll (CO)
Northwest Coll (WY)
The Ohio State U Ag Tech Inst (OH)
Scottsdale Comm Coll (AZ)

**ETHNIC, CULTURAL MINORITY,
GENDER, AND·GROUP STUDIES
RELATED**
Coll of Marin (CA)
Cosumnes River Coll, Sacramento
(CA)
Fullerton Coll (CA)
MiraCosta Coll (CA)
New Mexico State U–Alamogordo
(NM)

**EXECUTIVE ASSISTANT/
EXECUTIVE SECRETARY**
Alamance Comm Coll (NC)
Bellingham Tech Coll (WA)
Brookhaven Coll (TX)
Cape Fear Comm Coll (NC)
Cincinnati State Tech and Comm
Coll (OH)
Clark Coll (WA)
Crowder Coll (MO)
Dakota Coll at Bottineau (ND)
Danville Area Comm Coll (IL)
Edison Comm Coll (OH)
Elgin Comm Coll (IL)
Hawkeye Comm Coll (IA)
Hillsborough Comm Coll (FL)
Hopkinsville Comm Coll (KY)
Illinois Eastern Comm Colls, Frontier
Community College (IL)
Illinois Eastern Comm Colls, Wabash
Valley College (IL)
Ivy Tech Comm Coll–Bloomington
(IN)
Ivy Tech Comm Coll–Central Indiana
(IN)
Ivy Tech Comm Coll–Columbus (IN)
Ivy Tech Comm Coll–East Central
(IN)
Ivy Tech Comm Coll–Kokomo (IN)

Ivy Tech Comm Coll–Lafayette (IN)
Ivy Tech Comm Coll–North Central (IN)
Ivy Tech Comm Coll–Northeast (IN)
Ivy Tech Comm Coll–Northwest (IN)
Ivy Tech Comm Coll–Richmond (IN)
Ivy Tech Comm Coll–Southeast (IN)
Ivy Tech Comm Coll–Southern Indiana (IN)
Ivy Tech Comm Coll–Southwest (IN)
Ivy Tech Comm Coll–Wabash Valley (IN)
Jackson Coll (MI)
Kaskaskia Coll (IL)
Kilgore Coll (TX)
Lake Land Coll (IL)
Luzerne County Comm Coll (PA)
Mitchell Comm Coll (NC)
Northeast Texas Comm Coll (TX)
Northwest Florida State Coll (FL)
Owensboro Comm and Tech Coll (KY)
Owens Comm Coll, Toledo (OH)
Pensacola State Coll (FL)
Pima Comm Coll (AZ)
Quinsigamond Comm Coll (MA)
St. Clair County Comm Coll (MI)
Schoolcraft Coll (MI)
Somerset Comm Coll (KY)
Southern State Comm Coll (OH)
South Suburban Coll (IL)
Southwestern Michigan Coll (MI)
Waubonsee Comm Coll (IL)

FACILITIES PLANNING AND MANAGEMENT
Comm Coll of Philadelphia (PA)

FAMILY AND COMMUNITY SERVICES
Glendale Comm Coll (AZ)
Oxnard Coll (CA)
Phoenix Coll (AZ)
Snow Coll (UT)
Westmoreland County Comm Coll (PA)

FAMILY AND CONSUMER ECONOMICS RELATED
American Samoa Comm Coll (AS)
Los Angeles Mission Coll (CA)
Orange Coast Coll (CA)

FAMILY AND CONSUMER SCIENCES/HOME ECONOMICS TEACHER EDUCATION
Antelope Valley Coll (CA)
Copiah-Lincoln Comm Coll (MS)
Northwest Mississippi Comm Coll (MS)
South Florida State Coll (FL)
Vincennes U (IN)

FAMILY AND CONSUMER SCIENCES/HUMAN SCIENCES
Allen Comm Coll (KS)
Bainbridge State Coll (GA)
Butte Coll (CA)
Garden City Comm Coll (KS)
Hinds Comm Coll (MS)
Hutchinson Comm Coll and Area Vocational School (KS)
Iowa Lakes Comm Coll (IA)
Linn-Benton Comm Coll (OR)
Mesa Comm Coll (AZ)
Metropolitan Comm Coll–Kansas City (MO)
Mississippi Delta Comm Coll (MS)
Monroe Comm Coll (NY)
Mt. San Antonio Coll (CA)
Northeastern Jr Coll (CO)
Orange Coast Coll (CA)
Palomar Coll (CA)
Phoenix Coll (AZ)
Snow Coll (UT)
Tulsa Comm Coll (OK)
Tyler Jr Coll (TX)
Vincennes U (IN)

FAMILY RESOURCE MANAGEMENT
Gavilan Coll (CA)

FAMILY SYSTEMS
Goodwin Coll (CT)

FARM AND RANCH MANAGEMENT
Allen Comm Coll (KS)
Bismarck State Coll (ND)
Copiah-Lincoln Comm Coll (MS)
Crowder Coll (MO)

Eastern Wyoming Coll (WY)
Frank Phillips Coll (TX)
Hutchinson Comm Coll and Area Vocational School (KS)
Iowa Lakes Comm Coll (IA)
Lamar Comm Coll (CO)
Northeastern Jr Coll (CO)
Northwest Coll (WY)
Snow Coll (UT)
Treasure Valley Comm Coll (OR)
Trinity Valley Comm Coll (TX)

FASHION AND FABRIC CONSULTING
Harper Coll (IL)

FASHION/APPAREL DESIGN
Academy of Couture Art (CA)
The Art Inst of New York City (NY)
Ca&nnada Coll (CA)
Clary Sage Coll (OK)
Fashion Inst of Technology (NY)
FIDM/The Fashion Inst of Design & Merchandising, Los Angeles Campus (CA)
FIDM/The Fashion Inst of Design & Merchandising, Orange County Campus (CA)
FIDM/The Fashion Inst of Design & Merchandising, San Diego Campus (CA)
FIDM/The Fashion Inst of Design & Merchandising, San Francisco Campus (CA)
Fullerton Coll (CA)
Genesee Comm Coll (NY)
Harper Coll (IL)
Honolulu Comm Coll (HI)
Houston Comm Coll System (TX)
Lehigh Carbon Comm Coll (PA)
Metropolitan Comm Coll–Kansas City (MO)
Monroe Comm Coll (NY)
Nassau Comm Coll (NY)
Palomar Coll (CA)
Pasadena City Coll (CA)
Phoenix Coll (AZ)
Pima Comm Coll (AZ)
Santa Monica Coll (CA)
Santa Rosa Jr Coll (CA)
U of Hawaii Maui Coll (HI)
Wood Tobe–Coburn School (NY)

FASHION MERCHANDISING
Alexandria Tech and Comm Coll (MN)
Bay State Coll (MA)
Davis Coll (OH)
Fashion Inst of Technology (NY)
FIDM/The Fashion Inst of Design & Merchandising, Los Angeles Campus (CA)
FIDM/The Fashion Inst of Design & Merchandising, Orange County Campus (CA)
FIDM/The Fashion Inst of Design & Merchandising, San Diego Campus (CA)
FIDM/The Fashion Inst of Design & Merchandising, San Francisco Campus (CA)
Florida State Coll at Jacksonville (FL)
Genesee Comm Coll (NY)
Grand Rapids Comm Coll (MI)
Harper Coll (IL)
Herkimer County Comm Coll (NY)
Hinds Comm Coll (MS)
Houston Comm Coll System (TX)
Iowa Lakes Comm Coll (IA)
Kingsborough Comm Coll of the City U of New York (NY)
Lansing Comm Coll (MI)
Mesa Comm Coll (AZ)
Metropolitan Comm Coll–Kansas City (MO)
Mississippi Gulf Coast Comm Coll (MS)
Monroe Comm Coll (NY)
Mt. San Antonio Coll (CA)
Nassau Comm Coll (NY)
Northwest Mississippi Comm Coll (MS)
Orange Coast Coll (CA)
Pasadena City Coll (CA)
Phoenix Coll (AZ)
Pima Comm Coll (AZ)
San Diego City Coll (CA)
Santa Rosa Jr Coll (CA)
Scottsdale Comm Coll (AZ)
South Plains Coll (TX)
Tarrant County Coll District (TX)
Trinity Valley Comm Coll (TX)

Tunxis Comm Coll (CT)
Vincennes U (IN)

FASHION MODELING
Fashion Inst of Technology (NY)

FIBER, TEXTILE AND WEAVING ARTS
Antelope Valley Coll (CA)
FIDM/The Fashion Inst of Design & Merchandising, Orange County Campus (CA)

FILM/CINEMA/VIDEO STUDIES
Carl Albert State Coll (OK)
Coll of Marin (CA)
Cosumnes River Coll, Sacramento (CA)
De Anza Coll (CA)
Los Angeles Film School (CA)
Oakland Comm Coll (MI)
Orange Coast Coll (CA)
Palomar Coll (CA)
San Jacinto Coll District (TX)
Santa Monica Coll (CA)

FILM/VIDEO AND PHOTOGRAPHIC ARTS RELATED
Greenfield Comm Coll (MA)
Westchester Comm Coll (NY)

FINANCE
Broward Coll (FL)
Bunker Hill Comm Coll (MA)
Chipola Coll (FL)
Comm Coll of Philadelphia (PA)
Harper Coll (IL)
Iowa Lakes Comm Coll (IA)
Lake Tahoe Comm Coll (CA)
Lenoir Comm Coll (NC)
Lorain County Comm Coll (OH)
Los Angeles Mission Coll (CA)
Macomb Comm Coll (MI)
Mesa Comm Coll (AZ)
Miami Dade Coll (FL)
Mississippi Gulf Coast Comm Coll (MS)
Monroe County Comm Coll (MI)
Mt. San Antonio Coll (CA)
Northern Essex Comm Coll (MA)
NorthWest Arkansas Comm Coll (AR)
Norwalk Comm Coll (CT)
Oklahoma City Comm Coll (OK)
Salt Lake Comm Coll (UT)
San Diego City Coll (CA)
Scottsdale Comm Coll (AZ)
Seminole State Coll of Florida (FL)
Southeast Tech Inst (SD)
South Florida State Coll (FL)
Spoon River Coll (IL)
Springfield Tech Comm Coll (MA)
Stark State Coll (OH)
State U of New York Coll of Technology at Alfred (NY)
Trinity Valley Comm Coll (TX)
Tulsa Comm Coll (OK)
Vincennes U (IN)
Westchester Comm Coll (NY)
Wisconsin Indianhead Tech Coll (WI)

FINANCE AND FINANCIAL MANAGEMENT SERVICES RELATED
Bristol Comm Coll (MA)
Columbus State Comm Coll (OH)

FINANCIAL PLANNING AND SERVICES
Cecil Coll (MD)
Cincinnati State Tech and Comm Coll (OH)
Howard Comm Coll (MD)
Kilian Comm Coll (SD)
Raritan Valley Comm Coll (NJ)

FINE AND STUDIO ARTS MANAGEMENT
Dean Coll (MA)

FINE ARTS RELATED
Butler County Comm Coll (PA)
Carl Albert State Coll (OK)
Schoolcraft Coll (MI)
Seminole State Coll (OK)
Tulsa Comm Coll (OK)

FINE/STUDIO ARTS
Amarillo Coll (TX)
Anoka-Ramsey Comm Coll (MN)

Anoka-Ramsey Comm Coll, Cambridge Campus (MN)
Arizona Western Coll (AZ)
Berkeley City Coll (CA)
Bristol Comm Coll (MA)
Casper Coll (WY)
Cayuga County Comm Coll (NY)
Cecil Coll (MD)
Century Coll (MN)
Chandler-Gilbert Comm Coll (AZ)
Coconino Comm Coll (AZ)
Coll of the Mainland (TX)
County Coll of Morris (NJ)
Cumberland County Coll (NJ)
Delta Coll (MI)
East Central Coll (MO)
Elgin Comm Coll (IL)
Fashion Inst of Technology (NY)
Finger Lakes Comm Coll (NY)
Fiorello H. LaGuardia Comm Coll of the City U of New York (NY)
Genesee Comm Coll (NY)
Greenfield Comm Coll (MA)
Harford Comm Coll (MD)
Harper Coll (IL)
Hudson County Comm Coll (NJ)
Iowa Lakes Comm Coll (IA)
Jamestown Comm Coll (NY)
Lakes Region Comm Coll (NH)
Lake Superior Coll (MN)
Lansing Comm Coll (MI)
Lincoln Land Comm Coll (IL)
Manchester Comm Coll (CT)
McHenry County Coll (IL)
Minneapolis Comm and Tech Coll (MN)
New Mexico State U–Alamogordo (NM)
Niagara County Comm Coll (NY)
Normandale Comm Coll (MN)
Northampton Comm Coll (PA)
Northeastern Jr Coll (CO)
Norwalk Comm Coll (CT)
Oklahoma City Comm Coll (OK)
Oxnard Coll (CA)
Phoenix Coll (AZ)
Raritan Valley Comm Coll (NJ)
Rend Lake Coll (IL)
South Florida State Coll (FL)
South Suburban Coll (IL)
Southwestern Illinois Coll (IL)
Springfield Tech Comm Coll (MA)
Sussex County Comm Coll (NJ)
Truckee Meadows Comm Coll (NV)
U of New Mexico–Los Alamos Branch (NM)
Waubonsee Comm Coll (IL)
Westchester Comm Coll (NY)

FIRE PREVENTION AND SAFETY TECHNOLOGY
Antelope Valley Coll (CA)
Austin Comm Coll (TX)
Blackhawk Tech Coll (WI)
Bristol Comm Coll (MA)
Bucks County Comm Coll (PA)
Bunker Hill Comm Coll (MA)
Cape Fear Comm Coll (NC)
Catawba Valley Comm Coll (NC)
Cleveland Comm Coll (NC)
Coll of the Canyons (CA)
Coll of the Mainland (TX)
Collin County Comm Coll District (TX)
Comm Coll of Allegheny County (PA)
County Coll of Morris (NJ)
Delaware Tech & Comm Coll, Stanton/Wilmington Campus (DE)
Delta Coll (MI)
Fayetteville Tech Comm Coll (NC)
Florida State Coll at Jacksonville (FL)
Greenfield Comm Coll (MA)
Hillsborough Comm Coll (FL)
Houston Comm Coll System (TX)
Jamestown Comm Coll (NY)
Jefferson Coll (MO)
Jefferson Comm Coll (NY)
Lakeland Comm Coll (OH)
Lakes Region Comm Coll (NH)
Lake Superior Coll (MN)
Macomb Comm Coll (MI)
Middlesex County Coll (NJ)
Montgomery Coll (MD)
Montgomery County Comm Coll (PA)
Moraine Valley Comm Coll (IL)
Mott Comm Coll (MI)
Mount Wachusett Comm Coll (MA)
North Iowa Area Comm Coll (IA)
Ocean County Coll (NJ)
Oklahoma State U, Oklahoma City (OK)

Onondaga Comm Coll (NY)
Owens Comm Coll, Toledo (OH)
Oxnard Coll (CA)
Pasadena City Coll (CA)
Pensacola State Coll (FL)
Rogue Comm Coll (OR)
San Jacinto Coll District (TX)
South Florida State Coll (FL)
South Piedmont Comm Coll (NC)
Springfield Tech Comm Coll (MA)
Sullivan County Comm Coll (NY)
Treasure Valley Comm Coll (OR)
Tulsa Comm Coll (OK)
Victor Valley Coll (CA)
Waukesha County Tech Coll (WI)
Wayne County Comm Coll District (MI)
Western Nevada Coll (NV)
Westmoreland County Comm Coll (PA)

FIRE PROTECTION RELATED
Fox Valley Tech Coll (WI)
Sussex County Comm Coll (NJ)
Western Oklahoma State Coll (OK)

FIRE SCIENCE/FIREFIGHTING
Amarillo Coll (TX)
Arizona Western Coll (AZ)
Augusta Tech Coll (GA)
Barstow Comm Coll (CA)
Berkshire Comm Coll (MA)
Blackhawk Tech Coll (WI)
Bristol Comm Coll (MA)
Broward Coll (FL)
Butler County Comm Coll (PA)
Butte Coll (CA)
Casper Coll (WY)
Cecil Coll (MD)
Central Ohio Tech Coll (OH)
Central Oregon Comm Coll (OR)
Central Wyoming Coll (WY)
Chattahoochee Tech Coll (GA)
Cincinnati State Tech and Comm Coll (OH)
Clatsop Comm Coll (OR)
Cochise Coll, Sierra Vista (AZ)
Coconino Comm Coll (AZ)
Coll of Central Florida (FL)
Coll of Southern Maryland (MD)
Coll of the Desert (CA)
Collin County Comm Coll District (TX)
Columbia Coll (CA)
Columbus State Comm Coll (OH)
Comm Coll of Philadelphia (PA)
Comm Coll of Rhode Island (RI)
Copper Mountain Coll (CA)
Cosumnes River Coll, Sacramento (CA)
Crowder Coll (MO)
Danville Area Comm Coll (IL)
Daytona State Coll (FL)
Delaware Tech & Comm Coll, Stanton/Wilmington Campus (DE)
Delta Coll (MI)
East Central Coll (MO)
Eastern Arizona Coll (AZ)
Eastern Florida State Coll (FL)
Eastern Idaho Tech Coll (ID)
Elgin Comm Coll (IL)
Florida State Coll at Jacksonville (FL)
Fox Valley Tech Coll (WI)
Garden City Comm Coll (KS)
Gateway Comm and Tech Coll (KY)
Georgia Northwestern Tech Coll (GA)
Glendale Comm Coll (AZ)
Greenville Tech Coll (SC)
Harper Coll (IL)
Harrisburg Area Comm Coll (PA)
Helena Coll U of Montana (MT)
Hocking Coll (OH)
Honolulu Comm Coll (HI)
Hutchinson Comm Coll and Area Vocational School (KS)
Ilisagvik Coll (AK)
Illinois Eastern Comm Colls, Frontier Community College (IL)
Imperial Valley Coll (CA)
J. Sargeant Reynolds Comm Coll (VA)
Lakes Region Comm Coll (NH)
Lake Tahoe Comm Coll (CA)
Lanier Tech Coll (GA)
Lansing Comm Coll (MI)
Laramie County Comm Coll (WY)
Lincoln Land Comm Coll (IL)
Lone Star Coll–CyFair (TX)
Lone Star Coll–Montgomery (TX)
Lorain County Comm Coll (OH)
Lower Columbia Coll (WA)
Luzerne County Comm Coll (PA)

McHenry County Coll (IL)
Mercer County Comm Coll (NJ)
Mesa Comm Coll (AZ)
Metropolitan Comm Coll–Kansas City (MO)
Miami Dade Coll (FL)
Mid-Plains Comm Coll, North Platte (NE)
Mineral Area Coll (MO)
Mohave Comm Coll (AZ)
Monroe Comm Coll (NY)
Moraine Valley Comm Coll (IL)
Mt. San Antonio Coll (CA)
Mt. San Jacinto Coll (CA)
Northampton Comm Coll (PA)
Northeast Iowa Comm Coll (IA)
North Shore Comm Coll (MA)
Norwalk Comm Coll (CT)
Oakland Comm Coll (MI)
Oakton Comm Coll (IL)
Oklahoma State U, Oklahoma City (OK)
Owensboro Comm and Tech Coll (KY)
Owens Comm Coll, Toledo (OH)
Oxnard Coll (CA)
Ozarks Tech Comm Coll (MO)
Palomar Coll (CA)
Pensacola State Coll (FL)
Phoenix Coll (AZ)
Pima Comm Coll (AZ)
Pueblo Comm Coll (CO)
Rock Valley Coll (IL)
San Jacinto Coll District (TX)
San Juan Coll (NM)
Santa Rosa Jr Coll (CA)
Sauk Valley Comm Coll (IL)
Savannah Tech Coll (GA)
Schoolcraft Coll (MI)
Scottsdale Comm Coll (AZ)
Seminole State Coll of Florida (FL)
Southern Maine Comm Coll (ME)
South Plains Coll (TX)
Southwestern Illinois Coll (IL)
Southwestern Michigan Coll (MI)
Stark State Coll (OH)
Tallahassee Comm Coll (FL)
Tarrant County Coll District (TX)
Three Rivers Comm Coll (CT)
Treasure Valley Comm Coll (OR)
Truckee Meadows Comm Coll (NV)
Tyler Jr Coll (TX)
Umpqua Comm Coll (OR)
Victor Valley Coll (CA)
Vincennes U (IN)
Volunteer State Comm Coll (TN)
Walla Walla Comm Coll (WA)
Waubonsee Comm Coll (IL)
Western Dakota Tech Inst (SD)
West Georgia Tech Coll (GA)
West Kentucky Comm and Tech Coll (KY)
Wiregrass Georgia Tech Coll (GA)

FIRE SERVICES ADMINISTRATION
Delaware Tech & Comm Coll, Stanton/Wilmington Campus (DE)
Delta Coll (MI)
Dutchess Comm Coll (NY)
Erie Comm Coll, South Campus (NY)
Jefferson Comm Coll (NY)
Jefferson State Comm Coll (AL)
Mohawk Valley Comm Coll (NY)
Northampton Comm Coll (PA)
NorthWest Arkansas Comm Coll (AR)
Oxnard Coll (CA)
Quinsigamond Comm Coll (MA)
Tech Coll of the Lowcountry (SC)
Tulsa Comm Coll (OK)

FIRE SYSTEMS TECHNOLOGY
Coll of Western Idaho (ID)

FISHING AND FISHERIES SCIENCES AND MANAGEMENT
Bellingham Tech Coll (WA)
Central Oregon Comm Coll (OR)
Dakota Coll at Bottineau (ND)
Finger Lakes Comm Coll (NY)
Hocking Coll (OH)
Iowa Lakes Comm Coll (IA)

FLIGHT INSTRUCTION
Iowa Lakes Comm Coll (IA)

FLORICULTURE/FLORISTRY MANAGEMENT
Dakota Coll at Bottineau (ND)
Danville Area Comm Coll (IL)
Hinds Comm Coll (MS)
J. Sargeant Reynolds Comm Coll (VA)
MiraCosta Coll (CA)
The Ohio State U Ag Tech Inst (OH)
Santa Rosa Jr Coll (CA)
Westmoreland County Comm Coll (PA)

FOOD PREPARATION
Iowa Lakes Comm Coll (IA)
J. Sargeant Reynolds Comm Coll (VA)
Reading Area Comm Coll (PA)
San Jacinto Coll District (TX)

FOODS AND NUTRITION RELATED
Iowa Lakes Comm Coll (IA)

FOOD SCIENCE
Broward Coll (FL)
Grayson Coll (TX)
Greenfield Comm Coll (MA)
Hocking Coll (OH)
Miami Dade Coll (FL)
Missouri State U–West Plains (MO)
Normandale Comm Coll (MN)
Orange Coast Coll (CA)
South Florida State Coll (FL)
Vincennes U (IN)

FOOD SERVICE AND DINING ROOM MANAGEMENT
Iowa Lakes Comm Coll (IA)
Pasadena City Coll (CA)
Westmoreland County Comm Coll (PA)

FOOD SERVICE SYSTEMS ADMINISTRATION
Bishop State Comm Coll (AL)
Bucks County Comm Coll (PA)
Butler County Comm Coll (PA)
Comm Coll of Allegheny County (PA)
Florida State Coll at Jacksonville (FL)
Harper Coll (IL)
Harrisburg Area Comm Coll (PA)
Mott Comm Coll (MI)
Palomar Coll (CA)
Pensacola State Coll (FL)
Phoenix Coll (AZ)
San Jacinto Coll District (TX)
Wayne County Comm Coll District (MI)

FOODS, NUTRITION, AND WELLNESS
Antelope Valley Coll (CA)
Bossier Parish Comm Coll (LA)
Butte Coll (CA)
Carl Albert State Coll (OK)
Feather River Coll (CA)
Fullerton Coll (CA)
North Shore Comm Coll (MA)
Northwest Mississippi Comm Coll (MS)
Orange Coast Coll (CA)
Pensacola State Coll (FL)
Snow Coll (UT)

FOOD TECHNOLOGY AND PROCESSING
Butler County Comm Coll (PA)
Copiah-Lincoln Comm Coll (MS)
Honolulu Comm Coll (HI)
Lenoir Comm Coll (NC)
Luzerne County Comm Coll (PA)
Monroe Comm Coll (NY)
Orange Coast Coll (CA)
Stark State Coll (OH)
Tarrant County Coll District (TX)
U of Hawaii Maui Coll (HI)
Victor Valley Coll (CA)
Westchester Comm Coll (NY)

FOREIGN LANGUAGES AND LITERATURES
Austin Comm Coll (TX)
Bunker Hill Comm Coll (MA)
Casper Coll (WY)
Central Oregon Comm Coll (OR)
Coll of Marin (CA)
Coll of Southern Idaho (ID)
Comm Coll of Allegheny County (PA)
Darton State Coll (GA)

Eastern Arizona Coll (AZ)
Eastern Wyoming Coll (WY)
Fullerton Coll (CA)
Georgia Highlands Coll (GA)
Gordon State Coll (GA)
Grand Rapids Comm Coll (MI)
Hutchinson Comm Coll and Area Vocational School (KS)
Independence Comm Coll (KS)
Iowa Lakes Comm Coll (IA)
Lansing Comm Coll (MI)
Linn-Benton Comm Coll (OR)
Oklahoma City Comm Coll (OK)
Paris Jr Coll (TX)
San Jacinto Coll District (TX)
South Florida State Coll (FL)
South Georgia State Coll, Douglas (GA)
Texarkana Coll (TX)
Treasure Valley Comm Coll (OR)
Tulsa Comm Coll (OK)
Vincennes U (IN)

FOREIGN LANGUAGES RELATED
Genesee Comm Coll (NY)
Sauk Valley Comm Coll (IL)
Vincennes U (IN)

FOREIGN LANGUAGE TEACHER EDUCATION
Broward Coll (FL)
South Florida State Coll (FL)

FORENSIC SCIENCE AND TECHNOLOGY
American Samoa Comm Coll (AS)
Arkansas State U–Newport (AR)
Borough of Manhattan Comm Coll of the City U of New York (NY)
Broward Coll (FL)
Carroll Comm Coll (MD)
Casper Coll (WY)
Catawba Valley Comm Coll (NC)
Central Ohio Tech Coll (OH)
Coconino Comm Coll (AZ)
Comm Coll of Philadelphia (PA)
Cossatot Comm Coll of the U of Arkansas (AR)
Darton State Coll (GA)
Fayetteville Tech Comm Coll (NC)
Fox Valley Tech Coll (WI)
Grayson Coll (TX)
Herkimer County Comm Coll (NY)
ITT Tech Inst, Bessemer (AL)
ITT Tech Inst, Madison (AL)
ITT Tech Inst, Mobile (AL)
ITT Tech Inst, Tucson (AZ)
ITT Tech Inst (AR)
ITT Tech Inst, Culver City (CA)
ITT Tech Inst, Lathrop (CA)
ITT Tech Inst, National City (CA)
ITT Tech Inst, Orange (CA)
ITT Tech Inst, Oxnard (CA)
ITT Tech Inst, Rancho Cordova (CA)
ITT Tech Inst, San Bernardino (CA)
ITT Tech Inst, San Dimas (CA)
ITT Tech Inst, Sylmar (CA)
ITT Tech Inst, Torrance (CA)
ITT Tech Inst, Aurora (CO)
ITT Tech Inst, Westminster (CO)
ITT Tech Inst, Fort Lauderdale (FL)
ITT Tech Inst, Fort Myers (FL)
ITT Tech Inst, Jacksonville (FL)
ITT Tech Inst, Lake Mary (FL)
ITT Tech Inst, Miami (FL)
ITT Tech Inst, St. Petersburg (FL)
ITT Tech Inst, Tallahassee (FL)
ITT Tech Inst, Tampa (FL)
ITT Tech Inst, Atlanta (GA)
ITT Tech Inst, Duluth (GA)
ITT Tech Inst, Kennesaw (GA)
ITT Tech Inst (ID)
ITT Tech Inst, Arlington Heights (IL)
ITT Tech Inst, Oak Brook (IL)
ITT Tech Inst, Orland Park (IL)
ITT Tech Inst, Merrillville (IN)
ITT Tech Inst, Newburgh (IN)
ITT Tech Inst, Clive (IA)
ITT Tech Inst, Baton Rouge (LA)
ITT Tech Inst, St. Rose (LA)
ITT Tech Inst, Canton (MI)
ITT Tech Inst, Dearborn (MI)
ITT Tech Inst, Swartz Creek (MI)
ITT Tech Inst, Troy (MI)
ITT Tech Inst, Wyoming (MI)
ITT Tech Inst, Eden Prairie (MN)
ITT Tech Inst, Arnold (MO)
ITT Tech Inst , Earth City (MO)
ITT Tech Inst, Kansas City (MO)

ITT Tech Inst (NE)
ITT Tech Inst, Henderson (NV)
ITT Tech Inst, North Las Vegas (NV)
ITT Tech Inst (NM)
ITT Tech Inst, Getzville (NY)
ITT Tech Inst, Cary (NC)
ITT Tech Inst, Charlotte (NC)
ITT Tech Inst, High Point (NC)
ITT Tech Inst, Akron (OH)
ITT Tech Inst, Columbus (OH)
ITT Tech Inst, Dayton (OH)
ITT Tech Inst, Hilliard (OH)
ITT Tech Inst, Maumee (OH)
ITT Tech Inst, Norwood (OH)
ITT Tech Inst, Strongsville (OH)
ITT Tech Inst, Warrensville Heights (OH)
ITT Tech Inst , Youngstown (OH)
ITT Tech Inst, Tulsa (OK)
ITT Tech Inst, Portland (OR)
ITT Tech Inst, Columbia (SC)
ITT Tech Inst, Greenville (SC)
ITT Tech Inst, Chattanooga (TN)
ITT Tech Inst, Cordova (TN)
ITT Tech Inst, Johnson City (TN)
ITT Tech Inst, Knoxville (TN)
ITT Tech Inst, Nashville (TN)
ITT Tech Inst (UT)
ITT Tech Inst, Chantilly (VA)
ITT Tech Inst, Norfolk (VA)
ITT Tech Inst, Richmond (VA)
ITT Tech Inst, Salem (VA)
ITT Tech Inst, Springfield (VA)
ITT Tech Inst, Everett (WA)
ITT Tech Inst, Seattle (WA)
ITT Tech Inst, Spokane Valley (WA)
ITT Tech Inst (WV)
ITT Tech Inst , Greenfield (WI)
Macomb Comm Coll (MI)
Massachusetts Bay Comm Coll (MA)
Palomar Coll (CA)
Phoenix Coll (AZ)
South Florida State Coll (FL)
Sullivan County Comm Coll (NY)
Tompkins Cortland Comm Coll (NY)
Tunxis Comm Coll (CT)
U of Arkansas Comm Coll at Morrilton (AR)
Wayne Comm Coll (NC)

FOREST/FOREST RESOURCES MANAGEMENT
Broward Coll (FL)

FORESTRY
Allen Comm Coll (KS)
Bainbridge State Coll (GA)
Central Oregon Comm Coll (OR)
Coll of Southern Idaho (ID)
Columbia Coll (CA)
Copiah-Lincoln Comm Coll (MS)
Darton State Coll (GA)
Eastern Arizona Coll (AZ)
Gordon State Coll (GA)
Grand Rapids Comm Coll (MI)
Hinds Comm Coll (MS)
Hocking Coll (OH)
Iowa Lakes Comm Coll (IA)
Kilgore Coll (TX)
Miami Dade Coll (FL)
Monroe Comm Coll (NY)
Potomac State Coll of West Virginia U (WV)
Snow Coll (UT)
South Florida State Coll (FL)
Treasure Valley Comm Coll (OR)
Umpqua Comm Coll (OR)
Western Wyoming Comm Coll (WY)

FOREST TECHNOLOGY
Alabama Southern Comm Coll (AL)
Albany Tech Coll (GA)
Central Oregon Comm Coll (OR)
Dabney S. Lancaster Comm Coll (VA)
Hocking Coll (OH)
Jefferson Comm Coll (NY)
Lurleen B. Wallace Comm Coll (AL)
Mt. San Antonio Coll (CA)
Ogeechee Tech Coll (GA)
Okefenokee Tech Coll (GA)
Penn State Mont Alto (PA)
Potomac State Coll of West Virginia U (WV)
Southeastern Comm Coll (NC)
Wayne Comm Coll (NC)

FRENCH
Austin Comm Coll (TX)
Broward Coll (FL)

Coll of Marin (CA)
Coll of the Canyons (CA)
Coll of the Desert (CA)
Imperial Valley Coll (CA)
Lansing Comm Coll (MI)
Miami Dade Coll (FL)
MiraCosta Coll (CA)
Northwest Coll (WY)
Orange Coast Coll (CA)
Palomar Coll (CA)
Santa Rosa Jr Coll (CA)
Snow Coll (UT)
South Florida State Coll (FL)

FUNERAL SERVICE AND MORTUARY SCIENCE
Allen Comm Coll (KS)
Amarillo Coll (TX)
Arapahoe Comm Coll (CO)
Bishop State Comm Coll (AL)
The Comm Coll of Baltimore County (MD)
Fayetteville Tech Comm Coll (NC)
Fiorello H. LaGuardia Comm Coll of the City U of New York (NY)
Ivy Tech Comm Coll–Northwest (IN)
Jefferson State Comm Coll (AL)
John A. Gupton Coll (TN)
John Tyler Comm Coll (VA)
Luzerne County Comm Coll (PA)
Mercer County Comm Coll (NJ)
Miami Dade Coll (FL)
Monroe County Comm Coll (MI)
Nassau Comm Coll (NY)
Northampton Comm Coll (PA)
Ogeechee Tech Coll (GA)
Randolph Comm Coll (NC)
U of Arkansas Comm Coll at Hope (AR)
Vincennes U (IN)

FURNITURE DESIGN AND MANUFACTURING
Northcentral Tech Coll (WI)

GAME AND INTERACTIVE MEDIA DESIGN
Cayuga County Comm Coll (NY)
Collin County Comm Coll District (TX)
Fayetteville Tech Comm Coll (NC)
Hinds Comm Coll (MS)
Lehigh Carbon Comm Coll (PA)
Oklahoma City Comm Coll (OK)
Pima Comm Coll (AZ)
South Piedmont Comm Coll (NC)
Texas State Tech Coll Waco (TX)
Wayne Comm Coll (NC)

GENERAL STUDIES
Allen Comm Coll (KS)
Amarillo Coll (TX)
Ancilla Coll (IN)
Arizona Western Coll (AZ)
Arkansas State U–Newport (AR)
Austin Comm Coll (TX)
Berkeley City Coll (CA)
Bevill State Comm Coll (AL)
Bishop State Comm Coll (AL)
Blue Ridge Comm and Tech Coll (WV)
Bossier Parish Comm Coll (LA)
Bristol Comm Coll (MA)
Brookhaven Coll (TX)
Bunker Hill Comm Coll (MA)
Butler County Comm Coll (PA)
Carroll Comm Coll (MD)
Casper Coll (WY)
Catawba Valley Comm Coll (NC)
Cayuga County Comm Coll (NY)
Cecil Coll (MD)
Central Wyoming Coll (WY)
Chandler-Gilbert Comm Coll (AZ)
Cincinnati State Tech and Comm Coll (OH)
Cleveland Comm Coll (NC)
Cleveland State Comm Coll (TN)
Cochise Coll, Sierra Vista (AZ)
Coconino Comm Coll (AZ)
Coll of the Mainland (TX)
Colorado Northwestern Comm Coll (CO)
Columbia Gorge Comm Coll (OR)
Comm Coll of Allegheny County (PA)
Comm Coll of Rhode Island (RI)
Cossatot Comm Coll of the U of Arkansas (AR)
Crowder Coll (MO)
Dakota Coll at Bottineau (ND)
Danville Area Comm Coll (IL)

Darton State Coll (GA)
Delta Coll (MI)
Dutchess Comm Coll (NY)
Dyersburg State Comm Coll (TN)
East Central Coll (MO)
Eastern Wyoming Coll (WY)
Frank Phillips Coll (TX)
Gadsden State Comm Coll (AL)
Galveston Coll (TX)
Garden City Comm Coll (KS)
Gateway Comm and Tech Coll (KY)
Gavilan Coll (CA)
Genesee Comm Coll (NY)
Georgia Highlands Coll (GA)
Georgia Military Coll (GA)
Glen Oaks Comm Coll (MI)
Gordon State Coll (GA)
Grays Harbor Coll (WA)
Harford Comm Coll (MD)
Harrisburg Area Comm Coll (PA)
Helena Coll U of Montana (MT)
Herkimer County Comm Coll (NY)
Highland Comm Coll (IL)
Hinds Comm Coll (MS)
Howard Comm Coll (MD)
Illinois Eastern Comm Colls, Frontier
    Community College (IL)
Illinois Eastern Comm Colls, Lincoln
    Trail College (IL)
Illinois Eastern Comm Colls, Olney
    Central College (IL)
Illinois Eastern Comm Colls, Wabash
    Valley College (IL)
Iowa Lakes Comm Coll (IA)
Ivy Tech Comm Coll–Bloomington
    (IN)
Ivy Tech Comm Coll–Central Indiana
    (IN)
Ivy Tech Comm Coll–Columbus (IN)
Ivy Tech Comm Coll–East Central
    (IN)
Ivy Tech Comm Coll–Kokomo (IN)
Ivy Tech Comm Coll–Lafayette (IN)
Ivy Tech Comm Coll–North Central
    (IN)
Ivy Tech Comm Coll–Northeast (IN)
Ivy Tech Comm Coll–Northwest (IN)
Ivy Tech Comm Coll–Richmond (IN)
Ivy Tech Comm Coll–Southeast (IN)
Ivy Tech Comm Coll–Southern
    Indiana (IN)
Ivy Tech Comm Coll–Southwest (IN)
Ivy Tech Comm Coll–Wabash Valley
    (IN)
Jackson Coll (MI)
Jackson State Comm Coll (TN)
James Sprunt Comm Coll (NC)
Jefferson State Comm Coll (AL)
John Tyler Comm Coll (VA)
Kankakee Comm Coll (IL)
Kaskaskia Coll (IL)
Kent State U at Ashtabula (OH)
Kilgore Coll (TX)
Kirtland Comm Coll (MI)
Lake Land Coll (IL)
Lakes Region Comm Coll (NH)
Landmark Coll (VT)
Lane Comm Coll (OR)
Laramie County Comm Coll (WY)
Lawson State Comm Coll (AL)
Lehigh Carbon Comm Coll (PA)
Lincoln Land Comm Coll (IL)
Lurleen B. Wallace Comm Coll (AL)
Luzerne County Comm Coll (PA)
Macomb Comm Coll (MI)
Manchester Comm Coll (CT)
Marion Military Inst (AL)
Massachusetts Bay Comm Coll (MA)
McHenry County Coll (IL)
Miami Dade Coll (FL)
Mineral Area Coll (MO)
MiraCosta Coll (CA)
Missouri State U–West Plains (MO)
Mitchell Comm Coll (NC)
Mohawk Valley Comm Coll (NY)
Motlow State Comm Coll (TN)
Mott Comm Coll (MI)
Mount Wachusett Comm Coll (MA)
Nassau Comm Coll (NY)
New Mexico State U–Alamogordo
    (NM)
Niagara County Comm Coll (NY)
Northampton Comm Coll (PA)
Northcentral Tech Coll (WI)
Northern Essex Comm Coll (MA)
Northwest Coll (WY)
Northwest-Shoals Comm Coll (AL)
Norwalk Comm Coll (CT)
Nunez Comm Coll (LA)
Oakland Comm Coll (MI)
Ocean County Coll (NJ)

Oklahoma City Comm Coll (OK)
Oklahoma State U, Oklahoma City
    (OK)
Onondaga Comm Coll (NY)
Oregon Coast Comm Coll (OR)
Owens Comm Coll, Toledo (OH)
Panola Coll (TX)
Paris Jr Coll (TX)
Pennsylvania Highlands Comm Coll
    (PA)
Phoenix Coll (AZ)
Piedmont Comm Coll (NC)
Piedmont Virginia Comm Coll (VA)
Pima Comm Coll (AZ)
Pitt Comm Coll (NC)
Pueblo Comm Coll (CO)
Quinsigamond Comm Coll (MA)
Reading Area Comm Coll (PA)
River Valley Comm Coll (NH)
Roane State Comm Coll (TN)
Rogue Comm Coll (OR)
Salt Lake Comm Coll (UT)
San Jacinto Coll District (TX)
San Juan Coll (NM)
Schoolcraft Coll (MI)
Seminole State Coll (OK)
Shelton State Comm Coll (AL)
Sheridan Coll (WY)
Snead State Comm Coll (AL)
Southern U at Shreveport (LA)
South Florida State Coll (FL)
South Georgia State Coll, Douglas
    (GA)
South Louisiana Comm Coll (LA)
South Piedmont Comm Coll (NC)
Southwestern Illinois Coll (IL)
Southwestern Michigan Coll (MI)
Sowela Tech Comm Coll (LA)
Spoon River Coll (IL)
Springfield Tech Comm Coll (MA)
Treasure Valley Comm Coll (OR)
Truckee Meadows Comm Coll (NV)
Tulsa Comm Coll (OK)
The U of Akron–Wayne Coll (OH)
U of Arkansas Comm Coll at Hope
    (AR)
U of Arkansas Comm Coll at
    Morrilton (AR)
U of New Mexico–Los Alamos
    Branch (NM)
Volunteer State Comm Coll (TN)
Walters State Comm Coll (TN)
Waubonsee Comm Coll (IL)
Western Nevada Coll (NV)
Western Wyoming Comm Coll (WY)

GEOGRAPHIC INFORMATION SCIENCE AND CARTOGRAPHY
Austin Comm Coll (TX)
Bismarck State Coll (ND)
Brookhaven Coll (TX)
Casper Coll (WY)
Clark State Comm Coll (OH)
Collin County Comm Coll District
    (TX)
Greenville Tech Coll (SC)
Harrisburg Area Comm Coll (PA)
Hinds Comm Coll (MS)
Houston Comm Coll System (TX)
Lehigh Carbon Comm Coll (PA)
Mitchell Tech Inst (SD)
Oklahoma City Comm Coll (OK)
Southwestern Indian Polytechnic Inst
    (NM)

GEOGRAPHY
Allen Comm Coll (KS)
Austin Comm Coll (TX)
Broward Coll (FL)
Ca&nnada Coll (CA)
Cayuga County Comm Coll (NY)
Coll of Marin (CA)
Coll of Southern Idaho (ID)
Coll of the Canyons (CA)
Coll of the Desert (CA)
Coll of Western Idaho (ID)
The Comm Coll of Baltimore County
    (MD)
Cosumnes River Coll, Sacramento
    (CA)
Darton State Coll (GA)
Fullerton Coll (CA)
Holyoke Comm Coll (MA)
Lake Tahoe Comm Coll (CA)
Lansing Comm Coll (MI)
Los Angeles Mission Coll (CA)
MiraCosta Coll (CA)
Mississippi Delta Comm Coll (MS)
Montgomery Coll (MD)
Orange Coast Coll (CA)
Snow Coll (UT)
South Florida State Coll (FL)

GEOGRAPHY RELATED
Columbia Coll (CA)
Mt. San Jacinto Coll (CA)

GEOLOGICAL AND EARTH SCIENCES/GEOSCIENCES RELATED
Erie Comm Coll, North Campus (NY)
Truckee Meadows Comm Coll (NV)

GEOLOGY/EARTH SCIENCE
Amarillo Coll (TX)
Arizona Western Coll (AZ)
Austin Comm Coll (TX)
Broward Coll (FL)
Casper Coll (WY)
Central Wyoming Coll (WY)
Coll of Marin (CA)
Coll of Southern Idaho (ID)
Coll of the Desert (CA)
Coll of Western Idaho (ID)
Columbia Coll (CA)
Cosumnes River Coll, Sacramento
    (CA)
Eastern Arizona Coll (AZ)
Edison Comm Coll (OH)
Fullerton Coll (CA)
Georgia Highlands Coll (GA)
Grand Rapids Comm Coll (MI)
Grayson Coll (TX)
Great Basin Coll (NV)
Hinds Comm Coll (MS)
Iowa Lakes Comm Coll (IA)
Kilgore Coll (TX)
Lake Tahoe Comm Coll (CA)
Miami Dade Coll (FL)
Middlesex County Coll (NJ)
MiraCosta Coll (CA)
Orange Coast Coll (CA)
Palomar Coll (CA)
Pensacola State Coll (FL)
Potomac State Coll of West Virginia
    U (WV)
Salt Lake Comm Coll (UT)
San Jacinto Coll District (TX)
San Juan Coll (NM)
Snow Coll (UT)
South Florida State Coll (FL)
Treasure Valley Comm Coll (OR)
Trinity Valley Comm Coll (TX)
Tyler Jr Coll (TX)
Vincennes U (IN)
Western Wyoming Comm Coll (WY)

GERMAN
Austin Comm Coll (TX)
Broward Coll (FL)
Miami Dade Coll (FL)
MiraCosta Coll (CA)
Orange Coast Coll (CA)

GERMANIC LANGUAGES
Lansing Comm Coll (MI)

GERONTOLOGY
Genesee Comm Coll (NY)
Lakes Region Comm Coll (NH)
North Shore Comm Coll (MA)
South Florida State Coll (FL)

GLAZIER
Metropolitan Comm Coll–Kansas City
    (MO)

GOLF COURSE OPERATION AND GROUNDS MANAGEMENT
Anoka Tech Coll (MN)
Broward Coll (FL)
Harford Comm Coll (MD)
Owens Comm Coll, Toledo (OH)
Tech Coll of the Lowcountry (SC)
Walla Walla Comm Coll (WA)

GRAPHIC AND PRINTING EQUIPMENT OPERATION/ PRODUCTION
Central Maine Comm Coll (ME)
Columbus State Comm Coll (OH)
Erie Comm Coll, South Campus (NY)
Fox Valley Tech Coll (WI)
Fullerton Coll (CA)
Golden West Coll (CA)
Hinds Comm Coll (MS)
Houston Comm Coll System (TX)
Iowa Lakes Comm Coll (IA)
Lake Land Coll (IL)
Lakes Region Comm Coll (NH)
Lenoir Comm Coll (NC)
Luzerne County Comm Coll (PA)
Macomb Comm Coll (MI)
Mineral Area Coll (MO)
Mississippi Delta Comm Coll (MS)

Monroe Comm Coll (NY)
Northwest Coll (WY)
Ozarks Tech Comm Coll (MO)
Pasadena City Coll (CA)
Rock Valley Coll (IL)
San Diego City Coll (CA)
Shoreline Comm Coll (WA)
Sullivan Coll of Technology and
    Design (KY)
Tarrant County Coll District (TX)
Tulsa Comm Coll (OK)
Vincennes U (IN)

GRAPHIC COMMUNICATIONS
Bishop State Comm Coll (AL)
Central Maine Comm Coll (ME)
Clark Coll (WA)
Fox Valley Tech Coll (WI)
Gogebic Comm Coll (MI)
Hawkeye Comm Coll (IA)
Iowa Lakes Comm Coll (IA)
ITT Tech Inst, Bessemer (AL)
ITT Tech Inst, Tucson (AZ)
ITT Tech Inst (AR)
ITT Tech Inst, Lathrop (CA)
ITT Tech Inst, Rancho Cordova (CA)
ITT Tech Inst, Aurora (CO)
ITT Tech Inst, Jacksonville (FL)
ITT Tech Inst, Tallahassee (FL)
ITT Tech Inst, Atlanta (GA)
ITT Tech Inst, Duluth (GA)
ITT Tech Inst, Kennesaw (GA)
ITT Tech Inst, Arlington Heights (IL)
ITT Tech Inst, Baton Rouge (LA)
ITT Tech Inst, St. Rose (LA)
ITT Tech Inst, Owings Mills (MD)
ITT Tech Inst, Canton (MI)
ITT Tech Inst, Dearborn (MI)
ITT Tech Inst, Swartz Creek (MI)
ITT Tech Inst, Troy (MI)
ITT Tech Inst, Wyoming (MI)
ITT Tech Inst, Arnold (MO)
ITT Tech Inst , Earth City (MO)
ITT Tech Inst, Kansas City (MO)
ITT Tech Inst (NE)
ITT Tech Inst, Henderson (NV)
ITT Tech Inst (NM)
ITT Tech Inst, Getzville (NY)
ITT Tech Inst, Liverpool (NY)
ITT Tech Inst, High Point (NC)
ITT Tech Inst, Akron (OH)
ITT Tech Inst, Dayton (OH)
ITT Tech Inst, Hilliard (OH)
ITT Tech Inst, Maumee (OH)
ITT Tech Inst, Warrensville Heights
    (OH)
ITT Tech Inst , Youngstown (OH)
ITT Tech Inst, Tulsa (OK)
ITT Tech Inst, Portland (OR)
ITT Tech Inst, Columbia (SC)
ITT Tech Inst, Cordova (TN)
ITT Tech Inst, Knoxville (TN)
ITT Tech Inst, Nashville (TN)
ITT Tech Inst, Webster (TX)
ITT Tech Inst (UT)
ITT Tech Inst, Chantilly (VA)
ITT Tech Inst, Norfolk (VA)
ITT Tech Inst, Richmond (VA)
ITT Tech Inst, Everett (WA)
ITT Tech Inst, Seattle (WA)
ITT Tech Inst, Spokane Valley (WA)
ITT Tech Inst (WV)
ITT Tech Inst, Green Bay (WI)
ITT Tech Inst , Greenfield (WI)
MiraCosta Coll (CA)
Northcentral Tech Coll (WI)
Oklahoma City Comm Coll (OK)
Palomar Coll (CA)
Piedmont Comm Coll (NC)
Sullivan Coll of Technology and
    Design (KY)
Waukesha County Tech Coll (WI)

GRAPHIC COMMUNICATIONS RELATED
Carrington Coll California–Pleasant
    Hill (CA)
Eastern Florida State Coll (FL)
Middlesex County Coll (NJ)
Sullivan Coll of Technology and
    Design (KY)

GRAPHIC DESIGN
Antonelli Inst (PA)
Arapahoe Comm Coll (CO)
The Art Inst of New York City (NY)
Bradford School (OH)
Bradford School (PA)
Bristol Comm Coll (MA)
Brookhaven Coll (TX)
Broward Coll (FL)
Brown Mackie Coll–Birmingham (AL)

Brown Mackie Coll–Dallas/Ft. Worth
    (TX)
Brown Mackie Coll–Tucson (AZ)
Butte Coll (CA)
Casper Coll (WY)
Cayuga County Comm Coll (NY)
Central Wyoming Coll (WY)
Cloud County Comm Coll (KS)
Coll of the Canyons (CA)
Collin County Comm Coll District
    (TX)
Comm Coll of Vermont (VT)
Cosumnes River Coll, Sacramento
    (CA)
County Coll of Morris (NJ)
Davis Coll (OH)
Dunwoody Coll of Technology (MN)
Elgin Comm Coll (IL)
Florida Gateway Coll (FL)
Fox Coll (IL)
Fullerton Coll (CA)
Genesee Comm Coll (NY)
Glendale Comm Coll (AZ)
Great Falls Coll Montana State U
    (MT)
Harford Comm Coll (MD)
Harrisburg Area Comm Coll (PA)
Highland Comm Coll (IL)
Hinds Comm Coll (MS)
International Business Coll,
    Indianapolis (IN)
Iowa Lakes Comm Coll (IA)
Ivy Tech Comm Coll–Southwest (IN)
Jackson Coll (MI)
King's Coll (NC)
Kirtland Comm Coll (MI)
Lansing Comm Coll (MI)
Lehigh Carbon Comm Coll (PA)
Lincoln Land Comm Coll (IL)
Luzerne County Comm Coll (PA)
Minneapolis Business Coll (MN)
Moraine Park Tech Coll (WI)
Moraine Valley Comm Coll (IL)
Mott Comm Coll (MI)
New Mexico State U–Alamogordo
    (NM)
Northampton Comm Coll (PA)
Norwalk Comm Coll (CT)
Oakland Comm Coll (MI)
Oakton Comm Coll (IL)
Palomar Coll (CA)
Pasadena City Coll (CA)
Pensacola State Coll (FL)
Phoenix Coll (AZ)
Rend Lake Coll (IL)
Salt Lake Comm Coll (UT)
Santa Monica Coll (CA)
Santa Rosa Jr Coll (CA)
Sessions Coll for Professional Design
    (AZ)
South Florida State Coll (FL)
Southwestern Michigan Coll (MI)
Spoon River Coll (IL)
Sullivan Coll of Technology and
    Design (KY)
Texas State Tech Coll Waco (TX)
Waubonsee Comm Coll (IL)
Waukesha County Tech Coll (WI)
Westmoreland County Comm Coll
    (PA)
Wood Tobe–Coburn School (NY)

GREENHOUSE MANAGEMENT
Century Coll (MN)
Comm Coll of Allegheny County (PA)
Dakota Coll at Bottineau (ND)
The Ohio State U Ag Tech Inst (OH)

HAIR STYLING AND HAIR DESIGN
Inst of Business & Medical Careers
    (CO)

HAZARDOUS MATERIALS MANAGEMENT AND WASTE TECHNOLOGY
Butte Coll (CA)
Fullerton Coll (CA)
Palomar Coll (CA)
Pensacola State Coll (FL)

HEALTH AIDE
Allen Comm Coll (KS)
Texarkana Coll (TX)

HEALTH AND MEDICAL ADMINISTRATIVE SERVICES RELATED
Butler County Comm Coll (PA)
Carrington Coll California–Pleasant
    Hill (CA)

Carrington Coll California–San Leandro (CA)
Cumberland County Coll (NJ)
Hinds Comm Coll (MS)
Kent State U at Ashtabula (OH)
Kent State U at Salem (OH)
North Iowa Area Comm Coll (IA)
San Joaquin Valley Coll, Visalia (CA)
Westmoreland County Comm Coll (PA)
Wichita Area Tech Coll (KS)

HEALTH AND PHYSICAL EDUCATION/FITNESS
Allen Comm Coll (KS)
Antelope Valley Coll (CA)
Arapahoe Comm Coll (CO)
Austin Comm Coll (TX)
Barstow Comm Coll (CA)
Butte Coll (CA)
Ca&nnada Coll (CA)
Central Oregon Comm Coll (OR)
Cochise Coll, Sierra Vista (AZ)
Coll of Marin (CA)
Coll of the Canyons (CA)
Coll of the Desert (CA)
Columbia Coll (CA)
Comm Care Coll (OK)
Comm Coll of Allegheny County (PA)
Cosumnes River Coll, Sacramento (CA)
Dakota Coll at Bottineau (ND)
Darton State Coll (GA)
Eastern Arizona Coll (AZ)
Elgin Comm Coll (IL)
Feather River Coll (CA)
Fullerton Coll (CA)
Gavilan Coll (CA)
Genesee Comm Coll (NY)
Gordon State Coll (GA)
Holyoke Comm Coll (MA)
Houston Comm Coll System (TX)
Iowa Lakes Comm Coll (IA)
Lansing Comm Coll (MI)
Luzerne County Comm Coll (PA)
McHenry County Coll (IL)
MiraCosta Coll (CA)
Montgomery County Comm Coll (PA)
Mt. San Antonio Coll (CA)
Mt. San Jacinto Coll (CA)
Northeast Texas Comm Coll (TX)
Northwest Coll (WY)
Palomar Coll (CA)
Paris Jr Coll (TX)
Raritan Valley Comm Coll (NJ)
San Jacinto Coll District (TX)
San Juan Coll (NM)
Santa Monica Coll (CA)
Santa Rosa Jr Coll (CA)
Sheridan Coll (WY)
Vincennes U (IN)
Waubonsee Comm Coll (IL)

HEALTH AND PHYSICAL EDUCATION RELATED
Ancilla Coll (IN)
Coll of Southern Maryland (MD)
Columbus State Comm Coll (OH)
Fayetteville Tech Comm Coll (NC)
Garden City Comm Coll (KS)
Genesee Comm Coll (NY)
Herkimer County Comm Coll (NY)
Kingsborough Comm Coll of the City U of New York (NY)
Wright Career Coll, Overland Park (KS)
Wright Career Coll, Wichita (KS)
Wright Career Coll (NE)
Wright Career Coll, Oklahoma City (OK)
Wright Career Coll, Tulsa (OK)

HEALTH/HEALTH-CARE ADMINISTRATION
Brown Mackie Coll–Fort Wayne (IN)
Brown Mackie Coll–Indianapolis (IN)
Brown Mackie Coll–Kansas City (KS)
Brown Mackie Coll–Louisville (KY)
Brown Mackie Coll–Miami (FL)
Brown Mackie Coll–Northern Kentucky (KY)
Brown Mackie Coll–Salina (KS)
Brown Mackie Coll–South Bend (IN)
Brown Mackie Coll–Tulsa (OK)
Butler County Comm Coll (PA)
Carrington Coll California–Citrus Heights (CA)
Carrington Coll California–Pleasant Hill (CA)

Carrington Coll California–Sacramento (CA)
Carrington Coll California–San Jose (CA)
Carrington Coll California–San Leandro (CA)
Comm Care Coll (OK)
Harrisburg Area Comm Coll (PA)
Iowa Lakes Comm Coll (IA)
Kent State U at Trumbull (OH)
Luzerne County Comm Coll (PA)
Northwest Florida State Coll (FL)
Oakland Comm Coll (MI)
Oklahoma State U, Oklahoma City (OK)
Owens Comm Coll, Toledo (OH)
Pensacola State Coll (FL)
South Florida State Coll (FL)
South Plains Coll (TX)
Tyler Jr Coll (TX)
Wright Career Coll, Overland Park (KS)
Wright Career Coll, Wichita (KS)
Wright Career Coll (NE)
Wright Career Coll, Oklahoma City (OK)
Wright Career Coll, Tulsa (OK)

HEALTH INFORMATION/ MEDICAL RECORDS ADMINISTRATION
Alabama Southern Comm Coll (AL)
Amarillo Coll (TX)
Bowling Green State U-Firelands Coll (OH)
Broward Coll (FL)
Bunker Hill Comm Coll (MA)
Columbus State Comm Coll (OH)
Comm Coll of Philadelphia (PA)
Darton State Coll (GA)
Daytona State Coll (FL)
Florida Gateway Coll (FL)
Florida State Coll at Jacksonville (FL)
Georgia Highlands Coll (GA)
Hinds Comm Coll (MS)
Hocking Coll (OH)
Illinois Eastern Comm Colls, Lincoln Trail College (IL)
LDS Business Coll (UT)
Metropolitan Comm Coll–Kansas City (MO)
Miami Dade Coll (FL)
Mississippi Delta Comm Coll (MS)
Monroe Comm Coll (NY)
Mount Wachusett Comm Coll (MA)
Northern Essex Comm Coll (MA)
Oakton Comm Coll (IL)
Oklahoma City Comm Coll (OK)
Pensacola State Coll (FL)
Roane State Comm Coll (TN)
Shoreline Comm Coll (WA)
Southern U at Shreveport (LA)
South Florida State Coll (FL)
South Plains Coll (TX)
Southwestern Comm Coll (NC)
Stark State Coll (OH)
Tarrant County Coll District (TX)
Tulsa Comm Coll (OK)

HEALTH INFORMATION/ MEDICAL RECORDS TECHNOLOGY
Anoka Tech Coll (MN)
Arapahoe Comm Coll (CO)
Atlanta Tech Coll (GA)
Austin Comm Coll (TX)
Beal Coll (ME)
Bishop State Comm Coll (AL)
Borough of Manhattan Comm Coll of the City U of New York (NY)
Carrington Coll California–Pleasant Hill (CA)
Carroll Comm Coll (MD)
Catawba Valley Comm Coll (NC)
Central Oregon Comm Coll (OR)
Chippewa Valley Tech Coll (WI)
Cincinnati State Tech and Comm Coll (OH)
Coll of Central Florida (FL)
Coll of the Mainland (TX)
Collin County Comm Coll District (TX)
Columbus State Comm Coll (OH)
Columbus Tech Coll (GA)
Comm Coll of Allegheny County (PA)
Cosumnes River Coll, Sacramento (CA)
Crowder Coll (MO)
Danville Area Comm Coll (IL)

Darton State Coll (GA)
Dyersburg State Comm Coll (TN)
East Central Coll (MO)
Erie Comm Coll, North Campus (NY)
Fox Valley Tech Coll (WI)
Great Falls Coll Montana State U (MT)
Greenville Tech Coll (SC)
Highland Comm Coll (IL)
Hinds Comm Coll (MS)
Houston Comm Coll System (TX)
Hudson County Comm Coll (NJ)
Hutchinson Comm Coll and Area Vocational School (KS)
Illinois Eastern Comm Colls, Frontier Community College (IL)
ITT Tech Inst, Orange (CA)
ITT Tech Inst, San Bernardino (CA)
ITT Tech Inst, Sylmar (CA)
ITT Tech Inst, Lake Mary (FL)
ITT Tech Inst, Tampa (FL)
ITT Tech Inst (NM)
Jamestown Comm Coll (NY)
J. Sargeant Reynolds Comm Coll (VA)
Kaskaskia Coll (IL)
Kirtland Comm Coll (MI)
Lehigh Carbon Comm Coll (PA)
Lone Star Coll–CyFair (TX)
Lone Star Coll–North Harris (TX)
Montgomery Coll (MD)
Moraine Park Tech Coll (WI)
Moraine Valley Comm Coll (IL)
Mott Comm Coll (MI)
North Dakota State Coll of Science (ND)
Northeast Iowa Comm Coll (IA)
Northwest Florida State Coll (FL)
Ogeechee Tech Coll (GA)
Onondaga Comm Coll (NY)
Owens Comm Coll, Toledo (OH)
Ozarks Tech Comm Coll (MO)
Panola Coll (TX)
Paris Jr Coll (TX)
Pensacola State Coll (FL)
Phoenix Coll (AZ)
Pima Comm Coll (AZ)
Pitt Comm Coll (NC)
Raritan Valley Comm Coll (NJ)
Reading Area Comm Coll (PA)
Rend Lake Coll (IL)
Richmond Comm Coll (NC)
St. Clair County Comm Coll (MI)
San Jacinto Coll District (TX)
San Juan Coll (NM)
Schoolcraft Coll (MI)
Shawnee Comm Coll (IL)
Southern Maine Comm Coll (ME)
Southern U at Shreveport (LA)
Southwestern Comm Coll (NC)
Southwestern Illinois Coll (IL)
Southwestern Michigan Coll (MI)
State Fair Comm Coll (MO)
State U of New York Coll of Technology at Alfred (NY)
Tallahassee Comm Coll (FL)
TCI–The Coll of Technology (NY)
Tulsa Comm Coll (OK)
Tyler Jr Coll (TX)
Vincennes U (IN)
Volunteer State Comm Coll (TN)
Walters State Comm Coll (TN)
Waubonsee Comm Coll (IL)
Waukesha County Tech Coll (WI)
West Georgia Tech Coll (GA)
Williston State Coll (ND)
York County Comm Coll (ME)

HEALTH/MEDICAL PREPARATORY PROGRAMS RELATED
Arkansas State U–Newport (AR)
Darton State Coll (GA)
Eastern Arizona Coll (AZ)
Eastern Wyoming Coll (WY)
Edison Comm Coll (OH)
Fullerton Coll (CA)
Gavilan Coll (CA)
Gordon State Coll (GA)
Miami Dade Coll (FL)
MiraCosta Coll (CA)
Northwest Coll (WY)
South Georgia State Coll, Douglas (GA)
Treasure Valley Comm Coll (OR)
Western Wyoming Comm Coll (WY)

HEALTH PROFESSIONS RELATED
Berkshire Comm Coll (MA)

Bowling Green State U-Firelands Coll (OH)
Bucks County Comm Coll (PA)
Carl Albert State Coll (OK)
Carroll Comm Coll (MD)
Comm Coll of Allegheny County (PA)
Comm Coll of Philadelphia (PA)
Gateway Comm and Tech Coll (KY)
Genesee Comm Coll (NY)
Glen Oaks Comm Coll (MI)
Greenfield Comm Coll (MA)
Halifax Comm Coll (NC)
Herkimer County Comm Coll (NY)
Hinds Comm Coll (MS)
Lakeland Comm Coll (OH)
Lanier Tech Coll (GA)
Mercer County Comm Coll (NJ)
Miami Dade Coll (FL)
Middlesex County Coll (NJ)
Mineral Area Coll (MO)
Mitchell Comm Coll (NC)
Northeastern Jr Coll (CO)
North Shore Comm Coll (MA)
Northwestern Connecticut Comm Coll (CT)
Onondaga Comm Coll (NY)
Orange Coast Coll (CA)
Piedmont Comm Coll (NC)
Pitt Comm Coll (NC)
Reading Area Comm Coll (PA)
Richmond Comm Coll (NC)
Salt Lake Comm Coll (UT)
Spoon River Coll (IL)
Sussex County Comm Coll (NJ)
Tulsa Comm Coll (OK)
Volunteer State Comm Coll (TN)

HEALTH SERVICES ADMINISTRATION
Broward Coll (FL)
Florida Gateway Coll (FL)
Harrisburg Area Comm Coll (PA)

HEALTH SERVICES/ALLIED HEALTH/HEALTH SCIENCES
Alabama Southern Comm Coll (AL)
American Samoa Comm Coll (AS)
Ancilla Coll (IN)
Anoka-Ramsey Comm Coll (MN)
Anoka-Ramsey Comm Coll, Cambridge Campus (MN)
Arizona Western Coll (AZ)
Cambria-Rowe Business Coll, Johnstown (PA)
Carl Albert State Coll (OK)
Casper Coll (WY)
Cecil Coll (MD)
Central Wyoming Coll (WY)
Century Coll (MN)
Clark State Comm Coll (OH)
Columbia Coll (CA)
Dakota Coll at Bottineau (ND)
Dyersburg State Comm Coll (TN)
Garden City Comm Coll (KS)
Georgia Military Coll (GA)
Goodwin Coll (CT)
Hudson County Comm Coll (NJ)
Ilisagvik Coll (AK)
Lake Superior Coll (MN)
Middlesex County Coll (NJ)
Northwest Coll (WY)
Paris Jr Coll (TX)
Pitt Comm Coll (NC)
Quinsigamond Comm Coll (MA)
Raritan Valley Comm Coll (NJ)
Reading Area Comm Coll (PA)
Schoolcraft Coll (MI)
Sheridan Coll (WY)
South Florida State Coll (FL)
Western Wyoming Comm Coll (WY)
York County Comm Coll (ME)

HEALTH TEACHER EDUCATION
Austin Comm Coll (TX)
Bainbridge State Coll (GA)
Broward Coll (FL)
Copiah-Lincoln Comm Coll (MS)
Cosumnes River Coll, Sacramento (CA)
Georgia Military Coll (GA)
Harper Coll (IL)
Howard Comm Coll (MD)
Kilgore Coll (TX)
MiraCosta Coll (CA)
Mississippi Delta Comm Coll (MS)
South Florida State Coll (FL)
Umpqua Comm Coll (OR)

HEALTH UNIT COORDINATOR/ WARD CLERK
Comm Coll of Allegheny County (PA)
Southeast Tech Inst (SD)

HEATING, AIR CONDITIONING, VENTILATION AND REFRIGERATION MAINTENANCE TECHNOLOGY
Amarillo Coll (TX)
Antelope Valley Coll (CA)
Arizona Western Coll (AZ)
Bellingham Tech Coll (WA)
Bismarck State Coll (ND)
Blackhawk Tech Coll (WI)
Brown Mackie Coll–Fort Wayne (IN)
Butler County Comm Coll (PA)
Century Coll (MN)
Coll of the Desert (CA)
Columbus State Comm Coll (OH)
Comm Coll of Allegheny County (PA)
Delaware Tech & Comm Coll, Jack F. Owens Campus (DE)
Delta Coll (MI)
Dunwoody Coll of Technology (MN)
East Central Coll (MO)
Elgin Comm Coll (IL)
Fayetteville Tech Comm Coll (NC)
Galveston Coll (TX)
Grand Rapids Comm Coll (MI)
Grayson Coll (TX)
Harper Coll (IL)
Harrisburg Area Comm Coll (PA)
Hinds Comm Coll (MS)
Honolulu Comm Coll (HI)
Iowa Lakes Comm Coll (IA)
Ivy Tech Comm Coll–Bloomington (IN)
Ivy Tech Comm Coll–Central Indiana (IN)
Ivy Tech Comm Coll–Columbus (IN)
Ivy Tech Comm Coll–East Central (IN)
Ivy Tech Comm Coll–Kokomo (IN)
Ivy Tech Comm Coll–Lafayette (IN)
Ivy Tech Comm Coll–North Central (IN)
Ivy Tech Comm Coll–Northeast (IN)
Ivy Tech Comm Coll–Northwest (IN)
Ivy Tech Comm Coll–Richmond (IN)
Ivy Tech Comm Coll–Southern Indiana (IN)
Ivy Tech Comm Coll–Southwest (IN)
Ivy Tech Comm Coll–Wabash Valley (IN)
Jefferson Coll (MO)
Johnston Comm Coll (NC)
Kankakee Comm Coll (IL)
Kilgore Coll (TX)
Kirtland Comm Coll (MI)
Lansing Comm Coll (MI)
Laramie County Comm Coll (WY)
Lehigh Carbon Comm Coll (PA)
Lone Star Coll–North Harris (TX)
Luzerne County Comm Coll (PA)
Macomb Comm Coll (MI)
Manhattan Area Tech Coll (KS)
Miami Dade Coll (FL)
Mid-Plains Comm Coll, North Platte (NE)
Minneapolis Comm and Tech Coll (MN)
Minnesota State Coll–Southeast Tech (MN)
Mitchell Tech Inst (SD)
Mohave Comm Coll (AZ)
Mohawk Valley Comm Coll (NY)
Monroe Comm Coll (NY)
Moraine Valley Comm Coll (IL)
Mt. San Antonio Coll (CA)
Northampton Comm Coll (PA)
North Dakota State Coll of Science (ND)
North Iowa Area Comm Coll (IA)
Northwest Mississippi Comm Coll (MS)
Oklahoma State U Inst of Technology (OK)
Orange Coast Coll (CA)
Oxnard Coll (CA)
Ozarks Tech Comm Coll (MO)
Paris Jr Coll (TX)
Pitt Comm Coll (NC)
Richmond Comm Coll (NC)
Salt Lake Comm Coll (UT)
San Jacinto Coll District (TX)
San Joaquin Valley Coll, Hanford (CA)
San Joaquin Valley Coll, Hesperia (CA)

San Joaquin Valley Coll, Ontario (CA)
San Joaquin Valley Coll, Temecula (CA)
Sauk Valley Comm Coll (IL)
Southeast Tech Inst (SD)
Southern Maine Comm Coll (ME)
South Louisiana Comm Coll (LA)
South Piedmont Comm Coll (NC)
South Plains Coll (TX)
Southwestern Illinois Coll (IL)
Spartanburg Comm Coll (SC)
State U of New York Coll of Technology at Alfred (NY)
Tarrant County Coll District (TX)
Texarkana Coll (TX)
Triangle Tech, Inc.–Pittsburgh School (PA)
Trinity Valley Comm Coll (TX)
Tulsa Comm Coll (OK)
U of Arkansas Comm Coll at Morrilton (AR)
Walla Walla Comm Coll (WA)
Waubonsee Comm Coll (IL)
Wayne County Comm Coll District (MI)
Wenatchee Valley Coll (WA)
Western Dakota Tech Inst (SD)
Westmoreland County Comm Coll (PA)
Wichita Area Tech Coll (KS)

HEATING, VENTILATION, AIR CONDITIONING AND REFRIGERATION ENGINEERING TECHNOLOGY
Alamance Comm Coll (NC)
Arkansas State U–Newport (AR)
Austin Comm Coll (TX)
Bevill State Comm Coll (AL)
Blackhawk Tech Coll (WI)
Chippewa Valley Tech Coll (WI)
Clark State Comm Coll (OH)
The Comm Coll of Baltimore County (MD)
Delaware Tech & Comm Coll, Stanton/Wilmington Campus (DE)
Dunwoody Coll of Technology (MN)
Gadsden State Comm Coll (AL)
Georgia Piedmont Tech Coll (GA)
Iowa Lakes Comm Coll (IA)
Jackson Coll (MI)
Macomb Comm Coll (MI)
Manhattan Area Tech Coll (KS)
Mercer County Comm Coll (NJ)
Miami Dade Coll (FL)
Mineral Area Coll (MO)
Moraine Park Tech Coll (WI)
Mott Comm Coll (MI)
North Dakota State Coll of Science (ND)
North Georgia Tech Coll (GA)
Northwest Mississippi Comm Coll (MS)
Oakland Comm Coll (MI)
Oakton Comm Coll (IL)
Oklahoma Tech Coll (OK)
Raritan Valley Comm Coll (NJ)
San Joaquin Valley Coll, Bakersfield (CA)
San Joaquin Valley Coll, Fresno (CA)
San Joaquin Valley Coll, Visalia (CA)
Savannah Tech Coll (GA)
Shelton State Comm Coll (AL)
Southern Crescent Tech Coll (GA)
South Georgia Tech Coll (GA)
Springfield Tech Comm Coll (MA)
State U of New York Coll of Technology at Alfred (NY)
Sullivan Coll of Technology and Design (KY)
TCI—The Coll of Technology (NY)
Texas State Tech Coll Waco (TX)
Truckee Meadows Comm Coll (NV)

HEAVY EQUIPMENT MAINTENANCE TECHNOLOGY
Amarillo Coll (TX)
Coll of Western Idaho (ID)
Highland Comm Coll (IL)
Mesa Comm Coll (AZ)
Metropolitan Comm Coll–Kansas City (MO)
The Ohio State U Ag Tech Inst (OH)
Ozarks Tech Comm Coll (MO)
Rend Lake Coll (IL)
State U of New York Coll of Technology at Alfred (NY)
Western Wyoming Comm Coll (WY)

HEAVY/INDUSTRIAL EQUIPMENT MAINTENANCE TECHNOLOGIES RELATED
Bellingham Tech Coll (WA)
East Central Coll (MO)
Mineral Area Coll (MO)

HIGHER EDUCATION/HIGHER EDUCATION ADMINISTRATION
Lansing Comm Coll (MI)

HISPANIC-AMERICAN, PUERTO RICAN, AND MEXICAN-AMERICAN/CHICANO STUDIES
San Diego City Coll (CA)
San Jacinto Coll District (TX)

HISTOLOGIC TECHNICIAN
Comm Coll of Rhode Island (RI)
Darton State Coll (GA)
Goodwin Coll (CT)
Houston Comm Coll System (TX)
Lansing Comm Coll (MI)
Miami Dade Coll (FL)
Mott Comm Coll (MI)

HISTOLOGIC TECHNOLOGY/HISTOTECHNOLOGIST
Delaware Tech & Comm Coll, Stanton/Wilmington Campus (DE)
Oakland Comm Coll (MI)
Phoenix Coll (AZ)

HISTORY
Allen Comm Coll (KS)
Amarillo Coll (TX)
Ancilla Coll (IN)
Arizona Western Coll (AZ)
Austin Comm Coll (TX)
Bainbridge State Coll (GA)
Bronx Comm Coll of the City U of New York (NY)
Broward Coll (FL)
Bunker Hill Comm Coll (MA)
Ca&nnada Coll (CA)
Casper Coll (WY)
Coll of Marin (CA)
Coll of Southern Idaho (ID)
Coll of the Canyons (CA)
Coll of the Desert (CA)
Coll of Western Idaho (ID)
Copiah-Lincoln Comm Coll (MS)
Copper Mountain Coll (CA)
Dakota Coll at Bottineau (ND)
Darton State Coll (GA)
De Anza Coll (CA)
Eastern Arizona Coll (AZ)
Edison Comm Coll (OH)
Feather River Coll (CA)
Frank Phillips Coll (TX)
Fullerton Coll (CA)
Galveston Coll (TX)
Georgia Highlands Coll (GA)
Georgia Military Coll (GA)
Gordon State Coll (GA)
Great Basin Coll (NV)
Harford Comm Coll (MD)
Harper Coll (IL)
Hinds Comm Coll (MS)
Independence Comm Coll (KS)
Iowa Lakes Comm Coll (IA)
Kankakee Comm Coll (IL)
Kilian Comm Coll (SD)
Lamar Comm Coll (CO)
Lansing Comm Coll (MI)
Laramie County Comm Coll (WY)
Lorain County Comm Coll (OH)
Los Angeles Mission Coll (CA)
Miami Dade Coll (FL)
MiraCosta Coll (CA)
Mississippi Delta Comm Coll (MS)
Mohave Comm Coll (AZ)
Monroe Comm Coll (NY)
Northeastern Jr Coll (CO)
Northeast Texas Comm Coll (TX)
Northern Essex Comm Coll (MA)
Northwest Coll (WY)
Oklahoma City Comm Coll (OK)
Oklahoma State U, Oklahoma City (OK)
Orange Coast Coll (CA)
Otero Jr Coll (CO)
Oxnard Coll (CA)
Paris Jr Coll (TX)
Pasadena City Coll (CA)
Pensacola State Coll (FL)
Potomac State Coll of West Virginia U (WV)
Salt Lake Comm Coll (UT)
San Jacinto Coll District (TX)
Santa Rosa Jr Coll (CA)
Sauk Valley Comm Coll (IL)

Sheridan Coll (WY)
Snow Coll (UT)
South Florida State Coll (FL)
South Georgia State Coll, Douglas (GA)
Spoon River Coll (IL)
Texarkana Coll (TX)
Treasure Valley Comm Coll (OR)
Trinity Valley Comm Coll (TX)
Truckee Meadows Comm Coll (NV)
Umpqua Comm Coll (OR)
Vincennes U (IN)
Wenatchee Valley Coll (WA)
Western Wyoming Comm Coll (WY)

HISTORY TEACHER EDUCATION
Bucks County Comm Coll (PA)
Cochise Coll, Sierra Vista (AZ)
Darton State Coll (GA)

HOLISTIC HEALTH
Anoka-Ramsey Comm Coll (MN)
Anoka-Ramsey Comm Coll, Cambridge Campus (MN)

HOME HEALTH AIDE/HOME ATTENDANT
Allen Comm Coll (KS)

HOMELAND SECURITY
Butler County Comm Coll (PA)
Goodwin Coll (CT)
Harper Coll (IL)
Long Island Business Inst (NY)

HOMELAND SECURITY, LAW ENFORCEMENT, FIREFIGHTING AND PROTECTIVE SERVICES RELATED
Butler County Comm Coll (PA)
Central Wyoming Coll (WY)
Century Coll (MN)
Georgia Military Coll (GA)
Glendale Comm Coll (AZ)
Goodwin Coll (CT)
Lakeland Comm Coll (OH)
Laramie County Comm Coll (WY)
Miami Dade Coll (FL)
NorthWest Arkansas Comm Coll (AR)
Ocean County Coll (NJ)
Onondaga Comm Coll (NY)
Pittsburgh Tech Inst, Oakdale (PA)
San Joaquin Valley Coll, Bakersfield (CA)
Schoolcraft Coll (MI)
Westmoreland County Comm Coll (PA)

HOMELAND SECURITY RELATED
Fox Valley Tech Coll (WI)
Tallahassee Comm Coll (FL)

HORSE HUSBANDRY/EQUINE SCIENCE AND MANAGEMENT
Cecil Coll (MD)
Cosumnes River Coll, Sacramento (CA)
Highland Comm Coll (IL)
Linn-Benton Comm Coll (OR)
The Ohio State U Ag Tech Inst (OH)
Santa Rosa Jr Coll (CA)

HORTICULTURAL SCIENCE
Broward Coll (FL)
Butte Coll (CA)
Century Coll (MN)
Chattahoochee Tech Coll (GA)
Clark State Comm Coll (OH)
Coll of Western Idaho (ID)
Columbus Tech Coll (GA)
Cumberland County Coll (NJ)
Dakota Coll at Bottineau (ND)
Gwinnett Tech Coll (GA)
Lenoir Comm Coll (NC)
Luzerne County Comm Coll (PA)
Mesa Comm Coll (AZ)
Miami Dade Coll (FL)
Mississippi Delta Comm Coll (MS)
Mississippi Gulf Coast Comm Coll (MS)
Missouri State U–West Plains (MO)
Mt. San Antonio Coll (CA)
North Georgia Tech Coll (GA)
The Ohio State U Ag Tech Inst (OH)
Oklahoma State U, Oklahoma City (OK)
Orange Coast Coll (CA)
Potomac State Coll of West Virginia U (WV)

Shawnee Comm Coll (IL)
Sheridan Coll (WY)
Southeast Tech Inst (SD)
Southern Crescent Tech Coll (GA)
South Florida State Coll (FL)
South Georgia Tech Coll (GA)
Tarrant County Coll District (TX)
Treasure Valley Comm Coll (OR)
Trident Tech Coll (SC)
Trinity Valley Comm Coll (TX)
U of Hawaii Maui Coll (HI)
Victor Valley Coll (CA)
The Williamson Free School of Mecha Trades (PA)

HOSPITAL AND HEALTH-CARE FACILITIES ADMINISTRATION
Allen Comm Coll (KS)
Carrington Coll–Phoenix Westside (AZ)
Tulsa Comm Coll (OK)

HOSPITALITY ADMINISTRATION
Arizona Western Coll (AZ)
Austin Comm Coll (TX)
Berkshire Comm Coll (MA)
Broward Coll (FL)
Bunker Hill Comm Coll (MA)
Casper Coll (WY)
Cincinnati State Tech and Comm Coll (OH)
Coconino Comm Coll (AZ)
Coll of Southern Maryland (MD)
Coll of the Canyons (CA)
Coll of the Desert (CA)
Collin County Comm Coll District (TX)
Columbus State Comm Coll (OH)
Comm Coll of Vermont (VT)
Daytona State Coll (FL)
Florida State Coll at Jacksonville (FL)
Fox Valley Tech Coll (WI)
Genesee Comm Coll (NY)
Greenfield Comm Coll (MA)
Harper Coll (IL)
Harrisburg Area Comm Coll (PA)
Hillsborough Comm Coll (FL)
Hinds Comm Coll (MS)
Hocking Coll (OH)
Iowa Lakes Comm Coll (IA)
Ivy Tech Comm Coll–East Central (IN)
Ivy Tech Comm Coll–North Central (IN)
Ivy Tech Comm Coll–Northeast (IN)
Ivy Tech Comm Coll–Northwest (IN)
Jefferson Comm Coll (NY)
Jefferson State Comm Coll (AL)
J. Sargeant Reynolds Comm Coll (VA)
Lakeland Comm Coll (OH)
Lakes Region Comm Coll (NH)
Lincoln Land Comm Coll (IL)
Massachusetts Bay Comm Coll (MA)
Miami Dade Coll (FL)
MiraCosta Coll (CA)
Moraine Valley Comm Coll (IL)
Niagara County Comm Coll (NY)
Normandale Comm Coll (MN)
North Iowa Area Comm Coll (IA)
North Shore Comm Coll (MA)
Onondaga Comm Coll (NY)
Pasadena City Coll (CA)
Pensacola State Coll (FL)
Pima Comm Coll (AZ)
Potomac State Coll of West Virginia U (WV)
Quinsigamond Comm Coll (MA)
San Diego City Coll (CA)
Scottsdale Comm Coll (AZ)
Sheridan Coll (WY)
Southern U at Shreveport (LA)
South Florida State Coll (FL)
Sullivan County Comm Coll (NY)
Tech Coll of the Lowcountry (SC)
Three Rivers Comm Coll (CT)
Vincennes U (IN)
Wor-Wic Comm Coll (MD)

HOSPITALITY ADMINISTRATION RELATED
Bunker Hill Comm Coll (MA)
Butler County Comm Coll (PA)
Columbus State Comm Coll (OH)
Holyoke Comm Coll (MA)
Ivy Tech Comm Coll–Central Indiana (IN)
Ivy Tech Comm Coll–East Central (IN)
Ivy Tech Comm Coll–Northeast (IN)

J. Sargeant Reynolds Comm Coll (VA)
Long Island Business Inst (NY)
Penn State Beaver (PA)

HOSPITALITY AND RECREATION MARKETING
County Coll of Morris (NJ)
Dakota Coll at Bottineau (ND)
Flathead Valley Comm Coll (MT)
Florida State Coll at Jacksonville (FL)
Luzerne County Comm Coll (PA)
Montgomery County Comm Coll (PA)

HOTEL/MOTEL ADMINISTRATION
Albany Tech Coll (GA)
Athens Tech Coll (GA)
Atlanta Tech Coll (GA)
Bradford School (PA)
Bunker Hill Comm Coll (MA)
Cape Fear Comm Coll (NC)
Carl Albert State Coll (OK)
Central Georgia Tech Coll (GA)
Central Oregon Comm Coll (OR)
Central Wyoming Coll (WY)
Coll of Southern Idaho (ID)
Coll of the Canyons (CA)
Columbia Coll (CA)
Comm Coll of Allegheny County (PA)
The Comm Coll of Baltimore County (MD)
Comm Coll of Philadelphia (PA)
Daytona State Coll (FL)
Delaware Tech & Comm Coll, Stanton/Wilmington Campus (DE)
Delaware Tech & Comm Coll, Terry Campus (DE)
Finger Lakes Comm Coll (NY)
Florida State Coll at Jacksonville (FL)
Genesee Comm Coll (NY)
Gwinnett Tech Coll (GA)
Harrisburg Area Comm Coll (PA)
Hocking Coll (OH)
Houston Comm Coll System (TX)
International Business Coll, Indianapolis (IN)
Iowa Lakes Comm Coll (IA)
J. Sargeant Reynolds Comm Coll (VA)
King's Coll (NC)
Lane Comm Coll (OR)
Lansing Comm Coll (MI)
Luzerne County Comm Coll (PA)
Manchester Comm Coll (CT)
Mercer County Comm Coll (NJ)
Middlesex County Coll (NJ)
Minneapolis Business Coll (MN)
Mississippi Gulf Coast Comm Coll (MS)
Mohawk Valley Comm Coll (NY)
Monroe Comm Coll (NY)
Montgomery Coll (MD)
Moraine Park Tech Coll (WI)
Mt. San Antonio Coll (CA)
Nassau Comm Coll (NY)
Northampton Comm Coll (PA)
Northern Essex Comm Coll (MA)
Northwest Mississippi Comm Coll (MS)
Norwalk Comm Coll (CT)
Oakland Comm Coll (MI)
Ogeechee Tech Coll (GA)
Orange Coast Coll (CA)
Oxnard Coll (CA)
Ozarks Tech Comm Coll (MO)
Pittsburgh Tech Inst, Oakdale (PA)
Savannah Tech Coll (GA)
Scottsdale Comm Coll (AZ)
Southern U at Shreveport (LA)
Three Rivers Comm Coll (CT)
Tompkins Cortland Comm Coll (NY)
Trident Tech Coll (SC)
Tulsa Comm Coll (OK)
U of Hawaii Maui Coll (HI)
Vincennes U (IN)
Westmoreland County Comm Coll (PA)
Wood Tobe–Coburn School (NY)

HOTEL, MOTEL, AND RESTAURANT MANAGEMENT
Davis Coll (OH)
Fayetteville Tech Comm Coll (NC)
Pima Comm Coll (AZ)
Waukesha County Tech Coll (WI)

HOUSING AND HUMAN ENVIRONMENTS
Orange Coast Coll (CA)
Sullivan Coll of Technology and Design (KY)

HOUSING AND HUMAN ENVIRONMENTS RELATED
Comm Coll of Allegheny County (PA)
Hinds Comm Coll (MS)

HUMAN DEVELOPMENT AND FAMILY STUDIES
Bucks County Comm Coll (PA)
Georgia Military Coll (GA)
Imperial Valley Coll (CA)
Orange Coast Coll (CA)
Penn State Brandywine (PA)
Penn State DuBois (PA)
Penn State Fayette, The Eberly Campus (PA)
Penn State Mont Alto (PA)
Penn State New Kensington (PA)
Penn State Schuylkill (PA)
Penn State Worthington Scranton (PA)
Penn State York (PA)
Salt Lake Comm Coll (UT)
Shoreline Comm Coll (WA)

HUMAN DEVELOPMENT AND FAMILY STUDIES RELATED
Albany Tech Coll (GA)
Columbus State Comm Coll (OH)
Comm Coll of Allegheny County (PA)

HUMANITIES
Allen Comm Coll (KS)
Barstow Comm Coll (CA)
Bristol Comm Coll (MA)
Brookhaven Coll (TX)
Broward Coll (FL)
Bucks County Comm Coll (PA)
Ca&nnada Coll (CA)
Cayuga County Comm Coll (NY)
Central Oregon Comm Coll (OR)
Clinton Comm Coll (NY)
Cochise Coll, Sierra Vista (AZ)
Coll of Marin (CA)
Coll of the Canyons (CA)
Coll of the Desert (CA)
Columbia Coll (CA)
Columbia-Greene Comm Coll (NY)
Comm Coll of Allegheny County (PA)
Cosumnes River Coll, Sacramento (CA)
Dakota Coll at Bottineau (ND)
De Anza Coll (CA)
Dutchess Comm Coll (NY)
Erie Comm Coll (NY)
Erie Comm Coll, North Campus (NY)
Erie Comm Coll, South Campus (NY)
Feather River Coll (CA)
Finger Lakes Comm Coll (NY)
Fullerton Coll (CA)
Galveston Coll (TX)
Garden City Comm Coll (KS)
Genesee Comm Coll (NY)
Golden West Coll (CA)
Harper Coll (IL)
Herkimer County Comm Coll (NY)
Housatonic Comm Coll (CT)
Imperial Valley Coll (CA)
Iowa Lakes Comm Coll (IA)
Jamestown Comm Coll (NY)
Jefferson Comm Coll (NY)
John Tyler Comm Coll (VA)
Lake Tahoe Comm Coll (CA)
Lansing Comm Coll (MI)
Laramie County Comm Coll (WY)
Lehigh Carbon Comm Coll (PA)
Los Angeles Mission Coll (CA)
Luzerne County Comm Coll (PA)
Mercer County Comm Coll (NJ)
Miami Dade Coll (FL)
Mohawk Valley Comm Coll (NY)
Montgomery County Comm Coll (PA)
Mt. San Antonio Coll (CA)
Mt. San Jacinto Coll (CA)
Niagara County Comm Coll (NY)
Northeastern Jr Coll (CO)
Oklahoma City Comm Coll (OK)
Oklahoma State U, Oklahoma City (OK)
Onondaga Comm Coll (NY)
Orange Coast Coll (CA)
Otero Jr Coll (CO)
Palomar Coll (CA)
Pasadena City Coll (CA)
Salt Lake Comm Coll (UT)
Santa Rosa Jr Coll (CA)
Seminole State Coll (OK)
Snow Coll (UT)
South Florida State Coll (FL)

State U of New York Coll of Technology at Alfred (NY)
Texarkana Coll (TX)
Tompkins Cortland Comm Coll (NY)
Tulsa Comm Coll (OK)
Umpqua Comm Coll (OR)
Victor Valley Coll (CA)
Westchester Comm Coll (NY)
Western Wyoming Comm Coll (WY)

HUMAN NUTRITION
Broward Coll (FL)

HUMAN RESOURCES MANAGEMENT
Anoka-Ramsey Comm Coll (MN)
Anoka-Ramsey Comm Coll, Cambridge Campus (MN)
Beal Coll (ME)
Blackhawk Tech Coll (WI)
Broward Coll (FL)
Butler County Comm Coll (PA)
Cecil Coll (MD)
Chippewa Valley Tech Coll (WI)
Clark Coll (WA)
Clark State Comm Coll (OH)
Columbus State Comm Coll (OH)
Comm Coll of Allegheny County (PA)
Delaware Tech & Comm Coll, Terry Campus (DE)
Edison Comm Coll (OH)
Fayetteville Tech Comm Coll (NC)
Fox Valley Tech Coll (WI)
Harford Comm Coll (MD)
Hawkeye Comm Coll (IA)
Herkimer County Comm Coll (NY)
Illinois Eastern Comm Colls, Olney Central College (IL)
Lansing Comm Coll (MI)
Lehigh Carbon Comm Coll (PA)
Moraine Park Tech Coll (WI)
Moraine Valley Comm Coll (IL)
San Joaquin Valley Coll, Hanford (CA)
San Joaquin Valley Coll, Hesperia (CA)
San Joaquin Valley Coll, Temecula (CA)
San Joaquin Valley Coll, Visalia (CA)
Santa Rosa Jr Coll (CA)
South Florida State Coll (FL)
Tulsa Comm Coll (OK)
Umpqua Comm Coll (OR)
Waubonsee Comm Coll (IL)
Waukesha County Tech Coll (WI)
Westmoreland County Comm Coll (PA)

HUMAN RESOURCES MANAGEMENT AND SERVICES RELATED
Columbus State Comm Coll (OH)
Iowa Lakes Comm Coll (IA)
Pitt Comm Coll (NC)
San Joaquin Valley Coll–Online (CA)

HUMAN SERVICES
Alexandria Tech and Comm Coll (MN)
American Samoa Comm Coll (AS)
Austin Comm Coll (TX)
Beal Coll (ME)
Berkshire Comm Coll (MA)
Bismarck State Coll (ND)
Bowling Green State U-Firelands Coll (OH)
Bronx Comm Coll of the City U of New York (NY)
Bunker Hill Comm Coll (MA)
Ca&nnada Coll (CA)
Central Maine Comm Coll (ME)
Central Ohio Tech Coll (OH)
Century Coll (MN)
Clark State Comm Coll (OH)
Coll of Central Florida (FL)
Coll of Southern Idaho (ID)
Columbia Coll (CA)
Comm Coll of Philadelphia (PA)
Comm Coll of Vermont (VT)
Cosumnes River Coll, Sacramento (CA)
Daytona State Coll (FL)
Delaware Tech & Comm Coll, Jack F. Owens Campus (DE)
Delaware Tech & Comm Coll, Stanton/Wilmington Campus (DE)
Delaware Tech & Comm Coll, Terry Campus (DE)
Dutchess Comm Coll (NY)
Finger Lakes Comm Coll (NY)

Flathead Valley Comm Coll (MT)
Florida State Coll at Jacksonville (FL)
Genesee Comm Coll (NY)
Georgia Highlands Coll (GA)
Goodwin Coll (CT)
Grays Harbor Coll (WA)
Harper Coll (IL)
Harrisburg Area Comm Coll (PA)
Honolulu Comm Coll (HI)
Hopkinsville Comm Coll (KY)
Housatonic Comm Coll (CT)
Ivy Tech Comm Coll–Bloomington (IN)
Ivy Tech Comm Coll–Central Indiana (IN)
Ivy Tech Comm Coll–Columbus (IN)
Ivy Tech Comm Coll–East Central (IN)
Ivy Tech Comm Coll–Kokomo (IN)
Ivy Tech Comm Coll–Lafayette (IN)
Ivy Tech Comm Coll–North Central (IN)
Ivy Tech Comm Coll–Northeast (IN)
Ivy Tech Comm Coll–Northwest (IN)
Ivy Tech Comm Coll–Richmond (IN)
Ivy Tech Comm Coll–Southeast (IN)
Ivy Tech Comm Coll–Southern Indiana (IN)
Ivy Tech Comm Coll–Southwest (IN)
Ivy Tech Comm Coll–Wabash Valley (IN)
Jamestown Comm Coll (NY)
Jefferson Comm Coll (NY)
John Tyler Comm Coll (VA)
Kingsborough Comm Coll of the City U of New York (NY)
Lake Area Tech Inst (SD)
Lake Land Coll (IL)
Lakes Region Comm Coll (NH)
Laramie County Comm Coll (WY)
Lehigh Carbon Comm Coll (PA)
Lone Star Coll–Montgomery (TX)
Lorain County Comm Coll (OH)
Luzerne County Comm Coll (PA)
Manchester Comm Coll (CT)
Massachusetts Bay Comm Coll (MA)
Mesabi Range Comm and Tech Coll (MN)
Metropolitan Comm Coll–Kansas City (MO)
Miami Dade Coll (FL)
Minneapolis Comm and Tech Coll (MN)
MiraCosta Coll (CA)
Mississippi Gulf Coast Comm Coll (MS)
Mohawk Valley Comm Coll (NY)
Monroe Comm Coll (NY)
Mount Wachusett Comm Coll (MA)
New Mexico State U–Alamogordo (NM)
Niagara County Comm Coll (NY)
Northern Essex Comm Coll (MA)
Northwestern Connecticut Comm Coll (CT)
Norwalk Comm Coll (CT)
Ocean County Coll (NJ)
Oklahoma State U, Oklahoma City (OK)
Owensboro Comm and Tech Coll (KY)
Pasco-Hernando State Coll (FL)
Pennsylvania Highlands Comm Coll (PA)
Phoenix Coll (AZ)
Quinsigamond Comm Coll (MA)
Reading Area Comm Coll (PA)
River Valley Comm Coll (NH)
Rock Valley Coll (IL)
Santa Rosa Jr Coll (CA)
Shawnee Comm Coll (IL)
Southern State Comm Coll (OH)
Southern U at Shreveport (LA)
Stark State Coll (OH)
State U of New York Coll of Technology at Alfred (NY)
Sullivan County Comm Coll (NY)
Sussex County Comm Coll (NJ)
TCI–Tho Coll of Technology (NY)
Three Rivers Comm Coll (CT)
Trident Tech Coll (SC)
Tunxis Comm Coll (CT)
U of Arkansas Comm Coll at Hope (AR)
U of Hawaii Maui Coll (HI)
Western Wyoming Comm Coll (WY)

HYDRAULICS AND FLUID POWER TECHNOLOGY
The Comm Coll of Baltimore County (MD)
The Ohio State U Ag Tech Inst (OH)

HYDROLOGY AND WATER RESOURCES SCIENCE
Coll of Southern Idaho (ID)
Imperial Valley Coll (CA)
Iowa Lakes Comm Coll (IA)
Three Rivers Comm Coll (CT)

ILLUSTRATION
Collin County Comm Coll District (TX)
Fashion Inst of Technology (NY)
Oklahoma State U, Oklahoma City (OK)
Sessions Coll for Professional Design (AZ)

INDUSTRIAL AND PRODUCT DESIGN
Fiorello H. LaGuardia Comm Coll of the City U of New York (NY)
Kirtland Comm Coll (MI)
Luzerne County Comm Coll (PA)
Mt. San Antonio Coll (CA)
Orange Coast Coll (CA)
Owens Comm Coll, Toledo (OH)
Rock Valley Coll (CA)

INDUSTRIAL ELECTRONICS TECHNOLOGY
Bevill State Comm Coll (AL)
Big Bend Comm Coll (WA)
Danville Area Comm Coll (IL)
Dyersburg State Comm Coll (TN)
Eastern Arizona Coll (AZ)
John Tyler Comm Coll (VA)
J. Sargeant Reynolds Comm Coll (VA)
Kankakee Comm Coll (IL)
Lawson State Comm Coll (AL)
Lehigh Carbon Comm Coll (PA)
Lincoln Land Comm Coll (IL)
Lurleen B. Wallace Comm Coll (AL)
Moraine Valley Comm Coll (IL)
Northampton Comm Coll (PA)
Northwest-Shoals Comm Coll (AL)
Pasadena City Coll (CA)
Patrick Henry Comm Coll (VA)
Shelton State Comm Coll (AL)
South Louisiana Comm Coll (LA)
Spartanburg Comm Coll (SC)
Sullivan Coll of Technology and Design (KY)
Tech Coll of the Lowcountry (SC)
Wenatchee Valley Coll (WA)
Western Wyoming Comm Coll (WY)

INDUSTRIAL ENGINEERING
Blackhawk Tech Coll (WI)
Manchester Comm Coll (CT)
Northeast Texas Comm Coll (TX)
South Florida State Coll (FL)

INDUSTRIAL MECHANICS AND MAINTENANCE TECHNOLOGY
Alexandria Tech and Comm Coll (MN)
Bellingham Tech Coll (WA)
Big Bend Comm Coll (WA)
Bismarck State Coll (ND)
Bossier Parish Comm Coll (LA)
Casper Coll (WY)
Danville Area Comm Coll (IL)
Delta Coll (MI)
Dyersburg State Comm Coll (TN)
Eastern Arizona Coll (AZ)
Elgin Comm Coll (IL)
Gadsden State Comm Coll (AL)
Grayson Coll (TX)
Greenville Tech Coll (SC)
Illinois Eastern Comm Colls, Olney Central College (IL)
Ivy Tech Comm Coll–East Central (IN)
Kaskaskia Coll (IL)
Lower Columbia Coll (WA)
Macomb Comm Coll (MI)
Minnesota State Coll–Southeast Tech (MN)
Northwest-Shoals Comm Coll (AL)
Reading Area Comm Coll (PA)
Rend Lake Coll (IL)
San Joaquin Valley Coll, Ontario (CA)
San Juan Coll (NM)

Snow Coll (UT)
Somerset Comm Coll (KY)
South Louisiana Comm Coll (LA)
Southwestern Illinois Coll (IL)
Southwestern Michigan Coll (MI)
Sullivan Coll of Technology and Design (KY)
Texarkana Coll (TX)
Western Wyoming Comm Coll (WY)
Westmoreland County Comm Coll (PA)
Wichita Area Tech Coll (KS)

INDUSTRIAL PRODUCTION TECHNOLOGIES RELATED
Bismarck State Coll (ND)
Ivy Tech Comm Coll–Central Indiana (IN)
Ivy Tech Comm Coll–East Central (IN)
Ivy Tech Comm Coll–Lafayette (IN)
Ivy Tech Comm Coll–North Central (IN)
Ivy Tech Comm Coll–Northeast (IN)
Ivy Tech Comm Coll–Richmond (IN)
Ivy Tech Comm Coll–Southwest (IN)
Ivy Tech Comm Coll–Wabash Valley (IN)
Kent State U at Trumbull (OH)
Lansing Comm Coll (MI)
Middlesex County Coll (NJ)
Mountain Empire Comm Coll (VA)
St. Clair County Comm Coll (MI)
Seminole State Coll (OK)
Southwestern Michigan Coll (MI)

INDUSTRIAL RADIOLOGIC TECHNOLOGY
Amarillo Coll (TX)
Copiah-Lincoln Comm Coll (MS)
Daytona State Coll (FL)
Eastern Gateway Comm Coll (OH)
Lorain County Comm Coll (OH)
Mississippi Gulf Coast Comm Coll (MS)
Monroe Comm Coll (NY)
Mt. San Antonio Coll (CA)
Northern Essex Comm Coll (MA)
Orange Coast Coll (CA)
Roane State Comm Coll (TN)
Salt Lake Comm Coll (UT)
Southeastern Comm Coll (IA)
South Louisiana Comm Coll (LA)
South Plains Coll (TX)
Tarrant County Coll District (TX)
Tyler Jr Coll (TX)
Virginia Western Comm Coll (VA)
Wichita Area Tech Coll (KS)

INDUSTRIAL SAFETY TECHNOLOGY
Fox Valley Tech Coll (WI)
Northwest Tech Coll (MN)

INDUSTRIAL TECHNOLOGY
Albany Tech Coll (GA)
Allen Comm Coll (KS)
Arizona Western Coll (AZ)
Bismarck State Coll (ND)
Blackhawk Tech Coll (WI)
Bowling Green State U-Firelands Coll (OH)
Bucks County Comm Coll (PA)
Central Georgia Tech Coll (GA)
Central Oregon Comm Coll (OR)
Central Virginia Comm Coll (VA)
Cincinnati State Tech and Comm Coll (OH)
Clark State Comm Coll (OH)
Cleveland State Comm Coll (TN)
Clinton Comm Coll (NY)
Coll of the Ouachitas (AR)
Columbus Tech Coll (GA)
Comm Coll of Allegheny County (PA)
Comm Coll of Vermont (VT)
Crowder Coll (MO)
Cumberland County Coll (NJ)
Daytona State Coll (FL)
De Anza Coll (CA)
Eastern Gateway Comm Coll (OH)
Edison Comm Coll (OH)
Erie Comm Coll, North Campus (NY)
FIDM/The Fashion Inst of Design & Merchandising, Orange County Campus (CA)
Frank Phillips Coll (TX)
Gateway Comm and Tech Coll (KY)
Georgia Piedmont Tech Coll (GA)
Grand Rapids Comm Coll (MI)
Grays Harbor Coll (WA)

Great Basin Coll (NV)
Hagerstown Comm Coll (MD)
Highland Comm Coll (IL)
Hocking Coll (OH)
Hopkinsville Comm Coll (KY)
Illinois Eastern Comm Colls, Wabash Valley College (IL)
ITT Tech Inst, Bessemer (AL)
ITT Tech Inst, Madison (AL)
ITT Tech Inst, Mobile (AL)
ITT Tech Inst, Tucson (AZ)
ITT Tech Inst (AR)
ITT Tech Inst, Culver City (CA)
ITT Tech Inst, Lathrop (CA)
ITT Tech Inst, National City (CA)
ITT Tech Inst, Oakland (CA)
ITT Tech Inst, Orange (CA)
ITT Tech Inst, Oxnard (CA)
ITT Tech Inst, Rancho Cordova (CA)
ITT Tech Inst, San Bernardino (CA)
ITT Tech Inst, San Dimas (CA)
ITT Tech Inst, Sylmar (CA)
ITT Tech Inst, Fort Lauderdale (FL)
ITT Tech Inst, Fort Myers (FL)
ITT Tech Inst, Jacksonville (FL)
ITT Tech Inst, Miami (FL)
ITT Tech Inst, Orlando (FL)
ITT Tech Inst, St. Petersburg (FL)
ITT Tech Inst, Tampa (FL)
ITT Tech Inst (ID)
ITT Tech Inst, Fort Wayne (IN)
ITT Tech Inst, Newburgh (IN)
ITT Tech Inst, Clive (IA)
ITT Tech Inst, St. Rose (LA)
ITT Tech Inst, Canton (MI)
ITT Tech Inst, Dearborn (MI)
ITT Tech Inst, Swartz Creek (MI)
ITT Tech Inst, Troy (MI)
ITT Tech Inst, Wyoming (MI)
ITT Tech Inst, Arnold (MO)
ITT Tech Inst , Earth City (MO)
ITT Tech Inst, Kansas City (MO)
ITT Tech Inst, Akron (OH)
ITT Tech Inst, Columbus (OH)
ITT Tech Inst, Dayton (OH)
ITT Tech Inst, Hilliard (OH)
ITT Tech Inst, Maumee (OH)
ITT Tech Inst, Norwood (OH)
ITT Tech Inst, Strongsville (OH)
ITT Tech Inst, Warrensville Heights (OH)
ITT Tech Inst , Youngstown (OH)
ITT Tech Inst, Tulsa (OK)
ITT Tech Inst, Chattanooga (TN)
ITT Tech Inst, Cordova (TN)
ITT Tech Inst, Johnson City (TN)
ITT Tech Inst, Knoxville (TN)
ITT Tech Inst, Nashville (TN)
ITT Tech Inst, DeSoto (TX)
ITT Tech Inst, Houston (TX)
ITT Tech Inst (UT)
ITT Tech Inst, Chantilly (VA)
ITT Tech Inst, Norfolk (VA)
ITT Tech Inst, Richmond (VA)
ITT Tech Inst, Salem (VA)
ITT Tech Inst, Springfield (VA)
ITT Tech Inst, Seattle (WA)
ITT Tech Inst, Spokane Valley (WA)
Ivy Tech Comm Coll–Bloomington (IN)
Ivy Tech Comm Coll–Central Indiana (IN)
Ivy Tech Comm Coll–Columbus (IN)
Ivy Tech Comm Coll–East Central (IN)
Ivy Tech Comm Coll–Kokomo (IN)
Ivy Tech Comm Coll–Lafayette (IN)
Ivy Tech Comm Coll–North Central (IN)
Ivy Tech Comm Coll–Northeast (IN)
Ivy Tech Comm Coll–Northwest (IN)
Ivy Tech Comm Coll–Richmond (IN)
Ivy Tech Comm Coll–Southeast (IN)
Ivy Tech Comm Coll–Southern Indiana (IN)
Ivy Tech Comm Coll–Southwest (IN)
Ivy Tech Comm Coll–Wabash Valley (IN)
Jackson State Comm Coll (TN)
John Tyler Comm Coll (VA)
Kent State U at Trumbull (OH)
Kent State U at Tuscarawas (OH)
Lake Land Coll (IL)
Lanier Tech Coll (GA)
Lenoir Comm Coll (NC)
Lincoln Land Comm Coll (IL)
Lone Star Coll–CyFair (TX)
Lorain County Comm Coll (OH)
Macomb Comm Coll (MI)
Manchester Comm Coll (CT)
Mesa Comm Coll (AZ)

Miami Dade Coll (FL)
Mineral Area Coll (MO)
Missouri State U–West Plains (MO)
Monroe Comm Coll (NY)
Monroe County Comm Coll (MI)
Mountain Empire Comm Coll (VA)
Northeast Texas Comm Coll (TX)
North Georgia Tech Coll (GA)
Northwest Tech Coll (MN)
Nunez Comm Coll (LA)
Oakland Comm Coll (MI)
The Ohio State U Ag Tech Inst (OH)
Olympic Coll (WA)
Owens Comm Coll, Toledo (OH)
Ozarks Tech Comm Coll (MO)
Panola Coll (TX)
Patrick Henry Comm Coll (VA)
Penn State York (PA)
Piedmont Comm Coll (NC)
Rock Valley Coll (IL)
San Diego City Coll (CA)
San Joaquin Valley Coll, Hanford (CA)
San Joaquin Valley Coll, Hesperia (CA)
San Joaquin Valley Coll, Salida (CA)
San Joaquin Valley Coll, Temecula (CA)
San Joaquin Valley Coll, Visalia (CA)
San Juan Coll (NM)
Savannah Tech Coll (GA)
Seminole State Coll of Florida (FL)
Shoreline Comm Coll (WA)
Southeastern Comm Coll (NC)
Southeast Tech Inst (SD)
Southern Crescent Tech Coll (GA)
South Georgia Tech Coll (GA)
South Louisiana Comm Coll (LA)
Spoon River Coll (IL)
Stark State Coll (OH)
Three Rivers Comm Coll (CT)
Trident Tech Coll (SC)
Tulsa Comm Coll (OK)
Victoria Coll (TX)
Walters State Comm Coll (TN)
Western Nevada Coll (NV)
West Georgia Tech Coll (GA)
Westmoreland County Comm Coll (PA)

INFORMATION SCIENCE/ STUDIES

Alamance Comm Coll (NC)
Alexandria Tech and Comm Coll (MN)
Allen Comm Coll (KS)
Altamaha Tech Coll (GA)
Amarillo Coll (TX)
Athens Tech Coll (GA)
Augusta Tech Coll (GA)
Bainbridge State Coll (GA)
Bossier Parish Comm Coll (LA)
Bristol Comm Coll (MA)
Brookhaven Coll (TX)
Broward Coll (FL)
Bucks County Comm Coll (PA)
Catawba Valley Comm Coll (NC)
Cayuga County Comm Coll (NY)
Central Carolina Comm Coll (NC)
Central Georgia Tech Coll (GA)
Century Coll (MN)
Chattahoochee Tech Coll (GA)
Clark State Comm Coll (OH)
Cleveland Comm Coll (NC)
Cochise Coll, Sierra Vista (AZ)
Columbia-Greene Comm Coll (NY)
Columbus Tech Coll (GA)
Dabney S. Lancaster Comm Coll (VA)
Dakota Coll at Bottineau (ND)
De Anza Coll (CA)
Dutchess Comm Coll (NY)
Dyersburg State Comm Coll (TN)
Eastern Arizona Coll (AZ)
Fayetteville Tech Comm Coll (NC)
Florida State Coll at Jacksonville (FL)
Genesee Comm Coll (NY)
Georgia Northwestern Tech Coll (GA)
Georgia Piedmont Tech Coll (GA)
Grays Harbor Coll (WA)
Gwinnett Tech Coll (GA)
Howard Comm Coll (MD)
Imperial Valley Coll (CA)
ITI Tech Coll (LA)
Jefferson Comm Coll (NY)
Kaskaskia Coll (IL)
Kirtland Comm Coll (MI)
Lamar Comm Coll (CO)
Lamar State Coll–Orange (TX)
Lanier Tech Coll (GA)
Lone Star Coll–Kingwood (TX)

Lorain County Comm Coll (OH)
Manchester Comm Coll (CT)
Massachusetts Bay Comm Coll (MA)
Metropolitan Comm Coll–Kansas City (MO)
Miami Dade Coll (FL)
Mitchell Comm Coll (NC)
Monroe Comm Coll (NY)
Montgomery County Comm Coll (PA)
Moultrie Tech Coll (GA)
Niagara County Comm Coll (NY)
North Shore Comm Coll (MA)
Northwestern Connecticut Comm Coll (CT)
Norwalk Comm Coll (CT)
Oconee Fall Line Tech Coll (GA)
Ogeechee Tech Coll (GA)
Okefenokee Tech Coll (GA)
Oklahoma State U, Oklahoma City (OK)
Orange Coast Coll (CA)
Ozarks Tech Comm Coll (MO)
Panola Coll (TX)
Paris Jr Coll (TX)
Penn State DuBois (PA)
Penn State Hazleton (PA)
Penn State Lehigh Valley (PA)
Penn State New Kensington (PA)
Penn State Schuylkill (PA)
Pensacola State Coll (FL)
Pitt Comm Coll (NC)
Rappahannock Comm Coll (VA)
Salt Lake Comm Coll (UT)
Scottsdale Comm Coll (AZ)
Seminole State Coll of Florida (FL)
Shawnee Comm Coll (IL)
Sheridan Coll (WY)
Snow Coll (UT)
Southeastern Comm Coll (IA)
Southeastern Tech Coll (GA)
South Florida State Coll (FL)
South Georgia Tech Coll (GA)
South Piedmont Comm Coll (NC)
Southwestern Comm Coll (NC)
Southwest Georgia Tech Coll (GA)
Spoon River Coll (IL)
Sullivan County Comm Coll (NY)
Tompkins Cortland Comm Coll (NY)
Tunxis Comm Coll (CT)
Victoria Coll (TX)
Victor Valley Coll (CA)
Westchester Comm Coll (NY)
Western Wyoming Comm Coll (WY)
West Georgia Tech Coll (GA)
Wytheville Comm Coll (VA)

INFORMATION TECHNOLOGY

Atlanta Tech Coll (GA)
Barstow Comm Coll (CA)
Blue Ridge Comm and Tech Coll (WV)
Brown Mackie Coll–Boise (ID)
Brown Mackie Coll–Greenville (SC)
Brown Mackie Coll–Miami (FL)
Brown Mackie Coll–Northern Kentucky (KY)
Brown Mackie Coll–St. Louis (MO)
Brown Mackie Coll–Tulsa (OK)
Butte Coll (CA)
Catawba Valley Comm Coll (NC)
Central Carolina Comm Coll (NC)
Chandler-Gilbert Comm Coll (AZ)
Clark State Comm Coll (OH)
Cleveland Comm Coll (NC)
Coll of Central Florida (FL)
Coll of Southern Maryland (MD)
Coll of the Desert (CA)
Columbia Coll (CA)
Comm Coll of Vermont (VT)
Copper Mountain Coll (CA)
Cosumnes River Coll, Sacramento (CA)
Dakota Coll at Bottineau (ND)
Davis Coll (OH)
Daytona State Coll (FL)
Eastern Florida State Coll (FL)
Erie Comm Coll, North Campus (NY)
Erie Comm Coll, South Campus (NY)
Fayetteville Tech Comm Coll (NC)
Florida Gateway Coll (FL)
Florida State Coll at Jacksonville (FL)
Fullerton Coll (CA)
Galveston Coll (TX)
Georgia Military Coll (GA)
Gogebic Comm Coll (MI)
Gordon State Coll (GA)
Great Falls Coll Montana State U (MT)
Halifax Comm Coll (NC)
Hallmark Coll of Technology (TX)
Highland Comm Coll (IL)

Howard Comm Coll (MD)
Illinois Eastern Comm Colls, Olney Central College (IL)
Iowa Lakes Comm Coll (IA)
ITI Tech Coll (LA)
James Sprunt Comm Coll (NC)
Jamestown Comm Coll (NY)
Jefferson Coll (MO)
John Tyler Comm Coll (VA)
Kilian Comm Coll (SD)
Lake Land Coll (IL)
LDS Business Coll (UT)
Lone Star Coll–CyFair (TX)
Lone Star Coll–Montgomery (TX)
Lorain County Comm Coll (OH)
McHenry County Coll (IL)
Mesabi Range Comm and Tech Coll (MN)
Metropolitan Comm Coll–Kansas City (MO)
Miami Dade Coll (FL)
Mississippi Gulf Coast Comm Coll (MS)
Missouri State U–West Plains (MO)
Mitchell Comm Coll (NC)
Mohave Comm Coll (AZ)
Monroe Comm Coll (NY)
Monroe County Comm Coll (MI)
Mt. San Jacinto Coll (CA)
New Mexico State U–Alamogordo (NM)
Norwalk Comm Coll (CT)
Oakton Comm Coll (IL)
Oklahoma State U, Oklahoma City (OK)
Owens Comm Coll, Toledo (OH)
Palomar Coll (CA)
Panola Coll (TX)
Pasco-Hernando State Coll (FL)
Patrick Henry Comm Coll (VA)
Piedmont Comm Coll (NC)
Pitt Comm Coll (NC)
Potomac State Coll of West Virginia U (WV)
Randolph Comm Coll (NC)
Raritan Valley Comm Coll (NJ)
Richmond Comm Coll (NC)
Roane State Comm Coll (TN)
Salt Lake Comm Coll (UT)
Savannah Tech Coll (GA)
Seminole State Coll of Florida (FL)
South Piedmont Comm Coll (NC)
South Suburban Coll (IL)
Southwestern Illinois Coll (IL)
Stark State Coll (OH)
Sullivan Coll of Technology and Design (KY)
Tallahassee Comm Coll (FL)
Tyler Jr Coll (TX)
Wayne Comm Coll (NC)
Western Wyoming Comm Coll (WY)

INFORMATION TECHNOLOGY PROJECT MANAGEMENT

Cincinnati State Tech and Comm Coll (OH)

INSTITUTIONAL FOOD WORKERS

Greenville Tech Coll (SC)
Hinds Comm Coll (MS)
Iowa Lakes Comm Coll (IA)
James Sprunt Comm Coll (NC)
San Jacinto Coll District (TX)
Southwestern Indian Polytechnic Inst (NM)

INSTRUMENTATION TECHNOLOGY

Amarillo Coll (TX)
Bellingham Tech Coll (WA)
Bismarck State Coll (ND)
Butler County Comm Coll (PA)
Cape Fear Comm Coll (NC)
Central Carolina Comm Coll (NC)
Finger Lakes Comm Coll (NY)
Florida State Coll at Jacksonville (FL)
Georgia Piedmont Tech Coll (GA)
Hagerstown Comm Coll (MD)
Houston Comm Coll System (TX)
ITI Tech Coll (LA)
Lakeland Comm Coll (OH)
Lower Columbia Coll (WA)
Mesabi Range Comm and Tech Coll (MN)
Monroe Comm Coll (NY)
Moraine Valley Comm Coll (IL)
Nassau Comm Coll (NY)
Ozarks Tech Comm Coll (MO)
Salt Lake Comm Coll (UT)
San Jacinto Coll District (TX)
San Juan Coll (NM)

Southwestern Indian Polytechnic Inst (NM)
Sowela Tech Comm Coll (LA)
Texas State Tech Coll Waco (TX)
Western Wyoming Comm Coll (WY)

INSURANCE

Broward Coll (FL)
Clark State Comm Coll (OH)
Comm Coll of Allegheny County (PA)
Davis Coll (OH)
Florida State Coll at Jacksonville (FL)
Hinds Comm Coll (MS)
Mesa Comm Coll (AZ)
Nassau Comm Coll (NY)
North Iowa Area Comm Coll (IA)
Palomar Coll (CA)
San Diego City Coll (CA)
South Florida State Coll (FL)
Trinity Valley Comm Coll (TX)

INTEGRATED CIRCUIT DESIGN

Collin County Comm Coll District (TX)

INTELLIGENCE

Cochise Coll, Sierra Vista (AZ)

INTERDISCIPLINARY STUDIES

Bowling Green State U-Firelands Coll (OH)
Great Basin Coll (NV)
North Shore Comm Coll (MA)
Reading Area Comm Coll (PA)

INTERIOR ARCHITECTURE

Inst of Design and Construction (NY)
State U of New York Coll of Technology at Alfred (NY)
Tulsa Comm Coll (OK)

INTERIOR DESIGN

Alexandria Tech and Comm Coll (MN)
Amarillo Coll (TX)
Antelope Valley Coll (CA)
Arapahoe Comm Coll (CO)
Broward Coll (FL)
Butte Coll (CA)
Ca&nnada Coll (CA)
Cape Fear Comm Coll (NC)
Century Coll (MN)
Clary Sage Coll (OK)
Coll of Marin (CA)
Coll of the Canyons (CA)
Collin County Comm Coll District (TX)
Davis Coll (OH)
Daytona State Coll (FL)
Delaware Tech & Comm Coll, Terry Campus (DE)
Fashion Inst of Technology (NY)
FIDM/The Fashion Inst of Design & Merchandising, Los Angeles Campus (CA)
FIDM/The Fashion Inst of Design & Merchandising, Orange County Campus (CA)
FIDM/The Fashion Inst of Design & Merchandising, San Diego Campus (CA)
FIDM/The Fashion Inst of Design & Merchandising, San Francisco Campus (CA)
Florida State Coll at Jacksonville (FL)
Fox Valley Tech Coll (WI)
Fullerton Coll (CA)
Gwinnett Tech Coll (GA)
Harford Comm Coll (MD)
Harper Coll (IL)
Hawkeye Comm Coll (IA)
Houston Comm Coll System (TX)
Ivy Tech Comm Coll–North Central (IN)
Ivy Tech Comm Coll–Southwest (IN)
Lanier Tech Coll (GA)
Lansing Comm Coll (MI)
LDS Business Coll (UT)
Lehigh Carbon Comm Coll (PA)
Lone Star Coll–Kingwood (TX)
Mesa Comm Coll (AZ)
Miami Dade Coll (FL)
Monroe Comm Coll (NY)
Montgomery Coll (MD)
Mt. San Antonio Coll (CA)
Nassau Comm Coll (NY)
Northampton Comm Coll (PA)
Norwalk Comm Coll (CT)
Oakland Comm Coll (MI)
Ogeechee Tech Coll (GA)
Onondaga Comm Coll (NY)
Orange Coast Coll (CA)

Palomar Coll (CA)
Phoenix Coll (AZ)
Pima Comm Coll (AZ)
Randolph Comm Coll (NC)
Raritan Valley Comm Coll (NJ)
San Diego City Coll (CA)
San Jacinto Coll District (TX)
Santa Monica Coll (CA)
Santa Rosa Jr Coll (CA)
Scottsdale Comm Coll (AZ)
Seminole State Coll of Florida (FL)
State U of New York Coll of
    Technology at Alfred (NY)
Sullivan Coll of Technology and
    Design (KY)
Tulsa Comm Coll (OK)
Waukesha County Tech Coll (WI)
Wichita Area Tech Coll (KS)

INTERMEDIA/MULTIMEDIA
Bristol Comm Coll (MA)

**INTERNATIONAL BUSINESS/
TRADE/COMMERCE**
Austin Comm Coll (TX)
Broward Coll (FL)
Bunker Hill Comm Coll (MA)
Fullerton Coll (CA)
Harper Coll (IL)
Herkimer County Comm Coll (NY)
Houston Comm Coll System (TX)
Lansing Comm Coll (MI)
Luzerne County Comm Coll (PA)
Monroe Comm Coll (NY)
Owens Comm Coll, Toledo (OH)
Palomar Coll (CA)
Pasadena City Coll (CA)
Pitt Comm Coll (NC)
Raritan Valley Comm Coll (NJ)
San Jacinto Coll District (TX)
Shoreline Comm Coll (WA)
South Florida State Coll (FL)
Stark State Coll (OH)
Tompkins Cortland Comm Coll (NY)
Tulsa Comm Coll (OK)
Westchester Comm Coll (NY)

**INTERNATIONAL/GLOBAL
STUDIES**
Berkshire Comm Coll (MA)
Central Wyoming Coll (WY)
Delta Coll (MI)
Macomb Comm Coll (MI)
Oakland Comm Coll (MI)
Pasadena City Coll (CA)
Salt Lake Comm Coll (UT)
Tompkins Cortland Comm Coll (NY)

INTERNATIONAL MARKETING
Waukesha County Tech Coll (WI)

**INTERNATIONAL RELATIONS
AND AFFAIRS**
Bronx Comm Coll of the City U of
    New York (NY)
Broward Coll (FL)
Ca&nnada Coll (CA)
Casper Coll (WY)
Coll of Marin (CA)
De Anza Coll (CA)
Georgia Military Coll (GA)
Greenfield Comm Coll (MA)
Harrisburg Area Comm Coll (PA)
Lansing Comm Coll (MI)
Massachusetts Bay Comm Coll (MA)
Miami Dade Coll (FL)
Northern Essex Comm Coll (MA)
Northwest Coll (WY)
Salt Lake Comm Coll (UT)
South Florida State Coll (FL)
Western Wyoming Comm Coll (WY)

IRONWORKING
Ivy Tech Comm Coll–Lafayette (IN)
Ivy Tech Comm Coll–North Central
    (IN)
Ivy Tech Comm Coll–Northeast (IN)
Ivy Tech Comm Coll–Northwest (IN)
Ivy Tech Comm Coll–Southwest (IN)
Ivy Tech Comm Coll–Wabash Valley
    (IN)
Southwestern Illinois Coll (IL)

ITALIAN
Broward Coll (FL)
Coll of the Desert (CA)
Miami Dade Coll (FL)

JAPANESE
Austin Comm Coll (TX)
Lansing Comm Coll (MI)

MiraCosta Coll (CA)
Snow Coll (UT)

JAZZ/JAZZ STUDIES
Comm Coll of Rhode Island (RI)
Iowa Lakes Comm Coll (IA)
Santa Rosa Jr Coll (CA)
South Florida State Coll (FL)

JEWISH/JUDAIC STUDIES
Broward Coll (FL)

JOURNALISM
Allen Comm Coll (KS)
Amarillo Coll (TX)
Austin Comm Coll (TX)
Bainbridge State Coll (GA)
Broward Coll (FL)
Bucks County Comm Coll (PA)
Butte Coll (CA)
Carl Albert State Coll (OK)
Casper Coll (WY)
Cloud County Comm Coll (KS)
Cochise Coll, Sierra Vista (AZ)
Coll of the Canyons (CA)
Coll of the Desert (CA)
Comm Coll of Allegheny County (PA)
Copiah-Lincoln Comm Coll (MS)
Cosumnes River Coll, Sacramento
    (CA)
Darton State Coll (GA)
De Anza Coll (CA)
Delta Coll (MI)
Fullerton Coll (CA)
Georgia Highlands Coll (GA)
Golden West Coll (CA)
Hinds Comm Coll (MS)
Housatonic Comm Coll (CT)
Imperial Valley Coll (CA)
Iowa Lakes Comm Coll (IA)
Kilgore Coll (TX)
Kingsborough Comm Coll of the City
    U of New York (NY)
Lorain County Comm Coll (OH)
Luzerne County Comm Coll (PA)
Manchester Comm Coll (CT)
Miami Dade Coll (FL)
Monroe County Comm Coll (MI)
Mt. San Antonio Coll (CA)
Northampton Comm Coll (PA)
Northeastern Jr Coll (CO)
Northern Essex Comm Coll (MA)
Northwest Coll (WY)
Northwest Mississippi Comm Coll
    (MS)
Orange Coast Coll (CA)
Palomar Coll (CA)
Paris Jr Coll (TX)
Pensacola State Coll (FL)
Potomac State Coll of West Virginia
    U (WV)
San Diego City Coll (CA)
San Jacinto Coll District (TX)
Santa Monica Coll (CA)
South Florida State Coll (FL)
South Georgia State Coll, Douglas
    (GA)
South Plains Coll (TX)
Sussex County Comm Coll (NJ)
Texarkana Coll (TX)
Trinity Valley Comm Coll (TX)
Tulsa Comm Coll (OK)
Umpqua Comm Coll (OR)
Vincennes U (IN)
Westchester Comm Coll (NY)
Western Texas Coll (TX)
Western Wyoming Comm Coll (WY)

JUVENILE CORRECTIONS
Danville Area Comm Coll (IL)
Kaskaskia Coll (IL)
Lansing Comm Coll (MI)

KEYBOARD INSTRUMENTS
Iowa Lakes Comm Coll (IA)

**KINDERGARTEN/PRESCHOOL
EDUCATION**
Alabama Southern Comm Coll (AL)
Alamance Comm Coll (NC)
Bainbridge State Coll (GA)
Bristol Comm Coll (MA)
Butler County Comm Coll (PA)
Casper Coll (WY)
Central Carolina Comm Coll (NC)
Clark State Comm Coll (OH)
Cleveland State Comm Coll (TN)
Columbia-Greene Comm Coll (NY)
Comm Coll of Philadelphia (PA)
Comm Coll of Rhode Island (RI)

County Coll of Morris (NJ)
Daytona State Coll (FL)
Delaware Tech & Comm Coll, Jack F.
    Owens Campus (DE)
Delaware Tech & Comm Coll,
    Stanton/Wilmington Campus (DE)
Delaware Tech & Comm Coll, Terry
    Campus (DE)
Finger Lakes Comm Coll (NY)
Genesee Comm Coll (NY)
Grayson Coll (TX)
Great Basin Coll (NV)
Honolulu Comm Coll (HI)
Howard Comm Coll (MD)
Imperial Valley Coll (CA)
Iowa Lakes Comm Coll (IA)
Jamestown Comm Coll (NY)
Lake Tahoe Comm Coll (CA)
Lorain County Comm Coll (OH)
Manchester Comm Coll (CT)
Miami Dade Coll (FL)
Mississippi Gulf Coast Comm Coll
    (MS)
Mitchell Comm Coll (NC)
Mt. San Antonio Coll (CA)
Nassau Comm Coll (NY)
Northeastern Jr Coll (CO)
Northern Essex Comm Coll (MA)
North Shore Comm Coll (MA)
Northwest Coll (WY)
Northwestern Connecticut Comm
    Coll (CT)
Nunez Comm Coll (LA)
Orange Coast Coll (CA)
Otero Jr Coll (CO)
Ozarks Tech Comm Coll (MO)
Potomac State Coll of West Virginia
    U (WV)
Quinsigamond Comm Coll (MA)
Raritan Valley Comm Coll (NJ)
Roane State Comm Coll (TN)
St. Clair County Comm Coll (MI)
San Jacinto Coll District (TX)
Scottsdale Comm Coll (AZ)
Shoreline Comm Coll (WA)
Snow Coll (UT)
Southeastern Comm Coll (NC)
Southern State Comm Coll (OH)
Southern U at Shreveport (LA)
Spoon River Coll (IL)
Sullivan County Comm Coll (NY)
Three Rivers Comm Coll (CT)
Tompkins Cortland Comm Coll (NY)
Trinity Valley Comm Coll (TX)
Tunxis Comm Coll (CT)
Umpqua Comm Coll (OR)
Victor Valley Coll (CA)
Virginia Western Comm Coll (VA)
Wenatchee Valley Coll (WA)

**KINESIOLOGY AND EXERCISE
SCIENCE**
Broward Coll (FL)
Carroll Comm Coll (MD)
Central Oregon Comm Coll (OR)
Chandler-Gilbert Comm Coll (AZ)
Clark State Comm Coll (OH)
County Coll of Morris (NJ)
Delaware Tech & Comm Coll,
    Stanton/Wilmington Campus (DE)
Glendale Comm Coll (AZ)
Laramie County Comm Coll (WY)
Norwalk Comm Coll (CT)
Oakland Comm Coll (MI)
Orange Coast Coll (CA)
Raritan Valley Comm Coll (NJ)
Salt Lake Comm Coll (UT)
Santa Rosa Jr Coll (CA)
Sheridan Coll (WY)
South Florida State Coll (FL)
South Georgia State Coll, Douglas
    (GA)
South Suburban Coll (IL)
Western Wyoming Comm Coll (WY)

**LABOR AND INDUSTRIAL
RELATIONS**
Kingsborough Comm Coll of the City
    U of New York (NY)
San Diego City Coll (CA)

LANDSCAPE ARCHITECTURE
Hinds Comm Coll (MS)
MiraCosta Coll (CA)
Monroe Comm Coll (NY)
Mt. San Antonio Coll (CA)
Truckee Meadows Comm Coll (NV)
Western Texas Coll (TX)

**LANDSCAPING AND
GROUNDSKEEPING**
Anoka Tech Coll (MN)
Cape Fear Comm Coll (NC)
Century Coll (MN)
Cincinnati State Tech and Comm
    Coll (OH)
Clark Coll (WA)
Clark State Comm Coll (OH)
Coll of Central Florida (FL)
Coll of Marin (CA)
Comm Coll of Allegheny County (PA)
Dakota Coll at Bottineau (ND)
Danville Area Comm Coll (IL)
Florida Gateway Coll (FL)
Fullerton Coll (CA)
Harford Comm Coll (MD)
Harrisburg Area Comm Coll (PA)
Hinds Comm Coll (MS)
Iowa Lakes Comm Coll (IA)
Lincoln Land Comm Coll (IL)
Miami Dade Coll (FL)
MiraCosta Coll (CA)
Oakland Comm Coll (MI)
The Ohio State U Ag Tech Inst (OH)
Owens Comm Coll, Toledo (OH)
Pensacola State Coll (FL)
San Juan Coll (NM)
Santa Rosa Jr Coll (CA)
South Florida State Coll (FL)
Springfield Tech Comm Coll (MA)
The Williamson Free School of
    Mecha Trades (PA)

**LAND USE PLANNING AND
MANAGEMENT**
Dakota Coll at Bottineau (ND)
Hocking Coll (OH)

**LANGUAGE INTERPRETATION
AND TRANSLATION**
Allen Comm Coll (KS)
Cape Fear Comm Coll (NC)
Century Coll (MN)
Cleveland Comm Coll (NC)
Lake Region State Coll (ND)
Oklahoma State U, Oklahoma City
    (OK)
Pima Comm Coll (AZ)

**LASER AND OPTICAL
TECHNOLOGY**
Amarillo Coll (TX)
Central Carolina Comm Coll (NC)
Monroe Comm Coll (NY)
Roane State Comm Coll (TN)
Springfield Tech Comm Coll (MA)
Texas State Tech Coll Waco (TX)
Three Rivers Comm Coll (CT)

LATIN
Austin Comm Coll (TX)

LATIN AMERICAN STUDIES
Broward Coll (FL)
Miami Dade Coll (FL)
San Diego City Coll (CA)
Santa Rosa Jr Coll (CA)

**LEGAL ADMINISTRATIVE
ASSISTANT/SECRETARY**
Alamance Comm Coll (NC)
Alexandria Tech and Comm Coll
    (MN)
Alvin Comm Coll (TX)
Amarillo Coll (TX)
Anoka Tech Coll (MN)
Arizona Western Coll (AZ)
Bismarck State Coll (ND)
Blackhawk Tech Coll (WI)
Bradford School (PA)
Broward Coll (FL)
Butler County Comm Coll (PA)
Butte Coll (CA)
Cambria-Rowe Business Coll,
    Indiana (PA)
Cambria-Rowe Business Coll,
    Johnstown (PA)
Career Tech Coll, Monroe (LA)
Central Carolina Comm Coll (NC)
Clark Coll (WA)
Cleveland Comm Coll (NC)
Coll of the Ouachitas (AR)
Comm Coll of Allegheny County (PA)
Comm Coll of Rhode Island (RI)
Crowder Coll (MO)
Dabney S. Lancaster Comm Coll
    (VA)
Delaware Tech & Comm Coll, Jack F.
    Owens Campus (DE)

Delaware Tech & Comm Coll, Terry
    Campus (DE)
Eastern Gateway Comm Coll (OH)
Fullerton Coll (CA)
Georgia Piedmont Tech Coll (GA)
Golden West Coll (CA)
Harper Coll (IL)
Helena Coll U of Montana (MT)
Herkimer County Comm Coll (NY)
Howard Comm Coll (MD)
Inst of Business & Medical Careers
    (CO)
International Business Coll,
    Indianapolis (IN)
Iowa Lakes Comm Coll (IA)
Jefferson Coll (MO)
King's Coll (NC)
Kirtland Comm Coll (MI)
Lake Land Coll (IL)
Lake Superior Coll (MN)
Lane Comm Coll (OR)
Lincoln Land Comm Coll (IL)
Linn-Benton Comm Coll (OR)
Lower Columbia Coll (WA)
Manchester Comm Coll (CT)
Metropolitan Comm Coll–Kansas
    City (MO)
Miami Dade Coll (FL)
Minneapolis Business Coll (MN)
Minnesota State Coll–Southeast
    Tech (MN)
Monroe Comm Coll (NY)
Monroe County Comm Coll (MI)
Moraine Park Tech Coll (WI)
Mt. San Antonio Coll (CA)
Nassau Comm Coll (NY)
Northampton Comm Coll (PA)
Northeastern Jr Coll (CO)
Northeast Texas Comm Coll (TX)
North Iowa Area Comm Coll (IA)
North Shore Comm Coll (MA)
Oklahoma City Comm Coll (OK)
Olympic Coll (WA)
Otero Jr Coll (CO)
Palomar Coll (CA)
Pensacola State Coll (FL)
Pitt Comm Coll (NC)
Roane State Comm Coll (TN)
San Diego City Coll (CA)
Santa Monica Coll (CA)
Sauk Valley Comm Coll (IL)
Shawnee Comm Coll (IL)
South Plains Coll (TX)
Southwestern Illinois Coll (IL)
Spoon River Coll (IL)
Stark State Coll (OH)
Three Rivers Comm Coll (CT)
Treasure Valley Comm Coll (OR)
Trinity Valley Comm Coll (TX)
Tulsa Comm Coll (OK)
Tunxis Comm Coll (CT)
Tyler Jr Coll (TX)
Umpqua Comm Coll (OR)
Walla Walla Comm Coll (WA)
Wenatchee Valley Coll (WA)
Western Wyoming Comm Coll (WY)

LEGAL ASSISTANT/PARALEGAL
Alexandria Tech and Comm Coll
    (MN)
Alvin Comm Coll (TX)
Arapahoe Comm Coll (CO)
Athens Tech Coll (GA)
Atlanta Tech Coll (GA)
Austin Comm Coll (TX)
Bellingham Tech Coll (WA)
Bevill State Comm Coll (AL)
Blue Ridge Comm and Tech Coll
    (WV)
Bradford School (PA)
Bristol Comm Coll (MA)
Bronx Comm Coll of the City U of
    New York (NY)
Broward Coll (FL)
Brown Mackie Coll–Albuquerque
    (NM)
Brown Mackie Coll–Atlanta (GA)
Brown Mackie Coll–Birmingham (AL)
Brown Mackie Coll–Boise (ID)
Brown Mackie Coll–Greenville (SC)
Brown Mackie Coll–Indianapolis (IN)
Brown Mackie Coll–Louisville (KY)
Brown Mackie Coll–Merrillville (IN)
Brown Mackie Coll–Miami (FL)
Brown Mackie Coll–Oklahoma City
    (OK)
Brown Mackie Coll–Phoenix (AZ)
Brown Mackie Coll–San Antonio
    (TX)
Bunker Hill Comm Coll (MA)

Ca&nnada Coll (CA)
Casper Coll (WY)
Central Carolina Comm Coll (NC)
Central Georgia Tech Coll (GA)
Chippewa Valley Tech Coll (WI)
Clark Coll (WA)
Clark State Comm Coll (OH)
Cloud County Comm Coll (KS)
Coll of Southern Maryland (MD)
Coll of the Canyons (CA)
Coll of the Ouachitas (AR)
Collin County Comm Coll District (TX)
Columbus State Comm Coll (OH)
Comm Care Coll (OK)
Comm Coll of Allegheny County (PA)
The Comm Coll of Baltimore County (MD)
Comm Coll of Rhode Island (RI)
Cumberland County Coll (NJ)
Daytona State Coll (FL)
De Anza Coll (CA)
Delta Coll (MI)
Dutchess Comm Coll (NY)
Eastern Florida State Coll (FL)
Eastern Idaho Tech Coll (ID)
Edison Comm Coll (OH)
Elgin Comm Coll (IL)
Erie Comm Coll (NY)
Fayetteville Tech Comm Coll (NC)
Finger Lakes Comm Coll (NY)
Fiorello H. LaGuardia Comm Coll of the City U of New York (NY)
Florida State Coll at Jacksonville (FL)
Fox Valley Tech Coll (WI)
Fullerton Coll (CA)
Gadsden State Comm Coll (AL)
Genesee Comm Coll (NY)
Georgia Military Coll (GA)
Georgia Northwestern Tech Coll (GA)
Georgia Piedmont Tech Coll (GA)
Greenville Tech Coll (SC)
Halifax Comm Coll (NC)
Harford Comm Coll (MD)
Harper Coll (IL)
Harrisburg Area Comm Coll (PA)
Herkimer County Comm Coll (NY)
Hillsborough Comm Coll (FL)
Hinds Comm Coll (MS)
Houston Comm Coll System (TX)
Hudson County Comm Coll (NJ)
Hutchinson Comm Coll and Area Vocational School (KS)
Illinois Eastern Comm Colls, Wabash Valley College (IL)
Inst of Business & Medical Careers (CO)
International Business Coll, Indianapolis (IN)
Iowa Lakes Comm Coll (IA)
ITT Tech Inst, Fort Myers (FL)
ITT Tech Inst, Atlanta (GA)
ITT Tech Inst, Duluth (GA)
ITT Tech Inst, Kennesaw (GA)
ITT Tech Inst, Newburgh (IN)
ITT Tech Inst, Baton Rouge (LA)
ITT Tech Inst, Wyoming (MI)
ITT Tech Inst, Columbus (OH)
ITT Tech Inst, Myrtle Beach (SC)
ITT Tech Inst, Johnson City (TN)
ITT Tech Inst, Arlington (TX)
ITT Tech Inst, Austin (TX)
ITT Tech Inst, DeSoto (TX)
ITT Tech Inst, Houston (TX)
ITT Tech Inst, Richardson (TX)
ITT Tech Inst, San Antonio (TX)
ITT Tech Inst, Waco (TX)
ITT Tech Inst, Webster (TX)
ITT Tech Inst (WV)
ITT Tech Inst , Greenfield (WI)
Ivy Tech Comm Coll–Bloomington (IN)
Ivy Tech Comm Coll–Central Indiana (IN)
Ivy Tech Comm Coll–Columbus (IN)
Ivy Tech Comm Coll–East Central (IN)
Ivy Tech Comm Coll–Kokomo (IN)
Ivy Tech Comm Coll–Lafayette (IN)
Ivy Tech Comm Coll–North Central (IN)
Ivy Tech Comm Coll–Northeast (IN)
Ivy Tech Comm Coll–Northwest (IN)
Ivy Tech Comm Coll–Richmond (IN)
Ivy Tech Comm Coll–Southeast (IN)
Ivy Tech Comm Coll–Southern Indiana (IN)
Ivy Tech Comm Coll–Southwest (IN)
Ivy Tech Comm Coll–Wabash Valley (IN)
Jefferson Comm Coll (NY)
Johnston Comm Coll (NC)
J. Sargeant Reynolds Comm Coll (VA)
Kankakee Comm Coll (IL)
Kent State U at East Liverpool (OH)
Kent State U at Trumbull (OH)
Kilgore Coll (TX)
King's Coll (NC)
Lakeland Comm Coll (OH)
Lake Superior Coll (MN)
Lansing Comm Coll (MI)
Laramie County Comm Coll (WY)
Lehigh Carbon Comm Coll (PA)
Luzerne County Comm Coll (PA)
Macomb Comm Coll (MI)
Manchester Comm Coll (CT)
Massachusetts Bay Comm Coll (MA)
Mercer County Comm Coll (NJ)
Miami Dade Coll (FL)
Middlesex County Coll (NJ)
Minneapolis Business Coll (MN)
Minnesota School of Business–Brooklyn Center (MN)
Mississippi Gulf Coast Comm Coll (MS)
Missouri State U–West Plains (MO)
Mohave Comm Coll (AZ)
Montgomery Coll (MD)
Moraine Park Tech Coll (WI)
Mountain Empire Comm Coll (VA)
Mountain State Coll (WV)
Mt. San Antonio Coll (CA)
Mt. San Jacinto Coll (CA)
Mount Wachusett Comm Coll (MA)
Nassau Comm Coll (NY)
New Mexico State U–Alamogordo (NM)
New York Career Inst (NY)
Northampton Comm Coll (PA)
Northern Essex Comm Coll (MA)
North Shore Comm Coll (MA)
NorthWest Arkansas Comm Coll (AR)
Northwestern Connecticut Comm Coll (CT)
Northwest Florida State Coll (FL)
Northwest Mississippi Comm Coll (MS)
Norwalk Comm Coll (CT)
Nunez Comm Coll (LA)
Oakland Comm Coll (MI)
Ogeechee Tech Coll (GA)
Oxnard Coll (CA)
Palomar Coll (CA)
Pasadena City Coll (CA)
Pasco-Hernando State Coll (FL)
Patrick Henry Comm Coll (VA)
Pensacola State Coll (FL)
Phoenix Coll (AZ)
Pima Comm Coll (AZ)
Pitt Comm Coll (NC)
Raritan Valley Comm Coll (NJ)
Salt Lake Comm Coll (UT)
San Diego City Coll (CA)
San Jacinto Coll District (TX)
San Juan Coll (NM)
Santa Rosa Jr Coll (CA)
Seminole State Coll of Florida (FL)
Southern Crescent Tech Coll (GA)
Southern U at Shreveport (LA)
South Florida State Coll (FL)
South Georgia Tech Coll (GA)
South Piedmont Comm Coll (NC)
South Suburban Coll (IL)
Southwestern Comm Coll (NC)
Southwestern Illinois Coll (IL)
Sullivan County Comm Coll (NY)
Sussex County Comm Coll (NJ)
Tallahassee Comm Coll (FL)
Tarrant County Coll District (TX)
TCI–The Coll of Technology (NY)
Tech Coll of the Lowcountry (SC)
Tompkins Cortland Comm Coll (NY)
Trident Tech Coll (SC)
Truckee Meadows Comm Coll (NV)
Victoria Coll (TX)
Vincennes U (IN)
Volunteer State Comm Coll (TN)
Wayne County Comm Coll District (MI)
Westchester Comm Coll (NY)
Western Dakota Tech Inst (SD)
Westmoreland County Comm Coll (PA)

LEGAL PROFESSIONS AND STUDIES RELATED
Bristol Comm Coll (MA)
Bucks County Comm Coll (PA)

LEGAL STUDIES
Alvin Comm Coll (TX)
Broward Coll (FL)
Carroll Comm Coll (MD)
Harford Comm Coll (MD)
Iowa Lakes Comm Coll (IA)
Macomb Comm Coll (MI)
MiraCosta Coll (CA)
Palomar Coll (CA)
Trident Tech Coll (SC)

LIBERAL ARTS AND SCIENCES AND HUMANITIES RELATED
Bucks County Comm Coll (PA)
Cascadia Comm Coll (WA)
Chandler-Gilbert Comm Coll (AZ)
Cleveland Comm Coll (NC)
Cleveland State Comm Coll (TN)
Coll of Southern Maryland (MD)
Columbia-Greene Comm Coll (NY)
The Comm Coll of Baltimore County (MD)
Dakota Coll at Bottineau (ND)
Dutchess Comm Coll (NY)
Fayetteville Tech Comm Coll (NC)
Garrett Coll (MD)
Genesee Comm Coll (NY)
Great Falls Coll Montana State U (MT)
Hagerstown Comm Coll (MD)
Holyoke Comm Coll (MA)
Iowa Lakes Comm Coll (IA)
James Sprunt Comm Coll (NC)
Jamestown Comm Coll (NY)
J. Sargeant Reynolds Comm Coll (VA)
Kent State U at Ashtabula (OH)
Kent State U at East Liverpool (OH)
Kent State U at Salem (OH)
Kent State U at Trumbull (OH)
Kent State U at Tuscarawas (OH)
Luzerne County Comm Coll (PA)
Mitchell Comm Coll (NC)
Mohawk Valley Comm Coll (NY)
Montgomery Coll (MD)
Northampton Comm Coll (PA)
Oakland Comm Coll (MI)
Onondaga Comm Coll (NY)
Piedmont Comm Coll (NC)
Pitt Comm Coll (NC)
Pueblo Comm Coll (CO)
Randolph Comm Coll (NC)
Southern Maine Comm Coll (ME)
Southern U at Shreveport (LA)
South Florida State Coll (FL)
Tech Coll of the Lowcountry (SC)
Wayne Comm Coll (NC)
Wor-Wic Comm Coll (MD)
York County Comm Coll (ME)

LIBERAL ARTS AND SCIENCES/ LIBERAL STUDIES
Alabama Southern Comm Coll (AL)
Alamance Comm Coll (NC)
Alexandria Tech and Comm Coll (MN)
Alvin Comm Coll (TX)
Amarillo Coll (TX)
American Samoa Comm Coll (AS)
Anoka-Ramsey Comm Coll (MN)
Anoka-Ramsey Comm Coll, Cambridge Campus (MN)
Antelope Valley Coll (CA)
Arapahoe Comm Coll (CO)
Arkansas State U–Newport (AR)
Bainbridge State Coll (GA)
Berkeley City Coll (CA)
Berkshire Comm Coll (MA)
Bevill State Comm Coll (AL)
Big Bend Comm Coll (WA)
Bismarck State Coll (ND)
Blue Ridge Comm and Tech Coll (WV)
Borough of Manhattan Comm Coll of the City U of New York (NY)
Bossier Parish Comm Coll (LA)
Bowling Green State U-Firelands Coll (OH)
Bristol Comm Coll (MA)
Bronx Comm Coll of the City U of New York (NY)
Brookhaven Coll (TX)
Broward Coll (FL)
Bucks County Comm Coll (PA)
Butte Coll (CA)
Ca&nnada Coll (CA)
Cape Fear Comm Coll (NC)
Carroll Comm Coll (MD)
Cascadia Comm Coll (WA)
Casper Coll (WY)
Catawba Valley Comm Coll (NC)
Cayuga County Comm Coll (NY)
Cecil Coll (MD)
Central Carolina Comm Coll (NC)
Central Maine Comm Coll (ME)
Central Ohio Tech Coll (OH)
Central Oregon Comm Coll (OR)
Central Virginia Comm Coll (VA)
Century Coll (MN)
Chandler-Gilbert Comm Coll (AZ)
Chipola Coll (FL)
Chippewa Valley Tech Coll (WI)
Cincinnati State Tech and Comm Coll (OH)
Clark Coll (WA)
Clark State Comm Coll (OH)
Clatsop Comm Coll (OR)
Cleveland Comm Coll (NC)
Cleveland State Comm Coll (TN)
Clinton Comm Coll (NY)
Cloud County Comm Coll (KS)
Coll of Central Florida (FL)
Coll of Marin (CA)
Coll of Southern Idaho (ID)
Coll of Southern Maryland (MD)
Coll of the Canyons (CA)
Coll of the Desert (CA)
Coll of the Ouachitas (AR)
Coll of Western Idaho (ID)
Collin County Comm Coll District (TX)
Colorado Northwestern Comm Coll (CO)
Columbia Coll (CA)
Columbia Gorge Comm Coll (OR)
Columbia-Greene Comm Coll (NY)
Columbus State Comm Coll (OH)
Comm Coll of Allegheny County (PA)
The Comm Coll of Baltimore County (MD)
Comm Coll of Philadelphia (PA)
Comm Coll of Rhode Island (RI)
Comm Coll of Vermont (VT)
Copiah-Lincoln Comm Coll (MS)
Copper Mountain Coll (CA)
Cossatot Comm Coll of the U of Arkansas (AR)
Cosumnes River Coll, Sacramento (CA)
Cottey Coll (MO)
County Coll of Morris (NJ)
Crowder Coll (MO)
Cumberland County Coll (NJ)
Dabney S. Lancaster Comm Coll (VA)
Dakota Coll at Bottineau (ND)
Danville Area Comm Coll (IL)
Dean Coll (MA)
De Anza Coll (CA)
Delta Coll (MI)
Donnelly Coll (KS)
Dutchess Comm Coll (NY)
Dyersburg State Comm Coll (TN)
Eastern Arizona Coll (AZ)
Eastern Shore Comm Coll (VA)
Eastern Wyoming Coll (WY)
Edison Comm Coll (OH)
Elgin Comm Coll (IL)
Erie Comm Coll (NY)
Erie Comm Coll, North Campus (NY)
Erie Comm Coll, South Campus (NY)
Fayetteville Tech Comm Coll (NC)
Feather River Coll (CA)
Finger Lakes Comm Coll (NY)
Fiorello H. LaGuardia Comm Coll of the City U of New York (NY)
Flathead Valley Comm Coll (MT)
Florida Gateway Coll (FL)
Florida State Coll at Jacksonville (FL)
Frank Phillips Coll (TX)
Fullerton Coll (CA)
Gadsden State Comm Coll (AL)
Galveston Coll (TX)
Garden City Comm Coll (KS)
Garrett Coll (MD)
Gavilan Coll (CA)
Genesee Comm Coll (NY)
Georgia Highlands Coll (GA)
Golden West Coll (CA)
Goodwin Coll (CT)
Gordon State Coll (GA)
Grand Rapids Comm Coll (MI)
Grays Harbor Coll (WA)
Grayson Coll (TX)
Greenfield Comm Coll (MA)
Greenville Tech Coll (SC)
Hagerstown Comm Coll (MD)
Harford Comm Coll (MD)
Harper Coll (IL)
Hawkeye Comm Coll (IA)
Herkimer County Comm Coll (NY)
Highland Comm Coll (IL)
Hillsborough Comm Coll (FL)
Holyoke Comm Coll (MA)
Honolulu Comm Coll (HI)
Hopkinsville Comm Coll (KY)
Housatonic Comm Coll (CT)
Howard Comm Coll (MD)
Hudson County Comm Coll (NJ)
Hutchinson Comm Coll and Area Vocational School (KS)
Ilisagvik Coll (AK)
Illinois Eastern Comm Colls, Frontier Community College (IL)
Illinois Eastern Comm Colls, Lincoln Trail College (IL)
Illinois Eastern Comm Colls, Olney Central College (IL)
Illinois Eastern Comm Colls, Wabash Valley College (IL)
Imperial Valley Coll (CA)
Independence Comm Coll (KS)
Iowa Lakes Comm Coll (IA)
Ivy Tech Comm Coll–Bloomington (IN)
Ivy Tech Comm Coll–Central Indiana (IN)
Ivy Tech Comm Coll–Columbus (IN)
Ivy Tech Comm Coll–East Central (IN)
Ivy Tech Comm Coll–Kokomo (IN)
Ivy Tech Comm Coll–Lafayette (IN)
Ivy Tech Comm Coll–North Central (IN)
Ivy Tech Comm Coll–Northeast (IN)
Ivy Tech Comm Coll–Northwest (IN)
Ivy Tech Comm Coll–Richmond (IN)
Ivy Tech Comm Coll–Southeast (IN)
Ivy Tech Comm Coll–Southern Indiana (IN)
Ivy Tech Comm Coll–Southwest (IN)
Ivy Tech Comm Coll–Wabash Valley (IN)
Jackson Coll (MI)
Jackson State Comm Coll (TN)
James Sprunt Comm Coll (NC)
Jamestown Comm Coll (NY)
Jefferson Coll (MO)
Jefferson Comm Coll (NY)
Jefferson State Comm Coll (AL)
Johnston Comm Coll (NC)
John Tyler Comm Coll (VA)
Kaskaskia Coll (IL)
Kent State U at Salem (OH)
Kent State U at Trumbull (OH)
Kent State U at Tuscarawas (OH)
Kilian Comm Coll (SD)
Kingsborough Comm Coll of the City U of New York (NY)
Kirtland Comm Coll (MI)
Lake Land Coll (IL)
Lakeland Comm Coll (OH)
Lake Region State Coll (ND)
Lakes Region Comm Coll (NH)
Lake Superior Coll (MN)
Lake Tahoe Comm Coll (CA)
Lamar Comm Coll (CO)
Lamar State Coll–Orange (TX)
Landmark Coll (VT)
Lane Comm Coll (OR)
Lansing Comm Coll (MI)
Lawson State Comm Coll (AL)
LDS Business Coll (UT)
Lehigh Carbon Comm Coll (PA)
Lenoir Comm Coll (NC)
Lincoln Land Comm Coll (IL)
Linn-Benton Comm Coll (OR)
Lorain County Comm Coll (OH)
Los Angeles Mission Coll (CA)
Lower Columbia Coll (WA)
Lurleen B. Wallace Comm Coll (AL)
Luzerne County Comm Coll (PA)
Macomb Comm Coll (MI)
Manchester Comm Coll (CT)
Marion Military Inst (AL)
Massachusetts Bay Comm Coll (MA)
McHenry County Coll (IL)
Mercer County Comm Coll (NJ)
Mesabi Range Comm and Tech Coll (MN)
Mesa Comm Coll (AZ)
Metropolitan Comm Coll–Kansas City (MO)
Middlesex County Coll (NJ)
Mid-Plains Comm Coll, North Platte (NE)
Mid-South Comm Coll (AR)
Mineral Area Coll (MO)
Minneapolis Comm and Tech Coll (MN)
MiraCosta Coll (CA)
Mississippi Delta Comm Coll (MS)
Mississippi Gulf Coast Comm Coll (MS)
Mitchell Comm Coll (NC)
Mohave Comm Coll (AZ)

Monroe Comm Coll (NY)
Monroe County Comm Coll (MI)
Montgomery Coll (MD)
Montgomery County Comm Coll (PA)
Moraine Valley Comm Coll (IL)
Motlow State Comm Coll (TN)
Mott Comm Coll (MI)
Mountain Empire Comm Coll (VA)
Mountain View Coll (TX).
Mt. San Jacinto Coll (CA)
Mount Wachusett Comm Coll (MA)
Nassau Comm Coll (NY)
Niagara County Comm Coll (NY)
Normandale Comm Coll (MN)
Northampton Comm Coll (PA)
North Dakota State Coll of Science (ND)
Northeastern Jr Coll (CO)
Northeastern Tech Coll (SC)
Northeast Iowa Comm Coll (IA)
Northeast Texas Comm Coll (TX)
Northern Essex Comm Coll (MA)
North Iowa Area Comm Coll (IA)
North Shore Comm Coll (MA)
NorthWest Arkansas Comm Coll (AR)
Northwest Coll (WY)
Northwestern Connecticut Comm Coll (CT)
Northwest Florida State Coll (FL)
Northwest Mississippi Comm Coll (MS)
Northwest-Shoals Comm Coll (AL)
Norwalk Comm Coll (CT)
Oakland Comm Coll (MI)
Oakton Comm Coll (IL)
Ocean County Coll (NJ)
Oklahoma City Comm Coll (OK)
Orange Coast Coll (CA)
Oregon Coast Comm Coll (OR)
Otero Jr Coll (CO)
Owensboro Comm and Tech Coll (KY)
Ozarks Tech Comm Coll (MO)
Palomar Coll (CA)
Paris Jr Coll (TX)
Pasadena City Coll (CA)
Pasco-Hernando State Coll (FL)
Patrick Henry Comm Coll (VA)
Penn State Beaver (PA)
Penn State Brandywine (PA)
Penn State DuBois (PA)
Penn State Fayette, The Eberly Campus (PA)
Penn State Greater Allegheny (PA)
Penn State Hazleton (PA)
Penn State Lehigh Valley (PA)
Penn State Mont Alto (PA)
Penn State New Kensington (PA)
Penn State Schuylkill (PA)
Penn State Wilkes-Barre (PA)
Penn State Worthington Scranton (PA)
Penn State York (PA)
Pensacola State Coll (FL)
Phoenix Coll (AZ)
Piedmont Comm Coll (NC)
Piedmont Virginia Comm Coll (VA)
Pima Comm Coll (AZ)
Pitt Comm Coll (NC)
Potomac State Coll of West Virginia U (WV)
Pueblo Comm Coll (CO)
Quinsigamond Comm Coll (MA)
Rainy River Comm Coll (MN)
Randolph Comm Coll (NC)
Rappahannock Comm Coll (VA)
Raritan Valley Comm Coll (NJ)
Reading Area Comm Coll (PA)
Rend Lake Coll (IL)
Richmond Comm Coll (NC)
Rio Hondo Coll (CA)
River Valley Comm Coll (NH)
Roane State Comm Coll (TN)
Rock Valley Coll (IL)
Rogue Comm Coll (OR)
Saginaw Chippewa Tribal Coll (MI)
St. Clair County Comm Coll (MI)
San Diego City Coll (CA)
San Juan Coll (NM)
Santa Monica Coll (CA)
Santa Rosa Jr Coll (CA)
Seminole State Coll (OK)
Seminole State Coll of Florida (FL)
Shawnee Comm Coll (IL)
Shelton State Comm Coll (AL)
Shoreline Comm Coll (WA)
Snow Coll (UT)
Somerset Comm Coll (KY)
Southeastern Comm Coll (IA)

Southeastern Comm Coll (NC)
Southern State Comm Coll (OH)
South Florida State Coll (FL)
South Piedmont Comm Coll (NC)
South Plains Coll (TX)
South Suburban Coll (IL)
Southwestern Comm Coll (NC)
Southwestern Illinois Coll (IL)
Southwestern Indian Polytechnic Inst (NM)
Southwestern Michigan Coll (MI)
Southwest Virginia Comm Coll (VA)
Spartanburg Comm Coll (SC)
Spartanburg Methodist Coll (SC)
Spoon River Coll (IL)
Springfield Tech Comm Coll (MA)
State Fair Comm Coll (MO)
State U of New York Coll of Technology at Alfred (NY)
Sullivan County Comm Coll (NY)
Sussex County Comm Coll (NJ)
Tallahassee Comm Coll (FL)
Tarrant County Coll District (TX)
Tech Coll of the Lowcountry (SC)
Temple Coll (TX)
Texarkana Coll (TX)
Three Rivers Comm Coll (CT)
Tompkins Cortland Comm Coll (NY)
Trident Tech Coll (SC)
Trinity Valley Comm Coll (TX)
Tunxis Comm Coll (CT)
Tyler Jr Coll (TX)
Umpqua Comm Coll (OR)
The U of Akron–Wayne Coll (OH)
U of Arkansas Comm Coll at Hope (AR)
U of Arkansas Comm Coll at Morrilton (AR)
U of Hawaii Maui Coll (HI)
U of New Mexico–Los Alamos Branch (NM)
U of Wisconsin–Fox Valley (WI)
U of Wisconsin–Sheboygan (WI)
U of Wisconsin–Waukesha (WI)
Victoria Coll (TX)
Victor Valley Coll (CA)
Vincennes U (IN)
Virginia Western Comm Coll (VA)
Volunteer State Comm Coll (TN)
Walla Walla Comm Coll (WA)
Walters State Comm Coll (TN)
Waubonsee Comm Coll (IL)
Wayne Comm Coll (NC)
Wayne County Comm Coll District (MI)
Wenatchee Valley Coll (WA)
Westchester Comm Coll (NY)
Western Nevada Coll (NV)
Western Oklahoma State Coll (OK)
Western Texas Coll (TX)
Western Wyoming Comm Coll (WY)
Westmoreland County Comm Coll (PA)
Williston State Coll (ND)
Wor-Wic Comm Coll (MD)
Wytheville Comm Coll (VA)

LIBRARY AND ARCHIVES ASSISTING
Clark State Comm Coll (OH)
Ivy Tech Comm Coll–Bloomington (IN)
Ivy Tech Comm Coll–Columbus (IN)
Ivy Tech Comm Coll–East Central (IN)
Ivy Tech Comm Coll–Kokomo (IN)
Ivy Tech Comm Coll–Lafayette (IN)
Ivy Tech Comm Coll–North Central (IN)
Ivy Tech Comm Coll–Northeast (IN)
Ivy Tech Comm Coll–Northwest (IN)
Ivy Tech Comm Coll–Richmond (IN)
Ivy Tech Comm Coll–Southeast (IN)
Ivy Tech Comm Coll–Southern Indiana (IN)
Ivy Tech Comm Coll–Southwest (IN)
Ivy Tech Comm Coll–Wabash Valley (IN)
Minneapolis Comm and Tech Coll (MN)
Oakland Comm Coll (MI)
Palomar Coll (CA)
Pueblo Comm Coll (CO)
Waubonsee Comm Coll (IL)
Western Dakota Tech Inst (SD)

LIBRARY AND INFORMATION SCIENCE
Allen Comm Coll (KS)
Coll of Southern Idaho (ID)

Copiah-Lincoln Comm Coll (MS)
Grand Rapids Comm Coll (MI)
Mesa Comm Coll (AZ)
Westmoreland County Comm Coll (PA)

LIBRARY SCIENCE RELATED
Pasadena City Coll (CA)

LICENSED PRACTICAL/ VOCATIONAL NURSE TRAINING
Amarillo Coll (TX)
Anoka Tech Coll (MN)
Athens Tech Coll (GA)
Bainbridge State Coll (GA)
Big Bend Comm Coll (WA)
Bismarck State Coll (ND)
Butte Coll (CA)
Carrington Coll California–Sacramento (CA)
Carrington Coll California–San Jose (CA)
Carroll Comm Coll (MD)
Central Maine Comm Coll (ME)
Central Ohio Tech Coll (OH)
Central Oregon Comm Coll (OR)
Clark State Comm Coll (OH)
Coll of Southern Idaho (ID)
Coll of Southern Maryland (MD)
Coll of the Desert (CA)
Coll of the Ouachitas (AR)
Comm Coll of Allegheny County (PA)
Comm Coll of Rhode Island (RI)
Copper Mountain Coll (CA)
Dakota Coll at Bottineau (ND)
De Anza Coll (CA)
Delaware Tech & Comm Coll, Jack F. Owens Campus (DE)
Eastern Gateway Comm Coll (OH)
Feather River Coll (CA)
Fiorello H. LaGuardia Comm Coll of the City U of New York (NY)
Flathead Valley Comm Coll (MT)
Gavilan Coll (CA)
Grand Rapids Comm Coll (MI)
Great Falls Coll Montana State U (MT)
Harford Comm Coll (MD)
Helena Coll U of Montana (MT)
Hocking Coll (OH)
Howard Comm Coll (MD)
Imperial Valley Coll (CA)
Ivy Tech Comm Coll–Southeast (IN)
Jackson Coll (MI)
Jefferson Coll (MO)
J. Sargeant Reynolds Comm Coll (VA)
Kirtland Comm Coll (MI)
Lake Area Tech Inst (SD)
Lamar Comm Coll (CO)
Lansing Comm Coll (MI)
Manhattan Area Tech Coll (KS)
Mid-Plains Comm Coll, North Platte (NE)
MiraCosta Coll (CA)
North Dakota State Coll of Science (ND)
Northeastern Jr Coll (CO)
North Iowa Area Comm Coll (IA)
Northwest Mississippi Comm Coll (MS)
Northwest Tech Coll (MN)
Pasadena City Coll (CA)
Reading Area Comm Coll (PA)
San Diego City Coll (CA)
San Jacinto Coll District (TX)
San Joaquin Valley Coll, Hanford (CA)
San Joaquin Valley Coll, Hesperia (CA)
San Joaquin Valley Coll, Temecula (CA)
San Joaquin Valley Coll, Visalia (CA)
Santa Rosa Jr Coll (CA)
Schoolcraft Coll (MI)
Southeastern Comm Coll (IA)
Southeast Tech Inst (SD)
South Louisiana Comm Coll (LA)
South Plains Coll (TX)
Southwestern Comm Coll (NC)
Temple Coll (TX)
Texarkana Coll (TX)
Trinity Valley Comm Coll (TX)
Tyler Jr Coll (TX)
Wenatchee Valley Coll (WA)
Western Texas Coll (TX)
Western Wyoming Comm Coll (WY)

Westmoreland County Comm Coll (PA)
Williston State Coll (ND)

LINEWORKER
Bismarck State Coll (ND)
Chandler-Gilbert Comm Coll (AZ)
Coll of Southern Maryland (MD)
Harrisburg Area Comm Coll (PA)
Ivy Tech Comm Coll–Lafayette (IN)
Mitchell Tech Inst (SD)
Raritan Valley Comm Coll (NJ)

LINGUISTICS
Ca&nnada Coll (CA)
South Florida State Coll (FL)

LITERATURE
Oklahoma City Comm Coll (OK)

LITERATURE RELATED
Cayuga County Comm Coll (NY)

LIVESTOCK MANAGEMENT
The Ohio State U Ag Tech Inst (OH)

LOGISTICS, MATERIALS, AND SUPPLY CHAIN MANAGEMENT
Ancilla Coll (IN)
Arizona Western Coll (AZ)
Athens Tech Coll (GA)
Cecil Coll (MD)
Chattahoochee Tech Coll (GA)
Clark State Comm Coll (OH)
Cochise Coll, Sierra Vista (AZ)
Columbus State Comm Coll (OH)
Edison Comm Coll (OH)
Florida Gateway Coll (FL)
Fox Valley Tech Coll (WI)
Georgia Military Coll (GA)
Goodwin Coll (CT)
Houston Comm Coll System (TX)
Lone Star Coll–CyFair (TX)
Miami Dade Coll (FL)
Pima Comm Coll (AZ)
Pitt Comm Coll (NC)
Randolph Comm Coll (NC)
South Georgia State Coll, Douglas (GA)
Truckee Meadows Comm Coll (NV)
Westmoreland County Comm Coll (PA)

MACHINE SHOP TECHNOLOGY
Butler County Comm Coll (PA)
Cape Fear Comm Coll (NC)
Catawba Valley Comm Coll (NC)
Comm Coll of Allegheny County (PA)
Daytona State Coll (FL)
Delta Coll (MI)
Eastern Arizona Coll (AZ)
Fayetteville Tech Comm Coll (NC)
Florida State Coll at Jacksonville (FL)
Ivy Tech Comm Coll–Central Indiana (IN)
Metropolitan Comm Coll–Kansas City (MO)
Mitchell Comm Coll (NC)
Orange Coast Coll (CA)
Pasadena City Coll (CA)
Pitt Comm Coll (NC)
Pueblo Comm Coll (CO)
Randolph Comm Coll (NC)
San Juan Coll (NM)
Wayne Comm Coll (NC)
West Kentucky Comm and Tech Coll (KY)

MACHINE TOOL TECHNOLOGY
Alamance Comm Coll (NC)
Altamaha Tech Coll (GA)
Amarillo Coll (TX)
Bellingham Tech Coll (WA)
Butler County Comm Coll (PA)
Casper Coll (WY)
Central Maine Comm Coll (ME)
Clark Coll (WA)
Coll of Marin (CA)
Coll of the Ouachitas (AR)
Coll of Western Idaho (ID)
Columbus Tech Coll (GA)
De Anza Coll (CA)
East Central Coll (MO)
Elgin Comm Coll (IL)
Georgia Piedmont Tech Coll (GA)
Grayson Coll (TX)
Greenville Tech Coll (SC)
Gwinnett Tech Coll (GA)
Hawkeye Comm Coll (IA)
Hinds Comm Coll (MS)

Hutchinson Comm Coll and Area Vocational School (KS)
Illinois Eastern Comm Colls, Wabash Valley College (IL)
Ivy Tech Comm Coll–Bloomington (IN)
Ivy Tech Comm Coll–Central Indiana (IN)
Ivy Tech Comm Coll–Columbus (IN)
Ivy Tech Comm Coll–East Central (IN)
Ivy Tech Comm Coll–Kokomo (IN)
Ivy Tech Comm Coll–Lafayette (IN)
Ivy Tech Comm Coll–North Central (IN)
Ivy Tech Comm Coll–Northeast (IN)
Ivy Tech Comm Coll–Northwest (IN)
Ivy Tech Comm Coll–Richmond (IN)
Ivy Tech Comm Coll–Southern Indiana (IN)
Ivy Tech Comm Coll–Southwest (IN)
Ivy Tech Comm Coll–Wabash Valley (IN)
Jefferson Coll (MO)
Lake Area Tech Inst (SD)
Lansing Comm Coll (MI)
Linn-Benton Comm Coll (OR)
Lorain County Comm Coll (OH)
Lower Columbia Coll (WA)
Macomb Comm Coll (MI)
Mineral Area Coll (MO)
Moraine Park Tech Coll (WI)
Mt. San Antonio Coll (CA)
North Dakota State Coll of Science (ND)
Northeastern Tech Coll (SC)
Northern Essex Comm Coll (MA)
Northwest Mississippi Comm Coll (MS)
Orange Coast Coll (CA)
Ozarks Tech Comm Coll (MO)
Pima Comm Coll (AZ)
Reading Area Comm Coll (PA)
San Diego City Coll (CA)
Shelton State Comm Coll (AL)
Sheridan Coll (WY)
Shoreline Comm Coll (WA)
Southeastern Comm Coll (IA)
Southern Maine Comm Coll (ME)
South Louisiana Comm Coll (LA)
South Plains Coll (TX)
Southwestern Illinois Coll (IL)
Southwestern Michigan Coll (MI)
Spartanburg Comm Coll (SC)
State Fair Comm Coll (MO)
State U of New York Coll of Technology at Alfred (NY)
Tarrant County Coll District (TX)
Trident Tech Coll (SC)
Wayne County Comm Coll District (MI)
Western Nevada Coll (NV)
Westmoreland County Comm Coll (PA)
Wichita Area Tech Coll (KS)
The Williamson Free School of Mecha Trades (PA)
Wiregrass Georgia Tech Coll (GA)
Wytheville Comm Coll (VA)
York County Comm Coll (ME)

MAGNETIC RESONANCE IMAGING (MRI) TECHNOLOGY
Lansing Comm Coll (MI)
Owens Comm Coll, Toledo (OH)

MANAGEMENT INFORMATION SYSTEMS
Arkansas State U–Newport (AR)
Broward Coll (FL)
Cambria-Rowe Business Coll, Johnstown (PA)
Carl Albert State Coll (OK)
Carroll Comm Coll (MD)
Cecil Coll (MD)
Central Oregon Comm Coll (OR)
Coll of the Ouachitas (AR)
Columbia Gorge Comm Coll (OR)
Comm Coll of Allegheny County (PA)
The Comm Coll of Baltimore County (MD)
Cossatot Comm Coll of the U of Arkansas (AR)
County Coll of Morris (NJ)
Delaware Tech & Comm Coll, Jack F. Owens Campus (DE)
Delaware Tech & Comm Coll, Stanton/Wilmington Campus (DE)
Delaware Tech & Comm Coll, Terry Campus (DE)

East Central Coll (MO)
Garrett Coll (MD)
Gwinnett Tech Coll (GA)
Hagerstown Comm Coll (MD)
Hillsborough Comm Coll (FL)
Jackson State Comm Coll (TN)
John Tyler Comm Coll (VA)
Kilgore Coll (TX)
Kirtland Comm Coll (MI)
Lakeland Comm Coll (OH)
Lake Region State Coll (ND)
Lake Superior Coll (MN)
Lamar Comm Coll (CO)
Lane Comm Coll (OR)
Lansing Comm Coll (MI)
Manchester Comm Coll (CT)
Manhattan Area Tech Coll (KS)
Mercer County Comm Coll (NJ)
Miami Dade Coll (FL)
Mississippi Delta Comm Coll (MS)
Moraine Valley Comm Coll (IL)
Nassau Comm Coll (NY)
Normandale Comm Coll (MN)
Northwest Florida State Coll (FL)
Oklahoma City Comm Coll (OK)
Ozarks Tech Comm Coll (MO)
Pensacola State Coll (FL)
Raritan Valley Comm Coll (NJ)
River Valley Comm Coll (NH)
San Jacinto Coll District (TX)
South Florida State Coll (FL)
Treasure Valley Comm Coll (OR)
Victor Valley Coll (CA)
Western Nevada Coll (NV)
York County Comm Coll (ME)

MANAGEMENT INFORMATION SYSTEMS AND SERVICES RELATED
Bowling Green State U-Firelands Coll (OH)
Harrisburg Area Comm Coll (PA)
Hillsborough Comm Coll (FL)
Mid-South Comm Coll (AR)
Missouri State U–West Plains (MO)
Montgomery County Comm Coll (PA)
Pensacola State Coll (FL)
Seminole State Coll (OK)
Tulsa Comm Coll (OK)

MANAGEMENT SCIENCE
Cambria-Rowe Business Coll, Johnstown (PA)
Career Tech Coll, Monroe (LA)
Central Virginia Comm Coll (VA)
Delaware Tech & Comm Coll, Stanton/Wilmington Campus (DE)
Pensacola State Coll (FL)
Sauk Valley Comm Coll (IL)
South Florida State Coll (FL)

MANUFACTURING ENGINEERING
Bristol Comm Coll (MA)
Broward Coll (FL)
Mitchell Comm Coll (NC)
Penn State Fayette, The Eberly Campus (PA)
Penn State Greater Allegheny (PA)
Penn State Hazleton (PA)
Penn State Wilkes-Barre (PA)
Penn State York (PA)

MANUFACTURING ENGINEERING TECHNOLOGY
Albany Tech Coll (GA)
Altamaha Tech Coll (GA)
Bowling Green State U-Firelands Coll (OH)
Butler County Comm Coll (PA)
Casper Coll (WY)
Central Ohio Tech Coll (OH)
Central Oregon Comm Coll (OR)
Clark Coll (WA)
Coll of Southern Idaho (ID)
Coll of the Canyons (CA)
Crowder Coll (MO)
Danville Area Comm Coll (IL)
Delaware Tech & Comm Coll, Stanton/Wilmington Campus (DE)
Delta Coll (MI)
Edison Comm Coll (OH)
Fox Valley Tech Coll (WI)
Gadsden State Comm Coll (AL)
Garden City Comm Coll (KS)
Gateway Comm and Tech Coll (KY)
Hawkeye Comm Coll (IA)
Houston Comm Coll System (TX)
Hutchinson Comm Coll and Area Vocational School (KS)
Illinois Eastern Comm Colls, Wabash Valley College (IL)

ITI Tech Coll (LA)
Jefferson Coll (MO)
Lake Area Tech Inst (SD)
Lane Comm Coll (OR)
Lawson State Comm Coll (AL)
Lehigh Carbon Comm Coll (PA)
Macomb Comm Coll (MI)
Mid-South Comm Coll (AR)
Mitchell Comm Coll (NC)
Mohawk Valley Comm Coll (NY)
Normandale Comm Coll (MN)
Northcentral Tech Coll (WI)
North Dakota State Coll of Science (ND)
North Iowa Area Comm Coll (IA)
Northwest Florida State Coll (FL)
Northwest Tech Coll (MN)
Oakland Comm Coll (MI)
Oakton Comm Coll (IL)
Oklahoma City Comm Coll (OK)
Owens Comm Coll, Toledo (OH)
Pensacola State Coll (FL)
Pitt Comm Coll (NC)
Pueblo Comm Coll (CO)
Quinsigamond Comm Coll (MA)
Raritan Valley Comm Coll (NJ)
Rogue Comm Coll (OR)
Schoolcraft Coll (MI)
Southern Crescent Tech Coll (GA)
South Georgia Tech Coll (GA)
Southwestern Illinois Coll (IL)
Spartanburg Comm Coll (SC)
State Fair Comm Coll (MO)
Sullivan Coll of Technology and Design (KY)
Tallahassee Comm Coll (FL)
Texas State Tech Coll Waco (TX)
Truckee Meadows Comm Coll (NV)
Vincennes U (IN)
Waubonsee Comm Coll (IL)
Wayne County Comm Coll District (MI)
Westmoreland County Comm Coll (PA)

MARINE BIOLOGY AND BIOLOGICAL OCEANOGRAPHY
Broward Coll (FL)
Oregon Coast Comm Coll (OR)
Shoreline Comm Coll (WA)
Southern Maine Comm Coll (ME)
South Florida State Coll (FL)

MARINE MAINTENANCE AND SHIP REPAIR TECHNOLOGY
Cape Fear Comm Coll (NC)
Honolulu Comm Coll (HI)
Iowa Lakes Comm Coll (IA)
Kingsborough Comm Coll of the City U of New York (NY)
Lakes Region Comm Coll (NH)
Orange Coast Coll (CA)
Shoreline Comm Coll (WA)
State Fair Comm Coll (MO)

MARINE SCIENCE/MERCHANT MARINE OFFICER
American Samoa Comm Coll (AS)
San Jacinto Coll District (TX)

MARKETING/MARKETING MANAGEMENT
Albany Tech Coll (GA)
Alexandria Tech and Comm Coll (MN)
Altamaha Tech Coll (GA)
Alvin Comm Coll (TX)
Antelope Valley Coll (CA)
Arizona Western Coll (AZ)
Athens Tech Coll (GA)
Atlanta Tech Coll (GA)
Augusta Tech Coll (GA)
Austin Comm Coll (TX)
Bainbridge State Coll (GA)
Bellingham Tech Coll (WA)
Blackhawk Tech Coll (WI)
Bristol Comm Coll (MA)
Bronx Comm Coll of the City U of New York (NY)
Brookhaven Coll (TX)
Broward Coll (FL)
Casper Coll (WY)
Cecil Coll (MD)
Central Carolina Comm Coll (NC)
Central Georgia Tech Coll (GA)
Central Oregon Comm Coll (OR)
Century Coll (MN)
Chattahoochee Tech Coll (GA)
Chippewa Valley Tech Coll (WI)
Cincinnati State Tech and Comm Coll (OH)
Clark State Comm Coll (OH)

Cleveland Comm Coll (NC)
Coll of Central Florida (FL)
Coll of the Ouachitas (AR)
Coll of Western Idaho (ID)
Columbus State Comm Coll (OH)
Comm Coll of Allegheny County (PA)
Comm Coll of Rhode Island (RI)
Dakota Coll at Bottineau (ND)
Davis Coll (OH)
De Anza Coll (CA)
Delaware Tech & Comm Coll, Jack F. Owens Campus (DE)
Delaware Tech & Comm Coll, Stanton/Wilmington Campus (DE)
Delaware Tech & Comm Coll, Terry Campus (DE)
Delta Coll (MI)
Eastern Idaho Tech Coll (ID)
Edison Comm Coll (OH)
Elgin Comm Coll (IL)
Fayetteville Tech Comm Coll (NC)
FIDM/The Fashion Inst of Design & Merchandising, Orange County Campus (CA)
Finger Lakes Comm Coll (NY)
Florida State Coll at Jacksonville (FL)
Fox Valley Tech Coll (WI)
Genesee Comm Coll (NY)
Georgia Highlands Coll (GA)
Georgia Northwestern Tech Coll (GA)
Georgia Piedmont Tech Coll (GA)
Glendale Comm Coll (AZ)
Golden West Coll (CA)
Gwinnett Tech Coll (GA)
Harford Comm Coll (MD)
Harper Coll (IL)
Hinds Comm Coll (MS)
Hocking Coll (OH)
Houston Comm Coll System (TX)
Imperial Valley Coll (CA)
Iowa Lakes Comm Coll (IA)
Jackson Coll (MI)
Kingsborough Comm Coll of the City U of New York (NY)
Lake Area Tech Inst (SD)
Lake Land Coll (IL)
Lakeland Comm Coll (OH)
Lake Tahoe Comm Coll (CA)
Lamar Comm Coll (CO)
Lanier Tech Coll (GA)
Lenoir Comm Coll (NC)
Lone Star Coll–CyFair (TX)
Lone Star Coll–Kingwood (TX)
Lorain County Comm Coll (OH)
Macomb Comm Coll (MI)
Manchester Comm Coll (CT)
Mesa Comm Coll (AZ)
Metropolitan Comm Coll–Kansas City (MO)
Miami Dade Coll (FL)
Middlesex County Coll (NJ)
Minnesota School of Business–Brooklyn Center (MN)
Minnesota School of Business–Plymouth (MN)
Mississippi Gulf Coast Comm Coll (MS)
Monroe Comm Coll (NY)
Monroe County Comm Coll (MI)
Moraine Park Tech Coll (WI)
Mott Comm Coll (MI)
Moultrie Tech Coll (GA)
Mt. San Antonio Coll (CA)
Nassau Comm Coll (NY)
Normandale Comm Coll (MN)
Northampton Comm Coll (PA)
Northcentral Tech Coll (WI)
Northeastern Jr Coll (CO)
Northeastern Tech Coll (SC)
Northern Essex Comm Coll (MA)
North Shore Comm Coll (MA)
Northwest Florida State Coll (FL)
Norwalk Comm Coll (CT)
Oakton Comm Coll (IL)
Ogeechee Tech Coll (GA)
Orange Coast Coll (CA)
Oxnard Coll (CA)
Pasadena City Coll (CA)
Pasco-Hernando State Coll (FL)
Phoenix Coll (AZ)
Piedmont Virginia Comm Coll (VA)
Pitt Comm Coll (NC)
Raritan Valley Comm Coll (NJ)
Rock Valley Coll (IL)
Rogue Comm Coll (OR)
St. Clair County Comm Coll (MI)
Salt Lake Comm Coll (UT)
San Diego City Coll (CA)
Sauk Valley Comm Coll (IL)
Savannah Tech Coll (GA)
Schoolcraft Coll (MI)

Seminole State Coll of Florida (FL)
Shoreline Comm Coll (WA)
Southeastern Tech Coll (GA)
Southeast Tech Inst (SD)
Southern Crescent Tech Coll (GA)
South Florida State Coll (FL)
South Georgia Tech Coll (GA)
South Plains Coll (TX)
Southwestern Comm Coll (NC)
Springfield Tech Comm Coll (MA)
Stark State Coll (OH)
State U of New York Coll of Technology at Alfred (NY)
Sullivan County Comm Coll (NY)
Tarrant County Coll District (TX)
Texarkana Coll (TX)
Three Rivers Comm Coll (CT)
Trident Tech Coll (SC)
Trinity Valley Comm Coll (TX)
Tulsa Comm Coll (OK)
Tunxis Comm Coll (CT)
Umpqua Comm Coll (OR)
U of Hawaii Maui Coll (HI)
Vincennes U (IN)
Waukesha County Tech Coll (WI)
Westchester Comm Coll (NY)
Western Texas Coll (TX)
Western Wyoming Comm Coll (WY)
West Georgia Tech Coll (GA)
Williston State Coll (ND)
Wiregrass Georgia Tech Coll (GA)

MARKETING RELATED
Columbus State Comm Coll (OH)
Dakota Coll at Bottineau (ND)
Davis Coll (OH)

MASONRY
Florida State Coll at Jacksonville (FL)
Hinds Comm Coll (MS)
Ivy Tech Comm Coll–Central Indiana (IN)
Ivy Tech Comm Coll–Columbus (IN)
Ivy Tech Comm Coll–East Central (IN)
Ivy Tech Comm Coll–Lafayette (IN)
Ivy Tech Comm Coll–North Central (IN)
Ivy Tech Comm Coll–Northeast (IN)
Ivy Tech Comm Coll–Northwest (IN)
Ivy Tech Comm Coll–Southern Indiana (IN)
Ivy Tech Comm Coll–Southwest (IN)
Ivy Tech Comm Coll–Wabash Valley (IN)
Metropolitan Comm Coll–Kansas City (MO)
Mississippi Delta Comm Coll (MS)
Palomar Coll (CA)
Southwestern Illinois Coll (IL)
State U of New York Coll of Technology at Alfred (NY)
Tallahassee Comm Coll (FL)

MASSAGE THERAPY
Arizona Western Coll (AZ)
Butler County Comm Coll (PA)
Career Tech Coll, Monroe (LA)
Carrington Coll–Boise (ID)
Carrington Coll California–Pleasant Hill (CA)
Carrington Coll California–Sacramento (CA)
Carrington Coll California–San Jose (CA)
Carrington Coll California–San Leandro (CA)
Carrington Coll–Phoenix (AZ)
Central Oregon Comm Coll (OR)
Chandler-Gilbert Comm Coll (AZ)
Coll of Southern Maryland (MD)
Comm Care Coll (OK)
The Comm Coll of Baltimore County (MD)
Comm Coll of Rhode Island (RI)
Inst of Business & Medical Careers (CO)
Iowa Lakes Comm Coll (IA)
Ivy Tech Comm Coll–Northeast (IN)
Minnesota School of Business–Plymouth (MN)
Minnesota State Coll–Southeast Tech (MN)
Niagara County Comm Coll (NY)
Oakland Comm Coll (MI)
Owens Comm Coll, Toledo (OH)
Phoenix Coll (AZ)
Pima Comm Coll (AZ)
Pitt Comm Coll (NC)
St. Clair County Comm Coll (MI)
San Joaquin Valley Coll, Hanford (CA)

San Joaquin Valley Coll, Hesperia (CA)
San Joaquin Valley Coll, Salida (CA)
San Joaquin Valley Coll, Temecula (CA)
Schoolcraft Coll (MI)
Sheridan Coll (WY)
South Piedmont Comm Coll (NC)
Southwestern Comm Coll (NC)
Southwestern Illinois Coll (IL)
Spencerian Coll (KY)
Spencerian Coll–Lexington (KY)
Springfield Tech Comm Coll (MA)
Vincennes U (IN)
Williston State Coll (ND)

MASS COMMUNICATION/MEDIA
Amarillo Coll (TX)
Ancilla Coll (IN)
Arizona Western Coll (AZ)
Broward Coll (FL)
Bunker Hill Comm Coll (MA)
Casper Coll (WY)
Chipola Coll (FL)
Coll of Marin (CA)
Coll of the Desert (CA)
Crowder Coll (MO)
De Anza Coll (CA)
Finger Lakes Comm Coll (NY)
Fullerton Coll (CA)
Genesee Comm Coll (NY)
Georgia Military Coll (GA)
Grand Rapids Comm Coll (MI)
Harford Comm Coll (MD)
Harrisburg Area Comm Coll (PA)
Iowa Lakes Comm Coll (IA)
Lamar State Coll–Orange (TX)
Laramie County Comm Coll (WY)
Lorain County Comm Coll (OH)
Mercer County Comm Coll (NJ)
Miami Dade Coll (FL)
Monroe Comm Coll (NY)
Monroe County Comm Coll (MI)
Nassau Comm Coll (NY)
Niagara County Comm Coll (NY)
Oklahoma City Comm Coll (OK)
Orange Coast Coll (CA)
Salt Lake Comm Coll (UT)
Snow Coll (UT)
South Plains Coll (TX)
Spoon River Coll (IL)
Tulsa Comm Coll (OK)
Westchester Comm Coll (NY)
Western Texas Coll (TX)
Wytheville Comm Coll (VA)

MATERIALS ENGINEERING
Oakland Comm Coll (MI)
Southern Maine Comm Coll (ME)
South Florida State Coll (FL)

MATERIALS SCIENCE
Mt. San Antonio Coll (CA)
Northern Essex Comm Coll (MA)

MATHEMATICS
Alabama Southern Comm Coll (AL)
Allen Comm Coll (KS)
Alvin Comm Coll (TX)
Amarillo Coll (TX)
Antelope Valley Coll (CA)
Arizona Western Coll (AZ)
Austin Comm Coll (TX)
Bainbridge State Coll (GA)
Borough of Manhattan Comm Coll of the City U of New York (NY)
Bronx Comm Coll of the City U of New York (NY)
Broward Coll (FL)
Bucks County Comm Coll (PA)
Bunker Hill Comm Coll (MA)
Butler County Comm Coll (PA)
Butte Coll (CA)
Carl Albert State Coll (OK)
Casper Coll (WY)
Cecil Coll (MD)
Central Oregon Comm Coll (OR)
Central Wyoming Coll (WY)
Cochise Coll, Sierra Vista (AZ)
Coll of Marin (CA)
Coll of Southern Idaho (ID)
Coll of the Canyons (CA)
Coll of the Desert (CA)
Coll of the Mainland (TX)
Columbia Coll (CA)
Comm Coll of Allegheny County (PA)
Copper Mountain Coll (CA)
Cosumnes River Coll, Sacramento (CA)
Crowder Coll (MO)
Dakota Coll at Bottineau (ND)

Darton State Coll (GA)
De Anza Coll (CA)
Eastern Arizona Coll (AZ)
Eastern Wyoming Coll (WY)
Edison Comm Coll (OH)
Feather River Coll (CA)
Finger Lakes Comm Coll (NY)
Frank Phillips Coll (TX)
Fullerton Coll (CA)
Galveston Coll (TX)
Garden City Comm Coll (KS)
Gavilan Coll (CA)
Genesee Comm Coll (NY)
Golden West Coll (CA)
Gordon State Coll (GA)
Grayson Coll (TX)
Great Basin Coll (NV)
Harford Comm Coll (MD)
Harper Coll (IL)
Harrisburg Area Comm Coll (PA)
Hinds Comm Coll (MS)
Housatonic Comm Coll (CT)
Hutchinson Comm Coll and Area
   Vocational School (KS)
Imperial Valley Coll (CA)
Independence Comm Coll (KS)
Iowa Lakes Comm Coll (IA)
Jefferson Comm Coll (NY)
J. Sargeant Reynolds Comm Coll
   (VA)
Kankakee Comm Coll (IL)
Kilgore Coll (TX)
Kingsborough Comm Coll of the City
   U of New York (NY)
Lake Tahoe Comm Coll (CA)
Lamar State Coll–Orange (TX)
Lansing Comm Coll (MI)
Laramie County Comm Coll (WY)
Lehigh Carbon Comm Coll (PA)
Linn-Benton Comm Coll (OR)
Lorain County Comm Coll (OH)
Los Angeles Mission Coll (CA)
Luzerne County Comm Coll (PA)
Macomb Comm Coll (MI)
Mercer County Comm Coll (NJ)
Mesa Comm Coll (AZ)
Miami Dade Coll (FL)
Minneapolis Comm and Tech Coll
   (MN)
MiraCosta Coll (CA)
Mississippi Delta Comm Coll (MS)
Mohave Comm Coll (AZ)
Monroe Comm Coll (NY)
Monroe County Comm Coll (MI)
Montgomery County Comm Coll (PA)
Mt. San Antonio Coll (CA)
Mt. San Jacinto Coll (CA)
Nassau Comm Coll (NY)
Niagara County Comm Coll (NY)
Northampton Comm Coll (PA)
Northeastern Jr Coll (CO)
Northeast Texas Comm Coll (TX)
Northwest Coll (WY)
Northwestern Connecticut Comm
   Coll (CT)
Oklahoma City Comm Coll (OK)
Orange Coast Coll (CA)
Otero Jr Coll (CO)
Oxnard Coll (CA)
Palomar Coll (CA)
Paris Jr Coll (TX)
Pasadena City Coll (CA)
Pensacola State Coll (FL)
Potomac State Coll of West Virginia
   U (WV)
Roane State Comm Coll (TN)
San Diego City Coll (CA)
San Jacinto Coll District (TX)
San Juan Coll (NM)
Santa Rosa Jr Coll (CA)
Sauk Valley Comm Coll (IL)
Scottsdale Comm Coll (AZ)
Seminole State Coll (OK)
Sheridan Coll (WY)
Snow Coll (UT)
Southern U at Shreveport (LA)
South Florida State Coll (FL)
South Georgia State Coll, Douglas
   (GA)
Spoon River Coll (IL)
Springfield Tech Comm Coll (MA)
Sullivan County Comm Coll (NY)
Texarkana Coll (TX)
Treasure Valley Comm Coll (OR)
Trinity Valley Comm Coll (TX)
Truckee Meadows Comm Coll (NV)
Tulsa Comm Coll (OK)
Tyler Jr Coll (TX)
Umpqua Comm Coll (OR)
Victor Valley Coll (CA)

Vincennes U (IN)
Wenatchee Valley Coll (WA)
Western Nevada Coll (NV)
Western Wyoming Comm Coll (WY)

MATHEMATICS AND COMPUTER SCIENCE
Crowder Coll (MO)
Dean Coll (MA)

MATHEMATICS AND STATISTICS RELATED
Bristol Comm Coll (MA)
Georgia Highlands Coll (GA)

MATHEMATICS RELATED
Cayuga County Comm Coll (NY)
Genesee Comm Coll (NY)

MATHEMATICS TEACHER EDUCATION
Bucks County Comm Coll (PA)
Carroll Comm Coll (MD)
The Comm Coll of Baltimore County
   (MD)
Darton State Coll (GA)
Delaware Tech & Comm Coll, Jack F.
   Owens Campus (DE)
Delaware Tech & Comm Coll,
   Stanton/Wilmington Campus (DE)
Delaware Tech & Comm Coll, Terry
   Campus (DE)
Eastern Wyoming Coll (WY)
Harford Comm Coll (MD)
Highland Comm Coll (IL)
Kankakee Comm Coll (IL)
Kaskaskia Coll (IL)
Montgomery Coll (MD)
Moraine Valley Comm Coll (IL)
Northwest Mississippi Comm Coll
   (MS)
South Florida State Coll (FL)
Southwestern Illinois Coll (IL)
Vincennes U (IN)
Walla Walla Comm Coll (WA)

MECHANICAL DRAFTING AND CAD/CADD
Alexandria Tech and Comm Coll
   (MN)
Anoka Tech Coll (MN)
Blackhawk Tech Coll (WI)
Butler County Comm Coll (PA)
Cleveland Comm Coll (NC)
Commonwealth Tech Inst (PA)
Comm Coll of Allegheny County (PA)
Delaware Tech & Comm Coll, Jack F.
   Owens Campus (DE)
Edison Comm Coll (OH)
Fox Valley Tech Coll (WI)
Greenville Tech Coll (SC)
Hutchinson Comm Coll and Area
   Vocational School (KS)
Island Drafting and Tech Inst (NY)
Lake Superior Coll (MN)
Lane Comm Coll (OR)
Lansing Comm Coll (MI)
Macomb Comm Coll (MI)
MiraCosta Coll (CA)
Mitchell Comm Coll (NC)
Montgomery County Comm Coll (PA)
Moraine Park Tech Coll (WI)
Northcentral Tech Coll (WI)
North Iowa Area Comm Coll (IA)
Oakland Comm Coll (MI)
Ozarks Tech Comm Coll (MO)
St. Clair County Comm Coll (MI)
Southwestern Illinois Coll (IL)
State U of New York Coll of
   Technology at Alfred (NY)
Sullivan Coll of Technology and
   Design (KY)
Triangle Tech, Inc.–Pittsburgh
   School (PA)
Tulsa Comm Coll (OK)
Vincennes U (IN)
Waukesha County Tech Coll (WI)
Westmoreland County Comm Coll
   (PA)
Wichita Area Tech Coll (KS)

MECHANICAL ENGINEERING
Bristol Comm Coll (MA)
Broward Coll (FL)
Cayuga County Comm Coll (NY)
Fiorello H. LaGuardia Comm Coll of
   the City U of New York (NY)
Kilgore Coll (TX)
Northeast Texas Comm Coll (TX)

Pasadena City Coll (CA)
South Florida State Coll (FL)

MECHANICAL ENGINEERING/ MECHANICAL TECHNOLOGY
Alamance Comm Coll (NC)
Augusta Tech Coll (GA)
Benjamin Franklin Inst of Technology
   (MA)
Bowling Green State U-Firelands
   Coll (OH)
Cape Fear Comm Coll (NC)
Catawba Valley Comm Coll (NC)
Cayuga County Comm Coll (NY)
Central Ohio Tech Coll (OH)
Cincinnati State Tech and Comm
   Coll (OH)
Clark State Comm Coll (OH)
Columbus State Comm Coll (OH)
Columbus Tech Coll (GA)
County Coll of Morris (NJ)
Delaware Tech & Comm Coll,
   Stanton/Wilmington Campus (DE)
Delta Coll (MI)
Eastern Gateway Comm Coll (OH)
Edison Comm Coll (OH)
Erie Comm Coll, North Campus (NY)
Finger Lakes Comm Coll (NY)
Fullerton Coll (CA)
Greenville Tech Coll (SC)
Hagerstown Comm Coll (MD)
Harrisburg Area Comm Coll (PA)
Illinois Eastern Comm Colls, Lincoln
   Trail College (IL)
Jamestown Comm Coll (NY)
Kent State U at Trumbull (OH)
Kent State U at Tuscarawas (OH)
Lakeland Comm Coll (OH)
Lehigh Carbon Comm Coll (PA)
Macomb Comm Coll (MI)
Massachusetts Bay Comm Coll (MA)
Middlesex County Coll (NJ)
Mitchell Comm Coll (NC)
Mohawk Valley Comm Coll (NY)
Monroe Comm Coll (NY)
Montgomery County Comm Coll (PA)
Moraine Valley Comm Coll (IL)
Mott Comm Coll (MI)
Oakton Comm Coll (IL)
Onondaga Comm Coll (NY)
Penn State DuBois (PA)
Penn State Hazleton (PA)
Penn State New Kensington (PA)
Penn State York (PA)
Pitt Comm Coll (NC)
Potomac State Coll of West Virginia
   U (WV)
Richmond Comm Coll (NC)
Shoreline Comm Coll (WA)
Southeastern Comm Coll (IA)
Southeast Tech Inst (SD)
Southern U at Shreveport (LA)
South Piedmont Comm Coll (NC)
Spartanburg Comm Coll (SC)
Springfield Tech Comm Coll (MA)
Stark State Coll (OH)
State U of New York Coll of
   Technology at Alfred (NY)
Sullivan Coll of Technology and
   Design (KY)
Tarrant County Coll District (TX)
Texas State Tech Coll Waco (TX)
Three Rivers Comm Coll (CT)
Trident Tech Coll (SC)
Tulsa Comm Coll (OK)
Vincennes U (IN)
Virginia Western Comm Coll (VA)
Wayne Comm Coll (NC)
Westchester Comm Coll (NY)
Westmoreland County Comm Coll
   (PA)
Wichita Area Tech Coll (KS)
Wytheville Comm Coll (VA)

MECHANICAL ENGINEERING TECHNOLOGIES RELATED
Broward Coll (FL)
Glen Oaks Comm Coll (MI)
Jefferson Comm Coll (NY)
John Tyler Comm Coll (VA)
Middlesex County Coll (NJ)
Mohawk Valley Comm Coll (NY)
Moraine Park Tech Coll (WI)

MECHANIC AND REPAIR TECHNOLOGIES RELATED
Chandler-Gilbert Comm Coll (AZ)
Cloud County Comm Coll (KS)
Greenville Tech Coll (SC)

Ivy Tech Comm Coll–Bloomington
   (IN)
Ivy Tech Comm Coll–Columbus (IN)
Ivy Tech Comm Coll–Kokomo (IN)
Ivy Tech Comm Coll–Lafayette (IN)
Ivy Tech Comm Coll–North Central
   (IN)
Ivy Tech Comm Coll–Northwest (IN)
Ivy Tech Comm Coll–Southwest (IN)
Laramie County Comm Coll (WY)
Macomb Comm Coll (MI)
State Fair Comm Coll (MO)

MECHANICS AND REPAIR
Ivy Tech Comm Coll–Bloomington
   (IN)
Ivy Tech Comm Coll–Central Indiana
   (IN)
Ivy Tech Comm Coll–Columbus (IN)
Ivy Tech Comm Coll–Kokomo (IN)
Ivy Tech Comm Coll–Lafayette (IN)
Ivy Tech Comm Coll–North Central
   (IN)
Ivy Tech Comm Coll–Northeast (IN)
Ivy Tech Comm Coll–Northwest (IN)
Ivy Tech Comm Coll–Richmond (IN)
Ivy Tech Comm Coll–Southern
   Indiana (IN)
Ivy Tech Comm Coll–Southwest (IN)
Ivy Tech Comm Coll–Wabash Valley
   (IN)
Owensboro Comm and Tech Coll
   (KY)
Rogue Comm Coll (OR)
Western Oklahoma State Coll (OK)
Western Wyoming Comm Coll (WY)

MECHATRONICS, ROBOTICS, AND AUTOMATION ENGINEERING
Harrisburg Area Comm Coll (PA)
Randolph Comm Coll (NC)
Westmoreland County Comm Coll
   (PA)

MEDICAL ADMINISTRATIVE ASSISTANT AND MEDICAL SECRETARY
Alamance Comm Coll (NC)
Alexandria Tech and Comm Coll
   (MN)
Alvin Comm Coll (TX)
Amarillo Coll (TX)
Anoka Tech Coll (MN)
Antelope Valley Coll (CA)
Berkeley City Coll (CA)
Bismarck State Coll (ND)
Blackhawk Tech Coll (WI)
Bristol Comm Coll (MA)
Bronx Comm Coll of the City U of
   New York (NY)
Bunker Hill Comm Coll (MA)
Butte Coll (CA)
Cambria-Rowe Business Coll,
   Johnstown (PA)
Carrington Coll–Spokane (WA)
Central Carolina Comm Coll (NC)
Century Coll (MN)
Clark Coll (WA)
Clark State Comm Coll (OH)
Coll of Marin (CA)
Coll of the Ouachitas (AR)
Coll of Western Idaho (ID)
Columbia Coll (CA)
Comm Coll of Allegheny County (PA)
The Comm Coll of Baltimore County
   (MD)
Comm Coll of Philadelphia (PA)
Comm Coll of Rhode Island (RI)
Crowder Coll (MO)
Dabney S. Lancaster Comm Coll
   (VA)
Dakota Coll at Bottineau (ND)
Danville Area Comm Coll (IL)
Davis Coll (OH)
Daytona State Coll (FL)
Delta Coll (MI)
Eastern Gateway Comm Coll (OH)
Edison Comm Coll (OH)
Flathead Valley Comm Coll (MT)
Galveston Coll (TX)
Gavilan Coll (CA)
Genesee Comm Coll (NY)
Grand Rapids Comm Coll (MI)
Halifax Comm Coll (NC)
Hallmark Coll of Technology (TX)
Harper Coll (IL)
Hawkeye Comm Coll (IA)
Hocking Coll (OH)
Howard Comm Coll (MD)

Illinois Eastern Comm Colls, Olney
   Central College (IL)
Inst of Business & Medical Careers
   (CO)
Iowa Lakes Comm Coll (IA)
Jefferson Coll (MO)
Jefferson Comm Coll (NY)
Kirtland Comm Coll (MI)
Lake Land Coll (IL)
Lake Superior Coll (MN)
Lake Tahoe Comm Coll (CA)
LDS Business Coll (UT)
Lenoir Comm Coll (NC)
Linn-Benton Comm Coll (OR)
Lower Columbia Coll (WA)
Luzerne County Comm Coll (PA)
Manchester Comm Coll (CT)
Mesa Comm Coll (AZ)
Metro Business Coll, Jefferson City
   (MO)
Metropolitan Comm Coll–Kansas
   City (MO)
Minnesota School of Business–
   Brooklyn Center (MN)
Minnesota State Coll–Southeast
   Tech (MN)
Monroe County Comm Coll (MI)
Mt. San Antonio Coll (CA)
Nassau Comm Coll (NY)
Northampton Comm Coll (PA)
Northeastern Jr Coll (CO)
Northeast Texas Comm Coll (TX)
Northern Essex Comm Coll (MA)
North Iowa Area Comm Coll (IA)
North Shore Comm Coll (MA)
Northwest Mississippi Comm Coll
   (MS)
Northwest Tech Coll (MN)
Orange Coast Coll (CA)
Otero Jr Coll (CO)
Owensboro Comm and Tech Coll
   (KY)
Owens Comm Coll, Toledo (OH)
Palomar Coll (CA)
Piedmont Comm Coll (NC)
Potomac State Coll of West Virginia
   U (WV)
Quinsigamond Comm Coll (MA)
Reading Area Comm Coll (PA)
Roane State Comm Coll (TN)
St. Clair County Comm Coll (MI)
San Jacinto Coll District (TX)
San Joaquin Valley Coll, Visalia (CA)
Scottsdale Comm Coll (AZ)
Shawnee Comm Coll (IL)
Shelton State Comm Coll (AL)
Shoreline Comm Coll (WA)
Somerset Comm Coll (KY)
South Plains Coll (TX)
Spoon River Coll (IL)
Springfield Tech Comm Coll (MA)
State Fair Comm Coll (MO)
Treasure Valley Comm Coll (OR)
Trident Tech Coll (SC)
Tulsa Comm Coll (OK)
Tunxis Comm Coll (CT)
Tyler Jr Coll (TX)
Umpqua Comm Coll (OR)
Walla Walla Comm Coll (WA)
Wenatchee Valley Coll (WA)
Western Wyoming Comm Coll (WY)
West Virginia Jr Coll–Bridgeport
   (WV)
Williston State Coll (ND)
Wytheville Comm Coll (VA)

MEDICAL/CLINICAL ASSISTANT
Alamance Comm Coll (NC)
Anoka Tech Coll (MN)
Barstow Comm Coll (CA)
Bay State Coll (MA)
Beal Coll (ME)
Big Bend Comm Coll (WA)
Blue Ridge Comm and Tech Coll
   (WV)
Bossier Parish Comm Coll (LA)
Bradford School (OH)
Bradford School (PA)
Brown Mackie Coll–Atlanta (GA)
Brown Mackie Coll–Oklahoma City
   (OK)
Brown Mackie Coll–Salina (KS)
Brown Mackie Coll–Tulsa (OK)
Bucks County Comm Coll (PA)
Ca&nnada Coll (CA)
Career Tech Coll, Monroe (LA)
Carrington Coll–Boise (ID)
Carrington Coll California–Citrus
   Heights (CA)

Carrington Coll California–Pleasant Hill (CA)
Carrington Coll California–Sacramento (CA)
Carrington Coll California–San Jose (CA)
Carrington Coll California–San Leandro (CA)
Central Carolina Comm Coll (NC)
Central Maine Comm Coll (ME)
Central Oregon Comm Coll (OR)
Central Virginia Comm Coll (VA)
Clark Coll (WA)
Clark State Comm Coll (OH)
Cleveland Comm Coll (NC)
Coll of Marin (CA)
Columbus State Comm Coll (OH)
Comm Care Coll (OK)
Comm Coll of Allegheny County (PA)
Comm Coll of Vermont (VT)
Cossatot Comm Coll of the U of Arkansas (AR)
Cosumnes River Coll, Sacramento (CA)
Dakota Coll at Bottineau (ND)
Davis Coll (OH)
De Anza Coll (CA)
Delaware Tech & Comm Coll, Jack F. Owens Campus (DE)
Delaware Tech & Comm Coll, Stanton/Wilmington Campus (DE)
Delaware Tech & Comm Coll, Terry Campus (DE)
East Central Coll (MO)
Eastern Gateway Comm Coll (OH)
Eastern Idaho Tech Coll (ID)
Edison Comm Coll (OH)
Elmira Business Inst (NY)
Flathead Valley Comm Coll (MT)
Fox Coll (IL)
Georgia Piedmont Tech Coll (GA)
Goodwin Coll (CT)
Great Falls Coll Montana State U (MT)
Gwinnett Tech Coll (GA)
Hallmark Coll of Technology (TX)
Harford Comm Coll (MD)
Harper Coll (IL)
Harrisburg Area Comm Coll (PA)
Highland Comm Coll (IL)
Hinds Comm Coll (MS)
Hocking Coll (OH)
Hudson County Comm Coll (NJ)
Inst of Business & Medical Careers (CO)
International Business Coll, Indianapolis (IN)
Iowa Lakes Comm Coll (IA)
ITT Tech Inst, Rancho Cordova (CA)
ITT Tech Inst, Fort Lauderdale (FL)
ITT Tech Inst, Jacksonville (FL)
ITT Tech Inst, Lake Mary (FL)
ITT Tech Inst, Miami (FL)
ITT Tech Inst, St. Petersburg (FL)
ITT Tech Inst, Tampa (FL)
ITT Tech Inst, Louisville (KY)
ITT Tech Inst, Canton (MI)
ITT Tech Inst, Akron (OH)
ITT Tech Inst, Dayton (OH)
ITT Tech Inst, Hilliard (OH)
ITT Tech Inst, Norwood (OH)
ITT Tech Inst, Strongsville (OH)
ITT Tech Inst, Warrensville Heights (OH)
ITT Tech Inst , Youngstown (OH)
ITT Tech Inst, Tulsa (OK)
ITT Tech Inst, Richardson (TX)
ITT Tech Inst, Chantilly (VA)
ITT Tech Inst, Norfolk (VA)
ITT Tech Inst, Richmond (VA)
ITT Tech Inst, Salem (VA)
ITT Tech Inst, Springfield (VA)
Ivy Tech Comm Coll–Central Indiana (IN)
Ivy Tech Comm Coll–Columbus (IN)
Ivy Tech Comm Coll–East Central (IN)
Ivy Tech Comm Coll–Kokomo (IN)
Ivy Tech Comm Coll–Lafayette (IN)
Ivy Tech Comm Coll–North Central (IN)
Ivy Tech Comm Coll–Northeast (IN)
Ivy Tech Comm Coll–Northwest (IN)
Ivy Tech Comm Coll–Richmond (IN)
Ivy Tech Comm Coll–Southeast (IN)
Ivy Tech Comm Coll–Southern Indiana (IN)
Ivy Tech Comm Coll–Southwest (IN)
Ivy Tech Comm Coll–Wabash Valley (IN)
Jackson Coll (MI)

James Sprunt Comm Coll (NC)
Jamestown Business Coll (NY)
Johnston Comm Coll (NC)
Kankakee Comm Coll (IL)
King's Coll (NC)
Kirtland Comm Coll (MI)
Lake Area Tech Inst (SD)
Lake Tahoe Comm Coll (CA)
LDS Business Coll (UT)
Lehigh Carbon Comm Coll (PA)
Lenoir Comm Coll (NC)
Linn-Benton Comm Coll (OR)
Lower Columbia Coll (WA)
Macomb Comm Coll (MI)
Miami Dade Coll (FL)
Minneapolis Business Coll (MN)
Minnesota School of Business–Brooklyn Center (MN)
MiraCosta Coll (CA)
Mitchell Comm Coll (NC)
Mitchell Tech Inst (SD)
Mohave Comm Coll (AZ)
Mohawk Valley Comm Coll (NY)
Montgomery County Comm Coll (PA)
Mountain State Coll (WV)
Mt. San Jacinto Coll (CA)
Mount Wachusett Comm Coll (MA)
Niagara County Comm Coll (NY)
Northeast Texas Comm Coll (TX)
North Iowa Area Comm Coll (IA)
Northwestern Connecticut Comm Coll (CT)
Northwest-Shoals Comm Coll (AL)
Oakland Comm Coll (MI)
Oklahoma City Comm Coll (OK)
Olympic Coll (WA)
Orange Coast Coll (CA)
Palomar Coll (CA)
Panola Coll (TX)
Pasadena City Coll (CA)
Phoenix Coll (AZ)
Pitt Comm Coll (NC)
Randolph Comm Coll (NC)
Raritan Valley Comm Coll (NJ)
Richmond Comm Coll (NC)
St. Clair County Comm Coll (MI)
Salt Lake Comm Coll (UT)
San Joaquin Valley Coll, Bakersfield (CA)
San Joaquin Valley Coll, Fresno (CA)
San Joaquin Valley Coll, Hanford (CA)
San Joaquin Valley Coll, Hesperia (CA)
San Joaquin Valley Coll, Ontario (CA)
San Joaquin Valley Coll, Rancho Cordova (CA)
San Joaquin Valley Coll, Salida (CA)
San Joaquin Valley Coll, Temecula (CA)
San Joaquin Valley Coll, Visalia (CA)
San Joaquin Valley Coll–Online (CA)
Santa Rosa Jr Coll (CA)
Southeastern Comm Coll (IA)
Southern Maine Comm Coll (ME)
Southern State Comm Coll (OH)
South Piedmont Comm Coll (NC)
Southwestern Illinois Coll (IL)
Southwestern Michigan Coll (MI)
Springfield Tech Comm Coll (MA)
Stark State Coll (OH)
Sullivan County Comm Coll (NY)
Tulsa Comm Coll (OK)
Wayne Comm Coll (NC)
Wenatchee Valley Coll (WA)
Western Dakota Tech Inst (SD)
Western Wyoming Comm Coll (WY)
Westmoreland County Comm Coll (PA)
West Virginia Jr Coll–Bridgeport (WV)
Wichita Area Tech Coll (KS)
Wood Tobe–Coburn School (NY)
Wright Career Coll, Overland Park (KS)
Wright Career Coll (NE)
York County Comm Coll (ME)

MEDICAL/HEALTH MANAGEMENT AND CLINICAL ASSISTANT
CollAmerica–Flagstaff (AZ)
Owens Comm Coll, Toledo (OH)
Pittsburgh Tech Inst, Oakdale (PA)

MEDICAL INFORMATICS
The Comm Coll of Baltimore County (MD)
Dyersburg State Comm Coll (TN)
Mott Comm Coll (MI)

MEDICAL INSURANCE CODING
Berkshire Comm Coll (MA)
Bucks County Comm Coll (PA)
Butler County Comm Coll (PA)
Collin County Comm Coll District (TX)
Comm Care Coll (OK)
Dakota Coll at Bottineau (ND)
Davis Coll (OH)
Elmira Business Inst (NY)
Flathead Valley Comm Coll (MT)
Goodwin Coll (CT)
Hallmark Coll of Technology (TX)
Laramie County Comm Coll (WY)
North Dakota State Coll of Science (ND)
Paris Jr Coll (TX)
Southeast Tech Inst (SD)
Spencerian Coll (KY)
Spencerian Coll–Lexington (KY)
Springfield Tech Comm Coll (MA)
West Virginia Jr Coll–Bridgeport (WV)
Williston State Coll (ND)
Wright Career Coll, Overland Park (KS)

MEDICAL INSURANCE/MEDICAL BILLING
Carrington Coll–Boise (ID)
Carrington Coll California–Citrus Heights (CA)
Carrington Coll California–Pleasant Hill (CA)
Carrington Coll California–Sacramento (CA)
Carrington Coll California–San Jose (CA)
Carrington Coll California–San Leandro (CA)
Coconino Comm Coll (AZ)
Goodwin Coll (CT)
Great Falls Coll Montana State U (MT)
Jackson Coll (MI)
Northcentral Tech Coll (WI)
Pasadena City Coll (CA)
San Joaquin Valley Coll, Bakersfield (CA)
San Joaquin Valley Coll, Hanford (CA)
San Joaquin Valley Coll, Hesperia (CA)
San Joaquin Valley Coll, Temecula (CA)
Schoolcraft Coll (MI)
Spencerian Coll (KY)

MEDICAL MICROBIOLOGY AND BACTERIOLOGY
South Florida State Coll (FL)

MEDICAL OFFICE ASSISTANT
Beal Coll (ME)
Broward Coll (FL)
Butler County Comm Coll (PA)
Cambria-Rowe Business Coll, Indiana (PA)
Central Wyoming Coll (WY)
Cincinnati State Tech and Comm Coll (OH)
Coconino Comm Coll (AZ)
Commonwealth Tech Inst (PA)
Dakota Coll at Bottineau (ND)
Harford Comm Coll (MD)
Helena Coll U of Montana (MT)
Iowa Lakes Comm Coll (IA)
Kankakee Comm Coll (IL)
LDS Business Coll (UT)
Manhattan Area Tech Coll (KS)
Mitchell Tech Inst (SD)
New York Career Inst (NY)
Pasadena City Coll (CA)
Patrick Henry Comm Coll (VA)
Phoenix Coll (AZ)
Pittsburgh Tech Inst, Oakdale (PA)
San Joaquin Valley Coll, Fresno (CA)
San Joaquin Valley Coll, Ontario (CA)
San Joaquin Valley Coll, Salida (CA)
San Joaquin Valley Coll, Visalia (CA)
Sauk Valley Comm Coll (IL)
Schoolcraft Coll (MI)
Southwestern Illinois Coll (IL)
Western Wyoming Comm Coll (WY)
Westmoreland County Comm Coll (PA)

MEDICAL OFFICE COMPUTER SPECIALIST
Iowa Lakes Comm Coll (IA)
Lamar Comm Coll (CO)
Mississippi Delta Comm Coll (MS)

Normandale Comm Coll (MN)
Richmond Comm Coll (NC)
Rogue Comm Coll (OR)
Western Wyoming Comm Coll (WY)

MEDICAL OFFICE MANAGEMENT
Arapahoe Comm Coll (CO)
Bay State Coll (MA)
Big Bend Comm Coll (WA)
Brown Mackie Coll–Akron (OH)
Brown Mackie Coll–Albuquerque (NM)
Brown Mackie Coll–Atlanta (GA)
Brown Mackie Coll–Birmingham (AL)
Brown Mackie Coll–Cincinnati (OH)
Brown Mackie Coll–Dallas/Ft. Worth (TX)
Brown Mackie Coll–Greenville (SC)
Brown Mackie Coll–Hopkinsville (KY)
Brown Mackie Coll–Oklahoma City (OK)
Brown Mackie Coll–Phoenix (AZ)
Brown Mackie Coll–Quad Cities (IA)
Brown Mackie Coll–St. Louis (MO)
Brown Mackie Coll–San Antonio (TX)
Brown Mackie Coll–Tucson (AZ)
Cape Fear Comm Coll (NC)
Career Tech Coll, Monroe (LA)
Carrington Coll–Albuquerque (NM)
Carrington Coll–Boise (ID)
Carrington Coll California–Sacramento (CA)
Carrington Coll California–San Jose (CA)
Carrington Coll–Mesa (AZ)
Carrington Coll–Phoenix (AZ)
Carrington Coll–Spokane (WA)
Carrington Coll–Tucson (AZ)
Catawba Valley Comm Coll (NC)
Cleveland Comm Coll (NC)
Columbia-Greene Comm Coll (NY)
Columbus Tech Coll (GA)
Erie Comm Coll, North Campus (NY)
Fayetteville Tech Comm Coll (NC)
Florida State Coll at Jacksonville (FL)
Georgia Northwestern Tech Coll (GA)
Johnston Comm Coll (NC)
Kilian Comm Coll (SD)
Long Island Business Inst (NY)
Norwalk Comm Coll (CT)
Pennsylvania Inst of Technology (PA)
Pitt Comm Coll (NC)
Pueblo Comm Coll (CO)
Randolph Comm Coll (NC)
San Joaquin Valley Coll–Online (CA)
South Piedmont Comm Coll (NC)
Spencerian Coll–Lexington (KY)
The U of Akron–Wayne Coll (OH)
U of Arkansas Comm Coll at Hope (AR)
Wayne Comm Coll (NC)

MEDICAL RADIOLOGIC TECHNOLOGY
Albany Tech Coll (GA)
Athens Tech Coll (GA)
Augusta Tech Coll (GA)
Bellingham Tech Coll (WA)
Blackhawk Tech Coll (WI)
Bowling Green State U-Firelands Coll (OH)
Broward Coll (FL)
Bunker Hill Comm Coll (MA)
Cape Fear Comm Coll (NC)
Carolinas Coll of Health Sciences (NC)
Carrington Coll–Phoenix Westside (AZ)
Carrington Coll–Spokane (WA)
Catawba Valley Comm Coll (NC)
Central Georgia Tech Coll (GA)
Central Ohio Tech Coll (OH)
Chattahoochee Tech Coll (GA)
Chippewa Valley Tech Coll (WI)
Coll of Southern Idaho (ID)
Columbus State Comm Coll (OH)
Columbus Tech Coll (GA)
Comm Coll of Allegheny County (PA)
The Comm Coll of Baltimore County (MD)
Comm Coll of Philadelphia (PA)
Cumberland County Coll (NJ)
Delta Coll (MI)
Dunwoody Coll of Technology (MN)
East Central Coll (MO)
Eastern Florida State Coll (FL)
Erie Comm Coll (NY)
Fiorello H. LaGuardia Comm Coll of the City U of New York (NY)
Flathead Valley Comm Coll (MT)
Florida State Coll at Jacksonville (FL)

Galveston Coll (TX)
Greenville Tech Coll (SC)
Gwinnett Tech Coll (GA)
Hagerstown Comm Coll (MD)
Hillsborough Comm Coll (FL)
Holyoke Comm Coll (MA)
Hutchinson Comm Coll and Area Vocational School (KS)
Illinois Eastern Comm Colls, Olney Central College (IL)
Ivy Tech Comm Coll–Central Indiana (IN)
Ivy Tech Comm Coll–Columbus (IN)
Ivy Tech Comm Coll–East Central (IN)
Ivy Tech Comm Coll–Wabash Valley (IN)
Jackson Coll (MI)
Jackson State Comm Coll (TN)
Kent State U at Ashtabula (OH)
Kent State U at Salem (OH)
Kilgore Coll (TX)
Lakeland Comm Coll (OH)
Lanier Tech Coll (GA)
Lone Star Coll–CyFair (TX)
Massachusetts Bay Comm Coll (MA)
Mercer County Comm Coll (NJ)
Middlesex County Coll (NJ)
Mississippi Delta Comm Coll (MS)
Mitchell Tech Inst (SD)
Mohawk Valley Comm Coll (NY)
Montgomery Coll (MD)
Montgomery County Comm Coll (PA)
Moraine Park Tech Coll (WI)
Mott Comm Coll (MI)
Nassau Comm Coll (NY)
Niagara County Comm Coll (NY)
Northcentral Tech Coll (WI)
North Shore Comm Coll (MA)
Northwest Florida State Coll (FL)
Oakland Comm Coll (MI)
Owensboro Comm and Tech Coll (KY)
Owens Comm Coll, Toledo (OH)
Penn State New Kensington (PA)
Penn State Schuylkill (PA)
Pennsylvania Coll of Health Sciences (PA)
Pensacola State Coll (FL)
Pitt Comm Coll (NC)
Salt Lake Comm Coll (UT)
Somerset Comm Coll (KY)
Southeastern Tech Coll (GA)
Southern Crescent Tech Coll (GA)
Southern Maine Comm Coll (ME)
Southern U at Shreveport (LA)
South Florida State Coll (FL)
Southwestern Comm Coll (NC)
Southwest Georgia Tech Coll (GA)
Spartanburg Comm Coll (SC)
Tallahassee Comm Coll (FL)
Tech Coll of the Lowcountry (SC)
Treasure Valley Comm Coll (OR)
Tulsa Comm Coll (OK)
Vincennes U (IN)
Volunteer State Comm Coll (TN)
Waukesha County Tech Coll (WI)
Western Oklahoma State Coll (OK)
West Georgia Tech Coll (GA)
Wiregrass Georgia Tech Coll (GA)
Wor-Wic Comm Coll (MD)

MEDICAL RECEPTION
Iowa Lakes Comm Coll (IA)

MEDICAL STAFF SERVICES TECHNOLOGY
Rend Lake Coll (IL)

MEDICAL TRANSCRIPTION
Great Falls Coll Montana State U (MT)
Iowa Lakes Comm Coll (IA)
Jackson Coll (MI)
Mountain State Coll (WV)
Northern Essex Comm Coll (MA)
Oakland Comm Coll (MI)
Reading Area Comm Coll (PA)
Schoolcraft Coll (MI)
Western Dakota Tech Inst (SD)
Williston State Coll (ND)

MEDIUM/HEAVY VEHICLE AND TRUCK TECHNOLOGY
Edison Comm Coll (OH)

MEETING AND EVENT PLANNING
Fox Valley Tech Coll (WI)
Iowa Lakes Comm Coll (IA)
Northampton Comm Coll (PA)

Raritan Valley Comm Coll (NJ)
Southwestern Michigan Coll (MI)

MENTAL AND SOCIAL HEALTH SERVICES AND ALLIED PROFESSIONS RELATED
Coll of Southern Maryland (MD)
Columbus State Comm Coll (OH)
John Tyler Comm Coll (VA)
J. Sargeant Reynolds Comm Coll (VA)
Northcentral Tech Coll (WI)
Richmond Comm Coll (NC)
South Piedmont Comm Coll (NC)
Southwest Virginia Comm Coll (VA)
Waukesha County Tech Coll (WI)
Wayne Comm Coll (NC)
Wisconsin Indianhead Tech Coll (WI)

MENTAL HEALTH COUNSELING
Alvin Comm Coll (TX)
Comm Coll of Philadelphia (PA)
Comm Coll of Rhode Island (RI)
Housatonic Comm Coll (CT)
Kingsborough Comm Coll of the City U of New York (NY)
Macomb Comm Coll (MI)
Mt. San Antonio Coll (CA)
Northern Essex Comm Coll (MA)
North Shore Comm Coll (MA)
San Jacinto Coll District (TX)
Southern U at Shreveport (LA)
South Plains Coll (TX)
Southwestern Comm Coll (NC)
Tarrant County Coll District (TX)
Truckee Meadows Comm Coll (NV)
Virginia Western Comm Coll (VA)

MERCHANDISING
Delta Coll (MI)

MERCHANDISING, SALES, AND MARKETING OPERATIONS RELATED (GENERAL)
Herkimer County Comm Coll (NY)
Iowa Lakes Comm Coll (IA)
Lake Region State Coll (ND)
Northcentral Tech Coll (WI)
Northwest Florida State Coll (FL)
Southeast Tech Inst (SD)
State U of New York Coll of Technology at Alfred (NY)

MERCHANDISING, SALES, AND MARKETING OPERATIONS RELATED (SPECIALIZED)
Bay State Coll (MA)
Middlesex County Coll (NJ)

METAL AND JEWELRY ARTS
Fashion Inst of Technology (NY)
FIDM/The Fashion Inst of Design & Merchandising, Los Angeles Campus (CA)
Flathead Valley Comm Coll (MT)
Palomar Coll (CA)
Paris Jr Coll (TX)

METAL FABRICATOR
Helena Coll U of Montana (MT)
Waukesha County Tech Coll (WI)

METALLURGICAL TECHNOLOGY
Kilgore Coll (TX)
Linn-Benton Comm Coll (OR)
Macomb Comm Coll (MI)
Penn State DuBois (PA)
Penn State Fayette, The Eberly Campus (PA)
Penn State Hazleton (PA)
Penn State New Kensington (PA)
Penn State Schuylkill (PA)
Penn State Wilkes-Barre (PA)
Penn State York (PA)
Schoolcraft Coll (MI)

MICROBIOLOGY
Fullerton Coll (CA)

MIDDLE SCHOOL EDUCATION
Austin Comm Coll (TX)
Coll of the Mainland (TX)
Collin County Comm Coll District (TX)
Cossatot Comm Coll of the U of Arkansas (AR)
Darton State Coll (GA)
Delaware Tech & Comm Coll, Jack F. Owens Campus (DE)

Delaware Tech & Comm Coll, Stanton/Wilmington Campus (DE)
Delaware Tech & Comm Coll, Terry Campus (DE)
Gordon State Coll (GA)
Grayson Coll (TX)
Miami Dade Coll (FL)
Northampton Comm Coll (PA)
Panola Coll (TX)
San Jacinto Coll District (TX)
South Florida State Coll (FL)

MINING AND PETROLEUM TECHNOLOGIES RELATED
Pima Comm Coll (AZ)

MINING TECHNOLOGY
Casper Coll (WY)
Eastern Arizona Coll (AZ)
Illinois Eastern Comm Colls, Wabash Valley College (IL)
Sheridan Coll (WY)
Western Wyoming Comm Coll (WY)

MODERN LANGUAGES
Amarillo Coll (TX)
Imperial Valley Coll (CA)
Otero Jr Coll (CO)
San Diego City Coll (CA)
Tyler Jr Coll (TX)

MORTUARY SCIENCE AND EMBALMING
Wayne County Comm Coll District (MI)

MOTORCYCLE MAINTENANCE AND REPAIR TECHNOLOGY
Iowa Lakes Comm Coll (IA)

MOVEMENT AND MIND-BODY THERAPIES AND EDUCATION RELATED
Moraine Valley Comm Coll (IL)

MULTI/INTERDISCIPLINARY STUDIES RELATED
Alexandria Tech and Comm Coll (MN)
Anoka-Ramsey Comm Coll (MN)
Anoka-Ramsey Comm Coll, Cambridge Campus (MN)
Arkansas State U–Newport (AR)
Bishop State Comm Coll (AL)
Bismarck State Coll (ND)
Blue Ridge Comm and Tech Coll (WV)
Bucks County Comm Coll (PA)
Carroll Comm Coll (MD)
Central Maine Comm Coll (ME)
Century Coll (MN)
Chippewa Valley Tech Coll (WI)
Cincinnati State Tech and Comm Coll (OH)
Coll of Southern Maryland (MD)
Coll of the Desert (CA)
Columbus State Comm Coll (OH)
Cossatot Comm Coll of the U of Arkansas (AR)
County Coll of Morris (NJ)
Eastern Arizona Coll (AZ)
Fox Valley Tech Coll (WI)
Greenville Tech Coll (SC)
Harford Comm Coll (MD)
Hawkeye Comm Coll (IA)
Hopkinsville Comm Coll (KY)
Lake Superior Coll (MN)
Manhattan Area Tech Coll (KS)
Mid-South Comm Coll (AR)
Minnesota State Coll–Southeast Tech (MN)
Moraine Park Tech Coll (WI)
Normandale Comm Coll (MN)
Northcentral Tech Coll (WI)
North Dakota State Coll of Science (ND)
North Iowa Area Comm Coll (IA)
Northwest-Shoals Comm Coll (AL)
Oklahoma City Comm Coll (OK)
Raritan Valley Comm Coll (NJ)
San Jacinto Coll District (TX)
Sheridan Coll (WY)
Somerset Comm Coll (KY)
South Florida State Coll (FL)
Spartanburg Comm Coll (SC)
U of Arkansas Comm Coll at Hope (AR)
Waukesha County Tech Coll (WI)
Williston State Coll (ND)
Wisconsin Indianhead Tech Coll (WI)
York County Comm Coll (ME)

MUSEUM STUDIES
Casper Coll (WY)

MUSIC
Alabama Southern Comm Coll (AL)
Allen Comm Coll (KS)
Alvin Comm Coll (TX)
Amarillo Coll (TX)
American Samoa Comm Coll (AS)
Anoka-Ramsey Comm Coll (MN)
Anoka-Ramsey Comm Coll, Cambridge Campus (MN)
Antelope Valley Coll (CA)
Arizona Western Coll (AZ)
Austin Comm Coll (TX)
Bossier Parish Comm Coll (LA)
Bronx Comm Coll of the City U of New York (NY)
Brookhaven Coll (TX)
Broward Coll (FL)
Bucks County Comm Coll (PA)
Bunker Hill Comm Coll (MA)
Ca&nnada Coll (CA)
Carroll Comm Coll (MD)
Casper Coll (WY)
Central Wyoming Coll (WY)
Century Coll (MN)
Cochise Coll, Sierra Vista (AZ)
Coll of Marin (CA)
Coll of Southern Idaho (ID)
Coll of the Canyons (CA)
Coll of the Desert (CA)
Coll of the Mainland (TX)
Collin County Comm Coll District (TX)
Columbia Coll (CA)
Comm Coll of Allegheny County (PA)
Comm Coll of Philadelphia (PA)
Comm Coll of Rhode Island (RI)
Cosumnes River Coll, Sacramento (CA)
County Coll of Morris (NJ)
Crowder Coll (MO)
Darton State Coll (GA)
De Anza Coll (CA)
Eastern Arizona Coll (AZ)
Eastern Florida State Coll (FL)
Eastern Wyoming Coll (WY)
Elgin Comm Coll (IL)
Finger Lakes Comm Coll (NY)
Fullerton Coll (CA)
Galveston Coll (TX)
Gavilan Coll (CA)
Golden West Coll (CA)
Gordon State Coll (GA)
Grand Rapids Comm Coll (MI)
Grayson Coll (TX)
Harford Comm Coll (MD)
Harper Coll (IL)
Hinds Comm Coll (MS)
Holyoke Comm Coll (MA)
Howard Comm Coll (MD)
Imperial Valley Coll (CA)
Independence Comm Coll (KS)
Iowa Lakes Comm Coll (IA)
Jamestown Comm Coll (NY)
Kaskaskia Coll (IL)
Kilgore Coll (TX)
Kingsborough Comm Coll of the City U of New York (NY)
Lake Tahoe Comm Coll (CA)
Lansing Comm Coll (MI)
Laramie County Comm Coll (WY)
Lincoln Land Comm Coll (IL)
Lone Star Coll–CyFair (TX)
Lone Star Coll–Kingwood (TX)
Lone Star Coll–Montgomery (TX)
Lone Star Coll–North Harris (TX)
Lone Star Coll–Tomball (TX)
Lorain County Comm Coll (OH)
Los Angeles Mission Coll (CA)
Manchester Comm Coll (CT)
McHenry County Coll (IL)
Mercer County Comm Coll (NJ)
Mesa Comm Coll (AZ)
Miami Dade Coll (FL)
MiraCosta Coll (CA)
Mississippi Delta Comm Coll (MS)
Monroe Comm Coll (NY)
Moraine Valley Comm Coll (IL)
Mountain View Coll (TX)
Mt. San Antonio Coll (CA)
Mt. San Jacinto Coll (CA)
Niagara County Comm Coll (NY)
Normandale Comm Coll (MN)
Northeastern Jr Coll (CO)
Northeast Texas Comm Coll (TX)
Northern Essex Comm Coll (MA)
Northwest Coll (WY)
Oakton Comm Coll (IL)

Oklahoma City Comm Coll (OK)
Onondaga Comm Coll (NY)
Orange Coast Coll (CA)
Palomar Coll (CA)
Paris Jr Coll (TX)
Pensacola State Coll (FL)
Raritan Valley Comm Coll (NJ)
Salt Lake Comm Coll (UT)
San Diego City Coll (CA)
San Jacinto Coll District (TX)
Santa Monica Coll (CA)
Sauk Valley Comm Coll (IL)
Sheridan Coll (WY)
Shoreline Comm Coll (WA)
Snow Coll (UT)
Southeastern Comm Coll (NC)
South Florida State Coll (FL)
South Plains Coll (TX)
Southwestern Illinois Coll (IL)
Texarkana Coll (TX)
Treasure Valley Comm Coll (OR)
Trinity Valley Comm Coll (TX)
Truckee Meadows Comm Coll (NV)
Tulsa Comm Coll (OK)
Umpqua Comm Coll (OR)
Victor Valley Coll (CA)
Vincennes U (IN)
Waubonsee Comm Coll (IL)
Wenatchee Valley Coll (WA)
Western Wyoming Comm Coll (WY)

MUSICAL INSTRUMENT FABRICATION AND REPAIR
Orange Coast Coll (CA)

MUSICAL THEATER
Casper Coll (WY)

MUSIC HISTORY, LITERATURE, AND THEORY
Snow Coll (UT)
South Florida State Coll (FL)

MUSIC MANAGEMENT
Austin Comm Coll (TX)
Chandler-Gilbert Comm Coll (AZ)
Collin County Comm Coll District (TX)
Glendale Comm Coll (AZ)
Harrisburg Area Comm Coll (PA)
Houston Comm Coll System (TX)
The Inst of Production and Recording (MN)
Mt. San Jacinto Coll (CA)
Orange Coast Coll (CA)
Phoenix Coll (AZ)

MUSIC PERFORMANCE
Casper Coll (WY)
Dyersburg State Comm Coll (TN)
Greenfield Comm Coll (MA)
Houston Comm Coll System (TX)
Lansing Comm Coll (MI)
Macomb Comm Coll (MI)
Miami Dade Coll (FL)
Nassau Comm Coll (NY)
Oakland Comm Coll (MI)
South Florida State Coll (FL)
Walters State Comm Coll (TN)

MUSIC RELATED
Carl Albert State Coll (OK)
Cayuga County Comm Coll (NY)
Northwest Florida State Coll (FL)
Santa Rosa Jr Coll (CA)

MUSIC TEACHER EDUCATION
Amarillo Coll (TX)
Broward Coll (FL)
Casper Coll (WY)
Copiah-Lincoln Comm Coll (MS)
Darton State Coll (GA)
Eastern Wyoming Coll (WY)
Iowa Lakes Comm Coll (IA)
Miami Dade Coll (FL)
Mississippi Delta Comm Coll (MS)
Northeastern Jr Coll (CO)
Northwest Mississippi Comm Coll (MS)
Pensacola State Coll (FL)
Roane State Comm Coll (TN)
Snow Coll (UT)
South Florida State Coll (FL)
Southwestern Illinois Coll (IL)
Umpqua Comm Coll (OR)
Vincennes U (IN)
Wenatchee Valley Coll (WA)

MUSIC TECHNOLOGY
Mott Comm Coll (MI)
Owens Comm Coll, Toledo (OH)

MUSIC THEORY AND COMPOSITION
Houston Comm Coll System (TX)
Oakland Comm Coll (MI)
South Florida State Coll (FL)

MUSIC THERAPY
South Florida State Coll (FL)

NAIL TECHNICIAN AND MANICURIST
Inst of Business & Medical Careers (CO)

NANOTECHNOLOGY
Chippewa Valley Tech Coll (WI)
Harper Coll (IL)
Lehigh Carbon Comm Coll (PA)
North Dakota State Coll of Science (ND)
Oakland Comm Coll (MI)

NATURAL RESOURCE RECREATION AND TOURISM
Broward Coll (FL)
Wenatchee Valley Coll (WA)

NATURAL RESOURCES AND CONSERVATION RELATED
Snow Coll (UT)
Southwestern Indian Polytechnic Inst (NM)

NATURAL RESOURCES/ CONSERVATION
American Samoa Comm Coll (AS)
Central Oregon Comm Coll (OR)
Coll of the Desert (CA)
Colorado Northwestern Comm Coll (CO)
Columbia Coll (CA)
Dakota Coll at Bottineau (ND)
Feather River Coll (CA)
Finger Lakes Comm Coll (NY)
Florida Gateway Coll (FL)
Fox Valley Tech Coll (WI)
Grays Harbor Coll (WA)
Hocking Coll (OH)
Iowa Lakes Comm Coll (IA)
Mountain Empire Comm Coll (VA)
Niagara County Comm Coll (NY)
Santa Rosa Jr Coll (CA)
Tompkins Cortland Comm Coll (NY)
Treasure Valley Comm Coll (OR)
Vincennes U (IN)
Walla Walla Comm Coll (WA)

NATURAL RESOURCES/ CONSERVATION RELATED
Greenfield Comm Coll (MA)
Walla Walla Comm Coll (WA)

NATURAL RESOURCES LAW ENFORCEMENT AND PROTECTIVE SERVICES
Finger Lakes Comm Coll (NY)

NATURAL RESOURCES MANAGEMENT AND POLICY
Butte Coll (CA)
Finger Lakes Comm Coll (NY)
Hawkeye Comm Coll (IA)
Hocking Coll (OH)
Hutchinson Comm Coll and Area Vocational School (KS)
Northwest Coll (WY)
The Ohio State U Ag Tech Inst (OH)
Pensacola State Coll (FL)

NATURAL RESOURCES MANAGEMENT AND POLICY RELATED
Finger Lakes Comm Coll (NY)
Hocking Coll (OH)
The Ohio State U Ag Tech Inst (OH)

NATURAL SCIENCES
Amarillo Coll (TX)
Coll of the Mainland (TX)
Galveston Coll (TX)
Golden West Coll (CA)
Iowa Lakes Comm Coll (IA)
Lake Tahoe Comm Coll (CA)
Miami Dade Coll (FL)
Northeastern Jr Coll (CO)
Orange Coast Coll (CA)
Phoenix Coll (AZ)
Santa Rosa Jr Coll (CA)
Umpqua Comm Coll (OR)
Victor Valley Coll (CA)

NETWORK AND SYSTEM ADMINISTRATION
Big Bend Comm Coll (WA)
Broward Coll (FL)
Bucks County Comm Coll (PA)
Butler County Comm Coll (PA)
Butte Coll (CA)
Ca&nnada Coll (CA)
Central Maine Comm Coll (ME)
Cincinnati State Tech and Comm Coll (OH)
Coll of Western Idaho (ID)
Collin County Comm Coll District (TX)
Cosumnes River Coll, Sacramento (CA)
Dakota Coll at Bottineau (ND)
Florida State Coll at Jacksonville (FL)
Gavilan Coll (CA)
Genesee Comm Coll (NY)
Houston Comm Coll System (TX)
Island Drafting and Tech Inst (NY)
ITT Tech Inst, Bessemer (AL)
ITT Tech Inst, Madison (AL)
ITT Tech Inst, Mobile (AL)
ITT Tech Inst, Tucson (AZ)
ITT Tech Inst (AR)
ITT Tech Inst, Culver City (CA)
ITT Tech Inst, Lathrop (CA)
ITT Tech Inst, National City (CA)
ITT Tech Inst, Oakland (CA)
ITT Tech Inst, Orange (CA)
ITT Tech Inst, Oxnard (CA)
ITT Tech Inst, Rancho Cordova (CA)
ITT Tech Inst, San Bernardino (CA)
ITT Tech Inst, San Dimas (CA)
ITT Tech Inst, Sylmar (CA)
ITT Tech Inst, Torrance (CA)
ITT Tech Inst, Aurora (CO)
ITT Tech Inst, Westminster (CO)
ITT Tech Inst, Fort Lauderdale (FL)
ITT Tech Inst, Fort Myers (FL)
ITT Tech Inst, Jacksonville (FL)
ITT Tech Inst, Lake Mary (FL)
ITT Tech Inst, Miami (FL)
ITT Tech Inst, Orlando (FL)
ITT Tech Inst, Pensacola (FL)
ITT Tech Inst, St. Petersburg (FL)
ITT Tech Inst, Tallahassee (FL)
ITT Tech Inst, Tampa (FL)
ITT Tech Inst, Atlanta (GA)
ITT Tech Inst, Duluth (GA)
ITT Tech Inst, Kennesaw (GA)
ITT Tech Inst (ID)
ITT Tech Inst, Arlington Heights (IL)
ITT Tech Inst, Oak Brook (IL)
ITT Tech Inst, Orland Park (IL)
ITT Tech Inst, Fort Wayne (IN)
ITT Tech Inst, Merrillville (IN)
ITT Tech Inst, Newburgh (IN)
ITT Tech Inst, Clive (IA)
ITT Tech Inst, Louisville (KY)
ITT Tech Inst, Baton Rouge (LA)
ITT Tech Inst, St. Rose (LA)
ITT Tech Inst, Owings Mills (MD)
ITT Tech Inst, Canton (MI)
ITT Tech Inst, Dearborn (MI)
ITT Tech Inst, Swartz Creek (MI)
ITT Tech Inst, Troy (MI)
ITT Tech Inst, Wyoming (MI)
ITT Tech Inst, Brooklyn Center (MN)
ITT Tech Inst, Eden Prairie (MN)
ITT Tech Inst, Arnold (MO)
ITT Tech Inst, Earth City (MO)
ITT Tech Inst, Kansas City (MO)
ITT Tech Inst (NE)
ITT Tech Inst, Henderson (NV)
ITT Tech Inst, North Las Vegas (NV)
ITT Tech Inst (NM)
ITT Tech Inst, Albany (NY)
ITT Tech Inst, Getzville (NY)
ITT Tech Inst, Liverpool (NY)
ITT Tech Inst, Cary (NC)
ITT Tech Inst, Charlotte (NC)
ITT Tech Inst, High Point (NC)
ITT Tech Inst, Akron (OH)
ITT Tech Inst, Columbus (OH)
ITT Tech Inst, Dayton (OH)
ITT Tech Inst, Hilliard (OH)
ITT Tech Inst, Maumee (OH)
ITT Tech Inst, Norwood (OH)
ITT Tech Inst, Strongsville (OH)
ITT Tech Inst, Warrensville Heights (OH)
ITT Tech Inst, Youngstown (OH)
ITT Tech Inst, Tulsa (OK)
ITT Tech Inst, Portland (OR)
ITT Tech Inst, Columbia (SC)
ITT Tech Inst, Greenville (SC)
ITT Tech Inst, Myrtle Beach (SC)
ITT Tech Inst, North Charleston (SC)

ITT Tech Inst, Chattanooga (TN)
ITT Tech Inst, Cordova (TN)
ITT Tech Inst, Johnson City (TN)
ITT Tech Inst, Knoxville (TN)
ITT Tech Inst, Nashville (TN)
ITT Tech Inst, Arlington (TX)
ITT Tech Inst, Austin (TX)
ITT Tech Inst, DeSoto (TX)
ITT Tech Inst, Houston (TX)
ITT Tech Inst, Houston (TX)
ITT Tech Inst, Richardson (TX)
ITT Tech Inst, San Antonio (TX)
ITT Tech Inst, San Antonio (TX)
ITT Tech Inst, Waco (TX)
ITT Tech Inst, Webster (TX)
ITT Tech Inst (UT)
ITT Tech Inst, Chantilly (VA)
ITT Tech Inst, Norfolk (VA)
ITT Tech Inst, Richmond (VA)
ITT Tech Inst, Salem (VA)
ITT Tech Inst, Springfield (VA)
ITT Tech Inst, Everett (WA)
ITT Tech Inst, Seattle (WA)
ITT Tech Inst, Spokane Valley (WA)
ITT Tech Inst (WV)
ITT Tech Inst, Green Bay (WI)
ITT Tech Inst , Greenfield (WI)
ITT Tech Inst, Madison (WI)
Kaskaskia Coll (IL)
Lake Superior Coll (MN)
Linn-Benton Comm Coll (OR)
Manhattan Area Tech Coll (KS)
Metropolitan Comm Coll–Kansas City (MO)
Minneapolis Comm and Tech Coll (MN)
Mitchell Tech Inst (SD)
Montgomery County Comm Coll (PA)
North Iowa Area Comm Coll (IA)
Palomar Coll (CA)
Potomac State Coll of West Virginia U (WV)
Seminole State Coll of Florida (FL)
Southwestern Illinois Coll (IL)
Sullivan Coll of Technology and Design (KY)
Texas State Tech Coll Waco (TX)
Truckee Meadows Comm Coll (NV)

NEUROSCIENCE
Bucks County Comm Coll (PA)

NONPROFIT MANAGEMENT
Goodwin Coll (CT)
Miami Dade Coll (FL)

NUCLEAR ENGINEERING
Broward Coll (FL)
South Florida State Coll (FL)

NUCLEAR ENGINEERING TECHNOLOGY
Bismarck State Coll (ND)
Delaware Tech & Comm Coll, Jack F. Owens Campus (DE)
Delaware Tech & Comm Coll, Stanton/Wilmington Campus (DE)

NUCLEAR MEDICAL TECHNOLOGY
Amarillo Coll (TX)
Bronx Comm Coll of the City U of New York (NY)
Broward Coll (FL)
Central Maine Medical Center Coll of Nursing and Health Professions (ME)
Cincinnati State Tech and Comm Coll (OH)
Columbus State Comm Coll (OH)
Comm Coll of Allegheny County (PA)
Darton State Coll (GA)
Delaware Tech & Comm Coll, Stanton/Wilmington Campus (DE)
Fayetteville Tech Comm Coll (NC)
Galveston Coll (TX)
Harrisburg Area Comm Coll (PA)
Hillsborough Comm Coll (FL)
Houston Comm Coll System (TX)
Howard Comm Coll (MD)
Lakeland Comm Coll (OH)
Lorain County Comm Coll (OH)
Miami Dade Coll (FL)
Oakland Comm Coll (MI)
Orange Coast Coll (CA)
Owens Comm Coll, Toledo (OH)
Pennsylvania Coll of Health Sciences (PA)
Pitt Comm Coll (NC)
Southeast Tech Inst (SD)
Vincennes U (IN)

NUCLEAR/NUCLEAR POWER TECHNOLOGY
Allen Comm Coll (KS)
Cape Fear Comm Coll (NC)
Florida State Coll at Jacksonville (FL)
Texas State Tech Coll Waco (TX)
Three Rivers Comm Coll (CT)

NURSING ADMINISTRATION
Hinds Comm Coll (MS)
Paris Jr Coll (TX)
South Suburban Coll (IL)

NURSING ASSISTANT/AIDE AND PATIENT CARE ASSISTANT/AIDE
Allen Comm Coll (KS)
Barstow Comm Coll (CA)
Coconino Comm Coll (AZ)
Comm Coll of Allegheny County (PA)
North Iowa Area Comm Coll (IA)
Schoolcraft Coll (MI)
Tallahassee Comm Coll (FL)
Western Wyoming Comm Coll (WY)

NURSING EDUCATION
South Florida State Coll (FL)

NURSING PRACTICE
Coll of Western Idaho (ID)
Genesee Comm Coll (NY)

NUTRITION SCIENCES
Broward Coll (FL)
Casper Coll (WY)
Santa Rosa Jr Coll (CA)
Tulsa Comm Coll (OK)

OCCUPATIONAL HEALTH AND INDUSTRIAL HYGIENE
Niagara County Comm Coll (NY)

OCCUPATIONAL SAFETY AND HEALTH TECHNOLOGY
Central Wyoming Coll (WY)
Cincinnati State Tech and Comm Coll (OH)
Coll of the Mainland (TX)
The Comm Coll of Baltimore County (MD)
Honolulu Comm Coll (HI)
Ivy Tech Comm Coll–Central Indiana (IN)
Ivy Tech Comm Coll–Northeast (IN)
Ivy Tech Comm Coll–Northwest (IN)
Ivy Tech Comm Coll–Wabash Valley (IN)
Kilgore Coll (TX)
Lanier Tech Coll (GA)
Mt. San Antonio Coll (CA)
NorthWest Arkansas Comm Coll (AR)
Northwest Florida State Coll (FL)
Okefenokee Tech Coll (GA)
Oklahoma State U, Oklahoma City (OK)
San Diego City Coll (CA)
San Jacinto Coll District (TX)
San Juan Coll (NM)
Texas State Tech Coll Waco (TX)
Tulsa Comm Coll (OK)

OCCUPATIONAL THERAPIST ASSISTANT
Anoka Tech Coll (MN)
Augusta Tech Coll (GA)
Austin Comm Coll (TX)
Bristol Comm Coll (MA)
Brown Mackie Coll–Akron (OH)
Brown Mackie Coll–Albuquerque (NM)
Brown Mackie Coll–Atlanta (GA)
Brown Mackie Coll–Birmingham (AL)
Brown Mackie Coll–Boise (ID)
Brown Mackie Coll–Dallas/Ft. Worth (TX)
Brown Mackie Coll–Findlay (OH)
Brown Mackie Coll–Fort Wayne (IN)
Brown Mackie Coll–Greenville (SC)
Brown Mackie Coll–Hopkinsville (KY)
Brown Mackie Coll–Indianapolis (IN)
Brown Mackie Coll–Kansas City (KS)
Brown Mackie Coll–Louisville (KY)
Brown Mackie Coll–Merrillville (IN)
Brown Mackie Coll–Northern Kentucky (KY)
Brown Mackie Coll–Oklahoma City (OK)
Brown Mackie Coll–Phoenix (AZ)
Brown Mackie Coll–Quad Cities (IA)
Brown Mackie Coll–St. Louis (MO)
Brown Mackie Coll–Salina (KS)

Brown Mackie Coll–South Bend (IN)
Brown Mackie Coll–Tucson (AZ)
Brown Mackie Coll–Tulsa (OK)
Cape Fear Comm Coll (NC)
Carrington Coll–Phoenix Westside (AZ)
Casper Coll (WY)
Cincinnati State Tech and Comm Coll (OH)
Comm Coll of Allegheny County (PA)
Comm Coll of Philadelphia (PA)
Comm Coll of Rhode Island (RI)
Crowder Coll (MO)
Darton State Coll (GA)
Daytona State Coll (FL)
Delaware Tech & Comm Coll, Jack F. Owens Campus (DE)
Delaware Tech & Comm Coll, Stanton/Wilmington Campus (DE)
East Central Coll (MO)
Erie Comm Coll, North Campus (NY)
Fiorello H. LaGuardia Comm Coll of the City U of New York (NY)
Fox Valley Tech Coll (WI)
Goodwin Coll (CT)
Greenville Tech Coll (SC)
Hawkeye Comm Coll (IA)
Houston Comm Coll System (TX)
Ivy Tech Comm Coll–Central Indiana (IN)
Jamestown Comm Coll (NY)
Kaskaskia Coll (IL)
Kent State U at Ashtabula (OH)
Kent State U at East Liverpool (OH)
Lake Area Tech Inst (SD)
Lehigh Carbon Comm Coll (PA)
Lincoln Land Comm Coll (IL)
Macomb Comm Coll (MI)
Manchester Comm Coll (CT)
McHenry County Coll (IL)
Mott Comm Coll (MI)
North Dakota State Coll of Science (ND)
Oakland Comm Coll (MI)
Ocean County Coll (NJ)
Owens Comm Coll, Toledo (OH)
Ozarks Tech Comm Coll (MO)
Panola Coll (TX)
Penn State DuBois (PA)
Penn State Mont Alto (PA)
Pitt Comm Coll (NC)
Pueblo Comm Coll (CO)
Reading Area Comm Coll (PA)
Rend Lake Coll (IL)
River Valley Comm Coll (NH)
Salt Lake Comm Coll (UT)
San Juan Coll (NM)
Shawnee Comm Coll (IL)
South Suburban Coll (IL)
Springfield Tech Comm Coll (MA)
State Fair Comm Coll (MO)
Walters State Comm Coll (TN)
Wisconsin Indianhead Tech Coll (WI)
Wor-Wic Comm Coll (MD)

OCCUPATIONAL THERAPY
Amarillo Coll (TX)
Carrington Coll–Phoenix (AZ)
The Comm Coll of Baltimore County (MD)
Hinds Comm Coll (MS)
Lone Star Coll–Kingwood (TX)
Metropolitan Comm Coll–Kansas City (MO)
North Shore Comm Coll (MA)
Oklahoma City Comm Coll (OK)
Ozarks Tech Comm Coll (MO)
Quinsigamond Comm Coll (MA)
Roane State Comm Coll (TN)
Sauk Valley Comm Coll (IL)
South Florida State Coll (FL)
Stark State Coll (OH)
Trident Tech Coll (SC)
Tulsa Comm Coll (OK)

OCEAN ENGINEERING
Broward Coll (FL)
South Florida State Coll (FL)

OCEANOGRAPHY (CHEMICAL AND PHYSICAL)
Cape Fear Comm Coll (NC)
Shoreline Comm Coll (WA)

OFFICE MANAGEMENT
Anoka Tech Coll (MN)
Arizona Western Coll (AZ)
Berkeley City Coll (CA)
Big Bend Comm Coll (WA)
Brookhaven Coll (TX)
Catawba Valley Comm Coll (NC)
Cecil Coll (MD)

Cleveland Comm Coll (NC)
Coll of Central Florida (FL)
Coll of Marin (CA)
Coll of the Desert (CA)
Comm Coll of Allegheny County (PA)
Dakota Coll at Bottineau (ND)
Delaware Tech & Comm Coll, Jack F. Owens Campus (DE)
Delaware Tech & Comm Coll, Stanton/Wilmington Campus (DE)
Delaware Tech & Comm Coll, Terry Campus (DE)
Eastern Florida State Coll (FL)
Eastern Wyoming Coll (WY)
Erie Comm Coll, North Campus (NY)
Erie Comm Coll, South Campus (NY)
Fayetteville Tech Comm Coll (NC)
Florida Gateway Coll (FL)
Florida State Coll at Jacksonville (FL)
Fox Valley Tech Coll (WI)
Goodwin Coll (CT)
Grays Harbor Coll (WA)
Great Basin Coll (NV)
Halifax Comm Coll (NC)
Howard Comm Coll (MD)
Ilisagvik Coll (AK)
Iowa Lakes Comm Coll (IA)
Ivy Tech Comm Coll–Wabash Valley (IN)
Jamestown Business Coll (NY)
Jefferson Comm Coll (NY)
Jefferson State Comm Coll (AL)
Johnston Comm Coll (NC)
Lake Land Coll (IL)
Lake Superior Coll (MN)
Lane Comm Coll (OR)
Lansing Comm Coll (MI)
MiraCosta Coll (CA)
Mitchell Comm Coll (NC)
Moraine Park Tech Coll (WI)
Northwest Florida State Coll (FL)
Northwest Mississippi Comm Coll (MS)
Oakland Comm Coll (MI)
Owens Comm Coll, Toledo (OH)
Pensacola State Coll (FL)
Piedmont Comm Coll (NC)
Pitt Comm Coll (NC)
Richmond Comm Coll (NC)
St. Clair County Comm Coll (MI)
Santa Monica Coll (CA)
South Florida State Coll (FL)
South Suburban Coll (IL)
Spencerian Coll (KY)
Tallahassee Comm Coll (FL)
Treasure Valley Comm Coll (OR)
Wayne Comm Coll (NC)
Wayne County Comm Coll District (MI)
Wenatchee Valley Coll (WA)

OFFICE OCCUPATIONS AND CLERICAL SERVICES
Alamance Comm Coll (NC)
American Samoa Comm Coll (AS)
Butler County Comm Coll (PA)
Cloud County Comm Coll (KS)
Dakota Coll at Bottineau (ND)
Florida State Coll at Jacksonville (FL)
Gateway Comm and Tech Coll (KY)
Helena Coll U of Montana (MT)
Inst of Business & Medical Careers (CO)
Iowa Lakes Comm Coll (IA)
ITI Tech Coll (LA)
Jefferson Comm Coll (NY)
Lone Star Coll–CyFair (TX)
New Mexico State U–Alamogordo (NM)
San Joaquin Valley Coll, Fresno (CA)
San Joaquin Valley Coll, Ontario (CA)
San Joaquin Valley Coll, Salida (CA)
Southeast Tech Inst (SD)
Wichita Area Tech Coll (KS)

OPERATIONS MANAGEMENT
Blue Ridge Comm and Tech Coll (WV)
Bunker Hill Comm Coll (MA)
Central Carolina Comm Coll (NC)
Cleveland Comm Coll (NC)
Fayetteville Tech Comm Coll (NC)
Georgia Piedmont Tech Coll (GA)
Great Basin Coll (NV)
Hillsborough Comm Coll (FL)
Kilgore Coll (TX)
Macomb Comm Coll (MI)
McHenry County Coll (IL)
Mineral Area Coll (MO)
Mitchell Comm Coll (NC)
Northcentral Tech Coll (WI)
Northwest Florida State Coll (FL)

Oakton Comm Coll (IL)
Owens Comm Coll, Toledo (OH)
Pensacola State Coll (FL)
Pitt Comm Coll (NC)
Stark State Coll (OH)
Waukesha County Tech Coll (WI)
Wayne Comm Coll (NC)
Wisconsin Indianhead Tech Coll (WI)

OPERATIONS RESEARCH
Delaware Tech & Comm Coll, Stanton/Wilmington Campus (DE)

OPHTHALMIC AND OPTOMETRIC SUPPORT SERVICES AND ALLIED PROFESSIONS RELATED
Vincennes U (IN)

OPHTHALMIC LABORATORY TECHNOLOGY
Georgia Piedmont Tech Coll (GA)
Hocking Coll (OH)

OPHTHALMIC TECHNOLOGY
Lakeland Comm Coll (OH)
Miami Dade Coll (FL)
Volunteer State Comm Coll (TN)

OPTICIANRY
Benjamin Franklin Inst of Technology (MA)
Broward Coll (FL)
Comm Coll of Rhode Island (RI)
Erie Comm Coll, North Campus (NY)
Georgia Piedmont Tech Coll (GA)
Goodwin Coll (CT)
Hillsborough Comm Coll (FL)
Holyoke Comm Coll (MA)
J. Sargeant Reynolds Comm Coll (VA)
Ogeechee Tech Coll (GA)
Raritan Valley Comm Coll (NJ)
Southwestern Indian Polytechnic Inst (NM)

OPTOMETRIC TECHNICIAN
Hillsborough Comm Coll (FL)
Raritan Valley Comm Coll (NJ)
San Jacinto Coll District (TX)
TCI–The Coll of Technology (NY)
Tyler Jr Coll (TX)

ORGANIZATIONAL BEHAVIOR
Chandler-Gilbert Comm Coll (AZ)
Phoenix Coll (AZ)

ORGANIZATIONAL COMMUNICATION
Butler County Comm Coll (PA)

ORGANIZATIONAL LEADERSHIP
Olympic Coll (WA)

ORNAMENTAL HORTICULTURE
Antelope Valley Coll (CA)
Bronx Comm Coll of the City U of New York (NY)
Comm Coll of Allegheny County (PA)
Cumberland County Coll (NJ)
Dakota Coll at Bottineau (ND)
Finger Lakes Comm Coll (NY)
Golden West Coll (CA)
Gwinnett Tech Coll (GA)
Lenoir Comm Coll (NC)
Mercer County Comm Coll (NJ)
Mesa Comm Coll (AZ)
Miami Dade Coll (FL)
Mississippi Gulf Coast Comm Coll (MS)
Mt. San Antonio Coll (CA)
Orange Coast Coll (CA)
Pensacola State Coll (FL)
Victor Valley Coll (CA)
Walters State Comm Coll (TN)

ORTHOTICS/PROSTHETICS
Century Coll (MN)
Oklahoma City Comm Coll (OK)

PAINTING
Luzerne County Comm Coll (PA)

PAINTING AND WALL COVERING
Ivy Tech Comm Coll–Central Indiana (IN)
Ivy Tech Comm Coll–East Central (IN)

Ivy Tech Comm Coll–Lafayette (IN)
Ivy Tech Comm Coll–North Central (IN)
Ivy Tech Comm Coll–Northeast (IN)
Ivy Tech Comm Coll–Northwest (IN)
Ivy Tech Comm Coll–Southwest (IN)
Ivy Tech Comm Coll–Wabash Valley (IN)
Southwestern Illinois Coll (IL)

PARKS, RECREATION AND LEISURE
Central Wyoming Coll (WY)
Coll of Central Florida (FL)
Coll of the Canyons (CA)
The Comm Coll of Baltimore County (MD)
Dakota Coll at Bottineau (ND)
Feather River Coll (CA)
Fullerton Coll (CA)
Iowa Lakes Comm Coll (IA)
Kingsborough Comm Coll of the City U of New York (NY)
Miami Dade Coll (FL)
Monroe Comm Coll (NY)
Mt. San Antonio Coll (CA)
Niagara County Comm Coll (NY)
Northern Essex Comm Coll (MA)
Northwest Coll (WY)
Northwestern Connecticut Comm Coll (CT)
Norwalk Comm Coll (CT)
Onondaga Comm Coll (NY)
Palomar Coll (CA)
Phoenix Coll (AZ)
San Diego City Coll (CA)
San Juan Coll (NM)
Southeastern Comm Coll (NC)
South Georgia State Coll, Douglas (GA)
Sullivan County Comm Coll (NY)
Vincennes U (IN)

PARKS, RECREATION AND LEISURE FACILITIES MANAGEMENT
Allen Comm Coll (KS)
Arizona Western Coll (AZ)
Augusta Tech Coll (GA)
Broward Coll (FL)
Butler County Comm Coll (PA)
Butte Coll (CA)
Central Wyoming Coll (WY)
Chattahoochee Tech Coll (GA)
Coll of the Desert (CA)
Dakota Coll at Bottineau (ND)
Gogebic Comm Coll (MI)
Herkimer County Comm Coll (NY)
Mohawk Valley Comm Coll (NY)
Moraine Valley Comm Coll (IL)
Mt. San Antonio Coll (CA)
North Georgia Tech Coll (GA)
Northwestern Connecticut Comm Coll (CT)
Palomar Coll (CA)
Potomac State Coll of West Virginia U (WV)
Santa Rosa Jr Coll (CA)
Southeastern Comm Coll (NC)
South Florida State Coll (FL)
Tompkins Cortland Comm Coll (NY)
Western Texas Coll (TX)

PARKS, RECREATION, LEISURE, AND FITNESS STUDIES RELATED
Cincinnati State Tech and Comm Coll (OH)
Columbus State Comm Coll (OH)
The Comm Coll of Baltimore County (MD)
Dakota Coll at Bottineau (ND)
Genesee Comm Coll (NY)
Southwestern Comm Coll (NC)
Tompkins Cortland Comm Coll (NY)

PERCUSSION INSTRUMENTS
Iowa Lakes Comm Coll (IA)

PERIOPERATIVE/OPERATING ROOM AND SURGICAL NURSING
Comm Coll of Allegheny County (PA)

PERSONAL AND CULINARY SERVICES RELATED
Mohave Comm Coll (AZ)

PETROLEUM ENGINEERING
Kilgore Coll (TX)

PETROLEUM TECHNOLOGY
Panola Coll (TX)
South Plains Coll (TX)
Tulsa Comm Coll (OK)
U of Arkansas Comm Coll at Morrilton (AR)
Williston State Coll (ND)

PHARMACY
Broward Coll (FL)
Iowa Lakes Comm Coll (IA)
Lorain County Comm Coll (OH)
San Joaquin Valley Coll, Hesperia (CA)
South Florida State Coll (FL)

PHARMACY TECHNICIAN
Albany Tech Coll (GA)
Augusta Tech Coll (GA)
Bossier Parish Comm Coll (LA)
Brown Mackie Coll–Albuquerque (NM)
Brown Mackie Coll–Atlanta (GA)
Brown Mackie Coll–Cincinnati (OH)
Brown Mackie Coll–Findlay (OH)
Brown Mackie Coll–San Antonio (TX)
Carrington Coll–Boise (ID)
Carrington Coll California–Citrus Heights (CA)
Carrington Coll California–Pleasant Hill (CA)
Carrington Coll California–Sacramento (CA)
Carrington Coll California–San Jose (CA)
Carrington Coll California–San Leandro (CA)
Casper Coll (WY)
Coll of the Mainland (TX)
Columbus Tech Coll (GA)
Comm Care Coll (OK)
Comm Coll of Allegheny County (PA)
Cosumnes River Coll, Sacramento (CA)
Eastern Arizona Coll (AZ)
Fayetteville Tech Comm Coll (NC)
Hutchinson Comm Coll and Area Vocational School (KS)
Inst of Business & Medical Careers (CO)
J. Sargeant Reynolds Comm Coll (VA)
Kirtland Comm Coll (MI)
Lone Star Coll–North Harris (TX)
Mohave Comm Coll (AZ)
North Dakota State Coll of Science (ND)
Oakland Comm Coll (MI)
Pennsylvania Inst of Technology (PA)
Pensacola State Coll (FL)
Pima Comm Coll (AZ)
Roane State Comm Coll (TN)
San Joaquin Valley Coll, Bakersfield (CA)
San Joaquin Valley Coll, Fresno (CA)
San Joaquin Valley Coll, Hanford (CA)
San Joaquin Valley Coll, Hesperia (CA)
San Joaquin Valley Coll, Ontario (CA)
San Joaquin Valley Coll, Salida (CA)
San Joaquin Valley Coll, Temecula (CA)
San Joaquin Valley Coll, Visalia (CA)
Santa Rosa Jr Coll (CA)
Southern Crescent Tech Coll (GA)
Tallahassee Comm Coll (FL)
Texarkana Coll (TX)
Vincennes U (IN)
Wayne County Comm Coll District (MI)
Western Dakota Tech Inst (SD)
West Georgia Tech Coll (GA)
West Virginia Jr Coll–Bridgeport (WV)

PHILOSOPHY
Allen Comm Coll (KS)
Arizona Western Coll (AZ)
Austin Comm Coll (TX)
Broward Coll (FL)
Ca&nnada Coll (CA)
Cochise Coll, Sierra Vista (AZ)
Coll of the Canyons (CA)
Coll of the Desert (CA)
Copper Mountain Coll (CA)
Darton State Coll (GA)
De Anza Coll (CA)

Fiorello H. LaGuardia Comm Coll of the City U of New York (NY)
Fullerton Coll (CA)
Georgia Highlands Coll (GA)
Harford Comm Coll (MD)
Harper Coll (IL)
Harrisburg Area Comm Coll (PA)
Iowa Lakes Comm Coll (IA)
Lansing Comm Coll (MI)
Los Angeles Mission Coll (CA)
Miami Dade Coll (FL)
Minneapolis Comm and Tech Coll (MN)
MiraCosta Coll (CA)
Oklahoma City Comm Coll (OK)
Orange Coast Coll (CA)
Oxnard Coll (CA)
Pensacola State Coll (FL)
San Jacinto Coll District (TX)
Santa Rosa Jr Coll (CA)
Snow Coll (UT)
South Florida State Coll (FL)
South Georgia State Coll, Douglas (GA)
Truckee Meadows Comm Coll (NV)
Vincennes U (IN)

PHILOSOPHY AND RELIGIOUS STUDIES RELATED
Edison Comm Coll (OH)
South Florida State Coll (FL)

PHLEBOTOMY TECHNOLOGY
Coconino Comm Coll (AZ)
Schoolcraft Coll (MI)
Westmoreland County Comm Coll (PA)

PHOTOGRAPHIC AND FILM/VIDEO TECHNOLOGY
Catawba Valley Comm Coll (NC)
Cosumnes River Coll, Sacramento (CA)
Daytona State Coll (FL)
Herkimer County Comm Coll (NY)
Hinds Comm Coll (MS)
Miami Dade Coll (FL)
Minneapolis Comm and Tech Coll (MN)
MiraCosta Coll (CA)
Oklahoma City Comm Coll (OK)
Randolph Comm Coll (NC)
Salt Lake Comm Coll (UT)

PHOTOGRAPHY
Amarillo Coll (TX)
Antelope Valley Coll (CA)
Antonelli Inst (PA)
Barstow Comm Coll (CA)
Butler County Comm Coll (PA)
Butte Coll (CA)
Casper Coll (WY)
Cecil Coll (MD)
Coll of Southern Idaho (ID)
Coll of the Canyons (CA)
Columbia Coll (CA)
Comm Coll of Philadelphia (PA)
County Coll of Morris (NJ)
Dakota Coll at Bottineau (ND)
De Anza Coll (CA)
Delaware Tech & Comm Coll, Terry Campus (DE)
Gwinnett Tech Coll (GA)
Harford Comm Coll (MD)
Harrisburg Area Comm Coll (PA)
Howard Comm Coll (MD)
Iowa Lakes Comm Coll (IA)
Lansing Comm Coll (MI)
Luzerne County Comm Coll (PA)
Mercer County Comm Coll (NJ)
Miami Dade Coll (FL)
Mott Comm Coll (MI)
Mt. San Antonio Coll (CA)
Mt. San Jacinto Coll (CA)
Nassau Comm Coll (NY)
Oakland Comm Coll (MI)
Oklahoma State U Inst of Technology (OK)
Onondaga Comm Coll (NY)
Orange Coast Coll (CA)
Pasadena City Coll (CA)
Pensacola State Coll (FL)
San Diego City Coll (CA)
Scottsdale Comm Coll (AZ)
Shoreline Comm Coll (WA)
Sullivan County Comm Coll (NY)
Tompkins Cortland Comm Coll (NY)
Tyler Jr Coll (TX)
Western Wyoming Comm Coll (WY)

PHOTOJOURNALISM
Pasadena City Coll (CA)
Randolph Comm Coll (NC)
Vincennes U (IN)

PHYSICAL EDUCATION TEACHING AND COACHING
Alabama Southern Comm Coll (AL)
Alvin Comm Coll (TX)
Amarillo Coll (TX)
Broward Coll (FL)
Bucks County Comm Coll (PA)
Carl Albert State Coll (OK)
Casper Coll (WY)
Clinton Comm Coll (NY)
Coll of Southern Idaho (ID)
Coll of Western Idaho (ID)
Copiah-Lincoln Comm Coll (MS)
Cossatot Comm Coll of the U of Arkansas (AR)
Crowder Coll (MO)
Dean Coll (MA)
De Anza Coll (CA)
Dutchess Comm Coll (NY)
Eastern Wyoming Coll (WY)
Erie Comm Coll (NY)
Erie Comm Coll, North Campus (NY)
Erie Comm Coll, South Campus (NY)
Finger Lakes Comm Coll (NY)
Galveston Coll (TX)
Genesee Comm Coll (NY)
Grayson Coll (TX)
Harper Coll (IL)
Hinds Comm Coll (MS)
Imperial Valley Coll (CA)
Iowa Lakes Comm Coll (IA)
Jamestown Comm Coll (NY)
Kilgore Coll (TX)
Lake Tahoe Comm Coll (CA)
Laramie County Comm Coll (WY)
Linn-Benton Comm Coll (OR)
Lorain County Comm Coll (OH)
Luzerne County Comm Coll (PA)
Miami Dade Coll (FL)
Mississippi Delta Comm Coll (MS)
Monroe Comm Coll (NY)
Montgomery County Comm Coll (PA)
Niagara County Comm Coll (NY)
Northeastern Jr Coll (CO)
Northern Essex Comm Coll (MA)
North Iowa Area Comm Coll (IA)
Northwest Mississippi Comm Coll (MS)
Orange Coast Coll (CA)
Potomac State Coll of West Virginia U (WV)
Roane State Comm Coll (TN)
San Diego City Coll (CA)
Sauk Valley Comm Coll (IL)
Seminole State Coll (OK)
Snow Coll (UT)
South Plains Coll (TX)
Spoon River Coll (IL)
Treasure Valley Comm Coll (OR)
Trinity Valley Comm Coll (TX)
Tyler Jr Coll (TX)
Umpqua Comm Coll (OR)
Vincennes U (IN)

PHYSICAL FITNESS TECHNICIAN
Alexandria Tech and Comm Coll (MN)
Lake Region State Coll (ND)
Minnesota School of Business–Plymouth (MN)
Tallahassee Comm Coll (FL)

PHYSICAL SCIENCES
Alvin Comm Coll (TX)
Amarillo Coll (TX)
Antelope Valley Coll (CA)
Austin Comm Coll (TX)
Borough of Manhattan Comm Coll of the City U of New York (NY)
Butler County Comm Coll (PA)
Butte Coll (CA)
Carl Albert State Coll (OK)
Central Oregon Comm Coll (OR)
Central Wyoming Coll (WY)
Chandler-Gilbert Comm Coll (AZ)
Coll of Marin (CA)
Columbia Coll (CA)
Crowder Coll (MO)
Dakota Coll at Bottineau (ND)
Feather River Coll (CA)
Garden City Comm Coll (KS)
Gavilan Coll (CA)
Golden West Coll (CA)

Harper Coll (IL)
Harrisburg Area Comm Coll (PA)
Hinds Comm Coll (MS)
Howard Comm Coll (MD)
Hutchinson Comm Coll and Area Vocational School (KS)
Imperial Valley Coll (CA)
Independence Comm Coll (KS)
Iowa Lakes Comm Coll (IA)
Lehigh Carbon Comm Coll (PA)
Los Angeles Mission Coll (CA)
Miami Dade Coll (FL)
Middlesex County Coll (NJ)
MiraCosta Coll (CA)
Montgomery County Comm Coll (PA)
Northeastern Jr Coll (CO)
Northwestern Connecticut Comm Coll (CT)
Ozarks Tech Comm Coll (MO)
Paris Jr Coll (TX)
Phoenix Coll (AZ)
Reading Area Comm Coll (PA)
Roane State Comm Coll (TN)
Salt Lake Comm Coll (UT)
San Diego City Coll (CA)
San Jacinto Coll District (TX)
San Juan Coll (NM)
Seminole State Coll (OK)
Snow Coll (UT)
Spoon River Coll (IL)
Trinity Valley Comm Coll (TX)
Tulsa Comm Coll (OK)
Umpqua Comm Coll (OR)
U of New Mexico–Los Alamos Branch (NM)
Victor Valley Coll (CA)
Vincennes U (IN)
Wenatchee Valley Coll (WA)
Western Nevada Coll (NV)

PHYSICAL SCIENCES RELATED
Dakota Coll at Bottineau (ND)
Mt. San Antonio Coll (CA)

PHYSICAL SCIENCE TECHNOLOGIES RELATED
Westmoreland County Comm Coll (PA)

PHYSICAL THERAPY
Allen Comm Coll (KS)
Amarillo Coll (TX)
Athens Tech Coll (GA)
Blackhawk Tech Coll (WI)
Bossier Parish Comm Coll (LA)
Broward Coll (FL)
Central Oregon Comm Coll (OR)
Clark State Comm Coll (OH)
Daytona State Coll (FL)
De Anza Coll (CA)
Genesee Comm Coll (NY)
Gwinnett Tech Coll (GA)
Herkimer County Comm Coll (NY)
Hinds Comm Coll (MS)
Housatonic Comm Coll (CT)
Kilgore Coll (TX)
Kingsborough Comm Coll of the City U of New York (NY)
Metropolitan Comm Coll–Kansas City (MO)
Monroe County Comm Coll (MI)
NorthWest Arkansas Comm Coll (AR)
Oklahoma City Comm Coll (OK)
Roane State Comm Coll (TN)
Seminole State Coll of Florida (FL)
South Plains Coll (TX)
Southwestern Comm Coll (NC)
Stark State Coll (OH)
Tarrant County Coll District (TX)
Treasure Valley Comm Coll (OR)
Trident Tech Coll (SC)
Tulsa Comm Coll (OK)
Tunxis Comm Coll (CT)
Wytheville Comm Coll (VA)

PHYSICAL THERAPY TECHNOLOGY
Anoka-Ramsey Comm Coll (MN)
Arapahoe Comm Coll (CO)
Austin Comm Coll (TX)
Bay State Coll (MA)
Berkshire Comm Coll (MA)
Bishop State Comm Coll (AL)
Blackhawk Tech Coll (WI)
Blue Ridge Comm and Tech Coll (WV)
Bradford School (OH)
Brown Mackie Coll–Fort Wayne (IN)
Brown Mackie Coll–South Bend (IN)
Butler County Comm Coll (PA)
Carl Albert State Coll (OK)

Carrington Coll–Albuquerque (NM)
Carrington Coll–Boise (ID)
Carrington Coll California–Pleasant Hill (CA)
Carrington Coll–Las Vegas (NV)
Carrington Coll–Mesa (AZ)
Carroll Comm Coll (MD)
Chippewa Valley Tech Coll (WI)
Clark State Comm Coll (OH)
Coll of Central Florida (FL)
Coll of Southern Maryland (MD)
Comm Coll of Allegheny County (PA)
Comm Coll of Rhode Island (RI)
Darton State Coll (GA)
Delaware Tech & Comm Coll, Jack F. Owens Campus (DE)
Delaware Tech & Comm Coll, Stanton/Wilmington Campus (DE)
Delta Coll (MI)
Edison Comm Coll (OH)
Elgin Comm Coll (IL)
Fayetteville Tech Comm Coll (NC)
Fiorello H. LaGuardia Comm Coll of the City U of New York (NY)
Florida Gateway Coll (FL)
Florida State Coll at Jacksonville (FL)
Fox Coll (IL)
Genesee Comm Coll (NY)
Great Falls Coll Montana State U (MT)
Greenville Tech Coll (SC)
Gwinnett Tech Coll (GA)
Hawkeye Comm Coll (IA)
Hinds Comm Coll (MS)
Hocking Coll (OH)
Houston Comm Coll System (TX)
Howard Comm Coll (MD)
Hutchinson Comm Coll and Area Vocational School (KS)
Ivy Tech Comm Coll–East Central (IN)
Jackson State Comm Coll (TN)
Jefferson State Comm Coll (AL)
Kankakee Comm Coll (IL)
Kaskaskia Coll (IL)
Kent State U at Ashtabula (OH)
Kent State U at East Liverpool (OH)
Kilgore Coll (TX)
Kingsborough Comm Coll of the City U of New York (NY)
Lake Area Tech Inst (SD)
Lake Land Coll (IL)
Lake Superior Coll (MN)
Laramie County Comm Coll (WY)
Lehigh Carbon Comm Coll (PA)
Lone Star Coll–Montgomery (TX)
Lorain County Comm Coll (OH)
Macomb Comm Coll (MI)
Manchester Comm Coll (CT)
Massachusetts Bay Comm Coll (MA)
Mercer County Comm Coll (NJ)
Miami Dade Coll (FL)
Mohave Comm Coll (AZ)
Montgomery Coll (MD)
Mott Comm Coll (MI)
Mount Wachusett Comm Coll (MA)
Nassau Comm Coll (NY)
Niagara County Comm Coll (NY)
Northeast Texas Comm Coll (TX)
North Iowa Area Comm Coll (IA)
North Shore Comm Coll (MA)
Oakland Comm Coll (MI)
Oakton Comm Coll (IL)
Olympic Coll (WA)
Onondaga Comm Coll (NY)
Owens Comm Coll, Toledo (OH)
Ozarks Tech Comm Coll (MO)
Penn State DuBois (PA)
Penn State Hazleton (PA)
Penn State Mont Alto (PA)
Pennsylvania Inst of Technology (PA)
Pensacola State Coll (FL)
Pueblo Comm Coll (CO)
Randolph Comm Coll (NC)
Reading Area Comm Coll (PA)
River Valley Comm Coll (NH)
Salt Lake Comm Coll (UT)
San Jacinto Coll District (TX)
San Juan Coll (NM)
Somerset Comm Coll (KY)
Southern U at Shreveport (LA)
Southwestern Comm Coll (NC)
Southwestern Illinois Coll (IL)
Springfield Tech Comm Coll (MA)
State Fair Comm Coll (MO)
Tech Coll of the Lowcountry (SC)
Vincennes U (IN)
Volunteer State Comm Coll (TN)
Walters State Comm Coll (TN)
Waukesha County Tech Coll (WI)

West Kentucky Comm and Tech Coll (KY)
Williston State Coll (ND)

PHYSICIAN ASSISTANT
Georgia Highlands Coll (GA)
San Joaquin Valley Coll, Hanford (CA)
San Joaquin Valley Coll, Hesperia (CA)
San Joaquin Valley Coll, Temecula (CA)
San Joaquin Valley Coll, Visalia (CA)

PHYSICS
Allen Comm Coll (KS)
Amarillo Coll (TX)
Arizona Western Coll (AZ)
Austin Comm Coll (TX)
Broward Coll (FL)
Bunker Hill Comm Coll (MA)
Butte Coll (CA)
Ca&nnada Coll (CA)
Casper Coll (WY)
Cecil Coll (MD)
Cochise Coll, Sierra Vista (AZ)
Coll of Marin (CA)
Coll of Southern Idaho (ID)
Coll of the Canyons (CA)
Coll of the Desert (CA)
Comm Coll of Allegheny County (PA)
Cosumnes River Coll, Sacramento (CA)
Darton State Coll (GA)
De Anza Coll (CA)
Eastern Arizona Coll (AZ)
Finger Lakes Comm Coll (NY)
Frank Phillips Coll (TX)
Fullerton Coll (CA)
Georgia Highlands Coll (GA)
Gordon State Coll (GA)
Grayson Coll (TX)
Great Basin Coll (NV)
Harford Comm Coll (MD)
Kankakee Comm Coll (IL)
Kilgore Coll (TX)
Kingsborough Comm Coll of the City U of New York (NY)
Linn-Benton Comm Coll (OR)
Lorain County Comm Coll (OH)
Mercer County Comm Coll (NJ)
Miami Dade Coll (FL)
MiraCosta Coll (CA)
Monroe Comm Coll (NY)
Northampton Comm Coll (PA)
Northeast Texas Comm Coll (TX)
Northwest Coll (WY)
Oklahoma City Comm Coll (OK)
Oklahoma State U, Oklahoma City (OK)
Orange Coast Coll (CA)
Paris Jr Coll (TX)
Pensacola State Coll (FL)
Salt Lake Comm Coll (UT)
San Jacinto Coll District (TX)
San Juan Coll (NM)
Santa Rosa Jr Coll (CA)
Sauk Valley Comm Coll (IL)
Snow Coll (UT)
South Florida State Coll (FL)
South Georgia State Coll, Douglas (GA)
Spoon River Coll (IL)
Springfield Tech Comm Coll (MA)
Texarkana Coll (TX)
Treasure Valley Comm Coll (OR)
Truckee Meadows Comm Coll (NV)
Tyler Jr Coll (TX)

PHYSICS RELATED
South Florida State Coll (FL)

PHYSICS TEACHER EDUCATION
Broward Coll (FL)
The Comm Coll of Baltimore County (MD)
Harford Comm Coll (MD)
Montgomery Coll (MD)

PIPEFITTING AND SPRINKLER FITTING
Delta Coll (MI)
Ivy Tech Comm Coll–Bloomington (IN)
Ivy Tech Comm Coll–Central Indiana (IN)
Ivy Tech Comm Coll–Columbus (IN)
Ivy Tech Comm Coll–East Central (IN)
Ivy Tech Comm Coll–Kokomo (IN)
Ivy Tech Comm Coll–Lafayette (IN)

Ivy Tech Comm Coll–North Central (IN)
Ivy Tech Comm Coll–Northeast (IN)
Ivy Tech Comm Coll–Northwest (IN)
Ivy Tech Comm Coll–Richmond (IN)
Ivy Tech Comm Coll–Southern Indiana (IN)
Ivy Tech Comm Coll–Southwest (IN)
Ivy Tech Comm Coll–Wabash Valley (IN)
Oakland Comm Coll (MI)
Southwestern Illinois Coll (IL)

PLANT NURSERY MANAGEMENT
Coll of Marin (CA)
Comm Coll of Allegheny County (PA)
Cosumnes River Coll, Sacramento (CA)
Fullerton Coll (CA)
Miami Dade Coll (FL)
MiraCosta Coll (CA)
The Ohio State U Ag Tech Inst (OH)

PLANT SCIENCES
Mercer County Comm Coll (NJ)
Northwest Mississippi Comm Coll (MS)
Rend Lake Coll (IL)
South Florida State Coll (FL)

PLASTICS AND POLYMER ENGINEERING TECHNOLOGY
Cincinnati State Tech and Comm Coll (OH)
Daytona State Coll (FL)
Grand Rapids Comm Coll (MI)
Lorain County Comm Coll (OH)
Macomb Comm Coll (MI)
Mount Wachusett Comm Coll (MA)
West Georgia Tech Coll (GA)
Wichita Area Tech Coll (KS)

PLAYWRITING AND SCREENWRITING
Broward Coll (FL)
Minneapolis Comm and Tech Coll (MN)
Northwest Coll (WY)

PLUMBING TECHNOLOGY
Arizona Western Coll (AZ)
Delta Coll (MI)
Hinds Comm Coll (MS)
Luzerne County Comm Coll (PA)
Macomb Comm Coll (MI)
Northeast Iowa Comm Coll (IA)
Southeast Tech Inst (SD)
Southern Maine Comm Coll (ME)
Sowela Tech Comm Coll (LA)
State U of New York Coll of Technology at Alfred (NY)

POLITICAL SCIENCE AND GOVERNMENT
Allen Comm Coll (KS)
American Samoa Comm Coll (AS)
Arizona Western Coll (AZ)
Austin Comm Coll (TX)
Bainbridge State Coll (GA)
Broward Coll (FL)
Ca&nnada Coll (CA)
Casper Coll (WY)
Coll of Marin (CA)
Coll of Southern Idaho (ID)
Coll of the Canyons (CA)
Coll of the Desert (CA)
Coll of Western Idaho (ID)
Copper Mountain Coll (CA)
Darton State Coll (GA)
De Anza Coll (CA)
Eastern Arizona Coll (AZ)
Finger Lakes Comm Coll (NY)
Fullerton Coll (CA)
Georgia Highlands Coll (GA)
Gordon State Coll (GA)
Harford Comm Coll (MD)
Hinds Comm Coll (MS)
Iowa Lakes Comm Coll (IA)
Kankakee Comm Coll (IL)
Lansing Comm Coll (MI)
Laramie County Comm Coll (WY)
Lorain County Comm Coll (OH)
Miami Dade Coll (FL)
MiraCosta Coll (CA)
Mississippi Delta Comm Coll (MS)
Monroe Comm Coll (NY)
Northeast Texas Comm Coll (TX)
Northern Essex Comm Coll (MA)
Northwest Coll (WY)
Oklahoma City Comm Coll (OK)
Orange Coast Coll (CA)

Otero Jr Coll (CO)
Oxnard Coll (CA)
Paris Jr Coll (TX)
Pima Comm Coll (AZ)
Potomac State Coll of West Virginia U (WV)
Salt Lake Comm Coll (UT)
San Diego City Coll (CA)
San Jacinto Coll District (TX)
Santa Rosa Jr Coll (CA)
Sauk Valley Comm Coll (IL)
Snow Coll (UT)
South Florida State Coll (FL)
South Georgia State Coll, Douglas (GA)
Spoon River Coll (IL)
Texarkana Coll (TX)
Treasure Valley Comm Coll (OR)
Trinity Valley Comm Coll (TX)
Tyler Jr Coll (TX)
Umpqua Comm Coll (OR)
Vincennes U (IN)
Western Wyoming Comm Coll (WY)

POLYMER/PLASTICS ENGINEERING
Central Oregon Comm Coll (OR)

POLYSOMNOGRAPHY
Catawba Valley Comm Coll (NC)
Genesee Comm Coll (NY)
Minneapolis Comm and Tech Coll (MN)
Pueblo Comm Coll (CO)

PORTUGUESE
Broward Coll (FL)
Miami Dade Coll (FL)

POULTRY SCIENCE
Delaware Tech & Comm Coll, Jack F. Owens Campus (DE)
Northwest Mississippi Comm Coll (MS)

PRE-CHIROPRACTIC
Broward Coll (FL)

PRECISION METAL WORKING RELATED
Delta Coll (MI)
Oakland Comm Coll (MI)
Shelton State Comm Coll (AL)
Western Dakota Tech Inst (SD)

PRECISION PRODUCTION RELATED
Delta Coll (MI)
East Central Coll (MO)
Jefferson Coll (MO)
Mineral Area Coll (MO)
Mott Comm Coll (MI)
Sheridan Coll (WY)
Wichita Area Tech Coll (KS)

PRECISION PRODUCTION TRADES
Bucks County Comm Coll (PA)
Butler County Comm Coll (PA)
Mineral Area Coll (MO)
Owensboro Comm and Tech Coll (KY)

PRE-DENTISTRY STUDIES
Alabama Southern Comm Coll (AL)
Allen Comm Coll (KS)
Austin Comm Coll (TX)
Casper Coll (WY)
Darton State Coll (GA)
Eastern Wyoming Coll (WY)
Hinds Comm Coll (MS)
Howard Comm Coll (MD)
Iowa Lakes Comm Coll (IA)
Kilgore Coll (TX)
Pensacola State Coll (FL)
Treasure Valley Comm Coll (OR)
Vincennes U (IN)
Western Wyoming Comm Coll (WY)

PRE-ENGINEERING
Alabama Southern Comm Coll (AL)
Alexandria Tech and Comm Coll (MN)
Amarillo Coll (TX)
Anoka-Ramsey Comm Coll (MN)
Anoka-Ramsey Comm Coll, Cambridge Campus (MN)
Bronx Comm Coll of the City U of New York (NY)
Century Coll (MN)
Chipola Coll (FL)
Cleveland Comm Coll (NC)

Coll of the Canyons (CA)
Comm Coll of Philadelphia (PA)
Crowder Coll (MO)
Darton State Coll (GA)
De Anza Coll (CA)
Finger Lakes Comm Coll (NY)
Gordon State Coll (GA)
Housatonic Comm Coll (CT)
Imperial Valley Coll (CA)
Iowa Lakes Comm Coll (IA)
Lamar Comm Coll (CO)
Lenoir Comm Coll (NC)
Linn-Benton Comm Coll (OR)
Lorain County Comm Coll (OH)
Macomb Comm Coll (MI)
Mesabi Range Comm and Tech Coll (MN)
Mesa Comm Coll (AZ)
Metropolitan Comm Coll–Kansas City (MO)
Miami Dade Coll (FL)
Mississippi Gulf Coast Comm Coll (MS)
Monroe County Comm Coll (MI)
Mt. San Antonio Coll (CA)
New Mexico State U–Alamogordo (NM)
Normandale Comm Coll (MN)
Northeastern Jr Coll (CO)
North Shore Comm Coll (MA)
Northwestern Connecticut Comm Coll (CT)
Oklahoma City Comm Coll (OK)
Oklahoma State U, Oklahoma City (OK)
Otero Jr Coll (CO)
Pima Comm Coll (AZ)
Potomac State Coll of West Virginia U (WV)
Rainy River Comm Coll (MN)
Randolph Comm Coll (NC)
Roane State Comm Coll (TN)
Rock Valley Coll (IL)
San Diego City Coll (CA)
Seminole State Coll (OK)
Shoreline Comm Coll (WA)
Snow Coll (UT)
Southern Maine Comm Coll (ME)
South Plains Coll (TX)
Spoon River Coll (IL)
Three Rivers Comm Coll (CT)
Treasure Valley Comm Coll (OR)
Trinity Valley Comm Coll (TX)
Umpqua Comm Coll (OR)
U of New Mexico–Los Alamos Branch (NM)
Virginia Western Comm Coll (VA)
Wenatchee Valley Coll (WA)
Western Wyoming Comm Coll (WY)
Westmoreland County Comm Coll (PA)

PRE-LAW STUDIES
Alabama Southern Comm Coll (AL)
Allen Comm Coll (KS)
American Samoa Comm Coll (AS)
Carl Albert State Coll (OK)
Casper Coll (WY)
Central Oregon Comm Coll (OR)
Central Wyoming Coll (WY)
Coll of Southern Idaho (ID)
Darton State Coll (GA)
Garden City Comm Coll (KS)
Hinds Comm Coll (MS)
Iowa Lakes Comm Coll (IA)
Kilgore Coll (TX)
Laramie County Comm Coll (WY)
Paris Jr Coll (TX)
Pensacola State Coll (FL)
Treasure Valley Comm Coll (OR)
Western Wyoming Comm Coll (WY)

PREMEDICAL STUDIES
Alabama Southern Comm Coll (AL)
Allen Comm Coll (KS)
Austin Comm Coll (TX)
Broward Coll (FL)
Casper Coll (WY)
Central Oregon Comm Coll (OR)
Dakota Coll at Bottineau (ND)
Darton State Coll (GA)
Eastern Arizona Coll (AZ)
Eastern Wyoming Coll (WY)
Garden City Comm Coll (KS)
Hinds Comm Coll (MS)
Howard Comm Coll (MD)
Iowa Lakes Comm Coll (IA)
Kilgore Coll (TX)
Lansing Comm Coll (MI)
Paris Jr Coll (TX)

Pensacola State Coll (FL)
San Juan Coll (NM)
Sauk Valley Comm Coll (IL)
Springfield Tech Comm Coll (MA)
Treasure Valley Comm Coll (OR)
Vincennes U (IN)
Wayne County Comm Coll District (MI)
Western Wyoming Comm Coll (WY)

PRENURSING STUDIES
Cleveland Comm Coll (NC)
Dakota Coll at Bottineau (ND)
Edison Comm Coll (OH)
Garden City Comm Coll (KS)
Georgia Military Coll (GA)
Hinds Comm Coll (MS)
Iowa Lakes Comm Coll (IA)
Oklahoma State U, Oklahoma City (OK)
Paris Jr Coll (TX)
Pensacola State Coll (FL)
Randolph Comm Coll (NC)
Southwestern Michigan Coll (MI)
Treasure Valley Comm Coll (OR)
Western Wyoming Comm Coll (WY)

PRE-OCCUPATIONAL THERAPY
Broward Coll (FL)
Casper Coll (WY)
Georgia Highlands Coll (GA)
Gordon State Coll (GA)

PRE-OPTOMETRY
Broward Coll (FL)
Casper Coll (WY)

PRE-PHARMACY STUDIES
Alabama Southern Comm Coll (AL)
Allen Comm Coll (KS)
Amarillo Coll (TX)
Austin Comm Coll (TX)
Casper Coll (WY)
Central Oregon Comm Coll (OR)
Coll of Southern Idaho (ID)
Darton State Coll (GA)
Eastern Arizona Coll (AZ)
Eastern Wyoming Coll (WY)
Garden City Comm Coll (KS)
Georgia Highlands Coll (GA)
Gordon State Coll (GA)
Hinds Comm Coll (MS)
Howard Comm Coll (MD)
Iowa Lakes Comm Coll (IA)
Kilgore Coll (TX)
Laramie County Comm Coll (WY)
Luzerne County Comm Coll (PA)
Monroe Comm Coll (NY)
Northwest Coll (WY)
Paris Jr Coll (TX)
Pensacola State Coll (FL)
Quinsigamond Comm Coll (MA)
Schoolcraft Coll (MI)
South Florida State Coll (FL)
Treasure Valley Comm Coll (OR)
Tulsa Comm Coll (OK)
Vincennes U (IN)
Western Wyoming Comm Coll (WY)

PRE-PHYSICAL THERAPY
Broward Coll (FL)
Casper Coll (WY)
Georgia Highlands Coll (GA)
Gordon State Coll (GA)
Sauk Valley Comm Coll (IL)

PRE-VETERINARY STUDIES
Alabama Southern Comm Coll (AL)
Allen Comm Coll (KS)
Austin Comm Coll (TX)
Broward Coll (FL)
Casper Coll (WY)
Dakota Coll at Bottineau (ND)
Darton State Coll (GA)
Eastern Wyoming Coll (WY)
Garden City Comm Coll (KS)
Hinds Comm Coll (MS)
Howard Comm Coll (MD)
Iowa Lakes Comm Coll (IA)
Kilgore Coll (TX)
Pensacola State Coll (FL)
Treasure Valley Comm Coll (OR)
Vincennes U (IN)
Western Wyoming Comm Coll (WY)

PRINTING MANAGEMENT
Palomar Coll (CA)

PRINTING PRESS OPERATION
Dunwoody Coll of Technology (MN)

Iowa Lakes Comm Coll (IA)
Lake Land Coll (IL)

PRINTMAKING
De Anza Coll (CA)
Florida State Coll at Jacksonville (FL)

PROFESSIONAL, TECHNICAL, BUSINESS, AND SCIENTIFIC WRITING
Austin Comm Coll (TX)
De Anza Coll (CA)
Fox Valley Tech Coll (WI)
Linn-Benton Comm Coll (OR)
Oklahoma State U, Oklahoma City (OK)
Pima Comm Coll (AZ)
Southwestern Michigan Coll (MI)
Three Rivers Comm Coll (CT)

PROJECT MANAGEMENT
ITT Tech Inst, Lake Mary (FL)

PSYCHIATRIC/MENTAL HEALTH SERVICES TECHNOLOGY
Coll of Southern Idaho (ID)
Comm Coll of Allegheny County (PA)
The Comm Coll of Baltimore County (MD)
Fiorello H. LaGuardia Comm Coll of the City U of New York (NY)
Hagerstown Comm Coll (MD)
Hillsborough Comm Coll (FL)
Houston Comm Coll System (TX)
Ivy Tech Comm Coll–Bloomington (IN)
Ivy Tech Comm Coll–Central Indiana (IN)
Ivy Tech Comm Coll–Columbus (IN)
Ivy Tech Comm Coll–East Central (IN)
Ivy Tech Comm Coll–Kokomo (IN)
Ivy Tech Comm Coll–Lafayette (IN)
Ivy Tech Comm Coll–Northeast (IN)
Ivy Tech Comm Coll–Northwest (IN)
Ivy Tech Comm Coll–Richmond (IN)
Ivy Tech Comm Coll–Southeast (IN)
Ivy Tech Comm Coll–Southern Indiana (IN)
Ivy Tech Comm Coll–Southwest (IN)
Ivy Tech Comm Coll–Wabash Valley (IN)
Kingsborough Comm Coll of the City U of New York (NY)
Montgomery Coll (MD)
Montgomery County Comm Coll (PA)
North Dakota State Coll of Science (ND)
Pueblo Comm Coll (CO)
Williston State Coll (ND)

PSYCHOLOGY
Allen Comm Coll (KS)
Amarillo Coll (TX)
Austin Comm Coll (TX)
Bainbridge State Coll (GA)
Berkeley City Coll (CA)
Bronx Comm Coll of the City U of New York (NY)
Broward Coll (FL)
Bucks County Comm Coll (PA)
Bunker Hill Comm Coll (MA)
Butler County Comm Coll (PA)
Ca&nnada Coll (CA)
Carroll Comm Coll (MD)
Casper Coll (WY)
Central Wyoming Coll (WY)
Chandler-Gilbert Comm Coll (AZ)
Cochise Coll, Sierra Vista (AZ)
Coconino Comm Coll (AZ)
Coll of Marin (CA)
Coll of Southern Idaho (ID)
Coll of the Canyons (CA)
Coll of the Desert (CA)
Coll of Western Idaho (ID)
Comm Coll of Allegheny County (PA)
Comm Coll of Philadelphia (PA)
Copper Mountain Coll (CA)
Cossatot Comm Coll of the U of Arkansas (AR)
Crowder Coll (MO)
Dakota Coll at Bottineau (ND)
Darton State Coll (GA)
De Anza Coll (CA)
Eastern Arizona Coll (AZ)
Eastern Wyoming Coll (WY)
Edison Comm Coll (OH)
Finger Lakes Comm Coll (NY)

Fiorello H. LaGuardia Comm Coll of the City U of New York (NY)
Frank Phillips Coll (TX)
Fullerton Coll (CA)
Garden City Comm Coll (KS)
Genesee Comm Coll (NY)
Georgia Highlands Coll (GA)
Georgia Military Coll (GA)
Gogebic Comm Coll (MI)
Gordon State Coll (GA)
Grayson Coll (TX)
Great Basin Coll (NV)
Harford Comm Coll (MD)
Harper Coll (IL)
Harrisburg Area Comm Coll (PA)
Hinds Comm Coll (MS)
Howard Comm Coll (MD)
Hutchinson Comm Coll and Area Vocational School (KS)
Imperial Valley Coll (CA)
Iowa Lakes Comm Coll (IA)
Kankakee Comm Coll (IL)
Kilgore Coll (TX)
Kilian Comm Coll (SD)
Lake Tahoe Comm Coll (CA)
Lansing Comm Coll (MI)
Laramie County Comm Coll (WY)
Lehigh Carbon Comm Coll (PA)
Lorain County Comm Coll (OH)
Los Angeles Mission Coll (CA)
Miami Dade Coll (FL)
MiraCosta Coll (CA)
Mohave Comm Coll (AZ)
Monroe County Comm Coll (MI)
Montgomery County Comm Coll (PA)
Northeastern Jr Coll (CO)
Northeast Texas Comm Coll (TX)
Northwest Coll (WY)
Norwalk Comm Coll (CT)
Oklahoma City Comm Coll (OK)
Oklahoma State U, Oklahoma City (OK)
Otero Jr Coll (CO)
Oxnard Coll (CA)
Palomar Coll (CA)
Paris Jr Coll (TX)
Pasadena City Coll (CA)
Pensacola State Coll (FL)
Pima Comm Coll (AZ)
Potomac State Coll of West Virginia U (WV)
Reading Area Comm Coll (PA)
Salt Lake Comm Coll (UT)
San Diego City Coll (CA)
San Jacinto Coll District (TX)
San Juan Coll (NM)
Santa Rosa Jr Coll (CA)
Sauk Valley Comm Coll (IL)
Sheridan Coll (WY)
South Florida State Coll (FL)
South Georgia State Coll, Douglas (GA)
Spoon River Coll (IL)
Sullivan County Comm Coll (NY)
Treasure Valley Comm Coll (OR)
Trinity Valley Comm Coll (TX)
Truckee Meadows Comm Coll (NV)
Tyler Jr Coll (TX)
Umpqua Comm Coll (OR)
Vincennes U (IN)
Western Wyoming Comm Coll (WY)

PSYCHOLOGY RELATED
Cayuga County Comm Coll (NY)
Genesee Comm Coll (NY)
MiraCosta Coll (CA)
Seminole State Coll (OK)

PUBLIC ADMINISTRATION
Broward Coll (FL)
County Coll of Morris (NJ)
Fayetteville Tech Comm Coll (NC)
Housatonic Comm Coll (CT)
Houston Comm Coll System (TX)
Laramie County Comm Coll (WY)
Lehigh Carbon Comm Coll (PA)
Miami Dade Coll (FL)
Minneapolis Comm and Tech Coll (MN)
Northwest Florida State Coll (FL)
Palomar Coll (CA)
Scottsdale Comm Coll (AZ)
Southern U at Shreveport (LA)
South Florida State Coll (FL)
Three Rivers Comm Coll (CT)
Westchester Comm Coll (NY)

PUBLIC ADMINISTRATION AND SOCIAL SERVICE PROFESSIONS RELATED
Cleveland State Comm Coll (TN)
Erie Comm Coll (NY)
Oklahoma State U, Oklahoma City (OK)
Onondaga Comm Coll (NY)

PUBLIC HEALTH EDUCATION AND PROMOTION
Berkeley City Coll (CA)
Coll of Southern Idaho (ID)
Georgia Military Coll (GA)

PUBLIC HEALTH RELATED
Berkeley City Coll (CA)
Salt Lake Comm Coll (UT)

PUBLIC RELATIONS, ADVERTISING, AND APPLIED COMMUNICATION
Broward Coll (FL)
Oklahoma City Comm Coll (OK)

PUBLIC RELATIONS, ADVERTISING, AND APPLIED COMMUNICATION RELATED
Harper Coll (IL)

PUBLIC RELATIONS/IMAGE MANAGEMENT
Amarillo Coll (TX)
Bismarck State Coll (ND)
Cosumnes River Coll, Sacramento (CA)
Crowder Coll (MO)
Glendale Comm Coll (AZ)
South Florida State Coll (FL)
Vincennes U (IN)

PURCHASING, PROCUREMENT/ACQUISITIONS AND CONTRACTS MANAGEMENT
Cecil Coll (MD)
Columbus State Comm Coll (OH)
De Anza Coll (CA)
Greenville Tech Coll (SC)
Shoreline Comm Coll (WA)

QUALITY CONTROL AND SAFETY TECHNOLOGIES RELATED
Ivy Tech Comm Coll–Lafayette (IN)
Ivy Tech Comm Coll–Wabash Valley (IN)
Macomb Comm Coll (MI)

QUALITY CONTROL TECHNOLOGY
Central Carolina Comm Coll (NC)
Columbus State Comm Coll (OH)
Comm Coll of Allegheny County (PA)
Goodwin Coll (CT)
Grand Rapids Comm Coll (MI)
Illinois Eastern Comm Colls, Frontier Community College (IL)
Illinois Eastern Comm Colls, Lincoln Trail College (IL)
Ivy Tech Comm Coll–Lafayette (IN)
Lakeland Comm Coll (OH)
Lorain County Comm Coll (OH)
Macomb Comm Coll (MI)
Mesa Comm Coll (AZ)
Metropolitan Comm Coll–Kansas City (MO)
Monroe Comm Coll (NY)
Mt. San Antonio Coll (CA)
Northampton Comm Coll (PA)
Owens Comm Coll, Toledo (OH)
Palomar Coll (CA)
Rock Valley Coll (IL)
Salt Lake Comm Coll (UT)
Tarrant County Coll District (TX)
Tulsa Comm Coll (OK)

RADIATION PROTECTION/HEALTH PHYSICS TECHNOLOGY
Lone Star Coll–CyFair (TX)
Spartanburg Comm Coll (SC)

RADIO AND TELEVISION
Alvin Comm Coll (TX)
Amarillo Coll (TX)
Austin Comm Coll (TX)
Broward Coll (FL)
Butte Coll (CA)
Central Carolina Comm Coll (NC)
Central Wyoming Coll (WY)
Coll of the Canyons (CA)

Cosumnes River Coll, Sacramento (CA)
Daytona State Coll (FL)
De Anza Coll (CA)
Delta Coll (MI)
Fullerton Coll (CA)
Genesee Comm Coll (NY)
Golden West Coll (CA)
Hinds Comm Coll (MS)
Illinois Eastern Comm Colls, Wabash Valley College (IL)
Iowa Lakes Comm Coll (IA)
Lake Land Coll (IL)
Miami Dade Coll (FL)
Mt. San Antonio Coll (CA)
Northwest Coll (WY)
Northwest Mississippi Comm Coll (MS)
Onondaga Comm Coll (NY)
Oxnard Coll (CA)
Palomar Coll (CA)
Pasadena City Coll (CA)
San Diego City Coll (CA)
Santa Monica Coll (CA)
South Florida State Coll (FL)
Sullivan County Comm Coll (NY)
Virginia Western Comm Coll (VA)

RADIO AND TELEVISION BROADCASTING TECHNOLOGY
Arizona Western Coll (AZ)
Borough of Manhattan Comm Coll of the City U of New York (NY)
Cleveland Comm Coll (NC)
Cloud County Comm Coll (KS)
Genesee Comm Coll (NY)
Hinds Comm Coll (MS)
Houston Comm Coll System (TX)
Hutchinson Comm Coll and Area Vocational School (KS)
Iowa Lakes Comm Coll (IA)
Lansing Comm Coll (MI)
Lehigh Carbon Comm Coll (PA)
Luzerne County Comm Coll (PA)
Mercer County Comm Coll (NJ)
Miami Dade Coll (FL)
Mineral Area Coll (MO)
Mount Wachusett Comm Coll (MA)
Northampton Comm Coll (PA)
Northwest Mississippi Comm Coll (MS)
Oakland Comm Coll (MI)
Ozarks Tech Comm Coll (MO)
Pasadena City Coll (CA)
Salt Lake Comm Coll (UT)
San Jacinto Coll District (TX)
Schoolcraft Coll (MI)
Springfield Tech Comm Coll (MA)
Tompkins Cortland Comm Coll (NY)
Vincennes U (IN)
Waubonsee Comm Coll (IL)
Westmoreland County Comm Coll (PA)

RADIOLOGIC TECHNOLOGY/ SCIENCE
Amarillo Coll (TX)
Arizona Western Coll (AZ)
Austin Comm Coll (TX)
Blackhawk Tech Coll (WI)
Brookhaven Coll (TX)
Butler County Comm Coll (PA)
Ca&nnada Coll (CA)
Career Tech Coll, Monroe (LA)
Carl Albert State Coll (OK)
Carolinas Coll of Health Sciences (NC)
Carrington Coll–Phoenix (AZ)
Casper Coll (WY)
Central Maine Medical Center Coll of Nursing and Health Professions (ME)
Central Oregon Comm Coll (OR)
Central Virginia Comm Coll (VA)
Century Coll (MN)
Clark Coll (WA)
Cleveland Comm Coll (NC)
Comm Coll of Rhode Island (RI)
County Coll of Morris (NJ)
Danville Area Comm Coll (IL)
Delaware Tech & Comm Coll, Jack F. Owens Campus (DE)
Delaware Tech & Comm Coll, Stanton/Wilmington Campus (DE)
Elgin Comm Coll (IL)
Fayetteville Tech Comm Coll (NC)
Gadsden State Comm Coll (AL)
Galveston Coll (TX)
Gordon State Coll (GA)
Grayson Coll (TX)
Great Falls Coll Montana State U (MT)

Harper Coll (IL)
Harrisburg Area Comm Coll (PA)
Hinds Comm Coll (MS)
Houston Comm Coll System (TX)
Jefferson State Comm Coll (AL)
Kankakee Comm Coll (IL)
Kaskaskia Coll (IL)
Kilgore Coll (TX)
Lake Superior Coll (MN)
Lansing Comm Coll (MI)
Laramie County Comm Coll (WY)
Lincoln Land Comm Coll (IL)
Miami Dade Coll (FL)
Minnesota State Coll–Southeast Tech (MN)
Mitchell Tech Inst (SD)
Montgomery County Comm Coll (PA)
Moraine Valley Comm Coll (IL)
Northampton Comm Coll (PA)
Northeast Iowa Comm Coll (IA)
Northern Essex Comm Coll (MA)
Oklahoma State U, Oklahoma City (OK)
Paris Jr Coll (TX)
Pasadena City Coll (CA)
Pasco-Hernando State Coll (FL)
Pennsylvania Coll of Health Sciences (PA)
Piedmont Virginia Comm Coll (VA)
Pima Comm Coll (AZ)
Pitt Comm Coll (NC)
Pueblo Comm Coll (CO)
Quinsigamond Comm Coll (MA)
Randolph Comm Coll (NC)
St. Luke's Coll (IA)
San Jacinto Coll District (TX)
Santa Rosa Jr Coll (CA)
Sauk Valley Comm Coll (IL)
Southern Maine Comm Coll (ME)
Southern U at Shreveport (LA)
South Suburban Coll (IL)
Southwestern Illinois Coll (IL)
Southwest Virginia Comm Coll (VA)
Spencerian Coll (KY)
Spencerian Coll–Lexington (KY)
Springfield Tech Comm Coll (MA)
State Fair Comm Coll (MO)
Truckee Meadows Comm Coll (NV)
Virginia Western Comm Coll (VA)
Wenatchee Valley Coll (WA)
Westmoreland County Comm Coll (PA)

RADIO, TELEVISION, AND DIGITAL COMMUNICATION RELATED
Cayuga County Comm Coll (NY)
Fox Valley Tech Coll (WI)
Genesee Comm Coll (NY)
Mitchell Tech Inst (SD)
Montgomery County Comm Coll (PA)
Northwest Coll (WY)
Sullivan County Comm Coll (NY)

RANGE SCIENCE AND MANAGEMENT
Casper Coll (WY)
Central Wyoming Coll (WY)
Eastern Wyoming Coll (WY)
Northwest Coll (WY)
Sheridan Coll (WY)
Snow Coll (UT)
Treasure Valley Comm Coll (OR)
Trinity Valley Comm Coll (TX)

REAL ESTATE
Amarillo Coll (TX)
Antelope Valley Coll (CA)
Austin Comm Coll (TX)
Bristol Comm Coll (MA)
Broward Coll (FL)
Butte Coll (CA)
Cincinnati State Tech and Comm Coll (OH)
Coll of Marin (CA)
Coll of Southern Idaho (ID)
Coll of the Canyons (CA)
Collin County Comm Coll District (TX)
Columbus State Comm Coll (OH)
Comm Coll of Allegheny County (PA)
Cosumnes River Coll, Sacramento (CA)
De Anza Coll (CA)
Eastern Gateway Comm Coll (OH)
Florida State Coll at Jacksonville (FL)
Fullerton Coll (CA)
Gavilan Coll (CA)
Golden West Coll (CA)
Harrisburg Area Comm Coll (PA)
Hinds Comm Coll (MS)
Houston Comm Coll System (TX)

Iowa Lakes Comm Coll (IA)
J. Sargeant Reynolds Comm Coll (VA)
Lake Tahoe Comm Coll (CA)
Lamar State Coll–Orange (TX)
Lansing Comm Coll (MI)
Lorain County Comm Coll (OH)
Los Angeles Mission Coll (CA)
Luzerne County Comm Coll (PA)
Mesa Comm Coll (AZ)
MiraCosta Coll (CA)
Montgomery County Comm Coll (PA)
Mt. San Antonio Coll (CA)
Mt. San Jacinto Coll (CA)
Nassau Comm Coll (NY)
Northern Essex Comm Coll (MA)
Oakton Comm Coll (IL)
Palomar Coll (CA)
San Diego City Coll (CA)
San Jacinto Coll District (TX)
Santa Rosa Jr Coll (CA)
Scottsdale Comm Coll (AZ)
South Florida State Coll (FL)
South Plains Coll (TX)
Texarkana Coll (TX)
Trinity Valley Comm Coll (TX)
Tulsa Comm Coll (OK)
Victor Valley Coll (CA)
Waukesha County Tech Coll (WI)
Westmoreland County Comm Coll (PA)

RECEPTIONIST
Bristol Comm Coll (MA)
Dakota Coll at Bottineau (ND)
Iowa Lakes Comm Coll (IA)

RECORDING ARTS TECHNOLOGY
Bossier Parish Comm Coll (LA)
Comm Coll of Philadelphia (PA)
Finger Lakes Comm Coll (NY)
Fiorello H. LaGuardia Comm Coll of the City U of New York (NY)
Fullerton Coll (CA)
Glendale Comm Coll (AZ)
The Inst of Production and Recording (MN)
International Coll of Broadcasting (OH)
Lehigh Carbon Comm Coll (PA)
Los Angeles Film School (CA)
Miami Dade Coll (FL)
Minneapolis Comm and Tech Coll (MN)
MiraCosta Coll (CA)
Montgomery County Comm Coll (PA)
Phoenix Coll (AZ)
Schoolcraft Coll (MI)
Shoreline Comm Coll (WA)
South Plains Coll (TX)
Springfield Tech Comm Coll (MA)
Vincennes U (IN)

REGISTERED NURSING, NURSING ADMINISTRATION, NURSING RESEARCH AND CLINICAL NURSING RELATED
Genesee Comm Coll (NY)

REGISTERED NURSING/ REGISTERED NURSE
Alabama Southern Comm Coll (AL)
Alamance Comm Coll (NC)
Alexandria Tech and Comm Coll (MN)
Alvin Comm Coll (TX)
Amarillo Coll (TX)
Ancilla Coll (IN)
Anoka-Ramsey Comm Coll (MN)
Anoka-Ramsey Comm Coll, Cambridge Campus (MN)
Antelope Valley Coll (CA)
Arapahoe Comm Coll (CO)
Arkansas State U–Newport (AR)
Athens Tech Coll (GA)
Austin Comm Coll (TX)
Bainbridge State Coll (GA)
The Belanger School of Nursing (NY)
Bellingham Tech Coll (WA)
Berkshire Comm Coll (MA)
Bevill State Comm Coll (AL)
Big Bend Comm Coll (WA)
Bishop State Comm Coll (AL)
Bismarck State Coll (ND)
Blackhawk Tech Coll (WI)
Blue Ridge Comm and Tech Coll (WV)
Borough of Manhattan Comm Coll of the City U of New York (NY)
Bowling Green State U-Firelands Coll (OH)

Bristol Comm Coll (MA)
Bronx Comm Coll of the City U of New York (NY)
Brookhaven Coll (TX)
Broward Coll (FL)
Brown Mackie Coll–Albuquerque (NM)
Brown Mackie Coll–Findlay (OH)
Brown Mackie Coll–Fort Wayne (IN)
Brown Mackie Coll–Greenville (SC)
Brown Mackie Coll–Kansas City (KS)
Brown Mackie Coll–Miami (FL)
Brown Mackie Coll–North Canton (OH)
Brown Mackie Coll–Oklahoma City (OK)
Brown Mackie Coll–Phoenix (AZ)
Brown Mackie Coll–Salina (KS)
Brown Mackie Coll–Tulsa (OK)
Bucks County Comm Coll (PA)
Bunker Hill Comm Coll (MA)
Butler County Comm Coll (PA)
Butte Coll (CA)
Cape Fear Comm Coll (NC)
Carl Albert State Coll (OK)
Carolinas Coll of Health Sciences (NC)
Carrington Coll–Albuquerque (NM)
Carrington Coll–Boise (ID)
Carrington Coll California–Sacramento (CA)
Carrington Coll–Phoenix (AZ)
Carrington Coll–Phoenix Westside (AZ)
Carrington Coll–Reno (NV)
Carroll Comm Coll (MD)
Casper Coll (WY)
Catawba Valley Comm Coll (NC)
Cayuga County Comm Coll (NY)
Cecil Coll (MD)
Central Carolina Comm Coll (NC)
Central Maine Comm Coll (ME)
Central Maine Medical Center Coll of Nursing and Health Professions (ME)
Central Ohio Tech Coll (OH)
Central Oregon Comm Coll (OR)
Central Wyoming Coll (WY)
Century Coll (MN)
Chandler-Gilbert Comm Coll (AZ)
Chipola Coll (FL)
Chippewa Valley Tech Coll (WI)
Cincinnati State Tech and Comm Coll (OH)
Clark Coll (WA)
Clark State Comm Coll (OH)
Clatsop Comm Coll (OR)
Cleveland Comm Coll (NC)
Cleveland State Comm Coll (TN)
Clinton Comm Coll (NY)
Cloud County Comm Coll (KS)
Cochise Coll, Sierra Vista (AZ)
Coconino Comm Coll (AZ)
Coll of Central Florida (FL)
Coll of Marin (CA)
Coll of Southern Idaho (ID)
Coll of Southern Maryland (MD)
Coll of the Canyons (CA)
Coll of the Desert (CA)
Coll of the Mainland (TX)
Collin County Comm Coll District (TX)
Colorado Northwestern Comm Coll (CO)
Columbia Gorge Comm Coll (OR)
Columbia-Greene Comm Coll (NY)
Columbus State Comm Coll (OH)
Columbus Tech Coll (GA)
Comm Coll of Allegheny County (PA)
The Comm Coll of Baltimore County (MD)
Comm Coll of Philadelphia (PA)
Comm Coll of Rhode Island (RI)
Copiah-Lincoln Comm Coll (MS)
Copper Mountain Coll (CA)
County Coll of Morris (NJ)
Crowder Coll (MO)
Cumberland County Coll (NJ)
Dabney S. Lancaster Comm Coll (VA)
Dakota Coll at Bottineau (ND)
Danville Area Comm Coll (IL)
Darton State Coll (GA)
Daytona State Coll (FL)
De Anza Coll (CA)
Delaware Tech & Comm Coll, Jack F. Owens Campus (DE)
Delaware Tech & Comm Coll, Stanton/Wilmington Campus (DE)
Delaware Tech & Comm Coll, Terry Campus (DE)

Delta Coll (MI)
Dutchess Comm Coll (NY)
Dyersburg State Comm Coll (TN)
East Central Coll (MO)
Eastern Arizona Coll (AZ)
Eastern Florida State Coll (FL)
Eastern Idaho Tech Coll (ID)
Eastern Shore Comm Coll (VA)
Edison Comm Coll (OH)
Elgin Comm Coll (IL)
Erie Comm Coll (NY)
Erie Comm Coll, North Campus (NY)
Fayetteville Tech Comm Coll (NC)
Finger Lakes Comm Coll (NY)
Fiorello H. LaGuardia Comm Coll of the City U of New York (NY)
Flathead Valley Comm Coll (MT)
Florida Gateway Coll (FL)
Florida State Coll at Jacksonville (FL)
Fox Valley Tech Coll (WI)
Gadsden State Comm Coll (AL)
Galveston Coll (TX)
Garden City Comm Coll (KS)
Gateway Comm and Tech Coll (KY)
Gavilan Coll (CA)
Genesee Comm Coll (NY)
Georgia Highlands Coll (GA)
Glendale Comm Coll (AZ)
Glen Oaks Comm Coll (MI)
Gogebic Comm Coll (MI)
Golden West Coll (CA)
Goodwin Coll (CT)
Gordon State Coll (GA)
Grand Rapids Comm Coll (MI)
Grays Harbor Coll (WA)
Grayson Coll (TX)
Great Basin Coll (NV)
Greenfield Comm Coll (MA)
Greenville Tech Coll (SC)
Hagerstown Comm Coll (MD)
Halifax Comm Coll (NC)
Hallmark Coll of Technology (TX)
Harford Comm Coll (MD)
Harper Coll (IL)
Harrisburg Area Comm Coll (PA)
Hawkeye Comm Coll (IA)
Helena Coll U of Montana (MT)
Highland Comm Coll (IL)
Hillsborough Comm Coll (FL)
Hinds Comm Coll (MS)
Hocking Coll (OH)
Holyoke Comm Coll (MA)
Hopkinsville Comm Coll (KY)
Housatonic Comm Coll (CT)
Houston Comm Coll System (TX)
Howard Comm Coll (MD)
Hudson County Comm Coll (NJ)
Hutchinson Comm Coll and Area Vocational School (KS)
Illinois Eastern Comm Colls, Frontier Community College (IL)
Illinois Eastern Comm Colls, Olney Central College (IL)
Imperial Valley Coll (CA)
Iowa Lakes Comm Coll (IA)
ITT Tech Inst, Bessemer (AL)
ITT Tech Inst, Madison (AL)
ITT Tech Inst, Mobile (AL)
ITT Tech Inst, Rancho Cordova (CA)
ITT Tech Inst, Fort Lauderdale (FL)
ITT Tech Inst, Fort Myers (FL)
ITT Tech Inst, Jacksonville (FL)
ITT Tech Inst, Lake Mary (FL)
ITT Tech Inst, Miami (FL)
ITT Tech Inst, Orlando (FL)
ITT Tech Inst, St. Petersburg (FL)
ITT Tech Inst, Tallahassee (FL)
ITT Tech Inst, Tampa (FL)
ITT Tech Inst (ID)
ITT Tech Inst, Orland Park (IL)
ITT Tech Inst, Fort Wayne (IN)
ITT Tech Inst, Merrillville (IN)
ITT Tech Inst, Newburgh (IN)
ITT Tech Inst, Louisville (KY)
ITT Tech Inst, Canton (MI)
ITT Tech Inst , Earth City (MO)
ITT Tech Inst (NE)
ITT Tech Inst (NM)
ITT Tech Inst, High Point (NC)
ITT Tech Inst, Akron (OH)
ITT Tech Inst, Dayton (OH)
ITT Tech Inst, Hilliard (OH)
ITT Tech Inst, Norwood (OH)
ITT Tech Inst, Strongsville (OH)
ITT Tech Inst, Warrensville Heights (OH)
ITT Tech Inst , Youngstown (OH)
ITT Tech Inst, Tulsa (OK)
ITT Tech Inst, Portland (OR)
ITT Tech Inst, Nashville (TN)
ITT Tech Inst, Richardson (TX)

ITT Tech Inst, Norfolk (VA)
ITT Tech Inst, Salem (VA)
ITT Tech Inst (WV)
Ivy Tech Comm Coll–Bloomington (IN)
Ivy Tech Comm Coll–Central Indiana (IN)
Ivy Tech Comm Coll–East Central (IN)
Ivy Tech Comm Coll–Lafayette (IN)
Ivy Tech Comm Coll–North Central (IN)
Ivy Tech Comm Coll–Northwest (IN)
Ivy Tech Comm Coll–Richmond (IN)
Ivy Tech Comm Coll–Southeast (IN)
Ivy Tech Comm Coll–Southern Indiana (IN)
Ivy Tech Comm Coll–Southwest (IN)
Ivy Tech Comm Coll–Wabash Valley (IN)
Jackson Coll (MI)
Jackson State Comm Coll (TN)
James Sprunt Comm Coll (NC)
Jamestown Comm Coll (NY)
Jefferson Coll (MO)
Jefferson Comm Coll (NY)
Jefferson State Comm Coll (AL)
Johnston Comm Coll (NC)
John Tyler Comm Coll (VA)
J. Sargeant Reynolds Comm Coll (VA)
Kankakee Comm Coll (IL)
Kaskaskia Coll (IL)
Kent State U at Ashtabula (OH)
Kent State U at East Liverpool (OH)
Kent State U at Tuscarawas (OH)
Kilgore Coll (TX)
Kingsborough Comm Coll of the City U of New York (NY)
Kirtland Comm Coll (MI)
Lake Land Coll (IL)
Lakeland Comm Coll (OH)
Lake Region State Coll (ND)
Lakes Region Comm Coll (NH)
Lake Superior Coll (MN)
Lamar Comm Coll (CO)
Lamar State Coll–Orange (TX)
Lane Comm Coll (OR)
Lansing Comm Coll (MI)
Laramie County Comm Coll (WY)
Lawson State Comm Coll (AL)
Lehigh Carbon Comm Coll (PA)
Lenoir Comm Coll (NC)
Lincoln Land Comm Coll (IL)
Linn-Benton Comm Coll (OR)
Lone Star Coll–CyFair (TX)
Lone Star Coll–Kingwood (TX)
Lone Star Coll–Montgomery (TX)
Lone Star Coll–North Harris (TX)
Lone Star Coll–Tomball (TX)
Lorain County Comm Coll (OH)
Lower Columbia Coll (WA)
Lurleen B. Wallace Comm Coll (AL)
Luzerne County Comm Coll (PA)
Macomb Comm Coll (MI)
Manhattan Area Tech Coll (KS)
Massachusetts Bay Comm Coll (MA)
McHenry County Coll (IL)
Mercer County Comm Coll (NJ)
Mesa Comm Coll (AZ)
Metropolitan Comm Coll–Kansas City (MO)
Miami Dade Coll (FL)
Middlesex County Coll (NJ)
Mid-Plains Comm Coll, North Platte (NE)
Mineral Area Coll (MO)
Minneapolis Comm and Tech Coll (MN)
Minnesota State Coll–Southeast Tech (MN)
MiraCosta Coll (CA)
Mississippi Delta Comm Coll (MS)
Mississippi Gulf Coast Comm Coll (MS)
Missouri State U–West Plains (MO)
Mitchell Comm Coll (NC)
Mohave Comm Coll (AZ)
Mohawk Valley Comm Coll (NY)
Monroe Comm Coll (NY)
Monroe County Comm Coll (MI)
Montgomery Coll (MD)
Montgomery County Comm Coll (PA)
Moraine Park Tech Coll (WI)
Moraine Valley Comm Coll (IL)
Motlow State Comm Coll (TN)
Mott Comm Coll (MI)
Mountain Empire Comm Coll (VA)
Mt. San Antonio Coll (CA)
Mt. San Jacinto Coll (CA)

Mount Wachusett Comm Coll (MA)
Nassau Comm Coll (NY)
Niagara County Comm Coll (NY)
Normandale Comm Coll (MN)
Northampton Comm Coll (PA)
Northcentral Tech Coll (WI)
North Dakota State Coll of Science (ND)
Northeastern Jr Coll (CO)
Northeastern Tech Coll (SC)
Northeast Iowa Comm Coll (IA)
Northeast Texas Comm Coll (TX)
Northern Essex Comm Coll (MA)
North Iowa Area Comm Coll (IA)
North Shore Comm Coll (MA)
NorthWest Arkansas Comm Coll (AR)
Northwest Coll (WY)
Northwest Florida State Coll (FL)
Northwest Mississippi Comm Coll (MS)
Northwest-Shoals Comm Coll (AL)
Northwest Tech Coll (MN)
Norwalk Comm Coll (CT)
Oakland Comm Coll (MI)
Oakton Comm Coll (IL)
Ocean County Coll (NJ)
Oklahoma City Comm Coll (OK)
Oklahoma State U, Oklahoma City (OK)
Olympic Coll (WA)
Onondaga Comm Coll (NY)
Oregon Coast Comm Coll (OR)
Otero Jr Coll (CO)
Owensboro Comm and Tech Coll (KY)
Owens Comm Coll, Toledo (OH)
Palomar Coll (CA)
Panola Coll (TX)
Paris Jr Coll (TX)
Pasadena City Coll (CA)
Pasco-Hernando State Coll (FL)
Patrick Henry Comm Coll (VA)
Penn State Fayette, The Eberly Campus (PA)
Penn State Mont Alto (PA)
Penn State Worthington Scranton (PA)
Pennsylvania Coll of Health Sciences (PA)
Pensacola State Coll (FL)
Phoenix Coll (AZ)
Piedmont Comm Coll (NC)
Piedmont Virginia Comm Coll (VA)
Pima Comm Coll (AZ)
Pitt Comm Coll (NC)
Pittsburgh Tech Inst, Oakdale (PA)
Pueblo Comm Coll (CO)
Quinsigamond Comm Coll (MA)
Randolph Comm Coll (NC)
Rappahannock Comm Coll (VA)
Raritan Valley Comm Coll (NJ)
Reading Area Comm Coll (PA)
Richmond Comm Coll (NC)
Rio Hondo Coll (CA)
River Valley Comm Coll (NH)
Roane State Comm Coll (TN)
Rock Valley Coll (IL)
Rogue Comm Coll (OR)
St. Elizabeth Coll of Nursing (NY)
St. Luke's Coll (IA)
Salt Lake Comm Coll (UT)
San Diego City Coll (CA)
San Jacinto Coll District (TX)
San Joaquin Valley Coll, Hanford (CA)
San Joaquin Valley Coll, Hesperia (CA)
San Joaquin Valley Coll, Temecula (CA)
San Joaquin Valley Coll, Visalia (CA)
San Juan Coll (NM)
Santa Monica Coll (CA)
Santa Rosa Jr Coll (CA)
Sauk Valley Comm Coll (IL)
Schoolcraft Coll (MI)
Scottsdale Comm Coll (AZ)
Seminole State Coll (OK)
Seminole State Coll of Florida (FL)
Shawnee Comm Coll (IL)
Shelton State Comm Coll (AL)
Sheridan Coll (WY)
Shoreline Comm Coll (WA)
Snow Coll (UT)
Somerset Comm Coll (KY)
Southeastern Comm Coll (IA)
Southeastern Comm Coll (NC)
Southeast Tech Inst (SD)
Southern Maine Comm Coll (ME)
Southern State Comm Coll (OH)

Southern U at Shreveport (LA)
South Florida State Coll (FL)
South Georgia State Coll, Douglas (GA)
South Louisiana Comm Coll (LA)
South Piedmont Comm Coll (NC)
South Plains Coll (TX)
Southwestern Comm Coll (NC)
Southwestern Illinois Coll (IL)
Southwestern Michigan Coll (MI)
Southwest Georgia Tech Coll (GA)
Southwest Virginia Comm Coll (VA)
Spartanburg Comm Coll (SC)
Spencerian Coll (KY)
Spoon River Coll (IL)
Springfield Tech Comm Coll (MA)
Stark State Coll (OH)
State Fair Comm Coll (MO)
State U of New York Coll of Technology at Alfred (NY)
Sullivan County Comm Coll (NY)
Tallahassee Comm Coll (FL)
Tarrant County Coll District (TX)
Tech Coll of the Lowcountry (SC)
Temple Coll (TX)
Texarkana Coll (TX)
Three Rivers Comm Coll (CT)
Tompkins Cortland Comm Coll (NY)
Treasure Valley Comm Coll (OR)
Trident Tech Coll (SC)
Trinity Valley Comm Coll (TX)
Truckee Meadows Comm Coll (NV)
Tulsa Comm Coll (OK)
Tyler Jr Coll (TX)
Umpqua Comm Coll (OR)
U of Arkansas Comm Coll at Hope (AR)
U of Arkansas Comm Coll at Morrilton (AR)
U of Hawaii Maui Coll (HI)
Victoria Coll (TX)
Victor Valley Coll (CA)
Vincennes U (IN)
Virginia Western Comm Coll (VA)
Walla Walla Comm Coll (WA)
Walters State Comm Coll (TN)
Waubonsee Comm Coll (IL)
Waukesha County Tech Coll (WI)
Wayne Comm Coll (NC)
Wayne County Comm Coll District (MI)
Wenatchee Valley Coll (WA)
Westchester Comm Coll (NY)
Western Nevada Coll (NV)
Western Oklahoma State Coll (OK)
West Kentucky Comm and Tech Coll (KY)
Westmoreland County Comm Coll (PA)
Williston State Coll (ND)
Wor-Wic Comm Coll (MD)
Wytheville Comm Coll (VA)

REHABILITATION AND THERAPEUTIC PROFESSIONS RELATED
Central Wyoming Coll (WY)
Columbia-Greene Comm Coll (NY)
Columbus State Comm Coll (OH)
Iowa Lakes Comm Coll (IA)
Middlesex County Coll (NJ)
Nassau Comm Coll (NY)

RELIGIOUS STUDIES
Allen Comm Coll (KS)
Amarillo Coll (TX)
Broward Coll (FL)
Fullerton Coll (CA)
Kilgore Coll (TX)
Lansing Comm Coll (MI)
Laramie County Comm Coll (WY)
Orange Coast Coll (CA)
Pensacola State Coll (FL)
Santa Rosa Jr Coll (CA)
South Florida State Coll (FL)
Trinity Valley Comm Coll (TX)

RELIGIOUS STUDIES RELATED
Spartanburg Methodist Coll (SC)

RESORT MANAGEMENT
Coll of the Desert (CA)
Finger Lakes Comm Coll (NY)
Lehigh Carbon Comm Coll (PA)

RESPIRATORY CARE THERAPY
Alvin Comm Coll (TX)
Amarillo Coll (TX)
Athens Tech Coll (GA)
Augusta Tech Coll (GA)

Berkshire Comm Coll (MA)
Bossier Parish Comm Coll (LA)
Bowling Green State U-Firelands Coll (OH)
Broward Coll (FL)
Butte Coll (CA)
Carrington Coll–Mesa (AZ)
Carrington Coll–Phoenix (AZ)
Casper Coll (WY)
Catawba Valley Comm Coll (NC)
Central Virginia Comm Coll (VA)
Chippewa Valley Tech Coll (WI)
Cochise Coll, Sierra Vista (AZ)
Collin County Comm Coll District (TX)
Columbus State Comm Coll (OH)
Comm Coll of Allegheny County (PA)
The Comm Coll of Baltimore County (MD)
Comm Coll of Philadelphia (PA)
Comm Coll of Rhode Island (RI)
County Coll of Morris (NJ)
Cumberland County Coll (NJ)
Darton State Coll (GA)
Daytona State Coll (FL)
Delta Coll (MI)
East Central Coll (MO)
Eastern Gateway Comm Coll (OH)
Erie Comm Coll, North Campus (NY)
Fayetteville Tech Comm Coll (NC)
Florida State Coll at Jacksonville (FL)
Genesee Comm Coll (NY)
Goodwin Coll (CT)
Great Falls Coll Montana State U (MT)
Greenville Tech Coll (SC)
Gwinnett Tech Coll (GA)
Harrisburg Area Comm Coll (PA)
Hawkeye Comm Coll (IA)
Hillsborough Comm Coll (FL)
Hinds Comm Coll (MS)
Houston Comm Coll System (TX)
Hudson County Comm Coll (NJ)
Ivy Tech Comm Coll–Central Indiana (IN)
Ivy Tech Comm Coll–Lafayette (IN)
Ivy Tech Comm Coll–Northeast (IN)
Ivy Tech Comm Coll–Northwest (IN)
Ivy Tech Comm Coll–Southern Indiana (IN)
J. Sargeant Reynolds Comm Coll (VA)
Kankakee Comm Coll (IL)
Kaskaskia Coll (IL)
Kent State U at Ashtabula (OH)
Lakeland Comm Coll (OH)
Lake Superior Coll (MN)
Lane Comm Coll (OR)
Lincoln Land Comm Coll (IL)
Lone Star Coll–Kingwood (TX)
Luzerne County Comm Coll (PA)
Macomb Comm Coll (MI)
Manchester Comm Coll (CT)
Massachusetts Bay Comm Coll (MA)
Mercer County Comm Coll (NJ)
Metropolitan Comm Coll–Kansas City (MO)
Miami Dade Coll (FL)
Middlesex County Coll (NJ)
Mississippi Gulf Coast Comm Coll (MS)
Mohawk Valley Comm Coll (NY)
Monroe County Comm Coll (MI)
Moraine Park Tech Coll (WI)
Moraine Valley Comm Coll (IL)
Mott Comm Coll (MI)
Mountain Empire Comm Coll (VA)
Mt. San Antonio Coll (CA)
Nassau Comm Coll (NY)
Northeast Iowa Comm Coll (IA)
Northern Essex Comm Coll (MA)
North Shore Comm Coll (MA)
NorthWest Arkansas Comm Coll (AR)
Northwest Mississippi Comm Coll (MS)
Norwalk Comm Coll (CT)
Oakland Comm Coll (MI)
Oklahoma City Comm Coll (OK)
Onondaga Comm Coll (NY)
Orange Coast Coll (CA)
Ozarks Tech Comm Coll (MO)
Pennsylvania Coll of Health Sciences (PA)
Pima Comm Coll (AZ)
Pitt Comm Coll (NC)
Pueblo Comm Coll (CO)
Quinsigamond Comm Coll (MA)
Raritan Valley Comm Coll (NJ)

Reading Area Comm Coll (PA)
River Valley Comm Coll (NH)
Roane State Comm Coll (TN)
Rock Valley Coll (IL)
St. Luke's Coll (IA)
San Jacinto Coll District (TX)
San Joaquin Valley Coll, Bakersfield (CA)
San Joaquin Valley Coll, Hanford (CA)
San Joaquin Valley Coll, Hesperia (CA)
San Joaquin Valley Coll, Temecula (CA)
San Joaquin Valley Coll, Visalia (CA)
San Juan Coll (NM)
Santa Monica Coll (CA)
Seminole State Coll of Florida (FL)
Shelton State Comm Coll (AL)
Somerset Comm Coll (KY)
Southeastern Comm Coll (IA)
Southern Maine Comm Coll (ME)
Southern State Comm Coll (OH)
Southern U at Shreveport (LA)
South Florida State Coll (FL)
South Plains Coll (TX)
Southwestern Comm Coll (NC)
Southwestern Illinois Coll (IL)
Southwest Georgia Tech Coll (GA)
Spartanburg Comm Coll (SC)
Spencerian Coll (KY)
Springfield Tech Comm Coll (MA)
Stark State Coll (OH)
Sullivan County Comm Coll (NY)
Tallahassee Comm Coll (FL)
Tarrant County Coll District (TX)
Temple Coll (TX)
Trident Tech Coll (SC)
Tulsa Comm Coll (OK)
Tyler Jr Coll (TX)
U of Arkansas Comm Coll at Hope (AR)
Victoria Coll (TX)
Victor Valley Coll (CA)
Volunteer State Comm Coll (TN)
Walters State Comm Coll (TN)
Westchester Comm Coll (NY)
West Kentucky Comm and Tech Coll (KY)

RESPIRATORY THERAPY TECHNICIAN
Augusta Tech Coll (GA)
Borough of Manhattan Comm Coll of the City U of New York (NY)
Bunker Hill Comm Coll (MA)
Career Tech Coll, Monroe (LA)
Carrington Coll California–Pleasant Hill (CA)
Carrington Coll–Las Vegas (NV)
Carrington Coll–Mesa (AZ)
Carrington Coll–Phoenix Westside (AZ)
Columbus Tech Coll (GA)
Delaware Tech & Comm Coll, Jack F. Owens Campus (DE)
Delaware Tech & Comm Coll, Stanton/Wilmington Campus (DE)
Georgia Highlands Coll (GA)
Georgia Northwestern Tech Coll (GA)
Hutchinson Comm Coll and Area Vocational School (KS)
Miami Dade Coll (FL)
Mineral Area Coll (MO)
Missouri State U–West Plains (MO)
Northern Essex Comm Coll (MA)
Okefenokee Tech Coll (GA)
San Joaquin Valley Coll, Ontario (CA)
San Joaquin Valley Coll, Rancho Cordova (CA)
Southeastern Tech Coll (GA)
Southern Crescent Tech Coll (GA)

RESTAURANT, CULINARY, AND CATERING MANAGEMENT
Blackhawk Tech Coll (WI)
Blue Ridge Comm and Tech Coll (WV)
Broward Coll (FL)
Cincinnati State Tech and Comm Coll (OH)
Coll of Central Florida (FL)
Coll of the Canyons (CA)
Columbia Coll (CA)
Comm Coll of Allegheny County (PA)
Cosumnes River Coll, Sacramento (CA)
Culinary Inst LeNotre (TX)

Delaware Tech & Comm Coll, Stanton/Wilmington Campus (DE)
Elgin Comm Coll (IL)
Erie Comm Coll, North Campus (NY)
Hillsborough Comm Coll (FL)
Iowa Lakes Comm Coll (IA)
Lakeland Comm Coll (OH)
Lane Comm Coll (OR)
Linn-Benton Comm Coll (OR)
McHenry County Coll (IL)
MiraCosta Coll (CA)
Mohawk Valley Comm Coll (NY)
Moraine Valley Comm Coll (IL)
New England Culinary Inst (VT)
Orange Coast Coll (CA)
Pensacola State Coll (FL)
Pima Comm Coll (AZ)
Raritan Valley Comm Coll (NJ)
Reading Area Comm Coll (PA)
San Jacinto Coll District (TX)
Southwestern Illinois Coll (IL)
Vincennes U (IN)
Waukesha County Tech Coll (WI)
Westmoreland County Comm Coll (PA)

RESTAURANT/FOOD SERVICES MANAGEMENT
Broward Coll (FL)
Fiorello H. LaGuardia Comm Coll of the City U of New York (NY)
Hillsborough Comm Coll (FL)
Iowa Lakes Comm Coll (IA)
J. Sargeant Reynolds Comm Coll (VA)
Lakes Region Comm Coll (NH)
Minneapolis Comm and Tech Coll (MN)
Northampton Comm Coll (PA)
Norwalk Comm Coll (CT)
Oakland Comm Coll (MI)
Owens Comm Coll, Toledo (OH)
Oxnard Coll (CA)
Quinsigamond Comm Coll (MA)
Santa Rosa Jr Coll (CA)

RETAILING
Alamance Comm Coll (NC)
Bradford School (PA)
Bucks County Comm Coll (PA)
Butte Coll (CA)
Ca&nnada Coll (CA)
Casper Coll (WY)
Central Oregon Comm Coll (OR)
Clark Coll (WA)
Comm Coll of Allegheny County (PA)
Delta Coll (MI)
Elgin Comm Coll (IL)
Florida State Coll at Jacksonville (FL)
Garden City Comm Coll (KS)
Holyoke Comm Coll (MA)
Hutchinson Comm Coll and Area Vocational School (KS)
Iowa Lakes Comm Coll (IA)
Minnesota State Coll–Southeast Tech (MN)
MiraCosta Coll (CA)
Moraine Valley Comm Coll (IL)
Nassau Comm Coll (NY)
Orange Coast Coll (CA)
Wood Tobe–Coburn School (NY)

RETAIL MANAGEMENT
Collin County Comm Coll District (TX)
Davis Coll (OH)

RHETORIC AND COMPOSITION
Alabama Southern Comm Coll (AL)
Allen Comm Coll (KS)
Amarillo Coll (TX)
Austin Comm Coll (TX)
Bainbridge State Coll (GA)
Carl Albert State Coll (OK)
De Anza Coll (CA)
Gavilan Coll (CA)
Iowa Lakes Comm Coll (IA)
Linn-Benton Comm Coll (OR)
MiraCosta Coll (CA)
Monroe County Comm Coll (MI)
Palomar Coll (CA)
Paris Jr Coll (TX)
San Diego City Coll (CA)
San Jacinto Coll District (TX)
Santa Monica Coll (CA)
South Florida State Coll (FL)
Spoon River Coll (IL)
Trinity Valley Comm Coll (TX)

ROBOTICS TECHNOLOGY
Butler County Comm Coll (PA)
Casper Coll (WY)

Comm Coll of Allegheny County (PA)
Daytona State Coll (FL)
Dunwoody Coll of Technology (MN)
Ivy Tech Comm Coll–Columbus (IN)
Ivy Tech Comm Coll–Lafayette (IN)
Ivy Tech Comm Coll–North Central (IN)
Ivy Tech Comm Coll–Northeast (IN)
Ivy Tech Comm Coll–Richmond (IN)
Ivy Tech Comm Coll–Southwest (IN)
Ivy Tech Comm Coll–Wabash Valley (IN)
Kaskaskia Coll (IL)
Kirtland Comm Coll (MI)
Lake Area Tech Inst (SD)
Macomb Comm Coll (MI)
McHenry County Coll (IL)
Oakland Comm Coll (MI)
St. Clair County Comm Coll (MI)
Southern U at Shreveport (LA)
State U of New York Coll of Technology at Alfred (NY)
Sullivan Coll of Technology and Design (KY)
Texas State Tech Coll Waco (TX)
Vincennes U (IN)
Wichita Area Tech Coll (KS)

RUSSIAN
Austin Comm Coll (TX)

SALES AND MARKETING/MARKETING AND DISTRIBUTION TEACHER EDUCATION
Broward Coll (FL)
Northwest Mississippi Comm Coll (MS)

SALES, DISTRIBUTION, AND MARKETING OPERATIONS
Alexandria Tech and Comm Coll (MN)
Anoka-Ramsey Comm Coll (MN)
Anoka-Ramsey Comm Coll, Cambridge Campus (MN)
Butte Coll (CA)
Coll of the Canyons (CA)
Cosumnes River Coll, Sacramento (CA)
Fullerton Coll (CA)
Gadsden State Comm Coll (AL)
Greenfield Comm Coll (MA)
Greenville Tech Coll (SC)
Harper Coll (IL)
Harrisburg Area Comm Coll (PA)
Hawkeye Comm Coll (IA)
Iowa Lakes Comm Coll (IA)
Lake Area Tech Inst (SD)
Lansing Comm Coll (MI)
Minnesota State Coll–Southeast Tech (MN)
MiraCosta Coll (CA)
Montgomery County Comm Coll (PA)
Northeast Iowa Comm Coll (IA)
North Iowa Area Comm Coll (IA)
Northwest Tech Coll (MN)
Oakton Comm Coll (IL)
Owens Comm Coll, Toledo (OH)
Santa Monica Coll (CA)
U of New Mexico–Los Alamos Branch (NM)
Westmoreland County Comm Coll (PA)

SALON/BEAUTY SALON MANAGEMENT
Delta Coll (MI)
Mott Comm Coll (MI)
Oakland Comm Coll (MI)
Schoolcraft Coll (MI)

SCIENCE TEACHER EDUCATION
Darton State Coll (GA)
Iowa Lakes Comm Coll (IA)
Mississippi Delta Comm Coll (MS)
Moraine Valley Comm Coll (IL)
Northwest Mississippi Comm Coll (MS)
San Jacinto Coll District (TX)
Snow Coll (UT)
South Florida State Coll (FL)
Vincennes U (IN)

SCIENCE TECHNOLOGIES
Central Virginia Comm Coll (VA)
Harford Comm Coll (MD)
Waubonsee Comm Coll (IL)

SCIENCE TECHNOLOGIES RELATED
Blue Ridge Comm and Tech Coll (WV)
Cascadia Comm Coll (WA)
Cayuga County Comm Coll (NY)
Cleveland State Comm Coll (TN)
Comm Coll of Allegheny County (PA)
Dakota Coll at Bottineau (ND)
Delaware Tech & Comm Coll, Stanton/Wilmington Campus (DE)
Jackson State Comm Coll (TN)
Oakland Comm Coll (MI)
Pueblo Comm Coll (CO)
Reading Area Comm Coll (PA)
Sullivan County Comm Coll (NY)
Victor Valley Coll (CA)
Volunteer State Comm Coll (TN)

SCULPTURE
De Anza Coll (CA)
Mercer County Comm Coll (NJ)
Palomar Coll (CA)
Schoolcraft Coll (MI)

SECONDARY EDUCATION
Alabama Southern Comm Coll (AL)
Allen Comm Coll (KS)
Ancilla Coll (IN)
Arizona Western Coll (AZ)
Austin Comm Coll (TX)
Brookhaven Coll (TX)
Carl Albert State Coll (OK)
Cecil Coll (MD)
Central Wyoming Coll (WY)
Coll of the Mainland (TX)
Collin County Comm Coll District (TX)
Eastern Arizona Coll (AZ)
Eastern Wyoming Coll (WY)
Frank Phillips Coll (TX)
Georgia Highlands Coll (GA)
Georgia Military Coll (GA)
Gogebic Comm Coll (MI)
Gordon State Coll (GA)
Grayson Coll (TX)
Harford Comm Coll (MD)
Harrisburg Area Comm Coll (PA)
Hinds Comm Coll (MS)
Howard Comm Coll (MD)
Kankakee Comm Coll (IL)
Lansing Comm Coll (MI)
Montgomery County Comm Coll (PA)
Northampton Comm Coll (PA)
Northwest Coll (WY)
Paris Jr Coll (TX)
Reading Area Comm Coll (PA)
San Jacinto Coll District (TX)
San Juan Coll (NM)
Sauk Valley Comm Coll (IL)
Sheridan Coll (WY)
South Florida State Coll (FL)
Springfield Tech Comm Coll (MA)
State U of New York Coll of Technology at Alfred (NY)
Treasure Valley Comm Coll (OR)
Vincennes U (IN)
Western Wyoming Comm Coll (WY)

SECURITIES SERVICES ADMINISTRATION
TCI–The Coll of Technology (NY)
Vincennes U (IN)

SECURITY AND LOSS PREVENTION
Delta Coll (MI)
Palomar Coll (CA)
Tallahassee Comm Coll (FL)
Vincennes U (IN)

SELLING SKILLS AND SALES
Butler County Comm Coll (PA)
Clark Coll (WA)
Danville Area Comm Coll (IL)
Iowa Lakes Comm Coll (IA)
Lansing Comm Coll (MI)
McHenry County Coll (IL)
Minnesota State Coll–Southeast Tech (MN)
Northwest Florida State Coll (FL)
Orange Coast Coll (CA)
Santa Monica Coll (CA)
Southwestern Illinois Coll (IL)

SHEET METAL TECHNOLOGY
Coconino Comm Coll (AZ)
Comm Coll of Allegheny County (PA)
Delta Coll (MI)
Ivy Tech Comm Coll–Central Indiana (IN)
Ivy Tech Comm Coll–Lafayette (IN)

Ivy Tech Comm Coll–North Central (IN)
Ivy Tech Comm Coll–Northeast (IN)
Ivy Tech Comm Coll–Northwest (IN)
Ivy Tech Comm Coll–Southern Indiana (IN)
Ivy Tech Comm Coll–Southwest (IN)
Ivy Tech Comm Coll–Wabash Valley (IN)
Lake Superior Coll (MN)
Macomb Comm Coll (MI)
Palomar Coll (CA)
Rock Valley Coll (IL)
Southwestern Illinois Coll (IL)
Vincennes U (IN)

SIGN LANGUAGE INTERPRETATION AND TRANSLATION
Austin Comm Coll (TX)
Berkeley City Coll (CA)
Cincinnati State Tech and Comm Coll (OH)
Coconino Comm Coll (AZ)
Coll of the Canyons (CA)
Collin County Comm Coll District (TX)
Columbus State Comm Coll (OH)
Comm Coll of Allegheny County (PA)
The Comm Coll of Baltimore County (MD)
Comm Coll of Philadelphia (PA)
Florida State Coll at Jacksonville (FL)
Golden West Coll (CA)
Hinds Comm Coll (MS)
Houston Comm Coll System (TX)
J. Sargeant Reynolds Comm Coll (VA)
Lakeland Comm Coll (OH)
Lansing Comm Coll (MI)
Miami Dade Coll (FL)
Mohawk Valley Comm Coll (NY)
Mott Comm Coll (MI)
Mt. San Antonio Coll (CA)
Northcentral Tech Coll (WI)
Northern Essex Comm Coll (MA)
Northwestern Connecticut Comm Coll (CT)
Oakland Comm Coll (MI)
Ocean County Coll (NJ)
Oklahoma State U, Oklahoma City (OK)
Palomar Coll (CA)
Phoenix Coll (AZ)
Salt Lake Comm Coll (UT)
Southwestern Illinois Coll (IL)
Tarrant County Coll District (TX)
Tulsa Comm Coll (OK)
Tyler Jr Coll (TX)
Waubonsee Comm Coll (IL)

SMALL BUSINESS ADMINISTRATION
Borough of Manhattan Comm Coll of the City U of New York (NY)
Butte Coll (CA)
Ca&nnada Coll (CA)
Coll of the Canyons (CA)
Colorado Northwestern Comm Coll (CO)
Cosumnes River Coll, Sacramento (CA)
Dakota Coll at Bottineau (ND)
Delta Coll (MI)
Flathead Valley Comm Coll (MT)
Fullerton Coll (CA)
Harper Coll (IL)
Harrisburg Area Comm Coll (PA)
Helena Coll U of Montana (MT)
Independence Comm Coll (KS)
Iowa Lakes Comm Coll (IA)
J. Sargeant Reynolds Comm Coll (VA)
Lake Area Tech Inst (SD)
Middlesex County Coll (NJ)
MiraCosta Coll (CA)
Moraine Valley Comm Coll (IL)
Raritan Valley Comm Coll (NJ)
Schoolcraft Coll (MI)
South Suburban Coll (IL)
Southwestern Illinois Coll (IL)
Springfield Tech Comm Coll (MA)
Waubonsee Comm Coll (IL)

SMALL ENGINE MECHANICS AND REPAIR TECHNOLOGY
Coll of Western Idaho (ID)
Iowa Lakes Comm Coll (IA)
Mitchell Tech Inst (SD)
North Dakota State Coll of Science (ND)

SOCIAL PSYCHOLOGY
Broward Coll (FL)
Macomb Comm Coll (MI)
South Florida State Coll (FL)

SOCIAL SCIENCES
Alabama Southern Comm Coll (AL)
Amarillo Coll (TX)
Arizona Western Coll (AZ)
Barstow Comm Coll (CA)
Bristol Comm Coll (MA)
Broward Coll (FL)
Butte Coll (CA)
Carl Albert State Coll (OK)
Central Oregon Comm Coll (OR)
Central Wyoming Coll (WY)
Clinton Comm Coll (NY)
Cochise Coll, Sierra Vista (AZ)
Coll of Marin (CA)
Coll of Southern Idaho (ID)
Coll of the Canyons (CA)
Coll of the Desert (CA)
Comm Coll of Allegheny County (PA)
Comm Coll of Vermont (VT)
Copper Mountain Coll (CA)
Cosumnes River Coll, Sacramento (CA)
Dakota Coll at Bottineau (ND)
De Anza Coll (CA)
Eastern Wyoming Coll (WY)
Feather River Coll (CA)
Finger Lakes Comm Coll (NY)
Galveston Coll (TX)
Garden City Comm Coll (KS)
Gavilan Coll (CA)
Genesee Comm Coll (NY)
Georgia Military Coll (GA)
Greenfield Comm Coll (MA)
Harrisburg Area Comm Coll (PA)
Hinds Comm Coll (MS)
Housatonic Comm Coll (CT)
Howard Comm Coll (MD)
Hutchinson Comm Coll and Area Vocational School (KS)
Imperial Valley Coll (CA)
Independence Comm Coll (KS)
Iowa Lakes Comm Coll (IA)
J. Sargeant Reynolds Comm Coll (VA)
Kilgore Coll (TX)
Lake Tahoe Comm Coll (CA)
Lamar State Coll–Orange (TX)
Lansing Comm Coll (MI)
Laramie County Comm Coll (WY)
Lorain County Comm Coll (OH)
Los Angeles Mission Coll (CA)
Luzerne County Comm Coll (PA)
Massachusetts Bay Comm Coll (MA)
Miami Dade Coll (FL)
MiraCosta Coll (CA)
Monroe Comm Coll (NY)
Montgomery County Comm Coll (PA)
Mt. San Antonio Coll (CA)
Mt. San Jacinto Coll (CA)
Niagara County Comm Coll (NY)
Northeastern Jr Coll (CO)
Northwest Coll (WY)
Northwestern Connecticut Comm Coll (CT)
Orange Coast Coll (CA)
Otero Jr Coll (CO)
Palomar Coll (CA)
Paris Jr Coll (TX)
Reading Area Comm Coll (PA)
Roane State Comm Coll (TN)
San Diego City Coll (CA)
San Jacinto Coll District (TX)
Santa Rosa Jr Coll (CA)
Seminole State Coll (OK)
Sheridan Coll (WY)
South Florida State Coll (FL)
Spoon River Coll (IL)
Texarkana Coll (TX)
Treasure Valley Comm Coll (OR)
Tulsa Comm Coll (OK)
Tyler Jr Coll (TX)
Umpqua Comm Coll (OR)
Victor Valley Coll (CA)
Westchester Comm Coll (NY)
Western Wyoming Comm Coll (WY)

SOCIAL SCIENCES RELATED
Berkeley City Coll (CA)
Genesee Comm Coll (NY)
Greenfield Comm Coll (MA)

SOCIAL SCIENCE TEACHER EDUCATION
Northwest Mississippi Comm Coll (MS)
South Florida State Coll (FL)

SOCIAL STUDIES TEACHER EDUCATION
Broward Coll (FL)
Casper Coll (WY)
Northwest Mississippi Comm Coll (MS)

SOCIAL WORK
Allen Comm Coll (KS)
Amarillo Coll (TX)
Austin Comm Coll (TX)
Bismarck State Coll (ND)
Bowling Green State U–Firelands Coll (OH)
Bristol Comm Coll (MA)
Broward Coll (FL)
Casper Coll (WY)
Central Carolina Comm Coll (NC)
Chandler-Gilbert Comm Coll (AZ)
Chipola Coll (FL)
Clark State Comm Coll (OH)
Cochise Coll, Sierra Vista (AZ)
Comm Coll of Allegheny County (PA)
Comm Coll of Rhode Island (RI)
Cumberland County Coll (NJ)
Darton State Coll (GA)
Edison Comm Coll (OH)
Elgin Comm Coll (IL)
Galveston Coll (TX)
Garden City Comm Coll (KS)
Genesee Comm Coll (NY)
Gogebic Comm Coll (MI)
Gordon State Coll (GA)
Greenville Tech Coll (SC)
Harford Comm Coll (MD)
Harrisburg Area Comm Coll (PA)
Holyoke Comm Coll (MA)
Hopkinsville Comm Coll (KY)
Hudson County Comm Coll (NJ)
Illinois Eastern Comm Colls, Wabash Valley College (IL)
Iowa Lakes Comm Coll (IA)
Kilian Comm Coll (SD)
Lake Land Coll (IL)
Lakeland Comm Coll (OH)
Lawson State Comm Coll (AL)
Lehigh Carbon Comm Coll (PA)
Lorain County Comm Coll (OH)
Manchester Comm Coll (CT)
Miami Dade Coll (FL)
Mississippi Delta Comm Coll (MS)
Monroe County Comm Coll (MI)
Northampton Comm Coll (PA)
Northeastern Jr Coll (CO)
Northeast Iowa Comm Coll (IA)
Northeast Texas Comm Coll (TX)
Oakton Comm Coll (IL)
Paris Jr Coll (TX)
Pima Comm Coll (AZ)
Potomac State Coll of West Virginia U (WV)
Reading Area Comm Coll (PA)
Rogue Comm Coll (OR)
Salt Lake Comm Coll (UT)
San Diego City Coll (CA)
San Juan Coll (NM)
Sauk Valley Comm Coll (IL)
Shawnee Comm Coll (IL)
South Florida State Coll (FL)
South Plains Coll (TX)
South Suburban Coll (IL)
Southwestern Illinois Coll (IL)
Southwestern Michigan Coll (MI)
Treasure Valley Comm Coll (OR)
Tulsa Comm Coll (OK)
Umpqua Comm Coll (OR)
The U of Akron–Wayne Coll (OH)
Vincennes U (IN)
Waubonsee Comm Coll (IL)
Wayne County Comm Coll District (MI)
Western Wyoming Comm Coll (WY)
West Georgia Tech Coll (GA)
York County Comm Coll (ME)

SOCIAL WORK RELATED
Berkeley City Coll (CA)
Butler County Comm Coll (PA)
Genesee Comm Coll (NY)

SOCIOLOGY
Allen Comm Coll (KS)
Austin Comm Coll (TX)
Bainbridge State Coll (GA)
Berkeley City Coll (CA)
Broward Coll (FL)
Bunker Hill Comm Coll (MA)
Ca&nnada Coll (CA)
Casper Coll (WY)
Coconino Comm Coll (AZ)

Coll of Southern Idaho (ID)
Coll of the Canyons (CA)
Coll of the Desert (CA)
Coll of Western Idaho (ID)
Comm Coll of Allegheny County (PA)
Darton State Coll (GA)
De Anza Coll (CA)
Eastern Arizona Coll (AZ)
Finger Lakes Comm Coll (NY)
Frank Phillips Coll (TX)
Fullerton Coll (CA)
Georgia Highlands Coll (GA)
Gordon State Coll (GA)
Grayson Coll (TX)
Great Basin Coll (NV)
Harford Comm Coll (MD)
Hinds Comm Coll (MS)
Iowa Lakes Comm Coll (IA)
Kankakee Comm Coll (IL)
Kilian Comm Coll (SD)
Lansing Comm Coll (MI)
Laramie County Comm Coll (WY)
Lorain County Comm Coll (OH)
Los Angeles Mission Coll (CA)
Miami Dade Coll (FL)
MiraCosta Coll (CA)
Mohave Comm Coll (AZ)
Northeast Texas Comm Coll (TX)
Northwest Coll (WY)
Oklahoma City Comm Coll (OK)
Orange Coast Coll (CA)
Oxnard Coll (CA)
Paris Jr Coll (TX)
Pasadena City Coll (CA)
Pensacola State Coll (FL)
Pima Comm Coll (AZ)
Potomac State Coll of West Virginia U (WV)
Salt Lake Comm Coll (UT)
San Diego City Coll (CA)
San Jacinto Coll District (TX)
Santa Rosa Jr Coll (CA)
Sauk Valley Comm Coll (IL)
Snow Coll (UT)
Southern U at Shreveport (LA)
South Florida State Coll (FL)
South Georgia State Coll, Douglas (GA)
Spoon River Coll (IL)
Trinity Valley Comm Coll (TX)
Umpqua Comm Coll (OR)
Vincennes U (IN)
Wenatchee Valley Coll (WA)
Western Wyoming Comm Coll (WY)

SOCIOLOGY AND ANTHROPOLOGY
Harper Coll (IL)

SOIL SCIENCE AND AGRONOMY
Iowa Lakes Comm Coll (IA)
The Ohio State U Ag Tech Inst (OH)
Snow Coll (UT)
South Florida State Coll (FL)
Treasure Valley Comm Coll (OR)

SOLAR ENERGY TECHNOLOGY
Arizona Western Coll (AZ)
Coconino Comm Coll (AZ)
Comm Coll of Allegheny County (PA)
Crowder Coll (MO)
Pueblo Comm Coll (CO)
San Juan Coll (NM)
Texas State Tech Coll Waco (TX)
Treasure Valley Comm Coll (OR)

SPANISH
Arizona Western Coll (AZ)
Austin Comm Coll (TX)
Berkeley City Coll (CA)
Broward Coll (FL)
Ca&nnada Coll (CA)
Coll of Marin (CA)
Coll of the Canyons (CA)
Coll of the Desert (CA)
Copper Mountain Coll (CA)
Cosumnes River Coll, Sacramento (CA)
De Anza Coll (CA)
Fiorello H. LaGuardia Comm Coll of the City U of New York (NY)
Gavilan Coll (CA)
Grayson Coll (TX)
Imperial Valley Coll (CA)
Iowa Lakes Comm Coll (IA)
Lake Tahoe Comm Coll (CA)
Lansing Comm Coll (MI)
Laramie County Comm Coll (WY)
Los Angeles Mission Coll (CA)

Miami Dade Coll (FL)
MiraCosta Coll (CA)
Northeast Texas Comm Coll (TX)
Northwest Coll (WY)
Orange Coast Coll (CA)
Oxnard Coll (CA)
Pasadena City Coll (CA)
Santa Rosa Jr Coll (CA)
Snow Coll (UT)
South Florida State Coll (FL)
Trinity Valley Comm Coll (TX)
Western Wyoming Comm Coll (WY)

SPANISH LANGUAGE TEACHER EDUCATION
Carroll Comm Coll (MD)
The Comm Coll of Baltimore County (MD)
Harford Comm Coll (MD)
Montgomery Coll (MD)

SPECIAL EDUCATION
Alabama Southern Comm Coll (AL)
Broward Coll (FL)
Comm Coll of Rhode Island (RI)
Darton State Coll (GA)
Highland Comm Coll (IL)
Kankakee Comm Coll (IL)
Lehigh Carbon Comm Coll (PA)
Lincoln Land Comm Coll (IL)
McHenry County Coll (IL)
Moraine Valley Comm Coll (IL)
Normandale Comm Coll (MN)
Pensacola State Coll (FL)
Rend Lake Coll (IL)
San Juan Coll (NM)
Sauk Valley Comm Coll (IL)
South Florida State Coll (FL)
Truckee Meadows Comm Coll (NV)
Vincennes U (IN)

SPECIAL EDUCATION–EARLY CHILDHOOD
Mitchell Comm Coll (NC)
Motlow State Comm Coll (TN)
Santa Monica Coll (CA)

SPECIAL EDUCATION– ELEMENTARY SCHOOL
Truckee Meadows Comm Coll (NV)
Westmoreland County Comm Coll (PA)

SPECIAL EDUCATION– INDIVIDUALS WITH EMOTIONAL DISTURBANCES
Broward Coll (FL)
South Florida State Coll (FL)

SPECIAL EDUCATION– INDIVIDUALS WITH HEARING IMPAIRMENTS
Hillsborough Comm Coll (FL)

SPECIAL EDUCATION– INDIVIDUALS WITH INTELLECTUAL DISABILITIES
Broward Coll (FL)
South Florida State Coll (FL)

SPECIAL EDUCATION– INDIVIDUALS WITH SPECIFIC LEARNING DISABILITIES
Broward Coll (FL)
South Florida State Coll (FL)

SPECIAL EDUCATION– INDIVIDUALS WITH VISION IMPAIRMENTS
Broward Coll (FL)
South Florida State Coll (FL)

SPECIAL PRODUCTS MARKETING
Copiah-Lincoln Comm Coll (MS)
Metropolitan Comm Coll–Kansas City (MO)
Monroe Comm Coll (NY)
Orange Coast Coll (CA)
San Diego City Coll (CA)
Scottsdale Comm Coll (AZ)
South Plains Coll (TX)
State Fair Comm Coll (MO)
Three Rivers Comm Coll (CT)

SPEECH COMMUNICATION AND RHETORIC
Bristol Comm Coll (MA)
Brookhaven Coll (TX)
Bucks County Comm Coll (PA)
Bunker Hill Comm Coll (MA)

Ca&nnada Coll (CA)
Casper Coll (WY)
Central Oregon Comm Coll (OR)
Cochise Coll, Sierra Vista (AZ)
Coll of Marin (CA)
Coll of Southern Idaho (ID)
Coll of the Canyons (CA)
Coll of the Desert (CA)
Collin County Comm Coll District (TX)
Columbia Coll (CA)
Cosumnes River Coll, Sacramento (CA)
Dean Coll (MA)
Dutchess Comm Coll (NY)
Eastern Wyoming Coll (WY)
Edison Comm Coll (OH)
Erie Comm Coll, South Campus (NY)
Fiorello H. LaGuardia Comm Coll of the City U of New York (NY)
Fullerton Coll (CA)
Garden City Comm Coll (KS)
Harper Coll (IL)
Hinds Comm Coll (MS)
Hutchinson Comm Coll and Area Vocational School (KS)
Independence Comm Coll (KS)
Jamestown Comm Coll (NY)
Lansing Comm Coll (MI)
Laramie County Comm Coll (WY)
Lehigh Carbon Comm Coll (PA)
Lone Star Coll–CyFair (TX)
Lone Star Coll–U Park (TX)
Macomb Comm Coll (MI)
Manchester Comm Coll (CT)
Massachusetts Bay Comm Coll (MA)
Montgomery Coll (MD)
Montgomery County Comm Coll (PA)
Mountain View Coll (TX)
Nassau Comm Coll (NY)
Northampton Comm Coll (PA)
Northwest Coll (WY)
Norwalk Comm Coll (CT)
Onondaga Comm Coll (NY)
Oxnard Coll (CA)
Pasadena City Coll (CA)
Salt Lake Comm Coll (UT)
San Jacinto Coll District (TX)
Sauk Valley Comm Coll (IL)
South Florida State Coll (FL)
Tompkins Cortland Comm Coll (NY)
Treasure Valley Comm Coll (OR)
Tyler Jr Coll (TX)
Western Wyoming Comm Coll (WY)

SPEECH-LANGUAGE PATHOLOGY
Lake Region State Coll (ND)
Williston State Coll (ND)

SPEECH-LANGUAGE PATHOLOGY ASSISTANT
Alexandria Tech and Comm Coll (MN)
Fayetteville Tech Comm Coll (NC)
Mitchell Tech Inst (SD)
Oklahoma City Comm Coll (OK)

SPEECH TEACHER EDUCATION
Darton State Coll (GA)
Northwest Mississippi Comm Coll (MS)

SPORT AND FITNESS ADMINISTRATION/ MANAGEMENT
Bucks County Comm Coll (PA)
Butler County Comm Coll (PA)
Ca&nnada Coll (CA)
Cayuga County Comm Coll (NY)
Central Oregon Comm Coll (OR)
Clark Coll (WA)
Columbus State Comm Coll (OH)
Dean Coll (MA)
Delta Coll (MI)
Fullerton Coll (CA)
Garrett Coll (MD)
Holyoke Comm Coll (MA)
Howard Comm Coll (MD)
Hutchinson Comm Coll and Area Vocational School (KS)
Iowa Lakes Comm Coll (IA)
Jefferson Comm Coll (NY)
Kingsborough Comm Coll of the City U of New York (NY)
Lane Comm Coll (OR)
Lehigh Carbon Comm Coll (PA)
Lorain County Comm Coll (OH)
Niagara County Comm Coll (NY)

Northampton Comm Coll (PA)
North Iowa Area Comm Coll (IA)
Rock Valley Coll (IL)
Salt Lake Comm Coll (UT)
Springfield Tech Comm Coll (MA)
State U of New York Coll of Technology at Alfred (NY)
Sullivan County Comm Coll (NY)
Tompkins Cortland Comm Coll (NY)
Tulsa Comm Coll (OK)
Vincennes U (IN)

SPORTS STUDIES
Finger Lakes Comm Coll (NY)
Genesee Comm Coll (NY)

STATISTICS
Broward Coll (FL)
Eastern Wyoming Coll (WY)
South Florida State Coll (FL)

STATISTICS RELATED
Casper Coll (WY)

STRUCTURAL ENGINEERING
Bristol Comm Coll (MA)
Moraine Park Tech Coll (WI)

SUBSTANCE ABUSE/ ADDICTION COUNSELING
Alvin Comm Coll (TX)
Amarillo Coll (TX)
Austin Comm Coll (TX)
Beal Coll (ME)
Butte Coll (CA)
Casper Coll (WY)
Central Oregon Comm Coll (OR)
Century Coll (MN)
Chippewa Valley Tech Coll (WI)
Clark Coll (WA)
Coll of the Desert (CA)
Comm Coll of Allegheny County (PA)
The Comm Coll of Baltimore County (MD)
Comm Coll of Rhode Island (RI)
Delaware Tech & Comm Coll, Stanton/Wilmington Campus (DE)
Delaware Tech & Comm Coll, Terry Campus (DE)
Erie Comm Coll (NY)
Finger Lakes Comm Coll (NY)
Flathead Valley Comm Coll (MT)
Florida State Coll at Jacksonville (FL)
Fox Valley Tech Coll (WI)
Gadsden State Comm Coll (AL)
Garden City Comm Coll (KS)
Genesee Comm Coll (NY)
Grayson Coll (TX)
Housatonic Comm Coll (CT)
Howard Comm Coll (MD)
J. Sargeant Reynolds Comm Coll (VA)
Kilian Comm Coll (SD)
Lower Columbia Coll (WA)
Mesabi Range Comm and Tech Coll (MN)
Miami Dade Coll (FL)
Minneapolis Comm and Tech Coll (MN)
Mohave Comm Coll (AZ)
Mohawk Valley Comm Coll (NY)
Moraine Park Tech Coll (WI)
Moraine Valley Comm Coll (IL)
Mountain State Coll (WV)
Mt. San Jacinto Coll (CA)
North Shore Comm Coll (MA)
Northwestern Connecticut Comm Coll (CT)
Oakton Comm Coll (IL)
Oklahoma State U, Oklahoma City (OK)
Olympic Coll (WA)
Oxnard Coll (CA)
Palomar Coll (CA)
Pima Comm Coll (AZ)
Pitt Comm Coll (NC)
Reading Area Comm Coll (PA)
Shawnee Comm Coll (IL)
Southeastern Comm Coll (IA)
Southern State Comm Coll (OH)
Southwestern Comm Coll (NC)
Texarkana Coll (TX)
Three Rivers Comm Coll (CT)
Tompkins Cortland Comm Coll (NY)
Truckee Meadows Comm Coll (NV)
Tunxis Comm Coll (CT)
Tyler Jr Coll (TX)
Wenatchee Valley Coll (WA)

Westchester Comm Coll (NY)
Wor-Wic Comm Coll (MD)

SURGICAL TECHNOLOGY
Anoka Tech Coll (MN)
Athens Tech Coll (GA)
Augusta Tech Coll (GA)
Austin Comm Coll (TX)
Bellingham Tech Coll (WA)
Bismarck State Coll (ND)
Brown Mackie Coll–Albuquerque (NM)
Brown Mackie Coll–Birmingham (AL)
Brown Mackie Coll–Cincinnati (OH)
Brown Mackie Coll–Dallas/Ft. Worth (TX)
Brown Mackie Coll–Findlay (OH)
Brown Mackie Coll–Greenville (SC)
Brown Mackie Coll–Kansas City (KS)
Brown Mackie Coll–Merrillville (IN)
Brown Mackie Coll–North Canton (OH)
Brown Mackie Coll–Phoenix (AZ)
Brown Mackie Coll–Salina (KS)
Brown Mackie Coll–San Antonio (TX)
Brown Mackie Coll–Tucson (AZ)
Brown Mackie Coll–Tulsa (OK)
Cape Fear Comm Coll (NC)
Career Tech Coll, Monroe (LA)
Carrington Coll California–Citrus Heights (CA)
Carrington Coll California–San Jose (CA)
Central Ohio Tech Coll (OH)
Cincinnati State Tech and Comm Coll (OH)
Coll of Southern Idaho (ID)
Coll of Western Idaho (ID)
Collin County Comm Coll District (TX)
Columbus State Comm Coll (OH)
Columbus Tech Coll (GA)
Comm Care Coll (OK)
Comm Coll of Allegheny County (PA)
Delta Coll (MI)
Eastern Idaho Tech Coll (ID)
Fayetteville Tech Comm Coll (NC)
Flathead Valley Comm Coll (MT)
Georgia Northwestern Tech Coll (GA)
Georgia Piedmont Tech Coll (GA)
Great Falls Coll Montana State U (MT)
Harrisburg Area Comm Coll (PA)
Hinds Comm Coll (MS)
Hutchinson Comm Coll and Area Vocational School (KS)
Iowa Lakes Comm Coll (IA)
Ivy Tech Comm Coll–Central Indiana (IN)
Ivy Tech Comm Coll–Columbus (IN)
Ivy Tech Comm Coll–East Central (IN)
Ivy Tech Comm Coll–Kokomo (IN)
Ivy Tech Comm Coll–Lafayette (IN)
Ivy Tech Comm Coll–Northwest (IN)
Ivy Tech Comm Coll–Southwest (IN)
Ivy Tech Comm Coll–Wabash Valley (IN)
Kilgore Coll (TX)
Kirtland Comm Coll (MI)
Lakeland Comm Coll (OH)
Lake Superior Coll (MN)
Lanier Tech Coll (GA)
Lansing Comm Coll (MI)
Laramie County Comm Coll (WY)
Lincoln Land Comm Coll (IL)
Lorain County Comm Coll (OH)
Luzerne County Comm Coll (PA)
Macomb Comm Coll (MI)
Manchester Comm Coll (CT)
MiraCosta Coll (CA)
Mohave Comm Coll (AZ)
Montgomery Coll (MD)
Montgomery County Comm Coll (PA)
Moraine Park Tech Coll (WI)
Nassau Comm Coll (NY)
Niagara County Comm Coll (NY)
Northwest Florida State Coll (FL)
Oakland Comm Coll (MI)
Okefenokee Tech Coll (GA)
Oklahoma City Comm Coll (OK)
Owensboro Comm and Tech Coll (KY)
Owens Comm Coll, Toledo (OH)
Paris Jr Coll (TX)
Pennsylvania Coll of Health Sciences (PA)
Pittsburgh Tech Inst, Oakdale (PA)
Rock Valley Coll (IL)
San Jacinto Coll District (TX)

San Joaquin Valley Coll, Bakersfield (CA)
San Joaquin Valley Coll, Fresno (CA)
San Joaquin Valley Coll, Hanford (CA)
San Joaquin Valley Coll, Hesperia (CA)
San Joaquin Valley Coll, Temecula (CA)
San Juan Coll (NM)
Savannah Tech Coll (GA)
Somerset Comm Coll (KY)
Southeast Tech Inst (SD)
Southern Crescent Tech Coll (GA)
Southern Maine Comm Coll (ME)
Southern U at Shreveport (LA)
South Louisiana Comm Coll (LA)
South Plains Coll (TX)
Southwest Georgia Tech Coll (GA)
Spencerian Coll (KY)
Springfield Tech Comm Coll (MA)
Tallahassee Comm Coll (FL)
Tarrant County Coll District (TX)
Trinity Valley Comm Coll (TX)
Tulsa Comm Coll (OK)
Tyler Jr Coll (TX)
Vincennes U (IN)
Walters State Comm Coll (TN)
Waukesha County Tech Coll (WI)
Wayne County Comm Coll District (MI)
Western Dakota Tech Inst (SD)
West Kentucky Comm and Tech Coll (KY)
Wichita Area Tech Coll (KS)
Wright Career Coll, Overland Park (KS)
Wright Career Coll, Wichita (KS)
Wright Career Coll, Oklahoma City (OK)
Wright Career Coll, Tulsa (OK)

SURVEYING ENGINEERING
Comm Coll of Rhode Island (RI)

SURVEYING TECHNOLOGY
Austin Comm Coll (TX)
Bellingham Tech Coll (WA)
Bismarck State Coll (ND)
Clark Coll (WA)
Coll of the Canyons (CA)
The Comm Coll of Baltimore County (MD)
Delaware Tech & Comm Coll, Jack F. Owens Campus (DE)
Delaware Tech & Comm Coll, Stanton/Wilmington Campus (DE)
Flathead Valley Comm Coll (MT)
Lansing Comm Coll (MI)
Macomb Comm Coll (MI)
Middlesex County Coll (NJ)
Mohawk Valley Comm Coll (NY)
Moraine Valley Comm Coll (IL)
Mt. San Antonio Coll (CA)
Oklahoma State U, Oklahoma City (OK)
Penn State Wilkes-Barre (PA)
Phoenix Coll (AZ)
Salt Lake Comm Coll (UT)
Santa Rosa Jr Coll (CA)
Sheridan Coll (WY)
Southeast Tech Inst (SD)
South Florida State Coll (FL)
South Louisiana Comm Coll (LA)
Stark State Coll (OH)
State U of New York Coll of Technology at Alfred (NY)
Texas State Tech Coll Waco (TX)
Tulsa Comm Coll (OK)
Tyler Jr Coll (TX)
U of Arkansas Comm Coll at Morrilton (AR)
Vincennes U (IN)
Waubonsee Comm Coll (IL)

SYSTEM, NETWORKING, AND LAN/WAN MANAGEMENT
Arapahoe Comm Coll (CO)
Blue Ridge Comm and Tech Coll (WV)
Cloud County Comm Coll (KS)
Collin County Comm Coll District (TX)
Iowa Lakes Comm Coll (IA)
ITT Tech Inst, Orland Park (IL)
LDS Business Coll (UT)
Lone Star Coll–Tomball (TX)
Metropolitan Comm Coll–Kansas City (MO)
Mineral Area Coll (MO)
Moraine Valley Comm Coll (IL)
Oklahoma City Comm Coll (OK)

Paris Jr Coll (TX)
Pitt Comm Coll (NC)
Southwestern Comm Coll (NC)
Southwestern Indian Polytechnic Inst (NM)
Temple Coll (TX)
Texas State Tech Coll Waco (TX)
Williston State Coll (ND)

SYSTEMS ENGINEERING
Broward Coll (FL)
South Florida State Coll (FL)

TEACHER ASSISTANT/AIDE
Alamance Comm Coll (NC)
Antelope Valley Coll (CA)
Borough of Manhattan Comm Coll of the City U of New York (NY)
Central Wyoming Coll (WY)
Century Coll (MN)
Cloud County Comm Coll (KS)
Coll of Southern Idaho (ID)
Columbia-Greene Comm Coll (NY)
Comm Coll of Vermont (VT)
Dakota Coll at Bottineau (ND)
Danville Area Comm Coll (IL)
Fiorello H. LaGuardia Comm Coll of the City U of New York (NY)
Gateway Comm and Tech Coll (KY)
Genesee Comm Coll (NY)
Highland Comm Coll (IL)
Hopkinsville Comm Coll (KY)
Illinois Eastern Comm Colls, Lincoln Trail College (IL)
Jefferson Comm Coll (NY)
Kankakee Comm Coll (IL)
Kaskaskia Coll (IL)
Kingsborough Comm Coll of the City U of New York (NY)
Kirtland Comm Coll (MI)
Lansing Comm Coll (MI)
Lehigh Carbon Comm Coll (PA)
Lincoln Land Comm Coll (IL)
Linn-Benton Comm Coll (OR)
Manchester Comm Coll (CT)
Mercer County Comm Coll (NJ)
Mesa Comm Coll (AZ)
Miami Dade Coll (FL)
Middlesex County Coll (NJ)
Mitchell Comm Coll (NC)
Montgomery County Comm Coll (PA)
Moraine Park Tech Coll (WI)
Moraine Valley Comm Coll (IL)
Northampton Comm Coll (PA)
Northcentral Tech Coll (WI)
Owensboro Comm and Tech Coll (KY)
Patrick Henry Comm Coll (VA)
Phoenix Coll (AZ)
St. Clair County Comm Coll (MI)
Salt Lake Comm Coll (UT)
San Diego City Coll (CA)
Sheridan Coll (WY)
Shoreline Comm Coll (WA)
Somerset Comm Coll (KY)
Southeastern Comm Coll (NC)
Southern State Comm Coll (OH)
Southern U at Shreveport (LA)
Southwestern Illinois Coll (IL)
Southwestern Michigan Coll (MI)
State Fair Comm Coll (MO)
The U of Akron–Wayne Coll (OH)
Victor Valley Coll (CA)
Vincennes U (IN)
Waubonsee Comm Coll (IL)
Waukesha County Tech Coll (WI)

TECHNICAL TEACHER EDUCATION
East Central Coll (MO)
Greenville Tech Coll (SC)
Mineral Area Coll (MO)
State Fair Comm Coll (MO)

TECHNOLOGY/INDUSTRIAL ARTS TEACHER EDUCATION
Allen Comm Coll (KS)
Casper Coll (WY)
Delta Coll (MI)
Eastern Arizona Coll (AZ)
Fullerton Coll (CA)
Hinds Comm Coll (MS)
Iowa Lakes Comm Coll (IA)
Roane State Comm Coll (TN)

TELECOMMUNICATIONS TECHNOLOGY
Amarillo Coll (TX)
Carl Albert State Coll (OK)
Cayuga County Comm Coll (NY)
Central Carolina Comm Coll (NC)
Clark Coll (WA)

Collin County Comm Coll District (TX)
County Coll of Morris (NJ)
Erie Comm Coll, South Campus (NY)
Georgia Piedmont Tech Coll (GA)
Hinds Comm Coll (MS)
Howard Comm Coll (MD)
Illinois Eastern Comm Colls, Lincoln Trail College (IL)
Ivy Tech Comm Coll–North Central (IN)
Ivy Tech Comm Coll–Northwest (IN)
Lake Land Coll (IL)
Miami Dade Coll (FL)
Mitchell Tech Inst (SD)
Monroe Comm Coll (NY)
Northern Essex Comm Coll (MA)
Northwest Mississippi Comm Coll (MS)
Penn State DuBois (PA)
Penn State Fayette, The Eberly Campus (PA)
Penn State Hazleton (PA)
Penn State New Kensington (PA)
Penn State Schuylkill (PA)
Penn State Wilkes-Barre (PA)
Penn State York (PA)
Quinsigamond Comm Coll (MA)
Salt Lake Comm Coll (UT)
San Diego City Coll (CA)
Seminole State Coll of Florida (FL)
South Plains Coll (TX)
Springfield Tech Comm Coll (MA)
Texas State Tech Coll Waco (TX)
Trident Tech Coll (SC)

THEATER DESIGN AND TECHNOLOGY
Broward Coll (FL)
Carroll Comm Coll (MD)
Casper Coll (WY)
Central Wyoming Coll (WY)
Florida State Coll at Jacksonville (FL)
Gavilan Coll (CA)
Genesee Comm Coll (NY)
Harford Comm Coll (MD)
Howard Comm Coll (MD)
Lansing Comm Coll (MI)
MiraCosta Coll (CA)
Nassau Comm Coll (NY)
Normandale Comm Coll (MN)
Pasadena City Coll (CA)
San Juan Coll (NM)
Tulsa Comm Coll (OK)
Vincennes U (IN)
Western Wyoming Comm Coll (WY)

THEATER/THEATER ARTS MANAGEMENT
Genesee Comm Coll (NY)
Harper Coll (IL)

THERAPEUTIC RECREATION
Austin Comm Coll (TX)
Broward Coll (FL)
Comm Coll of Allegheny County (PA)
Northwestern Connecticut Comm Coll (CT)

TOOL AND DIE TECHNOLOGY
Bevill State Comm Coll (AL)
Delta Coll (MI)
Dunwoody Coll of Technology (MN)
Gadsden State Comm Coll (AL)
Ivy Tech Comm Coll–Bloomington (IN)
Ivy Tech Comm Coll–Central Indiana (IN)
Ivy Tech Comm Coll–Columbus (IN)
Ivy Tech Comm Coll–East Central (IN)
Ivy Tech Comm Coll–Kokomo (IN)
Ivy Tech Comm Coll–Lafayette (IN)
Ivy Tech Comm Coll–North Central (IN)
Ivy Tech Comm Coll–Northeast (IN)
Ivy Tech Comm Coll–Northwest (IN)
Ivy Tech Comm Coll–Richmond (IN)
Ivy Tech Comm Coll–Southern Indiana (IN)
Ivy Tech Comm Coll–Southwest (IN)
Ivy Tech Comm Coll–Wabash Valley (IN)
Macomb Comm Coll (MI)
North Iowa Area Comm Coll (IA)
Owens Comm Coll, Toledo (OH)
Rock Valley Coll (IL)
Shelton State Comm Coll (AL)
Vincennes U (IN)

TOURISM AND TRAVEL SERVICES MANAGEMENT
Albany Tech Coll (GA)
Amarillo Coll (TX)
Athens Tech Coll (GA)
Atlanta Tech Coll (GA)
Broward Coll (FL)
Bucks County Comm Coll (PA)
Bunker Hill Comm Coll (MA)
Butte Coll (CA)
Central Georgia Tech Coll (GA)
Cloud County Comm Coll (KS)
Columbus State Comm Coll (OH)
Daytona State Coll (FL)
Finger Lakes Comm Coll (NY)
Fiorello H. LaGuardia Comm Coll of the City U of New York (NY)
Genesee Comm Coll (NY)
Gwinnett Tech Coll (GA)
Harrisburg Area Comm Coll (PA)
Hinds Comm Coll (MS)
Hocking Coll (OH)
Houston Comm Coll System (TX)
Kingsborough Comm Coll of the City U of New York (NY)
Lakeland Comm Coll (OH)
Lansing Comm Coll (MI)
Lorain County Comm Coll (OH)
Luzerne County Comm Coll (PA)
Miami Dade Coll (FL)
Monroe Comm Coll (NY)
Moraine Valley Comm Coll (IL)
Niagara County Comm Coll (NY)
Northern Essex Comm Coll (MA)
North Shore Comm Coll (MA)
Ogeechee Tech Coll (GA)
San Diego City Coll (CA)
Savannah Tech Coll (GA)
Southern U at Shreveport (LA)
Sullivan County Comm Coll (NY)
Three Rivers Comm Coll (CT)
Tulsa Comm Coll (OK)
Westmoreland County Comm Coll (PA)

TOURISM AND TRAVEL SERVICES MARKETING
Bay State Coll (MA)
Florida State Coll at Jacksonville (FL)
Herkimer County Comm Coll (NY)
Luzerne County Comm Coll (PA)
MiraCosta Coll (CA)
Montgomery County Comm Coll (PA)

TOURISM PROMOTION
Comm Coll of Allegheny County (PA)
Genesee Comm Coll (NY)
Jefferson Comm Coll (NY)

TRADE AND INDUSTRIAL TEACHER EDUCATION
Broward Coll (FL)
Copiah-Lincoln Comm Coll (MS)
Darton State Coll (GA)
Iowa Lakes Comm Coll (IA)
Lenoir Comm Coll (NC)
Northeastern Jr Coll (CO)
Quinsigamond Comm Coll (MA)
Southeastern Comm Coll (IA)
South Florida State Coll (FL)
Southwestern Comm Coll (NC)
Victor Valley Coll (CA)

TRANSPORTATION AND MATERIALS MOVING RELATED
Cecil Coll (MD)
Mid-Plains Comm Coll, North Platte (NE)
Mt. San Antonio Coll (CA)
Nassau Comm Coll (NY)
St. Clair County Comm Coll (MI)
San Diego City Coll (CA)

TRANSPORTATION/MOBILITY MANAGEMENT
Cecil Coll (MD)
Hagerstown Comm Coll (MD)
South Florida State Coll (FL)

TRUCK AND BUS DRIVER/COMMERCIAL VEHICLE OPERATION/INSTRUCTION
Mohave Comm Coll (AZ)
Spoon River Coll (IL)

TURF AND TURFGRASS MANAGEMENT
Catawba Valley Comm Coll (NC)
Cincinnati State Tech and Comm Coll (OH)
Coll of the Desert (CA)
Comm Coll of Allegheny County (PA)

Danville Area Comm Coll (IL)
Delaware Tech & Comm Coll, Jack F. Owens Campus (DE)
Florida Gateway Coll (FL)
Harford Comm Coll (MD)
Hinds Comm Coll (MS)
Houston Comm Coll System (TX)
Iowa Lakes Comm Coll (IA)
MiraCosta Coll (CA)
Mt. San Jacinto Coll (CA)
North Georgia Tech Coll (GA)
The Ohio State U Ag Tech Inst (OH)
Oklahoma State U, Oklahoma City (OK)
Ozarks Tech Comm Coll (MO)
Sheridan Coll (WY)
Southeast Tech Inst (SD)
Texas State Tech Coll Waco (TX)
Walla Walla Comm Coll (WA)
Wayne Comm Coll (NC)
Westmoreland County Comm Coll (PA)
The Williamson Free School of Mecha Trades (PA)

URBAN FORESTRY
Dakota Coll at Bottineau (ND)
Kent State U at Trumbull (OH)
State U of New York Coll of Technology at Alfred (NY)

URBAN STUDIES/AFFAIRS
Lorain County Comm Coll (OH)

VEHICLE MAINTENANCE AND REPAIR TECHNOLOGIES
Coll of the Desert (CA)

VEHICLE MAINTENANCE AND REPAIR TECHNOLOGIES RELATED
North Dakota State Coll of Science (ND)
State U of New York Coll of Technology at Alfred (NY)
Victor Valley Coll (CA)
Western Dakota Tech Inst (SD)

VETERINARY/ANIMAL HEALTH TECHNOLOGY
Athens Tech Coll (GA)
Bradford School (OH)
Brown Mackie Coll–Akron (OH)
Brown Mackie Coll–Albuquerque (NM)
Brown Mackie Coll–Boise (ID)
Brown Mackie Coll–Cincinnati (OH)
Brown Mackie Coll–Findlay (OH)
Brown Mackie Coll–Fort Wayne (IN)
Brown Mackie Coll–Kansas City (KS)
Brown Mackie Coll–Louisville (KY)
Brown Mackie Coll–North Canton (OH)
Brown Mackie Coll–St. Louis (MO)
Brown Mackie Coll–Salina (KS)
Brown Mackie Coll–South Bend (IN)
Carrington Coll California–Citrus Heights (CA)
Carrington Coll California–Pleasant Hill (CA)
Carrington Coll California–Sacramento (CA)
Carrington Coll California–San Jose (CA)
Carrington Coll California–San Leandro (CA)
Carrington Coll California–Stockton (CA)
Central Carolina Comm Coll (NC)
Central Georgia Tech Coll (GA)
Coll of Central Florida (FL)
Coll of Southern Idaho (ID)
Columbus State Comm Coll (OH)
Comm Care Coll (OK)
The Comm Coll of Baltimore County (MD)
Cosumnes River Coll, Sacramento (CA)
County Coll of Morris (NJ)
Crowder Coll (MO)
Delaware Tech & Comm Coll, Jack F. Owens Campus (DE)
Eastern Florida State Coll (FL)
Eastern Wyoming Coll (WY)
Fiorello H. LaGuardia Comm Coll of the City U of New York (NY)
Florida Gateway Coll (FL)
Fox Coll (IL)
Genesee Comm Coll (NY)
Gwinnett Tech Coll (GA)

Hillsborough Comm Coll (FL)
Hinds Comm Coll (MS)
Holyoke Comm Coll (MA)
Independence Comm Coll (KS)
International Business Coll, Indianapolis (IN)
Jefferson Coll (MO)
Jefferson State Comm Coll (AL)
Kaskaskia Coll (IL)
Kent State U at Tuscarawas (OH)
Lansing Comm Coll (MI)
Lehigh Carbon Comm Coll (PA)
Lone Star Coll–Tomball (TX)
Macomb Comm Coll (MI)
Minnesota School of Business–Plymouth (MN)
Northampton Comm Coll (PA)
North Shore Comm Coll (MA)
Northwest Coll (WY)
Northwestern Connecticut Comm Coll (CT)
Oakland Comm Coll (MI)
Ogeechee Tech Coll (GA)
Oklahoma State U, Oklahoma City (OK)
Owensboro Comm and Tech Coll (KY)
Pensacola State Coll (FL)
Pima Comm Coll (AZ)
San Joaquin Valley Coll, Fresno (CA)
San Joaquin Valley Coll, Hanford (CA)
San Joaquin Valley Coll, Hesperia (CA)
San Joaquin Valley Coll, Temecula (CA)
San Juan Coll (NM)
Shawnee Comm Coll (IL)
State U of New York Coll of Technology at Alfred (NY)
Trident Tech Coll (SC)
Truckee Meadows Comm Coll (NV)
Tulsa Comm Coll (OK)
Vet Tech Inst (PA)
Vet Tech Inst at Bradford School (OH)
Vet Tech Inst at Fox Coll (IL)
Vet Tech Inst at Hickey Coll (MO)
Vet Tech Inst at International Business Coll, Fort Wayne (IN)
Vet Tech Inst at International Business Coll, Indianapolis (IN)
Vet Tech Inst of Houston (TX)
Volunteer State Comm Coll (TN)
Wayne County Comm Coll District (MI)
Westchester Comm Coll (NY)
Wright Career Coll, Overland Park (KS)

VISUAL AND PERFORMING ARTS
Amarillo Coll (TX)
Berkshire Comm Coll (MA)
Borough of Manhattan Comm Coll of the City U of New York (NY)
Bucks County Comm Coll (PA)
Chandler-Gilbert Comm Coll (AZ)
Coconino Comm Coll (AZ)
The Comm Coll of Baltimore County (MD)
Dutchess Comm Coll (NY)
Feather River Coll (CA)
Fiorello H. LaGuardia Comm Coll of the City U of New York (NY)
Frank Phillips Coll (TX)
Garden City Comm Coll (KS)
Gavilan Coll (CA)
Harford Comm Coll (MD)
Harrisburg Area Comm Coll (PA)
Herkimer County Comm Coll (NY)
Hutchinson Comm Coll and Area Vocational School (KS)
Kankakee Comm Coll (IL)
Middlesex County Coll (NJ)
MiraCosta Coll (CA)
Moraine Valley Comm Coll (IL)
Mott Comm Coll (MI)
Mt. San Antonio Coll (CA)
Mt. San Jacinto Coll (CA)
Nassau Comm Coll (NY)
Phoenix Coll (AZ)
Piedmont Virginia Comm Coll (VA)
Pima Comm Coll (AZ)
Rogue Comm Coll (OR)
Spartanburg Methodist Coll (SC)
Western Wyoming Comm Coll (WY)

VISUAL AND PERFORMING ARTS RELATED
Comm Coll of Allegheny County (PA)
Florida State Coll at Jacksonville (FL)
John Tyler Comm Coll (VA)
Northwest Coll (WY)
Northwest Florida State Coll (FL)

VITICULTURE AND ENOLOGY
Finger Lakes Comm Coll (NY)
Grayson Coll (TX)
Harrisburg Area Comm Coll (PA)
James Sprunt Comm Coll (NC)
Kent State U at Ashtabula (OH)
Santa Rosa Jr Coll (CA)
Texas State Tech Coll Waco (TX)
Walla Walla Comm Coll (WA)

VOCATIONAL REHABILITATION COUNSELING
South Florida State Coll (FL)

VOICE AND OPERA
Alvin Comm Coll (TX)
Iowa Lakes Comm Coll (IA)
Oakland Comm Coll (MI)

WATCHMAKING AND JEWELRYMAKING
Austin Comm Coll (TX)
Paris Jr Coll (TX)

WATER QUALITY AND WASTEWATER TREATMENT MANAGEMENT AND RECYCLING TECHNOLOGY
Bismarck State Coll (ND)
Bristol Comm Coll (MA)
Casper Coll (WY)
Coll of Southern Idaho (ID)
Coll of the Canyons (CA)
Delaware Tech & Comm Coll, Jack F. Owens Campus (DE)
Delta Coll (MI)
Florida State Coll at Jacksonville (FL)
Linn-Benton Comm Coll (OR)
Moraine Park Tech Coll (WI)
Mt. San Jacinto Coll (CA)
Ogeechee Tech Coll (GA)
Palomar Coll (CA)

WATER RESOURCES ENGINEERING
Bristol Comm Coll (MA)
Helena Coll U of Montana (MT)

WATER, WETLANDS, AND MARINE RESOURCES MANAGEMENT
Iowa Lakes Comm Coll (IA)
South Florida State Coll (FL)

WEB/MULTIMEDIA MANAGEMENT AND WEBMASTER
Casper Coll (WY)
Clark Coll (WA)
Comm Coll of Rhode Island (RI)
Delta Coll (MI)
Flathead Valley Comm Coll (MT)
Florida State Coll at Jacksonville (FL)
Fox Valley Tech Coll (WI)
ITT Tech Inst, Norwood (MA)
ITT Tech Inst, Wilmington (MA)
Kaskaskia Coll (IL)
Kirtland Comm Coll (MI)
Metropolitan Comm Coll–Kansas City (MO)
Mid-South Comm Coll (AR)
MiraCosta Coll (CA)
Monroe County Comm Coll (MI)
Montgomery County Comm Coll (PA)
Moraine Valley Comm Coll (IL)
Northern Essex Comm Coll (MA)
Oklahoma City Comm Coll (OK)
River Valley Comm Coll (NH)
St. Clair County Comm Coll (MI)
Seminole State Coll of Florida (FL)
Sheridan Coll (WY)
Southwestern Illinois Coll (IL)
Stark State Coll (OH)
Temple Coll (TX)
Tompkins Cortland Comm Coll (NY)
Trident Tech Coll (SC)
Truckee Meadows Comm Coll (NV)
Vincennes U (IN)
Walla Walla Comm Coll (WA)

Western Wyoming Comm Coll (WY)
West Virginia Jr Coll–Bridgeport (WV)

WEB PAGE, DIGITAL/ MULTIMEDIA AND INFORMATION RESOURCES DESIGN
The Art Inst of New York City (NY)
Berkeley City Coll (CA)
Bismarck State Coll (ND)
Blackhawk Tech Coll (WI)
Borough of Manhattan Comm Coll of the City U of New York (NY)
Bucks County Comm Coll (PA)
Bunker Hill Comm Coll (MA)
Butler County Comm Coll (PA)
Casper Coll (WY)
Cecil Coll (MD)
Central Georgia Tech Coll (GA)
Central Ohio Tech Coll (OH)
Chattahoochee Tech Coll (GA)
Cloud County Comm Coll (KS)
Coll of Southern Idaho (ID)
Coll of the Mainland (TX)
Coll of Western Idaho (ID)
Collin County Comm Coll District (TX)
Columbus Tech Coll (GA)
County Coll of Morris (NJ)
Davis Coll (OH)
Dunwoody Coll of Technology (MN)
Dyersburg State Comm Coll (TN)
Florida State Coll at Jacksonville (FL)
Genesee Comm Coll (NY)
Georgia Northwestern Tech Coll (GA)
Glendale Comm Coll (AZ)
Great Falls Coll Montana State U (MT)
Hagerstown Comm Coll (MD)
Harper Coll (IL)
Harrisburg Area Comm Coll (PA)
Hawkeye Comm Coll (IA)
Hutchinson Comm Coll and Area Vocational School (KS)
Independence Comm Coll (KS)
J. Sargeant Reynolds Comm Coll (VA)
Lake Superior Coll (MN)
Lanier Tech Coll (GA)
Lansing Comm Coll (MI)
LDS Business Coll (UT)
Lehigh Carbon Comm Coll (PA)
Mesabi Range Comm and Tech Coll (MN)
Metropolitan Comm Coll–Kansas City (MO)
Minneapolis Comm and Tech Coll (MN)
Minnesota State Coll–Southeast Tech (MN)
Mohawk Valley Comm Coll (NY)
Monroe County Comm Coll (MI)
Montgomery Coll (MD)
Motlow State Comm Coll (TN)
Mott Comm Coll (MI)
Moultrie Tech Coll (GA)
Mount Wachusett Comm Coll (MA)
Niagara County Comm Coll (NY)
Northampton Comm Coll (PA)
North Dakota State Coll of Science (ND)
Northern Essex Comm Coll (MA)
North Georgia Tech Coll (GA)
North Iowa Area Comm Coll (IA)
North Shore Comm Coll (MA)
Norwalk Comm Coll (CT)
Oklahoma State U, Oklahoma City (OK)
Oxnard Coll (CA)
Palomar Coll (CA)
Pasco-Hernando State Coll (FL)
Phoenix Coll (AZ)
Pittsburgh Tech Inst, Oakdale (PA)
Pueblo Comm Coll (CO)
Quinsigamond Comm Coll (MA)
Raritan Valley Comm Coll (NJ)
Reading Area Comm Coll (PA)
Schoolcraft Coll (MI)
Seminole State Coll of Florida (FL)
Sessions Coll for Professional Design (AZ)
Southeastern Tech Coll (GA)
Southern Crescent Tech Coll (GA)
South Louisiana Comm Coll (LA)
Spoon River Coll (IL)
Stark State Coll (OH)
State Fair Comm Coll (MO)

Sullivan Coll of Technology and Design (KY)
Tallahassee Comm Coll (FL)
Texas State Tech Coll Waco (TX)
Trident Tech Coll (SC)
Volunteer State Comm Coll (TN)
Walters State Comm Coll (TN)
Waubonsee Comm Coll (IL)
Western Wyoming Comm Coll (WY)
West Georgia Tech Coll (GA)
Westmoreland County Comm Coll (PA)
Wiregrass Georgia Tech Coll (GA)
Wisconsin Indianhead Tech Coll (WI)

WELDING ENGINEERING TECHNOLOGY
Mitchell Tech Inst (SD)

WELDING TECHNOLOGY
Alamance Comm Coll (NC)
American Samoa Comm Coll (AS)
Anoka Tech Coll (MN)
Antelope Valley Coll (CA)
Arizona Western Coll (AZ)
Austin Comm Coll (TX)
Bainbridge State Coll (GA)
Barstow Comm Coll (CA)
Beal Coll (ME)
Bellingham Tech Coll (WA)
Big Bend Comm Coll (WA)
Bismarck State Coll (ND)
Brown Mackie Coll–Kansas City (KS)
Brown Mackie Coll–Salina (KS)
Butte Coll (CA)
Casper Coll (WY)
Central Wyoming Coll (WY)
Clark Coll (WA)
Cochise Coll, Sierra Vista (AZ)
Coll of Southern Idaho (ID)
Coll of the Canyons (CA)
Comm Coll of Allegheny County (PA)
Crowder Coll (MO)
Delta Coll (MI)
Dunwoody Coll of Technology (MN)
East Central Coll (MO)
Eastern Arizona Coll (AZ)
Eastern Idaho Tech Coll (ID)
Eastern Wyoming Coll (WY)
Flathead Valley Comm Coll (MT)
Fox Valley Tech Coll (WI)
Galveston Coll (TX)
Garden City Comm Coll (KS)
Grand Rapids Comm Coll (MI)
Grays Harbor Coll (WA)
Grayson Coll (TX)
Great Basin Coll (NV)
Great Falls Coll Montana State U (MT)
Helena Coll U of Montana (MT)
Hinds Comm Coll (MS)
Honolulu Comm Coll (HI)
Hutchinson Comm Coll and Area Vocational School (KS)
Imperial Valley Coll (CA)
Iowa Lakes Comm Coll (IA)
Jamestown Comm Coll (NY)
Jefferson Coll (MO)
J. Sargeant Reynolds Comm Coll (VA)
Kankakee Comm Coll (IL)
Kaskaskia Coll (IL)
Kilgore Coll (TX)
Kirtland Comm Coll (MI)
Lake Area Tech Inst (SD)
Lane Comm Coll (OR)
Lansing Comm Coll (MI)
Lenoir Comm Coll (NC)
Linn-Benton Comm Coll (OR)
Lone Star Coll–CyFair (TX)
Lone Star Coll–North Harris (TX)
Lower Columbia Coll (WA)
Macomb Comm Coll (MI)
Manhattan Area Tech Coll (KS)
Mid-Plains Comm Coll, North Platte (NE)
Mississippi Gulf Coast Comm Coll (MS)
Mohave Comm Coll (AZ)
Mohawk Valley Comm Coll (NY)
Monroe County Comm Coll (MI)
Mountain View Coll (TX)
Mt. San Antonio Coll (CA)
North Dakota State Coll of Science (ND)
Northeast Texas Comm Coll (TX)
North Iowa Area Comm Coll (IA)
Northwest Coll (WY)
Northwest Florida State Coll (FL)
Oakland Comm Coll (MI)

Oklahoma Tech Coll (OK)
Olympic Coll (WA)
Orange Coast Coll (CA)
Owens Comm Coll, Toledo (OH)
Ozarks Tech Comm Coll (MO)
Palomar Coll (CA)
Paris Jr Coll (TX)
Pasadena City Coll (CA)
Pima Comm Coll (AZ)
Pitt Comm Coll (NC)
Pueblo Comm Coll (CO)
Richmond Comm Coll (NC)
Rock Valley Coll (IL)
Rogue Comm Coll (OR)
St. Clair County Comm Coll (MI)
Salt Lake Comm Coll (UT)
San Diego City Coll (CA)
San Jacinto Coll District (TX)
San Juan Coll (NM)
Schoolcraft Coll (MI)
Shawnee Comm Coll (IL)
Shelton State Comm Coll (AL)
Sheridan Coll (WY)
Southeastern Comm Coll (IA)
Southeastern Comm Coll (NC)
Southeast Tech Inst (SD)
South Louisiana Comm Coll (LA)
South Plains Coll (TX)
Southwestern Illinois Coll (IL)

State U of New York Coll of
    Technology at Alfred (NY)
Tallahassee Comm Coll (FL)
Tarrant County Coll District (TX)
Texarkana Coll (TX)
Treasure Valley Comm Coll (OR)
Trinity Valley Comm Coll (TX)
Truckee Meadows Comm Coll (NV)
Tyler Jr Coll (TX)
U of Hawaii Maui Coll (HI)
Victor Valley Coll (CA)
Walla Walla Comm Coll (WA)
Waubonsee Comm Coll (IL)
Wayne County Comm Coll District
    (MI)
Western Nevada Coll (NV)
Western Texas Coll (TX)
Western Wyoming Comm Coll (WY)
Westmoreland County Comm Coll
    (PA)
Wichita Area Tech Coll (KS)
Williston State Coll (ND)

**WILDLAND/FOREST
FIREFIGHTING AND
INVESTIGATION**
Coll of Western Idaho (ID)
Fox Valley Tech Coll (WI)

WILDLIFE BIOLOGY
Eastern Arizona Coll (AZ)
Iowa Lakes Comm Coll (IA)

**WILDLIFE, FISH AND
WILDLANDS SCIENCE AND
MANAGEMENT**
Casper Coll (WY)
Dakota Coll at Bottineau (ND)
Eastern Wyoming Coll (WY)
Feather River Coll (CA)
Flathead Valley Comm Coll (MT)
Garrett Coll (MD)
Hocking Coll (OH)
Iowa Lakes Comm Coll (IA)
Laramie County Comm Coll (WY)
Mt. San Antonio Coll (CA)
Ogeechee Tech Coll (GA)
Penn State DuBois (PA)
Potomac State Coll of West Virginia
    U (WV)
Shawnee Comm Coll (IL)
Treasure Valley Comm Coll (OR)
Western Wyoming Comm Coll (WY)

WINE STEWARD/SOMMELIER
Cayuga County Comm Coll (NY)
Niagara County Comm Coll (NY)

WOMEN'S STUDIES
Broward Coll (FL)
Bucks County Comm Coll (PA)
Casper Coll (WY)
Greenfield Comm Coll (MA)
Northern Essex Comm Coll (MA)
Palomar Coll (CA)
Santa Monica Coll (CA)
Santa Rosa Jr Coll (CA)

**WOOD SCIENCE AND WOOD
PRODUCTS/PULP AND PAPER
TECHNOLOGY**
Dabney S. Lancaster Comm Coll
    (VA)
Ogeechee Tech Coll (GA)
Potomac State Coll of West Virginia
    U (WV)

WOODWIND INSTRUMENTS
Iowa Lakes Comm Coll (IA)

WOODWORKING
Vincennes U (IN)

WORD PROCESSING
Florida State Coll at Jacksonville (FL)
Galveston Coll (TX)
Iowa Lakes Comm Coll (IA)
Lorain County Comm Coll (OH)

Mississippi Gulf Coast Comm Coll
    (MS)
Monroe County Comm Coll (MI)
Orange Coast Coll (CA)
Seminole State Coll of Florida (FL)
Stark State Coll (OH)
Western Wyoming Comm Coll (WY)

WORK AND FAMILY STUDIES
Antelope Valley Coll (CA)
Arizona Western Coll (AZ)

WRITING
Allen Comm Coll (KS)
Austin Comm Coll (TX)
Berkeley City Coll (CA)
Cayuga County Comm Coll (NY)

YOUTH SERVICES
Pima Comm Coll (AZ)

ZOOLOGY/ANIMAL BIOLOGY
Broward Coll (FL)
Dakota Coll at Bottineau (ND)
Garden City Comm Coll (KS)
Northeastern Jr Coll (CO)
Pensacola State Coll (FL)
Snow Coll (UT)
South Florida State Coll (FL)

Associate Degree Programs at Four-Year Colleges

ACCOUNTING
Abraham Baldwin Ag Coll (GA)
AIB Coll of Business (IA)
Baker Coll of Allen Park (MI)
Baker Coll of Auburn Hills (MI)
Baker Coll of Clinton Township (MI)
Baker Coll of Owosso (MI)
Broadview U–Boise (ID)
Broadview U–Layton (UT)
Broadview U–Orem (UT)
Broadview U–West Jordan (UT)
California U of Pennsylvania (PA)
Calumet Coll of Saint Joseph (IN)
Central Penn Coll (PA)
Champlain Coll (VT)
Clarke U (IA)
Coll of Mount St. Joseph (OH)
Davenport U, Grand Rapids (MI)
DeVry U, Bakersfield (CA)
DeVry U, Fremont (CA)
DeVry U, Colorado Springs (CO)
DeVry U, Jacksonville (FL)
DeVry U, Edina (MN)
DeVry U, Bellevue (WA)
Elizabethtown Coll School of
   Continuing and Professional
   Studies (PA)
Fisher Coll (MA)
Franklin U (OH)
Globe U–Appleton (WI)
Globe U–Eau Claire (WI)
Globe U–La Crosse (WI)
Globe U–Madison East (WI)
Globe U–Madison West (WI)
Globe U–Minneapolis (MN)
Globe U–Sioux Falls (SD)
Globe U–Wausau (WI)
Globe U–Woodbury (MN)
Gwynedd Mercy U (PA)
Harrison Coll, Indianapolis (IN)
Harrison Coll (OH)
Hawai`i Pacific U (HI)
Husson U (ME)
Immaculata U (PA)
Indiana Tech (IN)
Indiana Wesleyan U (IN)
Indian River State Coll (FL)
Inter American U of Puerto Rico,
   Aguadilla Campus (PR)
Inter American U of Puerto Rico,
   Bayamón Campus (PR)
Inter American U of Puerto Rico,
   Fajardo Campus (PR)
Inter American U of Puerto Rico,
   Guayama Campus (PR)
Inter American U of Puerto Rico,
   Metropolitan Campus (PR)
Inter American U of Puerto Rico,
   Ponce Campus (PR)
ITT Tech Inst, Indianapolis (IN)
Johnson State Coll (VT)
Keiser U, Fort Lauderdale (FL)
Keystone Coll (PA)
Lebanon Valley Coll (PA)
Lincoln Coll of New England,
   Southington (CT)
Maria Coll (NY)
Minnesota School of Business–
   Blaine (MN)
Minnesota School of Business–Elk
   River (MN)
Minnesota School of Business–
   Lakeville (MN)
Minnesota School of Business–
   Moorhead (MN)
Minnesota School of Business–
   Richfield (MN)
Minnesota School of Business–
   Rochester (MN)
Minnesota School of Business–St.
   Cloud (MN)

Minnesota School of Business–
   Shakopee (MN)
Missouri Southern State U (MO)
Monroe Coll, Bronx (NY)
Morrisville State Coll (NY)
Mount Aloysius Coll (PA)
Mount Marty Coll (SD)
Muhlenberg Coll (PA)
Northern Kentucky U (KY)
Palm Beach State Coll (FL)
Penn Foster Coll (AZ)
Pioneer Pacific Coll, Wilsonville (OR)
Point Park U (PA)
Rasmussen Coll Appleton (WI)
Rasmussen Coll Aurora (IL)
Rasmussen Coll Bismarck (ND)
Rasmussen Coll Blaine (MN)
Rasmussen Coll Bloomington (MN)
Rasmussen Coll Brooklyn Park (MN)
Rasmussen Coll Eagan (MN)
Rasmussen Coll Fort Myers (FL)
Rasmussen Coll Green Bay (WI)
Rasmussen Coll Kansas City/
   Overland Park (KS)
Rasmussen Coll Lake Elmo/
   Woodbury (MN)
Rasmussen Coll Land O' Lakes (FL)
Rasmussen Coll Mankato (MN)
Rasmussen Coll Mokena/Tinley Park
   (IL)
Rasmussen Coll Moorhead (MN)
Rasmussen Coll New Port Richey
   (FL)
Rasmussen Coll Ocala (FL)
Rasmussen Coll Romeoville/Joliet
   (IL)
Rasmussen Coll St. Cloud (MN)
Rasmussen Coll Tampa/Brandon
   (FL)
Rasmussen Coll Topeka (KS)
Rasmussen Coll Wausau (WI)
Rogers State U (OK)
Saint Francis U (PA)
Saint Mary-of-the-Woods Coll (IN)
Shawnee State U (OH)
Siena Heights U (MI)
Southern New Hampshire U (NH)
State Coll of Florida Manatee-
   Sarasota (FL)
Sullivan U (KY)
Thomas More Coll (KY)
Tiffin U (OH)
Trine U (IN)
Union Coll (NE)
Universidad del Turabo (PR)
U of Cincinnati (OH)
The U of Findlay (OH)
U of Rio Grande (OH)
U of the Potomac (DC)
U of the Virgin Islands (VI)
The U of Toledo (OH)
Utah Valley U (UT)
Walsh U (OH)
Webber International U (FL)
Wilson Coll (PA)
Youngstown State U (OH)

**ACCOUNTING AND BUSINESS/
MANAGEMENT**
AIB Coll of Business (IA)
Kansas State U (KS)

ACCOUNTING AND FINANCE
AIB Coll of Business (IA)

ACCOUNTING RELATED
AIB Coll of Business (IA)
Caribbean U (PR)
Franklin U (OH)
Montana State U Billings (MT)

**ACCOUNTING TECHNOLOGY
AND BOOKKEEPING**
American Public U System (WV)
Baker Coll of Flint (MI)
DeVry U, Pomona (CA)
DeVry U, Miramar (FL)
DeVry U, Orlando (FL)
DeVry U, Decatur (GA)
DeVry U, Federal Way (WA)
Ferris State U (MI)
Florida National U (FL)
Gannon U (PA)
Hickey Coll (MO)
International Business Coll, Fort
   Wayne (IN)
Kent State U at Geauga (OH)
Lewis-Clark State Coll (ID)
Mercy Coll (NY)
Miami U (OH)
Montana State U Billings (MT)
Montana Tech of The U of Montana
   (MT)
Morrisville State Coll (NY)
New York City Coll of Technology of
   the City U of New York (NY)
New York Inst of Technology (NY)
Pennsylvania Coll of Technology
   (PA)
Polk State Coll (FL)
State U of New York Coll of
   Agriculture and Technology at
   Cobleskill (NY)
State U of New York Coll of
   Technology at Canton (NY)
State U of New York Coll of
   Technology at Delhi (NY)
The U of Akron (OH)
U of Alaska Fairbanks (AK)
U of Cincinnati (OH)
U of Rio Grande (OH)
U of the District of Columbia (DC)
The U of Toledo (OH)

ACTING
Academy of Art U (CA)
Pacific Union Coll (CA)

**ADMINISTRATIVE ASSISTANT
AND SECRETARIAL SCIENCE**
Arkansas Tech U (AR)
Baker Coll of Auburn Hills (MI)
Baker Coll of Cadillac (MI)
Baker Coll of Clinton Township (MI)
Baker Coll of Jackson (MI)
Baker Coll of Muskegon (MI)
Baker Coll of Owosso (MI)
Ball State U (IN)
Black Hills State U (SD)
Campbellsville U (KY)
Clarion U of Pennsylvania (PA)
Clayton State U (GA)
Columbia Centro Universitario,
   Caguas (PR)
Columbia Centro Universitario,
   Yauco (PR)
Concordia Coll–New York (NY)
Dickinson State U (ND)
Dordt Coll (IA)
EDP U of Puerto Rico (PR)
EDP U of Puerto Rico–San
   Sebastian (PR)
Faith Baptist Bible Coll and
   Theological Seminary (IA)
Florida National U (FL)
Fort Hays State U (KS)
Fort Valley State U (GA)
Harrison Coll, Indianapolis (IN)
Harrison Coll (OH)
Hickey Coll (MO)
Indian River State Coll (FL)

Inter American U of Puerto Rico, San
   Germán Campus (PR)
International Business Coll, Fort
   Wayne (IN)
Lewis-Clark State Coll (ID)
Miami U (OH)
Montana State U Billings (MT)
Montana Tech of The U of Montana
   (MT)
Morrisville State Coll (NY)
Northern Michigan U (MI)
Oakland City U (IN)
Palm Beach State Coll (FL)
Rider U (NJ)
State Coll of Florida Manatee-
   Sarasota (FL)
Sul Ross State U (TX)
Tennessee State U (TN)
U of Rio Grande (OH)
U of the District of Columbia (DC)
Washburn U (KS)
Weber State U (UT)
Welch Coll (TN)

**ADULT AND CONTINUING
EDUCATION**
Fisher Coll (MA)

**ADULT AND CONTINUING
EDUCATION
ADMINISTRATION**
Concordia Coll–New York (NY)

**ADULT DEVELOPMENT AND
AGING**
Madonna U (MI)
The U of Toledo (OH)

ADVERTISING
Academy of Art U (CA)
The Art Inst of California–San Diego,
   a campus of Argosy U (CA)
Fashion Inst of Technology (NY)
State Coll of Florida Manatee-
   Sarasota (FL)

**AERONAUTICAL/AEROSPACE
ENGINEERING TECHNOLOGY**
Purdue U (IN)
Vaughn Coll of Aeronautics and
   Technology (NY)

**AERONAUTICS/AVIATION/
AEROSPACE SCIENCE AND
TECHNOLOGY**
Embry-Riddle Aeronautical U–
   Worldwide (FL)
Liberty U (VA)
Montana State U (MT)
Ohio U (OH)
Pacific Union Coll (CA)
U of Cincinnati (OH)
U of the District of Columbia (DC)
Vaughn Coll of Aeronautics and
   Technology (NY)

**AFRICAN AMERICAN/BLACK
STUDIES**
State Coll of Florida Manatee-
   Sarasota (FL)

AGRIBUSINESS
Southern Arkansas U–Magnolia
   (AR)
State U of New York Coll of
   Agriculture and Technology at
   Cobleskill (NY)
Vermont Tech Coll (VT)

**AGRICULTURAL BUSINESS
AND MANAGEMENT**
Abraham Baldwin Ag Coll (GA)

Coll of Coastal Georgia (GA)
Dickinson State U (ND)
Indian River State Coll (FL)
Michigan State U (MI)
Morrisville State Coll (NY)
North Carolina State U (NC)
State U of New York Coll of
   Agriculture and Technology at
   Cobleskill (NY)

**AGRICULTURAL BUSINESS
AND MANAGEMENT RELATED**
Penn State Abington (PA)
Penn State Altoona (PA)
Penn State Berks (PA)
Penn State Erie, The Behrend Coll
   (PA)
Penn State Shenango (PA)
Penn State U Park (PA)
U of Guelph (ON, Canada)

AGRICULTURAL ECONOMICS
Abraham Baldwin Ag Coll (GA)

AGRICULTURAL ENGINEERING
Morrisville State Coll (NY)

**AGRICULTURAL MECHANICS
AND EQUIPMENT
TECHNOLOGY**
Morrisville State Coll (NY)

AGRICULTURAL PRODUCTION
Eastern New Mexico U (NM)
Western Kentucky U (KY)

AGRICULTURE
Abraham Baldwin Ag Coll (GA)
Lubbock Christian U (TX)
Morrisville State Coll (NY)
North Carolina State U (NC)
South Dakota State U (SD)
State U of New York Coll of
   Agriculture and Technology at
   Cobleskill (NY)
U of Delaware (DE)
U of Guelph (ON, Canada)

**AGRICULTURE AND
AGRICULTURE OPERATIONS
RELATED**
Murray State U (KY)
U of New Hampshire (NH)

**AGRONOMY AND CROP
SCIENCE**
State U of New York Coll of
   Agriculture and Technology at
   Cobleskill (NY)

**AIRCRAFT POWERPLANT
TECHNOLOGY**
Embry-Riddle Aeronautical U–
   Daytona (FL)
Embry-Riddle Aeronautical U–
   Worldwide (FL)
Pennsylvania Coll of Technology
   (PA)
U of Alaska Fairbanks (AK)

**AIRFRAME MECHANICS AND
AIRCRAFT MAINTENANCE
TECHNOLOGY**
Kansas State U (KS)
Lewis U (IL)
Northern Michigan U (MI)

AIRLINE FLIGHT ATTENDANT
Liberty U (VA)

**AIRLINE PILOT AND FLIGHT
CREW**
Baker Coll of Flint (MI)

Baker Coll of Muskegon (MI)
Indian River State Coll (FL)
Kansas State U (KS)
Lewis U (IL)
Palm Beach State Coll (FL)
Polk State Coll (FL)
Southern Illinois U Carbondale (IL)
Southern Utah U (UT)
U of Alaska Fairbanks (AK)
Utah Valley U (UT)

AIR TRAFFIC CONTROL
LeTourneau U (TX)
Lewis U (IL)

ALLIED HEALTH AND MEDICAL ASSISTING SERVICES RELATED
Clarion U of Pennsylvania (PA)
Florida National U (FL)
Jones Coll, Jacksonville (FL)
National U (CA)
Nebraska Methodist Coll (NE)
Widener U (PA)

ALLIED HEALTH DIAGNOSTIC, INTERVENTION, AND TREATMENT PROFESSIONS RELATED
Ball State U (IN)
Cameron U (OK)
Gwynedd Mercy U (PA)
Pennsylvania Coll of Technology (PA)

AMERICAN GOVERNMENT AND POLITICS
State Coll of Florida Manatee-Sarasota (FL)

AMERICAN INDIAN/NATIVE AMERICAN STUDIES
Inst of American Indian Arts (NM)

AMERICAN NATIVE/NATIVE AMERICAN LANGUAGES
U of Alaska Fairbanks (AK)

AMERICAN SIGN LANGUAGE (ASL)
Bethel Coll (IN)
Madonna U (MI)

AMERICAN STUDIES
State Coll of Florida Manatee-Sarasota (FL)

ANIMAL/LIVESTOCK HUSBANDRY AND PRODUCTION
Michigan State U (MI)
North Carolina State U (NC)
Southern Utah U (UT)
U of Connecticut (CT)

ANIMAL SCIENCES
Abraham Baldwin Ag Coll (GA)
Becker Coll (MA)
Globe U–Woodbury (MN)
State U of New York Coll of Agriculture and Technology at Cobleskill (NY)
Sul Ross State U (TX)
U of Connecticut (CT)
U of New Hampshire (NH)

ANIMAL TRAINING
Becker Coll (MA)

ANIMATION, INTERACTIVE TECHNOLOGY, VIDEO GRAPHICS AND SPECIAL EFFECTS
Academy of Art U (CA)
Broadview Entertainment Arts U (UT)
Colorado Mesa U (CO)
Minnesota School of Business–Richfield (MN)
New England Inst of Technology (RI)

ANTHROPOLOGY
Indian River State Coll (FL)

APPAREL AND ACCESSORIES MARKETING
The Art Inst of California–Hollywood, a campus of Argosy U (CA)
The Art Inst of California–Inland Empire, a campus of Argosy U (CA)
The Art Inst of California–Orange County, a campus of Argosy U (CA)
The Art Inst of Charlotte, a campus of South U (NC)

The Art Inst of Raleigh-Durham, a campus of South U (NC)
The Art Inst of Seattle (WA)

APPAREL AND TEXTILE MANUFACTURING
Fashion Inst of Technology (NY)

APPAREL AND TEXTILE MARKETING MANAGEMENT
The Art Inst of Philadelphia (PA)
U of the Incarnate Word (TX)

APPAREL AND TEXTILES
Indian River State Coll (FL)
Palm Beach State Coll (FL)

APPLIED HORTICULTURE/HORTICULTURAL BUSINESS SERVICES RELATED
Morrisville State Coll (NY)
U of Massachusetts Amherst (MA)

APPLIED HORTICULTURE/HORTICULTURE OPERATIONS
Oakland City U (IN)
Pennsylvania Coll of Technology (PA)
State U of New York Coll of Technology at Delhi (NY)
U of Connecticut (CT)
U of Massachusetts Amherst (MA)
U of New Hampshire (NH)

APPLIED MATHEMATICS
Central Methodist U (MO)
Clarion U of Pennsylvania (PA)

AQUACULTURE
Morrisville State Coll (NY)

ARCHEOLOGY
Weber State U (UT)

ARCHITECTURAL DRAFTING AND CAD/CADD
Baker Coll of Flint (MI)
Baker Coll of Muskegon (MI)
Globe U–Woodbury (MN)
Indiana U–Purdue U Indianapolis (IN)
Indian River State Coll (FL)
Morrisville State Coll (NY)
New York City Coll of Technology of the City U of New York (NY)
Universidad del Turabo (PR)
Western Kentucky U (KY)

ARCHITECTURAL ENGINEERING TECHNOLOGY
Baker Coll of Clinton Township (MI)
Baker Coll of Owosso (MI)
Baker Coll of Port Huron (MI)
Bluefield State Coll (WV)
Ferris State U (MI)
Indiana U–Purdue U Fort Wayne (IN)
Morrisville State Coll (NY)
New England Inst of Technology (RI)
Norfolk State U (VA)
Northern Kentucky U (KY)
State U of New York Coll of Technology at Delhi (NY)
U of the District of Columbia (DC)
Vermont Tech Coll (VT)
Wentworth Inst of Technology (MA)

ARCHITECTURAL TECHNOLOGY
New York Inst of Technology (NY)
Pennsylvania Coll of Technology (PA)

ARCHITECTURE
Morrisville State Coll (NY)

ARCHITECTURE RELATED
Abilene Christian U (TX)

ART
Abraham Baldwin Ag Coll (GA)
Coll of Coastal Georgia (GA)
Coll of Mount St. Joseph (OH)
Eastern New Mexico U (NM)
Felician Coll (NJ)
Hannibal-LaGrange U (MO)
Indiana Wesleyan U (IN)
Kent State U at Stark (OH)
Lourdes U (OH)
Midland Coll (TX)
Northern Michigan U (MI)
Palm Beach State Coll (FL)
State Coll of Florida Manatee-Sarasota (FL)
State U of New York Empire State Coll (NY)
U of Rio Grande (OH)

ART HISTORY, CRITICISM AND CONSERVATION
Clarke U (IA)
Palm Beach State Coll (FL)
State Coll of Florida Manatee-Sarasota (FL)
Thomas More Coll (KY)

ART TEACHER EDUCATION
Indian River State Coll (FL)

ASIAN STUDIES
State Coll of Florida Manatee-Sarasota (FL)

ASTRONOMY
State Coll of Florida Manatee-Sarasota (FL)

ATHLETIC TRAINING
The U of Akron (OH)

AUDIOLOGY AND SPEECH-LANGUAGE PATHOLOGY
U of Cincinnati (OH)

AUTOBODY/COLLISION AND REPAIR TECHNOLOGY
Lewis-Clark State Coll (ID)
Montana State U Billings (MT)
Morrisville State Coll (NY)
New England Inst of Technology (RI)
Pennsylvania Coll of Technology (PA)
Utah Valley U (UT)

AUTOMOBILE/AUTOMOTIVE MECHANICS TECHNOLOGY
Baker Coll of Auburn Hills (MI)
Baker Coll of Cadillac (MI)
Baker Coll of Clinton Township (MI)
Baker Coll of Flint (MI)
Baker Coll of Owosso (MI)
Baker Coll of Port Huron (MI)
Colorado Mesa U (CO)
Dixie State U (UT)
Ferris State U (MI)
Indian River State Coll (FL)
Lewis-Clark State Coll (ID)
Midland Coll (TX)
Montana State U Billings (MT)
Montana Tech of The U of Montana (MT)
Morrisville State Coll (NY)
New England Inst of Technology (RI)
Northern Michigan U (MI)
Oakland City U (IN)
Pennsylvania Coll of Technology (PA)
Pittsburg State U (KS)
State U of New York Coll of Technology at Canton (NY)
State U of New York Coll of Technology at Delhi (NY)
U of the District of Columbia (DC)
Utah Valley U (UT)
Weber State U (UT)

AUTOMOTIVE ENGINEERING TECHNOLOGY
Farmingdale State Coll (NY)
Northern Kentucky U (KY)
Vermont Tech Coll (VT)

AVIATION/AIRWAY MANAGEMENT
Northern Kentucky U (KY)
Polk State Coll (FL)
U of the District of Columbia (DC)
Vaughn Coll of Aeronautics and Technology (NY)

AVIONICS MAINTENANCE TECHNOLOGY
Baker Coll of Flint (MI)
Excelsior Coll (NY)
U of the District of Columbia (DC)
Vaughn Coll of Aeronautics and Technology (NY)

BAKING AND PASTRY ARTS
The Art Inst of Atlanta (GA)
The Art Inst of Austin, a branch of The Art Institute of Houston (TX)
The Art Inst of California–Hollywood, a campus of Argosy U (CA)
The Art Inst of California–Inland Empire, a campus of Argosy U (CA)
The Art Inst of California–Los Angeles, a campus of Argosy U (CA)

The Art Inst of California–Orange County, a campus of Argosy U (CA)
The Art Inst of California–Sacramento, a campus of Argosy U (CA)
The Art Inst of California–San Diego, a campus of Argosy U (CA)
The Art Inst of California–San Francisco, a campus of Argosy U (CA)
The Art Inst of California–Silicon Valley, a campus of Argosy U (CA)
The Art Inst of Charleston, a branch of The Art Institute of Atlanta (SC)
The Art Inst of Colorado (CO)
The Art Inst of Dallas, a campus of South U (TX)
The Art Inst of Fort Lauderdale (FL)
The Art Inst of Houston (TX)
The Art Inst of Houston–North, a branch of The Art Institute of Houston (TX)
The Art Inst of Indianapolis (IN)
The Art Inst of Las Vegas (NV)
The Art Inst of Phoenix (AZ)
The Art Inst of Pittsburgh (PA)
The Art Inst of Salt Lake City (UT)
The Art Inst of San Antonio, a branch of The Art Institute of Houston (TX)
The Art Inst of Seattle (WA)
The Art Inst of Tampa, a branch of Miami International U of Art & Design (FL)
The Art Inst of Tennessee–Nashville, a branch of The Art Institute of Atlanta (TN)
The Art Inst of Tucson (AZ)
The Art Inst of Virginia Beach, a branch of The Art Institute of Atlanta (VA)
The Art Inst of Washington, a branch of The Art Institute of Atlanta (VA)
The Art Inst of Wisconsin (WI)
The Art Insts International–Kansas City (KS)
The Art Insts International Minnesota (MN)
The Culinary Inst of America (NY)
Harrison Coll, Indianapolis (IN)
Keiser U, Fort Lauderdale (FL)
Monroe Coll, Bronx (NY)
Newbury Coll (MA)
Pennsylvania Coll of Technology (PA)
Southern New Hampshire U (NH)
Sullivan U (KY)

BANKING AND FINANCIAL SUPPORT SERVICES
Harrison Coll, Indianapolis (IN)
Harrison Coll (OH)
Indian River State Coll (FL)
Universidad Metropolitana (PR)

BEHAVIORAL SCIENCES
Granite State Coll (NH)
Lewis-Clark State Coll (ID)
Midland Coll (TX)

BIBLICAL STUDIES
Alaska Bible Coll (AK)
Barclay Coll (KS)
Bethel Coll (IN)
Beulah Heights U (GA)
Boston Baptist Coll (MA)
Campbellsville U (KY)
Carolina Christian Coll (NC)
Cincinnati Christian U (OH)
Columbia International U (SC)
Corban U (OR)
Covenant Coll (GA)
Dallas Baptist U (TX)
Eastern Mennonite U (VA)
Emmaus Bible Coll (IA)
Faith Baptist Bible Coll and Theological Seminary (IA)
God's Bible School and Coll (OH)
Houghton Coll (NY)
Howard Payne U (TX)
Lincoln Christian U (IL)
Mid-Atlantic Christian U (NC)
Nazarene Bible Coll (CO)
Nyack Coll (NY)
Piedmont International U (NC)
Simpson U (CA)
Southern California Seminary (CA)
Southern Methodist Coll (SC)
Southwestern Assemblies of God U (TX)
Trinity Coll of Florida (FL)

Valley Forge Christian Coll (PA)
Welch Coll (TN)

BIOCHEMISTRY
Lake Superior State U (MI)
Saint Joseph's Coll (IN)

BIOLOGICAL AND BIOMEDICAL SCIENCES RELATED
Alderson Broaddus U (WV)
Gwynedd Mercy U (PA)
Roberts Wesleyan Coll (NY)

BIOLOGICAL AND PHYSICAL SCIENCES
Abraham Baldwin Ag Coll (GA)
Ferris State U (MI)
Jefferson Coll of Health Sciences (VA)
Ohio U–Zanesville (OH)
Oklahoma Wesleyan U (OK)
Penn State Altoona (PA)
Penn State Shenango (PA)
Trine U (IN)
Valparaiso U (IN)
Welch Coll (TN)

BIOLOGY/BIOLOGICAL SCIENCES
Abraham Baldwin Ag Coll (GA)
Cleveland U–Kansas City (KS)
Coll of Coastal Georgia (GA)
Dallas Baptist U (TX)
Immaculata U (PA)
Indiana Wesleyan U (IN)
Indian River State Coll (FL)
Lourdes U (OH)
Midland Coll (TX)
Oklahoma Wesleyan U (OK)
Palm Beach State Coll (FL)
Pine Manor Coll (MA)
Rogers State U (OK)
Shawnee State U (OH)
Siena Heights U (MI)
State Coll of Florida Manatee-Sarasota (FL)
State U of New York Coll of Agriculture and Technology at Cobleskill (NY)
Thomas More Coll (KY)
U of Cincinnati (OH)
U of New Hampshire at Manchester (NH)
U of Rio Grande (OH)
The U of Tampa (FL)
Utah Valley U (UT)
Welch Coll (TN)
Wright State U (OH)
York Coll of Pennsylvania (PA)

BIOLOGY/BIOTECHNOLOGY LABORATORY TECHNICIAN
State U of New York Coll of Agriculture and Technology at Cobleskill (NY)
Weber State U (UT)

BIOLOGY TEACHER EDUCATION
State Coll of Florida Manatee-Sarasota (FL)

BIOMEDICAL TECHNOLOGY
Baker Coll of Flint (MI)
Brown Mackie Coll–Birmingham (AL)
Brown Mackie Coll–Dallas/Ft. Worth (TX)
Penn State Altoona (PA)
Penn State Berks (PA)
Penn State Erie, The Behrend Coll (PA)
Penn State Shenango (PA)

BIOTECHNOLOGY
Indiana U–Purdue U Indianapolis (IN)
Inter American U of Puerto Rico, Guayama Campus (PR)
Keiser U, Fort Lauderdale (FL)
Universidad del Turabo (PR)

BLOOD BANK TECHNOLOGY
Rasmussen Coll St. Cloud (MN)

BOTANY/PLANT BIOLOGY
Palm Beach State Coll (FL)

BRASS INSTRUMENTS
McNally Smith Coll of Music (MN)

BROADCAST JOURNALISM
Evangel U (MO)
Ohio U–Zanesville (OH)

BUILDING/CONSTRUCTION FINISHING, MANAGEMENT, AND INSPECTION RELATED
Baker Coll of Flint (MI)
John Brown U (AR)
Palm Beach State Coll (FL)
Pratt Inst (NY)
Weber State U (UT)
Wentworth Inst of Technology (MA)

BUILDING/CONSTRUCTION SITE MANAGEMENT
State U of New York Coll of Technology at Canton (NY)
Wentworth Inst of Technology (MA)

BUILDING CONSTRUCTION TECHNOLOGY
Penn Foster Coll (AZ)
Wentworth Inst of Technology (MA)

BUILDING/HOME/ CONSTRUCTION INSPECTION
Utah Valley U (UT)

BUILDING/PROPERTY MAINTENANCE
State U of New York Coll of Technology at Canton (NY)
Utah Valley U (UT)

BUSINESS ADMINISTRATION AND MANAGEMENT
Abraham Baldwin Ag Coll (GA)
AIB Coll of Business (IA)
Alaska Pacific U (AK)
Albertus Magnus Coll (CT)
The American U of Rome (Italy)
Anderson U (IN)
Argosy U, Atlanta (GA)
Argosy U, Dallas (TX)
Argosy U, Denver (CO)
Argosy U, Hawai`i (HI)
Argosy U, Inland Empire (CA)
Argosy U, Los Angeles (CA)
Argosy U, Nashville (TN)
Argosy U, Orange County (CA)
Argosy U, Phoenix (AZ)
Argosy U, Salt Lake City (UT)
Argosy U, San Diego (CA)
Argosy U, San Francisco Bay Area (CA)
Argosy U, Sarasota (FL)
Argosy U, Seattle (WA)
Argosy U, Tampa (FL)
Argosy U, Twin Cities (MN)
Argosy U, Washington DC (VA)
Austin Peay State U (TN)
Baker Coll of Allen Park (MI)
Baker Coll of Auburn Hills (MI)
Baker Coll of Flint (MI)
Baker Coll of Owosso (MI)
Ball State U (IN)
Bay Path Coll (MA)
Beacon Coll (FL)
Benedictine U (IL)
Bethel Coll (IN)
Broadview U–Boise (ID)
Broadview U–Layton (UT)
Broadview U–Orem (UT)
Broadview U–West Jordan (UT)
Brown Mackie Coll–Birmingham (AL)
Bryan Coll (TN)
California U of Pennsylvania (PA)
Calumet Coll of Saint Joseph (IN)
Cameron U (OK)
Campbellsville U (KY)
Carroll Coll (MT)
Cazenovia Coll (NY)
Central Penn Coll (PA)
Chaminade U of Honolulu (HI)
Clarion U of Pennsylvania (PA)
Coll of Coastal Georgia (GA)
Coll of Mount St. Joseph (OH)
Coll of Saint Mary (NE)
Columbia Centro Universitario, Yauco (PR)
Columbia Southern U (AL)
Concordia Coll–New York (NY)
Concord U (WV)
Corban U (OR)
Cornerstone U (MI)
Dakota State U (SD)
Dallas Baptist U (TX)
Dallas Christian Coll (TX)
Davenport U, Grand Rapids (MI)
Dixie State U (UT)
Edinboro U of Pennsylvania (PA)
EDP U of Puerto Rico (PR)

EDP U of Puerto Rico–San Sebastian (PR)
Elizabethtown Coll School of Continuing and Professional Studies (PA)
Elmira Coll (NY)
Excelsior Coll (NY)
Fisher Coll (MA)
Five Towns Coll (NY)
Florida National U (FL)
Franklin U (OH)
Geneva Coll (PA)
Globe U–Appleton (WI)
Globe U–Eau Claire (WI)
Globe U–Green Bay (WI)
Globe U–La Crosse (WI)
Globe U–Madison East (WI)
Globe U–Madison West (WI)
Globe U–Minneapolis (MN)
Globe U–Sioux Falls (SD)
Globe U–Wausau (WI)
Globe U–Woodbury (MN)
Gwynedd Mercy U (PA)
Harrison Coll, Indianapolis (IN)
Harrison Coll (OH)
Hawai`i Pacific U (HI)
Husson U (ME)
Immaculata U (PA)
Indiana Tech (IN)
Indiana U–Purdue U Fort Wayne (IN)
Indiana Wesleyan U (IN)
Indian River State Coll (FL)
Inter American U of Puerto Rico, Aguadilla Campus (PR)
Inter American U of Puerto Rico, Bayamón Campus (PR)
Inter American U of Puerto Rico, Fajardo Campus (PR)
Inter American U of Puerto Rico, Guayama Campus (PR)
Inter American U of Puerto Rico, Metropolitan Campus (PR)
Inter American U of Puerto Rico, Ponce Campus (PR)
Inter American U of Puerto Rico, San Germán Campus (PR)
ITT Tech Inst, Phoenix (AZ)
ITT Tech Inst, Phoenix (AZ)
ITT Tech Inst, Tempe (AZ)
ITT Tech Inst, Clovis (CA)
ITT Tech Inst, Concord (CA)
ITT Tech Inst, Corona (CA)
ITT Tech Inst, Indianapolis (IN)
ITT Tech Inst, Indianapolis (IN)
ITT Tech Inst, South Bend (IN)
ITT Tech Inst, Wichita (KS)
ITT Tech Inst, Lexington (KY)
ITT Tech Inst, Southfield (MI)
ITT Tech Inst (MS)
ITT Tech Inst, Springfield (MO)
ITT Tech Inst, Charlotte (NC)
ITT Tech Inst, Oklahoma City (OK)
ITT Tech Inst, Salem (OR)
Johnson State Coll (VT)
Jones Coll, Jacksonville (FL)
Jones International U (CO)
Kansas Wesleyan U (KS)
Keiser U, Fort Lauderdale (FL)
Kent State U (OH)
Keystone Coll (PA)
King's Coll (PA)
Lake Superior State U (MI)
Lebanon Valley Coll (PA)
Lincoln U of New England, Southington (CT)
Lock Haven U of Pennsylvania (PA)
Long Island U–LIU Brooklyn (NY)
Madonna U (MI)
Maria Coll (NY)
Marian U (IN)
Marietta Coll (OH)
McKendree U (IL)
Medaille Coll (NY)
Medgar Evers Coll of the City U of New York (NY)
Mercy Coll (NY)
Minnesota School of Business–Blaine (MN)
Minnesota School of Business–Elk River (MN)
Minnesota School of Business–Lakeville (MN)
Minnesota School of Business–Moorhead (MN)
Minnesota School of Business–Rochester (MN)
Minnesota School of Business–St. Cloud (MN)
Missouri Baptist U (MO)
Missouri Western State U (MO)

Montana State U Billings (MT)
Montreat Coll, Montreat (NC)
Morrisville State Coll (NY)
Mount Aloysius Coll (PA)
Mount Marty Coll (SD)
Mount St. Mary's Coll (CA)
Muhlenberg Coll (PA)
National U (CA)
Newbury Coll (MA)
New England Inst of Technology (RI)
Newman U (KS)
New Mexico Inst of Mining and Technology (NM)
New York Inst of Technology (NY)
Niagara U (NY)
Northwood U, Michigan Campus (MI)
Nyack Coll (NY)
Oakland City U (IN)
Ohio Dominican U (OH)
Oklahoma Wesleyan U (OK)
Peirce Coll (PA)
Penn Foster Coll (AZ)
Pennsylvania Coll of Technology (PA)
Pioneer Pacific Coll, Wilsonville (OR)
Point Park U (PA)
Point U (GA)
Providence Coll (RI)
Rasmussen Coll Appleton (WI)
Rasmussen Coll Aurora (IL)
Rasmussen Coll Blaine (MN)
Rasmussen Coll Bloomington (MN)
Rasmussen Coll Brooklyn Park (MN)
Rasmussen Coll Eagan (MN)
Rasmussen Coll Fort Myers (FL)
Rasmussen Coll Green Bay (WI)
Rasmussen Coll Kansas City/ Overland Park (KS)
Rasmussen Coll Lake Elmo/ Woodbury (MN)
Rasmussen Coll Land O' Lakes (FL)
Rasmussen Coll Mankato (MN)
Rasmussen Coll Mokena/Tinley Park (IL)
Rasmussen Coll Moorhead (MN)
Rasmussen Coll New Port Richey (FL)
Rasmussen Coll Ocala (FL)
Rasmussen Coll Romeoville/Joliet (IL)
Rasmussen Coll St. Cloud (MN)
Rasmussen Coll Tampa/Brandon (FL)
Rasmussen Coll Topeka (KS)
Rasmussen Coll Wausau (WI)
Regent U (VA)
Rider U (NJ)
Robert Morris U Illinois (IL)
Rogers State U (OK)
Roger Williams U (RI)
Rust Coll (MS)
St. Francis Coll (NY)
Saint Francis U (PA)
St. Gregory's U, Shawnee (OK)
St. John's U (NY)
Saint Joseph's U (PA)
Saint Peter's U (NJ)
St. Thomas Aquinas Coll (NY)
Shawnee State U (OH)
Siena Heights U (MI)
Southern California Inst of Technology (CA)
Southern New Hampshire U (NH)
Southwestern Assemblies of God U (TX)
State Coll of Florida Manatee-Sarasota (FL)
State U of New York Coll of Agriculture and Technology at Cobleskill (NY)
State U of New York Coll of Technology at Delhi (NY)
Stevens–The Inst of Business & Arts (MO)
Taylor U (IN)
Thomas More Coll (KY)
Tiffin U (OH)
Toccoa Falls Coll (GA)
Trine U (IN)
Tulane U (LA)
Union Coll (NE)
Universidad del Turabo (PR)
The U of Akron (OH)
U of Alaska Fairbanks (AK)
U of Arkansas–Fort Smith (AR)
U of Cincinnati (OH)
The U of Findlay (OH)
U of Maine at Augusta (ME)
U of Maine at Fort Kent (ME)
The U of Montana Western (MT)

U of New Hampshire (NH)
U of New Hampshire at Manchester (NH)
U of New Haven (CT)
U of Pennsylvania (PA)
U of Pikeville (KY)
U of Rio Grande (OH)
The U of Scranton (PA)
U of the Incarnate Word (TX)
U of the Potomac (DC)
U of the Virgin Islands (VI)
The U of Toledo (OH)
Upper Iowa U (IA)
Utah Valley U (UT)
Vermont Tech Coll (VT)
Villa Maria Coll (NY)
Walsh U (OH)
Wayland Baptist U (TX)
Webber International U (FL)
Welch Coll (TN)
Wesley Coll (DE)
Western Kentucky U (KY)
Wilson Coll (PA)
Wright State U (OH)
Xavier U (OH)
York Coll of Pennsylvania (PA)
Youngstown State U (OH)

BUSINESS ADMINISTRATION, MANAGEMENT AND OPERATIONS RELATED
AIB Coll of Business (IA)
Columbia Centro Universitario, Caguas (PR)
Dixie State U (UT)
Embry-Riddle Aeronautical U–Worldwide (FL)
U of Cincinnati (OH)

BUSINESS AND PERSONAL/ FINANCIAL SERVICES MARKETING
Dixie State U (UT)

BUSINESS AUTOMATION/ TECHNOLOGY/DATA ENTRY
Baker Coll of Clinton Township (MI)
Colorado Mesa U (CO)
Montana State U Billings (MT)
Northern Michigan U (MI)
The U of Akron (OH)
U of Rio Grande (OH)
U of the District of Columbia (DC)
The U of Toledo (OH)
Utah Valley U (UT)

BUSINESS/COMMERCE
Adams State U (CO)
AIB Coll of Business (IA)
Alderson Broaddus U (WV)
Alvernia U (PA)
American Public U System (WV)
Baker Coll of Flint (MI)
Benedictine U at Springfield (IL)
Brown Mackie Coll–Dallas/Ft. Worth (TX)
Brown Mackie Coll–San Antonio (TX)
Caribbean U (PR)
Castleton State Coll (VT)
Champlain Coll (VT)
Coll of Staten Island of the City U of New York (NY)
Columbia Coll (MO)
Crown Coll (MN)
Ferris State U (MI)
Fisher Coll (MA)
Gannon U (PA)
Glenville State Coll (WV)
God's Bible School and Coll (OH)
Granite State Coll (NH)
Indiana U Northwest (IN)
Indiana U Southeast (IN)
Kent State U at Geauga (OH)
Limestone Coll (SC)
Lourdes U (OH)
Mayville State U (ND)
Metropolitan Coll of New York (NY)
Midland Coll (TX)
Missouri Southern State U (MO)
Montana State U Billings (MT)
Mount Vernon Nazarene U (OH)
Murray State U (KY)
New York U (NY)
Northern Kentucky U (KY)
Northern Michigan U (MI)
Olivet Nazarene U (IL)
Pacific Union Coll (CA)
Penn State Abington (PA)
Penn State Altoona (PA)

Penn State Berks (PA)
Penn State Erie, The Behrend Coll (PA)
Penn State Harrisburg (PA)
Penn State Shenango (PA)
Penn State York Park (PA)
Saint Leo U (FL)
Saint Mary-of-the-Woods Coll (IN)
Southern Arkansas U–Magnolia (AR)
Southern Nazarene U (MO)
Southwest Baptist U (MO)
Southwestern Assemblies of God U (TX)
Spalding U (KY)
State Coll of Florida Manatee-Sarasota (FL)
State U of New York Empire State Coll (NY)
Thomas More Coll (KY)
Troy U (AL)
Tulane U (LA)
U of Bridgeport (CT)
U of Cincinnati (OH)
U of Maine at Fort Kent (ME)
U of New Hampshire (NH)
U of Southern Indiana (IN)
The U of Toledo (OH)
Wright State U (OH)
Youngstown State U (OH)

BUSINESS/CORPORATE COMMUNICATIONS
AIB Coll of Business (IA)

BUSINESS, MANAGEMENT, AND MARKETING RELATED
AIB Coll of Business (IA)
Ball State U (IN)
Five Towns Coll (NY)
Florida National U (FL)
Oklahoma Wesleyan U (OK)
Purdue U North Central (IN)
Sacred Heart U (CT)
Sullivan U (KY)

BUSINESS/MANAGERIAL ECONOMICS
Campbellsville U (KY)
Saint Peter's U (NJ)
State Coll of Florida Manatee-Sarasota (FL)

BUSINESS TEACHER EDUCATION
Wright State U (OH)

CABINETMAKING AND MILLWORK
Utah Valley U (UT)

CAD/CADD DRAFTING/DESIGN TECHNOLOGY
The Art Inst of Las Vegas (NV)
Ferris State U (MI)
ITT Tech Inst, Springfield (IL)
Keiser U, Fort Lauderdale (FL)
Montana Tech of The U of Montana (MT)
Morrisville State Coll (NY)
Northern Michigan U (MI)
Shawnee State U (OH)
State U of New York Coll of Technology at Delhi (NY)
U of Arkansas–Fort Smith (AR)

CARDIOVASCULAR TECHNOLOGY
Arkansas Tech U (AR)
Gwynedd Mercy U (PA)
Mercy Coll of Ohio (OH)
Nebraska Methodist Coll (NE)
Polk State Coll (FL)

CARPENTRY
Indian River State Coll (FL)
Liberty U (VA)
Montana State U Billings (MT)
Montana Tech of The U of Montana (MT)
New England Inst of Technology (RI)
Southern Utah U (UT)
U of Alaska Fairbanks (AK)

CELL BIOLOGY AND ANATOMICAL SCIENCES RELATED
National U (CA)

CERAMIC ARTS AND CERAMICS
Palm Beach State Coll (FL)

CHEMICAL ENGINEERING
U of the District of Columbia (DC)

CHEMICAL TECHNOLOGY
Ball State U (IN)
Ferris State U (MI)
Indiana U–Purdue U Fort Wayne (IN)
Inter American U of Puerto Rico, Guayama Campus (PR)
Lawrence Technological U (MI)
Midland Coll (TX)
Millersville U of Pennsylvania (PA)
New York City Coll of Technology of the City U of New York (NY)
State U of New York Coll of Agriculture and Technology at Cobleskill (NY)
U of Cincinnati (OH)
Weber State U (UT)

CHEMISTRY
Abraham Baldwin Ag Coll (GA)
Castleton State Coll (VT)
Central Methodist U (MO)
Clarke U (IA)
Coll of Coastal Georgia (GA)
Immaculata U (PA)
Indiana U–Purdue U Indianapolis (IN)
Indiana Wesleyan U (IN)
Indian River State Coll (FL)
Lake Superior State U (MI)
Lindsey Wilson Coll (KY)
Midland Coll (TX)
Northern Kentucky U (KY)
Ohio Dominican U (OH)
Oklahoma Wesleyan U (OK)
Palm Beach State Coll (FL)
Siena Heights U (MI)
Southern Arkansas U–Magnolia (AR)
State Coll of Florida Manatee-Sarasota (FL)
Thomas More Coll (KY)
U of Cincinnati (OH)
U of Rio Grande (OH)
The U of Tampa (FL)
U of the Incarnate Word (TX)
Utah Valley U (UT)
Wright State U (OH)
York Coll of Pennsylvania (PA)

CHEMISTRY TEACHER EDUCATION
State Coll of Florida Manatee-Sarasota (FL)

CHILD-CARE AND SUPPORT SERVICES MANAGEMENT
Eastern New Mexico U (NM)
Ferris State U (MI)
Morrisville State Coll (NY)
Mount Vernon Nazarene U (OH)
Nicholls State U (LA)
Siena Heights U (MI)
Southeast Missouri State U (MO)
State U of New York Coll of Agriculture and Technology at Cobleskill (NY)
State U of New York Coll of Technology at Canton (NY)
Youngstown State U (OH)

CHILD-CARE PROVISION
American Public U System (WV)
Mayville State U (ND)
Pennsylvania Coll of Technology (PA)
Trevecca Nazarene U (TN)
U of Alaska Fairbanks (AK)

CHILD DEVELOPMENT
Abraham Baldwin Ag Coll (GA)
Arkansas Tech U (AR)
Evangel U (MO)
Indian River State Coll (FL)
Lewis-Clark State Coll (ID)
Lincoln Coll of New England, Southington (CT)
Madonna U (MI)
Midland Coll (TX)
Northern Michigan U (MI)
Ohio U (OH)
Polk State Coll (FL)
Southern Utah U (UT)
State Coll of Florida Manatee-Sarasota (FL)
U of the District of Columbia (DC)
Weber State U (UT)
Youngstown State U (OH)

CHRISTIAN STUDIES
Crown Coll (MN)
Heritage Bible Coll (NC)
Huntington U (IN)

Oklahoma Baptist U (OK)
Oklahoma Wesleyan U (OK)
Ouachita Baptist U (AR)
Regent U (VA)
Wayland Baptist U (TX)

CINEMATOGRAPHY AND FILM/VIDEO PRODUCTION
Academy of Art U (CA)
The Art Inst of Atlanta (GA)
The Art Inst of Charlotte, a campus of South U (NC)
The Art Inst of Colorado (CO)
The Art Inst of Dallas, a campus of South U (TX)
The Art Inst of Fort Lauderdale (FL)
The Art Inst of Ohio–Cincinnati (OH)
The Art Inst of Philadelphia (PA)
The Art Inst of Pittsburgh (PA)
The Art Inst of Seattle (WA)
The Art Inst of Tennessee–Nashville, a branch of The Art Institute of Atlanta (TN)
The Art Inst of Washington, a branch of The Art Institute of Atlanta (VA)
Fashion Inst of Technology (NY)
Inst of American Indian Arts (NM)
New England Inst of Technology (RI)
Pacific Union Coll (CA)

CIVIL ENGINEERING TECHNOLOGY
Bluefield State Coll (WV)
Fairmont State U (WV)
Ferris State U (MI)
Indiana U–Purdue U Fort Wayne (IN)
Indian River State Coll (FL)
Montana Tech of The U of Montana (MT)
Murray State U (KY)
New York City Coll of Technology of the City U of New York (NY)
Pennsylvania Coll of Technology (PA)
Point Park U (PA)
State Coll of Florida Manatee-Sarasota (FL)
State U of New York Coll of Technology at Canton (NY)
U of New Hampshire (NH)
U of Puerto Rico in Bayamón (PR)
U of the District of Columbia (DC)
Vermont Tech Coll (VT)
Youngstown State U (OH)

CLINICAL LABORATORY SCIENCE/MEDICAL TECHNOLOGY
Arkansas State U (AR)
Dixie State U (UT)
Ferris State U (MI)
Harrison Coll, Indianapolis (IN)
Lake Superior State U (MI)
Shawnee State U (OH)
U of Cincinnati (OH)

CLINICAL/MEDICAL LABORATORY ASSISTANT
New England Inst of Technology (RI)
U of Alaska Fairbanks (AK)
U of Maine at Augusta (ME)

CLINICAL/MEDICAL LABORATORY SCIENCE AND ALLIED PROFESSIONS RELATED
State U of New York Coll of Agriculture and Technology at Cobleskill (NY)
Youngstown State U (OH)

CLINICAL/MEDICAL LABORATORY TECHNOLOGY
Argosy U, Dallas (TX)
Argosy U, Twin Cities (MN)
Baker Coll of Owosso (MI)
Coll of Coastal Georgia (GA)
Farmingdale State Coll (NY)
Ferris State U (MI)
The George Washington U (DC)
Indian River State Coll (FL)
Keiser U, Fort Lauderdale (FL)
Marshall U (WV)
Mount Aloysius Coll (PA)
Our Lady of the Lake Coll (LA)
Rasmussen Coll Bismarck (ND)
Rasmussen Coll Green Bay (WI)
Rasmussen Coll Lake Elmo/Woodbury (MN)
Rasmussen Coll Mankato (MN)
Rasmussen Coll Moorhead (MN)
Rasmussen Coll St. Cloud (MN)
U of Maine at Presque Isle (ME)

U of Rio Grande (OH)
Weber State U (UT)
Youngstown State U (OH)

COMMERCIAL AND ADVERTISING ART
Academy of Art U (CA)
Baker Coll of Auburn Hills (MI)
Baker Coll of Clinton Township (MI)
Baker Coll of Muskegon (MI)
Baker Coll of Owosso (MI)
Baker Coll of Port Huron (MI)
California U of Pennsylvania (PA)
Creative Center (NE)
Fashion Inst of Technology (NY)
Mercy Coll (NY)
Mitchell Coll (CT)
Mount St. Mary's Coll (CA)
New York City Coll of Technology of the City U of New York (NY)
Northern State U (SD)
Palm Beach State Coll (FL)
Pennsylvania Coll of Technology (PA)
Pratt Inst (NY)
Robert Morris U Illinois (IL)
State Coll of Florida Manatee-Sarasota (FL)
State U of New York Coll of Agriculture and Technology at Cobleskill (NY)
U of Cincinnati (OH)
Villa Maria Coll (NY)

COMMERCIAL PHOTOGRAPHY
Academy of Art U (CA)
The Art Inst of Atlanta (GA)
The Art Inst of California–Hollywood, a campus of Argosy U (CA)
The Art Inst of California–Inland Empire, a campus of Argosy U (CA)
The Art Inst of California–Los Angeles, a campus of Argosy U (CA)
The Art Inst of California–Orange County, a campus of Argosy U (CA)
The Art Inst of California–San Francisco, a campus of Argosy U (CA)
The Art Inst of California–Silicon Valley, a campus of Argosy U (CA)
The Art Inst of Colorado (CO)
The Art Inst of Indianapolis (IN)
The Art Inst of Las Vegas (NV)
The Art Inst of Philadelphia (PA)
The Art Inst of Pittsburgh (PA)
The Art Inst of Seattle (WA)
Fashion Inst of Technology (NY)
The New England Inst of Art (MA)

COMMUNICATION
Elizabethtown Coll School of Continuing and Professional Studies (PA)
Keystone Coll (PA)
Midland Coll (TX)
National U (CA)
Thomas More Coll (KY)

COMMUNICATION AND JOURNALISM RELATED
Clarke U (IA)
Immaculata U (PA)
Madonna U (MI)
Tulane U (LA)
Valparaiso U (IN)

COMMUNICATION AND MEDIA RELATED
AIB Coll of Business (IA)
Keystone Coll (PA)

COMMUNICATION DISORDERS SCIENCES AND SERVICES RELATED
Granite State Coll (NH)

COMMUNICATIONS TECHNOLOGY
AIB Coll of Business (IA)
Colorado Mesa U (CO)
East Stroudsburg U of Pennsylvania (PA)

COMMUNITY HEALTH AND PREVENTIVE MEDICINE
National U (CA)
Utah Valley U (UT)

COMMUNITY HEALTH SERVICES COUNSELING
State Coll of Florida Manatee-Sarasota (FL)

COMMUNITY ORGANIZATION AND ADVOCACY
Metropolitan Coll of New York (NY)
Morrisville State Coll (NY)
State U of New York Empire State Coll (NY)
The U of Akron (OH)
U of Alaska Fairbanks (AK)
The U of Findlay (OH)
U of New Hampshire (NH)

COMPARATIVE LITERATURE
Palm Beach State Coll (FL)

COMPUTER AND INFORMATION SCIENCES
Baker Coll of Allen Park (MI)
Ball State U (IN)
Beacon Coll (FL)
Black Hills State U (SD)
California U of Pennsylvania (PA)
Calumet Coll of Saint Joseph (IN)
Caribbean U (PR)
Chaminade U of Honolulu (HI)
Clarke U (IA)
Columbia Coll (MO)
Edinboro U of Pennsylvania (PA)
Excelsior Coll (NY)
Fisher Coll (MA)
Husson U (ME)
Indiana Wesleyan U (IN)
Inter American U of Puerto Rico, Fajardo Campus (PR)
Inter American U of Puerto Rico, Ponce Campus (PR)
Jones Coll, Jacksonville (FL)
King's Coll (PA)
Lewis-Clark State Coll (ID)
Lincoln U (MO)
Manchester U (IN)
Midland Coll (TX)
Montana State U Billings (MT)
Morrisville State Coll (NY)
National U (CA)
New England Inst of Technology (RI)
New York City Coll of Technology of the City U of New York (NY)
Penn Foster Coll (AZ)
Rogers State U (OK)
St. John's U (NY)
State Coll of Florida Manatee-Sarasota (FL)
State U of New York Coll of Agriculture and Technology at Cobleskill (NY)
Troy U (AL)
Tulane U (LA)
Union Coll (NE)
U of Arkansas–Fort Smith (AR)
U of Cincinnati (OH)
U of Maine at Augusta (ME)
The U of Tampa (FL)
The U of Toledo (OH)
Utah Valley U (UT)
Washburn U (KS)
Webber International U (FL)

COMPUTER AND INFORMATION SCIENCES AND SUPPORT SERVICES RELATED
Indiana U–Purdue U Indianapolis (IN)
Inter American U of Puerto Rico, Guayama Campus (PR)
Montana State U Billings (MT)
Pace U (NY)
Palm Beach State Coll (FL)
U of the Potomac (DC)

COMPUTER AND INFORMATION SCIENCES RELATED
Limestone Coll (SC)
Lindsey Wilson Coll (KY)
Madonna U (MI)
State Coll of Florida Manatee-Sarasota (FL)

COMPUTER AND INFORMATION SYSTEMS SECURITY
Davenport U, Grand Rapids (MI)
St. John's U (NY)
U of Maine at Fort Kent (ME)
U of the Potomac (DC)

COMPUTER ENGINEERING
New England Inst of Technology (RI)
The U of Scranton (PA)

COMPUTER ENGINEERING TECHNOLOGIES RELATED
Universidad del Turabo (PR)

COMPUTER ENGINEERING TECHNOLOGY
Abraham Baldwin Ag Coll (GA)
Baker Coll of Owosso (MI)
California U of Pennsylvania (PA)
Indiana U–Purdue U Indianapolis (IN)
Indian River State Coll (FL)
ITT Tech Inst, Springfield (IL)
Morrisville State Coll (NY)
Northern Michigan U (MI)
Oakland City U (IN)
Polk State Coll (FL)
State Coll of Florida Manatee-Sarasota (FL)
U of Hartford (CT)
U of the District of Columbia (DC)
Vermont Tech Coll (VT)
Weber State U (UT)

COMPUTER GRAPHICS
Baker Coll of Cadillac (MI)
EDP U of Puerto Rico (PR)
Indiana Tech (IN)
State Coll of Florida Manatee-Sarasota (FL)

COMPUTER/INFORMATION TECHNOLOGY SERVICES ADMINISTRATION RELATED
Limestone Coll (SC)
Maria Coll (NY)
Mercy Coll (NY)
Pennsylvania Coll of Technology (PA)

COMPUTER INSTALLATION AND REPAIR TECHNOLOGY
Inter American U of Puerto Rico, Aguadilla Campus (PR)
Inter American U of Puerto Rico, Bayamón Campus (PR)
Inter American U of Puerto Rico, Fajardo Campus (PR)
Penn Foster Coll (AZ)
Sullivan U (KY)
Universidad Metropolitana (PR)
U of Alaska Fairbanks (AK)

COMPUTER PROGRAMMING
AIB Coll of Business (IA)
Baker Coll of Muskegon (MI)
Baker Coll of Owosso (MI)
Baker Coll of Port Huron (MI)
Black Hills State U (SD)
Caribbean U (PR)
Castleton State Coll (VT)
Champlain Coll (VT)
Coll of Staten Island of the City U of New York (NY)
Columbia Centro Universitario, Caguas (PR)
EDP U of Puerto Rico (PR)
EDP U of Puerto Rico–San Sebastian (PR)
Gwynedd Mercy U (PA)
Indian River State Coll (FL)
International Business Coll, Fort Wayne (IN)
Limestone Coll (SC)
Medgar Evers Coll of the City U of New York (NY)
Minnesota School of Business–Richfield (MN)
Missouri Southern State U (MO)
Morrisville State Coll (NY)
New England Inst of Technology (RI)
Oakland City U (IN)
Palm Beach State Coll (FL)
Polk State Coll (FL)
Rasmussen Coll Fargo (ND)
Saint Francis U (PA)
State Coll of Florida Manatee-Sarasota (FL)
U of Arkansas at Little Rock (AR)
Youngstown State U (OH)

COMPUTER PROGRAMMING RELATED
Florida National U (FL)
State Coll of Florida Manatee-Sarasota (FL)

COMPUTER PROGRAMMING (SPECIFIC APPLICATIONS)
Broadview U–Boise (ID)

Broadview U–Layton (UT)
Broadview U–Orem (UT)
Broadview U–West Jordan (UT)
Florida National U (FL)
Globe U–Eau Claire (WI)
Globe U–Green Bay (WI)
Globe U–La Crosse (WI)
Globe U–Madison East (WI)
Globe U–Madison West (WI)
Globe U–Minneapolis (MN)
Globe U–Sioux Falls (SD)
Globe U–Wausau (WI)
Globe U–Woodbury (MN)
Indiana U South Bend (IN)
ITT Tech Inst, Phoenix (AZ)
ITT Tech Inst, Phoenix (AZ)
ITT Tech Inst, Tempe (AZ)
ITT Tech Inst, Clovis (CA)
ITT Tech Inst, Concord (CA)
ITT Tech Inst, Corona (CA)
ITT Tech Inst, West Palm Beach (FL)
ITT Tech Inst, Indianapolis (IN)
ITT Tech Inst, South Bend (IN)
ITT Tech Inst, Wichita (KS)
ITT Tech Inst, Lexington (KY)
ITT Tech Inst, Southfield (MI)
ITT Tech Inst (MS)
ITT Tech Inst, Springfield (MO)
ITT Tech Inst, Oklahoma City (OK)
ITT Tech Inst, Salem (OR)
Kent State U at Geauga (OH)
Minnesota School of Business–Blaine (MN)
Minnesota School of Business–Elk River (MN)
Minnesota School of Business–Lakeville (MN)
Minnesota School of Business–Moorhead (MN)
Minnesota School of Business–Richfield (MN)
Minnesota School of Business–Rochester (MN)
Minnesota School of Business–St. Cloud (MN)
Minnesota School of Business–Shakopee (MN)
Palm Beach State Coll (FL)
The U of Toledo (OH)

COMPUTER SCIENCE
Abraham Baldwin Ag Coll (GA)
Alderson Broaddus U (WV)
Baker Coll of Allen Park (MI)
Baker Coll of Owosso (MI)
Black Hills State U (SD)
Carroll Coll (MT)
Central Methodist U (MO)
Central Penn Coll (PA)
Coll of Coastal Georgia (GA)
Creighton U (NE)
Farmingdale State Coll (NY)
Felician Coll (NJ)
Florida National U (FL)
Franklin U (OH)
Hawai'i Pacific U (HI)
Indian River State Coll (FL)
Inter American U of Puerto Rico, Aguadilla Campus (PR)
Inter American U of Puerto Rico, Bayamón Campus (PR)
Inter American U of Puerto Rico, Ponce Campus (PR)
Inter American U of Puerto Rico, San Germán Campus (PR)
Lake Superior State U (MI)
Madonna U (MI)
Midland Coll (TX)
Monroe Coll, Bronx (NY)
Morrisville State Coll (NY)
New England Inst of Technology (RI)
New York City Coll of Technology of the City U of New York (NY)
Oakland City U (IN)
Palm Beach State Coll (FL)
Southern California Inst of Technology (CA)
Southwest Baptist U (MO)
The U of Findlay (OH)
U of Maine at Fort Kent (ME)
U of New Haven (CT)
U of Rio Grande (OH)
U of the Virgin Islands (VI)
Utah Valley U (UT)
Walsh U (OH)
Weber State U (UT)

COMPUTER SOFTWARE AND MEDIA APPLICATIONS RELATED
American Public U System (WV)
Champlain Coll (VT)
Platt Coll San Diego (CA)

COMPUTER SOFTWARE ENGINEERING
Rasmussen Coll Appleton (WI)
Rasmussen Coll Bismarck (ND)
Rasmussen Coll Blaine (MN)
Rasmussen Coll Bloomington (MN)
Rasmussen Coll Brooklyn Park (MN)
Rasmussen Coll Eagan (MN)
Rasmussen Coll Fargo (ND)
Rasmussen Coll Fort Myers (FL)
Rasmussen Coll Green Bay (WI)
Rasmussen Coll Kansas City/Overland Park (KS)
Rasmussen Coll Lake Elmo/Woodbury (MN)
Rasmussen Coll Land O' Lakes (FL)
Rasmussen Coll Mankato (MN)
Rasmussen Coll Moorhead (MN)
Rasmussen Coll New Port Richey (FL)
Rasmussen Coll Ocala (FL)
Rasmussen Coll St. Cloud (MN)
Rasmussen Coll Tampa/Brandon (FL)
Rasmussen Coll Topeka (KS)
Rasmussen Coll Wausau (WI)
Vermont Tech Coll (VT)

COMPUTER SOFTWARE TECHNOLOGY
Globe U–Woodbury (MN)

COMPUTER SUPPORT SPECIALIST
Brown Mackie Coll–Birmingham (AL)
Brown Mackie Coll–Dallas/Ft. Worth (TX)
Brown Mackie Coll–San Antonio (TX)

COMPUTER SYSTEMS ANALYSIS
Davenport U, Grand Rapids (MI)
The U of Akron (OH)
The U of Toledo (OH)

COMPUTER SYSTEMS NETWORKING AND TELECOMMUNICATIONS
Baker Coll of Allen Park (MI)
Baker Coll of Flint (MI)
Broadview U–Boise (ID)
Broadview U–Layton (UT)
Broadview U–Orem (UT)
Broadview U–West Jordan (UT)
Clayton State U (GA)
DeVry Coll of New York (NY)
DeVry U, Phoenix (AZ)
DeVry U, Alhambra (CA)
DeVry U, Anaheim (CA)
DeVry U, Bakersfield (CA)
DeVry U, Daly City (CA)
DeVry U, Elk Grove (CA)
DeVry U, Fremont (CA)
DeVry U, Long Beach (CA)
DeVry U, Oakland (CA)
DeVry U, Oxnard (CA)
DeVry U, Palmdale (CA)
DeVry U, Pomona (CA)
DeVry U, San Diego (CA)
DeVry U, Sherman Oaks (CA)
DeVry U, Colorado Springs (CO)
DeVry U, Westminster (CO)
DeVry U, Jacksonville (FL)
DeVry U, Miami (FL)
DeVry U, Miramar (FL)
DeVry U, Orlando (FL)
DeVry U, Tampa (FL)
DeVry U, Alpharetta (GA)
DeVry U, Decatur (GA)
DeVry U, Duluth (GA)
DeVry U, Addison (IL)
DeVry U, Chicago (IL)
DeVry U, Tinley Park (IL)
DeVry U, Indianapolis (IN)
DeVry U (MI)
DeVry U, Edina (MN)
DeVry U, Kansas City (MO)
DeVry U, Kansas City (MO)
DeVry U, St. Louis (MO)
DeVry U (NV)
DeVry U, North Brunswick (NJ)
DeVry U, Paramus (NJ)

DeVry U, Charlotte (NC)
DeVry U, Columbus (OH)
DeVry U, Seven Hills (OH)
DeVry U (OK)
DeVry U (OR)
DeVry U, Fort Washington (PA)
DeVry U, King of Prussia (PA)
DeVry U, Philadelphia (PA)
DeVry U, Pittsburgh (PA)
DeVry U, Memphis (TN)
DeVry U, Nashville (TN)
DeVry U, Austin (TX)
DeVry U, Houston (TX)
DeVry U, Irving (TX)
DeVry U (UT)
DeVry U, Arlington (VA)
DeVry U, Chesapeake (VA)
DeVry U, Manassas (VA)
DeVry U, Bellevue (WA)
DeVry U, Federal Way (WA)
DeVry U, Milwaukee (WI)
Florida National U (FL)
Globe U–Eau Claire (WI)
Globe U–Green Bay (WI)
Globe U–La Crosse (WI)
Globe U–Madison East (WI)
Globe U–Madison West (WI)
Globe U–Minneapolis (MN)
Globe U–Wausau (WI)
Globe U–Woodbury (MN)
Harrison Coll, Indianapolis (IN)
Hickey Coll (MO)
Indiana Tech (IN)
International Business Coll, Fort Wayne (IN)
ITT Tech Inst, Springfield (IL)
Minnesota School of Business–Blaine (MN)
Minnesota School of Business–Elk River (MN)
Minnesota School of Business–Lakeville (MN)
Minnesota School of Business–Moorhead (MN)
Minnesota School of Business–Richfield (MN)
Minnesota School of Business–Rochester (MN)
Minnesota School of Business–St. Cloud (MN)
Minnesota School of Business–Shakopee (MN)
Montana Tech of The U of Montana (MT)
Pace U (NY)
Robert Morris U Illinois (IL)
The U of Akron (OH)
Weber State U (UT)

COMPUTER TEACHER EDUCATION
Baker Coll of Flint (MI)

COMPUTER TECHNOLOGY/COMPUTER SYSTEMS TECHNOLOGY
Harrison Coll, Indianapolis (IN)
Morrisville State Coll (NY)
New England Inst of Technology (RI)
Southeast Missouri State U (MO)
U of Cincinnati (OH)

COMPUTER TYPOGRAPHY AND COMPOSITION EQUIPMENT OPERATION
Baker Coll of Auburn Hills (MI)
Baker Coll of Cadillac (MI)
Baker Coll of Clinton Township (MI)
Baker Coll of Flint (MI)
Baker Coll of Jackson (MI)
Indian River State Coll (FL)
U of Cincinnati (OH)
The U of Toledo (OH)

CONSTRUCTION ENGINEERING TECHNOLOGY
Baker Coll of Owosso (MI)
Coll of Staten Island of the City U of New York (NY)
Ferris State U (MI)
Lawrence Technological U (MI)
New England Inst of Technology (RI)
New York City Coll of Technology of the City U of New York (NY)
Pennsylvania Coll of Technology (PA)
State Coll of Florida Manatee-Sarasota (FL)
State U of New York Coll of Technology at Canton (NY)

State U of New York Coll of Technology at Delhi (NY)
The U of Akron (OH)
Vermont Tech Coll (VT)

CONSTRUCTION MANAGEMENT
ITT Tech Inst, Durham (NC)
U of Alaska Fairbanks (AK)
U of the District of Columbia (DC)
Utah Valley U (UT)
Vermont Tech Coll (VT)

CONSTRUCTION TRADES
Colorado Mesa U (CO)
Morrisville State Coll (NY)
Northern Michigan U (MI)

CONSTRUCTION TRADES RELATED
John Brown U (AR)
Morrisville State Coll (NY)

CONSUMER MERCHANDISING/RETAILING MANAGEMENT
Baker Coll of Owosso (MI)
Indian River State Coll (FL)
Madonna U (MI)
The U of Toledo (OH)

COOKING AND RELATED CULINARY ARTS
Colorado Mesa U (CO)
Harrison Coll, Indianapolis (IN)
Hickey Coll (MO)

CORRECTIONS
Baker Coll of Muskegon (MI)
California U of Pennsylvania (PA)
Indian River State Coll (FL)
Lake Superior State U (MI)
Mercyhurst U (PA)
Mount Aloysius Coll (PA)
U of the District of Columbia (DC)
Xavier U (OH)

CORRECTIONS ADMINISTRATION
John Jay Coll of Criminal Justice of the City U of New York (NY)

CORRECTIONS AND CRIMINAL JUSTICE RELATED
Cameron U (OK)
Inter American U of Puerto Rico, Aguadilla Campus (PR)
Inter American U of Puerto Rico, Fajardo Campus (PR)
Morrisville State Coll (NY)
Rasmussen Coll Appleton (WI)
Rasmussen Coll Aurora (IL)
Rasmussen Coll Bismarck (ND)
Rasmussen Coll Blaine (MN)
Rasmussen Coll Bloomington (MN)
Rasmussen Coll Brooklyn Park (MN)
Rasmussen Coll Eagan (MN)
Rasmussen Coll Fort Myers (FL)
Rasmussen Coll Green Bay (WI)
Rasmussen Coll Kansas City/Overland Park (KS)
Rasmussen Coll Lake Elmo/Woodbury (MN)
Rasmussen Coll Land O' Lakes (FL)
Rasmussen Coll Mankato (MN)
Rasmussen Coll Mokena/Tinley Park (IL)
Rasmussen Coll Moorhead (MN)
Rasmussen Coll New Port Richey (FL)
Rasmussen Coll Ocala (FL)
Rasmussen Coll Rockford (IL)
Rasmussen Coll Romeoville/Joliet (IL)
Rasmussen Coll St. Cloud (MN)
Rasmussen Coll Tampa/Brandon (FL)
Rasmussen Coll Topeka (KS)
Rasmussen Coll Wausau (WI)

COSMETOLOGY
Indian River State Coll (FL)
Midland Coll (TX)

CREATIVE WRITING
Inst of American Indian Arts (NM)
National U (CA)
U of Maine at Presque Isle (ME)

CRIMINALISTICS AND CRIMINAL SCIENCE
Keiser U, Fort Lauderdale (FL)

CRIMINAL JUSTICE/LAW ENFORCEMENT ADMINISTRATION
Abraham Baldwin Ag Coll (GA)
American Public U System (WV)
Anderson U (IN)
Arkansas State U (AR)
Bemidji State U (MN)
Broadview U–Boise (ID)
Broadview U–Layton (UT)
Broadview U–Orem (UT)
Broadview U–West Jordan (UT)
Calumet Coll of Saint Joseph (IN)
Campbellsville U (KY)
Castleton State Coll (VT)
Clarion U of Pennsylvania (PA)
Coll of Coastal Georgia (GA)
Colorado Mesa U (CO)
Columbia Coll (MO)
Farmingdale State Coll (NY)
Fisher Coll (MA)
Fort Valley State U (GA)
Glenville State Coll (WV)
Globe U–Eau Claire (WI)
Globe U–Green Bay (WI)
Globe U–La Crosse (WI)
Globe U–Madison East (WI)
Globe U–Madison West (WI)
Globe U–Minneapolis (MN)
Globe U–Sioux Falls (SD)
Globe U–Wausau (WI)
Globe U–Woodbury (MN)
Hannibal-LaGrange U (MO)
Harrison Coll, Indianapolis (IN)
Harrison Coll (OH)
Hawai'i Pacific U (HI)
Husson U (ME)
Indian River State Coll (FL)
Keiser U, Fort Lauderdale (FL)
Keystone Coll (PA)
Lake Superior State U (MI)
Lincoln Coll of New England, Southington (CT)
Lincoln U (MO)
Lock Haven U of Pennsylvania (PA)
Mansfield U of Pennsylvania (PA)
Minnesota School of Business–Blaine (MN)
Minnesota School of Business–Elk River (MN)
Minnesota School of Business–Lakeville (MN)
Minnesota School of Business–Richfield (MN)
Minnesota School of Business–Rochester (MN)
Minnesota School of Business–St. Cloud (MN)
Monroe Coll, Bronx (NY)
Morrisville State Coll (NY)
National U (CA)
New England Inst of Technology (RI)
Northern Michigan U (MI)
Palm Beach State Coll (FL)
Peirce Coll (PA)
Penn Foster Coll (AZ)
Polk State Coll (FL)
Regent U (VA)
Roger Williams U (RI)
St. John's U (NY)
South U (NC)
South U, Glen Allen (VA)
Tiffin U (OH)
Trine U (IN)
U of Arkansas–Fort Smith (AR)
The U of Findlay (OH)
U of Maine at Fort Kent (ME)
U of Maine at Presque Isle (ME)
Utah Valley U (UT)
Washburn U (KS)
Wayland Baptist U (TX)
Webber International U (FL)
York Coll of Pennsylvania (PA)

CRIMINAL JUSTICE/POLICE SCIENCE
Abraham Baldwin Ag Coll (GA)
Arkansas State U (AR)
Armstrong Atlantic State U (GA)
Caribbean U (PR)
Columbia Southern U (AL)
Elizabethtown Coll School of Continuing and Professional Studies (PA)
Ferris State U (MI)
Indian River State Coll (FL)
John Jay Coll of Criminal Justice of the City U of New York (NY)
Lake Superior State U (MI)
Miami U (OH)

Missouri Southern State U (MO)
Missouri Western State U (MO)
Monroe Coll, Bronx (NY)
Northern Kentucky U (KY)
Palm Beach State Coll (FL)
Pioneer Pacific Coll, Wilsonville (OR)
Rasmussen Coll Blaine (MN)
Rasmussen Coll Bloomington (MN)
Rasmussen Coll Brooklyn Park (MN)
Rasmussen Coll Eagan (MN)
Rasmussen Coll Lake Elmo/
  Woodbury (MN)
Rasmussen Coll Mankato (MN)
Rasmussen Coll St. Cloud (MN)
Rogers State U (OK)
Southern Utah U (UT)
State U of New York Coll of
  Technology at Canton (NY)
Universidad del Turabo (PR)
The U of Akron (OH)
U of Arkansas at Little Rock (AR)
U of New Haven (CT)
U of the Virgin Islands (VI)

CRIMINAL JUSTICE/SAFETY
Arkansas Tech U (AR)
Ball State U (IN)
Bethel Coll (IN)
Brown Mackie Coll–San Antonio (TX)
Calumet Coll of Saint Joseph (IN)
Cazenovia Coll (NY)
Central Penn Coll (PA)
Clearwater Christian Coll (FL)
Colorado Mesa U (CO)
Columbus State U (GA)
Dixie State U (UT)
Edinboro U of Pennsylvania (PA)
Fisher Coll (MA)
Florida National U (FL)
Gannon U (PA)
Harrison Coll, Indianapolis (IN)
Husson U (ME)
Indiana Tech (IN)
Indiana U Northwest (IN)
Indiana U–Purdue U Indianapolis (IN)
Indiana Wesleyan U (IN)
Kent State U at Stark (OH)
King's Coll (PA)
Lake Superior State U (MI)
Liberty U (VA)
Lourdes U (OH)
Madonna U (MI)
Manchester U (IN)
Morrisville State Coll (NY)
New Mexico State U (NM)
Northern Kentucky U (KY)
Northern Michigan U (MI)
Penn State Altoona (PA)
St. Francis Coll (NY)
State Coll of Florida Manatee-
  Sarasota (FL)
Sullivan U (KY)
Thomas More Coll (KY)
Universidad Metropolitana (PR)
U of Cincinnati (OH)
U of Maine at Augusta (ME)
U of Pikeville (KY)
The U of Scranton (PA)
Weber State U (UT)
Xavier U (OH)
Youngstown State U (OH)

CRIMINOLOGY
Chaminade U of Honolulu (HI)
Elizabethtown Coll School of
  Continuing and Professional
  Studies (PA)

**CRISIS/EMERGENCY/DISASTER
MANAGEMENT**
Arkansas State U (AR)
Eastern New Mexico U (NM)
Universidad del Turabo (PR)

CROP PRODUCTION
North Carolina State U (NC)
U of Massachusetts Amherst (MA)

CULINARY ARTS
The Art Inst of Atlanta (GA)
The Art Inst of Austin, a branch of
  The Art Institute of Houston (TX)
The Art Inst of California–Hollywood,
  a campus of Argosy U (CA)
The Art Inst of California–Inland
  Empire, a campus of Argosy U
  (CA)
The Art Inst of California–Los
  Angeles, a campus of Argosy U
  (CA)

The Art Inst of California–Orange
  County, a campus of Argosy U
  (CA)
The Art Inst of California–
  Sacramento, a campus of Argosy
  U (CA)
The Art Inst of California–San Diego,
  a campus of Argosy U (CA)
The Art Inst of California–San
  Francisco, a campus of Argosy U
  (CA)
The Art Inst of California–Silicon
  Valley, a campus of Argosy U (CA)
The Art Inst of Charleston, a branch
  of The Art Institute of Atlanta (SC)
The Art Inst of Charlotte, a campus of
  South U (NC)
The Art Inst of Colorado (CO)
The Art Inst of Dallas, a campus of
  South U (TX)
The Art Inst of Fort Lauderdale (FL)
The Art Inst of Houston (TX)
The Art Inst of Houston–North, a
  branch of The Art Institute of
  Houston (TX)
The Art Inst of Indianapolis (IN)
The Art Inst of Jacksonville, a branch
  of Miami International U of Art &
  Design (FL)
The Art Inst of Las Vegas (NV)
The Art Inst of Michigan (MI)
The Art Inst of Ohio–Cincinnati (OH)
The Art Inst of Philadelphia (PA)
The Art Inst of Phoenix (AZ)
The Art Inst of Pittsburgh (PA)
The Art Inst of Portland (OR)
The Art Inst of Raleigh-Durham, a
  campus of South U (NC)
The Art Inst of St. Louis (MO)
The Art Inst of Salt Lake City (UT)
The Art Inst of San Antonio, a branch
  of The Art Institute of Houston (TX)
The Art Inst of Seattle (WA)
The Art Inst of Tampa, a branch of
  Miami International U of Art &
  Design (FL)
The Art Inst of Tennessee–Nashville,
  a branch of The Art Institute of
  Atlanta (TN)
The Art Inst of Tucson (AZ)
The Art Inst of Virginia Beach, a
  branch of The Art Institute of
  Atlanta (VA)
The Art Inst of Washington, a branch
  of The Art Institute of Atlanta (VA)
The Art Inst of Wisconsin (WI)
The Art Insts International–Kansas
  City (KS)
The Art Insts International Minnesota
  (MN)
Baker Coll of Muskegon (MI)
Bob Jones U (SC)
The Culinary Inst of America (NY)
Eastern New Mexico U (NM)
Harrison Coll, Indianapolis (IN)
The Illinois Inst of Art–Chicago (IL)
Indian River State Coll (FL)
Keiser U, Fort Lauderdale (FL)
Keystone Coll (PA)
Monroe Coll, Bronx (NY)
Newbury Coll (MA)
Nicholls State U (LA)
Oakland City U (IN)
Pennsylvania Coll of Technology (PA)
Robert Morris U Illinois (IL)
Southern New Hampshire U (NH)
State U of New York Coll of
  Agriculture and Technology at
  Cobleskill (NY)
State U of New York Coll of
  Technology at Delhi (NY)
Sullivan U (KY)
The U of Akron (OH)
U of Alaska Fairbanks (AK)
U of Charleston (WV)
Utah Valley U (UT)

CULINARY ARTS RELATED
Morrisville State Coll (NY)

**CURRICULUM AND
INSTRUCTION**
State U of New York Coll of
  Technology at Delhi (NY)

**DAIRY HUSBANDRY AND
PRODUCTION**
Morrisville State Coll (NY)

DAIRY SCIENCE
Michigan State U (MI)
Vermont Tech Coll (VT)

DANCE
Southern Utah U (UT)
Utah Valley U (UT)

**DATA ENTRY/
MICROCOMPUTER
APPLICATIONS**
Baker Coll of Allen Park (MI)

**DATA ENTRY/
MICROCOMPUTER
APPLICATIONS RELATED**
Baker Coll of Allen Park (MI)

**DATA MODELING/
WAREHOUSING AND
DATABASE ADMINISTRATION**
American Public U System (WV)
Limestone Coll (SC)

**DATA PROCESSING AND DATA
PROCESSING TECHNOLOGY**
Baker Coll of Auburn Hills (MI)
Baker Coll of Cadillac (MI)
Baker Coll of Clinton Township (MI)
Baker Coll of Flint (MI)
Baker Coll of Jackson (MI)
Baker Coll of Muskegon (MI)
Baker Coll of Owosso (MI)
Baker Coll of Port Huron (MI)
Campbellsville U (KY)
Dordt Coll (IA)
Miami U (OH)
Montana State U Billings (MT)
Mount Vernon Nazarene U (OH)
Northern Kentucky U (KY)
Northern State U (SD)
Palm Beach State Coll (FL)
Saint Peter's U (NJ)
The U of Toledo (OH)
Western Kentucky U (KY)
Youngstown State U (OH)

DENTAL ASSISTING
Lincoln Coll of New England,
  Southington (CT)
U of Alaska Fairbanks (AK)
U of Southern Indiana (IN)

DENTAL HYGIENE
Argosy U, Twin Cities (MN)
Baker Coll of Port Huron (MI)
Coll of Coastal Georgia (GA)
Dixie State U (UT)
Farmingdale State Coll (NY)
Ferris State U (MI)
Florida National U (FL)
Indiana U Northwest (IN)
Indiana U–Purdue U Fort Wayne (IN)
Indiana U–Purdue U Indianapolis (IN)
Indiana U South Bend (IN)
Indian River State Coll (FL)
Missouri Southern State U (MO)
New York City Coll of Technology of
  the City of New York (NY)
New York U (NY)
Palm Beach State Coll (FL)
Pennsylvania Coll of Technology (PA)
Rutgers, The State U of New Jersey,
  New Brunswick (NJ)
Shawnee State U (OH)
State U of New York Coll of
  Technology at Canton (NY)
Tennessee State U (TN)
U of Alaska Fairbanks (AK)
U of Arkansas–Fort Smith (AR)
U of Bridgeport (CT)
U of Cincinnati (OH)
U of Maine at Augusta (ME)
U of New Haven (CT)
Utah Valley U (UT)
Valdosta State U (GA)
Vermont Tech Coll (VT)
Weber State U (UT)
Western Kentucky U (KY)
West Liberty U (WV)

**DENTAL LABORATORY
TECHNOLOGY**
Florida National U (FL)
Indiana U–Purdue U Fort Wayne (IN)
New York City Coll of Technology of
  the City U of New York (NY)

**DESIGN AND APPLIED ARTS
RELATED**
U of Maine at Presque Isle (ME)
Washburn U (KS)

**DESIGN AND VISUAL
COMMUNICATIONS**
Academy of Art U (CA)

Inst of American Indian Arts (NM)
Keiser U, Fort Lauderdale (FL)
Utah Valley U (UT)

**DESKTOP PUBLISHING AND
DIGITAL IMAGING DESIGN**
Academy of Art U (CA)
Ferris State U (MI)
New England Inst of Technology (RI)
Platt Coll San Diego (CA)

**DIAGNOSTIC MEDICAL
SONOGRAPHY AND
ULTRASOUND TECHNOLOGY**
Adventist U of Health Sciences (FL)
Argosy U, Twin Cities (MN)
Arkansas State U (AR)
Baker Coll of Auburn Hills (MI)
Baker Coll of Owosso (MI)
Baker Coll of Port Huron (MI)
Ferris State U (MI)
Florida National U (FL)
Keiser U, Fort Lauderdale (FL)
Keystone Coll (PA)
Mercy Coll of Health Sciences (IA)
Midland Coll (TX)
Nebraska Methodist Coll (NE)
Polk State Coll (FL)
St. Catherine U (MN)
U of Charleston (WV)

**DIESEL MECHANICS
TECHNOLOGY**
Lewis-Clark State Coll (ID)
Midland Coll (TX)
Montana State U Billings (MT)
Morrisville State Coll (NY)
Pennsylvania Coll of Technology (PA)
State U of New York Coll of
  Agriculture and Technology at
  Cobleskill (NY)
Utah Valley U (UT)
Vermont Tech Coll (VT)
Weber State U (UT)

DIETETICS
Ferris State U (MI)
Life U (GA)
Lincoln Coll of New England,
  Southington (CT)
State Coll of Florida Manatee-
  Sarasota (FL)

DIETETIC TECHNOLOGY
Morrisville State Coll (NY)
Youngstown State U (OH)

DIETITIAN ASSISTANT
Youngstown State U (OH)

DIGITAL ARTS
Academy of Art U (CA)

**DIGITAL COMMUNICATION
AND MEDIA/MULTIMEDIA**
Florida National U (FL)
Indiana U–Purdue U Indianapolis (IN)
National U (CA)
Platt Coll San Diego (CA)
Vaughn Coll of Aeronautics and
  Technology (NY)

DIVINITY/MINISTRY
Carson-Newman U (TN)
Great Lakes Christian Coll (MI)
Nebraska Christian Coll (NE)
Providence Coll (RI)
Valley Forge Christian Coll (PA)

DOG/PET/ANIMAL GROOMING
Becker Coll (MA)

**DRAFTING AND DESIGN
TECHNOLOGY**
Baker Coll of Auburn Hills (MI)
Baker Coll of Clinton Township (MI)
Baker Coll of Owosso (MI)
Baker Coll of Port Huron (MI)
Black Hills State U (SD)
Brown Mackie Coll–Birmingham (AL)
California U of Pennsylvania (PA)
Caribbean U (PR)
Indian River State Coll (FL)
ITT Tech Inst, Phoenix (AZ)
ITT Tech Inst, Phoenix (AZ)
ITT Tech Inst, Tempe (AZ)
ITT Tech Inst, Clovis (CA)
ITT Tech Inst, Concord (CA)
ITT Tech Inst, Corona (CA)
ITT Tech Inst, West Palm Beach (FL)
ITT Tech Inst, Douglasville (GA)
ITT Tech Inst, Indianapolis (IN)
ITT Tech Inst, Indianapolis (IN)

ITT Tech Inst, South Bend (IN)
ITT Tech Inst, Overland Park (KS)
ITT Tech Inst, Wichita (KS)
ITT Tech Inst, Lexington (KY)
ITT Tech Inst, Southfield (MI)
ITT Tech Inst (MS)
ITT Tech Inst, Springfield (MO)
ITT Tech Inst, Charlotte (NC)
ITT Tech Inst, Durham (NC)
ITT Tech Inst, Oklahoma City (OK)
ITT Tech Inst, Salem (OR)
Kentucky State U (KY)
Langston U (OK)
LeTourneau U (TX)
Lewis-Clark State Coll (ID)
Lincoln U (MO)
Montana State U (MT)
Montana State U Billings (MT)
Morrisville State Coll (NY)
Palm Beach State Coll (FL)
Robert Morris U Illinois (IL)
State Coll of Florida Manatee-
  Sarasota (FL)
Universidad Metropolitana (PR)
The U of Akron (OH)
U of Alaska Fairbanks (AK)
U of Rio Grande (OH)
Utah Valley U (UT)
Weber State U (UT)
Wright State U (OH)
Youngstown State U (OH)

**DRAFTING/DESIGN
ENGINEERING TECHNOLOGIES
RELATED**
Morrisville State Coll (NY)
Pennsylvania Coll of Technology (PA)

DRAMATIC/THEATER ARTS
Adams State U (CO)
Clarke U (IA)
Indian River State Coll (FL)
Midland Coll (TX)
Palm Beach State Coll (FL)
Pine Manor Coll (MA)
State Coll of Florida Manatee-
  Sarasota (FL)
Thomas More Coll (KY)
Utah Valley U (UT)

DRAWING
Academy of Art U (CA)
Pratt Inst (NY)

**EARLY CHILDHOOD
EDUCATION**
Adams State U (CO)
Baker Coll of Allen Park (MI)
Baker Coll of Jackson (MI)
Bethel Coll (IN)
Chaminade U of Honolulu (HI)
Coll of Saint Mary (NE)
Cornerstone U (MI)
Dixie State U (UT)
Gannon U (PA)
Granite State Coll (NH)
Great Lakes Christian Coll (MI)
Keystone Coll (PA)
Lake Superior State U (MI)
Lincoln Christian U (IL)
Lincoln U (MO)
Lindsey Wilson Coll (KY)
Manchester U (IN)
Maranatha Baptist Bible Coll (WI)
Marian U (IN)
Morrisville State Coll (NY)
Mount Aloysius Coll (PA)
Mount St. Mary's Coll (CA)
National U (CA)
Nova Southeastern U (FL)
Oakland City U (IN)
Oklahoma Wesleyan U (OK)
Pacific Union Coll (CA)
Penn Foster Coll (AZ)
Pine Manor Coll (MA)
Rasmussen Coll Appleton (WI)
Rasmussen Coll Aurora (IL)
Rasmussen Coll Bismarck (ND)
Rasmussen Coll Blaine (MN)
Rasmussen Coll Bloomington (MN)
Rasmussen Coll Brooklyn Park (MN)
Rasmussen Coll Eagan (MN)
Rasmussen Coll Fargo (ND)
Rasmussen Coll Fort Myers (FL)
Rasmussen Coll Green Bay (WI)
Rasmussen Coll Kansas City/
  Overland Park (KS)
Rasmussen Coll Lake Elmo/
  Woodbury (MN)
Rasmussen Coll Land O' Lakes (FL)
Rasmussen Coll Mankato (MN)

Rasmussen Coll Mokena/Tinley Park (IL)
Rasmussen Coll Moorhead (MN)
Rasmussen Coll New Port Richey (FL)
Rasmussen Coll Ocala (FL)
Rasmussen Coll Rockford (IL)
Rasmussen Coll Romeoville/Joliet (IL)
Rasmussen Coll St. Cloud (MN)
Rasmussen Coll Tampa/Brandon (FL)
Rasmussen Coll Topeka (KS)
Rasmussen Coll Wausau (WI)
Rust Coll (MS)
St. Gregory's U, Shawnee (OK)
Southwestern Assemblies of God U (TX)
State U of New York Coll of Technology at Canton (NY)
Sullivan U (KY)
Taylor U (IN)
U of Arkansas–Fort Smith (AR)
U of Cincinnati (OH)
U of Great Falls (MT)
The U of Montana Western (MT)
U of Southern Indiana (IN)
U of the Virgin Islands (VI)
Utah Valley U (UT)
Valley Forge Christian Coll (PA)
Washburn U (KS)
Wayland Baptist U (TX)
Western Kentucky U (KY)
Xavier U (OH)

E-COMMERCE
Limestone Coll (SC)

ECONOMICS
Hawai`i Pacific U (HI)
Immaculata U (PA)
Indian River State Coll (FL)
Palm Beach State Coll (FL)
State Coll of Florida Manatee-Sarasota (FL)
Thomas More Coll (KY)
The U of Tampa (FL)

EDUCATION
Abraham Baldwin Ag Coll (GA)
Alderson Broaddus U (WV)
Baker Coll of Auburn Hills (MI)
Baker Coll of Cadillac (MI)
Cincinnati Christian U (OH)
Corban U (OR)
Florida National U (FL)
Indian River State Coll (FL)
Kent State U (OH)
Montana State U Billings (MT)
Montreat Coll, Montreat (NC)
Morrisville State Coll (NY)
National U (CA)
Palm Beach State Coll (FL)
Saint Francis U (PA)
Southwestern Assemblies of God U (TX)
State U of New York Empire State Coll (NY)
U of the District of Columbia (DC)

EDUCATIONAL/ INSTRUCTIONAL TECHNOLOGY
Cameron U (OK)

EDUCATION (MULTIPLE LEVELS)
Coll of Coastal Georgia (GA)
Midland Coll (TX)
St. Cloud State U (MN)

EDUCATION RELATED
The U of Akron (OH)

EDUCATION (SPECIFIC SUBJECT AREAS) RELATED
National U (CA)

ELECTRICAL AND ELECTRONIC ENGINEERING TECHNOLOGIES RELATED
Lake Superior State U (MI)
Lawrence Technological U (MI)
Northern Michigan U (MI)
Point Park U (PA)
Rochester Inst of Technology (NY)
Vaughn Coll of Aeronautics and Technology (NY)
Youngstown State U (OH)

ELECTRICAL AND ELECTRONICS ENGINEERING
New England Inst of Technology (RI)
Southern California Inst of Technology (CA)
The U of Scranton (PA)

ELECTRICAL AND POWER TRANSMISSION INSTALLATION
Polk State Coll (FL)
State U of New York Coll of Technology at Delhi (NY)

ELECTRICAL, ELECTRONIC AND COMMUNICATIONS ENGINEERING TECHNOLOGY
Baker Coll of Cadillac (MI)
Baker Coll of Owosso (MI)
Bluefield State Coll (WV)
California U of Pennsylvania (PA)
Cameron U (OK)
DeVry Coll of New York (NY)
DeVry U, Mesa (AZ)
DeVry U, Phoenix (AZ)
DeVry U, Alhambra (CA)
DeVry U, Anaheim (CA)
DeVry U, Bakersfield (CA)
DeVry U, Elk Grove (CA)
DeVry U, Fremont (CA)
DeVry U, Long Beach (CA)
DeVry U, Oxnard (CA)
DeVry U, Palmdale (CA)
DeVry U, Pomona (CA)
DeVry U, San Diego (CA)
DeVry U, Sherman Oaks (CA)
DeVry U, Colorado Springs (CO)
DeVry U, Westminster (CO)
DeVry U, Miramar (FL)
DeVry U, Orlando (FL)
DeVry U, Tampa (FL)
DeVry U, Decatur (GA)
DeVry U, Chicago (IL)
DeVry U, Tinley Park (IL)
DeVry U, Edina (MN)
DeVry U (NV)
DeVry U, North Brunswick (NJ)
DeVry U, Paramus (NJ)
DeVry U, Charlotte (NC)
DeVry U, Fort Washington (PA)
DeVry U, Philadelphia (PA)
DeVry U, Pittsburgh (PA)
DeVry U, Houston (TX)
DeVry U, Irving (TX)
DeVry U, Chesapeake (VA)
DeVry U, Federal Way (WA)
Fairmont State U (WV)
Fort Valley State U (GA)
Indiana U–Purdue U Fort Wayne (IN)
Indian River State Coll (FL)
Inter American U of Puerto Rico, Aguadilla Campus (PR)
Inter American U of Puerto Rico, San Germán Campus (PR)
ITT Tech Inst, Phoenix (AZ)
ITT Tech Inst, Phoenix (AZ)
ITT Tech Inst, Tempe (AZ)
ITT Tech Inst, Clovis (CA)
ITT Tech Inst, Concord (CA)
ITT Tech Inst, Corona (CA)
ITT Tech Inst, West Palm Beach (FL)
ITT Tech Inst, Douglasville (GA)
ITT Tech Inst, Indianapolis (IN)
ITT Tech Inst, Indianapolis (IN)
ITT Tech Inst, South Bend (IN)
ITT Tech Inst, Overland Park (KS)
ITT Tech Inst, Wichita (KS)
ITT Tech Inst, Lexington (KY)
ITT Tech Inst, Hanover (MD)
ITT Tech Inst, Southfield (MI)
ITT Tech Inst (MS)
ITT Tech Inst, Springfield (MO)
ITT Tech Inst, Charlotte (NC)
ITT Tech Inst, Durham (NC)
ITT Tech Inst, Oklahoma City (OK)
ITT Tech Inst, Salem (OR)
Kentucky State U (KY)
Lake Superior State U (MI)
Langston U (OK)
Lawrence Technological U (MI)
Michigan Technological U (MI)
Morrisville State Coll (NY)
New York City Coll of Technology of the City U of New York (NY)
New York Inst of Technology (NY)
Northern Kentucky U (KY)
Northern Michigan U (MI)
Northwestern State U of Louisiana (LA)
Palm Beach State Coll (FL)
Penn State Altoona (PA)

Penn State Berks (PA)
Penn State Erie, The Behrend Coll (PA)
Penn State Shenango (PA)
Pennsylvania Coll of Technology (PA)
Purdue U North Central (IN)
State Coll of Florida Manatee-Sarasota (FL)
State U of New York Coll of Technology at Canton (NY)
State U of New York Coll of Technology at Delhi (NY)
The U of Akron (OH)
U of Arkansas at Little Rock (AR)
U of Hartford (CT)
U of Massachusetts Lowell (MA)
U of the District of Columbia (DC)
Vermont Tech Coll (VT)
Weber State U (UT)
Youngstown State U (OH)

ELECTRICAL/ELECTRONICS EQUIPMENT INSTALLATION AND REPAIR
Lewis-Clark State Coll (ID)
New England Inst of Technology (RI)
Pittsburg State U (KS)
U of Arkansas–Fort Smith (AR)

ELECTRICIAN
Liberty U (VA)
Michigan State U (MI)
Pennsylvania Coll of Technology (PA)
Universidad del Turabo (PR)
Weber State U (UT)

ELECTROMECHANICAL AND INSTRUMENTATION AND MAINTENANCE TECHNOLOGIES RELATED
Excelsior Coll (NY)

ELECTROMECHANICAL TECHNOLOGY
Excelsior Coll (NY)
John Brown U (AR)
Midland Coll (TX)
New York City Coll of Technology of the City U of New York (NY)
Northern Michigan U (MI)
Pennsylvania Coll of Technology (PA)
Shawnee State U (OH)
State U of New York Coll of Technology at Delhi (NY)

ELECTRONEURODIAGNOSTIC/ ELECTROENCEPHALOGRAPHIC TECHNOLOGY
DeVry U, North Brunswick (NJ)

ELEMENTARY EDUCATION
Abraham Baldwin Ag Coll (GA)
Adams State U (CO)
Edinboro U of Pennsylvania (PA)
Ferris State U (MI)
God's Bible School and Coll (OH)
Morrisville State Coll (NY)
New Mexico Highlands U (NM)
Palm Beach State Coll (FL)
Rogers State U (OK)
Saint Mary-of-the-Woods Coll (IN)
U of Cincinnati (OH)
Weber State U (UT)
Wilson Coll (PA)

EMERGENCY MEDICAL TECHNOLOGY (EMT PARAMEDIC)
Baker Coll of Cadillac (MI)
Baker Coll of Clinton Township (MI)
Baker Coll of Muskegon (MI)
Colorado Mesa U (CO)
Creighton U (NE)
Dixie State U (UT)
EDP U of Puerto Rico (PR)
EDP U of Puerto Rico–San Sebastian (PR)
Indiana U–Purdue U Indianapolis (IN)
Indian River State Coll (FL)
Mercy Coll of Health Sciences (IA)
Midland Coll (TX)
Montana State U Billings (MT)
Pacific Union Coll (CA)
Pennsylvania Coll of Technology (PA)
Polk State Coll (FL)
Purdue U Calumet (IN)

Rogers State U (OK)
Saint Joseph's Coll (IN)
Shawnee State U (OH)
Southwest Baptist U (MO)
Spalding U (KY)
State U of New York Coll of Agriculture and Technology at Cobleskill (NY)
The U of Akron (OH)
U of Cincinnati (OH)
Weber State U (UT)
Western Kentucky U (KY)
Youngstown State U (OH)

ENERGY MANAGEMENT AND SYSTEMS TECHNOLOGY
Baker Coll of Flint (MI)
Montana State U Billings (MT)
U of Rio Grande (OH)

ENGINEERING
Coll of Staten Island of the City U of New York (NY)
Dixie State U (UT)
Ferris State U (MI)
Geneva Coll (PA)
Indian River State Coll (FL)
Lake Superior State U (MI)
Lindsey Wilson Coll (KY)
Morrisville State Coll (NY)
Palm Beach Atlantic U (FL)
Purdue U North Central (IN)
State Coll of Florida Manatee-Sarasota (FL)
State U of New York Coll of Technology at Canton (NY)
Union Coll (NE)
Weber State U (UT)

ENGINEERING SCIENCE
National U (CA)
Rochester Inst of Technology (NY)
U of Pittsburgh at Bradford (PA)

ENGINEERING TECHNOLOGIES AND ENGINEERING RELATED
Arkansas State U (AR)
Excelsior Coll (NY)
Missouri Southern State U (MO)
Morrisville State Coll (NY)
Rogers State U (OK)
State U of New York Coll of Agriculture and Technology at Cobleskill (NY)
State U of New York Coll of Technology at Canton (NY)
State U of New York Maritime Coll (NY)
U of Puerto Rico in Bayamón (PR)

ENGINEERING TECHNOLOGY
Austin Peay State U (TN)
Edinboro U of Pennsylvania (PA)
Fairmont State U (WV)
Indian River State Coll (FL)
Kansas State U (KS)
Lake Superior State U (MI)
Lincoln U (MO)
Miami U (OH)
Michigan Technological U (MI)
Morehead State U (KY)
National U (CA)
New Mexico State U (NM)
Northern Kentucky U (KY)
Penn Foster Coll (AZ)
Polk State Coll (FL)
Southern Utah U (UT)
The U of Toledo (OH)
Wright State U (OH)
Youngstown State U (OH)

ENGLISH
Abraham Baldwin Ag Coll (GA)
Calumet Coll of Saint Joseph (IN)
Carroll Coll (MT)
Central Methodist U (MO)
Coll of Coastal Georgia (GA)
Felician Coll (NJ)
Hannibal-LaGrange U (MO)
Immaculata U (PA)
Indiana Wesleyan U (IN)
Indian River State Coll (FL)
Liberty U (VA)
Lourdes U (OH)
Madonna U (MI)
Midland Coll (TX)
Palm Beach State Coll (FL)
Pine Manor Coll (MA)
Southwestern Assemblies of God U (TX)

State Coll of Florida Manatee-Sarasota (FL)
Thomas More Coll (KY)
U of Cincinnati (OH)
The U of Tampa (FL)
Utah Valley U (UT)
Xavier U (OH)

ENGLISH AS A SECOND/ FOREIGN LANGUAGE (TEACHING)
Cornerstone U (MI)
Lincoln Christian U (IL)
Union Coll (NE)

ENGLISH LANGUAGE AND LITERATURE RELATED
State U of New York Empire State Coll (NY)

ENGLISH/LANGUAGE ARTS TEACHER EDUCATION
State Coll of Florida Manatee-Sarasota (FL)

ENTREPRENEURSHIP
Baker Coll of Flint (MI)
Central Penn Coll (PA)
Universidad Metropolitana (PR)

ENVIRONMENTAL CONTROL TECHNOLOGIES RELATED
Montana Tech of The U of Montana (MT)

ENVIRONMENTAL ENGINEERING TECHNOLOGY
Baker Coll of Flint (MI)
Baker Coll of Owosso (MI)
Baker Coll of Port Huron (MI)
New York City Coll of Technology of the City U of New York (NY)

ENVIRONMENTAL STUDIES
Columbia Coll (MO)
Dickinson State U (ND)
State U of New York Coll of Agriculture and Technology at Cobleskill (NY)

EQUESTRIAN STUDIES
Centenary Coll (NJ)
Morrisville State Coll (NY)
Saint Mary-of-the-Woods Coll (IN)
The U of Findlay (OH)
U of Massachusetts Amherst (MA)
The U of Montana Western (MT)

EXECUTIVE ASSISTANT/ EXECUTIVE SECRETARY
Baker Coll of Allen Park (MI)
Baker Coll of Flint (MI)
Northern Kentucky U (KY)
U of Arkansas–Fort Smith (AR)
U of Cincinnati (OH)
Western Kentucky U (KY)

EXPLOSIVE ORDINANCE/BOMB DISPOSAL
American Public U System (WV)

FAMILY AND COMMUNITY SERVICES
Baker Coll of Flint (MI)

FAMILY AND CONSUMER SCIENCES/HOME ECONOMICS TEACHER EDUCATION
State Coll of Florida Manatee-Sarasota (FL)

FAMILY AND CONSUMER SCIENCES/HUMAN SCIENCES
Abraham Baldwin Ag Coll (GA)
Eastern New Mexico U (NM)
Indian River State Coll (FL)
Mount Vernon Nazarene U (OH)
Palm Beach State Coll (FL)

FARM AND RANCH MANAGEMENT
Abraham Baldwin Ag Coll (GA)

FASHION AND FABRIC CONSULTING
Academy of Art U (CA)

FASHION/APPAREL DESIGN
Academy of Art U (CA)
The Art Inst of California–Hollywood, a campus of Argosy U (CA)

The Art Inst of California–San Francisco, a campus of Argosy U (CA)
The Art Inst of Charlotte, a campus of South U (NC)
The Art Inst of Dallas, a campus of South U (TX)
The Art Inst of Fort Lauderdale (FL)
The Art Inst of Philadelphia (PA)
The Art Inst of Seattle (WA)
EDP U of Puerto Rico (PR)
Fashion Inst of Technology (NY)
Fisher Coll (MA)
Miami International U of Art & Design (FL)
Palm Beach State Coll (FL)
Parsons The New School for Design (NY)
Universidad del Turabo (PR)

FASHION MERCHANDISING
Abraham Baldwin Ag Coll (GA)
The Art Inst of Michigan (MI)
The Art Inst of Michigan–Troy (MI)
The Art Inst of Ohio–Cincinnati (OH)
The Art Inst of Philadelphia (PA)
Fashion Inst of Technology (NY)
Fisher Coll (MA)
Harrison Coll, Indianapolis (IN)
The Illinois Inst of Art–Chicago (IL)
The Illinois Inst of Art–Schaumburg (IL)
The Illinois Inst of Art–Tinley Park (IL)
Immaculata U (PA)
Indian River State Coll (FL)
LIM Coll (NY)
Lincoln Coll of New England, Southington (CT)
Miami International U of Art & Design (FL)
New York City Coll of Technology of the City U of New York (NY)
Palm Beach State Coll (FL)
Penn Foster Coll (AZ)
Southern New Hampshire U (NH)
Stevens–The Inst of Business & Arts (MO)
The U of Akron (OH)
U of Bridgeport (CT)
U of the District of Columbia (DC)

FASHION MODELING
Fashion Inst of Technology (NY)

FIBER, TEXTILE AND WEAVING ARTS
Academy of Art U (CA)

FINANCE
AIB Coll of Business (IA)
Davenport U, Grand Rapids (MI)
Franklin U (OH)
Harrison Coll, Indianapolis (IN)
Harrison Coll (OH)
Hawai`i Pacific U (HI)
Indiana Wesleyan U (IN)
Indian River State Coll (FL)
Palm Beach State Coll (FL)
Penn Foster Coll (AZ)
Saint Peter's U (NJ)
State Coll of Florida Manatee-Sarasota (FL)
The U of Findlay (OH)
Youngstown State U (OH)

FINE ARTS RELATED
Academy of Art U (CA)
Madonna U (MI)
Pennsylvania Coll of Technology (PA)
Saint Francis U (PA)

FINE/STUDIO ARTS
Academy of Art U (CA)
Adams State U (CO)
Beacon Coll (FL)
Fashion Inst of Technology (NY)
Inst of American Indian Arts (NM)
Keystone Coll (PA)
Lindsey Wilson Coll (KY)
Marian U (IN)
New Mexico State U (NM)
Pratt Inst (NY)
State Coll of Florida Manatee-Sarasota (FL)
Thomas More Coll (KY)
U of Maine at Augusta (ME)
Villa Maria Coll (NY)
York Coll of Pennsylvania (PA)

FIRE PREVENTION AND SAFETY TECHNOLOGY
Harrison Coll, Indianapolis (IN)

Montana State U Billings (MT)
Northern Kentucky U (KY)
The U of Akron (OH)
U of New Haven (CT)

FIRE SCIENCE/FIREFIGHTING
Columbia Southern U (AL)
Indian River State Coll (FL)
Keiser U, Fort Lauderdale (FL)
Lake Superior State U (MI)
Lewis-Clark State Coll (ID)
Madonna U (MI)
Midland Coll (TX)
Palm Beach State Coll (FL)
Polk State Coll (FL)
Providence Coll (RI)
State Coll of Florida Manatee-Sarasota (FL)
U of Alaska Fairbanks (AK)
U of Cincinnati (OH)
U of the District of Columbia (DC)
Utah Valley U (UT)
Vermont Tech Coll (VT)

FIRE SERVICES ADMINISTRATION
American Public U System (WV)
Columbia Coll (MO)

FISHING AND FISHERIES SCIENCES AND MANAGEMENT
Abraham Baldwin Ag Coll (GA)
State U of New York Coll of Agriculture and Technology at Cobleskill (NY)

FOOD PREPARATION
Washburn U (KS)

FOODS AND NUTRITION RELATED
U of Guelph (ON, Canada)

FOOD SERVICE SYSTEMS ADMINISTRATION
Inter American U of Puerto Rico, Aguadilla Campus (PR)
Morrisville State Coll (NY)
Northern Michigan U (MI)
U of New Hampshire (NH)

FOODS, NUTRITION, AND WELLNESS
Huntington Coll of Health Sciences (TN)
Indian River State Coll (FL)
Madonna U (MI)
Morrisville State Coll (NY)
Palm Beach State Coll (FL)

FOOD TECHNOLOGY AND PROCESSING
Arkansas State U (AR)

FOREIGN LANGUAGES AND LITERATURES
Coll of Coastal Georgia (GA)
Southwestern Assemblies of God U (TX)

FOREIGN LANGUAGES RELATED
U of Alaska Fairbanks (AK)

FOREIGN LANGUAGE TEACHER EDUCATION
State Coll of Florida Manatee-Sarasota (FL)

FORENSIC SCIENCE AND TECHNOLOGY
Arkansas State U (AR)
ITT Tech Inst, Phoenix (AZ)
ITT Tech Inst, Tempe (AZ)
ITT Tech Inst, Clovis (CA)
ITT Tech Inst, Concord (CA)
ITT Tech Inst, Corona (CA)
ITT Tech Inst, Douglasville (GA)
ITT Tech Inst, Indianapolis (IN)
ITT Tech Inst, South Bend (IN)
ITT Tech Inst, Wichita (KS)
ITT Tech Inst (MS)
ITT Tech Inst, Springfield (MO)
ITT Tech Inst, Charlotte (NC)
ITT Tech Inst, Durham (NC)
ITT Tech Inst, Oklahoma City (OK)
U of Arkansas–Fort Smith (AR)

FORESTRY
Abraham Baldwin Ag Coll (GA)
Coll of Coastal Georgia (GA)
Indian River State Coll (FL)

FOREST TECHNOLOGY
Abraham Baldwin Ag Coll (GA)
Glenville State Coll (WV)
Pennsylvania Coll of Technology (PA)
State U of New York Coll of Environmental Science and Forestry (NY)
State U of New York Coll of Technology at Canton (NY)
U of Maine at Fort Kent (ME)
U of New Hampshire (NH)

FRENCH
Indian River State Coll (FL)
State Coll of Florida Manatee-Sarasota (FL)
Thomas More Coll (KY)
The U of Tampa (FL)
Xavier U (OH)

FUNERAL SERVICE AND MORTUARY SCIENCE
Ferris State U (MI)
Lincoln Coll of New England, Southington (CT)
State U of New York Coll of Technology at Canton (NY)
U of the District of Columbia (DC)

GAME AND INTERACTIVE MEDIA DESIGN
Academy of Art U (CA)
Keiser U, Fort Lauderdale (FL)
National U (CA)

GENERAL STUDIES
Adventist U of Health Sciences (FL)
Alderson Broaddus U (WV)
Alverno Coll (WI)
American Baptist Coll of American Baptist Theological Seminary (TN)
American Public U System (WV)
Anderson U (IN)
Arkansas State U (AR)
Arkansas Tech U (AR)
Asbury U (KY)
Austin Peay State U (TN)
Barclay Coll (KS)
Belhaven U (MS)
Black Hills State U (SD)
Butler U (IN)
Cabarrus Coll of Health Sciences (NC)
Calumet Coll of Saint Joseph (IN)
Cameron U (OK)
Castleton State Coll (VT)
Chaminade U of Honolulu (HI)
Clearwater Christian Coll (FL)
Coll of Mount St. Joseph (OH)
Columbia Coll (MO)
Columbia Southern U (AL)
Concordia U, St. Paul (MN)
Concordia U Texas (TX)
Dakota State U (SD)
Dixie State U (UT)
Eastern Connecticut State U (CT)
Eastern Mennonite U (VA)
Ferris State U (MI)
Fisher Coll (MA)
Fort Hays State U (KS)
Friends U (KS)
God's Bible School and Coll (OH)
Granite State Coll (NH)
Great Lakes Christian Coll (MI)
Hope International U (CA)
Indiana Tech (IN)
Indiana U Northwest (IN)
Indiana U of Pennsylvania (PA)
Indiana U–Purdue U Indianapolis (IN)
Indiana U South Bend (IN)
Indiana U Southeast (IN)
Indiana Wesleyan U (IN)
John Brown U (AR)
Johnson State Coll (VT)
La Salle U (PA)
Lawrence Technological U (MI)
Lebanon Valley Coll (PA)
Liberty U (VA)
Lincoln Christian U (IL)
Lincoln Coll of New England, Southington (CT)
Lipscomb U (TN)
Louisiana Tech U (LA)
McNeese State U (LA)
Medaille Coll (NY)
Mercy Coll of Ohio (OH)
Miami U (OH)
Midland Coll (TX)
Monmouth U (NJ)
Montana State U Billings (MT)
Morehead State U (KY)
Morrisville State Coll (NY)

Mount Aloysius Coll (PA)
Mount Marty Coll (SD)
Mount Vernon Nazarene U (OH)
Newbury Coll (MA)
New Mexico Inst of Mining and Technology (NM)
New Mexico State U (NM)
Nicholls State U (LA)
Northern Michigan U (MI)
Northwest Christian U (OR)
Northwestern State U of Louisiana (LA)
Northwest U (WA)
Ohio Dominican U (OH)
The Ohio State U at Lima (OH)
Oklahoma Wesleyan U (OK)
Ouachita Baptist U (AR)
Our Lady of the Lake Coll (LA)
Pace U (NY)
Pacific Union Coll (CA)
Peirce Coll (PA)
Point U (GA)
Regent U (VA)
Rider U (NJ)
Shawnee State U (OH)
Siena Heights U (MI)
Simpson U (CA)
South Dakota School of Mines and Technology (SD)
South Dakota State U (SD)
Southern Arkansas U–Magnolia (AR)
Southern Nazarene U (OK)
Southern Utah U (UT)
Southwest Baptist U (MO)
Southwestern Adventist U (TX)
Southwestern Assemblies of God U (TX)
State U of New York Coll of Technology at Canton (NY)
State U of New York Coll of Technology at Delhi (NY)
Temple U (PA)
Tiffin U (OH)
Toccoa Falls Coll (GA)
Trevecca Nazarene U (TN)
Trinity Coll of Florida (FL)
U of Arkansas at Little Rock (AR)
U of Arkansas–Fort Smith (AR)
U of Bridgeport (CT)
U of Central Arkansas (AR)
U of Cincinnati (OH)
U of Hartford (CT)
U of Louisiana at Monroe (LA)
U of Maine at Fort Kent (ME)
U of Rio Grande (OH)
U of Wisconsin–Superior (WI)
Utah State U (UT)
Utah Valley U (UT)
Valley Forge Christian Coll Woodbridge Campus (VA)
Viterbo U (WI)
Wayland Baptist U (TX)
Weber State U (UT)
Western Kentucky U (KY)
Wichita State U (KS)
Widener U (PA)
York Coll of Pennsylvania (PA)

GEOGRAPHIC INFORMATION SCIENCE AND CARTOGRAPHY
The U of Akron (OH)

GEOGRAPHY
The U of Tampa (FL)
Wright State U (OH)

GEOGRAPHY RELATED
Adams State U (CO)

GEOLOGY/EARTH SCIENCE
Coll of Coastal Georgia (GA)
Midland Coll (TX)
Wright State U (OH)

GERMAN
State Coll of Florida Manatee-Sarasota (FL)
Xavier U (OH)

GERONTOLOGY
Holy Cross Coll (IN)
Madonna U (MI)
Manchester U (IN)
Ohio Dominican U (OH)
Siena Heights U (MI)
Thomas More Coll (KY)

GOLF COURSE OPERATION AND GROUNDS MANAGEMENT
Keiser U, Fort Lauderdale (FL)

GRAPHIC AND PRINTING EQUIPMENT OPERATION/PRODUCTION
Chowan U (NC)
Dixie State U (UT)
Lewis-Clark State Coll (ID)

GRAPHIC COMMUNICATIONS
ITT Tech Inst, Clovis (CA)
ITT Tech Inst, Indianapolis (IN)
ITT Tech Inst, South Bend (IN)
ITT Tech Inst, Hanover (MD)
New England Inst of Technology (RI)

GRAPHIC COMMUNICATIONS RELATED
Rasmussen Coll Moorhead (MN)
U of the District of Columbia (DC)

GRAPHIC DESIGN
Academy of Art U (CA)
The Art Inst of Austin, a branch of The Art Institute of Houston (TX)
The Art Inst of California–Hollywood, a campus of Argosy U (CA)
The Art Inst of California–Inland Empire, a campus of Argosy U (CA)
The Art Inst of California–Los Angeles, a campus of Argosy U (CA)
The Art Inst of California–Orange County, a campus of Argosy U (CA)
The Art Inst of California–Sacramento, a campus of Argosy U (CA)
The Art Inst of California–San Diego, a campus of Argosy U (CA)
The Art Inst of California–San Francisco, a campus of Argosy U (CA)
The Art Inst of California–Silicon Valley, a campus of Argosy U (CA)
The Art Inst of Charlotte, a campus of South U (NC)
The Art Inst of Dallas, a campus of South U (TX)
The Art Inst of Fort Lauderdale (FL)
The Art Inst of Fort Worth, a campus of South U (TX)
The Art Inst of Houston (TX)
The Art Inst of Houston–North, a branch of The Art Institute of Houston (TX)
The Art Inst of Indianapolis (IN)
The Art Inst of Jacksonville, a branch of Miami International U of Art & Design (FL)
The Art Inst of Michigan (MI)
The Art Inst of Michigan–Troy (MI)
The Art Inst of Ohio–Cincinnati (OH)
The Art Inst of Philadelphia (PA)
The Art Inst of Phoenix (AZ)
The Art Inst of Pittsburgh (PA)
The Art Inst of Portland (OR)
The Art Inst of Raleigh-Durham, a campus of South U (NC)
The Art Inst of Salt Lake City (UT)
The Art Inst of San Antonio, a branch of The Art Institute of Houston (TX)
The Art Inst of Seattle (WA)
The Art Inst of Tampa, a branch of Miami International U of Art & Design (FL)
The Art Inst of Tennessee–Nashville, a branch of The Art Institute of Atlanta (TN)
The Art Inst of Tucson (AZ)
The Art Inst of Wisconsin (WI)
The Art Inst of York–Pennsylvania (PA)
The Art Insts International–Kansas City (KS)
The Art Insts International Minnesota (MN)
Brown Mackie Coll–Birmingham (AL)
Brown Mackie Coll–Dallas/Ft. Worth (TX)
California U of Pennsylvania (PA)
Coll of Mount St. Joseph (OH)
Columbia Centro Universitario, Caguas (PR)
Ferris State U (MI)
Hickey Coll (MO)
The Illinois Inst of Art–Chicago (IL)
The Illinois Inst of Art–Schaumburg (IL)
The Illinois Inst of Art–Tinley Park (IL)
International Business Coll, Fort Wayne (IN)
Madonna U (MI)

Minnesota School of Business–
Richfield (MN)
Minnesota School of Business–St.
Cloud (MN)
Pacific Union Coll (CA)
Parsons The New School for Design
(NY)
Penn Foster Coll (AZ)
Platt Coll San Diego (CA)
Pratt Inst (NY)
South U, Columbia (SC)
State U of New York Coll of
Agriculture and Technology at
Cobleskill (NY)
State U of New York Coll of
Technology at Canton (NY)
Union Coll (NE)
U of the District of Columbia (DC)
Villa Maria Coll (NY)

HEALTH AIDE
National U (CA)

**HEALTH AND MEDICAL
ADMINISTRATIVE SERVICES
RELATED**
National U (CA)

**HEALTH AND PHYSICAL
EDUCATION/FITNESS**
Coll of Coastal Georgia (GA)
Midland Coll (TX)
Robert Morris U Illinois (IL)
State U of New York Coll of
Technology at Delhi (NY)
Universidad del Turabo (PR)
Utah Valley U (UT)

**HEALTH AND PHYSICAL
EDUCATION RELATED**
Pennsylvania Coll of Technology
(PA)

HEALTH AND WELLNESS
Howard Payne U (TX)

**HEALTH/HEALTH-CARE
ADMINISTRATION**
Baker Coll of Auburn Hills (MI)
Baker Coll of Flint (MI)
Mount St. Mary's Coll (CA)
National U (CA)
Park U (MO)
Penn Foster Coll (AZ)
Pioneer Pacific Coll, Wilsonville (OR)
State Coll of Florida Manatee-
Sarasota (FL)
The U of Scranton (PA)
Washburn U (KS)

**HEALTH INFORMATION/
MEDICAL RECORDS
ADMINISTRATION**
Baker Coll of Auburn Hills (MI)
Baker Coll of Cadillac (MI)
Baker Coll of Clinton Township (MI)
Baker Coll of Flint (MI)
Baker Coll of Jackson (MI)
Baker Coll of Port Huron (MI)
Indian River State Coll (FL)
Keiser U, Fort Lauderdale (FL)
Lincoln Coll of New England,
Southington (CT)
Montana State U Billings (MT)
Polk State Coll (FL)

**HEALTH INFORMATION/
MEDICAL RECORDS
TECHNOLOGY**
Baker Coll of Flint (MI)
Baker Coll of Jackson (MI)
Dakota State U (SD)
Davenport U, Grand Rapids (MI)
DeVry U, Pomona (CA)
DeVry U, Decatur (GA)
DeVry U, Chicago (IL)
DeVry U, North Brunswick (NJ)
DeVry U, Charlotte (NC)
DeVry U, Columbus (OH)
DeVry U, Seven Hills (OH)
DeVry U, Fort Washington (PA)
DeVry U, Houston (TX)
DeVry U, Irving (TX)
Ferris State U (MI)
Fisher Coll (MA)
Gwynedd Mercy U (PA)
Hodges U (FL)
Indiana U Northwest (IN)
ITT Tech Inst, Indianapolis (IN)
Keiser U, Fort Lauderdale (FL)
Louisiana Tech U (LA)

Mercy Coll of Ohio (OH)
Midland Coll (TX)
Missouri Western State U (MO)
Molloy Coll (NY)
National U (CA)
New England Inst of Technology (RI)
Northern Michigan U (MI)
Peirce Coll (PA)
Penn Foster Coll (AZ)
Pennsylvania Coll of Technology
(PA)
Rasmussen Coll Appleton (WI)
Rasmussen Coll Aurora (IL)
Rasmussen Coll Bismarck (ND)
Rasmussen Coll Blaine (MN)
Rasmussen Coll Bloomington (MN)
Rasmussen Coll Brooklyn Park (MN)
Rasmussen Coll Eagan (MN)
Rasmussen Coll Fort Myers (FL)
Rasmussen Coll Green Bay (WI)
Rasmussen Coll Kansas City/
Overland Park (KS)
Rasmussen Coll Lake Elmo/
Woodbury (MN)
Rasmussen Coll Land O' Lakes (FL)
Rasmussen Coll Mankato (MN)
Rasmussen Coll Mokena/Tinley Park
(IL)
Rasmussen Coll Moorhead (MN)
Rasmussen Coll New Port Richey
(FL)
Rasmussen Coll Ocala (FL)
Rasmussen Coll Rockford (IL)
Rasmussen Coll Romeoville/Joliet
(IL)
Rasmussen Coll St. Cloud (MN)
Rasmussen Coll Tampa/Brandon
(FL)
Rasmussen Coll Topeka (KS)
Rasmussen Coll Wausau (WI)
St. Catherine U (MN)
Sullivan U (KY)
U of Cincinnati (OH)
Washburn U (KS)
Weber State U (UT)
Western Kentucky U (KY)

**HEALTH/MEDICAL
PREPARATORY PROGRAMS
RELATED**
Immaculata U (PA)
Mount St. Mary's Coll (CA)
Ohio Valley U (WV)
U of Cincinnati (OH)

**HEALTH PROFESSIONS
RELATED**
Arkansas Tech U (AR)
Caribbean U (PR)
Ferris State U (MI)
Fisher Coll (MA)
Lock Haven U of Pennsylvania (PA)
Morrisville State Coll (NY)
Newman U (KS)
New York U (NY)
Northwest U (WA)
Saint Peter's U (NJ)
U of Cincinnati (OH)
U of Hartford (CT)
Villa Maria Coll (NY)

**HEALTH SERVICES
ADMINISTRATION**
Florida National U (FL)
Keiser U, Fort Lauderdale (FL)

**HEALTH SERVICES/ALLIED
HEALTH/HEALTH SCIENCES**
Cameron U (OK)
Fisher Coll (MA)
Howard Payne U (TX)
Keystone Coll (PA)
Lindsey Wilson Coll (KY)
Mercyhurst U (PA)
Pennsylvania Coll of Technology
(PA)
Pine Manor Coll (MA)
State U of New York Coll of
Agriculture and Technology at
Cobleskill (NY)
U of Hartford (CT)
U of Maine at Fort Kent (ME)
U of the Incarnate Word (TX)
Weber State U (UT)

**HEALTH TEACHER
EDUCATION**
Palm Beach State Coll (FL)
State Coll of Florida Manatee-
Sarasota (FL)

**HEATING, AIR CONDITIONING,
VENTILATION AND
REFRIGERATION
MAINTENANCE TECHNOLOGY**
Indian River State Coll (FL)
Lewis-Clark State Coll (ID)
Montana State U Billings (MT)
New England Inst of Technology (RI)
Oakland City U (IN)
State U of New York Coll of
Technology at Delhi (NY)

**HEATING, VENTILATION, AIR
CONDITIONING AND
REFRIGERATION ENGINEERING
TECHNOLOGY**
Ferris State U (MI)
Midland Coll (TX)
Northern Michigan U (MI)
Oakland City U (IN)
Pennsylvania Coll of Technology
(PA)
State U of New York Coll of
Technology at Canton (NY)

**HEAVY EQUIPMENT
MAINTENANCE TECHNOLOGY**
Ferris State U (MI)
Pennsylvania Coll of Technology
(PA)

HEBREW
Yeshiva U (NY)

HISTOLOGIC TECHNICIAN
Indiana U–Purdue U Indianapolis
(IN)
Northern Michigan U (MI)
The U of Akron (OH)

**HISTOLOGIC TECHNOLOGY/
HISTOTECHNOLOGIST**
Argosy U, Dallas (TX)
Argosy U, Twin Cities (MN)
Keiser U, Fort Lauderdale (FL)
Tarleton State U (TX)

**HISTORIC PRESERVATION AND
CONSERVATION**
Montana Tech of The U of Montana
(MT)

HISTORY
Abraham Baldwin Ag Coll (GA)
American Public U System (WV)
Clarke U (IA)
Coll of Coastal Georgia (GA)
Indiana Wesleyan U (IN)
Indian River State Coll (FL)
Lindsey Wilson Coll (KY)
Lourdes U (OH)
Midland Coll (TX)
Palm Beach State Coll (FL)
Regent U (VA)
Rogers State U (OK)
State Coll of Florida Manatee-
Sarasota (FL)
State U of New York Empire State
Coll (NY)
Thomas More Coll (KY)
U of Rio Grande (OH)
The U of Tampa (FL)
Utah Valley U (UT)
Wright State U (OH)
Xavier U (OH)

HOMELAND SECURITY
Keiser U, Fort Lauderdale (FL)

**HOMELAND SECURITY, LAW
ENFORCEMENT, FIREFIGHTING
AND PROTECTIVE SERVICES
RELATED**
Lake Superior State U (MI)
Universidad del Turabo (PR)

**HORSE HUSBANDRY/EQUINE
SCIENCE AND MANAGEMENT**
Michigan State U (MI)
Southern Utah U (UT)
U of Guelph (ON, Canada)

HORTICULTURAL SCIENCE
Abraham Baldwin Ag Coll (GA)
Andrews U (MI)
Morrisville State Coll (NY)
U of Connecticut (CT)
U of Guelph (ON, Canada)

**HOSPITAL AND HEALTH-CARE
FACILITIES ADMINISTRATION**
State Coll of Florida Manatee-
Sarasota (FL)

**HOSPITALITY
ADMINISTRATION**
Baker Coll of Flint (MI)
Baker Coll of Owosso (MI)
Colorado Mesa U (CO)
Florida National U (FL)
Keiser U, Fort Lauderdale (FL)
Lewis-Clark State Coll (ID)
Lexington Coll (IL)
Monroe Coll, Bronx (NY)
Morrisville State Coll (NY)
National U (CA)
New York City Coll of Technology of
the City U of New York (NY)
Penn Foster Coll (AZ)
Sullivan U (KY)
The U of Akron (OH)
U of Cincinnati (OH)
Utah Valley U (UT)
Webber International U (FL)
Western Kentucky U (KY)
Youngstown State U (OH)

**HOSPITALITY
ADMINISTRATION RELATED**
Morrisville State Coll (NY)
Penn State Berks (PA)
Purdue U (IN)
U of the District of Columbia (DC)

**HOSPITALITY AND
RECREATION MARKETING**
Ferris State U (MI)

**HOTEL/MOTEL
ADMINISTRATION**
Baker Coll of Muskegon (MI)
Baker Coll of Owosso (MI)
Baker Coll of Port Huron (MI)
Ferris State U (MI)
Indian River State Coll (FL)
Inter American U of Puerto Rico,
Fajardo Campus (PR)
International Business Coll, Fort
Wayne (IN)
Palm Beach State Coll (FL)
State U of New York Coll of
Agriculture and Technology at
Cobleskill (NY)
The U of Akron (OH)
U of the Virgin Islands (VI)

**HUMAN DEVELOPMENT AND
FAMILY STUDIES**
Penn State Abington (PA)
Penn State Altoona (PA)
Penn State Berks (PA)
Penn State Erie, The Behrend Coll
(PA)
Penn State Shenango (PA)

**HUMAN DEVELOPMENT AND
FAMILY STUDIES RELATED**
Utah State U (UT)

HUMANITIES
Abraham Baldwin Ag Coll (GA)
Aquinas Coll (TN)
Calumet Coll of Saint Joseph (IN)
Fisher Coll (MA)
Harrison Middleton U (AZ)
Indian River State Coll (FL)
Michigan Technological U (MI)
Ohio U (OH)
Saint Mary-of-the-Woods Coll (IN)
Saint Peter's U (NJ)
State Coll of Florida Manatee-
Sarasota (FL)
State U of New York Coll of
Agriculture and Technology at
Cobleskill (NY)
State U of New York Coll of
Technology at Delhi (NY)
Thomas More Coll (KY)
Utah Valley U (UT)
Valparaiso U (IN)
Washburn U (KS)

**HUMAN RESOURCES
DEVELOPMENT**
Northern Kentucky U (KY)
Park U (MO)

**HUMAN RESOURCES
MANAGEMENT**
Baker Coll of Owosso (MI)

Harrison Coll, Indianapolis (IN)
Harrison Coll (OH)
King's Coll (PA)
Marian U (IN)
Montana State U Billings (MT)
Penn Foster Coll (AZ)
Rasmussen Coll Appleton (WI)
Rasmussen Coll Blaine (MN)
Rasmussen Coll Bloomington (MN)
Rasmussen Coll Brooklyn Park (MN)
Rasmussen Coll Eagan (MN)
Rasmussen Coll Fargo (ND)
Rasmussen Coll Fort Myers (FL)
Rasmussen Coll Green Bay (WI)
Rasmussen Coll Kansas City/
Overland Park (KS)
Rasmussen Coll Lake Elmo/
Woodbury (MN)
Rasmussen Coll Land O' Lakes (FL)
Rasmussen Coll Mankato (MN)
Rasmussen Coll Moorhead (MN)
Rasmussen Coll New Port Richey
(FL)
Rasmussen Coll Ocala (FL)
Rasmussen Coll Tampa/Brandon
(FL)
Rasmussen Coll Topeka (KS)
Rasmussen Coll Wausau (WI)
U of Alaska Fairbanks (AK)
The U of Findlay (OH)
The U of Scranton (PA)

**HUMAN RESOURCES
MANAGEMENT AND SERVICES
RELATED**
American Public U System (WV)

HUMAN SERVICES
Alaska Pacific U (AK)
Arkansas Tech U (AR)
Baker Coll of Clinton Township (MI)
Baker Coll of Flint (MI)
Baker Coll of Muskegon (MI)
Beacon Coll (FL)
Bethel Coll (IN)
Caribbean U (PR)
Cazenovia Coll (NY)
Columbia Coll (MO)
Elizabethtown Coll School of
Continuing and Professional
Studies (PA)
Indian River State Coll (FL)
Mercy Coll (NY)
Morrisville State Coll (NY)
Mount St. Mary's Coll (CA)
Mount Vernon Nazarene U (OH)
New York City Coll of Technology of
the City U of New York (NY)
Rasmussen Coll Appleton (WI)
Rasmussen Coll Bismarck (ND)
Rasmussen Coll Blaine (MN)
Rasmussen Coll Bloomington (MN)
Rasmussen Coll Brooklyn Park (MN)
Rasmussen Coll Eagan (MN)
Rasmussen Coll Fargo (ND)
Rasmussen Coll Fort Myers (FL)
Rasmussen Coll Green Bay (WI)
Rasmussen Coll Kansas City/
Overland Park (KS)
Rasmussen Coll Lake Elmo/
Woodbury (MN)
Rasmussen Coll Land O' Lakes (FL)
Rasmussen Coll Mankato (MN)
Rasmussen Coll Moorhead (MN)
Rasmussen Coll New Port Richey
(FL)
Rasmussen Coll Ocala (FL)
Rasmussen Coll St. Cloud (MN)
Rasmussen Coll Tampa/Brandon
(FL)
Rasmussen Coll Topeka (KS)
Rasmussen Coll Wausau (WI)
U of Great Falls (MT)
U of Maine at Fort Kent (ME)
The U of Scranton (PA)
Valley Forge Christian Coll (PA)
Walsh U (OH)
Wayland Baptist U (TX)

**HYDROLOGY AND WATER
RESOURCES SCIENCE**
Indian River State Coll (FL)
Lake Superior State U (MI)
U of the District of Columbia (DC)

ILLUSTRATION
Academy of Art U (CA)
Fashion Inst of Technology (NY)
Pratt Inst (NY)

INDUSTRIAL AND PRODUCT DESIGN
Academy of Art U (CA)
The Art Inst of Pittsburgh (PA)
The Art Inst of Seattle (WA)
Oakland City U (IN)

INDUSTRIAL ELECTRONICS TECHNOLOGY
Ferris State U (MI)
Lewis-Clark State Coll (ID)
Penn Foster Coll (AZ)
Pennsylvania Coll of Technology (PA)

INDUSTRIAL ENGINEERING
Indiana Tech (IN)

INDUSTRIAL MECHANICS AND MAINTENANCE TECHNOLOGY
Northern Michigan U (MI)
Pennsylvania Coll of Technology (PA)
The U of West Alabama (AL)

INDUSTRIAL PRODUCTION TECHNOLOGIES RELATED
Austin Peay State U (TN)
California U of Pennsylvania (PA)
Clarion U of Pennsylvania (PA)
U of Alaska Fairbanks (AK)

INDUSTRIAL RADIOLOGIC TECHNOLOGY
Baker Coll of Owosso (MI)
The George Washington U (DC)
Indian River State Coll (FL)
Our Lady of the Lake Coll (LA)
Palm Beach State Coll (FL)
Widener U (PA)

INDUSTRIAL TECHNOLOGY
Arkansas Tech U (AR)
Baker Coll of Muskegon (MI)
Indiana U–Purdue U Fort Wayne (IN)
ITT Tech Inst, Phoenix (AZ)
ITT Tech Inst, Phoenix (AZ)
ITT Tech Inst, Tempe (AZ)
ITT Tech Inst, Clovis (CA)
ITT Tech Inst, Concord (CA)
ITT Tech Inst, Corona (CA)
ITT Tech Inst, West Palm Beach (FL)
ITT Tech Inst, Indianapolis (IN)
ITT Tech Inst, Wichita (KS)
ITT Tech Inst, Southfield (MI)
ITT Tech Inst (MS)
ITT Tech Inst, Springfield (MO)
ITT Tech Inst, Oklahoma City (OK)
Millersville U of Pennsylvania (PA)
Murray State U (KY)
Pittsburg State U (KS)
Southeastern Louisiana U (LA)
Southern Arkansas U–Magnolia (AR)
U of Puerto Rico in Bayamón (PR)
U of Rio Grande (OH)
Washburn U (KS)

INFORMATION RESOURCES MANAGEMENT
Rasmussen Coll Fort Myers (FL)
Rasmussen Coll Land O' Lakes (FL)
Rasmussen Coll New Port Richey (FL)
Rasmussen Coll Ocala (FL)
Rasmussen Coll Tampa/Brandon (FL)

INFORMATION SCIENCE/ STUDIES
Baker Coll of Clinton Township (MI)
Baker Coll of Owosso (MI)
Campbellsville U (KY)
Elizabethtown Coll School of Continuing and Professional Studies (PA)
Immaculata U (PA)
Indiana U–Purdue U Fort Wayne (IN)
Indian River State Coll (FL)
Johnson State Coll (VT)
Mansfield U of Pennsylvania (PA)
Morrisville State Coll (NY)
Newman U (KS)
Oakland City U (IN)
Penn State Abington (PA)
Penn State Altoona (PA)
Penn State Berks (PA)
Penn State Erie, The Behrend Coll (PA)
Penn State U Park (PA)
Pioneer Pacific Coll, Wilsonville (OR)
Saint Peter's U (NJ)
South U (NC)
State Coll of Florida Manatee-Sarasota (FL)

State U of New York Coll of Agriculture and Technology at Cobleskill (NY)
State U of New York Coll of Technology at Canton (NY)
State U of New York Coll of Technology at Delhi (NY)
Tulane U (LA)
U of Cincinnati (OH)
U of Massachusetts Lowell (MA)
U of Pittsburgh at Bradford (PA)
The U of Scranton (PA)
The U of Toledo (OH)
Wright State U (OH)

INFORMATION TECHNOLOGY
Argosy U, Atlanta (GA)
Argosy U, Dallas (TX)
Argosy U, Denver (CO)
Argosy U, Hawai`i (HI)
Argosy U, Inland Empire (CA)
Argosy U, Los Angeles (CA)
Argosy U, Nashville (TN)
Argosy U, Orange County (CA)
Argosy U, Phoenix (AZ)
Argosy U, Salt Lake City (UT)
Argosy U, San Diego (CA)
Argosy U, San Francisco Bay Area (CA)
Argosy U, Sarasota (FL)
Argosy U, Seattle (WA)
Argosy U, Tampa (FL)
Argosy U, Twin Cities (MN)
Argosy U, Washington DC (VA)
Arkansas Tech U (AR)
Cameron U (OK)
Ferris State U (MI)
Franklin U (OH)
Indiana U–Purdue U Fort Wayne (IN)
Keiser U, Fort Lauderdale (FL)
Keystone Coll (PA)
Limestone Coll (SC)
McNeese State U (LA)
Mercy Coll (NY)
Monroe Coll, Bronx (NY)
New England Inst of Technology (RI)
Peirce Coll (PA)
Regent U (VA)
Southern Utah U (UT)
Thomas More Coll (KY)
Tiffin U (OH)
Trevecca Nazarene U (TN)
Vermont Tech Coll (VT)
Youngstown State U (OH)

INSTITUTIONAL FOOD WORKERS
Immaculata U (PA)

INSTRUMENTATION TECHNOLOGY
U of Puerto Rico in Bayamón (PR)

INSURANCE
AIB Coll of Business (IA)
Caribbean U (PR)

INTERDISCIPLINARY STUDIES
Central Methodist U (MO)
John Brown U (AR)
Keiser U, Fort Lauderdale (FL)
Lesley U (MA)
U of North Florida (FL)

INTERIOR ARCHITECTURE
Villa Maria Coll (NY)

INTERIOR DESIGN
Academy of Art U (CA)
The Art Inst of Charlotte, a campus of South U (NC)
The Art Inst of Fort Lauderdale (FL)
The Art Inst of Michigan (MI)
The Art Inst of Ohio–Cincinnati (OH)
The Art Inst of Philadelphia (PA)
The Art Inst of Seattle (WA)
The Art Insts International Minnesota (MN)
Baker Coll of Allen Park (MI)
Baker Coll of Auburn Hills (MI)
Baker Coll of Clinton Township (MI)
Baker Coll of Muskegon (MI)
Baker Coll of Owosso (MI)
Baker Coll of Port Huron (MI)
Bay Path Coll (MA)
Chaminade U of Honolulu (HI)
EDP U of Puerto Rico (PR)
Fashion Inst of Technology (NY)
Indiana U–Purdue U Fort Wayne (IN)
Indiana U–Purdue U Indianapolis (IN)
Indian River State Coll (FL)
Interior Designers Inst (CA)

Montana State U (MT)
New England Inst of Technology (RI)
Palm Beach State Coll (FL)
Parsons The New School for Design (NY)
Robert Morris U Illinois (IL)
Stevens–The Inst of Business & Arts (MO)
Villa Maria Coll (NY)
Weber State U (UT)

INTERMEDIA/MULTIMEDIA
Academy of Art U (CA)
Platt Coll San Diego (CA)

INTERNATIONAL BUSINESS/ TRADE/COMMERCE
AIB Coll of Business (IA)
The American U of Rome (Italy)
Saint Peter's U (NJ)
Schiller International U (FL)
Schiller International U (France)
U of the Potomac (DC)

INTERNATIONAL/GLOBAL STUDIES
Holy Cross Coll (IN)
Thomas More Coll (KY)

JAZZ/JAZZ STUDIES
Five Towns Coll (NY)
State Coll of Florida Manatee-Sarasota (FL)
Villa Maria Coll (NY)

JEWISH/JUDAIC STUDIES
State Coll of Florida Manatee-Sarasota (FL)

JOURNALISM
Abraham Baldwin Ag Coll (GA)
Academy of Art U (CA)
Indian River State Coll (FL)
John Brown U (AR)
Madonna U (MI)
Manchester U (IN)
Morrisville State Coll (NY)
Palm Beach State Coll (FL)
State Coll of Florida Manatee-Sarasota (FL)

JOURNALISM RELATED
Adams State U (CO)
National U (CA)

KEYBOARD INSTRUMENTS
McNally Smith Coll of Music (MN)

KINDERGARTEN/PRESCHOOL EDUCATION
Abraham Baldwin Ag Coll (GA)
Baker Coll of Clinton Township (MI)
Baker Coll of Muskegon (MI)
Baker Coll of Owosso (MI)
California U of Pennsylvania (PA)
Fisher Coll (MA)
Indian River State Coll (FL)
Maria Coll (NY)
Miami U (OH)
Mitchell Coll (CT)
Mount St. Mary's Coll (CA)
Palm Beach State Coll (FL)
Piedmont International U (NC)
Shawnee State U (OH)
State Coll of Florida Manatee-Sarasota (FL)
Tennessee State U (TN)
U of Cincinnati (OH)
U of Great Falls (MT)
U of Rio Grande (OH)
Wilmington U (DE)

KINESIOLOGY AND EXERCISE SCIENCE
Southwestern Adventist U (TX)

LABOR AND INDUSTRIAL RELATIONS
Indiana U–Purdue U Fort Wayne (IN)
Rider U (NJ)
State U of New York Empire State Coll (NY)
Youngstown State U (OH)

LABOR STUDIES
Indiana U Bloomington (IN)
Indiana U Northwest (IN)
Indiana U–Purdue U Indianapolis (IN)

LANDSCAPE ARCHITECTURE
Academy of Art U (CA)
Keystone Coll (PA)
Morrisville State Coll (NY)

LANDSCAPING AND GROUNDSKEEPING
Abraham Baldwin Ag Coll (GA)
Farmingdale State Coll (NY)
Michigan State U (MI)
North Carolina State U (NC)
Pennsylvania Coll of Technology (PA)
State U of New York Coll of Technology at Delhi (NY)
U of Massachusetts Amherst (MA)
Vermont Tech Coll (VT)

LANGUAGE INTERPRETATION AND TRANSLATION
Indian River State Coll (FL)

LATIN AMERICAN STUDIES
State Coll of Florida Manatee-Sarasota (FL)

LAW ENFORCEMENT INVESTIGATION AND INTERVIEWING
U of the District of Columbia (DC)

LAY MINISTRY
Howard Payne U (TX)
Maranatha Baptist Bible Coll (WI)

LEGAL ADMINISTRATIVE ASSISTANT/SECRETARY
Baker Coll of Auburn Hills (MI)
Baker Coll of Clinton Township (MI)
Baker Coll of Flint (MI)
Baker Coll of Jackson (MI)
Baker Coll of Muskegon (MI)
Baker Coll of Owosso (MI)
Baker Coll of Port Huron (MI)
Clarion U of Pennsylvania (PA)
Dordt Coll (IA)
Florida National U (FL)
Hickey Coll (MO)
International Business Coll, Fort Wayne (IN)
Lewis-Clark State Coll (ID)
Palm Beach State Coll (FL)
Shawnee State U (OH)
Sullivan U (KY)
U of Rio Grande (OH)
U of the District of Columbia (DC)
Washburn U (KS)
Youngstown State U (OH)

LEGAL ASSISTANT/PARALEGAL
American Public U System (WV)
Broadview U–Boise (ID)
Broadview U–Layton (UT)
Broadview U–Orem (UT)
Broadview U–West Jordan (UT)
Brown Mackie Coll–Birmingham (AL)
Brown Mackie Coll–San Antonio (TX)
Calumet Coll of Saint Joseph (IN)
Central Penn Coll (PA)
Champlain Coll (VT)
Clayton State U (GA)
Coll of Mount St. Joseph (OH)
Coll of Saint Mary (NE)
Davenport U, Grand Rapids (MI)
Elms Coll (MA)
Ferris State U (MI)
Florida National U (FL)
Gannon U (PA)
Globe U–Appleton (WI)
Globe U–Eau Claire (WI)
Globe U–Green Bay (WI)
Globe U–Madison East (WI)
Globe U–Madison West (WI)
Globe U–Minneapolis (MN)
Globe U–Wausau (WI)
Globe U–Woodbury (MN)
Harrison Coll, Indianapolis (IN)
Hickey Coll (MO)
Hodges U (FL)
Husson U (ME)
Indian River State Coll (FL)
International Business Coll, Fort Wayne (IN)
ITT Tech Inst, Phoenix (AZ)
ITT Tech Inst, Springfield (IL)
ITT Tech Inst, Indianapolis (IN)
ITT Tech Inst, Indianapolis (IN)
ITT Tech Inst, Wichita (KS)
ITT Tech Inst, Lexington (KY)
ITT Tech Inst (MS)
ITT Tech Inst, Oklahoma City (OK)
Jones Coll, Jacksonville (FL)
Keiser U, Fort Lauderdale (FL)
Lewis-Clark State Coll (ID)
Lincoln Coll of New England, Southington (CT)
Madonna U (MI)
Maria Coll (NY)

McNeese State U (LA)
Midland Coll (TX)
Minnesota School of Business–Blaine (MN)
Minnesota School of Business–Elk River (MN)
Minnesota School of Business–Moorhead (MN)
Minnesota School of Business–Richfield (MN)
Minnesota School of Business–Rochester (MN)
Minnesota School of Business–St. Cloud (MN)
Missouri Western State U (MO)
Mount Aloysius Coll (PA)
National Paralegal Coll (AZ)
National U (CA)
Newman U (KS)
New York City Coll of Technology of the City U of New York (NY)
Peirce Coll (PA)
Penn Foster Coll (AZ)
Pennsylvania Coll of Technology (PA)
Pioneer Pacific Coll, Wilsonville (OR)
Rasmussen Coll Appleton (WI)
Rasmussen Coll Aurora (IL)
Rasmussen Coll Bismarck (ND)
Rasmussen Coll Blaine (MN)
Rasmussen Coll Bloomington (MN)
Rasmussen Coll Brooklyn Park (MN)
Rasmussen Coll Eagan (MN)
Rasmussen Coll Fargo (ND)
Rasmussen Coll Fort Myers (FL)
Rasmussen Coll Green Bay (WI)
Rasmussen Coll Kansas City/ Overland Park (KS)
Rasmussen Coll Lake Elmo/ Woodbury (MN)
Rasmussen Coll Land O' Lakes (FL)
Rasmussen Coll Mankato (MN)
Rasmussen Coll Mokena/Tinley Park (IL)
Rasmussen Coll Moorhead (MN)
Rasmussen Coll New Port Richey (FL)
Rasmussen Coll Ocala (FL)
Rasmussen Coll Rockford (IL)
Rasmussen Coll Romeoville/Joliet (IL)
Rasmussen Coll St. Cloud (MN)
Rasmussen Coll Tampa/Brandon (FL)
Rasmussen Coll Topeka (KS)
Rasmussen Coll Wausau (WI)
Robert Morris U Illinois (IL)
Saint Mary-of-the-Woods Coll (IN)
Shawnee State U (OH)
Southern Utah U (UT)
South U (AL)
South U, Royal Palm Beach (FL)
South U (GA)
South U (OH)
South U, Columbia (SC)
South U, Glen Allen (VA)
South U, Virginia Beach (VA)
State Coll of Florida Manatee-Sarasota (FL)
Stevens–The Inst of Business & Arts (MO)
Suffolk U (MA)
Sullivan U (KY)
Tulane U (LA)
The U of Akron (OH)
U of Alaska Fairbanks (AK)
U of Arkansas–Fort Smith (AR)
U of Cincinnati (OH)
U of Great Falls (MT)
U of Hartford (CT)
U of Louisville (KY)
U of the District of Columbia (DC)
Utah Valley U (UT)
Washburn U (KS)
Western Kentucky U (KY)
Widener U (PA)

LEGAL PROFESSIONS AND STUDIES RELATED
Florida National U (FL)

LEGAL STUDIES
Maria Coll (NY)
St. John's U (NY)
U of Hartford (CT)
U of New Haven (CT)

LIBERAL ARTS AND SCIENCES AND HUMANITIES RELATED
Adams State U (CO)
Ball State U (IN)
Colorado Mesa U (CO)
Ferris State U (MI)

Kent State U at Geauga (OH)
Kent State U at Stark (OH)
Long Island U–LIU Post (NY)
Marymount California U (CA)
Morrisville State Coll (NY)
Mount Aloysius Coll (PA)
New York U (NY)
Nyack Coll (NY)
Pennsylvania Coll of Technology (PA)
Sacred Heart U (CT)
Southern New Hampshire U (NH)
State U of New York Coll of Technology at Delhi (NY)
Taylor U (IN)
U of Maryland U Coll (MD)
U of Wisconsin–Green Bay (WI)
U of Wisconsin–La Crosse (WI)
Walsh U (OH)
Wayland Baptist U (TX)
William Penn U (IA)

LIBERAL ARTS AND SCIENCES/ LIBERAL STUDIES
Abraham Baldwin Ag Coll (GA)
Adams State U (CO)
Adelphi U (NY)
Alverno Coll (WI)
American U (DC)
The American U of Rome (Italy)
Amridge U (AL)
Aquinas Coll (MI)
Arizona Christian U (AZ)
Arkansas State U (AR)
Armstrong Atlantic State U (GA)
Ball State U (IN)
Bard Coll (NY)
Bard Coll at Simon's Rock (MA)
Bay Path Coll (MA)
Beacon Coll (FL)
Bemidji State U (MN)
Bethel Coll (IN)
Bethel U (MN)
Briar Cliff U (IA)
Bryan Coll (TN)
Bryn Athyn Coll of the New Church (PA)
California U of Pennsylvania (PA)
Calumet Coll of Saint Joseph (IN)
Cazenovia Coll (NY)
Centenary Coll (NJ)
Charter Oak State Coll (CT)
Chestnut Hill Coll (PA)
Christendom Coll (VA)
Clarke U (IA)
Clayton State U (GA)
Colby-Sawyer Coll (NH)
Coll of Coastal Georgia (GA)
Coll of Staten Island of the City U of New York (NY)
Colorado Mesa U (CO)
Columbia Coll (MO)
Columbus State U (GA)
Concordia Coll–New York (NY)
Concordia U (CA)
Concordia U Texas (TX)
Crossroads Coll (MN)
Dallas Baptist U (TX)
Dickinson State U (ND)
Dominican Coll (NY)
Eastern New Mexico U (NM)
Eastern U (PA)
Elmira Coll (NY)
Emmanuel Coll (GA)
Emory U (GA)
Endicott Coll (MA)
Excelsior Coll (NY)
Fairleigh Dickinson U, Metropolitan Campus (NJ)
Farmingdale State Coll (NY)
Felician Coll (NJ)
Ferris State U (MI)
Fisher Coll (MA)
Five Towns Coll (NY)
Florida A&M U (FL)
Florida Atlantic U (FL)
Florida Coll (FL)
Florida National U (FL)
Franklin U Switzerland (Switzerland)
Gannon U (PA)
Glenville State Coll (WV)
Gwynedd Mercy U (PA)
Holy Cross Coll (IN)
Houghton Coll (NY)
Indiana State U (IN)
Indiana U Northwest (IN)
Indiana U Southeast (IN)
Indian River State Coll (FL)
Johnson State Coll (VT)
Kent State U at Stark (OH)

Kentucky State U (KY)
Keystone Coll (PA)
Lake Superior State U (MI)
Laurel U (NC)
Lewis-Clark State Coll (ID)
Limestone Coll (SC)
Long Island U–LIU Brooklyn (NY)
Loras Coll (IA)
Lourdes U (OH)
Mansfield U of Pennsylvania (PA)
Maria Coll (NY)
Marian U (IN)
Marymount California U (CA)
Medaille Coll (NY)
Medgar Evers Coll of the City U of New York (NY)
Mercy Coll (NY)
MidAmerica Nazarene U (KS)
Midwestern State U (TX)
Minnesota State U Mankato (MN)
Minnesota State U Moorhead (MN)
Missouri Southern State U (MO)
Mitchell Coll (CT)
Molloy Coll (NY)
Montana State U (MT)
Montana State U Billings (MT)
Montreat Coll, Montreat (NC)
Morrisville State Coll (NY)
Mount Aloysius Coll (PA)
Mount Marty Coll (SD)
Mount St. Mary's Coll (CA)
Murray State U (KY)
Neumann U (PA)
Newman U (KS)
New England Coll (NH)
New Saint Andrews Coll (ID)
New York City Coll of Technology of the City U of New York (NY)
New York U (NY)
Niagara U (NY)
Northern State U (SD)
Nyack Coll (NY)
Oakland City U (IN)
The Ohio State U at Marion (OH)
The Ohio State U–Mansfield Campus (OH)
The Ohio State U–Newark Campus (OH)
Ohio U (OH)
Ohio Valley U (WV)
Okanagan Coll (BC, Canada)
Palm Beach State Coll (FL)
Penn State Abington (PA)
Penn State Altoona (PA)
Penn State Berks (PA)
Penn State Erie, The Behrend Coll (PA)
Penn State Harrisburg (PA)
Penn State Shenango (PA)
Penn State U Park (PA)
Polk State Coll (FL)
Providence Coll (RI)
Quincy U (IL)
Rivier U (NH)
Rocky Mountain Coll (MT)
Rogers State U (OK)
Roger Williams U (RI)
St. Catherine U (MN)
St. Cloud State U (MN)
St. Francis Coll (NY)
St. Gregory's U, Shawnee (OK)
St. John's U (NY)
Saint Joseph's U (PA)
Saint Leo U (FL)
Saint Louis Christian Coll (MO)
St. Thomas Aquinas Coll (NY)
Salve Regina U (RI)
San Diego Christian Coll (CA)
Schiller International U (FL)
Schiller International U (France)
Schreiner U (TX)
Spring Arbor U (MI)
State Coll of Florida Manatee-Sarasota (FL)
State U of New York Coll of Agriculture and Technology at Cobleskill (NY)
State U of New York Coll of Technology at Canton (NY)
State U of New York Coll of Technology at Delhi (NY)
Stephens Coll (MO)
Suffolk U (MA)
Syracuse U (NY)
Tabor Coll (KS)
Thomas More Coll (KY)
Trine U (IN)
Troy U (AL)
Unity Coll (ME)
The U of Akron (OH)

U of Alaska Fairbanks (AK)
U of Arkansas–Fort Smith (AR)
U of Cincinnati (OH)
U of Delaware (DE)
U of Hartford (CT)
U of Maine at Augusta (ME)
U of Maine at Fort Kent (ME)
U of Maine at Presque Isle (ME)
The U of Montana Western (MT)
U of New Hampshire at Manchester (NH)
U of North Georgia (GA)
U of Pittsburgh at Bradford (PA)
The U of South Dakota (SD)
U of the District of Columbia (DC)
U of the Incarnate Word (TX)
The U of Toledo (OH)
U of West Florida (FL)
U of Wisconsin–Eau Claire (WI)
U of Wisconsin–Superior (WI)
Upper Iowa U (IA)
Valdosta State U (GA)
Villa Maria Coll (NY)
Waldorf Coll (IA)
Washburn U (KS)
Wesley Coll (DE)
Western Connecticut State U (CT)
Western New England U (MA)
Wichita State U (KS)
Wilson Coll (PA)
Winona State U (MN)
Xavier U (OH)
Youngstown State U (OH)

LIBRARY AND ARCHIVES ASSISTING
U of Maine at Augusta (ME)

LIBRARY AND INFORMATION SCIENCE
Indian River State Coll (FL)

LICENSED PRACTICAL/ VOCATIONAL NURSE TRAINING
Campbellsville U (KY)
Dickinson State U (ND)
Indian River State Coll (FL)
Inter American U of Puerto Rico, Aguadilla Campus (PR)
Inter American U of Puerto Rico, Bayamón Campus (PR)
Inter American U of Puerto Rico, Metropolitan Campus (PR)
Inter American U of Puerto Rico, Ponce Campus (PR)
Inter American U of Puerto Rico, San Germán Campus (PR)
Lewis-Clark State Coll (ID)
Maria Coll (NY)
Medgar Evers Coll of the City U of New York (NY)
Monroe Coll, Bronx (NY)
Montana State U Billings (MT)
National U (CA)

LOGISTICS, MATERIALS, AND SUPPLY CHAIN MANAGEMENT
Park U (MO)
Sullivan U (KY)
The U of Toledo (OH)

MACHINE SHOP TECHNOLOGY
Missouri Southern State U (MO)

MACHINE TOOL TECHNOLOGY
Colorado Mesa U (CO)
Pennsylvania Coll of Technology (PA)

MANAGEMENT INFORMATION SYSTEMS
Arkansas State U (AR)
Columbia Centro Universitario, Yauco (PR)
Johnson State Coll (VT)
Lake Superior State U (MI)
Lindsey Wilson Coll (KY)
Lock Haven U of Pennsylvania (PA)
Morehead State U (KY)
Shawnee State U (OH)
Universidad del Turabo (PR)
U of the Virgin Islands (VI)
Weber State U (UT)
Wilson Coll (PA)
Wright State U (OH)

MANAGEMENT INFORMATION SYSTEMS AND SERVICES RELATED
Harrison Coll, Indianapolis (IN)

Mount Aloysius Coll (PA)
Purdue U North Central (IN)
Rasmussen Coll Appleton (WI)
Rasmussen Coll Aurora (IL)
Rasmussen Coll Bismarck (ND)
Rasmussen Coll Blaine (MN)
Rasmussen Coll Bloomington (MN)
Rasmussen Coll Brooklyn Park (MN)
Rasmussen Coll Eagan (MN)
Rasmussen Coll Fargo (ND)
Rasmussen Coll Fort Myers (FL)
Rasmussen Coll Green Bay (WI)
Rasmussen Coll Kansas City/ Overland Park (KS)
Rasmussen Coll Lake Elmo/ Woodbury (MN)
Rasmussen Coll Land O' Lakes (FL)
Rasmussen Coll Mankato (MN)
Rasmussen Coll Mokena/Tinley Park (IL)
Rasmussen Coll Moorhead (MN)
Rasmussen Coll New Port Richey (FL)
Rasmussen Coll Ocala (FL)
Rasmussen Coll Rockford (IL)
Rasmussen Coll Romeoville/Joliet (IL)
Rasmussen Coll St. Cloud (MN)
Rasmussen Coll Tampa/Brandon (FL)
Rasmussen Coll Wausau (WI)

MANAGEMENT SCIENCE
Hawai`i Pacific U (HI)

MANUFACTURING ENGINEERING TECHNOLOGY
Colorado Mesa U (CO)
Edinboro U of Pennsylvania (PA)
Excelsior Coll (NY)
Harrison Coll, Indianapolis (IN)
Harrison Coll (OH)
Lawrence Technological U (MI)
Lewis-Clark State Coll (ID)
Missouri Western State U (MO)
Morehead State U (KY)
New England Inst of Technology (RI)
Northern Kentucky U (KY)
Pennsylvania Coll of Technology (PA)
The U of Akron (OH)
Weber State U (UT)
Western Kentucky U (KY)
Wright State U (OH)

MARINE MAINTENANCE AND SHIP REPAIR TECHNOLOGY
New England Inst of Technology (RI)

MARINE SCIENCE/MERCHANT MARINE OFFICER
Indian River State Coll (FL)

MARKETING/MARKETING MANAGEMENT
Abraham Baldwin Ag Coll (GA)
Baker Coll of Allen Park (MI)
Baker Coll of Auburn Hills (MI)
Baker Coll of Cadillac (MI)
Baker Coll of Clinton Township (MI)
Baker Coll of Owosso (MI)
Broadview U–Boise (ID)
Broadview U–Layton (UT)
Broadview U–Orem (UT)
Broadview U–West Jordan (UT)
Central Penn Coll (PA)
Ferris State U (MI)
Globe U–Eau Claire (WI)
Globe U–Green Bay (WI)
Globe U–La Crosse (WI)
Globe U–Madison West (WI)
Globe U–Minneapolis (MN)
Globe U–Sioux Falls (SD)
Globe U–Wausau (WI)
Globe U–Woodbury (MN)
Harrison Coll, Indianapolis (IN)
Harrison Coll (OH)
Hawai`i Pacific U (HI)
Indian River State Coll (FL)
Madonna U (MI)
Marian U (IN)
Miami U (OH)
Minnesota School of Business–Blaine (MN)
Minnesota School of Business–Elk River (MN)
Minnesota School of Business–Lakeville (MN)
Minnesota School of Business–Moorhead (MN)

Minnesota School of Business–Richfield (MN)
Minnesota School of Business–Rochester (MN)
Minnesota School of Business–St. Cloud (MN)
Minnesota School of Business–Shakopee (MN)
New York City Coll of Technology of the City U of New York (NY)
Palm Beach State Coll (FL)
Penn Foster Coll (AZ)
Rasmussen Coll Appleton (WI)
Rasmussen Coll Bismarck (ND)
Rasmussen Coll Blaine (MN)
Rasmussen Coll Bloomington (MN)
Rasmussen Coll Brooklyn Park (MN)
Rasmussen Coll Eagan (MN)
Rasmussen Coll Fargo (ND)
Rasmussen Coll Fort Myers (FL)
Rasmussen Coll Green Bay (WI)
Rasmussen Coll Kansas City/ Overland Park (KS)
Rasmussen Coll Lake Elmo/ Woodbury (MN)
Rasmussen Coll Land O' Lakes (FL)
Rasmussen Coll Mankato (MN)
Rasmussen Coll Moorhead (MN)
Rasmussen Coll New Port Richey (FL)
Rasmussen Coll Ocala (FL)
Rasmussen Coll St. Cloud (MN)
Rasmussen Coll Tampa/Brandon (FL)
Rasmussen Coll Topeka (KS)
Rasmussen Coll Wausau (WI)
Saint Peter's U (NJ)
Southern New Hampshire U (NH)
Tulane U (LA)
Universidad del Turabo (PR)
The U of Akron (OH)
Walsh U (OH)
Webber International U (FL)
Wright State U (OH)
Youngstown State U (OH)

MARKETING RELATED
Sullivan U (KY)

MARKETING RESEARCH
Penn Foster Coll (AZ)

MASONRY
Pennsylvania Coll of Technology (PA)

MASSAGE THERAPY
Broadview U–Boise (ID)
Broadview U–Layton (UT)
Broadview U–Orem (UT)
Broadview U–West Jordan (UT)
Columbia Centro Universitario, Caguas (PR)
Globe U–Appleton (WI)
Globe U–Eau Claire (WI)
Globe U–Green Bay (WI)
Globe U–La Crosse (WI)
Globe U–Madison East (WI)
Globe U–Madison West (WI)
Globe U–Sioux Falls (SD)
Globe U–Wausau (WI)
Globe U–Woodbury (MN)
Harrison Coll, Indianapolis (IN)
Keiser U, Fort Lauderdale (FL)
Minnesota School of Business–Blaine (MN)
Minnesota School of Business–Elk River (MN)
Minnesota School of Business–Lakeville (MN)
Minnesota School of Business–Moorhead (MN)
Minnesota School of Business–Rochester (MN)
Minnesota School of Business–St. Cloud (MN)
Morrisville State Coll (NY)

MASS COMMUNICATION/ MEDIA
Adams State U (CO)
Black Hills State U (SD)
Elizabethtown Coll School of Continuing and Professional Studies (PA)
Palm Beach State Coll (FL)
Southwestern Assemblies of God U (TX)
State Coll of Florida Manatee-Sarasota (FL)

U of Rio Grande (OH)
U of the Incarnate Word (TX)
York Coll of Pennsylvania (PA)

MATERNAL AND CHILD HEALTH
Universidad del Turabo (PR)

MATHEMATICS
Abraham Baldwin Ag Coll (GA)
Clarke U (IA)
Coll of Coastal Georgia (GA)
Creighton U (NE)
Hawai`i Pacific U (HI)
Indiana Wesleyan U (IN)
Indian River State Coll (FL)
Midland Coll (TX)
Palm Beach State Coll (FL)
Shawnee State U (OH)
State U of New York Coll of Agriculture and Technology at Cobleskill (NY)
Thomas More Coll (KY)
Trine U (IN)
U of Great Falls (MT)
U of Rio Grande (OH)
The U of Tampa (FL)
Utah Valley U (UT)

MATHEMATICS AND COMPUTER SCIENCE
Immaculata U (PA)

MATHEMATICS TEACHER EDUCATION
State Coll of Florida Manatee-Sarasota (FL)

MECHANICAL DRAFTING AND CAD/CADD
Baker Coll of Flint (MI)
Globe U–Woodbury (MN)
Midland Coll (TX)
New York City Coll of Technology of the City U of New York (NY)

MECHANICAL ENGINEERING
New England Inst of Technology (RI)
Polytechnic U of Puerto Rico (PR)

MECHANICAL ENGINEERING/ MECHANICAL TECHNOLOGY
Baker Coll of Flint (MI)
Bluefield State Coll (WV)
Fairmont State U (WV)
Farmingdale State Coll (NY)
Ferris State U (MI)
Indiana U–Purdue U Fort Wayne (IN)
Lake Superior State U (MI)
Lawrence Technological U (MI)
Miami U (OH)
Michigan Technological U (MI)
Morrisville State Coll (NY)
New York City Coll of Technology of the City U of New York (NY)
Penn State Altoona (PA)
Penn State Berks (PA)
Penn State Erie, The Behrend Coll (PA)
Penn State Shenango (PA)
Point Park U (PA)
State U of New York Coll of Agriculture and Technology at Cobleskill (NY)
State U of New York Coll of Technology at Canton (NY)
Universidad del Turabo (PR)
The U of Akron (OH)
U of Arkansas at Little Rock (AR)
U of Rio Grande (OH)
Vermont Tech Coll (VT)
Weber State U (UT)
Youngstown State U (OH)

MECHANICAL ENGINEERING TECHNOLOGIES RELATED
Indiana U–Purdue U Indianapolis (IN)
Purdue U North Central (IN)

MECHANIC AND REPAIR TECHNOLOGIES RELATED
Pennsylvania Coll of Technology (PA)
Washburn U (KS)

MECHANICS AND REPAIR
Lewis-Clark State Coll (ID)
Utah Valley U (UT)

MECHATRONICS, ROBOTICS, AND AUTOMATION ENGINEERING
Utah Valley U (UT)

MEDICAL ADMINISTRATIVE ASSISTANT AND MEDICAL SECRETARY
Baker Coll of Auburn Hills (MI)
Baker Coll of Cadillac (MI)
Baker Coll of Clinton Township (MI)
Baker Coll of Flint (MI)
Baker Coll of Jackson (MI)
Baker Coll of Muskegon (MI)
Baker Coll of Owosso (MI)
Baker Coll of Port Huron (MI)
Broadview U–Boise (ID)
Broadview U–Layton (UT)
Broadview U–Orem (UT)
Broadview U–West Jordan (UT)
Dickinson State U (ND)
Florida National U (FL)
Globe U–Appleton (WI)
Globe U–Eau Claire (WI)
Globe U–Green Bay (WI)
Globe U–La Crosse (WI)
Globe U–Madison East (WI)
Globe U–Madison West (WI)
Globe U–Sioux Falls (SD)
Globe U–Wausau (WI)
Globe U–Woodbury (MN)
Indian River State Coll (FL)
Lincoln Coll of New England, Southington (CT)
Minnesota School of Business–Blaine (MN)
Minnesota School of Business–Elk River (MN)
Minnesota School of Business–Moorhead (MN)
Minnesota School of Business–Richfield (MN)
Minnesota School of Business–Rochester (MN)
Minnesota School of Business–St. Cloud (MN)
Monroe Coll, Bronx (NY)
Montana State U Billings (MT)
Morrisville State Coll (NY)
Rasmussen Coll Appleton (WI)
Rasmussen Coll Aurora (IL)
Rasmussen Coll Bismarck (ND)
Rasmussen Coll Blaine (MN)
Rasmussen Coll Bloomington (MN)
Rasmussen Coll Brooklyn Park (MN)
Rasmussen Coll Eagan (MN)
Rasmussen Coll Fargo (ND)
Rasmussen Coll Fort Myers (FL)
Rasmussen Coll Green Bay (WI)
Rasmussen Coll Kansas City/Overland Park (KS)
Rasmussen Coll Lake Elmo/Woodbury (MN)
Rasmussen Coll Land O' Lakes (FL)
Rasmussen Coll Mankato (MN)
Rasmussen Coll Mokena/Tinley Park (IL)
Rasmussen Coll Moorhead (MN)
Rasmussen Coll New Port Richey (FL)
Rasmussen Coll Ocala (FL)
Rasmussen Coll Rockford (IL)
Rasmussen Coll Romeoville/Joliet (IL)
Rasmussen Coll St. Cloud (MN)
Rasmussen Coll Tampa/Brandon (FL)
Rasmussen Coll Wausau (WI)
U of Cincinnati (OH)
U of Rio Grande (OH)

MEDICAL/CLINICAL ASSISTANT
Argosy U, Twin Cities (MN)
Arkansas Tech U (AR)
Baker Coll of Allen Park (MI)
Baker Coll of Auburn Hills (MI)
Baker Coll of Cadillac (MI)
Baker Coll of Clinton Township (MI)
Baker Coll of Flint (MI)
Baker Coll of Jackson (MI)
Baker Coll of Muskegon (MI)
Baker Coll of Owosso (MI)
Baker Coll of Port Huron (MI)
Broadview U–Boise (ID)
Broadview U–Layton (UT)
Broadview U–Orem (UT)
Broadview U–West Jordan (UT)
Cabarrus Coll of Health Sciences (NC)
Central Penn Coll (PA)
Davenport U, Grand Rapids (MI)
Florida National U (FL)
Globe U–Appleton (WI)
Globe U–Eau Claire (WI)
Globe U–Green Bay (WI)
Globe U–La Crosse (WI)

Globe U–Madison East (WI)
Globe U–Madison West (WI)
Globe U–Sioux Falls (SD)
Globe U–Wausau (WI)
Globe U–Woodbury (MN)
Harrison Coll, Indianapolis (IN)
Harrison Coll (OH)
Hodges U (FL)
International Business Coll, Fort Wayne (IN)
ITT Tech Inst, Lexington (KY)
ITT Tech Inst, Oklahoma City (OK)
Keiser U, Fort Lauderdale (FL)
Lincoln Coll of New England, Southington (CT)
Mercy Coll of Health Sciences (IA)
Minnesota School of Business–Blaine (MN)
Minnesota School of Business–Elk River (MN)
Minnesota School of Business–Lakeville (MN)
Minnesota School of Business–Richfield (MN)
Minnesota School of Business–Rochester (MN)
Minnesota School of Business–St. Cloud (MN)
Monroe Coll, Bronx (NY)
Montana State U Billings (MT)
Montana Tech of The U of Montana (MT)
Mount Aloysius Coll (PA)
New England Inst of Technology (RI)
Penn Foster Coll (AZ)
Pioneer Pacific Coll, Wilsonville (OR)
Rasmussen Coll Appleton (WI)
Rasmussen Coll Aurora (IL)
Rasmussen Coll Bismarck (ND)
Rasmussen Coll Blaine (MN)
Rasmussen Coll Bloomington (MN)
Rasmussen Coll Brooklyn Park (MN)
Rasmussen Coll Eagan (MN)
Rasmussen Coll Fort Myers (FL)
Rasmussen Coll Green Bay (WI)
Rasmussen Coll Kansas City/Overland Park (KS)
Rasmussen Coll Lake Elmo/Woodbury (MN)
Rasmussen Coll Land O' Lakes (FL)
Rasmussen Coll Mankato (MN)
Rasmussen Coll Mokena/Tinley Park (IL)
Rasmussen Coll Moorhead (MN)
Rasmussen Coll New Port Richey (FL)
Rasmussen Coll Ocala (FL)
Rasmussen Coll Rockford (IL)
Rasmussen Coll Romeoville/Joliet (IL)
Rasmussen Coll St. Cloud (MN)
Rasmussen Coll Tampa/Brandon (FL)
Rasmussen Coll Topeka (KS)
Rasmussen Coll Wausau (WI)
Robert Morris U Illinois (IL)
South U (AL)
South U (GA)
South U, Columbia (SC)
Sullivan U (KY)
The U of Akron (OH)
U of Alaska Fairbanks (AK)
U of Cincinnati (OH)
Youngstown State U (OH)

MEDICAL/HEALTH MANAGEMENT AND CLINICAL ASSISTANT
Florida National U (FL)
Lewis-Clark State Coll (ID)

MEDICAL INFORMATICS
Champlain Coll (VT)
Montana Tech of The U of Montana (MT)
National U (CA)
Southern New Hampshire U (NH)

MEDICAL INSURANCE CODING
Baker Coll of Allen Park (MI)
National U (CA)

MEDICAL INSURANCE/MEDICAL BILLING
Baker Coll of Allen Park (MI)
Harrison Coll, Indianapolis (IN)
Harrison Coll (OH)

MEDICAL MICROBIOLOGY AND BACTERIOLOGY
Florida National U (FL)

MEDICAL OFFICE ASSISTANT
Hickey Coll (MO)
Lewis-Clark State Coll (ID)

MEDICAL OFFICE COMPUTER SPECIALIST
Baker Coll of Allen Park (MI)

MEDICAL OFFICE MANAGEMENT
Brown Mackie Coll–Birmingham (AL)
Brown Mackie Coll–Dallas/Ft. Worth (TX)
Brown Mackie Coll–San Antonio (TX)
Sullivan U (KY)
The U of Akron (OH)

MEDICAL RADIOLOGIC TECHNOLOGY
Argosy U, Twin Cities (MN)
Arkansas State U (AR)
Ball State U (IN)
Bluefield State Coll (WV)
Coll of Coastal Georgia (GA)
Ferris State U (MI)
Gannon U (PA)
Indiana U–Purdue U Fort Wayne (IN)
Inter American U of Puerto Rico, Aguadilla Campus (PR)
Inter American U of Puerto Rico, Ponce Campus (PR)
Inter American U of Puerto Rico, San Germán Campus (PR)
Keiser U, Fort Lauderdale (FL)
Keystone Coll (PA)
La Roche Coll (PA)
Mercy Coll of Health Sciences (IA)
Mercy Coll of Ohio (OH)
Missouri Southern State U (MO)
Molloy Coll (NY)
Morehead State U (KY)
Mount Aloysius Coll (PA)
Newman U (KS)
New York City Coll of Technology of the City U of New York (NY)
Northern Kentucky U (KY)
Pennsylvania Coll of Technology (PA)
Polk State Coll (FL)
St. Catherine U (MN)
Shawnee State U (OH)
State Coll of Florida Manatee-Sarasota (FL)
The U of Akron (OH)
U of Charleston (WV)
U of Cincinnati (OH)
U of New Mexico (NM)
Weber State U (UT)

MEDICAL TRANSCRIPTION
Baker Coll of Flint (MI)
Baker Coll of Jackson (MI)
U of Cincinnati (OH)

MENTAL AND SOCIAL HEALTH SERVICES AND ALLIED PROFESSIONS RELATED
Clarion U of Pennsylvania (PA)
Northern Kentucky U (KY)
U of Alaska Fairbanks (AK)
U of Maine at Augusta (ME)
Washburn U (KS)

MERCHANDISING
The U of Akron (OH)

MERCHANDISING, SALES, AND MARKETING OPERATIONS RELATED (GENERAL)
Inter American U of Puerto Rico, Aguadilla Campus (PR)
Inter American U of Puerto Rico, San Germán Campus (PR)
State U of New York Coll of Technology at Delhi (NY)

METAL AND JEWELRY ARTS
Academy of Art U (CA)
Fashion Inst of Technology (NY)

METALLURGICAL TECHNOLOGY
Penn State Altoona (PA)
Penn State Berks (PA)
Penn State Erie, The Behrend Coll (PA)
Penn State Shenango (PA)

MIDDLE SCHOOL EDUCATION
U of Cincinnati (OH)
Wright State U (OH)

MILITARY HISTORY
American Public U System (WV)

MILITARY STUDIES
Hawai`i Pacific U (HI)

MINING AND PETROLEUM TECHNOLOGIES RELATED
U of the Virgin Islands (VI)

MISSIONARY STUDIES AND MISSIOLOGY
Faith Baptist Bible Coll and Theological Seminary (IA)
God's Bible School and Coll (OH)
Piedmont International U (NC)

MULTI/INTERDISCIPLINARY STUDIES RELATED
Arkansas Tech U (AR)
Liberty U (VA)
Miami U (OH)
Montana Tech of The U of Montana (MT)
Pennsylvania Coll of Technology (PA)
Providence Coll (RI)
State U of New York Empire State Coll (NY)
The U of Akron (OH)
U of Alaska Fairbanks (AK)
U of Arkansas–Fort Smith (AR)
U of Cincinnati (OH)
The U of Montana Western (MT)
The U of Toledo (OH)
Utah Valley U (UT)
Washburn U (KS)

MUSEUM STUDIES
Inst of American Indian Arts (NM)

MUSIC
Abraham Baldwin Ag Coll (GA)
Alderson Broaddus U (WV)
Clayton State U (GA)
Five Towns Coll (NY)
Hannibal-LaGrange U (MO)
Indian River State Coll (FL)
Midland Coll (TX)
Mount Vernon Nazarene U (OH)
Nyack Coll (NY)
Pacific Union Coll (CA)
Palm Beach State Coll (FL)
Southwestern Assemblies of God U (TX)
State Coll of Florida Manatee-Sarasota (FL)
Thomas More Coll (KY)
U of Maine at Augusta (ME)
U of Rio Grande (OH)
Utah Valley U (UT)
Villa Maria Coll (NY)
York Coll of Pennsylvania (PA)

MUSICAL INSTRUMENT FABRICATION AND REPAIR
Indiana U Bloomington (IN)

MUSIC MANAGEMENT
Broadview Entertainment Arts U (UT)
Ferris State U (MI)
Five Towns Coll (NY)
McNally Smith Coll of Music (MN)
U of Central Oklahoma (OK)
Villa Maria Coll (NY)

MUSIC PERFORMANCE
Five Towns Coll (NY)
Inter American U of Puerto Rico, Metropolitan Campus (PR)
State Coll of Florida Manatee-Sarasota (FL)
Villa Maria Coll (NY)

MUSIC RELATED
Academy of Art U (CA)
Alverno Coll (WI)
Five Towns Coll (NY)
Mercy Coll (NY)

MUSIC TEACHER EDUCATION
State Coll of Florida Manatee-Sarasota (FL)
U of the District of Columbia (DC)
Wright State U (OH)

MUSIC TECHNOLOGY
McNally Smith Coll of Music (MN)

MUSIC THEORY AND COMPOSITION
State Coll of Florida Manatee-Sarasota (FL)

NATURAL RESOURCES/ CONSERVATION
Morrisville State Coll (NY)

State U of New York Coll of Environmental Science and Forestry (NY)

NATURAL RESOURCES MANAGEMENT AND POLICY
Lake Superior State U (MI)
Morrisville State Coll (NY)
U of Alaska Fairbanks (AK)

NATURAL RESOURCES MANAGEMENT AND POLICY RELATED
State U of New York Coll of Technology at Delhi (NY)
Universidad Metropolitana (PR)
U of Guelph (ON, Canada)

NATURAL SCIENCES
Fresno Pacific U (CA)
Lourdes U (OH)
Madonna U (MI)
Roberts Wesleyan Coll (NY)
Universidad Metropolitana (PR)
U of Alaska Fairbanks (AK)
The U of Toledo (OH)
Washburn U (KS)

NETWORK AND SYSTEM ADMINISTRATION
Florida National U (FL)
Harrison Coll, Indianapolis (IN)
ITT Tech Inst, Phoenix (AZ)
ITT Tech Inst, Phoenix (AZ)
ITT Tech Inst, Tempe (AZ)
ITT Tech Inst, Clovis (CA)
ITT Tech Inst, Concord (CA)
ITT Tech Inst, Corona (CA)
ITT Tech Inst, West Palm Beach (FL)
ITT Tech Inst, Douglasville (GA)
ITT Tech Inst, Indianapolis (IN)
ITT Tech Inst, Indianapolis (IN)
ITT Tech Inst, South Bend (IN)
ITT Tech Inst, Overland Park (KS)
ITT Tech Inst, Wichita (KS)
ITT Tech Inst, Lexington (KY)
ITT Tech Inst, Hanover (MD)
ITT Tech Inst, Southfield (MI)
ITT Tech Inst (MS)
ITT Tech Inst, Springfield (MO)
ITT Tech Inst, Charlotte (NC)
ITT Tech Inst, Durham (NC)
ITT Tech Inst, Oklahoma City (OK)
ITT Tech Inst, Salem (OR)
Palm Beach State Coll (FL)

NUCLEAR ENGINEERING TECHNOLOGY
Arkansas Tech U (AR)

NUCLEAR MEDICAL TECHNOLOGY
Adventist U of Health Sciences (FL)
Ball State U (IN)
The George Washington U (DC)
Keiser U, Fort Lauderdale (FL)
U of Cincinnati (OH)

NUCLEAR/NUCLEAR POWER TECHNOLOGY
Excelsior Coll (NY)

NURSING ASSISTANT/AIDE AND PATIENT CARE ASSISTANT/AIDE
Cabarrus Coll of Health Sciences (NC)

NURSING EDUCATION
U of the District of Columbia (DC)

NURSING SCIENCE
Dixie State U (UT)
EDP U of Puerto Rico (PR)
EDP U of Puerto Rico–San Sebastian (PR)
Emmaus Bible Coll (IA)

NUTRITION SCIENCES
U of Cincinnati (OH)

OCCUPATIONAL SAFETY AND HEALTH TECHNOLOGY
Columbia Southern U (AL)
Fairmont State U (WV)
Indiana U Bloomington (IN)

OCCUPATIONAL THERAPIST ASSISTANT
Adventist U of Health Sciences (FL)
Arkansas Tech U (AR)

Baker Coll of Muskegon (MI)
Brown Mackie Coll–Birmingham (AL)
Brown Mackie Coll–Dallas/Ft. Worth (TX)
Cabarrus Coll of Health Sciences (NC)
California U of Pennsylvania (PA)
Central Penn Coll (PA)
Inter American U of Puerto Rico, Ponce Campus (PR)
Jefferson Coll of Health Sciences (VA)
Keiser U, Fort Lauderdale (FL)
Lincoln Coll of New England, Southington (CT)
Maria Coll (NY)
Mercy Coll (NY)
New England Inst of Technology (RI)
Newman U (KS)
Penn State Berks (PA)
Pennsylvania Coll of Technology (PA)
Polk State Coll (FL)
Rutgers, The State U of New Jersey, New Brunswick (NJ)
St. Catherine U (MN)
South U, Royal Palm Beach (FL)
South U, Tampa (FL)
State Coll of Florida Manatee-Sarasota (FL)
U of Charleston (WV)
U of Louisiana at Monroe (LA)
U of Southern Indiana (IN)
Washburn U (KS)

OCCUPATIONAL THERAPY
Coll of Coastal Georgia (GA)
Keystone Coll (PA)
Palm Beach State Coll (FL)
Shawnee State U (OH)
State Coll of Florida Manatee-Sarasota (FL)

OFFICE MANAGEMENT
Baker Coll of Jackson (MI)
Emmanuel Coll (GA)
Inter American U of Puerto Rico, Aguadilla Campus (PR)
Inter American U of Puerto Rico, Bayamón Campus (PR)
Inter American U of Puerto Rico, Fajardo Campus (PR)
Inter American U of Puerto Rico, Guayama Campus (PR)
Inter American U of Puerto Rico, Ponce Campus (PR)
Inter American U of Puerto Rico, San Germán Campus (PR)
Maranatha Baptist Bible Coll (WI)
Mercyhurst U (PA)
Miami U (OH)
Morrisville State Coll (NY)
Shawnee State U (OH)
Sullivan U (KY)
Universidad del Turabo (PR)
Universidad Metropolitana (PR)
The U of Akron (OH)
Washburn U (KS)

OFFICE OCCUPATIONS AND CLERICAL SERVICES
Bob Jones U (SC)
Midland Coll (TX)
Morrisville State Coll (NY)

OPERATIONS MANAGEMENT
Indiana U–Purdue U Fort Wayne (IN)
Indiana U–Purdue U Indianapolis (IN)
Northern Kentucky U (KY)
Polk State Coll (FL)

OPHTHALMIC LABORATORY TECHNOLOGY
Rochester Inst of Technology (NY)

OPTICAL SCIENCES
Indiana U of Pennsylvania (PA)

OPTICIANRY
New York City Coll of Technology of the City U of New York (NY)

OPTOMETRIC TECHNICIAN
Indiana U Bloomington (IN)
Inter American U of Puerto Rico, Ponce Campus (PR)

ORGANIZATIONAL BEHAVIOR
Hawai'i Pacific U (HI)
U of Cincinnati (OH)

ORGANIZATIONAL COMMUNICATION
Creighton U (NE)

ORGANIZATIONAL LEADERSHIP
AIB Coll of Business (IA)
Beulah Heights U (GA)
Harrison Coll, Indianapolis (IN)
Huntington U (IN)

ORNAMENTAL HORTICULTURE
Abraham Baldwin Ag Coll (GA)
Farmingdale State Coll (NY)
State U of New York Coll of Agriculture and Technology at Cobleskill (NY)
Vermont Tech Coll (VT)

ORTHOTICS/PROSTHETICS
Baker Coll of Flint (MI)

PAINTING
Academy of Art U (CA)
Pratt Inst (NY)

PALLIATIVE CARE NURSING
Madonna U (MI)

PARKS, RECREATION AND LEISURE
Eastern New Mexico U (NM)

PARKS, RECREATION AND LEISURE FACILITIES MANAGEMENT
Coll of Coastal Georgia (GA)
Indiana Tech (IN)
Webber International U (FL)

PARKS, RECREATION, LEISURE, AND FITNESS STUDIES RELATED
Southern Nazarene U (OK)

PASTORAL STUDIES/ COUNSELING
Indiana Wesleyan U (IN)
Marian U (IN)
Nebraska Christian Coll (NE)
William Jessup U (CA)

PERCUSSION INSTRUMENTS
McNally Smith Coll of Music (MN)

PERSONAL AND CULINARY SERVICES RELATED
U of Cincinnati (OH)

PETROLEUM TECHNOLOGY
Mansfield U of Pennsylvania (PA)
Montana State U Billings (MT)
Nicholls State U (LA)
U of Pittsburgh at Bradford (PA)

PHARMACOLOGY
Universidad del Turabo (PR)

PHARMACY
Indian River State Coll (FL)

PHARMACY, PHARMACEUTICAL SCIENCES, AND ADMINISTRATION RELATED
EDP U of Puerto Rico–San Sebastian (PR)

PHARMACY TECHNICIAN
Abraham Baldwin Ag Coll (GA)
Baker Coll of Flint (MI)
Baker Coll of Jackson (MI)
Baker Coll of Muskegon (MI)
Brown Mackie Coll–San Antonio (TX)
Cabarrus Coll of Health Sciences (NC)
Inter American U of Puerto Rico, Aguadilla Campus (PR)
Rasmussen Coll Appleton (WI)
Rasmussen Coll Aurora (IL)
Rasmussen Coll Blaine (MN)
Rasmussen Coll Bloomington (MN)
Rasmussen Coll Brooklyn Park (MN)
Rasmussen Coll Eagan (MN)
Rasmussen Coll Fort Myers (FL)
Rasmussen Coll Green Bay (WI)
Rasmussen Coll Kansas City/ Overland Park (KS)
Rasmussen Coll Lake Elmo/ Woodbury (MN)

Rasmussen Coll Land O' Lakes (FL)
Rasmussen Coll Mankato (MN)
Rasmussen Coll Mokena/Tinley Park (IL)
Rasmussen Coll Moorhead (MN)
Rasmussen Coll New Port Richey (FL)
Rasmussen Coll Ocala (FL)
Rasmussen Coll Rockford (IL)
Rasmussen Coll Romeoville/Joliet (IL)
Rasmussen Coll St. Cloud (MN)
Rasmussen Coll Tampa/Brandon (FL)
Rasmussen Coll Topeka (KS)
Rasmussen Coll Wausau (WI)
Robert Morris U Illinois (IL)
Sullivan U (KY)

PHILOSOPHY
Carroll Coll (MT)
Coll of Coastal Georgia (GA)
Indian River State Coll (FL)
Palm Beach State Coll (FL)
State Coll of Florida Manatee-Sarasota (FL)
Thomas More Coll (KY)
The U of Tampa (FL)
Utah Valley U (UT)

PHOTOGRAPHIC AND FILM/ VIDEO TECHNOLOGY
St. John's U (NY)
U of Cincinnati (OH)
Villa Maria Coll (NY)

PHOTOGRAPHY
Academy of Art U (CA)
The Art Inst of California–Orange County, a campus of Argosy U (CA)
The Art Inst of California–Sacramento, a campus of Argosy U (CA)
The Art Inst of California–San Diego, a campus of Argosy U (CA)
The Art Inst of Charlotte, a campus of South U (NC)
The Art Inst of Dallas, a campus of South U (TX)
The Art Inst of Fort Lauderdale (FL)
The Art Inst of Fort Worth, a campus of South U (TX)
The Art Inst of Washington, a branch of The Art Institute of Atlanta (VA)
Pacific Union Coll (CA)
Paier Coll of Art, Inc. (CT)
Palm Beach State Coll (FL)
Villa Maria Coll (NY)

PHYSICAL EDUCATION TEACHING AND COACHING
Abraham Baldwin Ag Coll (GA)
Fresno Pacific U (CA)
Indian River State Coll (FL)
Palm Beach State Coll (FL)
State Coll of Florida Manatee-Sarasota (FL)
U of Rio Grande (OH)

PHYSICAL FITNESS TECHNICIAN
Broadview U–West Jordan (UT)
Globe U–Madison West (WI)
Globe U–Woodbury (MN)
Minnesota School of Business–Richfield (MN)
Minnesota School of Business–St. Cloud (MN)

PHYSICAL SCIENCES
Abraham Baldwin Ag Coll (GA)
New York City Coll of Technology of the City U of New York (NY)
Oklahoma Wesleyan U (OK)
Palm Beach State Coll (FL)
Roberts Wesleyan Coll (NY)
Utah Valley U (UT)

PHYSICAL SCIENCES RELATED
State U of New York Empire State Coll (NY)

PHYSICAL THERAPY
Coll of Coastal Georgia (GA)
EDP U of Puerto Rico–San Sebastian (PR)
Indian River State Coll (FL)
Palm Beach State Coll (FL)
State Coll of Florida Manatee-Sarasota (FL)

PHYSICAL THERAPY TECHNOLOGY
Arkansas State U (AR)
Arkansas Tech U (AR)
Baker Coll of Flint (MI)
Baker Coll of Muskegon (MI)
California U of Pennsylvania (PA)
Central Penn Coll (PA)
Dixie State U (UT)
EDP U of Puerto Rico (PR)
EDP U of Puerto Rico–San Sebastian (PR)
Indian River State Coll (FL)
Inter American U of Puerto Rico, Ponce Campus (PR)
Jefferson Coll of Health Sciences (VA)
Keiser U, Fort Lauderdale (FL)
Louisiana Coll (LA)
Maria Coll (NY)
Mercy Coll of Health Sciences (IA)
Mercyhurst U (PA)
Missouri Western State U (MO)
Mount Aloysius Coll (PA)
Nebraska Methodist Coll (NE)
New England Inst of Technology (RI)
Our Lady of the Lake Coll (LA)
Penn State Shenango (PA)
Polk State Coll (FL)
St. Catherine U (MN)
Shawnee State U (OH)
Southern Illinois U Carbondale (IL)
South U (AL)
South U, Royal Palm Beach (FL)
South U, Tampa (FL)
South U (GA)
South U (MI)
South U (NC)
South U (OH)
South U (TX)
South U, Glen Allen (VA)
South U, Virginia Beach (VA)
State Coll of Florida Manatee-Sarasota (FL)
State U of New York Coll of Technology at Canton (NY)
U of Cincinnati (OH)
U of Evansville (IN)
U of Indianapolis (IN)
U of Maine at Presque Isle (ME)
Villa Maria Coll (NY)
Washburn U (KS)

PHYSICIAN ASSISTANT
Coll of Coastal Georgia (GA)
State Coll of Florida Manatee-Sarasota (FL)

PHYSICS
Coll of Coastal Georgia (GA)
Indian River State Coll (FL)
Midland Coll (TX)
Rogers State U (OK)
State Coll of Florida Manatee-Sarasota (FL)
Thomas More Coll (KY)
U of the Virgin Islands (VI)
Utah Valley U (UT)
York Coll of Pennsylvania (PA)

PHYSICS TEACHER EDUCATION
State Coll of Florida Manatee-Sarasota (FL)

PIPEFITTING AND SPRINKLER FITTING
New England Inst of Technology (RI)
State U of New York Coll of Technology at Delhi (NY)

PLANT PROTECTION AND INTEGRATED PEST MANAGEMENT
North Carolina State U (NC)

PLANT SCIENCES
Michigan State U (MI)
State U of New York Coll of Agriculture and Technology at Cobleskill (NY)

PLASTICS AND POLYMER ENGINEERING TECHNOLOGY
Ferris State U (MI)
Penn State Erie, The Behrend Coll (PA)
Pennsylvania Coll of Technology (PA)
Shawnee State U (OH)

PLAYWRITING AND SCREENWRITING
Pacific Union Coll (CA)

POLITICAL SCIENCE AND GOVERNMENT
Abraham Baldwin Ag Coll (GA)
Adams State U (CO)
Coll of Coastal Georgia (GA)
Holy Cross Coll (IN)
Immaculata U (PA)
Indian River State Coll (FL)
Liberty U (VA)
Midland Coll (TX)
Palm Beach State Coll (FL)
Thomas More Coll (KY)
The U of Tampa (FL)
The U of Toledo (OH)
Xavier U (OH)

POLYSOMNOGRAPHY
Mercy Coll of Health Sciences (IA)

POULTRY SCIENCE
Abraham Baldwin Ag Coll (GA)
State U of New York Coll of Agriculture and Technology at Cobleskill (NY)

PRACTICAL NURSING, VOCATIONAL NURSING AND NURSING ASSISTANTS RELATED
Rasmussen Coll Ocala School of Nursing (FL)

PRECISION METAL WORKING RELATED
Montana Tech of The U of Montana (MT)

PRE-DENTISTRY STUDIES
Coll of Coastal Georgia (GA)
Concordia U Wisconsin (WI)
U of Cincinnati (OH)

PRE-ENGINEERING
Abraham Baldwin Ag Coll (GA)
Coll of Coastal Georgia (GA)
Columbia Coll (MO)
Dixie State U (UT)
Fort Valley State U (GA)
Indian River State Coll (FL)
Newman U (KS)
Northern State U (SD)
Palm Beach State Coll (FL)
Siena Heights U (MI)
Southern Utah U (UT)
Utah Valley U (UT)
Weber State U (UT)

PRE-LAW STUDIES
Calumet Coll of Saint Joseph (IN)
Ferris State U (MI)
Immaculata U (PA)
Thomas More Coll (KY)
U of Cincinnati (OH)
Wayland Baptist U (TX)

PREMEDICAL STUDIES
Coll of Coastal Georgia (GA)
Concordia U Wisconsin (WI)
U of Cincinnati (OH)

PRENURSING STUDIES
Concordia U Wisconsin (WI)
Eastern New Mexico U (NM)
Keystone Coll (PA)
Lincoln Christian U (IL)
National U (CA)

PRE-PHARMACY STUDIES
Coll of Coastal Georgia (GA)
Edinboro U of Pennsylvania (PA)
Ferris State U (MI)
Keystone Coll (PA)
Madonna U (MI)
State Coll of Florida Manatee-Sarasota (FL)
U of Cincinnati (OH)

PRE-PHYSICAL THERAPY
Keystone Coll (PA)

PRE-THEOLOGY/PRE-MINISTERIAL STUDIES
Eastern Mennonite U (VA)
Nazarene Bible Coll (CO)

PRE-VETERINARY STUDIES
Coll of Coastal Georgia (GA)
U of Cincinnati (OH)

PRINTMAKING
Academy of Art U (CA)

PROFESSIONAL, TECHNICAL, BUSINESS, AND SCIENTIFIC WRITING
Ferris State U (MI)
Florida National U (FL)

PSYCHIATRIC/MENTAL HEALTH SERVICES TECHNOLOGY
Lake Superior State U (MI)
Pennsylvania Coll of Technology (PA)

PSYCHOLOGY
Abraham Baldwin Ag Coll (GA)
Argosy U, Atlanta (GA)
Argosy U, Dallas (TX)
Argosy U, Denver (CO)
Argosy U, Hawai`i (HI)
Argosy U, Inland Empire (CA)
Argosy U, Nashville (TN)
Argosy U, Orange County (CA)
Argosy U, Phoenix (AZ)
Argosy U, Salt Lake City (UT)
Argosy U, San Diego (CA)
Argosy U, San Francisco Bay Area (CA)
Argosy U, Sarasota (FL)
Argosy U, Seattle (WA)
Argosy U, Tampa (FL)
Argosy U, Twin Cities (MN)
Argosy U, Washington DC (VA)
Beacon Coll (FL)
Calumet Coll of Saint Joseph (IN)
Central Methodist U (MO)
Coll of Coastal Georgia (GA)
Eastern New Mexico U (NM)
Ferris State U (MI)
Fisher Coll (MA)
Fresno Pacific U (CA)
Indian River State Coll (FL)
Liberty U (VA)
Marian U (IN)
Midland Coll (TX)
Montana State U Billings (MT)
Muhlenberg Coll (PA)
Palm Beach State Coll (FL)
Regent U (VA)
Siena Heights U (MI)
Southwestern Assemblies of God U (TX)
State Coll of Florida Manatee-Sarasota (FL)
State U of New York Empire State Coll (NY)
Thomas More Coll (KY)
U of Cincinnati (OH)
U of Rio Grande (OH)
The U of Tampa (FL)
Utah Valley U (UT)
Valley Forge Christian Coll (PA)
Wright State U (OH)
Xavier U (OH)

PSYCHOLOGY RELATED
Morrisville State Coll (NY)

PUBLIC ADMINISTRATION
Central Methodist U (MO)
Ferris State U (MI)
Florida National U (FL)
Indiana U Bloomington (IN)
Indiana U Northwest (IN)
Indiana–Purdue U Indianapolis (IN)
Point Park U (PA)
State Coll of Florida Manatee-Sarasota (FL)
Universidad del Turabo (PR)
U of Maine at Augusta (ME)

PUBLIC ADMINISTRATION AND SOCIAL SERVICE PROFESSIONS RELATED
Point Park U (PA)
The U of Akron (OH)

PUBLIC HEALTH
American Public U System (WV)
U of Alaska Fairbanks (AK)

PUBLIC HEALTH EDUCATION AND PROMOTION
U of Cincinnati (OH)

PUBLIC POLICY ANALYSIS
Saint Peter's U (NJ)

PUBLIC RELATIONS, ADVERTISING, AND APPLIED COMMUNICATION RELATED
John Brown U (AR)
U of Maine at Presque Isle (ME)

PUBLIC RELATIONS/IMAGE MANAGEMENT
John Brown U (AR)
Xavier U (OH)

PURCHASING, PROCUREMENT/ACQUISITIONS AND CONTRACTS MANAGEMENT
Mercyhurst U (PA)

QUALITY CONTROL AND SAFETY TECHNOLOGIES RELATED
Madonna U (MI)
Rochester Inst of Technology (NY)

QUALITY CONTROL TECHNOLOGY
Baker Coll of Cadillac (MI)
Baker Coll of Flint (MI)
Baker Coll of Muskegon (MI)
Universidad del Turabo (PR)
Weber State U (UT)

RADIATION PROTECTION/HEALTH PHYSICS TECHNOLOGY
Keiser U, Fort Lauderdale (FL)

RADIO AND TELEVISION
Lawrence Technological U (MI)
Ohio U–Zanesville (OH)
State Coll of Florida Manatee-Sarasota (FL)
Xavier U (OH)

RADIO AND TELEVISION BROADCASTING TECHNOLOGY
Lincoln Coll of New England, Southington (CT)
New England Inst of Technology (RI)
State Coll of Florida Manatee-Sarasota (FL)

RADIOLOGIC TECHNOLOGY/SCIENCE
Adventist U of Health Sciences (FL)
Allen Coll (IA)
Alvernia U (PA)
Argosy U, Twin Cities (MN)
Baker Coll of Clinton Township (MI)
Baker Coll of Muskegon (MI)
Champlain Coll (VT)
Colorado Mesa U (CO)
Dixie State U (UT)
Fairleigh Dickinson U, Metropolitan Campus (NJ)
Florida National U (FL)
Fort Hays State U (KS)
Holy Family U (PA)
Indiana U Kokomo (IN)
Indiana U Northwest (IN)
Indiana U–Purdue U Indianapolis (IN)
Indiana U South Bend (IN)
Keystone Coll (PA)
Lewis-Clark State Coll (ID)
Mansfield U of Pennsylvania (PA)
Midland Coll (TX)
Montana Tech of The U of Montana (MT)
Nebraska Methodist Coll (NE)
Newman U (KS)
Northern Michigan U (MI)
Regis Coll (MA)
State Coll of Florida Manatee-Sarasota (FL)
U of Arkansas–Fort Smith (AR)
U of Rio Grande (OH)
Washburn U (KS)
Widener U (PA)
Xavier U (OH)

RADIO, TELEVISION, AND DIGITAL COMMUNICATION RELATED
Keystone Coll (PA)
Lawrence Technological U (MI)
Madonna U (MI)

REAL ESTATE
American Public U System (WV)
Caribbean U (PR)
National U (CA)
Northern Kentucky U (KY)
Saint Francis U (PA)

RECEPTIONIST
Baker Coll of Allen Park (MI)

RECORDING ARTS TECHNOLOGY
The Art Inst of California–Hollywood, a campus of Argosy U (CA)
The Art Inst of California–Inland Empire, a campus of Argosy U (CA)
The Art Inst of California–Los Angeles, a campus of Argosy U (CA)
The Art Inst of California–San Diego, a campus of Argosy U (CA)
The Art Inst of California–Silicon Valley, a campus of Argosy U (CA)
The Art Inst of Seattle (WA)
Broadview Entertainment Arts U (UT)
Columbia Centro Universitario, Caguas (PR)
Indiana U Bloomington (IN)
The New England Inst of Art (MA)

REGIONAL STUDIES
Arkansas Tech U (AR)

REGISTERED NURSING, NURSING ADMINISTRATION, NURSING RESEARCH AND CLINICAL NURSING RELATED
Rasmussen Coll Ocala School of Nursing (FL)

REGISTERED NURSING/REGISTERED NURSE
Abraham Baldwin Ag Coll (GA)
Alcorn State U (MS)
Aquinas Coll (TN)
Arkansas State U (AR)
Arkansas Tech U (AR)
Baker Coll of Allen Park (MI)
Baker Coll of Auburn Hills (MI)
Baker Coll of Cadillac (MI)
Baker Coll of Clinton Township (MI)
Baker Coll of Flint (MI)
Baker Coll of Muskegon (MI)
Baker Coll of Owosso (MI)
Becker Coll (MA)
Bethel Coll (IN)
Bluefield State Coll (WV)
Cabarrus Coll of Health Sciences (NC)
California U of Pennsylvania (PA)
Campbellsville U (KY)
Castleton State Coll (VT)
Clarion U of Pennsylvania (PA)
Coll of Coastal Georgia (GA)
Coll of Saint Mary (NE)
Coll of Staten Island of the City U of New York (NY)
Colorado Mesa U (CO)
Columbia Centro Universitario, Caguas (PR)
Columbia Centro Universitario, Yauco (PR)
Columbia Coll (MO)
Dixie State U (UT)
Excelsior Coll (NY)
Fairmont State U (WV)
Florida National U (FL)
Gardner-Webb U (NC)
Gwynedd Mercy U (PA)
Hannibal-LaGrange U (MO)
Harrison Coll, Indianapolis (IN)
Indian River State Coll (FL)
Inter American U of Puerto Rico, Guayama Campus (PR)
Inter American U of Puerto Rico, Ponce Campus (PR)
ITT Tech Inst, Phoenix (AZ)
ITT Tech Inst, West Palm Beach (FL)
ITT Tech Inst, Indianapolis (IN)
ITT Tech Inst, South Bend (IN)
ITT Tech Inst, Overland Park (KS)
ITT Tech Inst, Wichita (KS)
ITT Tech Inst, Lexington (KY)
ITT Tech Inst, Oklahoma City (OK)
Judson Coll (AL)
Keiser U, Fort Lauderdale (FL)
Kent State U (OH)
Kent State U at Geauga (OH)
Kentucky State U (KY)
Lamar U (TX)
La Roche Coll (PA)
Lincoln Memorial U (TN)
Lincoln U (MO)
Lock Haven U of Pennsylvania (PA)
Louisiana Tech U (LA)
Maria Coll (NY)
Marshall U (WV)
Mercy Coll of Health Sciences (IA)
Mercy Coll of Ohio (OH)
Mercyhurst U (PA)
Miami U (OH)
Midland Coll (TX)
Mississippi U for Women (MS)
Montana State U Billings (MT)
Montana Tech of The U of Montana (MT)
Morehead State U (KY)
Morrisville State Coll (NY)
Mount Aloysius Coll (PA)
Mount St. Mary's Coll (CA)
National U (CA)
New England Inst of Technology (RI)
New York City Coll of Technology of the City U of New York (NY)
Norfolk State U (VA)
Northern Kentucky U (KY)
Northwestern State U of Louisiana (LA)
Our Lady of the Lake Coll (LA)
Pacific Union Coll (CA)
Palm Beach State Coll (FL)
Park U (MO)
Penn State Altoona (PA)
Penn State Berks (PA)
Penn State Erie, The Behrend Coll (PA)
Penn State U Park (PA)
Pennsylvania Coll of Technology (PA)
Polk State Coll (FL)
Regis Coll (MA)
Rivier U (NH)
Robert Morris U Illinois (IL)
Rogers State U (OK)
Shawnee State U (OH)
Southern Arkansas U–Magnolia (AR)
Southwest Baptist U (MO)
State Coll of Florida Manatee-Sarasota (FL)
State U of New York Coll of Technology at Canton (NY)
State U of New York Coll of Technology at Delhi (NY)
Sul Ross State U (TX)
Tennessee State U (TN)
Troy U (AL)
Universidad Metropolitana (PR)
U of Arkansas at Little Rock (AR)
U of Charleston (WV)
U of Cincinnati (OH)
U of Guam (GU)
U of Maine at Augusta (ME)
U of North Georgia (GA)
U of Pikeville (KY)
U of Pittsburgh at Bradford (PA)
U of Rio Grande (OH)
The U of South Dakota (SD)
U of the Virgin Islands (VI)
The U of West Alabama (AL)
Utah Valley U (UT)
Vermont Tech Coll (VT)
Weber State U (UT)
Western Kentucky U (KY)

REHABILITATION AND THERAPEUTIC PROFESSIONS RELATED
National U (CA)
Rutgers, The State U of New Jersey, Newark (NJ)
Rutgers, The State U of New Jersey, New Brunswick (NJ)
U of Cincinnati (OH)

RELIGIOUS EDUCATION
Cincinnati Christian U (OH)
Dallas Baptist U (TX)
Heritage Bible Coll (NC)
Nazarene Bible Coll (CO)
Nebraska Christian Coll (NE)
Oakland City U (IN)
Piedmont International U (NC)
Southern Methodist Coll (SC)

RELIGIOUS/SACRED MUSIC
Cincinnati Christian U (OH)
Dallas Baptist U (TX)
God's Bible School and Coll (OH)
Immaculata U (PA)
Indiana Wesleyan U (IN)
Mount Vernon Nazarene U (OH)
Nazarene Bible Coll (CO)
Nebraska Christian Coll (NE)

RELIGIOUS STUDIES
Calumet Coll of Saint Joseph (IN)
Concordia Coll–New York (NY)
Corban U (OR)
Griggs U (MI)
Holy Apostles Coll and Seminary (CT)

Huntington U (IN)
Liberty U (VA)
Lourdes U (OH)
Madonna U (MI)
Mount Marty Coll (SD)
Mount Vernon Nazarene U (OH)
Northwest U (WA)
Palm Beach State Coll (FL)
State Coll of Florida Manatee-
    Sarasota (FL)
Thomas More Coll (KY)
Xavier U (OH)

RESORT MANAGEMENT
State U of New York Coll of
    Technology at Delhi (NY)

RESPIRATORY CARE THERAPY
Coll of Coastal Georgia (GA)
Dakota State U (SD)
Dixie State U (UT)
Ferris State U (MI)
Gannon U (PA)
Gwynedd Mercy U (PA)
Indian River State Coll (FL)
Jefferson Coll of Health Sciences
    (VA)
Keiser U, Fort Lauderdale (FL)
Mansfield U of Pennsylvania (PA)
Midland Coll (TX)
Molloy Coll (NY)
Morehead State U (KY)
Nebraska Methodist Coll (NE)
Newman U (KS)
Northern Kentucky U (KY)
Polk State Coll (FL)
Rutgers, The State U of New Jersey,
    New Brunswick (NJ)
Shawnee State U (OH)
State Coll of Florida Manatee-
    Sarasota (FL)
Universidad Metropolitana (PR)
U of Cincinnati (OH)
U of Southern Indiana (IN)
U of the District of Columbia (DC)
Vermont Tech U (VT)
Washburn U (KS)
Weber State U (UT)
York Coll of Pennsylvania (PA)

**RESPIRATORY THERAPY
TECHNICIAN**
Clarion U of Pennsylvania (PA)
Florida National U (FL)
Keiser U, Fort Lauderdale (FL)
Northern Michigan U (MI)

**RESTAURANT, CULINARY, AND
CATERING MANAGEMENT**
Arkansas Tech U (AR)
The Art Inst of Atlanta (GA)
The Art Inst of Austin, a branch of
    The Art Institute of Houston (TX)
The Art Inst of Charleston, a branch
    of The Art Institute of Atlanta (SC)
The Art Inst of Charlotte, a campus
    of South U (NC)
The Art Inst of Dallas, a campus of
    South U (TX)
The Art Inst of Houston (TX)
The Art Inst of Ohio–Cincinnati (OH)
The Art Inst of San Antonio, a branch
    of The Art Institute of Houston
    (TX)
Ferris State U (MI)
The Illinois Inst of Art–Chicago (IL)
The Illinois Inst of Art–Schaumburg
    (IL)
Morrisville State Coll (NY)
State U of New York Coll of
    Agriculture and Technology at
    Cobleskill (NY)
State U of New York Coll of
    Technology at Delhi (NY)
Sullivan U (KY)

**RESTAURANT/FOOD SERVICES
MANAGEMENT**
American Public U System (WV)
Morrisville State Coll (NY)
Pennsylvania Coll of Technology
    (PA)
The U of Akron (OH)

RETAILING
American Public U System (WV)
International Business Coll, Fort
    Wayne (IN)

Stevens–The Inst of Business & Arts
    (MO)
Weber State U (UT)

RETAIL MANAGEMENT
Penn Foster Coll (AZ)

RHETORIC AND COMPOSITION
Abraham Baldwin Ag Coll (GA)
Ferris State U (MI)
Indian River State Coll (FL)
Midland Coll (TX)
State Coll of Florida Manatee-
    Sarasota (FL)

ROBOTICS TECHNOLOGY
California U of Pennsylvania (PA)
Indiana U–Purdue U Indianapolis
    (IN)
Pennsylvania Coll of Technology
    (PA)
Purdue U (IN)
U of Rio Grande (OH)
Utah Valley U (UT)

ROOFING
Penn Foster Coll (AZ)

**RUSSIAN, CENTRAL
EUROPEAN, EAST EUROPEAN
AND EURASIAN STUDIES**
State Coll of Florida Manatee-
    Sarasota (FL)

RUSSIAN STUDIES
State Coll of Florida Manatee-
    Sarasota (FL)

**SALES AND MARKETING/
MARKETING AND
DISTRIBUTION TEACHER
EDUCATION**
Wright State U (OH)

**SALES, DISTRIBUTION, AND
MARKETING OPERATIONS**
AIB Coll of Business (IA)
Baker Coll of Flint (MI)
Baker Coll of Jackson (MI)
Inter American U of Puerto Rico,
    Aguadilla Campus (PR)
St. Cloud State U (MN)
The U of Findlay (OH)

**SCIENCE TEACHER
EDUCATION**
State Coll of Florida Manatee-
    Sarasota (FL)
Wright State U (OH)

SCIENCE TECHNOLOGIES
Washburn U (KS)

**SCIENCE TECHNOLOGIES
RELATED**
Madonna U (MI)
Maria Coll (NY)
Ohio Valley U (WV)
State U of New York Coll of
    Agriculture and Technology at
    Cobleskill (NY)
U of Alaska Fairbanks (AK)
U of Cincinnati (OH)

SCULPTURE
Academy of Art U (CA)

SECONDARY EDUCATION
Ferris State U (MI)
Rogers State U (OK)
U of Cincinnati (OH)

**SECURITY AND LOSS
PREVENTION**
John Jay Coll of Criminal Justice of
    the City U of New York (NY)

SELLING SKILLS AND SALES
AIB Coll of Business (IA)
Inter American U of Puerto Rico, San
    Germán Campus (PR)
The U of Akron (OH)
The U of Toledo (OH)

SHEET METAL TECHNOLOGY
Montana State U Billings (MT)

**SIGN LANGUAGE
INTERPRETATION AND
TRANSLATION**
Cincinnati Christian U (OH)
Mount Aloysius Coll (PA)

Nebraska Christian Coll (NE)
St. Catherine U (MN)
U of Arkansas at Little Rock (AR)

**SMALL BUSINESS
ADMINISTRATION**
Lewis-Clark State Coll (ID)
The U of Akron (OH)

SOCIAL PSYCHOLOGY
State Coll of Florida Manatee-
    Sarasota (FL)

SOCIAL SCIENCES
Abraham Baldwin Ag Coll (GA)
Campbellsville U (KY)
Divine Word Coll (IA)
Fisher Coll (MA)
Indian River State Coll (FL)
Long Island U–LIU Brooklyn (NY)
Midland Coll (TX)
Ohio U–Zanesville (OH)
Palm Beach State Coll (FL)
St. Gregory's U, Shawnee (OK)
Saint Peter's U (NJ)
Shawnee State U (OH)
Southwestern Assemblies of God U
    (TX)
State Coll of Florida Manatee-
    Sarasota (FL)
State U of New York Empire State
    Coll (NY)
Trine U (IN)
U of Cincinnati (OH)
U of Southern Indiana (IN)
Valparaiso U (IN)
Wayland Baptist U (TX)

SOCIAL SCIENCES RELATED
Concordia U Texas (TX)

**SOCIAL SCIENCE TEACHER
EDUCATION**
Montana State U (MT)

**SOCIAL STUDIES TEACHER
EDUCATION**
State Coll of Florida Manatee-
    Sarasota (FL)

SOCIAL WORK
Abraham Baldwin Ag Coll (GA)
Edinboro U of Pennsylvania (PA)
Elizabethtown Coll School of
    Continuing and Professional
    Studies (PA)
Ferris State U (MI)
Indian River State Coll (FL)
Northern State U (SD)
Palm Beach State Coll (FL)
State Coll of Florida Manatee-
    Sarasota (FL)
State U of New York Coll of
    Agriculture and Technology at
    Cobleskill (NY)
U of Cincinnati (OH)
U of Rio Grande (OH)
Wright State U (OH)
Youngstown State U (OH)

SOCIAL WORK RELATED
The U of Akron (OH)

SOCIOLOGY
Abraham Baldwin Ag Coll (GA)
Coll of Coastal Georgia (GA)
Fresno Pacific U (CA)
Holy Cross Coll (IN)
Indian River State Coll (FL)
Lourdes U (OH)
Marymount Manhattan Coll (NY)
Midland Coll (TX)
Montana State U Billings (MT)
Thomas More Coll (KY)
U of Rio Grande (OH)
The U of Scranton (PA)
The U of Tampa (FL)
Wright State U (OH)
Xavier U (OH)

**SOCIOLOGY AND
ANTHROPOLOGY**
Midland Coll (TX)

SOIL SCIENCES RELATED
Michigan State U (MI)

SOLAR ENERGY TECHNOLOGY
Pennsylvania Coll of Technology
    (PA)

SPANISH
Fresno Pacific U (CA)
Holy Cross Coll (IN)
Immaculata U (PA)
Indian River State Coll (FL)
Midland Coll (TX)
State Coll of Florida Manatee-
    Sarasota (FL)
Thomas More Coll (KY)
The U of Tampa (FL)
Xavier U (OH)

SPECIAL EDUCATION
Edinboro U of Pennsylvania (PA)
Montana State U Billings (MT)
U of Cincinnati (OH)

**SPECIAL EDUCATION–
INDIVIDUALS WHO ARE
DEVELOPMENTALLY DELAYED**
Saint Mary-of-the-Woods Coll (IN)

**SPECIAL EDUCATION
RELATED**
Minot State U (ND)

**SPECIAL PRODUCTS
MARKETING**
Indian River State Coll (FL)
Palm Beach State Coll (FL)

**SPEECH COMMUNICATION
AND RHETORIC**
American Public U System (WV)
Baker Coll of Jackson (MI)
Carroll Coll (MT)
Central Penn Coll (PA)
Coll of Mount St. Joseph (OH)
Indiana Wesleyan U (IN)
Lincoln Coll of New England,
    Southington (CT)
State U of New York Coll of
    Agriculture and Technology at
    Cobleskill (NY)
Trine U (IN)
Tulane U (LA)
U of Rio Grande (OH)
Utah Valley U (UT)
Wright State U (OH)

**SPEECH-LANGUAGE
PATHOLOGY**
Baker Coll of Muskegon (MI)
Elms Coll (MA)

**SPORT AND FITNESS
ADMINISTRATION/
MANAGEMENT**
AIB Coll of Business (IA)
Colorado Mesa U (CO)
Keiser U, Fort Lauderdale (FL)
Morrisville State Coll (NY)
Mount Vernon Nazarene U (OH)
National U (CA)
Southwestern Adventist U (TX)
State U of New York Coll of
    Technology at Delhi (NY)
U of Cincinnati (OH)
Webber International U (FL)

STATISTICS
State Coll of Florida Manatee-
    Sarasota (FL)

STRINGED INSTRUMENTS
McNally Smith Coll of Music (MN)

**SUBSTANCE ABUSE/
ADDICTION COUNSELING**
Indiana Wesleyan U (IN)
Midland Coll (TX)
National U (CA)
The U of Akron (OH)
U of Great Falls (MT)
Washburn U (KS)

SURGICAL TECHNOLOGY
Baker Coll of Clinton Township (MI)
Baker Coll of Flint (MI)
Baker Coll of Jackson (MI)
Baker Coll of Muskegon (MI)
Brown Mackie Coll–Birmingham (AL)
Brown Mackie Coll–Dallas/Ft. Worth
    (TX)
Brown Mackie Coll–San Antonio
    (TX)
Cabarrus Coll of Health Sciences
    (NC)
Harrison Coll, Indianapolis (IN)
Keiser U, Fort Lauderdale (FL)
Lincoln U (MO)

Mercy Coll of Health Sciences (IA)
Montana State U Billings (MT)
Mount Aloysius Coll (PA)
Nebraska Methodist Coll (NE)
New England Inst of Technology (RI)
Northern Michigan U (MI)
Our Lady of the Lake U (LA)
Pennsylvania Coll of Technology
    (PA)
Rasmussen Coll Brooklyn Park (MN)
Rasmussen Coll St. Cloud (MN)
Robert Morris U Illinois (IL)
The U of Akron (OH)
U of Arkansas–Fort Smith (AR)
U of Cincinnati (OH)
Washburn U (KS)

SURVEYING TECHNOLOGY
Ferris State U (MI)
Glenville State Coll (WV)
Indian River State Coll (FL)
Palm Beach State Coll (FL)
Pennsylvania Coll of Technology
    (PA)
Polytechnic U of Puerto Rico (PR)
State U of New York Coll of
    Environmental Science and
    Forestry (NY)
The U of Akron (OH)
Utah Valley U (UT)

**SYSTEM, NETWORKING, AND
LAN/WAN MANAGEMENT**
Baker Coll of Auburn Hills (MI)
Dakota State U (SD)
Midland Coll (TX)
Sullivan U (KY)

TEACHER ASSISTANT/AIDE
Alverno Coll (WI)
Dordt Coll (IA)
Eastern Mennonite U (VA)
Indian River State Coll (FL)
Johnson U (TN)
National U (CA)
Saint Mary-of-the-Woods Coll (IN)
State U of New York Coll of
    Agriculture and Technology at
    Cobleskill (NY)
U of Alaska Fairbanks (AK)
The U of Montana Western (MT)
Valparaiso U (IN)

**TECHNICAL TEACHER
EDUCATION**
Northern Kentucky U (KY)
Western Kentucky U (KY)

**TECHNOLOGY/INDUSTRIAL
ARTS TEACHER EDUCATION**
State Coll of Florida Manatee-
    Sarasota (FL)

**TELECOMMUNICATIONS
TECHNOLOGY**
New York City Coll of Technology of
    the City U of New York (NY)
Pace U (NY)
Penn State Shenango (PA)
St. John's U (NY)

**TERRORISM AND
COUNTERTERRORISM
OPERATIONS**
American Public U System (WV)

**THEATER DESIGN AND
TECHNOLOGY**
Johnson State Coll (VT)
U of Rio Grande (OH)
Utah Valley U (UT)

**THEOLOGICAL AND
MINISTERIAL STUDIES
RELATED**
Bob Jones U (SC)
California Christian Coll (CA)
Lincoln Christian U (IL)

THEOLOGY
Briar Cliff U (IA)
Creighton U (NE)
Griggs U (MI)
Immaculata U (PA)
Marian U (IN)
Missouri Baptist U (MO)
Ohio Dominican U (OH)
Piedmont International U (NC)
William Jessup U (CA)

THEOLOGY AND RELIGIOUS VOCATIONS RELATED
Anderson U (IN)

TOOL AND DIE TECHNOLOGY
Ferris State U (MI)

TOURISM AND TRAVEL SERVICES MANAGEMENT
AIB Coll of Business (IA)
Baker Coll of Flint (MI)
Baker Coll of Muskegon (MI)
Black Hills State U (SD)
Fisher Coll (MA)
Morrisville State Coll (NY)
Stevens—The Inst of Business & Arts (MO)
Sullivan U (KY)

TOURISM AND TRAVEL SERVICES MARKETING
Morrisville State Coll (NY)
State U of New York Coll of Agriculture and Technology at Cobleskill (NY)
State U of New York Coll of Technology at Delhi (NY)

TOURISM PROMOTION
St. Cloud State U (MN)

TRADE AND INDUSTRIAL TEACHER EDUCATION
Cincinnati Christian U (OH)
Murray State U (KY)
State Coll of Florida Manatee-Sarasota (FL)

TRANSPORTATION AND MATERIALS MOVING RELATED
Baker Coll of Flint (MI)

TRANSPORTATION/MOBILITY MANAGEMENT
Polk State Coll (FL)

TURF AND TURFGRASS MANAGEMENT
Michigan State U (MI)
North Carolina State U (NC)
U of Guelph (ON, Canada)
U of Massachusetts Amherst (MA)

URBAN STUDIES/AFFAIRS
Saint Peter's U (NJ)

VEHICLE AND VEHICLE PARTS AND ACCESSORIES MARKETING
Pennsylvania Coll of Technology (PA)

VETERINARY/ANIMAL HEALTH TECHNOLOGY
Argosy U, Twin Cities (MN)
Baker Coll of Cadillac (MI)
Baker Coll of Jackson (MI)
Baker Coll of Muskegon (MI)
Baker Coll of Port Huron (MI)
Becker Coll (MA)
Broadview U–Boise (ID)
Broadview U–Layton (UT)
Broadview U–Orem (UT)

Broadview U–West Jordan (UT)
Fort Valley State U (GA)
Globe U–Appleton (WI)
Globe U–Eau Claire (WI)
Globe U–Green Bay (WI)
Globe U–La Crosse (WI)
Globe U–Madison East (WI)
Globe U–Madison West (WI)
Globe U–Sioux Falls (SD)
Globe U–Wausau (WI)
Globe U–Woodbury (MN)
Harrison Coll, Indianapolis (IN)
Hickey Coll (MO)
International Business Coll, Fort Wayne (IN)
Lincoln Memorial U (TN)
Medaille Coll (NY)
Michigan State U (MI)
Minnesota School of Business–Blaine (MN)
Minnesota School of Business–Elk River (MN)
Minnesota School of Business–Lakeville (MN)
Minnesota School of Business–Moorhead (MN)
Minnesota School of Business–Rochester (MN)
Minnesota School of Business–St. Cloud (MN)
Minnesota School of Business–Shakopee (MN)
Morehead State U (KY)
New England Inst of Technology (RI)
Northwestern State U of Louisiana (LA)
Penn Foster Coll (AZ)
Purdue U (IN)
State U of New York Coll of Technology at Delhi (NY)
Sul Ross State U (TX)
Universidad del Turabo (PR)
U of Cincinnati (OH)
U of Guelph (ON, Canada)
U of Maine at Augusta (ME)
U of New Hampshire (NH)
Vermont Tech Coll (VT)

VISUAL AND PERFORMING ARTS
Pine Manor Coll (MA)

VITICULTURE AND ENOLOGY
Michigan State U (MI)

VOCATIONAL REHABILITATION COUNSELING
State Coll of Florida Manatee-Sarasota (FL)

VOICE AND OPERA
McNally Smith Coll of Music (MN)

WATER QUALITY AND WASTEWATER TREATMENT MANAGEMENT AND RECYCLING TECHNOLOGY
Colorado Mesa U (CO)
Lake Superior State U (MI)
Western Kentucky U (KY)

WEAPONS OF MASS DESTRUCTION
American Public U System (WV)

WEB/MULTIMEDIA MANAGEMENT AND WEBMASTER
American Public U System (WV)
Indiana Tech (IN)
Lewis-Clark State Coll (ID)
Montana Tech of The U of Montana (MT)

WEB PAGE, DIGITAL/ MULTIMEDIA AND INFORMATION RESOURCES DESIGN
Academy of Art U (CA)
The Art Inst of Atlanta (GA)
The Art Inst of Atlanta–Decatur, a branch of The Art Institute of Atlanta (GA)
The Art Inst of Austin, a branch of The Art Institute of Houston (TX)
The Art Inst of California–Hollywood, a campus of Argosy U (CA)
The Art Inst of California–Los Angeles, a campus of Argosy U (CA)
The Art Inst of California–Orange County, a campus of Argosy U (CA)
The Art Inst of California–Sacramento, a campus of Argosy U (CA)
The Art Inst of California–San Francisco, a campus of Argosy U (CA)
The Art Inst of California–Silicon Valley, a campus of Argosy U (CA)
The Art Inst of Charleston, a branch of The Art Institute of Atlanta (SC)
The Art Inst of Colorado (CO)
The Art Inst of Fort Lauderdale (FL)
The Art Inst of Houston (TX)
The Art Inst of Houston–North, a branch of The Art Institute of Houston (TX)
The Art Inst of Michigan (MI)
The Art Inst of Ohio–Cincinnati (OH)
The Art Inst of Philadelphia (PA)
The Art Inst of Pittsburgh (PA)
The Art Inst of St. Louis (MO)
The Art Inst of San Antonio, a branch of The Art Institute of Houston (TX)
The Art Inst of Seattle (WA)
The Art Inst of Virginia Beach, a branch of The Art Institute of Atlanta (VA)
The Art Inst of Washington, a branch of The Art Institute of Atlanta (VA)
The Art Inst of Washington–Dulles, a branch of The Art Institute of Atlanta (VA)
The Art Insts International Minnesota (MN)
Baker Coll of Allen Park (MI)
DeVry U, Phoenix (AZ)
DeVry U, Alhambra (CA)
DeVry U, Anaheim (CA)
DeVry U, Bakersfield (CA)

DeVry U, Daly City (CA)
DeVry U, Elk Grove (CA)
DeVry U, Fremont (CA)
DeVry U, Long Beach (CA)
DeVry U, Oakland (CA)
DeVry U, Oxnard (CA)
DeVry U, Palmdale (CA)
DeVry U, Pomona (CA)
DeVry U, San Diego (CA)
DeVry U, Sherman Oaks (CA)
DeVry U, Colorado Springs (CO)
DeVry U, Westminster (CO)
DeVry U, Jacksonville (FL)
DeVry U, Miami (FL)
DeVry U, Miramar (FL)
DeVry U, Orlando (FL)
DeVry U, Tampa (FL)
DeVry U, Alpharetta (GA)
DeVry U, Decatur (GA)
DeVry U, Duluth (GA)
DeVry U, Addison (IL)
DeVry U, Chicago (IL)
DeVry U, Gurnee (IL)
DeVry U, Tinley Park (IL)
DeVry U, Indianapolis (IN)
DeVry U, Merrillville (IN)
DeVry U (KY)
DeVry U, Edina (MN)
DeVry U, Kansas City (MO)
DeVry U, Kansas City (MO)
DeVry U, St. Louis (MO)
DeVry U (NV)
DeVry U, North Brunswick (NJ)
DeVry U, Paramus (NJ)
DeVry U, Columbus (OH)
DeVry U, Seven Hills (OH)
DeVry U (OK)
DeVry U (OR)
DeVry U, Fort Washington (PA)
DeVry U, King of Prussia (PA)
DeVry U, Philadelphia (PA)
DeVry U, Pittsburgh (PA)
DeVry U, Memphis (TN)
DeVry U, Nashville (TN)
DeVry U, Austin (TX)
DeVry U, Houston (TX)
DeVry U, Irving (TX)
DeVry U (UT)
DeVry U, Arlington (VA)
DeVry U, Chesapeake (VA)
DeVry U, Manassas (VA)
DeVry U, Bellevue (WA)
DeVry U, Federal Way (WA)
Florida National U (FL)
The Illinois Inst of Art–Schaumburg (IL)
Limestone Coll (SC)
New England Inst of Technology (RI)
Palm Beach State Coll (FL)
Polk State Coll (FL)
Rasmussen Coll Appleton (WI)
Rasmussen Coll Aurora (IL)
Rasmussen Coll Bismarck (ND)
Rasmussen Coll Blaine (MN)
Rasmussen Coll Bloomington (MN)
Rasmussen Coll Brooklyn Park (MN)
Rasmussen Coll Eagan (MN)
Rasmussen Coll Fargo (ND)
Rasmussen Coll Fort Myers (FL)
Rasmussen Coll Green Bay (WI)

Rasmussen Coll Kansas City/ Overland Park (KS)
Rasmussen Coll Lake Elmo/ Woodbury (MN)
Rasmussen Coll Land O' Lakes (FL)
Rasmussen Coll Mankato (MN)
Rasmussen Coll Mokena/Tinley Park (IL)
Rasmussen Coll Moorhead (MN)
Rasmussen Coll New Port Richey (FL)
Rasmussen Coll Ocala (FL)
Rasmussen Coll Romeoville/Joliet (IL)
Rasmussen Coll St. Cloud (MN)
Rasmussen Coll Tampa/Brandon (FL)
Rasmussen Coll Topeka (KS)
Rasmussen Coll Wausau (WI)
Thomas More Coll (KY)
Universidad del Turabo (PR)
Utah Valley U (UT)

WELDING TECHNOLOGY
Excelsior Coll (NY)
Ferris State U (MI)
Lewis-Clark State Coll (ID)
Liberty U (VA)
Midland Coll (TX)
Oakland City U (IN)
Pennsylvania Coll of Technology (PA)
State U of New York Coll of Technology at Delhi (NY)
Weber State U (UT)

WILDLIFE, FISH AND WILDLANDS SCIENCE AND MANAGEMENT
Abraham Baldwin Ag Coll (GA)
State U of New York Coll of Agriculture and Technology at Cobleskill (NY)

WOMEN'S STUDIES
Fisher Coll (MA)
Indiana U–Purdue U Fort Wayne (IN)
Nazarene Bible Coll (CO)
Shiloh U (IA)
State Coll of Florida Manatee-Sarasota (FL)

WOOD SCIENCE AND WOOD PRODUCTS/PULP AND PAPER TECHNOLOGY
Morrisville State Coll (NY)

WORD PROCESSING
Baker Coll of Allen Park (MI)
Palm Beach State Coll (FL)

WRITING
Carroll Coll (MT)
The U of Tampa (FL)

YOUTH MINISTRY
Piedmont International U (NC)
Valley Forge Christian Coll (PA)

ZOOLOGY/ANIMAL BIOLOGY
Palm Beach State Coll (FL)

Alphabetical Listing of Two-Year Colleges

NOTES

NOTES